Explanation of a Campsite Entry

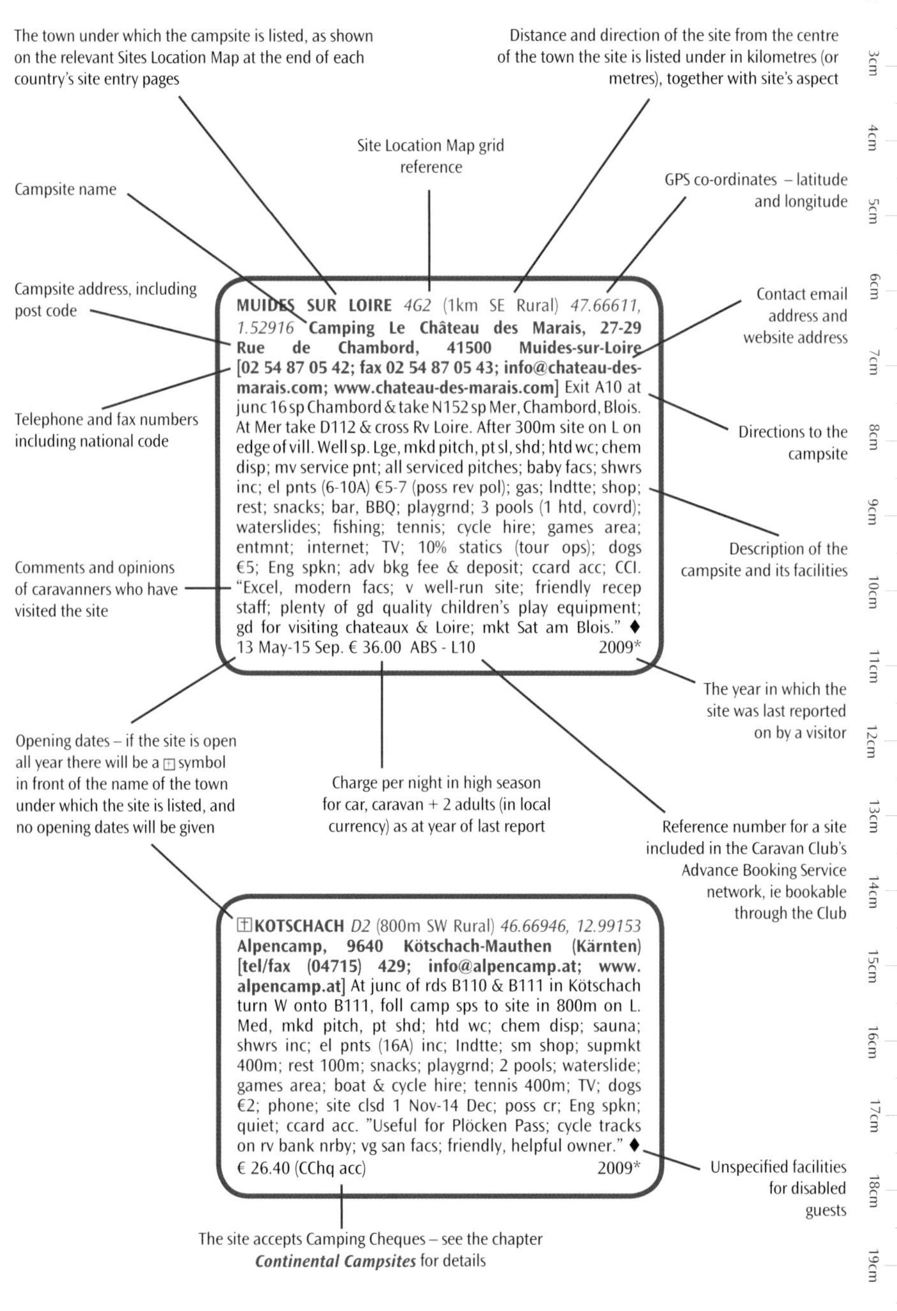
The town under which the campsite is listed, as shown on the relevant Sites Location Map at the end of each country's site entry pages
Distance and direction of the site from the centre of the town the site is listed under in kilometres (or metres), together with site's aspect
Site Location Map grid reference
Campsite name
GPS co-ordinates – latitude and longitude
Campsite address, including post code
Contact email address and website address
Telephone and fax numbers including national code
Directions to the campsite
Description of the campsite and its facilities
Comments and opinions of caravanners who have visited the site
MUIDES SUR LOIRE 4G2 (1km SE Rural) 47.66611, 1.52916 Camping Le Château des Marais, 27-29 Rue de Chambord, 41500 Muides-sur-Loire [02 54 87 05 42; fax 02 54 87 05 43; info@chateau-des-marais.com; www.chateau-des-marais.com] Exit A10 at junc 16 sp Chambord & take N152 sp Mer, Chambord, Blois. At Mer take D112 & cross Rv Loire. After 300m site on L on edge of vill. Well sp. Lge, mkd pitch, pt sl, shd; htd wc; chem disp; mv service pnt; all serviced pitches; baby facs; shwrs inc; el pnts (6-10A) €5-7 (poss rev pol); gas; Indtte; shop; rest; snacks; bar, BBQ; playgrnd; 3 pools (1 htd, covrd); waterslides; fishing; tennis; cycle hire; games area; entmnt; internet; TV; 10% statics (tour ops); dogs €5; Eng spkn; adv bkg fee & deposit; ccard acc; CCI. "Excel, modern facs; v well-run site; friendly recep staff; plenty of gd quality children's play equipment; gd for visiting chateaux & Loire; mkt Sat am Blois." ♦
13 May-15 Sep. € 36.00 ABS - L10 2009*
The year in which the site was last reported on by a visitor
Opening dates – if the site is open all year there will be a ⊞ symbol in front of the name of the town under which the site is listed, and no opening dates will be given
Charge per night in high season for car, caravan + 2 adults (in local currency) as at year of last report
Reference number for a site included in the Caravan Club's Advance Booking Service network, ie bookable through the Club
⊞KOTSCHACH D2 (800m SW Rural) 46.66946, 12.99153 Alpencamp, 9640 Kötschach-Mauthen (Kärnten) [tel/fax (04715) 429; info@alpencamp.at; www.alpencamp.at] At junc of rds B110 & B111 in Kötschach turn W onto B111, foll camp sps to site in 800m on L. Med, mkd pitch, pt shd; htd wc; chem disp; sauna; shwrs inc; el pnts (16A) inc; Indtte; sm shop; supmkt 400m; rest 100m; snacks; playgrnd; 2 pools; waterslide; games area; boat & cycle hire; tennis 400m; TV; dogs €2; phone; site clsd 1 Nov-14 Dec; poss cr; Eng spkn; quiet; ccard acc. "Useful for Plöcken Pass; cycle tracks on rv bank nrby; vg san facs; friendly, helpful owner." ♦
€ 26.40 (CChq acc) 2009*
Unspecified facilities for disabled guests
The site accepts Camping Cheques – see the chapter Continental Campsites for details

Caravan Europe 1

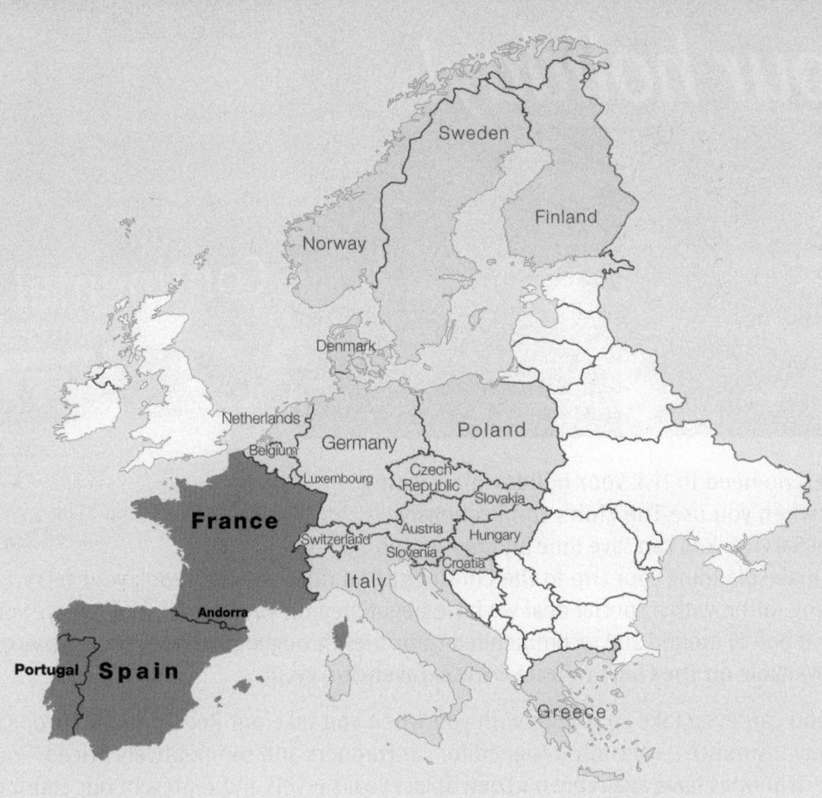

Published by The Caravan Club Limited
East Grinstead House, East Grinstead
West Sussex RH19 1UA

General Enquiries: 01342 326944
Travel Service Reservations: 01342 316101
Brochure Requests: 01342 327410
Club Shop: 01342 318813
General Fax: 01342 410258
Website: www.caravanclub.co.uk
Email: enquiries@caravanclub.co.uk

Editor: Bernice Hoare
Email: bernice.hoare@caravanclub.co.uk

Printed by Elanders Ltd
Newcastle-upon-Tyne

Maps and distance charts generated from Collins Bartholomew Digital Database

ISBN 978 1 85733 503 3

Front cover photo: House near Coulon, Poitou-Charentes, France

Contents

How To Use This Guide

Planning & Travelling

Contents

See also alphabetical index at the back of the guide

A warm welcome to the 2010 edition of **Caravan Europe**

Within these pages you'll find thousands of campsites of all kinds from small, away-from-it-all, rural retreats to busy city centre sites and vast beach holiday complexes with a full range of facilities, sports, excursions and entertainment to satisfy the most discerning family members.

Many campsites in this guide offer extremely good value for money and, as always, they have been visited and reported on by fellow caravanners during the course of their own holidays. Look at our website or telephone the Club to check our range of preferential ferry fares on many of the major routes and consider our Red Pennant holiday insurance, specially tailored for you, the caravanner. And don't forget to read the Handbook and Country Introduction chapters which contain a wealth of motoring advice and information covering all aspects of touring in Europe – whether with a caravan, motor caravan or trailer-tent – and which will go a long way to ensuring a relaxing and trouble-free trip.

Whatever your choice, you've made the right decision to pack up and head off to the Continent. Enjoy your holiday!

Bernice Hoare

Bernice Hoare
Editor

Palace of Versailles, France. © www.all-free-photos.com

www.caravanclub.co.uk

The Caravan Club's Travel

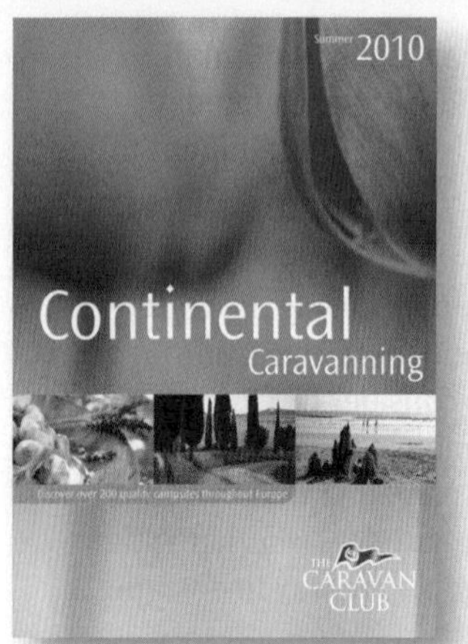

The Caravan Club offers members a comprehensive Travel Service that is second to none. Everything – from Continental site and ferry bookings to a superb Overseas Holiday travel insurance scheme – is handled with the customer-friendly approach you would expect from The Club. If you want to travel abroad, the Travel Service really is a good enough reason on its own to join **The Caravan Club**.

100,000 members can't be wrong!

Yes, that's right, 100,000 members use The Caravan Club's Travel Service each year. That figure alone gives you some idea of the confidence they have in The Club. One good reason for this trust is the dedication and efficiency of The Club's staff. Another is the financial security of The Caravan Club, at a time when many other operators are falling by the wayside. Many members use these services year after year, becoming firm friends not only with site owners overseas but The Club's Travel Service staff, too.

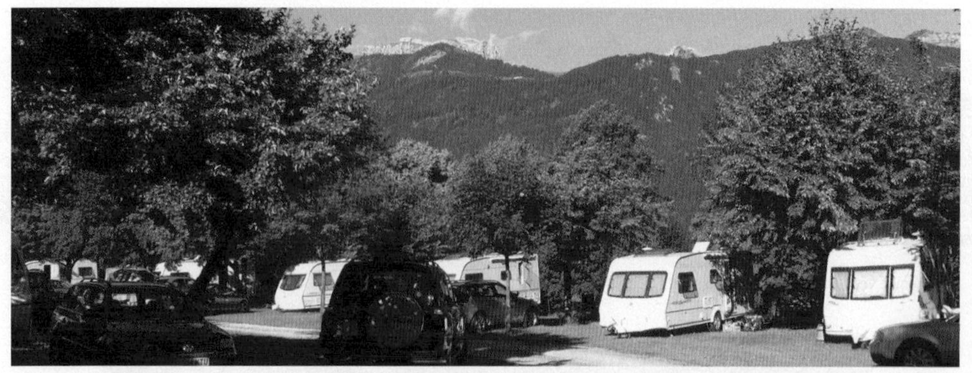

Travel & Save with The Club

Over many years The Club's Travel Service has established excellent relationships with most of the major ferry operators and a large number of overseas sites. That is how The Club can offer such favourable rates and, by working closely with these companies, can ensure members enjoy the best possible overseas holiday experiences available.

Unlike solely commercial operators, The Club, being a mutual organisation, can pass on considerable savings to its members.

With respected ferry companies such as Brittany Ferries, Stena Line, P&O Ferries, Norfolk Lines, SeaFrance and Eurotunnel all represented by The Club, you can be sure that almost any combination of route, time and destination will be available to you. Booking through The Club ensures that you will be offered the most appropriate crossing at a keen price every time.

Ferry fares can vary considerably by day of week and time of day, so even greater savings can be made if you are willing to be flexible in your travel arrangements. Travel Service staff are only too happy to discuss alternatives on the phone, so you can compare the cost of various options.

If you choose to book on The Club's website, the systems are specifically designed to make these comparisons easy.

Only the best will do...

The Club's experienced team of site inspectors regularly inspect and monitor over 200 sites in Europe. As members of The Caravan Club and regular overseas caravanners themselves, they really know what to look for, having a genuine interest in maintaining high standards.

Sites in The Club's Travel Service brochure are all pre-bookable by phone, with most also available from April on The Club website: **www.caravanclub.co.uk**

Watch the website and magazine for details of a new site booking facility coming online later in the year.

Plan ahead and reap rewards

As agents for all the major car ferry operators to the Continent, Ireland and Scandinavia The Club can make bookings for all their services. Special package fares are available to those members booking seven nights or more on one or more sites, including 'Camping Cheques'. These fares are often, but not always, cheaper than standard prices, but of course The Club will always offer its members the most suitable option for their circumstances.

Booking early is one of the best ways to ensure you achieve the lowest fare for your chosen sailing. Good planning is essential to take up any Club offers, so deciding your itinerary at the earliest possible date will bring appropriate rewards.

Save more out of season

If you really want to save money then it makes sense to tour abroad out of season, not in the peak months of July and August. The Club has a discount scheme on offer where members may pay in advance for a minimum of seven nights with 'Camping Cheque', which also enables them to take advantage of The Club's specially negotiated ferry fares.

NEW for 2010 will be the introduction by Camping Cheque of a "Silver Card". This will be available for a nominal charge and once registered, may be used to purchase "electronic" Cheques. This will then function in a similar way to the Camping Cheque Gold Card, but with fewer benefits. The good news is that for 2010 The Club will be able to sell Cheques to holders of both Gold and Silver cards, although initial Gold card purchase must still be made through Camping Cheque in the UK or France.

Camping Cheques, whether paper or electronic, will still only be available through The Club's Travel Service when sold in conjunction with an associated ferry booking.

Travel abroad with The Caravan Club...

For the latest Travel Service brochure simply phone **01342 327410*** or go online to **www.caravanclub.co.uk**

If you're not a member yet and would like to join The Caravan Club, simply phone **0800 328 6635***

quoting TS07 or visit the website **www.caravanclub.co.uk**

The complete Travel Service. From **The Caravan Club**.

When you book a complete holiday package with The Caravan Club's Travel Service you'll receive ticket wallets, GB stickers and an Overseas Campsite & Holiday Guide, listing Club recommended sites, plus maps, directions and driving regulations. Also available from The Club at very reasonable prices are yellow High Visibility vests, an essential accessory (along with Red Pennant insurance of course!) should you have the misfortune to break down.

Introduction

The information contained in this guide is presented in the following major categories:

Handbook

General information about touring in Europe, including legal requirements, advice and regulations, appears in the Handbook chapters at the front of the guide under the following section headings:

PLANNING AND TRAVELLING

DURING YOUR STAY

These two sections are divided into chapters in alphabetical order, not necessarily the order of priority. Where additional information is provided in another chapter, cross-references are provided.

Country Introductions

Following on from the Handbook chapters are the individual Country Introduction chapters containing information, regulations and advice specific to each country featured in the guide. You should read these Country Introductions carefully in conjunction with the Handbook chapters before you set off on holiday. Cross-references to other chapters are provided where appropriate.

Campsite Entries

After each Country Introduction you will find pages of campsite entries which are shown within an alphabetical list of towns and villages in or near which they are situated. Where several campsites are shown in and around the same town, they are given in clockwise order from the north.

A cross-reference system is incorporated within the campsite listings. Simply look for the name of the town or village where you wish to stay. If a campsite is not shown under the name of the particular town or village in which it is situated, then a cross-reference should indicate an alternative village or town name under which it may be found in the guide. For example, for Domme (France) the cross-reference will point you to the campsites listed under Sarlat-la-Canéda, or for Ceriale (Italy), look at the sites listed under Albenga.

To maintain consistency throughout the site entries listed in the guide, local versions of town or city names are used, eg:

Bruxelles instead of **Brussels**

Den Haag instead of **The Hague**

Dunkerque instead of **Dunkirk**

Firenze instead of **Florence**

Lisboa instead of **Lisbon**

Praha instead of **Prague**

Warszawa instead of **Warsaw**

Except in the case of those campsites included in the Club's Travel Services Advance Booking Service network and marked ABS at the end of their site entries, the Caravan Club has no contractual arrangements with any of the sites featured in this guide. Furthermore, even in the case of sites with which the Club is contracted, it has no direct control over day-to-day operations or administration. Only those sites marked ABS have been inspected by Caravan Club staff.

It is assumed by The Caravan Club Ltd, but not checked (except in the case of sites marked ABS), that all campsites fall under some form of local licensing, which may or may not take account of matters of safety and hygiene. Caravanners will be aware of the varying standards between countries and are responsible for checking such matters to their own satisfaction.

Campsite Fees

Campsite entries show high season charges per night in local currency for a car, caravan + 2 adults, as at the year of last report. In addition a deposit or booking fee may be charged – this may be non-refundable – and prices given do not necessarily include electricity or showers unless indicated, or local taxes. You are advised to check fees when booking, or at least before siting, as those shown can be used as a guide only.

Sites Location Maps

Each town and village listed alphabetically in the site entry pages has a map grid reference number, which relates to a Sites Location Map at the end of that country's site entries. Place names are shown on the maps in two colours; red where there is a site open all year (or for at least approximately eleven months of the year), or black where only seasonal sites have been reported. **Please note: these maps are for general campsite location purposes only; a detailed road map or atlas is essential for route planning and touring.**

The scale used for the Sites Location Maps means that it is not possible to pinpoint on them every town or village where a campsite exists. Where we cannot show an individual town or village on a Sites Location Map for reasons of space, we list it under another nearby town which then acts as a central point for campsites within that particular local area. With some exceptions, such as Paris or Berlin, sites are listed under towns up to a maximum of 15 kilometres away. The place names used as a central point are usually, but not always, the largest towns in each region; some may be only small villages. See the paragraph about cross-references earlier in this chapter.

Satellite Navigation

Many campsite entries in this guide now show a GPS (sat nav) reference and more will be added over time. The GPS reference is given after the Site Location Map grid reference and the distance and direction to the site in question and is in the format 12.34567 (latitude north) and 1.23456 (longitude east), ie decimal degrees. Readings shown as -1.23456 indicate that the longitude position in question is west of the 0 degrees Greenwich meridian. This is important to bear in mind when inputting co-ordinates into your sat nav device or recording co-ordinates of campsites in western France, most of Spain and all of Portugal.

Readings given in other formats such as degrees + minutes + seconds or degrees + decimal minutes can be converted using www.cosports.com then click on Cool Tools. Or simply use Google maps (http://maps.google.co.uk) and input a GPS reference in any format to locate a town, village or campsite.

The GPS co-ordinates given in this guide are derived from a number of reliable sources but it has not been possible to check them all individually. The Caravan Club cannot accept responsibility for any inaccuracies, errors or omissions or for their effects.

Site Report Forms

With the exception of campsites in the Advance Booking Service network, the Caravan Club does not inspect sites listed in this guide, nor, with a few exceptions, does it ask individual sites to update their own entries. Virtually all the site reports in these guides are submitted voluntarily by caravanners, whether or not members of the Caravan Club, during the course of their own holidays.

Sites which are not reported on for five years may be deleted from the guide. We rely very much, therefore, on you, the users of this guide, to tell us about old favourites re-visited as well as new discoveries.

You will find a small number of blank site report forms towards the back of the guide which we hope you will complete and return to us (freepost). An abbreviated site report form is provided if you are reporting no changes, or only minor changes, to a site entry. Additional loose forms are available on request, including a larger A4 version.

Alternatively you can complete both the full and abbreviated versions of site report forms online on our website. Simply go to www.caravanclub.co.uk/europereport and fill in the form. Or download blank forms for later completion and posting to the Club.

For an explanation of abbreviations used in site entries, refer to the following chapter ***Explanation of a Campsite Entry*** or use the tear-out bookmark at the front of the guide which shows the most common abbreviations used.

Please submit reports as soon as possible. Information received by **September** will be used, wherever possible, in the compilation of next year's edition of Caravan Europe. Reports received after that date are still very welcome and will be retained for entry in a subsequent edition. The editor is unable to respond individually to site reports submitted.

Win a Ferry Crossing

If you submit site reports to the editor during 2010 – whether by post, email or online – you will have your name entered into a prize draw to win one of two return Dover-Calais ferry crossings with P & O Ferries for a car, caravan or motor caravan and two adults during 2011 (terms and conditions apply), together with a copy of Caravan Europe 2011.

Tips for Completing Site Report Forms

- Try to fill in a form while at the campsite or shortly after your stay. Once back at home it can be difficult to remember details of individual sites, especially if you visited several during your trip.
- When giving directions to a site, remember to include the direction of travel, eg 'from north on D137, turn left onto D794 signposted Combourg' or 'on N83 from Poligny turn right at petrol station in village'. Where possible give road numbers together with junction numbers and/or kilometre post numbers where you exit from motorways or main roads. It is also helpful to mention useful landmarks such as bridges, roundabouts, traffic lights or prominent buildings, and whether the site is signposted. If you have a sat nav device please, wherever possible, include GPS co-ordinates recorded at a campsite entrance.
- When noting the compass direction of a site **this must be in the direction FROM THE TOWN the site is listed under, TO THE SITE and not the compass direction from the site to the town.** Distances are measured in a straight line and may differ significantly from the actual distance by road.
- If you are amending only a few details about a site there is no need to use the longer version form. You may prefer to use the abbreviated version but, in any event, do remember to give the campsite name and the town or village under which it is listed in the guide. Alternatively, use the online version of the form – www.caravanclub.co.uk/europereport
- If possible, give precise opening and closing dates, eg 1 April to 30 September. This information is particularly important for early and late season travellers.

The editor very much appreciates the time and trouble taken by caravanners in submitting reports on campsites you have visited; without your valuable contributions it would be impossible to update this guide.

Every effort is made to ensure that information contained in this publication is accurate and that details given in good faith by caravanners in site report forms are accurately reproduced or summarised. The Caravan Club Ltd has not checked these details by inspection or other investigation and cannot accept responsibility for the accuracy of these reports as provided by caravanners, or for errors, omissions or their effects. In addition The Caravan Club Ltd cannot be held accountable for the quality, safety or operation of the sites concerned, or for the fact that conditions, facilities, management or prices may have changed since the last recorded visit. Any recommendations, additional comments or opinions have been contributed by caravanners and are not generally those of the Caravan Club.

The inclusion of advertisements or other inserted material does not imply any form of approval or recognition, nor can The Caravan Club Ltd undertake any responsibility for checking the accuracy of advertising material.

Acknowledgements

The Caravan Club's thanks go to the AIT/FIA Information Centre (OTA), the Alliance Internationale de Tourisme (AIT), the Fédération International de Camping et de Caravaning (FICC) and to the national clubs and tourist offices of those countries who have assisted with this publication.

Explanation of a Campsite Entry

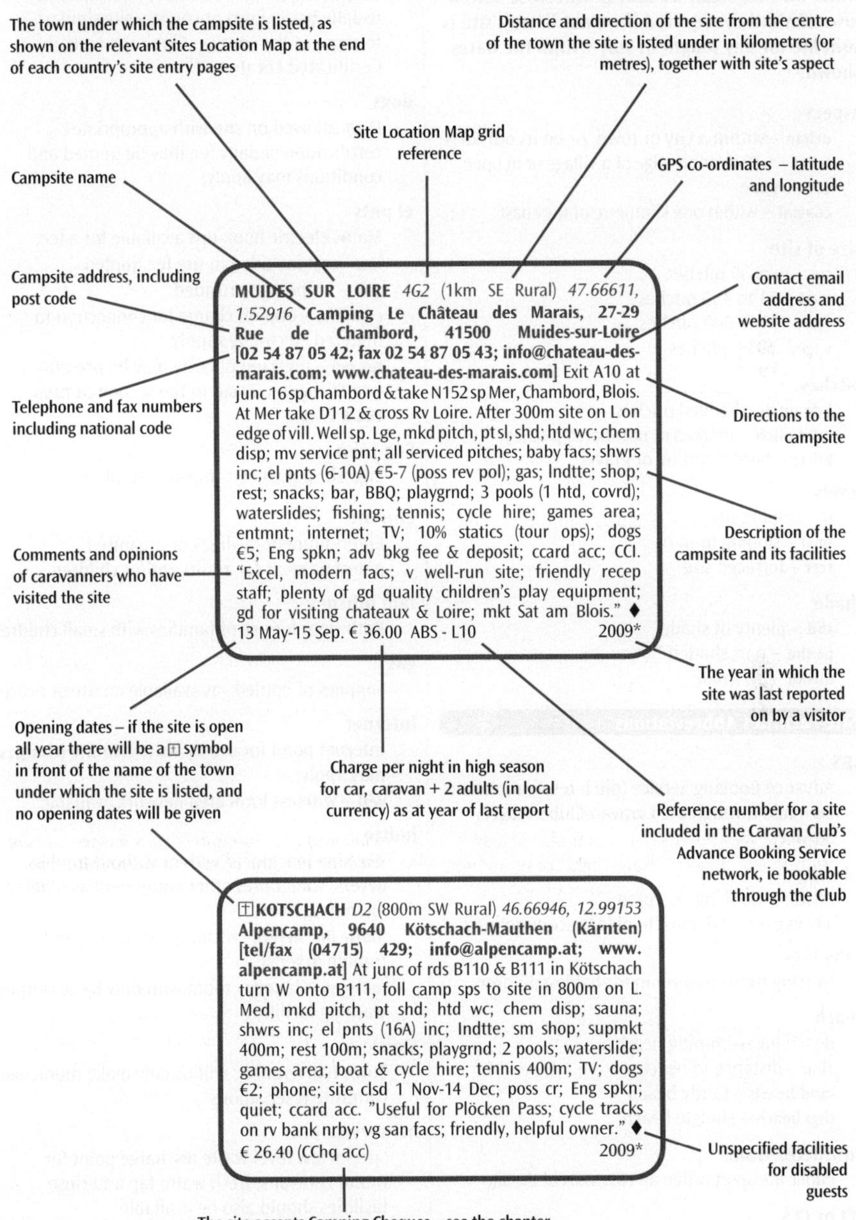

The town under which the campsite is listed, as shown on the relevant Sites Location Map at the end of each country's site entry pages
Distance and direction of the site from the centre of the town the site is listed under in kilometres (or metres), together with site's aspect
Site Location Map grid reference
Campsite name
GPS co-ordinates – latitude and longitude
Campsite address, including post code
Contact email address and website address
MUIDES SUR LOIRE 4G2 (1km SE Rural) 47.66611, 1.52916 Camping Le Château des Marais, 27-29 Rue de Chambord, 41500 Muides-sur-Loire [02 54 87 05 42; fax 02 54 87 05 43; info@chateau-des-marais.com; www.chateau-des-marais.com] Exit A10 at junc 16 sp Chambord & take N152 sp Mer, Chambord, Blois. At Mer take D112 & cross Rv Loire. After 300m site on L on edge of vill. Well sp. Lge, mkd pitch, pt sl, shd; htd wc; chem disp; mv service pnt; all serviced pitches; baby facs; shwrs inc; el pnts (6-10A) €5-7 (poss rev pol); gas; Indtte; shop; rest; snacks; bar, BBQ; playgrnd; 3 pools (1 htd, covrd); waterslides; fishing; tennis; cycle hire; games area; entmnt; internet; TV; 10% statics (tour ops); dogs €5; Eng spkn; adv bkg fee & deposit; ccard acc; CCI. "Excel, modern facs; v well-run site; friendly recep staff; plenty of gd quality children's play equipment; gd for visiting chateaux & Loire; mkt Sat am Blois." ♦
13 May-15 Sep. € 36.00 ABS - L10 2009*
Telephone and fax numbers including national code
Directions to the campsite
Description of the campsite and its facilities
Comments and opinions of caravanners who have visited the site
The year in which the site was last reported on by a visitor
Opening dates – if the site is open all year there will be a ⊞ symbol in front of the name of the town under which the site is listed, and no opening dates will be given
Charge per night in high season for car, caravan + 2 adults (in local currency) as at year of last report
Reference number for a site included in the Caravan Club's Advance Booking Service network, ie bookable through the Club
⊞ KOTSCHACH D2 (800m SW Rural) 46.66946, 12.99153 Alpencamp, 9640 Kötschach-Mauthen (Kärnten) [tel/fax (04715) 429; info@alpencamp.at; www.alpencamp.at] At junc of rds B110 & B111 in Kötschach turn W onto B111, foll camp sps to site in 800m on L. Med, mkd pitch, pt shd; htd wc; chem disp; sauna; shwrs inc; el pnts (16A) inc; Indtte; sm shop; supmkt 400m; rest 100m; snacks; playgrnd; 2 pools; waterslide; games area; boat & cycle hire; tennis 400m; TV; dogs €2; phone; site clsd 1 Nov-14 Dec; poss cr; Eng spkn; quiet; ccard acc. "Useful for Plöcken Pass; cycle tracks on rv bank nrby; vg san facs; friendly, helpful owner." ♦
€ 26.40 (CChq acc) 2009*
Unspecified facilities for disabled guests
The site accepts Camping Cheques – see the chapter Continental Campsites for details

Site Description Abbreviations

Each site entry assumes the following unless stated otherwise:

Level ground, open grass pitches, drinking water on site, clean wc unless otherwise stated (own sanitation required if wc not listed), site is suitable for any length of stay within the dates shown.

aspect
- **urban** – within a city or town, or on its outskirts
- **rural** – within or on edge of a village or in open countryside
- **coastal** – within one kilometre of the coast

size of site
- **sm** – max 50 pitches
- **med** – 51 to 150 pitches
- **lge** – 151 to 500 pitches
- **v lge** – 501+ pitches

pitches
- **hdg pitch** – hedged pitches
- **mkd pitch** – marked or numbered pitches
- **hdstg** – hard standing or gravel

levels
- **sl** – sloping site
- **pt sl** – sloping in parts
- **terr** – terraced site

shade
- **shd** – plenty of shade
- **pt shd** – part shaded
- **unshd** – no shade

Site Facilities Abbreviations

ABS
Advance Booking Service (pitch reservation can be made through the Caravan Club's Travel Service)

adv bkg
Advance booking accepted;
adv bkg rec – advance booking recommended

baby facs
Nursing room/bathroom for babies/children

beach
Beach for swimming nearby;
1km – distance to beach
sand beach – sandy beach
shgl beach – shingle beach

bus/metro/tram
Public transport within an easy walk of the site

CCI or CCS
Camping Card International or Camping Card Scandinavia accepted

chem disp
Dedicated chemical toilet disposal facilities;
(wc) – no dedicated point; disposal via wc only

CL-type
Very small, privately-owned, informal and usually basic, farm or country site similar to those in the Caravan Club's network of Certificated Locations

dogs
Dogs allowed on site with appropriate certification (a daily fee may be quoted and conditions may apply)

el pnts
Mains electric hook-ups available for a fee;
inc – cost included in site fee quoted
10A – amperage provided
conn fee – one-off charge for connection to metered electricity supply
rev pol – reversed polarity may be present (see ***Electricity and Gas*** in the section ***DURING YOUR STAY***)

Eng spkn
English spoken by campsite reception staff

entmnt
Entertainment facilities or organised entertainment for adults and/or children

fam bthrm
Bathroom for use of families with small children

gas
Supplies of bottled gas available on site or nearby

internet
Internet point for use by visitors to site (charges may apply);
wifi – wireless local area network available

lndtte
Washing machine(s) with or without tumble dryers, sometimes other equipment available, eg ironing boards;
lndtte (inc dryer) – washing machine(s) and tumble dryer(s)
lndry rm – laundry room with only basic clothes-washing facilities

Mairie
Town hall (France); will usually make municipal campsite reservations

mv service pnt
Special low level waste discharge point for motor caravans; fresh water tap and rinse facilities should also be available

NH
Suitable as a night halt

noisy
Noisy site with reasons given;
quiet – peaceful, tranquil site

open 1 Apr-15 Oct
Where no specific dates are given, opening dates are assumed to be inclusive, ie Apr-Oct – beginning April to end October **(NB: opening dates may vary from those shown; check in advance before making a long journey, particularly when travelling out of the main holiday season)**

phone
Public payphone on or adjacent to site

playgrnd
Children's playground

pool
Swimming pool (may be open high season only);
htd – heated pool
covrd – indoor pool or one with retractable cover

poss cr
During high season site may be crowded or overcrowded and pitches cramped

red CCI/CCS
Reduction in fees on production of a Camping Card International or Camping Card Scandinavia

rest
Restaurant;
bar – bar
BBQ – barbecues allowed (may be restricted to a separate, designated area)
cooking facs – communal kitchen area
snacks – snack bar, cafeteria or takeaway

serviced pitch
Electric hook-ups and mains water inlet and grey water waste outlet to pitch;
all – to all pitches
50% – percentage of pitches

shop(s)
Shop on site;
adj – shops next to site
500m – nearest shops
supmkt – supermarket
hypmkt – hypermarket
tradsmn – tradesmen call at the site, eg baker

shwrs
Hot showers available for a fee;
inc – cost included in site fee quoted

ssn
Season;
high ssn – peak holiday season
low ssn – out of peak season

50% statics
Percentage of static caravans/mobile homes/ chalets/fixed tents/cabins or long term seasonal pitches on site, including those run by tour operators

sw
Swimming nearby;
1km – nearest swimming
lake – in lake
rv – in river

TV
TV available for viewing by visitors (often in the bar);
TV rm – separate TV room (often also a games room)
cab/sat – cable or satellite connections to pitches

wc
Clean flushing toilets on site;
(cont) – continental type with floor-level hole
htd – sanitary block centrally heated in winter
own san – use of own sanitation facilities recommended

Other Abbreviations

AIT	Alliance Internationale de Tourisme
a'bahn	Autobahn
a'pista	Autopista
a'route	Autoroute
a'strada	Autostrada
adj	Adjacent, nearby
alt	Alternative
app	Approach, on approaching
arr	Arrival, arriving
avail	Available
Ave	Avenue
bdge	Bridge
bef	Before
bet	Between
Blvd	Boulevard
C	Century, eg 16thC
c'van	Caravan
ccard acc	Credit and/or debit cards accepted (check with site for specific details)
CChq acc	Camping Cheques accepted
cent	Centre or central
clsd	Closed
conn	Connection
cont	Continue or continental (wc)
conv	Convenient
covrd	Covered

dep	Departure
diff	Difficult, with difficulty
dir	Direction
dist	Distance
dual c'way	Dual carriageway
E	East
ent	Entrance/entry to
espec	Especially
ess	Essential
excel	Excellent
facs	Facilities
FIA	Fédération Internationale de l'Automobile
FICC	Fédération Internationale de Camping & de Caravaning
FKK/FNF	Naturist federation, ie naturist site
foll	Follow
fr	From
g'ge	Garage
gd	Good
grnd(s)	Ground(s)
hr(s)	Hour(s)
immac	Immaculate
immed	Immediate(ly)
inc	Included/inclusive
indus est	Industrial estate
INF	Naturist federation, ie naturist site
int'l	International
irreg	Irregular
junc	Junction
km	Kilometre
L	Left
LH	Left-hand
LS	Low season
ltd	Limited
mkd	Marked
mkt	Market
mob	Mobile (phone)
m'van	Motor caravan
m'way	Motorway
N	North
narr	Narrow
nr, nrby	Near, nearby
opp	Opposite
o'fits	Outfits
o'look(ing)	Overlook(ing)
o'night	Overnight
o'skts	Outskirts
PO	Post office
poss	Possible, possibly
pt	Part
R	Right
rd	Road or street
rec	Recommend/ed
recep	Reception
red	Reduced, reduction (for)
reg	Regular
req	Required
RH	Right-hand
rlwy	Railway line
rm	Room
rndabt	Roundabout
rte	Route
rv/rvside	River/riverside
S	South
san facs	Sanitary facilities ie wc, showers, etc
snr citizens	Senior citizens
sep	Separate
sh	Short
sp	Sign post, signposted
sq	Square
ssn	Season
stn	Station
strt	Straight, straight ahead
sw	Swimming
thro	Through
TO	Tourist Office
tour ops	Tour operators
traff lts	Traffic lights
twd	Toward(s)
unrel	Unreliable
vg	Very good
vill	Village
W	West
w/end	Weekend
x-ing	Crossing
x-rds	Cross roads

Symbols Used

◆	Unspecified facilities for disabled guests check before arrival
⊞	Open all year
*	Last year site report received (see Campsite Entries in Introduction)

Caravanning Abroad – Advice For First-Timers

You're seasoned caravanners around Britain but the time has come to make that trip you've been dreaming of, and understandably you feel a little apprehensive at the thought of taking your caravan or motor caravan across the Channel for the first time.

The advice in this chapter is a summary of the comprehensive information contained elsewhere in this guide, and is designed to give you the confidence to take that first trip, and make it one of many enjoyable and rewarding holidays. Laws, customs, regulations and advice differ from country to country and you are strongly advised to study all the chapters in this Handbook section carefully, together with the relevant Country Introduction chapters for the countries you are planning to visit.

Before You Travel

Choosing Your Campsite

The golden rule is not to be too ambitious. The south of France or southern Spain are exciting destinations but on your first visit you will probably not want to travel too far from your port of arrival and there are many good quality sites near the main French Channel ports. If France does not appeal, think about Belgium or the Netherlands where English is widely spoken.

The golden rule is not to be too ambitious

If you use a daytime ferry crossing it is a good idea to spend your first night at a campsite relatively near your port of arrival in order to give yourself a little time to get used to driving on the right. You will then be fresh for an early start the next morning when traffic is relatively light.

Decide whether you want a site near the seaside or in the country, quiet or lively, with facilities for children or near specific interests, such as vineyards, chateaux etc. During the peak holiday season the volume of traffic and tourists might be daunting, but remember that in low season not all site facilities will be open. Advance booking is recommended if you do travel during the peak school holiday period in July and August, or over

© Robert Paul Van Beets
Used under licence from Shutterstock.com

Easter, and this is particularly true if you are visiting a popular tourist resort.

The chapter in this guide entitled Continental Campsites tells you what to expect and has suitably-worded letters in five languages to help you make your own campsite bookings.

Advance Booking Service

For peace of mind you may prefer to use the Caravan Club's Advance Booking Service which offers Club members a booking service to over 200 campsites throughout Europe. This service gives freedom and flexibility of travel while eliminating any language problems, international deposit payments or waiting for replies by letter or email. Furthermore, you will have the reassurance of a confirmed pitch reservation and pitch fees paid in advance.

The Club's Continental Caravanning brochure (available from November) gives full details of the ABS and of those sites to which it applies, as well as information on the Club's range of 'package' inclusive holidays for caravanners. Sites in the ABS may be booked via the Club's website, www.caravanclub.co.uk/overseas

All the sites in the Club's Advance Booking Service are listed in this guide and are marked 'ABS' in their site entries. The Caravan Club cannot make advance reservations for any other campsites listed in this guide.

Choosing Your Ferry Crossing

There is a wide choice of ferry operators and routes to the Continent and the use of long or short ferry crossings, or the Channel Tunnel, is a matter of personal preference and convenience. The Channel Tunnel and crossings from Dover to Calais are the quickest, but if you have a long drive from home to your departure port, you may prefer the chance to relax for a few hours and enjoy a meal on an overnight crossing, which means you arrive fresh at the other end. The chapter ***Ferries and the Channel Tunnel*** contains a list of ferry routes and additional information.

Make sure you know the overall length as well as the height of your vehicle(s); vehicle decks on some ferries have areas where height is restricted, and this should be checked when making your booking.

The Club's website has a direct link through to a number of the most popular ferry operators' reservations systems and Club members can make their own reservations while still taking advantage of the Club's negotiated offers and the ferry companies' own early booking offers – see www.caravanclub.co.uk/overseas

Insurance

All UK motor vehicle policies give you the legal minimum of insurance for EU countries, but it is important to check whether your comprehensive cover becomes third-party only when you leave the UK. It may be necessary to pay an additional premium for comprehensive cover abroad.

Having insurance for your vehicles does not cover other risks which may arise on holiday, for example, emergency medical and hospital expenses, loss or theft of personal belongings. The Caravan Club's Red Pennant Overseas Holiday Insurance gives you maximum protection from a variety of mishaps which might otherwise ruin your holiday and is tailor-made for the caravanner and motor caravanner. This is backed by the Club's own helpline with multi-lingual staff available 24 hours a day, 365 days a year.

If you are going to leave your home unoccupied for any length of time, check your house and contents insurance policies regarding any limitations or regulations.

You will find further details, information and advice in the chapter ***Insurance*** or see www.caravanclub.co.uk/redpennant and www.caravanclub.co.uk/insurance

Documents

All members of your party must have a valid passport, including babies and children. The chapter ***Documents*** sets out the requirements and explains how to apply for a passport.

In some countries passports must be carried at all times as a form of photographic identification

A photocard driving licence or the pink EU version of the UK driving licence is universally acceptable. However, holders of an old-style green UK licence or a Northern Irish licence issued prior to 1991 are recommended to update it to a photocard licence, or obtain an International Driving Permit (IDP) to accompany their old-style UK licence in order to avoid any difficulties while abroad.

In some countries passports must be carried at all times as a form of photographic identification. In any event you should keep a separate photocopy of your passport details and leave a copy of the personal details page with a relative or friend.

You should carry your vehicle's Vehicle Registration Certificate (V5C), insurance certificate and MOT roadworthiness certificate, if applicable, together with a copy of your CRIS document in respect of your caravan.

See the chapter ***Documents*** in the section ***PLANNING AND TRAVELLING*** for full details.

Vehicles and Equipment

Ensure your car and caravan are properly serviced and ready for the journey, paying particular attention to tyres and tyre pressures. Ensure caravan tyres are suited to the maximum weight of the caravan and the maximum permitted speed when travelling abroad – see the chapter ***Motoring – Equipment*** and the Technical Information chapter of the Caravan Club's UK Sites Directory and Handbook.

Take a well-equipped spares and tool kit. Spare bulbs, a warning triangle (two are required in some countries), a fire extinguisher and a first-aid kit are legal requirements in many European countries. Nearside and offside extending mirrors are essential, together with a spare tyre/wheel for both car and caravan.

In many countries drivers who leave their vehicle when it is stationary on the carriageway must by law wear a reflective jacket or waistcoat, but it is sensible to do so in any country. A second jacket is a common-sense requirement for any passenger who also gets out of your vehicle to assist. Keep the jackets readily to hand inside your vehicle, not in the boot.

If they are likely to dazzle other road users, headlights must be adjusted to deflect to the right instead of the left using suitable beam deflectors or (in some cases) a built-in adjustment system. Even when not planning to drive at night, you will need to switch your headlights on in tunnels or if visibility is poor. Some countries require dipped headlights to be used during daylight hours. Bulbs are more likely to fail with constant use and you are recommended to carry spares, whether it is a legal requirement or not.

Money

It is a good idea to carry a small amount of foreign currency, including loose change, for countries you are travelling through in case of emergencies, or when shopping. In addition you may take travellers' cheques, a travel money card or use your credit or debit card on arrival at your destination to obtain cash from cash dispensers, which are often found in supermarkets as well as outside banks. The rate of exchange is often as good as anywhere else; look for the same symbol on the machine as on your debit or credit card.

Travellers' cheques are not welcome in some countries and credit cards issued by British banks may not be universally accepted, so it is wise to check before incurring expenditure. In some countries you may be asked to produce your passport for photographic identification purposes when paying by credit card.

*See the chapter **Money** and Country Introductions for further information.*

On the Journey

Ferries

Report to the check-in desk at the ferry port or Eurotunnel terminal allowing plenty of time, say an hour, before the scheduled boarding time. As you approach the boarding area after passport control and Customs, staff will direct you to the waiting area or the boarding lane for your departure. As you are driving a 'high vehicle' you may be required to board first, or last. While waiting to board stay with your vehicle(s) so that you can board immediately when instructed to do so. Virtually all ferries operate a 'drive on – drive off' system and you will not normally be required to perform any complicated manoeuvres, nor to reverse.

Eurotunnel will not accept vehicles powered by LPG or dual-fuel vehicles

While waiting, turn off the 12v electricity supply to your fridge to prevent your battery going flat. Most fridges will stay adequately cool for several hours, as long as they are not opened. If necessary, place an ice pack or two (as used in cool boxes) in the fridge. You may be required to show that your gas supply has been turned off correctly.

Neither the ferry companies nor Eurotunnel permit you to carry spare petrol cans, empty or full, and Eurotunnel will not accept vehicles powered by LPG or dual-fuel vehicles. However Eurotunnel will accept vehicles fitted with LPG tanks for the purposes of heating, lighting, cooking or refrigeration, subject to certain conditions.

If your vehicle has been converted and is powered by LPG, some ferry companies require a certificate showing that the conversion has been carried out to the manufacturer's specification.

You will be instructed when to drive onto the ferry and, once on board, will be directed to the appropriate position. Treat ferry access ramps with caution, as they may be steep and/or uneven. Drive slowly as there may be a risk of grounding of any low point on the tow bar or caravan hitch. If your ground clearance is low, consider whether removing your stabiliser and/or jockey wheel would help.

Once boarded apply your car and caravan brakes. Vehicles are often parked close together and many passengers leaving their vehicles will be carrying bags for the crossing. It may, therefore, be wise to remove extended rear view mirrors as they may get knocked out of adjustment or damaged.

Make sure your car and caravan are secure and that, wherever possible, belongings are out of sight. Ensure that items on roof racks or cycle carriers are difficult to remove – a long cable lock may be useful.

Note the number of the deck you are parked on and the number of the staircase you use. There is nothing more embarrassing than to discover, when you eventually return to find your vehicle(s) ready to disembark, that you are blocking other irate motorists in! You will not usually be permitted access to your vehicle(s) during the crossing so take everything you require with you, including passports, tickets and boarding cards.

On those ferry routes on which you are permitted to transport pets, animals are usually required to remain in their owners' vehicles or in kennels on the car deck. On longer ferry crossings you should make arrangements at the on-board Information Desk for permission to visit your pet at suitable intervals in order to check its well-being.

*See also **Pet Travel Scheme** under **Documents** in the section **PLANNING AND TRAVELLING**.*

If you have booked cabins or seats go to the Information Desk immediately after boarding to claim them. Many ferries have a selection of restaurants and cafés, a children's play area, even a cinema, disco or casino as well as a shop, to while away the time during the crossing. If you wish to use the main restaurant it may be advisable to make an early reservation.

Listen carefully to on-board announcements, one of which will be important safety information at the time of departure. A further announcement will be made when it is time to return to your vehicle(s). Allow plenty of time to get down to the car deck. Don't start your engine until vehicles immediately in front of you start to move. Once off the ferry you may want to pull over into a parking area to allow the queue of traffic leaving the ferry to clear.

Eurotunnel

If you have made an advance booking proceed to the signposted self check-in lanes. You will need to present the credit or debit card used when you made your booking. Having checked in you may, if you wish, visit the terminal to make any last minute purchases etc, and then follow signs to passport control and Customs. Your gas cylinder valves will be closed and sealed as a safety precaution and you will be asked to open the roof vents.

You will then join the waiting area allocated for your departure and will be directed onto the single-deck wagons of the train and told to park in gear with your brake on. You then stay in or around your car/motor caravan for the 35-minute journey but will not be allowed to use your caravan until arrival. Useful information and music are supplied via the on-board radio station. On arrival, close the roof vent and release the caravan brake and, when directed by the crew, drive off – remembering to drive on the right!

Motoring on the Continent

The chapters ***Motoring – Advice*** and ***Motoring – Equipment*** and the Country Introduction chapters cover all aspects of motoring on the Continent, but the following additional points may be helpful for nervous first-timers.

Most roads are not as busy as those in the UK, but avoid rush hours in larger towns. There are fewer lorries on the roads at weekends and, in France in particular, roads are quieter between noon and 2pm and good progress can often be made.

In your eagerness to reach your destination, don't attempt long distances in a single stint. Share the driving, if possible, and plan to break your journey overnight at a suitable campsite. There are thousands of sites listed in this guide and many are well-situated near motorways and main roads.

You are most likely to forget to drive on the right when pulling away from a parked position. It may be helpful to make yourself a sign and attach it to the dashboard to remind you to drive on the right. This can be removed before driving and replaced each time you stop. Alternatively, make a member of your party responsible for reminding the driver every time you start the car. Pay particular attention when turning left or when leaving a rest area, service station or campsite, and after passing through a one-way system.

Don't attempt long distances in a single stint

Make sure the road ahead is clear before overtaking. Stay well behind the vehicle in front and, if possible, have someone with good judgement in the left-hand seat to give you the 'all clear'.

Remember speed limit signs are in kilometres per hour, not miles per hour.

You will be charged tolls to use many European motorways. Credit cards are widely accepted in payment, but not always. The Country Introduction chapters contain details. Motorways provide convenient service stations and areas for a rest and a picnic en-route but, for your own safety, find an established campsite for an overnight stop.

Beware STOP signs. You will encounter more of them than you find in the UK. Coming to a complete halt is compulsory in most Continental countries and failure to do so may result in a fine.

The maximum legal level of alcohol in the blood in most European countries is much lower than that permitted in the UK. It is better not to drink at all when driving as penalties are severe.

If you are unfortunate enough to be involved in a road accident, take some photographs to back up the written description on your claim form.

During Your Stay

Arriving at the Campsite

Go to the site reception and fill in any registration forms required. You may need to leave your Camping Card International/Camping Card

Scandinavia or passport. In some countries where you must carry your passport at all times as a form of photographic identification, a CCI is essential.

If you have not booked in advance it is perfectly acceptable to ask to have a look around the site before deciding whether to stay or accept a particular pitch.

Pitches are usually available when the site re-opens after the lunch break and not normally before this time. Aim to arrive before 7pm or you may find site reception closed; if this is the case you will probably find a member of staff on duty in the bar. It is essential to arrive before 10pm as the gates or barriers on most sites are closed for the night at this time. If you are delayed, remember to let the site know so that they will keep your pitch. When leaving, you will usually need to vacate your pitch by midday at the latest.

If you have any complaints, take them up with site staff there and then

Many sites offer various sporting activities, such as tennis, fishing, watersports, horseriding and bicycle hire, as well as entertainment programmes for children and/or adults in high season. Many also have a snack bar, restaurant or bar. Restrictions may apply to the use of barbecues because of the risk of fire; always check with site staff before lighting up.

Dogs are welcome on many campsites but some sites will not allow them at all, or during the high season, or will require them to be on a lead at all times. Check in advance. In popular tourist areas local regulations may ban dogs from beaches during the summer months.

If you have any complaints, take them up with site staff there and then. It is pointless complaining after the event, when something could have been done to improve matters at the time.

Electricity and Gas

Calor Gas is not available on the Continent. Campingaz is widely available but, unless your caravan is relatively new and already fitted with a special bulkhead-mounted regulator, you will need an adaptor to connect to a Calor-type butane regulator. Alternatively carry sufficient gas for your stay, subject to the cross-Channel operator's regulations which may restrict you to three, two or even only one gas cylinder. Check when making your booking.

Voltage on most sites is usually 220v or 230v nominal but may be lower. Most UK mains appliances are rated at 220v to 240v and usually work satisfactorily. You will need your mains lead that you use in the UK as many sites have the European standard EN60309-2 connectors, (formerly known as CEE17) which your UK 3-pin connector will fit. On some sites you may need a continental 2-pin adaptor available from UK caravan accessory shops.

Caravanners may encounter the problem known as reverse polarity. This is where the site's 'live' line connects to the caravan's 'neutral' and vice versa and is due to different standards of plug and socket wiring that exist in other countries. The Club recommends checking the polarity immediately on connection, using a polarity tester, obtainable from a caravan accessory shop before you leave home.

The caravan mains electrical installation should not be used while a reversed polarity situation exists. Ask the site manager if you can use an alternative socket or bollard, as the problem may be restricted to that particular socket only. Frequent travellers to the Continent who are electrically competent often make themselves up an adaptor, clearly marked reversed polarity with the live and neutral wires reversed. This can be tried in place of the standard connector, to see if the electricity supply then reverts to 'normal'.

*See the chapter **Electricity and Gas** and **Country Introductions** for further information.*

Food and Water

There is a limit to the amount of food which may be imported into other countries, although Customs will rarely be interested unless their attention is drawn to it. But in the light of recent animal health concerns in the UK, authorities abroad will understandably take a cautious approach and there is no guarantee that meat and dairy products, if found, will not be confiscated by Customs officers.

You should, therefore, be reasonable in the amount of food you take with you. Experience of foreign cuisine is part of the enjoyment of a holiday and there is little point in taking large supplies of food other than basics or children's special favourites.

On the Continent generally it is sometimes difficult to obtain supplies of fresh milk, bread and cereals at campsite shops, particularly outside the summer season. It may be useful to pack a supply of basic items such as tea, coffee, fruit squash, cereals and powdered or long-life milk. When food shopping it may be helpful to take your own supply of carrier bags and a cool box in hot weather.

In the countries covered by this guide drinking water is clean and safe, but you may find the taste different from your own local mains supply. Bottled water is cheap and widely available.

Insect Control

Mosquitoes and flies can be a serious nuisance as well as a danger to health. Although an effective insect repellent is recommended as the simplest form of protection, insect screens on windows, door and roof vents will provide complete protection. Most modern caravans have fly screens installed as part of the window roller-blind system. Older caravans may be equipped using DIY kits available from most caravan accessory shops or DIY stores.

There are numerous sprays on the market to kill flies, ants and mosquitoes and insect repellent coils left burning at night are also an effective preventative device, as are anti-insect tablets which slot into a special electric heating element.

Medical Matters

Before leaving home obtain a European Health Insurance Card (EHIC) which entitles you to emergency health care in the EU and some other countries. An EHIC is required by each individual family member, so allow enough time before your departure to obtain them. You can apply online on www.ehic.org.uk or by telephoning 0845 6062030 or by obtaining an application form from a post office.

You are also recommended to obtain a copy of the Department of Health's leaflet, T7.1 Health Advice for Travellers which is downloadable from www.dh.gov.uk, email: dh@prolog.uk.com or call 08701 555455. Copies are also available in post offices. Alternatively, you will find advice and information for all the countries listed in this guide on the NHS Choices website, www.nhs.uk

Check with your GP the generic name of any prescription medicines you are taking. If you need more or lose your supply, the generic name will help a doctor or pharmacist to identify them. Keep receipts for any medication or treatment purchased abroad, plus the labels from the medicines, as these will be required if you make a claim on your travel insurance on returning home.

For further advice and information see the chapter ***Medical Matters****.*

Safety and Security

Safety is largely your own responsibility – taking sensible precautions and being aware of possible hazards won't spoil your holiday, but a careless attitude might.

A comprehensive chapter entitled Safety and Security, together with specific information relevant to particular countries in the appropriate Country Introduction chapters, cover all aspects of your own and your family's personal safety while on holiday. You are strongly advised to read these sections carefully and follow the advice contained in them.

Other Information

Tourist Boards

Many European countries maintain tourist offices in the UK which will supply information on their respective countries. In addition, a great deal of information can be obtained from tourist boards' websites. Address and contact details are given in each Country Introduction.

Route Planning

An organisation called Keep Moving (www.keepmoving.co.uk) provides information on UK roads including routes to ferry ports on 09003 401100 or 401100 from a mobile phone. Both the AA and RAC have useful websites offering a route planning service with access for non-members: www.theaa.com and www.rac.co.uk

Satellite Navigation

GPS co-ordinates are given for many site entries in this guide and others will be added over time. Your sat nav appliance is a valuable aid in finding a campsite in an area you are not familiar with, but it is important to realise that such systems are not perfect. It is probably wise, therefore, to use your sat nav in conjunction with the printed directions to sites in this guide which are often compiled using local knowledge to pinpoint the most appropriate route, together with an up-to-date map or atlas.

For further advice and information on the use of satellite navigation devices see the chapter ***Motoring – Equipment****.*

Checklist

It is assumed that users of this guide have some experience of caravanning and are well aware of the domestic and personal items necessary for trips away in their caravans, and of the checks to be made to vehicles before setting off. The Caravan Club's Technical Office will supply a copy of a leaflet 'Things to Take' to Club members on request, or you can download it from www.caravanclub.co.uk

The following is intended merely as an 'aide memoire' and covers some of those necessary items:

Car

Extending mirrors

Fire extinguisher

First aid kit

Fuses

Headlight converters/deflectors

Jack and wheelbrace

Mobile phone charger

Nationality stickers – GB or IRL (car and caravan)

Puncture kit (sealant)

Radiator hose

Reflective safety jacket(s)

Satellite navigation device

Snow chains (if winter caravanning)

Spare bulbs

Spare key

Spare parts, eg fan belt

Spare wheel/tyre

Stabiliser

Tool kit

Tow ball cover

Tow rope

Warning triangle (2 for Spain)

Caravan

Awning and groundsheet

Bucket

Chemical toilet and fluid/sachets

Corner steady tool and pads

Coupling lock

Electrical extension lead and adaptor(s)

Extra long motor caravan water hose pipe

Fire extinguisher

Gas cylinders

Gas regulator (Campingaz)

Gas adaptor and hoses (where regulator is fitted to the caravan)

Hitch and/or wheel lock

Insect screens

Levelling blocks

Mains polarity tester

Nose weight gauge

Peg mallet

Spare bulbs, fuses and lengths of wire

Spare key

Spare 7-pin plug

Spare water pump

Spare wheel/tyre

Spirit level

Step and doormat

Submersible water pump

Water containers - waste/fresh

Water hoses – waste/fresh

Wheel clamp

Documents and Papers

Address book, contact telephone numbers

Camping Card International/Camping Card Scandinavia

Car/caravan/motor caravan insurance certificates

Campsite booking confirmation(s)

Caravan Club membership card

Caravan Europe guide book

Copy of your CRIS document

Credit/debit cards, contact numbers in the event of loss

Driving licence (photocard or green/pink EU version)

European Health Insurance Card (EHIC)

European Accident Statement

Ferry ticket or booking reference and timetable

Foreign currency

Holiday travel insurance documents (Red Pennant)

International Driving Permit (if applicable)

International Motor Insurance Certificate, ie Green Card (if applicable)

Letter of authorisation from vehicle owner (if applicable)

Maps and guides

MOT roadworthiness certificate (if applicable)

NHS medical card

Passport (+ photocopy of details page) and visas (if applicable)

Pet's passport and addresses of vets abroad

Phrase books

Telephone card

Travellers' cheques and/or travel money card

Vehicle Registration Certificate V5C

Continental Campsites

Introduction

There are many thousands of excellent campsites throughout Europe, belonging to local municipalities, camping, touring or automobile clubs, families or companies. Most sites are open to all-comers but a few are reserved for their own members.

Compared with Caravan Club sites in the UK, pitches may be small and 80 square metres is not uncommon, particularly in Spain, Italy, Germany, Portugal and Switzerland. This may present problems for large outfits and/or with the erection of awnings. Elsewhere, for example in the south of France in summer, it may be difficult to erect an awning because of hard ground conditions.

Generally the approaches and entrances to campsites are well signposted, but often only with a tent or caravan symbol or with the word 'Camping', rather than the site's full name.

There are usually sinks for washing-up and laundry and many sites provide washing machines and dryers. Most have a shop in high season, even if only for basic groceries, but many stock a wide variety of items. Often they have a restaurant or snack bar, a swimming pool, playground, TV/games room and other leisure facilities. Occasionally there may be a car wash, petrol pumps, hairdresser, sauna, solarium, internet access point or wifi availability, bureau de change or a tourist information office.

In the high season all campsite facilities are usually open and some sites offer organised entertainment for children and adults as well as local excursions. However, bear in mind that in the months of July and August, toilets and shower facilities and pitch areas will be under the greatest pressure.

Booking A Campsite

It is advisable to pre-book pitches on campsites during the high season months of July and August. If you are planning a long stay then contact campsites early in the year (January is not too early). Some sites impose a minimum length of stay during this time in order to guarantee their business. Usually there are one or two unreserved pitches available for overnight tourers.

Often it is possible to book directly via a campsite's website using a credit or debit card to pay a deposit if required. Otherwise write, enclosing an

© Mark Lijesen
Used under licence from Shutterstock.com

International Reply Coupon, obtainable from main post offices and valid virtually all over the world, or letters may be ignored. A word of warning: **some campsites regard the deposit as a booking fee and will not deduct this amount from your final bill.**

Suitably-worded letters in English, German, French, Spanish and Italian are provided at the end of this chapter to assist you when communicating with campsites. Responses are also provided, in the same five languages, which should encourage site operators to reply. In any event it is worth remembering that rarely will a site reserve a special place for you. The acceptance of a reservation merely means you will be guaranteed a pitch; the best being allocated first or for repeat visitors. Not all campsites accept advance bookings.

Pre-booking sites en route to holiday destinations is not essential, but if you do not book ahead you should plan to arrive for the night no later than 4pm (even earlier at popular resorts), in order to secure a good pitch, since after that time sites fill up quickly.

Caravan Club Advance Booking Service

The Caravan Club's Travel Services offer Club members a campsite Advance Booking Service (to which terms and conditions apply) to over 200 campsites throughout Europe. This service gives freedom and flexibility of travel but with the reassurance of a confirmed pitch reservation and pitch fees paid in advance. Full details of this service, plus information on special offers with ferry operators, the Club's Tours and Excursions programme (some specifically aimed at motor caravanners) and details of Red Pennant Overseas Holiday Insurance appear in the Club's Continental

Caravanning brochure – telephone 01342 327410 to request a copy, or visit www.caravanclub.co.uk/overseas

Booking an ABS site through the Caravan Club gives you a price guarantee – whatever happens to exchange rates, there will be no surcharges.

All ABS sites are listed in this guide and are marked 'ABS' in their site entries. Many of them can be booked via the Club's website, www.caravanclub.co.uk. **The Caravan Club cannot make advance reservations for any other campsites listed in this guide.**

Camping Cheques

The Caravan Club operates a low season scheme in association with Camping Cheques offering Club members flexible touring holidays. The scheme covers approximately 560 sites in 23 European countries, plus Morocco.

Camping Cheques are supplied as part of a package which includes return ferry fare and a minimum of seven Camping Cheques. Each Camping Cheque is valid for one night's low season stay for two people, including car and caravan/motor caravan/trailer tent, electricity and one pet. Full details are contained in the Club's Continental Caravanning brochure.

Those sites which feature in the Camping Cheques scheme and which are listed in this guide are marked 'CChq' in their site entries.

Caravan Storage Abroad

The advantages of storing your caravan on a campsite on the Continent are obvious, not least being the avoidance of the long tow to your destination, and a saving in ferry and fuel costs. Some campsites advertise a long-term storage facility or you may negotiate with a site which appeals to you.

However, there are pitfalls and understandably insurers in the UK are reluctant to insure a caravan which will be out of the country most of the time. There is also the question of invalidity of the manufacturer's warranty for caravans less than three years old if the supplying dealer does not carry out annual servicing.

*See also **Insurance** in the section **PLANNING AND TRAVELLING.***

Electricity Supply

For your own safety you are strongly advised to read the chapter ***Electricity and Gas*** under ***DURING YOUR STAY***

Many campsites now include electricity and/or shower facilities in their 'per night' price and where possible this has been included in site entries. Where these are not included, a generous allowance should be made in your budget. It is not unknown for sites to charge up to the equivalent of £4 per night or more for electric hook-ups and £2 per shower. In winter sports areas, charges for electricity are generally higher in winter.

The system for charging for electricity varies from country to country and you may pay a flat daily rate or, notably in Germany and Austria, a connection charge plus a metered charge for electricity consumed. The Country Introduction chapters contain specific information on electricity supply.

Facilities and Site Description

Information is given about the characteristics of the campsite and availability of facilities on site or within a reasonable distance, as reported to the editor of this guide. Comments (in inverted commas) are those of caravanners visiting the site and it must be understood that people's tastes, opinions, priorities and expectations differ. Please also bear in mind that campsites change hands, opening dates and prices change and standards may rise or fall, depending on the season.

Facilities Out of Season

During the low season (this can be any time except July and early August) campsites may operate with limited facilities and shops, swimming pools, bars and restaurants may be closed. A municipal site warden may visit in the morning and/or evening only to collect fees which are often negotiable during the low season.

Sanitary Facilities

Facilities normally include toilet and shower blocks with shower cubicles, wash basins and razor sockets but toilets are not always fitted with seats, for ease of cleaning. The abbreviation 'wc' indicates the normal, pedestal type of toilet found in the UK. Some sites have footplate 'squatter' toilets and, where this is known, this is indicated by the abbreviation 'cont', ie continental.

It is recommended that you take your own universal flat plug (to fit all basin sizes) and toilet paper. During the low season it is not uncommon for only a few toilet and shower cubicles to be in use on a 'unisex' basis and they may not be cleaned as frequently as they are during the site's busy season. Hot water, other than for showers, may not be generally available.

In recent years many campsites have upgraded their sanitary facilities in line with visitors' expectations, but you may find that some are still unheated and may not offer items such as pegs on which to hang clothes/towels, or shelves for soap and shampoo. Rarely, there may be no shower curtains or shower cubicle doors and hence little or no privacy.

Waste Disposal

Site entries in this guide indicate (when known) where a campsite has a chemical disposal facility and/or motor caravan service point, which is assumed to include a waste (grey) water dump station and toilet cassette-emptying point.

European caravanners in general tend to prefer to use a site's toilet and shower facilities, together with its dishwashing and vegetable preparation areas, more than their British counterparts who prefer to use their own facilities. Caravanners used to the level of facilities for the disposal of waste water on Caravan Club sites may well find that facilities on Continental campsites are not of the same standard.

Wastemaster-style emptying points are not common

Chemical disposal points are occasionally difficult to locate and may be fixed at a high level requiring some strenuous lifting of cassettes in order to empty them. Or disposal may simply be down a toilet – continental or otherwise. Wastemaster-style emptying points are not common and you may have to empty your Wastemaster down the drain under a drinking water tap. On rare occasions, this is also the only place to rinse a toilet cassette! You may like to carry a bottle of disinfectant spray to use on water taps if necessary.

Formaldehyde-based chemical cleaning products are banned in many countries. If in doubt about the composition of the product you use and its use abroad, it is probably wiser to buy products which are commonly available in caravan accessory shops at your destination.

At some campsites, notably in Switzerland and Germany, you may have to purchase special plastic bags for the disposal of rubbish, or pay a daily 'rubbish' or 'environmental' charge. Generally you may find that you are expected to use recycling bins placed around the campsite.

Finding a Campsite

Detailed directions are given for all campsites listed in this guide and many also give GPS co-ordinates. Where GPS readings are not known full street addresses are given, wherever possible, to facilitate programming your own satellite navigation device.

*See the chapter **Motoring – Equipment** in the section **PLANNING AND TRAVELLING** for more information on satellite navigation.*

Lunch Breaks

Some campsites close for a lengthy lunch break, sometimes as long as three hours, and occasionally there is no access for vehicles during this period. In addition, use of vehicles within the site may be restricted during certain hours to ensure a period of quiet. Check individual campsite regulations on arrival.

Motor Caravanners

Increasingly towns and villages across Europe are providing dedicated overnight or short stay areas specifically for motor caravanners, many with good security, electricity, water and waste facilities. These are known as 'Aires de Services' or 'Stellplatz' and are usually well-signposted with a motor caravan pictogram.

Likewise, to cater for this growing market, many campsites in popular tourist areas have separate overnight areas of hard standing with appropriate facilities often just outside the main campsite area. Fees are generally very reasonable.

A number of organisations, for example ADAC (Germany), the Fédération Française de Camping et de Caravaning and Bel-air Camping-Caravaning (France) publish guides listing thousands of these sites in several countries. A publication, 'All the Aires – France' published by Vicarious Books lists 1,600 'aires' in towns and villages throughout France and is available from the Club's book shop – see www.caravanclub.co.uk/books and search for 'aires'. Vicarious Books also publish guides to 'aires' in Spain and Portugal, and Benelux and Scandinavia – see www.vicariousbooks.co.uk, tel 0131 208 3333.

For reasons of security the Caravan Club strongly advises against spending the night on petrol station service areas, ferry terminal car parks or isolated 'aires de repos' or 'aires de services' along motorways. *See the chapter **Safety and Security** in the section **DURING YOUR STAY.***

Where known, information on the availability of public transport within easy reach of a campsite, as reported by caravanners, is given in the site entries in this guide.

Municipal Campsites

Municipal sites are found in towns and villages all over Europe, in particular in France, and in recent years many municipalities have improved standards on their sites while continuing to offer good value for money. However, on some municipal sites you may still find that sanitary facilities are basic and old-fashioned, even though they may be clean. Bookings for a municipal site can usually be made during office hours through the local town hall ('Mairie' in France) or tourist office.

Outside the high season you may find significant numbers of seasonal workers, market traders and itinerants resident on sites – sometimes in a separate, designated area. In most cases their presence does not cause other visitors any problem but where they are not welcome some sites refuse entry to caravans with twin-axles ('deux essieux' in French) or restrict entry by caravan height, weight or length, or charge a hefty additional fee. Check if any restrictions apply if booking in advance. Recent visitors report that bona fide caravanners with twin-axle or over-height/weight/length caravans may be allowed entry, and/or may not be charged the higher published tariff, but this is negotiable with site staff at the time of arrival.

When approaching a town you may find that municipal sites are not always named and signposts may simply state 'Camping' or show a tent or caravan symbol.

Naturist Campsites

Details of several naturist sites are included in this guide, mainly in France, Spain, Germany and Croatia, and they are shown with the word 'naturist' after their site name. Some, shown as 'part naturist' simply have separate beach areas for naturists. Visitors to naturist sites aged 16 and over usually (but not always) require an INF card or Naturist Licence and this is covered by membership of British Naturism (tel 01604 620361 or www.british-naturism.org.uk). Alternatively, holiday membership is available on arrival at any recognised naturist site (a passport-size photograph is required). When looking for a site you will find that naturist campsites generally display the initials FNF, INF or FKK on their signs.

Opening Dates

Opening dates (where known) are given for campsites in this guide, many of which are open all year. Sometimes sites may close without notice for refurbishment work or because of a change of ownership or simply because of a lack of visitors or a period of bad weather. When a site is officially closed, owners who live on site may accept visitors for an overnight or short stay if, for example, they are working on site.

Outside the high season it is always best to contact campsites in advance as owners, particularly in Spain and the south of France, have a tendency to shut campsites when business is slack. Otherwise you may arrive to find the gates of an 'all year' campsite very firmly closed. Municipal campsites' published opening dates cannot always be relied on at the start and end of the season. It is advisable to phone ahead or arrive early enough to be able to find an alternative site if your first choice is closed.

Pets on Campsites

*See also **Pet Travel Scheme** under **Documents** and **Holiday Insurance for Pets** under **Insurance** in the section **PLANNING AND TRAVELLING.***

Dogs are welcome on many Continental campsites provided they conform to legislation and vaccination requirements, and are kept under control.

Be aware, however, that some countries' authorities may not permit entry to certain types or breeds of dogs and may have rules relating to the size or breed of dogs permitted entry or to matters such as muzzling. You are advised to contact the appropropriate authorities of the countries you plan to visit via their embassies in London before making travel arrangements for your dog.

Campsites usually make a daily charge for dogs, but this may be waived in low season. Dog owners must conform to site regulations concerning keeping dogs on a lead, dog-walking areas and fouling and may find restricted areas within a site where dogs are not permitted. There may also be limits on the number of dogs – often one per pitch – or type or breed of dog accepted. Some campsites will not allow dogs at all, or will require them to be on a lead at all times, or will not allow them during the peak holiday season. Be prepared to present documentary evidence of vaccinations on arrival at a campsite. In popular tourist areas local regulations may ban dogs from beaches during the summer.

Think very carefully before taking your pet abroad

Think very carefully before taking your pet abroad. Dogs used to the UK's temperate climate may find it difficult to cope with prolonged periods of hot weather. In addition, there are diseases transmitted by ticks, caterpillars, mosquitoes or sandflies, particularly in southern Europe, to which dogs from the UK have no natural resistance. Consult your vet about preventative treatment well in advance of your holiday. You need to be sure that your dog is healthy enough to travel and, if in any doubt, it may be in its best interests to leave it at home.

Visitors to southern Spain and Portugal, parts of central France and northern Italy from mid-winter onwards should be aware of the danger to dogs of pine processionary caterpillars. Dogs should be kept away from pine trees if possible or fitted with a muzzle that prevents the nose and mouth from touching the ground. This will also protect against poisoned bait sometimes used by farmers and hunters.

In the event that your pet is taken ill abroad a campsite will usually have information about local vets. Failing that, most countries have a telephone directory similar to the Yellow Pages, together with online versions such as www.pagesjaunes.fr for France or www.paginas-amarillas.es for Spain.

Most European countries require pets to wear a collar at all times identifying their owners. If your pet goes missing, report the matter to the local police and the local branch of that country's animal welfare organisation.

Prices

Campsite prices per night (for a car, caravan and two adults) are shown in local currencies. In those EU Member States included in this guide – Czech Republic, Denmark, Hungary and Poland – where euros are not the official currency they are usually readily accepted for payment of campsite fees and other goods and services, as they are in Croatia.

If you stay on site after midday you may be charged for an extra day

Payment of campsite fees should be made at least two hours before departure. Remember that if you stay on site after midday you may be charged for an extra day. Many campsites shown in this guide as accepting credit card payments may not do so for an overnight or short stay because of high transaction charges. Alternatively, a site will impose a minimum limit or will accept credit cards only in the peak season. It is always advisable to check the form of payment required when you check in.

On arrival at a campsite which has an automatic barrier at the entrance you may be asked for a deposit, returnable on departure, for the use of a swipe card to operate the barrier. The amount will vary from site to site; €25 or €30 is usual.

It is common for campsites to impose extra charges for the use of swimming pools and other leisure facilities, for showers and laundry facilities as well as the erection of awnings. Most impose a daily charge for dogs, at least in the high season.

Registering on Arrival

On arrival at a campsite it is usual to have to register in accordance with local authority requirements, and to produce an identity document which the campsite office may retain during your stay. Most campsites now accept the Camping Card International (or Camping Card Scandinavia) instead of a passport and, where known, their site entries are marked CCI or CCS. CCIs are available to Caravan Club members at a cost of £4.95 (free if you take out the Club's Red Pennant Overseas Holiday Insurance).

Alternatively, a photocopy of your passport may be acceptable and it is a good idea to carry a few copies with you to avoid depositing your passport and to speed up the check-in process.

If you do deposit your passport, make sure you have sufficient money for your stay if you are relying on travellers' cheques, as a passport must be produced when cashing them.

Sites' Contact Details

Telephone numbers are given for most campsites listed in this guide, together with fax numbers and website and email addresses where known. The telephone numbers assume you are in the country concerned and the initial zero should be dialled, where applicable. If you are telephoning from outside the country the initial zero is usually (but not always) omitted. For more details see individual Country Introductions or the chapter ***Keeping in Touch***.

General Advice

Most campsites close from 10pm until 7am or 8am. However, late night arrival areas are sometimes provided for late travellers. Motor caravanners, in particular, should check the gate/barrier closing time before going out for the evening in their vehicle. Check out time is usually between 10am and noon. Advise reception staff if you need to leave very early, for example to catch a ferry.

For security reasons many campsites have installed card operated entry gates or barriers. You will usually have to pay a deposit (usually cash) for a key or card to operate the barrier.

If possible inspect the site and facilities before booking in. If your pitch is allocated at check-in, ask to see it first, checking conditions and access, as marked or hedged pitches can sometimes be difficult for large outfits. Riverside pitches can be delightful but keep an eye on water levels; in periods of heavy rain these may rise rapidly and the ground become boggy.

It is usual for campsites to make a daily charge to accommodate children. It is quite common for site owners, particularly in France, to charge the full adult daily rate for children from as young as three years.

Local authorities in some countries impose a tourist tax on all people staying in hotels and on campsites during the peak holiday season. This averages around the equivalent of 50 pence per night per person. Similarly, VAT may be payable on top of your campsite fees. These charges are not usually included in prices listed in this guide.

Speed limits on site are usually restricted to 10 km/h (6 mph). You may be asked to park your car in an area away from your caravan.

French regulations ban the wearing of boxer shorts-style swimming trunks in pools on the grounds of hygiene. This rule may be strictly enforced by inspectors who have the power to close a site's swimming pool. As a result site owners have the right to insist on the wearing of conventional (brief-style) swimming trunks.

The use of the term 'statics' in the campsite reports in this guide in many instances refers to long-term seasonal pitches, chalets, cottages and cabins as well as mobile homes.

Complaints

If you have a complaint take it up with site staff or owners at the time so that it can be dealt with promptly. It is pointless complaining after the event, when action to improve matters could have been taken at the time. In France, if your complaint cannot be settled directly with the campsite, and if you are sure you are within your rights, you may take the matter up with the Préfecture of the local authority in question.

The Caravan Club has no control or influence over day to day campsite operations or administration. Except in the case of a small number of sites with which it is contracted (marked ABS in site entries) and on which it has made a booking for you it cannot intervene in any dispute you may have with a particular site.

Specimen Site Booking Letters

See the following pages and Booking a Campsite earlier in this section. The website http://uk.babelfish.yahoo.com/ allows simple translations into a number of languages which may be useful when communicating with campsites.

Site Booking Letter – English

Date: Address (block caps)..

....

....

Tel No: (0044) ....

Fax No: (0044) ....

Email ....

Dear Sir/Madam

I wish to make a reservation as follows:

Arriving (date and month)................ **Departing** (date and month)................ (........nights)

Adults .... **Children (+ ages)** ....

Car ☐ **Caravan** ☐ **Motor Caravan** ☐ **Trailertent** ☐

Electrical Hook-up ☐ **Awning** ☐ **Extra tent** ☐

I look forward to an early reply and enclose an International Reply Coupon and addressed envelope. When replying please advise all charges and deposit required. I look forward to meeting you and visiting your site.

Yours faithfully,

[Name in block capitals after signature]

Caravan Club Membership No......................

✂---

Reply

Date: Address...

....

....

Dear Mr/Mrs/Ms ....

Thank you for your reservation from .... to .... (........ nights).

- **YES, OK** – I am pleased to confirm your reservation (with/without electrical hook-up) and look forward to welcoming you.
- **NO, SORRY** – I regret that the site is fully booked for the dates you request.

Yours faithfully

....

Site Booking Letter – French

Date: Adresse (lettres majuscules)..

....

....

Tél : (0044)..

Fax : (0044)..

Email..

Monsieur/Madame

J'aimerais désire effectuer la réservation suivante :

Arrivée (jour et mois) .... **Départ** (jour et mois)..................... (.........nuits)

Adultes .... **Enfants (+ âges)** ....

Voiture ☐ **Caravane** ☐ **Camping car** ☐ **Tente-remorque** ☐

Branchement électrique ☐ **Auvent** ☐ **Tente supplémentaire** ☐

Ci-joint un coupon-réponse international et une enveloppe avec mon adresse. En vous remerciant par avance pour votre réponse je vous demanderais de bien vouloir me communiquer vos tarifs complets ainsi que le montant des arrhes à verser.

En attendant le plaisir de faire votre connaissance et de séjourner sur votre terrain, je vous prie de croire, Monsieur/Madame, à l'assurance de mes sentiments les meilleurs.

(Nom en lettres majuscules après la signature)

No. d'adhérent du Caravan Club ....

✂---

Réponse

Date: Adresse ....

....

....

Monsieur/Madame/Mademoiselle

J'accuse réception de votre bulletin de réservation pour la période

du...................... au ....(........nuits).

- **OUI** – Je confirme votre réservation (avec/sans branchement électrique) en attendant le plaisir de faire votre connaissance.
- **NON** – Je suis au regret de vous informer que le terrain est complet pendant la période de votre choix.

Veuillez croire, Monsieur/Madame/Mademoiselle, à l'assurance de mes sentiments les meilleurs.

....

Site Booking Letter – German

Datum: Anschrift (in Großbuchstaben)..

....

....

Telefonnummer.: (0044)..

Faxnummer: (0044)...

Email ....

Sehr geehrter Herr/sehr geehrte Dame

Ich möchte wie folgt reservieren:

Ankunft (Tag und Monat) .... **Abreise** (Tag und Monat).................... (... Nächte)

Erwachsene .... Kinder (in Alter von) ....

Auto ☐ **Caravan** ☐ **Wohnmobil** ☐ **Klappwohnwagen** ☐

Strom ☐ **Vordach** ☐ **Extra Zelt** ☐

Ich sehe einer baldigen Antwort entgegen und lege einen internationalen Antwortschein und addressierten Umschlag bei. Bitte führen Sie in Ihrem Antwortschreiben sämtliche erforderlichen Gebühren und Anzahlungen an. Ich freue mich auf den Aufenthalt auf Ihrem Campingplatz und hoffe, Sie dort zu treffen.

Mit freundlichen Grüßen

(Unterschrift und Name in Großbuchstaben)

Caravan Club Mitgliednummer ....

✂---

Antwort

Datum: Anschrift: ....

....

....

....

Herrn/Frau/Fräulein..

Vielen Dank für Ihre Reservierung von .... bis .... (.......Übernachtungen).

- **JA, OK** – Ich kann Ihre Reservierung (mit/ohne elektr. Anschluß) bestätigen und freue mich, Sie hier zu begrüßen.
- **NEIN, LEIDER** – Ich bedaure, daß der Campingplatz für die von Ihnen gewünschte Zeit voll belegt ist.

Mit freundlichen Grüßen

....

Site Booking Letter – Spanish

Fecha: Dirección (letra de imprenta)..

....

....

Nº de tel.: (0044) ....

Nº de fax: (0044) ....

Email ....

Estimado Sr/Estimada Sra/Srta

Deseo realizar la siguiente reserva:

Llegada (fecha y mes) .... **Salida** (fecha y mes) .... (.......... noches)

Adultos .... **Niños** (+ edades) ....

Coche ☐ **Caravana** ☐ **Caravana de motor** ☐ **Tienda con remolque** ☐

Enganche eléctrico ☐ **Toldo** ☐ **Tienda adicional** ☐

Espero con interés recibir su confirmación y tengo el gusto de adjuntar un cupón de respuesta internacional y un sobre con mi dirección. Cuando responda tenga la amabilidad de indicar todos los recargos y depósitos necesarios. Espero con ilusión conocerle y visitar su cámping.

Atentamente:

[Nombre en letra de imprenta después de la firma]

No de socio del Caravan Club ....

✂---

Respuesta

Fecha: Dirección...

....

....

Estimado Sr/Estimada Sra/Srta

Agradecemos su reserva del .... al .... (........... noches).

- **SI** – Tenemos el gusto de confirmar su reserva (con/sin enganche eléctrico) y esperamos con ilusión darle la bienvenida.
- **LO SENTIMOS** – Desafortunadamente le cámping está lleno durante las fechas que ha solicitado.

Atentamente:

....

Site Booking Letter – Italian

Data: Indirizzo (stampatello)...

....

....

Nº Tel: (0044)...

Nº Fax: (0044)...

Email..

Egregio Signore/Signora

Desidero fare una prenotazione come segue:

Arrivo (giorno e mese)...................... **Partenza** (giorno e mese)........................(...notti)

Adulti.............. **Bambini** (+ età)...................................

Automobile ☐ **Roulotte/Caravan** ☐ **Camper** ☐ **Tenda a rimorchio** ☐

Allacciamento elettrico ☐ **Tendone** ☐ **Tenda addizionale** ☐

Attendo un sollecito riscontro ed allego un Coupon di Risposta Internazionale con busta indirizzata. Quando risponde, la prego di farmi sapere tutte le tariffe ed il deposito richiesti. Attendendo di incontrarla e di visitare il suo campeggio, la prego di gradire i miei distinti saluti.

[Nome in stampatello dopo la firma]

No d'associazione al Caravan Club...............................

✂---

Risposta

Data: Indirizzo..

....

....

Egregio Signore/Signora...............

La ringrazio per il modulo di prenotazione da..............a.............. (......notti).

- **SI, OK** – Sono lieto di confermare la sua prenotazione (con/senza allacciamento elettrico) e attendo di incontrarla.
- **NO, MI DISPIACE** – Mi dispiace ma il campeggio è completamente prenotato per le date da lei richieste.

Distinti saluti.

....

Customs Regulations

Travelling to the UK from the European Union

On entry into the UK no tax or duty is payable on goods bought tax-paid in other EU countries which are for your own use and which have been transported by you. VAT and duty are included in the price of goods purchased and travellers can no longer buy duty-free or tax-free goods on journeys within the EU. Customs allowances for countries outside the EU apply to the following countries covered by this guide: Andorra, Croatia, Gibraltar, Norway and Switzerland.

The following are guidance levels for the import of alcohol and tobacco into the UK but Customs do not enforce any absolute limits. However, if you bring in more than the following quantities Customs may suspect that they are for a commercial purpose and may ask questions and make checks. If you break the rules Customs may seize the goods – and the vehicle(s) used to transport them – and may not return them to you.

3,200 cigarettes
400 cigarillos
200 cigars
3kg tobacco
10 litres of spirits
20 litres of fortified wine (such as port or sherry)
90 litres of wine
110 litres of beer

No one under 17 years is entitled to the tobacco or alcohol allowances.

No one under 17 years is entitled to the tobacco or alcohol allowances

When entering the UK from another member state of the EU without having travelled to or through a non-EU country, you should use the blue Customs channel or exit reserved for EU travellers, provided your purchases are within the limits for imports from that country and you are not importing any restricted or prohibited goods, details of which are given later in this chapter.

Travelling to/from Non-EU Countries to/from the UK

You may purchase goods free of duty if travelling from the UK direct to a country outside the EU.

© Charlie Bishop
Used under licence from Shutterstock.com

The allowances for goods you may take into non-EU countries covered by this guide are shown in the relevant Country Introductions.

Duty-free allowances for travellers returning to the UK (or entering any other EU country) from a non-EU country are as follows:

200 cigarettes, or 100 cigarillos, or 50 cigars, or 250 gms tobacco

1 litre of spirits, or 2 litres of fortified wine, sparkling wine or other liqueurs

4 litres of still wine

16 litres of beer

£340 worth of all other goods including perfume, gifts and souvenirs

No one under 17 years is entitled to the tobacco or alcohol allowances.

When entering the UK from a non-EU country, or having travelled to or through a non-EU country, you should go through the red Customs channel or use the telephone at the Red Point if you have exceeded your Customs allowances, or if you are carrying any prohibited, restricted or commercial goods. Use the green Customs channel if you have 'nothing to declare'.

All dutiable items must be declared to Customs on entering the UK; failure to do so may mean that you forfeit them and your vehicle(s). Customs officers are legally entitled to examine your baggage and your vehicles and you are responsible for packing and unpacking. Whichever Customs channel you use, you may be stopped by a Customs officer and you and your vehicles may be searched.

If you are caught with goods that are prohibited or restricted, or goods in excess of your Customs allowances, you risk a heavy fine and possibly a prison sentence.

For further information contact HM Revenue & Customs National Advice Service on 0845 010 9000 (+44 2920 501 261 from outside the UK).

Travelling Within the European Union

While there are no limits on what travellers can buy and take with them when travelling between EU countries (provided the goods are for personal use and not for re-sale), the guidance levels set by other countries in the EU are less generous than those set by the UK, namely:

800 cigarettes or 400 cigarillos or 200 cigars or 1 kg tobacco

10 litres spirits or 20 litres fortified wine

90 litres wine

110 litres beer

Boats

Virtually all boats of any size taken abroad must carry registration documents when leaving UK waters. Contact the Maritime and Coastguard Agency on 0870 6006505 or www.mcga.gov.uk for details. The Royal Yachting Association recommends that all boats have marine insurance and can provide details of the rules and regulations for taking a boat to countries bordering the Atlantic Ocean, and the Baltic, Mediterranean and Black Seas – tel 0845 345 0400, www.rya.org.uk. Some countries require owners of certain types of vessels to have an International Certificate of Competence and information is contained in RYA publications.

If planning to take a boat abroad check with the appropriate tourist office before departure as rules and regulations for boat use vary from country to country. Third party insurance is compulsory in most European countries and is advisable elsewhere.

Currency

Legislation on the control of funds entering or leaving the EU was introduced in 2007. Any person entering or leaving the EU will have to declare the money that they are carrying if this amounts to €10,000 (or equivalent in other currencies) or more. This includes cheques, travellers' cheques, money orders etc. This ruling does not apply to anyone travelling via the EU to a non-EU country, as long as the original journey started outside the EU, nor to those travelling within the EU.

Food and Plants

Travellers from within the EU may bring into the UK any food or plant products without restriction as long as they originate in the EU, are free from pests or disease and are for your own consumption. For animal products Andorra, the Canary Islands, the Channel Islands, the Isle of Man, Norway and San Marino are treated as part of the EU.

From most countries outside the EU you are not allowed to bring into the UK any meat or dairy products. Other animal products may be severely restricted or banned and it is important that you declare any such products on entering the UK.

HM Revenue & Customs publish leaflets broadly setting out the rules, entitled 'Bringing Food Products into the UK' and 'Bringing Fruit, Vegetable and Plant Products into the UK'. These can be downloaded from their website or telephone the National Advice Service on 0845 010 9000. If you are unsure about any item you are bringing in, or are simply unsure of the rules, you must go to the red Customs channel or use the phone provided at the Red Point to speak to a Customs officer. All prohibited and restricted items will be taken away and destroyed. No further action will be taken.

In the light of recent animal health concerns in the UK, authorities abroad will understandably take a cautious approach to the import of foodstuffs. There is no guarantee that such products, if found, will not be confiscated by Customs officers.

Medicines

If you intend to take medicines with you when you go abroad you should obtain a copy of HMRC Notice 4, 'Taking Medicines With You When You Go Abroad', from HM Revenue & Customs National Advice Service on 0845 010 9000 or download it from www.hmrc.gov.uk. Alternatively contact the Drugs Enforcement Policy Team, HM Revenue & Customs, New King's Beam House, 22 Upper Ground, London SE1 9PJ, tel 020 7865 5767, fax 020 7865 5910.

There is no limit to the amount of medicines obtained without prescription, but medicines prescribed by your doctor may contain controlled drugs (ie subject to control under the Misuse of Drugs legislation) and you should check the allowances for these – in good time – in case you need to obtain a licence from the Home Office. In general, the permitted allowance for each drug is calculated on an average 15 days' dose.

Motor Vehicles and Caravans

Travellers between member states of the EU are entitled to import temporarily a motor vehicle, caravan or trailer into other member states without any Customs formalities.

Motor vehicles and caravans may be temporarily imported into non-EU countries generally for a maximum of six months in any twelve month period, provided they are not hired, sold or otherwise disposed of in that country. Temporarily imported vehicles should not be left behind after the importer has left, should not be used by residents of the country visited and should not be left longer than the permitted period.

If you intend to stay longer than six months, take up employment or residence, or dispose of a vehicle you should seek advice well before your departure from the UK, for example from one of the motoring organisations. Anyone temporarily importing into another country a vehicle – either hired or borrowed – which does not belong to them should carry a letter of authority from the vehicle owner.

*See the chapter **Documents** in the section **PLANNING AND TRAVELLING** for further details.*

Use Of Caravan By Persons Other Than The Owner

Many caravan owners reduce the cost of a holiday by sharing their caravan with friends or relatives. Either the caravan is left on the Continent on a campsite or it is handed over at the port. In making these arrangements it is important to consider the following:

- The total time the vehicle spends abroad must not exceed the permitted period for temporary importation.
- The owner of the caravan must provide the other person with a letter of authority. It is not permitted to accept a hire fee or reward.
- The number plate on the caravan must match the number plate on the tow car used.
- Both drivers' motor insurers must be informed if a caravan is being towed and any additional premium must be paid. If travelling to a country where an International Motor Insurance Certificate (Green Card) is required, both drivers' Certificates must be annotated to show that a caravan is being towed.
- If using the Caravan Club's Red Pennant Overseas Holiday Insurance, both drivers must be members of the Caravan Club and both must take out a Red Pennant policy.

*See the chapter **Insurance** in the section **PLANNING AND TRAVELLING.***

Personal Possessions

Generally speaking, visitors to countries within the EU are free to carry reasonable quantities of any personal articles, including valuable items such as jewellery, cameras, laptops etc required for the duration of their stay. It is sensible to carry sales receipts for new items, particularly of a foreign manufacture, in case you need to prove that tax has already been paid.

Visitors to non-EU countries may temporarily import personal items on condition that the articles are the personal property of the visitor and that they are not left behind when the importer leaves the country.

Prohibited and Restricted Goods

Just because something is on sale in another country does not mean it can be freely brought back to the UK. The importation of some goods is restricted or banned in the UK, mainly to protect health and the environment. These include:

- Endangered animals or plants including live animals, birds and plants, ivory, skins, coral, hides, shells and goods made from them such as jewellery, shoes, bags and belts even though these items were openly on sale in the countries where you bought them.
- Controlled, unlicensed or dangerous drugs eg heroin, cocaine, cannabis, LSD, morphine etc.
- Counterfeit or pirated goods such as fake watches, CDs and sports shirts; goods bearing a false indication of their place of manufacture or in breach of UK copyright.
- Offensive weapons such as firearms, flick knives, knuckledusters, push daggers or knives disguised as everyday objects.
- Pornographic material depicting extreme violence or featuring children such as DVDs, magazines, videos, books and software.

This list is by no means exhaustive; if in doubt contact HM Revenue & Customs National Advice Service for more information or, when returning to the UK, go through the red Customs channel or use the telephone at the Red Point and ask a Customs officer. It is your responsibility to make sure that you are not breaking the law.

Never attempt to mislead or hide anything from Customs officers; penalties are severe.

Planning and Travelling

Documents

Camping Card International (CCI)

The Camping Card International (CCI) is a plastic credit card-sized identity card for campers and is valid worldwide (except in the USA and Canada). It is available to members of the Caravan Club and other clubs affiliated to the international organisations, the AIT, FIA and FICC.

A CCI may be deposited with campsite staff instead of a passport and is essential, therefore, in those countries where a passport must be carried at all times as a means of indentification, and is recommended elsewhere. However, it is not a legal document and campsite managers are within their rights to demand other means of identification. More than 1,100 campsites throughout Europe give a reduction to holders of a CCI, although this may not apply if you pay by credit card.

The CCI is provided automatically, free of charge, to Caravan Club members taking out the Club's Red Pennant Overseas Holiday Insurance, otherwise it costs £4.95. It provides extensive third party personal liability cover and is valid for any personal injury and material damage you may cause while staying at a campsite, hotel or rented accommodation. Cover extends to the Club member and his/her passengers (maximum eleven people travelling together) and is valid for one year. The policy excludes any claims arising from accidents caused by any mechanically-propelled vehicle, ie a car. Full details of the terms and conditions and level of indemnity are provided with the card.

When leaving a campsite, make sure it is your card that is returned to you, and not one belonging to someone else.

The CCI is no longer accepted at a number of campsites in Sweden.

*See individual **Country Introductions** for more information and www.campingcardinternational.com*

Driving Licence & International Driving Permit (IDP)

Driving Licence

A full, valid driving licence should be carried at all times when driving abroad as it must be produced on demand to the police and other authorities. Failure to do so may result in an immediate fine. If your driving licence is due to expire while you are away it can normally be renewed up to three months before the expiry date. If you need to renew your licence more than three months ahead of the expiry date write to the DVLA and they will advise you.

© Mark Yuill
Used under licence from Shutterstock.com

All European Union countries should recognise the pink EU-format paper driving licence introduced in the UK in 1990, subject to the minimum age requirements of the country concerned (18 years in all countries covered by this guide for a vehicle with a maximum weight of 3,500 kg and carrying not more than 8 people). However, there are exceptions, eg Slovenia, and the Country Introduction chapter contains details.

Holders of an old-style green UK paper licence or a licence issued in Northern Ireland prior to 1991, which is not to EU format, are strongly recommended to update it to a photocard licence before travelling in order to avoid any local difficulties with the authorities. Alternatively, obtain an International Driving Permit to accompany your UK licence. A photocard driving licence is also useful as a means of identification in other situations, eg when using a credit card, when the display of photographic identification may be required.

Driving licence – carry both the plastic card and its paper counterpart

If you have a photocard driving licence, remember to carry both the plastic card and its paper counterpart as you will need both parts if, for any reason, you need to hire a vehicle.

Application forms are available from most post offices or apply online at www.direct.gov.uk/motoring. Allow enough time for your application to be processed and do not apply if you plan to hire a car in the near future. Selected post offices and DVLA local offices offer a premium checking service for photocard applications but the service is not available for online applications.

International Driving Permit (IDP)

If you hold a British photocard driving licence, no other form of photographic identification is required to drive in any of the countries covered by this guide. If you plan to travel further afield then an IDP may still be required and you can obtain one over the counter at selected post offices and from motoring organisations, namely the AA, Green Flag or the RAC, whether or not you are a member. An IDP costs £5.50 and is valid for a period of 12 months from the date of issue but may be post-dated up to three months.

To apply for an IDP you will need to be resident in Great Britain, have passed a driving test and be over 18 years of age. When driving abroad you should always carry your full national driving licence with you as well as your IDP.

European Health Insurance Card – Emergency Medical Benefits

For information on how to apply for a European Health Insurance Card (EHIC) and the medical care to which it entitles you, see the chapter ***Medical Matters*** in the section ***DURING YOUR STAY.***

MOT Certificate

You are advised to carry your vehicle's MOT certificate of roadworthiness (if applicable) when driving on the Continent as it may be required by the local authorities if your vehicle is involved in an accident, or in the event of random vehicle checks. If your MOT certificate is due to expire while you are away you should have the vehicle tested before you leave home.

Passport

Many countries require you to carry your passport at all times and immigration authorities may, of course, check your passport on return to the UK or Ireland. While abroad, it will help gain access to assistance from British Consular services and to banking services. Enter next-of-kin details in the back of your passport, keep a separate record of your passport details and leave a copy of it with a relative or friend at home.

The following information applies only to British citizens holding, or entitled to hold, a passport bearing the inscription 'United Kingdom of Great Britain and Northern Ireland'.

Applying for a Passport

Each person (including babies) must hold a valid passport. It is not now possible to add or include children on a parent's British passport. A standard British passport is valid for ten years, but if issued to children under 16 years of age it is valid for five years.

All new UK passports are now biometric passports, also known as ePassports, which feature additional security features including a microchip with the holder's unique biometric facial features. Existing passports will remain valid until their expiry date and holders will not be required to exchange them for biometric passports before then.

Full information and application forms are available from main post offices or from the Identity & Passport Service's website, www.direct.gov.uk where you can complete an online application. Allow at least six weeks for first-time passport applications (for which you will probably need to attend an interview at your nearest IPS regional office – telephone the Passport Adviceline on 0300 2220000 to arrange one), three weeks for a renewal application and at least one week for the replacement of a lost, stolen or damaged passport.

Main post offices offer a 'Check & Send' service for passport applications costing £6.85 and priority is given to applications made using this service. To find your nearest 'Check & Send' post office call 08457 223344 or see www.postoffice.co.uk

Your passport is a valuable document – look after it!

Passport Validity

Most, but not all, countries covered by this guide merely require you to carry a passport valid for the duration of your stay. Where this requirement differs, mention is made in the relevant Country Introduction chapters. However, in the event that your return home is delayed for any reason and in order to avoid any local difficulties with immigration authorities, it is advisable to ensure that your passport has at least six months' validity left after your planned return travel date. You can renew your passport up to nine months before expiry, without losing the validity of the current one.

Schengen Agreement

All the countries covered by this guide except Andorra and Croatia are party to the Schengen Agreement which allows people and vehicles to pass freely without border checks from country to country within the Schengen area. While there are no longer any border checks you should not attempt to cross land borders without a full, valid passport. It is likely that random identity checks will continue to be made for the foreseeable future in areas surrounding land borders.

The United Kingdom and Republic of Ireland are not party to the Schengen Agreement.

Last but not least: your passport is a valuable document – look after it! It is expensive, time-consuming and inconvenient to replace and its loss or theft can lead to serious complications if your identity is later used fraudulently.

Pet Travel Scheme (PETS)

The Pet Travel Scheme (PETS) allows pet dogs, cats and a number of other animals from qualifying European countries to enter the UK without quarantine, providing they have an EU pet passport, and it also allows pets to travel from the UK to other EU qualifying countries. All the countries covered by this guide (including Gibraltar and Liechtenstein) are qualifying countries. However, the procedures to obtain the passport are lengthy and the regulations, of necessity, strict.

Be aware that some countries may not allow entry to certain types or breeds of dogs and may have rules relating to the size or breed of dogs permitted entry or to matters such as muzzling. You are advised to contact the appropropriate authorities of the countries you plan to visit via their embassies in London before making travel arrangements for your dog. You should also check with your vet for the latest available information or call the PETS Helpline on 0870 2411710, email: quarantine@animalhealth.gsi.gov.uk. More information is available from the website for the Department for the Environment, Food & Rural Affairs (Defra), www.defra.gov.uk

The PETS scheme operates on a number of ferry routes between the Continent and the UK as well as on Eurotunnel services and Eurostar passenger trains from Calais to Folkestone. Some routes may only operate at certain times of the year; routes may change and new ones may be added – check with the PETS Helpline for the latest information.

Pets normally resident in the Channel Islands, Isle of Man and the Republic of Ireland can also enter the UK under the PETS scheme if they comply with the rules. Pets resident anywhere in the British Isles (including the Republic of Ireland) will continue to be able to travel freely within the British Isles and will not be subject to PETS rules. Owners of pets entering the Channel Islands or the Republic of Ireland from outside the British Isles should contact the appropriate authorities in those countries for advice on approved routes and other requirements.

It is against the law in the UK to possess certain types of dogs (unless an exemption certificate is held) and the introduction of PETS does not affect this ban. Some European countries have laws about certain breeds of dogs and about transporting dogs in cars and, where known, this is covered in the relevant Country Introductions.

For a list of vets near Continental ports, look in the local equivalent of the Yellow Pages telephone directory, eg www.pagesjaunes.fr for France or www.paginas-amarillas.es for Spain. Or use the link to Pages Jaunes on the Defra website. Campsite owners or tourist offices located near Channel ports will be familiar with the requirements of British visitors and will probably be able to recommend a vet. Alternatively, the local British Consulate may be able to help, or the ferry company transporting your pet.

Adequate travel insurance for your pet is essential

Last but by no means least, adequate travel insurance for your pet is essential in the event of an accident abroad requiring veterinary treatment, emergency repatriation or long-term care if treatment lasts longer than your holiday. Travel insurance should also include liability cover in the event that your pet injures another animal, person or property while abroad. Contact the Caravan Club on 0800 0151396 or visit www.caravanclub.co.uk/petins for details of its Pet Insurance scheme, specially negotiated to take into account Club members' requirements both at home and abroad.

See ***Holiday Insurance for Pets*** *under* ***Insurance*** *in the section* ***PLANNING AND TRAVELLING.***

Travelling with Children

Some countries require documentary evidence of parental responsibility from single parents travelling alone with children before allowing lone parents to enter the country or, in some cases, before permitting children to leave the country. The authorities may want to see a birth certificate, a letter of consent from the other parent and some evidence as to your responsibility for the child.

If you are travelling with a minor under the age of 18 who is not your own you must carry a letter of authorisation, naming the adult in charge of the child, from the child's parent or legal guardian.

For further information on exactly what will be required at immigration, before you travel contact the Embassy or Consulate of the countries you intend to visit.

Vehicle Excise Licence

While driving abroad it is necessary to display a current UK vehicle excise licence (tax disc). If your vehicle's tax disc is due to expire while you are abroad you may apply to re-license the vehicle at a post office, or by post, or in person at a DVLA local office up to two months in advance. If you give a despatch address abroad the licence can be sent to you there.

Vehicle Registration Certificate (V5C)

You must always carry your Vehicle Registration Certificate (V5C) when taking your vehicle abroad. If you do not have one you should apply to a DVLA local office on form V62. If you need to travel abroad during this time you will need to apply for a Temporary Registration Certificate if you are not already recorded as the vehicle keeper. Telephone DVLA Customer Enquiries on 0870 2400009 for more information.

Caravan – Proof of Ownership (CRIS)

Britain and Ireland are the only European countries where caravans are not formally registered in the same way as cars. This may not be fully understood by police and other authorities on the Continent. You are strongly advised, therefore, to carry a copy of your Caravan Registration Identification Scheme (CRIS) document.

Hired or Borrowed Vehicles

If using a borrowed vehicle you must obtain from the registered owner a letter of authority to use the vehicle. You should also carry the Vehicle Registration Certificate (V5C).

In the case of hired or leased vehicles when the user does not normally possess the V5C, ask the company which owns the vehicle to supply a Vehicle On Hire Certificate, form VE103B, which is the only legal substitute for a V5C. Download a form from the RAC's website, www.rac.co.uk, or call them on 0870 1650979. Alternatively, see www.bvrla.co.uk or call them on 01452 887686 for more information.

If you are caught driving a hired vehicle abroad without this certificate you may be fined and/or the vehicle impounded.

Visas

British citizens holding a full UK passport do not require a visa for entry into any of the countries covered by this guide. EU countries normally require a permit for stays of more than three months and these can be obtained during your stay on application to the local police or civic authorities.

British subjects, British overseas citizens, British dependent territories citizens and citizens of other countries may need visas that are not required by British citizens. Check with the authorities of the country you are due to visit at their UK Embassy or Consulate. Citizens of other countries should apply to their own Embassy, Consulate or High Commission for information.

Ferries and the Channel Tunnel

Planning Your Trip

If travelling in July or August, or over peak weekends during school holidays, such as Easter and half-term, it is advisable to make a reservation as early as possible, particularly if you need cabin accommodation.

Space for caravans on ferries is usually limited especially during peak holiday periods. Off-peak crossings, which may offer savings for caravanners, are usually filled very quickly.

When booking any ferry crossing, account must be taken of boats, bicycles, skylights and roof boxes in the overall height/length of the car and caravan outfit or motor caravan, as ferry operators require you to declare total dimensions. It is important, therefore, to report the dimensions of your outfit accurately when making a ferry booking, as vehicles which have been under-declared may be turned away at boarding.

Individual ferry companies may impose vehicle length or height restrictions according to the type of vessel in operation on that particular sailing or route. Always check when making your booking.

Report the dimensions of your outfit accurately when making a ferry booking

Advise your booking agent at the time of making your ferry reservation of any disabled passengers or any who have special needs. Ferry companies can then make the appropriate arrangements for anyone requiring assistance at ports or on board ships.

For residents of both Northern Ireland and the Republic of Ireland travelling to the Continent via the British mainland Brittany Ferries, Irish Ferries and P & O Irish Sea offer special 'Landbridge' or 'Ferrylink' through-fares for combined crossings on the Irish Sea and the English Channel or North Sea, although the Club's own offers on the individual routes are often better value.

The table on the following page shows current ferry routes from the UK to the Continent and Ireland. Some ferry routes may not be operational all year and during peak holiday periods the transportation of caravans or motor caravans may be restricted. Current information on ferry timetables and

tariffs can be obtained from the Caravan Club's Travel Service or from a travel agent, or from ferry operators' websites.

Booking Your Ferry

The Caravan Club is an agent for most major ferry companies operating services to the Continent, Scandinavia, Ireland and the Isle of Wight, and each year provides thousands of Club members with a speedy and efficient booking service. The Club's Continental Caravanning brochure (available from November) features a range of special offers with ferry operators – some of them exclusive to the Caravan Club – together with full information on the Club's Advance Booking Service for campsites on the Continent, its Tours and Excursions programme, and Red Pennant Overseas Holiday Insurance. Telephone 01342 327410 for a brochure or see www.caravanclub.co.uk/overseas

During the course of the year, new special offers and promotions are negotiated and these are featured on the Travel Service News page of The Caravan Club Magazine and on the Club's website.

The Club's website has a direct link through to a number of ferry operators' reservations systems allowing Club members to make their own reservations and still take advantage of the Club's negotiated offers and the ferry companies' own early booking offers. A credit card deposit is taken and the balance collected ten weeks before departure date. Some ferry operators are imposing fuel surcharges but these will be included in all fares quoted by the Caravan Club.

Reservations may be made by telephoning the Caravan Club's Travel Service on 01342 316101 or on www.caravanclub.co.uk/overseas

Route	Operator	Approximate Crossing Time	Maximum Frequency
Belgium			
Hull – Zeebrugge	P & O Ferries	12½ hrs	1 daily
Ramsgate – Ostend†	Transeuropa Ferries	4½ hrs	4 daily
Rosyth – Zeebrugge	Norfolkline	20 hrs	3 per week
Denmark			
Harwich – Esbjerg	DFDS Seaways	18 hrs	3 per week
France			
Dover – Boulogne	LD Lines	1 hr	4 daily
Dover – Calais	P & O Ferries	1¼ hrs	22 daily
Dover – Calais	SeaFrance	1½ hrs	15 daily
Dover – Dunkerque	Norfolkline	2 hrs	12 daily
Folkestone – Calais	Eurotunnel	35 mins	3 per hour
Newhaven – Dieppe	LD Lines	4 hrs	2 daily
Plymouth – Roscoff	Brittany Ferries	5 / 9 hrs	3 daily
Poole – Cherbourg	Brittany Ferries	2¼ hrs / 6½ hrs	3 daily
Poole – St Malo (via Channel Islands)	Condor Ferries	4½ hrs	1 daily (May to Oct)
Portsmouth – Caen	Brittany Ferries	3¾ / 7½ hrs	4 daily
Portsmouth – Cherbourg*	Brittany Ferries	3 hrs	1 daily
Portsmouth – Cherbourg	Condor Ferries	5½ hrs	1 weekly (May to Sep)
Portsmouth – Le Havre	LD Lines	5½ / 8 hrs	2 daily
Portsmouth – St Malo	Brittany Ferries	9 / 10¾ hrs	1 daily
Weymouth – St Malo (via Channel Islands)	Condor Ferries	8¼ hrs	1 daily
Ireland – Northern			
Cairnryan – Larne	P & O Irish Sea	1 / 2 hrs	7 daily
Fleetwood – Larne	Stena Line	8 hrs	2 daily
Liverpool (Birkenhead) – Belfast	Norfolkline	8 hrs	2 daily
Stranraer – Belfast	Stena Line	2 / 3 hrs	7 daily
Troon – Larne	P & O Irish Sea	1 hr 50 mins	2 daily
Ireland – Republic			
Cork – Roscoff	Brittany Ferries	14 hrs	1 per week
Fishguard – Rosslare	Stena Line	2 / 3½ hrs	4 daily
Holyhead – Dublin	Irish Ferries	2 / 3¼ hrs	4 daily
Holyhead – Dublin	Stena Line	2 / 3¼ hrs	4 daily
Holyhead – Dun Loaghaire	Stena Line	2 hrs	1 daily
Liverpool – Dublin	P & O Irish Sea	7½ hrs	2 daily
Liverpool (Birkenhead) – Dublin	Norfolkline	7 hrs	2 daily
Pembroke – Rosslare	Irish Ferries	3¾ hrs	2 daily
Rosslare – Cherbourg†	Irish Ferries	18½ hrs	3 per week
Rosslare – Cherbourg	LD Lines	17 hrs	3 per week
Rosslare – Roscoff†	Irish Ferries	19 hrs	4 per week
Netherlands			
Harwich – Hook of Holland	Stena Line	6¼ hrs	2 daily
Hull – Rotterdam	P & O Ferries	10 hrs	1 daily
Newcastle – Amsterdam (Ijmuiden)	DFDS Seaways	15 hrs	1 daily
Spain			
Plymouth – Santander	Brittany Ferries	20 hrs	1 per week
Portsmouth – Bilbao	P & O Ferries	33 hrs	3 per week
Portsmouth – Santander	Brittany Ferries	24 hrs	1 per week

* *Cars and small motor caravans only.*

† *Not bookable through the Club's Travel Service.*

Channel Tunnel

The Channel Tunnel operator, Eurotunnel, accepts cars, caravans and motor caravans (except those running on LPG and dual-fuel vehicles) on their service between Folkestone and Calais. While they accept traffic on a 'turn up and go' basis, they also offer a full reservation service for all departures with exact timings confirmed on booking.

All information was current at the time this guide was compiled in the autumn of 2009 and may be subject to change during 2010.

Gas – Safety Precautions and Regulations on Ferries and in the Channel Tunnel

UK-based cross-Channel ferry companies usually allow up to three gas cylinders per caravan, including the cylinder currently in use. However some, eg Brittany Ferries, DFDS Seaways, SeaFrance and Stena Line restrict this to a maximum of two cylinders, providing they are securely fitted into your caravan. It is advisable to check with the ferry company before setting out.

Cylinder valves should be fully closed and covered with a cap, if provided, and should remain closed during the crossing. Cylinders should be fixed securely in or on the caravan in the manner intended and in the position designated by your caravan's manufacturer. Ensure gas cookers and fridges are fully turned off. Gas cylinders must be declared at check-in and ships' crew may wish to inspect each cylinder for leakage before shipment. They will reject leaking or inadequately secured cylinders.

Eurotunnel will allow vehicles fitted with LPG tanks for the purposes of heating, lighting, cooking or refrigeration to use their service but regulations stipulate that a total of no more than 47 kg of gas can be carried through the Channel Tunnel. Tanks must be switched off before boarding and must be less than 80% full; you will be asked to demonstrate this before you travel. **Vehicles powered by LPG or equipped with a dual-fuel system cannot be carried through the Channel Tunnel.**

Most ferry companies, however, are willing to accept LPG-powered vehicles provided they are advised at the time of booking. During the crossing the tank must be no more than 75% full and it must be turned off. In the case of vehicles converted to use LPG, some ferry companies also require a certificate showing that the conversion has been carried out to the manufacturer's specification.

The carriage of spare petrol cans, whether full or empty, is not permitted on ferries or through the Channel Tunnel.

Pets on Ferries and Eurotunnel

It is possible to transport your pet on a number of ferry routes to the Continent and Ireland as well as on Eurotunnel services from Folkestone to Calais. At the time this guide was compiled the cost of return travel for a pet was between £30 and £50, depending on the route used. Advance booking is essential as restrictions apply to the number of animals allowed on any one departure. Make sure you understand the carrier's terms and conditions for transporting pets.

Ensure that ferry staff know that your vehicle contains an animal

On arrival at the port ensure that ferry staff know that your vehicle contains an animal. Pets are normally required to remain in their owner's vehicle or in kennels on the car deck and, for safety reasons, access to the vehicle decks while the ferry is at sea may be restricted. On longer ferry crossings you should make arrangements at the on-board Information Desk for permission to visit your pet at suitable intervals in order to check its well-being. Information and advice on the welfare of animals before and during a journey is available on the website of the Department for Environment, Food and Rural Affairs (Defra), www.defra.gov.uk

*See also **Pet Travel Scheme** under **Documents** and **Holiday Insurance for Pets** under **Insurance** in the section **PLANNING AND TRAVELLING.***

Caravan Club Sites Near Ports

Once you have chosen your ferry crossing and worked out your route to the port of departure you may like to consider an overnight stop at one of the following Club sites, especially if your journey to or from home involves a long drive. Prior to the opening of seasonal sites before Easter you can book by using the Club's Advance Booking Service for Club sites on 01342 327490 or book online at www.caravanclub.co.uk/searchandbook

Otherwise contact the site direct. Advance booking is recommended, particularly if you are planning to stay during July and August or over Bank Holidays.

Port	Nearest Site and Town	Tel No.
Cairnryan, Stranraer	New England Bay, Drummore	01776 860275
Dover, Folkestone, Channel Tunnel	Bearsted*, Maidstone	01622 730018
	Black Horse Farm*, Folkestone,	01303 892665
	Daleacres, Hythe,	01303 267679
	Fairlight Wood, Hastings	01424 812333
Fishguard, Pembroke	Freshwater East, Pembroke	01646 672341
Harwich	Cherry Hinton*, Cambridge	01223 244088
	Commons Wood*, Welwyn Garden City	01707 260786
	Round Plantation, Mildenhall	01638 713089
Holyhead	Penrhos, Brynteg, Anglesey	01248 852617
Hull	Beechwood Grange, York	01904 424637
	Rowntree Park*, York	01904 658997
Newcastle upon Tyne	Old Hartley, Whitley Bay	0191 237 0256
Newhaven	Sheepcote Valley*, Brighton	01273 626546
Plymouth	Plymouth Sound, Plymouth	01752 862325
Poole	Hunter's Moon*, Wareham	01929 556605
Portsmouth	Rookesbury Park, Fareham	01329 834085
Rosslare	River Valley, Wicklow	00353 (0)404 41647
Weymouth	Crossways, Dorchester	01305 852032

** Site open all year*

When seasonal Club sites near the ports are closed, the following, which are open all year or most of the year (but may not be 'on the doorstep' of the ports in question) may be useful overnight stops for early and late season travellers using cross-Channel or Irish Sea ports. All 'open all year' sites offer a limited supply of hardstanding pitches.

Port	Nearest Site and Town	Tel No.
Dover, Folkstone, Channel Tunnel	Abbey Wood, London	020 8311 7708
	Alderstead Heath, Redhill	01737 644629
	Amberley Fields, Crawley	01293 524834
	Crystal Palace, London	020 8778 7155
Fishguard, Pembroke, Swansea	Pembrey Country Park, Llanelli	01554 834369
Portsmouth	Abbey Wood, London	020 8311 7708
	Alderstead Heath, Redhill	01737 644629
	Amberley Fields, Crawley	01293 524834
	Crystal Palace, London	020 8778 7155

NB Amberley Fields, Commons Wood, Daleacres, Fairlight Wood, Hunter's Moon, Old Hartley, Round Plantation and Rookesbury Park are open to Caravan Club members only. Non-members are welcome at all the other Caravan Club sites listed above.

Alternatively consider an overnight stay at a CL (Certificated Location) site within striking distance of your port of departure. Many CLs are open all year.

Full details of all these sites can be found in the Caravan Club's Sites Directory & Handbook 2009/10 and on the Club's website, www.caravanclub.co.uk

Insurance

Car, Motor Caravan and Caravan Insurance

Insurance cover for your car, caravan or motor caravan while travelling abroad is of the utmost importance. In addition, travel insurance, such as the Caravan Club's Red Pennant Overseas Holiday Insurance (available to members only), not only minimises duplication of cover offered by other motor and caravan insurance, but also covers contingencies which are not included, eg despatch of spare parts, medical and hospital fees, vehicle hire, hotel bills, vehicle recovery etc.

*See **Holiday Insurance** later in this section.*

In order to be covered for a period abroad the following action is necessary:

- **Caravan** – Inform your caravan insurer/broker of the dates of your holiday and pay any additional premium required. The Caravan Club's 5Cs Caravan Insurance gives free cover for up to 182 days.
- **Motor Car or Motor Caravan** – If your journey is outside the EU or EU Associated Countries (listed on the next page) inform your motor insurer/broker of the dates of your holiday, together with details of all the countries you will be visiting, and pay any additional premium. Also inform them if you are towing a caravan and ask them to include it on your Green Card if you need to carry one.

The Caravan Club's Car Insurance and Motor Caravan Insurance schemes extend to provide full policy cover for European Union or Associated Countries free of charge, provided the total period of foreign travel in any one annual period of insurance does not exceed 180 days for car insurance and 270 days for motor caravan insurance. It may be possible to extend this period, although a charge will be made. The cover provided is the same as a Club member enjoys in the UK, rather than just the minimum legal liability cover required by law in the countries you are visiting.

Should you be delayed beyond the limits of your insurance you must, without fail, instruct your insurer/broker to maintain cover.

For full details of the Caravan Club's caravan insurance telephone 01342 336610 or for car and motor caravan insurance products, telephone 0800 0284809 or visit our website, www.caravanclub.co.uk/insurance

© G Campbell
Used under licence from Shutterstock.com

Taking Your Car or Motor Caravan Abroad – Evidence of Insurance Cover (Green Card)

All countries oblige visiting motorists to have motor insurance cover for their legal liability to third parties. An International Motor Insurance Certificate, commonly known as a Green Card, is evidence of compliance with this requirement. However, motorists visiting EU and Associated Countries do not need a Green Card as, under EU legislation, a UK Motor Insurance Certificate is now accepted in all such countries as evidence that the obligatory motor insurance cover is in force.

Travellers outside the EU and Associated Countries will need to obtain a Green Card document, for which insurers usually make a charge. If a Green Card is issued, your motor insurers should be asked to include reference on it to any caravan or trailer you may be towing. If you do not have evidence of the obligatory insurance cover, you may have to pay for temporary insurance at a country's border.

Irrespective of whether a Green Card is required, it is advisable to notify your insurer/broker of your intention to travel outside the UK and obtain confirmation that your policy has been extended to include use of the insured vehicle abroad. Because of the potentially high cost of claims, your insurer may not automatically provide full policy cover when abroad. You should ensure that your vehicle and motor caravan policies provide adequate cover for your purposes, rather than the minimum cover that the country you are visiting obliges you to have.

European Accident Statement

You should also check with your motor insurer/broker to see if they provide a European Accident Statement to record details of any accident in which you may be involved with your motor vehicle. Travelling with your Vehicle Registration Certificate, (V5C), MOT certificate (if applicable), certificate of motor insurance, copy of your CRIS document, European Accident Statement and valid pink EU-format or photocard UK driving licence should be sufficient in the event that you are stopped for a routine police check or following an accident while travelling within the EU or an Associated Country. These documents should not be left in your vehicle when it is unattended.

European Union and Associated Countries

European Union: Austria, Belgium, Bulgaria, Cyprus, Czech Republic, Denmark, Estonia, Finland, France, Germany, Greece, Hungary, Ireland, Italy, Latvia, Lithuania, Luxembourg, Malta, Netherlands, Poland, Portugal, Romania, Slovakia, Slovenia, Spain, Sweden and the United Kingdom.

Associated EU Countries (ie non-EU signatories to the motor insurance Multilateral Guarantee Agreement): Andorra, Croatia, Iceland, Norway, Switzerland and Liechtenstein.

In spite of the foregoing, you may wish to obtain an actual Green Card if visiting Bulgaria or Romania so as to avoid local difficulties which can sometimes arise in these countries. If you do not take a Green Card you should carry your certificate of motor insurance. If you plan to visit countries outside the EU and Associated Countries, and in particular central and eastern European countries, you should check that your motor insurer will provide the necessary extension of cover.

If you are planning to visit Croatia and intend to drive through Bosnia and Herzegovina along the 20 km strip of coastline at Neum on the Dalmatian coastal highway to Dubrovnik you should obtain Green Card cover for Bosnia and Herzegovina. If you have difficulties obtaining such cover before departure contact the Club's Travel Service Information Officer for advice. Alternatively, temporary third-party insurance can be purchased at the country's main border posts, or in Split and other large cities. It is understood that it is not generally obtainable at the Neum border crossing itself.

For Club members insured under the Caravan Club's Car Insurance and Motor Caravan Insurance schemes full policy cover is available for the 20 km strip of coastline from Neum.

Caravans Stored Abroad

Caravan insurers will not normally insure caravans left on campsites or in storage abroad. In these circumstances specialist policies are available from Towergate Bakers on 01242 528844, www.towergatebakers.co.uk, email bakers@towergate.co.uk or Drew Insurance, tel 0845 4565758, www.drewinsurance.co.uk, email mail@kdib.co.uk

Legal Costs Abroad

A person who is taken to court following a road traffic accident in a European country runs the risk of being held liable for legal costs, even if cleared of any blame.

Motor insurance policies in the UK normally include cover for legal costs and expenses incurred with the insurer's consent and arising from any incident that is covered under the terms and conditions of the policy. The Caravan Club's Car Insurance and Motor Caravan Insurance schemes incorporate such cover, together with optional additional legal expenses cover for recovering any other losses that are not included in your motor insurance policy. Similar optional legal expenses insurance is also offered as an addition to the Club's 5Cs Caravan Insurance scheme.

Holiday Travel Insurance

Having insured your vehicles, there are other risks to consider and it is essential to take out adequate travel insurance. The Caravan Club's Red Pennant Overseas Holiday Insurance is designed to provide as full a cover as possible at a reasonable fee. The Club's scheme is tailor-made for the caravanner and motor caravanner and includes cover against the following:

- Recovery of vehicles and passengers
- Towing charges
- Emergency labour costs
- Chauffeured recovery
- Storage fees
- Spare parts location and despatch
- Continuation of holiday travel, ie car hire etc
- Continuation of holiday accommodation, ie hotels etc
- Emergency medical and hospital expenses
- Legal expenses
- Emergency cash transfers
- Loss of deposits/cancellation cover
- Personal accident benefits
- Personal effects and baggage insurance
- Loss of cash or documents
- Cost of telephone calls

If you are proposing to participate in dangerous sporting activities such as skiing, hang-gliding or mountaineering, check that your personal holiday insurance includes cover for such sports and that it also covers the cost of mountain and helicopter rescue.

Look carefully at the exemptions to your insurance policy, including those relating to pre-existing medical conditions or the use of alcohol. Be sure to declare any pre-existing medical conditions to your insurer.

Club members can obtain increased cover by taking out Red Pennant **Plus** cover. The Club also offers a range of annual multi-trip and long stay holiday insurance schemes for Continental and worldwide travel. For more details and policy limits refer to the Continental Caravanning and/or Overseas Holiday Insurance brochures from the Caravan Club. Alternatively see www.caravanclub.co.uk/redpennant for details or telephone 01342 336633.

Holiday Insurance for Pets

The Club's Red Pennant Overseas Holiday Insurance covers extra expenses in respect of your pet that may arise as part of a claim for an incident normally covered under the Red Pennant policy. It does not, however, cover costs arising from an injury to, or the illness of your pet, or provide any legal liability cover to you as a pet owner.

See our website, www.caravanclub.co.uk/petins for details of our Pet Insurance scheme

It is advisable, therefore, to ensure that you have adequate travel insurance for your pet in the event of an incident or illness abroad requiring veterinary treatment, emergency repatriation or long-term care in excess of the duration of your holiday.

Contact the Caravan Club on 0800 0151396 or see our website, www.caravanclub.co.uk/petins for details of the Club's Pet Insurance scheme, specially negotiated to take into account Club members' requirements both at home and abroad.

Home Insurance

Most home insurers require advance notification if you are leaving your home unoccupied for 30 days or more. They often require that mains services (except electricity) are turned off, water drained down and that somebody visits the home once a week. Check your policy documents or speak to your insurer/broker.

The Caravan Club's Home Insurance policy provides full cover for up to 90 days when you are away from home, for instance when touring, and requires only common sense precautions for longer periods of unoccupancy. Contact 0800 0284815 or see www.caravanclub.co.uk/homeins for details of our Home Insurance scheme, specially negotiated to suit the majority of Club members' requirements.

Marine Insurance

Car Ferries

Vehicles driven by their owner are normally conveyed in accordance with the terms of the carrying companies' published by-laws or conditions, and if damage is sustained during loading, unloading or shipment, this must be reported at the time to the carrier's representative. Any claim arising from such damage must be notified in writing to the carrier concerned within three days of the incident. Nonetheless it is unwise to rely upon the carrier accepting liability for your claim so it would be prudent to have separate transit insurance.

The majority of motor policies cover vehicles during short sea crossings up to 65 hours' normal duration – check with your insurer. The Caravan Club's 5Cs Caravan Insurance policy automatically covers you for crossings of any length within the area covered by Red Pennant Overseas Holiday Insurance.

Boats

The Royal Yachting Association recommends that all boats have marine insurance. Third party insurance is compulsory for some of the countries covered by this guide, together with a translation of the insurance certificate into the appropriate language(s). Check with your insurer/broker before taking your boat abroad.

Medical Insurance

*See the chapter **Medical Matters** in the section **DURING YOUR STAY**.*

Personal Belongings

The majority of travellers are able to cover their valuables such as jewellery, watches, cameras, bicycles and, in some instances, small boats under the All Risks section of their Householders' Comprehensive Policy.

Vehicles Left Behind Abroad

If you are involved in an accident or breakdown while abroad which prevents you taking your vehicle home, you must ensure that your normal insurance cover is maintained to cover the period that the vehicle remains abroad, and that you are covered for the cost of recovering it to your home address.

You should remove all items of baggage and personal belongings from your vehicles before leaving them unattended. If this is not possible you should check with your insurer/broker to establish whether extended cover can be provided. In all circumstances, you must remove any valuables and items which might attract Customs duty, including wine, beer, spirits and cigarettes.

International Holidays 2010 and 2011

International Holidays, Important Dates & UK Bank Holidays

2010				2011	
January	1	Friday	New Year's Day	1	Saturday
	6	Wednesday	Epiphany	6	Thursday
	14	Sunday	Chinese New Year	3 Feb	Thursday
February	17	Wednesday	Ash Wednesday	9 Mar	Wednesday
March	1	Monday	St David's Day	1	Tuesday
	17	Wednesday	St Patrick's Day	17	Thursday
	14	Sunday	Mother's Day	3 Apr	Sunday
	28	Sunday	British Summer Time begins	27	Sunday
April	28 Mar	Sunday	Palm Sunday	17	Sunday
	2	Friday	Good Friday	22	Friday
	4	Sunday	Easter Day	24	Sunday
	5	Monday	Easter Monday	25	Monday
	4	Sunday	Christian Orthodox Easter Day	24	Sunday
	23	Friday	St George's Day	23	Saturday
May	3	Monday	May Bank Holiday	2	Monday
	13	Thursday	Ascension Day	2 June	Thursday
	31	Monday	Spring Bank Holiday UK	30	Monday
	23	Sunday	Whit Sunday	12 June	Sunday
June	24 May	Monday	Whit Monday	13	Monday
	3	Thursday	Corpus Christi	23	Thursday
	20	Sunday	Father's Day	19	Sunday
August	15	Sunday	Assumption	15	Monday
	11	Wednesday	1st Day of Ramadan*	1	Monday
	30	Monday	Bank Holiday UK	29	Monday
September	9	Thursday	Jewish New Year (Rosh Hashanah)	29	Thursday
	9	Thursday	Ramadan Ends*	30 Aug	Tuesday
	18	September	Jewish Day of Atonement (Yom Kippur)	8 Oct	Saturday
October	31	Sunday	British Summer Time ends	30	Sunday
	31	Sunday	Halloween	31	Monday
November	1	Monday	All Saints' Day	1	Tuesday
	14	Sunday	Remembrance Sunday	13	Sunday
	30	Tuesday	St Andrew's Day	30	Wednesday
December	7	Tuesday	Al Hijra – Islamic New Year	26 Nov	Saturday
	25	Saturday	Christmas Day	25	Sunday
	26	Sunday	St Stephen's Day; Boxing Day UK	26	Monday
	27, 28	Mon, Tues	Bank Holiday	27	Tuesday

** Subject to the lunar calendar*

NOTES 1) *When a holiday falls on a Sunday it will not necessarily be observed the following day.*
2) *Public holidays in individual countries are listed in the relevant Country Introductions.*

Money

Take your holiday money in a mixture of cash, credit and debit cards and travellers' cheques or pre-paid travel cards and keep them separately. Do not rely exclusively on only one method of payment.

*See **Customs** in the section **DURING YOUR STAY** for information about declaring the amount of cash you carry when entering or leaving the EU.*

Local Currency

It is not necessary to carry a large amount of cash but it is a good idea to take sufficient foreign currency for your immediate needs on arrival, including loose change if possible. Even if you intend to use credit and debit cards for most of your holiday spending it makes sense to take some cash to tide you over until you are able to find a cash machine (ATM), and you may need change for parking meters or the use of supermarket trolleys.

You can change money at ports and on ferries but the rates offered do not generally represent the best value. Many High Street banks, exchange offices and travel agents offer commission-free foreign exchange, whereas some will charge a flat fee and some offer a 'buy back' service. Most stock the more common currencies, but it is wise to order in advance in case demand is heavy or if you require an unusual currency.

Shop around and compare commission and exchange rates

Currency can also be ordered by telephone or online for delivery to your home address on payment of a handling charge. Online providers such as the Post Office or Travelex and most of the High Street banks offer their customers an online ordering service which usually represents the best value. It can pay to shop around and compare commission and exchange rates, together with minimum charges.

If you pay for your currency with a credit or debit card the card issuer may charge a cash advance fee, in addition to the commission and/or handling charge.

Banks and money exchanges in central and eastern Europe may not be willing to accept Scottish and Northern Irish bank notes and may be reluctant to

© Matt Trommer
Used under licence from Shutterstock.com

change any sterling which has been written on, is creased or worn or is not in virtually mint condition.

Exchange rates (as at September 2009) are given in the Country Introductions in this guide. Up to date currency conversion rates can be obtained from your bank or national newspapers. Alternatively, www.oanda.com updates currency rates around the world daily and allows you to print a handy currency converter to take with you on your trip.

Foreign Currency Bank Accounts

Frequent travellers or those who spend long periods abroad may find a euro bank account useful. Most such accounts impose no currency conversion charges for debit or credit use and allow fee-free cash withdrawls at ATMs. Some banks may also allow you to spread your account across different currencies, depending on your circumstances. Your bank will advise you.

Travellers' Cheques

Travellers' cheques can be cashed or used as payment for goods or services in almost all countries, and are the safest way to carry large sums of money. They can be replaced quickly – usually within 24 hours – in the event of loss or theft. Travellers' cheques may be accepted where credit cards are not and are useful if you are travelling off the beaten track or in far-flung locations, but bear in mind that small bank branches may not offer foreign exchange services. Commission is payable when you buy the cheques and/or when you cash them in. See the Country Introductions for more information.

While it is now possible to buy euro travellers' cheques for use within the euro zone, in practice their use can be limited. Recent visitors report difficulties in finding a bank that will cash them for non-account holders, and where they are accepted high commission charges may be incurred. In addition retailers are often unwilling to handle them, many preferring debit or credit cards.

Outside the euro zone US dollar or euro travellers' cheques can be used for payment in countries which have a 'soft' currency, ie one which cannot be traded on the international markets. Your bank will advise you.

Travel Money Cards

An increasingly popular and practical alternative to travellers' cheques is a pre-paid, PIN protected travel money card offering the security of travellers' cheques with the convenience of plastic. Load the card with the amount you need (in euros, sterling or US dollars) before leaving home, and then simply use cash machines to make withdrawals and/or present the card to pay for goods and services in shops and restaurants as you would a credit or debit card. You can obtain a second card so that another user can access the funds and you can also top the card up over the telephone or on the internet while you are abroad.

These cards, which work like a debit card – except there are usually no loading or transaction fees to pay – can be cheaper to use than credit or debit cards for both cash withdrawals and purchases. They are issued by the Post Office, Travelex, Lloyds Bank and American Express amongst many others. For a comparison table see www.which-prepaid-card.co.uk

Credit and Debit Cards

Credit and debit cards offer a convenient and safe way of spending abroad. In addition to using a card to pay for goods and services wherever your card logo is displayed you can obtain cash advances from cash machines using your PIN. MasterCard and VISA list the location of their ATM/cash dispensers in countries throughout the world on www.mastercard.com and http://visa.via.infonow.net/locator/eur. More often than not ATMs will offer an English language option once you insert your card.

For the use of credit cards abroad most banks impose a foreign currency conversion charge (typically 2.75% per transaction) which is usually the same for both credit and debit cards. If you use your credit card to withdraw cash there will be a further commission charge of up to 3% and you may also be charged a higher interest rate.

In line with market practice, Barclaycard, which issues the Caravan Club's credit card, charges a 2.75% fee for all card transactions outside the UK. Cash withdrawals abroad are subject to a 2% handling charge as in the UK, with a minimum charge of £3, maximum £50.

Dynamic Currency Conversion

When you pay with a credit or debit card retailers may offer you the choice of currency for payment, eg a euro amount will be converted into sterling and then charged to your card account. You will be asked to sign an agreement to accept the conversion rate used and final amount charged and, having done so, there is no opportunity to change your mind or obtain a refund. This is known as a 'dynamic currency conversion' but the exchange rate used is unlikely to be as favourable as that used by your card issuer. You may also find retailers claiming that a sterling bill will automatically be generated when a UK-issued credit card is tendered and processed. If this is the case then you may prefer to pay cash.

Some ATMs particularly, it is reported, in Spain will give you the option to convert your withdrawal into sterling when you withdraw euros. Refuse and opt to pay in the national currency.

Contact your credit card issuer before you leave home to warn them that you are travelling abroad

Check the expiry date of your cards before you leave and memorise the PIN for each one. Even if you do not intend to withdraw cash with a card while you are away, you may need to key in your PIN at shops, restaurants or garages. If you have several cards, take at least two in case you come across gaps in acceptance of certain cards, eg shops which accept only MasterCard. If you are planning an extended journey arrange for your credit or charge card account to be cleared each month by variable direct debit, ensuring that bills are paid on time and no interest is charged.

Credit and debit 'chip and PIN' cards issued by UK banks may not be universally accepted abroad and it is wise to check before incurring expenditure.

Contact your credit or debit card issuer before you leave home to warn them that you are travelling abroad. In the battle against card fraud, card issuers are frequently likely to query transactions which they regard as unusual or suspicious. This may result in a cash withdrawal from an ATM being declined, or a retailer at the point of sale having to telephone for authorisation and/or confirmation of your details. Difficulties can occur if there is a language barrier or if the retailer is unwilling to bother with further checks. Your card may be declined or, worse still, temporarily stopped. In this instance you should insist that the retailer contacts the local authorisation centre but, in any event, it is a good idea to carry your card issuer's helpline number with you. You will also need this number to report the loss or theft of your card.

Emergency Cash

If an emergency or robbery means that you need cash in a hurry, then friends or relatives at home can use the MoneyGram instant money transfer service available at post offices and branches of Thomas Cook and Going Places travel agents. This service, which does not necessarily require the sender to use a bank account or credit card, enables the transfer of money to over 180,000 locations around the world. Transfers take approximately ten minutes and charges are levied on a sliding scale.

As a last resort, contact the nearest British Embassy or Consulate for help

Western Union operates a similar secure, worldwide service and has offices located in banks, post offices, travel agents, stations and shops. You can also transfer funds instantly by telephone on 0800 833833 or online at www.westernunion.co.uk

As a last resort, contact the nearest British Embassy or Consulate for help. The Foreign & Commonwealth Office in London can arrange for a relative or friend to deposit funds which will be authorised for payment by embassy staff. See individual Country Introductions for embassy and consulate addresses abroad.

Most travel insurance policies will cover you for only a limited amount of lost or stolen cash (usually between £250 and £500) and you will probably have to wait until you return home for reimbursement.

The Euro

The euro is now the only legal tender in the following countries covered by this guide: Austria, Belgium, Finland, France, Germany, Greece, Italy, Luxembourg, the Netherlands, Portugal, Slovakia, Slovenia and Spain. In addition, the Republic of Ireland, Cyprus, Malta and the states of Andorra, Monte Carlo, San Marino and the Vatican City have also adopted the euro. Each country's versions of banknotes and coins are valid in all the countries of the single currency euro zone.

Of the twelve member states which joined the EU in 2004 and 2007 only Cyprus, Malta, Slovakia and Slovenia have secured agreement to join the single currency and replace their former currencies with the euro. In the meantime, you will usually find euros readily accepted in other member states in payment for goods and services. Denmark, Sweden and the UK, although long-standing member states of the EU, do not currently participate in the euro.

Police have issued warnings that counterfeit euro notes are in circulation on the Continent. You should be aware and take all precautions to ensure that €10, €20 and €50 notes and €2 coins you receive from sources other than banks and legitimate bureaux de change, are genuine.

Holiday Money Security

Treat your cards as carefully as you would cash. Use a money belt, if possible, to conceal cards and valuables and do not keep all your cash and cards in the same place. Split cash between members of your party. Memorise your PINs and never keep them with your credit/debit cards.

If you keep a wallet in your pocket, place a rubber band around it, as it is then more difficult for a pickpocket to slide the wallet out without your noticing.

To avoid credit or debit card 'cloning' or 'skimming' never let your card out of your sight – in restaurants follow the waiter to the till or insist that the card machine is brought to your table. This is particularly important as you may frequently find that a signature on a transaction slip is not checked against the signature on your card. If you do allow your card to be taken and it is gone for more than a minute, become suspicious.

If you suspect your card has been fraudulently used, or if your card is lost or stolen, or if a cash machine retains it, call the issuing bank immediately. All the major card companies and banks operate a 24-hour emergency helpline. If you are unlucky enough to become a victim of fraud your bank should refund the money stolen, provided you have not been negligent or careless.

Keep your card's magnetic strip away from other cards and objects, especially if they are also magnetic. If the card is damaged in any way electronic terminals may not accept your transaction.

If you use travellers' cheques keep a separate note of their serial numbers in case of loss, and a record of where and when you cash them. If they are lost or stolen, contact the appropriate refund service immediately.

Join a card protection plan (the Caravan Club offers one to its members) so that in the event of loss or theft, one telephone call will cancel all your cards and arrange replacements. Carry your credit card issuer/bank's 24-hour UK helpline number with you.

Take care when using cash machines. If the machine is obstructed or poorly lit, avoid it. If someone near the machine is behaving suspiciously or makes you feel uneasy, find another one. If there is something unusual about the cash machine do not use it and report the matter to the bank or owner of the premises. Do not accept help from strangers and do not allow yourself to be distracted.

Be aware of your surroundings and if someone is watching you closely do not proceed with the transaction. Shield the screen and keyboard so that anyone waiting to use the machine cannot see you enter your PIN or transaction amount. Put your cash, card and receipt away immediately. Count your cash later and always keep your receipt to compare with your monthly statement.

If you bank over the internet and are using a computer in a public place such as a library or internet café, do not leave the PC unattended and ensure that no-one is watching what you type. Always log off from internet banking upon completion of your session to prevent the viewing of previous pages of your online session.

The cost of credit and debit card fraud is largely borne by banks and ultimately its customers, but the direct cost to cardholders should not be under-estimated in terms of inconvenience and frustration, not to mention the time taken for incidents to be investigated and fraudently withdrawn funds to be returned to your account. Learn more about card fraud and preventative measures to combat it on www.cardwatch.org.uk

*See also **Security and Safety** in the section **DURING YOUR STAY**.*

Motoring – Advice

Preparing For Your Journey

Adequate and careful preparation of your vehicles should be your first priority to ensure a safe and trouble-free journey. Make sure your car and caravan are properly serviced before you depart and take a well-equipped spares kit and a spare wheel and tyre for your caravan; the lack of this is probably the main single cause of disrupted holidays.

Re-read the Technical Information section of your UK Sites Directory & Handbook as it contains a wealth of information which is relevant to caravanning anywhere in the world.

The Caravan Club offers a free advice service to Club members, whether newcomers to caravanning or old hands, on technical and general caravanning matters and publishes information sheets on a wide range of topics, all of which members can download from the Club's website. Alternatively, write to the Club's Technical Department or telephone for more details. For advice on issues specific to countries other than the UK, Club members should contact the Travel Service Information Officer.

Driving On The Continent

Probably the main disincentive to travelling abroad, particularly for caravanners, is the need to drive on the right-hand side of the road. However, for most people this proves to be no problem at all after the first hour or so. There are a few basic, but important, points to remember:

- Buy a good road map or atlas and plan ahead to use roads suitable for towing. See ***Route Planning and GPS*** in the chapter ***Motoring – Equipment***.
- In your eagerness to reach your destination, don't attempt vast distances in a single stint. Share the driving, if possible, and plan to break your journey overnight at a suitable campsite. There are thousands of sites listed in this guide and many are well situated near motorways and main roads.
- Adjust all your mirrors for maximum rear-view observation. The vast majority of towed caravans – whatever the type of towing vehicle – will require extension mirrors to comply with legal requirements for an adequate rearwards view.
- Make sure the road ahead is clear before overtaking. Stay well behind the vehicle in front and, if possible, have someone with good judgement in the left-hand seat to give you the 'all clear'.
- If traffic builds up behind you, pull over safely and let it pass.
- Pay particular attention when turning left, when leaving a rest area/petrol station/campsite, or after passing through a one-way system to ensure that you continue to drive on the right-hand side of the road.
- If your headlights are likely to dazzle other road users, adjust them to deflect to the right instead of the left, using suitable beam deflectors or (in some cases) a built-in adjustment system. Some lights can have the deflective part of the lens obscured with tape or a pre-cut adhesive mask, but check in your car's handbook if this is permitted or not. Some lights run too hot to be partially obscured.
- While travelling, particularly in the height of the summer, it is wise to stop approximately every two hours (at the most) to stretch your legs and take a break.
- In case of breakdown or accident, use hazard warning lights and warning triangle(s).

Another disincentive for caravanners to travel abroad is the worry about roads and gradients in mountainous countries. Britain has steeper gradients on many of its main roads than many other European countries and traffic density is far higher.

The chapter ***Mountain Passes and Tunnels*** under ***PLANNING AND TRAVELLING*** gives detailed advice on using mountain passes.

Another worry involves vehicle breakdown and language difficulties. The Caravan Club's comprehensive and competitively priced Red Pennant Overseas Holiday Insurance is geared to handle all these contingencies with multi-lingual staff available at the Club's headquarters 24 hours a day throughout the year – see www.caravanclub.co.uk/redpennant

Some Final Checks

Experienced caravanners will be familiar with the checks necessary before setting off and the following list is a reminder:

- All car and caravan lights are working and a sets of spare bulbs are packed.
- The coupling is correctly seated on the towball and the breakaway cable is attached.
- All windows, vents, hatches and doors are shut.
- All on-board water systems are drained.
- All mirrors are adjusted for maximum visibility.
- Corner steadies are fully wound up and the brace is handy for your arrival on site.
- Any fires or flames are extinguished and the gas cylinder tap is turned off. Fire extinguishers are fully charged and close at hand.
- The over-run brake is working correctly.
- The jockey wheel is raised and secured, the handbrake is released.

Driving Offences

You are obliged to comply with the traffic rules and regulations of the countries you visit. Research shows that non-resident drivers are more like to take risks and break the law due to their feeling of impunity. Cross-border enforcement of traffic laws is the subject of a European Directive which is in the process of being ratified by EU member states. This will bring an end to flagrant disregard of traffic rules and make them equally enforceable throughout the EU. In the meantime, a number of bi-lateral agreements already exist between European countries which means that there is no escaping penalty notices and demands for payment for motoring offences.

Some foreign police officers can look rather intimidating to British visitors used to unarmed police. Needless to say, they expect you to be polite and show respect and, in return, they are generally helpful and may well be lenient to a visiting motorist. Never consider offering a bribe!

The authorities in many countries are hard on parking and speeding offenders. In Scandinavia, for example, fines for speeding are spectacularly high and speed traps so frequent that it is not worth taking the risk of driving over the speed limit. Visiting motorists should not be influenced by the speed at which locals drive; they often know where the speed traps are and can slow down in time to avoid being caught! In addition, driver education in some European countries – and consequently driving standards – is still poor. In general, it is no use protesting if caught, as those who refuse to pay may have their vehicle impounded.

The maximum legal level of alcohol in the blood in most Continental countries is lower than that in the UK, and many police forces are authorised to carry out random breath tests. It is wise to adopt the 'no drink when driving' rule at all times; offenders are heavily fined all over Europe and penalties can include confiscation of driving licence, vehicle(s) and even imprisonment.

Many police forces are authorised to carry out random breath tests

Be particularly careful if you have penalty points on your driving licence. If you commit an offence on the Continent which attracts penalty points, local police may well do checks on your licence to establish whether the addition of those points would render you liable to disqualification. You will then have to find other means to get yourself and your vehicle(s) home.

On-the-Spot Fines

Many countries allow their police officers to issue fines which must be paid immediately, up to certain limits. The fine may be a deposit for a larger fine which will be issued to your home address. In most countries credit cards are not accepted in payment of on-the-spot fines and you may find yourself accompanied to the nearest cash machine. Always obtain a receipt for money handed over.

Fuel

During ferry crossings make sure your petrol tank is not over-full. Don't be tempted to carry spare petrol in cans; the ferry companies and Eurotunnel forbid this practice and even the carriage of empty cans is prohibited.

Grades of petrol sold on the Continent are comparable to those sold in the UK with the same familiar brands; 3 Star is frequently known as 'Essence' and 4 Star as 'Super'. Diesel is sometimes called 'Gasoil' and is available in all the countries covered by this guide. The fuel prices given in the table at the end of this chapter were correct according to the latest information available in September 2009. Fuel prices and availability can also be checked on the AA's website, www.theaa.com

In sparsely populated regions, such as northern Scandinavia, it is a sensible precaution to travel with a full petrol tank and to keep it topped up. Similarly in remote rural areas in any country you may have difficulty finding a manned petrol station at night or on Sunday. Petrol stations offering a 24-hour service may involve an automated process which will only work with locally issued credit cards.

*See the **Fuel Price Guide Table** at the end of this chapter.*

Automotive Liquified Petroleum Gas (LPG)

The increasing popularity of LPG – known as 'autogas' or GPL – and use of dual-fuelled vehicles means that the availability of automotive LPG has become an important issue for some drivers, and the Country Introductions in this guide provide more information.

A Dutch guide, LPG Gids, listing the locations of LPG fuel stations in 22 countries across Europe, is sold by Vicarious Books – see www.vicariousbooks.co.uk or telephone 0131 208 3333.

There are different tank-filling openings in use in different countries. Pending the adoption of a common European filling system, UKLPG, the trade association for the LPG industry in the UK, and the major fuel suppliers recommend the use of either of the two types of Dutch bayonet fitting. UKLPG also recommends that vehicle-filling connections requiring the use of adaptors in order to fill with the Dutch bayonet filling guns, should not be used. However, the Club recognises that in some circumstances it may be necessary to use an adaptor and these are available from Autogas 2000 Ltd on 01845 523213, www.autogas.co.uk

Lead Replacement Petrol

Leaded petrol has been withdrawn from sale in many countries in Europe and, in general, is only available from petrol stations in the form of a bottled additive. Where lead replacement petrol is still available at the pump it is generally from the same pumps previously used for leaded petrol, ie red or black pumps, and may be labelled 'Super Plus', 'Super 98' or 'Super MLV', but it is advisable to check before filling up if this is not clear from information at the pump.

Low Emission Zones

More than 70 cities in eight countries around Europe have introduced 'Low Emission Zones' (LEZ) in order to regulate vehicle pollution levels. Some schemes require you to buy a windscreen sticker, pay a fee or register your vehicle before entering the zone and you may need to show proof that your vehicle meets the required standard.

At the time this guide was published, most LEZ legislation applied only to vans and lorries but in Germany, and to a lesser extent Italy, it applies to passenger cars and motor caravans. The appropriate Country Introductions contain further details; see also www.lowemissionzones.eu for maps showing the location of the LEZ and other information.

Motor Caravans Towing Cars

A motor caravan towing a small car is illegal in most European countries, although such units are sometimes encountered. Motor caravanners wishing to tow a small car abroad should transport it on a braked trailer so that all four of the car's wheels are off the road.

Motorway Tolls

For British drivers who may never, or rarely, have encountered a toll booth, there are a couple of points to bear in mind. First of all, you will be on the 'wrong' side of the car for the collection of toll tickets at the start of the motorway section and payment of tolls at the end. If you are travelling without a front seat passenger, this can mean a big stretch or a walk round to the other side of the car. Most toll booths are solidly built and you should be careful of any high concrete kerbs when pulling up to them.

On entering a stretch of motorway you will usually have to stop at a barrier and take a ticket from a machine to allow the barrier to rise. Avoid the lanes dedicated to vehicles displaying electronic season tickets. You may encounter toll booths without automatic barriers where it is still necessary to take a ticket and, if you pass through without doing so, you may be fined. On some stretches of motorway there are no ticket machines as you enter and you simply pay a fixed sum when you exit.

Your toll ticket will indicate the time you entered the motorway. Be warned that in some countries electronic tills at exit booths calculate the distance a vehicle has travelled and the journey time. The police are automatically informed if speeding has taken place and fines are imposed.

Payment can be made by credit cards in most, but not all countries covered by this guide.

*See **Country Introductions** for specific information.*

Parking

Make sure you check local parking regulations, as fines may be imposed and unattended vehicles clamped or towed away. Look out for road markings and for short-term parking zones. Ensure you are in possession of parking discs in towns where they are required. As a general rule, park on the right-hand side of the road in the direction of traffic flow, avoiding cycle and bus lanes and tram tracks. Vehicles should not cause an obstruction and should be adequately lit when parked at night.

The following are some signs that you may encounter.

No parking on Monday, Wednesday, Friday or Sunday

No parking on Tuesday, Thursday or Saturday

Fortnightly parking on alternative sides

No parking from the 1st-15th of the month

No parking from the 16th-end of the month

In parts of central Europe car theft may be a problem and you are advised to park only in officially designated, guarded car parks whenever possible.

Parking Facilities for the Disabled

The Blue Badge is recognised in most European countries and it allows disabled motorists to use the same parking concessions enjoyed by the citizens of the country you are visiting. Concessions differ from country to country, however, and it is important to know when and where you can and, more importantly, cannot park. If you are in any doubt about your rights, do not park.

An explanatory leaflet 'European Parking Card for People with Disabilities' describes what the concessions are in 29 countries and gives advice on how to explain to police and parking attendants in their own language that, as a foreign visitor, you are entitled to the same parking concessions as disabled residents. It is obtainable from www.iam.org.uk/motoringtrust. Alternatively the Department for Transport publishes a leaflet entitled 'The Blue Badge Scheme: Rights and Responsibilities in England' which also covers use abroad. Telephone 0300 1231102 to request a copy.

Priority and Roundabouts

*See also **Country Introductions**.*

When driving on the Continent it is essential to be aware of other vehicles which may have priority over you, particularly when they join from the right the road you are using. Road signs indicate priority or loss of priority and motorists must be sure that they understand the signs.

Care should be taken at intersections and you should never rely on being given right of way, even if you have priority, especially in small towns and villages where local, often slow-moving, traffic will take right of way. Always give way to public service and military vehicles and to buses, trams and coaches.

Never rely on being given right of way, even if you have priority

Generally, priority at roundabouts is given to vehicles entering the roundabout unless signposted to the contrary, for example in France (see Country Introduction). This is a reversal of the UK rule and care is needed when travelling anti-clockwise round a roundabout. Keep to the outside lane, if possible, to make your exit easier.

Public Transport

In general in built-up areas be prepared to stop to allow a bus to pull out from a bus stop when the driver is signalling his intention to do so. Take particular care when school buses have stopped and passengers are getting on and off.

Always overtake trams on the right; do not overtake near a tram stop. These may be in the centre of the road and when a tram or bus stops to allow passengers on and off, you should stop to allow them to cross to the pavement. Give way to trams which are turning across your carriageway.

Do not park so as to obstruct tram lines or force other drivers to do so; trams cannot steer round obstructions! Take care when crossing tram tracks, especially if the rails are wet, and be particularly careful when crossing them at shallow angles, on bends and at junctions.

Road Signs and Markings

*See also **Country Introductions**.*

You will often encounter STOP signs in situations which, in the UK, would probably be covered by a Give Way sign. Be particularly careful; coming to a complete halt is usually compulsory, even if local drivers seem unconcerned by it, and failure to do so may result in a fine. Be careful too in areas where maintenance of roads may be irregular and where white lines have worn away.

A solid single or double white line in the middle of the carriageway always means no overtaking.

Direction signs in general may be confusing, giving only the name of a town on the way to a larger city, or simply the road number and no place name. They may be smaller than you expect and not particularly easy to spot. The colours of signs indicating different categories of road may differ from those used in the UK. For example, motorway signs may be green (not blue) and non-motorway signs may be blue, rather than green as they are in the UK. This can be particularly confusing, for example when crossing from France where motorway signs are blue, into Switzerland or Italy where they are green.

Across the EU you will find that major routes have not only an individual road number, such as A6, but also a number beginning with an 'E' displayed on green and white signs. Routes running from east to west have even 'E' numbers, whereas routes running from north to south have odd 'E' numbers. This can be helpful when planning long-distance routes across international frontiers. In some countries, particularly in Scandinavia and Belgium, through routes or motorways may only show the 'E' road numbers, so it would be advisable to make a note of them when planning your route. The E road system is not recognised in the UK and there are no such road signs.

Pedestrian Crossings

Stopping to allow pedestrians to cross at zebra crossings is not nearly as common a practice on the Continent as it is in the UK. Pedestrians often do not expect to cross until the road is clear and may be surprised if you stop to allow them to do so. Check your mirrors carefully when braking as other drivers behind you, not expecting to stop, may be taken by surprise. The result may be a rear-end shunt or, worse still, vehicles overtaking you at the crossing and putting pedestrians at risk.

Speed Limits

Remember speed limit signs are in kilometres per hour, not miles per hour. General speed limits in each country are given in the table at the end of this chapter. Refer to individual Country Introductions for details of any variations.

Radar-detection devices, whether in use or not, are illegal in many countries on the Continent and should not be carried at all. If you have one in your vehicle remove it before leaving home.

Speed cameras are becoming more widespread throughout Europe but you should not expect them to be highly visible as they are in the UK. In many instances, for example on the German motorway network, they may be hidden or deliberately inconspicuous. The use of unmarked police cars using speed detection equipment is common.

Traffic Lights

Traffic lights may not be placed as conspicuously as they are in the UK , for instance they may be smaller, differently shaped or suspended across the road, with a smaller set on a post at the roadside. You may find that lights change directly from red to green, by-passing amber completely. Flashing amber lights generally indicate that you may proceed with caution if it is safe to do so but must give way to pedestrians and other vehicles. A green filter light should be treated with caution as you may still have to give way to pedestrians who have a green light to cross the road.

Be cautious when approaching a green light, especially in fast-moving traffic

You may find that drivers are not particularly well-disciplined about stopping as they approach a light as it turns red and if they are behind you in this situation, they will expect you to accelerate through the lights rather than brake hard to stop. Therefore be cautious when approaching a green light, especially if you are in a relatively fast-moving stream of traffic. Similarly, be careful when pulling away from a green light and check left and right just in case a driver on the road crossing yours has jumped a red light.

Fuel Price Guide

Prices in pence per litre as at September 2009

Country	Unleaded		Diesel	
	Unleaded	Translation of Unleaded	Diesel	Translation of Diesel
Andorra	89.00	Sans plomb or sin plomo	75.00	Gazole or gasóleo
Austria	98.70	Bleifrei	89.80	Diesel
Belgium	120.33	Sans plomb or loodvrije	92.47	
Croatia	82.70	Eurosuper or bez olova	87.27	Dizel
Czech Republic	99.16	Natural or bez olova	91.80	Nafta
Denmark	119.40	Blyfri	102.91	
Finland	111.51	Lyijyton polttoaine	99.23	
France	103.86	Essence sans plomb	95.69	Gazole
Germany	114.01	Bleifrei	94.34	Diesel
Gibraltar	75.00		75.00	-
Greece	98.08	Amoliwdi wensina	90.51	Petreleo
Hungary	97.47	Olommentes uzemanyag	91.54	Dizel or gázolaj
Italy	113.92	Sensa piombo	105.11	Gasolio
Luxembourg	95.94	Sans plomb	76.89	Gazole
Netherlands	112.35	Loodvrije	94.60	Diesel or gasolie
Norway	131.18	Blyfri	118.79	Diesel
Poland	94.08	Bezolowiu	80.15	
Portugal	115.79	Sem chumbo	92.02	Gasóleo or diesel
Slovakia	104.93	Natural or olovnatych prisad	98.70	Nafta
Slovenia	99.68	Brez svinca	92.56	
Spain	94.34	Sin plomo	83.66	Gasóleo A or Gas-oil
Sweden	105.01	Blyfri normal, premium	99.32	Diesel
Switzerland	92.55	Bleifrei or sans plomb or sensa piomba	94.90	Diesel or gazole or gasolio
United Kingdom	106.90		107.90	

Fuel prices courtesy of the Automobile Association (September 2009)

Prices shown are in pence per litre and use currency exchange rates at the time this guide was compiled. They should be used for guideline comparison purposes only. Differences in prices actually paid may be due to currency and oil price fluctuations as well as regional variations within countries. In general, the prices shown are for the lowest octane fuel available.

In many countries leaded petrol has been withdrawn and Lead Replacement Petrol (LRP) is becoming more difficult to find. Alternatively a lead substitute additive can be bought at petrol stations and added to the fuel tanks of cars which run on leaded petrol. It is understood that it is the same additive as used in the UK and that 10ml will treat 10 litres of petrol.

Speed Limits

Kilometres per hour (see Conversion Table below for equivalent miles per hour)

Country	Built-Up Areas	Open Road		Motorways		
		Solo	Towing	Solo	Towing	Minimum Speed
Andorra	50	60-90	60-90	n/a	n/a	n/a
Austria*	50	100	80	110-130	100	60
Belgium*	30-50	90	90	120	120	70
Croatia*	50	90	80	110-130	90	60
Czech Republic*	50	80-90	80	130	80	80
Denmark*	50	80-90	70	110-130	80	40
Finland*	50	80-100	80	100-120	80	-
France* Normal	50	90	80-90	110-130	90-130	80
France* Bad Weather	50	80	80	110	90-110	-
Germany*	50	100	80	130	80	60
Greece	50	90-110	80	130	80	-
Hungary	50	90-110	80	130	70-80	-
Italy*	50-70	90-110	70	130	80	40
Luxembourg*	50	90	75	130	90	-
Netherlands*	50	80-100	80	120	90	60
Norway*	50	80	80	90-100	80	-
Poland*	50-60	90-110	70-80	130	80	40
Portugal*	50	90-100	70-80	120	100	50
Slovakia*	50	90	90	130	90	65-80
Slovenia*	50	90-100	80	130	80	60
Spain*	50	90-100	70-80	120	80	60
Sweden*	30-60	70-100	70-90	110-120	80	-
Switzerland*	50	80	80	100-120	80	60

Converting Kilometres to Miles

km/h	20	30	40	50	60	70	80	90	100	110	120	130
mph	13	18	25	31	37	44	50	56	62	68	74	81

NOTES: 1) ** See Country Introductions for further details, including special speed limits, eg for motor caravans, where applicable.*

2) *In some countries speed limits in residential areas may be as low as 20 km/h*

European Distances

Distances are shown in kilometres and are calculated from town/city centres along the most practical roads, although not necessarily taking the shortest route.

1 km = 0.62 miles

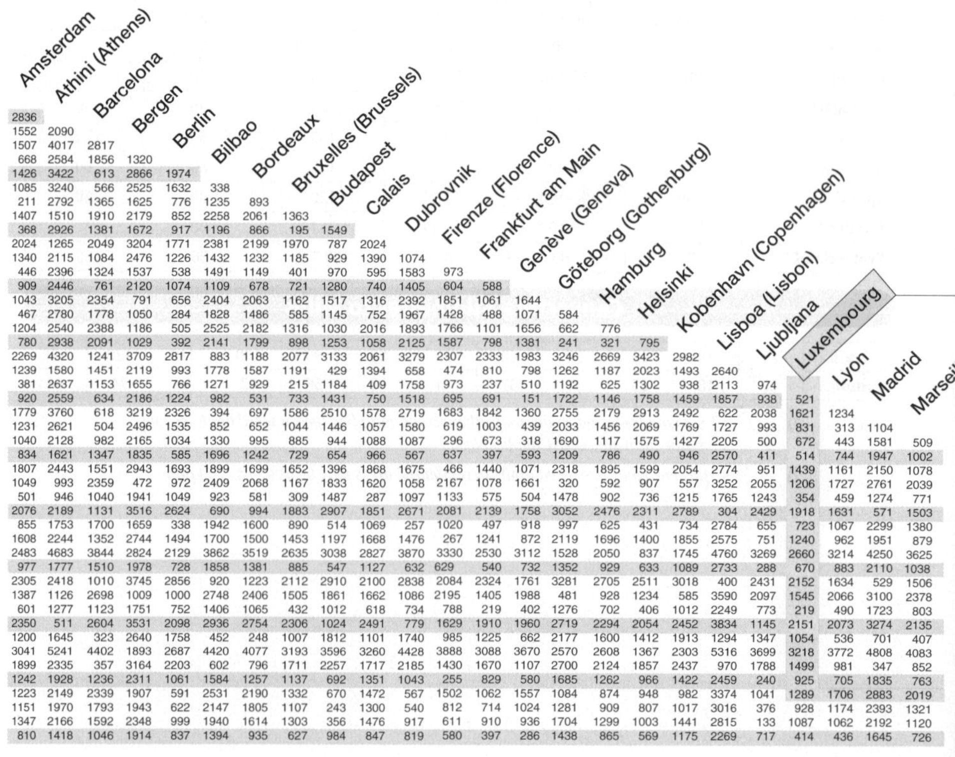

Amsterdam	Athini (Athens)	Barcelona	Bergen	Berlin	Bilbao	Bordeaux	Bruxelles (Brussels)	Budapest	Calais	Dubrovnik	Firenze (Florence)	Frankfurt am Main	Genève (Geneva)	Göteborg (Gothenburg)	Hamburg	Helsinki	Kobenhavn (Copenhagen)	Lisboa (Lisbon)	Ljubljana	Luxembourg	Lyon	Madrid	Marseill
2836																							
1552	2090																						
1507	4017	2817																					
668	2584	1856	1320																				
1426	3422	613	2866	1974																			
1085	3240	566	2525	1632	338																		
211	2792	1365	1625	776	1235	893																	
1407	1510	1910	2179	852	2258	2061	1363																
368	2926	1381	1672	917	1196	866	195	1549															
2024	1265	2049	3204	1771	2381	2199	1970	787	2024														
1340	2115	1084	2476	1226	1432	1232	1185	929	1390	1074													
446	2396	1324	1537	538	1491	1149	401	970	595	1583	973												
909	2446	761	2120	1074	1109	678	721	1280	740	1405	604	588											
1043	3205	2354	791	656	2404	2063	1162	1517	1316	2392	1851	1061	1644										
467	2780	1778	1050	284	1828	1486	585	1145	752	1967	1428	488	1071	584									
1204	2540	2388	1186	505	2525	2182	1316	1030	2016	1893	1766	1101	1656	662	776								
780	2938	2091	1029	392	2141	1799	898	1253	1058	2125	1587	798	1381	241	321	795							
2269	4320	1241	3709	2817	883	1188	2077	3133	2061	3279	2307	2333	1983	3246	2669	3423	2982						
1239	1580	1451	2119	993	1778	1587	1191	429	1394	658	474	810	798	1262	1187	2023	1493	2640					
381	2637	1153	1655	766	1271	929	215	1184	409	1758	973	237	510	1192	625	1302	938	2113	974				
920	2559	634	2186	1224	982	531	733	1431	750	1518	695	691	151	1722	1146	1758	1459	1857	938	521			
1779	3760	618	3219	2326	394	697	1586	2510	1578	2719	1683	1842	1360	2755	2179	2913	2492	622	2038	1621	1234		
1231	2621	504	2496	1535	852	652	1044	1446	1057	1580	619	1003	439	2033	1456	2069	1769	1727	993	831	313	1104	
1040	2128	982	2165	1034	1330	995	885	944	1088	1087	296	673	318	1690	1117	1575	1427	2205	500	672	443	1581	509
834	1621	1347	1835	585	1696	1242	729	654	966	567	637	397	593	1209	786	490	946	2570	411	514	744	1947	1002
1807	2443	1551	2943	1693	1899	1699	1652	1396	1868	1675	466	1440	1071	2318	1895	1599	2054	2774	951	1439	1161	2150	1078
1049	993	2359	472	972	2409	2068	1167	1833	1620	1058	2167	1078	1661	320	592	907	557	3252	2055	1206	1727	2761	2039
501	946	1040	1941	1049	923	581	309	1487	287	1097	1133	575	504	1478	902	736	1215	1765	1243	354	459	1274	771
2076	2189	1131	3516	2624	690	994	1883	2907	1851	2671	2081	2139	1758	3052	2476	2311	2789	304	2429	1918	1631	571	1503
855	1753	1700	1659	338	1942	1600	890	514	1069	257	1020	497	918	997	625	431	734	2784	655	723	1067	2299	1380
1608	2244	1352	2744	1494	1700	1500	1453	1197	1668	1476	267	1241	872	2119	1696	1400	1855	2575	751	1240	962	1951	879
2483	4683	3844	2824	2129	3862	3519	2635	3038	2827	3870	3330	2530	3112	1528	2050	837	1745	4760	3269	2660	3214	4250	3625
977	1777	1510	1978	728	1858	1381	885	547	1127	632	629	540	732	1352	929	633	1089	2733	288	670	883	2110	1038
2305	2418	1010	3745	2856	920	1223	2112	2910	2100	2838	2084	2324	1761	3281	2705	2511	3018	400	2431	2152	1634	529	1506
1387	1126	2698	1009	1000	2748	2406	1505	1861	1662	1086	2195	1405	1988	481	928	1234	585	3590	2097	1545	2066	3100	2378
601	1277	1123	1751	752	1406	1065	432	1012	618	734	788	219	402	1276	702	406	1012	2249	773	219	490	1723	803
2350	511	2604	3531	2098	2936	2754	2306	1024	2491	779	1629	1910	1960	2719	2294	2054	2452	3834	1145	2151	2073	3274	2135
1200	1645	323	2640	1758	452	248	1007	1812	1101	1740	985	1225	662	2177	1600	1412	1913	1294	1347	1054	536	701	407
3041	5241	4402	1893	2687	4420	4077	3193	3596	3260	4428	3888	3088	3670	2570	2608	1367	2303	5316	3699	3218	3772	4808	4083
1899	2335	357	3164	2203	602	796	1711	2257	1717	2185	1430	1670	1107	2700	2124	1857	2437	970	1788	1499	981	347	852
1242	1928	1236	2311	1061	1584	1257	1137	692	1351	1043	255	829	580	1685	1262	966	1422	2459	240	925	705	1835	763
1223	2149	2339	1907	591	2531	2190	1332	670	1472	567	1502	1062	1557	1084	874	948	982	3374	1041	1289	1706	2883	2019
1151	1970	1793	1943	622	2147	1805	1107	243	1300	540	812	714	1024	1281	909	807	1017	3016	376	928	1174	2393	1321
1347	2166	1592	2348	999	1940	1614	1303	356	1476	917	611	910	936	1704	1299	1003	1441	2815	133	1087	1062	2192	1120
810	1418	1046	1914	837	1394	935	627	984	847	819	580	397	286	1438	865	569	1175	2269	717	414	436	1645	726

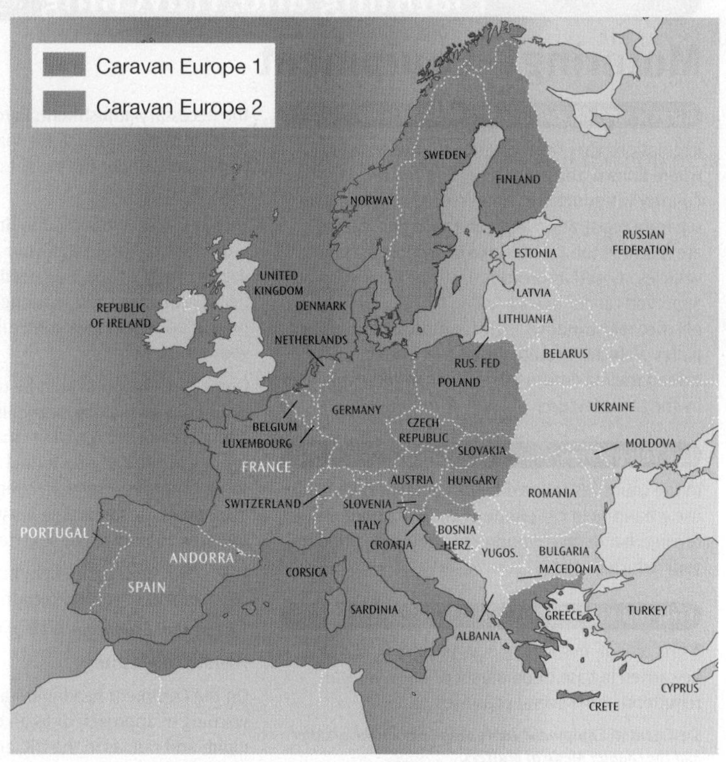

Luxembourg - Warszawa (Warsaw) = 1289 km

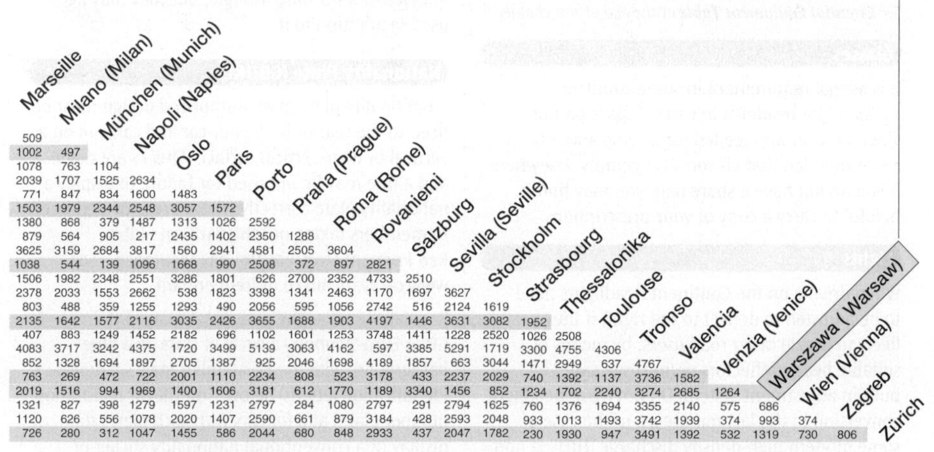

	Marseille	Milano (Milan)	München (Munich)	Napoli (Naples)	Oslo	Paris	Porto	Praha (Prague)	Roma (Rome)	Rovaniemi	Salzburg	Sevilla (Seville)	Stockholm	Strasbourg	Thessalonika	Toulouse	Tromso	Valencia	Venzia (Venice)	Warszawa (Warsaw)	Wien (Vienna)	Zagreb
Milano (Milan)	509																					
München (Munich)	1002	497																				
Napoli (Naples)	1078	763	1104																			
Oslo	2039	1707	1525	2634																		
Paris	771	847	834	1600	1483																	
Porto	1503	1979	2344	2548	3057	1572																
Praha (Prague)	1380	868	379	1487	1313	1026	2592															
Roma (Rome)	879	564	905	217	2435	1402	2350	1288														
Rovaniemi	3625	3159	2684	3817	1560	2941	4581	2505	3604													
Salzburg	1038	544	139	1096	1668	990	2508	372	897	2821												
Sevilla (Seville)	1506	1982	2348	2551	3286	1801	626	2700	2352	4733	2510											
Stockholm	2378	2033	1553	2662	538	1823	3398	1341	2463	1170	1697	3627										
Strasbourg	803	488	359	1255	1293	490	2056	595	1056	2742	516	2124	1619									
Thessalonika	2135	1642	1577	2116	3035	2426	3655	1688	1903	4197	1446	3631	3082	1952								
Toulouse	407	883	1249	1452	2182	696	1102	1601	1253	3748	1411	1228	2520	1026	2508							
Tromso	4083	3717	3242	4375	1720	3499	5139	3063	4162	597	3385	5291	1719	3300	4755	4306						
Valencia	852	1328	1694	1897	2705	1387	925	2046	1698	4189	1857	663	3044	1471	2949	637	4767					
Venzia (Venice)	763	269	472	722	2001	1110	2234	808	523	3178	433	2237	2029	740	1392	1137	3736	1582				
Warszawa (Warsaw)	2019	1516	994	1969	1400	1606	3181	612	1770	1189	3340	1456	852	1234	1702	2240	3274	2685	1264			
Wien (Vienna)	1321	827	398	1279	1597	1231	2797	284	1080	2797	291	2794	1625	760	1376	1694	3355	2140	575	686		
Zagreb	1120	626	556	1078	2020	1407	2590	661	879	3184	428	2593	2048	933	1013	1493	3742	1939	374	993	374	
Zürich	726	280	312	1047	1455	586	2044	680	848	2933	437	2047	1782	230	1930	947	3491	1392	532	1319	730	806

Motoring – Equipment

Bicycle and Motorbike Transportation

Regulations vary from country to country and, where known, these are set out in the relevant Country Introductions. As a general rule, however, separate registration and insurance documents are required for a motorbike or scooter and these vehicles, as well as bicycles, must be carried on an approved carrier in such a way that they do not obscure rear windows, lights, reflectors or number plates. Vehicles should not be overloaded, ie exceed the maximum loaded weight recommended by the manufacturer.

Car Telephones

In the countries covered by this guide it is illegal to use a hand-held car phone or mobile phone while driving; hands-free equipment should be fitted in your vehicle.

First Aid Kit

A first aid kit, in a strong dust-proof box, should be carried in case of emergency. This is a legal requirement in several countries.

*See **Essential Equipment Table** at the end of this chapter and the chapter **Medical Matters.***

Fire Extinguisher

As a recommended safety precaution, an approved fire extinguisher should be carried in all vehicles.

This is a legal requirement in several countries.

*See **Essential Equipment Table** at the end of this chapter.*

Glasses

It is a legal requirement in some countries, eg Spain, for residents to carry a spare pair of glasses if they are needed for driving and it is recommended that visitors also comply. Elsewhere, if you do not have a spare pair, you may find it helpful to carry a copy of your prescription.

Lights

When driving on the Continent headlights need to be adjusted to deflect to the right, if they are likely to dazzle other road users, by means of suitable beam deflectors or (in some cases) a built-in adjustment system. Do not leave headlight conversion to the last minute as, in the case of some modern high-density discharge (HID), xenon or halogen-type lights, a dealer may need to make the necessary adjustment. Remember also to adjust headlights according to the load being carried and to compensate for the weight of the caravan on the back of your car.

Even if you do not intend to drive at night, it is important to ensure that your headlights will not dazzle others as you may need to use them in heavy rain or fog and in tunnels. If using tape or a pre-cut adhesive mask remember to remove it on your return home.

Dipped headlights should be used in poor weather conditions such as fog, snowfall or heavy rain and in a tunnel even if it is well lit, and you may find police waiting at the end of a tunnel to check vehicles. In some countries dipped headlights are compulsory at all times, in others they must be used in built-up areas, on motorways or at certain times of the year.

Take a full set of spare light bulbs. This is a legal requirement in several countries.

*See **Essential Equipment Table** at the end of this chapter.*

Headlight-Flashing

On the Continent headlight-flashing is used as a warning of approach or as an overtaking signal at night, and not, as in the UK, an indication that you are giving way, so use with great care in case it is misunderstood. When another driver flashes you, make sure of his intention before moving.

Hazard Warning Lights

Generally hazard warning lights should not be used in place of a warning triangle, but they may be used in addition to it.

Nationality Plate (GB/IRL)

A nationality plate of an authorised design must be fixed to the rear of both your car and caravan on a vertical or near-vertical surface. Checks are made and a fine may be imposed for failure to display a nationality plate correctly. These are provided free to members taking out the Caravan Club's Red Pennant Overseas Holiday Insurance – see www.caravanclub.co.uk/redpennant

Regulations allow the optional display of the GB or Euro-Symbol – a circle of stars on a blue background, with the EU Member State's national identification letter(s) below – on UK car registration number plates and for cars with such plates the display of a conventional nationality sticker or plate is unnecessary when driving within the

EU and Switzerland. However, it is still required when driving outside the EU even when number plates incorporate the Euro-Symbol, and it is still required for all vehicles without Euro-Symbol plates. Registration plates displaying the GB Euro-Symbol must comply with the appropriate British Standard.

GB is the only permissible national identification code for cars registered in the UK.

Radar/Speed Camera Detectors

The possession or use of a radar-detection device, whether in use or not, is illegal in many countries on the Continent and you should not carry one in your vehicle. Penalties include fines, vehicle confiscation or a driving ban. Some countries also ban the use of GPS satellite navigation devices which pinpoint the position of fixed speed cameras and you must, therefore, deactivate the relevant Points of Interest (PoI) function .

Rear View External Mirrors

In order to comply with local regulations and avoid the attention of local police forces, ensure that your vehicle's external mirrors are adjusted correctly to allow you to view both sides of your caravan or trailer – over its entire length – from behind the steering wheel. Some countries stipulate that mirrors should extend beyond the width of the caravan but should be removed or folded in when travelling solo, and this is common-sense advice for all countries.

Reflective Jackets

Legislation has been introduced in some countries in Europe (see individual Country Introductions) requiring drivers to wear a reflective jacket or waistcoat if leaving a vehicle which is immobilised on the carriageway outside a built-up area. This is a common-sense requirement which will probably be extended to other countries and which should be observed wherever you drive. A second jacket is also recommended for a passenger who may need to assist in an emergency repair. Carry the jackets in the passenger compartment of your vehicle, rather than in the boot. The jackets should conform to at least European Standard EN471, Class 2 and are widely available from motor accessory shops and from the Club's shop – see www.caravanclub.co.uk/shop

Route Planning

An organisation called Keep Moving (www.keepmoving.co.uk) provides information on UK roads including routes to ferry ports , tel 09003 401100 or 401100 from a mobile phone. Both the AA and RAC have useful websites offering a route planning service with access for non-members: www.theaa.com and www.rac.co.uk. Other websites offering a European routes service and/or traffic information include www.viamichelin.com and www.mappy.com which, amongst other things, provides city centre maps for major towns across Europe.

Detailed, large-scale maps or atlases of the countries you are visiting are essential. Navigating your way around other countries can be confusing, especially for the novice, and the more care you take planning your route, the more enjoyable your journey will be. Before setting out, study maps and distance charts.

If you propose travelling across mountain passes check whether the suggested route supplied by the route-planning website takes account of passes or tunnels where caravans are not permitted or recommended.

*See the chapter **Mountain Passes and Tunnels.***

Before setting out, study maps and distance charts

Satellite Navigation

Continental postcodes do not, on the whole, pinpoint a particular street or part of a street in the same way as the system in use in the UK, and a French or German five-digit postcode, for example, can cover a very large area of many square kilometres. GPS co-ordinates are given for many site entries in this guide and others will be added over time. Otherwise, wherever possible full street addresses are given enabling you to programme your sat nav as accurately as possible.

Your sat nav device is a valuable aid in finding a campsite in an area you are not familiar with, but it is important to realise that such equipment is not perfect. For example, sat nav routes are unlikely to allow for the fact that you are towing a caravan or driving a large motor caravan. Use your common sense – if a road looks wrong, don't follow it.

It is probably wise, therefore, to use your sat nav in conjunction with the printed directions to campsites in this guide which are often compiled using local knowledge to pinpoint the most appropriate route, together with an up-to-date map or atlas. You may find it useful to identify a 'waypoint' (a nearby village, say) mentioned in these written directions and add it to your route definition when programming your sat nav to ensure you approach from a suitable direction.

Update your sat nav device regularly and remember that, in spite of detailed directions and the use of a sat nav, local conditions such as road closures and roadworks may, on occasion, make finding your destination difficult.

*See the chapter **Introduction** in the section **HOW TO USE THIS GUIDE** for more information on satellite navigation.*

Seat Belts

The wearing of seat belts is compulsory in all the countries featured in this guide. On-the-spot fines will be incurred for failure to wear them and, in the event of an accident and insurance claim, compensation for injury may be reduced by 50% if seat belts are not worn. As in the UK, legislation in most countries covered by this guide requires all children up to a certain age or height to use a child restraint appropriate for their weight or size and, in addition, some countries' laws prohibit them from sitting in the front of a car. Where local regulations differ from UK law, information is given in the relevant Country Introductions.

Rear-facing baby seats must never be used in a seat protected by a frontal airbag unless the airbag has been deactivated.

Snow Chains

Snow chains may be necessary on some roads in winter. They are compulsory in some countries during the winter where indicated by the appropriate road sign, when they must be fitted on at least two drive-wheels. Polar Automotive Ltd sells and hires out snow chains (20% discount for Caravan Club members), tel 01892 519933 www.snowchains.com, email: sales@snowchains.com

Spares

Caravan Spares

On the Continent it is generally much more difficult to obtain spares for caravans than for cars and it will usually be necessary to obtain spares from a UK manufacturer or dealer.

Car Spares Kits

Some motor manufacturers can supply spares kits for a selected range of models; contact your dealer for details. The choice of spares will depend on the vehicle, how long you are likely to be away and your own level of competence in car maintenance, but the following is a list of basic items which should cover the most common causes of breakdown:

Radiator top hose

Fan belt

Fuses and bulbs

Windscreen wiper blade

Length of 12v electrical cable

Tools, torch and WD40 or equivalent water repellent/dispersant spray

Spare Wheel

Your local caravan dealer should be able to supply an appropriate spare wheel. If you have any difficulty in obtaining one, the Caravan Club's Technical Department will provide Club members with a list of suppliers' addresses on request.

Tyre legislation across Europe is more or less fully harmonised and, while the Club has no specific knowledge of laws on the Continent regarding the use of space-saver spare wheels, there should be no problems in using such a wheel provided its use is strictly in accordance with the manufacturer's instructions.

Towing Bracket

The vast majority of cars registered after 1 August 1998 are legally required to have a European Type approved towing bracket (complying with European Directive 94/20) carrying a plate giving its approval number and various technical details, including the maximum noseweight. The approval process includes strength testing to a higher value than provided in the previous British Standard, and confirmation of fitting to all the car manufacturer's approved mounting points. Your car dealer or specialist towing bracket fitter will be able to give further advice. Checks may be made by foreign police. This requirement does not currently apply to motor caravans.

Tyres

Safe driving and handling when towing a caravan or trailer are very important and one major factor which is frequently overlooked is tyre condition. Your caravan tyres must be suitable for the highest speed at which you can legally tow (up to 81 mph in France), not for any lower speed at which you may choose to travel. Some older British caravans (usually over eight years old) may not meet this requirement and, if you are subject to a police check, this could result in an on-the-spot fine for each tyre, including the spare. Check your tyre specification before you leave and, if necessary, upgrade your tyres. The Caravan Club's technical advice leaflet 'Caravan Tyres and Wheels', available to members on the Club's website or by post, explains how to check if your tyres are suitable.

Most countries require a minimum tread depth of 1.6 mm over the central part of the whole tyre, but motoring organisations recommend at least 3 mm across the whole tyre. If you plan an extended trip and your tyres are likely to be more worn than this before you return home, replace them before you leave.

Winter tyres should be used in those countries with a severe winter climate to provide extra grip on snow and ice. If you intend to make an extended winter trip to alpine or Scandinavian areas or to travel regularly to them, it would be advisable to buy a set of winter tyres. Your local tyre dealer will be able to advise you. For information on regulations concerning the use of winter tyres and/or snow chains, see the appropriate Country Introductions.

Sizes

It is worth noting that some sizes of radial tyre to fit the 13" wheels commonly used on UK caravans are virtually impossible to find in stock at retailers abroad, eg 175R13C.

Tyre Pressure

Tyre pressure should be checked and adjusted when the tyres are cold; checking warm tyres will result in a higher pressure reading. The correct pressures will be found in your car handbook, but unless it states otherwise it is wise to add an extra four to six pounds per square inch to the rear tyres of a car when towing to improve handling and to carry the extra load on the hitch.

Make sure you know what pressure your caravan tyres should be. Some require a pressure much higher than that normally used for cars. Check your caravan handbook for details.

After a Puncture

The Caravan Club does not recommend the general use of liquid sealants for puncture repair. Such products should not be considered to achieve a permanent repair, and may indeed render the tyre irreparable. If sealant is used to allow the vehicle to be removed from a position of danger to one of safety, the damaged tyre should be removed from the vehicle, repaired and replaced as soon as practicable.

Following a caravan tyre puncture, especially on a single-axle caravan, it is advisable to have the opposite side (non-punctured) tyre removed from its wheel and checked inside and out for signs of damage resulting from overloading during the deflation of the punctured tyre. Failure to take this precaution may result in an increased risk of a second tyre deflation within a very short space of time.

Warning Triangles

In almost all European countries it is a legal requirement to use a warning triangle in the event of a breakdown or accident; some countries require two. It is strongly recommended that approved red warning triangles be carried as a matter of course.

A warning triangle should be placed on the road approximately 30 metres (100 metres on motorways) behind the broken down vehicle on the same side of the road. Always assemble the triangle before leaving your vehicle and walk with it so that the red, reflective surface is facing oncoming traffic. If a breakdown occurs round a blind corner, place the triangle in advance of the corner. Hazard warning lights may be used in conjunction with the triangle but they do not replace it.

*See **Essential Equipment Table** at the end of this chapter.*

Technical information compiled with the assistance of the Automobile Association.

Essential Equipment

See also the information contained in this Handbook chapter and in the relevant Country Introductions

Country	Warning Triangle	Spare Bulbs	First Aid Kit	Reflective Jacket	Additional Equipment to be Carried/Used
Andorra	Yes	Yes	Rec	Rec	Dipped headlights in poor daytime visibility. Winter tyres recommended; snow chains when road conditions dictate.
Austria	Yes	Rec	Yes	Yes	Winter tyres from 1 Nov to 15 April.*
Belgium	Yes	Rec	Rec	Yes	Dipped headlights in poor daytime visibility.
Croatia	Yes (2 for vehicle with trailer)	Yes	Yes	Yes	Dipped headlights at all times Oct-Mar.
Czech Rep	Yes	Yes	Yes	Yes	Dipped headlights at all times. Wearers of glasses when driving should carry a spare pair.
Denmark	Yes	Rec	Rec	Rec	Dipped headlights at all times. On motorways use hazard warning lights when queues or danger ahead.
Finland	Yes	Rec	Rec	Yes	Dipped headlights at all times. Winter tyres December to February.
France	Yes (2 rec)	Yes	Rec	Yes	Dipped headlights recommended at all times.
Germany	Yes	Rec	Yes	Rec	Dipped headlights recommended at all times. Winter tyres.
Greece	Yes	Rec	Yes	Rec	Fire extinguisher compulsory. Dipped headlights in towns at night and in poor daytime visibility.
Hungary	Yes	Rec	Yes	Yes	Dipped headlights at all times outside built-up areas and in built-up areas at night.
Italy	Yes	Rec	Rec	Yes	Dipped headlights at all times outside built-up areas.
Luxembourg	Yes	Rec	Rec	Yes	Dipped headlights at night and in daytime in bad weather.
Netherlands	Yes	Rec	Rec	Rec	Dipped headlights at night and in bad weather and recommended during the day.
Norway	Yes	Rec	Rec	Rec	Dipped headlights at all times. Vehicles over 3,500 kg must use snow chains in winter.
Poland	Yes	Rec	Rec	Rec	Dipped headlights at all times.
Portugal	Yes	Rec	Rec	Rec	Dipped headlights in poor daytime visibility, in tunnels and on main road linking Aveiro-Vilar Formoso at Spanish border (IP5).
Slovakia	Yes	Yes	Yes	Yes	Dipped headlights at all times.
Slovenia	Yes (2 for vehicle with trailer)	Yes	Yes	Yes	Dipped headlights at all times. Hazard warning lights when reversing. Use winter tyres between 15 Nov and 15 March or carry snow chains.
Spain	Yes (2 Rec)	Yes	Rec	Yes	Dipped headlights in tunnels and on 'special' roads (roadworks).* Wearers of glasses when driving recommended to carry a spare pair.
Sweden	Yes	Rec	Rec	Rec	Dipped headlights at all times. Winter tyres from 1 Dec to 31 March.
Switzerland (inc Liechtenstein)	Yes	Rec	Yes	Rec	Dipped headlights recommended at all times, compulsory in tunnels. Keep warning triangle in easy reach (not in boot).

NOTES:
1) *All countries: seat belts (if fitted) must be worn by all passengers.*
2) *Rec: not compulsory but strongly recommended.*
3) *Headlamp converters, spare bulbs, fire extinguisher, first aid kit and reflective waistcoat are recommended for all countries.*

* *See Country Introduction for further information.*

Mountain Passes and Tunnels

The mountain passes, rail and road tunnels listed in the following tables are shown on the maps within the chapter. Numbers and letters against each pass or tunnel in the following lists correspond with the numbers and letters on the maps.

Please read the following advice carefully.

Advice for Drivers

Mountain Passes

The conditions and comments in the following tables assume an outfit with good power/weight ratio. Even those mountain passes and tunnels which do not carry a 'not recommended' or 'not permitted' warning may be challenging for any vehicle, more so for car and caravan outfits. If in any doubt whatsoever, it is probably best to restrict yourself to those mountain passes which can be crossed by motorway. In any event, mountain passes should only be attempted by experienced drivers in cars with ample power and in good driving conditions; they should otherwise be avoided.

In the following table, where the entry states that caravans are not permitted or not recommended to use a pass, this generally – but not always – refers to towed caravans, and is based on advice originally supplied by the AA and/or local motoring organisations, but not checked by the Caravan Club. Motor caravans are seldom prohibited by such restrictions, but those which are relatively low powered or very large should find an alternative route. Always obey road signs at the foot of a pass, especially those referring to heavy vehicles, which may apply to some large motor caravans.

Do not attempt to cross passes at night or in bad weather. Before crossing, seek local advice if touring during periods when the weather is changeable or unreliable. Warning notices are usually posted at the foot of a pass if it is closed, or if chains or winter tyres must be used.

Caravanners are obviously particularly sensitive to gradients and traffic/road conditions on passes. Take great care when negotiating blind hairpins. The maximum gradient is usually on the inside of bends but exercise caution if it is necessary to pull out. Always engage a lower gear before taking a hairpin bend and give priority to vehicles ascending. Give priority to postal service vehicles – signposts usually show their routes. Do not go down hills in neutral gear.

Keep to the extreme right of the road and be prepared to reverse to give way to descending/ascending traffic.

On mountain roads it is not the gradient which taxes your car but the duration of the climb and the loss of power at high altitudes; approximately 10% at 915 metres (3000 feet), and 23% at 2133 metres (7000 feet). Turbo power restores much of the lost capacity.

To minimise the risk of engine-overheating, take high passes in the cool of the day, don't climb any faster than necessary and keep the engine pulling steadily. To prevent a radiator boiling, pull off the road, turn the heater and blower full on and switch off airconditioning. Keep an eye on water and oil levels. Never put cold water into a boiling radiator or it may crack. Check that the radiator is not obstructed by debris sucked up during the journey.

A long descent may result in overheating brakes; select the correct gear for the gradient and avoid excessive use of brakes. Note that even if using engine braking to control the outfit's speed, the caravan brakes may activate due to the action of the overrun mechanism, causing them to overheat. Use lay-bys and lookout points to stop and allow brakes to cool.

In alpine areas snow prevents road repairs during the winter resulting in increased road works during the summer which may cause traffic delays. At times one-way traffic only may be permitted on some routes. Information will be posted at each end of the road.

Precipitous slopes on main roads crossing major passes are rarely totally unguarded; but minor passes may be unguarded or simply have stone pillars placed at close intervals. Those without a good head for heights should consider alternative routes.

In mountainous areas always remember to leave the blade valve of your portable toilet open a fraction whilst travelling. This avoids pressure build-up in the holding tank. Similarly, a slightly open tap will avoid pressure build up in water pipes and fittings.

Tunnels

British drivers do not often encounter road tunnels but they are a common feature on the Continent, for example, along stretches of Italian coastline and lakes, and through mountain ranges. Tolls are usually charged for use of major tunnels. Ensure you have enough fuel before entering a tunnel. Emergency situations often involve vehicles stranded because of a lack of fuel.

In bright sunshine when approaching a tunnel, slow down to allow your eyes to adjust and look out for poorly-lit vehicles in front of you, and for cyclists. Take sunglasses off before entering a tunnel and take care again when emerging into sunshine at the other end.

Signposts usually indicate a tunnel ahead and its length. Once inside the tunnel, maintain a safe distance from the vehicle in front in case the driver brakes sharply. Minimum and maximum speed limits usually apply.

Dipped headlights are usually required by law even in well-lit tunnels. Switch them on before entering a tunnel. Some tunnels may be poorly or totally unlit.

Snow chains, if used, must be removed before entering a tunnel in lay-bys provided for this purpose.

'No overtaking' signs must be strictly observed.

Never cross central single or double lines. If overtaking is permitted in twin-tube tunnels, bear in mind that it is very easy to under-estimate distances and speed when driving in a tunnel.

In order to minimise the effects of exhaust fumes close all car windows and set the ventilator to circulate the air, or operate the air conditioning system coupled with the recycled air option.

Watch out for puddles caused by dripping or infiltrating water.

If there is a traffic jam, switch your hazard warning lights on and stop a safe distance from the vehicle in front. Sound the horn only in a real emergency. Never change driving direction unless instructed to do so by tunnel staff or a police officer.

If you break down, try to reach the next lay-by and call for help from the nearest emergency phone. Modern tunnels have video surveillance systems to ensure prompt assistance in an emergency. If you cannot reach a lay-by, place your warning triangle at least 100 metres behind your vehicle. Passengers should leave the vehicle through doors on the right-hand side only.

Mountain Pass Information

The dates of opening and closing given in the following table are approximate and inclusive. Before attempting late afternoon or early morning journeys across borders, check their opening times as some borders close at night.

Gradients listed are the maximum at any point on the pass and may be steeper at the inside of curves, particularly on older roads.

Gravel surfaces (such as dirt and stone chips) vary considerably; they are dusty when dry and slippery when wet. Where known to exist, this type of surface has been noted.

In fine weather wheel chains or winter tyres will only be required on very high passes, or for short periods in early or late summer. In winter conditions you will probably need to use them at altitudes exceeding 600 metres (approximately 2000 feet).

Abbreviations

MHV	Maximum height of vehicle
MLV	Maximum length of vehicle
MWV	Maximum width of vehicle
MWR	Minimum width of road
OC	Occasionally closed between dates stated
UC	Usually closed between dates stated
UO	Usually open between dates stated, although a fall of snow may obstruct the road for 24-48 hours.

Mountain Passes and Tunnels Report Form

The Caravan Club welcomes up-to-date information on mountain passes and tunnels from caravanners who use them during the course of their holidays. Please use the report forms at the end of this chapter. and complete and return them as soon as possible after your journey.

Converting Gradients

20% = 1 in 5	11% = 1 in 9
16% = 1 in 6	10% = 1 in 10
14% = 1 in 7	8% = 1 in 12
12% =1 in 8	6% =1 in 16

Much of the information contained in the following tables was originally supplied by The Automobile Association and other motoring and tourist organisations. Additional updates and amendments have been supplied by caravanners who have themselves used the passes and tunnels. The Caravan Club has not checked the information contained in these tables and cannot accept responsibility for their accuracy, or for errors, omissions or their effects.

Alpine Mountain Passes

Before using any of these passes, PLEASE READ CAREFULLY THE ADVICE AT THE BEGINNING OF THIS CHAPTER

	Pass Height In Metres (Feet)	From *To*	Max Gradient	Conditions and Comments
1	**Achenpass** (Austria – Germany) 941 (3087)	Achenwald *Glashütte*	4%	UO. Well-engineered road, B181/307. Gradient not too severe.
2	**Albula** (Switzerland) 2312 (7585)	Tiefencastel *La Punt*	10%	UC Nov-early Jun. MWR 3.5m (11'6") MWV 2.25m (7'6") Inferior alternative to the Julier; fine scenery. **Not rec for caravans**. Alternative rail tunnel. See ***Rail Tunnels*** in this section.
3	**Allos** (France) 2250 (7382)	Colmars *Barcelonette*	10%	UC early Nov-early Jun. MWR 4m (13'1") Very winding, narrow, mostly unguarded pass on D908 but not difficult otherwise; passing bays on southern slope; poor surface, MWV 1.8m (5'11"). **Not rec for caravans.**
4	**Aprica** (Italy) 1176 (3858)	Tresenda *Edolo*	9%	UO. MWR 4m (13'1") Fine scenery; good surface; well-graded on road S39. Narrow in places; watch for protruding rock when meeting oncoming traffic. Easier E to W.
5	**Aravis** (France) 1498 (4915)	La Clusaz *Flumet*	9%	OC Dec-Mar. MWR 4m (13'1"). Fine scenery; D909, fairly easy road. Poor surface in parts on Chamonix side. Some single-line traffic.
6	**Arlberg** (Austria) 1802 (5912)	Bludenz *Landeck*	13%	OC Dec-Apr. MWR 6m (19'8"). Good modern road B197/E60 with several pull-in places. Steeper fr W easing towards summit; heavy traffic. **Pass road closed to caravans/trailers.** Parallel road tunnel (tolls) available on E60 (poss long queues). See ***Road Tunnels*** in this section.
7	**Ballon d'Alsace** (France) 1178 (3865)	Giromagny *St Maurice-sur-Moselle*	11%	OC Dec-Mar. MWR 4m (13'1") Fairly straightforward ascent/descent; narrow in places; numerous bends. On road D465.
8	**Bayard** (France) 1248 (4094)	Chauffayer *Gap*	14%	UO. MWR 6m (19'8") Part of the Route Napoléon N85. Fairly easy, steepest on the S side with several hairpin bends. Negotiable by caravans from N-to-S via D1075 (N75) and Col-de-la-Croix Haute, avoiding Gap.
9	**Bernina** (Switzerland) 2330 (7644)	Pontresina *Poschiavo*	12.50%	OC Dec-Mar. MWR 5m (16'5") MWV 2.25m (7'6") Fine scenery. Good with care on open narrow sections towards summit on S-side; on road no. 29.
10	**Bracco** (Italy) 613 (2011)	Riva Trigoso *Borghetto di Vara*	14%	UO. MWR 5m (16'5") A two-lane road (P1) more severe than height suggests due to hairpins and volume of traffic; passing difficult. Rec cross early to avoid traffic. Alternative toll m'way A12 available.

Before using any of these passes, PLEASE READ CAREFULLY THE ADVICE AT THE BEGINNING OF THIS CHAPTER				
	Pass **Height In Metres (Feet)**	**From** ***To***	**Max Gradient**	**Conditions and Comments**
11	**Brenner (Europabrücke)** (Austria – Italy) 1374 (4508)	Innsbruck *Vipiteno/Sterzing*	14%	UO. MWR 6m (19'8") On road no. 182/12. Parallel toll m'way A13/A22/E45 (6%) suitable for caravans. Heavy traffic may delay at Customs. **Pass road closed to vehicles towing trailers.**
12	**Brouis** (France) 1279 (4196)	Nice *Col-de-Tende*	12.50%	UO. MWR 6m (19'8") Good surface but many hairpins on D6204 (N204)/S20. Steep gradients on approaches. Height of tunnel at Col-de-Tende at the Italian border is 3.8m (12'4) **Not rec for caravans.**
13	**Brünig** (Switzerland) 1007 (3340)	Brienzwiler Station *Giswil*	8.50%	UO. MWR 6m (19'8") MWV 2.5m (8'2") An easy but winding road (no. 4); heavy traffic at weekends; frequent lay-bys. On-going road improvement (2009) may cause delays – check before travel.
14	**Bussang** (France) 721 (2365)	Thann *St Maurice-sur-Moselle*	7%	UO. MWR 4m (13'1") A very easy road (N66) over the Vosges; beautiful scenery.
15	**Cabre** (France) 1180 (3871)	Luc-en-Diois *Aspres-sur-Buëch*	9%	UO. MWR 5.5m (18') An easy pleasant road (D93/D993), winding at Col-de-Cabre.
16	**Campolongo** (Italy) 1875 (6152)	Corvara-in-Badia *Arabba*	12.50%	OC Dec-Mar. MWR 5m (16'5") A winding but easy ascent on rd P244; long level stretch on summit followed by easy descent. Good surface, fine scenery.
17	**Cayolle** (France) 2326 (7631)	Barcelonnette *Guillaumes*	10%	UC early Nov-early Jun. MWR 4m (13'1") Narrow, winding road (D902) with hairpin bends; poor surface, broken edges with steep drops. Long stretches of single-track road with passing places. **Caravans prohibited.**
18	**Costalunga (Karer)** (Italy) 1745 (5725)	Bolzano *Pozza-di-Fassa*	16%	OC Dec-Apr. MWR 5m (16'5") A good well-engineered road (S241) but mostly winding with many blind hairpins. **Caravans prohibited.**
19	**Croix** (Switzerland) 1778 (5833)	Villars-sur-Ollon *Les Diablerets*	13%	UC Nov-May. MWR 3.5m (11'6") A narrow, winding route but extremely picturesque. **Not rec for caravans.**
20	**Croix Haute** (France) 1179 (3868)	Monestier-de-Clermont *Aspres-sur-Buëch*	7%	UO on N75. MWR 5.5m (18') Well-engineered road (D1075/N75); several hairpin bends on N side.
21	**Falzárego** (Italy) 2117 (6945)	Cortina-d'Ampezzo *Andraz*	8.50%	OC Dec-Apr. MWR 5m (16'5") Well-engineered bitumen surface on road R48; many blind hairpin bends on both sides; used by tour coaches.

Before using any of these passes, PLEASE READ CAREFULLY THE ADVICE AT THE BEGINNING OF THIS CHAPTER

	Pass Height In Metres (Feet)	From *To*	Max Gradient	Conditions and Comments
22	**Faucille** (France) 1323 (4341)	Gex *Morez*	10%	UO. MWR 5m (16'5") Fairly wide, winding road (N5) across the Jura mountains; negotiable by caravans but probably better to follow route via La Cure-St Cergue-Nyon.
23	**Fern** (Austria) 1209 (3967)	Nassereith *Lermoos*	8%	UO. MWR 6m (19'8") Obstructed intermittently during winter. An easy pass on road 179 but slippery when wet; heavy traffic at summer weekends. Connects with Holzleiten Sattel Pass at S end for travel to/from Innsbruck – see below.
24	**Flexen** (Austria) 1784 (5853)	Lech *Rauzalpe (nr Arlberg Pass)*	10%	UO. MWR 5.5m (18') The magnificent 'Flexenstrasse', a well-engineered mountain road (no. 198) with tunnels and galleries. The road from Lech to Warth, N of the pass, is usually closed Nov-Apr due to danger of avalanche. **Not rec for caravans.**
25	**Flüela** (Switzerland) 2383 (7818)	Davos-Dorf *Susch*	12.50%	OC Nov-May. MWR 5m (16'5") MWV 2.3m (7'6") Easy ascent from Davos on road no. 28; some acute hairpin bends on the E side; bitumen surface.
26	**Forclaz** (Switzerland – France) 1527 (5010)	Martigny *Argentière*	8.50%	UO Forclaz; OC Montets Dec-early Apr. MWR 5m (16'5") MWV 2.5m (8'2") Good road over the pass and to the French border; long, hard climb out of Martigny; narrow and rough over Col-des-Montets on D1506 (N506).
27	**Foscagno** (Italy) 2291 (7516)	Bormio *Livigno*	12.50%	OC Nov-May. MWR 3.3m (10'10") Narrow and winding road (S301) through lonely mountains, generally poor surface. Long winding ascent with many blind bends; not always well-guarded. The descent includes winding rise and fall over the Passo-d'Eira 2,200m (7,218'). **Not rec for caravans.**
28	**Fugazze** (Italy) 1159 (3802)	Rovereto *Valli-del-Pasubio*	14%	UO. MWR 3.5m (11'6") Very winding road (S46) with some narrow sections, particularly on N side. The many blind bends and several hairpin bends call for extra care. **Not rec for caravans.**
29	**Furka** (Switzerland) 2431 (7976)	Gletsch *Realp*	11%	UC Oct-Jun. MWR 4m (13'1") MWV 2.25m (7'6") Well-graded road (no. 19) with narrow sections (single track in place on E side) and several hairpin bends on both ascent and descent. Fine views of the Rhône Glacier. Beware of coaches and traffic build-up. **Not rec for caravans.** Alternative rail tunnel available. See ***Rail Tunnels*** in this section.
30	**Galibier** (France) 2645 (8678)	La Grave *St Michel-de-Maurienne*	12.50%	UC Oct-Jun. MWR 3m (9'10") Mainly wide, well-surfaced road (D902) but unprotected and narrow over summit. From Col-du-Lautaret it rises over the Col-du-Telegraphe then 11 more hairpin bends. Ten hairpin bends on descent then 5km (3.1 miles) narrow and rough; easier in N to S direction. Limited parking at summit. **Not rec for caravans.** (There is a single-track tunnel under the Galibier summit, controlled by traffic lights; caravans are not permitted).

Before using any of these passes, PLEASE READ CAREFULLY THE ADVICE AT THE BEGINNING OF THIS CHAPTER

	Pass Height In Metres (Feet)	From *To*	Max Gradient	Conditions and Comments
31	**Gardena (Grödner-Joch)** (Italy) 2121 (6959)	Val Gardena *Corvara-in-Badia*	12.50%	OC Dec-Jun. MWR 5m (16'5") A well-engineered road (S243), very winding on descent. Fine views. **Caravans prohibited.**
32	**Gavia** (Italy) 2621 (8599)	Bormio *Ponte-di-Legno*	20%	UC Oct-Jul. MWR 3m (9'10") MWV 1.8m (5'11") Steep, narrow, difficult road (P300) with frequent passing bays; many hairpin bends and gravel surface; not for the faint-hearted; extra care necessary. **Not rec for caravans.** Long winding ascent on Bormio side.
33	**Gerlos** (Austria) 1628 (5341)	Zell-am-Ziller *Wald im Pinzgau*	9%	UO. MWR 4m (13'1") Hairpin ascent out of Zell to modern toll road (B165); the old, steep, narrow and winding route with passing bays and 14% gradient is not rec but is negotiable with care. Views of Krimml waterfalls. **Caravans prohibited.**
34	**Gorges-du-Verdon** (France) 1032 (3386)	Castellane *Moustiers-Ste Marie*	9%	UO. MWR probably 5m (16'5") On road D952 over Col-d'Ayen and Col-d'Olivier. Moderate gradients but slow, narrow and winding. Poss heavy traffic.
35	**Grand St Bernard** (Switzerland – Italy) 2469 (8100)	Martigny *Aosta*	11%	UC Oct-Jun. MWR 4m (13'1") MWV 2.5m (8' 2") Modern road to entrance of road tunnel on road no. 21/E27 (UO), then narrow but bitumen surface over summit to border; also good in Italy. Suitable for caravans using tunnel. Pass road feasible but not recommended. See ***Road Tunnels*** in this section.
36	**Grimsel** (Switzerland) 2164 (7100)	Innertkirchen *Gletsch*	10%	UC mid Oct-late Jun. MWR 5m (16'5") MWV 2.25m (7'6") A fairly easy, modern road (no. 6) with heavy traffic at weekends. A long winding ascent, finally hairpin bends; then a terraced descent with six hairpins (some tight) into the Rhône valley. Good surface; fine scenery.
37	**Grossglockner** (Austria) 2503 (8212)	Bruck-an-der-Grossglocknerstrasse *Heiligenblut*	12.50%	UC late Oct-early May. MWR 5.5m (18') Well-engineered road (no. 107) but many hairpins; heavy traffic; moderate but very long ascent/descent. Negotiable preferably S to N by caravans. Avoid side road to highest point at Edelweissespitze if towing, as road is very steep and narrow. Magnificent scenery. Tolls charged. Road closed from 2200-0500 hrs (summer). Alternative Felbertauern road tunnel between Lienz and Mittersil (toll). See ***Road Tunnels*** in this section.
38	**Hahntennjoch** (Austria) 1894 (6250)	Imst *Elmen*	15%	UC Nov-May. A minor pass; **caravans prohibited.**
39	**Hochtannberg** (Austria) 1679 (5509)	Schröcken *Warth (nr Lech)*	14%	OC Jan-Mar. MWR 4m (13'1") A reconstructed modern road (no. 200). W to E long ascent with many hairpins. Easier E to W. **Not rec for caravans or trailers.**

Before using any of these passes, PLEASE READ CAREFULLY THE ADVICE AT THE BEGINNING OF THIS CHAPTER

	Pass Height In Metres (Feet)	From *To*	Max Gradient	Conditions and Comments
40	**Holzleiten Sattel** (Austria) 1126 (3694)	Nassereith *Obsteig*	12.50%	(12.5%), UO. MWR 5m (16'5") Road surface good on W side; poor on E. Light traffic; gradients no problem but **not rec for caravans or trailers.**
41	**Iseran** (France) 2770 (9088)	Bourg-St Maurice *Lanslebourg*	11%	UC mid Oct-late Jun. MWR 4m (13'1") Second highest pass in the Alps on road D902. Well-graded with reasonable bends, average surface. Several unlit tunnels on N approach. **Not rec for caravans.**
42	**Izoard** (France) 2360 (7743)	Guillestre *Briançon*	12.50%	UC late Oct-mid Jun. MWR 5m (16'5") Fine scenery. Winding, sometimes narrow road (D902) with many hairpin bends; care required at several unlit tunnels near Guillestre. **Not rec for caravans.**
43	**Jaun** (Switzerland) 1509 (4951)	Bulle *Reidenbach*	14%	UO. MWR 4m (13'1") MWV 2.25m (7'6") A modern but generally narrow road (no. 11); some poor sections on ascent and several hairpin bends on descent.
44	**Julier** (Switzerland) 2284 (7493)	Tiefencastel *Silvaplana*	13%	UO. MWR 4m (13'1") MWV 2.5m (8'2") Well-engineered road (no. 3) approached from Chur via Sils. Fine scenery. Negotiable by caravans, preferably from N to S, but a long haul and many tight hairpins. Alternative rail tunnel from Thusis to Samedan. See ***Rail Tunnels*** in this section.
45	**Katschberg** (Austria) 1641 (5384)	Spittal-an-der-Drau *St Michael*	20%	UO. MWR 6m (19'8") Good wide road (no. 99) with no hairpins but steep gradients particularly from S. Suitable only light caravans. Parallel Tauern/Katschberg toll motorway A10/E55 and road tunnels. See ***Road Tunnels*** in this section.
46	**Klausen** (Switzerland) 1948 (6391)	Altdorf *Linthal*	10%	UC late Oct-early Jun. MWR 5m (16'5") MWV 2.30m (7'6") Narrow and winding in places, but generally easy in spite of a number of sharp bends; **no through route for caravans** as they are prohibited from using the road between Unterschächen and Linthal (no. 17).
47	**Larche (della Maddalena)** (France – Italy) 1994 (6542)	La Condamine-Châtelard *Vinadio*	8.50%	OC Dec-Mar. MWR 3.5m (11'6") An easy, well-graded road (D900); long, steady ascent on French side, many hairpins on Italian side (S21). Fine scenery; ample parking at summit.
48	**Lautaret** (France) 2058 (6752)	Le Bourg-d'Oisans *Briançon*	12.50%	OC Dec-Mar. MWR 4m (13'1") Modern, evenly graded but winding road (D1091), and unguarded in places; very fine scenery; suitable for caravans but with care through narrow tunnels.
49	**Leques** (France) 1146 (3760)	Barrême *Castellane*	8%	UO. MWR 4m (13'1") On Route Napoléon (D4085). Light traffic; excellent surface; narrow in places on N ascent. S ascent has many hairpins.

Before using any of these passes, PLEASE READ CAREFULLY THE ADVICE AT THE BEGINNING OF THIS CHAPTER				
	Pass **Height In Metres (Feet)**	**From** ***To***	**Max Gradient**	**Conditions and Comments**
50	**Loibl (Ljubelj)** (Austria – Slovenia) 1067 (3500)	Unterloibl *Kranj*	20%	UO. MWR 6m (19'8") Steep rise and fall over Little Loibl pass (E652) to 1.6km (1 mile) tunnel under summit. **Caravans prohibited.** The old road over the summit is closed to through-traffic.
51	**Lukmanier (Lucomagno)** (Switzerland) 1916 (6286)	Olivone *Disentis*	9%	UC early Nov-late May. MWR 5m (16'5") MWV 2.25m (7'6") Rebuilt, modern road.
52	**Maloja** (Switzerland) 1815 (5955)	Silvaplana *Chiavenna*	9%	UO. MWR 4m (13'1") MWV 2.5m (8'2") Escarpment facing south; fairly easy, but many hairpin bends on descent; negotiable by caravans but possibly difficult on ascent. On road no. 3/S37.
53	**Mauria** (Italy) 1298 (4258)	Lozzo di Cadore *Ampezzo*	7%	UO. MWR 5m (16'5") A well-designed road (S52) with easy, winding ascent and descent.
54	**Mendola** (Italy) 1363 (4472)	Appiano/Eppan *Sarnonico*	12.50%	UO. MWR 5m (16'5") A fairly straightforward but winding road (S42), well-guarded, many hairpins. Take care overhanging cliffs if towing.
55	**Mont Cenis** (France – Italy) 2083 (6834)	Lanslebourg *Susa*	12.50%	UC Nov-May. MWR 5m (16'5") Approach by industrial valley. An easy highway (D1006/S25) with mostly good surface; spectacular scenery; long descent into Italy with few stopping places. Alternative Fréjus road tunnel available. See ***Road Tunnels*** in this section.
56	**Monte Croce-di-Comélico (Kreuzberg)** (Italy) 1636 (5368)	San Candido *Santo-Stefano- di-Cadore*	8.50%	UO. MWR 5m (16'5") A winding road (S52) with moderate gradients, beautiful scenery.
57	**Montgenèvre** (France – Italy) 1850 (6070)	Briançon *Cesana-Torinese*	9%	UO. MWR 5m (16'5") An easy, modern road (N94/S24) with some tight hairpin bends on French side; road widened & tunnels improved on Italian side. Much used by lorries; may be necessary to travel at their speed and give way to oncoming large vehicles on hairpins.
58	**Monte Giovo (Jaufen)** (Italy) 2094 (6870)	Merano *Vipiteno/Sterzing*	12.50%	UC Nov-May. MWR 4m (13'1") Many well-engineered hairpin bends on S44; good scenery. **Caravans prohibited.**
	Montets (See **Forclaz**)			
59	**Morgins** (France – Switzerland) 1369 (4491)	Abondance *Monthey*	14%	UO. MWR 4m (13'1") A lesser used route (D22) through pleasant, forested countryside crossing French/Swiss border. **Not rec for caravans.**

Before using any of these passes, PLEASE READ CAREFULLY THE ADVICE AT THE BEGINNING OF THIS CHAPTER				
	Pass **Height In Metres (Feet)**	**From** ***To***	**Max Gradient**	**Conditions and Comments**
60	**Mosses** (Switzerland) 1445 (4740)	Aigle *Château-d'Oex*	8.50%	UO. MWR 4m (13'1") MWV 2.25m (7'6") A modern road (no. 11). Aigle side steeper and narrow in places.
61	**Nassfeld (Pramollo)** (Austria – Italy) 1530 (5020)	Tröpolach *Pontebba*	20%	OC Late Nov-Mar. MWR 4m (13'1") The winding descent on road no. 90 into Italy has been improved but not rec for caravans.
62	**Nufenen (Novena) (Switzerland)** 2478 (8130)	Ulrichen *Airolo*	10%	UC Mid Oct-mid Jun. MWR 4m (13'1") MWV 2.25m (7'6") The approach roads are narrow, with tight bends, but the road over the pass is good; negotiable with care. Long drag from Ulrichen.
63	**Oberalp** (Switzerland) 2044 (6706)	Andermatt *Disentis*	10%	UC Nov-late May. MWR 5m (16'5") MWV 2.3m (7'6") A much improved and widened road (no. 19) with modern surface but still narrow in places on E side; many tight hairpin bends, but long level stretch on summit. Alternative rail tunnel during the winter. See ***Rail Tunnels*** in this section. **Caravans not recommended.**
64	**Ofen (Fuorn)** (Switzerland) 2149 (7051)	Zernez *Santa Maria-im-Münstertal*	12.50%	UO. MWR 4m (13'1") MWV 2.25m (7'6") Good road (no. 28) through Swiss National Park.
65	**Petit St Bernard** (France – Italy) 2188 (7178)	Bourg-St Maurice *Pré-St Didier*	8.50%	UC mid Oct-Jun. MWR 5m (16'5") Outstanding scenery, but poor surface and unguarded broken edges near summit. Easiest from France (D1090); sharp hairpins on climb from Italy (S26). **Closed to vehicles towing another vehicle.**
66	**Pillon** (Switzerland) 1546 (5072)	Le Sépey *Gsteig*	9%	OC Jan-Feb. MWR 4m (13'1") MWV 2.25m (7'6") A comparatively easy modern road.
67	**Plöcken (Monte Croce-Carnico)** (Austria – Italy) 1362 (4468)	Kötschach *Paluzza*	14%	OC Dec-Apr. MWR 5m (16'5") A modern road (no. 110) with long, reconstructed sections; OC to caravans due to heavy traffic on summer weekends; delay likely at the border. Long, slow, twisty pull from S, easier from N.
68	**Pordoi** (Italy) 2239 (7346)	Arabba *Canazei*	10%	OC Dec-Apr. MWR 5m (16'5") An excellent modern road (S48) with numerous blind hairpin bends; fine scenery; used by tour coaches. Long drag when combined with Falzarego pass.
69	**Pötschen** (Austria) 982 (3222)	Bad Ischl *Bad Aussee*	9%	UO. MWR 7m (23') A modern road (no. 145). Good scenery.

Before using any of these passes, PLEASE READ CAREFULLY THE ADVICE AT THE BEGINNING OF THIS CHAPTER

	Pass Height In Metres (Feet)	From *To*	Max Gradient	Conditions and Comments
70	**Radstädter-Tauern** (Austria) 1738 (5702)	Radstadt *Mauterndorf*	16%	OC Jan-Mar. MWR 5m (16'5") N ascent steep (road no. 99) but not difficult otherwise; but negotiable by light caravans using parallel toll m'way (A10) through tunnel. See ***Road Tunnels*** in this section.
71	**Résia (Reschen)** (Italy – Austria) 1504 (4934)	Spondigna *Pfunds*	10%	UO. MWR 6m (19'8") A good, straightforward alternative to the Brenner Pass. Fine views but no stopping places. On road S40/180.
72	**Restefond (La Bonette)** (France) 2802 (9193)	Barcelonnette *St Etienne-de-Tinée*	16%	UC Oct-Jun. MWR 3m (9'10") The highest pass in the Alps. Rebuilt, resurfaced road (D64) with rest area at summit – top loop narrow and unguarded. Winding with hairpin bends. **Not rec for caravans.**
73	**Rolle** (Italy) 1970 (6463)	Predazzo *Mezzano*	9%	OC Dec-Mar. MWR 5m (16'5") A well-engineered road (S50) with many hairpin bends on both sides; very beautiful scenery; good surface.
	Rombo (See **Timmelsjoch**)			
74	**St Gotthard (San Gottardo)** (Switzerland) 2108 (6916)	Göschenen *Airolo*	10%	UC mid Oct-early Jun. MWR 6m (19'8") MHV 3.6m (11'9") MWV 2.5m (8'2") Modern, fairly easy two- to three-lane road (A2/E35). Heavy traffic. Alternative road tunnel. See ***Road Tunnels*** in this section.
75	**San Bernardino** (Switzerland) 2066 (6778)	Mesocco *Hinterrhein*	10%	UC Oct-late Jun. MWR 4m (13'1") MWV 2.25m (7'6") Easy modern road (A13/E43) on N and S approaches to tunnel, narrow and winding over summit via tunnel suitable for caravans. See ***Road Tunnels*** in this section.
76	**Schlucht** (France) 1139 (3737)	Gérardmer *Munster*	7%	UO. MWR 5m (16'5") An extremely picturesque route (D417) crossing the Vosges mountains, with easy, wide bends on the descent. Good surface.
77	**Seeberg (Jezersko)** (Austria – Slovenia) 1218 (3996)	Eisenkappel *Kranj*	12.50%	UO. MWR 5m (16'5") An alternative to the steeper Loibl and Wurzen passes on B82/210; moderate climb with winding, hairpin ascent and descent. **Not rec for caravans.**
78	**Sella** (Italy) 2240 (7349)	Selva *Canazei*	11%	OC Dec-Jan. MWR 5m (16'5") A well-engineered, winding road; exceptional views of Dolomites; **caravans prohibited.**
79	**Sestriere** (Italy) 2033 (6670)	Cesana-Torinese *Pinarolo*	10%	UO MWR 6m (19'8") Mostly bitumen surface on road R23. Fairly easy; fine scenery.

Before using any of these passes, PLEASE READ CAREFULLY THE ADVICE AT THE BEGINNING OF THIS CHAPTER

	Pass Height In Metres (Feet)	From *To*	Max Gradient	Conditions and Comments
80	**Silvretta (Bielerhöhe)** (Austria) 2032 (6666)	Partenen *Galtur*	11%	UC late Oct-early Jun. MWR 5m (16'5") Mostly reconstructed road (188); 32 easy hairpin bends on W ascent; E side more straightforward. Tolls charged. **Caravans prohibited.**
81	**Simplon** (Switzerland – Italy) 2005 (6578)	Brig *Domodóssola*	11%	OC Nov-Apr. MWR 7m (23') MWV 2.5m (8'2") An easy, reconstructed, modern road (E62/S33), 21km (13 miles) long, continuous ascent to summit; good views, many stopping places. Surface better on Swiss side. Alternative rail tunnel fr Kandersteg in operation from Easter to September.
82	**Splügen** (Switzerland – Italy) 2113 (6932)	Splügen *Chiavenna*	13%	UC Nov-Jun. MWR 3.5m (11'6") MHV 2.8m (9'2") MWV 2.3m (7'6") Mostly narrow, winding road (S36), with extremely tight hairpin bends, not well guarded; care also required at many tunnels/galleries. **Not rec for caravans.**
83	**Stelvio** (Italy) 2757 (9045)	Bormio *Spondigna*	12.50%	UC Oct-late Jun. MWR 4m (13'1") MLV 10m (32') Third highest pass in Alps on S38; 40-50 acute hairpin bends either side, all well-engineered; good surface, traffic often heavy. Hairpin bends too acute for long vehicles. **Not rec for caravans.**
84	**Susten** (Switzerland) 2224 (7297)	Innertkirchen *Wassen*	9%	UC Nov-Jun. MWR 6m (19'8") MWV 2.5m (8'2") Very scenic and well-guarded road (no. 11); easy gradients and turns; heavy traffic at weekends. Eastern side easier than west. Negotiable by caravans (recommended for small/medium sized only) with care, but not for the faint-hearted. Large parking area at summit.
85	**Tenda (Tende)** Italy – France 1321 (4334)	Borgo-San Dalmazzo *Tende*	9%	UO. MWR 6m (19'8") Well-guarded, modern road (S20/ND6204) with several hairpin bends; road tunnel (height 3.8m) at summit narrow with poor road surface. Less steep on Italian side. **Caravans prohibited during winter.**
86	**Thurn** (Austria) 1274 (4180)	Kitzbühel *Mittersill*	8.50%	UO. MWR 5m (16'5") MWV 2.5m (8' 2") A good road (no. 161) with narrow stretches; N approach rebuilt. Several good parking areas.
87	**Timmelsjoch (Rombo)** (Austria – Italy) 2509 (8232)	Obergurgl *Moso*	14%	UC mid Oct-Jun. MWR 3.5m (11'6") Border closed at night 8pm to 7am. The pass (road no 186/S44b) is **open to private cars without trailers only** (toll charged), as some tunnels on Italian side too narrow for larger vehicles. Easiest N to S.
88	**Tonale** (Italy) 1883 (6178)	Edolo *Dimaro*	10%	UO. MWR 5m (16'5") A relatively easy road (S42); steepest on W; long drag. Fine views.
89	**Tre Croci** (Italy) 1809 (5935)	Cortina-d'Ampezzo *Auronzo-di-Cadore*	11%	OC Dec-Mar. MWR 6m (19'8") An easy pass on road R48; fine scenery.

Before using any of these passes, PLEASE READ CAREFULLY THE ADVICE AT THE BEGINNING OF THIS CHAPTER

	Pass Height In Metres (Feet)	From *To*	Max Gradient	Conditions and Comments
90	**Turracher Höhe** (Austria) 1763 (5784)	Predlitz *Ebene-Reichenau*	23%	UO. MWR 4m (13'1") Formerly one of the steepest mountain roads (no. 95) in Austria; now improved. Steep, fairly straightforward ascent followed by a very steep descent; good surface and mainly two-lane; fine scenery. **Not rec for caravans.**
91	**Umbrail** (Switzerland – Italy) 2501 (8205)	Santa Maria-im-Münstertal *Bormio*	9%	UC Nov-early Jun. MWR 4.3m (14'1") MWV 2.3m (7'6") Highest Swiss pass (road S38); mostly tarmac with some gravel surface. Narrow with 34 hairpin bends. **Not rec for caravans.**
92	**Vars** (France) 2109 (6919)	St Paul-sur-Ubaye *Guillestre*	9%	OC Dec-Mar. MWR 5m (16'5") Easy winding ascent and descent on D902 with 14 hairpin bends; good surface.
93	**Wurzen (Koren)** (Austria – Slovenia) 1073 (3520)	Riegersdorf *Kranjska Gora*	20%	UO. MWR 4m (13'1") Steep two-lane road (no. 109), otherwise not particularly difficult; better on Austrian side; heavy traffic summer weekends; delays likely at the border. **Caravans prohibited.**
94	**Zirler Berg** (Austria) 1009 (3310)	Seefeld *Zirl*	16.50%	UO. MWR 7m (23') South facing escarpment, part of route from Garmisch to Innsbruck; good, modern road (no. 171). Heavy tourist traffic and long steep descent with one hairpin bend into Inn Valley. Steepest section from hairpin bend down to Zirl. **Caravans not permitted northbound and not rec southbound.**

Technical information by courtesy of the Automobile Association

Major Alpine Rail Tunnels

Before using any of these passes, PLEASE READ CAREFULLY THE ADVICE AT THE BEGINNING OF THIS CHAPTER

	Tunnel	Route	Journey Time	General Information and Comments	Contact
A	**Albula** (Switzerland) 5.9 km (3.5 miles)	**Chur – St Moritz** Thusis to Samedan	90 mins	MHV 2.85m + MWV 1.40m or MHV 2.50m + MWV 2.20 Up to 11 shuttle services per day all year; advance booking required.	Thusis (081) 2884716 Samedan (081) 2885511 www.rhb.ch/autoverlad
B	**Furka** (Switzerland) 15.4 km (9.5 miles)	**Andermatt – Brig** Realp to Oberwald	15 mins	Hourly all year from 6am to 9pm weekdays; half-hourly weekends.	Realp (027) 9277676 Oberwald (027) 9277666 www.mgbahn.ch
C	**Oberalp** (Switzerland) 28 km (17.3 miles)	**Andermatt – Disentis** Andermatt to Sedrun	60 mins	MHV 2.50m 2-6 trains daily (Christmas-Easter only). Advance booking compulsory.	Andermatt (027) 9277707 Sedrun (027) 9277740 www.mgbahn.ch
D	**Lötschberg** (Switzerland) 14 km (8.7 miles)	**Bern – Brig** Kandersteg to Goppenstein	15 mins	MHV 2.90m Frequent all year half-hourly service. Journey time 15 minutes. Advance booking unnecessary; extension to Hohtenn operates when Goppenstein-Gampel road is closed.	Kandersteg (0900) 553333 www.bls.ch/autoverlad
E	**Simplon** (Switzerland – Italy)	**Brig – Domodossola** Brig to Iselle	20 mins	10 trains daily, all year.	(0900) 300300 http://mct.sbb.ch/mct/ autoverlad
	Lötschberg/Simplon Switzerland – Italy	**Bern – Domodossola** Kandersteg to Iselle	75 mins	Limited service March to October up to 3 days a week (up to 10 times a day) and at Christmas for vehicles max height 2.50m, motor caravans up to 5,000 kg. Advance booking required.	(033) 6504150 www.bls.ch
F	**Tauerbahn** (Austria)	**Bad Gadstein – Spittal an der Drau** Böckstein to Mallnitz	11 mins	East of and parallel to Grossglockner pass. Half-hourly service all year.	(05) 1717 http://autoschleuse. oebb.at
G	**Vereina** (Switzerland) 19.6 km (11.7 miles)	**Klosters – Susch** Selfranga to Sagliains	17 mins	MLV 12m Half-hourly daytime service all year. Journey time 18 minutes. Restricted capacity for vehicles over 3.30m high during winter w/ends and public holidays. Steep approach to Klosters.	(081) 2883737 (recorded) www.rhb.ch/ Autoverlad.63.0.html

NOTES: Detailed timetables are available from the appropriate tourist offices.

Major Alpine Road Tunnels

	Tunnel	Route and Height above Sea Level	General Information and Comments
			Before using any of these passes, **PLEASE READ CAREFULLY THE ADVICE AT THE BEGINNING OF THIS CHAPTER**
(H)	**Arlberg** (Austria) 14 km (8.75 miles)	**Langen to St Anton** 1220m (4000')	On B197 parallel and to S of Arlberg Pass which is closed to caravans/trailers. **Motorway vignette required; tolls charged.** www.arlberg.com
(I)	**Bosruck** (Austria) 5.5 km (3.4 miles)	**Spital am Pyhrn to Selzthal** 742m (2434')	To E of Phyrn pass; with Gleinalm Tunnel (see below) forms part of A9 a'bahn between Linz & Graz. Max speed 80 km/h (50 mph). Use dipped headlights, no overtaking. Occasional emergency lay-bys with telephones. **Motorway vignette required; tolls charged.**
(J)	**Felbertauern** (Austria) 5.3 km (3.25 miles)	**Mittersill to Matrei** 1525m (5000')	MWR 7m (23'), tunnel height 4.5m (14'9"). On B109 W of and parallel to Grossglockner pass; downwards gradient of 9% S to N with sharp bend before N exit. Wheel chains may be needed on approach Nov-Apr. **Tolls charged.**
(K)	**Frejus** (France – Italy) 12.8 km (8 miles)	**Modane to Bardonecchia** 1220m (4000')	MWR 9m (29'6"), tunnel height 4.3m (14'). Min/max speed 60/70 km/h (37/44 mph). Return tickets valid until midnight on 7th day after day of issue. Season tickets are available. Approach via A43 and D1006; heavy use by freight vehicles. Good surface on approach roads. **Tolls charged.** www.sftrf.fr
(L)	**Gleinalm** (Austria) 8.3 km (5 miles)	**St Michael to Fiesach (nr Graz)** 817m (2680')	Part of A9 Pyhrn a'bahn. **Motorway vignette required; tolls charged.**
(M)	**Grand St Bernard** (Switzerland – Italy) 5.8 km (3.6 miles)	**Bourg-St Pierre to St Rhémy (Italy)** 1925m (7570')	MHV 4m (13'1"), MWV 2.55m (8'2.5"), MLV 18m (60'). Min/max speed 40/80 km/h (24/50 mph). On E27. Passport check, Customs & toll offices at entrance; breakdown bays at each end with telephones; return tickets valid one month. Although approaches are covered, wheel chains may be needed in winter. Season tickets are available. **Motorway vignette required; tolls charged.** For 24-hour information tel: (027) 7884400 (Switzerland) or 0165 780902 (Italy). www.letunnel.com
(N)	**Karawanken** (Austria – Slovenia) 8 km (5 miles)	**Rosenbach to Jesenice** 610m (2000')	On A11. **Motorway vignette required; tolls charged.**
(O)	**Mont Blanc** (France – Italy) 11.6 km (7.2 miles)	**Chamonix to Courmayeur** 1381m (4530')	MHV 4.7m (15'5"), MWV 6m (19'6") On N205 France, S26 (Italy). Max speed in tunnel 70 km/h (44 mph) – lower limits when exiting; min speed 50 km/h. Leave 150m between vehicles; ensure enough fuel for 30km. Return tickets valid until midnight on 7th day after issue. Season tickets are available. **Tolls charged.** www.tunnelmb.net

Before using any of these passes, **PLEASE READ CAREFULLY THE ADVICE AT THE BEGINNING OF THIS CHAPTER**

	Tunnel	Route and Height above Sea Level	General Information and Comments
(P)	**Munt La Schera** (Switzerland – Italy) 3.5 km (2 miles)	**Zernez to Livigno** 1706m (5597')	MHV 3.6m (11'9"), MWV 2.5m (8'2"). Open 8am-8pm; single lane traffic controlled by traffic lights; roads from Livogno S to the Bernina Pass and Bormio closed Dec-Apr. On N28 (Switzerland). **Tolls charged** Tel: (081) 8561888.
(Q)	**St Gotthard** (Switzerland) 16.3 km (10 miles)	**Göschenen to Airolo** 1159m (3800')	Tunnel height 4.5m (14'9"), single carriageway 7.5m (25') wide. Max speed 80 km/h (50 mph). No tolls, but tunnel is part of Swiss motorway network (A2). **Motorway vignette required.** Tunnel closed 8pm to 5am Monday to Friday for periods during June and September. Heavy traffic and delays high season. www.gotthard-strassentunnel.ch
-	**Ste Marie-aux-Mines** 6.8 km (4.25 miles)	**St Dié to Ste-Marie-aux Mines** 772m (2533')	Re-opened October 2008. Also known as Maurice Lemaire Tunnel, through the Vosges in north-east France from Lusse on N159 to N59. Vehicle and vehicle combinations up to 3,500kg only. **Tolls charged.** Alternate route via Col-de-Ste Marie on D459.
(R)	**San Bernardino** (Switzerland) 6.6 km (4 miles)	**Hinterrhein to San Bernadino** 1644m (5396')	Tunnel height 4.8m (15'9"), width 7m (23'). On A13 motorway. No stopping or overtaking; keep 100m between vehicles; breakdown bays with telephones. Max speed 80 km/h (50 mph). **Motorway vignette required.**
(S)	**Tauern and Katschberg** (Austria) 6.4 km (4 miles) & 5.4km (3.5 miles)	**Salzburg to Villach** 1340m (4396') & 1110m (3642')	The two major tunnels on the A10, height 4.5m (14'9"), width 7.5m (25'). **Motorway vignette required; tolls charged.**

Technical information compiled with the assistance of the Automobile Association

NOTES: *Dipped headlights should be used (unless stated otherwise) when travelling through road tunnels, even when the road appears is well lit. In some countries police make spot checks and impose on-the-spot fines.*

During the winter wheel chains may be required on the approaches to some tunnels. These must not be used in tunnels and lay-bys are available for the removal and refitting of wheel chains.

For information on motorway vignettes, see the relevant Country Introductions.

GERMANY
SWITZERLAND
LIECHTENSTEIN
ITALY
Friedberg
Erding
Königsbrunn
Dachau
Olching
Waldkraiburg
Senden
Ehingen (Donau)
Albstadt
Bingen
Biberach an der Riß
Fürstenfeldbruck
Germering
München
Landsberg am Lech
Starnberg
Memmingen
Kaufbeuren
Geretsried
Rosenheim
Weingarten
Ravensburg
Leutkirch im Allgäu
Kempten (Allgäu)
Überlingen
Wangen im Allgäu
Konstanz
Friedrichshafen
Ursprungpass
Lindau (Bodensee)
Bregenz
Sonthofen
Oberjochpass
Garmisch-Partenkirchen
St Gallen
Dornbirn
Scharnitzpass
Herisau
Appenzell
Pass Thurn
Feldkirch
Innsbruck
Glarus
Chur
Merano
Bolzano
Sondrio
Belluno
Col Visentin
Trento
Vittorio Veneto
Conegliano
Rovereto
Lecco
Como
Cantù
Bassano del Grappa
Montebelluna
Castelfranco Veneto
Treviso
Bergamo
Schio
Valdagno
Vimercate
Lumezzane
Monza
Brescia
Vicenza
Mogliano Veneto
Mestre
Arzignano
Pioltello
Treviglio
Desenzano del Garda
Mirano
Spinea
Mira
Milano
Verona
San Donato Milanese
Padova
Venezia
Villafranca di Verona
Crema
Lodi

AUSTRIA
SLOVENIA
Salzburg
Villach
Klagenfurt
Graz
Leoben
Kapfenberg
Wolfsberg
Steyr
Wels
Traun
Amstetten
St Pölten
Traunreut
LJUBLJANA
Kranj
Jesenice
Maribor
Celje
Udine
Pordenone
Monfalcone
Nova Gorica
Gorizia
Portogruaro
San Donà di Piave
Jesolo
Piran
Izola
Motorway
Motorway (Proposed)
Motorway Road Tunnel
Major/Main Roads
Minor Mountain Passes (suitability for caravans not checked)
Major Mountain Passes Suitable for Caravans
Major Mountain Passes Unsuitable for Caravans
Major Rail Tunnels
Major Road Tunnels
These maps should be used in conjunction with the information in the Mountain Passes and Tunnels tables in this chapter.
2000m - +3000m
1000m - 2000m
100m - 1000m
0 - 100m
© Collins Bartholomew Ltd 2009

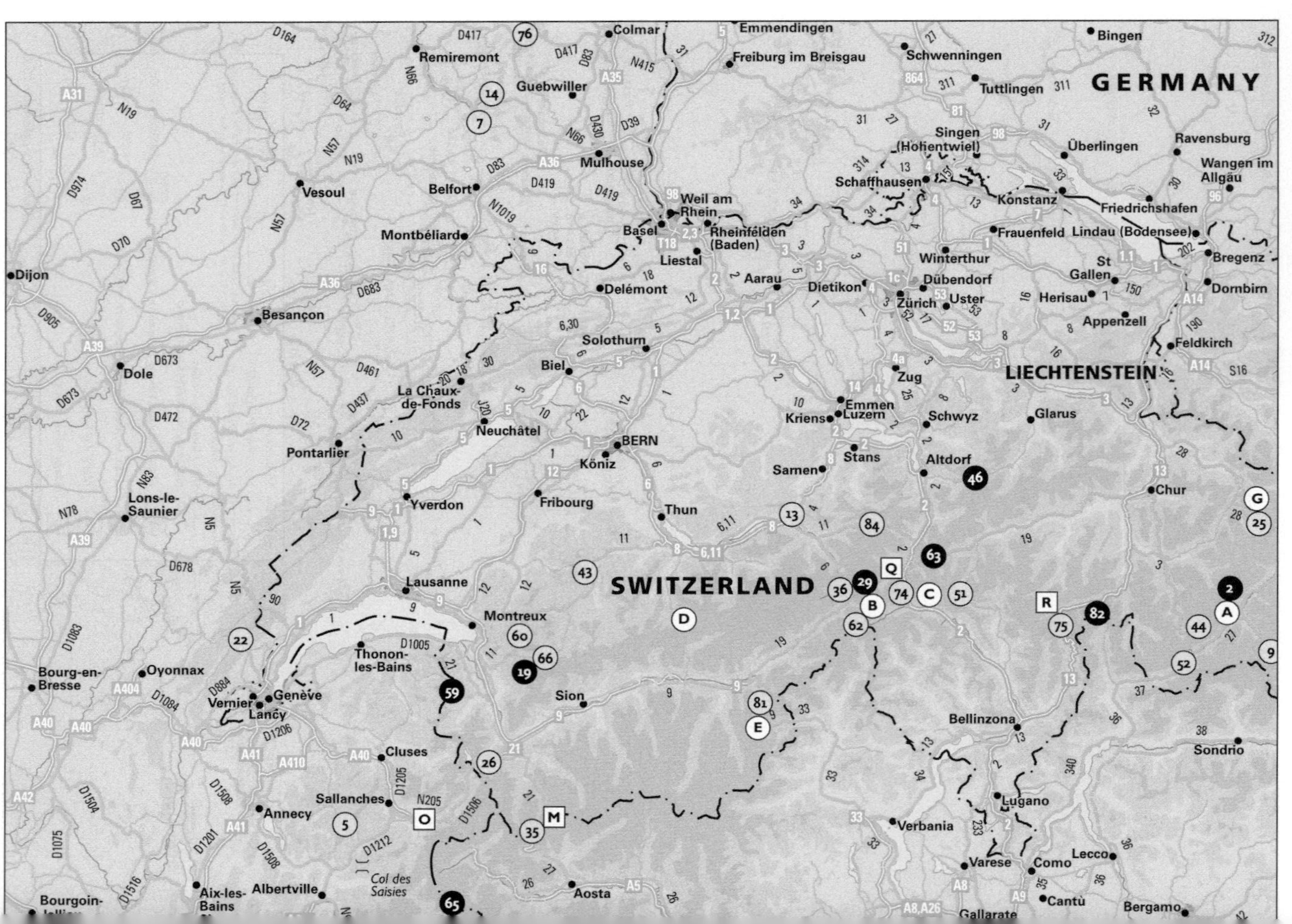
GERMANY
SWITZERLAND
LIECHTENSTEIN
Colmar
Emmendingen
Bingen
Remiremont
Freiburg im Breisgau
Schwenningen
Tuttlingen
Guebwiller
Singen (Hohentwiel)
Überlingen
Ravensburg
Wangen im Allgäu
Mulhouse
Vesoul
Belfort
Schaffhausen
Konstanz
Friedrichshafen
Weil am Rhein
Basel
Rheinfelden (Baden)
Liestal
Montbéliard
Frauenfeld
Lindau (Bodensee)
Bregenz
Winterthur
St Gallen
Dijon
Delémont
Aarau
Dietikon
Dübendorf
Zürich
Uster
Herisau
Dornbirn
Besançon
Appenzell
Solothurn
Feldkirch
Dole
Biel
Zug
La Chaux-de-Fonds
Emmen
Luzern
Kriens
Schwyz
Glarus
Neuchâtel
Pontarlier
BERN
Köniz
Stans
Sarnen
Altdorf
Chur
Yverdon
Fribourg
Lons-le-Saunier
Thun
Lausanne
Montreux
Thonon-les-Bains
Bourg-en-Bresse
Oyonnax
Genève
Vernier
Lancy
Sion
Bellinzona
Sondrio
Cluses
Sallanches
Annecy
Lugano
Verbania
Varese
Como
Lecco
Col des Saisies
Aix-les-Bains
Albertville
Aosta
Cantù
Bergamo
Gallarate
Bourgoin-

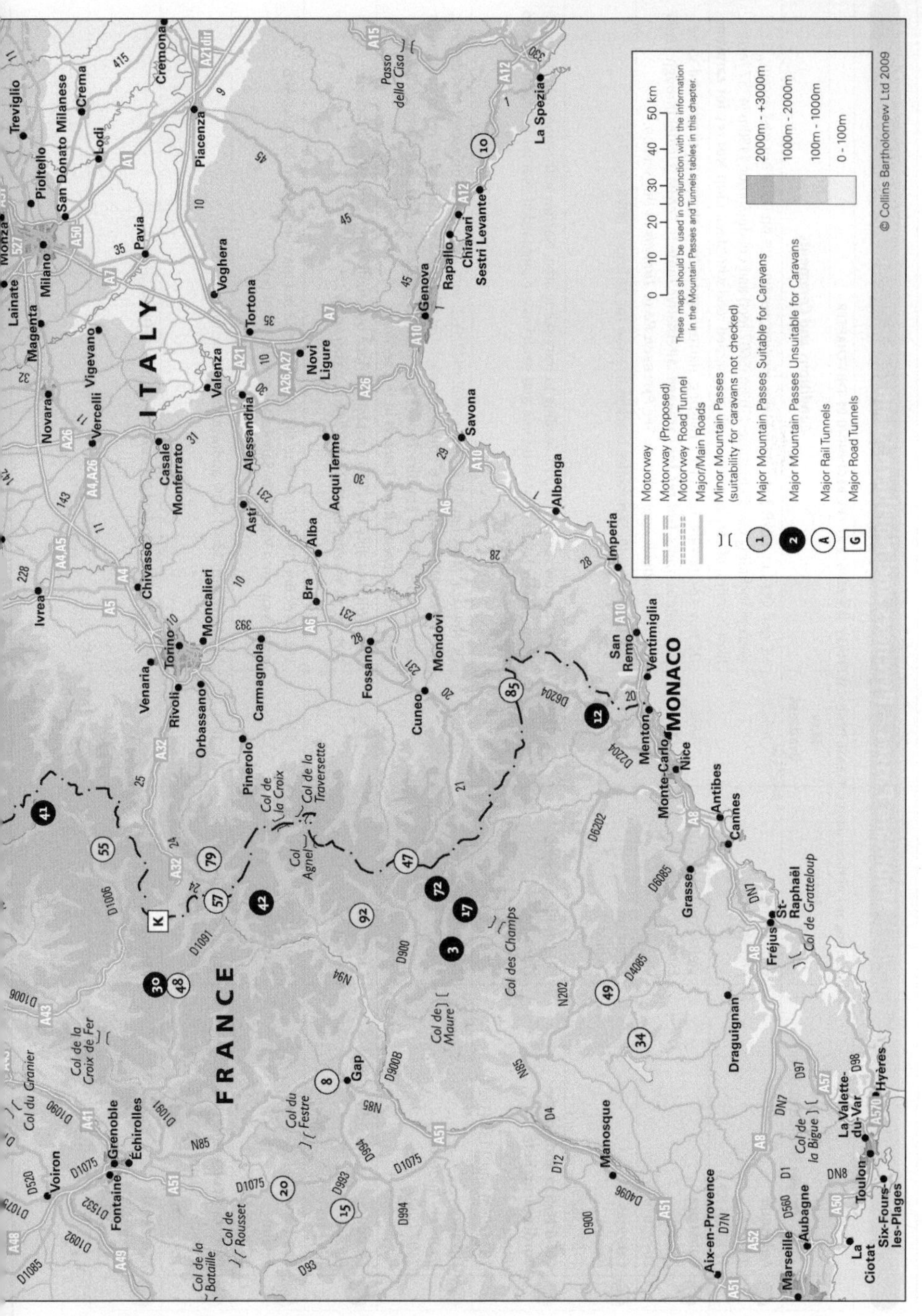
Motorway
Motorway (Proposed)
Motorway Road Tunnel
Major/Main Roads
Minor Mountain Passes (suitability for caravans not checked)
Major Mountain Passes Suitable for Caravans
Major Mountain Passes Unsuitable for Caravans
Major Rail Tunnels
Major Road Tunnels
0 10 20 30 40 50 km
These maps should be used in conjunction with the information in the Mountain Passes and Tunnels tables in this chapter.
2000m - +3000m
1000m - 2000m
100m - 1000m
0 - 100m
© Collins Bartholomew Ltd 2009
FRANCE
ITALY
MONACO

Mountain Passes – Pyrenees and Northern Spain

Before using any of these passes, PLEASE READ CAREFULLY THE ADVICE AT THE BEGINNING OF THIS CHAPTER

	Pass Height In Metres (Feet)	From To	Max Gradient	Conditions and Comments
101	**Aubisque** (France) 1710 (5610)	Eaux Bonnes *Argelés-Gazost*	10%	UC mid Oct-Jun. MWR 3.5m (11'6") Very winding; continuous on D918 but easy ascent; descent including Col-d'Aubisque 1709m (5607 feet) and Col-du-Soulor 1450m (4757 feet); 8km (5 miles) of very narrow, rough, unguarded road with steep drop. **Not rec for caravans** .
102	**Bonaigua** (Spain) 2072 (6797)	Viella (Vielha) *Esterri-d'Aneu*	8.5%	UC Nov-Apr. MWR 4.3m (14'1") Twisting, narrow road (C28) with many hairpins and some precipitous drops. **Not rec for caravans**. Alternative route to Lerida (Lleida) through Viella (Vielha) Tunnel is open all year. See ***Pyrenean Road Tunnels*** in this section.
103	**Cabrejas** (Spain) 1167 (3829)	Tarancon *Cuenca*	14%	UO. On N400/A40. Sometimes blocked by snow for 24 hours. MWR 5m (16')
104	**Col-d'Haltza and Col-de-Burdincurutcheta** (France) 782 (2565) and 1135 (3724)	St Jean-Pied-de-Port *Larrau*	11%	UO. A narrow road (D18/D19) leading to Iraty skiing area. Narrow with some tight hairpin bends; rarely has central white line and stretches are unguarded. Not for the faint-hearted. **Not rec for caravans**.
105	**Envalira** (France – Andorra) 2407 (7897)	Pas-de-la-Casa *Andorra*	12.5%	OC Nov-Apr. MWR 6m (19'8") Good road (N22/CG2) with wide bends on ascent and descent; fine views. MHV 3.5m (11'6") on N approach near l'Hospitalet. Early start rec in summer to avoid border delays. Envalira Tunnel (toll) reduces congestion and avoids highest part of pass. See ***Pyrenean Road Tunnels*** in this section.
106	**Escudo** (Spain) 1011 (3317)	Santander *Burgos*	17%	UO. MWR probably 5m (16'5") Asphalt surface but many bends and steep gradients. **Not rec in winter**. On N632; A67/N611 easier route.
107	**Guadarrama** (Spain) 1511 (4957)	Guadarrama *San Rafael*	14%	UO. MWR 6m (19'8") On NVI to the NW of Madrid but may be avoided by using AP6 motorway from Villalba to San Rafael or Villacastin (toll).
108	**Ibañeta (Roncevalles)** (France – Spain) 1057 (3468)	St Jean-Pied-de-Port *Pamplona*	10%	UO. MWR 4m (13'1") Slow and winding, scenic route on N135.
109	**Manzanal** (Spain) 1221 (4005)	Madrid *La Coruña*	7%	UO. Sometimes blocked by snow for 24 hours. On A6.

	Pass Height In Metres (Feet)	From *To*	Max Gradient	Conditions and Comments
	Before using any of these passes, PLEASE READ CAREFULLY THE ADVICE AT THE BEGINNING OF THIS CHAPTER			
110	**Navacerrada** (Spain) 1860 (6102)	Madrid *Segovia*	17%	OC Nov-Mar. On M601/CL601. Sharp hairpins. Possible but **not rec for caravans**.
111	**Orduna** (Spain) 900 (2953)	Bilbao *Burgos*	15%	UO. On A625/BU556; sometimes blocked by snow for 24 hours. Avoid by using AP68 motorway.
112	**Pajares** (Spain) 1270 (4167)	Oviedo *Léon*	16%	UO. On N630; sometimes blocked by snow for 24 hours. **Not rec for caravans**. Avoid by using AP66 motorway.
113	**Paramo-de-Masa** 1050 (3445)	Santander *Burgos*	8%	UO. On N623; sometimes blocked by snow for 24 hours.
114	**Peyresourde** (France) 1563 (5128)	Arreau *Bagnères-de-Luchon*	10%	UO. MWR 4m (13'1") D618 somewhat narrow with several hairpin bends, though not difficult. **Not rec for caravans**.
115	**Picos-de-Europa: Puerto-de-San Glorio, Puerto-de-Pontón, Puerto-de-Pandetrave** (Spain), 1609 (5279)	Unquera *Riaño* Riaño *Cangas-de-Onis* Portilla-de-la-Reina *Santa Marina-de-Valdeón*	12%	UO. MWR probably 4m (13'1") Desfiladero de la Hermida on N621 good condition. Puerto-de-San-Glorio steep with many hairpin bends. For confident drivers only. Puerto-de-Ponton on N625, height 1280 metres (4200 feet). Best approach fr S as from N is very long uphill pull with many tight turns. Puerto-de-Pandetrave, height 1562 metres (5124 feet) on LE245 not rec when towing as main street of Santa Marina steep & narrow.
116	**Piqueras** (Spain) 1710 (5610)	Logroño *Soria*	7%	UO. On N111; sometimes blocked by snow for 24 hours.
117	**Port** (France) 1249 (4098)	Tarascon-sur-Ariège *Massat*	10%	OC Nov-Mar. MWR 4m (13'1") A fairly easy, scenic road (D618), but narrow on some bends.
118	**Portet-d'Aspet** (France) 1069 (3507)	Audressein *Fronsac*	14%	UO. MWR 3.5m (11'6") Approached from W by the easy Col-des-Ares and Col-de-Buret; well-engineered but narrow road (D618); care needed on hairpin bends. **Not rec for caravans**.
119	**Pourtalet** (France – Spain) 1792 (5879)	Laruns *Biescas*	10%	UC late Oct-early Jun. MWR 3.5m (11'6") A fairly easy, unguarded road, but narrow in places. Easier from Spain (A136), steeper in France (D934). **Not rec for caravans**.

Before using any of these passes, PLEASE READ CAREFULLY THE ADVICE AT THE BEGINNING OF THIS CHAPTER

	Pass Height In Metres (Feet)	From To	Max Gradient	Conditions and Comments
120	**Puymorens** (France) 1915 (6283)	Ax-les-Thermes *Bourg-Madame*	10%	OC Nov-Apr. MWR 5.5m (18') MHV 3.5m (11'6") A generally easy, modern tarmac road (N20). Parallel toll road tunnel available. See ***Pyrenean Road Tunnels*** in this section.
121	**Quillane** (France) 1714 (5623)	Axat *Mont-Louis*	8.5%	OC Nov-Mar. MWR 5m (16'5") An easy, straightforward ascent and descent on D118.
122	**Somosierra** (Spain) 1444 (4738)	Madrid *Burgos*	10%	OC Mar-Dec. MWR 7m (23') On A1/E5; may be blocked following snowfalls. Snow-plough swept during winter months but wheel chains compulsory after snowfalls. Well-surfaced dual carriageway, tunnel at summit.
123	**Somport** (France – Spain) 1632 (5354)	Accous *Jaca*	10%	UO. MWR 3.5m (11'6") A favoured, old-established route; not particularly easy and narrow in places with many unguarded bends on French side (N134); excellent road on Spanish side (N330). Use of road tunnel advised – see ***Pyrenean Road Tunnels*** in this section. NB Visitors advise re-fuelling no later than Sabiñánigo when travelling south to north.
124	**Toses (Tosas)** (Spain) 1800 (5906)	Puigcerda *Ribes-de-Freser*	10%	UO MWR 5m (16'5") A fairly straightforward, but continuously winding, two-lane road (N152) with with a good surface but many sharp bends; some unguarded edges. Difficult in winter.
125	**Tourmalet** (France) 2114 (6936)	Ste Marie-de-Campan *Luz-St Sauveur*	12.5%	UC Oct-mid Jun. MWR 4m (13'1") The highest French Pyrenean route (D918); approaches good, though winding, narrow in places and exacting over summit; sufficiently guarded. Rough surface & uneven edges on west side. **Not rec for caravans.**
126	**Urquiola** (Spain) 713 (2340)	Durango (Bilbao) *Vitoria/Gasteiz*	16%	UO. Sometimes closed by snow for 24 hours. On BI623/A623. **Not rec for caravans.**

Major Pyrenean Road Tunnels

Before using any of these passes, **PLEASE READ CAREFULLY THE ADVICE AT THE BEGINNING OF THIS CHAPTER**

	Tunnel	Route and Height Above Sea Level	General Information and Comments
(AA)	**Bielsa** (France – Spain) 3.2 km (2 miles)	**Aragnouet to Bielsa** 1830m (6000')	Open 24 hours but possibly closed October-Easter. On French side (D173) generally good road surface but narrow with steep hairpin bends and steep gradients near summit. Often no middle white line. Spanish side (A138) has good width and is less steep and winding. Used by heavy vehicles. No tolls.
(BB)	**Cadi** (Spain) 5 km (3 miles)	**Bellver de Cerdanya to Berga** 1220m (4000')	W of Toses (Tosas) pass on E9/C16; link from La Seo de Urgel to Andorra; excellent approach roads; heavy traffic at weekends. **Tolls charged.**
(CC)	**Envalira** (France – Spain via Andorra) 2.8 km (1.75 miles)	**Pas de la Casa to El Grau Roig** 2000m (6562')	Tunnel width 8.25m. On N22/CG2 France to Andorra. **Tolls charged**.
(DD)	**Puymorens** (France –Spain) 4.8 km (2.9 miles)	**Ax-les-Thermes to Puigcerda** 1915m (6000')	MHV 3.5m (11'6"). Part of Puymorens pass on N20/E9. **Tolls charged**.
(EE)	**Somport** (France – Spain) 8.6 km (5.3 miles)	**Urdos to Canfranc** 1190m (3904')	Tunnel height 4.55m (14'9"), width 10.5m (34'). Max speed 90 km/h (56 mph); leave 100m between vehicles. On N134 (France), N330 (Spain). No tolls.
(FF)	**Vielha (Viella)** (Spain) 5 km (3.1 miles)	**Vielha (Viella) to Pont de Suert** 1635m (5390')	Single carriageway on N230; gentle gradients on both sides. Some rough sections with potholes on the approaches and in the tunnel. No tolls.

Santander
Torrelavega
Barakaldo
Bilbao
Donostia-San Sebastián
Llodio
Eibar
Arrasate
Vitoria-Gasteiz
Pamplona
Logroño
Burgos
Ponferrada
León
Palencia
Zamora
Valladolid
Aranda de Duero
Soria
Bragança
Salamanca
SPAIN
Segovia
Ávila
Colmenar Viejo
Guadalajara
Plasencia
MADRID
Arganda del Rey
Talavera de la Reina
Aranjuez
Toledo
Cuenca
Villanueva de la Serena
Don Benito
Alcázar de San Juan
Tomelloso
Villarrobledo
Ciudad Real
Valdepeñas
Puertollano
Albacete
Almansa
Hellín
Jumilla
Yecla
Andújar
Linares
Puerto de Rañadoiro
Puerto de Somiedo
Puerto de San Isidro
Puerto del Pontón
Puerto de Leitariegos
Porto de Piedrafita
Puerto de Tarna
Puerto de Piedrasluengas
Puerto de Palombera
Alto del Rabizo
La Collada
Alto de las Portillas
Puerto Pozazal
Puerto de la Mazorra
Puerto Echegárate
Puerto de Azáceta
Portilla del Padornelo
Puerto de la Brújula
Puerto de Oncala
Portilla Alta
Puerto de Menga
Puerto de la Paramera
Puerto de Tornavacas
Puerto de Navalmoral
Puerto del Pico
Puerto de Maranchón
Puerto de Pozondón
Puerto de la Serrana
Puerto de Miravete
Puerto de San Vicente
Puerto Llano
Puerto de Tórdiga
Puerto de los Carneros
Puerto de los Majales
Puerto del Rayo
Puerto Pulido
Puerto de Niefla
Puerto de Mestanza
Puerto Calatraveño
Puerto de Valderrepiso
Desfiladero de Despeñaperros
Puerto de los Pocicos
Puerto Los Altos
Puerto del Barrancazo
Puerto de las Crucetillas
Puerto del Arenal
Puerto de Jumilla

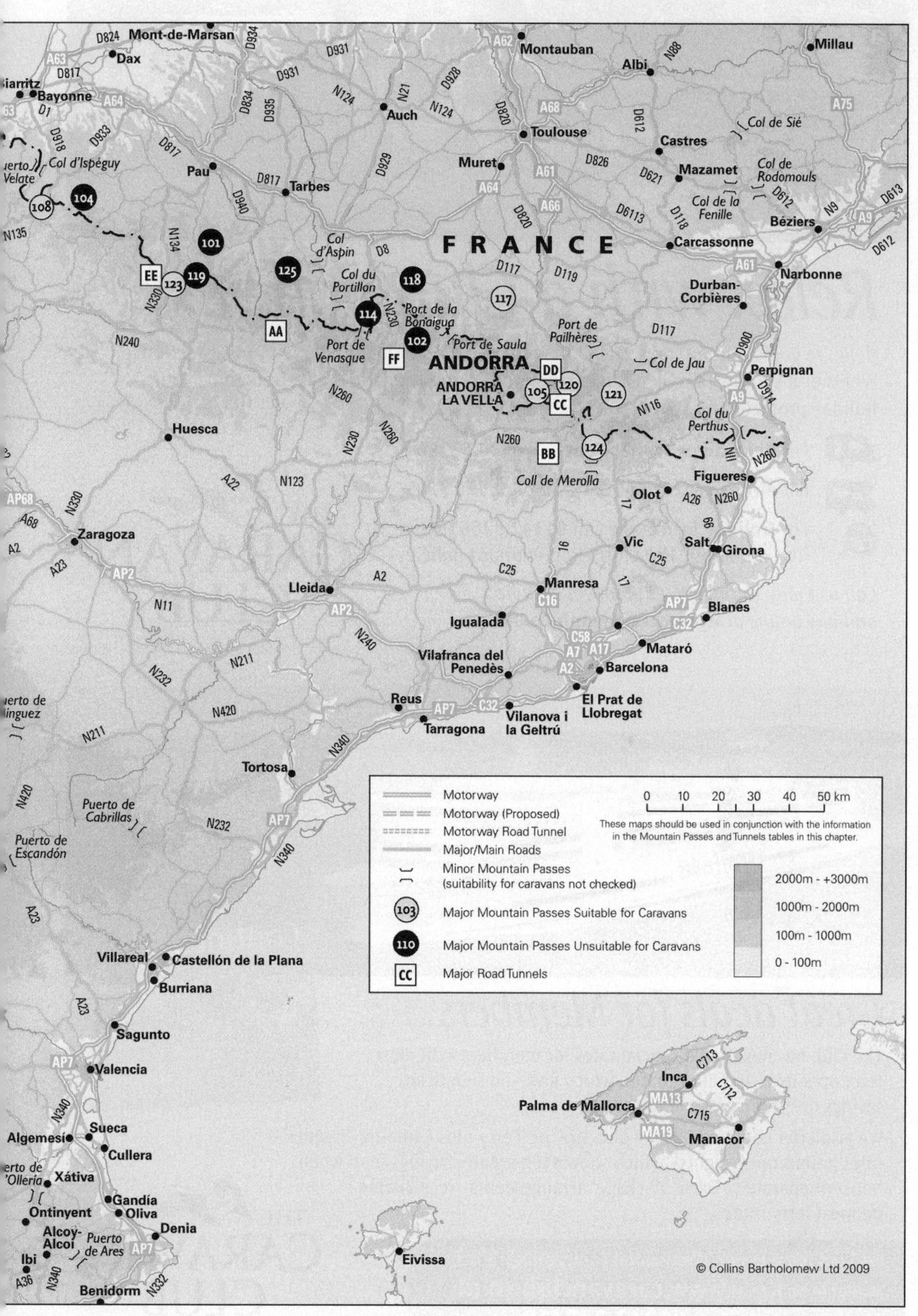
FRANCE
ANDORRA
ANDORRA LA VELLA
Mont-de-Marsan
Dax
Bayonne
Pau
Tarbes
Auch
Montauban
Toulouse
Muret
Albi
Millau
Castres
Mazamet
Carcassonne
Béziers
Narbonne
Durban-Corbières
Perpignan
Figueres
Olot
Vic
Salt
Girona
Blanes
Mataró
Barcelona
El Prat de Llobregat
Manresa
Igualada
Vilafranca del Penedès
Vilanova i la Geltrú
Reus
Tarragona
Tortosa
Lleida
Huesca
Zaragoza
Villareal
Castellón de la Plana
Burriana
Sagunto
Valencia
Algemesí
Sueca
Cullera
Xátiva
Gandía
Oliva
Ontinyent
Alcoy-Alcoi
Denia
Ibi
Benidorm
Palma de Mallorca
Inca
Manacor
Eivissa
Col d'Ispéguy
Col d'Aspin
Col du Portillon
Port de la Bonaigua
Port de Venasque
Port de Saula
Port de Pailhères
Col de Jau
Col du Perthus
Coll de Merolla
Col de Sié
Col de Rodomouls
Col de la Fenille
Puerto de Cabrillas
Puerto de Escandón
Puerto de Ares
Motorway
Motorway (Proposed)
Motorway Road Tunnel
Major/Main Roads
Minor Mountain Passes
(suitability for caravans not checked)
Major Mountain Passes Suitable for Caravans
Major Mountain Passes Unsuitable for Caravans
Major Road Tunnels
0 10 20 30 40 50 km
These maps should be used in conjunction with the information in the Mountain Passes and Tunnels tables in this chapter.
2000m - +3000m
1000m - 2000m
100m - 1000m
0 - 100m
© Collins Bartholomew Ltd 2009

Mountain Passes and Tunnels

Passes/Tunnel Report Form

Name of Pass/Tunnel ....

To/From ....

Date Travelled..

Comments (eg gradients, traffic, road surface, width of road, hairpins, scenery)

....

....

....

....

ARE YOU A Caravanner	Motor caravanner	Trailer-tenter?

==

Passes/Tunnel Report Form

Name of Pass/Tunnel ....

To/From ....

Date Travelled..

Comments (eg gradients, traffic, road surface, width of road, hairpins, scenery)

....

....

....

ARE YOU A: Caravanner	Motor caravanner	Trailer-tenter?

Mountain Passes and Tunnels

Passes/Tunnel Report Form)

Name of Pass/Tunnel ....

To/From ....

Date Travelled...

Comments (eg gradients, traffic, road surface, width of road, hairpins, scenery)

....

....

....

....

ARE YOU A: Caravanner	Motor caravanner	Trailer-tenter?

==

Passes/Tunnel Report Form

Name of Pass/Tunnel ....

To/From ....

Date Travelled...

Comments (eg gradients, traffic, road surface, width of road, hairpins, scenery)

....

....

....

ARE YOU A: Caravanner	Motor caravanner	Trailer-tenter?

Conversion Tables

Length & Distance

Centimetres/Metres	Inches/Feet/Yards	Inches/Feet/Yards	Centimetres/Metres
1 cm	0.4 in	1 in	2.5 cm
10 cm	4 in	1 ft	30 cm
25 cm	10 in	3 ft/1 yd	90 cm
1 m	3 ft 3 in	10 yds	9 m
100 m	110 yds	100 yds	91 m
Kilometres	**Miles**	**Miles**	**Kilometres**
1	0.6	1	1.6
10	6.2	10	16.1
25	15.5	25	40.2
50	31.1	50	80.5
100	62.2	100	160.9

Kilometres to Miles

km/h	20	30	40	50	60	70	80	90	100	110	120	130
mph	13	18	25	31	37	44	50	56	62	68	74	81

Weight

Grams/Kilograms	Ounces/Pounds	Ounces/Pounds	GramsKilograms
10 gm	0.3 oz	1 oz	28 gm
100 gm	3.5 oz	8 oz	226 gm
1 kg	2 lb 3 oz	1 lb	453 gm
10 kg	22 lb	10 lb	4.54 kg
25 kg	55 lb	50 lb	22.65 kg

Capacity

Millilitres/Litres	Fluid Ounces/ Pints/Gallon	Fluid Ounces/ Pints/Gallon	Millilitres/Litres
10 ml	0.3 fl oz	1 fl oz	28 ml
100 ml	3.5 fl oz	20 fl oz/1 pint	560 ml
1 litre	1.8 pints	1 gallon	4.5 litres
10 litres	2.2 gallons	5 gallons	22.7 litres
50 litres	11 gallons	10 gallons	45.5 litres

Area

Hectares	Acres	Acres	Hectares
1	2.5	1	0.4
5	12.4	5	2
10	24.7	10	4
50	123.5	50	20.2

Tyre Pressures

Bar	PSI (lb/sq.in)	Bar	PSI (lb/sq.in)
1.0	15	2.0	29
1.5	22	2.5	36

Map Scales

Scale	Equivalent Distance	
1:100 000	1 cm = 1 km	1 in = 1¾ miles
1: 200 000	1 cm = 2 km	1 in = 3¼ miles
1: 400 000	1 cm = 4 km	1 in = 6¼ miles
1: 500 000	1 cm = 5 km	1 in = 8 miles
1: 750 000	1 cm = 7.5 km	1 in = 12 miles
1:1 000 000	1 cm = 10 km	1 in = 16 miles
1:1 250 000	1 cm = 12.5 km	1 in = 20 miles
1: 2 000 000	1 cm = 20 km	1 in = 32 miles

Electricity and Gas

Electricity – General Advice

The nominal voltage for mains electricity has been 230 volts across the European Union for more than ten years, but varying degrees of 'acceptable tolerance' have resulted in significant variations in the actual voltage found. Harmonisation of voltage standards remains an on-going project. Most appliances sold in the UK are rated at 220-240 volts and usually work satisfactorily. However, some high-powered equipment, such as microwave ovens, may not function well and you are advised to consult the manufacturer's literature for further information.

Appliances which are 'CE' marked should work acceptably, as this marking indicates that the product has been designed to meet the requirements of relevant European directives.

The Country Introductions in this guide contain information on amperage supplied on campsites in individual countries (where known). Frequently you will be offered a choice of amperage and the following table gives an approximate idea of which appliances can be used (erring on the side of caution). You can work it out more accurately by noting the wattage of each appliance in your caravan. The kettle given is the caravan type, not a household kettle which usually has at least a 2000 watt element. Note that each caravan circuit also has a maximum amp rating which should not be exceeded.

Electrical Connections – EN60309-2 (CEE17)

Whilst there is a European Standard for connectors, EN60309-2 (formerly known as CEE17), this is not retrospective so you may find some Continental campsites where your UK 3-pin connector, which is to European Standard, will not fit. Accurate information is not easy to come by, but in Austria, Belgium, Denmark, Germany, Luxembourg, and the Netherlands most sites are fitted with CEE17 hook-ups, but not necessarily to all pitches. Spain, France, Italy and Switzerland have gradually changed over, but older style hook-ups may still occasionally be encountered. In some countries in Scandinavia and eastern Europe there may be few, if any CEE connections. See Country Introductions for more information.

© Mushakesa
Used under licence from Shutterstock.com

Different types of connector may be found within one campsite, as well as within one country. If you find your CEE17 connector does not fit, apply to campsite staff to borrow or hire an adaptor.

Different types of connector may be found within one campsite

Even with European Standard connections, poor electrical supplies are possible; the existence of the EN60309-2 (CEE17) standard should not be taken as an automatic sign of a modern system.

Amps	Wattage (Approx)	Fridge	Battery Charger	Air Conditioning	Colour TV	Water Heater	Kettle (750W)	Heater (1KW)
2	400	✓	✓					
4	800	✓	✓		✓	✓		
6	1200	✓	✓	*	✓	✓	✓	
8	1600	✓	✓	✓**	✓	✓	✓	✓**
10	2000	✓	✓	✓**	✓	✓	✓	✓**
16	3000	✓	✓	✓	✓	✓	✓	✓**

* *Possible, depending on wattage of appliance in question*
** *Not to be used at the same time as other high-wattage equipment*

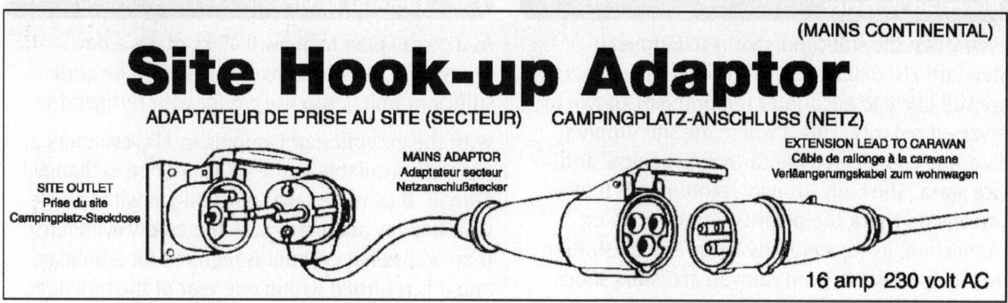

Other Connections

French – 2-pin, plus earth socket. Adaptors available from UK caravan accessory shops.

German – 2-pin, plus 2 earth strips, found in Norway and Sweden and possibly still Germany.

If the campsite does not have a modern EN60309-2 (CEE17) supply, ask to see the electrical protection for the socket outlet. If there is a device marked with IDn = 30mA, then the risk is minimised.

Hooking Up to the Mains

Connection

Connection should always be made in the following order:

- Check your caravan isolating switch is at 'off'.
- Uncoil the connecting cable from the drum. **A coiled cable with current flowing through it may overheat.** Take your cable and insert the connector (female end) into the caravan inlet.
- Insert the plug (male end) into the site outlet socket.
- Switch caravan isolating switch to 'on'.
- Preferably insert a polarity tester into one of the 13-amp sockets in the caravan to check all connections are correctly wired. **Never leave it in the socket.** Some caravans have these devices built in as standard.

It is recommended that the supply is not used if the polarity is incorrect *(see **Reversed Polarity** overleaf)*.

WARNING

In case of doubt or, if after carrying out the above procedures the supply does not become available, or if the supply fails, consult the campsite operator or a qualified electrician.

From time to time, you may come across mains supplies which differ in various ways from the common standards on most sites. The test equipment built into your caravan or readily available for everyday use may not be able to confirm that such systems are satisfactory and safe to use. While it is likely that such systems will operate your electrical equipment adequately in most circumstances, it is feasible that the protective measures in your equipment may not work effectively in the event of a fault.

To ensure your safety, the Club recommends that unless the system can be confirmed as safe, it should not be used.

Disconnection

- Switch your caravan isolating switch to 'off'.
- At the site supply socket withdraw the plug.
- Disconnect the cable from the caravan.
- Motor caravanners – if leaving your pitch during the day, do not leave your mains cable plugged into the site supply, as this creates a hazard if the exposed live connections in the plug are touched or if the cable is not seen during grass-cutting.

Reversed Polarity

Even when the site connector is to European Standard EN60309-2 (CEE17), British caravanners are still likely to encounter the problem known as reversed polarity. This is where the site supply's 'live' line connects to the caravan's 'neutral' and vice versa. The Club strongly recommends that you always check the polarity immediately on connection, using a polarity tester (see illustration overleaf) available from caravan accessory shops.

The caravan mains electrical installation **should not be used** while reversed polarity exists. Try using another nearby socket instead, which may cure the problem. Frequent travellers to the Continent who are electrically competent often make up an adaptor themselves, clearly marked 'reversed polarity', with the live and neutral wires reversed. (The 'German' plug can simply be turned upside down, so no further adaptor is required.) If these steps do not rectify the reversed polarity, the site supply may be quite different from that used in the UK and we recommend, for your own safety, that you disconnect from the mains and **do not use the electrical supply.**

Always check the polarity immediately on connection

Using a reversed polarity socket will probably not affect how an electrical appliance works BUT your protection in the event of a fault is greatly reduced. For example, a lamp socket may still be live as you touch it while replacing a blown bulb, even if the light switch is turned off.

Even when polarity is correct, it is always a wise precaution to check that a proper earth connection exists. This can be done with a proprietary tester such as a live-indicating neon screwdriver. If there is any doubt about the integrity of the earth system, **DO NOT USE THE SUPPLY.**

Shaver Sockets

Most campsites provide shaver sockets on which the voltage is generally marked as either 220V or 110V. Using an incorrect voltage may cause the shaver to become hot or to fail. The 2-pin adaptor obtainable in the UK is sometimes too wide for Continental sockets. It is advisable to buy 2-pin adaptors on the Continent, where they are readily available. Many shavers will operate on a range of voltages and these are most suitable when travelling abroad.

Gas – General Advice

As a guide, plan to allow 0.45 kg of gas a day for normal summer usage. This should be quite sufficient unless you use gas for your refrigerator.

With the exception of Campingaz, LPG cylinders normally available in the UK cannot be exchanged abroad. If possible take sufficient gas with you for your holiday and bring back the empty cylinder(s). If an additional cylinder is required for a holiday, and it is returned within one year of the hire date, then part of the hire charge will be refunded.

It is preferable to purchase a Campingaz regulator to use with Campingaz cylinders while you are abroad, especially if you are taking a long holiday. It is also wise to hold a spare Calor gas container in reserve in case you experience difficulty in renewing Campingaz supplies locally. With 130,000 stockists in 100 countries, however, these occasions should be rare, but prices may vary considerably from country to country. Alternatively, adaptors are available from Campingaz/Calor stockists to enable use of the normal Calor 4.5 kg regulator with a Campingaz cylinder.

Take sufficient gas with you for your holiday

Campingaz is marketed in the UK by The Coleman Company, Gordano Gate, Portishead, Bristol BS20 7GG tel. 01275 845024, www.campingaz.com. This product is widely available on the Continent.

BP Gaslight cylinders, which have been gaining in popularity in the UK, are available in several European countries. BP has a European exchange programme in which the UK does not yet participate. Moreover, Gaslight cylinders use different regulator fittings, depending on the country in which they are supplied. For news of further developments check the BP Gaslight website, www.bpgaslight.com

Cylinder gas under other brand names is widely distributed and is obtainable in most European countries. If you are touringin winter it is advisable to use propane gas and it may be necessary to purchase a cylinder of gas, plus the appropriate regulator or adaptor hose, at your destination. It is also advisable to compare prices carefully between the different brands and to check that cylinders fit into your gas cylinder locker.

When using other brands of gas a loan deposit is required, and when buying a cylinder for the first time you should also purchase the appropriate regulator or adaptor hose, as European pressures vary considerably. As in the UK, some operate at 28 mbar for butane and 37 mbar for propane; others at 30 or 50 mbar for both products, and in some parts of France and Belgium at even higher pressures.

The use of 30 mbar is being standardised for both types of gas. On later model caravans (2004 and later) a 30 mbar regulator suited to both propane and butane use is fitted. This is connected to the cylinder by an adaptor hose, and different hoses may be needed for different brands of gas. Availability of hoses and adaptors on the Continent is variable at present, and owners of new caravans may find it prudent to buy a Campingaz adaptor in the UK, to ensure at least that this commonly available make of gas can be used. Hoses and adaptors for other brands of gas used on the Continent are not currently available in the UK.

WARNING

Refilling your own UK standard cylinder is prohibited by law in most countries, unless it is carried out at certain designated filling plants. Since these plants are few and far between, are generally highly mechanised and geared for cylinders of a particular size and shape, the process is usually impracticable. Nevertheless, it is realised that many local dealers and site operators will fill your cylinders regardless of the prohibition.

The Caravan Club does not recommend the refilling of gas cylinders; there is real danger if cylinders are incorrectly filled.

- Cylinders must never be over-filled under any circumstances.
- Butane cylinders should only be filled with butane and not propane, which is a commonly used gas in Europe.
- Regular servicing of gas appliances is important. A badly adjusted appliance can emit carbon monoxide, which could prove fatal.
- Never use a hob or oven as a space heater.

*For information about the carriage of gas cylinders on ferries and in the Channel Tunnel, including safety precautions and regulations see the chapter **Ferries and the Channel Tunnel** in the section **PLANNING AND TRAVELLING.***

The editor of Caravan Europe welcomes information from members on the availability (or otherwise) of gas cylinders, especially in central Europe and Scandinavia.

Keeping in Touch

Emails and the Internet

On campsites increasingly wifi hotspots are the norm rather than a PC installed for clients' use and a wifi-enabled laptop is, therefore, a very useful accessory when travelling.

Alternatively there are internet cafés all over the world where you can log on to the internet and collect and send emails. You will be charged for the time you are logged on whereas public libraries in many countries offer free internet access.

WARNING: Wifi internet surfing abroad by means of a dongle (which uses a mobile phone network) is still prohibitively expensive. The reduction in international mobile phone roaming charges does not currently apply to data streaming.

Text Messages (SMS)

Using a mobile phone to send text messages is a cost-effective way of keeping in touch. There is a charge to send texts but receiving them abroad is free. There are numerous hand-held mobile phone devices available equipped with a keyboard or touch screen which enable the sending and receiving of emails, photos and video clips together with website browsing. They also have a multitude of other functions including organiser, address book, and instant messaging.

A number of websites offer a free SMS text message service to mobile phones, eg www.cbfsms.com or www.sendsmsnow.com

International Direct Dial Calls

International access codes for all the countries in this guide are given in the Country Introductions. To make an IDD call, first dial the international access code from the country you are in followed by the local number you wish to reach including its area code (if applicable), eg from the UK to France, dial 0033 – the international access code for France – then the local ten-digit number omitting the initial 0.

Most, but not all, countries include an initial 0 in the area code when telephone numbers are quoted. With the exception of Italy where the 0 must be dialled, this initial 0 should not be dialled when calling from outside the country in question. Some countries' telephone numbers do not have area codes at all (eg Denmark, Luxembourg, Norway). Simply dial the international access code and the

© Norman Chan
Used under licence from Shutterstock.com

number in full. The international access code to dial the UK from anywhere in the world is 0044.

International calls can be made from telephone boxes in countries covered by this guide using coins or, more commonly, phonecards or credit cards, and often instructions are given in English.

Ring Tones

Ring tones vary from country to country and the UK's double ring is not necessarily used in other countries. For example when dialling a number in France you will hear long, equal on and off tones, slower than the UK's engaged tone, and in Germany and Spain you will hear short, single tones separated by longer pauses.

Global Telephone Cards

Rechargeable global telephone cards offer rates for international calls which are normally cheaper than credit card or local phonecard rates. Payment methods vary, but are usually by monthly direct debit from your credit card or bank account. Also widely available are pre-paid international phonecards available on-line or locally from post offices, newsagents, kiosks or shops. There are many websites selling international phonecards for use all over the world, eg www.planetphonecards.com or www.thephonecardsite.com

Making Calls from your Laptop

Download Skype to your computer and you can make free calls to other Skype users anywhere in the world using a wifi broadband connection. Rates for calls to non-Skype users (landline or mobile phone) are also very competitively-priced. You will need a computer with a microphone and speakers, and a webcam is handy too. It is also possible to download Skype to an internet-enabled mobile phone to take advantage of the same low-cost calls – see www.skype.com

Radio and Television

Radio and Television Broadcasts

The BBC World Service broadcasts radio programmes 24 hours a day from a worldwide network of FM transmitters, via satellite and via the internet. In addition, many local radio stations broadcast BBC World Service programmes in English on FM frequencies. You can find programme schedules and links to a weekly email newsletter, at www.bbc.co.uk/worldservice

Listeners in Belgium, the Netherlands, Luxembourg, north-west Germany and northern France can currently listen to BBC Radio 5 Live on either 693 or 909 kHz medium wave or BBC Radio 4 on 198 kHz long wave. However, analogue television and radio signals will be switched off in the UK by 2012 and all radios, including car radios, will then use the DAB (digital) system. An adaptor is available, manufactured under the name of Pure Highway, which converts your analogue car radio to DAB.

BBC News Online is available on internet-enabled mobile phones, palmtop computers and other wireless handheld devices – text 81010 from your mobile phone for set-up information. Mobile phone network providers also have links to the BBC or Sky News from their own portals for breaking news and headlines.

Digital Terrestrial Television

As in the UK, television transmissions in most of Europe have been (or soon will be) converted to digital. The UK's high definition transmission technology will be more advanced than any currently implemented or planned in Europe and this means that digital televisions intended for use in the UK, whether for standard or high definition, will not be able to receive terrestrial signals in some countries.

Satellite Television

For English-language television the only realistic option is satellite. Satellite dishes are a common sight on caravans both at home and abroad. A satellite dish mounted on the roof or clamped to a pole fixed to the hitch or draw bar, or one mounted on a foldable, free-standing tripod, will provide good reception and minimal interference. Remember, however, that mountains or tall trees in the immediate vicinity of your dish, or heavy rain, may interfere with signals. As dishes become smaller and easier to use, numerous methods of fixing them have become available and a specialist dealer will be able to advise you. You will also need a receiver, sometimes called a digibox, and ideally a satellite-finding meter. Many satellite channels are 'free-to-air' which means they can be received by any make of receiver, but others are encrypted and require a viewing card and a Sky digibox. A number of portable 'free-to-air' systems are available which are suitable for the caravan market; contact a caravan accessory dealer or specialist electrical retailer. Such 'free-to-air' systems will not take a viewing card, for which a Sky digibox is needed.

There are hundreds of TV stations accessible both in the UK and in Europe, together with dozens of English-language radio stations including BBC broadcasts. The BBC's and ITV's satellite signals, while not as widespread throughout Europe as they used to be, are now 'free-to-air' and can be watched without the need for a viewing card throughout most of France, Belgium and the Netherlands, together with those parts of Germany, Switzerland and Spain bordering them. You should need only a 60 cm dish to access these 'free-to-air' channels but a larger dish will enable you to pick up the signals further afield.

In order to watch any encrypted channels you will need a Sky viewing card and, strictly speaking, it is contrary to Sky's terms and conditions to take it outside the UK. However, you are entitled to take your digibox because it is your personal property. Furthermore it will work perfectly well without the card as long as you restrict yourself to the 'free-to-air' channels such as those offered by the BBC and ITV.

If you prefer to have a second digibox for use in your caravan, Sky now offers a non-subscription digital satellite service, Freesat from Sky, for a one-off charge covering a digibox, dish, viewing card and installation – further details from www.freesatfromsky.co.uk or www.satelliteforcaravans.co.uk

There is also a non-Sky, non-subscription satellite service operated by the BBC in partnership with ITV, called Freesat, which carries all the main national channels and their digital variants, including the BBC, ITV, Channel 4 and Channel Five, together with many other independent 'free-to-air' channels and most national radio channels. Freesat is an alternative way of receiving satellite TV without the need for a Sky digibox. Receivers are readily available on the High Street.

See the website www.satelliteforcaravans.co.uk (operated by a Caravan Club member) for the latest changes and developments and for detailed information on TV reception throughout Europe plus a mine of other useful information.

Television via a Laptop Computer

With a modern laptop this is straightforward. In order to process the incoming signal the computer must, as a minimum, be fitted with a TV tuner and a TV-in connector – basically an aerial socket. Some modern laptops have them built in, but if not you can obtain a plug-in USB adaptor. An alternative connection is the HDMI socket (High Definition Multimedia Interface) which is fitted to some of the more expensive laptops, for which you will need an HD digital receiver. For more information see www.radioandtelly.co.uk

Be aware that in Europe it is not possible to use wifi to access 'catch-up' services such as the BBC iPlayer because these services are blocked to non-UK internet service providers to avoid breaching broadcasting rights. Theoretically it is possible to access such services via a mobile phone or broadband 'dongle' but connection charges are prohibitively expensive.

Using Mobile Phones Abroad

Mobile phones have an international calling option called 'roaming' which will automatically search for a local network when you switch your phone on, wherever you are in Europe. You should contact your service provider to obtain advice on the charges involved as these are partly set by the foreign networks you use and fluctuate with exchange rates. Most network providers offer added extras or 'bolt-ons' to your tariff to make the cost of calling to/from abroad cheaper.

There are no further formalities and the phone will work in exactly the same way as in the UK. When you arrive at your destination, your mobile will automatically select a network with the best service. You should also be able to access most of the features you use in the UK, including voicemail and pay-as-you-go top-up.

When calling UK landline or mobile phone numbers prefix the number with +44 and drop the initial 0 of the area code. Format telephone numbers in your phone's memory in this way, and you will get through to those numbers when dialling from the memory, whether you are in the UK or abroad.

Because mobile phones will only work within range of a base station, reception in some remote rural areas may be patchy, but coverage is usually excellent in main towns and near main roads and motorways. Approximate coverage maps can be obtained from many dealers.

If you are making calls to numbers within the country you are visiting, you only need to use the standard dialling code without the international code, rather like using your phone in the UK. To make a call to a country other than the UK from abroad, simply replace the +44 country code with the applicable country code, eg +33 for France or +49 for Germany.

You should note that if you receive an incoming call while abroad, the international leg of the call will be charged to your mobile phone account because the caller has no way of knowing that (s)he is making an international call. It is possible to bar or divert incoming calls when abroad and your service provider will supply a full list of options.

Mobile service providers have responded to pressure from the EU to reduce roaming charges but while mobile phone charges are coming down, sending and receiving video messages is still expensive – check with your network provider.

Global SIM Cards

As an alternative to paying your mobile service provider's roaming charges it is possible to buy a global SIM card which will enable your mobile phone to operate on a foreign mobile network more cheaply. When you go abroad you simply replace the SIM card in your phone with the new card, remembering to leave a voicemail message on the old card telling callers that you have temporarily changed number. This service is offered by a number of network providers as well as companies such as www.roameo.co.uk, www.SIM4travel.co.uk and www.0044.co.uk

You may, however, find it simpler to buy a SIM card abroad but before doing this, check with your UK service provider whether it has locked your phone against the use of a different SIM card and what, if anything, it will charge to unlock it. The website www.0044.co.uk has instructions on how to unlock mobile phones. If you plan to use a mobile phone a lot while abroad, eg to book campsites, restaurants etc then give some thought to buying a cheap 'pay-as-you-go' phone in the country you are visiting.

Internet-Enabled Phones

As technology advances VoIP (voice-over internet protocol) permits you to be contacted on your usual mobile phone number via a local number while abroad – see www.truphone.com for more details. You will need a wifi or 3G internet-enabled phone. Alternatively download software to your mobile phone to enable you to make Skype calls at local call rates.

Hands-Free

Legislation in Europe forbids the use of mobile or car phones while driving except when using hands-free equipment. **If you are involved in an accident while driving and, at the same time, using a hand-held mobile phone, your insurance company may refuse to honour the claim.**

Finally.....

Make a note of your mobile phone's serial number, your own telephone number and the number of your provider's customer services and keep them in a safe place separate from your mobile phone.

Remember to pack your charger and travel adaptor. Charging packs, available from major mobile phone retailers, provide a power source to recharge your phone if you do not have access to a mains supply. Whichever network you use, check that you have the instructions for use abroad.

Medical Matters

Very few countries offer such easy access to medical facilities as Britain. This chapter offers advice and information on what to do before you travel, how to avoid the need for health care when away from home and what to do when you return. Specific advice on obtaining emergency medical treatment in the countries covered by this guide is contained in the relevant Country Introductions.

Obtaining medical treatment abroad may seem complicated to UK residents used to the NHS and in most countries around the world you will have to pay, often large amounts, for relatively minor treatment.

Before leaving home obtain a copy of the Department of Health's leaflet, T7.1 Health Advice for Travellers which is downloadable from www.dh.gov.uk, email: dh@prolog.uk.com or call 08701 555455. Detailed advice about travel health matters in all the countries covered by this guide is also comprehensively covered by NHS Choices on www.nhs.uk/nhsengland/Healthcareabroad or at www.fitfortravel.scot.nhs.uk

Before You Travel

If you have any pre-existing medical conditions it is wise to check with your GP that you are fit to travel. If your medical condition is complex then ask your doctor for a written summary of your medical problems and a list of medications currently used, together with other treatment details, and have it translated into the language of the country you are visiting. This is particularly important for travellers whose medical conditions require them to use controlled drugs or hypodermic syringes, in order to avoid any local difficulties with Customs. The Caravan Club does not offer a translation service.

*See **Customs Regulations** in the section **PLANNING AND TRAVELLING**.*

Check the health requirements for your destination; these may depend not only on the countries you are visiting, but which parts, at what time of the year and for how long. If you are travelling to an unusual destination or heading well off the beaten track, or if you simply want to be sure of receiving the most up-to-date advice, the Medical Advisory Service for Travellers Abroad (MASTA) can supply you with a written personal Health Brief covering up to ten countries and designed to meet your specific travel needs, together with information on recommended

© Stasys Eidiejus
Used under licence from Shutterstock.com

health products. To obtain a Health Brief, which costs £3.99, log on to www.masta-travel-health.com or email enquiries@masta.org or telephone 0113 2387500.

Carry a card giving your blood group and details of any allergies

Always check that you have enough of your regular medications to last the duration of your holiday and carry a card giving your blood group and details of any allergies or dietary restrictions (a translation of these may be useful when visiting restaurants). Your doctor can normally prescribe only a limited quantity of medicines under the NHS so if you think you will run out of prescribed medicines while abroad, ask your doctor for the generic name of any drugs you use, as brand names may be different abroad. If you don't already know it, find out your blood group. In an emergency this may well ensure prompt treatment.

If you have any doubts about your teeth or plan to be away a long time, have a dental check-up before departure. An emergency dental kit is available from High Street chemists which will allow you temporarily to restore a crown, bridge or filling or to dress a broken tooth until you can get to a dentist.

European Heath Insurance Card (EHIC)

Before leaving home apply for a European Health Insurance Card (EHIC). British residents who are temporarily visiting another EU member state, as well as Iceland, Liechtenstein, Norway or

Switzerland, are entitled to receive state-provided emergency treatment during their stay on the same terms as a resident of the country being visited. As well as treatment in the event of an emergency, this includes on-going medical care for a chronic disease or pre-existing illness, ie medication, blood tests and injections. The card shows name and date of birth and a personal identification number. It holds no electronic or clinical data.

Apply online for your EHIC on www.ehic.org.uk or by telephoning 0845 6062030 or by obtaining an application form from a post office. An EHIC is required by each individual family member from the age of 16, so allow enough time before your departure for applications to be processed. Children under 16 must be included on a parent's card as dependants.

The EHIC is free of charge, is valid for up to five years and can be renewed up to six months before its expiry date. Before you travel remember to check that your EHIC is still valid.

Before you travel remember to check that your EHIC is still valid

Private treatment is generally not covered by your EHIC, and state-provided treatment may not cover everything that you would expect to receive free of charge from the NHS. If charges are made, these cannot be refunded by the British authorities but may be refundable under the terms of your holiday travel insurance policy.

An EHIC is not a substitute for travel insurance and **it is strongly recommended that you arrange additional travel insurance before leaving home (see below) regardless of the cover provided by your EHIC.**

An EHIC issued in the UK is valid provided the holder remains ordinarily resident in the UK and eligible for NHS services. Restrictions may apply to nationals of other countries resident in the UK. For enquiries about applications see www.ehic.org.uk or call EHIC Enquiries on 0845 6062030. For other enquiries call 0845 6050707.

If your EHIC is stolen or lost while you are abroad contact 0044 191 2127500 for help.

Holiday Travel Insurance

Despite the fact that you have an EHIC you may incur thousands of pounds of medical costs if you fall ill or have an accident, even in countries with which Britain has reciprocal health care arrangements. The cost of bringing a person back to the UK, in the event of illness or death, is **never** covered by reciprocal arrangements. Therefore, separate additional travel insurance adequate for your destination is essential, such as the Caravan Club's Red Pennant Overseas Holiday Insurance, available to Club members – see www.caravanclub.co.uk/redpennant

First Aid

A first aid kit containing at least the basic requirements is an essential item and in some countries it is compulsory to carry one in your vehicle (see the ***Essential Equipment Table*** in the chapter ***Motoring – Equipment***). Kits should contain items such as sterile pads, assorted dressings, bandages and plasters, hypo-allergenic tape, antiseptic wipes or cream, painkillers, gauze, cotton wool, scissors, finger stall, eye bath and tweezers. Add to that travel sickness remedies, a triangular bandage, medicated hand cleaner or wipes, a pair of light rubber gloves and a pocket mask in case you ever find yourself in a situation where you need to give mouth-to-mouth resuscitation. Above all, carry something for the treatment of upset stomachs, which spoil more holidays than anything else.

Carry something for the treatment of upset stomachs, which spoil more holidays than anything else

It is always wise to carry a good first aid manual containing useful advice and instructions. The British Red Cross publishes a comprehensive First Aid Manual in conjunction with St John Ambulance and St Andrew's Ambulance Association, which is widely available. First aid essentials are also covered in a number of readily-available compact guide books.

Emergency Multilingual Phrasebook

The British Red Cross, with the advice of the Department of Health, produces an Emergency Multilingual Phrasebook covering the most common medical questions and terms. It is aimed primarily at health professionals but the document can be downloaded as separate pages in a number of European languages from the Department of Health's website. See www.dh.gov.uk/publications and use the search facility.

Vaccinations

It is advisable to ensure that your tetanus and polio inoculations are up-to-date before going on holiday, ie booster shots within the last ten years.

The Department of Health advises long stay visitors to some eastern European countries to consider vaccination against hepatitis A. See the relevant Country Introductions.

Tick-Borne Encephalitis and Lyme Disease

Hikers and outdoor sports enthusiasts planning trips to forested, rural areas in some parts of central and eastern Europe including many countries popular with tourists such as Austria and Croatia, should seek medical advice well ahead of their planned departure date about preventative measures and immunisation against tick-borne encephalitis which is transmitted by the bite of an infected tick. TBE is a potentially life-threatening and debilitating viral disease of the central nervous system, with the risk highest between spring and autumn when ticks are active in long grass, bushes and hedgerows in forested areas and in scrubland and areas where animals wander, including in and around campsites and at rural motorway rest areas. It is endemic in many countries in mainland Europe.

There is no vaccine against Lyme disease, an equally serious tick-borne infection which, if left untreated, can attack the nervous system and joints. Early treatment with antibiotics will normally halt the progress of the disease, but you should be vigilant about checking yourself and your family for ticks and be aware of signs and symptoms of the disease.

For more information and advice on tick avoidance see www.tickalert.org or telephone 0113 2387500.

During Your Stay

When applying for medical treatment in a non-EU country, you may be asked for your NHS medical card. You are advised to take this with you if visiting a non-EU country. Residents of the Republic of Ireland, the Isle of Man and Channel Islands, should check with their own health authorities about reciprocal arrangements with other countries.

If you require treatment in an EU country but do not have an EHIC or are experiencing difficulties in getting your EHIC accepted telephone the Department for Work & Pensions in Newcastle-upon-Tyne for assistance on 0191 218 1999. The office is open from 8am to 8pm Monday to Friday. The department will fax documents if necessary.

Claiming Refunds

If you are entitled to a refund from the authorities of the country in which you received treatment you should make a claim in that country either in person or by post. You must submit the original bills, prescriptions and receipts (keep photocopies for your records). The booklet T7.1 contains details of how to claim refunds, as does NHS Choices on www.nhs.uk/nhsengland/Healthcareabroad

If you cannot claim until your return home you should contact the Department for Work & Pensions on 0191 218 1999. The DWP will liaise with overseas authorities on your behalf to obtain a refund, which may take some time.

Accidents and Emergencies

If you are unfortunate enough to be involved in, or witness a road accident, or become involved in an emergency situation, firstly summon help early by any means available, giving the exact location of the accident or emergency and the number of casualties. Notify the police; most police officers have first aid training.

If you witnessed an accident the police may question you about it. Before leaving the scene, make a brief note and a rough sketch to indicate details of the time you arrived and left, the position of the vehicles and the injured, the surface of the road, camber, potholes, etc, the weather at the time of the accident, skid marks and their approximate length – in fact anything you feel might be relevant – then date it and sign it. Take photographs if possible. You may never be called on to use these notes, but if you are, you have a written record made at the time which could be of great value.

Calling the Emergency Services

The telephone numbers for police, fire brigade and ambulance service are given in each Country Introduction. In all EU member states the number 112 can be used from landlines or mobile phones to call any of the emergency services. In most instances operators speak English.

In all EU member states the number 112 can be used to call any of the emergency services

Insect Bites

Most of the temperate parts of Europe have their fair share of nuisance insects such as mosquitoes and midges, particularly near lakes, and it is wise to carry insect repellant devices. A number of products are available including impregnated wrist and ankle bands and insect repellant sprays and coils. Covering exposed skin with long trousers and long-sleeved shirts is recommended after dark.

Also see information earlier in this chapter about tick-borne encephalitis and Lyme disease.

Rabies

Rabies incidence across Europe has reduced significantly in recent years, in large part due to EU-sponsored vaccination programmes. Apart from isolated incidents, rabies is now confined to a few member states in the east of the EU, principally Romania and Latvia.

Despite this, **DO NOT** bring any animals into the UK without first complying with the legal requirements.

Safe Bathing

Pollution of sea water at some Continental coastal resorts, including the Mediterranean, may still present a health hazard. Where the water quality may present risks, eg in rivers and lakes as well as at the coast, or where it is simply unsafe to bathe, signs are erected which forbid bathing:

French: Défense de se baigner or Il est défendu de se baigner

Italian: Vietato bagnarsi or Evietato bagnarsi

Spanish: Prohibido bañarse or Se prohibe bañarse

Sun Protection

Never under-estimate how ill careless exposure to the sun may make you. If you are not used to the heat it is very easy to fall victim to heat exhaustion or heat stroke. The symptoms include headache, tiredness, weakness and thirst, leading to confusion, disorientation and, in very extreme cases, coma and death. Anyone showing signs of serious over-exposure to the sun should be placed indoors or in the shade, encouraged to sip water and kept cool by fanning or sponging down with cool water. Call a doctor if the patient becomes unconscious.

Children need extra protection as they burn easily, tend to stay out in the sun longer and are unaware of the dangers of over-exposure. Most skin damage is caused in childhood.

Precautions

- Wear a broad-brimmed sun hat and light, loose-fitting clothing made of tightly woven fabrics. Swimming in shallow water does not protect from the sun as water and sand reflect rays onto your skin. Cover up with a cotton T-shirt when swimming. Wear good quality sunglasses which filter UV rays.
- Put children in sunsuits and hats. Use a total sun block cream and apply liberally half an hour before going out in the sun to allow time for it to develop. Keep babies out of the sun at all times.
- Use a good quality, broad-spectrum sun cream with balanced UVA/UVB protection suitable for your skin type and a high sun protection factor (SPF). Re-apply it frequently, especially if you are perspiring heavily or swimming. If possible store sun cream or lotion in a cool place or at least in the shade. Exposure to heat may damage it and it is probably not a good idea to use last year's leftover cream.
- Avoid strenuous exercise, drink plenty of water or soft drinks – alcohol, tea and coffee only increase dehydration.
- Avoid sitting in the sun during the hottest part of the day between 11am and 3pm. Take extra care when at high altitude especially in the snow, and in windy conditions.

Water and Food

Water from mains supplies throughout Europe is generally good but the level of chemical treatment may make it unpalatable and you may prefer to use bottled water.

Food poisoning is a potential risk anywhere in the world, but in extremely hot conditions a common-sense approach is called for. Avoid food that has been kept warm for prolonged periods or left unrefrigerated for more than two to four hours. If the source is uncertain, do not eat unpasteurised dairy products, ice-cream, under-cooked meat, fish or shellfish, salads, raw vegetables or dishes containing mayonnaise.

Returning Home

If you become ill on your return home do not forget to tell your doctor that you have been abroad and which countries you have visited. Even if you have received medical treatment in another country, always consult your doctor if you have been bitten or scratched by an animal while on holiday.

If you were given any medicines in another country, it may not be legal to bring them back into the UK. If in doubt, declare them at Customs when you return.

If you develop an upset stomach while away or shortly afterwards and your work involves handling food, tell your employer immediately. If after returning home you develop flu-like symptoms, a fever or rash contact your GP or NHS Direct.

Claim on your travel insurance as soon as possible for the cost of any medical treatment. Holders of an EHIC who have not been able to claim while abroad should put in a claim for a refund as soon as possible – see ***Claiming Refunds*** earlier in this chapter.

Safety and Security

The European Union has strong and effective safety legislation and Britain a tradition of closely following the law. Nevertheless, safety is largely your own responsibility; taking sensible precautions and being aware of possible hazards won't spoil your holiday, but a careless attitude might. The following advice will help you and your family have a safe and trouble-free holiday.

Overnight Stops

The Caravan Club strongly recommends that overnight stops should always be at campsites and not at motorway service areas, ferry terminal car parks, petrol station forecourts or isolated 'aires de services' or 'aires de repos' on motorways where robberies, muggings and encounters with illegal immigrants are occasionally reported. If you ignore this advice and decide to use these areas for a rest during the day or overnight, then you are advised to take appropriate precautions, for example, shutting all windows, securing locks and making a thorough external check of your vehicle(s) before departing.

Safeguard your property eg handbags while out of the caravan and beware of approaches by strangers.

Having said that, there is a wide network of 'Stellplätze', 'Aires de Services', 'Aree di Sosta' and 'Áreas de Servicio' in cities, towns and villages across Europe, many specifically for motor caravanners, and many with good security and overnight facilities. It is rare that you will be the only vehicle staying on such areas, but avoid any that are isolated, take sensible precautions and trust your instincts. For example, if there is a site for 'travellers' nearby or if the area appears run down and there are groups of young men hanging around, then you are probably wise to move on.

Around the Campsite

The Caravan Club gives safety a high priority at its UK sites but visitors to the Continent sometimes find that campsites do not always come up to Club standards on electrical safety, hygiene and fire precautions.

Take a few minutes when you arrive on site to ensure that everyone, from the youngest upwards, understands where everything is, how things work and where care is needed to avoid an accident. Once you've settled in, take a walk around the site to familiarise yourself with its layout and ensure that your children are familiar with it and know where their caravan is. Even if you have visited the site before, layout and facilities may have changed.

ION CAU
CAUTION
© Foto Factory
Used under licence from Shutterstock.com

Locate the nearest fire-fighting equipment and the nearest telephone box and emergency numbers.

Natural disasters are rare, but always think what could happen. A combination of heavy rain and a riverside pitch could lead to flash flooding, for instance, so make yourself aware of site evacuation procedures.

Be aware of sources of electricity and cabling on and around your pitch. Advice about electrical hook-ups is given in detail in the chapter ***Electricity and Gas*** in the section ***DURING YOUR STAY*** – read it carefully.

If staying at a farm site, remember that the animals are not pets. Do not approach any animal without the farmer's permission and keep children supervised. Make sure they wash their hands after touching any farm animal. Do not approach or touch any animal which is behaving oddly or any wild animal which appears to be tame.

A Club member has advised that, on occasion, site owners and/or farmers on whose land a site is situated, use poison to control rodents. Warning notices are not always posted and you are strongly advised to check if staying on a rural site and accompanied by your dog.

Common sense should tell you that you need to be careful if the site is close to a main road or alongside a river. Remind your children about the Green Cross Code and encourage them to use it. Adults and children alike need to remember that traffic is on the 'wrong' side of the road.

Incidents of theft from visitors to campsites are rare but when leaving your caravan unattended make sure you lock all doors and shut windows. Conceal valuables from sight and lock bicycles to a tree or to your caravan.

Children at Play

Watch out for children as you drive around the site and observe the speed limit (walking pace).

Children riding bikes should be made aware that there may be patches of sand or gravel around the site and these should be negotiated at a sensible speed. Bikes should not be ridden between or around tents or caravans.

Children's play areas are generally unsupervised. Check which installations are suitable for your children's ages and abilities and agree with them which ones they may use. Read and respect the displayed rules. Remember it is your responsibility to know where your children are at all times.

Be aware of any campsite rules concerning ball games or use of play equipment, such as roller blades and skateboards. Check the condition of bicycles which you intend to hire.

When your children attend organised activities, arrange when and where to meet afterwards.

Make sure that children are aware of any places where they should not go.

Fire

Caravans are perfectly safe provided you follow a few basic safety rules. Any fire that starts will spread quickly if not properly dealt with. Follow these rules at all times:

- Never use portable paraffin or gas heaters inside your caravan. Gas heaters should only be fitted when air is taken from outside the caravan.
- Never search for a gas leak with a naked flame! If gas is smelt, turn off the cylinder immediately, extinguish all naked flames and seek professional help.
- Never change your gas cylinder regulator inside the caravan. In the event of a fire starting in your caravan turn off the gas cylinder valve immediately.
- Never place clothing, tea towels or any other items over your cooker or heater to dry.
- Never leave children alone inside a caravan. Never leave matches where they can reach them.
- Never leave a chip pan or saucepan unattended.
- Keep heaters and cookers clean and correctly adjusted.
- Know where the fire points and telephones are on site and know the site fire drill. Establish a family fire drill. Make sure everyone knows how to call the emergency services.
- Where regulations permit the use of barbecues, take the following precautions to prevent fire:

  Never locate a barbecue near trees, hedges or accommodation. Have a bucket of water to hand in case of sparks.

  Only use recommended fire-lighting materials. Do not leave a barbecue unattended when lit and dispose of hot ash safely.

  Do not let children play near a lit or recently extinguished barbecue.

Swimming Pools

Make the first visit to the pool area a 'family exploration' not only to find out what is available, but also to identify features and check information which could be vital to your family's safety. Even if you have visited the site before, the layout may have changed, so check the following:

- Pool layout – identify shallow and deep ends and note the position of safety equipment. Check that poolside depth markings are accurate and whether there are any sudden changes of depth in the pool. The bottom of the pool should be clearly visible.
- Are there restrictions about diving and jumping into the pool? Are some surfaces slippery when wet? Ensure when diving into a pool that it is deep enough to do so safely.
- Check opening and closing times. For pools with a supervisor or lifeguard, note any times or dates when the pool is not supervised, eg lunch breaks or in low season. Read safety notices and rules posted around the pool. Check the location of any rescue equipment.
- Establish your own rules about parental supervision. Age and swimming ability are important considerations and at least one responsible adult who can swim should accompany and supervise children at the pool. Remember that even a shallow paddling pool can present a danger to young children. Even if a lifeguard is present, you are responsible for your children and must watch them closely.
- Do not swim just after a meal, nor after drinking alcohol.

Water Slides

Take some time to watch other people using the slides so that you can see their speed and direction when entering the water. Find out the depth of water in the landing area. Ensure that your children understand the need to keep clear of the landing area.

Consider and agree with your children which slides they may use. Age or height restrictions may apply.

Check the supervision arrangements and hours of use; they may be different from the main pool times.

Check and follow any specific instructions on the proper use of each slide. The safest riding position is usually feet first, sitting down. Never allow your children to stand or climb on the slide.

Do not wear jewellery when using slides.

Beaches, Lakes and Rivers

Check for any warning signs or flags before you swim and ensure that you know what they mean. Check the depth of water before diving and avoid diving or jumping into murky water as submerged swimmers or objects may not be visible. Familiarise yourself with the location of safety apparatus and/or lifeguards.

Children can drown in a very short time and in relatively small amounts of water. Supervise them at all times when they are in the water and ensure that they know where to find you on the beach.

Use only the designated areas for swimming, windsurfing, jetskiing etc. Use life jackets where appropriate. Swim only in supervised areas whenever possible.

Familiarise yourself with tides, undertows, currents and wind strength and direction before you or your children swim in the sea. This applies in particular when using inflatables, windsurfing equipment, body boards or sailing boats. Sudden changes of wave and weather conditions combined with fast tides and currents are particularly dangerous.

Establish whether there are submerged rocks or a steeply shelving shore which can take non-swimmers or weak swimmers by surprise. Be alert to the activities of windsurfers or jetskiers who may not be aware of the presence of swimmers.

On the Road

Do not leave valuable items on car seats or on view near windows in caravans, even if they are locked. Ensure that items on roof racks or cycle carriers are locked securely.

In view of recent problems with stowaways in vehicles on cross-Channel ferries and trains, check that your outfit is free from unexpected guests at the last practical opportunity before boarding.

Beware of a 'snatch' through open car windows at traffic lights, filling stations, in traffic jams or at 'fake' traffic accidents. When driving through towns and cities keep your doors locked. Keep handbags, valuables and documents out of sight at all times.

If flagged down by another motorist for whatever reason, take care that your own car is locked and windows closed while you check outside, even if someone is left inside. Be particularly careful on long, empty stretches of motorway and when you stop for fuel. Even if the people flagging you down appear to be officials (eg wearing yellow reflective jackets or dark, 'uniform-type' clothing) show presence of mind and lock yourselves in immediately. They may appear to be friendly and helpful, but may be opportunistic thieves prepared to resort to violence. Have a mobile phone to hand and, if necessary, be seen to use it. Keep a pair of binoculars handy for reading registration numbers too.

Road accidents are a significant risk in some countries where traffic laws may be inadequately enforced, roads may be poorly maintained, road signs and lighting inadequate and driving standards poor. The traffic mix may be more complex with animal-drawn vehicles, pedestrians, bicycles, cars, lorries, and perhaps loose animals, all sharing the same space. In addition you will be driving on the 'wrong' side of the road and should, therefore, be especially vigilant at all times. Avoid driving at night on unlit roads.

Pursuing an insurance claim abroad can be difficult and it is essential, if you are involved in an accident, to take all the other driver's details and complete an European Accident Statement supplied by your motor vehicle insurer.

It's a good idea to keep a fully-charged mobile phone with you in your car with the number of your breakdown organisation saved into it.

Personal Security

There is always the risk of being the victim of petty crime wherever you are in the world and as an obvious tourist you may be more vulnerable. But the number of incidents is very small and the fear of crime should not deter you from travelling abroad.

The Foreign & Commonwealth Office's Consular Division produces a range of material to advise and inform British citizens travelling abroad about issues affecting their safety, including political unrest, lawlessness, violence, natural disasters, epidemics, anti-British demonstrations and aircraft safety. Contact the FCO Travel Advice Unit on 0845 8502829, email: TravelAdvicePublicEnquiries@fco.gov.uk or see BBC2 Ceefax. The full range of notices is also available on the FCO's website, www.fco.gov.uk

Specific advice on personal security relating to countries covered by this guide is given in the relevant Country Introduction chapters, but the following are a few general precautions to ensure that you have a safe and problem-free holiday:

- Leave valuables and jewellery at home. If you do take them, fit a small safe in your caravan and keep them in the safe or locked in the boot of your car. Do not leave money or documents, such as passports, in a car glovebox, or leave handbags and valuables on view. Do not leave bags in full view when sitting outside at cafés or restaurants. Do not leave valuables unattended on the beach.
- When walking be security-conscious. Avoid unlit streets at night, walk well away from the kerb and carry handbags or shoulder bags on the side away from the kerb. The less of a tourist you appear, the less of a target you are. Never read a map openly in the street or carry a camera over your shoulder.
- Carry only the minimum amount of cash. Distribute cash, travellers' cheques, credit cards and passports amongst your party; do not rely on one person to carry everything. Never carry a wallet in your back pocket. A tuck-away canvas wallet, moneybelt or 'bumbag' can be useful and waterproof versions are available. It is normally advisable not to resist violent theft.
- Do not use street money-changers; in some countries it is illegal.
- Keep a separate note of bank account and credit card numbers and serial numbers of travellers' cheques. Join a card protection plan (the Caravan Club offers one to its members) so that in the event of loss or theft, one telephone call will cancel all your cards and arrange replacements. Carry your credit card issuer/ bank's 24-hour UK contact number with you.
- Keep a separate note of your holiday insurance reference number and emergency telephone number.
- Your passport is a valuable document; it is expensive to replace and its loss or theft can lead to serious complications if your identity is later used fraudulently. Keep a separate record of your passport details, preferably in the form of a certified copy of the details pages. Fill in the next-of-kin details in your passport. A photocopy of your birth certificate may also be useful.
- Many large cities have a drug problem with some addicts pickpocketing to fund their habit. Pickpockets often operate in groups, including children. Stay alert, especially in crowds, on trains and stations, near banks and foreign exchange offices, and when visiting well-known historical and tourist sites.
- Beware of bogus plain-clothes policemen who may ask to see your foreign currency and passport. If approached, decline to show your money or to hand over your passport but ask for credentials and offer instead to go with them to the nearest police station.
- Laws vary from country to country and so does the treatment of offenders; find out something about local laws and customs and respect them. Behave and dress appropriately, particularly when visiting religious sites, markets and rural communities. Be aware of local attitudes to alcohol consumption. Do not get involved with drugs.
- Do respect Customs regulations. Smuggling is a serious offence and can carry heavy penalties. Do not carry parcels or luggage through Customs for other people and do not cross borders with people you do not know in your vehicle, such as hitchhikers. If you are in someone else's vehicle do not cross the border in it – get out and walk across; you do not know what might be in the vehicle. Do not drive vehicles across borders for other people.
- Hobbies such as birdwatching and train, plane and ship-spotting, combined with the use of cameras or binoculars may be misunderstood (particularly near military installations) and you may risk arrest. If in doubt, don't.
- In the event of a natural disaster or if trouble flares up, contact family and friends to let them know that you are safe, even if you are nowhere near the problem area. Family and friends may not know exactly where you are and may worry if they think you are in danger.

The Risk of Terrorism

There is a global risk of indiscriminate terrorist attacks but it is important to remember that the overall risk of being involved in a terrorist incident is very low. Injury or death is far more likely through road accidents, swimming, alcohol-related occurrences, health problems or natural disasters.

Most precautions are simple common sense. Make sure you are aware of the situation in the country you are visiting and keep an eye on the news. Report anything you think is suspicious to the local police. The FCO Travel Advice for each country in this guide is summarised in the Country Introduction chapters, but situations can change so make a point of reading the FCO's advice before you travel and register for its email alerts.

British Consular Services Abroad

Consular staff offer practical advice, assistance and support to British travellers abroad. They can, for example, issue replacement passports, help Britons who have been the victims of crime, contact relatives and friends in the event of an accident, illness or death, provide information about transferring funds and provide details of local lawyers, doctors and interpreters. But there are limits to their powers and a British Consul cannot, for example, give legal advice, intervene in court proceedings, put up bail, pay for legal or medical bills, or for funerals or the repatriation of bodies, or undertake work more properly done by banks, motoring organisations and travel insurers.

Most British consulates operate an answerphone service outside office hours giving opening hours and arrangements for handling emergencies. If you require consular help outside office hours you may be charged a fee for calling out a Consular Officer.

In countries outside the European Union where there are no British consulates, you can get help from the embassies and consulates of other EU member states.

If you have anything stolen, eg money or passport, report it first to the local police and insist on a statement about the loss. You will need this in order to make a claim on your travel insurance. In the event of a fatal accident or death from whatever cause, get in touch with the nearest consulate at once.

If you commit a criminal offence you must expect to face the consequences. If you are charged with a serious offence, insist on the British Consul being informed. You will be contacted as soon as possible by a Consular Officer who can advise on local procedures, provide access to lawyers and insist that you are treated as well as nationals of the country which is holding you. However, (s)he cannot get you released as a matter of course.

If you need help because something has happened to a friend or relative abroad contact the Consulate Assistance Service on 020 7008 1500 (24 hours) or email consularassistance@fco.gov.uk

FCO's LOCATE Service

The FCO encourages ALL British nationals travelling abroad to register for this service, even for short trips. If a major catastrophe, crisis or natural disaster occurs the local British embassy or consulate will be able to contact you to check that you are all right and give advice, and if friends and family at home need to get in touch, you can be contacted easily. For more information see www.fco.gov.uk

British and Irish Embassy and Consular Addresses

These can be found in the relevant Country Introduction chapters.

France
(with Andorra)

© iStockphoto.com/Robert van Beets

Population: 62.1 million

Capital: Paris (population 12 million)

Area: 547,030 sq km

Bordered by: Andorra, Belgium, Germany, Italy, Luxembourg, Monaco, Spain, Switzerland

Terrain: Mostly flat plains or gently rolling hills in north and west; mountain ranges in south and east

Climate: Temperate climate with regional variations; generally warm summers and cool winters; harsh winters in mountainous areas; hot summers in central and Mediterranean areas

Coastline: 3,427 km

Highest Point: Mont Blanc 4,807 m

Language: French

Local Time: GMT or BST + 1, ie 1 hour ahead of the UK all year

Currency: Euro divided into 100 cents; £1 = €1.10, €1 = 90 pence (September 2009)

Telephoning: From the UK dial 0033 for France and omit the initial 0 of the 10-digit number you are calling. Mobile phone numbers start 06. The international dialling code for Andorra is 00376 plus the 6-digit number. For Monaco the code is 00377. To call the UK dial 0044 omitting the initial zero of the area code

Emergency Numbers: Police 112; Fire brigade 112; Ambulance 112. In Andorra dial 110 for police, 118 for fire brigade and ambulance or 112 from a mobile phone and specify the service you need

Public Holidays 2010

See under Country Information in the following chapter.

Tourist Offices

ATOUT FRANCE
FRENCH TOURIST BOARD
LINCOLN HOUSE
300 HIGH HOLBORN
LONDON WC1V 7JH
Tel: 09068 244123
Personal visits/written requests preferred
www.franceguide.com
info.uk@franceguide.com

EMBASSY OF THE PRINCIPALITY OF ANDORRA
63 WESTOVER ROAD
LONDON SW18 2RF
Tel: 020 8874 4806
www.andorra.com
andorra.embassyuk@btopenworld.com
(Visits by appointment only)

The following introduction to France should be read in conjunction with the important information contained in the Handbook chapters at the front of this guide.

Camping and Caravanning

General Information

There are approximately 11,000 campsites throughout France classified from 1 to 4 stars, including many small farm sites. All classified sites must display their classification, current charges, capacity and site regulations at the site entrance. Some sites have an inclusive price per pitch, whereas others charge per person + vehicle(s) + pitch. It is worth remembering that if you stay on site after midday you may be charged for an extra day.

In terms of site tariffs, high season dates and the qualifying age for charging for children vary from site to site and it is quite common for site owners to charge the full adult daily rate for children from seven years and sometimes from as young as three years of age.

Credit cards are widely accepted at campsites, but you may well find payment by this method refused for overnight or short stays because of high transaction charges.

Visitors are usually required to pay a tourism tax (taxe de séjour) which is imposed by local authorities and varies from 15 cents to over €1 per person per day, according to the quality and standard of accommodation. Children under 4 years of age are usually exempt and children under 10 may be charged a reduced rate. This tax usually applies in the high season only and is collected by campsite owners and will be included in your bill.

Casual/wild camping is prohibited in many state forests, national parks and nature reserves. It is also prohibited in all public or private forests in the départements of Landes and Gironde, along the Mediterranean coast including the Camargue, parts of the Atlantic and Brittany coasts, Versailles and Paris, and along areas of coast that are covered by spring tides.

A Camping Card International is recommended and accepted by most sites in lieu of a passport. Holders of a CCI may enjoy discounted fees at campsites.

The Camping Club de France owns a number of sites in France (some of which are listed in this guide and marked CC de F in their site entries) and has partnership agreements with others including the Campéole, Camping du Midi and Huttopia chains. Members of the CC de F enjoy a reduction with a CCI at these sites. Caravanners wishing to join the CC de F pay an annual fee of €46 per family (2009). Contact the CC de F at 5 bis Rue Maurice Rouvier, 75014 Paris, tel (0)1 58 14 01 23, email secretariat@campingclub.asso.fr, www.campingclub.asso.fr. In addition there are sites managed by, or operating in association with the Fédération Française de Camping & de Caravaning (marked FFCC in their site entries) which also give a discount to holders of a CCI.

July and August are the busiest holiday months and campsites in popular tourist areas, such as the Atlantic Coast, Brittany or the south of France, may be crowded. To be certain of a pitch, make an early booking yourself or use the Caravan Club's Advance Booking Service covering approximately 140 French sites. For details see the Club's Continental Caravanning brochure or visit www.caravanclub.co.uk/overseas. Campsites included in the Advance Booking Service network are marked ABS in their site entries in this guide. **The Caravan Club cannot make advance reservations for any other campsites listed in this guide.**

Many French campsites ban the wearing of boxer-style shorts in swimming pools on hygiene grounds. This rule may be strictly enforced by inspectors who have the power to close a site's swimming pool. As a result site owners have the right to insist on the wearing of conventional (brief-style) swimming trunks. Many sites also require swimmers to wear swimming caps.

During the low season it is not uncommon for only a few toilet and shower cubicles to be in use on a 'unisex' basis and they may not be cleaned as frequently as they are during the site's busy season. Hot water, other than for showers, may not be available. In addition, if the weather has been bad early in the season you may well find that site staff have not been able, for example, to cut grass or hedges and prepare the site fully for visitors.

Many sites are increasing their proportion of statics – bungalows, chalets and mobile homes – and these are often situated in premium positions thus reducing the choice of pitches for touring caravanners. However, in many instances these statics are only occupied during the main French holiday season.

Following incidents in recent years some authorities in southern France have introduced tighter regulations concerning sites which are potentially liable to flooding. It is understood many have been advised to limit their opening dates from mid-April/early May until end August/mid-September.

Recently certain areas of southern France have experienced severe water shortages with a consequent increased fire risk. This may result in some local authorities imposing restrictions at short notice on the use of barbecues. When they are used, you should be vigilant in ensuring that they do not pose a fire risk.

Motor Caravanners

There is a wide network of 'aires de services' in cities, towns and villages across France, many with good security and electricity, water and waste disposal facilities (called 'bornes'). Many 'aires' are specifically for motor caravanners. It is rare that yours will be the only motor caravan ('camping-car' in French) staying on such areas, but take sensible precautions and avoid any that are isolated.

*See **Safety and Security** later in this chapter and in the section **DURING YOUR STAY.***

Many campsites in popular tourist resorts have separate overnight areas of hardstanding with appropriate facilities often adjacent to or just outside the main campsite area. Fees are generally very reasonable. Look for the 'Stop Accueil Camping-Car' sign.

The Fédération Française de Camping et de Caravaning (FFCC) publishes a 'Guide Officiel Aires de Services Camping-Car', listing 'aires' and stopping places in France and in a number of other countries specifically set aside for motor caravans.

Bel-air Camping-Caravaning (France) also publishes a guide entitled 'Evasion Camping-Car' covering several countries. The website www.airecampingcar.com lists hundreds of 'aires' by French region and includes their GPS co-ordinates. Finally, Vicarious Books publishes a guide entitled 'All the Aires – France' listing 1600 'aires' in towns and villages throughout France – see www.vicariousbooks.co.uk, tel 0131 208 3333.

Motor caravanners are also welcome to park overnight free at approximately 1,100 vineyards and farms throughout France through an organisation called France Passion. Your motor caravan must be completely self-contained and you must have your own sanitation. In addition you must arrive and depart in daylight hours. Membership is open to motor caravanners only and costs €28 a year. Write for an application form to France Passion, BP 57, 84202 Carpentras or join online at www.france-passion.com, email: info@france-passion.com

It is illegal to spend the night in a (motor) caravan at the roadside.

Municipal Campsites

Municipal campsites are found in most towns and many villages in France. They can usually be booked in advance through the local town hall ('Mairie') or tourist office during office hours. Their published opening dates cannot always be relied on at the start and end of the season and it is advisable to phone ahead or arrive early enough to be able to find an alternative site if your first choice is closed.

When approaching a town you may find that municipal sites are not always named. Signposts may simply state 'Camping' or show a tent or caravan symbol.

Most municipal sites are clean, well-run and very reasonably priced but security may be rudimentary; at best there may be a barrier at the main entrance which is lowered at night. Occasionally a warden lives on site or nearby but more often (s)he will only call for an hour or so each morning and evening to clean and collect fees. When selecting a municipal site, therefore, try to take account of the character of the area in which it is situated – evident 'problem' urban areas are probably best avoided, as are isolated sites where yours is the only caravan.

In recent years in order to deter 'itinerants' from staying on municipal sites some local authorities have restricted entrance by caravan height or length and some sites refuse to accept caravans with twin-axles ('deux essieux'), or they make a large additional charge for them, possibly as high as €45 a night. It is advisable to check for restrictions when booking in advance and/or on arrival. You are, however, more likely to encounter groups of market traders or seasonal workers eg grape pickers, and in general their presence does not cause other visitors any problems.

Recent visitors report that bona fide caravanners with twin-axle caravans or over-height/weight/length caravans may be allowed entry, and/or may not be charged the higher published tariff, but this is negotiable with site staff at the time of arrival.

Naturism

The French Tourist Board, Atout France, has links to naturist centres approved by the French Federation of Naturism, or visit www.naturisme.fr and www.france4naturisme.com for details of naturist centres throughout the country. Visitors aged 15 and over are recommended to have a Naturist Licence, although this is no longer compulsory at many naturist centres. A licence can be obtained in advance from British Naturism (tel 01604 620361, www.british-naturism.org.uk, email headoffice@british-naturism.org.uk) or on arrival at any recognised naturist campsite (passport-size photo required). For further details contact the FFN at 5 Rue Regnault, 93500 Pantin, fax (0)1 48 45 59 05, email contact@ffn-naturisme.com, www.ffn-naturisme.com

Sites in Andorra, Corsica, Ile d'Oléron and Ile de Ré

Please note that campsites for these areas are listed separately at the end of the French site entry pages.

Country Information

Cycling

A number of French towns are actively promoting the use of bicycles. Initiatives include increasing the number of cycle paths, providing parking space for bicycles and constructing shelters and cycle hire points in car parks. You may hire bicycles at many local tourist offices and from some railway stations. The French Tourist Board has information on cycle routes and tours throughout France.

In Paris bicycles, known as 'Les Vélibs', are available for hire at very reasonable rates at approximately 750 self-service stations.

It is compulsory for cyclists to wear a reflective jacket when riding at night outside built-up areas and in poor daytime visibility. The wearing of safety helmets is not yet officially compulsory, but is highly recommended.

Transportation of Bicycles

Transportation on a support fixed to the rear of a vehicle is permitted provided the rear lights and number plate of the carrying vehicle are not obscured.

Electricity and Gas

Current on campsites is usually between 6 and 20 amps. Plugs have two round pins. Most campsites now have CEE connections. Visitors from the UK should be aware of the problem of reversed polarity which may be found on sites in France. If embarking on a tour of several campsites it may be useful to take two differently wired electric adaptors, one wired normally and one wired for reversed polarity.

The full range of Campingaz cylinders is widely available from large supermarkets and hypermarkets, although recent visitors report that at the end of the holiday season stocks may be low or shops may have run out altogether. Other popular brands of gas which visitors have found to be economical and easy to use are Primagaz, Butagaz, Totalgaz and Le Cube. A loan deposit is required and if you are buying a cylinder for the first time you may also need to buy the appropriate regulator or adaptor hose, as cylinder connections vary considerably. Compare prices carefully between the different brands and check that cylinders fit into your gas cylinder locker.

French and Spanish butane and propane gas cylinders are understood to be widely available in Andorra.

*See **Electricity and Gas** in the section **DURING YOUR STAY.***

Entry Formalities

British and Irish passport holders may stay in France for up to three months. Visitors remaining more than three months must obtain a 'carte de séjour' (residence permit) from the police station or town hall of their French place of residence.

On arrival at a hotel visitors are usually asked to complete a form for identification purposes. At campsites visitors presenting a Camping Card International do not have to complete such a form.

Regulations for Pets

*See **Pet Travel Scheme** under **Documents** in the section **PLANNING AND TRAVELLING.***

Campsites may impose a restriction of only one dog per pitch and in popular tourist areas local regulations may ban dogs from beaches during the summer months.

In preparation for your return home with your dog you can find the names and addresses of vets in France in the equivalent of the Yellow Pages ('Pages Jaunes') on www.pagesjaunes.fr or use the link under Wildlife and Pets on the website of the Department for Environment, Food & Rural Affairs, www.defra.gov.uk

Medical Services

British nationals requiring emergency treatment can take advantage of the French health service on production of a European Health Insurance Card (EHIC) which will allow you to claim reimbursement of around 70% of standard doctors' and dentists' fees and between 35% and 65% of the cost of most prescribed medicine. For the address of a doctor 'conventionné', ie working within the French national health system, ask at a pharmacy. After treatment you should be given a signed statement of treatment ('feuille de soins') showing the amount paid. You will need this in order to claim a refund once you are back in the UK.

Pharmacies dispense prescriptions and are able to dispense first aid. Your prescription will be returned to you and you should attach this, together with the stickers (vignettes) attached to the packaging of any medication or drugs, to the 'feuille de soins' in order to obtain a refund.

If you are admitted to hospital make sure you present your EHIC on admission. This will save you from paying any refundable costs up front and ensure that you only pay the fixed daily patient contribution.This charge is not refundable in France but you may be able to seek reimbursement when you are back in the UK.

Applications for refunds should be sent to a local sickness insurance office (Caisse Primaire d'Assurance-Maladie) and you should receive payment at your home address within about two months.

All visitors should take out comprehensive travel insurance to cover all eventualities, such as the Caravan Club's Red Pennant Overseas Holiday Insurance – see www.caravanclub.co.uk/redpennant

For sports activities such as skiing and mountaineering, travel insurance must include provision for covering the cost of mountain and helicoptor rescue. Visitors to the Savoie and Haute-Savoie areas should be aware that an accident or illness may result in a transfer to Switzerland for hospital treatment. There is a reciprocal health care agreement for British citizens visiting Switzerland but you will be required to pay the full costs of treatment and afterwards apply for a refund.

Andorra

The EHIC is not accepted in Andorra and there are no reciprocal emergency health care arrangements with Britain. You will be required to pay the full cost of medical treatment and, therefore, you are strongly advised to obtain comprehensive travel and medical insurance which includes cover for travel to non-EU countries, such as the Club's Red Pennant Overseas Holiday Insurance – see www.caravanclub.co.uk/redpennant

*See **Medical Matters** in the section **DURING YOUR STAY.***

Opening Hours

Banks – Tues-Sat 9am-1pm & 3pm-5pm; in Paris Mon-Fri 10am-5pm; in busy town centres some banks open on Saturday & close on Monday. Early closing the day before a public holiday.

Museums – Daily 10am-5pm; closed Monday or Tuesday, check locally. In Paris many have late opening once a week.

Post Offices – Mon-Fri 8am-7pm; Sat 8am-12 noon

Shops – Mon-Sat 9am/10am-7pm/8pm (supermarkets to 9pm/10pm); food shops generally close all or half-day on Monday; in small towns shops close for lunch from noon to 2 pm. Shops in tourist areas and very large towns may open on Sunday.

Public Holidays 2010

Jan 1; Apr 5; May 1, 8 (VE Day), 13, 24; Jul 14 (Bastille Day); Aug 15; Nov 1, 11 (Armistice Day); Dec 25. School summer holidays extend over July and August.

Andorra

Jan 1, 6; Feb 16 (Carnival); Mar 14 (Constitution Day); Apr 2, 5; May 1, 24; Jun 24 (St John's Day); Aug 15; Sep 8 (National Day); Nov 1, 4 (St Charles's Day); Dec 8 (Immaculate Conception); Dec 25.

Safety and Security

*See **Safety and Security** in the section **DURING YOUR STAY.***

In and around Calais and Dunkerque British-owned cars have been targetted by thieves, both while parked and on the move, eg by thieves flagging drivers down for a lift or indicating that a vehicle has a flat tyre. In some cases tyres have been punctured at service stations forcing drivers to stop soon afterwards on the road or motorway. If you stop in such circumstances be extremely wary of anyone offering help, ensure that car keys are not left in the ignition and that vehicle doors are locked while you investigate.

Pedestrians should beware of bag-snatchers operating on foot and from motorbikes. Avoid carrying passports, credit cards and money all together in handbags or pockets. Do not leave bags in full view when sitting outside at cafés or restaurants. Do not leave valuables unattended on the beach. Valuables, including tobacco and alcohol, should not be left unattended in parked cars and should be kept out of sight at all times.

Thieves and pickpockets operate on the Paris metro and RER (regional suburban rail network), especially RER line B, and you should be especially vigilant. Be particularly careful in and around shopping centres and car parks. Avoid illegal street vendors many of whom employ persistent and often intimidating techniques to sell their wares, and who are now to be found at many tourist sites and attractions in Paris.

Visitors to Commonwealth War Graves Commission cemeteries in northern France, many of which are in isolated areas, are advised not to leave handbags or other valuables in parked cars as they can be a target for thieves.

France shares with the rest of Europe a threat from international terrorism. Attacks could be indiscriminate and against civilian targets, including tourist attractions.

Overnight Motorway Stops

The Caravan Club strongly recommends that overnight stops should always be at recognised campsites and not at motorway service areas, ferry terminal car parks or 'aires de services' or 'aires de repos' along motorways where robberies, muggings and encounters with asylum-seekers are occasionally reported. This advice applies to all motorways but particularly to isolated rest areas (those without petrol stations or caféterias), especially those on the A10 between Paris and Bordeaux, the A16 between Calais and Dunkerque and the A25 between Dunkerque and Lille.

There have been several cases of burglary during the night at these rest areas while travellers are asleep inside their caravans, the victims first being rendered unconscious by the thieves using gas.

If you ignore this advice and decide to use these motorway areas for a rest during the day or overnight, then you are advised to take appropriate precautions. Avoid parking in isolated or dark areas, shut all windows, secure locks and make a thorough external check of your vehicle(s) before departing. Consider fitting an alarm to your caravan.

The South of France and Corsica

Always keep car doors locked and windows closed when driving in populated areas of the south of France, especially in the Marseille to Menton area. It is common for bags to be snatched from a front passenger seat, usually by individuals on motorbikes, often when the vehicle is stationary at traffic lights. Conceal bags and purses when driving and never leave valuables in a vehicle even for a short period of time when you are nearby.

In recent years there has been a number of bomb and other attacks on public buildings by the Corsican nationalist group, the FLNC. All the buildings were closed at the time of the attacks. While there is no specific threat to British tourists, visitors should take care, particularly in town centres and near public buildings, and be wary of unattended packages.

Fires can be a regular occurrence in forested areas along the Mediterranean coast and in Corsica during summer months. They are generally extinguished quickly and efficiently but short-term evacuations are sometimes necessary. Visits to forested areas will generally be trouble-free but you should familiarise yourself with local emergency procedures in the event of fire.

You are advised to avoid leaving your vehicle(s) unattended by the roadside, especially on coastal/ beach roads, as thefts are frequent.

Visitors to Corsica are warned that most road accidents occur during the tourist season. Many roads in Corsica are mountainous and narrow with numerous bends. Drivers should be extra vigilant and beware of wandering farm animals.

Andorra

Street crime is almost unknown but you should take the usual common-sense precautions to safeguard passports and money.

If you are planning a skiing holiday it is advisable to contact the Andorran Embassy in London (tel 020 8874 4806) for advice on safety and weather conditions before travelling. All safety instructions should be followed meticulously given the dangers of avalanches in some areas. See www.ski.andorra.com or www.avalanches.org for more information.

For Consular help while in Andorra contact the British Consulate-General in Barcelona – see ***Spain*** Country Introduction for contact details.

British Embassy

35 RUE DU FAUBOURG ST HONORE
BP 111-08, F-75383 PARIS CEDEX 08
Tel: 01 44 51 31 00
http://ukinfrance.fco.gov.uk/en/
public.paris@fco.gov.uk

There are also Consulates-General and Honorary Consulates in Amiens, Bordeaux, Boulogne-sur-Mer, Calais, Cherbourg, Clermont-Ferrand, Dunkerque, Le Havre, Lille, Lorient, Marseilles, Monaco, Montpellier, Nantes, Nice, Saumur, St Malo, Toulouse and Tours.

Irish Embassy

4 RUE RUDE, F-75116 PARIS
Tel: 01 44 17 67 00 Fax: 01 44 17 67 60
www.embassyofireland.fr

There is also Irish Consulates-General/Consulates in Cannes, Cherbourg, Lyon and Monaco.

Customs Regulations

Alcohol and Tobacco

For general import allowances for alcohol and tobacco products see ***Customs Regulations*** in the section ***PLANNING AND TRAVELLING.***

Duty-Free Imports from Andorra

Duty-free shopping is permitted in Andorra, which is not a member of the EU, but there are strict limits on the amount of goods which can be imported from there into France and Spain, and Customs checks are frequently made. Each person over 17 years of age is permitted to import the following items from Andorra free of duty or tax:

1.5 litre of spirits or 3 litres fortified wine

5 litres of table wine

16 litres beer

300 cigarettes or 150 cigarillos or 75 cigars or 400 gm of tobacco

Other items, including perfume, up to the value of €525

There are no Customs formalities when entering Andorra from France or Spain.

Caravans and Motor Caravans

A caravan, motor caravan or trailer imported into France from an EU country may remain indefinitely. The importer must be in possession of the purchase invoice showing that tax (VAT) has been paid in the country of purchase. The temporary importation of a caravan by persons other than the owner requires written authorisation from the owner.

Maximum permitted vehicle dimensions are: height 4 metres, width 2.55 metres, length 12 metres excluding the towbar, and total combined length of car + caravan 18.75 metres. In addition, caravans, trailers and motor caravans must not exceed the maximum authorised laden weight displayed on the vehicle's registration certificate.

There are no identity checks at the borders with other EU countries or with Switzerland but you may encounter Customs checks when entering or leaving Switzerland as well as when leaving Andorra.

Some border crossings in the Alps to Italy and in the Pyrénées to Spain close in winter. Border crossing posts with Germany are open continuously, except for those on ferries crossing the Rhine.

Documents

Driving Licence

You should carry your driving licence at all times when driving, together with original vehicle registration document (V5C), insurance certificate and MOT certificate (if applicable). If the vehicle is not registered in your name carry a letter of authorisation from the owner. A copy of your Caravan Registration Certificate (CRIS) document is also advisable. This advice applies to both France and Andorra.

Passport

Everyone, whatever their nationality, must carry identity papers, eg a passport, at all times as the police are empowered to check a person's identity at any time. This is also a requirement in Andorra.

Andorra – Green Card

Andorra is an Associated Country of the European Union and, therefore, an International Motor Insurance Certificate (Green Card) is no longer required.

*See **Documents** and **Insurance** in the section **PLANNING AND TRAVELLING.***

Money

*See **Money** in the section **PLANNING AND TRAVELLING.***

It is understood that French banks will not cash travellers' cheques for non-account holders. Therefore, their use is not recommended as a means of obtaining cash. You may be able to cash them at some post offices but handling charges and rates of commission for exchanging both travellers' cheques and bank notes may vary considerably and it is recommended that you check such charges before the transaction goes through. Pre-loadable travel money cards are a realistic alternative offering the security of travellers' cheques with the convenience of a cash card.

Frequent visitors may wish to consider opening a euro bank account in France in order to obtain a French credit/debit card. This will then avoid the problem of using credit cards at automated petrol stations (which may occasionally reject cards issued by foreign banks) and means that you will not have to pay any foreign exchange fees or commission charges to withdraw euros from cash machines or to use the card in shops, restaurants, campsites etc. Britline, a branch of Crédit Agricole is one bank which provides an English-speaking French banking service to residents of the UK and Ireland, tel 0033 231 55 67 89 or see www.britline.com

Major credit cards are widely accepted and cash dispensers are widespread – many allowing users to choose instructions in English. VISA cards are displayed as 'Carte Bleue' or 'CB'.

When shopping in supermarkets near the Channel ports and paying with a credit or debit card you will be offered the choice of paying in euros or sterling. You are recommended always to pay in euros as the exchange rate used is unlikely to be as favourable as that used by your card issuer.

Cardholders are recommended to carry their credit card issuers'/banks' 24-hour UK contact numbers in case of loss or theft.

Motoring

Accidents

A driver involved in an accident, or one who has committed a traffic offence may be required to take a saliva drugs test as well as a breathalyser test. In the event of an accident where people are injured or emergency assistance is required, dial 17 or 112 (police) from any phone. A European Accident Statement form should be completed and signed by all persons involved in an accident.

Alcohol

In both France and Andorra the maximum legal level of alcohol is 50 milligrams in 100 millilitres of blood, ie less than permitted in the UK (80 milligrams). It is advisable to adopt the 'no drink and drive' rule at all times. The police carry out random breath tests and penalties are severe.

Breakdown Service

Breakdown and accident assistance on motorways and on motorway service and rest areas can only be obtained by contacting the police direct. They can be called from one of the orange emergency telephones placed every 2 km along motorways. If you are in a service area ask service station staff to contact the police for you or dial 17 or 112 from a public phone and the police will be able to pinpoint your exact whereabouts. The police will arrange breakdown and towing assistance. No breakdown vehicle will enter a motorway without police authority.

Charges for motorway assistance are fixed by the government and vary according to category/weight of vehicle, time of day and whether the breakdown occurred over a weekend or public holiday. The basic cost (2009) of repairing a vehicle on the spot between Monday and Friday is €112. A further €112 is charged for towing a vehicle.

If you have taken out breakdown insurance (eg the Caravan Club's Red Pennant Overseas Holiday Insurance) you should contact your insurance provider once the breakdown service has arrived in order to establish a means of payment. Your insurance provider cannot summon the police on your behalf if you breakdown on a motorway. There are a number of expressways (N roads) where the same rules apply.

Essential Equipment

*See **Motoring – Equipment** in the section **PLANNING AND TRAVELLING.***

Lights

The use of dipped headlights is recommended at all times, day and night, but has not yet been made compulsory. Headlights must be adjusted for driving on the right if they are likely to dazzle other road users.

Bulbs are more likely to fail with constant use and you are required to carry spares at all times. Drivers able to replace a faulty bulb when requested to do so by the police may not avoid a fine, but may avoid the expense of calling out a garage.

If a driver flashes his headlights in France he is generally indicating that he has priority and you should give way, contrary to standard practice in the UK.

Reflective Jacket

It is now a legal requirement to wear a reflective jacket when getting out of a vehicle which is stationary on the carriageway or on the side of the road at any time of the day or night, regardless of visibility. It is common sense for any passenger who leaves the vehicle also to wear one. Keep the jacket(s) to hand in your vehicle, not in the boot.

Seat Belts – Andorra

No children under the age of 10 should sit in the front seat of a vehicle and small children should be in an approved child safety seat.

Warning Triangles

It is compulsory to carry a warning triangle which, in the event of vehicle breakdown or accident, must be placed (providing it is safe to do so) on the carriageway 30 metres from the vehicle so that it may be seen at a distance of 100 metres. The French Tourist Board recommends carrying two triangles, as do the authorities in Andorra.

Winter Driving

Snow chains must be fitted to vehicles using snow-covered roads in compliance with the relevant road signs. Fines may be imposed for non-compliance. Snow chains can be hired or purchased from Polar Automotive Ltd, tel 01892 519933, fax 01892 528142, www.snowchains.com, email: sales@snowchains.com (20% discount for Caravan Club members).

In Andorra winter tyres are recommended. Snow chains must be used when road conditions necessitate their use and/or when road signs indicate.

Fuel

Unleaded petrol pumps are marked 'Essence Sans Plomb'. Diesel pumps are marked Gas Oil or Gazole. Leaded petrol is no longer sold but lead replacement petrol is available under the name of Supercarburant or Super ARS.

Petrol stations may close on Sundays and those at supermarkets, where petrol is generally cheaper, may close for lunch. At supermarkets it is advisable to check the height and width clearance before towing past the pumps, or alternatively fill up when travelling solo.

Credit cards are accepted at petrol stations. Some automatic pumps at unmanned petrol stations are operated by credit cards and increasingly these accept cards issued outside France and have instructions in English, but you should not rely on this being the case.

To find the cheapest fuel in any area log on to www.zagaz.com. Simply click on the map of France on the home page to find the locations of petrol stations across the country, together with prices charged. Alternatively view the French government website, www.prix-carburants.gouv.fr which gives fuel prices all over the country.

In summer 2009 when this guide was compiled petrol prices in France were roughly the same as in the UK. Diesel was cheaper in France than petrol and, therefore, cheaper than in the UK.

LPG and Biofuel

LPG (also called Gepel or GPL) is widely available in petrol stations across the whole of France, especially on motorways. Maps showing their company's outlets are issued free by most LPG suppliers, eg Shell, Elf etc. A list of their locations is available online on http://stations.gpl.online.fr (English option).

Fuel containing 10% bioethanol has been on sale at many petrol stations in France since April 2009 alongside the regular Euro 95 unleaded fuel which it will eventually replace. Pumps are labelled SP95-E10. This fuel can be used in most modern vehicles manufactured since 2000 but if you are in any doubt about using it then Euro 98 Super Plus unleaded fuel is still available at most petrol stations. For a list of vehicles which can safely use SP95-E10 see www.carburante10.fr (in French only).

*See also **Fuel Price Guide** under **Motoring – Advice** in the section **PLANNING AND TRAVELLING.***

Mountain Passes and Tunnels

*See the chapter **Mountain Passes and Tunnels** in the section **PLANNING AND TRAVELLING.***

Following fires in 1999 and 2005, safety features in both the Mont Blanc and Fréjus tunnels have been significantly overhauled and improved. Both tunnels are heavily used by freight vehicles and traffic is subject to a number of restrictions including minimum and maximum speed limits. In the Fréjus tunnel vehicles over 3,500 kg are subject to one-hour alternate traffic flows, starting at 8am leaving France. All drivers should listen to the tunnels' radio stations and if your vehicle runs on LPG you should tell the toll operator before entering the tunnel. See www.tunnelmb.net and www.sftrf.fr

Overtaking and Passing

Overtaking where it means crossing a solid single or double centre line is heavily penalised.

On steep gradients vehicles travelling downhill must give way to vehicles travelling uphill. If one vehicle must reverse, it is the vehicle without a trailer (as opposed to a combination of vehicles) or the lighter weight vehicle which must do so. If both vehicles are of the same category the vehicle travelling downhill must reverse, unless it is clearly easier for the vehicle travelling uphill, eg if there is a convenient passing place nearby.

Outside built-up areas, outfits weighing more than 3,500 kg or more than 7 metres in length are required by law to leave at least 50 metres between themselves and the vehicle in front. They are only permitted to use the two right-hand lanes on roads with three or more lanes and, where overtaking is difficult, should slow down or stop to allow other smaller vehicles to pass.

Parking

As a general rule, all prohibitions are indicated by road signs or by yellow markings on the kerb. Stopping or parking on the left-hand side of the road is prohibited except in one-way streets. Parking meters and 'pay and display' machines are commonplace and in Paris machines do not take coins, only the 'Paris Carte' card available from tobacconists, or a credit or debit card. On public holidays and during August you can sometimes park free of charge in certain streets; this is indicated by yellow stickers placed on parking meters. Street parking is limited to two hours.

If you need to stop on the open road ensure that your vehicle(s) are driven off the road.

In Paris two red routes have been created on which stopping and parking are absolutely prohibited. Elsewhere, drivers must observe parking restrictions indicated by signs.

In Paris it is prohibited to leave a parked vehicle in the same place for more than 24 consecutive hours. This provision also applies to the following départements which surround Paris: Haut-de-Seine (92), Seine-St Denis (93) and Val-de-Marne (95).

Illegally parked vehicles, even if registered abroad, may be towed away, impounded or immobilised by wheel clamps.

*See also **Parking Facilities for the Disabled** under **Motoring – Advice** in the section **PLANNING AND TRAVELLING.***

Priority

Although the old rule of 'priority from the right' no longer applies at major junctions and roundabouts, it is still advisable to be watchful, particularly in some towns where the yellow lozenge signs still exist.

France

Outside built-up areas, all main roads of any importance have right of way, indicated by the following signs:

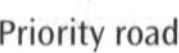

Priority road

End of priority road

Priority road

On entering towns, the same sign will often have a line through it, warning that vehicles may pull out from a side road on the right and will have priority.

Roundabouts

At roundabouts drivers must give way to traffic already on the roundabout, ie on the left. This is indicated by a red-bordered triangular sign showing a roundabout symbol with the words 'Vous n'avez pas la priorité' or 'Cédez le passage' underneath. However, in a few areas the old ruling of priority given to traffic entering the roundabout still applies and where the sign is not present you should approach with care.

Traffic on the roundabout has priority

See ***Priority and Roundabouts*** *under* ***Motoring – Advice*** *in the section* ***PLANNING AND TRAVELLING.***

Roads

France has a very extensive network of good quality roads falling into three categories: autoroutes (A) ie motorways; national (N) roads; and departmental (D) roads. There are over 8,000 kilometres of privately-owned motorways, on most of which tolls are levied. British motorists will find French roads relatively uncongested. Lorries are not allowed on the road for a 24-hour period from 11pm on Saturdays and the eve of public holidays.

Re-Numbering of French Roads

The French government has decided to transfer the administration of approximately 18,000 kilometres of national N roads to local authorities, resulting in the significant re-classification and re-numbering of roads. For example, the N21 has become the D821 and a part of the N20 is now the D820. The process started in January 2006 and will take several years to complete as each local authority chooses its own re-numbering system and changes road signs.

Where known at the time this guide was compiled, such road number changes have been incorporated into the directions contained in the campsite entries which follow.

Andorra

Travellers to Andorra from France should be aware that conditions on the road from Toulouse to Andorra, the N20/E9, can quickly become difficult in severe winter weather and you should be prepared for delays.

It is advisable to stick to main roads in Andorra when towing and not to attempt the many unsurfaced roads.

Road Signs and Markings

Directional signposting on major roads is generally good. Signs may be placed on walls pointing across the road they indicate and this may be confusing at first until you get the feel for them. The words 'tout droit' have nothing to do with turning right, instead they mean 'go straight ahead' or 'straight on'.

Although roads are clearly numbered, it is not advisable to plan your route solely by road numbers. Road signs on approach to roundabouts and at junctions usually do not show road numbers, merely the destination, with numbers being displayed once you are on the road itself. Make sure you know the names of places along your proposed route, and not just the road numbers. Once you have seen your destination town signposted continue along the road until directed otherwise. Intermediate junctions or roundabouts where you do not have to turn usually omit the destination name if the route to it is straight on.

Lines on the carriageway are generally white. A yellow zigzag line indicates a bus stop, blue markings indicate that parking is restricted and yellow lines on the edge of the roadway indicate that stopping and/or parking is prohibited. A solid single or double white line in the centre of the road indicates that overtaking is not permitted.

STOP signs mean stop. Your wheels must stop rolling; creeping slowly in a low gear will not do, even if local drivers do so. You must come to a complete halt otherwise you may be liable to a fine.

Whilst road signs conform to international standards, some other commonly used signs you may see include:

Allumez vos feux – *Switch on headlights*

Attention – *Caution*

Bouchon – *Traffic jam*

Chausée deformée – *Uneven road*

Chemin sans issue – *No through road*

Col – *Mountain pass*

Créneau de dépassement – *2-lane passing zone, dual carriageway*

Déviation – *Diversion*

Fin d'interdiction de stationner – *End of parking restrictions*

Gravillons – *Loose chippings*

Interdit aux piétons – *no pedestrians*

Itineraire bis – *Alternative route*

Nids de poules – *Potholes*

Péage – *Toll*

Poids lourds – *Lorries*

Ralentissez – *Slow down*

Rappel – *Continued restriction (eg no overtaking or speed limit)*

Rétrécissement – *Narrow lane*

Route barrée – *Road closed*

Sens interdit – *No entry*

Sens unique – *One-way street*

Serrez à gauche/droite – *Keep left/right*

Sortie d'usine – *Factory exit*

Stationnement interdit – *No parking*

Tout droit – *Straight on*

Toutes directions – *All directions*

Travaux – *Road works*

Virages – *Bends*

Voie unique – *Single-lane road*

Voitures – *Cars*

Andorra

Main roads are prefixed 'CG' (Carretera General) and side roads are prefixed 'CS' (Carretera Secundaria). CG road signs are white on red and CS signs are white on green.

Traffic Lights

There is no amber light after the red light in the traffic light sequence.

A flashing amber light indicates caution, slow down, proceed but give way to vehicles coming from the right. A flashing red light indicates no entry; it is also used to mark level crossings, obstacles, etc.

A yellow arrow at the same time as a red light indicates that drivers may turn in the direction of the arrow, traffic permitting, and providing they give way to pedestrians.

Watch out for traffic lights which may be mounted high above the road and hard to spot.

Speed Limits

*See **Speed Limits Table** under **Motoring – Advice** in the section **PLANNING AND TRAVELLING.***

Speed limits on motorways (in dry weather) are higher than in the UK – although they are lower on ordinary roads – and the accident rate is greater. Drivers undertaking long journeys in or through France should plan carefully and take sufficient breaks; a minimum of 15 minutes every two hours is recommended.

Fixed speed cameras are common on both motorways and major roads and they are usually prominently signposted well ahead of the actual camera position, but the cameras themselves may be hidden, or at best inconspicuous, in the form of brown/beige boxes mounted just off the ground. Unlike in parts of the UK where there are warning signs but no cameras, where you see a sign in France there will be a camera. The website http://english.controleradar.org allows you to look up the location of fixed speed cameras throughout France.

Speed camera ahead

The use of mobile speed cameras and radar traps is frequent, even on remote country roads. They may also be in use on exit slip roads from motorways or major roads where there is a posted speed limit. Mobile speed cameras may be operated from parked vans or motor bikes, or they may be hand-held. Oncoming drivers may flash warnings but headlight-flashing for this purpose is itself illegal, so do not be tempted to do it yourself.

Radar Detectors

Motorists should be aware that non-GPS radar detectors, laser detectors or speed camera jammers are illegal in France, whether in use in your vehicle or not. If caught carrying one you are liable to both a fine up to €1,500 and confiscation of the device, and possibly confiscation of your vehicle if unable to pay the fine. Such devices should be removed from your vehicle before travelling to France. GPS devices which pinpoint the position of speed cameras are legal but be warned that local law enforcement officers may not be aware of the difference between legal and illegal devices.

Inside Built-up Areas

The general speed limit is 50 km/h (31 mph) which may be raised to 70 km/h (44 mph) on important through-roads or as indicated by the appropriate sign. The beginning of a built-up area is marked by a road sign giving the name of the town or village in black letters on a light background with a red border. The end of the built-up area is indicated by the same sign with a red diagonal line through it – see below. Signs showing the name of a locality in white letters on a blue background do not indicate a built-up area for the purpose of this regulation.

Therefore, when you enter a town or village, even if there is no actual speed limit warning sign, the place name sign itself indicates that you are entering a 50 km/h zone. This is the point at which you may encounter the flash of a hidden speed camera, even as you attempt to slow down. The end of the 50 km/h zone is indicated by the place name sign crossed out, as described above. The word 'rappel' on a speed limit sign is a reminder of that limit.

The speed limit on stretches of motorway in built-up areas is 110 km/h (68 mph), except on the Paris ring road where the limit is 80 km/h (50 mph).

Outside Built-up Areas

General speed limits are as follows:

- On normal roads 90 km/h (56 mph)
- On dual-carriageways separated by a central reservation 110 km/h (68 mph)
- On motorways 130 km/h (81 mph)

These general speed limits also apply to private cars towing a trailer or caravan, provided the total weight of the vehicle or vehicle combination does not exceed 3,500 kg. According to new regulations which came into force in 2009, in a vehicle combination if the weight of the towing vehicle alone is less than 3,500 kg but the weight of the vehicle combination is over 3,500 kg the limits are 90 km/h (56 mph) on motorways, 80 km/h (50 mph) on priority roads (but 90 km/h on dual carriageways with a central reservation) and 50 km/h (31 mph) in towns).

To read the new regulations in full visit the Club's website, www.caravanclub.co.uk and click on 'News and Events' then 'Overseas News'. To request a hard copy call the Club's Travel Service Information Officer (Club members only).

Vehicles over 3,500 kg, such as large motor caravans, are classed as goods vehicles and their speed limit on motorways and dual carriageways is 90 km/h (56 mph) while on other roads it is 80 km/h (50 mph).

Speed Limit Stickers: The French highway code stipulates that stickers displaying the figures '80' or '90' must be displayed by vehicles required to drive at the lower limits detailed above. Stickers can be purchased from www.speedstickers.co.uk, telephone 0800 988 7329 between 10am and 2pm.

In case of rain or adverse weather conditions, the general speed limits are lowered as follows:

- On motorways 110 km/h (68 mph)
- On urban motorways and dual carriageways 100 km/h (62 mph)
- Outside built-up areas 80 km/h (50 mph)

A speed limit of 50 km/h (31 mph) applies on all roads in foggy conditions when visibility is less than 50 metres.

In long road tunnels there are lower maximum speed limits; in addition, minimum speeds are enforced.

Recently-Qualified Drivers

The minimum age to drive in France is 18 years and this also applies to foreign drivers. Driving on a provisional licence is not allowed. Visiting motorists who have held a full driving licence for less than two years must comply at all times with the wet weather speed limits shown above.

Rumble Strips and Sleeping Policemen

These means of slowing vehicles are becoming more prevalent particularly, it is reported, in the Massif Central. They are much more offensive than the British versions and should be shown the greatest respect. The advance warning sign shows 'Ralentissez' (slow down).

Traffic Jams

The busiest motorways in France are the A6/A7 (the Autoroute du Soleil) from Paris via Lyon to the south. Travelling from the north, bottlenecks are often encountered at Auxerre, Chalon-sur-Saône, Lyon, Valence and Orange. An alternative route to the south is the A20, which is largely toll-free, or the toll-free A75 via Clermont-Ferrand.

During periods of severe congestion on the A6, A7 and A10 Paris-Bordeaux motorways, traffic police close off junctions and divert holiday traffic onto alternative routes or 'Itinéraires Bis' which run parallel to main roads. Yellow and black signs indicate these routes. For a summer traffic calendar, indicating when certain areas are most prone to traffic jams, together with a real-time congestion map and regional telephone numbers to call for traffic and travel information, see www.bison-fute.equipement.gouv.fr (in English).

Alternative holiday routes

Information centre for holiday route

Information on traffic conditions on autoroutes can be found in English on www.autoroutes.fr. In addition, travel information may be obtained from orange emergency call boxes located every 4 km on main roads and every 2 km on motorways. Calls are free.

In general, Friday afternoons and Saturday mornings are busiest on roads leading to the south, and on Saturday and Sunday afternoons roads leading north may well be congested. It is still generally true that many French people drop everything for lunch and, therefore, between noon and 2pm roads are quieter and good progress can often be made.

At the start of the school holidays in early July, at the end of July and during the first and last few days of August roads are particularly busy. Avoid the changeover weekend at the end of July/beginning of August when traffic both north and southbound can be virtually at a standstill. Traffic can also be very heavy around the Christmas/New Year period and on the weekend of any public holiday.

Andorra

There is heavy traffic in Andorra-la-Vella town centre on most days of the year. During the peak summer holiday period you are likely to encounter queues of traffic on the Envalira pass from France on the N22. Traffic is at its worst in the morning from France and in the afternoon and evening from Andorra and you are recommended to use the Envalira Tunnel to avoid some of the congestion and reduce travel time.

*See **Mountain Passes – Pyrenees and Northern Spain** and **Major Pyrenean Road Tunnels** in the section **PLANNING AND TRAVELLING***

Violation of Traffic Regulations

Severe fines and penalties are in force for motoring offences and the police are authorised to impose and collect fines on the spot. Violations include minor infringements such as an excess at a parking meter, not wearing a seat belt or not respecting a STOP sign. More serious infringements such as dangerous overtaking, crossing a continuous central white line and driving at very high speeds can result in confiscation of your driving licence. If the offence committed is serious and likely to entail a heavy fine and the suspension of your driving licence or a prison sentence, a motorist who is not resident in France and has no employment there must deposit a guarantee. The police may hold a vehicle until payment is made.

In some cases instead of, or in addition to, a fine or prison sentence a vehicle may be confiscated. Although this measure is not often taken, the main offences for which it may be applied are hit and run, refusal to stop when requested or driving under the influence of alcohol or drugs. In such a case the vehicle becomes the property of the French government.

Drivers who are deemed to have deliberately put the lives of others in danger face a maximum fine of €15,000 and a jail sentence. Failure to pay may result in your car being impounded. Your driving licence may also be suspended for up to five years.

Police are particularly strict about speeding (*see **Speed Limits** earlier in this chapter*) and many automatic speed controls and speed cameras have been introduced and more are planned. Motorists caught doing more than 40 km/h (25 mph) over the speed limit face immediate confiscation of their driving licence. No distinction is made between French and foreign drivers. British motorists without a co-driver could be left stranded and face heavy costs to get their vehicle(s) home, which would not be covered by insurance.

Computerised tills at motorway toll booths tell the cashier not only how much a driver needs to pay, but also whether (s)he has been speeding. By calculating the distance a vehicle has travelled and the journey time, the computer will indicate by means of a red light whether the speed limit has been exceeded, prompting the cashier to call the police who will impose an immediate fine.

By paying fines on the spot (request a receipt) or within three days, motorists can avoid court action and even reduce the fine. Standard fines can now be paid electronically in post offices and newsagents equipped with a dedicated terminal or by visiting the following website: www.amendes.gouv.fr (in French only).

The authorities are concerned at the serious overloading of many British-registered vehicles touring in France. Drivers of overloaded vehicles may be prosecuted and held responsible for any accident in which they are involved.

Motorways

France has over 8,000 kilometres of excellent motorways and more are under construction or planned. Tolls are payable on most routes according to distance travelled and category of vehicle(s) and, because motorways are privately financed, prices per kilometre vary in different parts of the country.

Emergency telephones connected to the police are located every 2 km.

Motorway Service Areas

Stopping is allowed for a few hours at the service areas of motorways, called 'aires', and some have sections specially laid out for caravans. All have toilet facilities and a water supply but at 'aires' with only basic facilities, water may not be suitable for drinking, indicated by a sign 'eau non potable'. In addition 'aires de repos' have picnic and play areas, whereas 'aires de services' resemble UK motorway service areas with fuel, shop, restaurant and parking facilities for all types of vehicle. It should be noted that toll (péage) tickets are only valid for 24 or 48 hours depending on the particular autoroute used – check your ticket for details.

'Aires' along motorways are not campsites and, for reasons of security, the Caravan Club recommends that when seeking an overnight stop, you leave the motorway system and find a suitable campsite.

*See **Safety and Security** earlier in this chapter.*

Motorway Tolls

Motorways tolls are charged extensively throughout France by a number of different operating companies although there are numerous stretches, particularly around large cities, where no tolls are levied. Vehicles are classified as follows:

Class 1 – Vehicle up to 2 m in height (measured from the ground) with or without caravan/trailer up to height 2 m (excluding roof rack/antennae etc), and with total weight up to 3,500 kg.

Class 2 – Vehicle with height between 2 m and 3 m and total weight up to 3,500 kg; vehicles in Class 1 towing a caravan or trailer with height between 2 m and 3 m.

Class 3 – Vehicle with 2 axles and height over 3 m, or with total weight over 3,500 kg.

Class 4 – Vehicle or combination of vehicles with 3 axles or more, with height over 3 m, or with total weight over 3,500 kg.

Payments may be made in cash, by credit card, or by euro travellers' cheques but be aware that when paying with a credit card you will not be asked for a signature or required to key in a PIN. Pay booths marked as accepting credit cards only are usually geared to Class 1 vehicles and will have a height restriction which does not permit the passage of caravans.

On less frequently-used motorways toll collection is increasingly by automatic machines equipped with 'magic-eye' height detectors. It is probably simplest to pay with a credit card but there should be a cash/change machine adjacent. Avoid 'télépéage' toll booths which are for residents with pre-paid window stickers.

Motorists driving Class 2 vehicles adapted for the transport of disabled persons pay the toll specified for Class 1 vehicles. Holding a disabled person's Blue Badge does not automatically entitle foreign motorists to pay Class 1 charges, and the decision whether to downgrade from Class 2 to 1 will be made by the person at the toll booth, based on experience of similar vehicles registered in France.

To calculate the tolls payable on your planned route see www.viamichelin.com or, for more detailed information, consult the websites of the individual operating companies, a list of which can be found on www.autoroutes.fr/en/asfa (English option). Alternatively see the AA's website, www.theaa.com

Travelling for long distances on French motorways can prove expensive. For example, a vehicle or vehicle combination in Class 2 (car + caravan or motor caravan) will pay €31 to travel from Calais to Paris and €63.70 from Paris to Strasbourg.

Toll Bridges

Tolls are charged across the Pont de Tancarville on the River Seine estuary near Le Havre (A15) and the Pont de Normandie near Honfleur. Current charges (2009) are €2.90 and €5.80 respectively for car/caravan outfits and motor caravans.

The Pont de l'Ile-d'Oléron and Pont de la Seudre (linking La Tremblade with Marennes) south-west of Rochefort are toll-free, but a return charge is made on the Pont de l'Ile-de-Ré from La Rochelle.

The 2.5 km long Millau Viaduct opened in December 2004 on the A75 autoroute between Clermont-Ferrand and Béziers. The charge (2009) in summer is €11.60 for a car and caravan, or a motor caravan; a lower charge applies outside of July and August, see www.leviaducdemillau.com (English option).

Touring

France is divided administratively into 'régions', each of which consists of several 'départements'. There are 95 départements in total including

Corsica, and these are approximately equivalent to our counties, although with more autonomy.

Paris, the capital and hub of the region known as the Ile-de-France, remains the political, economic, artistic, cultural and tourist centre of France. Visit www.parisinfo.com for a wealth of information on what to see and do in the city. A Paris Pass, valid for 2 to 6 days, entitles you to free entrance (ahead of the queues) to over 60 Paris attractions and free unlimited public transport plus a range of discounts and free offers – see www.paris-pass.com

Visitors under the age of 26 are admitted free and visitors over 60 years old are entitled to reduced price entrance to permament collections in national museums; show your passport as proof of age. National museums, including the Louvre, are closed on Tuesday with the exception of Versailles and the Musée d'Orsay which are closed on Monday. Entrance to national museums, including the Louvre, is free on the first Sunday of every month. Municipal museums are usually closed on Monday and most museums close on public holidays.

Sunday lunch is an important occasion for French families; if you have found a restaurant that appeals to you it is advisable to book in advance. Many restaurants are not open on Sunday evening. Restaurants must display priced menus outside and most offer a set menu 'plat du jour' or 'table d'hôte' which usually represents good value. A service charge of 15% is included in restaurant bills but if you have received good service an additional tip may be left. Smoking is not allowed in bars and restaurants.

Information on shopping in Calais, including tips on where best to buy wine, beer, cigarettes etc and DIY supplies, as well as opening hours and price comparisons, can be found on www.day-tripper.net

Jersey and Guernsey

Ferry services operate for cars and passengers between Poole and Portsmouth and St Malo via Jersey and Guernsey. Caravans and motor caravans are permitted to enter Jersey between March and October, subject to certain conditions, including pre-booking direct with a registered campsite and the acquisition of a permit. For further information and a list of campsites on Jersey where caravans are permitted, see www.jersey.com or contact the Club's Travel Service Information Officer.

There are three campsites on Guernsey but, for the moment, the authorities in Guernsey do not accept trailer caravans. Motor caravans can only be taken onto the island if they are stored under cover and not used for human habitation. Trailer tents can be taken onto the island without restrictions.

Local Travel

Several large cities in addition to Paris have metro or tram systems and all have a comprehensive bus network. The Paris metro network comprises 15 lines and around 300 stations in eight zones, and has many connections to the RER (regional suburban rail network) and the SNCF national railway system. Tickets for the metro – also valid on RATP buses – can be bought singly from vending machines at the turnstiles or from ticket offices, but a 'carnet' of 10 tickets is a more economical option. Your ticket is valid for an hour and a half from the time it is validated at the machines on buses or at metro stations.

For tourists Paris Visite travel passes are available allowing unlimited travel for one to five days across some or all of the travel zones and a range of special offers on attractions. For further information see www.ratp.fr

Senior citizens aged 60 and over are entitled to a 25% discount when using French railways. Show your passport as proof of age.

Car ferry services operate all year across the Gironde estuary between Royan and Le Verdon eliminating a 155 km detour (approximately €56 single journey for car, caravan and 2 adults), and between Blaye and Lamarque north of Bordeaux (approximately €36 single journey) – see www.bernezac.com (English option) for more details.

Ferry services operate from Marseille, Nice and Toulon to Corsica. For information contact:

SOUTHERN FERRIES
30 CHURTON STREET
LONDON SW1V 2LP
Tel: 0844 8157785
www.southernferries.co..uk
mail@southernferries.com

Much of France remains undiscovered because visitors lack the time, inclination or courage to deviate from the prescribed checklist of what-to-see. Often it's just a question of taking N and D roads instead of autoroutes; many of the country's most appealing treasures, whether man-made or natural features, are sometimes within easy reach of more familiar sights. Ask at local tourist information offices (Syndicats d'Initiative) for leaflets about routes connecting points of interest and discover some of those 'off the beaten track' places.

All place names used in the Site Entry listings which follow can be found in Michelin's France Atlas, scale 1:200,000 (1 cm = 2 km).

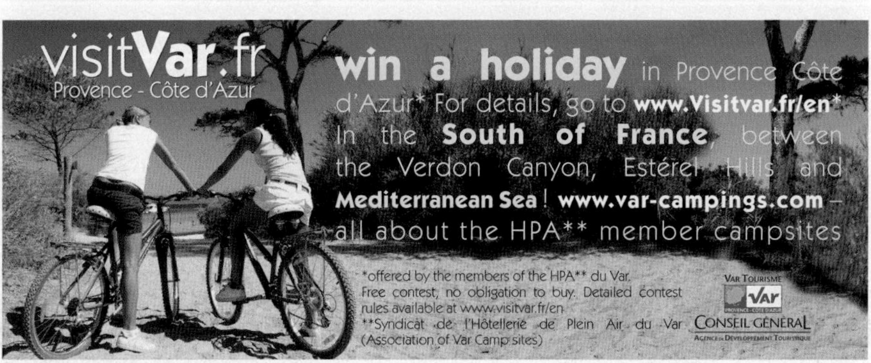

Sites in France

ABBEVILLE *3B3* (14km SE Rural) *50.03441, 1.98335* **Camp Municipal La Peupleraie, 80510 Long [03 22 31 84 27 or 03 22 31 80 21; fax 03 22 31 82 39; bacquet.lionel@free.fr; www.long.fr]** Exit A16 at junc 21 for D1001 (N1) N then turn L at Ailly-le-Clocher onto D32 for Long & foll sp. Med, mkd pitch, pt shd; wc (some cont); chem disp; shwrs inc; el pnts (6A) €2 (caution - poss rev pol & poss other elec concerns) (long lead req); Indry rm; tradsmn; shop, rest, snacks, bar in vill; BBQ; playgrnd; fishing adj; 90% seasonal statics; dogs; phone adj; poss cr; adv bkg; ccard not acc; CCI. "Pretty site; attractive, interesting area beside Rv Somme; san facs need update; gd walking/cycling by rv; site busy 1st week Sep - flea mkt in town; old power station museum; warden lives on site; conv en route Calais." 15 May-15 Nov. € 9.00 2009*

ABBEVILLE *3B3* (5km S Urban) *50.07826, 1.82378* **Camp Municipal du Marais-Talsac/Le Marais Communal, 62 Rue du Marais-Talsac, 80132 Mareuil-Caubert [03 22 31 62 37 or 03 22 24 11 46 (Mairie); fax 03 22 31 34 28; mairie.mareuilcaubert@wanadoo.fr]** Leave A28 at junc 3; at T-junc turn L onto D928; foll camping sp; in 4km turn sharp R onto D3 into Mareuil-Caubert; in 1km turn L thro houses to site by stadium. Well sp. Med, mkd pitch, hdstg, pt shd; wc; chem disp; mv service pnt; shwrs inc; el pnts (6A) €2.80 (poss rev pol); shop & 5km; rest 5km; playgrnd; 25% statics; quiet; CCI. "Clean, friendly site; sm pitches; helpful staff; clean dated facs, poss tired low ssn; no twin-axles or o'fits over 8m; hdstgs stony; gates clsd 2000-0800; interesting area; vg NH Calais." 1 Apr-30 Sep. € 10.90 2009*

ABBEVILLE *3B3* (10km SW Rural) *50.08581, 1.71482* **Camping Le Clos Cacheleux, Route de Bouillancourt, 80132 Miannay [03 22 19 17 47; fax 03 22 31 35 33; raphael@camping-lecloscacheleux.fr; www.camping-lecloscacheleux.fr]** Fr A28 exit junc 2 onto D925 sp Cambron. In 5km at Miannay turn S onto D86 sp Bouillancourt. Site thro vill on L adj Camping Le Val de Trie. Med, hdg/mkd pitch, pt shd; wc; chem disp; baby facs; fam bthrm; shwrs inc; el pnts (10A) €4.20; gas; Indtte; shop; tradsmn; rest 1km; snacks; bar; BBQ; playgrnd; htd, covrd pool; paddling pool; sand beach 20km; fishing pond; tennis 3km; games area; entmnt; farm animals; TV rm; dogs €1.50; Eng spkn; adv bkg; quiet; ccard acc; red low ssn; CCI. "Pleasant, peaceful, wooded site; lge pitches; charming, helpful owner; excel facs; gd walking & cycling; nice for dogs; excursions arranged." ♦ 15 Mar-15 Oct. € 20.60 2009*

See advertisement opposite

France

ABBEVILLE *3B3* (10km SW Rural) *50.08570, 1.71480* **Camping Le Val de Trie, Bouillancourt-sous-Miannay, 80870 Moyenneville [03 22 31 48 88; fax 03 22 31 35 33; raphael@camping-levaldetrie.fr; www.camping-levaldetrie.fr]** Fr A28 exit junc 2 onto D925 sp Cambron. In 5km at Miannay turn S onto D86 sp Bouillancourt. Site thro vill on L. Site sp fr A28. NB Last part of app narr & bendy. Med, hdg/mkd pitch, hdstg, pt sl, pt shd; htd wc; chem disp; mv service pnt; baby facs; shwrs inc; el pnts (6A) €4.20; gas; Indtte; shop; tradsmn; rest; snacks; bar; BBQ; playgrnd; htd, covrd pool; paddling pool; lake fishing; games rm; entmnt; wifi; TV rm; 1% statics; dogs €1.50; phone; Eng spkn; adv bkg; quiet but poss noise nr generator for bouncy castle; ccard acc; red long stay/low ssn; CCI. "Beautiful, well-run site; made v welcome by helpful, conscientious owner; excel clean san facs, ltd low ssn; poss boggy after heavy rain; gd family site; woodland walks; interesting area; conv Calais." ♦ 1 Apr-15 Oct. € 20.60 (CChq acc) 2009*

See advertisement above

ABBEVILLE *3B3* (7km NW Rural) *50.14166, 1.76237* **Camping Le Château des Tilleuls, Rue de la Baie, 80132 Port-le-Grand [03 22 24 07 75; fax 03 22 24 23 80; contact@chateaudestilleuls.com; www.chateaudestilleuls.com]** Fr N on A16 join A28 dir Rouen. At junc 1 take D40 dir St Valery-sur-Somme, site on R in approx 3km. Med, hdg/mkd pitch, hdstg, sl, terr, pt shd; htd wc; chem disp; mv service pnt; shwrs inc; el pnts (16A) €4; Indtte; shop & 5km; snacks; BBQ; playgrnd; htd pool; sand beach 7km; tennis; cycle hire; games rm; wifi; TV rm; dogs; Eng spkn; adv bkg; quiet; ccard acc; red long stay; CCI. "V pleasant site; lge pitches; new owners (2009) making improvements; rec." ♦ 1 Mar-30 Dec. € 16.00 2009*

See advertisement opposite

ABILLY see Descartes *4H2*

ABJAT SUR BANDIAT see Nontron *7B3*

ABRESCHVILLER *6E3* (Urban) *48.63573, 7.09341* **Camp Municipal du Moulin, 6 Rue du Moulin, 57560 Abreschviller [03 87 03 70 32; fax 03 87 03 75 90]** Exit N4 opp junc with D955 onto D41/D44 to Abreschviller. Or S fr Sarrebourg on D44 to Abreschviller. Sm, pt shd; wc (own san); chem disp; shwrs inc; el pnts €3; dogs. "Tourist train stn adj; walks; fishing; vg." ♦ 1 Apr-30 Oct. € 9.70 2007*

ABRETS, LES *9B3* (2km E Rural) *45.54065, 5.60834* **Kawan Village Le Coin Tranquille, 6 Chemin des Vignes, 38490 Les Abrets [04 76 32 13 48; fax 04 76 37 40 67; contact@coin-tranquille.com; www.coin-tranquille.com]** Fr N exit A43 at junc 10 Les Abrets & foll D592 to town cent. At rndbt at monument take D1006 (N6) twd Chambéry/Campings; cont for 500m then turn L sp Le Coin Tranquille; cross level x-ing & cont for 500m to site. Fr S on A48 exit junc 10 at Voiron onto D1075 (N75) to Les Abrets; turn R at rndabt onto D1006 twd Le Pont-de-Beauvoisin, then as above. Lge, hdg/mkd pitch, pt shd; wc (some cont); chem disp; mv service pnt; baby facs; shwrs inc; el pnts (6A) inc (poss rev pol & long lead poss req); gas; Indtte; shop; tradsmn; rest; snacks; bar; BBQ; playgrnd; pool + paddling pool in ssn; cycle hire; archery; horseriding & fishing 7km; golf 15km; games area; entmnt; TV rm; dogs €1; Eng spkn; adv bkg ess high ssn; noisy high ssn; ccard acc; red low ssn; CCI. "Well-kept, well-organised site in gd location; lge narr pitches; well-maintained, clean facs, ltd low ssn; helpful & friendly staff; busy/noisy site, but some quiet pitches avail; vg activities for children; poss flooding in wet weather; excel." ♦ 1 Apr-1 Nov. € 32.00 (CChq acc) ABS - M05 2009*

ABRETS, LES *9B3* (3km S Rural) *45.47079, 5.54688* **Camp Municipal Le Calatrin, 38850 Paladru [04 76 32 37 48; fax 04 76 32 42 02; lecalatrin@wanadoo.fr; www.paladru.com]** S on D1075 (N75) turn R onto D50 to Paladru; site 1km beyond vill on L on brow of hill. Med, mkd pitch, some terr, mainly sl, pt shd; wc (some cont); chem disp; shwrs inc; el pnts (5A) €2 (long lead poss req); gas; Indtte; shops 500m; BBQ; playgrnd; lake sw & shgl beach adj; fishing; watersports; TV; 50% statics; dogs €1; adv bkg; quiet; CCI. "Attractive site; helpful staff; gd lake access & recreational facs." 1 Apr-30 Sep. € 12.50 2007*

ABRETS, LES *9B3* (8km S Rural) *45.46736, 5.55857* **Camping International Le Lac, La Veronnière, 38620 Montferrat [04 76 32 31 67; fax 04 76 32 38 15; infos@camping-interdulac.com]** D1075 (N75) 5km S of Les Abrets turn R onto D50 dir Paladru. Turn L sp La Veronnière, site on R on lakeside. Lge, mkd pitch, pt shd; wc; chem disp; shwrs inc; el pnts (6A) inc; Indtte; tradsmn; rest; snacks; bar; BBQ; playgrnd; lake sw & shgl beach; fishing; sailing; wifi; 25% statics; dogs €1.30; phone; Eng spkn; adv bkg; quiet; ccard acc; CCI. "Lovely lake; plenty of activities; gd touring base & conv NH; beach poss cr w/end." ♦ 30 Apr-30 Sep. € 17.50 2009*

ABRETS, LES *9B3* (11km SW Rural) *45.44621, 5.53183* **Camp Municipal du Bord du Lac, 38850 Bilieu [04 76 06 67 00 or 04 76 06 62 41 (Mairie); fax 04 76 06 67 15; mairie.bilieu@pays-voironnais.com]** S on D1075 (N75) fr Les Abrets. Turn R onto D50. Just bef Paladru, turn L to Charavines. site on R on ent Bilieu, by lakeside. Med, mkd pitch, pt sl, terr, pt shd; htd wc; chem disp; shwrs inc; el pnts (10A) €3; Indtte; tradsmn; playgrnd; 70% statics; poss cr; quiet; CCI. "Nice site by lake; san facs v gd; staff helpful; no sw in lake fr site, only boat launch; pitch access poss diff; gd." 15 Apr-30 Sep. € 16.00 2008*

ABZAC see Coutras *7C2*

ACCOUS *8G2* (Rural) *42.97717, -0.60592* **Camping Despourrins, Route du Somport, 64490 Accous [05 59 34 71 16]** On N134 rte to & fr Spain via Somport Pass. Site sp on main rd. Sm, pt shd; wc (some cont); chem dis (wc); shwrs inc; el pnts (6A) €2.70; Indry rm; shop, rest, snacks, bar nrby; BBQ; 10% statics; dogs free; quiet but some rd noise. "Clean, tidy NH conv Col de Somport." 1 Mar-8 Nov. € 9.15 2007*

⊞ **ACY EN MULTIEN** *3D3* (700m SE Rural) *49.09842, 2.96144* **Caravaning L'Ancien Moulin (CC de F), 60620 Acy-en-Multien [tel/fax 03 44 87 21 28; ccdf_acy@cegetel.net; www.campingclub.asso.fr]** Leave A4 at junc 19 & turn L onto D401 to Lizy-sur-Ourcq. Cross rv & turn R then L onto D147 dir May-en-Multien. 1km then L onto D14 dir May. Cross D405 onto D420 (becomes D332) dir Rosoy-en-Multien & site is on L 2km after Rosoy, 500m bef Acy-en-Multien. Med, mkd pitch, pt shd; htd wc; chem disp; shwrs inc; el pnts (6A) inc; Indtte; shops, rest, snacks, bar, playgrnd 1km; fishing; games area; games rm; entmnt; TV rm; 90% statics; dogs €2.20; Eng spkn; adv bkg; quiet but poss aircraft noise; CCI. "Helpful, friendly staff; pitches by mill pool; 30km fr Disneyland Paris & nr 2 other theme parks; vg." ♦ € 22.40 2009*

ADRETS DE L'ESTEREL, LES see Napoule, La *10F4*

AGAY See also sites listed under St Raphaël.

AGAY *10F4* (700m E Coastal) *43.4328, 6.86868* **Camping Agay Soleil, Route de Cannes, 83700 Agay [04 94 82 00 79; fax 04 94 82 88 70; camping-agay-soleil@wanadoo.fr; www.agay-soleil.com/fr]** E fr St Raphaël on D559 (N98) site on R after passing Agay dir Cannes. Or (to avoid busy St Raphaël) fr A8 exit junc 38 on D37 & foll sp St Raphaël, then Agay/Valescure on D100 for approx 8 km; L at rndabt by beach in Agay; site far side of bay immed after watersports club. Med, mkd pitch, hdstg, pt sl, terr, pt shd; wc; chem disp; mv service pnt; baby facs; shwrs inc; el pnts (6A) €3.30; gas; Indtte; shop & 500m; rest, snacks, bar high ssn; playgrnd adj; sand beach adj; watersports; games area; wifi; some statics; dogs €2 (not acc high ssn); phone adj; train & bus 500m; poss cr; Eng spkn; adv bkg ess Easter to Aug; CCI. "Superb location on sea front; excel modern facs; many pitches too sm for awning; extra charge beach pitches; excel. " ♦ 1 Mar-1 Nov. € 27.90 (3 persons) 2007*

AGAY *10F4* (4km E Coastal) *43.43740, 6.89165* **Camping Azur Rivage, Blvd Eugène Brieux, 83530 Anthéor [04 94 44 83 12; fax 04 94 44 84 39; info@camping-azur-rivage.com; www.camping-azur-rivage.com]** On D559 (N98) heading NE dir Cannes pass Agay. Opp sandy cove at Anthéor, turn L under viaduct. Med, shd; wc (mainly cont); chem disp; mv service pnt; shwrs; el pnts (6A) €5; gas; Indtte; shop; rest; snacks; bar; cooking facs; BBQ; playgrnd; pool; paddling pool; dir access to sand beach across rd; fishing; wifi; some statics; dogs €2; poss cr; adv bkg; some rlwy noise; red low ssn. "Virtually under rlwy viaduct but excel, v clean site; pitches sm." 1 Apr-30 Sep. € 40.00 (4 persons) (CChq acc) 2009*

AGAY *10F4* (1.5km S Coastal) *43.41995, 6.85696* **Royal Camping, Plage de Camp-Long, 83530 Agay [tel/fax 04 94 82 00 20; contact@royalcamping.net; www.royalcamping.net]** On D559 (N98) twd St Raphaël. Turn at sp Tiki Plage & site. Stop in ent rd at recep bef ent site. Sm, mkd pitch, hdstg, pt shd; wc; chem disp; shwrs inc; el pnts (6A) €3.50; gas; Indtte; shops; tradsmn; rest, snacks, bar 300m; sand beach adj; wifi; some statics; dogs; phone; bus 200m; poss cr; Eng spkn; adv bkg; quiet but some rd/rlwy noise; CCI. "Gd walks; some pitches adj to beach in sep area; vg." ♦ 7 Feb-10 Nov. € 29.00 2009*

AGAY *10F4* (2km W Coastal) *43.41787, 6.84828* **CAMPEOLE Camping Le Dramont, 986 Blvd de la 36ème Division du Texas, 83530 Agay [04 94 82 07 68; fax 04 94 82 75 30; dramont@campeole.com; www.camping-mer.com or campeole.com]** W fr Agay on D559 (D1098/N98) dir St Raphaël; site on L in 1.8km. Or E fr St Raphaël on D559; site on R in 7km. Lge, mkd pitch, hdstg, pt sl, pt shd; wc; chem disp; mv service pnt; baby facs; shwrs inc; el pnts €4.10; gas adj; Indtte (inc dryer); shop; rest, snacks & bar adj; playgrnd; shgl beach adj; scuba diving adj; games area; games rm; entmnt; wifi; 50% statics; dogs €3.90; phone; bus adj; poss cr; Eng spkn; ccard acc; red low ssn. "Walking fr site; a great discovery on a crowded coast; gd." ♦ 20 Mar-10 Oct. € 38.90 2009*

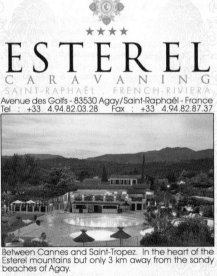

AGAY *10F4* (600m NW Coastal) *43.43376, 6.85245* **Camping des Rives de l'Agay, Ave de Gratadis, 83530 Agay [04 94 82 02 74; fax 04 94 82 74 14; reception@lesrivesdelagay.fr; www.lesrivesdelagay.fr]** Fr Agay take D100 dir Valescure, site in 400m on L. NB Dangerous bend & steep ent. Med, hdg/mkd pitch, shd; htd wc; chem disp; baby facs; shwrs inc; el pnts (6A) €3.50; gas; Indtte; shop; rest; snacks; bar; htd pool; paddling pool; sand beach 500m; entmnt; some statics; dogs €3; poss cr; Eng spkn; adv bkg; poss noisy; CCI. "San facs & pool v clean; gd pool with shade; excel site." ♦ 9 Mar-2 Nov. € 38.00 (3 persons) 2009*

I'll go online and tell the Club what we think of the campsites we've visited – www.caravanclub.co.uk/europereport

AGAY *10F4* (5km NW Rural) *43.45408, 6.83254* **Esterel Caravaning, Ave des Golfs, 83530 Agay/St Raphaël [04 94 82 03 28; fax 04 94 82 87 37; contact@esterel-caravaning.fr; www.esterel-caravaning.fr]** Fr A8 foll sps for St Raphaël & immed foll sp 'Agay (par l'interieur)/ Valescure' into D100/Ave des Golfs, approx 6km long. Pass golf courses & at end of rd turn L at rndabt twds Agay. Site ent immed after a L hand bend. Lge, hdg/mkd pitch, hdstg, terr, pt sl, pt shd; htd wc; chem disp; mv service pnt; shwrs inc; baby facs; indiv san facs to some pitches (extra charge); el pnts (10A) inc (poss rev pol); gas; Indtte; shop; rest; snacks; bar; no BBQ; playgrnd; htd, covrd pools inc padding pool; waterslide; sand beach 3km; lake sw 20km; tennis; squash; cycle hire; archery; games rm; fitness rm; entmnt; underground disco; wifi; TV rm; 50% statics; dogs €2; poss cr; Eng spkn; adv bkg; ccard acc; red low ssn/long stay; CCI. "Superbly situated, busy site adj Esterel forest; conv Gorges du Verdon, Massif de l'Estérel, Monaco, Cannes & St Tropez; gd for families - excel leisure activities; helpful staff; min stay 1 week high ssn (Sun to Sun); various pitch prices; ltd lge pitches avail; some pitches v sl & poss diff; excel rest; ltd facs low ssn; mkt Wed." ♦ 27 Mar-2 Oct. € 49.00 ABS - C21 2009*

See advertisement on previous page

⊞ **AGDE** *10F1* (2km NE Rural) **Camping Les Chalets du Rec de Rieu, Ave de Pomérols, 34510 Florensac [04 67 77 94 64; ortiz.freddy@wanadoo.fr]** Leave Florensac on D18 dir Pomérols & Montpellier; site on L in 2km. Sm, mkd pitch, pt shd; htd wc; chem disp; shwrs; el pnts (5A) inc; Indtte; shop; tradsmn; snacks; bar; BBQ; sm above grnd pool; adv bkg; quiet; CCI. "Welcoming owner; vg." ♦ € 15.00 2009*

AGDE *10F1* (1.5km E Coastal) *43.31091, 3.51158* **Camping Le Cap Agathois, Route de Sète, 34300 Agde [tel/fax 04 67 94 02 21; info@campingcapagathois.com; www.campingcapagathois.com]** Exit A9 junc 35; foll sp Agde & Sète onto D612 (N112); just bef Vias turn L onto D912 & cont thro Agde town dir Sète; 1km after supmkt complex site sp on L. Med, pt shd; wc; baby facs; shwrs inc; el pnts (6A) inc; Indtte; tradsmn; snacks; bar; BBQ (sep area); playgrnd; pool; waterpark; sand beach 3km; games area; child entmnt w/end; 40% statics (sep area); dogs €2; dog washing area; phone; Eng spkn; at times rlwy noise, track to side of site; red low ssn. "Newish site (2008) & expanding; excel pool; gd." ♦ May-Sep. € 23.00 2008*

AGDE *10F1* (3km SE Coastal) *43.27949, 3.48114* **Camping Le Rochelongue, Chemin des Ronciers, Route de Rochelongue, 34300 Le Cap d'Agde [04 67 21 25 51; fax 04 67 94 04 23; le.rochelongue@wanadoo.fr; www.camping-le-rochelongue.fr]** Exit A9 junc 34 sp Agde. Foll D612 to Le Cap d'Agde then thro Rochelongue. Site on L just bef rndabt. Med, mkd pitch, hdstg, pt shd; wc (cont); chem disp (wc); mv service pnt; baby facs; shwrs inc; el pnts (5A) inc; gas; Indtte; shop; rest; snacks; bar; BBQ; playgrnd; htd pool; sand beach 500m; cycle hire; golf 1.5km; internet; entmnt; 50% statics; dogs €2.50; phone; poss cr; Eng spkn; adv bkg; poss noisy high ssn; CCI. "Friendly, well-kept site; sh walk to vill & beach." ♦ 5 Apr-20 Sep. € 33.00 2007*

AGDE *10F1* (4.5km SE Coastal) *43.28514, 3.51941* **Camping de la Clape, 2 Rue du Gouverneur, 34300 Agde [04 67 26 41 32; fax 04 67 26 45 25; contact@camping-laclape.com; www.camping-laclape.com]** Foll sp Le Cap d'Agde, keep L at 1st gantry, L at 2nd gantry foll camping sp. Turn R at rndabt. Camp ent by lge free car pk. Lge, pt shd, mkd pitch; wc; mv service pnt; baby facs; shwrs; el pnts (10A) €3.70; Indtte; shop; rest; snacks; BBQ; pool adj; paddling pool; sand beach adj; games area; entmnt; some statics; dogs €2.65; poss cr; quiet; ccard acc; red low ssn; CCI. ♦ 1 Apr-30 Sep. € 21.80 2006*

AGDE *10F1* (5km SE Coastal) *43.29645, 3.52255* **Centre Hélio Marin René Oltra (Naturist), 1 Rue des Néréïdes, 34307 Le Cap-d'Agde [04 67 01 06 36 or 04 67 01 06 37; fax 04 67 01 22 38; infos@chm-reneoltra.fr; www.chm-reneoltra.com]** S fr m'way A9 Agde-Pézenas junc on N312/ D612 (N112) for 14km to Cap d'Agde turn-off; foll Camping Naturist sp to site on E side of Le Cap-d'Agde. V lge, hdg/ mkd pitch, pt shd; all serviced pitches; wc (some cont); mv service pnt; chem disp; shwrs inc; el pnts (5A) inc; gas 1km; Indtte; shop; tradsmn; rest; bar; pool; sand beach adj; 50% statics; dogs €2.80; poss cr high ssn; Eng spkn; adv bkg (rec high ssn); quiet; ccard acc; red low ssn. "Naturist area in Cap-d'Agde has all facs; lovely beach; gd size pitches; friendly atmosphere, modern san facs; gd family facs; excel." ♦ 15 Mar-15 Oct. € 28.00 2008*

AGDE *10F1* (1km S Rural) *43.29657, 3.47595* **FFCC Domaine des Champs Blancs, Route de Rochelongue, 34300 Agde [04 67 94 23 42; fax 04 67 21 36 75; champs-blancs@wanadoo.fr; www.champs-blancs.fr]** Exit fr A9 & foll sps to Agde (not Le Cap d'Agde). Thro cent of Agde foll sps to campsite & Rochelongue. Site on R after bdge over dual c'way. V lge, hdg pitch, shd; wc; chem disp; mv service pnt; individ san facs on pitches (extra charge); shwrs inc; el pnts inc (poss rev pol); gas; Indtte; shop, rest, snacks, bar adj; playgrnd; 2 htd pools; waterslide; sand beach adj; tennis; games area; golf 2km; 10% statics; dogs €2; adv bkg; quiet; CCI. "Friendly site; excel san facs; hot water to shwrs only; vg." ♦ 7 Apr-30 Sep. € 40.00 (CChq acc) 2007*

AGDE *10F1* (4km S Coastal) *43.28856, 3.44266* **Camping de la Tamarissière, 4 Rue du Commandant Malet, 34300 Agde [04 67 94 79 46; fax 04 67 94 78 23; contact@camping-tamarissiere.com; www.camping-tamarissiere.com]** At Agde bdge take D32E on R bank of Rv Hérault to La Tamarissière; sp. V lge, mkd pitch, pt sl, shd; wc; shwrs; el pnts (6A) €4.20; Indtte; shop; rest; snacks; bar; playgrnd; sand beach adj; games area; cycle hire; entmnt; harbour nr for boat owners; mkt every morning at site ent; 5% statics; dogs €3.20; poss cr; adv bkg; quiet; ccard acc; red long stay/low ssn; CCI. "Sandy site under pines; ferry across rv; ltd facs on site & in vill; lge areas flood after heavy rain; gate shut 2200-0700." ♦ 15 Apr-15 Sep. € 22.50 2009*

AGDE *10F1* (2km SW Rural) *43.29806, 3.45639* **Camping Le Neptune, 46 Boulevard du St Christ, 34300 Agde [04 67 94 23 94; fax 04 67 94 48 77; info@camping leneptune.com; www.campingleneptune.com]** Fr A9 exit junc 34 onto N312, then E on D612 (N112). Foll sp Grau d'Agde after x-ing bdge. Site on D32E on E bank of Rv Hérault on 1-way system. Lge, hdg/mkd pitch, pt shd; wc (some cont); chem disp; baby facs; fam bthrm; shwrs inc; el pnts (6-10A) inc; gas; Indtte; shop & bar in ssn; hypmkt 3km; rest 2km; bar; BBQ; playgrnd; htd pool; paddling pool; sand beach 2km; tennis; games area; entmnt; internet all pitches; TV; 40% statics; dogs €3 (no Pitbulls or Rottweillers); phone; bus 2km; poss cr; Eng spkn; adv bkg rec; quiet; ccard acc; red low ssn; CCI. "Peaceful, pleasant & clean site; helpful owners; modern facs, ltd low ssn; liable to flood after heavy rain; easy rvside walk/cycle to vill; gd cycleways; rv cruises avail; boat launch/slipway 500m." 1 Apr-29 Sep. € 27.20 (CChq acc) 2009*

AGEN *8E3* (12km SE Rural) *44.10456, 0.75061* **Camping au Lié, Aulié, 47220 Caudecoste [05 53 87 42 93 or 01473 832388 (UK); td.smith@aliceadsl.fr]** Fr N113 dir Toulouse, turn off sp Layrac approx 8km E of Agen. Do not use bdges across Rv Garonne at St Nicholas-de-la-Balerme (shut) or Sauveterre-St Denis (width restrict). Fr A62 exit junc 7 & turn R at 1st rndabt sp Layrac. Drive thro vill & turn L at 2nd traff lts (sharp turn) sp Caudecoste, cross bdge over Rv Gers & Caudecoste sp 1st R (silver horse at junc). In Caudecoste take D290 sp Miradoux, cross m'way in approx 1km, on L is farmhouse with pond, turn L just after this onto sm rd with grass growing in middle. At T-junc turn R, site on R. Sm, pt shd, wc; chem disp; shwrs inc; el pnts (6A) inc; shops, bar in vill; pool; dogs €1; c'van storage avail; quiet. "CL-type site in owner's garden; sm & lge pitches; san facs clean, dated; welcoming British owners; Indry facs; meals avail at farm house, inc coeliac & vegetarian; peaceful countryside; gd cycling area; excel." ♦ 1 Feb-1 Nov. € 20.00 2009*

AGEN *8E3* (8km NW Rural) *44.24368, 0.54290* **Camping Le Moulin de Mellet, Route de Prayssas, 47490 St Hilaire-de-Lusignan [05 53 87 50 89; fax 05 53 47 13 41; moulin. mellet@wanadoo.fr; www.camping-moulin-mellet.com]** NW fr Agen on N113 twd Bordeaux for 5km. At traff lts just bef Colayrac-St Cirq take D107 N twd Prayssas for 3km. Site on R. Sm, shd; wc; chem disp; baby facs; shwrs inc; el pnts (10-16A) €3; gas; Indry rm; shop 3km; tradsmn high ssn; rest; snacks; BBQ; snacks; playgrnd; 2 pools; dogs €2; adv bkg; quiet; Eng spkn; red low ssn; CCI. "Delightful, well-run site; helpful, friendly owners; small children's farm; RVs & twin-axles phone ahead; excel." ♦ 1 Apr-1 Oct. € 20.80 2009*

AGNAC see Eymet *7D2*

AGON COUTAINVILLE *1D4* (NE Urban/Coastal) *49.05105, -1.59112* **Camp Municipal Le Martinet, Blvd Lebel-Jehenne, 50230 Agon-Coutainville [02 33 47 05 20; fax 02 33 47 31 95; martinetmarais@wanadoo.fr]** Fr Coutances take D44 to Agon-Coutainville; site sp nr Hippodrome. Med, pt shd; wc; mv service pnt; shwrs inc; el pnts (5A) €2.30; Indtte; shop 250m; playgrnd; sand beach 1km; 55% statics; dogs €2.50; bus; poss cr; CCI. "V pleasant site; touring pitches ltd; ltd facs low ssn." ♦ 1 Apr-30 Oct. € 11.20 2006*

AGON COUTAINVILLE *1D4* (600m NE Urban/Coastal) *49.05163, -1.59136* **Camp Municipal Le Marais, Blvd Lebel-Jehenne, 50230 Agon-Coutainville [02 33 47 05 20; fax 02 33 47 31 95; martinetmarais@wanadoo.fr]** Fr Coutances take D44 to Agon-Coutainville. Site sp adj Hippodrome. Lge, unshd; wc; chem disp; shwrs inc; el pnts (5-10A) €2.30; Indtte; shops adj; tradsmn; playgrnd; sand beach 600m; sailing; fishing; dogs €2.50; adv bkg; quiet. ♦ 1 Jul-1 Sep. € 11.80 2006*

AGUESSAC see Millau *10E1*

AIGLE, L' *4E2* (12km NW Rural) *48.78841, 0.46533* **Camp Municipal des Saints-Pères, 61550 St Evroult-Notre-Dame-du-Bois [06 78 33 04 94 (mob) or 02 33 34 93 12 (Mairie); catherine-matte@orange.fr]** Fr L'Aigle on D13, on ent vill site on L by lake. Sm, hdstg, terr, pt shd; wc; chem disp; mv service pnt; shwrs inc; el pnts (4-10A) €1.50-2.50; shop, rest, snacks, bar 500m; playgrnd; lake sw adj; watersports; fishing; dogs €0.20; no adv bkg; poss noisy; CCI. "Pleasant lakeside vill; facs clean, ltd low ssn." ♦ 1 Apr-30 Sep. € 7.00 2009*

AIGNAN *8E2* (600m S Rural) *43.69290, 0.07528* **Camping Le Domaine du Castex, 32290 Aignan [05 62 09 25 13; fax 05 62 09 24 79; info@gers-vacances.com; www. gers-vacances.com]** Fr N on D924/N124 turn S on D20 thro Aignan onto D48; in 500m garage on R, immed after turn L; site sp. Fr S on D935 turn E at Monplaisir onto D3/D48 to Aignan; site on R bef vill. Sm, hdg/mkd pitch, pt shd; wc; chem disp; shwrs inc; el pnts (10A) €3; Indtte; shop 500m; tradsmn; rest; snacks; bar; BBQ; playgrnd; pool; lake sw 4km; tennis & squash adj; games area; TV rm; 4% statics; dogs €4; phone; poss cr; Eng spkn; adv bkg; quiet; red low ssn; ccard acc; CCI. "Lovely site in grnds of medieval farmhouse; helpful Dutch owners; modern san facs; excel pool & rest; gd touring cent for Bastide vills; mkt Mon; vg." ♦ 1 Apr-30 Oct. € 15.00 2008*

AIGREFEUILLE D'AUNIS *7A1* (2km N Rural) *46.14621, -0.94571* **Camp Municipal de la Garenne, Route de la Mazurie, 17220 St Christophe [05 46 35 51 79 or 05 46 35 16 15 (LS); fax 05 46 35 64 29; saintchristophe@ mairie17.com]** Fr Aigrefeuille-d'Aunis take D112 2.5km N to vill of St Christophe, site sp. Sm, hdg, mkd pitch, pt shd; wc; chem disp; mv service pnt; shwrs inc; el pnts (4A) €2.50; Indry rm; shop 250m; playgrnd; lake fishing 3km; tennis; horseriding; ldogs €0.85; quiet; CCI. "V clean site in sm vill; unreliable opening dates, phone ahead low ssn." ♦ 1 May-15 Sep. € 8.60 2007*

AIGREFEUILLE D'AUNIS *7A1* (500m SE Rural) *46.11430, -0.92687* **Camping La Taillée, 3 Rue du Bois Gaillard, 17290 Aigrefeuille-d'Aunis [tel/fax 05 46 35 50 88; vacances@lataillee.com; www.lataillee.com]** Exit D939 sp Aigrefeuille & fork R immed to 1st major R turn sp 'Equipement'. Take 1st L at mini-rndabt to site on L in 100m. Take care over hump. Med, pt shd; wc; chem disp; baby facs; shwrs inc; el pnts (6A) €3.10; Indtte; shops 500m; bar; BBQ; playground; pool adj; lake 900m; games rm; dogs €2.10; quiet; CCI. "V pleasant, clean site; ltd facs low ssn; excel pool adj; vg security; phone ahead low ssn to check open." ♦ 1 Jun-15 Sep. € 13.50 2007*

AIGUES MORTES See also sites listed under La Grande Motte and Le Grau-du-Roi.

AIGUES MORTES *10F2* (5km N Rural) *43.61130, 4.21010* **Camping Fleur de Camargue, 30220 St Laurent-d'Aigouze [04 66 88 15 42; fax 04 66 88 10 21; sarlaccv@aol.com; www.fleur-de-camargue.com]** Exit A9 junc 26 onto D6313/D979 dir Aigues-Mortes; turn L into St Laurent d'Aigouze; cont thro St Laurent onto D46; site on R in 2.5km. Or N fr Aigues-Mortes at junc with D58 over high-level bdge onto D46, site 2.5km on L on D46. NB Diff app thro St Laurent. Med, mkd pitch, pt shd; wc; chem disp; mv service pnt; shwrs inc; el pnts (10A) €4; gas; Indtte; shops 2km; tradsmn; rest, snacks & bar (high ssn); playgrnd; pool; paddling pool; sand beach 11km; rv & fishing 3km; entmnt; TV rm; 40% statics; dogs €4; phone; adv bkg; quiet; ccard acc; CCI. "Peaceful, relaxing site; lge pitches; pleasant owners; clean facs, poss stretched high ssn; site floods easily; gd." ♦ 4 Apr-26 Sep. € 25.00 (CChq acc) 2009*

AIGUES MORTES *10F2* (4km E Rural) **Camping à la Ferme (Loup), Le Mas de Plaisance, 30220 Aigues-Mortes [04 66 53 92 84 or 06 22 20 92 37 (mob)]** Site sp in Aigues-Mortes or foll D58 E dir Stes Maries-de-la-Mer, then R along farm road (v narr & potholed) at end of rv bdge. NB Fr town narr rd with much traff calming & sharp bends. Fr D58 4-5km potholed farm rd. Either way for v sm o'fits only. Sm, pt shd; wc; chem disp; mv service pnt; shwrs inc; el pnts inc; lndry rm; tradsmn; BBQ; quiet; CCI. "Excel CL-type site; superb san facs; helpful owners; rec not to use water at m'van service point as off irrigation system - other water points avail; video security at gate." 1 Apr-30 Sep. € 17.00 2009*

AIGUES MORTES *10F2* (3.5km W Rural) *43.56300, 4.15910* **Yelloh! Village La Petite Camargue, 30220 Aigues-Mortes [04 66 53 98 98; fax 04 66 53 98 80; info@yellohvillage-petite-camargue.com; www.yellohvillage-petite-camargue.com]** Heading S on N979 turn L onto D62 bef Aigues-Mortes & go over canal bdge twd Montpellier; site on R in 3km; sp. V lge, mkd pitch, pt shd; wc; mv service pnt; chem disp (wc); some serviced pitch; baby facs; shwrs inc; el pnts (10A) inc; gas; Indtte; shop; rest; snacks; bar; playgrnd; pool; paddling pool; jacuzzi; sand beach 3km; tennis; horseriding; cycle hire; entmnt; games rm; wifi; 50% statics; dogs €4; bus to beach high ssn; Eng spkn; adv bkg; ccard acc; red low ssn; CCI. "Lively, busy, youth-orientated commercial site with lots of sports facs; well-run & clean; excel pool complex; some sm pitches; take care o'head branches; gd cycling; mkt Wed & Sun." ♦ 23 Apr-19 Sep. € 43.00 ABS - C04 2009*

AIGUEZE see Pont St Esprit *9D2*

AIGUILLES *9D4* (1km NE Rural) *44.78783, 6.88849* **Camp Municipal Le Gouret, 05470 Aiguilles-en-Queyras [04 92 46 74 61 or 04 92 46 70 34; fax 04 92 46 79 05]** Fr Aiguilles on D947 dir Abriès, sp to site on R across rv bdge. Lge, shd; wc; chem disp; shwrs; el pnts (3-10A) inc; Indtte; shop, rest, snacks, bar 700m; dogs; phone; bus 100m; quiet. "Site on bank of Rv Guil; random pitching in lge area of larch forest; excel cent exploring Queyras National Park; vg." 15 Jun-15 Sep. € 10.00 2006*

AIGUILLON *7D2* (E Rural) *44.30467, 0.34491* **Camp Municipal du Vieux Moulin, Route de Villeneuve, 47190 Aiguillon [05 53 79 61 43; fax 05 53 79 82 01; mairie@ville-aiguillon.fr]** On ent town on D813 (N113), turn E onto D666 to site on bank of Rv Lot. Clearly sp. Or exit A62 junc 6 at Damazan onto D8 to Aiguillon. Med, mkd pitch, shd; wc (some cont)(own san rec); chem disp (wc); shwrs; el pnts (10A) €1.40; tradsmn; supmkt, rest & bar 1km; playgrnd; quiet, but some rd noise. "Site adj old mill house; san facs stretched; conv A62; NH only." 1 Jul-31 Aug. € 4.40 2008*

AIGUILLON SUR MER, L' *7A1* (S Coastal) *46.32942, -1.29846* **Camp Municipal de la Baie, Blvd du Communal, 85460 L'Aiguillon-sur-Mer [02 51 56 40 70; fax 02 51 97 11 57; camping.delabaie@aiguillonsurmer.fr]** On D46 fr La Tranche, cross bdge into Aiguillon-sur-Mer onto D746a. Foll rd to R; after it turns L site on R in 100m. Lge, mkd pitch, pt shd; wc; shwrs inc; el pnts (6A) inc; Indtte (inc dryer); shop; lge supmkt 500m; rest nr; snacks; bar; BBQ; playgrnd; pool; waterslide; lake sw & sand beach 600m; entmnt; TV; 50% statics; dogs; phone; bus adj; poss cr; Eng spkn; adv bkg (rec peak ssn); quiet; red long stay/low ssn. "Gd beaches in area; vg sailing, walking & cycling; gd birdwatching." 1 Apr-30 Sep. € 16.00 2008*

AIGUILLON SUR MER, L' *7A1* (1km W Coastal) *46.33218, -1.31764* **Camp Municipal La Côte de Lumière, Place du Dr Pacaud, 85460 La Faute-sur-Mer [02 51 97 06 16; fax 02 51 27 12 21]** On D46 E of La Tranche, thro town. Site bef bdge over rv. Lge, shd; wc (some cont); shwrs inc; el pnts (6A) €3; Indtte; shop; snacks; playgrnd; sand beach 300m; dogs; quiet; ccard acc; CCI. "Naturist beach adj; bird sanctuary, oyster/mussel beds adj; poss problem with insects; facs poss ltd & run down low ssn." ♦ 1 Apr-15 Oct. € 13.50 (3 persons) 2007*

AIGURANDE *7A4* (14km SW Rural) *46.38890, 1.61893* **Camp Municipal Fontbonne, Le Bourg, 23160 Crozant [05 55 89 80 12 or 06 85 96 53 79 (mob); fax 05 55 89 83 80]** Fr A20 take D36 to Eguzon R on D973 after 11km L on D30 to Crozant. Site sp in vill. Sm, mkd pitch, pt sl, pt shd; wc; shwrs inc; el pnts (6A) inc; Indry rm; shops, rest, snacks, bar 500m; BBQ; playgrnd; lake sw 7km; dogs €0.50; adv bkg; quiet; ccard not acc. "Attractive vill on Lake Chambon; rvside walk." 1 May-30 Sep. € 9.20 2006*

⊞ **AILLON LE JEUNE** *9B3* (3km NE Rural) *45.61020, 6.09658* **FFCC Camping Les Aillons, La Chapelle, 73340 Aillon-le-Jeune [04 79 54 60 32; fax 04 79 54 62 88; ggay@icor.fr]** Fr town hall/TO take rd to Aillon stn (winter sports development); site on L after bdge in 3km. Sm, pt shd; wc; shwrs inc; basic shop/bar/hotel in vill in summer, in winter at Aillon station; 30% statics; dogs; no twin-axles; CCI. "Mountain scenery; sm, basic site; conv orchid walk (May/Jun) & winter sports; local ski lift (winter & Jul/Aug); prize-winning cheese factory in old vill." € 9.80 2008*

AINHOA *8F1* (2.5km SW Rural) *43.29143, -1.50394* **Camping Xokoan, Quartier Dancharia, 64250 Ainhoa [05 59 29 90 26; fax 05 59 29 73 82]** Fr St Jean-de-Luz take D918 to St Pée-sur-Nivelle. Shortly after St Pée take D3 sp Dancharia then turn L at Spanish border post. Site is 25m on R. Long ent is narr & tortuous, poss diff for long o'fits. Sm, mkd pitch, pt sl, pt shd; wc; mv service pnt; shwrs inc; el pnts (6A) inc; Indtte; shop nr; rest; snacks; bar; playgrnd; adv bkg; quiet; CCI. "Conv for Spain & Pyrenees; gd walks; scenic site in grounds of sm hotel." 1 Feb-30 Nov. € 14.00 2007*

AINHOA *8F1* (NW) *43.30873, -1.50173* **Aire Naturelle Harazpy (Zaldua), 64250 Ainhoa [tel/fax 05 59 29 89 38 or 05 59 29 90 26 (LS)]** Take D918 E fr St Jean-de-Luz sp Espelette: in approx 20km turn R on D20 sp Ainhoa. App church in Ainhoa turn R thro open car park to rd at rear; site on R in 250m. Site sp. Sm, mkd pitch, terr, pt sl, pt shd; wc; chem disp; mv service pnt; shwrs; el pnts (10A) inc; Indtte; sm shop; tradsmn; lake sw 10km; dogs; phone; adv bkg; quiet; ccard not acc; CCI. "Beautiful location; conv Spanish border; helpful staff; excel walking area." ♦ 1 Apr-30 Sep. € 13.50 2009*

AIRE SUR LA LYS *3A3* (2km NE Urban) *50.64390, 2.40630* **Camp Municipal de la Lys, Bassin des Quatre Faces, Rue de Fort Gassion, 62120 Aire-sur-la-Lys [03 21 95 40 40; fax 03 21 95 40 41; camping@ville-airesurlalys.fr; www.ville-airesurlalys.fr]** Fr town cent, find main sq & exit to R of town hall. Thro traff lts turn R into narr lane just bef rv bdge dir of Hazebrouck. Site poorly sp. Sm, hdg/mkd pitch, hdstg, pt shd;htd wc; chem disp (wc); shwrs inc; some el pnts (6A) €2.10; quiet. "Ltd touring pitches; ltd but clean san facs; not suitable lge o'fits; NH." 1 Apr-31 Oct. € 7.60 2009*

AIRE SUR L'ADOUR *8E2* (E Urban) *43.70283, -0.25738* **Camping Les Ombrages de l'Adour, Rue des Graviers, 40800 Aire-sur-l'Adour [tel/fax 05 58 71 75 10; hetapsarl@yahoo.fr; www.camping-adour-landes.com]** Turn E on S side of bdge over Rv Adour in town. Site close to bdge & sp, past La Arena off rd to Bourdeaux. Med, pt shd; wc; chem disp; mv service pnt; shwrs inc; el pnts (10A) €3; Indtte; sm shop; snacks; BBQ; playgrnd; pool 500m; sports area; canoing, fishing, tennis 500m; dogs €1.80; poss cr; red low ssn. "Vg." 6 Apr-24 Oct. € 13.50 2009*

⊞ **AIRE SUR L'ADOUR** *8E2* (9km E Rural) **Camping Le Lahount, Hameau de Lahount, 32400 Lelin-Lapujolle [tel/fax 05 62 69 64 09 or 06 81 52 39 15 (mob); camping.de.lahount@wanadoo.fr; http://pagesperso-orange.fr/camping.de.lahount]** SE fr Aire-sur-l'Adour on D935, turn L in St Germé dir Lelin-Lapujolle. In 1.5km turn L, site on R, sp. Med, mkd pitch, terr, pt shd; wc; mv service pnt; baby facs; shwrs inc; el pnts (10A) €2.50; Indtte; shop; rest; snacks; bar; BBQ; playgrnd; pool; paddling pool; lake fishing; games area; cycle hire; entmnt; 60% statics; dogs €1; phone; adv bkg; ccard acc; CCI. "Ltd facs low ssn; pitches soft when set; barrier at ent awkward for long o'fits; suitable sm o'fits only." € 13.00 2008*

AIRES, LES see Lamalou les Bains *10F1*

AIRVAULT *4H1* (1km N Rural) *46.83200, -0.14690* **Camping de Courte Vallée, 8 Rue de Courte Vallée, 79600 Airvault [05 49 64 70 65; fax 05 49 94 17 78; info@caravanningfrance.com; www.caravanningfrance.com]** Fr N, S or W leave D938 sp Parthenay to Thouars rd at La Maucarrière twd Airvault & foll lge sp to site. Site on D121 twd Availles-Thouarsais. NB If app fr NE or E c'vans not permitted thro Airvault - watch carefully for sp R at Gendarmerie. Well sp fr all dirs. Med, hdg/mkd pitch, some hdstg, pt sl, pt shd; wc; chem disp; mv service pnt; shwrs inc; el pnts (8A) inc (poss long lead req); gas; Indtte; shop; tradsmn; rest/bar in town; snacks; bar; BBQ; playgrnd; htd pool; internet; fishing; cycling; walking; c'van storage; wifi; games/TV rm; 8% statics; dogs €1.50; adv bkg; quiet; ccard acc; red low ssn/long stay; CCI. "Peaceful, popular, well-kept site; helpful, pleasant British owners; excel, clean facs, poss stretched high ssn; conv Loire, Futuroscope, wine-tasting; mkt Sat." ♦ 15 Mar-31 Oct. € 33.00 ABS - L14 2009*

⊞ **AIX EN PROVENCE** *10F3* (9km E Rural) *43.51771, 5.54128* **FFCC Camping Ste Victoire, La Paradou, 13100 Beaurecueil [04 42 66 91 31; fax 04 42 66 96 43; campingvictoire@aol.com; www.campingsaintevictoire.com]** Exit A8/E80 junc 32 onto D7n (N7) dir Aix, then R onto D58 & foll sp for 3km. Sm, hdg/mkd pitch, hdstg, shd; htd wc (some cont); chem disp; mv service pnt; shwrs inc; el pnts (4-6A) €2.20-3.10 (some rev pol & poss no neutral); lndtte; shop 3km; tradsmn; playgrnd; pool 9km; rv 1km; archery; cycle hire; TV; dogs €1; phone; bus; site clsd end Nov to mid-Jan; some Eng spkn; adv bkg; quiet, some rd noise; red low ssn/long stay; no ccard acc; CCI. "Lovely, well-run site in attractive hilly, wooded country; friendly, helpful owners; clean, basic san facs, ltd low ssn; variable pitch sizes; lge o'fits poss diff manoeuvring; no lighting at night; gd walking & climbing." ♦ € 13.80 2009*

AIX EN PROVENCE *10F3* (2.5km SE Urban) *43.51250, 5.47196* **Camping L'Arc-en-Ciel, Ave Henri Malacrida, Pont des 3 Sautets, 13100 Aix-en-Provence [04 42 26 14 28; www.campingarcenciel.fr]** Fr E or W exit A8 at junc 31 for D7n (N7) dir SE; (turn N for 300m to 1st rndabt where turn R; in 200m at 2nd rndabt turn R again onto D7n dir SE); pass under m'way; site ent immed on R; sp. Take care at ent. NB Access easier if go past site for 1km to rndabt, turn round & app fr S. Sm, hdg/mkd pitch, terr, shd; htd wc; chem disp; shwrs inc; el pnts (6A) €3.20 (poss rev pol); gas; lndtte; shops nr; tradsmn; rest, snacks, bar 100m; BBQ; playgrnd; lge pool; fishing; canoeing; games area; golf 1km; TV; dogs; phone; bus; Eng library; poss cr; Eng spkn; adv bkg; m'way noise not too intrusive; ccard not acc; CCI. "Delightful, clean, well-supervised site; friendly, helpful staff; some pitches sm; gd clean facs; superb pool; if recep clsd use intercom in door; gd dog walk adj; bus to Marseille; poss no twin-axles; conv NH a'route; highly rec." 1 Apr-30 Sep. € 18.40 2009*

⊞ **AIX EN PROVENCE** *10F3* (3km SE Urban) *43.51556, 5.47431* **Airotel Camping Chantecler, Val-St André, 13100 Aix-en-Provence [04 42 26 12 98; fax 04 42 27 33 53; info@campingchantecler.com; www.campingchantecler.com]** Fr town inner ring rd foll sps Nice-Toulon, after 1km look for sp Chantecler to L of dual c'way. Foll camp sp past blocks of flats. Well sp in Val-St André. If on A8 exit at junc 31 sp Val-St André; site sp. If app fr SE on D7n turn R immed after passing under A8. Lge, hdg pitch, hdstg, sl, pt terr, pt shd; htd wc; chem disp; mv service pnt; shwrs inc; el pnts (6A) €3.90 (long lead poss req); gas; lndtte; shop; tradsmn; rest in ssn; snacks; bar; BBQ (gas/elec); playgrnd; pool; entmnt; TV; dogs €3.50; bus; poss cr; adv bkg; some rd noise; ccard acc; red long stay/low ssn; CCI. "Lovely, well-kept, wooded site; facs ltd low ssn & in need of refurb; some site rds steep - gd power/weight ratio rec; access poss diff some pitches; rec request low level pitch & walk to pitch bef driving to it; gd pool; conv city; vg touring base." ♦ € 20.30 2009*

AIX LES BAINS *9B3* (3km N Rural) *45.72770, 5.91838* **Camp Municipal Roger Milési, 23 Chemin de la Fontaine, 73100 Grésy-sur-Aix [04 79 88 28 21 or 04 79 34 80 50 (Mairie)]** Site on D1201 (N201) bet Aix-les-Bains & Albens-Annecy in vill of Grésy; exit A41 at junc 14 Aix N; turn L at supmkt flag sp to D1201; turn R & site on L in approx 1km. Sm, pt shd; wc (some cont); chem disp; 70% serviced pitches; shwrs; el pnts (10A) €3; gas 1km; lndtte, shop & rest in vill; lake sw 3km; tennis adj; dogs €1.30; quiet; adv bkg; CCI. "Higher charges for 1 night only; unreliable opening, rec phone ahead low ssn; vg." ♦ 1 Jun-30 Sep. € 8.70 2007*

AIX LES BAINS *9B3* (10km N) *45.78484, 5.94262* **FFCC Camping Beauséjour, La Rippe, 73410 Albens [04 79 54 15 20 or 06 43 33 01 93 (mob); www.camping beausejour-albens.com]** N fr Aix-les-Bains on D1201 dir Annecy to Albens; in Albens turn L at traff lts in town cent; site in 600m on left, over sm bdge. Site sp at traff lts. Med, pt sl, pt shd; wc (some cont); chem disp; mv service pnt; shwrs inc; el pnts (6A) €3; gas; lndtte; ice; shops & rest 500m; BBQ; playgrnd; games area; phone adj; bus 500m; adv bkg; some rd & rlwy noise; red low ssn; CCI. "Friendly, pleasant site; rarely full; no twin-axles; vg." 15 Jun-15 Sep. € 8.80 2009*

AIX LES BAINS *9B3* (7km SW Rural) *45.65511, 5.86142* **Camp Municipal L'Ile aux Cygnes, La Croix Verte, 501 Blvd Ernest Coudurier, 73370 Le Bourget-du-Lac [04 79 25 01 76; fax 04 79 25 32 94; camping@bourget dulac.com; www.bourgetdulac.com]** Fr N foll Bourget-du-Lac & Lac sp soon after Tunnel Le Chat. Fr Chambéry take D1504 (N504) dir Aix-les-Bains; foll sp to Le Bourget-du-Lac & Le Lac, bear R at Camping/Plage sp to site at end of rd. Lge, shd; wc; mv service pnt; baby facs; shwrs inc; el pnts (6A) €3.35; gas; lndtte (inc dryer); shop; tradsmn; rest; snacks; bar; playgrnd; private lake beach & sw; waterslide; boating; watersports; entmnt; TV; some statics; dogs €1.50; phone; bus; adv bkg; quiet; red low ssn; CCI. "On beautiful lake; mountain scenery; ground stoney." ♦ 26 Apr-28 Sep. € 16.70 2009*

AIX LES BAINS *9B3* (3km W Rural) *45.70005, 5.88666* **Camping International du Sierroz, Blvd Robert Barrier, Route du Lac, 73100 Aix-les-Bains [tel/fax 04 79 61 21 43; campingsierroz@aixlesbains.com; www.aixlesbains.com/campingsierroz]** Fr Annecy S on D1201 (N201), thro Aix-les-Bains, turn R at site sp. Keep to lakeside rd, site on R. Nr Grand Port. Lge, hdg/mkd pitch, shd; htd wc; chem disp; mv service pnt; baby facs; shwrs inc; el pnts (6A) inc; gas; lndtte; shop; tradsmn; rest; snacks; bar; playgrnd; pool 1km; games area; golf 4km; TV; 5% statics; dogs €1.60; bus (ask at recep for free pass); poss cr; adv bkg; quiet; ccard acc; red low ssn; CCI. "Pleasant location; lake adj for watersports; lge pitches; vg san facs; vg." ♦ 15 Mar-15 Nov. € 18.50 2009*

AIXE SUR VIENNE *7B3* (N Rural) *45.79887, 1.13928* **Camp Municipal Les Grèves, Ave des Grèves, 87700 Aixe-sur-Vienne [tel/fax 05 55 70 12 98 or 05 55 70 19 71 (TO); camping@mairie-aixesurvienne.fr; www.mairie-aixesur vienne.fr]** 13km SW fr Limoges, on N21 twds Périgueux, cross bdge over Rv Vienne & in about 600m turn to R (site sp) by rv. Steep down hill app & U-turn into site - take care gate posts! Med, shd; wc (some cont); chem disp; mv service pnt; shwrs inc; el pnts (10A) €2.50; Indtte; tradsmn; shops, rest, snacks & bar 300m; playgrnd; pool adj; fishing; quiet; poss cr; adv bkg; dogs free; "Pleasant, clean site by rv; spacious pitches; helpful, friendly warden; gd san facs inc disabled; conv Limoges area & Vienne valley; several chateaux easy reach; no twin-axles; vg." ♦ 20 May-30 Sep. € 11.50 2009*

AIZELLES *3C4* (500m N Rural) *49.49076, 3.80817* **Camping du Moulin, 16 Rue du Moulin, 02820 Aizelles [03 23 22 41 18 or 06 14 20 47 43 (mob); magali.merlo@ orange.fr; www.camping-du-moulin.fr]** Fr Laon take D1044 (N44) dir Reims; in 13km turn L on D88 to Aizelles; site sp in vill 'Camping à la Ferme'. Fr Reims on A26 exit junc 14 onto D925 then D1044 N. Turn R to Aizelles on D889 past Corbeny. Turn onto Rue du Moulin & site on R in 250m. Camping sp at church says 100m but allow 300m to see ent. NB Lge o'fits take care sharp R turn at ent to site. Sm, pt sl, pt shd; wc; chem disp; shwrs €1; el pnts (6A) €3.60 (poss rev pol, poss long lead req); shop 2km; tradsmn; playgrnd; fishing 800m; 70% statics (not visible); poss cr; little Eng spkn; quiet but poss noisy w/end; ccard acc; CCI. "Attractive, well-kept CL-type farm site; helpful owners; facs ltd but adequate; gates clsd 2200-0700; lovely quiet vill; conv Calais 3 hrs; a real gem." 15 Apr-15 Oct. € 11.40 2009*

AIZENAY *2H4* (1.5km SE Rural) *46.73410, -1.58950* **FFCC Camping La Forêt, Route de la Roche, 85190 Aizenay [tel/fax 02 51 34 78 12; rougier.francoise@wanadoo.fr; www.camping-laforet.com]** Exit Aizenay on D948 twd La Roche-sur-Yon. Site 1.5km on L. Med, mkd pitch, pt shd; wc; chem disp; mv service pnt; shwrs inc; el pnts (6A) €2.60; gas; Indtte; shop 1km; rest 1.5km; snacks; bar; BBQ; playgrnd; htd pool; lake beach & sw 1km; tennis; cycle hire; 10% statics; dogs €1.20; phone; adv bkg; quiet; ccard acc; red low ssn/CCI. ♦ Easter-30 Sep. € 15.50 2006*

AIZENAY *2H4* (6km NW Rural) *46.75282, -1.68645* **Camping Val de Vie, Rue du Stade, 85190 Maché [tel/ fax 02 51 60 21 02; campingvaldevie@aol.com; www. camping-val-de-vie.com]** Fr Aizenay on D948 dir Challans. After 5km turn L onto D40 to Maché. Fr vill cent cont twd Apremont. Sm, blue site sp 100m on L. Med, hdg/mkd pitch, pt sl, pt shd; wc; chem disp; 10% serviced pitches; baby facs; fam bthrm; shwrs inc; el pnts (6-10A) €3.30-3.60; Indtte; shops 200m; BBQ; playgrnd; pool; sand beach 20km; tennis adj; lake 300m; fishing; boat hire; cycle hire; 10% statics; dogs €2; phone in vill; adv bkg; quiet; red low ssn; CCI. "Lovely well-run, peaceful site in pretty vill; clean san facs; friendly, helpful British owners; gd touring base; not suitable teenagers (too quiet!); gd cycling; steel pegs useful; excel." ♦ 1 May-30 Sep. € 19.00 2009*

ALBAN *8E4* (Rural) *43.89386, 2.45416* **Camp Municipal La Franquèze, 81250 Alban [05 63 55 91 87 or 05 63 55 82 09 (Mairie); fax 05 63 55 01 97; mairie. alban@wanadoo.fr]** W of Albi on D999 turn L at ent to Alban. Site 300m on R, sp. Sm, hdg pitch, terr, pt sl, pt shd; wc; mv service pnt; shwrs; el pnts (6A) €2.10; Indtte; playgrnd; rv fishing; adv bkg; quiet; CCI. "In beautiful country, conv Tarn Valley; vg." 1 Jun-30 Sep. € 7.20 2008*

ALBEPIERRE BREDONS see Murat *7C4*

ALBERT *3B3* (500m N Urban) *50.01136, 2.65556* **Camp Municipal du Vélodrome, Rue Henry Dunant, 80300 Albert [03 22 75 22 53; fax 03 22 74 38 30; mairie@ ville-albert.fr; www.ville-albert.fr]** Fr town cent take Rue Godin E adjacent to Basilica & foll sp for site. Easiest access fr Bapaume (N) towards Albert; turn R at camping sp on edge of town. Med, mkd pitch, unshd; wc; chem disp; mv service pnt; shwrs €1.80; el pnts (4-10A) €2.40-3.60 (rev pol); shop 1km; 40% statics; dogs; poss cr in high ssn; Eng spkn; poss rwly noise; adv bkg; red long stay; CCI. "Pleasant, well-run, clean site with excel facs; friendly, helpful warden; fishing adj; poss security prob; conv for Lille, Arras & Amien by train & for WW1 battlefields etc." ♦ 28 Mar-27 Sep. € 8.20 2009*

ALBERT *3B3* (5km NE Rural) *50.04141, 2.66868* **International Camping Bellevue, 25 Rue d'Albert, 80300 Authuille [03 22 74 59 29; fax 03 22 74 05 14]** Take D929 Albert to Bapaume rd; in 3km turn L at La Boiselle, foll sp to Aveluy cont to Authuille. Site on R in vill cent. Med, hdg pitch, pt sl, pt shd; wc; chem disp; shwrs; el pnts (5A) inc (rev pol); rest; shop 7km; tradsmn; playgrnd; rv fishing 500m; 80% statics; adv bkg; quiet, poss noisy at w/end; CCI. "Helpful owner; gd, clean, quiet site; useful touring Somme WW1 battlefields; walking dist of Thiepval Ridge; gd NH." 1 Mar-31 Oct. € 17.20 2006*

ALBERT *3B3* (10km SW Rural) *49.91930, 2.57985* **FFCC Camping Les Puits Tournants, 6 Rue du Marais, 80800 Sailley-le-Sec [tel/fax 03 22 76 65 56; camping.puits tournant@wanadoo.fr; www.camping-les-puits-tournants. com]** Fr Bapaume on D929 dir Amiens, at Albert take D42 S to Sailly-Laurette then turn R onto D223 to Sailly-le-Sec & foll sp. Or fr A1 junc twd Albert onto N29. At Lamotte-Warfusée R onto D42 to Sailly-Laurette, turn L to Sailley-le-Sec. Med, some hdg pitch, some hdstg, pt shd; htd wc; chem disp; mv service pnt; shwrs inc; el pnts (4A) €3; gas; Indtte; shop & 7km; tradsmn; rest 2km; BBQ; playgrnd; htd pool; lake sw; fishing; sports area; canoe & cycle hire; tennis 2km; horseriding 5km; TV rm; 60% statics; dogs; adv bkg; quiet; ccard acc. "Pleasant, family-run site; gd clean san facs; grass pitches muddy when wet; tight ent, lge o'fits poss diff; gd pool; excel." ♦ 1 Apr-31 Oct. € 17.50 (3 persons) (CChq acc) 2008*

⊞ **ALBERTVILLE** *9B3* (2km SE Urban) *45.66501, 6.42232* **Camping La Maladière, 2263 Route de Tours, 73200 Albertville [tel/fax 04 79 37 80 44; camping@camping-lamaldiere.com]** SE fr cent Albertville take N90 twds Moûtiers. After approx 4km turn off sp La Bâthie & Tours-en-Savoie. Turn L under D90 & left onto D990 thro Tours-en-Savoie. Site 300m after exit sp on R. Sm, pt shd; htd wc; shwrs inc; el pnts (5-10A) €3-4.56; playgrnd; wifi; mostly statics; dogs €1.20; poss cr; adv bkg; quiet. "Well-kept site; friendly; gd clean san facs; conv Fréjus tunnel; gd NH." ♦ € 11.00 2008*

ALBERTVILLE *9B3* (6km SE Urban) *45.62527, 6.45074* **Camping Le Joli Mont, Rue Victor Hugo, 73540 La Bâthie [04 79 89 61 13 or 04 89 65 59 (LS); camping.joli.mont@wanadoo.fr]** Fr Albertville on N90 exit junc 33 sp La Bâthie; turn L under N90; then turn 1st R, then 1st L; site on L. Sm, pt shd; wc; chem disp (wc); shwrs inc; el pnts (10A) €2.50; lndry rm; playgrnd; 50% statics; dogs; adv bkg; quiet; CCI. "Mountain views; helpful, friendly staff; san facs dated but clean; gd." 1 Jun-1 Oct. € 10.45 2008*

ALBERTVILLE *9B3* (W Urban) *45.67922, 6.39636* **Camp Municipal Les Adoubes, Ave du Camping, 73200 Albertville [04 79 32 06 62 or 04 79 32 04 02; fax 04 79 32 87 09; tourisme@albertville.com; www.albertville.com]** Site is 200m fr town cent; over bdge on banks of Rv Arly. Med, unshd; wc (cont); own san; chem disp (wc); shwrs inc; el pnts (10A) €2.80; gas; lndtte; shop 200m; tradsmn; rest, bar 200m; playgrnd; pool 1km; entmnt; dogs €0.80; poss cr; Eng spkn; adv bkg; some rd noise; 20% red CCI. "Excel site; plenty of room, even high ssn; helpful warden." 9 Jun-15 Sep. € 9.63 2008*

ALBI *8E4* (1.5km E Urban) *43.93380, 2.16580* **FFCC Camping Caussels, Allée du Camping, 81000 Albi [tel/fax 05 63 60 37 06 or 05 63 76 78 75]** Fr Albi ring rd/bypass exit sp Lacause/St Juéry (do not turn twd Millau). Strt over & foll sp Géant-Casino hypmkt & 'Centre Ville', then foll camping/piscine sp. Med, mkd pitch, pt terr, shd; wc (some cont); chem disp; shwrs inc; el pnts (4-10A) €3-4.80; lndtte; supmkts adj; snacks; BBQ; playgrnd; pool adj; 5% statics; poss cr; bus; adv bkg; quiet; red CCI. "Conv position; helpful staff; basic, clean facs; pitches unlevelled - soft in wet & some poss diff lge o'fits due trees; gd walk by rv to town cent; Albi cathedral; Toulouse Lautrec exhibitions; 2km walk to town cent; fair NH." 1 Apr-15 Oct. € 12.00 2009*

ALBIAS see Montauban *8E3*

⊞ **ALBIES** *8G3* (Rural) *42.77444, 1.70328* **Camp Municipal La Coume, 09310 Albiès [tel/fax 05 61 64 98 99; camping.albies@wanadoo.fr]** Site sp fr N20 in vill. Med, hdg pitch, pt sl, terr, pt shd; htd wc; chem disp (wc); shwrs inc; el pnts (10A) inc; lndtte; shop, rest in vill; BBQ; Rv Ariège 100m; fishing; games area; some statics; quiet. "Gd san facs." ♦ € 10.10 2006*

The opening dates and prices on this campsite have changed. I'll send a site report form to the Club for the next edition of the guide.

ALBINE *8F4* (1km SW Rural) *43.45406, 2.52706* **Camping L'Estap Albine, Le Suc, 81240 Albine [05 63 98 34 74; enquiries@campinglestap.com; www.campinglestap.com]** Fr Mazamet on D612 (N112) dir Béziers for approx 12km; turn R onto D88 sp Albine. On app to vill turn R at sp 'Camping du Lac'. Site in 1km. Sm, hdg/mkd pitch, hdstg, terr, pt shd; wc; chem disp; baby facs; shwrs inc; el pnts (6A) €3.30; lndtte; tradsmn; snacks; bar; BBQ (gas); playgrnd; pool; fishing; games area; dogs €1.50; poss cr; Eng spkn; adv bkg; quiet; ccard acc; CCI. "Excel touring base; superb views; friendly, helpful British owner; vg." ♦ 1 Apr-31 Oct. € 17.00 2008*

ALBOUSSIERE *9C2* (300m N Rural) *44.95000, 4.73000* **Camp Municipal La Duzonne, 07440 Alboussière [04 75 58 20 91; camping-la-duzonne@camping-la-duzonne.com; www.camping-la-duzonne.com]** App fr Valence on D533 (Valence-Lamastre) turn L on ent vill of Alboussière onto D219 sp Vernoux. (Do not take D14 which is 1st Vernoux turn). Site well sp. Med, pt shd; wc; shwrs inc; el pnts (10A) €3; lndry rm; shops 1.2km; playgrnd; tennis; rv fishing; lake sw adj; dogs; adv bkg; quiet; red low ssn. "Peaceful site; gd walking; excel." 1 Apr-13 Oct. € 9.50 2008*

ALENCON *4E1* (1km SW Rural) *48.42566, 0.07321* **Camp Municipal de Guéramé, 65 Rue de Guéramé, 61000 Alençon [tel/fax 02 33 26 34 95; campingguerame@villealencon.fr]** Located nr town cent. Fr N on D38 (N138) take N12 W (Carrefour sp). In 5km take D1 L sp Condé-sur-Sarthe. At rndabt turn L sp Alençon then R immed after Carrefour supmkt, foll site sp. Site is sp fr D112 inner ring rd. Med, hdg pitches, hdstg, pt shd; htd wc (some cont); chem disp; mv service pnt; baby facs; shwrs inc; el pnts (5A) €3 (check el pnts carefully) (poss long lead req); Indtte; shop, snacks, bar adj; BBQ; playgrnd; pool complex 700m; tennis; boating; rv fishing; canoeing; cycle hire; horseriding; entmnt; TV rm; dogs €1.80; poss cr; Eng spkn; adv bkg; quiet but w/end disco noise; no ccard acc; CCI. "Pleasant site; helpful warden; gd, clean san facs; o'night area for m'vans; barrier/recep clsd 1800 low ssn; low ssn phone ahead to check site open; some pitches poss flood in heavy rain; poss itinerants low ssn; rvside walk to town thro arboretum; vg." ♦ 1 Apr-30 Sep. € 9.90 2009*

See advertisement

ALES *10E1* (13km SE Rural) *44.04705, 4.23024* **Camping Les Vistes, 30360 St Jean-de-Ceyrargues [04 66 83 29 56 or 04 66 83 28 09; info@lesvistes.com; www.lesvistes.com]** Fr Alès take D981 sp Uzès. After 12km take D7 S sp Brignon. At St Jean-de-Ceyrargues foll sp. Site S of vill on D7. Med, hdg/mkd pitch, pt sl, pt shd; wc; chem disp; baby facs; fam bthrm; shwrs inc; el pnts (4A) €3; Indtte; shops, rest, bar 2km; tradsmn; playgrnd; pool; TV rm; dogs free; quiet; CCI. "Excel views; excel pools; conv for Pont du Gard, Uzès; diff access some pitches; ltd facs low ssn." ♦ 1 Apr-30 Sep. € 16.50 2008*

ALES *10E1* (6km S Rural) *44.07912, 4.09700* **Camping Mas Cauvy, 30380 St Christol-lès-Alès [tel/fax 04 66 60 78 24; maurin.helene@wanadoo.fr; http://fermemascauvy.free.fr]** Fr Alès on D6110 (N110) S sp Montpellier. At S end of Christol-lès-Alès take 2nd rd on L after stone needle. Foll sp to site. Site in 1.5km. Sm, pt terr, pt shd; wc; chem disp (wc); shwrs inc; el pnts (6A) €3; gas 1.5km; Indtte; shop 1.5km; tradsmn; rest & snacks; 1.5km; BBQ; playgrnd; pool; tennis 3km; bus (1km); dogs €2; poss cr; adv bkg; quiet; red low ssn/CCI. "Attractive, CL-type site with lovely views; friendly, helpful owner; book early for shd pitch; excel." 1 Apr-30 Sep. € 15.00 2009*

ALES *10E1* (5km NW Rural) *44.15164, 4.04301* **Camping La Croix Clémentine, Route de Mende, 30480 Cendras [04 66 86 52 69; fax 04 66 86 54 84; clementine@clementine.fr; www.clementine.fr]** N fr Alès on N106, in 4 km turn L sp Cendras; site sp. Lge, pt sl, terr, pt shd; wc (some cont); chem disp (wc); mv service pnt; baby facs; shwrs inc; el pnts (10A) €4; gas; Indtte; shop; rest; snacks; bar; BBQ (gas); playgrnd; 3 pools (1 htd); rv 3km; tennis; games area; cycle hire; games rm; entmnt; wifi; TV rm; some statics; dogs €3; phone; bus adj; poss cr; Eng spkn; adv bkg rec high ssn; ltd facs low ssn; quiet; ccard acc; CCI. "Excel family-run, wooded site; friendly, helpful staff; tourers on flat, lower level; winter storage avail." ♦ 31 Mar-16 Sep. € 21.60 2007*

⊞ **ALET LES BAINS** *8G4* (Rural) *42.9949, 2.25525* **Camping Val d'Aleth, Ave Nicolas Pavillon, 11580 Alet-les-Bains [04 68 69 90 40; fax 04 68 69 94 60; info@valdaleth.com; www.valdaleth.com]** Fr Limoux S on D118 twd Quillan; in approx 8km ignore 1st L turn over Aude bdge into vill but take alt rte for heavy vehicles. Immed after x-ing rv, turn L in front of casino & ent town fr S; site sp on L. Sm, hdg/mkd pitch, hdstg, pt sl, shd; htd wc; chem disp; mv service pnt; baby facs; shwrs inc; el pnts (4-10A) €2.75-4; gas; Indtte (inc dryer); ice; shop & rest nrby; BBQ (gas only); playgrnd; pool 1km; rv/beach adj; cycle hire; wifi; 1% statics; dogs €1.45; phone; poss cr; adv bkg; rd & train noise, church bells daytime; ccard acc; red low ssn/long stay; CCI. "Rvside site in attractive vill; sm pitches (lge o'fits need to book); friendly British owner; gd clean san facs, inc disabled; v few facs in vill; conv Carcassonne & Cathar country." ♦ € 15.00 2009*

France

ALEX see Annecy *9B3*

ALLANCHE *7C4* (2km SE Rural) *45.21898, 2.93842* **Camp Municipal du Camp Vallat, 15160 Allanche [04 71 20 45 87; fax 04 71 20 49 26; mairie.allanche@wanadoo.fr]** Fr Clermont-Ferrand on A75 take exit Massiac, site on N side of D679. Med, pt sl, pt shd; htd wc (some cont); chem disp; mv service pnt 1km; shwrs; el pnts (6A) €1.85; Indtte; shops 2km; rest; snacks; bar; playgrnd; rv 5km; v quiet; CCI. "Steep steps to san facs; attractive rural surroundings; mkt Tues." ♦ 15 Jun-15 Sep. € 4.10 2007*

ALLAS LES MINES see Sarlat la Canéda *7C3*

ALLEGRE LES FUMADES *10E2* (2km NE Rural) *44.2089, 4.25665* **Camping Le Château de Boisson, 30500 Allègre-les-Fumades [04 66 24 85 61 or 04 66 24 82 21; fax 04 66 24 80 14; reception@chateaudeboisson.com; www.chateaudeboisson.com or www.les-castels.com]** Fr Alès NE on D904, turn R after Les Mages onto D132, then L onto D16 for Boisson. Fr A7 take exit 19 Pont l'Esprit, turn S on N86 to Bagnols-sur-Cèze & then D6 W. Before Vallérargues turn R onto D979 Lussan, then D37 & D16 to Boisson. Lge, hdg/mkd pitch, pt sl, shd; wc; chem disp; baby facs; shwrs inc; el pnts (6A) inc; gas; Indtte; shop; tradsmn; rest; snacks; bar; BBQ (gas & elec); playgrnd; 2 pools (1 htd & covrd); paddling pool; tennis; cycle hire; games rm; entmnt; wifi; 80% statics; dogs €2.50 (no dogs 10 Jul-14 Aug); phone; poss cr; Eng spkn; adv bkg; quiet; ccard acc; red low ssn/long stay. "Vg, well-run, peaceful site; some pitches v sm; excel rest & facs; few water pnts; superb pool complex." ♦ 3 Apr-25 Sep. € 34.50 ABS - C34 2009*

ALLEGRE LES FUMADES *10E2* (2km S Rural) *44.18538, 4.22918* **Camping Le Domaine des Fumades, 30500 Allègre-les-Fumades [04 66 24 80 78; fax 04 66 24 82 42; domaine.des.frumades@wanadoo.fr; www.domaine-des-fumades.com or www.camping-franceloc.fr]** Take Bollène exit fr A7 m'way, foll sps to Bagnols-sur-Cèze, take D6 twd Alès; 10km bef Alès turn R sp Allègre-les-Fumades on D7 to site in 5km. Easy to find fr Alès ring rd. Med, mkd pitch, pt shd; wc; chem disp; baby facs; shwrs inc; el pnts (4A) inc; gas; lndtte; shop; rest; bar; playgrnd; htd, covrd pool; paddling pool; waterslide; tennis; games rm; entmnt; golf & watersports nr; dogs €4; adv bkg. "Pleasant location; friendly staff; beautiful site; well-run." ♦ 15 Apr-3 Sep. € 31.00 2006*

This is a wonderful site.

I'll fill in a report online and let the Club know – www.caravanclub.co.uk/europereport

ALLEMANS DU DROPT see Miramont de Guyenne *7D2*

ALLEMONT/ALLEMOND see Bourg d'Oisans, Le *9C3*

ALLES SUR DORDOGNE see Bugue, Le *7C3*

ALLEVARD *9B3* (11km S Rural) *45.31869, 6.08430* **Camp Municipal Neige & Nature, Chemin de Montarmand, 38580 La Ferrière-d'Allevard [tel/fax 04 76 45 19 84; contact@neige.nature.fr; www.neige-nature.fr]** Fr Allevard take D525A S to La Ferrière; foll sp Collet & Le Pleynet. Sm, hdg/mkd pitch, pt sl, terr, pt shd; htd wc; chem disp; baby facs; shwrs; el pnts (10A) €3.90; gas 200m; lndtte; shop 200m; snacks; bar; playgrnd; rv & lake fishing; games area; entmnt; TV; dogs free; Eng spkn; adv bkg; quiet; ccard not acc; red long stay. "Excel, scenic site; helpful owners; many mkd walks." ♦ 15 May-15 Sep. € 16.10 2009*

ALLONNES see Saumur *4G1*

ALTKIRCH *6F3* (1km SE Rural) *47.61275, 7.23336* **Camp Municipal Les Acacias, Route de Hirtzbach, 68130 Altkirch [03 89 40 69 40 or 03 89 40 00 04 (Mairie); brahim.ighirri@free.fr]** Sp on D419 on app to town fr W. Sp in town. Sm, mkd pitch, shd; htd wc (some cont); chem disp; baby facs; shwrs inc; el pnts (10A) €3; shop in ssn & 1km; rest; snacks; bar; playgrnd; pool 1km; 20% statics; dogs; Eng spkn; adv bkg rec high ssn; CCI. "Lovely quiet site; gd, clean facs; office clsd until 1700 - site yourself & pay later; gd NH." 15 Apr-15 Oct. € 8.50 2009*

ALTKIRCH *6F3* (12.5km SW Rural) *47.53919, 7.18005* **Village Center Les Lupins, 1 Rue de la Gare, 68580 Seppois-le-Bas [03 89 25 65 37 or 04 99 57 21 21; fax 03 89 25 54 92; contact@village-center.com; www.village-center.com]** SW fr Altkirch on D432, after 3km turn R to Hirtzbach on D17 foll sp to Seppois-le-Bas. Site sp in vill. Med, mkd pitch, pt shd; htd wc; chem disp; shwrs inc; baby facs; el pnts (6A) inc; lndtte; shop 500m; supmkt nrby; tradsmn; rest, snacks, bar 100m; BBQ; playgrnd; pool; paddling pool; games area; TV; walking; fishing; golf 5km; wifi; 60% statics; dogs €3; phone; adv bkg; quiet midwk; noisy w/end; ccard acc; red low ssn/CCI. "Excel mod facs; Belfort worth visit; stork sanctuary adj; 1 hour Germany; 30 mins Switzerland; lge groups w/end." ♦ 30 Apr-13 Sep. € 20.00 2008*

ALZONNE *8F4* (3km N Rural) *43.26818, 2.16319* **Camping à la Ferme, Domaine de Contresty, 11170 Raissac-sur-Lampy [04 68 76 04 29; jh_cante@club.fr; www.aude-tourisme.com]** Take D6113 (N113) W fr Carcassonne; after 12km in Alzonne take 2nd R after traff lts, sp Camping à la Ferme. In 2km turn L sp Contresty. Sm, pt shd; wc; chem disp (wc); shwrs inc; el pnts (6A) €3; lndtte; tradsmn; BBQ; playgrnd; pool; no dogs; bus 2km; adv bkg; v quiet; CCI. "CL-type site on hilltop; helpful, friendly owner; clean san facs; conv Carcassonne (18km); gd birdwatching." ♦ 1 Apr-30 Oct. € 17.00 2008*

AMBAZAC *7B3* (1.8km NE Rural) *45.97158, 1.41315* **Camp Municipal de Jonas, 87240 Ambazac [05 55 56 60 25]** Fr A20 foll sp to Ambazac; site on D914. Med, terr, pt shd; wc (mainly cont); shwrs inc; el pnts (10A) €2.05; shop & 2km; playgrnd; lake sw, fishing, watersports & shgl beach adj; quiet but some noise at night. "Friendly staff; excel waterside site; san facs clean." 1 Jun-15 Sep. € 6.70 2007*

AMBERT *9B1* (1km S Urban) *45.53951, 3.72867* **Camping Les Trois Chênes, Rue de la Chaise-Dieu, 63600 Ambert [04 73 82 34 68 or 04 73 82 23 95 (LS); fax 04 73 82 44 00; tourisme@ville-ambert.fr; www.camping-ambert.com]** On main rd D906 S twd Le Puy on L bet Leisure Park & Aquacentre. Med, hdg/mkd pitch, pt shd, serviced pitch; wc (some cont); chem disp; shwrs inc; el pnts (10A) €3; gas 400m; Indtte; supermkt adj; tradsmn; snacks; rest nrby; playgrnd; htd pool adj; waterslide; many statics; dogs €1; poss cr; adv bkg; quiet but some traff noise; ccard not acc; CCI. "Excel, well-kept site; gd, clean san facs; rvside walk to town; rec arrive bef noon peak ssn; recep & barrier clsd 1900 low ssn; steam museum & working paper mill nr; steam train 1.5km; vg." ♦ 8 May-30 Sep. € 14.00 2009*

AMBERT *9B1* (9km S Rural) *45.47958, 3.73032* **Camp Municipal La Gravière, 63940 Marsac-en-Livradois [04 73 95 60 08 or 04 73 95 61 62 (Mairie); fax 04 73 95 66 87; mairie.marsac@cc-livradois.fr]** Ent vill fr Ambert foll sp to camp, turn L off D906. Med, mkd pitch, pt shd; wc; shwrs inc; el pnts (5A) inc (long lead poss req); Indry rm (no hot water); shop 500m; tennis; playgrnd; fishing adj; quiet. "Warden calls; unreliable opening dates, phone ahead." 15 Apr-15 Oct. 2007*

AMBERT *9B1* (10km W Rural) *45.57449, 3.63393* **Camp Municipal Saviloisirs, 63890 St Amant-Roche-Savine [tel/fax 04 73 95 73 60 or 04 73 95 70 22 (Mairie); saviloisirs@wanadoo.fr; www.saviloisirs.com]** W fr Ambert on D996 to St Amant, turn R onto D37 into vill. In vill cent turn R & foll site sp. Bear L at lge building facing, site on L. Sm, hdg/mkd pitch, pt shd; wc; shwrs inc; el pnts (16A) inc (rev pol); Indtte; shops adj; playgrnd; TV; dogs €0.30; quiet; CCI. "Tranquil vill site in wooded area; clean, modern facs; pleasant staff; easy walk to vill." 1 May-30 Oct. € 11.00 2009*

AMBIALET *8E4* (500m SE Rural) *43.94181, 2.38686* **Camping La Mise à l'Eau, Fédusse, 81430 Ambialet [05 63 79 58 29; fax 05 63 79 58 09; contact@camping-ambialet.com; www.camping-ambialet.com]** Fr Albi E on D999; in 15km, after Villefranche-d'Albigeois, turn L onto D74 to Ambialet; turn R at junc; in 100m bear L; site on L. NB Sharp turn, turning pnt avail down rd. Sm, mkd pitch, pt shd; wc; shwrs; el pnts (6-10A) €2.15; Indtte; shops, rest & bar 500m; snacks; dogs €1.50; playgrnd; pool; kayaking; poss cr; adv bkg; some rd noise; ccard not acc; CCI. "Easy walk to pretty vill; clean facs; excel." ♦ 15 Jun-30 Sep. € 12.00 2009*

AMBLETEUSE see Wimereux *3A2*

AMBOISE *4G2* (4km N Rural) *47.43113, 0.95430* **Camp Municipal des Patis, 37530 Nazelles-Négron [02 47 57 71 07 or 02 47 23 71 71; mairie.nazelles-negron@wanadoo.fr; www.ville-amboise.fr]** Fr Amboise, take D952 (N152) On N bank of rv twd Tours & turn R (N) onto D5 to Nazelles-Négron. Foll sp to vill. Site N of bdge over Rv Cisse, on R immed after x-ing bdge. Med, mkd pitch, pt shd; wc (some cont); chem disp; shwrs inc; el pnts (3-5A) €1.94-2.83 (long lead poss req); Indry rm; shops 100m; playgrnd; dogs €0.90; poss cr; quiet; CCI. "Peaceful, clean, well-kept site; some lge pitches; gd facs; no lge c'vans or twin-axles; boggy in wet weather; excel." 12 Apr-15 Sep. € 7.08 2008*

AMBOISE *4G2* (1km NE Rural) *47.41763, 0.98717* **Camp Municipal L'Ile d'Or, 37400 Amboise [02 47 57 23 37 or 02 47 23 47 38 (Mairie); fax 02 47 23 19 80; sports.loisirs@ville-amboise.fr; www.ville-amboise.fr]** Fr A10 exit junc 11 N on D31 dir Bléré & Amboise. In Amboise take D751 dir Blois & get in L lane to cross bdge to site on lge wooded island in Rv Loire. Fr N turn off D952 (N152) onto D431 across bdge to island. Site sp. Lge, mkd pitch, pt shd; own san; mv service pnt; shwrs inc; el pnts (6A) €2.15 (poss rev pol); Indtte; shop & 1km; rest; snacks; bar; playgrnd; pool & waterslide 2km (high ssn); tennis; fishing; crazy golf; entmnt; TV; no statics; dogs €1.10; phone; poss cr; Eng spkn; rd noise if pitched nr rd; ccard acc; red low ssn/long stay; CCI. "Lovely, spacious site clean in nice location adj Rv Loire; san facs old or in Portakabins (Sep 2009); interesting old town with gd rests; vg dog walking; conv Parc Léonardo Da Vinci (last place he lived); midsummer week music festival in adj park (v noisy) - check date; no twin-axles; m'van o'night area; easy walk to town; vg value." ♦ 21 Mar-5 Oct. € 8.50 2009*

⊞ **AMBOISE** *4G2* (6km NE Rural) *47.44580, 1.04669* **Camping Le Jardin Botanique, 9 bis, Rue de la Rivière, 37530 Limeray [02 47 30 13 50; fax 02 47 30 17 32; info@camping-jardinbotanique.com; www.camping-jardinbotanique.com]** Fr Amboise on D952 (N152) on N side of Rv Loire dir Blois, site sp in Limeray. Med, hdg/mkd pitch, hdstg, pt shd; htd wc; chem disp; mv service pnt; baby facs; fam bthrm; shwrs inc; el pnts (10A) €3.50 (poss rev pol); gas; Indtte; shop 2km; tradsmn; rest; snacks; bar; BBQ; playgrnd; pool; sand beach 15km; tennis; games area; cycle hire; TV; 20% statics; dogs €1; Eng spkn; adv bkg; rd & rlwy noise; red long stay/CCI. "NH for Loire chateaux; 500m fr rv; no lighting on rdways; friendly & helpful owner; gd for children; site muddy when wet; gd cycle rtes." ♦ € 15.50 2009*

See advertisement

AMBOISE *4G2* (5km E Rural) *47.43491, 1.02818* **Camp Municipal Le Verdeau, Rue du Verdeau, 37530 Chargé [02 47 57 04 22 or 02 47 57 04 01 (Mairie); fax 02 47 57 41 52; mairiedecharge@wanadoo.fr; www.amboise-valdeloire.com]** Fr Amboise take D751 twd Blois, site sp on L. Med, pt shd; wc; chem disp; mv service pnt; shwrs inc; el pnts (5A) €2.50; Indtte; tradsmn; playgrnd; rv fishing & boating; leisure/sports cent adj; dogs €1; no twin-axle c'vans; adv bkg rec high ssn; quiet; CCI. "Gd cent for Loire Valley; gd san facs." ♦ 30 Jun-2 Sep. € 7.50 2008*

Camping le Parc de Vaux ***
Ambrières-les-Vallées
Vallée du Loir
open from 02/04/2010 to 01/11/2010
At the beginning of the Normandie-Maine regional parc, where the rivers La Varenne and La Mayenne come together, you will find in idyllic surroundings the campside Parc de Vaux. Lots of activities like a swimming-pool, animation, horseriding, minigolf, electric boats etc. will guarantee you a relaxing and convivial holiday.
parcdevaux@camp-in-ouest.com
+33 (0)2 43 04 90 25
35 rue des Colverts
53300 Ambrières-les-Vallées
camp'in ouest
www. camp-in-ouest.com

AMBON PLAGES see Muzillac *2G3*

AMBRIERES LES VALLEES *4E1* (2km SW Rural) *48.39121, -0.61680* **Camping Le Parc de Vaux, 35 Rue des Colverts, 53300 Ambrières-les-Vallées [02 43 04 90 25; fax 02 43 08 93 28; parcdevaux@camp-in-ouest.com; www.camp-in-ouest.com]** Fr S on D23 turn R at sp 'Parc de Loisirs de Vaux'. Site in approx 400m on bank Rv Varenne. Check in at Office de Tourisme bef park ent. Med, hdg pitch, some hdstg, terr, pt shd; wc; shwrs inc; el pnts (10A) €3.10 (poss long lead req) (poss rev pol); Indtte; shops 2km; tradsmn; rest; bar; BBQ; playgrnd; htd pool; waterslide; lake adj; canoe hire; fishing; tennis; cycle hire; games area; wifi; entmnt; TV rm; 30% statics; dogs €1.30; Eng spkn; adv bkg; quiet; red long stay/CCI. "Excel site; beautiful surroundings." ♦ 2 Apr-15 Oct. € 12.90 2009*

See advertisement above

I'll fill in a report online and let the Club know – www.caravanclub.co.uk/europereport

AMIENS *3C3* (8km N Rural) *49.97240, 2.30150* **FFCC Camping du Château, Rue du Château, 80260 Bertangles [tel/fax 03 22 93 68 36; camping@chateaubertangles.com; www.chateaubertangles.com]** Foll N25 N of Amiens; after 8km turn W on D97 to Bertangles. Well sp in vill. Sm, hdg pitch, pt shd; wc; chem disp; shwrs inc; el pnts (5A) €3 (poss rev pol); tradsmn; tabac/bar in vill; bus; poss cr; quiet but slight rd noise; ccard notacc; red long stay; CCI. "Pleasant site by chateau wall; early arr rec; vg warden; clean san facs; ltd recep hrs, pitch yourself; grnd soft when wet; Amiens attractive city; gd walks; excel." ♦ 24 Apr-7 Sep. € 13.50 2009*

AMIENS *3C3* (8km NW Urban) *49.92091, 2.25883* **Camping Parc des Cygnes, 111 Ave des Cygnes, 80080 Amiens-Longpré [03 22 43 29 28; fax 03 22 43 59 42; camping.amiens@wanadoo.fr; www.parcdescygnes.com]** Exit A16 junc 20 or fr ring rd Rocade Nord exit junc 40. At 1st rndabt foll sp Amiens, Longpré D412; at 2nd rndabt foll sp Parc de Loisirs & in 800m strt over sm rndabt, site on R (take 1st ent). Med, mkd pitch, pt shd; htd wc; chem disp; baby facs; shwrs inc; el pnts (10A) €4.50; gas; Indtte; shop; snacks; bar; BBQ; playgrnd; fishing nrby; kayaking; cycle hire; games rm; wifi; TV; dogs €2.10; bus to city adj; adv bkg; quiet; ccard acc; red low ssn. "Lovely area; pleasant, well-kept site in parkland; helpful, welcoming staff; gd, clean facs, ltd low ssn; ring bell by recep if office clsd; gd canal-side cycling to city; Amiens cathedral worth visit (sound & light show in summer); conv Somme battlefields; excel." ♦ 1 Apr-15 Oct. € 20.30 ABS - P11 2009*

See advertisement opposite (above)

AMPILLY LE SEC see Châtillon sur Seine *6F1*

ANCENIS *2G4* (12km E Rural) *47.36702, -1.01275* **Camping de l'Ile Batailleuse, St Florent-le-Vieil, 44370 Varades [02 40 83 45 01; serge.rabec@aliceadsl.fr; http://campingilebatailleuse.com.chez-alice.fr]** On Ancenis-Angers rd D723 (N23) turn S in Varades onto D752 to St Florent-le-Vieil. After x-ing 1st bdge over Rv Loire site on L on island immed bef 2nd bdge. Med, pt shd; wc; chem disp; shwrs inc; el pnts (10A) €2; shops 1km; rest 20m; playgrnd; pool 1km; tennis 1km; cycle hire; games area; dogs €1; poss cr; Eng spkn; quiet but poss road noise; CCI. "Basic, clean site; main shwr facs up stone staircase; facs for disabled on grnd floor; panoramic views of Rv Loire in town; gd cycle rtes along rv." ♦ 28 Apr-15 Nov. € 11.00 2009*

ANCENIS *2G4* (5km SW Rural) *47.34400, -1.20693* **Camp Municipal de Drain (formerly Beauregret/La Pêche), 49530 Drain [02 40 98 20 30 or 02 40 98 20 16 (Mairie); fax 02 40 98 23 29]** Fr Ancenis take D763 S for 2km, turn R onto D751 & cont for 3km. Site on R bef vill of Drain on L. Sm, hdg pitch, pt shd; wc; own san rec; chem disp; mv service pnt; shwrs inc; el pnts (6-10A) €2.20-2.70 (poss rev pol); Indtte; shop nr; BBQ; playgrnd; lake nrby; games area; entmnt; TV rm; adv bkg; quiet. "Secluded, tranquil site; gd fishing; immac san facs up steps - ltd number; poss not suitable lge o'fits." ♦ 1 May-30 Sep. € 7.90 2008*

France

ANCENIS *2G4* (1km W Rural) *47.36201, -1.18721* **FFCC Camping de l'Ile Mouchet, La Davrays, 44150 Ancenis [02 40 83 08 43 or 06 83 52 73 44 (mob); fax 02 40 83 16 19; efberthelot@wanadoo.fr; www.camping-estivance.com]** Fr S turn L immed after x-ing Rv Loire & foll sp; site on banks of rv. Med, mkd pitch, pt shd; wc; chem disp; mv service pnt; shwrs inc; el pnts (6-10A) €2.80; Indtte; gas; shops adj; rest, snacks, bar high ssn; playgrnd; pool; waterslide; tennis 50m; games rm; TV; 12% statics; dogs; Eng spkn; adv bkg; quiet; ccard acc; red low ssn/CCI. "Rvside walks; ltd facs low ssn; excel." ♦ 1 Apr-10 Oct. € 12.80 2007*

ANCTEVILLE see Coutances *1D4*

ANDELOT BLANCHEVILLE *6F1* (1km W Rural) *48.25220, 5.29901* **Camping du Moulin, 5 Rue du Moulin, 52700 Andelot-Blancheville [03 25 32 61 28 or 03 25 01 33 31 (Mairie); fax 03 25 03 77 54; mairie.andelot@wanadoo.fr; www.camping-andelot.com]** Fr N on D974 (N74) site sp on ent Andelot-Blancheville. Foll sp & turn L onto D147. Site on R in 1km. Med, hdg/mkd pitch, shd; htd wc; chem disp; shwrs inc; el pnts (9A) €2 (poss rev pol); Indtte; shop 1km; tradsmn; snacks; bar; playgrnd; lake/rv fishing; games rm; wifi; TV rm; 10% statics; dogs free; phone; Eng spkn; quiet; red low ssn; CCI. "Peaceful, quiet site by rv; gd NH on journey S." ♦ 15 Jun-15 Sep. € 16.50 2009*

ANDELYS, LES *3D2* (1km S Rural) *49.23582, 1.40016* **FFCC Camping de L'Ile des Trois Rois, 27700 Les Andelys [02 32 54 23 79; fax 02 32 51 14 54; campingtroisrois@aol.com; www.camping-troisrois.com]** Fr Louviers after x-ing bdge over Rv Seine, R at junc of D135 & D313 S of Les Andelys. Site on R in 100m on rvside. Lge, hdg/mkd pitch, some hdstg, pt shd; htd wc (some cont); chem disp; mv service pnt; shwrs inc; el pnts (6A) inc; gas; Indtte; shop; tradsmn; snacks; bar; BBQ; playgrnd; sm htd pool; paddling pool; fishing; bowling alley; cycle hire; games rm; entmnt; TV rm; 50% statics sep; dogs €2; phone; poss cr; Eng spkn; quiet but some rd noise; ccard acc; red long stay/CCI. "Gd site on Rv Seine; extra lge pitches avail; clean san facs, but ltd number; friendly, helpful staff; gd security; conv Rouen, Evreux, Giverny, ruins of Château Gaillard opp." ♦ 15 Mar-15 Nov. € 20.00 2009*

See advertisement below

⊞ **ANDERNOS LES BAINS** *7D1* (3km NE Rural) *44.75777, -1.07194* **Camping Les Arbousiers, 134 Ave de Bordeaux, 33510 Andernos-les-Bains [05 56 82 12 46; fax 05 56 26 15 21; lesarbousiers@yahoo.fr; www.camping-les-arbousiers.fr]** 7km E of Arès fr Bordeaux on D106, take D215 sp Andernos. Site on L in 2km, ent rd to airport. Lge, hdg/mkd pitch, pt shd; htd wc; chem disp; baby facs; shwrs inc; el pnts (6A) inc (poss rev pol); Indtte; shop 2km; snacks; bar; BBQ; pool; sand beach 3km; 50% statics; dogs €1; Eng spkn; quiet; ccard acc. "Friendly staff; pleasantly situated site." € 19.50 2007*

ANDERNOS LES BAINS *7D1* (2.5km SE Coastal) *44.72568, -1.08083* **Camping Fontaine Vieille, 4 Blvd du Colonel Wurtz, 33510 Andernos-les-Bains [05 56 82 01 67; fax 05 56 82 09 81; contact@fontaine-vieille.com; www.fontaine-vieille.com]** Take D106 fr Bordeaux then D215 on L after 40km sp Andernos. Well sp. Site situated 600m off D3. V lge, hdg/mkd pitch, pt shd; wc (some cont); chem disp; mv service pnt; baby facs; shwrs inc; el pnts (5A) inc; gas; lndtte; shop & 3km; rest; snacks; bar; pool/waterpark; sand beach adj; watersports inc windsurfing; games area; tennis; entmnt; TV; dogs €3.20; adv bkg rec high ssn; quiet; ccard acc; red long stay/low ssn. "Nice site; some pitches sea view (extra charge); excel for families & beach holiday; organised bus trips & sports." ♦ 1 Apr-30 Sep. € 27.10 (CChq acc) 2008*

⊞ **ANDERNOS LES BAINS** *7D1* (5km SE Coastal) *44.70435, -1.04856* **Camping Domaine du Roumingue, 60 Ave de la Libération, 33138 Lanton [05 56 82 97 48; fax 05 56 82 96 09; info@roumingue.fr; www.roumingue.fr]** Approx 7km SE of Andernos-les-Bains on D3 bet Cassy & Lanton. Lge, hdg/mkd pitch, pt shd; htd wc (some cont); mv service pnt; chem disp; serviced pitches; shwrs inc; el pnts (6A) €3.50; gas; lndtte; shop; tradsmn; rest; snacks; bar; playgrnd; pool; guarded private sand beach adj; lake sw; fishing; windsurfing; tennis; archery; games/sports area; cycle hire; entmnt; sat TV; 30% statics; dogs €2; phone; site clsd Jan; Eng spkn; adv bkg; ccard acc; red low ssn/long stay; CCI. "Excel family site; many facs/activities; lge pitches avail; helpful, friendly staff; vg." ♦ € 22.00 2009*

ANDERNOS LES BAINS *7D1* (5km SE Coastal) *44.71425, -1.06029* **Camping Le Coq Hardi, Cassy, 33138 Lanton [05 56 82 01 80; fax 05 56 82 16 11; Violesgalyon@aol.com; www.campingcoq-hardi.com]** At Facture on N250 fr Bordeaux turn R on D3 twd Andernos. Site on L sp at Cassy. Lge, pt shd; wc (cont); chem disp; mv service pnt; shwrs inc; el pnts (6-10A) €3.70-4.70 (poss rev pol); gas; shop high ssn; snacks; playgrnd; htd pool; paddling pool; sand beach adj; indoor sports hall; entmnt; 15% statics; dogs €2.20; phone; bus adj; adv bkg (fee €16); quiet low ssn; CCI. "Gd rests, shops nrby; pleasant view; peaceful low ssn; helpful owners; gd pitches." 1 Apr-30 Sep. € 18.00 2007*

ANDERNOS LES BAINS *7D1* (6km W Coastal) *44.73443, -1.1960* **Airotel Camping Les Viviers, Ave Léon Lesca, Claouey, 33950 Lège-Cap-Ferret [05 56 60 70 04 or 01 76 76 70 10; fax 05 57 70 37 77; reception@lesviviers.com; www.airotel-les-viviers.com]** Fr N exit A10/A630 W of Bordeaux onto D106 sp Cap-Ferret. Foll D106 thro Arès & vill of Claouey on W side of Bassin d'Arcachon, site on L after LH bend (approx 1.5km after Claouey). Camp sp as being 1km away but ent on L after LH bend. V lge, hdg/mkd pitch, pt shd; htd wc; mv service pnt; chem disp; baby facs; sauna; shwrs inc; el pnts (10A) €9; gas; Indtte; supmkt; rest; snacks; bar; BBQ (gas/elec); playgrnd; htd, covrd pool; paddling pool; waterslide; sea water lagoon with private sand beach adj; fishing; sailing; windsurfing; tennis; cycle hire; games area; games rm; cinema; entmnt; TV rm; 27% statics; dogs €5; bus; Eng spkn; adv bkg ess; quiet; ccard acc; red long stay/low ssn/CCI. "Sand pitches; clean san facs; free night bus along peninsular; vg." ♦ 27 Mar-15 Oct. € 37.00 2009*

See advertisement

ANDERNOS LES BAINS *7D1* (6km W Coastal) *44.79809, -1.22566* **Camping Brémontier, Le Grand Crohot Océan 33950 Lège-Cap-Ferret [tel/fax 05 56 60 03 99; www.campingbremontier.fr]** Fr Andernos NW on D3 to Arès. Take Cap Ferret rd D106. 1km after Lège turn R on D106E sp Le Crohot. Site at end of rd in 5km. Fr Bordeaux stay on D106 thro Arès & Lège & on D106E. Site at end of rd in 6km. Med, shd; wc; shwrs inc; el pnts (5A) €3.30; gas; shop; sand beach 500m; no statics; dogs; quiet. "Simple site in pine woods; gd cycling." 1 Jun-30 Sep. € 15.00 2007*

ANDERNOS LES BAINS *7D1* (6km W Coastal) *44.75234, -1.18474* **Camping Les Embruns, Ave Edouard Branly, Clauouey, 33950 Lège-Cap-Ferret [05 56 60 70 76; fax 05 56 60 49 79; lesembruns4@wanadoo.fr; www.camping-lesembruns.fr]** Foll D106 Bordeaux to Cap-Ferret. On ent Claouey turn R at rndabt. Site sp. V lge, mkd pitch, pt sl, terr, shd; wc; chem disp; shwrs inc; el pnts (16A) €3; Indtte; shops adj; pizzeria; bar; playgrnd; htd pool; sand beach 700m; entmnt; some statics; dogs €1.50; quiet. "Well laid-out & organised; 20km cycle path adj; gd." ♦ 1 Apr-30 Sep. € 17.00 2008*

ANDERNOS LES BAINS *7D1* (5km NW Coastal) *44.77287, -1.14144* **Camping La Cigale, Route de Lège, 33740 Arès [05 56 60 22 59; fax 05 57 70 41 66; camping lacigaleares@wanadoo.fr; www.camping-lacigale-ares.com]** Fr Andernos proceed NW on D3 to Arès. Take Cap-Ferret rd D106. Site on L in 1km. Med, mkd pitch, shd; wc; shwrs inc; el pnts (6A) €5; gas; Indtte; shop; tradsmn; rest; snacks; bar; BBQ; playgrnd; pool; beach 900m; games area; entmnt; TV; some statics; poss cr; adv bkg rec high ssn; quiet. "Excel family-run site." ♦ 4 May-30 Sep. € 29.00 2007*

ANDERNOS LES BAINS *7D1* (5km NW Coastal) *44.77108, -1.14306* **Camping Les Abberts, Rue des Abberts, 33740 Arès [tel/fax 05 56 60 26 80; campinglesabberts@wanadoo.fr]** Fr town sq in Arès, take D106 twd Cap Ferrat, turn 1st L to site in 100m. Med, hdg/mkd pitch, pt shd; wc; chem disp; shwrs inc; el pnts (6A) €4.40; gas; Indtte; snacks; shops 400m; rest; snacks; playgrnd; pool; sand beach 600m; 25% statics; dogs €2; poss cr; adv bkg; quiet; CCI. "Nr cycle paths to Arès; mkt Tues; gd." ♦ 1 May-30 Sep. € 22.00 2006*

ANDERNOS LES BAINS *7D1* (5km NW Coastal) *44.75799, -1.11931* **Camping Les Goëlands, Ave de la Libération, 33740 Arès [05 56 82 55 64; fax 05 56 82 07 51; camping-les.goelands@wanadoo.fr; www.goelands.com]** Fr Bordeaux m'way by-pass take D106 for Cap-Ferret. At Arès take D3 SE twd Andernos. Site on R 200m after end of Arès town sp. Site sp. Lge, mkd pitch, shd; wc; chem disp; shwrs inc; el pnts (6A) inc; gas; Indtte; shop; rest; snacks; bar; playgrnd; sand beach 200m; seawater lake 200m; 90% statics; dogs; poss cr; adv bkg; poss noisy; red low ssn; CCI. "Many gd beaches." ♦ 1 Mar-31 Oct. € 21.00 2006*

ANDERNOS LES BAINS *7D1* (5km NW Coastal) *44.76207, -1.13729* **Camping Pasteur Vacances, 1 Rue du Pilote, 33740 Arès [05 56 60 33 33; pasteur.vacances@wanadoo.fr; www.atlantic-vacances.com]** Take D106 Bordeaux-Arès. At rndabt in Arès cent take D3 twd Andernos. Turn R at camp sp, site on L. Sm, pt shd; wc; mv service pnt; shwrs inc; el pnts (10A) €3.50; Indtte; snacks, shop adj; playgrnd; sm pool; beach adj & lake sw; dogs €2; poss cr; quiet; adv bkg; Eng spkn. "Friendly owners." ♦ 1 Apr-30 Sep. € 23.50 2006*

ANDERNOS LES BAINS *7D1* (5km NW Coastal) *44.77792, -1.14280* **FLOWER Camping La Canadienne, 82 Rue du Général de Gaulle, 33740 Arès [05 56 60 24 91; fax 05 57 70 40 85; info@lacanadienne.com; www.lacanadienne.com or www.flowercamping.com]** N fr town sq at Arès on D3 (Rue du Général de Gaulle) dir Cap Ferret. Site on R after 1km. Med, shd; wc; baby facs; shwrs inc; el pnts (15A) inc; gas; Indtte; shop; rest; snacks; bar; sand beach 2km; playgrnd; pool; paddling pool; cycle & canoe hire; fishing, sailing & windsurfing 1km; tennis; archery; entmnt; games/TV rm; dogs €2.50; adv bkg rec high ssn; quiet, but some rd noise; red low ssn. ♦ 2 Feb-30 Nov. € 30.90 2007*

ANDERNOS LES BAINS *7D1* (7.5km NW Rural) *44.80288, -1.13362* **Camping La Prairie, 93 Ave du Médoc, 33950 Lège-Cap-Ferret [tel/fax 05 56 60 09 75; camping-la-prairie@wanadoo.fr; www.campinglaprairie.com]** Site 1km N of Lège-Cap-Ferret on D3 dir Porge. Med, pt shd; htd wc; chem disp; shwrs inc; el pnts (10A) €3.10; Indtte; shop; snacks; BBQ; playgrnd; pool; sand beach 5km; games area; games rm; entmnt; some statics; dogs €1.50; Eng spkn; adv bkg; quiet; CCI. "Poss run down & unclean low ssn; friendly owner; long distance cycle paths; gd baker nrby." 1 Mar-1 Nov. € 14.70 2009*

France

ANDERNOS LES BAINS *7D1* (8km NW Rural) **FFCC Camping Mer et Forêt, 101 Ave du Médoc, 33950 Lège-Cap-Ferret [05 56 60 18 36 or 05 56 60 16 99; fax 05 56 60 39 47]** Fr Bordeaux take D106 W dir Arès. Fr cent Arès take D3 N sp Lège-Cap-Ferret. Site on L in 5km adj 'Camping Prairie'. Med, mkd pitch, pt shd; wc; chem disp; mv service pnt; shwrs €1; el pnts (3-6A) €1.25-2.50; shop 2km; tradsmn; sand beach 6km; dogs; phone; quiet; CCI. "Lovely site; generous pitches; warm welcome, friendly owner; excel, clean san facs; vg." ♦ 1 Jun-30 Sep. € 9.50 2009*

ANDORRA Campsites in Andorra are listed together at the end of the French site entry pages.

ANDOUILLE see Laval *2F4*

ANDRYES see Clamecy *4G4*

ANDUZE *10E1* (5km E Rural) *44.03585, 4.02390* **Kawan Village Domaine de Gaujac, 30140 Boisset-et-Gaujac [04 66 61 80 65; fax 04 66 60 53 90; gravieres@clubinternet.fr; www.domaine-de-gaujac.com]** S fr Alès on D6110 & turn R onto D910A dir Anduze. At Bagard (3km bef Anduze) turn L at mini rndabt onto D246 dir Boisset-et-Gaujac. At next rndbt turn R, then immed L. Foll vill & camping sp. Lge, pt terr, shd; htd wc (some cont); chem disp; mv service pnt; some serviced pitches; shwrs inc; baby facs; el pnts (4-6A) €4-4.50; gas; Indtte; shop; rest; snacks; bar; BBQ; playgrnd; 1 htd pool; paddling pool; rv adj; fishing; tennis; cycle hire; games area; games rm; internet; entmnt; wifi; TV; 30% statics; dogs €2.50; Eng spkn; adv bkg rec high ssn; quiet, but noisy until late in café area high ssn; red low ssn. "Tranquil site; friendly, helpful family owners; clean san facs; pitches poss unkempt; Trabuc caves, Tarn gorges nrby. ♦ 1 Apr-30 Sep. € 21.00 (CChq acc) 2009*

ANDUZE *10E1* (1.5km SE Rural) *44.03824, 3.99454* **Camping Le Bel Eté, 1870 Route de Nîmes, 30140 Anduze [tel/fax 04 66 61 76 04; contact@camping-bel-ete.com; www.camping-bel-ete.com]** S fr Alès on N110; W on D910A to Anduze. In Anduze take D907 SE twds Nîmes. Site on L, 200m after rlwy bdge. Med, mkd pitch, pt shd; wc; chem disp; serviced pitches; shwrs inc; el pnts (6A) €4.50; gas; Indtte; shop 1.5km; tradsmn; rest; playgrnd; pool; rv adj; 10% statics; dogs €1.50; phone; adv bkg ess; quiet but some rd noise; ccard acc; CCI. "Delightful, well-kept site in superb location; vg facs but ltd low ssn; helpful owner; gd base for Cévennes area; Thurs mkt." ♦ 8 May-17 Sep. € 22.50 2008*

ANDUZE *10E1* (5km SW Rural) *44.02733, 4.02736* **Camping Le Fief, 195 Chemin du Plan d'Eau, 30140 Massillargues-Attuech [04 66 61 81 71 or 04 66 61 87 80; fax 04 66 61 81 71; natbrunel@cegetel.net; www.campinglefiefdanduze.com]** Leave Anduze S on D982 dir Nîmes; site on L on leaving Attuech; sp. Med, mkd pitch, shd; wc; chem disp; baby facs; shws inc; el pnts (6A) €2.60 (poss no earth); Indtte; shops; tradsmn; rest; snacks; bar; playgrnd; pool; rv sw adj, shgl beach; 10% statics; dogs €1.50; phone; poss cr; adv bkg; quiet; ccard acc; CCI. "Clean facs; gd for cycling." 1 Apr-30 Sep. € 16.90 2006*

ANDUZE *10E1* (1.4km NW) *44.06430, 3.97694* **Camping Castel Rose, 30140 Anduze [04 66 61 80 15; castelrose@wanadoo.fr; www.castelrose.com]** Fr Alès S on D6110 (N110) & W on N910A to Anduze. Foll sp Camping L'Arche. Lge, shd; wc; shwrs inc; el pnts (6-10A) €3.20-4; gas; Indtte; shop; rest; snacks; bar; pool; fishing; boating; entmnt; TV; dogs €2; poss cr; Eng spkn; adv bkg rec high ssn. "Excel site by rv; friendly, helpful owners; attractive countryside; gd cent touring Cévennes." 1 Apr-30 Sep. € 12.00 2009*

ANDUZE *10E1* (1.7km NW Rural) *44.06025, 3.97379* **Camping Les Fauvettes, 1030 Route de St Jean-du-Gard, Quartier Labahou, 30140 Anduze [tel/fax 04 66 61 72 23; camping-les-fauvettes@wanadoo.fr; www.camping-les-fauvettes.fr]** Site sp fr D907 to St Jean-du-Gard. Med, mkd pitch, pt sl, terr, pt shd; wc; baby facs; shwrs inc; el pnts (6A) €2.60; gas; shop; snacks; bar; playgrnd; pool; paddling pool; waterslide; fishing; entmnt; TV; some statics; dogs; adv bkg; quiet. 24 Apr-25 Sep. € 15.25 2006*

ANDUZE *10E1* (2km NW Rural) *44.06785, 3.97336* **Camping L'Arche, Quartier de Labahou, 30140 Anduze [04 66 61 74 08; fax 04 66 61 88 94; contact@camping-arche.fr; www.camping-arche.fr]** Fr Alès S on N110/D910A to Anduze. On D907, sp on R. Access poss dff lge o'fits/m'vans. Lge, mkd pitch, shd; htd wc; chem disp; mv service pnt; baby facs; shwrs inc; el pnts (10A) €2; gas; Indtte; shop; tradsmn; rest; snacks; bar; BBQ; playgrnd; pool; waterslide; entmnt; wifi; TV; some statics; dogs €3.80; Eng spkn; adv bkg; quiet; red long stay; CCI. "Well-run site; gd san facs; beautiful area; bamboo gardens worth visit; 24hr security patrols." ♦ 1 Apr-30 Sep. € 28.50 2009*

ANDUZE *10E1* (4km NW Rural) *44.07814, 3.96533* **Camping Cévennes-Provence, Corbes-Thoiras, 30140 Anduze [04 66 61 73 10; fax 04 66 61 60 74; marais@camping-cevennes-provence.fr; www.camping-cevennes-provence.fr]** Fr Anduze D907 & D284 along rvside after bdge, site sp. Diff ent espec for lge o'fits. Lge, mkd pitch, terr, shd; wc (mainly cont); chem disp; some serviced pitches; mv service pnt; baby facs; shwrs inc; el pnts (3-15A) €3-4.30; gas; Indtte; shop, rest, snacks, bar; playgrnd; shgl beach & rv adj; games area; games rm; internet; TV; some statics; dogs €2; Eng spkn; adv bkg; quiet; red low ssn; CCI. "Variable pitch sizes; gd touring base; helpful recep; gd walking; vg site." ♦ 20 Mar-1 Nov. € 18.90 2006*

ANET *3D2* (500m N Urban) *48.86183, 1.44166* **Camp Municipal, Rue des Cordeliers, 28260 Anet [02 37 41 42 67 or 02 37 62 55 25 (Mairie); fax 02 37 62 20 99; martine.desrues@cegetel.net; www.ville-ivry-la-bataille.fr]** Take D928 NE fr Dreux; in Anet thro town & take 1st L after chateau; turn L on rd to Ezy & Ivry (camp sp on corner), site in 150m N of rv. Lge, pt shd; htd wc; chem disp (wc); mv service pnt; 75% serviced pitches; shwrs €0.90; el pnts (5A) inc; Indry rm; supmkt 1km; playgrnd; rv adj; lake sw & fishing 2km; tennis; 80% statics; dogs €0.80; poss cr; Eng spkn; ccard not acc; CCI. "Rvside pitches; ground soft in wet - site poss clsd early; helpful warden; clean, basic facs, poss stretched high ssn; gd walks in forest; chateau in vill; easy drive to Paris; conv NH." 1 Apr-31 Oct. € 7.30 2007*

ANET *3D2* (1km N Urban) *48.86278, 1.41552* **Camp Municipal Les Trillots, Chemin des Trillots, 27530 Ezy-sur-Eure [02 37 64 73 21 or 02 37 64 73 48 (Mairie)]** N fr Dreux on D928/D143. Site on N side of Rv Eure. Med, pt shd; htd wc; shwrs inc; el pnts (4A) inc; lndtte; supmkt nr; rest, snacks & bar 1km; BBQ; 60% statics; dogs; quiet. "Quiet site adj rvside walks; gd san facs; helpful warden." 1 Mar-15 Nov. € 11.40 2009*

ANGERS *4G1* (10km SE Rural) *47.44332, -0.40881* **Camping du Port Caroline, Rue du Pont, 49800 Brain-sur-l'Authion [02 41 80 42 18; www.campingduportcaroline.fr]** E fr Angers on D347 (N147) turn onto D113, site sp at ent to vill. Med, hdg/mkd pitch, hdstg, pt shd; htd wc; chem disp; shwrs inc; el pnts (10A) inc; lndtte; shop 300m; snacks; BBQ; playgrnd; htd pool; paddling pool; tennis, fishing nrby; games area adj; games rm; skateboarding; entmnt; TV rm; 5% statics; dogs €3; adv bkg; some rd & rlwy noise (& owls, woodpeckers); ccard acc. "Gd touring base." ♦ 16 Jun-2 Sep. € 12.00 2007*

ANGERS *4G1* (5km S Urban) *47.42438, -0.52720* **FFCC Camp Municipal de l'Ile du Château, Ave de la Boire Salée, 49130 Les Ponts-de-Cé [tel/fax 02 41 44 62 05; ile-du-chateau@wanadoo.fr; www.camping-ileduchateau.com]** Fr Angers take D160 (sp Cholet) to Les Ponts-de-Cé. Turn R at rndabt in town opp Hôtel de Ville, & site on R in 500m on banks of Rv Loire. Med, hdg pitch, pt shd; wc; chem disp; mv service pnt; child/baby facs; shwrs inc; el pnts (6A) €3; lndtte; shops 1km; tradsmn; snacks; bar; BBQ; playgrnd; pool, waterslide adj; sand beach 500m; tennis; golf 5km; wifi; TV; dogs €1.70; phone; poss cr; Eng spkn; quiet; ccard acc; red low ssn; CCI. "Well-kept site adj Rv Maine; excel views; access to site warden-controlled, off ssn recep opening times vary; excel pool adj; gd touring base for chateaux, vineyards; gd dog walking; open all year for m'vans; highly rec." ♦ 11 Apr-30 Sep. € 14.70 2009*

⊞ **ANGERS** *4G1* (6km SW Urban) *47.41878, -0.61160* **Camping Aire d'Accueil de Camping Cars, 25 Rue Chevrière, 49080 Bouchemaine [02 41 77 11 04 or 02 41 22 20 00 (Mairie); adm.generale@ville-bouchemaine.fr; www.ville-bouchemaine.fr]** Fr Angers take D160 S, at intersection with D112 W sp Bouchemaine. Cross Rv Maine via suspension bdge. At rndabt on W bank turn L, site on L in 100m dir La Pointe adj rv. Fr Château-Gontier take N162, then D106, then D102E. Bouchemaine well sp. Sm, hdstg, pt shd; wc; chem disp; mv service pnt; shwrs inc; el pnts (16A) €2.55 (poss rev pol); lndtte; shops 1km; tradsmn; rest 500m; pool 500m; games area; dogs; bus; phone; poss cr; adv bkg quiet; CCI. "M'vans & tents only; warden calls am & pm; free Oct-Apr but no el pnts; san facs upstairs; poss flooding nr rv; vg NH." € 7.50 2009*

ANGERS *4G1* (5km W Urban) *47.45434, -0.59595* **Camping du Lac de Maine, Ave du Lac de Maine, 49000 Angers [02 41 73 05 03; fax 02 41 73 02 20; camping@lacdemaine.fr; www.lacdemaine.fr]** W fr Angers on D723 (N23), exit at 'Quartier du Lac de Maine' then foll sp to site & Bouchemaine. After 4 rndabts site on L; sp W of Rv Maine. Fr S on D160 or A87, turn onto D4 at Les Ponts-de-Cé. In 6km, cross Rv Maine to Bouchemaine & turn R to Pruniers dir Angers. Site on R at Pruniers town exit sp. Lge, hdg/mkd pitch, hdstg, pt shd; htd wc; chem disp; mv service pnt; serviced pitches; baby facs; shwrs inc; el pnts (10A) €3.50 (rev pol); gas; lndtte; shop 1.5km; tradsmn; hypmkt 2km; rest, snacks & bar in ssn; BBQ; playgrnd; htd pool; jacuzzi; paddling pool; sand beach 800m; fishing; boating; windsurfing 500m; tennis 800m; games area; cycle hire; wifi; TV rm; 10% statics; dogs €2; bus; phone; Eng spkn; adv bkg rec high ssn; quiet; ccard acc; red low ssn/long stay/CCI. "Excel, well-run site in leisure park; some pitches suitable v l'ge o'fits; helpful managers; excel facs; height barrier at ent 3.20m; conv Loire chateaux." ♦ 25 Mar-10 Oct. € 17.50 (CChq acc) 2009*

See advertisement

France

ANGOULEME *7B2* (15km N Rural) *45.78194, 0.11915* **FFCC Camp Municipal Les Platanes, 16330 Montignac-Charente [05 45 39 89 16 or 05 45 39 70 09 (Mairie); fax 05 45 22 26 71]** Fr N, on N10, turn W on D11 then N on D737 thro vill onto D15. Narr rds on app, site on R by Rv Charente. Med, pt shd; wc (cont); chem disp; shwrs inc; el pnts (4-12A) €2.75-€4.90 (poss rev pol); gas 2km; lndry rm; shop 800m; rest, snacks in vill; bar; rv & fishing adj; canoeing; direct access to rv; dogs; poss cr; quiet; 25% red 16 days; ccard not acc; CCI. "Pleasant, grassy site in gd position; friendly staff; excel clean facs; many trees; no twin-axles; pleasant vill." ♦ 1 Jun-31 Aug. € 8.40 2009*

ANGOULEME *7B2* (11km SW Rural) *45.60773, 0.02365* **Camping Le Nizour, 2 Route de la Charente, 16440 Sireuil [05 45 90 56 27 or 06 87 54 64 05 (mob); fax 05 45 90 92 67; contact@campingdunizour.com; www.campingdunizour.com]** SW fr Angouleme on N10; in 11km exit N10 at junc with D7 sp Sireuil; cont on D7 for 3km; site on R just after x-ing rv. Site 1.5km bef Sireuil & sp throughout. Sm, pt shd; wc; chem disp; shwrs inc; el pnts €3.20; lndtte; shop 1.5km; rest; snacks; bar; playgrnd; pool; 5% statics, sep area; dogs € 1.30; poss cr; quiet. "Pleasant, well-run site nr Rv Charente; conv NH fr N10 & longer stay." 15 Apr-Sep. € 15.25 2009*

ANGOULEME *7B2* (5.5km NW Rural) **Camping du Plan d'Eau de la Grande Prairie, Impasse des Rouyères, 16710 St Yrieix-sur-Charante [tel/fax 05 45 92 14 64 or 05 45 95 16 84; info@angouleme-tourisme.com; www.angouleme-tourisme.com]** Fr N or S on N10/E606 turn NW & foll sp St Yrieix-sur-Charante, 'Plan d'Eau' & 'Nautilis - Centre Nautique'. Site sp. Med, hdg/mkd pitch, pt shd; htd wc; chem disp; mv service pnt; shwrs inc; el pnts €3.50; gas; lndtte; shop; tradsmn; rest; snacks; bar; BBQ; playgrnd; pool; lake sw & beach 500m; watersports; games area; wifi; TV rm; 10% statics; dogs; Eng spkn; adv bkg; quiet; ccard acc. "Superb location; excel." ♦ 1 Apr-31 Oct. € 18.00 2009*

See advertisement

⊞ **ANGOULEME** *7B2* (10km NW Rural) *45.79761, 0.06284* **Camping Marco de Bignac (formerly Les Sablons), Chemin de la Résistance, 16170 Bignac [05 45 21 78 41; fax 05 45 21 52 37; info@marcodebignac.com; www.marcodebignac.com]** Fr N10 approx 14km N Angoulême take exit La Touche & foll D11 W thro Vars; at Basse turn R onto D117 & foll sp in Bignac. Med, mkd pitch, pt shd; htd wc; chem disp; shwrs inc; child/baby facs; fam bthrm; el pnts (3-6A) €2-3; lndtte; shop or 10km; tradsmn; rest; snacks; bar; BBQ; playgrnd; pool high ssn; badminton; lake adj, fishing & watersports; tennis; games area; games rm; organised activities; wifi; few statics; dogs; phone; bus adj; Eng spkn; adv bkg; quiet; ccard acc; red low ssn/long stay; CCI. "Attractive, peaceful, tidy lakeside site; worth long drive; scenic area; lge pitches; welcoming, helpful British owners; clean san facs; gd rest; ideal for Angoulême Circuit des Remparts; vg." ♦ € 24.00 2009*

ANGOULINS SUR MER see Rochelle, La *7A1*

ANIANE *10E1* (1.5km SW Rural) *43.67550, 3.56542* **Camping La Source St Pierre (Naturist), 1 Route de Gignac, 34150 Aniane [tel/fax 04 67 57 76 95; campingstpierre@hotmail.com; www.campingstpierre.com]** Exit A750 at Gignac onto D32 dir Aniane; site on L in 2.5km (bef Aniane). Med, pt shd; wc (some cont); chem disp; shwrs inc; el pnts (5-10A) €3.30-3.90; gas; lndtte; ice; tradsmn; rest; snacks; bar; BBQ (sep area); playgrnd; rv adj; canoe & kayak hire; wifi; dogs € 2.50; phone; Eng spkn; quiet; ccard acc; red low ssn; CCI. "Friendly site - many regulars; vg rv bathing & rv sports; excel." ♦ 1 May-30 Sep. € 19.50 2009*

ANNECY *9B3* (8km SE Rural) *45.88990, 6.22367* **Camping La Ferme de Ferrières, 74290 Alex [04 50 02 87 09; fax 04 50 02 80 54; campingfermedesferrieres@wanadoo.fr; www.camping-des-ferrieres.com]** Take D909 on E side of lake out of Annecy twds Thônes; look out for sp on L after turn off to Château de Menthon. Med, pt sl, terr, pt shd; wc (cont); chem disp; baby facs; shwrs inc; el pnts (6A) €2.40; lndtte; shop & 2km; tradsmn; snacks; playgrnd; lake sw 6km; dogs €0.80; poss cr; quiet; phone; adv bkg; CCI. "Spectacular views; friendly owner; away fr crowds; v clean; mostly tents; pitches muddy when wet." ♦ 1 Jun-30 Sep. € 10.00 2006*

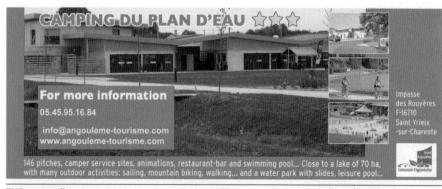

ANNECY *9B3* (8km SE Rural) *45.86305, 6.19690* **Camping Le Clos Don Jean, Route du Clos Don Jean, 74290 Menthon-St-Bernard [tel/fax 04 50 60 18 66; donjean74@wanadoo.fr; www.clos-don-jean.com]** Fr N site clearly sp fr vill of Menthon. L uphill for 400m. Med, hdg/mkd pitch, pt sl, pt shd; wc (some cont); chem disp; mv service pnt; shwrs inc; el pnts (3-10A) €2.30-2.75; gas; lndtte; shop; playgrnd; lake sw 900m; dogs €1; poss cr; Eng spkn; quiet; CCI; "Excel site; clean san facs; fine views chateau & lake; orchard setting." ♦ 1 Jun-15 Sep. € 16.80 2008*

ANNECY *9B3* (9km SE Urban) *45.82672, 6.18861* **Camp Municipal Les Champs Fleuris, 631 Voie Romaine, Les Perris, 74410 Duingt [04 50 68 57 31 or 04 50 68 67 07 (Mairie); fax 04 50 77 03 17; camping@duingt.fr; www.camping-duingt.com]** Fr Annecy take D1508 (N508) sp Albertville. Site on R bef Duingt vill (2km after St Jorioz). Site poorly sp - foll sp Camping Le Familial, over cycle path & turn L. Med, mkd pitch, pt sl, terr, pt shd; htd wc; chem disp; mv service pnt; shwrs inc; el pnts (3-6A) €2.40-3.60; gas 1km; lndtte; shops 1km; tradsmn; rest; snacks; bar; BBQ; playgrnd; lake sw 750m; wifi; 3% statics; dogs €1.80; phone; bus 200m; poss cr; Eng spkn; adv bkg; quiet; CCI. "Gd mountain scenery; busy high ssn; gd sized pitches; friendly, helpful warden; gd for walking, touring, cycling; vg lakeside beach; v cr if Tour de France in area; gd." ♦ 1 May-10 Sep. € 14.60 2009*

ANNECY *9B3* (10km SE Rural) *45.82423, 6.18523* **Camping Le Familial, Route de Magnonnet, 74410 Duingt [tel/fax 04 50 68 69 91; camping.lefamilial@laposte.net; www.annecy-camping-familial.com]** Fr Annecy on D1508 (N508) twd Albertville. 5km after St Jorioz turn R at site sp Entrevernes onto D8, foll sp past Camping Champs Fleuris. Sm, mkd pitch, some hdstg, pt sl, pt shd; wc; shwrs inc; el pnts (5-6A) €3.10-3.30; lndtte; tradsmn; playgrnd; lake & shgl beach 500m; TV rm; dogs €1.60; some Eng spkn; adv bkg rec Jul/Aug; quiet but rd noise; CCI. "Gd site in scenic area; gd atmosphere; generous pitches; friendly owner; communal meals & fondu evenings; conv lakeside cycle track." ♦ 1 Apr-30 Sep. € 13.10 2009*

ANNECY *9B3* (10km SE Rural) *45.84070, 6.16450* **Camping Le Solitaire du Lac, 615 Route de Sales, 74410 St Jorioz [tel/fax 04 50 68 59 30 or 06 88 58 94 24 (mob); campinglesolitaire@wanadoo.fr; www.campinglesolitaire.com]** Exit Annecy on D1508 (N508) twd Albertville. Site sp on N o'skts of St Jorioz. Med, hdg/mkd pitch, pt shd; wc (some cont); chem disp; mv service pnt; shwrs inc; el pnts (5A) €3.50 (poss rev pol); gas; lndtte; supmkts 2km; tradsmn; rest; snacks; bar & 2km; BBQ; playgrnd; lake sw; boat-launching; cycle hire; games areas; cycle track; internet rm; TV rm; 10% statics; dogs €2.20; poss v cr high ssn; Eng spkn; adv bkg; v quiet; red low ssn/long stay; ccard acc; CCI. "Well-run site; gd touring base in excel location; clean san facs; direct access to Lake Annecy & sh walk to public beach & water bus to Annecy; cycle path nr site; vg." 10 Apr-19 Sep. € 17.00 2009*

ANNECY *9B3* (14km SE Rural) *45.80153, 6.15166* **Aire Naturelle Le Combarut (Cottard), Chef-Lieu Le Verger, 74410 St Eustache [04 50 32 00 20]** Take D1508 (N508) S fr Annecy to Sévrier, turn R onto D912, site on farm just bef St Eustache. Sm, shd; wc (cont); mv service pnt; shwrs €1.20; el pnts (4A) €1.80; shop 5km; pool 15km; dogs €0.80; quiet. "Basic facs but clean; gd mountain views; tortuous access on winding rds, but not diff with care." 1 Jun-30 Sep. € 9.60 2006*

ANNECY *9B3* (1.5km S Rural) *45.89100, 6.13236* **Camp Municipal Le Belvédère, 8 Route du Semnoz, 74000 Annecy [04 50 45 48 30; camping@ville-annecy.fr; www.annecy.fr]** Fr A41 take D1508 (N508) at junc 16 & foll sp to Albertville & hospital thro Annecy, turn L at traff lts & up hill. Where main rd bends sharp L downhill bear R (hospital on L). Take next R up hill, Rte du Semnoz (D41); bear R then L & site on R in 250m. Lge, mkd pitch, pt sl, terr, pt shd; htd wc; chem disp; shwrs inc; el pnts (10A) inc (poss rev pol); gas; lndtte; shop; tradsmn; rest; snacks; playgrnd; cycle hire; sailing; fishing; forest walks; excursions; TV; sep statics area; dogs; phone; poss cr; Eng spkn; adv bkg; poss noisy; ccard acc; CCI. "Lovely, tidy site in beautiful setting; well lit at night; staff helpful; san facs OK; v steep footpath to old town; excel." ♦ 1 Apr 12 Oct. € 21.60 2009*

ANNECY *9B3* (5km S Urban) *45.85482, 6.14395* **Camping au Coeur du Lac, Les Choseaux, 74320 Sévrier [04 50 52 46 45; fax 04 50 52 19 01 45; info@aucoeurdulac.com; www.campingaucoeurdulac.com]** S fr Annecy on D1508 (N508) sp Albertville. Pass thro Sévrier cent. Site on L at lakeside 1km S of Sévrier. 300m after McDonald's. Med, mkd pitch, terr, pt sl, pt shd, some hdstg; wc (some cont); chem disp; mv service pnt; shwrs inc; el pnts (4-13A) €3.20-7.20, long cable rec; lndtte; shop; supmkt with petrol 2km; snacks; playgrnd; lake sw; yachting; grass & shgl beach; cycle/boat hire; entmnt; dogs €1 (low ssn only); bus nrby; info office 1km N; poss cr; some Eng spkn; adv bkg ess high ssn; quiet but some rd noise; ccard acc; red low ssn; CCI. "Busy site in lovely location; gd views fr upper terr o'looking lake; tight for lge o'fits - sm, sl pitches; gd san facs; gd access to lake beach & cycle path; excel, esp low ssn." ♦ 1 Apr-30 Sep. € 21.50 2009*

ANNECY *9B3* (6km S Rural) *45.84333, 6.14175* **Camping Le Panoramic, 22 Chemin des Bernets, Cessenaz, 74320 Sévrier [04 50 52 43 09; fax 04 50 52 73 09; info@camping-le-panoramic.com; www.camping-le-panoramic.com]** Exit A41 junc 16 Annecy Sud onto D1508 (N508) sp Albertville. Thro Sévrier to rndabt at Cessenaz (ignore all prior sp to site) & take 1st R onto D10. In 200m turn R up hill to site in 2km. Lge, mkd pitch, pt sl, terr, unshd; htd wc; chem disp; shwrs inc; el pnts (4-6A) €3.20-4.20 (some rev pol); lndtte; shop; supmkt 2km; tradsmn; rest; snacks; bar; playgrnd; pool; beach 2km; lake sw; games rm; TV; dogs €1.60; poss cr; Eng spkn; quiet; ccard acc; red low ssn; CCI. "Gd views; blocks/wedges ess for sl pitches; excel pool; rec for families." ♦ 26 Apr-30 Sep. € 19.20 2008*

ANNECY *9B3* (6.5km S Urban) *45.84412, 6.15354* **Camping de l'Aloua, 492 Route de Piron, 74320 Sévrier [tel/fax 04 50 52 60 06 or 04 50 52 64 54 (LS); camping.aloua@wanadoo.fr; http://campingaloua.free.fr]** Foll sp for Albertville D1508 (N508) S fr Annecy. Site on E side, approx 1.4km S of Sevrier vill. Turn L at Champion supmkt rndabt & foll sp twd lake. Lge, pt hdg/mkd pitch, shd; wc (some cont); chem disp; mv service pnt; shwrs inc; el pnts (2-6A) €2.50-3.50; gas 400m; Indtte; shop; supmkt 400m; tradsmn; rest; snacks; bar; playgrnd; shgl beach 300m; lake sw, fishing, boating & watersports adj; archery; entmnts; TV; sm dogs only €2; phone; poss cr; quiet, but rd noise; Eng spkn; adv bkg; red low ssn; CCI. "Gd base for lake (no dir access fr site); cycle track around lake; night security; poss noisy at night with youths & some rd noise; basic san facs; pleasant owners; vg." ♦ 20 Jun-10 Sep. € 17.50 2008*

ANNECY *9B3* (6.5km S Rural) *45.84806, 6.15129* **FFCC Camping Les Rives du Lac, Parc Claude Gelain, 331 Chemin du Communaux, 74320 Sévrier [04 50 52 40 14; fax 04 50 51 12 38; lesrivesdulac.sevrier@ffcc.fr; www.camp-in-france.com]** Take D1508 (N508) S fr Annecy sp Albertville, thro Sévrier sp FFCC. Turn L 100m past (S) Lidl supmkt, cross cycle path & turn R & foll sp FFCC keeping parallel with cycle path. Site on L in 400m. Med, mkd pitch, pt shd; wc; chem disp; mv service pnt; baby facs; shwrs inc; el pnts (6A) €3.80; Indtte; shops 500m; BBQ; playgrnd; private shgl beach; lake sw; sailing; fishing; walking; entmnt; wifi; 10% statics; dogs €0.95; bus nr; poss cr; Eng spkn; adv bkg; quiet but noise at night fr nrby disco; red CC members (not Jul/Aug); CCI. "Beautiful situation; generous pitches; helpful staff; water bus to Annecy nr; gd touring base; gd walking, sailing & cycling; cycle rte adj; san facs poss inadequate if site full." ♦ 10 Apr-15 Oct. € 19.90 2008*

ANNECY *9B3* (9km S Rural) *45.83077, 6.17837* **Camping International du Lac d'Annecy, 1184 Route d'Albertville, 74410 St Jorioz [tel/fax 04 50 68 67 93; contact@camping-lac-annecy.com; www.camping-lac-annecy.com]** Fr Annecy take D1508 (N508) sp Albertville. Site on R just after St Jorioz. Med, hdg/mkd pitch, some hdstg, pt shd; wc; chem disp; mv service pnt; shwrs inc; el pnts (6A) €3.80; gas; Indtte; shop 2km; tradsmn; rest; snacks; bar; BBQ; playgrnd; pool; lake sw; cycle hire; games area; TV rm; 30% statics; dogs €2.50; bus 500m; phone; poss cr; Eng spkn; red low ssn; CCI. "Excel for touring lake area; site ent tight for med/lge o'fits; sm pitches; gd rest nrby." 9 May-18 Sep. € 24.00 2009*

ANNECY *9B3* (9km S Rural) *45.82995, 6.18215* **Village Camping Europa, 1444 Route d'Albertville, 74410 St Jorioz [04 50 68 51 01; fax 04 50 68 55 20; info@camping-europa.com; www.camping-europa.com]** Fr Annecy take D1508 (N508) sp Albertville. Site on R 800m S of St Jorioz dir Albertville. Look for lge yellow sp on o'skirts of St Jorioz. Lge, hdg/mkd pitch, pt shd, wc; chem disp; mv service pnt; some serviced pitches; baby facs; shwrs inc; el pnts (6A) €3.80; Indtte; tradsmn; rest; snacks; bar; BBQ (gas); playgrnd; htd pool; waterslides; jacuzzi; beach (lake) 700m; windsurfing; boat hire; fishing; tennis 700m; cycle hire; cycle track adj; wifi; TV rm; dogs €3; Eng spkn; adv bkg; quiet but main rd adj; ccard acc; quiet; red long stay/low ssn; CCI. "Peaceful site; friendly staff; facs stretched high ssn; vg rest; excel for m'vans; conv Chamonix & Mont Blanc; variable pitch prices; some pitches tight lge o'fits; gd tourist base; excel." ♦ 30 Apr-13 Sep. € 28.00 2007*

ANNECY *9B3* (7km SW Rural) *45.86131, 6.05214* **Aire Naturelle La Vidome (Lyonnaz), 74600 Montagny-les-Lanches [tel/fax 04 50 46 61 31; j.lyonnaz@wanadoo.fr; www.lavidome.fr]** Exit Annecy on D1201 (N201) sp Aix-les-Bains/Chambéry; after 6km at Le Treige turn R sp Montagny-les-Lanches. In 1km turn R in Avulliens; site on R in 100m. Sm, pt sl, pt shd; wc; chem disp; shwrs; el pnts (3-10A) €2.10-4; Indtte; meals avail; hypermkt 3km; playgrnd; pool 3km; beach & mini-golf 10km; fishing 1km; horseriding 1km; dogs €0.80; quiet but some rd noise; adv bkg; gd views; CCI. "Excel site; friendly owners; vg san facs; access poss tight for lge o'fits; gd touring base." 1 May-30 Sep. € 11.60 2008*

ANNECY *9B3* (9km SW Rural) **Aire Naturelle Le Pré Ombragé (Metral), 74600 Montagny-les-Lanches [04 50 46 71 31; fax 04 50 57 20 04; lepreombrage@wanadoo.fr]** Exit Annecy on D1201 (N201) sp Aix-les-Bains/Chambéry, after 8km at Le Treige turn R sp Montagny-les-Lanches; site sp in vill. Sm, pt sl, pt shd; wc; chem disp; shwrs inc; el pnts €2; shops 3km; playgrnd; pool; dogs €0.50; Eng spkn; adv bkg; quiet; CCI. "Friendly, family-run farm in orchard; excel views." 15 Jun-30 Sep. € 9.50 2008*

ANNECY *9B3* (12km SW Rural) *45.81584, 6.02991* **Aire Naturelle Jouvenod (Mercier), 460 Route de Jouvenod, 74540 Alby-sur-Chéran [04 50 68 15 75]** Take A41 SW fr Annecy, turn off at junc 15 twds Alby-sur-Chéran. Foll sp in vill. Sm, pt sl, pt shd; wc; chem disp; mv service pnt; shwrs inc; el pnts (10A) €2; shop 3km; playgrnd; beach & boating 13km; lake sw & fishing 8km; tennis; 10% statics; dogs; phone; Eng spkn; ccard not acc. "Farm site; gd views & hill/woodland walks; Alby pretty, medieval town." 15 Jun-15 Sep. € 7.50 2007*

ANNECY *9B3* (8km NW Rural) *45.97811, 6.03564* **Camping La Caille, 18 Chemin de la Caille, 74330 La Balme-de-Sillingy [04 50 68 85 21; fax 04 50 68 74 56; contact@aubergedelacaille.com; www.aubergedelacaille.com]** Fr Annecy take D1508 (N508) dir Bellgarde-sur-Valserine. Strt on at rndabt at end of La Balme-de-Sillingy, foll sp. At mini rndabt strt on, site on R in 1km. Sm, hdg/mkd pitch, pt sl, shd; wc; chem disp; el pnts (4-12A) €3-5; Indtte; shop 750m; tradsmn; rest; snacks; bar; playgrnd; pool; 25% statics; dogs €3.70; adv bkg; quiet; CCI. "Gd, well-kept site." ♦ 1 May-30 Sep. € 20.00 2009*

ANNET SUR MARNE see Meaux *3D3*

ANNEYRON *9C2* (3km S Rural) *45.25469, 4.90350* **FLOWER Camping La Châtaigneraie, Route de Mantaille, 26140 Anneyron [tel/fax 04 75 31 43 33; contact@chataigneraie.com; www.chataigneraie.com or www.flowercamping.com]** Exit A7 junc 12 onto N7 S avoiding St Rambert; at La Creux de la Thine rndabt take D1 sp Anneyron; site sp at end of vill on D161. 3km S of Anneyron via narr, winding rd - poss dff lge o'fits. Med, hdg/mkd pitch, pt sl, terr, pt shd; wc; chem disp; fam bthrm; shwrs inc; el pnts (6-10A) €3.90-€4.50 (poss rev pol); Indtte; shop; tradsmn; rest; snacks; bar; BBQ (gas/elec); playgrnd; pool; tennis; games area; games rm; entmnt; 40% statics; dogs €2; phone; Eng spkn; adv bkg; quiet; ccard acc; red low ssn/CCI. "Attractive, peaceful site o'looking Rhône valley; friendly, helpful owner; gd size pitches; gd for children; gd walk to castle ruins." ♦ 1 Apr-30 Sep. € 17.60 2007*

ANNONAY *9C2* (Urban) *45.25799, 4.67426* **Camp Municipal de Vaure, 07100 Annonay [04 75 32 47 49 or 04 75 33 46 54; fax 04 75 32 28 22; www.mairie-annonay.fr]** Sp fr o'skts of town & foll sp St Etienne. Fr St Etienne & NW turn L at 1st rndabt & pass Intermarché, foll camping/piscine sp to site. Sm, pt shd; wc (some cont); shwrs inc; el pnts (6-10A) €1.85-2.80; Indtte; snacks; bar; supmkt adj; htd, covrd pool; games area; few statics; dogs €1.15; cr; quiet. "Helpful staff; poss itinerants; gd." 1 Apr-31 Oct. € 8.25 2006*

ANNOT *10E4* (1km N Rural) *43.97195, 6.65777* **Camping La Ribière, 04240 Annot [04 92 83 21 44]** On N202 exit at Les Scaffarels to Annot on D908. Site 1km beyond vill on L bank of rv. Med, mkd pitch, pt shd; wc; chem disp; shwrs €0.80; el pnts (5A) inc; Indtte; shops 1km; rest; snacks; playgrnd; fishing; 30% statics; adv bkg; quiet. "Interesting medieval vills & gorges." 15 Feb-5 Nov. € 12.90 2006*

ANNOVILLE *1D4* (1km SW Coastal) *48.95521, -1.54911* **Camp Municipal Les Peupliers, 50660 Annoville [02 33 47 67 73; fax 02 33 46 78 38; campinglespeupliers@orange.fr]** N fr Granville on D971 to Bréhal then take D20 for approx 6km dir Annonville, turn L at Hameau Hébert, site sp on R. Med, mkd pitch, unshd; wc; baby facs; shwrs inc; el pnts €3; supmkt in Bréhal; snacks; playgrnd; sand beach 500m; 10% statics; dogs €1.10; Eng spkn; adv bkg; quiet. "Gd walking, birdwatching; gd site." 1 May-13 Sep. € 8.00 2009*.

ANOULD see Corcieux *6F3*

ANSE see Villefranche sur Saône *9B2*

ANTIBES *10E4* (2km N Urban/Coastal) *43.60536, 7.11255* **Camping Caravaning Le Rossignol, Ave Jean Michard-Pelissier, Juan-les-Pins, 06600 Antibes [04 93 33 56 98; fax 04 92 91 98 99; campinglerossignol@wanadoo.fr; www.campingrossignol.com]** Turn W off N7 Antibes-Nice at sp to Hospitalier de la Fontonne then bear L along Chemin des Quatres past hospital & traff lts junc. In 400m turn R at rndabt into Ave Jean Michard Pelissier, site 200m on R. NB Narr ent off busy rd. Med, hdg/mkd pitch, hdstg, terr, shd; wc; chem disp; mv service pnt; baby facs; shwrs inc; el pnts (10A) €5; gas; Indtte; shop 400m; tradsmn high ssn; bar; BBQ (gas/elec); playgrnd; htd pool; paddling pool; shgl beach 1.2km; tennis 2km; games area; games rm; entmnt; TV rm; dogs €3.50; Eng spkn; adv bkg; quiet; ccard acc; red long stay/CCI. "Conv Antibes & surrounding area; peaceful site; sm pitches." ♦ 4 Apr-3 Oct. € 22.40 2008*

ANTIBES *10E4* (3.5km N Coastal) *43.61101, 7.11675* **Camping Antipolis, Ave du Pylone, La Brague, 06600 Antibes [04 93 33 93 99; fax 04 92 91 02 00; contact@camping-antipolis.com; www.camping-antipolis.com]** Exit A8 at Biot dir Marineland. In 800m turn R & foll site sp. Lge, hdg/mkd pitch, shd; wc (some cont); chem disp; shwrs; el pnts (10A) inc; gas; Indtte; shop; tradsmn; rest; snacks; bar; BBQ; playgrnd; 2 pools (1 htd); shgl beach 800m; tennis; games area; entmnt; 30% statics; no dogs; phone; train 1km; adv bkg; quiet; ccard acc; CCI. "Situated beside m'way, but pitches away fr rd; sm pitches; walk to beach along busy rds & across dual c'way; excel pool complex & activities." ♦ Easter-15 Sep. € 29.50 (CChq acc) 2009*

ANTIBES *10E4* (3.5km N Coastal) *43.61270, 7.12522* **Camping Les Embruns, 63 Route de Biot, Quartier de la Brague, 06600 Antibes [04 93 33 33 35; fax 04 93 74 46 70; www.campinglesembruns.com]** Fr Antibes take D6007 (N7) sp Nice, after 3.5km at rndabt with palm trees turn inland into Route de Biot; site sp on L. Sm, pt shd; wc; baby facs; shwrs inc; el pnts (5) €3.05; Indtte; snacks; bar; shop; shgl beach adj; fishing & watersports adj; cycle hire; tennis; TV; dogs €1; bus & metro adj; adv bkg; poss noise fr adj rd & rlwy; poss fairgrnd adj (Sep 2007); 5% red low ssn; ccard acc. "Lovely site; gd-sized pitches; well-supervised by owner; walking dist beach, bus & metro; no turning space - not suitable lge o'fits; some pitches waterlogged in wet weather; gd." 1 Jun-20 Sep. € 22.00 2008*

ANTIBES *10E4* (5km N Coastal) *43.61198, 7.11749* **Camping Les Frênes, Route du Pylone, La Brague, 06600 Antibes [04 93 33 36 52; fax 04 93 74 66 00; contact@camping-lesfrenes.com; www.camping-lesfrenes.com]** Fr Antibes on D6007 (N7), turn inland opp Biot rlwy, Rte de Biot. In approx 100m turn L, then R at T-junc, then L in approx 400m. Site 1st on R. Do not take coast rd fr Antibes/Nice, low bdge. Med, mkd pitch, shd; wc; chem disp; shwrs inc; el pnts (6A) inc; Indtte; shop (high ssn); tradsmn; rest; snacks; pizzaria; bar; Indtte; playgrnd; pool; paddling pool; sand beach 600m; entmnt; TV; 10% statics; dogs €1.80; train 600m; poss cr; Eng spkn; adv bkg; quiet but some m'way noise; ccard acc. "Friendly, helpful owner; conv Aquasplash & Marineland; conv train to Nice, Monte-Carlo, Monaco etc." 2 May-20 Sep. € 24.00 2007*

France

ANTONNE ET TRIGONANT see Périgueux *7C3*

APREMONT *2H4* (2km N Rural) *46.77848, -1.73394* **Camping Les Charmes, Route de la Roussière, 85220 Apremont [02 51 54 48 08 or 06 86 03 96 93 (mob); fax 02 51 55 98 85; contact@campinglescharmes.com; www.campinglescharmes.com]** Fr D948 Challans to Aizenay turn W onto D94 sp Commequiers; after 2km L, sp Les Charmes. Med, mkd pitch, pt shd; wc (some cont); chem disp; fam bthrm; shwrs inc; el pnts (6-10A) €3.20-4 (poss rev pol); gas; Indtte; shop; tradsmn; playgrnd; pool; lake sw with beach 3km; sand beach 18km; TV rm; 60% statics; dogs €2.80; poss cr; Eng spkn; adv bkg; quiet; ccard acc; red low ssn/long stay; CCI. "Beautiful, well-kept site; generous pitches but soft when wet; welcoming, helpful owners; excel, clean san facs; a great find." ♦ 1 Apr-12 Sep. € 16.80 2009*

APT *10E3* (9km N Rural) *43.92050, 5.34120* **Camping Les Chênes Blancs (Naturist), Route de Gargas, 84490 St Saturnin-les-Apt [04 90 74 09 20; fax 04 90 74 26 98; robert@les-chenes-blancs.com; www.les-chenes-blancs.com]** Fr W on D900 (N100) twd Apt, at NW o'skts of Apt turn N on D101, cont approx 2km turn R on D83 into Gargas; thro Gargas & in 4km turn L at camp sp; site on R in 300m. Narr rd. Lge, shd; wc; mv service pnt; shwrs inc; el pnts (6A) €5.40; Indtte; shop; rest; snacks; bar; playgrnd; htd pool; lake fishing 5km; games area; entmnt; TV rm; dogs €2.60; poss cr; Eng spkn; adv bkg rec; quiet; red low ssn; ccard acc. "Well-run, popular site in gd location; pitches amongst oaks poss diff lge outfits; stony ground, need steel pegs for awnings; friendly staff; san facs poss stretched high ssn; excel touring base." ♦ 15 Mar-3 Nov. € 16.80 (CChq acc) 2008*

APT *10E3* (500m NE Urban) *43.87753, 5.40302* **Camp Municipal Les Cèdres, Ave de Viton, 84400 Apt [tel/fax 04 90 74 14 61; lucie.bouillet@yahoo.fr]** In town turn N off D900 onto D22 twd Rustrel, site sp. Site on R in 200m immed after going under old rlwy bdge. Med, mkd pitch, pt shd; htd wc; chem disp; mv service pnt; shwrs inc; el pnts (6-10A) €3.50-4; gas; Indtte; shop & snacks (high ssn); cooking facs; playgrnd; entmnt; dogs €1; poss cr; adv bkg; ccard acc; CCI. "Excel, friendly site in lovely location; sm pitches; pitching poss haphazard low ssn; clean san facs; some pitches muddy when wet; cycle tracks; conv Luberon vills & ochre mines; mkt Sat." ♦ 15 Feb-11 Nov. € 11.00 2009*

APT *10E3* (2km SE Rural) *43.86636, 5.41275* **Camping Le Luberon, Route de Saignon, 84400 Apt [04 90 04 85 40; fax 04 90 74 12 19; leluberon@wanadoo.fr; www.camping-le-luberon.com]** Exit Apt by D48 sp Saignon & site on R in 2km. Sharp turn into site. Med, mkd pitch, pt sl, pt shd; wc; chem disp; baby facs; shwrs inc; el pnts (6A) €4.50; gas; Indtte; shops 2km; tradsmn; rest; snacks; bar; BBQ; playgrnd; pool (proper sw trunks only); fishing, sailing 3km; TV; 20% statics; dogs €3.50; phone; poss cr; Eng spkn; adv bkg; quiet; ccard acc; red low ssn; CCI. "Pitches well laid-out in woodland; well-run, clean site; helpful owners; poss not suitable teenagers; gd." ♦ 3 Apr-25 Sep. € 20.45 2009*

⊞ **ARAGNOUET** *8G2* (2km E Rural) *42.78650, 0.24671* **Camp Municipal du Pont de Moudang, 65170 Aragnouet [05 62 39 62 84 or 05 62 39 62 63 (Mairie); fax 05 62 39 60 47; infos@piau-engaly.com]** Site on L of D929, 9km SW fr St Lary, on rvside. Med, mkd pitch, hdstg, terr, pt shd; htd wc; chem disp; shwrs; el pnts (4-10A) €2.45-6.90; Indtte; shop 100m; playgrnd; TV rm; 25% statics; site clsd Oct; poss cr; quiet; CCI. "Excel, scenic site; sm pitches suitable sm o'fits/m'vans; jetons needed for use of hot water (no charge); mountain walking; conv for Aragnouet/Bielsa tunnel." € 9.00 2007*

ARAMITS *8F1* (1km SW Rural) *43.12135, -0.73215* **Camping Baretous-Pyrénées, Quartier Ripaude, 64570 Aramits [05 59 34 12 21; fax 05 59 34 67 19; atso64@hotmail.com; www.camping-baretous-pyrenees.com]** SW fr Oloron-Ste Marie take D919 sp Aramits, Arette. Fr Aramits cont on D919 sp Lanne; site on R; well sp. Sm, mkd pitch, pt shd; wc; chem disp; mv service pnt; serviced pitches; shwrs inc; el pnts (10A) €3.50; Indtte; supmkt 500m; tradsmn; snacks, bar high ssn; playgrnd; htd pool high ssn; cycle hire; games rm; TV; 50% statics; dogs €2.50; poss cr; Eng spkn; adv bkg; CCI. "Friendly, helpful owner; well-kept, clean site but muddy when wet; ltd facs low ssn; barrier clsd 2230-0800; twin-axles extra; gd base for Pyrenees; poss unreliable opening dates - phone ahead low ssn." ♦ 1 Feb-15 Oct. € 19.50 (CChq acc) 2008*

ARBOIS *6H2* (1.5km E Urban) *46.90331, 5.78691* **Camp Municipal Les Vignes, Ave du Général Leclerc, 39600 Arbois [tel/fax 03 84 66 14 12 or 03 84 25 26 19; reservation@rsl39.com; www.relaisoleiljura.com]** Fr N or S, ent town & at rndabt in cent foll camp sp on D107 dir Mesnay. Site adj stadium & pool. NB Steep slopes to terr & narr ent unsuitable lge o'fits. Med, some hdg pitch/mkd pitch, some hdstg, pt sl, terr, pt shd; wc; chem disp; serviced pitches; shwrs inc; el pnts (10A); gas; Indtte; shop & 1km; rest; snacks; bar; playgrnd; htd pool adj; tennis; fishing 1km; entmnt; TV; dogs €2; twin-axles €35; poss cr; Eng spkn; adv bkg; quiet; ccard acc; CCI. "Beautiful setting; clean san facs but poss stretched high ssn; site clsd 2200-0800 low ssn; ltd facs low ssn; pleasant sm town, home of Louis Pasteur; Roman salt works, grottoes nr; lge fair 1st w/end in Sep; excel." ♦ 1 May-27 Sep. € 15.00 2008*

ARC EN BARROIS *6F1* (W Rural) *47.95052, 5.00523* **Camp Municipal Le Vieux Moulin, 52210 Arc-en-Barrois [03 25 02 51 33 (Mairie); fax 03 25 03 82 89; mairie.arc.en.barrois@wanadoo.fr]** Exit A5 junc 24 onto D10 S to Arc-en-Barrois; turn R onto D3 thro vill; site on L on o'skirts. Or fr D65 turn L onto D6 about 4km S of Châteauvillain; site on R on D3 at ent to vill, adj rv. Sm, pt shd; htd wc; chem disp; mv service pnt; shwrs inc; el pnts (6A) €2.30; gas in vill; shops 500m; BBQ; sm playgrnd; tennis adj; TV; dogs; phone in vill; quiet; ccard not acc; CCI. "Attractive, peaceful, well-kept site adj vill sports field; basic, clean san facs; warden calls pm; beautiful vill; conv NH fr A5; a gem." 1 Apr-30 Sep. € 9.20 2009*

ARCACHON *7D1* (10km E Coastal) *44.64400, -1.11167* **Camp Municipal de Verdalle, 2 Allée de l'Infante, La Hume, 33470 Gujan-Mestras [tel/fax 05 56 66 12 62; www.village-center.com]** Fr A63 take A660 twd Arcachon. Turn R at rndabt junc with D652 sp La Hume. In vill at junc with D650 turn L, then R at rndabt; then 3rd turning on R after rlwy line. Med, hdg pitch, pt shd; wc (some cont); chem disp (wc); shwrs inc; el pnts (10A) inc; Indtte; BBQ; sand beach adj; dogs; phone; poss cr; some Eng spkn; red low ssn; CCI. "Excel position; friendly staff; cycling/walking; conv local attractions; vg." ♦ 1 May-30 Sep. € 22.40 2009*

⊞ **ARCACHON** *7D1* (2km S Coastal) *44.65089, -1.17381* **Camping Club d'Arcachon, 5 Allée de la Galaxie, Les Abatilles, 33120 Arcachon [05 56 83 24 15; fax 05 57 52 28 51; info@camping-arcachon.com; www.camping-arcachon.com]** Exit A63 ont A660 dir Arcachon. Foll sp 'Hôpital Jean Hameau' & site sp. Lge, terr, pt shd; htd wc; chem disp; mv service pnt; shwrs inc; el pnts (10A) €4; gas; Indtte; shop; tradsmn; rest; snacks; bar; BBQ some pitches; playgrnd; pool; sand beach 1.5km; lake sw 10km; cycle hire; entmnt; TV rm; 40% statics; dogs €4; site clsd 12 Nov-11 Dec; adv bkg; Eng spkn; quiet; ccard acc; red low ssn; CCI. "Vg site in pine trees; excel touring base; good facs; access rds narr, some manoeuvring into pitches not easy; gd network cycle tracks." ♦ € 31.00 2009*

ARCHIAC *7B2* (400m W Urban) *45.52322, -0.30452* **Camp Municipal, Rue des Voituriers, 17520 Archiac [05 46 49 10 46 or 05 46 49 10 82 (Mairie); fax 05 46 49 84 09; archiacmairie@free.fr]** Site sp fr D731 100m past sw pool. Sm, mkd pitch, terr, pt sl, pt shd; wc; mv service pnt; shwrs inc; el pnts (5A) €3.50; Indtte; tradsmn; shops 400m; 2 pools adj; tennis; games rm; dogs €0.75; quiet. "On arr check list on office door for allocated/free pitches; warden calls." 15 Jun-15 Sep. € 6.90 2009*

ARCIS SUR AUBE *4E4* (300m N Urban) *48.53907, 4.14270* **Camping de l'Ile, Rue des Châlons, 10700 Arcis-sur-Aube [03 25 37 98 79; fax 03 25 82 94 18; camping-arcis@hermans.cx; www.arcis-sur-aube.com]** Fr A26 junc 21 foll sp to Arcis. Fr town cent take D677 (N77) dir Châlons-en-Champagne. Turn R after rv bdge, site sp. Med, mkd pitch, shd, wc (some cont); chem disp; shwrs inc; el pnts (4-10A) inc (poss rev pol); rest, bar & shops 500m; playgrnd; rv adj; fishing; dogs €1.60; Eng spkn; poss cr w/end & noisy; no ccard acc; CCI. "Pleasant, well-kept site on island surrounded by rv; friendly, helpful Dutch owners; gd, clean san facs; narr site rds - diff to manoeuvre lge o'fits; popular NH, rec arr early." ♦ 15 Apr-30 Sep. € 19.00 2009*

⊞ **ARCIS SUR AUBE** *4E4* (8km S Rural) *48.46696, 4.12633* **FFCC Camping La Barbuise, 10700 St Remy-sous-Barbuise [03 25 37 50 95 or 03 25 37 41 11]** Fr Arcis-sur-Aube, take D677 (N77) twd Voué; site on L bef vill of Voué, sp. Fr S exit A26 junc 21 onto D441 W; then onto D677 S twd Voué & as bef. Sm, pt sl, pt shd; wc; chem disp; shwrs inc; el pnts (5A) €1.50 (poss rev pol); tradsmn; sm bar (high ssn); pool 8km; dogs; phone; adv bkg; quiet but some rd noise; red facs low ssn; ccard not acc; CCI. "Lovely, peaceful, spacious CL-type site; pleasant views; charming owners; san facs old but clean; early arr rec; easy access & pitching for lge o'fits; elec heaters not allowed; site yourself & owner collects payment in eve (cash only); conv NH/sh stay Champagne rtes/region; vg." ♦ € 6.50 2009*

ARDRES *3A3* (500m N Urban) *50.85726, 1.97551* **Camping Ardresien, 64 Rue Basse, 62610 Ardres [03 21 82 82 32]** Fr St Omer on D943 (N43) to Ardres, strt on at lights in town onto D231; site 500m on R - easy to o'shoot; v narr ent, not suitable twin-axles. Sm, hdg pitch, pt shd; wc; shwrs; el pnts (16A) inc; 95% statics; dogs free; poss cr; CCI. "Basic site; sm pitches; poss unkempt low ssn; friendly warden; san facs old & poss unclean; lge lakes at rear of site - fishing; ltd touring pitches; conv local vet; NH only." 1 May-30 Sep. € 12.00 2009*

ARDRES *3A3* (9km NE Rural) *50.88147, 2.08618* **Camp Municipal Les Pyramides, Rue Nord Boutillier, 62370 Audruicq [03 21 35 59 17 or 03 21 46 06 60 (Mairie)]** Fr Calais take A16 dir Dunkerque, after 8km exit S at junc 21 onto D219 to Audruicq; foll camp sp. Fr Ardres NE on D224 to Audruicq. Site on NE side of Audruicq nr canal. Med, hdg pitch, unshd; wc; chem disp; shwrs inc, el pnts (6A) inc; gas; Indtte; tradsmn; playgrnd; 80% statics; no ccard acc; quiet; CCI. "Conv Calais; few sm pitches for tourers; rec phone ahead." ♦ 1 Apr-30 Sep. € 18.80 2006*

ARDRES *3A3* (9km SE Rural) *50.82193, 2.07577* **Camping Le Relax, 318 Route de Gravelines, 62890 Nordausques [tel/fax 03 21 35 63 77; camping.le.relax@cegetel.net]** Fr N on D943 (N43) in vill 25km S of Calais at beginning of vill, turn L at sp. Site 200m on R. Or fr S on A26, leave at junc 2 & take D943 S for 1km into Nordausques, then as above. Med, hdg pitch, pt shd; wc; chem disp; shwrs €1.50; el pnts (6A) €2.20 (poss rev pol); Indry rm; shop 200m; tradsmn; snacks; playgrnd; 90% statics; poss cr; adv bkg ess; quiet; CCI. "Obliging owner; conv A26, Calais & war sites; not suitable lge o'fits, diff to manoeuvre; cheap & cheerful; OK NH." 1 Apr-30 Sep. € 11.45 2009*

France

⊞ **ARDRES** *3A3* (10km SE Rural) *50.80867, 2.05569* **Hôtel Bal Caravaning, 500 Rue du Vieux Château, 62890 Tournehem-sur-la-Hem [03 21 35 65 90; fax 03 21 35 18 57; philippe.baudens@wanadoo.fr]** Fr S on A26 leave at exit 2; turn R onto D217 then R onto D943 (N43) dir St Omer. Turn R in Nordausques onto D218 (approx 1km), pass under A26, site is 1km on L - ent thro Bal Parc Hotel gates. Fr N or S on D943, turn R or L in Nordausques, then as above. Med, hdg/mkd pitch, hdstg, pt sl, pt shd; htd wc (in hotel in winter); chem disp; shwrs inc; el pnts (10A) inc (poss rev pol); gas; tradsmn; rest, snacks, bar in adj hotel; playgrnd; sand beach 20km; sports ground & leisure cent adj; tennis; entmnt; 80% statics; poss cr; Eng spkn; adv bkg red; quiet; ccard acc; red low ssn/CCI. "25km Cité Europe shopping mall; friendly, helpful owner; low ssn poss open w/end only & poss clsd during bad weather; ltd pitches & facs low ssn; few touring pitches; gd rest adj; gd NH." ♦ € 23.40 2009*

ARDRES *3A3* (2km S Rural) *50.83865, 1.97612* **Camping St Louis, 223 Rue Leulène, 62610 Autingues [03 21 35 46 83; fax 03 21 00 19 78; www.campingstlouis.com]** Fr Calais S on D943 (N43) to Ardres; fr Ardres take D224 S twd Licques, after 2km turn L on D227; site well sp in 100m. Or fr junc 2 off A26 onto D943 dir Ardres. Turn L just after Total g'ge on R on app to Ardres. Well sp. If app fr S via Boulogne avoid Nabringhen & Licques as narr, steep hill with bends. NB Mkt Thurs am - avoid R turn when leaving site. Med, hdg/mkd pitch, pt shd; wc; chem disp; mv service pnt; baby facs; shwrs inc; el pnts (6A) €3 (long lead poss req; poss rev pol); gas; lndtte; sm shop & 1km; supmkt 3km; tradsmn; rest; snacks; bar; BBQ; playgrnd; lake 1km; games rm; entmnt; wifi; 20% statics; dogs free; phone; poss cr; Eng spkn; adv bkg ess high ssn; quiet; ccard acc; CCI. "Peaceful, well-kept site; conv Dunkerque, Calais ferries; gd grass pitches, some sm; clean san facs, far fr some pitches & stretched high ssn; chem disp inadequate high ssn; ltd touring pitches - phone ahead to check avail high ssn; early dep/late arr area; barrier opens 0600 high ssn; gd rest; conv NH." ♦
28 Mar-23 Oct. € 17.00 2009*

ARES see Andernos les Bains *7D1*

ARFEUILLES see Châtel Montagne *9A1*

ARGELES GAZOST *8G2* (500m N Rural) *43.01216, -0.09780* **Camping Sunêlia Les Trois Vallées, Ave des Pyrénées, 65400 Argelès-Gazost [05 62 90 35 47; fax 05 62 90 35 48; 3-vallees@wanadoo.fr; www.camping-les-3-vallees.fr]** S fr Lourdes on D821 (N21), turn R at rndabt sp Argelès-Gazost on D821A. Site off next rndabt on R. Lge, mkd pitch, pt shd; htd wc; chem disp; sauna; shwrs inc; el pnts (6A) inc (poss rev pol); lndtte; supmkt opp; tradsmn; bar; playgrnd; htd pool; waterslide; games rm; cycle hire; games area; golf 11km; entmnt; TV rm; 30% statics; dogs €2; poss cr; adv bkg ess high ssn; some rd noise nr site ent; ccard acc. "Interesting area; views of Pyrenees; conv Lourdes; excel touring base; red facs low ssn." ♦ 10 Mar-1 Nov. € 29.00 2006*

ARGELES GAZOST *8G2* (1km N Rural) *43.01725, -0.09670* **Camping La Bergerie, 54 Ave des Pyrénées, 65400 Ayzac-Ost [tel/fax 05 62 97 59 99; info@camping-labergerie.com; www.camping-labergerie.com]** Sp off D821 (N21). Sm, pt shd; wc; shwrs inc; el pnts (2-6A) €1.80-5.40; lndtte; rest, bar 100m; BBQ; playgrnd; htd pool; games area; entmnt; some statics; dogs €1; Eng spkn; adv bkg; quiet; ccard acc; red low ssn. "Clean, friendly site." ♦ 1 May-30 Sep. € 16.50 2009*

ARGELES GAZOST *8G2* (2km N Rural) *43.01885, -0.09167* **Camping Bellevue, 24 Chemin de la Plaine, 65400 Ayzac-Ost [tel/fax 05 62 97 58 81]** Fr Lourdes S on D821 (N21), foll sp for Ayzac-Ost then sp for 'Camping La Bergerie' but cont past ent for 200m. Site on R behind farm buildings. Sm, pt shd; wc; chem disp; mv service pnt; shwrs inc; el pnts (2-6A) €2; lndtte; shop, rest, snacks, bar 1km; tradsmn; playgrnd; fishing 300m; 2% statics; dogs €1; phone; quiet; CCI. "Surrounded by fields; gd san facs block; could be muddy; gd." ♦ 1 Jun-30 Sep. € 8.40 2007*

ARGELES GAZOST *8G2* (4km N Rural) *43.03560, -0.07086* **Camping Soleil du Pibeste, 65400 Agos-Vidalos [05 62 97 53 23; fax 05 61 06 67 73; info@campingpibeste.com; www.campingpibeste.com]** On D821 (N21), S of Lourdes. Exit at rndabt sp Agos-Vidalos, site on R on ent vill. Med, terr, pt shd; htd wc; chem disp; mv service pnt; shwrs inc; el pnts (6-10A) €4-6; gas; lndtte; shops adj; lndtte; tradsmn; rest; snacks; bar; playgrnd; sm pool; rv 500m; entmnt; TV; 10% statics; dogs €8; bus; Eng spkn; adv bkg rec high ssn; some rd noise; CCI. "Open outlook with views; beautiful area; warm welcome; guided mountain walks; excel, family-run site." ♦ 1 Apr-15 Oct. € 26.00 2009*

ARGELES GAZOST *8G2* (5km N Rural) *42.98120, -0.06535* **Camping Le Viscos, 16 Route de Préchac, 65400 Beaucens [05 62 97 05 45]** Fr Lourdes S twd Argelès-Gasost on D821 (N21). Cont twd Luz & Gavarnie to L of Argelès town, & turn L within 500m, sp Beaucens. Turn R to D13, site 2.5km on L. Med, pt sl, shd; wc; chem disp; shwrs inc; el pnts (2-10A) €2-4.50 (rev pol); gas; lndtte; shops 5km; tradsmn high ssn; snacks; BBQ; playgrnd; pool 4km; lake fishing 500m; dogs €1; quiet; adv bkg ess Jul-Aug; red long stay; ccard not acc; CCI. "Delightful site; landscaped grnds; clean san facs; gd rests in area." 10 May-30 Sep. € 10.90 2008*

ARGELES GAZOST *8G2* (1km S Rural) *42.98670, -0.08854* **Camping Les Frênes, 46 Route des Vallées, 65400 Lau-Balagnas [05 62 97 25 12; fax 05 62 97 01 41; http://campinglesfrenes.fr]** Site on R of D821 (N21) twd S. Med, pt terr, pt shd; htd wc; chem disp; baby facs; shwrs inc; el pnts (10A); gas; lndtte; shop 100m; BBQ; playgrnd; pool; rv & fishing 1km; entmnt; TV; some statics; adv bkg rec; quiet; red long stay. ♦ 15 Dec-15 Oct. € 18.25 2009*

⊞ **ARGELES GAZOST** *8G2* (2km S Rural) *42.98826, -0.08923* **Kawan Village Le Lavedan, 44 Route des Vallées, 65400 Lau-Balagnas [05 62 97 18 84; fax 05 62 97 55 56; contact@lavedan.com; www.lavedan.com]** Fr Lourdes S on D821 (N21) dir Argelès-Gazost/Cauterets; 2km after Argelès on D921 site on R after vill of Lau-Balagnas. Med, pt shd; htd wc; chem disp; baby facs; shwrs inc; el pnts (3-10A) €3-4 (poss rev pol); gas; Indtte (inc dryer); shops 2km; rest; snacks; bar; BBQ; playgrnd; htd, covrd pool; paddling pool; games/TV rm; 30% statics; dogs €2.50; Eng spkn; adv bkg; rd noise if pitched adj to rd; red low ssn. "In beautiful green valley; friendly, relaxed staff; gd clean san facs; excel cycle rte to Lourdes." ♦ € 24.00 (CChq acc) 2009*

ARGELES GAZOST *8G2* (2.5km S Rural) *42.9871, 0.1061* **Camping du Lac, 29 Chemin d'Azun, 65400 Arcizans-Avant [tel/fax 05 62 97 01 88; campinglac@campinglac65.fr; www.campinglac65.fr]** Fr Lourdes S thro Argelès-Gazost on D821 (N21) & D921. At 3rd rndabt take exit for St Savin/Arcizans-Avant. Cont thro St Savin vill & foll camp sp; site on L just thro Arcizans-Avant vill. NB: Dir rte to Arcizans-Avant is prohibited to c'vans. Med, hdg/mkd pitch, pt sl, pt shd; wc; chem disp; baby facs; shwrs inc; el pnts (5A) €4.30; gas; Indtte; shop; tradsmn; rest 500m; snacks; playgrnd; htd pool; games rm; cycle hire; TV rm; dogs €2; Eng spkn; adv bkg; quiet; red low ssn; CCI. "Excel, peaceful, scenic site; gd size pitches; clean san facs; gd for touring; vg." ♦ 15 May-30 Sep. € 21.80 2007*

ARGELES GAZOST *8G2* (5km S Rural) *42.98493, -0.10506* **Camping Les Châtaigniers, 65400 Arcizans-Avant [05 62 97 94 77 or 06 30 58 11 00 (mob); contact@camping-les-chataigniers.com; www.camping-les-chataigniers.com]** At rndabt on S side of Argelès-Gazost take D921 S dir Pierrefitte-Nestalas & foll sps to Arcizans-Avant & Les Châtaigniers. Med, hdg/mkd pitch, pt sl, pt shd; wc; chem disp; baby facs; el pnts (2-6A) €2-4; Indtte; tradsmn; playgrnd; pool; TV; some statics; dogs €1.20; no twin-axles; phone; poss cr; adv bkg; red low ssn; exce. "Immac site & facs; friendly, helpful owners; excel walking & cycling in mountains; excel." ♦ 15 May-15 Sep. € 13.50 2008*

ARGELES GAZOST *8G2* (2km SW Rural) *42.99502, -0.12076* **Camping L'Idéal, Route de Val d'Azun, 65400 Arras-en-Lavedan [05 62 97 03 13 or 05 62 97 02 12; info@camping-ideal-pyrenees.com; www.camping-ideal-pyrenees.com]** Leave Argelès Gazost SW on D918. Site on N side of rd on E o'skts of Arras-en-Lavedan. Ent on bend. Med, terr, pt shd; wc; chem disp; shwrs inc; el pnts (3-10A) €2.85-€9.50; sm shop; playgrnd; pool high ssn; tennis 1km; dogs free; adv bkg; quiet; CCI. "Vg, clean, scenic site; gd sized pitches; friendly owner; gd clean facs, v ltd low ssn; steel awning pegs rec; cooler than in valley." ♦ 1 Jun-15 Sep. € 12.00 2008*

ARGELES GAZOST *8G2* (10km SW Rural) *42.94139, -0.17714* **Camping Pyrénées Natura, Route du Lac, 65400 Estaing [05 62 97 45 44; fax 05 62 97 45 81; info@camping-pyrenees-natura.com; www.camping-pyrenees-natura.com]** Fr Lourdes take D821 (N21) to Argelès Gazost; fr Argelès foll sp Col d'Aubisque & Val d'Azun onto D918; after approx 7.5km turn L onto D13 to Bun; after Bun cross rv & turn R onto D103 twd Estaing; site in 3km - rd narr. Med, hdg/mkd pitch, terr, pt shd; htd wc; chem disp; mv service pnt; baby facs; sauna; shwrs inc; el pnts (10A) inc; gas; Indtte; shop; tradsmn; snacks; bar; BBQ (gas/elec/charcoal); playgrnd; pool 4km; solarium; internet; games/TV rm; 20% statics; dogs €2; Eng spkn; adv bkg; quiet; ccard acc; red low ssn; CCI. "Superb, well-kept, scenic site; friendly, helpful owners; clean facs; no plastic ground-sheets allowed; adj National Park; birdwatching area; organised walks; excel." ♦ 1 May-20 Sep. € 29.00 ABS - D22 2009*

ARGELES SUR MER *10G1* (1km N Coastal) *42.55726, 3.02893* **Camping de Pujol, Ave de la Ritirada, Route du Tamariguer, 66700 Argelès-sur-Mer [04 68 81 00 25; fax 04 68 81 21 21; www.campingdepujol.com]** Fr Perpignan on D914 (N114) exit junc 10 dir Argelès. L off slip rd foll sp Pujol, site on R - wide entrance. Lge, mkd pitch, pt shd; wc (some cont); chem disp; mv service pnt; baby facs; shwrs inc; el pnts (3-6A) inc; gas 2km; Indtte (inc dryer); shop; rest; snacks; bar; playgrnd; pool; paddling pool; sand beach 1km; car wash; entmnt; 30% statics; dogs free; phone; poss cr; Eng spkn; adv bkg rec high ssn; quiet but poss noisy disco; CCI. "Vg san facs but poss cold water shwrs only low ssn; vg pool; excel cycling." ♦ 1 Jun-30 Sep. € 27.80 2009*

ARGELES SUR MER *10G1* (1km N Rural) *42.57158, 3.02607* **Camping Les Galets, Route de Taxo d'Avall, Plage Nord, 66701 Argelès-sur-Mer [04 68 81 08 12; fax 04 68 81 68 76; lesgalets@campinglesgalets.fr; www.campmed.com]** Fr Perpignan take D914 (N114) dir Elne, Argelès, 4km after Elne pass Municipal Camping on L, sp listing many camp sites. Lge, pt shd; wc; baby facs; shwrs inc; el pnts (10A) inc; gas; Indtte; shop; rest; snacks; bar; playgrnd; htd pool; paddling pool; sand beach 1.5km; fishing, sailing & windsurfing 1.5km; rv sw 3km; equestrian cent nr; games area; entmnt; TV rm; 90% statics; dogs €4; poss cr; adv bkg rec all year; quiet; red low ssn. "Ltd touring pitches; gd for families." ♦ 1 Apr-30 Sep. € 33.00 2007*

ARGELES SUR MER *10G1* (1km N Coastal) *42.56320, 3.03498* **Camping Les Marsouins, Ave de la Retirada, 66702 Argelès-sur-Mer [04 68 81 14 81; fax 04 68 95 93 58; marsouin@campmed.com; www.campmed.com]** Fr Perpignan take exit 10 fr D914 (N114) & foll sp for Argelès until Shell petrol stn on R. Take next L just bef rv into Allée Ferdinand Buisson to T-junc, turn L at next rndabt dir Plage-Nord. Take 2nd R at next rndabt, site on L opp Spanish war memorial. V lge, hdg/mkd pitch, shd; wc; chem disp; mv service pnt; shwrs inc; el pnts (5A) inc; gas; Indtte; shops; rest; snacks; bar; BBQ; playgrnd; htd pool; sand beach 800m; sailing & windsurfing 1km; cycle hire; games area; entmnt; some statics; dogs €2; poss cr; Eng spkn; adv bkg (acc in writing Jan-May); quiet; red low ssn; ccard acc. "Excel, well-run site; busy rd to beach, but worth it; many sm coves; tourist office on site; gd area for cycling." 12 Apr-20 Sep. € 29.00 2008*

ARGELES SUR MER *10G1* (2km N Rural) *42.5724, 3.02171* **Camping Le Dauphin, Route de Taxo à la Mer, 66701 Argelès-sur-Mer [04 68 81 17 54; fax 04 68 95 82 60; info@campingledauphin.com; www.campingledauphin.com]** Fr Perpignan take D914 (N114) sp Elne & Argelès-sur-Mer. 4km after Elne, sp on L to Taxo d'Avall, turn L, site 2km on R. Lge, hdg/mkd pitches, pt shd; wc; chem disp; private bthrms avail some pitches - extra charge; baby facs; shwrs inc; el pnts (10A) €4.50; gas; Indtte; shop; rest; snacks; bar; BBQ (gas/elec); playgrnd; 2 pools; paddling pool; sand beach 3km; fishing; sailing; windsurfing; tennis; games area; games rm; internet; entmnt; TV rm; 80% statics; dogs €3.50; Eng spkn; adv bkg; ccard acc; quiet. "Gd for families; superb pool area; excel facs; free transport to beach high ssn; helpful staff; vg site." ♦ 15 May-18 Sep. € 27.70 2009*

See advertisement opposite

ARGELES SUR MER *10G1* (2km N Coastal) *42.55775, 3.03140* **Camping Paris Roussillon, Route de Tamariguer, Quartier Pujol, 66700 Argelès-sur-Mer [04 68 81 19 71; fax 04 68 81 68 77; contact@parisroussillon.com; www.parisroussillon.com or www.camping-franceloc.fr]** Fr Perpignan, take D914 (N114), junc 10 twds Pujol. Site 2km on R. Lge, mkd pitch, shd; wc, chem disp; shwrs inc; baby facs; el pnts (6A) €3.50; Indtte; shop 1km; rest; snacks; bar; BBQ; playgrnd; pool; beach 1.5km; tennis; games area; some statics; dogs €2.50; Eng spkn; quiet. ♦ 15 May-30 Sep. € 23.60 2007*

ARGELES SUR MER *10G1* (2km NE Coastal) *42.56728, 3.04425* **Camp Municipal Roussillonnais, Blvd de la Mer, 66700 Argelès-sur-Mer [04 68 81 10 42; fax 04 68 95 96 11; camping.rouss@infonie.fr; www.le-roussillonnais.com]** S fr Perpignan on D914 (N114) thro Elne to Argelès-sur-Mer, turn L in Argelès-sur-Mer foll coast rd & site on R in 1.5km. V lge, hdg/mkd pitch, pt shd; wc (some cont); chem disp; mv service pnt; baby facs; shwrs inc; el pnts (6A) €3.80; gas; Indtte; shop; rest; snacks; bar; playgrnd; sand beach 500m; boating; watersports; tennis; games area; entmnt; some statics; dogs €1.50; shuttle bus to beach; poss cr; Eng spkn; adv bkg; quiet; ccard acc; CCI. "Site open all yr for m'vans; ltd facs low ssn." 20 Apr-27 Sep. € 22.50 2009*

ARGELES SUR MER *10G1* (2km NE Coastal) *42.54819, 3.03617* **Camping du Stade, 8 Ave du 8 Mai 1945, 66702 Argelès-sur-Mer [04 68 81 04 40; fax 04 68 95 84 55; info@campingdustade.com; www.campingdustade.com]** S on D914 (N114) thro traff lts at Argelès; turn L after 400m at clearly mkd turn sp 'A la Plage'. Site 800m on L. Lge, shd; wc; baby facs; shwrs inc; el pnts (6A) inc; Indtte; shop 500m; rest; snacks; bar; playgrnd; sand beach 800m; sports complex adj; entmnt; TV rm; some statics; dogs €2; poss cr; adv bkg rec high ssn; quiet; red low ssn. "Lge pitches; gd walking area; mountain views; friendly owners." 1 Apr-30 Sep. € 23.00 2007*

France

ARGELES SUR MER *10G1* (2km NE Coastal) *42.57245, 3.04115* **Camping La Marende, Chemin de la Salanque, 66702 Argelès-sur-Mer [tel/fax 04 68 81 03 88; info@marende.com; www.marende.com]** Fr Perpignan S on D914 (N114) exit junc 10 Argelès-sur-Mer; foll sp Plage Nord; after 2km at rndabt turn L sp St Cyprian; at next rndabt turn R sp Plages Nord & Sud; site on L in 800m. L onto unmade rd. V lge, hdg/mkd pitch, shd; wc; chem disp; some serviced pitches; mv service pnt; baby facs; shwrs inc; el pnts (6-10A) inc; gas; Indtte; ice shop; rest & snacks (high ssn); bar; BBQ (el/gas); playgrnd; pool & paddling pool; jacuzzi; games area; sand beach adj; aquarobics, scuba-diving lessons Jul & Aug; internet; TV; 12% statics; dogs €2.50; phone; poss cr; Eng spkn; quiet; adv bkg; ccard acc; CCI. "Beautiful site; lge pitches; friendly, helpful family owners; 1st class facs; excel pool; many static tents high ssn; gd area for cycling & walking." ♦ 26 Apr-27 Sep. € 26.00 2007*

ARGELES SUR MER *10G1* (2km NE Rural) *42.56940, 3.02713* **Camping La Sirène, Route de Taxo, 66701 Argelès-sur-Mer [04 68 81 04 61; fax 04 68 81 69 74; contact@camping-lasirene.fr; www.camping-lasirene.fr]** Take D914 (N114) fr Perpignan twd Argelès. Cross Rv Tech & take 1st L twd Taxo d'Avall, site 1 of many about 2.5km on R. V lge, mkd pitch, shd; wc; baby facs; shwrs inc; el pnts (12A) €3; gas; Indtte; shop; rest; snacks; bar; BBQ; cooking facs; playgrnd; pool; waterslide; sand beach 1.5km; fishing, sailing & windsurfing 1km; tennis; horseriding; archery; cycle hire; games area; dogs €4; adv bkg; quiet; red low ssn. "Well-appointed site; gd pool complex." ♦ 18 Apr-28 Sep. € 43.00 2008*

ARGELES SUR MER *10G1* (2km NE Coastal) *42.56544, 3.03653* **Camping Le Neptune, Chemin de Tamariguer, Plage Nord, 66700 Argelès-sur-Mer [04 68 81 02 98 or 04 99 57 20 25; fax 04 68 81 00 41; www.village-center.com]** Fr Argelès-Plage take D81 coast rd to Argelès-Plage Nord & site sp on L. Lge, hdg/mkd pitch, hdstg, pt shd; wc; chem disp; baby facs; shwrs inc; el pnts (6A); gas; Indtte; shop; tradsmn; rest; snacks; bar; BBQ (gas); playgrnd; pool; paddling pool; waterslide; sand beach 350m; golf 7km; entmnt; dogs €3.50; golf 7km; cycle hire; entmnt; 60% statics; dogs; €3; poss cr; Eng spkn; adv bkg; ccard acc; red low ssn; CCI. "Busy, well-maintained site; gd san facs; vg." ♦ 21 Apr-16 Sep. € 38.00 2007*

ARGELES SUR MER *10G1* (3km NE Coastal) *42.55682, 3.04082* **Camping Beauséjour, Ave de Tech, Argelès-Plage, 66700 Argelès-sur-Mer [04 68 81 10 63; fax 04 68 95 75 08; contact@camping-lebeausejour.com; www.camping-lebeausejour.com]** Fr Perpignan, foll D914 (N114) to Argelès-sur-Mer. Turn L after Champion supmkt & Shell g'ge; foll sp to Plage Nord. At coast rd turn R to Argelès-Plage cent. Site on R shortly after supmkt. Lge, mkd pitch, shd; wc; chem disp; shwrs inc; el pnts (4A) inc; Indtte; shop adj; snacks, playgrnd; 2 pools; paddling pool; waterslide; jacuzzi; sand beach 300m; entmnt; 50% statics; dogs; phone; poss cr; Eng spkn; adv bkg rec; CCI. ♦ 1 Apr-30 Sep. € 34.00 (3 persons) 2006*

ARGELES SUR MER *10G1* (3.5km NE Coastal) *42.57543, 3.0431* **Camping Le Soleil, Route du Littoral, Plage-Nord, 66700 Argelès-sur-Mer [04 68 81 14 48 or 04 68 95 94 62 (LS); fax 04 68 81 44 34; camping.lesoleil@wanadoo.fr; www.campmed.com]** Exit D914 (N114) junc 10 & foll sp Argelès Plage-Nord. Turn L onto D81 to site. Site sp among others. V lge, mkd pitch, pt shd; wc (some cont); chem disp; mv service pnt; baby facs; shwrs inc; el pnts (6A) €3.70; gas; Indtte; ice; shop; tradsmn; rest; snacks; bar; no BBQ; playgrnd; pool; paddling pool; sand beach adj; rv fishing adj; tennis; cycle hire; horseriding; games area; entmnt; wifi; TV; 50% statics; no dogs; phone; Eng spkn; adv bkg (ess Aug); noisy nr disco; ccard acc; red low ssn. "Lovely views; excel site for partially-sighted & handicapped; rec visit to Collioure; vg." ♦ 16 May-30 Sep. € 32.50 2009*

ARGELES SUR MER *10G1* (500m E Coastal) *42.55072, 3.03120* **Camping La Massane, 25 Ave Molière (Zone Pujol), 66700 Argelès-sur-Mer [04 68 81 06 85; fax 04 68 81 59 18; camping.massane@infonie.fr; www.camping-massane.com]** Fr D914 (N114) exit junc 10, at traff island take 2nd exit, site sp further down rd. Site just bef municipal stadium on L. Lge, hdg/mkd pitch, pt shd; wc (some cont); chem disp; baby facs; shwrs inc; el pnts (6A) inc; gas; Indtte; shop & 500m; snacks; bar; BBQ (gas/elec only); playgrnd; htd pool; paddling pool; sand beach 1km; tennis adj; entmnt, excursions high ssn; dogs €2; poss cr; Eng spkn; adv bkg rec high ssn; red long stay/low ssn; quiet; ccard acc; CCI. "Vg site; friendly welcome; steel pegs req." ♦ 15 Mar-5 Oct. € 25.50 2008*

ARGELES SUR MER *10G1* (1km E Coastal) *42.54993, 3.04183* **Camping Europe, Ave du Général de Gaulle, 66700 Argelès-sur-Mer [04 68 81 08 10; fax 04 68 95 71 84; camping.europe@wanadoo.fr; www.camping-europe.net]** Fr Perpignan take D914 (N114) to Argelès-sur-Mer. Exit junc 12 to Argelès. At rndabt take last exit L to Argelès Ville. At next rndabt turn R, site on L after Dyneff g'ge 50m fr 'Tropical Golf'. Med, mkd pitch, shd; wc; chem disp; baby facs; shwrs inc; el pnts (10A) €4; gas; lndtte; shop; tradsmn; rest; snacks; bar; BBQ; playgrnd; pool 800m; sand beach 300m; 10% statics; dogs €1.65; phone; bus adj; poss cr; Eng spkn; adv bkg; quiet; CCI. "Friendly, secure, family-run site; gd san facs." Easter-27 Sep. € 17.00 2008*

ARGELES SUR MER *10G1* (2km E Urban/Coastal) *42.55317, 3.04375* **Camping La Chapelle, Ave du Tech, 66702 Argelès-sur-Mer [04 68 81 28 14; fax 04 68 95 83 82; contact@camping-la-chapelle.com; www.camping-la-chapelle.com]** Fr A9 exit junc 42 onto D900 (N9)/D914 (N114) to Argelès-sur-Mer. At junc 10 cont thro Argelès vill & foll sp Argelès-Plage. In 2.5km turn L at rndabt, bear L at Office de Tourisme, site immed L. Lge, hdg/mkd pitch, shd; wc (mainly cont); baby facs; shwrs inc; el pnts (6A) €6; lndtte; shop; rests, snacks, bar 100m; playgrnd; pool 2km; beach 200m; tennis 200m; entmnt; 30% statics; dogs €4; poss cr; Eng spkn; adv bkg; quiet; CCI. "Ltd facs low ssn; gd." ♦ 30 May-27 Sep. € 26.00 2008*

ARGELES SUR MER *10G1* (3km SE Coastal) *42.53311, 3.05200* **Camping La Coste Rouge, Route de Collioure, Zone Le Racou, 66700 Argelès-sur-Mer [04 68 81 08 94; fax 04 68 95 94 17; info@lacosterouge.com; www.lacoste rouge.com]** Exit junc 13 fr D914 (N114) dir Port-Argelès. At 2nd rndabt foll D114 to Racou, site on L. Med, pt sl, terr, shd; wc (some cont); chem disp; baby facs; shwrs inc; el pnts (6A) inc; lndtte; shop; rest; snacks; bar; no BBQ; playgrnd; pool; paddling pool; sand beach 1km; games rm; entmnt; some statics; dogs €2.30; phone; adv bkg; quiet; ccard acc. "Beautiful pool; gd touring base; aquarium at Banyuls-sur-Mer; cloisters at Elne." ♦ 1 Jun-15 Sep. € 25.80 2007*

ARGELES SUR MER *10G1* (4km SE Coastal) *42.53413, 3.06826* **Camping Les Criques de Porteils, Corniche de Collioure, 66701 Argelès-sur-Mer [04 68 81 12 73; fax 04 68 95 85 76; info@lescriques.fr; www.lescriques.com or www.les-castels.com]** Fr N on A9/E15 take exit junc 42 onto D914 (N114) Argelès-sur-Mer. Fr S exit junc 43 onto D914. At exit 13 leave D914 sp Collioure & foll site sp. Site by Hôtel du Golfe 1.5km fr Collioure. Lge, hdg/mkd pitch, pt sl, terr, pt shd; htd wc (some cont); chem disp; mv service pnt; baby facs; shwrs inc; el pnts (5A) inc; gas; lndtte; shop; rest; snacks; bar; playgrnd; htd pool; sand/shgl beach adj; boat excursions; fishing; watersports; scuba-diving; organised walks; games rm; games area; internet; TV rm; 15% statics; dogs €2; phone; Eng spkn; adv bkg; quiet; red low ssn/CCI. "Variable size pitches - not all suitable for lge o'fits; steps to beach; much improved/refurbished site." ♦ 5 Apr-28 Sep. € 38.00 2008*

ARGELES SUR MER *10G1* (2.5km SW Rural) *42.53999, 2.99515* **Camping Le Romarin, Route de Sorède, Chemin des Vignes,66702 Argelès-sur-Mer [04 68 81 02 63; fax 04 68 81 57 43; contact@camping-romarin.com; www.camping-romarin.com]** S fr Perpignon on D914 (N114); at rndabt junc with D618 foll sp St André on minor rd; in 500m L & immed L & foll sp to site. Or fr A9 exit junc 43; foll D618 to rndabt junc with D914; then as above. Med, pt sl, shd; wc (some cont); shwrs inc; el pnts (6A) €2-3.50; gas; lndtte; shop; rest; snacks; bar; playgrnd; pool; waterslide; beach 4km; sports activities; entmnt; some statics; dogs €3 (not acc Jul/Aug); train 2km; Eng spkn; adv bkg; quiet; red low ssn. "Pleasant site; conv Spanish border." 15 May-30 Sep. € 32.50 2009*

ARGELES SUR MER *10G1* (5km SW Urban) *42.53425, 2.95655* **Camping Les Micocouliers, Route de Palau, 66690 Sorède [04 68 89 20 27; fax 04 68 89 25 61; contact@camping-les-micocouliers.com; www.camping-les-micocouliers.com]** A9 S dir Le Boulou exit junc 43 onto D618 dir Argelès-sur-Mer; R onto D11 to Sorède, sp to site. Lge, hdg/mkd pitch, pt sl, shd; wc; chem disp; shrws inc; el pnts (6A) €3.80; gas; lndtte; shops & in vill; tradsmn; snacks; bar; BBQ; playgrnd; pool; beach 20km; tennis adj; cycle hire; TV rm; 5% statics; dogs €2.10; poss v cr; adv bkg ess Jul-Aug. "Lge pitches; conv N Spain, eg Figueres, Dali museum." ♦ 26 Jun-15 Sep. € 22.00 2007*

ARGELES SUR MER *10G1* (8km W Urban) *42.52667, 2.93515* **Camp Municipal Le Vivier, 31 Rue du Stade, 66740 Laroque-des-Albères [04 68 89 00 93 or 04 68 89 21 13; fax 04 68 95 42 58; camping.des.alberes@wanadoo.fr; www.campin-des-alberes.com]** D2 fr Argelès-sur-Mer to Laroque-des-Albères; foll sp in cent of vill. Lge, mkd pitch, pt sl, pt shd; wc; chem disp; shwrs inc; el pnts (6A) €4; lndtte; shop 300m; 5% statics; dogs €3; bus 300m; adv bkg; quiet; CCI. "Peaceful, simple site at edge Pyrenees, pleasant vill; vg." ♦ 15 Jun-15 Sep. € 22.00 2006*

ARGELES SUR MER *10G1* (8km W Rural) *42.52366, 2.94446* **Camping Les Albères, 66740 Laroque-des-Albères [04 68 89 23 64; fax 04 68 89 14 30; camping-des-alberes@wanadoo.fr; www.camping-des-alberes.com]** Fr A9 exit junc 43 onto D618 dir Argelès-sur-Mer/Port Vendres. Turn R onto D50 to Laroque-des-Albères. In vill at T-junc turn L, then turn R at rndabt & foll sp to site on D11. Lge, mkd pitch, terr, pt shd; wc (some cont); chem disp; mv service pnt; baby facs; shwrs inc; el pnts (6-10A) €4; lndtte; shop; rest; snacks; bar; BBQ (gas only); playgrnd; pool (high ssn); sand beach 8km; tennis; TV; rm; entmnt; 5% statics; dogs €3; phone; quiet; poss cr; red low ssn; CCI. "Attractive site under slopes of Pyrenees; gd walking area; peaceful (apart fr cockerel!); friendly owners; excel." ♦ 1 Apr-30 Sep. € 23.00 2008*

ARGELES SUR MER *10G1* (8km W Rural) *42.52547, 2.91412* **Camping-Caravaning Las Planes, 117 Ave du Vallespir, 66740 Laroque-des-Albères [04 68 89 21 36 or 06 24 49 06 46 (mob); fax 04 68 89 01 42; info@lasplanes.com; www.lasplanes.com]** Exit A9 junc 43 onto D618 dir Argelès. In 8.5km take D2 S dir Laroque. In vill turn W onto D11, site on L in 2km - steep ent. Med, pt sl, shd, mkd pitch; wc; chem disp; shwrs inc; el pnts (4-6A) €4; gas; Indtte; shop; snacks; bar; BBQ (el/gas); playgrnd; 2 pools; sand beach 8km; cycle hire; dogs €2.50; poss cr; adv bkg rec high ssn; quiet; CCI. "Friendly owners & staff; gd security; pitches tight due o'hanging trees." 15 Jun-31 Aug. € 20.00 2008*

ARGELES SUR MER *10G1* (2km NW Rural) *42.57018, 3.01239* **Camping Etoile d'Or, Route de Taxo d'Avall, 66701 Argelès-sur-Mer [04 68 81 04 34; fax 04 68 81 57 05; info@aletoiledor.com; www.aletoiledor.com]** Fr D914 (N114) exit junc 10 dir Taxo-Plage. Site in 1km on R. Lge, mkd pitch, shd; wc (cont); baby facs; shwrs inc; el pnts (4A) inc; gas; Indtte; shop; rest; snacks; bar; el/gas BBQ; playgrnd; pool; sand beach 2.5km; tennis; games rm; entmnt; TV rm; many statics; dogs €3; adv bkg; quiet. ♦ 15 Mar-15 Sep. € 31.00 2007*

ARGENTAN *4E1* (500m SE Urban) *48.73991, -0.01668* **Camp Municipal du Parc de la Noë, 34 Rue de la Noë, 61200 Argentan [02 33 36 05 69; fax 02 33 36 52 07; tourisme.argentan@wanadoo.fr; www.argentan.fr]** S fr Caen on N158/D958 foll camping sp fr by-pass. Sm, shd; htd wc; chem disp; mv service pnt; shwrs; el pnts (10A) €2.30; Indtte; shop 1km; playgrnd; pool 1km; rv & pond; sports area; TV; few statics; poss cr; adv bkg ess high ssn; quiet. "Superb, clean, tidy site adj town park; helpful warden; excel, clean san facs; gd disabled facs; lovely town." ♦ 1 Apr-30 Sep. € 8.30 2009*

🅃 **ARGENTAN** *4E1* (2km S Rural) *48.71841, -0.01077* **FFCC Aire Naturelle du Val de Baize (Huet des Aunay), 18 Rue de Mauvaisville, 61200 Argentan [02 33 67 27 11; fax 02 33 35 39 16]** Take D958 (N158) fr Argentan twd Sées & Alençon; site clealy sp on D958 - turn R just bef leaving Argentan boundary. Site adj T-junc N of farm buildings. Sm, some hdstg, pt shd; wc; chem disp; mv service pnt; shwrs inc; el pnts (3-6A) €2.50-4.60; gas; shops 1.5km; snacks; playgrnd; pool 2.5km; B&B; 10% statics; dogs; Eng spkn; adv bkg; quiet; ccard not acc; CCI. "Charming, well-kept site; lge pitches in orchard; clean but dated facs, ltd low ssn; friendly welcome; NH only." € 10.00 2008*

ARGENTAT *7C4* (10km N Rural) *45.16601, 1.97861* **Camp Municipal La Croix de Brunal, 19320 St Martin-la-Méanne [05 55 29 11 91 or 05 55 29 12 75 (Mairie); fax 05 55 29 28 48]** Fr Argentat take D18 to St Martin-la-Méanne. Site well sp on ent to vill. Sm, hdg pitch, pt shd; wc; shwrs inc; el pnts (5A); gas, Indtte; shop 1km; rest, snacks, bar 1km; BBQ; htd pool 1km; sand beach 15km; rv sw 8km; tennis 1km; games area; some statics; dogs; phone; quiet. "Simple site; warden calls am & pm; gd walking; fishing, horseriding, watersports within 15km." ♦ 15 Jun-15 Sep. 2006*

ARGENTAT *7C4* (1km NE Urban) *45.10205, 1.94390* **Camp Municipal Le Langour, Route d'Egletons, 19400 Argentat [05 55 28 13 84; fax 05 55 28 81 26; mairie.argentat@wanadoo.fr; www.argentat.fr]** Fr cent of Argentat head N dir Egletons on D18. Med, pt shd; wc; chem disp; shwrs inc; el pnts €2.90; Indtte; shops 1km; tradsmn; playgrnd; htd pool & sports complex adj; tennis; fishing; dogs €1.20; phone; poss cr; quiet. "Efficiently run, clean site; pleasant rvside walk to old quay & cafés; gd touring base Dordogne; excel." 15 Jun-14 Sep. € 9.70 2009*

ARGENTAT *7C4* (4km NE Rural) *45.11151, 1.95908* **Camping Château de Gibanel, 19400 St Martial-Entraygues [05 55 28 10 11; fax 05 55 28 81 62; contact@camping-gibanel.com; www.camping-gibanel.com]** Exit Argentat on D18 twd Egletons & fork R on lakeside past hydro-electric dam. Sp fr all dir. Site in grounds of sm castle on N bank of Rv Dordogne. App rd narr but satisfactory. Lge, mkd pitch, pt sl, pt shd; wc (some cont); chem disp; child/baby facs; fam bthrm; shwrs inc; el pnts (6A) €3.20; gas; Indtte; shop; tradsmn; rest; snacks; bar; BBQ; playgrnd; pool; paddling pool; lake sw; sports area; boating; fishing; entmnt; games rm; TV; 15% statics; dogs €1.50 (free low ssn); Eng spkn; adv bkg; quiet; red low ssn; ccard acc; CCI. "Excel, well-managed site in beautiful location; helpful owner; gd san facs, ltd low ssn; various pitch sizes; lovely sm town." ♦ 31 May-7 Sep. € 17.20 2008*

ARGENTAT *7C4* (3km SW Rural) *45.08135, 1.92945* **Camping Europe, Le Chambon, 19400 Monceaux-sur-Dordogne [05 55 28 07 70; fax 05 55 28 19 60; camping-europe@wanadoo.fr; www.camping-europe.fr]** Fr Argentat take D12 twd Beaulieu-sur-Dordogne. Site 2km fr D1120 (N120). Ent on L by awkward RH bend in Le Chambon. Med, mkd pitch, pt sl, pt shd; wc; chem disp; mv service pnt; shwrs inc; el pnts (5A) €3.10; gas; Indtte; shops 1km; rest 500m; snacks 1km; playgrnd; pool; tennis; games area; entmnt; some statics; dogs €1.60; poss cr; quiet. "Lovely rvside site; interesting town." 5 Apr-8 Nov. € 17.40 2007*

ARGENTAT *7C4* (4km SW Rural) *45.07531, 1.91689* **Camping Sunêlia au Soleil d'Oc, 19400 Monceaux-sur-Dordogne [05 55 28 84 84 or 05 55 28 05 97 (LS); fax 05 55 28 12 12; info@dordogne-soleil.com; www.dordogne-soleil.com]** Fr N exit A20 junc 46a dir Tulle, then D1120 (N120) to Argentat. Fr Argentat take D12 sp Beaulieu. In 4km in Laygues turn L over bdge x-ing Rv Dordogne, site in 300m. Med, hdg/mkd pitch, terr, pt shd; wc (some cont); chem disp; mv service pnt; baby facs; shwrs inc; el pnts (6A) €4.10; gas; Indtte (inc dryer); shop; rest; snacks; bar; BBQ; playgrnd; pool & paddling pool; rv & shgl beach; canoeing; games area; games rm; cycle hire; archery; entmnt; wifi; TV; some statics; dogs €3 (free low ssn); phone; Eng spkn; adv bkg; quiet; ccard acc; red low ssn/long stay/CCI. "Ideal family site high ssn & quiet, peaceful low ssn; some pitches on rv bank; gd walking & other activities; many beautiful vills in area; tours arranged." ♦ 4 Apr-14 Nov. € 20.70 (CChq acc) 2008*

France

ARGENTAT *7C4* (6km SW Rural) *45.05736, 1.91479* **Camping du Saulou, Vergnolles, 19400 Monceaux-sur-Dordogne [05 55 28 12 33; fax 05 55 28 80 67; le.saulou@wanadoo.fr; www.saulou.net]** S on D1120 (N120), turn at N o'skts of Argentat onto D12, sp Beaulieu. Foll rv L sp Vergnolles & camp sp. Lge, hdg/mkd pitch, pt shd; wc (some cont); chem disp; shwrs inc; el pnts (4-13A) €2.60-3.55; gas; lndtte; shop & 1km; tradsmn; rest; snacks; bar; playgrnd; htd pool; paddling pool; boating; fishing; games area; entmnt; TV rm; 10% statics; dogs €2.05; phone; poss cr; Eng spkn; adv bkg; quiet low ssn; red low ssn; ccard acc; CCI. "Early dep arrange el pts disconnect night bef; facs constantly cleaned; friendly, helpful owners." 1 Apr-30 Sep. € 18.65 2007*

ARGENTAT *7C4* (9km SW Rural) *45.04583, 1.88388* **Camping Le Vaurette, 19400 Monceaux-sur-Dordogne [05 55 28 09 67; fax 05 55 28 81 14; info@vaurette.com; www.vaurette.com]** SW fr Tulle on D1120 (N120); fr Argentat SW on D12 sp Beaulieu; site sp on banks of Rv Dordogne. Med, mkd pitch, pt shd; wc; chem disp; mv service pnt; baby facs; shwrs inc; el pnts (6A) €3.30; gas; lndtte; shop; snacks; bar; BBQ; playgrnd; htd pool; shgl beach & rv sw adj; tennis; badminton; fishing; canoe expeditions; games area; games rm; wifi; TV rm; statics; dogs €3.50; Eng spkn; adv bkg; quiet; ccard acc; red low ssn; CCI. "Lovely setting; helpful, friendly owners; many sports avail." ♦ 1 May 21 Sep. € 23.50 2009*

ARGENTIERE LA BESSEE, L' *9C3* (6km N Rural) *44.85758, 6.58979* **Camping de l'Iscle de Prelles, Hameau de Prelles, 05120 St Martin-de-Queyrieres [04 92 20 28 66; contact@camping-iscledeprelles.com; www.camping-iscledeprelles.com]** S fr Briançon on N94; in 5km turn L opp Intermarché supmkt, go over unguarded level x-ing (quiet line), track turns R & site in 500m. Foll sp. Med, mkd pitch, pt shd; (htd winter) wc (some cont); chem disp; baby facs; shwrs inc; el pnts (4-10A) €3.70-7.10; gas; lndtte; sm shop; rest; snacks; bar; BBQ; playgrnd; htd pool; shgl beach 400m; rv adj; climbing; gd walking; skiing; quad bikes; rafting; horseriding; games area; tennis; paint ball; entmnt; internet; 25% statics; no twin axles; TV; dogs €1.60; phone; train 5km; Eng spkn; adv bkg; quiet; no ccard acc; CCI. "Attractive mountain aspects; cable car; gd long stay for children; new owners 2007 with plans; vg." ♦ 1 Dec-30 Sep. € 17.00 2007*

ARGENTIERE LA BESSEE, L' *9C3* (2.5km S Rural) *44.77775, 6.55798* **Camp Municipal Les Ecrins, 05120 L'Argentière-la-Bessée [04 92 23 03 38; fax 04 92 23 07 71; contact@camping-les-ecrins.com; www.camping-les-ecrins.com]** Fr L'Argentière on N94, turn R onto D104, site sp. Med, some mkd pitch, pt shd, htd wc (some cont); shwrs inc; el pnts (10A) €2.40; lndtte; shop; snacks; playgrnd; walking; kayaking; games area; dogs €1; phone; adv bkg; rd/rlwy noise. "Mountain scenery." ♦ 18 Apr-15 Sep. € 12.50 2006*

⊞ **ARGENTIERE LA BESSEE, L'** *9C3* (5km S Rural) *44.75765, 6.57995* **FFCC Camping Le Verger, 05310 La Roche-de-Rame [tel/fax 04 92 20 92 23; info@campingleverger.com; www.campingleverger.com]** S fr Briançon on N94; site 500m L of road bef vill; sp. Sm, hdg pitch, terr, shd; wc; chem disp; mv service pnt; shwrs inc; el pnts (3-10A) €2.10-3.60; lndtte; shop 5km; rest, snacks, bar 1km; lake sw 1km; TV; 25% statics; dogs; phone; bus 5km; Eng spkn; adv bkg; quiet; red low ssn. "Grass pitches in orchard; excel, well-maintained facs; excel." € 15.00 2009*

ARGENTIERE LA BESSEE, L' *9C3* (4km NW Rural) *44.82455, 6.52575* **CAMPEOLE Camping Le Courounba, Le Village, 05120 Les Vigneaux [04 92 23 02 09; fax 04 92 23 04 69; courounba@campeole.com or campeolelesvigneaux@orange.fr; www.camping-courounba.com or www.campeole.com]** Take N94 S fr Briançon to L'Argentiere-la-Bessée, turn R onto D994E dir Vallouise. Site on L over rv bdge. Lge, hdstg, pt shd; htd wc; chem disp; mv service pnt; baby facs; shwrs inc; el pnts (6A) €4.10 (poss long lead req); lndtte (inc dryer); shop 500m; tradsmn; rest; snacks; bar; BBQ; playgrnd; htd pool; paddling pool; waterslide; fishing; tennis; cycle hire; horseriding nr; wifi; entmnt; TV; 20% statics; dogs; phone; Eng spkn; adv bkg; quiet; ccard acc; red low ssn; CCI. "Gd site, beautifully situated in woods by rv in mountains; gd clean san facs; no site lighting." ♦ 29 May-19 Sep. € 20.60 2009*

See advertisement

ARGENTIERE LA BESSEE, L' *9C3* (8km NW Rural) *44.84354, 6.48989* **Camping Les Chambonnettes, 05290 Vallouise [tel/fax 04 92 23 30 26 or 06 82 23 65 09 (mob); campingvallouise@hotmail.fr; http://camping chambonnettesvallouise.chez-alice.fr]** Take N94 Briançon-Gap, on N o'skts of L'Argentière-la-Bessée take D994 W dir Vallouise. In cent of Vallouise turn L over bdge & immed L, site in 200m on rvside. Lge, mkd pitch, pt sl, pt shd; htd wc (some cont); chem disp; mv service pnt; shwrs inc; el pnts (3-6A) €3.30; gas 1.5km; Indtte; shops 200m; tradsmn, rest, snacks, bar 500m; playgrnd; pool 3km; tennis; TV; 50% statics; dogs €1.80; phone; poss cr; Eng spkn; adv bkg; quiet; red low ssn "Mountain scenery; basic facs; gd cent for walking, skiing, canoeing; white-water rafting at nrby rv; interesting vill; fair." 15 Dec-1 Oct. € 13.50 2009*

ARGENTON LES VALLEES (FORMERLY ARGENTON CHATEAU) *4H1* (500m N Rural) *46.9877, -0.4504* **Camp Municipal du Lac d'Hautibus, Rue de la Sablière, 79150 Argenton-les-Vallées [05 49 65 95 08 or 05 49 65 70 22 (Mairie); fax 05 49 65 70 84; mairie-argenton-chateau@cegetel.net]** Fr E or W on D759, site well sp in town, on lakeside. Med, hdg pitch, pt sl, terr; wc (some cont); chem disp; mv service pnt; shwrs inc; el pnts (10A) €2.35; Indtte; shops in town; playgrnd; pool 100m; lake sw 500m; some statics; quiet; CCI. "Beautifully-situated, well-kept site; interesting town; vg." ♦ 1 Apr-30 Sep. € 8.10 2009*

ARGENTON SUR CREUSE *7A3* (12km SE Rural) *46.50709, 1.58355* **La Chaumerette Camping Club à Tou Vert, 36190 Gargilesse-Dampierre [02 54 47 73 44; camping lachaumerette@wanadoo.fr]** Fr A20 take exit 17 for D48 to Badecon-le-Pin then R onto D40. Turn R sp Barsize then foll sp to site. Sm, shd; wc; chem disp; baby facs; shwrs inc; el pnts (6A) inc; tradsmn; snacks; bar; playgrnd; fishing; adv bkg; quiet; CCI. "Superb location in wooded valley adj rv; gd san facs; additional overflow area when site full; pay at sm bar/rest adj; excel." 1 Apr-31 Oct. € 7.50 2009*

ARGENTON SUR CREUSE *7A3* (12km SW Rural) *46.54192, 1.40328* **Camping La Petite Brenne (Naturist), La Grande Metairie, 36800 Luzeret [02 54 25 05 78; fax 02 54 25 05 97; info@lapetitebrenne.com; www.lapetite brenne.com]** Fr A20 exit junc 18 sp Luzeret/Prissac; foll D55 to Luzeret vill. After bdge in vill turn L, then next L to site. Lge, pt sl, unshd; wc; chem disp; sauna; shwrs inc; el pnts (10A) €4 (long leads poss req); Indtte; shop 12km; tradsmn; rest; bar; playgrnd; 2 pools (1 htd); horseriding; wifi; no dogs; Eng spkn; adv bkg rec high ssn; quiet; ccard acc; red long stay/low ssn. "Friendly Dutch owners; lge pitches; excel san facs; ideal for children; pools excel; gd rest; gd walking in National Park; excel." 27 Apr-27 Sep. € 24.00 2009*

ARGENTON SUR CREUSE *7A3* (2km NW Rural) *46.59636, 1.50619* **Camp Municipal Les Chambons, Route des Chambons, 36200 Argenton-sur-Creuse [02 54 24 15 26 or 02 54 22 26 61; fax 02 54 22 58 80; entreprisefrery@ orange.fr; www.ot-argenton-sur-creuse.fr]** Fr A20 exit junc 17 onto D937 dir Argenton; turn R at rndabt, then L at mini rndabt nr supmkt sp St Marcel; foll rd downhill over rlwy bdge; then 1st R in 100m. But best app fr N on D927 to avoid traff calming rd humps; at town sp cross rlwy bdge & turn R immed past LH turn for Roman archaeological museum; foll camping sp on narr, busy app rd. Med, mkd pitch, some hdstg, pt sl, shd; wc; chem disp; shwrs inc; el pnts (5A) €3.40 (poss long lead req); gas; shop 1.5km; tradsmn; bar; rest 1km; playgrnd; quiet but some rd noise. "Beautiful, well-kept, peaceful site by rv; helpful warden; v muddy after heavy rain & poss uneven pitches by rv; rvside walk into old town; no need to unhitch so useful for early start; quiet in day, busy in evening as NH high ssn; interesting town; excel." 15 May-15 Sep. € 13.20 2009*

ARGENTON SUR CREUSE *7A3* (6km NW Rural) *46.62965, 1.47882* **Camp Municipal des Rives de la Bouzanne, 36800 Le Pont Chrétien-Chabenet [02 54 25 80 53 or 02 54 25 81 40 (Mairie); fax 02 54 25 87 59]** Exit A20 junc 17 onto D927; site well sp over rv bdge. Or fr St Gaultier on D927 dir Argenton-sur-Creuse; turn R in Le Pont Chrétien-Chabenet, bef rv bdge, site 50m on L. Med, pt shd; wc (some cont); chem disp (wc); shwrs inc; el pnts €2.50; Indtte; shop, bar adj; playgrnd; rv adj; games rm; dogs €0.50; adv bkg rec; quiet; CCI. "Picturesque, quiet site; gd, drained pitches; immac san facs; conv A20." 15 Jun-15 Sep. € 7.00 2009*

ARLANC *9C1* (1km W Rural) *45.41344, 3.71866* **Camp Municipal Le Metz, Loumas, 63220 Arlanc [04 73 95 15 62; fax 04 73 95 78 31; jardin-terre.arlanc@ wanadoo.fr; www.arlanc.fr]** Fr Ambert on D906 to Arlanc, turn R (W) onto D300 (D999A) dir St Germain-l'Herm. Site on R in 800m, sp. Med, some hdg pitch, pt shd; wc (some cont); chem disp (wc); shwrs inc; el pnts (6A) inc (long lead poss req); Indtte (inc dryer); shop 800m; rest, snacks & bar 150m; playgrnd; pool 100m; games area; 10% statics; dogs; phone; adv bkg; quiet. "Lace-making museum in Arlanc." ♦ 15 Jun-30 Sep. € 11.40 2009*

ARLES *10E2* (8km NE Rural) *43.72336, 4.71861* **Camp Municipal des Pins, Rue Michelet, 13990 Fontvieille [04 90 54 78 69; fax 04 90 54 81 25; campmunicipal. lespins@wanadoo.fr]** Take D570 (N570) fr Arles to Avignon; in 2km turn R on D17 to Fontvieille; at far end of vill turn R & foll sp. Med, pt sl, shd; wc; shwrs inc; el pnts (6A) €3; gas fr Shell g'ge in vill; shops 1km; pool 500m high ssn; dogs €1.30; bus; poss cr; Eng spkn; adv bkg; red long stay: CCI. "Delightful, quiet site in pines; friendly staff; vg facs; 15-20 mins walk to lively vill; quiet forest walks; tight access/exit long o'fits." 1 Apr-30 Sep. € 12.00 2009*

⊞ **ARLES** *10E2* (7km E Rural) *43.64799, 4.70625* **Camping La Bienheureuse, 13280 Raphèle-les-Arles [04 90 98 48 06; fax 04 90 98 37 62; contact@labienheureuse.com; www.labienheureuse.com]** Fr Arles E on D453, site on L 5km after Pont-de-Crau. W fr Salon-de-Provence on D113 or A54 (exit junc 12) to St Martin-de-Crau & take D453 dir to site. Med, hdg pitch, pt shd; wc; chem disp; shwrs inc; el pnts (10A) €3.50; Indtte; tradsmn; snacks; bar; playgrnd; pool; paddling pool; tennis, horseriding nr; entmnt; some statics; dogs €2.50; phone; bus adj; Eng spkn; adv bkg; quiet; CCI. "Pleasant site; obliging British owners; 700m to shops/bar in vill; gd facs." ♦ € 16.70 2009*

ARLES *10E2* (2km SE Urban) *43.66981, 4.64422* **Camping Le City, 67 Route de la Crau, 13200 Arles [04 90 93 08 86; fax 04 90 93 91 07; contact@camping-city.com; www.camping-city.com]** Fr town cent foll rd to Pont-de-Crau. Site well sp on L in 2km. Or exit N113 at junc 7 sp Arles & Pont de Crau; at rndabt go R alongside arches; site on R in 350m; well sp. Med, mkd pitch, pt shd; wc (some cont); chem disp; mv service pnt; baby facs; shwrs inc; el pnts (5A) €4; gas 1km; Indtte; shop; supmkt 1km; tradsmn; rest; snacks; bar; playgrnd; pool; paddling pool; sand beach 25km; tennis; cycle hire; entmnt; TV; many statics; dogs €2; bus; some Eng spkn; quiet; CCI. "Vg site; modern, clean san facs - low ssn ltd & poss upstairs; walk to town cent." ♦ 1 Mar-30 Sep. € 18.00 2009*

⊞ **ARLES** *10E2* (4km SE Urban) *43.65942, 4.65416* **Camping Les Rosiers, Pont-de-Crau, 13200 Arles [04 90 96 02 12; fax 04 90 93 36 72; lesrosiers.arles@wanadoo.fr; www.arles-camping-club.com]** Exit Arles E by D453 sp Pont-de-Crau or junc 7 fr N113 dir Raphèle-les-Arles; 200m after exit vill take 1st exit at rndabt then R at Flor Hotel sp on D83E. Site in 50m on R adj hotel. Med, pt shd; htd wc (some cont); mv service pnt; shwrs inc; chem disp; el pnts (6A) €4; Indtte; shop 500m; rest; bar; playgrnd; pool; games area; entmnt; TV; many statics; dogs €1.50; bus fr rndabt; no o'fits over 5.50m allowed (but poss not enforced); poss cr; Eng spkn; some rd & rlwy noise; red low ssn. "Many mosquitoes; red facs low ssn; v muddy after rain; visit Les Baux citadel early morning bef coach parties arr; gd birdwatching; poss no site lighting low ssn; conv Arles." € 17.00 2008*

ARLES *10E2* (14km W Rural) *43.66200, 4.47380* **Camping Caravaning Crin-Blanc, Hameau de Saliers, 13123 L'Albaron [04 66 87 48 78; fax 04 66 87 18 66; camping-crin.blanc@wanadoo.fr; www.camping-crin-blanc.com]** E fr St Gilles on N572 twd Arles; in 3km turn R onto D37 sp Saliers; site sp. Lge, pt shd; wc; chem disp; mv service pnt; baby facs; shwrs; el pnts (10A) inc; gas; Indtte; shop; tradsmn; rest; snacks; bar; playgrnd; htd pool; paddling pool; tennis; horseriding; 70% statics; dogs €2; Eng spkn; adv bkg; quiet; red low ssn; ccard acc; CCI. "Poss muddy; mosquitoes; bird reserve."♦ 1 Apr-30 Sep. € 23.00 2006*

ARLES SUR TECH *8H4* (2km NE Rural) *42.46646, 2.65150* **Camping Le Vallespir, Route d'Amélie-les-Bains, 66150 Arles-sur-Tech [04 68 39 90 00; fax 04 68 39 90 09; info@campingvallespir.com; www.campingvallespir.com]** Site on D115 mid-way between Amélie-les-Bains & Arles-sur-Tech. Clearly sp on RH side of rd. Avoids narr vill. Med, some hdg pitch, pt shd; wc; chem disp; mv service pnt; baby facs; shwrs inc; el pnts (6-10A) €3.20-4.95; Indtte; tradmn; rest; snacks; bar; playgrnd; pool; paddling pool; tennis; entmnt; golf 2km; TV rm; 50% statics; dogs €2.20; phone; poss cr; poss noisy by rd. "Pleasant, quiet site; well-organised & maintained; lovely area for hiking & cycling; ltd facs low ssn." ♦ 1 Apr-31 Oct. € 17.60 2008*

⊞ **ARLES SUR TECH** *8H4* (1km W Urban) *42.45783, 2.62563* **Camping du Riuferrer, 66150 Arles-sur-Tech [04 68 39 11 06; fax 04 68 39 12 09; pascal.larreur@campingduriuferrer.fr; www.campingduriuferrer.fr]** Take D115 fr Le Boulou thro Arles-sur-Tech (v narr but poss). Twd town exit just bef rv bdge, turn R. Foll sp 500m to site. Ent across narr footbdge. O'fits width across wheels over 2.19m ask for guidance to rear ent. Med, pt sl, shd, mkd pitch, hdstg; wc (some cont); chem disp; shwrs inc; el pnts (4-6A) €2.50-2.80; gas; Indtte; rest, snacks, bar in ssn; shops 500m; tradsmn; playgrnd; pool adj; poss cr; adv bkg; 20% statics; dogs €1; quiet; ccard not acc; red low ssn/long stay; Eng spkn; red CCI. "Helpful owner; some sm pitches diff for manoeuvring; beautiful area; vg." ♦ € 13.00 2006*

⊞ **ARMENTIERES** *3A3* (3km E Rural) *50.68774, 2.93279* **Camping L'Image, 140 Rue Brune, 59116 Houplines [tel/fax 03 20 35 69 42 or 06 81 61 56 82 (mob); campimage@wanadoo.fr; www.campingimage.com]** Exit A25 junc 8 sp Armentières, onto D945 N twd Houplines. After approx 3km after 2nd traff lts take 1st R at x-rds, site in 1km on R. Ent not v clearly sp. Med, hdg pitch, shd; htd wc; chem disp; mv service pnt; serviced pitches; shwrs inc; el pnts (6-10A) inc; Indtte; shop high ssn & 4km; snacks; playgrnd; tennis; entmnt; 90% statics; poss cr; adv bkg; quiet; red low ssn; CCI. "Mainly statics." € 19.00 2009*

ARNAY LE DUC *6H1* (1km E Rural) *47.13388, 4.49835* **Camping L'Etang de Fouché, Rue du 8 Mai 1945, 21230 Arnay-le-Duc [03 80 90 02 23; fax 03 80 90 11 91; info@campingfouche.com; www.campingfouche.com]** App by D906 (N6) to Arnay (site sp); turn E onto D17, site on R in 2km. Lge, hdg/mkd pitch, hdstg, pt shd; htd wc; chem disp; baby facs; shwrs inc; el pnts (6A) €4; Indtte; shop; tradsmn; rest; snacks; bar; BBQ; playgrnd; htd pool; paddling pool; waterslide; lake sw & beach adj; fishing; tennis; cycle hire; games rm; TV; entmnt; wifi; sat TV/TV rm; dogs €2; Eng spkn; adv bkg; quiet; ccard acc; red low ssn; CCI. "Excel lakeside site with pleasant views; lge pitches; gd san facs; friendly staff; attractive sm town; gd touring base S Burgundy; gd for young families." ♦ 15 Apr-15 Oct. € 17.80 2009*

ARRADON see Vannes *2F3*

ARRAS *3B3* (12km SE Rural) *50.27347, 2.94852* **Camping La Paille Haute, 145 Rue de Seilly, 62156 Boiry-Notre-Dame [03 21 48 15 40; fax 03 21 22 07 24; lapaillehaute@wanadoo.fr; www.la-paille-haute.com]** Fr Calais take A26/A1 twd Paris, exit junc 15 onto D939 twd Cambrai; in 3km take D34 NE to Boiry-Notre-Dame & foll camp sp. Fr D950 (N50) Douai-Arras rd, at Fresnes turn S onto D43, foll sp to Boiry in 7km, site well sp in vill. Med, pt hdg pitch, hdstg, terr, pt shd; wc; chem disp; mv service pnt; shwrs inc; el pnts (10A) €3 (poss rev pol); Indtte; rest & snacks high ssn; bar; BBQ; playgrnd; htd pool; lake fishing; tennis; games rm; entmnt; internet; 60% statics in sep area; dogs; site open w/ends in winter; poss cr; Eng spkn; quiet; red long stay/low ssn; ccard acc; CCI. "Popular NH; useful & reliable; pretty site with views; rec arr early; lge pitches; friendly, helpful owner; gd for children; facs stretched high ssn, basic low ssn; Calais under 2hrs; conv WW1 sites." ♦ 1 Apr-31 Oct. € 18.50 2009*

See advertisement

⊞ **ARREAU** *8G2* (7km N Rural) *42.97176, 0.37710* **Camp Municipal d'Esplantats, 65410 Sarrancolin [05 62 98 79 20 or 06 07 09 35 65; camping.esplantats.sarrancolin@wanadoo.fr; http://pagesperso-orange.fr/camping.international.arreau/]** Site on E side of D929 at N end of vill; ent by Total petrol stn, sp. Med, mkd pitch, pt shd; htd wc; mv service pnt; shwrs inc; el pnts (2-8A) €2.50-5.60 (long lead poss req); Indtte; shops, rest in vill; pool; some statics; dogs €2; quiet. "Site on rv bank; warden calls am & pm; clean san facs; gd facs for disabled." ♦ € 10.40 2009*

⊞ **ARREAU** *8G2* (12km SE Rural) *42.79631, 0.40674* **FLOWER Camping Pène Blanche, 65510 Loudenvielle [05 62 55 68 85; fax 05 62 99 98 20; info@peneblanche.com; www.peneblanche.com or www.flowercamping.com]** S fr Arreau on D618 in dir of Avajan. Take D25 thro Genos. Site on W of D25 just bef turn over bdge to Loudenvielle. Avoid app fr E over Col de Peyresourde. Med, some mkd pitch, terr, pt shd; htd wc; chem disp; shwrs inc; el pnts (5-10A) €3.15-7; Indtte; shop 500m; rest; snacks; bar; BBQ; playgrnd; htd pool opp; lake 1km; 20% statics; dogs €1.90; clsd Nov; adv bkg; ccard acc. "Lge sports complex opp; quiet low ssn." ♦ € 21.50 2007*

⊞ **ARREAU** *8G2* (500m SW Urban) *42.90098, 0.35478* **Camp Municipal Beuse Debat, 8 Rue de la Courbère, 65240 Arreau [05 62 98 65 56 (Mairie); fax 05 62 98 68 78]** Foll sp fr D929 across bdge (D618 sp Luchon) immed turn R on D19 & foll sp to site on banks of Rv Neste. Med, terr, pt sl, pt shd; htd wc; chem disp; baby facs; shwrs; el pnts (4-10A) €3-5.90 (rev pol); Indtte; shops 1km; rest; snacks; playgrnd; rv fishing adj; tennis; entmnt; TV rm; some statics; dogs €1; site poss clsd Oct; poss cr; adv bkg; quiet. "Gd facs." € 11.50 2008*

⊞ **ARRENS MARSOUS** *8G2* (800m E Rural) *42.9613, -0.2034* **Camping La Hèche, 54 Route d'Azun, 65400 Arrens-Marsous [05 62 97 02 64; laheche@free.fr; www.campinglaheche.com]** Fr Argelès-Gazost foll D918. Site on L immed bef Arrens. If towing c'van do not app fr Col d'Aubisque. Lge, mkd pitch, pt shd; htd wc; baby facs; shwrs inc; el pnts (3-6A) €2.60; gas; Indtte (inc dryer); shop; tradsmn; playgrnd; pool in vill high ssn; waterslide; tennis; games area; TV; 10% statics; dogs €0.50; phone; no adv bkg; quiet; CCI. "Gd for wintersports; beautiful location; gd san facs." ♦ € 6.60 2008*

ARROMANCHES LES BAINS *3D1* (3km E Coastal) *49.33963, -0.58188* **Camp Municipal Quintefeuille, Ave Maurice Schumann, 14960 Asnelles [02 31 22 35 50; fax 02 31 21 99 45; campingquintefeuille@wanadoo.fr]** Site sp on D514, but visible fr vill sq in Asnelles. Med, mkd pitch, unshd; wc; chem disp; shwrs; el pnts; Indtte; shops adj; rest, snacks, bar 300m; playgrnd; sand beach 300m; fishing; tennis; games area; quiet. ♦ 1 Apr-30 Sep. 2008*

ARROMANCHES LES BAINS *3D1* (W Urban/Coastal) *49.33793, -0.62647* **Camp Municipal, Ave de Verdun, 14117 Arromanches-les-Bains [02 31 22 36 78; fax 02 31 21 80 22; campingarromanches@wanadoo.fr]** App fr Bayeux on D516. Turn R on onto D65 on app to Arromanches to site on L. Med, pt sl, terr, pt shd; wc; shwrs inc; el pnts (10A) inc; gas; sand beach 500m; poss cr. "Conv Mulberry Harbour exhibition & invasion beaches; friendly warden; levelling blocks req most pitches; ground soft when wet; sh/stay pitches stony." 1 Apr-3 Nov. € 16.00 2009*

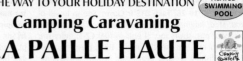

ARROU *4F2* (NW Rural) *48.10189, 1.11556* **Camp Municipal du Pont de Pierre, 28290 Arrou [02 37 97 02 13 (Mairie); fax 02 37 97 10 28]** Take D15 fr Cloyes. Site sp in vill of Arrou. Med, hdg/mkd pitch, pt sl, unshd; wc; chem disp; mv service pnt; shwrs inc; el pnts (6-10A) €2-3; Indry rm; supmkt nr; rest, bar, snacks in vill; BBQ; playgrnd; pool adj; lake fishing & sand beach adj; tennis; horseriding; cycle hire; 10% statics; phone; adv bkg; quiet; CCI. "Lovely, peaceful, well-kept site; lge pitches; old but well-kept, clean san facs; gd security; phone warden (or call at house) if office & barrier clsd; gd rvside walks/cycle rides." ♦ 1 May-30 Sep. € 4.60 2009*

ARS SUR FORMANS see Villefranche sur Saône *9B2*

ARTAIX see Marcigny *9A1*

ARTEMARE see Virieu le Grand *9B3*

ARZAL *2G3* (4.5km W Rural) *47.5143, -2.4343* **Camping de Kernéjeune, 56190 Arzal [02 97 45 01 60 or 06 18 79 65 10 (mob); fax 02 97 45 05 42; contact@camping-de-kernejeune.com; www.camping-de-kernejeune.com]** Fr E on N165 exit onto D139 sp Arzal. Opp town hall turn L sp Billiers & foll sp to site. Site on rd on R after vill of Bourgerelle. Med, mkd pitch, pt shd; htd wc; shwrs; el pnts (6-10A) €3.05; Indtte; shop; tradsmn; BBQ; playgrnd; htd pool high ssn; fishing; games area; entmnt; TV; 30% statics; dogs €1.50; phone; red low ssn; quiet. "Gd base for interesting area; helpful, friendly owners; rec." ♦ 1 Apr-1 Nov. € 13.80 2009*

ASCAIN see St Jean de Luz *8F1*

ASCOU see Ax les Thermes *8G4*

ASNIERES SUR OISE *3D3* (1km NE Rural) *49.14083, 2.38861* **Camping Domaine Les Princes, Route des Princes, 95270 Asnières-sur-Oise [tel/fax 01 30 35 40 92; lesprinces@club internet.fr; www.lesprinces.fr]** Site sp fr D909, nr Abbaye de Royaumont. Med, hdg/mkd pitch, pt shd; htd wc; shwrs inc; el pnts (3A) €3.50; Indtte; shop, rest 1km; playgrnd; fishing 500m; games area, golf, horseriding nr; BBQ; 90% statics; dogs €2.50; adv bkg; quiet; red long stay. "Pleasant, attractive, secure site; conv Parc Astérix & Paris." 1 Mar-30 Nov. € 13.00 2008*

ASPET *8G3* (Rural) *43.00969, 0.79665* **Camp Municipal Le Cagire, 31160 Aspet [05 61 88 51 55; fax 05 61 88 44 03; camping.aspet@wanadoo.fr]** Exit A64 at junc 18 St Gaudens & take D5 S. In 14km, site sp on R in vill of Aspet. Sp 'Camping, Stade.' Sm, mkd pitch, shd; wc; chem disp (wc); shwrs; el pnts (6A) €2.50; Indtte; shop, rest, snacks, bar 500m; pool, tennis 300m; games area; 30% statics; dogs €0.50; quiet; adv bkg; CCI. "Pleasant, well kept site nr lively, sm town; rec arr bef 1800 hrs high ssn; basic facs; some pitches muddy when wet." 1 Apr-30 Sep. € 8.30 2009*

ASPRES SUR BUECH *9D3* (3km S Rural) *44.51497, 5.74347* **Camping L'Adrech, Route de Sisteron, 05140 Aspres-sur-Buëch [04 92 58 60 45; fax 04 92 58 78 63; ladrech.camping@wanadoo.fr; http://camping.ladrech.chez-alice.fr]** Site on L of D1075 (N75) fr Aspres. Med, hdg pitch, hdstg, pt sl, pt shd; wc; chem disp; shwrs; el pnts (3-10A) €2.50-6; gas; Indtte; shop & 1km; tradsmn; snacks; BBQ; playgrnd; fishing; rv/lake 5km; entmnt; 50% statics; dogs €1; phone; poss cr; Eng spkn; adv bkg; quiet; CCI. "Lge pitches; helpful American owner; also poss open 21-31 Dec; ltd facs low ssn; useful NH." 1 Apr-1 Nov. € 10.00 2007*

ASPRES SUR BUECH *9D3* (8km NW Rural) *44.53048, 5.68371* **FFCC Aire Naturelle La Source (Pardoe), 05140 St Pierre-d'Argençon [tel/fax 04 92 58 67 81; info@lasource-hautesalpes.com; www.lasource-hautesalpes.com]** Fr D1075 (N75) at Aspres-sur-Buëch turn onto D993 dir Valence to St Pierre-d'Argençon; site sp. Or fr N on D93, cont onto D993 over Col de Cabre; site sp on L bef St Pierre-d'Argençon. Sm, mkd pitch, pt sl, pt shd; wc; chem disp; mv service pnt; shwrs inc; el pnts (10A) €2.50; Indtte; tradsmn; BBQ; playgrnd; wifi; dogs €1; adv bkg; quiet; ccard acc; red long stay; CCI. "Lovely clean, scenic, peaceful CL-type site in woodland/open field; helpful British owners; chambre d'hôte on site; highly rec." 15 Apr-15 Oct. € 9.00 2008*

ASSERAC *2G3* (5km NW Coastal) *47.44533, -2.44766* **Camping Le Moulin de l'Eclis, Pont Mahé, 44410 Assérac [02 40 01 76 69; fax 02 40 01 77 75; info@camping-moulin-de-leclis.fr; www.camping-moulin-de-leclis.fr]** Fr D774 turn N onto D83 to Assérac. Take D82 two coast to Pont Mahé, site sp. Lge, hdg/mkd pitch, pt shd; wc; chem disp; mv service pnt; baby facs; shwrs inc; el pnts (4-10A) €2.80-4; Indtte; shop high ssn; rest 100m; snacks; bar; BBQ (gas/elec only); playgrnd; htd, covrd pool; dir access to sand beach adj; watersports; sailing school; windsurfing; games area; cycle hire; entmnt; TV rm; 20% statics; dogs €2; phone; adv bkg; Eng spkn; quiet; ccard acc. "Excel family site; conv Guérande; vg touring base." ♦ 1 Apr-12 Nov. € 22.00 2006*

⊞ **ATTICHY** *3C4* (500m SW Rural) *49.40664, 3.05295* **Camp Municipal Fleury, Rue de la Fontaine-Aubier, 60350 Attichy [03 44 42 15 97 or 06 62 83 79 35 (mob); francoise.camping-municipal-mme-lysak@wanadoo.fr]** Fr Compiègne E on N31. After 16km turn L at traff lts sp Attichy & site. Over iron bdge & turn R to site on lakeside. Med, hdg pitch, pt shd; htd wc; chem disp; mv service pnt; shwrs inc; el pnts (5A) inc; shop 1km; tradsmn; rests in town; BBQ; playgrnd; pool; fishing; 80% statics; dogs €0.50; poss cr; quiet; CCI. "Attractive, clean site in pleasant vill; many w/end statics, few touring pitches; helpful wardens live on site; modern san facs, stretched high ssn; gd security; excel NH low ssn." € 11.50 2009*

ATTIGNY see Rethel *5C1*

ATUR see Périgueux *7C3*

AUBAS see Montignac *7C3*

AUBAZINES *7C3* (4km E Rural) *45.18620, 1.70730* **CAMPEOLE Camping Le Coiroux, Parc Touristique du Coiroux, 19190 Aubazines [05 55 27 21 96; fax 05 55 27 19 16; coiroux@campeole.com; www.camping-coiroux.com or www.campeole.com]** Fr Brive-La-Gaillarde take N89 NE twd Tulle. At Cornil turn R onto D48 & foll sp. Site in 8km - long, fairly steep climb. Med, pt hdg/mkd pitch, pt shd; wc; chem disp; mv service pnt; baby facs; shwrs inc; el pnts (5A); gas; Indtte; shop; rest; snacks; bar; playgrnd; htd pool; paddling pool; lake sw & sand beach; fishing; boating; tennis; golf; cycle hire; entmnt; TV rm; 50% statics; dogs; poss cr; Eng spkn; adv bkg; quiet; red low ssn; CCI. "Excel, wooded site." ♦ 15 Mar-15 Oct. € 20.30 2007*

AUBENAS *9D2* (3km N Rural) *44.64268, 4.37925* **Camping Domaine de Gil, Route de Vals-les-Bains, 07200 Ucel [04 75 94 63 63; fax 04 75 94 01 95; raf.garcia@wanadoo.fr; www.domaine-de-gil.com]** Fr Aubenas NE on D104 to St Privat. Cross bdge over Rv Ardèche 1km. At Pont d'Ucel, turn L along D578 twds Ucel; site 3km on L. Med, hdg/mkd pitch, pt shd; wc; chem disp; mv service pnt; serviced pitch; baby facs; shwrs inc; el pnts (10A) €5 (poss rev pol); Indtte; shop; tradsmn; rest; snacks; bar; BBQ (gas & elec); playgrnd; htd pool; tennis; canoeing; entmnt; wifi; TV; 75% statics; dogs €3; phone; adv bkg ess in Aug; quiet; ccard acc; red low ssn; CCI. "Neat, clean site in scenic area; lge pitches; excel, family site; efficient, helpful staff; gd, clean san facs; vg." ♦ 18 Apr-20 Sep. € 31.00 2009*

AUBENAS *9D2* (7km N Urban) *44.66920, 4.36343* **Camping au Fil de la Volane, Quartier du Stade, 07600 Vals-les-Bains [04 75 37 46 85; camping.aufildelavolane@wanadoo.fr; www.campingaufildelavolane.com]** Fr Aubenas NW on N102 dir Le Puy-en-Velay; in 3.5km take D578 to Vals-les-Bains. Clearly sp at N end of town by sports complex. Med, mkd pitch, terr, shd; wc (cont); chem disp (wc); mv service pnt; fam bthrm; shwrs inc; el pnts (10A) inc; Indtte (inc dryer); shops 500m; snacks; bar; BBQ; playgrnd; pool; entmnt; rv fishing & sw adj; few statics; dogs €1; phone; quiet; red low ssn. "Lovley, peaceful site; helpful owners; rv walk to spa town; vg." 1 Apr-30 Sep. € 17.60 2009*

AUBENAS *9D2* (2km E Rural) *44.61885, 4.43220* **Camping Le Plan d'Eau, Route de Lussas, 07200 St Privat [tel/fax 04 75 35 44 98; info@campingleplandeau.fr; www.campingleplandeau.fr]** Exit A7 at Montélimar dir Aubenas. Bef Aubenas turn R at rndabt onto D104 dir St Privat. In approx 1km turn R twd Lussas & foll site sp. Site on R on rvside. Med, mkd pitch, pt shd; wc; chem disp; baby facs; shwrs inc; el pnts (8A) €4.20; Indtte (inc dryer); shop adj; rest; snacks; bar; BBQ (gas only); cooking facs; playgrnd; htd pool; games rm; wifi; entmnt; TV rm; 25% statics; dogs €2.70; phone; Eng spkn; adv bkg; quiet; red long stay/CCI. "Vg, peaceful site; gd san & sports facs." 26 Apr-13 Sep. € 26.00 2009*

AUBENAS *9D2* (7km E Rural) *44.60495, 4.47126* **Ludocamping, Route de Lavilledieu, 07170 Lussas [04 75 94 21 22; fax 04 75 88 60 60; ludocamping@infonie.fr; www.ludocamping.com]** SE fr Aubenas on N102 twd Montélimar. Turn L after 10km in vill Lavilledieu onto D224 sp Lussas. Site sp on R in 4km. Med, mkd pitch, terr, pt shd; wc; chem disp; shwrs inc; el pnts (6A) €3 (poss rev pol); gas; Indtte; shop; rest in vill 600m; bar; playgrnd; htd pool; dogs €1.50; poss cr; Eng spkn; adv bkg; quiet. "Gd walking country; peaceful; facs poss stretched in high ssn; Dutch owned - all notices in Dutch only; excel." ♦ 1 Apr-15 Oct. € 25.00 2006*

AUBENAS *9D2* (7km SE Rural) *44.56401, 4.46119* **Camping Les Rives d'Auzon, Route de St Germain, 07170 Lavilledieu [tel/fax 04 75 94 70 64; contact@camping-rivesdauzon.fr; www.camping-rivesdauzon.fr]** Fr Aubenas on N102 turn R immed after Lavilledieu, sp St Germain (D103) site on L. Sm, pt shd; wc (some cont); mv service pnt; shwrs; el pnts (6A) €3.50; Indry rm; shop; rest; snacks; bar; playgrnd; pool; TV rm; entmnt; dogs €2; Eng spkn; adv bkg; some rd noise. "Friendly owner; beautiful location; poss diff for lge o'fits due trees." 6 Apr-30 Sep. € 17.00 2009*

AUBENAS *9D2* (8km SE Rural) *44.55315, 4.44855* **Camping à la Ferme Le Bardou (Boule), 07170 St Germain [tel/fax 04 75 37 71 91; info@lebardou.com; www.lebardou.com]** On N102 Aubenas-Montélimar turn S at Lavilledieu on D103, site on L in 2km. Site ent fairly narr bet stone houses in St Germain. Sm, pt shd; wc (some cont); chem disp; shwrs inc; el pnts (6A) €3; shops 150m; pool; fishing adj; some statics; dogs; adv bkg; red low ssn; quiet. "Lovely views; helpful owners; pleasant site low ssn; clean, basic facs but poss inadequate high ssn; gd." 1 Apr-31 Oct. € 15.00 2008*

AUBENAS *9D2* (3km S) *44.59671, 4.37644* **Camping Les Acacias, 07200 St Etienne-de-Fontbellon [04 75 93 67 87; fax 04 75 93 71 77; camping-les-acacias@wanadoo.fr; http://campinglesacacias.monsite.wanadoo.fr]** Fr Aubenas travel thro cent of St Etienne. Turn 2nd R at rndabt S of Leclerc hypmkt & foll sps. Fr S turn off D104 N of Lachapelle to St Etienne. At next rndabt turn L & foll sp. Sm, mkd pitch, pt shd; wc (cont); chem disp; mv service pnt; baby facs; shwrs inc; el pnts (6A) €2.50; Indtte; shops 1.5km; rest, snacks, bar high ssn; BBQ; playgrnd; pool; wifi; entmnt; dogs €0.70; Eng spkn; adv bkg; quiet; red low ssn; CCI. "Gd touring cent." 1 Apr-8 Oct. € 10.50 2007*

AUBENAS *9D2* (8km S Rural) *44.54113, 4.41495* **Camping Les Roches, 07200 Vogüé [tel/fax 04 75 37 70 45; hm07@free.fr; www.campinglesroches.fr]** Fr Aubenas take D104 S. Then L onto D579 to Vogüé. Site on L 1.5km past Vogüé - do not turn twd Vogüé, but cont in dir Vogüé Gare. Med, pt sl, shd; wc (most cont); mv service pnt; baby facs; shwrs inc; el pnts (6-10A) €3.80; Indtte; shop; rest; snacks; bar; playgrnd; pool; tennis; games area; entmnt; TV; some statics; adv bkg; quiet. "Nice site; pitch yourself, warden calls." ♦ 28 Apr-2 Sep. € 19.50 2006*

AUBENAS *9D2* (10km S Rural) *44.53693, 4.41039* **Camping Les Peupliers, 07200 St Maurice-d'Ardèche [04 75 37 71 47; fax 04 75 37 70 83; girard.jean-jacques@club-internet.fr; www.campingpeupliers.com]** Fr Aubenas take D104 S twd Alès. In 2km, turn L onto D579 dir Vogüé/Vallon Pont d'Arc. In 9km, pass L turn to Vogüé. Immed after crossing rv, turn R at rndabt. Site on R in 300m, (2nd site of 3 on rd). Lge, mkd pitch, pt shd; wc (some cont); chem disp; mv service pnt; baby facs; shwrs inc; el pnts (6A) €3.85; gas; Indtte; shop; rest; snacks; bar; BBQ; playgrnd; pool; rv & shgl beach adj; entmnt; some statics; dogs €1.40; phone; poss cr; adv bkg; quiet; ccard acc; CCI. "Gd touring base; access to rv for canoeing & fishing." 1 Apr-30 Sep. € 19.45 2007*

AUBENAS *9D2* (10km S Rural) *44.53416, 4.40690* **Domaine du Cros d'Auzon, 07200 St Maurice-d'Ardèche [04 75 37 75 86; fax 04 75 37 01 02; camping.auzon@wanadoo.fr; www.camping-cros-auzon.com]** Take D104 S fr Aubenas for 2km; at island turn L onto D579. After 9km, pass L turn to Vogüé vill, cross rv & turn R immed. Site 600m on R, 1km fr Vogüé stn. Lge, hdg/mkd pitch, pt shd; htd wc; chem disp; mv service pnt; serviced pitch; child/baby facs; shwrs inc; el pnts (4-6A) €4.20; gas; Indtte; shop 1km; tradsmn; rest; snacks; bar; playgrnd; pool; waterslide; fishing; cycle hire; tennis; entmnt; games/TV rm; cinema; 70% statics; dogs €2.50; Eng spkn; adv bkg; quiet; red low ssn/long stay; ccard acc; CCI. "Gd touring base; when office clsd check in at hotel at top of hill; poss long walk to shwrs; excel." ♦ 3 Apr-11 Sep. € 24.00 2006*

AUBENAS *9D2* (7km NW Rural) *44.65157, 4.32384* **Camp Municipal du Pont des Issoux, Allée de Vals, 07380 Lalevade-d'Ardèche [04 75 94 14 09 or 04 75 38 00 51 (Mairie); fax 04 75 94 01 92]** Fr Aubenas, N102 sp Mende & Le Puy-en-Velay; Lalevade in 10km; R in vill; well sp. Med, mkd pitch, pt shd; wc (mostly cont); chem disp (wc); shwrs inc; el pnts (10A) inc (poss rev pol); gas; Indtte; supmkt adj; rest, snacks & bar 250m, playgrnd; lake sw & shgl beach adj; tennis & children's park nrby; dogs; bus 250m; poss cr; Eng spkn; adv bkg; quiet; CCI. "Pleasant, shady beside Rv Ardèche; friendly, helpful warden; san facs dated but clean, poss scruffy low ssn; no twin-axles; many tatty statics; close to vill; conv touring base; vg." ♦
1 Apr-15 Oct. € 13.50 2009*

AUBENCHEUL AU BAC *3B4* (500m E Rural) *50.25576, 3.16264* **FFCC Camping Les Colombes, Route de Fressies, 59265 Aubencheul-au-Bac [03 27 89 25 90; fax 03 27 94 58 11; campinglescolombes@club-internet.fr]** Fr S on D643 (N43) dir Douai, on ent vill of Aubencheul-au-Bac, turn R at camp sp onto D71, site on L down lane. Site app thro housing estate. Med, hdg pitch, pt shd; wc; chem disp; shwrs inc; el pnts (4-6A) €2-€4; shops 1km; tradsmn; BBQ; playgrnd; lake fishing; 90% statics; dogs; poss cr; adv bkg; quiet; CCI. "Pretty, clean, tidy site; friendly, helpful staff; excel facs, poss stretched high ssn; ltd touring pitches; poss aircraft noise; gate locked 2200-0700." ♦ 1 Apr-31 Oct. € 11.00 2008*

AUBENCHEUL AU BAC *3B4* (2km W Rural) *50.26134, 3.14042* **Camping aux Roubaisiens, Rue de l'Abbeye, 62860 Oisy-le-Verger [03 21 59 51 54; pascallage@aol.com]** Fr Cambrai take D643 (N43) NW twd Douai. In 10km immed bef canal bdge turn L (W) twd Oisy-le-Verger. Go under rlwy bdge after 100m then R in 1km: cross canal & site on L in 200m. Sm, pt shd; wc; own san rec; chem disp; shwrs; el pnts (6A) €2; shop; fishing; 95% statics; quiet. "Run down, NH as last resort." 1 Apr-15 Oct. € 8.40 2006*

AUBERIVE *6F1* (SE Rural) *47.78445, 5.06488* **Camp Municipal Les Charbonnières, 52160 Auberive [tel/fax 03 25 86 21 13 (Mairie); mairie.auberive@wanadoo.fr]** Leave A31 at junc 6 W twds Châtilion-sur-Seine on D428 for 12km, site on L bef vill. Site sp. Sm, mkd pitch, sl, pt shd; htd wc (some cont); chem disp (wc); shwrs inc; el pnts (6A) €1.60; Indry rm; shops in vill; rest in vill; playgrnd; phone; quiet; CCI. "Pleasant, clean, well-maintained site in forestry area with gd walks; site yourself; friendly warden calls; ltd el pnts; attractive vill adj; music festival in abbey early Jul; gd." 15 Apr-1 Oct. € 7.40 2009*

When we get home I'm going to post all these site report forms to the Club for next year's guide. The deadline's September.

AUBERIVES SUR VAREZE *9B2* (8km E Rural) *45.42830, 4.92823* **Kawan Village Camping Le Bontemps, 5 Impasse du Bontemps, 38150 Vernioz [04 74 57 83 52; fax 04 74 57 83 70; info@campinglebontemps.com; www.camping-lebontemps.com]** Take N7 S fr Vienne. At Le Clos turn L onto D37 thro Cheyssieu & Vernioz, site approx 9km E of Vernioz. Fr S, on N7 N of vill of Auberives R onto D37, site on R in 8km. Tight ent - rec swing wide. NB Also sp Hotel de Plein Air. Med, mkd pitch; terr, pt shd; wc; mc service pnt; baby facs; shwrs inc; el pnts (6A) inc; Indtte; shop; rest; snacks; bar; BBQ (charcoal & gas); playgrnd; pool; games area; child entmnt; wildlife sanctuary; wifi; TV; 30% statics; dogs €2; adv bkg; quiet; ccard acc; red low ssn; CCI. "Attractive, peaceful site; excel sports facs; twin-axles welcome; excel." ♦ 28 Mar-31 Oct. € 28.00 (CChq acc) ABS - M10 2009*

⊞ **AUBERIVES SUR VAREZE** *9B2* (1km S Rural) *45.41284, 4.81358* **Camping des Nations, 38550 Clonas-sur-Varèze [04 74 84 95 13 or 04 74 84 97 17; fax 04 74 79 93 75; jacquet.g@wanadoo.fr]** Fr Vienne S on N7; site sp on R in 12km. Or fr S exit A7 junc 12 onto N7 dir Vienne; do not go into Clonas vill; site on L, just S of Auberives adj Hotel des Nations. Med, hdg/mkd pitch, shd; htd wc; chem disp; shwrs inc; el pnts (5A) inc; tradsmn; rest nr; snacks; pool; dogs €1; adv bkg (ess high ssn); quiet; no ccard acc; Eng spkn; CCI. "Pleasant, well-laid out site; gd sized pitches; muddy when wet; gd, clean san facs; useful transit site for Spain & the Med; gd touring base/NH." ♦ € 17.00 2009*

AUBETERRE SUR DRONNE *7C2* (500m E Urban) *45.26975, 0.17566* **Camp Municipal, Route de Ribérac, 16390 Aubeterre-sur-Dronne [05 45 98 60 17 or 05 45 98 50 33 (Mairie); fax 05 45 98 57 82; aubeterre-tourisme@wanadoo.fr; http://aubeterresurdronne.free.fr]** On D2 fr Chalais, take D17 around S end of town. Turn R over rv & site on R adj sports ground. Med, pt shd; wc (cont); chem disp (wc); shwrs inc; el pnts (7-10A) €2.20-2.50; shop 250m; rest in town; café 500m; bar; playgrnd; beach & rv adj; fishing & boating adj; tennis; cycle hire; dogs; poss cr; Eng spkn; quiet. "Excel site; gd for children; friendly staff; picturesque town; conv touring Périgord." 1 May-30 Sep. € 10.50 2007*

AUBIGNAN see Carpentras *10E2*

AUBIGNY SUR NERE *4G3* (1.5km E Rural) *47.48435, 2.45703* **FLOWER Camping des Etangs, Route de Sancerre, 18700 Aubigny-sur-Nère [02 48 58 02 37 or 02 48 81 50 07 (LS); fax 02 48 81 50 98; camping.aubigny@orange.fr; www.camping-aubigny.com or www.flowercamping.com]** D940 fr Gien, turn E in vill of Aubigny onto D923, foll sp fr vill; site 1km on R by lake, after Camp des Sports & just bef End of Village sp. Best to avoid town cent due congestion. Med, mkd pitch, pt shd; wc; chem disp; shwrs inc; el pnts (6A) inc; lndry rm; shop, rest & bar nr; tradsmn; BBQ; playgrnd; fishing; 10% statics; dogs free; phone; poss cr; adv bkg; quiet; red low ssn/CCI. "Excel, well-kept site with lake views; clean san facs; pretty vill; mkt Sat." ♦ 1 Apr-30 Sep. € 17.80 (3 persons) 2009*

AUBURE see Ribeauville *6E3*

⊞ **AUBUSSON** *7B4* (10km N Rural) *46.02133, 2.13928* **Camping La Perle, Fourneaux, 23200 St Médard-la-Rochette [05 55 83 01 25; fax 05 55 83 34 18; info@camping-laperle.nl; www.camping-laperle.nl]** On D942 N fr Aubusson dir Guéret; site on R bef Fourneaux. Sm, hdg/mkd pitch, some hdstg, terr, pt shd; wc; shwrs inc; el pnts (10A) inc; lndtte; shops 10km; tradsmn; rest; bar; BBQ; playgrnd; htd pool; cycle hire; wifi; TV rm; some statics; dogs; Eng spkn; adv bkg; quiet; red low ssn; CCI. "Tapestry museum in Aubusson & other historical attractions; vg site." € 18.50 2007*

AUBUSSON *7B4* (1.5km S Urban) *45.94652, 2.17608* **Camp Municipal La Croix Blanche, Route de Felletin, 23200 Aubusson [05 55 66 18 00]** Site on D982 on banks of Rv Creuse; sp fr all dir. NB Do not drive thro town cent to site - narr main street with iron pillars. Med, shd; wc (some cont); shwrs inc; el pnts (6A) inc; lndry rm; tradsmn; snacks; playgrnd; pool 1km; wifi; phone; adv bkg; quiet; CCI. "Vg site in pleasant location by rv; excel shwrs; park on site rds if pitches waterlogged; conv tapestry factories." 1 Apr-30 Sep. € 13.70 2009*

AUCH *8F3* (7km N Rural) *43.71275, 0.56455* **Camping Le Talouch, 32810 Roquelaure [05 62 65 52 43; fax 05 62 65 53 68; info@camping-talouch.com; www.camping-talouch.com]** Head W on N124 fr Auch, then N on D148 for 7km to site. Med, mkd pitch, pt shd; wc; chem disp; mv service pnt; shwrs; baby facs; el pnts (4-6A) €2.70-7.10; gas; lndtte; shop; rest; snacks; bar; playgrnd; pool; paddling pool; tennis; golf driving range; games area; internet; entmnt; 25% statics; dogs €2.20; adv bkg; quiet; red low ssn; CCI. "Poss liable to flooding; gd walking & nature trails; friendly owners." ♦ 1 Apr-30 Sep. € 22.05 (CChq acc) 2006*

AUCH *8F3* (1.5km SW Rural) *43.63664, 0.58858* **Camp Municipal d'Ile St Martin, Rue de Mouzon, Parc des Sports, 32000 Auch [05 62 05 00 22]** Fr S on N21 approx 750m after business area, turn R at traff lts into Rue Général de Gaulle which runs into Rue du Mouzon, site in 500m adj rv. NB There is also a Parc des Sports on N side of Auch. Med, hdg pitch, hdstg, shd; wc; shwrs inc; el pnts (6-10A) €2.35-4.70; shops 300m; pool 250m; few statics; poss cr; quiet but some rd noise. "Sm pitches; not suitable disabled due facs up stairs; rec arr bef 1700; lovely walk along rv; site generally scruffy, NH only (2009)." 15 Apr-15 Nov. € 6.55 2009*

⊞ **AUDENGE** *7D1* (1km E Rural) *44.68400, -1.00501* **Camping Le Braou, Route de Bordeaux, 33980 Audenge [tel/fax 05 56 26 90 03; info@camping-audenge.com; www.camping-audenge.com]** SW fr Bordeaux turn R off D1250 (N250) twd Andernos onto D3; at traff lts in Audenge turn R; site 750m on R. Lge, mkd pitch, pt shd; wc; mv service pnt; shwrs inc; el pnts (3A) €3.50; lndtte; shops 1km; tradsmn; snacks; pool; beach 1.5km; cycle hire; games area; entmnt; some statics; dogs €3.50; bus 1km; quiet; CCI. ♦ € 16.50 2006*

AUDENGE *7D1* (10km SE Urban) *44.60486, -0.94225* **Camp Municipal de l'Eyre, Allée de la Plage, 33380 Mios [05 56 26 42 04; fax 05 56 26 41 69]** Fr N or S on A63, join A660 sp Arcachon; leave at junc 1 to Mios. After vill turn L after traff lts (sm sp) bet tourist & post offices. Site adj Rv Eyre. Med, mkd pitch, pt shd; htd wc; shwrs inc; el pnts (5A) €3; lndtte; shop 500m; sports hall adj; canoe hire; cycle hire for adj rte; many statics; dogs €1.50; CCI. "Excel touring base; helpful warden; ltd facs low ssn; park outside site to book in; phone ahead low ssn to check if open; san facs poss stretched if site full; poss noisy at night." ♦ 1 Apr-30 Oct. € 13.00 2006*

AUDENGE *7D1* (5km S Urban) *44.65076, -0.97914* **Camping Marache, 25 Rue Gambetta, 33380 Biganos [05 57 70 61 19; fax 05 56 82 62 60; contact@marache vacances.com; www.marachevacances.com]** Exit A660 junc 2 sp Facture; take D3 dir Audenge, site clearly sp. NB Height restriction 2.6m in Facture, use ring rd. Med, mkd pitch, pt shd; wc; mv service pnt; baby facs; shwrs inc; el pnts (6A) €3.80; lndtte; shops 1km; rest; snacks; playgrnd; htd pool; rv & fishing 1km; tennis 1km; entmnt; TV; dogs €3.50; adv bkg; quiet. "Pleasant management; twin-axles pay extra; basic facs, ltd low ssn; NH only." ♦ 1 Mar-31 Oct. € 20.50 2007*

AUDIERNE *2F1* (4.5km NE Rural) *48.04924, -4.48235* **Camp Municipal de Langroas, 29790 Pont-Croix [02 98 70 40 66 (Mairie) or 06 85 79 18 18 (mob); fax 02 98 70 53 62; pontcroix.mairie@wanadoo.fr; www.pont-croix.info]** Site sp at ent to Pont-Croix on D765; also sp fr town cent. Med, pt shd; wc; chem disp (wc); shwrs inc; el pnts €2.20; gas 700m (in Super U); Indtte; shop; rest; snacks; bar; BBQ; playgrnd; beach 4km; 6% statics; dogs; bus; phone (card only); adv bkg; quiet; CCI. "Beautiful site with some magnificent trees; pretty sm town; gd." ♦ 15 Jun-15 Sep. € 9.20 2008*

AUDIERNE *2F1* (700m SE Coastal/Rural) *48.02458, -4.52863* **Camping Le Loquéran, Bois de Loquéran, 29770 Audierne [02 98 74 95 06; fax 02 98 74 91 14; http://campgite.loqueran.free.fr]** Fr Quimper on D784 thro Plozévet & Plouhinec dir Audierne. Look out for sm, yellow/purple camping sp on R, site 500m on L. Sm, mkd pitch, terr, pt shd; wc; chem disp; shwrs inc; el pnts (6A) €2; Indtte; shop & 600m; playgrnd; beach 1km; dogs €1; ccard acc; quiet; CCI. "Gd san facs; peaceful site." 15 May-30 Sep. € 10.50 2007*

AUDIERNE *2F1* (3km SE Coastal) *48.00723, -4.50799* **Camping de Kersiny-Plage, 1 Rue Nominoé, 29780 Plouhinec [02 98 70 82 44; mail@camping-kersiny.com; www.camping-kersiny.com]** Fr Audierne on D784 turn R at 2nd traff lts in Plouhinec, cont for 1km; turn L into Rue Nominoé (sp diff to see) for 100m. Or fr Quimper on D784 to Plouhinec, turn L at 1st traff lts & as bef. Med, hdg pitch, terr, pt shd; wc; chem disp; mv service pnt; baby facs; shwrs; el pnts (8A) €2.80; gas; Indtte; tradsmn high ssn; BBQ; playgrnd; direct access to sand beach; dogs €2; Eng spkn; quiet; barrier clsd 2300-0730; red low ssn; CCI. "Beautiful location & beach; most pitches sea views; welcoming, friendly owner; clean facs; not much in area for children except beach; peaceful low ssn; vg." 8 May-15 Sep. € 14.50 2009*

AUDIERNE *2F1* (8km W Coastal) *48.02527, -4.61830* **Camp Municipal de Kermalero, 29770 Primelin [tel/fax 02 98 74 84 75 or 02 98 74 81 19 (LS); campingkermalero@wanadoo.fr]** D784 Audierne-Pointe du Raz, after Ecomarché supmkt at Primelin turn L, site sp. Med, hdg pitch, terr, pt shd; wc; chem disp; mv service pnt; shwrs inc; el pnts (6A) €2.50; Indtte; supmkt 1km; tradsmn; playgrnd; games area; sand beach 1km; tennis; TV; 5% statics; quiet. "Pleasant site; gd outlook/views; helpful warden; clean facs; gd." ♦ 3 Mar-24 Oct. € 10.00 2008*

AUDIERNE *2F1* (1.5km NW Urban) *48.02859, -4.55675* **FFCC Camping de Kerivoas, Route de la Pointe du Raz, 29770 Audierne [02 98 70 26 86 or 02 98 70 27 75 (LS); camping.kerivoas@wanadoo.fr]** W fr Audierne on D784 sp Pointe du Raz; site on L at top of hill opp Leclerc supmkt. Sm, pt sl, pt shd; wc; chem disp (wc); shwrs inc; el pnts (6-10A) €2.60-3.20 (poss long lead req); dogs €1; Indry rm; shops & rests nrby; beach 1.5km; dogs €1.20; bus; no twin-axles; adv bkg; some rd noise; red long stay; CCI. "Sm pitches poss diff long o'fits." 1 Apr-31 Oct. € 11.10 2009*

AUDRUICQ see Ardres *3A3*

AUGIGNAC see Nontron *7B3*

AUGIREIN *8G3* (S Rural) *42.93151, 0.91917* **Camping La Vie en Vert, 09800 Augirein [05 61 96 82 66; fax 05 61 04 73 00; daffis@lavieenvert.com; www.lavieenvert.com]** Fr St Girons on D618 twd Castillon. On app Castillon turn R foll sp to Luchon. 1km after vill Orgibet turn L into vill of Augirein. Site on L over bdge. Sm, hdg/mkd pitch, pt shd; wc; baby facs; shwrs inc; el pnts (3-10A) €2.50-5; Indtte; shop; tradsmn; rest in vill; BBQ; playgrnd; dogs €1; Eng spkn; adv bkg; quiet; 5% red 5+ days; CCI. "Charming owners who own bar/café in vill; excel little site." ♦ 15 May-15 Sep. € 14.00 2006*

⊞ **AULUS LES BAINS** *8G3* (NW Rural) *42.79402, 1.33197* **Camping Le Coulédous, 09140 Aulus-les-Bains [05 61 96 02 26; fax 05 61 96 06 74; couledous@wanadoo.fr; www.couledous.com]** Take D618 fr St Girons. After 13km cross rv; turn R onto D3 sp Aulus-les-Bains. On app to Oust turn L onto D32, site approx 17km on R at ent to vill on rvside. Med, mkd pitch, hdstg, sl, pt shd; htd wc; chem disp; mv service pnt; shwrs inc; el pnts (6-10A) €4.30-6.30; Indtte; shop 500m; bar 300m, playgrnd; some statics; dogs €4; site clsd last week Nov & 1st week Dec; poss cr; Eng spkn; adv bkg; quiet; CCI. "Gd walking & skiing (16km); sm spa in vill; excel." ♦ € 18.00 2006*

AUMALE *3C3* (1km W) *49.76618, 1.74618* **Camp Municipal Le Grand Mail, 76390 Aumale [02 35 93 40 50; fax 02 35 93 86 79; communeaumale@wanadoo.fr; www.aumale.com]** Clearly sp in town; long steep climb to ent. Med, pt shd; wc; mv service pnt; shwrs €1.80; el pnts (6A) €2.40; Indtte; shops 1km; playgrnd; pool 1km; cycle hire €1; fishing 1km; dogs €2; noise fr rd. "Gd site; clean, modern san facs; conv Channel ports; steep slope fr town to site." ♦ 10 Apr-30 Sep. € 9.60 2009*

AUNAC see Mansle *7B2*

AUNAY SUR ODON see Villers Bocage *3D1*

⊞ **AUPS** *10E3* (300m SE Rural) *43.62525, 6.23103* **Camping Les Prés, 181 Route de Tourtour, 83630 Aups [04 94 70 00 93; fax 04 94 70 14 41; lespres.camping@wanadoo.fr; www.campinglespres.com]** Fr cent of Aups on rd to Tourtour, site on R. Rough rd. Med, hdg/mkd pitch, pt shd; htd wc; baby facs; fam bthrm; shwrs inc; el pnts (4-6A) €3.70; gas; Indtte; shop 300m; tradsmn; rest; snacks; bar; playgrnd; pool; entmnt; TV rm; some statics; adv bkg; quiet. "Peaceful, friendly site." € 15.50 2008*

AUPS *10E3* (500m W Rural) *43.62455, 6.21760* **International Camping, Route de Fox-Amphoux, 83630 Aups [04 94 70 06 80; fax 04 94 70 10 51; info@internationalcamping-aups.com; www.internationalcamping-aups.com]** Site on L on D60 nr vill cent. Lge, hdg/mkd pitch, pt shd; wc; chem disp; shwrs inc; el pnts (16A) €5.30; Indtte; shop; tradsmn; snacks & rest high ssn; bar; pool; tennis; games rm; disco; entmnt; many statics (sep area); dogs €1; Eng spkn; rec adv bkg high ssn; quiet; ccard acc; red low ssn. "Vg site in beautiful area; lge pitches; gd rest." 1 Apr-30 Sep. € 19.10 2009*

AUPS *10E3* (1km NW Rural) *43.63631, 6.20793* **Camping St Lazare, Route de Moissac, 83630 Aups [04 94 70 12 86; fax 04 94 70 01 55; camping.caravaning.st-lazare@orange.fr]** NW fr Aups twd Régusse on D9, site sp. Med, pt sl, pt shd, hdg/mkd pitch; wc (some cont); chem disp; baby facs; shwrs inc; el pnts (10A) €4; gas; Indtte; shop 1.5km; snacks; playgrnd; pool; paddling pool; games area; 25% statics; dogs €1; phone; TV; entmnts; mountain bike hire; 10% statics; adv bkg rec; CCI. "Excel touring base; poss unkempt low ssn; vg, quiet site." 1 Apr-30 Sep. € 16.10 2009*

AURAY *2F3* (5km SE Coastal) *47.64909, -2.92540* **Camp Municipal Kergouguec, 56400 Plougoumelen [02 97 57 88 74]** Site is S of N165, 13km W of Vannes; sp fr vill sq 500m S on R, nr stadium. Med, pt sl, pt shd; wc (some cont); chem disp; shwrs; el pnts (6A) €2.55; playgrnd; beach & windsurfing 300m; tennis; dogs €1.35; adv bkg; quiet; CCI. "Well-run site; gd touring base." ♦ 15 Jun-15 Sep. € 8.40 2008*

AURAY *2F3* (7km SE Rural) *47.64320, -2.89890* **Aire Naturelle La Fontaine du Hallate (Le Gloanic), 8 Chemin du Poul Fétan, La Hallate, 56400 Plougoumelen [09 64 04 90 16 or 06 16 30 08 33 (mob); clegloanic@orange.fr; www.camping-hallate.fr]** Fr N165 Vannes-Lorient, turn S onto D101E to Plougoumelen; watch for sp after Plougoumelen, site in La Hallate. Narr, bumpy app rd. Sm, hdg/mkd pitch, pt sl, pt shd; shwrs inc; el pnts (6A) €2.80 (poss rev pol); Indtte; shops 2km; playgrnd; golf/tennis adj; 2% statics; dogs €1; phone; adv bkg ess Jul/Aug; CCI. "Gd alternative to lge/noisier sites; gd coast paths; conv local boat trips & Ste Anne-d'Auray; vg." 29 Mar-24 Oct. € 12.00 2009*

AURAY *2F3* (5km S Rural) *47.64402, -2.93774* **FFCC Camping du Parc-Lann, 52 Rue Thiers, Le Varquez, 56400 Le Bono [02 97 57 93 93 or 02 97 57 83 91; campingduparclann@wanadoo.fr; www.auray-tourisme.com]** S fr Auray on D101 sp Le Bono. Site well sp in Le Bono. Med, hdg/mkd pitch, pt shd; wc; chem disp; mv service pnt; baby facs; shwrs inc; el pnts (6A) €2.30; Indtte; ice; shop 2km; tradsm; rest; snacks; bar; BBQ; playgrnd; pool 5km; sand beach 9km; games area; dogs €0.70; bus; phone; red low ssn; CCI. "Lovely quiet site in pretty area; gd, clean san facs poss stretched high ssn & ltd low ssn; warden on site 1800-1900 only low ssn; gd walking." ♦ 1 May-30 Sep. € 13.20 2009*

AURAY *2F3* (7km SW Rural) *47.64256, -3.05406* **FFCC Camping Le Kergo, 56400 Ploemel [tel/fax 02 97 56 80 66; campingdekergo@wanadoo.fr]** Fr Auray take D768 SW sp Carnac. After 4km turn NW on D186 twd Ploemel & foll sp. Med, mkd pitch, pt shd; wc; chem disp; shwrs inc; el pnts (6-10A) inc; Indtte; shops 2km; tradsmn; playgrnd; sand beach 5km; dogs €0.70; some statics; adv bkg rec high ssn; red low ssn/CCI. "Lovely, peaceful site, lots of trees; excel san facs, ltd low ssn." ♦ 1 May-30 Sep. € 15.40 2007*

⊞ **AURAY** *2F3* (8km W Rural) *47.66368, -3.10019* **FFCC Camping Le St Laurent, Kergonvo, 56400 Ploemel [tel/fax 02 97 56 85 90; camping.saint.laurent@wanadoo.fr; www.ploemel.com]** Fr Auray on D22 twd Belz/Etel; after 8km turn L on D186 to Ploemel & site on L in 200m. Med, some hdstg, shd; wc; chem disp; mv service pnt; baby facs; shwrs inc; el pnts (10A) €2.30; Indtte; shop & 3km; rest; bar; BBQ; playgrnd; htd pool; sand beach 6km; dogs €0.80; adv bkg; quiet. "Peaceful site; friendly staff; red facs low ssn." € 12.60 2006*

AUREILHAN see Mimizan *7D1*

AURIBEAU SUR SIAGNE see Grasse *10E4*

AURILLAC *7C4* (2km NE Urban) *44.93551, 2.45596* **Camp Municipal de l'Ombrade, Chemin du Gué Bouliaga, 15000 Aurillac [tel/fax 04 71 48 28 87; www.caba.fr/camping]** Take D17 N fr Aurillac twd Puy-Mary; site on banks of Rv Jordanne. Well sp fr town. Lge, mkd pitch, shd; wc; shwrs inc; el pnts (10A) €2.10; Indry rm; shops adj; TV & games rm; quiet. "Well-managed, spacious site; lge pitches; gd clean facs, inc disabled; poss not well-kept low ssn; interesting, lge mkt town; vg." ♦ 15 Jun-15 Sep. € 10.50 2009*

AURILLAC *7C4* (2km S Urban) *44.89858, 2.46265* **Camp Municipal de la Cère, Rue Félix Ramond, 15130 Arpajon-sur-Cère [tel/fax 04 71 64 55 07; sebastienpradel@yahoo.fr]** Fr Rodez take D920 twd Aurillac. Site sp 2km bef Aurillac on S side of Arpajon. Med, hdg pitch, pt shd; wc; shwrs inc; el pnts (10A) €2; gas; Indtte; shops adj; pool 4km; rv fishing adj; beach 20km; sports facs adj; golf 5km; adv bkg; some rd noise; ccard acc; CCI. "Pleasant site in pretty area; public access to site - not secure; generous pitches." ♦ 1 Jun-30 Sep. € 11.00 2006*

AUSSOIS see Modane *9C4*

⊞ **AUTERIVE** *8F3* (1km S Rural) *43.34228, 1.48084* **Camp Municipal du Ramier, Allée Ramier, 31190 Auterive [05 61 50 65 73 or 05 61 08 33 98]** Turn E off N20 onto D622; cross rv bdge & immed turn R into no-thro-rd. Site at end. Sm, pt shd; wc; shwrs; el pnts (6A) €3.50; shop 1km; pool adj; tennis; rv fishing; many statics; quiet but poss noise fr disco. "Space found even when 'Complet' sign up but rec arr by 1730; fair NH." € 6.30 2008*

⊞ **AUTERIVE** *8F3* (7km NW Rural) *43.43109, 1.43504* **Camp Municipal Le Ramier, 31810 Vernet [05 61 08 33 98 or 05 61 08 50 47 (Mairie)]** Site at S exit of Vernet, sp fr N20/D820 Toulouse-Pamiers rd. Med, shd; wc (some cont); chem disp; shwrs; el pnts (5A); shops adj; quiet. "Conv NH for Andorra; gd location by rv." 2008*

AUTHUILLE see Albert *3B3*

AUTRANS *9C3* (E Rural) *45.17520, 5.54770* **Camping au Joyeux Réveil, Le Château, 38880 Autrans [04 76 95 33 44; fax 04 76 95 72 98; contact@camping-au-joyeux-reveil.fr; www.camping-au-joyeux-reveil.fr]** Fr Villard-de-Lans take D531 to Lans-en-Vercors & turn L onto D106 to Autrans. On E side of vill site sp at 1st rndabt. NB App on D531 fr W fr Pont-en-Royans not rec - v narr rd & low tunnels. Med, mkd pitch, pt sl, pt shd; htd wc; chem disp; mv service pnt; baby facs; shwrs inc; el pnts (2-10A) €2-8; gas; Indtte; shop 300m; tradsmn; rest 100m; snacks; bar; BBQ; playgrnd; htd pool & paddling pool; waterslide; rv fishing; tennis 300m; cycle hire; golf 20km; games area; TV rm; cab TV to pitches; 60% statics; dogs; bus 300m; phone; quiet; adv bkg; Eng spkn; red low ssn; ccard acc; CCI. "Site in Vercors National Park with excel views; winter sport facs, 1050m altitude; modern san facs; excel." ♦ 1 Dec-31 Mar & 1 May-30 Sep. € 30.00 (CChq acc) 2009*

AUTRECHE *4G2* (200m NE Rural) *47.52639, 0.99934* **FFCC Camp Municipal de l'Etang, Rue du Général de Gaulle, 37110 Autrèche [02 47 29 59 64 or 02 47 56 22 03 (Mairie)]** Exit A10 junc 18 onto D31 S to Autrèche, turn L into vill for 600m, site sp. Sm, unshd; wc (cont for men); shwrs inc; el pnts inc; playgrnd; tennis; poss cr; quiet; CCI. "Useful/vg NH fr m'way." 1 May-25 Sep. € 7.60 2007*

AUTUN *6H1* (1km N Rural) *46.96968, 4.29402* **Camp Municipal de la Porte d'Arroux, Les Chaumottes, 71400 Autun [03 85 52 10 82; fax 03 85 52 88 56; contact@camping-autun.com; www.camping-autun.com]** Foll sp fr town on D980 dir Saulieu & site on L; only site in Autun. Med, some hdg pitch, some hdstg, pt shd; wc (some cont); mv service pnt; baby facs; shwrs inc; el pnts (6A) €2.95; (poss rev pol); gas high ssn; Indry rm; shop; snacks; rest high ssn; playgrnd; rv sw & fishing; canoe & cycle hire; wifi; dogs €1.30; phone; Eng spkn; adv bkg; ccard acc; red low ssn; CCI. "Lovely, quiet, clean site; views fr some pitches; friendly, helpful staff; sm pitches; no twin-axles; v muddy when wet (tow avail); vg lively rest; medieval architecture & Roman walls around town - m'van Aire de Service nr lake in town; mkt Wed/Fri." ♦ 1 Apr-31 Oct. € 13.71 2009*

AUVERS SUR OISE see Pontoise *3D3*

AUXERRE *4F4* (3km SE Urban) *47.78678, 3.58721* **Camp Municipal, 8 Rue de Vaux, 89000 Auxerre [03 86 52 11 15; fax 03 86 51 17 54; camping.mairie@auxerre.com; www.auxerre.com]** Exit A6 at Auxerre; at junc N6 ring rd foll sp Vaux & 'Stade'; site sp by Rv Yonne. Or fr N6 (N) take ring rd, site/stadium sp. Site also well sp fr town cent as 'L'Arbre Sec'. Lge, mkd pitch, pt shd; wc; chem disp; mv service pnt; shwrs inc; el pnts (6A) €2.55 (long lead poss req); Indtte; shop; supmkt 400m; bar/café; playgrnd; pool 250m; fishing 300m; TV; 10% statics; dogs; adv bkg; quiet; ccard acc; CCI. "Popular NH; lge pitches; friendly staff; gd clean san facs; poss cr & noisy during football ssn; site poss flooded stormy weather; no c'vans over 5m; ltd el pnts for site size; no vehicles 2200-0700." 15 Apr-30 Sep. € 9.05 2009*

AUXERRE *4F4* (10km S Rural) *47.70704, 3.63563* **FFCC Camping Les Ceriselles, Route de Vincelottes, 89290 Vincelles [33 86 42 50 47; fax 03 86 42 39 39; camping@cc-payscoulangeois.fr; www.campingceriselles.com]** Leave A6 at Auxerre Sud. Fr Auxerre, take D606 S twd Avallon. 10km fr Auxerre turn L into vill. In 400m immed after 'Maxi Marche', turn L into site access rd, sp as Camping/Base de Loisirs. Site is approx 16km fr a'route exit. Med, mkd pitch, some hdstg, pt shd; htd wc; chem disp; mv service pnt; shwrs inc; el pnts (6-10A) inc (poss rev pol); gas adj; Indtte; sm supmkt adj; tradsmn; rest adj; snacks; bar; BBQ; playgrnd; rv adj; cycle hire; TV rm; 10% statics; dogs €1.50; phone; no twin-axles; poss cr; some Eng spkn; adv bkg; quiet but noise fr N6; ccard acc; red long stay/low ssn; CCI. "Excel site by canal in lovely countryside; friendly & helpful owner; gd facs poss stretched high ssn & ltd low ssn; cycle track to Auxerre; highly rec." ♦ 1 Apr-30 Sep. € 18.00 (CChq acc) 2009*

AUXI LE CHATEAU *3B3* (500m NW Rural) *50.2341, 2.1058* **Camp Municipal des Peupliers, 22 Rue de Cheval, 62390 Auxi-le-Château [03 21 41 10 79]** Take D928 S fr Hesdin. In 11km take D119 to Auxi-le-Château. Or fr S on D925, turn N onto D933 at Bernaville to Auxi-le-Château, then take D938 twds Crécy, site sp on R in 300m by football stadium. Med, hdg pitch; unshd wc; chem disp; shwrs inc; el pnts (3-6A); Indtte; shops, rest, snacks, bar 500m; playgrnd; fishing; sailing; dir access to rv; 80% statics; poss cr; adv bkg; quiet; ccard acc. 1 Apr-30 Sep. 2008*

⊞ **AUXONNE** *6G1* (500m NW Rural) *47.19838, 5.38120* **Camping L'Arquebuse, Route d'Athée, 21130 Auxonne [03 80 31 06 89; fax 03 80 31 13 62; camping.arquebuse@wanadoo.fr; www.campingarquebuse.com]** On D905 (N5) Dijon-Geneva, site sp on L bef bdge at ent to Auxonne. Med, pt shd; htd wc (some cont); chem disp; mv service pnt; shwrs inc; el pnts (10A) €3.70 (poss rev pol); gas; Indry rm; shop 500m; rest; snacks; bar; playgrnd; htd pool adj; fishing; sailing; windsurfing; entmnt; wifi; TV rm; 20% statics; dogs €1.80; adv bkg; quiet; clsd 2200-0700; CCI. "Rvside site; friendly staff; san facs poss tatty (2008); poss busy w/ends as NH; interesting town; gd." € 12.30 2009*

AVAILLES LIMOUZINE see Pressac *7A3*

AVALLON *4G4* (2km SE Rural) *47.48030, 3.91246* **Camp Municipal Sous Roches, 89200 Avallon [tel/fax 03 86 34 10 39; campingsousroche@ville-avallon.fr]** App town fr a'route or fr SE on N6. Turn sharp L at 2nd traff lts in town cent, L in 2km at sp Vallée du Cousin (bef bdge), site 250m on L. If app fr S care needed when turning R after bdge. Med, some hdstg pitches, terr, pt shd; wc; mv service pnt; shwrs inc; el pnts (6A) €3; Indtte; shop; tradsmn (to order); BBQ; playgrnd; pool 1km; rv & fishing adj; dogs; phone adj; Eng spkn; CCI. "Popular, clean site in lovely location; helpful staff; modern san facs; conv Morvan National Park; poss flood warning after heavy rain; no twin-axles or o'fits over 2,500kg." ♦ 1 Apr-15 Oct. € 10.00 2008*

AVANTON see Poitiers *7A2*

AVIGNON *10E2* (2km N Rural) *43.97063, 4.79928* **Camp Municipal de la Laune, Chemin St Honoré, 30400 Villeneuve-lès-Avignon [04 90 25 76 06 or 04 90 25 61 33; fax 04 90 25 91 55; campingdelalaune@wanadoo.fr; www.camping-villeneuvelezavignon.com]** Fr Avignon, take N100 twd Nîmes over rv bdge. At W end of 2nd part of rv bdge, turn R onto N980 sp Villeneuve-lès-Avignon. Site is 3km on R just past old walled town battlements on L. Adj sports complex. Med, hdg/mkd pitch, hdstg, shd; wc; chem disp; mv service pnt; shwrs inc; el pnts (6A) €3.20 (poss rev pol); Indtte; shop; snacks; bar; pool & sports complex adj (free to campers); dogs €1; phone; bus; Eng spkn; quiet; ccard acc; red low ssn; CCI. "Lovely, well-run site; gd, clean facs; helpful staff; excel security; vg local mkt; sports facs adj; gd walks/cycle rides." ♦ 1 Apr-15 Oct. € 18.00 2009*

AVIGNON *10E2* (4km NE Rural) *43.97651, 4.88475* **Camping du Grand Bois, 14 Chemin du Grand Bois, Quartier La Tapy, 84130 Le Pontet [04 90 31 37 44; fax 04 90 31 46 53; campinglegrandbois@orange.fr]** Exit A7/E714 at junc 23 onto D53 S, Chemin du Pont Blanc. At rndabt turn onto Chemin du Grand Bois, site on R, sp. Med, hdg pitch, pt shd; wc; chem disp; shwrs inc; el pnts (5A) €3; Indtte; shop; hypmkt 3km; tradsmn; rest; snacks; playgrnd; cycle hire; wifi; TV; dogs €2; phone; Eng spkn; adv bkg; quiet; ccard acc; CCI. "Superb location; plenty of rm; family-run alt to main Avignon sites; ltd facs; helpful staff; insects poss a problem." ♦ 1 May-15 Sep. € 26.00 2009*

AVIGNON *10E2* (9km NE Rural) *43.99057, 4.91340* **FFCC Camping Flory, Route d'Entraigues, 84270 Vedène [04 90 31 00 51; fax 04 90 23 46 19; infos@campingflory.com; www.campingflory.com]** Exit A7 junc 23 NE onto D942 twd Carpentras. In 3km foll sp on R for Camping Flory. Med, mkd pitch, pt sl, pt shd; wc (some cont); chem disp; shwrs inc; el pnts (10A) €4 (poss rev pol); gas; Indtte; shop & 1km; tradsmn; rest & 3km; snacks; bar & 3km; playgrnd; pool (high ssn); dogs €2.50; phone; 15% statics; poss cr; quiet; adv bkg; Eng spkn; 10% red low ssn; CCI. "Conv touring base Vaucluse; uneven pitches & paths (2007); facs poss stretched high ssn & ltd low ssn; lovely pool." ♦ 15 Mar-30 Sep. € 18.00 2007*

AVIGNON *10E2* (8km S Urban) *43.88361, 4.87010* **Camping de la Roquette, 746 Ave Jean Mermoz, 13160 Châteaurenard [tel/fax 04 90 94 46 81; contact@camping-la-roquette.com; www.camping-la-roquette.com]** Exit A7/D907 (N7) Avignon S to Noves; take D28 to Châteaurenard 4km; foll sp to site & Piscine Olympic/Complex Sportiv. Poss awkward access/exit lge o'fits. Med, hdg/mkd pitch, pt shd; wc; chem disp; some serviced pitches; mv service pnt; baby facs; shwrs inc; el pnts (6A) €3; Indtte; shops 1.5km; tradsmn; rest; snacks; bar; playgrnd; pool; paddling pool; tennis; dogs €1; phone; TV; Eng spkn; adv bkg rec; quiet but some rd noise; 5% red 30+ days; ccard acc; CCI. "Gd touring cent; sm pitches; owners kind, friendly & helpful; clean facs; gd walks." ♦ 1 Mar-31 Oct. € 15.20 2008*

The opening dates and prices on this campsite have changed. I'll send a site report form to the Club for the next edition of the guide.

⊞ **AVIGNON** *10E2* (12km W Rural) *43.95155, 4.66451* **Camping Le Bois des Ecureuils, Plateau de Signargues, 30390 Domazan [tel/fax 04 66 57 10 03; infos@boisdesecureuils.com; www.boisdesecureuils.com]** Exit A9/E15 at Remoulins junc 23 twd Avignon on N100. Site on R in 6km. Fr S on N7 foll sp for Nîmes onto N100. Go over 2 lge rndabts, site about 6km on L at rndabt. Sm, mkd pitch, all hdstg, shd; wc (some cont); chem disp (wc); baby facs; shwrs inc; el pnts (6A) inc; gas; Indtte; shop; rest adj; snacks, bar high ssn; BBQ; playgrnd; htd pool; entmnt; TV; 5% statics; dogs free; phone; poss cr; Eng spkn; adv bkg (rec high ssn); quiet but some rd noise; red low ssn CCI. "Ideal for touring Avignon & Pont du Gard; friendly owners; clean facs; steel awning pegs ess; many long-stay residents low ssn." € 18.00 2008*

⊞ **AVIGNON** *10E2* (500m NW Urban) *43.95216, 4.79946* **FFCC Camping Bagatelle, Ile de la Barthelasse, 84000 Avignon [04 90 86 30 39; fax 04 90 27 16 23; camping.bagatelle@wanadoo.fr; www.campingbagatelle.com]** Exit D907 (A7) at Avignon Nord. After passing end of old bdge bear L, then onto new Daladier bdge & take immed R turn over bdge foll sp to Barthelasse & Villeneuve-lès-Avignon. Caution - do not foll Nîmes sp at more southerly bdge (Pont d'Europe). Lge, mkd pitch, pt shd; htd wc; mv service pnt; baby facs; shwrs inc; el pnts (6-10A) €3-4.50; gas; Indtte; shop; rest; pool 100m; playgrnd; entmnt; TV; boating; fishing; tennis 2km; games area; TV rm; dogs €2.40; some traffic noise at night; ccard acc; red low ssn/CCI. "Busy site on rv bank; sm pitches; helpful staff; facs dated but clean, ltd low ssn; narr site rds, suggest find pitch bef driving in; if recep unmanned, go to bar or supmkt to check in; free ferry to town; site low lying & poss damp; poss unkempt low ssn; poss o'night tented school parties; poor security." ♦ € 21.92 2009*

France

AVIGNON *10E2* (1km NW Urban) *43.95670, 4.80222* **Camping du Pont d'Avignon, 10 Chemin de la Barthelasse, Ile de la Barthelasse, 84000 Avignon [04 90 80 63 50; fax 04 90 85 22 12; info@camping-avignon.com; www.camping-avignon.com]** Exit A7 junc 23 Avignon Nord dir Avignon Centre (D225) then Villeneuve-les-Avignon. Go round wall & under Pont d'Avignon; then cross rv dir Villeneuve, Ile de la Barthelasse. Turn R onto Ile de la Barthelasse. Lge, hdg/mkd pitch, mostly shd; wc; chem disp; mv service pnt; shwrs inc; el pnts (6-10A) €2.90; gas; Indtte; shop; rest; snacks; bar; BBQ; cooking facs; playgrnd; pool; paddling pool; tennis; games area; games rm; entmnt; wifi; TV; statics; dogs €2.50; phone; car wash; poss cr; Eng spkn; adv bkg ess high ssn; quiet but some rd, rlwy & rv barge noise; ccard acc; red low ssn/long stay; CCI. "Superb, well-run, well-lit, busy site; views city & bdge; welcoming staff; clean, dated facs, ltd number; lovely pool; gd sized pitches but most with high kerbs; poss flooded low ssn; extra for c'vans over 5.50m; Avignon festival Jul/Aug; best site for Avignon - 20 mins walk or free ferry; rec arr early even low ssn." ♦ 16 Mar-1 Nov. € 23.82 (CChq acc) 2009*

See advertisement

AVIGNON *10E2* (5km NW Rural) *43.99573, 4.81843* **CAMPEOLE Camping L'Ile des Papes, Quartier l'Islon, 30400 Villeneuve-lès-Avignon [04 90 15 15 90; fax 04 90 15 15 91; ile-des-papes@campeole.com; www.avignon-camping.com or www.campeole.com]** Fr A9 exit sp Roquemaure; head S on D980. Site adj to rv 2km NW of city. Fr D907 (A7) exit Avignon Nord, twds Avignon cent & cross bdge twds Villeneuve. Turn off after x-ing rv before x-ing canal. Site bet rv & canal. Lge, pt shd; wc; shwrs; el pnts (6A) €4; Indtte; cooking facs; rest; supmkt; playgrnd; pool; archery; lake fishing adj; hiking; entmt; TV; statics 35%; dogs €3.50; adv bkg; quiet but some rlwy noise; Eng spkn; red low ssn; ccard acc; red low ssn/CCI. "Lovely area; well-run site; pleasant staff; lge pitches; excel disabled facs & access to pool; gd site rest." ♦ 27 Mar-6 Nov. € 25.10 2007*

AVRANCHES *2E4* (6km S Rural) **FFCC Camping Rural Avallonn (Martinet), La Caufetière, 50220 Céaux [02 33 68 39 47]** Fr Avranches on N175 exit La Buvette & W onto D43. Site in approx 2km. Sm, pt shd; wc; shwrs inc; el pnts (5A) €3.50; rest; snacks; playgrnd; pool; sand beach 20km; dogs; Eng spkn; adv bkg; quiet. "In apple orchard; friendly, helpful owners; clean, rustic san facs; goats & horses in pens on site; many activities, museums nrby; 10km fr Mont-St Michel; uneven grnd, steep & narr ent but gd NH." ♦ 15 Apr-30 Sep. € 14.10 2009*

AVRANCHES *2E4* (10km W Rural) *48.68775, -1.48454* **Camping Les Coques d'Or, Route du Bec-d'Andaine, 50530 Genêts [02 33 70 82 57 or 06 85 21 13 01 (mob LS); fax 02 33 70 86 83; information@campinglescoquesdor.com; www.campinglescoquesdor.com]** Fr Avranches foll Granville rd. In 1km turn L on D911 sp Vains to Genêts. At Genêts take D35E for 500m & site on R. Med, hdg/mkd pitch, pt shd; wc; shwrs inc; el pnts (3-10A) €2-4; Indtte; shops 1km; tradsmn; snacks; bar; playgrnd; sm pool; sand beach 800m; fishing; TV rm; entmnt; 80% statics (sep area); dogs €2; poss cr; Eng spkn; quiet; red low ssn. "Gd views Mont-St Michel nrby." ♦ 1 Apr-30 Sep. € 14.80 2007*

This is a wonderful site.

I'll fill in a report online and let the Club know – www.caravanclub.co.uk/europereport

AVRANCHES *2E4* (10km W Rural) *48.69663, -1.47434* **FFCC Camping La Pérame, 50530 Genêts [02 33 70 82 49]** Fr Avranches on N175; in 1km turn L on D911 thro Genêts. Turn R onto D35 immed after passing thro Genêts, site on R in 1km. Sm, pt shd; wc; shwrs inc; el pnts (10A) €2.70 (rev pol); tradsmn; farm produce; playgrnd; 60% statics; dogs €0.90; phone; poss cr; red low ssn; quiet; CCI. "CL-type site in apple orchard nr sm vill; pleasant owner; gd views of Mont-St Michel fr vill; poss ltd & unkempt low ssn; guided walks to Mont St Michel; rec." 1 Apr-31 Oct. € 11.60 2009*

⊞ **AVRILLE** *7A1* (500m N Rural) *46.47641, -1.49373* **Camping Le Domaine des Forges, Rue des Forges, 85440 Avrillé [02 51 22 38 85; fax 02 51 90 98 70; contact@campingdomainedesforges.com; www.campingdomaine desforges.com or www.les-castels.com]** In Avrillé on D949 turn N into Rue des Forges, site sp. Med, mkd pitch, pt shd; wc; chem disp; baby facs; shwrs; el pnts (10A) inc; gas; lndtte (inc dryer); shop; takeaway; snacks; bar; BBQ; playgrnd; htd pool; paddling pool; lake fishing; sand beach 10km; cycle hire; tennis; games area; games rm; entmnt; wifi; TV; dogs €4; adv bkg; ccard acc; red low ssn. "Spacious pitches; lovely setting." ♦ € 27.00 ABS - A43 2009*

AVRILLE *7A1* (1km E Rural) *46.47005, -1.48691* **Camping Le Beauchêne, Ave de Lattre de Tassigny, 85440 Avrillé [02 51 22 30 49; fax 02 51 22 37 60; campinglebeauchene@wanadoo.fr; www.lebeauchene.com]** On E o'skts of Avrillé, on D949, visible fr rd. Med, mkd pitch, unshd, wc; chem disp; baby facs; shwrs inc; el pnts (6A) €3; lndtte; shops 500m; tradsmn; snacks; rest adj; BBQ; playgrnd; htd pool; sand beach 9km; games area; entmnt; TV rm; 40% statics; dogs €3; poss cr; Eng spkn; adv bkg; rd noise; CCI. "On o'skts of Avrillé; friendly, helpful owners; pitches well packed in; gd facs; fair." ♦ 1 May-6 Sep. € 14.00 2008*

AVRILLE *7A1* (1km S Rural) *46.45578, -1.48365* **Camping Les Mancellières, Route de Longeville-sur-Mer, 85440 Avrillé [02 51 90 35 97; fax 02 51 90 39 31; camping.mancellieres@wanadoo.fr; www.lesmancellieres.com]** Fr Avrillé take D105 S twd Longeville-sur-Mer. Site on L in 1.5km. Med, hdg/mkd pitch, pt sl; wc (some cont); chem disp; baby facs; shwrs inc; el pnts (6A) €3.90; gas; lndtte; shop; snacks; BBQ (charcoal/gas); playgrnd; htd pool; paddling pool; waterslide; beach 5km; fishing 2km; tennis 800m; cycle hire, horseriding 3km; games rm; entmnt; 30% statics; dogs €2; some Eng spkn; adv bkg; quiet; 30% red low ssn; ccard not acc. "Friendly owners; peaceful; ent gates set on angle & poss diff lge o'fits." ♦ 1 May-15 Sep. € 17.00 2009*

⊞ **AX LES THERMES** *8G4* (2km NE Rural) *42.73308, 1.85386* **FFCC Camp Municipal La Prade, 09110 Sorgeat [05 61 64 36 34 or 05 61 64 21 93; fax 05 61 64 63 38; camping@sorgeat.com; www.sorgeat.com]** In cent of Ax-les-Thermes turn E off N20 onto D613. In 5km in Sorgeat turn R & foll sp thro vill to site, 800m on R. V steep, winding, narr app with hairpins - not rec lge car/c'van o'fits. Sm, hdg/mkd pitch, terr, pt shd; htd wc (some cont); chem disp; shwrs inc; el pnts (5-10A) €2.80-5.40; gas 5km; lndtte; shop 1km; rest 5km; snacks; playgrnd; pool 5km; 15% statics; dogs €0.60; phone; poss cr; adv bkg; quiet; ccard not acc; CCI. "Clean site 1150m high o'looking Ariège valley; ski lifts at Ax; gd walks; not suitable lge o'fits." € 10.00 2008*

⊞ **AX LES THERMES** *8G4* (7km E Rural) *42.72421, 1.89311* **FFCC Camping Ascou La Forge, 09110 Ascou [05 61 64 60 03; fax 05 61 64 60 06; mountain.sports@wanadoo.fr; www.mountain-sports.net]** On N20 S turn L at rndabt by church in Ax sp Ascou. In 4km turn R sp Ascou-Pailhères. Foll site sp to site on R in 3km after lake & hamlet Goulours. Rd narr & mountainous, not rec med/lge o'fits. Sm, mkd pitch, pt sl, pt shd; wc; chem disp; shwrs inc; el pnts (4-10A) €3-5; lndtte; shop & 7km; tradsmn; bar; playgrnd; fishing; entmnt; dogs €1.50; adv bkg; red low ssn; CCI. "Mountain scenery; simple, immac facs; gd walking; charming, helpful Dutch owners." ♦ € 15.00 2008*

⊞ **AX LES THERMES** *8G4* (4km SE Rural) *42.70245, 1.88345* **Camp Municipal d'Orlu, 09110 Orlu [05 61 64 30 09 or 05 61 64 21 70; fax 05 61 64 64 23]** On N20 S foll sp for Spain thro town cent. On exit town turn L immed bef bdge sp Orlu. Site on R in 3km. Med, mkd pitch, pt shd; htd wc; shwrs inc; el pnts (2-10A) €1.85-5.30; gas; lndtte; shop 3km; rest, snacks, bar 500m; playgrnd; pool high ssn; rv adj; fishing; games area; entmnt; 30% statics; dogs €0.95; phone; poss cr; adv bkg; quiet; CCI. "Gd, friendly, scenic site; poss floods in bad weather; excel walks; conv Andorra or Spain." ♦ € 10.80 2006*

⊞ **AX LES THERMES** *8G4* (1km NW Rural) *42.72870, 1.82541* **Camping Sunêlia Le Malazéou, 09110 Ax-les-Thermes [05 61 64 69 14; fax 05 61 64 05 60; camping.malazeou@wanadoo.fr; www.campingmalazeou.com]** Sp on N20 to Foix. Lge, hdg pitch, pt sl, shd; htd wc (some cont); chem disp; mv service pnt; baby facs; shwrs inc; el pnts (6A) inc; gas; lndry rm; shop 1km; tradsmn; playgrnd; 70% statics; dogs €2.50; train 500m; site clsd Nov; Eng spkn; adv bkg; quiet but some rd noise; CCI. "Fair NH; lovely scenery & gd fishing; rvside walk to town." ♦ € 23.00 2008*

⊞ **AX LES THERMES** *8G4* (8km NW Rural) *42.75880, 1.76319* **Camp Municipal Le Castella, 09250 Luzenac [05 61 64 47 53; fax 05 61 64 40 59; campingcastella@wanadoo.fr; www.campingcastella.com]** Site on W of N20 bet Ax-les-Thermes & Foix. Med, mkd pitch, terr, pt shd; htd wc; shwrs inc; el pnts (4-10A) €2.05-5.20; lndtte; shop, bar 300m; playgrnd; pool in ssn; fishing; tennis; archery; entmnt; quiet; ccard acc. "Gd walking; prehistoric caves at Niaux; mountain views; barrier locked until 0900 when office opens." ♦ € 8.95 2007*

AXAT *8G4* (2km E Rural) *42.80775, 2.25408* **Camping de la Crémade, 11140 Axat [tel/fax 04 68 20 50 64; www.lacremade.com]** S fr Quillan on D117, cont 1km beyond junc with D118 twd Perpignan. Turn R into site, sp, narr access. Med, hdg pitch, pt sl, pt shd; wc; shwrs inc; el pnts (6A) inc; lndtte; shop & 3km; BBQ; playgrnd; games rm; 5% statics; dogs €1; Eng spkn; adv bkg; quiet; CCI. "Pleasant, well-maintained site in beautiful location; few level pitches." ♦ Easter-30 Sep. € 13.70 2008*

AYDAT *9B1* (2km NE Rural) *45.66777, 2.98943* **Camping du Lac d'Aydat, Forêt du Lot, 63970 Aydat [04 73 79 38 09; fax 04 73 79 34 12; info@camping-lac-aydat.com; www.camping-lac-aydat.com]** Exit A75 S fr Clermont-Ferrand at junc 5 onto D13 W. Foll sp Lake Aydat. At x-rds at end of Rouillas-Bas, turn L at rndabt & foll site sp. Med, mkd pitch, some hdstg, terr, shd; wc (some cont); chem disp; mv service pnt; serviced pitches; shwrs inc; el pnts (10A) €4; Indtte; shop 1km; tradsmn high ssn; rest 500m; snacks; bar 500m; playgrnd; lake sw 500m; fishing; entmnt; 30% statics; dogs €1.50; phone; poss cr; adv bkg; quiet; red low ssn; CCI. "On shore of Lake Aydat; gd for m'vans." ♦ 1 Apr-30 Sep. € 16.00 2007*

AYDAT *9B1* (3km W Rural) *45.66195, 2.94857* **Camping Les Volcans, La Garandie, 63970 Aydat [tel/fax 04 73 79 33 90; keith_harvey@compuserve.com]** Exit A73 junc 5 onto D213 W. In 16km turn S in Verneuge onto D5. After 2km turn W onto D788 sp La Garandie. In vill turn R just after phone box, site on L in 200m. Sm, mkd pitch, pt sl, pt shd; wc; chem disp; shwrs inc; el pnts (6A) €2.60; Indtte; sm shop; tradsmn; rest, snacks 4km; bar 3km; lake sw & sand beach 4km; dogs €0.60; phone adj; adv bkg; quiet. "Excel walking & cycle rtes nr; relaxing site; lge pitches; beautiful area; gd touring base." 1 Jun-31 Aug. € 10.10 2009*

I'm going to fill in some site report forms and post them off to the Club; we could win a ferry crossing – it's here on page 12.

⊞ **AZAY LE FERRON** *4H2* (8km N Rural) *46.91949, 1.03679* **Camping Le Cormier, Route de St Flovier, 36290 Obterre [02 54 39 27 95 or 0844 232 7271 (UK); mike.smith51@orange.fr; www.loireholidays.biz]** Fr Azay-le-Ferron N on D14, site on R just N of Obterre. Or fr Loches S on D943 for 3.5km, turn onto D41 to St Flovier then turn L onto D21 sp Obterre. In 1km turn R onto D14, site on L in 4km. Sm, hdg/mkd pitch, hdstg, pt shd; htd wc; chem disp; shwrs inc; el pnts (8A) €4; Indry rm; ice; tradsmn; rest, snacks & bar 5km; BBQ; pool; games area; games rm; TV; dogs free; Eng spkn; adv bkg; quiet; red low ssn. "Friendly, helpful British owners (C'van Club members); lge pitches; excel touring/walking base; nr Brenne National Park; excel birdwatching; vg." € 12.00 2009*

AZAY LE FERRON *4H2* (E Rural) *46.85086, 1.07306* **Camp Municipal Le Camp du Château, Rue Hersent-Luzarche, 36290 Azay-le-Ferron [02 54 39 21 91 (Mairie); mairieazayleferron@mcom.fr]** On D975 Châtillon-sur-Indre to Le Bland, turn R in vill onto D925, site on R in 100m. Sm, pt shd; wc (some cont); shwrs inc; el pnts (10A) inc; shops 100m; rest; playgrnd; tennis; fishing; tennis; quiet. "Warden calls pm." 15 Apr-15 Oct. € 10.00 2008*

AZAY LE RIDEAU *4G1* (300m E Urban) *47.25919, 0.46992* **FFCC Camp Municipal Le Sabot, Rue du Stade, 37190 Azay-le-Rideau [02 47 45 42 72 or 02 47 45 42 11 (Mairie); fax 02 47 45 49 11; camping.lesabot@wanadoo.fr; http://monsite.orange.fr/azaylerideau.camping]** Fr town cent foll D84 (N bank of rv) sp Artannes; after chateau on R, cont to mini rndabt & turn sharp R. Parked cars hide ent to site. Best app is fr by-pass to avoid narr town - turn off at rndabt nr Champion supmkt & downhill to site. Lge, mkd pitch, pt shd; wc (some cont); chem disp; mv service pnt; shwrs inc; el pnts (10A) €4 (poss rev pol); gas 1km; shop, snacks, rest in town; BBQ; htd pool adj; playgrnd; fishing; boat & canoe hire; wifi; TV; phone; dogs; poss cr fr Son et Lumière in high ssn; Eng spkn; adv bkg rec; quiet; ccard acc; red low ssn/long stay; CCI. "Pleasant, spacious, well-kept site by rv & chateau; poss long dist to san facs fr some pitches - central facs have steps; red facs low ssn; site prone to flooding; when site clsd m'vans can stay on car park by rv o'night - no facs but well lit (enq at tourist office)." ♦ 10 Apr-1 Oct. € 11.00 2009*

AZAY SUR THOUET see Parthenay *4H1*

AZUR see Soustons *8E1*

BACCARAT *6E2* (1km SE Rural) *48.44360, 6.74360* **Camp Municipal Pré de Hon, 54120 Baccarat [03 83 76 35 35 or 03 83 75 13 37 (LS); fax 03 83 75 36 76; info-baccarat@orange.fr; www.ot-baccarat.fr]** Fr Baccarat cent opp town hall take D158 S past church twd Lachapelle. Site in 500m down lane on L. Sm, pt shd, wc; chem disp; shwrs; el pnts (10A); shop 200m; pool nr; bus 400m; poss cr; adv bkg; quiet, some rd noise; CCI. "Pleasant, quiet rvside site; helpful warden, if absent site yourself; rvside walk to interesting town; gd NH." ♦ 1 May-15 Sep. € 9.40 2009*

BADEN *2F3* (500m SW Rural) *47.61410, -2.92540* **Camping Mané Guernehué, 52 Rue Mané er Groëz, 56870 Baden [02 97 57 02 06; fax 02 97 57 15 43; info@camping-baden.com; www.camping-baden.com]** Exit N165 sp Arradon/L'Ile aux Moines onto D101 to Baden (10km); in Baden vill turn R at camp sp immed after sharp L-hand bend; in 200m bear R at junc; site on R. Sp at both ends of vill. Lge, hdg/mkd pitch, terr, pt shd; htd wc; chem disp; mv service pnt; sauna; baby facs; shwrs inc; el pnts (10A) €4.70; gas 1km; Indtte; sm shop; rest/snacks; bar; BBQ; playgrnd; lge htd pool complex (covrd & outdoor); waterslide; jacuzzi; sand beach 3km; fishing; tennis 600m; fitness rm; games area; games rm; cycle hire; golf 1.5km; wifi; entmnt; TV rm; 35% statics; dogs €3.80; phone; Eng spkn; quiet; ccard acc; red low ssn/long stay. "Mature, pleasant site; gd views; some larger open pitches at bottom of site fully serviced; excel san facs; excel." ♦ 30 Apr-31 Oct. € 36.00 (CChq acc) 2008*

BAERENTHAL *5D3* (500m N Rural) *48.98170, 7.51230* **Camp Municipal Ramstein-Plage, Rue de Ramstein, 57230 Baerenthal [03 87 06 50 73; fax 03 87 06 50 26; camping.ramstein@wanadoo.fr; www.baerenthal.eu]** Fr N62 turn onto D36 sp Baerenthal, site sp on lakeside. Lge, hdg/mkd pitch, pt sl, pt shd; htd wc; chem disp; mv service pnt; baby facs; shwrs inc; el pts (12A) €4.20; Indtte; shop 1km; rest; snacks; bar; playgrnd; htd pool; lake sw, sand beach adj; tennis; games area; entmnt; 60% statics (sep area); dogs €1.10; m'van o'night area; poss cr; Eng spkn; adv bkg; quiet. "Attractive location in important ecological area; generous pitches; excel clean, modern san facs; gd walks; birdwatching; conv Maginot Line; excel." ♦ 1 Apr-30 Sep. € 17.10 2007*

BAGNEAUX SUR LOING see Nemours *4F3*

BAGNERES DE BIGORRE *8F2* (9km NE Rural) *43.11196, 0.04931* **Aire Naturelle Le Cerf Volant (Dhom), 7 Cami de la Géline, 65380 Orincles [tel/fax 05 62 42 99 32; lecerfvolant1@yahoo.fr]** Fr Bagnères-de-Bigorre on D935; turn L onto D397 dir Lourdes; site on L opp D407. Single track app rd for 150m. Sm, pt shd; wc (cont); chem disp; shwrs inc; el pnts (15A) €1.50; Indtte; tradsmn; playgrnd; no statics; dogs free; poss cr; no ccard acc; CCI. "Farm site - produce sold Jul-Aug; conv Lourdes & touring Pyrenees gd."♦ 15 May-15 Oct. € 6.70 2007*

BAGNERES DE BIGORRE *8F2* (1km E Urban) *43.07158, 0.15692* **Camping Les Fruitiers, 9 Rue de Toulouse, 65200 Bagnères-de-Bigorre [tel/fax 05 62 95 25 97; daniellevillemur@wanadoo.fr; www.camping-les-fruitiers.com]** On D938 fr town cent dir Toulouse. Site sp at traff lits at x-rds with D8. Site well sp on app; take care on final app to ent. Med, mkd pitch, pt sl, pt shd; htd wc; chem disp; baby facs; shwrs inc; el pnts (2-6A) €2-5; Indtte; shops 200m; rest 300m; snacks 200m; playgrnd; pool 200m; tennis; dogs €1; phone; bus; poss cr; adv bkg; quiet/some traff noise; CCI. "Lovely, well-kept site; helpful staff; excel facs; sharp bends on site rds & o'hanging trees poss diff lge o'fits; attractive town; vg mkt; vg." ♦ Apr-Oct. € 12.00 2009*

⊞ **BAGNERES DE BIGORRE** *8F2* (3km E Rural) *43.08180, 0.15139* **Camping Le Monlôo, 6 Route de la Plaine, 65200 Bagnères-de-Bigorre [tel/fax 05 62 95 19 65; campingmonloo@yahoo.com; www.lemonloo.com]** Fr A64 exit junc 14 onto D20/D938 to Bagnères-de-Bigorre. At traff lts on ent turn R onto D8, site on R in 1km, sp at ent. Fr Tarbes (N) on D935 turn L at 1st rndabt, L again over old rlwy line, site in R. Med, sl, pt shd; wc; chem disp; mv service pnt; shwrs inc; el pnts (3-10A) €3-8; Indtte; shop 1km; playgrnd; pool (high ssn); waterslide; tennis; TV; entmnt; 30% statics; phone; dogs €1; adv bkg; quiet; ccard acc; red low ssn; CCI. "Peaceful, spacious, scenic, well-kept site; friendly, welcoming owner; ltd water points; gd facs, poss stretched high ssn; pleasant town." € 15.30 (3 persons) 2009*

⊞ **BAGNERES DE BIGORRE** *8F2* (2km SE Rural) *43.05566, 0.16510* **Camping La Pommeraie, 2 Ave Philadelphe, 65200 Gerde [05 62 91 32 24; fax 05 62 95 16 42]** App fr E, exit A64 junc 14 (Tournay) onto D20/D938 to Bagnères-de-Bigorre; on ent town turn L at traff lts & foll sp to site. App fr W, exit A64 junc 12 (Tarbes); leave ring rd at junc with D935 & cont to Bagnères-de-Bigorre; foll site sps fr town. Sm, mkd pitch, some hdstg, pt sl, pt shd; wc; chem disp; shwrs inc; el pnts (6A) inc; gas 2km; Indry area; shop 2km; BBQ; sm playgrnd; htd, covrd pool 2km; cycle hire in Bagnères; some statics; dogs; phone; Eng spkn; adv bkg; quiet; CCI. "Mountain views; friendly owners; excel walking, mountain biking & touring base; vg." € 16.80 2008*

⊞ **BAGNERES DE BIGORRE** *8F2* (6km S Rural) *43.01777, 0.17567* **Camping FFCC Le Layris, Quartier Bourg, 65710 Campan [05 62 91 75 34; lelayris@campan-pyrenees.com; www.campan-pyrenees.com]** Exit A64 junc 14 S on D20/D938 to Bagnères. Fr Bagnères, take D935 S, site on R after ent to Campan, sp. Sm, mkd pitch, pt shd; htd wc (cont); chem disp; shwrs inc; el pnts (8A) €7.50; Indtte; shops adj; playgrnd; pool 5km; fishing; tennis adj; wintersports 12km; dogs; poss cr; adv bkg; quiet; CCI. "Gd site for walkers." € 12.10 2008*

BAGNOLES DE L'ORNE *4E1* (3km SE Rural) *48.53738, -0.40141* **Camping Le Clos Normand, Route de Bagnoles de l'Orne, 61410 Couterne [02 33 37 92 43 or 06 07 17 44 94 (mob); www.camping-clos-normand.fr]** On D916 approx midway bet Couterne & La Ferté Macé; well sp. Med, hdg/mkd pitch, pt sl, shd; wc; chem disp; shwrs inc; el pnts (5-10A) €2.55-3.40; gas; Indtte; shops 2km; tradsmn; rest, bar 2km; snacks; BBQ; playgrnd; canoeing; entmnt; TV; 20% statics; dogs €0.53; phone; Eng spkn; adv bkg; some rd noise. "Attractive, well-maintained, friendly site; in National Park Normandie-Maine - gd walks; san facs need update; poss long stay workers on site; close to thermal spa & excel sports facs, boating lake & casino; 1 hour fr car ferry; unreliable opening dates low ssn - phone ahead." 1 May-30 Sep. € 7.80 2007*

BAGNOLES DE L'ORNE *4E1* (1.3km SW Rural) *48.54746, -0.42026* **Camping de la Vée, Rue du President Coty, 61140 Bagnoles-de-l'Orne [02 33 37 87 45; fax 02 33 30 14 32; camping-de-la-vee@wanadoo.fr; www.bagnoles-de-lorne.com]** Access fr D335 in vill of Bagnoles-Château. Or fr La Ferté-Macé on D916 for 6km sp Couterne. Well sp fr all dirs. Lge, hdg/mkd pitch, pt shd; htd wc (some cont); chem disp; mv service pnt; baby facs; shwrs inc; el pnts (6-10A) €3.25-4.10 (poss rev pol); gas 1km; Indtte; shop 1km; tradsmn; rest; snacks; bar; BBQ; playgrnd; htd pool 1.5km; rv & lake nrby; golf, archery, tennis & mini-golf nrby; wifi; TV; 10% statics; dogs €1.45; phone; free bus to town cent at site ent; poss cr; Eng spkn; no adv bkg; quiet; no ccard acc; CCI. "Excel, well-run site in vg location; vg, clean facs; beautiful thermal spa town; forest walks; gd for dogs." ♦ 20 Mar-6 Nov. € 10.85 2009*

See advertisement on next page

France

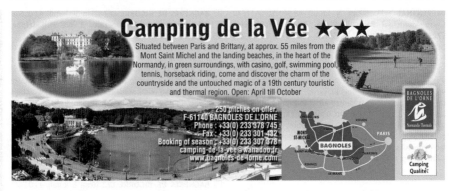

BAGNOLS SUR CEZE *10E2* (2km NE Rural) *44.17378, 4.63643* **Camping Les Genêts d'Or, Route de Carmigan, 30200 Bagnols-sur-Cèze [tel/fax 04 66 89 58 67; info@camping.genets-dor.com; www.camping-genets-dor.com]** N fr Bagnols on N86 over rv bdge, turn R into D360 immed after Total stn. Foll sp to site on rv. Med, pt sl, pt shd; wc (some cont); shwrs inc; el pnts (3-8A) €2.86-3.70 (rev pol); gas; lndtte; shop; rest; snacks; bar; pool; playgrnd; sports area; canoeing, fishing 2km; games rm; no dogs Jul/Aug; poss cr; Eng spkn; adv bkg ess; quiet; ccard acc. "Excel, clean site; welcoming Dutch owners; nice pool; wildlife in rv; gd rest; highly rec." ♦ 1 Apr-30 Sep. € 21.20 2006*

⊞ **BAGNOLS SUR CEZE** *10E2* (7km S Rural) *44.08434, 4.59177* **Camping Le Vieux Verger, Ave des Platanes, 30330 Connaux [04 66 82 91 62; fax 04 66 82 60 02; campinglevieuxverger@wanadoo.fr; www.campinglevieuxverger.com]** Fr S on D6086 (N86) turn L into vill fr bypass to x-rds in 200m & then L into Ave des Platanes. Site on R. S fr Bagnols-sur-Cèze on D6086 to Connaux. Look for green site sp 1km after turn. Site sp. Sm, hdg/mkd pitch, pt sl, terr, pt shd; wc; chem disp; shwrs; el pnts (10A) €3; lndtte; shop; snacks; bar; playgrnd; 2 htd pools; games area; 25% statics; dogs €1.90; poss cr; Eng spkn; adv bkg; quiet; ccard acc; red low ssn; CCI. "Well-maintained steep, sloping site; excel san facs; not suitable v lge o'fits; no twin-axles; excel." ♦ € 14.90 2008*

BAGNOLS SUR CEZE *10E2* (8km NW Rural) *44.18865, 4.52448* **Camping Les Cascades, Route de Donnat, 30200 La Roque-sur-Cèze [04 66 82 72 97; fax 04 66 82 68 51; info@campinglescascades.com; www.campinglescascades.com]** Fr Bagnols take D6 W twd Alès. After 4km turn N on D143 & foll sp to La Roque-sur-Cèze. Site on R in 7km. App fr N not rec. Long narr bdge (2.3m). Med, pt sl, pt shd; wc (cont); chem disp; shwrs inc; el pnts (6-10A) €3.30-3.50; gas; lndtte; shop; rest; snacks; bar; playgrnd; pool; shgl beach & rv adj; tennis; fishing; boating; internet; entmnt; TV; dogs €1.50; poss cr; adv bkg; quiet. "Tranquil site; poss ltd facs when full." 1 Apr-30 Sep. € 17.80 (CChq acc) 2007*

BAGUER PICAN see Dol de Bretagne *2E4*

BAIGNES STE RADEGONDE *7B2* (500m SW Rural) *45.38187, -0.23862* **FFCC Camp Municipal, Le Plein, 16360 Baignes-Ste-Radegonde [05 45 78 79 96 or 05 45 78 40 04 (Mairie); fax 05 45 78 47 41; point.i.baignes@orange.fr; www.baignes-sainte-radegonde.fr]** Fr N10 turn W onto D2 to Baignes; site well sp on rvside. Sm, pt shd; wc; chem disp; shwrs inc; el pnts (5A) €2.50; shops 100m; tennis; adv bkg; ccard acc. "Warden calls pm; attractive sm town; quiet; gd." 1 May-30 Sep. € 7.00 2009*

BAILLEUL *3A3* (3km N Rural) *50.76160, 2.74956* **Camping Les Saules (Notteau), 453 Route du Mont Noir, 59270 Bailleul [03 28 49 13 75]** N fr Lille on A25 exit junc 10 & head N into Bailleul cent; in town at traff lts turn R onto D23/N375; in 2km just bef Belgian border turn L onto D223. Site on L in 300m. Sm, hdstg, pt shd; wc; chem disp; shwrs inc; el pnts (6A) €3; lndtte; farm shop; BBQ; playgrnd; 90% statics; dogs; Eng spkn; quiet but some rd noise; CCI. "Excel farm site; friendly owner; clean, modern san facs; conv Calais, Dunkerque, WW1 sites." 1 Apr-31 Oct. € 9.30 2009*

BAILLEUL *3A3* (4km N Rural) *50.77909, 2.73692* **Camping Domaine de la Sablière, Mont-Noir, 59270 St Jans-Cappel [03 28 49 46 34; fax 03 28 42 62 90]** Fr A25 exit junc 10, N on D10 thro Bailleul to St Jans-Cappel. Thro vill turn R at x-rds onto D318 to Mont-Noir. Site on R at top of hill. Med, hdg/mkd pitch, terr, shd; wc; chem disp; some serviced pitches; shwrs inc; el pnts (6A) inc; lndtte; shop, rest & bar 3km; bar; playgrnd; fishing 2km; tennis; mini-golf 100m; 80% statics; phone. "Well-kept site; new owners (2009); clean san facs; pitch access poss diff lge o'fits due steep gradients & tight turns; conv WW1 battlefields, Dunkerque & Calais; gd." 15 Mar-15 Oct. € 18.00 2009*

BAILLEUL *3A3* (8km NE Rural) *50.79397, 2.67311* **Camping Les 5 Chemins Verts, 689 Rue des 5 Chemins Verts, 59299 Boeschepe [tel/fax 03 28 49 42 37; cinq.chemins.verts@gmail.com; www.5-chemins-verts.ovh.org]** Fr N exit A25 junc 13 onto D948 W; in 5km turn R onto D10 to Boeschepe; turn R in vill. Or fr S exit A25 at Bailleul; N onto D10 to Boeschepe; turn L in vill. Site sp. V narr app rds, not suitable lge o'fits. Med, pt sl, pt shd; wc (some cont); chem disp; fam bthrm; shwrs inc; gas; el pnts (10A) €2.80; gas; Indtte; tradsmn; rest; snacks; bar; BBQ; playgrnd; games area; games rm; entmnt; wifi; 98% statics; dogs; phone; some Eng spkn; adv bkg; ccard acc; CCI. "Well-kept gardens; just a few touring pitches; clean, roomy modern san facs up steps, inc disabled; fishing in pond with ducks; gd rests around Mont des Cats; conv WWI sites, Calais; gd." ♦ 15 Mar-31 Oct. € 9.00 2009*

BAIN DE BRETAGNE *2F4* (1km SE Urban) *47.8300, -1.67083* **Camp Municipal du Lac, Route de Launay, 35470 Bain-de-Bretagne [02 99 43 85 67 or 02 99 43 70 24 (Mairie); contact@camping-dulac.fr]** Take N137 take D777 E, then N772 E dir Châteaubriant, foll sp. Up hill & turn R into narr lane; at bottom of himm over x-rds, L at T-junc & R into site rd. Site sp. Not rec to tow thro Bain-de-Bretagne. Med, hdg/mkd pitch, pt shd; wc; chem disp; mv service pnt; shwrs inc; el pnts (10A) €2; shop 1km; tradsmn; rest; snacks; bar; playgrnd; htd pool 500m; lake sw, sailing school nr; statics; dogs €1.50; phone; poss cr; Eng spkn; quiet; CCI. "Pretty site with views over lake; fees collected each eve; go to bar/café if gates locked or phone warden on number displayed at office; old but clean facs; attractive sm town; many leisure facs in walking dist; poss itinerants; conv NH." ♦ 1 Apr-30 Oct. € 13.00 2009*

BAIN DE BRETAGNE *2F4* (11km W Rural) *47.8200, -1.8299* **Camp Municipal Le Port, Rue de Camping, 35480 Guipry [02 99 34 72 90 (Mairie) or 02 99 34 28 26]** W fr Bain-de-Bretagne on D772, cross rv at Messac; cont on D772 sharp L at Leader supmkt into Ave du Port; site sp bef ent Guipry. NB Do not app after dark as rv is at end of app rd. Med, hdg/mkd pitch, pt shd; wc; mv service pnt; shwrs; el pnts (6A) €2.65 (poss long lead req); shop & rest nrby; playgrnd; pool nrby; rv fishing; train noise; CCI. "Excel site; friendly; warden on duty am & late pm; barrier 1.90m locked at times but phone for help or go to pitch 30; delightful rv walks & cycle paths; cruising & hire boats avail; nr classic cars museum." ♦ Easter-15 Oct. € 9.80 2009*

BAIX *9D2* (2km W Rural) *44.70527, 4.73794* **Camping Le Merle Roux, 07210 Baix [04 75 85 84 14; fax 04 75 85 83 07; lemerleroux@hotmail.com; www.lemerleroux.com]** Fr A7/E15 exit junc 16. Foll sp Le Pouzin, x-ing Rv Rhône. Turn L onto D86 (S), go thro Le Pouzin, in 2km immed bef rlwy x-ing, turn R twd Privas; in 500m turn L at sp & foll rd approx 2km. Single track rd to site, not rec low powered car + lge c'van Med, pt sl, terr, pt shd; wc; chem disp; shwrs inc; el pnts (6A) €3.50; Indtte; shop; tradsmn; rest; snacks; bar; no BBQ; playgrnd; pool; 15% statics; dogs €2.50; adv bkg; quiet; red low ssn; CCI. "Scenic site; gd facs & pitches; poss diff to reverse onto pitch; welcoming Dutch owners; excel." 1 Apr-30 Sep. € 27.00 2009*

BALARUC LES BAINS *10F1* (300m NE Coastal) *43.44084, 3.68320* **Camp Municipal Pech d'Ay, Ave de la Gare, 34540 Balaruc-les-Bains [04 67 48 50 34]** Exit N113 to Balaruc-les-Bains; foll sp Centre Commercial & then head for prom. Site on prom. Lge, mkd pitch, pt sl, pt shd; htd wc; chem disp; mv service pnt; shwrs; el pnts (10A) €3.40; Indtte in town; shops, rest & bar adj; playgrnd; shgle beaches nrby; bus; poss cr; adv bkg rec (even low ssn); poss noisy; CCI. "Delightful holiday resort; busy all ssn, rec arr early; vg, clean san facs; many gd rests adj; thermal baths in vill; bus to Sète." 28 Feb-12 Dec. € 13.00 2009*

BALARUC LES BAINS *10F1* (500m NE Coastal) *43.45203, 3.69237* **Camping Le Mas du Padre, 4 Chemin du Mas du Padre, 34540 Balaruc-les-Bains [04 67 48 53 41; fax 04 67 48 08 94; info@mas-du-padre.com; www.mas-du-padre.com]** Fr Sète N on D2. In Balaruc turn R after traff lts 1km fr vill, then 2nd on R onto local rd for 500m. Well sp. Fr A9 exit junc 33 on N300 sp Sète; foll sp Balaruc-les-Bains on D2 for 2 rndabts, then turn R on D2E6 sp campings. Med, hdg/mkd pitch, pt sl, terr, shd; wc; chem disp; baby facs; shwrs inc; el pnts (6A) inc; gas; Indtte; shops 3km; tradsmn; playgrnd; pool; lake sw, fishing & boating 2km; tennis; entmnt; TV; 10% statics; dogs €2.15; poss cr; Eng spkn; adv bkg rec high ssn; quiet; ccard acc; red low ssn; CCI. "Pretty, well-equipped & well-kept site nr beaches; immac facs; extra for lger pitches; site rds narr; owner helpful; poss unkempt low ssn; excel." ♦ 5 Apr-12 Oct. € 28.55 2007*

BALARUC LES BAINS *10F1* (500m NE Coastal) *43.45344, 3.68802* **Camping Les Vignes, 34540 Balaruc-les-Bains [04 67 48 04 93; fax 04 67 18 74 32; camping.lesvignes@free.fr; www.camping-lesvignes.com]** Fr N113 take D2 sp Sète, turn W sp Balurac-les-Bains, after 2nd rndabt turn R, well sp in 100m on R. Med, hdg/mkd pitch, pt shd; wc (some cont); chem disp; mv service pnt; shwrs inc; el pnts (6-10A) €3-3.50; Indtte; shops 1km; snacks; bar; playgrnd; pool; shgl beach 1km; sand beach 7km; fishing, horseriding & tennis nr; 30% statics; dogs €2; poss cr; adv bkg rec high ssn; quiet; ccard acc; CCI. "Narr site rds tight for long o'fits; Sète worth a visit; gd touring base." ♦ 1 Apr-31 Oct. € 17.00 2007*

BALAZUC *9D2* (1km N Rural) *44.51199, 4.38667* **FFCC Camping La Falaise, Hameau Les Silles, 07120 Balazuc [tel/fax 04 75 37 72 33 or 04 75 37 74 27; camping.falaise@wanadoo.fr]** Sp on D579 on rvside. Sm, hdg pitch, pt sl, shd; wc; chem disp; baby facs; shwrs inc; el pnts (6A); gas; Indtte; shop; tradsmn; snacks; bar; playgrnd; rv beach; canoe hire; poss cr; Eng spkn; adv bkg; CCI. "Site beside Rv Arèche; helpful owners; vg." 1 Apr-30 Sep. € 15.00 2006*

BALAZUC *9D2* (2km N Rural) *44.50778, 4.40340* **Camping Le Chamadou, Mas de Chaussy, 07120 Balazuc [04 75 37 00 56; fax 04 75 37 70 61; infos@camping-le-chamadou.com; www.camping-le-chamadou.com]** Fr Ruoms foll D579 dir Aubenas. After approx 9km turn R under viaduct, site sp. Keep R up narr rd to site. App recep on foot fr car pk. Med, hdg pitch, hdstg, pt sl, pt shd; htd wc; chem disp; baby facs; fam bthrm; shwrs inc; el pnts (5A) €4 (some rev pol); lndtte; shop & 3km; tradsmn; snacks; bar; BBQ; playgrnd; pool; rv & beach 1.5km; canoe & kayak hire; entmnt; TV rm; dogs €1.80; phone; poss cr; Eng spkn; adv bkg rec; v quiet; ccard acc; CCI. "Excel, well-run, family site; panoramic views; most pitches spacious." 1 Apr-30 Sep. € 18.50 2006*

BALBIGNY *9B1* (3km NW Rural) *45.82558, 4.16196* **Camping La Route Bleue, Route du Lac de Villerest, Pralery, 42510 Balbigny [04 77 27 24 97 or 06 78 69 51 54 (mob); camping.balbigny@wanadoo.fr]** Fr N on D1082 (N82), take 1st R after a'route (A89/72) junc N of Balbigny onto D56. Fr S on D1082, turn L at RH bend on N o'skirts of Balbigny, D56, sp Lac de Villerest & St Georges-de-Baroille. Well sp. Med, hdg/mkd pitch, pt sl, pt shd; chem disp; mv service pnt; wc; shwrs inc; el pnts (6-10A) inc (poss long lead req); lndtte; shops 1.5km; tradsmn; rest; snacks; bar; playgrnd; pool & paddling pool; rv adj; fishing; games rm; sports complex adj; adv bkg; quiet; red long stay; ccard acc; CCI. "Excel site on rv bank; conv for A72; helpful & welcoming staff; san facs need update (2009); extra for twin-axles." ♦ 1 Apr-30 Sep. € 14.80 2009*

BALLEROY *1D4* (5km SW Rural) *49.15677, -0.92287* **Camping Domaine de Litteau, Le Perron, 14490 Litteau [02 31 22 22 08 or 05 56 07 90 17; domainedelitteau@siblu.fr; www.siblu.fr/litteau]** Fr St Lô, take D972 to Bayeux. After 14km, at La Malbreche, turn R onto D209 to Litteau. Site on L in approx 500m. Med, some hdg/mkd pitch, pt sl, unshd; wc; chem disp; baby facs; shwrs inc; el pnts (6A) inc; lndtte; shop & 4km; snacks; bar; playgrnd; htd covrd pool; lake fishing adj; sand beach 25km; horseriding; child entmnt; TV; 90% statics; dogs; phone; poss cr; eng spkn; adv bkg; ccard acc; CCI. "Busy high ssn; forest adj; conv D-Day beaches, museums, Bayeux tapestry." 4 Apr-1 Nov. € 40.00 2009*

BAN DE SAPT see Raon l'Etape *6E3*

BANDOL *10F3* (3km NW Rural) *43.15980, 5.72905* **Camping Le Clos Ste Thérèse, Route de Bandol, 83270 St Cyr-sur-Mer [tel/fax 04 94 32 12 21; camping@clos-therese.com; www.clos-therese.com]** Fr Bandol take D559 twd St Cyr & Marseilles. Site on R after 3km. Caution - site ent sharp U turn fr rd. Site service rds steep & narr; not suitable lge vans. Med, terr, shd; htd wc; chem disp; shwrs; el pnts (6-10A) €4-5.20; gas; lndtte; supmkt 1km; rest; snacks; bar; playgrnd; 2 pools (1 htd); paddling pool; sand beach 4km; golf, tennis, horseriding nr; entmnt; TV rm; 30% statics; dogs €2.30; adv bkg rec; some daytime rd noise. "Many beaches & beauty spots in area; tractor will site c'vans." ♦ 1 Apr-30 Sep. € 22.50 2008*

BANDOL *10F3* (6km NW Coastal) *43.17236, 5.69641* **Camping Les Baumelles, 1 Roiute de la Madrague, 83270 St Cyr-sur-Mer [04 94 26 21 27; fax 04 94 88 76 13; baumellesloisirs@aol.com]** Fr Bandol take coast rd D559 NW to St Cyr. Turn L by statue on rd to La Madrague. Foll this coast rd 1.5km. Site on L at junc of coast rd. V lge, some mkd pitch; pt sl, shd; wc; baby facs; shwrs inc; el pnts (10A) €3.50; gas adj; lndtte; shop; rest; snacks; bar; playgrnd; sand beach adj; golf 2km; entmnt; TV; 60% statics; dogs €2; poss cr; Eng spkn; quiet; ccard acc. ♦ 1 Apr-30 Oct. € 26.00 2009*

BANNALEC see Pont Aven *2F2*

BANNES see Langres *6F1*

BANYULS SUR MER *10H1* (700m S Rural) *42.47665, 3.11904* **Camp Municipal La Pinède, 66650 Banyuls-sur-Mer [04 68 88 32 13 or 04 68 88 00 62 (Mairie); fax 04 68 88 32 48; camping.banyuls@wanadoo.fr; www.banyuls-sur-mer.com]** On D914 (N114) foll sp to Banyuls-sur-Mer; turn R at camping sp at cent of sea-front by town hall; foll sp to site. Lge, hdg/mkd pitch, pt sl, pt terr; pt shd; wc; chem disp; mv service pnt; shwrs; el pnts (4-13A) €2-3; lndtte; snacks; supmkt 100m; playgrnd; shgl beach 1km; dogs; Eng spkn; quiet; ccard acc; red low ssn; CCI. "Busy, friendly site; spacious pitches, narr site rds; gd views fr top; vg, clean facs; sh walk into Banyuls." ♦ 4 Apr-5 Nov. € 12.50 2009*

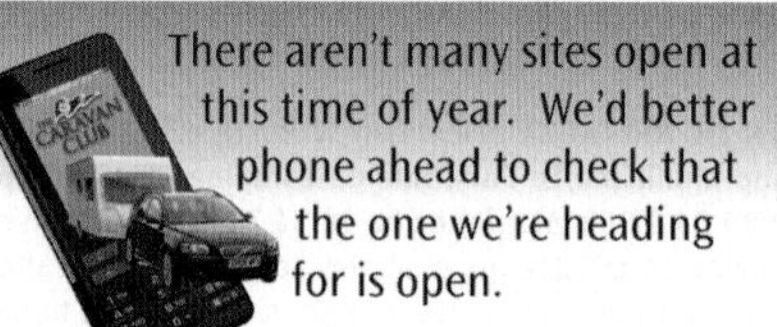
There aren't many sites open at this time of year. We'd better phone ahead to check that the one we're heading for is open.

BAR LE DUC *6E1* (1km E Urban) *48.77433, 5.17415* **FFCC Camp Municipal du Château de Marbeaumont, Rue du Stade, off Rue de St Mihiel, 55000 Bar-le-Duc [03 29 79 17 33 (TO) or 03 29 79 11 13 (LS)); fax 03 29 79 21 95]** Fr town cent foll Camping sps. Rue de St Mihiel is part of D1916 dir Verdun. Fr NW on D994/D694 or fr SE on N1135, at rndabt turn E onto D1916 sp Metz, Verdun & St Mihiel. In 200m turn L into Rue du Stade sp Camping. Site on L in 100m. Sm, pt shd; wc; chem disp; shwrs inc; el pnts (8A) €2.62 (poss long lead req); lndtte (inc dryer); shops adj; no twin-axles; Eng spkn; some rd noise. "Delightful site in grounds of chateau; friendly & helpful warden; clean, modern san facs; clsd 1200-1500; lovely walk into historic town; gd NH." 15 May-30 Sep. € 10.50 2009*

BAR SUR LOUP, LE see Grasse *10E4*

BARBATRE see Noirmoutier en l'Ile *2H3*

BARBIERES *9C2* (1km NE Rural) *44.97942, 5.16357* **Camping Combe d'Oyans, 26300 Rochefort-Samson [04 75 47 33 23; fax 04 75 82 90 57; combe-doyans@orange.fr; www.combedoyans.fr]** Exit A49 junc 7 onto D149 to Chatuzange; cont on D149 for 5.5km to rndabt just bef Barbières; turn L onto D125 to Rochfort-Samson; cont thro vill; in 600m cont over x-rds; site on R in 500m. Sm, hdg/mkd pitch, terr, pt shd; wc; chem disp (wc); shwrs inc; el pnts €3; shops 3km; tradsmn; snacks; playgrnd; htd pool; 15% statics; dogs €1; phone adj; adv bkg; ccard not acc; red low ssn; CCI. "Conv Vercors Massif; gd walking, cycling, rockclimbing; children's activity camping adj; vg." ♦ 6 May-29 Sep. € 17.00 2009*

BARBIERES *9C2* (1km SE Rural) *44.94470, 5.15100* **Camping Le Gallo-Romain, Route de Col de Tourniol, 26300 Barbières [tel/fax 04 75 47 44 07; info@legalloromain.net; www.legalloromain.net]** Exit A49 junc 7 onto D149 dir Marches & Barbières. Go thro vill & ascend Rte du Col de Tourniol for 2km, site on R, well sp. Med, mkd pitch, pt sl, terr, pt shd; wc; chem disp; baby facs; shwrs inc; el pnts (6A) €3.75; Indtte; shop & 1km; rest; snacks; bar; BBQ; playgrnd; pool; entmnt; internet; TV; 15% statics; dogs €4; phone; poss cr; Eng spkn; adv bkg; quiet; no ccard acc; red low ssn; CCI. "Mountain setting; welcoming, friendly, helpful Dutch owners; ltd facs low ssn; gd." ♦ 25 Apr-13 Sep. € 24.00 2009*

BARBOTAN LES THERMES *8E2* (1km S Rural) *43.94027, -0.04557* **Camping Le Lac de l'Uby, Cazaubon, 32150 Barbotan-les-Thermes [05 62 09 53 91; fax 05 62 09 56 97; balia-vacances@wanadoo.fr; www.camping-uby.com]** Fr Eauze take D626/N524 sp Cazaubon, immed bef Cazaubon turn R sp Barbotan. Site on R in 2km. Lge, mkd pitch, some hdstg, pt shd; htd wc; chem disp; el pnts (5-10A) €6; Indtte; shop & 2km; cooking facs; playgrnd; pool; lake sw & beach 300m; fishing; sailing; windsurfing; tennis; games area; cycle hire; entmnt; some statics; dogs €1.80; adv bkg rec; ccard acc; red low ssn; CCI. "Gd, well-kept, well-run site; interesting Bastide towns nrby." ♦ 15 Mar-30 Nov. € 16.00 2009*

BARCARES, LE *10G1* (1.5km S Coastal) *42.77607, 3.02435* **Camping L'Oasis, Route de St Laurent, 66423 Le Barcarès [04 68 86 12 43; fax 04 68 86 46 83; camping.loasis@wanadoo.fr; www.camping-oasis.com]** Fr N exit A9/E15 junc 40 Leucate onto D627 & D83 twd Le Barcarès. Exit junc 9 dir Canet & take 1st R sp St Laurent-de-la-Salanque. Pass St Laurent & go under bdge dir Le Barcarès, site sp on L. Lge, shd; wc (some cont); chem disp; baby facs; shwrs; el pnts (10A) inc; Indtte; supmkt; rest; snacks; bar; playgrnd; 3 pools; waterslide; sand beach 1km; tennis; games area; internet; entmnt; TV; dogs €4.50; red low ssn; CCI. ♦ 24 Apr-17 Sep. € 35.00 (CChq acc) 2009*

BARCARES, LE *10G1* (2km S Coastal) *42.77570, 3.02300* **Camping California, Route de St Laurent, 66420 Le Barcarès [04 68 86 16 08; fax 04 68 86 18 20; camping-california@wanadoo.fr; www.camping-california.fr]** Exit A9 junc 41 onto D627 sp Leucate. Ignore sp Le Barcarès & Port Barcarès; exit junc 9 sp Canet onto D81; then at D90 intersection turn R dir St Laurent-de-la-Salangue & go under D81; site on L. Lge, hdg/mkd pitch, shd; wc; chem disp; baby facs; shwrs inc; el pnts (10A) inc (poos rev pol); Indtte; supmkt 1km; shop, rest, snacks, bar high ssn; BBQ (gas/elec only); playgrnd; 3 pools; waterslide; paddling pool; sand beach 1.5km; watersports 1km; tennis; games area; entmnt; wifi; games/TV rm; 20% statics; dogs €5; Eng spkn; adv bkg; noisy high ssn; ccard acc; red low ssn/long stay; CCI. "Vg reception; various pitch sizes, some poss diff; friendly, helpful, hardworking owners; excel, modern san facs, ltd low ssn; mosquito repellant useful; busy rd thro site; highly rec." ♦ 4 Apr-18 Sep. € 32.00 ABS - C02 2009*

⊞ **BARCARES, LE** *10G1* (1km SW Coastal) *42.77462, 3.02207* **Camping L'Europe, Route de St Laurent, 66420 Le Barcarès [04 68 86 15 36; fax 04 68 86 47 88; reception@europe-camping.com; www.europe-camping.com]** Exit A9 at Perpignan N & take D83 sp Le Barcarès. After 9km turn R on D81 sp Canet Plage, L on D90 sp Le Barcarès. Site on R. Lge, hdg/mkd pitch, shd; wc; shwrs inc; el pnts (16A) €4.20; gas; Indtte; shop & 2km; rest; snacks; bar; playgrnd; 2 pools high ssn; waterslides; rv & beach 500m; tennis; archery; entmnts; disco; 50% statics; dogs €7; Eng spkn; adv bkg; poss noisy; red long stay/low ssn; CCI. "Gd location; all pitches have individ san facs; resident dogs (& mess) nuisance; gd value low ssn but ltd facs & unkempt pitches; gd cycle rte to beach & shops; vg winter NH/sh stay." ♦ € 41.00 2008*

BARCARES, LE *10G1* (1km SW Coastal) *42.78094, 3.02267* **Yelloh! Village Le Pré Catalan, Route de St Laurent, 66420 Le Barcarès [04 68 86 12 60; fax 04 68 86 40 17; info@precatalan.com; www.precatalan.com or www.yellohvillage.com]** Exit A9 junc 41 onto D83; app Le Barcarès turn R onto D81, then L onto D90 to Le Barcarès, site sp. Lge, shd; wc; shwrs inc; el pnts (6A) €4; gas; shop; rest; snacks; sand beach 1km; pool; playgrnd; tennis; TV; entmnt; dogs €3; quiet; adv bkg. 30 Apr-20 Sep. € 32.00 2007*

BARCARES, LE *10G1* (1km W Coastal) *42.78624, 3.02527* **Camping Las Bousigues, Ave des Corbières, 66420 Le Barcarès [04 68 86 16 19; fax 04 68 86 28 44; info@camping-barcares.com; www.camping-barcares.com or www.camping-franceloc.fr]** Fr N exit A9/E15 junc 40 Leucate onto D627 & D83 twd Le Barcarès & exit junc 10. Turn R at rndabt, site sp on L. Lge, hdg/mkd pitch, shd; wc; chem disp; mv service pnt; individual san facs some pitches (extra charge); baby facs; shwrs; el pnts (6-10A) inc; Indtte; shop; rest; snacks; bar; BBQ; playgrnd; pool; paddling pool; waterslide; sand beach 900; games area; entmnt; car wash; 50% statics; dogs €3.50; phone; poss cr; €3.20; Eng spkn; adv bkg; quiet; CCI. "No twin-axles; helpful staff; excel." ♦ 1 Apr-30 Sep. € 32.00 2007*

BARCELONNETTE *9D4* (8km NE Urban) *44.42027, 6.73639* **Camping Le Planet, 04850 Jausiers [04 92 81 06 57]** N fr Barcelonnette on D900; at N end of Jausiers on E side of D900, just bef turn to Col de la Bonette. Sm, pt shd; wc (some cont); chem disp (wc); shwrs €0.90; el pnts €3; shop, rest & bar 200m; snacks; quiet. "Simple, CL-type site nr all facs; gd cent for mountain walking/cycling; fair." 15 Jun-15 Sep. € 8.50 2008*

⊞ **BARCELONNETTE** *9D4* (2km S Urban) *44.38294, 6.63470* **Tampico Camping Caravaneige, Ave de Nice, 04400 Barcelonnette [tel/fax 04 92 81 02 55; le-tampico@wanadoo.fr; http://letampico.free.fr]** Exit Barcelonnette onto D902 sp Col d'Allos & Col de la Cayolle; site on R in 1.3km. NB Do not app fr Col d'Allos or Col de la Cayolle. Med, mkd pitch, pt shd; htd wc; chem disp; baby facs; fam bthrm; shwrs inc; el pnts (6A) €2.90-5.80; gas; Indtte; ice; tradsmn; rest; snacks; bar; BBQ (gas, charcoal); playgrnd; white water canoeing/rafting; htd pool 2km; games area; TV; 10% statics; dogs €1.50; phone; bus; poss cr; Eng spkn; adv bkg; quiet; ccard acc; red long stay. "Lovely wooded site, mountain views; friendly owner; walk to town by rv; vg walking & outdoor activities; vg." ♦ € 14.10 2009*

BARCELONNETTE *9D4* (500m W Rural) *44.38393, 6.64281* **Camping du Plan, 52 Ave Emile Aubert, 04400 Barcelonnette [tel/fax 04 92 81 08 11; www.camping duplan.fr]** Exit town on D902 sp Col d'Allos & Col de la Cayolle. Site on R. Sm, mkd pitch, pt shd; wc; shwrs inc; el pnts (3-10A) €2.85-4.15 gas; Indtte; shop; tradsmn; rest; dogs €1; adv bkg; quiet. "Lovely views & walks; helpful owners; unisex san facs; excel." 25 May-30 Sep. € 19.30 2008*

BARCELONNETTE *9D4* (6km W Rural) *44.39229, 6.57340* **Camping Le Fontarache, 04580 Les Thuiles [tel/fax 04 92 81 90 42; reception@camping-fontarache.fr; www.camping-fontarache.fr]** Site sp fr D900 on ent Les Thuiles fr Barcelonnette. Lge, mkd pitch, pt shd; wc (some cont); chem disp; mv service pnt; shwrs inc; el pnts (6A) €3; Indtte; shop 100m; tradsmn; snacks; BBQ; playgrnd; htd pool; paddling pool; fishing; kayaking; tennis; games area; entmnt; TV; some statics; dogs €3; poss cr; Eng spkn; adv bkg; quiet. "Pleasant, scenic site." ♦ 1 Jun-6 Sep. € 16.00 2006*

BARCELONNETTE *9D4* (6km W Rural) *44.39686, 6.54605* **Domaine Loisirs de l'Ubaye, Vallée de l'Ubaye, 04340 Barcelonnette [04 92 81 01 96; fax 04 92 81 92 53; info@loisirsubaye.com; www.loisirsubaye.com]** Site on S side of D900. Lge, mkd pitch, terr, shd; wc; shwrs inc; el pnts (6A) €3.50; Indry rm; gas; shop; rest; snacks; bar; playgrnd; htd pool; rv adj; watersports; cycle hire; entmnt; TV rm; statics; dogs €3.50; phone; red low ssn/long stay; CCI. "Magnificent scenery." ♦ 1 Apr-30 Oct. € 21.00 2009*

BAREGES see Luz St Sauveur *8G2*

BARFLEUR *1C4* (500m NW Urban/Coastal) *49.67564, -1.26645* **Camp Municipal La Blanche Nef, 50760 Barfleur [02 33 23 15 40; fax 02 33 23 95 14; infos@lablanchenef.com; www.lablanchenef.com]** Foll main rd to harbour; half-way on L side of harbour & turn L at mkd gap in car pk; cross sm side-street & foll site sp on sea wall; site visible on L in 300m. Med, pt sl, unshd; htd wc; chem disp; mv service pnt; shwrs inc; el pnts (6-10A) €3.10-4.75; Indtte; shops 1km; tradsmn; snacks; bar; playgrnd; sand beach adj; 45% statics; dogs €1.30; Eng spkn; quiet; adv bkg; ccard acc; red low ssn; CCI. "Gd sized pitches; sea views; gd birdwatching, walking, cycling; vg facs; gd beach; m'vans all year." ♦ Mid Feb-Mid Nov. € 13.70 2009*

⊞ **BARFLEUR** *1C4* (1km NW Coastal) *49.67971, -1.27364* **Camping La Ferme du Bord de Mer, 50760 Gatteville-le-Phare [02 33 54 01 77; fax 02 33 54 78 99; fdbm@caramail.com]** On D901 fr Cherbourg; on o'skts of Barfleur turn L onto D116 for Gatteville-Phare. Site on R in 1km. Sm, hdg/md pitch, pt sl, pt shd; wc; chem disp; shwrs inc; Indry rm; some serviced pitches; el pnts (3-10A) €2.60-4.40; gas; Indry rm; shop 1.5km; rest, snacks & bar high ssn or 1.5km; playgrnd; sm sand beach adj; entmnt; games rm; 25% statics; dogs €1.45; phone; poss cr; quiet; red low ssn. "CL-type site; sheltered beach; coastal path to vill & lighthouse; conv ferries (30 mins); WARNING: Sep 2002 member reported site owner using high-strength poison against rodents in field adj site - no warning notices displayed - site not rec children or dogs; gd." ♦ € 10.85 2009*

BARJAC (GARD) *9D2* (3km S Rural) *44.26685, 4.35170* **Domaine de la Sablière (Naturist), 30430 St Privat-de-Champclos [04 66 24 51 16; fax 04 66 24 58 69; contact@villagesabliere.com; www.villagesabliere.com]** Fr Barjac S on D901 twd Bagnols. At 3km R onto D266, foll sp. Steep ent. Lge, hdg/mkd pitch, pt sl, shd; wc; chem disp; sauna; shwrs; el pnts (6-10A) inc; gas; Indtte; shop; rest; snacks; bar; playgrnd; 2 pools (1 htd, covrd); paddling pool; rv & beach; fishing; canoeing; tennis; games area; archery; entmnt; internet; TV rm; 40% statics; dogs €2.50; bus; sep car park; Eng spkn; adv bkg; quiet; red low ssn. "Helpful owners; gd facs; steep rds, narr bends & sm pitches - poss diff access lge o'fits; risk of flooding after heavy rain; gd shopping & excel local mkt; many naturist trails in forest." 28 Mar-5 Oct. € 37.15 (CChq acc) 2009*

BARJAC (GARD) *9D2* (9km S Rural) *44.26738, 4.37041* **Naturissimo La Génèse (Naturist), Route de la Génèse, 30430 Méjannes-le-Clap [04 66 24 51 73 or 04 66 24 51 82; fax 04 66 24 50 38; info@lagenese.com; www.lagenese.com]** Fr A7 exit junc 19, take dir Bagnols-sur-Cèze (D994 & N86) then in Bagnols head twd Alès on D6. Exit twd Lusanne onto D979 & foll sp for Méjannes-le-Clap. Site on banks of Rv Cèze. Lge, hdg/mkd pitch, pt sl, shd; wc; chem disp; shwrs inc; el pnts (6A) inc; gas; Indtte; shop & 5km; rest; snacks; bar; playgrnd; htd pool; fishing; sailing; canoe & cycle hire; tennis; archery; entmnt; TV rm; 10% statics; dogs €4; phone; adv bkg; quiet; ccard acc; red low ssn; INF card. 1 Apr-9 Oct. € 26.00 2008*

BARJAC (LOZERE) see Mende *9D1*

BARNEVILLE CARTERET *1C4* (6km N Coastal) *49.42963, 1.80472* **Camping Bel Sito, Le Caumont de la Rue, 50270 Baubigny [02 33 04 32 74 or 06 75 80 72 80 (mob); camping@bel-sito.com; www.camping-normandie-belsito.com]** Fr Cherbourg take D950 twd Coutances thro Les Pieux & on twd Carteret. 10km S of Les Pieux turn R onto D131 sp Baubigny to site 1km on L. Med, pt sl, pt shd; wc; shwrs inc; el pnts (6A) €3.50; gas; lndtte; shop; tradsmn; sand beach 900m; wifi; some statics; dogs €3; quiet. 15 Apr-13 Sep. € 22.00 2008*

⊞ **BARNEVILLE CARTERET** *1C4* (3km SE Coastal/Rural) *49.36211, -1.74644* **Camping Les Mimosas (formerly Camping L'Ermitage), 1 Chemin de Coutances, 50210 St Jean-de-la-Rivière [02 33 04 78 90; fax 02 33 04 06 62; www.les-mimosas-normandie.com]** Take D650 fr Cherbourg to Barneville-Carteret, site sp. Med, mkd pitch, pt shd; wc; mv service pnt; baby facs; shwrs inc; el pnts (6A) €4.20; lndtte; shop; snacks; bar; BBQ; playgrnd; htd pool; sand beach 500m; solarium; tennis; games area; games rm; wifi; entmnt; TV; 60% statics; dogs €3; adv bkg; quiet. "Pleasant site; roomy pitches; vg touring base." ♦ € 22.60 2008*

BARNEVILLE CARTERET *1C4* (2.5km S Coastal) *49.36383, -1.75386* **Yelloh! Village Les Vikings, St Jean-de-la-Rivière, 50270 Barneville-Cartaret [02 33 53 84 13; fax 02 33 53 08 19; www.campingviking.com or www.yellohvillage.com]** Fr D650 foll sp dir St Jean-de-la-Rivière. Site well sp. Lge, mkd pitch, pt shd; wc; chem disp; baby facs; shwrs inc; el pnts (4A) €3 (poss rev pol); lndtte; shop; rest; snacks; bar; BBQ; playgrnd; htd pool high ssn; sand beach 500m; games rm; games area; golf, tennis nr; entmnt high ssn; excursions; TV; 50% statics; dogs €1.71; Eng spkn; adv bkg; quiet; red low ssn; ccard acc; CCI. "Gd site; helpful owner; vg touring base; gd walking." ♦ 1 Apr-4 Oct. € 23.73 2006*

BARNEVILLE CARTERET *1C4* (2.5km SW Coastal) *49.36758, -1.75773* **Camping Les Bosquets, Rue du Capitaine Quenault, 50270 Barneville-Plage [02 33 04 73 62; fax 02 33 04 35 82; lesbosquets@orange.fr; www.camping-lesbosquets.com]** Fr D650 at Barneville-Carteret turn S dir Barneville-Plage, site sp. Lge, terr, pt shd; wc; chem disp; shwrs inc; el pnts (10A) €3.80; lndtte; shop; bar; playgrnd; htd pool; paddling pool; sand beach 400m; horseriding nrby; games rm; TV; 50% statics; dogs €1.80; bus; poss cr; adv bkg; quiet; CCI. "Pleasant site; beach ideal for children." ♦ 1 Apr-15 Sep. € 17.40 2009*

BARNEVILLE CARTERET *1C4* (10km SW Coastal) *49.30323, 1.68825* **Camping L'Espérance, 36 Rue de la Gamburie, 50580 Denneville-Plage [02 33 07 12 71; fax 02 33 07 58 32; camping.esperance@wanadoo.fr; www.camping-esperance.fr]** S fr Cherbourg on D950 thro Barneville-Carteret; in 7km fork R & cont on D650 & then R onto D137 sp Denneville-Plage & camping. Med, hdg/mkd pitch, pt shd; wc; chem disp; shwrs inc; el pnts (4-6A) €2.90-3.80; gas; lndtte; shop; snacks; bar; playgrnd; htd pool; sand beach 300m; tennis; cycle hire; entmnt; 50% statics; dogs €2; phone; poss cr; Eng spkn; adv bkg; quiet; ccard acc; CCI. "Helpful owners." 1 Apr-30 Sep. € 21.00 2009*

BARNEVILLE CARTERET *1C4* (2.5km W Urban/Coastal) *49.38081, -1.78614* **Camping du Bocage, Rue du Bocage, Carteret, 50270 Barneville-Carteret [02 33 53 86 91; fax 02 33 04 35 98]** Fr Cherbourg take D650 to Carteret, turn R onto D902, site by disused rlwy stn & nr tourist office. Med, hdg pitch, shd; wc (some cont); chem disp; baby facs; shwrs inc; el pnts (3-6A) €2.30-2.90; lndtte; shops adj; rest 200m; snacks; playgrnd; sand beach 500m; 40% statics; poss cr; adv bkg; quiet; CCI. "Pleasant seaside resort with excel beaches; pitches soft in wet weather; well-kept site." Easter-30 Sep. € 20.80 2008*

BARREME *10E3* (S Urban) *43.95225, 6.37316* **Camping Napoléon, Le Bas Paraire, 04330 Barrême [tel/fax 04 92 34 22 70 or 06 72 90 42 74 (mob); camping napoleon@hotmail.com; www.camping-napoleon.com]** Fr Digne-les-Bains on N85; strt ahead at rndabt on ent Barrême; site on L over bdge, site sp. Med, mkd pitch, shd; wc; chem disp; mv service pnt; baby facs; shwrs inc; el pnts (10A) inc; gas; lndtte; shop & rest 300m; snacks; bar; playgrnd; pool; rv fishing & sw adj; entmnt; TV; some statics; dogs €1.50; bus; phone; Eng spkn; adv bkg; quiet; red low ssn; CCI. "Nice position; helpful owners; OK facs; narr gauge rlwy adj site so some noise; vg." ♦ 11 Apr-29 Sep. € 20.00 2008*

BARROU *4H1* (Rural) *46.86500, 0.77100* **FFCC Camping Les Rioms, Les Rioms, 37350 Barrou [02 47 94 98 43 or 06 87 66 87 60 (mob); campinglesrioms@orange.fr; www.lesrioms.com]** Fr D750 Descartes to La Roche-Posay rd turn R at sp Camping at ent to Barrou vill. Site sp. NB Site has barriers, phone if clsd. Sm, hdg/mkd pitch, pt shd; wc; chem disp (wc); shwrs inc; el pnts (16A) €4; lndry rm; tradsmn; shop, rest & snacks nr; BBQ; playgrnd; htd pool; sand rv beach 2km; 20% statics; dogs free; Eng spkn; adv bkg; quiet; red low ssn; CCI. "Pleasant, peaceful site on bank of Rv Creuse; clean san facs; friendly owners; gd pool; excel." ♦ 4 Apr-24 Oct. € 9.00 2009*

BARZAN PLAGE see Cozes *7B1*

BASTIDE DE SEROU, LA *8G3* (1km S Rural) *43.00150, 1.44472* **Camping L'Arize, Route de Nescus, 09240 La Bastide-de-Sérou [05 61 65 81 51; fax 05 61 65 83 34; camparize@aol.com; www.camping-arize.com]** Fr Foix on D117 on ent La Bastide-de-Sérou turn L at Gendarmerie on D15 sp Nescus, site 1km on R. Med, hdg/mkd pitch, pt shd; wc; chem disp; mv service pnt; baby facs; shwrs inc; el pnts 6A) inc (poss rev pol); gas; lndtte; shop & 2km; tradsmn; rest adj; snacks; playgrnd; pool; lake sw 5km; fishing; golf 5km; horseriding adj; golf nr; 10% statics; dogs €1.50; poss cr; Eng spkn; adv bkg; ccard acc; CCI. "Pleasant, scenic site on bank Rv Arize; modern facs; gd mkd walking/cycle rtes." ♦ 10 Mar-6 Nov. € 23.70 2006*

France

BASTIDE SOLAGES, LA *8E4* (1km N Rural) *43.95660, 2.52157* **Domaine de la Libaudié (Wijnen), 12550 La Bastide-Solages [05 65 99 70 33; contact@libaudie.com; www.libaudie.com]** Fr Albi take D999 W dir St Sernin-sur-Rance; take D33 N to La Bastide-Solanges; in vill turn L & foll site sp. NB Twisting rds not suitable car+c'vans. Sm, pt shd; wc; chem disp; shwrs; el pnts (16A) €3.50; Indtte; shops 5km; rest; bar; playgrnd; pool; rv 500m; canoeing; cycling; walking; TV rm; poss open all year; dogs €2; bus; Eng spkn; adv bkg ess high ssn; no ccard acc. "Stunning views; vg family-run, friendly CL-type site; conv Tarn valley."
1 May-31 Oct. € 15.50 2007*

BATHIE, LA see Albertville *9B3*

BATZ SUR MER see Croisic, Le *2G3*

BAUBIGNY see Barneville Carteret *1C4*

BAUD *2F3* (3.5km S Rural) *47.84613, -3.01354* **Camp Municipal du Petit Bois, Route de Lambel-Camors, 56330 Camors [02 97 39 18 36 or 02 97 39 22 06; fax 02 97 39 28 99; commune.de.camors@wanadoo.fr; www.camors56.com]** S fr Baud on D768 to Camors. Sp in vill on D189. Sm, mkd pitch, pt sl, terr, unshd; wc; chem disp; mv service pnt; shwrs inc; el pnts (6A) €2.20; Indtte; playgrnd; horseriding adj; adv bkg; quiet; CCI. "Pleasant surroundings; vg facs; well-managed site." ♦ 1 Jul-31 Aug. € 8.40 2006*

BAUD *2F3* (7km W Rural) **Camping Base de Loisirs de Pont Augan, Pont Augan, 56150 Baud [02 97 51 04 74 or 02 97 51 09 37 (LS); fax 02 97 39 07 23]** Fr N24 exit onto D172 & foll sp Bubry & Quistinic; fr S on D768 to Baud, turn W onto D3, foll sp Bubry & Quistinic. Sm, hdg/mkd pitch, pt shd; htd wc; chem disp (wc); mv service pnt; baby facs; shwrs inc; el pnts (10A); Indtte; rest, snacks, bar 200m; playgrnd; pool; fishing, canoeing in lake on site or in Rv Blavet adj; dogs; adv bkg; quiet; no ccard acc; CCI. "Peaceful site; barrier & office ltd opening hrs but parking area avail." ♦ 1 Apr-30 Sep. 2008*

BAUGE *4G1* (1km E Rural) *47.53889, -0.09637* **Camp Municipal du Pont des Fées, Chemin du Pont des Fées, 49150 Baugé [02 41 89 14 79 or 02 41 89 18 07 (Mairie); fax 02 41 84 12 19; camping@ville-bauge.fr; www.ville-bauge.fr]** Fr Saumur traveling N D347/D938 turn 1st R in Baugé onto D766. Foll camping sp to site by sm rv; ent bef rv bdge. Sm, hdg pitch, shd; wc; chem disp; shwrs inc; el pnts (4A) €2.30; Indtte; shops 1km; BBQ; 2 pools & 2 tennis courts 150m; fishing; no twin-axles; phone; adv bkg; quiet. "Excel countryside; pleasant, well-kept site; obliging wardens." 15 May-15 Sep. € 8.40 2008*

BAULE, LA *2G3* (2km NE Rural) *47.29833, -2.35722* **Airotel Camping La Roseraie, 20 Ave Jean Sohier, Route du Golf, 44500 La Baule-Escoublac [02 40 60 46 66; fax 02 40 60 11 84; camping@laroseraie.com; www.laroseraie.com]** Take N171 fr St Nazaire to La Baule. In La Baule-Escoublac turn R at x-rds by church, site in 300m on R; sp fr La Baule cent. Lge, hdg/mkd pitch, pt shd; wc (some cont); chem disp; mv service pnt; baby facs; fam bthrm; shwrs inc; el pnts (6-10A) €5; gas; Indtte; shop 200m; tradsmn; rest; snacks; bar; BBQ; playgrnd; htd, covrd pool; paddling pool; waterslide; sand beach 2km; fishing; watersports; tennis; games area; games rm; fitness rm; wifi; entmnt; TV rm; 80% statics; dogs €2.50; phone; Eng spkn; adv bkg; quiet; ccard acc; red long stay; CCI. "Well-kept, pleasant site; clean san facs; ltd facs low ssn; vg." ♦ 4 Apr-27 Sep. € 31.00 (CChq acc) 2009*

See advertisement

BAULE, LA *2G3* (8km NE Rural) *47.32102, -2.30817* **Camping Les Chalands Fleuris, Rue du Stade, 44117 St André-des-Eaux [02 40 01 20 40; fax 02 40 91 54 24; chalfleu@club-internet.fr]** W fr St Nazaire on N171. Take 1st exit to St André-des-Eaux; fr town cent foll site sp 800m. Lge, hdg/mkd pitch, pt shd; htd wc; mv service pnt; chem disp; serviced pitches; shwrs inc; el pnts (8A) €4.40; gas; Indtte; ice, shop, tradsmn high ssn; rest, snacks, bar 100m; playgrnd; htd, covrd pool; sand beach 8km; fishing; tennis; golf 2km; games rm; entmnt; TV; 50% statics; dogs €2.70; adv bkg; quiet; red long stay/low ssn; ccard acc; red CCI. "Site adj to 'Village Fleuris', beautiful display all thro vill." ♦ 1 Apr-15 Oct. € 20.00 2007*

BAULE, LA *2G3* (1km E Coastal) *47.28864, -2.37236* **Camping Le Bois d'Amour, Allée de Diane, 44500 La Baule [02 40 60 17 40 or 04 73 77 05 05 (LS); fax 04 73 73 05 06; contact@lesbalconsverts.com; www.lesbalconsverts.com]** Fr Ave du Bois d'Amour bear L & immed under rlwy bdge, turn R at traff lts. Ent to site on R. Lge, mkd pitch, shd; wc; chem disp; shwrs inc; el pnts (6A) inc; gas; Indtte; shop; rest; playgrnd; sand beach 800m; wifi; 50% statics; dogs €2; phone; bus & railway adj; no dogs high ssn; poss cr; Eng spkn; adv bkg; quiet, but some rd/rlwy noise at site perimeter; red low snn; CCI. "Useful NH, some pitches v sm; sm area for tourers." ♦ 1 Apr-3 Oct. € 25.00 2009*

BAULE, LA *2G3* (1km W Rural) *47.29372, -2.37916* **Camping Les Ajoncs d'Or, Chemin du Rocher, 44500 La Baule [02 40 60 33 29; fax 02 40 24 44 37; contact@ajoncs.com; www.ajoncs.com]** Fr D13 foll sp for La Baule cent & turn L at rndabt nr Champion supmkt, site sp. Lge, mkd pitch, pt shd; wc; chem disp; baby facs; shwrs; el pnts inc; Indtte; shop; supmkt 1km; rest; snacks; bar; playgrnd; sand beach 1.5km; games area; entmnt; TV; 25% statics; dogs €0.95; adv bkg; quiet. "Peaceful, well-run site; vg." ♦ 1 Apr-30 Sep. 2007*

BAUME LES DAMES *6G2* (12km N Rural) *47.43918, 6.34191* **Camping du Bois de Reveuge, Route de Rougemont, 25680 Huanne-Montmartin [03 81 84 38 60; fax 03 81 84 44 04; info@campingduboisdereveuge.com; www.campingduboisdereveuge.com]** Exit A36 junc 5 Baume-les-Dames onto D50 dir Rougemont-Villersexel. Foll sp Huanne & site for 9km. Site is 1km N of Huanne-Montmartin. Lge, mkd pitch, pt sl, terr, pt shd; wc (some cont); mv service pnt; chem disp; baby facs; shwrs inc; el pnts (6A) inc; gas; Indtte; shop & 4km; tradsmn; snacks; pizzeria; bar; playgrnd; 3 htd pools, (1 covrd); waterslides; fishing lake with pedaloes; sand beach 15km; sailing school; cycle hire; archery; horseriding; rockclimbing; games area; entmnt; excursions; TV rm; some statics; dogs €2; Eng spkn; adv bkg; quiet; ccard acc; red low ssn; CCI. "Superb staff & management; beautiful site; lge pitches; clean san facs; wonderful countryside; gd walking, birdwatching, watersports; free activities, many for children; gd touring base." ♦ 23 Apr-15 Sep. € 30.00 2007*

BAUME LES DAMES *6G2* (500m S Rural) **Camp Municipal, Quai du Canal, 25110 Baume-les-Dames [03 81 84 38 89; camping-baume-les-dames@orange.fr]** Fr D683 (N83) in Baume-les-Dames turn S onto D50, cross canal & turn W. Site sp. Sm, some hdstg, pt shd; wc; chem disp; shwrs; el pnts (16A) inc; Indtte; some cabins; quiet. "Peaceful site; development in hand 2008/09." 2008*

BAUME LES DAMES *6G2* (5km S Rural) *47.32506, 6.36127* **Camping L'Ile, 1 Rue de Pontarlier, 25110 Pont-les-Moulins [03 81 84 15 23; info@campingdelile.fr; www.campingdelile.fr]** S fr Baume-les-Dames on D50, site on L on ent Pont-les-Moulins. Sm, pt shd; wc (some cont); chem disp; mv service pnt; shwrs inc; el pnts (6A) €2.50; gas; Indtte; shops 5km; bread 100m; rest & bar 500m; playgrnd; pool 6km; 10% statics; dogs free; Eng spkn; adv bkg; rd noise; red long stay; CCI. "Tidy, basic site in pleasant setting by Rv Cusancin; helpful, friendly owner; clean, basic facs; gd." 1 May-7 Sep. € 11.50 2009*

BAUME LES MESSIEURS see Lons le Saunier *6H2*

BAYAS see Coutras *7C2*

BAYEUX *3D1* (1km N Urban) *49.2840, 0.6977* **Camp Municipal, Blvd Périphérique d'Eindhoven, 14400 Bayeux [tel/fax 02 31 92 08 43; d.poupinel@libertysurf.fr; www.mairie-bayeux.fr]** Site sp off Périphérique d'Eindhoven (Bayeux by-pass, N13); fr W site almost opp Briconaut DIY store. Fr E turn N of N13 Formigny & immed L over N13 sp Trevières. Site on R. Fr Bayeux, site N off inner ring rd. Lge, pt shd, some hdg pitch, some hdstg; wc (some cont); chem disp; mv service pnt; shwrs inc; el pnts (4-10A) €1.50-3 (poss rev pol); gas; Indtte; shop (Jul/Aug); playgrnd; indoor pool adj; sand beach 10km; dogs; phone; some; adv bkg ess high ssn; rd noise; 10% red 5+ days; CCI. "Gd, well-kept site; clean facs; avoid perimeter pitches (narr hdstgs & rd noise); no twin-axles; conv for ferries; no access to site 1000-1700 low ssn; lge mkt Sat; Bayeux festival 1st w/end July." ♦ 29 Apr-30 Sep. € 10.50 2008*

BAYEUX *3D1* (7km SE Rural) *49.24840, -0.60245* **Camping Le Château de Martragny, 14740 Martragny [02 31 80 21 40; fax 02 31 08 14 91; chateau.martragny@wanadoo.fr; www.chateau-martragny.com or www.les-castels.com]** Fr Caen going NW on N13 dir Bayeux/Cherbourg, leave at Martragny/Carcagny exit. Strt on & take 2nd R (past turn for Martragny/Creully) into site & chateau grounds. Fr Bayeux after leaving N13 (Martragny/Carcagny), go L over bdge to end of rd, turn L then take 2nd R into Chateau grounds. Lge, some mkd pitch, pt sl, pt shd; wc; chem disp (ltd in ssn); baby facs; shwrs inc; el pnts (10A) inc (long lead poss req, poss rev pol); gas; Indtte; shop; tradsmn; rest; snacks; bar; BBQ; playgrnd; htd pool; paddling pool; sand beach 10km; fishing; tennis; cycle hire; horseriding 500m; entmnt; wifi; games/TV rm; dogs; poss cr; Eng spkn; adv bkg; quiet; ccard acc; red low ssn; CCI. "Popular site in attractive area; pleasant staff; poss long trek to san facs, stretched high ssn; site poss v muddy when wet; D-Day beaches 15km; Sat mkt in Bayeux; vg." ♦ 1 May-10 Sep. € 32.00 (CChq acc) ABS - N06 2009*

France

⊞ **BAYEUX** *3D1* (8km SE Rural) *49.25041, -0.59251* **Camping Le Manoir de l'Abbaye (Godfroy), 15 Rue de Creully, 14740 Martragny [tel/fax 02 31 80 25 95; yvette.godfroy@libertysurf.fr; http://pagesperso-orange.fr/godfroy]** Take N13 Bayeux, Caen dual c'way for 7km, fork R sp Martagny. Over dual c'way L at T-junc, then 1st R sp D82 Martragny & Creully site on R 500m. Sm, pt shd; wc; chem disp; shwrs inc; el pnts (15A) €3.20 (poss rev pol); Indtte; tradsmn; dogs €2.30; Eng spkn; adv bkg; red low ssn; CCI. "Peaceful, well-kept site; lovely grounds; helpful, welcoming owners; steps to san facs; meals & wine avail on request; winter storage; conv Ouistreham ferries; highly rec." ♦ € 16.00 2009*

BAYEUX *3D1* (9km NW Rural) *49.33120, -0.80240* **Camping Reine Mathilde, 14400 Etréham [02 31 21 76 55; fax 02 31 22 18 33; camping.reine.mathilde@wanadoo.fr; www.campingreinemathilde.com]** NW fr Bayeux on D6 turn L to Etréham (D100); site 3km (sp). Or W fr Bayeux on N13 for 8km, exist junc 38. At x-rds 1.5km after vill of Tour-en-Bessin turn R on D206 to Etréham & bear L at Etréham church. Med, hdg/mkd pitch, pt shd; htd wc; chem disp; baby facs; shwrs inc; el pnts (6A) €4.70; Indtte; sm shop & 4km; tradsmn; rest, snacks & pizza van (high ssn); bar; playgrnd; pool; htd paddling pool; sand beach 5km; cycle hire; fishing 1km; entmnts; free wifi; TV; 15% statics; dogs €3; phone; Eng spkn; adv bkg; quiet; ccard not acc; CCI. "Well-kept site; lge pitches; friendly, helpful warden; gd, clean san facs; conv D-Day beaches etc; excel." ♦
1 Apr-30 Sep. € 18.50 2009*

BAYON *6E2* (500m NW Rural) *48.47898, 6.30645* **Camp Municipal du Passetemps, Rue de la Moselle, 54290 Bayon [tel/fax 03 83 72 45 60 or 03 83 72 51 52 (Mairie)]** Fr N57 N fr Charmes or S fr Nancy; turn onto D9 sp Bayon; in 2.5km strt on at x-rds & over bridge; site on L in 500m by Rv Moselle. Med, pt shd; wc (some cont); chem disp; shwrs €0.90; el pnts (8A) inc; rest 500m; playgrnd; rv & sports facs adj; 50% statics; quiet. "Rv adj liable to dry out & also flood - care in wet weather; barrier clsd 2200-0700; sep area for tourers." 15 Apr-15 Oct. € 12.00 2009*

BAYONNE *8F1* (8km NE Rural) *43.54858, -1.40381* **Aire Naturelle L'Arrayade (Barret), 280 Chemin Pradillan, 40390 St Martin-de-Seignanx [05 59 56 10 60]** On D26 midway bet D810 (N10) & D817 (N117), 3km W of St Martin. (Opp tall crenellated building). Sm, pt sl, pt shd; wc (some cont); shwrs; el pnts €2.50 (long lead rec); Indry rm; BBQ; playgrnd; dogs; quiet. "Delightful little site; warm welcome; helpful owner; simple facs poss stretched high ssn."
1 Jun-30 Sep. € 10.50 2009*

⊞ **BAYONNE** *8F1* (10km NE Rural) *43.55588, -1.36115* **FFCC Camping Le Ruisseau, 40390 St André-de-Seignanx [05 59 56 71 92; campingle@aol.com; www.campingleruisseau.fr]** Fr Bayonne, take D817 (N117) dir Orthez. Turn L after 10km at traff lts in St Martin & foll sp for 5km to site. Sp fr all dir. Take care on ent - by rd junc. Med, hdg/mkd pitch, terr, pt shd; wc; chem disp; 15% serviced pitches; shwrs inc; el pnts (6A) €4; Indtte; shop; tradsmn; rest, snacks & bar 1km; playgrnd; pool; sand beach 10km; TV; 20% statics; dogs €2.50; adv bkg; quiet; red long stay/low ssn; CCI ess. "Away fr busy coastal area; helpful owner; not suitable lge o'fits." € 24.50 (3 persons) 2009*

BAYONNE *8F1* (11km NE Rural) *43.52820, -1.39157* **Camping Lou P'tit Poun, 110 Ave du Quartier Neuf, 40390 St Martin-de-Seignanx [05 59 56 55 79; fax 05 59 56 53 71; contact@louptitpoun.com; www.louptitpoun.com]** Fr Bordeaux exit A63 junc 6 dir Bayonne Nord; then take D817 (N117) dir Pau & St Martin-de-Seignanx; site sp on R in 7km. Lge, mkd pitch, terr, pt shd; wc; chem disp; mv service pnt; serviced pitch; baby facs; shwrs inc; el pnts (10A) inc; gas; Indtte; shop high ssn & 4km; tradsmn; rest (high ssn); snacks; bar; BBQ (el/gas); playgrnd; pool; paddling pool; sand beach 10km; tennis; games area; entmnt; games/TV rm; 17% statics; dogs €5; phone; Eng spkn; adv bkg; quiet; ccard acc; red low ssn; CCI. "Charming, friendly, spacious, family-run site; ltd facs low ssn; conv Biarritz, St Jean-de-Luz & a'route; excel." ♦
1 Jun-11 Sep. € 33.50 ABS - A39 2009*

BAZAS *7D2* (2km SE Rural) *44.43139, -0.20167* **Camping Le Grand Pré, Route de Casteljaloux, 33430 Bazas [05 56 65 13 17; fax 05 56 25 90 52; legrandpre@wanadoo.fr; http://pagesperso-orange.fr/legrandpre]** Exit A62 junc 3 onto N524 (D932) twd Bazas, then D655. Cont thro town cent & foll sp Casteljaloux/Grignols. Site sp on R. Sm, hdg/mkd pitch, pt sl, pt shd; wc; chem disp; mv service pnt; baby facs; fam bthrm; shwrs inc; el pnts (6-16A) €3.25-4.90; gas; Indtte; shop 2km; tradsmn; bar; playgrnd; htd pool; TV rm; 6% statics; dogs €3 (free low ssn); Eng spkn; adv bkg; quiet; red long stay/low ssn; CCI. "Pleasant, relaxed, well-kept site in picturesque location; views of chateau & town; friendly, helpful staff; san facs v smart but poss stretched high ssn; pleasant walk/cycle track to interesting, walled town; vineyards nr." ♦ 1 Apr-29 Sep. € 19.45 2009*

BAZINVAL see Blangy sur Bresle *3C2*

BAZOUGES SUR LE LOIR see Flèche, La *4G1*

BEAUCENS see Argelès Gazost *8G2*

BEAUFORT *9B3* (10km SE Rural) *45.65252, 6.58201* **Camping Les Amis, 73270 Arèches [04 79 38 14 65 or 04 79 38 12 07; info@campinglesamis.com; www.campinglesamis.com]** Fr Albertville take D925 to Beaufort cent; turn R onto D218A sp Arèches; site 5km beyond Arèches on rd to Barrage de St Guérin. Narr, winding rds. Sm, pt sl; pt shd, wc (some cont); chem disp (wc); mv service pnt; shwrs inc; el pnts (12A) €2.20; Indtte; tradsmn; shops, rest, snacks & bar 5km; lake fishing 1km; chair lifts to mountains; games rm; TV; 5% statics; dogs free; phone; bus 5km; quiet. "V remote, scenic site in mountains; vg walking; gd." ♦ 20 Jun-15 Sep. € 12.20 2007*

BEAUFORT *9B3* (300m NW Rural) *45.72160, 6.56418* **Camp Municipal Le Domelin, Domelin, 73270 Beaufort [tel/fax 04 79 38 33 88 or 04 79 38 33 15 (LS)]** Fr Albertville take D925 dir Beaufort & Bourg-St Maurice; site on L just bef ent Beaufort 100m up side rd (after passing D218B); clearly sp. NB App fr E (Bourg-St Maurice) rd v diff for towing. Med, mkd pitch, pt sl, pt shd; htd wc (some cont); chem disp; baby facs; shwrs inc; el pnts (10A) €2.65; Indtte; shops, rest, snacks & bar 1km; playgrnd; htd pool 1km; dogs; phone; bus 1km; poss cr; adv bkg; ccard acc; CCI. "Quiet, pleasant site; vg walking; attractive town; gd touring base." 1 Jun-30 Sep. € 11.84 2009*

BEAUGENCY *4F2* (500m E Rural) *47.77628, 1.64294* **Camp Municipal du Val de Flux, Route de Lailly-en-Val, 45190 Beaugency [02 38 44 50 39 or 02 38 44 83 12; fax 02 38 46 49 10; mairie.de.beaugency@wanadoo.fr]** Exit A10 junc 15 onto N152. In Beaugency turn L at traff lts nr water tower onto D925 & again over rd bdge. Site sp on S bank of Rv Loire. Med, mkd pitch, pt shd; htd wc; chem disp; shwrs inc; el pnts (10A) €3.05; Indry rm; shop & 500m; rest 1km; snacks; bar; playgrnd; sand beach; fishing; watersports; entmnts; 10% statics; dogs €0.55; poss cr w/end in ssn; quiet; Eng spkn; red long stay; CCI. "Basic facs stretched high ssn & poss unclean low ssn; views over Loire; helpful staff; poss itinerants & unruly youths; free 1 night site for m'vans over rv on other side of town." ♦ 1 Apr-31 Aug. € 9.75 2009*

⊞ **BEAUGENCY** *4F2* (8km S Rural) *47.68679, 1.55802* **Camping de l'Amitié, Nouan-sur-Loire, 41220 St Laurent-Nouan [02 54 87 01 52 or 03 86 37 95 83 (reservations); fax 02 54 87 09 93; aquadis1@wanadoo.fr; www.aquadis-loisirs.com]** On D951 SW fr Orléans cont past power stn into Nouan-sur-Loire. Site on R sp. Med, mkd pitch, pt shd; htd wc; mv service pnt; shwrs; el pnts (10A) €4.30; Indtte; shop 500m; rest 500m; pools & sports activities nr; direct access to rv; 50% statics; dogs €2.10; adv bkg; quiet; 10% red CCI. "Interesting area; view of Rv Loire; workers poss resident on site; friendly staff; phone ahead low ssn to check open." € 10.60 2008*

BEAULIEU SUR DORDOGNE *7C4* (E Urban) *44.97950, 1.84040* **FLOWER Camping des Iles, Blvd Rodolphe-de-Turenne, 19120 Beaulieu-sur-Dordogne [05 55 91 02 65; fax 05 55 91 05 19; info@campingdesiles.fr; www.campingdesiles.fr or www.flowercamping.com]** Exit A20 junc 52 ont D158/D38 dir Collonges-la-Rouge; cont on D38 & turn R onto D940 to Beaulieu-sur-Dordogne; site sp fr o'skts of town. Or on D940 N fr Bretenoux, turn R in Beaulieu town sq, site about 200m on island in Rv Dordogne. NB 3m height limit at ent. Med, mkd pitch, shd; htd wc; chem disp; baby facs; fam bthrm; shwrs inc; el pnts (10A) inc (poss long lead req); Indtte; shops 500m; rest; snacks; bar; BBQ (gas); playgrnd; pool; rv & fishing; cycling; sports area; entmnt high ssn; cycle, canoe hire; archery; games rm; wifi; 15% statics; dogs €1.60; poss cr; Eng spkn; adv bkg rec; quiet; red long stay/low ssn. "Delightful, wooded site; facs stretched high ssn, ltd low ssn; attractive medieval town; highly rec." 17 Apr-25 Sep. € 21.90 2009*

BEAULIEU SUR LOIRE *4G3* (300m E Rural) *47.54407, 2.82167* **FFCC Camp Municipal du Canal, Route de Bonny, 45630 Beaulieu-sur-Loire [02 38 35 89 56 or 02 38 35 32 16 (LS); fax 02 38 35 86 57; renault.campingbeaulieu@orange.fr; www.beaulieu-sur-loire.fr]** Exit A77 junc 21 Bonny-sur-Loire, cross rv to Beaulieu-sur-Loire on D296. On E o'skirts of vill on D926, nr canal. Sm, hdg/mkd pitch, pt shd; wc; chem disp; mv service pnt; shwrs inc; el pnts (6A) €2.70; Indry rm; shop 2km; rest adj; snacks, bar 500m; playgrnd; poss cr; Eng spkn; adv bkg; CCI. "Clean site; direct access to canal; gd walking along canal & Rv Loire; boat trips; mkt Wed." ♦ Easter-1 Nov. € 6.00 2009*

BEAUMES DE VENISE see Carpentras *10E2*

BEAUMONT DE LOMAGNE *8E3* (800m E Urban) *43.88406, 0.99800* **Camping Le Lomagnol (formerly Municipal Le Lac), Ave du Lac, 82500 Beaumont-de-Lomagne [05 63 26 12 00; fax 05 63 65 60 22; villagedeloisirslelomagnol@wanadoo.fr; www.villagelelomagnol.fr]** On SE of D928 at E end of vill. Sp 'Centre de Loisirs, Plan d'Eau'. Med, mkd pitch, pt shd; wc; chem disp; baby facs; sauna; shwrs inc; el pnts (10A) €3 (poss long lead req); Indtte; shop; rest; snacks; bar; playgrnd; pool; waterslide; jacuzzi; lake sw; fishing; tennis; cycle & canoe hire; golf; sailing; 25% statics; dogs €2; poss cr; quiet; red low ssn. "Gd quality, modern site; interesting old town; mkt Sat." ♦ Easter-30 Sep. € 13.00 2008*

BEAUMONT DU PERIGORD *7D3* (6km W Rural) *44.75603, 0.70216* **Centre Naturiste de Vacances Le Couderc (Naturist), 24440 Naussannes [05 53 22 40 40; fax 05 53 23 90 98; info@lecouderc.com; www.lecouderc.com]** Fr D660 at D25 W thro Naussannes & hamlet of Leydou. Just beyond Leydou turn R into site, well sp. Lge, mkd pitch, pt sl, pt shd; wc; chem disp; sauna; shwrs inc; el pnts (5A) €4.50; shop; rest; snacks; bar; playgrnd; htd pool; paddling pool; jacuzzi; sm lake; cycle hire; entmnt; wifi; some statics; dogs €4.65; adv bkg, ess high ssn; quiet; ccard acc; red long stay/low ssn. "Beautiful site with relaxed atmosphere; friendly, helpful Dutch owners; gd san facs; superb pool; naturist walks on site; gd walking/cycling area; Bastide towns nrby." ♦ 1 Apr-1 Oct. € 27.90 2009*

France

BEAUMONT HAGUE *1C4* (5km N Rural/Coastal) *49.70442, -1.84116* **Camp Municipal du Hable, 50440 Omonville-la-Rogue [tel/fax 02 33 52 86 15 or 02 33 01 86 00]** W fr Cherbourg on D901 to Beaumont-Hague; turn N onto D45 dir Omonville-la-Rogue. Med, hdg/mkd pitch, hdstg, pt shd; wc; chem disp; mv service pnt; shwrs €1; el pnts (5-10A) €2.95-4.80; lndtte; shop, gas adj; rest; bar; playgrnd; beach 100m; dogs €0.95; quiet; CCI. "In pretty vill with gd harbour; 30 mins fr Cherbourg; gd NH." 1 Apr-30 Sep. € 8.50 2009*

BEAUMONT SUR OISE *3D3* (8km SW Rural) *49.12805, 2.18318* **Parc de Séjour de l'Etang, 10 Chemin des Belles Vues, 95690 Nesles-la-Vallée [01 34 70 62 89; brehinier1@hotmail.com; www.campingparcset.com]** Fr D927 Méru-Pontoise rd, turn L onto D64 at sp L'Isle Adam. After passing thro Nesles-la-Vallée camp sp on L. Med, hdg pitch, pt shd; htd wc (cont); chem disp; serviced pitches (extra charge); shwrs inc; el pnts (3A) inc (rev pol); lndtte; shops 1km; playgrnd; lake fishing adj; dogs €2; Eng spkn; quiet; red CCI. "Lovely, peaceful, out-of-the way setting; spacious pitches; friendly, helpful staff; gd facs; conv day trips to Paris & Versailles; excel." 1 Feb-9 Dec. € 18.50 2009*

BEAUMONT SUR SARTHE *4F1* (500m E Rural) *48.22382, 0.13651* **FFCC Camp Municipal de Beaumont/Val de Sarthe, Rue de l'Abreuvoir, 72170 Beaumont-sur-Sarthe [02 43 97 01 93; fax 02 43 97 02 21; beaumont.sur.sarthe@wanadoo.fr; www.ville-beaumont-sur-sarthe.fr]** Fr D338 (N138) Alençon-Le Mans, turn L at traff lts in cent of Beaumont & foll site sp twd E of town. Fr Le Mans on A28 exit 21 onto D6, R onto D338 & R at traff lts & foll sp. NB Narr app thro town rds & steep app rd fr town with blind corners. Narr site access. Med, hdg/mkd pitch, pt shd; wc; chem disp; mv service pnt; shwrs inc; el pnts (6A) €3; (long cable poss req)(poss rev pol); lndtte; shops & rest 500m; playgrnd; pool 500m; rv boating & fishing adj; dogs €0.35; poss cr w/end; adv bkg rec high ssn; ccard acc; CCI. "Beautiful, peaceful, well-run rvside site; lge pitches, some by rv; immac san facs; no twin-axles & poss no c'vans over 2,000 kg; barrier clsd 2200; interesting, pretty town; mkt Tues." ♦ 1 May-30 Sep. € 7.40 2009*

BEAUMONT SUR SARTHE *4F1* (9.5km S Rural) *48.14267, 0.18428* **FFCC Camp Municipal Le Pont d'Orne, 72380 Montbizot [02 43 27 60 44 or 02 43 27 62 16 (LS); mairie.montbizot@wanadoo.fr]** Exit A28 junc 21 onto D47 to Montbizot; cont on D47, site 300m S of vill on L. Sm, hdg/mkd pitch, shd; wc; mv service pnt; shwrs inc; el pnts inc; snacks; bar; playgrnd. "Quiet site with access to rv; warden calls am/pm." 15 May-27 Sep. € 9.30 2009*

BEAUNE *6H1* (1km NE Urban) *47.03304, 4.83911* **Camp Municipal Les Cent Vignes, 10 Rue Auguste Dubois, 21200 Beaune [03 80 22 03 91; campinglescentvignes@mairie-beaune.fr; www.beaune.fr]** Fr N on A31 & fr S on A6 at junc with m'ways A6/A31 take A6 sp Auxerre-Paris; after 1km leave at junc 24 to join D974 (N74) twd Beaune; after approx 1.5km, turn R at 2nd traff lts fr a'route to site (sp) in 200m. If app fr S on D974 site well sp fr inner ring rd & foll sp to Dijon (not a'route sps). Also sp fr Mersault/L'Hôpital x-rds. Med, hdg/mkd pitch, hdstg, pt shd; htd wc; chem disp; mv service pnt; shwrs inc; el pnts (6A) €3.70 (some rev pol); gas; lndtte (inc dryer); shop; hypmkt 2km; rest; snacks; bar; BBQ; playgrnd; pool 800m; tennis; cycle hire; games area; wifi; TV rm; dogs; phone; Eng spkn; adv bkg in writing only bef 30 May; quiet; red long stay; ccard acc; CCI. "Well-run, clean, busy site; a few pitches for lge o'fits; no twin-axles; narr access rds, tight turns & low trees poss diff for lge o'fits; gd san facs; rec arr early even low ssn; vg." 15 Mar-30 Oct. € 11.80 2009*

⊞ **BEAUNE** *6H1* (3.5km NE Rural) *47.02458, 4.88711* **Camping Les Bouleaux, 11 Rue Jaune, 21200 Vignoles [03 80 22 26 88]** Do not leave A6 at new Beaune exit (24) but use old exit (junc 24.1); 500m after toll turn R at rndabt, in 1.5km turn R sp Dole rndabt. Immed after x-ing m'way turn L sp Vignoles. L again at next junc then R & foll camping sp. Site in approx 1.5km in cent Chevignerot; fr town cent take D973 (E) sp Dole. In 2km cross a'route & 1st L (N) sp Vignoles. Well sp. Sm, hdg/mkd pitch, pt shd; htd wc; chem disp; shwrs inc; el pnts (3-6A) €2.20-3.50 (rev pol altered on request); shop; tradsmn; supmkt 2km; dogs; adv bkg rec; quiet but some rd noise; CCI. "Attractive, well-kept, busy site; rec arr early high ssn; some gd sized pitches, most sm; helpful & friendly owners; superb clean san facs, poss stretched high ssn & ltd low ssn; poss muddy after rain - park on rdways; conv Beaune & NH fr a'route." ♦ € 13.10 2009*

BEAUNE *6H1* (8km SW Rural) *46.98573, 4.76855* **Kawan Village La Grappe d'Or, 2 Route de Volnay, 21190 Meursault [03 80 21 22 48; fax 03 80 21 65 74; info@camping-meursault.com; www.camping-meursault.com]** SW on D974 (N74)/D973 fr Beaune, fork R on D973 sp Autun, fork L on D111 sp Mersault; camp at ent to Meursault, 300m past motel; care needed at ent - almost U-turn. Med, mkd pitch; terr, pt shd; wc; chem disp; shwrs inc; el pnts (15A) €3.50 (poss rev pol); gas; lndtte; shop; rest; snacks; bar; playgrnd; pool; waterslide; tennis; cycle hire; wifi; phone; dogs €1.30; poss cr; Eng spkn; adv bkg ess in ssn; some rd noise; red low ssn; CCI. "Busy family site high ssn & busy NH - arr early; superb views over vineyards; basic facs stretched; site poss tired end of ssn; some pitches uneven, sm or obstructed by trees; barrier clsd 2200-0730; poss muddy when wet; sh walk to lovely town; conv famous wine vills; gd cycle paths; gd food adj motel; vg." ♦ 1 Apr-15 Oct. € 18.00 (CChq acc) 2009*

BEAUNE *6H1* (5km NW Rural) *47.06861, 4.80292* **FFCC Camping Les Premiers Prés, Route de Bouilland, 21420 Savigny-lès-Beaune [tel/fax 03 80 26 15 06 or 06 30 17 98 85 (mob); www.camping-savigny-les-beaune.fr]** Fr Beaune ring rd turn N on D974 (N74) sp Dijon; in 200m at traff lts turn L sp Savigny; in 100m ignore camping sp & bear R to Savigny (3km); site 1km thro vill on L. Med, mkd pitch, pt sl, pt shd; wc; chem disp; mv service pnt; shwrs inc; el pnts (6-16A) inc (some rev pol); gas 1.3km; shops 1km; supmkt 3km; tradsmn; BBQ; playgrnd; dogs €1; adv bkg; quiet; CCI. "Pleasant, busy NH in beautiful area; pleasant staff; facs not adequate if site full & ltd low ssn; no twin-axles; conv A6, A31, A36 & Beaune; poss itinerant workers at grape harvest; vg." ♦ 1 May-30 Sep. € 14.50 2007*

BEAURAINVILLE see Hesdin *3B3*

BEAURECUEIL see Aix en Provence *10F3*

BEAUREPAIRE *9C2* (S Urban) *45.33825, 5.06101* **Camp Municipal, Ave Charles de Gaulle, 38270 Beaurepaire [04 74 84 64 89 or 04 74 84 67 29; fax 04 74 79 24 14; ccpb@pays-de-beaurepaire.com]** Sp in town on L of Beaurepaire-Romans rd, adj pool & stadium. Med, shd; wc (some cont); shwrs inc; el pnts (6A) €2; shops 250m; 2 supmkts nr; rv fishing; quiet. 1 May-15 Sep. € 7.00 2007*

BEAUREPAIRE *9C2* (10km S Rural) *45.25332, 5.02803* **Camping du Château, Route de Romans, 26390 Hauterives [04 75 68 80 19; fax 04 75 68 90 94; contact@camping-hauterives.com; www.camping-hauterives.com]** Take D538 S to Hauterives, site sp in vill adj Rv Galaure. Med, mkd pitch, pt shd; wc; mv service pnt; shwrs; el pnts (6-10A) €2.50-3; Indtte; snacks; sm supmkt adj; playgrnd; htd pool; paddling pool; rv & fishing adj; tennis; games area; some statics; dogs €1; adv bkg; quiet. "Gd NH; friendly; gd pool." ♦ 1 Apr-30 Sep. € 14.00 2009*

BEAUREPAIRE *9C2* (9km SW Rural) *45.28250, 4.97833* **Camping Château de la Pérouze, Le Meyerie, 26210 St Sorlin-en-Valloire [04 75 31 70 21 or 06 70 00 04 74 (mob); fax 04 75 31 75 75; contact@campingfrance.info]** Exit Beaurepaire on D130/D139 sp Manthes for approx 1km; bef St Sorlin turn L at site sp in 1.5km. Narr site ent. Med, mkd pitch, pt shd; shwrs; htd wc; chem disp; baby facs; sauna; jacuzzi; shwrs inc; chem disp; baby facs; el pnts (6-10A) €2.30-4.20; gas; Indtte; shop 2km; tradsmn; rest; bar; pool; fishing; tennis; 30% statics; no dogs; quiet; adv bkg; CCI. "Friendly, helpful warden; in 14thC chateau grounds; sep, shd car park; gates clsd 2100-0900; access to pitches poss diff; winter c'van storage." 15 Jun-15 Sep. € 18.90 2008*

BEAUVAIS *3C3* (S Urban) *49.42440, 2.07991* **Camp Municipal, Rue Camard, 60000 Beauvais [03 44 02 00 22]** On S edge of town. Take Paris rd fr town cent over Pont de Paris; after 200m turn R at lts up Rue Binet (steep). 1st R & site on R. Well sp. Uphill app - can turn in car park at top of hill. Med, pt sl, pt shd; wc (some cont); shwrs inc; el pnts (4A) €1.90; shop 300m; rest, bar adj; playgrnd; htd pool, tennis adj; poss cr; quiet; CCI. "Spacious site, choice of pitch; gates close 2100." 1 Jun-30 Aug. € 8.60 2009*

BEAUVILLE *7D3* (500m SE Rural) *44.27210, 0.88850* **Camping Les Deux Lacs, 47470 Beauville [tel/fax 05 53 95 45 41; camping-les-2-lacs@wanadoo.fr; www.les2lacs.info]** Fr D656 S to Beauville, site sp on D122. NB Steep descent to site - owners help when leave if nec. Med, hdg/mkd pitch, terr, shd; wc; chem disp; mv service pnt; shwrs inc; el pnts (6A) €2.45; Indtte; rest; snacks; bar; shop 600m; playgrnd; lake sw adj; games area; fishing; watersports; wifi; 10% statics; dogs €2.15; Eng spkn; adv bkg; quiet; ccard acc; red long stay/low ssn; CCI. "Peaceful; gd fishing; pleasant walk to vill; vg." ♦ 1 Apr-31 Oct. € 14.90 2009*

France

BEAUVOIR see Mont St Michel, Le *2E4*

BEAUVOIR EN ROYANS see St Marcellin *9C2*

BEAUVOIR SUR MER *2H3* (4km E Rural) *46.89984, -1.98840* **Camp Municipal, 85230 St Gervais [02 51 68 73 14 (Mairie) or 06 12 16 32 (mob); fax 02 51 68 48 11]** On D948, 1km E of St Gervais on R. Sm, mkd pitch, pt shd; wc; chem disp; shwrs; el pnts (10A) €2.50; gas; Indry rm; shop; BBQ; quiet; CCI. "Facs basic but clean." ♦ 1 Apr-15 Sep. € 8.50 2009*

BEAUVOIR SUR MER *2H3* (4km E Rural) *46.92298, -1.99036* **Camping Le Fief d'Angibaud, 85230 St Gervais [02 51 68 43 08; camping.fief.angibaud@orange.fr; www.campinglefiefangibaud.com]** Fr Beauvoir-sur-Mer E on D948 to St Gervais turn L after PO/Mairie onto D59 twd Bouin (narr ent easy to miss); in 2km pass sm chapel; take 2nd rd on L; site on R after 500m. Sm, unshd; wc; shwrs inc; chem disp; el pnts (6A) inc; gas 4km; basic Indry rm; shops 2km; tradsmn; sand beach 5km; fishing/golf nrby; dogs €1; adv bkg rec high ssn; quiet; red CCI. "Excel, simple site adj farm; lge pitches; pleasant, helpful British owners; clean facs; variety of bird life; conv Ile de Noirmoutier; ferry to Ile d'Yeu, coastal resorts; free parking close to beach (blue flag); gd cycling area; vg value." ♦ 1 Mar-31 Oct. € 15.50 2009*

BEC HELLOUIN, LE see Brionne *3D2*

BEDARIEUX *10F1* (8km N Rural) *43.67313, 3.17265* **FFCC Camping La Sieste, 34260 La Tour-sur-Orb [04 67 23 72 96; fax 04 67 23 75 38; campinglasieste@orange.fr; http://pagesperso-orange.fr/campinglasieste]** Fr Bédarieux, take D35 N twd Lodève; site 3km N of La Tour-sur-Orbe at sm vill of Vereilles. Med, pt shd; wc; chem disp; shwrs inc; el pnts (4-8A) €2.30-4; Indtte; shop; tradsmn; rest; bar; BBQ; pool open June; dogs €2.50; phone; adv bkg; Eng spkn; quiet; poss v cr high ssn; ccard acc; 20% red low ssn; 5% red CCI. "Well-kept site; charming owners; unspoilt countryside." ♦ 1 Jun-31 Aug. € 14.00 2007*

⊞ **BEDENAC** *7C2* (1km E Rural) **Camping Louvrignac, 17210 Bedenac [05 46 70 31 88; lcarpenter@freenet.co.uk]** Fr N10 exit sp Bedenac onto D145. Thro Bedenac vill take D158 sp Montguyon & in 500m take 1st L sp Bernadeau. Site on L in 100m - narr rd. Sm, pt shd; own san; chem disp; el pnts (10A) inc; tradsmn; shop, rest, snacks, bar 10km; BBQ; htd pool; adv bkg; quiet. "CL-type site with 5 pitches; friendly British owners; rec phone in advance." € 12.00 2008*

BEDOIN *10E2* (1.5km NE Rural) *44.13363, 5.18738* **Domaine de Bélézy (Naturist), 84410 Bédoin [04 90 65 60 18; fax 04 90 65 94 45; info@belezy.com; www.belezy.com]** Fr Carpentras D974 to Bédoin. Go thro vill & turn R at rndabt sp Mont Ventoux. In 300m turn L & foll sp to site. Lge, pt sl, shd; htd wc (some cont); chem disp; mv service pnt; sauna; steam rm; shwrs inc; el pnts (12A) €5; gas; Indtte; shop; rest; snacks; bar; cooking facs; playgrnd; 2 htd pools; paddling pool; tennis; games area; horseriding 2km; golf 20km; wifi; entmnt; TV rm; 20% statics; no dogs; phone; sep car park high ssn; poss cr; Eng spkn; adv bkg; quiet; red long stay/low ssn; ccard acc; INF card. "Delightful, welcoming, peaceful site; lovely location; extensive facs; some sm & awkward pitches; gd base for Mt Ventoux, Côtes du Rhône." ♦ 23 Mar-2 Oct. € 38.00 (3 persons) (CChq acc) 2009*

BEDOIN *10E2* (1km S Rural) *44.11380, 5.18134* **Camping Ménèque, Chemin de Ménèque, 84410 Bédoin [04 90 65 93 50; fax 04 90 12 83 61; lemeneque@orange.fr; www.lemeneque.eu]** S fr Malaucène on D939, turn E onto D19 to Bédoin. S of Bédoin at fork in rd, bear L. Site on L. Med, pt sl, pt shd; wc; chem disp; shwrs inc; el pnts (6A) €3; gas; Indtte; shop; tradsmn; rest, snacks, bar; BBQ; playgrnd; pool; no statics; dogs €1.50; phone; poss cr; quiet; CCI. "Basic site in beautiful area; rec NH." ♦1 Apr-30 Sep. € 12.00 2006*

BEDOIN *10E2* (1km W Rural) *44.12468, 5.17249* **Camp Municipal de la Pinède, Chemin des Sablières, 84410 Bédoin [04 90 65 61 03; fax 04 90 65 95 22; la-pinede.camping.municipal@wanadoo.fr]** Take D938 S fr Malaucène for 3km, L onto D19 for 9km to Bédoin. Site adj to vill & sp. Med, sl, terr, shd; htd wc; shwrs inc; el pnts (16A) €2.50; Indtte; shops in vill; snacks; playgrnd; pool (high ssn); dogs €1; quiet; ccard not acc; CCI. "Pool clsd Mon; 5 min walk to vill & gd mkt on Mon." 15 Mar-31 Oct. € 11.50 2006*

BEDUER see Figeac *7D4*

BEGARD *2E2* (2km S Rural) *48.61666, -3.28227* **Camping du Donant, Gwenezhan, 22140 Bégard [02 96 45 46 46; fax 02 96 45 46 48; camping.begard@wanadoo.fr; www.camping-donant-bretagne.com]** Fr N12 at Guingamp take D767 dir Lannion, Perros-Guirec. S of Bégard foll sp Armoripark, site sp. Med, hdg/mkd pitch, hdstg, terr, pt shd; wc; chem disp; mv service pnt; baby facs; shwrs inc; el pnts (12A) €2.80; gas 1km; Indtte (inc dryer); shop & bar adj; BBQ; playgrnd; htd pool & leisure facs adj; tennis adj; TV rm; statics; dogs €1.35; Eng spkn; adv bkg; quiet; ccard acc. "Pleasant countryside; friendly, helpful staff; san facs poss not well-maintained low ssn & stretched high ssn; conv coast; gd touring base." ♦ Easter-15 Sep. € 12.60 2008*

BELCAIRE *8G4* (SW Rural) *42.81598, 1.95098* **Camp Municipal La Mousquière, 4 Chemin Lac, 11340 Belcaire [04 68 20 39 47 or 04 68 20 31 23 (Mairie); fax 04 68 20 39 48; mairie.belcaire@wanadoo.fr]** Site on D613 bet Ax-les-Thermes & Quillan. Sm, mkd pitch, pt sl, shd; wc; chem disp; shwrs inc; el pnts €1,50; gas 1km; Indtte; lake sw adj; dogs; phone; quiet; CCI. "Site by lake; gd cent for walking; tennis & horseriding nrby; historic vill of Montaillou nr; excel." ♦ 1 Jun-30 Sep. € 10.50 2006*

BELFORT *6G3* (1.5km N Urban) *47.65335, 6.86445* **FFCC Camping de l'Etang des Forges, 11 Rue du Général Béthouart, 90000 Belfort [03 84 22 54 92; fax 03 84 22 76 55; contact@camping-belfort.com; www.camping-belfort.com]** Exit A36 junc 13; go thro cent of Belfort; then foll sp Offemont on D13, then site sp. Or fr W on N19 site well sp. Med, hdg/mkd pitch, pt shd; htd wc; chem disp; mv service pnt; baby facs; shwrs inc; el pnts (6A) €3.50; Indtte; shop 500m; tradsmn high ssn; rest 200m; snacks, bar high ssn; BBQ; playgrnd; pool; fishing & watersports 50m; archery; internet; entmnt; TV rm; 5% statics; dogs €1.50; extra for twin-axles; Eng spkn; adv bkg; quiet; red low ssn/long stay; ccard acc; CCI. "Clean, modern san facs; friendly recep; conv for Corbusier's chapel at Ronchamp; well-kept but slightly scruffy & unkempt low ssn; fair." ♦ 7 Apr-30 Sep. € 16.10 (CChq acc) 2008*

BELGENTIER see Cuers *10F3*

⊞ **BELLAC** *7A3* (700m N Urban) *46.12744, 1.05052* **Camp Municipal Les Rochettes, Rue des Rochettes, 87300 Bellac [05 55 68 13 27; camping.bellac@wanadoo.fr; www.camping-limousin.com]** On N147 ent Bellac fr Poitiers take sharp L at 1st traff lts onto D675. Cont to rndabt & turn L. Foll sp, site on L in 400m adj football pitch. Fr Limoges on N147 take R at 3rd traff lts after ent Bellac onto D675 then foll sp as above. NB Sl ent to site. Med, mkd pitch, pt sl, pt shd, terr; htd wc; chem disp; mv service pnt; shwrs inc; el pnts (10A) €2.50 (long lead poss req); gas; Indry rm; shops 500m; supmkt 1km; bar 500m; playgrnd; pool & waterslide 1km; games area; dogs €1.10; quiet; ccard not acc; red long stay/low ssn. "Pleasant, spacious, clean site but poss diff if wet; pleasant warden; coded barrier clsd 2000-0800; facs poss ltd low ssn & site run down; phone ahead to check open low ssn; gd NH." € 10.30 2009*

⊞ **BELLAC** *7A3* (9km SE Rural) **Camping Fonclaire, 87300 Blond [tel/fax 05 55 60 88 26; fontclair@neuf.fr; http://limousin-gites.com]** Fr Bellac take D675 S dir St Junien. Site on L in approx 7km, 2km bef Mortemart. Sm, hdstg, pt shd, wc; chem disp; shwrs inc; (own san facs Nov-Mar) el pnts (6A) €4; gas 1km; lndtte; shop 4km; rest & bar 2km; sm htd pool; lake sw; fishing; golf 2km; horseriding 3km; no statics; dogs; phone 2km; Eng spkn; adv bkg; quiet; ccard not acc; CCI. "Lovely, peaceful, spacious CL-type site; friendly, helpful British owners; gd facs; nr Oradour-sur-Glane martyr vill; conv Futuroscope; gd cycling; excel." ♦ € 13.00 2009*

BELLEME *4E2* (SW Urban) *48.37420, 0.55370* **Camp Municipal Le Val, Route de Mamers, 61130 Bellême [02 33 85 31 00 (Mairie); fax 02 33 83 58 85; mairie.bellame@wanadoo.fr; www.lepaysbellemois.com]** Fr Mortagne, take D938 S to Bellême; turn R ent town on D955 Alençon rd; site sp on L half-way down hill. Sm, hdg pitch, pt sl, pt shd; wc (some cont); chem disp (wc); shwrs inc; el pnts (10A) inc (poss long lead req); shops 1km by footpath; supmkt nrby; playgrnd, pool, fishing; tennis adj; dogs €0.50; adv bkg rec high ssn. "Pretty, well-kept, comfortable site; some pitches v sl; warden visits twice daily; gd san facs; poss mkt traders; poss long water hoses req; pitches poss soft when wet; steep walk into town." 15 Apr-15 Oct. € 7.90 2009*

BELLENTRE *9B4* (2km E Rural) *45.57576, 6.73553* **Camping L'Eden, 73210 Landry [04 79 07 61 81; fax 04 79 07 62 17; info@camping-eden.net; www.camping-eden.net]** Fr N90 Moûtiers to Bourg-St Maurice at 20km turn R sp Landry; site on L after 500m adj Rv Isère. Med, mkd pitch, hdstg, pt shd; htd wc; chem disp; shwrs inc; el pnts (10A) €4-6; gas; lndtte (inc dryer); shop; tradsmn; snacks; bar; playgrnd; htd pool; games rem; TV; dogs €1.50; phone; ski bus; poss cr; quiet; adv bkg; ccard acc; Eng spkn. "Gd cent mountain sports; helpful, friendly owner; red facs low ssn; ltd site lighting; poss unkempt end of ssn." 15 Dec-5 May & 25 May-15 Sep. € 21.40 2008*

⊞ **BELLENTRE** *9B3* (3km SE Rural) *45.56065, 6.73941* **Camping de Montchavin, 73210 Bellentre [04 79 07 83 23; fax 04 79 07 80 18; info@montchavin-lescoches.com; www.montchavin-lescoches.com]** On N90 fr Moûtiers to Bourg-St Maurice (ignore site sps on N90); at 20km turn R onto D87E sp Landry & Montchavin-les-Coches; in 1km turn R onto D220, in 500m turn L onto D225; site in 7km on L at Montchavin. Med, mkd pitch, terr, pt shd; htd wc; mv service pnt; shwrs inc; el pnts (4-10A) €3.80-€7.60; gas; lndtte; shops 500m; pool in vill; games area; chairlift 200m; 60% statics; site clsd Oct; adv bkg (ess Jul/Aug & winter); quiet; ccard acc. "Site at 1200m; steep hill to shops; walking in summer, skiing in winter; magnificent setting." € 13.20 2009*

BELLEY *9B3* (8km E Rural) *45.76860, 5.76985* **Camping du Lac du Lit du Roi, La Tuilière, 01300 Massignieu-de-Rives [04 79 42 12 03; fax 04 79 42 19 94; info@camping-savoie.com; www.camping-savoie.com]** Fr D1504 (N504) turn E onto D992 to Massignieu-de-Rives, site sp. Site on NE of lake nr Les Mures. Med, hdg/mkd pitch, terr, pt shd; htd wc; chem disp; mv service pnt; shwrs inc; el pnts (10A) €5 (long lead req); gas; lndtte; shop 8km; tradsmn; snacks; bar; BBQ; playgrnd; pool; lake sw & beach; boating; tennis; cycle hire; TV rm; 20% statics; dogs €4; phone; Eng spkn; adv bkg (fee); ccard acc; red long stay/low ssn; CCI. "Superb site; many pitches on lake with lovely views; some v sm pitches; excel facs; few water pnts (2009)." ♦ 14 Apr-4 Oct. € 20.50 (CChq acc) 2009*

BELMONT SUR RANCE *8E4* (500m W Rural) *43.81777, 2.75108* **Camping Val Fleuri du Rance, Route de Lacaune, 12370 Belmont-sur-Rance [05 65 99 04 76; marjandejong@wanadoo.fr; http://campingfleuri.monsite.orange.fr/]** On D32 on ent vill fr SW; on L side of rd on sh unmade service rd. Sm, hdg/mkd pitch, pt shd; wc; chem disp; shwrs inc; el pnts (6A) €3.50; gas; lndry rm; shop 500m; rest; pool 500m; rv fishing; tennis; dogs €1; Eng spkn; adv bkg; quiet; CCI. "Attractive valley setting; helpful Dutch owners; attractive sm town; diff ent/exit to/fr south." ♦ 1 Jun-15 Sep. € 12.50 2008*

BELUS see Peyrehorade *8F1*

BELVES *7D3* (4km N Rural) *44.82560, 0.98902* **Camping du Port, 24170 Siorac-en-Périgord [05 53 28 63 81 or 06 18 12 64 75 (mob); contact@campingduport.net; www.campingduport.net]** On D25 in vill turn down beside Intermarché supmkt. Site ent strt ahead. Med, hdg/mkd pitch, shd; wc; shwrs; el pnts (10A) inc; lndtte; shops 1km; snacks; bar; playgrnd; rv beach, sw & fishing; adv bkg rec; quiet. "Friendly owners; pleasant site." ♦ 20 Apr-15 Nov. € 15.00 2008*

BELVES *7D3* (7km SE Rural) *44.74150, 1.04518* **Camping Les Hauts de Ratebout, 24170 Ste Foy-de-Belvès [05 53 29 02 10; fax 05 53 29 08 28; ratebout@franceloc.fr; www.camping-hauts-ratebout.fr or www.camping-franceloc.fr]** Turn E fr D710 onto D54 2km S of Belvès & foll camp sp. NB Do not ent Belvès. Lge, pt sl, terr, pt shd; htd wc; chem disp; shwrs inc; el pnts inc (6-10A); rest; snacks; bar; shop; gas; lndtte; covr'd pool & paddling pool; waterslide; tennis; golf; fishing; horseriding; entmnt; adv bkg Jul/Aug; Eng spkn; ccard acc; red low ssn; CCI. "Excel hilltop site; lge pitches; gd cent for touring." ♦ 12 May-9 Sep. € 34.00 2008*

BELVES *7D3* (2km S Rural) *44.76192, 1.01457* **Camping Le Moulin de la Pique, 24170 Belvès [05 53 29 01 15; fax 05 53 28 29 09; info@rcn-lemoulindelapique.fr; www.rcn-campings.fr]** Site sp S of Belvès on L. Med, shd; htd wc; chem disp; baby facs; shwrs inc; el pnts (6A) inc; Indtte; shop; rest; snacks; bar; BBQ; playgrnd; 3 pools (1 htd); paddling pool; waterslides; boating; fishing; tennis; games area; entmnt; TV; some statics; dogs €4; Eng spkn; adv bkg; red low ssn. "Site vg for children; clean & well-maintained; poss soft in wet weather; gd Sat mkt." ♦ 12 Apr-11 Oct. € 45.50 (CChq acc) 2008*

BELVES *7D3* (4km SW Rural) *44.75258, 0.98330* **FLOWER Caming Les Nauves, Le Bos-Rouge, 24170 Belvès [05 53 29 12 64; campinglesnauves@hotmail.com; www.lesnauves.com or www.flowercamping.com]** On D53 fr Belvès. Site on L just after junc to Larzac. Avoid Belves cent - use lorry rte dir Monpazier. Med, hdg pitch, pt sl, pt shd; wc; chem disp; mv service pnt; baby facs; shwrs inc; el pnts (6A) inc; Indtte; shop adj; rest; snacks; bar; BBQ; playgrnd; pool; paddling pool; games rm; horseriding; cycle hire; games rm; internet; entmnt; TV; some statics; dogs €2.30; adv bkg; quiet. "Excel site; gd views fr some pitches; Belvès lovely town." ♦ 11 Apr-21 Sep. € 19.50 2007*

BELVES *7D3* (8km SW Rural) *44.75813, 0.90222* **Camping Terme d'Astor (Naturist), St Avit-Rivière, 24480 Bouillac [05 53 63 24 52; fax 05 53 63 25 43; termdastor@wanadoo.fr; www.termedastor.com]** Leave D710 at Belvès onto D53; in 4km turn R onto D26 to Bouillac; pass thro vill; then turn 2nd L. Well sp. Med, mkd pitch, pt sl, shd; wc (some cont); chem disp; shwrs inc; el pnts (6A) €4; gas; Indtte; shop; tradsmn; rest; snacks; bar; BBQ; playgrnd; pool; paddling pool; waterslide; excursions; rafting; archery; tennis, horserding & canoeing nrby; games rm; internet; entmnt; TV; 10% statics; dogs free; phone; Eng spkn; adv bkg; quiet; ccard acc; INF. "Gd cent for Dordogne rv & chateaux; vg." ♦ 14 Apr-30 Sep. € 26.00 2007*

BELVES *7D3* (2km NW Rural) *44.79567, 1.00753* **Camping FFCC La Lenotte, 24170 Monplaisant [tel/fax 05 53 30 25 80 or 06 89 33 05 60 (mob); campinglalenotte@libertysurf.fr; www.la-lenotte.com]** Fr Sarlat take D57 twds Beynac, turn R in vill onto D703, at Siorac turn L onto D710 twd Belvès. Site on L in 2km. Med, hdg/mkd pitch, pt shd; wc; chem disp; mv service pnt; baby facs; shwrs inc; el pnts (10A) €3; gas; Indtte; shop; tradsmn; snacks; BBQ; playgrnd; pool; shgl beach 3km; rv & fishing 3km; cycling; 5% statics; dogs €1.60; phone; Eng spkn; adv bkg; quiet but some rd noise; red CCI. "Beautiful scenery; Belvès magnificent medieval town; helpful owner." ♦ 1 Apr-31 Oct. € 11.60 2007*

BELZ *2F3* (W Coastal) *47.68288, -3.18869* **Camping St Cado, Port de St Cado, 56550 Belz [02 97 55 31 98; fax 02 97 55 27 52; info@camping-saintcado.com; www.camping-saintcado.com]** W fr Auray on D22 then D16. Well sp fr Belz. Med, hdg pitch, pt shd; wc; el pnts (3-6A) €2.30-3.30; Indtte; tradsmn; shop, rest 300m; playgrnd; tennis; games area; fishing, boat hire 300m; games rm; some statics; dogs €1.50; adv bkg; quiet. "Popular site in picturesque location; rec phone ahead for pitch high ssn; helpful owner." 1 Apr-30 Sep. € 12.00 2008*

BENODET *2F2* (1.5km E Coastal) *47.86670, -4.09080* **Camping Le Letty, 29950 Bénodet [02 98 57 04 69; fax 02 98 66 22 56; reception@campingduletty.com; www.campingduletty.com]** Fr N ent town on D34, foll sp Fouesnant D44. Le Letty sp R at rndabt. Fr E on N165 take D44 sp Fouesnant & foll rd to outskirts Bénodet. After town sp, site is sp. Lge, hdg/mkd pitches, hdstg, pt sl, pt shd; wc (some cont); chem disp; mv service pnt; baby facs; sauna; shwrs €0.60; el pnts (10A) €4; gas; Indtte; shop; takeaway snacks; bar; BBQ (gas); playgrnd; pool 500m; sand beach adj; kayak hire; tennis; squash; games area; games rm; gym; golf & horseriding nr; library; entmnt; wifi; TV rm; 2% statics; dogs €2.30; phone; poss cr; Eng spkn; adv bkg; quiet; ccard acc; red low ssn; CCI. "Excel, well-run, beautifully laid-out site; clean & well-equipped; lovely beach adj; excel playgrnd; many activities; friendly, helpful staff; highly rec." ♦ 12 Jun-6 Sep. € 24.40 2009*

See advertisement below

Fine sandy beach 300 m away
Camping ☆☆☆
Le Helles
55, rue du Petit Bourg
Saint-Marine - 29120 COMBRIT
Tel./Fax +33(0)2 98 56 31 46
contact@le-helles.com
www.le-helles.com

BENODET *2F2* (500m SE Coastal) *47.86780, -4.09750* **Camping du Poulquer, Route de Letty, 29950 Bénodet [02 98 57 04 19; fax 02 98 66 20 30; campingdupoulquer@wanadoo.fr; www.campingdupoulquer.com]** Fr N ent town on D34. At rndabt after junc with D44 strt onto Rue Penfoul. At next rndabt (tourist info office on R after rndabt) go strt dir La Plage until reach seafront; turn L at seafront then turn L at end of prom at camping sp; site in 100m on R. Fr E on N165 take D44 sp Fouesnant & foll rd to outskirts Bénodet. After town sp, site is sp. Med, hdg/mkd pitch, pt sl, pt shd; wc; chem disp; baby facs; shwrs inc; el pnts (10A) inc (long lead poss req)(poss rev pol); gas; Indtte; shop, snacks & bar high ssn; rest 600m; BBQ; playgrnd; htd pool & paddling pool; waterslide; aqua park; sand beach adj; tennis; golf nr; cycle hire 1km; entmnt; wifi; games/TV rm; dogs €2; c'vans over 7.50m not acc high ssn; adv bkg; quiet; ccard not acc; red low ssn; CCI. "Friendly, helpful owner; gd, clean san facs, poss tired end of ssn; pitches tight for lge o'fits; mkt Mon." ♦ 15 May-30 Sep. € 26.40 ABS - B16 2009*

BENODET *2F2* (2km SE Coastal) *47.86290, -4.09600* **Camping Sunêlia La Pointe St Gilles, Corniche de la Mer, 29950 Bénodet [02 98 57 05 37; fax 02 98 57 27 52; sunelia@stgilles.fr; www.camping-stgilles.fr]** Fr N ent town on D34. At rndabt after junc with D44 (Pont l'Abbé) strt onto Rue Penfoul. At next rndabt (tourist info office on R after rndabt) go strt dir La Plage until reach seafront. Turn L at end of prom twd Le Letty & L after Les Horizons development into Rue du Poulquer; site in 200m on L. Fr E on N165 take D44 sp Fouesnant & foll rd to outskirts Bénodet. After town sp, site is sp. Lge, hdg pitch, pt shd; wc; baby facs; shwrs inc; el pnts (10A) inc; gas; Indtte; shop; snacks; BBQ; 2 pools (1 covrd); paddling pool; jacuzzi; waterslide; sand beach adj; watersports; games area; games rm; wifi; entmnt; sat TV; 90% statics; no dogs; phone; poss cr; adv bkg; quiet; ccard acc; red long stay/low ssn. "Pleasant town, gd beaches; busy, well-run site; helpful staff; modern san facs; ltd touring pitches in sep area." 30 Apr-7 Sep. € 38.00 2007*

BENODET *2F2* (7km W Coastal) *47.86903, -4.12848* **Camping Le Helles, 55 Rue du Petit-Bourg, 29120 Combrit-Ste Marine [tel/fax 02 98 56 31 46; contact@le-helles.com; www.le-helles.com]** Exit D44 S dir Ste Marine, site sp. Med, mkd pitch, pt sl, pt shd; htd wc; chem disp; baby facs; fam bthrm; shwrs inc; el pnts (6-10A) €3.50-4.40; Indtte; shop; tradsmn; snacks; BBQ; playgrnd; htd pool; paddling pool; sand beach 300m; some statics; dogs €2.60; Eng spkn; adv bkg; quiet; ccard acc; red low ssn; CCI. "Vg site with lge pitches; gd, clean san facs; friendly, helpful staff; excel beach." ♦ 1 May-12 Sep. € 21.50 2009*

See advertisement above

The opening dates and prices on this campsite have changed. I'll send a site report form to the Club for the next edition of the guide.

BENODET *2F2* (1km NW Rural) *47.88237, -4.10334* **Yelloh! Village Port de Plaisance, Route de Quimper, Clohars-Fouesnant, 29950 Bénodet [tel/fax 02 98 57 02 38; info@campingbenodet.fr; www.campingbenodet.fr or www.yellohvillage.com]** Fr Bénodet take D34 twd Quimper, site on R 200m bef rndabt at ent to town. Lge, hdg pitch, pt sl, pt shd; wc; chem disp; mv service pnt; shwrs inc; child/baby facs; el pnts (6A) inc; Indtte; shop; tradsmn; rest; snacks; bar; playgrnd; htd pool; sand/shgl beach 1.5km; tennis; games area; cycle hire; internet; entmnt; 80% statics; dogs €4; phone; poss cr; Eng spkn; poss noisy (disco); adv bkg; ccard acc; red low ssn; CCI. "Many tour ops on site; some pitches poss diff lge o'fits; excel." ♦ 3 Apr-20 Sep. € 39.00 2009*

BENON see Courçon *7A2*

BENOUVILLE see Ouistreham *3D1*

BERAUT see Condom *8E2*

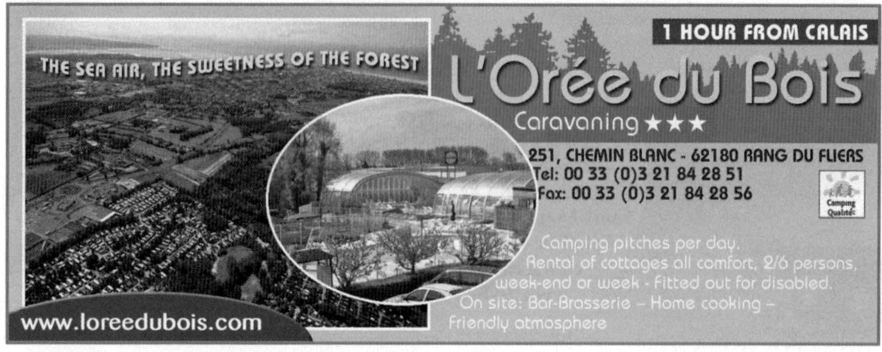

THE SEA AIR, THE SWEETNESS OF THE FOREST
1 HOUR FROM CALAIS
L'Orée du Bois
Caravaning ★★★
251, CHEMIN BLANC - 62180 RANG DU FLIERS
Tel: 00 33 (0)3 21 84 28 51
Fax: 00 33 (0)3 21 84 28 56
Camping pitches per day.
Rental of cottages all comfort, 2/6 persons,
week-end or week - Fitted out for disabled.
On site: Bar-Brasserie – Home cooking –
Friendly atmosphere
www.loreedubois.com

BERCK *3B2* (4km E Rural) *50.41861, 1.60556* **Camping L'Orée du Bois, 251 Chemin Blanc, 62180 Rang-du-Fliers [03 21 84 28 51; fax 03 21 84 28 56; oree.du.bois@wanadoo.fr; www.loreedubois.fr]** Exit A6 junc 25 onto D140 & D917. Thro Rang-du-Fliers, turn R bef pharmacy into Chemin Blanc, site sp. V lge, hdg/mkd pitch, pt shd; wc (some cont); chem disp; mv service pnt; serviced pitches; shwrs inc; el pnts (6A) inc; gas; shop adj; lndtte; tradsmn; rest; snacks; bar; playgrnd; pools; sand beach 4km; tennis; games area; fishing lake; cycle hire; entmnt; 80% statics; dogs €4; Eng spkn; adv bkg; quiet; ccard acc; red low ssn/long stay/CCI. "Conv Le Touquet, Boulogne, Montreuil & Calais; peaceful site in woodland; ltd facs low ssn; ltd space for tourers." ♦ 3 Apr-4 Nov. € 26.00 2009*

See advertisement above

BERGERAC *7C3* (500m S Urban) *44.84898, 0.47636* **Camp Municipal La Pelouse, 8 bis Rue Jean-Jacques Rousseau, 24100 Bergerac [tel/fax 05 53 57 06 67; population@mairie-bergerac.fr; www.ville-bergerac.com]** On S bank of Rv Dordogne 300m W of old bdge opp town cent. Do not ent town, foll camping sp fr bdge, ent on R after L turn opp block of flats. Well sp, on Rv Dordogne. Med, mkd pitch, pt sl, pt shd; wc; chem disp; mv service pnt; shwrs inc; el pnts (6A) €3.20-4.50; gas; lndtte; shop in town; playgrnd; rv fishing adj; dogs €1.20; poss cr; adv bkg; Eng spkn; quiet; CCI. "Peaceful site on rv bank; san facs need update (2008) & ltd low ssn; friendly warden; easy walk by rv into attractive old town; no twin-axles & c'vans over 6m; site poss clsd earlier if weather bad; rec arr bef 1400 high ssn." ♦ 1 Apr-31 Oct. € 11.70 2009*

BERGERAC *7C3* (8km W Rural) *44.83849, 0.33052* **Camping Parc Servois, 11 Rue du Bac, 24680 Gardonne [05 53 57 27 46]** Fr D936 Bergerac to Bordeaux, R in vill of Gardonne. Site 250m after traff lts. Sm, mkd pitch, pt shd; wc; chem disp; shwrs inc; el pnts (10A) €1.90-2.10; shops 200m; rest 300m; dogs €0.60; phone 200m; Eng spkn; quiet; CCI. "Pretty, CL-type site on bank of Rv Dordogne; lge pitches; helpful staff; facs immac but dated & poss stretched in ssn; sm mkt Wed & Sun; excel." 1 Apr-30 Sep. € 7.80 2009*

BERGUES *3A3* (7km N Rural) *50.96500, 2.43300* **Aire de Camping-Car Municipal, 59380 Bergues** Exit A25 junc 16 twd Bergues (N) on D916 then R onto D110. When town ramparts appear on L turn L twd town ent arch. Turn R bef drawbridge, site in 200m. NB m'vans only. Med, all hdstg, unshd; no facs; own san; shop, rest, snacks, bar in town; BBQ; dogs; bus adj; quiet. "Only avail when all-weather, winter sports pitch adj not in use; no charge; gd views of town; clean & tidy; pleasant walks." 2009*

BERGUES *3A3* (500m NE Urban) *50.97248, 2.43420* **Camping Le Vauban, Ave Vauban, 59380 Bergues [03 28 68 65 25; fax 03 28 63 52 60; cassiopee.tourisme@wanadoo.fr; www.bergues.fr]** Exit A16 junc 60 twd Bergues on D916. In 2km turn L onto D2 dir Coudekerque vill. In 2km turn R at rndabt onto D72 to Bergues, turn R immed bef canal, site strt on at foot of town ramparts. Med, hdg/mkd pitch, terr, pt shd; wc (cont); chem disp; mv service pnt; baby facs; fam bthrm; shwrs €1.30; el pnts (6A) €3.60 (poss rev pol); lndtte; tradsmn; shop, rest, snacks & bar in town; playgrnd; pool nr; 60% statics; no twin-axles; dogs €1.05; poss cr; adv bkg; quiet; no ccard acc; red low ssn; CCI. "Lovely fortified town; sm pitches poss diff lge o'fits; ltd manoeuvring in site rds; basic, v dated san facs housed in WW2 bunker!; gates clsd 2130-0700; conv Dunkerque & Calais; NH only." ♦ 1 Apr-31 Oct. € 17.20 2008*

⊞ **BERGUES** *3A3* (4km NE Rural) *50.97720, 2.50447* **FFCC Parc Les Résidences La Becque, 791 Rue de l'Est, 59380 Warhem [03 28 62 00 40; fax 03 28 62 05 65; www.residences-la-becque.com]** Exit A25 at junc 16 sp Bergues. At top of slip rd turn L D916 then turn R at rndabt onto D110; L in 4km to Warhem. Site well sp in vill. Med, hdg/mkd pitch, hdstg, pt shd, wc (cont); own san; shwrs €1.55; el pnts (6A) €2.50; gas; lndry rm; shop 1km; supmkt in Hoymille; playgrnd; rv fishing 2km; tennis; 99% statics; dogs €1.55; quiet. "Only 2 pitches for tourers; low ssn ltd office opening (clsd Mon & Fri) & access/exit diff (Jun 08) - not rec to arr on these days; otherwise last resort NH; clean facs." ♦ € 17.00 2008*

BERNAY *3D2* (1.5km S Urban) *49.08020, 0.58703* **Camp Municipal, Rue des Canadiens, 27300 Bernay [02 32 43 30 47; camping@bernay27.fr; www.ville-bernay27.fr]** Site sp fr S'most (Alençon) rndabt off Bernay by-pass D438 (N138); twd France Parc Exposition then 1st L & on R. Well sp. Sm, hdg/mkd pitch, pt shd; wc; chem disp; mv service pnt; shwrs inc; el pnts (10A) €3.60 (poss rev pol); Indry rm; shop 500m; tradsmn; rest, bar 1km; playgrnd; pool 300m; table tennis; TV rm; dogs; phone; adv bkg; no ccard acc; CCI. "Nice, quiet, well-kept site; well set-out pitches, diff sizes; helpful & friendly; gd clean facs; 20 mins walk to town cent; barrier clsd 2200-0700; excel." ♦ 1 May-30 Sep. € 14.65 2009*

BERNERIE EN RETZ, LA see Pornic *2G3*

BERNEVAL LE GRAND *3B2* (500m N Coastal) *49.96158, 1.1933* **FFCC Camp Municipal Le Val Boisé, 56 Ave Capitaine Porthéous, 76340 Berneval-le-Grand [02 35 85 29 18; camping-berneval@wanadoo.fr; http://bernevallegrand.fr/camping]** Fr Dieppe take D925 for 6km, turn L at Graincourt onto D54 past Silo on R. Site sp. Sm, mkd pitch, hdstg, terr, pt shd; wc; chem disp; mv service pnt; shwrs; el pnts (16A) €2.70; shop 2km; playgrnd; shgl beach 700m; entmnt; some statics; dogs €0.80; Eng spkn; adv bkg rec; quiet, but rd noise some pitches; CCI. "Lovely quiet spot; v hilly area, poss diff lge o'fits; gd." 1 Apr-1 Nov. € 9.40 2009*

BERNY RIVIERE *3C4* (1.5km S Rural) *49.40603, 3.12860* **Camping La Croix du Vieux Pont, Route de Fontenoy, 02290 Berny-Rivière [03 23 55 50 02; fax 03 23 55 05 13; info@la-croix-du-vieux-pont.com; www.la-croix-du-vieux-pont.com]** On N31 bet Soissons & Compiègne. At site sp turn onto D13, then at Vic-sur-Aisne take next R, R again then L onto D91. Foll sp to site on o'skts of Berny. V lge, hdg pitch, hdstg, pt shd; htd wc; chem disp; mv service pnt; some serviced pitch; baby facs; shwrs inc; el pnts (6A) €2.50 (poss rev pol & no earth); gas; Indtte; supmkt; tradsmn; rest; snacks; bar; playgrnd; 4 htd pools (2 covrd); waterslide; aquatic park; tennis; games rm; lake beach & sw; fishing; boating; tennis; games rm; horseriding; archery; golf; cycle hire; beauty cent; gym; excursions to Paris & Disneyland; wifi; entmnt; TV rm; many tour op statics high ssn; dogs; poss cr; Eng spkn; adv bkg rec; quiet; ccard acc; CCI. "V pleasant, family site; lge pitches, some rvside; helpful staff; vg san facs, ltd low ssn; vg rest; gd entment; some sh stay pitches up steep bank; some pitches liable to flood; site open all yr but no services Nov-Mar; excel." ♦ 1 Apr-31 Oct. € 22.00 (CChq acc) 2009*

See advertisement below

France

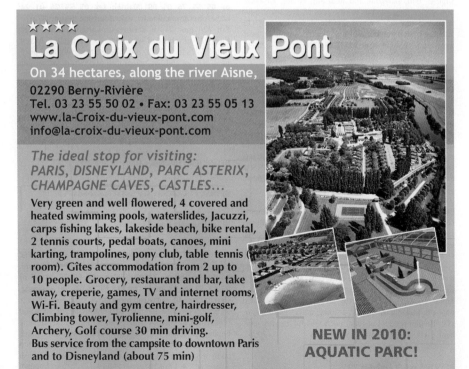

⊞ **BERNY RIVIERE** *3C4* (2km W Urban) *49.39280, 3.15161* **Camping La Halte de Mainville, 18 Rue de Routy, 02290 Ressons-le-Long [03 23 74 26 69; fax 03 23 74 03 60; lahaltedemainville@wanadoo.fr; www.lahaltedemainville.com]** On L of N31 Soissons to Compiègne rd 10km W of Soissons, clearly sp. Lge, hdg/mkd pitch, pt shd; wc; chem disp; shwrs inc; el pnts (6A) €3 (poss rev pol); Indtte; shop 4km; tradsmn; playgrnd; htd pool; fishing; tennis; 60% statics; dogs; phone; Eng spkn; adv bkg rec; quiet but poss some rd noise; no ccard acc; red CCI. "Pleasant, clean, conv NH; friendly staff; 1 hr fr Disneyland; vg." € 15.00 2009*

BERT see Donjon, Le *9A1*

BERTANGLES see Amiens *3C3*

BESANCON *6G2* (5km NE Rural) *47.26472, 6.07255* **FFCC Camping La Plage, 12 Route de Belfort, 25220 Chalezeule [03 81 88 04 26; fax 03 81 50 54 62; laplage.besancon@ffcc.fr; www.laplage-besancon.com]** Exit A36 junc 4 S; foll sp Montbéliard & Roulons onto D683 (N83); site in 1.5km on R, 200m after rlwy bdge; well sp fr D683. Fr Belfort 2.65m height restriction; foll sp to Chalezeule & 300m after supmkt turn L to rejoin D683, site in 200m on rvside. Med, mkd pitch, terr, pt shd; htd wc; chem disp; mv service pnt; shwrs inc; el pnts (6A) €3.60 (poss rev pol); Indtte (inc dryer); supmkt 1km; playgrnd; htd pool adj; rv adj; kayaking; 50% statics; dogs €1; bus to city; poss cr; Eng spkn; quiet but some rd & rlwy noise; ccard acc; red low ssn; CCI. "Helpful staff; dated but well-kept san facs adequate; twin-axles extra." ♦ 1 Apr-30 Sep. € 13.65 (CChq acc) 2009*

BESANCON *6G2* (11km NW Rural) *47.32933, 5.97165* **Camping Les Peupliers, 25870 Geneuille [03 81 57 72 04]** Fr Besançon take N57 towards Vesoul then take L into D1 & fork R to Geneuille. Site sp thro vill. Sm, mkd pitch, pt shd; wc (some cont); chem disp (wc); el pnts (10A) inc; shops 1km, rest, snacks, bar 500m; rv; 10% statics; quiet; dogs. "Fairly run down, old fashioned but peaceful site nr rv; friendly welcome; some refurbed san facs; access to facs by stairs, diff for disabled; poss mosquitoes." 23 Jun-15 Sep. € 10.90 2008*

BESSE SUR BRAYE *4F2* (S Rural) *47.83114, 0.75394* **Camping Le Val de Braye, 25 Rue du Val de Braye, 72310 Bessé-sur-Braye [02 43 35 31 13; fax 02 43 35 58 86; camping.bessesurbraye@orange.fr; www.besse-sur-braye.fr.st]** Fr D357 at St Calais take D303 to Bessé-sur-Braye; ignore Centre Ville sp & cont on by-pass. Site on L 300m beyond traff lts by sw pool. NB Avoid town cent. Med, pt shd; htd wc; chem disp; mv service pnt; shwrs inc; el pnts (13A) €2 (some rev pol); Indtte; shop adj; BBQ; playgrnd; htd, covrd pool adj; walking; fishing; TV; adv bkg; quiet; red long stay; CCI; "Helpful resident warden; pitch area ltd low ssn; well-kept, excel site." ♦ 15 Apr-15 Sep. € 8.00 2008*

BESSEGES see St Ambroix *9D2*

⊞ **BESSINES SUR GARTEMPE** *7A3* (4km N Rural) *46.14777, 1.36505* **Camp Municipal, 87250 Morterolles-sur-Semme [05 55 76 60 18 or 05 55 76 05 09 (Mairie); fax 05 55 76 68 45; ot.bessines@wanadoo.fr]** S on A20 take exit 23.1 sp Châteauponsac. Take 1st turn R, site on L in vill of Morterolles by stadium. N on A20 take exit 24.2 sp Bessines, turn under a'route & take 1st R sp Châteauponsac to Morterolles in 3km. Sm, mkd pitch, pt shd; htd wc; shwrs inc; el pnts (5A) inc (poss rev pol); Indry rm; playgrnd; covrd pool 200m; cycle hire; dogs; poss cr; Eng spkn; quiet; CCI. "Delightful farm site nr Limoges; gd low ssn as htd shwr blocks old-fashioned but clean; helpful warden - if absent on arr, pitch yourself & will call later; poss itinerants; conv A20, excel NH." ♦ € 10.00 2009*

This is a wonderful site.

I'll fill in a report online and let the Club know – www.caravanclub.co.uk/europereport

BESSINES SUR GARTEMPE *7A3* (1.5km SW Urban) *46.10013, 1.35423* **Camp Municipal Lac de Sagnat, Route de St Pardoux, 87250 Bessines-sur-Gartempe [05 55 76 17 69 or 05 55 76 05 09 (Mairie); fax 05 55 76 01 24; ot.bessines@wanadoo.fr; www.tourisme-bessines87.fr]** Exit A20 junc 24 sp Bessines-sur-Gartempe onto D220; then D27 sp lake. Foll sp to Bellevue Restaurant. At rest, turn R foll site sp. Well sp fr junc 24. Med, hdg/mkd pitch, pt sl, terr, pt shd; wc; chem disp (wc); shwrs inc; el pnts (6A) inc; Indtte; shops 1km; tradsmn high ssn; rest 500m; snacks high ssn; playgrnd adj; sand beach & lake sw adj; TV rm; Eng spkn; poss cr; quiet. "Pretty site with lake views; peaceful location; friendly staff; gd, clean san facs; poss unkempt low ssn (Jun 2009); hotel for meals nrby; conv NH A20." ♦ 1 May-30 Sep. € 15.00 2009*

BEUZEC CAP SIZUN see Douarnenez *2E2*

BEYNAC ET CAZENAC see Sarlat la Canéda *7C3*

BEZ, LE see Brassac *8F4*

BEZIERS *10F1* (8km NE Rural) *43.36254, 3.31924* **FFCC Aire Naturelle Domaine de Clairac (Philippon), Route de Bessan, 34500 Béziers [04 67 76 78 97 or 06 11 19 98 13 (mob); fax 04 67 76 78 98; camping.clairac@free.fr; www.campingclairac.com]** Exit A9 junc 35 Béziers Est; after toll take dir 'Centre Ville'; at 1st & 2nd rndabts foll sp Pézenas onto N9; in 5km turn R to Domaine de Clairac. Sm, pt shd; wc; chem disp; shwrs inc; el pnts (6A) €3; Indtte; tradsmn; snacks; bar; BBQ; playgrnd; htd pool; dogs; Eng spkn; quiet. "Friendly, helpful Swedish owner; gd." ♦ 1 Apr-30 Sep. € 15.00 2009*

⊞ **BEZIERS** *10F1* (10km NE Rural) *43.39849, 3.37338* **Camping Le Rebau, 34290 Montblanc [04 67 98 50 78; fax 04 67 98 68 63; gilbert@camping-lerebau.fr; www.camping-lerebau.fr]** NE on N9 fr Béziers-Montpellier, turn R onto D18. Site sp, narr ent 2.50m. Lge, hdg/mkd pitch, hdstg, pt shd; wc; chem disp; baby facs; shwrs inc; el pnts (5A) €4.50; gas 2km; Indtte; shop in vill; snacks & bar high ssn; playgrnd; pool; entmnt; TV; 10% statics; dogs €2.80; phone; bus 1km; poss cr; Eng spkn; adv bkg; quiet; red low ssn; CCI. "Gd site; tight ent & manoeuvring onto pitches; some facs old, but modern shwrs; ltd facs low ssn, but clean; helpful owner; gd pool; gd touring base; low ssn phone ahead to check open." € 19.50 2007*

BEZIERS *10F1* (6km SE Urban) *43.3169, 3.2842* **Camping Les Berges du Canal, Promenade des Vernets, 34420 Villeneuve-les-Béziers [04 67 39 36 09; fax 04 67 39 82 07; contact@lesbergesducanal.com; www.lesbergesducanal.com]** Fr A9 exit junc 35 & foll sp for Agde. Exit 1st rndabt for D612 (N112) dir Béziers then 1st L onto D37 sp Villneuve-les-Béziers. Foll site sp to site adj canal. Med, hdg/mkd pitch, shd; wc; chem disp; mv service pnt; baby facs; shwrs inc; el pnts inc (poss rev pol); Indtte; shop; rest; snacks; playgrnd; htd pool; beach 10km; cycle hire; 45% statics; dogs €3; poss cr; Eng spkn; adv bkg; CCI. "Pleasant site; facs clean but poss stretched in ssn; some pitches tight lge o'fits." 15 Apr-15 Sep. € 24.00 2008*

⊞ **BEZIERS** *10F1* (7km SW Rural) *43.31864, 3.14276* **Camping Les Peupliers, 7 Promenade de l'Ancien Stade, 34440 Colombiers [04 67 37 05 26; fax 04 67 37 67 87; contact@camping-colombiers.com; www.camping-colombiers.com]** SW fr Béziers on D609 (N9) turn R on D162E & foll sp to site using heavy vehicle rte. Cross canal bdge & fork R; turn R & site on L. Easier ent fr D11 (Béziers-Capestang) avoiding narr vill rds, turn L at rndabt at end of dual c'way sp Colombiers; in 1km at rlwy bdge, go strt on; in 100m turn L (bef canal bdge) where rd turns sharp R. Med, mkd pitch, pt shd; wc; chem disp; fam bthrm; shwrs inc; el pnts (10A) €3.10 (inc in high ssn); gas; Indtte; shop, rest 1km; snacks; bar; BBQ; playgrnd; sand beach 15km; wifi; 10% statics; dogs €2.50; adv bkg; quiet, some rlwy noise; red low ssn/long stay; CCI. "Nr Canal du Midi away fr busy beach sites; poss resident workers; excel walking & cycling." ♦ € 21.90 2009*

BEZINGHEM *3A3* (1km S Rural) *50.58431, 1.82607* **FFCC Camping Les Aulnes, Hameau d'Egranges, 62650 Bezinghem [03 21 90 93 88; fax 03 21 86 07 88; campinglesaulnes@orange.fr; www.campinglesaulnes.com]** S fr Desvres or N fr Montreuil on D127. Site at S end of vill on W side of rd, v narr app rds. Med, pt shd; wc (some cont); shwrs inc; el pnts (10A) €3; gas; Indtte; shop; snacks; bar; BBQ; playgrnd; fishing; some statics; rd noise; CCI. "Sm pitches." Easter-15 Oct. € 14.00 2007*

BIARRITZ *8F1* (3.5km E Rural) *43.46416, -1.53222* **Camping Le Parme, 2 Allée Etchécopar, 64600 Anglet [05 59 23 03 00; fax 05 59 41 29 55; campingdeparme@wanadoo.fr; www.campingdeparme.com]** On D810 (N10) fr St Jean-de-Luz to Bayonne. Site sp on R bef Biarritz aerodrome, 500m down tarmac app rd. Lge, pt sl, terr, shd; htd wc (some cont); shwrs inc; el pnts (6-10A) €4-4.50; gas; Indtte; shops 3km; rest; snacks; bar; playgrnd; pool; paddling pool; sand beach 3km; tennis; golf 2km; entmnt; wifi; TV; dogs €3; ccard acc. "Diff exit up steep slope & by blind corner - owner will advise alt R-turn rte; pleasant site." ♦ 4 Apr-7 Nov. € 28.00 2009*

BIARRITZ *8F1* (3km S Coastal) *43.43838, -1.58184* **Village Camping Sunêlia Berrua, Rue Berrua, 64210 Bidart [05 59 54 96 66; fax 05 59 54 78 30; contact@berrua.com; www.berrua.com]** Exit A63 junc 4 dir Bidart, fr Bidart on D810 (N10) sp St Jean de Luz, L at 1st traff lts, site sp. Lge, pt sl, pt shd; wc; chem disp; mv service pnt; shwrs inc; baby facs; el pnts (6A) €5.30; (poss long lead req); gas; Indtte; shop; tradsmn; rest; snacks; bar; BBQ; playgrnd; htd pool & paddling pool; waterslides; beach 1km; tennis; cycle hire; archery; golf 2km; wifi; TV; 50% statics; dogs €3.70; phone; bus 1km; poss cr; Eng spkn; adv bkg; some rd & rlwy noise; ccard acc; red low ssn; CCI. "Busy, well-kept site in attractive location; excel, clean facs; pitches tight lge o'fits; site rds narr, low trees, some high kerbs; muddy after rain; gd rest; sh walk to vill; gd." ♦ 15 Apr-4 Oct. € 33.00 (CChq acc) 2009*

BIARRITZ *8F1* (3km S Coastal) *43.45305, -1.57277* **Yelloh! Village Ilbarritz (formerly Airotel Camping Résidence des Pins), Ave de Biarritz, 64210 Bidart [05 59 23 00 29; fax 05 59 41 24 59; contact@campingdespins.com; www.campingdespins.com www.camping-ilbarritz.com or www.yellohvillage.com]** S fr Bayonne on D810 (N10), by-pass Biarritz. 1km after A63 junc turn R at rndabt immed after Intermarché on R; sp to Pavillon Royal. Site 1km on R sp. Lge, mkd pitch, pt sl, terr, shd; wc; chem disp; shwrs inc; baby facs; el pnts (10A) inc; gas; Indtte; shop; tradsmn; rest & snacks high ssn; bar; playgrnd; htd pool; sand beach 600m; tennis; games area; cycle hire; golf nr; horseriding; internet; TV; many statics & tour ops; dogs €4; phone; poss cr; Eng spkn; adv bkg over 15 days & high ssn; ccard acc; red low ssn; CCI. "Attractive, mature site; lge pitches; narr access rds poss diff long o'fits; excel pool; gd beaches nrby; gd." ♦ 4 Apr-19 Sep. € 39.00 2009*

BIARRITZ *8F1* (5km S Rural) *43.43678, -1.56780* **Camping Le Ruisseau des Pyrénées, Route d'Arbonne, 64210 Bidart [05 59 41 94 50; fax 05 59 41 95 73; francoise.dumont@wanadoo.fr; www.camping-le-ruisseau.fr or www.les-castels.com]** Exit D810 (N10), at Bidart take rd sp Arbonne, site sp. Rds twisty & narr. Lge, some hdg pitch, pt sl, terr, pt shd; wc; chem disp (wc); mv service pnt; shwrs inc; el pnts (6A) inc; gas; Indtte; shop; rest; snacks; bar; playgrnd; 3 pools (1 covrd) & paddling pool; waterslide; lake fishing; boating; sand beach 2.5km; tennis; games area; cycling; 90% statics; dogs €1.50; poss cr; adv bkg ess high ssn; poss noisy; red low ssn; golf nr; CCI. "Steep slope/short run to barrier poss diff; best pitches by lake; site muddy after rain; excel for children & teenagers." 24 Apr-14 Sep. € 37.00 2008*

France

BIARRITZ *8F1* (5km S Coastal) *43.43371, -1.59040* **Camping Ur-Onéa, Rue de la Chapelle, 64210 Bidart [05 59 26 53 61; fax 05 59 26 53 94; contact@uronea.com; www.uronea.com]** Exit A63 junc 4 dir Bidart, fr Bidart on D810 (N10) sp St Jean de Luz, L at 2nd traff lts nr church, then immed R, site is 500m on L. Access fr main rd a bit tricky, 2nd access further S is easier. Lge, mkd pitch, hdstg, terr, pt shd; wc (some cont); chem disp; serviced pitches; baby facs; fam bthrm; shwrs inc; el pnts (5-10A) €3.50-5; gas; Indtte; shop high ssn; tradsmn; rest; snacks; bar, BBQ; playgrnd; pool; sand beach 600m; lake sw 12km; wifi; entmnt; TV; 20% statics; dogs €2.50; phone; Eng spkn; adv bkg; quiet, some rail noise; ccard acc; red low ssn; CCI. "Conv Pays Basque vills; 600m fr Bidart; staff friendly & helpful; excel, clean san facs." ♦ 3 Apr-18 Sep. € 26.50 2009*

BIARRITZ *8F1* (2km SW Coastal) *43.4625, -1.5672* **Camping Biarritz, 28 Rue Harcet, 64200 Biarritz [05 59 23 00 12; fax 05 59 43 74 67; biarritz.camping@wanadoo.fr; www.biarritz-camping.fr]** S fr Bayonne on D810 (N10), by-pass Biarritz & cont to junc of D810 coast rd sp Bidart & Biarritz; double back on this rd, take 1st exit at next rndabt, 1st L dir Biarritz Cent, foll sp to site in 2km. Lge, mkd pitch, pt sl, terr, pt shd; wc; chem disp; mv service pnt; shwrs inc; el pnts (10A) €4; gas; Indtte; shop; tradsmn; rest; snacks; bar; playgrnd; htd pool; padddling pool; sand beach 1km; tennis 4km; entmnt; 10% statics; no dogs; bus at gate; poss cr; adv bkg; ccard acc; noisy in high ssn; red low ssn/CCI. "One of better sites in area, espec low ssn." ♦ 6 May-16 Sep. € 21.50 2007*

BIARRITZ *8F1* (3.5km SW Coastal) *43.45525, -1.58119* **Camping Pavillon Royal, Ave du Prince-de-Galles, 64210 Bidart [05 59 23 00 54; fax 05 59 23 44 47; info@pavillon-royal.com; www.pavillon-royal.com]** Exit A63/E4 junc 4; then take N10 S dir Bidart. At rndabt after "Intermarche" supmkt turn R (SP Biarritz). After 600m turn left at campsite sign. Lge, hdg/mkd pitch, pt sl, pt shd, wc (some cont); chem disp; serviced pitch; baby facs; shwrs inc; el pnts (5A) inc (long lead poss req); gas; Indtte; shop; tradsmn; rest; snacks; bar; BBQ; playgrnd; pool & paddling pool; sand beach adj; tennis nr; fitness rm; games rm; cycle hire; golf 500m; horseriding 2km; wifi; no dogs; poss cr; Eng spkn; adv bkg (ess Jul/Aug); ccard acc; red low ssn. "Lovely, well-run, busy site; friendly; various pitch sizes, some with sea views, some sm & diff lge o'fits; direct access via steps to excel beach; excel surfing area; excel for families, but not young families - powerful breakers; gd pool & paddling pool; san facs poss irreg cleaning low ssn; conv Spanish border & Pyrenees; mkt Sat; excel." ♦ 15 May-30 Sep. € 49.00 ABS - A06 2009*

BIARRITZ *8F1* (4km SW Coastal) *43.44431, -1.58166* **Camping Erreka, Ave de Cumba, 64210 Bidart [05 59 54 93 64; fax 05 59 47 70 46; campingerreka@laposte.net; www.camping-erreka.com]** Site at junc of D810 (N10) Biarritz by-pass & main rd into town cent; well sp. Lge, terr, pt sl, pt shd; wc (some cont); chem disp; mv service pnt; baby facs; shwrs; el pnts (6A) €4; gas; Indtte; shop; snacks; playgrnd; pool; paddling pool; sand beach 800m; wifi; entmnt; TV; 75% statics; no dogs; red low ssn; adv bkg; ccard acc; quiet; CCI. "Some pitches sl & poss v diff to get into, rec adv bkg to ensure suitable pitch; access rds v steep." 16 Jun-16 Sep. € 22.00 2007*

BIARRITZ *8F1* (5km SW Coastal) *43.43584, -1.58295* **Camping Oyam, Chemin Oyamburua, 64210 Bidart [05 59 54 91 61; fax 05 59 54 76 87; accueil@camping-oyam.com; www.camping-oyam.com]** Leave A63 at junc 4 onto D810 (N10); 150m after Bidart boundary sp turn L at traff lts sp Arbonne. In 600m at brow of hill turn R & then immed L. Med, mkd pitch, pt sl, terr, pt shd; wc; chem disp; baby facs; shwrs inc; el pnts (3A) €4.50; Indtte; shop; rest; snacks; bar; BBQ; playgrnd; pool; paddling pool; sand beach 1.2km; games area; entmnt; TV; 90% statics; dogs €2.50; free bus to vill; Eng spkn; adv bkg; some rd & rlwy noise; CCI. "Well-managed site in lovely surroundings; clean, modern san facs; pitches sm & awkward." ♦ 1 Jun-30 Sep. € 26.00 2008*

BIDART see Biarritz *8F1*

BIERT see Massat *8G3*

BIESHEIM see Neuf Brisach *6F3*

BIGANOS see Audenge *7D1*

BIGNAC see Angoulême *7B2*

BILIEU see Abrets, Les *9B3*

BILLOM *9B1* (NE Urban) *45.72860, 3.34573* **Camp Municipal Le Colombier, Allée des Tennis, 63160 Billom [04 73 68 91 50; fax 04 73 73 37 60; billom@billom.com; www.billom.com]** Exit A72 junc 2 onto D906 sp Pont-de-Dore; turn R onto N89; in 1km turn L onto D212/D229 to Billom; at rndabt junc with D997 cont on D229 & take 1st L into Route de Lezoux, then L into Rue des Tennis. Site sp. Sm, hdg/mkd pitch, pt sl, shd; wc (cont); chem disp (wc); shwrs inc; el pnts (10A) €2.70; gas 500m; Indry rm; shop; rest 500m; snacks 200m; bar; BBQ; pool & tennis adj; games rm; entmnt; TV; 30% statics; dogs; phone 200m; no twin axles; adv bkg; quiet; CCI. "Clean, spacious facs; disabled the only non-cont wc (unisex); helpful warden; historic town & interesting area; unreliable opening dates." ♦ 1 Jun-15 Sep. € 7.00 2007*

BINIC *2E3* (500m NE Urban/Coastal) *48.60641, -2.82137* **Camp Municipal des Fauvettes, Rue des Fauvettes, 22520 Binic [02 96 73 60 83 or 02 96 73 61 15 (Mairie); fax 02 96 73 72 38; ville.binic@wanadoo.fr; www.ville-binic.fr]** Fr D786 foll sp to Binic & site. Narr ent. Med, mkd pitch, terr, pt sl, pt shd; wc; chem disp (wc); mv service pnt; shwrs; el pnts (6A) €4; Indtte; shop; snacks; BBQ; playgrnd; pool; waterslide nr; sand beach adj; some statics; dogs €2; poss cr; Eng spkn; quiet; CCI. "Clifftop site with gd sea viewsl; vg." ♦ 1 Apr-30 Sep. € 18.30 (3 persons) 2007*

BINIC *2E3* (1km S Coastal) *48.59216, -2.8238* **Camping Le Panoramic, Rue Gasselin, 22520 Binic [02 96 73 60 43; fax 02 96 69 27 66; camping.le.panoramic@wanadoo.fr; www.lepanoramic.net]** D786 St Brieuc-Paimpol. 1st slip rd for Binic & 1st R up hill 100m, site sp. Med, mkd pitch, pt sl, terr, pt shd; htd wc; chem disp; shwrs; el pnts (10A) €5 (poss rev pol); gas; Indtte; shop; snacks; bar; BBQ; htd pool; paddling pool; sand beach 500m; golf adj; entmnt; many statics; dogs €2.50; quiet; red low ssn. "Pleasant site; clean facs; coastal path nr." 1 Apr-30 Sep. € 18.70 2008*

BINIC *2E3* (2.5km S Coastal) *48.58269, -2.80477* **Camping Les Madières, Rue du Vau Madec, 22590 Pordic [02 96 79 02 48; fax 02 96 79 46 67; campinglesmadieres@wanadoo.fr; www.campinglesmadieres.com]** Site at E end of Pordic vill, sp. Med, pt sl, shd; htd wc (mainly cont); shwrs inc; el pnts (10A) €3.50; gas; Indtte; sm shop; rest; snacks; bar; htd pool; shgl beach 800m; sand beach & watersports 3km; entmnt; 10% statics; dogs €2; adv bkg; quiet; red CCI. "Pleasant, clean, child-friendly site; immac facs; friendly, helpful owners; poss diff access to shgl beach & not suitable children, Binic beach OK; highly rec." ♦ 29 Mar-2 Nov. € 17.10 2007*

BINIC *2E3* (4km S Coastal) *48.57875, -2.78498* **Camping Le Roc de l'Hervieu, 19 Rue d'Estienne d'Orves, 22590 Pordic [02 96 79 30 12; le.roc.de.lhervieu@wanadoo.fr; www.campinglerocdelhervieu.fr]** Site on E side of vill off N786, Binic-St Brieuc rd. Turn E in cent of vill, sp to Les Madières then sp Le Roc de l'Hervieu. Med, hdg pitch, pt shd; wc (some cont); chem disp; mv service pnt; shwrs inc; el pnts (10A) €3.30; Indtte; shop; playgrnd; sand beach 2km; fishing; some statics; quiet. "Gd walking; pleasant site." ♦ 20 May-30 Sep. € 14.85 2006*

BINIC *2E3* (8km SW Rural) **Camping à la Ferme (Hello), La Corderie, 22170 Plélo [02 96 74 21 21; fax 02 96 74 31 64; hello.odile@22.wanadoo.fr]** Fr Binic take D4 dir Châtelaudren, site on R at La Corderie. Sm, pt shd; wc; chem disp; shwrs inc; el pnts (10A) €2; Indtte; playgrnd; sand beach 8km; 20% statics; quiet. "CL-type site." 25 Jun-10 Sep. € 8.50 2007*

BINIC *2E3* (1.2km W Rural) *48.60539, -2.84124* **Camping des Palmiers, Ker Viarc'h, 22520 Binic [tel/fax 02 96 73 72 59 or 06 67 32 78 66 (mob); campingpalmiers.chantal@laposte.net; www.campingpalmiers.com]** N fr St Brieuc on D786 dir Pordic/Paimpol on coast rd. Foll sp to site on o'skts on Binic. Sm, mkd pitch, hdstg, terr, pt shd; htd wc; chem disp; mv service pnt; baby facs; shwrs inc; el pnts (10A) €6; Indtte; gas; shop; supmkt 1km; tradsmn; rest 1.5km; snacks; bar; BBQ; playgrnd; htd, covrd pool; paddling pool; sand beach 1.5km; tennis 1km; games rm; wifi; entmnt; TV; 6% statics; dogs €2; Eng spkn; adv bkg; quiet; red low ssn/CCI. "Warm welcome; excel site in gd situation." ♦ 1 Jun-30 Sep. € 21.00 2009*

France

BINIC *2E3* (6km W Rural) *48.60640, -2.86160* **FFCC Camping Les Etangs, Pont de la Motte, Route de Châtelaudren, 22410 Lantic [02 96 71 95 47; contact@campinglesetangs.com; www.campinglesetangs.com]** D786 fr Binic twd Paimpol; turn L approx 1km on D4 sp Châtelaudren & Lantic; in 3km at x-rds turn L foll camping sp; site in 50m on R. Fr N12 Guingamp-St Brieuc take D4 at Châtelaudren. Med, mkd pitch, pt sl, pt shd; wc (cont); chem disp; mv service pnt; shwrs inc; el pnts (6A) €2.60; gas; Indtte; sm shop; tradsmn; snacks; playgrnd; pool; beach 3km; TV; 2% statics; dogs €1.20; phone; poss v cr; Eng spkn; adv bkg; quiet; ccard acc; CCI. "Gd base slightly away fr cr coast sites; helpful, friendly owners; gd pool; boat excursions fr St Brieuc; excel." ♦ 1 Apr-30 Sep. € 17.00 2006*

BIRON *7D3* (4km S Rural) *44.60035, 0.87111* **Camping Le Moulinal, 24540 Biron [05 53 40 84 60; fax 05 53 40 81 49; lemoulinal@perigord.com; www.lemoulinal.com or www.camping-franceloc.fr]** Fr Bergerac S dir Agen, then E Issigeac & Villeréal; fr Villeréal dir Lacapelle-Biron, site sp. Fr Monpazier take D104 twd Villeréal; in 4km S on D53 thro Biron & onto Lacapelle-Biron. Head W twd Villeréal for 2km to site. Lge, mkd pitches, terr, pt shd; htd wc (some cont); baby facs; shwrs; el pnts (6A) inc; gas; Indtte; shop; rest; snacks; bar; BBQ; playgrnd; htd pool; sand beach for lake sw; boating; tennis; games area; games rm; internet; entmnt; dogs €5; poss cr; Eng spkn; adv bkg; quiet; ccard acc; red low ssn; CCI. "Lovely site; extra for lakeside & 'super' pitches." ♦ 7 Apr-23 Sep. € 35.00 2008*

BIRON *7D3* (4km SW Rural) *44.61394, 0.83535* **Camping Laborde (Naturist), 47150 Paulhiac [05 53 63 14 88; fax 05 53 61 60 23; domainelaborde@wanadoo.fr; www.domainelaborde.com]** Leave Montpazier on D2 sp Monflanquin/Villeréal; in 5.6km at Source de la Brame turn L onto D2E sp Monflanquin. Turn R onto D255 at sp Laborde FFN dir Lacapelle-Born. Med, pt sl, pt shd; wc; chem disp; sauna; shwrs inc; el pnts (3-10A) €3.50-4.50 (poss long lead req); gas; Indtte; tradsmn; ltd shop; supmkt 14km; rest; snacks; bar; playgrnd; 2 tropical indoor pools & outdoor pool; lake sw adj; tennis; games rm; dogs €3; Eng spkn; adv bkg; quiet; ccard acc; red low ssn; INF card not req. ♦ 31 Mar-1 Oct. € 23.00 2008*

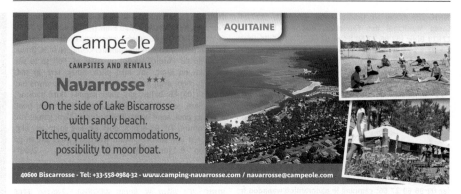

BIRON *7D3* (W Rural) *44.6305, 0.8733* **Aire Communale, Route de Vergt de Biron, 24540 Biron [05 53 63 15 23; fax 05 53 24 28 12]** Fr Villeréal or Monpazier on D104/D2 turn onto D53 to Biron, foll sp for Information. M'vans only. Sm, unshd; own san; chem disp; mv service pnt; water €2; el pnts €2; shop 8km; rest, snacks & bar 100m; dogs; poss cr; quiet. "Extensive views fr site; gd NH." 1 Apr-31 Oct. € 2.00 2009*

BISCARROSSE See also sites listed under Gastes, Sanguinet and Parentis en Born.

BISCARROSSE *7D1* (3km N Coastal) *44.42955, -1.16792* **CAMPEOLE Camping Navarrosse, 712 Chemin de Navarosse, 40600 Biscarrosse [05 58 09 84 32; fax 05 58 09 86 22; navarrosse@campeole.com; www.camping-navarrosse.com or www.campeole.com]** Fr Biscarrosse N on D652 dir Sanguinet; 1km beyond turning to L to Biscarosse Plage, turn L onto D305 & foll sp to Navarosse. V lge, mkd pitch, pt shd; htd wc; baby facs; mv service pnt; baby facs; shwrs inc; el pnts (10A) inc; lndtte (inc dryer); tradsmn; supmkt adj; rest 200m; snacks; bar; BBQ: playgrnd; sand beach & lake sw adj; fishing; sailing; tennis; cycle hire; games area; games rm; wifi; entmnt; TV; 40% statics; dogs; late arrivals area; Eng spkn; quiet; ccard acc; red low ssn/CCI. "Pleasant site; vg for children; helpful staff; gd walking; sailing lessons; cycle rtes." ♦ 30 Apr-12 Sep. € 30.60 2009*

See advertisement

BISCARROSSE *7D1* (5km N Rural) *44.43996, -1.14068* **Aire Naturelle Le Frézat (Dubourg), 2583 Chemin de Mayotte, 40600 Biscarrosse [06 22 65 57 37]** Fr Biscarrosse on D652 dir Sanguinet; after 5km turn L at water tower onto D333; site 2nd on R in 1km. Med, shd; wc (some cont); chem disp (wc); shwrs €1.20; el pnts (6A) inc; shops 4km; tradsmn; BBQ; playgrnd; lake & sand beach 3km; dogs; Eng spkn; adv bkg; quiet; CCI. "Lovely site; friendly owners; clean facs; cycle paths." 15 Apr-15 Oct. € 14.00 2009*

BISCARROSSE *7D1* (5km N Rural) *44.43535, -1.15496* **FFCC Camping Village Mayotte Vacances, Chemin des Roseaux, 40600 Biscarrosse [05 58 78 00 00; fax 05 58 78 83 91; camping@mayottevacances.com; www.mayottevacances.com]** Twd NE fr Biscarosse on D652 L sp Navarosse & at 1st fork R to Mayotte, foll camping sp. V lge, mkd pitch, hdstg, pt shd; wc; chem disp; mv service pnt; shwrs inc; el pnts (10A) inc (poss rev pol); snacks; gas; lndtte; shop; rest; snacks; bar; BBQ; playgrnd; pool; waterslide; jacuzzi; lake sw adj; sailing school; sand beach 9km; tennis; cycle hire; games rm; entmnt; TV; 25% statics; dogs €5; Eng spkn; adv bkg (ess Jul/Aug); quiet; ccard acc; red low ssn/CCI. "Excel leisure facs; vg for families; rec." ♦ 4 Apr-19 Sep. € 43.00 2009*

BISCARROSSE *7D1* (3km NE Rural) *44.43374, -1.13064* **Aire Naturelle Camping Les Bruyères, 3725 Route de Bordeaux, 40600 Biscarrosse [05 58 78 79 23]** N fr Biscarrosse on D652 twd Arcachon; site on L visible fr rd, just bef sm concrete water tower. Sm, shd; wc; chem disp (wc); shwrs €1.10; baby facs; el pnts (3-10A) inc (poss rev pol); shop adj; BBQ; cooking facs; sand beach 10km; lake sw & watersports 3km; adv bkg; quiet. "Helpful owners; CL-type site; beach 10km excel for surfing; rec Latécoère seaplane museum." 1 Apr-30 Sep. 2008*

BISCARROSSE *7D1* (8km NE Rural) *44.46230, -1.12900* **Camping du Domaine de la Rive, Route de Bordeaux, 40600 Biscarrosse [05 58 78 12 33; fax 05 58 78 12 92; info@larive.fr; www.larive.fr]** Fr Bordeaux on A63 dir Bayonne/San Sebastian; at junc 22 turn off onto A660; cont until 1st junc where turn L onto D216; cont for 17km to Sanguinet; cont on A652 for 3km; site sp on R nr Lake Cazaux. V lge, hdg/mkd pitch, pt shd; htd wc; chem disp; baby facs; shwrs inc; el pnts (6A) inc; gas; lndtte; shop; rest; snacks; bar; BBQ (gas only); playgrnd; 2 pools (1 htd, covrd); waterslide; jacuzzi; lake sw & private, sand beach adj; ocean beach 18km; watersports; tennis; cycle, canoe, surf hire; archery; games area; organised activities; games rm; horseriding; entmnt; wifi; games/TV rm; 30% statics; dogs €6; poss cr; phone; Eng spkn; adv bkg; some noise fr entmnt; ccard acc; red low ssn; CCI. "Delightful area; well-run site; clean facs; some pitches diff lge o'fits due trees; gd beaches; gd cycling." ♦ 3 Apr-5 Sep. € 44.00 (CChq acc) ABS - A38 2009*

BISCARROSSE *7D1* (1.5km S Rural) *44.38869, -1.18170* **Camping Latécoère, 265 Rue Louis Bréguet, 40600 Biscarrosse [05 58 78 13 01; fax 05 58 78 16 26; latecoere.biscarrosse@wanadoo.fr; www.camping-latecoere.com]** S on D652 Sanguinet-Biscarrosse rd to cent of town. Strt in front of church by mkt sq; site in 1.5km adj lake. Lge, mkd pitch, pt shd; wc; shwrs inc; el pnts (10A) inc; Indtte; shop; snacks; bar; BBQ; playgrnd adj; pool; lake sw & sand beach adj; watersports; 40% statics; quiet. "Yacht club adj; museums opp; seaplanes." 1 May-30 Sep. € 25.00 2008*

BISCARROSSE *7D1* (8km NW Coastal) *44.45804, -1.23968* **CAMPEOLE Camping Le Vivier, 681 Rue du Tit, 40600 Biscarrosse-Plage [05 58 78 25 76; fax 05 58 78 35 23; vivier@campeole.com; www.camping-biscarrosse.info or www.campeole.com]** Fr Arcachon & Pyla-sur-Mer, take D218, D83 to Biscarrosse Plage. Town o'skts site sp to R. Foll sps. Lge, pt shd; wc; chem disp; shwrs; el pnts €3.90; shop; snacks; playgrnd; htd pool; paddling pool; sand beach 800m; tennis; boating; fishing; horseriding nr; cycle hire; entmnt; dogs €3.50; quiet; red low ssn. "Access to beach via path thro dunes." 12 May-12 Sep. € 23.10 2006*

BISCARROSSE *7D1* (9km NW Coastal) *44.44133, -1.24558* **CAMPEOLE Camping Plage Sud, 230 Rue des Bécasses, 40600 Biscarrosse-Plage [05 58 78 21 24; fax 05 58 78 34 23; plage-sud@campeole.com; www.landes-camping.net or www.campeole.com]** Clearly sp on D146 on ent to Biscarrosse-Plage in pine forest. V lge, mkd pitch, pt sl, pt shd; wc; chem disp; baby facs; shwrs inc; el pnts (6A) €3.90; Indtte; shop adj; tradsmn; snacks; bar; BBQ; playgrnd; htd pool; paddling pool; sand beach 800m; cycle hire; entmnt; 20% statics; dogs €3.50; Eng spkn; adv bkg; noise fr disco high ssn; red low ssn; CCI. "Sm, modern town; lots of rests; gd beach inc surfing." 12 May-12 Sep. € 23.10 2006*

BIZANET see Narbonne *10F1*

BIZE MINERVOIS *8F4* (300m SW Urban) *43.31584, 2.87070* **Camping La Cesse, 11120 Bize-Minervois [tel/fax 04 68 46 14 40]** Exit N fr D5/D11 Béziers-Carcassonne rd onto D26 to Bize-Minervois (D26 is 800m to E of D607); site in 1.8km on L, just bef rv bdge in S of vill. Sm, mkd pitch, pt shd; wc; chem disp (wc); shwrs inc; el pnts (5A) €2.30; Indtte; shops, rest & snacks nrby; BBQ; rv 400m; dogs €1.20; phone; poss cr; adv bkg; quiet; red low ssn; CCI. "Peaceful site; in need of TLC but relaxing; vg." 1 May-30 Sep. € 10.90 2009*

BLACERET see Villefranche sur Saône *9B2*

BLAIN *2G4* (1km S Rural) *47.46782, -1.76787* **Camp Municipal Le Château, Route de St Nazaire, 44130 Blain [02 40 79 11 00 or 02 40 79 00 08 (Mairie); fax 02 40 78 83 72; otsi.blain@free.fr; www.ville-blain.fr]** Fr N on N137 turn W onto N171; fr S on N137 turn W onto D164 to Blain. On app town, take L at rndabt on N171 dir St Nazaire/Bouvron. Immed after x-ing Brest-Nantes canal bdge, site on L adj to chateau. Sm, mkd pitch, pt shd; wc; shwrs inc; chem disp; mv service pnt; el pnts (10A) €2.30; Indry rm; shops 500m; tradsmn; rest, bar 500m; playgrnd; pool 1km; fishing; boating; dogs €0.80; phone adj; adv bkg; quiet but some rd noise; CCI. "Super, well-managed site; gd pitch size; helpful staff; immac san facs; chateau museum adj; no twin-axles; no access for vehicles after 2000 high ssn." ♦ 1 May-30 Sep. € 7.10 2009*

BLAMONT *6E3* (1km E Rural) *48.58890, 6.85051* **Camp Municipal de la Vezouze, Route de Cirey, 54450 Blâmont [03 83 76 28 28 (Mairie) or 06 07 70 27 39 (mob); fax 03 83 76 28 32]** Fr Sarrebourg on N4 dir Blâmont; foll sps Town Cent, then turn L onto D74/ D993 dir Cirey-sous-Vezouze & foll sp for site. Sm, pt shd; wc; shwrs inc; el pnts (16A) €2; shop, rest, snacks, bar 300m; playgrnd; sports area; sw, fishing adj; dogs €0.80; quiet. "Gd rvside site; gd walking, cycling; phone ahead bef arr." 15 May-15 Sep. € 6.50 2008*

BLANC, LE *4H2* (2km E Rural) *46.63202, 1.09389* **Camping L'Ile d'Avant, Route de Châteauroux, 36300 Le Blanc [02 54 37 88 22; fax 02 54 36 35 42; a.tou.vert@wanadoo.fr; www.atouvert.com]** Fr town cent take D951 (N151) twd St Gaultier/Argenton; site on R 1km after supmkt. Med, hdg/mkd pitch, pt shd; wc; mv service pnt; shwrs inc; el pnts (6A) inc; Indtte; shops 1km; rest, snacks, bar 2km; BBQ; playgrnd; htd pool adj inc; fishing; tennis adj; adv bkg; quiet but some rd noise. "Gd pitches; adj sports field & club house." 1 May-30 Sep. € 14.00 2009*

BLANDY *4E3* (1.5km E) *48.56622, 2.78219* **FFCC Camping Le Pré de l'Etang, 34 Rue St Martin, 77115 Blandy-les-Tours [tel/fax 01 60 66 96 34; campingdupredeletang@orange.fr; http://camping.blandy.77.monsite.orange.fr]** Fr Paris on A5 take exit 16 onto D47 dir Blandy, or fr D215 take D68. In Blandy foll dir St Méry, site on R in 200m. Site is 2.5km fr a'route. NB Site has narr ent & vill rds tricky with parked cars. Med, hdg/mkd pitch, pt sl, pt shd; htd wc (some cont); chem disp; shwrs inc; el pnts (5A) €2; bar, shop, rest 500m; BBQ; playgrnd 500m; 60% statics; dogs €1.30; phone; adv bkg; quiet; CCI. "V picturesque; pond on site; lge pitches but poss unkempt; conv Fontainebleau & Disneyland; conv Château de Vaux-le-Vicomte 5km; trains for Paris 10km." ♦ 15 Mar-30 Oct. € 17.00 2008*

France

BLANGY LE CHATEAU *3D1* (500m N Rural) *49.24670, 0.27370* **Camping Le Domaine du Lac, 14130 Blangy-le-Château [02 31 64 62 00; fax 02 31 64 15 91]** Fr Pont-l'Evêque & A13 S on D579 twd Lisieux. In 5km turn L onto D51 to Blangy where at fountain (rndabt) turn L, taking care. In 200m at end of vill turn L onto D140 Rte de Mesnil & site 200m on R. Site is 5km SE of Pont-l'Evêque. Med, mkd pitch, pt sl, pt shd; wc; chem disp; baby facs; shwrs inc; el pnts (6A) inc (long lead poss req); gas; Indtte; shop & 1km; rest; snacks; bar; BBQ; beach 22km; lake fishing; tennis; games rm; wifi; 70% statics; dogs; adv bkg; some rd noise; ccard acc; CCI. "Peaceful NH in lovely area; friendly British owner; poss uneven pitches; tired, old facs in dire need of refurb; access to pitches diff when wet; pretty vill; gd walks; conv Honfleur; 1hr to Le Havre ferry; NH only." 1 Apr-31 Oct. € 20.00 2008*

BLANGY LE CHATEAU *3D1* (3km SE Rural) *49.22525, 0.30438* **Camping Le Brévedent, 14130 Le Brévedent [02 31 64 72 88 or 02 31 64 21 50 (LS); fax 02 31 64 33 41; contact@campinglebrevedent.com; www.camping lebrevedent.com or www.les-castels.com]** Fr Pont l'Evêque & A13 go S on D579 twd Lisieux; after 5km turn L onto D51 twd Blangy-le-Château. In Blangy bear R at rndabt to stay on D51 & foll sp to Le Brévedent & Moyaux; site on L in 3km. Med, mkd pitch, pt sl, pt shd; htd wc; chem disp; mv service pnt; baby facs; shwrs inc; el pnts (5-10A) inc (poss long leads req); gas; Indtte; shop & 3km; tradsmn; rest; snacks; bar; BBQ (gas/elec); playgrnd; 2 htd pools; paddling pool; sand beach 22km; lake fishing; tennis 100m; sports area; cycle hire; horseriding 2km; golf 11km; entmnt; excursions; wifi; games rm; internet; many statics & tour ops; no dogs; phone; sep car park after 2230; poss cr; Eng spkn; adv bkg; quiet; ccard acc; red low ssn; CCI. "Pleasant site around lake; welcoming, helpful staff; some modern san facs, ltd low ssn; sm pitches; no c'vans over 8m acc; rallies welcome; excel." ♦ 1 May-18 Sep. € 29.10 ABS - N01 2009*

BLANGY SUR BRESLE *3C2* (2.5km E Rural) *49.92378, 1.65693* **Camp Municipal Les Etangs, 76340 Blangy-sur-Bresle [02 35 94 55 65; fax 02 35 94 06 14]** Leave A28 at junc 5, R at T-junc onto D49, site on L in approx 1km. Med, mkd pitch, unshd; wc (some cont); chem disp; shwrs inc (clsd 1130-1400 & 2100-0700); el pnts (5-10A) €1.55-2.60 (poss rev pol); Indry rm; supmkt nr; rest, snacks, bar 2km; BBQ; playgrnd; tennis & mini-golf nrby; ccard not acc; CCI. "Attractive site adj lakes; san facs need update (2009); adv bkg rec lge o'fits high ssn; no twin-axles; rec wait for warden for pitching; poss waterlogged in wet (& entry refused); conv Calais, A28 & D928; excel NH but not rec due security probs (2008) & intimidating behaviour fr visitors to site." ♦ 1 Apr-30 Sep. € 8.95 2009*

BLANGY SUR BRESLE *3C2* (8km W Rural) *49.95430, 1.55098* **Camp Municipal La Forêt, 76340 Bazinval [tel/fax 02 32 97 04 01; bazinval2@wanadoo.fr]** NW fr Blangy on D49 for 6km, then D149 to Bazinval. Site sp. Sm, hdg pitch, pt sl, pt shd; wc; chem disp (wc); shwrs inc; el pnts (10A) €4 (poss rev pol); Eng spkn; quiet; CCI. "Gd san facs, poss inadequate; site yourself, warden calls early eve; poss itinerants on site; NH only." 1 Apr-30 Oct. € 8.00 2007*

BLAUVAC see Carpentras *10E2*

BLAVOZY see Puy en Velay, Le *9C1*

BLAYE *7C2* (5km NE Rural) *45.16708, -0.61666* **Aire Naturelle Les Tilleuls (Paille), Domaine Les Alberts, 33390 Mazion [05 57 42 18 13; fax 05 57 42 13 01; chateau-alberts@hotmail.com]** Fr Blaye on D937 N, sp to site on L. Sm, pt sl, pt shd; own san; el pnts (3-10A) €2.50; BBQ; dogs; rd noise; CCI. "Pleasant, family-run site in vineyards; wine-tasting; cycle track to Blaye." 15 Apr-15 Oct. € 10.50 2008*

BLAYE *7C2* (W Urban) *45.12936, -0.66621* **Camp Municipal La Citadelle, 33390 Blaye [05 57 42 00 20 or 05 57 42 16 79 (LS)]** Fr N ent town, over x-rds, sp in town; ent thro narr gateways in fortifications; access by narr track, single in places. Fr S on D669 cont thro town passing citadel on L; turn L at mini rndabt, go over bdge & take 1st L; sp strt on thro arches. NB Site access unsuitable m'vans higher than 2.7m due to narr, curved arches. Sm, terr, pt shd; wc (some cont); serviced pitches; shwrs inc; el pnts (10-15A) €2.60; shops 500m; tradsmn high ssn; pool 250m; phone adj; poss cr; quiet; no ccard acc. "Lovely site within ancient monument, partly o'lookng rv; spacious pitches; pitch yourself, warden visits pm; clean but basic san facs; vineyards nr." 1 May-30 Sep. € 9.90 2009*

BLENEAU *4G3* (600m N Rural) *47.70473, 2.94891* **Camp Municipal La Pépinière, Rue du Lieutenant Travers, 89220 Bléneau [03 86 74 93 73 or 03 86 74 91 61 (Mairie); fax 03 86 74 86 74; mairiedebleneau@wanadoo.fr; www.bleneau.fr]** At junc of D47/D22 & D90 in Bléneau take D64 twd Champcevrais & site. Sp in Bléneau. Sm, hdg pitch, shd; wc (cont); chem disp; shwrs inc; el pnts (10A) €2; shops, rest, snacks, bar 600m; pool adj; games rm; fishing adj; poss cr; adv bkg; quiet; CCI. "Set in orchard; gd." 1 Apr-30 Sep. € 5.30 2006*

⊞ **BLENEAU** *4G3* (12km NE Rural) *47.75759, 3.09998* **Camping Le Bois Guillaume, 89350 Villeneuve-les-Genêts [03 86 45 45 41; fax 03 86 45 49 20; camping@bois-guillaume.com; www.bois-guillaume.com]** Fr W on D965 dir St Fargeau. At Mézilles take D7 thro Tannerre-en-Puisaye; stay on D7 & after 3.5km foll sp for site. Or fr A6 exit junc 18 onto D16 thro Charny, then turn L onto D119 to Champignelles; take D7 dir Tannere for approx 2km; turn R & foll sp to site. Med, hdg/mkd pitch, some hdstg, shd; htd wc; chem disp; mv service pnt; shwrs inc; el pnts (5-10A) €2.80-3.50; gas; rest; bar; playgrnd; htd pools; sports area; cycle hire; tennis; dogs €1.30; poss cr; Eng spkn; CCI. "Friendly staff; clean, tidy site; facs ltd low ssn; vg rest." € 12.70 2007*

BLERE *4G2* (500m NE Urban) *47.32791, 0.99685* **Camp Municipal La Gâtine, Rue de Cdt Lemaître, 37150 Bléré [tel/fax 02 47 57 92 60; marie@blere-touraine.com; www.blere-touraine.com]** Exit A10 S of Tours onto A85 E. Exit A85 junc 11 dir Bléré. Site in 5km adj sports cent on S side of Rv Cher. Lge, mkd pitch, pt shd; wc; chem disp; mv service pnt; shwrs inc; el pnts (6-16A) €3.50-5.90 (poss rev pol & long lead poss req); lndtte (inc dryer); shops 300m; supmkt 400m; htd pool adj; rv fishing adj; dogs €2; no adv bkg; quiet; ccard acc; CCI. "Gd site; sm pitches; helpful warden; clean san facs, some dated (2009); cycle rte to Chenonceau; gd security; gd cent for wine rtes & chateaux; unreliable opening dates low ssn; rec." ♦ 10 Apr-15 Oct. € 9.80 2009*

BLESLE see Massiac *9C1*

BLET *4H3* (400m S Rural) *46.89294, 2.73079* **Camp Municipal Le Gouffre, 18350 Blet [tel/fax 02 48 74 78 24 or 02 48 74 71 04 (Mairie)]** SE fr Bourges on D2076 (N76). In 35km turn R onto D6 in cent of Blet sp Chalivoy-Milon. Site 400m on R just past sm lake. NB no sp at ent. Med, pt shd; wc; shwrs; el pnts (5A) €2.90; shop 500m; dogs €1; quiet. "Gd NH; facs basic but adequate." ♦ 1 Apr-1 Nov. € 6.30 2006*

BLIGNY SUR OUCHE *6H1* (500m NW Rural) *47.10858, 4.66000* **Camping des Isles, 2 Allée de la Gare, 21360 Bligny-sur-Ouche [03 80 20 00 64 or 06 62 97 19 28 (mob)]** On D17/D970 fr Arnay-le-Duc, site on L on ent vill. Med, pt shd; wc (mainly cont); shwrs inc; el pnts (15A) €2.35; shop 500m; café/rest 300m; playgrnd; quiet; red long stay. "Peaceful, clean & tidy; helpful owner; in reach of Côte d'Or wine areas; steam rlwy 100m; noise fr cornmill at harvest time; poss flooding in adverse weather; gd." 1 May-30 Sep. € 11.75 2009*

BLOIS *4G2* (12km NE Rural) *47.68666, 1.48583* **Camping Le Château de la Grenouillère, 41500 Suèvres [02 54 87 80 37; fax 02 54 87 84 21; la.grenouillere@wanadoo.fr; www.camping-loire.com or www.les-castels.com]** Exit A10 junc 16 sp Chambord, Mer; take rd to Mer; go thro Mer on D2152 (N152) dir Blois; site in 5km, 2km NE of Suèvres. Lge, mkd pitch, pt shd; wc; chem disp; mv service pnt; sauna; baby facs; shwrs inc; el pnts (10A) inc; gas; lndtte; shop; pizzeria; snacks; bar; BBQ (gas/charcoal); playgrnd; 2 pools (1 covrd); paddling pool; waterslide; boating; fishing; tennis; cycle hire; entmnt; wifi; games/TV; statics (tour ops); dogs €4; Eng spkn; adv bkg (min 3 nts); some pitches some rd & rlwy noise; ccard acc; red low ssn; CCI. "Ideal for Loire area; gates clsd 2230-0700; modern san facs, poss ltd low ssn; mkt Wed & Sat Blois." ♦ 17 Apr-11 Sep. € 39.00 ABS - L04 2009*

BLOIS *4G2* (10km E Rural) *47.59149, 1.45894* **FFCC Aire Naturelle (Delaboissière), 6 Rue de Châtillon, 41350 Huisseau-sur-Cosson [02 54 20 35 26]** Fr Blois cross Rv Loire on D765 dir Vineuil. 1km S turn L onto D33. Site at E end of vill of Huisseau on R. Sm, hdg/mkd pitch, pt sl, pt shd; wc; chem disp; mv service pnt; shwrs inc; el pnts (6A) €3.50 (poss rev pol); gas; shops 400m, supmkt 4km; dogs €1; site clsd 16-22 Jul 08; poss cr; adv bkg; quiet; ccard not acc; CCI. "Sm, peaceful garden site; gd basic san facs; some pitches no hdg & no el pnts; friendly owner; local wine & fruit for sale; conv Loire Valley chateaux; cycle rte thro forest to Chambord Château, vg Son et Lumière show in town." ♦ 1 May-20 Sep. € 12.00 2009*

BLOIS *4G2* (8km S Rural) *47.52539, 1.38675* **Camp Municipal, Rue du Conon, 41120 Cellettes [02 54 70 48 41 or 02 54 70 47 54 (Mairie)]** On D956, Blois to Châteauroux rd, pass almost thro Cellettes, site 120m fr D956 down 1st L after rv bdge, site on L in 100m, well sp. NB Turn-in narr fr v busy main rd. Med, pt shd; wc; chem disp; shwrs inc; el pnts (6A) inc; snacks; shops, pool, playgrnd & tennis adj; fishing; games area; poss cr; phone; quiet, some daytime rd noise; ccard acc; CCI. "Lovely, peaceful site in pleasant rvside location; lge pitches; poss boggy after rain; friendly, helpful warden; poor shwrs; excel for Loire chateaux; rec." ♦ 1 Jun-30 Sep. € 11.70 2009*

BLOIS *4G2* (6km SW Rural) *47.54379, 1.31114* **FFCC Camping Le Cosson, 1 Rue de la Forêt, 41120 Chailles [02 54 79 46 49]** Fr Blois foll sp dir Montrichard (D751); after x-ing rv bdge at rndabt take 1st exit sp Montrichard/Chailles (D751); after x-ing sm rv bdge in Chailles take 1st L onto Rue de la Forêt; site in 50m; sm sp easily missed. Sm, hdg pitch, pt shd; wc (cont); chem disp (wc); shwrs inc; baby facs; el pnts (6A) €3.50; shops 1km; baker 500m; games area; playgrnd; dogs; phone; poss cr; adv bkg; rd noise; CCI. "Well-maintained, quiet site nr chateaux; pleasant, helpful owners; walks & cycle paths in local forest; poss tired pitches & facs end of ssn." 1 May-7 Sep. € 11.35 2009*

BOIRY NOTRE DAME see Arras *3B3*

BOIS DE CENE *2H4* (S Rural) *46.93395, -1.88728* **Camping Le Bois Joli, 2 Rue de Châteauneuf, 85710 Bois-de-Céné [02 51 68 20 05; fax 02 51 68 46 40; contact@camping-leboisjoli.com; www.camping-leboisjoli.com]** Fr D21 turn R at church in cent of vill, site on R in 500m on rd D28. Med, mkd pitch; shd; wc; chem disp; shwrs inc; el pnts (6A) inc; gas; lndtte; shop adj; snacks; playgrnd; pool; sand beach 18km; fishing; tennis; games area; entmnt; some statics; dogs €3.50; Eng spkn; adv bkg; ltd facs low ssn; CCI. "Friendly, helpful owner; clean san facs; gd walks." 1 Apr-24 Sep. € 16.90 2006*

BOIS PLAGE EN RE, LE see Couarde sur Mer, La *7A1*

BOISSE PENCHOT see Decazeville *7D4*

BOISSIERE DU MONTAIGU, LA see Montaigu *2H4*

⊞ **BOLLENE** *9D2* (5.5km E Rural) *44.29811, 4.78645* **FFCC Camping de la Simioune, Quartier Guffiage, 84500 Bollène [04 90 30 44 62; fax 04 90 30 44 77; la-simioune@wanadoo.fr; www.la-simioune.fr]** Exit A7 junc 19 onto D994/D8 dir Carpentras (Ave Salvatore Allende D8). At 3rd x-rd 900m bef fire stn take L turn (Ave Alphonse Daudet) foll rd 3km to sp for camping on L, then site 1km. Sm, pt sl, shd; wc; chem disp; baby facs; shwrs €1; el pnts (6A) €4.50; Indtte; shops & supmkt 4km; tradsmn; rest; bar; BBQ; playgrnd; pool; paddling pool; horseriding; entmnt; 10% statics; dogs €2; adv bkg rec high ssn; quiet; red CCI. "In pine forest; facs need upgrading - ltd in winter; excel pony club for children & adults; NH only." € 13.00 2008*

BOLLENE *9D2* (7km E Rural) *44.29124, 4.83837* **FFCC Camping Le Pont du Lez, Ave es Côtes du Rhône, 26790 Suze-la-Rousse [tel/fax 04 75 98 82 83; camping-lepontdulez@wanadoo.fr; www.campinglepontdulez.fr]** E fr Bollène on D94 to Suze-la-Rousse; L in vill sq; R immed bef rv bdge. Sm, pt shd; wc; shwrs inc; el pnts (6-10A) €3.40 (long lead poss req); Indtte; shop 300m; supmkt 7km; snacks; bar; playgrnd; fishing; games area; TV; dogs €1.40; no twin-axles; red low ssn; CCI. "Lovely but decrepit (2009); basic, clean facs - hot water to shwrs only; lovely area." 1 Apr-30 Sep. € 12.80 2009*

BOLLENE *9D2* (6km SW Rural) *44.24335, 4.72931* **FFCC Camping La Pinède en Provence (formerly Municipal), Quartier des Massanes, 84430 Mondragon [04 90 40 82 98; fax 09 59 92 16 56; contact@camping-pinede-provence.com; www.camping-pinede-provence.com]** Exit A7 junc 19 dir Bollène & take D26 S, site 1.5km N of Mondragon. Steep access. Med, mkd pitch, pt sl, terr, pt shd; htd wc; chem disp; mv service pnt; baby facs; shwrs inc; el pnts (8-13A) €3.90-4.50; Indtte; shop; BBQ; playgrnd; pool; some statics; dogs €1.50; adv bkg; quiet; red low ssn; CCI. "Gd, clean site; gd touring base; conv Ardèche Gorge." 14 Feb-14 Nov. € 14.00 2009*

BONLIEU see St Laurent en Grandvaux *6H2*

BONNAC LA COTE *7B3* (1km S Rural) *45.93238, 1.28977* **Camping Le Château de Leychoisier, 1 Route de Leychoisier, 87270 Bonnac-la-Côte [tel/fax 05 55 39 93 43; contact@leychoisier.com; www.leychoisier.com or www.les-castels.com]** Fr S on A20 exit junc 27 & L at T-junc onto D220. At rndabt take 3rd exit then 1st L onto D97. At mini-rndabt in Bonnac take 2nd exit, site on L in 1km. Fr N exit A20 junc 27, turn R at T-junc onto D97, then as above. Med, mkd pitch, pt sl, shd; wc; chem disp; baby facs; shwrs inc; el pnts (10A) inc; Indtte; ltd shop; rest; snacks; bar; BBQ (gas & charcoal); playgrnd; pool; tennis; wifi; games rm/TV; dogs €1; Eng spkn; adv bkg; ccard not acc; red low ssn; CCI. "Peaceful site; welcoming, friendly & helpful staff; gd san facs; excel rest; extra for m'vans; blocks req some pitches; rallies welcome; conv NH nr m'way; excel." ♦ 15 Apr-20 Sep. € 29.00 ABS - L11 2009*

BONNAL *6G2* (3.5km N Rural) *47.50777, 6.35583* **Camping Le Val de Bonnal, Rue de Moulin, 25680 Bonnal [03 81 86 90 87; fax 03 81 86 03 92; val-de-bonnal@wanadoo.fr; www.camping-valdebonnal.fr or www.les-castels.com]** Fr N on D9 fr Vesoul or Villersexel to Esprels, turn S onto D49 sp "Val de Bonnal'. Fr S exit A36 junc 5 & turn N onto D50 sp Rougemont, site sp to N of Rougemont. Lge, mkd pitches, pt shd; wc; chem disp; baby facs; shwrs inc; el pnts (5-10A) inc (poss rev pol); gas; Indtte; shop; rest; snacks; bar; BBQ (charcoal/gas); playgrnd; pool; waterslide; paddling pool; lake sw & sand beach adj; fishing (permit); canoeing; watersports; cycle hire; gym; golf 6km; entmnt high ssn; wifi; games/TV rm; 40% statics; dogs €1.50; poss cr; Eng spkn; adv bkg; quiet; ccard acc; red low ssn; CCI. "Attractive site; busy & popular high ssn; excel welcome; lge accessible pitches; ultra-modern, clean facs; gd child activities; ltd facs low ssn; tour ops." ♦ 30 Apr-5 Sep. € 38.00 ABS - J01 2009*

BONNARD see Joigny *4F4*

BONNES see Chauvigny *7A3*

BONNEUIL MATOURS *4H2* (1km S Rural) *46.67600, 0.57640* **Camp Municipal du Parc de Crémault, 8 Allée du Stade, 86210 Bonneuil-Matours [tel/fax 05 49 85 20 47]** Fr D910 (N10) 20km N of Poitiers take D82 E to Bonneuil-Matours. Site sp in vill next to stadium & Rv Vienne but site ent not well sp. Med, mkd pitch, shd; htd wc; chem disp; mv service pnt; shwrs €1; el pnts €2.70; Indry rm; shops 1km; tradsmn; rest; snacks; bar; BBQ; playgrnd; rv & fishing adj; tennis; archery; entmnt; TV; quiet, but some traff noise fr across rv. "Nature reserve adj; clean facs; lovely site." Mid Apr-Mid Sep. € 9.15 2008*

BONNEVAL *4F2* (1km SE Rural) *48.17080, 1.38640* **Camping Le Bois Chièvre, Route de Vouvray, St Maurice, 28800 Bonneval [02 37 47 54 01; fax 02 37 96 26 79; camping-bonneval-28@orange.fr; http://monsite.orange.fr/camping-bonneval-28]** Rec app fr N (Chartres), or SE (D27 fr Patay/Orléans) as app fr S thro town is narr & diff. Fr Chartres take N10 into Bonneval & foll camp sp (mainly to L). Med, hdg/mkd pitch, hdstg, pt sl, shd; htd wc; chem disp; mv service pnt; shwrs inc; el pnts (6A) inc (rev pol); Indtte; shop 1km; tradsmn; rest; snacks; bar; BBQ; playgrnd; htd pool adj inc; some statics; dogs €1; Eng spkn; adv bkg; quiet; red long stay/low ssn; CCI. "Well-run, well-kept site in woodland; gd, lge pitches; friendly, helpful staff; vg facs but poss stretched in ssn; no twin-axles over 5.60m; vg NH for Le Havre or Dieppe." ♦ 1 Apr-31 Oct. € 15.00 2009*

BONNEVILLE *9A3* (500m NE Rural) *46.08206, 6.41288* **Camp Municipal Le Bois des Tours, 314 Rue des Bairiers, 74130 Bonneville [04 50 97 04 31 or 04 50 25 22 14 (Mairie)]** Fr A40 junc 16 take D1203 (N203), or fr Cluses take D1205 (N205) to Bonneville. Cross rv bdge into town cent; site sp. Med, pt shd; wc (some cont); chem disp; shwrs; el pnts (10A); shops 500m; playgrnd; poss cr; adv bkg; quiet. "Well-maintained, immac site; gd san facs." 15 Jun-15 Sep. € 6.50 2006*

⊞ **BONNIERES SUR SEINE** *3D2* (2km N Rural) *49.05804, 1.61224* **Camping Le Criquet, 42 Rue du Criquet, 78840 Freneuse [tel/fax 01 30 93 07 95; www.camping-le-criquet.fr]** Fr D915 (N15) at Bonnières to Freneuse on D37. Thro vill, site sp at end of vill past cemetary. Lge, pt shd; wc; chem disp; shwrs €3; el pnts (10A) €3; BBQ; playgrnd; games area; mainly statics; adv bkg; quiet. "V run down (May 2008) - san facs unclean & need refurb, pitches unkempt; Monet's garden 12km" € 12.30 2008*

BONNIERES SUR SEINE *3D2* (5km E Rural) *49.04646, 1.66256* **Camping Loisirs des Groux, Chemin de Vétheuil, 78270 Mousseaux-sur-Seine [01 34 79 33 86; campingloisirsdesgroux@wanadoo.fr; www.camping desgroux.com]** Fr W exit A13 junc 15 onto D113 (N13) dir Bonnières. Cont thro Bonnières, turn L onto D37 Mousseaux/Base de Loisirs. Cont strt on D37/D124/D125 & then turn R & foll site sp. Fr E exit A13 junc 14 sp Bonnières & foll sp Zone Industrielle. At rndabt take D113 Bonnières, then as above. Med, hdg/mkd pitch, pt shd; wc (some cont); chem disp (wc); mv service pnt; shwrs inc; el pnts (10A) €2; Indtte; BBQ; leisure cent inc pool 500m; lake sw & beach 500m; games area; wifi; 90% statics; dogs; Eng spkn; adv bkg rec; quiet; ccard acc; CCI. "Basic san facs; friendly, helpful staff; ltd touring pitches; excel walks or cycling along Seine; conv Paris (65km), Versailles, Rouen, Giverny." ♦ 1 Apr-30 Nov. € 15.00 2009*

See advertisement

BONNIEUX *10E2* (1km W Rural) *43.81893, 5.31170* **Camp Municipal du Vallon, Route de Ménerbes, 84480 Bonnieux [tel/fax 04 90 75 86 14; campingvallon@ wanadoo.fr]** Fr Bonnieux take D3 twd Ménerbes, site sp on L on leaving vill. Med, mkd pitch, terr, pt shd; wc (some cont); chem dsip; shwrs inc; el pnts (10A) €3.50; Indtte; shop; tradsmn; snacks; bar; playgrnd; dogs €1; some Eng spkn; quiet; red low ssn; CCI. "Quaint, 'olde worlde' site in wooded area; friendly warden; basic facs but clean; gd walking & mountain biking; attractive hilltop vill; gd touring base." 15 Mar-30 Oct. € 18.00 2009*

BONO, LE see Auray *2F3*

BONZEE *5D1* (E Rural) *49.09539, 5.61173* **Base de Loisirs du Colvert Les Eglantines, 55160 Bonzée [03 29 87 31 98; fax 03 29 87 30 60; blcv@wanadoo.fr; www.campings-colvert.com]** Fr Verdun take D903 twd Metz for 18km; in Manheulles, turn R to Bonzée in 1km; at Bonzée turn L for Fresnes; site on R, adj Camping Marguerites. Or fr A4 exit junc 32 to Fresnes; then foll sp Bonzée. Med, hdg/ mkd pitch, pt shd; wc; chem disp; mv service pnt; shwrs inc; el pnts (4-6A) €3.71-5.30; gas & 1km; Indtte; shop & 1km; tradsmn; BBQ; rest; snacks; bar; playgrnd; lake sw & boating adj; waterslide; fishing; tennis 1.5km; many statics; dogs €1.26; phone; extra €14.36 for twin-axles; adv bkg; noisy high ssn; ccard acc; CCI. "Spacious pitches in well-planned sites (2 sites together); facs ltd low ssn." ♦ 1 Apr-30 Sep. € 12.81 2007*

BOOFZHEIM see Rhinau *6E3*

⊞ **BORDEAUX** *7C2* (7km N Rural) *44.89782, -0.58388* **Camping de Bordeaux Lac, Blvd Jacques Chaban Delmas, 33520 Bordeaux-Bruges [05 57 87 70 60; contact@ camping-bordeaux.com; www.camping-bordeaux.com]** On ring rd A630 take exit 5 twd lake; site sp on N side of lake, 500m N of Parc des Expositions. Med, mkd pitch, pt shd; htd wc; chem disp; mv service pnt; shwrs inc; el pnts inc; Indtte; snacks; playgrnd; lake sw & fishing adj; wifi; TV; some statics; dogs €4; adv bkg; quiet; CCI. "New site 2009." € 29.00 2009*

⊞ **BORDEAUX** *7C2* (4km S Urban) *44.75529, -0.62772* **Camping Beau Soleil, 371 Cours du Général de Gaulle, 33170 Gradignan [tel/fax 05 56 89 17 66; camping beausoleil@wanadoo.fr; www.camping-gradignan.com]** Fr N take exit 16 fr Bordeaux ring rd onto D1010 (N10). Site on S of Gradignan on R after Beau Soleil complex. Sm, mkd pitch, hdstg, pt sl, pt shd; htd wc; chem disp; shwrs inc; el pnts (6-10A) inc (poss rev pol); Indtte; shops adj; snacks; bar; gas/elec BBQ; htd pool & waterslides 5km; rv/ lake sw 2km; 70% statics; dogs €1; bus/tram 250m; poss cr; Eng spkn; adv bkg rec; quiet; red low ssn; CCI. "Pleasant, clean, family-run site; helpful owners; vg clean san facs; ltd touring pitches; sm pitches not suitable lge o'fits; adv bkg rec; excel." ♦ € 17.50 2009*

BORMES LES MIMOSAS see Lavandou, Le *10F3*

BORT LES ORGUES *7C4* (4km N Rural) *45.43213, 2.50461* **Camping La Siauve, Rue du Camping, 15270 Lanobre [04 71 40 31 85 or 05 46 55 10 01; fax 04 71 40 34 33 or 05 46 55 10 10; www.village-center.com]** On D992 Clermont-Ferrand to Bort-les-Orgues, site on R 3km S of Lanobre. Site sp. Lge, hdg/mkd pitch, terr, pt shd; wc; chem disp; mv service pnt; shwrs inc; el pnts (6A) inc; lndtte; shop & 3km; tradsmn; rest; snacks; bar; playgrnd; lake sw adj; fishing; tennis nr; games area; cycle hire; entmnt; TV rm; dogs €3; phone; Eng spkn; adv bkg; noisy high ssn; ccard acc; red low ssn; CCI. "Footpaths (steep) to lake; gd sw, boating etc; excel touring base; v scenic." 21 Jun-31 Aug. € 18.00 2008*

BORT LES ORGUES *7C4* (6km S Rural) *45.33671, 2.47379* **Camp Municipal de Bellevue, 15240 Saignes [04 71 40 68 40 or 04 71 40 62 80 (Mairie); saignes-mairie@wanadoo.fr]** Fr Bort-les-Orgues take D922 S twd Mauriac. In 5km, turn L onto D22. Site sp on R after ent vill. Foll sp 'Piscine/Stade'. Sm, hdg/mkd pitch, pt shd; wc (some cont); chem disp; shwrs inc; el pnts (6-10A) €2.20; lndtte; shops, rest 500m; snacks; bar; BBQ; playgrnd; 3 pools adj; 2 tennis courts adj; dogs; Eng spkn; adv bkg; quiet; no ccard acc; CCI. "Pleasant situation with views; roomy pitches; vill in walking dist; gd touring base." 1 Jul-31 Aug. € 6.20 2009*

BORT LES ORGUES *7C4* (7km SW Rural) *45.33249, 2.48713* **Camping à la Ferme (Chanet), Domaine de la Vigne, 15240 Saignes [tel/fax 04 71 40 61 02 or 06 83 12 39 32 (mob); chanetcollete@wanadoo.fr]** Take D922 S fr Bort-les-Orgues sp Mauriac. After 5.5km at junc with D15 take sharp L sp Saignes; then turn R onto D22. In cent of Saignes turn L at T-junc onto D30. After 200m turn L onto C14 sp La Vigne & Camping. Farmhouse on L after 400m, site on R. Sm, pt sl, pt shd; wc; cold shwrs inc; el pnts (6A) €2.30 (rev pol); shops 800m; sm pool; poss cr; adv bkg; quiet. "Beautiful, peaceful setting; CL-type site; friendly owners; ltd facs; san facs poss neglected low ssn." Mar-Nov. € 10.50 2009*

BOUCHEMAINE see Angers *4G1*

BOUGE CHAMBALUD see St Rambert d'Albon *9C2*

BOULANCOURT see Malesherbes *4E3*

BOULOGNE SUR GESSE *8F3* (6km NE Rural) *43.33135, 0.68046* **Camping Le Canard Fou, Laron, 31350 Lunax [05 61 88 26 06]** Fr Boulogne-sur-Gesse N on D632 sp Toulouse. In 6km turn L sp Lunax, foll site sp for 1km. Turn L at x-rds, site 300m on R. Sm, pt sl, pt shd; wc; chem disp (wc); shwrs inc; el pnts (9A) inc; gas; lndtte; shop 6km; BBQ; pool 6km; reservoir adj; some statics; phone 800m; Eng spkn; adv bkg; quiet. "Peaceful CL-type site; friendly owners; san facs clean but open to elements; breakfast & eve meals avail; perfect site for walking, cycling." ♦ 15 Mar-15 Dec. € 11.00 (4 persons) 2009*

BOULOGNE SUR GESSE *8F3* (1.3km SE Rural) *43.28323, 0.65544* **Camp Municipal du Lac, Ave du Lac, 31350 Boulogne-sur-Gesse [05 61 88 20 54; fax 05 61 88 62 16; villagevacancesboulogne@wanadoo.fr; www.ville-boulogne-sur-gesse.fr]** Fr Boulogne-sur-Gesse, take D633 for 1km. Foll sp, turn L to site. Lake (watersports cent) adj ent. Lge, mkd pitch, pt sl, pt shd; wc (some cont); chem disp; shwrs inc; el pnts (10A) €3.70; gas; shops 1km; rest; bar; playgrnd; htd pool 300m; boating; fishing; tennis; golf; entmnt; 90% statics; dogs €1; phone; Eng spkn; quiet. "High kerbs poss diff lge o'fits; clean facs; phone ahead to check open early ssn." ♦ 1 Apr-30 Sep. € 10.30 2009*

BOULOGNE SUR MER *3A2* (8km E Rural) *50.73111, 1.71582* **Camp Municipal Les Sapins, 62360 La Capelle-les-Boulogne [03 21 83 16 61]** Exit A16 junc 31 E onto N42 to La Capelle vill; cont to next rndabt & take sp Crémarest; site on R. Sm, pt shd; wc; shwrs inc; el pnts (4-6A) €2.35-4.60 (poss rev pol); lndtte; hypmkt, rest, snacks & bar 2km; playgrnd; sand beach 4km; few statics; bus 1km; poss cr; adv bkg; poss rd noise & fr adj horseriding school; no ccard acc; CCI. "Basic san facs, dated but clean; friendly, helpful warden; TLC needed (2009); gd NH for Calais." 15 Apr-15 Sep. € 10.15 2009*

⊞ **BOULOGNE SUR MER** *3A2* (16km E Rural) **Camping à la Ferme Le Bois Grout (Leclercq), Le Bois de Grout, Le Plouy, 62142 Henneveux [03 21 33 32 16; www.leboisgroult.fr]** Take N42 fr Boulogne twd St Omer, take exit S dir Desvres (D127). Immed at rndabt foll sp Colembert. On ent Le Plouy turn R at the calvary & foll sp to site. Sm, some hdstg, pt sl, pt shd; wc; shwrs €2; el pnts (10A) €4 (poss long lead req); shops 6km; dogs €1; adv bkg; quiet; ccard not acc. "Lovely, well-kept CL-type site; pleasant owner; basic facs ltd in winter; twin-axles acc; no barrier; WWI places of interest; easy access fr N42; excel." € 7.00 2009*

BOULOGNE SUR MER *3A2* (6km S Coastal) *50.67128, 1.57079* **FFCC Camp Municipal La Falaise, Rue Charles Cazin, 62224 Equihen-Plage [03 21 31 22 61; fax 03 21 80 54 01; mairie.equihen.plage@wanadoo.fr; www.ville-equihen-plage.fr]** Exit A16 junc 28 onto D901 (N1) dir Boulogne, then D940 S. Turn R to Condette then foll sp Equihen-Plage, site sp in vill. Access fr D901 via narr rds. Med, hdg pitch, sl, terr, pt shd; wc; chem disp; mv service pnt; shwrs inc; el pnts (10-16A) €4.90-6.40; lndtte; playgrnd; sand beach 200m; watersports; games rm; 85% statics (sep area); dogs €2.20; phone; adv bkg; ccard acc; red low ssn; CCI. "Pleasant, well-run site in excel location, but poss windy; excel clean facs; sl pitches poss diff long o'fits." 1 Apr-5 Nov. € 16.00 2009*

BOULOGNE SUR MER *3A2* (7km S Urban) *50.67698, 1.64245* **Camping Les Cytises, Rue de l'Eglise, 62360 Isques [tel/fax 03 21 31 11 10; campcytises@orange.fr; www.lescytises.fr]** S fr Boulogne on D901 (N1) to Isques; site 150m fr D901. Or on A16 exit junc 28 & foll sp Isques & camp sp. Med, hdg pitch, terr, pt shd; htd wc; chem disp; baby facs; shwrs inc; el pnts (3-6A) €3; gas; Indtte; shop 100m; snacks; playgrnd; pool & sand beach 4km; rv adj; archery; 50% statics; dogs free; Eng spkn; adv bkg; some rlwy noise; ccard not acc; red low ssn; CCI. "Gd site; clean, modern san facs; poss sm pitches - poss unkempt low ssn; barrier clsd 2300-0700; conv Channel Tunnel & 5 mins fr Nausica; vg NH nr m'way." ♦ 1 Apr-15 Oct. € 14.20 2009*

BOULOU, LE *8G4* (2km N Rural) *42.54157, 2.83431* **Camping Le Mas Llinas, 66160 Le Boulou [04 68 83 25 46; info@camping-mas-llinas.com; www.camping-mas-llinas.com]** Fr Perpignan, take D900 (N9) S; 1km N of Le Boulou turn R at Intermarché supmkt 100m to mini rndabt, turn L & foll sp to Mas-Llinas to site in 2km. Or fr A9 exit 43 & foll sp Perpignan thro Le Boulou. L at rndabt adj Leclerc supmkt, site well sp. Med, terr, pt shd; wc; shwrs inc; chem disp; el pnts (5-10A) €3.50-4.50; gas; Indtte; shops adj; tradsmn; snacks; playgrnd; pool; some statics; dogs €2; phone; adv bkg; Eng spkn; quiet; red low ssn; CCI. "Friendly, welcoming owners; peaceful in hillside setting with views fr top levels; golden orioles on site; beware poss high winds on high pitches; ltd water points at top levels; ltd facs low ssn; facs clean; gd sized pitches." ♦ 1 Feb-30 Nov. € 18.30 2006*

⊞ **BOULOU, LE** *8G4* (1km SE Rural) *42.52088, 2.84509* **Camping Les Oliviers, Route d'Argelès-sur-Mer, 66160 Le Boulou [04 68 83 12 86 or 06 15 43 99 89; fax 04 68 87 60 08; infos@lesoliviers.com; www.lesoliviers.com]** Exit A9 junc 43 at Le Boulou. Foll sp onto D618 twds Argelès-sur-Mer. Site on R in 1km, well sp fr D618. Med, mkd pitch, pt shd; htd wc; chem disp; mv service pnt; shwrs inc; el pnts (6-10A) €3.50; gas 1km; Indtte; shop 1km; tradsmn; bar; playgrnd; shgl beach 12km; 40% statics; dogs €1.50; site clsd mid-Dec to mid-Jan; poss cr; adv bkg; quiet; red low ssn; CCI. "Helpful, friendly owner; san facs basic but adequate, poss stretched peak ssn; dog-friendly; conv juncs of A9 & N9; popular NH en rte Spain." ♦ € 18.00 2009*

BOULOU, LE *8G4* (S Urban) *42.50964, 2.82680* **Camping L'Olivette, Route du Perthus, 66160 Le Boulou [04 68 83 48 08; fax 04 68 87 46 00; info@camping-olivette.fr; www.camping-olivette.fr]** D900 (N9) twd Spanish border, site on R alongside main D900, v busy rd. Med, hdg/mkd pitch; pt sl, pt shd; wc; baby facs; shwrs inc; el pnts (10A) €2.50; Indtte; shops; snacks; bar; many statics; dogs €1.60; poss cr; Eng spkn; some rd noise. "Conv for Salvador Dali Museum & ruins at Empurias; security gate; poss tired pitches; clean san facs; helpful owners; gd NH." 15 Mar-31 Oct. € 14.50 2009*

BOULOU, LE *8G4* (5km S Rural) *42.49083, 2.79777* **Camping Les Pins/Le Congo, Route de Céret, 66480 Maureillas-las-Illas [04 68 83 23 21; fax 04 68 83 45 64; lespinslecongo@hotmail.fr; www.camping-lespinslecongo.com]** Fr Le Boulou take D900 (N9) S, fork R after 2km onto D618 dir Céret. Site on L 500m after Maureillas. Med, hdg pitch, shd; htd wc (cont); chem disp (wc); shwrs inc; el pnts (10A) €3.50; gas; Indtte; shop 500m; tradsmn; rest; snacks; BBQ; playgrnd; pool; sand beach 20km; 10% statics; dogs; phone; adv bkg; Eng spkn; ccard acc. ♦ 1 Feb-30 Nov. € 16.50 2009*

BOULOU, LE *8G4* (4km SW Rural) *42.50664, 2.79502* **Camping de la Vallée/Les Deux Rivières, Route de Maureillas, 66490 St Jean-Pla-de-Corts [04 68 83 23 20; fax 04 68 83 07 94; campingdelavallee@yahoo.fr; www.campingdelavallee.com]** Exit A9 at Le Boulou. Turn W on D115. Turn L after 3km at rndabt, into St Jean-Pla-de-Corts, thro vill, over bdge, site on L. Med, mkd pitch, pt shd, htd wc; chem disp; mv service pnt; baby facs; shwrs inc; el pnts (5A) €4; gas 800m; Indtte; shop 800m; tradsmn; rest; snacks; bar; playgrnd; pool; sand beach 20km; lake sw & fishing 1km; archery; entmnt; internet; TV; 50% statics (sep area); dogs €2.50; phone; bus adj; poss cr; Eng spkn; adv bkg; quiet; ccard acc; red long stay/low ssn; CCI. "Lovely well-kept site; easy access lge pitches; excel san facs; owners with gd local info; conv NH fr A9 or longer; highly rec." ♦ May-Sep. € 17.00 2009*

BOULOU, LE *8G4* (5km SW Rural) *42.47853, 2.80399* **Camping La Clapère (Naturist), Route de Las Illas, 66400 Maureillas-las-Illas [04 68 83 36 04; fax 04 68 83 34 44; info@clapere.com; www.clapere.com]** Exit Le Boulou S on D900 (N9) twd Le Perthus; after 3km take N618 twd Maureillas, D13 for 2km twd Las Illas. Lge, terr, pt shd; wc; chem disp; shwrs inc; el pnts (6-10A) €5-8; Indtte; shop; rest; snacks; bar; playgrnd; pool; rv adj; fishing; tennis; archery; games area; entmnt; TV; dogs €2.50; poss cr; Eng spkn; adv bkg; quiet. "Excel with easy access for c'vans; INF card req or may be purchased; vg for children; friendly recep." ♦ 1 May-30 Sep. € 23.00 2006*

⊞ **BOULOU, LE** *8G4* (4km W Rural) *42.50908, 2.78429* **FFCC Camping Les Casteillets, 66490 St Jean Pla-de-Corts [04 68 83 26 83; fax 04 68 83 39 67; jc@campinglescasteillets.com; www.campinglescasteillets.com]** Exit A9 at Le Boulou; turn W on D115; after 3km turn L immed after St Jean-Pla-de-Corts; site sp on R in 400m. NB Narr app last 200m. Med, mkd pitch, pt shd; wc; chem disp; some serviced pitches; shwrs inc; el pnts (6A) €3.30 (poss rev pol); gas; Indtte; shop; rest; snacks; bar; playgrnd; pool; tennis; sand beach 20km; games area; entmnt; internet; TV; 10% statics; poss cr; Eng spkn; adv bkg ess high ssn; quiet; red low ssn/long stay. "Lovely, friendly, scenic site; lge pitches; conv for touring & en rte NE Spain." ♦ € 18.00 2009*

France

BOURBON LANCY *4H4* (Urban) *46.62098, 3.76557* **Camping St Prix, Rue de St Prix, 71140 Bourbon-Lancy [tel/fax 03 85 89 20 98 or 03 86 37 95 83; aquadis1@wanadoo.fr; www.camping-chalets-bourbon-lancy.com]** Fr N turn L fr D979 on D973 & foll into Bourbon-Lancy. Where D973 veers L (sp Autun) strt on to x-rds in about 100m. Turn R, then next R. Site well sp. Med, hdg pitch, hdstg, terr, pt sl, shd; htd wc; chem disp; shwrs inc; el pnts (10A) inc; lndry rm; shop; snacks; playgrnd; htd pool adj; lake sw/fishing; 25% statics; dogs €3.10; Eng spkn; quiet; CCI. "Well-managed site in gd condition; helpful staff; lovely old town 10 min walk; rec." ♦ 1 Apr-31 Oct. € 18.00 2008*

BOURBON L'ARCHAMBAULT *9A1* (10km NE Rural) *46.66050, 3.09490* **Camping Les Fourneaux (Naturist), Route Limoise, 03160 Couzon [tel/fax 04 70 66 23 18; lesfourneaux@wanadoo.fr; www.lesfourneaux.org]** Fr Bourbon NE on D139 to Couzon, then L onto D13, site in 2.5km on L. Med, pt sl, pt shd; wc; chem disp; shwrs el pnts (4-6A) €4; tradsmn; bar; playgrnd; pool; cycle hire; no dogs; phone; Eng spkn; quiet; red long stay; INF card req. "V lge pitches; helpful Dutch owners; site not suitable children; conv touring base; many pitches o'grown/unkempt (2009)." ♦ 1 Jun-30 Aug. € 22.25 2009*

BOURBON L'ARCHAMBAULT *9A1* (1km W Rural) *46.58058, 3.04804* **Camp Municipal de Bignon, 03160 Bourbon-l'Archambault [04 70 67 08 83; fax 04 70 67 35 35; mairie-bourbon-archambault@wanadoo.fr]** Take D953 (sp) to Montluçon fr town cent. Turn R nr top of hill at camping sp bef town cancellation sp. Lge, sl, pt shd; wc (some cont); shwrs inc; el pnts (6-10A) €2-2.20; lndtte; shops 1km; htd pool & waterslide 300m; tennis nr; 75% statics; poss cr; quiet. "Beautifully laid-out in park surroundings; dated san facs; gd pitches; charming town; excel." 1 Mar-31 Oct. € 5.60 2008*

BOURBONNE LES BAINS *6F2* (500m NW Urban) *47.95723, 5.74011* **Camping Le Montmorency, Rue du Stade, 52400 Bourbonne-les-Bains [03 25 90 08 64; fax 03 25 84 23 74; c.montmorency@wanadoo.fr; www.camping-montmorency.com]** Sp on ent town either way on D417. After exit D417, sp at 1st turn L at telephone box. Site adj to pool & stadium. Med, hdg/mkd pitch, pt sl, unshd; wc; mv service pnt; shwrs inc; el pnts (6A) €3; gas; lndry rm; shops 500m; snacks; pool adj; tennis; dogs €0.80; adv bkg; quiet. "Pleasant site; helpful warden; popular with visitors to spa cent; gd NH." 5 Mar-20 Nov. € 9.90 2007*

BOURBOULE, LA *7B4* (1km N Rural) *45.59680, 2.75130* **FFCC Camping Le Panoramique, Le Pessy, 63150 Murat-le-Quaire [04 73 81 18 79; fax 04 73 65 57 34; camping.panoramique@wanadoo.fr; http://membres.lycos.fr/campingpanoramique]** Exit A89 junc 25; cont strt until junc with D922; turn R; in 3km turn R onto D219 dir Mont-Dore; in 5km pass thro Murat-le-Quaire; in 1km turn L in Le Pessy; site on L in 300m. Site well sp fr D922. Med, mkd pitch, terr, pt shd; htd wc; chem disp; mv service pnt; baby facs; shwrs inc; el pnts (6-10A) €4.30-5.60; gas; lndtte; shop & snacks 2km; tradsmn; rest 1km; bar; playgrnd; pool; games rm; 30% statics; dogs €1.70; phone; adv bkg; quiet; CCI. "Site well set-out; mountain views; friendly, helpful recep; clean facs; pets corner; vg." 15 May-30 Sep. € 14.80 2007*

BOURBOULE, LA *7B4* (500m NE Rural) *45.59399, 2.75699* **Camping Le Poutie, 750 Ave de Maréchal Leclerc, 63150 La Bourboule [04 73 81 04 54; fax 04 73 81 04 54; campingpoutie@aol.com; www.camping-poutie.com]** Fr La Bourboule on D996, 500m past rlwy stn. Med, hdg/mkd pitch, hdstg, terr, pt shd; wc (some cont); chem disp (wc); baby facs; shwrs inc; el pnts (4-10A) €4-5.50 (poss rev pol); gas; lndtte; shop & 500m; tradsmn; rest 500m; snacks; playgrnd; htd pool; lge games rm; entmnt; wifi; 50% statics; dogs €2; phone adj; poss full; adv bkg; quiet; CCI. "Superb views; friendly British owners; san facs need update." ♦ 15 May-31 Oct. € 12.50 2007*

BOURBOULE, LA *7B4* (1km E Rural) *45.58980, 2.75257* **Camp Municipal des Vernières, Ave de Lattre de Tassigny, 63150 La Bourboule [04 73 81 10 20 or 04 73 81 31 00 (Mairie); fax 04 73 65 54 98]** Fr N on N89 or S on D922 turn E onto D130 dir Le Mont-Dore, site sp. Lge, some hdg pitch; pt terr, pt shd; htd wc (some cont); chem disp; shwrs inc; el pnts (10A) €3.60; lndtte; supmkt nr; playgrnd; pool nr; fishing nr; dogs €1; poss cr; no adv bkg; some rd noise daytime. "Lovely setting in mountains; gd clean facs; short walk to fine spa town; rec." ♦ Easter-30 Sep. € 9.10 2009*

BOURBOULE, LA *7B4* (4km E Rural) *45.59456, 2.76347* **Camping Les Clarines, 1424 Ave Maréchal Leclerc, Les Planches, 63150 La Bourboule [04 73 81 02 30; fax 04 73 81 09 34; www.camping-les-clarines.com]** Fr La Bourboule take D996 (old rd sp Piscine & Gare); fork L at exit fr town. Site sp on R. Lge, terr, pt shd; htd wc (some cont); baby facs; shwrs inc; el pnts (3-10A) €2.15-€5.80; gas; lndtte; shop & adj; bar; BBQ; htd pool; playgrnd; wifi; entmnt; TV rm; dogs €1.90; poss cr; adv bkg (ess high ssn); quiet; 15% red low ssn. "Gd winter sports cent; excel htd facs." ♦ 21 Dec-20 Oct. € 13.20 2007*

BOURDEAUX *9D2* (3km E Rural) *44.59572, 5.16203* **Aire Naturelle Le Moulin (Arnaud), 26460 Bézaudun-sur-Bine [tel/fax 04 75 53 37 21 or 04 75 53 30 73; arnocamp moulin26@aol.com]** Exit A7 junc 16; D104 to Crest then D538 to Bourdeaux; just bef bdge L to Bézaudun-sur-Bine. Site on R in 3km. Sm, pt sl, pt shd; wc; chem disp (wc); shwrs €1; el pnts (6A) €2.50; lndtte; shop 3km; tradsmn; snacks; bar; pool; no statics; dogs €1.50; quiet; CCI. "Lovely area; wonderful views; pretty vills; gd walking; vg." ♦ 15 Apr-30 Sep. € 12.00 2008*

BOURDEAUX *9D2* (1.5km SE Rural) *44.57825, 5.12795* **Camping Les Bois du Chatelas, 26460 Bourdeaux [04 75 00 60 80; fax 04 75 00 60 81; bois.du.chatelas@infonie.fr; www.chatelas.com]** A7 m'way exit at Valence Sud, head twd Crest then twd Bourdeaux. In Bourdeaux sp Dienlefit, site in 1km on L. Med, mkd pitch, terr, pt shd; htd wc; chem disp; mv service pnt; baby facs; shwrs inc; el pnts (10A) €4.50; gas; Indtte; shop; tradsmn; rest; snacks; bar; cooking facs; playgrnd; htd covrd pool; rv 5km; entmnt; TV rm; 30% statics; dogs €4; phone; Eng spkn; adv bkg ess high ssn; red low ssn; ccard acc; CCI. "In lovely,scenic area; gd walking; site on steep slope." 7 Apr-30 Sep. € 23.00 2006*

BOURDEAUX *9D2* (300m S Rural) *44.58389, 5.13615* **FFCC Camp Municipal Le Gap des Tortelles, 26460 Bourdeaux [tel/fax 04 75 53 30 45; info@campingdebourdeaux.com; www.campingdebourdeaux.com]** Foll camping/piscine sp in vill. Gd app fr S via D94 & D70 fr Nyons. Sm, terr, pt shd; wc; mv service pnt; shwrs inc; el pnts (6A) €2.80; Indtte; shop, 600m; rest; bar; playgrnd; sw rv; tennis adj; few statics; dogs €2; adv bkg; quiet. "Attractive area away fr tourist scene; helpful warden; sh path into vill." ♦ 1 Apr-30 Sep. € 11.00 2009*

BOURDEAUX *9D2* (4km NW Rural) *44.59583, 5.11127* **Kawan Village Le Couspeau, Quartier Bellevue, 26460 Le Poët-Célard [04 75 53 30 14; fax 04 75 53 37 23; info@couspeau.com; www.couspeau.com]** Fr D538 Crest-Bourdeaux; pass thro Saou & after several kms turn R over bdge to Le Poët-Célard, site sp in vill. Med, terr, mkd pitch, sl, pt shd; wc; chem disp; serviced pitches; shwrs inc; el pnts (6A) €3 (poss rev pol); gas; Indtte; sm shop; tradsmn; rest, snacks, bar high ssn; playgrnd; 2 htd pools (1 covrd); rv & fishing; canoeing; tennis; horseriding 4km; TV rm; 20% statics; dogs €1; Eng spkn; adv bkg; quiet; ccard acc; min 6 days high ssn; red low ssn; CCI. "On steep hillside; gd views; facs for disabled but site rds steep; tractor assistance avail on arr/dep; excel." ♦ 15 Apr-30 Sep. € 26.00 (CChq acc) 2006*

BOURG see Langres *6F1*

BOURG ACHARD *3D2* (1km W Rural) *49.35330, 0.80814* **Camping Le Clos Normand, 235 Route de Pont Audemer, 27310 Bourg-Achard [02 32 56 34 84 or 06 03 60 36 26 (mob); www.leclosnormand.eu]** 1km W of vill of Bourg-Achard, D675 (N175) Rouen-Pont Audemer or exit A13 at Bourg-Achard junc. Med, hdg/mkd pitch, pt sl, pt shd; wc (chem clos); shwrs inc; el pnts (6A) €3.20 (poss rev pol & poss long lead req); gas; shop; supmkt nr; playgrnd; pool; paddling pool; 10% statics; dogs free; poss cr; adv bkg; some rd noise; ccard acc; CCI. "Clean san facs but need refurb; plenty hot water; many pitches uneven; gd." ♦ 1 Apr-30 Sep. € 15.80 2009*

BOURG ACHARD *3D2* (10km NW Rural) **Camping Les Cerisiers, Quai Eduard Salmon Marie, 76940 Heurteauville [tel/fax 02 35 37 41 37; alain.planes.405@orange.fr]** Exit A13 junc 25 onto D313/D490 N dir La Mailleraye-sur-Seine; then turn R onto D65 to Heurteauville. Site on bank of Seine nr ferry. Sm, mkd pitch, hdstg, pt shd; own san; chem disp; mv service pnt; no shwrs; no el pnts; shops 5km; dogs; no twin-axles; adv bkg; CCI. "Sm CL-type site (12 pitches) aimed at m'vans; sm c'vans accepted; gd location by Rv Seine; friendly owner; vg." 1 May-31 Oct. € 10.00 2008*

⊞ **BOURG ARGENTAL** *9C2* (S Rural) **Camping Domaine de l'Astrée, L'Allier, 42220 Bourg-Argental [tel/fax 04 77 39 72 97 or 04 77 39 63 49 (OT); prl@bourgargental.fr]** S fr St Etienne on D1082 (N82) to Bourg-Argental, thro town, site well sp on R soon after rndabt & opp filling stn. Fr Annonay or Andance site on L of D1082 at start of Bourg-Argental, adj rv. Sm, pt shd; wc; chem disp (wc); shwrs inc; el pnts (4-6A) €3.50-5.50 (long cable poss req); gas; Indtte; shop 250m; snacks; playgrnd; pool 600m; rv adj; waterslide; fishing; cycle hire; 60% statics; dogs €1.50; phone; poss cr; some rd noise; red low ssn; ccard acc; CCI. "Pleasant site with modern facs; vg." ♦ € 15.00 2006*

BOURG DES COMPTES see Guichen *2F4*

BOURG D'OISANS, LE *9C3* (1.5km NE Rural) *45.06557, 6.03980* **Camping à la Rencontre du Soleil, Route de l'Alpe-d'Huez, La Sarenne, 38520 Le Bourg-d'Oisans [04 76 79 12 22; fax 04 76 80 26 37; rencontre.soleil@wanadoo.fr; www.alarencontredusoleil.com]** Fr D1091 (N91) approx 800m E of town turn N onto D211, sp 'Alpe d'Huez'. In approx 500m cross sm bdge over Rv Sarennes, then turn immed L to site. (Take care not to overshoot ent, as poss diff to turn back.) Med, hdg/mkd pitch, pt shd; htd wc (some cont); chem disp; mv service pnt; baby facs; shwrs inc; el pnts (10A) inc; Indtte; supmkt 300m; tradsmn; rest; snacks; bar; BBQ; playgrnd; htd pool; fishing; tennis; games area; horseriding 1.5km; entmnt; internet; TV/games rm; 45% statics; dogs €0.80; adv bkg ess; rd noise; ccard acc; red low ssn; CCI. "Wonderful scenery; various pitch sizes/shapes; excel san facs; helpful staff; La Marmotte cycle race (early Jul) & Tour de France usually pass thro area & access poss restricted; excel rest; organised walks; pitches poss flooded after heavy rain, but staff excel at responding; mkt Sat; highly rec." ♦ 1 May-30 Sep. € 31.65 (CChq acc) ABS - M01 2009*

BOURG D'OISANS, LE *9C3* (1.5km NE Rural) *45.06401, 6.03895* **Camping La Cascade, Route de l'Alpe d'Huez, 38520 Le Bourg-d'Oisans [04 76 80 02 42; fax 04 76 80 22 63; lacascade@wanadoo.fr; www.lacascadesarenne.com]** Fr W drive thro Le Bourg-d'Oisans & cross bdge over Rv Romanche. Approx 800m E of town turn onto D211, sp Alpe-d'Huez. Site on R in 600m. Med, mkd pitch, pt shd; htd wc; chem disp; baby facs; shwrs; el pnts (16A) €4.30; Indtte; supmkt 1km; snacks; bar high ssn; playgrnd; htd pool high ssn; some statics; dogs free; poss cr; Eng spkn; adv bkg; quiet; ccard acc; CCI. "Friendly site; discounts for ski passes fr recep." 15 Dec-30 Sep. € 25.00 2008*

⊞ **BOURG D'OISANS, LE** *9C3* (1.5km NE Rural) *45.06357, 6.03772* **Camping La Piscine, Route de l'Alpe d'Huez, 38520 Le Bourg-d'Oisans [04 76 80 02 41; fax 04 76 11 01 26; infos@camping-piscine.com; www.camping-piscine.com]** Fr D1091 (N91) approx 800m E of town, take D211 sp Alpe d'Huez. After 1km turn L into site. Fountains at ent. Med, mkd pitch, pt shd; htd wc (some cont); chem disp; shwrs inc; el pnts (16A) €3.50; Indtte; shops 1.5km; tradsmn; snacks; bar; BBQ; playgrnd; htd pool (summer); paddling pool; rv adj; tennis 2km; entmnt; TV; 10% statics; dogs €1; phone; poss cr; Eng spkn; adv bkg; quiet but with some rd noise; 10% red 7+ days/low ssn; ccard acc; CCI. "Excel site; excel lge pool; conv town cent; facs stretched high ssn & when La Marmotte cycle race (early Jul) & Tour de France in area; ski slopes 10-18km." ♦ € 21.00 2007*

BOURG D'OISANS, LE *9C3* (500m SE Rural) *45.05258, 6.03561* **Camping Le Colporteur, Le Mas du Plan, 38520 Le Bourg-d'Oisans [04 76 79 11 44 or 06 85 73 29 19 (mob); fax 04 76 79 11 49; info@camping-colporteur.com; www.camping-colporteur.com]** W fr Briançon on D1019 (N91) to Le Bourg-d'Oisans. Ent town, pass Casino supmkt, site sp on L; 150m to sw pool - 2nd site sp, site 50m - sp on side of house. Fr Grenoble on A480 exit 8 onto N85, cont on D1019 (N91) to Le Bourg-d'Oisans. Foll sp R in cent of town. Med, hdg/mkd pitch, hdstg, shd; htd wc; chem disp; baby facs; shwrs inc; el pnts (6-15A) €4.20; Indtte; shops 500m; tradsmn; rest; snacks; bar; BBQ; playgrnd; htd pool 150m; waterslide; lake sw 10km; fishing; tennis; squash; mountain bikes; rockclimbing; horseriding; cycle hire 200m; entmnt; games rm; wifi; TV; 10% statics; dogs €1.70; Eng spkn; adv bkg; quiet; red long stay/low ssn; ccard acc; CCI. "Site to v high standard; well-organised; lge pitches; gd security; mountain scenery; many activities; conv National Park des Ecrins." ♦ 15 May-19 Sep. € 25.00 2009*

See advertisement

BOURG D'OISANS, LE *9C3* (13km SE Rural) *44.98611, 6.12027* **Camping Le Champ du Moulin, Bourg d'Arud, 38520 Vénosc [04 76 80 07 38; fax 04 76 80 24 44; info@champ-du-moulin.com; www.champ-du-moulin.com]** On D1091 (N91) SE fr Le Bourg-d'Oisans sp Briançon for about 6km; turn R onto D530 twd La Bérarde & after 8km site sp. Turn R to site 350m after cable car stn beside Rv Vénéon. NB Site sp bef vill; do not cross rv on D530. Med, mkd pitch, pt shd; wc; chem disp; baby facs; shwrs inc; el pnts (10A) inc (extra charge in winter; poss rev pol); gas; Indtte: tradsmn; rest; snacks; bar; BBQ; playgrnd nr; htd pool adj; fishing, tennis, rafting, horseriding, archery nr; wifi; games/TV rm; 20% statics; dogs €1.50; poss cr; Eng spkn; adv bkg ess; quiet; ccard acc; red long stay/low ssn; CCI. "Lovely, well-run site by alpine torrent (unguarded); friendly, helpful owners; ltd facs low ssn; ideal walking & climbing; cable car to Les Deux Alpes adj (closes end Aug); mkt Tue Vénosc (high ssn); highly rec." ♦ 15 Dec-24 Apr & 1 Jun-15 Sep. € 24.70 ABS - M03 2009*

BOURG D'OISANS, LE *9C3* (4km NW Rural) *45.09000, 6.00750* **Camping Ferme Noémie, Chemin Pierre Polycarpe, Les Sables, 38520 Le Bourg-d'Oisans [tel/fax 04 76 11 06 14 or 06 87 45 08 75 (mob); fermenoemie@aliceadsl.fr; www.fermenoemie.com]** On D1091 (N91) Grenoble to Briançon; Les Sables is 4km bef Le Bourg-d'Oisans; turn L next to church, site in 400m. Sm, mkd pitch, unshd; htd wc; chem disp; mv service pnt; shwrs inc; el pnts (16A) €2.50; Indtte; tradsmn; shop, rest, snacks & bar 3km; BBQ (gas communal); playgrnd; rock climbing; skiing; cycling; walking; fishing; pool 3km; games area; internet; 25% statics; dogs free; phone; bus 500m; poss cr; adv bkg; quiet; red long stay; ccard acc; CCI. "Simple site in superb location with excel facs; helpful British owners; lots of sports; gd touring base lakes & Ecrins National Park." ♦ May-Oct. € 15.00 2009*

BOURG D'OISANS, LE *9C3* (7km NW Rural) *45.11388, 6.00785* **Camping Belledonne, Rochetaillée, 38520 Le Bourg-d'Oisans [04 76 80 07 18; fax 04 76 79 12 95; info@rcn-belledonne.fr; www.rcn-campings.fr/belledonne/fr]** Fr S of Grenoble take N85 to Vizille then D1091 (N91) twd Le Bourg-d'Oisans; in approx 25km in Rochetaillée turn L onto D526 sp Allemont. Site 100m on R. Med, hdg pitch, shd; wc (some cont); chem disp; sauna; baby facs; sauna; shwrs inc; el pnts (6A) inc; gas; Indtte; shop; rest; snacks; bar; BBQ; playgrnd; 2 htd pools & paddling pool; tennis; horseriding, fishing 500m; rafting, climbing, paragliding; entmnt; wifi; games/TV rm; dogs €6; Eng spkn; quiet; ccard acc; red low ssn; CCI. "Access to most pitches v tight; no twin-axles; san facs dated; La Marmotte cycle race (early Jul) & Tour de France usually pass thro area & access poss restricted; gd for families with teenagers; walks; mkt Sat." ♦ 24 Apr-25 Sep. € 39.50 (CChq acc) ABS - M02 2009*

BOURG D'OISANS, LE *9C3* (7km NW Rural) *45.11595, 6.00591* **Camping Le Château de Rochetaillée, Chemin de Bouthéon, 38520 Rochetaillée [04 76 11 04 40; fax 04 76 80 21 23; jcp@camping-le-chateau.com; www.camping-le-chateau.com or www.les-castels.com]** On D1091 (N91) fr Grenoble turn 7km bef Le Bourg-d'Oisans onto D526 sp Allemont. Site is 50m on L. Med, pt shd; wc; chem disp; baby facs; shwrs inc; el pnts (6A) inc; Indtte; shop; rest; snacks; bar; BBQ; playgrnd; sports area; pool; dogs €0.80; 5% statics; quiet; red low ssn; CCI. "Vg; san facs clean & modern; helpful staff; mountain views." ♦ 13 May-13 Sep. € 31.00 2009*

⊞ **BOURG D'OISANS, LE** *9C3* (7km NW Rural) *45.12579, 6.03586* **Camping Le Grand Calme, Le Plan, 38114 Allemont/Allemond [04 76 80 70 03; fax 04 76 80 73 13; hotel-ginies@wanadoo.fr; www.hotel-ginies.com]** Fr Grenoble on D1091 (N91), at Rochetailée turn L (N) on D526 to Allemont. Site on R in 1.5km opp Hotel Ginies. Med, pt shd; pt htd wc; chem disp; shwrs €1; el pnts (10A) €3.20; Indtte; shops 500m; tradsmn; rest; bar; playgrnd; 10% statics; dogs €0.50; phone nr; poss cr; Eng spkn; adv bkg; quiet; ccard acc; CCI. "Vg, well-maintained site run by hotel opp (gd rest); call at hotel recep if site recep clsd; phone ahead to check site open low ssn; beautiful, scenic area gd for skiers & walkers." ♦ € 12.00 2007*

France

BOURG D'OISANS, LE *9C3* (7km NW Rural) *45.12075, 6.01326* **Camping Les Bouleaux, La Pernière Basse, 38114 Allemont/Allemond [04 76 80 71 23 or 06 87 56 17 48 (mob); fax 04 76 80 70 75; philippe.vincent27@wanadoo.fr]** Take D1091 (N91) fr Bourg-d'Oisans, then turn onto D526 dir Allemont/Allemond. After x-ing 1st bdge, turn immed L at x-rds over another bdge, site on R, well sp. Recep up narr lane beside stream. Sm, pt shd; wc; chem disp; shwrs inc; el pnts inc; tradsmn; pool 2km; dogs; poss cr; Eng spkn; quiet; red 7+ days & low ssn; CCI. "Vg sheltered, peaceful, much improved, delightful farm site; helpful owners." ♦ 15 Jun-15 Sep. 2008*

BOURG D'OISANS, LE *9C3* (8km NW Rural) *45.12914, 6.04130* **Camp Municipal Le Plan, 38114 Allemont/Allemond [04 76 80 76 88 or 04 76 80 70 30 (Mairie); fax 04 76 79 80 28; info@camping-leplan-allemont.com; www.camping-leplan-allemont.com]** At Rochetaillée on D1091 (N91) fr Grenoble turn N 7km bef Le Bourg-d'Oisans on D526 sp Allemont site on R at N end of vill below dam. Med, mkd pitch, hdstg; pt shd; htd wc; chem disp; shwrs inc; el pnts (16A) €2; Indtte; snacks; shops in vill; pool adj high ssn only; no statics; dogs €0.50; adv bkg; quiet; ccard acc high ssn; CCI. "In quiet vill with lovely mountain scenery; excel, clean facs; helpful staff." ♦ 1 May-30 Sep. € 9.70 2008*

BOURG DUN, LE see Veules les Roses *3C2*

BOURG EN BRESSE *9A2* (1km NE Urban) *46.20943, 5.24013* **FFCC Camp Municipal de Challes, Ave de Bad Kreuznach, 01000 Bourg-en-Bresse [04 74 45 37 21; fax 04 74 22 40 32; camping-municipal-bourgenbresse@wanadoo.fr; www.bourg-en-bresse.org]** Fr N or S ON N83 foll sp Camping/Piscine/Stade. Site opp stadium. Med, hdstg, shd; wc (most cont); chem disp; shwrs inc; el pnts (6A) €2.30 (poss rev pol); Indry rm; hypermkt nr; snacks; rest; BBQ; htd, covrd pool & sports ground adj; lake sw 2km; 10% statics; bus adj; poss cr; adv bkg; some rd noise; red long stay; ccard acc; 10% red CCI. "Suitable lge o'fits; site poss full by 1800; gd shwr block; gd touring base; daytime noise fr stadium; poss itinerants; mkt Wed; vg." 1 Apr-15 Oct. € 13.20 2009*

BOURG EN BRESSE *9A2* (11km NE Rural) *46.29078, 5.29078* **Camp Municipal du Sevron, Chemin du Moulin, 01370 St Etienne-du-Bois [04 74 30 50 65 or 04 74 30 50 36 (Mairie); fax 04 74 25 85 72; st-etienne-du-bois-01@wanadoo.fr; www.st-etienne-du-bois.fr]** On D1083 (N83) at S end of vill of St Etienne-du-Bois on E side of rd. Sm, hdg pitch, shd; wc; chem disp; shwrs inc; el pnts (10A) €2.05; shops 300m; tennis; rv fishing; dogs €1.06; Eng spkn; ccard not acc. "Gd NH; clean facs; friendly; sm pitches; late arrivals get v sm pitches; poss rd & rlwy noise; gd shwrs & plenty hot water." 1 Mar-25 Oct. € 9.90 2008*

BOURG EN BRESSE *9A2* (13km SE) *46.14705, 5.33159* **Camp Municipal de Journans, Rue de Boisserolles/Montée de Lachat, 01250 Journans [04 74 42 64 71 or 04 74 51 64 45; fax 04 74 42 64 83; mairiejournans@wandadoo.fr]** Exit A40 junc 7, turn L onto D1075 (N75), then L onto D64 dir Tossiat & Journans. Or SE fr Bourg-en-Bresse on D1075 (N75) for 9.5km E onto D64 to Journans. Site sp on D52 Sm, mkd pitch, sl terr, pt shd; wc (some cont); shwrs inc; el pnts (5-10A) €2.60; shops 1km (Tossiat); dog €1; poss cr; quiet; CCI. "Pleasant setting; helpful warden calls pm; some pitches diff for c'vans; gd views; excel value; v quiet low ssn; poss mkt traders." 1 May-15 Sep. € 7.00 2009*

BOURG EN BRESSE *9A2* (20km SE Rural) *46.12775, 5.4282* **Camping de l'Ile Chambod, Route du Port, 01250 Hautecourt-Romanèche [04 74 37 25 41; fax 04 74 37 28 28; camping.chambod@free.fr; http://camping.chambod.free.fr]** Fr S exit A42 junc 9 onto D1075 (N75) dir Geneva. In 1km turn L onto N84 dir Nantua. At Poncin turn L at traff lts dir Ile Chambod & site. Fr N turn S off D979 in Hautecourt at x-rds (site sp). Site sp in 4km off D59. At rvside cont for 500m. Med, mkd pitch; pt shd; wc; mv service pnt; baby facs; shwrs inc; el pnts (5-10A) €2.80-3.80 (poss rev pol); gas; Indtte; shop; snacks; BBQ; playgrnd; pool; lake 100m; fishing/boat hire 400m; cycle hire; games area; games rm; entmnt; internet; 10% statics; dogs €1.10; poss cr; Eng spkn; adv bkg; quiet; ccard acc; red low ssn. "Lovely, picturesque, remote site; superb san facs; helpful manager; gd for families; 2 nights min w/end; conv Geneva; highly rec." ♦ 1 Apr-27 Sep. € 15.70 2009*

BOURG EN BRESSE *9A2* (15km SW Rural) *46.08655, 5.15192* **Camping Etang du Moulin, Etang du Moulin, 01240 St Paul-de-Varax [04 74 42 53 30; fax 04 74 42 51 57; moulin@campingendombes.fr; www.camping-etang-du-moulin.fr]** Fr N on D1083 (N83) fr Bourg-en-Bresse turn L into St Paul-de-Varax under narr rlwy bdge, thro vill on D70B twd St Nizier-le-Désert. In 2km turn L into lane with 45km/h speed limit, site on R in 2km. Lge, hdg/mkd pitch, pt shd; htd wc (some cont); mv service pnt; baby facs; shwrs inc; el pnts (6A) inc; Indtte; shops; tradsmn; rest; snacks; bar; BBQ; playgrnd; pool; paddling pool; waterslide; shgl beach on lake; fishing; watersports; tennis; archery; TV rm; 10% statics; dogs €2.40; quiet low ssn; ccard acc; red long stay/CCI. "Many sports & activities; huge pool & waterslides; gd for children; gd security; excel for birdwatching."
1 May-31 Aug. € 20.00 2008*

⊞ **BOURG ET COMIN** *3D4* (500m NE Rural) *49.39871, 3.66072* **Camping de la Pointe, 5 Rue de Moulins, 02160 Bourg-et-Comin [03 23 25 87 52; fax 03 23 25 06 02; michel.pennec@9online.fr; www.tourisme-paysdelaon.com]** Leave A26/E17 at junc 14 & turn W along D925 dir Soissons for 15km. Site on R on ent vill. Sm, hdg pitch, pt shd; htd wc; shwrs inc; el pnts (6A) €3; Indtte; baker 500m; tradsmn; crêperie adj; rest; bar 500m; BBQ; playgrnd; htd, covrd pool; dogs €2; phone; bus 500m; adv bkg; quiet; CCI. "CL-type site in orchard; narr ent & acces to pitches poss diff lge o'fits; most pitches not suitable lge o'fits; san facs poss stretched; excel rest; gd walking area; 10 mins fr Parc Nautique de l'Ailette with watersports; conv Aisne Valley; gd touring base." € 12.00 2008*

⊞ **BOURG MADAME** *8H4* (200m N Urban) *42.43531, 1.94469* **Camping Le Sègre, 8 Ave Emmanuel Brousse, 66760 Bourg-Madame [04 68 04 65 87; fax 04 68 04 91 82; camping.lesegre@free.fr]** N on N20 site on R immed under rlwy bdge. Med, pt shd; wc; shwrs inc; el pnts (3-6A) €2.25; Indtte; shops adj; playgrnd; sports cent nr; poss cr; some rd & rlwy noise. "V ltd touring pitches in winter, rec arr early." ♦ € 11.50 2006*

⊞ **BOURG MADAME** *8H4* (1km N Rural) *42.43878, 1.94391* **Camping Mas Piques, Rue du Train Jaune, 66760 Bourg-Madame [04 68 04 62 11; fax 04 68 04 68 36; campiques@wanadoo.fr; www.campingmaspiques.fr]** Last camp site in France bef Spain & Cadí Tunnel. App via N20 or N116. Med, pt shd; htd wc; chem disp; baby facs; shwrs inc; el pnts (6A) inc; shop 500m; Indtte; playgrnd; 95% statics; dogs €1.50; poss v cr; adv bkg ess high ssn. "Vg; organised rambling; popular with w/end skiers in winter; can walk to Puigcerda in Spain; gd san facs & el pnts." ♦
€ 18.90 2008*

⊞ **BOURG MADAME** *8H4* (5km NE Rural) *42.46902, 1.99870* **Camping L'Enclave, 66800 Estavar [04 68 04 72 27; fax 04 68 04 07 15; contact@camping-lenclave.com; www.camping.lenclave.com]** Leave Saillagouse on D33 sp Estavar vill. Lge, pt sl, terr, pt shd; htd wc; chem disp; mv service pnt; baby facs; shwrs inc; el pnts (3A) inc; gas; Indtte; shop, rest adj; snacks; bar; playgrnd; htd, covrd pool; tennis; cycle hire; entmnt; dogs €1.52; site clsd Oct; adv bkg; quiet; red low ssn; CCI. "Nr ski resorts & Spanish border, friendly."
♦ € 26.00 2008*

⊞ **BOURG MADAME** *8H4* (7km NE Rural) *42.43983, 2.03193* **Camping Las Closas, 1 Place St Genis, 66800 Err [04 68 04 71 42; fax 04 68 04 07 20; camping.las.closas@wanadoo.fr; www.camping-las-closas.com]** On N116 fr Bourg-Madame immediate after vill of Err take D33A on R. Site well sp. Med, pt sl, unshd; htd wc; shwrs; el pnts (3-10A) €3.70-6.80; gas; Indtte; shop; BBQ; playgrnd; entmnt; dogs €1.30; adv bkg; quiet; red low ssn. € 12.00
2007*

⊞ **BOURG MADAME** *8H4* (6km NW Rural) *42.45979, 1.91075* **Camping Le Robinson, Ave Gare Internationale, 66760 Enveitg [tel/fax 04 68 04 80 38; www.robinson-cerdagne.com]** Fr Bourg-Madame, take N20 N twd Foix. Thro vill of Enveitg & turn L down Chemin de la Gare & L at camping sp. Lge, mkd pitch, pt sl, shd; wc; chem disp; baby facs; shwrs inc; el pnts (4-13A) €3-9; gas; Indtte; shops adj; tradsmn; rest adj; snacks; BBQ; playgrnd; pool; games rm; entmnt; TV rm; some statics; dogs €1.50; phone; adv bkg; quiet. "Beautiful setting; winter sports cent; conv Barcelona, Andorra; conv scenic rte train (Train Jaune)." ♦
€ 16.00 2006*

BOURG ST ANDEOL *9D2* (1.5km N Rural) *44.38131, 4.64840* **Camping Le Lion, Chemin du Chenevrier, 07700 Bourg-St Andéol [tel/fax 04 75 54 53 20; contact@campingdulion; www.campingdulion.com]** Exit A7 at junc 18 or 19 onto N7. At Pierrelatte turn W on D59 to Bourg-St Andéol. Site sp fr cent town dir Viviers. Med, mkd pitch, shd; wc; shwrs inc; el pnts (6A) €3; Indtte; shop; snacks; bar; playgrnd; pool; games area; games rm; dir access to rv; some statics; dogs €1.70; poss cr; adv bkg; quiet; red low ssn. "Peaceful site in woodland setting; modern san facs; highly rec."
1 Apr-15 Sep. € 20.00 2008*

⊞ **BOURG ST MAURICE** *9B4* (2km NE Rural) *45.62578, 6.79386* **FFCC Camp Municipal Le Reclus, Pont du Reclus, 73700 Séez [04 79 41 01 05; fax 04 79 40 18 54; campinglereclus@wanadoo.fr; www.campinglereclus.com]** Site on R of D1090 (N90) bet Bourg-St Maurice & St Bernard Pass, bef vill of Séez. Med, terr, pt sl, shd; htd wc; chem disp; shwrs inc; el pnts (4-10A) €4-4.70; Indtte; shops 300m; tradsmn; BBQ; playgrnd; pool 350m; wifi; dog €1; quiet; CCI. "Busy site high ssn, rec arr bef midday; helpful warden; diff exit fr site due slope up to rd & bend." ♦ € 12.40
2008*

BOURG ST MAURICE *9B4* (1km E Rural) *45.62241, 6.78503* **Camping Le Versoyen, Route des Arcs, 73700 Bourg-St Maurice [04 79 07 03 45; fax 04 79 07 25 41; leversoyen@wanadoo.fr; www.leversoyen.com]** Fr SW on N90 thro town turn R to Les Arcs. Site on R in 1km. Do not app fr any other dir. Lge, hdstg, pt shd; wc; chem disp; mv service pnt; sauna; shwrs inc; el pnts (4-10A) €4.60-5.20; Indtte; shops 200m; playgrnd; 2 pools adj; tennis adj; games area; entmnt; fishing, canoeing; dogs €1; Eng spkn; quiet; red low ssn; red CCI. "Excel for touring mountains & winter sports; mountain views; mkd walks fr site; rvside walk to town; well-organised site; dated but clean facs; ."
♦ 13 Dec-2 May & 25 May-5 Nov. € 13.90 2007*

BOURG ST MAURICE *9B4* (8km S Rural) *45.53100, 6.77530* **Camping Les Lanchettes, 73210 Peisey-Nancroix [04 79 07 93 07; fax 04 79 07 88 33; lanchettes@free.fr; www.camping-lanchettes.com]** Fr Moûtiers foll N90 NE twds Bourg-St Maurice. In 20km turn R sp Landry & Peisey-Nancroix. Up v steep rd with hairpin bends for 6km. Site 1km beyond Nancroix. Long steep ascent with many hairpin bends, not rec for closely rated o'fits. Med, pt sl, terr, pt shd; htd wc; chem disp; mv service pnt; shwrs inc; el pnts (3-10A) €3-7.30; gas adj; lndtte; shop 200m (summer); rest; snacks; bar; playgrnd; tennis 100m; ski cent in winter; TVrm; some statics; dogs €1.20; adv bkg; CCI. "Lovely setting in National Park; superb location for outdoor pursuits; excel walking." ♦ 17 Dec-30 Sep. € 13.10 (CChq acc) 2006*

BOURG SUR GIRONDE *7C2* (Urban) *45.03880, -0.56065* **Camp Municipal La Citadelle, 33710 Bourg-sur-Gironde [05 56 68 40 06; fax 05 57 68 39 84; commune-de-bourg@wanadoo.fr]** Take D669 fr St André-de-Cubzac (off A10) to Bourg. Foll sp Halte Nautique & Le Port into Rue Franklin on L twd town cent & foll sp to site. Or fr Blaye, foll Camping sp on app Bourg, cont round by-pass to other end of town to Rue Franklin. NB Do not attempt to take c'van thro town. Sm, mkd pitch, pt shd; wc; chem disp; mv service pnt; shwrs inc; el pnts (3-10A) €3-6 (poss long lead req); shops in town; BBQ; pool, playgrnd adj; dogs; no statics; adv bkg; quiet; CCI. "Scenic, CL-type rvside site; well-maintained but basic facs; poss variable opening dates; excel." ♦ 15 May-30 Sep. € 7.00 2008*

BOURGES *4H3* (1km S Urban) *47.07246, 2.39480* **Camp Municipal Robinson, 26 Blvd de l'Industrie, 18000 Bourges [02 48 20 16 85; fax 02 48 50 32 39; www.ville-bourges.fr]** Exit A71/E11 at junc 7, foll sp Bourges Centre & bear R at 'Autres Directions' sp; foll site sp; site at traff lts on N side of S section of inner ring rd half-way bet junc with D2144 (N144) & D2076 (N76). NB: site access is via a loop - no L turn at traff lts, but rndabt just past site if turning missed. If on outer ring rd D400, app city on D2144 & then as above. Sp on app rds to site gd. Med, hdg/mkd pitch, hdstg, pt shd; htd wc; chem disp; some serviced pitches; shwrs inc; el pnts (6-10A) €3.20-4.70 (poss rev pol); gas 3km; lndtte; no BBQ; playgrnd; pool 300m inc; dogs; poss cr; Eng spkn; quiet; €25.50 extra twin-axle; ccard acc; red long stay; CCI. "Attractive, well-kept, busy, rvside site in gd location; friendly staff; gd facs for disabled; some v lge pitches, some sm & poss diff entry; most pitches hdstg; twin-axles extra; excel NH." ♦ 15 Mar-15 Nov. € 12.80 2009*

BOURGET DU LAC, LE see Aix Les Bains *9B3*

BOURGUEIL *4G1* (700m S Rural) *47.26991, 0.16873* **Parc Municipal Capitaine, 37140 Bourgueil [02 47 97 85 62 or 02 47 97 25 00 LS]** N on D749 fr junc 5 of A85, site 1km on R. Fr W (Longue) via D10 & by-pass, S at rndabt on D749 to site on L in 200m. Do not app fr N via D749 thro town cent. Med, hdg/mkd pitch, pt shd; wc; chem disp; mv service pnt; shwrs inc; el pnts (10A) €2.10; gas; lndtte; shops 1km; supmkt nrby; playgrnd; sw lake; dogs €1.22; quiet; CCI. "Gd san facs; ideal cent Loire châteaux & wine rtes; long lead poss req some pitches; 2 sites - one on R for tourers." ♦ 15 May-15 Sep. € 10.00 2009*

BOURNEL see Villereal *7D3*

BOURNEZEAU *2H4* (500m N Rural) **Camp Municipal Les Humeaux, Rue de la Gare, 85480 Bournezeau [02 51 40 01 31 or 02 51 40 71 29 (Mairie); fax 02 51 40 79 30; mairie@bournezeau.fr; www.bournezeau.fr]** Exit A83 junc 6 to Bournezeau cent. Take D7 sp St Martin-des-Noyers. Site on R in 500m, well sp. Sm, mkd pitch, pt shd; wc; chem disp; mv service pnt; shwrs; el pnts (6A) €2.90; lndtte; shop, rest, snacks, bar 500m; playgrnd; dogs €1; adv bkg; quiet. "Vg, conv NH; gd facs; easy walk to town." 1 Jun-15 Sep. € 8.60 2008*

BOUSSAC *7A4* (2km NE Rural) *46.37192, 2.20036* **Camping Le Château de Poinsouze, Route de la Châtre, 23600 Boussac-Bourg [05 55 65 02 21; fax 05 55 65 86 49; info.camping-de.poinsouze@orange.fr; www.camping-de-poinsouze.com or www.les-castels.com]** Fr junc 10 on A71/E11 by-pass Montluçon via N145 dir Guéret; in 22km turn L onto D917 to Boussac; cont on D917 dir La Châtre; site 3km on L. Or fr Guéret on N145, exit Gouzon, at rndabt take D997 to Boussac, then as above. Med, mkd pitch, sl, unshd; wc; chem disp; mv service pnt; serviced pitch; baby facs; shwrs inc; el pnts (10A) inc (poss rev pol); lndtte; shop & 3km; tradsmn; rest; snacks; bar; BBQ; playgrnd; pool; paddling pool; waterslide; course-fishing lake; boating; horseriding; golf 20km; cycle hire; entmnt; internet; games/TV rm; 10% statics; dogs €3 (not 11/7-14/8); Eng spkn; adv bkg ess high ssn & booking fee; quiet; ccard acc; red low ssn; CCI. "Super, well-run, peaceful site by lakeside; lge pitches, some sl; relaxed atmosphere; welcoming, helpful owners; superb san facs; excel rest & snacks." ♦ 12 May-11 Sep. € 33.00 (CChq acc) ABS - L16 2009*

BOUSSAC *7A4* (3km W Rural) *46.34938, 2.18662* **Camping Creuse-Nature (Naturist), Route de Bétête, 23600 Boussac [05 55 65 18 01; fax 05 55 65 81 40; creuse-nature@wanadoo.fr; www.creuse-nature.com]** Fr Boussac take D917 N twd La Châtre. In 500m turn L (W) on D15 sp Bétête. Site on R in 2.5km, clearly sp. Med, hdg/mkd pitch, pt sl, pt shd; wc; shwrs; el pnts (10A) €4.50; lndtte; sm shop; rest; snacks; bar; playgrnd; 2 htd pools (1 covrd); paddling pool; fishing; games area; entmnt; some statics; dogs €5.50; Eng spkn; adv bkg; v quiet; ccard acc; red low ssn; INF card req. "Excel site in lovely area; great pitches; charming & helpful owners; clean facs; poss insect prob; interesting château in town." ♦ 11 Apr-31 Oct. € 24.00 2009*

BOUZIGUES see Meze *10F1*

BOUZONVILLE AUX BOIS see Pithiviers *4F3*

BRACH *7C1* (SW Rural) *45.04069, -0.94283* **Aire Naturelle Le Bois de Geai (Douat), 16 Route de Lacanau, 33480 Brach [05 56 58 70 54]** N on D1 fr Bordeaux. At Castelnau-de-Médoc cent turn L onto D207. After 11km in vill of Brach fork L. Sm, pt shd; own san; shwrs; el pnts (6A) €2; gas; lndtte; shop; tradsmn; playgrnd; fishing, sailing & beaches nr; some statics; dogs €2; adv bkg; CCI. "Peaceful site; poss v cr with pickers at grape harvest time." 1 May-31 Oct. € 11.50 2007*

France

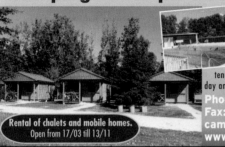

BRACIEUX *4G2* (500m N Urban) *47.55060, 1.53743* **Camp Municipal des Châteaux, 11 Rue Roger Brun, 41250 Bracieux [02 54 46 41 84; fax 02 54 46 41 21; campingdebracieux@wanadoo.fr; www.campingdeschateaux.com]** Fr S take D102 to Bracieux fr Cour-Cheverny. Fr N exit Blois on D765 dir Romorantin; after 5km take D923 to Bracieux & site on R on N o'skts of town opp church, sp. Lge, pt hdg/mkd pitch, hdstg, pt shd; wc (some cont); chem disp; shwrs inc; el pnts (3A) €2.70 (poss long lead req); gas 300m; Indtte; shop 300m; supmkt 1km; tradsmn high ssn; rest, snacks 300m; playgrnd; htd pool high ssn; tennis; cycle hire & tracks; games rm; TV; 10% statics; dogs €2.80; Eng spkn; adv bkg; quiet; ccard acc; red long stay/low ssn; CCI. "Peaceful spot; attractive forest area; busy high ssn; excel disabled facs; gd security; gd touring base; excel." ♦ 27 Mar-29 Nov. € 16.00
2009*

See advertisement

BRAIN SUR L'AUTHION see Angers *4G1*

BRAIZE see Urcay *4H3*

BRAMANS LE VERNEY see Modane *9C4*

BRANTOME *7C3* (1km E Rural) *45.36074, 0.66035* **Camping Peyrelevade, Ave André Maurois, 24310 Brantôme [05 53 05 75 24; fax 05 53 05 87 30; info@camping-dordogne.net; http://www.camping-dordogne.net]** Fr N on D675 foll sp Centre Ville; ent vill & turn L onto D78 Thiviers rd, site sp at turn; in 1km on R past stadium adj g'ge. Fr S D939 foll sp 'Centre Ville' fr rndabt N of town. Then L onto D78 Thiviers rd & foll sp. Do not foll 'Centre Ville' sp fr rndabt S of town, use by-pass. Lge, hdg/mkd pitch, pt shd; wc; chem disp; mv service pnt; baby facs; shwrs inc; el pnts (10A) inc (poss long lead req); Indtte; shop 1km; tradsmn; snacks & bar high ssn; BBQ; playgrnd; htd pool; paddling pool; rv sw; tennis nr; games area adj; entmnt; wifi; 3% statics; dogs €2 (2 max); no twin-axles; Eng spkn; adv bkg; quiet; ccard acc; red low ssn/CCI. "Well laid-out, spacious rvside site; beautiful countryside; lge pitches; friendly, helpful owners; grnd poss soft after heavy rain; sh walk to pleasant town; excel." ♦ 5 May-31 Oct. € 18.00
2009*

BRANTOME *7C3* (4km SW Rural) *45.32931, 0.63690* **Camping du Bas Meygnaud, 24310 Valeuil [05 53 05 58 44; camping-du-bas-meygnaud@wanadoo.fr; www.basmeygnaud.fr]** Fr Brantôme, take D939 S twd Périgueux; in 4.5km turn R at sp La Serre. In 1km turn L to in 500m, well sp. Winding, narr app thro lanes; poss diff lge o'fits. Sm, pt sl, pt shd; wc; chem disp; shwrs inc; el pnts (6A) €3; gas 4km; Indtte; shop; tradsmn; rest 4km; snacks; bar; BBQ; playgrnd; pool; entmnt; dogs €2; phone; Eng spkn; quiet, entmnt poss noisy some eves; CCI. "Most pitches shaded by pine trees; helpful & friendly owner; dated san facs; unspoilt countryside." 1 Apr-30 Sep. € 15.00
2009*

BRASSAC *8F4* (11km SE Rural) *43.59700, 2.60732* **Camping Le Rouquié, Lac de la Raviège, 81260 Lamontélarie [05 63 70 98 06; fax 05 63 50 49 58; camping.rouquie@wanadoo.fr; www.campingrouquie.fr]** Fr Brassac take D62 to N side of Lac de la Raviège; site on lakeside. Med, mkd pitch, terr, pt shd; wc; baby facs; shwrs; el pnts (3-6A) €4; Indtte; shop; tradsmn; snacks; bar; playgrnd; lake sw; fishing; sailing & watersports adj; games area; cycle hire; entmnt; TV; poss cr; quiet; CCI. "Ltd facs low ssn; gd lake views." 15 Apr-31 Oct. € 11.20 2007*

BRASSAC *8F4* (5km S Rural) *43.60835, 2.47148* **FFCC Camping Le Plô, Le Bourg, 81260 Le Bez [tel/fax 05 63 74 00 82; info@leplo.com; www.leplo.com]** Fr Castres on D622 to Brassac; then D53 S to Le Bez, site sp W of Le Bez. Med; pt shd; wc; chem disp; shwrs inc; el pnts (4A) €2.30; Indry rm; playgrnd; pool; cycle hire; games area; trampoline; games rm; dogs €1.40; Eng spkn; red low ssn. "Lovely location; excel, clean san facs; friendly, helpful Dutch owners; beautiful, historical area with National Park; much wildlife; cafés & gd rest nrby; vg." 20 May-30 Sep. € 13.00 2008*

BRASSAC *8F4* (500m W Urban) *43.63101, 2.49194* **Camp Municipal La Lande, Ave de Sidobre, 81260 Brassac [tel/fax 05 63 74 00 82; lalande@sidobretouristique.com]** Fr Castres on D622, turn sharp L just bef rv bdge in Brassac. Sm, pt shd; wc; shwrs inc; el pnts inc; Indtte; shops, rest, bar 500m; BBQ; playgrnd; rv fishing; dogs €1.40; quiet; CCI. "Pleasant site; gd facs, poss unclean early ssn (2009); access poss diff lge o'fits due parked cars & other traffic." ♦ 1 May-30 Sep. € 10.10 2007*

⊞ **BRAUCOURT** *6E1* (9km W Rural) *48.55754, 4.70629* **Camping Le Clos du Vieux Moulin, 33 Rue du Lac, 51290 Châtillon-sur-Broué [03 26 41 30 43; fax 03 26 72 75 13; eclosduvieuxmoulin@wanadoo.fr; www.leclosduvieuxmoulin.fr]** Fr N take D13 fr Vitry-le-François. Turn R at sp for Châtillion-sur-Broué; site 100m on R. Fr S 2nd L fr Giffaumont (1km); site 100m on R. Med, hdg/mkd pitch, hdstg, pt sl, pt shd; htd wc; chem disp; baby facs; shwrs inc; el pnts (5A) €3.70; gas; Indtte; shops; tradsmn; rest 400m; snacks; bar; playgrnd; pool; lake 400m; watersports; birdwatching; 50% statics; dogs; phone; quiet; ccard acc; red low ssn; CCI. "Peaceful, green site; gd san facs; paths for disabled; early ssn poss unkempt." ♦ € 16.00 2008*

BRAUCOURT *6E1* (3km NW Rural) *48.55425, 4.79235* **Camping Presqu'île de Champaubert, Lac du Der, 52290 Braucourt [03 25 04 13 20; fax 03 25 94 33 51; camping-de-braucourt@wanadoo.fr; www.lacduder.com]** Fr St Dizier take D384 SW twd Montier-en-Der & Troyes. In Braucourt R onto D153 sp Presq'ile de Champaubert, site on L in 2km. Site situated on Lac du Der-Chantecoq. Lge, hdg/mkd pitch, shd; wc (some cont); chem disp; mv service pnt; serviced pitch; shwrs inc; el pnts (10A) €4 (rev pol); gas; Indtte; basic shop; tradsmn; rest; snacks; bar; playgrnd; htd pool; lake sw & sand beach nrby; watersports, boating, fishing, bird-watching; TV; dogs €1; poss cr; quiet; 60% statics; dogs; phone; quiet; ccard acc; red low ssn; CCI. "Beautiful lge beach; lge pitches; improved san facs; gates clsd 2230." ♦ 1 Apr-30 Nov. € 22.00 2009*

BRAY DUNES see Dunkerque *3A3*

BRAY SUR SEINE *4E4* (200m E Rural) *48.41425, 3.24623* **Camping La Peupleraie, Rue des Pâtures, 77480 Bray-sur-Seine [01 60 67 12 24 or 06 83 93 33 89 (mob); camping.lapeupleraie@wanadoo.fr; www.lapeupleraie.com]** Exit A5 at junc 18 onto D41, in 20km turn N to Bray. Turn L bef bdge, foll rd down under bdge, cont on rvside to site. Foll 'complex sportif' & camping sp. Lge, hdg/mkd pitch, pt shd; wc (cont); shwrs inc; el pnts (6A); Indtte; supmkt adj; snacks; playgrnd; pool adj; boating; tennis; 80% statics; dogs; adv bkg; quiet. "Diff to exit bef 0900 when office opens; clean site; helpful warden; site adapted for handicapped." ♦ 1 Apr-31 Oct. € 14.40 2009*

BRECEY *2E4* (1km S Rural) *48.72110, -1.15199* **Camp Municipal Le Pont Roulland, 50370 Brécey [02 33 48 60 60; fax 02 33 89 21 09; mairie-brecey@wanadoo.fr]** Fr Villedieu-les-Poêles S on D999. In Brécey cent L by church on D911; after 1km turn S on D79 sp Les Cresnays. Site in 50m on L thro car park. Med, terr, pt sl, pt shd; wc; chem disp; shwrs; el pnts (16A) €2.50; (rev pol); shops 1km; tradsmn; Indtte; tennis; playgrnd; htd pool adj; dogs €0.50; adv bkg; quiet but noisy tractors at harvest time, inc at night; CCI. "Lovely, well-kept orchard site; excel, clean san facs; friendly staff; nr fishing lake; grnd soft after prolonged rain." 1 Jun-30 Sep. € 8.00 2008*

BREHAL *1D4* (4km N Coastal) *48.90863, -1.56473* **FFCC Camp Intercommunal de la Vanlée, 50290 Bréhal [02 33 61 63 80; fax 02 33 61 87 18; contact@camping-vanlee.com; www.camping-vanlee.com]** Turn W off D971 onto D20 thro Bréhal to coast, then N. Site sp, nr 'route submersible'. Lge, mkd pitch, pt sl, unshd; wc; chem disp; mv service pnt; baby facs; shwrs inc; el pnts (6A) €3.80; Indtte; shop high ssn; supmkt nr; rest; snacks; bar; playgrnd; pool; paddling pool; sand beach adj; games area; entmnt; TV rm; dogs €2.60; poss cr; Eng spkn; ccard acc; quiet; CCI. "Beware soft sand when pitching." ♦ 1 May-30 Sep. € 13.90 2009*

BREIL SUR ROYA *10E4* (500m N Urban) *43.94026, 7.51634* **Camp Municipal Azur et Merveilles, 06540 Breil-sur-Roya [04 93 62 47 04 or 04 93 04 99 76 (LS); fax 04 93 04 99 80; contact@camping-azur-merveilles.com; www.camping-azur-merveilles.com]** On D6204, 500m N of Breil-sur-Roya. Sp fr town & fr N. Med, hdg/mkd pitch, hdstg, pt shd; wc; chem disp; shwrs inc; el pnts €3; Indtte; shop & rest 500m; BBQ (communal); pool adj; kayaking; canoeing; 15% statics; dogs €2; train 300m (to Nice); ccard acc; CCI. "Site beside Rv Roya; gd canoeing etc; gd." 1 May-14 Sep. € 16.00 2008*

BRENGUES *7D4* (1.5km N Rural) *44.58683, 1.83738* **Camping Le Moulin Vieux, Route de Figeac, 46320 Brengues [05 65 40 00 41; fax 05 65 40 05 65; blasquez.a@wanadoo.fr; www.brengues.com]** Fr Figeac on D13, in 6km L onto D41. In approx 17km site well sp on L bef Brengues vill. Med, shd; wc; chem disp; shwrs inc; el pnts (10A) €2.60; Indtte; shop; snacks; bar; playgrnd; pool; entmnt; archery; some statics; adv bkg; some rd noise; ccard acc; red low ssn; CCI. "Beautiful site; helpful owners; facs stretched high ssn; poss scruffy/unkempt early ssn (2009); excel." ♦ 1 Apr-30 Sep. € 13.00 2009*

BRENGUES *7D4* (S Rural) *44.57550, 1.83334* **Camp Municipal de Brengues, 46320 Brengues [tel/fax 05 65 40 06 82 or 05 65 40 05 71 (Mairie)]** W fr Figeac on D13. After 6km turn L onto D41. After 17km, turn L at x-rds with D38, site ent 100m on R bef bdge over Rv Célé. Sm, mkd pitch, pt shd; wc; shwrs; el pnts (10A) €1.10 (rev pol); Indtte; shop 300m; rest; bar; playgrnd; tennis; CCI. "Warden visits." 15 Jun-30 Sep. € 9.85 2006*

BRENGUES *7D4* (8km SW Rural) *44.55571, 1.77079* **Camp Municipal Le Pré de Monsieur, 46160 Marcilhac-sur-Célé [tel/fax 05 65 40 77 88; lepredemonsieur@gmail.com; www.camping-marcilhac.com]** W fr Figeac on D802; L onto D41; site on L on ent Marcilhac. App fr E, site on R at far end of vill. Med, pt shd; wc; baby facs; fam bthrm; shwrs inc; el pnts €2.35; Indtte; shop 200m; rest; snacks; bar; BBQ; playgrnd; sm play pool; rv adj; fishing; canoeing; tennis; cycle hire; games area; games rm; wifi; TV; 2% statics; dogs €0.95; phone; Eng spkn; adv bkg; quiet; CCI. "Vg." ♦ 1 Apr-30 Sep. € 10.05 2008*

France

⊞ **BRESSE, LA** *6F3* (3.2km E Rural) *47.99895, 6.91770* **FFCC Camp Municipal Le Haut des Bluches, 5 Route des Planches, 88250 La Bresse [03 29 25 64 80; fax 03 29 25 78 03; hautdesbluches@labresse.fr; www.domainehautdesbluches.labresse.fr]** Leave La Bresse on D34 Rte de la Schlucht. Site on R in 3km. Med, mkd pitch, terr, pt shd; htd wc; chem disp; mv service pnt; child/baby facs; shwrs inc; el pnts (4-13A) €2-4.80; Indtte; shop; tradsmn; rest; snacks; takeaway; bar; BBQ; playgrnd; pool in vill; games area; games rm; internet; TV; 10% statics; dogs free; NH area for m'vans; site clsd Nov-mid Dec; Eng spkn; adv bkg; red low ssn; ccard acc; red low ssn/CCI. "Excel site in attractive setting; excel san facs; gd walks fr site; conv winter sports." ♦ € 12.80 2009*

BRESSUIRE *4H1* (1km S Rural) *46.82981, -0.50326* **Camping Le Puy Rond, Cornet, 79300 Bressuire [05 49 72 43 22 or 06 85 60 37 26 (mob); info@puyrondcamping.com; www.puyrondcamping.com]** Fr N149 foll site sp on rte 'Poids Lourds' to site on D38. Fr 'Centre Ville' foll sp for Fontenay-Le-Comte; turn R 100m after overhead bdge & go across junc to site. Well sp. Sm, mkd pitch, pt sl, pt terr, pt shd; htd wc; chem disp (wc); mv service pnt; baby facs; shwrs inc; el pnts (10A) €3.50; gas 1.50m; Indtte; shop & 1.5km; tradsmn; snacks; rest, bar 1.5km; BBQ; playgrnd; pool; fishing 1km; 15% statics; dogs €2; bus 2km; adv bkg; quiet; red low ssn/long stay; ccard acc; CCI. "Gd touring base; British owners; basic facs; adv bkg ess for twin-axles; winter storage avail." ♦ 1 Apr-30 Oct. € 16.50 2008*

BREST *2E2* (4km E Coastal) *48.39821, -4.39498* **Camp Municipal de Camfrout, 29480 Le Relecq-Kerhuon [02 98 28 37 84 or 02 98 28 14 18 (Mairie); fax 02 98 28 61 32; secretariat.mairie@mairie-relecq-kerhuon.fr; www.mairie-relecq-kerhuon.fr]** Fr Brest take N165 dir Quimper, at city o'skts becomes Relecq-Kerhuon. In 2km turn L onto D67, site on L opp foreshore. Fr S on N165/E60, cross Rv Elorn twd Brest & R onto D67. Med, hdg pitch, pt shd; wc; shwrs; el pnts (8A) €1.85; Indtte; shops 3km; playgrnd; sand beach adj; fishing; boating; dogs €1.40; quiet. "Ent open all day; many places of interest in area." ♦ 24 Jun-3 Sep. € 10.10 2007*

⊞ **BREST** *2E2* (6km W Coastal) *48.36544, -4.54163* **Camping du Goulet, Ste Anne-du-Porzic, 29200 Brest [tel/fax 02 98 45 86 84; campingdugoulet@wanadoo.fr; www.campingdugoulet.com]** On D789 turn L at site sp. Approx 4km fr Brest after R bend at T junc, turn L & L again at site sp; down hill to site. Med, pt sl, terr, unshd; htd wc; chem disp; shwrs inc; el pnts (6-10A) €2.50-3; Indtte; shop high ssn; snacks; playgrnd; pool complex; waterslides; sand beach 1km; 15% statics; dogs €1.30; adv bkg; quiet; CCI. ♦ € 15.00 2006*

⊞ **BRETENOUX** *7C4* (Urban) *44.91650, 1.83816* **Camping La Bourgnatelle, 46130 Bretenoux [05 65 10 89 04; fax 05 65 10 89 18; contact@dordogne_vacances.fr; www.dordogne-vacances.fr]** In town 100m fr D940. Lge, pt shd; wc; mv service pnt; shwrs inc; el pnts (5-10A) €3; Indtte; shops adj; rest; snacks; playgrnd; pool; rv & fishing; canoe hire; entmnt; dogs €1.50; adv bkg; quiet; red low ssn. "On banks of Rv Cère; clean site; gd fishing; lovely town." € 16.00 2009*

BRETENOUX *7C4* (4km W Rural) *44.91937, 1.80262* **Camping Les Chalets sur La Dordogne, Pont de Puybrun, 46130 Girac [05 65 10 93 33; contact@camping-leschalets.com; www.camping-leschalets.com]** Fr Bretenoux on D803 dir Puybrun. Site on L on rvside - sp on rd barrier easily missed. Sm, mkd pitch, shd; wc; chem disp; shwrs inc; el pnts (6A) inc; Indtte; shop; tradsmn; rest; snacks; bar; playgrnd; pool; rv & shgl beach adj; canoeing; TV rm; 20% statics; dogs €1.50; Eng spkn; quiet; ccard acc. "Gd, clean family site; helpful owners." ♦ 10 Apr-30 Sep. € 18.30 2009*

BRETIGNOLLES SUR MER *2H3* (2km N Coastal) *46.63024, -1.86048* **Camping Les Vagues, 85470 Bretignolles-sur-Mer [02 51 90 19 48 or 02 40 02 46 10; fax 02 40 02 49 88; lesvagues@free.fr; www.campinglesvagues.fr]** Well sp on D38. Lge, hdg pitch, pt shd; wc; chem disp; sauna; baby facs; shwrs inc; el pnts (6A) €4; Indtte (inc dryer); rest; snacks; bar; BBQ; playgrnd; 2 pools (1 htd, covrd); paddling pool; waterslide; sand beach 900m; games area; games rm; entmnt; TV; 50% statics; dogs €2.50; adv bkg; red low ssn; CCI. "Gd sized pool; close to town cent with shops & rests." ♦ 1 Apr-30 Sep. € 25.00 2009*

BRETIGNOLLES SUR MER *2H3* (1km E Coastal) **Camping La Haute Rivoire, 85470 Bretignolles-sur-Mer [03 76 84 49 59 or 020 7193 6613 (UK); hauterivoire@gmail.com; www.restandrelaxfrance.com]** Fr St Gilles Croix-de-Vie take D38 S twd Les Sables. Cross bdge over Rv Jaunay. Turn L on D12 sp Chaize-Giraud. Site 3rd turning on R sp Chambres. Site in 300m. Take ent after barns. Sm, unshd; wc; chem disp; shwrs inc; el pnts (6A) €4.50 (poss rev pol); snacks; shop 2km; sand beach 2km; pool; golf; fishing; horseriding; watersports adj; sep car park; adv bkg; red low ssn. "British-owned, peaceful CL-type farm site; san facs v clean; no children or dogs; twin-axles extra; phone bef arrival to check open; payment on arr." € 28.50 2007*

BRETIGNOLLES SUR MER *2H3* (1km E Urban) *46.63583, -1.85861* **CHADOTEL Camping La Trévillière, Route de Bellevue, 85470 Bretignolles-sur-Mer [02 51 90 09 65 or 02 51 33 05 05 (LS); fax 02 51 33 94 04; info@chadotel.com; www.chadotel.com]** S along D38 fr St Gilles Croix-de-Vie twd Olonne-sur-Mer, site is sp to L in Bretignolles-sur-Mer. Site 1km fr town cent nr football stadium. Sp from town cent. Lge, hdg/mkd pitch, shd; wc; 50% serviced pitches; baby facs; shwrs inc; el pnts (6A) inc (rev pol); gas; Indtte; shop; tradsmn; snacks; bar; BBQ (charcoal/gas); playgrnd; htd pool; paddling pool; waterslide; sand beach 2km; fishing; watersports 3km; horseriding 5km; cycle hire; entmnt; wifi; games/TV rm; 70% statics; dogs €3; phone; c'van max 8m high ssn; Eng spkn; adv bkg; ccard acc; red long stay/low ssn; CCI. "Friendly, family site; pleasant walk to local shops & rests; less pitch care low ssn; salt marshes worth a visit; mkt Thu & Sun." ♦ 3 Apr-25 Sep. € 29.50 ABS - A26 2009*

BRETIGNOLLES SUR MER *2H3* (5km E Rural) *46.64817, -1.83334* **Camping Les Alouettes, Route de St Gilles, 85220 La Chaize-Giraud [02 51 22 96 21; fax 02 51 22 92 68; contact@lesalouettes.com; www.lesalouettes.com]** Take D38 N fr Bretignolles; in 2.5km take D12 to La Chaize-Giraud. Site on L in 5km. Med, pt sl, pt shd; wc (some cont); chem disp; shwrs inc; el pnts (6A) inc; gas; Indtte; shop; tradsmn; snacks; playgrnd; htd pool; sand beach 5km; lake sw 14km; games area; 75% statics; dogs €2.20; adv bkg; quiet; ccard acc; CCI. "Few touring pitches; gd san facs." ♦ 1 Apr-31 Oct. € 23.00 2008*

BRETIGNOLLES SUR MER *2H3* (5km E Rural) *46.63502, -1.79735* **Camping L'Evasion, Route des Sables, 85220 Landevieille [tel/fax 02 51 22 90 14; contact@camping-levasion.fr]** Site sp in Landevieille. Med, hdg/mkd pitch, pt shd; wc; chem disp; baby facs; shwrs inc; el pnts (10A) €3; gas; Indtte; shop; supmkt 750m; rest; snacks; bar; BBQ; playgrnd; 3 htd pools; waterslides; jacuzzi; beach 5km; fishing lake; games area; 75% statics; dogs €2; dog exercise area; phone; some Eng spkn; quiet except for bar/disco high ssn; ccard acc; CCI. "Vg." 1 Apr-15 Oct. € 17.00 2006*

BRETIGNOLLES SUR MER *2H3* (5km E Rural) *46.64021, -1.80708* **Camping L'Oree de l'Océan, Rue Capitaine de Mazenod, 85220 Landevieille [02 51 22 96 36; fax 02 51 22 29 09; info@camping-oreedelocean; www.camping-oreedelocean.com]** Take D12 fr La Mothe-Achard to St Julien-des-Landes & cont to x-rds bef La Chaize-Giraud. Turn L onto D32, take 1st R in Landevieille to site on L in 50m. Adj Mairie. Med, hdg/mkd pitch, pt sl, pt shd; wc; chem disp; shwrs inc; el pnts (10A) €4; Indtte; shops 500m; bar; playgrnd; htd pool; tennis; sand beach 5km; TV rm; phone; 40% statics; dogs €3; phone; poss cr; quiet; adv bkg; Eng spkn; 15% red 7+ days; ccard acc; CCI. "Gd, friendly, family site; many gd beaches & mkd cycle tracks nr." ♦ 1 Apr-30 Sep. € 23.00 2008*

BRETIGNOLLES SUR MER *2H3* (5km E Urban) *46.64220, -1.79950* **Camping Pong, Rue du Stade, 85220 Landevieille [02 51 22 92 63; fax 02 51 22 99 25; info@lepong.com; www.lepong.com]** Fr Challans S on D32. Pass Landevieille church on L, then rd bends R; turn L immed after sm bdge into Rue de la Stade; foll rd, site on L. Fr Vaire N on D32, soon after ent Landevieille & immed bef sm bdge turn R into Rue de la Stade, then as above. Lge, pt sl, pt shd; wc (some cont); chem disp; serviced pitches; baby facs; shwrs inc; el pnts (6A) inc; gas; Indtte; shop; rest; snacks; bar; BBQ (charcoal/gas); playgrnd; htd pool; paddling pool; waterslide; sand beach 5km; lake 2.5km; fishing; tennis; cycle hire; entmnt; wifi; games/TV rm; some statics; dogs €3.50; adv bkg; quiet; ccard acc; red low ssn. "Beautiful site with great facs; extra charge for lger pitches; pleasant, helpful staff; Lac d'Apremont with 16thC château 13.5km; vineyards & winetasting in area." ♦ 1 Apr-15 Sep. € 25.70 ABS - A24 2009*

BRETIGNOLLES SUR MER *2H3* (4km S Coastal) *46.60413, -1.83231* **Camping Le Chaponnet, 16 Rue du Chaponnet, 85470 Brem-sur-Mer [02 51 90 55 56; fax 02 51 90 91 67; campingchaponnet@wanadoo.fr; www.le-chaponnet.com]** Fr La Roche-sur-Yon on N160 dir Les Sables-d'Olonne. Turn R onto D87 thro St Mathurin vill & take 1st R (just after church) D38 dir L'Ile d'Olonne. Foll sp Brem-sur-Mer, go thro vill & foll sp 'Océan' (nr bakery & bar); turn L opp hairdresser, site in 50m along 1-way rd. Lge, hdg pitch, pt shd; wc; chem disp; baby facs; sauna; shwrs inc; el pnts (6A) inc; gas; Indtte; sm shop; supmkt 200m; rest; snacks; bar; BBQ; playgrnd; htd covrd pool; waterslides; sand beach 1km; jacuzzi; gym; games area; tennis; cycle hire; entmnt; games rm; TV rm; 75% statics; dogs; €3; phone; poss cr; adv bkg; quiet; red low ssn; ccard acc; CCI. "Gd beaches adj; vg." ♦ 1 May-30 Sep. € 33.90 (3 persons) 2007*

BRETIGNOLLES SUR MER *2H3* (W Coastal) *46.62708, -1.86488* **Camping La Motine, 4 Rue des Morinières, 85470 Bretignolles-sur-Mer [02 51 90 04 02; fax 02 51 33 80 52; campinglamotine@wanadoo.fr; www.lamotine.com]** Foll sp fr D38 in Bretignolles-sur-Mer dir Plage de la Parée along Ave de la Plage, then turn R into Rue des Morinières. Med, hdg pitch, pt sl, pt shd; wc; chem disp; mv service pnt; serviced pitches; baby facs; shwrs inc; el pnts (6A) inc; Indtte; rest; bar; playgrnd; htd, covrd pool; sand beach 600m; 60% statics; dogs €3; adv bkg; quiet; ccard acc; CCI. "Unisex san facs low ssn; vg site." ♦ 1 Apr-30 Sep. € 27.00 2009*

BRETTEVILLE see Cherbourg *1C4*

BREUILLET *7B1* (1.5km S Rural) *45.67839, -1.05166* **Camping Transhumance, Chemin des Métairies, Route de Royan, 17920 Breuillet [05 46 22 72 15; fax 05 46 22 66 47; contact@transhumance.com; www.transhumance.com]** Fr Saujon take D14 NW dir St Sulphice-de-Royan & La Tremblade. After approx 8km turn L at junc with D140 sp Breuillet & Camping Transhumance; site well sp on L. Or fr Rochefort S on D733; turn R onto D14 to Breuillet & as above. Lge, hdg pitch, unshd; wc; chem disp; baby facs; shwrs inc; el pnts (10A) €4.50; gas; Indtte; shop; rest; snacks; bar; BBQ; playgrnd; 2 pools; paddling pool; waterslide; beach 3.5km; watersports 6km; fishing; tennis; games rm; cycle hire; archery; horseriding 4km; golf 7km; entmnt; statics; dogs €3; adv bkg; quiet; ccard acc; CCI. "Facs poss stretched high ssn." ♦ Easter-9 Sep. € 18.00 2008*

BREUILLET *7B1* (1.5km NW Rural) *45.69998, -1.06576* **Camping à la Belle Etoile, 27 Route des Renouleaux, 17920 Breuillet [tel/fax 05 46 02 14 07; camping.a.la.belle.etoile@wanadoo.fr; www.alabelle-etoile.com]** Fr Saujon on D14 W dir La Tremblade, turn L onto D242 dir St Augustin then 1st R after 800m. Site sp. Med, mkd pitch, pt shd; wc (cont); chem disp; mv service pnt; shwrs inc; el pnts (10A) €4.30; gas; Indtte; shop 1.5km; tradsmn; rest 500m; snacks; bar 1.5km; playgrnd; pool; sand beach 10km; 60% statics; dogs €2; adv bkg; quiet; ccard acc; red low ssn/CCI. "Gd cycle rtes nr; conv Royan, Ile d'Oléron, La Rochelle; insufficient facs for size of site." ♦ 4 Apr-27 Sep. € 17.20 2008*

France

BREVEDENT, LE see Blangy le Château *3D1*

BREVILLE SUR MER see Granville *1D4*

⊞ **BRIANCON** *9C4* (3km NE Rural) *44.91731, 6.67517* **Camping Les Gentianes, La Vachette, 05100 Val-des-Prés [02 92 21 21 41; fax 04 92 21 24 12; campinglesgentianes@wanadoo.fr; www.campinglesgentianes.com]** Fr Briançon take N94 dir Montgenèvre. At La Vachette site sp in vill. Med, pt sl, pt shd; htd wc; chem disp; mv service pnt; shwrs inc; el pnts (6-10A) €5-7; Indtte; shops, rest in vill; snacks; bar; playgrnd; pool; canoeing; fishing; x-country skiing; wifi; 40% statics; dogs €1; adv bkg; quiet; CCI. "Suitable winter sports users; mountain stream runs thro site; still awaiting renovation (2008); NH only." € 14.10 2008*

BRIANCON *9C4* (5km NE Rural) *44.93905, 6.68323* **Camp Municipal l'Iscle du Rosier, Le Rosier, 05100 Val-des-Prés [04 92 21 06 01; fax 04 92 21 46 46; www.ifrance.com/campingdurosier]** Fr Briançon on N94 E & take 3rd L after leaving Briançon (5km) sp Le Rosier. Foll rd thro until Le Rosier, site on L after bdge. Med, pt shd; wc (some cont); chem disp; shwrs inc; el pnts (5-10A) €3.50-5.20; gas; Indtte; shop; snacks; bar; BBQ; playgrnd; 5% statics; dogs €1.70; phone; bus adj; Eng spkn; quiet. "Nice, well-kept site by rv; friendy, helpful staff; superb walking, cycling & climbing nrby; conv Col de Montgenèvre rd; gd bus service." ♦ 15 Jun-15 Sep. € 10.10 2009*

⊞ **BRIANCON** *9C4* (6km NE Rural) *44.93034, 6.68169* **Camp Municipal du Bois des Alberts, 05100 Montgenèvre [04 92 21 16 11 or 04 92 21 92 88; fax 04 92 21 98 15]** Take N94 fr Briançon sp Italie. In 4km turn L onto D994, site 200m past Les Alberts vill on L. Lge, hdstg, shd; htd wc (some cont); chem disp; mv service pnt; baby facs; shwrs inc; el pnts (6-10A) inc (rev pol); Indtte; shop; tradsmn; rest, snacks, bar high ssn; playgrnd; tennis; games area; kayak tuition; cycle & walking paths; fishing; x-country skiing; 30% statics; adv bkg; quiet; ccard acc; CCI. "Pleasant, friendly site in pine trees; random pitching; facs dated but clean, ltd low ssn; lge pine cones can fall fr trees - park away fr tall ones; gd touring base." ♦ € 12.85 2008*

BRIARE *4G3* (7km S Rural) *47.59713, 2.76617* **Camping Hortus - L'Ecluse des Combles, Chemin de L'Oire, 45360 Châtillon-sur-Loire [tel/fax 02 38 36 35 94; info@camping-hortus.com; www.camping-hortus.com]** SE fr Briare on N7, in 4km turn SW onto D50. Site immed bef rv bdge on R. Care needed over bdge after ent. Med, terr, pt shd; htd wc; chem disp; mv service pnt; shwrs inc; el pnts (5A) inc; gas; Indtte; shops 4km; tradsmn; rest, takeaway & bar adj; BBQ; playgrnd; fishing; games rm; 5% statics; no twin-axles; dogs; Eng spkn; quiet; ccard not acc; CCI. "Lovely location; pleasant, quiet site by Rv Loire; delightful warden; OK san facs; nr historic canals; no twin-axles; mkt day 2nd Thurs of month; vg." ♦ 1 Mar-30 Sep. € 14.00 2009*

BRIARE *4G3* (500m W Rural) *47.64137, 2.72560* **Camping Le Martinet, Quai Tchékof, 45250 Briare [02 38 31 24 50 or 02 38 31 24 51; fax 02 38 31 39 10; campingbriare@recrea.fr; www.recrea.fr/campingbriare]** Exit N7 into Briare. Fr N immed R after canal bdge; fr S L bef 2nd canal bdge; sp. Lge, mkd pitch, unshd; wc (some cont); shwrs; el pnts (10A) €3.50; Indry rm; shops 500m; rest, snacks, bar 500m; fishing adj; poss cr; adv bkg; quiet. "Gd views some pitches; pretty bars & rests along canal; gd walking & cycling; gates close 2200." ♦ 1 Apr-30 Sep. € 10.50 2009*

⊞ **BRIENNE LE CHATEAU** *6E1* (6km S Rural) *48.34835, 4.53265* **Camping Le Colombier, 8 Ave Jean-Lanez, 10500 Dienville [tel/fax 03 25 92 23 47; lecolombier10500@wanadoo.fr; www.lacs-champagne.fr]** On D443 S fr Brienne; in Dienville town cent turn L immed after church & bef bdge, site on R thro archway. Sm, hdg pitch, pt shd; htd wc; chem disp; mv service pnt; shwrs inc; el pnts (6A) €3.50; gas; Indry rm; shop 400m; rest; snacks (high ssn); bar; playgrnd; rv adj; lake 500m; watersports; dogs €2.50; Eng spkn; adv bkg; quiet. "Pretty rvside site - pitches away fr bdge quieter; rv view extra; some sm pitches; pleasant, friendly owner; facs poss stretched high ssn & ltd low ssn; access poss diff lge o'fits if site busy; site poss tired end of ssn; church clock strikes 24 hrs." ♦ € 16.00 2009*

BRIENNE LE CHATEAU *6E1* (6km S Rural) *48.34800, 4.5270* **Camping Le Tertre, Route de Radonvilliers, 10500 Dienville [tel/fax 03 25 92 26 50; campingdutertre@wanadoo.fr; www.campingdutertre.fr]** On D443 S fr Brienne-le-Château; at Dienville turn R at rndabt onto D11; site on R in 200m, sp. NB Site opp Lake Amance harbour, foll sp 'Le Port'. Med, hdg/mkd pitch, hdstg, pt shd; wc; chem disp; mv service pnt; 50% serviced pitches; baby facs; shwrs inc; el pnts (6-10A) €3 (poss long lead req); gas; Indtte (inc dryer); shop; tradsmn; rest; snacks; bar; BBQ; playgrnd; htd pool; paddling pool; sand rv beach 200m; man-made lake with sailing, fishing; gym; games area; games rm; entmnt; internet; TV rm; 5% statics; dogs €1; phone; bus 500m; poss cr; Eng spkn; adv bkg; quiet; ccard acc; red low ssn/CCI. "Pleasant site 2 mins fr vill; excel site for all watersports & other activities; cycle tracks; vg." ♦ 1 Apr-15 Oct. € 20.90 2009*

BRIENNE LE CHATEAU *6E1* (5km SW Rural) *48.35865, 4.50174* **Camping Le Garillon, Rue des Anciens Combattants, 10500 Radonvilliers [03 25 92 21 46; fax 03 25 92 21 34]** Exit Brienne S on D443 & at Brienne-Le-Ville turn R onto D11B to Radonvilliers. Site well sp. Med, pt shd; wc (some cont); chem disp; shwrs inc; el pnts (3-10A) inc; Indry rm; shops 2km; tradsmn; snacks, bar 2km; playgrnd; pool planned 2007; lake 1.5km; mainly statics; poss cr Jul/Aug; Eng spkn; adv bkg; quiet; red CCI. "Pleasant, friendly, family site in Parc Regional de la Forêt d'Orient; ltd touring pitches; modern, clean facs block but unisex washbasin/wc area; some pitches boggy when wet; 2 golf courses within 40km; Nigoland theme park 5km S; gd cycle track around lake." ♦ 1 May-15 Sep. € 15.00 2006*

BRIEY *5D2* (1km NW Rural) **Camping Intercommunal Plan d'Eau de la Sangsue, 54150 Briey [03 82 20 96 22; fax 03 82 21 83 70; marilyne.nicollet@cc-paysdebriey.fr; www.cc-paysdebriey.fr]** Exit A4 junc 33 to Briey, site sp. Sm, hdstg, terr; wc; chem disp; shwrs inc; el pnts (16A) €1.50; snacks; playgrnd; CCI. "Gd site adj lake; gd walks." 1 May-31 Oct. € 9.00 2007*

BRIGNOGAN PLAGES *1D2* (Coastal) *48.67278, -4.32916* **Camping de la Côte des Légendes, Keravezan, 29890 Brignogan-Plages [02 98 83 41 65; fax 02 98 83 59 94; camping-cote-des-legendes@wanadoo.fr; www.campingcotedeslegendes.com]** Fr Roscoff on D10, fr Brest on D788/770 or fr N12 exit dir Lesneven. In Brignogan foll sp Brignogan-Plages & 'Centre Nautique'. Lge, hdg/mkd pitch, some hdstg, pt shd; wc; chem disp; mv service pnt; baby facs; shwrs inc; el pnts (5A) €2.50 (poss rev pol); Indtte; shop; tradsmn; snacks; bar; BBQ; playgrnd; dir access to sand beach adj; sailing & watersports; sailing; entmnt; TV rm; site guarded 24 hrs; 30% statics; dogs €1.10; phone; Eng spkn; adv bkg; quiet; ccard acc; red long stay/low ssn/CCI. "On beautiful sandy cove; some sea view pitches; friendly, helpful staff; ltd facs low ssn; vg touring base in interesting area; vg." ♦ 1 Apr-1 Nov. € 13.90 2008*

BRIGNOGAN PLAGES *1D2* (2km NW Coastal) *48.67535, -4.34534* **Camping du Phare, Plage du Phare, 29890 Brignogan-Plages [02 98 83 45 06; fax 02 98 83 52 19; camping.du.phare@orange.fr; www.camping-du-phare.com]** Take D770 N fr Lesneven to Brignogan-Plages; take L fork in town cent & foll site sp dir Kerverven. Med, some hdg pitch, some hdstg, pt shd; wc; chem disp; mv service pnt; shwrs €1; el pnts (6A) €2.80; gas; Indtte; shop 1km; tradsmn; snacks; playgrnd; sand beach adj; wifi; 10% statics; dogs €1.80; poss cr; adv bkg; quiet; CCI. "Next to pretty bay & gd beach; helpful owner; vg site nr walking rte GR34." 1 Apr-30 Sep. € 11.00 2009*

See advertisement

BRIGNOLES *10F3* (500m E) *43.40573, 6.07885* **Camp Municipal, 786 Route de Nice, 83170 Brignoles [tel/fax 04 94 69 20 10; campingbrignoles@aol.com; http://campingdebrignoles.ifrance.com]** Exit A8 junc 35 onto DN7 (N7) E dir Le Luc/Nice; site just bef Intermarché supmkt rndabt. Med, hdg pitch, pt shd; wc; chem disp; shwrs inc; el pnts (10A) €3; gas; Indtte; supmkt 100m; snacks; playgrnd; municipal pool adj; 10% statics; phone; dogs €1.50; Eng spkn; some rd noise; adv bkg; ccard acc; CCI. "NH; well-managed site by friendly family." 15 Mar-15 Oct. € 12.50 2007*

BRIGNOLES *10F3* (9km SE Rural) *43.33919, 6.12579* **Camping La Vidaresse, 83136 Ste Anastasie-sur-Issole [04 94 72 21 75; fax 04 98 05 01 21; lavidaresse@wanadoo.fr; www.campinglavidaresse.com]** On DN7 (N7) 2km W of Brignoles at rndabt take D43 dir Toulon. In about 10km turn L at rndabt to D15. Do not ent vill, go strt & site is approx 250m on R. Med, hdg/mkd pitch, terr, pt shd; wc (some cont); chem disp; mv service pnt; shwrs inc; el pnts (6-10A) €3.50-4.50 (poss rev pol); gas; Indtte; shop in vill 1km & 5km; rest high ssn; snacks & bar (all ssn); BBQ (gas/elec only); playgrnd; htd, covrd pool; paddling pool; sand beach 40km; tennis; games area; fishing 200m; 40% statics; dogs €2; poss cr; adv bkg; red long stay; ccard acc; CCI. "Well-managed, family site in lovely area; peaceful; friendly & helpful; facs adequate; excel pool; gd touring base Haute Provence, Gorges du Verdon & Riviera; vineyard adj; gd." ♦ 15 Apr-30 Sep. € 23.00 2007*

BRILLANE, LA *10E3* (8km NE Rural) *43.95787, 6.00622* **Camping Les Matherons, 04700 Puimichel [tel/fax 04 92 79 60 10; lesmatherons@wanadoo.fr; www.campinglesmatherons.com]** Exit D4096 (N96) or A51 junc 19 at La Brillane. Take D4B across Rv Durance to Oraison. Foll camp sps on D12 twd Puimichel; site on L 6km. Sm, pt sl, terr, pt shd; wc; chem disp; shwrs inc; el pnts (3A) €2.50; shop 6km; tradsmn; rest; snacks; playgrnd; dogs €1.10; Eng spkn; adv bkg ess; quiet; red low ssn; CCI. "Unspoilt site in depths of country; gd walks." 20 Apr-30 Sep. € 15.00 2007*

France

⊞ **BRILLANE, LA** *10E3* (2km E Rural) *43.92282, 5.92369* **Camping Les Oliviers, Chemin St Sauveur, 04700 Oraison [tel/fax 04 92 78 20 00; camping-oraison@wanadoo.fr; www.camping-oraison.com]** Exit A51 junc 19; take rd E to Oraison in 2km; site sp in vill. Med, mkd pitch, pt sl, pt terr, pt shd; wc; chem disp; mv service pnt; baby facs; fam bthrm; shwrs inc; el pnts (16A) €3.80; gas; lndtte; tradsmn (in ssn); shops, snacks & bar (in ssn) or 500m; playgrnd; pool; cycle hire; games area; games rm; TV rm; 10% statics; dogs €2.50; Eng spkn; adv bkg; quiet; ccard acc; CCI. "Pleasant, family-run site among olive trees; nice views; friendly, helpful owners; walks fr site; conv Verdon gorge; adj elec sub-station, elec cables run over site; gd." € 16.00 2008*

BRILLANE, LA *10E3* (3km W Rural) *43.93305, 5.86777* **Camping Le Moulin de Ventre, 04300 Niozelles [04 92 78 63 31; fax 04 92 79 86 92; moulindeventre@aol.com; www.moulin-de-ventre.com]** Exit A51 junc 19 at La Brillane; turn R onto D4096 (N96), then L onto D4100 (N100) sp Niozelles & Forcalquier. Site in 3km on L just after bdge, adj Rv Lauzon. Med, mkd pitch, pt sl, pt shd; htd wc; chem disp; mv service pnt; serviced pitches; baby facs; shwrs inc; el pnts (10A) inc; gas; lndtte; shop 2km; tradsmn; rest; snacks; bar; BBQ (gas/elec); playgrnd; pool; rv beach, fishing, boat hire adj; wifi; games/TV rm; 10% statics; dogs €3; phone; Eng spkn; adv bkg (bkg fee + dep); quiet; ccard acc; red low ssn/long stay; CCI. "Well-run, pleasant site; some pitches adj stream; excel touring base." ♦ 3 Apr-30 Sep. € 29.00 ABS - M09 2009*

BRIONNE *3D2* (500m N Urban) *49.20256, 0.71554* **Camp Municipal La Vallée, Rue Marcel Nogrette, 27800 Brionne [02 32 44 80 35; fax 02 32 46 25 61; secretariat-mairie-brionne@wanadoo.fr; www.ville-brionne.fr]** Fr D438 (N138) N or S on by-pass, turn N at D46 junc, pass Carrefour supmkt on L & take 1st R, site on L. Sm, hdg pitch, pt shd; wc; chem disp; mv service pnt; shwrs inc; el pnts (8A) €3.20; gas; lndtte; shop, rest etc nrby; BBQ; playgrnd; some statics; dogs; poss cr; quiet; CCI. "Excel site in lovely vill; gd san facs; poss ltd low ssn; excel disabled facs; poss smell fr sewage works (2009)." 30 Apr-30 Sep. € 8.15 2009*

BRIONNE *3D2* (5km N Rural) *49.23648, 0.72265* **FFCC Camp Municipal St Nicolas, 15 Rue St Nicolas, 27800 Le Bec-Hellouin [tel/fax 02 32 44 83 55 or 02 32 44 86 40 (Mairie); info@lebec-hellouin.com; www.lebec-hellouin.com]** Exit A28 junc 13 onto D438 (N138) then take D581 to Malleville-sur-le-Bec; site on R 1km after Malleville. Well sp. Med, pt shd; htd wc; chem disp; mv service pnt; shwrs inc; el pnts (10A) €3.30; lndtte; tradsmn (excel bakeries); rest, snacks, bar in vill; BBQ; playgrnd; tennis, horseriding nr; a few statics; 1 dog free (2nd €1.05); poss cr; quiet; CCI. "Attractive, well-kept site in pleasant area; conv NH nr Calais; spacious pitches; friendly, helpful warden; vg, clean san facs; gate clsd 2200; gd dog walks; vg cycling; a gem." ♦ 1 Apr-30 Sep. € 8.90 2009*

⊞ **BRIONNE** *3D2* (6km N Rural) *49.2420, 0.7030* **Camp Municipal Les Marronniers, Rue Louise Givon, 27290 Pont-Authou [02 32 42 75 06; fax 02 32 56 34 51; campingmunicipaldesmarroniers27@orange.fr]** Heading S on D438 (N138) take D130 just bef Brionne sp Pont-Audemer (care req at bdge & rndabts). Site on L in approx 5km, well sp on o'skts of Pont-Authou; foll sp in vill. Med, mkd pitch, some hdstg, pt shd; htd wc; chem disp; mv service pnt; shwrs; el pnts (10A) €3.15 (poss rev pol); lndtte; shops 500m; tradsmn; rest, bar in vill; BBQ; playgrnd; fishing; 50% statics; dogs €1.30; adv bkg; quiet; CCI. "Useful, pleasant, clean stop nr Rouen & m'way; friendly recep; clean san facs; best pitches far side of lake; beautiful valley with many historic towns & vills; excel walking; vg NH." € 9.30 2009*

BRIOUDE *9C1* (2km S Rural) *45.2813, 3.4045* **Camping La Bageasse, Ave de la Bageasse, 43100 Brioude [04 71 50 07 70; fax 04 73 34 70 94; aquadis1@wanadoo.fr; www.aquadis-loisirs.com]** Turn off N102 & foll sp for Brioude town centre; then foll site sp. Narr app rd. Site on Rv Allier. Med, mkd pitch, terr, pt shd; wc (some cont); chem disp (wc); shwrs inc; el pnts (6A) inc (some rev pol); lndtte; sm shop; tradsmn; snacks; bar; BBQ; playgrnd; pool 2km; fishing & boating adj; canoe hire; 8% statics; dogs €1.50; phone; Eng spkn; adv bkg; quiet; red long stay; CCI. "Clean site; phone ahead to check open low ssn; interesting basilica." ♦ 1 Apr-30 Sep. € 19.00 2009*

BRIOUX SUR BOUTONNE see Melle *7A2*

BRISSAC see Ganges *10E1*

BRISSAC QUINCE *4G1* (2km NE Rural) *47.35944, -0.43388* **Camping de l'Etang, Route de St Mathurin, 49320 Brissac-Quincé [02 41 91 70 61; fax 02 41 91 72 65; info@campingetang.com; www.campingetang.com]** Fr N on A11, exit junc 14 onto N260 passing E of Angers, following sp for Cholet/Poitiers. After x-ing Rv Loire, foll sp to Brissac-Quincé on D748. Foll sp for St Mathurin/Domaine de l'Etang on D55 to site. Med, hdg/mkd pitch, hdstg, pt shd; htd wc; mv service pnt; chem disp; baby facs; some serviced pitches (€3 extra charge); shwrs inc; el pnts (10A) inc; gas; lndtte; shop; tradsmn; rest; snacks; bar; BBQ (charcoal/gas); playgrnd; 2 pools (1 htd, covrd); paddling pool; waterslide; lake fishing; cycle hire; golf 8km; leisure park; entmnt; wifi; games/TV; dogs €4; Eng spkn; adv bkg; quiet; ccard acc; red long stay/low ssn; CCI. "Excel, well-cared for site amongst vineyards, wine-tastings & visits; lge pitches; staff pleasant & helpful; clean, modern facs & gd disabled facs; gd touring base Loire valley; leisure facs gd for children; 15 min rvside walk to Brissac; mkt Thu." ♦ 15 May-11 Sep. € 30.00 ABS - L15 2009*

BRISSAC QUINCE *4G1* (1km S Rural) *47.33317, -0.43664* **Camping à la Ferme Domaine de la Belle Etoile, La Belle Etoile, 49320 Brissac-Quincé [02 41 54 81 18]** Take D748 S fr Angers dir Poitiers. At D761 rndabt cont on D748 sp N-D-d'Allençon. Site sp at 2nd turn on L in 500m. Sm, pt shd; wc; chem disp; shwrs €1; el pnts (5A) €2; Indtte; BBQ; playgrnd; quiet. "Vg CL-type site in vineyard with wine-tasting & farm produce; clean, modern facs; troglodyte caves, mushroom farms & château nrby." 1 Apr-1 Nov. € 7.90 2009*

⊞ **BRIVE LA GAILLARDE** *7C3* (8km S Rural) *45.10049, 1.52423* **FFCC Camping à la Ferme (Delmas), Malfarges, 19600 Noailles [tel/fax 05 55 85 81 33]** Fr A20/E9 take exit 52 sp Noailles; immed after tunnel take 1st R across yellow paving at vill café/shop (to avoid steep dangerous hill), turn R at T-junc, site on L. Sp fr m'way. Sm, mkd pitch, terr, pt shd; wc; chem disp; mv service pnt; shwrs inc; el pnts (5A) €2.50-5 (poss rev pol); shop 500m; farm meals & produce; fishing 200m; dogs €2.50; few statics; adv bkg; quiet; CCI. "Conv NH/sh stay adj A20; friendly, helpful farmer; if owner not around choose a pitch; basic san facs; parking on terr poss awkward; fly problem in hot weather; strict silence after 2200; excel." € 8.20 2009*

BRIVE LA GAILLARDE *7C3* (6km SW Rural) *45.09975, 1.45115* **Camping Intercommunal La Prairie, 19600 Lissac-sur-Couze [05 55 85 37 97; fax 05 55 85 37 11; lecausse.correzien@wanadoo.fr]** A20 exit 51; D1089 (N89) to Larche; L onto D19 sp Lissac; L onto D59 round N side of Lac de Causse, then bear L over dam; R to site in 2km. Site sp as 'Camping Nautica'. Med, mkd pitch, hdstg, terr, pt shd; wc; serviced pitches; shwrs inc; el pnts (16A) €3; gas 4km; Indtte; shop; snacks; bar; playgrnd; pool; lake sw; boating; windsurfing; 5% statics; dogs €3; quiet; adv bkg; no ccard acc; CCI. "Beautiful setting o'looking lake; red facs low ssn & poss unclean; recep 1030-1200 & 1700-1900 but poss clsd Tues & Sun - site inaccessible when recep clsd, phone ahead rec; many outdoor activities." ♦ 1 Apr-4 Oct. € 14.00 2008*

⊞ **BRIVE LA GAILLARDE** *7C3* (10km SW Rural) *45.06942, 1.43060* **Camping La Magaudie, La Magaudie Ouest, 19600 Chartrier-Ferrière [tel/fax 05 55 85 26 06; camping@lamagaudie.com; www.lamagaudie.com]** Exit A20 junc 53 onto D920/D19 dir Chasteaux. After rlwy bdge take 2nd L to Chartrier & foll blue sps to site. NB Diff app climbing up narr lane with no passing paces for 1km. Sm, mkd pitch, sl, pt shd; htd wc; chem disp; shwrs inc; el pnts (10A) €2.75; Indtte; shop 2km; tradsmn; rest; snacks; bar; gas BBQ; playgrnd; pool; lake sw 3km; 5% statics; dogs €1.25; Eng spkn; adv bkg; quiet; red low ssn; CCI. "Dutch owners; vg site & facs but v ltd low ssn; rec arr early high ssn." ♦ € 14.00 2008*

BROU *4F2* (1km W Rural) *48.20787, 1.14637* **Parc de Loisirs de Brou, Route des Moulins, 28160 Brou [02 37 47 02 17; fax 02 37 47 86 77; contact@parc-loisirs-brou.fr; www.parc-loisirs-brou.fr]** Sp in town on D13. Lge, hdg/mkd pitch, shd; wc; chem disp; shwrs inc; el pnts (10A) €6; Indtte; shops 2km; rest; playgrnd; htd pool; waterslide; lake adj; fishing; golf; many statics; quiet; red low ssn; CCI. "Ent to site by card, so no ent when office clsd (winter office clsd Mon & Wed); vg san facs." ♦ 16 Feb-14 Dec. € 11.00 2008*

BROUSSES ET VILLARET *8F4* (500m S Rural) *43.33932, 2.25201* **Camping Le Martinet Rouge, 11390 Brousses-et-Villaret [tel/fax 04 68 26 51 98; campinglemartinetrouge@orange.fr; www.camping-lemartinetrouge.com]** Fr D118 Mazamet-Carcassonne, turn R 3km after Cuxac-Carbades onto D103; turn L in Brousses & foll sp. Sm, mkd pitch, pt sl, shd; wc; baby facs; shwrs inc; el pnts (6A) €2.50; Indtte; shop; snacks; bar; playgrnd; pool; trout-fishing; horseriding; canoeing; 20% statics; dogs €2; adv bkg; quiet; CCI. "Helpful owners." ♦ 15 May-8 Sep. € 15.00 2007*

BRUERE ALLICHAMPS see St Amand Montrond *4H3*

BRUGHEAS see Vichy *9A1*

BRULON *4F1* (500m SE Rural) *47.96275, -0.22773* **Camping Le Septentrion, 72350 Brûlon [02 43 95 68 96; fax 02 43 92 60 36; le.septentrion@wanadoo.fr; www.campingleseptentrion.com]** Exit A81 junc 1; foll D4 S to Brûlon; site sp on ent to town to L; turn on L down narr rd (Rue de Buet); then turn R in 300m. Site well sp. Sm, pt sl, shd; wc; mv service pnt; shwrs inc; el pnts (6A) €3; Indtte; shop 600m; tradsmn; rest; snacks; bar; BBQ; playgrnd; pool (high ssn); lake sw; boating; fishing; cycle hire; games/TV rm; 50% statics; dogs €1.20; phone; adv bkg; quiet; red long stay/low ssn. "V spacious pitches; gd welcome; clean, modern san facs - unisex low ssn; gd cycling & walking area; vg." 11 Apr-30 Sep. € 13.50 (CChq acc) 2009*

BRUNIQUEL *8E3* (4km NW Rural) *44.07660, 1.61103* **FFCC Camping Le Clos Lalande, Route de Bioule, 82800 Montricoux [tel/fax 05 63 24 18 89; contact@camping-lecloslalande.com; www.camping-lecloslalande.com]** Fr A20 exit junc 59 to Caussade; fr Caussade take D964 to Montricoux where site well sp. Med, hdg/mkd pitch, pt shd; wc; chem disp; mv service pnt; baby facs; shwrs inc; el pnts (6A) €3.50; Indtte; shop 1km; tradsmn; snacks; bar & 1km; BBQ; playgrnd; pool; rv & shgl beach 400m; tennis; basketball; fishing; watersports; cycle & canoe hire; internet; TV rm; 10% statics; dogs €2; phone; bus 400m; poss full; some Eng spkn; adv bkg (rec high ssn); CCI. "Peaceful, quiet, well-kept site by rv at mouth of Aveyron gorges; beautiful area, inc Bastide vills; great family site; friendly, helpful owners; mkt Weds; highly rec." ♦ 25 Apr-15 Sep. € 14.20 2009*

BRUYERES *6E2* (6km SE Rural) *48.18987, 6.77508* **Camping Les Pinasses, La Chapelle-devant-Bruyères, 88600 Bruyères [03 29 58 51 10; fax 03 29 58 54 21; info@camping-les-pinasses.com; www.camping-les-pinasses.com]** Fr Bruyères, take D423 twd Gérardmer. In 3km turn L on D60 sp Corcieux, Site on R in 3km at La-Chapelle-devant-Bruyères. Med, hdg/mkd pitch, pt shd; wc (some cont); chem disp; shwrs inc; el pnts (4-6A) €3.70-4.70; gas; Indtte; shop; tradsmn; rest; snacks; bar; BBQ; playgrnd; htd pool; paddling pool; tennis; TV rm; 30% statics; dogs €1.30; adv bkg; some rlwy noise; CCI. "Beautiful area." Apr-15 Sep. € 18.10 2008*

France

BRUYERES *6E2* (6km S Rural) *48.17870, 6.74309* **Camping Domaine des Messires, 1 La Feigne, 88600 Herpelmont [03 29 58 56 29 or 0031 321 331456 (N'lands); fax 03 29 51 62 86; mail@domainedesmessires.com; www.domainedesmessires.com]** SE fr Bruyères on D423; at Laveline turn R sp Herpelmont & foll site sp. Site 1.5km N of Herpelmont. Med, pt shd; wc; mv service pnt; chem disp; serviced pitches; child/baby facs; shwrs inc; el pnts (6A) inc; gas; Indtte; shop; tradsmn; rest; snacks; bar; BBQ; playgrnd; lake sw; fishing; boating; dogs €4; Eng spkn; adv bkg; quiet; ccard acc; red low ssn/long stay; CCI. "Attractive, peaceful, lakeside site; gd touring base Alsace & Vosges; friendly, helpful staff." ♦ 23 Apr-18 Sep. € 25.50 2009*

See advertisement

BUGEAT *7B4* (3km NW Rural) *45.60608, 1.88446* **Camp Municipal Puy de Veix, 19170 Viam [05 55 95 52 05 (Mairie); fax 05 55 95 21 86; viam.mairie@wanadoo.fr; www.viam.correze.net]** Fr Bugeat NW on D979; in 4km L onto D160; foll sp to Viam. Sm, mkd pitch, pt sl, terr, pt shd; wc; chem disp; mv service pnt; el pnts (6-10A) €1.90; Indtte (inc dryer); shop 4km; rest 500m; playgrnd; lake sw & shgl beach adj; fishing; games area; phone; poss cr; Eng spkn; adv bkg; CCI. "On lakeside; beautiful views; vg." 1 Jun-30 Sep. € 7.00 2008*

When we get home I'm going to post all these site report forms to the Club for next year's guide. The deadline's September.

BUGUE, LE *7C3* (4km NE Rural) *44.93436, 0.93571* **Camping La Linotte, Route de Rouffignac, 24260 Le Bugue [05 53 07 17 61; fax 05 53 54 16 96; infos@campinglalinotte.com; www.campinglalinotte.com]** E off D710 onto D32E after passing thro town heading N twd Périgueux on rd to Rouffignac. Site sp fr D710. Med, hdg pitch, pt sl, terr, pt shd; wc; chem disp; baby facs; fam bthrm; shwrs inc; el pnts (6A) €3.30; Indtte; shop; rest; snacks; playgrnd; htd pool; waterslide; entmnt; quiet; adv bkg; CCI. "Splendid views; lovely site; gd mkt Tues." 5 Apr-13 Sep. € 22.15 2008*

BUGUE, LE *7C3* (1km SE Urban) *44.90980, 0.93160* **Camping Les Trois Caupain (formerly Municipal Le Port), 24260 Le Bugue [05 53 07 24 60; info@camping-bugue.com; www.camping-des-trois-caupain.com]** Exit Le Bugue town cent on D703 twd Campagne. Turn R at sp after 400m to site in 600m. Med, mkd pitch, pt shd; wc; chem disp; mv service pnt; shwrs inc; el pnts (6-10A) €3-3.60; gas; shops 1km; rest & snacks (high ssn); bar; playgrnd; pool; rv & games area adj; wifi; 40% statics, sep area; dogs free; adv bkg; quiet. "Beautiful site; pleasant, helpful owners; pretty town; excel." 1 Apr-30 Oct. € 16.50 2009*

BUGUE, LE *7C3* (3km SE Rural) *44.90663, 0.97412* **Camping Le Val de la Marquise, 24260 Campagne [05 53 54 74 10; fax 05 53 54 00 70; val-marquise@wanadoo.fr; www.levaldelamarquise.com]** Fr D703 bet Le Bugue & Les Eyzies take D35 at Campagne dir St Cyprien, site sp. Med, mkd pitch, terr, pt shd; wc; chem disp; mv service pnt; baby facs; shwrs inc; el pnts (15A) €4; Indtte; shops 4km; tradsmn, rest high ssn; snacks; bar; BBQ; playgrnd; pool; paddling pool; fishing lake; games aea; 5% statics; dogs €2; phone; Eng spkn; adv bkg; quiet; CCI. "Peaceful, attractive site; poss diff access to pitches for lge c'vans due narr site rds & low terrs; clean san facs; beautiful pool; Michelin starred rest nrby." 1 Apr-15 Oct. € 17.80 2008*

BUGUE, LE *7C3* (7km SE Rural) *44.86199, 0.98150* **Camping Le Clou, Meynard, 24220 Coux-et-Bigaroque [05 53 31 63 32; fax 05 53 31 69 33; info@camping-le-clou.com; www.camping-le-clou.com]** S fr Le Bugue on D703 twd Belvès; site 8km on R. Med, mkd pitch, pt sl, pt shd; htd wc; chem disp; mv service pnt; serviced pitches; baby facs; fam bthrm; shwrs inc; el pnts (6A) €3.50; gas; Indtte; tradsmn; rest; snacks; bar; BBQ; playgrnd; 2 pools & paddling pool; fishing; canoeing; horseriding; entmnt; games rm; TV; phone; 10% statics; dogs €2.50; Eng spkn; adv bkg; quiet; ccard acc; red long stay/low ssn/CCI. "Pleasant owners; ideal base for Dordogne; lovely wooded site with much wildlife." ♦ 28 Apr-15 Sep. € 19.75 2007*

BUGUE, LE *7C3* (8km S Rural) *44.85416, 0.91208* **Camping Le Pont de Vicq, 24480 Le Buisson-de-Cadouin [05 53 22 01 73; fax 05 53 22 06 70; le.pont.de.vicq@wanadoo.fr; www.campings-dordogne.com/pontdevicq]** Fr Le Bugue foll sp to Le Buisson. Site immed S of bdge over Rv Dordogne on rd D51E. Sp fr all dir in Le Buisson. Med, hdg/mkd pitch, pt shd; wc; baby facs; shwrs inc; el pnts (6A) €3.50 (poss rev pol); Indtte; shops 1.5km; rest adj; snacks in ssn; playgrnd; shgl beach & rv; games area; games rm; entmnt; TV; 60% statics; dogs €1.10; phone adj; poss cr; adv bkg; quiet; CCI. "Pleasant site on rv; poss mosquitoes." 21 Mar-1 Oct. € 20.40 2009*

BUGUE, LE *7C3* (5km SW Rural) *44.89323, 0.87955* **Camping La Ferme des Poutiroux, 24510 Limeuil [05 53 63 31 62; fax 05 53 58 30 84; camping.les.poutiroux@tiscali.fr; www.poutiroux.com]** W fr Le Bugue on D703 twd Bergerac; in 2km take D31 S for 4km; bef bdge take R fork twd Trémolat/Lalinde; in 300m fork R (sp), site well sp. Sm, mkd, pt sl, terr, pt shd; wc; chem disp; mv service pnt; baby facs; shwrs; el pnts (6A) €3.80; Indtte; shops 2km; playgrnd; pool; canoes & rv sw nrby; some statics; dogs €1; phone; Eng spkn; adv bkg; quiet; ccard not acc; CCI. "Peaceful, well-kept, well-positioned, family-run site; friendly, helpful farmer; facs clean; vg value low ssn; highly rec." ♦ 3 Apr-19 Oct. € 15.50 2009*

France

BUGUE, LE *7C3* (6km SW Rural) *44.87990, 0.88576* **Camping du Port de Limeuil, 24480 Alles-sur-Dordogne [05 53 63 29 76; fax 05 53 63 04 19; didierbonvallet@aol.com; www.leportdelimeuil.com]** Exit Le Bugue on D31 sp Le Buisson; in 4km turn R on D51 sp Limeuil; at 2km turn L over rv bdge; site on R after bdge. Med, hdg/mkd pitch, pt sl, pt shd; wc; chem disp; 50% serviced pitches; shwrs inc; el pnts (5A) €3.50; gas; Indtte; shop & 1km; bar; snacks; BBQ; playgrnd; htd pool; shgl beach & rv adj; games rm; canoe & cycle hire; 40% statics (tour ops); dogs €2; poss cr; Eng spkn; adv bkg; quiet; red low ssn; CCI. "Superb location & site for all ages; lge pitches; clean san facs, ltd low ssn; tour ops." ♦ 1 May-30 Sep. € 24.90 2008*

BUGUE, LE *7C3* (9km SW Rural) *44.87909, 0.82751* **Camping de Trémolat, Centre Nautique, Route de Mauzac, 24510 Trémolat [05 53 22 81 18 or 05 53 05 65 65 (res); fax 05 53 06 30 94; semitour@perigord.tm.fr]** Fr Le Bugue, take D703 W twd Pezuls. In vill, turn L onto D30 twd Trémolat. Site 700m N of Trémolat, well sp fr all dir. Med, hdg pitch, pt shd; wc; chem disp; shwrs inc; el pnts (10A) inc; Indtte; shops 700m; rest; snacks; BBQ; pool; rv adj; fishing; canoeing; 20% statics; dogs; phone; poss cr; Eng spkn; adv bkg; quiet; CCI. "Peaceful site; most touring pitches have rv frontage, excel for fishing & canoeing; facs poss stretched high ssn." ♦ 1 May-30 Sep. € 21.40 2009*

BUGUE, LE *7C3* (10km W Rural) *44.91527, 0.82083* **Camping La Forêt, Ste Alvère, 24510 Pezuls [05 53 22 71 69; camping.laforet@wanadoo.fr; www.camping-la-foret.com]** Off D703 fr Le Bugue to Lalinde rd, sp on L 1.5km bef Pezuls. In Le Bugue do not foll sp to Lalinde but cont thro town on D703, turn R, L & R, passing fire stn. Med, pt sl, pt shd; wc; chem disp; baby facs; shwrs inc; el pnts (3A) inc; gas; Indtte; sm shop; snacks; BBQ (gas/charcoal only); playgrnd; pool; tennis; games area; disco weekly high ssn away fr vans; games/TV rm; dogs free; no c'vans over 6m high ssn; poss cr; adv bkg; quiet; ccard not acc; red low ssn; CCI. "Beautiful, simple, peaceful site; nature lovers' paradise - wild orchids, butterflies, etc; underused low ssn; helpful, friendly owner; gd san facs, ltd low ssn; gd touring base; excel." ♦ 1 Apr-15 Oct. € 19.70 ABS - D03 2009*

BUGUE, LE *7C3* (5km NW Rural) *44.95130, 0.85070* **Camping St Avit Loisirs, 24260 St Avit-de-Vialard [05 53 02 64 00; fax 05 53 02 64 39; contact@saint-avit-loisirs.com; www.saint-avit-loisirs.com or www.les-castels.com]** Leave N89/E70 SE of Périgueux & turn S onto D710 for approx 32km; about 3km N of Le Bugue turn R sp St Avit-de-Vialard. Turn R in vill & conf for approx 1.5km, site on R. NB Narr, twisting app rd. Lge, hdg pitch, pt sl, pt shd; wc; chem disp; baby facs; shwrs inc; el pnts (6A) inc; gas; Indtte; shop; rest; snacks; bar; BBQ; playgrnd; 2 pools (1 htd, covrd); waterslide; paddling pool; tennis; crazy golf; golf, watersports, archery & horseriding nr; cycle hire; entmnt; wifi; games/TV rm; dogs €4.90; many static tents/vans; poss cr; adv bkg; quiet; ccard acc; red low ssn; CCI. "Excel, well-run, busy site; friendly welcome; gd san facs; conv for Lascaux" ♦ 31 Mr-18 Sep. € 40.40 ABS - D10 2009*

BUIS LES BARONNIES *9D2* (300m N Urban) *44.27558, 5.27830* **Camp Municipal, Quartier du Jalinier, 26170 Buis-les-Baronnies [04 75 28 04 96 or 06 60 80 40 53 (mob)]** Fr Vaison-la-Romaine S on D938; turn L onto D54/D13/D5 to Buis-les-Baronnies; cont N onto D546; at bend turn R over rv bdge; turn L along rv, then 1st R. Site split into 2 either side of sw pool; recep in upper site. Med, hdg/mkd pitch, pt sl, pt shd; wc; chem disp; shwrs inc; el pnts (6A) €3; Indry rm; pool nrby; 5% statics; dogs €1.20; phone; bus 300m; poss cr; quiet, but poss noise fr pool; CCI. "Lovely views; san facs dated but clean; not suitable lge o'fits but lger, more accessible pitches on lower level; attractive town; gd mkt Wed & Sat; fair." 1 Mar-11 Nov. € 11.20 2008*

BUIS LES BARONNIES *9D2* (3km N Rural) *44.30364, 5.27250* **Camping Le Romegas (Naturist), 26170 Buis-les-Baronnies [tel/fax 04 75 28 10 78; http://leromegas.free.fr/]** S fr Nyons on D938, E on D46/D4/D5 to Buis-les-Baronnies. On D546 turn N on D108 sp St Jalle. Site on L bef summit of Col d'Ey. Rd access gd although high altitude. Med, terr, pt shd; wc (some cont); shwrs; el pnts (6A) €3.50; Indtte; shop; rest; playgrnd; pool & paddling pool; TV; some statics; dogs €3; quiet; red low ssn; CCI. "Beautiful situation; gd walking; friendly staff; access round site diff due tight bends & steep hillside." 1 Apr-30 Sep. € 20.00 (3 persons) 2008*

BUIS LES BARONNIES *9D2* (7km E Rural) **Camping/Gîte du Lièvre (Taponnier), La Roche-sur-les-Buis, 26170 Buis-les-Baronnies [04 75 28 11 49; fax 04 75 28 19 26; gitedulievre@wanadoo.fr; www.gitedulievre.com]** In Buis-les-Baronnies travel N on D546; at edge of town after x-ing rv turn R onto D159; foll for 10km to Poët-en-Percip; site sp on L; 3km down unmade rd. Sm, mkd pitch, hdstg, terr, pt shd; wc (some cont); chem disp (wc); shwrs inc; el pnts (10A) €2 (poss long lead req); tradsmn; rest; snacks; bar; playgrnd; pool; mountain bike trails; horseriding; some statics; adv bkg; quiet; no ccard acc; CCI. "Site on farm; scenic but v isolated at 3,000 feet; views of Mt Ventoux; walks; climbing." May-Oct. € 15.00 2007*

BUIS LES BARONNIES *9D2* (1.5km SW Rural) *44.26882, 5.26781* **Camping Les Ephélides, Quartier Tuves, 26170 Buis-les-Baronnies [04 75 28 10 15; fax 04 75 28 13 04; ephelides@wanadoo.fr; www.ephelides.com]** Fr S of Vaison D54 or D13 E to Entrechaux, then D5 & D147 to vill. Sp in main rd S across rv, turn R, site in 1.5km. Normal exit in main rd blocked; access fr SW end of town to 'Parking Sud' by Rv L'Ouvèze. Med, pt shd; wc; shwrs; el pnts (3-10A) €2.70-3.30; Indtte; snacks; tennis adj; horseriding; some statics; dogs; phone; adv bkg; quiet; red low ssn; ccard acc. "Site in cherry orchard; excel views; mkt in town Wed; take care when x-ing bdge." 15 May-1 Sep. € 16.60 2007*

BUIS LES BARONNIES *9D2* (4km SW Rural) *44.25190, 5.24370* **Camping La Gautière, La Penne-sur-l'Ouvèze, 26170 Buis-les-Baronnies [04 75 28 02 68; fax 04 75 28 24 11; accueil@camping-lagautiere.com; www.camping-lagautiere.com]** On D5 Vaison-la-Romaine to Buis-les-Baronnies rd, on L. Sm, mkd pitch, pt shd; htd wc; shwrs inc; el pnts (3-10A) €3-4.60; gas; Indtte; shop & 4km; snacks; bar; BBQ; playgrnd; pool; climbing at Rocher St Julien & Gorges d'Ubrieux; horseriding & fishing nr; games area; games rm; 5% statics; dogs €2.50; phone; bus adj; Eng spkn; adv bkg; quiet; ccard acc; CCI. "Beautiful situation; haphazard pitch size; diff for o'fits over 6m; helpful owners." 1 Apr-1 Oct. € 15.50 2009*

BUISSON DE CADOUIN, LE see Bugue, Le *7C3*

BUJALEUF see St Léonard de Noblat *7B3*

BULGNEVILLE *6F2* (750m SE Rural) *48.20250, 5.84400* **Camping Porte des Voges, 15 Chemin des Curtilles, 88140 Bulgnéville [03 29 09 12 00; fax 03 29 09 15 71; camping.portedesvosges@wanadoo.fr; www.camping-portedesvosges.com]** Exit A31 junc 9; 1st rndabt foll sp Bulgnéville; Chemin des Curtilles 2nd turning to L (off D164). Site sp. Med, unshd; wc; chem disp; baby facs; shwrs inc; el pnts (10A) inc; Indtte; shop 2km; rest; playgrnd; dogs €2; phone; Eng spkn; adv bkg; quiet; ccard acc. "Conv NH fr A31; vg." 17 Apr-30 Sep. € 17.00 2008*

BURNHAUPT LE HAUT see Cernay *6F3*

The opening dates and prices on this campsite have changed. I'll send a site report form to the Club for the next edition of the guide.

BURTONCOURT *5D2* (1km W Rural) *49.22485, 6.39929* **FFCC Camping La Croix du Bois Sacker, 57220 Burtoncourt [tel/fax 03 87 35 74 08; camping.croixsacker@wanadoo.fr; www.campingcroixsacker.com]** Exit A4 junc 37 sp Argancy; at rndabt foll sp Malroy; at 2nd rndabt foll sp Chieuilles & cont to Vany; then take D3 for 12km dir Bouzonville; turn R onto D53A to Burtoncourt. Lge, hdg/mkd pitch, some hdstg, terr, pt shd; wc (mainly cont); mv service pnt; shwrs €1; el pnts (6A) inc; gas; Indtte; shop; tradsmn; rest, snacks 1km; bar; playgrnd; games area; lake sw, sand beach; fishing; tennis; entmnt; TV; 2% statics; dogs €1.50; phone; bus 300m; Eng spkn; adv bkg; quiet; CCI. "Lovely, wooded site in beautiful location; lge pitches; pleasant, friendly owners; clean san facs; forest walks; gd security; gd NH or sh stay en rte Alsace/Germany; conv Maginot Line; excel." ♦ 1 Apr-31 Oct. € 15.00 2008*

BUSSEROLLES see St Mathieu *7B3*

BUYSSCHEURE see St Omer *3A3*

BUZANCAIS *4H2* (500m N Urban) *46.89309, 1.41801* **Camp Municipal La Tête Noire, Allée des Sports, 36500 Buzançais [02 54 84 17 27 or 06 15 85 53 04 (mob); fax 02 54 02 13 45; buzancais@wanadoo.fr]** D943 (N143) fr Châteauroux thro town cent, cross rv, immed turn R into sports complex. Lge, some hdstg, pt shd; wc (some cont); mv service pnt; shwrs inc; el pnts (16A) inc; Indtte; shop, rest, snacks, bar 500m; playgrnd; pool 500m; entmnt; some statics; adv bkg; quiet; red low ssn/long stay; CCI. "Pleasant, peaceful situation on rv; lovely, well-kept site; clean facs; gd disabled facs; no access when office clsd but ample parking; no twin-axles; gd fishing." ♦ 1 May-30 Sep. € 11.60 2009*

BUZANCY *5C1* (1.5km SW Rural) *49.42647, 4.93891* **Camping La Samaritaine, 08240 Buzancy [03 24 30 08 88; fax 03 24 30 29 39; info@campinglasamaritaine.com; www.campinglasamaritaine.com]** Fr Sedan take D977 dir Vouziers for 23km. Turn L onto D12, cont to end & turn L onto D947 for Buzancy. On ent Buzancy in 100m turn 2nd R immed after g'ge on R sp Camping Stade. Foll sp to site on L past football pitches. Med, hdg/mkd pitch, some hdstg, pt shd; wc; chem disp (wc); mv service pnt; 45% serviced pitches; mv service pnt; baby facs; shwrs inc; el pnts (10A) inc; Indtte; sm shop; tradsmn; rest 1.6km; snacks, bar high ssn; BBQ (gas/charcoal); playgrnd; lake sw & sand beach adj; fishing; horseriding; tennis; games/TV rm; 10% statics; dogs €2.50; phone; Eng spkn; adv bkg; quiet; ccard not acc; red low ssn; CCI. "Beautiful area for walking/cycling; excel renovated site; helpful, pleasant staff; no site lighting; ltd san facs low ssn & poss not cleaned regularly." ♦ 1 May-20 Sep. € 18.50 ABS - P10 2009*

BUZY see Louvie Juzon *8F2*

CABOURG *3D1* (1km E Coastal) *49.28618, -0.09024* **Camp Municipal Les Tilleuls, Route de Lisieux, 14160 Dives-sur-Mer [02 31 91 25 21; fax 02 31 91 72 13; campinglestilleuls@wanadoo.fr; www.dives-sur-mer.com]** Fr Cabourg cross bdge to Dives-sur-Mer, turn R at traff lts (Rue Gaston Manneville) & foll camping sp past church at bottom of hill up to D45. Turn L, site on R in 300m. Or fr A13 take D400 sp Cabourg, pass Super U & Intermarché supmkts & turn R sp Camping Touristique, site on R in 1.2km. Lge, pt sl, pt shd; htd wc (mainly cont); shwrs inc; el pnts (6A) inc; Indry rm; shops 500m; playgrnd; sand beach 3km; horseriding; dogs; quiet. Easter-15 Sep. € 16.00 2008*

CABOURG *3D1* (8km SW Rural) *49.25210, -0.18823* **Camping Le Clos Tranquille, 17 Route de Troarn, 14810 Gonneville-en-Auge [02 31 24 21 36; fax 02 31 24 28 80; contact@campingleclostranquille.fr; www.campingleclostranquille.fr]** Fr Cabourg, take D513 twd Caen. 2km after Varaville turn R to Gonneville-en-Auge (by garden cent) D95A. Foll sp to vill, site ent on R after LH bend. Med, pt shd; wc; chem disp; el pnts (4-10A) €3-€5 (poss rev pol & long lead req); shwrs inc; gas; Indtte; tradsmn; snacks; shop; playgrnd; cycle hire; sand beach 5km; 12% statics €2; poss cr; Eng spkn; adv bkg; quiet; ccard acc; CCI. "Excel." 1 Mar-31 Dec. € 15.00 2007*

CABOURG *3D1* (1km W Coastal) *49.28166, -0.13795* **Camping La Pommeraie, Le Bas Cabourg, 14390 Cabourg [02 31 91 54 58 or 06 07 15 84 67; fax 02 31 91 66 57]** Take D513 fr Cabourg twd Caen. Site on L 1km after Bas-Cabourg sp. Med, pt shd; wc; shwrs €1; el pnts (5A) €4; gas; Indtte; shop; sand beach 800m; 90% statics; dogs; adv bkg; ccard acc. "Few touring pitches; san facs being updated (2009); mkt Sat." 1 Apr-30 Sep. € 18.00 2009*

CABOURG *3D1* (2km W Coastal) *49.28326, -0.17053* **Camping Les Peupliers, Allée des Pins, 14810 Merville-Franceville-Plage [tel/fax 02 31 24 05 07; contact@camping-peupliers.com; www.camping-peupliers.com]** Exit A13 to Cabourg onto D400, take D513 W, turn R sp Le Hôme, site sp, 2km E of Merville-Franceville. Med, pt sl, unshd; htd wc; chem disp; baby facs; shwrs inc; el pnts (10A) €5.50; Indtte; shop 2km; tradsmn; rest high ssn; snacks; bar; BBQ; playgrnd; htd pool; sand beach 300m; games area; tennis 2km; entmnt; TV; 50% statics; dogs €3.10; phone; poss cr; Eng spkn; adv bkg; ccard acc; red low ssn; CCI. "Pleasant, friendly, well-run, busy site; some lge pitches; clean, modern san facs; vg facs for children; conv ferries." ♦ 1 Apr-31 Oct. € 21.30 2009*

CABOURG *3D1* (6km W Coastal) *49.28319, -0.19098* **Camping Le Point du Jour, Route de Cabourg, 14810 Merville-Franceville-Plage [02 31 24 23 34; fax 02 31 24 15 54; camp.lepointdujour@wanadoo.fr; www.camping-lepointdujour.com]** Fr Ouistreham on D514 turn E at Bénouville onto D224, cross bdge onto D514, site on L dir Cabourg. Or fr A13/D675 (N175) exit Dozulé dir Cabourg, then D514 to site. Med, hdg pitch, pt shd; htd wc; chem disp; mv service pnt; baby facs; shwrs inc; el pnts (10A) €5 (poss rev pol); gas; Indtte; shop; tradsmn; rest; snacks; BBQ; playgrnd; htd, covrd pool; sand beach adj; games rm; entmnt; TV rm; wifi; 10% statics; dogs €3; bus; poss cr; adv bkg; quiet; ccard acc; red low ssn/long stay; CCI. "Excel site with sea views; direct access to Sword beach (D-Day) & sand dunes; conv Pegasus Bridge." ♦ 1 Mar-15 Nov. € 24.40 2009*

See advertisement

CABOURG *3D1* (6km W Coastal) *49.28296, -0.19072* **Camping Village Ariane, 100 Route de Cabourg, 14810 Merville-Franceville-Plage [02 31 24 52 52; fax 02 31 24 52 41; info@loisirs-ariane.com; www.camping-ariane.com]** Fr Ouistreham on D514 turn E at Bénouville onto D224, cross bdge onto D514 to site dir Cabourg. Or fr A13/D675 (N175) exit Dozulé dir Cabourg, then D514 to site. Lge, mkd pitch, pt shd; htd wc; chem disp; baby facs; fam bthrm; shwrs inc; el pnts (6-10A) €4; gas; Indtte; shop 500m; tradsmn; snacks; playgrnd; sand beach 300m; watersports & tennis nr; games area; games rm; wifi; entmnt; TV rm; 10% statics; dogs €3; Eng spkn; adv bkg; quiet; red long stay/low ssn; CCI. ♦ 1 Apr-5 Nov. € 19.20 2009*

See advertisement

CABRERETS *7D3* (1km NE Rural) *44.50771, 1.66234* **Camping Cantal, 46330 Cabrerets [05 65 31 26 61; fax 05 65 31 20 47]** Fr Cahors take D653 E for approx 15km bef turning R onto D662 E thro Vers & St Géry. Turn L onto D41 to Cabrerets. Site 1km after vill on R. Sm, pt sl, pt shd; wc; chem disp (wc); 50% serviced pitch; shwrs inc; el pnts €2; rv canoeing nrby; quiet; CCI. "Superb situation; peaceful site; warden calls; ground slightly bumpy; excel san facs; not suitable lge o'fits; conv Pech Merle; excel." 1 May-30 Oct. € 10.00 2008*

CABRIERES D'AIGUES see Pertuis *10E3*

CADENET *10E3* (10km NE Rural) *43.76871, 5.44970* **Camping Lou Badareu, La Rasparine, 84160 Cucuron [04 90 77 21 46; fax 04 90 77 27 68; contact@loubadareu.com; www.loubadareu.com]** In Cadenet foll sp for church (église) onto D45 dir Cucuron; S of Cucuron turn onto D27 (do not go into town); site is E 1km. Well sp fr D27. Sm, mkd pitch, pt sl, pt shd; ltd wc (own san rec); chem disp; shwrs inc; el pnts (4-10A) €3-4 (long lead poss req); Indtte; shop & 1km; tradsmn; playgrnd; pool; few statics; dogs €1.80; phone; quiet; CCI. "Pretty farm site in cherry orchard; friendly, helpful warden; sep access for high vans." ♦ 1 Apr-15 Oct. € 10.60 2008*

CADENET *10E3* (10km NE Rural) *43.75667, 5.44448* **FFCC Camping Le Moulin à Vent, Chemin de Gastoule, 84160 Cucuron [04 90 77 25 77; fax 04 90 77 28 12; bressier@aol.com; www.avignon-et-provence.com/campings/moulin-vent]** Fr A51 exit junc 15 to Pertuis. N on D56 fr Pertuis to Cucuron. Site sp S fr Cucuron vill dir Villelaure. Sm, mkd pitch, terr, pt shd; wc; mv service point; baby facs; shwrs inc; spa; el pnts inc (6-10A) €3-4; shop; tradsmn; snacks; Indtte; playgrnd; htd pool 4km; 10% statics; dogs €2.50; Eng spkn; quiet; CCI. "Spacious pitches, but access poss diff; friendly, helpful staff." ♦ 1 Apr-6 Oct. € 14.00 2009*

CADENET *10E3* (2km SW Rural) *43.71968, 5.35479* **Camping Val de Durance, Les Routes, 84160 Cadenet [04 90 68 37 75 or 04 42 20 47 25 (LS); fax 04 90 68 16 34; info@homair.com; www.homair.com]** Exit A7 at Cavaillon onto D973 dir Cadenet. In Cadanet take D59, site sp. Lge, hdg pitch, unshd; wc; chem disp; shwrs inc; el pnts (4-10A) €5 (long lead req); gas; Indtte; shop & 2km; rest; snacks; bar; playgrnd; pool; rv sw & beach; archery; canoeing; cycling; games area; entmnt; TV; 70% statics; dogs €5; adv bkg; red low ssn; ccard acc; CCI. "Dir access to lake; adj Luberon Park; san facs need update (2006); few mature trees; noisy entmnt till late most evenings high ssn." ♦ 28 Mar-4 Oct. € 26.00 2006*

CADENET *10E3* (5km SW Rural) *43.72073, 5.30223* **Camping de Silvacane, Ave de la Libération, 13640 La Roque-d'Anthéron [04 42 50 40 54; www.silvacaneenprovence.com]** Fr A7 take Sénas exit onto N7 twd Aix-en-Provence. In 10km take D561 E to La Roque-d'Anthéron. Site sp & visible fr rd. Med, terr, shd; wc; shwrs inc; el pnts (10A) inc; Indtte; shop; supmkt nr; snacks; bar; BBQ; playgrnd; pool; waterslide; fishing; tennis; entmnt; TV; many statics; dogs €3; poss cr; adv bkg; quiet but some rd noise; red low ssn; ccard acc; CCI. "Beautiful scenery in Durance Valley." ♦ 16 Jun-2 Sep. € 23.00 2007*

CADENET *10E3* (5km SW Rural) *43.72788, 5.32076* **Caravaning Domaine des Iscles, 13640 La Roque-d'Anthéron [04 42 50 44 25; fax 04 42 50 56 29; www.domaine-des-iscles.com or www.village-center.com]** Fr A7 at junc 26 take N7 sp Lambesc; At Pont Royal turn L onto D561 to La Roque-d'Anthéron; at rndabt on edge of vill stay on D561; immed R on slip rd, foll sp thro tunnel under canal. Lge, hdg pitch, pt shd; wc (cont); chem disp; mv service pnt; shwrs inc; el pnts (10A) inc; (long lead poss req); Indtte; shop; tradsmn; rest; snacks; bar; playgrnd; pool; lake adj; fishing; golf; tennis; games area; 10% statics; dogs €3; poss cr; Eng spkn; adv bkg; red low ssn; CCI. "Gd site for children; lge pitches; pleasant setting; san facs clean." ♦ 21 Apr-16 Sep. € 29.00 2007*

CADENET *10E3* (10km W Rural) *43.71360, 5.24664* **Camping L'Orée du Bois, Ave du Bois, 13350 Charleval [04 42 28 41 75; fax 04 42 28 47 48; www.oree-des-bois.com]** Fr Cadenet take D561 to La Roque-d'Anthéron, cont to Charleval. Site sp in vill. Lge, hdg/mkd pitch, pt sl, pt shd; htd wc; chem disp; shwrs inc; el pnts (10A) inc; gas; Indtte; shop high ssn; rest, snacks, bar 500m; playgrnd; pool adj; waterslide; entmnt; 30% statics; dogs €3; phone; poss cr; Eng spkn; adv bkg; poss noisy; ccard acc; CCI. 10 Mar-11 Nov. € 23.00 2007*

CAEN *3D1* (14km N Coastal) *49.32551, 0.39010* **Yelloh! Village Côte de Nacre, Rue du Général Moulton, 14750 St Aubin-sur-Mer [02 31 97 14 45; fax 02 31 97 22 11; camping-cote-de-nacre@wanadoo.fr; www.camping-cote-de-nacre.com or www.yellohvillage.com]** Fr Caen on D7 dir Douvres-la-Délivrande, Langrune-sur-Mer & St Aubin. Site in St Aubin-sur-Mer on S side of D514; clearly sp on o'skts. Lge, mkd pitch, hdstg, unshd; wc; chem disp; mv service pnt; baby facs; shwrs inc; el pnts (10A) inc; Indtte; shop high ssn; tradsmn; rest; snacks; bar; BBQ; playgrnd; htd pool; waterslide; sand beach 500m; tennis 200m; cycle hire; games rm; entmnt; TV; internet; 15% statics; dogs €4; quiet; phone; poss cr; Eng spkn; adv bkg rec; ccard acc; CCI. "Conv Normandy beaches, Mont St Michel, Honfleur; helpful staff; vg, modern san facs; vg." ♦ 3 Apr-27 Sep. € 44.00 2009*

See advertisement

CAGNES SUR MER *10E4* (2km N Rural) *43.67855, 7.12593* **Camping Caravaning St Paul, 637 Chemin du Malvan, 06570 St Paul [04 93 32 93 71; fax 04 93 32 01 97; booking@caravaningsaintpaul.fr; www.caravaningsaintpaul.fr]** Fr W exit A8 junc 47 dir Vence; fr E exit junc 48; in cent of Cagnes take D36 sp St Paul. At 3rd rndabt in 2km turn R & in 100m L to site in further 1km. Site sp. Med, hdg/mkd pitch, shd; wc; chem disp; mv service pnt; baby facs; shwrs inc; el pnts (6-10A) €3-4; gas; Indtte; shop 500m; tradsmn; rest; snacks; bar; playgrnd; pool; shgl beach 4.5km; cycle hire; entmnt; dogs €1.50; poss cr; Eng spkn; adv bkg; quiet; CCI. "Attractive, family-run site; well-kept & clean; conv Côte d'Azur." ♦ 1 Apr-30 Sep. € 24.00 2008*

France

CAGNES SUR MER *10E4* (3km N Rural) *43.68944, 7.15666* **Camping Green Park, 159 Vallon-des-Vaux, 06800 Cagnes-sur-Mer [04 93 07 09 96 or 06 80 48 25 74 (mob); fax 04 93 14 36 55; info@greenpark.fr; www.greenpark.fr]** Exit A8 junc 47 onto D6007 (N7) sp Villeneuve-Loubet, Cagnes-sur-Mer & Nice; at Cagnes at 1st traff lts (do not foll sp Centre Ville) - racecourse on R; go strt for 1.5km (8 sets of traff lts); then turn L onto Chemin du Val Fleuri; cont strt for 4km. Fr Nice take D6098 coast rd dir Cannes. Shortly after Cagnes turn R opp Le Port & foll sp Camping. Turn R then L at traff lts, site 3rd on L in 3km opp Camping Le Todos (same owner). Med, mkd pitch, pt shd; wc; chem disp; mv service pnt; baby facs; shwrs inc; el pnts (16A) inc; gas; lndtte; sm shop; rest; snacks; bar; BBQ (gas/elec); playgrnd; 2 htd pools; shgl beach 4.3km; fishing 4.5km; horseriding 12km; tennis 400m; sports area; cycle hire; disco; entmnt; wifi; games/TV rm; mainly statics; dogs €2.50-3.60; adv bkg rec; quiet; red low ssn; CCI. "Friendly; well-run; gd pool; excel; v ltd touring pitches." ♦ 31 Mar-18 Oct. € 57.90 (4 persons) 2008*

CAGNES SUR MER *10E4* (3km N Rural) *43.69018, 7.15643* **Camping Le Todos, 159 Vallon-des-Vaux, 06800 Cagnes-sur-Mer [04 93 31 20 05; fax 04 92 12 81 66; info@letodos.fr; www.letodos.fr]** Fr Aix on A8 exit junc 47 & foll dir Cagnes-sur-Mer/Nice on D6007 (N7) (do not foll sp 'Centre Ville'). After 1st traff lts beside racecourse strt on for 2km, then turn L dir Val Fleuri, site in 3km. Fr Nice take D6098 (N98) coast rd dir Cannes. Shortly after Cagnes turn R opp Le Port & foll sp Camping. Turn R then L at traff lts, site on L in 3km opp Camping Green Park. Med, mkd pitch, some terr, pt shd; wc; chem disp; mv service pnt; shwrs inc; el pnts (6-10A) €4.10-5.70; lndtte; tradmsn; shop; rest, snacks, bar at adj Camping Green Park; BBQ (gas/elec); playgrnd; pool & use of htd pool at Green Park; sand beach 4.5km; tennis 400m; cycle hire; games area; internet; TV; mainly statics; dogs €5; poss cr; adv bkg; quiet; red low ssn. "Owners also own Camping Green Park - some facs shared; v ltd touring pitches." ♦ 22 Mar-12 Oct. € 36.00 2009*

CAGNES SUR MER *10E4* (3.5km N Rural) *43.69468, 7.14323* **Camping La Rivière, 168 Chemin des Salles, 06800 Cagnes-sur-Mer [tel/fax 04 93 20 62 27; www.campinglariviere06.fr]** Fr D6007 N on D18 sp Val de Cagne. Site on rvside. Med, hdg/mkd pitch, pt shd; wc; shwrs inc; el pnts (4-6A) €2.90-€3.30; gas; lndtte; shop; rest; bar; playgrnd; pool; sand beach 4.5km; entmnt; 10% statics; dogs €1.50; poss cr; quiet; adv bkg; ccard acc. ♦ 1 Mar-31 Oct. € 20.50 2008*

CAGNES SUR MER *10E4* (3.5km N Rural) *43.69850, 7.14212* **Camping Le Val de Cagnes, 179 Chemin des Salles, 06800 Cagnes-sur-Mer [tel/fax 04 93 73 36 53; valdecagnes@wanadoo.fr; www.camping-leval-cagnes.com]** On A8 exit Cagnes sur Mer, foll sp for Centre Ville. In town foll sp 'Haut de Cagnes' to Rue Jean Féraud, then R fork onto Chemin des Salles & foll for approx 3km to site on L, past La Rivière. Sm, hdg/mkd pitch, terr, shd; wc; chem disp; shwrs inc; el pnts (6A) €3.50; Indtte; rest & snacks 3.5km; BBQ; htd pool; shgl beach 4km; some statics; dogs €3; Eng spkn; adv bkg; quiet; ccard not acc; red low ssn; CCI. "Pleasant, peaceful, family-run site; sm pitches; clean san facs, ltd low ssn; trains to Monaco & Italy fr town." 1 Feb-31 Oct. € 22.00 2009*

CAGNES SUR MER *10E4* (3.5km N Rural) *43.68717, 7.15589* **Camping Le Val Fleuri, 139 Vallon-des-Vaux, 06800 Cagnes-sur-Mer [tel/fax 04 93 31 21 74; valfleuri2@wanadoo.fr; www.campingvalfleuri.fr]** Fr Nice take D6007 (N7) W twd Cannes. On app Cagnes turn R & foll sp Camping; site on R after 3km, well sp. NB 3.3m height restriction on this rte. Sm, terr, pt shd; wc (some cont); shwrs; el pnts (3-10A) €4 shop 3km; tradsmn; rest; shgl beach 4km; playgrnd; htd pool; entmnt; wifi; dogs €1.50; poss cr; Eng spkn; adv bkg; red low ssn. "Gd, improving site, divided by rd (not busy); some sm pitches; helpful, friendly owners; gd." 14 Feb-31 Oct. € 19.50 2008*

CAGNES SUR MER *10E4* (8km NE Rural) *43.71466, 7.17775* **Camping Magali, 1814 Route de la Baronne, 06700 St Laurent-du-Var [04 93 31 57 00; fax 04 92 12 01 33; info@camping-magali.com; www.camping-magali.com]** Exit A8 junc 49 to St Laurent-du-Var. Site sp fr town cent. Or fr Digne S on D6202 bis (N202), turn R onto D2210 at Pont-de-la-Manda; foll sp to St Laurent-du-Var for approx 7km, site on L. Med, mkd, pitch pt shd; htd wc (mainly cont); chem disp; shwrs inc; baby facs; el pnts (2-4A) €2.70-3.50; gas; Indtte; shop; rest; snacks; bar; pool; shgl beach 6km; sailing; fishing; tennis; horseriding; some statics; dogs €2; bus nrby; poss cr; adv bkg; quiet; ccard acc; red low ssn. "Conv Nice ferry (25 mins to port), Nice carnival/Menton Lemon Fair; sm pitches." ♦ 1 Feb-31 Oct. € 22.30 2008*

CAGNES SUR MER *10E4* (2km S Coastal) *43.63128, 7.12993* **Camping Parc des Maurettes, 730 Ave du Docteur Lefebvre, 06270 Villeneuve-Loubet [04 93 20 91 91; fax 04 93 73 77 20; info@parcdesmaurettes.com; www.parcdesmaurettes.com]** Fr Nice exit A8 junc 47, turn L onto D6007 (N7) dir Antibes; foll sp Intermarché, then R into Rue des Maurettes; site in 250m. N fr Cannes on A8 exit Villeneuve-Loubet-Plage junc 46; foll D241 over D6007 & rwly line, U-turn back over rwly line, then R onto D6007 dir Antibes as above. NB Site on steep cliff with narr winding rds packed with trees; diff ent. Med, mkd pitch, terr, pt shd; htd wc; chem disp; mv service pnt; some serviced pitches; shwrs inc; el pnts (3-10A) €3.20-5.30; gas; Indtte; shops adj; snacks; playgrnd; htd, covrd pool; shgl beach 500m; wifi; sat TV; dogs €1.90; train Nice 400m; poss cr; Eng spkn; adv bkg; quiet; red long stay; ccard acc; CCI. "Well-kept site with clean facs (facs poor Jun 2008 & many uneven steps); variable pitch size/price." ♦ 10 Jan-15 Nov. € 27.15 2008*

⊞ **CAGNES SUR MER** *10E4* (7km S Rural) *43.62027, 7.12583* **Camping La Vieille Ferme, 296 Blvd des Groules, 06270 Villeneuve-Loubet-Plage [04 93 33 41 44; fax 04 93 33 37 28; info@vieilleferme.com; www.vieilleferme.com or www.les-castels.com]** Fr W (Cannes) take Antibes exit 44 fr A8, foll D35 dir Antibes 'Centre Ville'. At lge junc turn onto D6007 (N7), Ave de Nice, twd Biot & Villeneuve-Loubet sp Nice (rlwy line on R). Just after Marineland turn L onto Blvd des Groules. Fr E (Nice) leave A8 at junc 47 to join D6007 twd Antibes, take 3rd turning after Intermarché supmkt; site well sp fr D6007. Med, hdg/mkd pitch, pt terr, pt sl, pt shd; htd wc; chem disp; mv service pnt; serviced pitches; baby facs; shwrs inc; el pnts (10A) inc; gas; Indtte; sm shop; supmkt 800m; snacks; BBQ (gas/elec only); playgrnd; 2 pools (1 htd/covrd); shgl beach 1km (busy rd & rlwy to cross); archery; games rm; wifi; games/TV rm; 40% statics; dogs €2; c'vans over 8m not acc; bus, train nrby; Eng spkn; adv bkg; some aircraft & rd noise; ccard acc; red long stay/low ssn. "Well-kept, popular, family-run site; gd sized pitches; beach not suitable children & non-swimmers; excel pool; gd for walking, cycling & dogs as lge park adj; well-drained, lge pitches; vg value low ssn; excel." ♦ € 38.00 ABS - C22 2009*

CAGNES SUR MER *10E4* (2km SW Rural) *43.61944, 7.12565* **Caravaning L'Oree de Vaugrenier, Blvd des Groules, 06270 Villeneuve-Loubet [tel/fax 04 93 33 57 30]** Take D6007 (N7) fr Antibes, strt over rndabt at Biot & turn L in 500m. Site ent 100m past Camping La Vieille Ferme. C'vans only. Sm, hdg pitch, hdstg, pt shd; chem disp; 75% serviced pitch; wc; shwrs inc; el pnts (2-10A) €2.05-3.25; gas; Indtte; shops 3km; playgrnd; shgl beach 1.5km; dogs €2.80; adv bkg; quiet; ccard acc; CCI. "Excel, secure, clean, family-run site; lge pitches; hdstg suitable for awnings; adj Vaugrenier National Park." Easter-15 Oct. € 20.00 (3 persons) 2006*

CAGNES SUR MER *10E4* (4km SW Rural) *43.66001, 7.1000* **Parc Saint James Le Sourire, Route de Grasse, 06270 Villeneuve-Loubet [04 93 20 96 11; fax 04 93 22 07 52; lesourire@camping-parcsaintjames.com; www.camping-parcsaintjames.com]** Exit A8 at junc 47; take D2 to Villeneuve; at rndbt take D2085 sp Grasse. Site on L in 2km. Sp Le Sourire. Med, hdg pitch, hdstg, pt shd; htd wc; shwrs inc; el pnts (6A) inc; Indtte; tradsmn; rest; bar; playgrnd; htd pools; shgl beach 5km; tennis, golf & horseriding nr; games area; entmnt; 70% statics; dogs €5; Eng spkn; adv bkg; some rd noise; red long stay/low ssn; ccard acc. "Vg; red facs low ssn; park in visitors' car park bef registering; conv Nice, Cannes & beaches." ♦ 3 Apr-25 Sep. € 30.00 2009*

See advertisement opposite

CAGNES SUR MER *10E4* (1km NW Urban) *43.67159, 7.13845* **Camping Le Colombier, Collines de la Route de Vence, 35 Chemin de Ste Colombe, 06800 Cagnes-sur-Mer [tel/fax 04 93 73 12 77; campinglecolombier06@wanadoo.fr; www.campinglecolombier.com]** N fr Cagnes cent foll 1-way system dir Vence. Half way up hill turn R at rndabt dir Cagnes-sur-Mer & R at next island. Site on L 300m, sp fr town cent. Sm, hdg/mkd pitch, pt shd; htd wc; chem disp; mv service pnt; shwrs inc; el pnts (2-6A) €1.80-3.30; Indry rm; shop 400m; rest 800m; snacks; bar; no BBQ; playgrnd, sm pool adj; TV; beach 2.5km; cycle hire; some statics; no dogs Jul/Aug; phone; Eng spkn; quiet; red long stay/CCI. "Friendly, family-run site." 1 Apr-30 Sep. € 22.20 2007*

CAGNES SUR MER *10E4* (4km NW Rural) *43.68449, 7.07297* **Camping Le Vallon Rouge, Route de Gréolières, 06480 La Colle-sur-Loup [04 93 32 86 12 or 06 82 90 93 05 (mob); fax 04 93 32 80 08; info@auvallonrouge.com; www.auvallonrouge.com]** Exit A8 junc 47 onto D6007 (N7) dir Nice then D2 to Villeneuve-Loubet. Foll sp Villeneuve-Loubet over rv & thro sh tunnel to rndabt. Turn L at rndabt & foll sps for D6 La Colle-sur-Loup; site on R in 2.5km. NB Lge o'fits park in lay-by & ask at recep bef tackling steep downhill ent driveway. NB Ask recep for code for rear gate on leaving. Med, mkd pitch, hdstg, shd; wc; chem disp; mv service pnt; baby facs; shwrs inc; solarium; el pnts (10A) inc; Indtte; tradsmn; rest; snacks; BBQ (gas/elec); playgrnd; pool; paddling pool; shgl beach 9km; fishing; games area; entmnt; wifi; games/TV rm; 40% statics; dogs €3.50; adv bkg; ccard acc; red low ssn; CCI. "Conv Nice, Cannes, St Paul-de-Vence & Grasse; Sat mkt; vg site." ♦ 5 Apr-26 Sep. € 33.00 (CChq acc) ABS - C20 2009*

CAGNES SUR MER *10E4* (4km NW Rural) *43.68272, 7.08391* **Camping Les Pinèdes, Route de Pont de Pierre, 06480 La Colle-sur-Loup [04 93 32 98 94; fax 04 93 32 50 20; camplespinedes06@aol.com; www.lespinedes.com]** Exit A8 junc 47; take D6007 (N7) dir Nice, then D2 sp Villeneuve-Loubet; turn R at rndabt sp Villeneuve-Loubet & cross rv bdge; go thro sh tunnel, other side is Cagnes-sur-Mer & rndabt; turn L onto D6 to Colle-sur-Loup; site on R sh dist after Colle-sur-Loup. NB Take 2nd turning into site (1st leads to restaurant). Lge, hdg/mkd pitch, hdstg, pt sl, terr, pt shd; wc; chem disp; mv service pnt; serviced pitches; shwrs inc; el pnts (10A) inc; Indtte; shop (high ssn) & 1.5km; tradsmn; rest; snacks; bar; BBQ (gas/elec); playgrnd; pool; paddling pool; solarium; sand beach 3km; fishing adj; tennis, horseriding 1.5km; cycle hire; archery; games area; entmnt; wifi; games/TV rm; 20% statics; dogs €3.20; c'vans over 6m & m'vans over 8m not acc high ssn; Eng spkn; adv bkg; quiet; ccard acc over €50; red long stay/low ssn/CCI. "Excel, family-run site; pleasant, helpful & friendly; spacious pitches; steep access to pitches but gd rd surface; not suitable for disabled; luxurious san facs; highly rec." 15 Mar-30 Sep. € 36.50 ABS - C30 2009*

See advertisement above

CAHAGNES see Villers Bocage *3D1*

CAHORS *7D3* (8km N Rural) *44.52585, 1.46048* **Camping Les Graves, 46090 St Pierre-Lafeuille [tel/fax 05 65 36 83 12; infos@camping-lesgraves.com; www.camping-lesgraves.com]** Leave A20 at junc 57 Cahors Nord onto D820 (N20). Foll sp St Pierre-Lafeuille; at N end of vill, site is opp L'Atrium wine cave. Med, hdg pitch, sl, pt shd; wc, chem disp; mv service pnt; shwrs inc; el pnts (6-10A) €2.50-3.50 (poss rev pol); Indtte; shop 10km; tradsmn; rest; snacks; bar; playgrnd; pool; cycle hire; 5% statics; dogs €1.50; adv bkg rec high ssn; rd noise; ccard acc; red low ssn/CCI. "Clean, scenic site; lge pitches; poss clsd during/after wet weather due boggy ground; disabled facs over stony rd & grass; ltd facs low ssn; poss unkempt & pools dirty low ssn; conv for a'route." ♦ 1 Apr-31 Oct. € 14.50 2009*

CAHORS *7D3* (8km N Rural) *44.53136, 1.45926* **Quercy-Vacances, Mas de la Combe, 46000 St Pierre-Lafeuille [05 65 36 87 15; fax 05 65 36 02 39; quercyvacances@wanadoo.fr; www.quercy-vacances.com]** Heading N on D820 (N20), turn L at N end of St Pierre-Lafeuille turn W at site sp N of vill, site in 700m down lane; new site opened adj so care needed to spot correct sp. Fr A20 exit junc 57 & foll sp N20. Med, pt sl, pt shd; wc; chem disp; baby facs; shwrs inc; el pnts (6-10A) €3.30-5.30; gas; Indtte; shops 10km; tradsmn; rest; snacks; bar; playgrnd; pool; tennis; TV; some statics; dogs €1.50; phone; Eng spkn; adv bkg; quiet; ltd facs low ssn; ccard acc; red low ssn; CCI. "Pretty site; most pitches slightly sloping; clean, modern san facs; poss unkempt low ssn; lge pool needs overhaul (2008); helpful owner; vg." ♦ 1 Apr-31 Oct. € 18.80 2008*

CAHORS *7D3* (1.5km E Urban) *44.46318, 1.44226* **Camping Rivière de Cabessut, Rue de la Rivière, 46000 Cahors [05 65 30 06 30; fax 05 65 23 99 46; camping-riviere-cabessut@wanadoo.fr; www.cabessut.com]** Fr N or S on D820 (N20), at S end Cahors by-pass take D911 sp Rodez. At traff lts by bdge do not cross rv but bear R on D911. In 1km at site sp turn L. Site on E bank of Rv Lot, well sp fr town. 1.8km to site fr bdge (Pont Cabessut). Med, hdg/mkd pitch, pt shd; wc; chem disp; mv service pnt; some serviced pitches; baby facs; shwrs inc; el pnts (10A) €2 (poss rev pol); gas; Indtte; shop; hypmkt 1.5km; tradsmn; rest; snacks; bar; BBQ (gas only); playgrnd; pool (no shorts); rv adj; 5% statics; dogs €2; phone; frequent 'park & ride' bus to Cahors 600m approx; poss cr; adv bkg rec - ess high ssn; quiet; CCI. "Excel, well-run site; pleasant, helpful owners; some v lge pitches, sm pitches diff access when site full; gd san facs, ltd low ssn; gd for children; food mkt Wed, full mkt Sat." ♦ 1 Apr-30 Sep. € 16.00 2009*

CAHORS *7D3* (7km E Rural) *44.46681, 1.48469* **Camp Municipal Lamagdelaine, 46090 Lamagdelaine [05 65 35 05 97 (Mairie); fax 05 65 22 64 93]** Fr Cahors take D653 sp Figeac; site on R at Lamagdelaine rndabt. Fr Figeac on D802 (D653) sp Cahors; rndabt is 9km after Vers. Sm, pt shd; wc (some cont); shwrs inc; el pnts €1.80; shops 1.5km; pool 7km; dogs €1; quiet; CCI. "Lovely, quiet site; warden 0800-0930 & 1730-2000, barrier locked outside these hrs; chain across ent 2200; key fr Mairie adj if warden absent, but office infrequently open (3 afternoons p/w); rec arrive when warden present." 15 Jun-Aug. € 9.50 2007*

CAJARC *7D4* (300m SW Urban) *44.48374, 1.83928* **Camp Municipal Le Terriol, Rue Le Terriol, 46160 Cajarc [05 65 40 72 74 or 05 65 40 65 20 (Mairie); fax 05 65 40 39 05; mairie.cajarc@wanadoo.fr]** Fr Cahors dir Cajarc on D662 on L foll sp to site. Sm, hdg/mkd pitches, some hdstg, pt shd; wc (cont); chem disp; baby facs; fam bthrm; shwrs inc; el pnts (10A) inc (poss rev pol); Indtte; shop, rest, bar in vill; BBQ; playgrnd; pool & tennis 500m; dogs; phone; no twin-axles; Eng spkn; adv bkg; some rd noise; CCI. "Gd sized pitches; clean, basic facs; lovely sm town on Rv Lot has gd rests & facs." 1 May-30 Sep. € 14.00 2008*

CAJARC *7D4* (6km SW Rural) *44.46630, 1.75077* **Camp Municipal Le Grand Pré, 46330 Cénevières [05 65 30 22 65 or 05 65 31 28 16 (Marie); fax 05 65 31 37 00; mairie.cenevieres@wanadoo.fr]** Fr Villefranche on D911 twd Cahors turn R onto D24 at Limogne for Cénevières. Foll sp. Fr St Cirq-Lapopie on D24 thro vill & over rlwy. Sm, hdg/mkd pitch, pt shd; wc; chem disp (wc); mv service pnt; shwrs inc; el pnts (10A) inc; rest, snacks, bar 1km; BBQ; dogs; bus; phone; quiet. "Peaceful site with vg san facs; site self & warden calls pm; wonderful views of cliffs." 1 Jun-28 Sep. € 11.30 2008*

CAJARC *7D4* (6km W Rural) *44.4735, 1.7835* **Camping Ruisseau de Treil, 46160 Larnagol [05 65 31 23 39; fax 05 65 31 23 27; lotcamping@wanadoo.fr; www.lotcamping.com]** Exit A20 junc 57 onto D49 sp St Michel; in 4km turn R onto D653; after 5.5km in Vers at mini-rndabt turn L onto D662; site on L immed after leaving Larnagol. Or fr Figeac foll D19 thro Cajarc. At top of hill leaving Cajarc turn R onto D662 sp Cahors & Larnagol. Site sp on R 300m bef Larnagol on blind bend. Sm, mkd pitch, pt sl, pt shd; wc; chem disp; baby facs; shwrs inc; el pnts (6A) €3.60; Indtte; tradsmn; rest; snacks; bar; BBQ; playgrnd; 2 pools; rv sw, fishing, canoeing adj; horseriding; cycle hire; TV rm; 4% statics; dogs €3.60; poss cr; Eng spkn; adv bkg; quiet; 20-30% red low ssn & snr citizen; CCI. "Spacious, British-owned site in lovely area; friendly, helpful owners; clean san facs but ltd when site full; pitches poss uneven; guided walks; vg touring base; excel." ♦ 12 May-15 Sep. € 19.30 2008*

⊞ **CALAIS** *3A3* (8km E Rural) *50.98730, 2.04199* **Camping Bouscarel, 448 Rue du Lac, Le Tap-Cul, 62215 Oye-Plage [03 21 36 76 37; fax 03 21 35 68 19; bouscarel62@aol.com]** Fr W exit A16 at junc 49 & foll D940 twd Oye-Plage; at traff lts in cent of Oye-Plage turn L; at junc with D119 turn R, site on R in 200m. Fr E exit A16 junc 50 onto D219 to Oye-Plage. At traff lts strt on then R onto D119, site on R in 200m. Med, hdg/mkd pitch, hdstg, pt shd; wc; chem disp; mv service pnt; shwrs inc; el pnts (6A) €3; Indtte; shops 1.5km; playgrnd; sand beach 2km; games/TV rm; 60% statics; dogs €1.90; phone; poss cr; adv bkg rec; ccard not acc; CCI. "Neat, well-kept site; gd sized pitches; friendly owners; san facs clean, poss stretched high ssn; poss noisy high ssn due to constant arr/dep of campers; late arrivals welcome; conv for Calais & Dunkerque ferries/tunnel/Cité Europe or to tour area; gd." ♦ € 15.80 2009*

CALAIS *3A3* (8km E Rural) *50.98020, 2.01393* **Camping Les Petits Moulins, 1634 Rue des Petits Moulins, 62215 Oye-Plage [03 21 85 12 94]** Fr A16 junc 21 proceed to Oye-Plage. Strt thro traff lts & take 2nd L to site past derelict windmill. Sm, unshd; wc (own facs low ssn); chem disp (wc); shwrs inc; el pnts (10A) inc; shops 2km; sw beach 2km; 90% statics; dogs; poss cr; quiet. "Busy, well-kept CL-type site at end of statics site; open view; friendly, helpful owner; gd, basic san facs; ltd el pnts; poss run down low ssn; find pitch, book in house adj; ltd touring pitches; phone ahead; conv ferries; NH only." 15 Apr-30 Sep. € 12.00 2009*

⊞ **CALAIS** *3A3* (12km E Coastal) *50.99657, 2.05062* **Camping Clairette, 525 Route des Dunes, 62215 Oye-Plage [tel/fax 03 21 35 83 51; camping.clairette.sarl@cegetel.net]** Exit A16 junc 50 & foll sp Oye-Plage. At traff lts at D940 cont strt. At junc with D119 turn R then L, site on L in 2km. Foll sp 'Réserve Naturelle'. Med, mkd pitch, pt sl, unshd; htd wc (own san rec); chem disp (wc); mv service pnt; shwrs inc; el pnts (6-10A) inc; gas 5km; Indtte; shops 5km; tradsmn; BBQ; sm playgrnd; htd, covrd pool 5km; beach 500m; 90% statics; dogs €1.30; clsd 16 Dec-14 Jan; poss cr; Eng spkn; adv bkg; quiet, some rd noise; ccard acc; CCI. "Warm welcome; helpful owners; basic, dated facs; security barrier; v ltd touring pitches; nature reserve nrby; conv ferries; fair." € 19.00 2009*

This is a wonderful site.

I'll fill in a report online and let the Club know – www.caravanclub.co.uk/europereport

⊞ **CALAIS** *3A3* (12km E Rural) *50.96613, 2.05270* **Camping Le Pont d'Oye, 300 Rue de la Rivière, 62215 Oye-Plage [03 21 35 81 25 or 06 67 56 43 46 (mob); campingpontdoye@aol.com]** Exit A16 at junc 50 onto D219 to Oye-Plage; cross rv & immed turn R sp camping; foll rv; site on L. Sm, unshd; wc; chem disp (wc); shwrs €0.80; el pnts (6A) €2; gas; Indtte; shop 2km; tradsmn; playgrnd; mainly statics; dogs; CCI. "Basic CL-type site; few touring pitches; grassed field for c'vans; site scruffy (2009); friendly, helpful owners; san facs adj statics park - v dated but clean; conv ferries; NH only." ♦ € 10.60 2009*

⊞ **CALAIS** *3A3* (1km SW Coastal) *50.96603, 1.84370* **Aire Communale, Plage de Calais, Ave Raymond Poincaré, 62100 Calais [03 21 46 66 41; tourisme-patrimonie@marie-calais.fr]** A16 exit junc 43 dir Blériot-Plage/Calais cent & foll sp for beach (plage). Site nr harbour wall & Fort Risban. Well sp fr town cent. Med; wc; water; shop, rest nrby; obtain token/pass fr Camp Municipal adj; wc part-time & have attendant & charge; warden calls to collect fee pm or pay at Camp Municipal; noise fr ferries; m'vans only. "Well-kept, busy site; gd NH to/fr ferries; bracing walks." € 7.00 2009*

CALAIS *3A3* (1km SW Coastal) *50.96490, 1.84339* **Camp Municipal, Plage de Calais, Ave Raymond Poincaré, 62100 Calais [03 21 34 73 25 or 03 21 97 89 79 (Mairie); tourisme-patrimonie@marie-calais.fr; www.calais.fr]** A16 exit junc 43 dir Blériot-Plage/Calais cent & foll sp for beach (plage). Site nr harbour wall & Fort Risban. If barrier down during day, call at building adj site office. Lge, unshd; wc; shwrs; el pnts (10A) €2.50 (poss rev pol); Indtte; sand beach 200m; 70% statics; poss cr; Eng spkn; adv bkg for 3+ nights only high ssn; noise fr ferries daytime but quiet at night; ccard acc. "Helpful recep; some sm pitches; rec arr early to secure a pitch high ssn; clean, OK san facs; barrier should open 0700 but poss down low ssn at w/end & warden poss diff to find after 1700 or absent altogether - check if req early dep; gd rests nr; conv ferries & beach; gd NH." Easter-31 Oct. € 10.20 2009*

CALAIS *3A3* (4km SW Coastal) *50.95677, 1.81101* **Camp Municipal du Fort Lapin, 62231 Sangatte-Blériot Plage [03 21 97 67 77 or 03 21 97 89 79 (Mairie)]** Fr E exit junc 43 fr A16 Calais cent, dir beach (Blériot-Plage). Turn L along coast onto D940 dir Sangatte; site on R in dunes shortly after water tower, opp sports cent; site sp fr D940. Fr S exit A16 junc 41 to Sangatte; at T-junc turn R onto D940; site on L just bef water tower. Lge, mkd pitch, pt sl, unshd; wc (some cont); own san high ssn; chem disp; baby facs; shwrs inc poss clsd 2130; el pnts (10A) inc (poss rev pol)(take care elecs); Indtte; shop 1km; rest; snacks; bar; BBQ; playgrnd; sand beach adj; 50% statics; dogs; phone; bus; poss cr; adv bkg; quiet; CCI. "Warden lives on site - if recep unmanned; rec arr bef 1700 high ssn; gates clsd 2300-0700; ltd parking outside espec w/end - phone ahead for access code; poss youth groups high ssn; adequate san facs; gd bus service; conv Auchan & Cité Europe shops; conv NH." ♦ 21 May-31 Aug. € 17.90 2008*

CALAIS *3A3* (8km SW Rural) *50.91160, 1.75127* **Camping Les Epinettes, Mont-Pinet, 62231 Peuplingues [03 21 85 22 24 or 03 21 85 21 39; fax 03 21 85 26 95; info@lesepinettes.fr; www.lesepinettes.fr]** A16 fr Calais to Boulogne, exit junc 40 W on D243 sp Peuplingues, go thro vill & foll sp; site on L in 3km. Med, hdg pitch, pt sl, pt shd; wc; chem disp; shwrs €1; el pnts (4A) €1.50; Indtte; sm shop & 3km; hypmkt 5km; tradsmn; rest 1.5km; playgrnd; sand beach 3km; 80% statics; dogs €1; phone; poss cr; adv bkg; quiet; ccard acc; CCI. "Pleasant, easy-going site; san facs clean but insufficient for site size; adv bkg doesn't guarantee pitch high ssn; when bureau clsd, site yourself - warden calls eve or call at cottage to pay; if arr late, park on grass verge outside main gate; use facs excl elec - pay half price; some pitches sm; conv NH for ferries & tunnel." 1 Apr-30 Oct. € 10.90 2009*

France

CALAIS *3A3* (5km W Coastal) *50.94610, 1.75798* **Camping des Noires Mottes (formerly Cassiopée), Rue Pierre Dupuy, 62231 Sangatte [tel/fax 03 21 82 04 75; www.ville-sangatte.fr]** Fr A16 exit junc 41 sp Sangatte onto D243, at T-junc in vill turn R then R again bef monument. Lge, hdg/mkd pitch, pt sl, pt shd; wc (some cont); chem disp; mv service pnt; shwrs inc (clsd 2130-0800); el pnts (10A) €3.70; Indtte; shop 200m; tradsmn; playgrnd; sand beach 500m; many statics; dogs €1.30; bus 500m; poss cr; some Eng spkn; adv bkg rec high ssn; ccard not acc; CCI. "Conv ferries & Eurotunnel; lge pitches; new owners (2009); san facs need update & poss unclean (2009); barrier - no arrival bef office opens 1500 (1600 low ssn); san facs clsd o'night & poss 1200-1600; some pitches boggy when wet; windy spot; OK NH." ♦ 15 Mar-15 Nov. € 14.20 2009*

CALLAC *2E2* (1km SW Rural) *48.40150, -3.43609* **Camp Municipal La Verte Vallée, Rue de la Verte Vallée, 22160 Callac [02 96 45 58 50 or 02 96 45 81 30 (Mairie); fax 02 96 45 91 70; commune@mairie-callac.fr]** Sp fr all town app rds, on D28 to Morlaix. Off Ave Ernest Renan. Med, mkd pitch, terr, pt shd, unshd; wc; shwrs; el pnts (16A) €1.80; gas; shop 1km; lake sw 500m; fishing; quiet but some traff noise." 15 Jun-15 Sep. € 7.60 2007*

CALVIAC EN PERIGORD see Sarlat la Canéda *7C3*

CAMARET SUR MER *2E1* (500m Urban) *48.27698, -4.60430* **Camp Municipal du Lannic, Rue du Grouanoc'h, 29570 Camaret-sur-Mer [02 98 27 91 31 or 02 98 27 94 22; www.camaret-sur-mer.com]** On ent town foll sp to Port, on quayside to L turn sp Camping-Golf Miniature/m'van parking. Foll sp to site in 500m behind sports cent. Lge, pt sl, pt shd; wc; chem disp; mv service pnt; baby facs; shwrs €2; Indtte; shops 500m; el pnts €2.50; sand beach 1km; some statics; dogs €1; poss cr; quiet. "Excel site bet town & beach; sections for vans & tents." 1 May-30-Sep. € 9.10 2006*

CAMARET SUR MER *2E1* (2km NE Coastal) *48.28070, -4.56490* **Camping Le Grand Large, Lambézen, 29570 Camaret-sur-Mer [02 98 27 91 41; fax 02 98 27 93 72; contact@campinglegrandlarge.com; www.campinglegrandlarge.com]** On D8 bet Crozen & Camaret, turn R at ent to Camaret onto D355, sp Roscanvel. Foll sps to site in 3km. Med, hdg/mkd pitch, pt sl, pt shd; wc; chem disp; baby facs; shwrs inc; el pnts (10A) inc; gas; Indtte (inc dryer); shop; snacks; bar; BBQ; playgrnd; htd pool; sandy & shgl beach 450m; tennis; boating; TV; dogs €1.50; adv bkg; quiet; ccard acc; red low ssn. "Coastal views fr some pitches; pleasant, helpful owners; cliff top walk to town; excel." ♦ 29 Mar-30 Sep. € 26.50 (CChq acc) 2009*

CAMARET SUR MER *2E1* (3.5km NE Coastal) *48.28788, -4.56540* **Camping Plage de Trez-Rouz, 29160 Camaret-sur-Mer [02 98 27 93 96; fax 02 98 27 84 54; camping-plage-de-trez-rouz@wanadoo.fr; www.trezrouz.com]** Foll D8 to Camaret-sur-Mer & at rndabt turn N sp Roscanvel/D355. Site on R in 3km. Med, hdg/mkd pitch, pt sl, pt shd; wc; chem disp; mv service pnt; baby facs; shwrs inc; el pnts (16A) €3; Indtte; shop; tradsmn; rest; snacks; playgrnd; sand beach; tennis 500m; horseriding 2km; 10% statics; poss cr; adv bkg; poss cr; quiet; CCI. "Great position opp beach; conv for Presqu'île de Crozon; gd facs but stretched high ssn; site scruffy low ssn; friendly owner." 15 Mar-15 Oct. € 15.20 2006*

CAMBIAC see Caraman *8F4*

CAMBO LES BAINS *8F1* (1.3km SW Rural) *43.35526, -1.41484* **Camping Bixta-Eder, Route de St Jean-de-Luz, 64250 Cambo-les-Bains [05 59 29 94 23; fax 05 59 29 23 70; contact@camping-bixtaeder.com; www.camping-bixtaeder.com]** Fr Bayonne on D932 (ignore 1st sp Cambo-les-Bains) exit at junc with D918 L twd Cambo. Site on L nr top of hill (Intermarché supmkt at by-pass junc). Med, mkd pitch, pt sl, pt shd; wc; baby facs; shwrs inc; el pnts (6-10A) €3.55-4; Indtte; shops 500m; rest, bar 100m; sand beach 20km; playgrnd; pool, tennis 400m; wifi; TV; dogs €1; poss cr; adv bkg; ccard acc. "Clean facs; muddy when wet." ♦ 15 Apr-15 Oct. € 14.50 2009*

⊞ **CAMBO LES BAINS** *8F1* (3km SW Rural) *43.33863, -1.40129* **Camping L'Hiriberria, 64250 Itxassou [05 59 29 98 09; fax 05 59 29 20 88; hiriberria@wanadoo.fr; www.hiriberria.com]** Fr Cambo-les-Bains on D932 to Itxassou. Site on L 200m fr D918. Lge, hdg/mkd pitch, hdstg, pt sl, pt shd; htd wc (some cont); chem disp; mv service pnt; shwrs inc; baby facs; el pnts (5A) €3.25; gas; Indtte; shops 2km; tradsmn; rest, bar 1km; snacks 3km; BBQ; playgrnd; htd, covrd pool; rv 2km; games area; wifi; TV rm; 20% statics; dogs €1; Eng spkn; phone; quiet; 10% red 21+ days; CCI. "Popular site, phone ahead rec; gd views Pyrenees; pretty vill in 1km." ♦ € 17.75 2009*

CAMBO LES BAINS *8F1* (5km W Rural) *43.33969, -1.47000* **Camping Alegera, 64250 Souraïde [05 59 93 91 80; www.camping-alegera.com]** Fr St Jean-de-Luz take D918 to Souraïde, site sp on L on rvside. Lge, hdg/mkd pitch; pt shd; wc (cont); chem disp; mv service pnt; baby facs; shwrs inc; el pnts (4-10A) €3.20-3.90 (poss rev pol); gas; Indtte; ice, shop (high ssn) & 150m; snacks; BBQ (gas/elec); playgrnd; pool; fishing 4km; games rm; tennis; golf; 10% statics; dogs €1.20; poss cr; adv bkg; quiet. "Excel for coast & Pyrenees; spacious pitches; v quiet low ssn & red facs; pretty vill." ♦ 15 Mar-31 Oct. € 14.50 2007*

CAMBRAI *3B4* (1km W Urban) *50.17533, 3.21534* **FFCC Camp Municipal Les Trois Clochers, 77 Rue Jean Goudé, 59400 Cambrai [03 27 70 91 64; campinglestrois clochers@villecambrai.com]** Site sp fr all dirs on ent town. Sm, hdg pitch, unshd; htd wc; chem disp; mv service pnt; baby facs; shwrs inc; el pnts €2.50; shop, rest adj; Eng spkn; noise fr busy rd adj & early cockerel. "Beautiful, well-kept site; gd, spacious pitches; conv Calais; helpful, friendly manager; gd san facs (inc for disabled) but ltd & stretched when site full; interesting town; excel." ♦ 15 Apr-15 Oct. € 12.00 2009*

CAMIERS see Touquet Paris Plage, Le *3B2*

CAMON see Mirepoix (Ariege) *8F4*

CAMPAN see Bagnères de Bigorre *8F2*

CAMPOURIEZ see Entraygues sur Truyère *7D4*

CAMPSEGRET *7C3* (Rural) *44.93455, 0.56173* **Camping Le Bourg, 24140 Campsegret [05 53 61 87 90; fax 05 53 24 22 36]** On N21, sp & clearly visible on E of main rd. Sm, mkd pitch, pt shd; wc; shwrs inc; el pnts (10A) €2; shop; playgrnd; paddling pool; fishing; tennis; dogs €0.50; rd & farm noise, church bells. "NH only." ♦ 1 Jun-30 Sep. € 6.40 2007*

CANCALE *2E4* (3km N Coastal) *48.70369, -1.84829* **Camp Municipal La Pointe du Grouin, 35260 Cancale [02 99 89 63 79 or 02 99 89 60 15; mairie@ville-cancale.fr; www.ville-cancale.fr]** Take D76 twd Cancale & cont on D201 sp Pointe de Grouin; site on R in 3km on cliffs above sea, on N side of Cancale (diff to see, on RH bend mkd with chevrons); sp 'Camp Municipal'. Care req at ent. Lge, pt sl, terr; wc (mainly cont); mv service pnt; shwrs inc; el pnts (8-13A) €3.10-4.10 (poss long lead req); lndtte; shop; rest in town; BBQ; playgrnd; rocky beach adj; watersports; fishing; dogs €1.35; Eng spkn; quiet; ccard acc. "Well-maintained site in gd location; some pitches uneven; excel san facs; gates clsd 2300-0700; conv Dinan, Mont-St Michel, St Malo; sea views; gd walking." 1 Mar-24 Oct. € 12.10 2008*

CANCALE *2E4* (6km S Coastal) *48.61893, -1.84946* **Camp Municipal des Ondes, Rue Bord de la Mer, 35114 St Benoît-des-Ondes [02 99 58 65 21]** In vill cent on D155. Med, unshd; wc; chem disp (wc); mv service pnt; shwrs inc; el pnts (6A) €2.55; lndtte; shop, rest, snacks adj; playgrnd; sand/shgl beach adj; dogs; phone; rd noise; CCI. "Site adj main rd; gd san facs; gd walking & cycling." 1 Jun-30 Sep. € 12.75 2009*

CANCALE *2E4* (6km S Coastal) *48.61592, -1.85151* **Camping de l'Ile Verte, 35114 St Benoît-des-Ondes [02 99 58 62 55]** Site on S side of vill. Fr Cancale, take D76 SW for approx 4km, then turn L onto D155 into St Benoît. Foll site sp. Sm, hdg pitch, pt shd; htd wc (cont); chem disp; mv service pnt; shwrs inc; el pnts (6A) inc (poss rev pol); gas; lndtte; shop; rest, bar adj; playgrnd; sand beach adj; 3% statics; phone; adv bkg; quiet; red low ssn; CCI "Well-kept site on edge of vill; facs poss stretched high ssn." 1 Jun-7 Sep. € 21.70 2008*

CANCALE *2E4* (1km W Coastal) *48.68322, -1.86881* **Camping Les Genêts, La Ville Gueurie, 35260 Cancale [02 99 89 76 17; fax 02 99 89 96 31; les.genets.camping@wanadoo.fr; www.camping-genets.com]** Fr Cancale take D355 St Malo rd; go across supmkt rndabt; then take 1st rd on R (about 200m) & site on R in 200m. Med, mkd pitch, pt shd; wc; chem disp (wc); shwrs inc; el pnts (6A) €4; gas 500m; lndtte; shop & supmkt 500m; rest in town; snacks; bar; playgrnd; sand beach 1.5km; 80% statics; dogs €2; phone; adv bkg; CCI. "Clean, well-kept site bet town & beach; helpful staff; gd." ♦ 2 Apr-15 Sep. € 19.00 2007*

CANCALE *2E4* (6.5km NW Coastal) *48.69076, -1.87396* **Camping Notre Dame du Verger, La Ville Aumont, 35260 Cancale [02 99 89 72 84; fax 02 99 89 60 11; info@camping-verger.com; www.camping-verger.com]** Take D201 E fr St Malo, site on L after La Pointe du Grouin. Med, hdg pitch, pt sl, terr, pt shd; wc; chem disp; mv service pnt; shwrs inc; el pnts (6A) €4; lndtte; tradsmn; snacks, bar in ssn; playgrnd; htd pool; sand beach 400m; 50% statics; dogs €2.50; poss cr; adv bkg; quiet; 20% red low ssn; ccard acc; CCI. "Dir access gd beach; friendly owners; gd touring base; lovely walks." 2 Apr-26 Sep. € 22.00 2007*

CANCALE *2E4* (7km NW Coastal) *48.68861, -1.86833* **Camping Le Bois Pastel, 13 Rue de la Corgnais, 35260 Cancale [02 99 89 66 10; fax 02 99 89 60 11; camping.bois-pastel@wanadoo.fr; www.campingboispastel.fr]** Fr Cancale take D201 dir Pointe du Grouin & St Malo by Rte Touristique. Site sp on L 2.5km after Pointe du Grouin. Med, pt shd; wc; shwrs inc; mv service pnt; shwrs inc; el pnts (6A) €4; lndtte; shop; bar; BBQ; playgrnd; htd, covrd pool; sand beach 800m; 25% statics; dogs €2.50; adv bkg; quiet; red long stay/low ssn. "Conv Mont-St Michel, St Malo; gd touring base." 1 Apr-30 Sep. € 22.00 2009*

See advertisement on next page

CANCALE *2E4* (2km W Rural) *48.68823, -1.86061* **Camping La Ville ès Poulain, 35260 Cancale [02 99 89 87 47; www.ville-cancale.fr]** Leave Cancale town cent on D355; after 1km cross D201 & turn immed R by bar & foll sp; site in 1km. Sm, hdg pitch, pt shd; wc; chem disp; shwrs; el pnts (10A) €2.60; lndry rm; supmkt 1.5km; sand beach 2km; dog €1; quiet; no ccard acc; CCI. "CL-type site; lge pitches; gd base but no views - entire site surrounded by high hedge; conv St-Malo ferry & Mont St Michel; excel fish rests in port." 15 Apr-30 Sep. € 13.00 2007*

France

CANCON *7D3* (5km N Rural) *44.57728, 0.62128* **Camp Municipal de St Chavit, 47290 Lougratte [05 53 01 70 05; fax 05 53 41 18 04; mairie.lougratte@wanadoo.fr]** N on N21 fr Cancon, site at lake, L turn 50m bef church, site seen fr rd 500m fr turn. Med, pt hdg pitch, pt shd; wc; chem disp (wc); shwrs; el pnts (6A) €2.60; Indtte; shop 500m; bar; BBQ; playgrnd; games rm; sand beach; boating; fishing; tennis nr; phone; v quiet. "Nice position; spacious; clean san facs high ssn; warden calls eves; gd touring base; highly rec." ♦ 1 Jun-15 Sep. € 8.30 2008*

I'm going to fill in some site report forms and post them off to the Club; we could win a ferry crossing – it's here on page 12.

CANCON *7D3* (2km E Rural) **Camp Municipal du Lac, 47290 Cancon [05 53 36 54 30 or 05 53 01 60 24 (Mairie); fax 05 53 01 64 70; mairie.cancon@wanadoo.fr; www.cancon.fr/cancon_cadre.htm]** Sp fr N21 on both sides of Cancon & in town. Med, mkd pitch, pt sl, shd; wc; shwrs inc; el pnts (10A) €3.30; Indtte; shop 2km; rest, snacks; bar; playgrnd; pool; fishing; games area; dogs €1; CCI. "Peaceful site in woodland & lake setting; no twin axles; opening dates poss unreliable." 15 Jun-15 Sep. € 8.45 2008*

⊞ **CANCON** *7D3* (8km W Rural) **Camping Le Moulin, Lassalle, 47290 Monbahus [05 53 01 68 87; info@lemoulin-monbahus.com; www.lemoulin-monbahus.com]** Fr N21 turn W at Cancon on D124 sp Miramont. In 7.5km at Monbahus pass thro vill cent take L turn, still on D124 sp Tombeboeuf. In 3km lge grain silos on L, site next on R. Sm, mkd pitch, hdstg, pt shd; wc; chem disp; shwrs inc; fam bthrm; el pnts (10A) €3; Indtte; tradsmn; shop 3km; bistro; snacks; BBQ; playgrnd; htd pool; lake 5km; cycle hire; wifi; dogs; Eng spkn; adv bkg; some rd noise; CCI. "CL-type site in garden; friendly British owners; facs spotless; vg pool; B & B avail; extra for twin-axles over 5m; excel." € 13.00 2008*

CANCON *7D3* (12km NW Rural) *44.61653, 0.51841* **Camping La Vallée de Gardeleau, 47410 Sérignac-Péboudou [tel/fax 05 53 36 96 96; valleegardeleau@wanadoo.fr; http://pagesperso-orange.fr/camping.valleegardeleau.fr]** Fr Cancon take N21 N; turn L twds Montauriol & Sérignac-Péboudou; foll camping sp. Sm, hdg pitch, pt sl, pt shd; wc; chem disp; shwrs inc; el pnts (5A) €3.15 (poss rev pol); gas 5km; Indtte; shop & 5km; tradsmn; rest; snacks; bar; playgrnd; pool; lake fishing 2km; entmnt; 8% statics; dogs €2.50; phone; poss cr; Eng spkn; adv bkg; quiet; ccard acc; red low ssn; CCI. "Calm & peaceful atmosphere; v shady; sm pitches; friendly, helpful owners; grnd soft after heavy rain; nr Bastide towns." ♦ 22 Mar-31 Oct. € 14.05 2008*

CANDE SUR BEUVRON *4G2* (500m S Rural) *47.48952, 1.25834* **Kawan Village La Grande Tortue, 3 Route de Pontlevoy, 41120 Candé-sur-Beuvron [02 54 44 15 20; fax 02 54 44 19 45; info@la-grande-tortue.com; www.la-grande-tortue.com]** Exit A10 junc 17 at Blois dir Vierzon. Cross rv on D751 (sp Chaumont/Amboise). In 14km cross Rv Beuvron at Candé-sur-Beuvron & 400m after bdge take L fork & site immed on L. Fr Onzain cross rv to Chaumont, then NE on D751; in 4km turn sharp R (S) & site on L. Lge, hdg/mkd pitch, pt sl, pt shd; htd wc; chem disp; mv service pnt; baby facs; shwrs inc; el pnts (10A) €3.50; gas; lndtte (inc dryer); shop; tradsmn; rest; snacks; bar; BBQ; playgrnd; htd, covrd pool; paddling pool; cycle hire; horseriding; entmnt; internet; TV rm; 20% statics; dogs €3.70; Eng spkn; adv bkg; quiet; ccard acc; red low ssn/CCI. "Excel, rustic site amongst trees; poss diff access due to trees; helpful staff; gd cycling; conv Loire chateaux; gd for children; vg, clean, modern san facs & gd pool." ♦ 14 Apr-25 Sep. € 28.00 (CChq acc) 2009*

See advertisement opposite (below)

CANET DE SALARS see Pont de Salars *7D4*

CANET EN ROUSSILLON see Canet Plage *10G1*

CANET PLAGE *10G1* (3km N Coastal) *42.70808, 3.03332* **Yelloh! Village Le Brasilia, 2 Ave des Anneux du Roussillon, 66140 Canet-en-Roussillon [04 68 80 23 82; fax 04 68 73 32 97; camping-le-brasilia@wanadoo.fr; www.brasilia.fr or www.yellohvillage.com]** Exit A9 junc 41 sp Perpignan Nord & Rivesaltes onto D83 dir Le Barcarès & Canet for 10km; then take D81 dir Canet for 6km. At Canet cont across rndabts until reaching the very big rndabt, turning R dir Ste-Marie, then follow sps to Le Brasilia on R. V lge, hdg/mkd pitch, pt shd, wc (some cont); chem disp; all serviced pitch; baby facs; shwrs inc; el pnts (10A) inc; gas; lndtte; supmkt; tradsmn; rest; snacks; bar; BBQ (gas/elec); playgrnd; htd pool high ssn; paddling pool; sand beach 150m; fishing; tennis; cycle hire; archery; entmnt; excursions; wifi; games/TV rm; 35% statics; dogs €4.50; bus to Canet; Eng spkn; quiet but poss noisy disco & entmnt on adj campsite; ccard acc; red low ssn; CCI. "Excel, well-managed, well laid-out site; gd sized pitches; friendly staff; excel facs; in Jul & Aug identity card for pool - passport size photo needed; rvside walk adj; conv day trips to Andorra; daily mkt in Canet except Mon." ♦ 24 Apr-25 Sep. € 47.97 ABS - C01 2009*

CANET PLAGE *10G1* (4km N Coastal) *42.73897, 3.03355* **Camp Municipal de la Plage, 66470 Ste Marie-Plage [04 68 80 68 59; fax 04 68 73 14 70; contact@camping-municipal-de-la-plage.com; www.camping-municipal-de-la-plage.com]** Exit A9 junc 41 onto D83, then D81 to Ste Marie-Plage. Look for sm red sp, site adj Camping La Palais de la Mer. Lge, hdg pitch, pt shd; wc; chem disp; mv service pnt; shwrs; el pnts (6A) €3.30; lndtte; shop; rest; snacks; bar; playgrnd; pool; paddling pool; sand beach adj; games area; games rm; cycle hire; TV; 30% statics; dogs €2.40; poss cr; Eng spkn; adv bkg; quiet; CCI. "Direct access to beach; v busy high ssn; san facs run down." ♦ 1 Mar-31 Oct. € 24.00 2006*

CANET PLAGE *10G1* (500m S Coastal) *42.67540, 3.03120* **Camping Club Mar Estang, Route de St Cyprien, 66140 Canet-en-Roussillon [04 68 80 35 53; fax 04 68 73 32 94; marestang@wanadoo.fr; www.marestang.com]** Exit A9 junc 41 Perpignan Nord dir Canet, then foll sp St Cyprien, site sp. Site on D81A bet Canet-Plage & St Cyprien-Plage. V lge, mkd pitch, hdstg, pt shd; wc; chem disp; mv service pnt; baby facs; shwrs inc; el pnts (5A) €7; gas; lndtte; shop; tradsmn; rest; snacks; bar; playgrnd; htd pool; waterslide; private sand beach adj; tennis; cycle hire; fitness rm; TV rm; 50% statics; dogs €4; Eng spkn; adv bkg; quiet; ccard acc; red low ssn/long stay/low ssn/CCI. "Conv Spanish border & Pyrenees; gd birdwatching." ♦ 28 Apr-23 Sep. € 30.00 2006*

CANET PLAGE *10G1* (4km W Urban) *42.70114, 2.99850* **Camping Ma Prairie, Ave des Coteaux, 66140 Canet-en-Roussillon [04 68 73 26 17; fax 04 68 73 28 82; ma.prairie@wanadoo.fr; www.maprairie.com]** Leave A9/E15 at junc 41, sp Perpignan Centre/Canet-en-Roussillon. Take D83, then D81 until Canet-en-Roussillon. At rndabt, take D617 dir Perpignan & in about 500m leave at exit 5. Take D11 dir St Nazaire, pass under bdge & at rndabt turn R. Site on L. Lge, hdg pitch, shd; wc; serviced pitches; chem disp; baby facs; shwrs inc; el pnts (10A) inc; gas; lndtte; supmkt adj; tradsmn; rest; snacks; bar; BBQ (gas/elec only); playgrnd; pool; paddling pool; waterslide; solarium; sand beach 2km; waterskiing; sailing, canoeing; cycle hire; archery; entmnt; wifi; games/TV rm; 20% statics; dogs €5; no c'vans over 7m high ssn; bus to town nr; poss cr; Eng spkn; adv bkg ess Aug; quiet; ccard acc; red low ssn; CCI. "Friendly, helpful owners; disabled facs not open until Jun; shuttle bus to beach (Jul/Aug); daily mkt Perpignan; gd." ♦ 5 May-25 Sep. € 38.50 (CChq acc) ABS - C05 2009*

CANET PLAGE *10G1* (4km W Rural) *42.68914, 2.99877* **FFCC Camping Les Fontaines, Route de St Nazaire, 66140 Canet-en-Roussillon [tel/fax 04 68 80 22 57 or 06 77 90 14 91 (mob); campinglesfontaines@wanadoo.fr; www.camping-les-fontaines.com]** Take D11 fr Canet dir St Nazaire; site sp on L in 1.5km. Easy access. Med, hdg/mkd pitch, unshd; wc; chem disp; mv service pnt; baby facs; fam bathrm; shwrs inc; el pnts (10A) €3.50; gas 2km; lndtte; shop & 1km; tradsmn; snacks; bar; BBQ (gas/elec); playgrnd; pool; sand beach 2.5km; 30% statics; dogs €3; bus; phone; Eng spkn; adv bkg; quiet. "Pitches lge; Etang de Canet et St Nazaire nature reserve with flamingos; birdwatching; excel." 1 May-30 Sep. € 22.00 2006*

CANNES *10F4* (3km NE Urban) *43.55610, 6.96060* **Camping Parc Bellevue, 67 Ave Maurice Chevalier, 06150 Cannes [04 93 47 28 97; fax 04 93 48 66 25; contact@parcbellevue.com; www.parcbellevue.com]** A8 exit junc 41 twd Cannes. Foll N7 & at junc controlled by traff lts, get in L lane. Turn L & in 100m turn L across dual c'way, foll sp for site. Site in 400m on L after sports complex - steep ramp at ent. Lge, mkd pitch, pt shd; wc; chem disp; shwrs; el pnts (6A) €4; gas; lndtte; shops; rest; snacks; bar; htd pool; sandy beach 1.5km; sat TV; many statics; dogs €2; phone; bus/train nr; poss cr; Eng spkn; adv bkg; rd noise; red low ssn; CCI. "Vg, site on 2 levels; gd security; gd san facs; some pitches long way fr facs; many steps to gd pool; helpful, friendly staff; conv beaches & A8; green oasis in busy area; gd bus to prom; no m'van facs." ♦ 1 Apr-30 Sep. € 24.00 (CChq acc) 2009*

CANNES *10F4* (4km NW Urban) *43.56469, 6.97765* **Ranch Camping, L'Aubarède, Chemin de St Joseph, 06110 Le Cannet [04 93 46 00 11; fax 04 93 46 44 30; www.leranchcamping.fr]** Exit A8 at junc 42 Le Cannet. Foll sp L'Aubarède & then La Bocca. Site well sp via D9. Med, hdg pitch, pt sl, terr, pt shd; htd wc (some cont); baby facs; shwrs inc; el pnts (6A) €3; lndtte; shop; tradsmn; playgrnd; covrd pool; sand beach 2km; wifi; 10% statics; dogs €1; bus; adv bkg summer ssn ess by March; some rd noise; quiet. "Fairly basic site but conv location; pitches at cent or top of site quieter; gd." ♦ 1 Apr-30 Oct. € 25.00 2007*

CANNES *10F4* (5.5km NW Rural) *43.58802, 6.93810* **Camping St Louis, Domaine des Chênes, 06550 La Roquette-sur-Siagne [04 92 19 23 13; fax 04 92 19 23 14; caravaning.st-louis@wanadoo.fr; www.homair.com & www.campingsaintlouis.com]** Exit A8 at Cannes/Mandelieu & take D6007 (N7) twd Mandelieu. Fr Mandelieu take D109/D9 N twd Grasse. Turn R in Pégomas, site on L on leaving vill. Med, mkd/hdg pitch, v sl, terr, pt shd; wc; chem disp; shwrs inc; el pnts (6A) inc; gas; lndtte; shop; supmkt 100m; pizzeria; snack; bar; pool; waterslide; beach 5km; pool; tennis nr; entmnt; 25% statics; dogs; adv bkg; quiet; red low ssn. "Friendly staff; sm, sl pitches; facs ltd low ssn; conv Nice, Cannes." ♦ 1 Apr-30 Sep. € 37.00 (3 persons) 2007*

CANNES *10F4* (9km NW) *43.59005, 6.92376* **FFCC Caravaning Les Mimosas, Quartier Cabrol, 06580 Pégomas [04 93 42 36 11; fax 04 93 60 92 74]** Site on L of D109 Mandelieu to Grasse. Exit A8 junc 41 at Mandelieu turn R & foll sp to Pégomas on D9. Turn L immed bef rv bdge app Pégomas. Med, hdg/mkd pitch, shd; wc; chem disp; mv service pnt; baby facs; shwrs inc; el pnts (5A) inc; lndtte; shop; rest, bar 1km; snacks; playgrnd; pool; sand beach 8km; fishing in rv adj; games area; entmnt; 40% statics; dogs €1.60; adv bkg; quiet; ccard acc; CCI. "Pleasant site; convenient for Cannes, Côte d'Azur & mountain vills; poor san facs (2008); dogs roaming site; night security guard in ssn; barrier clsd 2300-0600." ♦ Easter-31 Oct. € 20.00 2008*

CANNET DES MAURES, LE *10F3* (4km N Rural) *43.42140, 6.33655* **FFCC Camping Domaine de la Cigalière, Route du Thoronet, 83340 Le Cannet-des-Maures [04 94 73 81 06; fax 04 94 73 81 06; campinglacigaliere@wanadoo.fr; www.campings-var.com]** Exit A8 at Le Cannet-des-Maures onto D17 N dir Le Thoronet; site in 4km on R, sp. Med, hdg/mkd pitch, hdstg, pt shd; wc; baby facs; shwrs inc; el pnts (10A) €3; lndtte; shop; tradsmn; snacks; takeaway; bar; BBQ (gas/elec); playgrnd; pool; paddling pool; games rm; 60% statics; dogs €2; quiet; CCI. "Peaceful site; lge pitches; St Tropez 44km; gd." ♦ 1 Apr-31 Oct. € 17.00 2007*

CANOURGUE, LA *9D1* (2km E Rural) *44.40789, 3.24178* **Camping Le Val d'Urugne, Route des Gorges-du-Tarn, 48500 La Canourgue [04 66 32 84 00; fax 04 66 32 88 14; lozereleisure@wanadoo.fr; www.lozereleisure.com]** Exit A75 junc 40 dir La Canourgue; thro vill dir Gorges-du-Tarn. In 2km site on R 600m after golf clubhouse Sm, hdg pitch, pt sl, pt shd; wc; chem disp; mv service pnt; shwrs inc; el pnts (6A) €3.50; lndtte; shop (high ssn) & 2km; tradsmn; rest, snacks, bar at golf club; TV rm; some chalets adj; dogs €2; Eng spkn; adv bkg; quiet; ccard acc; red low ssn; CCI. "Vg site; golf adj; conv A75 & Gorges-du-Tarn; low ssn stop at golf club for key to site; site poss tired end of ssn." ♦ 1 May-30 Sep. € 14.50 2009*

CANOURGUE, LA *9D1* (1km SE Rural) *44.44238, 3.19646* **Camping La Mothe, 75 Route d'Espagne, 48500 Banassac [04 66 32 88 11 or 04 66 32 97 37; fax 04 66 32 97 37]** Leave A75 at junc 40, foll sp D998 La Canourgue. Take 2nd exit at each of 2 rndabts sp St Geniez-d'Olt N9 twds La Mothe. Site on L in 300m immed over Rv Lot. Med, shd; wc (some cont); chem disp (wc); shwrs inc; el pnts (6A) €3; lndtte; supmkt 1.5km; rest 2km; snacks; bar; BBQ; playgrnd; rv sw & fishing 1.5km; dogs €1; some rd noise; CCI. "Basic site by Rv Lot; gd for birdwatchers & fishing; interesting area; phone ahead to check opening dates; no warden on site end ssn." ♦ 1 Apr-30 Oct. € 11.00 2008*

⊞ **CANY BARVILLE** *3C2* (3km N Rural) *49.80375, 0.64960* **Camping Maupassant, 12 Route de la Folie, 76450 Vittefleur [tel/fax 02 35 97 97 14; campingmaupassant@orange.fr; www.camping-maupassant.com]** S fr St Valery-en-Caux on D925 dir Cany-Barville; site sp turning to R 700m bef Cany-Barville. Med, hdg/mkd pitch, hdstg, pt shd; htd wc; chem disp; mv service pnt; baby facs; shwrs €1.70; el pnts (6A) inc; gas; lndtte (inc dryer); shop, rest, snacks & bar 6km; BBQ (charcoal); some statics; dogs; phone; adv bkg; quiet; CCI. "Friendly staff." € 14.50 2008*

CANY BARVILLE *3C2* (500m S Urban) *49.78335, 0.64214* **Camp Municipal, Route de Barville, 76450 Cany-Barville [02 35 97 70 37; fax 02 35 97 72 32; mairie-de-cany-barville@wanadoo.fr]** Sp fr town cent, off D268 to S of town, adj stadium. Med, hdg/mkd pitch, hdstg, pt shd; htd wc; chem disp; mv service pnt; shwrs inc; el pnts (10A) €2.80 (poss rev pol); lndtte; shop 500m; playgrnd; pool 1km; lake 2km; 25% statics; dogs €0.95; adv bkg; poss noisy; 10% red 14+ days; ccard acc; CCI. "Vg facs but poss stretched at high ssn; poss no check-in on Sun; within reach of Dieppe & Fécamp chateau; gd cycling." ♦ 1 Apr-30 Sep. € 9.65 2006*

CAPELLE LES BOULOGNE, LA see Boulogne sur Mer *3A2*

CAPESTANG *10F1* (W Urban) *43.32759, 3.03865* **Camp Municipal Tounel, Ave de la République, 34310 Capestang [04 67 49 85 95 or 04 67 93 30 05 (Mairie); ot-capestang@wanadoo.fr; www.capestango-t.com]** Fr Béziers on D11, turn R twd vill of Capestang, approx 1km after passing supermarket. Site on L in leisure park opp Gendamarie. Med, hdg pitch, pt shd; wc (cont); mv service pnt; shwrs; el pnts (6A) €3; shops, rest 500m; playgrnd; dogs free; quiet. "300m fr Canal de Midi, excel walks or cycle rides; lovely rest in vill; low ssn site yourself, fees collected." ♦ 1 May-30 Sep. € 9.00 2009*

CAPVERN LES BAINS see Lannemezan *8F2*

CARAMAN *8F4* (5km SE Rural) **FFCC Camping La Ferme du Tuillié, 31460 Cambiac [05 61 83 30 95 or 06 88 16 27 14 (mob); fax 05 62 18 52 48; www.couleur-lauragais.fr/camping-tuillie]** Fr Toulouse E onto D826 (N126); in 30km turn R onto D11 to Caraman; cont thro vill onto D25; in 4km turn L onto D18; site on L in 5km. Sm, hdg/mkd pitch, hdstg, unshd; wc; chem disp; mv service pnt; shwrs inc; el pnts (6A) inc; lndry rm; tradsmn; BBQ; playgrnd; cycle hire; fishing; TV; 5 statics; phone adj; adv bkg; quiet; no ccard acc. "Beautiful, remote site by lake; friendly owners; excel." ♦ 1 Apr-30 Oct. € 13.00 2008*

CARAMAN *8F4* (1.5km SW Rural) *43.52967, 1.74783* **Camp Municipal L'Orme Blanc, 31460 Caraman [05 62 18 81 60 or 05 61 83 10 12 (Mairie); fax 05 61 83 98 83; mairie-caraman@wanadoo.fr]** Site sp on D1 & D11 fr all dirs. Steep, narr, unfenced app track & sharp R turn not rec lge o'fits or lge m'vans. Sm, mkd pitch, pt sl, shd; wc; chem disp; shwrs; el pnts €2.50; gas, shop 1km; rest, snacks, bar 1km; BBQ; lake fishing, sw & watersports adj; tennis; phone; adv bkg; quiet; CCI. "Rural site 20km fr Toulouse." ♦ 20 Jun-15 Sep. € 9.00 2007*

CARANTEC see St Pol de Léon *1D2*

CARCANS *7C1* (8km W Rural) *45.06657, -1.13903* **Camping Le Maubuisson, 81 Ave de Maubuisson, 33121 Carcans [05 56 03 30 12; fax 05 56 03 47 93; camping-maubuisson@wanadoo.fr; www.camping-maubuisson.com]** Fr D1215 (N215) at Castelnau-de-Médoc turn W onto D207 to Carcans & onto Maubuisson, in vill camp ent on L, sp. V lge, mkd pitch, pt sl, shd; wc; baby facs; shwrs inc; el pnts (5A) €3.50; gas; lndtte; shop; rest; snacks; bar; playgrnd; sand beach 3km; lake sw 100m; fishing; watersports; windsurfing; tennis; some statics; dogs €1.50; poss cr; adv bkg; quiet. "Site in wooded park; conv Médoc wine region & many sandy beaches." ♦ 1 Mar-30 Nov. € 19.60 2007*

CARCASSONNE *8F4* (5km N Rural) *43.25999, 2.36509* **FFCC Camping Das Pinhiers, Chemin du Pont Neuf, 11620 Villemoustaussou [04 68 47 81 90; fax 04 68 71 43 49; campingdaspinhiers@wanadoo.fr; www.camping-carcassonne.net]** Exit A6 junc 23 Carcassonne Ouest & foll sp Mazamet on D118; R at rndabt with filling stn; turn R & foll camping sp. Med, hdg pitch, pt sl, shd; wc; chem disp; mv service pnt; shwrs inc; el pnts (10A) inc; shop (high ssn) & 1km; rest; snacks; bar; playgrnd; pool; 10% statics; no twin-axles; dogs €2.60; bus 1 km; Eng spkn; adv bkg; quiet; ccard acc; red low ssn; CCI. "Diiff to pitch lge vans due to hdg pitches & slope; san facs basic & stretched high ssn; general area rather run down (2009)." ♦ 1 Mar-31 Oct. € 16.20 2009*

CARCASSONNE *8F4* (17km N Rural) *43.33820, 2.32627* **Camping La Royale, Rue La Royale, 11600 Villardonnel [04 68 77 51 13; reception2008@laroyale.net; www.laroyale.net]** For lge o'fits exit D118 onto D73 dir Salsigne; in 3.7km sp Camping on R; turn R onto tarmac la Rue La Royale opp farm with horses; Domaine La Royale is down hill on L. Or for smaller o'fits poss exit D118 onto D111 to Villardonnel & turn L after vill. Rue La Royale joins D73 & D111. Sm, terr, pt shd; htd wc; chem disp (wc); shwrs inc; el pnts (10A) €3; gas; lndtte (inc dryer); shop 4.5km; tradsmn; rest; BBQ; internet; some statics; dogs €2; phone; Eng spkn; adv bkg; quiet; red long stay. "Vg site; British owners." 25 May-24 Aug. € 18.00 2008*

CARCASSONNE *8F4* (10km NE Rural) *43.28305, 2.44166* **Camping Le Moulin de Ste Anne, Chemin de Ste Anne, 11600 Villegly-en-Minervois [04 68 72 20 80; fax 04 68 72 27 15; campingstanne@wanadoo.fr; www.moulindesainteanne.com]** Leave A61 junc 23 Carcassone Ouest dir Mazamet; after approx 14km onto D620 to Villegly, site sp at ent to vill. NB Turning R off D620 hidden by trees, then over narr bdge; long o'fits need wide swing in. Med, hdg/mkd pitch, pt sl, terr, unshd; htd wc; chem disp (wc); mv service pnt; baby facs; shwrs inc; el pnts (10A) inc; lndtte; shop 300m; tradsmn; snacks; bar; playgrnd; htd pool; sand beach 60km; games area; 25% statics; dogs €2; poss cr; adv bkg; Eng spkn; quiet; ccard acc; min 3 nights high ssn; red long stay/low ssn; CCI. "Pretty, clean site; lge pitches; friendly, helpful owner; ltd san facs; pitches poss diff/muddy in wet; gd touring base; poss local youths congregate on motorbikes nrby in eve; vg." ♦ 1 Mar-15 Nov. € 20.00 2009*

CARCASSONNE *8F4* (6km E Rural) *43.20700, 2.44258* **FFCC Camping à l'Ombre des Micocouliers, Chemin de la Lande, 11800 Trèbes [04 68 78 61 75 or 04 68 78 88 77 (LS); fax 04 68 78 88 77; infos@campingmicocouliers.com; www.campingmicocouliers.com]** Fr Carcassonne, take D6113 (N113) E for 6km to Trèbes; go under rlway bdge; fork L onto D610; turn R immed bef rv bdge; site on L in 200m. Site sp. Med, mkd pitch, shd; wc; chem disp; mv service pnt; shwrs (up steps); el pnts (16A) €3; lndtte; shop; rest; snacks; BBQ; htd, covrd pool nr; rv fishing; TV; no statics; dogs €1.50; phone; poss cr; some Eng spkn; red low ssn; CCI. "Pleasant, sandy site; gd san facs, 1 block up steps; ltd el pnts; walking dist to sm town; gd base Canal du Midi, with vg cycling." ♦ 1 Apr-30 Sep. € 17.00 2009*

France

CARCASSONNE *8F4* (2km SE Rural) *43.19994, 2.35271* **CAMPEOLE Camping La Cité, Route de St Hilaire, 11000 Carcassonne [04 68 25 11 77; fax 04 68 47 33 13; cite@campeole.com; www.camping-carcassonne.info or www.campeole.com]** Fr N & W exit Carcassonne by D6113 (N113) twd Narbonne; cross rv & turn S on D104 foll sp. Fr S (D118) take D104 to E & foll sp. Fr E (D6113) take D342 S to D104; foll sp. NB Site (La Cité) well sp fr all dirs & easy access fr A61 junc 23. Lge, hdg/mkd pitch, pt shd; wc (some cont); chem disp; mv service pnt; shwrs inc; el pnts (10A) inc (poss rev pol); lndry rm; shops 1.5km; tradsmn; rest; snacks; bar; playgrnd; pool (high ssn); tennis; internet; entmnt; some statics; dogs €3.50; bus; Eng spkn; adv bkg (rec high ssn - fewer than 7 days not accepted); quiet with some rd noise; ccard acc; red low ssn; CCI. "Delightful, well-kept site in gd location adj woods; popular - rec arr bef 1600; mixed pitch sizes & types; friendly, helpful staff; san facs need refurb & stretched high ssn, poss irreg cleaning low ssn; poss untidy low ssn; ltd water pnts & waste water pnts; many leisure facs; pleasant walk along rv to La Cité; no twin-axles; high ssn o'spill area without el pnts; site closes 2nd Monday of Oct (variable date)." ♦ 15 Mar-15 Oct. € 28.40 2009*

⊞ **CARCASSONNE** *8F4* (5km S Rural) *43.17938, 2.37024* **Camping à l'Ombre des Oliviers, Ave du Stade, 11570 Cazilhac [tel/fax 04 68 79 65 08 or 06 81 54 96 00 (mob); florian.romo@wanadoo.fr; www.alombredesoliviers.com]** Fr N & W exit Carcassonne by D6113 (N113) dir Narbonne. Cross rv & turn S onto D104, then D142/D56 to Cazilhac, site sp. Sm, pt shd; wc; baby facs; shwrs inc; el pnts (6-10A) €2 (poss rev pol); lndry rm; supmkt in vill; bar; BBQ; playgrnd; pool; tennis; games area; TV; 10% statics; dogs €1.50; site clsd 1st week Jan; poss v cr; adv bkg; quiet; red low ssn. "Site in pleasant position; pitches poss muddy/soft & diff for med/lge o'fits to manoeuvre; few water points; v ltd facs low ssn; long c'vans check with recep, then ent via exit, as corners tight; if office clsd on arr phone owner on mobile, or site yourself; insufficient san facs when site full & ltd other facs; bus to old city nrby; helpful owners." € 18.00 2009*

CARCASSONNE *8F4* (7km S Rural) *43.1588, 2.2930* **Airotel Camping Grand Sud, Route de Limoux, 11250 Preixan [04 68 26 88 18; fax 04 68 26 85 07; sudfrance@wanadoo.fr; www.camping-grandsud.com]** A61 exit junc 23 at Carcassonne Ouest onto D118 dir Limoux. Site visible fr rd on lakeside at end of dual-carriageway section. Med, hdg/mkd pitch, hdstg, pt shd; wc; chem disp; mv service pnt; baby facs; shwrs inc; el pnts (6A) inc (poss rev pol); lndtte (inc dryer); shop; tradsmn; rest; snacks; bar; BBQ; playgrnd; 2 pools high ssn; waterslide; fishing; boating; horseriding; tennis; games area; games rm; entmnt; TV; 50% statics; dogs €4; adv bkg; quiet; ccard acc; red low ssn; CCI. "Pleasant, attractive site; easy access A61; friendly, helpful owners; wild fowl reserve; conv beautiful city of Carcassonne; gd walking; gd rest; excel." 1 Apr-15 Sep. € 30.00 2009*

CARCASSONNE *8F4* (12km SW Rural) *43.12410, 2.26080* **Yelloh! Village Domaine d'Arnauteille, 11250 Montclar [04 68 26 84 53; fax 04 68 26 91 10; www.arnauteille.com or www.yellohvillage.com]** Fr Carcassonne take D118 S twd Limoux. Turn R bef end of sm section dual c'way (not 1st section) & foll sp to Montclar. Site approx 2.5km on L. NB Site app along single track - site ent steep & narr & sp v insignificant on gatepost & driveway appears to be to private house. V lge, hdg/mkd pitch, pt sl, terr, pt shd; htd wc; chem disp; mv service pnt; some serviced pitches; baby facs; fam bthrm; shwrs inc; el pnts (6-10A) inc; gas; lndtte; shop; tradsmn; rest; snacks; bar; playgrnd; pool; waterpark; horseriding, fishing 2km; golf 14km; games rm; games area; entmnt; internet; TV rm; 70% statics; dogs €3.50; Eng spkn; adv bkg; v quiet; ccard acc; red low ssn; CCI. "Huge & impersonal; superb pool complex & facs; excel rest; siting poss diff in wet weather; site muddy after rain; views of Corbières; vg site." ♦ 20 Mar-30 Oct. € 38.00 2008*

CARCASSONNE *8F4* (15km NW Rural) *43.29861, 2.22277* **Camping de Montolieu (formerly Camping Les Oliviers), L'Olivier, 11170 Montolieu [04 68 76 95 01 or 06 31 90 31 92 (mob); nicole@camping-de-montolieu.com; www.camping-de-montolieu.com]** Fr D6113 (N113) 4km W Carcassonne, take D629 twd Montolieu; site on R in 2.5km after Moussoulens. Sp fr D6113, approx 5km dist. App thro Montolieu not rec. Sm, hdg/mkd pitch, pt shd; wc; chem disp; shwrs inc; el pnts (6A) inc; gas; lndtte; shops 1.5km; tradsmn; rest, snacks, bar 100m; BBQ; pool 100m; games area; games rm; wifi; few statics; dogs €2; phone; adv bkg; quiet; red low ssn; CCI. "Well-managed site in lovely countryside; manoeuvering tight; new owners (2009); gd san facs; conv Carcassonne." ♦ Apr-Nov. € 15.00 2009*

CARCES *10F3* (500m SE Urban) *43.47350, 6.18826* **Camping Les Fouguières, Quartier Les Fouguières, 83570 Carcès [34 94 59 96 28 or 06 74 29 69 02 (mob); fax 34 94 59 96 28; info@camping-les-fouguieres.com; www.camping-les-fouguieres.com]** Exit A8 junc 35 at Brignoles onto D554 to Le Val; then take D562 to Carcès. Site sp off D13. Med, pt shd; wc; mv service pnt; shwrs inc; el pnts (4-12A) €2.30-3.50; gas; lndtte; snacks; playgrnd; pool; Rv Caramy runs thro site; rv sw, fishing & canoeing nrby; wifi; TV; dogs €2; phone; bus; Eng spkn; quiet; red low ssn. "Pleasant, clean, well-shaded site; friendly; interesting, medieval town; Lake Carcès 2km; mkt Sat; excel." ♦ 1 Mar-1 Nov. € 16.00 2009*

CARDET *10E1* (500m NW Rural) *44.02780, 4.07416* **Camping Beau Rivage, 22 Rue du Bosquet, 30350 Cardet [04 66 83 02 48; fax 04 66 83 80 55; reception@campingbeaurivage.com; www.campingbeaurivage.com]** Fr Alès take N106 dir Nîmes. Exit at sp Lédignan onto D982 dir Anduze & cont for 7km & cross D6110 (N110). On app Cardet take 3rd exit to vill avoid narr rds. Med, level, shd; htd wc; chem disp; baby facs; shwrs inc; el pnts (6A) €2.90; gas; lndry rm; tradsmn; rest; snacks; BBQ; playgrnd; pool; rv sw adj; canoe hire; games rm; TV rm; disco; dogs €3; poss cr; Eng spkn; adv bkg ess Jul/Aug; quiet; red low ssn; red CCI. "Pleasant parkland setting by rv; well-organised; helpful staff; gd pizzeria; if office clsd site yourself; excel." 1 Apr-1 Oct. € 19.75 2007*

CARENTAN *1D4* (500m E Urban) *49.30988, -1.2388* **Camp Municipal Le Haut Dick, 30 Chemin du Grand-Bas Pays, 50500 Carentan [tel/fax 02 33 42 16 89; lehautdick@aol.com; www.camping-municipal.com]** Exit N13 at Carentan; clearly sp in town cent, nr pool, on L bank of canal, close to marina. Ask for "Le Port". Med, hdg/mkd pitch, pt shd; wc; chem disp; mv service pnt; shwrs inc; el pnts (6A) €3.40 (rev pol); gas; shop 500m; tradsmn; rest, snacks, bar 500m; BBQ; playgrnd; htd pool adj; sand beach 10km; cycle hire; games rm; 5% statics; dogs; phone; poss cr; Eng spkn; adv bkg; quiet; ccard not acc; CCI. "Immac site & facs, poss ltd in low ssn; some pitches tight for lge o'fits; gd security; gates locked 2200-0700; mkt Mon; conv Cherbourg ferry & D-Day beaches; gd bird-watching & cycling." ♦
15 Jan-31 Oct. € 10.60 2009*

CARENTAN *1D4* (6km SE Rural) **FFCC Camping à la Ferme (Duval), 50620 Montmartin-en-Graignes [02 33 56 84 87]** On N13 by-pass Carantan going S; join N174; site on L in 4km. Sm, unshd; wc; shwrs inc; el pnts inc; chem disp; playgrnd; adv bkg; quiet. "Charming CL-type site, also B&B; pleasant owner; 1 hr fr Cherbourg." 15 Jun-15 Sep. € 12.60 2007*

CARHAIX PLOUGUER *2E2* (1.5km W Rural) *48.27763, -3.60183* **Camp Municipal La Vallée de l'Hyères, Rue de Kerniguez, 29270 Carhaix-Plouguer [02 98 99 10 58; fax 02 98 99 15 92; tourismecarhaix@wanadoo.fr; www.ville-carhaix.com]** SE fr Huelgoat on D794 for 17km, sm site sp on all apps to Carhaix Med, pt shd; wc (some cont); chem disp (wc); shwrs inc; el pnts (10A) inc; lndtte; shop 1.5km; tradsmn, snacks; bar; playrnd nr; pool 1.5km; canoe/kayak hire; 5% statics; adv bkg; quiet; CCI. "Pleasantly situated in parkland on rv; muddy after rain, poss waterlogged adj rv." ♦ 1 Jun-30 Sep. € 9.15 2007*

CARLEPONT see Noyon *3C3*

CARLUCET *7D3* (1.5km NW Rural) *44.72881, 1.59804* **Camping Château de Lacomte, 46500 Carlucet [05 65 38 75 46; fax 05 65 33 17 68; chateaulacomte@wanadoo.fr; www.campingchateaulacomte.com]** Fr Gramat SW on D677/D807. After approx 14km turn R onto D32 sp Carlucet, foll site sp (narr rd). Or fr A20 exit junc 56 & foll D802/D807 sp Gramat. In 5km turn L onto D32 as bef. Med, hdg pitch, some hdstg, pt sl, terr, pt shd; wc; chem disp; all serviced pitches; shwrs; el pnts (10A) €5; gas 7km; lndtte; shops 12km; rest; snacks; bar; playgrnd; 3 pools; tennis; cycle hire; golf 9km; 5% statics; dogs €3; adv bkg; quiet; ccard acc; red low ssn/CCI. "British owners; excel facs & rest; some pitches diff long o'fits; 'freedom' pitches for m'vanners inc use of sm car, bookable daily; conv Rocamadour & Lot & A20; excel walking in area." ♦
15 May-15 Sep. € 32.00 2008*

CARLUX see Sarlat la Canéda *7C3*

CARNAC *2G3* (1km N Rural) *47.59683, -3.06035* **Camping La Grande Métairie, Route des Alignements de Kermario, 56342 Carnac [02 97 52 24 01; fax 02 97 52 83 58; info@lagrandemetairie.com; www.lagrandemetairie.com or www.les-castels.com]** Fr Auray take N768 twd Quiberon. In 8km turn L onto D119 twd Carnac. La Métairie site sp 1km bef Carnac (at traff lts) turn L onto D196 to site on R in 1km. V lge, hdg/mkd pitch, pt shd; htd wc; chem disp; mv service pnt; baby facs; shwrs inc; el pnts (6A) inc; gas; lndtte; shop; rest; snacks; bar; playgrnd; 2 pools (1 htd, covrd); paddling pool; waterslide; sand beach 2.5km; watersports, sailing 2.5km; tennis; entmnt; TV; 80% statics; dogs €4; Eng spkn; adv bkg; quiet; ccard acc; red low ssn. "Excel facs; vg pool complex; friendly, helpful staff; rec." ♦
27 Mar-4 Sep. € 43.40 2009*

See advertisement

CARNAC *2G3* (1km N Rural) *47.60225, -3.07869* **Camping Les Ombrages, Kerlann, 56340 Carnac [02 97 52 16 52 (Jul & Aug) or 02 97 52 14 06]** Exit Auray SW on N168. After 9.5km L on D119. After 3km R at carwash, site 600m on R sp fr D119. Med, mkd pitch, shd; wc; shwrs; el pnts (6A) €2.50; lndtte; shops 1km; playgrnd; sand beach 3km; tennis; dogs €1; some statics; poss cr; quiet. "Well-kept site in wooded area." 15 Jun-15 Sep. € 13.10 2006*

CARNAC *2G3* (1km N Rural) *47.5964, -3.0617* **Camping Le Moulin de Kermaux, Route de Kerlescan, 56340 Carnac [02 97 52 15 90; fax 02 97 52 83 85; moulin-de-kermaux@wanadoo.fr; www.camping-moulinkermaux.com]** Fr Auray take D768 S sp Carnac, Quiberon. In 8km turn L onto D119 twds Carnac. 1km bef Carnac take D196 (Rte de Kerlescan) L to site in approx 500m opp round, stone observation tower for alignments. Med, hdg/mkd pitch, pt shd; htd wc; chem disp; mv service pnt; baby facs; sauna; shwrs inc; el pnts (6A) €4 (poss rev pol); gas; Indtte; shop; tradsmn; snacks; bar; BBQ; playgrnd; htd, covrd pool; waterslide; jacuzzi; sand beach 3km; games area; wifi; entmnt; TV; 50% statics; dogs €2; phone; bus adj; Eng spkn; adv bkg; quiet; ccard acc; CCI. "Well-kept, friendly, attractive site nr standing stones; peaceful & comfortable low ssn; many repeat visitors; excel." ♦ 1 May-12 Sep. € 25.00 2009*

See advertisement below

CARNAC *2G3* (2km N Rural) *47.60110, -3.08211* **Camping L'Etang, 67 Route de Kerlann, 56340 Carnac [02 97 52 14 06; fax 02 97 52 23 19]** Exit Auray on D768 Carnac-Quiberon. In 9.5km L onto D119 & in 3km R immed after petrol stn to site in 700m on R. Sp Les Ombrages, de l'Etang & Les Pins. Lge, hdg/mkd pitch, hdstg, pt shd; wc (some cont); chem disp; shwrs inc; el pnts (6A) €3; gas; Indtte; shop; tradsmn; snacks; bar; BBQ; playgrnd; htd, covrd pool; waterslide; sand beach 3km; sailing; fishing; tennis; games rm; TV; 10% statics; dogs €1; phone; Eng spkn; adv bkg; quiet; CCI. "Lge pitches; helpful owner; well-placed for 'Alignements'." ♦ 1 Apr-15 Oct. € 18.00 2007*

CARNAC *2G3* (1.5km NE Rural) *47.60198, -3.03672* **Camping de Kervilor, Route du Latz, 56470 La Trinité-sur-Mer [02 97 55 76 75; fax 02 97 55 87 26; ebideau@camping-kervilor.com; www.camping-kervilor.com]** Sp fr island in cent of Trinité-sur-Mer. Lge, hdg/mkd pitch, hdstg, pt shd; wc; chem disp; mv service pnt; shwrs inc; el pnts (6-10A) €3.60-4.10; gas; Indtte; shop; snacks; bar; BBQ; playgrnd; htd, covrd pool & paddling pool; waterslides; solarium; sand beach 4km; tennis; games area; cycle hire; entmnt; internet; 10% statics; dogs €2.90; poss cr; Eng spkn; adv bkg; ccard acc; red low ssn; CCI. "Busy, family site; vg facs." ♦ 1 Apr-20 Sep. € 28.15 2009*

See advertisement opposite

CARNAC *2G3* (2km NE Rural) *47.60820, -3.06605* **Kawan Village Le Moustoir, 71 Route du Moustoir, 56340 Carnac [02 97 52 16 18; fax 02 97 52 88 37; info@lemoustoir.com; www.lemoustoir.com]** Fr N165 take D768 at Auray dir Carnac & Quiberon. In 5km take D119 dir Carnac, site on L at ent to Carnac. Lge, hdg/mkd pitch, pt sl, pt shd; wc; chem disp; mv service pnt; shwrs inc; el pnts (6A) €4.80; Indtte; shop; tradsmn; snacks; bar; BBQ; playgrnd; 2 htd pools; paddling pool; waterslide; sand beach 3km; tennis; games area; cycle hire; wifi; TV rm; 30% statics (tour ops); dogs; phone; poss cr & noisy; Eng spkn; adv bkg; red low ssn; ccard acc; CCI. "Attractive, friendly, well-run site; facs clean but stretched; megaliths nrby; Sun mkt." ♦ 1 Apr-30 Sep. € 26.80 (4 persons) (CChq acc) 2008*

CARNAC *2G3* (8km NE Rural) *47.61538, -2.98965* **Camping Le Fort Espagnol, Route de Fort Espagnol, 56950 Crac'h [02 97 55 14 88; fax 02 97 30 01 04; fort-espagnol@wanadoo.fr; www.fort-espagnol.com]** Fr Auray take D28 S; in Crac'h turn L at rndabt; site sp in 1km on R. Lge, pt shd; htd wc (some cont); chem disp; baby facs; shwrs inc; el pnts (10A) €4; gas; Indtte; shops 1km; tradsmn; snacks; bar; playgrnd; pool; waterslide; sand beach 5km; tennis; sports facs; entmnt; 30% statics; dogs €3.50; poss cr; adv bkg rec high ssn; quiet; ccard acc; CCI. "Helpful, pleasant management; popular with British; some lge pitches." 1 May-7 Sep. € 28.00 2009*

France

CARNAC *2G3* (2km E Rural/Coastal) *47.5810, -3.0576* **Camping Les Druides, 55 Chemin de Beaumer, 56340 Carnac [02 97 52 08 18; fax 02 97 52 96 13; contact@camping-les-druides.com; www.camping-les-druides.com]** Go E on seafront Carnac Plage to end; turn N onto Ave d'Orient; at junc with Rte de la Trinité-sur-Mer, turn L, then 1st R; site 1st on L in 300m. Med, hdg pitch, pt sl, pt shd; wc; chem disp; mv service pnt; baby facs; shwrs inc; el pnts (6A) €3.70; Indtte; shop 1km; rest adj; playgrnd; htd pool; sand beach 500m; entmnts; games/TV rm; 5% statics; dogs €2.30; phone adj; Eng spkn; adv bkg; quiet; ccard acc; CCI. "Friendly welcome." ♦ 24 May-13 Sep. € 29.00 2008*

CARNAC *2G3* (2km E Coastal) *47.58806, -3.04331* **Camping Park Plijadur, 94 Route de Carnac, 56470 La Trinité-sur-Mer [02 97 55 72 05; fax 02 72 68 95 06; parkplijadur@hotmail.com; www.parkplijadur.com]** Take D781 Route de Carnac W fr La Trinité-sur-Mer, site 1km on R. Lge, hdg/mkd pitch, pt shd; wc; chem disp; mv service pnt; baby facs; sauna; shwrs inc; el pnts (6A) €2.75; Indtte; shop; tradsmn; supmkt nr; rest 1km; snacks; bar; BBQ; playgrnd; htd pool; paddling pool; jacuzzi; sand beach 1km; games rm; fitness rm; cycle hire; golf 10km; entmnt; internet; TV rm; 3% statics; dogs €3.05; phone; poss cr; Eng spkn; adv bkg; quiet; ccard acc; red low ssn/long stay/CCI. ♦
1 Apr-30 Sep. € 25.75 2007*

CARNAC *2G3* (3km E Rural) *47.61122, -3.02908* **Camping du Lac, 56340 Carnac [02 97 55 78 78 or 02 97 55 82 60; fax 02 97 55 86 03; camping.dulac@wanadoo.fr; www.camping-carnac.com]** Fr Auray (by-pass) take D768 sp Carnac; in 4km turn L on D186; after 4km look for C105 on L & foll sp to site. Fr E end of quay-side in La Trinité-sur-Mer take main Carnac rd & in 100m turn R onto D186; in 2km R on C105, R on C131; sp. Med, hdg pitch, pt sl, pt shd; wc; chem disp; mv service pnt; serviced pitches; baby facs; shwrs inc; el pnts (6A) €3.60; gas; Indtte; shop; tradsmn; rest 3km; BBQ; playgrnd; trampoline; htd pool; sand beach 3km; cycle hire; multi-sport court; exercise equip rm; TV rm; entmnt; 50% statics; dogs €2; phone; poss cr; Eng spkn; adv bkg; quiet; ccard acc; red low ssn; CCI. "Excel woodland site o'looking tidal lake; helpful owner; clean, well-cared for; superb pool; gd cycling & walking; vg." 12 Apr-20 Sep. € 19.40 2008*

CARNAC *2G3* (1.5km SE Coastal) *47.58116, -3.05804* **Camping Le Dolmen, 58 Chemin de Beaumer, 56340 Carnac [02 97 52 12 35; fax 02 97 52 63 91; contact@campingledolmen.com; www.campingledolmen.com]** Fr N on D768 twd Quiberon; turn L onto D781 twd La Trinité-sur-Mer. At Montauban turn R at rndabt dir Kerfraval & Beaumer, site in 700m, sp. Med, hdg/mkd pitch, hdstg, pt sl, pt shd; htd wc (some cont); chem disp; mv service pnt; baby facs; shwrs inc; el pnts (6-10A) €3.60-4.20; Indtte; shop 800m; tradsmn; rest; snacks; BBQ; playgrnd; htd pool; paddling pool; sand beach 600m; games rm; games area; wifi; entmnt; 2% statics; dogs €2; Eng spkn; adv bkg; ccard acc; quiet; red low ssn/CCI. "Excel, pleasant site." ♦
1 Apr-26 Sep. € 27.00 2009*

See advertisement on next page

CARNAC *2G3* (2km SE Coastal) *47.5810, -3.0572* **Camping Le Men Dû, Chemin de Beaumer, 56340 Carnac [tel/fax 02 97 52 04 23; contact@camping-mendu.com; www.camping-mendu.fr]** Go E on seafront (Carnac Plage) to end; N on Ave d'Orient; at junc with Rte de la Trinité-sur-Mer turn L & 1st R; 2nd site on R. Med, hdg/mkd pitch, pt sl, pt shd; wc; chem disp; shwrs inc; el pnts (6-10A) €3-4; gas; Indtte; shop 500m; rest, snacks, bar high ssn; sand beach 150m; 50% statics; dogs €2; bus 100m; poss cr; adv bkg; poss noisy; CCI. "Friendly staff; mkd pitches not rec for manoeuvring twin-axles; manhandling req for long or heavy vans; narr rds on site; yachting (inc school)." ♦
Easter-30 Sep. € 22.00 2008*

CARNAC *2G3* (3km SE Coastal) *47.57565, -3.0289* **Camping de la Plage, Plage de Kervillen, 56470 La Trinité-sur-Mer [02 97 55 73 28; fax 02 97 55 88 31; camping@camping-plage.com; www.camping-plage.com]** Fr Auray on D28 & D781 dir La Trinite. Foll sp Kervillen Plage to S. Lge, hdg pitch, pt shd; wc; chem disp; mv service pnt; chem disp; serviced pitches; baby facs; shwrs inc; el pnts (6A) €3.10; gas; Indtte; shop 200m; rest; snacks; bar; BBQ; playgrnd; htd pool; waterslide; jacuzzi; sand beach adj; fishing; tennis adj; boat hire; cycle hire; 80% statics; dogs €1.20; poss cr; Eng spkn; adv bkg; quiet; red long stay/low ssn; ccard acc; CCI. "Pleasant site; friendly staff; tight ent; variable pitch sizes." ♦ 30 Apr-14 Sep. € 33.70 2006*

CARNAC *2G3* (4km SE Coastal) *47.57396, -3.02653* **Camping La Baie, Plage de Kervillen, 56470 La Trinité-sur-Mer [02 97 55 73 42; fax 02 97 55 88 81; contact@campingdelabaie.fr; www.campingdelabaie.fr]** Fr Carnac take D186. Turn R after causeway, keep R, past Camping de la Plage site, & site on L. Fr E app vill along seafront sp Carnac, cont strt thro traff lts, after 2nd traff lts take 1st L & foll rd for 1km. Site ent on L. Lge, hdg/mkd pitch, hdstg, pt shd; wc; chem disp; mv service pnt; baby facs; serviced pitches; shwrs inc; el pnts (6-10A) €2.20-3.25; lndtte; shops, snacks, rest, bar 500m; playgrnd; entmnt; htd pool; sand beach 50m; fishing; boat hire, mini-golf & tennis 250m; TV rm; 30% statics; dogs €1.20; phone; poss cr; Eng spkn; adv bkg; quiet; red low ssn; ccard acc. "Excel, well-maintained site in superb location; excel recep & san facs; some narr site rds - pitching poss diff lge o'fits; vg family beach; highly rec." ♦ 17 May-14 Sep. € 35.35 2007*

CARNAC *2G3* (9km SW Coastal) *47.57169, -3.12638* **Camp Municipal Les Sables Blancs, Route de Quiberon, 56340 Plouharnel [02 97 52 37 15 or 02 97 52 30 90 (Mairie); fax 02 97 52 48 49; mairie@plouharnel.fr]** Fr Auray take by-pass to Quiberon (clearly mkd), cont thro Plouharnel (D768) twd Quiberon - site clearly mkd after Plouharnel. Lge, mkd pitch, unshd; wc; shwrs inc; el pnts (4-13A) €2.45-3.45; gas; lndtte; shops; rest, snacks, bar in ssn; sand beach; 30% statics; dogs €1.05; Eng spkn; quiet. "Situated on a sand spit, care needed over soft sand." 1 Apr-30 Sep. € 12.00 2008*

CARNAC *2G3* (1.5km NW Rural) *47.59468, -3.09659* **Camping Les Goélands, Kerbachic, 56340 Plouharnel [02 97 52 31 92; angelina.oliviero@wanadoo.fr]** Take D768 fr Auray twd Quiberon. In Plouharnel turn L at rndabt by supmkt onto D781 to Carnac. Site sp to L in 500m. Med, pt shd; wc (some cont); chem disp; shwrs inc; el pnts (3-5A) €2-3; gas; lndtte; shops 1km; playgrnd; sand beach 3km; dogs €1; poss cr; adv bkg. "Friendly owners; excel facs; gd-sized pitches; gate clsd at 2200; nr beaches with bathing & gd yachting; bells fr adj abbey not too intrusive; conv for megalithic sites; high standard site." 1 Jun-15 Sep. € 15.00 2008*

CARNAC *2G3* (8km NW Rural) *47.63282, -3.14743* **Camping Kerzerho, 56410 Erdeven [tel/fax 02 97 55 63 16; info@camping-kerzerho.com; www.camping-kerzerho.com]** N fr Carnac on D781, site sp 400m S of Erdeven. Med, hdg/mkd pitch, pt shd; wc; baby facs; sauna; shwrs; el pnts (10A) €5; lndtte; shop; tradsmn; rest; snacks; bar; playgrnd; htd pool; paddling pool; waterslide; beach 2.5km; cycle hire; excursions; entmnt; some statics; dogs €3; adv bkg; quiet; red low ssn. "Busy site; some sm pitches diff lge o'fits." 1 Jun-3 Sep. € 23.00 2006*

CARNAC *2G3* (8km NW Rural) *47.63200, -3.15831* **Camping La Croëz Villieu, Route de Kerhillio, 56410 Erdeven [02 97 55 90 43; fax 02 97 55 64 83; la-croez-villieu@wanadoo.fr; www.la-croez-villieu.com]** Fr Carnac take D781 to Erdeven, turn L opp Marché des Menhirs. Site 1km on R. Med, hdg pitch, pt shd; wc; chem disp (wc); baby facs; shwrs inc; el pnts (4-6A) €2.50-3.50; gas; lndtte; shops 1km; snacks; bar; playgrnd; htd pool; sand beach 2km; 65% statics; dogs €1.65; poss cr; Eng spkn; adv bkg; quiet; red low ssn; CCI. "Friendly & helpful owners." ♦ 1 May-30 Sep. € 17.75 2007*

I'll go online and tell the Club what we think of the campsites we've visited – www.caravanclub.co.uk/europereport

CARNAC *2G3* (8km NW Coastal) *47.62165, -3.16462* **Idéal Camping, Route de la Plage de Kerhilio, Lisveur, 56410 Erdeven [02 97 55 67 66; contact@camping-l-ideal.com; www.camping-l-ideal.com]** Fr Carnac take D781 to Erdeven, turn L at rndabt. Site 2km on R at hotel/cafe. Sm, hdg pitch, pt shd; wc; chem disp (wc); baby facs; shwrs inc; el pnts (6A) €5; gas; lndtte; rest; shops 500m; tradsmn; rest; snacks; bar; BBQ; playgrnd; htd, covrd pool; paddling pool; sand beach 800m; sailing; fishing; tennis nr; games rm; TV; 90% statics; dogs €4; sep parking area for cars; Eng spkn; no adv bkg; quiet; ccard acc; red low ssn; CCI. "Peaceful site nr excel beach & cent of mkt town; not rec twin-axles or lge o'fits dur narr site rds." ♦ 1 Apr-30 Oct. € 23.00 (3 persons) 2009*

CARNAC *2G3* (12.5km NW) *47.65500, -3.17194* **Camping Les Sept Saints, 56410 Erdeven [02 97 55 52 65; fax 02 97 55 22 67; info@septsaints.com; www.septsaints.com]** Fr Erdeven on D781 going NW dir Lorient; site on L in 2km. Lge, hdg/mkd pitch, pt sl, pt shd; wc; chem disp; baby facs; shwrs inc; el pnts (10A) inc; gas; lndtte; shop; snacks; bar; BBQ (charcoal/gas); playgrnd; htd pool; paddling pool; waterslide; sand beach 4km; watersports 1.5km; cycle hire; entmnt; internet; games/TV rm; many statics; dogs €5; c'vans over 8m not acc high ssn; adv bkg; quiet; ccard acc; red low ssn; CCI. "V pleasant site; gd lge pitches; superb unspoilt beaches nrby; excel cycling rtes; Etel 3km worth visit; vg." ♦ 1 May-15 Sep. € 37.50 2009*

CAROMB see Malaucène *10E2*

CARPENTRAS *10E2* (5km N Rural) *44.09723, 5.03682* **Camping Le Brégoux, Chemin du Vas, 84810 Aubignan [04 90 62 62 50 or 04 90 67 10 13 (LS); camping-lebregoux@wanadoo.fr; www.camping-lebregoux.fr]** Exit Carpentras on D7 sp Bollène. In Aubignan turn R immed after x-ing bdge, 1st R again in approx 250m at Club de Badminton & foll site sp at fork. Lge, hdg/mkd pitch, hdstg, pt shd; wc; chem disp; mv service pnt; baby facs; shwrs inc; el pnts (6-10A) €3.10 (poss long lead req); gas 1km; lndtte; shops, rest, bars etc 1km; BBQ; sm playgrnd; pool 5km in ssn; tennis; go-karting & golf nrby; entmnt (high ssn); games rm; sm library; wifi; TV; 2% statics; dogs €1.40; phone; poss v cr; Eng spkn; adv bkg; poss noisy high ssn; ccard acc; red low ssn; CCI. "Populer site in beautiful area; lge pitches & gd access; helpful, friendly staff; gd san facs; gates clsd 2200-0700; poss flooding in heavy rain; owner prefers stays of 4+ nights; excel walking & cycling nrby; gd." ♦ 1 Mar-31 Oct. € 12.55 2009*

CARPENTRAS *10E2* (7km N Rural) *44.12246, 5.03437* **Camp Municipal de Roquefiguier, 84190 Beaumes-de-Venise [04 90 62 95 07 or 04 90 62 94 34 (Mairie)]** Leave A7 exit 22, take N7 S then L onto D950 sp Carpentras. At rndabt after Sarrians sp turn L onto D21 to Beaumes-de-Venise. Cross Beaumes & foll site sp. Turn L bef Crédit Agricole to site on R. Med, hdg/mkd pitch, pt sl, terr, pt shd; wc (some cont); chem disp; mv service pnt; baby facs; shwrs inc; el pnts (6A) €2.55; lndtte; BBQ; pool in vill; wifi; dogs €1.20; phone; no adv bkg; quiet; ccard acc; CCI. "Facs clean; steel pegs req for pitches; poss diff access lge o'fits; steep access some pitches; gate clsd 1900-0900, key avail; 5 mins walk to town; gd views; wine caves adj; mkd walks & cycle ways; conv for Mt Ventoux, Orange & Avignon; gd." ♦ 1 Mar-31 Oct. € 9.55 2009*

CARPENTRAS *10E2* (7km E Rural) *44.08057, 5.11385* **Camping Le Ventoux, Chemin La Combe, 84380 Mazan [tel/fax 04 90 69 70 94; info@camping-le-ventoux.com; www.camping-le-ventoux.com]** Take D974 twd Bédoin; after 7km turn R at x-rds on D70 sp Mazan. Site on R in 300m. Sm, mkd pitch, pt shd; wc (some cont); chem disp; mv service pnt; baby facs; shwrs inc; el pnts (6A) €3.50 (poss rev pol); gas; lndtte (inc dryer); shop (high ssn) & 3km; tradsmn; rest (all ssn); snacks; bar; BBQ; playgrnd; pool; lake fishing 4km; entment; some statics; dogs €2.50; phone; poss cr; Eng spkn; adv bkg (ess high ssn); quiet; ccard acc; CCI. "New Dutch owners (2008); friendly & helpful; wine-tasting area; excel site in every way." ♦ 1 Mar-15 Nov. € 19.00 2008*

CARPENTRAS *10E2* (12km E Rural) *44.02904, 5.19974* **Camp Municipal Aéria, Le Portail, 84570 Blauvac [tel/fax 04 90 61 81 41 (Mairie)]** E fr Carpentras on D942; E of Mazan fork onto D150. Site 100m N of Blauvac vill cent. Sm, mkd pitch, pt shd; wc (some cont); shwrs; el pnts (10A) €2; shop; rest; snacks; bar; playgrnd. "Superb, quiet site on hilltop with view; basic facs; warden calls am & pm; may be exposed in bad weather." 15 Mar-15 Oct. € 8.00 2009*

CARPENTRAS *10E2* (10km SE Rural) *44.01428, 5.17098* **Camping Font Neuve, Rte de Méthamis, 84570 Malemort-du-Comtat [04 90 69 90 00 or 04 90 69 74 86; fax 04 90 69 91 77; camping.font-neuve@libertysurf.fr; http://camping.font.neuve.free.fr]** Fr Malemort take Méthanis rd D5; as rd starts to rise look for sp on L to site. Med, hdg pitch, terr, pt shd; wc (some cont); chem disp; serviced pitches; baby facs; shwrs inc; el pnts (10A) €4.50; lndtte; tradsmn; rest; snacks; bar; playgrnd; pool; tennis; entmnt; TV; some statics; dogs €1.70; adv bkg req high ssn; quiet. "Friendly, family-run site; gd rest; immac san facs." ♦ 1 May-30 Sep. € 12.50 2008*

CARPENTRAS *10E2* (500m S Urban) *44.04379, 5.05363* **FLOWER Camp Municipal Lou Comtadou, Ave Pierre de Coubertin, Route de Saint-Didier, 84200 Carpentras [04 90 67 03 16 or 06 09 36 67 56 (mob); fax 04 90 46 01 81; info@campingloucomtadou.com; www.campingloucomtadou.com or www.flowercamping.com]** Exit A7 junc 22 or 23 to Carpentras; foll sp dir St Didier thro one-way system onto D4; in 200m turn L into Ave Pierre de Coubertin. Site sp in 500m. Med, hdg/mkd pitch, hdstg, shd; htd wc; chem disp; baby facs; shwrs inc; el pnts (6A) €3; lndtte; ice; shop; tradsmn; rest; snacks; BBQ; playgrnd; pool; wifi; dogs €3; phone; bus adj; Eng spkn; quiet; ccard acc; red low ssn; CCI. "Well-kept, clean site; lge pitches; attractive walled town; excel." ♦ 1 Mar-31 Oct. € 19.60 2009*

CARPENTRAS *10E2* (6km S Urban) *43.99917, 5.06591* **Camp Municipal Coucourelle, Ave René Char, 84210 Pernes-les-Fontaines [04 90 66 45 55 or 04 90 61 31 67 (Mairie); fax 04 90 61 32 46; camping@ville-pernes-les-fontaines.fr; www.ville-pernes-les-fontaines.fr]** Take D938 fr Carpentras to Pernes-les-Fontaines; then take D28 dir St Didier (Ave René Char pt of D28). Site sp (some sps easily missed). Foll sp sports complex, site at rear of sw pool. Sm, hdg/mkd pitch, shd; wc; chem disp; mv service pnt; shwrs inc; el pnts (10A) €2.80; gas 1km; lndtte; shops & rests 1km; BBQ; playgrnd; pool, sw & fishing 2.5km; tennis adj; dogs €0.50; poss cr; adv bkg; quiet; ccard acc; CCI. "Well-run, pleasant, functional site; views of Mont Ventoux; most pitches lge but some sm & narr; gd, clean facs; m'vans can park adj to mv point free when site clsd; gates close 1930; no twin-axles; free use of adj pool; v attractive old town, easy parking; vg." ♦ 1 Apr-30 Sep. € 13.40 2009*

France

CARPENTRAS *10E2* (4km SW Rural) *44.0398, 5.0009* **Camp Municipal de Bellerive, 54 Chemin de la Ribière, 84170 Monteux [04 90 66 81 88 or 04 90 66 97 52 (TO); camping.bellerive@orange.fr]** Site on N edge of Monteux cent, sp off ring rd Monteux N, immed after rlwy x-ing. Sm, hdg/mkd pitch, pt shd; some serviced pitches; wc; chem disp; shwrs inc; el pnts (6A) €2.50; lndry rm; shops 500m; rest, snacks, bar 500m; playgrnd; pool 4km; some statics; phone; bus; poss cr; quiet, but poss noise fr park adj (music); red long stay; CCI. "Excel site; rec arr early high ssn; warden lives adj; gd security; vg, clean san facs; trees a problem for sat TV - choose pitch carefully; park adj gd for children; 5 min walk to vill; gd touring base; Mistral blows early ssn." ♦ 1 Apr-15 Oct. € 9.50 2009*

CARPENTRAS *10E2* (7km NW Urban) *44.07981, 4.97693* **Camp Muncipal de la Sainte Croix, Quartier Ste Croix, 84260 Sarrians [tel/fax 04 90 65 43 72; camping destecroix@orange.fr; www.camping-sainte-croix.com]** Fr Carpentras on D950 dir Orange; in 7km turn L at rndabt on o'skts of Sarrians onto D221; site in 200m on R. Sm, hdg/mkd pitch, some hdstg, pt shd; wc; chem disp; shwrs inc; el pnts €3.50; lndtte; shop 500m; snacks; bar; BBQ; playgrnd; pool; rv sw 5km; tennis; 20% statics; dogs €2; phone; poss cr; adv bkg; red low ssn; CCI. "Pleasant site; helpful warden; clean facs; gd touring base." ♦ 30 Mar-31 Oct. € 17.50 2009*

CARPENTRAS *10E2* (11km NW Rural) *44.14269, 4.98646* **Camp Municipal Les Queyrades, Route de Vaison, 84190 Vacqueyras [04 90 12 39 02 (TO); fax 04 90 65 83 28; tourisme.vacqueyras@wanadoo.fr; www.vacqueyras.tm.fr]** Site on W of D7 at N end of Vacqueyras, clearly sp. Sm, pt shd, hdg pitch; wc; shwrs inc; el pnts (6-10A) €3; shops 1km; playgrnd; rv sw 3km; tennis adj; Eng spkn; adv bkg; quiet, but some rd noise; CCI. "Clean, popular site; wine caves opp; D7 v fast & busy." Easter-Sep. € 9.40 2008*

CARQUEIRANNE see Hyères *10F3*

⊞ **CARRY LE ROUET** *10F2* (Coastal) *43.33024, 5.13747* **Camping Lou Souleï, 13620 Carry-le-Rouet [04 42 44 75 75; fax 04 42 44 57 24; lousoulei@wanadoo.fr; www.lousoulei.com]** Fr Martigues take A55 & exit dir Carry-le-Rouet. Site on beach rd. V lge, hdg/mkd pitch, hdstg, pt shd; htd wc; chem disp; serviced pitch; shwrs inc; el pnts (6A) inc; lndtte; shop adj; rest; snacks; bar; playgrnd; htd pool; beach adj; games rm; games area; entmnt; TV rm; 60% statics; dogs; phone; poss cr; Eng spkn; adv bkg; red low ssn. "Gd base for Marseille, Camargue, Aix, etc; red facs low ssn." € 45.00 (4 persons) 2006*

CARSAC AILLAC see Sarlat la Canéda *7C3*

CASSAGNABERE TOURNAS *8F3* (S Rural) *43.22583, 0.78920* **Camping Pré Fixe, 31420 Cassagnabère-Tournas [05 61 98 71 00 or 06 48 23 46 79 (mob); camping@instudio4.com; www.instudio4.com/pre-fixe]** Exit A64 at junc 21 onto D635 dir Aurignac. Cont thro vill on D635 sp Cassagnabère for 8km, sp in vill. Sm, hdg/mkd pitch, terr, pt shd; wc (some cont); chem disp; mv disposal; baby facs; shwrs inc; el pnts (6-10A) €4; gas; lndtte; shop 500m; tradsmn; rest; snacks; bar; BBQ; playgrnd; pool; entmnt; TV rm; 10% statics; no dogs; phone; Eng spkn; adv bkg; quiet; CCI. "Friendly owners; beautiful landscape; gd touring base; excel." ♦ 15 Apr-30 Sep. € 18.00 2009*

CASSANIOUZE *7D4* (10km SW Rural) *44.64265, 2.36656* **Camping de Coursavy, 15340 Cassaniouze [tel/fax 04 71 49 97 70; camping.coursavy@wanadoo.fr; www.campingcoursavy.com]** Fr Entraygues (E) foll D107 along Rv Lot dir Conques. 6km after Vieillevie, site on L on rvside. Cont to next rd junc (500m) after site ent to turn & return. Sm, mkd pitch, terr, pt sl, pt shd; wc; chem disp, shwrs inc; el pnts (5A) €2.50; lndtte; shop 2km; tradsmn; rest, snacks, bar 1km; playgrnd; pool; fishing; cycle hire; games area; TV rm; dogs €1.50; phone adj; Eng spkn; adv bkg; quiet; red low ssn; CCI. "Excel site in beautiful, unspoilt area; gd touring base; friendly Dutch owners; diff lge m'vans due trees." ♦ 20 Apr-20 Sep. € 17.60 2007*

CASSIS *10F3* (1.5km N Coastal) *43.22417, 5.54126* **Camping Les Cigales, Ave de la Marne, 13260 Cassis [04 42 01 07 34; fax 04 42 01 34 18; www.campingcassis.com]** App Cassis on D41E, then at 2nd rndabt exit D559 sp Cassis, then turn 1st R sp Les Calanques into Ave de la Marne, site immed on R. Avoid town cent as rds narr. Lge, hgd/mkd pitch, hdstg, pt sl, pt shd; wc (some cont); chem disp; mv service pnt; shwrs inc; el pnts (3A) €2.60 (poss long lead req); gas; lndtte; shop; tradsmn; rest; snacks; bar; playgrnd; shgl beach 1.5km; 30% statics; dogs €1.10; phone; rd noise some pitches; Eng spkn; ccard acc; CCI. "Gd base for Calanques; v busy w/ends; attractive resort, but steep walk to camp site; poss tired san facs end ssn; poss diff lge o'fits due trees; v strong pegs req to penetrate hardcore." 15 Mar-15 Nov. € 16.50 2009*

CASTELFRANC *7D3* (9km N Rural) *44.57710, 1.19283* **Camping La Pinède, Le Bourg, 46250 Goujounac [05 65 36 61 84; camping-goujounac@orange.fr; http://monsite.orange.fr/camping-de-goujounac]** Fr Gourdon take D673 SW. At Frayssinet-le-Gelet turn L onto D660 for 2.5km. Site on L at ent to vill. Sm, mkd pitch, terr, pt shd; wc; chem disp; shwrs inc; el pnts (20A) €2; lndtte; shop 1km; bar; pool; tennis; quiet. "Attractive vill & site in pine wood; gd rest 1km." 15 Jun-15 Sep. € 12.00 2008*

CASTELFRANC *7D3* (6km SE Rural) *44.48095, 1.28160* **Camp Municipal de l'Alcade, 46140 Luzech [05 65 30 72 32 (Mairie); fax 05 65 30 76 80; mairie.luzech@wanadoo.fr; www.ville-luzech.fr]** Fr Cahors take D811 NW, turn L onto D8 foll sp to Luzech; cross both bdges in Luzech; site on R in 1km on D8; do not foll camp sp on D88 to Sauzac. Sm, pt shd; wc (cont); sauna; shwrs inc; el pnts (6-10A) €3 (rev pol); shops 1km; bar; playgrnd; dogs €2; some rd noise; red low ssn. "Peaceful site on Rv Lot; rv not suitable for sw, sluice gates of dam upstream liable to be opened, causing rv to rise sharply; warden visits am & pm - arrange for barrier to be open; peaceful site."
1 Jun-30 Sep. € 16.00 2006*

CASTELFRANC *7D3* (2km SW Rural) *44.47636, 1.19942* **Camping Base Nautique Floiras, 46140 Anglars-Juillac [05 65 36 27 39; fax 05 65 21 41 00; info@campingfloiras.com; www.campingfloiras.com]** Fr Castelfranc head S on D45; cross rv, then turn R onto D8 to Anglars-Juillac; in vill turn R just after rest on L; site at end of lane; site sp. Or fr W on D811 (formerly D911) turn R at main sq Prayssac sp Mont Cuq. In 2km cross rv at Pont Juillac, turn 1st R & foll sp to site. Sm, mkd pitch, pt shd; htd wc; chem disp; mv service pnt; shwrs inc; el pnts (10A) €3.50 (rev pol); gas; lndtte (inc dryer); sm shop; tradsmn; rest adj; snacks; sm bar; BBQ; pool 2km; cycle & canoe hire; dogs €1.30; phone adj; poss cr; Eng spkn; adv bkg ess high ssn (bkg fee); quiet but poss youth groups; ccard acc; CCI. "Well-kept site on Rv Lot set in vineyards; v lge pitches; vg, clean san facs; helpful Dutch owner; nr mkts & rests; super site." ♦ 1 Apr-15 Oct. € 16.40 2008*

CASTELJALOUX *7D2* (500m N Urban) *44.31472, 0.09153* **Camp Municipal de la Piscine, Rue du Souvenir Français, Route de Marmande, 47700 Casteljaloux [05 53 93 54 68; fax 05 53 89 48 07; www.casteljaloux.com]** On N side of town on D933 visible fr rd. Sm, pt shd; wc; shwrs inc; el pnts (10A) €2.15; shops 750m; rest; bar; pool adj inc; rv & lake sw; fishing; rd noise. "Gd, old-fashioned site; sm park nr; helpful warden; gd san facs; conv for town; useful NH; extra charge c'vans over 4m." ♦ 1 Apr-11 Nov. € 7.35 2009*

CASTELJALOUX *7D2* (8km SE Rural) *44.27262, 0.18969* **Camping Moulin de Campech, 47160 Villefranche-du-Queyran [05 53 88 72 43; fax 05 53 88 06 52; campech@orange.fr; www.moulindecampech.co.uk]** Fr A62 exit junc 6 (sp Damazan & Aiguillon). Fr toll booth take D8 SW sp Mont-de-Marsan. In 3km turn R in Cap-du-Bosc onto D11 twd Casteljaloux. Site on R in 4km. Or fr Casteljaloux S on D655 then SW on D11 after 1.5km. Site on L after 9.5km. Med, hdg/mkd pitch, pt shd; wc (some cont); chem disp; shwrs inc; el pnts (6A) inc; lndtte; sm shop; tradsmn; rest; snacks; bar; BBQ; htd pool; lake fishing; games area; golf nr; guided tours; dogs €2.40; phone; poss cr; adv bkg; quiet but rd noise; ccard acc; red low ssn; CCI. "Superb, rvside site; interesting & picturesque area; British owners; helpful, friendly staff; san facs OK, a bit tired low ssn (2008); gd pool; excel, gd value rest; ideal for nature lovers; a little gem." 1 Apr-15 Oct. € 26.50 ABS - D16 2009*

CASTELJALOUX *7D2* (2.5km S Rural) **Camping Club de Clarens, Lac de Clarens, Route de Mont-de-Marsan, 47700 Casteljaloux [tel/fax 05 53 93 07 45; location-chalets@cegetel.net; www.castel-chalets.com]** Sp fr D933. Sm, hdg/mkd pitch, hdstg, pt shd; wc; mv service pnt; shwrs; el pnts (6A) inc; shop, rest nrby; playgrnd; lake sw; fishing; watersports; golf opp; mainly chalets; dogs; Eng spkn; adv bkg; quiet; CCI. "Lakeside pitches in beautiful location; vg for families & walkers." 1 Apr-30 Nov. € 10.00 2006*

CASTELLANE *10E3* (1.5km N Rural) *43.85598, 6.49563* **Camping Le Provençal, Route de Digne, 04120 Castellane [tel/fax 04 92 83 65 50; accueil@camping-provencal.com; www.camping-provencal.com]** Fr N on D4085 (N85) at foot of Col de Lècques site on R on LH bend. Fr Castellane site on D4085 in 1km on L. Med, mkd pitch, pt sl, pt shd; wc; chem disp; baby facs; shwrs inc; el pnts (6A) inc; lndtte; shop; supmkt 500m; tradsmn; snacks; bar; pool, tennis 1.5km; dogs €2; some rd noise; red low ssn. "Gd, clean site; fine scenery, friendly owners; conv Gorges du Verdon." 1 May-15 Sep. € 18.00 2009*

CASTELLANE *10E3* (8km N Rural) *43.88354, 6.51455* **Camping Castillon de Provence (Naturist), La Grande Terre, La Baume, 04120 Castellane [04 92 83 64 24; fax 04 92 83 68 79; info@castillondeprovence.com; www.castillondeprovence.com]** Fr Castellane take D955 at Casino supmkt & after 5km turn L on D402 (up narr mountain rd) site in 7km. NB up access for car & vans only after 1400, down before 1300. Med, pt sl, pt shd; wc (some cont); chem disp (wc); shwrs inc; el pnts (2-6A) €3.50-4.50; gas; lndtte; shop; tradsmn; rest; snacks; bar; playgrnd; htd pool; paddling pool; lake sw, fishing, watersports 2km; TV rm; 20% statics; dogs €2; phone; poss cr; Eng spkn; adv bkg; quiet; ccard not acc; INF card. "Site 1000m high & cold at night; mountain views o'looking Lac de Castillon; friendly, family owners; v lge pitches." ♦ 14 Apr-4 Oct. € 24.00 2008*

CASTELLANE *10E3* (5km SE Rural) *43.81631, 6.57296* **RCN Camping Les Collines de Castellane, Route de Grasse, 04120 La Garde [04 92 83 68 96; fax 04 92 83 75 40; info@rcn-lescollinesdecastellane.fr; www.rcn-campings.fr]** Fr Castellane, take D4085 (N85) for 5km to La Garde, go thro vill & foll sp. Site on R in 1km. Lge, terr, pt shd; wc; mv service pnt; baby facs; shwrs inc; el pnts (10A) inc; gas; lndtte; shop; rest; snacks; bar; playgrnd; pool; lake sw 5km; games area; organised activites inc watersports, rock climbing, paragliding, hiking; entmnt, TV; dogs €6; Eng spkn; adv bkg; red low ssn. "Friendly owners; peaceful site on steep hillside with stunning views; main site rd v steep." ♦ 17 Apr-25 Sep. € 39.50 2009*

France

⊞ **CASTELLANE** *10E3* (SW Urban) *43.84623, 6.50995* **Camping Frédéric Mistral, 12 Ave Frédéric Mistral, 04120 Castellane [04 92 83 62 27; contact@camping-fredericmistral.com; www.camping-fredericmistral.com]** In town turn onto D952 sp Gorges-du-Verdon, site on L in 100m. Med, mkd pitch, pt shd; htd wc; chem disp; some serviced pitches; shwrs inc; el pnts (6A) €3 (poss rev pol); gas 200m; shops adj; supmkt nr; rest; bar; snacks; pool 200m; 2% statics; poss cr; adv bkg; quiet; red low ssn; CCI. "Friendly owners; gd san facs but poss stretched in ssn; poss music fr adj community cent till late w/end; gd base for gorges etc." ♦ € 14.00 2008*

CASTELLANE *10E3* (500m SW Rural) *43.84570, 6.50447* **Camping Notre Dame, Route des Gorges du Verdon, 04120 Castellane [tel/fax 04 92 83 63 02; camping-notredame@wanadoo.fr; www.camping-notredame.com]** N fr Grasse on D6085 (N85), turn L in Castellane at sq onto D952 to site on R in 500m. Sm, pt shd; wc; chem disp; mv service pnt; shwrs inc; el pnts (6A) €3.50; gas; Indtte; sm shop; rest 600m; playgrnd; 20% statics; dogs free; phone; poss cr; Eng spkn; adv bkg; some rd noise; red low ssn; CCI. "Ideal touring base; helpful owners; poss unkempt early ssn; excel." ♦ 1 Apr-15 Oct. € 16.00 2009*

CASTELLANE *10E3* (1.5km SW Rural) *43.83921, 6.49370* **Camping Le Camp du Verdon, Domaine du Verdon, 04120 Castellane [04 92 83 61 29; fax 04 92 83 69 37; contact@camp-du-verdon.com; www.camp-du-verdon.com or www.les-castels.com]** Fr Castellane take D952 SW twd Grand Canyon du Verdon & Moustiers-Ste Marie. After 1.5km turn L into site. NB To avoid Col de Lèques with hairpins use N202 & D955 fr Barrême instead of D6085 (N85). V lge, hdg/mkd pitch; pt shd; wc (some cont); chem disp; mv service pnt; ltd baby facs; shwrs inc; el pnts (6A) inc; gas; Indtte; shop; rest; snacks; bar; BBQ (gas only); playgrnd; 2 pools (1 htd); waterslides; paddling pool; rv fishing adj; canoeing, kayaking, rafting, horseriding nrby; archery; games area; entmnt; wifi; games/TV rm; dogs €3; poss cr; Eng spkn; poss noisy; ccard acc; red low ssn; CCI. "Excel site; gd pitches; gd clean facs; many facs high ssn only; quiet, rural walk to town; guided walks to gorge; mkt Wed & Sat." ♦ 15 May-15 Sep. € 42.20 (3 persons) (CChq acc) ABS - C15 2009*

CASTELLANE *10E3* (2km SW Rural) *43.83790, 6.49051* **Camping de la Colle, Route des Gorges du Verdon, Quartier de la Colle, 04120 Castellane [tel/fax 04 92 83 61 57; contact@camping-gorges-verdon.com; www.campinglacolle.com]** Leave Castellane on D952 heading W. In 2km, take R fork. Site is on a narr rd, sp. Sm, terr, shd; wc; chem disp; mv service pnt; baby facs; shwrs inc; el pnts (6-10A) €3.90; Indtte; sm shop & 2km; tradsmn; rest; snacks; bar; playgrnd; pool 2km; lake & rv sw 5km; 15% statics; dogs €2.30; phone; adv bkg; quiet; CCI. "Not suitable for v lge c'vans or m'vans; family-run; unspoilt natural setting well above town; dir access to Gorges du Verdon; vg." ♦ 1 Apr-30 Oct. € 16.30 2007*

CASTELLANE *10E3* (8.5km SW Rural) *43.82842, 6.42743* **FFCC Domaine de Chasteuil-Provence, Route de Moustiers, Chasteuil, 04120 Castellane [04 92 83 61 21; fax 04 92 83 75 62; contact@chasteuil-provence.com; www.chasteuil-provence.com]** Take D952 W fr Castellane; site by rv on L. Lge, mkd pitch, pt terr, shd; wc; chem disp; shwrs inc; el pnts (6-10A) €3.30-5.40; gas; Indtte; shop; tradsmn; rest; snacks; bar; playgrnd; htd pool; paddling pool; rv beach; boating; fishing; games area; entmnt high ssn; 10% statics; dogs free; poss cr; adv bkg; quiet; red low ssn; ccard acc; CCI. "Lovely location by rv; dated facs & poss not clean; excel touring & walking base; access OK for lge o'fits." 1 May-15 Sep. € 22.80 (3 persons) 2008*

CASTELLANE *10E3* (12km SW Rural) *43.79596, 6.43733* **Camp Municipal de Carajuan, 04120 Rougon [04 92 83 70 94 or 04 92 83 66 32 (Mairie); fax 04 92 83 66 49; camping.carajuan@wanadoo.fr; www.rougon.fr]** Fr N on D4085 (N85) turn R on D952 & foll sps for 16km to rv bank of Gorges du Verdon nr Carajuan bdge; site on L. Fr E on D952 ignore turning to Rougon; site sp in 5km. Med, mkd pitch, pt shd; wc; chem disp (wc); shwrs inc; el pnts (6A) €2.70; Indtte; shop 10km; tradsmn; snacks; playgrnd; 10% statics; dogs €1.20; phone; bus Jul/Aug; poss cr; quiet; Eng spkn; adv bkg; quiet; red long stay; CCI. "Natural, unspoilt site nr rvside with shingle beach (no sw); friendly staff; basic, dated facs, poss unclean low ssn; gd walking; fair." 21 Mar-30 Sep. € 11.40 2008*

CASTELLANE *10E3* (W Urban) *43.84608, 6.50715* **Camping Les Lavandes, Route des Gorges du Verdon, 04120 Castellane [04 92 83 68 78 or 04 92 78 33 51 (LS); fax 04 92 83 69 92; accueil@camping-les-lavandes.com; www.camping-les-lavandes.com]** Head W on D952 sp Gorges du Verdon to site on R. Med, mkd pitch, pt shd; wc; chem disp; sauna, solarium; baby facs; shwrs €1; el pnts (3-10A) €2.90-3.90; supmkt 500m; playgrnd; entmnt; rv adj; some statics; poss cr; adv bkg; quiet; red low ssn; no ccard acc. "Lovely site; sm pitches; beautiful mountain scenery; excel view of Notre Dame du Roc; conv town cent; site yourself if office clsd; poss unkempt low ssn." 1 Apr-15 Oct. € 12.50 2007*

CASTELLANE *10E3* (9km W Rural) *43.82276, 6.43143* **Camp des Gorges du Verdon, Clos d'Aremus, 04120 Castellane [04 92 83 63 64; fax 04 92 83 74 72; aremus@camping-gorgesduverdon.com; www.camping-gorgesduverdon.com]** On D6085 (N85) fr Grasse turn L on D952 in Castellane. Camp in 9km on L. Look for sp Chasteuil on R of rd; site in 500m. Lge, mkd pitch, shd; wc; chem disp; mv service pnt; shwrs inc; el pnts (6A) inc; gas; Indtte; sm shop; rest; snacks; bar; playgrnd; htd pool; fishing; boating; canoeing; games area; games rm; entmnt; wifi; TV; 10% statics; dogs free; poss cr; Eng spkn; adv bkg ess; red low ssn; CCI. "Some sm pitches; rd along Gorges du Verdon poss diff for lge o'fits." ♦ 26 Apr-15 Sep. € 28.50 (3 persons) 2008*

CASTELLANE *10E3* (2km NW Rural) *43.85861, 6.49795* **Kawan Village Camping International, Route Napoléon, La Palud, 04120 Castellane [04 92 83 66 67; fax 04 92 83 77 67; info@camping-international.fr; www.camping-international.fr]** Site sp fr D4085 (N850) & D602. Lge, hdg pitch, pt sl, pt shd; wc; chem disp; mv service pnt; serviced pitches; baby facs; shwrs inc; el pnts (6A) €4.50; gas; Indtte; gd sm supmkt; tradsmn; rest; snacks; bar; playgrnd; pool; lake sw & sand beach 5km; games area; golf; horseriding; entmnt; internet; TV rm; 50% statics; dogs €2; adv bkg; Eng spkn; ccard acc; red low ssn; CCI. "Busy site; friendly, helpful owners; main san facs vg, some dated; most pitches on gentle slope; conv Gorges de Verdon; gd walking; gd." ♦ 31 Mar-30 Sep. € 19.00 (CChq acc) 2009*

CASTELLANE *10E3* (8km NW Rural) *43.86532, 6.46447* **Camping Les Sirènes, Col des Lècques, Route Napoléon, 04120 Castellane [04 92 83 70 56; fax 04 92 83 72 72; accueil@les-sirenes.com; www.les-sirenes.com]** On D4085 (N85) 8km NW of Castellane. Sm, pt sl, shd; wc; shwrs; el pnts (6A) €3; shop 8km; rest; snacks; bar; BBQ; playgrnd; htd pool; some statics; dogs €1.50; quiet; adv bkg; CCI. "Gd views; scenic walks; conv heritage fossil site." Easter-22 Sep. € 13.50 2007*

CASTELNAU MAGNOAC *8F2* (2km SE Rural) *43.26610, 0.52140* **Camping L'Eglantière (Naturist), 65230 Aries-Espénan [05 62 99 83 64 or 05 62 39 88 00; fax 05 62 39 81 44; infos@leglantiere.com; www.leglantiere.com]** Fr Castelnau-Magnoac take D929 S sp Lannemezan; in 2.5km L on D9 sp Monléon; in 1km L on unclass rd for 500m; L at T-junc & foll L'Eglantiere sp to site; app fr D632 not rec. Lge, hdg/mkd pitch, pt sl, pt shd; wc; chem disp; mv service pnt; serviced pitch; sauna; shwrs inc; el pnts (16A) €5.20 (rev pol); gas; Indtte; shop; tradsmn; rest; snacks; bar; playgrnd; htd pool; paddling pool; fishing; canoeing; archery; cycle hire; golf nrby; 15% statics; dogs €4.20; adv bkg; Eng spkn; quiet; various pitch prices; ccard acc; red low ssn; CCI. "Beautiful, relaxing site on rv; helpful staff; pitches poss soft after rain; plenty naturist walks; conv Pyrenees; fantastic site." ♦ 3 Apr-26 Sep. € 34.00 (CChq acc) 2009*

CASTELNAUD LA CHAPELLE see Sarlat la Canéda *7C3*

CASTELNAUDARY *8F4* (4km E Rural) *43.31723, 2.01582* **FFCC Camping à la Ferme Domaine de la Capelle (Sabatte), St Papoul, 11400 St Martin-Lalande [04 68 94 91 90; lacapelle1@orange.fr; http://la-capelle.site.voila.fr]** Fr D6113 (N113) Castelnaudary/Carcasonne, take D103 E & foll sp to St Papoul & site in 2km. Well sp. NB Ent poss awkward lge o'fits. Sm, hdg/mkd pitch, pt sl, pt shd; htd wc; chem disp (wc); shwrs inc; el pnts (16A) €2.50; Indtte (inc dryer); shop 2km; tradsmn; BBQ; no statics; dogs €1; phone; Eng spkn; quiet; CCI. "Delightful, peaceful, spacious CL-type site; friendly, helpful owner; clean facs, poss stretched when site full; gd walking; nr St Papoul, a Cathar vill with abbey; ideal NH for Spain; excel." 1 Apr-30 Sep. € 12.00 2009*

CASTETS *8E1* (800m E Urban) *43.88069, -1.13768* **Camp Municipal Le Galan, 73 Rue du Stade, 40260 Castets [05 58 89 43 52 or 05 58 89 40 09; fax 05 58 55 00 07; contact@camping-legalan.com; www.camping-legalan.com]** Exit N10 junc 12 onto D42. Site on L at end of wide cul-de-sac. Lge, pt sl, shd; wc; hot water & shwrs inc; el pnts (6A) inc; gas; Indtte; shop high ssn & 1km; tradsmn; rest 100m; playgrnd; paddling pool; tennis; few statics; dogs €1.70; bus to Dax; adv bkg; quiet but some rd noise; CCI. "Excel, peaceful, clean site in nice vill; extra for twin-axles; NH area poss cr; rv walks." ♦ 1 Feb-30 Nov. € 14.35 2009*

CASTIES LABRANDE *8F3* (Rural) *43.32502, 0.99046* **Camping Le Casties, Bas de Lebrande, 31430 Casties-Labrande [05 61 90 81 11; fax 05 61 90 81 10; lecasties@wanadoo.fr; www.camping-lecasties.com]** S fr Toulouse, exit A64 junc 26 onto D626; after Pouy-de-Touges turn L onto new rd & foll camping sp. Med, hdg pitch, pt shd; wc; chem disp; shwrs inc; el pnts (5A) €1; Indtte; tradsmn; snacks; bar; BBQ; playgrnd; pool; fishing; 10% statics; dogs; phone; Eng spkn; adv bkg; quiet; ccard acc; CCI. "In the middle of nowhere!; lge pitches; san facs basic but clean; staff friendly & helpful; lovely pool; excel." ♦ 1 May-30 Sep. € 8.00 2006*

CASTILLON LA BATAILLE *7C2* (E Urban) *44.85350, -0.03550* **Camp Municipal La Pelouse, Chemin de Halage, 33350 Castillon-la-Bataille [05 56 40 04 22 or 05 56 40 00 06 (Mairie)]** Site in town on N bank of Rv Dordogne; not well sp in town. After x-ing rv on D17 fr S to N, take 1st avail rd on R to rv. Sm, shd; wc; shwrs inc; el pnts (15A) inc; shop; poss cr; adv bkg; quiet; CCI. "Peaceful site by rv; busy high ssn; pitches poss rough & muddy when wet; helpful warden; facs dated but clean; conv St Emillion & wine area; gd NH." 1 May-15 Oct. € 11.00 2009*

CASTILLONNES *7D3* (300m N Urban) *44.65566, 0.59111* **Camp Municipal La Ferrette, Route de Bergerac, 47330 Castillonnès [05 53 36 94 68 or 05 58 36 80 49 (Mairie); fax 05 53 36 88 77; rouquet47@hotmail.fr]** On N21, 27km S of Bergerac, on N side of Castillonnès. Easily seen fr main rd. Med, mkd pitch, pt sl, pt shd; wc (cont); el pnts (6A) inc; Indtte; shops 300m; playgrnd; tennis adj; some statics; quiet. "Beautiful situation; interesting town; gd san facs." ♦ 1 Jul-31 Aug. € 11.00 2006*

⊞ **CASTILLONNES** *7D3* (5km NW Rural) **Camping Le Bost, Le Bost, 24560 Plaisance [05 53 22 84 98 or 06 75 54 18 44 (mob); camping@lebost.com; www.lebost.com]** S fr Bergerac on N21 to Plaisance in 16km; cont thro vill, going up hill, to lane in 500m sp Le Bost; site set back off rd just after sp. Sm, hdstg, pt sl, pt shd; wc; chem disp; shwrs; el pnts (10A) €3.50; shop 5km; rest, sancks & bar 2km; BBQ; wifi; dogs €1; red long stay. "CL-type site; ideal base for Bergerac wine area; friendly, helpful British owners; gd NH en rte Spain." € 12.00 2008*

France

CASTRES *8F4* (2km NE Urban) *43.62054, 2.25401* **Camping Gourjade (formerly Municipal), Ave de Roquecourbe, 81100 Castres [tel/fax 05 63 59 33 51; contact@campingdegourjade.com; http://camping degourjade.perso.cegetel.net]** Leave Castres NE on D89 sp Rocquecourbe; site on R in 2km. Well sp. Ave de Roquecourbe is part of D89. Med, hdg pitch, pt terr, pt shd; wc; chem disp; mv service pnt; shwrs; el pnts (6-10A) inc (poss rev pol); gas; lndtte; shop in ssn; rest adj; snacks; bar; BBQ; playgrnd; pool; 9 hole golf course adj; cycling; boat fr site to town; 5% statics; dogs €2; bus; quiet; ccard acc; red low ssn; CCI. "Lovely site in beautiful park; lge pitches; helpful staff; gd, clean san facs; some lower pitches sl & poss soft; extra charge twin-axles; gd security; poss groups of workers on site low ssn; leisure cent adj; vg cycling; highly rec." ♦ 1 Apr-3 Oct. € 15.50 2009*

⊞ **CASTRIES** *10E1* (1.5km NE Rural) *43.69406, 3.99585* **FLOWER Camping Domaine de Fondespierre, 277 Route de Fontmarie, 34160 Castries [04 67 91 20 03; fax 04 67 16 41 48; accueil@campingfondespierre.com; www.campingfondespierre.com or www.flowercamping.com]** Fr A9 exit junc 28 dir Castries onto N110; site 1.5km after vill on L. Not well sp. Med, hdg/mkd pitch, hdstg, terr, ptshd; htd wc; chem disp; mv service pnt; baby facs; shwrs inc; el pnts (10A) inc (poss long lead req); gas 5km; lndtte; shops 1.5km; tradsmn; rest, snacks 1.5km; bar; BBQ (sep area); playgrnd; pool; lake sw 5km; tennis adj; golf 2.5km; cycle hire; 40% statics; dogs €3; phone; poss cr; Eng spkn; quiet; ccard acc; red CCI. "Gd walking area; poss itinerants & site poss unkempt low ssn; site rds narr with sharp, tree-lined bends - poss diff access to pitches for lge o'fits; NH." € 24.00 2008*

CAUDEBEC EN CAUX *3C2* (6km S Urban) *49.48373, 0.77247* **Camp Municipal du Parc, Rue Victor Hugo, 76940 La Mailleraye-sur-Seine [02 35 37 12 04; mairie-sg.lamailleraysurseine@wanadoo.fr]** Fr N on D131/D490 turn E onto D65. Or fr S on D913. Site sp in cent of town close to rv bank. Sm, hdg pitch, pt sl, pt shd; wc; chem disp; shwrs; el pnts (6A) €3; shop, rest, bar 200m; playgrnd; poss cr; quiet. "Pleasant NH; site yourself, warden calls; gd walking area." 1 Apr-30 Sep. € 8.00 2009*

CAUDEBEC EN CAUX *3C2* (1.5km W Rural) *49.52303, 0.70606* **Camping Barre-y-Va, Route de Villequier, 76490 Caudebec-en-Caux [02 35 96 26 38 or 02 35 95 90 10 (Mairie); campingbarreyva@orange.fr; www.camping-barre-y-va.com]** Fr Caudebec take D81 W twd Villequier & site on R in 1.5km next to Rv Seine. Med, pt shd; wc (some cont); chem disp; shwrs inc; el pnts (10A) €4.10 (poss rev pol); lndtte; shops 1.5km; tradsmn; snacks & takeaway; playgrnd; pool 300m; rv fishing & boating adj; cycle hire; games rm; TV; some statics; dogs €2.50; phone; Eng spkn; noise fr rd, rv & nrby disco; red low ssn/CCI. "Popular, clean & well-kept site in interesting area; unisex san facs; barrier clsd 2200-0700." 1 Apr-31 Oct. € 16.95 2009*

CAUDECOSTE see Agen *8E3*

CAUNES MINERVOIS *8F4* (1km S Rural) **Camp Municipal Les Courtals, 11160 Caunes-Minervois [04 68 78 07 83 or 04 68 78 00 28 (Mairie); fax 04 68 78 05 78]** Sp fr D620 at stadium & adj rv. Sm, pt shd; wc; shwrs; el pnts (4A) inc; shops adj; playgrnd; pool 6km; games area; rv adj; quiet. "Pleasantly situated site; office opens 1800; gate locked 2100; site self, warden calls; interesting town." 1 Jun-31 Aug. € 12.10 2007*

CAUREL see Mûr de Bretagne *2E3*

CAUSSADE *8E3* (750m NE Urban) *44.16582, 1.54446* **Camp Municipal de la Piboulette, 82300 Caussade [05 63 93 09 07]** S on D820 (N20) fr Cahors (40km), turn L off D820 on ent Caussade onto D17 (Rte de Puylaroque). About 750m turn L (sp), site on R in 100m; lge grass stadium. Med, mkd pitch, pt shd; wc (some cont); chem disp; serviced pitches; shwrs inc; el pnts (3-6A) €1.50-2.80; lndtte; shop 500m; tradsmn; playgrnd; sports centre adj; pool on far side of stadium; adv bkg; quiet; CCI. "Spacious pitches; pleasant warden; excel clean san facs, poss tired low ssn; conv for Gorges de l'Aveyron; gd cycling round adj lake; mkt Mon; excel value; vg." ♦ 1 May-30 Sep. € 5.95 2009*

CAUSSADE *8E3* (7km NE Rural) *44.18273, 1.60305* **Camping de Bois Redon, 10 Chemin de Bonnet, 82240 Septfonds [05 63 64 92 49; info@campingdeboisredon.com; www.campingdeboisredon.com]** Exit A20 junc 59 to Caussade, then onto D926 to Septfonds; after rndabt turn 3rd L; site sp. Site in 2km. One-way system when leaving site. Sm, mkd pitch, pt sl, pt shd; wc; chem disp; baby facs; shwrs inc; el pnts (10A) €3; lndtte; shop; tradsmn; snacks; bar; playgrnd; pool; cycle hire; 10% statics; dogs €2; Eng spkn; adv bkg (dep); quiet; CCI. "Well-shaded spacious site in ancient oak forest with walks; charming Dutch owners; immac facs; Septfonds nr with all facs." ♦ 1 Apr-1 Oct. € 14.00 2009*

⊞ **CAUSSADE** *8E3* (10km NE Rural) *44.2167, 1.6116* **Camping Le Clos de la Lère, Clergue, Route de Septfonds, 82240 Cayriech [05 63 31 20 41; contact@camping-leclos delalere.com; www.camping-leclosdelalere.com]** Take D17 fr Caussade. Turn R at junc with D103 (sp Cayriech/ Septfonds). In Cayriech vill turn R at T-junc by church, site on R in 200m. Foll sp only for Camping Le Clos de la Lère. Fr Septfonds turn N off D926, site in 5.3km on L just bef Cayriech sp. Sm, hdg/mkd pitch, hdstg, pt shd; htd wc; mv service pnt; baby facs; shwrs inc; el pnts (6-10A) €2.10-3.80; gas; lndtte; shop 4km; tradsmn; snacks; no BBQ; playgrnd; pool; few statics; dogs €1.60; adv bkg; quiet; red low ssn/ long stay; ccard acc; CCI. "Well-maintained site; clean san facs; helpful staff; excel winter site & NH; ltd facs low ssn; excel games facs; rec arr bef dark." ♦ € 12.30 2009*

France

CAUSSADE *8E3* (11km SW) *44.07200, 1.51805* **FFCC Camp Municipal Le Colombier, 82800 Nègrepelisse [05 63 64 20 34; fax 05 63 64 26 24]** Fr A20 exit junc 59 dir Nègrepelisse. Fr Montauban, take D958 to Nègrepelisse, turn L into vill then 1st L after Total/Citroën g'ge, foll sp to site. Site nr prominent water tower in town. Well sp. Med, mkd pitch, terr, pt shd; wc; mv service pnt; shwrs inc; el pnts (6A) €2.20; supmkt 300m; gas; pool adj; playgrnd; dogs €1.15; quiet; red long stay. "Pool open school hols - free with 3+ days stay." 10 Jun-30 Sep. € 7.00 2007*

CAUSSADE *8E3* (10km NW Rural) *44.24323, 1.47735* **Camping Le Faillal, 82270 Montpezat-de-Quercy [05 63 02 07 08; fax 04 73 93 71 00; lefaillal@wanadoo.fr; www.revea-vacances.fr]** N on D820 (N20), turn L onto D20, site clearly sp on R in 2km. (Do not take D38 bef D20 fr S). Med, hdg pitch, pt sl, terr, pt shd; wc; chem disp; shwrs inc; el pnts (4-6A) €3.50; Indtte; shops 200m; playgrnd; pool high ssn; tennis adj; few statics; dogs €1.50; phone; adv bkg; quiet; red low ssn/CCI. "Pretty, well-kept site; friendly, helpful staff; gd, clean san facs, poss ltd; super pool; many pitches unavailable after heavy rain; old town a 'must'; rec pay night bef departure; excel." ♦
4 Apr-10 Oct. € 14.30 (CChq acc) 2009*

⊞ **CAUTERETS** *8G2* (500m N Urban) *42.89402, -0.11255* **Camping Les Glères, 19 Route de Pierrefitte, 65110 Cauterets [05 62 92 55 34; fax 05 62 92 03 53; camping-les-gleres@wanadoo.fr; www.gleres.com]** Fr N on N920 ent town; site on R with sharp turn but sp. Narr ent (take care long o'fits). Med, hdg/mkd pitch, hdstg, pt shd; htd wc; chem disp; mv service pnt nr; some serviced pitches; shwrs inc; el pnts (6A) inc; gas; Indtte; rest, snacks, bar, shop, pool 500m; playgrnd; 10% statics; dogs €1.20; phone; site clsd 21 Oct-30 Nov; Eng spkn; quiet; red low ssn; CCI. "Conv town cent; gd walking area with cable car 500m; superb san facs; friendly & helpful; tight access to pitches; municipal m'van site adj; excel." € 17.90 2007*

CAUTERETS *8G2* (1km N Rural) *42.90254, -0.10605* **Camping Le Péguère, Route de Pierrefitte, 65110 Cauterets [tel/fax 05 62 92 52 91; campingpeguere@wanadoo.fr; www.lescampings.com/peguere]** Fr Lourdes on N21 foll sp for Cauterets. On app Cauterets site on R immed after rv bdge. Med, pt sl, pt shd; wc; mv service pnt; shwrs inc; el pnts (6A) inc; Indtte; tradsmn; snacks; playgrnd; rv fishing adj; entmnt; TV rm; some statics; dogs €0.85; adv bkg; quiet; ccard acc; CCI. "Clean facs; beautiful setting; ideal base for walking in Pyrenees." ♦ 1 May-30 Sep. € 13.00 2007*

CAUTERETS *8G2* (1.5km N Rural) *42.90319, -0.10730* **Camping Le Cabaliros, Pont de Secours, 65110 Cauterets [tel/fax 05 62 92 55 36; info@camping-cabaliros.com; www.camping-cabaliros.com]** App Cauterests fr Argelès-Gazost on D921/D920, site 1st on R over bdge. Med, pt sl, pt shd wc; chem disp; mv service pnt; shwrs inc; el pnts (3A) €3.15; Indtte; shop 200m; rest; snacks; bar; playgrnd; pool 1km; fishing; 10% statics; dogs €0.90; poss cr; adv bkg ess; quiet. "Conv Pyrenees National Park; gd walking." ♦
1 Jun-30 Sep. € 12.60 2007*

CAUTERETS *8G2* (2.5km NE Rural) *42.91092, -0.09934* **Camping GR10, Route de Pierrefitte, 65110 Cauterets [06 70 72 05 02 or 06 20 30 25 85 (LS); contact@gr10camping.com; www.gr10camping.com]** N fr Cauterets on D920; site in 2.5km on R. Med, mkd pitch, terr, shd; htd wc; chem disp; shwrs inc; el pnts €4; Indtte; supmkt nrby; playgrnd; htd pool; tennis; canyoning (guide on site); games area; games rm; TV; 25% statics; dogs €1.30; poss cr; Eng spkn; quiet. "Pretty site; excel." Jun-Sep. € 14.30 2009*

CAVAILLON *10E2* (8km E Rural) *43.84220, 5.13284* **Camp Municipal Les Royères du Prieuré, La Combe-St Pierre, 84660 Maubec [04 90 76 50 34; fax 04 32 52 91 57; camping.maubec.provence@wanadoo.fr; www.camping maubec-luberon.com]** Heading E fr Cavaillon on D2, thro vill of Robion, in 400m at end vill sp turn R to Maubec. Site on R in 1km bef old vill. (Avoid any other rte with c'van). Diff access at ent, steep slope. Sm, terr, pt shd; wc (mainly cont); shwrs inc; shops 1km; el pnts (6-10A) €3-4; Indtte; playgrnd; 30% statics; dogs €2; poss cr; quiet; CCI. "Awkward site for lge o'fits - otherwise vg; san facs stretched high ssn; conv A7." 1 Apr-15 Oct. € 10.00 2009*

CAVAILLON *10E2* (10km E Rural) *43.85568, 5.16803* **Camping Les Boudougnes (Guiraud), Les Chênes, Petit-Coustellet, 84580 Oppède [tel/fax 04 90 76 96 10]** Fr N180 in Coustellet, take D2 dir Cavaillon. After 1km turn L onto D3 sp Ménerbes. Site on L in approx 2km just after hamlet of Petit-Coustellet. Take care, hump at ent to lane leading to site, danger of grounding. Sm, pt shd; wc; shwrs inc; el pnts (6A) €1; shop 700m; snacks; playgrnd; dogs free; adv bkg; CCI. "Pleasant farm site on edge Luberon National Park; parking among oak trees; levelling blocks req; old facs but clean; nr lavender museum; rec."
10 Apr-1 Oct. € 8.80 2008*

CAVAILLON *10E2* (1km S Urban) *43.82107, 5.03723* **Camp Municipal de la Durance, 495 Ave Boscodomini, 84300 Cavaillon [04 90 71 11 78; fax 04 90 71 98 77; camping.cavaillon@wanadoo.fr]** S of Cavaillon, nr Rv Durance. Fr A7 junc 25 foll sp to town cent. In 200m R immed after x-ing rv. Site sp (Municipal Camping) on L. Lge, pt shd; wc; chem disp; shwrs; el pnts (4-10A) €2.40- 6.15; shops 1.5km; snacks; pool 100m; fishing; tennis; TV; some statics; dogs €1.05; poss cr; adv bkg; some noise during early am. "NH only." 1 Apr-30 Sep. € 13.20 2006*

CAVAILLON *10E2* (3km S Rural) *43.78182, 5.04040* **Camping de la Vallée Heureuse, Quartier Lavau, 13660 Orgon [04 90 44 17 13; fax 04 90 55 16 49; information@camping-lavalleheureuse.com; www.camping-lavallee heureuse.com]** Sp in Organ town cent. Med, mkd pitch, terr, shd; wc; chem disp; mv service pnt; baby facs; shwrs inc; el pnts €3.50; gas 1km; Indtte; tradsmn; rest & snacks 1km; bar; BBQ, playgrnd; pool; lake sw 500m; wifi; TV; dogs €1.70; poss cr; Eng spkn; adv bkg; v quiet; red low ssn; CCI. "Site in old quarry in beautiful position; friendly, helpful staff; superb san facs; gd pool; gd walking; interesting area; conv m'way." 15 Mar-15 Oct. € 19.00 2009*

The opening dates and prices on this campsite have changed. I'll send a site report form to the Club for the next edition of the guide.

CAVAILLON *10E2* (12km SW Rural) *43.76058, 4.95154* **FFCC Camping Les Oliviers, Ave Jean Jaurès, 13810 Eygalières [04 90 95 91 86; fax 04 90 95 91 86; reservation@camping-les-oliviers.com; www.camping-les-oliviers.com]** Exit A7 junc 25; D99 dir St Rémy-de-Provence; in 8km camping sp on L; in vill well sp. Sm, hdg pitch, pt shd; htd wc; el pnts (6A) inc; shop, rest, snacks, bar 250m; BBQ; playgrnd; dogs €1; bus 3km; adv bkg; quiet. "Lovely, friendly site in olive grove nr scenic vill." 30 Mar-15 Oct. € 14.00 2008*

⊞ **CAVAILLON** *10E2* (7km W Rural) *43.83331, 4.94650* **Camp Municipal St Andiol, 13670 St Andiol [tel/fax 04 90 95 01 13]** Exit Avignon on N7 & D7n to St Andiol, site on R of D7n past vill. NB No advance warning of site. Sm, hdg pitch, pt shd; wc; shwrs inc; el pnts (6-10A) €3.50-4.50; gas; Indtte; snacks; shop in vill; bar; pool; tennis 1km; golf 15km; dogs €1; some rd noise; CCI. "Facs adequate; unkempt low ssn; NH only." € 13.00 2006*

CAVALAIRE SUR MER *10F4* (Urban/Coastal) *43.16956, 6.53005* **Camping La Baie, Blvd Pasteur, 83240 Cavalaire-sur-Mer [04 94 64 08 15 or 04 94 64 08 10; campbaie@club-internet.fr; www.camping-baie.com]** Exit A8 sp Ste Maxime/St Tropez & foll D25 & D559 to Cavalaire. Site sp fr seafront. Lge, mkd pitch, pt sl, pt shd; htd wc; baby facs; shwrs inc; el pnts (10A) €5; Indtte; shop; rest; snacks; bar; BBQ; playgrnd; htd pool; paddling pool; jacuzzi; sand beach 400m; sailing; watersports; diving 500m; games area; games rm; internet; 10% statics; dogs €4; poss cr; Eng spkn; adv bkg; quiet; ccard acc; red low ssn. "Well-run, busy site; pleasant staff; excel facs; nr shops, beach, marina & cafes." ♦ 15 Mar-15 Nov. € 45.60 (3 persons) 2009*

CAVALAIRE SUR MER *10F4* (1.5km NE Rural) *43.18220, 6.51610* **Kawan Village Cros de Mouton, Chemin de Cros de Mouton, 83240 Cavalaire-sur-Mer [04 94 64 10 87 or 04 94 05 46 38; fax 04 94 64 10 87; info@crosdemouton.com; www.crosdemouton.com]** Exit A8 junc 36 dir Ste Maxime on D125/D25, foll sp on D559 to Cavalaire-sur-Mer. Site sp on coast app fr Grimaud/St Tropez & Le Lavandou; diff access. Lge, mkd pitch, terr, mainly shd; wc; chem disp; mv service pnt; 20% serviced pitches; shwrs inc; el pnts (10A) €4.50; gas; Indtte; shop; rest; snacks; bar; playgrnd; htd pool; paddling pool; sand beach 1.8km; wifi; TV; some statics; dogs €2; phone; Eng spkn; adv bkg (ess Jul/Aug book by Jan; quiet; red low ssn; ccard acc; CCI. "Attractive, well-run, popular site in hills behind town - rec adv bkg even low ssn; lge pitches avail; pleasant, welcoming staff; gd san facs; gd pool; superb rest & bar; excel." ♦ 15 Mar-9 Nov. € 23.70 (CChq acc) 2008*

CAVALAIRE SUR MER *10F4* (3km NE Coastal) *43.19450, 6.55495* **Sélection Camping, 12 Blvd de la Mer, 83420 La Croix-Valmer [04 94 55 10 30; fax 04 94 55 10 39; camping-selection@wanadoo.fr; www.selectioncamping.com]** Off N559 bet Cavalaire & La Croix-Valmer, 2km past La Croix at rndabt turn R sp Barbigoua, site in 200m. Lge, hdg/mkd pitch, terr, shd; htd wc; chem disp; mv service pnt; baby facs; private bthrms avail; shwrs inc; el pnts (10A) €5; gas; Indtte; shop; tradsmn; rest; snacks; bar; playgrnd; htd pool; paddling pool; sand beach 400m; games area; internet; entmnt; TV rm; 20% statics; dogs (not acc Jul/Aug) €3.50; phone; bus; poss cr; Eng spkn; adv bkg ess high ssn; quiet. "In excel location; sm pitches; vg san facs; excel pool." ♦ 15 Mar-15 Oct. € 32.50 (3 persons) (CChq acc) 2008*

CAVALAIRE SUR MER *10F4* (500m SW Coastal) *43.17203, 6.52461* **Camping La Pinède, Chemin des Mannes, 83240 Cavalaire-sur-Mer [04 94 64 11 14; fax 04 94 64 19 25; contact@le-camping-la-pinede.com; www.le-camping-la-pinede.com]** Sp on R (N) of N559 on S o'skts of Cavalaire. Lge, mkd pitch, pt sl, shd; wc; shwrs inc; el pnts (5A) €3; shop; gas; Indtte; tradsmn; snacks; playgrnd; sand beach 500m; poss cr; adv bkg ess; quiet but noisy nr rd; red low ssn. "Cavalaire pleasant, lively resort." ♦ 15 Mar-15 Oct. € 21.00 2007*

CAVALAIRE SUR MER *10F4* (1km W Coastal) *43.16681, 6.51910* **Camping Bonporteau, 83240 Cavalaire-sur-Mer [04 94 64 03 24; fax 04 94 64 18 62; contact@bonporteau.fr; www.camping-bonporteau.com]** Sp on S side of N559 Cavalaire-Toulon rd, approx 100m on R after rndabt. Lge, sl, terr, shd; htd wc; shwrs inc; el pnts (10A) €5; gas; Indtte; shop; supmkt 500m; rest; snacks; bar; playgrnd; htd pool; jacuzzi; sand beach 200m; cycle hire; TV; some statics; dogs €4.50; min 1 week's stay Jul/Aug; adv bkg; red low ssn; quiet. "Gd cycle rte to town, beach & port." 15 Mar-15 Oct. € 41.50 (3 persons) 2009*

CAVALAIRE SUR MER *10F4* (1km W Rural) *43.17034, 6.52138* **Camping La Treille, 83240 Cavalaire-sur-Mer [04 94 64 31 81; fax 04 94 15 40 64; campingdelatreille@wanadoo.fr; www.campingdelatreille.com]** Fr St Tropez foll promenade into Cavalaire to rndabt. Take Toulon/Lavandou exit, 1 way rd. 50m after passing x-rd sp Pompiers, Camping Pinède, turn R at next junc; phone box on corner. Site on R in 50m. Lge, mkd pitch, terr, pt shd; wc; chem disp; baby facs; shwrs; el pnts (5A) €4; gas; lndtte; shop; supmkt; rest; snacks; bar; BBQ (gas only); playgrnd; pool 2km; sand beach 1.5km; some statics; dogs €2; phone; Eng spkn; adv bkg; poss noisy; red long stay/low ssn; CCI. "Well-run, friendly family site; nr sandy cove & lively town." ♦ 15 Mar-15 Oct. € 22.50 2006*

CAYEUX SUR MER *3B2* (2km NE Coastal) *50.19765, 1.51675* **Camping Le Bois de Pins, Rue Guillaume-le-Conquérant, Brighton, 80410 Cayeux-sur-Mer [tel/fax 03 22 26 71 04; info@campingleboisdepins.com; www.campingleboisdepins.com]** Take D940 out of St Valery to Cayeux, then D102 NE for 2km & foll sp. Lge, mkd pitch, pt shd; htd wc; shwrs; chem disp; mv service pnt; el pnts (6-10A) inc; lndtte; shop; playgrnd; beach 500m; sailing & fishing adj; cycle hire; horseriding; games rm; entmnt; 50% statics; dogs €3; adv bkg; quiet. "Friendly, clean, busy site; attractive sm town; gd cycling & birdwatching area; gd." ♦ 1 Apr-1 Nov. € 28.50 (3 persons) 2009*

See advertisement

CAYEUX SUR MER *3B2* (3km NE Coastal) *50.20291, 1.52641* **Camping Les Galets de la Mollière, Rue Faidherbe, 80410 La Mollière-d'Aval [03 22 26 61 85; fax 03 22 26 65 68; info@campinglesgaletsdelamolliere.com; www.campinglesgaletsdelamolliere.com]** Fr Cayeux-sur-Mer take D102 N along coast for 3km. Site on R. Lge, mkd pitch, pt shd; wc; chem disp; mv service pnt; shwrs inc; el pnts (10A) inc; gas; lndtte; shop; snacks; bar; BBQ; playgrnd; htd pool; sand beach 500m; games area; games rm; 25% statics; dogs €3; phone adj; quiet; CCI. "Spacious, much improved, wooded site with lge pitches; barrier clsd 2300-0700; pleasant staff." 1 Apr-1 Nov. € 29.00 2009*

See advertisement

CAYLAR, LE *10E1* (4km SW Rural) *43.83629, 3.29045* **Aire Naturelle Mas de Messier, St Félix-de-l'Héras, 34520 Le Caylar [tel/fax 04 67 44 52 63; info@masdemessier.com; www.masdemessier.com]** Fr N exit A75 junc 49 onto D9 thro Le Caylar. Turn R sp St Félix & foll sp St Félix-de-l'Héras; at x-rds in St Félix turn R, site in 1km on L. Fr S exit A75 junc 50; foll sp to St Félix-de-l'Héras; at x-rds turn R & as bef. Sm, hdg pitch, pt sl, pt shd; wc; chem disp; mv service pnt; shwrs; el pnts (6A) €3; lndtte; shop 4km; tradsmn; playgrnd; pool; wifi; dogs free; adv bkg, ess high ssn; quiet; Eng spkn; red low ssn; CCI. "Excel views fr some pitches; friendly & helpful Dutch owner; facs fair; access unsuitable lge o'fits; meals avail some eves; gd walking; excel." ♦ 15 Apr-15 Oct. € 14.50 2009*

CAYLUS *8E4* (NE Rural) *44.23368, 1.77636* **FFCC Camping La Vallée de la Bonnette, 82160 Caylus [tel/fax 05 63 65 70 20]** In vill by rv. Med, hdg/mkd pitch, pt shd; wc; chem disp; mv service pnt; baby facs; shwrs inc; el pnts (6A) €3.40; Indtte; shop 1km; tradsmn; snacks; BBQ; playgrnd; pool 1km; rv sw & fishing 500m; games area; entmnt; dogs €1.90; Eng spkn; adv bkg (rec high ssn); quiet; red 7 days; CCI. "Nice, tidy, scenic site on edge of medieval vill." ♦ 1 Apr-30 Sep. € 13.50 2006*

CAYRIECH see Caussade *8E3*

CAZALS *7D3* (Rural) *44.64186, 1.22179* **Camp Municipal du Plan d'Eau, La Cayré, 46250 Cazals [05 65 22 84 45 or 05 65 22 82 84 (Mairie); fax 05 65 22 87 15; mairiecazals@wanadoo.fr]** Fr Frayssinet-le-Gélat N on D673 dir Gourdon; site on L immed after ent Cazals. Ent just past red/white 'No Entry' sp. Med, mkd pitch, pt shd; wc; mv service pnt; shwrs; el pnts; Indtte; shops 500m; rest; bar; playgrnd; lake sw; entmnt; some statics; poss cr; quiet. "Basic, clean facs; friendly warden; tractor/machinery museum nrby open Sun. 1 May-30 Sep. € 9.80 2009*

CAZOULES see Souillac *7C3*

CELLES SUR BELLE see Melle *7A2*

CELLES SUR PLAINE see Raon l'Etape *6E3*

CELLETTES see Blois *4G2*

CENAC ET ST JULIEN see Sarlat la Canéda *7C3*

CENDRAS see Alés *10E1*

CENEVIERES see Cajarc *7D4*

CERCY LA TOUR *4H4* (Urban) *46.86680, 3.64328* **Camp Municipal Le Port, 58360 Cercy-la-Tour [03 86 50 55 27 or 03 86 50 07 11 (Mairie)]** At Decize take D981 E; in 12 km L onto D37, then L onto D10 to Cercy-la-Tour; site sp in vill. Adj municipal pool, Rv Aron & canal. Med, hdstg, pt shd; wc; chem disp; shwrs inc; el pnts inc; pool nrby; dogs; phone; quiet; CCI. "Clean & tidy site; immac san facs; gd cycling/walking along canal; great value; excel." 15 May-15 Sep. € 8.50 2008*

CERESTE *10E3* (2.5km SW Rural) *43.84564, 5.56394* **Camping Bois de Sibourg (Vial-Ménard), 04280 Céreste [04 92 79 02 22 or (mobs) 06 30 88 63 29 or 06 70 64 62 01; campingsibourg@orange.fr; www.sibourg.com]** W fr Céreste on D900/D4100 (N100); turn L in 2km (site sp); site on L in 1km. Sm, pt shd; wc (cont); shwrs inc; el pnts (6A) €2.80; dogs free; phone; Eng spkn; CCI. "Delightful 'green' farm site; St Michel l'Observatoire 15km; gd NH or longer; excel." 15 Apr-15 Oct. € 8.70 2009*

CERET *8H4* (7km N Rural) *42.54833, 2.75361* **Camp Municipal Al Comu, Route de Fourques, 66300 Llauro [04 68 39 42 08; alcomu@wanadoo.fr; www.village-llauro.com/camping]** Fr N on A9 exit junc 43. Take D115 dir Céret. Bef bdge R onto D615 to Llauro. Site on L after vill. Sm, mkd pitch, hdstg, terr, pt shd; wc; chem disp; baby facs; fam bthrm; shwrs inc; el pnts (16A) €2.68; Indtte; shop in vill; tradsmn; playgrnd; pool 10km; lake sw 6km; dogs; Eng spkn; quiet; red low ssn; CCI. "Attractive setting in lower Pyrenees; gd views; friendly & helpful owners live on site; vg." ♦ Apr-Nov. € 13.43 2008*

CERET *8H4* (500m E Urban) *42.48421, 2.75871* **Camp Municipal Bosquet de Nogarède, Ave d'Espagne, 66400 Céret [04 68 87 26 72]** Exit A9 junc 43 onto D115 twd Céret, then foll sp Maureillas D618. Site clearly sp 500m fr cent Céret. Med, mkd pitch, terr, shd; wc; chem disp; shwrs inc; el pnts (6A) inc; gas 1km; Indtte; shop 1km; rest; snacks; bar 1km; BBQ; playgrnd; htd, covrd pool 800m; sand beach 27km; 10% statics; dogs; phone; poss cr; some rd noise; CCI. "Attractive town with modern art museum; san facs fair; gd NH." ♦ 1 Apr-30 Oct. € 11.80 2009*

⊞ **CERET** *8H4* (1km E Rural) *42.48981, 2.76305* **Camping Les Cerisiers, Mas de la Toure, 66400 Céret [tel/fax 04 68 87 00 08]** Exit A9 junc 43 onto D115, turn off for cent of Céret. Site is on D618 approx 800m E of Céret twd Maureillas, sp. Tight ascent for lge o'fits. Med, mkd pitch, shd; wc; chem disp; baby facs; fam bthrm; shwrs inc; el pnts (4A) €2.90; gas; Indtte; shop, rest, snacks, bar 1km; playgrnd; pool 600m; lake sw 2km; sand beach 28km; 60% statics; dogs; phone; site clsd Jan; quiet; CCI. "Site in cherry orchard; gd size pitches; facs dated & ltd low ssn; poss seasonal workers & old scrap c'vans; footpath to attractive vill with excel modern art gallery; conv Andorra, Perpignan, Collioure; 1 night stays not allowed." ♦ € 10.80 2006*

CERILLY *4H3* (8km N Rural) *46.68210, 2.78630* **Camping des Ecossais, La Salle, 03360 Isle-et-Bardais [04 70 66 62 57 or 04 70 67 55 89 (LS); fax 04 70 66 63 99; ecossais@campingstroncais.com; www.campingstroncais.com]** Fr Lurcy-Lévis take D978A SW, turn R onto D111 N twd Isle-et-Bardais & foll camp sp. Ent tight. Med, pt sl, pt shd; wc; shwrs inc; el pnts (10A) €2.95; Indtte; playgrnd; rest nr; lake sw; fishing; dogs €0.76; adv bkg; quiet; red low ssn; CCI. "V busy high ssn; ltd facs low ssn; gd cycling; site in oak forest; rec." 1 Apr-30 Sep. € 8.00 2008*

CERILLY *4H3* (11km NW Rural) *46.65683, 2.68837* **FFCC Camping de Champ Fossé, 03360 St Bonnet-Tronçais [04 70 06 11 30; fax 04 70 06 15 01; champfosse@campingstroncais.com; www.campingstroncais.com]** Fr D2144 (N144) turn E on D978A sp Forêt de Tronçais; after 8km foll sp to vill of St Bonnet-Tronçais. Med, sl, some hdstg, pt shd; wc (some cont); mv service pnt; shwrs inc; el pnts (10A) inc; Indtte; shops 1km; snacks; bar; playgrnd; sand beach; bathing; boat hire; fishing; walking; dogs €0.80; quiet; adv bkg. "Poor supervision; sl, so blocks req; idyllic location; excel walks; sh walk to vill." 1 Apr-31 Oct. € 10.30 2008*

CERNAY *6F3* (5km N Rural) *47.8324, 7.16833* **Camping Les Sources, Route des Crêtes, 68700 Wattwiller [03 89 75 44 94; fax 03 89 75 71 98; camping.les.sources@wanadoo.fr; www.camping-les-sources.com]** Fr Cernay take D5 NE to Soultz; thro Uffholtz & turn L foll sp to Wattwiller; turn L immed after vill sp & foll camp sp. Park outside bef check-in. Some site rds steep. Lge, mkd pitch, hdstg, terr, pt shd; wc (v steep app to facs - 25% gradient); chem disp; mv service pnt; serviced pitches; baby facs; shwrs inc; el pnts (5A) €3.50 (poss rev pol); gas; Indtte; shop; tradsmn; rest; BBQ (gas/charcoal only); playgrnd; htd, covrd pool; tennis; games rm; games area; horseriding adj; entmnt; internet; 25% statics; dogs €2; Eng spkn; adv bkg ess high ssn; quiet; ccard acc; CCI. "Steep wooded app to site; diff getting on & off some pitches; tractor avail; not suitable lge o'fits; on 'wine rte'; barrier clsd 2200; mkt Tue & Fri Cernay." ♦ 3 Apr-10 Oct. € 28.50 2008*

CERNAY *6F3* (500m S Urban) *47.80448, 7.16999* **FFCC Camping Les Acacias, 16 Rue René Guibert, 68700 Cernay [03 89 75 56 97; fax 03 89 39 72 29; www.camping-les-acacias.com]** Fr N on D83 (N83) by-pass, exit Cernay Est. Turn R into town at traff lts, immed L bef rv bdge, site sp on L; well sp. Lge, mkd pitch, pt shd; wc; chem disp; mv service pnt; shwrs inc; el pnts (5A) €3.50 (poss rev pol); Indtte; shop, rest, bar & pool (high ssn); entmnt; 25% statics; dogs €1.20; poss cr; quiet; red long stay; 10% red CCI (pitch only). "Friendly staff; clean, tidy campsite but dated san facs; storks nesting over some pitches; sh walk to town." ♦ 1 Apr-1 Oct. € 12.00 2009*

CERNAY *6F3* (6km S Rural) *47.74684, 7.12423* **Camping Les Castors, 4 Route de Guewenheim, 68520 Burnhaupt-le-Haut [03 89 48 78 58; fax 03 89 62 74 68; camping.les.castors@wanadoo.fr]** Exit A36 junc 15 sp Burnhaupt-le-Haut onto D83 (N83), then D466 sp Masevaux. Site on R. Med, mkd pitch, pt shd; htd wc; chem disp; baby facs; shwrs inc; el pnts (5-10A) inc; gas; Indtte; tradsmn; rest; bar; BBQ; playgrnd; games rm; 40% statics; dogs €1.20; phone; poss cr; Eng spkn; adv bkg; quiet; CCI. "Conv German & Swiss borders, Black Forest; wine route; Mulhouse motor museum; gd san facs; vg." ♦ 1 Apr-1 Oct. € 16.20 2006*

CESSERAS see Olonzac *8F4*

CEYRAT see Clermont Ferrand *9B1*

CHABEUIL see Valence *9C2*

CHABLIS *4F4* (600m W Rural) *47.81376, 3.80563* **Camp Municipal Le Serein, Route des Sept Miraux, 89800 Chablis [03 86 42 44 39; fax 03 86 42 49 71; ot-chablis@chablis.net; www.chablis.net]** On D965 Tonnerre-Chablis turn L at camping sp bef x-ing Rv Serein. Med, hdg/mkd pitch, shd; wc (some cont); shwrs inc; el pnts (3-5A) €1.80; gas, shops, rest & snacks 1km; tradsmn; playgrnd; rv adj; some statics; no dogs; poss cr; Eng spkn; adv bkg; quiet; CCI. "Vineyards & cellars nrby; facs stretched high ssn." ♦ 1 Jun-15 Sep. € 8.20 2009*

CHAGNY *6H1* (W) *46.91187, 4.74567* **Camp Municipal du Pâquier Fané, 20 Rue du Pâquier Fané, 71150 Chagny [03 85 87 21 42; paquierfane@aol.com]** Clearly sp in town. Med, hdg pitch, pt shd; wc; chem disp; mv service pnt; shwrs inc; el pnts (6A) €3.60 (rev pol); gas; Indtte; shop, rest, snacks & bar 500m; playgrnd; htd pool adj; fishing; tennis adj; dogs €1; Eng spkn; adv bkg (ess Jul/Aug); quiet except rlwy noise adj; CCI. "Well laid-out site; friendly, helpful resident wardens; clean san facs; gd night lighting; on wine rte; gd cycling nrby canals (voie verte)." ♦ 15 Apr-31 Oct. € 13.40 2009*

CHAGNY *6H1* (6km W Rural) *46.90770, 4.68715* **Camping des Sources, Ave des Sources, 21590 Santenay [03 80 20 66 55; fax 03 80 20 67 36; info@campingsantenay.com; www.campingsantenay.com]** Site sp fr N6 & at D974 (N74) junc, foll sp adverts for Santenay Casino & campsite. Do not drive into Chagny. Med, hdg/mkd pitch, pt shd; wc; chem disp; mv service pnt; baby facs; shwrs inc; el pnts (6A) inc (poss rev pol; long lead poss req); gas; Indtte; shop & rest 250m; tradsmn; snacks; BBQ; playgrnd; htd pool & tennis adj; games rm; wifi; TV; 30% statics (tour ops); dogs €1.30; phone; Eng spkn; adv bkg; ccard acc; red low ssn; CCI. "Excel, popular site on edge of Santenay; arr early or bkg rec; boggy when wet; no twin-axles; excel, clean facs; gates clsd 2200-0730; helpful owner; gd walks & cycling (Voie Verte)." ♦ 10 Apr-31 Oct. € 20.00 (CChq acc) 2009*

⊞ **CHAILLAC** *7A3* (SW Rural) *46.43260, 1.29602* **Camp Municipal Les Vieux Chênes, 36310 Chaillac [02 54 25 61 39 or 02 54 25 74 26 (Mairie); fax 02 54 25 65 41; chaillac-mairie@wanadoo.fr]** Exit N20 S of Argenton-sur-Creuse at junc 20 onto D36 to Chaillac. Thro vill, site 1st L after sq by 'Mairie', adj Lac du Rochegaudon. Sm, hdg/mkd pitch, pt sl, pt shd; htd wc (some cont); chem disp; shwrs inc; el pnts (16A) inc (poss rev pol); Indry rm; shop, rest, bar 200m; BBQ; playgrnd; lake sw & fishing adj; waterslide; tennis adj; 35% statics; dogs; phone adj; poss cr; adv bkg; quiet; CCI. "Well-kept site in beautiful setting; clean facs; friendly warden; conv fr a'route; excel walks." ♦ € 9.60 2009*

CHAILLES see Blois *4G2*

CHAISE DIEU, LA *9C1* (2km NE Rural) *45.33526, 3.70388* **Camp Municipal Les Prades, 43160 La Chaise-Dieu [04 71 00 07 88; fax 04 71 00 03 43]** Site well sp fr D906. Med, pt sl, shd; wc (some cont); chem disp; shwrs inc; el pnts (10A) €2.80 (long lead poss req); Indtte; shops 2km; playgrnd; lake sw 300m; 10% statics; quiet. "Fair sh stay/NH; tourist info office in vill; 14thC church; vg for mushrooms in ssn!" 1 Jun-30 Sep. € 9.50 2006*

CHAIZE GIRAUD, LA see Bretignolles sur Mer *2H3*

CHALANDRAY *4H1* (750m N Rural) *46.66728, -0.00214* **Camping du Bois de St Hilaire, Rue de la Gare, 86190 Chalandray [tel/fax 05 49 60 20 84 or 01246 852823 (UK); acceuil@camping-st-hilaire.com; www.camping-st-hilaire.com]** Foll N149 bet Parthenay & Vouille; at xrds in vill, turn N into Route de la Gare (D24); site 750m on R over rlwy line. Sm, mkd pitch, pt shd; wc; chem disp; shwrs inc; el pnts (10A) €3.75; Indtte; shop; rest, snacks, bar in vill; BBQ; playgrnd; pool; tennis; games rm; TV rm; dogs; bus 750m; c'van storage; adv bkg; ccard acc; quiet; CCI. "Friendly, helpful British owners; situated in mature forest area, sh walk fr vill; 20 mins fr Futuroscope; lge pitches; excel, clean site & pool; poss muddy & unkept wet weather." ♦ 1 May-26 Sep. € 15.40 2009*

CHALARD, LE see St Yrieix la Perche *7B3*

⊞ **CHALLANS** *2H4* (3km S Rural) *46.81869, -1.88874* **FFCC Camping Le Ragis, Chemin de la Fradinière, 85300 Challans. [tel/fax 02 51 68 08 49; info@camping-leragis.com; www.camping-leragis.com]** Fr Challans go S on D32 Rte Les Sables, turn R onto Chemin de la Fradinière & foll sp. Med, hdg/mkd pitch, pt sl, pt shd; wc; chem disp (wc); baby facs; shwrs inc; el pnts (6A) €2; gas; Indtte; shop; tradsmn, rest, snacks high ssn; bar 3km; playgrnd; htd pool; waterslide; sand beach 12km; games area; entmnt; TV; 60% statics; dogs €2; phone; Eng spkn; adv bkg; quiet. "Vg." ♦ € 18.00 2007*

CHALLES LES EAUX see Chambéry *9B3*

CHALON SUR SAONE *6H1* (1km E Rural) *46.78411, 4.87136* **Camping du Pont de Bourgogne, Rue Julien Leneveu, 71380 St Marcel [03 85 48 26 86 or 03 85 94 16 90 (LS); fax 03 85 48 50 63; campingchalon71@wanadoo.fr; www.camping-chalon.com]** Fr A6 exit junc 26 (sp Chalon Sud) onto N80 E; foll sp Chalon-sur-Saône; at 1st rndabt go strt over (sp Louhans & St Marcel) & over flyover; take 4th exit on 2nd rndbt (sp Roseraie & St Nicolas); immed after this rndabt fork R thro Les Chavannes (still on N80). Strt on at next rndabt onto D5a, site sp. Turn R at traff lts. (DO NOT CROSS BRIDGE). Site in 500m. Med, hdg/mkd pitch, hdstg, terr, pt shd; htd wc; chem disp; mv service pnt; shwrs inc; el pnts (6A) inc; gas; Indtte; shop; hypmkt nr; tradsmn; rest; snacks; bar; BBQ; playgrnd; pool 500m; rv fishing; cycle hire; wifi; game/TV rm; 20% statics; dogs €2.50; Eng spkn; some noise fr rd & rv pathway; ccard acc; red low ssn; CCI. "Charming, well-run rvside site; lge pitches, some by rv; friendly staff; gd, modern san facs, ltd low ssn; vg rest/bar; rv walks; lovely town; vg." ♦ 1 Apr-30 Sep. € 24.70 ABS - L17 2009*

CHALON SUR SAONE *6H1* (12km SE Rural) *46.69813, 4.92751* **Mini-Camping Les Tantes, 29 Route de Grigny, 71240 Marnay [03 85 44 23 88]** On D978 SE fr Chalon-sur-Saône, turn R in vill of Ouroux-sur-Saône onto D6 twd Marnay. Over bdge, foll site sp. Sm, hdg pitch, pt shd; wc; chem disp; shwrs inc; el pnts (5A) inc; Indry rm; tradsmn; snacks; BBQ; sm playgrnd; pool; games area; 30% statics; dogs; phone; no twin-axles; quiet. "New unshd pitches for NH (2008); gd. ♦ 15 Mar-31 Oct. € 11.60 2008*

CHALONNES SUR LOIRE *2G4* (1km E Rural) *47.35013, -0.74951* **Camping Le Candais, Route de Rochefort, 49290 Chalonnes-sur-Loire [02 41 78 02 27 or 02 41 78 26 21 (OT); camping@chalonnes-sur-loire.fr; www.chalonnes-sur-loire.fr]** Turn E in Chalonnes to D751. Site on L in 1km on S bank of Loire. Med, mkd pitch, hdstg, pt shd; wc; shwrs inc; chem disp (wc); mv service pnt; el pnts (5A) €2.50; gas 1km; ice; Indtte; shop adj; tradsmn; snacks; bar; BBQ; playgrnd; pool 200m; fishing, cycle hire; games area; entmnt; TV rm; 2% statics; dogs €1.50; Eng spkn; adv bkg; quiet; CCI. "Peaceful rvside site in beautiful location; lge pitches; gd touring base; liable to flooding; gd." ♦ 1 Jun-16 Sep. € 7.50 2009*

CHALONNES SUR LOIRE *2G4* (8km SE Rural) *47.32285, -0.71428* **Camp Municipal Les Patisseaux, Route de Chalonnes, 49290 Chaudefonds-sur-Layon [02 41 78 04 10 (Mairie); fax 02 41 78 66 89; mairie.chaudefondsurlayon@wanadoo.fr]** Fr Chalonnes on D961 S dir Cholet. Turn L onto D125. At narr rlwy bdge after 3km, foll sp to site on Rv Layon. Sm, mkd pitch, pt shd; wc; shwrs €1; el pnts €2.50; shop, bar 500m; quiet. "V basic, clean site nr rv; lots of interest in area." ♦ 1 May-31 Aug. € 5.50 2006*

CHALONNES SUR LOIRE *2G4* (9km SE Urban) *47.32803, -0.67134* **Camp Municipal du Layon, Rue Jean de Pontoise, 49190 St Aubin-de-Luigné [02 41 78 33 28 (Mairie); fax 02 41 78 68 55; mairie-sg.staubin@wanadoo.fr]** Exit N160 Angers-Chemillé at sp St Aubin or turn S off D751 at sp St Aubin. Site sp in vill. Sm, hdg/mkd pitch, pt shd; wc; mv service pnt in adj car pk with access to facs; shwrs inc; el pnts €4.90; shop 150m; playgrnd; rv adj; quiet. "Pleasant, historic vill; warden calls 0800-0945 or pay at Mairie nrby; unsuitable lge o'fits due diff manoeuvring; san facs adequate; public footpath thro site; gd walking/cycling; wine-tasting area; boats for hire on rv high ssn." ♦ 1 May-30 Sep. € 7.00 2009*

CHALONNES SUR LOIRE *2G4* (9km NW) *47.39211, -0.87082* **Camping La Promenade, Quai des Mariniers, 49570 Montjean-sur-Loire [02 41 39 02 68; fax 02 40 83 16 19; efberthelot@wanadoo.fr; www.camping.montjean.net]** Exit Angers on N23 twd Nantes. Exit 1km beyond St Germain-des-Prés dir Montjean-sur-Loire. Cross rv then R on D210 to site in 500m. Med, pt shd; wc (some cont); shwrs inc; el pnts (6-9A) €2.60; gas 5km; Indtte; shops adj; rest; snacks; BBQ; playgrnd; pool; sand beach 600m; entmnt; TV; 30% statics; dogs €1.05; Eng spkn; adv bkg; quiet; CCI. "Friendly, young owners; interesting sculptures in vill & at Ecomusée." 1 Apr-7 Oct. € 11.40 2007*

France

CHALONS EN CHAMPAGNE *5D1* (3km S Urban) *48.93579, 4.38299* **Camp Municipal, Rue de Plaisance, 51000 Châlons-en-Champagne [tel/fax 03 26 68 38 00; camping.mairie.chalons@wanadoo.fr; www.chalons-tourisme.com]** Fr N on A26 exit junc 17 take D3 to Châlons, site sp. Fr S exit junc 18 onto D977, then D5 over rv & canal nr town cent; then foll site sp to R. Fr N44 S of Châlons sp St Memmie; foll site sp. D977 fr N into Châlons, cont on main rd to traff lts at 6 x-rds & turn R, site well sp. Or exit A4 junc 27 onto N44; turn R at St Memmie; site sp. NB some sps in area still show old town name 'Châlons-sur-Marne'. Med, hdg/mkd pitch, gd hdstg (pebbled), pt shd; htd wc; chem disp; mv service pnt; shwrs inc; el pnts (10A) inc (poss long lead req) gas; lndtte; shop 100m; hypmkt 1km; tradsmn; snacks; bar; BBQ; playgrnd; pool 2km; sm lake; tennis; wifi; TV rm; dogs €1.50; bus; c'van cleaning area; poss cr; Eng spkn; adv bkg; quiet but poss noisy high ssn; ccard acc; red long stay; CCI. "Popular, clean, tidy & well-run site adj park; generous pitches, inc hdstg; friendly, helpful & efficient staff; gd, clean san facs, but stretched/tired if site busy; gd disabled shwr; rec arr early or phone ahead; check barrier arrangements if need early departure; gates shut 2130 low ssn & 2300 high ssn; ltd bus service; lovely, interesting town; conv touring base; reliable; excel site & NH." ♦ 1 Apr-31 Oct. € 21.30 2009*

CHALUS *7B3* (12km S Rural) *45.54711, 0.95487* **FFCC Camping Le Périgord Vert, Fardoux, 24450 La Coquille [05 53 52 85 77; fax 05 53 55 14 25; leperigordvert@aol.com]** On N21 Périgueux/Châlus rd bet Thiviers & Châlus, turn L in vill of La Coquille at traff lts foll sps for Mialet. In 1.5km turn R, site 500m on L; sp. Sm, pt shd, pt sl; wc; chem disp; mv service pnt; shwrs inc; el pnts (6A) €2.50; gas; lndtte; shops 2km; tradsmn; rest, snacks, bar high ssn; playgrnd; pool high ssn; free fishing; tennis; 5% statics; dogs; phone; poss cr; Eng spkn; adv bkg; quiet; red low ssn; CCI. "Nice nice; helpful staff; choice of meadow or woodland pitch; poor facs (2008), ltd low ssn." ♦ 15 Apr-30 Oct. € 9.90 2008*

⊞ **CHALUS** *7B3* (9km NW Rural) **Camping Parc Verger, Le Poteau, 87150 Champagnac-la-Rivière [05 55 01 22 83 or 06 72 35 86 88 (mob); info@parcverger.com; www.parcverger.com]** N fr Châlus on D901, turn L at sp Champagnac-la-Rivière, site on L in 150m. Sm, some mkd pitch, hdstg, unshd; htd wc; chem disp; mv service pnt; shwrs inc; el pnts (16A) €4.50; gas 1km; lndtte (inc dryer); shop 1km; tradsmn; rest, snacks & bar 1km; BBQ; no playgrnd (2009); sm pool; lake sw & sand beach 10km; wifi; dogs; bus 150m; Eng spkn; adv bkg; v quiet; ccard acc; red grass pitch; red long stay; CCI. "Welcoming, friendly, helpful British owners; lge pitches suitable for RVs; gd clean san facs, poss stretched high ssn; walk/cycle path adj (old rwly track); gem of a site." € 14.50 2009*

CHAMBERY *9B3* (5km E Rural) *45.55151, 5.98416* **Camp Municipal Le Savoy, Parc des Loisirs, Chemin des Fleurs, 73190 Challes-les-Eaux [tel/fax 04 79 72 97 31; camping73challes-les-eaux@wanadoo.fr]** On o'skts of town app fr Chambéry on D1006 (N6). Pass airfield, lake & tennis courts on L, L at traff lts just before cent of Challes-les Eaux sp Parc de Loisirs, at Hôtel Les Neiges de France foll camp sp to site in 100m. Fr A41 exit junc 20, foll sp Challes-les-Eaux, then 'Centre Ville', then D1006 N. Med, mkd pitch, hdstg, shd; wc; chem disp; serviced pitches; shwrs; el pnts (6-10A) €2.60-2.85; gas; lndtte; shop, rest adj; snacks in ssn; lake sw, fishing, tennis adj; dogs €1; bus; adv bkg; quiet but some rd noise; ccard acc. "Well-designed, well-run, clean, level site (suitable wheelchairs) in beautiful setting; friendly, helpful staff; excel modern san facs inc disabled; excel walking." ♦ 1 May-30 Sep. € 12.75 2009*

CHAMBERY *9B3* (10km SW Rural) *45.53804, 5.79973* **Camping Les Peupliers, Lac d'Aiguebelette, 73610 Lépin-le-Lac [04 79 36 00 48; fax 04 79 44 12 48; info@camping-lespeupliers.net; www.camping-lespeupliers.net]** Exit A43 junc 12 & foll sp Lac d'Aiguebelette (D921). Turn L at rndabt & foll rd on L of lake. Site on R after sm vill. Lge, hdg/mkd pitch, pt shd; wc; chem disp; shwrs inc; el pnts (6A) €3.10; lndtte; shop 3km; tradsmn; rest 3km; snacks; bar; playgrnd; lake sw adj; fishing; dogs €1; poss cr; quiet; ccard acc; red low ssn; CCI. "V pleasant site in beautiful setting, espec lakeside pitches; friendly, helpful owner." 1 Apr-31 Oct. € 11.30 2008*

CHAMBERY *9B3* (11km SW Rural) *45.53990, 5.77940* **Camping Le Curtelet, 73610 Lépin-le-Lac [tel/fax 04 79 44 11 22; lecurtelet@wanadoo.fr; www.camping-le-curtelet.com]** Fr A43 E to Chambéry exit junc 12 onto D921 bef Tunnel L'Epine sp Lac d'Aiguebelette. Foll rd round lake, turn L on D921D to Lépin-le-Lac. Site sp after stn on L over level x-ing. Med, mkd pitch, pt sl, pt shd; wc; chem disp; baby facs; shwrs inc; el pnts (2-6A) €2.30-3; lndtte; shop 1km; tradsmn; bar; BBQ; playgrnd; lake sw; sand beach adj; dogs €1.40; Eng spkn; adv bkg; some rlwy noise at top of site; red low ssn; CCI. "Beautiful scenery; well-maintained site; no twin-axles due terrain; public beach adj poss scruffy low ssn; highly rec." 15 May-30 Sep. € 15.00 2009*

CHAMBERY *9B3* (12km W Rural) *45.55582, 5.79095* **Camping Le Sougey, 73610 St Alban-de-Montbel [04 79 36 01 44; fax 04 79 44 19 01; info@camping-sougey.com; www.camping-sougey.com]** Fr A43 E to Chambéry take D921 sp Lac d'Aiguebelette. On W side of lake 3km to site on L. Med, hdg/mkd pitch, some hdstg, pt sl, pt shd; wc; chem disp; 30% serviced pitches; baby facs; shwrs inc; el pnts (6A) inc; gas; lndtte; shop; rest; snacks; bar; playgrnd; lake sw & fishing adj; tennis; horseriding; cycle hire; archery; entmnts; TV; 20% statics; dogs €1.60; Eng spkn; adv bkg rec high ssn; quiet; red low ssn; ccard acc. "Attractive area; spacious site; helpful staff." ♦ 1 May-10 Sep. € 19.00 2006*

CHAMONIX MONT BLANC *9B4* (2km NE Rural) *45.9378, 6.8925* **Camping La Mer de Glace, 200 Chemin de la Bagna, Praz de Chamonix, 74400 Chamonix [04 5 53 44 03; fax 04 50 53 60 83; info@chamonix-camping.com; www.chamonix-camping.com]** Foll sp on D1506 (N506) thro Chamonix dir Argentière & Swiss Frontier; site well sp on R in 3km but ent under bdge 2.6m. Rec, to avoid low bdge cont to 1st rndabt in Praz-de-Chamonix & foll sp to site (R at rndabt). Med, hdg/mkd pitch, hdstg, pt sl, pt shd; htd wc (some cont); chem disp; mv service pnt; baby facs; shwrs inc; el pnts (3-10A) €2.80-3.60; gas 500m; Indtte (inc dryer); shop, rest & bar 500m; tradsmn; snacks; BBQ; playgrnd; htd pool 2km; sports cent nr; wifi; dogs free; phone adj; bus & train 500m; poss cr; Eng spkn; no adv bkg, arr early high ssn; quiet but helicopter noise; ccard not acc; red low ssn; CCI. "Wooded site with superb views; helpful staff; vg facs; v conv trains/buses; close to Flégère lift; path to town via woods & rv; excel." ♦ 25 Apr-5 Oct. € 20.90 2009*

CHAMONIX MONT BLANC *9B4* (7km NE Rural) *45.97552, 6.92224* **Camping Le Glacier d'Argentière, 161 Chemin des Chosalets, 74400 Argentière [04 50 54 17 36; fax 04 50 54 03 73; www.campingchamonix.com]** On Chamonix-Argentière D1506 (N506) rd bef Argentière take R fork twd Argentière cable car stn. Site immed on R. Med, pt sl, pt shd; wc; chem disp; shwrs inc; el pnts (2-10A) €2.60-5; Indtte; shops 1km; tradsmn; BBQ; dogs €0.50; phone adj; poss cr; adv bkg; quiet; CCI. "Alpine excursions; cable cars adj; mountain views; friendly, helpful owners." ♦ 20 Jun-30 Sep. € 15.20 2009*

CHAMONIX MONT BLANC *9B4* (1km SW Rural) *45.91466, 6.86138* **Camping Iles des Barrats, 185 Chemin de l'Ile des Barrats, 74400 Chamonix [tel/fax 04 50 53 51 44]** Fr Mont Blanc tunnel take 1st L on app Chamonix, foll sp to hospital, site opp hospital. Do not go into town. Sm, mkd pitch, pt sl, unshd; wc; chem disp; mv service pnt; shwrs inc; el pnts (5-10A) €3.30-4.30; gas; Indtte; shops 1km; tradsmn; sw 250m; dogs €1; poss cr; Eng spkn; adv bkg; quiet; CCI. "Great little site; superb mountain views; friendly family owners; immac facs; 10 mins level walk to town; 10 mins cable car Mont Blanc; excel." 15 May-20 Sep. € 20.20 2009*

CHAMONIX MONT BLANC *9B4* (3km SW Rural) *45.90578, 6.83673* **Camping Les Ecureuils, Rue Chemin des Doux, Les Bossons, 74400 Chamonix [tel/fax 04 50 53 83 11; contact@campingdesecureuils.fr; www.campingdesecureuils.fr]** Fr St Gervais on D1205 (N205) twd Chamonix. L fork to vill. L at x-rd. Under rlwy, sharp R. Site at end of rd. Sm, mkd pitch, hdstg, pt shd; wc; shwrs inc; el pnts (6A) €3; Indtte; shop 3km tradsmn; some statics; poss v cr; adv bkg; quiet; ccard acc; CCI. "Warm welcome; v sm pitches - not suitable lge o'fits; vg." 1 Apr-30 Sep. € 11.90 2008*

CHAMONIX MONT BLANC *9B4* (3.5km SW Rural) *45.90233, 6.83672* **Camping Les Cimes, 28 Route des Tissières, Les Bossons, 74400 Chamonix [04 50 53 19 00 or 04 50 53 58 93; infos@campinglescimesmontblanc.com; www.campinglescimesmontblanc.com]** Exit Mont Blanc tunnel foll sps Geneva turn L on D1506 (N506) (Chamonix-Geneva rd), in 2km turn R for Les Bossons & L under bdge. Fr Sallanches foll sps Chamonix & Mont Blanc tunnel. On dual c/way turn R at sp `Les Bossons' & site after Novotel adj to Les Deux Glaciers site. Med, pt sl, pt shd; wc (cont); shwrs inc; el pnts (3A) €2.80; Indtte; shop 4km; tradsmn; rest 500m; snacks; BBQ; playgrnd; dogs; poss cr; adv bkg; rd noise; CCI. "Fair site; poss diff lge o'fits." 1 Jun-30 Sep. € 14.80 2008*

⊞ **CHAMONIX MONT BLANC** *9B4* (3.5km SW Rural) *45.90203, 6.83716* **Camping Les Deux Glaciers, 80 Route des Tissières, Les Bossons, 74400 Chamonix [04 50 53 15 84; fax 04 50 55 90 81; info@les2glaciers.com; www.les2glaciers.com]** Exit Mont Blanc tunnel foll sps Geneva turn L on D1506 (N506) (Chamonix-Geneva rd), in 2km turn R for Les Bossons & L under bdge. Fr W foll sps Chamonix & Mont Blanc tunnel. On dual c/way turn R at sp `Les Bossons' & site after Mercure Hotel; adj Les Cimes site; site clearly sp from D1205 (N205). Med, terr, pt shd; htd wc; chem disp; shwrs inc; el pnts (2-10A) €2.50-7; Indtte (inc dryer); shop; tradsmn; rest; snacks; bar; playgrnd; pool & skating rink 4km; games rm; wifi; dogs free; bus; Eng spkn; quiet but some rd noise; site clsd 16/11- 14/12; red low ssn/long stay; CCI. "Pleasant, well-kept, tidy site in wonderful location just under Mont Blanc; roomy pitches; clean facs; poss diff site for lge o'fits over 6m; if recep clsd pitch & wait until 1730; ideal for walking; funicular adj to Mer de Glace; rec arr early high ssn; highly rec." ♦ € 14.30 2008*

CHAMPAGNAC LA RIVIERE see Chalus *7B3*

CHAMPAGNAT (SAONE ET LOIRE) see Cuiseaux *9A2*

CHAMPAGNE SUR LOUE see Mouchard *6H2*

CHAMPAGNOLE *6H2* (1km NW Urban) *46.7484, 5.9018* **Camp Municipal de Boÿse, 20 Rue Georges Vallerey, 39300 Champagnole [03 84 52 00 32; fax 03 84 52 01 16; camping.boyse@wanadoo.fr; www.camping.champagnole.com]** Turn W onto D5, N of town off D5 to Dijon. Look for sp. Site adj to sw pool. Lge, mkd pitch, pt sl, pt shd; wc (cont); chem disp; mv service pnt; baby facs; shwrs inc; el pnts (10A) inc; Indtte; shops 5km; tradsmn; rest; snacks; bar; htd sw pools adj; dogs €1.60; phone; adv bkg; no admissions 1200-1400; quiet; ccard acc; CCI. "Friendly warden; poss ltd facs low ssn; vg rest; early arr rec." ♦ 1 Jun-15 Sep. € 16.80 2008*

CHAMPANGES see Thonon les Bains *9A3*

CHAMPDOR *9A3* (800m NW Rural) *46.02298, 5.59120* **Camp Municipal Le Vieux Moulin, Route de Corcelles, 01110 Champdor [04 74 36 01 79; www.champdor.com]** Exit junc 8 on A404 & foll sp for St-Martin-du-Frêne. At ent to St-Martin-du-Frêne turn R onto D31 sp Brénod. After 10km turn R onto D21. Site 7km on R on o'skts of Champdor. Med, mkd pitch, some hdstg, unshd; htd wc; chem disp; mv service pnt; shwrs inc; el pnts (4-16A) €1.50; gas; Indry rm; shop, snacks, bar 1km; playgrnd; rv sw & fishing nrby; 20% statics; dogs; phone; quiet; CCI. "Modern san facs; gd walks adj." € 8.70 2007*

CHAMPFROMIER *9A3* (500m S Rural) *46.18877, 5.81357* **Camp Municipal Les Géorennes, 01410 Champfromier [04 50 56 92 40 (Mairie); fax 04 50 56 96 05; marire.champfromier@wanadoo.fr]** Fr Bellegarde foll D1084 (N84) twds Nantua. In 8km turn sharp R onto D14 sp Pont-des-Pierres/Mont-Rond. Site sp R on ent vill of Champfromier. Sm, terr, pt shd; wc; shwrs; el pnts (16A) €2; shop 500m; playgrnd; fishing; quiet; CCI. "Gd walking & scenery; site yourself, warden calls; excel." ♦ 1 Jun-15 Sep. € 11.00 2007*

CHAMPIGNY SUR MARNE see Paris *3D3*

CHAMPS ROMAIN see Nontron *7B3*

CHANAC *9D1* (500m S Urban) *44.46519, 3.34670* **Camp Municipal La Vignogue, 48230 Chanac [tel/fax 04 66 48 24 09 or 06 82 93 60 68 (mob)]** Exit A75 junc 39 onto N88 to Chanac; site well sp in vill. Sm, mkd pitch, pt sl, pt shd; htd wc (some cont); chem disp; shwrs inc; el pnts (6A) inc; Indtte; shops, rest, bar 500m; BBQ; pool adj; dogs €1; Eng spkn; adv bkg; quiet. "Excel." ♦ 16 Apr-30 Sep. € 11.00 2006*

CHANAS see St Rambert d'Albon *9C2*

CHANTEMERLE LES BLES see Tain l'Hermitage *9C2*

CHANTILLY *3D3* (5km W Rural) *49.21225, 2.40270* **Camping L'Abbatiale, 39 Rue Salvador Allendé, 60340 St Leu-d'Esserent [tel/fax 03 44 56 38 76; camping-de-l-abbatiale@wanadoo.fr; http://pagesperso-orange.fr/camping.l-abbatiale]** S twds Paris on A1 exit Senlis; cont W fr Senlis on D924/D44 thro Chantilly x-ing Rv Oise to St Leu-d'Esserent; cont on D44, x-ing D603 (D92) which becomes Rue Salvador Allendé in 700m; foll site sps; avoid rv x-ing on D17 fr SW; v narr bdge. Lge, pt shd; htd wc; shwrs €1; el pnts (3A) €2; Indtte; shop; playgrnd; some statics; dogs €0.50; red long stay. "Chantilly & chateau interesting; site mainly statics." € 10.00 2008*

CHANTILLY *3D3* (5km NW Rural) *49.22571, 2.42862* **Camping Campix, 60340 St Leu d'Esserent [03 44 56 08 48; fax 03 44 56 28 75; campix@orange.fr; www.campingcampix.com]** Exit A1 junc 8 to Senlis; cont W fr Senlis on D924 thro Chantilly, x-ing Rv Oise to St Leu-d'Esserent; leave town on D12 NW twd Cramoisy thro housing est; foll site sp for 1km, winding app. Med, mkd pitch, hdstg, terr, shd; htd wc; chem disp; mv service pnt; baby facs; shwrs inc; el pnts (6A) €3.50 (min 25m cable poss req); gas; Indtte; tradsmn; rest & shops 500m; pizza delivery; BBQ; playgrnd; pool complex; sand beach & lake sw 1km; fishing; games rm; some statics; dogs €2; phone; Eng spkn; adv bkg; quiet; red long stay/low ssn; ccard acc; CCI. "Site in former quarry - poss unguarded, vertical drops; helpful owner & friendly staff; san facs OK; variety of pitches - narr, steep access & o'hanging trees on some; conv Paris Parc Astérix & Disneyland (Astérix tickets fr recep); sh walk to vill; rec." ♦ 7 Mar-30 Nov. € 16.50 (CChq acc) 2009*

See advertisement

CHANTONNAY *2H4* (12km NE Rural) **Camping La Baudonnière, 85110 Monsireigne [02 51 66 43 79; bannigan.tom@orange.fr; www.paysdepouzauges.fr]** Fr Chantonnay take D960B NE dir St Prouant & Pouzauges. In St Prouant take D23 to Monsireigne. In 1.1km L onto D113; in 400m L onto Rue des Salinières. Site on L in 800m. Sm, pt sl, pt shd; wc; chem disp; shwrs inc; el pnts (10A) inc; shops, rest, snacks, bar 3km; BBQ; pool, tennis 2km; lake 5km; adv bkg; quiet. "V relaxing, CL-type site; welcoming, friendly, helpful Irish owners; excel san facs; vg." € 18.00 2008*

France

CHANTONNAY *2H4* (7km NW Rural) *46.74516, -1.11817* **Camp Municipal La Rivière, 25 Rue du Stade, 85110 Ste Cécile [02 51 40 24 07; fax 02 51 40 25 59; mairiestececile85@wanadoo.fr]** Fr Chantonnay NW on D137; in St Vincent-Sterlanges turn onto D39 to Ste Cécile (2.5km); site sp clearly fr main rd. Sm, hdg/mkd pitch, pt shd; wc; shwrs inc; el pnts (10A) €2.50; Indtte; playgrnd; pool; paddling pool; rv fishing adj; tennis; statics; adv bkg rec high ssn; quiet. "Part of larger complex of holiday bungalows; some facs dated & poor." 1 Jun-30 Sep. € 9.00 2006*

CHAPELLE AUX FILTZMEENS, LA see Combourg *2E4*

CHAPELLE D'ANGILLON, LA *4G3* (1 km SE Rural) **Camp Municipal Les Murailles, Route d'Henrichemont, 18380 La Chapelle-d'Angillon [02 48 73 40 12 (Mairie); fax 02 48 73 48 67]** Fr Bourges or Aubigny-sur-Nère on D940, turn E onto D926; turn onto D12 in vill, site on R, sp. Sm, pt sl, pt shd; wc (some cont); chem disp (wc); shwrs inc; el pnts (6A) €3.20; gas, shop, rest, & bar 1km; BBQ; playgrnd; lake fishing adj; some statics; dogs; ccard acc; CCI. "Lake adj with huge castle o'looking; v quiet; facs dated but adequate; site yourself, warden calls; vg." ♦ 25 Jun-17 Sep. € 7.15 2006*

CHAPELLE EN VERCORS, LA *9C3* (N Urban) *44.9695, 5.4156* **Camp Municipal Les Bruyères, Ave des Bruyères, 26420 La Chapelle-en-Vercors [04 75 48 21 46; camping lesbruyeres@wanadoo.fr; http://pagesperso-orange.fr/les bruyeres.camping]** Take D518 N fr Die over Col de Rousset. Fr N on A49 exit 8 to N532 St Nazaire-en-Royans, then D76 thro St Thomas-en-Royans, then D216 to St Laurent-en-Royans. Take D2 round E flank of Combe Laval (2 short 2-lane tunnels). Fr Col de la Machine foll D76 S 1km, then D199 E over Col de Carri to La Chapelle. (D531 fr Villard de Lons, D76 over Combe Laval & D518 Grandes Goulet not suitable for c'vans & diff lge m'vans due narr rds & tunnels & 5km of o'hanging ledges.) Med, pt sl, pt shd; htd wc; chem disp; mv service pnt; shwrs inc; el pnts €3.50; Indtte; shops adj; rest, snacks, bar 200m; playgrnd; pool 2km; fishing; climbing; horseriding; cycling; TV; some statics; dogs €1; adv bkg; quiet; CCI. "Excel base for beautiful Vercors plateau." ♦ 1 May-1 Oct. € 12.00 2008*

CHAPELLE EN VERCORS, LA *9C3* (6.5km N Rural) *45.02534, 5.44370* **Camping La Porte St Martin, 26420 St Martin-en-Vercors [04 75 45 51 10; infos@camping-laportestmartin.com; www.camping-laportestmartin.com]** Sp 200m N of vill on D103. (D531 fr Villard-de-Lans W not rec for c'vans.) Med, mkd pitch, pt terr, pt shd; wc; shwrs inc; el pnts (6-10A) €2.80; Indtte; shops, rest, snacks & bar 500m; pool; paddling pool; some statics; dogs €2; phone; Eng spkn; quiet; red low ssn; CCI. "Superb mountain views fr most pitches; excel walking." ♦ 1 May-24 Sep. € 13.50 2006*

CHAPELLE EN VERCORS, LA *9C3* (2km E Rural) *44.96808, 5.43048* **Camping Les Myrtilles, Les Chaberts, 26420 La Chapelle-en-Vercors [tel/fax 04 75 48 20 89; camping.des.myrtilles@wanadoo.fr; http://pagesperso-orange.fr/camping.des.myrtilles/]** Fr A49/E713 exit 8 to N532 St Nazaire-en-Royans, then D76 thro St Thomas-en Royans, then D216 to St Laurent-en-Royans. Take D2 around E flank of Combe Laval (2 short 2-lane tunnels). Fr Col de la Machine foll D76 S 1km, then D199 E over Col de Carri to La Chapelle. Fr S fr Die, foll D518 over Col de Rousset. (D76 over Combe Laval, D531 fr Villard-de-Lans & D518 fr Pont-en-Royans over Grandes Goulet not suitable for c'vans.) Med, pt sl, pt shd; wc; chem disp; shwrs inc; el pnts (6A) €3; Indtte; shop 1km; snacks; bar; playgrnd; htd pool; rv fishing 2km; 20% statics; dogs €1.50; adv bkg; v quiet; CCI. "Beautiful setting; excel walking, caves & gorges; gates locked 2200-0700." ♦ 1 May-15 Sep. € 14.25 2009*

CHAPELLE HERMIER, LA *2H4* (4km SW Rural) *46.66652, -1.75543* **Camping Le Pin Parasol, Châteaulong, 85220 La Chapelle-Hermier [02 51 34 64 72; fax 02 51 34 64 62; contact@campingpinparasol.fr; www.campingpinparasol.fr]** Exit A83 junc 4 onto D763/D937 dir La Roche-sur-Yon; turn R onto D948; at Aizenay turn R onto D6 twd St Gilles Croix-de-Vie; after 10km at x-rds turn L onto D21; in La Chapelle-Hermier foll D42 twds L'Aiguillon-sur-Vie; site sp in 4km. Lge, hdg/mkd pitch, pt sl, terr, unshd; wc; chem disp; mv service pnt; baby facs; shwrs inc; el pnts (10A) inc; gas; Indtte; sm shop; tradsmn; rest 500m nr lake; snacks; bar; BBQ; playgrnd; 2 pools (1 htd); paddling pool; waterslide; sand beach 12km; lake sw, boating, fishing, canoeing 200m; cycle hire; archery; fitnss rm; games area; entmnt; wifi; games/TV rm; 70% statics; dogs €4.20; poss v cr; Eng spkn; adv bkg; quiet; ccard acc (Visa only); red low ssn; CCI. "Excel staff & facs; lge pitches; lovely pools; away fr crowds but close to beaches; pleasant walks & cycle tracks around lake; many British tourers." ♦ 23 Apr-26 Sep. € 32.00 ABS - A36 2009*

CHAPELLE TAILLEFERT, LA see Guéret *7A4*

CHARAVINES *9B3* (600m N Rural) *45.44167, 5.51503* **Camping Robert, Rue Principale, 38850 Charavines [04 76 55 66 77]** S fr Les Abrets on D1075; in 4km turn R onto D50; cont on D50 past Paladru; turn L at rndabt at W end of lake sp Charavines; site on R in 500m. Fr Charavines, foll Rue Principale N for 600m; site on L. Med, hdg/mkd pitch, pt sl, pt shd; wc (some cont); chem disp; shwrs inc; el pnts (3-10A) €3-6; snacks; lake sw & beach adj; Eng spkn; CCI. "San facs clean but old; gd." 1 Apr-30 Sep. € 17.50 2009*

CHARCHIGNE see Lassay les Châteaux *4E1*

CHARETTE VARENNES *6H1* (500m N Rural) *46.92601, 5.16980* **Aire Naturelle Municipale La Jeanette, 5 Rue de la Chapelle, 71270 Charette-Varennes [tel/fax 03 85 76 23 58; mairiecharettevarennes@wanadoo.fr]** Exit N73 by bdge at Navilly onto D996. In 3km, turn L onto D73 to Charette-Varennes. Site sp in vill by rv. Sm, pt sl, pt shd; wc (one cont); chem disp (wc); shwrs inc; el pnts (16A) inc; lndry rm; shop 10km; BBQ; dogs €0.80; phone; quiet. "Peaceful CL-type site adj rv; poss problem with flooding in wet weather low ssn." 1 Jun-1 Sep. € 8.75 2006*

CHARITE SUR LOIRE, LA *4G4* (500m W Urban) *47.17683, 3.01058* **FFCC Camp Municipal La Saulaie, Quai de la Saulaie, 58400 La Charité-sur-Loire [03 86 70 00 83 or 03 86 70 16 12; fax 03 86 70 32 00; contact@ lacharitesurloire-tourisme.com]** Fr old N7 (Montargis-Nevers) turn W over bdge sp Bourges; take 2nd R bef next bdge. Fr Bourges on N151, turn L immed after x-ing 1st bridge over Rv Loire. Foll sp. NB Take care when turn R over narr rv bdge when leaving site - v high kerb. Med, mkd pitch, pt shd; wc; chem disp; shwrs inc; el pnts (10A) €3; lndtte; shop 500m; tradsmn; snacks; playgrnd & pool adj inc (pool opens 1 Jul); rv beach & sw adj; sandy rv banks; dogs €2; no twin-axles; quiet; ccard not acc; red long stay; CCI. "Lovely, well-kept rvside site; warm welcome, helpful staff; vg san facs, ltd low ssn; gd security; low ssn phone to check open." ♦ 27 Apr-22 Sep. € 13.10 2009*

CHARLEVAL see Cadenet *10E3*

CHARLEVILLE MEZIERES *5C1* (500m N Urban) *49.77813, 4.72245* **Camp Municipal Mont Olympe, Rue des Pâquis, 08000 Charleville-Mézières [03 24 33 23 60 or 03 24 32 44 80; fax 03 24 33 37 76; camping-charlevillemezieres@wandadoo.fr]** Fr N43/E44 head for Hôtel de Ville, with Hôtel de Ville on R, cont N along Ave des Arches, turn R at 'Gare' sp & cross rv bdge. Turn sharp L immed along Rue des Pâquis, site on L in 500m, visible fr rd. Well sp from town cent. Med, hdg/mkd pitch, some hdstg, pt shd; htd wc (some cont); chem disp; mv service pnt; all serviced pitches; baby facs; fam bthrm; shwrs inc; el pnts (10A) €3.60; gas; lndtte; shops 500m; tradsmn; bar; BBQ; playgrnd; htd covrd pool adj; fishing & boating; wifi; TV/games rm; some statics; dogs €1.60; poss cr; Eng spkn; quiet; ccard acc; CCI. "Well-kept, spacious site on Rv Meuse; excel san facs but inadequate when site full; excel." 1 Apr-15 Oct. € 12.60 2009*

CHARLEVILLE MEZIERES *5C1* (12km N Urban) *49.87757, 4.74187* **Camp Municipal au Port à Diseur, Rue André Combain, 08800 Monthermé [03 24 53 01 21; fax 03 24 53 01 15]** Fr D988 at Revin turn E onto D1 sp Monthermé. Site is on D1 S of town. Med, hdg/mkd pitch, pt sl, pt shd; wc (some cont); chem disp (wc); shwrs inc; el pnts (4-10A) inc; gas 100m; lndtte; shop 100m; rest, snacks, bar 1km; few statics; dogs; phone; poss cr; quiet but some rd noise; CCI. "Pleasant, rvside site in conv location; lge pitches; excel, clean san facs, poss stretched if site full; gd rvside walks; 20 min easy walk to Monthermé; gd cycling & walking; popular with fishermen & canoeists." 10 Apr-31 Aug. € 10.80 2009*

⊞ **CHARLEVILLE MEZIERES** *5C1* (12km NE Rural) *49.85655, 4.79235* **Camping Departemental d'Haulmé, Pont Semoy, 08800 Haulmé [03 24 32 81 61; fax 03 24 32 37 66]** Fr Charleville, take N43 & turn R at sp to Nouzonville. Turn onto D988, D989 to Monthermé. In town turn R over bdge onto D31. In 5km turn R sp Haulmé, site in 1.5km on rvside. Lge, mkd pitch, pt shd; wc (cont); mv service pnt; shwrs inc; el pnts (6-10A) €2.65-4.60; gas; shop 5km; tradsmn; rest, bar 500m; fishing; tennis; cycle hire; dogs €0.90; poss cr; adv bkg; fairly quiet; ccard acc. "Vg; excel for fishing; top end of site noisy due to semi-perm tents; rec pitch mid-site as lower site is adj public park; v wet pitches in rain; gd san facs; sh walk to town cent." ♦ € 11.30 2008*

CHARLIEU *9A1* (E Urban) *46.15851, 4.18088* **FFCC Camp Municipal de la Douze, Rue Riottier, 42190 Charlieu [04 77 69 01 70 or 06 65 34 77 39 (mob); fax 04 77 69 07 28; camp-charlieu@voila.fr]** N fr Roanne on D482 to Pouilly-sous-Charlieu, then E on D487 to Charlieu town cent, site sp in town, by sw pool. NB Do not confuse with Camp Municipal Pouilly-sous-Charlieu which is sp fr main rd. Med, hdg/mkd pitch, pt shd; wc; chem disp; mv service pnt; shwrs inc; el pnts (6A) inc; lndtte; shops 1km; snacks; bar; playgrnd; pool adj; sports area; fishing, boating adj; entmnt; 40% statics; poss cr; Eng spkn; adv bkg; CCI. "Gd clean san facs; facs poss stretched high ssn, excel low ssn; vg value." ♦ 1 Apr-30 Sep. € 11.00 2009*

CHARLIEU *9A1* (4km W Rural) *46.15003, 4.11204* **FFCC Camp Municipal Les Ilots, Rue de Marcigny, 42720 Pouilly-sous-Charlieu [04 77 60 80 67; fax 04 77 60 79 44; mairie.pouilly-sous-charlieu42@wanadoo.fr]** N fr Roanne on D482 sp Pouilly-sous-Charlieu. Site sp on ring rd 1km N of town, turn E into stadium. Med, mkd pitch, pt shd; htd wc (cont); mv service pnt; shwrs inc; el pnts (6A) €3; gas; lndtte; shops 1km; rest, bar 500m; playgrnd; pool; fishing; games area; poss cr; Eng spkn; quiet; ccard not acc; red CCI. "Lge pitches grouped in circles." 15 May-15 Sep. € 7.00 2009*

CHARLY SUR MARNE *3D4* (S Urban) *48.97363, 3.28210* **Camp Municipal Les Illettes, Route de Pavant, 02310 Charly-sur-Marne [03 28 82 12 11 or 03 23 82 00 32 (Mairie); fax 03 23 82 13 99; mairie.charly@wanadoo.fr; www.charly-sur-marne.fr]** Exit A4 junc 18 onto D603 (N3) dir La Ferté; then take D402/D969 NE to Charly. Site sp in town. Sm, hdg pitch, pt shd; wc; chem disp; shwrs; el pnts (5-10A) €2-3; lndry rm; supmkt adj; dogs €2.50; quiet; no twin-axles; red long stay/low ssn. "Lovely, well-kept site; pleasant warden; conv for touring Champagne route; rec arr early to secure pitch during grape harvest; excel." ♦ 1 Apr-30 Sep. € 14.50 2009*

France

CHARMES *6E2* (500m NE Rural) *48.37706, 6.28974* **Camp Municipal Les Iles, 20 Rue de l'Ecluse, 88130 Charmes [tel/fax 03 29 38 87 71 or 03 29 38 85 85; andre.michel@tiscali.fr; www.ville-charmes.fr/camping.htm]** Exit N57 for Charmes, site well sp on Rv Moselle. Do not confuse with sp for 'Camping Cars'. Med, mkd pitch, pt shd; wc; chem disp; mv service pnt; shwrs inc; el pnts (10A) €3.25; gas; Indtte; shop 300m; tradsmn; rest; snacks; bar; BBQ; playgrnd; fishing; kayak hire; dogs; phone; Eng spkn; adv bkg; quiet; red long stay; CCI. "Lovely site bet rv & canal; lge pitches; friendly staff; footpath to town; m'van o'night area in town; vg value; gd." 1 Apr-30 Sep. € 9.45 2009*

CHARMES SUR L'HERBASSE see St Donat sur l'Herbasse *9C2*

CHARNY *4F3* (500m N Rural) *47.89078, 3.09419* **FFCC Camping des Platanes, 41 Route de la Mothe, 89120 Charny [tel/fax 03 86 91 83 60; campingdesplatanes@wanadoo.fr; www.campingdesplatanes.com]** Exit A6 junc 18 onto D943 to Montargis. Turn S onto D950 to Charny, site on R as ent vill; sp. Med, hdg/mkd pitch, pt shd; htd wc; chem disp; mv service pnt; serviced pitch; shwrs inc; el pnts (10A) inc; gas; Indtte; shop 500m; tradsmn; snacks; BBQ; playgrnd; pool; rv fishing 150m; tennis 500m; cycle hire; wifi; TV rm; 60% statics; dogs €1; Eng spkn; adv bkg; quiet; red low ssn/long stay; CCI. "Pleasant site; gd sized pitches; friendly, helpful owner; excel, clean san facs; short walk to vill; gd walking; gd touring base." ♦ 15 Mar-30 Oct. € 16.50 (CChq acc) 2009*

CHARNY-SUR-MEUSE see Verdun *5D1*

CHAROLLES *9A2* (500m E Rural) *46.43972, 4.28208* **FFCC Camp Municipal, Route de Viry, 71120 Charolles [03 85 24 04 90; fax 03 85 24 08 20; camping.charolles@orange.fr]** Exit N79 at E end of by-pass sp Vendenesse-lès-Charolles; at rndabt foll camping sp; then sharp R bottom hill bef town; site on L, next to Municipal pool. Med, hdg/mkd pitch, hdstg, pt sl, pt shd; htd wc; chem disp; mv service pnt; shwrs inc; el pnts (6A) €2; Indtte; shops 300m; rest; snacks; bar; playgrnd; pool adj high ssn (proper sw trunks req); TV; dogs €1; adv bkg rec; quiet, but faint rd noise; CCI. "Well-kept site; sm pitches; friendly, helpful warden; gd, modern san facs; m'van area outside site; negligible security." ♦ 1 Apr-5 Oct. € 9.00 2009*

CHARRIN see Decize *4H4*

CHARTRE SUR LE LOIR, LA *4F2* (500m W Rural) *47.73220, 0.57451* **Camping Le Vieux Moulin, Chemin des Bergivaux, 72340 La Chartre-sur-le Loir [02 43 44 41 18; camping@lachartre.com; www.le-vieux-moulin.fr or www.loir-valley.com]** Sp fr D305 in town. Fr S exit A28 junc 27 onto D766 dir Beaumont-la-Ronce; then take D29 to La Chartre-sur-le Loir; go over rv, turn L immed after bdge. Med, hdg/mkd pitch, pt shd; htd wc (some cont); chem disp; mv service pnt; baby facs; fam bthrm; shwrs inc; el pnts (5-10A) €4-5 (poss rev pol); gas 500m; Indtte; sm shop & 500m; tradsmn; snacks; bar; BBQ; playgrnd; htd pool; rv fishing, canoeing adj; cycle hire; wifi; entmnt; TV; 20% statics; dogs €1.50; poss cr; Eng spkn; adv bkg rec high ssn; quiet; red low ssn & CCI. "Beautiful, well-kept rvside site; helpful, friendly staff; excel pool; gd for dogs; v lge m'vans acc; gd base for chateaux, forest & Loir Valley; excel." ♦ 1 Apr-30 Sep. € 13.20 2009*

See advertisement on page 130

CHARTRES *4E2* (1km SE Urban) *48.43433, 1.49914* **FFCC Camping Les Bords de l'Eure, 9 Rue de Launay, 28000 Chartres [tel/fax 02 37 28 79 43; camping-roussel-chartres@wanadoo.fr; www.auxbordsdeleure.com]** Exit N123 ring rd at D935, R at T-junc dir Chartres; then R at 2nd traff lts dir Chartres immed after rlwy bdge; site on L in 400m; inside of ring rd. Also sp fr town cent on N154 fr N, foll sp town cent under 2 rlwy bdges, L at traff lts sp Orléans, after 1km site sp. Fr SE on N154 cross ring rd, foll site sp & turn L at 2nd traff lts; site on R. Med,some hdg/mkd pitch, pt shd; htd wc (some cont); chem disp; mv service pnt; baby facs; shwrs inc; el pnts (6A) €3.11 (poss rev pol); Indry rm; shop; tradsmn; BBQ; shop in ssn; supmkt 1km; playgrnd; fishing; wifi; some statics; dogs €1; poss cr; Eng spkn; adv bkg; quiet; ccard acc; red low ssn; CCI. "Spacious, well laid-out, well-kept, busy site; friendly, helpful staff; san facs poss stretched high ssn; ltd el pnts when site busy; some pitches diff lge o'fits; gates clsd 2200-0800; site poss tired end of ssn; poss itinerants & long-stay workers; walk along rv to Chartres; excel 'Son et Lumière' in Chartres; ideal NH & longer; vg." ♦ 10 Apr-30 Oct. € 11.13 2009*

CHARTRES *4E2* (9km S Rural) *48.40100, 1.48918* **Camp Municipal, 28630 Morancez [02 37 30 02 80 or 02 37 28 49 71 (Mairie); mairie.morancez@wanadoo.fr]** S on Chartres by-pass (N123) take exit D935; L at T-junc twd Morancez; R on D114/Base de Loisirs at S end of vill (abrupt turn); cross bdge; after 200m turn R onto track, site at end of lake 300m. Travelling N on N10/D910 turn R onto D114 sp Morancez; strt over at x-rds at La Varenne; cont on narr rd for 1.5km; cross rv bdge, site on L. Sm, hdg/mkd pitch, shd; wc (some cont); chem disp (wc); shwrs inc; el pnts (6A) €2.75 (poss rev pol); shops & supmkt 2km; playgrnd adj; fishing adj; 20% statics; adv bkg; quiet but some rd noise; CCI. "Pleasant, peaceful site; surrounded by woods, lakes & rvs; friendly, helpful warden; san facs could be improved (2009); site locked 2200-0700; unreliable opening dates; bus fr vill to Chartres every hr (high ssn); excel NH." 17 May-31 Aug. € 11.95 2009*

CHASSENEUIL DU POITOU see Jaunay Clan *4H1*

CHASSENEUIL SUR BONNIEURE *7B3* (Urban) *45.82389, 0.44415* **Camp Municipal Les Charmilles, Rue des Ecoles, 16260 Chasseneuil-sur-Bonnieure [05 45 39 55 36; jctelemaque@free.fr]** On N141 Angoulême-Limoges leave by-pass sp Chasseneuil. In town turn L onto D27 sp Mémorial de la Résistance. Turn R at camping sp, site ahead. Med, hdg/mkd pitch, pt shd; wc; chem disp; shwrs inc; el pnts (10A) inc; Indtte; gas 200m; shop; supmkt 100m; rest, snacks, bar 50m; playgrnd; htd, covrd pool adj; dogs; quiet. "Warden calls pm or key fr Mairie; diff to ent/leave site without key to bollard; gd san facs; vg value." ♦ Easter-30 Sep. € 9.00 2009*

⊞ **CHASSENEUIL SUR BONNIEURE** *7B3* (9km E Rural) *45.83283, 0.55811* **Camping Le Paradis, Mareuil, 16270 Mazières [tel/fax 05 45 84 92 06; rosie@le-paradis-camping.com; www.le-paradis-camping.com]** Fr Limoges W on N141 twd Angoulême, turn L at 1st traff lts in Roumazières-Loubert D161. Site sp in 5km at t-junc. Sm, hdg/mkd pitch, hdstg, pt shd; wc; chem disp; mv service pnt; fam bthrm; shwrs inc; el pnts (10-16A) €4.50-7.50; gas 3km; Indtte; shop; tradsmn; rest, snacks & bar 3km; BBQ; playgrnd; lake sw & watersports 5km; fishing nrby; tennis nr; games area; 20% statics; dogs free; phone; bus 1km; adv bkg rec; quiet; CCI. "Clean, tranquil site; gd sized pitches; vg, immac san facs; welcoming British owners, helpful & friendly; gd touring base; adv bkg rec lge o'fits; rallies welcome; stays bet 1 Nov & 28 Feb by adv bkg only; excel." ♦ € 13.50 2009*

CHATAIGNERAIE, LA *2H4* (5km E Rural) **Camping La Viollière, 85120 Breuil-Barret [02 51 87 44 82; vendee vacances@gmail.com; http://vendeevacances.googlepages.com/]** Take D949 E dir Poitiers thro La Châtaigneraie for 5km. Cont thro Breuil-Barret & site 2nd R after pasing under rlwy bdge. Sm, pt sl, pt shd; wc; chem disp; shwrs inc; el pnts (6A) inc (poss long lead req); shop 2km; supmkt 6km; rest, bar 2km; tradsmn; htd, covrd pool 8km; adv bkg; quiet. "Peaceful, relaxing CL-type site; 6 spacious pitches & 5 el pnts only; helpful British owners." Apr-Oct. € 14.00 2008*

CHATEAU ARNOUX *10E3* (3km NE Rural) *44.10611, 6.01556* **Camping Sunêlia L'Hippocampe, Route Napoléon, 04290 Volonne [04 92 33 50 00; fax 04 92 33 50 49; camping@l-hippocampe.com; www.l-hippocampe.com]** Exit A51 junc 21 onto D4085 (N85) 12km S of Sisteron twd Volonne vill over rv. Turn R on D4 on ent vill & foll camp sp 1km. Lge, hdg/mkd pitch, some hdstg, pt shd; wc; chem disp; mv service pnt; child/baby facs; serviced pitches; shwrs inc; el pnts (10A) inc (poss rev pol); Indtte; shop; tradsmn; rest; bar; BBQ (elec/gas); playgrnd; 2 pools (1 htd); rv sw & beach 150km; fishing; canoeing; rafting; tennis; cycle hire; games rm; entmnt; wifi; TV rm; some statics; dogs €2; Eng spkn; adv bkg; quiet but poss noisy nr recep; red low ssn/long stay; ccard acc; red low ssn/long stay; CCI. "Pleasant, busy, well-run site; spacious, well-screened pitches; various pitch sizes/prices, some by lake; some pitches poss diff due trees; excel." ♦ 3 Apr-30 Sep. € 40.00 (CChq acc) 2009*

CHATEAU CHINON *4H4* (1km S Urban) *47.05513, 3.92626* **Camp Municipal du Gargouillat, Rue de Pertuy d'Oiseau, 58120 Château-Chinon [03 86 85 08 17; fax 03 86 85 01 00]** Sp fr D978 rndabt at E end town. Med, hdg/mkd pitches, sl, pt shd; wc (some cont); shwrs inc; el pnts (10A) €2.50; shops, rest, bar 1km; tradsmn; dogs free; poss cr; quiet. "Gd location; some pitches diff; san facs need refurb & ltd low ssn; poss itinerants; conv Morvan National Park; levelling blocks rec; gd NH." 1 May-30 Sep. € 7.50 2008*

CHATEAU CHINON *4H4* (6km S Rural) *47.00587, 3.90548* **FFCC Camping L'Etang de la Fougeraie, Hameau de Champs, 58120 St Léger-de-Fougeret [03 86 85 11 85; fax 03 86 79 45 72; campingfougeraie@orange.fr; www.campingfougeraie.com]** Fr Château-Chinon foll sps to St Léger-de-Fougeret; in vill foll sps to site in 2km. Med, hdg/mkd pitch, terr, pt shd; wc; chem disp; baby facs; shwrs inc; el pnts (6A) €3.20; Indtte; shop; tradsmn; rest; snacks; bar; BBQ; playgrnd; cycle hire; lake sw & fishing; donkey rides; games area; games rm; TV; dogs €1.70; Eng spkn; quiet; red low ssn; CCI. "Beautiful, tranquil situation; most pitches lge & face lake; facs at top of terr & poss stretched high ssn; poss diff lge o'fits; welcoming, efficient owners; gd rest; excel." 4 Apr-3 Oct. € 13.50 2009*

CHATEAU D'OLONNE see Sables d'Olonne, Les *7A1*

CHATEAU DU LOIR *4G1* (6km E Rural) *47.71250, 0.49930* **Camping du Lac des Varennes, Route de Port Gauthier, 72340 Marçon [02 43 44 13 72; fax 02 43 44 54 31; lacdesvarennes@camp-in-ouest.com; www.camp-in-ouest.com or www.lacdesvarennes.com]** Fr N on D338 (N138) fr Château-du-Loir dir Vendôme for 3km. Turn L onto D305 sp Marçon. In vill turn L onto D61 over bdge. Site on R by lake. Lge, hdg/mkd pitch, hdstg, pt shd; htd wc; chem disp; mv service pnt; baby facs; shwrs inc; el pnts (10A) €3.10 (poss rev pol, poss long lead req); Indtte; shop high ssn; tradsmn; rest; snacks; bar; BBQ; playgrnd; lake sw & sand beach adj; boat hire; watersports; tennis; cycle hire; horseriding; cycle hire; wifi; entmnt; 15% statics; dogs €1.80; Eng spkn; adv bkg rec; quiet; ccard acc; red long stay/CCI. "Pretty site in lovely situation bet lake & rv; friendly, helpful staff; gd security; gd walks & cycling." ♦ 26 Mar-14 Nov. € 14.50 2009*

See advertisement on next page

⊞ **CHATEAU GONTIER** *4F1* (1km N Urban) *47.83851, -0.69965* **Camping Le Parc, Route de Laval, 53200 Château-Gontier [02 43 07 35 60; fax 02 43 70 38 94; camping.parc@cc-chateau-gontier.fr; www.sudmayenne.com]** App Château-Gontier fr N on N162, at 1st rndabt on bypass take 1st exit. Site on R in 250m. Sm, mkd pitch, sl, pt shd; wc; chem disp; mv service pnt; shwrs inc; el pnts (10A) inc (rev pol); Indtte; shops 1km; tradsmn; bar; playgrnd; pool 800m; fishing; tennis; entmnt; games rm; TV; 20% statics; dogs; quiet; ccard acc; red low ssn; CCI. "V pleasant site; most pitches sloping; excel san facs; rvside path to attractive town; mkt Thurs." ♦ € 18.50 2009*

France

Camping du Lac des Varennes ***
Marçon
Loir Valley
open from 26/03/2010 to 14/11/2010
In the heart of the Loir Valley, in edge of a splendid lake of 50ha, you have found the ideal place for an unforgettable stay. You will be allured by this area with the richest architectural, wine and gastronomical heritage.
lacdesvarennes@camp-in-ouest.com
+33 (0)2 43 44 13 72
Route de port Gauthier
72340 Marçon
camp'in ouest
www. camp-in-ouest.com

CHATEAU GONTIER *4F1* (11km N Rural) *47.92109, -0.68334* **Camping Village Vacances et Pêche, Rue des Haies, 53170 Villiers-Charlemagne [02 43 07 71 68; fax 02 43 07 72 77; vvp.villiers.charlemagne@wanadoo.fr; www.sud-mayenne.com]** N fr Château-Gontier on N162; turn R onto D20 to Villiers-Charlemagne; site on R. Sm, pt shd; wc; chem disp; shwrs inc; el pnts (6A) inc; lndtte; playgrnd; cycle hire; lake 200m; fishing; tennis; games rm; entmnt; dogs. 1 Mar-30 Nov. € 17.00 2007*

CHATEAU GONTIER *4F1* (11km SE Rural) *47.74985, -0.64258* **Camping Communautaire des Rivières, Rue du Bac, 53200 Daon [02 43 06 94 78 or 02 43 70 42 74; fax 02 43 70 36 05; tourisme@sud-mayenne.com]** On town side of rv bdge, turn down lane & site ent on R at bottom of hill. Med, pt shd; wc; chem disp; shwrs inc; el pnts (10A) €3; lndtte; shop in town; playgrnd, tennis, mini-golf & sw nrby; adv bkg; quiet; CCI. "Vg clean & well-cared for site; some pitches diff to access; boating on adj Rv Mayenne." ♦ 1 May-1 Oct. € 10.00 2007*

CHATEAU GONTIER *4F1* (6km S Rural) *47.77500, -0.67334* **Camp Municipal du Bac, Rue de Port, 53200 Ménil [02 43 70 24 54; fax 02 43 70 25 25; menil@cc-chateau-gontier.fr]** On N162 dir Château-Gontier, turn off at Ménil & foll sp. Sm, hdg pitch, pt shd; wc; mv service pnt; shwrs inc; el pnts (10A) €2.20; lndtte; snacks; bar 250m; playgrnd; 5% statics; dogs; phone; bus; Eng spkn; adv bkg; CCI. "Beside Rv Mayenne; gd fishing, walks, cycling; lge vans by request." ♦ 15 Apr-15 Sep. € 7.50 2007*

CHATEAU LA VALLIERE *4G1* (500m W Rural) *47.54565, 0.31354* **FFCC Camp Municipal du Val Joyeux, 37330 Château-la-Vallière [02 47 24 00 21 or 02 47 24 04 93; fax 02 47 24 06 13; www.chateaulavalliere.com]** Turn L off D959, in vill 1km S on D749. Site on R after x-ing bdge with lake on L. Med, hdg/mkd pitch, pt shd; wc; chem disp; mv service pnt; serviced pitch; shwrs inc; el pnts (5A) €2.50; shops 1km; tradsmn; playgrnd; lake beach & fishing adj; dogs €0.80; Eng spkn; adv bkg rec high ssn; quiet; CCI. "Friendly welcome; modern, clean san facs; mkd walks; handy for Loire chateaux; v soft ground after heavy rain; unreliable opening dates." ♦ 27 Apr-17 Sep. € 10.50 2007*

CHATEAU RENAULT *4G2* (6km S Urban) *47.54471, 0.88786* **Camp Municipal du Moulin, Rue du Lavoir, 37110 Villedômer [02 47 55 05 50 or 02 47 55 00 04 (Mairie); fax 02 47 55 06 27; mairie.villedomer@wanadoo.fr]** Fr A10 exit junc 18 onto D31 (N10) dir Château-Renault. Turn W onto D73 sp to Auzouer & Villedômer. Fr Château-Renault S on D910 (N10), site sp dir Villedômer. Sm, hdg pitch, shd; wc (male cont); chem disp; shwrs inc; el pnts (10A) €3; shops, rest, bar adj; rv fishing; lake & fishing 2km; dogs €1; adv bkg. "Gd, clean facs but old-fashioned; pitch yourself if warden not present." 15 Jun-15 Sep. € 6.50 2006*

CHATEAU RENAULT *4G2* (500m W Urban) *47.59283, 0.90687* **Camp Municipal du Parc de Vauchevrier, Rue Paul-Louis-Courier, 37110 Château-Renault [02 47 29 54 43 or 02 47 29 85 50 (LS); fax 02 47 56 87 50]** At Château-Renault foll sp to site 800m fr D910 (N10). If app fr a'route turn L on ent town & site on R of main rd adj Rv Brenne. Med, mkd pitch, pt shd; wc; chem disp; mv service pnt; shwrs inc; el pnts (6A) €2.20 (long lead poss req); shops 800m; rest 600m; bar 300m; playgrnd; htd pool; fishing; tennis; some rd noise; ccard not acc; CCI. "Pleasant site by rv in park; lge pitches; friendly, helpful warden; clean san facs, ltd low ssn; gd NH nr D910." ♦ 1 May-15 Sep. € 8.90 2009*

CHATEAUBRIANT *2F4* (1.5km S) *47.70305, -1.37789* **Camp Municipal Les Briotais, Rue de Tugny, 44110 Châteaubriant [02 40 81 14 38 or 02 40 81 02 32; mairie.chateaubriant@wanadoo.fr]** App fr Nantes (D178) site sp on S end of town. Or fr Angers on D963/D163 foll sp at 1st rndabt; fr town cent, foll sps thro town. Sm, hdg pitch, pt shd; wc; mv service pnt; shwrs; el pnts €2.70; shops, rest, snacks, bar 1km; pool in town; games area; dogs; €0.35; quiet. "11thC chateau in town; site locked overnight; site on municipal playing field; gd NH." ♦ 2 May-30 Sep. € 6.00 2009*

CHATEAUDUN *4F2* (1km N Urban) *48.08008, 1.33141* **Camp Municipal Le Moulin à Tan, Rue de Chollet, 28200 Châteaudun [02 37 45 05 34 or 02 37 45 11 91 (LS); fax 02 37 45 54 46; tourisme-chateaudun@wanadoo.fr]** App Châteaudun fr N on N10; turn R at rndabt (supmkt on L); L at next rndabt & foll site sp. Site adj Rv Loir. Med, mkd pitch, pt shd; wc (some cont); chem disp; mv service pnt; shwrs inc; el pnts (5A) €2.05; Indtte; shops, rest, snacks 2km; playgrnd; htd, covrd pool 2km; fishing; canoeing; games area; TV; 5% statics; CCI. "Gd base for touring; helpful warden; some night flying fr nrby military airfield; security gate 2.10m height; no twin-axles." 1 Apr-30 Sep. € 6.10 2009*

CHATEAULIN *2E2* (1.5km S Rural) *48.18754, -4.08515* **La Pointe Superbe Camping, Route de St Coulitz, 29150 Châteaulin [tel/fax 02 98 86 51 53; lapointecamping@aol.com; www.lapointesuperbecamping.com]** Fr N165 foll sp to Châteaulin; in town cent, cross bdge & turn L along rv on D770. After approx 750m, turn L at sp for St Coulitz; 100m turn R into site. If travelling N on D770 do not turn R (tight turn), go into town & turn round. Med, hdg/mkd pitch, some hdstg, pt sl, pt shd; wc; chem disp; mv service pnt; baby facs; shwrs inc; el pnts (10A) €3; Indtte (inc dryer) (planned for 2009); supmkt 1.5km; tradsmn; rest, snacks & bar 1km; BBQ; playgrnd; covrd pool 1km; sand beach 15km; rv fishing nr; games rm; wifi; dogs €1; phone; bus 1.5km; Eng spkn; adv bkg; quiet but some rd noise; no ccard acc; red low ssn; CCI. "Excel, peaceful, well-organised, spacious site in wooded setting; helpful & friendly British owners making improvements; immac facs; rvside path to town; gd cycling, walking & fishing; 1 of best sites in Brittany if you don't req a pool." ♦ 15 Mar-31 Oct. € 16.00 (CChq acc) 2009*

CHATEAULIN *2E2* (500m SW Urban) *48.19099, -4.08597* **Camping de Rodaven (formerly Municipal), 29150 Châteaulin [02 98 86 32 93; fax 02 98 86 31 03; campingderodaven@orange.fr]** Fr canal/rv bdge in town cent take Quai Moulin (SE side of rv) for about 350m; site down track on R opp sw pool. Med, pt shd; wc; chem disp; mv service pnt; shwrs inc; el pnts (10A) €2.70; shops 200m; snacks; playgrnd; htd, covrd pool 300m; direct rv access, fishing; sand beah 5km; wifi; entmnt; dogs €1; phone; poss cr; Eng spkn; adv bkg; quiet; CCI. "Well-managed, refurbished site (2008); pleasant owner; gd touring base." ♦ 1 May-15 Oct. € 10.40 2009*

CHATEAUMEILLANT *7A4* (500m NW Rural) *46.56807, 2.18823* **Camp Municipal L'Etang Merlin, 18370 Châteaumeillant [02 48 61 31 38; fax 02 48 61 39 89; camping.chateaumeillant.chalets@wanadoo.fr; http://monsite.wanadoo.fr/chalets.etang.merlin]** Rec app fr W to avoid narr town rds. Site sp fr rndabt at W end of town on D80 N of Châteaumeillant on lakeside. Fr Culan by pass town on D943, then as above. Sm, hdg/mkd pitch, pt shd; wc; serviced pitches; chem disp; shwrs inc ; el pnts (5A) inc; Indry rm; shop 3km; playgrnd; pool; lake adj (no sw); fishing; tennis & basketball at sports complex adj; dogs €1; Eng spkn; adv bkg; quiet; no ccard acc; CCI. "Superb, well-kept site; lge pitches; friendly & helpful staff; rec arr early high ssn to secure pitch; easy walk to town." ♦ 1 May-30 Sep. € 11.45 2009*

CHATEAUNEUF D'ILLE ET VILAINE *2E4* (1.5km NE Rural) *48.57589, -1.91941* **Camping Le Bel Event, 35430 St Père [02 99 58 83 79; fax 02 99 58 82 24; contact@camping-bel-event.com; www.camping-bel-event.com]** Fr terminal at St Malo, at 1st rndabt foll sp Toutes Directions; at 2nd traff lts turn R & cont foll dir Toutes Directions, then sp Rennes; cont twd Rennes on D137 for approx 10km & take exit for Dinan/Châteauneuf; take immed L twds Cancale; past an old rlwy stn on R & take 1st little rd on L (500m fr stn) opp rest; site 100m further on L. Fr S on D137 at Châteauneuf junc turn R onto D74 sp Cancale, then as above. Med, mkd pitch, pt sl, pt shd; wc; chem disp; shwrs inc; el pnts (10A) €4.20 (rev pol poss); Indtte; tradsmn; sm shop; snacks; bar; htd pool (high ssn); playgrnd; lake sw, fishing & watersports adj; sand beach 5km; cycle hire; tennis; TV; 75% statics (sep area); dogs €2.10; quiet, some rd noise; adv bkg; red low ssn . "Excel NH for St Malo & ferry; clean & tidy site; immac facs, ltd low ssn; some sm pitches - 4 per enclave; gd touring base." 22 Mar-12 Oct. € 18.50 2008*

CHATEAUNEUF DU FAOU *2E2* (4km SE Rural) *48.16853, -3.77578* **Camp Municipal du Goaker, Moulin du Pré, 29520 St Goazec [02 98 26 84 23; fax 02 98 26 86 48]** D36 fr Châteauneuf-du-Faou, turn L sp St Goazec & foll sps to site 800m N of vill nr rv. Sm, pt shd; wc (cont); shwrs inc; el pnts €1.50; shops 750m; playgrnd; rest & bar 1km; quiet. "Pleasantly situated on Rv Aulne adj Goaker lock on Nantes-Brest canal; clean san facs." 15 Jun-15 Sep. € 7.00 2008*

CHATEAUNEUF LES BAINS see St Gervais d'Auvergne *7A4*

CHATEAUNEUF SUR LOIRE *4F3* (500m S Rural) *47.85673, 2.23009* **Camping La Maltournée, Sigloy, 45110 Châteauneuf-sur-Loire [02 38 58 42 46; fax 02 38 58 54 11; contact@revea-vacances.com; www.revea-vacances.fr]** S fr Chateauneuf cent, cross rv on D11; take 1st L, site in 300m on S bank of Rv Loire. Lge, pt shd; htd wc; chem disp; mv service pnt; shwrs inc; el pnts (10A) €3.80; Indtte; shops 1.5km; tradsmn; snacks; playgrnd; pool 2km; canoeing; 75% statics in sep area; dogs; security barrier; poss cr; adv bkg; quiet; CCI. "Well-kept site; clean, modern san facs; chem disp v basic; m'van pitches beside rv; helpful, pleasant staff; excel." ♦ 1 Apr-31 Oct. € 10.60 2008*

CHATEAUNEUF SUR LOIRE *4F3* (7km W Urban) *47.86884, 2.11597* **Camping de l'Isle aux Moulins, Rue du 44ème Régiment d'Infanterie, 45150 Jargeau [tel/fax 02 38 59 70 04 or 02 54 22 26 61 (LS)]** On D952 thro Châteauneuf & N60 twd Orléans. At St Denis-de l'Hôtel take sharp L onto D921 to Jargeau over Loire bdge. Site clearly visible on R of bdge on W bank of rv. Turn R immed at end of bdge. Lge, mkd pitch, pt sl, pt shd; htd wc (mainly cont); chem disp; mv service pnt; baby facs; shwrs inc; el pnts (5A) €3.50; Indtte; tradsmn; shop, rest, bar 500m; playgrnd; pool adj; rv fishing adj; cycle hire; games area; entmnt; 2% statics; dogs; bus 500m; poss cr; Eng spkn; adv bkg; quiet; ccard acc; red long stay/CCI. "Pleasant rvside site; dated facs but clean; friendly farming family." ♦ 1 Apr-31 Oct. € 11.95 2009*

CHATEAUNEUF SUR SARTHE *4G1* (E Rural) *47.67745, -0.48673* **Camp Municipal du Port, Rue de la Gare, 49330 Châteauneuf-sur-Sarthe [02 41 69 82 02 or 02 41 96 15 20; fax 02 41 96 15 29; tourismechateauneufsursarthe@wanadoo.fr]** Site clearly sp in vill, 18km E of Le Lion-d'Angers. Access to site fr bdge. Sm, pt shd; wc; chem disp; shwrs inc; el pnts (10A) €2.70 (long lead poss req); lndtte; shops & rest in vill; playgrnd; rv adj; fishing; sailing; v quiet but some rd noise; CCI. "Attractive area; lge pitches; clean facs but poss stretched high ssn; warden on site am & pm." 1 May-30 Sep. € 7.15 2009*

⊞ **CHATEAUPONSAC** *7A3* (200m SW Rural) *46.13163, 1.27083* **Camp Municipal La Gartempe - Le Ventenat, Ave de Ventenat, 87290 Châteauponsac [05 55 76 55 33 or 05 55 76 31 55 (Mairie); fax 05 55 76 98 05; chateauponsac.tourisme@wanadoo.fr; www.holidayschateauponsac.com]** Fr N exit A20 junc 23.1 sp Châteauponsac; go thro vill, well sp on L on rvside. Fr S exit A20 junc 24 sp Châteauponsac & then as above. Sm, hdg/mkd pitch, terr, pt shd; htd wc; chem disp; shwrs inc; el pnts (6A) €3 (poss rev pol); lndtte; supmkt 500m; rest, snacks, bar (Jul.Aug); playgrnd; pool; kayaking; lake 10km; archery; children's activites; adj to holiday bungalows/gites; dogs €1; poss cr; Eng spkn; poss noise fr parties in rest; adv bkg; red low ssn; CCI. "Pleasant site; helpful staff; gd san facs; pitches muddy in wet; not suitable lge m'vans; activities down steep hill; low ssn warden visits eves only." € 15.00 2009*

CHATEAURENARD see Avignon *10E2*

CHATEAUROUX *4H2* (1km N Rural) *46.82368, 1.69496* **FFCC Camp Municipal Le Rochat-Belle Isle, Rue du Rochat, 36000 Châteauroux [02 54 34 26 56 or 02 54 08 33 00; fax 02 54 07 03 11; camping-le-rochat@orange.fr]** Site on banks of Rv Indre, sp in town. Med, pt shd; wc (cont); chem disp; mv service pnt; baby facs; shwrs inc; el pnts (5-10A) €3.30-4.50; gas; lndtte; shops 300m; rest, snacks, bar 100m; playgrnd; dogs free; Eng spkn; poss noise fr low-flying aircraft. "Leisure park adj with pool & windsurfing on lake; modern, clean san facs; poss music noise till late w/end high ssn; poss itinerants; pleasant walk into town." ♦ 1 May-30 Sep. € 14.00 2008*

CHATEAUROUX *4H2* (9km SW Rural) *46.74214, 1.61983* **Camping Les Grands Pins, Les Maisons-Neuves, 36330 Velles [02 54 36 61 93; contact@les-grands-pins.fr; www.les-grands-pins.fr]** Fr N exit A20 junc 14 dir Châteauroux; in 500m turn R onto D920 parallel with m'way. Foll sp Maisons-Neuves & site. Fr S exit A20 junc 15, turn R then L onto D920, site on R. Med, pt sl, pt shd; wc (some cont); chem disp; some serviced pitches; shwrs inc; el pnts (10A) €4.30 (poss rev pol) (long lead req if in open field); lndtte; shop 8km; rest; bar; playgrnd; pool; tennis; entmnt; dogs €1.50; site clsd w/end 1 Nov-14 Dec; Eng spkn; adv bkg; quiet; ccard acc; CCI. "Gd, tidy site in pine forest; clean facs; gd rest; low ssn recep in rest only; max weight m'van 3,500kg Oct-Apr - heavier acc in summer; no site lighting; vet in Châteauroux; excel NH nr m'way." ♦ 11 Mar-14 Dec. € 14.70 2009*

See advertisement

CHATEL *9A4* (1.5km SW Rural) *46.25768, 6.83023* **Camping Caravaneige L'Oustalet, 1428 Route des Freinets, 74390 Châtel [04 50 73 21 97; fax 04 50 73 37 46; oustalet@valdabondance.com; www.oustalet.com]** Fr Thonon-les-Bains, take D902 & D22 to Châtel. Site sp fr church in cent. Med, hdg/mkd pitch, pt shd; htd wc; mv service pnt; sauna; shwrs inc; el pnts (10A) inc; gas; lndtte; shop, rest, bar 100m; playgrnd; htd, covrd pool high ssn; tennis; games rm; entmnt; some statics; dogs €2.10; adv bkg rec winter; quiet. "Excel site; conv for ski lifts; ski bus stop adj; excel clean facs; vg pool; gd mountain walks." ♦ 23 Jun-1 Sep & 19 Dec-5 Apr. € 30.00 2009*

CHATEL CENSOIR see Coulanges sur Yonne *4G4*

CHATEL DE NEUVRE *9A1* (N Rural) *46.4131, 3.31884* **Camping Deneuvre, Les Graves, 03500 Châtel-de-Neuvre [tel/fax 04 70 42 04 51; campingdeneuvre@wanadoo.fr; www.deneuvre.com]** S fr Moulins on D2009 (N9); sp N of vill on E side of D2009. Med, mkd pitch, hdstg, pt shd; wc; chem disp; mv service pnt; baby facs; shwrs inc; el pnts (4A) inc; gas; lndtte; tradsmn; rest; snacks; bar; playgrnd; canoe hire; dogs €1; adv bkg; Eng spkn; quiet; ccard not acc; CCI. "Excel, clean facs; Dutch management; friendly welcome; at border of Rv Allier in nature reserve; splendid place for walking, fishing, biking & birdwatching; ltd facs low ssn; diff ent/exit for lge o'fits; no twin-axles." ♦ 1 Apr-1 Oct. € 16.35 2009*

⊞ **CHATEL DE NEUVRE** *9A1* (400m W Rural) *46.40320, 3.31350* **FFCC Camping de la Courtine, 7 Rue de St Laurant, 03500 Châtel-de-Neuvre [04 70 42 06 21; fax 04 70 42 82 89; camping-lacourtine@club-internet.fr; www.camping-lacourtine.fr]** Fr N on D2009 (N9) to cent of vill, turn L at x-rds onto D32; site in 500m. Sm, mkd pitch, hdstg, pt shd; htd wc; chem disp; mv service pnt; baby facs; shwrs inc; el pnts (6A) €2.50 (poss rev pol); lndtte; shop 400m; tradsmn; rest 400m; snacks; bar; playgrnd; wifi; dogs €1; poss cr; Eng spkn; adv bkg; quiet; CCI. "Basic but pleasant site; friendly welcome; poss facs poorly maintained & site unkempt low ssn; site liable to flood & poss clsd low ssn, phone ahead to check; access to Rv Allier for canoeing, fishing; walking in nature reserve; NH only." ♦ € 8.70 2008*

CHATEL MONTAGNE *9A1* (10km NE Rural) *46.15938, 3.73506* **Camp Municipal La Boulère, 03120 Arfeuilles [04 70 55 50 11 (Mairie); fax 04 70 55 53 28]** Site off D207 at NE exit to Arfeuilles 50m fr town name sp. 8km fr N7. Sm, pt sl, pt shd; wc; chem disp; shwrs inc; el pnts (6-10A) €3-3.50; lndry rm; shops, rest, snacks, bar 500m; dogs; quiet; CCI. "Peaceful, under-used site set in beautiful countryside; local fishing; gd walking; excel." ♦ 1 May-1 Oct. € 8.00 2009*

CHATEL MONTAGNE *9A1* (1km NW Rural) *46.11526, 3.67700* **FFCC Camping La Croix Cognat, 03250 Châtel-Montagne [tel/fax 04 70 59 31 38 or 06 65 53 91 93 (mob); campinglacroixcognat@wanadoo.fr; http://campinglacroixcognat.monsite.wanadoo.fr]** SW fr Lapalisse on D7; in 15km L on D25 to Châtel-Montagne in 5km & foll sp; site on L bef vill. 'Sleeping policemen' at ent. Sm, mkd pitch, terr, sl, pt shd; wc (some cont); chem disp; mv service pnt; baby facs; shwrs inc; el pnts (6A) €3; gas; Indtte; supmkt 6km; rest; snacks; playgrnd; pool (high ssn); paddling pool; fishing; tennis 100m; mountain bike hire; horseriding & windsurfing adj; 5% statics; dogs €0.50; adv bkg; quiet; CCI. "Sm pitches poss diff o'fits over 6m." 1 May-30 Sep. € 11.00 2006*

CHATEL SUR MOSELLE *6E2* (5km E Rural) *48.32568, 6.42556* **Camping Châtel-sur-Moselle (Perrin), Route de Hadigny, 88330 Châtel-sur-Moselle [03 29 67 94 56]** Exit N57 to Châtel-sur-Moselle, foll sp Hadigny-les-Verrières on minor rd D52. After approx 5km turn L at x-rds, farm on L Sm, hdg pitch, pt shd; htd wc; chem disp; shwrs inc; el pnts (10A) inc; Indtte; shop 5km; quiet. "Farm site in lovely setting; gd area for walking, cycling; WW1 battle site at Epinal." € 15.00 2007*

CHATELAILLON PLAGE *7A1* (2km N Urban) *46.08632, -1.09489* **Camping L'Océan, Ave d'Angoulins, 17340 Châtelaillon-Plage [05 46 56 87 97; www.campingocean17.com]** Fr La Rochelle take D602 to Châtelaillon-Plage, site sp on L in 300m (after passing g'ge & L'Abbaye camp site). Med, hdg/mkd pitch, shd; wc (some cont); chem disp (wc); baby facs; shwrs inc; el pnts (10A) €4.50; Indry rm; tradsmn; ice; shops, rest, snacks & bar 1km; BBQ; waterslide; sand beach 500m; dogs €2; bus; park & ride 400m; phone; poss cr; some Eng spkn; occasional noise fr rlwy & clay pigeon range; ccard acc; red low ssn. "Gd, clean san facs; daily covrd mkt in town; excel." ♦ 6 Jun-20 Sep. € 23.00 2009*

CHATELAILLON PLAGE *7A1* (2.5km SE Coastal) *46.05491, -1.08331* **Camping Port Punay, Les Boucholeurs, Allée Bernard Moreau, 17340 Châtelaillon-Plage [05 46 56 01 53; fax 05 46 56 86 44; contact@camping-port-punay.com; www.camping-port-punay.com]** Fr N exit D137 (N137) La Rochell-Rochefort rd onto D109; strt on at 1st rndabt, L at 2nd rndabt; then cont for 2.8km to end (harbour); turn L, keep R along narr one-way st; at next junc to L, site sp. Fr S exit D137 onto D203 sp Les Boucholeurs; at rndabt in 1km foll site sp to edge of Châtelaillon & turn R, foll sp. Site in 500m. Lge, pt shd; wc; baby facs; shwrs inc; el pnts (10A) €5; gas; Indtte; Indry rm; shops adj; rest; snacks; bar; playgrnd; pool; sand beach 500m; games area; cycle hire; entmnt; wifi; TV; 25% statics; dogs €2.50; poss cr; Eng spkn; adv bkg; quiet; red low ssn. "Immac san facs; friendly, energetic, helpful owners; steel pegs req; sm pitches; excel." 4 Apr-27 Sep. € 23.00 (3 persons) 2009*

CHATELGUYON see Riom *9B1*

We can fill in site report forms on the Club's website – www.caravanclub.co.uk/europereport

CHATELLERAULT *4H1* (1km N Rural) *46.83850, 0.53443* **FFCC Le Relais du Miel, Route d'Antran, 86100 Châtellerault [05 49 02 06 27; fax 05 49 93 25 76; camping@lerelaisdumiel.com; www.lerelaisdumiel.com]** On A10 exit junc 26 at Châtellerault-Nord. Foll sp twd Antran; site on R fr rndabt, well sp (easy to find). Med, hdstg, terr, shd; wc; chem disp; mv service pnt; serviced pitches; shwrs inc; el pnts (10A) inc; Indtte; shop 400m; tradsmn; bar; BBQ; playgrnd; pool; tennis; wifi; dogs €5; Eng spkn; adv bkg; some rd & rlwy noise; ccard acc; red long stay; CCI. "Beautifully situated rvside site in Château de Valette park; friendly owners; clean san facs - ltd low ssn & need updating; extra charge over 5m; conv Futuroscope, Chinon, Loches; conv A10." ♦ 15 May-30 Sep. € 26.00 (2 nights) 2009*

CHATILLON COLIGNY *4F3* (S Rural) *47.81717, 2.84447* **Camp Municipal de la Lancière, Rue André Henriat, 45230 Châtillon-Coligny [02 38 92 54 73 or 06 16 09 30 26 (mob); lalanciere@wanadoo.fr]** N fr Briare twd Montargis on N7; E fr Les Bézards on D56 twd Châtillon-Coligny; site sp on ent town on R immed bef canal bdge. Fr town cross Canal de Briare on D93 twd Bléneau; immed turn S along canal rd sp Camping & Marina. Sm, pt shd; wc (some cont); chem disp (wc); shwrs inc; el pnts (3-6A) €1.90-2.95 (poss long lead req & rev pol); shops adj; pool high ssn; rv fishing; quiet; 25% statics; no ccard acc; CCI. "Attractive, peaceful, tidy site; many lge pitches; clean, dated facs; site would benefit fr some upgrading (2009); site yourself, warden calls; easy walk to historic vill; gd walking/cycling along canal." 1 Apr-30 Sep. € 8.70 2009*

CHATILLON EN DIOIS *9D3* (Urban) *44.69450, 5.48817* **Camp Municipal Les Chaussières, 26410 Châtillon-en-Diois [04 75 21 10 30 or 04 75 21 14 44 (Mairie); fax 04 75 21 18 78; camping.chatillonendiois@wanadoo.fr; www.camping-chatillonendiois.com]** Fr Die take D93 S for 6km then L on D539 to Châtillon (8km) site sp on R on ent to town. Lge, mkd pitch, pt shd; wc (some cont) chem disp (wc); mv service pnt; shwrs; el pnts (10A) €2.65 shop 200m; snacks; rest, bar 200m; BBQ; playgrnd; pool; canoeing; horseriding; cycling; entmnts; 30% statics; dogs €1.58; phone; Eng spkn; adv bkg; quiet; ccard acc; CCI. "On rv bank; attractive old town; gd walking; spectacular mountain scenery; helpful, friendly staff; facs basic but clean; low branches on some pitches." 1 Apr-1 Nov. € 11.98 2007*

CHATILLON EN VENDELAIS see Vitre *2F4*

CHATILLON SUR CHALARONNE *9A2* (500m SE Urban) *46.11622, 4.96172* **FFCC Camp Municipal du Vieux Moulin, Ave Jean Jaurès, 01400 Châtillon-sur-Chalaronne [04 74 55 04 79; fax 04 74 55 13 11; campingvieuxmoulin@orange.fr; www.camping-vieuxmoulin.com]** Take D936 SW out of Bourg-en-Bresse to Châtillon-sur-Chalaronne; pick up D7 on S site of vill; site on R in 400m. Ave Jean Jaurès is part of D7. Sp on ent town. Med, hdg pitch, hdstg, shd; wc (some cont); baby facs; shwrs inc; el pnts (10A) €4 (long lead req on some pitches]; lndry rm; supmkt adj; rest adj; snacks; playgrnd; pool adj inc; fishing; leisure cent adj; 50% statics; dogs €2; phone; adv bkg; quiet, noisy eves high ssn; ccard acc; 10% red CCI. "Lovely site; immac facs; helpful warden; check office opening hrs for early departure; red facs low ssn; lovely town; excel model railway; mkt Sat; excel." ♦ 1 May-30 Sep. € 15.70 2009*

CHATILLON SUR INDRE *4H2* (N Rural) *46.99116, 1.17382* **Camp Municipal de la Ménétrie, Rue de Moulin la Grange, 36700 Châtillon-sur-Indre [06 78 27 16 39 or 02 54 38 75 44 (Mairie)]** Site well sp in vill. N twd Loches then foll sp. Med, some hdg/mkd pitch, pt shd; wc; shwrs inc; el pnts (6-10A) €1.80; gas, shop & rest 400m; BBQ; playgrnd adj; paddling pool; htd pool adj (proper sw trunks only); dogs; no adv bkg; quiet; CCI. "Lovely relaxed site; well-kept; gd bird-watching area; sh walk to old town; conv Loire chateaux; mkt Fri; gd, clean san facs; no twin-axle vans; excel value; vg." ♦ 15 May-15 Sep. € 5.80 2008*

CHATILLON SUR LOIRE see Briare *4G3*

CHATILLON SUR SEINE *6F1* (1km Urban) *47.85955, 4.57975* **Camp Municipal Louis Rigoly, Esplanade Saint Vorles, 21400 Châtillon-sur-Seine [03 80 91 03 05 or 03 80 91 13 19 (LS); fax 03 80 91 21 46; tourism-chatillon-sur-seine@wanadoo.fr]** Fr N, cross rv bdge (Seine); cont approx 400m twd town cent; at lge fountain forming rndabt turn L into street with Bureau de Tourisme on corner; foll sp to site. Fr S ignore all camping sp & cont into town cent to fountain, turn R & cont as above. Med, hdg/mkd pitch, pt sl, pt shd; wc; chem disp; mv service pnt; shwrs inc; el pnts (4-6A) €2.30-4.65; gas; lndtte; shops 500m; snacks adj municipal pool; playgrnd; htd pool adj; dogs; Eng spkn; adv bkg; quiet; CCI. "Pretty site next to lovely park; clean, tidy, well-spaced pitches; helpful, welcoming warden; excel, clean san facs; easy walk to ancient town; ruined chateau; no twin-axles; vg." ♦ 1 Apr-30 Sep. € 11.05 2009*

⊞ **CHATILLON SUR SEINE** *6F1* (6km S Rural) *47.81390, 4.53896* **Camping de la Forge, La Forge, 21400 Ampilly-le-Sec [tel/fax 03 80 91 46 53; campinglaforge@orange.fr; www.campinglaforge.com]** S fr Châtillon-sur-Seine on D971(N71), on leaving Buncey take 1st turn R immed after layby (narr rd); site on R in 1km, on bend immed bef rv bdge, sp. Or app fr S on D971, after passing Chamesson, Ampilly-le-Sec & site sp - note sharp R turn in Ampilly. Sm, pt shd; wc; chem disp; shwrs inc; el pnts (6-16A) inc; lndtte; shop 2km; tradsmn; rest 2.5km; BBQ; playgrnd; rv sw adj; fishing; dogs; phone; Eng spkn; adv bkg rec high ssn; ltd facs winter - phone ahead Dec to Feb to check open; quiet; red long stay; CCI. "Beautiful, secluded, CL-type site in woodland by rv; helpful, friendly British owners; clean, basic ltd san facs; area for lge m'vans across rd; access poss tight v lge o'fits; levelling blocks poss req; popular NH, phone ahead rec." ♦ € 14.70 2009*

CHATRE, LA *7A4* (3km N Rural) *46.60131, 1.97808* **Camp Municipal Solange-Sand, Rue du Pont, 36400 Montgivray [02 54 06 10 34 or 02 54 06 10 36; fax 02 54 06 10 39; mairie.montgivray@wanadoo.fr]** Fr La Châtre take rd to Montgivray, foll camping sp. Fr Châteauroux on D943 SE twd La Châtre turn R 2km S of Nohant on D72. Site behind church. Med, mkd pitch, pt shd; wc; chem disp; shwrs inc; el pnts (3-10A) €1.60-2.40 (poss rev pol); lndry rm; BBQ; dogs; quiet; CCI. "Pleasant site in chateau grounds; san facs old but clean; gd access; warden calls am & pm; gd rest adj; gd walks." ♦ 15 Mar-15 Oct. € 6.67 2009*

CHATRE, LA *7A4* (2km SE Rural) *46.56862, 1.99921* **Camping Intercommunal Le Val Vert, Vavres, 36400 La Châtre [02 54 48 32 42 or 02 54 62 10 10; fax 02 54 48 32 87]** Fr La Châtre take D943 dir Montluçon. On o'skts La Châtre turn R to Briantes, site sp at this junc. Or fr Montluçon on D943, turn L just bef La Châtre; site sp. Sm, hdg pitch, terr, pt shd; wc; chem disp; mv service pnt; shwrs inc; el pnts (10A) €2.35; Indry rm; shop 1km; tradsmn; BBQ; playgrnd; htd pool 5km; statics; adv bkg; quiet; ccard not acc; CCI. "Spacious, pleasant site; excel grounds; san facs poor quality & looking old; walk/cycle to shops; poss itinerants." ♦ 1 Jun-15 Sep. € 7.80 2006*

CHATRES SUR CHER see Villefranche sur Cher *4G3*

CHAUDEFONDS SUR LAYON see Chalonnes sur Loire *2G4*

CHAUDES AIGUES *9C1* (5km N) *44.89500, 3.00157* **Camping Le Belvédère, Le Pont-de-Lanau, 15260 Neuvéglise [04 71 23 50 50; fax 04 71 23 58 93; belvedere.cantal@wanadoo.fr; www.campinglebelvadere.com]** S on A75/E11 exit junc 28 at St Flour; take D921 S twd Chaudes-Aigues; site at Pont-de-Lanau 300m off D921. Steep acc poss diff lge o'fits. Med, terr, pt shd; wc (some cont); chem disp; baby facs; sauna; shwrs inc; el pnts (6A) inc; gas; Indtte; shop; rest; snacks; bar; BBQ; playgrnd; htd pool; paddling pool; canoeing; fishing; sailing 15km; fitness rm; climbing; horseriding 20km; entmnt; wifi; games/TV rm; 25% statics; dogs free; adv bkg; quiet; ccard acc; red low ssn; CCI. "Views over Rv Truyere; friendly, peaceful, family-run site; steep terrs & tight pitches poss diff; not rec for disabled; mkt Neuvéglise Fri." ♦ 24 Apr-16 Oct. € 24.00 ABS - D12 2009*

CHAUDES AIGUES *9C1* (3km SW Rural) *44.84583, 3.00039* **Camp Municipal Le Château du Couffour, 15110 Chaudes-Aigues [tel/fax 04 71 23 57 08 or 04 71 23 52 47 (Mairie); www.chaudesaigues.com]** Sp on L of D921 N dir Laguiole. Lge, pt shd; wc; shwrs inc; el pnts (6A) €2.50; Indtte; shops, rest, snacks, bar 2.5km; BBQ; playgrnd; pool 3km; sports area; tennis; fishing 1km; golf 2km; TV; quiet. "V picturesque area; attractive family-run site with fine views; gd walking; 1000m altitude; thermal spa in town; excel." ♦ 1 May-20 Oct. € 8.00 2009*

CHAUFFAILLES see Clayette, La *9A2*

CHAUMARD *4H4* (Rural) *47.14428, 3.90658* **Camp Municipal Les Iles, 58120 Chaumard [03 86 78 03 00; fax 03 86 78 05 83]** Fr Château-Chinon take D944 dir Pannecière-Chaumard; in 500m turn R onto D37 to Corancy; then D12 to Chaumard; foll camping sp, then turn L into site 100m after cemetary. Sm, hdg pitch, hdstg, pt shd; wc (some cont); chem disp (wc); shwrs €1.20; el pnts €1.50; lake sw adj; fishing; bus 250m. "Access poss diff lge o'fits." € 7.60 2006*

CHAUMONT *6F1* (800m NW Urban) *48.11790, 5.13334* **Camp Municipal Parc Ste Marie, Rue des Tanneries, 52000 Chaumont [03 25 32 11 98 or 03 25 30 60 27 (Mairie); fax 03 25 30 59 50; sports@ville-chaumont.fr]** Site on Chaumont W by-pass joining N19 Troyes rd to N67 St Dizier rd. Do not try to app fr town cent. Sm, hdg/mkd pitch, pt sl, pt shd; wc (cont); chem disp; shwrs inc; el pnts (10A) inc (poss long lead req); shops 1km; tradsmn; snacks; playgrnd; 20% statics; dogs €1.50; poss cr; some traff noise; CCI. "Rec arr early; care needed with steep access to some sl pitches; friendly warden; ent barrier under warden control at all times; gd NH." 2 May-30 Sep. € 13.55 2009*

CHAUMONT SUR LOIRE *4G2* (500m NE Rural) *47.48491, 1.19462* **Camp Municipal Grosse Grève, Ave des Trouillas, 41150 Chaumont-sur-Loire [02 54 20 95 22 or 02 54 20 98 41 (Mairie); fax 02 54 20 99 61]** Site sp in vill on D751. E of vill, rd to L just bef bdge. Fr rvside turn E under bdge. Med, terr, pt shd; htd wc; chem disp; shwrs inc; el pnts (5A) €1.80 (poss long lead req); Indry rm; rest & bar 1km; BBQ; playgrnd; fishing; horseriding; canoeing; tennis; cycle hire; quiet; no ccard acc; CCI. "Pleasant, relaxed site by rv; gd, clean san facs; no twin-axles; interesting chateau; cycle track along Loire; excel." ♦ 15 May-30 Sep. € 9.90 2009*

CHAUNY *3C4* (1km NW Urban) *49.62469, 3.20009* **Camp Municipal, Auberge de Jeunesse, Boulevard de Bad-Köstritz, 02300 Chauny [03 23 52 09 96; fax 03 23 38 70 46; animation@ville-chauny.fr; www.ville-chauny.fr]** Fr S (Soissons) on D1 until junc with D1032 (N32) sp Compiègne. Take D1032 SW until junc with D56. Site sp 100m on L. Sm, hdg/mkd pitch, hdstg, pt sl, pt shd; htd wc (cont); shwrs inc; el pnts (4-10A) €2-50-5.50; shop, rest, bar 1km; playgrnd; sports area; watersports 2km; adv bkg; quiet; ccard not acc. "Fair NH; poss itinerant workers on site." ♦ 1 Jul-31 Aug. € 7.00 2006*

CHAUVIGNY *7A3* (1km E Urban) *46.57072, 0.65326* **Camp Municipal de la Fontaine, Rue de la Fontaine, 86300 Chauvigny [tel/fax 05 49 46 31 94; chauvigny@cg86.fr; www.chauvigny.fr]** Fr N on D2. On ent vill turn L into Rue Vital Guérin & site on R. Site well sp fr Chauvigny. Med, pt shd; htd wc (some cont); chem disp; mv service pnt; baby facs; shwrs; el pnts (15A) inc; Indtte; shop 500m; tradsmn; BBQ; playgrnd; pool & tennis 1km; rv 1km; cycle hire; dogs €1.15; adv bkg; red low ssn; CCI. "Popular, well-run site adj park & lake; views of castle; immac facs; friendly staff; extra for twin-axles; delightful walk to cent; mkts Tue, Thur & Sat." ♦ 5 Apr-5 Oct. € 11.45 2009*

CHAUVIGNY *7A3* (7km NW Rural) *46.60189, 0.59838* **Camp Municipal, 13 Rue de la Varenne, 86300 Bonnes [05 49 56 44 34 or 05 49 56 40 17 (Mairie); fax 05 49 56 48 51; camping_bonnes86@hotmail.com]** Sp fr D951 (N151) & D749. Sp to site easily missed in vill. Site on rvside. Med, hdg pitch, pt shd; wc; chem disp; mv service pnt; shwrs inc; el pnts (10A) inc; Indtte; shop adj in vill; tradsmn; rest & bar 500m; pool adj; waterslide; playgrnd; rv adj; sand beach adj; dogs €1.05; poss cr; adv bkg; quiet; Eng spkn; dogs; CCI. "Friendly, helpful staff; clean & welcoming; vg pool; vg value rest adj; poss itinerants." 15 May-15 Sep. € 13.90 2006*

CHAVANNES SUR SURAN *9A2* (500m E Rural) *46.26601, 5.42819* **Camp Municipal, Le Village, 01250 Chavannes-sur-Suran [04 74 51 70 52; fax 04 74 51 71 83; mairie chavannessuran@wanadoo.fr]** Turn E off N83 at St Etienne-du-Bois onto D3, cross D52 bef Treffort (v narr rds). Then steep climb & bends & after 6km turn N onto D936 sp Chavannes. Turn E at town hall (Mairie), site sp. Fr Bourg-en-Bresse turn E onto D936 sp Jasseron about 1km after joining N83 in Bourg. Foll D936 for approx 18km to Chavannes. Sm, hdg/mkd pitch, pt shd; wc; chem disp (wc); shwrs inc; el pnts (10A) inc (poss rev pol); shop 500m; BBQ; quiet. "Clean san facs; excel cycling, fishing, walking; pretty rvside site nr attractive vill; site self, warden calls; lge pitches; highly rec." ♦ 1 May-30 Sep. € 8.80 2007*

⊞ **CHEF BOUTONNE** *7A2* (2km W Rural) *46.11277, -0.09888* **Camping Le Moulin, 1 Route de Niort, 79110 Chef-Boutonne [05 49 29 73 46; campinglemoulin.chef@aliceadsl.fr; www.campingchef.com]** Fr D950 to or fr Poitiers, turn E onto D740 to Chef-Boutonne, site on R. Fr N10 turn onto D948 to Sauzé-Vaussais then L onto D1 to Chef-Boutonne; then take D740 dir Brioux-sur-Boutonne; site on L. Sm, hdg/mkd pitch, ltd hdstg, pt shd; htd wc; chem disp; mv service pnt 1km; shwrs inc; el pnts (10A) €4; Indtte; ice; shop 2km; tradsmn; rest; snacks; bar; BBQ; playgrnd; pool; entmnt; wifi; dogs €1.20; bus 2km; poss cr; Eng spkn; adv bkg; quiet; ccard acc; red long stay/low ssn; CCI. "Well-kept site; lge pitches; friendly, helpful British owners; gd, clean facs; gd rest on site (ltd opening in winter); much bird life; conv Futuroscope & La Rochelle; highly rec." ♦ € 15.50 2009*

CHEMERY see Contres *4G2*

CHEMILLE *2G4* (1km SW Rural) *47.20001, -0.73442* **FFCC Camping Coulvée, Route de Cholet, 49120 Chemillé [02 41 30 42 42 or 02 41 30 39 97 (Mairie); fax 02 41 30 39 00; camping-chemille-49@wanadoo.fr; www.camping-coulvee-chemille.com]** Fr Chemillé dir Cholet on D160, turn R in 1km. Sm, hdg pitch, terr, pt shd; wc; chem disp; mv service pnt; shwrs inc; el pnts (10A) €3.60; Indtte; tradsmn; bar; BBQ; playgrnd; sm sand beach; lake sw; pedaloes; dogs €1.70; some Eng spkn; adv bkg; quiet; ccard not acc; red long stay; CCI. "Clean facs; helpful staff; gd pitches; poss unreliable opening dates; mkt Thurs." ♦ 25 Apr-15 Sep. € 9.90 2007*

CHENAC ST SEURIN D'UZET see Cozes *7B1*

CHENERAILLES *7A4* (2km SW Rural) *46.10337, 2.16059* **Camp Municpal de la Forêt, 23130 Chénérailles [05 55 62 38 26 or 05 55 62 37 22; fax 05 55 62 95 55; mairie.chenerailles@wanadoo.fr]** SW fr Chénérailles on D55; site in 2km on R. Sm, mkd pitch, pt sl, pt shd; wc (some cont); chem disp (wc); shwrs inc; el pnts (10A) €2.25; Indry rm; shop, rest, bar 2km; BBQ; lake sw adj; dogs €1.56; Eng spkn; adv bkg; CCI. "Sand beach on lake adj; warden on site 0730-1000 & 1530-1930." ♦ 15 Jun-15 Sep. € 7.15 2006*

CHENONCEAUX *4G2* (1.5km E Rural) *47.32905, 1.08816* **Camping de l'Ecluse, Route de la Plage, 37150 Chisseaux [02 47 23 87 10 or 06 15 83 21 20 (mob); sandrine@campingdelecluse-37.fr; www.campingdelecluse-37.fr]** E fr Chenonceaux on D176; cross bdge; immed hard R & foll rv bank; site in 300m. Med, mkd pitch, pt shd; wc; chem disp; mv waste; shwrs inc; el pnts (16A) €3.90 (rev pol); Indtte; shop 1km; supmkt 6km; tradsmn; snacks; bar; playgrnd; fishing; canoeing; watersports; dogs €1.50; phone; poss cr; Eng spkn; adv bkg; quiet tho some rd/rlwy noise; ccard acc; CCI. "Rv trips; fishing; gd walking; gd." ♦ 1 Mar-31 Oct. € 11.55 2009*

CHENONCEAUX *4G2* (S Rural) *47.33033, 1.06947* **Camp Municipal, Fontaine les Prés, 37150 Chenonceaux [02 47 23 90 13 (Mairie); fax 02 47 23 94 46]** In town cent foll sp Château de Chenonceaux & site. Ent as if visiting chateau & attendants will direct you. Site ent narr & twisting, poss not suitable long o'fits. Sm, pt sl, pt shd; wc (some cont); chem disp; mv service pnt; shwrs inc; el pnts (6A) €2.20; shop, rest, bar 500m; BBQ; sm playgrnd; dogs €1; phone; bus adj; poss cr; no adv bkg; some rlwy noise; CCI. "Simple site conv for chateau." ♦ Easter-30 Sep. € 7.20 2006*

CHENONCEAUX *4G2* (1.5km S Rural) *47.32765, 1.08936* **Camping Le Moulin Fort, Pont de Chisseaux, 37150 Francueil [02 47 23 86 22; fax 02 47 23 90 83; lemoulinfort@wanadoo.fr; www.lemoulinfort.com]** Exit A85 junc 11 N, then take D976 (N76) E dir Montrichard; site on S bank of Rv Cher just off D976. Fr Tours take D976 sp Vierzon; keep on D976 by-passing Bléré until sm rndabt (5km) where site sp to L twd rv. Ttake sm rd on R to site, bef actually x-ing bdge. Site well sp. Med, hdg/mkd pitch, pt shd; wc; chem disp; baby facs; shwrs inc; el pnts (6A) inc (long lead poss req); gas; Indtte; shop; tradsmn; rest; snacks; bar; BBQ (gas/charcoal); playgrnd; pool; paddling pool; fishing; cycle hire; entmnt; wifi; games/TV rm; dogs €2.30; Eng spkn; adv bkg ess (min 3 nts); rd noise & a little rlwy noise; ccard acc; red low ssn; CCI. "Lovely, well-kept site on rv bank; beautiful area; friendly, helpful, hard-working British owners; gd san facs (but shwrs poss cold); easy access most pitches; many sm & v shady pitches; poss security probs due access to site fr rv bank; Fri mkt Montrichard; excel." ♦ 1 Apr-30 Sep. € 26.00 ABS - L08 2009*

CHENONCEAUX *4G2* (2km W Rural) *47.32684, 1.04016* **Camp Municipal de l'Ile, Route de Bléré, 37150 Civray-de-Touraine [02 47 23 62 80 or 02 47 29 90 75 (Mairie); fax 02 47 23 62 88; civraydetouraine@wanadoo.fr]** On D976 (N76) bet Bléré & Montrichard site on N bank of Rv Cher, sp fr both dirs; ent 100m after x-ing narr bdge. V diff for car & c'van to make R turn into narr ent. Instead pass ent, turn around & turn L into ent. Sm, pt shd; wc; chem disp; mv service pnt; shwrs inc; el pnts (5A); shop 1km; tradsmn; rest, bar 1km; playgrnd; pool 3km; rv adj; quiet but poss noise fr nrby rd & rlwy; CCI. "Gd well-maintained site; v attractive rv lock & weir 500m." ♦ 18 Jun-31 Aug. 2007*

CHENS SUR LEMAN see Douvaine *9A3*

CHERBOURG *1C4* (5km NE Urban/Coastal) *49.65405, -1.56675* **Camp Municipal Espace Loisirs de Collignon, Plage Collignon, 50110 Tourlaville [02 33 54 80 68; fax 02 33 20 53 03; camping-collignon@wanadoo.fr; www.mairie-tourlaville.fr]** Foll sp fr ferry terminal for Espace Loisirs Collignon or Tourlaville-Plage; site on D116; turn L at lge rndabt beyond Tourlaville boundary. Med, mkd pitch, unshd; wc; chem disp; shwrs inc; el pnts (10A) €3.75; gas; lndtte; shops 500m; rest 2km; bar 500m; covrd pool adj; sand beach adj; fishing, sw & watersports adj; games rm; entmnt; TV; 30% statics; dogs; poss cr; adv bkg (rec high ssn); poss noisy high ssn (youth groups); some rd noise; ccard acc; CCI. "Lge landscaped complex; generous pitches; poss poor security; conv ferries." ♦ 1 May-30 Sep. € 15.90 2009*

CHERBOURG *1C4* (12km NE Coastal) *49.6928, -1.4387* **Camping La Plage, 2 Village de Fréval, 50840 Fermanville [02 33 54 38 84; fax 02 33 54 74 30; contact@camping-femanville.com; www.camping-fermanville.com]** Fr Cherbourg on D116 dir Barfleur, site in 12km on L. Med, some hdg pitch, unshd; wc; chem disp; shwrs inc; el pnts (5A) €2.50; snacks; bar; playgrnd; beach 300m; 70% statics; dogs €2; poss cr; adv bkg ess summer, rec winter; quiet. "Friendly owner; conv for ferry & D-Day landing beaches; poss unreliable opening dates." 1 Mar-30 Nov. € 13.00 2008*

CHERBOURG *1C4* (10km E Coastal) *49.65703, -1.52645* **Camp Municipal du Fort, 47 Route du Fort, 50110 Bretteville [02 33 22 27 60]** Immed exit car ferries in Cherbourg, turn L on D116. On leaving Bretteville turn sharp L at junc of D116 & D611, 1st turn R. App poss diff lge o'fits. Med, pt sl, unshd; wc; chem disp; shwrs; el pnts (10A) €2.30; shops 4km; BBQ; playgrnd; shgl beach adj; 90% statics; quiet. "Sep area tourers, sm pitches; some pitches view of coast; locked 2200-0700; poss diff in wet; some pitches diff lge o'fits; sh stay only." 1 May-30 Sep. € 8.50 2006*

CHERBOURG *1C4* (10km E Coastal) *49.66750, -1.48685* **Camping L'Anse du Brick, 18 L'Anse du Brick, 50330 Maupertus-sur-Mer [02 33 54 33 57; fax 02 33 54 49 66; welcome@anse-du-brick.com; www.anse-du-brick.com or www.les-castels.com]** At rndabt at port take 2nd exit sp Caen, Rennes & Mont St Michel; at 2nd rndabt take 3rd exit sp Caen & Mont St Michel (N13); at 3rd rndabt take 2nd exit onto dual c'way sp St Lô, Caen (N13), Bretteville-sur-Mer; exit on D116 & foll sp thro Bretteville-en-Saire (take care massive speed hump in Le Becquet); turn R for site just after R-hand blind bend & turning for Maupertus; up v steep incline. Med, hdg/mkd pitch, terr, sl, shd; wc; chem disp; mv service pnt; baby facs; serviced pitches; shwrs inc; el pnts (10A) inc (poss rev pol); gas; lndtte; shop & 3km; tradsmn; rest; snacks; bar; BBQ; playgrnd; 2 htd pools; paddling pool; waterslide; sand beach adj; tennis; cycle hire; archery; wifi; games/TV rm; dogs €2.60; poss cr; adv bkg; quiet; ccard acc; red low ssn; CCI. "Attractive, well-kept site in beautiful setting; conv ferry; gd clean san facs; some pitches for lge o'fits; excel for dogs - allowed on adj beach; cliff behind so no sat TV recep; conv Landing Beaches, Barfleur, coastal nature reserve." ♦ 1 Apr-30 Sep. € 36.80 ABS - N14 2009*

⊞ **CHERBOURG** *1C4* (6km S Rural) *49.58951, -1.59433* **Camping Le Village Vert, 50470 Tollevast [02 33 43 00 78; fax 02 33 43 03 38; le-village-vert@wanadoo.fr; www.le-village-vert.com]** S'bound take N13 sp Caen out of town. Cont on N13 fr Auchan rndabt for approx 5km to D56 slip rd sp Delasse. Turn L at x-rds over N13 onto N13 sp Cherbourg. Site on R approx 3.5km, sp nr Auchan hypmkt. N'bound exit sp Tollevast & site. Lge, some hdstg, pt sl, pt shd; wc; chem disp; mv service pnt; shwrs inc; baby facs; el pnts (10A) €1.50 (check rev pol); gas; sm shop & 1km; tradsmn; rest 200m; playgrnd; tennis; golf & horseriding 2km; 95% statics (sep); dogs €2; Eng spkn; adv bkg; quiet but poss rd noise at front of site; ccard acc; red CCI. "Conv NH for ferries in woodland setting; ltd space for tourers but spacious pitches; friendly & efficient; poss waterlogged pitches; poss itinerants; office closes 1930, night arrivals area." ♦ € 13.00 2009*

⊞ **CHERBOURG** *1C4* (3km NW Urban/Coastal) *49.65576, -1.65257* **Camp Municipal de la Saline, Rue Jean Bart, 50120 Equeurdreville-Hainneville [02 33 93 88 33 or 02 33 53 96 00 (Mairie); fax 02 33 93 12 70; mairie-equeurdreville@dialoleane.com; www.equeurdreville.com]** Fr ferry terminal foll D901 & sp Beaumont-Hague. On dual c'way beside sea look out for site sp to L. Med, hdg/mkd pitch, hdstg, pt sl, terr, pt shd; htd wc; chem disp; mv service pnt in 100m; shwrs inc; el pnts (10A) €4.34; lndry rm; shop, rest, snacks & bar 500m; sand beach adj; fishing; 50% statics; dogs €0.50; phone; rd noise; adv bkg; CCI. "Sea views; boules & skateboard park adj; aquatic cent 500m; cycle path to town; secured at night; gd NH." ♦ € 9.00 2008*

CHERRUEIX see Dol de Bretagne *2E4*

⊞ **CHESNE, LE** *5C1* (2km NE Rural) *49.53166, 4.77430* **Camp Departmental du Lac de Bairon, 08390 Le Chesne [03 24 30 11 66]** Leave A203 exit Sedan, W on D764, in 500m L on D977 sp Vouziers. 2km bef Le Chesne R on D12, in 500m L on D312. Site 2km on L. Lge, mkd pitch, some hdstg, pt shd; wc; chem disp; mv service pnt; shwrs inc; el pnts (6-10A) €3-5; lndtte; shop 2km; tradsmn; snacks; bar; playgrnd; tennis; cycle hire; watersports; entmnts; lake sw, sand beach, fishing, boat & canoe hire; TV rm; entmnt; 20% statics; dogs €1.20; phone; CCI. "V pleasant, quiet site; gd, clean san facs; poss diff site ent with lge o'fits; forest walks; excel." ♦ € 11.00 2009*

CHEVENON see Nevers *4H4*

France

CHEVERNY *4G2* (2km S Rural) *47.47798, 1.45070* **Camping Les Saules, 102 Route de Contres, 41700 Cheverny [02 54 79 90 01; fax 02 54 79 28 34; contact@camping-cheverny.com; www.camping-cheverny.com]** Exit A10 junc 17 dir Blois Sud onto D765 to Romorantin. At Cour-Cheverny foll sp Cheverny & chateau. Fr S on D956 turn R onto D102 just N of Contres, site on L just bef Cheverny. Well sp fr all dirs. Lge, mkd pitch, shd; htd wc; chem disp; mv service pnt; baby facs; shwrs inc; el pnts (10A) €3.50 (poss long lead req); gas; lndtte; shop; tradsmn; rest; snacks; bar; BBQ; playgrnd; htd pool; paddling pool; fishing; tennis, golf nr; excursions; games rm; cycle hire; internet; 2% statics; TV; dogs €2; Eng spkn; adv bkg; quiet but some rd noise; ccard acc; red long stay/low ssn; CCI. "Well-run site; excel facs; friendly, welcoming, helpful owners; excel pool; all pitches under trees; muddy after heavy rain; many cycle & walking rtes nr; conv many chateaux." ♦ 1 Apr-26 Sep. € 29.90 2009*

See advertisement above

CHEYLARD, LE *9C2* (1km E Rural) *44.90721, 4.43198* **Camping La Chèze, Route de St Christol, 07160 Le Cheylard [tel/fax 04 75 29 09 53; mosslercat@wanadoo.fr; www.camping-de-la-cheze.com]** Fr Le Cheylard take D264 SE & foll camping sp. App up steep hill & sharp bend into final app. Less steep app fr Valence on N86 & D120. Site 25km fr St Agrève by rd. NB If overshoot acute L-hand bend proceed thro Le Cheylard & turn in car park. Med, mkd pitch, terr, pt shd; wc (some cont); chem disp (wc); shwrs inc; el pnts (10A) €2.50; lndtte; shops 1.2km; tradsmn; rest; playgrnd; rv sw 2km; some statics; dogs €0.50; phone; security barrier; poss cr; Eng spkn; adv bkg; v quiet; 10% red CCI. "In grounds of château; lovely views over attractive town & mountains; gd walks nrby; poss unkempt early ssn (2008)." ♦ Easter-1 Nov. € 10.50 2008*

CHEZERY FORENS *9A3* (500m S Rural) *46.21770, 5.86378* **Camp Municipal Le Valserine, Route de Confort, 01410 Chézery-Forens [tel/fax 04 50 56 20 88; camping.valserine@orange.fr; www.chezery.fr/camping/]** Site off D991 on app to vill. Sm, pt shd; wc; chem disp; shwrs inc; el pnts (5-10A) €3-3.50; lndtte; shops adj; rv adj; dogs €1; quiet. "Gd walks." 1 Apr-31 Oct & 1 Dec-15 Mar. € 12.00 2008*

CHILLY LE VIGNOBLE see Lons le Saunier *6H2*

CHINON *4G1* (500m SW Rural) *47.16397, 0.23377* **Camping de L'Ile Auger, Quay Danton, 37500 Chinon [02 47 93 08 35; fax 02 47 98 47 92; communaute.r.c.s.b@wanadoo.fr; www.ville-chinon.com]** On S side of rv at bdge. Fr S foll sp Chinon St Jacques; when app 2nd bdge on 1-way 'loop', avoid R lane indicated for x-ing bdge & cont strt past S end of main bdge to site on R. Fr N foll sp 'Centre Ville' round castle, cross bdge, site on R. Well sp in town & opp castle. Lge, hdg/mkd pitch, pt shd; wc (some cont); chem disp (wc); mv service pnt; baby facs; shwrs inc; el pnts (4-12A) €2.10-3.60 (poss rev pol) lndtte; shop 200m; snacks adj; playgrnd; htd pool 300m; sat TV; dogs €0.90; phone; quiet; ccard acc; CCI. "Excel, well-kept site in gd location; gd clean san facs, poss stretched if site busy; elec connected by warden; twin-axles discretionary; poss midge prob; poss itinerants; views of chateau." ♦ 15 Mar-15 Oct. € 9.20 2009*

CHINON *4G1* (14km NW Rural) *47.20693, 0.08127* **Camping Belle Rive, 2 Route de Chinon, 37500 Candes-St Martin [02 47 95 98 11; fax 02 47 95 80 95; cte.de.cnes.RGV@wanadoo.fr; www.cdc-rivegauchevienne.com]** Fr Chinon take D751. Site on R bef junc with D7, on S bank of Rv Vienne. Med, mkd pitch, pt shd; wc; shwrs; el pnts (10A) €1.95; lndtte; shops 1km; tradsmn; rvside café; bar; rv sw 1km; playgrnd; fishing adj; dogs €0.90; adv bkg; quiet; CCI. "Pleasant rvside site, conv Saumur & chateaux; poor san facs, on 2 floors." ♦ Mid Apr-Mid Sep. € 6.50 2007*

CHOLET *2H4* (5km SE Rural) *47.03699, -0.84171* **Camping Village Vacances Le Lac de Ribou, Allée Léon Mandin, 49300 Cholet [02 41 49 74 30; fax 02 41 58 21 22; info@lacderibou.com; www.lacderibou.com]** Fr Cholet ring rd foll sp Parc des Loisirs de Ribou. Sp fr Cholet. Lge, hdg/mkd pitch, hdstg, terr, pt shd; htd wc; chem disp; mv service pnt; serviced pitches; shwrs inc; el pnts (10A) €3.85 (long lead req); lndtte; tradsmn; shop; hypmkt 1.5km; rest; snacks; bar; BBQ; playgrnd; 2 htd pools; waterslides; lake sw & sand beach 500m; fishing; boating; windsurfing; skating; tennis; archery; golf nr; entmnt; TV rm; dogs €2.10; extra for twin-axles; poss cr; Eng spkn; adv bkg ess; quiet; ccard acc; 5% red CCI. "Excel touring area; excel site." ♦ 1 Apr-30 Sep. € 18.90 2009*

CHOLET *2H4* (8km SE Rural) *47.01915, -0.82976* **Camping du Verdon, Le Bois Neuf, Route du Verdon, 49280 La Tessoualle [02 41 49 74 61; fax 02 41 58 21 22; www.cholet-sports-loisirs.com]** On D258 fr Cholet ring rd, turn L in 6km. Site well sp at Barrage du Verdon & La Tessoualle vill. Sm, hdg pitch, pt shd; wc; chem disp; shwrs; el pnts (3-5A) €2.05-3 (long lead req some pitches) shop; rest, snacks, bar adj (poss lunchtime only); lake sw & land beach; dogs €1; Eng spkn; adv bkg; quiet; CCI. "Peaceful location, lovely pitches; facs dated but clean; windsurfing on Lac du Verdon; excel walking, cycling." 1 Jul-31 Aug. € 9.65 2007*

CHORGES *9D3* (9km NE Rural) *44.56169, 6.34642* **CAMPEOLE Camping Le Clos du Lac, Route des Lacs, 05160 St Apollinaire [04 92 44 27 43; fax 04 92 43 46 93; clos-du-lac@campeole.com; www.camping-closdulac.com or www.campeole.com]** N94 to Chorges, then take D9 to St Apollinaire. Take D509 to NW of vill, site in 2.2km, sp. Med, terr, pt shd; htd wc; chem disp; baby facs; shwrs inc; el pnts (7A) €4.10; Indtte; shop; tradsmn; playgrnd; lake sw & beach adj; fishing; watersports; games area; some statics; dogs €1.80; Eng spkn; adv bkg; quiet; ccard acc; red low ssn. "Pleasant, peaceful, well-kept site in lovely location; gd facs." ♦ 22 May-25 Sep. € 14.20 2009*

See advertisement below

CHORGES *9D3* (2.5km E Rural) *44.53515, 6.30231* **Camping Le Rio Claret, Les Chabes, 05230 Chorges [tel/fax 04 92 50 62 16; rio-claret@wanadoo.fr; www.camping-lerioclaret.com]** Fr Gap foll N94 E dir Embrun; take main rd by-passing Chorges & 4km past traff lts look for sp to site. Turn L at junc (narr lane), turn R & R again to site. Sm, mkd pitch, pt shd; wc (some cont); chem disp; mv service pnt; shwrs inc; el pnts (3-10A) €2.50-3.80; lndry rm; tradsmn; shop 2.4km; rest; snacks; bar; playgrnd; lake sw & beach 2km; TV; 10% statics; dogs €2; phone; adv bkg; some rd noise at lower level. "Conv touring base; day trip to Italy via Briançon; boat excursions; spectacular views; gd san facs; excel meals; helpful, pleasant owners." ♦ 1 Jun-30 Sep. € 16.00 2008*

CHORGES *9D3* (5km E Rural) *44.52289, 6.34125* **Camping Club Le Roustou, 05230 Prunières [04 92 50 62 63; fax 04 92 50 90 48; info@campingleroustou.com; www.campingleroustou.com]** E fr Gap on N94. Site on side of Lac de Serre-Ponçon. Do not attempt to go to Prunières vill, always stay on N94. Lge, mkd pitch, hdstg, terr, pt shd; wc; own san rec; chem disp; mv service pnt; baby facs; shwrs inc; el pnts (4A) inc; Indtte; shops 10km; tradsmn; snacks; bar; playgrnd; pool (no shorts); beach adj; ; lake sw; canoe hire; tennis; cycle hire; games area; TV; dogs €0.80; poss cr; Eng spkn; quiet; red low ssn; ccard acc; CCI. "Beautiful views; excel scenery; relaxing area; always park on E side in case of poss problem with wind; excel." 1 May-30 Sep. € 22.70 2006*

CHORGES *9D3* (6km E Rural) *44.52701, 6.35876* **Camping Le Nautic, Lac de Serre-Ponçon, 05230 Prunières [04 92 50 62 49; fax 04 92 53 58 42; info@campinglenautic.com; www.campinglenautic.com]** Fr Gap or Embrun take N94, site sp bet Savines & Chorges. Med, terr, shd; wc; chem disp; shwrs; el pnts (6A) €3; gas; shop; snacks; playgrnd; pool; shgl beach & lake sw; boating; dogs €1.50; adv bkg; quiet. "Beautiful location, lake sw excel in sheltered bay; vg san facs." 15 May-15 Sep. € 17.80 (CChq acc) 2006*

CHORGES *9D3* (10km SW Rural) *44.47581, 6.26330* **Camping La Viste, Le Belvédère de Serre-Ponçon, 05190 Rousset [04 92 54 43 39; fax 04 92 54 42 45; camping@laviste.fr; www.laviste.fr]** N on A51 or D1085 (N85) twds Gap; take D942 sp Barcelonnette; after Espinasses turn L onto D3 to Barrage de Serre-Ponçon; then L onto D103. Site on L. NB D3 long, v steep climb, hairpin bends. Med, hdg/mkd pitch, pt sl, pt shd; wc; chem disp; mv service pnt; shwrs inc; el pnts (5A) €3.30; gas; Indtte; shop & 4km; tradsmn; rest; snacks; bar; BBQ; playgrnd; pool; lake sw 2km; some statics; dogs €2.40; phone; adv bkg; quiet; ccard acc; CCI. "Ltd facs low ssn; site o'looks Lac de Serre-Poncon (amenity area); cool at night; gd walking; site rds narr; access diff lge o'fits." ♦ 15 May-15 Sep. € 18.20 2009*

France

CIOTAT, LA *10F3* (4km NE Coastal) *43.18733, 5.65810* **Camping Les Oliviers, Le Liouquet, Route de Toulon, 13600 La Ciotat [04 42 83 15 04; fax 04 42 83 94 43; www.camping-lesoliviers.com]** Fr La Ciotat, foll D559 coast rd sp Bandol & Toulon. Site in 4km, look for lge sp on L. Caution x-ing dual c'way. V lge, pt sl, terr, shd; wc; chem disp; shwrs inc; el pnts (6A) €2.80 (poss rev pol); gas; lndtte; shops 300m; rest, snacks, bar 300m; playgrnd; pool; sand/shgle beach 4km; tennis; 5% statics; dogs €1; bus 300m; poss v cr; Eng spkn; adv bkg; quiet but some noise fr main rd & rlwy adj; ccard acc; CCI. "Many pitches have sea views; friendly staff; tired san facs & poss unclean; v sm shwrs; care on ent due to lge boulders; gd touring base." ♦ 15 Mar-15 Sep. € 16.70 2006*

⊞ **CIOTAT, LA** *10F3* (3km E Coastal) *43.18938, 5.64605* **Camping Santa Gusta, Domaine de Fontsainte, 13600 La Ciotat [04 42 83 14 17; fax 04 42 08 90 93; santagusta@wanadoo.fr; www.santagusta.com]** Foll D559 coast rd fr La Ciotat twd Les Lecques to Total filling stn on R. Site down by filling stn. Lge, pt sl, pt shd; wc (cont); chem disp (wc); shwrs inc; el pnts (5A) €2.90; lndtte; shop; rest, snacks, bar high ssn; playgrnd; rocky beach adj; boat-launching facs; wifi; entmnt; 95% statics; dogs €4; poss cr; quiet; CCI. "San facs open 0730-2000; adj beach not suitable for bathing; ltd facs low ssn; smart card access; NH only." € 18.20 2006*

CIVRAY *7A2* (1km NE Urban) *46.15835, 0.30169* **FFCC Camping Les Aulnes, Les Coteaux de Roche, 86400 Civray [05 49 87 17 24; campingaulnes@yahoo.fr; www.camping-les-aulnes.com]** Civray 9km E of N10 halfway bet Poitiers & Angoulême. Site outside town SE of junc of D1 & D148. Sp on D148 & on S by-pass. Avoid town cent narr rds. Med, pt sl, pt shd; wc (cont); chem disp (wc); shwrs; el pnts (6-10A) €3 (poss long lead req); lndtte; shop 500m; rest; snacks; bar; BBQ; playgrnd; htd pool 1km; rv sw & fishing adj; cycle hire; golf; few statics; dogs €1; Eng spkn; quiet; ccard acc; CCI. "V pleasant rvside site; gd san facs, poss irreg cleaning low ssn; pitches soft when wet; vg rest; conv town cent; mkt Wed; vg." 1 Apr-15 Oct. € 7.50 2009*

CLAIRVAUX LES LACS *6H2* (1.2km SE Rural) *46.56431, 5.7562* **Yelloh! Village Le Fayolan, Chemin de Langard, 39130 Clairvaux-les-Lacs [03 84 25 26 19; reservation@rsl39.com; www.relaisoleiljura.com or www.yellohvillage.com]** Fr town foll campsite sp, last site along lane adj to lake. V lge, hdg/mkd pitch, terr, pt shd; wc; serviced pitches; chem disp; sauna; some serviced pitches; shwrs inc; el pnts (6A) inc; gas; lndtte; shop; rest; snacks; bar; playgrnd; htd pools (1 covrd); waterslide; sand lake beach adj; games rm; tennis 1km; cycle hire; entmnt; TV; 16% statics; dogs €3.50; extra for twin axles; Eng spkn; adv bkg rec; quiet; red low ssn; ccard acc; CCI. "Excel, clean site; extra for lakeside pitches high ssn; v pleasant sm town in easy walking dist; lovely area." ♦ 30 Apr-14 Sep. € 36.00 2008*

CLAIRVAUX LES LACS *6H2* (1km S Rural) *46.56761, 5.75480* **Camping La Grisière et Europe Vacances, Chemin Langard, 39130 Clairvaux-les-Lacs [03 84 25 80 48; fax 03 84 25 22 34; bailly@la-grisiere.com; www.la-grisiere.com]** Turn S off D678 (N78) in Clairvaux opp church onto D118; fork R in 500m & foll site sps to lake. Sp in vill. Camping La Grisière ent after Camping Les Lacs. V lge, mkd pitch, pt sl, pt shd; htd wc (some cont); chem disp; mv service pnt; baby facs; shwrs inc; el pnts (6-10A) €2.60; lndry rm; shop; tradsmn; snacks; bar; BBQ; playgrnd; lake sw & beach adj; rv sw 5km; fishing; watersports; cycle & canoe hire; tennis 1km; wifi; TV; 5% statics; dogs €1; phone; bus 700m; Eng spkn; no adv bkg; quiet; ccard acc; red low ssn; CCI. "Lovely views in beautiful area; lge pitches; excel site." ♦ 1 May-30 Sep. € 17.30 2009*

CLAIRVAUX LES LACS *6H2* (1km S Rural) *46.56822, 5.75513* **Camping Le Grand Lac, Chemin du Langard, 39130 Clairvaux-les-Lacs [03 84 25 22 14 or 03 84 25 26 19; reservation@rsl39.com; www.relaisoleiljura.com]** SE on D678 (N78) fr Lons-le-Saunier; in Clairvaux vill turn R opp church on L, 1st R then fork R, foll sp. Ent 2.7m wide. Lge, hdg/mkd pitch, terr, pt shd; wc; mv service pnt; baby facs; shwrs inc; el pnts (6A) inc; lndtte; shop; tradsn; BBQ; sand beach; fishing; boating; 30% statics; dogs €2; Eng spkn; ccard acc. "Lovely country nr Jura mountains; gd site." ♦ 31 May-5 Sep. € 19.00 2008*

CLAIRVAUX LES LACS *6H2* (10km S Rural) *46.50922, 5.79300* **Camping Le Val d'Eté, 100 Rue du Champ-Coubet, 39130 Etival [tel/fax 03 84 44 87 31; camping.etival@cegetel.net]** E fr Lons-le-Saunier on D678 (N78) to Clairvaux-les-Lacs. In Clairvaux foll camping sp thro town. Then ignore them & take D118 to Châtel-de-Joux & Etival. Site on L on ent to vill. Sm, mkd pitch, terr, pt sl, pt shd; htd wc (cont); chem disp (wc); mv service pnt; shwrs inc; el pnts (6-10A) €2; llndtte; shop & 10km; tradsmn; snacks; bar 10km; playgrnd; lake sw 500m; games area; 30% statics; adv bkg; quiet; red low ssn. CCI. "Lovely position; helpful owner; guided walks - superb wild flowers." 1 Jul-31 Aug. € 12.50 (3 persons) 2007*

CLAIRVAUX LES LACS *6H2* (10km SW Rural) *46.52311, 5.67350* **Camping de Surchauffant, Pont de la Pyle, 39270 La Tour-du-Meix [03 84 25 41 08; fax 03 84 35 56 88; info@camping-surchauffant.fr; www.camping-surchauffant.fr]** Fr Clairvaux S on D27 or D49 to D470. Foll sp Lac de Vouglans, site sp. Med, mkd pitch, pt sl, pt shd; wc; chem disp; mv service pnt; shwrs inc; el pnts (6A) €3; lndtte; shops adj; rest; snacks; bar; BBQ; playgrnd; pool; paddling pool; dir access to lake 120m; sailing; watersports; entmnt; TV rm; some statics; dogs €1.60; Eng spkn; adv bkg; quiet; ccard acc. "Vg facs; lovely location; hiking trails." ♦ 29 Apr-14 Sep. € 19.00 2009*

CLAIRVAUX LES LACS *6H2* (4km W Rural) *46.58625, 5.70194* **Camping Le Moulin, 39130 Patornay [03 84 48 31 21; fax 03 84 44 71 21; contact@camping-moulin.com; www.camping-moulin.com]** Exit A39 junc 8 to Lons-le-Saunier, then take D52/D678 (N78) SE to Pont-de-Poitte. After x-ing bdge over Rv Ain, ent to site on L. Lge, hdg/mkd pitch, hdstg, pt terr, shd; wc; chem disp; mv service pnt; baby facs; shwrs inc; el pnts (6A) inc; gas; lndtte; shop; tradsmn; snacks; bar; BBQ; playgrnd; htd pool; waterslide; rv sw & sand beach 5km; fishing; games area; games rm; wifi; entmnt; TV; dogs €2; phone; poss cr; Eng spkn; adv bkg; ccard acc; red low ssn; CCI. "Site clsd 1200-1400, do not arr during this time as narr app rd poss blocked with queuing traff; excel cent for touring Jura; vg site." ♦ 25 Apr-13 Sep. € 28.00 2008*

CLAIRVAUX LES LACS *6H2* (7km W Rural) *46.59976, 5.68824* **Camping Beauregard, 2 Grande Rue, 39130 Mesnois [tel/fax 03 84 48 32 51; reception@juracampingbeauregard.com; www.juracampingbeauregard.com]** S fr Lons-le-Saunier on D52/D678 (N78), about 1km bef Pont-de-Poitte turn L on D151. Site 1km on L opp rd junc to Pont-de-Poitte. Lge, hdg/mkd pitch, hdstg, pt sl, terr, pt shd; htd wc (some cont); chem disp; baby facs; shwrs inc; el pnts (6A) €3 (poss long lead req); gas; lndtte; shop 1km; tradsmn; rest; playgrnd; htd pool high ssn; sand beach 800m; kayaking nr; tennis; cycle hire; games rm; 10% statics; dogs €2; poss cr; Eng spkn; adv bkg; quiet. "Super site, clean & well-run; diff sized pitches; excel san facs, ltd low ssn; excel rest; narr site rds poss muddy when wet." ♦ 1 Apr-30 Sep. € 21.50 2008*

CLAMECY *4G4* (5km NE Rural) *47.51665, 3.48001* **Camping Le Bois Joli, Route de Villeprenoy, 89480 Andryes [tel/fax 03 86 81 70 48; info@campingauboisjoli.com; www.campingauboisjoli.com]** S on N151 fr Auxerre to Coulanges-sur-Yonne. W on D39 sp Andryes, foll sps `Camping Andryes', site 3km after vill. Med, mkd pitch, terr, shd; htd wc; chem disp; baby facs; baby facs; fam bthrm; shwrs inc; el pnts (6A) €3 (poss rev pol); gas; lndry rm; shop; tradsmn; BBQ; playgrnd; pool inc; rv sw, fishing & boat hire 2km; tennis; cycle hire; wifi; TV; 10% statics; dogs €2; phone; Eng spkn; quiet; red low ssn; CCI. "Dutch owners; beautiful countryside; gd pitches; muddy in rain; excel facs." ♦ 1 Apr-1 Nov. € 18.00 2008*

CLAMECY *4G4* (8km SE Rural) *47.41390, 3.60828* **Camp Municipal Les Fontaines, 58530 Brèves [tel/fax 03 86 24 25 26; mairie-breves@wanadoo.fr; www.vaux-yonne.com]** On D985 (Clamecy-Corbigny) at Brèves. Both app clearly sp. Med, pt sl, unshd; wc; chem disp (wc); shwrs inc; el pnts (6A) €2; lndtte; tradsmn; shop; BBQ; playgrnd; 4% statics; dogs; phone. CCI. "Quiet site in pretty area nr Rv Yonne & canal; friendly staff; grnd soft after heavy rain; vg." ♦ 1 Jun-30 Sep. € 8.60 2009*

CLAMECY *4G4* (S Urban) *47.45231, 3.52772* **Camp Municipal du Pont-Picot, Rue de Chevroche, 58500 Clamecy [03 86 27 05 97; tourism.clamecy@wanadoo.fr; www.vaux-yonne.com]** On N151 fr S, exiti N151 at rndabt 3km SW of town cent, cross level x-ing then R at rndabt on D23, take 1st L, site sp in 2.4km. Narr app rd. App fr N or E thro town not rec. Med, pt sl, pt shd; wc; chem disp; shwrs inc; el pnts (6A) €2.90; lndry rm; shops 1km; tradsmn; playgrnd; sw; no twin-axles; poss cr; Eng spkn; quiet: CCI. "Pleasant, peaceful site b et rv & canal in beautiful location; friendly, helpful staff; facs poss inadequate when busy; town 10 min walk on towpath; gd cycling; gd NH." ♦ 19 Apr-4 Oct. € 11.20 2009*

CLAYETTE, LA *9A2* (8km NE Rural) *46.33667, 4.38185* **Camping Château de Montrouant, 71800 Gibles [03 85 84 51 13; fax 03 85 84 54 30; campingdemontrouant@wanadoo.fr]** Fr N79 at Trivy take D41 to Dompierre-les-Ormes & Montmelard, then Gibles. Site sp fr Gibles. Sm, hdg/mkd pitch, pt sl, pt shd; htd wc; chem disp; shwrs inc; el pnts (6A) €5; lndtte (inc dryer); basic shop & 2km; rest 1.5km; snacks; bar; BBQ; playgrnd; htd pool; paddling pool; fishing lake; tennis; entment; TV; dogs; phone; Eng spkn; adv bkg; v quiet. "Pretty location; charming owners; unsuitable lge o'fits/m'vans due steep rds; some pitches sm & tight access; gd." ♦ 1 Jun-8 Sep. € 23.00 (CChq acc) 2008*

CLAYETTE, LA *9A2* (500m E Urban) *46.29159, 4.32020* **Camping des Bruyères (formerly Municipal), 9 Route de Gibles, 71800 La Clayette [03 85 28 09 15; fax 03 85 28 17 16; aquadis1@wanadoo.fr; www.aquadis-loisirs.com]** Site on D79, 100m fr D987 & lake. Med, hdg/mkd pitch, hdstg, pt sl, shd; htd wc; chem disp; mv service pnt; shwrs inc; el pnts (6A) inc; gas; lndtte; shops adj; tradsmn; snacks, bar 500m; BBQ; playgrnd; htd pool adj Jun-Aug; boating; tennis; games area; entmnt; 10% statics; dogs €1.60; phone; poss cr; adv bkg; quiet; CCI. "Excel, clean, pleasant & well-maintained site; o'looks lake & chateau; friendly, helpful staff; gd-sized pitches, mostly sloping; many wine cellars." ♦ 1 Apr-31 Oct. € 14.60 2007*

CLAYETTE, LA *9A2* (13km S Rural) *46.2011, 4.3391* **FFCC Camp Municipal Les Feuilles, Rue de Châtillon, 71170 Chauffailles [03 85 26 48 12; fax 03 85 26 55 02; campingchauffailles@orange.fr]** S fr La Clayette on D985 (dir Les Echarmeaux), turn R at camp sp down hill & cross Rv Botoret to site. Med, mkd pitch, hdstg, pt shd; htd wc; chem disp; mv service pnt; shwrs; el pnts (5A) inc; lndtte; supmkt 500m; playgrnd; pool adj; fishing; tennis; games rm; TV; Eng spkn; adv bkg ess; quiet; 10% red CCI. "Attractive site; popular with rallies May/June & Sep (poss noisy); gd san facs but hot water to shwrs & dishwashing only; easy walk to interesting town; sep m'van Aire de Service adj rear ent." 1 May-30 Sep. € 12.00 2009*

CLAYETTE, LA *9A2* (5km NW Rural) *46.30583, 4.26461* **Camping à la Ferme Les Noues, 71800 Vareilles [03 85 28 09 78]** Fr La Clayette on D989 to Vareilles, then foll site sp & sp 'fromage'. Sm, pt sl, pt shd; wc; chem disp; shwrs inc; el pnts; lndtte; quiet. "Excel CL-type site; friendly, helpful owners." 1 Apr-31 Oct. € 10.00 2006*

France

CLECY *3D1* (E Rural) *48.91366, -0.47399* **FFCC Camping Les Rochers des Parcs, La Cour, 14570 Clécy [02 31 69 70 36; fax 02 31 66 96 08; campingclecy@ocampings.com; www.ocampings.com]** Fr Condé take D562 dir Caen; turn R onto D133a sp Clécy & Le Vey; do not take turning to Clécy cent but cont downhill, past museum on L & then over bdge; turn R in 150m at campsite sp; site on R. Med, mkd pitch, some hdstg, pt sl, pt shd; wc; shwrs inc; el pnts (16A) €3.15; Indtte; shop 1km; tradsmn; snacks; playgrnd; fishing; canoeing; games area; some statics; dogs €1; phone; poss cr; quiet. "Lovely rvside situation; friendly staff; facs stretched high ssn, ltd & poss unclean low ssn; excel cent for walking." 1 Apr-30 Sep. € 12.00 (CChq acc) 2008*

CLELLES *9C3* (4km N Rural) *44.85118, 5.62478* **FFCC Camp Municipal de la Chabannerie, 38930 St Martin-de-Clelles [tel/fax 04 76 34 00 38; camping.chabannerie@yahoo.fr; www.camping-isere.fr]** D1075 (N75) fr Grenoble, after St Michel-les-Portes look for rest on R. Turn L after 300m to St Martin-de-Clelles, site sp. Site well sp fr N & S. Sm, mkd pitch, hdstg, terr, shd; wc; chem disp; baby facs; shwrs inc; el pnts (10A) €3; gas 5km; Indtte; shop 5km; rest; snacks; bar; no BBQs; playgrnd; pool; games area; TV rm; 4% statics; dogs €1.50; phone; Eng spkn; adv bkg; quiet; ccard acc; red low ssn/long stay/CCI. "Conv Vercours National Park & mountains; sm pitches & steep site rds, access diff lge o'fits; ltd facs low ssn; gd walking; v quiet site with 38 species of orchids in ssn." ♦ 1 May-30 Sep. € 15.00 2009*

CLEON D'ANDRAN *9D2* (Rural) *44.60985, 4.93715* **Camp Municipal Les Cigales, Rue de Piscine, 26450 Cléon-d'Andran [04 75 90 29 51 or 04 75 90 12 73 (Mairie); fax 04 75 90 43 73]** Fr A7 leave at junc 16 sp Privas/Crest. S fr Crest on D538. In 5km take D6. In 11km at Cléon-d'Andran turn L in vill, in 100m turn R. Sm, shd; wc (cont); shwrs inc; el pnts €2.50; Indtte; shop 500m; pool; quiet; CCI. 1 Jun-31 Aug. € 10.80 2006*

CLERE SUR LAYON see Vihiers *4G1*

CLEREY see Troyes *4E4*

CLERGOUX *7C4* (300m E Rural) *45.27871, 1.96566* **FFCC Camping La Petite Rivière, 19320 Clergoux [05 55 27 68 50; jcbakker@xs4all.nl; www.compumess.nl/lapetiteriviere]** Exit A89 junc 21 onto D1089. Go E until next rndabt, turn R & after approx 5km turn L onto D978 to Clergoux. Site on R just bef W end of vill. Or fr Tulle on D978 site in approx 20km, sp. Sm, mkd pitch, pt sl, pt shd; wc; chem disp; mv service pnt; baby facs; shwrs inc; el pnts (6A) €2.25; Indtte; tradsmn; lake sw & sand beach 1.5km; 20% statics; dogs €1.30; Eng spkn; adv bkg; quiet; red low ssn; CCI. "Helpful Dutch owner; 25 planned walks in area; excel." 1 Apr-15 Sep. € 10.20 2009*

CLERMONT EN ARGONNE *5D1* (6km SW Rural) *49.07665, 5.00285* **Camp Municipal Pierre Cochenet, 55120 Futeau [03 29 88 27 06 (Mairie)]** Leave A4 at Ste Ménéhould & proceed E on N3 for 9km to Les Islettes; turn S on D2 for 4km to Futeau; site behind church. Sm, pt shd; htd wc (some cont); chem disp (wc); shwrs inc; el pnts (10A) inc (poss rev pol); shops 4km; tradsmn; BBQ; dogs; phone; quiet bu church bells early am; CCI. "Site yourself; warden calls; gd for walking; vg NH." ♦ 1 Apr-1 Sep. € 10.00 2007*

⊞ **CLERMONT FERRAND** *9B1* (7km SE Rural) *45.70018, 3.16902* **Camping Le Clos Auroy, Rue de la Narse, 63670 Orcet [tel/fax 04 73 84 26 97; camping.le.clos.auroy@wanadoo.fr; www.camping-le-clos-auroy.com]** S on A75 take exit 5 sp Orcet; foll D213 to Orcet for 2km, at rndabt onto D52, take 1st L, site on R, sp. Med, hdg/mkd pitch, hdstg, terr, pt shd; htd wc; chem disp; mv service pnt; shwrs inc; el pnts (5-10A) €3.25-€4.75 (poss rev pol); gas; Indtte; sm shop 500m; tradsmn; snacks; bar; playgrnd; htd pool; paddling pool; rv fishing 500m; tennis; horseriding; entmnt; 15% statics; dogs €2; phone; Eng spkn; adv bkg; quiet; red low ssn/long stay; CCI. "Tidy, well-kept site; easy access; lge pitches, poss v high hedges; clean san facs, ltd low ssn; pitches by rv poss liable to flood; extra charge for sh stay m'vans; ltd fresh water points & diff to use for refill; vg winter site; interesting town; gd dog walks adj." ♦ € 19.00 2008*

CLERMONT FERRAND *9B1* (9km SE Urban) *45.74015, 3.22247* **Camp Municipal Le Pré des Laveuses, Rue des Laveuses, 63800 Cournon-d'Auvergne [04 73 84 81 30; fax 04 73 84 90 65; camping@cournon-auvergne.fr; www.cournon-auvergne.fr]** Fr S o'skts Clermont-Ferrand take D212 E to Cournon & foll sp in town; by Rv Allier, 1km E of Cournon. Lge, mkd pitch, pt shd; wc (some cont); chem disp; baby facs; shwrs inc; el pnts (5-10A) €3.30; Indtte; shop; supmkt nrby; snacks; bar; playgrnd; htd pool; slide paddling pool; rv sw/lake adj; fishing & boating; 40% statics; dogs €2.10; poss cr; Eng spkn; quiet low ssn; red low ssn; ccard acc; CCI. "Well-kept site - even low ssn; lge pitches; helpful manager; sports grnd adj; excel." ♦ 4 Apr-31 Oct. € 17.60 2009*

⊞ **CLERMONT FERRAND** *9B1* (15km SE Rural) *45.67887, 3.20454* **Camping La Font de Bleix, Le Lot, 63730 Les Martres-de-Veyre [04 73 39 26 49 or 06 87 75 42 74 (mob); fax 04 73 39 20 11; ailes_libres@infonie.fr]** Fr Clermont-Ferrand exit A75 junc 5. Turn E onto D213, then R onto D978 at rndabt & sharp L at camping sp to go thro vill. Site on L after traff lts over rlwy x-ing. Sm, mkd pitch, pt sl, unshd; wc (cont); chem disp; shwrs inc; el pnts (10A) €3.50; Indtte; shop 1km; snacks; rv adj; dogs €1.60; quiet; adv bkg; CCI. ♦ € 11.50 2009*

⊞ **CLERMONT FERRAND** *9B1* (6km SW Urban) *45.73866, 3.06168* **Camp Municipal Le Chanset, Ave Jean-Baptiste Marrou, 63122 Ceyrat [tel/fax 04 73 61 30 73 or 04 73 61 42 55 (Mairie); camping.lechanset@wanadoo.fr; www.campingdeceyrat63.com]** Exit A75 junc 2 onto D2089 (N189) dir Aubière/Beaumont. Foll sp Beaumont then in approx 7km at rndabt junc foll sp Ceyrat. Uphill into Ceyrat; curve R to traff lts; cross main rd & take L fork up hill. Site at top on R - turn poss diff so cont 50m for U-turn back to site. Lge, hdg/mkd pitch, terr, pt sl, pt shd; htd wc (some cont); chem disp; mv service pnt; baby facs; shwrs inc; el pnts (10A) €3.90 (poss rev pol); gas; lndtte; shop; rest; snacks; bar; BBQ; playgrnd; htd pool high ssn; games & TV rm; 10% statics; dogs €1.50; bus; phone; security barrier; poss cr; some Eng spkn; adv bkg; poss noisy when cr; red low ssn/long stay; ccard acc; CCI. "Excel views; busy site but vg for families; friendly staff; pool used by public at w/end (poss cr); some sm pitches; san facs old & poss unclean low ssn; gd base for Auvergne, Puy de Dôme & Volcania Park; conv a'route; unreliable opening in winter - phone ahead." ♦ € 12.70 2009*

CLERMONT FERRAND *9B1* (5km W Rural) *45.75845, 3.05453* **Camping Indigo Royat, Route de Gravenoire, 63130 Royat [04 73 35 97 05; fax 04 73 35 67 69; royat@camping-indigo.com; www.camping-indigo.com]** Site diff to find fr Clermont-Ferrand cent. Fr N, leave A71 at Clermont-Ferrand. Foll sp Chamalières/Royat, then sp Royat. Go under rlwy bdge & pass thermal park on L. At mini-rndabt go L & up hill. At statue, turn L & go up long hill. Look for site sp & turn R. Site on R. NB Do not go down steep rd with traff calming. NB Sat Nav directs up v narr rds & steep hills. Lge, mkd/hdstg pitch, terr, pt shd; htd wc; chem disp; mv service pnt; some serviced pitches; baby facs; shwrs inc; el pnts (6-10A) €4.60-6.80; gas; lndtte; sm shop; tradsmn; rest, snacks high ssn; bar; BBQ; playgrnd; htd pool; tennis; cycle hire; internet; entmnt; TV rm; some statics; dogs €4; phone; Eng spkn; adv bkg; quiet; ccard acc; red low ssn; CCI. "Excel, clean, spacious site; views at top levels over Clermont; vg clean san facs; conv touring base." ♦ 3 Apr-25 Oct. € 20.90 (CChq acc) 2009*

CLERMONT L'HERAULT *10F1* (7km SE Rural) *43.61450, 3.49221* **Camping Les Rivières, Route de la Sablière, 34800 Canet [04 67 96 75 53; fax 04 67 96 58 35; camping-lesrivieres@wanadoo.fr; www.camping-lesrivieres.com]** On D2 sp Clermont-l'Hérault/Canet. At Canet foll sp approx 2km. Med, hdg/mkd pitch, pt shd; wc; shwrs inc; el pnts (5A) €4; gas; lndtte; tradsmn; rest; snacks; playgrnd; pool; solarium; rv fishing; TV rm; 5% statics; sm dogs only €5; Eng spkn; adv bkg; quiet. "Well-laid out; nice pool with rest/bar; friendly; young, hardworking & helpful owners; gd area for touring; nr to Lac du Salagou; highly rec." ♦ 8 Apr-15 Sep. € 22.00 2007*

⊞ **CLERMONT L'HERAULT** *10F1* (5km NW Rural) *43.64491, 3.38982* **Camp Municipal du Lac du Salagou, 34800 Clermont-l'Hérault [04 67 96 13 13; fax 04 67 96 32 12; centretouristique@wanadoo.fr; www.le-salagou.fr]** Fr N9 S take D909 to Clermont-l'Hérault, foll sp to Lac du Salagou 1.5km after town sp. Fr by-pass foll sp Bédarieux. Well sp. Lge, mkd pitch, pt sl, pt shd; htd wc (some cont); chem disp; mv service pnt; shwrs inc; el pnts (5-10A) €2.80-3.40; lndtte; shops 4km; tradsmn; rest; snacks; BBQ; playgrnd; shgl beach & lake 300m; fishing; watersports; entmnt; TV; many statics; dogs €1.60; phone; poss cr; adv bkg; noise fr disco some nights; red low ssn; CCI. "Unique location; poss muddy low ssn & poss windy; facs dated; gd undeveloped beaches around lake." ♦ € 13.20 2009*

CLERY SUR SOMME see Péronne *3C3*

CLISSON *2H4* (S Urban) *47.09582, -1.28216* **Camp Municipal du Vieux Moulin, Rue de la Fontaine Câlin, Route de Nantes, 44190 Clisson [02 40 54 44 48 or 02 40 54 02 95 (LS)]** 1km NW of Clisson cent on main rd to Nantes, at rndabt. Look for old windmill nr ent on L of rd. Leclerc hypmkt on opp side of rd; site sp fr town cent. Narr ent. Sm, hdg pitch, pt sl, pt shd; wc; chem disp; shwrs inc; el pnts (6A) €3; hypmkt, rest, snacks & bar 500m; tradsmn; fishing, tennis, horseriding adj; boating; dogs €1.12; phone (card only); Eng spkn; adv bkg; quiet but some rd noise. "Gd municipal site; lge pitches; gd clean san facs; if office clsd pitch self, book in later; picturesque town 15 min walk; mkd walks." 15 Apr-15 Oct. € 14.55 2009*

CLOYES SUR LE LOIR *4F2* (1km N Rural) *48.00240, 1.23304* **Parc de Loisirs Le Val Fleuri, Route de Montigny, 28220 Cloyes-sur-le-Loir [02 37 98 50 53; fax 02 37 98 33 84; info@parc-de-loisirs.com; www.val-fleuri.fr]** Located on L bank of Rv Loir off N10; site sp. Med, hdg pitch, pt shd; wc (some cont); chem disp; shwrs inc; el pnts (5A) inc; shop; rest; snacks; bar; playgrnd; pool; waterslide; cycle hire; 50% statics; dogs €1.80; adv bkg; quiet. "Facs gd for children but ltd low ssn; well-run, pleasant site in wooded valley; site fees inc use of sm leisure park, pedaloes & rowing boats on Rv Loir." 15 Mar-15 Nov. € 24.60 2009*

CLOYES SUR LE LOIR *4F2* (2km S Rural) *47.97326, 1.23292* **FFCC Aire Naturelle Camping Les Fouquets (Fetter), 41160 St Jean-Froidmentel [02 54 82 66 97; lesfouquets@aol.com]** Off N10 twd Vendôme. Sp Les Fouquets 200m SE of N10. Sm, shd; wc; shwrs inc; el pnts (15A) inc; lndry rm; shop, rest 2km; pool; fishing, tennis & sailing 2km; dogs €1; quiet; CCI. "Lovely family-run site in woodland; friendly, welcoming owner; nice pool." ♦ 1 Apr-30 Sep. € 12.00 2009*

France

CLUNY *9A2* (500m E Rural) *46.43138, 4.66695* **Camp Municipal St Vital, Rue de Griottons, 71250 Cluny [tel/fax 03 85 59 08 34; cluny-camping@wanadoo.fr]** Fr Cluny take D15 sp Azé, cross narr rv bdge. Site 1st R adj to pool. Lge, mkd pitch, sl, pt shd; htd wc; chem disp; shwrs inc; el pnts (6A) €3.25 (poss rev pol); gas; Indtte; shops 500m; playgrnd; pool adj (free to campers); poss cr; adv bkg rec high ssn; frequent rlwy noise daytime. "Well-run, tidy site; helpful staff; clean san facs; cycle & walking rte adj (Voie Verte); interesting town; excel, reliable site." ♦ 1 May-1 Oct. € 12.00 2009*

CLUNY *9A2* (10km S Rural) *46.81195, 6.30285* **Camp Municipal Le Lac de St Point-Lamartine, 8 Rue du Port, 71520 St Point [03 81 69 61 64 or 03 81 69 62 08 (Mairie); camping-saintpointlac@wanadoo.fr; www.camping-saint pointlac.com]** Turn S off N79, Mâcon/Paray-le-Monial rd, turn L bef Ste Cécile on D22; site sp at junc; site 100m on R after St Point vill. Med, hdg/mkd pitch, pt terr, pt sl (gd blocks needed), pt shd; htd wc; chem disp; mv service pnt; shwrs inc; el pnts (16A) inc; gas 800m; Indtte; shop 800m; rest; snacks; bar; BBQ; playgrnd; TV; lake sw adj; fishing; boat hire; tennis 4km; 30% statics; dogs; phone; adv bkg; quiet; CCI. "Some sm pitches for long o'fits; poss no hot water for washing up; ltd facs low ssn; Cluny attractive town & abbey; lovely scenery & pleasant lake; on edge of Beaujolais; sp walks fr site; unreliable opening dates low ssn." 1 May-30 Sep. € 14.50 (4 persons) 2008*

CLUNY *9A2* (11km NW Rural) *46.51775, 4.59865* **Camp Municipal de la Clochette, Place de la Clochette, 71250 Salornay-sur-Guye [03 85 59 90 11; fax 03 85 59 47 52; mairie.salornay@wanadoo.fr]** Sp fr N or S on D980; turn E on D14 sp Cormatin & Taizé. Ent opp PO within 300m. Med, mkd pitch, pt shd; wc; shwrs €1; chem disp; mv service pnt; el pnts (8-10A) €2-3; Indry rm; shop adj; BBQ; playgrnd; rv adj; fishing; adv bkg; quiet; CCI. "Pleasant, tidy site on sm rv & mill pond; site yourself, recep open morning & evening; well sp walks around vill; rvside pitches poss subject to flooding." 10 May-12 Sep. € 6.00 2009*

CLUSAZ, LA *9B3* (6km N Rural) *45.94021, 6.44245* **Camping Le Clos du Pin, 74450 Le Grand-Bornand [tel/fax 04 50 02 70 57; contact@le-clos-du-pin.com; www.le-clos-du-pin.com]** Foll sps fr La Clusaz &/or St Jean-de-Sixte to Grand Bornand. Thro vill dir Vallée du Bouchet; site on R in 1km. Med, mkd pitch, unshd; htd wc; chem disp; shwrs inc; el pnts (2-10A) €2.90-5; gas 1km; Indtte; shops 1km; BBQ; playgrnd; rv sw & fishing 100m; pool 1km; TV/games rm; 30% statics; dogs €1.30; adv bkg; quiet; ccard acc; CCI. "Base for ski stn; ski & boot rm; friendly owner; clean san facs; high fees in winter; excel." ♦ 15 Jun-20 Sep & 1 Dec-10 May. € 13.00 2007*

CLUSAZ, LA *9B3* (6km N Rural) *45.93972, 6.42777* **Camping L'Escale, 74450 Le Grand-Bornand [04 50 02 20 69; fax 04 50 02 36 04; contact@campinglescale.com; www.campinglescale.com]** Exit A41 junc 17 onto D16/D909 E dir La Clusaz. At St Jean-de-Sixt turn L at rndabt sp Le Grand Bornand. After 1.5km foll camping sp on main rd & at junc turn R sp for site & 'Vallée du Bouchet'. Site is 1st exit R at rndabt at end of this rd. D4 S fr Cluses not rec while towing as v steep & winding. Med, mkd pitch, pt sl, terr, pt shd; htd wc; chem disp; mv service pnt; serviced pitch in summer; baby facs; shwrs inc; el pnts (10A) inc (poss rev pol); gas; Indtte; shop; tradsmn; rest; snacks; bar; BBQ; playgrnd; 2 pools (1 htd, covrd); paddling pool; fishing; wintersports; cycle hire 200m; tennis; archery; wifi; games/TV rm; 20% statics; dogs €2.23; skibus; poss cr; adv bkg ess; ccard acc; red low ssn; CCI. "Scenic area; family-run site; vg rest; free use htd ski/boot rm in winter; boggy in wet weather; vg mkt Wed." ♦ 21 May-26 Sep & 4 Jan-18 Apr. € 29.40 ABS - M07 2009*

CLUSAZ, LA *9B3* (12km NE) *46.00449, 6.39449* **Camp Municipal Les Marronniers, 74130 Le Petit-Bornand-Les-Glieres [04 50 03 54 74; maptbo@mairie-petit-bornand.fr; www.mairie-petit-bornand.fr]** E fr Annecy on D909 for 28km to St Jean-de-Sixt. N on D4 for 1km, turn W on D12 for 11km to Le Petit Bornand. Site thro vill on L. Sm, pt sl, pt shd; wc; chem disp; shwrs €0.70; el pnts (3A) €2.50; Indtte; fishing; tennis nr; dogs €1; adv bkg; quiet; CCI. "Vg site in National Park; shop 500m walk uphill." 1 Jun-15 Sep. € 9.20 2008*

CLUSAZ, LA *9B3* (2km E Rural) *45.90921, 6.45208* **Camping Le Plan du Fernuy, 1800 Route des Confins, 74220 La Clusaz [04 50 02 44 75; fax 04 50 32 67 02; info@plandufernuy.com; www.plandufernuy.com or www.camping-franceloc.fr]** Fr Annecy take D909 to La Clusaz (32km). Turn L for Les Confins & site on R in 2km. Med, mkd pitch, pt sl, unshd; wc; chem disp; shwrs inc; baby rm; el pnts (13A) inc; gas; lndtte; shop; snacks; bar; playgrnd; htd, covrd pool; paddling pool; wifi; TV; some statics; dogs €2.20; free ski bus; poss cr; quiet. "Site at 1200m alt; excel site & facs; poss diff lge o'fits." ♦ 17 Jun-3 Sep & 17 Dec-30 Apr. € 27.70 2006*

CLUSES *9A3* (1km N Urban) *46.06896, 6.57390* **Camping La Corbaz, Ave des Glières, 74300 Cluses [04 50 98 44 03; fax 04 50 96 02 15; camping.lacorbaz@wanadoo.fr; www.camping-lacorbaz.com]** Take D1205 (N205) W fr Chamonix or fr Annecy D1203 (N203) NE to Bonneville & D1205 E to Cluses; take D902 N dir Taninges; after x-ing rlwy turn L onto D19 beside rlwy; site on R in 500m. Med, pt shd; htd wc; chem disp; mv service pnt; shwrs; el pnts (4-10A) €2.50; shop; rest; bar; playgrnd; pool; lake sw 2km; TV; 70% statics; dogs €1.50; adv bkg; quiet but some rd & rlwy noise. "Excel touring base; pleasant park setting; lge pitches; helpful staff; facs dated but clean; conv A40." 1 Apr-15 Oct. € 14.50 2008*

COEX *2H4* (2.5km W Rural) *46.67679, -1.76899* **Camping La Ferme du Latois, 85220 Coëx [02 51 54 67 30; fax 02 51 60 02 14; info@rcn-lafermedulatois.fr; www.rcn-campings.fr]** Exit D948 at Aizenay onto D6 dir St Gilles-Croix-de-Vie; at Coëx take D40 SW sp Brétignolles; site in 1.5km on L. Lgd, pt shd; htd wc; chem disp; shwrs inc; el pnts inc (poss rev pol); lndry rm; shop; tradsmn; rest; snacks; bar; BBQ (gas); playgrnd; pool; lake fishing; cycle hire; games area; games rm; wifi; 20% statics; dogs €5; phone; Eng spkn; adv bkg; quiet; red low ssn. "Spacious pitches; cycle rtes adj; conv Lac du Jaunay & Lac du Gué-Gorand; excel - a gem." ♦ 11 Apr-10 Oct. € 43.50 2008*

COGNAC *7B2* (200m N Urban) **Aire Communautaire, Place de la Levade, Quartier St Jaques, 16700 Cognac [05 45 36 64 30; contact@cc-cognac.fr]** M'vans only. N fr Cognac, cross rv bdge & foll m'van sp on L. Opp Hennessy Cognac House. Chem disp, mv service pnt, el pnts; lndtte; shop; rest. "Free NH adj rv." 1 Jun-15 Sep. 2006*

COGNAC *7B2* (2.5km NE Rural) *45.70906, -0.31287* **Camping de Cognac, Blvd de Châtenay, 16100 Cognac [05 45 32 13 32 or 05 45 36 64 30 (LS); fax 05 45 32 15 82; info@campingdecognac.com; www.campingdecognac.com]** Foll 'Camping' sp fr town cent, on R of D24 by Rv Charente just S of rv. Take care ent barrier. Poor sp fr town cent. Med, hdg/mkd pitch, pt shd; wc (some cont); chem disp; mv service pnt; shwrs inc; el pnts (6A) inc (poss long leads req); lndtte; shop high ssn & 2km; tradsmn; rest, snacks high ssn; bar; BBQ; playgrnd; htd pool; rv boating & fishing; dogs €1.50; phone; poss cr; Eng spkn; adv bkg; rd noise; ccard acc; red long stay/low ssn; CCI. "Excel lge park with many facs; dated san facs; gates clsd 2200-0700; no twin axles; footpath to town; conv Cognac distilleries (vouchers fr site recep)." ♦ 25 Apr-30 Sep. € 20.00 2008*

COGNAC *7B2* (10km E Rural) *45.67160, -0.22718* **Camping du Port (formerly Municipal), 16200 Bourg-Charente [06 03 98 60 19 (mob)]** Exit N141 onto D158 dir Bourg-Charente; turn L in 800m & site on R. Site sp fr D158. Chicane-type ent gates. Sm, pt sl, pt shd; wc (some cont); chem disp; mv service pnt; shwrs; el pnts (6A) €2.50; rest & shop 500m; fishing; poss cr; ccard acc; red long stay. "Delightful little site on banks of Rv Charante; facs basic but clean, poss stretched high ssn; site on 2 levels, lower one sl; gd walks & cycle path to Jarnac & Cognac; gd." 15 Jun-15 Sep. € 7.50 2009*

COGNAC *7B2* (14km E Urban) *45.67606, -0.17349* **FFCC Camping de l'Ile Madame, 16200 Jarnac [05 45 81 18 54 or 05 45 81 68 02; fax 05 45 81 24 98; camping.jarnac@wanadoo.fr; www.camping-jarnac.com]** Turn E at S end of rv bdge at S end of town. Fr Angoulême on N141, exit junc sp 'Jarnac Est'; foll sp Jarnac thro 2 rndabts into Jarnac; at traff lts (LH lane) turn L sp Tourist Info/Camping; cross rv brge & immed turn L to site. Lge, pt shd; wc; shwrs inc; el pnts (6-10A) €2.60 (rev pol); lndtte; shops & rest adj; playgrnd; pool inc; games area; golf, canoe & cycle hire nrby; entmnt; TV; dogs €0.50; poss cr; adv bkg; poss noise fr adj sports ground & disco; red long stay/low ssn; CCI. "Pleasant, well-run site; gd sized pitches; san facs clean but update needed; no twin-axles; easy walk into Jarnac with shops & rests; gd walks along rv; nr Courvoisier bottling plant." 1 Apr-30 Sep. € 13.00 2009*

The opening dates and prices on this campsite have changed. I'll send a site report form to the Club for the next edition of the guide.

⊞ **COGNAC** *7B2* (8km S Rural) **Camping Le Chiron (Chainier), Le Chiron, Celles, 16130 Salles-d'Angles [05 45 83 72 79; fax 05 45 83 64 80; mchainier@voila.fr]** Fr Cognac D731 Barbezieux to Salles-d'Angles, R at bottom hill then in 3km turn L & 1km on R (foll Chambres d'Hôtes sps). Sm, pt sl, pt shd; htd wc (1 cont); chem disp; shwrs inc; el pnts (10A) €4 (rev pol); shop 3km; no dogs; Eng spkn; quiet; ccard not acc. "Vg; meals avail at farm." € 10.00 2009*

COGNAC LA FORET *7B3* (1.5km W Rural) *45.82494, 0.99674* **Camping des Alouettes, Les Alouettes, 87310 Cognac-la-Forêt [05 55 03 26 93; info@camping-des-alouttes.com; www.camping-des-alouettes.com]** Fr Aixe-sur-Vienne on D10, site W of Cognac-la-Forêt on D10, sp to L. Med, hdg pitch, pt shd; wc; chem disp; shwrs inc; el pnts (5-10A) €2-3; lndtte; shop 1.5km; shop 1km; tradsmn; rest; snacks; bar; BBQ; playgrnd; lake sw & sand beach 1km; tennis 700m; 8% statics; dogs €1; Eng spkn; adv bkg; quiet; CCI. "Beautiful location; friendly owners; conv war vill Oradour-sur-Glane & Richard Lion Heart sites; vg site & facs." ♦ 1 Apr-1 Oct. € 13.60 2009*

See advertisement

France

COGNIN LES GORGES *9C3* (E Rural) **Aire Naturelle La Chatonnière (Boucher), Route de Malleval, 38470 Cognin-les-Gorges [04 76 38 18 76; info@la-chato.com; www.la-chato.com]** Exit A49 junc 10 S onto N532, turn 1st L after Cognin-les-Gorges sp at service stn. Fr vill cent, take 1st R past church. In 50m turn L at stop sp, site 100m on L. Sm, pt shd; wc; chem disp; chem disp; mv service pnt; baby facs; shwrs inc; el pnts (10A) €3 (rev pol); shop 500m; tradsmn; pool 6km; no statics; dogs; bus; phone 100m; Eng spkn; adv bkg; quiet; red +7 days; CCI. "Welcoming, helpful owners; bread baked on site; meals avail; picturesque mountain setting; conv Grenoble & Vercours." Jun-Sep. € 15.00 2008*

COLLE SUR LOUP, LA see Cagnes sur Mer *10E4*

COLLIAS see Remoulins *10E2*

COLMAR *6F3* (2km E Urban) *48.07942, 7.38665* **Camping de l'Ill, 1 Allée de Camping, 68180 Horbourg-Wihr [tel/fax 03 89 41 15 94; campingdelill@calixo.net; www.campingdelill.com]** Exit A35 junc 25 onto D415, foll Freibourg sp. At 2nd rndabt turn L to Colmar cent, site on L bef bdge. Lge, hdg/mkd pitch, hdstg, pt sl, terr, shd; htd wc; chem disp; mv service pnt; shwrs; el pnts (3-10A) €3.30-4.30 (poss rev pol); Indtte (inc dryer); shop & tradsmn (high ssn); supmkt nr; rest; snacks & bar (high ssn); playgrnd; cycle hire; wifi; 10% statics; dogs €1.90; bus to city cent; poss cr; some Eng spkn; adv bkg; noise fr a'route; ccard acc (over €20); CCI. "Lovely, clean, rvside site; friendly staff; excel san facs; some pitches req steel pegs; sep area for NH; gd rest." ♦ 21 Mar-21 Dec. € 14.40 2009*

COLMAR *6F3* (7km S Rural) *48.01613, 7.34983* **Camping Clair Vacances, Route de Herrlisheim, 68127 Ste Croix-en-Plaine [03 89 49 27 28; fax 03 89 49 31 37; clairvacances@wanadoo.fr; www.clairvacances.com]** Exit D83 (N83) at sp Herrlisheim onto D1 bis. Take 2nd rd to vill sp camping, foll site sp thro vill. NB Rd thru vill narr with traff calming bollards. Fr A35 turn off at junc 27 sp Herrlisheim/Ste Croix-en-Plaine onto D1 dir Herrlisheim to site in 1km. Med, hdg/mkd pitch, some hdstg, pt shd; htd wc; chem disp; mv service pnt; baby facs; shwrs inc; el pnts (4-13A) €3-5 (long lead poss req); gas; service wash; shop 2km; tradsmn; snacks high ssn; BBQ (no charcoal); playgrnd; htd pool; paddling pool; cycle hire; 10% statics; no dogs; phone; poss cr; Eng spkn; adv bkg; quiet; ccard acc; red low ssn; CCI. "Beautiful site, well-maintained & supervised; helpful, friendly owners; gd size pitches; excel, clean san facs; gd touring base Alsace wine rte; excel." ♦ 1 Apr-17 Oct. € 20.00 2009*

See advertisement

COLMAR *6F3* (7km SW Rural) *48.04238, 7.29935* **Camp Municipal Les Trois Châteaux, 10 Rue du Bassin, 68420 Eguisheim [03 89 23 19 39; fax 03 89 24 10 19; camping.eguisheim@wanadoo.fr; www.camping-eguisheim.fr]** Foll D83 (N83) S (Colmar by-pass) R at sp Eguisheim. R into vill to site at top of vill, foll camp sp. Med, mkd pitch, pt sl, terr, pt shd; wc; chem disp; mv service pnt; shwrs inc; el pnts (6-10A) €3-5 (poss rev pol); gas; Indtte; shops, rest & bars in vill 300m; hypmkt 5km; playgrnd; dogs €2; phone adj; poss cr; clsd 1230-1400; adv bkg (tel 2 days bef arr); poss noisy; ccard acc; red low ssn; CCI. "Populer, well-run, busy site; sm pitches poss cramped; no c'vans over 7m (inc draw bar); mv pitches flat but some c'van pitches sl & poss diff; weekly wine-tasting events; stork park adj; rec arr early; excel." ♦ 1 Apr-18 Oct. € 13.00 2009*

COLMAR *6F3* (7km W Urban) *48.08517, 7.27253* **FFCC Camp Municipal Les Cigognes, Quai de la Gare, 68230 Turckheim [03 89 27 02 00; fax 03 89 80 86 93; ot.turckheim@wanadoo.fr; www.camping-turckheim.com]** Fr D83 (N83) twd Turchkeim turn W onto D11 to Turckheim. On ent vill, turn immed L down 1-way rd after x-ing rlwy lines. Do not cross rv bdge. Site on L bef bdge, adj stadium. Med, hdg pitch, pt shd; wc; chem disp; mv service pnt; baby facs; shwrs inc; el pnts (5-10A) €3.20-5; Indtte; shop 500m; playgrnd; entmnt; TV; 50% statics; dogs €1.55; bus 500m; train 250m; poss cr; quiet; red low ssn; CCI. "Lovely site with spacious pitches; gd san facs, ltd low ssn; cycle rtes nr; resident storks; short walk to interesting, beautiful old vill with rests; on wine route; highly rec." ♦ 15 Mar-31 Oct. € 11.10 2009*

COLMARS *9D4* (400m S Rural) *44.17731, 6.62151* **Aire Naturelle Les Pommiers, Chemin des Mélèzes, 04370 Colmars-les-Alpes [04 92 83 41 56; fax 04 92 83 40 86; contact@camping-pommier.com; www.camping-pommier.com]** Fr N on D908 on ent Colmars take 1st R over rd bdge & foll site sp. Sm, pt terr, pt shd; wc (some cont); chem disp; mv service pnt; shwrs inc; el pnts (10A) €2; Indtte; shop 400m; tradsmn; rest, snacks, bar 400m; BBQ; htd pool 800m; dogs €1; phone; adv bkg; CCI. "Beautifully-situated, well-maintained CL-type site nr medieval town; friendly owner; gd walking." ♦ 1 May-1 Oct. € 12.00 2008*

COLMARS *9D4* (1km S Rural) *44.17472, 6.61629* **Camping Le Bois Joly, Chemin des Buissières, 04370 Colmars-les-Alpes [04 92 83 40 40; fax 04 92 83 50 60; camping-le-bois-joly@club-internet.fr; www.colmars-les-alpes.fr]** Fr S on D955 & D908 twds Colmars, go thro Beauvezer & Villars-Colmars. Ignore two other sites en rte. Site sp. Sm, mkd, hdstg, shd; wc (some cont); chem disp (wc); mv service pnt; shwrs inc; el pnts (6A) €2.43; gas; Indtte; rest, snacks, bar & shop 1km; BBQ; tradsmn high ssn; rv fishing adj; no dogs; phone; adv bkg; quiet; CCI. "Well-kept wooded site with gd atmosphere; gd facs; ideal base for walking in Haute Provence; friendly owners." 1 May-1 Oct. € 11.10 2008*

COLMARS *9D4* (2km SW Rural) *44.19148, 6.59690* **Camping Le Haut Verdon, 04370 Villars-Colmars [04 92 83 40 09; fax 04 92 83 56 61; campinglehautverdon@wanadoo.fr; www.lehautverdon.com]** Only app fr S on D955 & D908 fr St André-les-Alps thro Beauvezer. Clearly sp on ent Villars-Colmars on R. (Do not confuse with Municipal site approx 5km bef this site). Med, hdg/mkd pitch, pt shd; htd wc; chem disp; mv service pnt; shwrs inc; el pnts (6-10A) €3-4; gas; Indtte; shop & 2km; tradsmn; rest 1km; snacks; bar; playgrnd; pool; rv fishing; TV rm; dogs €2; poss cr; Eng spkn; adv bkg; quiet; CCI. "Superb setting on Rv Verdon; gd, clean san facs; helpful staff; conv Colmars, flower meadows, Allos Lake." ♦ 3 May-14 Sep. € 25.00 2007*

COMBOURG *2E4* (8km NE Rural) *48.45304, -1.65031* **Camping Le Bois Coudrais, 35270 Cuguen [02 99 73 27 45; fax 02 99 73 13 08; info@vacancebretagne.com; www.vacancebretagne.com]** Fr Combourg take D796 twd Pleine-Fougères, 5km out of Combourg turn L on D83 to Cuguen; 500m past Cuguen, turn L, site sp. Or fr Dol-de-Bretagne, take D795 then turn L onto D9 to Cuguen. Sm, hdg/mkd pitch, pt sl, pt shd; wc; chem disp; shwrs inc; el pnts (10A) €3; shop 500m; snacks; bar; BBQ; playgrnd; pool; fishing, watersports, golf, zoo, adventure park nr; cycle hire; wifi; dogs €1; Eng spkn; adv bkg; v quiet; red long stay; no ccard acc; CCI. "CL-type site; friendly British owners; gd clean facs; great for young children; sm animal-petting area; gd touring base." ♦ 1 Apr-30 Sep. € 16.00 2009*

COMBOURG *2E4* (1.5km SE Rural) *48.40449, -1.74271* **Camp Municipal Le Vieux Châtel, Route de Lanrigan, 35270 Combourg [02 99 73 07 03; fax 02 99 73 29 66; ot@combourg.org]** Fr W, N & E foll sp fr town cent. Fr S on D795, turn R at lake. Site on L in approx 500m. Med, hdg/mkd pitch, pt shd; wc; chem disp; shwrs; el pnts (5A) €1.85; Indtte; shop, rest, snacks, bar 500m; BBQ; playgrnd; htd pool 1km; lake fishing nrby; phone; Eng spkn; adv bkg; quiet; CCI. "Forests, chateaux & churches nrby; 20 mins to Emerald Coast; castle in Combourg." 1 Jun-15 Sep. € 8.50 2006*

COMBOURG *2E4* (6km SW Rural) *48.38090, -1.83290* **FFCC Camping Domaine du Logis, 35190 La Chapelle-aux-Filtzméens [02 99 45 25 45 or 06 85 78 69 71 (mob); fax 02 99 45 30 40; domainedulogis@wanadoo.fr; www.domainedulogis.com]** Fr N176 at junc for Dol-de-Bretagne branch R onto D155 sp Dol & take D795 S to Combourg. Then take D13 twd St Domineuc, go thro La Chapelle-aux-Filtzméens & site on R in 1km. Lge, hdg/mkd pitch, pt shd; wc; chem disp; mv service pnt; shwrs inc; el pnts (10A) inc; gas; Indtte; sm shop & 5km; tradsmn; rest; snacks; bar; BBQ; playgrnd; 2 htd pools; sand beach 20km; fitness rm; canoes 800m; fishing nr; cycle hire; golf 15km; games area; games rm; entmnt; wifi; TV rm; 10% statics; dogs €2 (some breeds not acc - check with site); phone; Eng spkn; adv bkg; quiet; ccard acc; red low ssn/long stay/CCI. "Helpful staff; new san facs planned (2010); conv St Malo, Mont St Michel, Dinan & Channel Islands; mkt in Combourg Mon; excel." ♦ 1 Apr-31 Oct. € 27.40 (CChq acc) ABS - B02 2009*

This is a wonderful site.

I'll fill in a report online and let the Club know – www.caravanclub.co.uk/europereport

COMBRIT STE MARINE see Bénodet *2F2*

COMPEYRE see Millau *10E1*

COMPREIGNAC *7B3* (2.5km N Rural) *46.01402, 1.27814* **Camp Municipal de Montimbert, 87140 Compreignac [05 55 71 04 49 or 05 55 71 00 23 (Mairie)]** S on A20 to Limoges, turn W at exit 26 Le Crouzill. Foll D5 W to Compreignac, turn N by church onto D60, fork L, foll sp 'Montimbert' for site. Sm, pt sl, pt shd; wc; chem disp; shwrs inc; el pnts (5A) (poss rev pol); shop in vill; playgrnd; lake sw, fishing & boating 1km; CCI. "Facs ltd; unreliable opening dates." 1 Jun-15 Sep. 2008*

Campsite le Cabellou Plage
www.le-cabellou-plage.com
A peninsula in front of Concarneau
South Britany
Tél : 00 33 2 98 97 37 41

COMPREIGNAC *7B3* (6km N Rural) *46.03282, 1.29559* **Camping Santrop, Lac de St-Pardoux, 87640 Razès [05 55 71 08 08 or 05 55 71 04 40 (LS); fax 05 55 71 23 93; lacsaintpardoux@wanadoo.fr; www.lac-saint-pardoux.com]** N fr Limoges on A20, exit junc 25 Razès, sp Lac de St Pardoux; foll sp 4km to site. Lge, hdg pitch, pt sl, shd; wc; baby facs; shwrs inc; el pnts (16A) €3.80; Indtte (inc dryer); shop; rest; bar; playgrnd; pool; waterslide; lake adj; watersports; games area; entmnt; TV rm; dogs €1.10; poss cr; Eng spkn; poss noisy. "Popular, busy site on lake beach; random pitching under trees in woodland; gd rest on lakeside; poss late night noise fr revellers on beach; pitches unkempt & site tired end ssn (2009)." 1 May-20 Sep. € 16.40 2009*

CONCARNEAU *2F2* (3km W Coastal) *47.88910, -3.94070* **Camping Les Prés Verts, Kernous-Plage, 29186 Concarneau [02 98 97 09 74; fax 02 98 97 32 06; info@presverts.com; www.presverts.com]** Exit N165 onto D70 dir Concarneau. At rndabt by Leclerc supmkt foll sp 'Centre Ville' (Town Centre) with Leclerc on L. At x-rds with traff lts go strt over, then fork R into Rue de Kerneach & down slope. Bear L at 1st rndabt & R at next. Keep R to join coast rd & foll sp La Forêt-Fouesnant; pass Hôtel Océans; site 3rd rd on L in 1.5km. Med, hdg/mkd pitch, pt sl, pt shd; wc; chem disp; mv service pnt; serviced pitch; shwrs inc; el pnts (6A) inc (poss rev pol & long lead req); gas 2km; Indtte; shop; rest 3km; BBQ (charcoal/gas); playgrnd; htd pool; paddling pool; dir access to sand beach 300m; sailing 1km; horseriding 1km; games rm; 10% statics; dogs €1.70; c'vans over 8m not acc high ssn; poss cr; adv bkg; quiet; ccard acc; red low ssn. "Friendly staff; gd facs, ltd low ssn & poss unkempt; mkt Mon & Fri; gd touring base." 15 Apr-30 Sep. € 24.90 ABS - B24 2009*

I'm going to fill in some site report forms and post them off to the Club; we could win a ferry crossing – it's here on page 12.

CONCARNEAU *2F2* (2km S Coastal) *47.85628, -3.89999* **Camping Le Cabellou Plage, Ave de Cabellou, Kersaux, 29900 Concarneau [02 98 97 37 41; fax 02 98 60 78 57; info@le-cabellou-plage.com; www.le-cabellou-plage.com]** Fr N165 turn onto D70 dir Concarneau. At 5th rndabt (Leclerc supmkt) foll dir Tregunc. After Moros bdge take 2nd exit a next rndabt dir Le Cabellou-Plage. Site sp on L. Lge, mkd/hdg pitch, hdstg, pt shd; wc (cont); chem disp; baby facs; shwrs; el pnts (10A) inc; Indtte; tradsmn; snacks; bar; playgrnd; htd pool; paddling pool; sand beach adj; watersports; cycle hire; games area; games rm; wifi; TV; 16% statics; dogs €2; bus at site ent; Eng spkn; adv bkg; quiet; ccard acc. "Pleasant seaside site; vg san facs; gd walking fr site." ♦ 25 May-18 Sep. € 27.00 2009*

See advertisement above

CONCARNEAU *2F2* (1km NW Urban/Coastal) *47.8807, -3.9311* **Camping Les Sables Blancs, Ave du Dorlett, 29900 Concarneau [tel/fax 02 98 97 16 44; contact@camping-lessablesblancs.com; www.camping-lessablesblancs.com]** Exit N165 to Concarneau dir 'Centre Ville'. Then foll sp 'La Côte' 300m after traff lts. Site on R, sp. Med, hdg/mkd pitch, hdstg, pt sl, terr, pt shd; htd wc; chem disp; mv service pnt; baby facs; fam bthrm; shwrs inc; el pnts (10A) €3.50; Indtte; shop 1.5km; tradsmn; rest; snacks; bar; BBQ; playgrnd; htd pool; paddling pool; sand beach 300m; games area; games rm; wifi; entmnt; TV rm; 3% statics; dogs €1; phone; bus 300m; poss cr; Eng spkn; adv bkg; quiet; ccard acc; red low ssn/long stay; CCI. "Nice, cean, family site in woodland; many sm pitches; excel san facs; vg." ♦ 1 Apr-30 Oct. € 18.00 2009*

See advertisement opposite

CONCHES EN OUCHE *3D2* (8km NE Urban) *49.00228, 1.03462* **Camping Les Sapins, 2 La Mare Hue, 27190 La Bonneville-sur-Iton [02 32 37 11 03 or 06 29 98 15 17 (mob); arlette.mercier@wanadoo.fr; www.labonnevillesuriton.fr]** Fr Evreux W on D830 dir Conches-en-Ouche; site on R in 6km; sp. Sm, pt shd; wc; no chem disp; shwrs; el pnts (6A) €4.50; Indtte; shop; snacks; playgrnd; fishing; poss cr; quiet. "NH only; rv 900m, lake 1km." 14 Feb-14 Nov. € 14.00 2009*

CONCORET *2F3* (300m S Rural) *48.06086, -2.20495* **Camp Municipal du Val-aux-Fées, Rue Renan-le-Cunff, 56430 Concoret [02 97 22 64 82 or 02 97 22 61 19 (Mairie); fax 02 97 22 93 17; mairie-concoret@wanadoo.fr; www.cc-mauron-broceliande.com]** Site sp fr cent of Concoret. Lge, mkd pitch, pt sl, pt shd; wc; chem disp (wc); mv service pnt; shwrs inc; el pnts (10A) €2.35; shops 500m; playgrnd; fishing; tennis; 5% statics; dogs; Eng spkn; quiet. "V basic; san facs clean but dated, poss stretched high ssn; 'Enchanted Forest' of King Arthur adj; gd." 28 Mar-30 Sep. € 8.60 2007*

CONDAMINE CHATELARD, LA *9D4* (1km W Rural) *44.46487, 6.75247* **Camping Base de Loisirs Champ Félèze, 04530 La Condamine-Châtelard [04 92 84 39 39; fax 04 92 84 37 90; syflor@infonie.fr]** 15 km NE of Barcelonnette on D900. Lge sp on D900 visible fr rd. Sm, pt shd; wc; chem disp; serviced pitch; shwrs inc; el pnts (4-6A) €2.50-3.50; Indtte; shops 1km; rest; snacks; bar; BBQ; playgrnd; lake & rv adj; canoe hire; 5% statics; dogs €0.50; Eng spkn; adv bkg; quiet; CCI. "Gd site; lge pitches; easy access to sm private lake; gd base for touring Alps, fishing & walking." 15 Jun-15 Sep. € 12.70 2006*

CONDE SUR NOIREAU *3D1* (10km E Rural) *48.87142, -0.41104* **Camp Municipal, Rue du Stade René Vallée, 14690 Pont-d'Ouilly [02 31 69 80 20 or 02 31 69 46 12]** Fr Cherbourg take N13 to Vire, D512 for Condé-sur-Noireau & D562/D1 twd Falaise to site in 11km on W side of vill. On ent Pont-d'Ouilly turn R, site bef bdge over rv. Well sp in vill. Med, hdg/mkd pitch, pt sl, pt shd; wc (some cont); own san rec; chem disp; shwrs inc; el pnts (7A) €2.50; shops, rest, snacks, bar in vill; BBQ; playgrnd; tennis; canoeing & leisure cent adj; phone; poss cr; adv bkg; quiet; CCI. "Gd walking; conv WW2 battle areas; facs poss stretched high ssn." Easter-15 Sep. € 8.00 2008*

CONDE SUR NOIREAU *3D1* (500m W Urban) *48.85146, -0.55703* **Camp Municipal du Stade, Rue de Vire, 14110 Condé-sur-Noireau [02 31 69 45 24]** On D562 (Flers to Caen rd). In town, turn W on D512 twd Vire. After Zone Industrielle, sports complex on L, no L turn. Go 1 block further & foll lge white sp 'Espace Aquatique' to site. Site 500m on R in grounds of sports cent. Sm, pt shd; wc; chem disp; shwrs inc; el pnts (6-10A) €3; Indry rm; shops, rest, snacks, bar 300m; playgrnd; htd pool adj; tennis; dogs; quiet; CCI. "Well-maintained, clean site in grounds of leisure cent; gd size pitches; clean san facs but old; staff friendly & helpful; pleasant town; gd NH." 1 May-30 Sep. € 8.50 2008*

CONDETTE see Hardelot Plage *3A2*

CONDOM *8E2* (4km NE Rural) *43.97491, 0.42038* **Camping à la Ferme (Rogalle), Guinland, 32100 Condom [05 62 28 17 85; http://campingdeguinland.monsite.wanadoo.fr]** NE fr Condom on D931, turn R onto D41. Pass water tower on R, site ent on L at bottom of hill just bef sm lake on R. Sm, shd; wc; chem disp; shwrs inc; el pnts (6-10A) €2.50; shop, rest etc 4km; BBQ; playgrnd; tennis & canoe hire nrby; 10% statics; dogs; quiet. "Vg CL-type site in pine grove; friendly owner; clean facs." 1 Apr-30 Oct. € 7.50 2008*

We can fill in site report forms on the Club's website – www.caravanclub.co.uk/europereport

⊞ **CONDOM** *8E2* (6km SE Rural) **Camping à la Ferme (Vignaux), Bordeneuve, 32100 Béraut [05 62 28 08 41]** E fr Condom on D7 to Caussens; far end of vill turn R on D204, sp St Orens; in 1.2km turn R sp Béraut, bear R at fork, site on L in 400m. Also sp fr D654. Sm, pt sl, pt shd; wc; chem disp; shwrs inc; el pnts (12A) €2 (long lead poss req); Indtte; shops 2.5km; adv bkg; clsd Nov; quiet. "Peaceful & secluded CL-type site; friendly owners; basic san facs; waymkd trails nr." € 6.00 2008*

CONDOM *8E2* (1.5km SW Rural) *43.94813, 0.36435* **Camp Municipal de l'Argenté, Chemin de l'Argenté, Gauge 32100 Condom [tel/fax 05 62 28 17 32; camping.municipal@condom.org]** Fr Condom, take D931 twd Eauze; site ent on L opp municipal sports grnd. Med, pt shd, wc; chem disp; baby facs; shwrs inc; el pnts (6A) €3.50; shop 500m; tradsmn; rest & bar adj; playgrnd; pool 200m; fishing; tennis adj; dogs €1.10; phone; red low ssn. "Well-kept, spacious site adj rv; well shaded; friendly staff; excel san facs but ltd low ssn; levelling blocks useful; lge pitches; no twin-axle c'vans; lots for older children to do; interesting, unspoilt town nr pilgrim rte; rec visit Armagnac distilleries; excel." 1 Apr-30 Sep. € 11.60 2009*

CONDOM *8E2* (2km SW Rural) *43.93638, 0.35711* **Camping La Ferme de Laillon (Danto), Route d'Eauze, 32100 Condom [tel/fax 05 62 28 19 71 or 06 07 69 14 19 (mob); www.calaf32.free.fr/laillon/fr]** Site sp fr D931 dir Vopillon. Bumpy lane to site. Sm, pt sl, shd; wc; chem disp; shwrs inc; el pnts inc; lndry rm; farm produce; playgrnd; some statics; dogs; Eng spkn; quiet. "Delightful, wooded site; helpful owner; pleasant area." 21 Mar-19 Dec. € 9.20 2007*

CONDRIEU *9B2* (4km N Rural) *45.50949, 4.77330* **Camping Domaine du Grand Bois (Naturist), Tupin et Semons, 69420 Condrieu [04 74 87 89 00 or 04 74 87 04 29; fax 04 74 87 88 48; www.domainedugrandbois.fr]** Fr Vienne take D502 dir Rive-de-Gier; site well sp after x-ing Rv Rhône. NB Do not app fr Condrieu - v steep with hairpins. Lge, sl, pt shd; wc (most cont); chem disp (wc); shwrs inc; el pnts (6A) €4.50; shop 6km; snacks; bar; playgrnd; pool; TV; 75% statics; phone; poss cr; adv bkg; quiet; INF card. "Spectacular views; v basic san facs." ♦ 15 Apr-15 Oct. € 16.00 2006*

CONDRIEU *9B2* (750m E Rural) *45.46021, 4.77701* **Camping Belle Rive, Chemin de la Plaine, 69420 Condrieu [tel/fax 04 74 59 51 08]** Heading S on D386 (N86) fr Vienne after ent vill turn L immed bef Elf g'ge on R. Site in 600m. NB Headroom under rlwy 2.60m. Alt rte avoiding bdge after vill. Lge, mkd pitch, unshd; wc; shwrs; el pnts (3-6A) €2-4; gas; lndtte; shop; rest adj; snacks; bar; BBQ; playgrnd; pool; paddling pool; waterslide; lake fishing 2km; tennis; cycle hire; games area; 60% statics; dogs €1.20; poss cr; some rlwy noise. "C'vans over 6.50m poss need manhandling." 1 Apr-30 Sep. € 14.40 2008*

CONDRIEU *9B2* (2km SE Rural) *45.42413, 4.78251* **Camping Le Daxia, Route du Péage, 38370 St Clair-du-Rhône [04 74 56 39 20; fax 04 74 56 93 46; info@campingledaxia.com; www.campingledaxia.com]**
S fr Vienne on D386 (N86); turn L in Condieu sp D28 Les Roches-de-Condrieu & Le Péage-de-Roussillon; foll sp A7 Valance & 'Camping' onto D4. Site on L well sp fron Condrieu. Med, hdg/mkd pitch, pt shd; wc; chem disp; mv service pnt; baby facs; shwrs inc; el pnts (5-6A) €2.40-2.85; lndtte; shop 1km; sm rest; snacks; bar; BBQ; playgrnd; pool; paddling pool; games rm; dogs €1.85; adv bkg; quiet; CCI. "Vg site; on edge of sm rv with beach." ♦ 1 Apr-30 Sep. € 14.80 2007*

CONFOLENS *7A3* (500m N Rural) *46.01905, 0.67531* **Camp Municipal des Ribières, Ave de St Germain, 16500 Confolens [05 45 85 35 27 or 05 45 84 01 97 (Mairie); fax 05 45 85 34 10; mairie.confolens@free.fr]** Fr N foll D951 dir Confolens turn L sp St Germain-de-Confolens, site on R in 7km at edge of town bet rd & rv. NB Diff app fr S thro vill. Med, mkd pitch, pt shd; wc (most cont); shwrs inc; gas; el pnts (16A) €2; lndry rm; shop 700m; tradsmn; BBQ; pool 200m; rv sw adj; fishing & boating; no statics; dogs; phone; m'van o'night area outside site; some rd noise; cc & CCI not acc. "Interesting, pretty town; facs neglected (2008) & ltd low ssn; warden calls am & pm." ♦ 1 May-1 Sep. € 7.00 2009*

CONFOLENS *7A3* (7km S Rural) *45.96605, 0.70888* **Camp Municipal Moulin de la Cour, 16500 St Maurice-des-Lions [05 45 85 55 99; fax 05 45 85 52 89]** Fr Confolens take D948 S. In 6.5km turn L thro vill, site 700m, well sp. Sm, hdg/mkd pitch, terr, pt shd; wc (some cont); chem disp (wc); shwrs inc; el pnts (6A) €2; shop, rest, bar 500m; BBQ; adv bkg; quiet. "Pleasant site in quiet location; pitch yourself, warden calls pm; old, inadequate facs (2008); height limitations when site clsd (see sp at ent to sports cent & site); ent thro stone pillars - care req with wide o'fits; site used by Boules Club & football; nr pretty vill with 12thC church & old houses; Confolens folk festival mid-Aug." 1 Jun-30 Sep. € 6.00 2009*

CONNERRE *4F1* (8km SE) *48.03945, 0.59302* **Camp Municipal La Piscine, Rue de la Piscine, 72390 Dollon [02 43 93 42 23; fax 02 43 71 53 88; mairie.dollon@wanadoo.fr]** Fr Connerré take D302 sp Vibraye & Thorigné-sur-Dué. In Dollon foll 'La Piscine' sp to sports complex at E end of vill. Sm, pt shd; wc; chem disp; shwrs; el pnts (10A) €3.35; gas; shops 300m; playgrnd; pool; tennis; fishing; adv bkg rec; quiet. "Site part of sports complex; popular - rec arr early high ssn." 15 May-15 Sep. € 6.00 2006*

CONQUES *7D4* (8km E Rural) *44.55948, 2.46184* **Camping L'Etang du Camp, 12320 Sénergues [05 65 46 01 95; info@etangducamp.fr; www.etangducamp.fr]** Fr S on D901 dir Conques; at St Cyprien turn R onto D46 sp Sénergues; foll sp Sénergues up hill for 6km; 2nd L at the top; foll Camping sp. Med, hdg/mkd pitch, pt shd; wc; chem disp; mv service pnt; baby facs; fam bthrm; shwrs inc; el pnts (6A) €3.50; lndtte; ice; sm shop; supmkt 3km; rest,bar 6km; tradsmn; BBQ (charcoal); playgrnd; htd pool 6km; fishing in private lake; cycle hire; canoeing nrby; cycle hire; games area; games rm; wifi; dogs €1.50; Eng spkn; adv bkg; quiet; red low ssn; CCI. "Well-situated, well-kept site; quiet & relaxing; warm welcome, British owners; gd walking; conv Conques; excel." ♦ 1 Apr-30 Sep. € 16.00 2009*

CONQUES *7D4* (8km SE Rural) *44.54671, 2.40773* **Camp Municipal, 12320 St Cyprien-sur-Dourdou [05 65 72 80 52 or 05 65 69 83 16 (Mairie); fax 05 65 69 89 31; mairie-stcyprien12@wanadoo.fr; www.conques.fr]** Fr Conques on D901 S, turn L onto D46 to St Cyprien-sur-Dourdou & foll sp to site. Sm, hdg pitch, shd; wc; shwrs inc (no sep cubicles); el pnts €2; lndry rm; shops, rest, snacks, bar 500m; playgrnd; htd pool & tennis adj; dogs; phone; adv bkg; CCI. "Well-maintained site; sports field nrby; sh walk to vill; gd walking, touring area." ♦ 15 Jun-15 Sep. € 7.00 2007*

CONQUES *7D4* (1km W Rural) *44.60041, 2.39461* **Camping Beau Rivage, 12320 Conques [05 65 69 82 23 or 05 65 72 89 29 (LS); fax 05 67 72 89 29; camping.conques@wanadoo.fr; www.campingconques.com]** Site on D901 Rodez-Aurillac rd on Rv Dourdou. Med, mkd pitch, pt sl, pt shd; wc (some cont); mv service pnt; shwrs inc; el pnts (6-10A) €3.50; gas; lndry rm; shop; tradsmn; rest; snacks; bar; playgrnd; pool; fishing; rv adj; some statics; adv bkg; quiet; red low ssn; CCI. "Gd position by rv bank; poss run down low ssn; sm pitches; some modern san facs, others v dated; tight for lge o'fits due trees & narr pathways; gd." ♦ 1 Apr-30 Sep. € 16.50 2008*

CONQUES *7D4* (5km NW Rural) *44.62222, 2.36101* **Camping Le Moulin, Les Passes, 12320 Grand-Vabre [tel/fax 05 65 72 87 28; contact@grand-vabre.com; www.grand-vabre.com]** N fr Conques on D901, site sp on banks Rv Dourdou. Sm, mkd pitch, terr, shd; wc; shwrs; el pnts (10A) €2; tradsmn; snacks; bar; playgrnd; htd pool; tennis 1km; poss cr; quiet. "Pleasant rvside site; gd." 1 Apr-31 Oct. € 11.00 2006*

CONQUET, LE *2E1* (2km N Coastal) *48.36748, -4.75990* **Camping Les Blancs Sablons, 29217 Le Conquet [tel/fax 02 98 89 06 90; cledelles.reservations@wanadoo.fr; www.lescledelles.com]** Exit Brest on D789 to Le Conquet. Turn R after 22km (1.8km bef Le Conquet) on D67 twd St Renan, turn L after 700m on D28 twd Ploumoguer. After 2km, turn L at x-rds twd Plage des Blancs Sablons, site on L in 1km. Lge, mkd pitch, unshd; wc; chem disp; mv service pnt; shwrs inc; el pnts (16A) €3 (long lead poss req); lndtte; shop in ssn & 1km; rest, snacks 1km; bar 500m; playgrnd; htd pool; sand beach 100m; adv bkg; ccard acc; CCI. "Vg; excel shwrs; some soft pitches; ltd facs low ssn; gd views fr some pitches; lovely old fishing town." ♦ 1 Apr-31 Oct. € 16.40 2007*

⊞ **CONQUET, LE** *2E1* (7km SE Coastal) *48.34154, -4.70749* **Camping Les Terrasses de Bertheaume, Rue de Perzel, 29217 Plougonvelin [tel/fax 02 98 48 32 37; camping-lesterrassesdebertheaume@wanadoo.fr; www.camping-brest.com]** Sp nr town. Sm, mkd pitch, pt sl, terr, unshd; wc (some cont); chem disp (wc); shwrs €1; el pnts €2.50; lndtte; shop 1km; snacks; bar; BBQ; playgrnd; htd pool; sand beach adj (steps); TV rm; 80% statics; dogs €1; poss cr; CCI. "Some sea views; Le Fort de Bertheaume 500m interesting; cliff walk; steep access poss diff lge o'fits." ♦ € 17.00 2006*

CONTIS PLAGE *8E1* (Coastal) *44.08895, -1.31678* **Yelloh! Village Lous Seurrots, 40170 Contis-Plage [05 58 42 85 82; fax 05 58 42 49 11; info@lous-seurrots.com; www.lous-seurrots.com or www.yellohvillage.com]** S fr Mimizan take D652; 14km turn R onto D41 sp Contis-Plage; site on L. Or fr N10/E5/E70 exit junc 14 onto D38/D41 to Contis. V lge, hdg pitch, shd; htd wc; chem disp; baby facs; fam bthrm; shwrs inc; el pnts (6A) €4; gas; lndtte; shop; rest; snacks; bar; playgrnd; pools; sand beach 400m; tennis; cycle hire; games area; entmnt; internet; TV; 30% statics; dogs €3; adv bkg; quiet; Eng spkn; ccard acc; red low ssn. "Pitches vary in size, some req levelling blocks; excel." ♦ 5 Apr-6 Sep. € 32.00 2006*

CONTRES *4G2* (9km S Rural) *47.34567, 1.47411* **Camp Municipal Le Gué, Route de Couddes, 41700 Chémery [02 54 71 37 11 or 02 54 71 31 08; fax 02 54 71 31 08; ot.chemery@wanadoo.fr]** S fr Contres on D956 turn NW in Chémery cent sp Couddes. Site on R over bdge. Med, mkd pitch, pt shd; htd wc; chem disp; mv service pnt; shwrs inc; el pnts (6A) €3.20 (rev pol); shop; tradsmn; rest, bar 500m; playgrnd; pool high ssn; cycle hire; rv fishing adj; dogs €1; quiet; adv bkg; CCI. "Warden only on site Mon-Fri low ssn, otherwise can find warden's home in vill; chateau in vill." 15 Apr-15 Sep. € 10.20 2007*

CONTRES *4G2* (6km SW Rural) *47.38261, 1.36251* **Camping à la Ferme La Presle (Degroite), 41700 Oisly [02 54 79 52 69 or 06 15 70 74 02; fax 02 54 79 80 44; lapresle@lapost.net; www.gites-centre-loire.com]** Fr Contres take D675 SW for 3km D21 to just past Oisly. Well sp. Sm, pt sl, pt shd; wc; shwrs €1; el pnts (4A) €2.20 (poss no earth); shops 1.5km; lake fishing; v quiet. "Excel CL-type site; owner helpful." Easter-15 Oct. € 6.60 2009*

CONTREXEVILLE *6F2* (1km SW Rural) *48.18005, 5.88519* **Camp Municipal du Tir aux Pigeons, Rue du 11 Septembre, 88140 Contrexéville [03 29 08 15 06; secretariat@ville.contrexeville.fr; www.ville-contrexeville.fr]** Off D164. App town fr NW on D164 turn R onto D13 & foll sp. 200m W of level x-ing, adj to stadium. Med, mkd pitch, pt shd; wc; chem disp; shwrs inc; el pnts (5A) €2.50; lndtte; shops 1km; tradsmn; paddling pool; lake fishing 2km; tennis adj; games area; games rm; poss cr; some rd noise. "Popular NH." ♦ 1 Apr-31 Oct. € 13.00 2008*

COQUILLE, LA see Chalus *7B3*

CORBIGNY *4G4* (3.5km W Rural) *47.25858, 3.64131* **Camp Intercommunal L'Ardan, Route de Germeney, 58800 Chaumot [03 86 20 07 70; campingdelardan@wanadoo.fr; www.camping-bourgogne.com]** D977 fr Corbigny to Chaumot. Turn on D130 sp Germenay. Site on R after 50m. Med, shd; wc (some cont); chem disp; shwrs inc; el pnts €3; shop 3.5km; rest; bar; playgrnd; lake adj; fishing; boat hire; some statics; dogs €1; Eng spkn; adv bkg; quiet. "Dutch owned." 1 Apr-1 Oct. € 12.00 2009*

France

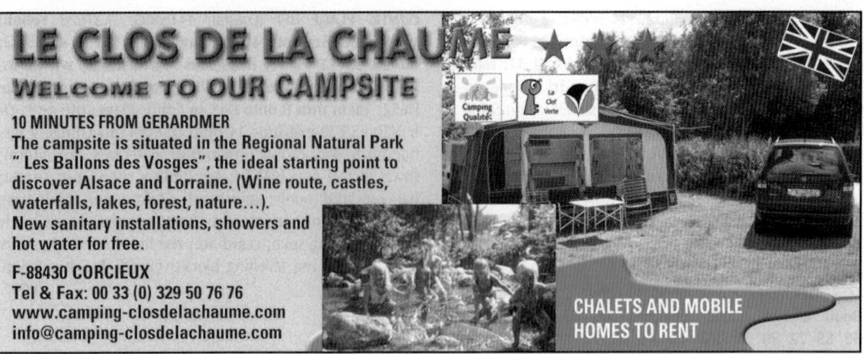

CORCIEUX *6F3* (8km NE Urban) *48.18436, 6.95784* **Camping Les Acacias, 191 Rue L de Vinci, 88650 Anould [tel/fax 03 29 57 11 06; contact@acaciascamp.com; www.acaciascamp.com]** Site in vill of Anould sp fr all dir; just off main rd. (Annexe Camping Nature Les Acacias 800m fr this site open 15 Jun-15 Sep, terr in woods.) Med, pt shd; wc (some cont); chem disp; mv service pnt; baby facs; shwrs inc; el pnts (3A) €2.60; gas; Indtte; shops 500m; supmkt 2km; rest; snacks; takeaway; sm bar; playgrnd; sm pool; rv fishing nrby; games rm; tennis & karting 2km; cycle trails; excursions; 10% statics; dogs €1; poss cr; Eng spkn; adv bkg; quiet; CCI. "Gd standard site; helpful owners; gd clean san facs; excel." ♦ 5 Dec-5 Oct. € 10.80 2008*

CORCIEUX *6F3* (600m E Rural) *48.16806, 6.89044* **Camping Le Clos de la Chaume, 21 Rue d'Alsace, 88430 Corcieux [tel/fax 03 29 50 76 76 or 06 85 19 62 55 (mob); info@camping-closdelachaume.com; www.camping-closdelachaume.com]** Take D145 fr St Dié, then D8 thro Anould onto D60. Site in 3km on R at ent to vill. Med, hdg/mkd pitch, hdstg, pt shd; wc (some cont); chem disp; mv service pnt; some serviced pitches; fam bthrm; shwrs inc; el pnts (6-10A) €3.90; gas; Indtte; shop 800m; tradsmn, rest, snacks, bar 600m; BBQ; playgrnd; pool; sand beach & lake sw 12km; fishing; games area; games rm; cycle hire 800m; wifi; 15% statics; dogs €1.40; phone; Eng spkn; adv bkg; quiet; ccard acc; red low ssn/long stay/CCI. "Beautiful area; conv Gérardmer & Alsace wine rte; excel, peaceful, high quality site." ♦ 10 Apr-18 Sep. € 16.30 2009*

See advertisement

CORCIEUX *6F3* (1km E Rural) *48.16631, 6.89366* **Camping au Mica, 8 Route de Gérardmer, 88430 Corcieux [tel/fax 03 29 50 70 07; info@campingaumica.com; www.campingaumica.com]** Take D415 fr St Dié, then D8 thro Anould onto D60. Site in 5km on L. Med, hdg/mkd pitch, shd; wc (come cont); chem disp; mv service pnt; serviced pitches; shwrs inc; el pnts (6A) €2.50; gas; Indtte; shop; tradsmn; bar; BBQ; playgrnd; pool 150m; rv fishing adj; games rm; cycle hire; TV; some statics; dogs €1; phone; Eng spkn; adv bkg; quiet; red low ssn/long stay; ccard acc; CCI. "Walking rtes; beautiful area in National Park." 15 Apr-1 Nov. € 11.00 2006*

CORCIEUX *6F3* (S Rural) *48.1690, 6.88023* **Yelloh! Village Le Domaine des Bans, La Rochotte, 88430 Corcieux [03 29 51 64 67; fax 03 29 51 64 65; info@domaine-des-bans.com; www.domaine-des-bans.com or www.yellohvillage.com]** Fr St Dié by-pass join D415 S to Anould. After approx 10km turn R on D8 & in 5km R on D60 to Corcieux. Or fr S take D8 N fr Gérardmer thro Gerbépal. In 2km turn L onto D60 twd Corcieux, site on L. V lge, hdg/mkd pitch, terr, pt shd; wc; chem disp; baby facs; shwrs inc; el pnts (6A) inc; gas; Indtte; sm shop, rest, snacks, bar high ssn; BBQ; playgrnd; pool high ssn; sm lake; tennis; games rm; horseriding; entmnt; 75% tour ops static tents/vans; dogs €3; poss cr; Eng spkn; adv bkg ess high ssn (min 7 days); poss noisy; ccard acc; CCI. "Pitches by lake quieter than nr vill; gd site with gd facs, poss stretched high ssn; care needed on narr site rds with speed control ditches; mkt Mon." ♦ 25 Apr-5 Sep. € 39.00 2008*

CORDELLE see Roanne *9A1*

CORDES SUR CIEL *8E4* (1.5km SE Rural) *44.05429, 1.97201* **Camping Moulin de Julien, Livers-Cazelle, 81170 Cordes-sur-Ciel [tel/fax 05 63 56 11 10; contact@campingmoulindejulien.com; www.campingmoulindejulien.com]** Exit Cordes E on D600 in Albi dir. Turn R on D922 Gaillac. Site on L in 100m. Fr Gaillac heading N site on R 100m bef junc with D600 & site sp bef tricolour shield on R advertising Hôtel Ecuyer. Med, pt sl, pt shd; wc; chem disp; shwrs inc; el pnts (5A) €4; Indtte; supmkt 1km; snacks & bar in ssn; playgrnd; 2 pools in ssn; waterslide; lake for fishing; red low ssn; CCI. "V pleasant, peaceful site in interesting area; lge pitches; friendly owners; conv Albi Cathedral, Bastide towns/vills & medieval town of Cordes." 1 May-30 Sep. € 19.00 2008*

CORDES SUR CIEL *8E4* (5km SE Rural) *44.04158, 2.01722* **Camping Redon, Livers-Cazelles, 81170 Cordes-sur-Ciel [tel/fax 05 63 56 14 64; info@campredon.com; www.campredon.com]** Off D600 Albi to Cordes rd. Exit on D107 to E nr water tower. Site sp. Sm, hdg pitch, pt sl, pt shd; wc; chem disp; mv service pnt; baby facs; shwrs inc; el pnts (6-16A) €4.10; gas; Indtte; shops 5km; tradsmn; sm playgrnd; pool; TV rm; dogs €1.75; phone; bus 1km; poss cr; Eng spkn; adv bkg; quiet; red long stay/low ssn/CCI. "Well-run site; views fr some pitches; friendly, helpful Dutch owner; excel facs, poss stretched high ssn; conv Bastides in area; highly rec." ♦ 1 Apr-1 Nov. € 18.50 2009*

CORDES SUR CIEL *8E4* (2km W Rural) *44.06681, 1.92408* **Camping Le Garissou, 81170 Cordes-sur-Ciel [05 63 56 27 14; fax 05 63 56 26 95; legarissou@wanadoo.fr]** Take D600 fr Cordes thro Les Cabanes, site sp on L. Med, mkd pitch, terr, unshd; wc; shwrs inc; el pnts (6A) inc; Indtte; sm shop; playgrnd; pool complex adj; dogs €1.50; quiet; red low ssn. "Hilltop site; excel views; clean facs." 1 Apr-31 Oct. € 12.50 2009*

CORMATIN *9A2* (500m N Rural) *46.54841, 4.68351* **Camping Le Hameau des Champs, 71460 Cormatin [03 85 50 76 71; fax 03 85 50 76 98; camping.cormatin@wandoo.fr; www.le-hameau-des-champs.com]** Fr Cluny N on D981 dir Cormatin for approx 14km, site N of town sp on L, 300m after chateau. Look for line of European flags. Sm, hdg/mkd pitch, pt sl, unshd; htd wc; chem disp; mv service pnt; shwrs inc; el pnts (13A) €3.20 (long lead poss req); gas 500m; Indtte; shop 500m; tradsmn; rest; snacks; bar; BBQ (gas/elec); cooking facs; playgrnd; rv sw 1km; shgle beach 7km; cycle hire; TV rm; 10% statics; dogs €1; phone; Eng spkn; adv bkg; quiet; ccard acc; red low ssn; CCI. "Clean, secure site in lovely countryside; welcoming, friendly owner; lge grassy pitches; gd facs, poss stretched high ssn; rest open low ssn; WW1 museum nrby; Voie Verte cycling rte adj." ♦ 4 Apr-30 Sep. € 12.80 2009*

CORMATIN *9A2* (6km NW Rural) *46.57139, 4.66245* **Camping Le Gué, Meusseugne, 71460 Savigny-sur-Grosne [03 85 92 56 86; camping-savigny@wanadoo.fr; www.chalon-sur-saone.net]** Fr Cluny N on D981, 2km N of Cormatin fork L sp Malay. Site 3km on R bef rv bdge. Med, mkd pitch, shd; htd wc; chem disp (wc); shwrs €0.80; el pnts €2; tradsmn; snacks; bar; BBQ; playgrnd; games area; dir access to rv; fishing; many statics; dogs; CCI. "Pleasant, friendly site; nr St Genoux-le-National (national monument), Cluny & Taizé; on Burgundy wine rd." 1 May-31 Oct. € 7.10 2007*

CORMEILLES *3D1* (4km E Rural) *49.24623, 0.44954* **Camping Les Pommiers, La Febvrerie, 27260 St Sylvestre-de-Cormeilles [02 32 42 29 69; cmaraisc@aol.com; www.campinglespommiers.com]** Exit A13 junc 28 Beuzeville onto N175 then D27 S sp Epaignes & Bernay twds Lieurey. Cont on D27 for approx 15km & at rndabt with D139 at Epaignes strt on for 5.6km, turn off R down narr lane sp St Sylvestre, Camping. Site on R in 1.5km. Sm, hdg pitch, pt shd; wc; chem disp (wc); shwrs inc; el pnts inc (6A) €2.50 (poss rev pol); Indry rm; shops 4km, rest, snacks, bar 4km; BBQ; playgrnd; some statics; dogs free; phone; poss cr; Eng spkn; adv bkg; quiet. "Pleasant, friendly, family-run, secluded site in orchard; excel clean facs." 1 Apr-31 Oct. € 8.10 2008*

CORMORANCHE SUR SAONE see Macon *9A2*

CORNY SUR MOSELLE *5D2* (Rural) *49.03768, 6.05736* **Camping Le Pâquis, 57680 Corny-sur-Moselle [03 87 52 03 59 or 03 87 60 68 67; fax 03 87 60 71 96]** SW fr Metz on D657 (N57); site sp on ent to vill. Or S on A31 take junc 29 Féy & turn R onto D66 into Corny-sur-Moselle. At rndabt in vill turn R & cross rv. Site 300m on L. Lge, unshd; htd wc; chem disp; shwrs inc; el pnts (6A) €2.80 (long cable poss req); Indtte; snacks; bar; shops 1km; tradsmn; playgrnd; rv sw adj; TV; entmnt; dogs €0.92; poss cr; adv bkg; poss rlwy noise; ccard acc; CCI. "Gd, well-run site on Rv Moselle; friendly, helpful owners; rec arr early for quieter pitch at far end site; many pitches long, drive-thro so no need unhitch." 1 May-30 Sep. € 10.80 2009*

CORREZE *7C4* (400m E Urban) **Camp Municipal La Chapelle, 19800 Corrèze [05 55 21 29 30 or 05 55 21 25 21 (Mairie); mairie.correze@wanadoo.fr]** N fr Tulle on D1089 (N89) dir Egletons, turn L at La Gare de Corrèze onto D26 sp to Corrèze. Site 400m fr town cent on D143. Med, mkd pitch, pl sl, terr, pt shd; wc; chem disp; shwrs inc; el pnts (5A) €2.08; gas; Indtte; shop, rest, shops; snacks; playgrnd; htd pool 500m; canoeing & rv fishing; phone; Eng spkn; quiet; CCI. "Lovely area; old vill; areas for c'vans on opp side of rv fr recep." ♦ 15 Jun-15 Sep. € 8.65 2008*

CORSICA Campsites in towns in Corsica are listed together at the end of the French site entry pages.

COSNE COURS SUR LOIRE *4G3* (SW Rural) *47.40923, 2.91792* **Camping de l'Ile, Ile de Cosne, 18300 Bannay [03 86 28 27 92; fax 03 86 28 18 10; contact@restaurantcamping.com; www.restaurantcamping.com]** Fr Cosne take Bourges rd, D955, over 1st half of bdge, ent immed on L, 500m strt. On rv island. Lge, shd; htd wc; chem disp; shwrs inc; el pnts (10A) €4; Indtte; ltd shop; rest; snacks; bar; BBQ; playgrnd; paddling pool; entmnts; cycle hire; TV; some statics; dogs €0.90; quiet; ccard acc; CCI. "Helpful staff; views of Rv Loire; gd san facs; gd NH." ♦ 1 Apr-30 Oct. € 14.00 2009*

COUBON see Puy en Velay, Le *9C1*

COUCHES see Nolay *6H1*

COUCOURDE, LA see Montélimar *9D2*

COUHE *7A2* (1km N Rural) *46.31254, 0.18216* **Camping Les Peupliers, 86700 Couhé [05 49 59 21 16; fax 05 49 37 92 09; info@lespeupliers.fr; www.lespeupliers.fr]** Site 35km S of Poitiers on N10 bis (old rd off by-pass); ent by bdge over Rv Dive. Fr N or S on N10 take N exit for Couhé. Site on R in 800m. Lge, hdg/mkd pitch, pt shd; wc; 30% serviced pitch; chem disp; mv service pnt; shwrs inc; el pnts (10A) €4.50; gas; Indtte; shop & 1.5km; tradsmn; rest; snacks; bar; BBQ; playgrnd; 2 htd pools & paddling pools high ssn; waterslides; jacuzzis; fishing; sports area; games rm; entmnt; internet; TV rm; some statics; dogs free; Eng spkn; adv bkg; quiet; ccard acc; red low ssn/long stay/CCI. "Beautiful, friendly, well-organised & maintained; immac san facs; easy access fr N10; conv Futuroscope." ♦ 2 May-30 Sep. € 25.50 2009*

See advertisement on next page

France

COULANGES SUR YONNE *4G4* (9km E Rural) **Camp Municipal Le Petit Port, 89660 Châtel-Censoir [03 86 81 01 98 (Mairie) or 06 37 13 68 26 (mob); www.chatel-censoir.com]** Fr Auxerre or Clamecy on N151 at Coulanges turn E onto D21, S side of rv & canal to Châtel-Censoir; site sp. Med, pt shd; wc (some cont); chem disp; shwrs inc; el pnts (16A) €2 (poss rev pol); Indry rm; basic shop 400m rest; bar; BBQ; playgrnd; rv sw & fishing adj; wifi; some statics; dogs €0.50; phone; Eng spkn; some slight rlwy noise; CCI. "Attractive, peaceful site bet rv & canal; resident warden; some pitches soggy when wet; beautiful area with gd cycling; no twin-axles." 1 May-30 Sep. € 7.50 2009*

COULANGES SUR YONNE *4G4* (S Rural) *47.52269, 3.53817* **Camping des Berges de l'Yonne, 89480 Coulanges-sur-Yonne [03 86 81 76 87]** On N151 dir Nevers. Med, pt shd; wc; chem disp; shwrs; el pnts (10A) €2.80; shop; snacks; playgrnd; tennis. "V pleasant site in beautiful area; dated facs but adequate & clean." 1 May-15 Sep. € 10.30 2009*

COULLONS *4G3* (1km W Rural) *47.62319, 2.48444* **Camp Municipal Plancherotte, Route de la Brosse, 45720 Coullons [02 38 29 20 42 or 06 86 73 94 94 (mob)]** Fr cent of Coullons foll sp twd Cerdon (D51). Bef leaving vill & after passing lake, take 1st rd on L. Site in 500m on L side of lake. Med, pt shd, hdg/mkd pitch; wc (cont); chem disp; some serviced pitches; shwrs; el pnts; gas 1km; shop 1km; playgrnd; tennis; 50% statics; phone; adv bkg; CCI. "Vg." ♦ 1 Apr-31 Oct. 2008*

COULON *7A2* (N Rural) *46.32739, -0.58437* **Camp Municipal La Niquière, Route de Benet, 79510 Coulon [05 49 35 81 19 or 05 49 35 90 26 (Mairie); fax 05 49 35 82 75; tourisme.coulon79@orange.fr; www.ville-coulon.fr]** Fr N148 at Benet take D1 to Coulon to site on L at ent to Coulon. Sm, pt shd; wc (some cont); chem disp (wc); shwrs inc; el pnts (15A) €2.80; gas; shops 1km; sports facs adj; boats for hire; dogs €0.40; poss cr. "Well-kept site; dated but clean san facs; ent only with barrier card - collect fr Mairie when office clsd; 10 min walk to vill." 1 Apr-30 Sep. € 8.10 2008*

COULON *7A2* (3km N Rural) **Camping à la Ferme La Planche, 79510 Coulon [05 49 35 93 17]** Fr N148, foll main rd thro Benet, then foll sp (bus & lorry) Coulon. Take 1st L sp Coulon, then 1st R, site sp. Site on L in 1.5km. Sm, pt shd; wc; shwr; el pnts (10A) inc; supmkt 1.5km; tradsmn; rest 1.5km; BBQ; horse & carriage rides; some statics; adv bkg; quiet. "Excel CL-type farm site; sm pitches; friendly owners; ltd, old but clean facs; busy high ssn." € 13.00 2009*

COULON *7A2* (2km S Rural) *46.30468, -0.59665* **Camping L'Ilot du Chail, Rue des Gravées, 79270 La Garette [05 49 35 00 33; fax 05 49 35 00 31; www.marais-poitevin.com/la-garette]** Fr Niort take dir to Coulon & La Venise-Verte; at Coulon rndbt turn L; site thro vill on R. Med, mkd pitch, pt shd; wc; shwrs inc; el pnts (6A) €2.50; rest/bar 300m; shop & 3km; tradsmn; pool; fishing; boat rides; horseriding; tennis; games rm; some statics; dogs €0.80; quiet; red long stay; ccard acc; CCI. "Many rests within 1km; vg." ♦ 8 Apr-8 Sep. € 12.50 2007*

COULON *7A2* (2km W Rural) *46.31444, -0.60888* **Camping La Venise Verte, 178 Route des Bordes de Sèvre, 79510 Coulon [05 49 35 90 36; fax 05 49 35 84 69; accueil@camping-laveniseverte.com; www.camping-la-venise-verte.com]** Exit A83 junc 9 onto D148 thro Benet. Turn R at rndabt onto D1 sp Coulon & in Coulon turn R at rndabt with D123 & keep canal on L. Site on R bef bdge. Drive along rv & foll sp to site. Med, mkd pitch, pt shd; wc; chem disp; baby facs; shwrs inc; el pnts (10A) inc (poss rev pol); Indtte; tradsmn; rest, snacks, bar (high ssn); BBQ (charcoal/gas); playgrnd; pool; boating; fishing; canoe/cycle hire; entmnt; wifi; 25% statics; dogs €2; phone; poss cr; adv bkg; poss noisy high ssn; ccard acc; red low ssn; CCI. "Superb site in park-like setting; helpful, friendly owner & relaxed atmosphere; gd facs; good sized pitches, but some sm & diff due trees & posts; excel touring base for nature lovers; gd walking & cycle rtes; pretty town; much revisited site." ♦ 1 Apr-11 Nov. € 29.00 ABS - A37 2009*

COULON *7A2* (6km W Rural) *46.33020, -0.67524* **Camping Le Relais du Pêcheur, 85420 Le Mazeau [02 51 52 93 23 or 02 51 52 91 14 (Mairie); fax 02 51 52 97 58]** Fr Fontenay-le-Comte take N148 SE. At Benet turn R onto D25 thro vill to Le Mazeau. Turn L in vill then R over canal bdge. Site on L in 500m. Med, hdg pitch, pt shd; wc (most cont); chem disp; shwrs inc; el pnts (16A) €2; Indtte; shop 500m; supmkt 5km; playgrnd; paddling pool; boat hire nrby; adv bkg; quiet; CCI. "Pleasant site in delightful location; gd cyling & walks." ♦ 1 Apr-15 Oct. € 8.00 2008*

COULONGES SUR L'AUTIZE *7A2* (500m S Rural) *46.4794, -0.5990* **Camp Municipal Le Parc, Rue du Calvaire, 79160 Coulonges-sur-l'Autize [05 49 06 27 56; fax 05 49 06 13 26; mairie-coulanges-sur-lautize@wanadoo.fr; www.ville-coulanges-sur-lautize.fr]** Fr Fontenay take D745 sp Parthenay/St Hilaire E to Coulonges, site sp nr 'piscine' on D1. Fr Niort take D744 N to Coulonges. Sm, hdg/mkd pitch, pt shd; wc; chem disp (wc); shwrs inc; el pnts €1.80; Indry rm; shop adj; tradsmn; playgrnd; pool nr; rv sw & fishing 4km; cycle hire; 80% statics; dogs; phone; quiet; CCI. "Site yourself; warden calls." ♦ May-Oct. € 7.40 2008*

⊞ **COURBIAC** *7D3* (S Rural) *44.37818, 1.01807* **FFCC Le Pouchou, 47370 Courbiac [tel/fax 05 53 40 72 68 or 06 80 25 15 13 (mob); le.pouchou@wanadoo.fr; www.camping-le-pouchou.com]** S fr Fumel on D102 thro Tournon-d'Agenais; Courbiac sp to L on S side of town; site on R in 2.5km (1.5km bef Courbiac). Sm, pt sl, pt shd; wc; mv service pnt; shwrs inc; el pnts (10A) €3.50 (poss rev pol); Indry rm; shop; snacks; bar; playgrnd; pool & paddling pool; cycle hire; fishing; horseriding; archery; internet; sat TV; some statics; dogs €1.80; site clsd 21 Dec-9 Jan; Eng spkn; adv bkg ess high ssn; quiet; CCI. "Vg site in lovely setting; lge pitches each with picnic table; many sl pitches poss diff; gd, clean facs; gd views; friendly, hospitable owners; gd cycling; vg." ♦ € 13.00 2009*

COURCON *7A2* (6km N Rural) *46.30089, -0.80782* **Camping du Port (Naturist), Rue du Port, 17170 La Ronde [05 46 41 65 58 or 06 26 06 72 37 (mob); jean-jacques.faudoire@wanadoo.fr; www.camping-naturiste-du-port.com]** Fr Marans E on D114, bef Courçon head N on D116 dir Maillezais. Site on R after leaving vill of La Ronde. Sm, hdg/mkd pitch, hdstg, pt shd; wc; chem disp; shwrs inc; el pnts (6-10A) €3.50; gas; Indtte; shops adj; BBQ; playgrnd; pool high ssn; sand beach 30km; few statics; dogs €2; poss cr; adv bkg; quiet. "Excel, well looked-after site; helpful owner; facs clean; site poss open outside dates shown." ♦ 1 May-30 Sep. € 17.00 2009*

COURCON *7A2* (500m SE Rural) *46.24060, -0.80635* **Camp Municipal La Garenne, 12 Rue du Collège, 17170 Courçon [05 46 01 60 19 or 05 46 01 60 50 (Mairie); fax 05 46 01 63 59; mairie.courcon@mairie17.com]** Fr E on N11 turn N at La Laigne on D114 to Courçon. Site on L on app to vill. Fr W turn N onto D116 to Courçon. Sm, pt shd; wc; mv service pnt; shwrs; el pnts (3A) €3.50; Indtte; shops 500m; htd pool adj; rv sw 5km; fishing 5km; dogs €1.50; adv bkg rec high ssn; quiet. 1 Jun-31 Aug. € 8.50 2006*

COURCON *7A2* (5km S Urban) *46.20365, -0.81619* **Camp Municipal du Château, 17170 Benon [06 66 90 35 59 (mob) or 05 46 01 61 48 (Mairie); fax 05 46 01 01 19; mairie-benon@smic17.fr; www.smic17.fr/mairie-benon/camping.htm]** Fr N11 turn S to Benon onto D116. On S side of Benon turn E onto D206 twd St Georges-du-Bois, site immed on R thro tall, narr, metal gateway; take wide sweep on ent (or use easier access at rear - foll wall round to L). Site also sp in Benon. Sm, pt sl, mainly shd; wc; chem disp; shwrs inc; el pnts (10A) €2.20; Indtte; tradsmn; playgrnd; pool 6km; tennis; dogs €1; quiet; adv bkg; ccard acc; CCI. "Attractive site adj Mairie; no lighting; site tired, refurb planned (2009); oyster beds at Châtelaillon; gd cycling area; 20 mins La Rochelle; poss itinerants." 1 May-30 Sep. € 8.60 2008*

COURNON D'AVERGNE see Clermont Ferrand *9B1*

COURPIERE *9B1* (5km NE Rural) *45.7838, 3.6004* **Camping Le Grün du Chignore, Les Plaines, 63120 Vollore-Ville [tel/fax 04 73 53 73 37; camping-du-chignore@hotmail.fr; www.campingauvergne.fr]** D906 S fr Thiers; at Courpière turn L onto D7 dir Vollore-Ville; take D45 N fr vill; site on R in 500m. Sm, hdg/mkd pitch, pt shd; wc (some cont); chem disp (wc); shwrs inc; el pnts (10A) €3.10: Indtte; shop 500m; tradsmn; rest; snacks; bar; BBQ (sep area); playgrnd; shallow pool; games area; some statics; dogs €1.50; a little English spkn; adv bkg; quiet; ccard acc. "Situated above fishing lake; rolling hills; v quiet; lovely owners; gd walks; chateau in Vollore-Ville; bar part of vill life; highly rec." ♦ 1 Apr-31 Oct. € 9.30 2007*

COURSEULLES SUR MER *3D1* (500m NE Coastal) *49.33417, -0.44433* **Camp Municipal Le Champ de Course, Ave de la Libération, 14470 Courseulles-sur-Mer [02 31 37 99 26 (Mairie); fax 02 31 37 96 37; camping-courseulles@wanadoo.fr; www.courseulles-sur-mer.com]** Fr N814 by-pass thro Caen, take exit 5 onto D7 & D404 dir Courseulles-sur-Mer. On ent to town, foll sp 'Campings' at 1st rndabt, then sp 'Centre Juno Beach'. Site on D514 on R. Lge, hdg/mkd pitch, unshd; wc; chem disp; mv service pnt; baby facs; shwrs inc; el pnts (10A) €4.50; Indtte; tradsmn; rest, snacks, bar adj; BBQ; playgrnd; pool adj; sand beach; sports area; boat hire; tennis, mini-golf & horseriding nr; TV rm; 15% statics; dogs €1.90; phone; poss cr; Eng spkn; adv bkg; quiet; ccard acc; CCI. "Nice site adj beach; friendly staff; facs clean; early 6am dep for ferry OK; conv Juno (D-Day landings) beach; flat walk to town; gd dog walks; oyster beds & daily fish mkt; vg." ♦ 1 Apr-30 Sep. € 14.00 2009*

COURSEULLES SUR MER *3D1* (2km E Coastal) *49.33225, -0.42820* **Camping Le Havre de Bernières, Chemin de Quintefeuille, 14990 Bernières-sur-Mer [02 31 96 67 09; fax 02 31 97 31 06; info@camping-normandie.com; www.camping-normandie.com]** W fr Ouistreham on D514 for 20km. Site well sp. Lge, mkd pitch, pt sl, pt shd; wc; chem disp; 50% serviced pitches; shwrs inc; el pnts (20A) €6; Indtte; shop; rest; snacks; bar; playgrnd; pool; sand beach adj; tennis; games area; entmnt; many statics; dogs €4.20; poss v cr; Eng spkn; adv bkg; poss noisy; red low ssn; CCI. "Gd beaches & watersports; conv Ouistreham ferries; busy site, poss untidy; inadequate san facs high ssn & poss unclean; pool unclean (8/09); when site cr c'vans poss need manhandling; gates clsd 2200-0730." ♦ 28 Mar-31 Oct. € 27.50 2009*

COURSEULLES SUR MER *3D1* (8km SW Rural) *49.28949, -0.52970* **Camp Municipal des Trois Rivières, Route de Tierceville, 14480 Creully [tel/fax 02 31 80 12 00 or 02 31 80 90 17]** Fr Caen ring rd, exit junc 5 onto D7 twd N; at rndabt at Courseulles-sur-Mer turn L onto D12 dir Bayeux. At Tierceville turn S, sp Creully; site 1km on L on D93 to Creully. NB only app is fr Tierceville as c'vans not permitted on other rds. Med, hdg pitch, pt sl, pt shd; htd wc; chem disp (wc); shwrs inc; chem disp; el pnts (6-10A) €3.40-3.80 (long leads req, poss rev pol); Indtte; shops, rest, snacks, bar 1km; BBQ; playgrnd; pool 5km; games area; games rm; sand beach 5km; dogs €1.05; Eng spkn; adv bkg; quiet; ccard acc; CCI. "Well-maintained, clean site; gd pitches; friendly warden; excel facs, stretched high ssn; conv D-Day beaches, Bayeux; gd cycling." ♦ 1 Apr-30 Sep. € 10.10 2008*

COURTILS see Mont St Michel, Le *2E4*

COURVILLE SUR EURE *4E2* (S Urban) *48.44629, 1.24157* **Camp Municipal Les Bords de l'Eure, Ave Thier, 28190 Courville-sur-Eure [02 37 23 76 38 or 02 37 18 07 90 (Mairie); fax 02 37 18 07 99; jean-claude.larcher@courville-sur-eure.fr; www.courville-sur-eure.fr]** Turn N off D923 (N23) 19km W of Chartres. Site on bank of rv. Foll sp. Med, hdg pitch, pt shd; wc (some cont); chem disp (wc); shwrs; el pnts (6A) €2.81; supmkt 1km; rest in town; pool 200m; dogs; poss cr; quiet. "Lovely site; san facs clean, poss stetched high ssn; poss no twin-axles; conv Chartres; mkt Thurs." 1 Jun-15 Sep. € 10.20 2009*

⊞ **COUTANCES** *1D4* (1km W Urban) *49.05172, -1.45927* **FFCC Camp Municipal Les Vignettes, 27 Rue de St Malo, 50200 Coutances [02 33 45 43 13; fax 02 33 45 74 98]** Fr N on D971 or D2 turn R onto Coutances by-pass, sp St Malo & Avranches. At rndabt turn L. Site 200m on R after Cositel ent. Fr S foll sp for Valognes or Cherbourg. Site in Coutances on L immed after Logis sp. Med, hdg/mkd pitch, pt sl, pt shd; wc (some cont); chem disp; mv service pnt; shwrs inc; ltd el pnts (6A) €2.50; shops 500m; snacks; bar; BBQ; playgrnd; htd pool adj; sports stadium adj; few statics; dogs €1.05; poss cr; some rd noise; CCI. "Pretty site; gd, clean san facs; friendly warden; access poss diff to some pitches; muddy when wet; gd NH for Cherbourg." € 9.15 2008*

⊞ **COUTANCES** *1D4* (6.5km NW Rural) *49.09951, -1.48421* **Camping La Renaudière Féret, 50200 Ancteville [02 33 45 57 53; enquiries@renaudiere-feret.com; www.renaudiere-feret.com]** N fr Coutances on D2; in 6.5km take 1st R after R turn for Servigny; site on R in 200m. App fr N on D2, take 1st L turn after L turn for Ancteville (site on rd bet turnings for Ancteville & Servigny). Sm, unshd; wc; chem disp; mv service pnt; fam bthrm; shwrs inc; el pnts (10-16A) inc; shops nrby; BBQ area; wifi; dogs; adv bkg; quiet; red long stay. CCI. "Tranquil à la ferme site with nice views; British owners; conv NH or longer; vg. ♦ € 15.00 2009*

COUTRAS *7C2* (3km SW Rural) *45.01335, -0.10856* **Camping Résidential de Loisir Le Paradis, 8 Champ des Ardouins, Port-du-Mas, 33230 Abzac [05 57 49 05 10; fax 05 57 49 18 88; campingleparadis@free.fr; www.residentiel-leparadis.com]** Fr Coutras on S on D17 to Abzac, site well sp. Sm, pt shd; htd wc; mv service pnt; baby facs; shwrs inc; el pnts (6A) €3; gas; Indtte; shop; tradsmn; rest; snacks; BBQ; playgrnd; pool; lake sw, sand beach; fishing; games rm; entmnt;TV rm; 90% statics; dogs €1.50; ccard acc; m'vans only; CCI. "Excel site; san facs need refurb; gd for vineyards." 1 May-15 Sep. € 15.20 2009*

⊞ **COUTRAS** *7C2* (7.5km NW Rural) *45.07944, -0.20622* **Camping Le Chêne du Lac, 3 Lieu-dit Chateauneuf, 33230 Bayas [05 57 69 13 78 or 06 07 98 92 65 (mob); le-chene-du-lac@wanadoo.fr; www.camping-lechenedulac.com]** Fr Coutras W on D10 to Guitres; N fr Guitres on D247 to Bayas; site 2km N of Bayas, sp. Sm, mkd ptch, pt shd; wc (some cont); chem disp; shwrs inc; el pnts (10A) €4.30-5; gas; Indry rm; shop; tradsmn; snacks; bar; BBQ sep area; playgrnd; internet; 25% statics; no twin-axles; dogs €2; adv bkg; quiet; CCI. "Helpful owner; pedalos for hire adj; vg." ♦ € 12.10 2009*

COUTURES *4G1* (1km NE Rural) *47.37440, -0.34690* **Yelloh! Village Parc de Montsabert, 49320 Coutures [02 41 57 91 63; fax 02 41 57 90 02; camping@parcdemontsabert.com; www.parcdemontsabert.com or www.yellohvillage.com]** Easy access on R side of Rv Loire bet Angers & Saumur. Take D751 to Coutures & fr town cent foll sp for site. First R after 'Tabac' & foll rd to site (first on R bef chateau). Med, hdg/mkd pitch, hdstg, pt sl, pt shd; htd wc; chem disp; 50% serviced pitches; child/baby facs; shwrs inc; el pnts (5-10A) €2.95-4.10; Indtte; shop 1.5km; tradsmn; rest; snacks; bar; playgrnd; htd, covrd pool; paddling pool with slide; tennis; games area; games hall; cycle hire; crazy golf; gym; entmnt; TV; 15% statics; dogs €3.20; phone; bus 1km; Eng spkn; adv bkg; quiet; ccard acc; CCI. "Ideal for chateaux & wine cellars; lge pitches." ♦ 29 Apr-15 Sep. € 23.80 2006*

COUX see Montendre *7C2*

COUX ET BIGAROQUE see Bugue, Le *7C3*

COUZON see Bourbon L'Archambault *9A1*

COZES *7B1* (8km NE Rural) *45.61100, 0.74300* **Camping Vacances St Jacques, Allée de la Mirolle, 17260 St André-de-Lidon [tel/fax 05 46 90 11 05]** D129 fr St André-de-Lidon dir Montpellier-de-Médillan, at junc turn R onto D143 sp Cravans. Site on R in 100m. Sm, mkd pitch, pt shd; wc; shwrs; el pnts (16A) inc; gas 7km; Indtte; shops, rest, snacks 2km; bar; BBQ; playgrnd; paddling pool; sand beach 20km; TV rm; quiet; adv bkg; Eng spkn; no ccard acc. "Friendly British owners; CL-type site; gd for disabled; gd cycling; gd rests in vill; nrby beaches, medieval towns." ♦ May-Oct. € 12.00 2009*

COZES *7B1* (9km S Rural) *45.50148, -0.83518* **Camp Municipal St Seurin-d'Uzet, 12 Quai Esturgeon, 17120 Chenac-St Seurin-d'Uzet [05 46 90 45 31 or 05 46 90 44 03 (Mairie); fax 05 46 90 40 02; chenac-saint-seurin.duzet@mairie17.com]** SE fr Royan take D25/D145 thro St Georges-de-Didonne, Meschers-sur-Gironde & Talmont to St Seurin-d'Uzet. Site sp in vill. Med, hdg/mkd pitch, pt shd; wc; chem disp (wc); shwrs inc; el pnts (5A) €1.55 (poss rev pol & poss long lead req); Indtte; shop 100m; playgrnd; rv sw & sand beach adj; dogs €0.80; adv bkg rec high ssn; quiet. "Rec; pretty, well-maintained site beside creek; lge pitches; gd views & walks; pleasant staff; poss mosquito prob; gd vill shop." ♦ 1 May-30 Sep. € 7.10 2008*

COZES *7B1* (4km SW Rural) *45.54536, -0.88901* **Camping Fleur des Champs, Le Coudinier, 17120 Arces-sur-Gironde [05 46 90 40 11; fax 05 46 97 64 45; contact@campingfdc.com; www.campingfdc.com]** Site on D114 on R 1km fr Arces to Talmont. Sm, mkd pitch, pt sl, pt shd; wc; shwrs inc; el pnts (6A) €3.20; gas; tradsmn; Indtte; shop 1km; tradsmn; playgrnd; pool 4km; lake sw & beach; cycle hire; entmnts; 70% statics; dogs €1.50; quiet. "Nice, quiet rural site; ideal for seaside holiday away fr typical coastal sites." 1 Jun-15 Sep. € 9.00 2008*

COZES *7B1* (W Urban) *45.58650, -0.83568* **Camp Municipal Le Sorlut, Rue de Stade, 17120 Cozes [05 46 90 75 99 or 05 46 90 90 97 (Mairie); fax 05 46 90 75 12]** Clearly sp in Cozes, 150m fr D730 (N730). Turn into app rd on R of Champion supmkt. Med, mkd pitch, pt shd; wc; chem disp; shwrs inc; el pnts (5A) €2.53; Indry rm; shops adj; supmkt 500m; playgrnd; pool; sand beach 6km; tennis; poss cr; quiet; CCI. "Pleasant site close to Royan; helpful warden; ltd facs when only few o'fits; no arr 1200-1500; no twin-axles; popular with long stay British." 15 Apr-15 Oct. € 6.45 2009*

CRAC'H see Carnac *2G3*

CRAON *2F4* (E Urban) *47.84819, -0.94409* **Camp Municipal du Mûrier, Rue Alain Gerbault, 53400 Craon [02 43 06 96 33 or 02 43 06 13 09 (Mairie); fax 02 43 06 39 20; contact@ville-craon53.fr; www.ville-craon53.fr]** Fr Laval take D771 (N171) S to Craon. Site sp fr town cent. Sm, hdg pitch, pt shd; wc; shwrs inc; el pnts (6A) €2.10; Indtte; snacks; playgrnd; pool 200m; tennis; entmnt; wifi; no twin-axles; adv bkg; quiet; red long stay. "Lge pitches; san facs poss stretched when site full; easy walk to town; local chateau gardens." 1 May-22 Sep. € 10.00 2009*

CRAYSSAC *7D3* (500m SW Rural) *44.50694, 1.32416* **CAMPEOLE Camping Les Reflets du Quercy, Mas de Bastide, 46150 Crayssac [05 65 30 00 27; fax 05 17 47 50 80; reflets-du-quercy@campeole.com; www.camping-lot.info or www.campeole.com]** Take D911 W fr Cahors; 1km after steep winding climb foll camp sp on L sp Luzech for 1km. NB: D9 to Crayssac not rec. Med, hdg pitch, hdstg, pt sl, pt shd; htd wc; chem disp; mv service pnt; baby facs; shwrs inc; el pnts (10A) €4.10; gas; Indtte (inc dryer); shop; tradsmn; rest; bar; BBQ; playgrnd; pool; paddling pool; fishing, canoeing nr; tennis; horseriding nr; games area; games rm; wifi; entmnt; games/TV rm; 60% statics; dogs €2.60; Eng spkn; adv bkg; quiet; ccard acc; red low ssn; CCI. "Beautiful touring & walking area; pleasant, helpful staff." ♦ 3 Apr-19 Sep. € 20.00 2009*

See advertisement

CRECHES SUR SAONE see Mâcon *9A2*

CREISSAN *10F1* (Urban) *43.37550, 3.00909* **Camp Municipal Les Oliviers, 34370 Creissan [04 67 93 81 85 or 04 67 93 75 41 (Mairie); fax 04 67 93 85 28; mairie@creissan.com; www.creissan.com]** Fr D612 (N112) foll sp Creissan & site. Sm, mkd pitch, pt shd; shwrs inc; el pnts €3; Indtte; shop, rest, bar in vill; BBQ; playgrnd; municipal pool adj; tennis; entmnt; adv bkg; quiet. "Pleasant site located in housing estate (30 pitches); helpful & friendly; key req to immac san facs - warden's hrs ltd (2009); excel." 1 Apr-30 Sep. € 10.25 2009*

⊞ **CREMIEU** *9B2* (5km NW Rural) *45.74829, 5.22486* **Camping à la Ferme des Epinettes, 11 Rue de l'Eglise, 38460 St Romain-de-Jalionas [tel/fax 04 74 90 94 90 or 06 19 31 03 50 (mob); cochet38@wanadoo.fr]** N fr Crémieu on D517; in 3km site sp on R, immed bef rndabt on edge of St Romain-de-Jalionas. Sm, mkd pitch, pt shd; htd wc; chem disp (wc); shwrs inc; el pnts (5A) €3; Indry rm; shops etc 5km; 20% statics; dogs €1; no twin-axles; quiet; red low ssn. "Rec NH for interesting & historic town of Crémieu; ltd facs low ssn." ♦ € 11.00 2008*

⊞ **CREON** *7D2* (3km NW Rural) *44.78372, -0.37108* **FFCC Camping Caravaning Bel Air, 33670 Créon [05 56 23 01 90; fax 05 56 23 08 38; info@camping-bel-air.com; www.camping-bel-air.com]** Fr A10/E70 at junc 24 take D936 E fr Bordeaux sp Bergerac. Approx 15km E turn SE onto D671 sp Créon & cont for 5km. Site on L, 1.5km after Lorient. Med, hdg/mkd pitch, hdstg, pt shd; wc (some cont); chem disp; mv service pnt; shwrs inc; el pnts (5A) €3.50; gas; Indtte; shop high ssn; tradsmn; supmkt 1km; rest; snacks; bar; playgrnd; pool; 10% statics; dogs €2.50; clsd to vehicles 2200-0800; Eng spkn; adv bkg; quiet; red long stay; CCI. "Helpful owners; no twin-axle vans; phone ahead to check open low ssn; rest sm & ltd; facs v ltd low ssn; Bordeaux 20km; sh stay/NH only." ♦ € 13.00 2007*

CRESPIAN *10E1* (S Rural) *43.87850, 4.09590* **Camping Le Mas de Reilhe, 30260 Crespian [04 66 77 82 12; fax 04 66 80 26 50; info@camping-mas-de-reilhe.fr; www.camping-mas-de-reilhe.fr]** Exit A9 at Nîmes Ouest N onto N106 dir Alès for 5km. Fork R, then L over bdge onto D999 dir Le Vigan. Foll rd for 24km, R at x-rds onto D6110 (N110) to site on R just on ent Crespian. Take care - ent on a bend on busy rd. Med, mkd pitch, pt sl, terr, pt shd; wc; chem disp; baby facs; shwrs inc; el pnts (6A) inc; Indtte; shop; rest; snacks; bar; BBQ (gas/elec); playgrnd; htd pool & paddling pool; tennis; fishing & horseriding 10km; games rm; entmnt high ssn; wifi; TV; dogs €2.60; poss cr; Eng spkn; quiet but poss some rd noise; ccard acc; red low ssn; CCI. "Quiet & relaxing site; friendly staff; conv Nîmes, Uzès & Cévennes National Park; excel." ♦ 3 Apr-19 Sep. € 25.40 (CChq acc) ABS - C10 2009*

CREST *9D2* (5km E Rural) *44.71095, 5.08960* **Gervanne Camping, Bellevue, 26400 Mirabel-et-Blacons [04 75 40 00 20; fax 04 75 40 03 97; info@gervanne-camping.com; www.gervanne-camping.com]** Exit A7 junc 16 Loriol onto D104/D164, turn off onto D93. Site E of Mirabel-et-Blacons on both sides or rd. Recep by shop. Med, pt sl, pt shd; htd wc; chem disp; mv service pnt; shwrs inc; baby facs; el pnts (4-6A) €3.20-3.90; gas; Indtte; shop adj; rest; snacks; bar; BBQ (gas/elec); playgrnd; htd pool; rv sw & beach adj; games area; internet; TV; 7% statics; dogs €2.50; poss cr; Eng spkn; adv bkg (ess high ssn); quiet; ccard acc; red low ssn; CCI. "Excel, family-run site in beautiful area on Rv Drôme; gd size pitches but poss soft after rain - no hdstg; lovely pool complex; vg rest." ♦ 1 Apr-30 Sep. € 19.00 2009*

CREST *9D2* (500m S Urban) *44.72410, 5.02755* **Camping Les Clorinthes, 26400 Crest [04 75 25 05 28; fax 04 75 76 75 09; lecampinglesclorinthes@minitel.net]** S fr Crest twd Nyons on D538 turn L immed after x-ing bdge over rv. Site sp. Lge, hdg/mkd pitch, pt sl, pt shd; wc (some cont); own san rec; chem disp; shwrs; el pnts (6A) €3.60; gas; Indtte; shop & 500m; tradsmn; snacks; bar; pool; rv sw adj; sports complex 500m; TV; entmnt; fishing; 20% statics; dogs €2.10; phone; poss cr; adv bkg; poss cr; quiet, some train noise; CCI. "Well-maintained; dir access rv; beautiful situation; muddy when wet." ♦ 1 Apr-30 Sep. € 15.80 2006*

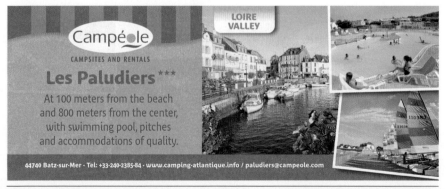

CREST *9D2* (8km W Rural) *44.72717, 4.92664* **Camping Les Quatre Saisons, Route de Roche-sur-Grane, 26400 Grane [04 75 62 64 17; fax 04 75 62 69 06; contact@camping-4-saisons.com; www.camping-4saisons.com]** Exit A7 at junc for Loriol or Crest, take D104 E for 18km. Turn R thro vill twd Roche-sur-Grane, site well sp. If a lge unit, access thro 4th junc to Grane. Site well sp fr Crest. Med, pt sl, terr, pt shd; wc; chem disp; mv service pnt; baby facs; shwrs inc; el pnts (6A) €3.50; Indtte; shop; tradsmn; snacks; bar; BBQ; pool; tennis; games area; some statics; dogs; phone; poss cr; adv bkg; Eng spkn; quiet; red long stay/low ssn; ccard acc; CCI. "Beautiful views; well-run site; pleasant, helpful owner; sm & lge pitches; excel san facs; nice pool; Grane (supmkt, rest etc.) in walking dist; gd." ♦ 1 Apr-30 Sep. € 20.00 (CChq acc) 2008*

CREULLY see Courseulles sur Mer *3D1*

CREVECOEUR EN BRIE see Fontenay Trésigny *4E3*

⊞ **CREVECOEUR LE GRAND** *3C3* (7km SE Rural) **Camping à la Ferme (Fontana), 8 Hameau de la Neuve Rue, 60480 Ourcel-Maison [03 44 46 81 55]** NE fr Beauvais on D1001 (N1) to Froissy; turn W at traff lts onto D151. Avoid 1st sp to Francastel but cont to x-rds & turn into vill on D11. Francastel adjoins Ourcel-Maison & site at far end. Or fr A16 exit junc 16 W onto D930 & foll sp. Sm, pt shd; wc (some cont); chem disp; shwrs inc; el pnts (5A) inc (rev pol); shop 6km; tradsmn; rest; BBQ; playgrnd; quiet; ccard not acc. "Farm produce & occasional eve meals avail; no hdstg & poss muddy/diff in wet; gd NH." € 8.00 2008*

CREVECOEUR LE GRAND *3C3* (10km SW Rural) **Camping du Vieux Moulin, 9 Rue Larris Boissy, 60690 Roy-Boissy [03 44 46 33 06]** Fr Marseille-en-Beauvasis SW onto D930 dir Gournay-en-Bray; in 1.5km site sp to R at Roy-Boissy. Sm, pt shd; wc; chem disp; shwrs inc; el pnts inc (poss rev pol); playgrnd; 90% statics; phone; v quiet. "Farm site in area with few sites; beautiful countryside; pitch yourself, owner calls eves; excel." ♦ 1 Apr-31 Oct. € 8.00 2009*

CREYSSE see Martel *7C3*

⊞ **CRIEL SUR MER** *3B2* (2km N Coastal) *50.02568, 1.30855* **FFCC Camp Municipal Le Mont Joli Bois, 29 Rue de la Plage, 76910 Criel-sur-Mer [02 35 50 81 19; fax 02 35 50 22 37; camping.criel@wanadoo.fr]** Fr D925 take D222 into Criel cent. Turn R opp church into D126 for 1.6km to beach. Turn L then immed R & foll beach rd to site in 1.5km. Med, hdg/mkd pitch, pt sl, terr, pt shd; htd wc; chem disp; mv service pnt; shwrs inc; el pnts (4-6A) €3-4.50; Indtte; tradsmn; shops, rest, snacks & bar 2km; playgrnd; shgl beach 500m; TV rm; 50% statics; dogs €1.50; bus; poss cr; quiet; CCI. "Fair." ♦ € 10.40 2007*

CRIEL SUR MER *3B2* (1.5km NW Coastal) *50.03048, 1.30815* **Camping Les Mouettes, 43 Rue de la Plage, 76910 Criel-sur-Mer [tel/fax 02 35 86 70 73; contact@camping-lesmouettes.fr; www.camping-lesmouettes.fr]** Fr D925 take D222 thro Criel to coast, site sp. Care needed with narr, steep access. Sm, mkd pitch, terr, unshd; wc; chem disp; shwrs; el pnts (6A) €3.50; Indtte; shop; supmkt 5km; snacks; bar; BBQ; games area; games rm; TV; some statics; dogs €2; Eng spkn; adv bkg; quiet. "V nice little site; well-kept; friendly, helpful owner; gd san facs; sea views." 1 Apr-1 Nov. € 13.50 2009*

CRIQUETOT L'ESNEVAL see Etretat *3C1*

CROISIC, LE *2G3* (1km SE Coastal) *47.29415, -2.53846* **Camping Le Paradis, 44490 Le Croisic [02 40 23 07 89; www.camping-paradis.com]** Fr La Baule take D245 to Le Croisic; on ent Le Croisic cont on D245 (R fork), which then becomes the D45 coast rd; cont on coast rd anti-clockwise for approx 4km until site sp on L. Med, hdg/mkd pitch, pt shd; wc; chem disp; shwrs inc; el pnts (3-6A) €2.90-€3.60; gas; Indtte; shop 2km; rest; snacks; bar; BBQ; playgrnd; sand/shgl beach adj; golf adj; dogs €2; poss cr; adv bkg; red low ssn; CCI. "Beaches sm bet rocks; gd cycling; gd mkt; vg." 1 May-30 Sep. € 12.00 2009*

CROISIC, LE *2G3* (3.5km SE Coastal) *47.27888, -2.49138* **CAMPEOLE Camping Les Paludiers, Rue Nicolas Appert, 44740 Batz-sur-mer [02 40 23 85 84; fax 02 40 23 75 55; paludiers@campeole.com; www.camping-atlantique.info or www.campeole.com]** Fr Guérande take D774/D245 to Batz-sur-Mer. Thro Batz sp Le Croisic, site is opp windmill. Lge, hdg/mkd pitch, unshd; wc; mv service pnt; baby facs; shwrs; el pnts inc; Indtte (inc dryer); tradsmn; rest; snacks; bar; BBQ; playgrnd; htd pool; paddling pool; sand beach 100m; watersports; cycle hire; games area; games rm; wifi; TV rm; 50% statics; dogs €2.50-3.20; Eng spkn; adv bkg; quiet; ccard acc; red low ssn; CCI. "Vg, family site; helpful, friendly staff." ♦ 1 Apr-30 Sep. € 26.60 2009*

See advertisement opposite

CROISIC, LE *2G3* (2km S Coastal) *47.29272, -2.52850* **Camping La Pierre Longue, Rue Henri Dunant, 44490 Le Croisic [02 40 23 13 44; fax 02 40 23 23 13; contact@campinglapierrelongue.com; www.camping lapierrelongue.com]** Turn L off Le Pouliguen-Le Croisic rd at g'ge at Le Croisic sp; foll camp sps. Lge, hdg/mkd pitch, pt shd; htd wc; chem disp; mv service pnt; baby facs; shwrs inc; el pnts (6-10A) €3.50-5; gas; Indtte; shop; rest; snacks; bar; BBQ; playgrnd; htd pool; sand beach 500m; entmnt; TV; 60% statics; phone; dogs; Eng spkn; adv bkg; quiet; ccard acc; red low ssn; CCI. "Warm welcome; excel facs; excel beaches." ♦ 1 Mar-30 Nov. € 20.00 2009*

See advertisement on next page

France

CROISIC, LE *2G3* (1km W Coastal) *47.29558, -2.53605* **Camping de l'Océan, 15 Route de la Maison Rouge, 44490 Le Croisic [02 40 23 07 69; fax 02 40 15 70 63; info@camping-ocean.com; www.camping-ocean.com]** Foll N171/D213 to Guérande. At junc take D774 to La Baule, Batz-sur-Mer, then D245 to Le Croisic. At rndabt foll site sp. Lge, hdg/mkd pitch, pt shd; wc; chem disp; mv service pnt; serviced pitches; baby facs; shwrs inc; el pnts (6A) €4-6; gas; lndtte; shop; rest; snacks; bar; BBQ; playgrnd; 2 htd pools, (1 covrd); waterslide; jacuzzi; shgl beach 150m; tennis; games area; fitness rm; wifi; entmnt; 30% statics; dogs €6.50; adv bkg; Eng spkn; quiet; red low ssn; ccard acc; red low ssn/CCI. "Interesting coast line nr La Baule; caves & rocky headlands; salt flats at ent to Le Croisic; pleasant walk to walled city of Guérande adj; excel pools complex." ♦ 3 Apr-30 Sep. € 40.00 2009*

CROIX EN TERNOIS see St Pol sur Ternoise *3B3*

CROIXILLE, LA see Ernée *2E4*

CROMARY see Rioz *6G2*

CROTOY, LE *3B2* (Urban/Coastal) *50.22226, 1.61804* **Camping La Prairie, 2 Rue de Mayocq, 80550 Le Crotoy [tel/fax 03 22 27 02 65; info@camping-laprairie.fr; www.camping-laprairie.fr]** Fr S exit A16 at Abbeville onto D86/D940 to Le Crotoy to rndabt at ent to town. Cont strt for 1.5km then 2nd L, site on L in 500m. Fr N exit A16 for Rue onto D32, then D940, then as above. Lge, hdg pitch, pt shd; wc (some cont); chem disp (wc); shwrs; el pnts (3A) inc; tradsmn; playgrnd; sand beach 400m; 90% statics; dogs €1; phone; poss cr; quiet. "Busy site; ltd pitches for tourers; conv beach & town; gd san facs; gd cycle paths." ♦ 1 Apr-30 Sep. € 18.60 2009*

CROTOY, LE *3B2* (1.5km N Rural) *50.22968, 1.64140* **Camping La Ferme de Tarteron, Route de Rue, 80550 Le Crotoy [03 22 27 06 75; fax 03 22 27 02 49; contact@letarteron.fr; www.letarteron.fr]** Fr A16 exit junc 24 onto D32, then D940 around Rue twd Le Crotoy. Pass D4 dir St Firmin site on L. Med, hdg/mkd pitch, pt shd; wc; chem disp; shwrs inc; el pnts (4A) €3.40; gas; shop; tradsmn; snacks; bar; playgrnd; htd pool; sand beach 1.5km; many statics; quiet. "Conv Marquenterre bird park & steam train fr Le Crotoy." 1 Apr-31 Oct. € 17.90 2007*

CROTOY, LE *3B2* (3km N Rural/Coastal) *50.23905, 1.63182* **Kawan Club Camping Le Ridin, Mayocq, 80550 Le Crotoy [03 22 27 03 22; fax 03 22 27 70 76; leridin@baiedesommepleinair.com; www.baiedesommepleinair.com]** Fr A16 exit junc 24 dir Rue & Le Crotoy. At rndabt on D940 on app to Le Crotoy take D4 (due W) sp St Firmin, take 2nd rd to R, site sp. Do not ent Le Crotoy town with c'van. Lge, hdg/mkd pitch, hdstg, unshd; htd wc; chem disp; mv service pnt; baby facs; fam bthrm; shwrs inc; el pnts (6-10A) €3-5; gas; lndtte (inc dryer); shop; supmkt 1km; tradsmn; rest; snacks; bar; playgrnd; htd pool; paddling pool; sand beach 1km; tennis 4km; cycle hire; fitness rm; games rm; golf 10km; wifi; entmnt; TV rm; 60% statics; dogs €2; poss cr; Eng spkn; adv bkg; quiet except noise fr adj gravel pit/lorries; ccard acc; red long stay/CCI. "Some sm, tight pitches bet statics; narr site rds not suitable lge o'fits; clean san facs, unisex low ssn; bird sanctuary at Marquenterre; Le Crotoy beautiful town; vg site." ♦ 1 Apr-5 Nov. € 22.00 (CChq acc) 2009*

See advertisement opposite

CROTOY, LE *3B2* (4km N Coastal) *50.24941, 1.61145* **Camping Les Aubépines, 800 Rue de la Maye, St Firmin, 80550 Le Crotoy [03 22 27 01 34; fax 03 22 27 13 66; lesaubepines@baiedesommepleinair.com; www.baiedesommepleinair.com]** Exit A16 junc 23 to Le Crotoy via D40 & D940; then foll sp St Firmin; site sp. Or exit A16 junc 24 onto D32 dir Rue; by-pass Rue but take D4 to St Firmin; after church look for site sp. Site on rd to beach on W of D4. Med, hdg/mkd pitch, pt shd; htd wc; chem disp; baby facs; shwrs inc; el pnts (3-10A) €3-8 (poss long lead req); gas; lndtte; shop; tradsmn; BBQ; playgrnd; htd pool; paddling pool; sand beach 1km; horseriding; games rm; entmnt; 40% statics; dogs €1.50; phone; poss cr; Eng spkn; adv bkg; quiet; ccard acc; red low ssn; CCI. "Well-run site; tourers sited with statics; some pitches sm; gd cycling & walking; Marquenterre ornithological park 3km; steam train 3km; excel." ♦ 1 Apr-7 Nov. € 21.50 2009*

See advertisement opposite

CROUY SUR COSSON see Muides sur Loire *4G2*

⊞ **CROZON** *2E2* (5km E Coastal) *48.24204, -4.42932* **Camping L'Aber, Tal-ar-Groas, Route de la Plage de l'Aber, 29160 Crozon [02 98 27 02 96 or 06 75 62 39 07 (mob); contact@camping-aber.com; www.camping-aber.com]** On F887 turn S in Tal-ar-Groas foll camp sp to site in 1km on R. Med, mkd pitch, pt sl, terr, pt shd; wc; shwrs inc; el pnts (6A) €2; gas; Indtte; snacks; bar; htd pool; sand beach 1km; sailing; fishing; windsurfing; dogs €1.50; adv bkg; quiet. ♦ € 13.20 2008*

CROZON *2E2* (3km SW) *48.22138, -4.52285* **Camping Les Bruyères, Le Bouis, 29160 Crozon [tel/fax 02 98 26 14 87; camping.les.bruyeres@presquile-crozon.com]** Take D887 then D255 SW fr Crozon (sp Cap de la Chèvre). In 1.5km turn R & site on R in 700m. Lge, mkd pitch, pt shd; wc (mainly cont); shwrs inc; gas; shop in ssn; el pnts (5A) €2.80; playgrnd; sand beach 1.8km; dogs €1; Eng spkn; adv bkg; quiet; red 2+ days. "Gd san facs; conv beaches & mkt town." 1 Jun-15 Sep. € 13.00 2006*

CUBJAC *7C3* (1.5km S Rural) *45.2167, 0.9333* **Camping L'Ilot, 24640 Cubjac [05 53 05 39 79; fax 05 53 05 37 82; musitelli@wanadoo.fr]** Take D5 E fr Périgueux to Cubjac (21km). Fork R off D5 into vill. At x-rds in vill turn S & site on R in 1.5km. Sm, mkd pitch, pt shd; wc (some cont); baby facs; shwrs inc; el pnts (5A) €3; Indtte; shop adj; rest; snacks; bar; BBQ; playgrnd; pool 4km; fishing; canoes; tennis adj; games area; entmnt; dogs free; adv bkg. ♦ 1 Apr-30 Sep. € 12.00 2008*

CUCURON see Cadenet *10E3*

CUERS *10F3* (6km W Rural) *43.23243, 6.00645* **Camping Les Tomasses, 83210 Belgentier [04 94 48 92 70; fax 04 94 48 94 73]** Exit A8 junc 34 St Maximin onto N7. After Tourves take D205 then D5/D554 sp Solliès-Pont. After Belgentier in 1.5km turn R at yellow sp, site in 200m on L. Or N fr Toulon onto D554. Well sp on R in vill. Med, hdg/mkd pitch, pt shd; wc (mainly cont); chem disp (wc); shwrs inc; el pnts (6A) €3.50; gas; Indtte; shop; snacks; bar; BBQ; playgrnd; pool; tennis; entmnt; 10% statics; dogs €2; phone; bus 300m; adv bkg; quiet, poss dog noise; red low ssn; CCI. "Pretty CL-type site; friendly management; twin-axles welcome; acces poss diff lge o'fits" ♦ 1 Apr-30 Sep. € 13.30 2006*

CUISEAUX *9A2* (5km W Rural) *46.49570, 5.32662* **Camping Le Domaine de Louvarel, 71480 Champagnat [tel/fax 03 85 76 62 71; contact@domainedelouvarel.com; www.domainedelouvarel.com]** Exit A39 junc 9 dir Cuiseaux; foll sp 'Base de Loisirs de Louvarel'. Or fr D1083 (N83) exit Champagnat & foll sp to site on lakeside. Med, hdg/mkd, terr, pt shd (planted 2007); htd wc; chem disp; mv service pnt; baby facs; fam bthrm; shwrs inc; el pnts (10A) €4; Indtte; tradsmn; rest; snacks; bar; BBQ; playgrnd; lake sw adj, sand beach; fishing; boating; games area; cycle hire; 7% statics; dogs €1; phone; o'night area for m'vans; Eng spkn; adv bkg; quiet; CCI. "Helpful manager; excel, immac san facs; gd walking; gd rest in ssn." 22 Mar-5 Nov. € 14.00 (CChq acc) 2008*

CULAN *7A4* (7km E Rural) *46.54123, 2.42675* **Camp Municipal Les Bergerolles, 18360 Vesdun [02 48 63 03 07 (Mairie); fax 02 48 63 12 62; mairie.vesdun.cher@wanadoo.fr]** Exit Culan S on D943 twd Montluçon; in 200m turn L onto D4 to Vesdun. Site sp in vill adj stadium. Sm, mkd pitch, pt shd; wc; shwrs inc; el pnts; shop, rest, snacks, bar 500m; playgrnd; games area; quiet. "Vill has monument/garden `Centre of France'; pay site fees at Mairie 300m." Whitsun-30 Sep. 2006*

CULOZ see Ruffieux *9B3*

CUVILLY *3C3* (1.5km N Rural) *49.56750, 2.70790* **Camping de Sorel, 24 Rue de St Claude, 60490 Orvillers-Sorel [03 44 85 02 74; fax 03 44 42 11 65; contact@aestiva.fr; www.aestiva.fr]** Exit A1/E15 at junc 12 (Roye) S'bound or 11 (Ressons) N'bound. Site on E of D1017. Med, mkd pitch, pt shd; htd wc; chem disp; shwrs inc; el pnts (6A) €3; Indry rm; shop; tradsmn; rest; snacks; bar; playgrnd; games area; TV; 50% statics; poss cr; quiet. "Pleasant situation; conv NH nr a'route & Calais; gd facs; friendly staff; rec early arr in ssn; busy at w/end; 30 mins Parc Astérix." 2 Feb-14 Dec. € 15.00 (CChq acc) 2009*

France

DAGLAN *7D3* (3km Rural) *44.76762, 1.17590* **Camping Le Moulin de Paulhiac, 24250 Daglan [05 53 28 20 88; fax 05 53 29 33 45; francis.armagnac@wanadoo.fr; www.moulin-de-paulhiac.com]** D57 SW fr Sarlat, across rv into St Cybranet & site in 2km. Fr Souillac W on D703 alongside Rv Dordogne; x-ing rv onto D46 (nr Domme) & D50, to site. Med, hdg/mkd pitch, shd; wc (some cont); chem disp; mv service pnt; shwrs; el pnts (6-10A) €3.60-4.30; gas; Indtte; shop; rest; snacks; bar; playgrnd; 4 htd pools; waterslide; TV rm; entmnt; shgl beach/rv adj with canoeing/fishing; 20% statics; dogs €1.90; poss cr; Eng spkn; adv bkg; quiet with some rd noise; red low ssn; ccard acc; CCI. "V pretty site; friendly, helpful staff; vg fruit/veg mkt Sun in vill." ♦ 15 May-16 Sep. € 24.20 2009*

DAMAZAN *7D2* (2km S Rural) **Camp Municipal du Lac, Route de Buzet-sur-Baïse, 47160 Damazan [05 53 79 40 15; fax 05 53 79 26 92]** Fr A62 take junc 6, turn R at rndabt. Almost immed take slip rd sp Damazan/Buzet-dur-Baïse. At top turn R sp Buzet. Site 1km on R (2nd turning goes to lake only); adj cricket club. Med, some hdg/mkd pitch, pt sl, pt shd; wc (some cont); chem disp (wc); shwrs inc; el pnts (10A) €2; gas 2km; Indtte; shops, rest, snacks, bar 2km; BBQ; playgrnd adj; lake sw adj; 2% statics; dogs; phone adj; poss cr; adv bkg; quiet but nr a'route; CCI. "Pretty site by lake; helpful staff; warden calls am & pm; if office clsd, pitch self; clean basic san facs; attractive Bastide town; conv NH; excel." ♦ 1 Jun-30 Sep. € 10.00 2009*

DAMBACH *5D3* (500m E Rural) *48.32271, 7.44320* **Aire Naturelle Municipal du Hohenfels, Rue du Stade, 67110 Dambach [03 88 09 24 08; fax 03 88 09 21 81]** Fr N on D35 turn S onto D853, site sp. Med, pt sl, terr, pt shd; wc; chem disp; shwrs inc; el pnts (6A) €3; quiet. "Delightfully peaceful setting; lovely area; warden calls 0900-0930, site yourself; access poss diff lge o'fits; walk fr site to Maginot Line relics." 1 Apr-31 Oct. € 10.30 2008*

DAMBACH LA VILLE see Sélestat *6E3*

DAMGAN see Muzillac *2G3*

DAMPIERRE SUR BOUTONNE *7A2* (Rural) *46.06642, -0.41459* **Camp Municipal, 17470 Dampierre-sur-Boutonne [05 46 24 02 36 (Mairie); fax 05 46 33 95 49; dampierre-sur-boutonne@mairie17.com]** S fr Niort on D150 twds St Jean-d'Angély; in vill of Tout-y-Faut turn E on D115 sp Dampierre; turn N in vill on D127 twds Rv Boutonne, site behind vill hall; well sp. Sm, hdg pitch, shd; wc (some cont); shwrs inc; el pnts (6A) €2; shop, rest, snacks, bar 500m; rv fishing; dogs €0.80; quiet. "Clean site; san facs outside camp boundary & wc's open to public; poss noisy, local youths congregate nrby; rec sh stay/NH only." 30 Apr-30 Sep. € 7.90 2009*

DAMVIX see Maillezais *7A2*

DANGE ST ROMAIN *4H2* (3km N Rural) *46.96944, 0.60399* **Camp Municipal, 8 Rue des Buxières, 86220 Les Ormes [05 49 85 61 30 (Mairie); fax 05 49 85 66 17; les-ormes@cg86.fr; www.lesormes.fr]** Turn W off D910 (N10) in cent Les Ormes onto D1a sp Vellèches & Marigny-Marmande, foll site sp to site on rv. Sm, mkd pitch, pt sl, pt shd; wc; chem disp (wc); shwrs inc; el pnts (10A) inc; Indtte; shop, rest, bar 800m; playgrnd; tennis 100m; dogs €1.20; quiet, but some rlwy noise; adv bkg; Eng spkn; dogs; CCI. "Lovely, quiet setting on rv bank; friendly & helpful warden; clean san facs; quiet vill; chateau in walking dist." 1 Apr-30 Sep. € 8.30 2008*

DAON see Château Gontier *4F1*

DARBRES *9D2* (Rural) *44.64788, 4.50372* **Camping Les Lavandes, 07170 Darbres [tel/fax 04 75 94 20 65; sarl.leslavandes@online.fr; www.les-lavandes-darbres.com]** SE fr Aubenas on N102 twds Montélimar. Turn L after 10km in vill Lavilledieu onto D224 sp Lussas. Cont 5km to Darbres, site sp. Med, mkd pitch, terr, pt shd; wc; chem disp; baby facs; shwrs inc; el pnts (6A) €3.50; Indtte; shop; rest; snacks; bar; BBQ (gas/charcoal only); playgrnd; pool; waterslide; games area; cycle hire; entmnt; TV; some statics; dogs €2.50; poss cr; Eng spkn; quiet; ccard acc. "Attractive site; gd san facs." Easter-30 Sep. € 17.00 2007*

DARDILLY see Lyon *9B2*

⊞ **DAX** *8E1* (3.5km NE Urban) *43.74707, -0.99539* **Camping Les Jardins de l'Adour, 848 Rue de Pouy, 40990 St Vincent-de-Paul [tel/fax 05 58 89 99 60 or 06 03 03 09 77 (mob); info@camping-jardinsdeladour.fr; www.camping-jardinsdeladour.fr]** NE on D824 (N124) fr Dax twd Mont-de-Marsan on dual c'way, take exit to St Vincent-de-Paul at rndabt; site in 200m on L, sp. Med, hdg/mkd pitch, shd; wc; chem disp; mv service pnt; shwrs inc; el pnts (6A) €3; gas; Indtte; shop 1km & 5km; rest; snacks; pool; sand beach 30km; 50% statics; dogs €1.50; phone; barrier clsd 2230-0730; Eng spkn; adv bkg; CCI. "Pretty, well-kept site; friendly, helpful owners; clean san facs; excel." ♦ € 14.00 2008*

DAX *8E1* (1.5km W Rural) *43.71189, -1.07304* **Camping Les Chênes, Allée du Bois de Boulogne, 40100 Dax [05 58 90 05 53; fax 05 58 90 42 43; camping-chenes@wanadoo.fr; www.camping-les-chenes.fr]** Fr D824 (N124) to Dax, foll sp Bois de Boulogne, cross rlwy bdge & rv bdge & foll camp sp on rv bank. Well sp. Lge, mkd pitch, shd; htd wc (cont); chem disp; some serviced pitches; shwrs inc; el pnts (5A) inc; gas; Indtte; shop; tradsmn; rest adj; snacks; takeaway; bar; playgrnd; pool; beach 20km; TV rm; cycle hire; many statics; dogs €1.50; poss cr; Eng spkn; adv bkg; ccard acc; red low ssn; CCI. "Excel position; gd san facs; easy walk along rv into town; poss noise fr school adj; conv thermal baths at Dax." ♦ 22 Mar-1 Nov. € 17.90 2008*

DAX *8E1* (6km W Rural) *43.72680, -1.12302* **Camping L'Etang d'Ardy, Route de Bayonne, 40990 St Paul-lès-Dax [05 58 97 57 74; info@etangardy.com; www.etangardy.com]** Fr E on D824 (N124) dir Dax; turn R onto D16 dir Magescq; then L sp Ardy; foll camping sp. Fr W leave D824 sp La Pince/Dax/Magescq; at rndabt U-turn onto D824 going E; take 1st exit & foll site sp. Med, hdg pitch, shd; wc; chem disp; serviced pitches; shwrs inc; el pnts (5-10A) €2.20-3.15; Indtte; shops; tradsmn; playgrnd; pool; lake fishing; 30% statics; dogs €1.50; adv bkg; quiet; red long stay. "Friendly site." ♦ 5 Apr-25 Oct. € 18.20 2006*

DAX *8E1* (9km W Rural) *43.68206, -1.14974* **Camping Lou Bascou, 40180 Rivière-Saas-et-Gourby [05 58 97 57 29; fax 05 58 97 59 52; loubascou@orange.fr; www.camping loubascou.fr]** Leave N10 at junc 9 for D824 (N124) twd Dax. In 3.5km turn R onto D13 sp Rivière-Saas-et-Gourby. Well sp fr D824. Beware speed humps in Rivière vill. Med, hdg/mkd pitch, pt shd; htd wc; chem disp; mv service pnt; shwrs inc; el pnts (6-10A) €3-5; Indtte; shop 300m; tradsmn; snacks; bar; BBQ; playgrnd; pool 9km; sand beach 25km; tennis; entmnt; 50% statics in sep area; dogs €1.50; Eng spkn; adv bkg; red long stay/low ssn. "Quiet, friendly site; excel, clean facs; thermal facs in Dax; nrby wetlands wildlife inc storks worth seeing; vg NH." ♦ 1 Apr-31 Oct. € 16.00 2009*

⊞ **DAX** *8E1* (11km W Rural) *43.68706, -1.14687* **FFCC Camping à la Ferme Bertranborde (Lafitte), 975 Route des Clarions, 40180 Rivière-Saas-et-Gourby [05 58 97 58 39; bertranborde@orange.fr]** Turn S off D824 (N124) 5km W of Dax onto D113, sp Angoumé; at x-rd in 2km turn R (by water tower); then immed L; site on R in 100m, well sp. Or fr N10/A63, exit junc 9 onto D824 dir Dax; in 5km turn R onto D113, then as bef. Sm, pt shd, pt sl; wc (own san); chem disp; mv service pnt; shwrs inc; el pnts (4-10A) €2.50-4; Indtte; ice; shops 3km; BBQ; playgrnd; rv sw 7km; dogs €0.50; poss cr; Eng spkn; quiet; adv bkg; CCI. "Peaceful CL-type site; beautiful garden; friendly, helpful owners; meals on request; min 2 nights high ssn; poss itinerants festival time; excel." € 9.50 2009*

DAX *8E1* (3km NW Rural) *43.72020, -1.09365* **FFCC Camping Les Pins du Soleil, Route des Minières, La Pince, 40990 St Paul-les-Dax [05 58 91 37 91; fax 05 58 91 00 24; info@pinsoleil.com; www.pinsoleil.com]** Exit N10 junc 11 sp Dax onto D16. Cross D824 (N124) & turn R onto D459 S. Cross rndabt & cont on D459, Route des Minières. Site sp in pine forest. Med, hdg/mkd pitch, pt sl, pt shd; htd wc, chem disp; mv service pnt; serviced pitches; baby facs; shwrs inc; el pnts (5A) €2; gas; Indtte; shop; tradsmn; rest 1km; snacks; bar; playgrnd; pool; tennis 2km; cycle hire; entmnt; internet; TV rm; 25% statics; dogs €2; phone; Eng spkn; some rd noise; red long stay/low ssn; ccard acc. "Nice, quiet site (low ssn); various pitch sizes, some spacious; soft, sandy soil poss problem when wet; helpful, friendly staff; excel pool; spa 2km; conv Pyrenees & Biarritz; vg." ♦ 29 Mar-7 Nov. € 24.00 (CChq acc) 2007*

DAX *8E1* (12km NW Rural) *43.82364, -1.15103* **FFCC Camping Aire Naturelle Le Toy (Fabas), 40990 Herm [05 58 91 55 16; fax 05 58 91 09 50; vincent.fabas@laposte.net; www.camping-du-toy.com]** Exit N10 junc 11 at Magescq; foll sps for cent vill & then Herm on D150; at Herm x-rds by church turn L onto rd to Castets. Site 1km on R. Sm, hdg/mkd pitch, shd; wc; shwrs inc; el pnts (4-10A) €2.20-4; shops 1km; Indtte; playgrnd; sand beach 20 mins; games area; trampolines; dogs €0.80; Eng spkn; quiet. "Pleasant woodland site." Easter-31 Oct. € 9.00 2006*

DEAUVILLE *3D1* (2km NE Rural) *49.34946, 0.11172* **Camping des Haras, Chemin du Calvaire, 14800 Touques [02 31 88 44 84; fax 02 31 88 97 08; les.haras@wanadoo.fr]** N on D677 (N177) Pont l'Evêque-Deauville rd, ignore 1st slip rd sp Touques (too narr, vans prohibited); stay on by-pass & turn R at traff lts by g'ge sp Trouville. Turn R again at next rndabt sp Touques then L on D62; fork L to site after church. Also sp fr D513 Deauville-Caen rd. Lge, hdg/mkd pitch, pt sl, pt shd; wc; own san; chem disp; shwrs; el pnts (10A) €4.12; gas; Indtte; shop; rest; snacks; bar; playgrnd; pool 2km; sand beach 2km; entmnt; 60% statics; dogs €1.55; poss cr; adv bkg; red low ssn. "Some pitches poss diff lge o'fits; in winter phone ahead; conv Honfleur & WW2 sites; office clsd fr 1830 low ssn & Sun; san facs run down; c'vans sited nr playgrnd." ♦ 1 Feb-30 Nov. € 16.35 2008*

DEAUVILLE *3D1* (3km S Urban) *49.32903, 0.08593* **Camping La Vallée de Deauville, Ave de la Vallée, 14800 St Arnoult [02 31 88 58 17; fax 02 31 88 11 57; campinglavalleedeauville@wanadoo.fr; www.camping-deauville.com]** Fr Deauville take D27 dir Caen, turn R onto D278 to St Arnoult, foll site sp. Lge, hdg/mkd pitch, hdstg, pt shd; htd wc (some cont); baby facs; shwrs inc; el pnts (10A) €4; gas; Indtte; shop; tradsmn; rest; snacks; bar; playgrnd; htd pool; waterslide; sand beach 4km; fishing lake; games rm; entmnt; wifi; 80% statics; dogs €4; phone; Eng spkn; some rlwy noise; red low ssn; ccard acc; CCI. "Easy access to beaches & resorts; conv Le Havre using Pont de Normandie; lake walks & activities on site; excel san facs." ♦ 1 Apr-2 Nov. € 30.00 2009*

DEAUVILLE *3D1* (6km S Rural) *49.32216, 0.06048* **Camping du Lieu Rôti, 14800 Vauville [tel/fax 02 31 87 96 22; info@deauville-camping.com; www.deauville-camping.com]** Fr Deauville, take D27 S twd Caen. Site on R 200m after Tourgéville church. Well sp. Med, mkd pitch, pt shd; htd wc; chem disp; shwrs inc; el pnts (5A) €4; Indtte; shop; tradmn; rest; snacks; bar; playgrnd; htd pool; paddling pool; sand beach 3.5km; games area; 50% statics; dogs €3; phone; Eng spkn; adv bkg; quiet; ccard acc; CCI. "Pleasant location; helpful recep; excel." ♦ 15 Apr-15 Oct. € 27.00 2007*

France

DECAZEVILLE *7D4* (9km NE Rural) *44.62920, 2.32030* **Camping La Plaine, Le Bourg, 12300 St Parthem [tel/fax 05 65 64 05 24 or 05 65 43 03 99; infos@camping-laplaine.fr; www.camping-laplaine.fr]** N fr Decazeville on D963; in 6km turn R onto D42 to St Parthem. Site 1km past vill on R. Med, hdg/mkd pitch, pt shd; wc; chem disp; shwrs inc; el pnts (6A) inc; lndtte; tradsmn; rest; snacks; bar; BBQ; playgrnd; pool; tennis; 5% statics; dogs €1; phone; poss cr; Eng spkn; adv bkg; quiet; CCI. "Idyllic setting on banks of Rv Lot; friendly Dutch owners; excel walking; vg." ♦ Mid Apr-30 Sep. € 12.50 2008*

⊞ **DECAZEVILLE** *7D4* (3km NW Rural) *44.58819, 2.22145* **FFCC Camping Le Roquelongue, 12300 Boisse-Penchot [tel/fax 05 65 63 39 67; info@camping-roquelongue.com; www.camping-roquelongue.com]** Fr D963 N fr Decazeville turn W onto D140 & D42 to Boisse-Penchot. Rte via D21 not rec (steep hill & acute turn). Site mid-way bet Boisse-Penchot & Livinhac-le-Haut on D42. Med, hdg/mkd pitch, pt shd; wc; chem disp; shwrs inc; el pnts (6-10A) 3.60-4.30; gas; lndtte; shop; tradsmn; supmkt 5km; snacks; bar; playgrnd; htd pool; fishing; canoeing; tennis; cycle hire; entmnt; internet; 10% statics; dogs free; phone; adv bkg; quiet; CCI. "Direct access Rv Lot; pitches gd size; san facs clean; no twin-axles; excel base for Lot Valley." ♦ € 15.80 2009*

DECIZE *4H4* (500m NE Urban) *46.83487, 3.45552* **Camping des Halles (formerly Municipal), Allée Marcel Merle, 58300 Decize [03 86 25 14 05 or 03 86 25 03 23 (Mairie); fax 03 86 77 11 48; aquadis1@wanadoo.fr; www.des-vacances-vertes.com or www.aquadis-loisirs.com]** Fr Nevers take D981 (N81) to Decize, look for sp for 'Stade Nautique Camping'. Lge, mkd pitch, pt shd; wc (some cont); snacks; shwrs inc; el pnts (6A) inc; gas; shop; rv & sand beach adj; sat TV; dogs €1.60; poss cr; some Eng spkn; quiet; ccard acc; CCI. "Lge pitches, some by rv; helpful staff; gd san facs, poss tired high ssn; extra for twin-axles; poss diff access pitches due trees." ♦ 1 Apr-31 Oct. € 13.40 2008*

DECIZE *4H4* (12km SE Rural) **Camping La Varenne à la Ferme, Rue de Tanjeat, 58300 Charrin [tel/fax 03 86 50 30 14]** Fr Decize take D979 twd Digoin & foll sp Camping la Ferme; site off to R thro vill of Charrin. In vill foll sp for Chambres d'Hôtes. Sm, pt shd; wc; chem disp; shwrs inc; el pnts inc (long lead req); fishing 2km; adv bkg; quiet. "Lovely, quiet CL-type site; friendly owners; basic facs; breakfast & some farm produce avail; gd touring base for Nivernais canal." 1 Jun-30 Sep. € 8.00 2007*

DELLE *6G3* (5km N Rural) *47.53220, 7.01719* **Camp Municipal du Passe-Loup, Rue des Chênes, 90100 Joncherey [03 84 56 32 63; fax 03 84 56 27 66; www.joncherey.fr]** Exit A75 junc 11 Sevenans onto N1019 (N19) S dir Delle. Turn L onto D3 N dir Boron, site on R in approx 3km. Med, sl, pt shd; wc; chem disp; shwrs inc; el pnts (6A) €3.50; playgrnd; lake fishing adj; 45% statics; dogs €1.25; quiet; CCI. "Pleasant, spacious site; basic san facs." 1 Apr-31 Oct. € 10.50 2008*

DENNEVILLE PLAGE see Barneville Carteret *1C4*

DESCARTES *4H2* (5km SE Rural) *46.94090, 0.72248* **Camp Municipal Ile de la Claise, 37169 Abilly [02 47 59 78 01 (Mairie); fax 02 47 59 89 93; mairie.abilly@wanadoo.fr]** Fr Descartes take D750 S for 3km; SE on D42 to Abilly. Site sp adj Rv Claise. Sm, shd; wc; shwrs; el pnts; shop; rest, snacks, bar 500m; playgrnd; pool 6km; fishing; tennis; dogs; quiet. ♦ 1 May-15 Sep. € 5.40 2006*

DESCARTES *4H2* (S Urban) *46.97152, 0.69586* **Camp Municipal La Grosse Motte, Allée Léo Lagrange, 37160 Descartes [02 47 59 85 90 or 02 47 92 42 20; fax 02 47 59 72 20; otm-descartes@wanadoo.fr; www.ville-descartes.fr]** Fr S on D750 turn L just bef Descartes sp, cross rlwy line & in 500m turn L into site. Fr N turn R after Descartes sp. V narr turn into site due stone house walls. Sm, hdg pitch, pt sl, shd; wc (some cont); baby facs; shwrs inc; shops in town; el pnts (10A) €2.10 (poss rev pol); pool adj; playgrnd, tennis, mini-golf nr; boating on rv; dogs €1; adv bkg; quiet; ccard not acc; CCI. "Beautiful site; public gardens adj; spacious pitches; clean facs; friendly staff; popular with school parties; gd NH." 1 Jun-30 Sep. € 6.75 2009*

DEUX CHAISES see Montmarault *9A1*

DEVILLAC see Villéreal *7D3*

DEVILLE LES ROUEN see Rouen *3C2*

⊞ **DEYME** *8F3* (500m NE Rural) *43.48672, 1.5322* **Camping Les Violettes, Porte de Toulouse, 31450 Deyme [05 61 81 72 07; fax 05 61 27 17 31; camping lesviolettes@wanadoo.fr]** SE fr Toulouse to Carcassonne on N113, sp on L, 12km fr Toulouse (after passing Deyme sp). Med, mkd pitch, hdstg, pt shd; htd wc; mv service pnt; shwrs inc; el pnts (6A) €4; lndtte; shop; rest; snacks; bar; BBQ; playgrnd; TV; 60% statics; dogs €0.70; poss cr; quiet but rd noise; CCI. "Helpful, friendly staff; facs v run down (Jun 2009); poss v muddy when wet (except hdstg); 800m fr Canal du Midi & 10km fr Space City; Park & Ride 2.5km & metro to Toulouse." € 12.00 2009*

DIE *9D2* (N Urban) *44.75123, 5.36604* **Camp Municipal Le Justin (formally de la Piscine), Rue de Chabestar, 26150 Die [tel/fax 04 75 22 14 77 or 04 75 22 06 19 (Mairie); camping-municipal-die@wanadoo.fr]** Ent town fr W on D93, fork R D751, sp Gap & 'rugby stade' (not football); foll sps for Camp Municipal & piscine; site on S of rlwy line bef sw pool 'piscine'. Poss diff bdge for long o'fits. Med, pt sl, pt shd; wc (some cont); chem disp; mv service pnt; shwrs inc; el pnts (10A) €2.90; lndtte; shops, rest 500m; tradsmn; snacks; playgrnd; rv sw adj; entmnts; dogs €1.50; Eng spkn; adv bkg; ccard acc; red low ssn; CCI. "Site in beautiful setting in Drôme valley; gd facs; poor security - vehicles use track thro site as short cut; easy walk to Die - interesting town." 15 May-30 Sep. € 12.00 2008*

DIE *9D2* (400m N Urban) *44.75444, 5.37778* **FFCC Camping La Riou-Merle, Route de Romeyer, 26150 Die [tel/fax 04 75 22 21 31; lerioumerle@aol.com; www.camping-lerioumerle.com]** Fr Gap on D93 heading twd Valence. Cont on D93 twd town cent; R on D742 to Romeyer. Site on L in 200m. On D93 fr Crest foll sp round town cent onto D742. Sharp turn at ent. Med, pt sl, pt shd; wc (some cont); chem disp; mv service pnt; shwrs inc; el pnts (5A) €3.70; Indtte; shops in town; playgrnd; pool; fishing; 30% statics; dogs €1.50; quiet; red low ssn. "Clean site; gd san facs." 1 Apr-15 Oct. € 16.00 2009*

DIE *9D2* (2km W Rural) *44.75890, 5.35095* **Camping La Pinède, Quartier du Pont Neuf, 26150 Die [04 75 22 17 77; fax 04 75 22 22 73; info@camping-pinede.com; www.camping-pinede.com]** W fr Die on D93 dir Crest, site sp on L. Access diff for lge vans - narr rv bdge 2.75m wide. Med, mkd pitch, terr, pt shd; wc; shwrs inc; el pnts (5-10A) €3.50-5; gas; Indtte; rest; shop; playgrnd; pool; shgl beach & rv sw adj; fishing; canoeing; tennis; entmnt; TV; dogs €2; adv bkg ess; noisy; red low ssn. ♦ 20 Apr-15 Sep. € 24.00 2007*

DIE *9D2* (2km NW Rural) *44.76250, 5.34674* **Camping de Chamarges, Route de Crest, 26150 Die [tel/fax 04 75 22 14 13 or 04 75 22 06 77; campingchamarges@orange.fr]** Foll D93 twd Valence, site on L by Rv Drôme. Med, mkd pitch, pt shd; wc (some cont); chem disp; shwrs inc; el pnts (3-6A) €2.90-3.60; gas; shop 1km; rest; snacks; bar; BBQ (gas); playgrnd; pool; rv sw, fishing & canoeing adj; entmnt; TV; dogs €1.60; phone; Eng spkn; rec adv bkg high ssn; quiet; ccard acc; CCI. "Beautiful mountainous area; vg." ♦ 1 Apr-13 Sep. € 12.10 2008*

DIE *9D2* (12km NW Urban) *44.83264, 5.28236* **Aire Naturelle Le Moulin du Rivet (Szarvas), 26150 St Julien-en-Quint [tel/fax 04 75 21 20 43; contact@moulindurivet.com; www.moulindurivet.com]** On D93 E fr Crest twd Die, turn L onto D129 dir Ste Croix/St Julien. Foll sp St Julien. Site on L in 9km. Sm, some hdstg, terr, pt shd; wc; chem disp (wc); shwrs inc; el pnts (6A) €3; shop 9km; tradsmn; rest; playgrnd; rv sw adj; dogs; poss cr; Eng spkn; adv bkg; quiet; CCI. "Attractive, peaceful CL-type site on Rv Sûre; gd views; friendly owners." 1 Apr-1 Nov. € 10.00 2007*

⊞ **DIENNE** *7A3* (800m NE Rural) *46.44613, 0.56023* **Camping Domaine de Dienné, 86410 Dienné [05 49 45 87 63; fax 05 49 54 17 96; info@domaine-de-dienne.fr; www.domaine-de-dienne.fr or www.les-castels.com]** Fr Poitiers on N147/E62 S thro Fleuré & in 2.5km turn R to Dienné. Foll site sp. Med, pt shd; wc; sauna; shwrs; el pnts inc; Indtte; rest; snacks; playgrnd; 2 pools (1 htd, covrd); fishing; horseriding; games area; statics; site clsd 5-26 Jan; adv bkg; quiet. € 43.00 2009*

DIENVILLE see Brienne Le Château *6E1*

DIEPPE *3C2* (4km S Urban) *49.90040, 1.07472* **Camping Vitamin, 865 Chemin des Vertus, 76550 St Aubin-sur-Scie [02 35 82 11 11; camping-vitamin@wanadoo.fr; www.camping-vitamin.com]** Foll dir to Formule 1 & Hotel B&B. Lge, hdg pitch, unshd; wc; chem disp; mv service pnt; shwrs inc; el pnts (10A) inc; Indtte; shops 1km; bar; playgrnd; pool; shgl beach 2km; adv bkg; many statics; dogs €1.50; quiet; CCI. "Lovely, well-maintained site; san facs immac; poss boggy in wet; conv ferries; excel." 1 Apr-15 Oct. € 19.90 2009*

The opening dates and prices on this campsite have changed. I'll send a site report form to the Club for the next edition of the guide.

DIEPPE *3C2* (5km S Rural) *49.87063, 1.14426* **Camping des 2 Rivières, 76880 Martigny [02 35 85 60 82; fax 02 35 85 95 16; martigny.76@wanadoo.fr; www.camping-2-rivieres.com]** Martigny vill on D154 S fr Dieppe. Med, pt shd; wc; el pnts €2.75; Indtte; shop; playgrnd; covrd pool, watersports, mountain biking, horseriding & Arques forest nrby; dogs €1.45; adv bkg; quiet. "Attractive, spacious site by lge lake; access poss diff long o'fits due parked vehicles; conv Dieppe; cycle paths; highly rec." 27 Mar-11 Oct. € 11.00 2009*

DIEPPE *3C2* (4km SW Rural) *49.89820, 1.05705* **Camping La Source, 63 Rue Tisserands, Petit-Appeville, 76550 Hautot-sur-Mer [02 35 84 27 04; fax 02 35 82 25 02; info@camping-la-source.fr; www.camping-la-source.fr]** Fr Dieppe ferry terminal foll sp Paris, take D925 W dir Fécamp. In 2km at Petit Appeville turn L, site in 800m on rvside. Med, mkd pitch, hdstg, pt shd; wc (some cont); chem disp; mv service pnt; shwrs inc; el pnts (6A) €3; Indtte; shop 3km; tradsmn; snacks; bar; playgrnd; htd pool; sand beach 3km; rv sw, fishing & boating adj; games area; games rm; cycle hire; golf 4km; entmnt; TV rm; few statics; dogs €1.50; Eng spkn; some rlwy & rd noise; adv bkg; quiet; ccard acc; red low ssn; CCI. "Excel site in attractive setting; pleasant, helpful staff; vg, clean san facs; footpath to Le Plessis vill; gd cycling; excel NH for ferry." ♦ 15 Mar-15 Oct. € 19.40 (CChq acc) 2009*

DIEPPE *3C2* (4km SW Urban) *49.9075, 10.4200* **Camping Relais Motard, 1015 Rue de la Mer, 76550 Pourville-sur-Mer [02 35 83 92 49; www.relais-motard.com]** Fr Dieppe ferry terminal foll sp Paris. Take D925 W dir Fécamp. In 2km at Petit Appeville turn R to Pourville, site in approx 1km (behind permanent c'van park). Sm, mkd pitch, unshd; wc; chem disp; mv service pnt; shwrs inc; el pnts (6-10A) €2; Indry rm; rest 1km; snacks; bar; BBQ; sand beach 1km; 10% statics; dogs; quiet; CCI. "Modern san facs; pleasant site; beach nrby with oyster farm & rest." ♦ 14 Apr-31 Oct. € 10.50 2007*

France

DIEPPE *3C2* (6km SW Urban) *49.87297, 1.04497* **Camp Municipal du Colombier, 453 Rue Loucheur, 76550 Offranville [02 35 85 21 14; fax 02 35 04 52 67]** W fr Dieppe on D925, take L turn on D55 to Offranville, site clearly sp in vill to Parc du Colombier. NB Part of site cul-de-sac, explore on foot bef towing in. Med, hdg/mkd pitch, pt shd; wc; chem disp; shwrs inc; el pnts (10A) €2.20 (poss rev pol); gas; Indtte; shop & supmkt 500m; rest; shgl beach 5km; many statics; ltd Eng spkn; CCI. "Pleasant setting in ornamental gardens; vg clean site & facs; helpful staff; gates clsd 2200-0700; ask warden how to operate in his absence; conv ferries; easy walk to town; rec." ♦ 1 Apr-15 Oct. € 14.10 2008*

DIGNE LES BAINS *10E3* (1km NE Rural) *44.10011, 6.24915* **Camping Notre Dame du Bourg, Route de Barcelonnette, 04000 Digne-les-Bains [04 92 31 04 87; contact@campingdubourg-alpes-provence.com; www.campingdubourg-alpes-provence.com]** Fr rndabt by rv bdge take main st (Boulevard Gassendi) thro cent town, sp D900 La Javie, Barcelonnette. Camp sp on R. Med, unshd; wc; shwrs inc; el pnts (4A) inc; Indrtte; shops 1.5km; playgrnd; pool 1.5km; tennis; games area; entmnt; TV; 40% statics; dogs €1.50; quiet. "Views fr terr areas but poss diff access lge o'fits; recep manned ltd hrs; pleasant town; thermal baths; beautiful & fascinating area." ♦ 1 Apr-31 Oct. € 16.50 2009*

DIGNE LES BAINS *10E3* (1.5km SE Rural) *44.08646, 6.25028* **Camping Les Eaux Chaudes, 32 Ave des Thermes, 04000 Digne-les-Bains [04 92 32 31 04; fax 04 92 34 59 80; info@campingleseauxchaudes.com; www.campingleseauxchaudes.com]** Fr S foll N85 sp 'Centre Ville' over bdge keeping L to rndabt, turn 1st R sp Les Thermes (D20). Past Intermarché, site on R 1.6km after leaving town. Med, mkd pitch, pt shd; htd wc; chem disp; shwrs inc; el pnts (4-10A) €2-3.50 (poss rev pol); gas; Indtte; shops 1.5km; snacks; pool 1.5km; pool; lake sw 3km; games area; 30% statics; dogs €1; poss cr; adv bkg; quiet; red low ssn; CCI. "Pleasant site; gd touring base; vg facs; 500m fr thermal baths; National Geological Reserve in town cent; phone ahead low ssn to check open." ♦ 1 Apr-31 Oct. € 18.00 2008*

DIGOIN *9A1* (500m W Urban) *46.47985, 3.96780* **Camping de la Chevrette, Rue de la Chevrette, 71160 Digoin [03 85 53 11 49; fax 03 85 88 59 70; info@lachevrette.com; www.lachevrette.com]** Fr S exit N79/E62 at junc 24 sp Digoin-la-Grève D994, then on D979 cross bdge over Rv Loire. Take 1st L, sp campng/piscine. Sm, some hdg pitch, hdstg, terr, pt shd; htd wc (some cont); chem disp; shwrs inc; el pnts (10A) €3.20; tradsmn; Indry rm; shops 500m; rest 500m; snacks; playgrnd; htd pool adj; fishing; dogs €1; sep car park; Eng spkn; adv bkg; some rd noise; red low ssn; CCI. "Pleasant, well-run site by rv; gd sized pitches; friendly, helpful owner; ltd facs low ssn; gd disabled facs; barrier clsd 2200-0700; nice walk by rv to town; vg." ♦ 1 Mar-31 Oct. € 14.20 2009*

DIJON *6G1* (2km W Urban) *47.32127, 5.01108* **Camping du Lac Kir, 3 Blvd Chanoine Kir, 21000 Dijon [tel/fax 03 80 43 54 72; info@camping-dijon.com; www.camping-dijon.com]** Site situated nr N5, Lac Kir. Fr Dijon ring rd take N5 exit (W) sp A38 twd Paris. At traff lts L sp A31, site immed on R under 3m high bdge. Do not tow thro town cent. Med, mkd pitch, pt hdstg, pt shd; htd wc (mainly cont); chem disp; shwrs inc; el pnts (6A) €3.50; (poss rev pol); gas; Indtte; shop; supmkt nr; tradsmn; rest; snacks; sw lake 1km; fishing, sw & boating; dogs €2; bus adj; poss cr; Eng spkn; quiet but some rd noise; ccard acc; red low ssn; CCI. "Attractive, well-run, busy, friendly site adj lake; various pitch sizes; san facs adequate; rvside path to town; gd site but some updating req; poss 'tired' low ssn; gd security; poss flooding; gd." 1 Apr-12 Oct. € 12.40 2009*

DINAN *2E3* (3km N Rural) *48.48903, -2.00855* **Camp Municipal Beauséjour, La Hisse, 22100 St Samson-sur-Rance [02 96 39 53 27 or 02 96 39 16 05 (Mairie); fax 02 96 87 94 12; beausejour-stsamson@orange.fr; www.beausejour-camping.com]** Fr Dinan take N176/D766 N twd Dinard. In 3km turn R onto D12 dir Taden then foll sp thro Plouer-sur-Rance to La Hisse; site sp. Fr N exit N176/E401 dir Plouer-sur-Rance, then foll sp La Hisse. Med, hdg/mkd pitch, hdstg, pt sl, pt shd; wc; chem disp; mv service pnt; baby facs; shwrs inc; el pnts (10A) €3.20 (poss rev pol); Indtte; sm shop; supmkt 5km; tradsmn; rest; snacks; bar; playgrnd; htd pool; tennis; games area; sailing; 5% statics; dogs €1.95; phone; poss cr; Eng spkn; adv bkg; quiet; red low ssn/long stay; CCI. "V pleasant, well-kept, clean site; helpful, friendly staff; quiet & spacious Jun & Sep; no twin-axles; gd pool; excel rv walks. " ♦ 1 Jun-30 Sep. € 13.30 2009*

DINAN *2E3* (3km NE Rural) *48.47138, -2.02277* **Camp International de la Hallerais, 22100 Taden [02 96 39 15 93 or 02 96 87 63 50 (Mairie); fax 02 96 39 94 64; camping.la.hallerais@wanadoo.fr; www.wdirect.fr/hallerais.htm]** Fr Dinan take N176/D766 N twd Dinard. In 3km turn R onto D12 to Taden. Foll La Hallerais & Taden sp to site. Fr N176 take exit onto D166 dir Taden; turn onto D766 dir Taden, then L onto D12A sp Taden & Camping. At rndabt on ent Taden take 1st exit onto D12 sp Dinan; site rd is 500m on L. Do not ent Dinan. Site adj Rv Rance. Lge, mkd pitch, terr, pt shd; wc; chem disp; mv service pnt; serviced pitches; shwrs inc; el pnts (6A) inc (rev pol); gas; Indtte; shop; tradsmn; rest; snacks (high ssn); bar; BBQ; playgrnd; htd pool; paddling pool; shgl beach 10km; tennis; fishing; horseriding 500m; wifi; games/TV rm; statics (sep area); dogs free; storage facs; Eng spkn; adv bkg; quiet; ccard acc; red low ssn. "Pleasant site; excel, spacious san facs; phone ahead if arr late at night low ssn; ltd office hours low ssn - report to bar; sh walk to Taden, mkt Fri eve; rvside walk to Dinan medieval town, mkt Thur am; rv trips; rec." ♦ 8 Mar-14 Nov. € 20.60 ABS - B01 2009*

DINAN *2E3* (10km NE Coastal) *48.52466, -1.96617* **Camping Ville Ger, 22690 Pleudihen-sur-Rance [02 96 83 33 88]** Fr Dinan take D675/D676 in dir Dol de Bretagne; turn L on D29 after 6km; site sp after 4km on L. Sm, mkd pitch; pt shd; wc (cont); rec own san high ssn; shwrs €1; el pnts (3A) €2.10; Indtte; shops 1.5km; rest; bar; playgrnd; dogs €0.50; poss cr; adv bkg ess high ssn; quiet; CCI. "Lovely area; close to rv; gd for dog-walking." 1 Apr-15 Oct. € 8.00 2007*

DINAN *2E3* (200m S Urban) *48.44743, -2.04631* **Camp Municipal Châteaubriand, 103 Rue Châteaubriand, 22100 Dinan [02 96 39 11 96 or 02 96 39 22 43 (LS); fax 02 96 85 06 97; campingmunicipaldinan@wanadoo.fr]** Fr N176 (E or W) take slip rd for Dinan cent; at lge rndbt in cent take 2nd R; down hill to site on L (500m). Sm, mkd pitch, pt sl, pt shd; wc; chem disp; mv service pnt; shwrs inc; el pnts (6A) €2.70; gas 500m; Indry rm; shop, rest, snacks 500m; bar adj; BBQ; sand beach 18km; games area; dogs €1.50; phone; poss cr; Eng spkn; adv bkg; daytime rd noise; ccard not acc; CCI. "Basic/dated facs poss unclean; pleasant, helpful staff; high kerb onto pitches; poss market traders; opening dates vary each year; check time barrier locked espec low ssn; gd cent for Rance valley, St Malo & coast." 15 Jun-15 Sep. € 9.30 2009*

DINARD *2E3* (6km S Rural) *48.58113, -2.05622* **Camp Municipal L'Estuaire, Rue Jean Boyer, 35730 Pleurtuit [tel/fax 02 99 88 44 06; contact@campingdelestuaire.com; www.campingdelestuaire.com]** Fr N on D266 or fr S on D766 in cent of vill, sp fr each dir. Med, hdg pitch, pt shd; wc (cont); baby facs; shwrs inc; el pnts (10A) €3.50; Indtte; shops adj; tradsmn; rest; snacks; bar; playgrnd; sand beach 4km; games area; entmnt; 50% statics; dogs €2.50; quiet. "Friendly site." 1 Apr-30 Sep. € 9.80 2007*

DINARD *2E3* (1.5m W Coastal) *48.6309, -2.08413* **Camping La Touesse, 171 Rue de la Ville Gehan, La Fourberie, 35800 St Lunaire [02 99 46 61 13; fax 02 99 16 02 58; camping.la.touesse@wanadoo.fr; www.campinglatouesse.com]** Exit Dinard on St Lunaire coast rd D786, site sp. Med, mkd pitch, pt shd; wc; mv service pnt; baby facs; shwrs inc; el pnts (5-10A) €3.20-3.60; Indtte; shop; snacks; bar; playgrnd; 2 pools (1 htd, covrd); sand beach 300m; tennis 1.5km; golf 2km; entmnt; TV rm; dog €1.50; adv bkg (dep); quiet, some late night noise; red low ssn; CCI. "Gd beach & rocks nr; friendly recep; clean." ♦ 1 Apr-30 Sep. € 19.00 2007*

DINARD *2E3* (1km W Coastal) *48.63486, -2.07928* **Camping Le Port Blanc, Rue de Sergent Boulanger, 35800 Dinard [02 99 46 10 74; fax 02 99 16 90 91; info@camping-port-blanc.com; www.camping-port-blanc.com]** Fr Dinard foll sp to St Lunaire on D786 for 1.5km. Turn R at traff lts by football ground to site. Lge, mkd pitch, pt sl, terr, pt shd; wc (some cont); chem disp; child/baby facs; shwrs inc; el pnts (10A) €3.95; Indtte; sm shop; supmkt 800m; rest 500m; snacks; bar; playgrnd; sand beach adj; 40% statics; dogs €1.90; phone; bus; poss cr; adv bkg; quiet at night; ccard acc; CCI. "Overlooks sand beach; gd san facs." ♦ 1 Apr-30 Sep. € 19.00 2009*

DINARD *2E3* (4km W Coastal) *48.63406, -2.12039* **Camping Longchamp, Blvd St Cast, 35800 St Lunaire [02 99 46 33 98; fax 02 99 46 02 71; contact@camping-longchamp.com; www.camping-longchamp.com]** Fr St Malo on D168 turn R sp St Lunaire, In 1km turn R at g'ge into St Lunaire, site sp to W of vill on D786 dir St Briac. Lge, hdg/mkd pitch, pt shd; wc; chem disp; mv service pnt; baby facs; shwrs inc; el pnts (4-10A) €2.90-4; gas; Indtte; shop; tradsmn; rest; snacks; bar; BBQ; playgrnd; sand beach 300m; 30% statics; dogs €1.50; phone adj; bus 500m; Eng spkn; adv bkg rec; quiet; red low ssn. "Excel, well-run site; clean facs; friendly, helpful staff; clean beach 300m; conv Brittany Ferries at St Malo." ♦ 1 May-10 Sep. € 21.00 2009*

DIOU see Dompierre sur Besbre *9A1*

DISNEYLAND PARIS see Meaux *3D3*

DISSAY see Jaunay Clan *4H1*

DIVONNE LES BAINS *9A3* (3km N Rural) *46.37487, 6.12143* **Camping Le Fleutron, Quartier Villard, 01220 Divonne-les-Bains [04 50 20 01 95 or 04 42 20 47 25 (LS); fax 04 50 20 00 35; info@homair.com; www.homair.com]** Exit E62 dir Divonne-les-Bains approx 12km N of Geneva. Fr town on D984, foll sp to site. Lge, hdg/mkd pitch, sl, terr, shd; htd wc; shwrs inc; chem disp; el pnts (4A) €5; gas; Indtte; shop, snacks & rest in ssn; bar; supmkts 3km; lake sw 3km; htd pool; paddling pool; lake sw 3km; tennis; games area; entmnt in ssn; TV rm; 50% statics; dogs €5; Eng spkn; adv bkg; quiet; ccard acc; red low ssn; CCI. "Helpful owner; levellers req; Lake Geneva 8km." 4 Apr-18 Oct. € 26.00 2009*

DOL DE BRETAGNE *2E4* (6km N Coastal) *48.60290, -1.77241* **Camp Municipal L'Abri des Flots, 35960 Le Vivier-sur-Mer [02 99 48 91 57; fax 02 99 48 98 43]** On sea front in Le Vivier-sur-Mer at E end of town; sp. Med, mkd pitches, pt shd; wc; mv service pnt; shwrs €1.35; el pnts (6A) €2.30 (long lead poss req); Indtte; sm shop & in vill; tradsmn; dogs €1; poss cr; no adv bkg; noise fr adj port; Eng spkn; CCI. "Clean site in vill cent & on sea front; resident warden; friendly; muddy beach not suitable for sw; gd NH to see mussel/oyster beds; tours fr museum nrby." 25 Apr-30 Sep. € 11.80 2008*

DOL DE BRETAGNE *2E4* (7km NE Coastal) *48.60052, -1.71182* **Camping de l'Aumône, 35120 Cherrueix [02 99 48 95 11; fax 02 99 80 87 37; breizhid@wanadoo.fr; www.camping-de-laumone.com]** On L of D797, opp rd leading into vill of Cherrueix. Med, unshd; wc; baby facs; shwrs inc; el pnts (10A) €2.50; gas; Indtte; shops 300m; snacks; sand beach 500m (not suitable for bathing); TV; dogs €0.50; adv bkg rec high ssn. "Friendly, sm farm with modern san facs; sand yachting nrby." 15 Jun-15 Sep. € 9.00 2006*

France

DOL DE BRETAGNE *2E4* (8km NE Coastal) *48.60503, -1.70797* **Camping Le Tenzor de la Baie, 10 Rue Théophile Blin, 35120 Cherrueix [02 99 48 98 13; www.tenzor-de-la-baie.com]** Fr Dol-de-Bretagne, take D155 N to Le Vivier-sur-Mer; turn R onto D797, L onto D82 to Cherrueix; site in vill 150m E of church, just beyond 'Mairie', sp. Sm, pt shd; wc; shwrs; el pnts (6A) €3.50; shop adj; playgrnd; pool; beach 150m; rv fishing & sw 14km; 75% statics; dogs €1.50; poss cr; adv bkg; quiet; ccard not acc. "V pleasant, clean, flat site in interesting bay of Mont St Michel; sand yachting, mussel & oyster beds nr; basic facs." 6 Jun-15 Oct. € 14.00 2007*

DOL DE BRETAGNE *2E4* (4km E Rural) *48.54941, -1.68386* **FFCC Camping du Vieux Chêne, Le Motais, 35120 Baguer-Pican [02 99 48 09 55; fax 02 99 48 13 37; vieux.chene@wanadoo.fr; www.camping-vieuxchene.fr]** Leave N176 E of Dol on slip rd sp Baguer-Pican. At traff lts turn L thro vill, site on R of D576 at far end vill adj lake. Lge, hdg pitch, pt sl, pt shd; wc; chem disp; mv service pnt; baby facs; shwrs inc; el pnts (10A) inc (poss rev pol & poss long cable req); gas; lndtte; shop; supmkt nr; rest; snacks; bar; BBQ (charcoal & gas); playgrnd; 2 htd pools; paddling pool; lake fishing; horseriding; tennis; games area; games rm; entmnt; interneti; TV rm; dogs €3; phone; Eng spkn; adv bkg; quiet; ccard acc; red low ssn/long stay; CCI. "Friendly & helpful site; fruit trees on pitches; conv Mont St Michel; basic facs stretched high ssn; clean site; shop & rest ltd low ssn; poss sm pitches; gates clsd 2100-0900; mkt in Dol Sat." ♦ 13 May-26 Sep. € 35.00 ABS - B10 2009*

DOL DE BRETAGNE *2E4* (7km SE Rural) *48.49150, -1.72990* **Camping Le Domaine des Ormes, 35120 Epiniac [02 99 73 53 60 or 02 99 73 53 01; fax 02 99 73 53 55; info@lesormes.com; www.lesormes.com or www.les-castels.com]** Exit N176/E401 at W end of Dol-de-Bretagne; then S fr Dol on D795 twd Combourg & Rennes, in 7km site on L of rd, clearly sp. V lge, hdg/mkd pitch, pt sl, pt shd; wc; chem disp; baby facs; shwrs inc; el pnts (6A) inc (poss long lead req); gas; lndtte; shop; tradsmn; rest; snacks; bar; BBQ; playgrnd; htd pool complex; waterslide; paddling pool; lake fishing, canoeing; sand beach 25km; tennis; cycle hire; horseriding; archery; golf course adj (discount to campers); cycle hire; entmnt; wifi; games/TV rm; 80% statics; dogs €2; poss cr; adv bkg; Eng spkn; poss noisy (disco); ccard acc; red low ssn; CCI. "Excel all round; suitable RVs; helpful staff; few bins or water taps; conv Mont St Michel, St Malo & Dinan; disco at night; mkt Sat." ♦ 15 May-4 Sep. € 44.60 ABS - B08 2009*

DOLE *6H2* (6km NE Rural) *47.12557, 5.58825* **Camping Les Marronniers, Rue Chaux, 39700 Rochefort-sur-Nenon [03 84 70 50 37; fax 03 84 70 55 05; reservation@camping-les-marronniers.com; www.camping-les-marronniers.com]** NE fr Dole on D673 (N73) twds Besançon. Turn R on D76 & pass thro vill of Rochefort-sur-Nenon. Site in 2km, well sp. Med, hdg pitch, pt shd; wc; mv service pnt; serviced pitches; shwrs inc; el pnts (6A) €2.50; lndtte; tradsmn; snacks; bar; playgrnd; pool; cycle hire; entmnt; 10% statics; dogs €1; Eng spkn; adv bkg; poss noisy; red low ssn; CCI. "Poss noisy disco; fair sh stay/NH." ♦ 1 Apr-31 Oct. € 18.50 2008*

DOLE *6H2* (300m E Rural) *47.08937, 5.50339* **FFCC Camping Le Pasquier, 18 Chemin Georges et Victor Thévenot, 39100 Dole [03 84 72 02 61; fax 03 84 79 23 44; lola@camping-le-pasquier.com; www.camping-le-pasquier.com]** Fr A39 foll sp dir Dole & Le Pasquier. Fr all dir foll sp 'Centre ville' then foll site name sp & 'Stade Camping' in town; well sp. Site on rvside private rd. Narr app. Lge, hdg/mkd pitch, pt shd; htd wc; chem disp; mv service pnt; shwrs inc; el pnts (10A) €3.20 (rev pol); lndry rm; shop & 1km; tradsmn; snacks; bar; playgrnd; pool; aqua park 2km; dir access rv 500m; fishing; entmnt; internet; 10% statics; dogs €1; extra for twin-axle c'vans; poss cr; Eng spkn; quiet; ccard acc; red long stay/low ssn; CCI. "Well-kept site; generous pitches; friendly recep; gd clean san facs, ltd low ssn; poss mosquito problem; nice pool; rv walk into Dole; mkt Tues, Thur, Sat; gd NH or longer; rec." 15 Mar-25 Oct. € 14.50 2009*

DOLE *6H2* (8km SE Rural) *47.01660, 5.48160* **FFCC Camping Les Bords de Loue, 39100 Parcey [03 84 71 03 82; fax 03 84 71 03 42; contact@jura-camping.fr; www.jura-camping.fr]** Leave A39 at junc 6 onto D905 (N5) dir Chalon-sur-Saône. Turn L (SE) at rndabt after going under A39 & in 6km turn R into vill of Parcey at 'Camping' sp. Lge, pt shd; wc; chem disp; 10% serviced pitches; shwrs inc; el pnts (5A) €3; lndtte; tradsmn; rest; snacks; bar; BBQ; playgrnd; pool; paddling pool; beach adj; fishing; boating; 20% statics; dogs €1.50; phone; poss cr; Eng spkn; adv bkg; poss some noise when busy; ccard acc; red low ssn; CCI. "Pleasant site." ♦ 15 Apr-15 Sep. € 18.00 2009*

DOLLON see Connerré *4F1*

DOLUS D'OLERON *7B1* (4km SE Coastal) *45.91288, -1.22386* **Camping Ostréa, Route des Huîtres, 17550 Dolus d'Oléron [05 46 47 62 36 or 06 14 35 01 20 (mob); fax 05 46 75 20 01; www.camping-ostrea.com]** After x-ing viaduc bdge to Ile d'Oléron turn R to Château d'Oléron; cont thro vill & foll coast rd Blvd Phillippe Dasté which becomes Route des Huîtres; site on L in 4km. Med, mkd pitch, pt shd; htd wc; chem disp; mv service pnt; baby facs; shwrs (inc); gas; lndtte; el pnts (3-6A) €3.50-4.50; shop, snacks high ssn; tradsmn; BBQ; playgrnd; pool (htd covrd); golf nrby; fishing; archery; games rm; entmnt; TV; dogs €2.30; red low ssn; ccard acc; CCI. "Friendly, family-run site in oyster production region; facs immac; vg." ♦ 1 Apr-30 Sep. € 21.00 2007*

DOMAZAN see Avignon *10E2*

DOMFRONT *4E1* (6km N Rural) *48.61490, -0.60119* **Camping La Nocherie, 61700 St Bômer-les-Forges [02 33 37 60 36; fax 02 33 38 16 08]** S fr Flers on D962 1km after Les Forges turn L. Site sp Camping à la Ferme, narr rd with long hill. Sm, pt shd; wc; shwrs inc; el pnts (6A) €1.50; shop 4km; rest; bar; playgrnd; fishing; tennis 3km; quiet. "Farm site in apple orchard; gd walking; gd tourist base." 15 Mar-15 Dec. € 10.50 2006*

⊞ **DOMFRONT** *4E1* (7km SE Rural) **Camping La Belle Arrivée, Rue La Belle Arrivée, 61700 Perrou [02 33 66 18 36; labellearrivee@gmail.com; http://labelle arrivee-perrou.com]** SE fr Domfront take D976 (N176), turn L onto D15 thro Perrou to junc with D52, site on L. Sm, pt shd; htd wc; chem disp (wc); shwrs inc; el pnts (6A) €2; Indtte; shop 2km; rest; snacks; bar; playgrnd; games area; no statics; dogs; poss cr; Eng spkn; quiet. "Adj GR22 walking rte in forest park; helpful, friendly owners." ♦ € 5.00 2007*

DOMFRONT *4E1* (500m S Urban) *48.58808, -0.65045* **Camp Municipal, 4 Rue du Champ Passais, 61700 Domfront [02 33 37 37 66 or 02 33 38 92 24 (LS); mairie@ domfront.com; www.domfront.com]** Fr N on D962 foll Laval sps into Domfront; then take D976 (N176) W dir Mont-St Michel; site turning in 400m on L; well sp bet old quarter & town cent. Fr S on D962 well sp fr edge of town. Sm, hdg/mkd pitch, hdstg, terr, pt shd; wc; chem disp; shwrs inc; el pnts (10A) €4; Indtte; shops, rest, snacks, bar 1km; playgrnd; rv fishing nr; TV rm; dogs €0.80; phone; Eng spkn; some rd noise; red low ssn; CCI. "V pleasant, well-kept terr site with views; helpful, charming staff; few shady pitches; gd security; sh, steep walk to medieval town; no twin-axles; vg." ♦ 1 Apr-30 Sep. € 11.00 2009*

DOMFRONT *4E1* (12km SW Rural) *48.48840, -0.69704* **Camp Municipal des Chauvières, 61350 St Fraimbault [02 33 30 69 60 or 02 33 38 32 22 (Mairie); st.fraimbault@ wanadoo.fr]** S fr Domfront on D962 sp Mayenne. At Ceaucé turn R on D24 sp St Fraimbault, site on R past lake on ent to vill. Sm, mkd pitch, unshd; wc; mv service pnt; shwrs; el pnts (3A) €2; Indry rm; shop adj; mini-mkt, rest, snacks, bar in vill; playgrnd; lake adj; sw 8km; tennis; cycle hire; games area; some statics; quiet. "Picturesque site in lge park with excel floral displays; warden calls; vg." 20 Mar-31 Oct. € 3.00 2007*

DOMME see Sarlat la Canéda *7C3*

DOMPIERRE LES ORMES *9A2* (Rural) *46.36369, 4.47460* **Camp Municipal Le Village des Meuniers, 71520 Dompierre-les-Ormes [03 85 50 36 60; fax 03 85 50 36 61; levillagedesmeuniers@wanadoo.fr; www.villagedesmeuniers.com]** Fr A6 exit Mâcon Sud onto N79 dir Charolles. After approx 35km take slip rd onto D41 for Dompierre-les-Ormes. Well sp nr stadium. Med, hdg/ mkd pitch, terr, pt shd; wc; chem disp; mv service pnt; 50% serviced pitch; shwrs inc; el pnts (16A) €4.50; gas; Indtte; shops 2km; tradsmn; rest; snacks; bar; playgrnd; htd pools; waterslide; cycle hire; tennis; entmnt; dogs €1.50; adv bkg (ess high ssn); quiet; ccard acc; red low ssn; CCI. "Excel, clean site with views; v lge pitches; o'flow field at cheaper rates with full facs high ssn; facs stretched high ssn; excel for children; gd sp walks in area; pools, rest, bar etc used by public; free m'van hdstg outside site ent." ♦ 29 Apr-30 Sep. € 24.00 2006*

DOMPIERRE SUR BESBRE *9A1* (E Urban) *46.51378, 3.68276* **Camp Municipal, La Madeleine, Parc des Sports, 03290 Dompierre-sur-Besbre [04 70 34 55 57 or 04 70 48 11 30 (Mairie)]** At E end of town nr rv behind stadium; sp. Med, hdg pitch, shd, pt sl; htd wc; chem disp; mv service pnt; baby facs; shwrs inc; el pnts (10A) €2; Indtte; shop 500m; BBQ; full sports facs adj; dogs; phone; poss cr; Eng spkn; adv bkg; quiet; CCI. "Smart, well-run, busy site; clean san facs, but poss stretched high ssn; excel sports complex; gd for Loire Valley, vineyards & chateaux; highly rec low ssn; excel." ♦ 15 May-15 Sep. € 5.90 2008*

DOMPIERRE SUR BESBRE *9A1* (5km E Rural) *46.53523, 3.74359* **Camping du Gué de Loire, 03290 Diou [03 85 53 11 49 (Mairie); info@lachevrette.com]** Sp in cent of vill in both dirs on rvside, off N79. Sm, hdg/mkd pitch, pt sl, shd; wc; mv service pnt; shwrs inc; el pnts; Indry rm; shop 800m; rest, bar 500m; rd noise; no ccard acc; CCI. "Simple site; gd touring base." 1 Jul-15 Sep. 2006*

This is a wonderful site.
I'll fill in a report online and let the Club know – www.caravanclub.co.uk/ europereport

DONJON, LE *9A1* (500m N Urban) *46.35317, 3.79188* **Camp Municipal, Route de Monétay-sur-Loire, 03130 Le Donjon [04 70 99 56 35 or 04 70 99 50 25 (Mairie); fax 04 74 99 58 02]** Fr Lapalisse N on D994. Site sp fr town cent on D166 Rte de Monétay-sur-Loire. Sm, pt sl, pt shd; wc (some cont); mv service pnt; shwrs inc; el pnts (10A) €2; shop 500m; rest, bar 400m; playgrnd; fishing, sailing & windsurfing 900m; quiet; CCI. ♦ 1 May-31 Oct. € 5.50 2006*

DONJON, LE *9A1* (7km SW Rural) *46.32415, 3.70996* **Camp Municipal La Grande Ouche, 03130 Bert [04 70 99 61 92 or 04 70 99 60 90 (Mairie); fax 04 70 99 64 28; mairie-bert@pays-allier.com]** Fr D994 exit Le Donjon on D989 to NW, after 1km turn L onto D23, after 7km turn L onto D124 to Bert in 3km. Site on E edge of vill alongside sm lake & Rv Têche. Sm, mkd pitch, pt shd; wc (cont); shwrs inc; el pnts (3-5A) €1.70; shops adj; rest, bar 200m; playgrnd; htd pool adj; lake fishing adj; tennis; cycle hire; dogs; quiet. "Clean facs." 1 May-15 Sep. € 6.50 2007*

⊞ **DONZENAC** *7C3* (1km S Rural) *45.21800, 1.51900* **Aire Communale, Route d'Ussac, 19270 Donzenac [05 55 85 72 33 or 06 11 04 28 14 (mob); mairie-donzenac@ wanadoo.fr]** Exit A20 at junc 47; take 1st exit at rndabt dir Donzenac; site on L in 3km. NB Avoid app thro Donzenac as narr & diff for lge o'fits. Adj Camping La Rivière. Sm, mkd pitch, hdstg, unshd; wc; chem disp; mv service pnt; el pnts (3A); Indtte; shop & 100m; rest, snacks, bar 100m; bus 100m; phone; quiet. "El pnts not avail Jul/Aug." € 5.80 2007*

France

DONZENAC *7C3* (1.5km S Rural) *45.21937, 1.51804* **Village de Vacances Municipal La Rivière, Route d'Ussac, 19270 Donzenac [tel/fax 05 55 85 63 95 or 06 03 11 98 69; mairie-donenac@wanadoo.fr]** Fr N exit A20 at junc 47 (do not use junc 48); take exit at rndabt dir Donzenac D920. In 3km on ent Donzenac keep on D920 & don't go down hill to rndabt. Take 2nd exit D170 sp Uzzac, site on R in 500m. NB Avoid app thro Donzenac as narr & diff for lge o'fits. Fr S exit junc 49 to Ussac. Med, mkd pitch, pt shd; wc; chem disp; shwrs inc; el pnts (5A) €2.70; lndtte; shops 1km; snacks; bar; htd pool Jul/Aug; rv adj; fishing 5km; cycle hire; dogs €1.10; adv bkg rec high ssn. "Excel facs; resident warden." ♦ 1 Jun-30 Sep. € 14.30 2008*

DORAT, LE *7A3* (600m S Urban) *46.21161, 1.08237* **Camp Municipal, Route de la Planche des Dames, 87210 Le Dorat [05 55 60 72 20 (Mairie) or 05 55 60 76 81 (TO); fax 05 55 68 27 87]** Site sp fr D675 & in town cent. Sm, hdg/mkd pitch, pt shd; wc; shwrs inc; el pnts (16A) inc; shop, rest, bar 600m; quiet; CCI. "Excel, basic site; permanent barrier, code fr tourist office; clean facs, but ltd & own san rec high ssn (2007); warden calls eves; public uses footpath as short-cut." 1 May-30 Sep. € 7.50 2009*

⊞ **DORCEAU** *4E2* (2km N Rural) *48.43717, 0.82742* **Camping Forest View, L'Espérance, 61110 Dorceau [tel/fax 02 33 25 45 27 or 06 89 24 49 62 (mob); petej.wilson@wanadoo.fr; www.forestviewleisurebreaks.co.uk]** Fr D920 (ring rd) in Rémalard take D38 sp Bretoncelles; site in 4km on corner on L. Sm, pt sl, pt shd; wc; chem disp; shwrs inc; el pnts (10A) inc; lake fishing; painting workshops; wifi; dogs €1.40; some statics; adv bkg; quiet; red low ssn; CCI. "Simple, well-kept site in beautiful countryside; helpful, friendly British owners; vill 2km; gd touring base or NH; excel." € 16.00 2009*

DORMANS *3D4* (7km NE Rural) *49.10638, 3.73380* **Camping Rural (Nowack), 10 Rue Bailly, 51700 Vandières [03 26 58 02 69 or 03 26 58 08 79; fax 03 26 58 39 62; champagne.nowack@wanadoo.fr; www.champagne-nowack.com]** Fr N3, turn N at Port Binson, over Rv Marne, then turn W onto D1 for 3km, then N into Vandières. Site on R about 50m fr start of Rue Bailly, sp 'Champagne Nowack' or 'Camping Nowack.' Sm, pt sl, pt shd; wc; shwrs inc; el pnts (6A) inc; lndtte; tradsmn; BBQ; playgrnd; pool 8km; fishing 1km; rv sw & boating 6km; tennis 2km; TV; adv bkg; ccard acc; CCI. "Charming, peaceful, CL-type site in orchard; friendly owner; facs excel but fresh water tap used for rinsing chem disp; grape pickers on site Sep; excel value." 1 Mar-31 Oct. € 15.00 2009*

DORMANS *3D4* (1km W Urban) *49.07830, 3.63530* **Camping Sous Le Clocher, Route de Vincelles, 51700 Dormans [03 26 58 21 79; fax 03 26 57 29 62; dom.ribaille@wanadoo.fr]** On D1003 (N3) E fr Château-Thierry; in Dormans foll sp, over Rv Marne; camp site 50m fr end of bdge. Med, hdg pitch, pt shd; wc (some cont); shwrs; el pnts (6A) €3 (rev pol); shop 200m; rest, bar 1km; playgrnd; htd pool adj high ssn; games area; TV; some statics; dogs €2; poss cr; rlwy noise & noisy at w/end; ccard acc. "Ideal for Champagne area; sm pitches; basic facs, poss stretched high ssn; unreliable opening low ssn, phone ahead." Easter-15 Sep. € 8.00 2008*

DORTAN *9A3* (3km N Rural) *46.34129, 5.63028* **Camp Municipal Les Cyclamens, La Presqu'île, 01590 Chancia [tel/fax 04 74 75 82 14; campinglescyclamens@wandadoo.fr; www.camping-chancia.com]** Fr N on D436 to Dortan; R at traff lts sp Bourg-en-Bresse; in 1.5km R (furniture shop) onto D60 sp Chancia; foll sp. NB go past Camping du Lac. Lge, mkd pitch, pt shd; wc; chem disp; mv service pnt; shwrs inc; el pnts (6A) €2.10; gas; lndtte; shop 6km; tradsmn; rest,bar 1km; playgrnd; lake sw & shgl beach 100m; fishing, tennis, walking & watersports near; 50% statics; dogs €1.40; phone; poss cr; adv bkg; quiet; CCI. "Beautiful area; clean, friendly; few tourists; excel." 1 May-30 Sep. € 7.80 2008*

DOSCHES see Troyes *4E4*

DOUAI *3B4* (10km S Rural) *50.27374, 3.10565* **Camp Municipal Les Biselles, Chemin des Bisselles, 59151 Arleux [03 27 89 52 36 or 03 27 93 10 00; fax 03 27 94 37 38; office.tourisme@arleux.com]** Exit A2 junc 14 at Cambrai & take D643 (N43) twd Douai, after 5km turn W at Bugnicourt to Arleux. Site sp in vill adj canal La Sensée. Lge, hdg/mkd pitch, shd; wc (some cont); shwrs inc; el pnts €6.85; playgrnd; pool; rv fishing; tennis 200m; games area; 96% statics; dogs; phone; poss cr; adv bkg; quiet. "Very few touring pitches." ♦ 1 Apr-31 Oct. € 13.95 2009*

DOUAI *3B4* (10km S Rural) *50.29004, 3.04945* **FFCC Camp Municipal de la Sablière, Rue du 8 Mai 1945, 62490 Tortequesne [03 21 24 14 94; fax 03 21 07 46 07; camping@tortequesne.fr; www.tortequesne.fr]** Fr D643 (N43) Douai-Cambrai rd; turn S onto D956 to Tortequesne where site sp. Sm, hdg/mkd pitch, hdstg; pt shd; wc (some cont); shwrs inc; el pnts (6A) €3; supmkt 5 mins; playgrnd; walking in La Valée de la Sensée; tennis; games area; 80% statics; dogs €0.50; CCI. "San facs clean but need update; park & fishing adj; late night arrivals area; gd." 1 Apr-30 Sep. € 11.20 2008*

DOUARNENEZ *2E2* (2km W Urban) *48.09270, -4.35220* **Camping de Trézulien, Route de Trézulien, 29100 Douarnenez [02 98 74 12 30 or 02 98 92 81 40; fax 02 98 74 01 16; contact@camping-trezulien.com; www.camping-trezulien.com]** Ent Douarnenez fr E on D7; foll sp 'Centre Ville'; turn L at traff lts sp to Tréboul. Cross rv bdge into Ave de la Gare, at post office turn L, then 1st L. Turn R at island, foll site sp. Lge, pt terr, pt shd; wc; baby facs; shwrs inc; el pnts (6-10A) €2.50-3.10; gas; lndtte; shops 1km; playgrnd; sand beach 1.5km; dogs €1; quiet. "Pleasant site; steep hill fr ent to recep; 1km by foot to Les Sables Blancs; conv Pointe du Raz." 1 Apr-30 Sep. € 10.50 2006*

DOUARNENEZ *2E2* (6km W Rural) *48.08166, -4.40722* **FLOWER Camping Le Pil Koad, Route de Douarnenez, 29100 Poullan-sur-Mer [02 98 74 26 39; fax 02 98 74 55 97; info@pil-koad.com; www.pil-koad.com or www.flower camping.com]** Fr E take circular rd around Douarnenez on D7/D765 dir Audierne. After x-ing rv estuary, turn R at traff lts (D7) sp Poullan-sur-Mer, Tréboul & Pointe-du-Van; at 1st rndabt turn L sp Tréboul onto Blvd Jean Moulin; cont strt over rndabts foll sp Tréboul; at 3rd rndabt turn L sp Poullan-sur-Mer & Beuzec; site off D7 1km fr Poullan-sur-Mer vill on L, shortly after church spire becomes visible. Med, hdg/mkd pitch, pt shd; htd wc; chem disp; baby facs; shwrs inc; el pnts (10A) inc; gas; lndtte; shop; rest; snacks; bar; BBQ (charcoal/gas); playgrnd; htd pool; paddling pool; sand beach 5km; watersports 4km; lake fishing; tennis; cycle hire; games area; entmnt; wifi; games/TV rm; statics (tour ops); dogs €3.50; Eng spkn; adv bkg; quiet; ccard acc; red low ssn; CCI. "Tranquil site; staff friendly; ltd facs low ssn; guided walks high ssn; typical Breton ports nr; mkt Mon & Fri." ♦ 1 May-19 Sep. € 29.50 ABS - B04 2009*

See advertisement

DOUARNENEZ *2E2* (11km W Coastal) *48.08416, -4.48194* **Camping Pors Péron, 29790 Beuzec-Cap-Sizun [02 98 70 40 24; fax 02 98 70 54 46; info@campingporsperon.com; www.campingporsperon.com]** W fr Douarnenez take D7 sp Poullan-sur-Mer. Thro Poullan & in approx 4km turn R sp Pors-Piron, foll site & beach sp. Site bef Beuzec-Cap-Sizun vill. Med, hdg/mkd pitch, pt shd; wc; chem disp; mv service pnt; baby facs; shwrs inc; el pnts (10A) €2.60; gas; lndtte; shop & 3km; snacks; BBQ; playgrnd; sand beach 200m; games area; cycle hire; wifi; 5% statics; dogs €1.60; phone 200m; adv bkg; quiet; red low ssn; CCI. "1st class site nr beautiful sandy cove; friendly, helpful & efficient British owners; gd san facs; highly rec." ♦ 1 Apr-30 Sep. € 13.00 2009*

DOUCIER *6H2* (3km N Rural) *46.67755, 5.78080* **Camping La Pergola, 1 Rue des Vernois, Lac de Chalain, 39130 Marigny [03 84 25 70 03; fax 03 84 25 75 96; contact@lapergola.com; www.lapergola.com]** Fr D471 Lons-le-Saunier to Champagnole rd, turn S on D27 twd Marigny, site on L in 6km on N shore of Lac de Chalain. Lge, hdg/mkd pitch, pt sl, terr, pt shd; wc; chem disp; baby facs; some serviced pitches; shwrs inc; baby facs; el pnts (12A) inc; gas; lndtte; shop; rest; snacks; bar; BBQ; playgrnd; htd pool; paddling pool; lake sand beach adj; fishing; games rm; games area; entmnt; internet; TV; 50% statics; dogs €4; phone; poss cr; Eng spkn; adv bkg; red long stay; ccard acc; CCI. "Beautiful gorges nrby; naturist beach on lake 500m; superb san facs; some sm pitches; busy, popular site." ♦ 8 May-20 Sep. € 36.00 (CChq acc) 2009*

DOUCIER *6H2* (6km N Rural) *46.71221, 5.79709* **Camping Le Git, Monnet-le-Bourg, 39300 Montigny-sur-l'Ain [03 84 51 21 17 or 03 84 37 87 58 (LS); christian.olivier22@wanadoo.fr]** W fr Champagnole on D471 foll sp Monnet-la-Ville, foll camp sp thro vill, turn L at x-rds to church; site immed afterwards on R behind church in Monnet-la-Ville (also known as Monnet-le-Bourg). Med, mkd pitch, pt sl, pt shd; wc; chem disp; shwrs inc; el pnts (5A) €2.50; lndtte; lndry rm; supmkt 800m; rest; snacks; bar; playgrnd; lake sw 4km; sports area; fishing, kayaking 1.5km; dogs €1.50; adv bkg; quiet; CCI. "Peaceful site; beautiful views; lge pitches; gd san facs. "♦ 1 Jun-31 Aug. € 12.00 2009*

DOUCIER *6H2* (7km N Rural) *46.72244, 5.79934* **Camping Sous Doriat, 34 Rue Marcel Hugon, 39300 Monnet-la-Ville [03 84 51 21 43; camping.sousdoriat@wanadoo.fr; www.camping-sous-doriat.com]** Take D471 fr Champagnole to Pont-du-Navoy. After 10km fork L to Monnet-la-Ville. Site on L. Sm, unshd; wc; baby facs; shwrs inc; el pnts (10A) €2.50; lndtte; shops 300m; lake sw 6km; some statics; dogs free; adv bkg; quiet. ♦ 1 May-30 Sep. € 13.10 2007*

France

DOUCIER *6H2* (8km N Rural) *46.72383, 5.78463* **Camping Le Bivouac, Route du Lac de Chalain, 39300 Pont-du-Navoy [03 84 51 26 95; fax 03 84 51 29 70; camping-lebivouac-jura.fr; www.bivouac-jura.com]** D471 to Pont-du-Navoy, S over bdge & immed fork R onto D27; 2nd site on R. Med, mkd pitch, pt shd; htd wc; chem disp; shwrs inc; el pnts (16A) €2.80 (poss rev pol/no earth); Indtte; shops 1km; tradsmn; rest; snacks; bar; playgrnd; rv adj; lake sw 6km; TV; 20% statics; dogs €0.50; adv bkg; quiet; ccard not acc; CCI. "In beautiful countryside; friendly owners; poss unreliable opening dates." 15 Mar-15 Oct. € 12.10 2008*

DOUCIER *6H2* (3km NE Rural) *46.66361, 5.81333* **Camping Domaine de Chalain, 39130 Doucier [03 84 25 78 78; chalain@chalain.com; www.chalain.com]** Fr Lons-le-Saunier take D39 E. In Doucier, site sp to L. Fr Champagnole take D471 for 11km, L onto D27 at Pont-du-Navoy to Doucier & foll sp to site. V lge, pt shd; wc (some cont); mv service pnt; chem disp; sauna; shwrs inc; el pnts (7A) €3; gas; Indtte; shops; rest; snacks; bar; htd, covrd pools; waterslide & aquatic cent; lake sw adj; boating; fishing; watersports; cycle hire; tennis; horseriding; games area; entmnt; internet; statics; dogs €2; poss cr; adv bkg ess. "Extra for lakeside pitches; famous caves Grottes des Beaume adj; vg site." 29 Apr-21 Sep. € 33.00 (3 persons) 2009*

DOUCIER *6H2* (6km SE Rural) *46.61429, 5.84780* **Camping Le Relais de l'Eventail, Route de la Vallée du Hérisson, 39130 Menétrux-en-Joux [03 84 25 71 59; fax 03 84 25 76 66; relais-de-leventail@club-internet.fr]** Fr Doucier take D326 E (site not accessable fr D39). Adj tourist office. Med, mkd pitch, pt shd; wc; chem disp; mv service pnt; shwrs inc; el pnts (6A) €2.70 Indtte; rest; bar; tradsmn; pool; dogs €1.50; quiet. "Lovely, peaceful site; helpful staff; site in limestone gorge nr dramatic waterfall 'Herisson Cascades'; gd walks." 26 Jun-31 Aug. € 14.30 2008*

DOUCIER *6H2* (1.5km S Rural) *46.65260, 5.72119* **Kawan Village Domaine de l'Epinette, 15 Rue de l'Epinette, 39130 Châtillon-sur-Ain [03 84 25 71 44; fax 03 84 25 71 25; info@domaine-epinette.com; www.domaine-epinette.com]** Exit A39 junc 7 to Poligny, then N5 to Champagnole & D471 W. Turn S onto D27 to Lac de Chalain then D39 to Châtillon. Med, mkd pitch, mainly sl, terr, pt shd; wc (some cont); chem disp; shwrs inc; el pnts (6A) inc; Indtte; shop; tradsmn; rest; snacks; bar; playgrnd; pool; paddling pool; rv sw & fishing; canoeing, kayaking & horseriding 3km; games rm; 30% statics; dogs €2; phone; adv bkg; quiet. "Gd base for Jura area; vg." ♦ 10 Jun-15 Sep. € 27.00 (CChq acc) 2009*

DOUE LA FONTAINE *4G1* (1km N Rural) *47.20338, -0.28165* **Camp Municipal Le Douet, Rue des Blanchisseries, 49700 Doué-la-Fontaine [02 41 59 14 47; mairie@ville-doue-la-fontaine.fr]** Fr Doué N on D761 twd Angers; site in sports ground on o'skts of town adj zoo; sp. Med, mkd pitch, pt shd; wc; chem disp; shwrs inc; el pnts (6A) €3; Indtte; shop 1km; rests nr; htd pool high ssn adj; tennis; few statics; poss cr; quiet but some factory noise at E end; no ccard acc; 5% red CCI. "Clean, well-organised site; gd, flat pitches; gd san facs; helpful warden; poss itinerant workers in old c'vans low ssn; lovely park & museum; conv zoo, rose gardens & Cadre Noir Equestrian Cent." ♦ 1 Apr-30 Sep. € 9.00 2008*

DOUE LA FONTAINE *4G1* (2km SW Rural) *47.17390, -0.34750* **Camping La Vallée des Vignes, 49700 Concourson-sur-Layon [02 41 59 86 35; fax 02 41 59 09 83; campingvdv@wanadoo.fr; www.campingvdv.com]** D960 fr Doué-la-Fontaine (dir Cholet) to Concourson-sur-Layon; site 1st R 250m after bdge on leaving Concourson-sur-Layon. Or fr Angers foll sp dir Cholet & Poitiers; then foll sp Doué-la-Fontaine. Med, mkd pitch, pt shd; htd wc; chem disp; serviced pitches; baby facs & fam bthrm; shwrs inc; el pnts (10A) €4; gas; Indtte; shop; tradsmn; rest; snacks; bar; BBQ; playgrnd; htd pool; paddling pool; lake sw 10km; cycle hire; entmnt; TV rm; 5% statics; dogs €3; bus; poss cr; Eng spkn; adv bkg; quiet, some rd noise; ccard acc; red long stay low ssn; ccard acc; CCI. "Peaceful site poss open all year weather permitting - phone to check; friendly, helpful British owners; vg, clean, well-maintained facs but owners' dog roaming site (mess 9/07); pool open & htd early ssn; some pitches diff lge o'fits due o'hanging trees; conv for Loire chateaux & Futuroscope." ♦ 1 Apr-30 Sep. € 23.00 2009*

DOUE LA FONTAINE *4G1* (8km W Rural) *47.19355, -0.37075* **Camping Les Grésillons, Chemin des Grésillons, 49700 St Georges-sur-Layon [02 41 50 02 32; fax 02 41 50 03 16; camping.gresillon@wanadoo.fr; www.camping-gresillons.com]** Fr Doué-la-Fontaine on D84, site sp. Sm, hdg pitch, hdstg, terr, pt shd; htd wc; chem disp; baby facs; shwrs inc; el pnts (6-10A) €2.90-3.50; Indtte; shop & 500m; rest; snacks, bar 500m; playgrnd; htd pool; rv fishing 200m; games area; entmnt; 28% statics; dogs free; Eng spkn; adv bkg; quiet; ccard acc; red long stay/CCI. "Delightful site in area of vineyards; friendly, helpful owner." ♦ 1 Apr-30 Sep. € 11.00 2009*

DOUE LA FONTAINE *4G1* (15km W Rural) **Camping KathyDave, Les Beauliers, 49540 La Fosse-de-Tigné [02 41 67 92 10 or 06 14 60 81 63 (mob); bookings@camping-kathydave.co.uk; www.camping-kathydave.co.uk]** Fr Doué-la-Fontaine on D84 to Tigne, turn S thro La Fosse-de-Tigné. Pass chateau, site sp on R. Sm, pt shd; htd wc; chem disp; shwrs inc; el pnts (8A) €3 (poss rev pol); Indtte; tradsmn; rest nr; BBQ (gas); dogs; adv bkg; quiet; CCI. "Tranquil orchard site in picturesque area; welcoming, helpful British owners; gd san facs; access poss diff lge o'fits; gd touring base; adults only preferred; phone ahead rec." 1 May-31 Oct. € 10.50 2009*

DOUHET, LE *7B2* (2km S Rural) *45.81080, -0.55288* **Camping La Roulerie, 17100 Le Douhet [05 46 96 40 07 or 06 75 24 91 96 (mob); www.camping-laroulerie.fr]** Fr Niort to Saintes, site on W side of D150 in vill of La Roulerie. Sm, some hdg/mkd pitch, some hdstdg, pt shd; wc; chem disp; mv service pnt; shwrs inc; el pnts (16A) €3; Indtte; shop; supmkt 9km; playgrnd; pool; games area; some statics; Eng spkn; adv bkg; quiet but some rd noise; ccard not acc; CCI. "Sm pitches; full by early eve; friendly, helpful owner; gd san facs; vg value; gd NH." 1 May-15 Oct. € 7.50 2009*

DOURDAN *4E3* (700m NE Urban) *48.52572, 2.02878* **Camping Les Petits Prés, 11 Rue Pierre Mendès France, 91410 Dourdan [01 64 59 64 83 or 01 60 81 14 17; fax 01 60 81 14 29; loisirs.dourdan@wanadoo.fr]** Exit A10 junc 10 dir Dourdan; foll by-pass sp Arpajon; after 5th rndabt site 200m on L. Med, pt sl, pt shd; wc; shwrs; el pnts (4A) €3.10; gas & supmkt 500m; rest 1km; playgrnd; pool 500m; poss cr; 75% statics; Eng spkn; adv bkg; poss noisy. "Gd NH; ltd facs low ssn; town worth visit." 1 Apr-30 Sep. € 11.60 (3 persons) 2008*

DOUSSARD *9B3* (1.5km N Rural) *45.79120, 6.21599* **Camping International de Lac Bleu, Route de la Plage, 74210 Doussard [04 50 44 30 18 or 04 50 44 38 47; fax 04 50 44 84 35; contact@camping-lac-bleu.com; www.camping-lac-bleu.com]** S fr Annecy on D1508 (N508) twd Albertville. Site on L in 20km just past Bout-du-Lac & bef Camp La Nublière. Lge, hdg/mkd pitch, pt sl, pt shd; wc; chem disp; mv service pnt; some serviced pitches; shwrs inc; el pnts (8A) €3.90; gas adj; Indtte; shop 2km; hypmkt 4km; rest & snacks in high ssn; bar; playgrnd; pool; lake beach adj; watersports; wifi; dogs €4; phone; bus adj; poss cr; Eng spkn; adv bkg; rd noise some pitches; red low ssn/long stay; ccard acc; CCI. "Excel lakeside location; some lge pitches; gd watersports; cycle path into Annecy; ltd facs low ssn." ♦ 4 Apr-26 Sep. € 28.90 2009*

DOUSSARD *9B3* (2.5km N Rural) *45.79534, 6.20589* **Camping L'Idéal, 715 Route de Chaparon, 74210 Lathuile [04 50 44 32 97; fax 04 50 44 36 59; info@camping-ideal.com; www.camping-ideal.com]** Take Annecy Sud exit fr A41, foll Albertville sp on D1508 (N508) on W side of lake. In vill of Brédannaz R at traff lts, immed L on narr rd for 100m; site on R after 2km. Lge, mkd pitch, pt sl, pt shd; wc; chem disp; shwrs inc; el pnts (6A) €3.90; gas; Indtte; shop; rest; snacks; bar; BBQ: playgrnd; htd, covrd pool; waterslide; lake sw 800m; games area; entmnt; TV; 15% statics; dogs €3.20; phone; poss cr high ssn; adv bkg; quiet; red long stay; CCI. "Pleasant, family-run site; less cr than lakeside sites; views of mountains & lake." 1 May-23 Sep. € 23.00 2009*

DOUSSARD *9B3* (3km N Rural) *45.80256, 6.20960* **Camping La Ravoire, Route de la Ravoire, Bout-du-Lac, 74210 Doussard [04 50 44 37 80; fax 04 50 32 90 60; info@camping-la-ravoire.fr; www.camping-la-ravoire.fr]** On D1508 (N508) S fr Annecy twd Doussard, keep lake to your L; at Bredannaz cont past traff lts & turn R after vill opp rest & boat landing stage (site sp); turn R again immed after cycle track; site on R in 300m. Med, hdg/mkd pitch, pt shd; wc; chem disp; mv service pnt (poss diff access); serviced pitches; shwrs inc; el pnts (5A) inc (poss rev pol); gas; Indtte; sm shop; tradsmn; supmkt 5km; rest 800m; snacks; bar; playgrnd; htd pool; paddling pool; waterslide; lake sw 800m; fishing, golf, horseriding, sailing & windsurfing adj; cycle hire; games area; TV; some statics; dogs; phone; poss cr; Eng spkn; adv bkg rec Jul/Aug; quiet; ccard acc; red low ssn; CCI. "Excel, well-kept, busy site with mountain views; immac facs; friendly staff & atmosphere; lake ferry fr Doussard; cycle paths adj." ♦ 15 May-7 Sep. € 30.00 (CChq acc) 2009*

DOUSSARD *9B3* (3km N Rural) *45.80302, 6.20608* **Camping Le Taillefer, 1530 Route de Chaparon, 74210 Doussard [tel/fax 04 50 44 30 30; info@campingletaillefer.com; www.campingletaillefer.com]** Fr Annecy take D1508 (N508) twd Faverges & Albertville. At traff lts in Bredannaz turn R, then immed L for 1.5km; site immed on L by vill sp 'Chaparon'. Do NOT turn into ent by Bureau but stop on rd & ask for instructions as no access to pitches fr Bureau ent. Or, to avoid Annecy, fr Faverges, along D1508, turn L (sp Lathuile) after Complex Sportif at Bout-du-Lac. Turn R at rndabt (sp Chaparon), site is on R after 2.5km. Sm, mkd pitch, pt sl, terr, pt shd; wc; chem disp; mv service pnt; shwrs inc; el pnts (6A) inc (check rev pol); Indtte; sm shop & 3km; tradsmn; snacks, bar (high ssn); BBQ (gas/charcoal only); playgrnd; lake sw 1km; shgl beach 3km; tennis 100m; watersports 2km; cycle hire; TV rm; dogs €1.80; Eng spkn; adv bkg; some rd noise; ccard not acc; red low ssn/long stay. "Mains water & waste disp only avail fr wc block at recep; helpful, friendly owners; clean facs; vg rest within easy walking dist; mkt Mon; highly rec." ♦ 1 May-30 Sep. € 18.80 ABS - M06 2009*

DOUSSARD *9B3* (3.1km N Rural) *45.79967, 6.20545* **Camping La Ferme, 1170 Route de Chaparon, 74210 Lathuile [04 50 44 33 10 or 06 80 72 68 74 (mob); fax 04 50 44 39 50; info@campinglaferme.com; www.campinglaferme.com]** Fr Annecy take D1508 (N508) dir Faverges & Albertville; at traff lts in Brédannaz turn R then immed L for 1.5km; site on L by vill sp 'Chaparon' & adj Camping Le Taillefer. Or fr Faverges, along D1508, turn L (sp Lathuile) after Complex Sportif at Bout-du-Lac; turn R at rndabt (sp Chaparon), site is on R after 2.5km. Med, mkd pitch, terr, pt shd; wc (cont); chem disp; baby facs; shwrs inc; el pnts (6-10A) €3.30-4.80; Indtte; sm shop; tradsmn; snacks; takeaway; bar; BBQ; playgrnd; 2 pools (1 htd covrd); lake sw, fishing & watersports 1km; games area; games rm; entmnt; wifi; dogs €2; bus 1km; poss cr; Eng spkn; adv bkg; ccard acc; CCI. "Gd views; family-run site; vg." 1 Apr-30 Sep. € 20.00 2007*

France

DOUSSARD *9B3* (500m NW Rural) *45.79115, 6.21298* **Camping Le Polé, 1430 Route du Bout du Lac, 74210 Lathuile [04 50 44 32 13 or 06 88 04 68 70 (mob); contact@camping-le-pole.fr; www.camping-le-pole.fr]** S fr Annecy on D1508 dir Albertville; in 14km at Bout-du-Lac turn R dir Lathuile; site on L in 70m, just after cylce track. Or N fr Faverges on D1508; in 8km turn sharp L after passing Camping International du Lac Bleu; site on L. Med, hdg/mkd pitch, pt shd; wc; chem disp; baby facs; shwrs inc; el pnts (2-6A) €3.50-7; Indry rm; ice; shops 3km; tradsmn rest 2km; snacks 500m; bar 200m; BBQ; playgrnd; pool; paddling pool; lake sw adj; games area; games rm; TV; 50% statics; dogs €2.50; phone; Eng spkn; adv bkg; quiet. "Quiet, scenic site in busy area high ssn; helpful manager; gd pool; cycle path adj; gd walks; vg." ♦ 1 Jun-30 Sep. € 15.50 2009*

DOUVAINE *9A3* (8km NE Rural) *46.36812, 6.32809* **Camping Mathieu Le Léman 1, 74140 Yvoire [04 50 72 84 31; fax 04 50 72 96 33; www.campingsmathieu.com]** Exit D1005 (N5) at Sciez (bet Geneve & Thonon) onto D25 sp Yvoire; site in 10km; at Yvoire foll camping sp. NB Narr ent to site. Med, mkd pitch, pt sl, pt shd; wc (mainly cont); chem disp; shwrs inc; el pnts (6A) €2.50; Indtte; tradsmn; shop, snacks & bar 500m; BBQ; playgrnd; lake sw 500m; 75% statics; dogs €1; Eng spkn; adv bkg; quiet; red low ssn; CCI. "Excel site above medieval vill; friendly owner; v lge pitches, some v sloping; clean san facs; gd lake sw; adj site Mathieu Le Léman 2 open Jul-Aug only - same ownership, sep recep & facs; conv Geneva & Thonon-les-Bains." 1 Apr-28 Oct. € 14.50 2008*

DOUVAINE *9A3* (4km NW Rural) *46.32441, 6.26101* **Camp Municipal Le Lémania, Plage de Tougues, 74140 Chens-sur-Léman [04 50 94 22 43; fax 04 50 94 22 43; machens@chens-leman.mairies74.org; www.camping-nautique.com]** Fr Geneva dir Thonon on D1005 (N5) turn L onto D20 dir Tougues at Douvaine. Site sp. Med, pt shd; wc (some cont); chem disp; shwrs inc; el pnts (5A); Indtte; shop 300m; rest 200m; shgl beach on lake 200m; some statics; dogs €1; red low ssn. "Gd lake sw nr; gd NH." 1 May-30 Sep. € 15.00 2006*

DOUVILLE *7C3* (2km S Rural) *44.99271, 0.59853* **Camping Lestaubière, Pont-St Mamet, 24140 Douville [05 53 82 98 15; fax 05 53 82 90 17; lestaubiere@cs.com; www.lestaubiere.com]** Foll sp for 'Pont St Mamet' fr N21; then watch for camping sp. Med, mkd pitch, pt sl, pt shd; wc; chem disp; baby facs; fam bthrm; shwrs inc; el pnts (6-10A) €3.50; gas; Indtte; shop in ssn; tradsmn; rest & snacks (high ssn); bar; BBQ; playgrnd; pool; paddling pool; lake sw, sm sand beach; fishing; tennis 5km; games area; games rm; child entmnt (high ssn); wifi; TV; dogs €2; phone; twin-axles (high ssn only); Eng spkn; adv bkg; quiet; ccard acc; red low ssn; CCI. "Spacious, park-like site run by friendly Dutch couple; superb out of ssn; v lge pitches; vg modern san facs; excel." ♦ 1 May-30 Sep. € 23.00 2008*

DOUZE, LA *7C3* (3km E Rural) *45.06493, 0.88817* **Camping Laulurie en Périgord (Naturist), 24330 La Douze [05 53 06 74 00; fax 05 53 06 77 55; toutain@laulurie.com; www.laulurie.com]** Fr Périgueux S on N221; in 8km turn S on D710 twd Le Bugue. Or exit A89 onto D710 S. On ent La Douze turn L & foll arrow signs. Sm, hdg/mkd pitch, pt sl, pt shd; wc (some cont); chem disp; shwrs inc; el pnts (3-10A) €3-6.50; gas; shop; rest; snacks; bar; playgrnd; pool; dogs €3; sep car park; adv bkg; quiet; red low ssn; ccard acc. "Excel; friendly owners; gd touring base for Dordogne & Périgueux; INF card req." ♦ 15 May-15 Sep. € 20.50 2009*

DOUZE, LA *7C3* (6km SE Rural) *45.00765, 0.93039* **FFCC Camping Roc de Lavandre, Le Bourychou, 24620 St Félix-de-Reillac-et-Mortemart [tel/fax 05 53 03 23 47 or 06 81 12 52 71 (mob); contact@camping-roc-lavandre.com; www.camping-roc-lavandre.com]** Fr Les Eyzies-de-Tayac N on D47 dir Périgueux; site on R just bef St Félix-de-Reillac. Med, hdg/mkd pitch, pt shd; wc (some cont); chem disp; shwrs inc; el pnts (6A) €2.50; Indry rm; shops over 5km; tradsmn; rest; snacks; bar; playgrnd; lake sw; fishing; cycle hire; entmnt; 15% statics; dogs €1; Eng spkn; adv bkg; quiet, some rd noise; red low ssn; CCI. "Friendly, helpful owners; excel food in rest." 22 Mar-28 Oct. € 12.00 2008*

DOUZY see Sedan *5C1*

DRAGUIGNAN *10F3* (2km S Rural) *43.51796, 6.47836* **Camping La Foux, Quartier La Foux, 83300 Draguignan [tel/fax 04 94 68 18 27; camp.foux@wanadoo.fr]** Fr A8, take Le Muy intersection onto N555 N to Draguignan. Site ent on R at ent to town sp Sport Centre Foux. Fr Draguignan, take N555 S; just after 'End of Draguignan' sp, double back at rndabt & turn R. Lge, pt sl, unshd; wc; shwrs inc; el pnts (4-10A); Indtte; shop; rest; bar; playgrnd; sand beach 20km; rv adj; fishing; entmnt; TV rm; dogs; poss cr; quiet. "Clean san facs; care needed long vehicles on ent site; easy access to Riviera coast." 20 Jun-30 Sep. 2008*

⊞ **DREUX** *4E2* (6km W Rural) *48.76149, 1.29041* **Camping Les Etangs de Marsalin, 3 Place du Général de Gaulle, 28500 Vert-en-Drouais [02 37 82 92 23; fax 02 37 82 85 47; camping.etangs.de.marsalin@wanadoo.fr; www.campingdemarsalin.com]** Fr W on N12 dir Dreux, cross dual c'way bef petrol stn onto D152 to Vert-en-Drouais; on ent turn R to church, site on L. Well sp. Med, hdg/mkd pitch, some hdstg, pt sl, pt shd; htd wc (some cont); chem disp; shwrs inc; el pnts (20A) €4.10 (poss rev pol, long leads poss req, avail at recep); shop; tradsmn; rest 4km; snacks; bar 100m; lake fishing 2km; wifi; 80% statics; dogs; phone adj; poss cr; Eng spkn; quiet; CCI. "Peaceful location; friendly, helpful staff; gd basic san facs; site untidy/scruffy (2009); muddy when wet; touring pitches at far end far fr facs; conv Versailles & NH." ♦ € 10.20 2009*

DUCEY see Pontaubault *2E4*

DUN SUR MEUSE *5C1* (10km SE Rural) *49.32071, 5.26589* **Camping Le Brouzel, 55110 Sivry-sur-Meuse [03 29 85 86 45]** On D964 11km S of Dun twd Verdun, site sp in vill of Sivry. Sm, some hdstg, unshd; wc (cont); chem disp; shwrs inc; gas; el pnts (6A) €3.15; shop adj; rest; snacks; bar; playgrnd; games area; dir access to rv; fishing; sailing 2km; 80% statics; Eng spkn; adv bkg; quiet. "Clean site; friendly owner; gd san facs." 1 Apr-1 Oct. € 10.40 2009*

DUN SUR MEUSE *5C1* (10km S Rural) *49.32112, 5.08136* **Camping La Gabrielle, Ferme de la Gabrielle, 55110 Romagne-sous-Montfaucon [03 29 85 11 79; La-Gabrielle@wanadoo.fr; www.antenna.nl/la-gabrielle]** Site is on D998, 800m beyond end of Romagne. Well sp. Sm, pt sl, pt shd; wc; chem disp (wc); shwrs inc; el pnts (6A) €2 (rev pol); playgrnd; TV; 10% statics; dogs €1; Eng spkn; adv bkg; quiet; CCI. "Restful site in pretty setting; friendly Dutch owners; meals by arrangement; nr WW1 monuments; gd." ♦ 1 Apr-30 Sep. € 12.00 2009*

DUNKERQUE *3A3* (3km NE Coastal) *51.05171, 2.42025* **Camp Municipal La Licorne, 1005 Blvd de l'Europe, 59240 Dunkerque [03 28 69 26 68; fax 03 28 69 56 21; campinglalicorne@ville-dunkerque.fr]** Leave A16 sp 'Malo'. At end of slip rd traff lts turn L sp Malo-les-Bains. In 2km (at 5th traff lts) turn R at camping sp. At 2nd traff lts past BP g'ge turn L. Site on L (cont strt to rndabt & return on opp side of dual c'way to ent). Lge, mkd pitch, pt sl, unshd; htd wc; chem disp; mv service pnt; shwrs; el pnts (8A) €4.25 (poss long lead); gas; Indtte; sm shop; supmkt 500m; rest; snacks; bar; playgrnd; pool in high ssn; sand beach adj; 50% statics; dogs €0.90; bus fr site ent; clsd 2200-0700; poss cr; Eng spkn; adv bkg; quiet; CCI. "Gd NH for Calais; pitches uneven; many site rd humps; promenade to town cent; lge supmkts nr with petrol; owners give code for gate if dep early for ferry; poss windy." ♦ 1 Apr-30 Nov. € 17.10 2009*

⊞ **DUNKERQUE** *3A3* (11km NE Coastal) *51.07941, 2.52177* **Camp Municipal des Dunes, 222 Rue de l'Eglise, 59123 Bray-Dunes [03 28 26 61 54 or 03 28 26 57 63]** Fr Dunkerque-Ostend on D601 (N1), take R slip rd sp Bray-Dunes (approx 100m bef Belgian border), foll rd over D601 for 3km into Bray-Dunes. Foll Camping Municipal sp in town. Or exit A16 junc 36 to Bray-Dunes. V lge, mkd pitch, pt sl, unshd; wc; chem disp (wc); shwrs €1; el pnts (5A) inc (long lead poss req); shop 200m; playgrnd; sand beach 300m; 99% statics; dogs €0.50. "Ltd space for tourers; low ssn untidy & cats roaming site; poss long way to water point; conv for ferry but poss clsd low ssn - phone ahead." € 20.00 2007*

DUNKERQUE *3A3* (12km NE Coastal) *51.07600, 2.55524* **Camping Perroquet Plage Frontière, 59123 Bray-Dunes [03 28 58 37 37; fax 03 28 58 37 01; camping-perroquet@wanadoo.fr; www.camping-perroquet.com]** On Dunkerque-Ostend D601 (N1), about 100m fr Belgian frontier, thro vill on D947; cont 1km to traff lts, R on D60 thro vill, past rlwy stn to site on L. V lge, hdg pitch, hdstg, pt shd; htd wc; chem disp; sauna; shwrs €1; el pnts (4-10A) €4.50; Indtte (inc dryer); shop; rest; snacks; bar; playgrnd; sand beach adj; watersports; tennis; entmnt; wifi; 85% statics; dogs €0.50; poss cr; adv bkg (ess high ssn); Eng spkn; CCI. "Busy, well-kept site; lge pitches; if parked nr site ent, v long walk to beach; san facs poss far; many local attractions; gd." ♦ 1 Apr-30 Sep. € 14.80 2009*

⊞ **DUNKERQUE** *3A3* (6km S Urban) *51.00340, 2.40670* **Camping Les Bois des Forts, 59380 Coudekerque [03 28 61 04 41 or 06 73 83 28 81 (mob)]** Exit A16 junc 60 onto D916, in 2km turn L onto D2 dir Coudekerque. In 2km at rndabt turn L, site on R. Med, hdg pitch, unshd; wc; shwrs; el pnts (10A) 1.90; Indtte; shop adj; bar; playgrnd; games area; 70% statics; quiet. € 9.70 2008*

⊞ **DURAS** *7D2* (500m N Rural) *44.68293, 0.18602* **Camping Le Cabri, Malherbe, Route de Savignac, 47120 Duras [05 53 83 81 03; fax 05 53 83 08 91; holidays@lecabri.eu.com; www.lecabri.eu.com]** On ent Duras fr N turn R onto D203. Site well sp fr D708. Sm, hdg pitch, some hdstg, pt shd; htd wc; chem disp; baby facs; shwrs inc; el pnts (6-16A) €5-7; gas 500m; Indtte; shop 500m; rest; snacks; bar; playgrnd; pool; tennis 1km; 50% statics; dogs €2; bus 500m; Eng spkn; adv bkg; quiet; ccard acc; red long stay; CCI. "Excel, clean, spacious site; British owners (Caravan Club members); gd, modern san facs; hdstg pitches lge." ♦ € 19.00 2009*

DURAVEL see Puy l'Evêque *7D3*

DURTAL *4G1* (200m W Urban) *47.67115, -0.23798* **Camping L'Internationale Les Portes de l'Anjou, 9 Rue de Camping, 49430 Durtal [02 41 76 31 80; lesportesdelanjou@camp-in-ouest.com; www.lesportesdelanjou.com or www.camp-in-ouest.com]** Exit A11 junc 11 dir La Flèche, by-passing Durtal. At D323 (N23) turn R for Durtal, site on L at ent to town. Sps not readily visible, look out for 'Motor Caravan Parking'. Med, hdg/mkd pitch, pt shd; wc (mainly cont); chem disp; baby facs; shwrs inc; el pnts (6A) €2.60; gas; Indtte (inc dryer); shops 500m; tradsmn; snacks; bar; playgrnd; htd pool; paddling pool; fishing; canoeing; games rm; wifi; entmnt; TV rm; 12% statics; dogs €1.80; Eng spkn; adv bkg; quiet; ccard acc; red long stay/CCI. "Vg site in pleasant position on Rv Loir; helpful staff; interesting vill." ♦ 2 Apr-1 Nov. € 14.70 2009*

See advertisement on next page

EAUX BONNES see Laruns *8G2*

⊞ **EAUX PUISEAUX** *4F4* (1km S Rural) *48.11587, 3.88508* **Camping à la Ferme des Haut Frênes (Lambert), 6 Voie de Puiseaux, 10130 Eaux-Puiseaux [03 25 42 15 04; fax 03 25 42 02 95; les.hauts.frenes@wanadoo.fr; www.les-hauts-frenes.com]** N fr St Florentin or S fr Troyes on N77. Ignore D374 but take next turning D111 in NW dir. Site in 2km; well sp. Long o'fits take care at ent gate. Med, hdg/mkd pitch, hdstg, pt shd; htd wc; chem disp; shwrs inc; el pnts (10A) €2 (some rev pol); Indtte; shop 2km; tradsmn; rest 3km; BBQ; playgrnd; tennis 3km; TV & games rm; dogs €1.50; poss cr; adv bkg; quiet; red 10+ days; CCI. "Well-kept farm site in beautiful, quiet setting; v lge, level pitches; helpful & friendly owners; gd san facs; meals on request; cider museum in vill; conv m'way; excel value." ♦ € 10.00 2009*

EAUZE *8E2* (Urban) *43.87043, 0.10671* **Camp Municipal Le Moulin du Pouy, 32800 Eauze [05 62 09 86 00; fax 05 62 09 79 20; camplinglemoulin@tiscali.fr]** On D931 on N o'skts, sp. Site in 2 parts, connected by bdge. Sm, well shd; wc (cont); shwrs inc; el pnts (6-10A) inc; rest; snacks; bar; supmkt 500m; pool; library; TV rm; quiet; red low ssn/CCI. "Noise fr pool during day; facs basic but clean; gd rest & pool; friendly staff; gd." 15 May-30 Sep. € 18.50 2008*

EBREUIL see Gannat *9A1*

ECHELLES, LES *9B3* (6km NE Rural) *45.45679, 5.81327* **Camping La Bruyère, Hameau Côte Barrier, 73160 St Jean-de-Couz [tel/fax 04 79 65 74 27; bearob@libertysurf.fr; www.camping-labruyere.com]** Heading S on D1006 (N6) Chambéry-Lyon rd, after x-ing Col de Coux 15km S of Chambéry take D45 to St Jean-de-Couz; site sp. Med, pt sl, pt shd; wc (cont); chem disp; shwrs inc; el pnts (6A) €2.90; gas; shop; tradsmn; rest, snacks high ssn; bar; BBQ; playgrnd; TV; 30% statics; dogs €0.90; adv bkg; quiet. "Vg, clean facs; helpful owner; magnificent scenery; peaceful site; Chartreuse caves open to public adj; gd walking area." 1 May-30 Sep. € 12.20 2006*

ECHELLES, LES *9B3* (200m SE Urban) *45.43462, 5.75615* **Camping L'Arc-en-Ciel, Chemin des Berges, 38380 Entre-Deux-Guiers [04 76 66 06 97; info@camping-arc-en-ciel.com; www.camping-arc-en-ciel.com]** Fr D520 turn W sp Entre-Deux-Guiers. On ent vill turn R into Ave de Montcelet dir Les Echelles & R again in 100m. Site sp fr D520. Med, some hdg/mkd pitch, pt sl, pt shd; wc (some cont); chem disp; shwrs inc; el pnts (2-4A) €2.50-4.30; gas; Indtte; shops, rest, snacks & bar nrby; 40% statics; dogs €1.10; poss cr; red low ssn; CCI. "Conv La Chartreuse area with spectacular limestone gorges; gd." ♦ 1 Mar-15 Oct. € 15.10 2009*

ECHELLES, LES *9B3* (5km SE Rural) *45.42977, 5.70161* **Camping Le Balcon de Chartreuse, 950 Chemin de la Forêt, 38380 Miribel-les-Echelles [04 76 55 28 53; fax 04 76 55 25 82; balcondechartreuse@wanadoo.fr; www.camping-balcondechartreuse.com]** Fr D520 out of Voiron to St Etienne-de-Crossey take D49 to Mirabel. Rec do not app with c'van fr Les Echelles. Med, terr, pt shd; wc; chem disp; shwrs inc; el pnts (6A) €4; Indtte; shop 4km; rest; snacks; bar; playgrnd; pool; paddling pool; horseriding; tennis 1km; games area; entmnt; TV; 30% statics; dogs €1.50; poss cr; adv bkg rec; quiet; CCI. "Few touring pitches." 1 Apr-30 Oct. € 14.00 2007*

ECHELLES, LES *9B3* (6km S Rural) *45.39107, 5.73656* **Camp Municipal Les Berges du Guiers, Le Revol, 38380 St Laurent-du-Pont [04 76 55 20 63 or 04 76 06 22 55 (LS); fax 04 76 06 21 21; mairie.st-laurent-du-pont@wanadoo.fr]** On D520 Chambéry-Voiron S fr Les Echelles. On ent St Laurent-du-Pont turn R just bef petrol stn on L. Sm, mkd pitch, pt shd; wc; chem disp; baby facs; shwrs; el pnts (5A) €3; shops 1km; rest, bar 600m; playgrnd; pool 200m; rv adj; tennis 100m; dogs €1; ccard not acc; CCI. "Clean & well-kept; nice area; gates clsd 1100-1530." 15 Jun-15 Sep. € 11.50 2006*

ECLARON BRAUCOURT STE LIVIERE *6E1* (2km SW Rural) *48.57142, 4.84936* **Yelloh! Village en Champagne les Sources du Lac, 52290 Eclaron-Braucourt-Ste Livière [03 25 06 34 24; fax 03 25 06 96 47; info@yellohvillage-en-champagne.com; www.lacduder.com]** S fr St Dizier on D2/D384 dir Troyes; site on R, 2km S of Eclaron-Braucourt-Ste Livière. Med, mkd pitch, pt shd; htd wc; chem disp; shwrs inc; el pnts (6A) inc; shop; tradsmn; rest; snacks; BBQ; pool; direct access to beach; watersports; fishing; cycle hire; games rm; entmnt; 40% statics; dogs; Eng spkn; poss cr; quiet; ccard acc; red low ssn; CCI. "Wooded site nr Lake Der; sm pitches; vg." 24 Apr-11 Sep. € 39.00 2009*

ECLASSAN see St Vallier *9C2*

ECOMMOY *4F1* (400m NE Urban) *47.83367, 0.27985* **Camp Municipal Les Vaugeons, Rue de la Charité, 72220 Ecommoy [02 43 42 14 14 or 02 43 42 10 14 (Mairie); fax 02 43 42 62 80; mairie.ecommoy@wanadoo.fr]** Heading S on D338 (N138) foll sp. Turn E at 2nd traff lts in vill; sp Stade & Camping. Also just off A28. Med, pt sl, pt shd; wc (some cont); chem disp; shwrs €1.30; el pnts (6A) €2.30; Indtte; shops 1km; playgrnd; tennis; poss cr; Eng spkn; adv bkg; quiet; ccard not acc; red low ssn; CCI. "Site full during Le Mans week as close to circuit; excel facs; recep 1600-2000 low ssn & 1500-2100 high ssn, new arrivals no access when recep clsd; coarse sand/grass surface." ♦ 1 May-30 Sep. € 8.20 2009*

ECOMMOY *4F1* (4km SE Rural) *47.81564, 0.33358* **Camp Municipal Le Chesnaie, 72220 Marigné-Laillé [02 43 42 12 12 (Mairie); fax 02 43 42 61 23; mairie.marigne-laille@wanadoo.fr]** S on D338 (N138) Le Mans-Tours, turn E 3km after Ecommoy twds Marigné-Laillé. Site in 1.5km. Sm, pt shd, mkd pitch; wc; shwrs; el pnts (10A) €1.20; shops 300m; playgrnd; pool 5km; lake & fishing adj; tennis; poss cr; v quiet; CCI. "If height barrier down, use phone at ent for vehicles over 2m high; barrier clsd except 1 hr am & pm, w/end open 0900-0930 & 1830-1900; pleasant warden." 1 Apr-1 Oct. € 7.00 2007*

ECOMMOY *4F1* (8km S Rural) *47.75641, 0.28780* **Camp Municipal Plan d'Eau du Fort des Salles, 72360 Mayet [02 43 46 68 72; fax 02 43 46 07 61]** On D338 (N138) Le Mans-Tours rd turn W at St Hubert onto D13 to Mayet & site. Sp 'Camping Plan d'Eau'. Or exit A28 sp Ecommoy & then as above. Med, mkd pitch, pt shd; wc, chem disp (wc); shwrs inc; el pnts (10A) €2.32; gas; Indtte; shops 500m; playgrnd; pool nrby; lake fishing; cycle hire; statics; quiet; CCI. "Well-maintained, clean site; mkd walks nrby; card operated barrier; recep open 0830-1130 & 1600-1900; arr only bet these times as no waiting area." ♦ 15 Apr-17 Sep. € 7.00 2006*

ECUEILLE *4H2* (1km SE Urban) *47.08238, 1.35257* **Camp Municipal de la Potinière, Ave de la Gare, 36240 Ecueillé [02 54 40 21 10; fax 02 54 40 27 51; mairie.ecueille@wanadoo.fr]** Well sp fr town cent in Ave de la Gare - 1st part of D8 SE fr Ecueillé. Site adj lake. Sm, hdg/mkd pitch, pt sl, pt shd; wc (some cont); chem disp; mv service pnt; shwrs inc; el pnts (6A) €2; gas 1km; dogs; no twin-axles; some Eng spkn; quiet; CCI. "Immac site in lovely setting; do not arr after 1700, no site office; park in lake car park & tel Mairie to open height barrier; lake fishing Wed & w/end; excel." ♦ 1 Jun-30 Sep. € 6.00 2008*

⊞ **EGLETONS** *7C4* (2km NE Rural) *45.41852, 2.06431* **Camping Le Lac, 19300 Egletons [tel/fax 05 55 93 14 75; campingegletons@orange.fr; www.camping-egletons.com]** Site off D1089 (N89) nr Hôtel Ibis. Med, mkd pitch, terr, pt shd; wc; chem disp; baby facs; fam bthrm; shwrs inc; el pnts (4-8A) €2.50-3.40; gas; Indtte; shops 2km; tradsmn; rest; snacks; bar; lake sw, fishing & watersports 300m; playgrnd; entmnt; TV; 30% statics; dogs €1.30; phone; Eng spkn; quiet; CCI. € 11.00 2008*

EGUISHEIM see Colmar *6F3*

⊞ **EGUZON CHANTOME** *7A3* (300m N Urban) *46.44562, 1.58331* **Camping La Garenne, 1 Rue Yves Choplin, 36270 Eguzon-Chantôme [02 54 47 44 85; info@campinglagarenne.eu; www.campinglagarenne.eu]** Exit A20 junc 20 onto D36 to Eguzon; on ent vill sq cont strt on, foll sp; site on L in 300m. Med, hdg pitch, pt sl, pt shd; wc; chem disp; baby facs; shwrs inc; el pnts (6A) €3; gas 300m; Indtte; shop & rest 300m; snacks; bar; htd pool; cycling; lake sw & water sports 4km; wifi; TV rm; 20% statics; dogs €.1.50; phone; site clsd 16 Dec-14 Jan; poss cr; Eng spkn; adv bkg; quiet; red long stay/CCI. "All you need on site or in vill; excel." ♦ € 15.00 2008*

⊞ **EGUZON CHANTOME** *7A3* (3km SE Rural) *46.43372, 1.60399* **Camp Municipal du Lac Les Nugiras, Route de Messant, 36270 Eguzon-Chantôme [02 54 47 45 22; fax 02 54 47 47 22; nugiras@orange.fr; www.eguzonlaccreuse.com]** Fr A20 exit junc 20, E on D36 to Eguzon; in vill turn R & foll site sp. Lge, hdg/mkd pitch, pt sl, terr, pt shd; htd wc; shwrs inc; el pnts (10A) €3 (rev pol); Indtte; shop; tradsmn; rest; snacks; bar; playgrnd; sand beach 300m; watersports; waterski school; entmnt; games rm; some statics; security barrier; quiet but poss noise fr statics or entmnt; red low ssn; CCI. "Scenic site & region; ample, clean facs but v ltd low ssn; site yourself on arr; warden avail early eves; gd winter site; muddy after heavy rain." ♦ € 8.00 2009*

France

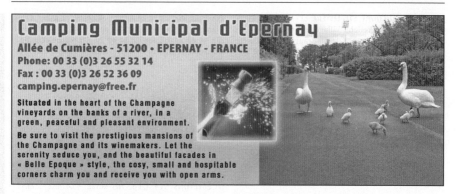

ELNE *10G1* (1.8km NE Rural) *42.60701, 2.99021* **Camp Municipal Al Mouly, Blvd d'Archimède, 66200 Elne [04 68 22 08 46; fax 04 68 37 95 05; cpg.elmoli@orange.fr]** Exit A9 at Perpignan Sud dir Argelès. Site well sp fr Elne cent in dir St Cyprien on D40. Lge, pt shd; wc; chem disp; baby facs; shwrs inc; el pnts (10A) €3; Indtte; shop; rest & snacks high ssn; playgrnd; pool; sand beach 5km; tennis; horseriding; games area; entmnt; TV; poss cr; quiet; adv bkg; CCI. ♦ 1 Jun-30 Sep. € 19.90 2008*

ELNE *10G1* (4km S Rural) *42.57570, 2.96514* **Kawan Village Le Haras, Domaine St Galdric, 66900 Palau-del-Vidre [04 68 22 14 50; fax 04 68 37 98 93; haras8@wanadoo.fr; www.camping-le-haras.com]** Exit A9 junc 42 sp Perpignan S dir Argelès-sur-Mer on D900 (N9) & then D914 (N114); then exit D914 junc 9 onto D11 to Palau-del-Vidre. Site on L at ent to vill immed after low & narr rlwy bdge. Med, shd; wc; chem disp; mv service pnt; baby facs; shwrs inc; el pnts (6A) inc; Indtte (inc dryer); supmkt 6km; tradsmn; rest, snacks in ssn; bar; BBQ (gas/elec only); pool; sand beach 6km; fishing 50m; tennis 1km; archery; entmnt; wifi; games/TV rm; some statics; dogs €3.50; no c'vans over 6.50m acc high ssn; poss cr; Eng spkn; adv bkg; some rlwy noise; ccard acc; red low ssn; CCI. "Lovely, peaceful, family site in wooded parkland; helpful, friendly staff; some corners on site rds narr for lge o'fits; staff can tow lge o'fits to pitch; rds around site poss liable to flood in winter; red facs low ssn; gd rest & pool; 5 mins walk to delightful vill with gd rest; conv Spanish border; excel." ♦ 20 Mar-20 Oct. € 31.00 (CChq acc) ABS - C26 2009*

EMBRUN *9D3* (6km N Rural) *44.60290, 6.52150* **FFCC Camping Les Cariamas, 05380 Châteauroux-les-Alpes [04 92 43 22 63 or 06 65 00 32 88 (mob); p.tim@free.fr; http://les.cariamas.free.fr]** Fr Embrun on N94; in 6km slip rd R to Châteauroux & foll sp to site. Site in 1km down narr but easy lane. Med, mkd pitch, pt sl, terr, pt shd; wc; chem disp; mv service pnt; shwrs inc; el pnts (6A) €3.15; Indtte; shop 1km; rest; snacks; bar; BBQ; playgrnd; htd pool; lake sw adj; beach 6km; sailing; rafting; canoeing; tennis 500m; 20% statics; dogs €2.50; phone; Eng spkn; adv bkg; some rd noise; red low ssn; CCI. "Excel for watersports & walking; mountain views; National Park 3km." 1 Apr-31 Oct. € 15.00 2006*

EMBRUN *9D3* (1km SE Urban) *44.55440, 6.48610* **Camping de la Vieille Ferme, La Clapière, 05200 Embrun [04 92 43 04 08; fax 04 92 43 05 18; info@campingembrun.com; www.campingembrun.com]** On N94 fr Gap, cross Rv Durance just bef Embrun town, take 1st R sp La Vieille Ferme. Med, mkd pitch, pt shd; wc; chem disp; mv service pnt; shwrs inc; el pnts (6-10A) €3-5; Indtte; supmkt nr; rest; snacks; playgrnd; rv 200m, lake 400m; watersports; entmnt; some statics; dogs €3; Eng spkn; adv bkg; red long stay; quiet. "Friendly, family-run site; gd facs; pretty town." ♦ 1 May-30 Sep. € 23.00 2007*

⊞ **EMBRUN** *9D3* (4km S Rural) *44.53818, 6.48725* **Camping Le Verger, 05200 Baratier [04 92 43 15 87; fax 04 92 43 49 81; camping.leverger@wanadoo.fr; www.campingleverger.fr]** Fr Embrun N94 twd Gap. L at rndabt onto D40. Ignore 1st sp to Baratier & take 2nd after 1km, thro vill & fork L by monument. Site on R next to trout farm. Med, hdg pitch, hdstg, terr, pt sl, pt shd; htd wc; chem disp; baby facs; shwrs; el pnts (10A) €5.10; Indtte; shop; snacks; bar; BBQ; playgrnd; htd pool; lake 1km; entmnts; TV; 30% statics; dogs €1.50; poss cr; adv bkg; red low ssn; CCI. "Lge pitches, gd views; pleasant site." € 13.00 2007*

EMBRUN *9D3* (4km S Rural) *44.54808, 6.49638* **Camping Les Grillons, Route de la Madeleine, 05200 Embrun [tel/fax 04 92 43 32 75; info@lesgrillons.com; www.lesgrillons.com]** Fr Embrun take N94 twds Gap; over bdge; L at rndabt onto D40. Turn L at 1st sharp bend; site on L in 400m. Med, mkd pitch, pt sl, pt shd; wc; chem disp; shwrs inc; el pnts (3-10A) €2.60-3.96; Indtte; tradsmn; snacks high ssn; playgrnd; 2 pools; tennis; lake sw & fishing 2km; 5% statics; dogs €1.60; Eng spkn; adv bkg; red low ssn; CCI. "Helpful, pleasant owners." 15 May-6 Sep. € 12.98 2006*

⊞ **EMBRY** *3B3* (200m NW Rural) *50.49365, 1.96463* **Aire de Service Camping-Cars d'Embryère, 62990 Embry [03 21 86 77 61]** N fr Embry site is just off D108 dir Hucqueliers & Desvres. Sm, hdstg; wc; shwrs; el pnts; mv service pnt; el pnts £2; Indry sinks; picnic area & gardens; BBQ; m'vans only. "Modern, well-kept site; jetons fr credit card-operated dispenser for services; conv Boulogne & Calais." ♦ € 6.00 2009*

ENTRAIGUES see Mure, La (Isère) *9C3*

ENTRAINS SUR NOHAIN *4G4* (200m N Rural) *47.46574, 3.25870* **Camp Municipal St Cyre, Route d'Etais, 58410 Entrains-sur-Nohain [03 86 29 22 06 (Mairie); fax 03 86 29 25 99; mairie-entrains-sur-nohain@wanadoo.fr]** On D1 fr Entrains-sur-Nohain, sp on R. Sm, hdg pitch, pt shd; wc (some cont); chem disp (wc); shwrs inc; el pnts (10A) inc; lndry rm; shop, rest, bar 300m; BBQ; htd pool 500m; 1% statics; dogs; phone 300m; quiet; CCI. "Warden calls twice a day; basic, clean san facs." ♦ 1 Jun-30 Sep. € 5.30
2006*

ENTRAUNES *9D4* (500m E Rural) *44.18896, 6.75011* **Camping Le Tellier, Route des Grandes Alpes, 06470 Entraunes [04 93 05 51 83; roche.grande@wanadoo.fr]** 15km N of Guillaumes on D2202; sp fr top end of vill. Sm, mkd pitch, pt sl, terr, pt shd; wc (some cont); chem disp (wc); shwrs inc; el pnts €3.50; shops etc 500m; quiet. "Beautiful mountain setting at foot of Col de la Cayolle; gd walking base; vg." 1 Jun-30 Sep. € 13.00 2008*

ENTRAYGUES SUR TRUYERE *7D4* (4km NE Rural) *44.67777, 2.58279* **Camping Le Lauradiol, Banhars, 12460 Campouriez [05 65 44 53 95; fax 05 65 44 81 37; info@camping-lelauradiol.com; www.camping-lelauradiol.com]** On D34, sp on rvside. Sm, hdg/mkd pitch, pt shd; wc; el pnts (6A) inc; lndtte; shop 5km; htd pool; paddling pool; rv adj; tennis; some statics; dogs 1.50; quiet; CCI. "Beautiful setting & walks; excel." ♦ 1 Jul-31 Aug. € 16.00 2009*

ENTRAYGUES SUR TRUYERE *7D4* (1.6km S Rural) *44.64218, 2.56406* **Camping Le Val de Saures (formerly Municipal), 12140 Entraygues-sur-Truyère [05 65 44 56 92; fax 05 65 44 27 21; info@camping-valdesaures.com; www.camping-valdesaures.com]** Fr town cent take D920 & in 200m turn R over narr bdge onto D904, foll site sp. Med, mkd pitch, pt shd; wc; shwrs; el pnts (6A) €3; lndtte; shops in town; playgrnd; pool adj; entmnt; some statics; dogs €1.50; Eng spkn; quiet; red low ssn. "Pleasant, friendly site; footbdge to town over rv; vg, well-kept san facs; recep clsd Sun & pm Mon low ssn; gd touring base." ♦ 1 May-30 Sep. € 17.00 2008*

ENTRECHAUX see Vaison la Romaine *9D2*

ENVEITG see Bourg Madame *8H4*

EPERLECQUES see St Omer *3A3*

EPERNAY *3D4* (1km NW Urban) *49.05734, 3.95042* **Camp Municipal d'Epernay, Allée de Cumières, 51200 Epernay [03 26 55 32 14; fax 03 26 52 36 09; camping.epernay@free.fr]** Fr Reims take D951 (N51) twd Epernay, cross rv & turn R at rndabt onto D301 sp Cumières (look for sp 'Stade Paul Chandon'), site sp. Site adj Stadium. Avoid town at early evening rush hour. NB Beware kerb at ent, espec if you have movers. Med, hdg/mkd pitch, pt shd; htd wc; chem disp; mv service pnt; shwrs inc; el pnts (5A) €3.10; lndtte; tradsmn; supmkt 300m; snacks; bar; BBQ; playgrnd; htd, covrd pool & waterslide 2km; fishing; canoeing; tennis; cycle hire; games area; internet; dogs free; phone; poss cr; Eng spkn; adv bkg; quiet; ccard acc; red long stay/low ssn/CCI. "Attractive site on banks of Rv Marne; conv location; friendly, helpful staff; gd spacious san facs; barrier clsd 2200-0700 high ssn; entry 0800-2000 - parking outsite; footpaths along rv into town; conv Champagne area; Mercier train tour with wine-tasting; gd walks; NB no twin-axles or o'fits over 6m acc; vg." ♦ 30 Apr-1 Oct. € 13.50 2009*

See advertisement

EPESSES, LES *2H4* (500m N Rural) *46.88920, -0.89950* **FFCC Camping La Bretèche, La Haute Bretèche, 85590 Les Epesses [02 51 57 33 34; fax 02 51 57 41 98; contact@camping-la-bretache.com; www.camping-la-breteche.com]** Fr Les Herbiers foll D11 to Les Epesses. Turn N on D752, site sp on R by lake - sp fr cent Les Epesses. Med, hdg/mkd pitch, pt shd; wc, chem disp; mv service pnt; shwrs inc; el pnts (10A) €2.75 (poss rev pol); lndtte; shop 1km; tradsmn; rest; snacks; bar; playgrnd; htd pool adj; tennis; fishing; horseriding; entmnt; TV; dogs €1.75; Eng spkn; adv bkg (fee €8); poss cr; ccard acc; red low ssn; CCI. "Clean, well-run site; busy high ssn; helpful staff; plenty of attractions nr; conv for Puy du Fou." ♦ 1 Apr-30 Sep. € 15.30 2007*

EPINAC *6H1* (500m SW Rural) *46.98577, 4.50617* **Camp Municipal du Pont Vert, Rue de la Piscine, 71360 Epinac [03 85 82 00 26; fax 03 85 82 13 67; info@campingdupontvert.com; www.campingdupontvert.com]** On D973 Autun dir Beaune for 16km. Turn L on D43 to Epinac, site nr public sports facs, sp in town. Med, pt shd; wc; chem disp; shwrs inc; el pnts (10A) €3.70; lndtte; shops in vill; snacks; cycle hire; wifi; some statics; dogs €1.05; extra charge for twin axles (€44 in 2009); quiet. 1 Apr-1 Nov. € 11.65
2009*

EPINAL *6F2* (1km E Urban) *48.17930, 6.46780* **Camping Parc du Château, 37 Rue du Petit Chaperon Rouge, 88000 Epinal [03 29 34 43 65 or 03 29 82 49 41 (LS); fax 03 29 31 05 12; parcduchateau@orange.fr; www.parcduchateau.com]** Sp fr town cent. Or fr N57 by-pass take exit sp Razimont, site sp in 1km. Med, hdg/mkd pitch, some hdstg, terr, pt shd; htd wc (some cont); chem disp; mv service pnt; shwrs inc; el pnts (6-10A) €5-6; gas; lndtte; shop; snacks; BBQ; playgrnd; pool; lake sw 8km; tennis; TV; 20% statics; dogs €3; Eng spkn; adv bkg; quiet but stadium adj; ccard acc; red low ssn/long stay; CCI. "Lge pitches; ltd facs low ssn; slightly run down - like the town!" ♦
1 Apr-30 Sep. € 17.00 2009*

France

Camping ★★★
Les Pins
22430 Erquy Phone. : 33 (0) 296 72 31 12Fax : 33 (0) 296 63 67 94
camping.des.pins@wanadoo.fr - yellohvillage.co.uk/camping/les_pins
GPS: N 48° 38' 18.276" W 2° 27' 20.34"
NEW COVERED SWIMMING POOL
yelloh!
ERQUY will change your life!! Rental, fitness room, Jacuzzi, solarium, bar, pub, restaurant.

⊞ **EPINAL** *6F2* (8km W Rural) *48.16701, 6.35975* **Camping Club Lac de Bouzey, 19 Rue du Lac, 88390 Sanchey [03 29 82 49 41; fax 03 29 64 28 03; camping.lac.de.bouzey@wanadoo.fr; www.camping-lac-de-bouzey.com]** Fr Epinal take D460 sp Darney. In vill of Bouzey turn L at camp sp. Site in few metres, by reservoir. Lge, hdg/mkd pitch, hdstg, pt sl, terr, pt shd; htd wc (some cont); chem disp; mv service pnt; baby facs; shwrs inc; el pnts (6A) €4; gas; lndtte; shop; tradsmn; rest; snacks; bar; BBQ; playgrnd; htd pool; paddling pool; sand beach & lake adj; fishing; games area; cycle hire; horseriding; child/teenager entmnt; internet; TV rm; 15% statics; dogs €3; phone; adv bkg; Eng spkn; quiet; ccard acc; red low ssn/long stay; CCI. "Attractive site; san facs need attention & poss unclean; gd shop & excel pool; gd touring base." ♦ € 25.00 (CChq acc) 2007*

ERQUY *2E3* (1km N Coastal) *48.63838, -2.45561* **Yelloh! Village Les Pins, Le Guen, Route des Hôpitaux, 22430 Erquy [02 96 72 31 12; fax 02 96 63 67 94; camping.des.pins@wanadoo.fr; www.yellohvillage.co.uk/camping/les_pins]** Site sp on all app rds to Erquy. Lge, hdg/mkd pitch, pt sl, pt shd; wc (some cont); chem disp; sauna; baby facs; shwrs inc; el pnts (6A) €2; lndtte; shop; tradsmn; rest; snacks; bar; BBQ; playgrnd; htd, covrd pool; paddling pool; waterslide; sand beach 600m; tennis; fitness rm; jacuzzi; games rm; games area; entmnt & TV rm; 40% statics; dogs €4; Eng spkn; adv bkg; quiet; ccard acc; CCI. "Gd family holiday site; excel facs." ♦ 23 Apr-12 Sep. € 34.00 2009*

See advertisement

EPINIAC see Dol de Bretagne *2E4*

ERDEVEN see Carnac *2G3*

ERNEE *2E4* (E Urban) **Camp Municipal d'Ernée, 53500 Ernée [02 43 05 19 90]** Site sp on app to town, off Fougères-Mayenne rd on E side of town. Head for 'Centre Ville', turn L for Fougères, round rndabt & site on R. Med, pt sl, pt shd, hdg pitch; serviced pitch; wc; shwrs inc; el pnts (6A) inc; shops 300m; pool adj; quiet. 15 Jun-15 Sep. € 12.00 2007*

ERNEE *2E4* (10km SW Rural) *48.19301, -0.99519* **Camping-Caravaning à la Ferme (Jarry), La Lande, 53380 La Croixille [02 43 68 57 00]** SW fr Ernée on D29 to La Croixille. In vill L onto D30 twds Laval. In 2.5km L onto D158, dir Juvigne, then R at next x-rds, sp Le Bourgneuf-le-Forêt. Site in 2km. Fr A81 exit junc 4 onto D30. Sm, pt shd; wc; shwrs €1.20; el pnts (10A) €1.70 (rev pol); lndtte; supmkt 4km; playgrnd; dogs €0.50; Eng spkn. "Excel CL-type farm site with orchard; quiet & beautiful; friendly owners; farm produce for sale; Ernée mkt Tues, Vitré mkt Mon; Laval mkt Sat." 15 May-15 Sep. € 8.00 2007*

ERQUY *2E3* (3km NE Coastal) *48.64201, -2.42456* **Camping Les Hautes Grées, Rue St Michel, Les Hôpitaux, 22430 Erquy [02 96 72 34 78; fax 02 96 72 30 15; hautesgrees@wanadoo.fr; www.camping-hautes-grees.com]** Fr Erquy NE D786 dir Cap Fréhel & Les Hôpitaux sp to site. Med, hdg/mkd pitch, hdstg, pt shd; wc (some cont); chem disp; mv service pnt; shwrs inc; el pnts (10A) €4.50 (rec long lead); gas; lndtte; shop; tradsmn; rest & snacks or 2km; bar; BBQ; playgrnd; htd pool; sand beach 400m; fishing; tennis; horseriding; gym; child entment; TV rm; some statics; dogs €1.70; adv bkg; ccard acc; red low ssn; CCI. "Lovely, well-run site; well-kept pitches, extra charge lge ones; helpful staff." ♦ 4 Apr-3 Oct. € 18.85 2009*

ERQUY *2E3* (1km E Coastal) *48.63828, -2.44233* **Camping Le Vieux Moulin, 14 Rue des Moulins, 22430 Erquy [02 96 72 34 23; fax 02 96 72 36 63; camp.vieux.moulin@wanadoo.fr; www.camping-vieux-moulin.com]** Sp fr all dirs on D786. Lge, mkd pitch, sl, pt shd; wc; mv service pnt; shwrs inc; el pnts (6-9A) €4.50-5; gas; lndtte; shop; rest; snacks; bar; htd pools; waterslide; sand beach 1km; games rm; entmnt; TV; statics; dogs €4; poss cr; quiet. "Site set in pine woods; plenty of beaches in 20 mins drive; ideal for family holiday; poss diff access lge o'fits; lower pitches subject to flooding." ♦ Easter-9 Sep. € 29.70 2006*

ERQUY *2E3* (5km S Rural) *48.59410, -2.48530* **Camping Bellevue, Route de Pléneuf-Val-André, La Couture, 22430 Erquy [02 96 72 33 04; fax 02 96 72 48 03; campingbellevue@yahoo.fr; www.campingbellevue.fr]** Fr Erquy, take D786 twd Le Val-André, site sp. Med, hdg/mkd pitch, hdstg, pt shd; wc; chem disp; mv service pnt; baby facs; shwrs inc; el pnts (6-10A) €3.30-4.80; gas; lndtte; shop; tradsmn; snacks; bar; BBQ; 3 playgrnds; htd, covrd pool; paddling pool; sand beach 2km; watersports; tennis 2km; games area; games rm; entmnt; child entmnt high ssn; TV rm; 40% statics; dogs €1.70; phone; Eng spkn; adv bkg; quiet; red low ssn/long stay; ccard acc; CCI. "Excel for families; rec." ♦ 12 Apr-15 Sep. € 19.50 2007*

⊞ **ERQUY** *2E3* (700m SW Coastal) *48.61821, -2.47638* **Aire Communale Erquy, Ave de Caroual, 22430 Erquy [02 96 63 64 64]** Take D786 fr Erquy dir Pleneuf-Val-André. Site on R at Plage de Carouel, sp. Med, chem disp; mv service pnt; el pnts €2; water fill €2 for 100 litres; rest; beach 100m; poss cr; m'vans only. "Rec arr early as full by 1700." € 3.00 2008*

ERQUY *2E3* (2.5km SW Coastal) *48.6094, 2.4769* **Camping Les Roches, Caroual, 22430 Erquy [02 96 72 32 90; fax 02 96 63 57 84; info@camping-les-roches.com; www.camping-les-roches.com]** Sp fr D786 fr Erquy or Le Val-André. Med, hdg/mkd pitch, pt sl, pt shd, wc; baby facs; mv service pnt; shwrs inc; el pnts (10A) €3.20; lndtte; sm shop; bar; playgrnd; sand beach 900m; games rm; wifi; some statics; dogs €1.20; phone; adv bkg; quiet. "Pleasant site; sea views; gd walking." 1 Apr-15 Sep. € 14.20 2007*

ERQUY *2E3* (4km SW Rural/Coastal) *48.60695, -2.49723* **Camping de la Plage de St Pabu, 22430 Erquy [02 96 72 24 65; fax 02 96 72 87 17; camping@saintpabu.com; www.saintpabu.com]** Sp on D786 bet Erquy & Le Val-André at St Pabu. Narr rd, restricted passing places. Lge, hdg/mkd pitch, hdstg, terr, pt shd; wc; chem disp; mv service pnt; baby facs; shwrs inc; el pnts (10A) €4.80; gas; lndtte; shop; tradsmn; snacks; bar; BBQ; playgrnd; sand beach adj; wind surfing; cycle hire; entmnt; games/TV rm; some statics; dogs €1.60; Eng spkn; adv bkg; quiet; ccard acc; red long stay/low ssn; CCI. "In beautiful location; vg beach adj; lge pitches; upper terrs poss diff lge o'fits; friendly; san facs gd; vg touring base; conv St Malo, Dinan, Granit Rose coast; excel." ♦ 1 Apr-10 Oct. € 19.50 2009*

ERR see Bourg Madame *8H4*

ERVY LE CHATEL *4F4* (2km E Rural) **Camp Municipal Les Mottes, 10130 Ervy-le-Châtel [tel/fax 03 25 70 07 96 or 03 25 70 50 36 (Mairie); mairie-ervy-le-chatel@wanadoo.fr]** Exit N77 sp Auxon (int'l camping sp Ervy-le-Châtel) onto D374, then D92; site clearly sp. Med, pt shd; wc; shwrs inc; el pnts (5A) €2.50; lndtte; shops adj; playgrnd; rv fishing 300m; tennis; dogs €1.50; adv bkg; quiet; CCI. "Pleasant, well-kept, grassy site; lge pitches; vg facs; friendly, helpful warden; no twin-axles; rests in vill; rec." ♦ 15 May-15 Sep. € 9.00 2007*

ESCALLES see Wissant *3A2*

ESNANDES see Rochelle, La *7A1*

ESPALION *7D4* (300m E Urban) *44.52176, 2.77098* **Camp Municipal Le Roc de l'Arche, 12500 Espalion [tel/fax 05 65 44 06 79; campingrocdelarche@wanadoo.fr; http://pagesperso-orange.fr/camping-rocdelarche]** Sp in town off D920 & D921. Site on S banks of Rv Lot 300m fr bdge in town. Med, hdg/mkd pitch, pt shd; wc; mv service pnt; baby facs; shwrs inc; el pnts (6-10A); lndtte; shops 250m; snacks; BBQ; playgrnd; pool adj inc; tennis; fishing; canoeing; dogs €0.50; poss cr; adv bkg; quiet; red low ssn. "Well-kept site; gd sized pitches, water pnts to each; service rds narr; friendly, helpful warden; clean, modern san facs; excel." 1 Apr-15 Oct. € 17.30 2009*

ESPALION *7D4* (4km E Rural) *44.51376, 2.81849* **Camping Belle Rive, Rue de Terral, 12500 St Côme-d'Olt [05 65 44 05 85; bellerive12@voila.fr; http://bellerive.site.voila.fr]** Fr Espalion take D987 E to St Côme-d'Olt; in 6km, just bef vill, turn R onto D6. Site on N bank of Rv Lot, site sp. NB Avoid vill cent, v narr rds. Med, pt shd; wc; shwrs inc; el pnts (5-10A) inc (poss rev pol & long lead may be req); lndtte; shop, rest in vill; 10% statics; dogs €0.70; poss cr; Eng spkn; quiet. "Pleasant rvside site; friendly, helpful owner; delightful medieval vill; excel." 1 May-30 Sep. € 12.50 2009*

ESSARTS, LES *2H4* (800m W Urban) *46.77285, -1.23558* **Camp Municipal Le Pâtis, Rue de la Piscine, 85140 Les Essarts [02 51 62 95 83 or 02 51 62 83 26 (Mairie); fax 02 51 62 81 24; camping.lepatis@wanadoo.fr]** Exit A83 junc 5 onto D160. On ent Les Essarts, foll sp to site. Site on L just off rd fr Les Essarts to Chauché. Sm, pt shd; htd wc; baby facs; shwrs inc; el pnts (16A) €2.80; lndtte; supmkt, rests in town; tradsmn; snacks; BBQ (gas/charcoal); playgrnd; 2 pools (1 Olympic size), paddling pool, tennis & sports cent adj; 40% statics; dogs €1.60; some statics; v quiet. "Gd NH off A83; superb, clean san facs; warden resident; opening dates uncertain - poss open longer." ♦ 1 May-7 Sep. € 11.24 2009*

ESSAY *4E1* (S Rural) *48.53799, 0.24649* **FFCC Camp Municipal Les Charmilles, Route de Neuilly, 61500 Essay [02 33 28 40 52; fax 02 33 28 59 43; si-paysdessay@wanadoo.fr]** Exit A28 junc 18 (Alençon Nord) onto D31 to Essay (sp L'Aigle); turn R in vill dir Neuilly-le-Bisson; site on R in 200m. Sm, hdg pitch, pt shd; wc; shwrs €1.60; el pnts (6A) €1.60; lndry rm; playgrnd; adv bkg. "V quiet on edge of vill; lge pitches, some diff to access; park, then find tourist office to pay; interesting historical vill; fair NH." 1 Apr-30 Sep. € 5.80 2009*

France

ESTAGEL *8G4* (6km NE Rural) *42.81497, 2.73955* **Camping Le Priourat, Rue d'Estagel, 66720 Tautavel [tel/fax 04 68 29 41 45; j.ponsaille@libertysurf.fr; www.le-priourat.fr]** W fr Estagel on D117. In 2km turn R onto D611 & keep R onto D9 to Tautavel. Site on R bef cent of vill (2nd rd on R after vill sign). NB Sloping exit fr site onto narr lane. Sm, hdg/mkd pitch, pt sl, pt shd; wc; shwrs inc; el pnts (6A) €3 (rev pol); lndry rm; shop in vill; rest; bar; BBQ; playgrnd; pool high ssn; rv 500m; beach 40km; no statics; Eng spkn; adv bkg ess high ssn; quiet; ccard acc; red low ssn; CCI. "Lovely, friendly, sm site; sm pitches; ltd facs low ssn; poss muddy." 1 Apr-30 Sep. € 17.00 2007*

ESTAGEL *8G4* (3km W Rural) *42.76566, 2.66583* **Camping La Tourèze, Route d'Estagel, 66720 Latour-de-France [tel/fax 04 68 29 16 10; camping.latoureze@wanadoo.fr; http://campinglatoureze.monsite.wanadoo.fr]** Fr D117 at Estagel turn S onto D612 then R onto D17 to Latour. Site on R on ent to vill. Med, mkd pitch, shd; wc; chem disp; mv service pnt; baby facs; shwrs inc; el pnts (10A) €3.50; lndtte; tradsmn; shop, rest, bar 500m; playgrnd; htd pool 3km; rv sw adj; 13% statics; dogs €1.80; phone; Eng spkn; adv bkg; quiet; ccard acc. "Pretty vill & wine 'cave' in walking dist; rec visit Rv Agly barrage nrby; helpful staff; excel." 11 Apr-10 Oct. € 14.00 2008*

ESTAING (AVEYRON) *7D4* (2km N Rural) *44.56211, 2.67826* **Camp Municipal La Chantellerie, 12190 Estaing [05 65 44 72 77 or 05 65 44 70 32; fax 05 65 44 03 20; mairie-estaing@wanadoo.fr]** Fr D920 in Estaing nr rv bdge take D167; fork R onto D97; site on L. Well sp fr Estaing cent adj stadium. Med, hdg/mkd pitch; pt shd; wc (some cont); shwrs inc; el pnts €2; shop 2km; rest, snacks & bar 2km; pool 2km; rv sw 2km; phone; quiet; CCI. "Gd walking country; vg rest in Logis Hotel in Estaing; warden calls am & pm; NH only." 22 May-30 Sep. € 9.10 2008*

ESTAING (HAUTES PYRENEES) see Argelès Gazost *8G2*

ESTANG *8E2* (500m E Rural) *43.86493, -0.10321* **Camping Les Lacs de Courtès, Courtès, 32240 Estang [05 62 09 61 98; fax 05 62 09 63 13; contact@lacs-de-courtes.com; www.lacs-de-courtes.com]** W fr Eauze site sp fr D30. Fr Mont-de-Marsan D932 take D1 to Villeneuve-de-Marsan, then D1/D30 to Estang. Med, mkd pitch, pt shd; wc; chem disp; mv service pnt; el pnts (6A) €3; lndtte; tradsmn; supmkt 5km; rest 400m; snacks; bar; playgrnd; pool; paddling pool; lake fishing; tennis; games area; internet; entmnt; TV; some statics; dogs €2.50; area for m'vans open all yr; adv bkg; quiet. "Gd family site." ♦ Easter-31 Oct. € 23.00 (CChq acc) 2008*

ESTAVAR see Bourg Madame *8H4*

ETABLES SUR MER *2E3* (1km S Coastal) *48.63555, -2.83526* **Camping L'Abri Côtier, Rue de la Ville-ès-Rouxel, 22680 Etables-sur-Mer [02 96 70 61 57 or 06 07 36 01 91 (mob LS); fax 02 96 70 65 23; camping.abricotier@wanadoo.fr; www.camping-abricotier.fr]** Fr N12 round St Brieuc take D786 N thro Binic & 500m after Super U supmkt turn L to Etables. Go thro vill for approx 3 km & turn L into Rue de la Ville-es-Rouxel just after R turning for Plage-du-Moulin. Site ent just after sm x-rds. NB Long c'vans & big m'vans (to avoid going thro vill): cont on D786, past Chapel, down hill & turn L at boatyard dir Etables; take 2nd turn on R. To avoid manoevering, park on rd & go to recep on foot. Med, mkd pitch, pt sl, pt shd; htd wc; chem disp; mv service pnt; 15% serviced pitch; baby facs; shwrs inc; el pnts (6A) inc; gas; lndtte; shop; tradsmn; snacks; bar; BBQ; playgrnd; htd pool & paddling pool; jacuzzi; sand beach 500m; watersports 2km; tennis in vill; golf 4km; games rm; entmnt; wifi; TV; 10% statics; dogs €2; British owned; c'vans over 7.50m not acc high ssn; adv bkg; quiet; ccard acc; red low ssn; CCI. "Popular, immac site; excel beach; entry narr & steep, narr corners on site rds diff lge o'fits; mkt Tues & Sun; vg." ♦ 1 May-12 Sep. € 20.60 ABS - B09 2009*

⊞ **ETAMPES** *4E3* (3km S Rural) *48.41015, 2.14413* **FFCC Caravaning Le Vauvert, 91150 Ormoy-la-Rivière [01 64 94 21 39; fax 01 69 92 72 59]** Fr Etampes S on N20 take D49 sp Saclas. Site on L in approx 1.5km. NB acess on a loop to cross rd. Med, hdg pitch, shd; wc; shwrs inc; el pnts (6-10A) €3-3.50; gas; shop & hypmkt 3km; bar; pool 3km; tennis; fishing; rv adj; games area; many statics; quiet; site clsd 16 Dec-14 Jan; red long stay; ccard not acc; CCI. "If travelling in winter phone to check site open; few touring pitches; gd san facs; wcs in touring area clsd winter; conv train to Paris; excel." € 14.00 2009*

ETANG SUR ARROUX *4H4* (S Rural) *46.86170, 4.19230* **FFCC Camping des 2 Rives, 26 Route de Toulon, 71190 Etang-sur-Arroux [03 85 82 39 73]** Fr Autun on N81 SW for 11km; turn L onto D994 to Etang-sur-Arroux; site on R after passing thro main part of town. Med, shd; wc; chem disp; mv service pnt; shwrs inc; el pnts (6-10A) inc; lndtte; shop 1km; rest, snacks & bar high ssn or 1km; playgrnd; pool 500m; rv sw adj; canoeing; kayaking; 20% statics; dogs €1.80; phone; Eng spkn; adv bkg; CCI. "Well-kept site bet two rvs; Dutch owners; dated but adequate san facs; gd rv sports; ltd opening Jan & Feb." 1 Apr-31 Oct. € 17.10 2008*

ETAPLES *3B2* (2km N Rural) *50.53238, 1.6257* **Camp Municipal La Pinède, Rue de Boulogne, 62630 Etaples [tel/fax 03 21 94 34 51]** Take D940 S fr Boulogne-sur-Mer for 25km, site on R after war cemetary & bef Atac supmkt. Or N fr Etaples for 2km on D940. Med, hdg pitch, terr, pt sl, pt shd; wc; mv service pnt; shwrs; el pnts (5A) inc; gas 500m; Indtte; rest, snacks & bar high ssn; shop high ssn 500m & 1km; playgrnd; beach 4km; rv 500m; 50% statics; dogs; phone; 15% statics; poss cr; adv bkg; some rd/rlwy noise; CCI. "No twin-axles; dated, poss tired san facs, ltd low ssn; helpful warden; war cemetery 200m." ♦
15 Feb-15 Dec. € 15.60 2009*

ETIVAL see Clairvaux les Lacs *6H2*

ETREAUPONT see Vervins *3C4*

ETREHAM see Bayeux *3D1*

ETRETAT *3C1* (6km E Rural) *49.69880, 0.27580* **FFCC Camping de l'Aiguille Creuse, 24 Rue de l'Aiguille, 76790 Les Loges [02 35 29 52 10; fax 02 35 10 86 64; camping@aiguillecreuse.com; www.campingaiguillecreuse.com]** On S side of D940 in Les Loges; sp. Med, unshd; wc (some cont); chem disp; shwrs inc; el pnts (10A) €4.30; Indtte; shops 500m; bar; BBQ; playgrnd; pool (no shorts); beach 3km; tennis; games rm; dogs €2.50; adv bkg; quiet. "Facs ltd low ssn." ♦ 1 Apr-30 Sep. € 15.10 (CChq acc) 2007*

ETRETAT *3C1* (2km SE Urban/Coastal) *49.70053, 0.21428* **Camp Municipal, 69 Rue Guy de Maupassant, 76790 Etretat [tel/fax 02 35 27 07 67]** Fr Fécamp SW on D940 thro town cent of Etretat & site on L. Or fr Le Havre R at 2nd traff lts; site on L in 1km on D39. Med, mkd pitch, some hdstg, pt sl, pt shd; htd wc (some cont); chem disp; mv service pnt; shwrs inc; el pnts (5-6A) €3.70-5.40 (poss rev pol); gas; Indtte; shop 1km; BBQ; playgrnd; shgl beach 1km; no statics; phone; poss cr; no adv bkg; quiet; ccard acc; CCI. "Busy, well-maintained site; lge pitches; clean san facs; friendly staff; gate clsd 2200-0730; pleasant seaside resort, attractive beach nr; conv Le Havre ferry; gd cliff top walks nr; level walk to town; m'van o'night area adj (no el pnts) open all yr; excel."
♦ 1 Apr-15 Oct. € 13.00 2009*

ETRETAT *3C1* (3km S Rural) *49.68302, 0.21319* **Camping Les Tilleuls, Hameau de Grosse Mare, Impasse Dom-Filastre, 76790 Le Tilleul [tel/fax 02 35 27 11 61]** Fr Le Havre N on D940 18km to vill of Le Tilleul. Turn R after filling stn, site sp. Med, shd; wc (some cont); chem disp; shwrs inc; el pnts inc; Indtte; shop; snacks; BBQ; playgrnd; beach 3km; adv bkg; quiet. 1 Apr-30 Sep. € 12.75 2009*

ETRETAT *3C1* (10km SW Rural) *49.62271, 0.24904* **Camping Le Beau Soleil, 76280 Criquetot-l'Esneval [02 35 20 24 22; fax 02 35 20 82 09; lebeausoleil@wanadoo.fr; www.etretat.net]** S fr Etretat on D39 to Criquetot-l'Esneval. Site is 3km SW of Criquetot-l'Esneval on D79 twd Turretot. Med, pt shd; wc; chem disp; mv service pnt; shwrs €1; el pnts (2-10A) €1.10-5.50; bar; playgrnd; beach 8km; 70% statics; dogs €0.60; Eng spkn; CCI. "Pleasant site, friendly owners; conv Le Havre ferry." 1 Apr-30 Sep. € 7.00 2006*

ETRIGNY see Tournus *9A2*

EU *3B2* (Urban) **Camp Municipal du Parc Château, 76260 Eu [02 35 86 20 04]** App fr Blangy on D1015 turn L at junc with D925 & foll camp sp to site in grounds of Hôtel de Ville (chateau). Fr Abbeville on D925 fork R at 1st rndabt in town S of rlwy then immed strt on over cobbled rd right up to chateau walls. Turn R at chateau walls into long, narr app rd thro trees. Ignore sp to Stade. Med, some hdg pitch, hdstg, mainly terr, pt shd; wc; chem disp; shwrs inc; el pnts (6-16A) €3.90-6 (poss rev pol); gas; Indtte; shops 250m; shgl beach 3km; 10% statics; poss cr. "Louis-Philippe museum in chateau; clean san facs; vg Fri mkt." 1 Apr-31 Oct. € 9.20 2009*

EVAUX LES BAINS *7A4* (N Urban) *46.17841, 2.49009* **Camp Municipal, 23110 Evaux-les-Bains [05 55 65 55 82 or 05 55 65 55 38]** Fr N on D993/D996 sp 'International'. Also site sp fr other dirs. Sm, pt sl, pt shd; wc (some cont); chem disp (wc); shwrs inc; el pnts (3A) €3.20; shops 500m; playgrnd; pool 500m; 10% statics; dogs €0.45; quiet. "Evaux attractive health spa; friendly & informal site; well run; gd facs." ♦ 1 Apr-31 Oct. € 5.80 2006*

EVAUX LES BAINS *7A4* (5km W Rural) *46.18597, 2.43391* **Camp Municipal La Pouge, Rue du Stade, 23170 Chambon-sur-Voueize [05 55 82 13 21]** Take D915 fr Evaux-les-Bains; at ent to Chambon-sur-Voueize turn R bef x-ing rv. Site adj municipal stadium. Sm, mkd pitch, pt shd; wc; chem disp; shwrs inc; el pnts (10A) €1.30; Indtte; shops, rest & bar 150m; BBQ; playgrnd; tennis; games rm; 10% statics; dogs €0.50; phone; bus 1.5km; adv bkg; quiet; no ccard acc; CCI. "Pleasant rural area; sm pitches; gd walking & cycling; golf at Gouzon; vg." 1 Apr-31 Oct. € 6.20 2008*

EVIAN LES BAINS *9A3* (4km E Rural) *46.40033, 6.64546* **Camping de Vieille Eglise, Route des Prés Parrau, 74500 Lugrin [04 50 76 01 95; campingvieilleeglise@wanadoo.fr; www.camping-vieille-eglise.com]** D21 fr Evian via Maxilly, or turn S off D1005 (N5) at Tourronde, sp. Med, hdg/mkd pitches, pt terr, pt sl, pt shd; wc; chem disp; baby facs; shwrs inc; el pnts (4-10A) €3-4.05; gas; Indtte; shop; supmkt 400m; rest, bar 400m; playgrnd; htd pool; paddling pool; shgl beach & lake 1km; games area; internet; 50% statics; dogs €1.70; adv bkg; quiet; ccard acc; red long stay; CCI. "View of Lac Léman." ♦ 10 Apr-20 Oct. € 18.30 2008*

France

EVIAN LES BAINS *9A3* (6km W Rural) *46.39388, 6.52805* **FFCC Camping Les Huttins, Rue de la Plaine, Amphion-les-Bains, 74500 Publier [tel/fax 04 50 70 03 09; camping leshuttins@club-internet.fr; www.camping-leshuttins.com]** Fr Thonon on D1005 (N5) twds Evian, at start of Amphion turn L onto Rte du Plaine sp; ent 200m on R after rndabt. Fr Evian on D1005 twds Thonon, at end of Amphion turn R & foll sp. Med, mkd pitch, shd; wc (some cont); chem disp; mv service pnt; shwrs inc; el pnts (3-6A) €2.50-4; gas; lndtte; shop; hypermkt 300m; rest, bar 400m; BBQ; playgrnd; pool & sports complex 200m; lake sw 400m; tennis adj; TV; 5% statics; dogs €1; Eng spkn; adv bkg; quiet; red low ssn. "Spacious, relaxed, simple site; enthusiastic, helpful owners; basic, clean san facs; gd base for Lake Léman area & boat trips; poss unreliable opening dates - phone ahead; vg." 10 Apr-30 Sep. € 14.00 2009*

EVRON *4F1* (7km SE Rural) *48.09423, -0.35642* **Camp Municipal la Croix Couverte, La Croix Couverte, 53270 Ste Suzanne [02 43 01 41 61 or 02 43 01 40 10 (Mairie); fax 02 43 01 44 09]** Take D7 SW fr Evron sp Ste Suzanne. Site 800m S (downhill) after this sm fortified town. Sm, some hdg/mkd pitch, pt shd; wc; shwrs inc; el pnts (3-5A) €2.10; shops 800m; playgrnd; htd pool; walking & horseriding adj; quiet; CCI. "Clean, simple site in lovely area; sm pitches; unspoilt town & castle with historic Eng connections; excel NH." ♦ 1 May-30 Sep. € 6.25 2009*

⊞ **EVRON** *4F1* (W Urban) *48.15077, -0.41223* **Camp Municipal de la Zone Verte, Blvd du Maréchal Juin, 53600 Evron [02 43 01 65 36; fax 02 43 37 46 20; camping@evron.fr; www.camping-evron.fr]** Site on ring rd in clockwise dir fr Super-U supmkt; clearly sp fr all rds into town. Med, some hdg pitch, pt shd; htd wc (some cont); chem disp; mv service pnt; shwrs inc; el pnts (6-10A) €1.55-2.40; lndtte; shops 1km; playgrnd; htd pool & sports complex adj; 50% statics; dogs €0.85; adv bkg; quiet. "Triangular hdg pitches - enter tow bar 1st & manhandle; well-kept; friendly, pleasant site with lots of flowers; restricted recep hrs in winter - warden on site lunchtime & early eve only; no twin-axle vans." ♦ € 9.45 2006*

EXCENEVEX see Thonon les Bains *9A3*

EYMET *7D2* (6.5km N Rural) *44.70379, 0.39911* **Camping Lou Tuquet, Le Mayne, 24500 Fonroque [05 53 74 38 32 or 06 85 18 23 01 (mob); loutuquet@wanadoo.fr; www.campingloutuquet.com]** Take D933 SW of Bergerac dir Eymet. In vill of Fonroque turn R & foll sp. Site well sp. Sm, mkd pitch, pt sl, pt shd: wc; chem disp (wc); mv service pnt; shwrs; el pnts (6A) €2.50; lndtte; shop, rest, snacks, bar 2km; BBQ; playgrnd; lake fishing 150m; 15% statics; dogs €1; Eng spkn; quiet; red long stay. "Ideal for walking & cycling on deserted rds; basic but peaceful organic farm site." ♦ 1 May-1 Nov. € 8.60 2007*

EYMET *7D2* (5km SW Rural) *44.63211, 0.39977* **Camping Le Moulin Brûlé, 47800 Agnac [tel/fax 05 53 83 07 56; thebeales@wanadoo.fr; www.eymetguide.com]** Fr D933 at Miramont-de-Guyenne (6km S of Eymet) turn E onto D1; in 4km turn L onto C501 dir Eymet; site on L in 2km. Sm, mkd/mkd pitch, hdstg, pt shd; wc; chem disp (wc); el pnts (16A) €3; shwrs inc; lndtte; shops, rest, snacks & bar 6km; BBQ; playgrnd; pool; games area; 2 statics; no twin axles; Eng spkn; adv bkg; CCI. "Lovely, peaceful site in pleasant surroundings; friendly British owners; gd clean san facs; gd cycling; gd touring base; excel." 1 May-1 Oct. € 12.00 2009*

EYMET *7D2* (500m W Urban) *44.66923, 0.39615* **Camp Municipal du Château, Rue de la Sole, 24500 Eymet [05 53 23 80 28; fax 05 53 22 22 19; eymetcamping@aol.com; www.eymet-dordogne.fr]** Go thro Miramont onto D933 to Eymet. Turn opp Casino supmkt & foll sp to site. Sp on ent to Eymet fr all dirs. Sm, hdg/mkd pitch, pt shd, wc; chem disp; mv service pnt; shwrs inc; el pnts (10A) €3 (poss rev pol); gas 300m; lndtte; shops, rest, snacks & bar 300m; playgrnd; pool 1.5km; lake & rv sw nrby; wifi; dogs; poss cr; Eng spkn; adv bkg; no twin-axles; quiet; red long stay; CCI. "Well-kept site behind ruined medieval chateau by rv; friendly, helpful owner; clean san facs; lovely old Bastide town; Thur mkt; excel." ♦ 1 Apr-30 Sep. € 10.00 2009*

EYMOUTHIERS see Montbron *7B3*

EYMOUTIERS *7B4* (8km N) *45.80560, 1.84342* **Camp Municipal Les Peyrades, Auphelle, Lac de Vassivière, 87470 Peyrat-le-Château [05 55 69 41 32 or 05 55 69 40 23 (Mairie); fax 05 55 69 49 24]** Fr Peyrat E on D13, at 5km sharp R onto D222 & foll sp for Lac de Vassivière. At wide junc turn L, site on R. Med, pt sl, pt shd; wc cont; shwrs inc; el pnts (5A) €2.30; lndry rm; shop, rest, snacks, bar adj; BBQ; lake sw adj; sand beach adj; dogs; phone; poss v cr; adv bkg; quiet. "Helpful warden; some pitches overlook lake." 2 May-10 Sep. € 8.50 2006*

EYMOUTIERS *7B4* (8km N Rural) *45.82584, 1.76599* **Camp Municipal Moulin de l'Eau, 87470 Peyrat-le-Château [05 55 69 41 01 or 05 55 69 40 23]** 1.5km N of Peyrat on D940 to Bourganeuf, site on L immed bef bdge. Med, pt sl, pt terr, pt shd; wc; shwrs; el pnts €2.29; shops 2km; fishing; no adv bkg; quiet; CCI. "Pleasant site; beautiful area; pay at Mairie in town." 1 Jul-15 Sep. € 6.00 2006*

EYMOUTIERS *7B4* (2km S) *45.73061, 1.75249* **Camp Municipal, St Pierre-Château, 87120 Eymoutiers [05 55 69 10 21; fax 05 55 69 27 19; mairie-eymoutiers@wanadoo.fr; www.mairie-eymoutiers.fr]** On E of D940 S fr Eymoutiers site sp on R. Diff sharp bend bef ent. Sm, pt sl, terr, pt shd; wc; shwrs; el pnts (6A) €2 (long lead poss req); shops 2km; adv bkg; quiet. "Gd views; clean site; site yourself, warden calls; attractive town & area." 1 Jun-30 Sep. € 6.90 2009*

⊞ **EYMOUTIERS** *7B4* (10km W Rural) *45.71633, 1.60127* **FFCC Camping Le Cheyenne, Ave Michel Sinibaldi, Rue Torrade, 87130 Châteauneuf-la-Forêt [tel/fax 05 55 69 63 69 or 05 55 69 39 29 (LS); campinglecheyenne@neuf.fr; www.campinglecheyenne.com]** Fr Limoges E on D979 for 33km. Turn R at Lattée D15 & in 4km foll sp to site fr vill of Châteauneuf. Med, mkd pitch, pt shd; htd wc; chem disp; mv service pnt; shwrs inc; el pnts (6A) €3.50; Indtte; tradsmn; bar/rest; takeaway; lake sw adj; phone; site clsd Feb; Eng spkn. "Lovely position by lake & woods but nr town; gd size pitches; reasonable facs; poss unkempt/untidy low ssn; factory on 24hr shift gives cont background hum, but not obtrusive; gd walks; gd." € 11.00 2007*

EYZIES DE TAYAC, LES *7C3* (4km N Rural) *44.98070, 1.04457* **Camping Bouyssou, Lespinasse, 24620 Tursac [05 53 06 98 08; campingbouyssou@wanadoo.fr; http://pagesperso-orange.fr/campingbouyssou24]** N fr Les Eyzies on D707, turn L across rv bdge sp La Madelaine. Take R fork, site sp on L. Sm, hdg pitch, pt shd; wc; chem disp; shwrs inc; el pts (10A) €2; shop, rest 1km; playgrnd; pool; paddling pool; rv fishing 200m; some statics; poss cr; adv bkg; quiet. "Pleasant site with views; friendly, helpful owner; vg modern, unisex san facs; excel touring base." 2 Jun-29 Sep. € 10.00 2006*

EYZIES DE TAYAC, LES *7C3* (4km NE Rural) *44.95633, 1.04410* **Camping La Ferme du Pelou, 24620 Tursac [05 53 06 98 17; info@leseyzies.com; www.lafermedupelou.com]** Fr Les Eyzies-de-Tayac take D706 dir Tursac. In 3km turn R, site sp. 1km up hill on L. Ent poss diff for lge o'fits. Med, hdg pitch, pt shd; wc; chem disp; mv service pnt; shwrs inc; el pnts (6A) €2.80 (long lead poss req); Indtte; shop, rest & bar 4km; BBQ; playgrnd; htd pool; mainly statics; dogs free; phone; adv bkg; quiet low ssn; CCI. "Well-kept, clean site; views fr part of site without el pnts; friendly, helpful owners; gd san facs, poss too few high ssn; vg pool; gd walking; many dogs, inc owner's; site too sm for v lge o'fits; highly rec." ♦ 15 Mar-15 Nov. € 10.50 2009*

EYZIES DE TAYAC, LES *7C3* (5km NE Rural) *44.96935, 1.04623* **Camping Le Pigeonnier, Le Bourg, 24620 Tursac [tel/fax 05 53 06 96 90; campinglepigeonnier@wanadoo.fr; http://campinglepigeonnier.monsite.wanadoo.fr]** NE fr Les Eyzies for 5km on D706 to Tursac; site is 200m fr Mairie in vill cent; ent tight. Sm, hdg/mkd pitch, pt sl, terr, shd; wc; chem disp in vill; shwrs inc; el pnts (10A) €3; gas; Indtte; tradsmn; shop 5km; snacks; bar; playgrnd; sm pool; shgl beach, rv sw, fishing & canoeing 1km; horseriding; cycle hire; dogs €1; adv bkg; quiet; no ccard acc; CCI. "Freshwater pool (v cold); spacious, grass pitches; facs poss stretched high ssn; v quiet hideaway site in busy area; close to prehistoric sites." 1 Jun-30 Sep. € 14.50 2008*

⊞ **EYZIES DE TAYAC, LES** *7C3* (6km NE Rural) *44.95277, 1.08820* **FFCC Camping Auberge (Veyret), Bardenat, 24620 Marquay [05 53 29 68 44; fax 05 53 31 58 28; contact@auberge-veyret.com; www.auberge-veyret.com]** Leave Les Eyzies dir Sarlat on D47; in 4km go L onto D48 (dir Tamniès); in 3.5km turn L & foll sp for Auberge Veyret. Sm, sl, pt shd; wc; chem disp (wc); shwrs inc; el pnts (16A) €2.30; tradsmn; rest; snacks; playgrnd; pool; adv bkg low ssn ess; quiet; CCI. "Excel rest; simple CL-type site with sl grass pitches & views." € 9.15 2006*

France

EYZIES DE TAYAC, LES *7C3* (2km S Rural) *44.92370, 1.02910* **Camping Le Pech Charmant, 24620 Les Eyzies-de-Tayac [05 53 35 97 08; fax 05 53 35 97 09; info@lepech.com; www.lepech.com]** Fr Sarlat take D47 to Les Eyzies then take D706 dir Le Bugue. Turn L immed after g'ge & foll sm site sps round 1-way system. Med, mkd pitch, terr, pt shd; wc; chem disp; shwrs; el pnts (10A) €3; gas; Indtte; shop; tradsmn; snacks; bar; playgrnd; pool; paddling pool; rv sw 2km; games area; horseriding; children's farm; entmnt; 10% statics; dogs €1.80; Eng spkn; adv bkg; quiet; ccard acc; CCI. ♦ 1 Apr-1 Oct. € 21.00 2009*

EYZIES DE TAYAC, LES *7C3* (2km SW Rural) *44.92361, 1.00327* **Camping Le Queylou, 24620 Les Eyzies-de-Tayac [05 53 06 94 71; henri.appels@wanadoo.fr; www.vacances24queylou.com]** Take D706 fr Les Eyzies dir Le Bugue; after 2km turn L (after sharp L hand bend) up hill on narr rd to Le Queylou in 1km sp on app. Sm, pt sl, pt shd; wc; shwrs inc; el pnts (16A); shops 3km; BBQ; some statics; dogs; poss cr; Eng spkn; adv bkg; quiet; red long stay/CCI. "Helpful owner; pleasant CL-type site; woodland walks." 2008*

EYZIES DE TAYAC, LES *7C3* (1km NW Rural) *44.93695, 1.00563* **Camping La Rivière, 3 Route du Sorcier, 24620 Les Eyzies-de-Tayac [05 53 06 97 14; fax 05 53 35 20 85; la-riviere@wanadoo.fr; www.lariviereleseyzies.com]** Site off D47 Rte de Périgueux. Lge o'fits use 2nd ent by sw pool & walk to recep. Med, hdg/mkd pitch, pt shd; wc; chem disp; mv service pnt; shwrs; el pnts (6-10A) €3.50-4; Indtte; shop; rest; snacks; bar; playgrnd; pool; paddling pool; canoe hire 500m; tennis; internet; TV rm; 5% statics; dogs €1; phone; Eng spkn; adv bkg; quiet; ccard acc; red low ssn; CCI. "Pleasant site; sm pitches; gd clean facs; walking dist many prehistoric caves." ♦ 4 Apr-1 Nov. € 18.40 2009*

FALAISE *3D1* (500m W Urban) *48.89545, -0.20476* **FFCC Camp Municipal du Château, 3 Rue du Val d'Ante, 14700 Falaise [02 31 90 16 55 or 02 31 90 30 90 (Mairie); fax 02 31 90 53 38; camping@falaise.fr]** Fr N on N158, at rndabt on o'skirts of town, turn L into vill; at next rndabt by Super U go strt on; at 2nd mini-rndabt turn R; then sp on L after housing estate. Or fr S on D958, at 1st rndabt foll sp town cent & site. Cont down hill thro town then turn L (avoid 1st site sp as v narr bdge) foll site sp as rd starts to climb (poss diff for lge o'fits). Cont approx 1km then as above fr castle. Med, hdg/mkd pitch, pt sl, terr, pt shd; wc (some cont); chem disp; mv service pnt; shwrs inc; el pnts (6-10A) €2.50-4; gas 500m; lndry rm; tradsmn; shops, rest, snacks, bar 500m; BBQ; playgrnd; htd pool in town; tennis; wifi; TV rm; sat TV some pitches; dogs €2.20; poss cr; some Eng spkn; adv bkg; quiet; ccard acc; red long stay/CCI. "Lovely, peaceful, well-kept site in pleasant surroundings; pitches poss diff lge o'fits; clean facs poss ltd low ssn & stretched high ssn & clsd 2200-0800; pitch self & pay later; town is birthplace of William the Conqueror; vet in Falaise." ♦ 1 May-30 Sep. € 12.60 2009*

FANJEAUX *8F4* (2.5km S Rural) *43.18070, 2.03301* **FFCC Camping à la Ferme Les Brugues (Vialaret), 11270 Fanjeaux [04 68 24 77 37; fax 04 68 24 60 21; http://lesbrugues.free.fr]** Exit A61 junc 22 onto D4/D119 (dir Mirepoix) to Fanjeaux; cont on D119 dir Mirepoix; at top of hill turn L onto D102 sp La Courtète (past rest La Table Cathare & fuel station) & in 100m turn R to site in 2.5km. Site well sp fr Fanjeaux. Sm, hdg/mkd pitch, pt sl, terr, shd; wc; chem disp; shwrs inc; el pnts (10A) inc (rev pol); lndtte (inc dryer); shop 2km; tradsmn; rest, bar 2.5km; playgrnd; games rm; wifi; few statics; dogs; Eng spkn; adv bkg; quiet; CCI. "Delightful, under-used, well-kept site adj sm lake; care req sm children; v lge pitches; friendly, helpful owners; gd clean san facs; excel touring base." ♦ 1 Jun-30 Sep. € 15.98 2009*

FAOUET, LE *2F2* (2km SE Rural) *48.01826, -3.47142* **Camp Municipal Beg er Roch, Route de l'Orient, 56320 Le Faouët [02 97 23 15 11 or 06 89 33 75 70 (mob); fax 02 97 23 11 66; camping.lefaouet@wanadoo.fr]** SE fr Le Faouët on D769 site sp on L. Med, hdg/mkd pitch, pt shd; wc; mv service pnt; chem disp; shwrs inc; el pnts (10A) €3; gas 2km; lndtte; shops, tradsmn; rest, bar 2km; playgrnd; htd pool; lake sw 2km; fishing; tennis; games area; golf; games/TV rm; 25% statics; dogs €1.05; Eng spkn; adv bkg; ccard acc; red long stay/CCI. "Pleasant, clean, quiet rvside site with many mkd walks; lovely, historic area; helpful warden." ♦ 10 Mar-30 Sep. € 16.50 2009*

See advertisement

⊞ **FARAMANS** *9C2* (500m E Rural) *45.39355, 5.17401* **Camp Municipal des Eydoches, 515 Ave des Marais. 38260 Faramans [04 74 54 21 78 or 04 74 54 22 97 (Mairie); fax 04 74 54 20 00; mairie.faramans@wanadoo.fr]** Fr Beaurepaire take D73 to Faramans. Site sp. Med, pt shd; wc; chem disp; mv service pnt; shwrs; el pnts (5A) €3.10; lndtte; shop 500m; rest 100m; snacks; bar 200m; lake sw; fishing; 50% statics; dogs €1.50; adv bkg; quiet. ♦ € 12.50 2007*

FAUTE SUR MER, LA see Aiguillon sur Mer, L' *7A1*

FAVERGES *9B3* (2km N Rural) *45.76676, 6.30941* **Camp Municipal Les Pins, 90 Rue Pré de Foire, 74210 St Ferréol [04 50 32 47 71 or 04 50 44 56 36 (Mairie); fax 04 50 44 49 76; st.ferreol@wanadoo.fr; www.pays-de-faverges.com]** Fr D1508 (N508) nr Faverges go N on D12 for 2km to site on rvside. Med, mkd pitch, pt sl, pt shd; wc (some cont); chem disp; shwrs inc; el pnts (10A) €2.25; gas; lndtte; shop 2km; tradsmn; rest; snacks; bar; playgrnd; dogs €1.15; phone; poss cr; Eng spkn; adv bkg; quiet; ccard not acc; CCI. "Well-equipped site; gd walking; no twin-axles or 4x4s; poss boggy in heavy rain; barrier - low ssn may need to contact Mairie." ♦ 15 Jun-15 Sep. € 10.45 2008*

FAVERGES *9B3* (2km N Urban) *45.79090, 6.21630* **CAMPEOLE Camping La Nublière, 74210 Doussard [04 50 44 33 44; fax 04 50 44 31 78; nubliere@campeole.com; www.camping-nubliere.com or www.campeole.com]** Fr Annecy take D1508 (N508) twd Albertville, site on L in 20km, 300m after Camp du Lac Bleu. Fr Faverges NW on D1508. Lge, mkd pitch, pt shd, wc (some cont); chem disp; mv service pnt; shwrs inc; el pnts (6A) €4.10; gas; lndtte; shop; rest; snacks; bar; playgrnd; lake sw adj; boating; golf; cycle hire; games area; entmnt; dogs €3.50; poss cr; adv bkg; poss noisy; ccard acc; red low ssn. "Helpful staff; gd san facs." ♦ 30 Apr-19 Sep. € 22.50 2006*

FAVEROLLES *9C1* (S Rural) *44.93932, 3.14759* **Camp Municipal, 15320 Faverolles [04 71 23 49 91 or 04 71 23 40 48 (Mairie); fax 04 71 23 49 65; faverolles.mairie@wanadoo.fr]** Fr A75 exit junc 30 & take D909 S, turn L onto D13 at Viaduct de Garabit & foll sp for Faverolles for 5km, then sp to site dir St Chély-d'Apcher. Sm, mkd pitch, pt sl, pt shd; htd wc (some); chem disp; shwrs inc; el pnts (6A) inc (rev pol); shops 500m; lndtte; playgrnd; some statics; phone; ccard not acc; quiet. "Nr pretty lake; excel, spotless san facs; vg rest in vill." ♦ 1 Jun-15 Oct. € 11.40 2009*

FAVEROLLES SUR CHER see Montrichard *4G2*

⊞ **FAYENCE** *10E4* (3km E Rural) *43.60659, 6.74855* **Camping Les Prairies, Chemin des Maures, 83440 Callian [04 94 76 48 36; fax 04 94 85 72 21; info@campingdesprairies.com; http://campingdesprairies.com]** Site on D562 Grasse - Draguignan rd, 3km W fr junc with D37. Site next to Renault g'ge. Fr A8 exit junc 39 onto D37 to D562 (gd rd) & as bef. Med, mkd pitch, pt sl, pt shd; wc; chem disp; shwrs inc; el pnts (10A) €4; lndtte; shops 400m; supmkt 800m; playgrnd; pool; fishing, sailing 5km; wifi; 70% statics; dogs €2; poss noisy; Eng spkn; adv bkg; CCI. "New san facs under construction (2009)." ♦ € 21.00 2009*

⊞ **FAYENCE** *10E4* (5km E Rural) *43.60139, 6.77278* **FFCC Camp de Loisirs du Lac, Domaine de la Chesnaie, 83440 Montauroux [04 94 76 46 26; fax 04 94 47 66 16; contact@campingdulac.fr; www.campingdulac.fr]** Fr A8 exit junc 39 onto D37; turn L onto D562 sp Draguignan; site on L in 1km soon after rndabt. Lge, hdg/mkd pitch, shd; wc (some cont); chem disp; shwrs inc; el pnts (2-10A) €1.50; gas; Indtte; shop 500m; snacks; bar; BBQ (gas/elec); playgrnd; pool; mainly statics; dogs €3-4; bus; phone; Eng spkn; adv bkg; quiet; ccard acc; CCI. "Ltd facs & poss unkempt low ssn; poss diff access for c'vans due trees/shrubs (Sep 2008); friendly, helpful staff." € 18.50 2008*

FAYENCE *10E4* (10km S Rural) *43.58449, 6.69016* **Camping Le Parc, Quartier Trestaure, 83440 St Paul-en-Forêt [04 94 76 15 35; fax 04 94 84 71 84; campingleparc@wanadoo.fr; www.campingleparc.com]** Fr D562 midway bet Draguinan & Grasse turn S onto D4. Site sp on L. Exit A8 junc 39, N on D37 for 11km, at junc with D562 turn L for 10km; L onto D4 for 900m; sm sp, L into sm lane, site on bend. Med, mkd pitch, terr, shd; htd wc; chem disp; mv service pnt; shwrs inc; el pnts (10A) inc; gas; Indtte; shop; tradsmn; rest; snacks, bar high ssn; playgrnd; pool; lake 6km; beach 30km; tennis; fishing; lake sw 15km; 10% statics; poss cr; adv bkg; quiet; red low ssn; CCI. "Conv hill vills of Provence; gd rests in St Paul; vg." 1 Apr-30 Sep. € 23.10 2006*

FAYENCE *10E4* (6km W Rural) *43.58487, 6.66627* **Camping La Tuquette (Naturist), 83440 Fayence [04 94 76 21 78; fax 04 94 76 23 95; robert@tuquette.com; www.tuquette.com]** Fr Fayence take N562. At km 64.2 sp turn R, site ent 100m. Sm, mkd pitch, terr, pt shd; wc; chem disp; shwrs ind; el pnts (6A) €4.60; Indtte; shop 6km; tradsmn; snacks; bar; BBQ; playgrnd; 2 htd pools; wifi; some statics; dogs €1.80; poss cr; Eng spkn; adv bkg; quiet; INF card. "Vg, clean site; friendly owners." ♦ 10 Apr-26 Sep. € 29.20 2009*

FECAMP *3C1* (6km SE Rural) *49.74041, 0.41660* **Camp Municipal du Canada, 76400 Toussaint [02 35 29 78 34; fax 02 35 27 48 82; mairie.toussaint@wanadoo.fr]** On D926 N of Toussaint (sharp turn at side of golf course). Med, hdg pitch, pt sl, shd; htd wc (some cont); shwrs inc; el pnts (4-10A) €2.10-2.65; Indtte; shop; BBQ; playgrnd; games area; 70% statics; dogs €0.35; quiet; CCI. "Gd." ♦ 15 Mar-15 Oct. € 7.35 2006*

FECAMP *3C1* (500m SW Coastal) *49.75712, 0.36200* **Camping Le Domaine de Renéville, Chemin de Nesmond, 76400 Fécamp [02 35 28 20 97 or 02 35 10 60 00; fax 02 35 29 57 68; camping-de-reneville@tiscali.fr; http://campingdereneville.free.fr]** Site off Etretat rd (D940) on o'skts of Fécamp; sp. NB Steep cliff site, access poss diff lge o'fits; narr bends. NB Lge o'fits best app fr dir Etretat & not Fécamp town. Lge, hdg/mkd pitch, terr, pt sl, shd; htd wc; chem disp; mv service pnt; shwrs inc; el pnts (6A) inc (poss long cable req)(poss rev pol); Indtte; shop 1km; tradsmn; rest, snacks & bar in town; playgrnd; pool adj; shgl beach 500m; 15% statics; phone; Eng spkn; adv bkg fr 10.00am on same day - rec peak ssn; CCI. "Vg site with sea views; ltd water pnts; gd san facs - poss steep walk to reach; interesting town; sep m'van o'night area on harbour adj tourist office; highly rec." ♦ 21 Mar-12 Nov. € 16.30 2008*

FEINS *2E4* (2km N Rural) *48.33923, -1.63816* **Camp Municipal L'Etang de Boulet/La Bijouterie, La Bijouterie, 35440 Feins [02 99 69 63 23 or 02 99 69 70 52 (Mairie); fax 02 99 69 70 52; feins@wanadoo.fr; www.feins.fr]** N fr Feins on D91; site on L in 1.5km. Sp fr Feins & fr Marcillé-Raoul. Sm, hdg/mkd pitch, pt shd; wc; chem disp (wc); shwrs inc; el pnts €3; Indtte; shops, rest & snacks nrby; playgrnd; lake & beach adj; sailing & canoe hire; 40% statics; dogs; quiet; CCI. "Cycle track; vg." ♦ May-30 Sep. € 11.10 2009*

FELLETIN *7B4* (4km N Rural) **Camping des Combes, 23500 Felletin [05 55 66 77 29]** Take D982 N fr Felletin. Turn L bet level x-ing & cemetary L & foll sp on unclassified rd along lake 4km to site. Sm, hdg/mkd pitch, pt sl, terr, pt shd; wc; chem disp; mv service pnt; shwrs inc; el pnts (10A) inc; gas 4km; Indtte; shop & 2km; playgrnd; lake sw adj; fishing; boating; dogs; Eng spkn; adv bkg. "V quiet site on edge Lake Combes; ideal touring base; vg`." ♦ 1 Mar-30 Sep. € 14.00 2008*

FENOUILLER, LE see St Gilles Croix de Vie *2H3*

Camping Caravaning LES RIVES DU CÉLÉ ★★★
Domaine du Surgié - 46100 FIGEAC • Tel: 05 61 64 88 54 • Fax: 05 61 64 89 17
www.lesrivesducele.com
Mobile homes to let
The campsite is situated on the Domaine du Surgié, a leisure park with lodgings. It has 100 pitches on 2 ha of land and three sanitary blocks with all modern facilities. Situated on the banks of the river Célé, with many services and activities, the medieval village of Figeac nearby and a gentle climate and delicious gastronomy, the LOT department invites you to come and enjoy your relaxing holidays here.

FERE, LA *3C4* (400m N Urban) *49.66554, 3.36205* **Camp Municipal du Marais de la Fontaine, Rue Vauban, 02800 La Fère [03 23 56 82 94; fax 03 23 56 40 04]** S on D1044 (N44) (St Quentin to Laon); R onto D338; turn E at rndabt; ignore 1st camping sp; turn N at next rndabt; site sp. Or Exit A26 junc 12 onto D1032 (N32) SW; in 2km turn R onto D35; in 4km pass under D1044; in 400m turn R; in 800m turn R at traff lts; foll over bdge to sports complex. Sm, hdg/mkd pitch, pt shd; wc; chem disp (wc); shwrs inc; el pnts (6-15A) €3; shop; tradsmn; rest, snacks & bar 1km; BBQ; htd, covrd pool adj; dogs €1.20; adv bkg rec; rd & rlwy noise; red long stay; CCI. "Well-kept site adj leisure cent; clean san facs; pitching awkward due sm pitches & narr site rds; warden lives adj site; gates shut 2200-0700 - no vehicle/person access; gd NH." ♦ 1 Apr-30 Sep. € 7.50 2009*

FERMANVILLE see Cherbourg *1C4*

FERRIERE D'ALLEVARD, LA see Allevard *9B3*

FERRIERES EN GATINAIS see Montargis *4F3*

FERRIERES SUR SICHON *9B1* (Rural) **Camp Municipal, 03250 Ferrières-sur-Sichon [04 70 41 10 10; fax 04 70 41 15 22]** Well sp in Ferrières-sur-Sichon. At x-rds of D995 & D122. Sm, pt sl, pt shd; htd wc; shwrs inc; el pnts €2.20; shop 500m; playgrnd; dogs; quiet. "CL-type site; gd san facs; friendly warden visits 1930; excel NH." 1 Jun-30 Sep. € 7.70 2008*

FERTE BERNARD, LA *4F2* (1km S Rural) *48.17595, 0.64792* **Camp Municipal Le Valmer, Espace du Lac, 72400 La Ferté-Bernard [tel/fax 02 43 71 70 03; camping@la-ferte-bernard.com; www.la-ferte-bernard.com]** Fr A11/E50 junc 5, take D1 to La Ferté-Bernard. At 1st rndabt in town cent, take 3rd exit. Join D323 (N23) & at next rndabt, take 3rd exit. Foll sp Le Valmer. Site off D323 by Rv Huisne & lake. Med, hdg/mkd pitch, pt sl, shd; wc; chem disp; mv service pnt; shwrs inc; el pnts (6A) €2.10; lndry rm; shop 1km; playgrnd; sand beach 500m; watersports; child entmnt Jul/Aug; 10% statics; dogs €1.30; Eng spkn; quiet; CCI. "Vg, friendly, clean site; excel facs; well-lit at night; pitches v muddy after rain; some pitches diff for lge o'fits; no twin-axles; mkt Mon; vg." ♦ 1 May-15 Sep. € 9.00 2007*

FERTE GAUCHER, LA *4E4* (700m E Urban) *48.77912, 3.31074* **Camp Municipal Joël Teinturier, 77320 La Ferté-Gaucher [01 64 20 20 40]** On D634 (N34) bet Coulommiers & Sézanne; site opp leisure cent. Lge, hdg/mkd pitch, pt shd; htd wc (some cont); chem disp (wc); shwrs inc; el pnts (5A) inc; gas; lndry rm; shop, rest, snacks, bar 700m; playgrnd; htd pool 100m; 30% statics; dogs; bus 500m; phone; adv bkg; quiet; red CCI. "Attractive parkland site by leisure cent; san facs dated but clean; gd touring base." ♦ 1 Mar-31 Oct. € 21.00 2006*

FERTE MACE, LA *4E1* (500m N Urban) *48.59869, -0.36143* **Camp Municipal La Saulaie, Blvd André Hamonic, 61600 La Ferté-Macé [06 76 86 67 20 (mob)]** Fr town cent foll D18 to Flers & turn R onto dual c'way in 500m. Site on L adj stadium. Sp. Sm, pt shd; htd wc; shwrs inc; el pnts (10A) €1.75; shops 1km; BBQ (gas); playgrnd; rv 2km; dogs; phone; quiet but little rd noise. "Excel site; call at house adj when recep clsd." ♦ 15 Apr-1 Oct. € 4.90 2008*

FERTE ST AUBIN, LA *4F3* (1km N Urban) *47.72553, 1.93565* **Camp Municipal Le Cosson, Ave Löwendal, 45240 La Ferté-St Aubin [02 38 76 55 90]** S fr Orléans on N20; ent on R on N o'skts twd Municipal pool. NB Access fr S poss diff for lge o'fits thro narr rds in business hrs. Sm, pt shd; wc; chem disp (wc); shwrs inc; el pnts (10A) €5.50 (poss rev pol); shops 1km; tradsmn; rest 100m; pool adj; fishing adj; wifi; dogs; phone; Eng spkn; train noise; ccard not acc; red low ssn; CCI. "Agreeable, spacious site; friendly, helpful recep; clean, ltd facs; easy walk to delightful town & gd rests; nr park & chateau; poss itinerants low ssn; conv A71; NH only." 1 Apr-31 Oct. € 12.00 2009*

FEUILLERES see Péronne *3C3*

FEURS *9B2* (1km N Urban) *45.75457, 4.22595* **Camp Municipal Le Palais, Route de Civens, 42110 Feurs [tel/fax 04 77 26 43 41]** Site sp fr D1082 (N82) on N o'skts of town. Lge, pt shd; htd wc; chem disp (wc); mv service pnt; shwrs inc; el pnts (6A) €3.05; gas; sm shop; tradsmn; snacks; playgrnd; pool adj; mostly statics; dogs €0.61; phone; quiet; CCI. "Pleasant, spacious, beautifully-kept site; busy, espec w/ends; clean san facs." ♦ 1 Apr-31 Oct. € 10.07 2009*

FIGEAC *7D4* (1.5km E Rural) *44.60989, 2.05015* **Camping Les Rives du Célé, Domaine du Surgié, 46100 Figeac [05 61 64 88 54; fax 05 61 64 89 17; contact@marc-montmija.com; www.lesrivesducele.com]** Fr all dirs foll sp Rodez to site by Rv Célé adj leisure complex. Foll sps 'Base Loisirs de Surgie'. Narr ent, light controlled. NB fr E on N140 v sharp R turn at 1st traff lts. NB Recep at beginning of rd to leisure cent & camping. Med, hdg/mkd pitch, pt shd, wc; chem disp; mv service pnt; shwrs inc; el pnts (10A) inc; gas 1km; Indtte; shop; rest; snacks; bar; playgrnd; htd pool & waterslide adj; boating; rv sw adj; tennis; cycle hire; entmnt; 30% statics; dogs €2.50; Eng spkn; adv bkg; quiet; red low ssn/long stay. "Excel pool complex at leisure cent adj (free to campers); peaceful low ssn; nice walk to beautiful town; adj rv unfenced; mkt Sat; vg." ♦ 1 Apr-30 Aug. € 22.00 2009*

See advertisement opposite

FIGEAC *7D4* (7km SE Urban) *44.57328, 2.07296* **Camp Municipal Les Rives d'Olt, Blvd Paul-Ramadier, 12700 Capdenac-Gare [05 65 80 88 87 or 05 65 80 22 22 (Mairie); camping.capdenac@wanadoo.fr]** Fr Figeac on N140 dir Rodez; at Capdenac turn R over rv bdge. Site on R in 200m. Med, hdg/mkd pitch, shd; wc; chem disp; mv service pnt; shwrs inc; el pnts (9A) €2.80; gas adj; Indtte; shop, rest, snacks, bar adj; playgrnd; pool 1km; tennis adj; TV rm; 5% statics; dogs; quiet, a little rd noise; CCI. "Well-cared for site beside Rv Lot; ent clsd 1200-1600 low ssn; gd fishing, walking & cycling; vg." ♦ 10 Apr-30 Sep. € 10.65 2009*

FIGEAC *7D4* (7km SW Rural) **FFCC Camping de Pech-Ibert, Route de Cajarc, 46100 Béduer [05 65 40 05 85; fax 05 65 40 08 33; contact@camping-pech-ibert.com; www.camping-pech-ibert.com]** SW fr Figeac on D662/D19 twds Cajarc. Site well sp on R after Béduer. Sm, pt shd; htd wc; chem disp; mv service pnt; baby facs; shwrs inc; el pnts (16A) €3.20 (poss rev pol); Indtte; snacks high ssn; BBQ; playgrnd; pool; tennis; cycle hire; fishing & sw 1km; dogs €1.70; Eng spkn; adv bkg ess high ssn; quiet; red low ssn; CCI. "Peaceful, relaxing CL-type site; pleasant, helpful owners; gd clean san facs; gd walking fr site (mkd trails); on pilgrimage rte; Sat mkt Figeac; absolute gem." ♦
15 Mar-15 Dec. € 10.50 2009*

FIQUEFLEUR EQUAINVILLE see Honfleur *3C1*

FISMES *3D4* (800m W Urban) *49.30944, 3.67138* **Camp Municipal de Fismes, Allée des Missions, 51170 Fismes [03 26 48 10 26; fax 03 26 48 82 25; mairie-fismes@wanadoo.fr; www.fismes.fr]** Fr Reims NW on N31. At Fismes do not ent town, but stay on N31 dir Soissons. Site on L down little lane at end of sports stadium wall. Or exit A4 junc 22 sp Soissons & Fismes & as bef. Sm, hdstg, unshd; wc; chem disp; baby facs; shwrs; el pnts (12A) inc (poss rev pol); shop 250m; supmkt 250m; BBQ (gas & el); games area; horseriding 5km; dogs; train; no twin-axles; adv bkg; ccard not acc; CCI. "Conv for Laon, Epernay, Reims; noisy due to busy rd & position on indus est; san facs usually immac but old; gates locked 2200-0700; warden on site ltd hrs; train to Reims nr; mkt Sat am; gd NH." ♦ 2 May-15 Sep. € 10.30 2009*

FLECHE, LA *4G1* (10km E Rural) *47.70230, 0.07330* **Camp Municipal La Chabotière, Place des Tilleuls, 72800 Luché-Pringé [02 43 45 10 00; fax 02 43 45 10 00; contact@lachabotiere.com; www.lachabotiere.com or www.loir-valley.com]** SW fr Le Mans on D323 (N23) twd La Flèche. At Clermont-Créans turn L on D13 to Luché-Pringé. Site sp. Med, hdg/mkd pitch, pt sl, pt shd; wc (some cont); chem disp; mv service pnt; baby facs; shwrs; el pnts (10A) inc (poss rev pol); Indtte; shops 100m; playgrnd; pool adj high ssn; cycle hire; TV; 10% statics; dogs €1.50; phone; sep car park high ssn; poss cr; Eng spkn; adv bkg; quiet; red low ssn; CCI. "Lovely site by Rv Loir; helpful, friendly warden; clean, modern facs; gd site for children; conv chateaux; excel." ♦ 1 Apr-15 Oct. € 12.30 2009*

See advertisement on page 130

FLECHE, LA *4G1* (500m S Urban) *47.69527, -0.07611* **Camping La Route d'Or, Allée du Camping, 72200 La Flèche [tel/fax 02 43 94 55 90; info@camping-laroutedor.com; www.camping-laroutedor.com or www.loir-valley.com]** Fr NW dir Laval D306, keep to W of town, leave S on D306 twd Bauge; site on L after x-ing rv; sp. Fr S take dir for A11 & Laval, site clearly sp on R on rvside. Lge, hdg/mkd pitch, some hdstg, pt shd; htd wc; chem disp; mv service pnt; shwrs inc; el pnts (10A) €3.60 (poss long lead req); gas; Indtte; shop 500m; supmkt nr; tradsmn; rest nr; playgrnd; pool; paddling pool; sand beach 1km; canoeing, fishing adj; tennis; games area; cycle hire; wifi; dogs €1; phone; Eng spkn; ccard acc; red long stay; CCI. "Busy, well-run site in beautiful location; lge pitches; helpful, welcoming staff; facs ltd low ssn; gd disabled facs; ring for entry code if office clsd; no twin-axles; conv ferries; mkt Wed." ♦
1 Mar-31 Oct. € 10.60 2009*

See advertisement on page 130

FLECHE, LA *4G1* (7km W Rural) *47.68696, -0.16993* **Camp Municipal Le Vieux Pont, 72200 Bazouges-sur-Le Loir [02 43 45 03 91 or 02 43 45 32 20 (Mairie); fax 02 43 45 38 26]** Off D323 (N23) fr Le Mans to Angers turn L over rv at 2nd traff lts in cent Bazouges. Sp to site on R after x-ing rv. Sm, hdg pitch, pt shd; wc (some cont); shwrs inc; el pnts (10A) inc; Indtte; playgrnd; pool 7km; fishing, horseriding adj; red low ssn. "Pleasant site on rv bank; san facs need update - wc's v sm (2009)." 15 May-30 Oct. € 14.00 2009*

⊞ **FLEURAT** *7A4* (500m E Rural) **Camping Les Boueix, Les Boueix, 23320 Fleurat [05 55 41 86 81; info@campinglesboueix.com; www.campinglesboueix.com]** Fr N145 N onto D5 to Fleurat. Foll sp La Boueix & site. Sm, pt hdg/mkd pitch, pt sl; wc; chem disp; shwrs inc; el pnts (10A) €3.50; shops, rest, snacks & bar 6km; BBQ; fishing; dogs €1.50; phone; adv bkg; quiet; no ccard acc. "Beautiful, quiet & relaxing CL-type site; views fr pitches; immac; v welcoming & helpful British owners; vg san facs; well-stocked fishing lake nrby; lovely walks; ideal for beautiful Creuse Valley; rallies welcome; conv A20; highly rec." € 12.50 2008*

FLEURIE *9A2* (500m SE Rural) *46.18758, 4.69895* **Camp Municipal La Grappe Fleurie, 69820 Fleurie [04 74 69 80 07 or 04 74 04 10 44 (Mairie); fax 04 74 69 85 71; camping@fleurie.org; www.camping-beaujolais.fr]** S dir Lyon on D306 (N6) turn R (W) at S end of Romanèche onto D32; 4km to vill of Fleurie (beware sharp turn in vill & narr rds) & foll site sp. Med, hdg/mkd pitch, terr, pt shd; wc (some cont); chem disp; mv service pnt; serviced pitches; shwrs inc; baby facs; el pnts (10A) inc; gas; lndtte; tradsmn; shop, rest, snacks, bar 500m; playgrnd; pool; tennis; wifi; entmnt; some statics; poss cr; Eng spkn; adv bkg rec Jul/Aug; ccard acc; red low ssn/CCI. "Clean, well-run, busy site; friendly staff; excel facs; lovely pool; gates & wash rms clsd 2200-0700; path to town thro vineyards (uphill); mkt Fri; excel." ♦ 23 Mar-17 Oct. € 16.50 2009*

FLORAC *9D1* (1km N Rural) *44.33569, 3.59002* **FFCC Camp Municipal Le Pont du Tarn, Route de Pont de Montvert, 48400 Florac [04 66 45 18 26 or 04 66 45 17 96 (LS); fax 04 66 45 26 43; contact@camping-florac.com; www.camping-florac.com]** Exit Florac N on N106 & turn R in 500m by by-pass on D998; site on L in 300m. Lge, pt shd, mkd pitch; htd wc (some cont); chem disp; mv service pnt; shwrs inc; el pnts (10A) inc; lndtte; supmkt 2km; tradsmn; rest, snacks, bar 2km; BBQ (no gas); playgrnd; pool; rv fishing adj; wifi; 60% statics; dogs €1.30; phone; poss v cr; some Eng spkn; adv bkg rec; quiet; red low ssn; CCI. "Nice, well-run site in beautiful area; san facs poor & need update; no twin-axles; gd base for area; mv service pnt poss diff to use; 20 min walk to town, gd shops & lge mkt Thurs; excel." ♦ 1 Apr-6 Nov. € 19.50 2009*

FLORAC *9D1* (2.5km NE Rural) *44.34528, 3.61008* **FFCC Camping Chantemerle, La Pontèze, 48400 Bédouès [04 66 45 19 66 or 06 73 86 53 16 (mob); chante-merle@wanadoo.fr; http://monsite.wanadoo.fr/camping chantemerle]** Exit Florac N on N106; in 500m turn R onto D998; in 2.5km site on L, past Bédouès vill cent. Med, mkd pitch, pt sl, pt shd; wc; chem disp (wc); shwrs inc; el pnts (6A) €2.80; lndry rm; sm shop; tradsmn; snacks; playgrnd; rv sw adj; games rm; wifi; 10% statics; dogs €1.50; poss cr; Eng spkn; quiet; red low ssn; CCI. "Lovely location; helpful owner; gd walking; conv Gorges du Tarn, Cévennes National Park; vg." 15 Apr-15 Sep. € 13.00 2009*

FLORAC *9D1* (4km NE Rural) *44.34433, 3.60533* **Camping Chon du Tarn, 48400 Bédouès [04 66 45 09 14; fax 04 66 45 22 91; info@camping-chondutarn.com; www.camping-chondutarn.com]** Exit Florac N on N106, turn R in 500m onto D998 (sp Pont de Monvert), site on L in 3km in vill. Med, mkd pitch, pt sl, terr, pt shd; wc; chem disp; mv service pnt; shwrs inc; el pnts (6A) 2.10 (poss rev pol); gas; lndtte; shop & 4km; rest & bar adj; playgrnd; rv sw & sand beach; games area; dogs €1; adv bkg; quiet; ccard not acc; red low ssn; CCI. "Beautiful rvside site with views; helpful staff; clean san facs dated, ltd low ssn; conv Tarn Gorges, Causses & Cévennes National Park; excel." ♦ 1 Apr-20 Oct. € 9.90 2009*

FLORAC *9D1* (500m S Urban) *44.31760, 3.59968* **FFCC Camping Velay, Le Pont Neuf, 48400 Florac [04 66 45 19 23 or 04 66 45 12 19]** Site on Rv Tarn adj to bdge connecting D907 & N106; ent fr N106. At S end of bypass; do not go thro town. Sm, pt sl, pt shd; wc; shwrs inc; el pnts (8A) €2.20; gas; lndtte; shop 300m; tradsmn; rests nr; rv sw & shgl beach adj; dogs €1; some rd noise. "Friendly recep; gd walks; conv Gorges du Tarn & Cévennes National Park; sh walk to town cent." 1 Jul-30 Sep. € 9.20 2008*

FLORENSAC see Agde *10F1*

⊞ **FLUMET** *9B3* (1.5km NE Rural) *45.82216, 6.53512* **Camping Le Vieux Moulin, 73590 Flumet [tel/fax 04 79 31 70 06; amrey@hotmail.fr]** Fr Albertville go N on D1212 (N212) & cont past Flumet for 1km. Turn R, watch for sp. Med, mkd pitch, hdstg, pt shd; htd wc; chem disp; mv service pnt; shwrs inc; el pnts (3-10A) €5-9.50; lndtte; tradsmn; rest nr; playgrnd; ski lifts 200m; 20% statics; dogs €1.20; phone; clsd 15 Apr-30 May; poss cr; Eng spkn; some rd noise; CCI. "Superb san block but ltd; friendly staff; gd touring cent; highly rec; v ltd facs low ssn outside ski ssn." ♦ € 13.50 2008*

⊞ **FOIX** *8G3* (2km N Rural) *42.98911, 1.61565* **Camping du Lac, Quartier Labarre, 09000 Foix [05 61 65 11 58; fax 05 61 05 32 62; camping-du-lac@wanadoo.fr; www.campingdulac.com]** Fr N on N20 foll sp for 'Centre Ville', site on R in 2km opp Peugeot g'ge in Labarre. Fr S onto on N20 thro tunnel & take 1st exit N of Foix & foll sp 'Centre Ville', then as above. Lge, mkd pitch, pt shd; wc (some cont); chem disp; mv service pnt; shwrs inc; baby facs; el pnts (6A) inc; lndtte; supmkt adj; tradsmn; rest; snacks; bar; BBQ; playgrnd; pool (high ssn); paddling pool; lake fishing adj; boating; windsurfing; tennis; entmnts; TV; 30% statics; dogs €1.50; Eng spkn; poss cr; adv bkg rec high ssn; quiet but some rd (N20) noise; ccard acc; red low ssn; CCI. "Quiet, spacious pitches on L of camp; facs poss stretched high ssn; gd disabled facs, others need refurb; gates clsd 2300-0700; busy w/end; gd." ♦ € 21.00 (CChq acc) 2009*

FOIX *8G3* (4km S Urban) *42.93081, 1.63883* **FFCC Camping Roucateille, 15 Rue du Pradal, 09330 Montgaillard [tel/fax 05 61 64 05 92; info@camping-roucateille.com; www.camping-roucateille.com]** Fr N exit N20 junc 11, fr S exit N20 junc 12; foll sp Montgaillard; site sp fr main rd thro vill. NB Swing wide at ent. Med, hdg/mkd pitch, pt shd; wc; chem disp; mv service pnt; shwrs inc; el pnts (4-10A) €2.30-4.90; lndtte; shop 500m, hypmkt 2km; playgrnd; pool 3km; some statics in sep area; dogs free; adv bkg; quiet; red low ssn/long stay; CCI. "Picturesque, informal site; charming, helpful young owners; excel facs; care needed to avoid trees; garden produce in ssn; gd touring base; excel." ♦ 1 May-30 Sep. € 13.60 2009*

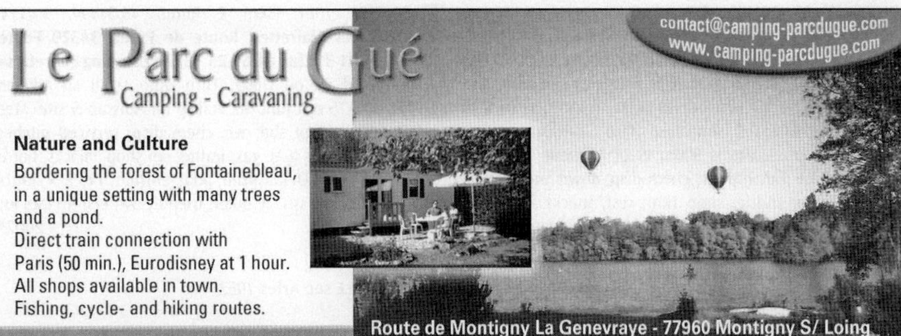

Le Parc du Gué
Camping - Caravaning
contact@camping-parcdugue.com
www.camping-parcdugue.com
Nature and Culture
Bordering the forest of Fontainebleau, in a unique setting with many trees and a pond.
Direct train connection with Paris (50 min.), Eurodisney at 1 hour.
All shops available in town.
Fishing, cycle- and hiking routes.
OPEN: 15 MARCH TILL 30 NOVEMBER
Route de Montigny La Genevraye - 77960 Montigny S/ Loing
Tel: 00 33 (0) 1 64 45 87 79 - Fax: 00 33 (0) 1 64 78 31 46

France

⊞ **FOIX** *8G3* (5km NW Rural) **Camp Municipal de Rieutort, 09000 Cos [05 61 65 39 79 or 06 80 85 07 75 (mob); mairiecos@neuf.fr]** Fr Foix take D117 dir Tarbes. Foll sp Cos onto D617, site on L in 3km. Sm, pt sl, pt shd; htd wc (some cont); chem disp; 25% serviced pitches; baby facs; fam bthrm; shwrs inc; el pnts (15A) €3.30; Indtte; shop 5km; rest, snacks, bar 5km; playgrnd; pool; tennis; dogs; quiet; CCI. "Pleasant site amongst trees with gd views; no c'vans over 6m; gd facs, ltd low ssn; sm step into disabled facs." ♦ € 10.00 2009*

FONTAINE DE VAUCLUSE see Isle sur la Sorgue, L' *10E2*

FONTAINE SIMON *4E2* (800m N Rural) *48.51314, 1.01941* **Camp Municipal, Rue de la Ferrière, 28240 Fontaine-Simon [02 37 81 88 11 or 06 81 67 78 79 (mob); fax 02 37 81 83 47; fontaine-simon@wanadoo.fr; www.mairie-fontaine-simon.fr]** Fr La Loupe on D929 take D25 N to Fontaine-Simon, site sp. Med, hdg pitch, pt sl, pt shd; wc (some cont); chem disp; shwrs inc; el pnts inc (poss long lead req); Indtte; tradsmn; BBQ; playgrnd; covrd pool adj; lake sw adj; fishing; few statics; dogs €1.10; adv bkg; quiet; CCI. "Undulating, lakeside site; warden friendly; gd." ♦ 1 Apr-30 Oct. € 13.00 2008*

FONTAINEBLEAU *4E3* (5km NE Rural) *48.42215, 2.74872* **Camp Municipal Grange aux Dîmes, Chemin de l'Abreuvoir, 77210 Samoreau [01 64 23 72 25; fax 01 64 23 98 31; mairie-de-samoreau@wanadoo.fr]** Fr cent of Fontainebleau take D210 (dir Provins); in approx 4km at rndabt cross bdge over Rv Seine; take R at rndabt; site sp at end of rd thro Samoreau vill; site twd rv. Med, hdg/mkd pitch, pt sl, pt shd; htd wc; chem disp; mv service pnt; shwrs inc; el pnts (10A) inc (poss rev pol); Indtte; shop 250m; snacks & bar 100m; rest 500m; phone; bus; poss v cr; adv bkg; rlwy & barge noise; CCI. "Attractive location by Rv Seine; peaceful; gd sized pitches; helpful managers; gd, immac san facs; adj vill hall poss noisy w/end; jazz festival late Jun; conv palace, Paris (by train) & Disneyland; clsd 2200-0700; excel site." ♦ 15 Mar-30 Sep. € 15.20 2008*

FONTAINEBLEAU *4E3* (10km S Rural) *48.33362, 2.75386* **Camping Le Parc du Gué, Route de Montigny, 77690 Montigny-sur-Loing [01 64 45 87 79; fax 01 64 78 31 46; contact@camping-parcdugue.com; www.camping-parcdugue.com]** On D607 (N7) foll sp S to Montigny-sur-Loing, site sp. Lge, hdg/mkd pitch, pt shd; htd wc (some cont); chem disp; shwrs inc; el pnts (6A) €3.50; Indtte; tradsmn; BBQ; playgrnd; rv sw adj; watersports; kayaks; fishing; wifi; 10% statics; dogs €3.50; mkt Sat 2km; Eng spkn; adv bkg; quiet; ccard acc; red CCI. "Beautiful, wooded country; excel walking & cycling." ♦ 15 Mar-30 Nov. € 16.00 2009*

See advertisement

FONTAINEBLEAU *4E3* (10km S Rural) *48.31740, 2.69650* **Camping Les Prés, Chemin des Prés, 77880 Grez-sur-Loing [tel/fax 01 64 45 72 75; camping-grez@wanadoo.fr; www.camping-grez-fontainebleau.info]** Fr Fontainebleau on D607 (N7) twd Nemours (S) for 8km; look for camping sps. At traff island turn L onto D40D, in 1km immed after x-ing bdge turn R; site on L. Do not tow into Grez-sur-Loing. Med, pt shd; wc; chem disp; shwrs inc; el pnts (5A) €2.95; gas; Indtte; shop; rest, bar 200m; snacks; playgrnd; htd, covrd pool 10km; fishing; canoe hire; cycle hire; 70% statics; dogs; phone; poss cr; Eng spkn; adv bkg; quiet but half touring pitches nr busy rd; ccard acc; red long stay; CCI. "In v attractive area; mainly statics - many old/tatty (2008); site poss unkempt/scruffy end of ssn (2008); helpful British manager." ♦ 21 Mar-11 Nov. € 10.05 2009*

FONTENAY LE COMTE *7A2* (7km NE Rural) *46.52140, -0.76906* **FFCC Camping La Joletière, 85200 Mervent [02 51 00 26 87 or 06 14 23 71 31 (mob LS); fax 02 51 00 27 55; contact@campinglajoletiere.fr; www.campinglajoletiere.fr]** Fr Fontenay-le-Comte N on D938; after 6.5km, turn R onto D99; in 3km enter vill of Mervent; site on R. Or fr A83 exit junc 8 & take bypass to W of Fontenay-le-Comte. Med, hdg/mkd pitch, some hdstg, pt sl, pt shd; wc; mv service pnt; shwrs inc; el pnts (5A) €3.70 (rev pol); gas; Indtte; shop 1km; rest; snacks; bar; playgrnd; htd pool high ssn; sw 2km; fishing; boating/windsurfing 2km; forest walks 500m; 25% statics; dogs €1.70; poss cr; adv bkg; ccard acc. "Quiet & pleasant site; gd lge pitches; friendly owners; poss ltd facs low ssn; san facs old & unclean (Jul 2008)." ♦ 15 Jun-15 Sep. € 13.70 2009*

FONTENAY LE COMTE *7A2* (7km NE Rural) *46.52454, -0.76983* **FFCC Camping Le Chêne Tord, Route du Chêne-Tord, 85200 Mervent [02 51 00 20 63; fax 02 51 00 27 94]** Exit A83 junc 8 & foll D938 N fr Fontenay-Le-Comte twd La Châtaigneraie for 6km to vill of Fourchaud. Turn E to Mervent on D99 & foll camp sps, sharp L turn immed bef vill at stone cross. Site is 500m W of Mervent. Sm, mkd pitch, pt sl, pt shd; htd wc; chem disp; shwrs inc; el pnts (6A) €4.50; gas; Indtte; shop 1km; rest, snacks, bar 1km; BBQ (gas only); rv/lake sw & fishing 2km; games area; 90% statics; dogs €1.30; phone; Eng spkn; adv bkg rec high ssn; v quiet; red low ssn; CCI. "Nice area; third of site forest adventure park - poss noisy high ssn; poss scruffy low ssn; welcoming & friendly; mainly statics; gd NH." Easter-31 Oct. € 12.00 2009*

FONTENAY TRESIGNY *4E3* (6km NE Rural) *48.75340, 2.89446* **Camping des Quatre Vents, 77610 Crèvecoeur-en-Brie [01 64 07 41 11; fax 01 64 07 45 07; contact@caravaning-4vents.fr; www.caravaning-4vents.fr]** At Calais take A26/E15 dir Arras; at Arras take A1/E15 dir Paris; next take A104 dir A4 Metz/Nancy/Marne-la-Vallée, then A4 dir Metz/Nancy, exit junc 13 dir Provins (onto D231); turn R dir Crèvecoeur-en-Brie & foll site sp. Site in 13km. Lge, hdg/mkd pitch, pt shd; htd wc; chem disp; mv service pnt; baby facs; serviced pitches; shwrs inc; el pnts (6A) inc; Indtte; shops 2km; tradsmn; snacks; BBQ; playgrnd; pool; horseriding; games area; wifi; games/TV rm; 50% statics sep area; dogs €3; phone; poss cr; Eng spkn; adv bkg ess in ssn; quiet but some aircraft noise; ccard acc; CCI. "Friendly, well-run site; gd, lge pitches; san facs clean but v basic; helpful, welcoming staff; excel pool; conv Disneyland & Paris by car/train; poss muddy when wet; poss late access to site; superb." ♦ 1 Mar-1 Nov. € 27.00 ABS - P09 2009*

FONTENOY LE CHATEAU *6F2* (2km S Rural) *47.95637, 6.21157* **Camping Le Fontenoy, Route de la Vierge, 88240 Fontenoy-le-Château [03 29 36 34 74 or 06 84 48 51 48 (mob); marliesfontenoy@hotmail.com; www.campingfontenoy.com]** SE fr Bains-les-Bains on D434 to Fontenoy-le-Château (6km). In cent of vill turn L onto D40 for 2km to site. Med, mkd pitch, pt shd; wc; chem disp; shwrs inc, el pnts (4A) €2.25; Indtte; tradsmn; rest; snacks; bar; playgrnd; pool 5km; 10% statics; dogs €0.60; poss cr; Eng spkn; adv bkg; quiet, ccard not acc; red long stay; CCI. "Attractive site; lovely area." 15 Apr-30 Sep. € 11.55 2009*

FONTES *10F1* (800m N Rural) *43.54734, 3.37999* **FFCC Camping L'Evasion, Route de Cabrières, 34320 Fontès [04 67 25 32 00; fax 04 67 25 31 96; campingevasion34@yahoo.fr; http://camping.evasion.free.fr]** Fr A75 exit junc 59 (Pézenas). At rndabt take D124 to Lézignan-la-Cèbe then fork L, cont on D124 to Fontès. In vill foll sp to site. Sm, hdg/mkd pitch, pt sl, pt shd; wc; chem disp; mv service pnt; baby facs; showrs inc; el pnts (6A) €2; gas; Indtte; rest; snacks; bar; BBQ; playgrnd; pool; beach 30km; 50% statics; dogs €2.70; phone; adv bkg; quiet; CCI. "Excel san facs; touring pitches amongst statics." ♦ 1 Apr-30 Oct. € 12.00 2008*

⊞ **FONTES** *10F1* (3km E Rural) *43.54491, 3.41743* **Camping Les Clairettes, Route de Péret, 34320 Fontès [04 67 25 01 31; fax 04 67 25 38 64; camping-clairettes@wanadoo.fr]** Sp on D609. Turn onto D128 sp Adissan, Fontès. Fr A75 exit junc 58. Foll sp for Adissan & site. Med, hdg/mkd pitch, pt shd; wc; chem disp; serviced pitches; shwrs inc; el pnts (6A); gas; Indtte; sm shop, snacks, bar in ssn; rest 4km; BBQ; playgrnd; pool; entmnt; TV; 50% statics; adv bkg; red low ssn. "V quiet; friendly owners; ltd facs low ssn." ♦ 2007*

FONTVIEILLE see Arles *10E2*

FORCALQUIER *10E3* (500m E Urban) *43.96206, 5.78718* **Camping Indigo Forcalquier, Route de Sigonce, 04300 Forcalquier [04 92 75 27 94; fax 04 92 75 18 10; forcalquier@camping-indigo.com; www.camping-indigo.com]** Fr town cent foll sp Digne/Sisteron; in 400m turn L at petrol stn, then 1st R. Site on R in 200m. Med, mkd pitch, pt sl, pt shd; wc (some cont); chem disp; mv service pnt; baby facs; some serviced pitches; shwrs inc; el pnts (6-10A) €4.60-6.80 (long lead poss req); Indtte; shop 500m; tradsmn; rest; snacks; bar; playgrnd; htd pool; paddling pool; games area; internet; TV rm; some statics; dogs €4; phone; Eng spkn; adv bkg; quiet; red low ssn; CCI. "Pleasant site in lovely location; san facs ltd/inadequate low ssn; excel m'van facs; access diff due v narr rds & awkward corners; poss high untrimmed hedges (2007)." ♦ 3 Apr-18 Oct. € 20.60 (CChq acc) 2009*

FORCALQUIER *10E3* (6km S Urban) *43.91096, 5.78210* **FFCC Camping l'Eau Vive, 04300 Dauphin [tel/fax 04 92 79 51 91; info@leauvive.fr; www.leauvive.fr]** S fr Forcalquier on D4100 (N100) dir Apt; in 2.5km turn L onto D13 (at Mane); site on R in 3km. Or fr D4096, turn onto D13 at Volx; site on L in 6km (800m past Dauphin). Med, mkd pitch, shd; htd wc; chem disp; shwrs inc; el pnts (3-6A) €3.50-4.50; Indtte; shop; supmkt 6km; snacks; BBQ (gas, sep area); playgrnd; 2 pools; paddling pool; tennis; cycle hire; games area; games rm; child entmnt; TV; dogs €3.50; bus 800m; Eng spkn; adv bkg; quiet; ccard not acc; red low ssn. "Well-run site; helpful owners; vg pools; vg for children; excel. 1 Apr-31 Oct. € 21.00 2009*

FORCALQUIER *10E3* (4km NW Rural) *43.97235, 5.73800* **Camping Le Domaine des Lauzons (Naturist), 04300 Limans [04 92 73 00 60; fax 04 92 73 04 31; leslauzons@wanadoo.fr; www.camping-lauzons.com]** Exit A51 junc 19 onto N100 dir Avignon; in Forcalquier at rndabt turn L onto D950/D313 sp Banon; site on R in approx 6km. Lge site sp. Diff app. Med, mkd pitch, pt sl, terr, pt shd; wc; chem disp; baby facs; sauna; shwrs inc; el pnts (6A) €4.50; gas; Indtte (inc dryer); ice; sm shop; supmkt 6km; tradsmn; rest; snacks; bar; BBQ (gas or charcoal sep area); playgrnd; 2 htd pools; pony rides; archery; games area; games rm; many activities; entmnt; wifi; TV; 25% statics; dogs €4; phone; poss cr; some Eng spkn; adv bkg; quiet; ccard acc; INF req. "Pleasant site in wooded valley; wonderful scenery; helpful, friendly staff; excel family site; san facs ltd low ssn; Forcalquier lovely town; walks fr site." ♦ 1 Apr-30 Sep. € 28.00 2009*

FORET FOUESNANT, LA *2F2* (500m N Rural) *47.91136, -3.97979* **Camping Manoir de Penn Ar Ster, 2 Chemin de Penn Ar Ster, 29940 La Forêt-Fouesnant [02 98 56 97 75; fax 02 98 56 80 49; info@camping-pennarster.com; www.camping-pennarster.com]** Fr Concarneau take D783 twd Quimper. In 8km after sp Kerlevan L to La Forêt-Fouesnant. After 1km R at bottom of hill opp car park to site in 100m. Med, hdg pitch, pt sl, terr, unshd; wc (some cont); chem disp; mv service pnt; shwrs inc; el pnts (6-10A) €3.20-3.50; lndtte; shop adj; rest 500m; playgrnd; sand beach 2km; golf adj; entmnt; 60% statics (sep area); dogs €2; adv bkg; fairly quiet; CCI. "Well-kept site; close to gd beaches; nice welcome; excel." ♦ 10 Feb-10 Nov. € 22.00 2007*

FORET FOUESNANT, LA *2F2* (2.5km SE Coastal) *47.89936, -3.95493* **Camping de Kéranterec, Route de Port la Forêt, Kerleven, 29940 La Forêt-Fouesnant [02 98 56 98 11; fax 02 98 56 81 73; info@camping-keranterec.com; www.camping-keranterec.com]** Fr Quimper take D783 SE. Turn R onto D44 twds La Forêt-Fouesnant; in vill cent foll sp for Beg Menez for 200m, then take 1st R twds Kerleven; turn L at Kerleven seafront rndabt, cont for 500m & at next rndabt foll site sp. (NB: Kéranterec shares same ent with Camping St Laurent.) Lge, hdg/mkd pitch, terr, pt shd; wc; serviced pitches; chem disp; baby facs; shwrs inc; el pnts (6A) €4; gas; lndtte; shop; tradsmn; snacks; bar; playgrnd; htd pool; waterslide; sand beach 400m; tennis; games area; fishing & watersports adj; entmnt; TV; 30% statics; dogs €3; adv bkg (ess high ssn); Eng spkn; ccard acc; red low ssn/CCI. "Lovely views fr most pitches; clean, modern san facs; many lge pitches; tight turn into sm hedged pitches on steep terr poss diff lge o'fits." ♦ 5 Apr-15 Sep. € 30.00 2008*

FORET FOUESNANT, LA *2F2* (2.5km SE Coastal) *47.89611, -3.95446* **Camping Domaine du St Laurent, Kerleven, 29940 La Forêt-Fouesnant [02 98 56 97 65; fax 02 98 56 92 51; saintlaurent@franceloc.fr; www.camping-franceloc.fr]** Fr Quimper take D783 SE. Turn R onto D44 to La Forêt-Fouesnant; in vill cent foll sp for Plage de Kerleven; turn L at Kerleven seafront rndabt, cont for 500m & at next rndabt foll site sp. (NB: Camping St Laurent shares same ent with Kéranterec.) Lge, hdg/mkd pitch, pt shd; wc; mv service pnt; chem disp; shwrs inc; el pnts (6A) inc (long lead req); gas; lndtte; shop; tradsmn; snacks; bar; playgrnd; htd pool; paddling pool; waterslide; jacuzzi; sauna; sand beach adj; tennis; gym; entmnt; TV; 50% statics; dogs €4.50; poss cr; adv bkg; phone; Eng spkn; ccard acc; red low ssn; CCI. "Friendly, well-run site with excel facs; lge pitches; many excel, quiet beaches within 10km; beautiful coast, sea views; highly rec. " ♦ End Apr-end Sep. € 37.00 2008*

⊞ **FORGES LES EAUX** *3C2* (1km S) **Aire de Service (M'vans only), 76440 Forges-les-Eaux [02 32 89 94 20; mairie@ville-forges-les-eaux.fr]** Fr Forges-les-Eaux cent, take D921 S sp Lyons-la-Forêt. In 500m turn R foll sp, camp on L in 250m opp municipal site. Med, hdstg, unshd; mv service pnt; water points; el pnts (poss rev pol). "Free 1st night, 2nd night €5; max 2 nights; warden visits or pay at Municipal site opp; town cent easy walk; views of open countryside; excel." 2007*

FORGES LES EAUX *3C2* (1km S Urban) *49.60603, 1.54302* **Camp Municipal La Minière, 3 Blvd Nicolas Thiese, 76440 Forges-les-Eaux [02 35 90 53 91]** Fr Forges-les-Eaux cent, take D921 S sp Lyons-la-Forêt. In 750m turn R foll sp, camp on R in 150m. Med, hdg pitch, pt sl, pt shd; wc (some cont); mv service pnt opp; shwrs inc; el pnts (4-8A) €2.70 (rev pol); lndry rm; shops nr; htd pool in town; 85% statics (sep area); poss cr; quiet; CCI. "Well-presented site; friendly warden; basic, clean san facs; excel disabled facs; poss diff access some pitches; m'van o'night area opp; pleasant town with excel WWII Resistance Museum; useful NH." ♦ 1 Apr-30 Oct. € 7.80 2009*

The opening dates and prices on this campsite have changed. I'll send a site report form to the Club for the next edition of the guide.

FORT MAHON PLAGE *3B2* (1km E Rural) *50.33230, 1.57990* **Airotel Camping Le Royon, 1271 Route de Quend, 80120 Fort-Mahon Plage [03 22 23 40 30; fax 03 22 23 65 15; info@campingleroyon.com; www.campingleroyon.com]** Exit A16 at junc 24 Forest-Montiers onto D32 to Rue, then dir Quend & Fort-Mahon-Plage, site sp. Lge, hdg/mkd pitch, pt shd; wc (some cont); mv service pnt; chem disp; shwrs inc; el pnts (6A) inc; gas; lndtte; shop; tradsmn; snacks; bar; playgrnd; htd, covrd pool; paddling pool; sand beach 2km; games area; sailing, fishing, golf nr; cycle hire; wifi; entmnt; 50% statics; dogs €3; phone; Eng spkn; adv bkg; ccard acc; red low ssn/long stay/CCI. "Discount voucher given on departure for next visit; modern san facs; conv Mercanterre nature reserve; site staff connect/disconnect el pnt; vg. ♦ 13 Mar-4 Nov. € 29.00 (3 persons) 2009*

See advertisement on next page

FORT MAHON PLAGE *3B2* (8km S Rural) *50.31950, 1.60583* **FLOWER Camping Les Vertes Feuilles, 25 Route de la Plage, Monchaux, 80120 Quend Plage-les-Pins [03 22 23 55 12; fax 03 22 19 07 52; lesvertesfeuilles@baiedesommepleinair.com; www.baiedesommepleinair.com]** Exit A16 junc 24 onto D32/D940 N. Turn W dir Quend onto D32, site sp. Med, hdg/mkd pitch, pt shd; htd wc; chem disp; baby facs; shwrs inc; el pnts (4-10A) €2-6.50; gas; lndtte; tradsmn; snacks; BBQ; playgrnd; htd, covrd pool; paddling pool; sand beach 4km; tennis 6km; cycle hire; games area; games rm; entmnt; internet; TV rm; 40% statics; dogs €1.50; poss cr; Eng spkn; adv bkg; quiet; ccard acc; red low ssn. "Pleasant, family site." ♦ 1 Apr-7 Nov. € 23.90 2009*

See advertisement on page 295

ROYON
www.campingleroyon.com
Enjoy great comfort in a warm environment on the border of a protected nature park.
Rental of mobile homes from March till November.
Covered and heated swimming pool opened from mid May to mid September.
Summer animations.
CAMPING LE ROYON
Loisirs ****
1271, route de Quend
80120 FORT-MAHON-PLAGE
Phone: (0033) 03 22 23 40 30
Fax (0033) 03 22 23 65 15

FORT MOVILLE see Pont Audemer *3D2*

FOUESNANT *2F2* (3km S Rural) *47.88202, -4.01863* **Camping Les Hortensias, La Grande Allée, 29170 Fouesnant [02 98 56 52 95; fax 02 98 71 55 07; information@campingleshortensias.com; www.campingleshortensias.com]** Fr Quimper on D34 dir Fouesnant, then S twds Mousterlin, site sp. Med, hdg pitch, pt shd; htd wc; chem disp; mv service pnt; baby facs; shwrs; el pnts (6A) €2.90; gas; lndtte; tradsmn; snacks; BBQ; playgrnd; games area; games rm; entmnt; TV; dogs €2; phone; adv bkg; quiet. "Guided walks & cycle rides." Easter-30 Sep. € 13.50 2006*

FOUESNANT *2F2* (4km S Coastal) *47.85992, -3.98850* **Camping Le Kervastard, Hent-Kervastard, Beg-Meil, 29170 Fouesnant [02 98 94 91 52; fax 02 98 94 99 83; camping.le.kervastard@wanadoo.fr; www.campinglekervastard.com]** Foll rd fr Quimper thro Beg-Meil. Site sp on R immed after rd bends sharply to L. Med, hdg/mkd pitch, pt shd; wc; chem disp; mv service pnt; baby facs; serviced pitches; shwrs; el pnts (6-10A) €3.60-3.90; gas; lndtte; shops adj; playgrnd; htd pool; paddling pool; sand beach 300m; sailing, watersports nr; entmnt; TV; 30% statics; dogs €2.20; phone; adv bkg (fee); Eng spkn; quiet; ccard acc; red low ssn/CCI. "Quiet part of Brittany with several sheltered coves; excel site." ♦ 23 May-9 Sep. € 23.50 2008*

FOUESNANT *2F2* (5km S Coastal/Rural) *47.85456, -3.99585* **Camping Le Vorlen, Plage de Kerambigorn, Beg-Meil, 29170 Fouesnant [02 98 94 97 36; fax 02 98 94 97 23; info@vorlen.com; www.vorlen.com]** Fr Fouesnant on D45 to Beg-Meil. Fr cent of Beg-Meil turn R at hotel Le Bretagnel & foll sp Kerambigorn; site 300m W of this beach & sp at most rd juncs. V lge, hdg/mkd pitch, pt shd; wc (some cont); mv service pnt; chem disp; baby facs; shwrs inc; el pnts (5-10A) €3; gas; lndtte; shop; tradsmn; snacks; playgrnd; htd pool & paddling pool; waterslide; sand beach 200m; games area; fishing; watersports; golf nr; TV; 15% statics; dogs €2; phone; Eng spkn; adv bkg; red low ssn; ccard acc; CCI. "Pleasant wooded site; gd, modern san facs; friendly; Beg-Meil excel resort; excel site, espec autumn." ♦ 15 May-15 Sep. € 26.00 2008*

FOUESNANT *2F2* (3.5km SW Rural) *47.86667, -4.01556* **Camping La Piscine, 51 Hent Kerleya, 29170 Fouesnant [02 98 56 56 06; fax 02 98 56 57 64; contact@campingdelapiscine.com; www.campingdelapiscine.com]** Turn R off D45 on exit Fouesnant onto D145 sp Mousterlin; in 1km L at site sp. Lge, hdg/mkd pitch, some hdstg, pt shd; wc; chem disp; mv service pnt; baby facs; sauna; shwrs inc; el pnts (6-10A) €4-4.60; gas; lndtte; shop; tradsmn; rest 2km; snacks; BBQ; playgrnd; htd pool; paddling pool; waterslide; sand beach 1.5km; lake adj; golf, tennis nr; golf 7km; games rm; wifi; entmnt; 30% statics; dogs €2.20; Eng spkn; adv bkg; quiet; ccard acc; red low ssn; CCI. "Highly rec, family-run site; gd walking, cycling." ♦ 13 May-12 Sep. € 26.00 2009*

I'll fill in a report online and let the Club know – www.caravanclub.co.uk/europereport

FOUESNANT *2F2* (4.5km SW Coastal) *47.85851, -4.02009* **Camping Sunêlia L'Atlantique, Hent Poul an Corre, 29170 Fouesnant [02 98 56 14 44; fax 02 98 56 18 67; sunelia@latlantique.fr; www.camping-bretagne-atlantique.com]** Exit Quimper on D34 sp Fouesnant, take D45 L to Fouesnant & after lge intersection with D44 look for next R to Mousterlin, site sp. Lge, hdg/mkd pitch, pt shd; htd wc; chem disp; mv service pnt; baby facs; shwrs inc; el pnts (6-10A) inc; gas; lndtte (inc dryer); shop; rest; snacks; bar; BBQ; playgrnd; htd pools (1 covrd); paddling pool; waterslide; sand beach 400m; watersports; spa, fitness rm & beauty treatments; lake fishing 200m; tennis; cycle hire; games rm; games area; golf 12km; internet; entmnt; TV rm; 70% statics; no dogs; phone; poss cr; adv bkg rec; ccard acc; red long stay; CCI. "Excel leisure facs; helpful, friendly staff; ideal for families." ♦ 23 Apr-12 Sep. € 39.00 (CChq acc) 2009*

See advertisement opposite

FOUESNANT *2F2* (5km SW Coastal) *47.85055, -4.03444* **Camping Kost-Ar-Moor, Route du Grande Large, 29170 Mousterlin [02 98 56 04 16; fax 02 98 56 65 02; kost-ar-moor@wanadoo.fr; www.camping-fouesnant.com]** S fr Fouesnant on D145, site sp. Lge, hdg/mkd pitch, pt shd; htd wc; chem disp; baby facs; fam bthrm; shwrs inc; el pnts (10A) €3.50; gas; Indtte; shop; tradsmn; snacks; bar; playgrnd; pools; waterpark; sand beach 400m; lake adj; cycle hire; games area; golf, horseriding nr; entmnt; wifi; TV rm; 10% statics; dog €2.50; phone; Eng spkn; adv bkg; quiet; ccard acc; CCI. "Vg clean site; helpful owner; gd for beach holiday & walking, cycling." ♦ 24 Apr-11 Sep. € 21.00 2009*

FOUESNANT *2F2* (6km SW Coastal) *47.84878, -4.03707* **Camping Le Grand Large, Route du Grand Large, Mousterlin, 29170 Fouesnant [02 98 56 04 06 or 04 66 73 97 39; fax 02 98 56 58 26; grandlarge@franceloc.fr; www.camping-franceloc.fr]** Site sp fr D145. Lge, hdg/mkd pitch, pt shd; wc; some serviced pitches; shwrs inc; el pnts (5A) inc; gas; Indtte; shop; tradsmn; rest; snacks; bar; playgrnd; htd pool; waterslide; sand beach adj; tennis; TV; watersports; cycle hire; internet; entmnt; cinema high ssn; 30% statics; dogs €3.50; poss cr; quiet; adv bkg ess Jul & Aug; red low ssn; CCI. "Excel, well-kept site." ♦ 31 Mar-16 Sep. € 37.00 2007*

FOUGERES *2E4* (1.5km E Urban) *48.3544, -1.1795* **Camp Municipal de Paron, Route de la Chapelle-Janson, 35300 Fougères [02 99 99 40 81; fax 02 99 94 27 94; campingmunicipal35@orange.fr or sports@fougeres.fr; www.ot-fougeres.fr]** Fr A84/E3 take junc 30 then ring rd E twd N12. Turn L at N12 & foll sp. Site on D17 sp R after Carrefour. Well sp on ring rd. Med, hdg pitch, hdstg, pt sl, pt shd; wc; serviced pitches; chem disp; shwrs inc; el pnts (5-10A) €3-3.50 (poss rev pol); Indtte; shops 1.5km; hypmkt 800m; tradsmn high ssn; rest 600m; playgrnd; pool 1km; tennis; horseriding adj; internet; dogs; adv bkg; quiet; ccard acc; red low ssn; CCI. "Well-kept site in pleasant parkland setting; popular NH; helpful warden; gd clean facs; gates clsd to vehicles 2200-0700; tours of 12thC castle; old town worth visit; Sat mkt." 2 May-30 Sep. € 13.50 2009*

I'm going to fill in some site report forms and post them off to the Club; we could win a ferry crossing – it's here on page 12.

FOUILLOUX, LE see Montguyon *7C2*

France

⊞ **FOURAS** *7A1* (Coastal) *45.99264, -1.08680* **Camp Municipal du Cadoret, Blvd de Chaterny, 17450 Fouras [05 46 82 19 19; campinglecadoret@mairie17.com; www.campings-fouras.com]** Fr Rochefort take N137, L onto D937 at Fouras, fork R at sp to site in 1km. At next rndabt take 3rd exit into Ave du Cadoret, then 1st R at next rndabt. Lge, hdg/mkd pitch, pt sl, pt shd; wc (some cont); chem disp; baby facs; shwrs inc; el pnts (6-10A) €2.90-4.70 (poss long lead req); gas; Indtte; shop 800m; rest; takeaway; bar; htd pool; paddling pool; sand beach adj; pool; fishing; boating; tennis 1km; golf 5km; games area; entment; 50% statics; dogs €2.30; bus to La Rochelle, Rochefort, ferry to Ile d'Aix; poss cr; adv bkg; red low ssn; CCI. "Popular, clean site; lge pitches; poorly lit except for wc block; ltd facs low ssn; a favourite." ♦ € 19.90 2009*

FOURAS *7A1* (1km E Rural) *45.99023, -1.05184* **Camping Domaine Les Charmilles, Route de l'Océan, 17450 Fouras [05 46 80 00 05 or 0820 20 23 27; fax 02 46 84 02 84 or 0820 20 19 49; charmilles17@wanadoo.fr; www.domainedescharmilles.com]** N fr Rochefort on N137, after 2km L onto D937. Site on L in 2km bef ent Fouras. Lge, hdg/mkd pitch, pt shd; htd wc; chem disp; mv service pnt; shwrs inc; el pnts (6A) €4; gas; Indtte; shop 1km; snacks; bar; BBQ (gas); playgrnd; htd, covrd pool; paddling pool; waterslide; sand beach 3km; cycle hire; entmnt; bus to beach high ssn; 20% statics; no dogs; poss cr; adv bkg; ccard acc; red long stay/low ssn; CCI. "Gd; some pitches tight for sm o'fits." ♦ 5 May-22 Sep. € 30.00 2007*

FOURAS *7A1* (3km NW Coastal) *46.00210, -1.11819* **Camp Municipal de la Fumée, Pointe de la Fumée, 17450 Fouras [05 46 84 26 77 or 05 46 84 60 11 (Mairie); fax 05 46 84 51 59; www.camping-fouras.com]** Fr N137, take D214E twd Fouras. Foll sps La Fumée/Ile d'Aix to end of peninsula. Ent on L immed in front of car park ent for ferry. Med, mkd pitch, pt shd; wc; chem disp; shwrs inc; el pnts (4-10A) €1.80-3.80; gas 3km; Indtte; shop & 3km; rest, bar 100m; snacks; pool 2km; sand beach; tennis 2km; fishing; 25% statics; dogs €1.70; phone; poss cr; Eng spkn; quiet; red long stay; CCI. "Great situation; clean site; sm pitches; friendly staff; excel facs; diff to manoeuvre lge o'fits; excel beaches; conv La Rochelle, Rochefort; ferry to Ile d'Aix; free NH for m'vans; gd." ♦ 27 Mar-25 Oct. € 8.80 2009*

FOURCHAMBAULT see Nevers *4H4*

FOURMIES see Hirson *3C4*

FRAISSE SUR AGOUT see Salvetat sur Agout, La *8F4*

FRANGY *9A3* (4km E Rural) *46.01060, 5.97610* **Camping Le Chamaloup, 74270 Contamine-Sarzin [04 50 77 88 28 or 06 72 80 09 84 (mob); fax 04 50 77 99 79; camping@chamaloup.com; www.chamaloup.com]** Exit A40 junc 11 onto D1508 (N508) dir Annecy, thro Frangy. Site sp on L in 10km. Med, hdg/mkd pitch, pt shd; htd wc; chem disp; serviced pitches; mv service pnt; baby facs; shwrs inc; el pnts (16A) €4; gas; Indtte; shop; tradsmn; snacks; bar; BBQ; htd pool; wifi; 20% statics; dogs €2; poss cr; Eng spkn; some noise fr bar music; adv bkg; ccard acc; CCI. "Friendly owners; rv & fish pond (fenced-off) on site." ♦ 1 May-15 Sep. € 22.00 2009*

FRASNOIS, LE *6H2* (Rural) *46.64095, 5.90584* **Camp Municipal Le Lac de Narlay, 39130 Le Frasnois [03 84 25 58 74 (Mairie)]** On N5 fr Champagnole dir St Laurent-en-Grandvaux turn R onto D75 at Pont-de-la-Chaux; cont to Le Frasnois, site sp in vill. Lge, pt sl, pt terr, pt shd; wc (some cont); chem disp (wc); shwrs inc; el pnts €3; Indry rm; shops 500m; tradsmn; snacks; playgrnd; lake sw adj; tennis; cycle hire; 5% statics; dogs; phone; poss cr; Eng spkn; CCI. "Site yourself warden calls each pm; only terr pitches have el pnts; Cascades du Hérisson & gd walks nrby." 15 May-15 Sep. € 10.00 2007*

FREJUS *10F4* (2.5km N Urban) *43.46290, 6.7257* **Camping Les Pins Parasols, 3360 Rue des Combattants d'Afrique du Nord, 83600 Fréjus [04 94 40 88 43; fax 04 94 40 81 99; lespinsparasols@wanadoo.fr; www.lespinsparasols.com]** Fr A8 exit junc 38 sp Fréjus cent. Fr E'bound dir foll Bagnols sp at 2 rndabts & Fréjus cent/Cais at 3rd. Fr W'bound dir foll Bagnols at 3 rndabts & Fréjus cent/Cais at 4th. Site on L in 500m. Lge, hdg/mkd pitch, terr, pt sl, pt shd, htd wc; chem disp; san facs on individual pitches; baby facs; shwrs inc; el pnts (6A) inc; gas; Indtte; shop; tradsmn; rest; snacks; bar; playgrnd; pool; paddling pool; waterslide; sand beach 6km; tennis; entmnt; TV rm; 30% statics; dogs €2.80; phone; adv bkg; quiet; Eng spkn; red low ssn; CCI. "Pleasant, family-run site; clean san facs; tractor to terr pitches; some lge pitches; excel." ♦ 3 Apr-25 Sep. € 27.30 2009*

See advertisement below

France

FREJUS *10F4* (5km SW Rural) *43.39890, 6.67531* **Camping Domaine de la Bergerie, Vallée-du-Fournel, Route du Col-du-Bougnon, 83520 Roquebrune-sur-Argens [04 98 11 45 45; fax 04 98 11 45 46; info@domainelabergerie.com; www.domainelabergerie.com]** On DN7 (N7) twd Fréjus, turn R onto D7 sp St Aygulf & Roquebrune-sur-Argens; after passing Roquebrune, site sp in approx 6km on R. V lge, hdg/mkd pitch, terr, pt sl, pt shd; wc; chem disp; sauna; some serviced pitches; baby facs; shwrs inc; el pnts (6A) inc (extra for 10A); gas; lndtte; supmkt; rest; snacks; bar; playgrnd; 2 pools (1 htd, covrd); paddling pool; waterslide; jacuzzi; lake fishing; sand beach 7km; tennis; games area; mini-farm; archery; wifi; entmnt; 70% statics in sep area; dogs €3.50-5; Eng spkn; adv bkg; quiet; ccard acc; CCI. "Well-organised site; entmnt/activities for all ages; early bkg ess for summer; excel." ♦
24 Apr-30 Sep. € 41.50 2009*

See advertisement above

FREJUS *10F4* (8km W Rural) *43.46890, 6.65981* **Camping Domaine J Bousquet (CC de F), Route de la Bouverie, 83520 Roquebrune-sur-Argens [04 94 45 42 51; fax 04 94 81 61 06; ccdf_bousquet@cegetel.net; www.campingclub.asso.fr]** Exit A8 at Puget-sur-Argens, onto DN7 (N7) dir Le Muy, R onto minor rd at rndabt in about 2km. Site on R after 'Goelia'. Lge, pt sl, shd; wc (cont); chem disp; baby facs; shwrs inc; el pnts (6A) inc; gas; shop; rest; bar; playgrnd; pool; sand beach 10km; entmnt; statics; dogs €2.10; poss cr; adv bkg; quiet but some rd & rlwy noise; CCI. ♦ 1 Jan-3 Nov. € 22.05 2007*

FREJUS *10F4* (8km W Rural) *43.44535, 6.65790* **Camping Le Moulin des Iscles, 83520 Roquebrune-sur-Argens [04 94 45 70 74; fax 04 94 45 46 09; moulin.iscles@wanadoo.fr; www.provence-campings.com/sttropez/moulin-des-iscles]** Twd Fréjus on DN7 (N7), turn R onto D7 to St Aygulf sp Roquebrune. Site on L after passing thro Roquebrune vill. Med, shd; wc (some cont); baby facs; shwrs inc; el pnts (6A) €2.70; lndtte; shop; rest; snacks; bar; playgrnd; sand beach 12km; games rm; internet; entmnt; TV; 10% statics; dogs €1.30; adv bkg; quiet; red low ssn/long stay; ccard acc. "Gd security; helpful owners; excel family site; clean, well-managed." ♦ 1 Apr-30 Sep. € 19.80 (3 persons) (CChq acc) 2008*

FREJUS *10F4* (8km W Rural) *43.47866, 6.63991* **Camping Leï Suves, Quartier du Blavet, 83520 Roquebrune-sur-Argens [04 94 45 43 95; fax 04 94 81 63 13; camping.lei.suves@wanadoo.fr; www.lei-suves.com]** Exit A8 junc 36 at Le Muy, thro Le Muy twd Fréjus on DN7 (N7). After 5km turn L (under a'route, not into Roquebrune-sur-Argens) at sp. Foll sp to camp 4km N of Roquebrune. Lge, mkd pitch, terr, pt shd; wc; chem disp; baby facs; shwrs inc; el pnts (6A) €4.50; gas; lndtte; shop; rest; snacks; bar; BBQ (gas only); playgrnd; htd pool; paddling pool; sand beach 15km; lake sw & fishing 3km; tennis; games rm; entmnt; excursions; wifi; 45% statics; dogs €3.50; phone; Eng spkn; adv bkg; quiet; ccard acc; red low ssn; CCI. "V nice location in pine forest; well-maintained, family-run site; facs clean; excel pool; some sm pitches; conv Côte d'Azur." ♦
3 Apr-15 Oct. € 38.50 2009*

See advertisement on next page

FREJUS *10F4* (10km W Rural) *43.45070, 6.63320* **Kawan Village Les Pêcheurs, Quartier Verseil, 83520 Roquebrune-sur-Argens [04 94 45 71 25; fax 04 94 81 65 13; info@camping-les-pecheurs.com; www.camping-les-pecheurs.com]** Exit A8 dir Le Muy, onto DN7 (N7) then D7 sp Roquebrune; camp 800m on L (bef bdge over Rv Argens) at ent to vill. Lge, hdg/mkd pitch, hdstg, pt shd; htd wc; chem disp; mv service pnt; baby facs; sauna; spa; jacuzzi; shwrs inc; el pnts (6-10A) €4.20-5.50; gas; lndtte; shop; rest; snacks; bar; BBQ (gas/elec); playgrnd; htd pool; sand beach 12km; lake sw, fishing, canoeing adj; spa & jacuzzi; tennis 2km; horseriding; cycle hire 1km; entmnt; wifi; TV rm; 45% statics; dogs €3.10; phone; Eng spkn; adv bkg; quiet; ccard acc; red low ssn/CCI. "Pleasant views; helpful staff; lovely site but getting tired & in need refurb (2007); most pitches no grass due use; some site rds/pitch access tight for lge outfits, OK with mover; popular with families high ssn; conv St Tropez, St Raphaël; gd walking, cycling." ♦ 1 Apr-30 Sep. € 36.20 (CChq acc) 2009*

⊞ **FREJUS** *10F4* (3km NW Rural) *43.46335, 6.7247* **Camping Le Fréjus, Route de Bagnols, 83600 Fréjus [04 94 19 94 60; fax 04 94 19 94 69; contact@lefrejus.com; www.lefrejus.com]** Exit A8 junc 38, at 1st rndabt turn L, then L at 2nd rndabt & L again at 3rd rndabt, Site on R in 200m. Lge, mkd pitch, pt sl, pt terr, pt shd; htd wc (some cont); chem disp; mv service pnt; baby facs; shwrs inc; el pnts (6A) inc; gas high ssn; Indtte; shop high ssn & 500m; tradsmn, rest & snacks high ssn; bar; playgrnd; htd pool; waterslide; sand beach 6km; tennis; games rm; entmnt; internet; 10% statics; dogs €4; site clsd 16 Dec-14 Jan; Eng spkn; adv bkg; quiet; ccard acc; red low ssn; CCI. "Ideal position for coast bet Cannes & St Tropez; lge pitches; pleasant, friendly staff; gd san facs; quiet low ssn." ♦ € 31.50 2009*

FREJUS *10F4* (4km NW) *43.46616, 6.72203* **Camping Village La Baume, Route de Bagnoles, Rue des Combattants d'Afrique du Nord, 83600 Fréjus [04 94 19 88 88; fax 04 94 19 83 50; reception@labaume-lapalmeraie.com; www.labaume-lapalmeraie.com]** Fr A8 exit junc 38 sp Fréjus cent. Fr E'bound dir foll Bagnols sp at 2 rndabts & Fréjus cent/Cais at 3rd. Fr W'bound dir foll Bagnols at 3 rndabts & Fréjus cent/Cais at 4th. Site on L in 300m. V lge, pt sl, pt shd; htd wc; shwrs; el pnts (6A) inc; gas; Indtte; shop; rest; snacks; bar; playgrnd; 5 pools (1 htd, 2 covrd); sand beach 5km; waterslide; tennis; horseriding; entmnt; many tour ops statics; dogs €4; adv bkg ess Jul/Aug; quiet (except N part of site adj to m'way); 15% red low ssn. ♦ 1 Apr-30 Sep. € 38.00 (3 persons) 2006*

FREJUS *10F4* (4km NW Coastal) *43.44545, 6.72683* **Yelloh! Domaine du Colombier, 1052 Rue des Combattants d'Afrique du Nord, 83600 Fréjus [04 94 51 56 01 or 04 94 51 52 38 (LS); fax 04 94 51 55 57; info@clubcolombier.com; www.clubcolombier.com or www.yellohvillage.com]** Fr E (Nice) on A8 exit junc 38 sp Fréjus. Go strt over 3 rndabts, turn R at 4th rndabt, then R again at next rndabt, site on R. Fr W (Aix-en-Provence) exit A8 junc 38 & turn R at 1st rndabt, then L at intersection. Site on L. Lge, hdg/mkd pitch, hdstg, terr, pt shd; htd wc (some cont); chem disp; mv service pnt; 30% serviced pitches; baby facs; shwrs inc; el pnts (16A) inc; gas; Indtte; supmkt; tradsmn; rest; snacks; bar; BBQ (elec); playgrnd; htd pool & waterslides; sand beach 4km; tennis; sports area; games rm; excursions; entmnt high ssn; wifi; TV rm; 85% statics/tour ops; dogs €4; poss cr; Eng spkn; adv bkg; quiet but poss noise fr disco; ccard acc; red low ssn; CCI. "Well-organised, clean site in pine forest with exotic trees; excel." ♦ 1 Apr-11 Oct. € 49.00 (3 persons) 2008*

We can fill in site report forms on the Club's website – www.caravanclub.co.uk/europereport

FREJUS *10F4* (5km NW Rural) *43.45904, 6.69324* **Camping Caravaning des Aubrèdes, 408 Chemin des Aubrèdes, 83480 Puget-sur-Argens [04 94 45 51 46; fax 04 94 45 28 92; campingaubredes@wanadoo.fr; www.campingaubredes.com]** Sp on R of DN7 (N7) W fr Fréjus. Fr A8 exit junc 37 dir Fréjus/Puget-sur-Argens. Lge, mkd pitch, pt sl, pt shd; wc (some cont); chem disp; mv service pnt; shwrs inc; el pnts (8A) €4.50; gas; lndtte; shop; tradsmn; rest, snacks, bar high ssn; playgrnd; pool; sand beach 5km; tennis; games rm; entmnt; 30% statics; dogs €2; poss cr; Eng spkn; adv bkg rec high ssn; quiet; ccard acc; red long stay/low ssn; CCI. "Excel, esp low ssn; conv m'way." 1 May-15 Sep. € 25.00 2007*

FREJUS *10F4* (6km NW Rural) *43.46944, 6.67805* **Camping La Bastiane, 1056 Chemin des Suvières, 83480 Puget-sur-Argens [04 94 55 55 94; fax 04 94 55 55 93; info@labastiane.com; www.labastiane.com]** Exit A8 at junc 37 Puget/Fréjus. At DN7 (N7) turn R dir Le Muy & in 1km turn R immed after 2nd bdge. Foll sp to site. Fr DN7 turn L at traff lts in Puget, site is 2km N of Puget. Lge, hdg/mkd pitch, pt sl, shd; wc; chem disp; baby facs; fam bthrm; shwrs inc; el pnts (6A) inc; lndtte; shop; tradsmn; rest; snacks; bar; BBQ (elec); playgrnd; htd pool; paddling pool; sand beach 7km; watersports; tennis; cycle hire; games area; games rm; cinema; disco; entmnt; internet; TV; car wash area; 40% statics; dogs €4; phone; poss cr; Eng spkn; adv bkg; quiet; ccard acc; red long stay/low ssn/CCI. "Excel; family-run, friendly site." ♦ 26 Mar-17 Oct. € 38.50 2008*

FREJUS *10F4* (6km NW Rural) **Parc Saint James Oasis, Route de la Bouverie, 83480 Puget-sur-Argens [04 98 11 85 60; fax 04 98 11 85 79; info@camping-parcsaintjames.com; www.camping-parcsaintjames.com]** Exit A8 at junc 37 for Puget-sur-Argens onto DN7 (N7) dir Le Muy, in 2.5km turn R into Rte de la Bouverie, site in 1km on R. Lge, pt shd; wc; shwrs; el pnts; gas; lndtte; shop; tradsmn; rest; snacks; bar; htd pool; beach 7km; tennis; games area; entmnt; all statics; phone; dogs €5; adv bkg. 3 Apr-25 Sep. 2009*

See advertisement on page 567

FREJUS *10F4* (7km NW Rural) *43.4835, 6.7190* **Camping La Pierre Verte, Route de Bagnols-en-Forêt, 83600 Fréjus [04 94 40 88 30; fax 04 94 40 75 41; info@campinglapierreverte.com; www.campinglapierreverte.com]** Exit A8 junc 38 onto D4 dir Bagnols-en-Forêt. Site N of military camp. Lge, mkd pitch, hdstg, pt sl, terr, pt shd; wc; chem disp; baby facs; fam bthrm; shwrs inc; el pnts (6A) €4; gas; lndtte; shop; tradsmn; rest; bar; snacks; no BBQ; htd pool; waterslide; sand beach 8km; tennis; games area; cycle hire; games rm; entmnt; internet; TV rm; 50% statics; dogs €4; phone; adv bkg; quiet; Eng spkn; ccard acc; red long stay/low ssn; CCI. "Well-situated for local attractions; vg." ♦ 4 Apr-27 Sep. € 28.00 2008*

FRELAND see Kaysersberg *6F3*

FRENEUSE see Bonnières sur Seine *3D2*

FRESNAY SUR SARTHE *4E1* (Rural) *48.28297, 0.0158* **Camp Municipal Le Sans Souci, Allée André Chevalier, Ave Victor Hugo, 72130 Fresnay-sur-Sarthe [02 43 97 32 87; fax 02 43 33 75 72; camping-fresney@wanadoo.fr]** Fr Alençon S on D338 (N1380; in 14km at La Hutte turn R on D310 to Fresnay; sp in town on traff lts bef bdge; fr Beaumont-sur-Sarthe NW on D39 to Fresnay. Med, hdg/mkd pitch, pt sl, terr, pt shd; wc; chem disp; shwrs; el pnts (6A) inc (poss rev pol); lndtte; shops high ssn & 500m; htd pool adj; rv adj; fishing; canoe hire; cycle hire; entmnt; dogs €1.05; Eng spkn; adv bkg; quiet; CCI. "V pleasant, clean site adj to Rv Sarthe; gd rvside pitches; facs poss stretched high ssn; office opens 1600; gd cycling; excel value; vg." 1 Apr-30 Sep. € 12.20 2009*

FRETEVAL see Morée *4F2*

FRONCLES BUXIERES *6E1* (500m N Urban) *48.3004, 5.1476* **Camp Municipal Les Deux Ponts, Rue des Ponts, 52320 Froncles-Buxières [03 25 02 38 35 or 03 25 02 31 21 (Mairie); fax 03 25 02 09 80]** Fr Chaumont take N67 twd Joinville, ignore sp to Vouécourt but take R turn E on D253 sp Froncles. Site sp fr main rd. Sm, hdg pitch, pt shd; wc (some cont); chem disp (wc); shwrs; el pnts (6A) inc; shops in vill; rv fishing; dogs €0.75; adv bkg; quiet. "Pleasant situation; facs clean; friendly; warden calls pm; gd." 15 Mar-15 Oct. € 10.60 2009*

FRONTIGNAN *10F1* (5km NE Urban) *43.49173, 3.77932* **Camping L'Europe, 31 Route de Frontignan, 34110 Vic-la-Gardiole [04 67 78 11 50; www.campingleurope.com or www.village-center.com]** Exit A9 junc 32 & foll sp D612 dir Sète; in 10km turn L onto D14 to Vic-la-Gardiole. Lge, pt shd; wc; shwrs inc; el pnts (6A) inc; lndtte; shop; rest; takeaway; bar; playgrnd; 3 pools; aqua gym; beach 2km; archery; games area; games rm; internet; dogs €3; red low ssn. 9 Jun-9 Sep. € 32.00 2007*

⊞ **FRONTIGNAN** *10F1* (6km NE Rural) *43.50038, 3.78683* **Camping Le Clos Fleuri, Route de la Mer, 34110 Vic-la-Gardiole [04 67 78 15 68; fax 04 67 78 77 62; reception@camping-clos-fleuri.fr; www.camping-clos-fleuri.fr]** Fr A9 dir Montpellier exit junc 33 for D600 twd Sète. At Sète take D612 (N112) for 13km then R into D114 sp Vic-la-Gardiole. Ignore 1st turn & go round vill & foll sp. Med, hdg/mkd pitch, shd; wc; chem disp; mv service pnt; shwrs inc; el pnts (3-6A) €3-3.80; lndtte; shops in ssn or 1km; rest; snacks; bar; htd pool; shgl beach 2km; cycle hire; 30% statics; dogs €2.80; phone adj; poss cr; adv bkg; quiet but noise fr bar; CCI. "Friendly but not suitable for sm children or lge o'fits; san facs tired but clean; chem disp facs poor; sheltered fr Mistral." € 17.50 (3 persons) 2008*

France

Rental of
Mobile Hom
and Chalets

FRONTIGNAN *10F1* (3.5km E Coastal) *43.44563, 3.79815* **Camping Club Le Soleil, 60 Ave d'Ingrill, 34110 Frontignan-Plage [04 67 43 02 02; fax 04 67 53 34 69; campingdusoleil@wanadoo.fr; www.logassist.fr/soleil]** Fr A9/E15 exit junc 32 at St Jean-de-Védas onto D612 & foll sp Sète; in 8km turn L onto D114 sp Vic-la-Gardiole; cross rlwy & Canal du Rhône; pass Les Aresquiers-Plages & then turn L in 500m, site sp on L in 500m. Fr N on D613 (N113), take D600 to Sète, then D612 to Frontignan-Plage. Sm, hdg pitch, hdstg, pt shd; wc; chem disp; mv service pnt; baby facs; shwrs inc; el pnts (6A) €6; Indtte; sm supmkt adj; rest; snacks; bar; BBQ (gas); playgrnd; htd pool; paddling pool; beach 100m; cycle hire; games rm; entmnt; wifi; 50% statics; dogs €5; dog shwr; phone; bus; poss cr; Eng spkn; red low ssn; CCI. "Sheltered fr wind; gd, clean san facs; gates locked 2300-0800; vg." ♦
3 Apr-15 Sep. € 32.00 2009*

FRONTIGNAN *10F1* (1km S Coastal) *43.42998, 3.75968* **Camping Méditerranée, 11 Ave des Vacances, Quartier L'Entrée, 34110 Frontignan-Plage [tel/fax 04 67 48 12 32 or 04 42 58 11 19 (LS)]** 3km fr Sète on D612 to Montpellier, turn R at rlwy bdge, in approx 1km L at x-rds to site. Or on D129 fr Frontignan to Frontignan-Plage site on R 100m past reclamation area. Med, unshd; wc; shwrs inc; el pnts (6A) €3.50; Indtte; shop; rest; snacks; bar; playgrnd; sand beach 100m; tennis; lake 500m; games area; entmnt; dogs €1.50; bus adj; adv bkg rec high ssn; quiet but some rlwy & rd noise; red low ssn. 30 Mar-29 Sep. € 16.00 (3 persons)
2009*

FRONTIGNAN *10F1* (6km S Coastal) *43.44970, 3.80540* **Camping Les Tamaris, 140 Ave d'Ingril, 34110 Frontignan-Plage [04 67 43 44 77 or 04 78 04 67 92 (LS); fax 04 67 18 97 90; les-tamaris@wanadoo.fr; www.les-tamaris.fr]** Fr A9/E15 exit junc 32 St Jean-de-Védas & foll sp Sète. At next rndbt foll sp Sète N112. After approx 8km turn L sp Vic-la-Gardiole onto D114. Cross rlwy & Canal du Rhône. Pass Les Aresquiers-Plages & turn L in 500m, site sp on L in 500m. Fr N on D613 (N113), take N300 to Sète; then N112 to Frontignan-Plage. Lge, hdg pitch, pt shd; wc (some cont); chem disp; mv service pnt; baby facs; shwrs inc; el pnts (10A) inc (pos rev pol); Indtte; shop; tradsmn; rest; snacks; bar; BBQ; playgrnd; pool; paddling pool; sand beach adj; watersports; lake fishing; cycle hire; horseriding nrby; archery; weights rm; entmnt; wifi; games/TV rm; many statics; dogs €3; phone; poss cr; adv bkg; quiet; ccard acc; red long stay/low ssn; CCI. "Excel, popular, family-run site; direct access to beach; excel for families; friendly, helpful staff; gd clean san facs; excel pool; different sized pitches, some sm & poss tight for lge o'fits; lovely town; mkt Thu & Sat am." ♦ 2 Apr-24 Sep. € 43.00 (CChq acc) ABS - C11 2009*

See advertisement opposite

FUILLA see Vernet les Bains *8G4*

FUMEL *7D3* (2km E Rural) *44.48929, 0.99704* **Camping de Condat/Les Catalpas, Route de Cahors, 47500 Fumel [05 53 71 11 99 or 06 30 24 20 04; fax 05 53 71 36 69; les-catalpas@wanadoo.fr; www.les-catalpas.com]** Take D811 fr Fumel E twd Cahors. Clearly sp after Condat. Med, mkd pitch, hdstg, pt sl, pt shd; htd wc; chem disp (wc); mv service pnt; shwrs inc; el pnts (10A) €2; Indtte; shops 1km; rest in vill; snacks; BBQ; playgrnd; pool; fishing adj; entmnt high ssn; wifi; 15% statics; dogs; Eng spkn; adv bkg; red low ssn; CCI. "Helpful, friendly owner." ♦
1 Apr-31 Oct. € 17.00 2009*

⊞ **FUMEL** *7D3* (4km E Rural) **Aire Naturelle Le Valenty (Baillargues), 46700 Soturac [05 65 36 59 50 or 06 72 57 69 80 (mob); campingdevalenty@gmail.com; http://members.lycos.nl/brightday]** Fr Fumel take D811 dir Cahors. Thro Soturac, site immed on L outside vill. Sm, terr, pt shd; wc; shwrs inc; el pnts (4-10A) €2.50; gas 3km; Indtte; shops, snacks, bar 2.5km; tradsmn; rest 1km; playgrnd; pool; minigolf; pony rides; games rm; 20% statics; dogs €1; bus 200m; Eng spkn; adv bkg; quiet; CCI. "Delightful CL-type site; helpful owners; tranquil but secure; organic produce for sale." € 13.00 2007*

FUMEL *7D3* (8km E Rural) *44.49810, 1.06670* **Camping Le Ch'Timi, La Roque, 46700 Touzac [05 65 36 52 36; fax 05 65 36 53 23; info@campinglechtimi.com; www.campinglechtimi.com]** Fr N20-E9 at Cahors, turn R at rndabt onto D811 sp Villeneuve-sur-Lot. In Duravel, take 3rd exit at rndabt, sp Vire-sur-Lot & foll rd to L. After about 3km, cross bdge & turn R at rndabt, sp Touzac. Site on R on rvside, on hill, in about 2km, well sp. Med, mkd pitch, pt sl, pt shd; wc; baby facs; shwrs inc, chem disp; el pnts (6A) inc; gas; Indtte; shop & 700m; tradsmn; rest; snacks; bar; BBQ (charcoal/gas); playgrnd; pool; paddling pool; canoeing; fishing 100m; cycle hire; tennis; archery; games area; entmnt; wifi; games/TV rm; 20% statics; dogs €1.75; poss cr; Eng spkn; adv bkg; quiet; ccard acc; red low ssn; CCI. "Gd position; Dutch owners; clean facs, ltd low ssn; gd local rests; wine-tasting tours; mkt Puy l'Evêque Tue." 1 Apr-30 Sep. € 20.90 ABS - D05 2009*

FUMEL *7D3* (10km E Rural) *44.48023, 1.05204* **Camping Le Clos Bouyssac, 46700 Touzac [05 65 36 52 21; fax 05 65 24 68 51; camping.leclosbouyssac@wanadoo.fr; www.campingbytheriver.eu]** Fr Fumel on D911/D811, turn R to Touzac. Cross bdge over Rv Lot, turn R in vill to site in 2km on rvside. Site sp. Med, mkd pitch, terr, shd; wc; chem disp; mv service pnt; baby facs; shwrs inc; el pnts (10A) €3.50; gas; Indtte; shop 8km; snacks; bar; BBQ; playgrnd; pool; paddling pool; fishing; canoe hire; games area; games rm; entmnt; wifi; TV rm; 15% statics; dogs €1.75; phone; poss cr; Eng spkn; adv bkg; quiet; ccard acc; red low ssn/CCI. "Pleasant, tranquil site on S bank of Rv Lot; friendly, welcoming British/Dutch owners; recent refurbs; gd, clean facs; plenty of activities high ssn, inc wine-tasting; vg cycling; guided walks; vg wine area; gd." 1 Apr-30 Sep. € 15.00
2009*

See advertisement on next page

France

FUTEAU see Clermont en Argonne *5D1*

GABARRET *8E2* (E Rural) *43.98250, 0.01562* **Camp Municipal La Chêneraie, 40310 Gabarret [05 58 44 92 62; fax 05 58 44 35 38]** Fr cent of vill take D656 dir Mézin & Nérac. After 300m turn R onto C35, site in 300m on R. Look for bright orange site sp. Sm, hdg pitch, pt sl, pt shd; htd wc; chem disp; shwrs inc; el pnts (10A) €1.70; Indtte; shops, rest, bar 500m; playgrnd; htd pool; adv bkg ess Jul/Aug; quiet; CCI. ♦ 1 Mar-31 Oct. € 8.94 2007*

GACE *4E1* (200m E Urban) *48.79475, 0.29926* **Camp Municipal Le Pressoir, 61230 Gacé [02 33 35 50 24 or 02 33 35 50 18; fax 02 33 35 92 82; ville.gace@wanadoo.fr]** Exit A28 junc 16 onto D932/D438; turn off D438 (N138) E opp Intermarché; foll sp. Sm, hdg/mkd pitch, sl, pt shd; wc; chem disp (wc); mv service pnt in vill; shwrs inc; el pnts inc (poss long lead req); Indry rm; supmkt & rest 100m; playgrnd; rv 500m; poss cr; quiet. "Clean, well-managed site; most pitches gd size; warden calls am & pm; rec early arrival; sm pitches poss diff for lge o'fits; ltd el pnts (2006); conv NH fr A28." 1 Jun-1 Sep. € 9.00 2009*

GACILLY, LA *2F3* (200m E Rural) *47.76325, -2.12544* **FFCC Camp Municipal Le Bout du Pont, 35550 Sixt-sur-Aff [02 99 08 10 59 or 02 99 08 10 18 (Mairie); fax 02 99 08 25 38; mairie.lagacilly@wanadoo.fr]** On ent La Gacilly exit rv bdge onto D777 dir Sixt-sur-Aff. Site on L outside town sp. Well sp fr town cent. Sm, mkd pitch, pt shd; wc; mv service pnt; shwrs inc; el pnts (6A) €1.50; shops 500m; tradsmn; rests 200m; playgrnd; rv adj; Eng spkn; quiet. "V pretty town; vg facs; easy walk to town; poss unreliable opening dates." ♦ 1 Jun-31 Aug. € 7.50 2006*

GAILLAC *8E4* (8km N Rural) *43.98373, 1.91432* **Camp Municipal au Village, Route de Cordes, 81140 Cahuzac-sur-Vère [05 63 33 91 94 or 05 63 33 90 18 (Mairie); fax 05 63 33 94 03]** Fr Gaillac, take D922 N twd Cordes. Site on L of rd, clearly sp thro vill of Cahuzac. Sm, pt sl, pt shd; wc; shwrs; el pnts (3A) €2.40 (rev pol); shops, rest, snacks, bar nr; playgrnd; pool; tennis; games area; cycle hire; phone; adv bkg; quiet. "Gd, clean site; call warden on arr; barrier at entry - poss to remove post to ease entry." 1 Jun-30 Sep. € 8.25 2007*

GAILLAC *8E4* (5km E Urban) *43.90929, 1.98311* **Camping Les Pommiers, Aigueleze, 81600 Rivières [05 63 33 02 49; info@camping-lespommiers.com; www.camping-lespommiers.com]** Fr Gaillac on D988 dir Albi to Rivières. Or fr Albi W on N88/D988. Site (& adj 'Parc des Loisirs') well sp fr D988. Med, hdg/mkd pitch, hdstg, pt shd; wc; chem disp (wc); baby facs; shwrs inc; el pnts (8A) €3; Indtte; sm shop Jul/Aug; tradsmn; playgrnd; pool nrby; canoe & cycle hire 150m; dogs €1.50; phone; Eng spkn; quiet; red low ssn/long stay. "Visit Albi by sightseeing boat on Rv Tarn or by train; vg." ♦ 3 May-30 Sep. € 13.00 2008*

GAILLAC *8E4* (2km W Urban) *43.89674, 1.88522* **FFCC Camping des Sources, 9 Rue Guynemer, 81600 Gaillac [05 63 57 18 30; fax 05 49 52 28 58]** Exit A68 junc 9 onto D999 then in 3.5km at rndabt turn onto D968 dir Gaillac. In 100m turn R immed past Leclerc petrol stn, then L by Aldi. Site 200m on R, well sp fr town cent. Med, hdg/mkd pitch, hdstg, terr, unshd; htd wc; chem disp; mv service pnt; chem disp (wc); baby facs; shwrs inc; el pnts (10A) inc; gas 300m; Indtte; shop 500m; tradsmn; snacks; bar; playgrnd; pool; entmnt; TV; 10% statics; dogs €1; quiet; ccard acc (over €15); CCI. "Helpful staff; peaceful, clean, tidy site; gd, modern san facs; purpose-made dog-walk area; steep walk to recep & bar but san facs at pitch level; gd touring base Tarn & Albi region & circular tour Bastides; cent of wine area; not suitable lge o'fits; gd." ♦ 1 Apr-31 Oct. € 20.00 2007*

GALLARGUES LE MONTUEUX see Lunel *10E2*

GAMACHES *3B2* (1km NW Rural) *49.99397, 1.54366* **Camping Les Marguerites, Rue Antonin Gombert, 80220 Gamaches [tel/fax 03 22 30 89 51; camping.les.marguerites@wanadoo.fr]** A28 exit 5 onto D1015 dir Eu & Le Treport to Gamaches in 8km. Site sp fr town, 200m fr stadium, Lge, mkd pitch, hdstg, pt shd; wc (cont); chem disp; shwrs inc; el pnts (6-10A) €5-6.50; Indtte; tradsmn; rest; snacks; bar; BBQ; playgrnd; pool; paddling pool; rv adj; games area; 75% statics; dogs; poss cr; quiet; adv bkg; red long stay/CCI. "Nr forest of Eu, & Somme coast; gd fishing, riding." ♦ 15 Mar-15 Sep. € 15.00 2006*

GANGES *10E1* (2km S Rural) *43.84685, 3.70488* **Camping Le Val d'Hérault, 34190 Brissac [04 67 73 72 29; fax 04 67 73 30 81; info@camping-levaldherault.com; www.camping-levaldherault.com]** Fr D999 at Ganges take D4 S to Brissac; on D4 by rv. Med, hdg/mkd pitch, pt sl, shd; wc; chem disp; shwrs inc; el pnts (6A) €4.10; gas; Indtte; tradsmn; rest; snacks; bar; playgrnd; htd pool; rv beach 250m; canoeing; games area; wifi; 60% statics; dogs €2.20; poss cr; quiet; red low ssn; CCI. "Conv Hérault Gorge; unsuitable red mobility due steps to san facs; vg."
15 Mar-31 Oct. € 19.90 2008*

GANNAT *9A1* (7km N Rural) *46.16588, 3.18975* **Camp Municipal Champ de la Sioule, Route de Chantelle, 03800 Jenzat [04 70 56 86 35 or 04 70 56 81 77 (Mairie); fax 04 70 56 85 38; mairie-jenzat@pays-allier.com]** D2009 (N9) N fr Gannat for 4.5km, turn L onto D42, site in 3km in Jenzat on R just after rv bdge. Med, pt shd; wc; shwrs inc; el pnts (6-10) €1.90-2.95; Indtte; shops 250m; playgrnd; rv sw adj; Eng spkn; spotless facs; quiet; CCI. "Pleasant site on rv bank; helpful warden; clean facs, poss stretched high ssn; muddy after heavy rain." ♦ 19 Apr-21 Sep. € 8.60 2009*

GANNAT *9A1* (1km SW Rural) *46.09106, 3.19385* **Camp Municipal Le Mont Libre, 10 Route de la Bâtisse, 03800 Gannat [04 70 90 12 16 or 06 73 86 04 95 (mob); fax 04 70 90 12 16; camping.gannat@wanadoo.fr; www.bassin-gannat.com]** App Gannat fr S on D2009 (N9); at rndabt just after town name sp, turn L for 150m. Turn R (stadium on R) for 700m. Turn L uphill for 200m, turn R to site. Site sp. Med, pt sl, terr, hdstg, pt shd; wc; chem disp; mv service pnt; el pnts (10A) €2.40; Indtte; shop & 500m, supmkt 1km; tradsmn; playgrnd; sm pool; rv 5km; games area; games/TV rm; some statics; dogs; no o'fits over 5m; poss cr; adv bkg; quiet; ccard acc. "Pretty, well-kept site; gd sized pitches; helpful warden; spotless facs, but poss tired end of ssn; grnd soft after heavy rain; pleasant town; popular, busy NH." ♦ 1 Apr-31 Oct. € 10.00 2009*

GANNAT *9A1* (10km W Rural) *46.10880, 3.07348* **Camp Municipal Les Nières, 03450 Ebreuil [04 70 90 70 60 or 04 70 90 71 33 (Mairie); fax 04 70 90 74 90; mairie-ebreuil@wanadoo.fr]** Site 1km SW of Ebreuil, sp fr D915. Sm, shd; wc (cont); chem disp; shwrs; el pnts (4-8A) €1.95-2.80; Indtte; shops 1km; snacks; playgrnd; fishing; access to rv; quiet. "Nice setting; san facs dated but clean, poss stretched high ssn; warden present 0700-0800 only low ssn; sh walk into vill." 1 Jun-15 Sep. € 8.10 2009*

GANNAT *9A1* (10km W Rural) *46.10838, 3.07347* **Camping La Filature de la Sioule, Route de Chouvigny, 03450 Ebreuil [04 70 90 72 01; camping.filature@aliceadsl.fr; www.campingfilature.com]** Fr A71 exit 12 (avoid 12.1); foll sp to Ebreuil N 500m, then W for 5km thro vill. Turn W onto D915 dir Chouvigny, site in 1km. Med, hdg/mkd pitch, pt shd; wc (some cont); chem disp; mv service pnt 800m; baby facs; shwrs inc; el pnts (6A) €3.50; gas; Indtte; shop; tradsmn; snacks; bar; BBQ; playgrnd; canoes; trout-fishing; tennis 800m; cycle hire; table tennis; horseriding; TV rm; some statics; dogs free; Eng spkn; adv bkg; v quiet; ccard acc; red long stay/low ssn; CCI. "Peaceful, pleasant site in orchard; lge pitches; helpful British owners; clean facs, ltd low ssn; vg value food high ssn (gd home cooking); vg walking area; conv A71." ♦ 31 Mar-1 Oct. € 18.00 2009*

See advertisement below

GAP *9D3* (1.5km N Rural) *44.58030, 6.08270* **Camping Alpes-Dauphiné, Route Napoléon, 05000 Gap [04 92 51 29 95; fax 04 92 53 58 42; info@alpesdauphine.com; www.alpesdauphine.com]** On N85, sp. Med, mkd pitch, some hdstg, pt sl, terr, pt shd; htd wc; chem disp; mv service pnt; baby facs; shwrs inc; el pnts (6A) €3; gas; Indtte; shop; tradsmn; vg rest; snacks; bar; playgrnd; htd pool; paddling pool; games area; wifi; sat TV; 20% statics; dogs €2.10; phone; poss cr; Eng spkn; adv bkg rec high ssn; quiet; ccard acc; red low ssn; CCI. "M'vans need levellers; pleasant site with views; modern san facs; gd touring base; conv NH." ♦ 1 Apr-1 Nov. € 18.70 (CChq acc) 2008*

GAP *9D3* (10km S Rural) *44.45708, 6.04785* **Camp Municipal Le Chêne, Route de Marseille, 05130 Tallard [04 92 54 13 31 or 04 92 54 10 14 (Mairie); fax 04 92 54 00 81; mairie.tallard@wanadoo.fr]** Fr S take N85 twds Gap; turn R at traff lts onto D942; site on R after 3km. Fr Gap take N85 S; turn L at traff lts, D942; site on R 3km. Med, mkd pitch, hdstg, sl, terr, pt shd; wc (some cont); shwrs inc; el pnts (6A) €4; Indtte; shop 2km; rest; bar; playgrnd; htd pool; tennis; BBQ; entmnts; phone; dogs; adv bkg; CCI. "Poss unsuitable for lgs o'fits, sm pitches." 1 Jun-15 Sep. 2008*

GAP *9D3* (8km SW Rural) *44.49914, 6.02901* **Camping Les Bonnets, Le Haut-du-Village, 05000 Neffes [04 92 57 93 89 or 06 88 73 13 59; camping.les.bonnets@wanadoo.fr; www.camping-les-bonnets.com]** N85 SW fr Gap, turn R onto D46, site sp 1km fr vill. Med, mkd pitch, pt shd; htd wc; baby facs; shwrs; el pnts (6-10A) €3.30-4; Indtte; shop; supmkt 5km; rest, bar 1km; playgrnd; pool; fishing 3km; games area; entmnt; TV rm; some statics; dogs €1.50; quiet. "Well-kept farm site in beautiful area; excel pool; friendly owner." 1 Apr-30 Sep. € 13.50 2009*

GARDONNE see Bergerac *7C3*

GASSIN see St Tropez *10F4*

GASTES *7D1* (N Rural) *44.32905, -1.14603* **FFCC Camping Les Prés Verts, Ave du Lac, 40160 Gastes [tel/fax 05 58 09 74 11; camping@presverts.net; www.presverts.net]** S fr Bordeaux on N10 exit junc 17 & turn W on D43 to Parentis-en-Born & foll D652 to Gastes; site sp in vill. Med, shd; wc; shwrs inc; el pnts (10A) €2.95; gas; Indtte; shop; rest; snacks; bar; playgrnd; htd pool; lake sw; watersports; fishing; cycle hire; tennis; 99% statics; dogs €2; adv bkg; quiet; CCI. "Gd walking; important ecological site; 2 touring pitches only." 1 Mar-30 Nov. € 15.00 2007*

GASTES *7D1* (3km SW Rural) *44.31331, -1.16856* **Camping La Réserve, 1229 Ave Félix Ducourneau, 40160 Gastes [05 58 09 74 79 or 05 58 09 79 23; fax 05 58 09 78 71; lareserve@siblu.fr; www.siblu.com/lareserve]** At traff lts in cent Parentis-en-Born, turn L sp Pontenx & Gastes on D652. After 3km turn R dir Gastes, Ste Eulalie & Mimizan-Plage. Cont onto rndabt & take 2nd exit D652, then turn immed R sp La Réserve. Site sp. V lge, pt shd; wc; chem disp; shwrs inc; el pnts (6A) inc; gas; Indtte; rest; snacks; bar; shop; BBQ (gas only); playgrnd; pools (1 htd, covrd); waterslide; lake sw & private beach adj; watersports high ssn; windsurfing; cycle hire; tennis; games area; archery; wifi; entmnt; 70% statics; no dogs; Eng spkn; adv bkg ess high ssn; ccard acc; red low ssn; CCI. "Situated in pine forest & by lakeside; lge pitches; watersports & sailing school avail; children's club inc in site fee." ♦ 25 Apr-26 Sep. € 70.00 2009*

GAUDONVILLE see St Clar *8E3*

GAUGEAC see Monpazier *7D3*

GAVARNIE *8G2* (2km N Rural) *42.75896, 0.00069* **Camping Le Pain de Sucre, 65120 Gavarnie [tel/fax 05 62 92 47 55 or 06 75 30 64 22 (mob); info@camping-gavarnie.com; www.camping-gavarnie.com]** N of Gavarnie, across rv by sm bdge; clearly visible & sp fr rd. Med, pt shd; wc; mv service pnt; shwrs inc; el pnts (6-10A) €4.15-6.25 (long lead poss req); Indtte; shops, rest, snacks, bar 3km; BBQ; playgrnd; dogs €1.65; quiet; ccard acc. "Gd base for walking; gd facs; access to national park; vg." 1 Jun-30 Sep & 15 Dec-15 Apr. € 12.20 2009*

GEMAINGOUTTE see St Die *6E3*

GEMOZAC *7B2* (400m W) *45.56825, -0.68086* **Camp Municipal, Place de Champ de Foire, 17260 Gémozac [05 46 94 50 16; fax 05 46 94 16 25]** Exit A10 junc 36 (or turn W off off N137) onto D732 sp Gémozac. In 7km foll site sp. Turn L immed after Elan/Renault garage at end of vill. Sm, mkd pitch, pt shd; wc; chem disp; mv service pnt adj; baby facs; shwrs inc; el pnts (10A) inc (poss rev pol); Indtte; shop, pizzeria & snacks 500m; tradsmn; rest & bar 100m; BBQ; htd pool adj; dogs; adv bkg; Eng spkn; phone in vill; ccard not acc; quiet; CCI. "Excel site; pool free to campers; pleasant sm town; gate clsd 1300-1600; no twin-axles." 15 Jun-2 Sep. € 12.45 2006*

GENETS see Avranches *2E4*

GENNES *4G1* (Rural) *47.34239, -0.22966* **Camping Le Bord de Loire, Rue des Cadets-de-Saumur, 49350 Gennes [02 41 38 04 67 or 02 41 38 07 30; fax 02 41 38 07 12; auborddeloire@free.fr; www.camping-auborddeloire.com]** At Rv Loire bdge cross S to Gennes on D751B. Site 200m on L. Ent to site thro bus terminus/car park on ent to Gennes. Med, pt sl, pt shd; wc (some cont); chem disp; shwrs inc; el pnts (10A) €2.80; Indtte; shop in vill; snacks; bar; BBQ; shop in vill; tradsmn; snacks; playgrnd; htd pool in vill; entmnt; 2% statics; dogs €0.80; rd noise; CCI. "Delightful, relaxing, well-maintained site; excel san facs; vg." 1 May-30 Sep. € 8.30 2009*

GERARDMER See also sites listed under Corcieux, Granges-sur-Vologne, La Bresse and Le Tholy.

⊞ **GERARDMER** *6F3* (3km E Rural) *48.07826, 6.94261* **Camp Municipal du Domaine de Longemer, 121 Route de la Plage, 88400 Xonrupt-Longemer [03 29 63 07 30; fax 03 29 63 27 10; camping.dudomaine@wanadoo.fr]** Fr W thro Gérardmer on D417. immed after sp Xonrupt-Longemer turn R & cont thro vill. Site 1st one; turn L over bdge. App fr E (Colmar), turn L opp hotel Auberge du Lac. Site on both sides of rd. V lge, pt shd; htd wc; mv service pnt; shwrs inc; el pnts (6A) €3; shop; rest; snacks; bar; playgrnd; lake sw; fishing; x-country skiing; 10% statics; phone; poss cr; quiet; 5% red for long stays; CCI. "Attractive, clean lakeside site; gd walking." € 10.80 2009*

France

GERARDMER *6F3* (5km E Rural) *48.07815, 6.94246* **Camping Belle Rive, 2493 Route du Lac, 88400 Xonrupt-Longemer [03 29 63 31 12]** W fr Gérardmer on D417 (sp Colmar) in approx 1km over bdge, turn R at T-junc (still on D417). After 2km turn R opp hotel Auberge du Lac & immed R round W side of lake to S bank where site located. Med, mkd pitch, pt sl, terr, pt shd; wc; chem disp; shwrs €0.70; el pnts (1-6A) €1.20-3; Indtte; shops adj & 2km; snacks; bar adj; playgrnd; pool 8km; lake sw adj; 10% statics; dogs €0.80; phone adj; quiet. "Clean san facs; lakeside beautiful area; lovely position." 15 May-15 Sep. € 8.80 2007*

GERARDMER *6F3* (6km E Rural) *48.06755, 6.94830* **FFCC Camping Les Jonquilles, Route du Lac, 88400 Xonrupt-Longemer [03 29 63 34 01; fax 03 29 60 09 28]** Sp off D417 SE of Xonrupt-Longemer. Fr W thro Gérardmer on D417 (sp Colmar) in approx 1km over bdge & turn R at T-junc (still on D417). After 3km turn R opp hotel Auberge du Lac & almost immed R round W end of lake for 500m to T-junc, turn L, site on S bank 1km. Lge, mkd pitch, pt sl, unshd; wc (some cont); chem disp; mv service pnt; baby facs; shwrs inc; el pnts (6-10A) €3-4.50; gas; Indtte; shop; rest; snacks; bar; playgrnd; lake beach & sw adj; fishing; sailing; entmnt; TV; few statics; dogs €1.10; phone; bus 1km; Eng spkn; adv bkg; quiet but some noise fr entmnt at night; ccard acc; red low ssn; CCI. "Friendly, well-maintained, family-run site; gd views; poss uneven pitches; excel for Alsace wine region/Colmar." ♦ 15 Apr-10 Oct. € 12.00 2009*

GERARDMER *6F3* (7km E Rural) *48.06318, 6.95640* **Camping du Lac, 88400 Xonrupt-Longemer [03 29 57 52 91 or 06 73 64 15 76 (mob); fax 03 29 57 51 31; agnes.albiser@wanadoo.fr; www.campinglaclongemer.fr]** Fr Gérardmer on D417 twd Colmar, in 6km opp Hotel du Lac turn R sp La Bresse. In 200m turn R, then in 500m turn L at T-junc & cont for 1.5km on S side of lake. Site on R. Med, mkd pitch, pt sl, pt shd; htd wc; chem disp; mv service pnt; shwrs inc; el pnts (6-10A) €2.80-4; Indtte; tradsmn; snacks; bar; playgrnd; lake sw & beach adj; cycle hire; dogs €1; adv bkg; daytime rd noise. "Well-maintained site with views." 15 Apr-15 Oct. € 9.70 2007*

GERARDMER *6F3* (1.5km SW Rural) *48.0636, 6.8561* **Camping Les Sapins, 18 Chemin de Sapois, 88400 Gérardmer [tel/fax 03 29 63 15 01 or 06 37 35 36 20 (mob); les.sapins@camping-gerardmer.com; www.camping-gerardmer.com]** On S side of lake 150m up C17 rd sp Col de Sapois. Med, pt shd; wc; mv service pnt; shwrs inc; el pnts (4-6A) €3-4.70; sm shop; rest; snacks; bar; BBQ; playgrnd; lake with beach 200m; fishing & watersports adj; games area; TV rm; 10% statics; dogs €1.20; adv bkg rec; quiet; red low ssn. "Well-kept site in lovely area; lge pitches but o'looked by sports stadium; no lake views; walk along lake into pretty town." 1 Apr-10 Oct. € 13.50 2009*

GERE BELESTEN see Laruns *8G2*

GERSTHEIM *6E3* (1km NE Rural) *48.38891, 7.71244* **Camp Municipal au Clair Ruisseau, Rue de Ried, 67150 Gerstheim [03 88 98 30 04; fax 03 88 98 43 26; info@clairruisseau.com; www.clairruisseau.com]** Site sp on D924. Med, mkd pitch; pt shd; wc; mv service pnt; shwrs inc; el pnts (16A) €3.40; gas; shop; playgrnd; 60% statics; dogs €1; quiet. 30 Mar-28 Oct. € 12.10 2006*

GEX *9A3* (500m E Urban) *46.33430, 6.06744* **Camping Les Genêts, 400 Ave des Alpes, 01170 Gex [04 50 42 84 57 or 06 79 17 13 69 (mob)]** Fr all dir head for 'Centre Ville'; at rndabt take D984 twd Divonne/Lausanne. Site sp to R (tight turn) after rlwy sheds (poor sp in town) & Musée Sapeurs Pompiers. Med, hdg pitch, hdstg, pt sl, pt shd; wc (some cont); chem disp; shwrs inc; el pnts (16A) €2.90; gas 500m; Indtte; shops 500m; tradsmn; snacks; bar; playgrnd; games area; TV rm; dogs €1; phone; gates clsd 2200-0800; Eng spkn; adv bkg; quiet; ccard acc; CCI. "Excel site; excel games facs/playgrnd; friendly, helpful staff; clean facs; quiet with lots of privacy; conv Geneva." ♦ 25 May-30 Sep. € 12.50 2009*

GIBLES see Clayette, La *9A2*

GICQ, LE see Matha *7B2*

GIEN *4G3* (1km SW Rural) *47.68233, 2.62289* **Camping Touristique de Gien, Rue des Iris, 45500 Poilly-lez-Gien [02 38 67 12 50; fax 02 38 67 12 18; camping-gien@wanadoo.fr; www.camping-gien.com]** Off D952 Orléans-Nevers rd; turn R over old rv bdge in Gien & then R again onto D951; site on R on Rv Loire. Lge, hdg/mkd pitch, hdstg, pt sl, pt shd; htd wc; chem disp; mv service pnt; baby facs; shwrs inc; el pnts (4-10A) €3.50-5; gas adj; Indtte; shop; rest; snacks; bar adj; BBQ; playgrnd; covrd pool; paddling pool; lake sw 3km; canoeing; tennis; cycle hire; games rm; entmnt; wifi; TV rm; 20% statics; dogs €2; phone; adv bkg; Eng spkn; quiet; ccard acc; red long stay/CCI. "Lovely rvside site but no sw allowed; gd san facs; easy walk to town across bdge; porcelain factory 'seconds'." ♦ 6 Mar-14 Nov. € 18.00 2009*

See advertisement on next page

CAMPING TOURISTIQUE DE GIEN ***
Rue des iris - 45500 Poilly lez Gien (GIEN)
Tél : 02 38 67 12 50 - Fax : 02 38 67 12 18
Email : camping-gien@wanadoo.fr - www.camping-gien.com
Wi Fi
Plenty touristic and cultural sites
Trips,canoes and montain bikes (to let),fishing
Covered swimming pool,mini golf,maxi trampoline
Entertainment and theme evenings
Mobile homes and Roulottes to let
Restaurant-Bar-Ice cream
Supermarket,Laundry

GIEN *4G3* (5km SW Rural) *47.64152, 2.61528* **Domaine Les Bois du Bardelet, Route de Bourges, 45500 Poilly-lez-Gien [02 38 67 47 39; fax 02 38 38 27 16; contact@bardelet.com; www.bardelet.com]** Fr Gien take D940 dir Bourges; turn R onto D53, then R again onto unclassified rd to go back across D940; foll sp to site on L side of this rd. Site well sp fr D940. Lge, hdg/mkd pitch, some hdstg, pt shd; htd wc; chem disp; mv service pnt; baby facs; shwrs inc; el pnts (6A) inc (some rev pol); gas; lndtte; shop; rest; snacks; bar; BBQ; playgrnd; 3 pools (2 htd/covrd); paddling pool; jacuzzi; lake fishing; canoeing; tennis; games area; games rm; fitness rm; cycle hire; archery; entmnt; wifi; TV; 17% statics; dogs €4; phone; adv bkg; quiet; ccard acc; red snr citizen/low ssn/long stay; CCI. "V pleasant site; friendly welcome; modern facs; full site facs all ssn; beautiful o'door pools; trips & guided walks arranged." ♦
1 Apr-30 Sep. € 32.00 (CChq acc) ABS - L05 2009*

See advertisement opposite

GIGNAC *10F1* (1km NE Rural) *43.66192, 3.55887* **Camp Municipal La Meuse, Chemin de la Meuse, Route d'Aniane, 34150 Gignac [04 67 57 92 97; camping.meuse@wanadoo.fr; www.campinglameuse.fr]** Exit A75 onto A750 sp Montpellier & Gignac. In Gignac foll D32 sp Aniane. Site sp to L in 1km at town name cancellation sp. Med, hdg pitch, pt shd; wc; chem disp; mv service pnt; shwrs inc; el pnts (16A) €2.40; gas 1km; lndtte; shop 1km; bar; tennis; dogs €1.50; Eng spkn; adv bkg; quiet; ccard acc; red long stay; CCI. "Pleasant, clean site; easy access; lge pitches; warden connects/disconnects el pnts; poss flooding on some pitches in heavy rain; gd cycling; unreliable opening low ssn; rec." ♦ 1 Jun-15 Sep. € 13.10 2009*

GIGNAC *10F1* (1.5km W Rural) *43.65395, 3.54056* **Camping du Pont, 730 Blvd Moulin, 34150 Gignac [tel/fax 04 67 57 52 40; www.campingdupont.com]** Foll sp fr town cent. Sm, pt shd; wc; chem disp; shwrs inc; el pnts (6A) €2.70; lndtte; shop; tradsmn; rest; snacks; BBQ; playgrnd; pool; fishing; tennis adj; entmnt; 20% statics; dogs €2; adv bkg; quiet. "Friendly welcome." ♦ 1 Apr-30 Sep. € 22.00 2009*

GIGNAC *10F1* (5km W Rural) *43.64056, 3.49521* **Camping Le Septimanien, Route de Cambous, 34725 St André-de-Sangonis [04 67 57 84 23; fax 04 67 57 54 78; info@camping-leseptimanien.com; www.camping-leseptimanien.com]** Exit A75 junc 57. At rndabt on E side of a'route take D128 to Brignac. In Brignac turn L at T-junc, then fork R on D4 twd St André-de-Sangonis. Site on R in 3km. Med, hdg pitch, pt shd; wc; chem disp; shwrs inc; el pnts (5A) inc; gas; lndtte; shop & 1km; tradsmn; rest; snacks; bar; playgrnd; pool; paddling pool; entmnt; 15% statics; dogs €2.15; phone; adv bkg; quiet; ccard acc; CCI. "Well-organised site; vg sh stay/NH." ♦ 29 Apr-25 Sep. € 22.50 2009*

GIGNY SUR SAONE see Sennecey le Grand *6H1*

⊞ **GISAY LA COUDRE** *3D2* (500m S Rural) **Aire Communale La Villette, 27330 Gisay-la-Coudre [02 32 44 38 86; mairie.gisaylacoudre@wanadoo.fr]** Turn S of N138 at Bernay onto D833 to La Barre-en-Ouche. In town turn R onto D49 dir Broglie & in 200m turn L onto D35, site on R in 3km, sp. M'vans only. Sm, hdstg, unshd; own san; chem disp; mv service pnt; el pnts €2 for 2 hrs; water €2 for 100 litres; shop, rest, snacks, bar 200m; quiet. "Payment for services with jeton obtainable fr Bar-Rest La Tortue 500m further on fr site; car/c'vans probably acc; vg NH." 2007*

GISORS *3D3* (7km SW Rural) *49.25639, 1.70174* **Camp Municipal de l'Aulnaie, Rue du Fond-de-l'Aulnaie, 27720 Dangu [02 32 55 43 42]** On ent Gisors fr all dirs, take ring rd & exit dir Vernon D10, then L onto D181 dir Dangu. Site on L bef Dangu. Site sp fr D10. NB speed humps. Lge, mkd pitch, pt shd; htd wc; chem disp; mv service pnt; shwrs inc; el pnts (10A) €2.60; gas; lndtte; tradsmn; rest, snacks, bar 800m; playgrnd; lake sw; fishing; 90% statics; dogs €2.50; poss cr; adv bkg; some rd noise; CCI. "Conv Giverny & Gisors local attractions; Gisors attractive town; lakeside site." ♦
1 Apr-31 Oct. € 13.60 2009*

⊞ **GIVET** *5B1* (500m N Urban) *50.14345, 4.82614* **Caravaning Municipal La Ballastière, 16 Rue Berthelot, 08600 Givet [03 24 42 30 20; fax 03 24 40 10 70]** Site at N end of town on lake. Foll 'Caravaning' sp fr W end of rv bdge or Dinant rd. Med, some hdg pitch, hdstg, pt shd; htd wc; chem disp; shwrs; el pnts (10A) inc; lndtte; shop, rest, snacks, bar 1km; pool adj; 70% statics (sep area); dogs €0.85; quiet; CCI. "Nr Rv Meuse; adj sports & watersports complex; picturesque town; gd." € 8.50 2009*

GIVET *5B1* (2km SW Rural) *50.12993, 4.80721* **Camping Le Sanglier, 63 Rue des Grands Jardins, 08600 Rancennes [03 24 42 72 61]** Off D949 Givet to Beauraing. Immed after x-ing rv bdge turn R. Turn R again foll sp to site at end narr access rd on rvside. Sm, pt sl, terr, pt shd; wc; chem disp; shwrs; el pnts (4A); shop 2km; snacks; fishing; watersports; 60% statics; phone; Eng spkn; adv bkg; quiet; CCI. "Gd touring base; clean, basic facs; gd NH." 1 Jun-30 Sep. 2008*

GIVORS *9B2* (7km NW Urban) *45.61498, 4.67068* **Camp Municipal de la Trillonnière, Monts du Lyonnais, Rue de la Loire, 69440 Mornant [04 78 44 16 47 or 04 78 44 00 46 (Mairie); fax 04 78 44 91 70; mairie mornant@wanadoo.fr; www.ville-mornant.fr]** Exit A7 at Givors & foll sp for St Etienne via D488, thro Givors onto D2 till sp seen for Mornant via D34, cont on D34 up hill for 7km, cross D342 (D42) & cont 1km to o'skts of Mornant, L at junc island & site on L. Med, pt sl, pt shd; wc; chem disp; shwrs; el pnts (10A) inc; shops, rest, snacks bar 500m; pool 250m; dogs €1; adv bkg; some rd noise; access for vans 0815-1015 & 1700-2200. 1 May-30 Sep. € 14.00 2009*

GIVRAND see St Gilles Croix de Vie *2H3*

GIVRE, LE *7A1* (Rural) *46.44472, -1.39832* **Camping Aire Naturelle La Grisse (Martineau), 85540 Le Givre [02 51 30 83 03; lagrisse@wanadoo.fr]** Fr Luçon take D949 & turn L at junc with D747 (La Tranche rd). Turn L in 3km & foll sps. Sm, pt shd; wc; chem disp; shwrs inc; el pnts (5A) €3; Indry rm; sand beach 10km; dogs €2; Eng spkn; adv bkg; ccard not acc; CCI. "Peaceful, friendly, farm site; lge pitches; clean, modern facs; beautiful area/beach; gd for dogs." ♦ 15 Apr-15 Oct. € 13.00 2007*

GIVRY EN ARGONNE *5D1* (200m S Rural) *48.94835, 4.88545* **Camp Municipal du Val d'Ante, Rue du Pont, 51330 Givry-en-Argonne [03 26 60 04 15 or 03 26 60 01 59 (Mairie); fax 03 26 60 18 22; mairie.givryenargonne@wanadoo.fr]** Exit A4 junc 29 at Ste Menéhould; S on D382 to Givry-en-Argonne; site sp on R on lakeside. Sm, pt sl, pt shd; wc (some cont); chem disp; shwrs inc; el pnts (3A) inc; shops 200m; playgrnd; shgl lake beach sw; boats for hire adj; dogs €1.20; poss cr; quiet; no ccard acc. "Attractive, basic, pleasant site; clean san facs; warden calls am & pm; gd bird-watching; not suitable lge m'vans." 1 May-15 Sep. € 8.00 2009*

GLUIRAS see Ollières sur Eyrieux, Les *9D2*

GONDREXANGE see Héming *6E3*

GONDRIN *8E2* (E Rural) *43.88214, 0.23895* **FFCC Camping Le Pardaillan, Rue du Pardaillon, 32330 Gondrin-en-Armagnac [05 62 29 16 69; fax 05 62 29 11 82; cample pardaillan@wanadoo.fr; www.camping-le-pardaillan.com]** Fr Condom take D931 S for 12km to Gondrin. Site clearly sp. Med, hdg/mkd pitch, hdstg, pt shd; htd wc; chem disp; mv service pnt; baby facs; shwrs inc; el pnts (6-10A) inc; gas; Indtte; shop; tradsmn; rest; snacks; bar; playgrnd; paddling pool; lake sw adj; games rm; entmnt; TV rm; many statics; dogs €2; phone; poss cr; Eng spkn; adv bkg; CCI. "Excel site; lovely region; red facs & NH only low ssn; highly rec." ♦ 30 Apr-11 Sep. € 21.00 2006*

GONDRIN *8E2* (2km S Rural) *43.86936, 0.25844* **Camping La Brouquère, Betbézé, 32330 Gondrin [05 62 29 19 44; camping@brouquere.com; www.brouquere.com]** Fr Condom S on D931; pass thro Gondrin & turn S onto D113 dir Courrensan; site sp in 2km. Sm, mkd pitch, pt sl, sp shd; wc; chem disp; fam bthrm; shwrs inc; el pnts (10A) €2.25; Indry rm (owner will do washing); tradsmn; bar; BBQ; playgrnd; pool 2km; wifi; TV; dogs €1; Eng spkn; adv bkg; quiet; red low ssn. "V quiet, 6-pitch site; friendly Dutch owners; clean san facs; wine-tasting; local produce, inc Armagnac; excel." 26 Apr-30 Sep. € 13.15 2008*

GORDES *10E2* (2km N Rural) *43.92689, 5.20207* **Camping Les Sources, Route de Murs, 84220 Gordes [04 90 71 12 48; fax 04 90 72 09 43; www.campingdessources.com]** Fr A7 junc 24, E on D973; then D22; then D900 (N100) twds Apt. After 18km at Coustellet turn N onto D2 then L on D15 twds Murs; site on L in 2km beyond Gordes. Med, mkd pitch, hdstg, terr, pt shd; wc (some cont); chem disp; mv service pnt; baby facs; shwrs inc; el pnts (6A) €4.10 (long lead poss req); Indtte; shop & 2km; rest; snacks; takeaway; bar; playgrnd; pool; cycles hire; games areas; games rm; entmnt; 25% statics; dogs €5; Eng spkn; adv bkg; quiet; red low ssn/long stay; ccard acc; CCI. "Lovely location & views; access rd narr; modern, clean san facs; friendly staff; 24 hr security barriers; sm pitches v diff lge o'fits; ask for easy pitch & inspect on foot; some steep rds to pitches as site on hillside; gd pool; gd walking; mkt Tues." 23 Mar-27 Sep. € 19.80 2008*

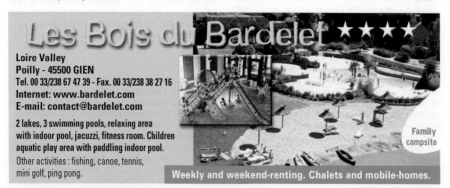

France

GORDES *10E2* (10km NE Rural) *43.94069, 5.22925* **Camp Municipal Les Chalottes, 84220 Murs [04 90 72 60 84 or 04 90 72 60 00 (Mairie); fax 04 90 72 61 73]** W on D900 (N100) fr Avignon, L onto D2 at Coustellet. Do not turn L sp Gordes but cont 3.5km & turn L D102 sp Joucas/Mura. Or fr Apt twd Avignon on D900, R to D4 after 4km site sp to Murs. Do not app site thro Gordes. NB 2.5t weight restriction on southern app. Sm, mkd pitch, pt sl, pt shd; wc (some cont); chem disp; shwrs inc; el pnts (6A) €2; tradsmn; playgrnd; dogs; phone; quiet; CCI. "Peaceful, pretty site among pines; gd walks; vill 1.8km." Easter-15 Sep. € 10.00 2009*

GOUAREC *2E3* (SW Rural) *48.22555, -3.18307* **Camping Tost Aven, Au Bout du Pont, 22570 Gouarec [tel/fax 02 96 24 85 42; baxter.david@wanadoo.fr; http://brittany camping.com]** Sp fr town cent bet rv & canal. Med, mkd pitch, pt shd; wc (some cont); chem disp; shwrs inc; el pnts (10A) €2.25; gas adj; lndry rm; shops adj; supmkt nr; rest, snacks, bar 500m; BBQ; sm playgrnd; sw adj (rv & canal); cycle, canoe hire; entmnt; dogs; bus 200m; poss cr; Eng spkn; adv bkg; quiet. "Helpful, friendly British owners; clean, tidy gem of a site bet Nantes-Brest canal & rv on edge of vill; towpath for cycling." ♦ 4 Apr-30 Sep. € 9.45 2008*

GOUDARGUES *10E2* (1km NE Rural) *44.22056, 4.47884* **Camping Les Amarines, La Vérune Cornillon, 30630 Goudargues [04 66 82 24 92; fax 04 66 82 38 64; contact@campinglesamarines.com; www.campingles amarines.com]** Fr D928 foll sp onto D23 & site between Cornillon & Goudargues. Med, hdg/mkd pitch, shd; htd wc; baby facs; shwrs inc; el pnts (6A) €3.50; lndtte; snacks; bar; playgrnd; htd pool; rv fishing; entmnt; statics; dogs €1.50; adv bkg; quiet; red low ssn. "Lge pitches; site liable to flood after heavy rain; excel." ♦ 1 Apr-15 Oct. € 17.90 2006*

GOUDELIN *2E3* (3km NE Rural) *48.61433, -2.99288* **Camping à la Ferme Kérogel (Faucheur), 22290 Goudelin [tel/fax 02 96 70 03 15; kerogel@wanadoo.fr; www.kerogel.com]** NE fr Guingamp on D9 to Goudelin. Fr cent of vill take rd dir Lanvollon, site sp on R. Sm, pt sl, pt shd; wc; chem disp (wc); shwrs inc; el pnts (10A) €1.85; lndry rm; tradsmn; rest, snacks, bar 3km; BBQ; playgrnd; games rm; dogs €0.50; Eng spkn; adv bkg; quiet; CCI. "Well-kept farm site; lge pitches; clean facs; helpful owner; gd touring base away fr cr coastal sites." ♦ 1 Apr-30 Sep. € 8.00 2008*

GOUEX see Lussac Les Châteaux *7A3*

GOURDON *7D3* (4km E Rural) *44.77304, 1.44097* **Camping Le Rêve, 46300 Le Vigan [05 65 41 25 20; fax 05 65 41 68 52; info@campinglereve.com; www.campinglereve.com]** On D820 (N20), 3km S of Payrac. R onto D673, sp Le Vigan & Gourdon. After 2km turn R onto sm lane, foll camp sp for 2.5km. Med, pt sl, pt terr, pt shd; wc; chem disp; baby facs; shwrs inc; el pnts (6A) €2.70; gas; lndtte; sm shop & 4km; bar; playgrnd; pool & paddling pool; games area; TV rm; entmnt; cycle hire; dogs €0.80; Eng spkn; adv bkg ess Jun-mid Aug; v quiet; red long stay/low ssn; ccard not acc; CCI. "Welcoming, helpful Dutch owners; gd walking; excel." ♦ 25 Apr-21 Sep. € 16.15 2008*

GOURDON *7D3* (11km S Rural) *44.64954, 1.43508* **Camp Municipal Le Moulin Vieux, 46310 St Germain-du-Bel-Air [05 65 31 00 71 or 05 65 31 02 12; contact@camping-moulin-vieux-lot.com; www.camping-moulin-vieux-lot.com]** W fr D820 (N20) Cahors-Souillac rd on D23 sp St Germain-du-Bel Air. On ent vill turn R at camping sp. After 150m turn R & foll narr rd, over sm bdge then imm turn L for site. Lge, shd; wc; chem disp; shwrs; el pnts (6-16A) €3-5; gas; lndtte; rest; shops 1km; pool adj; playgrnd; lake sw & fishing; entmnt; some statics; dogs €2; quiet. "Excel, clean site; friendly recep & helpful warden; vg walks in valley; highly rec." 1 Apr-15 Sep. € 13.00 2009*

GOURDON *7D3* (2km SW Rural) *44.72214, 1.37381* **Aire Naturelle Le Paradis (Jardin), La Peyrugue, 46300 Gourdon [tel/fax 05 65 41 65 01 or 06 72 76 32 60 (mob); contact@campingleparadis.com; www.campingleparadis.com]** S on D673 Gourdon/Fumel rd, after Intermarché supmkt on L, turn L onto track sp site. Track shares ent to supmkt. Sm, pt sl, terr, pt shd; wc; shwrs inc; el pnts (6A) €1.60; lndtte; supmkt adj; rest; pool; dogs €2; quiet; adv bkg; gd. "Gd welcome; farm produce; facs poss stretched if full." 1 May-10 Sep. € 8.25 2006*

GOURDON *7D3* (5km W Rural) *44.73507, 1.29533* **Camping Le Marcassin de St Aubin (Naturist), Les Grèzes, 24250 St Aubin-de-Nabirat [tel/fax 05 53 28 57 30; campinglemarcassin@gmail.com; www.lemarcassin.fr]** Fr Gourdon foll sp for hospital. At hospital take R fork sp Nabirat (D1) & in about 8km turn L at Renault tractor g'ge & foll sp for site in 1.5km. Site on R immed past speed limit sp. Sm, hdg pitch, pt shd; wc; shwrs inc; el pnts (6A) €3; lndtte; tradsmn; BBQ; pool; TV rm; some statics; Eng spkn; adv bkg; no ccard acc; INF card. "Beautiful area; helpful, friendly Dutch owners." ♦ 12 Apr-18 Oct. € 25.00 2008*

GOURDON *7D3* (10km W Rural) **Camping Calmésympa, La Grèze, 24250 St Martial-de-Nabirat [05 53 28 43 15; fax 05 53 30 23 65; duarte-jacqueline@wanadoo.fr; www.tourisme-ceou.com/calmesympa.htm]** SW fr Gourdon take D673 twd Salviac; at Pont Carrat turn R onto D46 sp Sarlat. Site 1.5km N of St Martial on L. Sm, hdg pitch, pt sl, pt shd; htd wc; chem disp; baby facs; shwrs inc; el pnts (8A) inc; lndtte; sm shop; playgrnd; pool; paddling pool; fishing; games area; games rm; entmnt; some statics; dogs €1.50; adv bkg; quiet; CCI. "Spacious site off the tourist track; friendly, welcoming owners; gd." ♦ 31 Mar-15 Sep. € 13.00 2007*

GOURDON *7D3* (10km W Rural) *44.74262, 1.26504* **Camping Le Carbonnier, 24250 St Martial-de-Nabirat [05 53 28 42 53 or 0825 13 85 85; fax 05 53 28 51 31 or 02 51 33 91 31; lecarbonnier@aol.com; www.lecarbonnier.fr]** On D46, sp in St Martial-de-Nabirat. Lge, mkd pitch, pt sl, pt shd; wc; chem disp; shwrs inc; el pnts (6A) inc; lndtte; shop; rest; snacks; bar; playgrnd; htd, covrd pool; waterslides; lake adj; tennis; horseriding adj; canoeing 8km; 50% statics; dogs €4.20; poss cr; adv bkg; quiet. "Excel." ♦ 31 Mar-27 Oct. € 26.60 2007*

GOURDON *7D3* (1.5km NW Rural) *44.74637, 1.37700* **Camp Municipal La Quercy, Domaine Ecoute S'il Pleut, 46300 Gourdon [05 65 41 06 19; fax 05 65 41 09 88]** Fr N site on R of D704 1.5km bef Gourdon. Lge, mkd pitch, pt sl, shd; wc; shwrs inc; el pnts (6A) €3; shop & 4km; lndtte; cooking facs; playgrnd; pool; lake beach; fishing; sailing, watersports 200m; tennis; games area; 50% statics; adv bkg rec high ssn; quiet; red low ssn. "50% tented vill; recep clsd early am, rec pay eve bef dep to avoid waiting; Gourdon attractive town; NH only." 15 Jun-15 Sep. € 10.00 2006*

GOUZON *7A4* (300m SW Urban) *46.18785, 2.23913* **Camp Municipal de la Voueize, 1 Ave de la Marche, 23230 Gouzon [05 55 81 73 22; www.lavoueize.com]** On E62/N145 Guéret/Montluçon exit at sp for Gouzon. In cent of vill bear R past church & site is sp on edge of Rv Voueize. Sm, pt shd; wc; chem disp; shwrs inc; el pnts (10A) inc (poss rev pol); gas adj; lndry rm; shop, rest, bar in vill; playgrnd; fishing; cycle hire; golf 2km; birdwatching on lake 8km; adv bkg; quiet. "Lovely aspect; friendly recep; clean site; facs poss tired high ssn; gd walking & cycling rtes; gd NH." 1 May-31 Oct. € 15.70 2009*

GRACAY see Vatan *4H3*

⊞ **GRAMAT** *7D4* (7km SE Rural) *44.74767, 1.79954* **Camping Le Teulière, L'Hôpital Beaulieu, 46500 Issendolus [05 65 40 86 71; fax 05 65 33 40 89; http://laparro.mcv.free.fr]** Site on R on D840 (N140) at L'Hôpital, clearly sp. Access fr ent narr & tight corners, not for underpowered. Sm, pt sl, pt shd; wc; shwrs inc; el pnts (20A) €2.65 (poss rev pol); lndtte; shop; rest; snacks; bar; BBQ; playgrnd; pool; tennis; fishing; TV; some statics; poss cr; adv bkg; quiet. "Conv Rocamadour; basic san facs; ltd facs low ssn; site rds unmade, steep & narr - gd traction req; pitches muddy when wet." € 8.00 2009*

GRAND BORNAND, LE see Clusaz, La *9B3*

GRAND FORT PHILIPPE see Gravelines *3A3*

GRAND PRESSIGNY, LE *4H2* (200m S Rural) *46.91723, 0.80600* **Camp Municipal Croix Marron, Rue St Martin, 37350 Le Grand-Pressigny [02 47 94 06 55 or 02 47 94 90 37 (Mairie); fax 02 47 91 04 77]** Fr Descartes take D750 S for 3km, L onto D42 to Le Grand-Plessigny. Site at SE end of vill by rv. Sm, mkd pitch, pt shd; wc; chem disp; shwrs inc; el pnts inc; shop, rest, bar in vill; playgrnd; pool adj; quiet. "Pleasant location; prehistoric sites nr; access to site by key fr Mairie (town hall) in vill, during office hrs." Easter-31 Oct. € 7.00 2006*

GRANDCAMP MAISY *1C4* (500m W Coastal) *49.38814, -1.05204* **Camping Le Joncal, Le Petit Nice, 14450 Grandcamp-Maisy [02 31 22 61 44; fax 02 31 22 73 99; info@campingdujoncal.com; www.campingdujoncal.com]** Ent on Grandcamp port dock area; visible fr vill. Fr N13 take D199 sp Grandcamp-Maisy & foll Le Port & Camping sps. Lge, mkd pitch, unshd; mv service pnt; wc; shops, rest adj; gas; el pnts (3-6A) €2.50-4; many statics; dogs €1; bus; quiet. "Conv for D Day beaches." ♦ 1 Apr-30 Sep. € 13.50 2006*

GRANDE MOTTE, LA *10F1* (Coastal) *43.56440, 4.07528* **FFCC Camping La Petite Motte à La Grande-Motte, 195 Allée des Peupliers, 34280 La Grande-Motte [04 67 56 54 75; fax 04 67 29 92 58; camping.lagrandemotte@ffcc.fr; www.camp-in-france.com]** Exit A9 for Lunel or Montpellier Est to La Grande Motte, site sp on D59 & D62 coast rd. Lge, shd, wc; shwrs; mv service pnt; el pnts (4A) €4.50; lndtte (no dryer); shop; rest; snacks; bar; playgrnd; sand beach 700m; tennis, horseriding, golf & water sports nrby; games area; entmnt; 10% statics; dogs free; poss cr; adv bkg; red low ssn/long stay/CCI. "Walk to beach thro ave of trees & footbdge over rds; vg." 1 Apr-30 Sep. € 16.30 2008*

GRANDE MOTTE, LA *10F1* (700m W Coastal/Urban) *43.56334, 4.07275* **Camping Le Garden, Ave de la Petite Motte, 34280 La Grande-Motte [04 67 56 50 09; fax 04 67 56 25 69; jc.mandel@wanadoo.fr; www.legarden.fr]** Fr La Grande Motte W on D59, site sp. Lge, hdg/mkd pitch, hdstg, pt shd; htd wc; chem disp; mv service pnt; baby facs; fam bthrm; shwrs inc; el pnts (10A) inc; gas; lndtte; shop; rest; snacks; bar; BBQ (gas); pool; paddling pool; sand beach 300m; entmnt; 30% statics; dogs €2; phone; bus; poss cr; Eng spkn; adv bkg; ccard acc; red low ssn (30-40%); CCI. "Easy access to beach, town & bus; some soft sand on pitches; highly rec." 1 Apr-15 Oct. € 39.50 (3 persons) 2009*

GRANDE MOTTE, LA *10F1* (2km W Coastal) *43.56703, 4.07576* **Camp Intercommunal Les Cigales, Allée des Pins, 34280 La Grande-Motte [tel/fax 04 67 56 50 85; camping.lescigales@wanadoo.fr; www.sivom-etang-or.fr]** Ent La Grande-Motte fr D62. Turn R at 1st traff lts; 1st on R to site. Lge, mkd pitch, pt shd; htd wc (cont); shwrs inc; el pnts (10A) inc; lndtte; shop 200m; snacks; bar; playgrnd; sand beach 900m; quiet, but faint rd noise; red low ssn. "Quiet low ssn & ltd facs; pleasant seaside town." 10 Apr-15 Oct. € 19.50 2009*

GRANDE PAROISSE, LA see Montereau Fault Yonne *4E3*

GRAND'LANDES see Legé *2H4*

GRANDPRE *5D1* (300m S Rural) *49.33924, 4.87314* **FFCC Camp Municipal, Rue André Bastide, 08250 Grandpré [03 24 30 50 71 or 03 24 30 52 18 (Mairie)]** Fr D946 in Grandpré turn S onto D6 at vill sq by church twd rv, site in 300m on rvside. Med, mkd pitch, pt shd; wc; mv service pnt; shwrs €0.60; el pnts (6-10A) €2.40-3.30; lndtte; shops, rest, bar 300m; playgrnd; fishing; dogs €0.55; poss cr; quiet. "Pleasant site; two ents to site: 1st to newer part with new facs, 2nd to office & older part." 1 Apr-30 Sep. € 7.05 2008*

GRANE see Crest *9D2*

GRANGES SUR VOLOGNE *6F3* (5km S Rural) *48.12123, 6.82857* **Camping La Sténiole, 1 Le Haut Rain, 88640 Granges-sur-Vologne [03 29 51 43 75; steniole@wanadoo.fr; www.steniole.fr]** D423 fr Gérardmer NW to Granges-sur-Vologne & foll sp. Well sp. Med, hdg pitch, terr, pt shd; wc (some cont); chem disp; shwrs inc; el pnts (4-10A) €3-5; gas; lndtte; shop; supmkt 3km; tradsmn; rest; snacks; bar; BBQ; playgrnd; lake sw & shgl beach adj; fishing, tennis; walking rte; horseriding 4km; games rm; TV rm; 10% statics; dogs €1; Eng spkn; adv bkg rec high ssn; quiet; CCI. "Pleasant, wooded, relaxing site; vg rest." 15 Apr-30 Oct. € 11.00 2009*

GRANGES SUR VOLOGNE *6F3* (200m W Rural) *48.14217, 6.78708* **Camping Les Peupliers, 12 Rue de Pré Dixi, 88640 Granges-sur-Vologne [03 29 57 51 04 or 03 29 51 43 36; fax 03 29 57 51 04]** D423 fr Gérardmer NW to Granges-sur-Vologne. On entering town look for sm park with bandstand on L; shortly after turn L into sm rd just bef rv bdge nr town cent. Well sp. Sm, mkd pitch, pt shd; wc; chem disp; shwrs €1; el pnts (6A) €3; shop & rest adj; playgrnd; fishing; TV rm; dogs €0.70; phone; poss cr high ssn; no Eng spkn; adv bkg; quiet; no ccard acc; CCI. "Friendly owner; modern, clean san facs, poss ltd high ssn; attractive site; gd walking." ♦ 1 May-15 Sep. € 8.00 2007*

GRANVILLE *1D4* (2km NE Coastal) *48.85206, -1.58090* **Camping L'Ermitage, Rue de l'Ermitage, 50350 Donville-les-Bains [02 33 50 09 01; fax 02 33 50 88 19; camping-ermitage@wanadoo.fr; www.camping-ermitage.com]** Turn off D971E in Donville at sm rndabt, site sp. Fr Bréhal turn R immed after post office on R. Lge, pt sl, pt shd; wc; chem disp; shwrs; el pnts (10A) €2.90; lndtte; shop 1km; rest, snacks, bar adj; sand beach; tennis adj; 10% statics; dogs €1.90; phone; poss cr; adv bkg; quiet, CCI. ♦ 15 Apr-15 Oct. € 11.90 2007*

GRANVILLE *1D4* (6km NE Coastal) *48.86976, -1.56380* **Kawan Village La Route Blanche, 6 La Route Blanche, 50290 Bréville-sur-Mer [02 33 50 23 31; fax 02 33 50 26 47; larouteblanche@camping-breville.com; www.camping-breville.com]** Exit A84 junc 37 onto D924 dir Granville. Bef Granville turn L onto D971, then L onto D114 which joins D971e. Site on R bef golf club. Nr Bréville sm airfield. Lge, hdg/mkd pitch, hdstg, pt shd; htd wc (some male cont); chem disp; mv service pnt; baby facs; serviced pitches; shwrs inc; el pnts (6-10A) €4-5; gas; lndtte; shop; tradsmn; snacks; bar; BBQ; playgrnd; htd pools; paddling pool; waterpark; waterslide; sand beach 500m; sailing school; golf & tennis nr; games area; wifi; entmnt; TV rm; 40% statics; dogs €2.50; phone; poss cr; Eng spkn; adv bkg; quiet; ccard acc; red long stay/CCI. "Pleasant, busy site with vg clean facs; staff friendly & helpful; vg disabled facs inc seatlift in pool; gd walking, cycling & beach; pleasant old walled town & harbour; vg." ♦ 1 Apr-15 Oct. € 28.00 (CChq acc) 2009*

See advertisement above

GRANVILLE *1D4* (2.5km SE Coastal) *48.8227, -1.5700* **Camping La Vague, 126 Route Vaudroulin, St Nicholas, 50400 Granville [02 33 50 29 97]** On D911 coast rd S fr Granville, or on D973 dir Avranches, site sp. Med, hdg/mkd pitch, pt shd; wc; chem disp; mv service pnt; shwrs inc; el pnts (4A) €4.30; gas; lndtte; shop 1km; tradsmn; rest, bar 1km; snacks; playgrnd; covrd pool; sand beach adj; fishing; TV; dogs €1.90; poss cr; adv bkg; quiet; CCI. ♦ 1 Jun-30 Sep. € 21.40 2008*

GRANVILLE *1D4* (3km SE Rural) *48.80033, -1.5517* **Camping de l'Ecutot, Route de l'Ecutot, 50380 St Pair-sur-Mer [02 33 50 26 29; fax 02 33 50 64 94; camping.ecutot@wanadoo.fr; www.ecutot.com]** Fr Avranches NW on D973 twds Granville. 5km S of Granville turn onto D309 sp St Pair-sur-Mer; site on R (wide rear ent). Lge, hdg pitch, indiv san facs some pitches; wc; chem disp; shwrs inc; el pnts (2-10A) €1.60-4; lndtte; sm shop; snacks; bar; playgrnd; htd pool; beach 1.2km; games area; entmnt; TV rm; 80% statics; dogs €1.20; Eng spkn; adv bkg; quiet; ccard acc. "Soft ground early ssn; san facs OK; chem disp facs poor; conv ferry to Channel Is, Bayeux Tapestry, Mont St Michel." 1 Jun-15 Sep. € 23.00 2008*

GRANVILLE *1D4* (3.5km SE Rural) *48.79054, -1.52598* **Camping Angomesnil, 50380 St Pair-sur-Mer [02 33 51 64 33; info@angomesnil.com; http://pagesperso-orange.fr/angomesnil/]** Take D973 SE fr Granville twd Avranches. At D154 exit to R sp Kairon-Bourg & site in 1km. Sm, hdg/mkd pitch, pt sl, pt shd; wc; chem disp; mv service pnt; shwrs inc; el pnts (6A) €3; Indtte; shops 3km; tradsmn; playgrnd; sand beach 3.5km; tennis; games room; TV; no dogs; adv bkg; quiet. "Nice little site; roomy pitches; helpful warden." ♦ 20 Jun-10 Sep. € 13.35 2009*

GRANVILLE *1D4* (6km SE Rural) *48.79790, -1.5244* **Camping Le Château de Lez-Eaux, 50380 St Pair-sur-Mer [02 33 51 66 09; fax 02 33 51 92 02; bonjour@lez-eaux.com; www.lez-eaux.com or www.les-castels.com]** App site on D973 Granville to Avranches rd (not via St Pair). Fr rndabt at Intermarché cont for 2km, site sp on R. Med, mkd pitch, pt sl, pt shd; wc; chem disp; mv service pnt; serviced pitches; baby facs; shwrs inc; el pnts (10A) inc; Indtte; shop & 4km; snacks; bar; BBQ; playgrnd; 2 pools (1 htd covrd); paddling pool; waterslide; sand beach 4km; lake fishing; tennis; cycle hire; boat hire 7km; horseriding 4km; wifi; games/TV rm; 80% statics; dogs free; poss cr; quiet; ccard acc; red low ssn; CCI. "Lovely site; v easy access; spacious pitches, various prices; helpful & friendly staff; clean, modern san facs; gd for children; gd cycling; gd cycle rte to beach; conv Mont St Michel, Dol & landing beaches; mkt Thu St Pair; highly rec." ♦ 1 Apr-20 Sep. € 43.00 ABS - N02 2009*

See advertisement below

GRANVILLE *1D4* (5km S Coastal) *48.78130, -1.56720* **Camping La Chaussée, 1 Ave de la Libération, 50610 Jullouville [02 33 61 80 18; fax 02 33 61 45 26; jmb@camping-lachaussee.com; www.camping-lachaussee.com]** On coast rd D911 fr Granville to Jullouville. Site on L heading S, sp. Lge, mkd pitch, hdstg, pt shd; wc (some cont); chem disp; mv service pnt; baby facs; fam bthrm; shwrs inc; el pnts (6-10A) €3.80-5; gas; Indtte; shop; tradsmn; snacks; bar; BBQ; playgrnd; htd pool; sand beach 100m; tennis 500m; games area; games rm 400m; archery; games rm; TV rm; dogs €1.50; phone; bus adj; Eng spkn; adv bkg; quiet; ccard acc; red low ssn; CCI. "Pleasant site on attractive coast; lge pitches; old & poss unclean san facs (July 2008); lovely pool; promenade walk; conv Mont St Michel." 4 Apr-14 Sep. € 25.50 2008*

GRANVILLE *1D4* (7km S Urban) *48.77783, -1.56618* **Camp Municipal du Docteur Lemonnier, Ave du Dr Lemonnier, 50610 Jullouville [02 33 51 42 60]** S on D911 Granville-Avranches coast rd. On on ent Jullouville turn L in mkt sq. Ent in far L corner. Med, unshd; wc; mv service pnt; shwrs inc; el pnts (6A); gas; Indtte; shop 200m; snacks; BBQ; playgrnd; sand beach 100m; 10% statics; dogs; poss cr high ssn; adv bkg; CCI. "Gd." 1 Apr-30 Sep. 2008*

GRASSE *10E4* (8km NE Rural) *43.70230, 6.99515* **FFCC Camping des Gorges du Loup, Chemin des Vergers, 06620 Le Bar-sur-Loup [04 93 42 45 06; info@lesgorgesduloup.com; www.lesgorgesduloup.com]** E fr Gasse on D2085 sp Chateauneuf-Grasse; in 4km turn L onto D2210 to Le Bar-sur-Loup. Site well sp. Med, mkd pitch, some hdstg, terr, pt shd; wc (some cont); chem disp; shwrs inc; el pnts (6-10A) €3.20-4.20 (poss rev pol); gas; Indtte; ice: shop; tradsmn; playgrnd; pool; shgl beach; TV rm; 20% statics; dogs €2.50; phone; bus 1km; Eng spkn; adv bkg; quiet; ccard not acc; red low ssn; CCI. "Peaceful, well-kept site with superb views; helpful, pleasant owners; clean san facs; steep access rds; owner will site c'van; not suitable disabled; not rec for lge o'fits; gd hilly cycling; highly rec. " 1 Apr-26 Sep. € 22.20 2009*

GRASSE *10E4* (7km E Rural) *43.65939, 6.99219* **Camping l'Orée d'Azure, 18 Route de Cannes, 06860 Opio [04 93 77 32 00; fax 04 93 77 71 89; accueil@camping-loreedazur.fr; www.camping-loreedazur.fr]** Exit A8 at Cannes/Grasse, foll sp for Grasse & to Valbonne, D3. (Can also exit A8 at Antibes, foll D103 to D3 & Valbonne). On D9 thro Valbonne, turn R at N end of vill sq. Cont on D3 sp Opio. After 3km site on L. Med, low hdg pitch, sl (terr vineyard), shd; wc; chem disp; shwrs inc; el pnts (2-4A) €2.60; shops 1km; gas; Indtte; rest; snacks; bar; playgrnd; pool; sand beach 14km; tennis, horseriding; golf 1km; TV rm; 90% statics; dogs; phone; poss cr; Eng spkn; adv bkg; v quiet; CCI. "Beautiful location conv Côte d'Azur & Provence Alps; helpful owner; vg." 1 Jun-1 Sep. € 25.00 2007*

France

GRASSE *10E4* (S Urban) *43.63507, 6.94859* **Camping Caravaning La Paoute, 160 Route de Cannes, 06130 Grasse [04 93 09 11 42; fax 04 93 40 06 40; camppaoute@hotmail.com; www.campinglapaoute.com]** Sp fr Grasse town cent on Route de Cannes (secondary rd to Cannes, NOT D6185), a 10 min drive. Med, hdg/mkd pitch, pt shd; wc; chem disp; mv service pnt; shwrs inc; el pnts (10A) €4; Indtte (inc dryer); tradsmn; supmkt nr; snacks; bar; playgrnd; htd pool; games rm; wifi; 40% statics; dogs; bus 500m; red low ssn/ long stay; CCI. "Gd site." 1 Apr-30 Sep. € 20.00 2008*

GRASSE *10E4* (8km S Rural) *43.60650, 6.90216* **Camping Le Parc des Monges, 635 Chemin du Gabre, 06810 Auribeau-sur-Siagne [tel/fax 04 93 60 91 71; contact@parcdesmonges.fr; www.parcdesmonges.com]** Exit A8 junc 40 or 41 onto D6007 dir Grasse; then onto D109 becoming D9; foll sp to Auribeau-sur-Siagne; site on rd to Le Gabre. Med, hdg pitch, shd; htd wc (some cont); chem disp; mv service pnt; baby facs; fam bthrm; shwrs inc; el pnts (4-10A) €3.50-5.50; gas 2km; Indtte (inc dryer); ice; shop 600m; tradsmn; rest, snacks & bar 2km; playgrnd; htd pool; rv sw adj; fishing nrby; activities & entment; 7% statics; dogs €2.50; phone; bus adj; poss cr; Eng spkn; adv bkg; quiet; ccard acc; red low ssn; CCI. "Vg site by Rv Siagne; rv not accessible fr site." ♦ 4 Apr-26 Sep. € 23.00 2009*

⊞ **GRASSE** *10E4* (8km NW Rural) *43.69088, 6.86450* **Camping Parc des Arboins, 755 Route Napoléon, 06460 St Vallier-de-Thiey [04 93 42 63 89; fax 04 93 09 61 54]** N fr Cannes on D6085 (N85) foll sp thro Grasse for Digne; approx 1.5km bef vill of St Vallier-de-Thiey, site located on R of rd. Med, mkd pitch, hdstg, shd; htd wc; mv service pnt; shwrs; el pnts (3A) €2.40; gas; Indtte; shop; supmkt 1.5km; rest; snacks; bar; playgrnd; htd pool; paddling pool; sand beach 30km; tennis 1.5km; golf 10km; games area; entmnt; TV rm; 95% statics; dogs €1.20; adv bkg; quiet but poss rd noise; CCI. "Lovely position on hillside; ltd touring pitches; ltd space to manoeuvre; 'quaint' san facs (own san rec); vg rest adj." € 17.40 2006*

GRAU DU ROI, LE *10F2* (1km N Coastal) *43.55450, 4.10720* **Camping Le Boucanet, Route de Carnon, 30240 Le Grau-du-Roi [04 66 51 41 48; fax 04 66 51 41 87; contact@campingboucanet.fr; www.campingboucanet.fr or www.camping-franceloc.fr]** Fr A9 fr N exit junc 26, fr S exit junc 29 Montpellier Airport dir Aigues-Mortes. Fr Aigues-Mortes take D62/D62A to Le Grau-du-Roi, twd La Grande-Motte. Site clearly sp off rndabt after area called Le Boucanet (on L). Lge, hdg/mkd pitch, some hdstg, pt shd; wc (some cont); chem disp; mv service pnt; shwrs inc; el pnts (6A) inc; gas; Indtte; shop; tradsmn; rest; snacks; bar; no BBQs; playgrnd; htd pool & paddling pool; dir access to sand beach adj; surf school; tennis; horseriding; golf 2km; creche; entmnt; no dogs; Eng spkn; adv bkg; quiet; ccard acc; red low ssn/ long stay; CCI. "Excel, popular site; some sm pitches poss diff lge o'fits; some pitches sandy; m'van parking on rd opp site; no waiting area outside site." ♦ 11 Apr-4 Oct. € 39.00 2009*

GRAU DU ROI, LE *10F2* (1km S Coastal) *43.52186, 4.14979* **Camping Les Jardins de Tivoli, Route de l'Espiguette, 30240 Le Grau du Roi [04 66 53 97 00; fax 04 66 51 09 81; contact@lesjardinsdetivoli.com; www.lesjardinsdetivoli.com]** Fr A9 take exit 26 to Aigues-Mortes. Then foll D979 twds Le Grau-du-Roi, Port Camargue & Espiguette. Site sp. Lge, hdg/mkd pitch, shd; wc; shwrs inc; each pitch has individ san facs inc shwr; el pnts (6-10A) inc; gas; Indtte; shop; rest; snacks; bar; gas; BBQ (gas); playgrnd; 3 pools; paddling pool; waterslides; sand beach 600m; tennis; sports activities; cycle hire; entmnt; TV; 20% statics; dogs €7; phone; adv bkg; ccard acc; red low ssn; CCI. "Excel site; superb individ san facs; lge pitches." ♦ 1 Apr-30 Sep. € 54.00 (4 persons) 2006*

GRAU DU ROI, LE *10F2* (4km SW Coastal) *43.50609, 4.12975* **Camping L'Espiguette, Route de l'Espiguette, 30240 Le Grau-du-Roi [04 66 51 43 92; fax 04 66 53 25 71; reception@campingespiguette.fr; www.campingespiguette.fr]** Fr A9 exit junc 26 onto D979 S to Aigues-Mortes & La Grande-Motte. Foll sps to Port Camargue & L'Espiguette & site sp on R fr rndabt; access via L bank of Le Grau-du-Roi; 3km fr Port Camargue & lighthouse. NB Caution on app due to height barrier. V lge, mkd pitch, pt shd; wc; mv service pnt; baby facs; shwrs inc; el pnts (5A) inc; gas; Indtte; shops; rest; snacks; bar; playgrnd; water park/play pool; waterslides into shallow sea water; sand beach adj & access to naturist beach 3km; cycle hire; games area; gym; wifi; entmnt; 10% statics; dogs €3; adv bkg; quiet; ccard acc; red long stay/low ssn; CCI. "Vg family site; beautiful beach adj; some pitches on sand poss diff in wet; many facs high ssn; helpful staff; dated but clean san facs, stretched high ssn; gd security." ♦ 27 Mar-3 Nov. € 32.80 2009*

See advertisement opposite

GRAVE, LA *9C3* (1km E Rural) *45.04508, 6.31052* **Camping de la Meije, 05320 La Grave [tel/fax 04 76 79 93 34 or 06 08 54 30 84 (mob); nathalie-romagne@wanadoo.fr; www.camping-delameije.com]** On D1091 (N91) travelling fr W site ent end of vill immed after last building. Site sp easily missed, by stream below vill. Fr E awkward app fr Briançon (sharp L-hand turn) cont & turn in parking area 150m. NB Rec app fr W. Sm, mkd pitch, pt sl, pt shd; wc (cont); chem disp (wc); baby facs; fam bthrm; shwrs €1; el pnts (4A) €3; Indtte; shop 500m; tradsmn; rest, snacks, bar 500m; BBQ; playgrnd; htd pool high ssn; tennis; games area; dogs €1; bus; poss cr; Eng spkn; adv bkg; quiet; red 5 days+; CCI. "Well-kept site in superb setting; mountain views; poss cr early & mid-July due La Marmotte cycle race & Tour de France." ♦ 15 May-20 Sep. € 11.00 2006*

GRAVE, LA *9C3* (1km W Rural) *45.04355, 6.29665* **Camping Le Gravelotte, La Meije, 05320 La Grave [04 76 79 93 14; fax 04 76 79 92 39; info@camping-le-gravelotte.com; www.camping-le-gravelotte.com]** On D1091 (N91), sp. Med, mkd pitch, pt sl, pt shd; wc; chem disp; shwrs inc; el pnts (5A) €2.50; gas; Indtte; shop; tradsmn; bar; htd pool; rv rafting/sw; games area; dogs €1; phone; poss cr; quiet; CCI. "Friendly welcome; spacious & open situation." ♦ 15 Jun-15 Sep. € 12.10 2008*

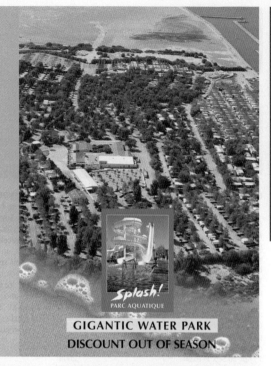

GRAVELINES *3A3* (1km N Coastal) *51.00777, 2.11777* **Camping des Dunes, Rue Victor-Hugo, Plage de Petit-Fort-Philippe, 59820 Gravelines [03 28 23 09 80; fax 03 28 65 35 99; campingdesdunes@campingvpa.fr; www.camping-des-dunes.com]** E fr Calais on D940 foll sp to Gravelines. Heading W fr Dunkerque exit D601 (N1) E of Gravelines; turn R into Blvd de L'Europe & foll sp for Petit-Fort-Philippe & site. Site on both sides of rd. Lge, hdg/mkd pitch, hdstg, pt shd; htd wc; chem disp; shwrs inc; el pnts (10A) €3.95; Indtte; shop (high ssn); shop, rest, snacks & bar 1km; playgrnd; direct access to sand beach adj; entmnt; games rm; TV; 15% statics; dogs €2; phone; bus; Eng spkn; adv bkg; ccard acc; red low ssn/CCI. "Site in 2 parts, various prices; gd site rds; helpful, friendly staff; poss uneven pitches & raised manhole covers; conv Dunkerque ferries (15km)." ♦ 1 Apr-31 Oct. € 17.30 2009*

See advertisement on next page

GRAVELINES *3A3* (3km W Coastal) *51.00250, 2.09694* **Camping de la Plage, 115 Rue du Maréchal-Foch, 59153 Grand-Fort-Philippe [03 28 65 31 95 or 03 28 23 09 80; fax 03 28 65 35 99; campingdelaplage@campingvpa.fr; www.camping-de-la-plage.info]** Exit A16 junc 51 dir Grand-Fort-Philippe; at o'skts of town turn R sp Camping ***; cont into town cent; foll rd along quayside; foll rd to L past lge crucifix; turn R at next x-rds; site on R. Med, hdg pitch, hdstg, pt shd; htd wc; chem disp; mv service pnt; shwrs inc; el pnts (10A) €3.35 (poss long lead req); Indtte; shop 2km; sand beach 300m; playgrnd; pool 3km; entmnt; 7% statics; dogs €1.80; Eng spkn; adv bkg; quiet; ccard acc; red low ssn/CCI. "Various pitch sizes; ltd el pnts; nice walk to sea front; night security guard; conv ferries; vg." ♦ 1 Apr-31 Oct. € 14.15 2009*

See advertisement on next page

GRAVESON *10E2* (1km SE Rural) *43.84408, 4.78080* **Camping Les Micocouliers, 445 Route de Cassoulen, 13690 Graveson [04 90 95 81 49; micocou@free.fr; http://micocou.free.fr]** Leave A7 junc 25 onto D99 St Rémy-de-Provence then D5 N past Maillane, site on R. Med, hdg/mkd pitch, unshd; wc; chem disp; mv service pnt; shwrs inc; el pnts (4-13A) €3.80-6.80; Indtte; shop, rest, bar 1km; BBQ; pool; tennis 1km; wifi; 8% statics; dogs €2; phone; Eng spkn; adv bkg; red low ssn; CCI. "Pretty, well-kept site; friendly, helpful owners; excel, immac san facs; gd pool; interesting area." ♦ 15 Mar-15 Oct. € 18.80 (CChq acc) 2009*

Camping de la Plage
Camping des Dunes
118 rue du Maréchal Foch
59153 Grand-Fort-Philippe
Phone: 00 33 03 28 65 31 95
E-mail: campingdelaplage@campingvpa.fr
Website: www.camping-de-la-plage.info
Quiet camping at 20 minutes from the ferry.
Rue Victor Hugo
59820 Gravelines
Phone: 00 33 03 28 23 09 80 Fax: 03 28 65 35 99
E-mail: campingdesdunes@campingvpa.fr
Website: www.camping-des-dunes.com
Direct access to the beach

GRAVIERS see Vans, Les *9D1*

GRAY *6G2* (1km E Rural) *47.45207, 5.59999* **Camp Municipal Longue Rive, Rue de la Plage, 70100 Gray [03 84 64 90 44; fax 03 84 65 46 26; tourisme-gray@wanadoo.fr; www.ville-gray.fr]** S on D67 to Gray. cross rv bdge, L at rndabt, after 300m sp La Plage. Well sp fr all rtes. Med, hdg/mkd pitch, pt shd; wc (mainly cont); mv service pnt; shwrs inc; el pnts (10A) €2.25; gas; lndtte; shop 1.5km; rest, bar, & pool opp; playgrnd; boating & fishing; tennis; dogs €0.85; poss cr; Eng spkn; poss noisy; ccard not acc; CCI. "Lovely setting on Rv Saône; friendly recep; basic facs, poss stretched high ssn; several Bastide vills within cycling dist; many pitches waterlogged early ssn; NH only."
15 Apr-30 Sep. € 10.00 2008*

GRAYAN ET L'HOPITAL see Soulac sur Mer *7B1*

GRENOBLE *9C3* (12km SE Rural) *45.15431, 5.83758* **Camping de Luiset, Allée de l'Eglise, 38410 St Martin-d'Uriage [04 76 89 77 98; fax 04 76 59 70 91; camping@leluiset.com]** Take D524 SE fr Grenoble to Uriage-les-Bains; turn L on D280 to St Martin-d'Uriage; site behind church in vill; steep climb fr Uriage-les-Bains. Med, mkd pitch, pt terr, pt shd; wc (cont); shwrs; el pnts (2-6A); lndtte; shop, rest 200m; BBQ; playgrnd; rv fishing 100m; games area; quiet. "Beautiful setting; basic facs." ♦ 1 May-30 Sep. 2008*

GRENOBLE *9C3* (10km S Rural) *45.08553, 5.69872* **Camping à la Ferme Le Moulin de Tulette (Gaudin), Route du Moulin de Tulette, 38760 Varces-Allières-et-Risset [04 76 72 55 98; tulette@wanadoo.fr; http://pagesperso-orange.fr/moulindetulette]** Fr A51, exit junc 12 to join D1075 (N75) N, Varces in approx 2km. Turn R at traff lts & foll sp to site, (approx 2km fr D1075). If driving thro Grenoble look for sp Gap - D1075 diff to find; on ent Varce foll site sp. Sm, mkd pitch, pt sl, pt shd; wc; chem disp; baby facs; shwrs inc; el pnts (5-10A) €2.50; shop 1km; tradsmn; dogs €1; poss cr; Eng spkn; adv bkg; quiet; CCI. "Peaceful, picturesque, well-kept site with views; friendly, helpful owners; facs ltd but clean - stretched high ssn; gd base for touring/x-ing Alps." ♦ 1 May-31 Oct. € 13.00 2009*

⊞ **GRENOBLE** *9C3* (7km SW Urban) *45.16687, 5.69897* **Camping Caravaning Les 3 Pucelles, Rue des Allobroges, 38180 Seyssins [04 76 96 45 73; fax 04 76 21 43 73; contact@camping-trois-pucelles.com; www.camping-trois-pucelles.com]** On A480 in dir of rocade (by-pass) S exit 5B, on R after supmkt then foll sp to R then L. Clearly sp. Well sp fr m'way. Sm, hdg pitch, hdstg, pt shd; htd wc (some cont); chem disp; shwrs inc; el pnts (6A) €2.50; lndtte; ice shop; tradsmn; rest; snacks; bar; playgrnd; pool; 70% statics; phone; bus nr; poss cr; Eng spkn; noise fr indus area; CCI. "Site part of hotel campus run by friendly family; sm pitches; san facs need refurb; site grubby (Jun 2008); conv Grenoble by bus/tram; NH only." € 16.00 2009*

GREOUX LES BAINS *10E3* (600m S Rural) *43.75262, 5.89588* **Yelloh! Village Verdon Parc, Domaine de la Paludette, 04800 Gréoux-les-Bains [04 92 78 08 08; fax 04 92 77 00 17; info@yellohvillage-verdon-parc.com; www.yellohvillage-verdon-parc.com]** On D952 to Gréoux, turn S onto D8 dir St Pierre. Cross bdge over Rv Verdon (v narr) turn L immed. Site in 500m. Lge, mkd pitch, hdstg, terr, pt shd; wc; chem disp; baby facs; fam bthrm; shwrs inc; el pnts (10A) €4; gas 1km; lndtte; shop & 1km; rest; snacks; bar; playgrnd; pool; paddling pool; lake sw & fishing 3km; tennis; games area; entmnts; internet; TV rm; 60% statics; dogs €2 (acc low ssn only); phone; bus 1km; Eng spkn; adv bkg; quiet; CCI. "Helpful manager; clean facs; all gravel standings; barrier clsd 2230-0700; pleasant (hilly) spa town; excel." ♦ 1 Apr-28 Oct. € 33.00 2008*

GREOUX LES BAINS *10E3* (1.2km S Rural) *43.75158, 5.88185* **Camping Le Verseau, Route de St Pierre, 04800 Gréoux-les-Bains [tel/fax 04 92 77 67 10]** Fr W on D952 to Gréoux. Go under bdge then bear L just bef petrol stn. Cross rv (narr bdge), site on R in 500m. Med, hdg pitch, pt sl, pt shd; wc; chem disp; mv service pnt; baby facs; shwrs inc; el pnts (10A) €3; lndtte; shop 1km; rest; snacks; bar; BBQ (gas/elec); playgrnd; pool; tennis 1km; entmnt; dogs €1.80; phone; adv bkg; quiet; CCI. "Friendly owners; interesting spa town; great views." 1 Apr-31 Oct. € 16.00 2006*

GREZ SUR LOING see Fontainebleau *4E3*

GRIGNAN see Valréas *9D2*

GRIMAUD *10F4* (2km E Rural) *43.27924, 6.56409* **Aire Naturelle (Gerard), Les Cagnignons, 83310 Grimaud [04 94 56 34 51; fax 04 94 56 51 26; lyons.cagnignons@wanadoo.fr]** Leave A8 at junc 36 onto D125/D25 at Le Muy sp Ste Maxime then onto D559 (N98) dir St Tropez. Take R onto D14 sp Grimaud & 3rd rd on R to site. Sm, terr, shd; wc; chem disp; shwrs inc; el pnts (3-6A) €3-3.50; Indtte; basic playgrnd; pool adj, tennis 500m; sand beach 2km; horseriding 2km; phone; 30% statics; dogs €1.60; adv bkg; quiet; no ccard acc; CCI. "Clean site; away fr bustle of St Tropez; not rec teenagers; some pitches ltd for long o'fits." ♦ Easter-30 Sep. € 18.00 2006*

The opening dates and prices on this campsite have changed. I'll send a site report form to the Club for the next edition of the guide.

GRIMAUD *10F4* (3km E Coastal) *43.28527, 6.57972* **Domaine des Naïades ACF, St Pons-les-Mûres, 83310 Grimaud [04 94 55 67 80; fax 04 94 55 67 81; info@lesnaiades.com; www.lesnaiades.com]** Exit A8 junc 36 (for Le Muy) onto D125/D25 dir St Maxime; join D559 (N98) W dir St Tropez & Grimaud. After 5km at rndabt opp Camping Prairies de la Mer turn R sp St Pons-les-Mûres; site sp & ent 500m on L. Lge, terr, shd, mkd pitch; wc (some cont); chem disp; baby facs; shwrs inc; el pnts (10A) inc (poss rev pol); Indtte; shops; rest; snacks; bar; playgrnd; htd pool + paddling pool; waterslides; sand beach 900m; watersports; cycle hire; games area; entmnt; wifi; games/TV rm; some statics; dogs €5; min 7 nights Jul/Aug; poss cr; adv bkg ess; quiet except noisy disco & dog kennels adj; ccard acc; red low ssn/long stay; CCI. "Gd views; gd recep; vg, clean san facs; 24hr security." ♦ 27 Mar-23 Oct. € 50.00 ABS - C27 2009*

GRIMAUD *10F4* (4km E Coastal) *43.27080, 6.57320* **Camping Club Holiday Marina, Le Ginestel, 83310 Grimaud [04 94 56 08 43; fax 04 94 56 23 88; info@holiday-marina.com; www.holiday-marina.com]** Exit A8 junc 36 onto D125/D25 dir Ste Maxime; turn R onto D559 (N98) dir St Tropez (sea on your L); in approx 6km pass under sm flyover at Port Grimaud. Site on R in approx 500m past flyover just after Villa Verde garden cent. Lge, hdg/mkd pitch, pt shd; htd wc; chem disp; serviced pitches; pitches have private bthrms; shwrs inc; el pnts (20A) inc; gas; Indtte; shop; tradsmn; rest; snacks; bar; BBQ (el only); playgrnd; 2 htd pools; jacuzzi; sand beach 950m; fishing; cycle & scooter hire; games rm; entmnt; wifi; sat TV; 70% statics; dogs €3; deposit for barrier card & bathrm; sep car park; British owners; poss cr; adv bkg ess high ssn; rd noise; ccard acc; min 3 nights; red low ssn/long stay; CCI. "Helpful staff; lovely pool area with jacuzzi; excel sports facs; pitches poss tight & diff manoeuvring for lge o'fits; conv for all Côte d'Azur." ♦ 1 Mar-31 Oct. € 53.00 ABS - C23 2009*

See advertisement below

GRIMAUD *10F4* (4km E Coastal) *43.28205, 6.58614* **Camping de la Plage, 98 Route National, St Pons-les-Mûres, 83310 Grimaud [04 94 56 31 15; fax 04 94 56 49 61; campingplagegrimaud@wanadoo.fr; www.camping-de-la-plage.fr]** Fr St Maxime turn onto D559 (N98) sp to St Tropez; site 3km on L on both sides of rd (subway links both parts). Lge, pt shd; wc; chem disp; mv service pnt; shwrs inc; el pnts (4-10A) €4.50-8.50; gas; Indtte; shop; rest; snacks; bar; playgrnd; sand beach adj; tennis; wifi; entmnt; dogs €2; poss cr; some rd noise; adv bkg ess high ssn (rec bkg in Jan - non-rtnable bkg fee); ccard acc; CCI. "Pitches nr beach or in shd woodland - some sm; excel situation & views; clean facs but need refurb; cycle tracks; site poss flooded after heavy rain; used every year for 40 yrs by 1 C'van Club member." ♦ 15 Mar-13 Oct. € 30.00 2009*

GRIMAUD *10F4* (4km E Coastal) *43.28375, 6.59165* **Camping Les Mûres, St Pons-les-Mûres, 83310 Grimaud [04 94 56 16 17; fax 04 94 56 37 91; info@camping-des-mures.com; www.camping-des-mures.com]** Exit Ste Maxime on D559 (N98) twd St Tropez, site in 5km visible on both sides of rd midway bet Ste Maxime & Grimaud. V lge, mkd pitch, pt sl, pt shd; wc (some cont); chem disp; shwrs inc; el pnts (6A) inc (poss rev pol); gas; Indtte; shop; rest; snacks; bar; playgrnd; sand beach adj; boat hire; water-skiing; games area; entmnt; some statics; dogs €2; poss cr; quiet but rd noise & disco (high ssn); adv bkg; red low ssn; CCI. "Well-run, clean site; site has own beach, beach pitches with views avail; v ltd facs low ssn." 4 Apr-3 Oct. € 35.00 2009*

GRIMAUD *10F4* (4km E Coastal) *43.28083, 6.58250* **Camping Les Prairies de la Mer, St Pons-les-Mûres, 83360 Grimaud [04 94 79 09 09; fax 04 94 79 09 10; prairies@riviera-villages.com; www.riviera-villages.com]** Leave A8/E80 at Ste Maxime/Draguignan exit. Take DD125/D25 twd Ste Maxime. Site on L of D559 (N98) heading SW, 400m bef St Pons-les-Mûres with rndabt at ent. Site opp Marina Village. V lge, mkd pitch, hdstg, pt shd, wc; chem disp; mv service pnt; shwrs inc; el pnts (6-10A) inc; gas; Indtte; shop; supmkt; rest; snacks; bar; playgrnd; sand beach adj; fishing; watersports; entmnt; 60% statics; dogs; phone; bus; poss cr; adv bkg ess high ssn; poss noisy - family site; ccard acc; red low ssn; CCI. "Popular beach site; well organsied; gd recep; pitches tight for med to lge o'fits; pitches poss dusty high ssn; gd san facs; Port Grimaud sh walk; gd." ♦ 20 Mar-11 Oct. € 35.00 2008*

⊞ **GRIMAUD** *10F4* (2km SE Rural) *43.26414, 6.53365* **FFCC Camping Domaine du Golfe de St Tropez, Chemin des Vignaux, 83310 Grimaud [04 94 43 26 95; fax 04 94 43 21 06; info@golfe-st-tropez.com; www.golfe-st-tropez.com]** Sp down lane, Carraire de St Pierre, nr junc of D14 & D61 or off D558. Med, hdg/mkd pitch, pt shd; wc; chem disp; shwrs inc; el pnts (6-10A) €4-5; rest; snacks; playgrnd; pool; beach 3.5km; 40% statics; dogs €3; phone; ccard acc. "Conv for Port Grimaud & beaches." € 20.00 2009*

GROLEJAC see Sarlat la Canéda *7C3*

⊞ **GROS THEIL, LE** *3D2* (3km SW Rural) *49.21207, 0.81533* **Camp de Salverte, Route de Brionne, 27370 Le Gros-Theil [02 32 35 51 34; fax 02 32 35 92 79; david.farah@wanadoo.fr; www.camping-salverte.com]** Fr Brionne take D26 E twd Le Gros-Thiel. After 10km turn R at Salverte, site sp. Lge, hdg pitch, terr, pt shd; htd wc; shwrs inc; el pnts (4A) inc (poss rev pol); el pnts (6A) €5 compulsory charge Nov-Mar; Indry rm; shop; snacks; bar; playgrnd; covrd pool; tennis; entmnt; many statics; quiet; CCI. "Conv NH Le Havre/Caen ferries; attractive site but v ltd facs low ssn; sm area for tourers diff when wet." € 17.90 2008*

GRUISSAN *10F1* (5km NE Coastal) *43.1358, 3.1424* **Camping Les Ayguades, Ave de la Jonque, 11430 Gruissan [04 68 49 81 59; fax 04 68 49 05 64; loisirs-vacances-languedoc@wanadoo.fr; www.loisirs-vacances-languedoc.com]** Exit A9 junc 37 onto D168/D32 sp Gruissan. In 10km turn L at island sp Les Ayguades, foll site sp. Lge, hdg/mkd pitch, unshd; htd wc; chem disp; mv service pnt; baby facs; shwrs inc; el pnts (6A) inc; Indtte; shop; rest; bar; playgrnd; sand beach adj; entmnt; TV; 75% statics; dogs €2.50; Eng spkn; adv bkg; quiet; ccard acc; CCI. "Pleasant site." ♦ 28 Mar-8 Nov. € 26.10 2008*

GUDAS *8G3* (2km S Rural) *42.99269, 1.67830* **Camping Mille Fleurs (Naturist), Le Tuilier, 09120 Gudas [tel/fax 05 61 60 77 56; info@camping-millefleurs.com; www.camping-millefleurs.com]** Fr S at Foix town on N20, turn R onto D1 at traff lts sp Laroque d'Olmes, Lieurac and l'Herm. In 6.5km sharp bend L onto D13 sp Mirepoix. In 500m fork L at sp Gudas & Varihles. Site in 2km over bdge on L. NB Do not app fr Varilhes thro Dalou & Gudas, rd too narr for c'vans. Sm, hdg/mkd pitch, terr, pt shd; wc; chem disp; shwrs inc; child/baby facs; fam bthrm; sauna; el pnts (6-10A) €3.25-3.75; gas 10km; shop 8km; tradsmn; bar; BBQ; pool; no statics; dogs €1.80; phone; Eng spkn; adv bkg; quiet; red low ssn; INF card req. "Excel site; lovely owners; gd pitches; clean facs; gd base Andorra, Toulouse & Carcassonne; gd views; adv bkg rec high ssn." ♦ 1 Apr-1 Nov. € 18.00 2009*

GUEBWILLER *6F3* (2km E Rural) *47.90050, 7.23663* **Camping Le Florival, Route de Soultz, 68500 Issenheim [tel/fax 03 89 74 20 47; contact@camping-leflorival.com; www.camping-leflorival.com]** Fr Mulhouse take D430 N. Then take D5 twd Issenhiem. Site well sp. Med, hdg/mkd pitch, pt shd; wc; chem disp; shwrs inc; baby facs; el pnts (6A) €3; Indtte, shop & 200m; tradsmn; playgrnd; pool, waterslide 100m; TV rm; 30% statics; dogs €1.50; phone; Eng spkn; quiet; red 7 days; ccard acc; CCI. "Vg NH; friendly recep." 1 Apr-31 Oct. € 14.50 2007*

GUEGON see Josselin *2F3*

GUEMENE PENFAO *2G4* (1km SE Rural) *47.62575, -1.81857* **Camping L'Hermitage, 36 Ave du Paradis, 44290 Guémené-Penfao [02 40 79 23 48; fax 02 40 51 11 87; contact@campinglhermitage.com; www.campinglhermitage.com]** On D775 fr cent of Guémené-Penfao, dir Châteaubriant for 500m, turn R, site sp. Med, mkd pitch, hdstg, pt shd; wc; chem disp; mv service pnt; baby facs; shwrs inc; el pnts (6A) €2.50; gas; Indtte; shop 1.5km; tradsmn; rest; snacks; bar; BBQ; playgrnd; htd, covrd pool adj; paddling pool; waterslide; jacuzzi; rv sw & fishing 300m; canoeing; tennis; games area; games rm; cycle hire; entmnt; TV; 20% statics; dogs €1; phone; some Eng spkn; adv bkg; quiet; red low ssn; CCI. "Gd walking in area; excel." ♦ 1 Apr-31 Oct. € 10.30 2006*

GUENROUET *2G3* (E Rural) *47.52215, -1.95008* **Camp Municipal St Clair, Route de Plessé, 44530 Guenrouet [tel/fax 02 40 87 61 52 or 06 98 86 89 90; chabliny@wanadoo.fr; www.campingsaintclair.com]** S fr Redon take D164 dir Blain, turn R onto D2 to Guenrouet, over bdge & site directly on L after bdge. Med, hdg/mkd pitch, pt sl, pt shd; wc; chem disp; mv service pnt; 50% serviced pitches; shwrs inc; el pnts (10A) €3; gas 1km; shop & 1km; tradsmn; rest 100m; playgrnd; htd pool adj; waterslide; fishing; canoe hire; dogs €1.50; Eng spkn; quiet; CCI. "On banks of canal; special area for late arrivals; excel." ♦ 1 May-27 Sep. € 18.20 2009*

GUERANDE *2G3* (2km N Rural) *47.34954, -2.43170* **Camping La Fontaine, Kersavary, Route de St-Molf, 44350 Guérande [02 40 24 96 19 or 06 08 12 80 96 (mob)]** Fr Guérande take N774 N sp La Roche-Bernard; opp windmill, fork L sp St-Molf; site on L in 500m. Med, mkd pitch; pt shd; wc; chem disp (wc); shwrs inc; el pnts (6A) €3; Indtte; snacks; shop, rest & bar 4km; playgrnd; sand beach 4km; statics sep; dogs €1.50; phone; adv bkg rec high ssn; quiet; red low ssn/CCI. "Pleasant, peaceful site in orchard; helpful staff." ♦ 1 Apr-30 Sep. € 12.00 2009*

GUERANDE *2G3* (2km E Rural) *47.33352, -2.39060* **Camping Le Domaine de Léveno, Route de Sandun, 44350 Guérande [02 40 24 79 30; fax 02 40 62 01 23; contact@camping-leveno.com; www.camping-leveno.com]** Fr Guérande foll sps to l'Etang de Sandun. Med, pt shd; wc; serviced pitches; shwrs; el pnts (6A) inc; gas; Indtte; shop; rest; snacks, bar; BBQ; playgrnd; htd, covrd pool; paddling pool; waterslide; sand beach 5km; tennis; games area; entmnt; TV rm; 60% statics; dogs €5; adv bkg; quiet; red low ssn. "Conv La Baule; vg site in lovely park." 4 Apr-30 Sep. € 35.00 2008*

⊞ **GUERANDE** *2G3* (7km E Rural) *47.34621, -2.34613* **FFCC Camping de l'Etang en Kerjacob, 47 Rue des Chênes, Sandun, 44350 Guérande [02 40 61 93 51; fax 02 40 61 96 21; camping-etang@wanadoo.fr; www.camping-etang.com]** Fr Guérande take D51 NE for approx 5km, turn R onto D48 for 3km. Turn L to site on lakeside. Sp fr each junc on Guérande by-pass. Med, hdg/mkd pitch, pt shd; wc; chem disp; baby facs; shwrs inc; el pnts (10A) €3.60; Indtte; shop, rest, snacks, bar high ssn; BBQ; playgrnd; htd pool & paddling pool; sand beach 9km; watersports 9km; lake fishing; cycle hire; games rm; wifi; many statics; dogs €2.50; poss cr; Eng spkn; adv bkg; ccard acc; red low ssn; CCI. "Pleasant, peaceful site; friendly staff; dated, clean san facs, ltd low ssn; plenty of shade; poss resident workers; mkt Wed & Sat." ♦ € 19.50 2008*

GUERANDE *2G3* (1km S Urban/Rural) *47.29797, -2.39988* **Camping Trémondec, 48 Rue du Château de Careil, 44350 Guérande [02 40 60 00 07; fax 02 40 60 91 10; info@camping-tremondec.com; www.camping-tremondec.com]** Fr Nantes on N165/N171/D213 dir La Baule. Take D192 dir La Baule cent, turn W in 800m dir Brenave, Careil. Site sp. Med, mkd pitch, hdstg, pt sl, pt shd; wc; chem disp; baby facs; shwrs inc; el pnts (6A) €3.80; gas 1km; Indtte; tradsmn; supmkt 900m; rest, snacks, bar high ssn; BBQ; playgrnd; htd pool; sand beach 2km; games area; entmnt; 50% statics; dogs €2.50; adv bkg; Eng spkn; quiet; ccard acc; red low ssn/long stay/CCI. "Lovely beaches & coast; pleasant walks thro salt marshes; cycle rtes; reported unkempt & san facs unclean (Aug 2007)." ♦ 1 Apr-30 Sep. € 20.20 2007*

GUERANDE *2G3* (7km W Coastal) *47.32856, -2.49907* **Camp Municipal Les Chardons Bleus, Blvd de la Grande Falaise, 44420 La Turballe [02 40 62 80 60; fax 02 40 62 85 40; camping.les.chardons.bleus@wanadoo.fr]** Foll D99 to La Turballe. Site well sp fr town cent along D92. Lge, hdg/mkd pitch, unshd; wc; chem disp; mv service pnt adj; shwrs inc; el pnts (6-10A) €2.90-4.10 (poss rev pol, long lead poss req); gas; Indtte; shop; tradsmn; rest in ssn; snacks; bar; playgrnd; htd pool; sand beach adj (pt naturist) & 2km; entmnt; dogs €2.30; phone; Eng spkn; ccard acc; red low ssn; CCI. "Well-run, well-kept site in great location; warm welcome; gd, clean san facs, poss stretched high ssn; ltd el pnts when full; variable opening dates - phone ahead to check early ssn; superb beach; nature reserve adj with bird life." ♦ 30 Apr-30 Sep. € 15.90 2009*

GUERANDE *2G3* (7km NW Rural) *47.34252, -2.47159* **Camping Le Parc Ste Brigitte, Manoir de Bréhet, 44420 La Turballe [02 40 24 88 91; fax 02 40 15 65 72; saintebrigette@wanadoo.fr; www.campingsaintebrigitte.com]** Take D99 NW fr Guérande twd La Turballe thro vill of Clis. Sp on R in 900m. Lge, mkd pitch, shd; wc; chem disp; mv service pnt; serviced pitch; shwrs inc; baby facs; el pnts (6-10A) inc; gas; Indtte; shop; rest; snacks; bar; playgrnd; htd, covrd pool; sand beach 2km; fishing; cycle hire; entmnt; TV rm; some statics; dogs €1.50; phone; poss cr; adv bkg; poss noisy; ccard not acc; CCI. "V peaceful; excel rest & bar; some sm pitches; poss unkempt, untidy & poor pitch maintenance low ssn; gd." ♦ 1 Apr-1 Oct. € 28.30 2007*

GUERANDE *2G3* (7km NW Coastal) *47.35388, -2.51722* **Camping-Caravaning La Falaise, 1 Blvd de Belmont, 44220 La Turballe [02 40 23 32 53; fax 02 40 62 87 07; info@camping-de-la-falaise.com; www.camping-de-la-falaise.com]** Fr Guérande exit on D99 sp La Turballe/Piriac-sur-Mer; pass La Turballe; site easily seen on L 200m after Intermarché. Med, hdg/mkd pitch, pt shd; htd wc (some cont); chem disp; some serviced pitches; shwrs inc; el pnts (10A) inc; Indtte; shop 200m; tradsmn; rest 100m; bar; BBQ; playgrnd; sand beach adj; watersports; naturist beach 2km; horseriding & mini-golf 3km; entmnts; TV; 5% statics; dogs €2.25; Eng spkn; adv bkg; quiet (some rd noise); CCI. "V pleasant site." ♦ 25 Mar-31 Oct. € 28.30 (3 persons) 2008*

France

GUERANDE *2G3* (8km NW Coastal) *47.36045, -2.51473* **Camping Le Refuge, 56 Rue de Brandu, 44420 La Turballe [02 40 23 37 17; fax 02 40 11 85 10]** On D99 thro La Turballe twd Piriac. Ikm after Intermarché supmkt turn R into Rue de Brandu. Site on R in 800m, sp. Lge, hdg pitch, shd; wc; chem disp (wc); mv service pnt; shwrs inc; el pnts (6A) €3.50; Indtte; shop 1km; tradsmn; BBQ (gas); playgrnd; sand beach 300m; fishing; sailing; tennis; no dogs; adv bkg; quiet; CCI. "Excel, well-kept site; lge pitches; easy access to gd beach & town; gd cycling area." ♦
1 Jun-30 Sep. € 17.00 2009*

⊞ **GUERCHE DE BRETAGNE, LA** *2F4* (6km E Rural) *47.94383, -1.17233* **Camp Municipal, 35130 La Selle-Guerchaise [02 99 96 26 81; fax 02 99 96 46 72]** Fr N on D178 Vitré to Châteaubriant rd 3km N of of La Guerche-de-Bretagne; turn L onto D106 to Availles-sur-Seiche, then foll sp La Selle-Guerchaise; site behind Mairie in vill. Sm, hdg/mkd pitch, pt sl, pt shd; htd wc; chem disp (wc); shwrs inc; el pnts (4A) €2; (rev pol, poss long cable req); Indtte; playgrnd, multisports area; fishing adj; 50% statics; dogs; adv bkg; poss noisy; CCI. "Welcoming; excel san facs; site poss untidy low ssn; poss noisy church bells & barking dogs; locked barrier poles OK for cars but too low 4x4s or similar; fair NH." ♦ € 6.80 2006*

GUERCHE SUR L'AUBOIS, LA *4H3* (2km SE Rural) *46.94029, 2.95852* **Camp Municipal Robinson, 2 Rue de Couvache, 18150 La Guerche-sur-l'Aubois [02 48 74 18 86 or 02 48 77 53 53; fax 02 48 77 53 59; vangeluwe.laurence@orange.fr; www.mairie-la-guerche-sur-laubois.com]** Site sp fr D976 opp church in vill cent. Sm, hdg/mkd pitch, pt shd; wc; shwrs inc; el pnts (10A) €3; Indry rm; shop; tradsmn; rest, bar 300m; playgrnd; lake sw adj; fishing; pedalo boating; entmnt; dogs; phone; poss cr; quiet, some rlwy noise; CCI. "Pleasantly situated; v welcoming; clean san facs; gd cycling area; excel." ♦ 15 Apr-15 Oct. € 8.50
2008*

GUERET *7A4* (8km S Rural) *46.10257, 1.83528* **Camp Municipal Le Gué Levard, 5 Rue Gué Levard, 23000 La Chapelle-Taillefert [05 55 51 09 20 or 05 55 52 36 17 (Mairie); www.ot-gueret.fr]** Take junc 48 from N145 sp Tulle/Bourganeuf (D33 thro Guéret); S on D940 fr Guéret, turn off at site sp. Foll sp thro vill, well sp. Sm, hdstg, pt sl, terr, shd; wc; mv service pnt; shwrs inc; el pnts (16A) €2; Indtte; shop; tradsmn; rest, snacks, bar 500m; tradsmn; playgrnd; fishing in Rv Gartempe; sports facs nr; some statics; dogs; phone; quiet; ccard not acc; CCI. "Attractive, peaceful, well-kept site hidden away; new, vg san facs; trout stream runs thro site; gd walking; ltd facs low ssn; warden calls 1900; gd auberge in vill; phone ahead to check open low ssn." ♦
1 Apr-1 Nov. € 7.00 2007*

GUERET *7A4* (3km W Rural) *46.16387, 1.85882* **Camp Municipal du Plan d'Eau de Courtille, Route de Courtille, 23000 Guéret [05 55 81 92 24 or 05 55 52 99 50 (LS)]** Fr W on N145 take D942 to town cent; then take D914 W; take L turn bef lake sp; site in 1.5km along lakeside rd with speed humps. Site sp 'L'Aire de Loisirs de Courtille'. Med, hdg/mkd pitch, pt sl, pt shd; wc (some cont); chem disp; mv service pnt; baby facs; shwrs inc; el pnts (10A) inc; shops 2km; rest, bar 500m; playgrnd; pool 1.5km; sand beach & lake sw; watersports; dogs €0.95; phone; poss cr; no adv bkg; quiet; CCI; "Pleasant scenery; well-managed site; narr ent to pitches; mkd walks nrby; poss noisy w/end." ♦
1 Jun-30 Sep. € 11.00 2006*

GUERNO, LE see Muzillac *2G3*

GUICHEN *2F4* (8km SE Rural) *47.92741, -1.75354* **Camp Municipal La Courbe, 11 Rue du Camping, 35580 Bourg-des-Comptes [06 77 04 37 47 (mob) or 02 99 05 62 62 (Mairie); fax 02 99 05 62 69; bourg-des-comptes@wanadoo.fr]** Fr Rennes take N137 S dir Nantes. At Crévin take rd W dir Guichen. Site sp on L bef bdge over Rv Vilaine. Sm, mkd pitch, pt shd; wc; chem disp; shwrs €0.91; el pnts (10A); shops 800m; rest 1km; bar 200m; playgrnd; lake & rv 100m; fishing; some long-stay statics; dogs; adv bkg; quiet. "Rough field." 1 Apr-31 Oct. 2008*

GUIDEL see Pouldu, Le *2F2*

GUIGNICOURT *3C4* (SE Urban) *49.43209, 3.97035* **Camp Municipal de Guignicourt, Rue des Godins, 02190 Guignicourt [03 23 79 74 58 or 03 23 25 36 60; fax 03 23 79 74 55; camping-guignicourt@wanadoo.fr]** Exit A26 at junc 14 Guignicourt/Neufchâtel & foll sp for Guignicourt (3km). Site sp in vill on rv bank. Turn R at g'ge down narr rd to site (12% descent at ent & ramp). Med, pt mkd pitch, pt shd; htd wc (some cont); chem disp; mv service pnt; shwrs; el pnts (6-16A) €3-7 (poss rev pol, poss long cable req); shops 300m; tradsmn; rest, snacks & bar 600m; BBQ; playgrnd; fishing; tennis; 50% statics (sep area); dogs €1.50; train 500m; poss cr; Eng spkn; adv bkg; quiet; red long stay; ccard acc; CCI. "Pretty, well-kept, well-guarded site; popular NH, conv A26; friendly, helpful staff; clean dated san facs, poss tired high ssn; site poss muddy when wet; pleasant town; excel touring base Reims, Epernay; poss itinerants; no twin-axles; easy access despite gradient; excel." 1 Apr-30 Sep. € 10.60 2009*

⊞ **GUILLESTRE** *9D4* (1km S Rural) *44.65677, 6.63306* **Camping St James Les Pins, 05600 Guillestre [04 92 45 08 24; fax 04 92 45 18 65; camping@lesaintjames.com; www.lesaintjames.com]** Exit N94 onto D902A; in 1km foll Camping sps. Med, mkd pitch, shd; wc; chem disp; mv service pnt; shwrs; el pnts (5A) €2.50-4.50; gas; Indtte; sm shop; rest, snacks & bar 1km; playgrnd; pool & tennis 300m; canoeing nrby; games area; games rm; TV rm; 15% statics; dogs €1; phone; CCI. "Vg." € 12.75
2007*

GUILLESTRE *9D4* (800m SW Rural) *44.65854, 6.63836* **Camp Municipal La Rochette, 05600 Guillestre [tel/fax 04 92 45 02 15; guillestre@aol.com; www.campingguillestre.com]** Exot N94 onto D902A to Guillestre. In 1km fork R on side rd at camp sps. Site on L in 1km. Lge, mkd pitch, pt shd; wc (some cont); shwrs inc; el pnts (4-10A) €2.50-3.40; gas; Indtte; shop; snacks; BBQ; playgrnd; pool, tennis adj; fishing; dir access to rv; sports area; entmnt; poss cr; adv bkg; quiet. "Modern san facs; helpful, friendly manager." ♦ 15 May-22 Sep. € 14.00 2007*

⊞ **GUILLESTRE** *9D4* (3km W Rural) *44.65910, 6.62653* **Camping Le Villard, 05600 Guillestre [04 92 45 06 54; fax 04 92 45 00 52; camping-le-villard@wanadoo.fr; www.camping-levillard.com]** Exit N94 onto D902 twd Guillestre. Site on R in 1km. Ent few metres down side rd with site sp at corner. Med, mkd pitch, shd; wc (some cont); chem disp; shwrs inc; el pnts (2-10A) €1.40-2.80; gas; Indry rm; shop 500m; tradsmn; rest; snacks; bar; playgrnd; sports area; pool; rv adj; fishing; lake 2km; tennis; wintersports; TV rm; entmnt; 10% statics; dogs €1; adv bkg; red low ssn; CCI. "Poss run down low ssn; vg." ♦ € 16.50 2007*

GUILVINEC *2F2* (2.5km W Coastal) *47.80388, -4.31222* **Yelloh! Village la Plage, 29730 Guilvinec [02 98 58 61 90; fax 02 98 58 89 06; info@yellohvillage-la-plage.com; www.villagelaplage.com or www.yellohvillage.com]** Fr Pont l'Abbé on D785 SW to Plomeur; cont S on D57 sp Guilvinec. Bear R on app to town & head W along coast rd twd Penmarch. Site on L in approx 1.5km. Lge, pt shd; wc; chem disp; mv service pnt; baby facs; sauna; shwrs inc; el pnts (5A) inc; gas; Indtte; shop; rest; snacks; bar; BBQ; playgrnd; htd pool; paddling pool; waterslide; sand beach adj; tennis; archery; games rm; fitness rm; cycle hire; wifi; entmnt; 70% statics; dogs €4; c'vans over 8m not acc; poss cr; adv bkg; quiet; ccard acc; red low ssn. "Ideal for families; spacious pitches; site rds poss diff lge o'fits; excel touring base; excursions booked; mkt Tue & Sun." ♦ 2 Apr-12 Sep. € 40.00 ABS - B15 2009*

GUILVINEC *2F2* (3.5km NW Coastal) *47.81819, -4.30942* **Camping Les Genêts, Rue Gouesnac'h Nevez, 29760 Penmarc'h [02 98 58 66 93 or 06 83 15 85 92 (mob); fax 02 98 58 64 15; rohart@wanadoo.fr; www.camping-lesgenets.com]** S fr Pont-l'Abbé on D785 to Plomeur; cont on D785 for another 4km, then turn L onto D53 sp Guilvinec; in 300m turn L into Rue Gouesnac'h Nevez to site. Med, hdg/mkd pitch, pt shd; wc; chem disp; baby facs; shwrs inc; el pnts (10A) €3; gas; Indte; ice; tradsmn; rest; snacks; bar; BBQ; playgrnd, htd pool; sand beach 1.5km; cycle hire nrby; horseriding 800m; TV rm; 25% statics; dogs €1.50; bus; phone; poss cr; Eng spkn; adv bkg; red low ssn/long stay; CCI. "Friendly, family-run site; excel san facs; excel." ♦ 1 Apr-30 Sep. € 16.30 2009*

GUINES *3A3* (2km W Rural) *50.86611, 1.85694* **Camping La Bien Assise, 62340 Guînes [03 21 35 20 77; fax 03 21 36 79 20; castels@bien-assise.com; www.camping-bien-assise.fr or www.les-castels.com]** Exit A16 at junc 40 dir Fréthun Gare TGV; turn L onto D215 dir Fréthun Gare TGV & foll sp Guînes thro St Tricat & Hamas-Boucres (NB 30km/h zone & must give way on R) to rndabt at site ent. Fr S exit A26 junc 2; foll sp to Ardres then take D231 thro Guîes to rndabt to site. NB Arr bet 1000 & 2200 rec; phone ahead if early or late arr anticipated. Lge, hdg/mkd pitch, pt sl, pt shd; htd wc (some cont); chem disp; mv service pnt; baby facs; shwrs inc; el pnts (6A) inc (poss rev pol); gas; Indtte; shop; supmkt 3km; tradsmn; rest (clsd Mon); snacks & bar (high ssn); BBQ; playgrnd; 2 pools (1 htd, covrd); paddling pool; waterslide; beach 12km; tennis; cycle hire; horseriding 3km; wifi; entmnt; TV/games rm; 50% statics (tour ops); dogs €2; v cr high ssn; Eng spkn; adv bkg, rec all times; some rd noise; red long stay/low ssn; ccard acc; CCI. "Well-run, well-kept, busy site in grnds of chateau; lge pitches - some soft low ssn; pleasant, cheerful staff; clean san facs, stretched high ssn; gd rest; vg dog walk; vet in Ardres (9km); late arrivals area - conv ferries; even if notice says 'Complet' check availability for sh stay; mkt Fri; excel." ♦ 30 Mar-25 Sep. € 31.50 ABS - P05 2009*

See advertisement

GUINES *3A3* (1km NW Urban) *50.88562, 1.87080* **Camping La Belle Pêche, 62340 Hames-Boucres [03 21 35 21 07 or 03 21 35 97 00; fax 03 21 82 51 50; camping-belle-peche@wanadoo.fr; www.bellepeche.com]** Fr Guînes foll sp Calais on D127; site on L in 1km. Med, hdg pitch, hdstg, pt shd; wc; chem disp; shwrs inc; el pnts €2.50; shop 500m, rest; bar; playgrnd; rv fishing; tennis; entmnt; 80% statics; Eng spkn; quiet; no cc. "Some pitches flood in wet weather; fishing instruction; conv ferries; Eurotunnel 15 mins." 1 May-30 Oct. € 16.30 2009*

GUIPRY see Bain de Bretagne *2F4*

GUISE *3C4* (SE Urban) *49.89488, 3.63372* **FFCC Camp de la Vallée de l'Oise, Rue du Camping, 02120 Guise [03 23 61 14 86; fax 03 23 61 21 07]** Foll Vervin sp in town & camp clearly sp fr all dirs in town. Med, pt shd; wc (some cont); shwrs inc; el pnts (3-6A) €3-5 (rev pol); lndry rm; shops 500m; tradsmn; playgrnd; rv fishing & canoe hire adj; cycle hire; games rm; TV; entmnt; 50% statics; dogs; some Eng spkn; adv bkg; v quiet; red low ssn; CCI. "Spacious, beautifully kept, friendly site; busy w/ends; gd san facs; interesting old town; if arr late, pitch & pay next morning." 1 Apr-20 Oct. € 10.00 2008*

GUISSENY see Plouguerneau *2E2*

GUJAN MESTRAS see Arcachon *7D1*

HAGETMAU *8E2* (200m S Urban) *43.65020, -0.59190* **Camp Muncipal de la Cité Verte, 40700 Hagetmau [tel/fax 05 58 79 79 79]** On D933 S fr Mont-de-Marsan, go thro St Sever & cont on D933 to Hagetmau. Take ring rd & ent town fr S, sp 'Cité Verte'. Heading N fr Orthez on D933, also foll sp 'Cité Verte'. Sm, hdg pitch, pt shd; wc; chem disp (wc); mv service pnt; serviced pitch; fam bthrm; sauna; shwrs inc; el pnts (16A) inc; shops 500m; rest, snacks, bar 1km; BBQ; playgrnd; htd, covrd pool; jacuzzi; gym; dogs; phone; adv bkg ess; quiet. "A unique site associated with sports cent inc Olympic-sized pool; 24 pitches with personal facs; gd base for touring area; v attractive town; excel." 1 Jun-30 Sep. € 20.00 2006*

HAGUENAU *5D3* (2km S Urban) *48.80289, 7.76911* **Camp Municipal Les Pins, Rue de Strasbourg, 67500 Haguenau [03 88 73 91 43 or 03 88 93 70 00; fax 03 88 93 69 89; tourisme@ville-haguenau.fr; www.ville-haguenau.fr]** N fr Strasbourg; after passing town sp turn L at 2nd set of traff lts; foll camping sp along D263. Med, mkd pitch, terr, pt shd; wc; chem disp; shwrs inc; el pnts (6A) inc; gas; lndry rm; shop & rest 2km; playgrnd; dogs €0.90; phone; adv bkg; quiet; CCI. "Lge pitches; very clean; modern san facs; helpful staff; meals avail fr warden; grnd remains firm even after heavy rain; gd." 1 May-30 Sep. € 12.00 2008*

⊞ **HAMBYE** *1D4* (1.5km N Rural) *48.9600, -1.2600* **Camping aux Champs, 1 Rue de la Ripaudière, 50450 Hambye [02 33 90 06 98; michael.coles@wanadoo.fr]** Exit A84 junc 38 onto D999 to Percy; then turn L at town cent rndabt onto D58 to Hambye; at mkt sq proceed to junc, strt sp Le Guislain, past Mairie; site on R in 1.5 km on D51. Sm, some hdstg, unshd; htd wc; chem disp; fam bthrm; shwrs inc; el pnts (10A) €3; lndtte; shop, rest, snacks, bar 2km; adv bkg; red long stay; quiet; red long stay; CCI. "Friendly, helpful British owners; excel, clean san facs; Abbaye de Hambye nrby; conv ferry ports." € 12.00 2009*

HANNONVILLE SOUS LES COTES *5D2* (3km W Rural) *49.02093, 5.63802* **Camping Le Longeau, 55210 Hannonville-sous-les-Côtes [03 29 87 30 54; fax 03 29 88 84 40]** Fr Hannonville on D908. Foll sp 'Etang du Longeau.' Narr, steep forest tracks to site not rec trailer c'vans. Med, pt shd; wc; chem disp; shwrs inc; el pnts (3-6A) €2.50-4; rest; snacks; bar; fishing; no Eng spkn; quiet. "Gd." Easter-15 Sep. € 8.00 2007*

HARDELOT PLAGE *3A2* (3km NE Urban) *50.64661, 1.62539* **Caravaning du Château d'Hardelot, 21 Rue Nouvelle, 62360 Condette [tel/fax 03 21 87 59 59; contact@camping-caravaning-du-chateau.com; www.camping-caravaning-du-chateau.com]** Take D901 (N1) S fr Boulogne, R turn onto D940 dir Le Touquet; then R at rndabt on D113 to Condette; take 2nd turning to Château Camping, R at next rndabt & site 400m on R. Fr S leave A16 at exit 27 to Neufchâtel-Hardelot, take D940 twd Condette & turn L at 1st rndabt onto D113, then as above. Not well sp last 3km. Tight turn into site ent. Med, hdg/mkd pitch, pt sl, pt shd; wc; chem disp; mv service pnt; baby facs; shwrs inc; el pnts (10A) €4.70 (poss rev pol); lndtte; shop 500m; playgrnd; sand beach 3km; tennis 500m; sm multi-gym; horseriding; games rm; golf; 30% statics; dogs free; poss cr; some Eng spkn; adv bkg (rec high ssn); some rd noise; no ccard acc; red low ssn; CCI. "Lovely, well-run, wooded site; popular & busy high ssn; sm pitches; helpful, friendly owner; clean, modern san facs; conv Calais (site barrier opens 0800)." ♦ 1 Apr-31 Oct. € 20.60 2009*

HAULME see Charleville Mézières *5C1*

HAUTECOURT ROMANECHE see Bourg en Bresse *9A2*

HAUTEFORT *7C3* (3km NE Rural) *45.28081, 1.15917* **Camping La Grenouille, Brégérac, 24390 Hautefort [tel/fax 05 53 50 11 71; info@lagrenouillevacances.com; www.lagrenouillevacances.com]** Fr N on D704 at Cherveil-Cubas take D77 dir Boisseuilh/Teillots. In 4km turn R & in 800m turn L to site. Fr S on D704 at St Agnan take D62 sp Hautefort/Badefols d'Ans. Pass 'Vival' (sm shop on L) in Hautefort & turn L dir Boisseuilh. After 1st bdge turn L to La Besse & site in 2km. Sm, pt sl, pt shd; wc; chem disp; shwrs inc; el pnts (8A) €3.50; lndtte; ice; shop & 3km; tradsmn; rest; bar 3km; BBQ; playgrnd; pool; wifi; dogs free; Eng spkn; adv bkg; v quiet; ccard not acc; CCI. "Tranquil, scenic, well-kept site; friendly, helpful, Dutch owners; vg san facs; meals avail; goats, guinea pigs, chickens in pens on site; gd walking; highly rec." 15 Apr-15 Oct. € 18.00 2009*

HAUTEFORT *7C3* (8km W Rural) *45.28032, 1.04845* **Camping Les Tourterelles, 24390 Tourtoirac [05 53 51 11 17; les-trouterelles@tiscali.com; www.les-tourterelles.com]** Fr N or S on D704 turn W at Hautefort on D62/D5 to Tourtoirac. In Tourtoirac turn R over rv then L. Site in 1km. Med, hdg/mkd pitch, terr, pt shd; wc; chem disp; mv service pnt; baby facs; shwrs; el pnts (6A) inc; gas; Indtte; shop 2km; rest; snacks; bar; playgrnd; pool; tennis; horseriding; TV rm; 20% statics; dogs €4; bus 1km; phone; poss cr; Eng spkn; adv bkg; quiet; low ssn/snr citizens red; ccard acc; CCI. "Beautiful Auvézère valley; rallies welcome; owners helpful; equestrian cent; gd walks." ♦ 25 Apr-27 Sep. € 29.00 2008*

HAUTERIVES see Beaurepaire *9C2*

⊞ **HAUTEVILLE LOMPNES** *9B3* (500m SW Rural) *45.97266, 5.59543* **Camp Municipal Les Aberreaux, 125 Chemin des Lésines, 01110 Hauteville-Lompnes [tel/fax 04 74 35 36 73; mairie.hauteville.01@wanadoo.fr]** Site sp fr only rndabt in Hauteville-Lompnes; adj casino. Access via lane L fr Chemin des Lésines immed after lge terracotta-coloured building. Sm, hdg/mkd pitch, pt shd; wc chem disp (wc); shwrs inc; el pnts €1.80; gas 1km; Indry rm; shop, rest, snacks & bar 1km; htd covrd pool adj; 30% statics; CCI. "Clean, basic site adj sports complex; calm & pleasant; lge pitches; vg touring base; winter sports vill; vg." € 6.30 2008*

HAUTOT SUR MER see Dieppe *3C2*

HAYE DU PUITS, LA *1D4* (1km N Rural) *49.29980, -1.54495* **Camping L'Etang des Haizes, 50250 St Symphorien-le-Valois [02 33 46 01 16; fax 02 33 47 23 80; info@campingetangdeshaizes.com; www.campingetangdeshaizes.com]** Heading N fr La Haye-du-Puits on D900 under rlwy bdge & site 3rd on L, well sp. Med, hdg pitch, some hdstg, pt sl, pt shd; wc; chem disp; mv service pnt; baby facs; shwrs inc; el pnts (10A) €2-6; gas; Indtte; supmkt 1km; shop; tradsmn; rest; snacks; bar; playgrnd; htd pool complex; waterslide; beach 15km; archery; fishing; cycle hire; games area; entmnt; TV rm; 50% statics (sep area); dogs €2; bus; phone; poss cr; Eng spkn; adv bkg rec; quiet; red low ssn; CCI. "Pretty, well-kept, well-run site in nature park; helpful, pleasant owners; ltd facs low ssn; barrier clsd 2300-0700; conv Cherbourg ferry (1hr)." ♦ 1 Apr-15 Oct. € 27.00 (CChq acc) 2009*

HAYE DU PUITS, LA *1D4* (6km N Urban) *49.38725, -1.52755* **FFCC Camp Municipal du Vieux Château, Ave de la Division-Leclerc, 50390 St Sauveur-le-Vicomte [02 33 41 72 04 or 02 33 21 50 44; fax 02 33 95 88 85; ot.ssv@wanadoo.fr; www.saintsauveurlevicomte.fr.tc]** Fr Cherbourg on N13/D2 site on R after x-ing bdge at St Sauveur-le-Vicomte, sp. Med, mkd pitch, pt sl, pt shd; wc; chem disp; shwrs inc; el pnts (6A) €1.80 (poss rev pol); Indtte; shop 500m; tradsmn; rest adj; BBQ; playgrnd adj; pool, tennis 1km; games area; games rm; TV; dogs €1.10; phone; adv bkg; quiet; ccard acc; CCI. "Excel site in chateau grounds; friendly warden; gd facs; ideal 1st stop fr Cherbourg; office open until 2200 for late arr; barrier clsd 2200-0800." 1 Jun-15 Sep. € 9.10 2009*

HEIMSBRUNN see Mulhouse *6F3*

HEMING *6E3* (5km SW Rural) *48.69130, 6.92769* **Camping Les Mouettes, 57142 Gondrexange [03 87 25 06 01; fax 03 87 25 01 13]** Exit Héming on N4 Strasbourg-Nancy. Foll sp Gondrexange & site sp. App fr W on D955 turn to site sp on L about 1km bef Héming. Lge, mkd pitch, pt sl, unshd; htd wc; chem disp; mv service pnt; shwrs inc; el pnts (2-6A) €2-4.50 (rev pol); Indtte; shop, rest, snacks, bar 200m; playgrnd; lake beach, sw, fishing & sailing adj; tennis; cycle hire; 60% statics; phone; poss cr; quiet; CCI. "Pleasant site by lake; poss noisy w/end; basic facs but clean." 1 Apr-30 Sep. € 11.50 2007*

HENDAYE *8F1* (2km N Rural) *43.3719, -1.7470* **Camping Les Acacias, Route de la Glacière, 64700 Hendaye-Plage [tel/fax 05 59 20 78 76; info@les-acacias.com; www.les-acacias.com]** Exit A63 junc 2 or N10 onto D913 twd coast. Then foll D912 Route de la Corniche dir Hendaye. At Aizpurdi rndabt turn L, site sp. Lge, sl, shd; wc; mv service pnt; shwrs; el pnts (6A) €4.80 (rev pol); gas; Indtte; shop; supmkt 3km; rest; snacks; bar in high ssn; playgrnd; sand beach 1.4km (free shuttle); lake sw & waterslide 1.5km; 50% statics; dogs €2.80; poss cr; adv bkg; quiet but some rlwy noise. "Helpful management; 5km to Spanish frontier; many tours in mountains; easy access shops & beaches; own lake for trout fishing." 1 Apr-30 Sep. € 21.50 2007*

HENDAYE *8F1* (2km W Urban/Coastal) *43.37335, -1.75608* **Camping Ametza, Blvd de l'Empereur, 64700 Hendaye-Plage [05 59 20 07 05; fax 05 59 20 32 16; contact@camping-ametza.com; www.camping-ametza.com]** Exit A63 junc 2 St Jean-de-Luz S onto D192. Foll sp to site. Turn L on hill down to seafront, cross rlwy, site immed on L. Lge, sl, shd; wc; chem disp; baby facs; shwrs inc; el pnts (6A) €5 (poss rev pol); Indry rm; shop; snacks; bar; playgrnd; pool; sand; beach 900m; games area; entmnt; wifi; 30% statics; dogs €2; poss cr; Eng spkn; quiet but rd & rlwy noise; red low ssn; CCI. "Lovely relaxed site; some gd sized pitches, some sm; excel facs; Henday pleasant resort; excel beach in walking dist; excel." 1 May-30 Sep. € 24.50 2009*

HENNEBONT see Lorient *2F2*

HENNEVEUX see Boulogne sur Mer *3A2*

HENRIDORFF see Phalsbourg *5D3*

HENVIC see St Pol de Léon *1D2*

HERBIGNAC *2G3* (300m E Rural) *47.44802, -2.31073* **Camp Municipal Le Ranrouet, Rue René Guy Cadou, 44410 Herbignac [02 40 88 96 23]** Site at intersection D774 & D33 on E edge of vill. Med, mkd pitch, pt shd; wc; chem disp; mv service pnt; shwrs; el pnts (6A); Indtte; supmkt, bar adj; rest 1km; playgrnd; beach 10km; entmnt; TV; CCI. "Immac san facs; gd cent for Guérande." Easter-30 Oct. 2008*

France

⊞ **HERIC** *2G4* (2km W Rural) *47.41329, -1.67050* **Camping La Pindière, La Denais, Route de la Fay-de-Bretagne, 44810 Héric [tel/fax 02 40 57 65 41; camping.pindiere@free.fr; www.camping-la-pindiere.com]** Exit N137 twd Héric at traff lts in town, leave town & turn W onto D16 (sp Camping). Site on L after rndabt supmkt, turn at sp Notre Dames-des-Landes. Med, hdg pitch, hdstg, pt shd; wc; chem disp; mv service pnt; baby facs; shwrs inc; el pnts (6-10A) €3.20-4.80; gas; lndtte; shop or 1.5km; tradsmn; rest; bar; playgrnd; htd pool; paddling pool; sports facs; tennis; horseriding 200m; TV; 80% statics; dogs €1.40; phone; Eng spkn; adv bkg rec, site poss clsd w/end low ssn; some noise fr rd on N side; red low ssn; CCI. "Pleasant site; lge, grass pitches, soft in wet weather; warm welcome; gd clean san facs; gd NH; vg." ♦ € 14.00 2009*

HERICOURT EN CAUX see Yvetot *3C2*

HERISSON *7A4* (500m NW Rural) *46.51055, 2.70576* **Camp Municipal de l'Aumance, Rue de Crochepot, 03190 Hérisson [04 70 06 80 45 or 04 70 06 85 93]** Exit A71 junc 9 onto D2144 (N144) N; turn R onto D11 dir Hérisson; immed bef T-junc with D3 turn L at blue sp (high on L) into Rue de Crochepot; site on R down hill. Med, mkd pitch, pt shd; wc; shwrs inc; el pnts (10A) inc; playgrnd; games area; rv adj; phone. "Idyllic setting; delightful rvside site; warden calls eves; rec." 1 Apr-30 Oct. € 6.94 2009*

HERMENT *7B4* (N Rural) *45.75481, 2.56683* **Camp Municipal de Herment, Rue de la Chapelle, 63470 Herment [04 73 22 11 98]** Fr main rd thro vill, foll sp upwards thro older part of town. No name on rd of site. Sm, hdg/mkd pitch, pt shd; wc; el pnts (6A) €0.76; shops 500m; quiet. "Pitches poss diff access lge o'fits; el pnts hidden behind bushes on pitch." ♦ € 5.50 2009*

HERPELMONT see Bruyères *6E2*

HESDIN *3B3* (6km SE Rural) *50.35982, 2.06826* **Camping de la Route des Villages Fleuris, 98 Rue de Frévent, 62770 St Georges [03 21 03 11 01 or 03 21 41 97 45]** Fr Hesdin, SE on D340 for 5.5km. Site on L in vill, in same rd as Camping St Ladre. Look for correct sp. Med, mkd pitch, pt sl, pt shd; wc (some cont); chem disp; shwrs €1; el pnts (4A) €2.30; gas; shops 6km; tradsmn; BBQ; playgrnd; 90% statics; adv bkg; quiet; CCI. "Space for approx 7 tourers at rear of site; security barrier; friendly warden - can find him in bungalow to L of site ent; gd." 1 Apr-30 Sep. 2006*

HESDIN *3B3* (6km SE Rural) *50.35979, 2.07116* **Camping St Ladre, 66 Rue Principale, 62770 St Georges [03 21 04 83 34; bd-martin@wanadoo.fr; http://monsite.wanadoo.fr/martinbernard]** Fr Hesdin SE on D340 for 5.5km. Site on L after St Georges, ent narr lane next cottage on bend. Fr W on D939 (N39) or D349 foll sp Frévent, then St Georges. Sp to site poor. Sm, hdg/mkd pitch, pt shd; wc; chem disp; shwrs inc; el pnts (5A) €2.50; lndtte; tradsmn; no statics; adv bkg; quiet; ccard not acc; CCI. "Sm, family-run, peaceful site in orchard; basic facs but clean; welcoming, pleasant owner; conv Channel ports, Agincourt & Crécy; usual agricultural noises; gd rests in Hesdin." 1 Apr-30 Oct. € 8.00 2006*

⊞ **HESDIN** *3B3* (12km NW Rural) *50.41971, 1.91243* **Camp Municipal La Source, Rue des Etangs, 62990 Beaurainville [03 21 81 40 71 or 06 80 32 17 25 (mob); fax 03 21 90 02 88]** Fr Hesdin take D349 NW to Beaurainville. Site on R bef cent of town, 1.5km E of town cent nr lake; sp. Med, mkd pitch, pt shd; htd wc; shwrs inc; el pnts (10A) inc (poss rev pol); lndtte; shop 1km; bar; playgrnd; fishing; boating; games area; horseriding; 90% statics; 10% red long stay; CCI. "Ltd touring pitches; site poss clsd in winter - phone ahead; pleasant area with plenty wildlife; poss cold shwrs low ssn; gd NH." ♦ € 12.60 2006*

HEUDICOURT see St Mihiel *5D2*

HEURTEAUVILLE see Bourg Achard *3D2*

HILLION see St Brieuc *2E3*

HIRSON *3C4* (3km N Rural) *49.94344, 4.08796* **Camping de la Cascade, Blangy, 02500 Hirson [03 23 58 18 97; fax 03 23 58 74 51; lousoulei@wanadoo.fr]** Exit Hirson W twd La Capelle & turn R on D963; at rndabt (site sp) fork R immed; foll site sp. Long, narr access rd. Med, hdg/mkd pitch, pt sl, pt shd; wc; chem disp; mv service pnt; shwrs inc; el pnts (6-13A) €3-4; lndtte; shop; tradsmn; rest, snacks 2km; bar; BBQ; playgrnd; pool high ssn; 25% statics; dogs €0.50; Eng spkn; adv bkg ess high ssn; quiet but some rlwy noise; CCI. "Clean site & facs; 2,500kg weight limit; pitches uneven; rec arr bet 1000-1200 & 1700-1900; popular with youth groups - rec do not stay if gangs of youths on site as poss intimidating behaviour & threats + noise into small hours (July 2008); conv NH." ♦ 15 Apr-15 Sep. € 9.60 2009*

HIRSON *3C4* (10km N Rural) *50.00585, 4.06195* **Camping Les Etangs des Moines, 59610 Fourmies [03 27 60 04 32; fourmies@atouvert.com; www.atouvert.com]** Fr Hirson head N on D964 to Anor. Turn L to Fourmies, site sp on R on ent town. Med, hdg pitch, hdstg, pt shd; wc; chem disp; shwrs €1; el pnts (10A) €3.20; lndtte (inc dryer); shop 1km; tradsmn; playgrnd; htd pool; 80% statics; dogs €1; no twin-axles; poss cr; Eng spkn; some rlwy noise; CCI. "Textile & eco museum in town; shwrs run down, other facs gd; vg." 1 Apr-31 Oct. € 10.80 2007*

⊞ **HOHWALD, LE** *6E3* (1km W Urban) *48.40626, 7.32340* **Camp Municipal Herenhause, 28 Rue du Herrenhaus, 67140 Le Hohwald [tel/fax 03 88 08 30 90]** Site on W o'skts of town on D425 300m fr cent. Med, pt sl, terr, shd; htd wc; shwrs inc; lndtte; shops adj; el pnts (10A) €2-4; snacks; playgrnd; tennis 300m; many statics; dogs €1.65; adv bkg; quiet. "Beautiful setting in pine woodland; san facs dated but immac." € 10.45 2007*

France

HONFLEUR *3C1* (5km S Rural) *49.40083, 0.30638* **Camping Domaine Catinière, Route d' Honfleur, 27210 Fiquefleur-Equainville [02 32 57 63 51; fax 02 32 42 12 57; info@camping-catiniere.com; www.camping-catiniere.com]** Fr A29/Pont de Normandie (toll) bdge exit junc 3 sp Le Mans, pass under m'way onto D580/D180. In 3km go strt on at rndabt & in 100m bear R onto D22 dir Beuzeville; site sp on R in 500m. Med, hdg/mkd pitch, pt shd; wc (some cont); chem disp; shwrs inc; baby facs; el pnts (4A) inc (long lead poss req)(poss rev pol), extra charge for 8-13A; Indtte; sm shop & 3km; tradsmn; snacks, takeaway & bar in high ssn; BBQ; playgrnd; htd pool; waterslide; rv fishing; games rm; entmnt; wifi; TV rm; 15% statics; dogs €2; phone; poss cr; Eng spkn; adv bkg rec high ssn & w/end; quiet; ccard acc only over €70; CCI. "Attractive, well-kept site; lge & sm pitches; friendly staff; gd san facs, ltd low ssn; gate clsd 2200-0800 (2300 high ssn); poss school groups; gd walks; easy parking for m'vans nr town; 20 mins to Le Havre ferry via Normandy bdge; conv A13; highly rec." ♦ 2 Apr-20 Sep. € 26.00 ABS - N16 2009*

See advertisement

HONFLEUR *3C1* (2.5km SW Rural) *49.39777, 0.20861* **Camping La Briquerie, 14600 Equemauville [02 31 89 28 32; fax 02 31 89 08 52; info@campinglabriquerie.com; www.campinglabriquerie.com]** Fr E ent town cent keeping harbour on R. Turn L onto D279 then in 2km turn R at rndabt at Intermarché. Site on R, N of water tower, E of Equemauville. Site well sp fr town cent. Fr S take D579 dir Honfleur Centre. At water tower on R turn L at Intermarché rndabt, site on R in 300m. Lge, hdg pitch, pt shd; wc; chem disp; mv service pnt; baby facs; fam bthrm; shwrs inc; el pnts (5-10A) €4-5 (poss rev pol); gas; Indtte; supmkt adj; rest, snacks & bar (high ssn); BBQ; playgrnd; 3 htd pools; waterslide (high ssn); sand beach 2.5km; tennis, horseriding 500m; games rm; fitness rm; wifi; TV rm; entmnt; 50% statics; dogs €3; poss cr; Eng spkn; adv bkg (fee for Jul/Aug); quiet; red low ssn; ccard not acc; CCI. "Gd pitches; clean facs; staff helpful late/early ferry arrivals; local vets geared up for dog inspections, etc; gd." ♦ 1 Apr-30 Sep. € 22.80 2009*

HONFLEUR *3C1* (800m NW Coastal) *49.42445, 0.22753* **Camp du Phare, Blvd Charles V, 14600 Honfleur [02 31 24 22 12 (Central Reservations); fax 02 31 96 06 05; vival-cabourg@wanadoo.fr; www.campings-plage.com/phare_honfleur]** Fr N fr Pont de Normandie on D929 take D144; at ent to Honfleur keep harbour in R; turn R onto D513 sp Trouville-sur-Mer & Deauville (avoid town cent); fork L past old lighthouse to site entry thro parking area. Or fr E on D180; foll sp 'Centre Ville' then Vieux Bassin dir Trouville; at rectangular rndabt with fountain turn R sp Deauville & Trouville, then as above. Med, hdg pitch, pt shd; wc (some cont); chem disp; mv service pnt; shwrs €1.20; el pnts (2-10A) €4.05-5.80; gas; Indtte; shop 800m; tradsmn; rest 1km; snacks; bar; BBQ; playgrnd; htd, covrd pool nr; sand beach 100m; fishing; 10% statics; dogs €2.50; phone; poss cr; Eng spkn; rd noise; no ccard acc; red low ssn; CCI. "Gd clean site in excel location; conv NH Le Havre ferry; friendly owners; m'van pitches narr & adj busy rd; some soft, sandy pitches; facs ltd low ssn; barrier clsd 2200-0700; easy walk to town/harbour; sep m'van Aire de Service nr harbour." 30 Mar-30 Sep. € 18.70 2009*

HONNECOURT SUR ESCAUT *3B4* (Urban) *50.03834, 3.19940* **FFCC Camping de l'Escaut, 12 Rue de L'Eglise, 59266 Honnecourt-sur-Escaut [tel/fax 03 27 74 32 22; camping.de.lescaut@orange.fr; www.campingdelescaut.fr]** Fr Cambrai on D644 (N44) S twd St Quentin. Turn R onto D16 dir Honnecourt. Or fr A26 exit junc 9 onto D917 then D644. In Honnecourt after x-ing canal turn L in 150m; site behind church. Well sp. Med, hdg/mkd pitch, pt shd; wc; chem disp (wc); shwrs €1.20; mv service pnt; el pnts (6A) €3 (poss rev pol); Indtte; snacks; BBQ; playgrnd; fishing; 80% statics; dogs; adv bkg; CCI. "Lovely, peaceful site; lge pitches; gd, clean san facs; resident warden; gd NH." 1 Feb-30 Nov. € 11.00 2009*

HOSPITALET, L' *8G4* (600m N Rural) *42.59121, 1.80333* **Camp Municipal, 09390 L'Hospitalet-près-l'Andorre [05 61 05 21 10; fax 05 61 05 23 08; mairie.lhospitalet-pres-landorre@wanadoo.fr]** Site clearly sp on N20 fr Ax-les-Thermes to Andorra. Med, terr, unshd; wc; mv service pnt; shwrs inc; el pnts (5A) €2.30; Indtte; shops 200m; dogs; adv bkg; quiet but some rd noise. "Mainly tents, ltd space for tourers; vg walking; immac facs; conv day trips to Andorra & Spain; friendly warden; excel views." 1 Jun-31 Oct. € 9.80 2008*

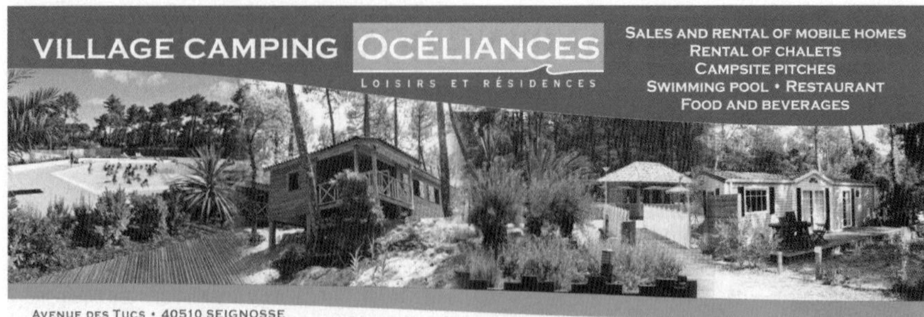

HOSSEGOR *8E1* (6km N Coastal) *43.69490, -1.42953* **Village Camping Océliances, Ave des Tucs, 40510 Seignosse [05 58 43 30 30; fax 05 58 41 64 21; oceliances@wanadoo.fr; www.oceliances.com]** Take D79 N fr Hossegor. After 6km turn L at rndabt. Site sp. Lge, mkd pitch, pt sl, pt shd; htd wc; chem disp; baby facs; shwrs inc; el pnts (6A) €3.90; gas; Indtte; shop; rest; snacks; bar; BBQ; playgrnd; pool; paddling pool; sand beach 600m; windsurfing; lake 2km; games area; games rm; cycle hire; entmnt; 65% statics; dogs €3.40; Eng spkn; adv bkg; quiet; ccard acc; red long stay/low ssn. "Pleasant site in pine forest." ♦ 29 Apr-29 Sep. € 26.60 2009*

See advertisement above

HOSSEGOR *8E1* (1.5km NE Urban) *43.67212, -1.42035* **Camping Le Lac, 580 Routes des Lacs, 40150 Hossegor [05 58 43 53 14; fax 05 58 43 55 83; info@camping-du-lac.com; www.camping-du-lac.com]** Exit A63 junc 8 or N10 onto D28 sp Hossegor/Capbreton & foll sp for town cent. Site well sp at Soorts-Hossegor. Lge, hdg/mkd pitch, pt shd; wc (some cont); chem disp (wc); mv service pnt; shwrs inc; el pnts (6A) inc; gas; Indtte (inc dryer); shop; tradsmn; rest; snacks; bar; playgrnd; pool; paddling pool; sand beach 2km; lake 300m; games area; cycle hire; wifi; 80% statics; dogs €4; poss cr; Eng spkn; adv bkg; some rd noise; ccard acc; CCI. "Ltd space for tourers." ♦ 1 Apr-30 Sep. € 34.00 2009*

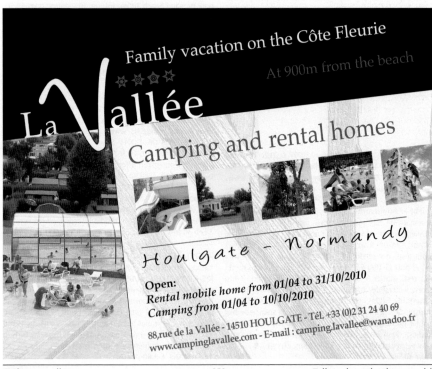

HOSSEGOR *8E1* (2km S Coastal) *43.62947, -1.43270* **Camping La Civelle (formerly Municipal), Rue des Biches, 40130 Capbreton [05 58 72 15 11]** Fr N on A63, take exit 8 & foll sps to Capbreton; cont twds cent. At 1st rndabt, turn L past Intermarché. Strt on at 2nd rndabtat. At 3rd rndabt take 3rd exit & foll sp for site. Lge, mkd pitch, shd; wc (some cont); chem disp; 10% serviced pitches; el pnts inc; gas; lndtte; shop 1.5km; snacks; rest; pool; many statics; phone; ccard acc; CCI. "Busy site; no arrivals bef 1500 - poss queues lunchtime high ssn when office clsd; some sandy pitches; conv for area; cycle rte dir to beach." 1 Jun-30 Sep. € 20.95 2006*

⊞ **HOSSEGOR** *8E1* (3km S Coastal) *43.65168, -1.42998* **Camp Municipal Bel Air, Ave de Bourret, 40130 Capbreton [05 58 72 12 04; secretariat-general@capbreton.fr]** Fr N10 or A63, take D28 to Capbreton; turn R onto D152; turn L at 4th rndabt, site on L in 200m. Med, hdg pitch, pt sl, pt shd; wc; chem disp; shwrs; el pnts (10A) inc; gas; lndtte; shops 500m; tradsmn; playgrnd; sand beach 1km; cycle hire adj; dogs €2.05; quiet; 10% red low ssn; CCI. "No arr bef 1500; card-op barrier, rec phone ahead to arrange access; arr bef 2000 unless late arr agreed in advance; vg winter NH/sh stay but phone ahead to check open; marina nrby, gd fishing; network of cycle paths; excel surfing; conv Biarritz." ♦ € 24.40 2009*

HOSSEGOR *8E1* (4km S Coastal) *43.62164, -1.44044* **Camping de la Pointe, Ave Jean Lartigau, 40130 Capbreton [05 58 72 14 98 or 05 58 72 35 34; info@camping-lapointe.com; www.camping-lapointe.com or www.homair.com]** Fr N10 at Labenne, take D652 twd Capbreton. In 5km turn L at camp sp. Site in 1km on R. Lge, shd; wc; chem disp; shwrs inc; el pnts €3; gas; lndtte; shop; rest; snacks; playgrnd; htd pool; paddling pool; sand beach 800m; entmnt; TV; mainly statics; dogs €2; Eng spkn; quiet; ccard acc. 1 Apr-31 Oct. € 23.00 2007*

HOULGATE *3D1* (3.5km NE Coastal) *49.30699, -0.04382* **Camping Les Falaises, Route de la Corniche, 14510 Gonneville-sur-Mer [02 31 24 81 09; fax 02 31 28 04 11; camping.lesfalaises@voila.fr; www.lesfalaises.com]** Fr D513 take D163; site clearly sp close to Auberville. Lge, pt sl, pt shd, wc; chem disp (wc); shwrs inc; el pnts (4-6A) €3.90-4.60 (poss v long lead req); snacks; shop; gas; htd pool; playgrnd; 30% statics; dogs €2.50; poss cr. "Nice site, different areas sep by trees; most pitches sl & poss uneven; pleasant, helpful staff; gd, clean facs, red low ssn." ♦ 1 Apr-15 Oct. € 18.15 2009*

HOULGATE *3D1* (1km E Urban) *49.29223, -0.07428* **Camp Municipal des Chevaliers, Chemin des Chevaliers, 14510 Houlgate [02 31 24 37 93; fax 02 31 28 37 13; camping-chevaliers.houlgate@orange.fr; www.ville-houlgate.fr]** Fr Deauville take D513 SW twds Houlgate; 500m after 'Houlgate' town sp, turn L & foll camping sps to site, 250m after Camping de la Vallée. Lge, mkd pitch, pt sl, pt terr, unshd; wc; shwrs inc; el pnts (6-10A) €2.70-4.40; tradsmn; sand beach, fishing & boating 800m; dogs €0.75; adv bkg (rec high ssn); v quiet. "Facs simple but adequate & clean; barrier clsd 1800-0700 (low ssn), key avail; conv for town; excel." ♦ 1 Apr-30 Sep. € 9.05 2009*

HOULGATE *3D1* (1km E Coastal) *49.29390, -0.06820* **Camping La Vallée, 88 Rue de la Vallée, 14510 Houlgate [02 31 24 40 69; fax 02 31 24 42 42; camping.lavallee@wanadoo.fr; www.campinglavallee.com]** Exit junc 29 or 29a fr A13 onto D45 to Houlgate. Or fr Deauville take D513 W. Before Houlgate sp, turn L & foll sp to site. Lge, hdg/mkd pitch, pt sl, terr, pt shd; htd wc; chem disp; mv service pnt; some serviced pitches; shwrs inc; el pnts (4A) inc; gas; lndtte; supmkt; tradsmn; rest; snacks; bar; playgrnd; htd, covrd pool; paddling pool; waterslide; sand beach 900m; lake fishing 2km; tennis; cycle hire; golf 1km; games rm; entmnt; internet; TV rm; 30% statics; dogs €5; Eng spkn; adv bkg; ccard acc; red low ssn; CCI. "Superb, busy site; clean san facs; friendly recep; some pitches sm for lge o'fits & sl; sep area m'vans." ♦ 1 Apr-10 Oct. € 30.00 (CChq acc) 2009*

See advertisement opposite (below)

HOUMEAU, L' see Rochelle, La *7A1*

HOUPLINES see Armentières *3A3*

HOURTIN *7C1* (1.5km N Rural) *45.17242, -1.05337* **Camping L'Orée du Bois, Route d'Aquitaine, 33990 Hourtin [tel/fax 05 56 09 15 88 or 06 09 65 48 96 (mob); loree-du-bois@wanadoo.fr; www.camping-loreedubois.fr.st]** Fr Hourtin, take D101E twd beach, site in 1.5km. Med, shd; wc; shwrs inc; el pnts (3-6A) €3; gas; lndtte; shop; snacks; bar; playgrnd; pool; sand beach 8km; entmnt; dogs €1.50; adv bkg; quiet; red low ssn. "In Médoc area with its chateaux & wines." May-Sep. € 18.00 2007*

HOURTIN *7C1* (1.5km W Rural) *45.17935, -1.07451* **Camping La Rotonde - Le Village Western, Chemin de Bécassine, 33990 Hourtin [05 56 09 10 60; fax 05 56 73 81 37; la-rotonde@wanadoo.fr; www.village-western.com]** In Hourtin, foll sp Hourtin Port; in 1.5km L at sp; site on L 200m. Lge, pt shd; wc; chem disp; shwrs inc; el pnts (4-6A) €3.80-4.15; gas; lndtte; shop & 2km; Tex-Mex rest; snacks; bar; playgrnd; pool in ssn; lake sw & beach 500m; watersports; tennis; games area; games rm; entmnt; internet; 30% statics; dogs €2.05; adv bkg; quiet; ccard acc; CCI. "In pine forest nr largest lake in France; gates shut 2230-0730 high ssn. " ♦ 1 Apr-30 Sep. € 24.25 2007*

HOURTIN *7C1* (1.5km W Rural) *45.17919, -1.07502* **Camping Les Ourmes, 90 Ave du Lac, 33990 Hourtin [05 56 09 12 76; fax 05 56 09 23 90; info@lesourmes.com; www.lesourmes.com]** Fr vill of Hourtin (35km NW Bordeaux), foll sp Houtin Port. In 1.5km, L at sp to site. Lge, mkd pitch, pt shd; wc; chem disp; mv service pnt; baby facs; shwrs inc; el pnts (6A) inc; gas; lndtte; shops 1.5km; tradsmn; rest, snacks, bar 1.5km; BBQ; playgrnd; pool; lake sw 1km; sand beach (sea) 10km; watersports; fishing; horseriding; games rm; entmnt; TV; 10% statics; dogs €2; phone; bus; poss cr in ssn; Eng spkn; adv bkg; quiet; CCI. "Excel for family holiday; Lake Hourtin shallow & excel for bathing, sailing etc; vg beaches nrby; nr Les Landes & Médoc vineyards." 1 Apr-30 Sep. € 23.00 2007*

France

HOURTIN *7C1* (10km W Coastal) *45.22296, -1.16472* **Airotel Camping de la Côte d'Argent, 33990 Hourtin-Plage [05 56 09 10 25; fax 05 56 09 24 96; info@camping-cote-dargent.com; www.camping-cote-dargent.com]** On D1215 (N215) at Lesparre-Médoc take D3 Hourtin, D101 to Hourtin-Plage, site sp. V lge, mkd pitch, pt sl, some terr, shd; wc; chem disp; mv service pnt; baby facs; fam bthrm; shwrs inc; el pnts (6A) inc; gas; Indry rm; ice; shop; rest; snacks; bar; BBQ; playgrnd; 3 htd, pools (1 covrd); waterslide; jacuzzi; huge sand beach 300m; watersports; lake sw & fishing 4km; horseriding; cycle hire; games area; games rm; wifi; entmnt; 30% statics; dogs €5.50; phone; Eng spkn; adv bkg; quiet; ccard acc; red low ssn/long stay; CCI. "Pleasant, peaceful site in pine trees & dunes; poss steel pegs req; conv Médoc region chateaux & vineyards; ideal for surfers & beach lovers." ♦ 12 May-19 Sep. € 46.00 (CChq acc) 2009*

See advertisement

HOURTIN PLAGE see Hourtin *7C1*

HUANNE MONTMARTIN see Baume les Dames *6G2*

HUELGOAT *2E2* (3km E Rural) *48.36275, -3.71532* **FFCC Camping La Rivière d'Argent, La Coudraie, 29690 Huelgoat [02 98 99 72 50; fax 02 98 99 90 61; campriviere@wanadoo.fr; www.larivieredargent.com]** Sp fr town cent on D769A sp Poullaouen & Carhaix. Med, some hdg/mkd pitch, shd; wc; chem disp; shwrs inc; el pnts (6-10A) €3.60-4.30; Indtte; shops 3km; rest, snacks, playgrnd; pool, tennis & entmnt high ssn; dogs €1.60; adv bkg; quiet; red long stay/low ssn. "Lovely wooded site on rv bank; some rvside pitches; helpful owner; ltd facs low ssn; gd walks with maps provided." 12 Apr-12 Oct. € 13.50 2009*

HUELGOAT *2E2* (800m W Rural) *48.36388, -3.76361* **Camp Municipal du Lac, Le Faô, 29690 Huelgoat [02 98 99 78 80; fax 02 98 99 75 72; mairie.huelgoat@wanadoo.fr]** Fr cent of Huelgoat foll unnumbered rd W sp La Feuillée/Brest; foll site sp. Med, pt hdstg pitch, pt shd; wc; chem disp; shwrs inc; el pnts (3-10A) €2.10; Indry rm; shops 600m; rest, bar 500m; playgrnd; htd pool adj; dogs €1.20; no adv bkg; quiet; no ccard acc; CCI. "Peaceful site at end of lake (no sw); gd size pitches; gd san facs; gd walking." Jul-Aug. € 11.40 2009*

HUISSEAU SUR COSSON see Blois *4G2*

HUMES JORQUENAY see Langres *6F1*

HYERES *10F3* (4km E Coastal) *43.12050, 6.18464* **Camping Port Pothuau, 101 Chemin des Ourlèdes, 83400 Hyères [04 94 66 41 17; fax 04 94 66 33 09; pothuau@free.fr; www.campingportpothuau.com]** Fr Hyères E twds Nice on D98, turn R on D12 sp Salins d'Hyères. Site 2nd on R. Lge, mkd pitch, shd; wc; some serviced pitches; shwrs; el pnts (6-10A) inc (check rev pol/earth & poss long lead req); gas; Indtte; shop; rest; snacks; bar; playgrnd; pool; sand beach 1km; tennis; games area; cycle hire; TV; 90% statics; dogs €3; red low ssn. "Nr interesting town of Hyères; excursions to peninsula of Giens; basic facs; vg." 1 Apr-22 Oct. € 35.00 2006*

HYERES *10F3* (8km E Rural) *43.13017, 6.21650* **Camping La Pascalinette, 83250 La Londe-les-Maures [04 94 66 82 72 or 04 94 87 46 62; fax 04 94 87 55 75]** Site sp on D98 E of Hyères. Lge, mkd pitch, shd; wc; baby facs; shwrs inc; el pnts (6A) €3.80; gas; Indtte; shop; snacks; playgrnd; sand/shgl beach 3km; games rm; entmnt; TV; adv bkg; CCI. ♦ 1 Jun-15 Sep. € 17.00 2006*

HYERES *10F3* (8km E Coastal) *43.12240, 6.23542* **Camping Les Moulières, Route de Port-de-Miramar, 83250 La Londe-les-Maures [04 94 01 53 21; fax 04 94 01 53 22; camping.les.moulieres@wanadoo.fr; www.campingles moulieres.com]** On D98, in cent La Londe-les-Maures turn S at traff lts. After 1km turn R over white bdge & foll rd for 1km. Camping sp on R. Lge, pt shd; wc; baby facs; shwrs inc; el pnts (6A) €5; Indtte; shop; rest; snacks; bar; playgrnd; sand beach 800m; entmnt; TV; dogs €3.50; poss cr; adv bkg rec high ssn; quiet. "Pleasant shaded pitches; security barrier with code; gd." ♦ 14 Jun-6 Sep. € 24.50 2008*

France

HYERES *10F3* (8km E Coastal) *43.1186, 6.24693* **Miramar Camping, 1026 Blvd Louis Bernard, 83250 La Londes-les-Maures, [04 94 66 80 58 or 04 94 66 83 14; camping.miramar.lalonde@wanadoo.fr; www.provence-campings.com/azur/miramar]** On D98 in cent of La Londes-les-Maures, turn S at traff lts; in 1km turn R over white bdge & foll rd for 1.5km dir Port Miramar; site on R 150m bef port. Lge; hdg/mkd pitch, shd; wc; chem disp; snacks; shwrs inc; el pnts (4-10A) €4.50-6.50; Indtte; v sm shop & 2km; rest; snacks; bar; sand beach 200m; games rm; 25% statics; no dogs; phone; bus 2km; poss cr; Eng spkn; quiet; ccard acc; CCI. "Vg shade; beach, port, rests & shops 200m, but food shops 2km; vg boat marina; excel site out of ssn; vg." ♦ 1 May-30 Sep. € 22.00 2008*

HYERES *10F3* (4km SE Coastal) *43.05604, 6.14707* **CAMPEOLE Camping Eurosurf, Plage de la Capte, 83400 Hyères [04 94 58 00 20; fax 04 94 58 03 18; eurosurf@campeole.com; www.camping-hyeres.com or www.campeole.com]** Fr A8 take A57 as far as Hyères, foll sps to Giens & Les Iles, site is just outside La Capte vill on L on D97. V lge, mkd pitch, pt sl, pt shd; wc; chem disp; mv service pnt; baby facs; shwrs inc; el pnts (10A) €3.90; gas; Indtte; shop; tradsmn; rest; snacks; bar; no BBQ; playgrnd; sand beach adj; watersports; diving cent; 50% statics; dogs €3.90; phone; poss cr; no adv bkg; some rd noise; ccard acc; red low ssn. "Some areas of soft sand & pitches not mkd; excel for watersports; excel location." ♦ 13 Mar-3 Nov. € 32.50 2006*

HYERES *10F3* (5km SE Coastal) *43.10103, 6.16955* **Camping Domaine du Ceinturon III, Rue du Ceinturon, L'Ayguade, 83400 Hyères [04 94 66 32 65; fax 04 94 66 48 43; ceinturon3@securmail.net; www.provence-campings.com/azur/ceinturon3.htm]** Fr Hyères take L'Ayguade rd sp airport. At T-junc in L'Ayguade turn R. Site 400m twd Hyères harbour & adj airport on D42. Fr NE on D42 drive thro L'Ayguade, turn R at traff lts just after end of vill sp. Lge, mkd pitch, shd; htd wc (some cont); chem disp; serviced pitch; shwrs inc; el pnts (2-10A) €2-3.50; gas; Indtte; shop high ssn; tradsmn; rest; snacks; bar; playgrnd; beach adj, tennis; TV rm; excursions; TV; 15% statics; dogs €3.50; bus; poss cr; Eng spkn; adv bkg ess Jul/Aug; quiet but some daytime noise fr adj airport; no ccard acc; CCI. "Excel, popular site; v busy high ssn; sm pitches; helpful owners; smart shwrs; excel cycle paths in area. ♦ 30 Mar-30 Sep. € 16.35 2006*

HYERES *10F3* (5km SE Coastal) *43.04480, 6.14601* **Camping La Bergerie, 4231 Route de Giens, 83400 Hyères [04 94 58 91 75; fax 04 94 58 14 28; info@camping-de-la-bergerie.com; www.camping-de-la-bergerie.com]** On L of D97 fr Hyères to Giens on Presqu'île de Giens. Med, pt shd; htd wc; mv service pnt; shwrs; el pnts (5A) €6.50; Indtte; shop; tradsmn; snacks (high ssn); bar; playgrnd; sand beach 200m; 50% statics; dogs €3; adv bkg; quiet. "Fair sh stay low ssn." 1 Mar-10 Jan. € 25.50 2007*

HYERES *10F3* (8km S Coastal) *43.04100, 6.14340* **Camping La Presqu'île de Giens, 153 Route de la Madrague, Giens, 83400 Hyères [04 94 58 22 86 or 04 94 57 20 18; fax 04 94 58 11 63; info@camping-giens.com; www.camping-giens.com]** Fr Toulon A570 dir Hyères. Thro palm-lined main street in Hyères dir Giens-les-Iles & foll sp to La Capte & Giens past airport on L, thro La Capte, turn R at rndabt to site on L, sp. Lge, pt sl, terr, pt shd; htd wc; mv service pnt; baby facs; shwrs inc; el pnts (15A) €4.90; gas; Indtte; shop; tradsmn; snacks; playgrnd; TV; games rm; entmnt; sand beach 600m; fishing & boat excursions; 75% statics; dogs €2.80; poss cr; adv bkg; quiet; red low ssn. "Sm pitches, layout cramped; access to pitches awkward/steep lge o'fits; sister site La Tour Fondue much better access; ltd water pnts; gd clean san facs; pleasant, helpful staff." ♦ 22 Mar-5 Oct. € 20.90 (CChq acc) 2008*

HYERES *10F3* (9km S Coastal) *43.02980, 6.15490* **Camping La Tour Fondue, Ave des Arbanais, 83400 Giens [04 94 58 22 86; fax 04 94 58 11 63; info@camping-latourfondue.com; www.camping-latourfondue.com]** D97 fr Hyères, site sp. Med, hdg pitch, pt sl, pt terr, pt shd; wc; chem disp; mv service pnt; shwrs inc; el pnts (6A) €4.70; Indtte; rest; snacks; bar; beach adj; games area; entmnt; some statics; dogs €2.90 (not allowed on beach); no adv bkg; ccard acc. "Pleasant, sister site of Camping Presqu'île de Giens with easier access." 28 Mar-1 Nov. € 20.90 2008*

HYERES *10F3* (13km S Coastal) *43.04156, 6.12799* **Camping International, 1737 Route de la Madrague, 83400 Hyères [04 94 58 90 16; fax 04 94 58 90 50; Thierry.Coulomb@wanadoo.fr; www.international-giens.com]** S fr Hyères on D97 dir Giens, once past La Capte foll sp La Bergerie & La Madrague, site sp. Lge, mkd pitch, hdstg, terr, pt shd; wc; chem disp; mv service pnt; shwrs inc; el pnts (6A) €5; gas; Indtte; shop; rest; snacks; bar; no BBQ; playgrnd; sand beach 300m; tennis adj; watersports; windsurfing; skin-diving; solarium; horseriding; internet; entmnt; some statics; no dogs; Eng spkn; adv bkg; quiet. "Excel family site; many activities." 1 Apr-31 Oct. € 24.00 2006*

HYERES *10F3* (6km W Rural) *43.11442, 6.05609* **FLOWER Camping Le Beau Vezé, Route de la Moutonne, 83320 Carqueiranne [tel/fax 04 94 57 65 30; info@camping-beauveze.com; www.camping-beauveze.com or www.flowercamping.com]** Fr Toulon take D559 E dir Carqueiranne. Approx 2km after Le Pradet turn L onto D76 twd La Moutonne. Site on R in 1.5km. Med, mkd pitch terr, pt shd; htd wc (some cont); chem disp; baby facs; shwrs inc; el pnts (4A) €4; gas; Indtte; shop; rest; snacks; bar; BBQ (gas only); playgrnd; 2 pools & paddling pool; beach 4km; tennis; cycle hire; entmnt; few statics; dogs €2.50; poss cr; adv bkg; quiet but some rd noise; red low ssn; ccard not acc. "Poss diff access some pitches for lge o'fits; no twin-axle c'vans; mkt Thu." 1 May-19 Sep. € 27.00 (CChq acc) 2007*

IGOVILLE see Pont de l'Arche *3D2*

ILE BOUCHARD, L' *4H1* (500m N Urban) *47.12166, 0.42857* **Camping Les Bords de Vienne, 4 Allée du Camping, 37220 L'Ile-Bouchard [02 47 95 23 59; fax 02 47 98 45 29; info@campingbordsdevienne.com; www.campingbordsdevienne.com]** On N bank of Rv Vienne 100m E of rd bdge nr junc of D757 & D760. Med, mkd pitch, pt sl, pt shd; wc; chem disp; shwrs inc; el pnts (6-16A) €4; gas; lndtte; supmkt adj; snacks; playgrnd; pool & tennis 500m; rv sw adj; dogs €2; phone adj; Eng spkn; adv bkg; quiet; red low ssn/long stay; CCI. "Lovely, clean rvside site; v attractive location; no twin-axles; conv Loire chateaux." Easter-Mid Oct. € 16.00 2009*

ILE DE RE Campsites in towns on the Ile de Ré are listed together at the end of the French site entry pages.

ILE D'OLERON Campsites in towns on the Ile d'Oléron are listed together at the end of the French site entry pages.

ILLIERS COMBRAY *4E2* (2km SW Rural) *48.28667, 1.22697* **FLOWER Camping le Bois Fleuri, Route de Brou, 28120 Illiers-Combray [02 37 24 03 04; fax 02 37 24 16 21; infos@camping-chartres.com; www.camping-chartres.com or www.flowercamping.com]** S on D921 fr Illiers for 2km twd Brou. Site on L. Med, hdg pitch, pt shd; htd wc; chem disp; some serviced pitches; shwrs inc; el pnts (6-8A); gas; lndry rm; shop 2km; htd pool 500m; fishing adj; 30% statics; dogs €1.50; poss cr; adv bkg; quiet; red low ssn; CCI. "Many pitches wooded & with flowers; excel san facs; ltd water/ el pnts; uneven grnd makes access diff - but new owners (2009); gd security; excel cycle path to vill." ♦ 4 Apr-31 Oct. € 16.90 (CChq acc) 2009*

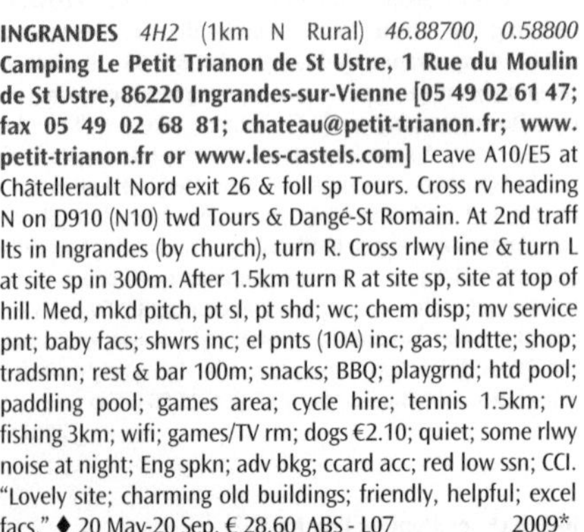
We can fill in site
report forms on the
Club's website –
www.caravanclub.co.uk/
europereport

INGRANDES *4H2* (1km N Rural) *46.88700, 0.58800* **Camping Le Petit Trianon de St Ustre, 1 Rue du Moulin de St Ustre, 86220 Ingrandes-sur-Vienne [05 49 02 61 47; fax 05 49 02 68 81; chateau@petit-trianon.fr; www.petit-trianon.fr or www.les-castels.com]** Leave A10/E5 at Châtellerault Nord exit 26 & foll sp Tours. Cross rv heading N on D910 (N10) twd Tours & Dangé-St Romain. At 2nd traff lts in Ingrandes (by church), turn R. Cross rlwy line & turn L at site sp in 300m. After 1.5km turn R at site sp, site at top of hill. Med, mkd pitch, pt sl, pt shd; wc; chem disp; mv service pnt; baby facs; shwrs inc; el pnts (10A) inc; gas; lndtte; shop; tradsmn; rest & bar 100m; snacks; BBQ; playgrnd; htd pool; paddling pool; games area; cycle hire; tennis 1.5km; rv fishing 3km; wifi; games/TV rm; dogs €2.10; quiet; some rlwy noise at night; Eng spkn; adv bkg; ccard acc; red low ssn; CCI. "Lovely site; charming old buildings; friendly, helpful; excel facs." ♦ 20 May-20 Sep. € 28.60 ABS - L07 2009*

ISIGNY SUR MER *1D4* (500m NW Rural) *49.31872, -1.10825* **Camping Le Fanal, Rue du Fanal, 14230 Isigny-sur-Mer [02 31 21 33 20; fax 02 31 22 12 00; info@camping-lefanal.com; www.camping-lefanal.com]** Fr N13 exit into Isigny, site immed N of town. Foll sp to 'Stade' in town, (just after sq & church on narr street just bef R turn). Med, hdg/ mkd pitch, pt shd; wc; chem disp; mv service pnt; shwrs inc; el pnts (10A) €3.30 (long cable poss req); lndtte; shop; snacks; bar; playgrnd; pool; aquapark; sand beach 10km; lake fishing adj; horseriding; tennis; games area; games rm; entmnt; TV; 50% statics; dogs €4; phone; adv bkg; quiet; ccard acc; red low ssn; CCI. "Friendly staff; poss boggy in wet weather; vg site." ♦ 1 Apr-30 Sep. € 25.00 2008*

ISLE ET BARDAIS see Cérilly *4H3*

ISLE JOURDAIN, L' *7A3* (500m N Rural) *46.24065, 0.68502* **Camp Municipal du Lac de Chardes, Rue de Chardes, 86150 L'Isle-Jourdain [05 49 48 72 46 or 05 49 48 70 54 (Mairie); fax 05 49 48 84 19; isle-jourdain@wanadoo.fr]** Fr N147 in Lussac take D11 S to L'Isle-Jourdain. Site sp on R. Sm, mkd pitch, terr, pt shd; wc (some cont); shwrs inc; el pnts inc; lndtte; shops, rest, snacks, bar 700m; tradsmn; htd pool adj; boating; sand beach & fishing 100m; tennis; dogs; adv bkg; quiet. "Lovely peaceful site nr rv; excel san facs; sh walk to Rv Vienne; site yourself, warden calls am & pm." ♦ 1 May-31 Aug. € 9.20 2009*

ISLE SUR LA SORGUE L' *10E2* (2km E Rural) *43.91451, 5.07181* **Camping Airotel La Sorguette, Route d'Apt, 84800 L'Isle-sur-la-Sorgue [04 90 38 05 71; fax 04 90 20 84 61; info@camping-sorguette.com; www.camping-sorguette.com]** Fr Isle-sur-la-Sorgue take D901 twd Apt, on L site in 1.5km, sp. Med, hdg/mkd pitch, pt shd; wc; chem disp; mv service pnt; shwrs inc; el pnts (6A) €4.40; gas; lndtte; shop; tradsmn; rest nr; BBQ; playgrnd; beach adj; trout fishing adj; canoeing (not for faint-hearted!); tennis; games area; wifi; 10% statics; dogs €2.90; adv bkg; poss cr; Eng spkn; quiet; ccard acc; red low ssn; CCI. "Lovely, well-run site; useful & busy; friendly, helpful staff; beware low trees; dated but clean san facs; rvside walk to attractive town; Sun mkt (shuttle fr site); highly rec." ♦ 15 Mar-15 Oct. € 20.90 2009*

ISLE SUR LA SORGUE L' *10E2* (3km E Rural) **Aire Naturelle de Sorgiack, Route de Lagnes, 84800 L'Isle-sur-la-Sourge [04 90 38 13 95]** 2.5km SE of L'Isle-sur-la-Sorgue on D901; take D99 twd Lagnes; site sp. Sm, mkd pitch, hdstg, pt shd; htd wc; chem disp; shwrs inc; el pnts (10A) inc; lndtte; shop, rest, snacks, bar 2.5km; paddling pool; sw 3km; rv & fishing 500m; games rm; phone; adv bkg; quiet; ccard not acc; CCI. "Delightful site in cherry orchard; friendly hosts; excel facs, inc for disabled; gd mkts in area, esp antiques; excel touring base." ♦ 1 Apr-15 Oct. € 15.75 2009*

⊞ **ISLE SUR LA SORGUE L'** *10E2* (5km E Rural) *43.91931, 5.11683* **Aire Communale Vergnes, Ave Robert Garcin, 84800 Fontaine-de-Vaucluse [04 90 20 31 79]** D25 fr Isle-sur-la-Sorgue; site on R after vill boundary; or on D24 fr Cavaillon then join D25. Sm, hdstg, unshd; wc; own san; chem disp; shops, rest, snacks & bar 500m; dogs; poss cr; ccard acc. "Pleasant location next to rv; mainly for m'vans but spaces for c'vans; gd NH." € 3.00 2008*

ISLE SUR LA SORGUE L' *10E2* (5km NW Rural) *43.92980, 4.98320* **Camping Domaine du Jantou, 535 Chemin des Coudelières, 84250 Le Thor [04 90 33 90 07; fax 04 90 33 79 84; jantou@franceloc.fr; www.camping-franceloc.fr]** Exit A7 at Avignon Nord onto D942 sp Carpentras. Turn S onto D6; in 8km join D901 E sp Le Thor. Site sp bef vill. App fr E fork R at sharp bend, thro town gate take L turn after passing church & L. Med, hdg pitch, pt shd; wc; chem disp; mv service pnt; shwrs inc; el pnts (3-10A) €3-5.70; Indtte; shop; snacks; playgrnd; 2 pools; paddling pool; cycle hire; games rm; entmnt; wifi; TV rm; some statics; dogs €5; adv bkg; quiet; ccard acc. "Attractive site by Rv Sorgue; sm pitches, ltd access." ♦ 1 Apr-30 Sep. € 26.50 2009*

ISLE SUR LA SORGUE, L' *10E2* (5km E Rural) *43.91087, 5.10665* **Camping La Coutelière, Route de Fontaine de Vaucluse, 84800 Lagnes [04 90 20 33 97; fax 04 90 20 27 22; info@camping-lacouteliere.com; www.camping-lacouteliere.com]** Leave L'Isle-sur-la-Sorgue by D900 (N100) dir Apt, fork L after 2km sp Fontaine-de-Vaucluse. Site on L on D24 bef ent Fontaine. Med, hdg pitch, shd; wc; shwrs inc; el pnts (10A) €4; Indtte; rest; snacks; bar; playgrnd; pool; canoeing nr; tennis, entmnt; 40% statics; dogs €3.10; phone; Eng spkn; adv bkg; quiet; CCI. "Gd site; 2km easy cycle ride to Fontaine." ♦ 1 Apr-15 Oct. € 15.30 2007*

ISLE SUR LE DOUBS, L' *6G2* (400m N Rural) *47.45288, 6.58338* **Camping Les Lûmes, 10 Rue des Lûmes, 25250 L'Isle-sur-le-Doubs [tel/fax 03 81 92 73 05; contact@les-lumes.com; www.les-lumes.com]** Well sp fr town edge on D683 (N83) bef rv bdge. Med, pt shd; wc; chem disp; shwrs; el pnts (10A) €3.30 (long lead req & poss rev pol; shop; tradsmn; playgrnd; rv sw; 20% statics; dogs €1.20; poss cr; Eng spkn; adv bkg; CCI. "Busy site; san facs need upgrade (2008) & not suitable disabled as up steps; sh walk to town; gd." 1 May-30 Sep. € 11.70 2009*

ISLE SUR SEREIN, L' *4G4* (Rural) *47.58011, 4.00561* **Camp Municipal Le Parc de Château, 89440 L'Isle-sur-Serein [03 86 33 93 50 or 03 86 33 80 74 (Mairie); fax 03 86 33 91 81; www.isle-sur-serein.com]** Exit A6 junc 21 or 22 & foll sp Noyers or Montréal & L'Isle-sur-Serein on D117. Or fr Avallon, take D957 twd Sauvigny-le-Bois; then D86 to L'Isle-sur-Serein; site on L on ent to vill. Sm, hdg/mkd pitch, shd; wc; chem disp; shwrs inc; el pnts (6A) 2.60; Indtte; shop 1km; rest; bar; BBQ; playgrnd; tennis & boating adj; games area; dogs; adv bkg; quiet, some rd noise; CCI. "Basic, well-kept site in attractive area; helpful warden; dated facs; vg." 15 Apr-30 Sep. € 7.70 2009*

⊞ **ISOLA** *9D4* (1km NW Rural) *44.18881, 7.03957* **Camping Lac des Neiges, Quartier Lazisola, 06420 Isola [04 93 02 18 16; fax 04 93 02 19 40]** SE fr St Etienne-de-Tinée on D2205. site on R after approx 13km, site sp. Med, hdg/mkd pitch, hdstg, pt shd; htd wc; chem disp; mv service pnt; shwrs inc; el pnts (3-6A) inc; Indtte; shops 1km; tradsmn; playgrnd; sw pool 1km; lake adj; ski stn 20 mins; fishing; kayaking; tennis; TV rm; 25% statics; dogs €1; phone; Eng spkn; adv bkg; quiet; ccard not acc; CCI. ♦ € 20.20 2008*

ISPAGNAC *9D1* (2km E Rural) *44.37722, 3.54648* **Camping de l'Aiguebelle, 48320 Ispagnac [04 66 44 20 26]** N fr Florac on N106 for approx 6km; take turning for Ispagnac & foll sp for site; site on L 1km after Faux bet rd & Rv Tarn. Med, pt sl, pt shd; wc; chem disp; shwrs inc; el pnts (10A) €3.05; Indtte; shop & rest 1km; snacks; bar; BBQ; playgrnd; pool; tennis; no statics; dogs; phone; adv bkg; quiet but a little rd noise; CCI. "Uncrowded, shady site; poss unkempt; vg base for Tarn Gorge, Cévennes, etc." 1 Apr-30 Sep. € 11.00 2007*

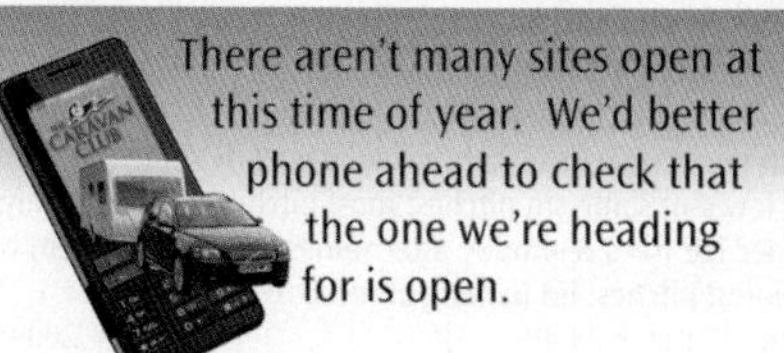
There aren't many sites open at
this time of year. We'd better
phone ahead to check that
the one we're heading
for is open.

ISPAGNAC *9D1* (1km W Rural) *44.37232, 3.53035* **FFCC Camp Municipal Le Pré Morjal, 48320 Ispagnac [04 66 44 23 77 or 04 66 44 20 50 (Mairie); fax 04 66 44 23 84; contact@lepremorjal.fr; www.lepremorjal.fr]** On D907B 500m W of town, turn L off D907B & then 200m on R, sp. Med, hdg pitch, pt shd; htd wc; chem disp; mv service pnt; baby facs; shwrs inc; el pnts (10-16A) inc; Indtte; shops 200m; rest; playgrnd; pool 50m; paddling pool; rv sw 200m; games area; games rm; internet; TV; dogs €1; quiet; red low ssn. "Lovely family site; gd size pitches on rocky base, poss muddy when wet; friendly staff; gd rvside walks; vg base for Tarn & Joute Gorges." ♦ 1 Apr-31 Oct. € 17.00 2008*

ISQUES see Boulogne sur Mer *3A2*

ISSAMBRES, LES see St Aygulf *10F4*

ISSENDOLUS see Gramat *7D4*

ISSOIRE *9B1* (2.5km E Rural) *45.55113, 3.27423* **FFCC Camp Municipal du Mas, Ave du Dr Bienfait, 63500 Issoire [04 73 89 03 59 or 04 73 89 03 54 (LS); fax 04 73 89 41 05; camping-mas@wanadoo.fr; http://monsite.orange.fr/campingmasenglish]** Fr Clermont-Ferrand S on A75/E11 take exit 12 sp Issoire; turn L over a'route sp Orbeil; at rndabt, take 1st exit & foll site sp. Med, hdg/mkd pitch, pt shd; htd wc (mostly cont); chem disp; shwrs inc; el pnts (10-13A) inc (long lead poss req); gas; Indtte; supmkt 500m; shops 2km; tradsmn; snacks; playgrnd; fishing in adj lake; TV rm; 5% statics; dogs free; phone; poss cr; adv bkg (rec high ssn); quiet but some rd noise; ccard acc; red long stay/low ssn; CCI. "Well-run, basic site in lovely park-like location surrounded by hills; lge pitches; helpful warden; modern but open-sided san facs; site poss boggy after rain; excel NH." ♦ 1 Apr-1 Nov. € 16.40 2009*

France

ISSOIRE *9B1* (6km SE Rural) *45.50908, 3.2848* **FFCC Camping Château La Grange Fort, 63500 Les Pradeaux [04 73 71 05 93 or 04 73 71 02 43; fax 04 73 71 07 69; chateau@lagrangefort.com; www.lagrangefort.com]** S fr Clermont Ferrand on A75, exit junc 13 onto D996 sp Parentignat. At 1st rndabt take D999 sp St Rémy-Chargnat (new rd); at next rndabt take 1st exit onto D34 & foll sp to site on hill-top. Narr app rd & uphill ent. Med, hdg/mkd pitch, shd; htd wc; chem disp; mv service pnt; baby facs; sauna; shwrs inc; el pnts (6A) €3.50; Indtte; gas; shop in vill; tradsmn; rest in chateau; snacks; bar; playgrnd; htd, covrd pool & outdoor pool; paddling pool; rv fishing; tennis; canoe & mountain bike facs; internet; TV rm; some statics; dogs €3; phone; Eng spkn; adv bkg (fee); quiet; ccard acc; CCI. "Pleasant, peaceful Dutch-run site in chateau grounds with views; excel san facs but long walk fr some pitches & ltd low ssn; some sm pitches; most pitches damp & gloomy under lge trees & muddy after rain; mosquito problem on shadiest pitches; ltd parking at recep; conv A75; gd."
4 Apr-17 Oct. € 24.40 2009*

ISSOIRE *9B1* (11km S Rural) *45.47373, 3.27161* **Camping Les Loges, 63340 Nonette [04 73 71 65 82; fax 04 73 71 67 23; les.loges.nonette@wanadoo.fr; www.lesloges.com]** Exit 17 fr A75 onto D214 sp Le Breuil, dir Nonette. Turn L in 2km, cross rv & turn L to site. Site perched on conical hill. Steep app. Med, hdg/mkd pitch, pt shd; wc; chem disp; child/baby facs; shwrs inc; el pnts (10A) €3.50; gas; Indtte; shop; tradsmn; rest; snacks; bar; playgrnd; htd pool; rv sw & fishing adj; entmnt; TV; 30% statics; dogs €1.80; quiet; red low ssn; CCI. "Friendly site; conv Massif Central & A75."
Easter-10 Sep. € 16.90 2008*

ISSOUDUN *4H3* (1.5km N Rural) *46.96361, 1.99011* **Camp Municipal Les Taupeaux, 37 Route de Reuilly, 36100 Issoudun [02 54 03 13 46 or 02 54 21 74 02; tourisme@issoudun.fr; www.issoudun.fr]** Fr Bourges SW on N151, site sp fr Issoudun on D16 nr Carrefour supmkt. Sm, hdg/mkd pitch, pt shd; wc; shwrs inc; el pnts inc; no adv bkg; rd noise.
Jun-31 Aug. € 8.00 2007*

ISSY L'EVEQUE *4H4* (S Rural) *46.70760, 3.95970* **Camping L'Etang Neuf, 71760 Issy-l'Evêque [03 85 24 96 05; info@camping-etang-neuf.com; www.camping-etang-neuf.com]** Fr Luzy take D973 S for 2km. Then take D25 to Issy-l'Evêque. Site off D42 well sp in town cent. Med, hdg/mkd pitch, terr, pt shd; wc (some cont); chem disp; mv service pnt; shwrs inc; el pnts (6A) inc; gas; Indtte; shop 800m; tradsmn; rest; bar; playgrnd; pool; paddling pool; lake sw, fishing adj; tennis; wifi; TV rm; dogs €2; phone; Eng spkn; adv bkg; quiet; ccard acc; CCI. "Nice, peaceful setting in unspoilt area; helpful staff; some san facs run down (2007)." ♦
28 Apr-15 Sep. € 21.00 2007*

ISTRES *10F2* (6km S Coastal) *43.46958, 5.02420* **Camping Félix de la Bastide, Allée Plage d'Arthur, 13920 St Mitre-les-Remparts [04 42 80 99 35; fax 04 42 49 96 85; info@campingfelix.com; www.campingfelix.com]** S fr Istres on D5 to end of built up area. At 2nd rndabt turn L (foll sp); approx 2km on L. Med, hdg/mkd pitch, pt shd; wc; chem disp; shwrs inc; el pnts (6A) €3 (poss rev pol); gas 2km; Indry service; shop; tradsmn; rest; bar; BBQ; playgrnd; pool; paddling pool; shgl beach & lake adj; watersports; games area; wifi; dogs €1.50; phone; poss cr; Eng spkn; adv bkg; poss noise fr dogs barking & club nrby; red long stay. "Spacious pitches; poss strong winds; friendly Dutch owners; san facs poss stretched high ssn; beautiful scenery."
1 Apr-1 Nov. € 17.50 2009*

JABLINES see Meaux *3D3*

JARD SUR MER *7A1* (Urban/Coastal) *46.42098, -1.56997* **CHADOTEL Camping L'Océano d'Or, Rue Georges Clémenceau, 85520 Jard-sur-Mer [02 51 33 65 08 or 02 51 33 05 05 (LS); fax 02 51 33 94 04; chadotel@wanadoo.fr; www.chadotel.com]** D21 & D19 to Jard-sur-Mer. Site sp. Lge, hdg/mkd pitch, pt shd; htd wc; chem disp; baby facs; shwrs inc; el pnts (6A) inc; gas; Indtte; shop; snacks; bar; playgrnd; htd pool; waterslide; sand beach 900m; tennis; cycle hire; entmnt; dogs €3; adv bkg; quiet; red long stay/low ssn; CCI. "Vg; gd walking." ♦ 4 Apr-27 Sep.
€ 29.90 2008*

JARD SUR MER *7A1* (2km NE Rural) *46.42740, -1.56800* **Camping La Mouette Cendrée, Les Malécots, 85520 St Vincent-sur-Jard [02 51 33 59 04; fax 02 51 20 31 39; camping.mc@orange.fr; www.mouettecendree.com]** Fr Les Sables-d'Olonne take D949 SE to Talmont-St-Hilaire; then take D21 to Jard-sur-Mer; at rndabt stay on D21 (taking 2nd exit dir La Tranche-sur-Mer & Maison-de-Clemanceau); in 500m turn L onto D19 sp St Hilaire-la-Forêt & foll site sps. Site on L in 700m. Med, hdg/mkd pitch, pt shd; wc (some cont); chem disp; shwrs inc; el pnts (10A) inc; Indtte; supmkt nr; tradsmn; BBQ (gas/elec); playgrnd; pool; waterslide; paddling pool; sand beach 2km; fishing; windsurfing 2km; table tennis; horseriding 500m; golf 10km; wifi; 30% statics; dogs €2.50; c'van max 7.50m high ssn; Eng spkn; adv bkg; quiet; ccard acc; red low ssn; CCI. "Friendly, peaceful site; gd pitches; v welcoming & helpful owners; gd san facs; vg pool; gd woodland walks & cycle routes nr; mkt Mon." ♦ 1 Apr-31 Oct. € 27.00 ABS - A20
2009*

JARD SUR MER *7A1* (1km E Coastal) *46.41433, -1.55181* **Camp Municipal du Pied Girard, 9 Rue de la Forêt, 85520 St Vincent-sur-Jard [tel/fax 02 51 33 65 11; camping.pg@wanadoo.fr]** Fr Talmont-St-Hilaiare take D21 S to Jard-sur-Mer & on to St Vincent-sur-Jard. Site sp fr edge of vill. Med, mkd pitch, sl, pt shd; wc; chem disp (wc); shwrs inc; el pnts (10A) inc; Indtte; shop & rest 1km; snacks & bar 500m; playgrnd; sand beach 500m; dogs; poss cr; adv bkg; ccard acc. "Vg site in pine wood; uneven pitches; gd clean san facs." 15 Apr-15 Sep. € 14.00 2009*

JARD SUR MER *7A1* (SE Coastal) *46.41088, -1.57269* **CHADOTEL Camping La Pomme de Pin, Rue Vincent Auriol, 85520 Jard-sur-Mer [02 51 33 43 85 or 02 51 33 05 05 (LS); fax 02 51 33 94 04; chadotel@wanadoo.fr; www.chadotel.com]** Foll sp fr town. Lge, hdg/mkd pitch, shd; htd wc; serviced pitches; baby facs; shwrs inc; el pnts (6A) inc; gas; lndtte; shop; snacks; bar; BBQ (gas); playgrnd; pool; waterslide; sand beach 150m; games rm; TV rm; entmnt; mainly statics; dogs €3; Eng spkn; adv bkg; quiet; ccard acc; CCI. "Well-maintained site; early arrival rec; ltd facs low ssn; vg." ♦ 5 Apr-27 Sep. € 29.90 2008*

JARD SUR MER *7A1* (2km SE Coastal) *46.41980, -1.52580* **CHADOTEL Camping La Bolée d'Air, Route du Bouil, Route de Longeville, 85520 St Vincent-sur-Jard [02 51 90 36 05 or 02 51 33 05 05 (LS); fax 02 51 33 94 04; chadotel@wanadoo.fr; www.chadotel.com]** Fr A11 junc 14 dir Angers. Take N160 to La Roche-sur-Yon & then D747 dir La Tranche-sur-Mer to Moutier-les-Mauxfaits. At Moutiers take D19 to St Hilaire-la-Forêt & then L to St Vincent-sur-Jard. In St Vincent turn L by church sp Longeville-sur-Mer, site on R in 1km. Lge, hdg/mkd pitch, pt shd; htd wc; chem disp (wc); serviced pitches; baby facs; sauna; shwrs inc; el pnts (6A) inc; gas; lndtte; shop; snacks; bar; BBQ (charcoal/gas); playgrnd; 2 pools (1 htd covrd); waterslide; paddling pool; sand beach 900m; tennis; cycle hire; entmnt; internet; games/TV rm; 25% statics; dogs €3; no c'vans over 8m high ssn; Eng spkn; adv bkg; quiet; ccard acc; red long stay/low ssn; CCI. "Popular, busy site; ltd facs fr end Aug; excel." ♦ 3 Apr-25 Sep. € 29.50 ABS - A31 2009*

JARD SUR MER *7A1* (S Coastal) *46.41184, -1.58355* **Camping La Ventouse, Rue Pierre Curie, 85520 Jard-sur-Mer [02 51 33 58 65 or 02 51 33 40 17 (Mairie); fax 02 51 33 91 00; campings-parfums-ete@wanadoo.fr; www.campings-parfums-ete.com]** Fr Talmont St-Hilaire take D21 to Jard turn R on app & foll sps. Look for blue sp Port de Plaisance; pass Camping Les Ecureuils, site shortly after. Lge, pt sl, pt shd; wc; baby facs; shwrs inc; el pnts (10A) €3.60 (poss rev pol & poss long lead req); gas; lndtte; shops, rest, snacks, bar 500m; playgrnd; htd pool; paddling pool; sand beach 500m; some statics; dogs €1.90; poss cr; quiet. "Gd site with plenty of pine trees; adj vill & harbour." 1 May-30 Sep. € 15.60 2008*

JARD SUR MER *7A1* (S Coastal) *46.41169, -1.57932* **Camping Le Bosquet, Rue de l'Océan, 85520 Jard-sur-Mer [02 51 33 56 57 or 02 51 33 06 72; fax 02 51 33 03 69; campings-parfums-ete@wanadoo.fr; www.campings-parfums-ete.com]** Exit D949 at Talmont St Hilaire onto D21 to Jard-sur-Mer. In town look for sp Port de Plaisance, pass Camping Les Ecureuils & La Ventouse on L & take 2nd rd, Rue de l'Ocean, to R. Sm, pt sl, shd; wc; baby facs; shwrs inc; el pnts (10A) €3; lndry rm; shops adj; playgrnd; pool 1.5km; sand beach; tennis adj; entmnt; 30% statics; dogs €1.50; Eng spkn; adv bkg; quiet. "Gd location nr harbour; picturesque boating cent with man-made harbour; few pitches." 1 Apr-30 Sep. € 14.00 2009*

JARD SUR MER *7A1* (1km SW Coastal) *46.41130, -1.58960* **Camping Les Ecureuils, Route des Goffineaux, 85520 Jard-sur-Mer [02 51 33 42 74; fax 02 51 33 91 14; camping-ecureuils@wanadoo.fr; www.camping-ecureuils.com]** Fr Talmont St Hilaire take D21 to Jard-sur-Mer. Turn R app vill, site sp. Lge, mkd pitch, shd; wc; chem disp; serviced pitches; baby facs; shwrs inc; el pnts (10A) inc (rev pol); gas; lndtte; sm shop & 1km; snacks; bar; BBQ (gas); playgrnd; htd indoor pool, outdoor pool; rocky beach 400m, sand beach 1km; tennis adj; TV rm; 33% statics; no dogs; poss cr; Eng spkn; adv bkg; quiet; ccard acc; red low ssn; CCI. "Gd site with helpful staff; gd rds & lighting; gd, clean san facs; night security guard; boating cent & man-made tidal harbour 1km." ♦ 5 Apr-27 Sep. € 29.80 2008*

JARGEAU see Châteauneuf sur Loire *4F3*

JARNAC see Cognac *7B2*

JAULNY *5D2* (500m S Rural) *48.96578, 5.88524* **Camping La Pelouse, 54470 Jaulny [tel/fax 03 83 81 91 67; lapelouse@aol.com]** SW fr Metz on D657, cross rv at Corny-sur-Moselle & turn W onto D28 dir Thiaucourt-Regniéville. Site sp, easy to find off D28. Med, sl, pt shd; wc; chem disp; shwrs inc; el pnts (4-6A) €2.05-2.65; lndtte; tradsmn; rest; bar; BBQ; playgrnd; 25% statics; rv sw 100m; fishing; quiet; CCI. "Friendly owner & staff; san facs poss overstretched high ssn; no fresh or waste water facs for m'vans; vg site." 1 Apr-30 Sep. € 8.80 2007*

JAUNAY CLAN *4H1* (1km N Rural) *46.68302, 0.35851* **Camping La Croix du Sud, Route de Neuville, 86130 Jaunay-Clan [05 49 62 58 14 or 05 49 62 57 20; fax 05 49 62 57 20; camping@la-croix-du-sud.fr; www.la-croix-du-sud.fr]** On A10 fr N or S, take Futuroscope exit. Take last exit at rndabt sp Neuville & after 1.5km turn L onto D20/D62. Site on L immed after x-ing m'way. Also clearly sp fr D910 (N10) at traff lts in Jaunay-Clan. Lge, hdg/mkd pitch, pt shd, 20% serviced pitches; wc; chem disp; mv service pnt; shwrs inc; el pnts (10A) €3; gas; lndtte; shop & hypmkt 1km; tradsmn; rest, snacks & bar high ssn; playgrnd; pool; entmnt; 15% statics; dogs; Eng spkn; adv bkg; some rd noise & dogs barking; ccard acc; red low ssn/CCI. "Conv position & NH; clean, tidy site; 3km to Futuroscope - mini-bus fr site high ssn; 10km to Poitiers; san facs poss unclean; poss itinerants." ♦ 1 Feb-11 Nov. € 10.70 2009*

JAUNAY CLAN *4H1* (6km NE Rural) *46.69807, 0.42619* **Camp Municipal du Parc, 86130 Dissay [05 49 62 84 29 or 05 49 52 34 56 (Mairie); fax 05 49 62 58 72]** N on D910 (N10) Poitiers dir Châtellerault. At rndabt turn R on D15 sp Dissay. Turn R ent Dissay & site on R 50m. Med, mkd pitch, pt shd; wc; chem disp; shwrs inc; el pnts (10A) €2.50; lndtte; shop 100m; quiet; CCI. "Friendly warden; clean modern facs; conv Futuroscope; 15thC chateau adj; gate locked 2200 but can request key." ♦ 15 Jun-15 Sep. € 9.50 2007*

France

JAUNAY CLAN *4H1* (7km NE Rural) *46.72015, 0.45982* **FLOWER Camping du Lac de St Cyr, 86130 St Cyr [05 49 62 57 22; fax 05 49 52 28 58; contact@camping lacdesaintcyr.com; www.campinglacdesaintcyr.com or www.flowercamping.com]** Fr A10 take Châtellerault Sud exit & take D910 (N10) dir Poitiers; at Beaumont turn L at traff lts for St Cyr; foll camp sp in leisure complex (Parc Loisirs) by lakeside - R turn for camping. Or fr S take Futuroscope exit to D910. Lge, hdg/mkd pitch, pt sl, pt shd; wc; chem disp; mv service pnt; serviced pitches; shwrs inc; el pnts (10A) inc (poss rev pol); gas; Indtte; shop; rest; snacks; bar; BBQ; playgrnd; sand beach & lake sw; watersports; tennis; boat & cycle hire; fitness rm; games area; golf course adj; entmnt; wifi; TV rm; 15% statics; dogs €1.50; poss cr; some Eng spkn; adv bkg; quiet, some rlwy sound; ccard acc; red low ssn/long stay; CCI. "Excel, well-kept site; lovely setting; gd, clean san facs but poss stretched high ssn & ltd low ssn; rec long o'fits unhitch at barrier due R-angle turn; gd golf nr; gd rest; beautiful lake; public access to site fr lakeside beach; Futuroscope approx 13km; highly rec." ♦ 1 Apr-30 Sep. € 25.00 ABS - L09 2009*

⊞ **JAUNAY CLAN** *4H1* (2km SE Urban) *46.66401, 0.39466* **Camping Le Futuriste, Rue du Château, 86130 St Georges-les-Baillargeaux [05 49 52 47 52; fax 05 49 37 23 33; camping-le-futuriste@wanadoo.fr; www.camping-le-futuriste.fr]** On A10 fr N or S, take Futuroscope exit 28; fr toll booth at 1st rndabt take 2nd exit. Thro tech park twd St Georges. At rndabt under D910 (N10) take slip rd N onto D910. After 150m exit D910 onto D20, foll sp. At 1st rndabt bear R, over rlwy, cross sm rv & up hill, site on R. Med, hdg/mkd pitch, pt shd; htd wc; chem disp; mv service pnt; some serviced pitches; shwrs inc; el pnts (6A) €3.90 (check earth & poss rev pol); gas; Indtte; shop; hypmkt 2km; tradsmn; rest, snacks high ssn; bar; BBQ; playgrnd; 2 htd pools; waterslide; lake fishing; games area; games rm; entmnt; excursions; TV rm; some statics; dogs €2.10; poss cr; Eng spkn; adv bkg; quiet; red low ssn; ccard acc; CCI. "Excel, vg value, busy, secure site, espec in winter; friendly, helpful family owners; ltd facs low ssn - facs block clsd 2200-0700; do not arr bef 1200; ideal touring base for Poitiers & Futuroscope (tickets fr recep); conv fr a'route." ♦ € 21.80 (3 persons) (CChq acc) 2009*

See advertisement

JAUNAY CLAN *4H1* (4km SE Rural) *46.65464, 0.37786* **Camp Municipal Parc des Ecluzelles, 86360 Chasseneuil-du-Poitou [05 49 52 77 19; fax 05 49 52 52 23; chasseneuil-du-poitou@cg86.fr]** Fr A10 or D910 (N10) N or Poitiers take Futuroscope exit 28/18. Take Chasseneuil rd, sp in town to site. Sm, mkd pitch, some hdstg, pt shd; wc; chem disp; mv service pnt; shwrs inc; el pnts (8A) inc; shop 1km; tradsmn; BBQ; playgrnd; htd pool adj inc; dogs; poss cr; no adv bkg; quiet. "Vg, clean site; v lge pitches; conv Futuroscope; excel." 1 Apr-30 Sep. € 12.85 2006*

JAUSIERS see Barcelonnette *9D4*

JOIGNY *4F4* (1.5km N Rural) *47.98143, 3.37439* **FFCC Camp Municipal, 68 Quai d'Epizy, 89300 Joigny [03 86 62 07 55; fax 03 86 62 08 03; villedejoigny3@wanadoo.fr; www.joigny.com]** Fr A6 exit junc 18 or 19 to Joigny cent. Fr cent, over brdg, turn L onto D959; turn L in filter lane at traff lts. Foll sp to site. Sm, hdg pitch, hdstg, pt shd; wc; chem disp; mv service pnt; shwrs; el pnts (10A) €2.07; shops 500m; rest, bar 3km; pool 4km; sw 3km; fishing adj; tennis; horseriding; many statics; poss cr; quiet; CCI. "V busy site; helpful warden; liable to flood in wet weather; interesting town." 1 Apr-31 Oct. € 5.11 2008*

JOIGNY *4F4* (8km E Urban) *47.95646, 3.50657* **Camping Les Confluents, Allée Léo Lagrange, 89400 Migennes [tel/fax 03 86 80 94 55; planethome2003@yahoo.fr; www.les-confluents.com]** A6 exit at junc 19 Auxerre Nord onto N6 & foll sp to Migennes & site, well sp. Med, hdg/mkd pitch, hdstg, pt shd; htd wc (some cont); chem disp; mv service pnt; baby facs; fam bthrm; shwrs inc; el pnts (6-10A) €3-4.25; gas; Indtte; shop; rest; snacks; bar; BBQ; playgrnd; pool; watersports 300m; lake sand beach; canoe, cycle hire; sports area; entmnt; TV rm; 8% statics; dogs €0.65; phone; bus 10 mins; quiet; red long stay; ccard acc; CCI. "Friendly, family-run, clean site nr canal & indust area; lge pitches; medieval castle, wine cellars, potteries nrby; walking dist to Migennes; mkt Thurs; excel." ♦ 28 Mar-2 Nov. € 11.50 2009*

JOIGNY *4F4* (12km SE Rural) *47.92802, 3.51932* **Camp Municipal Le Patis, 28 Rue du Porte des Fontaines, 89400 Bonnard [03 86 73 26 25 or 03 86 73 25 55 (Mairie); mairie.bonnard@wanadoo.fr]** Exit A6 junc 19; N on N6 dir Joigny; in 8.5km at Bassou turn R & foll sp Bonnard. Site on L immed after rv bdge. Sm, mkd pitch, shd; wc; chem disp; shwrs inc; el pnts (10A) €2; Indtte; shop 1km; rest 500m; playgrnd; rv sw, fishing, boating, tennis adj; dogs; phone; poss cr; adv bkg; quiet. "Well-kept site on banks of Rv Yonne; friendly, helpful warden; immac san facs; gd security; vg fishing; excel." ♦ 15 May-30 Sep. € 7.00 2007*

JOIGNY *4F4* (3.5km NW Rural) *47.99550, 3.34468* **Camp Municipal L'Ile de L'Entonnoir, Route de St Aubin-sur-Yonne, 89410 Cézy [03 86 63 17 87 or 03 86 63 12 58 (LS); fax 03 86 63 02 84; info@camping-cezy.com]** Site sp off N6 N & S-bound (Joigny by-pass). Thro St Aubin vill, cross bdge over Rv Yonne. Site on L bank of rv. Or exit N6 Joigny by-pass at N of rndabt onto N2006 twd St Aubin. After St Aubin turn R to Cézy & site in 1km. Rec app via St Aubin - narr bdge 3.5t weight restriction. Sm, mkd pitch, pt shd; wc; shwrs inc; chem disp; mv service pnt; el pnts (6-10A) inc; Indtte; shop 1km; rest, snacks, bar, BBQ; playgrnd; rv sw & beach 100m; dogs €1; Eng spkn; adv bkg; quiet; CCI. "V pleasant, quiet site; helpful staff; conv Chablis area; barrier clsd 2200." 1 May-31 Oct. € 15.40 2009*

JOINVILLE *6E1* (6km E Rural) **Camp Municipal Poissons, 52230 Poissons** Fr N67 to Joinville 'Centre Ville'; then onto D60 dir Thonnance; after supmkt turn R onto D427 to Poissons; site on L as exit vill. Site sp in vill. Sm, pt sl, pt shd; htd wc (cont); own san; chem disp (wc); shwrs inc; el pnts inc; shop 1km; rest 6km, snacks, bar 1km; BBQ; 20% statics; dogs; quiet; CCI. "V basic, peaceful CL-type site; warden calls evening or call at No 7 same rd to pay; uneven pitches; facs & el pnts poor; san facs poss unclean & need refurb; easy to find; poss open all yr; NH only." € 6.70 2006*

JONQUIERES see Orange *10E2*

JONZAC *7B2* (Urban) *45.44366, -0.43358* **Camp Municipal des Mégisseries, Parc des Expositions, 17500 Jonzac [05 46 48 49 29; fax 05 46 48 51 07; Tourisme.Jonzac@wanadoo.fr; www.jonzac.fr]** Fr A10/N137 to Bordeaux exit D699 to Jonzac, site well sp in all dirs in town past school & sports complex, adj Rv Seugne - foll sp to football stadium. Sm, mkd pitch, all hdstg, pt shd; wc; own san; mv service pnt; shwrs; el pnts (6-16A) €3.45-5.15; Indtte; shop 2km; tradsmn; pool adj; dogs €1.10; lake fishing 1km; poss cr - pitches close; adv bkg. "Excel situation; pleasant warden; facs clean but basic; pitches well-drained in wet at end ssn but site liable to sudden flooding; public footpath thro site; leisure complex nr." ♦ 1 Apr-30 Oct. € 8.50 2008*

JONZAC *7B2* (2km SW Rural) *45.42916, -0.44833* **FFCC Camping Les Castors, St Simon de Bordes, 17500 Jonzac [05 46 48 25 65; fax 05 46 04 56 76; camping-les-castors@wanadoo.fr; www.campingcastors.com]** Fr Jonzac take D19 S twds Montendre, after approx 2km, immed after ring rd rndabt, turn R into minor rd. Site ent adj. Med, hdg pitch, hdstg, pt shd; wc; chem disp; mv service pnt; shwrs inc; el pnts (6-10A) €4.20-4.90; Indtte; tradsmn; snacks; bar; playgrnd; covrd pool; rv sw 2km; entmnts; TV; 50% statics; dogs €1.60; no twin-axles; quiet; red low ssn; CCI. "Peaceful & well-maintained site; gd facs; friendly; excel pool; gd." ♦ 15 Mar-30 Oct. € 13.40 2008*

JOSSELIN *2F3* (1.5km W Rural) *47.95230, -2.57338* **FFCC Camp Municipal du Bas de la Lande, 56120 Guégon [02 97 22 22 20 or 02 97 22 20 64; fax 02 97 73 93 85; campingbasdelalande@wanadoo.fr; www.guegon.fr]** Exit N24 by-pass W of town sp Guégon; foll sp 1km; do not attempt to cross Josselin cent fr E to W. Site on D724 just S of Rv Oust (canal). Med, hdg pitch, terr, pt shd; wc; chem disp; mv service pnt; baby facs; shwrs inc; el pnts (5A) €3.10; Indtte; shops 2km; bar high ssn; playgrnd; quiet but some rd noise; red low ssn; CCI. "Barrier clsd 1200-1400; walk to Josselin, chateau & old houses; vg, clean san facs; gd cycling." ♦ 1 Apr-31 Oct. € 11.00 2007*

JUGON LES LACS *2E3* (S Rural) *48.40166, -2.31678* **Camping au Bocage du Lac, 22270 Jugon-les-Lacs [02 96 31 60 16; fax 02 96 31 75 04; contact@campingjugon.com; www.campingjugon.com]** Bet Dinan & Lamballe by N176. Foll 'Camping Jeux' sp on D52 fr Jugon-les-Lacs. Situated by lakes, sp fr cent of Jugon. Lge, pt sl, pt shd; wc; mv service pnt; baby facs; shwrs inc; el pnts (5A) €3.10; Indtte; shops adj; tradsmn; bar; playgrnd; htd pool; paddling pool; waterslide; fishing & watersports in lake/rv adj; games area; games rm; entmnts; TV; some statics; dogs €2.50; adv bkg; red low ssn. "Well-situated nr pretty vill; many sports & activities; vg, modern san facs; vg, attractive site." 5 Apr-27 Sep. € 19.80 2008*

JULLOUVILLE see Granville *1D4*

France

JUMIEGES *3C2* (1km E Rural) *49.43490, 0.82970* **Camping de la Forêt, Rue Mainberthe, 76480 Jumièges [02 35 37 93 43; info@campinglaforet.com; www.campinglaforet.com]** Exit A13 junc 25 onto D313 N to Pont de Brotonne. Cross Pont de Brotonne & immed turn R onto D982 sp Yainville & Jumièges, then R onto D143. Turn L in Jumièges & foll site sp. Turn L at x-rds after cemetary & church, site on R in 1km. NB M'vans under 3.5t & 3m height can take ferry fr Port Jumièges - if towing do not use sat nav directions. Med, hdg/mkd pitch, pt shd; htd wc; chem disp; mv service pnt; baby facs; shwrs inc; el pnts (10A) inc (poss rev pol); gas; lndtte; shop; supmkt, tradsmn; rest & bar nr; BBQ; playgrnd; htd pool; paddling pool; lake beach 2.5km; watersports; fishing; cycle hire; tennis nrby; games area; wifi; games/TV rm; 30% statics; dogs free; phone; bus to Rouen; poss cr; adv bkg; quiet; ccard accp red low ssn. "Well-situated, well-run, busy site; lge pitches but some sm, generally tight access; gd, clean san facs but poss stretched high ssn; adj Abbey of Jumièges; interesting vill; conv Paris & Giverny; gd walking, cycling; gd for dogs; excel." ♦ 1 Apr-31 Oct. € 23.50 (CChq acc) ABS - N15 2009*

JUMIEGES *3C2* (3km S Rural) **Camping Boucles de la Seine-Normande, Base de Plein Air du Parc de Brotonne, 76480 Jumièges [02 35 37 31 72; fax 02 35 37 99 97; jumieges@uepa.asso.fr]** E fr Le Havre on N15; foll D131 S fr Yvetot by-pass twd Pont de Brotonne (toll). Bef bdge turn SE on D982, thro Le Trait. Turn S on D143 at Yainville for Jumièges. Cont thro Jumièges on D65, site well sp on R on lake in 3km. Fr S fr Bourg-Achard take D313 twd Pont de Brotonne; turn off after bdge on D982 as above. Med, hdg pitch, pt sl, shd; wc; chem disp; shwrs inc; el pnts (6A) inc (check pol); lndtte; shops 3km; tradsmn; rest, snacks, bar 3km; playgrnd; lake sw adj; watersports; tennis; games area; archery; golf, 30% statics; dogs €1.05; barrier clsd 2200-0800; poss cr; adv bkg; quiet; red long stay; CCI. "Lovely area; helpful warden; lge pitches; poss itinerants low ssn; poss youth camps; san facs stretched high ssn; gd." ♦ 1 Mar-31 Oct. € 17.20 2006*

JUSSAC *7C4* (W Rural) *44.99231, 2.41945* **FFCC Camp Municipal du Moulin, Impasse du Moulin, 15250 Jussac [tel/fax 04 71 46 69 85; s.pradel@laba.fr; www.caba.fr/camping]** On D922 8km N of Aurillac; on L immed after bdge. Med, mkd pitch, pt shd; wc; chem disp; shwrs inc; el pnts (10A) €2; lndry rm; shop & rest 150m; pool 150m; tennis & riding nr; quiet. "Quiet, country-style, vg value site nr lge vill; clean, well-kept, grassy; excel san facs; pleasant, helpful owners; gd walking." ♦ 15 Jun-1 Sep. € 8.50 2007*

KAYSERSBERG *6F3* (Urban) *48.13580, 7.26233* **Aire Communale Erlenbad, Rue Rocade, 68240 Kaysersberg [03 89 78 11 12 (Mairie)]** On D415 foll sp P1, site clearly visible. Med, hdstg, unshd; wc; chem disp; mv service pnt; shop, rest, snacks, bar 300m; poss cr; some rd noise. "Gd NH; m'vans only; pay at machine." 15 Mar-31 Dec. € 6.00 2008*

KAYSERSBERG *6F3* (1km NW Rural) *48.14899, 7.25405* **Camp Municipal, Rue des Acacias, 68240 Kaysersberg [tel/fax 03 89 47 14 47 or 03 89 78 11 11 (Mairie); camping@ville-kaysersberg.fr; www.kaysersberg.com]** Fr A35/N83 exit junc 23 onto D4 sp Sigolsheim & Kaysersberg; bear L onto N415 bypass dir St Dié; site sp 100m past junc with D28. Or SE fr St Dié on N415 over Col du Bonhomme; turn L into Rue des Acacias just bef junc with D28. Med, hdg/mkd pitch, pt shd; wc; chem disp; shwrs inc; baby facs; el pnts (8-13A) €3.35-4.25; gas; lndtte; shops 150m; supmkt 700m; pool 1km; playgrnd; TV; fishing, tennis adj; dogs €2 (no dogs Jul/Aug); quiet. "Vg, busy, clean site; rec arr early high ssn; many gd sized pitches; barrier locked 2200; rv walk to lovely town, birth place Albert Schweitzer; many mkd walks/cycle rts; Le Linge WWI battle grnd nr Orbey." 1 Apr-30 Sep. € 12.25 2009*

KAYSERSBERG *6F3* (7km NW Rural) *48.18148, 7.18449* **Camping Les Verts Bois, 3 Rue de la Fonderie, 68240 Fréland [tel/fax 03 89 71 91 94 or 03 89 47 57 25; lacabane.thai@orange.fr; www.camping-lesvertsbois.com]** Sp off N415 Colmar/St Dié rd bet Lapoutroie & Kaysersberg. Site approx 5km after turn fr main rd on D11 at far end of vill. Turn L into rd to site when D11 doubles back on itself. Sm, pt sl, terr, pt shd; htd wc; chem disp; shwrs inc; el pnts (10A) inc; gas; lndtte; shop & bank in vill; rest; snacks, bar; dogs €0.50; poss cr; Eng spkn; poss cr; adv bkg; quiet; ccard acc; red low ssn; CCI. "Beautiful setting adj rv; lovely site; friendly welcome; clsd 2230-0700; excel." 1 Apr-31 Oct. € 13.80 2009*

⊞ **KESKASTEL** *5D3* (700m NE Rural) *48.97684, 7.05354* **Camp Municipal Les Sapins, Centre des Loisirs, 67260 Keskastel [03 88 00 19 25 (Mairie); fax 03 88 00 34 66; camping.keskastel@orange.fr]** Exit A4 junc 42 fr N or junc 43 fr S dir Sarralbe/Keskastel. In Keskastel cent turn onto D338 twds Herbitzheim. Cont for approx 1km; turn R for approx 400m; site on L, well sp on lakeside. Med, hdg/mkd pitch, pt shd; htd wc (some cont); chem disp; shwrs inc; el pnts (10A) inc (poss rev pol); lndtte; shop 1km; tradsmn; rest & snacks (high ssn); bar; BBQ; playgrnd; sand beach adj; lake sw & fishing; tennis nr; 60% statics; site clsd 22 Feb-7 Mar, 24 Oct-6 Nov & 19-31 Dec; dogs; phone; poss cr; some Eng spkn; quiet; adv bkg; ccard acc; CCI. "Relaxing location; conv m'way; spacious pitches; helpful warden lives above recep, ring bell if office clsd; basic san facs, ltd low ssn; office poss clsd Sun morn; barrier clsed 2300; vg." ♦ € 18.00 2009*

LABENNE *8E1* (4km S Coastal) *43.56950, -1.46033* **Airotel Camping Lou Pignada, 741 Ave de la Plage, 40440 Ondres [05 59 45 30 65; fax 05 59 45 25 79; info@camping-loupignada.com; www.camping-loupignada.com]** Turn R off N10 at N end of Ondres vill, sp Ondres-Plage, site immed after rlwy level x-ing on L. Med, shd; wc; baby facs; shwrs; el pnts (6-8A) €5; gas; lndtte; shop; rest; snacks; bar; BBQ; playgrnd; pool; paddling pools; waterslide; spa/jacuzzi; sand beach 1.7km; games area; tennis; cycle hire; horseriding, golf nrby; entmnts; TV; 50% statics; dogs €5; adv bkg; red low ssn; v quiet; ccard acc. "Tight manoeuvring amongst trees." 21 Mar-30 Sep. € 27.00 2008*

⊞ **LABENNE** *8E1* (4km S Rural) *43.56470, -1.45240* **Camping du Lac, 518 Rue de Janin, 40440 Ondres [05 59 45 28 45 or 06 80 26 91 51 (mob); fax 05 59 45 29 45; contact@camping-du-lac.fr; www.camping-du-lac.fr]** Fr N exit A63 junc 8 onto N10 S. Turn R just N of Ondres sp Ondres-Plage, at rndabt turn L & foll site sp. Fr S exit A63 junc 7 onto N10 to Ondres. Cont thro town cent & turn L at town boundary, then as above; tight turns thro housing est. Med, hdg/mkd pitch, terr, pt shd; htd wc; chem disp; baby facs; shwrs inc; el pnts (10A) inc; gas; lndtte; shop 500m; rest in ssn; snacks; bar; playgrnd; pool in ssn; sand beach 4km; fishing; boating; games area; entmnt; cycle hire; 60% statics; dogs €4; phone; twin-axles acc low ssn only; Eng spkn; adv bkg (dep); quiet; red long stay/low ssn; CCI. "Peaceful, charming lakeside site; gd welcome; helpful staff; ltd facs low ssn; vg pool; excel." ♦ € 32.00 2009*

LABENNE *8E1* (3km SW Coastal) *43.59533, -1.45651* **Yelloh! Village Le Sylvamar, Ave de l'Océan, 40530 Labenne [05 59 45 75 16; fax 05 59 45 46 39; camping@sylvamar.fr; www.sylvamar.fr or www.yellohvillage.com]** Exit A63 junc 7 onto D85; then take N10 N to Labenne; turn L onto D126; site sp. Lge, hdg/mkd pitch, pt shd; wc; chem disp; serviced pitches; shwrs inc; el pnts (10A) inc; lndtte; shop adj; tradsmn; rest; snacks; bar; pool; waterslide; playgrnd; sand beach 800m; fitness rm; dogs €5.50; adv bkg; quiet; Eng spkn; red low ssn; ccard acc; CCI. ♦ 26 Apr-17 Sep. € 40.00 2007*

LABENNE *8E1* (2km W Coastal) *43.59547, -1.45695* **Camping La Côte d'Argent, 60 Ave de l'Océan, 40530 Labenne-Océan [05 59 45 42 02; fax 05 59 45 73 31; info@camping-cotedargent.com; www.camping-cotedargent.com]** Fr N10 take D126 W fr Labenne to Labenne-Plage & site. Lge, hdg/mkd pitch, shd; htd wc; 10% serviced pitches; mv service pnt; chem disp; baby facs; shwrs inc; el pnts (6A) €3.80; gas 300m; lndtte; shop 200m; tradsmn, rest, snacks, bar high ssn; BBQ; playgrnd; pool; paddling pool; sand beach 900m; fishing 300m; games rm; archery; tennis 500m; entmnt high ssn; TV rm; cycle hire; 50% statics; dogs €2.50; poss cr; Eng spkn; adv bkg rec; quiet; ccard acc; CCI. "Nice pool area; children's park; gd cycle tracks; ltd facs low ssn; conv Biarritz; excel for family hols." ♦ 1 Apr-31 Oct. € 24.90 (CChq acc) 2007*

LABENNE *8E1* (2km W Coastal) *43.59596, -1.46157* **Camping La Mer, Route de la Plage, 40530 Labenne-Océan [05 59 45 42 09; fax 05 59 45 43 07; campinglamer@wanadoo.fr; www.campinglamer.com]** Turn W off N10 in Labenne at traff lts in town cent onto D126 to Labenne-Plage. Site 2km on L. Lge, shd; wc; baby facs; shwrs inc; el pnts (6A) €3.60; gas; lndtte; shop; rest; snacks; bar; BBQ; playgrnd; htd, covrd pool; jacuzzi; sand/shgl beach 500m; games area; some statics; dogs €2.50; adv bkg; quiet; red long stay/low ssn. 1 Apr-30 Sep. € 17.80 2007*

LABLACHERE *9D2* (4km NW Rural) *44.47955, 4.17096* **Camping Le Ch'ti Franoi, Route de Planzolles, 07230 Lablachère [04 75 36 64 09; info@campinglechti.com; www.campinglechti.com]** Exit D104 to Lablachère; cont thro vill onto D4 dir Planzolles; site on L in 4km, just bef Cédat. Sm, pt sl, pt shd; wc; chem disp (wc); shwrs inc; el pnts (3A) inc (10-16A extra); lndry rm; shop; tradsmn; rest; snacks; bar; BBQ; playgrnd; pool; entmnt; TV rm; 75% statics; dogs €4; adv bkg. "Welcoming, friendly, helpful British owners." 1 Apr-31 Oct. € 24.00 2009*

LAC D'ISSARLES, LE *9C1* (Rural) *44.82382, 4.07104* **Camp Municipal Les Bords du Lac, 07470 Le Lac-d'Issarlès [04 66 46 20 70 or 04 66 46 20 06 (Mairie); fax 04 66 46 49 73; mairielacissarles@orange.fr]** On N88 S fr Le Puy-en-Velay, take D16 N sp Coucouron. Foll sp for Lac-d'Issarlès. Site on L well sp. Lge, mkd pitch, pt sl, terr, pt shd; wc; chem disp (wc); mv service pnt; shwrs inc; el pnts inc; lndtte; shop, rest, snacks, bar 200m; playgrnd; sand beach; lake sw, fishing, boating; dogs; Eng spkn; quiet. "Pleasant views with dir access to lake; poss diff for long o'fits." ♦ 1 May-15 Sep. € 12.90 2007*

LAC D'ISSARLES, LE *9C1* (2km E Rural) *44.81805, 4.05352* **Camping La Plaine de la Loire, Pont-de-Laborie, 07470 Le Lac-d'Issarlès [04 66 46 25 77 or 06 24 49 22 79 (mob); fax 04 66 46 21 55; campinglaplainedelaloire@ifrance.com; http://campinglaplainedelaloire.ifrance.com]** Fr S on N102 take D16 sp Le Lac-d'Issarles. After Coucouron (5km) site on R after Pont-de-Laborie. Med, mkd pitch, pt shd; wc (cont); chem disp; shwrs inc; el pnts (6A) inc; gas; lndtte; shop; tradsmn; snacks; playgrnd; rv sw adj; games area; 5% statics; adv bkg; quiet; CCI. "Lovely, tranquil site - a real gem." ♦ 5 Jun-15 Oct. € 12.00 2007*

LACANAU OCEAN *7C1* (1km N Coastal) *45.00823, -1.19322* **Airotel Camping de l'Océan, 24 Rue du Repos, 33680 Lacanau-Océan [05 56 03 24 45; fax 05 57 70 01 87; airotel.lacanau@wanadoo.fr; www.airotel-ocean.com]** On ent town at end of sq in front of bus stn turn R, fork R & foll sp to site (next to Camping Grand Pins). Lge, pt sl, pt shd; wc; chem disp; shwrs inc; el pnts (15A) inc; gas; lndtte; shop; rest; snacks; bar; pool; sand beach 600m; tennis; entmnt; fishing; watersports; cycle hire; TV; statics; dogs €4; poss cr; adv bkg; quiet; red low ssn. "Attractive site/holiday vill in pine woods behind sand dunes; surf school nrby; care in choosing pitch due soft sand; gd, modern san facs; some pitches tight access." Easter-27 Sep. € 33.00 2008*

LACANAU OCEAN *7C1* (1km N Coastal) *45.01166, -1.19305* **Yelloh! Village Les Grands Pins, Plage Nord, Ave des Grands Pins, 33680 Lacanau-Océan [05 56 03 20 77; fax 05 57 70 03 89; reception@lesgrandspins.com; www.lesgrandspins.com or www.yellohvillage.com]** On ent town, by bus stn at sq turn R, fork R & foll sp 'Plage Nord' & site. V lge, hdg/mkd pitch, terr, pt shd; htd wc; serviced pitches; chem disp; mv service pnt; baby facs; shwrs inc; el pnts (10A) inc; gas; lndtte; shop; rest; snacks; bar; playgrnd; htd pool; sand beach 500m; cycle hire; internet; entmnt; TV; 20% statics; dogs €4; poss cr; adv bkg red high ssn; quiet; red low ssn. "Excel well organised site; lge pitches; doesn't feel overcr - even when full." 26 Apr-20 Sep. € 43.00 2008*

France

LACANAU OCEAN *7C1* (7km E Rural) *45.00808, -1.11230* **Camping Talaris Vacances, Route de L'Océan, 33680 Lacanau [05 56 03 04 15; fax 05 56 26 21 56; www.talaris-vacances.fr]** Fr Lacanau-Océan towards Lake Lacanau, site on R. Lge, mkd pitch, hdstg, shd; wc (some cont); chem disp; mv service pnt; baby facs; shwrs inc; el pnts (6A) €3.90; gas; Indtte; shop; rest; snacks; bar; BBQ area; playgrnd; pool; waterslide; lake sw 2km; tennis; 50% statics; dogs €4; bus adj; Eng spkn; adv bkg; some rd noise; red low ssn; CCI. "Nr Lake Lacanau, sw & watersports; excel network cycle tracks." ♦ 4 Apr-26 Sep. € 32.00 2009*

LACANAU OCEAN *7C1* (5km SE Rural) *44.98620, -1.13410* **Camping Le Tedey, Par Le Moutchic, Route de Longarisse, 33680 Lacanau-Océan [05 56 03 00 15; fax 05 56 03 01 90; camping@le-tedey.com; www.le-tedey.com]** Fr Bordeaux take D6 to Lacanau & on twd Lacanau-Océan. On exit Moutchic take L fork twd Longarisse. Ent in 2km well sp on L. V lge, mkd pitch, shd; wc (some cont); chem disp; mv service pnt; baby facs; shwrs inc; el pnts (10A) €4; gas; Indtte; shop; snacks; bar; playgrnd; lake sw & sand beach adj; boating; cycle hire; golf 5km; entmnt; internet; TV rm; some statics; no dogs; poss cr; Eng spkn; adv bkg (ess Jul/Aug); quiet, but poss live music Sat night high ssn; red low ssn; ccard acc; CCI. "Set in pine woods - avoid tree sap; peaceful, friendly, family-run site; golf nr; gd cycle tracks; no el pnts for pitches adj to beach; access diff to some pitches; excel site." ♦ 26 Apr-20 Sep. € 20.50 2007*

LACAPELLE MARIVAL *7D4* (1km NW Rural) *44.73331, 1.91764* **Camp Municipal Bois de Sophie, Route d'Aynac, 46120 Lacapelle-Marival [tel/fax 05 65 40 82 59; lacapelle.mairie@wanadoo.fr; http://lacapelle-marival.site.voila.fr]** NE fr N140 onto D940 dir St Céré; site at far end of Lacapelle-Marival on W side of D940. Visible fr rd. Med, mkd pitch, pt sl, pt shd; wc; chem disp; mv service pnt; shwrs inc; el pnts (10A) €2.75; shops 1km; playgrnd; pool adj; tennis; some statics; quiet; CCI. "Vg sh stay/NH." ♦ 15 May-30 Sep. € 11.00 2007*

LACAPELLE VIESCAMP *7C4* (1.6km SW Rural) *44.91272, 2.24853* **Camping La Presqu'île du Puech des Ouilhes, 15150 Lacapelle-Viescamp [04 71 46 42 38 or 06 80 37 15 61 (mob); contact@cantal-camping.fr; www.camping-lac-auvergne.com]** W fr Aurillac on D120; at St Paul-des-Landes turn S onto D53 then D18 to Lacapelle-Viescamp. Foll sp Base de Loisirs, Plage-du-Puech des Ouilhes & Camping. Site beside Lake St Etienne-Cantalès. Med, hdg/mkd pitch, hdstg, pt shd; wc; chem disp; baby facs; shwrs inc; el pnts (16A) €3; Indtte; shop 200m; rest; snacks; bar; playgrnd; pool; sand beach adj; lake sw adj; water sports; canoeing; fishing; tennis; games rm; some statics; dogs €2; Eng spkn; quiet; red low ssn/long stay. "Friendly, helpful young owners; excel." ♦ 15 May-15 Sep. € 16.00 2008*

⊞ **LACAUNE** *8E4* (5km E Rural) *43.69280, 2.73790* **Camping Le Clôt, Les Vidals, 81230 Lacaune [tel/fax 05 63 37 03 59; campingleclot@orange.fr; www.pageloisirs.com/le-clot]** Fr Castres to Lacaune on D622. Cont on D622 past Lacaune then turn R on D62 for Les Vidals. Site sp 500m on L after Les Vidals. Sm, terr, pt shd; htd wc; chem disp; shwrs inc; el pnts (10A) €3; Indtte; shop 5km; rest; snacks; playgrnd; lake sw, fishing, sailing, windsurfing 12km; dogs €1.50; Eng spkn; quiet; CCI. "Excel site; gd views; gd walking in Monts de Lacaune; friendly Dutch owner; vg rest." ♦ € 17.15 2009*

LACAUNE *8E4* (10km SE Rural) *43.64806, 2.78155* **Camping Indigo Rieu-Montagné, Lac du Laouzas, 81320 Nages [05 63 37 24 71; fax 05 63 37 15 42; rieumontagne@camping-indigo.com; www.camping-indigo.com]** E fr Lacaune on D622 for 8km. R on D62 twds Nages. 2km after Nages turn E on shore of Lac de Laouzas. Sp fr junc D662/D62. Lge, hdg/mkd pitch, terr, pt shd; wc (some cont); serviced pitches; baby facs; shwrs inc; el pnts (6-10A) €4-6; gas; Indtte; shop; rest, snacks high ssn; bar; BBQ; playgrnd; htd pool; lake sw; cycle hire, archery, tennis & mini-golf nr; games area; some statics; dogs €3.30; Eng spkn; adv bkg; ccard acc; CCI. ♦ 14 Jun-14 Sep. € 21.70 2007*

LADIGNAC LE LONG see St Yrieix la Perche *7B3*

LAFFREY see Vizille *9C3*

LAGRASSE *8F4* (1km NE Rural) *43.09516, 2.61893* **Camp Municipal de Boucocers, 11220 Lagrasse [04 68 43 10 05 or 04 68 43 15 18; fax 04 68 43 10 41; mairielagrasse@wanadoo.fr; www.lagrasse.fr]** 1km on D212 fr Lagrasse to Fabrezan (N). Sm, hdstg, pt sl, pt shd; wc; chem disp; mv service pnt; shwrs inc; el pnts (15A) €2.70; shops, rest 500m; rv sw 1km; dogs €1.50; phone; adv bkg; CCI. "At cent of off-the-beaten-track beautiful touring area; helpful warden; simple but gd san facs; gd walking; o'looks superb medieval town; rec arr early." ♦ 15 Mar-15 Oct. € 10.60 2008*

LAGUENNE see Tulle *7C4*

LAGUEPIE *8E4* (1km E Rural) *44.14780, 1.97892* **Camp Municipal Les Tilleuls, 82250 Laguépie [05 63 30 22 32 or 05 63 30 20 81 (Mairie); mairie.laguepie@info82.com; www.laguepie.com]** Exit Cordes on D922 N to Laguépie; turn R at bdge, still on D922 sp Villefranche; site sp to R in 500m; tight turn into narr lane. NB App thro Laguépie poss diff lge o'fits. Med, pt terr, pt shd; wc (some cont); shwrs inc; el pnts (10A) €2.50; shops 1km; bar/café adj; playgrnd; pool; paddling pool; canoe hire; tennis; 4% statics; dogs; phone; adv bkg; quiet. "V attractive setting on Rv Viaur; friendly welcome; excel playgrnd; gd touring base; conv Aveyron gorges." ♦ 4 May-30 Sep. € 10.50 2009*

LAGUIOLE *7D4* (500m NE Rural) *44.68158, 2.85440* **Camp Municipal Les Monts D'Aubrac, 12210 Laguiole [05 65 44 39 72 or 05 65 51 26 30 (LS); fax 05 65 51 26 31]** E of Laguiole on D15 at top of hill. Fr S on D921 turn R at rndabt bef ent to town. Site sp. Med, hdg/mkd pitch, pt sl, pt shd; wc; chem disp; mv service pnt; shwrs inc; el pnts inc; lndtte; shops, rest, snacks & bar 500m; dogs; phone; quiet; CCI. "Clean & well-cared for; pleasant vill; a gem." 15 May-15 Sep. € 9.30 2009*

⊞ **LAIGNES** *6F1* (500m N Rural) **Aire Communale, Le Moulin Neuf, 21300 Laignes [03 80 81 43 03; mairie@laignes.fr]** Fr E or W to Laignes on D965; in town foll sp "Camping pour camping cars", N on D953. Sm (10 m'vans), pt shd; own san; chem disp; mv service pnt; water points; el pnts; picnic tables; shops & rest 15 min walk; m'vans only. "Free of charge; delightful site by mill-pond." 2009*

LAISSAC *7D4* (500m N Urban) *44.38500, 2.82100* **Camping Aire de Service Camping Car, 12310 Laissac [05 65 69 60 45; fax 05 65 70 75 14; mairie-de-laissac@wanadoo.fr]** Exit N88 sp Laissac. Foll sp to site. Site adj livestock mkt. Sm, mkd pitch, hdstg, unshd; wc (some cont); chem disp; mv service pnt; lndtte; shop, bar 200m; rest, snacks 500m; phone 500m; rd noise. "Gd NH only; room for 6 m'vans only." ♦ 1 Mar-30 Nov. 2008*

LAISSAC *7D4* (3km SE) *44.36525, 2.85090* **FLOWER Camping La Grange de Monteillac, 12310 Sévérac-l'Eglise [05 65 70 21 00; fax 05 65 70 21 01; info@le-grange-de-monteillac.com; www.la-grange-de-monteillac.com or www.flowercamping.com]** Fr A75, at junc 42, go W on N88 twds Rodez; after approx 22km; bef Laissac; turn L twds Sévérac-l'Eglise; site sp. Med, hdg/mkd pitch, pt sl, terr, unshd; wc; chem disp (wc); mv service pnt; shwrs inc; el pnts (6A) inc (long lead poss req); lndtte; rest, bar & shops high ssn; playgrnd; 2 pools; archery; horseriding; cycle hire; walking; tennis; entmnts; TV; dogs €1.50; phone; Eng spkn; adv bkg rec high ssn; quiet; CCI. "Beautiful site." ♦ 1 May-15 Sep. € 23.50 2006*

LAIVES see Sennecey le Grand *6H1*

LALINDE *7C3* (1.5km E) *44.83956, 0.76298* **Camping Moulin de la Guillou, Route de Sauveboeuf, 24150 Lalinde [05 53 61 02 91 or 05 53 73 44 60 (Mairie); fax 05 53 57 81 60; la-guillou@wanadoo.fr]** Take D703 E fr Lalinde (Rv Dordogne on R) & keep strt where rd turns L over canal bdge. Site in 300m; sp. Med, shd; wc; shwrs inc; el pnts (5A) €1.90; shops 1km; tradsmn; pool; playgrnd; rv sw & fishing adj; entmnt; tennis adj; dogs €1.85; adv bkg. "Beside Rv Dordogne; basic, clean facs; poss itinerants; vg." 1 May-30 Sep. € 10.80 2009*

LALINDE *7C3* (4km E Rural) *44.84129, 0.78553* **Camping Les Bö-Bains, 24150 Badefols-sur-Dordogne [05 53 73 52 52; fax 05 53 73 52 55; info@bo-bains.com; www.bo-bains.com]** Take D29 E fr Lalinde, site sp on L immed after vill sp for Badefols, on rvside. Med, shd, hdg pitch; wc; chem disp; shwrs inc; el pnts (6A) inc; lndtte; shop & 4km; rest; snacks; bar; entmnt; playgrnd; pool; waterslide; tennis; games area; canoe hire; archery; boules; entmnt; some statics; dogs €3; quiet; adv bkg; ccard acc. "Delightful site on banks of Rv Dordogne." ♦ Easter-30 Sep. € 31.00 2007*

LALINDE *7C3* (8.5km SE Rural) *44.7944, 0.8336* **Camping La Grande Veyière, Route de Cadouin, 24480 Molières [05 53 63 25 84; fax 05 53 63 18 25; la-grande-veyiere@wanadoo.fr; www.lagrandeveyiere.com]** Fr Bergerac take D660 E for 19km to Port-de-Couze. Turn SW still on D660 sp Beaumont. In 6km turn L on D27. Site sp fr here. In approx 6km, ent on R. Med, hdg/mkd pitch, pt sl, terr, pt shd; wc (some cont); chem disp; shwrs inc; el pnts (6A) €2.75; gas; shop; tradsmn; snacks; bar; playgrnd; pool; games/TV rm; some statics; dogs €1; Eng spkn; adv bkg (rec Jul/Aug); phone; CCI. "Off beaten track, worth finding; owners friendly & helpful; tractor tow avail in wet weather." ♦ 1 Apr-2 Nov. € 15.35 2007*

LALINDE *7C3* (4km W Urban) *44.82604, 0.79583* **Camping des Moulins, Route de Cahors, 24150 Couze-et-St Front [05 53 61 18 36; fax 05 53 24 99 72; camping-des-moulins@wanadoo.fr; www.campingdesmoulins.com]** Fr Lalinde take D703 dir Bergerac. In 2km turn L on D660 sp Port-de-Couze; over bdge (Dordogne Rv) into Couze. Turn R on D37 sp Lanquais, turn immed L, site sp. (NB Do not take D37E.) Sm, hdg pitch, pt sl, pt shd; wc; chem disp; mv service pnt; shwrs inc; el pnts (10A) €4.50; gas; lndtte; snacks; bar; BBQ; playgrnd; 3 pools; lake sw 3km; games area; games rm; 40% statics; dogs €2; phone adj; poss cr; Eng spkn; adv bkg; quiet; ccard acc; CCI. "Generous pitches; friendly, helpful owner; ltd facs low ssn & poss unclean; gd pools; conv Bergerac; excel." 18 Mar-5 Nov. € 17.00 (4 persons) 2007*

LALLEY *9D3* (300m S Rural) *44.75490, 5.67940* **Camping Belle Roche, 38930 Lalley [tel/fax 04 76 34 75 33 or 06 86 36 71 48 (mob); www.campingbelleroche.com]** Off D1075 (N75) at D66 for Mens; down long hill into Lalley. Site on R thro vill. Med, some hdg pitch, hdstg, pt sl, pt shd; wc; chem disp; mv service pnt; baby facs; shwrs inc; el pnts (10A) €3.60 (poss rev pol); gas; lndtte; shop 500m; tradsmn Jul-Aug; rest; snacks; bar; playgrnd; htd pool; tennis 500m; entmnt; wifi; dogs €1.50; poss cr; adv bkg; quiet; ccard acc over €20; red low ssn; CCI. "Mountain views; spacious pitches; friendly, welcoming owners; clean site, san facs & pool; gd for alpine flowers; excel walks nrby; nr Vercors National Park; also conv NH to S; highly rec." ♦ 4 Apr-27 Sep. € 15.40 (CChq acc) 2009*

France

LAMALOU LES BAINS *10F1* (400m NE Rural) *43.60074, 3.08314* **Camp Municipal Le Verdale, Blvd de Mourcairol, 34240 Lamalou-les-Bains [04 67 95 86 89; fax 04 67 95 64 52; omt.lamalou@wanadoo,fr; www.ot-lamaloulesbains.fr]** S fr Bédarieux on D908 twds Lamalou. Turn N off D908 at traff lts into Lamalou. At 2nd rndbt turn E foll sp to site on NE side of town. Med, mkd pitch, pt shd; htd wc; mv service pnt; shwrs; el pnts (6A) €2.30; shop, pool, tennis & golf in town; games area; 30% statics; dogs; phone; poss cr; adv bkg rec. "San facs clean; helpful, friendly warden; sm pitches; nr thermal baths; easy walk to town & shops." ♦ 1 Mar-31 Oct. € 11.20 2008*

LAMALOU LES BAINS *10F1* (2km SE Rural) *43.57631, 3.06842* **Camping Domaine de Gatinié, Route de Gatinié, 34600 Les Aires [04 67 95 71 95 or 04 67 28 41 69 (LS); fax 04 67 95 65 73; gatinie@wanadoo.fr; www.domainegatinie.com]** Fr D908 fr Lamalou-les-Bains or Hérépian dir Poujol-sur-Orb, site sp. Fr D160 cross rv to D908 then as above. Med, hdg/mkd pitch, pt sl, pt shd; wc (some cont); chem disp; baby facs; shwrs inc; el pnts (6A) inc; Indtte; tradsmn; rest; snacks; bar; BBQ; playgrnd; pool; paddling pool; rv sw 100m; canoeing; fishing; games area; golf, horseriding, tennis 2km; entmnt; some statics; dogs €2; Eng spkn; adv bkg; quiet; red low ssn/long stay/CCI. "Beautiful, peaceful situation; many leisure activities; vg." ♦ 5 Apr-31 Oct. € 19.00 2009*

LAMASTRE *9C2* (5km NE Rural) **Camping Les Roches, 07270 Le Crestet [04 75 06 20 20; fax 04 75 06 26 23; camproches@club-internet.fr; www.campinglesroches.com]** Take D534 fr Tournon-sur-Rhône dir Lamastre. Turn R at Le Crestet & foll sp for site, 3km fr vill. Sm, mkd pitch, hdstg, terr, pt shd; wc (some cont); chem disp; mv service pnt; baby facs; shwrs inc; el pnts (4-6A) €3.20-3.50; Indtte; shop; tradsmn; rest; snacks; bar; BBQ; playgrnd; htd pool; rv sw adj; fishing; tennis 3km; games area; TV rm; 30% statics; dogs €1.50; bus 1km; adv bkg; quiet; ccard acc; 5% red CCI. "Family-run site; clean facs; lovely views; gd base for touring medieval vills; gd walking." ♦ 15 Apr-30 Sep. € 15.50 2008*

LAMASTRE *9C2* (2km NW Rural) *44.99161, 4.56497* **Camping Le Retourtour, 1 Rue de Retourtour, 07270 Lamastre [tel/fax 04 75 06 40 71; campingderetourtour@wanadoo.fr; www.campingderetourtour.com]** Fr Lamastre take D533 W. Site well sp. Med, mkd pitch, pt shd; wc (some cont); chem disp; mv service pnt; baby facs; shwrs inc; el pnts (4-13A) €2.90-€4.60; gas; Indtte; shop; tradsmn; rest; snacks; bar; BBQ; playgrnd; rv sw 500m; games area; games rm; entmnt; 10% statics; dogs €2; phone; Eng spkn; adv bkg; quiet; ccard not acc; CCI. "Friendly, helpful owners." ♦ 7 Apr-29 Sep. € 14.90 2007*

LAMBALLE *2E3* (700m NE Urban) *48.47576, -2.50472* **Camp Municipal, Rue St Sauveur, 22400 Lamballe [tel/fax 02 96 34 74 33 or 02 96 50 13 50 (LS)]** NE side of town beyond church; nr water tower. Clearly sp. Sm, terr, pt shd; wc; shwrs inc; el pnts (5A) €3; shops 700m; htd pool 700m; quiet. "Interesting town, historical 17thC church." 1 Jul-4 Sep. € 9.00 2006*

LAMONTELARIE see Brassac *8F4*

LANDEBIA see Plancoët *2E3*

LANDEDA *2E1* (2km NW Coastal) *48.59333, -4.60333* **Camping des Abers, 51 Toull-Tréaz, Plage de Ste Marguerite, 29870 Landéda [02 98 04 93 35; fax 02 98 04 84 35; camping-des-abers@wanadoo.fr; www.camping-des-abers.com]** NW fr Brest on D13/D10 to Landéda via Bourg-Blanc & Lannilis; go thro Landéda & foll sps 'Plages' (beach will be on R); then foll sps to 'Camping des Abers'. Lge, some hdg/mkd pitch, terr, pt shd; wc; chem disp; mv service pnt; baby facs; fam bthrm; shwrs €0.80; el pnts (10A) inc (long lead poss req); gas; Indtte; shop & snacks in ssn; rest 200m; bar 100m; BBQ; playgrnd; sand beach adj; fishing; cycle hire; entmnt; wifi; games/TV rm; 10% statics; dogs €1.90; Eng spkn; adv bkg (rec high ssn); quiet; ccard acc; red low ssn; CCI. "Attractive site adj spectacular wild coast; highest pitches have views; site well landscaped; friendly, helpful manager; san facs clean, some new others old; shop adj site am only; some pitches muddy when wet; gd walks, cycling; unspoilt area; excel." ♦ 1 May-30 Sep. € 17.20 ABS - B30 2009*

LANDEDA *2E1* (3km NW Coastal) *48.60310, -4.59882* **Camp Municipal de Penn-Enez, 29870 Landéda [02 98 04 99 82; info@camping-penn-enez.com; www.camping-penn-enez.com]** Proceed NW thro Landéda, turn R in 1km sp Penn-Enez then L in 600m. Site sp. Med, pt hdg pitch, pt sl, unshd; wc; chem disp (wc); shwrs inc; el pnts (16A) €2.80; playgrnd; sand beach 500m; 2% statics; dogs €1.30; Eng spkn; quiet. "Friendly, helpful management; grassy headland site; beach views fr some pitches; san facs poss stretched high ssn; site self if warden absent; gd walks." ♦ 25 Apr-30 Sep. € 10.30 2007*

LANDERNEAU *2E2* (SW Urban) *48.44575, -4.25854* **Camp Municipal Les Berges de l'Elorn, Route de Calvaire, 29800 Landerneau [02 98 85 44 94 or 02 98 85 00 66 (Mairie); fax 02 98 85 43 35; ti-ker-landerne@mairie-landerneau.fr; www.ville-landerneau.fr]** Site S of rv. Foll sps to pool, sports stadium & site. Sm, hdg pitch, hdstg, pt shd; wc; chem disp; mv service pnt; shwrs €0.50; el pnts (7A) €3.35; shops, rest, snacks bar 250m; BBQ; playgrnd adj; pool 500m; tennis; dogs €1.15; phone adj; Eng spkn; adv bkg; quiet, some rd noise; CCI. "Historic, pretty town on tidal rv; conv touring base. Note: An Aire de Service for m'vans 100m E of site on same rd." ♦ Apr-Oct. € 9.60 2008*

LANDEVIEILLE see Bretignolles sur Mer *2H3*

LANDIVISIAU *2E2* (7km NE) *48.57724, -4.03006* **Camp Municipal Lanorgant, 29420 Plouvorn [02 98 61 32 40 (Mairie); fax 02 98 61 38 87; commune-de-plouvorn@wanadoo.fr; www.plouvorn.com]** Fr Landivisiau, take D69 N twd Roscoff. In 8km turn R onto D19 twd Morlaix. Site sp, in 700m turn R. NB Care req entry/exit, poss diff lge o'fits. Sm, hdg/mkd pitch, terr, pt shd; wc (cont for men); mv service pnt; shwrs; el pnts (10A) €2; Indtte; shops, snacks, bar 500m; rest 1km; BBQ; playgrnd; sand beach; lake sw; sailboards & canoes for hire; fishing; tennis; adv bkg; quiet. "Ideal NH for ferries; lge pitches; nr lake." 26 Jun-15 Sep. € 10.00 2009*

LANDUDEC *2F2* (2km SW Rural) *47.99190, -4.35353* **Camping Domaine de Bel-Air, Keridreuff, 29710 Landudec [02 98 91 50 27; fax 02 98 91 55 82; camping-dubelair@wanadoo.fr; www.belaircamping.com]** Fr N165 exit dir Quimper Cent. On ring rd foll sp Douarnenez & Audierne & exit ring rd onto D765 immed after Carrefour supmkt sp Douarnenez. Turn L at rndabt onto D784 dir Audierne/Landudec. Strt on at traff lts in Landudec, site on L in 750m. Lge, hdg/mkd pitch, terr, pt shd; wc; chem disp; shwrs inc; el pnts (10A) inc; gas; Indtte; shop; tradsmn; rest; snacks; playgrnd; htd pool; paddling pool; beach 10km; lake adj; waterslide; watersports; tennis; games rm; entmnt; TV; dogs €2; poss cr; Eng spkn; adv bkg; quiet; ccard acc; red low ssn; CCI. "Well-situated, family site; excel." ♦ 1 May-30 Sep. € 24.00 2009*

LANGEAC *9C1* (1km N Rural) *45.10251, 3.49980* **Camp Municipal du Pradeau/Des Gorges de l'Allier, 43300 Langeac [04 71 77 05 01; fax 04 71 77 27 34; infos@campinglangeac.com; www.campinglangeac.com]** Exit N102 onto D56 sp Langeac; in 7km join D585 into Langeac; pass under rlwy; at 2nd rndabt in 1km turn L to site, just bef junc with D590. Fr S on D950 to Langeac, take 1st R after rv bdge; then 1st exit at rndabt in 100m. Lge, pt shd; wc (some cont); chem disp; mv service pnt; shwrs inc; el pnts (10A) €2.50 (poss long lead req); gas 500m; Indtte; shop 1km; tradsmn; rest 500m; snacks; playgrnd; pool (high ssn); rv sw, fishing, canoeing & walking rtes adj; cycle hire; entmnt; TV rm; some statics; dogs €1; phone; bus 1km; poss cr; Eng spkn; quiet; red low ssn; CCI. "Beautiful location on Rv Allier; tourist train thro Gorges d'Allier fr Langeac; ltd facs low ssn; gd local mkt." ♦ 1 Apr-31 Oct. € 12.50 2009*

LANGEAIS *4G1* (1km E Urban) *47.32968, 0.41848* **Camp Municipal du Lac, 37130 Langeais [02 47 96 85 80; fax 02 47 96 69 23; contact@langeais.fr; www.langeais.fr]** Exit A85 junc 7 onto D952 dir Langeais & foll 'Camping Municipal' sp. Med, mkd pitch, pt shd; wc; chem disp; shwrs inc; el pnts (6A) €3; shop; rest; snacks; bar; playgrnd; htd pool; fishing nr; 5% statics; dogs; rlwy noise; ccard acc; CCI. "Easy walk to shops; nr Rv Loire cycle path; gd." 1 Jun-15 Sep. € 8.50 2009*

LANGOGNE *9D1* (1km S Urban) *44.72781, 3.86466* **Camp Municipal de l'Allier, 9 Route de St Alban-en-Montagne, 48300 Langogne [04 66 69 28 98 or 04 66 69 10 33 (Mairie)]** Fr Le Puy take N88 dir Mende. At Langogne over rv bdge & 1st L. Foll sp, site in 1km. Med, mkd pitch, pt sl, pt shd; wc (some cont); chem disp (wc); shwrs inc; el pnts (6A) €2.40; Indtte; shops 500m; rest; snacks; bar; pool 500m; phone; poss cr; quiet; adv bkg; CCI. "Gd walking area; lake for sailing 2km; close to walking routes." ♦ 1 Jun-15 Sep. € 6.60 2006*

LANGOGNE *9D1* (2km W Rural) *44.73180, 3.83995* **Camping Les Terrasses du Lac, 48300 Naussac [04 66 69 29 62; fax 04 66 69 24 78; info@naussac.com; www.naussac.com]** S fr Le Puy-en-Velay on N88. At Langogne take D26 to lakeside, site sp. Lge, terr, pt shd; wc; chem disp; baby facs; shwrs; el pnts (6A) €2.50; Indtte; Indry rm; shop 2km; rest; snacks; bar; BBQ; playgrnd; pool; lake sw & sand beach adj; watersports adj; sailing school; games area; cycle hire; golf 1km, horseriding 3km; entmnt; excursions; TV rm; 10% statics; dogs €1.80; phone; Eng spkn; adv bkg; quiet; red low ssn; CCI. "Vg views; steep hill bet recep & pitches; vg cycling & walking." ♦ 15 Apr-30 Sep. € 14.50 (CChq acc) 2008*

⊞ **LANGRES** *6F1* (6km NE Rural) *47.89505, 5.39510* **Camping Hautoreille, 52360 Bannes [tel/fax 03 25 84 83 40; campinghautoreille@orange.fr; www.campinghautoreille.com]** N fr Dijon on D974/D674 (N74) to Langres; foll rd around Langres to E; onto D74 NE to Bannes; site on R on ent vill. Or exit A31 junc 7 Langres Nord onto D619 (N19), then D74 NE to Bannes. Med, mkd pitch, some hdstg, pt sl, pt shd; htd wc; chem disp; mv service pnt; shwrs inc; el pnts (6A) €3 (rev pol); Indtte; shops 5km; tradsmn; rest (summer only); snacks; bar; playgrnd; lake sw 2.5km; horseriding & tennis 5km; dogs €1; phone; poss cr; Eng spkn; adv bkg; quiet; CCI. "Peaceful, clean, tidy site; basic facs, ltd low ssn & poss inadequate high ssn; pleasant owner; gd site rest; site muddy when wet - parking on hdstg or owner will use tractor; on Sundays site yourself - recep opens 1700; gd NH." ♦ € 14.00 2009*

LANGRES *6F1* (5km E Rural) *47.87190, 5.38120* **Kawan Village Le Lac de la Liez, Rue des Voiliers, 52200 Peigney [03 25 90 27 79; fax 03 25 90 66 79; campingliez@free.fr; www.campingliez.com]** Exit A31 at junc 7 (Langres Nord) onto DN19l; at Langres turn L at traff lts onto D74 sp Vesoul, Mulhouse, Le Lac de la Liez; at rndabt go strt on sp Epinal, Nancy; after Champigny-lès-Langres cross over rlwy bdge & canal turning R onto D52 sp Peigney, Lac de la Liez; in 3km bear R onto D284 sp Langres Sud & Lac de la Liez; site on R in 800m. Med, hdg/mkd pitch, some hdstg, terr, pt shd; htd wc; chem disp; mv service pnt; sauna; baby facs; shwrs inc; el pnts (10A) inc; lndtte; shop; tradsmn; rest; snacks; bar; BBQ; playgrnd; 2 pools (1 htd covrd); paddling pool; spa; lake sw & sand beach adj; fishing, watersports; tennis; cycle hire; horseriding, golf 10km; entmnt; wifi; games/TV rm; 15% statics; dogs €3; phone; poss v cr; Eng spkn; quiet; ccard acc; red low ssn; CCI. "Lovely, well-run, popular site; lake views fr some pitches; helpful, friendly staff; excel, clean facs, ltd low ssn; secure site; slightly sloping, blocks poss req; some sm pitches diff manoeuvre lge o'fits; vg rest; rec arr bef 1600 high ssn; interesting town; vg NH." ♦ 1 Apr-10 Oct. € 31.00 (CChq acc) ABS - J05 2009*

LANGRES *6F1* (5km S Rural) *47.81210, 5.32080* **FFCC Camp Municipal La Croix d'Arles, 52200 Bourg [tel/fax 03 25 88 24 02; croix.arles@wanadoo.fr]** Site is 4km S of Langres on W side of D674 (N74) S of junc of D674 with D428. Fr Dijon no L turn off N74 - can pull into indust est N of site & return to site. Med, hdg/mkd pitch, ltd hdstg, pt sl, pt shd; wc; chem disp; mv service pnt; shwrs inc; el pnts (10A) €4 (poss rev pol) (long cable req); lndtte; shop; tradsmn; rest; snacks; bar; playgrnd; pool; statics; dogs; phone; poss cr; Eng spkn; ccard acc; red low ssn; CCI. "Popular site, fills up quickly after 1600; friendly staff; some lovely secluded pitches in woodland; gd san facs; muddy after rain; unkempt low ssn; poss haphazard pitching when full; conv NH Langres historic town." ♦ 15 Mar-31 Oct. € 15.00 2009*

LANGRES *6F1* (500m SW Urban) *47.86038, 5.32894* **Camp Municipal Navarre, 9 Blvd Maréchal de Lattre de Tassigny, 52200 Langres [03 25 87 37 92 or 06 10 74 10 16; fax 03 25 87 37 92; campingnavarre@free.fr]** App fr N or S on D619 (N19)/D674, cont on main rd until lge rndabt at top of hill & go thro town arched gateway; site well sp fr there. NB Diff access for lge o'fits thro walled town but easy access fr D619. Med, pt sl, pt shd; htd wc; chem disp; shwrs inc; el pnts (6-10A) €3-3.50 (long lead req & poss rev pol); lndry rm; playgrnd nr; dogs free; phone; poss cr in high ssn & w/end; Eng spkn; quiet, some rd noise; ccard not acc; CCI. "Busy, well-situated NH; gd views fr some pitches; recep open 1800-2200; on arr site self & see warden; rec arr bef 1630; helpful staff; excel, modern san facs; no twin-axles; part of site muddy after rain; no barrier but security number for locked san facs." ♦ 15 Mar-31 Oct. € 11.60 2009*

LANGRES *6F1* (4km NW Rural) *47.90213, 5.30238* **Camp Municipal La Mouche, Rue de la Mouche, 52200 Humes-Jorquenay [03 25 87 50 65 (Mairie)]** Exit A31 at junc 7, foll N19 S for 4km; site on W of N19 over rv bdg; sp in vill cent. Or S fr Chaumont on N19, into vill of Humes. Sm, unshd; wc; shwrs inc; el pnts (8A) €2 (poss long cable rec); tradsmn; rest 2km; snacks; playgrnd; poss cr; quiet. "Pretty site; basic but busy; early arr rec; no staff on site, fees collected each pm; no apparent security; interesting area; gd NH." 15 Apr-30 Sep. € 9.00 2008*

LANILDUT *2E1* (1km N Coastal) *48.48012, -4.75184* **Camping du Tromeur, 11 Route du Camping, 29840 Lanildut [02 98 04 31 13; tromeur@vive-les-vacances.com; www.vive-les-vacances.com/tromeur]** Site well sp on app rds to vill. Med; wc; chem disp (wc); shwrs inc; el pnts €2 (poss long lead req & poss rev pol); lndry rm; tradsmn; shop, bar, crêperie & gd rest in vill; BBQ; dogs €1; phone; quiet. "Clean, sheltered site; san facs gd; harbour & sm beach; low ssn warden am & pm only - site yourself." 1 May-30 Sep. € 9.00 2008*

LANLOUP *2E3* (W Rural) *48.71369, -2.96711* **FFCC Camping Le Neptune, Kerguistin, 22580 Lanloup [02 96 22 33 35 or 06 75 44 39 69 (mob); fax 02 96 22 68 45; contact@leneptune.com; www.leneptune.com]** Take D786 fr St Brieuc or Paimpol to Lanloup, site sp. Med, hdg/mkd pitch, pt shd; wc (some cont); chem disp; baby facs; shwrs inc; el pnts (6-16A) €3.90; gas; lndtte; shop (high ssn) or 500m; tradsmn; snacks, bar (high ssn) or 500m; BBQ; playgrnd; htd, covrd pool; sand beach 2.5km; tennis 300m; horseriding 4km; cycle hire; TV rm; 15% statics; dogs €2.50; phone; poss cr; Eng spkn; adv bkg; quiet, rd noise some pitches; red low ssn; CCI. "Excel, well-maintained site nr beautiful coast; various pitch sizes; spotless san facs; friendly, helpful owner; highly rec." ♦ 5 Apr-20 Oct. € 19.10 (CChq acc) 2008*

LANNE *8F2* (1km NW Rural) *43.17067, 0.00186* **Camping La Bergerie, 79 Rue des Chênes, 65380 Lanne [tel/fax 05 62 45 40 05; camping-la-bergerie@orange.com; www.camping-la-bergerie.com]** Fr Lourdes take N21 twd Tarbes. Turn R on D216, site sp. Med, mkd pitch, shd; htd wc; shwrs; el pnts (10A) €3 (poss rev pol); gas; shop; snacks & bar (high ssn); playgrnd; pool high ssn; tennis; dogs €1; bus 200m; Eng spkn; adv bkg; quiet but some rd noise & aircraft noise at night; red low ssn; CCI. "Well-run site; friendly owners; gd san facs; poss unkempt low ssn; poss flooding wet weather; no turning area." ♦ 1 Feb-30 Sep. € 14.50 2009*

LANNEMEZAN *8F2* (6km W Rural) *43.10544, 0.32333* **FFCC Camping Les Craouès, Rue du 8 Mai 1945, 65130 Capvern [tel/fax 05 62 39 02 54; demande@camping-les-craoues.net; www.camping-les-craoues.net]** Exit A64 junc 15. At rndabt at ent to Capvern foll sp Capvern Village. Site also sp fr Lannemezan on D817 (N117). Med, mkd pitch, pt sl, shd; wc; mv service pnt; baby facs; shwrs inc; el pnts (3-8A) €2.75-5; gas; lndtte; shops 500m; playgrnd; pool, paddling pool 100m; games rm; dogs €1; poss cr; adv bkg; red low ssn. "V basic site; not clearly mkd pitches; scruffy overall (low ssn report); NH only." ♦ 1 May-15 Oct. € 12.60 2007*

LANNION *1D2* (2km SE) *48.72300, -3.44600* **Camp Municipal Les Deux Rives, Rue du Moulin du Duc, 22300 Lannion [02 96 46 31 40 or 02 96 46 64 22; fax 02 96 46 53 35; infos@ville.lannion.fr]** SW fr Perros-Guirec on D788 to Lannion; fr Lannion town cent; foll dir Guincamp on D767; site well sp approx 1.5km just bef Leclerc supmkt (do not confuse with hypmkt). Fr S on D767 sp at rndabts; turn L at Leclerc supmkt. Med, mkd pitch, unshd; wc; chem disp; shwrs inc; el pnts (6A) €2; Indtte; shop high ssn & 1km; bar high ssn; playgrnd; security barrier; dogs €1; adv bkg; CCI. "Rvside walk to old town; gd san facs but ltd low ssn; poss unkempt low ssn; phone ahead low ssn to check open; warden lives on site but poss no arrivals acc Sun." ♦ 1 Mar-30 Sep. € 13.10 2008*

LANNION *1D2* (7km NW Coastal) *48.73764, 3.5437* **FFCC Camping Les Plages de Beg Léguer, Route de la Côte, 22300 Lannion [02 96 47 25 00 or 02 99 83 34 81 (LS); fax 02 96 47 27 77; info@campingdesplages.com; www.campingdesplages.com]** Fr Lannion take rd out of town twd Trébeurden then twd Servel on D65, then head SW off that rd twd Beg Léguer (sp). Lge, hdg/mkd pitch, pt shd; wc (some cont); chem disp; ltd mv service pnt; baby facs; shwrs inc; el pnts (6-10A) €3-4.50 (poss long lead req); gas; Indtte; sm shop & 5km; tradsmn; rest; snacks; bar; playgrnd; htd pool; paddling pool; sand beach 350m; fishing; sailing; windsurfing; tennis; wifi; TV; 30% statics; dogs €1; phone; bus 400m; Eng spkn; adv bkg; quiet; red long stay/low ssn; ccard acc; CCI. "Pleasant, peaceful, family-run site; lge pitches; immac, modern san facs." ♦ Easter-1 Nov. € 20.00 2008*

LANOBRE see Bort les Orgues *7C4*

LANSLEBOURG MONT CENIS *9C4* (Rural) *45.28417, 6.87380* **Camp Municipal Les Balmasses, 73480 Lanslebourg-Mont-Cenis [04 79 05 82 83; fax 04 79 05 91 56; burdin61@club-internet.fr; www.camping-les-balmasses.com]** Fr Modane, site on R on rv on ent to town. Med, mkd pitch, pt shd; wc (some cont); shwrs inc; el pnts (6-10A) €4.30-5.40; Indtte; shop 500m; BBQ; playgrnd; dogs; phone; Eng spkn; CCI. "Pleasant, quiet site by rv; lovely mountain views; clean facs; conv NH bef/after Col du Mont-Cenis." ♦
1 Jun-20 Sep. € 12.80 2009*

LANSLEBOURG MONT CENIS *9C4* (2.5km E Rural) *45.29038, 6.90928* **Camp Municipal Caravaneige, 73480 Lanslevillard [tel/fax 04 79 05 90 52 or 06 86 11 66 86 (mob); www.camping-valcenis.com]** Fr Lanslebourg, take sp rd D902 to Lanslevillard. Site on L at ent to vill. Med, mkd pitch, pt sl, unshd; htd wc; chem disp; mv service pnt; shwrs inc; el pnts (6-10A) €5.80-7.80 (ensure staff reset bef connection); gas 500m; Indtte; shops 500m; bar/rest; playgrnd; tennis nr; some statics; phone; poss cr (winter ski); adv bkg only in winter; quiet; CCI. "Winter ski-resort, summer walking & cycling; ltd recep hrs; vg." ♦ 15 Jun-15 Sep & 16 Dec-1 May. € 12.40 2007*

LANTON see Andernos les Bains *7D1*

LANVEOC *2E2* (1km N Coastal) *48.29176, -4.46072* **Camp Municipal La Cale, Route de la Grève, 29160 Lanvéoc [02 98 27 58 91]** N fr Crozon dir Roscanvel. After approx 5.5km turn R onto D55 for Lanvéoc. Site sp. Med, mkd pitch, terr, unshd; shwrs inc; el pnts (10A) €2.90; Indtte; rest; snacks; bar; dir access to coast; fishing; no statics; dogs €1; quiet; CCI. "Sea views; low ssn unisex san facs; site rd steep with sharp bends to upper levels." 1 Jun-15 Sep. € 8.00 2009*

LAON *3C4* (2.5km W Rural) *49.56190, 3.59583* **Camp Municipal La Chênaie, Allée de la Chênaie, 02000 Laon [tel/fax 03 23 20 25 56; aaussel@ville-laon.fr; www.ville-laon.fr]** Exit A26 junc 13 onto N2 sp Laon; in 10km at junc with D1044 (N44) (rndabt) turn sp Semilly/Laon, then L at next rndabt. Site well sp. Med, hdg/mkd pitches, pt shd; htd wc; chem disp; mv service pnt; baby facs; shwrs inc; el pnts (6A) €3.10 (poss rev pol); Indry rm; ice; ltd shop & 500m; tradsmn; rest; snacks; bar; BBQ; playgrnd; fishing lake 500m (no sw); dogs €2; phone; poss cr; Eng spkn; adv bkg; quiet with some rd noise; ccard not acc; CCI. "Peaceful, popular NH in gd location; well-mkd pitches - lgest at end of site rd; vg, clean san facs; poss unkempt low ssn; no twin-axles; gates close 2200; if travelling Sep phone to check site open; m'van parking nr cathedral; vg." ♦
1 May-29 Sep. € 10.40 2009*

LAPALISSE *9A1* (250m S Urban) *46.24322, 3.63950* **Camp Municipal, Rue des Vignes, 03120 Lapalisse [04 70 99 26 31; fax 04 70 99 33 53; office.tourismet@cc-paysdelapalisse.fr; www.ville-lapalisse.fr]** N7 fr Moulins, site on R 50m bef Lapalisse cancellation sp. Med, mkd pitch, pt shd; htd wc (some cont); shwrs inc; el pnts (6-9A) €2.10; Indtte; shops 300m; tradsman; playgrnd; dogs €1; quiet; Eng spkn; ccard acc; CCI. "Popular NH; no twin-axle vans." ♦
1 Apr-30 Sep. € 8.00 2008*

LAPEYROUSE *7A4* (2km SE Rural) *46.22159, 2.88339* **Camp Municipal Les Marins, La Loge, 63700 Lapeyrouse [04 73 52 02 73 or 04 73 52 00 79 (Mairie); fax 04 73 52 03 89; http://63lapeyrouse.free.fr]** Fr Montluçon S on D2144 (N144) sp Montaigut. In 24km turn L on D13 sp Lapeyrouse. In 7km turn R onto D998, site on R at end of vill, well sp. Med, hdg/mkd pitch, pt shd; wc; chem disp; baby facs; shwrs inc; el pnts (10-16A) inc; Indtte; bar nr; playgrnd; lake sw adj; windsurfing; fishing; tennis; games area; cycle hire; TV; adv bkg; quiet; CCI. "Delightful countryside; barrier access." 15 Jun-1 Sep. € 15.00 (3 persons) 2006*

LARGENTIERE *9D2* (4km SE Rural) *44.50347, 4.29430* **Camping Les Châtaigniers, Le Mas-de-Peyrot, 07110 Laurac-en-Vivarais [04 75 36 86 26; chataigniers@hotmail.com; www.chataigniers-laurac.com]** Fr Aubenas S on D104 dir Alès; site sp fr D104. Site on one of minor rds leading to Laurac-en-Vivarais. Med, mkd pitch, pt sl, pt shd; wc, chem disp (wc); baby facs; shwrs; el pnts (10A) €2.50; Indtte; BBQ (gas); playgrnd; pool & sun area; 15% statics; dogs €2; poss cr; adv bkg; quiet, but rd noise on lower terr; red low ssn. "Attractive site; some pitches deep shade; nice pool; sh uphill walk to vill shops & auberge; vg." ♦
1 Apr-30 Sep. € 15.50 2009*

LARGENTIERE *9D2* (1.6km NW Rural) *44.56120, 4.28615* **Kawan Village Les Ranchisses, Route de Rocher, Chassiers, 07110 Largentière [04 75 88 31 97; fax 04 75 88 32 73; reception@lesranchisses.fr; www.lesranchisses.fr]** Fr Aubenas S on D104. 1km after vill of Uzer turn R onto D5 to Largentière. Go thro Largentière on D5 in dir Rocher/Valgorge; site on L in 1.5km. DO NOT use D103 bet Lachapelle-Aubenas & Largentière - too steep & narr for lge vehicles & c'vans. NB Not advisable to use sat nav directions to this site. Med, mkd pitch, pt shd; wc; chem disp; baby facs; shwrs inc; el pnts (10A) inc; gas; Indtte; shop; rest; snacks; bar; BBQ (gas/elec only) playgrnd; 2 htd pools (1 covrd); wellness centre; paddling pool; rv sw, fishing; canoeing; tennis; archery; games area; entmnt; wifi; games/ TV rm; 30% statics; dogs €3.20; poss cr; adv bkg ess; ccard acc; red low ssn. "Lovely, well-managed site adj vineyard; helpful, hard-working staff; excel rest; poss muddy when wet; noisy rd adj to S end of site." ♦ 3 Apr-25 Sep. € 42.00 (CChq acc) ABS - C32 2009*

LARGENTIERE *9D2* (8km NW Rural) *44.56631, 4.22888* **FFCC Camping La Marette, Les Marches du Tanargues, Route de Valgorge, 07110 Joannas [04 75 88 38 88; fax 04 75 88 36 33; reception@lamaratte.com; www. lamarette.com]** Fr Aubenas D104 SW to Largentière. Foll D5 3km N of Largentière then W on D24 to Valgorge. Site 3km past vill of Joannas. Med, mkd pitch; pt sl, terr, pt shd; wc; chem disp; mv service pnt; shwrs; el pnts (10A) €3.70; Indtte; shop; tradsmn; snacks; bar; playgrnd; pool; 5% statics; dogs €2; quiet; adv bkg; Eng spkn; CCI. "Friendly family-run site; excel for children; organised tours, canoe hire, walking; gd san facs; not rec for lge trailer o'fits." ♦ Easter-30 Sep. € 22.30 2008*

LARNAGOL see Cajarc *7D4*

LARNAS *9D2* (2.5km SW Rural) *44.43674, 4.57728* **Camping Le Domaine d'Imbours, 07220 Larnas [04 75 54 39 50; fax 04 75 54 39 20; info@domaine-imbours.com; www. domaine-imbours.com or www.camping-franceloc.fr]** Fr Bourg-St Andéol on D86 (N86) take D4 to St Remèze. Do not exit on D462 which has sp for tourists for Imbours site. In St Remèze turn R on D362 to Mas-du-Gras & D262 twd Larnas & site. Do not attempt app to site via D262 thro St Montant. Lge, mkd pitch, some hdstg, pt sl, pt shd; wc; shwrs inc; el pnts inc; Indtte; shop; rest; snacks; bar; playgrnd; htd, pool complex; waterslide; tennis; cycle hire; entmnt; some statics; dogs €4.30; poss cr; adv bkg (ess Jul/Aug); quiet. "Many sports activities; beautiful area." ♦ 31 Mar-6 Oct. € 26.00 (3 persons) 2006*

LAROQUE DES ALBERES see Argelès sur Mer *10G1*

⊞ **LARUNS** *8G2* (6km N Rural) *43.02085, -0.42043* **Camp Municipal de Monplaisir, Quartier Monplaisir, 64260 Gère-Bélesten [05 59 82 61 18; fax 05 59 82 60 71]** Site sp on E side of D934 S of Gère-Bélesten. Med, mkd pitch, pt shd, htd wc; shwrs €0.82; el pnts (3-16A) €1.95-6.30; tradsmn; shops 4km; rest, bar 100m; playgrnd; htd pool 4km; fishing; TV; 50% statics; adv bkg; quiet. € 8.50 2006*

LARUNS *8G2* (2km E Rural) *42.97991, -0.41430* **Camping du Valentin, Quartier Pon, 64440 Laruns [05 59 05 39 33; fax 05 59 05 65 84; campingduvalentin@wanadoo.fr; www.ossau-camping-valentin.com]** Fr Laruns take D934 dir Col de Pourtalet. Site well sp on L Med, hdg/mkd pitch, terr, pt shd; wc; shwrs inc; el pnts (3-6A) €2.50-3.20; Indtte; shop; tradsmn; rest, snacks high ssn; bar; playgrnd; pool 3km; 20% statics; dogs €1.10; adv bkg; quiet at night but some rd noise; red low ssn/long stay; CCI. "Pleasant, well-managed site; some pitches cramped for awning; facs ltd low ssn; conv Spanish border, cable car & mountain train; gd sh stay/NH." ♦ 19 Apr-11 Nov. € 14.55 2008*

LARUNS *8G2* (6km SE Rural) *42.96972, -0.38220* **Camping d'Iscoo, 64440 Eaux-Bonnes [05 59 05 36 81 or 06 98 23 54 93 (mob); http://iscoo.free.fr]** Site is on R 1.4km fr Eaux-Bonnes on climb to Col d'Aubisque (site sp says Camping * *, no name). Site ent in middle of S-bend so advise cont 500m & turn on open ground on L. Sm, mkd pitch, pt sl, pt shd; wc (some cont); shwrs; el pnts (2-5A) €2.50; shops 1.5km; playgrnd; pool 3km; dogs; quiet; ccard not acc; CCI. "V pleasant location; pleasant owner." 1 Jun-30 Sep. € 12.00 2008*

⊞ **LARUNS** *8G2* (1km S Rural) *42.98241, -0.41591* **Camping Les Gaves, Pon, 64440 Laruns [05 59 05 32 37; fax 05 59 05 47 14; campingdesgaves@wanadoo.fr; www. campingdesgaves.com]** Site on S edge of town, N of Hôtel Le Lorry & bdge. Fr town sq cont on Rte d'Espagne (narr exit fr sq) to end of 1-way system. After Elf & Total stns turn L at site sp immed bef bdge (high fir tree each side of bdge ent). Ignore 1st site on L. At v constricted T-junc at ent to quartier 'Pon', turn R & foll rd into site. Med, mkd pitch, pt shd; htd wc; chem disp; serviced pitch; shwrs inc; el pnts (3-10A) €2.60-4.50; Indtte; shops 1.5km; tradsmn; bar; playgrnd; pool 800m; fishing; rv fishing adj; games area; TV; 75% statics; dogs €3; quiet; CCI. "Beautiful site; excel facs; level walk to vill." € 18.80 2008*

LARUSCADE *7C2* (4km SW Rural) **Aire Naturelle Le Lac Vert (Saumon), 33620 Laruscade [tel/fax 05 57 68 64 43]** N on N10 fr Bordeaux for 28km, about 1km S of Cavignac, sp off to R. Access over narr bdge. Sm, pt shd; wc; chem disp; shwrs inc; ltd el pnts €2.70 (long cable req); shops 1km; rest; snacks; bar; lake sw; playgrnd; dogs; Eng spkn; CCI. "V pretty site nr lake; v quiet but some rlwy noise; Auberge rest on site; fair NH." 1 May-30 Sep. € 8.10 2009*

⊞ **LASSAY LES CHATEAUX** *4E1* (2km N Rural) **Camping La Cloue, La Cloue, 53110 Ste Marie-du-Bois [02 43 00 10 80; cheryl_carter@hotmail.co.uk]** Fr D976 turn S onto D34. In 8km turn R at top of hill bef sm church & in 1km turn R bef junc to site. Sm, pt sl, pt shd; own san req; mv service pnt in vill car park; shop, rest, bar 2km; no statics; dogs €1; quiet; ccard not acc; CCI. "Fair, basic CL-type area for self-contained o'fits; British owners; water avail but empty bef arrival (in Couterne); vet in town speaks Eng." € 5.00 2009*

⊞ **LASSAY LES CHATEAUX** *4E1* (6.5km E Rural) *48.41768, -0.40105* **Camping Le Malidor, 53250 Charchigné [02 43 03 99 88 or 07799 032995 (UK mob); le-malidor@orange.fr; www.fcmholidays.com]** N fr Mayenne on N12/D34 to Lassay-les-Châteaux. Turn E onto D33 to Charchigné, site sp. Sm, hdg pitch, pt shd; wc; shwrs inc; el pnts inc; shops in vill; rest; bar; BBQ; pool; lake fishing; games area; some statics; dogs; adv bkg; quiet. "Welcoming British owners; excel, peaceful site; conv NH/sh stay bet Channel ports & Bordeaux or longer stay." € 15.00 2009*

LATHUILE see Doussard *9B3*

LATTES see Montpellier *10F1*

⊞ **LAUBERT** *9D1* (Rural) *44.58262, 3.63552* **Camp Municipal La Pontière, 48170 Laubert [04 66 47 71 37 or 04 66 47 72 09; fax 04 66 47 73 08; pms.laubert@wanadoo.fr]** Site on R in hamlet of Laubert on N88. 7% hill descent fr Laubert to Mende. Sm, sl, pt shd; wc; shwrs inc; el pnts inc; lndtte; bar; snacks; quiet. "Peaceful; site at 1000m - can be chilly." ♦ € 10.00 2006*

⊞ **LAURENS** *10F1* (1km S Rural) *43.53620, 3.18583* **Camping L'Oliveraie, Chemin de Bédarieux, 34480 Laurens [04 67 90 24 36; fax 04 67 90 11 20; oliveraie@free.fr; www.oliveraie.com]** Clearly sp on D909 Béziers to Bédarieux rd. Sp reads Loisirs de L'Oliveraie. Med, mkd pitch, hdstg, terr, pt shd; htd wc; chem disp; baby facs; sauna high ssn; shwrs inc; el pnts (6-10A) €3.20-4.60 (poss rev pol); lndtte; shop high ssn; tradsmn; rest & bar high ssn; snacks; playgrnd; pool high ssn; games rm; beach 30km; TV rm; 30% statics; dogs free, €2 (high ssn); phone; adv bkg; quiet; red low ssn; ccard acc; CCI. "Site in wine-growing area; gd san facs; gd winter NH." ♦ € 23.60 2007*

LAVAL *2F4* (10km N Rural) *48.17467, -0.78785* **Camp Municipal Le Pont, 53240 Andouillé [02 43 69 72 72 (Mairie); fax 02 43 68 77 77]** Fr Laval N on D31 dir Ernée. In 8km turn R onto D115 to Andouillé. Site on L bef hill to vill cent. Sm, hdg pitch, pt shd; wc; chem disp; shwrs inc; el pnts (3A) inc; lndtte; shops 300m; playgrnd; pool 10km; rv adj; 50% statics; poss cr; quiet; no ccard acc. "Pretty, busy site; vg, clean san facs; warden on am & pm for 1 hr; site liable to flood." 1 Apr-31 Oct. € 5.50 2008*

LAVAL *2F4* (4km W Rural) *48.06428, -0.83140* **Camp Municipal Le Moulin de Coupeau, 53940 St Berthevin [02 43 68 30 70; fax 02 43 69 20 88; office.tourisme@mairie-laval.fr; www.ville.saint-berthevin.fr]** Fr Laval W on D57 (N157) twd Rennes. Site sp at St Berthevin. Sm, hdg/mkd pitch, terr, pt shd; wc; shwrs inc; el pnts (10A) €1.60; shops 2km; rest in ssn; bar adj; BBQ; htd pool adj; paddling pool; 50% statics; dogs €1; bus; adv bkg; quiet; no ccard acc; CCI. "Attractive, well-kept site on hillside by rv; helpful staff; grnd v soft after heavy rain; poss itinerant workers; poss diff access lge o'fits." 25 Apr-27 Sep. € 9.70 2009*

LAVANDOU, LE *10F3* (2km E Coastal) *43.14471, 6.38084* **Caravaning St Clair, Ave André Gide, 83980 Le Lavandou [04 94 01 30 20; fax 04 94 71 43 64; patrick.martini@wanadoo.fr]** N559 thro Le Lavandou twd St Raphaël; after 2km at sp St Clair turn R immed after bend 50m after blue 'caravaning' sp (easy to overshoot). Med, mkd pitch, shd; htd wc (cont); mv service pnt; shwrs inc; el pnts (16A) €3.50 (rev pol); lndtte; shops 100m; rest, bar nrby; playgrnd; sand beach adj; fishing; boat hire; TV rm; dogs €1; no tents; poss cr; adv bkg ess Jul-Aug; some noise fr rd; no ccard acc. "Popular with British; pitch & ent screened by trees; conv beach & rests." ♦ 1 Apr-15 Oct. (3 persons) 2008*

LAVANDOU, LE *10F3* (5km E Coastal) **Parc-Camping, Ave du Capitaine Ducourneau, Pramousquier, 83980 Le Lavandou [04 94 05 83 95; fax 04 94 05 75 04; camping-lavandou@wanadoo.fr; www.campingpramousquier.com]** Take D559 E fr Le Lavandou. At Pramousquier site sp on main rd; awkward bend. Lge, terr on steep hillside, pt shd; wc; shwrs inc; el pnts (3-6A) €3.304; gas; lndtte; shop; snacks; bar; playgrnd; sand beach 400m; dogs €2.10; poss cr; Eng spkn; red low ssn. "Pleasant, relaxing, clean site; site lighting poor; gd cycle track to Le Lavandou; not rec for disabled; excel." 26 Apr-30 Sep. € 21.70 2008*

LAVANDOU, LE *10F3* (2km S Coastal) *43.11800, 6.35210* **Camping du Domaine, La Favière, 2581 Route de Bénat, 83230 Bormes-les-Mimosas [04 94 71 03 12; fax 04 94 15 18 67; mail@campdudomaine.com; www.campdudomaine.com]** App Le Lavandou fr Hyères on D98 & turn R on o'skts of town clearly sp La Favière. Site on L in 2.3km about 200m after ent to Domaine La Favière (wine sales) - ignore 1st lge winery. If app fr E do not go thro Le Levandou, but stay on D559 until sp to La Favière. V lge, sl, pt shd, 75% serviced pitch; wc; chem disp; mv service pnt; baby facs; shwrs inc; el pnts (10A) inc (long lead poss req); gas; lndtte; shop; supmkt; tradsmn; rest; snacks; bar; BBQ (gas); playgrnd; sand beach adj; tennis; games rm; wifi; entmnt; TV rm; dogs (not acc Jul/Aug); phone; poss cr; Eng spkn; adv bkg ess high ssn; quiet; ccard acc; red low ssn; CCI. "Lge pitches, some with many trees; well-organised site with excel facs; direct access to beautiful beach; gd walking & attractions in area." ♦ 27 Mar-31 Oct. € 39.00 2009*

See advertisement on next page

LAVANDOU, LE *10F3* (1.5km SW Coastal) *43.13386, 6.35224* **Camping Beau Séjour, Quartier St Pons, 83980 Le Lavandou [04 94 71 25 30]** Take Cap Bénat rd on W o'skts of Le Lavandou. Site on L in approx 500m. Lge, mkd pitch, pt shd; wc; shwrs inc; el pnts (6A); shop; rest; snacks; bar; beach adj; poss cr; no adv bkg; rd noise on W side. "Fixed height barrier 2.60m at ent to site; sm pitches." ♦ Easter-30 Sep. 2006*

France

LAVANDOU, LE *10F3* (W Urban/Coastal) *43.13630, 6.35439* **Camping St Pons, Ave Maréchal Juin, 83960 Le Lavandou [04 94 71 03 93; info@campingsaintpons.com; www.campingstpons.com]** App fr W on D98 via La Londe. At Bormes keep R onto D559. At 1st rndabt turn R sp La Favière, at 2nd rndabt turn R, then 1st L. Site on L in 200m. Med, mkd pitch, shd; wc (some cont); chem disp; shwrs inc; el pnts (6A) inc; lndtte; shop adj; rest, snacks, bar high ssn; sand beach 800m; playgrnd; entmnt; 10% statics; dogs €3.90; phone; poss cr; Eng spkn; some rd noise; red low ssn; CCI. "Much improved site; helpful owner." 25 Apr-3 Oct. € 26.20 2009*

⊞ **LAVANDOU, LE** *10F3* (9km W Rural) *43.16262, 6.32152* **Camping Manjastre, 150 Chemin des Girolles, 83230 Bormes-les-Mimosas [04 94 71 03 28; fax 04 94 71 63 62; manjastre@infonie.fr; www.campingmanjastre.com]** App fr W on D98 about 3km NE of where N559 branches off SE to Le Lavandou. Fr E site is 2km beyond Bormes/Collobrières x-rds; sp. Lge, hdg/mkd pitch, v sl, terr, pt shd; htd wc; chem disp; mv service pnt; shwrs inc; el pnts (10A) €4.60; lndtte; shop; rest; snacks; bar; playgrnd; pool; paddling pool; sand beach 8km; 10% statics; dogs €1.50 (not acc Jul/Aug); poss cr; Eng spkn; adv bkg; quiet; red low ssn; CCI. "Site in vineyard on steep hillside - not for unfit or disabled; c'vans taken in & out by tractor; facs poss stretched in ssn; winter storage avail." € 26.80 (3 persons) (CChq acc) 2009*

LAVELANET *8G4* (1km SW Urban) *42.92340, 1.84477* **Camping Le Pré Cathare, Rue Jacquard, 09300 Lavelanet [tel/fax 05 61 01 55 54; camping.avelana@wanadoo.fr; www.campinglavelanet.com]** Fr Lavelanet, take D117 twd Foix & foll sp. Adj 'piscine'. Med, hdg/mkd pitch, pt shd; wc (mainly cont); chem disp; shwrs; el pnts (16A) €3; lndtte; shops 1km; tradsmn; snacks; BBQ; playgrnd; pool adj; tennis 800m; games area; rv 4km; entmnt; TV rm; some statics; dogs free; adv bkg; quiet; CCI. "Gd sized pitches, some with mountain views; poss open in winter with adv bkg; gates locked 2200; quiet town; vg." ♦ 1 Jun-30 Sep. € 14.00 2007*

LAVIT *8E3* (500m NE Urban) *43.96212, 0.92409* **Camp Municipal Le Bertranon, Route d'Asques, 82120 Lavit [05 63 94 05 54; fax 05 63 94 11 10; mairie-lavit-de-lomagne@info82.com; www.tourisme-en-lomagne.com]** Fr N, exit A62 junc 8 onto D953 S; in 5km turn L onto D3 sp Lavit; on ent town turn L onto D15; Rte d'Asques is 3rd turning on L. Site adj stadium. Well sp on o'skts. Sm, hdg pitch, pt shd; wc; chem disp (wc); shwrs inc; el pnts (6A) €2.30; shops, rest & snacks nrby; playgrnd; 5% statics; dogs €1; bus 500m; no twin-axles; quiet. "Lge pitches; pay at Mairie (not open w/end!); gd." ♦ 15 Jun-30 Sep. € 8.00 2009*

LAVOUTE SUR LOIRE see Puy en Velay, Le *9C1*

LECTOURE *8E3* (2.5km SE Rural) *43.91260, 0.64500* **Yelloh! Village Le Lac des Trois Vallées, 32700 Lectoure [05 62 68 82 33; fax 05 62 68 88 82; contact@ lacdes3vallees.fr; www.lacdes3vallees.fr or www.yelloh village.com]** Site sp fr N21, on lake bet Lectour & Fleurance. App fr N, look for & foll sps to L after leaving Lectoure; take this rd for 2.4km & site on L. NB Narr app rd with steep gradient. Lge, hdg/mkd pitch, pt sl, pt shd; wc; chem disp; baby facs; shwrs inc; el pnts (10A) inc; gas; lndtte; shop; bar; rest; snacks; bar; BBQ (gas/charcoal only); playgrnd; htd pool; paddling pool; waterslide; lake sw; waterslides; fishing; watersports; tennis; cycle hire; skateboard course; entmnt; wifi; games/TV rm; 60% statics; dogs €4; poss cr; adv bkg; quiet (some disco noise); ccard acc; red low ssn. "Excel lake pool; excursions to Pau, Lourdes, Andorra; mkt Tue Fleurance." ♦ 5 Jun-12 Sep. € 46.00 ABS - D18 2009*

LEGE *2H4* (7km S Rural) *46.82899, -1.59368* **Camp Municipal de la Petite Boulogne, 12 Rue du Stade, 85670 St Etienne-du-Bois [02 51 34 52 11 or 02 51 34 54 51; fax 02 51 34 54 10; la.petite.boulogne@wanadoo.fr]** S fr Legé on D978 dir Aizenay. Turn E onto D94 twd St Etienne-du-Bois. Foll sp to site. Sm, mkd pitch, pt sl, terr, pt shd; wc; chem disp (wc); shwrs inc; el pnts (10A) €2.70; gas 7km; lndtte; shops 500m; bar in vill; pool; sand beach 30km; TV rm; dogs €2.10; Eng spkn; adv bkg; quiet; CCI. "Pleasant, clean site; helpful warden; san facs would be stretched if site full." ♦ 1 Apr-30 Sep. € 12.50 2008*

⊞ **LEGE** *2H4* (8km SW Rural) *46.82121, -1.64844* **Camp Municipal Les Blés d'Or, 85670 Grand'Landes [02 51 98 51 86; fax 02 51 98 53 24; mairiegrandlandes@ wanadoo.fr]** Take D753 fr Legé twd St Jean-de-Monts. In 4km turn S on D81 & foll sp. Fr S on D978, turn W sp Grand-Landes. 3km N of Palluau. Sm, pt sl, pt shd; wc; chem disp; shwrs inc; el pnts (16A) €2.30; gas; shop, rest & bar adj; playgrnd adj; 30% statics; Eng spkn; adv bkg; quiet; ccard not acc. "V pleasant site; ent barrier clsd 2000 (poss earlier); height barrier only, cars 24hr access; rec arr early but helpful warden lives on site (pitch 4 in 2008) & will open up." € 8.40 2009*

LEGE CAP FERRET see Andernos les Bains *7D1*

LELIN LAPUJOLLE see Aire sur l'Adour *8E2*

LEMPDES SUR ALLAGNON *9C1* (N Rural) *45.38699, 3.26598* **Camp Municipal au Delà de l'Eau (formerly Camping A Tou Vert), Route de Chambezon, 43410 Lempdes-sur-Allagnon [04 71 76 53 69]** Going S on A75 exit junc 19 (ltd access) onto D909; turn R on D654 bef vill, site sp at junc. Or fr junc 20 going N; foll sp. Site just outside vill. Med, hdg pitch, pt shd; wc (some cont); chem disp (wc); mv service pnt; shwrs inc; baby facs; el pnts (10A) €3.60; lndtte; shops 500m; bar; playgrnd; pool 100m; phone; dogs €1; adv bkg; quiet; ccard acc. "Pleasant site in v beautiful area - poss a bit scruffy in early ssn; helpful warden; conv NH A75; gd." ♦ 1 Apr-30 Sep. € 12.00 2009*

LEON *8E1* (6km N Rural) *43.90260, -1.31030* **Camping Sunêlia Le Col Vert, Lac de Léon, 40560 Vielle-St Girons [08 90 71 00 01; fax 05 58 42 91 88; contact@colvert. com; www.colvert.com]** Exit N10 junc 12; at Castets-des-Landes turn R onto D42 to Vielle-St Girons. In vill turn L onto D652 twd Léon sp Soustons. In 4km, bef Vielle, take 2nd of 2 RH turns twd Lac de Léon. Site on R at end of rd in 1.5km. V lge, shd; wc; chem disp; baby facs; serviced pitches; shwrs inc; Wellness Beauty Centre; el pnts (3A) inc; gas; lndtte; shop; tradsmn; rest; snacks; bar; BBQ (gas/ elec); playgrnd; 2 pools (1 htd, covrd); paddling pool; sand beach 6km; lake sw, fishing, sailing nrby; tennis; fitness rm; wellness cent; archery; horseriding; cycle hire; entmnt; wifi; games/TV rm; 60% statics; dogs €4.40; max 6m c'van length high ssn; poss cr; adv bkg; poss noisy (nightclub); ccard acc; red low ssn/long stay; CCI. "Lakeside site in pine forest; some pitches 800m fr facs; daily mkt in Léon in ssn; ideal for children & teenagers." ♦ 3 Apr-19 Sep. € 40.20 ABS - A08 2009*

France

LEON *8E1* (5km NE Rural) **Camping Aire Naturelle Le Cayre (Capdupuy), 751 Route de Chevreuils, 40550 St Michel-Escalus [05 58 49 23 85]** Fr N10 exit Castets & St Girons onto D42 sp St Girons/Linxe. In Linxe turn L onto D374 sp Escalus & camping. In 1km R sp Léon, site on L in 1km. Sm, pt shd; wc; shwrs inc; el pnts €2.60; gas; lndtte; shops 4km; playgrnd; pool 5km; sand beach 10km; some statics; dogs €1; poss cr; ccard acc. "In pine forest; friendly, helpful owner; ltd facs low ssn." ♦ 15 Apr-15 Sep. € 12.20 2008*

LEON *8E1* (1.5km NW Rural) *43.88528, -1.31510* **Camping Lou Puntaou, 1315 Route du Lac, 40550 Léon [05 58 48 74 30; fax 05 58 48 70 42; reception@ louputaou.com; www.louputaou.com]** Site sp fr D142 on Etang de Léon. V lge, mkd pitch, pt shd; wc; chem disp; mv service pnt; shwrs inc; el pnts (15A) inc; lndtte; supmkt; rest 100m; snacks; bar; playgrnd; 2 pools (1 htd, covrd); paddling pool; waterslide; jacuzzi; lake sw 100m; sand beach 5km; tennis; watersports; games area; cycle hire; fitness rm; cash machine; entmnt; 20% statics; dogs €4; adv bkg; quiet. "Excel sports facs; lovely location." ♦ 3 Apr-4 Oct. € 35.00 2009*

LEON *8E1* (10km NW Coastal) *43.90830, -1.36380* **Domaine Naturiste Arna (Naturist), Arnaoutchot, 40560 Vielle-St Girons [05 58 49 11 11; fax 05 58 48 57 12; contact@ arna.com; www.arna.com]** Fr St Girons turn R onto D328 at Vielle sp Pichelèbe. Site in 5km on R. Lge, pt sl, shd; wc (some cont); chem disp; baby facs; shwrs inc; Arna Forme Spa; el pnts (3A) inc; gas; lndtte; shop; rest; snacks; bar; BBQ (gas/elec); playgrnd; 2 pools (1 htd covrd); paddling pool; sand beach adj; lake adj; watersports 5km; tennis; cycle hire; golf nr; archery; games area; entmnt; wifi; games/TV rm; many statics (sep area); dogs €3.40; Eng spkn; adv bkg; quiet; ccard acc; red long stay/low ssn; INF card req. "Excel site in pine forest; some pitches sandy; facs ltd low ssn; c'vans over 6m not acc high ssn; vg beach; daily mkt in Léon in ssn." ♦ 3 Apr-26 Sep. € 41.50 (CChq acc) ABS - A07 2009*

LERAN *8G4* (2km E Rural) *42.98368, 1.93516* **Camping La Régate, Route du Lac, 09600 Léran [tel/fax 05 61 01 92 69]** Fr Lavelanet go N on D625, turn R onto D28 & cont to Léran. Site sp fr vill. Ent easily missed - rd past it is dead end. Med, hdg/mkd pitch, terr, shd; wc; chem disp; baby facs; shwrs; el pnts (8A) €3.70; lndtte; shop 2km; tradsmn; rest adj; bar; BBQ; playgrnd; pool adj; lake adj; watersports; leisure cent nr; cycle hire & pony trekking nrby; entmnt; 10% statics; dogs €1; phone; quiet; adv bkg; ccard acc. "Conv Montségur chateau; clean san facs; gd location." 1 Apr-30 Oct. € 14.00 2008*

LESCAR see Pau *8F2*

LESCHERAINES *9B3* (2.5km SE Rural) *45.70279, 6.11158* **Camp Municipal de l'Ile, Base de Loisirs, Les Iles du Chéran, 73340 Lescheraines [tel/fax 04 79 63 80 00; contact@iles-du-cheran.com; www.iles-du-cheran.com]** Fr Lescheraines foll sp for Base de Loisirs. Lge, mkd pitch, pt shd; wc; chem disp; mv service pnt; baby facs; shwrs inc; el pnts (6-10A) €2-2.85; gas 1km; lndtte; shop; rest 500m; snacks; bar; BBQ; playgrnd; lake sw; canoe & boat hire; fishing; entmnt; wifi; 5% statics; dogs €1.50; phone; Eng spkn; quiet; red low ssn; CCI. "Beautiful setting; ♦ 18 Apr-27 Sep. € 13.20 2009*

LESCONIL see Pont l'Abbé *2F2*

LESCUN *8G2* (1.5km SW Rural) *42.92805, -0.64147* **Camp Municipal Le Lauzart, 64490 Lescun [tel/fax 05 59 34 51 77; campinglauzart@wanadoo.fr]** Turn L (W) off N134 8km N of Urdos on D239 sp Lescun & foll camping sp for 5km; app rd gd but steep with hairpins; foll Camping sp to fork L - do not ent Lescun vill, v narr & steep, unsuitable for c'vans. Sm, mkd pitch, terr, pt shd; htd wc; chem disp; mv service pnt; shwrs inc; el pnts (10A) €2.80; gas; lndtte; shop; rest & bar nr; dogs €0.80; adv bkg; quiet. "Mountain views; basic san facs, poss stretched high ssn; gd walks; vg." ♦ 15 Apr-30 Sep. € 10.20 2008*

LESPERON *8E1* (4km SW Rural) *43.96657, -1.12940* **FFCC Parc de Couchoy, Route de Linxe, 40260 Lesperon [tel/fax 05 58 89 60 15; info@parcdecouchoy.com; www.parcdecouchoy.com]** Exit N10 junc 13 to D41 sp Lesperon; in 1km turn L, thro vill of Lesperon; L at junc onto D331; bottom of hill turn R & immed L; site on R in 3km dir Linxe. Med, mkd pitch, pt shd; wc; chem disp; child/baby facs; shwrs inc; el pnts (6A) €3; gas; lndtte; shops 3km; tradsmn; snacks; bar; playgrnd; pool; sand beach 8km; lake sw 5km; 10% statics; dogs €1; phone; poss cr; adv bkg; quiet; ccard acc high ssn; 10% red long stay; CCI. "Lovely but isolated site on edge of wine country; gd facs on lakes for sailing, windsurfing; British owners; clean san facs; vg." 1 Jun-15 Sep. € 22.00 2009*

LEUCATE PLAGE *10G1* (200m S Coastal) *42.90316, 3.05178* **Camp Municipal du Cap Leucate, Chemin de Mouret, 11370 Leucate-Plage [04 68 40 01 37; fax 04 68 40 18 34; cap.leucate@wanadoo.fr; www.mairie-leucate.fr/capleucate]** Exit A9 junc 40 onto D627 thro Leucate vill to Leucate-Plage approx 9km. Site sp. Lge, hdg pitch, shd; wc (some cont); chem disp; mv service pnt; baby facs; fam bthrm; shwrs inc; el pnts (6A) €2.10; lndtte; shop 200m; tradsmn; rest, snacks, bar 300m; BBQ; playgrnd; htd pool 100m; sand beach 100m; games area; entmnt; TV; 60% statics; dogs €2; phone; adv bkg; quiet; red low ssn; CCI. "Nice, spacious, sandy site in gd position; popular with surfers; m'van area outside; gd NH." 1 Feb-30 Nov. € 13.40 2008*

LEVIER *6H2* (1km NE Rural) *46.95974, 6.13289* **FFCC Camping La Forêt, Route de Septfontaine, 25270 Levier [tel/fax 03 81 89 53 46; camping@camping-dela-foret.com; www.camping-dela-foret.com]** Fr D72 turn L at rndabt by supmkt onto D41, site on L in 700m. Med, mkd pitch, pt sl, terr, shd; wc; mv service pnt; baby facs; shwrs inc; el pnts (6A) €3.50; gas; lndtte; supmkt 500m; snacks; playgrnd; htd pool; dogs €0.50; poss cr; adv bkg; quiet. ♦ 11 Apr-20 Sep. € 16.50 2008*

LEVIGNAC DE GUYENNE see Miramont de Guyenne *7D2*

LEZIGNAN CORBIERES *8F4* (10km S Rural) *43.11727, 2.73609* **Camping Le Pinada, 11200 Villerouge-la-Crémade [04 68 43 32 29; contact@camping-le-pinada.com; www.camping-le-pinada.com]** Fr Lézignan-Corbières on D611 S, pass airfield & fork L thro Ferrals-les-Corbières (steep, narr) on D106. Site sp & on L after 4km. Alt rte to avoid narr rd thro Ferrals: exit A61 junc 25 & foll D611 thro Fabrezan. At T-junc turn L onto D613 & after 2km turn L onto D106. Site on R after Villerouge-la-Crémade. Med, hdg/mkd pitch, pt sl, terr, shd; wc; chem disp (wc); baby facs; shwrs inc; el pnts (6A) €5; lndtte; shop; tradsmn; snacks; bar; playgrnd; pool; rv sw & fishing 3km; tennis; entmnt; TV rm; 25% statics; dogs €2; poss cr; Eng spkn; adv bkg, bkg fee; quiet; ccard not acc; CCI. "Friendly owners; gd base for Carcassonne & Med coast; well-run site; dated san facs; excel." ♦ 1 Feb-30 Nov. € 16.00 2008*

LEZIGNAN CORBIERES *8F4* (500m NW Urban) *43.20475, 2.75255* **Camp Municipal de la Pinède, Ave Gaston Bonheur, 11200 Lézignan-Corbières [tel/fax 04 68 27 05 08; campinglapinede@wanadoo.fr; www.campinglapinede.fr]** On D6113 (N113) fr Carcassonne to Narbonne on N of rd; foll 'Piscine' & 'Restaurant Le Patio' sp. Med, all hdg/hdstg pitch, pt sl, terr, pt shd; wc; chem disp; mv service pnt; shwrs inc; el pnts (6A) inc; gas; lndtte; shop 1km; rest; snacks; bar; BBQ (gas only); htd pool adj; tennis; 5% statics; dogs €2; no c'vans/m'vans over 5m; adv bkg; quiet; ccard not acc; red low ssn/CCI. "Well-run, clean, popular site; helpful, friendly staff; gd san facs; gd m'van facs; some pitches diff due high kerb; superb pool; gd touring base; mkt Wed; vg NH."♦ 1 Mar-30 Oct. € 16.70 2009*

LICQUES *3A3* (1km E Rural) *50.77974, 1.94766* **Camping Les Pommiers des Trois Pays, 253 Rue du Breuil, 62850 Licques [tel/fax 03 21 35 02 02; denis.lamce@wanadoo.fr; www.pommiers-3pays.com]** Fr Calais to Guînes on D127 then on D215 to Licques; take D191 fr vill & foll sp; site on L in 1km. Or exit A26 junc 2 onto D217 to Licques; turn L onto D215; cont strt on & site on L on far side of vill. NB sloping ent, long o'fits beware grounding. Med, hdg/mkd pitch, sl, pt shd; wc; chem disp; mv service pnt; baby facs; shwrs inc; el pnts (16A) €4.40; Indtte; shops 1km; rest; snacks; bar; BBQ; playgrnd; htd, covrd pool; sand beach, golf, sailing 25km; fishing 2km; games area; games rm; wifi; TV rm; 65% statics; dogs €1; adv bkg; quiet; ccard acc; red long stay/low ssn. "Gd beaches nr; lge pitches; friendly, helpful owners; gd quality facs, ltd low ssn; gd walking; conv Calais/Dunkerque ferries; gd." ♦ 21 Apr-31 Oct. € 17.10 2009*

LICQUES *3A3* (2.5km E Rural) *50.77905, 1.95567* **Camping-Caravaning Le Canchy, Rue de Canchy, 62850 Licques [tel/fax 03 21 82 63 41; camping.lecanchy@wanadoo.fr; www.camping-lecanchy.com]** Fr Calais D127 to Guînes, then D215 sp Licques; site sp in vill on D191; site on L in 1km with narr app rd. Or fr Ardres take D224 to Liques then as above. Or A26 fr Calais exit junc 2 onto D217 dir Zouafques/Tournehem/Licques. Foll site sp in vill. Med, hdg/mkd pitch, pt shd; wc (some cont); chem disp; shwrs inc; el pnts (6A) €3.50; Indtte; shops 2km; snacks; bar; BBQ; playgrnd; fishing nrby; entmnt; 50% statics; Eng spkn; adv bkg; quiet; CCI. "Busy, comfortable site; friendly, helpful staff; san facs ltd low ssn; gd walking/cycling; conv Calais & ferries." 15 Mar-31 Oct. € 12.10 2009*

LIEPVRE see Seléstat *6E3*

LIGNY EN BARROIS *6E1* (500m W Rural) *48.68615, 5.31666* **Camp Municipal Chartel, Rue des Etats-Unis, 55500 Ligny-en-Barrois [03 29 77 09 36 or 03 29 78 02 22 (Mairie)]** If app fr E, leave N4 at Ligny-en-Barrois N exit, turn S twd town; in approx 500m turn R at junc (before rd narr); foll sm sp, site 500m on L. If app fr W, leave N4 at exit W of town onto N135 (Rue des Etats-Unis); site sp on R. Sm, hdstg, terr, pt shd; wc (some cont), own san facs; chem disp (wc); shwrs; el pnts inc; shop 500m; pool 1km; rv sw & fishing 500m; dogs; rd noise; Eng spkn; CCI. "Poss diff lge o'fits; gd NH." 1 Jun-30 Sep. € 10.50 2008*

LIGNY LE CHATEL *4F4* (500m SW Rural) *47.89542, 3.75288* **Camp Municipal La Noue Marrou, 89144 Ligny-le-Châtel [03 86 47 56 99 or 03 86 47 41 20 (Mairie); fax 03 86 47 44 02]** Exit A6 at junc 20 Auxerre S onto D965 to Chablis. In Chablis cross rv & turn L onto D91 dir Ligny. On ent Ligny turn L onto D8 at junc after Maximart. Cross sm rv, foll sp to site on L in 200m. Sm, mkd pitch, pt shd; wc; chem disp (wc); mv service pnt; shwrs inc; el pnts (10A) €3 (poss rev pol, poss long lead req); Indtte; shop; rest; snacks; bar; playgrnd; rv sw adj; tennis; dogs; phone; bus 200m; quiet; CCI. "Well-run site; lge pitches; no twin-axles; friendly warden lives on site; san facs dated but clean; pleasant vill with gd rests; excel." ♦ Easter-30 Sep. € 13.50 2009*

⊞ **LIGUEIL** *4H2* (2km N Rural) *47.05469, 0.84615* **Camping de la Touche, Ferme de la Touche, 37240 Ligueil [02 47 59 54 94; booklatouche@hotmail.co.uk; www.theloirevalley.com]** Fr Loches SW on D31; turn L at x-rds with white cross on R 2km after Ciran; in 500m turn R, site on R bef hotel. Fr A10 exit junc 25 Ste Maure-de-Touraine & foll sp to Ligueil; then take D31 dir Loches; turn L at white cross. Sm, mkd ptch, hdstg, pt shd; wc; chem disp (wc); shwrs inc; el pnts €4-5; Indtte; sm shop; snacks; playgrnd; pool; cycle hire; fishing; dogs free; adv bkg; ccard acc; quiet; CCI. "Well-maintained, relaxed CL-type site; lge pitches; welcoming, helpful British owners; c'van storage; excel san facs; gd walking & touring base; much wild life; conv m'way; excel." € 12.00 2009*

⊞ **LILLEBONNE** *3C2* (4km W Rural) *49.53024, 0.49763* **Camping Hameau des Forges, 76170 St Antoine-la-Forêt [02 35 39 80 28 or 02 35 91 48 30]** Fr Le Havre take rd twds Tancarville bdge, D982 into Lillebonne, D81 W to site on R in 4km, sp (part winding rd). Fr S over Tancarville bdge onto D910 sp Bolbec. At 2nd rndabt turn R onto D81, site 5km on L. Med, pt shd; wc; chem disp; shwrs €1.20; el pnts (5A) €3.10; tradsmn; 90% statics; dogs; poss cr; adv bkg; quiet; no ccard acc; CCI. "Basic, clean site; staff welcoming & helpful; poss statics only low ssn & facs ltd; site muddy when wet; conv NH for Le Havre ferries late arr & early dep; Roman amphitheatre in town worth visit." € 6.60 2009*

LIMERAY see Amboise *4G2*

LIMEUIL see Bugue, Le *7C3*

LIMOGES *7B3* (10km N Rural) *45.86951, 1.27370* **FFCC Camp Municipal d'Uzurat, 40 Ave d'Uzurat, 87280 Limoges [tel/fax 05 55 38 49 43; contact@campinglimoges.fr; www.campinglimoges.fr]** Fr N twd Limoges on A20 take exit 30 sp Limoges Nord Zone Industrielle, Lac d'Uzurat; foll sp to Lac d'Uzarat & site. Fr S twd Limoges on A20 exit junc 31 & foll sp as above. Well sp fr A20. Lge, hdstg, pt shd; htd wc (some cont); chem disp; mv service pnt; serviced pitches; baby facs; shwrs inc; el pnts (10A) €3.40; Indtte; hypmkt 500m; playgrnd adj; lake fishing; wifi; some statics; dogs €1; bus; phone; twin-axles acc; m'van o'night area; Eng spkn; quiet but some rd noise; ccard acc; red low ssn; CCI. "Excel, refurbished site; gd sized pitches; gd, clean facs; pitch on chippings; awnings diff; friendly & helpful; conv martyr vill Oradour-sur-Glane; poss reduced opening dates - phone ahead low ssn; poss market traders." ♦ 1 Mar-31 Oct. € 14.20 2009*

LIMOGNE EN QUERCY *7D4* (600m W Rural) *44.39571, 1.76396* **Camp Municipal Bel-Air, 46260 Limogne-en-Quercy [05 65 24 32 75; fax 05 65 24 73 59; camping.bel-air@orange.fr]** E fr Cahors on D911 just bef Limogne vill. W fr Villefranche on D911 just past vill; 3 ents about 50m apart. Sm, mkd pitch, sl, shd; wc; shwrs inc; el pnts (6A) inc; Indtte; shops & bar 600m; pool; quiet; adv bkg rec high ssn. "Friendly welcome; if warden absent, site yourself; pleasant vill." 1 Apr-1 Oct. € 14.30 2009*

France

LIMOGNE EN QUERCY *7D4* (6km NW Rural) *44.42344, 1.69609* **Camping Lalbrade (Naturist), Lalbrade, 46260 Lugagnac [05 65 31 52 35 or 06 20 05 98 57 (mob); fax 05 65 24 36 21; le-camping-de-lalbrade@wanadoo.fr; http://lalbrade.free.fr/]** Fr D911 Cahors to Villefranche-de-Rouergue rd; at Limogne-en-Quercy take D40 sp Lugagnac (narr rd); site sp after Lugagnac; 2km of single-track ent rd. Diff to find. Sm, pt shd; wc (some cont); shwrs inc; el pnts (10A) €2.50; pool; dogs €3; Eng spkn; quiet. "In interesting area; gd walking within site boundaries." ♦ 31 Mar-30 Sep. € 20.00 2007*

The opening dates and prices on this campsite have changed. I'll send a site report form to the Club for the next edition of the guide.

LIMOUX *8G4* (200m SE Urban) *43.04734, 2.22280* **Camp Municipal du Breil, Ave Salvador Allende, 11300 Limoux [tel/fax 04 68 31 13 63]** Fr D118 cross bdge to E side of Rv Aude, then S on D129 Ave De Corbié & foll sp. Sm, pt sl; wc; shwrs; el pnts (6A) €2.80; shops adj; pool adj; fishing; boating; quiet but some rd noise. "Basic rvside site, walking dist pleasant town." 1 Jun-30 Sep. € 8.00 2008*

LINDOIS, LE see Montbron *7B3*

LINXE *8E1* (1km N Rural) *43.93203, -1.25770* **Camp Municipal Le Grandjean, 190 Route de Mixe, 40260 Linxe [05 58 42 90 00 or 05 58 42 92 27; fax 05 58 42 94 67; mairie.linxe@wanadoo.fr]** Exit N10 junc 12 dir Castets; take D42 to Linxe; turn R & R into site. Site well sp at N of Linxe cent. Med, mkd pitch, pt shd; wc, chem disp; baby facs; shwrs inc; el pnts (4-6A) inc; lndtte; supmkt 5km; rest, snacks, bar 1km; playgrnd; cycle hire, tennis 1 km; Eng spkn; adv bkg; quiet. "Vg." 1 Jul-31 Aug. € 11.35 2006*

LION D'ANGERS, LE *2G4* (500m N Rural) *47.63068, -0.71190* **Camp Municipal Les Frênes, Route de Château-Gontier, 49220 Le Lion-d'Angers [02 41 95 31 56; fax 02 41 95 34 87; mairie.lelionangers@wanadoo.fr]** On N162 Laval-Angers rd, site on R bef bdge over Rv Oudon app Le Lion-d'Angers, easily missed. Med, mkd pitch, pt shd; wc; chem disp; shwrs inc; el pnts (10A); lndry rm; shops adj; rest; BBQ; playgrnd; rv fishing adj; phone; card operated barrier; no twin-axle vans; poss cr; Eng spkn; adv bkg; quiet but some rd noise; CCI. "Excel site; friendly staff; gd location; wc block up 2 flights steps; no m'vans; unreliable opening dates - phone ahead." ♦ 1 Jun-31 Aug. 2008*

LISIEUX *3D1* (2km N Rural) **Camp Municipal de La Vallée, 9 Rue de la Vallée, 14100 Lisieux [02 31 62 00 40 or 02 31 48 18 10 (LS); fax 02 31 48 18 11; tourisme@cclisieuxpaysdauge.fr; www.lisieux-tourisme.com]** N on D579 fr Lisieux twd Pont l'Evêque. Approx 500m N of Lisieux take L to Coquainvilliers onto D48 & foll sp for Camping (turn L back in Lisieux dir). Site on D48 parallel to main rd. Med, hdstg, pt shd; wc (some cont); chemp disp; shwrs inc; el pnts (6A) €2 gas; shop 1km; rest, snacks, bar 2km; htd pool, waterslide nrby; 20% statics; poss cr; ccard not acc; rd noise & dogs barking all day (animal refuge adj); CCI. "Interesting town, childhood home of St Thérèse; gates locked 2200-0700; helpful warden; gd." Easter-30 Sep. € 10.00 2007*

LISIEUX *3D1* (10km NE Rural) *49.18009, 0.33238* **Aire Naturalle Le Mont Criquet (Bernard), Clos du Mont Criquet, 14590 Ouilly-du-Houley [tel/fax 02 31 62 98 98 or 06 08 93 19 63 (mob); bernard.ocjh@orange.fr; http://pagesperso-orange.fr/rmc14]** Fr D613 (N13) turn N onto D137 to Ouilly-du-Houley; foll D137 after x-rds in vill by church; site sp. NB App narr single track rd - owner assists, just phone. Sm, pt sl, pt shd; wc; shwrs inc; el pnts (2-6A) €2.40; lndtte; tradsmn; BBQ; playgrnd; games area; 60% statics; dogs; poss cr; Eng spkn; adv bkg; quiet; CCI. "Beautiful site in orchard; helpful, knowledgable owner; gd modern facs; m'vans not acc in periods wet weather." 30 Apr-14 Sep. € 9.00 2009*

LIT ET MIXE *8E1* (2km N Rural) *44.02401, -1.27818* **Airotel Camping Les Vignes, Route de la Plage du Cap de l'Homy, 40170 Lit-et-Mixe [05 58 42 85 60; fax 05 58 42 74 36; www.village-center.com]** N10 S to exit 13 onto D41 twd Lit-et-Mixe. S on D652 dir St Girons. W on D88 twd Cap de l'Homy Plage. Lge, pt shd; wc; chem disp; serviced pitches; shwrs inc; el pnts (10A) inc; gas; lndtte; supmkt; rest; snacks; bar; playgrnd; pool; waterslide; jacuzzi; beach 3km; tennis; cycle hire; games rm; fitness rm; entmnt; internet; dogs €3; quiet; adv bkg; red low ssn/CCI. "Wonderful site - everything you need; immac san facs." ♦ 12 May-16 Sep. € 37.00 2007*

LIT ET MIXE *8E1* (8km W Coastal) *44.03861, -1.33477* **Camp Municipal de la Plage du Cap de l'Horny, Ave de l'Océan, 40170 Lit-et-Mixe [05 58 42 83 47; fax 05 58 42 49 79; contact@camping-cap.com; www.camping-cap.com]** S fr Mimizan on D652. In Lit-et-Mixe R on D88 to Cap de l'Homy Plage. Site on R when rd becomes 1-way. Lge, hdg/mkd pitch, pt sl, shd; wc (some cont); chem disp; mv service pnt; shwrs inc; el pnts (10A) €6.50 (poss rev pol); lndtte; shop, rest high ssn; playgrnd; beach 300m; surfing; dogs €2.60; poss cr; quiet. "Gd position for beach holiday; site in pine woods on sandy soil; gd walks; interesting flora & fauna; Aire de Service for m'vans at ent; vg." 1 May-30 Sep. € 17.70 2009*

LITTEAU see Balleroy *1D4*

LIVERDUN see Nancy *6E2*

LLAURO see Ceret *8H4*

LOCHES *4H2* (800m S Urban) *47.12255, 1.00175* **Kawan Village La Citadelle, Ave Aristide Briand, 37600 Loches [02 47 59 05 91 or 06 21 37 93 06 (mob); fax 02 47 59 00 35; camping@lacitadelle.com; www.lacitadelle.com]** Easiest app fr S. Fr any dir take by-pass to S end of town & leave at Leclerc rndabt for city cent; site well sp on R in 800m. Lge, hdg/mkd pitch, pt shd; htd wc (some cont); chem disp; mv service pnt; shwrs inc; el pnts (10A) inc (poss rev pol) (poss long lead req); gas; lndtte; shop & 2km; tradsmn; rests, snacks; bar; BBQ; playgrnd; pool on site & 2 htd pools adj; fishing; boating; games area; tennis nr; cycle hire; golf 9km; entmnt; internet; wifi; sat TV rm; 30% statics; dogs €2.30; poss cr; Eng spkn; adv bkg rec (bkg fee); poss night noise fr entmnts; ccard acc; red long stay/low ssn; CCI. "Attractive, well-kept, busy site nr beautiful old town; gd sized pitches, poss uneven; helpful staff; facs poss stretched; barrier clsd 2200-0800; site muddy after heavy rain; no waiting area." ♦ 23 Mar-4 Oct. € 31.50 (CChq acc) 2009*

LOCMARIAQUER *2G3* (800m N Rural) *47.57339, -2.95774* **Camping La Ferme Fleurie, Kerlogonan, 56740 Locmariaquer [tel/fax 02 97 57 34 06; www.campinglafermefleurie.com]** Sp off D781. Sm, mkd pitch, pt shd; wc; shwrs inc; el pnts (10A) €2.50; shop; lndtte; playgrnd; beach 1km; fishing; sailing; entmnt; some statics; dogs €1; adv bkg ess high ssn; quiet. "Lovely, friendly, CL-type site in attractive area; coastal path nr; excel, clean facs but poss stretched when site full; midge repellent rec; unreliable opening dates - phone ahead low ssn." 1 Feb-15 Nov. € 13.00 2009*

LOCMARIAQUER *2G3* (2km S Coastal) *47.55598, -2.93939* **Camp Municipal de la Falaise, Route de Kerpenhir, 56740 Locmariaquer [02 97 57 31 59 or 02 97 57 32 32 (LS); fax 02 97 57 32 85; campinglafalaise@wanadoo.fr; www.ot-locmariaquer.com]** Site sp fr Locmariaquer. On ent vill, site sp R avoiding narr cent (also sp fr vill cent). Lge, mkd pitch, pt sl; wc; shwrs; chem disp; mv service pnt; el pnts (6A) inc; gas; lndtte; shop 300m; rest 500m; playgrnd; sand beach adj; entmnt (high ssn); dogs €1; poss cr; ccard acc. "Gd, quiet site in pleasant countryside; san facs need update & poss unclean low ssn (2008); archaeological remains; gd fishing, boating, cycling & coastal walking." ♦ 15 Mar-15 Oct. € 12.00 2008*

LOCRONAN *2E2* (E Urban) *48.09657, -4.19774* **Camping de Locronan, Rue de la Troménie, 29180 Locronan [02 98 91 87 76; contact@camping-locronan.fr; www.camping-locronan.fr]** Fr Quimper/Douarnenez foll sp D7 Châteaulin; ignore town sp, take 1st R after 3rd rndabt. Fr Châteaulin, turn L at 1st town sp & foll site sp at sharp L turn. NB Foll gd sp around town, do not enter Locronan. Med, hdg pitch, steeply terr, pt shd; wc; chem disp; baby facs; fam bathrm; shwrs; el pnts (3-6A) €3; lndtte (inc dryer); shops 1.5km; tradsmn; rest & bar 400m; playgrnd; htd covrd pool; paddling pool; games area; wifi; dogs €1.20; phone; Eng spkn; adv bkg (rec indicate o'fit size when bkg); quiet; ccard acc; CCI. "Gd touring cent with gd views; gd walks; historic town; excel." 19 Apr-15 Nov. € 14.70 2008*

LOCRONAN *2E2* (5km S Rural) *48.09868, -4.18302* **Camping Ar Voden, La Motte, 29136 Plogonnec [tel/fax 02 98 51 80 02; contact@camping-ar-voden.fr; www.camping-ar-voden.fr]** Fr Locronan take D7 twd Châteaulin. By side of church, foll sp. La Motte at top of hill by La Chapelle Ar-Zonj. Med, hdg/mkd pitch, pt sl, terr, pt shd; wc; chem disp; shwrs inc; el pnts (6A) €3; shop 3km; tradsmn; rest 1km; BBQ; playgrnd; htd covrd pool 800m; sand beach 5km; horseriding 500m; mountain bike tracks; dogs €1.10; Eng spkn; poss cr; adv bkg; quiet; CCI. "Rallies accepted; mkt Sat." 28 Jun-31 Aug. € 12.80 2008*

LOCUNOLE see Quimperle *2F2*

LODEVE *10E1* (5km NE Rural) *43.76110, 3.36000* **Camping des Sources, Chemin d'Aubaygues, 34700 Soubès [tel/fax 04 67 44 32 02 or 06 86 38 91 31 (mob); camping-sources@orange.fr; www.camping-sources.com]** Exit A75 junc 52 to Soubès; then 1st R dir Fozières; foll sp. Sm, terr, pt shd; wc; chem disp; shwrs inc; el pnts (6A) inc; lndtte; tradsmn; shop 1km; snacks; playgrnd; children pool; rv sw, sailing & fishing adj; dogs €3; adv bkg rec high ssn; quiet; ccard acc; red low ssn; CCI. "Peaceful site with relaxed atmosphere; helpful, pleasant owner; immac facs; not suitable lge o'fits as app rd v narr & some pitches sm; lovely bar/rest; excel." ♦ 29 Mar-11 Nov. € 20.00 2009*

⊞ **LODEVE** *10E1* (6km SE Rural) *43.69198, 3.35030* **Camping Les Peupliers, Les Casseaux, 34700 Le Bosc [tel/fax 04 67 44 38 08]** Take exit 54 on A75; sp Le Bosc. Med, mkd pitch, pt sl, terr, pt shd; wc; shwrs inc; el pnts (5A) €3; gas; shop 4km; tradsmn Jul-Aug; snacks; bar; playgrnd; pool; sand beach 40km; lake 5km; 90% statics; dogs €0.80; Eng spkn; adv bkg; some rd noise; CCI. "Friendly staff; ltd facs low ssn; windsurfing Lac du Salagou; easy access fr m'way; fair winter NH." ♦ € 11.90 2008*

LODEVE *10E1* (7km S Rural) *43.67182, 3.35429* **Camp Municipal Les Vailhés, Lac du Salagou, 34702 Lodève [04 67 44 25 98 or 04 67 44 86 00 (LS); fax 04 67 44 65 97; mairie@lodeve.com]** Fr N exit A75 junc 43 onto D148 dir Octon & Lac du Salagou. Foll site sp. Fr S exit A75 junc 55. Lge, hdg pitch, terr, pt shd; wc; chem disp; shwrs inc; el pnts (16A) €2.50; lndtte; tradsmn; playgrnd; beach by lake; watersports; 20% statics; dogs; poss cr; quiet; CCI. "Peaceful, remote site by lake; pleasant staff; no facilities nrby; excel walks; gd." 1 Apr-30 Sep. € 10.48 2009*

LODEVE *10E1* (5km W Rural) *43.73631, 3.26443* **Camping Domaine de Lambeyran (Naturist), Lambeyran, 34700 Lodève [04 67 44 13 99; fax 04 67 44 09 91; lambeyran@wanadoo.fr; www.lambeyran.com]** Fr N or S on N9 take sliprd to Lodève. Leave town on D35 W twd Bédarieux. In 2km take 2nd R, sp L'Ambeyran & St Martin. Foll sp 3.7km up winding hill to site. Lge, hdg/mkd pitch, terr, pt sl, pt shd; wc; chem disp; shwrs inc; el pnts (6A) €4.20; gas; lndtte; shop & supmkt 4km, rest, snacks, bar high ssn; BBQ; playgrnd; pool; sailing, windsurfing 10km; 5% statics; dogs; phone; Eng spkn; adv bkg; quiet; ccard acc; red low ssn; CCI. "Superb location with views; lge pitches; gd walking, inc on site; gates clsd 2000; Lac du Salagou with sports facs 12km." 15 May-15 Sep. € 24.40 2009*

LODS see Ornans *6G2*

LONG see Abbeville *3B3*

LONGCHAUMOIS see Morez *9A3*

LONGEAU PERCEY *6F1* (3km S Rural) *47.73978, 5.30807* **FFCC Camp Municipal du Lac, 52190 Villegusien-le-Lac [03 25 88 47 25 or 03 25 88 45 24]** Exit A31 junc 6 dir Longeau. Site sp fr both D67 & D674 (N74) S of Longeau. Visible fr D674 & rec app. Med, pt shd; wc (some cont); chem disp; mv service pnt; shwrs inc; el pnts (6A) inc; shop; tradsmn; snacks; playgrnd; tennis; fishing, boating & sw in lake; poss cr; adv bkg; rd & rlwy noise; "Conv NH." ♦ 15 Apr-30 Sep. € 19.00 2007*

LONGEVILLE SUR MER *7A1* (2km S Coastal) *46.40402, -1.50673* **Camp Le Petit Rocher, 1250 Ave du Dr Mathevet, 85560 Longeville-sur-Mer [02 51 90 31 57; fax 02 51 96 17 93; info@campinglepetitrocher.com; www.campinglepetitrocher.com]** Fr La Tranche-sur-Mer take D105 N. In 8km site clearly sp 'Le Rocher' at 3rd exit fr rndabt (Ave du Dr Mathevet). Site on R in 1km at beginning of beach rd. Lge, hdg/mkd pitches, pt sl, shd; wc; chem disp; shwrs inc; el pnts (6A) inc; gas; shops adj; rest & snacks nrby; playgrnd; sand beach 150m; games area; games rm; cycle hire; entmnt; some statics; dogs €3; adv bkg; quiet; CCI. "Gd beach holiday; gd facs." 1 May-20 Sep. € 23.00 2008*

LONGEVILLE SUR MER *7A1* (2km S Coastal) *46.39499, -1.48736* **Camping Le Sous-Bois, La Haute Saligotière, 85560 Longeville-sur-Mer [02 51 33 36 90; fax 02 51 33 32 73]** Sp fr D105 fr La Tranche-sur-Mer. Med, hdg pitch, shd; wc; chem disp; shwrs inc; el pnts (10A) €3.80 (poss rev pol); Indtte; shop; tradsmn; playgrnd; sand beach 1km; tennis; TV; 15% statics; dogs €1.60; phone; quiet; ccard not acc; CCI. "Nice, well-managed, family site; pleasant 1km woodland walk to beach; gd walks; cycle track network; excel." ♦ 1 Jun-15 Sep. € 17.00 2009*

LONGEVILLE SUR MER *7A1* (3km S Coastal) *46.38830, -1.48777* **Camping Les Clos des Pins, Les Conches, 85560 Longeville-sur-Mer [02 51 90 31 69; fax 02 51 90 30 68; info@campingclosdespins.com; www.campingclosdespins.com]** Fr La Tranche-sur-Mer take D105 coast rd N, turn L in Les Conches into Ave de la Plage, site on R in 1km. Med, mkd pitch, pt sl, shd; wc; chem disp; baby facs; shwrs inc; el pnts (6A) €4; gas; Indtte; shop; tradsmn; rest; snacks; bar; BBQ (gas/elec only); playgrnd; htd pool; paddling pool; waterslide; sand beach 200m; watersports; cycle hire; games area; activities inc silk painting, jogging, canoeing, aerobics; wifi; entmnt; 60% statics; dogs €3.30; phone; bus; Eng spkn; adv bkg; quiet; red low ssn/CCI. "Set among pine trees; some pitches in soft sand - adv bkg rec to ensure a suitable pitch; friendly, helpful staff; excel leisure facs; vg." ♦ 3 Apr-26 Sep. € 25.00 2009*

See advertisement on page 519

LONGEVILLE SUR MER *7A1* (3km SW Coastal) *46.4131, -1.5228* **Camping Les Brunelles, Le Bouil, 85560 Longeville-sur-Mer [02 51 33 50 75; fax 02 51 33 98 21; camping@les-brunelles.com; www.les-brunelles.com]** Site bet Longeville-sur-Mer & Jard-sur-Mer; foll D21. Lge, mkd pitch, pt sl, pt shd; wc; baby facs; shwrs inc; el pnts (6A) inc; Indtte; shop; rest 500m; snacks; bar; playgrnd; 2 htd pools (1 covrd) & paddling pool; waterslide; sand beach 700m; watersports; tennis; cycle hire; games area; horseriding 2km; golf 15km; internet; entmnt; TV rm; 75% statics; dogs €5; adv bkg; ccard acc. "Gd san facs." ♦ 25 May-18 Sep. € 25.00 (CChq acc) 2008*

⊞ **LONGNY AU PERCHE** *4E2* (1km SW Rural) *48.51749, 0.74177* **Camping Monaco Parc, Route de Monceau, 61290 Longny-au-Perche [02 33 73 59 59; fax 02 33 25 77 56; monacoparc@wanadoo.fr; www.camping monacoparc.com]** Fr N on N12 take D918 to Longny, then D111 S to site, sp. Med, pt shd; htd wc; chem disp; mv service pnt; baby facs; sauna; shwrs; el pnts; Indtte; shop; rest; snacks; bar; BBQ; playgrnd; htd, covrd pool; lake fishing; games area; fitness rm; TV; 80% statics; adv bkg; quiet. "Conv NH to/fr Paris; ltd touring pitches." ♦ (CChq acc) 2009*

LONS LE SAUNIER *6H2* (1km NE Rural) *46.68437, 5.56843* **Camping La Marjorie, 640 Blvd de l'Europe, 39000 Lons-le-Saunier [03 84 24 26 94; fax 03 84 24 08 40; info@camping-marjorie.com; www.camping-marjorie.com]** Site clearly sp in town on D1083 (N83) twd Besançon. Fr N bear R dir 'Piscine', cross under D1083 to site. Lge, hdg pitch, some hdstg, pt sl, pt shd; wc; baby facs; chem disp; shwrs inc; el pnts (6A) inc (poss rev pol); gas; Indtte; shop; tradsmn; rest; bar; playgrnd; 2 htd pools (1 covrd) & aquatic centre adj; games area; golf 8km; entmnt; wifi; dogs €1; phone; Eng spkn; rd noise; red low ssn; ccard acc; CCI. "Beautiful area; lge pitches; excel san facs; welcoming, friendly staff; conv location; 20 mins walk to town; excel." ♦ 1 Apr-15 Oct. € 19.60 2009*

LONS LE SAUNIER *6H2* (8km NE Rural) *46.71213, 5.64034* **Camp Municipal de la Toupe, 39210 Baume-les-Messieurs [03 84 44 63 16; fax 03 84 44 95 40; baumelesmessieurs@wandoo.fr]** On D471 Lons-le-Saunier to Champagnole rd, take L onto D4 then D70 to Baume-les-Messieurs. Site 500m thro vill on D70 - narr, steep app rd not suitable lge o'fits. Or, fr D1083 (N83) turn E onto D120 at St Germain-lès-Arlay to Voiteur then onto D70. Sm, pt shd; wc (some cont); shwrs inc; el pnts (6A) €2.80; playgrnd; rv adj; dogs €1; quiet. "Beautiful location nr lovely vill; some outdated facs." 1 Apr-30 Sep. € 7.50 2008*

LONS LE SAUNIER *6H2* (8km SW Rural) *46.65854, 5.49934* **Camp Municipal, Grande Rue, 39570 Chilly-le-Vignoble [03 84 43 09 34 or 03 84 43 09 32 (Mairie); fax 03 84 47 34 09]** Fr A39 exit junc 8 onto D678 (N78). After approx 5km turn R to Courlans & Chilly-le-Vignoble. Site sp 2km. Med, pt shd; wc (most cont); shwrs inc; el pnts (5A) inc; supmkt 3km; tradsmn; rest; snacks; playgrnd; games rm; golf nrby; quiet; CCI. "V pleasant site in quiet vill; ent for c'vans fr 1530 only; gd." 1 Jun-15 Sep. € 12.60 2007*

France

⊞ **LORIENT** *2F2* (6km N Rural) *47.82041, -3.40689* **Camping Ty Nénez, Route de Lorient, 56620 Pont-Scorff [02 97 32 51 16; fax 02 97 32 43 77; contact@camping-tynenez.com; www.lorient-camping.com]** N fr N165 on D6, look for sp Quéven in approx 5km on R. If missed, cont for 1km & turn around at rndabt. Site sp fr Pont-Scorff. Med, hdg pitch, pt shd; htd wc; chem disp; mv service pnt; baby facs; shwrs inc; el pnts (16A) €2.75; Indtte; supmkt 1km; bar; games area; some statics; dogs €0.65; adv bkg; quiet. "Site barrier locked 2200-0800; zoo 1km; peaceful NH." ♦ € 7.70 2007*

LORIENT *2F2* (10km NE Rural) *47.80582, -3.28347* **Camp Municipal St Caradec, Quai St Caradec, 56700 Hennebont [02 97 36 21 73; camping.municipal.stcaradec@wanadoo.fr]** Fr S on D781 to Hennebont. In town cent turn L & cross bdge, then sharp R along Rv Blavet for 1km. On R on rv bank. Med, mkd pitch, pt shd; wc; chem disp; shwrs inc; el pnts inc; Indtte; shop 2km; playgrnd; sand beach 12km; some statics; adv bkg; quiet; CCI. "Pretty site." 15 Jun-15 Sep. 2009*

LORIENT *2F2* (3km SW Coastal) *47.70367, -3.38494* **Camp Municipal des Algues, 21 Blvd de Port Maria, 56260 Larmor-Plage [02 97 65 55 47; fax 02 97 84 26 27; camping@larmor-plage.com; www.larmor-plage.com]** Fr N165, take Lorient exit, foll D29 for Larmor-Plage. Site adj beach, turn R after Tourist Info office. Lge, mkd pitch, pt shd; wc; chem disp; mv service pnt; shwrs inc; el pnts (10A) €3; Indtte; shop adj; rest, playgrnd; sand beach adj; fishing, sailing; dogs €1.20; poss cr; quiet. ♦ 15 Jun-15 Sep. € 13.90 2007*

⊞ **LORIENT** *2F2* (4km SW Coastal) *47.70955, -3.39228* **Camping La Fontaine, Rue de Québello, Kerderff, 56260 Larmor-Plage [02 97 33 71 28 or 02 97 65 11 11; fax 02 97 33 70 32; contact@campingdelafontaine.com; www.camping-la-fontaine.com]** At Larmor-Plage 300m fr D152. Well sp. Med, hdg pitch, pt sl, pt shd; htd wc; mv service pnt; chem disp; baby facs; shwrs inc; el pnts (10A) €2.45 (rev pol); Indtte; shop adj; snacks; bar; playgrnd; beach 800m; tennis adj; horseriding; sailing; sports; dogs €1.55; Eng spkn. "Excel site; gd facs." ♦ € 15.00 2009*

⊞ **LORIENT** *2F2* (8km W Coastal) *47.72814, -3.49401* **FFCC Camping L'Atlantys, Blvd des Sables Blancs, Fort Bloqué, 56270 Ploemeur [02 97 05 99 81; fax 02 97 05 95 78; info@camping-atlantys.com; www.camping-atlantys.com]** Fr cent Lorient take rd D162 in dir of Ploemeur then coast rd D152 dir Guidel-Plage. Site ent on R adj to sp Fort Bloqué. Or D29 fr Lorient then onto D152 & site on R at ent Fort Bloqué. Lge, mkd pitch, terr, pt sl, unshd; wc; shwrs inc; el pnts (6-10A) €3-4 (rev pol); Indry rm; shop; snacks; bar; playgrnd; pool, sand beach & golf adj; fishing; horseriding 2km; 85% statics; dogs €2; poss cr; Eng spkn; adv bkg; quiet; CCI. "Sea views fr many pitches - sunsets; ltd facs low ssn; vg." € 17.00 2007*

LORMES *4G4* (500m S Rural) *47.28260, 3.82241* **Camp Municipal L'Etang du Goulot, 2 Rue des Campeurs, 58140 Lormes [03 86 22 82 37; fax 03 86 85 19 28; http://etangdugoulot.free.fr]** Fr Château-Chinon on D944 site on R on lakeside 250m after junc with D17 fr Montsauche, 500m bef town cent. Med, hdg pitch, pt shd, pt sl; wc (some cont); chem disp; mv service pnt; shwrs inc; el pnts (4A) €2.50; shop 500m; snacks; BBQ; playgrnd; lake sw; fishing; 1% statics; dogs €0.50; Eng spkn; adv bkg; quiet; red low ssn; CCI. "O'looking lake with gd walks; friendly, helpful warden." ♦ 1 May-15 Sep. € 12.90 2007*

LOUBRESSAC *7C4* (200m S Rural) *44.86999, 1.80077* **Camping La Garrigue, 46130 Loubressac [tel/fax 05 65 38 34 88; infos@camping-lagarrigue.com; www.camping-lagarrigue.com]** Fr D940 S to Bretenoux, then D14 to Loubressac. Fr cent vill foll sp 200m. Sm, hdg/mkd pitch, pt sl, terr, pt shd; wc; chem disp; shwrs inc; el pnts (6A) €2.80; gas; Indtte; shop; tradsmn high ssn; snacks; bar; BBQ; playgrnd; pool; paddling pool; entmnt; TV rm; 20% statics; dogs €1.20; phone; quiet; Eng spkn; adv bkg; CCI. "Access poss diff for lge vans; pretty vill." ♦ 1 Apr-30 Sep. € 14.00 2007*

LOUDEAC *2E3* (2km E Rural) *48.17827, -2.73010* **Camp Municipal Pont es Bigots, 22600 Loudéac [02 96 28 14 92 or 02 96 66 85 00 (Mairie); fax 02 96 66 08 93; mairie.loudeac@wanadoo.fr; www.ville-loudeac.fr]** Fr Loudéac, take N164 twd Rennes, site on L by lake in 1km, sp. Height barrier into site 1.8m. Med, hdg pitch, pt shd; wc; shwrs; el pnts €2; shops 1km; playgrnd; entmnt; lake sw; fishing; horseriding; quiet. "V pleasant; site clsd 1100-1700." 15 Jun-15 Sep. € 6.35 2009*

LOUDENVIELLE see Arreau *8G2*

LOUDUN *4H1* (1km W Rural) *47.00379, 0.06337* **Camp Municipal de Beausoleil, Chemin de l'Etang, 86200 Loudun [05 49 98 14 22; fax 05 49 98 12 88]** On main rte fr Poitiers to Saumur/Le Mans; N on D347 (N147) around Loudun, foll sp; turn L just N of level x-ing, then on R approx 250m. Sm, hdg/mkd pitch, terr, pt shd; wc, chem disp; shwrs inc; el pnts €2.95; Indry rm; shop 1km; playgrnd; lake adj for fishing; bus adj; Eng spkn; CCI. "Beautiful, quiet, well-kept site; low ssn site yourself, warden calls am & pm; friendly & helpful; unguarded; excel." ♦ 15 May-31 Aug. € 10.25 2009*

LOUE *4F1* (Urban) *47.99606, -0.14777* **Camping Village Loisirs (Au Fil de l'Eau), Place Hector Vincent, 72540 Loué [02 43 88 65 65; fax 02 43 88 59 46; village.dhotes@orange.fr; www.villageloisirs.com]** Exit A81 junc 1 to Loué. Site in cent of town adj sw pool. Sm, unshd; htd wc; chem disp; shwrs inc; el pnts (6A) €4; Indtte (inc dryer); rest; bar; playgrnd; htd pool; waterslide; paddling pool; cycle hire & fishing adj; games rm; TV; 50% statics; dogs €1; phone; bus; Eng spkn; adv bkg; quiet; CCI. "Friendly staff; conv Le Mans (rec adv bkg race w/ends); vg." ♦ 1 Apr-31 Oct. € 12.00 2008*

LOUHANS *6H1* (2km W Urban) *46.62286, 5.21733* **Camp Municipal de Louhans, 10, Chemin de la Chapellerie, 71500 Louhans [03 85 75 19 02 or 03 85 76 75 10 (Mairie); fax 03 85 76 75 11; mairiedelouhanschateaurenaud@yahoo.fr]** In Louhans foll sp for Romenay on D971. Go under rlwy & over rv. Site on L just after stadium. Med, hdg/mkd pitch, hdstg, shd; wc (some cont); chem disp (wc); mv service pnt; shwrs inc; el pnts €3.60; Indtte; snacks; playgrnd; pool & tennis courts adj; sw rv adj; poss cr; adv bkg; some rlwy noise; CCI. "Rv location; clean & well-appointed; sports complex adj; lovely cycling area; lge town mkt Mon am; poss itinerants; vg." ♦ 1 Apr-30 Sep. € 7.40 2007*

LOUPIAC see Payrac *7D3*

LOURDES *8F2* (1km N Urban) *43.11425, -0.03661* **Caravaning Plein-Soleil, Route de Tarbes, 65100 Lourdes [05 62 94 40 93; fax 05 62 94 51 20; camping.plein.soleil@wanadoo.fr; www.camping-pleinsoleil.com]** Fr N site sp on N21. Turn R imm opp aquarium sp. Sm, terr, pt shd; htd wc; chem disp; shwrs inc; el pnts (4A) inc; Indtte; snacks; playgrnd; pool; dogs; poss cr; Eng spkn; adv bkg; poss noise fr adj builders' yard; CCI. "Pleasant site; gd facs; gd security; helpful staff; ltd access lge o'fits; muddy when wet; conv hypmkt." Easter-10 Oct. € 21.50 2007*

LOURDES *8F2* (2km N) *43.11569, -0.03225* **FFCC Camping Le Moulin du Monge, Ave Jean Moulin, 65100 Lourdes [05 62 94 28 15; fax 05 62 42 20 54; camping.moulin.monge@wanadoo.fr]** S on N21 fr Tarbes, site on L of rd 2km bef Lourdes, visible fr rd. Med, pt shd; htd wc; mv service pnt; sauna; shwrs inc; el pnts (2-6A) €2-4; Indtte; shops & farm produce; playgrnd; htd, covrd pool; some rd & rlwy noise. "Pleasant site." 1 Apr-10 Oct. € 14.40 2009*

LOURDES *8F2* (2.1km E Rural) *43.09316, -0.02091* **Camping du Ruisseau Blanc, Route de Bagnères-Anclades, 65100 Lourdes [05 62 42 94 83; fax 05 62 42 94 62]** Exit Lourdes on D937 twd Bagnères & foll sp. Site has 2 ents. C'vans ignore 1st sp for site on R & cont on D937 foll next sp. Med, pt shd; wc (most cont); chem disp; mv service pnt; shwrs; el pnts (2-6A) €4; Indtte; shop (local produce); playgrnd; TV rm; no dogs; "Gd views; beautiful site but facs poss stretched high ssn." Easter-10 Oct. € 7.60 2008*

LOURDES *8F2* (2.5km W Urban) *43.09773, -0.06986* **Camp du Loup, Route de la Forêt, 65100 Lourdes [tel/fax 05 62 94 23 60]** Fr Lourdes take D937 sp Pau, Bétharram. Turn L at level x-ing into Rue de Pau, then immed R. Foll rd & turn L over rv bdge, site sp. Sm, pt shd; wc; chem disp; mv service pnt; shwrs €1; el pnts (6A) €2.50; Indtte; shop 1km; tradsmn; playgrnd; rv 300m; dogs €1; poss cr; adv bkg ess; quiet; CCI. "Excel CL-type site; basic facs; friendly, helpful host; gd atmosphere; gd security; adv bkg rec high ssn; rvside walk to shrine." ♦ Easter-15 Oct. € 11.00 2008*

LOURDES *8F2* (4km W Rural) *43.10461, -0.06782* **Camping d'Arrouach, 9 Rue des Trois Archanges, Biscaye, 65100 Lourdes [05 62 42 11 43; fax 05 62 42 05 27; camping.arrouach@wanadoo.fr; www.camping-arrouach.com]** Fr Lourdes take D940 twd Pau. As you leave Lourdes take L fork D937 (sp) Bétharram. Site on R 200m. Med, hdg/mkd pitch, hdstg, pt sl, pt shd; wc; chem disp; mv service pnt; shwrs inc; el pnts (3-6A) €2.50-5; gas; Indtte; shop 2km; tradsmn; bar; BBQ; playgrnd; 10% statics; phone; poss cr; quiet; adv bkg; Eng spkn; CCI; red 15 days. "Pleasant, elevated site with views; poss flooding in v wet weather; clean san facs; easy access parking for Lourdes via Rte de Pau." ♦ 15 Mar-31 Dec. € 11.80 2006*

LOURDES *8F2* (4km W Rural) *43.09561, -0.07463* **Camping La Forêt, Route de la Forêt, 65100 Lourdes [05 62 94 04 38 or 05 62 45 04 57 (LS); fax 05 62 42 14 86]** Fr Lourdes take D937 twd Pau; turn L on level x-ing; foll sp to site. Med, mkd pitch, pt shd; wc; mv service pnt; shwrs €1; el pnts (3-10A) €2.60-7.60; gas; Indtte; shop; rest; snacks; bar; playgrnd; few statics; dogs €1.30; poss cr; Eng spkn; adv bkg; quiet; ccard acc; CCI. "Lovely site; helpful owners; conv town cent & grotto; poss to stay bef official opening date by arrangement." 1 Apr-31 Oct. € 12.00 2008*

LOURDES *8F2* (6km W Rural) *43.10133, -0.12888* **FFCC Camping Le Prat Dou Rey, 31 Route de Pau, 65270 Peyrouse [05 62 41 81 54; fax 05 62 41 89 76; lepradourey@orange.fr; www.camping-lepratdourey.com]** Take D940 fr Lourdes then in 2km take D937 E sp Bétharram. Cont thro Peyrouse vill & site on L in 500m. Med, pt shd; wc; mv service pnt; shwrs inc; el pnts (6-10A) €3.20-4.20 inc; Indtte; shop in ssn & 6km; snacks; BBQ; playgrnd; pool; rv 100m; fishing; 10% statics; dogs €0.95; CCI. "Various sports activities; san facs unclean (2008)." 15 Mar-15 Oct. € 12.40 2008*

LOURES BAROUSSE see Montréjeau *8F3*

LOUROUX, LE *4G2* (N Rural) *47.16270, 0.78697* **Camping à la Ferme La Chaumine (Baudoin), 37240 Le Louroux [tel/fax 02 47 92 82 09 or 06 85 45 68 10 (mob); bruno.baudoin@free.fr]** Fr Tours, take D50 S for 30km. Site immed on R bef Le Louroux. Sm, hdg pitch, shd; wc; chem disp; shwrs inc; el pnts (10A) inc; BBQ; playgrnd; dogs; bus 200m; Eng spkn; adv bkg; quiet. "Superb CL-type site nr quaint vill; helpful owners; gd, clean san facs; gd walks fr site."
1 May-15 Oct. € 14.50 2008*

⊞ **LOUVIE JUZON** *8F2* (1km E Rural) *43.08940, -0.41019* **FFCC Camping Le Rey, Quartier Listo, Route de Lourdes, 64260 Louvie-Juzon [05 59 05 78 52; fax 05 59 05 78 97; campinglerey@club-internet.fr; www.camping-pyrenees-ossau.com]** Site on L at top of hill E fr Louvie; v steep app. Sm, mkd pitch, pt sl, pt shd; htd wc; chem disp; shwrs inc; el pnts (6A) €3.30; Indtte; shops 1km; tradsmn; rest 1km; snacks; bar; playgrnd; sm pool; watersports, fishing nr; games area; entmnt; 50% statics; dogs €2; phone; site clsd last 2 weeks Nov & last 2 weeks Jan; adv bkg; quiet; CCI. "Fascinating area; chateau nr." ♦ € 13.25 2009*

LOUVIE JUZON *8F2* (3km S Rural) *43.06324, -0.42411* **FFCC Camping L'Ayguelade, 64260 Bielle [05 59 82 66 50 or 06 31 23 06 48 (mob); camping-ayguelade@orange.fr; http://perso.orange.fr/ayguelade]** S fr Louvie-Juzon on D934, site clearly sp on L. Med, mkd pitch, pt shd; wc; mv service pnt; shwrs inc; el pnts (3-9A) €2.50-4.50; Indtte; shop 4km; tradsmn; rest adj; snacks; bar; playgrnd; entmnt; TV; 75% statics; dogs €1.80; Eng spkn; adv bkg; quiet; CCI. "Rv runs thro site, pleasant setting." ♦ 1 Mar-1 Nov. € 12.50 2008*

⊞ **LOUVIE JUZON** *8F2* (6km NW Rural) **FFCC Aire Naturelle Les Jardins d'Ossau (Dunan), 2 Chemin de Départ, 64250 Buzy [05 59 21 05 71; dunan.pascal@wanadoo.fr]** S fr Pau on N134; approx 12 km past Gan sp Camping; after restaurant at Belair turn L onto D34 sp Buzy; in 2km turn L after going under 1st rlwy bdge. Site on R, sp. Sm, pt shd; wc; chem disp (wc); shwrs inc; el pnts (6A) €2.10 (long lead poss req); Indtte; games area; games rm; dogs €0.50; Eng spkn; adv bkg; quiet; no ccard acc; CCI. "Peaceful site on fruit farm; san facs v basic but clean; views of Pyrenees; easy access; helpful owners; NH only to/fr Spain." ♦ € 11.40 2009*

LOUVIERS *3D2* (2km W Rural) *49.21490, 1.13279* **Camping Le Bel Air, Route de la Haye-Malherbe, Hameau de St-Lubin, 27400 Louviers [tel/fax 02 32 40 10 77; contact@camping-lebelair.fr; www.camping-lebelair.fr]** Site well sp in Louviers (bottom line on sps). Fr cent foll D81 W for 2.5km dir La Haye-Malherbe; twisting rd uphill; site on R. Or if travelling S leave A13 at junc 19 to Louviers & as bef. NB In town cent look for sm green sp after Ecole Communale (on L) and bef Jardin Public - a v narr rd (1-way) & easy to miss. Med, hdg/mkd/hdstg pitch, shd; wc (chem clos - own san rec); chem disp; mv service pnt; shwrs inc; el pnts (6A) €4.20; gas; Indtte; tradsmn; playgrnd; htd pool; 30% statics; dogs €1.80; poss cr; Eng spkn; adv bkg; quiet; ccard acc; red low ssn/CCI. "Barrier clsd at 2200; facs need update (2008) & poss unclean (2009); access to pitches diff long o'fits, poss mover req; conv Le Havre; NH only." 1 Mar-31 Oct. € 15.40 (CChq acc) 2009*

LOYAT see Ploërmel *2F3*

LUBERSAC *7B3* (300m E Rural) *45.44244, 1.40899* **Camp Municipal La Vézénie, 19210 Lubersac [05 55 73 50 14 (Mairie); fax 05 55 73 67 99; mairie@ville-lubersac.fr; www.chalets-decouverte.com]** Fr A20 N of Uzerche exit junc 44 & turn W onto D902 to Lubersac. At far end of mkt sq take rd L of Hôtel de Commerce; turn immed L; then 1st L; at T-junc turn R; then L at mini-rndabt onto site. Sm, mkd pitch, pt sl, terr, pt shd; htd wc (some cont); shwrs inc; el pnts (5A) €2.30; Indtte; shop adj; rest, snacks; playgrnd; htd pool; paddling pool; sand beach & lake sw, fishing 400m; tennis; horseriding; poss cr; quiet. "Modern, clean site overlkg lake." 1 Jun-15 Sep. € 9.10 2008*

LUBERSAC *7B3* (2km SE Urban) *45.42976, 1.45564* **Camping Le Domaine Bleu, Bourg, 19210 St Pardoux-Corbier [tel/fax 35 55 73 59 89; www.ledomainebleu.eu]** Exit A20 junc 44; take D920 S for 1.5km; turn W onto D902; in 9km turn S to St Pardoux-Corbier. Sm, pt shd; wc; chem disp; shwrs inc; el pnts (10A) €2.50; Indtte; tradsmn; local rest, snacks, pool & tennis; dogs €1.50; Eng spkn; CCI. "Clean site; Dutch owners; vg." ♦ 1 Jun-1 Sep. € 10.00 2007*

LUC EN DIOIS *9D3* (Rural) *44.61565, 5.44618* **Camp Municipal Les Foulons, Rue de la Piscine, 26310 Luc-en-Diois [04 75 21 36 14 or 04 75 21 31 01 (Mairie); fax 04 75 21 35 70; contact@camping-luc-en-diois.com; www.camping-luc-en-diois.com/foulons]** Sp in vill off D93. Med, pt shd; wc; shwrs; el pnts (10-16A) €3-4.50; Indtte; shops & rest 500m; playgrnd; pool, rv adj; games area adj; tennis; dog €2; Eng spkn; adv bkg; quiet; red low ssn; CCI. "Excel site in scenic area; modern & well-maintained; gates clsd 2200-0700; attractive sm town; gd walking/cycling; canoeing, horseriding, hang-gliding avail in area; mkt Fri." ♦ 15 Apr-15 Oct. € 13.00 2008*

LUC EN DIOIS *9D3* (5km NW Rural) *44.65910, 5.40970* **Camping Le Couriou, 26310 Recoubeau-Jansac [04 75 21 33 23; fax 04 75 21 38 42; camping.lecouriou@wanadoo.fr; www.campinglecouriou.com]** Fr Die on D93 twds Luc-en-Diois for 13 km. Turn R at D140 & foll sp. Med, mkd pitch, some hdstg, terr, pt shd; wc; chem disp; baby facs; shwrs inc; el pnts (6A) €4.20; gas; Indtte; shop high ssn; rest; snacks; bar; playgrnd; htd pool; 5% statics; dogs €2; phone; poss cr; adv bkg ess high ssn; quiet; CCI. "Mountain views." ♦ 1 May-31 Aug. € 23.50 2008*

LUC SUR MER see Ouistreham *3D1*

LUC, LE *10F3* (4km SE Rural) *43.35838, 6.32778* **Camping Les Bruyères, Route de Mayons, 83340 Le Luc [04 94 73 47 07; fax 04 94 60 99 26; Yvonraboin@aol.com]** Fr D97 at sports stadium in Le Luc turn L on D33. Site in 3.5km. Med, mkd pitch, hdstg, pt shd; htd wc; shwrs inc; el pnts (6A) inc; gas; Indtte; shop 4km; snacks; bar; playgrnd; pool; games area; TV; some statics; dogs free; quiet, poss some noise fr nrby race circuit. "Friendly owner; fair NH." 1 Mar-15 Nov. € 16.50 2008*

LUCAY LE MALE *4H2* (4km SW Rural) *47.11066, 1.40504* **Camp Municipal La Foulquetière, 36360 Luçay-le-Mâle [02 54 40 52 88 or 02 54 40 43 31 (Mairie); fax 02 54 40 42 47; mairie@ville-lucaylemale.fr]** SW fr Valençay & thro Luçay, on D960, then fork L onto D13, site on R in 1km. Sm, hdg/mkd pitch, pt sl, pt shd; htd wc; chem disp; mv service pnt; shwrs inc; el pnts (6A) €1.50; Indtte; shop 3km; rest; snacks; bar; playgrnd; watersports; canoeing; fishing; tennis; games area; no dogs; Eng spkn; adv bkg; v quiet; CCI. "Excel lakeside site but isolated; gd sized pitches; basic facs; gd walking country; if recep unmanned, pay at Mairie or at rest." 1 Apr-15 Oct. € 6.50 2008*

France

LUCENAY L'EVEQUE *6H1* (S Rural) *47.07668, 4.24675* **Camping du Ternin, 71540 Lucenay-l'Evêque [03 85 82 61 86; camping@bourgogne-morvan.com; www.camping.bourgogne-morvan.com]** On D980 Autun to Saulieu rd, 300m S of Lucenay site ent immed bef vill sp. Ent narr; easier when warden opens 2nd gate. Sm, hdg/mkd pitch, pt shd; wc (some cont); shwrs inc; el pnts €3; playgrnd; shops 300m; dogs €1.50; tennis; quiet; ccard acc; CCI. "Neat site with brook running thro; gd walking country; v quiet low ssn; warden visits am & pm - site yourself; narr ent to pitches with el pnts." 1 May-1 Sep. € 10.00 2007*

LUCHE PRINGE see Flèche, La *4G1*

LUCHON *8G3* (2km N Rural) *42.80806, 0.59667* **Camping Pradelongue, 31110 Moustajon [05 61 79 86 44; fax 05 61 79 18 64; camping-pradelongue@wanadoo.fr; www.camping-pradelongue.com]** Site is on D125c on W of D125 main rd fr Luchon. Ent at Moustajon/Antignac going S. Site adj Intermarché; sp. Lge, hdg/mkd pitch, pt shd; wc; chem disp; mv service pnt; baby facs; shwrs inc; el pnts (2-10A) €2-4; Indtte; shop 100m; BBQ; playgrnd; htd pool; games area; wifi;10% statics; dogs €2; Eng spkn; adv bkg; quiet; ccard acc; red low ssn; CCI. "Excel, well-run site; mountain views; gd sized pitches; friendly, helpful owners; rec." ♦ 1 Apr-30 Sep. € 17.40 2009*

⊞ **LUCHON** *8G3* (4km N Rural) *42.82233, 0.60649* **FFCC Camping Le Pyrénéen, 31110 Salles-et-Pratviel [05 61 79 59 19; fax 05 61 79 75 75; campinglepyreneen@wanadoo.fr; www.campinglepyreneen-luchon.com]** Fr Luchon, take N125 twd Montréjeau; in 4km exit on D125 to Salles; thro vill & site sp on R. Med, pt shd; htd wc; chem disp; baby facs; shwrs inc; el pnts (10A) inc; Indtte; shop & 4km; bar; htd pool; paddling pool; games rm; games area; TV; 50% statics; no dogs; adv bkg; quiet. "Some sm pitches; neat, clean site; gd san facs; wintersports." ♦ € 18.00 (3 persons) 2007*

LUCHON *8G3* (1km NE Rural) *42.79472, 0.60826* **Camping La Lanette/Arome Vanille, 31110 Montauban-de-Luchon [05 61 79 00 38; info@camping-aromevanille.com; www.camping-aromevanille.com]** Exit A64 junc 17 at Montréjeau onto D825/N125/D33/D125; at end of new section of D125 turn L at rndabt sp Luzet-de-Luchon; turn R in vill; site on R in 1km. Lge, hdg/mkd pitch, pt shd; htd wc; baby facs; shwrs inc; el pnts (6-10A) €4-5; gas; Indtte; rest; snacks; bar; playgrnd; games area; child entmnt; 30% statics; dogs €3; poss cr; adv bkg; quiet; ccard acc; red low ssn; CCI. "Vg site; high level hiking rtes 20-30 mins by car." 1 Apr-30 Oct. € 15.00 2009*

LUCON *7A1* (11km E Rural) *46.46745, -1.02792* **Camp Municipal Le Vieux Chêne, Rue du Port, 85370 Nalliers [02 51 30 91 98 or 02 51 30 90 71; fax 02 51 30 94 06; nalliers.mairie@wanadoo.fr]** Fr Luçon E on D949 dir Fontenay-le-Comte; 500m after ent Nalliers turn R onto D10 (Rue de Brantome); after level x-ing cont strt on for 50m (leaving D10); then Rue du Port on L. Site sp on D949 but easy to miss. Sm, hdg/mkd pitch, pt shd; wc; chem disp; shwrs inc; el pnts (4-13A) €3; shop 500m; tradsmn; playgrnd; adv bkg; quiet; site yourself on lge pitch; CCI. "Excel, clean site; in low ssn contact Mairie for ent to site; vg NH." 15 May-15 Sep. € 9.00 2008*

LUCON *7A1* (10km SW Rural) *46.41170, -1.26527* **Camping La Fraignaye, Rue de Beau Laurier, 85580 St Denis-du-Payré [02 51 27 21 36; fax 02 51 27 27 74; camping.fraignaye@wanadoo.fr; www.camping-lafraignaye.com]** Fr A8 exit junc 7 onto D137 dir La Rochelle. Turn L after Ste Gemme onto D949 to Luçon, then take D746 to Triaize. Take D25 to St Denis-du-Payré, in vill turn L bef church & foll sp. Sm, mkd pitch, pt shd; wc; chem disp; shwrs inc; el pnts (6-10A) €2.50-4; gas; Indry rm; shop & 7km; rest; snacks; bar; playgrnd; sand beach 12km; games rm; cycle hire; TV; 20% statics; dogs €1.50; phone; poss cr; Eng spkn; adv bkg; quiet; ccard acc; red long stay/low ssn. "Pleasant owner; nr nature reserve; site liable to flooding." ♦ 1 Apr-30 Sep. € 13.00 2006*

LUDE, LE *4G1* (1km NE Rural) *47.65094, 0.16221* **Camp Municipal au Bord du Loir, Route du Mans, 72800 Le Lude [02 43 94 67 70; fax 02 43 94 93 82; contact@camping-auborddulor.fr; www.ville-lelude.fr or www.loir-valley.com]** Fr town cent take D305 (E); in 1km take D307 (N) sp 'Le Mans'; site immed on L. Well sp. Med, hdg/mkd pitch, pt shd; wc; chem disp; mv service pnt; shwrs inc; el pnts (5A) inc; Indtte; shops 300m; tradsmn; rests 100m; snacks adj (high ssn); BBQ (gas only); playgrnd; free pool adj; waterslide; tennis; beach 6km; canoeing; fishing; entmnt; TV; 10% statics; phone; poss cr; Eng spkn; adv bkg; poss traff noise far end of site; ccard acc; CCI. "Clean; modern site & facs; warm welcome, helpful staff; Château du Lude worth visit; highly rec." ♦ 1 Apr-30 Sep. € 10.00 2009*

See advertisement on page 130

LUGAGNAC see Limogne en Quercy *7D4*

LUGNY see Pont de Vaux *9A2*

LUNEL *10E2* (2km NE Rural) *43.69000, 4.14800* **FFCC Camping du Pont de Lunel, Chemin du Mas de Viala, 34400 Lunel [04 67 71 10 22; contact@campingdupontdelunel.com; www.camping-du-pontdelunel.com]** Fr N on N113, cross Rv Vidourle & turn R at rndbt onto D34. Site on R in 400m. Sm, hdg/mkd pitch, shd; wc; mv service pnt; shwrs; el pnts (5A) inc; Indtte; shops adj; rest; snacks; bar; BBQ; playgrnd; pool 4km; sand beach 12km; games area; entmnt; dogs €1.50; adv bkg. "Pleasant, family-run site." 15 Mar-15 Sep. € 17.00 2009*

LUNEL *10E2* (5km NE Rural) *43.71675, 4.16704* **Camping Les Amandiers, Clos de Manset, 30660 Gallargues-le-Montueux [04 66 35 28 02; fax 04 66 51 48 57; camping-lesamandiers@orange.fr; www.camping-lesamandiers.com]** Exit A9 at junc 26 Gallargues/Les Plages. Turn R after toll, site in 2km. Med, mkd pitch, pt shd; wc; chem disp; mv service pnt; baby facs; shwrs inc; el pnts (16A) €4; gas; Indtte; shops adj; snacks; bar; playgrnd; pool; sand beach 15km; fishing 800m; tennis; games area; entmnt; TV; 20% statics; dogs €2.50; adv bkg; quiet; ccard acc; CCI. "Conv NH en rte to Spain; gd touring area." ♦ 30 Apr-1 Sep. € 18.00 2009*

LUNEL *10E2* (6km SW) *43.65180, 4.06611* **FFCC Camping Le Fou du Roi, Chemin des Codoniers, 34130 Lansargues [04 67 86 78 08; fax 04 67 86 78 06; reservation@campinglefouduroi.com; www.campinglefouduroi.fr]** SW fr Lunel on D24 to Lansargues, 100m past vill turn N. Site 50m on R. Med, hdg pitch, pt shd; wc; chem disp; mv service pnt; shwrs inc; el pnts (10A) €4; Indtte; shop; supmkt 4km; snacks; bar; playgrnd; pool; tennis; horseriding; wifi; 75% statics; dogs €4; poss cr; adv bkg rec high ssn; quiet; red low ssn; CCI. ♦ 15 Mar-15 Oct. € 18.60 2008*

LUNEVILLE *6E2* (1km NE Urban) *48.59650, 6.49871* **Camping Les Bosquets, Chemin de la Ménagerie, 54300 Lunéville [03 83 73 37 58; camping@cc-lunevillois.fr; www.cc-lunevillois.fr]** Exit N333 Lunéville by-pass sp `Lunéville-Château' & foll sp to Lunéville. Fr traff lts in sq in front of chateau, take rd to L of chateau (Quai des Bosquets). At sm rndabt do not ent site on R but cont round rndabt to L to yard opp warden's house. Warden will open barrier. Sm, mkd pitch, terr, pt shd; wc; chem disp; shwrs inc; el pnts (10-15A) €2.55; Indtte; shops 500m; tradsmn; pool 200m; playgrnd nrby; internet; dogs; rd noise; CCI. "Friendly staff; rec visit adj chateau gardens; rd noise on bottom pitches; vg." ♦ 1 Apr-31 Oct. € 9.25 2008*

LURE *6F2* (1.5km SE Urban) *47.66798, 6.50500* **Camp Intercommunal de Lure/Les Ecuyers, Route de la Saline, 70200 Lure [03 84 30 43 40 or 03 84 89 00 30; fax 03 84 89 00 31; magalie-sarre@pays-delure.fr]** Well sp fr town cent on D18. Sm, hdg pitch, pt shd; wc; chem disp; shwrs inc; el pnts (6A) €2; Indtte; supmkt 500m; rest, bar 1km; playgrnd; htd, covrd pool 3km; archery; adv bkg; quiet; no ccard acc; CCI. "Delightful, clean, well-kept site; friendly staff; Le Corbusier church worth visit 8km in Ronchamp; rec." ♦ 1 Jun-30 Sep. € 8.60 2008*

LUREUIL *4H2* (3km N Rural) **Camping La Maloterie, 36220 Lureuil [02 54 37 41 25; domainedelamaloterie@tele2.fr]** N fr Le Blanc on D975; take 2nd L after vill sp La Maloterie; foll lane for 1km, farm on R. Sm, pt sl; own san; chem disp; tradsmn; BBQ; dogs €1; adv bkg; CCI. "Lovely, quiet CL-type site in National Park; lge pitches; British owner; vg." 1 Apr-31 Oct. € 8.50 2008*

LUS LA CROIS HAUTE see St Julien en Beauchêne *9D3*

LUSIGNAN *7A2* (500m NE Rural) *46.43712, 0.12369* **Camp Municipal de Vauchiron, Chemin de la Plage Charles Clerc, 86600 Lusignan [05 49 43 30 08 or 05 49 43 31 48 (Mairie); fax 05 49 43 61 19; lusignan@cg86.fr]** Site sp fr D611, 22km SW of Poitiers; foll camp sp in Lusignan to rvside. Med, pt shd; wc; chem disp; baby facs; shwrs inc; el pnts (15A) €2.05 (poss rev pol); Indtte; Indtte; ice; shops 2km; tradsmn; snacks high ssn; bar 1km; BBQ; playgrnd; rv sw adj; fishing; boat hire; entmnt; dogs free; phone; no twin-axles; adv bkg; quiet; ccard acc; CCI. "Beautiful, peaceful site in spacious park; lge pitches; forest & rv walks adj; friendly, helpful resident warden; excel clean san facs; steep walk to historic old town; highly rec." ♦ 15 Apr-30 Sep. € 9.40 2009*

LUSSAC LES CHATEAUX *7A3* (6km SW Rural) *46.36912, 0.69330* **Camp Municipal du Moulin Beau, 86320 Gouex [05 49 48 46 14; fax 05 48 84 50 01]** Fr Lussac on N147/E62 dir Poitiers, cross rv bdge sp Poitiers & immed turn L on D25; foll sp to Gouex; site on L in 4km at swimming pool/camping sp. Sm, pt shd; wc (some cont); chem disp; shwrs inc; el pnts (15A) €1.60 (check pol); bakery 500m in vill; pool 300m; v quiet; no ccard acc; CCI. "Excel site on bank of Rv Vienne; facs clean but ltd; bollards at site ent, care needed if van over 7m or twin-axle; highly rec." 15 Jun-15 Sep. € 4.20 2009*

This is a wonderful site.

I'll fill in a report online and let the Club know – www.caravanclub.co.uk/europereport

LUSSAC LES CHATEAUX *7A3* (11km SW Rural) *46.32231, 0.67384* **Camp Municipal du Renard, 86150 Queaux [05 49 48 48 32 or 05 49 48 48 08 (Mairie); fax 05 49 48 30 70; contact@queaux.fr; www.queaux.fr]** Fr Lussac cross rv bdge sp Poitiers & immed turn L. Foll sp to Gouex & Queaux. Site on D25 S of vill. Med, mkd pitch, pt sl, pt shd; wc; mv service pnt; shwrs inc; el pnts (6A) €2.50; tradsmn; shops, rest 500m; bar; playgrnd; paddling pool; quiet. "Lovely rvside site nr pleasant vill; manned high ssn or apply to Mairie." 15 Jun-15 Sep. € 5.50 2009*

LUSSAC LES CHATEAUX *7A3* (3km W Rural) *46.39636, 0.70531* **Camp Municipal Mauvillant, 86320 Lussac-les-Châteaux [tel/fax 05 49 48 03 32]** W fr Lussac on N147/E62 dir Poitiers; in 1km (shortly bef bdge) turn L at Municipal sp & foll to site 800m on L. Site parallel to Rv Vienne. Exit L turn onto N147 can be diff for lge o'fits Med, hdg/mkd pitch, hdstg, pt shd; wc (mainly cont); chem disp; baby facs; shwrs inc; el pnts (10A) inc; Indtte; BBQ; playgrnd; pool nr; rv 200m; no dogs; Eng spkn; adv bkg; quiet; CCI. "Warden calls 0800-1200 & 1700-1900, if office clsd site yourself & register later; height barrier - o'fits above 2m cannot ent if office clsd; NH only." 1 Jul-15 Oct. € 11.95 2008*

LUXEUIL LES BAINS *6F2* (500m N Rural) *47.82315, 6.38200* **FFCC Camping du Domaine de Chatigny, 14 Rue Grammont, 70300 Luxeuil-les-Bains [03 84 93 97 97; fax 03 84 93 61 01; camping.ot-luxeuil@wanadoo.fr; www.camping.luxeuil.fr]** N fr Vesoul on N57; turn L at rndabt into Luxeuil-les-Bains; foll Camping sp. Vehicular access fr Rue Ste Anne. Med, hdg/mkd pitch, hdstg, terr, pt shd; htd wc; chem disp; mv service pnt; baby facs; shwrs inc; el pnts (16A) €3.50-4.50; gas; lndtte; ice; shop; supmkt 100m; tradsmn; rest; snacks; bar; BBQ; playgrnd; pool; indoor tennis court; TV rm; 20% statics; dogs €1.70; bus 300m; no twin-axles; Eng spkn; adv bkg; quiet; ccard acc; red low ssn/long stay; CCI. "New (2009), high standard site." 28 Mar-7 Nov. € 16.50 2009*

LUYNES see Tours *4G2*

LUZ ST SAUVEUR *8G2* (1km N Rural) *42.88140, -0.01258* **Airotel Camping Pyrénées, 46 Ave du Barège, La Ferme Theil, 65120 Esquièze-Sère [05 62 92 89 18; fax 05 62 92 96 50; airotel.pyrenees@wanadoo.fr; www.airotel-pyrenees.com]** On main rd fr Lourdes to Luz on L past International Campsite. L U-turn into ent archway needs care - use full width of rd & forecourt. Med, mkd pitch, pt sl, pt shd; htd wc (some cont); mv service pnt; chem disp (wc); sauna; shwrs inc; fam bthrm; el pnts (3-10A) €3.50-6.50 (rev pol); gas; lndtte; shop; supmkt 800m; tradsmn, rest & snacks in high ssn; bar; playgrnd; indoor & o'door pools; ski in winter; fishing; walking; horseriding; rafting; TV; entmnts; dogs €1.50; 30% statics; poss cr; quiet but some rd noise; Eng spkn; adv bkg; site clsd Oct & Nov; ccard acc; CCI. "Beautiful area; facs poss stretched high ssn; excel walking & wildlife; lovely vill." ♦ 1 Dec-30 Sep. € 26.00 2008*

LUZ ST SAUVEUR *8G2* (1.5km N Rural) *42.88285, -0.01354* **Camping International, 50 Ave de Barège, 65120 Esquièze-Sère [05 62 92 82 02; fax 05 62 92 96 87; camping.international.luz@wanadoo.fr; www.international-camping.fr]** On E side of D921, clearly sp. Ave de Barège is part of D921. Lge, hdg/mkd pitch, pt sl, pt shd; htd wc; chem disp; mv service pnt; baby facs; shwrs inc; el pnts (2-6A) €2-5; lndtte (inc dryer); shop; supmkt 800m; tradsmn; snacks; bar; playgrnd; htd pool; waterslide; tennis; horseriding; skiing; games area; games rm; entmnt; wifi; TV; 10% statics; dogs free; phone; poss cr; Eng spkn; adv bkg; quiet, some rd noise; red low ssn; CCI. "Beautiful views fr site; friendly, helpful owners; excel walking; ltd facs low ssn; vg." ♦ 15 Dec-20 Apr & 20 May-30 Sep. € 21.10 (CChq acc) 2009*

LUZ ST SAUVEUR *8G2* (500m E Rural) *42.87362, 0.00293* **Camping Le Bergons, Route de Barègas, 65120 Esterre [05 62 92 90 77; info@camping-bergons.com; www.camping-bergons.com]** On D918 to Col du Tourmalet, site on R. Med, mkd pitch, pt sl, terr, pt shd; htd wc; shwrs inc; chem disp; el pnts (2-6A) €1.90-4.80; gas; lndtte; shops adj; tradsmn; BBQ; playgrnd; pool 500m; 10% statics; dogs €0.75; phone; rd noise; red long stay/low ssn; CCI. "Well-kept site; friendly, helpful owner; gd san facs; levelling blocks poss req; v tight ent for lge o'fits; excel walking; Donjon des Aigles at Beaucens worth visit; mkt Mon; vg." ♦ 15 Dec-20 Oct. € 9.40 2009*

LUZ ST SAUVEUR *8G2* (8km E Rural) *42.89451, 0.05741* **Camping La Ribère, 65120 Barèges [tel/fax 05 62 92 69 01 or 06 80 01 29 51 (mob); contact@laribere.com; www.laribere.com]** On N side of rd N618 on edge of Barèges, site sp as `Camping Caraveneige'. Phone kiosk at ent. Sm, pt sl, pt shd; htd wc ltd; chem disp; shwrs inc; el pnts (6A) €6; lndtte; shops, tradsmn; rest adj; some statics; dogs €0.95; poss cr; quiet. "Gd facs; magnificent views." 5 May-21 Oct. € 12.80 2006*

LUZECH see Castelfranc *7D3*

LUZENAC see Ax les Thermes *8G4*

LUZERET see Argenton sur Creuse *7A3*

LUZY *4H4* (1km NE Rural) *46.79622, 3.97685* **Camp Municipal La Bédure, Route d'Autun, 58170 Luzy [03 86 30 02 34 (Mairie)]** Foll sps on D981 (N81) to site. Med, mkd pitch, pt sl, pt shd; wc (some cont); shwrs; shops 1km; el pnts (6A) €1.50 (poss rev pol); pool adj; quiet. "Pleasant site; gd walking; poss itinerants; gd touring base." 1 Jul-1 Sep. € 6.00 2006*

LUZY *4H4* (7km NE Rural) *46.81680, 4.05650* **Camping Domaine de la Gagère (Naturist), 58170 Luzy [03 86 30 48 11; fax 03 86 30 45 57; info@la-gagere.com; www.la-gagere.com]** Fr Luzy take D981 (N81) dir Autun. In 6.5km over rlwy, turn R onto unclassified rd sp 'La Gagère'. Site at end of rd in 3.5km on L. Med, mkd pitch, hdstg, pt sl, terr, pt shd; wc; chem disp; mv service pnt; child/baby facs; fam bthrm; sauna; shwrs inc; el pnts (6A) inc; gas 10km; lndtte; sm shop & shops 10km; tradsmn; rest; snacks; bar; BBQ; playgrnd; 2 htd pools; lake, shgle beach 12km; entment; wifi; TV rm; 20% statics; dogs €2.45; bus 10km; phone; poss cr; Eng spkn; adv bkg; quiet; ccard acc; red low ssn; INF card req. "Excel, wooded site with views in beautiful area; friendly, helpful owners; superb san facs; gd touring base." ♦ 1 Apr-30 Sep. € 34.00 2009*

LUZY *4H4* (2km SW Rural) *46.75790, 3.94472* **Camping Château de Chigy, 58170 Tazilly [03 86 30 10 80; fax 03 86 30 09 22; reception@chateaudechigy.com.fr; www.chateaudechigy.com.fr]** Fr Luzy take D973 S twd Bourbon-Lancy, in 4km turn L on minor rd sp Chigy, site sp. Fr S turn R onto rd to Chigy. Site is E of D973 - do not take sp rd to Tazilly vill. V lge, pt sl, pt terr, pt shd; wc; chem disp; baby facs; shwrs inc; private san facs some pitches; el pnts (6A) €4; gas; lndtte; rest, snacks (high ssn); bar; playgrnd; htd covrd pool; paddling pool; fishing; games area; entmnt; TV; some statics; dogs €2; adv bkg; quiet; red low ssn/long stay/snr citizens; CCI. "Lovely site in large grounds of château with lovely walks; v lge pitches; gd." ♦ 26 Apr-30 Sep. € 22.00 2009*

France

LYON *9B2* (12km E Rural) *45.79082, 4.99223* **Camping Le Grand Large, 81 Rue Victor Hugo, 69330 Meyzieu [04 78 31 42 16; fax 04 72 45 91 78; camping.grand. large@wanadoo.fr]** Exit N346 junc 6, E onto D6 dir Jonage. In approx 2 km turn L twd Le Grand Large (lake), site in 1km. Lge, pt shd; htd wc (mainly cont); chem disp; mv service pnt; shwrs inc; el pnts (5A) inc; gas; Indtte; shop 2km; snacks; pool 2km; lake sw & beach adj; boating, fishing in lake; games area; entmnt; TV; 90% statics; dogs €1; bus 1km; train 2km; poss cr; quiet; adv bkg; ccard acc; CCI. "Minimal, poss scruffy san facs; stn 2km for trains to Lyon; fair." 1 Apr-31 Oct. € 17.70 (3 persons) 2007*

⊞ **LYON** *9B2* (10km SW Urban) *45.68702, 4.78636* **Camping des Barolles, 88 Ave Foch, 69230 St Genis-Laval [04 78 56 05 56; fax 04 72 67 95 01]** Exit A7 at Pierre-Bénite cent onto A450 & exit at Basses Barolles; foll sp. Or fr D342 (D42) to St Genis-Laval cent main sq (Place Joffre) then take Ave Foch SW to site. Poorly sp. Sm, hdstg, terr, pt shd; wc (own san rec); shwrs; el pnts (6-10A) €3.30-6.90; gas; Indtte; snacks; bar; playgrnd; dogs €2; quiet. "Ungated; poss itinerants; recep unreliable opening; NH only." € 14.50 2006*

⊞ **LYON** *9B2* (8km NW Urban) *45.81948, 4.76168* **Camping Indigo Lyon, Ave de la Porte de Lyon, 69570 Dardilly [04 78 35 64 55; fax 04 72 17 04 26; lyon@camping-indigo.com; www.camping-indigo.com]** Fr D306 (N6) Paris rd, take Limonest-Dardilly-Porte de Lyon exit at Auchan supmkt. Fr A6 exit junc 33 Porte de Lyon. Site on W side of A6 adj m'way & close to junc, foll sp (poss obscured by trees) for 'Complexe Touristique'. Fr E take N ring rd dir Roanne, Paris, then as above. Lge, hdg/mkd pitch, hdstg, pt shd; htd wc; chem disp; mv service pnt; serviced pitches; mv service pnt; baby facs; shwrs inc; el pnts (6-10A) €4.30-6.80; gas 100m; Indtte; hypmkt 200m; rest, bar 100m; playgrnd; pool; games rm; internet; TV rm; some statics; dogs €3; phone; bus/train to city nr; extra for twin-axle c'vans; Eng spkn; adv bkg; rd noise; ccard acc; red low ssn; CCI. "Well-run, secure site; Lyon easily accessible by bus & metro; gd touring base for interesting area; helpful recep; gd clean san facs." ♦ € 18.40 (CChq acc) 2009*

LYONS LA FORET *3D2* (500m NE Rural) *49.40334, 1.47954* **FFCC Camp Municipal St Paul, 27480 Lyons-la-Forêt [02 32 49 42 02; camping-saint-paul@wanadoo.fr; www. camping-saint-paul.fr]** Fr Rouen E on N31/E46 for 33km; at La Feuillie, S on D921/321 for 8km; site on L at ent to town adj Rv Lieure. Med, hdg/mkd pitch, pt shd; htd wc (cont); chem disp; shwrs inc; el pnts (6A) inc (poss rev pol); Indtte; shops 1km; tradsmn; rest, snacks, bar 1km; playgrnd; pool adj; fishing; tennis; horseriding; poss cr; 50% statics; dogs €1; adv bkg; quiet; CCI. "Gd site but liable to flood after heavy rain; facs poss inadequate for site size & ltd low ssn; statics graveyard off-putting (2008); Lyons-la-Forêt lovely town, conv Dieppe ferry; walking & cycling in forests." 1 Apr-31 Oct. € 18.00 2008*

MACHE see Aizenay *2H4*

MACHECOUL *2H4* (500m SE Urban) *46.98987, -1.81562* **Camp Municipal La Rabine, Allée de la Rabine, 44270 Machecoul [tel/fax 02 40 02 30 48; camprabine@ wanadoo.fr]** Sp fr most dirs. Look out for prominent twin-spired church in cent; take sm one-way street that leads away fr spire end; site on R in 400m. Med, pt shd; wc; chem disp; shwrs €1; el pnts (4-13A) €2-3.20; Indtte; shops 500m; tradsmn; BBQ (gas only) playgrnd; pool adj; sand beach 14km; entmnt; some statics; dogs €0.90; adv bkg; quiet. "V nice site with lge pitches & gd facs; excel base for birdwatching & cycling over marshes; pleasant town; mkt Wed & Sat." 15 Apr-30 Sep. € 7.60 2008*

MACON *9A2* (3km N Urban) *46.33023, 4.84491* **Camp Municipal Les Varennes, 1 Route des Grandes Varennes, Sancé, 71000 Mâcon [03 85 38 16 22 or 03 85 38 54 08; fax 03 85 39 39 18; camping@ville-macon.fr; www. macon.fr]** Fr both N & S exit A6 junc 28 & cont S on N6 twd Mâcon; site on L in approx 3km, sp. (Fr S, leaving A6 at junc 28 avoids long trip thro town). Lge, mkd pitch, pt sl, pt shd; htd wc (some cont); chem disp; mv service pnt; baby facs; shwrs inc; el pnts (5-10A) €2.70 (rev pol); gas; Indtte; shop; supmkt nr; hypmkt 1km; rest; snacks; bar; playgrnd; 2 pools; tennis 1km; golf 6km; TV; dogs €0.75; phone; bus; poss cr; Eng spkn; adv bkg; quiet but some rd & rlwy noise; ccard acc; red low ssn/long stay; CCI. "Well-maintained, busy NH nr A6; rec arr early as poss full after 1800; friendly staff; superb facs (plenty); poss too few el pnts high ssn; excel rest; gates clsd 2200-0630; poss flooding bottom end of site; twin-axles extra; long level walk to town; excel." ♦ 15 Mar-31 Oct. € 12.70 2009*

MACON *9A2* (8km S Rural) *46.25167, 4.82610* **Base de Loisirs Cormoranche, Luizant, 01290 Cormoranche-sur-Saône [03 85 23 97 10; fax 03 85 23 97 11; contact@ lac-cormoranche.com; www.lac-cormoranche.com]** Exit A26 junc 29 sp Mâcon Sud onto N6 S to Crêches-sur-Saône. Turn L in town at traff lts onto D31 sp Cormoranche, then D51A. Cross rv (height restriction on bdge 2.6m), site sp on L. Alt rte: exit N6 in Mâcon & turn E onto D1079 dir St Laurent-sur-Saône then take D933 S to Pont-de-Veyle. Cont on D933 & foll sp to Cormoranche. Med, hdg/mkd pitch, pt shd; wc; chem disp; mv service pnt; shwrs inc; el pts inc; Indtte; shop; tradsmn; rest; snacks; bar; playgrnd; lake sw & sand beach adj; fishing; cycle hire; entmnt; TV rm; 25% statics; dogs €2; poss cr; Eng spkn; adv bkg; quiet; ccard acc; CCI. "Spacious pitches, some with narr access; vg." ♦ 1 May-30 Sep. € 22.50 2007*

MACON *9A2* (8km S Rural) *46.24106, 4.80643* **Camp Municipal du Port d'Arciat, Route du Port d'Arciat, 71680 Crêches-sur-Saône [03 85 36 57 91 or 03 85 37 48 32 (LS); fax 03 85 36 51 57; camping-creches.sur.saone@wanadoo.fr; http://pagesperso-orange.fr/campingduportdarciat/]** S fr Mâcon on N6 to Crêches-sur-Saône. Site sp (1 sm sp) at 3rd set of traff lts in cent vill on N6, turn E, cross m'way bdge; site on R by rv, sp on rndabt. NB Adj rv bdge has 2.6m height limit (just after site turning if app fr W). Lge, mkd pitch, pt sl, pt shd; wc (some cont); chem disp; mv service pnt; shwrs inc; el pnts (6A) €3.80; gas; lndtte; shop; supmkt 1km; rest; snacks; bar; playgrnd; pool 1km; fishing & boating; entmnt; dogs €1.40; gates clsd 2200-0700; some Eng spkn; adv bkg; ccard acc; CCI. "Gd touring base; gd facs; gate to lake/beach clsd bef 1900; conv a'route; ideal NH, espec low ssn; vg." ♦ 15 May-15 Sep. € 10.90 2009*

MADIRAN *8F2* (Urban) *43.54955, -0.05712* **FFCC Camp Municipal Le Madiran, Route de Vignoble, 65700 Madiran [tel/fax 05 62 31 92 83 or 06 84 67 26 13 (mob); irma.hofstede@aliceadsl.fr; http://monsite.orange.fr/madiran]** S fr Riscle on D935 after approx 12km turn R onto D58 to Madiran. Site in middle of town. Sm, mkd pitch, pt sl, unshd; wc; chem disp; shwrs inc; el pnts €2.50; gas, shop, snacks, bar 50m; playgrnd; pool; dogs; Eng spkn; quiet; ccard acc; CCI. "Excel site." ♦ 15 Jun-15 Oct. € 10.00 2008*

MAGNAC BOURG *7B3* (Urban) *45.61965, 1.42864* **FFCC Camp Municipal Les Ecureuils, 87380 Magnac-Bourg [05 55 00 80 28 (Mairie); fax 05 55 00 49 09; mairie.magnac-bourg@wanadoo.fr]** Leave A20 at junc 41 sp Magnac-Bourg; foll sps to site in vill. Site behind town hall. Sm, pt sl, some hdg pitch, pt shd; wc; mv service pnt; shwrs inc; el pnts (5A) €3; supmkt, petrol & rest nr; playgrnd; fishing 2km; CCI. "Quiet & peaceful; coded barrier access if arr at lunchtime; warden calls at 1600; mkt Sat am; gd." 1 Apr-30 Sep. € 10.50 2007*

MAGNIERES *6E2* (300m W Rural) *48.4463, 6.5588* **FFCC Camping du Pré Fleury, 18 Rue de la Barre, 54219 Magnières [03 83 73 82 21; fax 03 83 72 32 77; kern.christian@wanadoo.fr; www.campingduprefleury.com]** Fr N333 exit junc 4 S onto D914 to Magnières. Site sp. Or on D22 fr Bayon or Baccarat go to Magnières. Site sp. Sm, mkd pitch, hdstg, pt sl, pt shd; wc; chem disp; mv service pnt; shwrs inc; el pnts (5-10A) €2.50-4.50; lndtte; shops 1km; rest, bar adj; playgrnd; fishing; quiet. "Gd touring base; gd cycling, birdwatching, walks." ♦ 1 Apr-15 Oct. € 9.00 2007*

⊞ **MAICHE** *6G3* (1km S Rural) *47.24705, 6.79952* **Camp Municipal St Michel, 23 Rue St Michel, 25120 Maîche [03 81 64 12 56 or 03 81 64 03 01 (Mairie); fax 03 81 64 12 56; camping.maiche@wanadoo.fr; www.mairie-maiche.fr]** Fr S turn R off D437 onto D442. App on D464 L on o'skts of town. Sp fr both dir. Med, hdstg, sl, terr, pt shd; htd wc; chem disp; shwrs inc; el pnts (6A) €2.40; lndtte; shops 1km; playgrnd; pool adj; games area; games rm; a few statics; dogs; phone; site clsd 3rd week Nov & Dec; adv bkg; rd noise. "Attractive, neat, well-run site with views; clean facs; phone ahead low ssn to check open; gd walks in woods." ♦ € 9.80 2008*

MAICHE *6G3* (10km SW Rural) *47.16304, 6.72469* **Camp Municipal Les Sorbiers, Rue Foch, 25210 Le Russey [03 81 43 75 86]** On D437 Maîche-Morteau, 1st R after vill church, site sp on L in 250m. Sm, hdstg, pt shd; htd wc (men cont); chem disp; shwrs €2; el pnts (10A) €2.55; gas; lndtte; shop 1km; rest, snacks, bar 500m; playgrnd; tennis; games rm; 20% statics; adv bkg; quiet; ccard not acc. "Excel, scenic cent; high altitude, poss cold nights." 15 Jun-15 Sep. € 6.10 2006*

MAILLE see Maillezais *7A2*

MAILLERAYE SUR SEINE, LA see Caudebec en Caux *3C2*

MAILLEZAIS *7A2* (Rural) *46.36912, -0.74027* **Camp Municipal de l'Autize, Rue du Champ de Foire, Route de Maillé, 85420 Maillezais [02 51 00 70 79 or 06 31 43 21 33 (mob); fax 02 51 00 70 79; mairie-maillezais@wanadoo.fr; www.maillezais.fr]** Fr Fontenay take D148 twd Niort; after 9km, turn R onto D15 to Maillezais; at church in vill on L, site on R after 200m. Or fr A83, exit junc 9 onto D148, then D15 (do not use v minor rds, as poss directed by sat nav). Sm, hdg pitch, pt shd; wc; chem disp; shwrs inc; el pnts (4-13A) €3-5; lndtte; shops 200m; playgrnd; games area; games rm; TV: 30% statics; adv bkg; quiet; ccard not acc; red low ssn; CCI. "Lovely, clean site; spacious pitches, gd views fr some; excel san facs, inc for disabled; warden calls am & pm; friendly & helpful; twin-axles extra; conv Marais Poitevin area; vg NH fr A83; excel." ♦ 1 Apr-30 Sep. € 9.00 2009*

MAILLEZAIS *7A2* (6km S Rural) *46.31308, -0.73342* **FFCC Camping Les Conches, Route d'Arçais, 85420 Damvix [tel/fax 02 51 87 17 06; didier.vezin@wanadoo.fr; http://campingdesconches.free.fr]** Fr Fontenay-le-Comte exit D148 at Benet then W on D25 thro Le Mazeau to sp on L for Damvix. Or exit A83 junc 8 then S on D938 & E on D25 dir Benet. Site 1km thro vill on R over bdge (sp). Med, mkd, shd; wc; chem disp; mv service pnt; shwrs; el pnts (6-10A) €3; lndry rm; shops adj; rest adj; playgrnd; pool; tennis; golf; horseriding; rv fishing & boating adj; dogs €1; adv bkg rec; quiet but some noise fr disco opp high ssn; CCI. "Gd rest; friendly staff; gd cycling." 1 May-30 Sep. € 11.00 2009*

MAILLEZAIS *7A2* (5km SW Rural) *46.34037, -0.79640* **Camp Municipal La Petite Cabane, 85420 Maillé [02 51 87 05 78 (Mairie); fax 02 51 87 02 48; mairiedemaille@wanadoo.fr]** Site is 500m W of Maillé, clearly sp. Sm, pt shd; wc; shwrs inc; el pnts (6-15A) inc; gas 500m; lndry rm; shops 500m; playgrnd; paddling pool; boat & canoe hire; adv bkg; quiet; CCI. "Site by canal in cent of Marais Poitevin National Park; diff access lge o'fits; elec unreliable (2008); gd cycle rtes." 1 Apr-30 Sep. € 11.00 2008*

MAILLY LE CHATEAU *4G4* (S Rural) *47.58906, 3.65332* **Camp Municipal Le Pré du Roi, Pertuis des Bouchets, 89660 Mailly-le-Château [03 86 81 44 85 or 03 86 81 40 37 (Mairie); fax 03 86 81 40 37; mairie-maillylechateau@wanadoo.fr]** NW on N6 fr Avallon twd Auxerre, turn W in Voutenay-sur-Cure on D950 to Mailly-la-Ville. Cross bdge twd Mailly-le-Château, site sp. Heading S fr Auxerre, turn R off N6 SE of Vincelles on D100 to Bazarnes & Mailly-le-Château. Med, mkd pitch, pt shd; wc; shwrs; el pnts (20A) €3; shops 2km; fishing; dogs; quiet. "Pleasant, peaceful situation by Rv Yonne; gd san facs." 25 May-3 Sep. € 8.40 2007*

MAILLY LE CHATEAU *4G4* (5km S Rural) *47.56267, 3.64671* **Camp Municipal Escale, 5 Impasse de Sables, 89660 Merry-sur-Yonne [03 86 81 01 60; fax 03 86 81 06 14; gite.merrysuryonne@wanadoo.fr]** Fr Auxerre, take N151. Turn E onto D21 at Coulanges. Thro Châtel-Censoir turn L over rv into Merry-sur-Yonne. Site sp. Med, mkd pitch, hdstg, pt shd; wc; mv service pnt (some cont); shwrs €2; el pnts (10A) €4; gas; Indtte; shop 5km; rest, bar 500m; rv sw adj; canoe hire, fishing; tennis, dogs €1; phone; quiet; CCI. "Gd site." ♦ 10 Apr-15 Oct. € 6.70 2007*

⊞ **MAINTENON** *4E2* (4km NW Rural) *48.60890, 1.54760* **Camping Les Ilots de St Val, 28130 Villiers-le-Morhier [02 37 82 71 30; fax 02 37 82 77 67; lesilots@campinglesilotsdestval.com; www.campinglesilotsdestval.com]** Take D983 N fr Maintenon twd Nogent-le-Roi, in 5km 2nd L onto D101 sp Néron/Vacheresses-les-Basses/Camping to site in 1km on L at top of hill. NB App fr N on D929 not rec as rds in Nogent-le-Roi narr. Lge, some hdg/mkd pitch, hdstg, pt shd; htd wc; chem disp; baby facs; shwrs inc; el pnts (6-10A) €3.80-6.40; gas; Indtte; shops 4km; tradsmn; BBQ; playgrnd; pool 4km; rv fishing 1km; tennis; 10% statics; dogs €2; train 4km; little Eng spkn; adv bkg; quiet but some aircraft noise; red long stay/CCI. "Pleasant, peaceful site in open countryside; lge private pitches; some vg, modern san facs; helpful staff; take care electrics; conv Chartres, Versailles, Maintenon Château, train to Paris." ♦ € 15.60 2009*

See advertisement

MAISONS LAFFITTE see Paris *3D3*

MALARCE SUR LA THINES see Vans, Les *9D1*

MALAUCENE *10E2* (4km N Rural) *44.20101, 5.12535* **FFCC Camping Aire Naturelle La Saousse (Letilleul), La Madelaine, 84340 Malaucène [04 90 65 14 02]** Fr Malaucène take D938 N dir Vaison-la-Romaine & after 3km turn R onto D13 dir Entrechaux where site sp. After 1km turn R,site 1st on R. Sm, hdg pitch, terr, shd; wc; chem disp; shwrs inc; el pnts (5A) €2.50; Indry rm; tradsmn high ssn; shop, rest, snacks, bar, pool 4km; no statics; dogs; adv bkg rec; quiet; ccard not acc; red low ssn; CCI. "CL-type site o'looking vineyards with views to Mt Ventoux; some pitches in woods with steep incline to reach; friendly, helpful owners; basic, clean facs; rec pitch on lower level for easy access; excel." 1 Apr-30 Oct. € 12.50 2009*

MALAUCENE *10E2* (8km S Rural) *44.12383, 5.10968* **Camping Le Bouquier, Route de Malaucène, 84330 Caromb [tel/fax 04 90 62 30 13; lebouquier@wanadoo.fr; www.lebouquier.com]** NE fr Carpentras on D974 then D13; site on R 1.5km after Caromb cent. Fr Malaucène S on D938 for 8km; turn L D13 sp Caromb. Site 800m on L just bef vill. Med, hdg/mkd pitch, hdstg, terr, pt shd, htd wc; chem disp; shwrs inc; el pnts (10A) inc; Indtte; shops 1.5km; tradsmn; snacks; bar; BBQ (gas/elec); playgrnd; htd pool; lake sw 1km; gd walking/cycling; wifi; 5% statics; dogs €1.60; phone; poss cr; Eng spkn; adv bkg; quiet but some rd noise; CCI. "Well-kept site; attractive scenery; helpful staff; excel san facs; steps to disabled facs; steel pegs req; gd touring base; no twin-axles; vg." ♦ 31 Mar-15 Oct. € 15.00 2008*

MALAUCENE *10E2* (500m NW Rural) *44.17789, 5.12533* **Camping Le Bosquet, Route de Suzette, 84340 Malaucène [04 90 65 24 89 or 04 90 65 29 09; fax 04 90 65 12 52; camping.lebosquet@wanadoo.fr; www.guideweb.com/provence/camping/bosquet]** Fr S on D938 dir Vaison-la-Romaine turn L onto D90 at Malaucène dir Suzette. Site on R in 300m. Sm, hdg pitch, all hdstg, terr, pt shd; htd wc; chem disp; baby facs; shwrs inc; el pnts (10A) €2.80 (poss rev pol); gas; Indtte; shop 600m; tradsmn; snacks; bar; playgrnd; pool; 2% statics; dogs free; phone; adv bkg; quiet; ccard not acc; red low ssn; CCI. "Clean san facs; friendly owner; gd touring base Mt Ventoux." ♦ 1 Apr-30 Sep. € 14.60 2008*

MALBUISSON *6H2* (S Urban) *46.79223, 6.29377* **Camping Les Fuvettes, 24 Route de la Plage et des Perrières, 25160 Malbuisson [03 81 69 31 50; fax 03 81 69 70 46; les-fuvettes@wanadoo.fr; www.camping-fuvettes.com]** Site 19km S of Pontarlier on N57 & D437 to Malbuisson, thro town, R down rd to Plage. Lge, pt sl, pt shd; htd wc (some cont); shwrs inc; el pnts (4-6A) €3.60-4; gas; lndtte (inc dryer); shop; rest; snacks; bar; playgrnd; shgl beach for lake sw; fishing; boating; games rm; 30% statics; dogs €1,50; poss cr; quiet; CCI. "Popular, lakeside, family site; mkd walks/cycle paths in adj woods; petting zoo (llamas etc) nrby." 1 Apr-30 Sep. € 21.00 2008*

MALBUISSON *6H2* (2km S Rural) *46.77449, 6.27370* **Camping du Lac, 10 Rue du Lac, 25160 Labergement-Ste Marie [03 81 69 31 24; camping.lac.remoray@wanadoo.fr; www.camping-lac-remoray.com]** Exit N57/E23 junc 2 onto D437 thro Malbuisson to Labergement. Site sp to R of D437 after x-ing Rv Doubs. Med, mkd pitch, pt shd; wc; chem disp; mv service pnt; baby facs; shwrs inc; el pnts (6A) €3.50; gas; lndtte; tradsmn; rest; snacks; bar; playgrnd; lake beach adj; fishing; walking; cycling; sports area; tennis nrby; internet; TV; 5% statics; dogs €1.50; phone; Eng spkn; adv bkg; quiet; ccard acc; CCI. "Forest views by Lake Remoray; excel, roomy site; kind & helpful owner; clean san facs; vill 500m with gd shops; vg." ♦ 1 May-30 Sep. € 14.50 2008*

MALEMORT DU COMTAT see Carpentras *10E2*

MALENE, LA *9D1* (200m W Rural) *44.30120, 3.31923* **FFCC Camp Municipal Le Pradet, 48210 La Malène [04 66 48 58 55 or 04 66 48 51 16 (LS); fax 04 66 48 58 51; la.malene.mairie@wanadoo.fr]** W fr La Malène on D907B dir Les Vignes. Site on L in 200m. Well sp. Sm, mkd pitch, some hdstg, pt sl, pt shd; wc (some cont); chem disp; mv service pnt; shwrs inc; el pnts (10A) €2.50; lndtte; shops, rest, snacks & bar 200m; BBQ; playgrnd; rv sw & fishing; dogs €0.30; phone; poss cr; adv bkg; quiet; ccard acc; red low ssn; CCI. "Kayak hire; boat trips fr vill; helpful warden; excel." 1 Apr-30 Sep. € 11.60 2009*

⊞ **MALESHERBES** *4E3* (5km S Rural) *48.25659, 2.43574* **FFCC Camping Ile de Boulancourt, 6 Allée des Marronniers, 77760 Boulancourt [01 64 24 13 38; fax 01 64 24 10 43; camping-ile-de-boulancourt@wanadoo.fr; www.camping-iledeboulancourt.com]** Exit A6 at junc 14 Ury & Fontainebleau. SW on D152 to Malesherbes; S on D410 for 5km into Boulancourt. Site sp fr D410 & in vill. Med, pt shd; htd wc (many cont); chem disp; mv service pnt; shwrs inc; el pnts (3-6A) €2; lndtte; shop 3km; rest; BBQ; playgrnd; pool nr; tennis; rv adj; fishing 3km; waterslide 5km; 90% statics; dogs €1; sep field for tourers; Eng spkn; quiet; red low ssn; CCI. "Attractive rv thro site; well-maintained facs, ltd low ssn; friendly, helpful staff; golf course in vill; chateau nr; excel." € 13.00 2008*

MALESTROIT *2F3* (500m E Urban) *47.80865, -2.37922* **Camp Municipal de la Daufresne, Chemin des Tanneurs, 56140 Malestroit [02 97 75 13 33 or 02 97 75 11 75 (Mairie); fax 02 97 73 71 13; tourisme@malestroit.com; www.malestroit.com]** S fr Ploërmel on N166 dir Vannes for 9km. Turn L onto D764 to Malestroit; site sp just off D776 on E bank of Rv Oust. Sm, some hdg pitch, pt shd; wc; chem disp (wc); mv service pnt; shwrs inc; el pnts (6A) €2.50 (poss long lead req); lndtte; shop, rest, snacks, bar 300m; playgrnd; tennis; adv bkg; rv & fishing adj; canoeing nr; dogs free; ccard not acc; CCI. "Pleasant, peaceful site in excel location; clean san facs poss stretched high ssn; canal towpath adj; gd cycle rtes; no twin-axles; Museum of Breton Resistance in St Marcel; highly rec." ♦ 1 May-15 Sep. € 6.80 2009*

MALICORNE SUR SARTHE *4F1* (Urban) *47.81736, -0.08791* **Camp Municipal Porte Ste Marie, 72270 Malicorne-sur-Sarthe [02 43 94 80 14; fax 02 43 94 57 26; mairie.malicorne@wanadoo.fr; www.ville-malicorne.fr]** Fr A11/E501 take D306 exit twds La Flèche. Turn E onto D23 twds Malicorne. Site across rv on W of town adj stadium. Med, pt shd; wc; chem disp; mv service pnt, shwrs inc; el pnts (4-13A) €1.45-2.50; lndtte; shops, rest, bar 500m; BBQ; playgrnd; pool; tennis adj; dogs €0.50; poss cr; quiet; red low ssn; "Quiet position by rv; gd san facs & lndry facs; no access when recep clsd 1230-1430 & after 1930; poss noise (church bell); no waiting area; diff turning; gd." 1 Apr-31 Oct. € 8.70 2006*

MALLEMORT see Salon de Provence *10E2*

⊞ **MAMERS** *4E1* (500m N Rural) *48.35778, 0.37181* **Camp Municipal du Saosnois, Route de Contilly, 72600 Mamers [02 43 97 68 30; fax 02 43 97 38 65; mairie.mamers@wanadoo.fr; www.mairie-mamers.fr]** Fr W on D311, at rndabt at top of hill on circular rd, turn R (sp); then easy L (sp). Fr E on D311, strt thro rndabt (at Super U), ignore 1st camping sp, turn R at traff its & 2nd camping sp; at mini-rndabt turn L, sp Contilly; see lake & site. Sm, hdg pitch, hdstg, pt sl, terr, pt shd; htd wc; mv service pnt; shwrs inc; el pnts (10A) €3-4.20 (long lead poss req); lndtte; shop & 500m; snacks; pool 200m; lakeside beach; games area; TV rm; 30% statics; dogs €0.50; poss cr; adv bkg; quiet; CCI. "Well-kept, secure site; admittance low ssn 1700-1900 only; Mamers pretty; poss itinerants." ♦ € 8.60 2008*

MANDEURE *6G3* (500m NW Urban) *47.45633, 6.80575* **Camping Les Grands Ansanges, Rue de l'Eglise, 25350 Mandeure [03 81 35 23 79; fax 03 81 30 09 26; mairie.mandeure@ville-mandeure.com; www.ville-mandeure.com]** Exit A36 sp Exincourt, site sp fr cent Mandeure, adj Rv Doubs. Med, mkd pitch, pt shd; wc; chem disp; shwrs inc; el pnts (4-10A) €4; lndry rm; sm shop; supmkt 1.4km; tradsmn; rest; bar; playgrnd; games rm; archery & golf nrby; 10% statics; poss cr; CCI. "Beautifully laid-out site facing open farmland; helpful staff; basic san facs (disabled up steps)." 1 May-30 Sep. € 10.90 2008*

MANDRES AUX QUATRE TOURS *5D2* (2km S Rural) *48.82739, 5.78936* **Camp Municipal Orée de la Forêt de la Reine, Route Forêt de la Reine, 54470 Mandres-aux-Quatre-Tours [03 83 23 17 31]** On D958 Commercy to Pont-à-Mousson, sp as Camping Mandres. Turn R at sp in Beaumont & foll sp to vill Mandres-aux-Quatre-Tours. Sm, mkd/hdg pitch, pt shd; wc; chem disp (wc); shwrs inc; el pnts (10A) €1.70; tradsmn; playgrnd; tennis; watersports, sailing 500m; horseriding adj; some statics; dogs; quiet; CCI. "Gd, peaceful site; basic san facs; site poss muddy in wet weather; gd birdwatching, walking, cycling." 1 Apr-31 Oct. € 8.50 2009*

MANOSQUE *10E3* (8.5km NE Rural) *43.86942, 5.83145* **Camp Municipal de la Vandelle, Chemin de Pietramal, 04130 Volx [04 92 79 35 85 or 04 92 70 18 00; fax 04 92 79 32 27; infos@camping-volx.com; www.camping-volx.com]** Fr D4096 (N96) turn W at traff lts in Volx, foll sp to site in 1km. Sm, pt sl, terr, pt shd; htd wc; shwrs inc; el pnts (3A) €3.40; lndtte; shops 1.3km; playgrnd; sm pool; paddling pool; games area; entmnt; dogs free; adv bkg; quiet. ♦ 1 May-30 Sep. € 10.00 2007*

MANOSQUE *10E3* (1.5km W Rural) *43.82986, 5.76384* **FFCC Camping Les Ubacs, 1138 Ave de la Repasse, 04100 Manosque [04 92 72 28 08; fax 04 92 87 75 29; lesubacs.manosque@ffcc.fr; www.camp-in-france.com]** Exit A51 junc 18 onto D907 dir Manosque; then D907 dir Apt; site sp at last rndabt on W side of Manosque. NB easy to overshoot. Med, hdg/mkd pitch, pt shd; wc (cont); mv service pnt; shwrs inc; el pnts (3-9A) €3.34-4.20; lndtte; shop; rest, snacks (high ssn); bar; playgrnd; pool (high ssn); tennis; lake sw 5km; entmnt; dogs €1; ccard acc; red long stay/low ssn/CCI. "Conv Gorges du Verdon; helpful." 1 Apr-30 Sep. € 12.65 2007*

MANS, LE *4F1* (8km N Rural) *48.07179, 0.18934* **FFCC Camping Le Vieux Moulin, 72190 Neuville-sur-Sarthe [02 43 25 31 82; fax 02 43 25 38 11; info@lemans camping.net; www.lemanscamping.net]** Leave D338 (N138) 6km N of Le Mans at St Saturnin; turn E onto D197 to Neuville & foll sp for 3km to site nr Rv Sarthe. Med, pt shd, hdg/mkd pitch, serviced pitch; wc (some cont); chem disp; mv service pnt; baby facs; shwrs inc; el pnts (10A) €3 (poss rev pol); gas; lndtte; sm shop (high ssn) & 500m; tradsmn; rest adj; playgrnd; sm htd pool; tennis; 5% statics; dogs €1; Eng spkn; adv bkg; quiet; ccard acc; red low ssn/CCI. "Open for Le Mans 24 hours race ssn only - phone to confirm opening dates; lge, grassy pitches; friendly, helpful owner; clean san facs; sm lake & watermill/rest adj; peaceful setting; gates clsd 2200-0730; highly rec." € 13.00 2009*

MANS, LE *4F1* (6km NE Rural) *48.01904, 0.27996* **Camping Le Pont Romain, Allée des Ormeaux, Lieu-dit La Châtaigneraie, 72530 Yvré-l'Evêque [02 43 82 25 39; info@lepontromain.com; www.lepontromain.com]** Fr Le Mans take D314 to Yvré-l'Evêque - but do not ent town; just after rv bdge take 1st L into Allée des Ormeaux; site on L in 800m. Or exit A28 junc 23 onto D314 dir 'Le Mans Centre'; site on R just bef Yvré-l'Evêque. Med, mkd pitch, hdstg, pt shd; htd wc; chem disp; baby facs; shwrs inc; el pnts (16A) inc; lndtte (inc dryer); shop; rest; snacks; playgrnd; htd pool; games rm; wifi; TV rm; 10% statics; dogs €1; phone, bus 500m; sep car park; no twin-axles; poss cr; Eng spkn; adv bkg; red low ssn; CCI. "New site (2009); san facs ltd & poss stretched when busy; conv Le Mans & m'way; gd." ♦ 1 Mar-30 Oct. € 19.60 2009*

MANSIGNE *4F1* (500m N Rural) *47.75188, 0.13153* **Camp Municipal La Plage, Route du Plessis, 72510 Mansigné [02 43 46 14 17; fax 02 43 46 16 65; camping-mansigne@wanadoo.fr; www.ville-mansigne.fr or www.loir-valley.com]** N fr Le Lude on D307 to Pontvallain. Take D13 E for 5km to Mansigné, thro vill & foll site sp. Lge, pt shd; wc; chem disp; shwrs inc; el pnts (10A) €2.40; lndtte (inc dryer); shop 200m; rest; snacks; bar; BBQ; htd pool; sand beach & lake sw adj; watersports; tennis; some statics; dogs €1.60; adv bkg; quiet; red long stay; CCI. "Pleasant lakeside position; conv for Loir Valley & Le Mans 24-hour race; ltd facs & office hrs low ssn." ♦ Easter-15 Oct. € 11.65 2009*

See advertisement on page 130

MANSLE *7B2* (NE Urban) *45.87841, 0.18175* **Camp Municipal Le Champion, Rue de Watlington, 16230 Mansle [05 45 20 31 41 or 05 45 22 20 43; fax 05 45 22 86 30; mairie.mansle@wanadoo.fr]** N on N10 fr Angoulême, foll sp Mansle Ville. Leave N10 at exit to N of town, site rd on L, well sp. Rec ent/leave fr N as rte thro town diff due to parked cars. Site beside Rv Charente. Med, hdg pitch, pt shd; wc; chem disp; mv service pnt; shwrs inc; el pnts (16A) inc (poss long lead req); gas in town; lndtte; shops 200m; shop 800m; rest; snacks, bar adj; BBQ; playgrnd; rv sw & boating adj; fishing; entmnt; 5% statics; phone; poss cr; quiet but some rd noise; adv bkg; phone 1km; Eng spkn; ccard not acc; CCI. "Popular, peaceful, well-maintained NH nr N10; lge pitches, choose own; helpful warden; immac san facs; grnd poss boggy after heavy rain; mkt Tues, Fri am; vg." ♦ 15 May-15 Sep. € 15.30 2009*

MANSLE *7B2* (8km NE Rural) *45.90904, 0.25247* **Camp Municipal Le Magnerit, Les Maisons Rouges, 16460 Aunac [05 45 22 24 38; fax 05 45 22 23 17; mairie.aunac@wanadoo.fr]** N on N10 fr Mansle, exit onto D27 to Bayers & Aunac. Site 1km SE vill, well sp. Sm, pt shd; wc; chem disp; shwrs; el pnts (8A) €2.50; shop 1km; playgrnd; rv sw adj; fishing; quiet; CCI. "Peaceful, simple, CL-type site beside Rv Charente; ltd, dated facs but clean; warden visits; vg NH." 15 Jun-15 Sep. € 7.80 2009*

⊞ **MANSLE** *7B2* (10km SE Rural) *45.84137, 0.27319* **Camping Devezeau, 16230 St Angeau [tel/fax 05 45 39 21 29; bookings@campingdevezeau.com; www.campingdevezeau.com]** N or S on N10 exit Mansle; in cent vill at traff lts foll sp twd La Rochefoucauld (D6); past Champion supmkt; over bdge; 1st R onto D6. In approx 9km at T-junc turn R, site sp. App down narr rd. Sm, some hdstg, pt sl, pt shd; wc; chem disp; shwrs inc; el pnts (10A) €2; gas; lndtte; shop 1.5km; tradsmn; supmkt in Mansle; rest 5km; snacks & bar; BBQ; playgrnd; pool; cycling; walking; canoeing; fishing; horseriding; 10% statics; dogs; phone 1km; Eng spkn; adv bkg; quiet; red low ssn; CCI. "Nice CL-type site; friendly British owners; old san facs need gd clean (2009); traction diff in wet (4x4 avail); gd cycling country; phone ahead in winter." ♦ € 18.00 2009*

MANTENAY MONTLIN *9A2* (400m W Rural) *46.42218, 5.09208* **Camp Municipal du Coq, 01560 Mantenay-Montlin [04 74 52 66 91 or 04 74 52 61 72 (Mairie); cdec.sainttrivierdecourtes@wanadoo.fr]** Exit A40 junc 5 Bourg-en-Bresse Nord onto D975 to Mantenay-Montlin; site sp in vill on D46. Or exit A39 junc 10 to St Trivier-de-Courtes, then S to Mantenay. Sm, hdg/mkd pitch, pt shd; wc; chem disp; shwrs inc; el pnts (6A) €1.70; shop, rest & bar 400m; playgrnd; tennis; dogs €1; bus 400m; quiet; red long stay; ccard acc. "Vg rvside site in pretty area; lge pitches; san facs old but clean; warden calls pm; conv NH just off D975." 1 Jun-15 Sep. € 7.50 2007*

MARANS *7A1* (2km N Rural) *46.31682, -0.99158* **Camp Municipal Le Bois Dinot, Route de Nantes, 17230 Marans [05 46 01 10 51; fax 05 46 01 01 72; campingboisdinot.marans@wanadoo.fr; www.ville-marans.fr]** Heading S, site on L of D137 bef ent Marans. Heading N, site is well sp on R 300m after supmkt on L. Lge, shd; wc; shwrs inc; el pnts (10A) €3.50; shops adj; rest, snacks, bar 200m; pool adj; fishing; boat hire; wifi; dogs €1; Eng spkn; poss cr; some rd noise; red long stay/low ssn; CCI. "Well-kept site; helpful warden; facs poss stretched; quieter pitches at back of site; vg pool adj; gd cycling; mkt Tues & Sat; excel." 1 Apr-30 Sep. € 11.60 2009*

MARCENAY *6F1* (1km N Rural) *47.87070, 4.40560* **Camping Les Grèbes du Lac de Marcenay, 5 Route du Lac, 21330 Marcenay [03 80 81 61 72; fax 03 25 81 02 64; info@campingmarcenaylac.com; www.campingmarcenaylac.com]** On D965 bet Laignes & Châtillon-sur-Seine. Fr Châtillon sp on R 8km after vill of Cérilly. Foll sp to lake & camp. Med, hdg/mkd pitch, hdstg; shd; htd wc; chem disp; mv service pnt; baby facs; shwrs inc; el pnts (10A) €3; gas; lndtte (inc dryer); shop; rest adj; snacks; bar adj; BBQ; playgrnd; lake sw adj; fishing; watersports; boat, canoe & cycle hire; golf; horseriding; games rm; games area; wifi; TV rm; 5% statics; dogs €0.50; phone; Eng spkn; adv bkg rec; quiet; ccard acc; red low ssn; CCI. "Lovely, peaceful, well-run lakeside site in beautiful area; friendly, helpful Dutch owners; excel san facs; pitches poss soft after rain; gd touring base; gd walking & cycling; Châtillon museum & Abbey de Fontenay outstanding; well worth finding." ♦ 1 May-30 Sep. € 15.00 2009*

MARCHAINVILLE *4E2* (N Rural) **Camp Municipal Les Fosses, 61290 Marchainville [tel/fax 02 33 73 65 80 (Mairie); mairiemarchainville@wanadoo.fr]** Fr Verneuil-sur-Avre take D941 S to La Ferté-Vidame & at start of town turn R onto D4/D11 SW to Marchainville; site sp at x-rds in vill on D243. Sm, hdg/mkd pitch, pt sl, pt shd; wc; shwrs; el pnts (10A); shop, rest, snacks, bar 8km; tennis; no statics; phone; adv bkg; quiet; CCI. "Warden visits." ♦ 1 Apr-30 Oct. 2008*

MARCIAC *8F2* (1.5km NW Rural) *43.53228, 0.16633* **FFCC Camping du Lac, Bezines, 32230 Marciac [tel/fax 05 62 08 21 19; camping.marciac@wanadoo.fr; www.camping-marciac.com]** E fr Maubourguet take D943 to Marciac. Take D3 to lake dir Plaisance. At lake turn R & R again at sp. Site on L in 200m. Fr N exit A62 at junc 3 & foll D932 sp Pau to Aire-sur-Adour then E on D935 & D3 & foll sp. Med, mkd pitch, some hdstg, pt shd; wc chem disp; mv service pnt; baby facs; shwrs inc; el pnts (6A) inc; gas; lndtte; shop & 800m; tradsmn; rest 300m; snacks; bar; BBQ; playgrnd; pool; lake adj; wifi; 8% statics; dogs €1.50; phone; adv bkg; red long stay/low ssn; ccard acc; CCI. "Friendly British owners improving site; lge pitches with easy access; interesting old town; jazz festival 1st 2 weeks Aug (extra charge); Wed mkt." ♦ 28 Mar-17 Oct. € 16.00 2009*

MARCIGNY *9A1* (7km W Rural) *46.26489, 3.95756* **Camping La Motte aux Merles, 71110 Artaix [03 85 25 37 67]** Leave D982 (Digoin-Roanne) at Marcigny by-pass. Take D989 twd Lapalisse. In 2km at Chambilly cont on D990, site sp in 5km on L, 200m down side rd. Sm, pt sl, pt shd; wc; shwrs inc; el pnts (8A) €2.40; lndry rm; snacks; playgrnd; pool (high ssn); fishing, tennis; golf nrby; dogs €1; quiet. " Friendly owners; gd sightseeing in peaceful area; excel." ♦ 1 Apr-31 Oct. € 9.80 2009*

MARCILLAC LA CROISSILLE *7C4* (2km SW Rural) *45.26896, 2.00838* **Camp Municipal Le Lac, 28 Route du Viaduc, 19320 Marcillac-la-Croisille [tel/fax 05 55 27 81 38 or 05 55 27 82 05 (Mairie); campingdulac19@wanadoo.fr; www.campingdulac19.com]** S fr Egletons on D16 & D18. Site sp at S end of vill at intersection with D978. Lge, pt sl, shd, wc; shwrs; el pnts (6A) €2.40; lndtte; shops 2km; snacks; playgrnd; lake & sand beach adj; tennis adj; entmnt; TV; some statics; dogs €0.80; adv bkg; quiet; red low ssn. 1 Jun-1 Oct. € 10.20 2007*

MARCILLAC ST QUENTIN see Sarlat la Canéda *7C3*

MARCILLAC VALLON *7D4* (300m NW Urban) *44.47721, 2.45575* **Camp Municipal, 24 Ave Gustave Bessières, 12330 Marcillac-Vallon [05 65 71 74 96]** App Marcillac-Vallon fr N on D901; on ent town, site on L immed after x-ing rv bdge. Sm, hdg/mkd pitch, pt sl, shd; htd wc; chem disp; shwrs inc; shops nrby; some statics; quiet. "Otters in sm rv; NH only." € 7.90 2009*

MARCON see Château du Loir *4G1*

MARENNES *7B1* (5km SE Rural) *45.81083, -1.06027* **Camping Séquoia Parc, La Josephtrie, 17320 St Just-Luzac [05 46 85 55 55; fax 05 46 85 55 56; info@sequoiaparc.com; www.sequoiaparc.com or www.les-castels.com]** Fr A10/E05 m'way exit at Saintes, foll sp Royan (N150) turning off onto D728 twd Marennes & Ile d'Oléron; site sp to R off D728, just after leaving St Just-Luzac. Or fr Rochefort take D733 & D123 S; just bef Marennes turn L on D241 sp St Just-Luzac. Best ent to site fr D728, well sp fr each dir. Lge, hdg/mkd pitch, sl, unshd; wc; chem disp; mv service pnt; baby facs; shwrs inc; el pnts (6A) inc (poss rev pol); gas; lndtte; shop; rest; snacks; bar; BBQ; playgrnd; 3 htd pools; paddling pool; waterslides; sand beach 5km; fishing 1.5km; watersports 3km; horseriding; tennis; cycle hire; games area; games rm; entmnt; wifi; TV rm; 50% statics (tour ops); dogs €5; barrier clsd 2230; adv bkg (bkg fee); ccard acc; red long stay/low ssn; CCI. "High standard site; lge pitches; clean san facs; superb pools; excel free club for children; some pitches flood in v heavy rain; wonderful flowers." ♦ 12 May-5 Sep. € 45.00 ABS - A28 2009*

See advertisement

MARENNES *7B1* (10.5km SE Rural) *45.77324, -0.96301* **Camping Le Valerick, La Mauvinière, 17600 St Sornin [tel/fax 05 46 85 15 95; camplevalerick@aol.com; www.marennes.fr]** Fr Marennes take D728 sp Saintes for 10km; L to St Sornin; site sp in vill. Fr Saintes D728 W for 26km; take 2nd R turn R in vill D118, site on L sp La Gripperie. Sm, mkd pitch, pt sl, pt shd; wc; chem disp (wc); shwrs inc; el pnts (4-6A) €3-€3.50 (poss rev pol); lndtte; shop; rest; snacks; bar; BBQ; playgrnd; sand beach 18km; entmnt; dogs €1.40; adv bkg; CCI. "Nice, friendly site; gd san facs; plenty of bird life - herons, storks etc; poss mosquito problem." 1 Apr-30 Sep. € 12.50 2008*

MARENNES *7B1* (2km SW Coastal) **Camping La Ferme de la Prée, 17320 Marennes [05 46 85 03 61]** Fr Saintes on D123 & Marennes N by-pass, foll sps for Ile d'Oléron to concrete water tower. In 150m turn L on C15 (sp Marennes-Plage 2km). Site on L in 1km. Sm, mkd pitch, pt shd; wc (some cont); shwrs €0.80; el pnts (6A) inc; gas; lndry rm; shops 2.5km, supmkt 4km; tradsmn; BBQ; sand beach 500m; few statics; adv bkg; quiet; CCI. "Gd farm site; friendly & helpful owners." 15 Jun-15 Sep. € 6.70 2008*

MARENNES *7B1* (2km NW Coastal) *45.83139, -1.15092* **Camp Municipal La Giroflée, 17560 Bourcefranc-le-Chapus [05 46 85 06 43 or 05 46 85 02 02 (Mairie); fax 05 46 85 48 58; camping-lagiroflee-bourcefranc@mairie17.com]** Fr Saintes on D728/D26 to Boucefranc, turn L at traff lts. Site on L after 1km (after sailing school) opp beach. Med, pt shd; wc (few cont); shwrs €0.80; el pnts (8A) €2.90; lndry rm; shops 2km; snacks; playgrnd; beach adj; poss cr; quiet. 1 May-30 Sep. € 7.20 2008*

MAREUIL *7B2* (5km N Rural) *45.49504, 0.44860* **FFCC Camping Les Graulges, Le Bourg, 24340 Les Graulges [tel/fax 05 53 60 74 73; info@lesgraulges.com; www.lesgraulges.com]** Fr D939 at Mareuil turn L onto D708 & foll sp to Les Graulges in 5km. Sm, mkd pitch, pt sl, terr, pt shd; wc; chem disp (wc); baby facs; shwrs inc; el pnts (6A) €3.50; lndtte; tradsmn; rest; snacks; bar; BBQ; playgrnd; pool; lake fishing; some statics; dogs €2; phone 300m; poss cr; Eng spkn; adv bkg; quiet; red 7+ days. "Tranquil site in forested area; ideal touring base; friendly Dutch owners; excel rest." ♦ 1 Apr-15 Sep. € 16.25 2009*

MAREUIL *7B2* (4km SE Rural) *45.44481, 0.50474* **Camping L'Etang Bleu, 24340 Vieux-Mareuil [05 53 60 92 70; fax 05 53 56 66 66; marc@letangbleu.com; www.letangbleu.com]** On D939 Angoulême-Périgueux rd, after 5km turn L cent of Vieux-Mareuil onto D93, foll camping sp to site in 2km. Narr app thro vill. Lge, hdg/mkd pitch, pt shd; wc; chem disp; mv service pnt; baby facs; fam bthrm; shwrs inc; el pnts (10A) €4.25 (poss rev pol); gas; lndtte; shop; tradsmn; rest; snacks; bar; BBQ; playgrnd; pool; paddling pool; lake fishing 500m; TV; entmnt; 10% statics; dogs €3; adv bkg; ccard acc; red low ssn; CCI. "Pleasant site in unspoilt countryside; lge pitches, but narr site rds access diff lge o'fits without mover; friendly British owners; gd san facs, ltd low ssn; gd walking/cycling area; excel." ♦ 19 Mar-20 Oct. € 18.25 2009*

France

MAREUIL *7B2* (6km SE Rural) *45.42465, 0.53012* **Camping La Charrue, Les Chambarrières, 24340 Vieux-Mareuil [tel/fax 05 53 56 65 59; info@la-charruefrance.com; www.la-charruefrance.com]** SE fr Angoulême on D939 sp Périgueux to Mareuil. Fr Mareuil stay on D939 twds Brantôme, thro Vieux-Mareuil then in 2km site immed on L after passing a lge lay-by on R with white stone chippings. Awkward turn. Sm, mkd pitch, pt shd; wc; chem disp; shwrs inc; el pnts (4A) €3; gas 3km; Indtte; shop 2km; tradsmn; rest & bar 500m; snacks; BBQ; playgrnd; pool; sand beach, lakes & watersports nr; fishing 3km; cycle hire; golf nr; dogs (low ssn only); adv bkg (full payment req); some rd noise; red long stay/low ssn; CCI. "CL-type site in Regional Park; friendly, helpful British owners; immac facs; gd touring base for beautiful area; B&B & gites avail; excel." 1 May-31 Oct. € 13.00 2009*

MAREUIL *7B2* (500m SW Rural) *45.44680, 0.45153* **Camp Municipal Vieux Moulin, Rue des Martyrs/Rue Arnaud de Mareuil; 24340 Mareuil [05 53 60 91 20 (Mairie) or 05 53 60 99 80; fax 05 53 60 51 72; mariemareuil@wanadoo.fr]** Fr town cent take D708 (sp Ribérac); after 300m turn L on D99 (sp 'La Tour Blanche'); after 100m turn L opp lge school, site 100m ahead. Well sp all dirs. Sm, mkd pitch, shd; wc; shwrs; el pnts (6A) €1.70; shop 500m; rest, snacks, bar 400m; playgrnd; rv 1km; dogs €0.50; adv bkg; quiet. "Clean, tidy site; friendly warden; ltd, well-kept facs; lovely walk by stream to vill; interesting chateau; vg." ♦ 1 Jun-30 Sep. € 8.00 2009*

MARIGNY see Doucier *6H2*

MARNAY (HAUTE SAONE) *6G2* (500m SE Urban) *47.28975, 5.77628* **Camp Municipal Vert Lagon, Route de Besançon, 70150 Marnay [03 84 31 71 41 or 03 84 31 73 16; sidmarnay@wanadoo.fr; www.camping-vertlagon.com]** Fr N stay on D67 Marnay by-pass; ignore old camping sp into town. Proceed to S of town on by-pass then turn L at junc. Bef bdge in 1km take gravel rd on S side, round under bdge to site (app thro town fr N v narr). Med, some hdg/mkd pitch, pt shd; wc; chem disp; mv service pnt; baby facs; shwrs inc; el pnts (10A) €4; Indtte; shops & rest 500m; snacks (high ssn); BBQ; playgrnd; fishing; canoeing; 40% statics; dogs €1; poss cr; adv bkg; quiet; ccard acc; red low ssn; CCI. "Pleasant, popular, family site by Rv Ognon; gd san facs; lake adj; tree-top walks; gd." 1 May-30 Sep. € 13.40 2009*

MARNAY (SAONE ET LOIRE) see Chalon sur Saône *6H1*

MARNE LA VALLEE see Meaux *3D3*

MARQUAY see Eyzies de Tayac, Les *7C3*

MARQUION *3B4* (2km N Rural) *50.22280, 3.10863* **FFCC Camping de l'Epinette, 7 Rue du Calvaire, 62860 Sauchy-Lestrée [03 21 59 50 13; epinette62@wanadoo.com; www.lepinette62.com]** Fr A26 exit junc 8 onto D939 to Marquion. On ent Marquion turn R at x-rds to Sauchy-Lestrée; on ent vill turn R at 1st T-junc & site on L in 100m. Fr Cambrai take D939 twd Arras, then as above. Sm, pt sl, pt shd; wc (own san rec); chem disp; shwrs €1.50; el pnts (4-6A) €2.50-3 (poss rev pol); gas; Indtte; shops 3km; playgrnd; games area; many statics; dogs free; adv bkg; quiet but some military aircraft noise; ccard not acc; CCI. "Pretty, well-kept site; helpful owner; sm CL-type area for tourers; simple but adequate facs, ltd low ssn; levelling blocks ess for m'vans; conv Calais/Dunkerque; WW1 cemetary nr; popular NH." 1 Apr-31 Oct. € 9.00 2009*

MARQUISE *3A3* (4km S Rural) *50.78316, 1.67035* **FFCC Camping L'Escale, 62250 Wacquinghen [tel/fax 03 21 32 00 69; camp-escale@wanadoo.fr; www.escale-camping.com]** Fr A16 S fr Calais exit junc 34. Fr A16 N fr Boulogne exit junc 33. Foll sp. Lge, pt shd; wc (cont); chem disp; mv service pnt; shwrs €1; el pnts (4A) €3.20 (poss rev pol); gas; Indtte; shop; supmkt 3km; rest; snacks; bar; playgrnd; entmnt; 90% statics; dogs; poss cr; quiet; ccard acc. "Open 24 hrs; conv NH nr ferries, Channel tunnel & WW2 coastal defences; o'fits staying 1 night pitch on meadow at front of site for ease of exit (but some noise fr m'way); m'van 'aire' open all yr; pleasant site; vg." ♦ 15 Mar-15 Oct. € 16.00 2009*

MARSAC EN LIVRADOIS see Ambert *9B1*

MARSANNE *9D2* (2.5km NE Rural) *44.64870, 4.87930* **Camping Les Bastets, Quartier Les Bastets, 26740 Marsanne [04 75 90 35 03; fax 04 75 90 35 05; contact@campinglesbastets.com; www.campinglesbastets.com]** Exit A7 junc 17 onto N7; pass thro Les Tourettes & La Coucourde to Marsanne. In La Coucourde turn L onto D74 & in 6km L onto D105 thro Marsanne. Site sp fr D105. App fr N on D57 not rec. Med, hdg/mkd pitch, sl, terr, pt shd; wc; chem disp; mv service pnt; baby facs; fam bthrm; shwrs inc; el pnts (10A) €4; Indtte; shop; tradsmn; rest; snacks; bar; BBQ; playgrnd; pool; archery; games area; games rm; golf 10km; entmnt; TV rm; 10% statics; dogs €4; Eng spkn; adv bkg; quiet; red low ssn. "Tractor tow to pitches - not rec to attempt under own steam; pleasant site with gd views; beautiful area; vg." ♦ 1 Apr-15 Oct. € 22.00 (CChq acc) 2009*

MARSEILLAN PLAGE *10F1* (Coastal/Urban) *43.31365, 3.54779* **Camping Beauregard-Est, Chemin de l'Airette, 34340 Marseillan-Plage [04 67 77 15 45; fax 04 67 01 21 78; campingbeauregardest@wanadoo.fr; www.camping-beauregard-est.com]** On N112 Agde-Sète rd, turn S at rndabt to Marseillan-Plage onto D51 & foll camping sp thro town. Site immed on leaving town cent. Lge, hdg pitch, pt shd; wc; chem disp; mv service pnt; baby facs; shwrs inc; el pnts (6A) inc; Indtte; shop, rest & bar adj; rest-bar high ssn; playgrnd; sand beach adj; entmnt; TV; 5% statics; Eng spkn; adv bkg; poss cr; quiet; red low ssn. "Superb sand beach sheltered by dunes." ♦ 1 Apr-30 Sep. € 29.00 (CChq acc) 2008*

France

MARSEILLAN PLAGE *10F1* (1km NE Coastal) *43.32158, 3.55932* **Camping Le Paradou, 2 Impasse Ronsard, 34340 Marseillan-Plage [04 67 21 90 10; info.paradou@wanadoo.fr; www.paradou.com]** Exit A9 junc 34 or 35 onto N113/N312 dir Agde & Sète. Fr Agde foll sp Sète to Marseillan-Plage. Site well sp on N112. Med, hdg pitch, pt shd; htd wc; chem disp; baby facs; shwrs inc; el pnts (10A) €3.20; gas; Indtte; shop 1km; tradsmn; rest, bar 1km; snacks; playgrnd; dir access sand beach adj; 5% statics; dogs; phone; bus 1km; poss cr; CCI. "Gd area for cycling; ltd pitches avail for long o'fits." ♦ 26 Mar-29 Oct. € 21.00 2006*

MARSEILLAN PLAGE *10F1* (500m SW Coastal) *43.30648, 3.53924* **Camping Europ 2000, 960 Ave des Campings, 34340 Marseillan-Plage [tel/fax 04 67 21 92 85; contact@camping-europ2000.com; www.camping-europ2000.com]** Fr cent of Marseillan-Plage S on coast rd D51e, site on L. Med, hdg/mkd pitch, hdstg, pt shd; wc; chem disp; mv service pnt; shwrs inc; el pnts (10A) €3.50; gas; Indtte; shop & 500m; tradsmn; snacks; BBQ; playgrnd; sand beach adj; games area; 10% statics; dogs €2; phone; poss cr; Eng spkn; adv bkg; quiet; red low ssn CCI. "Easy access to beach; friendly, helpful owner; gd family-run site." ♦ 1 Apr-20 Oct. € 28.00 2009*

MARSEILLAN PLAGE *10F1* (500m SW Coastal) *43.31036, 3.54601* **Camping La Plage, 69 Chemin du Pairollet, 34340 Marseillan-Plage [04 67 21 92 54; fax 04 67 01 63 57; info@laplage-camping.net; www.laplage-camping.net]** On N112 Agde to Sète, turn S at rndabt dir Marseillan-Plage. Foll sp for site at 2nd rndabt. Site on L in 150m. Med, hdg pitch, pt shd; wc; chem disp; mv service pnt; shwrs inc; child/baby facs; el pnts (10A) inc; gas; Indtte; rest; snacks; bar; BBQ; playgrnd; sand beach adj; watersports; games area; entmnt; TV; 1% statics; dogs €3; phone; extra for beachfront pitches; poss cr; Eng spkn; adv bkg; quiet; ccard acc, CCI. "Excel, popular, family-run site; superb beach; sm pitches; gd, friendly atmosphere." ♦ 15 Mar-31 Oct. € 30.00 2008*

MARSEILLAN PLAGE *10F1* (1km SW Coastal) *43.31275, 3.54638* **Camping La Créole, 74 Ave des Campings, 34340 Marseillan-Plage [04 67 21 92 69; fax 04 67 26 58 16; campinglacreole@wanadoo.fr; www.campinglacreole.com]** Fr Agde-Sète rd N112, turn S at rndabt onto D51 & foll sp thro town. Narr ent easily missed among lger sites. Med, hdg/mkd pitch, hdstg, pt shd; wc; chem disp; mv service pnt; baby facs; shwrs inc; el pnts (6A) €2.85; Indtte; shop; rest, snacks, bar adj; playgrnd; sand beach adj; tennis 1km; games area; entmnt; 10% statics; dogs €3; phone; adv bkg; quiet; red long stay; CCI. "Dir access to excel beach; naturist beach 600m; well-maintained, quiet site." ♦ 1 Apr-15 Oct. € 25.75 2007*

MARSEILLAN PLAGE *10F1* (1km SW Coastal) *43.30586, 3.53788* **Camping Les Sirènes, 1078 Ave des Campings, 34340 Marseillan-Plage [04 67 21 92 83]** On N112 Agde-Sète rd, turn S onto D51 at rndabt, & foll sps in town. Site at end of rd thro lge area of camp sites. V lge, hdg/mkd pitch, hdstg, pt shd; wc; chem disp; shwrs inc; el pnts (10A) inc; gas 300m; Indtte; shop 100m; tradsmn; playgrnd; pool complex; waterslides; sand beach adj; watersports; tennis 1km; cycle hire; horseriding; games area; games rm; entmnt; sat TV; no statics; dogs €2.80; Eng spkn; no adv bkg; quiet; red low ssn; CCI. "Vg site in excel location; gd facs; seaside town nr with all facs; excel beach." ♦
15 May-15 Sep. € 40.00 2009*

See advertisement

MARSEILLAN PLAGE *10F1* (1.5km SW Coastal) *43.30905, 3.54263* **Yelloh! Village La Nouvelle Floride, 262 Ave des Campings, 34340 Marseillan-Plage [04 67 21 94 49; fax 04 67 21 81 05; info@yellohvillage-mediterranees.com; www.yellohvillage-mediterranees.com]** Exit A9 sp Agde/Bessan junc 34 or 35 onto N312/N112 & foll sps to site. Turn R at traff lts in Marseillan-Plage, site 1.5km. Lge, shd; htd wc; mv service pnt; shwrs inc; baby facs; el pnts (6A) inc; gas; Indtte; supmkt; rest; snacks; bar; BBQ; playgrnd; htd pool; paddling pool; waterslide; sand beach adj; games area; horseriding; entmnt; 20% statics; dogs €4; adv bkg; quiet; red long stay/low ssn; ccard acc; CCI. "Excel family site." ♦ 25 Apr-2 Sep. € 44.00 (3 persons) 2007*

MARSEILLAN PLAGE *10F1* (1.5km SW Coastal) *43.31031, 3.54305* **Yelloh! Village Le Charlemagne, Ave des Campings, 34340 Marseillan-Plage [04 67 21 92 49; fax 04 67 21 86 11; info@yellohvillage-mediterranees.com; www.yellohvillage-mediterranees.com]** In Marseillan-Plage, off N112 Sète-Agde rd, take D51e SW to site. Lge, hdg/mkd pitch, shd; wc; chem disp; mv service pnt; baby facs; shwrs inc; el pnts (6A) inc; Indtte; shop; rest; snacks; bar; playgrnd; 3 htd pools; waterslide; sand beach 200m; games area; golf 5km; internet; entmnt; 50% statics; dogs €4; phone; poss cr; Eng spkn; adv bkg; red low ssn for 14+ days; quiet; ccard acc. "Site also owns Nouvelle Floride opp on beach of similar standard; lge pitches; lots of shops, rests nrby; many tour ops; poss mosquitoes; excel." ♦ 3 Apr-3 Oct. € 44.00 (3 persons) 2008*

MARTEL *7C3* (5km SE Rural) *44.88538, 1.59929* **Camping du Port, 46600 Creysse [05 65 32 20 82 or 05 65 32 27 59; fax 05 65 38 78 21; contact@campingduport.com; www.campingduport.com]** Fr Souillac take D803 to Martel. On ent Martel turn R on D23 on rd to Creysee. Alt app on D840 (N140) S fr Martel to Gluges not rec. Narr, twisty rd fr Gluges to site. Med, pt sl, pt shd by rv; wc (some cont); shwrs inc; el pnts (6A) inc; Indtte; shops in Martel; rest in Creysse; playgrnd; pool; canoe & cycle hire; dogs €1.50; adv bkg; quiet. "Lovely grounds; gd access to rv; friendly; v peaceful low ssn; ltd facs low ssn; Creysse beautiful vill." 1 May-20 Sep. € 16.30 2009*

MARTEL *7C3* (500m NW Rural) *44.93852, 1.60805* **Camp Municipal de la Callopie, Ave de Turenne, 46600 Martel [05 65 37 30 03 (Mairie); fax 05 65 37 37 27; mairiedemartel@wanadoo.fr]** On NW o'skts of vill of Martel on D23, 100m fr rndabt on L, ent opp Auberge des 7 Tours. Sm, shd; wc; shwrs inc; el pnts (10A) €1.80; shops, rest, bar 200m; rv 5km; no statics; poss cr; no adv bkg; rd noise. "Attractive, well-kept site in beautiful medieval vill; gd, clean, modern facs; warden calls pm or pay at Mairie; no twin-axles." 1 May-30 Sep. € 5.80 2008*

MARTIGNE FERCHAUD *2F4* (500m NE Rural) *47.83354, -1.31636* **Camp Municipal Le Bois Feuillet, Rue de la Vieille-Chaussée, 35640 Martigné-Ferchaud [02 99 47 84 38; fax 02 99 47 84 65; mairie-de-martigne-ferchaud@wanadoo.fr]** After ent Martigné-Ferchaud on E of D178; fr N cross level x-ing, site on L in 400m; fr S, thro vill, site on R after bend at bottom of hill. Site sp fr town cent. Med, terr, unshd; wc; chem disp; shwrs inc; el pnts (16A) €2; Indtte; shop adj; rest, snacks, bar 1km; BBQ; playgrnd; lake sw with sm shgl beach; fishing & boating; sports area; tennis; quiet; CCI. "Attractive, lakeside site; Jun & Sep barrier opened at 0900 & 1900 - foll instructions in Eng on office door or report to town hall to gain ent (parking diff); lge pitches; gd san facs; 2nd week Aug excel water spectacular." ♦ 1 Jun-30 Sep. € 8.50 2007*

MARTRAGNY see Bayeux *3D1*

MARTRES DE VEYRE, LES see Clermont Ferrand *9B1*

⊞ **MARTRES TOLOSANE** *8F3* (2km E Rural) *43.19684, 1.06721* **Camp Municipal Le Plantaurel, Les Pesquès, 31220 Palaminy [05 61 97 03 71; fax 05 61 90 62 04]** Exit A64 at junc 23 onto D6 to Cazères, cross rv bdge. Turn W (R) on D62, foll rv for 1.5km. Site well sp, Lge, mkd pitch, shd; htd wc; chem disp; mv service pnt; shwrs inc; el pnts (10A); gas; Indtte; shop, rest 2km; snacks; playgrnd; entmnt; TV; 40% statics; phone; dir access to rv; dogs; adv bkg; red long stay; CCI." (4 persons) 2008*

MARTRES TOLOSANE *8F3* (1.5km S Rural) *43.19060, 1.01840* **Camping Le Moulin, 31220 Martres-Tolosane [05 61 98 86 40; fax 05 61 98 66 90; info@campinglemoulin.com; www.campinglemoulin.com]** Exit A64 junc 22 (fr N or S) & foll camping sps. Site sp adj Rv Garonne. Med, pt sl, pt shd; htd wc (some cont); baby facs; shwrs inc; el pnts (6-10A) €3.50-5; Indtte; shops 1.5km; snacks; bar; playgrnd; htd pool; paddling pool; rv fishing adj; tennis; cycle hire; games area; games rm; entmnt; TV; 20% statics; dogs €2; adv bkg rec high ssn; quiet; red long stay; red low ssn; ccard acc; CCI. "Excel, well-maintained site; friendly welcome; gd, modern san facs; gd touring base for Spain, Lourdes, etc." 23 Mar-30 Sep. € 22.00 2008*

MARTRES TOLOSANE *8F3* (7km SW Rural) *43.13447, 0.93240* **Camp Municipal, 31360 St Martory [05 61 90 44 93 or 05 61 90 22 24; cccsm@wanadoo.fr]** Leave A64 at junc 20. Turn N onto D117 twd St Martory. In 1km turn L (sp) soon after Gendarmerie. Sm, hdg pitch, pt shd; htd wc (some cont); chem disp (wc); shwrs inc; el pnts inc; dogs €1.50; quiet; CCI. ♦ 15 Jun-15 Sep. € 9.90 2006*

MARVAL *7B3* (3.5km N Rural) *45.65445, 0.78913* **Camping La Nozillière, L'Age de Milhaguet, 87440 Marval [05 55 78 25 60; adriaan.von-bekkum@wanadoo.fr; www.nozilliere.nl]** Fr Marval N on D67 sp Milhaguet; take D73 to St Barthélemy, turn L in 500m, site sp. Sm, pt sl, pt shd; wc; chem disp; shwrs inc; el pnts (6A) inc; gas 3.5km; shop 3.5km, rest; snacks, bar 3.5km; tradsmn; BBQ; playgrnd; pool; lake sw 3km; dogs; Eng spkn; adv bkg; quiet; ccard acc; CCI. "Excel." ♦ 1 May-31 Oct. € 18.00 2006*

MARVEJOLS *9D1* (1km NE Rural) *44.55077, 3.30440* **Camping Village Le Coulagnet, Quartier de l'Empery, 48100 Marvejols [04 66 32 03 69]** Exit A75 junc 38 onto D900 & N9. Foll E ring rd onto D999, cont over rv & foll sp to site; no R turn into site, cont 500m to Aire de Retournement, & turn L into site. Foll sp 'VVF', camping part of same complex. Sm, hdg pitch, pt shd; wc (mainly cont); shwrs inc; el pnts (5A) €3 (poss rev pol); Indtte (inc dryer); shop & 1km; BBQ (sep area); playgrnd; pool; rv adj; tennis; games area; games rm; TV rm; 50% statics; no dogs; phone; Eng spkn; adv bkg; quiet; ccard acc. "Sep area for tourers; san facs immac; interesting walled town; excel." ♦ 19 Jun-10 Sep. € 13.90 2009*

MARVILLE *5C1* (1km N Rural) *49.46294, 5.45859* **Camp Syndicat Mixte de la Vallée de l'Othain, 55600 Marville [03 29 88 19 06 or 03 29 88 15 15; fax 03 29 88 14 60; marville.accueil@wanadoo.fr]** Sp on D643 on app Marville fr both dirs. Med, hdg pitch, pt shd; wc (some cont); shwrs; el pnts (3A); Indtte; sm shop; snacks; rest; playgrnd; htd covrd pool adj; entmnt; 20% statics; quiet; CCI. "Easy access adj lake; gd NH." 1 Feb-30 Nov. 2008*

⊞ **MASEVAUX** *6F3* (N Urban) *47.77820, 6.99090* **Camping Masevaux, 3 Rue du Stade, 68290 Masevaux [tel/fax 03 89 82 42 29; contact@camping-masevaux.com; www.camping-masevaux.com]** Fr N83 Colmar-Belfort rd take N466 W to Masevaux; site sp. NB D14 fr Thann to Masevaux narr & steep - not suitable c'vans. Med, mkd pitch, pt shd; htd wc; chem disp; mv service pnt; baby facs; shwrs inc; el pnts (3-6A) €3.20-3.80; Indtte; shop 1km; tradsmn; snacks; bar; playgrnd; htd pool & sports complex adj; entmnt; internet; TV rm; 40% statics; dogs €0.50; no twin-axles; poss cr; Eng spkn; adv bkg; quiet; some rd noise; ccard acc; red long stay; CCI. "Pleasant walks; interesting town - annual staging of Passion Play; helpful, friendly owners; excel facs; gd cycle rtes; excel." ♦ € 10.40 2008*

MASSAT *8G3* (4km W Rural) *42.89214, 1.31251* **Aire Naturelle L'Azaigouat (Gouaze), Route du Col de Saraillé, 09320 Biert [tel/fax 05 61 96 95 03; camping.azaigouat@club-internet.fr; www.azaigouat.com]** Take D618 S fr St Girons dir Massat. At Biert turn R onto D118 dir Oust & Col de Saraille, site sp. Sm, pt sl, pt shd; wc; shwrs inc; el pnts (6-10A) €2.50; Indry rm; shop, rest, snacks 800m; BBQ; games area; games rm; horseriding 3km; fishing nr; dogs; adv bkg; quiet; CCI. "Excel CL-type site beside stream; friendly owners; gd wildlife walks." 15 Jun-15 Sep. € 10.00 2007*

MASSERET *7B3* (9km N Rural) *45.61142, 1.50110* **Camping de Montréal, Rue du Petit Moulin, 87380 St Germain-les-Belles [05 55 71 86 20; fax 05 55 71 00 83; contact@campingdemontreal.com; www.campingdemontreal.com]** S on N20/A20 fr Limoges, turn L onto D7bis, junc 42. Vill is 4.5km. Site sp in vill. Care needed due narr rds. Med, hdg/mkd pitch, terr, pt shd; htd wc; chem disp; mv service pnt; shwrs inc; el pnts (10A) €3; Indtte; sm shop 1km; tradmn; rest, snacks, bar 250m; BBQ; playgrnd; lake sw adj; fishing; watersports; tennis; cycle hire 1km; wifi; entmnt; 12% statics; dogs €1.50; phone; poss cr; Eng spkn; adv bkg; quiet; ccard acc; red low ssn; CCI. "Peaceful site in attractive setting; excel san facs." ♦ 1 Apr-31 Oct. € 13.00 2008*

MASSERET *7B3* (5km E Rural) *45.53880, 1.57790* **Camping Plan l'Eau, Complexe Touristique Bourg, 19510 Lamongerie [05 55 73 44 57; fax 05 55 73 49 69]** Exit A20 at junc 43 sp Masseret & foll sp Lamongerie. At rndabt turn R, site sp. Site ent bet 2 lge stone pillars. Med, sl, shd; wc; chem disp; shwrs; el pnts (5A) €2.30 (poss long lead req some pitches); Indtte; sm shop; snacks; playgrnd; lake beach & sw; fishing; tennis; golf nrby; fitness course thro woods & round lake; TV; poss cr; quiet. "V pleasant situation; clean facs; gd NH & longer." ♦ 1 Apr-30 Sep. € 10.30 2009*

MASSEUBE *8F3* (12km NE Rural) *43.50199, 0.68585* **Camping Domaine Naturiste du Moulin de Faget (Naturist), Au Grange, 32450 Faget-Abbatial [05 62 65 49 09; fax 05 62 66 29 21; info@moulin-faget.com; www.moulin-faget.com]** Fr Masseube D929 for 7 km; in Seissan R on D104 sp Faget-Abbatial; in 8.5km R at T-junc onto D40; site sp on L in 300m; at top of track after 500m. Sm, pt sl, unshd; wc; chem disp (wc); shwrs inc; el pnts (6A) €3.50; Indtte; tradsmn; rest; bar; lake adj; games area; cycle hire; 10% statics; no dogs; B & B avail all yr; Eng spkn; adv bkg; quiet; CCI. "Extremely quiet & secluded site in beautiful area; no play facilities for children; friendly, helpful Dutch owners; modern san facs; gd walking, cycling; attractive vill nrby; excel." ♦ 1 May-1 Oct. € 22.00 2009*

MASSIAC *9C1* (7km N Rural) *45.31217, 3.17278* **Camp Municipal La Bessière, 43450 Blesle [04 71 76 25 82; fax 04 71 76 25 42; mairie.de.blesle@wanadoo.fr; http://blesle-camping.ifrance.com/]** Fr Massiac take D909 N. In 5km at Babory turn L onto D8. In 2km turn L immed after x-ing rv bdge. Site sp. Sm, some hdg/mkd pitch, terr, pt shd; wc (some cont); chem disp (wc); mv service pnt; shwrs inc; el pnts (10A) €2.30; Indry rm; BBQ; playgrnd; tennis; wifi; 30% statics; dogs €1; phone 200m; poss cr; quiet; red long stay; CCI. "Pretty vill; pleasant, clean site; helpful, friendly warden; gd touring base; vg." ♦ 4 Apr-4 Oct. € 8.30 2009*

MASSIAC *9C1* (800m SW Rural) *45.24703, 3.18765* **Camping de l'Allagnon, Ave de Courcelles, 15500 Massiac [tel/fax 04 71 23 03 93]** Exit A75 at Massiac onto N122 or N122e; cont on N122 dir Murat; site sp on L on rvside 800m along Ave de Courcelles (part of N122). Med, mkd pitch, shd; wc; shwrs; el pnts (6-10A) €2.20; gas; Indtte; shops adj; playgrnd; pool adj; fishing; tennis; wifi; dogs €0.60; poss cr; ccard acc; CCI. "Nice, simple, popular site; sh walk to town cent; conv A75; vg." ♦ 1 May-31 Oct. € 7.70 2009*

MASSIAC *9C1* (6km SW Rural) *45.23353, 3.13432* **Camp Municipal, Pré Mongeal, 15500 Molompize [04 71 73 62 90 or 04 71 73 60 06; fax 04 71 73 60 24; mairie.molompize@wanadoo.fr]** Fr N exit A75 junc 23 onto N122 dir Aurillac; site on L just bef Molompize. Or fr S exit A75 junc 24 onto N122e to Massiac; then join N122 dir Aurillac; then as bef. Med, pt shd; wc; chem disp (wc); shwrs inc; el pnts (10A); Indry rm; shops 500m; playgrnd; 6% statics; quiet; CCI. "Rvside site behind stadium; tennis courts; friendly warden; super vill; gd." ♦ 15 Jun-15 Sep. € 5.00 2008*

MATEMALE *8G4* (1.7km SW Rural) *42.58209, 2.10563* **Camping Le Lac, Forêt de la Matte, 66210 Matemale [04 68 30 94 49; fax 04 68 04 35 16; www.camping-lac-matemale.com]** N on D118 fr Mont Louis; do not turn into Matemale, turn L on D52 sp Les Angles; site on L in 500m. Sm, pt sl, pt shd; htd wc; mv service pnt; baby facs; shwrs; el pnts (3-6A) €2.60-4.20; Indtte; tradsmn; snacks; bar; BBQ; lake 200m; fishing; watersports; games area; games rm; dogs €1; open w/end & school hols rest of yr; quiet. "Friendly site amid pine trees." ♦ 1 Jun-30 Sep. € 15.00 2008*

France

MATHA *7B2* (9km NE Rural) *45.93342, -0.24284* **Camping La Forge, 10B Rue de la Forge, 17160 Le Gicq [tel/fax 05 46 32 48 42 or 01733 252089 (UK); mail@la-forge-holidays.com; www.la-forge-holidays.com]** Fr Matha take D131 thro Les Touches-de-Périgny. In 5km turn R at x-rds sp Le Gicq & foll sp to site. Sm, hdg pitch, pt shd; wc; chem disp; mv service pnt; shwrs inc; el pnts (10A) €3; gas 5km; lndtte; tradsmn; shop, rest, snacks, bar 5km; BBQ; htd pool; lake sw 10km; no dogs; phone; adv bkg; quiet. "Peaceful CL-type site on farm; helpful British owners; vg touring base Cognac, La Rochelle & coast; gd cycling area." ♦ 19 May-29 Sep. € 24.00 2007*

MATHA *7B2* (5km S Rural) *45.83584, -0.30747* **Camping Le Relais de l'Etang, Route de Matha, La Vernïouze, 17160 Thors [05 46 58 26 81 or 05 46 58 75 36; paysmatha@cc-matha.fr]** Fr Matha take D121 S twd Cognac. Site on L in 5km. Sm, hdg/mkd pitch, pt shd; wc (some cont); chem disp; shwrs inc; el pnts (10A) inc; rest; snacks; bar; playgrnd; lake sw; adv bkg; quiet; CCI. "Gd for visiting Cognac." 1 Jun-30 Sep. € 9.00 2006*

MATHES, LES *7B1* (2.5km N Rural) *45.72333, -1.17451* **FFCC Camping La Palombière, 1551 Route de la Fouasse, 17570 Les Mathes [05 46 22 69 25; fax 05 46 22 44 58; camping.lapalombiere@wanadoo.fr; www.camping-lapalombiere.com]** Fr La Tremblade bypass foll sp Dirée on D268; site on R in 5km just past Luna Park. Med, pt shd; htd wc; chem disp; mv service pnt; baby facs; fam bthrm; shwrs inc; el pnts (6A) €4.50; gas; lndtte (inc dryer); ice; shop; tradsmn; rest; snacks; bar; BBQ; playgrnd; pool; sand beach 5km; games area; 10% statics; dogs €3; phone; bus; Eng spkn; quiet; ccard not acc; red low ssn; CCI. "Spacious, tranquil site under oaks & pines; lge pitches; palatial san facs high ssn, ltd low ssn; superb beaches 5km (some naturist); excel." ♦ 1 Apr-31 Oct. € 22.00 2009*

MATHES, LES *7B1* (3.5km N Rural) *45.72980, -1.17929* **Camping L'Orée du Bois, 225 Route de la Bouverie, La Fouasse, 17570 Les Mathes [05 46 22 42 43; fax 05 46 22 54 76; info@camping-oree-du-bois.fr; www.camping-oree-du-bois.fr]** Fr A10 to Saintes, then dir Royan. Fr Royan take D25 thro St Palais & La Palmyre twd Phare de la Coubre. Cont 4km past Phare & turn R on D268 to La Fouasse. Site on R in 4km. Lge, hdg/mkd pitch, hdstg, pt shd; wc (some cont); 40 pitches with own san; chem disp; baby facs; shwrs inc; el pnts (6A) inc; gas; lndtte; shop; rest; snacks; bar; BBQ; playgrnd; 3 htd pools; waterslide; sand beach 4km; tennis; cycle hire; golf 20km; games area; games rm; entmnt/child ent Jul & Aug; internet; sat TV rm; 50% statics; dogs €3.60; Eng spkn; adv bkg rec high ssn; quiet; ccard acc; red low ssn/CCI. "Well-kept site in pine wood; local beaches ideal for sw & surfing; helpful staff; excel pool area; zoo in La Palmyre worth visit; min stay 7 days high ssn; excel." ♦ 1 May-12 Sep. € 38.00 (CChq acc) 2008*

MATHES, LES *7B1* (4km SW Coastal) *45.69805, -1.19960* **Camping Bonne Anse Plage, 17570 La Palmyre [05 46 22 40 90; fax 05 46 22 42 30; bonneanseplage@siblu.fr; www.siblu.fr/bonneanse]** N fr Royan on D25 thro St Palais-sur-Mer to La Palmyre, after zoo at rndbt site sp; site on L after x-rds D25 & D141 in 600m. Lge, mkd pitch, terr, pt sl, shd; wc; chem disp; mv service pnt; shwrs inc; el pnts (6A) €6.80; gas; lndtte; shops; rest; snacks; bar; playgrnd; htd pool complex; paddling pool; waterslides; sand beach 600m; games area; cycle hire; internet; entmnt; sat TV; many tour ops statics; no dogs; poss cr; Eng spkn; some rd noise; ccard acc; CCI. "Superb pool complex; friendly, family site; clean san facs; cycle path." ♦ 1 May-19 Sep. € 40.00 (3 persons) 2008*

MATHES, LES *7B1* (6km SW Coastal) *45.6974, -1.2286* **Camping Parc de la Côte Sauvage, Phare de la Coubre, 17570 La Palmyre [05 46 22 40 18 or 05 49 35 83 60; contact@parc-cote-sauvage.com; www.parc-cote-sauvage.com]** D25 fr Royan, thro La Palmyre, at rndabt foll sp 'Phare de la Coubre'. Turn L at junc sp as bef, turn L on R-hand bend. Lge, mkd pitch, pt terr, pt shd; wc (some cont); chem disp; mv service pnt; baby facs; shwrs inc; el pnts (6-10A) €5; gas; lndtte; shop; rest/bar adj; snacks; playgrnd; pool complex; sand beach 500m - can be v windy; tennis; cycle hire adj; boating; surf school; entmnt; internet; TV; 25% statics; dogs €3 (not acc Jul/Aug); poss v cr (NH area); Eng spkn; no adv bkg; ccard acc; red low ssn; CCI. "Lge pitches." ♦ 1 May-15 Sep. € 34.00 2008*

MATHES, LES *7B1* (2km W Rural) *45.72826, -1.17593* **Camping La Pinède, La Palmyre, 17570 Les Mathes [05 46 22 45 13; fax 05 46 22 50 21; contact@campinglapinede.com; www.campinglapinede.com]** Fr La Tremblade, take D141 twd Les Mathes. Turn W after vill onto D141 E twd La Fouasse, foll sp. Site in 2km. Lge, mkd pitch, pt shd; wc; chem disp; shwrs inc; el pnts (5A) €6.90; lndtte; shop; rest; snacks; bar; BBQ; playgrnd; 2 pools (1 htd, covrd); waterslides; sand beach 4km; tennis; cycle hire; archery; games area; games rm; entmnt; mini-farm; 75% statics; dogs (sm only) €6.50; private san facs avail for extra charge; adv bkg; quiet. "Dir access to rv; excel for children." 1 May-20 Sep. € 39.00 2009*

MATHES, LES *7B1* (2km NW Rural) *45.73473, -1.17713* **Camping Atlantique Forêt, La Fouasse, 17570 Les Mathes [05 46 22 40 46 or 05 46 36 82 77 (LS); www.camping-atlantique-foret.com]** Fr La Tremblade by-pass, foll sp Diree (D268). Drive thro vill & cont for 2km. Site on L. Or fr La Palmyre on D141 twd Les Mathes; at rndabt take dir La Fouasse. Last site on R. Med, pt shd; wc (a few cont); chem disp; baby facs; shwrs inc; el pnts (6A) €4.30; gas; lndtte; shop; tradsmn; rest, snacks, bar 500m; BBQ (gas only); playgrnd; pool, tennis 300m; beach 2km; 2% statics; dogs free; phone; poss cr; Eng spkn; adv bkg; quiet; CCI. "Pleasant, peaceful wooded site in beautiful area; roomy, clean & well-run; family-run; gd alt to nrby lge sites; excel for young children; cycle paths thro forest; great place to stay." ♦ 15 Jun-15 Sep. € 19.60 2009*

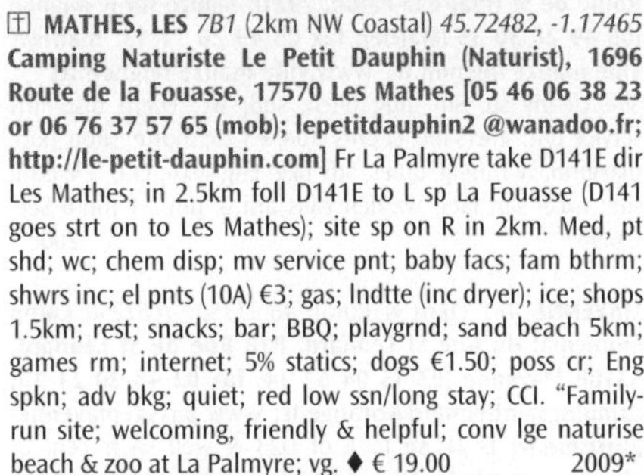

⊞ **MATHES, LES** *7B1* (2km NW Coastal) *45.72482, -1.17465* **Camping Naturiste Le Petit Dauphin (Naturist), 1696 Route de la Fouasse, 17570 Les Mathes [05 46 06 38 23 or 06 76 37 57 65 (mob); lepetitdauphin2 @wanadoo.fr; http://le-petit-dauphin.com]** Fr La Palmyre take D141E dir Les Mathes; in 2.5km foll D141E to L sp La Fouasse (D141 goes strt on to Les Mathes); site sp on R in 2km. Med, pt shd; wc; chem disp; mv service pnt; baby facs; fam bthrm; shwrs inc; el pnts (10A) €3; gas; lndtte (inc dryer); ice; shops 1.5km; rest; snacks; bar; BBQ; playgrnd; sand beach 5km; games rm; internet; 5% statics; dogs €1.50; poss cr; Eng spkn; adv bkg; quiet; red low ssn/long stay; CCI. "Family-run site; welcoming, friendly & helpful; conv lge naturise beach & zoo at La Palmyre; vg. ♦ € 19.00 2009*

MATHES, LES *7B1* (2.5km NW Rural) *45.72098, -1.17165* **Camping La Clé des Champs, 1188 Route de la Fouasse, 17570 Les Mathes [05 46 22 40 53; fax 05 46 22 56 96; contact@la-cledeschamps.com; www.la-cledeschamps.com]** S of La Tremblade, take D141 twd La Palmyre, site sp. Lge, mkd pitch, pt shd; wc (some cont); chem disp; baby facs; shwrs; el pnts (6-10A) €4.30-4.60; gas; lndtte; shop; rest; snacks; bar; BBQ; playgrnd; htd, covrd pool; paddling pool; sand beach 3.5km; cycle hire; fishing & watersports 3km; cycle hire; games area; games rm; TV rm; entmnt; 30% statics; dogs €2.70; Eng spkn; adv bkg; ccard acc; quiet; CCI. "Well-equipped, busy site; many excel beaches in area; local oysters avail; Cognac region; Luna Park nrby - poss noise at night." ♦ 1 Apr-30 Sep. € 20.30 2009*

See advertisement

MATHES, LES *7B1* (3km NW Rural) *45.73229, -1.17655* **Camping L'Estanquet, 2596 Route de la Fouasse, 17570 Les Mathes [05 46 22 47 32 or 05 46 93 93 51 (LS); fax 05 46 22 51 46; contact@campinglestanquet.com; www.campinglestanquet.com]** Fr Royan take D25 to La Palmyre. Turn R in town cent onto D141 dir Les Mathes; cont on D141 passing racecourse on R; turn L bef Les Mathes along La Fouasse. Site in 2.5km on L. Lge, hdg/mkd pitch, pt shd; wc; chem disp; baby facs; shwrs inc; el pnts (10A) inc; gas; lndtte; shop; rest; snacks; bar; BBQ (gas only); playgrnd; pool; paddling pool; waterslide; sand beach 5km; fishing, windsurfing 5km; tennis; cycle hire; horseriding 1km; golf 9km; entmnt; games/TV rm; 85% statics; dogs €3; poss cr; adv bkg; quiet ♦ 1 May-30 Sep. € 29.50 2006*

MATIGNON see St Cast le Guildo *2E3*

MATOUR *9A2* (1km W) *46.30475, 4.47858* **Camp Municipal Le Paluet, 71520 Matour [03 85 59 70 58; fax 03 85 59 74 54; mairie.matour@wanadoo.fr; www.matour.com]** On W o'skts of Matour off Rte de la Clayette. Med, hdg/mkd pitch, pt shd; wc; chem disp; shwrs inc; el pnts (10A) inc; lndtte; shop 500m; bar; snacks; BBQ; playgrnd; pool high ssn; waterslide; lake fishing adj; tennis; games area; entmnt; TV; adv bkg; quiet; CCI. "Conv touring vineyards; highly rec; facs poss inadequate high ssn." ♦ 1 May-30 Sep. € 15.90 2006*

MAUBEC see Cavaillon *10E2*

MAUBEUGE *3B4* (1km N Rural) *50.29545, 3.97696* **Camp Municipal du Clair de Lune, 212 Route de Mons, 59600 Maubeuge [03 27 62 25 48; fax 03 27 60 25 94; camping@ville-maubeuge.fr; www.ville-maubeuge.fr]** Fr Mons head S on N2 twd Maubeuge, site on L about 1.5km bef town cent, sp. Med, hdg/mkd pitch, some hdstg, pt sl, pt shd; htd wc; chem disp; baby facs; shwrs inc; el pnts (10A) €4.35 (rev pol); shops 500m; hypmkt 1km; tradsmn; rest, snacks, bar 2km; BBQ; playgrnd; watersports 25km; cycle hire; internet; few statics; dogs; phone adj; bus adj; adv bkg; some rd noise; ccard acc. "Attractive, well-kept, busy transit site; spacious pitches; friendly, helpful staff; excel san facs; barrier clsd 2300-0700; mkt Sat am; excel." ♦ 6 Feb-18 Dec. € 10.40 ABS - P07 2009*

MAUBEUGE *3B4* (8km NE Rural) *50.34525, 4.02842* **Camping Les Avallées, 19 Rue du Faubourg, 59600 Villers-Sire-Nicole [03 27 67 92 56; fax 03 27 67 45 18; loisirs-les-avallees@wanadoo.fr; www.loisirs-les-avallees.fr]** N fr Maubeuge on N2; in 5km R onto D159 to Villers-Sire-Nicole. Site well sp. Lge, pt sl, terr, pt shd; wc; chem disp; el pnts (4A) €2; shwrs inc; shop (high ssn); rest; snacks; bar; BBQ; playgrnd; mainly statics; dogs; quiet. "Friendly owners; lake fishing; no twin-axles; vg." 1 Apr-14 Oct. € 7.00 2008*

MAUBOURGUET *8F2* (SW Urban) *43.4658, 0.0349* **Camp Municipal de l'Echez, Rue Jean Clos Pucheu, 65700 Maubourguet [05 62 96 37 44 or 06 12 90 14 55 (mob)]** On D935 (NW of Tarbes), sp in Maubourguet, on bank of Rv Echez. Sm, pt shd; wc; shwrs inc; mv service pnt; el pnts; shops 200m; lndtte; playgrnd; TV; rv fishing 300m; quiet. "Pleasantly situated; nice country town." 15 Jun-15 Sep. € 10.40 2006*

MAULEON LICHARRE *8F1* (1km S Rural) *43.20795, -0.89695* **Camping Uhaitza Le Saison, Route de Libarrenx, 64130 Mauléon-Licharre [05 59 28 18 79; fax 05 59 28 00 78; camping.uhaitza@wanadoo.fr; www.camping-uhaitza.com]** Fr Sauveterre take D936 twd Oloron. In 500m turn R onto D23 to Mauléon, then take D918 dir Tardets, site on R. Sm, hdg/mkd pitch, pt sl, pt shd; wc; chem disp; baby facs; shwrs inc; el pnts (4-6A) €2.50-3.20; lndtte; shops 1.5km; bar high ssn; BBQ; playgrnd; pool 4km; rv fishing adj; some statics; dogs €1; adv bkg; quiet; CCI. "Lovely quiet site beside rv - steep access; friendly owners." ♦ Easter-30 Oct. € 13.20 2006*

MAUPERTUS SUR MER see Cherbourg *1C4*

MAURIAC *7C4* (1km SW Rural) *45.21865, 2.31639* **Camping Le Val St Jean, 15200 Mauriac [04 71 67 31 13; fax 04 73 93 71 00; e.foure@revea-vacances.com; www.revea-vacances.fr]** Site adj lake; well sp. Med, hdg/mkd pitch, terr, unshd; htd wc; chem disp; shwrs inc; el pnts (10A) €3.60; lndry rm; shop; tradsmn; snacks; playgrnd; htd pool; waterslide; paddling pool; sand beach & lake sw adj; fishing; golf adj; TV rm; some statics; dogs €1.50; adv bkg; quiet; red low ssn; CCI. "Excel, clean, tidy site; ltd facs low ssn; gd touring base." ♦ 25 Apr-27 Sep. € 20.50 2009*

MAURIAC *7C4* (1.5km SW Rural) *45.21110, 2.32356* **Camp Municipal La Roussilhe, 15200 Mauriac [04 71 68 06 99]** Foll sp for Ally & Pleux on D681; downhill, past supmkt, sp to R, 1st L. Med, pt shd; wc; 50% serviced pitches; shwrs; el pnts (3A) €1.80; quiet. "Nice site adj football pitch; plenty of shade." 7 Jun-7 Sep. € 6.00 2008*

MAUROUX see St Clar *8E3*

MAURS *7D4* (6km SE) *44.68140, 2.26050* **FFCC Camping Le Moulin de Chaules, Route de Calvinet, 15600 St Constant [04 71 49 11 02; fax 04 71 49 13 63; camping@moulin-de-chaules.com; www.moulin-de-chaules.com]** Fr N122 in Maurs, foll sp to St Constant on D663. Take by-pass round St Constant & turn L to Calvinet, well sp fr Maurs. Med, mkd pitch, terr, shd; wc; chem disp; baby facs; shwrs inc; el pnts (4A) €3; lndtte (inc dryer); sm shop; tradsmn; rest; snacks; bar; BBQ (gas); playgrnd; pool; games area; games rm; wifi; some statics; no twin-axles; dogs €1.50; Eng spkn; adv bkg; quiet; red low ssn/long stay; CCI. "Friendly Dutch owner; excel facs; excel for young children; terr access steep - care needed (tractor tow avail); gd." ♦ 11 Apr-11 Oct. € 21.50 2009*

MAURS *7D4* (800m S Rural) *44.70522, 2.20586* **Camp Municipal du Vert, Route de Decazeville, 15600 Maurs [04 71 49 04 15; fax 04 71 49 00 81; mairie@ville-maurs.fr]** Fr Maurs take D663 dir Decazeville. Site on L 400m after level x-ing thro sports complex. Narr ent. Med, mkd pitch, shd; wc; chem disp; baby facs; shwrs inc; el pnts (15A) inc; lndtte; shops 1km; playgrnd; pool; tennis; rv fishing; poss cr; adv bkg; quiet. "V pleasant on side of rv; sports complex adj." ♦ 1 May-30 Sep. € 11.10 2008*

MAURY see St Paul de Fenouillet *8G4*

MAUSSANE LES ALPILLES see Mouriès *10E2*

MAUZE SUR LE MIGNON *7A2* (1km NW Rural) *46.20063, -0.68186* **Camp Municipal Le Gué de La Rivière, Route de St Hilaire-la-Palud, 79210 Mauzé-sur-le-Mignon [05 49 26 30 35 (Mairie); fax 05 49 26 71 13; mairie@ville-mauze-mignon.fr; www.ville-mauze-mignon.fr]** Site clearly sp. Sm, hdg pitch, shd; wc; chem disp; mv service pnt; shwrs inc; el pnts (10A) €3.25; lndtte; shop 1km; playgrnd; rv fishing; quiet; adv bkg; Eng spkn; CCI. "Pleasant site; excel san facs; warden calls am & pm." 1 Jun-6 Sep. € 6.90 2008*

MAYENNE *4E1* (1km N Rural) *48.31350, -0.61296* **Camp Municipal du Gué St Léonard, 818 Rue de St Léonard, 53100 Mayenne [02 43 04 57 14; fax 02 43 30 21 10; campingsaintleonard@orange.fr; www.paysdemayenne-tourisme.fr]** Fr N, sp to E of D23 & well sp fr cent of Mayenne on rvside. Med, hdg/mkd pitch, pt shd; htd wc; chem disp; some serviced pitches; shwrs inc; el pnts (10A) €2.05; lndtte; shop (high ssn) & 1km; tradsman high ssn; snacks; rest 1km; BBQ; playgrnd; htd pool high ssn inc; rv fishing adj; 8% statics; phone; extra for twin-axles; adv bkg; some noise fr adj factory; red low ssn; CCI. "Peaceful, well-kept site by rv; pleasant location adj parkland walks; clean, dated facs; some pitches sm & access poss diff; vg value." ♦ 15 Mar-30 Sep. € 11.00 (3 persons) 2009*

MAYET see Ecommoy *4F1*

MAYRES *9D1* (500m S Rural) *44.66723, 4.08965* **Camping La Chataigneraie, Hameau de Cautet, 07330 Mayres [tel/fax 04 75 87 20 40 or 04 75 87 20 97]** Fr Aubenas on N102; L after Mayres vill, over Ardèche bdge, up hill in 500m. Sm, mkd pitch, terr, pt shd; wc (cont); shwrs inc; el pnts (3-6A) €2.50-4; tradsmn; rv sw 2km; dogs €1; quiet; ccard acc. "Vg CL-type site; secluded by tributary of Rv Ardèche; helpful owners." ♦ Easter-1 Nov. € 13.00 2009*

MAZAMET *8F4* (1.5km E Urban) *43.49634, 2.39075* **FFCC Camp Municipal de la Lauze, Chemin de la Lauze, 81200 Mazamet [tel/fax 05 63 61 24 69; camping.mazamet@imsnet.fr; www.ville-mazamet.com/camping]** Exit Mazamet dir St Pons on D612 (N112), site on R past rugby grnd. Med, hdstg, pt sl, pt shd; wc (mainly cont); chem disp; mv service pnt; baby facs; shwrs inc; el pnts (15A) €3.50; lndtte; BBQ; htd pool adj; tennis; dogs; poss cr; adv bkg; some rd noise; red long stay/CCI. "Well-kept site in 2 adj parts, 1 flat & other sl; office thro gateway - warden needed for access; san facs excel; gd touring base 'Black Mountain' region." ♦ 1 Jun-30 Sep. € 13.00 2009*

France

MAZAMET *8F4* (8km E Urban) *43.48061, 2.48664* **Camping La Vallée du Thoré, La Lamberthe, 81240 St Amans-Soult [05 63 98 30 20; camping-valleethore@wanadoo.fr]** Fr Mazamet take D612 (N112) dir Béziers; site on L in 8km, clearly sp in vill by nursery school. Sm, pt sl, pt shd; wc; chem disp; shwrs inc; el pnts (6A) inc; gas; Indtte; tradsmn; shops, rest, snacks & bar 500m; 30% statics; dogs free; Eng spkn; adv bkg; quiet; CCI. "Lovely vill site close to rv; church bells stop at night; vg." 1 May-30 Sep. € 13.20 2008*

MAZAN see Carpentras *10E2*

MAZERES *8F3* (1km SE Rural) *43.24901, 1.68271* **Camp Municipal La Plage, Ave de Belpech, 09270 Mazères [05 61 69 38 82 or 05 61 69 42 04 (Mairie); fax 05 61 69 37 97; danielle@camping-mazeres.com; www.camping-mazeres.com]** Exit A66 junc 2; foll sp Mazères; on ent vill turn R onto lorry rte; site sp on D11 just bef leaving vill. Med, hdg/mkd pitch, pt shd; wc; chem disp; fam bthrm; shwrs inc; el pnts (10A) inc; Indtte; shop 100m; tradsmn; rest; snacks; bar; playgrnd; 2 pools (1 htd); tennis; fishing & canoeing nr; games rm; entmnt; dogs; phone; adv bkg; noise fr peacocks; CCI. "Several san blocks, poss not all cleaned regularly low ssn (Jun 2007); gd." ♦ 1 Jun-30 Sep. € 14.00 2007*

MAZIERES see Chasseneuil sur Bonnieure *7B3*

MAZURES, LES see Rocroi *5C1*

MEAUDRE see Villard de Lans *9C3*

MEAULNE *7A4* (S Urban) *46.59667, 2.61352* **Camp Municipal Le Cheval Blanc, Route de Montluçon, 03360 Meaulne [04 70 06 91 13 or 04 70 06 95 34; fax 04 70 06 91 29; mairie.meaulne@wanadoo.fr; www.meaulne-ami.com]** Site off D2144 (N144) on bank Rv Aumance. Sm, pt shd; wc; chem disp (wc); shwrs inc; el pnts (12A) €2; Indtte; shop, rest, bar 300m; BBQ; playgrnd; rv fishing; canoeing; dogs; phone; quiet, some rd noise; CCI. "Pleasant, well-kept, basic site in beautiful rvside position; clean san facs; site yourself, warden calls 1300 & 1900 or put money in letterbox; poss flooding in high rainfall; excel NH." ♦ 1 May-30 Sep. € 10.00 2009*

MEAUX *3D3* (4km NE Rural) *49.00301, 2.94139* **Camping Village Parisien, Route de Congis, 77910 Varreddes [01 64 34 80 80; fax 01 60 22 89 84; leslie@villageparisien.com; www.villageparisien.com]** Fr Meaux foll sp on D405 dir Soissons then Varreddes, site sp on D121 dir Congis. Med, hdg/mkd pitch, pt shd; wc; chem disp; mv service pnt; baby facs; shwrs inc; el pnts (6A) €2; gas; Indtte (inc dryer); sm shop (high ssn); tradsmn; rest & snacks (high ssn); bar; BBQ; playgrnd; pool; paddling pool; waterslide; fishing; tennis; games area; cycle hire; golf 5km; games rm; entmnt; TV rm; 85% statics; dogs free; poss cr; Eng spkn; adv bkg; aircraft noise; ccard acc; red low ssn/long stay/CCI. "Conv Paris cent (drive to metro), Parc Astérix & Disneyland - tickets avail fr site; friendly, helpful staff; sm pitches; narr site rds; v busy, well-used site." 15 Mar-1 Nov. € 27.00 (CChq acc) 2009*

MEAUX *3D3* (10km SW Rural) *48.91333, 2.73416* **Camping L'International de Jablines, 77450 Jablines [01 60 26 09 37; fax 01 60 26 43 33; welcome@camping-jablines.com; www.camping-jablines.com]** Fr N on A1 then A104 exit Claye-Souilly. Fr E on A4 then A104 exit Meaux. Fr S on A6, A86, A4, A104 exit Meaux. Site well sp 'Base de Loisirs de Jablines'. Lge, mkd pitch, pt sl, pt shd; htd wc; chem disp; mv service pnt; shwrs inc; el pnts (10A) inc; Indtte; shop; tradsmn; rest; snacks; bar; playgrnd; sand beach & lake sw 500m; fishing; sailing; windsurfing; tennis 500m; horseriding; cycle hire; dogs €2; bus to Eurodisney; Eng spkn; adv bkg; quiet; red low ssn; ccard acc; CCI. "Clean, well-run, well-guarded site; ideal for Disneyland (tickets for sale), Paris & Versailles; pleasant staff." ♦ 27 Mar-24 Oct. € 25.00 (CChq acc) 2009*

See advertisement

⊞ **MEAUX** *3D3* (10km SW Urban) *48.87723, 2.78663* **Motor Caravan Park at Disneyland Paris, 77777 Marne-la-Vallée** Fr all dirs foll sp to Disneyland & foll sp to m'van (camping car) park. Easy to find. Lge, hdstg, unshd; htd wc; mv service pnt; shwrs inc; no el pnts; picnic area; rest etc in Disney Village; dogs; phone; bus, train adj; Eng spkn; quiet; ccard acc; m'vans only. € 13.00 2009*

MEAUX *3D3* (14km W Rural) *48.92136, 2.72217* **Camping L'Ile Demoiselle, Chemin du Port, 77410 Annet-sur-Marne [01 60 26 03 07 or 01 60 26 18 15; ile.demoiselle@wanadoo.fr; www.chez.com/demoiselles]** Fr Meaux take D603 (N3) W, then turn L onto D404 twd Annet. Foll sp to 'Base de Loisirs de Jablines'. Fr Annet take D45 twd Jablines. Site on R immed bef bdge over rv. Med, some hdg pitch, pt shd; wc; chem disp (wc); shwrs €1.50; el pnts (4A) inc; gas 4km; lndry rm; shops 1km; BBQ; lake sw, sand beach 1km; 25% statics; dogs €1.50; some Eng spkn; adv bkg; rd noise; ccard acc; CCI. "V nice site; conv Paris & Disneyland Paris; many other attractions in area; gd sh stay/NH." 1 Apr-31 Oct € 16.50 2007*

MEES, LES *10E3* (9km S Rural) *43.95377, 5.93304* **Camping L'Olivette, Hameau Les Pourcelles, 04190 Les Mées [tel/fax 04 92 34 18 97; campingolivette@club-internet.fr; http://campingolivette.free.fr]** Exit A51 junc 20 (fr N) or 19 (fr S) & cross Rv Durance onto D4. Site bet Oraison & Les Mées. Turn onto D754 to Les Pourcelles & foll site sp. Sm, hdg/mkd pitch, pt sl, terr, pt shd; wc; chem disp; shwrs inc; el pnts (6A) €3.50; playgrnd; pool; 5% statics; dogs €1.50; Eng spkn; adv bkg; quiet. "Views over beautiful area; friendly owners; occasional out of ssn pitches avail; unreliable opening (2008); vg." ♦ 15 Jun-15 Sep. € 15.00 2008*

MEGEVE *9B3* (2km SW Rural) *45.84120, 6.58887* **FFCC Camping Gai Séjour, 332 Route de Cassioz, 74120 Megève [tel/fax 04 50 21 22 58]** On D1212 (N212) Flumet-Megève rd, site on R 1km after Praz-sur-Arly, well sp. Med, mkd pitch, sl (blocks needed), pt shd; wc; chem disp; shwrs inc; el pnts (4A); lndry rm; shops, rest, bar 1km; dogs; Eng spkn; adv bkg; quiet; CCI. "Pleasant site with gd views, lge pitches; gd walks; 40km fr Mont Blanc; helpful owners." 20 May-15 Sep. € 10.90 2009*

MEHUN SUR YEVRE *4H3* (500m N Urban) **Camp Municipal, Ave Jean Châtelet, 18500 Mehun-sur-Yèvre [02 48 57 44 51 or 02 48 57 30 25 (Mairie); fax 02 48 57 34 16]** Leave A71 junc 6 onto D2076 (N76) dir Bourges. App Mehun & turn L into site at 2nd traff lts. Ave Jean Châtelet is part of D2076. Sm, mkd pitch, pt shd; wc; chem disp; mv service pnt; shwrs inc; el pnts (6A) inc (poss rev pol & long lead req some pitches); lndtte; shop, rest & bar 600m; playgrnd; pool & tennis adj; quiet with some rd noise; ccard not acc. "Excel NH conv for m'way; clean, modern san facs; water pnts poss long walk; gates locked 2200-0700 (high ssn); twin-axles extra charge." ♦ Mid May-30 Sep. € 9.80 2009*

MEHUN SUR YEVRE *4H3* (6km NE Rural) *47.09648, 2.18165* **Camp Municipal Pierre Sicard, 18120 Preuilly [02 48 57 12 04 or 02 48 51 30 08 (Mairie); fax 02 48 51 06 28; mairie.preuilly@wanadoo.fr]** S fr Vierzon on D27 sp Brinay & Quincy to Preuilly; take 2nd L to site in 500m; on R just past rv bdge. Med, hdg/mkd pitch, pt shd; wc; chem disp; shwrs inc; el pnts (5A) inc; lndtte; shop; snacks; bar; playgrnd; games area; tennis opp; a few statics; dogs €0.80; phone adj; adv bkg; quiet, but poss noise fr rest adj; CCI. "Gd touring base for wine rte; san facs old but clean; direct access to rv fishing & boating; fair." ♦ 1 May-30 Sep. € 9.80 2009*

MEILHAN SUR GARONNE *7D2* (N Rural) *44.52439, 0.03589* **Camp Municipal au Jardin, 47200 Meilhan-sur-Garonne [06 08 03 54 77 (mob) or 05 53 94 30 04 (Mairie); fax 05 53 94 31 27; communedemeilhan.47@wanadoo.fr]** On N side of Canal Latéral, below Meilhan; exit A62 at junc 4 onto D9; or turn off N113 at Ste Bazeille; foll sp. Med, mkd pitch, pt shd; wc; shwrs €1; el pnts (10A) €1.35; lndtte; shops 500m; playgrnd; pool 500m; rv sw, fishing 100m; quiet; CCI. "If barrier down & no warden, key is in elect cupboard." 1 Jun-30 Sep. € 7.00 2007*

MEIX ST EPOING, LE see Sézanne *4E4*

MEJANNES LE CLAP see Barjac (Gard) *9D2*

MELE SUR SARTHE, LE *4E1* (500m SE Rural) *48.50831, 0.36298* **Camp Intercommunal La Prairie, La Bretèche, St Julien-Sarthe, 61170 Le Mêle-sur-Sarthe [02 33 27 18 74]** Turn off N12 onto D4; site sp in vill. Med, mkd pitch, pt shd; wc; chem disp; mv service pnt; shwrs; el pnts (6A) inc; lndtte; supmkt 300m; playgrnd; sand beach/lake 300m; sailing; tennis; adv bkg; CCI. "Part of excel municipal sports complex; vg." 1 May-30 Sep. € 9.40 2009*

MELISEY *6F2* (500m E Rural) *47.75484, 6.58683* **Camping La Bergereine, 17bis Route des Vosges, 70270 Mélisey [tel/fax 06 23 36 87 16 (mob); isabelle.schweizer0704@orange.fr]** Fr Lure (or by-pass) take D486 dir Le Thillot; site sp. Sm, pt shd; wc; chem disp; shwrs; el pnts inc; gas; leisure cent & pool 500m; fishing in adj rv; 25% statics; adv bkg; v quiet; CCI. "Gd NH; simple farm site; attractive scenery." 1 Apr-30 Sep. € 8.00 2008*

MELISEY *6F2* (7km E Rural) *47.75525, 6.65273* **Camping La Broche, Le Voluet, 70270 Fresse [tel/fax 03 84 63 31 40; www.camping-broche.com]** Fr Lure head NE on D486 twd Melisey. Fr Mélisey stay on D486 twd Le Thillot, in 2.5km turn R onto D97 dir Plancher-les-Mines. In approx 5.5km site sp on R in Fresse. Sm, mkd pitch, pt sl, terr, pt shd; wc; chem disp; shwrs inc; el pnts (10A) €2; lndtte; ice; shop 200m; BBQ; playgrnd; lake sw & fishing adj; games area; games rm; some statics; dogs €1; phone; poss cr; adv bkg; quiet apart fr double-chiming church bells; CCI. "Secluded, relaxing site in attractive setting in regional park; friendly owner; conv Rte of 1000 lakes; great site." ♦ 15 Apr-15 Oct. € 8.00 2009*

MELLE *7A2* (1km N Urban) **Camp Municipal La Fontaine de Villiers, Route de Villiers, 79500 Melle [05 49 29 18 04 or 05 49 29 15 10 (TO); fax 05 49 29 19 83; tourismemelle@wanadoo.fr; www.ville-melle.fr]** Fr N on D150 (D950) on ent Melle turn R at 1st rndabt, site is 1km fr Super U, well sp. Sm, hdg/mkd pitch, pt sl, pt shd; wc (some cont); chem disp; mv service pnt; shwrs inc; el pnts (3-10A) €2.45-3.90; shop, rest, snacks, bar 1km; BBQ; playgrnd; htd pool 500m; tennis 1km; phone; adv bkg; quiet; CCI. "NH only." 15 Apr-30 Sep. € 8.85 2007*

⊞ **MELLE** *7A2* (8km S Rural) **Camping La Maison de Puits, 14 Rue de Beauchamp, 79110 Tillou [05 49 07 20 28; mark.hall@sfr.fr; www.hallmarkholidays.eu]** Fr Niort on D948. At Melle foll sp Angoulême, R turn (to ring rd & avoids Melle cent). At Total stn rndabt turn R onto D948 dir Chef-Boutonne. In 3.5km turn R onto D737 sp Chef-Boutonne. After approx 5km at x-rds of D111 & D737, strt over & take 2nd turn R in 1km (sm sp to Tillou) along narr rd sp Tillou. In 1.6km site on L. Sm, sl, unshd; wc; chem disp; shwr; el pnts (6A) €3; BBQ; splash pool; adv bkg; quiet. "CL-type site in meadow/orchard (6 vans only); quiet & peaceful; friendly, helpful British owners - help with house-hunting avail; ring ahead to book; interesting area; a real gem." € 11.00 2009*

MELLE *7A2* (10km SW Rural) *46.14421, -0.21983* **Camp Municipal, Rue des Merlonges, 79170 Brioux-sur-Boutonne [05 49 07 50 46; fax 05 49 07 27 27]** On ent Brioux fr Melle on D150 (D950) turn R immed over bdge; site on R in 100m. Sm, pt shd; wc; shwrs inc; el pnts (6A) €0.85; lndry rm; shops 300m; playgrnd adj; quiet, some rd noise. "Pleasant rural setting; tidy, well-cared for site; ltd facs but clean; choose own pitch & pay at Mairie on departure if no warden; vg sh stay/NH." 1 Apr-31 Oct. € 6.00 2009*

MELLE *7A2* (6km NW Rural) *46.25877, -0.21463* **Camp Municipal La Boissière, Route de Chizé, 79370 Celles-sur-Belle [05 49 32 95 57 or 05 49 79 80 17 (Mairie); fax 05 49 32 95 10; mairie-cellessurbelle@wanadoo.fr]** Fr Melle or Niort on D948. Exit by-pass into Celles & in town foll sp to Sports Complex & camping. Sm, pt sl, pt shd; htd wc (some cont); shwrs inc; el pnts (6A) €2.10; gas, shop 500m; BBQ; playgrnd; pool adj; rv 200m; lake 400m; tennis; 20% statics; dogs €0.85; adv bkg rec high ssn. "Warden calls am & pm; quiet apart fr football ground adj; gd NH."♦ 15 Apr-15 Oct. € 6.75 2006*

MELUN *4E3* (3km S Rural) *48.52569, 2.66930* **Camping La Belle Etoile, Quai Joffre, 77000 La Rochette [01 64 39 48 12; fax 01 64 37 25 55; info@camping labelleetoile.com; www.campinglabelleetoile.com]** On ent La Rochette on D606 (N6) fr Fontainbleu pass Total stn on L; turn immed R into Ave de la Seine & foll site sp; turn L at Rv Seine & site on L in 500m. Lge, hdg/mkd pitch, pt shd; wc; chem disp; mv service pnt; shwrs; el pnts (6A) €3.30 (poss rev pol); gas; lndtte; shop 1km; snacks (high ssn); bar; playgrnd; htd pool; rv fishing; tennis 500m; golf 8km; internet; 10% statics; phone; dogs €1.50; Eng spkn; adv bkg; some rlwy & rv noise; ccard acc; red low ssn; CCI. "Pretty site; helpful owners; san facs tired; gates locked 2300; conv Paris, Fontainebleau & Disneyland (ticket fr recep); sports complex nrby; gd walking & cycling in forest; mkt Melun Wed; gd." ♦ 30 Mar-19 Oct. € 18.70 (CChq acc) 2008*

MEMBROLLE SUR CHOISILLE, LA *4G2* (Urban) *47.43613, 0.63771* **Camp Municipal, Route de Fondettes, 37390 La Membrolle-sur-Choisille [02 47 41 20 40]** On D938 (N138) Tours to Le Mans rd. Site on L on ent La Membrolle, sp. Med, pt shd; wc (some cont); chem disp; mv service pnt; shwrs inc; el pnts (3A) inc; lndtte; shop 5mins; hypmkt 3km; playgrnd; fishing, tennis, rv walks; dogs; bus 5min; phone; adv bkg; a little rd noise; CCI. "Clean, well-maintained site; gd san facs; wardens friendly, helpful." ♦ 1 May-30 Sep. € 10.60 2008*

MENAT *7A4* (2km E Rural) *46.09579, 2.92899* **Camp Municipal des Tarteaux, 63560 Menat [04 73 85 52 47 or 04 73 85 50 29 (Mairie); fax 04 73 85 50 22]** Heading SE fr St Eloy-les-Mines on D2144 (N144) foll sp Camping Pont de Menat. Exit D2144 at Menat opp Hôtel Pinal. Site alongside Rv Sioule. Med, terr, pt sl, shd; wc (cont); shwrs inc; el pnts (5A) inc; lndtte; shop 2km; playgrnd; rv adj; fishing & boating 2km; adv bkg; quiet; CCI. "Beautiful position beside rv; basic san facs clean but in need of update - own san facs rec; Chateau Rocher ruins nrby; OK NH." 1 Apr-30 Sep. € 10.80 2009*

We can fill in site report forms on the Club's website – www.caravanclub.co.uk/europereport

⊞ **MENDE** *9D1* (2km S Rural) *44.51409, 3.47363* **Camping Tivoli, Route des Gorges du Tarn, 48000 Mende [tel/fax 04 66 65 00 38; camping.tivoli0601@orange.fr; www.camping-tivoli.com]** Sp fr N88, turn R 300m downhill (narr but easy rd). Site adj Rv Lot. Med, pt shd; wc (some cont); chem disp; mv service pnt; htd shwrs inc; el pnts (6A) inc; lndtte; shop; hypmkt 1km; bar; playgrnd; pool; rv fishing; TV rm; some statics; dogs €1; quiet but rd noise; adv bkg. "Gd site nr town at back of indust est; v narr ent with little room to park." € 18.60 2009*

MENDE *9D1* (8km SW Rural) *44.50104, 3.40717* **Camping Le Clos des Peupliers, 48000 Barjac [04 66 47 01 16; leclosdespeupliers@wanadoo.fr]** On N88 in dir of Mende turn N on D142 sp Barjac & Camping. Site ent almost immed on R thro sh narr but not diff tunnel (max height 3.4m), adj Rv Lot. Lge, mkd pitch, pt shd; wc; chem disp; shwrs inc; el pnts (6-10A) €2.50-3; lndtte; rest 300m; snacks; playgrnd; rv fishing adj; TV; dogs €1.30; quiet. "Pleasant rvside site; poss unkempt low ssn; helpful warden; basic, clean facs, ltd low ssn; gd walks." ♦ 1 May-15 Sep. € 9.00 2009*

MENESPLET see Montpon Ménestérol *7C2*

MENETRUX EN JOUX see Doucier *6H2*

MENIL see Château Gontier *4F1*

MENITRE, LA see Rosiers sur Loire, Les *4G1*

MENNETOU SUR CHER see Villefranche sur Cher *4G3*

MENS *9C3* (500m S Urban) *44.81493, 5.74860* **Camping du Pré Rolland, Rue de la Piscine, Place Richard-Wilm, 38710 Mens [04 76 34 65 80; fax 04 76 34 65 80; contact@camping-prerolland.fr; www.camping-prerolland.fr]** Turn E fr N75 onto D526 sp Celles & Mens; site in 14km. Turn R at ent to town. Well sp. Med, hdg/mkd pitch, pt shd; wc; chem disp; mv service pnt; shwrs inc; el pnts (10A) €3; Indtte; snacks; sw nrby; entmnt; TV; 5% statics; dogs €1.50; phone; Eng spkn; adv bkg; quiet, but poss noise fr pool nr ent; red low ssn/long stay; CCI. "Refurbished site (2008) in beautiful area; mountain views; friendly owners; excel walking; painting courses high ssn; vg." ♦ 1 May-30 Sep. € 14.50 2008*

MENTON *10E4* (1km N Urban/Coastal) *43.78005, 7.49821* **Camp Municipal du Plateau St Michel, Route de Ciappes, 06500 Menton [04 93 35 81 23; fax 04 93 57 12 35]** Fr A8 Menton exit foll sp to town cent. After 2km with bus stn on L & rlwy bdge ahead turn L at rndabt, then R at T-junc. L at next T-junc, foll sp to site & Auberge Jeunesse. Rd is v steep & narr with hairpins - not rec trailer c'vans. Med, mkd pitch, terr, pt shd; wc (some cont); shwrs inc; el pnts (16A) €2.90; shop; rest; snacks; bar; sand beach 1km; dogs €2.75; bus; poss v cr with tents; noisy; ccard acc; CCI. "Pleasant site; helpful staff; clean, dated san facs; steep walk to town." 1 Apr-31 Oct. € 18.80 2009*

⊞ **MEOUNES LES MONTRIEUX** *10F3* (500m S Rural) *43.27672, 5.97036* **FFCC Camping aux Tonneaux, Les Ferrages, 83136 Méounes-lès-Montrieux [04 94 33 98 34; contact@camping-aux-tonneaux.com; www.camping-aux-tonneaux.com]** D43/D554 fr Brignoles to Toulon. Site sp off D554 at exit to vill - busy, narr rd. Sm, mkd pitch, shd; wc; chem disp; shwrs inc; el pnts (6A) inc; gas; Indtte; shop; snacks; bar; playgrnd; pool; tennis; 20% statics; dogs; Eng spkn; no adv bkg; quiet; 25% red low ssn; CCI. € 16.00 2007*

⊞ **MERENS LES VALS** *8G4* (1km W Rural) *42.64633, 1.83083* **Camp Municipal Ville de Bau, 09110 Mérens-les-Vals [05 61 02 85 40 or 05 61 64 33 77; fax 05 61 64 03 83; camping.merens@wanadoo.fr]** Fr Ax-les-Thermes on N20 sp Andorra past Mérens-les-Vals turn R nr start of dual c'way sp Camp Municipal. Site on R in 800m. Med, hdg pitch; wc (some cont); shwrs inc; el pnts (6-10A) €2.30-4 (poss rev pol); shop; playgrnd; pool 8km; 20% statics; dogs €0.50; poss cr; quiet; ccard acc; CCI. "Conv Andorra, Tunnel de Puymorens; excel facs; gd walks fr site; vg value." € 10.40 2006*

MERIBEL *9B3* (2km N Rural) **Camping Le Martagon, Le Raffort, Route de Méribel, 73550 Les Allues [04 79 00 56 29; fax 04 79 00 44 92]** Fr Moûtiers on D915 S to Brides-les-Bains then D90 S dir Méribel. Site on L at Le Raffort. Park in public car park & go to rest. Sm, hdstg, terr, unshd; htd wc; chem disp; shwrs inc; el pnts (10A) €5; gas 200m; Indtte; shop 2km; tradsmn; rest; bar; no statics; dogs; adv bkg; rd noise; ccard acc. "Ski bus every 20 mins at site ent; skilift 100m; htd boot room; mountain-biking in summer." ♦ 26 Apr-Nov. € 25.00 2007*

MERINCHAL *7B4* (S Urban) **Camp Municipal La Mothe, Château de Mérinchal, 23420 Mérinchal [05 55 67 25 56 (TO); fax 05 55 67 23 71; tourisme.merinchal@wanadoo.fr]** E fr Pontaumur on D941twds Aubusson. R onto D27 to Mérinchal. Site in vill. Sm, pt sl, pt shd; wc; shwrs inc; el pnts €2; Indtte; shop, rest, bar nr; playgrnd; TV; fishing 500m; quiet. "Excel site in chateau grounds but poss clsd w/end if weddings etc in chateau - phone ahead to check." ♦ 1 May-30 Oct. € 8.50 2007*

MERS LES BAINS *3B2* (1.5km NE Coastal/Rural) *50.07709, 1.41430* **FLOWER Camping Le Rompval, Lieu-Dit Blengues, 154 Rue André Dumont, 80350 Mers-les-Bains [02 35 84 43 21 or 06 50 02 79 57; campinglerompval@gmail.com; www.campinglerompval.com]** Fr Calais on A16, exit junc 23 at Abbeville onto A28. In 5km exit junc 2 dir Friville-Escarbotin, Le Tréport & cont to Mers-les-Bains. Site sp. Fr S on A28 exit junc 5 onto D1015 to Mers-les-Bains & foll sp Blengues & site. Med, hdg/mkd pitch, pt shd; htd wc; chem disp; baby facs; shwrs inc; el pnts (8A) inc; gas; Indtte; shop; tradsmn; snacks; bar; BBQ; playgrnd; htd pool; paddling pool; sand beach 3km; tennis 3km; cycle hire; games area; wifi; 25% statics; dogs €1.50; Eng spkn; adv bkg; quiet; ccard acc; red long stay; CCI. "Vg site; gd facs." ♦ 1 Apr-31 Oct. € 24.00 2009*

See advertisement on page 295

MERVANS *6H1* (NE Rural) *46.80179, 5.19171* **Camp Municipal du Plan d'Eau, Route de Pierre-de-Bresse, 71310 Mervans [03 85 76 16 63 (Mairie); fax 03 85 76 16 93; mairie-de-mervans@wanadoo.fr]** E on N78 fr Chalon-sur-Saône. At Thurey fork L onto D204; at x-rds turn L onto D996 to Mervans. In vill take D313 dir Pierre-de-Bresse, site sp by lake. Sm, pt shd; wc (some cont); shwrs inc; el pnts (10A) inc; shop, rest adj; fishing nr; quiet; CCI. "Well-kept site, clean facs; lovely countryside; pleasant vill." ♦ 1 Jun-15 Sep. € 6.60 2008*

MERVENT see Fontenay le Comte *7A2*

MERVILLE FRANCEVILLE PLAGE see Cabourg *3D1*

MERY SUR SEINE *4E4* (W Rural) *48.51067, 3.88502* **Camp Municipal au Bout de la Ville, Rue de Grèves, 10170 Méry-sur-Seine [03 25 21 23 72 or 03 25 21 20 42 (Mairie); fax 03 25 21 13 19]** Turn N off D619 (N19) Troyes to Romilly onto D373 sp Méry-sur-Seine; in vill turn 1st L after x-ing Rv Seine; site on L in 500m on rv bank. Med, hdg/mkd pitch, hdstg, pt sl, pt shd; wc (cont); chem disp; shwrs inc; el pnts (3-10A) €1.40-2.70; Indtte; shops 50m; BBQ; playgrnd; fishing; 75% statics; phone; poss cr; Eng spkn; adv bkg; quiet; CCI. "Peaceful site; vg clean san facs; friendly warden on site for initial access (0900-1200 & 1700-1900); access for m'vans outside office hrs; pleasant town with Sat mkt; vg." ♦ 1 Apr-30 Sep. € 7.00 2009*

MESCHERS SUR GIRONDE see Royan *7B1*

MESLAND see Onzain *4G2*

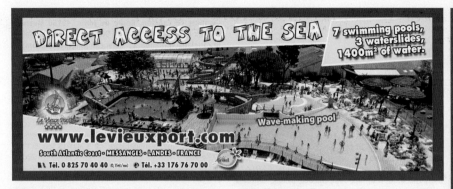

MESLAY DU MAINE *4F1* (2.5km NE Rural) *47.96409, -0.52979* **Camp Municipal La Chesnaie, 53170 Meslay-du-Maine [02 43 98 48 08 or 02 43 64 10 45 (Mairie); fax 02 43 98 75 52; camping-lachesnaie@wanadoo.fr]** Take D21 SE fr Laval to Meslay. Turn L in cent of vill onto D152. Site on R in 2.5km. Med, hdg/mkd pitch, pt shd; wc (some cont); shwrs inc; el pnts (6-12A) €2.30 (poss long lead req); lndtte; shop 2.5km; rest 200m; snacks; bar; playgrnd; lake adj; watersports, leisure cent adj; 10% statics; poss cr; adv bkg; ccard acc; CCI. "Excel; clean & quiet." ♦ 1 Apr-30 Sep. € 8.60 2008*

MESNIL ST PERE *6F1* (1km NE Rural) *48.25000, 4.34000* **Kawan Village Camping Lac d'Orient, Rue du Lac, 10140 Mesnil-St Père [tel/fax 03 25 40 61 85; info@camping-lacdorient.com; www.camping-lacdorient.com]** On D619 (N19) foll sps Lac de la Forêt d'Orient. Approx 10km fr Vendeuvre or 20km fr Troyes turn N on D43A, to Mesnil-St Père; site sp. Lge, pt sl, pt shd; wc (some cont); chem disp; mv service pnt; private san facs some pitches; baby facs; shwrs inc; el pnts (10A) inc; lndtte; shop; tradsmn; rest; snacks; bar; BBQ; playgrnd; 2 htd pools (1 covrd); paddling pool; lake sw/shgl beach & watersports 500m; fishing; games area; wifi; some statics; dogs €2; phone; Eng spkn; adv bkg; quiet; ccard acc; red low ssn; CCI. "Newly reopened, improvements in hand (2009); 1st class san facs; conv Nigloland theme park & Champagne area; vg." ♦ 27 Mar-2 Oct. € 33.00 (CChq acc) ABS - J07 2009*

MESNOIS see Clairvaux les Lacs *6H2*

MESSANGES *8E1* (2km S Coastal) *43.80070, -1.39220* **Camping La Côte, Route de Vieux-Boucau, 40660 Messanges [05 58 48 94 94; fax 05 58 48 94 44; lacote@wanadoo.fr; www.campinglacote.com]** On D652 2km S of Messanges. Med, pt shd; wc; chem disp; mv service pnt; serviced pitches; shwrs inc; el pnts (6-10A) €3.50-4.60; lndtte; sm shop; supmkt 1km; tradsmn; snacks; playgrnd; pool complex; paddling pool; sand beach 1km; horseriding 300m; golf 2km; 5% statics; dogs €2; phone; adv bkg; Eng spkn; quiet but poss early noise fr builders yard adj; red low ssn; CCI. "Peaceful, clean, tidy site adj pine woods; lge pitches; gd access to beaches; gd cycle tracks; excel." ♦ 1 Apr-30 Sep. € 18.20 2009*

MESSANGES *8E1* (2km SW Coastal) *43.79790, -1.40135* **Airotel Camping Le Vieux Port, Plage Sud, 40660 Messanges [01 76 76 70 00 or 0825 70 40 40; fax 05 58 48 01 69; contact@levieuxport.com; www.levieuxport.com]** Fr S take D652 past Vieux-Boucau; site sp. Turn W at Super U rndabt. V lge, mkd pitch, hdstg, pt shd; wc (some cont); chem disp; mv service pnt; shwrs inc; el pnts (6-8A) €8.30; gas 1km; lndtte; shop; tradsmn; rest; snacks; bar; BBQ; playgrnd; htd, pt cvrd pool + pool complex; paddling pool; waterslides; dir access to sand beach 500m; tennis; games area; cycle hire; horseriding; quadbikes; boules; beach train; internet; entmnt; TV; 10% statics; dogs €5.20; Eng spkn; adv bkg; poss cr; quiet; red low ssn; ccard acc; CCI. "V pleasant, clean site; superb pool complex; excel touring base." ♦ 1 Apr-26 Sep. € 46.00 (CChq acc) 2009*

See advertisement above

METZ *5D2* (500m NW Urban) *49.12402, 6.16917* **Camp Municipal Metz-Plage, Allée de Metz-Plage, 57000 Metz [03 87 68 26 48; fax 03 87 38 03 89; campingmetz@mairie-metz.fr; www.mairie-metz.fr]** Exit A31 junc 33 Metz-Nord/Pontiffroy exit. Foll 'Autres Directions' sp back over a'route & Rv Moselle; site sp on S bank of rv, bet Pont de Thionville & Pont des Morts. Lge, mkd pitch, hdstg, pt sl, pt shd; wc; chem disp; mv service pnt; baby facs; shwrs inc; el pnts (10A) inc (poss rev pol); lndtte; shop, snacks; playgrnd; pool adj; rv fishing adj; internet; dogs €0.50; twin-axles extra; poss cr; Eng spkn; adv bkg; traff noise fr rv bdge at far end; ccard acc; CCI. "Beautifully situated on rv with views; some gd sized pitches; helpful staff; poss long walk to san facs; facs stretched if site full; early arr ess high ssn; vg." ♦ 23 Apr-4 Oct. € 16.00 2009*

MEURSAULT see Beaune *6H1*

MEYRAS see Thueyts *9D2*

MEYRIEU LES ETANGS *9B2* (800m SE Rural) *45.50790, 5.20850* **Camping Base de Loisirs du Moulin, Route de Châtonnay, 38440 Meyrieu-les-Etangs [04 74 59 30 34; fax 04 74 58 36 12; contact@camping-meyrieu.com; www.camping-meyrieu.com]** Exit A43 at junc 8. Enter Bourgoin & foll sp for La Gare to pick up D522 SW twd St Jean-de-Bournay. Site next to lake 1km fr D522, sp. Med, mkd pitch, hdstg, terr, pt shd; wc; shwrs; el pnts (6-10A) €3.60-4.80; lndry rm; shop; rest; lake sw; pedaloes; fishing; canoeing; archery; games rm; entmnt in ssn; TV; dogs €1.60; phone; adv bkg; quiet. "Views across lake; sm pitches; hdstg on all pitches for car; clean san facs & site; vg." ♦ 15 Apr-30 Sep. € 15.40 2007*

MEYRUEIS *10E1* (3km N Rural) *44.19633, 3.45724* **FFCC Camping La Cascade, Salvinsac, 48150 Meyrueis [04 66 45 45 45 or 06 85 84 07 15 (mob); fax 04 66 45 48 48; contact@camping-la-cascade.com; www.camping-la-cascade.com]** N of Meyrueis on D996, on R. NB Do not app fr N - narr rd. Rec app fr Millau dir only. Sm, mkd pitch, pt sl, terr, pt shd; wc; chem disp; mv service pnt; baby facs; shwrs inc; el pnts (10A) €2.90; gas; lndtte; shop; tradsmn; BBQ; playgrnd; canoeing; fishing; horseriding; walking; 20% statics; dogs; poss cr; Eng spkn; adv bkg; ccard acc. "Friendly owners." ♦ 8 Apr-1 Nov. € 12.50 2006*

MEYRUEIS *10E1* (1km NE Rural) *44.18590, 3.43856* **Camping Le Pré de Charlet, Route de Florac, 48150 Meyrueis [04 66 45 63 65; fax 04 66 45 63 24; contact@camping-lepredecharlet.com; www.camping-lepredecharlet.com]** Exit Meyrueis on rd to Florac (D996). Site on R on bank of Rv Jonte. Med, mkd pitch, pt sl, terr, pt shd, pt sl; wc (some cont); chem disp; mv service pnt; baby facs; shwrs inc; el pnts (16A) €2.60; gas; lndtte; shop & 11km; tradsmn; bar; BBQ; playgrnd; pool 400m; rv fishing; phone; adv bkg; phone; quiet; ccard acc; CCI. "Friendly owner; excel." ♦ 15 Apr-10 Oct. € 12.00 2007*

MEYRUEIS *10E1* (500m E Rural) *44.18075, 3.43540* **Camping Le Champ d'Ayres, Route de la Brèze, 48150 Meyrueis [tel/fax 04 66 45 60 51; campinglechampdayres@wanadoo.fr; www.campinglechampdayres.com]** Fr W on D907 dir Gorges de la Jonte into Meyrueis. Foll sp Château d'Ayres & site. Med, hdg/mkd pitch, pt sl, pt shd; wc (some cont); chem disp; mv service pnt; baby facs; fam bthrm; shwrs inc; el pnts (6A) €3; lndtte; shop; tradsmn; snacks; bar; BBQ; playgrnd; htd pool; cycle hire; games area; games rm; wifi; 15% statics; dogs €1; phone; poss cr; Eng spkn; adv bkg; red low ssn; ccard acc; CCI. "Helpful owners; rec." ♦ 11 Apr-19 Sep. € 21.00 2009*

MEYRUEIS *10E1* (800m NW Rural) *44.18580, 3.41977* **Camping Le Capelan, Route de Jonte, 48150 Meyrueis [tel/fax 04 66 45 60 50 or 04 90 53 34 45 (LS); camping.le.capelan@wanadoo.fr; www.campingcapelan.com]** Site sp on D996 on banks of Rv Jonte. Med, mkd pitch, shd; wc; chem disp; mv service pnt; baby facs; fam bthrm; shwrs inc; el pnts (4-10A) €3; gas; lndtte; shop; tradsmn; supmkt 500m; BBQ; rest 1km; snacks; bar; playgrnd; 2 htd pools (no shorts); fishing; tennis 1km; games rm; games area; rockclimbing; internet; entmnt; sat TV; 70% statics; private bthrms avail; Eng spkn; adv bkg; quiet; red low ssn; ccard acc; CCI. "Gd, scenic, rvside site; conv touring Gorges du Tarn & Cévennes National Park." ♦ 1 May-15 Sep. € 19.00 (CChq acc) 2007*

MEYSSAC *7C3* (2km NE Rural) *45.06150, 1.66402* **Intercommunal Moulin de Valane, Route de Collonges-la-Rouge, 19500 Meyssac [05 55 25 41 59; fax 05 55 84 07 28; mairie@meyssac.fr; www.meyssac.fr]** Well sp on D38 bet Meyssac & Collonges-la-Rouge. Med, mkd pitch, pt sl, pt shd; wc; chem disp; shwrs; el pnts (10A) €2.80; lndtte; shop; rest; snacks; bar; playgrnd; pool; tennis; many statics; adv bkg; CCI. "Within walking dist of attractive vill; fair only." ♦ 1 May-30 Sep. € 13.00 2007*

MEYZIEU see Lyon *9B2*

MEZE *10F1* (1km N Coastal) *43.43019, 3.61070* **Kawan Village Beau Rivage, 113 Route Nationale, 34140 Mèze [04 67 43 81 48; fax 04 67 43 66 70; reception@camping-beaurivage.fr; www.camping-beaurivage.fr]** Fr Mèze cent foll D613 (N113) dir Montpellier, site on R 100m past rndabt on leaving town; well sp. Lge, mkd pitch, pt shd; wc; chem disp; mv service pnt; shwrs inc; el pnts (3-6A) inc; lndtte; shop; supmkt 200m; rest; snacks; bar (high ssn); BBQ; playgrnd; htd pool & paddling pool; sand beach 700m; fishing; sailing; tennis 900m; entmnt; TV rm; 50% statics; phone; dogs €3; poss cr; Eng spkn; adv bkg; quiet; ccard acc; CCI. "Lovely site; trees & narr access rds poss diff lge o'fits; vg modern san facs; poor security - rear of site open to public car park; conv Sète & Noilly Prat distillery; excel." ♦ 5 Apr-19 Sep. € 35.00 (CChq acc) 2008*

MEZE *10F1* (3km N Rural) *43.44541, 3.61595* **Camp Municipal Loupian, Route de Mèze, 34140 Loupian [04 67 43 57 67; camping@loupian.fr; www.loupian.fr]** Fr Mèze tak D613 (N113) & turn L at 1st Loupian sp, then foll sp for site. Med, hdg/mkd pitch, pt shd; wc; chem disp; shwrs; el pnts (5A) €2.40; lndtte; snacks; bar; BBQ; playgrnd; sand beach 3km; entmnt; dogs €0.75; poss cr; Eng spkn; adv bkg; quiet; red low ssn; CCI. "Pleasant site in popular area; plenty shade; friendly welcome; gd san facs; gd beaches; gd rests near Mèze; old rlwy rte fr site to Mèze." ♦ 25 Apr-4 Oct. € 12.90 2009*

MEZE *10F1* (5.5km NE Coastal) *43.45070, 3.66562* **Camping Lou Labech, Chemin du Stade, 34140 Bouzigues [04 67 78 30 38; fax 04 67 78 35 46; contact@lou-labech.fr; www.lou-labech.fr]** Exit A9 junc 33 onto D660/D613 S to Bouzigues; site sp. Part of Chemin du Stade borders sea. Sm, hdstg, terr, pt shd; wc; chem disp; baby facs; shwrs; el pnts (5A) £3; lndtte; tradsmn; rest 800m; bar; BBQ (charcoal sep area); playgrnd; wifi; TV; dogs free; poss cr; Eng spkn; quiet; red low ssn. "Delightful site; friendly, helpful staff; Bouzigues lovely vill." ♦ Apr-Oct. € 21.00 2009*

MEZEL *10E3* (W Rural) *43.99634, 6.19678* **Camp Municipal Le Claux, 04270 Mézel [04 92 35 53 87 (Mairie); fax 04 92 35 52 86]** Sp fr N85 fr both dir. Heading S fr Digne onto D907; turn R to site on L. Sm, pt sl, pt shd; wc (cont); shwrs; el pnts (3-6A); shops adj; snacks nr; poss cr; quiet. "Private rlwy to Nice v nr." 1 Jul-31 Aug. 2007*

MEZIERES EN BRENNE *4H2* (500m E Rural) *46.81909, 1.22253* **Camp Municipal La Cailauderie, Route de l'Eglise, 36290 Mézières-en-Brenne [02 54 38 12 24 or 02 54 38 09 23]** On D925 to Châteauroux, sp Stade. Sm, mkd pitch, pt shd; wc; chem disp; shwrs inc; el pnts (6A) €2.65; shop, rest, bar 500m; playgrnd; rv adj; dogs; quiet; CCI. "Site yourself, warden calls am & pm; rv fishing on site; gd birdwatching; poss itinerants; poss vicious mosquitoes." 1 May-30 Sep. € 9.00 2007*

MEZIERES EN BRENNE *4H2* (6km E Rural) *46.79817, 1.30595* **Camping Bellebouche, 36290 Mézières-en-Brenne [02 54 38 32 36; fax 02 54 38 32 96; v.v.n@orange.fr; www.village-vacances-bellebouche.com]** Sp on D925. Med, mkd pitch, pt sl, pt shd; wc (cont); chem disp (wc); baby facs; shwrs inc; el pnts inc; lndtte; shop 6km; rest high ssn; bar 6km; playgrnd; lake sw adj; watersports; fishing; no statics; no dogs high ssn; phone; quiet; ccard acc; CCI. "In country park; gd walking, cycling, bird-watching; vg." 1 Mar-30 Nov. € 14.00 2006*

MEZIN *8E2* (4km NW Rural) *44.07281, 0.20774* **FLOWER Camping du Lac de Lislebonne, Le Bétous, 47170 Mézin-Réaup-Lisse [05 53 65 65 28; fax 05 53 65 34 05; domainelislebonne@free.fr; www.domainelislebonne.com]** Exit A62 junc 6 (Agen) dir Nérac on D656; cont on D656 to Mézin; then foll site sps. Sm, mkd pitch, pt shd; htd wc; shwrs inc; el pnts (12A) inc; gas; lndtte; shop; tradsmn; rest; snacks; bar; BBQ; playgrnd; lake sw & beach adj; cycle hire; games area; games rm; entmnt; wifi; TV; 45% statics; dogs €1.50; quiet; Eng spkn; adv bkg; ccard acc; red low ssn; CCI. "Vg touring base; gd walking; vg site." ♦ 25 Apr-27 Sep. € 18.50 2008*

MEZOS *8E1* (1km SE Rural) *44.07980, -1.16090* **Le Village Tropical Sen Yan, 40170 Mézos [05 58 42 60 05; fax 05 58 42 64 56; reception@sen-yan.com; www.sen-yan.com]** Fr Bordeaux on N10 in 100km at Laharie turn W onto D38 dir Mimizan; in 12km turn L onto D63 to Mézos; turn L at mini-rndabt; site on L in approx 2km. Site 1.5km fr D63/D38 junc NE of Mézos. Lge, hdg/mkd pitch, shd; wc (some cont); chem disp; baby facs; sauna; shwrs inc; el pnts (6A) inc; gas; lndtte; shop; rest; snacks; bar; BBQ (gas only); playgrnd; 3 pools (1 htd & covrd); paddling pool; waterslides sand beach 12km; rv adj; fishing; canoe hire 1km; watersports 15km; tennis; cycle hire; many sports & games; fitness cent; entmnt; wifi; games/TV (cab/sat) rm; 80% statics; dogs €5; phone; max c'van 7m high ssn; Eng spkn; adv bkg; quiet; ccard acc; red low ssn; CCI. "Pleasant & restful; excel facs for families; mkt Mimizan Fri." ♦ 1 Jun-15 Sep. € 36.50 ABS - A09 2009*

MIANNAY see Abbeville *3B3*

MIGENNES see Joigny *4F4*

⊞ **MILLAS** *8G4* (3km W Rural) *42.69067, 2.65785* **FLOWER Camping La Garenne, 66170 Néfiach [04 68 57 15 76; fax 04 68 57 37 42; camping.lagarenne.nefiach@wanadoo.fr; www.camping-lagarenne.fr or www.flowercamping.com]** Fr Millas on R of D916, sp. Med, shd; htd wc (some cont); chem disp; baby facs; shwrs inc; el pnts (6-10A) €5; gas; lndtte; shop; snacks; bar; BBQ; playgrnd; pool high ssn; tennis 500m; games area; entmnt; 50% statics; dogs free; adv bkg rec high ssn; rd noise & poss noisy disco; red low ssn. "Friendly owners; gd facs." ♦ € 18.50 2008*

MILLAU *10E1* (1km NE Urban) *44.10500, 3.08833* **Camping du Viaduc, Millau-Cureplat, 121 Ave du Millau-Plage, 12100 Millau [05 65 60 15 75; fax 05 65 61 36 51; info@camping-du-viaduc.com; www.camping-du-viaduc.com]** Exit Millau on N991 (sp Nant) over Rv Tarn via Cureplat bdge. At rndabt take D187 dir Paulhe, 1st campsite on L. Lge, hdg/mkd pitch, shd; htd wc; chem disp; some serviced pitches (extra charge); baby facs; shwrs inc; el pnts (6A) €4 (poss long lead req); gas; lndtte; shop; rest; snacks; bar; BBQ; playgrnd; htd pool; paddling pool; rv sw & private sand beach; entmnt; wifi; dogs €3; Eng spkn; some rd noise; ccard acc; red low ssn/long stay/CCI. "Well-run, peaceful site; helpful, welcoming staff; excel clean san facs; barrier clsd 2200-0700; many sports & activities in area; conv for gorges & viaduct tours; quiet low ssn; super site." ♦ 23 Apr-26 Sep. € 27.00 2009*

MILLAU *10E1* (1km NE Urban) *44.11044, 3.08712* **Camping Larribal, Ave de Millau Plage, 12100 Millau [05 65 59 08 04; camping.larribal@wanadoo.fr; www.campinglarribal.com]** Exit Millau on D991 (sp Nant), cross rv & at rndabt take 3rd exit, site on L. Med, mkd pitch, shd; htd wc; chem disp; shwrs inc; el pnts (6A) €2; gas; lndtte; shop; tradsmn; playgrnd; rv sw adj; shgl beach; TV; 5% statics; phone; adv bkg; quiet but poss noise fr stadium across rv; red low ssn/long stay; CCI. "Excel, well-kept, quiet site on Rv Tarn; friendly, helpful staff; excel, clean san facs; lge o'fits poss diff access; high m'vans poss diff under trees; gd access to gorges; severe tree fluff in May." ♦ 23 Apr-30 Sep. € 11.50 2009*

France

MILLAU *10E1* (1km NE Rural) *44.10640, 3.08800* **Camping Les Erables, Route de Millau-Plage, 12100 Millau [05 65 59 15 13; fax 05 65 59 06 59; camping-les-erables@orange.fr; www.campingleserables.fr]** Exit Millau on D991 (sp Nant) over Rv Tarn bdge; take L at island sp to Millau-Plage & site on L immed after Camping du Viaduc & bef Camping Larribal. On ent Millau fr N or S foll sps 'Campings'. Med, hdg/mkd pitch, shd; wc; chem disp; baby facs; shwrs inc; el pnts (6A) €3 (rev pol); Indtte; shop; snacks high ssn; bar; BBQ; playgrnd; rv sw, canoeing adj; wifi; entmnt; TV; dogs €1.20; phone; Eng spkn; adv bkg; some rd noise; ccard acc; CCI. "Clean site; friendly, helpful owners; beavers nrby; gd." ♦ 5 Apr-30 Sep. € 15.60 2009*

MILLAU *10E1* (2km NE Urban) *44.10240, 3.09100* **Camping Côte-Sud, Ave de l'Aigoual, 12100 Millau [tel/fax 05 65 61 18 83; camping-cotesud@orange.fr; www.campingcotesud.com]** Fr N exit A75 junc 45 to Millau. Turn L at 2nd traff island sp 'Camping'. Site on R over bdge in 200m. Fr S exit A75 junc 47 onto D809 (N9) & cross rv on by-pass, turn R at 1st traff island sp Nant on D991, cross bdge, site on R in 200m, sp. Site a S confluence of Rv Dourbie & Rv Tarn. Med, mkd pitch, pt sl, shd; wc; chem disp; shwrs inc; el pnts (5A) €3.50; gas; Indtte; shop; snacks; playgrnd; pool; rv sw adj; fishing, canoe hire & hang-gliding nrby; some statics; dogs €1.50; Eng spkn; adv bkg; red low ssn; CCI. "Excel site; gd san facs; pleasant, helpful owner; conv Tarn Gorges; lge mkt Fri." 1 Apr-30 Sep. € 20.50 2008*

MILLAU *10E1* (6km NE Rural) *44.15188, 3.09899* **Camping d'Aguessac, Chemin des Prades, 12520 Aguessac [05 65 59 84 67 or 06 22 57 54 99 (mob); fax 05 65 59 08 72]** Site on N907 in vill; ent on R v soon after level x-ing when app fr Millau - adj g'ge forecourt. Med, mkd pitch, pt shd; wc; chem disp; shwrs inc; el pnts (6A) €2.50; gas; Indtte; shops adj; bar; rv adj; fishing; canoeing; games area; sports grnd adj; wifi; entmnt; dogs €1; quiet; red long stay/low ssn; CCI. "Nice, spacious, clean rvside site; gd position with mountain views; gd sized pitches; helpful & friendly staff; public footpath thro site along rv; picturesque vill & local viaduct; poss youth groups high ssn - but no problem; excel touring base; unreliable opening dates." ♦ 1 Apr-30 Sep. € 12.50 2009*

MILLAU *10E1* (8.5km NE Rural) *44.16861, 3.11944* **Camping Les Cerisiers, Pailhas, 12520 Compeyre [05 65 59 87 96 or 05 65 59 10 35 (LS); contact@campinglescerisiers.com; www.campinglescerisiers.com]** Fr Millau N on D809 (N9) for 4km, then D907 to Pailhas; site at exit to vill on R. Med, mkd pitch, pt shd; wc; chem disp; shwrs inc; el pnts (6A) €3; Indry rm; shop; tradsmn; snacks; playgrnd; private beach on Rv Tarn; pool 3km; rock climbing; canoeing, mountain biking, paragliding & horseriding nrby; games rm; entmnt; wifi; 5% statics; dogs €1.50; phone; poss cr; Eng spkn; adv bkg; quiet; ccard acc; red low ssn; CCI. "Vg, clean site; helpful staff; bird-watching; Millau tourist train; conv Tarn gorges." ♦ 1 May-15 Sep. € 14.00 2009*

MILLAU *10E1* (1km E Rural) *44.11552, 3.08692* **Camping Club Le Millau-Plage, Route de Millau-Plage, 12100 Millau [05 65 60 10 97; fax 05 65 60 16 88; info@campingmillauplage.com; www.campingmillauplage.com]** Exit Millau on D991 (sp Nant) over Rv Tarn; at rndabt take final exit onto D187 sp Paulhe; site is 4th on L. Lge, mkd pitch, pt shd; wc; chem disp; shwrs inc; el pnts (5A) inc; gas; Indtte; shop; tradsmn; rest; snacks; bar; playgrnd; pool; multi-sports area; TV; play rm; 40% statics; dogs €3; poss cr; Eng spkn; adv bkg; quiet; ccard acc; red low ssn; CCI. "Magnificent scenery." ♦ 1 Apr-30 Sep. € 26.00 2008*

MILLAU *10E1* (1km E Urban) *44.10287, 3.08732* **Camping Les Deux Rivières, 61 Ave de l'Aigoual, 12100 Millau [05 65 60 00 27 or 06 07 08 41 41 (mob); fax 05 65 60 76 78; camping.deux-rivieres@orange.fr; www.ot-millau.fr]** Fr N on D911 foll sp for Montpellier down to rv. At rndabt by bdge turn L over bdge, site immed on L well sp. Fr S on D992 3rd bdge, sp camping. Sm, mkd pitch, shd; htd wc (50% cont); shwrs inc; el pnts (8-10A) €2.40; gas; Indry rm; shops adj; tradsmn; snacks; playgrnd; fishing; phone; poss cr; quiet; CCI. "Basic site in gd situation by rv; san facs dated but clean; poss a bit unkempt low ssn; gd base for touring gorges." 1 Apr-31 Oct. € 13.80 2009*

MILLAU *10E1* (1km E Rural) *44.10166, 3.09611* **Camping Les Rivages, Ave de l'Aigoual, 12100 Millau [05 65 61 01 07 or 06 89 78 50 33 (mob); fax 05 65 59 03 56; camping lesrivages@wanadoo.fr; www.campinglesrivages.com]** Fr Millau take D991 dir Nant (sp Gorges de la Dourbie & Campings). Cross Rv Tarn & cont on this rd, site is 500m after bdge on R. Lge, pt shd; htd wc (some cont); chem disp (wc); serviced pitches (additional charge); baby facs; shwrs inc; el pnts (6A) inc (poss rev pol); gas; lndtte; sm shop; supmkt 2km; tradsmn; rest; snacks; bar; BBQ; playgrnd; 2 pools; paddling pool; tennis; fishing; canoeing nr; cycle hire; hang-gliding; entmnt; wifi; games/TV rm; 10% statics; dogs €3.50; phone; poss cr; Eng spkn; adv bkg; quiet; ccard acc over €30; red low ssn; CCI. "Pleasant, busy, scenic site - esp rv/side pitches; helpful & friendly staff; gd san facs; gd security; mkt Wed & Fri." ♦ 29 Apr-30 Sep. € 30.00 ABS - D20 2009*

MILLAU *10E1* (2.5km E Rural) *44.10029, 3.11099* **FFCC Camping St Lambert, Ave de l'Aigoual, 12100 Millau [05 65 60 00 48; fax 05 65 61 12 12; camping.saintlambert@orange.fr; www.campingsaintlambert.fr]** Fr N on either D809 (N9) or D11 foll dir D992 St Affrique/Albi. Turn L at rndabt over bdge onto D991 dir Nant. Site on R, sp. Fr S on D992 turn R at rndabt & dir as above. Med, mkd pitch, shd; wc (some cont); chem disp; mv service pnt; shwrs inc; el pnts (6A) €2.80; gas; lndtte; shop; bar; playgrnd; sand/shgl beach & rv sw adj; 10% statics; dogs €1; poss cr; adv bkg; quiet; CCI. "Particularly gd low ssn; owners helpful; twin-axles not acc." 1 May-30 Sep. € 14.00 2009*

MILLY LA FORET *4E3* (4km SE Rural) *48.39569, 2.50380* **Camping La Musardière, Route des Grandes Vallées, 91490 Milly-la-Forêt [tel/fax 01 64 98 91 91; lamusardiere@infonie.fr]** Fr S exit A6 junc 14 onto D152 then D16 dir Milly; Rte des Grande Vallées is R turn 2km after Noisy-sur-Ecole (4km bef Milly). Look for 'Domain Regional' sps (not easy to read). Fr N exit A6 junc 13 onto D372 to Milly; exit Milly S on D16; Rte des Grandes Vallées turning to L in 1.5km. Site on L 1km along Rte des Grandes Vallées. Best app fr N. Lge, mkd pitch, hdstg, pt sl, pt shd; htd wc (some cont); chem disp; baby facs; fam bthrm; shwrs inc; el pnts (6A) inc; lndtte; shop 4km; tradsmn (w/end only low ssn); BBQ; playgrnd; htd pool high ssn; paddling pool; cycle hire; 70% statics; dogs free; Eng spkn; adv bkg; ccard acc; red long stay; CCI. "Wooded site; excel pool; helpful, friendly staff; gd walks in nrby forest." ♦ 16 Feb-1 Dec. € 22.10 2009*

See advertisement opposite

MIMIZAN *7D1* (2km N Rural) *44.21997, -1.22968* **Camping du Lac, Ave de Woolsack, 40200 Mimizan [05 58 09 01 21; fax 05 58 09 43 06; lac@mimizan-camping.com; www.mimizan-camping.com]** Fr Mimizan N on D87, site on R. Lge, mkd pitch; pt shd; wc; chem disp; mv service pnt; baby facs; shwrs inc; el pnts (3A) inc; gas; lndtte; shop; rest; snacks; bar; BBQ; playgrnd; sand beach 6km; lake adj - no sw; boating; fishing; entmnt; some statics; dogs €1.70; poss cr; adv bkg; quiet; red low ssn. "Nice site in lovely location; o'night area for m'vans; rec." ♦ 3 Apr-20 Sep. € 17.80 2009*

MIMIZAN *7D1* (3km E Rural) *44.22296, -1.19445* **Camping Aurilandes, 1001 Promenade de l'Etang, 40200 Aureilhan [05 58 09 10 88 or 05 46 55 10 01; fax 05 46 55 10 00; www.village-center.com]** Fr N10 S of Bordeaux take D626 W fr Labouheyre twds Mimizan. Site 1km fr D626 by Lake Aureilhan. V lge, mkd pitch, pt shd; wc; mv service pnt; sauna; shwrs inc; el pnts (6-10A) inc; lndtte; shop; tradsmn; rest; playgrnd; htd pool complex; paddling pool; spa; sand beach 10km; dir access to lake; watersports; tennis; games rm; entmnt; statics; dogs €3; Eng spkn; adv bkg; ccard acc; quiet; ccard acc. ♦ 12 May-19 Sep. € 29.00 2007*

MIMIZAN PLAGE *7D1* (1km E Coastal) *44.21629, -1.28584* **Camping de la Plage, Blvd d'Atlantique, 40200 Mimizan-Plage [05 58 09 00 32; fax 05 58 09 44 94; contact@mimizan-camping.com; www.mimizan-camping.com]** Turn off N10 at Labouheyre on D626 to Mimizan (28km). Approx 5km after Mimizan turn R. Site in approx 500m. V lge, pt sl, shd; wc; mv service pnt; baby facs; shwrs; el pnts (10A) €2; lndtte; shops 500m; playgrnd; sand beach 850m; games area; entmnt; 15% statics; dogs €1.80; poss cr; noisy. Easter-30 Sep. € 16.00 2006*

MIMIZAN PLAGE *7D1* (3km E Coastal) *44.20420, -1.2908* **Club Marina-Landes, Rue Marina, 40202 Mimizan-Plage-Sud [05 58 09 12 66; fax 05 58 09 16 40; contact@clubmarina.com; www.marinalandes.com]** Turn R off N10 at Labouheyre onto D626 to Mimizan (28km). Approx 5km fr Mimizan-Plage turn L at Camping Marina sp on dual c'way. Site sp on S bank of rv. V lge, hdg pitch, hdstg, pt shd; wc; chem disp; mv service pnt; baby facs; shwrs inc; el pnts (10A) €5; gas; lndtte; ice; shop; rest; snacks; bar; BBQ; playgrnd; 2 pools (1 htd, covrd); paddling pool; waterslide; sand beach 500m; tennis; horseriding; games area; cycle hire; games rm; fitness rm; golf 7km; entmnt; wifi; TV rm; some statics; dogs €4; poss cr; Eng spkn; adv bkg; ccard acc; quiet; red CCI. "Excursions to Dax, Biarritz & Bordeaux areas; excel leisure facs; vg." ♦ 30 Apr-13 Sep. € 39.00 (3 persons) 2009*

See advertisement on next page

MIOS see Audenge *7D1*

MIRAMBEAU *7C2* (1km N Urban) *45.37822, -0.56874* **Camp Municipal Le Carrelet, 92 Ave de la République, 17150 Mirambeau [05 46 70 26 99]** Exit 37 fr A10 onto D730/D137 dir Mirambeau. Site opp Super U supmkt, behind tourist office. Sm, pt shd; wc; chem disp (wc); washing cubicles; shwrs inc; el pnts (10A) €4 (poss rev pol); shops, rest adj; mostly statics; dogs €1.50; quiet. "Basic site; clean but tired facs; obliging warden; site yourself & warden calls evening; v muddy when wet; poss neglected low ssn; conv A10." 1 Apr-31 Dec. € 11.00 2009*

⊞ **MIRAMBEAU** *7C2* (8km S Rural) *45.31430, -0.60290* **Camping Chez Gendron, 33820 St Palais [tel/fax 05 57 32 96 47; info@chezgendron.com; www.chezgendron.com]** N fr Blaye on N137; turn to St Palais, past church 1km; turn L twd St Ciers. Site sp R down narr lane. Or N fr Bordeaux on A10 exit juncs 37 or 38 onto N137 to St Palais & as above. Sm, mkd pitch, terr, pt sl, pt shd; htd wc; chem disp; shwrs; fam bthrm; el pnts (6A) inc; lndtte; shops 3km; tradsmn; rest; snacks; bar; BBQ; playgrnd; pool; paddling pool; games area; tennis 3km; games rm; wifi; TV; dogs free; phone; Eng spkn; adv bkg rec; quiet; red low ssn; CCI. "Peaceful & relaxed - lovely ambience; friendly, helpful Dutch owners; sep car park high ssn; superb san facs; ltd facs low ssn; pitches nr bar/recep poss noisy till late peak ssn; poss waterlogged after heavy rain; chem disp poor; excel Sun mkt." ♦ € 17.50 2008*

⊞ **MIRAMONT DE GUYENNE** *7D2* (13km W Rural) *44.62918, 0.22126* **Camping Parc St Vincent, 47120 Lévignac-de-Guyenne [05 53 83 75 17 or 01425 275080 (UK); sara.psv@wanadoo.fr; www.psv47.com]** Fr Miramont take D668 to Allemans-du-Dropt, then D211. At junc D708 turn S to Lévignac, site sp. Fr Marmande N on D708 sp St Foy & Duras. Turn E at Lévignac church to further green site sp on D228. Sm, pt shd; wc; chem disp; mv service pnt; shwrs inc; el pnts (5A); gas; lndtte; shops 2.5km; tradsmn; rest; snacks; BBQ; playgrnd; pool; lake sw 6km; entmnt; TV rm; 90% statics; dogs; phone; adv bkg; quiet; CCI. "Peaceful site; British owners make visitors welcome." ♦ 2006*

MIRAMONT DE GUYENNE *7D2* (6km NW Rural) **Camp Municipal Le Dropt, Rue du Pont, 47800 Allemans-du-Dropt [05 53 20 68 61 or 05 53 20 23 37 (Mairie); fax 05 53 20 68 91]** Fr D668 site well sp in vill. Sm, shd; wc (some cont); chem disp (wc); shwrs inc; el pnts (20A) €2; shop 400m; rest, snacks & bar 400m; playgrnd; quiet; CCI. "Attractive site on opp side of Rv Dropt to vill; friendly warden; ltd pitches for c'vans & lge o'fits due trees & o'hanging branches; excel." 1 May-31 Oct. € 7.00 2008*

MIRANDE *8F2* (1km NE Rural) *43.55235, 0.31371* **Camping Pouylebon (Devroome), Pouylebon, 32320 Montesquiou [05 62 66 72 10; campingpouylebon2@wanadoo.fr; http://pagesperso-orange.fr/campingpouylebon]** Exit N21 NW at Mirande onto D159; in 10km, at Pouylebon, turn R onto D216; in 900m site on R, 600m down track. Sm, pt sl, pt shd; wc; chem disp; shwrs inc; el pnts (6A) €2.85; lndtte; ice; sm shop & 12km; snacks; bar; BBQ; playgrnd; pool; tennis, fishing & horseriding nr; games area; games rm; wifi; TV rm; dogs free; poss cr; Eng spkn; adv bkg; ccard not acc; red low ssn. "Rural retreat; charming, Dutch owners; meals on request; excel." 1 May-1 Oct. € 14.70 2009*

MIRANDE *8F2* (500m E Rural) *43.51432, 0.40990* **Camp Municipal L'Ile du Pont, 32300 Mirande [05 62 66 64 11; fax 05 62 66 69 86; info@camping-iledupont.com; www.camping-gers.com]** On N21 Auch-Tarbes, foll sp to site on island in Rv Grande Baise. Med, pt shd; wc (cont); chem disp; mv service pnt; shwrs inc; el pnts (10A) inc; lndtte; tradsmn; snacks; bar; playgrnd; pool; waterslides; canoeing; sailing; windsurfing; fishing; tennis; entmnt; 20% statics; dogs €1; adv bkg rec; quiet; red low ssn; ccard not acc; CCI. "Excel site; helpful staff." 15 May-15 Sep. € 14.00 2006*

⊞ **MIRANDE** *8F2* (3km SW Rural) *43.48384, 0.37744* **FFCC Aire Naturelle La Hourguette, 32300 Berdoues [tel/fax 05 62 66 58 47]** Exit Mirande on N21 S dir Tarbes. 1st L after 'Intermarché' onto D524 to Berdoues, sp 'Camping La Ferme'. After 600m, turn R at fork in rd. Site in 2km. Sm, pt sl, pt shd; htd wc; chem disp; shwrs inc; el pnts (10A) €2; lndtte; shop 1.5km; rest, snacks & bar 3km; playgrnd; pool 3km; 10% statics; dogs; Eng spkn; quiet; CCI. "Pleasant, CL-type site; gd san facs; gd." ♦ € 18.00 2007*

MIRANDE *8F2* (10km NW Rural) *43.56500, 0.31972* **Camping Château Le Haget, Route de Mielan, 32320 Montesquiou [05 62 70 95 80; fax 05 62 70 94 83; info@lehaget.com; www.lehaget.com]** SW fr Mirande on N21 for 9km. At Renault g'ge turn R onto D16, then immed R onto D34 sp Montesquiou. Site on L in 11km. Rec do not use D943 fr Auch. Med, hdg/mkd pitch, pt sl, pt shd; htd wc (some cont); chem disp; shwrs inc; el pnts (10A) inc; Indtte; rest; snacks; bar; playgrnd; pool; games area; games rm; 60% statics; dogs €2; Eng spkn; adv bkg; quiet; cc acc; CCI. "V welcoming, friendly, helpful owners; wooded site full of wildlife, flowers; lge pitches; excel rest; a gem."
12 Apr-17 Oct. € 22.00 (3 persons) 2008*

MIRANDOL BOURGNOUNAC *8E4* (5km N Rural) *44.17709, 2.17874* **Camping Les Clots, 81190 Mirandol-Bourgnounac [tel/fax 05 63 76 92 78; campclots@wanadoo.fr; www.campinglesclots.info]** Fr Carmaux N on N88; L onto D905 to Mirandol, site sp; last 2-3km narr private rd - rough with steep hairpin. Sm, terr, pt shd; wc; chem disp; shwrs inc; el pnts (6-10A) €2.80; gas; Indtte; sm shop, tradsmn, bar high ssn; playgrnd; 2 pools; rv sw & fishing adj; games rm; TV; 10% statics; dogs €1; Eng spkn; adv bkg; quiet; red 5+ days; CCI. "Helpful Dutch owners; poss diff ent to site - not rec for towed c'vans; interesting area." 1 May-1 Oct.
€ 22.00 (3 persons) 2007*

MIREPOIX (ARIEGE) *8F4* (1km E Rural) *43.08871, 1.88585* **Camping Les Nysades (formerly Municipal Dynam'eau), Route de Limoux, 09500 Mirepoix [05 61 68 28 63; fax 05 61 68 89 48; campinglesnysades@orange.fr; www.camping-mirepoix-ariege.com]** E fr Pamiers on D119 to Mirepoix. Site well sp on D626. Med, hdg/mkd pitch, shd; wc; chem disp; shwrs; el pnts (6A) €3; shops 1km; pool; fishing 1km; tennis; some statics; dogs €2; quiet; red low ssn. "Lge pitches; gd, renovated san facs; interesting medieval town; mkt Mon." ♦ 25 Apr-4 Oct. € 13.00 2009*

MIREPOIX (ARIEGE) *8F4* (10km SE Rural) *43.03055, 1.93605* **Camping La Pibola, Le Cazalet, 09500 Camon [05 61 68 12 14; fax 05 61 68 10 59; pibolacamping@orange.fr; www.lapibola.com]** E fr Pamiers to Mirepoix. S on D625 twds Lavelanet. L after 4km sp Lagarde. Foll D7 for 4km sp on R, 1km to site. App is steep & narr. Med, terr, pt shd, mkd pitch; wc; chem disp; shwrs inc; el pnts (5A) €4; Indtte; shop; rest; snacks; BBQ; playgrnd; pool; lake fishing 5km; games area; cycle hire; TV; some statics; dogs €1; adv bkg; quiet; red low ssn. "Gd." 1 May-30 Sep. € 14.00
2006*

MIRMANDE *9D2* (3km SE Rural) *44.68705, 4.85444* **Camping La Poche, 26270 Mirmande [04 75 63 02 88; fax 04 75 63 14 94; camping@la-poche.com; www.la-poche.com]** Fr N on N7, 3km after Loriol turn L onto D57 sp Mirmande. Site sp in 7km on L. Fr S on N7 turn R onto D204 in Saulce & foll sp. Med, hdg/mkd pitch, some hdstg, terr, shd; wc; chem disp; baby facs; shwrs inc; el pnts (6A) €3; Indtte; shop; snacks; rest & bar high ssn; playgrnd; pool; paddling pool; games area; entmnt; TV; poss cr; 90% statics; adv bkg; quiet; red low ssn; CCI. "Pleasant, scenic site in wooded valley; gd walking/cycling; friendly, helpful owner."
15 Apr-15 Oct. € 17.00 2007*

MITTLACH see Munster *6F3*

⊞ **MODANE** *9C4* (7km NE Rural) *45.22455, 6.74572* **Camp Municipal La Buidonnière, Route de Cottériat, 73500 Aussois [tel/fax 04 79 20 35 58; camping@aussois.com; www.camping-aussois.com]** Fr Modane on D125 to Aussois; in vill foll sp camping. Lge, mkd pitch, hdstg, pt sl, terr, unshd; htd wc (cont); chem disp; shwrs inc; el pnts (6-10A) €4.45-6.15; Indtte; shops 500m; playgrnd; shuttle bus to ski lifts; 50% statics; dogs; adv bkg; CCI. "Mountain views; skiing resort; v exposed site; poss unkempt low ssn; gd rest in vill." ♦ € 10.70 2007*

MODANE *9C4* (10km NE Rural) *45.22870, 6.78116* **Camp Municipal Val d'Ambin, Plan de l'Eglise, 73500 Bramans-le-Verney [04 79 05 22 88 or 04 79 05 03 05 or 06 16 51 90 91 (mob); fax 04 79 05 23 16; camping dambin@aol.com; www.camping-bramansvanoise.com]** 10km after Modane on D1006 (N6) twd Lanslebourg, take 2nd turning R twd vill of Bramans, & foll camping sp, site by church. App fr Lanslebourg, after 12km turn L at camping sp on D306 at end of vill. Med, unshd; wc; shwrs; el pnts (12-16A) inc; shops 5km; playgrnd; pool 10km; dogs €1.60; no adv bkg; v quiet. "Away-from-it-all site worth the climb; beautiful area; gd dog walk adj." 5 May-10 Oct.
€ 16.60 2007*

⊞ **MODANE** *9C4* (1km W Rural) *45.19437, 6.66413* **Camping Les Combes, Refuge de La Sapinière, Route de Bardonnèche, 73500 Modane [04 79 05 00 23 or 06 10 16 54 61 (mob); fax 04 79 05 00 23; camping-modane@wanadoo.fr; http://camping-modane.chez-alice.fr]** Exit A43 junc 30 twd Modane. Take D216 on R, site on bend on hill. Fr Fréjus tunnel site on L 1km bef Modane. Med, pt sl, pt shd; htd wc (some cont); chem disp; shwrs inc; el pts (6A) €3; Indtte; shop 1km; tradsmn; snacks; bar; playgrnd; pool 1km; tennis; winter sports; wifi; 10% statics; dogs €1.50; quiet. "Excel & conv NH for Fréjus tunnel; warm welcome; superb scenery; low ssn recep opens 1700 - site yourself." € 13.00 2008*

MOELAN SUR MER see Pont Aven *2F2*

MOIRANS EN MONTAGNE *9A3* (900m S Rural) *46.41980, 5.72381* **Camping Le Champ Renard, Ave de St Claude, 39260 Moirans-en-Montagne [03 84 42 34 98; fax 03 84 42 60 50; camping.champ.renard@wanadoo.fr; http://pagesperso-orange.fr/champ.renard]** Fr St Claude foll Lons-Lyon rd (D436 to D470) to Moirans-en-Montagne (approx 25km by rd). Site opp sm indus est. Steep access rds. Med, mkd pitch, mainly sl, terr, pt shd; wc; shwrs inc; el pnts (6A) €2.60; shops 2km; tradsmn; snacks; bar; BBQ; playgrnd; pool; shgl beach & lake 6km; games area; dogs €1.20; adv bkg; some rd noise; CCI. "Friendly, helpful staff; one of nicer sites in area; attractive town & lake; pleasant sp walks." 15 Mar-15 Oct. 2008*

MOIRANS EN MONTAGNE *9A3* (5km NW Rural) *46.46833, 5.68864* **Camping Trélachaume, Lac de Vouglans, 39260 Maisod [tel/fax 03 84 42 03 26; www.trelachaume.com]** Fr St Claude take D436 NW past Moirans-en-Montagne; turn L onto D301 to Maisod; site well sp. Lge, mkd pitch, pt sl, pt shd; wc; chem disp; baby facs; shwrs inc; el pnts (5A) €2.70; Indtte; shop; tradsmn; rest; snacks; bar; BBQ; adventure playgrnd; paddling pool; lake sw/sand beach 800m; games rm; entmnt; 10% statics; dogs €1.50; phone; poss cr; Eng spkn; adv bkg; quiet; ccard acc; CCI. "Beautiful, uncrowded part of France; helpful owners; excel." ♦ 19 Apr-6 Sep. € 14.10 2008*

MOISSAC *8E3* (1.5km S Rural) *44.09664, 1.08878* **Camp Municipal L'Ile de Bidounet, St Benoît, 82200 Moissac [tel/fax 05 63 32 52 52; info@camping-moissac.com; www.camping-moissac.com]** Exit A62 at junc 9 at Castelsarrasin onto N113 dir Moissac, site sp. Or fr N on N113 cross Rv Tarn, turn L at 1st rndabt & foll camp sp, site on L by rv. NB Height restriction 3.05m for tunnel at ent & tight turn lge o'fits. Med, hdg/mkd pitch, some hdstg, shd; wc (some cont); chem disp; mv service pnt; baby facs; shwrs inc; el pnts (6A) €3; gas 2km; Indtte; shop, rest & snacks 2km; tradsmn; bar; BBQ; playgrnd; pool (high ssn); fishing; watersports; boat & canoe hire; cycle hire; entmnt; 10% statics; dogs €1.50; phone; Eng spkn; adv bkg; quiet; ccard acc; red low ssn/long stay; CCI. "Excel rvside site in lovely area; extra for twin-axles; pitches tight lge o'fits; helpful staff; basic, clean san facs; conv lovely town & abbey; gd fishing; walking/cycling." ♦ 1 Apr-30 Sep. € 15.80 2009*

See advertisement

MOLIERES (DORDOGNE) see Lalinde *7C3*

MOLIERES (TARN ET GARONNE) *8E3* (1.5km E Rural) *44.18480, 1.38790* **Camping Domaine des Merlanes, 82220 Molières [05 63 67 64 05; fax 05 63 24 28 96; simone@domaine-de-merlanes.com; www.domaine-de-merlanes.com]** Fr N on N20, exit on D20 to Montpezat-de-Quercy & Molières; sp in vill. Sm, terr, pt shd; wc; chem disp; baby facs; shwrs; el pnts (6A) inc; tradsmn; rest; bar; playgrnd; htd pool; 10% statics; dogs €3; poss cr; Eng spkn; quiet; red low ssn; ccard acc; CCI. "Pleasant, Dutch owners; clean, well-kept site; excel children's facs; adv bkg ess high ssn; excel." 25 Apr-5 Sep. € 32.80 2009*

MOLIETS ET MAA *8E1* (2km W Coastal) *43.85210, -1.38730* **Airotel Camping St Martin, Ave de l'Océan 40660 Moliets-Plage [05 58 48 52 30; fax 05 58 48 50 73; contact@camping-saint-martin.fr; www.camping-saint-martin.fr]** On N10 exit for Léon, Moliets-et-Maa. At Moliets foll sp to Moliets-Plage. Camp site after Les Cigales, by beach. V lge, hdg/mkd pitches, pt sl, terr, pt shd; htd wc (some cont); chem disp; some serviced pitches; baby facs; sauna; shwrs inc; el pnts (10A) €4.50; gas; Indtte; shops; supmkt; rests; snacks; bar; playgrnd; 3 pools (1 htd, covrd); paddling pool; jacuzzi; dir access to sand beach 300m; rv 250m; watersports; tennis, golf nr; games area; cycle paths; entmnt; TV rm; dogs €4 (free low ssn); Eng spkn; adv bkg rec high ssn (fee); quiet; ccard acc; red low ssn; CCI. "Excel family site; vg san facs; gd for teenagers; gd cycling, walking." 8 Apr-11 Nov. € 44.50 2009*

MOLIETS ET MAA *8E1* (2km W Coastal) *43.85166, -1.38375* **Camping Les Cigales, Ave de l'Océan, 40660 Moliets-Plage [05 58 48 51 18; fax 05 58 48 53 27; reception@camping-les-cigales.fr; www.camping-les-cigales.fr]** In Moliets-et-Maa, turn W for Moliets-Plage, site on R in vill. Lge, pt sl, shd; wc; chem disp; mv service pnt; shwrs inc; el pnts (5A) €3.50; Indtte; shop; tradsmn; rest; snacks; bar; BBQ; playgrnd; sand beach 300m; games area; TV; many statics; dogs €2; adv bkg; quiet; ccard acc; CCI. "Site in pine wood - sandy soil; narr access tracks; excel beach & surfing; many shops, rests 100m." 1 Apr-30 Sep. € 25.00 2009*

MOLOMPIZE see Massiac *9C1*

MOLSHEIM see Obernai *6E3*

MONBALEN *7D3* (Rural) **Ferme Equestre Crinière au Vent, Bouillon, 47340 Monbalen [05 53 95 18 61; http://monsite.wanadoo.fr/criniereauvent]** Site 15km N Agen & 13km S Villeneuve-sur-Lot. Fr Agen, take N21 N dir Villeneuve-sur-Lot. In approx 15km turn R onto D110 sp Laroque-Timbaut & foll 'Camping' sp. Fr Villeneuve-sur-Lot, take N21 S dir Agen. In approx 10km turn L onto D110 sp Laroque-Timbaut & foll 'Camping' sp. Sm, pt sl, shd; wc (some cont); chem disp; shwrs inc; el pnts (10A) €2; Indry rm; tradsmn; bar (soft drinks only); horseriding; no statics; dogs €1; little Eng spkn; no ccard acc; CCI. "Owner v pleasant; horseriding for all ages on site; vg." ♦ 15 Apr-30 Sep. € 8.20 2006*

France

MONCEAUX SUR DORDOGNE see Argentat *7C4*

MONDRAGON see Bollène *9D2*

MONESTIER DE CLERMONT *9C3* (700m SW Urban) *44.91515, 5.62809* **Camp Municipal Les Portes du Trièves, Chemin de Chambons, 38650 Monestier-de-Clermont [04 76 34 01 24; fax 04 76 34 19 75; campinglesportesdutrieves@wanadoo.fr]** Turn W off D1075 (N75). Sp in vill. 700m up steep hill adj sw pool & school. Fr Grenoble take A51 to S end of vill & foll sps to site. Sm, hdg/mkd pitch, hdstg, terr, pt shd; htd wc; chem disp; mv service pnt; shwrs inc; el pnts (6A) €2.70; Indtte (inc dryer); shop, rest, snacks & bar 800m; playgrnd; htd pool 200m; tennis adj; lake 10km; games rm; wifi; dogs free; bus 500m; quiet; Eng spkn; adv bkg; red long stay; CCI. "Attractive, immac, well-run site; helpful staff; watersports at lake; spectacular countryside; train to Grenoble; vg." 1 May-30 Sep. € 11.10 2009*

MONETIER LES BAINS, LE *9C3* (1km NW Rural) *44.98010, 6.49515* **Camp Municipal Les Deux Glaciers, 05220 Le Monêtier-les-Bains [04 92 46 10 08 or 06 83 03 70 72; fax 04 92 24 52 18; camping.monetier@orange.fr; www.monetier.com]** On D1091 (N91) 12km NW of Briançon; pass thro Le Monêtier-les-Bains, in 1km site sp on L. Med, mkd pitch, hdstg, terr, unshd (trees planted 2008); htd wc; chem disp; mv service pnt; baby facs; shwrs inc; el pnts (16A) €3.50; Indtte; tradsmn; shop, rest, snacks bar in vill 1km; playgrnd; dogs €1; phone 500m; bus 1km; adv bkg; red low ssn; CCI. "Excel, scenic site bef x-ing Montgenèvre pass; gd base for Ecrins National Park; easy access fr D1091; footpath to vill; vg." ♦ Dec-Apr & Jun-Sep. € 14.00 2008*

MONFORT *8E3* (Urban) *43.79628, 0.82315* **Camp Municipal de Monfort, 32120 Monfort [tel/fax 05 62 06 83 26 (Mairie)]** SE fr Fleurance on D654 to Monfort, then foll sp to 'Centre Ville' & camping sp. Town has narr rds so foll sp. Sm, hdg pitch, pt sl, pt shd; wc; chem disp (wc); shwrs inc, el pnts (5A) €1.50; shop, rest & bar 200m; BBQ; playgrnd; no twin-axles; dogs €0.50; quiet; ccard not acc; CCI. "Excel, well-kept, scenic, CL-type site on ramparts of attractive Bastide town; pitch yourself, warden calls am & pm." 1 May-15 Oct. € 8.40 2008*

MONISTROL D'ALLIER *9C1* (4km N Rural) *44.99148, 3.67781* **Camp Municipal Le Marchat, 43580 St Privat-d'Allier [04 71 57 22 13; fax 04 71 57 25 50; info@mairie-saintprivatdallier.fr; www.mairie-saintprivatdallier.fr]** Fr Le Puy-en-Velay W on D589. Turn R in cent of vill at petrol stn, site on R in 200m. Sm, hdg pitch, terr, shd; wc; chem disp; shwrs inc; el pnts (10A) €1.10; shops, bar in vill; playgrnd; quiet. "Beautifully-kept site; poss unkempt low ssn; not suitable lge o'fits." ♦ 1 May-1 Nov. € 6.10 2009*

MONISTROL D'ALLIER *9C1* (S Rural) *44.96912, 3.64793* **Camp Municipal Le Vivier, 43580 Monistrol-d'Allier [04 71 57 24 14 or 04 71 57 21 21 (Mairie); fax 04 71 57 25 03; mairie-monistroldallier@wanadoo.fr; www.monistroldallier.com]** Fr Le Puy-en-Velay W on D589 to Monistrol-d'Allier. Turn L in vill immed after rlwy stn & cont down steep entry rd bef x-ing bdge. Site sp in town cent. Sm, mkd pitch, pt shd; wc; chem disp; shwrs inc; el pnts (5-10A) €2.60; shops, rest, snacks; bar 200m; BBQ; dogs; phone; train 500m; quiet; CCI. "Vg site steep valley." ♦ 15 Apr-15 Sep. € 12.00 2008*

MONISTROL SUR LOIRE *9C1* (7km SE Rural) *45.21630, 4.21240* **Camping de Vaubarlet, 43600 Ste Sigolène [04 71 66 64 95; fax 04 71 66 11 98; camping@vaubarlet.com; www.vaubarlet.com]** Fr Monistrol take D44 SE twd Ste Sigolène & turn R into vill. In vill take D43 dir Grazac for 6km. Site by Rv Dunière, ent L bef bdge. Site well sp fr vill. Med, mkd pitch, pt shd; wc; chem disp; mv service pnt; shwrs inc; el pnts (6A) €3 (poss rev pol); Indtte; shop & 6km; tradsmn; rest; snacks; bar; playgrnd; htd pool; paddling pool; rv sw adj; trout fishing; cycle hire; games area; entmnt; TV rm; 15% statics; phone; dogs €1; Eng spkn; adv bkg; quiet; red low ssn; ccard acc; CCI. "Friendly, helpful staff; well-run site; excel san facs; interesting museums nrby." ♦ 1 May-30 Sep. € 18.00 (CChq acc) 2006*

MONISTROL SUR LOIRE *9C1* (500m W Rural) *45.2937, 4.1616* **Camp Municipal La Chaud/Beau Sejour, Chemin de Chaponas, 43120 Monistrol-sur-Loire [04 71 66 53 90]** Site on N88, on W edge of town, sp. Exit by-pass at 1 of exits to Monistrol - head for casino, then Intermarché. Med, hdg pitch, pt sl, shd; htd wc; shwrs inc; el pnts (6A) €2.44; Indtte; supmkt adj; playgrnd; pool, tennis adj; 90% statics; adv bkg; quiet. "Gd NH." ♦ 1 Apr-31 Oct. € 10.00 2007*

MONNERVILLE *4E3* (2km S Rural) *48.3325, 2.04722* **Camping Le Bois de la Justice, Méréville, 91930 Monnerville [01 64 95 05 34; fax 01 64 95 17 31; picquetfredo@orange.fr; http://pagesperso-orange.fr/campingboislajustice/]** Fr N20 S of Etampes, turn onto D18 at Monnerville, site well sp. Long narr app rd. Med, hdg/mkd pitch, pt sl, pt shd; htd wc; chem disp (wc); shwrs inc; el pnts (5A) €2.50; Indtte; tradsmn; snacks high ssn; bar; BBQ; cooking facs; playgrnd; htd pool high ssn; tennis; games area; TV rm; 50% statics; dogs €1; phone; Eng spkn; adv bkg; quiet; red low ssn; ccard acc. "Delightful woodland oasis in open countryside; friendly welcome; clean san facs; ideal for Chartres, Fontainebleau, Orléans, Paris or excel NH just off N20." ♦ 4 Feb-26 Nov. € 19.50 2009*

See advertisement on next page

MONPAZIER *7D3* (3km SW Rural) *44.65875, 0.87925* **Camping Moulin de David, Route de Villeréal, 24540 Gaugeac-Monpazier [05 53 22 65 25 or 04 99 57 20 25; fax 05 53 23 99 76; www.moulin-de-david.com or www.village-center.com]** Fr Monpazier, take D2 SW twd Villeréal, site sp on L after 3km. Narr app rds. Lge, hdg/mkd pitch, pt shd; htd wc; chem disp; mv service pnt; serviced pitches; baby facs; shwrs inc; el pnts (3-10A) inc gas; Indtte; shop; tradsmn; rest; snacks; bar; BBQ; playgrnd; pool; paddling pool; lake sw & waterslide high ssn; fishing adj; tennis; games area; wifi; games/TV rm; cycle hire; archery; internet; entmnt; many statics; dogs €3; poss cr; Eng spkn; adv bkg; quiet; ccard acc; red low ssn; CCI. "Charming site nr lovely town; welcoming, helpful owners; excel facs, ltd low ssn; poss mosquitoes nr rv thro site; mkt Thu Monpazier; highly rec." ♦ 30 Apr-7 Sep. € 24.00 2009*

MONSIREIGNE see Chantonnay *2H4*

MONT DORE, LE *7B4* (500m NW Urban) *45.57711, 2.80387* **Camp Municipal des Crouzets, 4 Ave des Crouzets, 63240 Le Mont-Dore [tel/fax 04 73 65 21 60 or 04 73 65 22 00 (Mairie); camping.crouzets@orange.fr; www.mairie-mont-dore.fr]** Take D130 fr Bourboule to Le Mont-Dore; site ent just on L after entering town. Poor sps. Lge, mkd pitch, hdstg, pt sl, unshd; htd wc; chem disp; mv service pnt adj; shwrs inc; el pnts (10A) €3.90 (poss rev pol); Indtte; tradsmn; shops & rests adj; BBQ; playgrnd; pool 4km; sports area; dogs €1.45; poss cr; Eng spkn; ccard acc. "Well-run in town cent, but quiet; gd sized pitches; excel san facs; helpful warden; gd touring base; cable car to Puy de Sancy." ♦ 2 Dec-18 Oct. € 9.10 2009*

MONT DORE, LE *7B4* (1.5km NW Urban) *45.58685, 2.80098* **Camp Municipal L'Esquiladou, Le Queureuilh, Route des Cascades, 63240 Le Mont-Dore [04 73 65 23 74 or 04 73 65 20 00 (Mairie); fax 04 73 65 23 74; camping.esquiladou@orange.fr; www.mairie-mont-dore.fr]** Fr Mont-Dore cent, take D996 dir La Bourboule (not D130). Pass 'La Poste' on L & at rlwy stn app turn R, then L at T-junc onto D996. In Queureuilh fork R at 'Route Cascades' sp, then foll camping sp. Med, hdg/mkd pitch, hdstg, terr, pt shd; htd wc; chem disp; mv service pnt; shwrs inc; el pnts (6-10A) €2.80-4.10; gas; Indtte; shops 1km; tradsmn; BBQ; playgrnd; pool; dogs €1.50; phone; adv bkg; ccard acc; red low ssn; CCI. "V pleasant, well-run, quiet site; gd views; excel san facs; gd mountain walks; poss itinerants; run down (Jun 2008) - like lge carpark, but conv." ♦ 26 Apr-18 Oct. € 9.85 2008*

MONT LOUIS *8G4* (3.5km N Rural) **Camping Rural du Pla de Barrès, Route des Bouillouses, 66210 La Llagonne [04 68 04 26 04 or 04 68 04 21 97 (TO); otmontlouis@wanadoo.fr; www.mont-louis.net/camping.htm]** Leave Mont-Louis on D118 dir Formiguères; site sp on L at top of hill; cont for 1km. Lge, pt shd; wc (cont); shwrs; el pnts (6A) €3; playgrnd; paddling pool; rv sw adj; fishing; quiet. "Most of site in pine forest; ground poss boggy; beautiful area." ♦ 15 Jun-15 Sep. € 7.90 2007*

MONT LOUIS *8G4* (5km W Rural) *42.50636, 2.04671* **Camping Huttopia Font-Romeu, Route de Mont-Louis, 66120 Font-Romeu [04 68 30 09 32; fax 04 68 04 56 39; fontromeu@huttopia.com; www.huttopia.com]** W fr Mont-Louis on D618. Site on L bef Font-Romeu, opp stadium. Fr Aix-les-Thermes or Puigcerdà turn E at Ur up longish hill, thro town to site on R at o'skts. Lge, sl, pt shd; htd wc; shwrs; el pnts (6-10A) €4.20-6.20; Indtte; shop; rest, bar (w/ends); htd pool; paddling pool; tennis 500m; horserieing 1km; internet; entmnt; some statics; dogs €3.50; phone; adv bkg; quiet. "New site Jul 2008; gd cent for mountain walks; site at 1800m altitude." Easter-28 Sep. € 22.00 2008*

MONT ST MICHEL, LE *2E4* (8km E Rural) *48.62820, -1.41450* **Camping St Michel, Route du Mont-St Michel, 50220 Courtils [02 33 70 96 90; fax 02 33 70 99 09; infos@campingsaintmichel.com; www.campingsaintmichel.com]** Fr E exit A84 junc 33 to N175. Take D43 coast rd fr Pontaubault twds Le Mont-St Michel. Site in vill of Courtils on L. Med, hdg/mkd pitch, some hdstg, pt sl, pt shd; htd wc; chem disp; mv service pnt; baby facs; shwrs inc; el pnts (6A) €3; gas; Indtte; shop; rest; snacks; bar; BBQ; playgrnd; htd pool; sand beach 8km; cycle hire; games rm; internet; entmnt; some statics; dogs €1; phone; bus adj; poss cr; Eng spkn; adv bkg; noisy (farm adj); ccard acc; CCI. "Excel, flat site; clean facs; helpful owner; new san facs planned 2008; cycle paths adj; gd NH for St Malo." ♦ 8 Feb-11 Nov. € 18.00 2007*

MONT ST MICHEL, LE *2E4* (2km S Rural) *48.61476, -1.50887* **Camping du Mont St Michel, 50150 Le Mont St Michel [02 33 60 22 10; fax 02 33 60 20 02; contact@camping-montsaintmichel.com; www.le-mont-saint-michel.com]** Located at junc of D976 (Pontorson/Le Mont St Michel) with D275, behind Hotel Vert. Lge, hdg/mkd pitch, pt shd; wc; chem disp; mv service pnt; shwrs inc; baby facs; el pnts (5A) €2.80 (poss long lead req); gas; Indtte; supmkt, rest adj; snacks; bar; playgrnd; sand beach 2km; fishing; TV; dogs; phone; adv bkg; Eng spkn; ccard acc; red low ssn/CCI. "Well-located, well-kept site; excel san facs, inc for disabled; no provision to fill Aquaroll etc; vg shady pitches behind hotel; poss noisy - m'van area on opp side D275 quieter, closes end Sep; beach at 2km reported unsafe for sw (quicksand); pitches poss muddy after heavy rain; diff to get onto some pitches due trees; gd walking & cycling to the mount." ♦ 15 Feb-10 Nov. € 14.80 2009*

MONT ST MICHEL, LE *2E4* (4km S Rural) *48.59622, -1.51244* **Camping aux Pommiers, 28 Route du Mont-St Michel, 50170 Beauvoir [tel/fax 02 33 60 11 36; pommiers@aol.com; www.camping-auxpommiers.com]** N fr Pontorson foll D976 sp Le Mont St Michel. Site 5km on R on ent vill of Beauvoir. Med, hdg/mkd pitch, hdstg, pt shd; htd wc (some cont); chem disp; mv service pnt; shwrs inc; el pnts (6A) €4; gas; Indtte; shop; supmkt 4km; tradsmn; rest; snacks; bar; BBQ; playgrnd; htd pool; waterslide; sand/shgl beach 2km; tennis 900m; games area; games rm; cycle hire; wifi; entmnt; TV; 30% statics; dogs €1.20; Eng spkn; adv bkg; quiet; ccard acc; red long stay/low ssn/CCI. "Busy site, rec arr early; friendly, helpful staff & owner; clean facs; gd touring base; easy cycle ride to Mont St Michel or nice walk." 1 Apr-8 Nov. € 18.80 2009*

See advertisement

MONTAGNAC *10F1* (500m E Rural) *43.48200, 3.48893* **Camp Municipal La Piboule, 9 Chemin de la Piboule, 34530 Montagnac [04 67 24 01 31]** Exit A75 junc 59 Pézenas onto D613 (N113) E to Montagnac. Site sp to E of Montagnac. Narr app rds & parked cars unsuitable/v diff lge o'fits. Best app fr E on D5. Med, hdg/mkd pitch, pt sl, pt shd; wc (cont); shwrs inc; el pnts (10A) €3.20; Indry; shop, rest, snacks, bar 800m; playgrnd; phone; CCI. "Clean san facs; short walk to pretty vill; diff lge o'fits." 15 May-31 Oct. € 10.00 2009*

MONTAGNAC *10F1* (4km SE Rural) *43.45175, 3.51600* **Camping Domaine St Martin-du-Pin (Crebassa), 34530 Montagnac [04 67 24 00 37; fax 04 67 24 47 50; elise_crebassa@yahoo.fr; www.saint-martin-du-pin.com]** Exit A75 junc 59 onto D113 to Montagnac; 2km past Montagnac turn R immed past picnic site at end of dual c'way, site sp. Sm, hdg pitch, pt sl, pt shd; wc; chem disp; baby facs; shwrs inc; el pnts €3; Indtte; shop 4km; tradsmn; BBQ; playgrnd; pool; sand beach 9km; few statics; no dogs; Eng spkn; adv bkg; quiet; CCI. "Delightful, relaxing site; lge pitches; friendly owners; clean facs; gd touring base." 1 Jun-30 Sep. € 21.00 2008*

MONTAGNAC MONTPEZAT see Riez *10E3*

MONTAGNY LES LANCHES see Annecy *9B3*

MONTAIGU *2H4* (10km SE Rural) *46.93769, -1.21975* **Camping L'Eden, La Raillière, 85600 La Boissière-de-Montaigu [02 51 41 62 32; fax 02 51 41 56 07; contact@domaine-eden.fr; www.domaine-eden.fr]** Fr Montaigu S on D137, in 8km turn E on D62, thro Le Pont-Legé. Site sp on L off D62. Med, mkd pitch, shd; wc (some cont); shwrs inc; el pnts (10A) inc; gas; Indtte; shop & 4km; rest; snacks; bar; playgrnd; htd pool; tennis; entmnt; TV; 40% statics; dogs €2; poss cr; adv bkg; site poss open all year; red low ssn CCI. "Nice, quiet site in woodlands; clean facs; motor mover useful; excel." ♦ 1 Mar-15 Nov. € 19.00 2009*

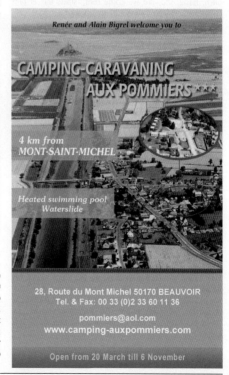

France

MONTALIEU VERCIEU *9B2* (1.5km NE Rural) *45.82756, 5.42052* **Camp Municipal La Vallée Blue, 38390 Montalieu-Vercieu [04 74 88 63 67; fax 04 74 88 62 11; camping.valleebleue@wanadoo.fr; www.camping-valleebleue.com]** S fr Ambérieu-en-Bugey on D1075; in 15km (nr Porcieu-Amblagnieu) site sp on L. Med, pt sl, pt shd; wc (some cont); chem disp; mv service pnt; shwrs; el pnts (6A) €3; gas; Indtte; sm shop; tradsmn; snacks; playgrnd; htd pool; aquapark; paddling pool; games area; dogs €1.90; phone; bus; ccard acc; red low ssn/long stay; CCI. "Immed access to Rv Rhône; conv NH fr D1075; vg." ♦ 4 Apr-25 Oct. € 15.00 2009*

MONTARGIS *4F3* (12km N Rural) *48.09198, 2.78482* **Camp Municipal Le Perray/Les Ferrières, Rue du Perray, 45210 Ferrières-en-Gâtinais [06 71 43 25 65 (mob) or 02 38 96 52 90 (Mairie); fax 02 38 96 62 76; ferrieres.mairie@wanadoo.fr; www.ferrieres-en-gatinais.com]** N fr Mantargis on N7. R onto D32 sp Ferrières & foll camp sp. Med, mkd pitch, pt shd; wc; chem disp; mv service pnt; shwrs inc; el pnts (10A) €2.50 (poss rev pol); playgrnd; pool & sports facs adj; rv fishing adj; entmnt; 5% statics; quiet. "Vg." 1 Apr-30 Sep. € 7.00 2009*

MONTARGIS *4F3* (2km NE Urban) *48.00821, 2.74965* **Camp Municipal de la Forêt, 38 Ave Chautemps, 45200 Montargis [02 38 98 00 20]** Heading N on N7 at town boundary take R fork sp with camping symbol. Med, mkd pitch, hdstg, shd; htd wc (some cont); shwrs inc; el pnts (5-10A) €2.90-5.80; shop 200m; playgrnd; pool adj; 50% statics; quiet. "Spacious pitches; facs dated but clean; poss muddy when wet; gate/recep closes 1900; no o'fits over 6m; conv for train to Paris; NH only." 1 Feb-30 Nov. € 9.50 2008*

MONTAUBAN *8E3* (10km NE Rural) *44.08927, 1.45598* **Camping La Forge, 85 Route de Nègrepelisse, 82350 Albias [tel/fax 05 63 31 00 44 or 06 76 38 81 22 (mob); contact@camping-laforge.com]** Fr S turn R at traff lts on D820 (N20) in Albias onto D65 sp Nègrepelisse. Site clearly sp 1km on L adj cemetary extension. Sm, pt shd; wc; chem disp; shwrs inc; el pnts (3-6A) €1.85-3.65; Indtte; shops 500m; supmkt & fuel 7km; tradsmn; 10% statics; dogs €0.75; adv bkg; quiet; red low ssn; CCI. "Quiet, simple, woodland site; helpful & friendly owner; facs v dated & poss unclean low ssn; poss unsuitable for sm children due steep bank to fast-flowing rv; no twin-axles; useful stopover; NH only." 1 Apr-30 Sep. € 10.50 2009*

MONTAUBAN DE BRETAGNE *2E3* (500m N Rural) *48.20357, -2.04697* **Camp Municipal de la Vallée St Eloi, 35360 Montauban-de-Bretagne [02 99 06 42 55; fax 02 99 06 59 89]** Fr N12 foll sp to Montauban cent on D61. Site in 500m on R at ent to town by sm lake. Sm, mkd pitch, pt shd; wc; shwrs inc; el pnts (6A); shop 500m; quiet; CCI. "Basic but clean san facs; picturesque location; unreliable opening dates, phone ahead." 16 Jun-15 Sep. 2007*

MONTAUROUX see Fayence *10E4*

MONTBARD *6G1* (1km W Urban) *47.6314, 4.33303* **Camp Municipal Les Treilles, Rue Michel Servet, 21500 Montbard [tel/fax 03 80 92 69 50; camping.montbard@wanadoo.fr; www.montbard.com]** Lies off N side D980. Camping sp clearly indicated on all app including by-pass. Turn onto by-pass at traff lts at rndabt at junc of D905 & D980. Site nr pool. Med, hdg pitch, pt shd, wc; chem disp; shwrs inc; el pnts (16A) €4; Indry rm; shop 1km; supmkt 300m; tradsmn; BBQ; snacks; playgrnd; pool complex adj inc; cycle hire; rv sw 100m; dogs €1; phone; poss cr; quiet but rd/rlwy noise at far end; CCI. "V pleasant & well-kept, but poss shabby low ssn; gd pitches; lge, smart san facs; poss a few contract worker campers; v quiet low ssn; interesting area; excel NH." ♦ 2 Mar-24 Oct. € 15.00 2009*

MONTBAZON *4G2* (300m N Rural) *47.29044, 0.71595* **Camping de la Grange Rouge, 37250 Montbazon [02 47 26 06 43; fax 02 47 26 03 13; infos@camping-montbazon.com; www.camping-montbazon.com]** On D910 (N10) thro Montbazon fr S to N, after x-ing bdge (part of D910) immed turn L to site. Clearly visible & clearly sp on W side of rd at N end of town. Med, mkd pitch, pt shd; wc (male cont); chem disp; shwrs inc; el pnts (6A) €3.95; Indtte; shops 300m; tradsmn; rest & bar adj; playgrnd; sm htd pool; fishing; tennis; TV rm; some statics; dogs €1.05; Eng spkn; adv bkg; quiet; ccard acc; CCI. "Lovely, rvside site in pretty town; helpful, friendly owner; facs adequate only; conv Tours." ♦ 25 Apr-26 Sep. € 13.00 2009*

MONTBAZON *4G2* (2km E Rural) *47.28924, 0.73436* **Camping de la Plage, 37250 Veigné [02 47 26 23 00; fax 02 47 73 11 47; campingveigne@aol.com; www.touraine-vacance.com]** Exit A10 junc 23 dir Montbazon onto D910 (N10). N of Montbazon after 'Les Gues' turn SE onto D50 to Veigné & site. Site in 2km on R at rvside. Med, mkd pitch, pt shd; htd wc; chem disp; mv service pnt; baby facs; shwrs, el pnts (10A) €4.50; gas 200m; Indtte; shop 200m; rest; snacks; BBQ; playgrnd; htd pool high ssn; canoeing; fishing; games area; entmnt; 13% statics; dogs €1.20; phone; Eng spkn; adv bkg; quiet, some rd/rwly noise; ccard acc; red low ssn/long stay; CCI. "Rvside site nr vill; gd san facs; gd for Loire chateaux & Tours; gd walking & cycling; site used as short cut by locals (2008); poss clsd Oct, phone ahead." ♦ 1 Apr-31 Oct. € 13.10 2009*

MONTBERT *2H4* (500m SE Rural) *47.05133, -1.47930* **Camping Le Relais des Garennes (Gendron), La Bauche Coiffée, 44140 Montbert [tel/fax 02 40 04 78 73; phgendron@wanadoo.fr; www.gites-de-france-44.fr/relais_garennes]** Fr Nantes on N937 dir La Roche, at Geneston turn L dir Montbert & foll site sp. Or fr Nantes on N137 dir La Rochelle turn R at Aigrefeuille-sur-Maine for Montbert. Sm, mkd pitch, pt shd; htd wc; baby facs; fam bthrm; shwrs inc; el pnts (10A) €2.50; htd pool 1km; tennis, sports facs nrby; sm lake; lake fishing adj; dogs; Eng spkn; adv bkg; quiet; CCI. "V peaceful & picturesque; friendly owners; immac facs; rabbits & hens on site; toys for children; many attractions nrby; nice walk to town; highly rec." ♦ 1 Jun-30 Sep. € 8.50 2009*

France

MONTBIZOT see Beaumont sur Sarthe *4F1*

MONTBLANC see Béziers *10F1*

MONTBRISON *9B1* (1.5km S Urban) *45.59133, 4.07806* **Camp Municipal Le Surizet, 31 Rue du Surizet, Moingt, 42600 Montbrison [04 77 58 08 30; fax 04 77 58 00 16]** Fr St Etienne on D8, at rndabt junc with D204 turn L sp St Anthème & Ambert. Cross rlwy & turn R in 400m, site sp. Med, pt shd; wc; chem disp; mv service pnt; shwrs; el pnts (5-10A) inc; Indtte; shop 1km; BBQ sep area; playgrnd; pool; fishing; pool, tennis 2km; 60% statics; dogs €0.85; bus (every hr); quiet; adv bkg; CCI. "Pleasant, well-kept site; no twin-axles; vg value; highly rec NH or sh stay." 15 Apr-15 Oct. € 12.70 2009*

MONTBRISON *9B1* (2km W Rural) *45.59896, 4.04259* **Camping Le Bigi, Vinols, 42600 Bard [tel/fax 04 77 58 06 39; andre.drutel@orange.fr; www.camping-le-bigi.fr]** Fr Montbrison cent take D113 twd Bard, site sp. Sm, hdg/mkd pitch, sl, terr, pt shd; wc; chem disp; mv service pnt; shwrs inc; el pnts (5A) inc; Indtte; tradsmn; playgrnd; htd pool; tennis; 60% statics; dogs €1.10; poss cr; CCI. "Helpful owner; well-run, delightful site in landscaped garden nr medieval town; no twin-axle c'vans." ♦
31 May-15 Sep. € 14.50 2008*

MONTBRON *7B3* (11km NE Rural) *45.74042, 0.58678* **Camping de l'Etang, Les Geloux, 16310 Le Lindois [05 45 65 02 67; fax 05 45 65 08 96; www.camping deletang.com]** Fr S take D16 N fr Montbron, in 9km turn R onto D13, in 3km turn R onto D27. Site sp in vill opp lake. Sm, hdg/mkd pitch, pt sl, pt shd; htd wc; chem disp; baby facs; shwrs inc; el pnts (16A) €3.50; Indtte; sm shop; rest; snacks; bar; playgrnd; lake sw & beach adj; fishing; dogs €1.50; phone; Eng spkn; adv bkg rec high ssn; ccard acc; quiet; CCI. "Beautiful, peaceful, wooded site by sm lake; lge pitches in indiv clearings in trees; friendly Dutch owners; excel." 1 Apr-1 Nov. € 16.50 2008*

MONTBRON *7B3* (500m E Urban) *45.66643, 0.50851* **Camp Municipal Les Moulins de Tardoire, Route de Limoges, 16220 Montbron [05 45 70 74 67 or 05 45 63 15 15 (Mairie); info@ot-montbron.com; www.ot-montbron.com]** On D699, foll sp fr vill cent. Sm, hdg pitch, pt shd; wc (cont); chem disp; shwrs inc; el pnts (16A) €2.50: shop 500m; pool 100m; playgrnd; dogs free; quiet; adv bkg; Eng spkn; CCI. "Basic site but OK sh stay."
15 May-15 Sep. € 6.30 2007*

MONTBRON *7B3* (6km SE Rural) *45.65972, 0.55805* **Camping Les Gorges du Chambon, Le Chambon, 16220 Eymouthiers [05 45 70 71 70; fax 05 45 70 80 02; info@gorgesduchambon.fr; www.gorgesduchambon.fr or www.les-castels.com]** Fr N141 turn SE onto D6 at La Rochefoucauld; cont on D6 out of Montbron; after 5km turn L at La Tricherie onto D163; foll camp sp to site in approx 1.9km. NB Fr La Tricherie narr in places & some sharp bends. Med, mkd pitch, pt sl, pt shd; htd wc; chem disp; mv service pnt; baby facs; shwrs inc; el pnts (10A) €3.70; gas; Indtte; shop; tradsmn; rest; snacks; bar; BBQ (gas/charcoal only); playgrnd; pool; paddling pool; sand/shgl beach 15km; fishing, canoe hire; tennis; cycle hire; walking; horseriding, golf nrby; entmnt; internet; games/TV rm; 25% statics; no dogs; Eng spkn; adv bkg; quiet; ccard acc; red long stay/low ssn; CCI. "Beautiful, 'away from it all' site in scenic location; exceptional staff - welcoming, helpful & friendly; lge pitches but some sl; excel san facs; superb rest; gd marked walks; bird-watching & wildlife; a site to return to; excel." ♦ 24 Apr-18 Sep. € 30.85 (CChq acc)
ABS - D11 2009*

See advertisement

MONTBRUN LES BAINS *10E3* (500m E Rural) *44.17621, 5.44767* **Camp Municipal Le Pré des Arbres, 26570 Montbrun-les-Bains [04 75 28 85 41 or 04 75 28 82 49; fax 04 75 28 81 16]** Site well sp in Montbrun. Sm, mkd pitch, terr, pt shd; wc; shwrs; el pnts (15A) €3.25; pool, tennis adj; some statics; dogs; quiet. "Gd, clean site; walking dist to pleasant town & spa; thermal baths; interesting area; warden visits." 1 Apr-31 Oct. € 9.20 2006*

MONTCABRIER *7D3* (2km NE Rural) *44.54865, 1.08229* **Camping Le Moulin de Laborde, 46700 Montcabrier [05 65 24 62 06; fax 05 65 36 51 33; moulindelaborde@ wanadoo.fr; www.moulindelaborde.com]** Fr Fumel take D673 NE & site 1km past Montcabrier on L. Med, hdg pitch, pt shd; wc; chem disp; baby facs; shwrs inc; el pnts (6A) €2.80; gas; Indtte; shop; tradsmn; rest; snacks; bar; playgrnd; pool; sm lake; games area; cycle hire; entmnt; wifi; TV rm; no dogs; phone; poss cr; Eng spkn; adv bkg; quiet; red low ssn. "Pleasant, peaceful site; friendly owners; gd facs; gd rest; many attractions & activities nrby; vg." ♦ 25 Apr-8 Sep. € 21.80 2009*

MONTCLAR (ALPES DE HAUTE PROVENCE) *9D3* (2km N Rural) *44.40925, 6.34811* **Yelloh! Village Etoile des Neiges, St Jean, 04140 Montclar [04 92 35 01 29 or 04 92 35 07 08; fax 04 92 35 12 55; contact@etoile-des-neiges.com; www.etoile-des-neiges.com or www.yelloh village.com]** On D900 turn S at St Vincent-les-Forts twd Col St Jean & Digne, site sp at the Col. Med, terr, shd; htd wc; mv service pnt; sauna; steam rm; shwrs inc; el pnts (6A) inc; Indtte; supmkt 200m; tradsmn; rest; bar; snacks; playgrnd; htd, covrd pools; rv fishing; tennis; games area; entmnt; TV rm; dogs €3; adv bkg rec winter & summer; quiet. "Ski stn in winter; steep access rds to pitches poss diff; excel." ♦ 1 May-15 Sep & 22 Dec-25 Mar. € 31.00 2008*

MONTCLAR (AUDE) see Carcassonne *8F4*

MONTCUQ *7D3* (Rural) *44.34050, 1.20179* **Camp Municipal St Jean, 46800 Montcuq [05 65 22 93 73 or 05 65 31 80 05 (Mairie); communaute.communes-montcuq@wanadoo.fr]** Fr Cahors S on D820 (N20) twd Montauban & in 3km take D653 to Montcuq. Site sp on R in vill. Sm, mkd pitch, shd; wc; mv service pnt; shwrs inc; el pnts (10-15A) €1.25-1.90; Indtte; supmkt, rest 300m; bar 200m; playgrnd; pool, tennis adj; lake fishing, lake sw & watersports 800m; tennis; horseriding; adv bkg rec high ssn; quiet. ♦ 15 Jun-15 Sep. € 7.10 2007*

⊞ **MONTDIDIER** *3C3* (1km W Urban) *49.64737, 2.55303* **Camping Le Pré Fleuri, 46 Route d'Ailly-sur-Noye, 80500 Montdidier [03 22 78 93 22]** App Montdidier fr Breteuil (W) on D930; on W o'skts, foll site sp & turn L onto D26. Site 1km on R. Or leave A1 at junc 11 onto D935 Montdidier. In town foll sp for Breteuil until rlwy x-ing & turn R onto D26. Sm, hdg/mkd pitch, pt sl, pt shd; wc (some cont); chem disp; mv service pnt; shwrs inc; el pnts (6-10A) inc (poss rev pol); gas; Indtte; shop 1km; tradsmn; rest, snacks, bar 1km; playgrnd; pool 1km; fishing, tennis nr; horseriding; 75% statics; dogs; adv bkg; rd noise; red long stay; CCI. "Helpful, friendly owners; insufficient san facs; diff to level m'van; conv Amiens, Compiègne & Somme; vg." ♦ € 16.00 2006*

MONTECH *8E3* (1km E Rural) *43.96608, 1.24003* **FFCC Camping Le Canal, Rue de la Mouscane, 82700 Montech [05 63 27 00 51; fax 05 63 27 00 52; cplcanal@atciat. com]** Exit A20 junc 65 Montauban Sud onto D928 dir Auch. In Montech turn R just bef canal, site well sp. Lge, hdg/mkd pitch, unshd; wc; chem disp; mv service pnt; shwrs inc; el pnts (16A) €4; Indtte; shop high ssn; rest; snacks; bar; BBQ; playgrnd; pool; lake fishing nr; games area; entmnt; 60% statics; dogs €2.80; extra for twin-axles; Eng spkn; adv bkg; CCI. "Gd cycle paths." 1 May-28 Sep. € 20.30 2007*

⊞ **MONTELIMAR** *9D2* (12km N Rural) *44.63716, 4.77319* **Camping Floral, Derbières, 26740 La Coucourde [04 75 90 06 69; info@campingfloral.com; www.camping floral.com]** Exit A7 at junc 17 Montélimar Nord, S on N7 for 4km. Site sp S of vill. Steep, rough app. NB Across rv fr power station cooling towers. NB If app fr Montélimar on N7, camp sp pt obscured. Sm, mkd pitch, hdstg, pt sl, pt shd; wc; mv service pnt; shwrs inc; el pnts (6A) €2; gas; Indtte; sm shop; rest; snacks; bar; playgrnd; pool; entmnt; dogs €1; Eng spkn; rd & some rlwy noise; red low ssn; CCI. "Friendly, welcoming owners; clean, tidy site; facs poss stretched high ssn; hdstg poss too sm lge o'fits; san facs poss unclean early ssn & site run down (May/Jun 2008); many resident workers (Jun 2008); NH only." € 13.00 2008*

⊞ **MONTENDRE** *7C2* (5km N Rural) **The Vines Camping, Chez Penaud, 17130 Coux [05 46 48 95 55; barry.playford@orange.fr; www.caravanineurope.co.uk/site-43.html]** Exit A10 at Mirambeau onto D730 dir Montendre; then D19 dir Jonzac; then D253 dir Coux; do not turn into Coux vill but cont on D253; cross rlwy & then over x-rds; turn L at sp Chez Penaud; foll sps. NB D253 is long & winding. Sm, some hdstg, unshd; htd wc; chem disp; shwrs inc; el pnts (16A) inc; gas 4km; lndtte; shops etc 4km; BBQ; lake fishing & golf nrby; dogs; Eng spkn; adv bkg; quiet; red long stay. "Well-kept, CL-type 5-pitch site; lge pitches; friendly British owners; gd touring base; wine tasting; vg." € 12.00 2009*

The opening dates and prices on this campsite have changed. I'll send a site report form to the Club for the next edition of the guide.

⊞ **MONTENDRE** *7C2* (4km NW Rural) *45.30037, -0.43495* **Camping Twin Lakes, La Faiencérie, 17130 Souméras [tel/fax 05 46 49 77 12 or 0114 2463800 (UK); twinlakesinfo@hotmail.co.uk; www.twinlakesfrance.com]** Exit N10/E606 at Montlieu-la-Garde onto D730 thro Montendre dir Mirambeau; go past Souméras vill on R, site sp on L. Or exit A10 junc 37; turn R onto D730; at rndabt turn R onto N137; in Mirambeau turn L onto D730; site on R in approx 14 km. Sm, hdg pitch, pt sl, pt shd; wc; chem disp (wc); fam bthrm; shwrs inc; el pnts (10-16A) €3; gas; shops 2.5km; tradsmn; snacks; bar; BBQ; playgrnd; htd pool; paddling pool; lake fishing; games rm; TV rm; 15% statics; dogs €1.50; Eng spkn; adv bkg; quiet; red long stay; clsd 15 Dec-5 Jan. "Vg British-owned site; meals on site poss arranged; gd touring base; vg." ♦ € 17.00 2008*

MONTERBLANC see Vannes *2F3*

MONTEREAU FAULT YONNE *4E3* (3km W Rural) *48.37472, 2.90382* **Camping La Grande Paroisse, La Noue Notre-Dame, 77130 La Grande-Paroisse [01 60 57 02 02; fax 01 60 74 28 93; basedeloisirs.lagrandeparoisse@wanadoo.fr; www.cc-deuxfleuves.fr]** Exit A5 junc 17 onto D210 then D605 S to Montereau. In Montereau take D39 W & foll sp La Grand-Paroisse & site on rvside. Med, hdg/mkd pitch, hdstg, pt shd; wc; chem disp; mv service pnt; shwrs; el pnts (4-13A) €3-6; shop; supmkt 2km; rest 5km; bar 2km; BBQ; playgrnd; pool 5km; sand beach 8km; sw & fishing adj; sailing, windsurfing & watersports; sailing school; games area; entmnt; 60% statics; dogs; adv bkg; quiet. "Well-situated site; conv Fontainebleau; excel fishing, walking & sailing; vg." ♦ 16 Mar-31 Oct. € 10.00 2009*

See advertisement

MONTESQUIOU see Mirande *8F2*

MONTESTRUC SUR GERS *8E3* (2km NE Rural) *43.79257, 0.64291* **Camping en Saubis (Daguzan), Route de Céran, 32390 Montestruc-sur-Gers [05 62 62 26 12]** S fr Fleurance on N21; after Montestruc-sur-Gers (immed past level x-ing) turn L onto D240; then turn R onto D251 for 1.5km, take R fork. Farm ent on L in 500m with conifer drive, site on L 50m. Sm, shd; wc; chem disp (wc); shwrs inc; el pnts (6A) €2.50 (long cable poss req); shops 2km; BBQ; playgrnd; golf 4km; 2 statics; poss cr; quiet. "Gd CL-type site with gd facs; peaceful farm with pleasant walks; friendly farmer." 1 Jun-30 Sep. € 6.50 2006*

MONTEUX see Carpentras *10E2*

MONTFAUCON *7D3* (2km N Rural) *44.69197, 1.53480* **Kawan Village Domaine de la Faurie, 46240 Séniergues [05 65 21 14 36; fax 05 65 31 11 17; contact@camping-lafaurie.com; www.camping-lafaurie.com]** Fr N20 turn E onto D2 sp Montfaucon, or fr A20 exit junc 56. In 5km site sp. Rd to site (off D2) is 500m long, single-track with passing places & steep but passable. Med, mkd pitch, pt sl, pt shd; wc; chem disp; mv service pnt; shwrs inc; el pnts (6-10A) €3.50-6; lndtte; shop; rest; playgrnd; pool; paddling pool; cycle hire; games area; wifi; TV rm; 30% statics; dogs €2.50; Eng spkn; adv bkg; quiet; ccard acc; red low ssn. "Superb, pretty site in lovely location; quiet & peaceful; lge pitches; v welcoming owners; excel facs & rest; gd touring base; narr, sl site rds - some pitches poss diff l'ge o'fits; conv A20." ♦ 5 Apr-26 Sep. € 20.00 (CChq acc) 2009*

MONTFERRAND *8F4* (2km N Rural) *43.3902, 1.8277* **FFCC Domaine St Laurent, Les Touzets, 11320 Montferrand [tel/fax 04 68 60 15 80 or 06 76 60 58 42 (mob); info@campingdomainesaintlaurent.fr; www.campingdomainesaintlaurent.fr]** S fr Toulouse on N113/D1113 past Villefranche-de-Lauragais. Turn L onto D43 for 4.2km; then R to St Laurent. Or turn L onto D218 bypassing Montferrand & cont directly to St Laurent; turn L at church. Site well sp. Sm, some hdg pitch, pt shd; wc; chem disp; sauna; shwrs inc; el pnts (3-6A) €4-5; lndtte; shop; rest; snacks; bar; playgrnd; pool; tennis; archery; cycle hire; entmnt; TV rm; dogs €2.50; Eng spkn; adv bkg; quiet; ccard not acc; red low ssn; INF card req. "Attractive, peaceful, well-kept site; clean san facs; friendly owners; gd views; woodland walks; goats & ducks." 1 Apr-25 Oct. € 18.00 2007*

MONTFERRAND *8F4* (6km SE Rural) *43.31451, 1.80246* **Camping Le Cathare, Château de la Barthe, 11410 Belflou [04 68 60 32 49; fax 04 68 60 37 90; info@auberge-lecathare.com; www.auberge-lecathare.com]** Fr Villefranche-de-Lauragais on N113/D6113, foll D622 sp Toulouse/Carcassonne over rlwy, canal, then immed L on D625 for 7km. Thro St Michel-de-Lanes then take D33 to Belflou; foll sp to Le Cathare. Sm, mkd pitch, pt shd; wc (some cont); chem disp; shwrs inc; el pnts (3-10A) €3-7.50; shops 12km; tradsmn; rest in ferme auberge; snacks, bar 4km; lake sw 3km; sand/shgl beach; some statics; dogs €1.20; v quiet; CCI. "Poss long walk to v basic san facs & poss sh timer for lts at san facs - might prefer own san facs; Centre Nautique on lake." 15 Apr-1 Nov. € 11.90 2008*

France

MONTFERRAT see Abrets, Les *9B3*

MONTFRIN *10E2* (500m NW Urban) *43.87980, 4.58917* **Camping Belle Rive, Cours Antelme, 30490 Montfrin [tel/fax 04 66 57 20 79 or 06 20 89 57 04 (mob); fredbissiere@hotmail.fr; www.campingbellerive.fr]** Fr Pont-du-Gard on D986 dir Beaucaire. Or on D2 SW fr Avignon. Well sp in vill; by rv & sw pool. Med, mkd pitch, pt shd; wc; chem disp; mv service pnt; shwrs inc; el pnts (10A) €3; Indtte; rest; snacks; bar; BBQ; playgrnd; pool adj; rv fishing; canoeing; tennis nrby; games area; games rm; entmnt; wifi; TV; 20% statics; dogs €1; no twin-axles; Eng spkn; adv bkg; quiet; red low ssn; CCI. "Peaceful site on Rv Gardon; welcoming owrner; nr interesting vill with bullring; conv Avignon, Arles, Nimes; vg." ♦ 1 May-15 Sep. € 15.50 2008*

MONTGAILLARD see Foix *8G3*

MONTGEARD see Villefranche de Lauragais *8F3*

MONTGENEVRE see Briançon *9C4*

MONTGUYON *7C2* (3km E Rural) *45.21193, -0.13653* **FFCC Aire Naturelle La Motte, La Motte, 17270 Le Fouilloux [05 46 04 08 39; enquiries@lamottecamping.com; www.lamottecamping.com]** Exit N10 at Montlieu-la-Garde onto D730 to Montguyon where site sp. La Motte bet vills Le Gat & Lampiat on D270. Sm, mkd pitch, pt sl, pt shd; wc; chem disp; mv service pnt; shwrs inc; el pnts (10A) inc; Indtte; shop; BBQ; playgrnd; cycle hire; games area; wifi; 5% statics; dogs €1.80; quiet; adv bkg. "Helpful British owners; nr medieval castle; twin-axles by prior arrangement; excel." ♦ 1 Mar-30 Oct. € 23.00 2008*

MONTHERME see Charleville Mézières *5C1*

MONTIGNAC *7C3* (7km E Rural) *45.05375, 1.23980* **Yelloh! Village Lascaux Vacances, 24290 St Amand-de-Coly [05 53 50 81 57; fax 05 53 50 76 26; mail@campinglascauxvacances.com; www.campinglascauxvacances.com]** Exit A89 junc 17 (Peyrignac) SE onto D6089 to Le Lardin-St Lazare. Join D62 S to Coly & then foll sp to Saint Amand-de-Coly. Site well sp. Med, mkd pitch, pt shd; wc; chem disp; mv service pnt; sauna; shwrs; el pnts; Indtte; supmkt; rest; snacks; bar; BBQ; playgrnd; pool complex; paddling pool; waterslides; fishing nr; cycle hire nr; games area; games rm; wifi; entmnt; TV; 60% statics; dogs €4; phone; adv bkg; quiet; ccard acc. "Excel, peaceful, renovated site in superb location; warm welcome; excel touring base." ♦ 16 Apr-20 Sep. € 30.00 2009*

See advertisement

MONTIGNAC *7C3* (6.5km SE Rural) *45.07211, 1.23431* **Camping La Tournerie Ferme, La Tournerie, 24290 Aubas [05 53 51 04 16; la-tournerie@orange.fr; www.la-tournerie.com]** Fr Montignac on D704 dir Sarlat-la-Canéda; in 5.5km turn L onto C1 sp St Amand-de-Coly; in 1.6km at x-rds turn L sp Malardel & Drouille; in 400m at Y-junc foll rd to R sp Manardel & La Genèbre; cont on this rd ignoring minor rds; in 1.6km at elongated junc take rd to R of post box; immed after passing Le Treuil farm on R turn R at x-rds La Tournerie. Site opp farm. Sm, terr, hdstg, terr, sl, unshd; htd wc; chem disp; shwrs inc; el pnts (6A) inc; Indtte; shop 6.5km; rest, bar 2.5km; dogs; adv bkg ess. "Quiet, scenic site; adults only; lge pitches, inc 2 for dog-owners; British owners; request detailed directions or see website - sat nav not rec; gd san facs; poor site lighting; excel touring base." ♦ 1 Mar-30 Nov. € 20.00 2009*

MONTIGNAC *7C3* (500m S Urban) *45.05980, 1.15860* **Camping Le Moulin du Bleufond, Ave Aristide Briand, 24290 Montignac [05 53 51 83 95; fax 05 53 51 19 92; le.moulin.du.bleufond@wanadoo.fr; www.bleufond.com]** S on D704, cross bdge in town & turn R immed of rv on D65; site sp in 500m nr stadium, adj Rv Vezere. Med, hdg pitch, pt shd; wc (some cont); shwrs inc; el pnts (10A) €3.30; shops 500m; rest; snacks; bar; BBQ; htd pool high ssn; paddling pool; tennis adj; fishing; entmnt; wifi; dogs €1.80; poss cr; quiet; ccard acc. "Pleasant site; poss diff lge o'fits due trees; pleasant, helpful owners; facs excel; conv Lascaux caves & town; gd walking area." Easter-15 Oct. € 18.10 2009*

MONTIGNAC *7C3* (7km S Rural) *45.01744, 1.18808* **FFCC Camping La Fage, 24290 La Chapelle-Aubareil [05 53 50 76 50; fax 05 53 50 79 19; camping.lafage@wanadoo.fr; www.camping-lafage.com]** Fr Montignac take D704 twd Sarlat. In approx 7km turn R to La Chapelle-Aubareil & foll camp sp to site ent 1km bef La Chapelle. Long winding drive thro woods to site. Med, pt sl, pt shd; wc; mv service pnt; baby facs; shwrs inc; el pnts (6A) €3; Indtte; shop; snacks; bar; playgrnd; pool; padding pool; games area; wifi; entmnt; TV; 30% statics; dogs €1.50; adv bkg; red low ssn/CCI. "Excel site; helpful owners; vg, clean san facs; red facs low ssn; gd rest; conv Lascaux 2 & other pre-historic sites." 1 May-30 Sep. € 18.00 (CChq acc) 2008*

MONTIGNAC *7C3* (8km SW Rural) *45.04107, 1.11895* **Camping La Castillonderie, 24290 Thonac [05 53 50 76 79; fax 05 53 51 59 13; castillonderie@wanadoo.fr; www.castillonderie.nl]** Take D706 dir Les Eyzies. At rndabt in Thonac turn R onto D65 sp Fanlac in 1km after x-rd take R, site is sp 1.5km. Med, hdg/mkd pitch, hdstg, pt sl, pt shd; htd wc; chem disp; mv service pnt; baby facs; fam bthrm; shwrs inc; el pnts (16A) €3.50; gas 5km; Indtte; sm shop & 2km; tradsmn; rest; snacks; bar; BBQ; playgrnd; pool; paddling pool; canoeing 3km; entmnt; TV rm; 10% statics; dogs; phone; Eng spkn; adv bkg; quiet; ccard acc; red low ssn; CCI. "Dutch owners friendly & helpful; gd cent for historic visits." ♦ Easter-30 Sep. € 16.50 2007*

MONTIGNAC *7C3* (9km SW Rural) *45.00178, 1.07155* **Camping Le Paradis, 24290 St Léon-sur-Vézère [05 53 50 72 64; fax 05 53 50 75 90; le-paradis@perigord.com; www.le-paradis.com]** On W bank of Rv Vézère on D706 Montignac-Les Eyzies rd, 1km fr Le Moustier. D706 poss rough rd. Med, hdg pitch, pt shd; htd wc; chem disp; mv service pnt; baby facs; shwrs inc; el pnts (10A) €3.50; Indtte; shop; tradsmn; rest; snacks; bar; BBQ; playgrnd; htd, covrd pool; paddling pool; beach adj; boat hire; rv sw & fishing; tennis; cycle hire; games area; entmnt; wifi; TV rm; 25% statics; dogs €2; phone; poss cr; Eng spkn; adv bkg; poss rd noise; ccard acc; red low ssn/long stay; CCI. "Gd site in gd location; vg for families; conscientious Dutch owners; immac san facs & gd pool; rest & takeaway vg; tropical vegetation around pitches; excel, espec low ssn." ♦ 1 Apr-19 Oct. € 27.00 (CChq acc) 2009*

MONTIGNAC CHARENTE **see Angoulême** *7B2*

MONTIGNY EN MORVAN *4H4* (2km E Rural) *47.15627, 3.87476* **Camp Municipal Plat du Lac, Bonin, 58120 Montigny-en-Morvan [03 86 84 75 76; fax 03 86 84 73 05; montignyenmorvan@free]** N fr Château-Chinon on D944. At Montigny take D303 on R sp Barrage de Pannecière. Foll sp Bonin & site. Access fr D303 narr & not rec lge o'fits. Med, pt sl, shd; wc; chem disp; shwrs; el pnts (10A) inc (poss rev pol); tradsmn; lake sw; fishing; CCI. "Pitches poss soft after rain." 1 May-30 Sep. € 11.90 2009*

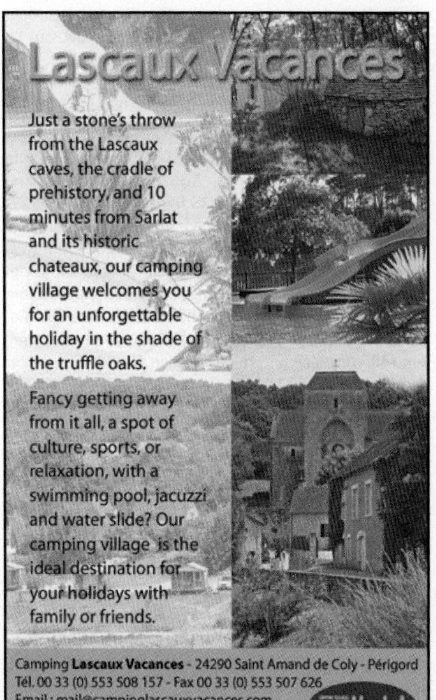

Lascaux Vacances
Just a stone's throw from the Lascaux caves, the cradle of prehistory, and 10 minutes from Sarlat and its historic chateaux, our camping village welcomes you for an unforgettable holiday in the shade of the truffle oaks.
Fancy getting away from it all, a spot of culture, sports, or relaxation, with a swimming pool, jacuzzi and water slide? Our camping village is the ideal destination for your holidays with family or friends.
Camping Lascaux Vacances - 24290 Saint Amand de Coly - Périgord
Tél. 00 33 (0) 553 508 157 - Fax 00 33 (0) 553 507 626
Email : mail@campinglascauxvacances.com
Site : www.campinglascauxvacances.com
yelloh!

MONTIGNY LE ROI *6F2* (1km N Rural) *48.00084, 5.49637* **Camping du Château, Rue Hubert Collot, 52140 Montigny-le-Roi [tel/fax 03 25 87 38 93; campingmontigny52@wanadoo.fr; www.campingduchateau.com]** Fr A31 junc 8 for Montigny-le-Roi. Site well sp in cent vill on D74. Med, terr, pt shd; htd wc; chem disp; mv service pnt; baby facs; shwrs inc; el pnts (5A) €3; Indry rm; shop; snacks; bar; BBQ; playgrnd; tennis; cycle hire; entmnt. "Modern facs; steep ent; rests & shops in vill." ♦ 15 Apr-15 Oct. € 12.00 2008*

MONTJEAN SUR LOIRE **see Chalonnes sur Loire** *2G4*

MONTLIEU LA GARDE *7C2* (8km N Rural) *45.30233, -0.23228* **Camp Municipal Bellevue, 17210 Chevanceaux [05 46 04 60 03 or 05 46 04 60 09 (Mairie)]** N fr Montlieu on N10 to Chevanceaux in 7km; site by church & primary school in vill. Sm, mkd pitch, pt sl, pt shd; wc; chem disp; shwrs inc; el pnts (6A) inc; shops, rest, bar in vill; snacks high ssn; BBQ (gas, elec); playgrnd; pool adj; tennis; quiet; CCI. "Peaceful, clean site in pleasant vill; lge pitches; warden visits am; no security; easy walk to vill; gd NH." 1 Apr-30 Oct. € 11.00 2009*

MONTLIEU LA GARDE *7C2* (1km NE Rural) *45.24849, -0.25097* **Camp Municipal des Lilas, Roch, 17210 Montlieu-la-Garde [05 46 04 44 12 (Mairie); fax 05 46 04 50 91; montlieulagarde@mairie17.com]** On L N10 sp Montlieu-la-Garde; take D730 into vill. Turn L at multiple sp on corner (diff to see) & in 1km turn R & foll site sp. Site along vill lane. Sm, pt sl, pt shd; wc; shwrs; el pnts €2.10; tradsmn; shop in vill; pool 1km; quiet. "Vg NH; clean san facs; some rd noise." 1 May-30 Sep. € 5.70 2008*

MONTLUCON *7A4* (12km NW Rural) *46.37795, 2.46695* **Camp Municipal Le Moulin de Lyon, 03380 Huriel [06 11 75 05 63 or 04 70 28 60 08 (Mairie); fax 04 70 28 94 90; mairie.huriel@wanadoo.fr; http://huriel.planet-allier.com]** Exit A71 junc 10 & foll sp Domérat, then D916 to Huriel. Site well sp. Or fr N D943 turn SW at La Chapelaude to Huriel on D40, foll sp to site. Last km single track (but can pass on level grass) with steep incline to site ent. Site adj Rv Magieure. Med, hdg pitch, pt sl, pt shd; wc (some cont); chem disp; shwrs; el pnts (10A) €2.25 (poss rev pol); gas; Indry rm; shops, tradsmn; snacks, bar 1km; BBQ; playgrnd; lake/rv fishing; tennis; TV; few statics; Eng spkn; quiet. "Peaceful, friendly, clean, wooded site in lovely setting; site yourself, warden calls am & pm; no apparent security; 10 mins uphill walk to vill." 15 Apr-15 Oct. € 5.30 2009*

France

MONTMARAULT *9A1* (5km N Rural) *46.36698, 2.95234* **Camping La Ferme La Charvière, 03390 St Priest-en-Murat [04 70 07 38 24; fax 04 70 02 91 27; robert.engels@wanadoo.fr; www.lacharviere.nl]** Exit A71 junc 11 at Montmarault onto D68 dir Sazeret/Chappes. Site 4km beyond Sazeret, sp. Sm, pt shd; wc; shwrs inc; el pnts (10A) €3.50; Indtte; rest; playgrnd; pool; dogs €1; adv bkg; quiet; red low ssn; CCI. "Helpful Dutch owner; v ltd facs low ssn; san facs, stretched if busy; poss open in winter - phone to check; easy access to m'way." 1 Apr-31 Oct. € 16.00 2008*

MONTMARAULT *9A1* (4.5km NE Rural) *46.35995, 2.99213* **Camping La Petite Valette, La Vallette, 03390 Sazeret [04 70 07 64 57 or 06 80 23 15 54 (mob); fax 04 70 07 25 48; la.petite.valette@wanadoo.fr; www.valette.nl]** Leave A71 at junc 11 & take 3rd exit at 1st rndabt onto D46; after 400m turn L at next rndabt, site sp on L in 3km. Or N of Montmarault in vill of Sazeret site well sp. Narr rd fr vill to site poss diff lge o'fits. Med, hdg/mkd pitch, pt shd; htd wc; chem disp; baby facs; fam bthrm; shwrs inc; el pnts (6A) €2.95; gas; Indtte; tradsmn; rest (high ssn); snacks; bar; playgrnd; htd pool & paddling pool; cycle hire; fishing; games area; dogs €1.70; Eng spkn; adv bkg (fee req); quiet; red low ssn. "Attractive, well-run, improving site; lge pitches; gd, clean facs; pleasant walks; vg." ♦ 1 Apr-31 Oct. € 14.15 2008*

MONTMARAULT *9A1* (9km NE) *46.38107, 3.03926* **Camp Municipal, 03240 Deux-Chaises [04 70 47 12 33]** Exit A71 junc 11 onto N79 dir Moulins; in 8km turn off N79 to Deux-Chaises. Site in vill, well sp. Sm, hdg pitch, terr, pt sl, unshd; wc; shwrs; el pnts (16A) €2; shop; rest & bar 200m; playgrnd; tennis; lake fishing adj. "Well-kept, site in beautiful setting; gd, basic facs; warden calls for fees pm; phone to check open bef arr, esp low ssn; vg rest nrby; gd NH." 25 Mar-15 Oct. € 6.50 2009*

MONTMAUR see Veynes *9D3*

MONTMEDY *5C1* (500m NW Urban) *49.52126, 5.36090* **Camp Municipal La Citadelle, Rue Vauban, 55600 Montmédy [03 29 80 10 40 (Mairie); fax 03 29 80 12 98; mairie.montmedy@wanadoo.fr]** Fr D643 (N43) foll sp to Montmédy cent & foll site sp. Steep app. Sm, hdg pitch, pt sl, pt shd; wc; chem disp; shwrs inc; el pnts (5-10A) €2.80-3.97; Indry facs; shops 1km; tradsmn; playgrnd; dogs €1.90; phone; quiet; red long stay; CCI. "Warden calls am & pm; facs clean, ltd low ssn; nr Montmedy Haut fortified town; 10A hook-up not avail high ssn; vg." 1 May-30 Sep. € 11.90 2009*

MONTMELIAN *9B3* (12km NE Rural) *45.55861, 6.16944* **FLOWER Camping Le Lac de Carouge, 73250 St Pierre-d'Albigny [tel/fax 04 79 28 58 16; campinglacdecarouge@orange.fr; www.campinglacdecarouge.fr or www.flowercamping.com]** Exit A43 junc 23 dir St Pierre-d'Albigny; site ent on 2nd rndabt 3km bef vill. Med, hdg/mkd pitch, pt shd, wc; chem disp; baby facs; shwrs inc; el pnts (10A) €3; Indtte; shop 1km; tradsmn; rest, snacks & bar adj; playgrnd; rv sw adj; 20% statics; dogs €1.50; phone; Eng spkn; adv bkg; some rlwy noise; ccard acc; red low ssn; CCI. "By lake surrounded by mountains; v lge pitches; friendly owners; excel facs; vg." ♦ 25 Apr-15 Sep. € 15.00 2008*

MONTMELIAN *9B3* (5km SE Rural) *45.47745, 6.04111* **FFCC Camping L'Escale, 73800 Ste Hélène-du-Lac [tel/fax 04 79 84 04 11; campingescale@wanadoo.fr; www.camping-savoie-escale.com]** Exit A43 junc 22 onto D923 dir Pontcharra & Les Mollettes; after x-ing A43 site on R. Med, hdg pitch, pt shd; wc; baby facs; shwrs inc; el pnts (6A) inc; gas; Indtte; rest; snacks; bar; BBQ; playgrnd; pool; 30% statics; dogs €1; poss cr; adv bkg; some rd & rlwy noise; CCI. "Gd san facs." 15 Feb-15 Oct. € 14.00 2006*

MONTMEYAN *10E3* (500m S Rural) *43.63830, 6.06080* **Camping Le Château de L'Eouvière, 83670 Montmeyan [tel/fax 04 94 80 75 54; leouviere@wanadoo.fr; www.leouviere.com]** Fr Montmeyan take D13 dir Fox-Amphoux; site 500m on R out of Montmeyan. Med, mkd pitch, terr, pt shd; wc; chem disp; shwrs inc; el pnts (10A) €4; Indtte; shop; tradsmn; rest; snacks; bar; BBQ (el only on pitch); playgrnd; pool; tennis; games rm; TV rm; no statics; dogs €4; Eng spkn; adv bkg; Eng spkn; quiet; red low ssn; no ccard acc. "Peaceful site in lovely area; diff access; steep slopes/uneven steps poss diff for disabled; poorly lit; adequate san facs." ♦ 15 Apr-15 Oct. € 23.00 2006*

MONTMIRAIL *3D4* (1km E Rural) *48.87299, 3.55147* **Camp Municipal Les Châtaigniers, Rue du Petit St Lazare, 51210 Montmirail [03 26 81 25 61; fax 03 26 81 14 27; mairie.montmirail@wanadoo.fr]** Site sp at junc of D933 & D373 at E o'skts of town. By sports stadium 150m twds town by Gendarmerie. Sm, mkd pitch, pt shd; wc (cont); own san rec; shwrs inc; el pnts (20A) €4; shops 500m; playgrnd; pool 500m; tennis; golf; ccard not acc; CCI. "Gd, clean, peaceful site approx 1 hr fr Paris; warm welcome; fees collected each pm; call at warden's house L of ent for removal of barrier." 1 Apr-31 Oct. € 4.35 2008*

MONTMORILLON *7A3* (500m E Urban) *46.42035, 0.87554* **Camp Municipal de l'Allochon, 31 Ave Fernand Tribot, 86500 Montmorillon [05 49 91 02 33 or 05 49 91 13 99 (Mairie); fax 05 49 91 58 26; marie@ville-montmorillon.fr]** On D54 to Le Dorat, approx 400m SE fr main rd bdge over rv at S of town. Site on L. Fr S v sharp RH turn into site. Med, mkd pitch, terr, pt shd; htd wc (some cont); mv service pnt; shwrs inc; el pnts (6-10A) €1.80-4.75; Indtte; shop 1km; rest, snacks, bar 500m; BBQ; playgrnd; htd, covrd pool adj; fishing; games area; wifi; TV; dogs; poss cr; adv bkg; some rd noise; CCI. "Delightful, peaceful, well-kept site; lge pitches; friendly, hard-working warden; gd touring base; vg value." ♦ 1 Mar-31 Oct. € 5.00 2009*

MONTOIRE SUR LE LOIR *4F2* (500m S Rural) *47.74750, 0.86351* **Camp Municipal Les Reclusages, Ave des Reclusages, 41800 Montoire-sur-le Loir [tel/fax 02 54 85 02 53; mairie.montoire@wanadoo.fr]** Foll site sp, out of town sq, over rv bdge & 1st L on blind corner at foot of old castle. Med, some mkd pitch, pt shd; wc (some cont); chem disp; mv service pnt; shwrs inc; el pnts (10A) €3.50; Indtte; shops 500m; bar; snacks (am only); playgrnd; htd pool adj; playgrnd; canoeing; fishing; 5% statics; adv bkg; quiet; no ccard acc; CCI. "Lovely location nr Rv Loir; peaceful, well-kept, secure site; some rvside pitches; friendly & helpful warden; excel clean san facs, v ltd low ssn; gd cycling; conv troglodyte vills; vg value; excel." ♦
1 May-15 Sep. € 7.25 2009*

MONTPELLIER *10F1* (8km N Rural) *43.65135, 3.89630* **Camping Sunêlia Le Plein Air des Chênes, Route de Castelnau, 34830 Clapiers [04 67 02 02 53; fax 04 67 59 42 19; contact@pleinairdeschenes.net; www.pleinairdeschenes.net]** Exit A9 junc 28 onto N113/D65 twd Montpellier. Leave at junc with D21 sp Jacou & Teyran, site sp on L. Tight ent. Med, mkd pitch, pt sl, terr, pt shd; wc (cont); shwrs inc; private san facs some pitches (extra charge); el pnts (10A) inc; gas; Indtte; shops 800m; rest (high ssn); snacks; bar; playgrnd; pool (high ssn); paddling pool; waterslides; sand beach 16km; tennis; games area; horseriding; 60% statics; dogs €6; quiet; red long stay/low ssn. "Improved site; site rds tight for lge o'fits; pitches muddy in wet." ♦ 1 Mar-31 Dec. € 37.00 (CChq acc) 2007*

MONTPELLIER *10F1* (6km SE Rural) *43.57625, 3.92580* **Camping Le Parc, Route de Mauguio, 34970 Lattes [04 67 65 85 67; fax 04 67 20 20 58; camping-le-parc@wanadoo.fr; www.leparccamping.com]** Exit A9 junc 29 for airport onto D66. In about 4km turn R onto D172 sp Lattes & campings, cross over D21. Site ent in 200m on R. Med, hdg pitch, shd; wc; chem disp; shwrs inc; el pnts (10A) inc; gas; Indtte; sm shop; huge shopping cent 1km; tradsmn; snacks high ssn; playgrnd; pool; sand beach 4km; 15% statics; dogs €2.80; Eng spkn; adv bkg (dep); quiet; CCI. "Friendly, helpful owners; lge pitches but dusty; gd facs, excel pool & snack bar; conv Cévennes mountains & Mediterranean beaches; hiking & mountain biking; barrier locked 2200." ♦ 25 Mar-11 Nov. € 23.40 2006*

MONTPELLIER *10F1* (4km S Rural) *43.55426, 3.89353* **Camping L'Oasis Palavasienne, Route de Palavas, 34970 Lattes [04 67 15 11 61; fax 04 67 15 10 62; oasis.palavasienne@wanadoo.fr; www.oasis-palavasienne.com]** Leave A9 at exit Montpellier Sud. Take D986 sp Palavas. About 1.5km after Lattes take slip rd sp Camping; turn under dual c'way. Site opp. Lge, hdg pitch, pt shd; wc; gym & sauna; shwrs inc; el pnts inc; Indtte; shop; rest; snacks; bar; playgrnd; htd pool; rv adj; sand beach, watersports 4km; cycle hire; horseriding 2km; entmnt; disco; TV; statics; dogs €4; free bus to beach; Eng spkn; adv bkg ess; some traff noise; CCI. "Bus to Palavas & Montpellier."
5 Apr-13 Sep. € 29.00 2008*

MONTPEZAT DE QUERCY see Caussade *8E3*

MONTPON MENESTEROL *7C2* (300m N Rural) *45.01280, 0.15828* **Camping Port Vieux, 1 Rue de la Paix, Route de Ribérac, 24700 Montpon-Ménestérol [05 53 80 22 16; daniel.taillez455@orange.fr]** Fr Montpon town cent traff lts take D730 N to Ménestérol. Site on L bef bdge beside Rv Isle. Med, hdg/mkd pitch, pt shd; wc; chem disp; shwrs inc; el pnts (10A) €3; gas 500m; Indtte; shop 100m; tradsmn; rest; snacks; bar; BBQ; playgrnd; lake sw 200m; boat hire; fishing; tennis 200m; cycle hire 500m; leisure park nrby; TV rm; 2% statics; dogs; Eng spkn; adv bkg (30% dep); quiet; ccard acc; CCI. "Gd touring base for St Emilion region; gd walking, cycling; vg." ♦ 1 Apr-30 Sep. € 9.00 2007*

MONTPON MENESTEROL *7C2* (10km SE Rural) *44.94153, 0.21260* **Domaine de Chaudeau (Naturist), 24700 St Géraud-de-Corps [05 53 82 49 64; fax 05 53 81 18 94; chaudeau.naturiste@wanadoo.fr; www.domainedechaudeau.com]** Fr Montpon take D708 S; after 8km turn E on D33 for St Géraud-de-Corps; foll black & white sp Chaudeau. Fr St Foy-la-Grande take D708 N; after 11km on exit St Méard-de-Gurçon turn E & foll sp as above. Med, hdg/mkd pitch, shd; wc; chem disp; shwrs inc; el pnts (5A) €3.90; Indtte; shop; snacks; bar; pool; lake sw; fishing; games area; entmnt; some statics; dogs €2.40; phone; quiet; ccard not acc; red low ssn. "Excel naturist site; INF card req but holiday membership avail; v lge pitches."
1 Apr-30 Sep. € 19.00 2009*

MONTPON MENESTEROL *7C2* (4km S Rural) *44.96046, 0.16506* **Camping La Tuilière, 24700 St Rémy-sur-Lidoire [tel/fax 05 53 82 47 29 or 06 87 26 28 04 (mob); contact@campinglatuiliere.com; www.campinglatuiliere.com]** On W side of D708 4km S of Montpon-Ménestérol. Med, hdg/mkd pitch, shd; wc; chem disp; shwrs inc; el pnts (10A) €3.20; gas; Indtte; sm shop 3km; tradsmn; rest; snacks; bar; playgrnd; pool;lake adj; tennis; 20% statics; dogs €1.20; poss cr; Eng spkn; adv bkg; quiet; red long stay; ccard acc; CCI. "Excel rest." ♦ 1 May-16 Sep. € 12.40 2008*

⊞ **MONTPON MENESTEROL** *7C2* (9km W Rural) *44.99857, 0.07228* **Camping Les Loges, 24700 Ménesplet [05 53 81 84 39; fax 05 53 81 62 74]** At Ménesplet turn S of N89 onto D10 sp Minzac. Turn L after level x-ing, foll sp. Sm, hdg pitch, pt shd; wc; mv service pnt; shwrs inc; el pnts (16A) inc (take care electrics); gas 7km; Indtte; shops 2.5km; playgrnd; rv sw 5km; games area; 5% statics; dogs €2; adv bkg; quiet; CCI. "Peaceful site in pleasant countryside." ♦
€ 17.00 2006*

MONTREAL *8E2* (2km NW Rural) *43.96378, 0.18514* **FFCC Camping Rose d'Armagnac, Moulierous, 32250 Montréal [tel/fax 05 62 29 47 70; campingrosedarmagnac@free.fr; http://campingrosedarmagnac.free.fr]** Exit Montréal in dir of Fources; L turn to Sos, v sharp turn off D29; after sm bdge 1st L, uphill 1km. Sm, some mkd pitch, pt terr, pt shd; wc; chem disp; mv service pnt; shwrs inc; el pnts (6A) €2.50; gas; Indtte; tradsmn; BBQ; rest, snacks & bar 2km; sm playgrnd; unhtd paddling pool; waterslide & sand beach 2km; dogs €0.50; poss cr; adv bkg; quiet; ccard not acc; CCI. "V quiet, British-owned site in scenic area; choice of pitches in woods or on open terr; gd san facs; Roman villa nr." ♦ 1 Apr-31 Oct. € 9.50 2007*

France

⊞ **MONTREJEAU** *8F3* (1.5km N Rural) *43.09234, 0.55457* **Camping Midi-Pyrénées, Chemin de Loubet, 31210 Montréjeau [05 61 95 86 79; fax 05 61 95 90 67; camping-midi-pyrenees@wanadoo.fr; www.camping midipyrenees.com]** Exit A64 junc 17 Montréjeau. Outside town take R fork onto D34 sp Cugeron & cont past Champion & Gamm Vert. At rndabt diff RH turn off curve to lane behind cemetary, then immed L & up hill, site well sp. Med, hdstg, pt sl, some terr, pt shd; htd wc; mv service pnt; shwrs inc; el pnts (6A) €3; rest; snacks; bar; playgrnd; htd pool; rv & lake 2km; wifi; entmnt; 70% statics; dogs €1; extra for twin-axles; quiet; CCI. "Lovely site; excel views Pyrenees; gd welcome; gd, modern san facs; excel infinity pool; site diff for disabled; poss not open for tourers until Jun-Jul; gd." € 12.00 2009*

MONTREJEAU *8F3* (7km S Rural) *43.02864, 0.57852* **Camping Es Pibous, Chemin de St Just, 31510 St Bertrand-de-Comminges [05 61 94 98 20 or 05 61 88 31 42; fax 05 61 95 63 83; es-pibous@wanadoo.fr; www.es-pibous.fr]** Turn S fr D817 (N117) onto D825 (N125) sp Bagnères-de-Luchon & Espagne. Foll past 'Super U' to lge rndabt & turn R sp St Bertrand-de-Comminges/Valcabrère then at 1st traff lts turn R & foll sp for St Bertrand & site. Or exit A64 junc 17 onto A645 sp Bagnères-de-Luchon to lge rndabt, then as above. Med, hdg/mkd pitches, pt shd; htd wc; chem disp; mv service pnt; shwrs inc; el pnts (6A) inc; gas; Indtte; shop; rest, bar 300m; playgrnd; pool; fishing, tennis 3km; TV; 20% statics; dogs; poss cr; adv bkg; quiet; ccard acc; red low ssn. "Peaceful, friendly site; pitches among trees; facs need update (2009) & poss unclean, ltd low ssn; gd touring area nr mountains; picturesque town in walking dist." ♦ 1 Mar-30 Sep. € 16.00 2009*

MONTREJEAU *8F3* (8km S Rural) *43.02898, 0.60859* **Camp Municipal Bords de Garonne, Chemin du Camping, 65370 Loures-Barousse [05 62 99 29 29 or 06 87 56 19 32 (mob)]** Exit A64 junc 17 onto A645 by-passing Montréjeau. Or fr Montréjeau take D825 sp Luchon & 'Espagne'. In 5km cont onto D33. Site on R in 3km, visible fr rd. Med, shd; htd wc (some cont); chem disp (wc); mv service pnt; shwrs; el pnts (4A) €2.50; shop 500m; rest, bar 400m; shops 500m; 80% statics; adv bkg; some Eng spkn; quiet but some rd noise; CCI. "Touring pitches on rvside; clean san facs; friendly, helpful staff; ideal as NH to/fr Spain; pleasant site; easy walk to vill." ♦ 1 Mar-31 Oct. € 6.50 2009*

MONTREJEAU *8F3* (6km W Rural) *43.0714, 0.4779* **FFCC Camping La Neste, 7 Chemin Gleize Bieille, 65150 St Laurent-de-Neste [05 62 39 73 38 or 05 62 99 01 49]** Exit A64/E80 junc 17 to Montréjeau or S fr Toulouse on D817 (N117). At W end of Montréjeau keep L on D938 sp La Barthe-de-Neste; in 6km turn S in vill of St Laurent-de-Neste & immed W on N bank of rv at camp sp; site on L in 1km. Sm, mkd pitch, pt shd; wc; chem disp; mv service pnt; shwrs inc; el pnts (6A) inc; Indry rm; shop 1km; playgrnd; rv sw & beach; phone; dogs; quiet; adv bkg; CCI. "Unreliable opening dates low ssn - phone ahead." 1 May-30 Sep. € 15.60 2009*

MONTRESOR *4H2* (3km NE Rural) *47.15782, 1.16026* **Camping Les Coteaux du Lac, 37460 Chemillé-sur-Indrois [02 47 92 77 83; fax 02 47 92 72 95; lescoteauxdulac@wanadoo.fr; www.lescoteauxdulac.com]** Fr Loches on D764; then D10 dir Montrésor; cont to Chemillé-sur-Indrois. Med, pt sl; wc; chem disp; baby facs; shwrs inc; el pnts (6A) €3.70; Indtte; sm shop; rest & bar 200m; playgrnd; htd pool; lake fishing & boating; trekking in Val d'Indrois; child activities; games rm; internet; TV rm; dogs €1.50; phone; v quiet. "Excel site by lake; clean san facs." ♦ 7 Apr-30 Sep. € 16.50 2006*

⊞ **MONTREUIL** *3B3* (500m N Rural) *50.46848, 1.76287* **FFCC Camping La Fontaine des Clercs, 1 Rue de l'Eglise, 62170 Montreuil [tel/fax 03 21 06 07 28; desmarest.mi@wanadoo.fr]** Fr N or S turn W off D901 (N1) at traff lts. Turn R after rlwy x-ing & in 100m fork R to site, site sp on Rv Canche. Med, mkd pitch, hdstg, pt sl, terr, pt shd; wc; chem disp; mv service pnt; shwrs inc; el pnts (6A) inc; shops 500m; tradsmn; pool 1.5km; rv adj; fishing; games rm; 40% statics; dogs €1; site clsd over New Year; adv bkg rec high ssn; quiet; red long stay; no ccard acc; CCI. "Busy site; generous pitches beside rv, some on steep terr with tight turns; helpful owner; basic site & san facs; conv NH Le Touquet, beaches & ferry; vet in Montreuil; attractive, historic town - uphill walk." € 19.00 2009*

⊞ **MONTREUIL BELLAY** *4H1* (4km E Rural) *47.15263, -0.13599* **FFCC Camping Le Thouet, Les Côteaux-du-Chalet, 49260 Montreuil-Bellay [02 41 38 74 17; fax 02 41 50 92 83; Brian.Senior@wanadoo.fr; www.camping-le-thouet.co.uk]** Fr D347 (N147) N of Montreuil-Bellay take dir 'Centre Ville'; turn L immed bef rv bdge & foll sp to Les Côteaux-du-Chalet. Access via narr, rough rd for 1km. Med, pt shd; wc; chem disp; shwrs inc; el pnts (10A) inc; gas; shop 4km; tradsmn; bar; BBQ; playgrnd; pool; fishing; boating; dogs; phone; 5% statics; adv bkg; quiet; ccard acc; red long stay; ccard acc; CCI. "Peaceful, spacious, British-owned site; lge area grass & woods surrounded by vineyards; pitches in open grass field; poss unkempt low ssn; gd walks; vill not easily accessed by foot; unguarded rv bank poss not suitable children." ♦ € 20.00 2009*

MONTREUIL BELLAY *4H1* (1km W Urban) *47.13191, -0.15897* **Camping Les Nobis, Rue Georges Girouy, 49260 Montreuil-Bellay [02 41 52 33 66; fax 02 41 38 72 88; contact@campinglesnobis.com; www.campinglesnobis.com]** Fr S on D938 turn L immed on ent town boundary & foll rd for 1km to site; sp fr all dir. Fr N on D347 (N147) ignore 1st camping sp & cont on D347 to 2nd rndabt & foll sp. Fr NW on D761 turn R onto D347 sp Thouars to next rndabt, foll site sp. Lge, hdg/mkd pitch, pt shd; wc (some cont); chem disp; mv service pnt; shwrs inc; el pnts (10A) €3 (poss long cable req); gas; Indtte; shop; tradsmn; rest; snacks; bar; playgrnd; htd pool; cycle hire; TV rm; 7% statics; dogs; phone; poss cr; Eng spkn; adv bkg; quiet; 10% red 15+ days/low ssn; ccard acc; CCI. "Spacious site between castle & rv; vg rest; local chateaux & town worth exploring; 'aire de service' for m'vans adj." ♦ 22 Mar-5 Oct. € 20.00 2009*

France

MONTREVEL EN BRESSE *9A2* (500m E Rural) *46.33911, 5.13615* **Camping La Plaine Tonique, Base de Plein Air, 01340 Montrevel-en-Bresse [04 74 30 80 52; fax 04 74 30 80 77; plaine.tonique@wanadoo.fr; www.laplainetonique.com]** Exit A40 junc 5 Bourg-en-Bresse N onto D975; at Montrevel-en-Bresse turn E onto D28 dir Etrez & Marboz; site sp on L in 400m. Or exit A6 junc 27 Tournus S onto D975. V lge, hdg/mkd pitch, shd; wc; chem disp; mv service pnt; baby facs; shwrs inc; el pnts (10A) inc; lndtte; shop; rest; snacks; bar; BBQ; playgrnd; 3 htd, covrd pools; 2 paddling pools; 2 waterslides; lake beach & sw adj; watersports; fishing; tennis; cycle hire; games area; archery; mountain biking; entmnt; TV; dogs €2.10; Eng spkn; adv bkg; quiet; ccard acc; red low ssn. "Excel, busy, family site; superb leisure facs; vg clean san facs; some pitches boggy after rain." ♦ 11 Apr-25 Sep. € 23.30 2009*

MONTRICHARD *4G2* (1km S Rural) *47.33384, 1.18766* **Camping Couleurs du Monde, Bas de Montparnasse, 41400 Faverolles-sur-Cher [02 54 32 06 08 or 06 74 79 56 29 (mob); fax 02 54 32 61 35; touraine-vacances@wanadoo.fr; www.camping-couleurs-du-monde.com]** E fr Tours on D796 (N76) thro Bléré; at Montrichard turn S on D764 twd Faverolles-sur-Cher, site 200m fr junc, adj to Champion supmkt - on L by 2nd rndabt. Med, mkd pitch, hdstg, pt shd; wc; chem disp; baby facs; sauna; shwrs inc; el pnts (10A) €3.50 (rev pol); lndtte; supmkt adj; rest; snacks; bar; BBQ; playgrnd; htd pool; paddling pool; beach & sw 600m; games area; games rm; wifi; entmnt; TV; 5% statics; dogs €2; Eng spkn; adv bkg; quiet, but some rd noise; gate clsd 2200-0800; ccard acc; red low ssn/CCI. "Gd sports activities; ltd facs low ssn; vg." ♦ 18 Apr-26 Sep. € 19.00 2009*

See advertisement

MONTRICHARD *4G2* (1km W Rural) *47.33827, 1.16991* **Camp Municipal L'Etourneau, Rue Vieille de Tours, 41400 Montrichard [02 54 32 10 16 or 02 54 32 00 46 (Mairie); fax 02 54 32 05 87]** Fr D150 site sp twd rv. Med, mkd pitch, pt shd; wc; chem disp; mv service pnt; shwrs inc; el pnts (13A) inc (poss long leads req); supmkt & shops, rest, snacks 1km; bar; playgrnd; pool 2km; rv sw 2km; poss cr; Eng spkn; CCI. "Well-run site; helpful staff; card operated barrier." 1 Jun-15 Sep. € 12.00 2007*

MONTROLLET *7B3* (NE Rural) **Camping Auberge La Marchadaine, Beaulieu, 16420 Montrollet [05 45 71 09 88 or 06 22 46 35 64 (mob); aubergedelamarchadaine@yahoo.fr; www.auberge-camping-16.com]** N fr St Junien on D675, turn W onto D2 to Montrollet. Auberge sp in vill. Sm, pt shd; wc; chem disp (wc); shwr; el pnts (6A) inc; gas; shop 4km; tradsmn; rest; bar; playgrnd; fishing; internet; dogs; phone; Eng spkn; adv bkg; quiet; CCI. "Delightful CL-type site o'looking lake; vg rest." € 9.00 2007*

MONTSALVY *7D4* (800m S Rural) *44.70029, 2.50674* **Camp Municipal de la Grangeotte, Route d'Entraygues, 15120 Montsalvy [04 71 49 26 00 or 04 71 49 20 10 (Mairie); fax 04 71 49 26 93; mairie-montsalvy@wanadoo.fr; www.montsalvy.fr]** On W of D920 behind sports complex. Sm, mkd pitch, pt sl, pt shd; wc; shwrs; el pnts (3-6A) €2.50-3.70; lndtte; shops in vill; rest; snacks; bar; playgrnd; htd pool adj (Jun-Aug); fishing 2km; games area; adv bkg; quiet but some rd noise. "Pleasant vill; entmnt; views fr some pitches; friendly warden." 1 Jun-15 Sep. € 12.10 2008*

MONTSAUCHE LES SETTONS *4G4* (5km SE Rural) **Camp Municipal de la Baie de la Faye, Lac des Settons, 58230 Montsauche-les-Settons [03 86 84 55 83; fax 03 86 84 54 99; mairie-de-montsauche-les-settons@wanadoo.fr]** Foll sp 'Rive Droite' off D193 fr Montsauche-les-Settons. Sm, hdg pitch, terr, pt shd; wc; chem disp (wc); shwrs inc; el pnts (6A) €3; lndry rm; tradsmn; lake sw; watersports; boat hire 1km; 3% statics; dogs; poss cr; adv bkg; quiet; CCI. "Lakeside access dir fr site; Morvan National Park; gd." ♦ 1 Jun-15 Sep. € 11.00 2006*

MONTSAUCHE LES SETTONS *4G4* (5km SE Rural) *47.17114, 4.06037* **Camping L'Hermitage de Chevigny, 58230 Moux-en-Morvan [03 86 84 50 97]** Fr Montsauche take D520 S & after approx 5km turn L on D290; at T-junc in 3km turn L & in further 800m turn L into Chevigny & foll sp to L'Hermitage. App rds narr & twisting. Med, hdg/mkd pitch, pt shd; wc (mainly cont); chem disp; shwrs inc; el pnts (3-6A) €3.20; gas; Indtte; sm shop; tradsmn; snacks, bar; playgrnd; lake sw; watersports; fishing; games area; dogs €1.80; adv bkg; Eng spkn; quiet; ccard not acc; CCI. "Peaceful, secluded woodland site; clean facs; friendly, helpful owner; gd cycling & walking; less well-known part of France - a real gem; excel." 1 Apr-30 Sep. € 15.60 2007*

MONTSAUCHE LES SETTONS *4G4* (5km SE Rural) *47.18175, 4.05293* **FFCC Camping Les Mésanges, 58230 Montsauche-les-Settons [tel/fax 03 86 84 55 77 or 03 86 84 54 74]** Fr Montsauche take D193 to Les Settons, then D520 dir Chevigny. Foll sp to site on W side of lake. Med, mkd pitch, terr, pt sl, pt shd; wc (some cont); chem disp; mv service pnt; baby facs; shwrs inc; el pnts (4A) €3.20; gas; shop; rest 1km; snacks; playgrnd; lake sw; fishing; games area; dogs €0.80; poss cr; Eng spkn; quiet; adv bkg; CCI. "Beautiful, lakeside site; well-maintained; gd for families - lge play areas; excel." ♦ 1 May-15 Sep. € 13.00 2006*

MONTSAUCHE LES SETTONS *4G4* (7km SE Rural) *4.0705* **Camping Plage du Midi, Lac des Settons Les Branlasses, 58230 Montsauche-les-Settons [03 86 84 51 97; fax 03 86 84 57 31; campplagedumidi@aol.com; www.settons-camping.com]** Fr Salieu take D977 bis to Montsauche, then D193 'Rive Droite' to Les Settons for 5km. Cont a further 3km & take R fork sp 'Les Branlasses' Centre du Sport. Site on L after 500m at lakeside. Med, mkd pitch, terr, pt shd; wc (few cont); chem disp; baby facs; shwrs inc; el pnts (10A) €3.40; gas; shop; rest; snacks; bar; playgrnd; lake sw; sand beach adj; watersports; horseriding 2km; entmnt; dogs €1; phone; poss cr; Eng spkn; adv bkg; poss noisy; red low ssn; ccard acc; CCI. ♦ Easter-15 Oct. € 13.90 (CChq acc) 2007*

MONTSOREAU *4G1* (500m NE Rural) *47.21805, 0.05270* **Kawan Village L'Isle Verte, Ave de la Loire, 49730 Montsoreau [02 41 51 76 60 or 02 41 67 37 81; fax 02 41 51 08 83; isleverte@cvtloisirs.fr; www.camping isleverte.com]** At Saumur on S side of rv turn R immed bef bdge over Rv Loire; foll sp to Chinon & site. Fr N foll sp for Fontevraud & Chinon fr Rv Loire bdge; site on D947 in vill on banks of Loire opp 'Charcuterie' shop. Med, mkd pitch, pt shd; wc; chem disp; mv service pnt; shwrs inc; el pnts (6A) inc (poss long lead req); gas; Indry rm; shops 200m; tradsmn; rest & in vill; snacks; bar; playgrnd; pool; paddling pool; rv fishing/watersports; tennis; games area; golf 13km; entmnt high ssn; wifi; TV rm: bus to Saumur; poss cr; Eng spkn; adv bkg rec high ssn; rd noise, poss disco noise; red low ssn; ccard acc; CCI. "Gd rvside site in beautiful situation; various sized/shaped pitches; gd clean san facs, poss irreg cleaning low ssn (2009); barrier clsd 2200-0700; gd security; vg rest; twin-axles extra." ♦ 1 Apr-30 Sep. € 21.50 (CChq acc) 2009*

MONTSURS *4F1* (500m N Rural) *48.13784, -0.55170* **Camp Municipal de la Jouanne, Rue de la Jouanne, 53150 Montsûrs [02 43 01 00 31 (Mairie); fax 02 43 02 21 42; commune.montsurs@wanadoo.fr]** Well sp fr town cent. Med, pt shd; wc; chem disp (wc); shwrs inc; el pnts (6A) inc; Indry rm; shop, rest, snacks, bar 500m; playgrnd; rv fishing adj; phone; adv bkg rec; quiet; no ccard acc; CCI. "Pretty, well-kept rvside site in pleasant situation; peaceful; conv many medieval vills; ask at house opp if barrier clsd; highly rec." 1 Jun-30 Sep. € 8.61 2008*

MOOSCH see Thann *6F3*

MORCENX *8E1* (3km SE Rural) *44.00901, -0.89215* **Camping Le Clavé, 40110 Morcenx [58 07 83 11; contact@camping-leclave.com; www.camping-leclave.com]** Exit junc 14 fr N10 onto D38 thro Morcenx. Site on o'skts of vill on D27 bordering rv in chateau grounds. Med, pt sl, pt shd; wc; shwrs; el pnts (10A) €3; Indtte; shop; snacks; supmkt 2km; BBQ; sm pool; cycle hire; nr National Park; games rm; dogs €1.50; quiet. 1 Apr-31 Oct. € 18.00 2007*

MORCENX *8E1* (2km S Rural) *44.00735, -0.89612* **Camping à La Ferme Fortanier (Labadie), 1180 Route de Rion, 40110 Morcenx [05 58 07 82 59; mauricette.labadie@wanadoo.fr]** Fr N10 turn E at junc 14 onto D38 dir Mont-de-Marsan. At Morcenx turn R on D27. Site on R 1km past Camping Le Clavé. Well sp. Sm, hdg/mkd pitch, shd; wc; chem disp (wc); shwrs inc; el pnts (6A) €2.50-3.50; gas; Indtte; shop, rest, bar 1km; BBQ; playgrnd; pool, lake 3km; 5% statics; dogs; phone 500m; adv bkg; quiet; CCI. "Friendly owners; well-kept, clean, tidy site; peaceful & relaxing." 1 Mar-30 Sep. € 10.00 2008*

MORCENX *8E1* (7km W Rural) *44.03433, -0.94285* **Aire Naturelle La Réserve (Lemercier), 1870 Ave de l'Océan, 40110 Garrosse [dlemercier@club-internet.fr; www.camping-lareserve.com]** Exit N10 junc 14 onto D38 dir Morcenx; foll camping sps for 5km; site on L. Sm, pt sl, shd; wc; chem disp (wc); shwrs inc; el pnts (6-10A) €4; playgrnd; sm pool; snacks; games area; dogs €1; quiet. "Site in pine trees; conv N10." ♦ 1 Apr-30 Sep. € 9.10 2007*

MOREE *4F2* (2km W Rural) *47.88885, 1.21101* **Camp Municipal, Rue de l'Etang, 41160 Fréteval [02 54 82 63 52 (Mairie); fax 02 54 82 07 15; freteval.mairie@wanadoo.fr]** Site 100m fr N157 by Rv Loir in vill cent, 500m fr lake. NB Chicane ent/exit thro concrete posts & fencing - not for lge o'fits. Med, mkd pitch, pt shd; wc (some cont); shwrs inc; el pnts inc; shops 500m; playgrnd; fishing; quiet, some rd noise. "Lovely, location on Rv Loir; diff ent/exit, esp med/lge o'fits; facs need update; conv beautiful town of Vendôme; site run down (2009)." 1 Jun-31 Aug. € 7.50 2009*

MOREE *4F2* (500m NW Rural) *47.90643, 1.22755* **Camp Municipal La Varenne, Plan d'Eau de la Varenne, 41160 Morée [02 54 82 06 16 or 02 54 89 15 15; fax 02 54 89 15 10; mairie-de-moree@wanadoo.fr]** W fr Orléans on N157/D357 or N fr Vendôme on D910 (N100) & foll sp in vill onto D19 to site. Sm, pt shd; htd wc; chem disp; mv service pnt; shwrs inc; el pnts (8A) €3; gas, shops 400m; snacks; bar; playgrnd; lake sw & beach adj; fishing; canoeing; tennis 500m; golf 5km; adv bkg; red long stay; CCI. "Lovely, lakeside site; ltd san facs stretched if site full; popular with school parties high ssn; poss unreliable opening dates." 1 May-1 Sep. € 11.50 2008*

MOREE *4F2* (600m NW Urban) *47.88932, 1.20109* **Camping La Maladrerie, 41160 Fréteval [tel/fax 02 54 82 62 75; campingdelamaladrerie@aliceadsl.fr]** E fr Le Mans on D357 (N157) to Fréteval; turn L in vill. Sp. Med, mkd pitch, pt shd; wc; chem disp; shwrs inc; el pnts (4-6A) €1.55-2.30; gas; lndtte; shops 800m; bar; BBQ; playgrnd; pool; rv sw 200m; lake fishing on site; 5% statics; ccard acc; CCI. "Well-kept, quiet site; friendly owner; poss ltd facs low ssn; site was a medieval leper colony; highly rec." ♦ 15 Mar-31 Oct. € 8.45 2009*

MORESTEL *9B3* (8km S Urban) *45.63521, 5.57231* **Camping Les Epinettes, 6 Rue du Stade, 38630 Les Avenières [tel/fax 04 74 33 92 92; infos@camping-les-avenieres.com]** S fr Morestel on D1075, turn onto D40 to Les Avenières, site well sp. Med, hdg/mkd pitch, hdstg, pt shd; htd wc; chem disp; mv service pnt; baby facs; shwrs inc; el pnts (10A); lndtte; shop; tradsmn; rest; snacks; bar; BBQ; playgrnd; pool adj; rv sw 2km; entmnt; TV rm; 35% statics; dogs; phone; adv bkg; noise fr adj stadium; red low ssn; ccard acc; CCI. "Phone ahead low ssn to check open." ♦ 1 May-30 Sep. 2008*

MORESTEL *9B3* (NW Urban) *45.67694, 5.46587* **Camp Municipal La Rivoirette, Rue François Perrin, 38510 Morestel [04 74 80 14 97; mairie@morestel.com; www.morestel.com]** Foll camping sps in town. Site by sports complex on D517. (NB No Entry sps do not apply to campers). Med, pt shd; wc; shwrs inc; el pnts (8A) €2.70; supmkt 1km; pool & sports complex adj; dogs; quiet. "Sm, poss awkward pitches; twin-axles extra charge; ent barrier operated by adj sw pool staff; excel NH." 1 May-30 Sep. € 10.70 2009*

MORET SUR LOING *4E3* (2km NW Rural) *48.38333, 2.80194* **Camping Les Courtilles du Lido, Chemin du Passeur, 77250 Veneux-les-Sablons [01 60 70 46 05; fax 01 64 70 62 65; lescourtilles-dulido@wanadoo.fr; www.les-courtilles-du-lido.fr]** Use app fr N6 sp Veneux-les-Sablons & foll sp. 1km fr N6. Or fr Moret foll sp; long, tortuous rte; narr streets; 35m, 1-width tunnel. NB sp say 'Du Lido' only. Lge, mkd pitch, pt shd; wc; chem disp; mv service pnt; shwrs inc; el pnts (10A) €3; gas; lndtte; shops 1km; tradsmn; rest; snacks; bar; playgrnd; sm pool; tennis; wifi; 75% statics; dogs €1.50; poss cr; Eng spkn; adv bkg; rlwy noise at night; CCI. "Early arr rec; lge pitches; clean facs but poss insufficient high ssn; friendly owners; vg for children; lovely old town; conv Fontainebleau & train to Paris; excel." 11 Apr-20 Sep. € 14.00 2009*

MOREZ *9A3* (3km N Rural) *46.54218, 6.01907* **Camp Municipal La Bucle, 54 Route Germain Paget, 39400 Morbier [tel/fax 03 84 33 48 55; info.bucle@wanadoo.fr; www.euro-tourisme.com/pub/bucle]** Fr N on N5 look for sps 10km after St Laurent. Pass supmkt & lge car pk on R, take sharp L turn after L bend in rd. Fr S turn R 50m past bdge. Med, some hdstg, pt sl, pt terr, unshd; wc; shwrs inc; el pnts (10A) €2.30; shops 1km; pool; dogs €0.60; quiet; red low ssn; gd NH. "Lovely site & town; site poss unkempt." 1 Jun-15 Sep. € 14.50 2006*

MOREZ *9A3* (9km S Rural) *46.48368, 5.94885* **Camping Le Baptaillard, 39400 Longchaumois [03 84 60 62 34; camping-lebaptaillard@orange.fr]** Foll D69 S, site sp on R. Med, mkd pitch, pt sl, pt shd; htd wc; chem disp; shwrs inc; el pnts (6A) €2.50; lndtte; shop; rest, snacks, bar 3km; playgrnd; paddling pool; fishing 3km; tennis; skiing; games rm; some statics; adv bkg essential winter; quiet. "Beautiful CL-type site; views; lge pitches." 1 Jan-30 Sep & Dec. € 12.30 2007*

MORHANGE *5D2* (6.5km N Rural) *48.95745, 6.63474* **Camp Municipal La Mutche, Harprich, 57340 Morhange [03 87 86 21 58; fax 03 87 86 24 88; mutche@orange.fr; www.mutche.fr]** Fr D674 (N74) turn N onto D78 sp Harprich, site sp on shore of Etang de la Mutche. Med, mkd pitch, hdstg, pt sl, pt shd; htd wc; chem disp; shwrs €0.70; el pnts (16A) €2.80; lndtte; shop 2km; tradsmn; rest 2km; bar; BBQ; playgrnd; pool; sand beach; lake sw; watersports; fishing; tennis; games area; entmnt; 20% statics; Eng spkn; adv bkg; quiet; red long stay. "Modern san facs, poss insufficient high ssn." ♦ 1 Apr-31 Oct. € 11.50 2008*

MORLAIX *2E2* (6km NE Rural) *48.61583, -3.76822* **Camping Vert de Morlaix (Berric), Ferme de Kerroyal, Bois de La Roche, 29610 Garlan [02 98 79 12 54 or 06 14 39 21 61 (mob); fax 02 98 63 24 47; nills.bretagne@wanadoo.fr]** Fr Morlaix take D786 dir Lannion; in 6km turn R; farm on L in 1km. Foll blue & white camping sps. Clearly sp fr D786. Sm, hdg pitch, pt shd; wc; chem disp forbidden (2009); shwrs inc; el pnts €2; bar (in season); lndtte; playgrnd; htd pool 5km; TV; dogs; quiet; ccard not acc. "Pleasant CL-type site; goats, pony & duckpond; conv Roscoff & Marlaix; gd." ♦ Easter-31 Oct. € 10.00 2009*

MORLAIX *2E2* (11km E Rural) *48.60283, -3.73833* **Camping Aire Naturelle la Ferme de Croas Men (Cotty), Garlan, 29610 Plouigneau [tel/fax 02 98 79 11 50; fermecroasmen@free.fr; http://pagesperso-orange.fr/camping.croamen]** Fr D712 rndabt W of Plouigneau twd Morlaix (exit from N12) 2km R sp Garlan; thro Garlan site 1km on L, well sp. Sm, hdg pitch, pt shd; wc; 50% serviced pitches; chem disp; baby facs; shwrs; el pnts (6A) €3.20; playgrnd; horseriding 200m; farm museum; donkey/tractor rides; some statics; dogs €1; quiet; CCI. "Super CL-type farm site; clean, well-presented; ideal for children; excel facs; produce avail inc cider & crêpes." ♦ 1 Apr-31 Oct. € 11.40 2009*

France

MORLAIX *2E2* (15km S Rural) *47.91293, -4.23981* **Aire Naturelle Les Bruyères, 29410 Le Cloître-St Thégonnec [02 98 79 71 76 or 01736 362512 (UK); www.caravan campingsites.co.uk/france/29/bruyeres.htm]** Fr Morlaix take D769 S twd Huelgoat/Carhaix & Le Cloître-St Thégonnec. At Le Plessis after 14.5km turn L for Le Cloître-St Thégonnec. When ent vill, take L fork at Musée des Loups, 1st L, 500m then R to camp. Sm, mkd pitch, pt sl, pt shd; wc; chem disp; shwrs inc; gas; lndry rm; shop 500m; rest; bar; BBQ; playgrnd; dogs €2; quiet; adv bkg; CCI. "Helpful British owners; NB no electricity/el pnts; water htd by gas; oil lamps in san block (2008); camp fires; enjoy camping like it used to be; for stays outside of Jul/Sep tel to request." 1 Jul-15 Sep. € 16.00 2008*

MORMOIRON *10E2* (4km E Rural) *44.05531, 5.23725* **Camp Municipal, Route de la Nesque, 84570 Villes-sur-Auzon [04 90 61 82 05 or 06 10 48 91 15 (mob)]** E on D942 fr Carpentras; at T-junc in Villes-sur Auzon turn R; foll sp Gorge de la Nesque & sports complex 400m. R into site. Med, pt shd; wc; shwrs inc; el pnts (5A); shop nrby; playgrnd; pool 500m; quiet. "Friendly, helpful staff; clean facs; gd walking." 1 Apr-30 Sep. 2007*

MORMOIRON *10E2* (4km E Rural) *44.05713, 5.22798* **Camping Les Verguettes, Route de Carpentras, 84570 Villes-sur-Auzon [04 90 61 88 18; fax 04 90 61 97 87; info@provence-camping.com; www.provence-camping.com]** E on D942 fr Carpentras dir Sault. Site at ent to Villes-sur-Auzon beyond wine cave. Or at Veulle-les-Roses turn E onto D68. Cont thro Sottenville-sur-Mer. Site on L in 2km. Lge, hdg/mkd pitch, pt sl, pt shd; htd wc; chem disp; shwrs inc; el pnts (6A) inc; lndry rm; shops 1km; rest; pool; paddling pool; tennis; games rm; fishing 300m; tennis; internet; TV rm; dogs €2.60; adv bkg rec all times; quiet; red low ssn. "Lovely location - view Mont Ventoux; gd walking & cycling; friendly & helpful owner; families with children sited nr pool, others at end of camp away fr noise; poss muddy when it rains; sm pitches & poor access, not suitable lge o'fits; red facs low ssn." ♦ 1 Apr-12 Oct. € 22.40 (CChq acc) 2008*

MORMOIRON *10E2* (2km SE Rural) *44.05975, 5.18191* **Camping de l'Auzon, Quartier de la Rode, 84570 Mormoiron [tel/fax 04 90 61 80 42]** Fr Carpentras or Sault on D942, turn S off D942 onto D14. Foll sp. Sm, mkd pitch, terr, shd; wc; chem disp (wc); shwrs inc; el pnts (6A); lndtte; shop, rest, snacks, bar 1km; playgrnd; 50% statics; dogs; quiet "Asparagus fair last w/end in Apr; m'vans poss extra." ♦ 15 Apr-15 Oct. 2007*

MORNAS *10E2* (2km E Rural) *44.21540, 4.74530* **Camping Beauregard, Route d'Uchaux, 84550 Mornas [04 90 37 02 08; fax 04 90 37 07 23; beauregard@franceloc.fr; www.camping-beauregard.com or www.camping-franceloc.fr]** Exit A7 at Bollène, then N7 twd Orange. On N end of Mornas turn L on D74 to Uchaux, site after 1.7km, sp. Lge, pt sl, shd; htd wc (some cont); chem disp; mv service pnt; shwrs inc; el pnts (6-10A) €3.30-4.40; gas; lndtte; shop; rest; snacks; bar; playgrnd; 3 htd pools; games rm; tennis; golf; horseriding; cycle hire; entmnt; dogs €4.15; 80% statics; adv bkg rec high ssn; quiet; Eng spkn; ccard acc; red CCI. "Open until 2230; phone ahead to check open low ssn; gd san facs; many derelict vans; poorly maintained & ltd facs low ssn" ♦ 25 Mar-4 Nov. € 21.00 (3 persons) 2006*

MORNAY SUR ALLIER see St Pierre le Moûtier *4H4*

⊞ **MORTAGNE SUR GIRONDE** *7B2* (1km SW Coastal) *45.47600, -0.79400* **Aire Communale Le Port, 17120 Mortagne-sur-Gironde [05 46 90 63 15; fax 05 46 90 61 25; mairie-mortagne@smic17.fr]** Fr Royan take D730 dir Mirambeau for approx 28km. Turn R in Boutenac-Touvent onto D6 to Mortagne, then foll sp Le Port & Aire de Camping-Car. M'vans only. Sm, unshd; chem disp; mv service pnt; shwrs €1; el pnts (10A) inc; shop 500m; rest, snacks, bar 600m; dogs; poss v cr; quiet. "Car/c'vans poss acc; shwrs & mv service pnt 800m fr site; fees collected 0900; gd." € 6.00 2008*

⊞ **MORTAIN** *2E4* (8km S Rural) **Camping Les Taupinières, La Raisnais, 50140 Notre-Dame-du-Touchet [02 33 69 49 36 or 06 33 26 78 82 (mob); belinfrance@fsmail.net; www.lestaupinieres.com]** Fr Mortain S on D977 sp St Hilaire-du-Harcouët; shortly after rndabt take 2nd L at auberge to Notre-Dame-deTouchet. In vill turn L at post office, sp Le Teilleul D184, then 2nd R sp La Raisnais. Site at end of lane on R (haycart on front lawn). Sm, hdstg, pt sl, pt shd; wc; chem disp; shwrs inc; el pnts (10A) inc (poss long lead req); NB no wc or shwrs Dec-Feb but water & el pnts all year; shop, rest 1km; htd pool 8km; dogs; adv bkg; quiet. "Pleasant, tranquil CL-type site adj farm; lovely outlook; friendly, helpful British owners; adults only; adv bkg rec." € 15.00 2009*

MORTAIN *2E4* (500m W Urban) *48.64808, -0.94350* **Camp Municipal Les Cascades, Place du Château, 50140 Mortain [06 23 90 42 65; mairie.de.mortain@wanadoo.fr]** On D977 S fr Vire twd St Hilaire-du-Harcouët; site in cent of Mortain, sp to R. Sm, pt shd; wc; chem disp; mv service pnt; shwrs inc; el pnts (6A) €2; shop 200m; sm playgrnd; no statics; dogs; m'van parking area outside site; CCI. "Sm extra charge for twin-axles." ♦ Easter-1 Nov. € 6.00 2006*

MORTEAU *6H2* (Urban) *47.05304, 6.59908* **Camping Le Cul de la Lune, Rue du Pont Rouge, 25500 Morteau [03 81 67 17 52 or 03 81 67 18 53; fax 03 81 67 62 34; otsi.morteau@wanadoo.fr; www.morteau.org]** Fr Besançon take N57 E then D461. In Morteau foll sps to Pontarlier then 'Toutes Directions'. Site on R over rlwy/rv bdge sp Montlebon (D48). Clearly sp thro'out town. Across rv bdge. Sm, pt shd; wc (some cont); shwrs inc; el pnts (10A) €3; shops 300m; tradsmn; rv sw, fishing & boating; cycling; dogs €1; poss v cr; adv bkg; noise fr rd & rlwy; red low ssn. "Beautiful location on rv bank; modern san facs; pt of site v wet after heavy rain; poss v cold at nights (altitude)." 1 Jun-15 Sep. € 13.00 2008*

MORZINE *9A3* (3km NW Rural) *46.19510, 6.67715* **Camping-Caravaneige Les Marmottes, 74110 Essert-Romand [tel/fax 04 50 75 74 44 or 06 12 95 00 48 (mob); contact@campinglesmarmottes.com; www.campinglesmarmottes.com]** Exit A40 junc 18 or 19 onto D902 twd Morzine, then turn L onto D328 to Essert-Romand. Fr A40 take junc 18 to Morzine. Sm, hdstg, unshd; wc; chem disp; serviced pitches; baby facs; shwrs inc; el pnts (3-10A) €4.50-8; Indtte; shop 2km; tradsmn; playgrnd; lake sw 3km; TV; some statics; dogs €1; ski-bus; Eng spkn; adv bkg; quiet; red long stay; CCI. "Specialises in winter c'vanning for skiers; tractor to tow to pitch in snow." ♦ 21 Jun-7 Sep & 22 Dec-13 Apr. € 16.50 2009*

MOSNAC *7B2* (Rural) *45.50557, -0.52304* **Camp Municipal Les Bords de la Seugne, 17240 Mosnac [05 46 70 48 45; fax 05 46 70 49 13]** Fr Pons S on N137 for 4.5km; L on D134 to Mosnac; foll sp to site behind church. Sm, pt shd; wc; shwrs inc; el pnts (6A) €2.10; gas; 10% statics; dogs; Eng spkn; adv bkg; no ccard acc; quiet; red long stay; CCI. "Charming, clean, neat site in sm hamlet; site yourself, warden calls; helpful staff; excel facs; conv Saintes, Cognac & Royan." 15 Apr-15 Oct. € 6.30 2008*

MOSTUEJOULS **see Peyreleau** *10E1*

MOTHE ACHARD, LA *2H4* (5km NW Rural) *46.64107, -1.71046* **Camping Domaine de la Forêt, Rue de la Forêt, 85150 St Julien-des-Landes [02 51 46 62 11; fax 02 51 46 60 87; camping@domainelaforet; www.domainelaforet.com]** Take D12 fr La Mothe-Achard to St Julien. Turn R onto D55 at x-rds & site sp on L. Med, hdg/mkd pitch, pt shd; wc; all serviced pitches; shwrs inc; el pnts (6A) €3.80; gas; Indtte; shop & in vill; rest; snacks; bar; BBQ; 2 htd pools (no shorts); gd playgrnd; games rm; sand beach 12km; cycle hire; tennis; lake fishing adj; entmnt; dogs €2.60; 60% statics; poss cr; adv bkg rec high ssn; quiet; red low ssn; CCI. "Part of private chateau estate, popular with British visitors; gd for families; excel facs; gates clsd 2200-0800." 15 May-15 Sep. € 28.00 (3 persons) 2006*

MOTHE ACHARD, LA *2H4* (5km NW Rural) *46.65285, -1.74759* **Camping La Guyonnière, 85150 St Julien-des-Landes [02 51 46 62 59; fax 02 51 46 62 89; info@laguyonniere.com; www.laguyonniere.com]** Leave A83 junc 5 onto D160 W twd La Roche-sur-Yon. Foll ring rd N & cont on D160 twd Les Sables-d'Olonne. Leave dual c'way foll sp La Mothe-Achard, then take D12 thro St Julien-des-Landes twd La Chaize-Giraud. Site sp on R. Lge, hdg pitch, pt sl, pt shd; wc; chem disp; shwrs inc; el pnts (6A) €3.50 (long lead rec); gas; Indtte; shop; tradsmn; rest; snacks; bar; BBQ; playgrnd; 2 pools (1 htd, covrd); water park; waterslide; sand beach 10km; lake fishing, canoe hire, windsurfing 400m; cycle hire; internet; cab/sat TV rm; some statics; dogs €3; phone; Eng spkn; adv bkg; ccard acc; red low ssn. "V lge pitches; gd views; friendly owners; gd walking area." ♦ 12 Apr-26 Sep. € 23.50 2008*

MOTHE ACHARD, LA *2H4* (6km NW Rural) *46.64469, -1.73346* **FLOWER Camping La Bretonnière, 85150 St Julien-des-Landes [02 51 46 62 44 or 06 14 18 26 42 (mob); fax 02 51 46 61 36; camp.la-bretonniere@wanadoo.fr; www.la-bretonniere.com or www.flowercamping.com]** Fr La Roche-sur-Yon take D160 to La Mothe-Achard, then D12 dir St Gilles-Croix-de-Vie. Site on R 2km after St Julien. Med, mkd pitch, pt sl, pt shd; wc (some cont); chem disp; mv service pnt; baby facs; shwrs inc; el pnts (6-12A) €2-4.50; Indtte; ice; shops 7km; tradsmn; bar 1km; BBQ; playgrnd; 2 pools, htd covrd; sand beach 12km; fishing; sailing & lake sw 2km; tennis; cycle hire; games area; games rm; child entmnt; wifi; TV rm; 20% statics; dogs €2; Eng spkn; adv bkg; quiet; ccard acc; red low ssn; CCI. "Excel, friendly site adj dairy farm; lge pitches; 10 mins fr Bretignolles-sur-Mer sand dunes." ♦ 1 Apr-15 Oct. € 26.00 2009*

MOTHE ACHARD, LA *2H4* (7km NW Rural) *46.66280, -1.71380* **Camping La Garangeoire, 85150 St Julien-des-Landes [02 51 46 65 39; fax 02 51 46 69 85; info@garangeoire.com; www.camping-la-garangeoire.com or www.les-castels.com]** Site sp fr La Mothe-Achard. At La Mothe-Achard take D12 for 5km to St Julien, D21 for 2km to site. Or fr Aizenay W on D6 turn L dir La Chapelle-Hermier. Site on L, well sp. Lge, hdg/mkd pitch, pt sl, shd; serviced pitch; wc; chem disp; mv service pnt; shwrs inc; el pnts (8A) inc; gas; Indtte; shop; rest; snacks; bar; playgrnd; htd pool complex; waterslide; lake fishing; sand beach 12km; horseriding; tennis; wifi; 50% statics (tour ops); dogs €3.50; phone; poss cr; Eng spkn; adv bkg (ess Aug); ccard acc; red low ssn; CCI. "Busy site; lge pitches; pleasant helpful owners; vg, clean facs; gd for families & all ages; super site." ♦ 24 Apr-25 Sep. € 36.50 (CChq acc) ABS - A42 2009*

MOUCHAMPS *2H4* (1km SE Rural) *46.77493, -1.05510* **Camp Municipal Le Hameau du Petit Lay, Route de St Prouant, 85640 Mouchamps [tel/fax 02 51 66 25 72 or 02 51 66 28 02]** Fr Chantonnay to D137 NW; 1km past St Vincent-Sterlanges turn R sp Mouchamps; turn R onto D113 sp St Prouant & camping; site on L in 1 km. Sm, hdg/mkd pitch, pt shd; wc, chem disp; shwrs inc; el pnts €2; shop, rest, snacks & bar 1km; playgrnd adj; htd pool adj; quiet, but traff noise am; CCI. "Barrier clsd 2200-7000; vg." ♦ € 9.90 2006*

France

MOUCHARD *6H2* (8km N Rural) *47.04080, 5.8156* **FFCC Camp Municipal La Louve, Rue du Pont, 39600 Champagne-sur-Loue [tel/fax 03 84 37 69 12; camping. champagne@valdamau.com; http://monsite.wanadoo.fr/ camping_champagne]** Fr Mouchard NW on D121 to Cramans then NE on D274 to Champagne-sur-Loue; pass thro vill, site well sp on R. Care needed thro vill. Sm, shd; wc (some cont); mv service pnt; shwrs inc; el pnts (6A) €2.50; shops 2km; tradsmn; rest 1km; BBQ; playgrnd; fishing; dogs €0.80; adv bkg; quiet; CCI. "Beautiful situation on rv; all grass, poss diff for m'vans if wet; used by groups canoeists; vg." ♦ 1 Apr-30 Sep. € 6.50 2009*

MOULIHERNE see Vernantes *4G1*

MOULINS *9A1* (500m SW Rural) *46.55806, 3.32460* **Camping de la Plage, 03000 Moulins [04 70 44 19 29]** Fr Moulins turn W across Rv Allier at town bdge sp Clermont-Ferrand. Turn L on D2009 (N9) & in 100m turn L & foll sp to site on rvside. Med, some hdstg, pt shd; wc; own san facs rec high ssn; chem disp (m'van area); shwrs inc; el pnts (10A) inc (ltd & poss rev pol, poss long lead req); gas; Indtte; shop 500m; rest adj; snacks; bar; playgrnd; pool 1km; rv fishing & boat hire; entmnt; TV; phone; poss cr; poss noisy high ssn; ccard acc; CCI. "Ltd water pnts; basic san facs, poss ltd/run down low ssn & stretched high ssn; helpful staff; gates clsd 2200-0700; mkt Sat am; NH only." 1 May-15 Sep. € 10.00 2008*

MOURIES *10E2* (2km E Rural) **Camping à la Ferme Les Amandaies (Crouau), 13890 Mouriès [04 90 47 50 59; fax 04 90 47 61 79]** Fr Mouriès take D17 E sp Salon-de-Provence. Site sp 200m past D5 rd to R. Foll site sp to farm in 2km. Sm, pt shd; wc; shwrs inc; el pnts €2.50 (rec long lead) (poss rev pol); tradsmn; dogs; quiet. "Simple CL-type site; a few lge pitches; friendly owners; dated, dimly-lit san facs; conv coast & Avignon; book in using intercom on LH wall at ent to shwr block." 15 Mar-10 Oct. € 11.00 2006*

MOURIES *10E2* (2km NW Rural) *43.70008, 4.85738* **Camping Le Devenson, Route du Férigoulas, 13890 Mouriès [04 90 47 52 01; fax 04 90 47 63 09; devenson@ libertysurf.fr; www.camping-devenson.com]** Exit St Rémy by D5 for Maussane-les-Alpilles, turn L on app to vill onto D17 (sps), after 5km (NW edge of vill) bef g'ge on o'skts of Mouriès, sharp L to D5, site on R, approach narr. Med, hdstg, pt sl, terr, pt shd; wc; chem disp; shwrs inc; el pnts (5A) €3.50 (rec long cable); Indtte; shop; BBQ (gas); pool; playgrnd; TV; dogs €2; Eng spkn; adv bkg; quiet; red low ssn; CCI. "Simple but v special site; spacious; attractive situation in pine & olive trees; simple, spotless facs; tractor tow to pitch if necessary; gd pool; min 1 week stay high ssn." 4 Apr-15 Sep. € 15.00 2009*

MOURIES *10E2* (7km NW Urban) *43.72138, 4.80950* **Camp Municipal Les Romarins, Route de St Rémy-de-Provence, 13520 Maussane-les-Alpilles [04 90 54 33 60; fax 04 90 54 41 22; camping-municipal-maussane@ wanadoo.fr; www.maussane.com]** Fr Mouriès N on D17, turn onto D5 on o'skts of vill dir St Rémy-de-Provence, turn immed L site on R adj municipal pool. Med, hdg pitch, pt shd; wc; chem disp; baby facs; shwrs inc; el pnts (4A) €3.50; gas 200m; Indtte; shops 200m; BBQ; playgrnd; pool adj inc; tennis free; cycle hire; internet; TV; dogs €2.50; buses in ssn; adv bkg rec; quiet, but some rd noise; red long stay; ccard acc; CCI. "Well-kept, well-run site in lovely area; on edge of vill; excel san facs; some pitches diff m'vans due low trees; gd security; excel." ♦ 15 Mar-15 Oct. € 19.50 2009*

MOUSSEAUX SUR SEINE see Bonnières sur Seine *3D2*

MOUSTERLIN see Fouesnant *2F2*

MOUSTIERS STE MARIE *10E3* (6km N Rural) *43.89836, 6.18011* **Camping à la Ferme Vauvenières (Sauvaire), 04410 St Jurs [04 92 74 72 24; fax 04 92 74 44 18; contact@ferme-de-vauvenieres.fr; www.ferme-de-vauvenieres.fr]** Fr Riez take D953 N to 1km beyond Puimoisson then fork R onto D108 sp St Jurs & site sp. Sm, pt shd; wc; chem disp; shwrs; el pnts €2.60; shops 2km; lake sw 2.5km; sports area; dogs €0.65; Eng spkn; adv bkg; quiet; CCI. "Peaceful & quiet; off beaten track; wonderful views; clean san facs; gd for mountain walking; lavender production area; gd Sunday mkt in Riez." 1 Apr-1 Oct. € 9.60 2007*

MOUSTIERS STE MARIE *10E3* (300m S Rural) *43.83963, 6.22150* **Camping Le Vieux Colombier, Quartier St Michel, 04360 Moustiers-Ste Marie [tel/fax 04 92 74 61 89 or 04 92 74 61 82 (LS); Contact@lvcm.fr; http://pagesperso-orange.fr/camping.vieux.colombier/]** Fr Moustiers go E on D952 dir Castellane. Site on R in 300m opp garage. NB Steep, winding access rd. Med, mkd pitch, sl, terr, pt shd; htd wc; 80% serviced pitches; chem disp; mv service pnt; baby facs; shwrs inc; el pnts (3-6A) €2.70-3.40 (rev pol); gas; Indtte; shop 600m; snacks; bar; BBQ; playgrnd; lake sw 5km; wifi; canoeing; windsurfing; dogs €2; Eng spkn; adv bkg ess high ssn; quiet; ccard acc; CCI. "Helpful staff; steep terrs, park at top & walk down; gd, clean san facs; steep uphill walk to lovely vill; conv Gorges du Verdon; gd walking; vg." ♦ 1 Apr-30 Sep. € 14.00 2009*

MOUSTIERS STE MARIE *10E3* (1km SW Rural) *43.84371, 6.21475* **Camping St Jean, Route de Riez, 04360 Moustiers-Ste Marie [tel/fax 04 92 74 66 85; camping-saint-jean@wanadoo.fr]** On D952 opp Renault g'ge. Med, some hdg pitch, pt sl, pt shd; wc (some cont); mv service pnt; shwrs inc; el pnts (3-6A) €2.60-3.30; gas; Indtte; shop 700m; tradsmn; sand beach & lake sw 4km; 3% statics; dogs €1.40; poss cr; Eng spkn; adv bkg; quiet; ccard acc; CCI. "Excel site in lovely location; conv Gorges du Verdon." ♦ 1 Apr-29 Oct. € 12.90 2007*

MOUSTIERS STE MARIE *10E3* (500m W Rural) *43.84497, 6.21555* **Camping Manaysse, 04360 Moustiers-Ste Marie [04 92 74 66 71; fax 04 92 74 62 28; www.camping-manaysse.com]** Fr Riez take D952 E, pass g'ge on L & turn L at 1st rndabt for Moustiers; site on L off RH bend; strongly advised not to app Moustiers fr E (fr Castellane, D952 or fr Comps, D71) as these rds are diff for lge vehicles/c'vans - not for the faint-hearted. Med, mkd pitch, pt sl, pt shd; wc (some cont); chem disp; mv service pnt; shwrs inc; el pnts (6-10A) €2.50-3.30; shops 500m; tradsmn; playgrnd; dogs €0.50; adv bkg; quiet; CCI. "Welcoming, family-run site; super views; gd san facs; cherry trees on site - avoid parking under during early Jun; steep walk into vill; lge o'fits do not attempt 1-way system thro vill, park & walk; gd." ♦ 15 Mar-2 Nov. € 9.90 2009*

MOUTIERS *9B3* (3km N Rural) *45.50700, 6.49097* **Camping Eliana, 205 Ave de Savoie, 73260 Aigueblanche [tel/fax 04 79 24 11 58]** Fr Albertville take N90 S & exit 38 for Aigueblanche. Foll sp in vill for 'Camping' on D97 dir La Léchère. Site on L 700m after supmkt; well sp. NB Final L turn from D97 is through a NO ENTRY sign. Sm, mkd pitch, terr, shd; htd wc; chem disp; mv service pnt; shwrs inc; el pnts (4-10A) €1.90-3.50; gas 1km; Indtte; shop 1km; tradsmn; rest; snacks; bar; BBQ; htd pool 500m; phone; dogs €0.30; quiet; CCI. "Well-managed site in orchard; gd, clean facs; warden calls 1800 - lives nr; sm pitches poss diff lge o'fits; gd walking & cycling." ♦ 1 Apr-31 Oct. € 8.50 2006*

MOUTIERS *9B3* (4km S Rural) *45.45294, 6.56232* **Camping La Piat, Ave Greyffié de Bellecombe, 73570 Brides-les-Bains [04 79 55 22 74; fax 04 79 55 28 55; campinglapiat@wanadoo.fr]** Fr Moûtiers on D915 to Brides-les-Bains into town cent. Turn R onto Ave Greyffié de Bellecombe & foll sp to site. Med, mkd pitch, some hdstg, pt sl, terr, pt shd; wc (some cont); chem disp; mv service pnt; baby facs; shwrs inc; el pnts (3-10A) €1.70-3.60; gas; Indtte; shops, rest, snacks, bar 500m; tradsmn; playgrnd; pool adj; 10% statics; dogs €0.80; phone adj; bus 500m; ski lift 500m; poss cr; Eng spkn; adv bkg; quiet but some rd noise; ccard acc; CCI. "Gd mountain base; Brides-les-Bains is thermal spa town specialising in obesity treatments; some pitches v muddy in wet weather." ♦ 15 Apr-15 Oct. € 10.00 2007*

MOUTIERS EN RETZ, LES see Pornic *2G3*

MOYAUX *3D1* (3km NE Rural) *49.20860, 0.39230* **Camping Château Le Colombier, Le Val Séry, 14590 Moyaux [02 31 63 63 08; fax 02 31 63 15 97; mail@camping-lecolombier.com; www.camping-lecolombier.com]** Fr Pont de Normandie on A29, at junc with A13 branch R sp Caen. At junc with A132 branch R & foll sp Lisieux to join A132, then D579. Turn L onto D51 sp Blangy-le-Château. Immed on leaving Moyaux turn L onto D143 & foll sp to site on R in 3km. Lge, mkd pitch, pt shd; wc; chem disp; mv service pnt; baby facs; shwrs inc; el pnts (10A) inc (poss lead req); gas; Indtte; shop; tradsmn; rest; snacks; bar; BBQ; playgrnd; htd pool; tennis; cycle hire; excursions; games area; library; entmnt; wifi; games/TV rm; some static tents/tour ops; dogs free; phone; Eng spkn; adv bkg; quiet; ccard acc; red long stay/low ssn; CCI. "Beautiful, spacious, well-kept, family-run site in chateau grounds; immac san facs; vg for children; friendly, helpful owners; gd shop & crêperie; shgl paths poss diff some wheelchairs etc; mkt Sun; barrier clsd 2230-0800." ♦ 1 May-15 Sep. € 34.00 ABS - N04 2009*

MOYENNEVILLE see Abbeville *3B3*

MUIDES SUR LOIRE *4G2* (6km E Rural) *47.64803, 1.61165* **Camp Municipal du Cosson, 41220 Crouy-sur-Cosson [02 54 87 08 81 or 02 54 87 50 10; fax 02 54 87 59 44]** Fr Muides-sur-Loire, take D103 E dir Crouy-sur-Cosson. In vill, turn R onto D33 dir Chambord. Site 200m fr village, well sp. Med, mkd pitch, pt shd; wc; shwrs inc; el pnts (5A) €3.15 (poss rev pol); lndry rm; shops 500m; tradsmn; rest 300m; snacks; bar 300m; BBQ; playgrnd; rv fishing nr; few statics; dogs; adv bkg; quiet; CCI. "Pleasant site; woodland setting; nr Rv Loire; poss long-stay workers." Easter-1 Nov. € 6.85 2006*

MUIDES SUR LOIRE *4G2* (1km S Rural) *47.66611, 1.52916* **Camping Le Château des Marais, 27 Rue de Chambord, 41500 Muides-sur-Loire [02 54 87 05 42; fax 02 54 87 05 43; info@chateau-des-marais.com; www.chateau-des-marais.com]** Exit A10 at junc 16 sp Chambord & take D2152 (N152) sp Mer, Chambord, Blois. At Mer take D112 & cross Rv Loire onto D103; at Muides-sur-Loire x-rds cont strt on for 800m; then turn R at Camping sp; site on R in 800m. Lge, mkd pitch, pt sl, shd; htd wc; chem disp; mv service pnt; all serviced pitches; baby facs; sauna; shwrs inc; el pnts (6A) inc (poss rev pol); gas; Indtte; shop; rest; snacks; bar, BBQ; playgrnd; 3 pools (1 htd, covrd); waterslides; water park; fishing; tennis; cycle hire; games area; games rm; wifi; TV; 50% statics (tour ops); dogs €5; Eng spkn; adv bkg; ccard acc; red low ssn; CCI. "Well-run site; excel, modern facs; friendly recep staff; plenty of gd quality children's play equipment; sh walk to rv; gd for visiting chateaux & Loire; mkt Sat am Blois." ♦ 13 May-15 Sep. € 41.00 ABS - L10 2009*

See advertisement on next page

France

41500 Muides sur Loire
Château des Marais
★★★★
Wi Fi
FREE ZONE
Tel. : +33 2 54 87 05 42
Fax : +33 2 54 87 05 43
www.chateau-des-marais.com
chateau.des.marais@wanadoo.fr

MUIDES SUR LOIRE *4G2* (W Rural) *47.67326, 1.52763* **Camp Municipal Belle Vue, Ave de la Loire, 41500 Muides-sur-Loire [02 54 87 01 56 or 02 54 87 50 08 (Mairie); fax 02 54 87 01 25; mairie.muides@wanadoo.fr; www.muides.fr]** Fr A10/E5/E60 exit junc 16 S onto D205. Turn R onto N152 then D112 over rv. Site on S bank of rv on D112 W of bdge. Tight U-turn into site fr N. Med, mkd pitch, pt shd; wc; chem disp/mv service pnt; shwrs inc; el pnts (5A) €2.20 (poss long lead req)(poss rev pol); gas in vill; lndtte; shops 200m; rest, snacks adj; playgrnd; rv fishing adj; sw 4km; cycling; dogs €1.40; vehicle barrier; quiet; no ccard acc; CCI. "Neat, clean, basic, spacious site; gd views over rv; some pitches by fast-flowing (unfenced) rv; little shade; excel cycling." ♦ 1 May-15 Sep. € 7.70 2008*

⊞ **MULHOUSE** *6F3* (4km NE Urban) *47.78267, 7.39453* **Camping Le Safary, 35 Rue de la Forêt-Noire, 68390 Sausheim [tel/fax 03 89 61 99 29; contact@campinglesafary.com; www.campinglesafary.com]** Exit A36/E54 junc 20 onto D201 N dir Battenheim & Baldersheim, site on E of D201, sp. Med, hdg/mkd pitch, pt shd; wc; chem disp; shwrs inc; el pnts (6-10A) €3; lndtte; shops 2km; bar; 60% statics; dogs €1; CCI. "Barrier clsd 2200-0800; few facs for size of site, poss inadequate if site full; poss itinerants." € 11.00 2006*

MULHOUSE *6F3* (2km SW Rural) *47.73405, 7.3235* **Camping de l'Ill, 1 Rue de Pierre Coubertin, 68100 Mulhouse [03 89 06 20 66; fax 03 89 61 18 34; campingdelill@wanadoo.fr; www.camping-de-lill.com]** Fr A36 take Mulhouse/Dornach exit & foll sp Brunstatt at 1st traff lts. At 2nd traff lts turn R, foll University/Brunstatt/Camping sps, site approx 2.5km on rvside. Lge, some mkd pitch, pt sl, pt shd; wc; chem disp; mv service pnt; baby facs; shwrs inc; el pnts (5A) €3.70; gas; supmkt & rest 1km; tradsmn; snacks; pool; internet; dogs €1.50; tram 500m; quiet but some rlwy noise; red low ssn/CCI. "Welcoming recep; cycle along rv to town cent; OK NH." 1 Apr-17 Oct. € 14.70 2009*

⊞ **MULHOUSE** *6F3* (10km SW Rural) *47.72225, 7.22590* **FFCC Camping Parc La Chaumière, 62 Rue de Galfingue, 68990 Heimsbrunn [tel/fax 03 89 81 93 43 or 03 89 81 93 21; accueil@camping-lachaumiere.com; www.camping-lachaumiere.com]** Exit A36 junc 15; turn L over m'way; at rndabt exit on N466 sp Heimsbrunn; in vill turn R at rndabt; site end of houses on R. Med, hdg pitch, hdstg, pt sl, shd; htd wc; chem disp; mv service pnt; shwrs inc; el pnts (10A) €2.50 (rev pol); lndry rm; shop 1km; tradsmn; snacks; playgrnd; pool; 50% statics; dogs €1; quiet; ccard acc; CCI. "Sm pitches not suitable long o'fits; beautiful wine vills on La Route des Vins; museum of trains & cars in Mulhouse." € 10.50 2008*

MUNSTER *6F3* (10km N Rural) *48.13436, 7.15529* **Camp Municipal Lefébure, 68370 Orbey [tel/fax 03 89 71 37 42 or 03 89 71 33 18; www.camping-orbey.com]** Fr Colmar take N415 to St Dié. At rndabt just beyond Hachimette, turn L onto D48 to Orbey. Turn R after supmkt at site sp. Site on L after 2km climb. Med, mkd pitch, terr, pt shd; wc; chem disp (wc); mv service pnt; shwrs inc; el pnts (5-10A) inc (long cable req some pitches); lndtte; shops 1km; tradsmn; snacks; playgrnd; 5% statics; dogs €1; phone; quiet; ccard not acc; CCI. "Peaceful site 300m above Rhine valley; helpful staff." 1 May-30 Sep. € 12.20 2007*

MUNSTER *6F3* (500m E Rural) *48.03944, 7.14250* **Camping Le Parc de la Fecht, Route de Gunsbach, 68140 Munster [03 89 77 31 68 or 08 10 12 21 83 (LS); www.village-center.com]** Clear site sp on all app to Munster & in town. Site on D10. Lge, hdg/mkd pitch, pt shd; wc; chem disp; shwrs inc; el pnts (6A) inc; lndtte; shops adj; rest; snacks; bar; BBQ; playgrnd; htd pool, waterslide adj; entmnt; TV; some statics; dogs €3; Eng spkn; quiet; CCI. "Pleasant site; friendly & helpful staff; gd walking & cycling; o'night waiting area." ♦ 5 Dec-31 Oct. € 16.00 2007*

MUNSTER *6F3* (3km E Rural) *48.0453, 7.1798* **Camping Beau Rivage, 8 Rue des Champs, 68140 Gunsbach [tel/fax 03 89 77 44 62; beaurivagecamping@wanadoo.fr; www.beau-rivage-gunsbach.com]** Site on rv off D417 Colmar to Munster rd. Med, pt shd; htd wc; chem disp; shwrs inc; el pnts (3-6A) €2.20-3.20; gas; lndtte; shop (high ssn); supmkt 2.5km; snacks; bar; playgrnd; rv adj; fishing; sports area; 50% statics; dogs €0.70; adv bkg; quiet; CCI. "Excel for visiting Albert Schweitzer house & memorial." 1 Apr-20 Oct. € 10.00 2008*

MUNSTER *6F3* (4km E Rural) *48.05160, 7.20527* **Camping La Route Verte, 13 Rue de la Gare, 68230 Wihr-au-Val [03 89 71 10 10; info@camping-routeverte.com; www.camping-routeverte.com]** Take D417 out of Colmar twd Munster & turn R int Wihr-au-Val. Site on L 800m. Well sp. Med, mkd pitch, pt sl, shd; wc; chem disp; mv service pnt; shwrs inc; el pnts (4-6A) €2.65-3.80; Indtte; shops, rest, bar 50m; pool 4km; games rm; dogs €1.30; phone; poss cr; adv bkg; quiet; 10% red long stay; CCI. "Delightful, clean site amid vineyards; owner helpful & friendly; not suitable lge c'vans (6m max); excel san facs; highly rec." ♦ 25 Apr-30 Sep. € 9.05 2008*

MUNSTER *6F3* (9km SW Rural) *47.98250, 7.01865* **Camp Municipal de Mittlach Langenwasen, 68380 Mittlach [03 89 77 63 77; fax 03 89 77 74 36; mairiemittlach@wanadoo.fr; www.mittlach.fr]** Fr Munster on D10 to Metzeral then R onto D10. Site at end rd in 6km. Med, hdg/mkd pitch, pt sl, pt shd, serviced pitch; wc; chem disp; shwrs inc; el pnts (6-10A) €2.45-6: gas; Indtte; sm shop & 6km; tradsmn; playgrnd; 10% statics; dogs €0.80; Eng spkn; adv bkg; quiet; red low ssn; CCI. "Peaceful, wooded site at bottom of valley; helpful staff; san facs gd & clean; gd walking base." ♦ 1 May-30 Sep. € 10.10 2008*

⊞ **MUR DE BRETAGNE** *2E3* (6km N Rural) *48.25568, -2.98801* **Camping Le Boterff d'en Haut, 22320 St Mayeux [02 96 24 02 80 or 06 64 81 62 22 (mob); victor.turner@wanadoo.fr; www.brittanyforholidays.com]** N fr Mur-de-Bretagne on D767 to St Mayeux. Turn R into vill & R after vill hall (Salle Municipal); to T-junc, turn R & site on L. App via 750m single-track lane. Car parking in rd outside. Sm, unshd; wc; chem disp; shwrs inc; el pnts (6A) inc; gas 8km; shops, rest, bar 2km; lake sw & watersports 8km; adv bkg; dogs €2.20 (2 max); quiet; ccard not acc; red low ssn. "Excel, remote CL-type site; friendly British owners; gd san facs; gd touring cent; gd walks & cycling; when wet, cars parked off site." € 19.00 2009*

MUR DE BRETAGNE *2E3* (2km SW Rural) *48.19872, -3.01282* **Camp Municipal Le Rond Point du Lac, Rond-Point de Guerlédan, 22530 Mur-de-Bretagne [02 96 26 01 90 or 02 96 28 51 32 (LS); fax 02 96 26 09 12]** Fr Mur-de-Bretagne take D18 & foll site sp; ent opp view point of Lake Guerlédan. Med, terr, pt sl, pt shd; wc (mainly cont); chem disp; shwrs inc; el pnts; Indry rm; shops, rest 1.5km; bar 50m; playgrnd; sand beach/lake 500m; poss cr; quiet; CCI. "Gd walking & watersports." ♦ 15 Jun-15 Sep. 2007*

MUR DE BRETAGNE *2E3* (4km NW Rural) *48.20670, -3.04907* **Camping Beau Rivage Les Pins, Le Guerlédan, 22530 Caurel [02 96 28 52 22]** Fr Mur-de-Bretagne foll Caurel sp W on N164. Fork L after church in Caurel & foll sp to site past Camping Nautic to bottom of hill & turn L. Narr access rd & site ent. Med, mkd pitch, pt sl, terr, pt shd; wc; chem disp; shwrs inc; el pnts (6A) €2.20; Indtte; shop; rest; bar; playgrnd; lake sw adj; boating; watersports; some statics; dogs €1; adv bkg; quiet. "Friendly owners." 1 Apr-30 Sep. € 11.90 2008*

MUR DE BRETAGNE *2E3* (4km NW Rural) **Camping Le Guerlédan, 22530 Caurel [02 96 26 08 24; fax 02 96 26 08 24]** Fr Mur-de-Bretagne foll Caurel sp W on N164. Fork L after church in Caurel & foll sp to site past Camping Nautic to bottom of hill & turn L. Narr access rd & site ent. Med, mkd pitch, pt sl, pt shd; wc; shwrs inc; el pnts (poss rev pol); gas; playgrnd; lake sw adj; quiet; CCI. "Vg; attractive lakeside setting; friendly, helpful owners." 1 Jul-31 Aug. € 10.80 2006*

MUR DE BRETAGNE *2E3* (4km NW Rural) *48.20950, -3.05150* **Camping Nautic International, Route de Beau Rivage, 22530 Caurel [02 96 28 57 94; fax 02 96 26 02 00; contact@campingnautic.fr; www.campingnautic.fr]** Fr Loudéac on N164 into Caurel. Fork L 100m past church, site is 1st on L, beside Lac de Guerlédan. NB App fr Pontivy on D767 via Mur-de-Bretagne v steep in places & not rec when towing. Med, mkd pitch, terr, pt shd; wc (some cont); chem disp; baby facs; shwrs inc; el pnts (10A) inc; Indtte; shop (high ssn); BBQ; playgrnd; htd pool; paddling pool; jacuzzi; lake fishing; watersports & horseriding nr; cycle hire; tennis; games/TV rm; dogs €1.80; adv bkg; quiet; ccard acc; red low ssn; CCI. "Peaceful site in attractive countryside; gd pitches, poss diff lge o'fits; dated facs, poss stretched when site full; wonderful pool & lake." ♦ 15 May-25 Sep. € 27.60 ABS - B22 2009*

MURAT *7C4* (10km NE Rural) *45.12926, 2.96745* **Camping La Prade, Route de Murat, 15150 Neussargues-Moissac [04 71 20 50 21; camping@neussargues-moissac.fr; http://campingneussargues.monsite.wanadoo.fr]** Site sp on N122. Sm, hdg/mkd pitch, terr, unshd; htd wc; chem disp; baby facs; shwrs inc; el pnts (10A) inc; Indtte; shop 700m; tradsmn; rest, snacks, bar 700m; playgrnd; 40% statics; dogs €0.60; phone; bus 700m; adv bkg; quiet; CCI. "Clean, modern facs; excel views." ♦ 15 Jun-15 Sep. € 9.25 2008*

MURAT *7C4* (1km SW Urban) *45.10303, 2.86599* **Camp Municipal de Stalapos, 8 Rue de Stade, 15300 Murat [04 71 20 01 83 or 04 71 20 03 80; fax 04 71 20 20 63; agyl@camping-murat.com; www.murat.fr]** Fr N122 site sp fr cent of Murat dir Aurillac, adj Rv Alagnon. Lge, some hdstg, pt sl, pt shd; wc (cont); chem disp; shwrs inc; el pnts (6A) inc; Indtte; shops 1km; playgrnd; rv fishing adj; poss cr; no adv bkg; also winter season, phone ahead; quiet; red CCI. "Peaceful location; basic but clean san facs; warden lives on site; excel touring base; gd views medieval town." ♦ 1 May-30 Sep. € 9.60 2009*

MURAT *7C4* (5km SW Rural) *45.07781, 2.83047* **Aire Naturelle Municipal, 15300 Albepierre-Bredons [04 71 20 20 49]** SW fr Murat on D39 dir Prat-de-Bouc; site sp fr cent of Albepierre. Sm, pt shd; wc (some cont); chem disp (wc); shwrs inc; el pnts (10A) €2; shops, rest & bar 300m; dogs free; quiet; ccard not acc; CCI. "Excel, peaceful location; basic, clean facs; warden visits am & pm; vg walking amidst extinct volcanoes; gd." 15 Jun-15 Sep. € 6.80 2009*

France

MURAT *7C4* (5km SW Rural) **Camping Les Trois Pierres (à la Ferme), Le Bourg, 15300 Albepierre-Bredons [04 71 20 12 23; pascale.martres@libertysurf.fr]** Fr Murat take D39 sp Prat de Bouc. Site sp fr cent of vill of Albepierre-Bredons. Sm, pt sl, pt shd; wc; chem disp (wc); shwrs inc; el pnts inc; shop, rest, bar 500m; dogs; Eng spkn; adv bkg; quiet; CCI. "Excel, peaceful location for mountains, touring or walking; helpful owner." ♦ 1 Jul-30 Aug. € 9.00 2006*

MURE ARGENS, LA see St André les Alpes *10E3*

MURE, LA (ISERE) *9C3* (13km E Rural) *44.90064, 5.94606* **Camp Municipal Les Vigneaux, 38740 Entraigues [04 76 30 24 44 or 06 10 78 16 36 (mob); fax 04 73 60 20 18]** S on N85 fr La Mure, turn L on D114, fork R on D26 to Valbonnais. This rd becomes D526. Site on L on ent Entraigues, 4km beyond Lake Valbonnais. Ent on bend in rd, more diff if ent fr Bourg-d'Oisans. Sm, mkd pitch, pt shd; wc; mv service pnt; shwrs inc; el pnts (5A) inc (poss rev pol); shops 100m; rv 100m; lake 3km; fishing; 15% statics; dogs; adv bkg; quiet; red long stay; CCI. "Clean facs; National Park adj; warden visits am & pm." ♦ 1 May-30 Sep. € 12.00 2007*

MURE, LA (ISERE) *9C3* (7km SE Rural) *44.87593, 5.83710* **Camping Belvédère de l'Obiou, Les Egats, 38350 St Laurent-en-Beaumont [tel/fax 04 76 30 40 80; info@camping-obiou.com; www.camping-obiou.com]** Clearly sp on N85. Sm, pt sl, pt terr, pt shd; htd wc; chem disp; mv service pnt; shwrs; el pnts (4-10A) €3-5 (poss rev pol); Indtte; shop 7km; tradsmn; rest; snacks; playgrnd; htd, covrd pool; cycle hire; wifi; TV; English library; 5% statics; dogs €2; poss cr; Eng spkn; rd noise; red long stay/low ssn; CCI. "Superb, immac, family-run site; excel facs; helpful owners; picturesque & interesting area; gd local walks." 1 Apr-30 Sep. € 18.90 (CChq acc) 2008*

MUROL *7B4* (1km S Rural) *45.56275, 2.93825* **Camping Sunêlia La Ribeyre, Route de Jassat, 63790 Murol [04 73 88 64 29; fax 04 73 88 68 41; info@laribeyre.com; www.camping-laribeyre.com]** Exit 6 fr A75 onto D978 S sp Champeix/St Nectaire, then D996 to Murol. In Murol take D5 S sp Besse-et-St Anastaise. In approx 500m take D618 twd Jassat & site in 500m on rvside. Sp fr Murol. Lge, mkd pitch, pt shd; wc (some cont); chem disp; serviced pitches; baby facs; shwrs inc; el pnts (6A) €6.90 (poss rev pol); Indtte; shop 1km; tradsmn; rest; bar; BBQ; playgrnd; pools (1 htd, covrd) & aqua park; paddling pool; waterslides; lake sw & sand beach adj; fishing; boat hire; tennis; horseriding; hiking; games area; games rm; wifi; entmnt; TV rm; 30% statics; dogs €2.60; Eng spkn; adv bkg; quiet; ccard acc; red low ssn; CCI. "Beautiful setting by lake; spacious pitches, some by lake; gd san facs; excel sw complex; ideal touring base & family site; great walks fr site; activities for all ages; barrier operated 2300-0700; quiet low ssn; groups welcome low ssn; vg." ♦ 1 May-15 Sep. € 25.30 2009*

See advertisement

MUROL *7B4* (1km S Rural) *45.57400, 2.95735* **FFCC Camp Le Repos du Baladin, Groire, 63790 Murol [04 73 88 61 93; fax 04 73 88 66 41; reposbaladin@free.fr; http://reposbaladin.free.fr]** Fr D996 at Murol foll sp 'Groire' to E, site on R in 1.5km just after vill. Med, hdg/mkd pitch, pt sl, shd; wc (some cont); chem disp; shwrs inc; el pnts (5A) €4; Indtte; shop 1.5km; tradsmn; snacks; playgrnd; htd pool; lake sw 5km; dogs €2; poss cr; poss noise high ssn; Eng spkn; CCI. "Lovely site with immac san facs; friendly & helpful owners." 1 May-22 Sep. € 16.90 2006*

MUROL *7B4* (2km W Rural) *45.57516, 2.91428* **Camping Le Pré Bas, 63790 Chambon-sur-Lac [04 73 88 63 04; fax 04 73 88 65 93; prebas@campingauvergne.com; www.campingauvergne.com]** Take D996 W fr Murol twd Mont-Dore. Site 1.5km on L, twd lake. Lge, hdg/mkd pitch, pt sl, pt shd; wc; chem disp; mv service pnt; serviced pitches; baby facs; shwrs inc; el pnts (6A) €4.70; gas 1km; Indtte; ice/freezer; shop & 1km; tradsmn; snacks; bar (high ssn); BBQ; playgrnds; 2 pools (I htd, covrd); waterslides; lake sw; games area; library; entmnt; TV rm; 40% statics; dogs €2.10; phone; poss cr; Eng spkn; adv bkg; quiet; CCI. "Excel, friendly, family-run site; helpful staff; superb views; immac san facs; excel walking area; access to sm pitches poss diff lge o'fits." ♦ 1 May-30 Sep. € 22.90 2008*

MUROL *7B4* (5km W Rural) *45.56979, 2.90185* **Camping Les Bombes (formerly Municipal), Chemin de Pétary, 63790 Chambon-sur-Lac [04 73 88 64 03 or 06 88 33 25 94 (mob); les-bombes-camping@orange.fr; www.camping-les-bombes.com]** Site is on D996. Nr exit fr vill Chambon. Well sp. Med, mkd pitch, pt shd; wc (some cont); chem disp; mv service pnt; shwrs; el pnts (6A) €4.50; Indtte; shops; tradsmn; rest 500m; snacks; bar; BBQ; playgrnd; pool; lake sw 1km; TV rm; 5% statics; dogs €2.20; phone; quiet; Eng spkn; adv bkg; ccard acc; red low ssn; CCI. "Beautiful area; gd, clean, well-maintained facs; lge pitches; friendly, helpful owners; excel." ♦ 15 May-30 Sep. € 16.60 2008*

MUSSIDAN *7C2* (7km S Rural) *44.98058, 0.34027* **Camping Jardin Biologique de la Contie, La Contie, 24400 St Géry [tel/fax 05 53 58 64 31; migama@wanadoo.fr]** Fr Mussidan on D6089 take D20 S sp Ste Foy-la-Grande. At St Géry turn L, then L again in 500m. Site on R in 500m. Sm, pt sl, pt shd; wc; own san; chem disp (wc); shwrs €3; el pnts (10A) €3; Indtte; meals on request; cooking facs; playgrnd; no statics; dogs; Eng spkn; quiet. "Friendly, basic CL-type site; rural walks; fruit & veg fr garden." 1 Apr-31 Oct. € 10.00 2007*

MUY, LE *10F4* (1km E Rural) *43.46832, 6.59202* **RCN Camping Domaine de la Noguière, 1617 Route de Fréjus, 83490 Le Muy [04 94 45 13 78; fax 04 94 45 92 95; info@rcn-domainedelanoguiere.fr; www.rcn-campings.fr]** Exit A8 junc 37 dir Roquebrune-sur-Argens & Puget-sur-Argens & take DN7 for 8km. Site on R. V lge, mkd pitch, pt shd; htd wc; shwrs inc; el pnts inc; Indtte; shop; tradsmn; rest; snacks; bar; playgrnd; pool complex; waterslides; sand beach 15km; tennis; games area; wifi; entmnt; TV rm; statics; dogs €5; adv bkg; quiet. Easter-1 Nov. € 21.00 (CChq acc) 2008*

Les plaisirs de l'eau au pied des volcans
AUVERGNE
Sunêlia
La Ribeyre
La Clef Verte
Camping Qualité
JASSAT - 63790 MUROL
Tel. 04 73 88 64 29 - Fax : 04 73 88 68 41
email: info@laribeyre.com - www.camping-laribeyre.com

MUY, LE *10F4* (3km W Rural) *43.45872, 6.54638* **Camping Les Cigales, 721 Chemin des Oliviers, 83490 Le Muy [04 94 45 12 08; fax 04 94 45 92 80; contact@les-cigales.com; www.les-cigales.com]** Exit A8 at Le Muy, keep in L hand lane & take 1st L across dual c'way after Péage (toll), foll lge sp at sm lane ent to site. Fr DN7 (N7) W of Le Muy take A8 access rd, turn R into lane 250m bef toll booth & foll lane past toll to site in 1km. Lge, hdg/mkd pitch, hdstg, pt sl, terr, shd; wc (some cont); chem disp; mv service pnt; shwrs inc; el pnts (6-10A) €3-4.50; gas; Indtte; sm shop & 3km; rest; snacks; bar; playgrnd; htd pool; sand beach 20km; rv sw 2km; tennis; games area; horseriding; entmnt; TV rm; 20% statics; dogs free; Eng spkn; adv bkg (rec); quiet; red long stay; ccard acc; CCI. "Conv for St Raphaël & a'route to Nice; beautiful, clean san facs; excel pool; helpful staff; some pitches diff for lge o'fits but tractor avail; peaceful site; nightingales!" ♦ 31 Mar-28 Sep. € 29.50 2007*

MUZILLAC *2G3* (12km N Rural) *47.66220, -2.46837* **Camp Municipal de l'Etang de Célac, Route de Damgan, 56230 Questembert [02 97 26 11 24 or 02 97 26 11 38 (LS)]** Site on D7 W of Questembert on o'skts of town. Med, mkd pitch, pt shd; htd wc (some cont); chem disp; mv service pnt; shwrs; el pnts (12A) €2.25; lndry rm; shop; tradsmn; rest; playgrnd; fishing; TV; dogs €1.05; CCI. "Clean facs, attractive location by lake; Monday mkt sp fr vill; no twin-axles; diff access lge o'fits as ent zig-zags around concrete flower tubs." 15 Jun-15 Sep. € 7.60 2006*

MUZILLAC *2G3* (5km NE Rural) *47.61394, -2.50140* **Camping Le Moulin de Cadillac, Route de Berric, 56190 Noyal-Muzillac [02 97 67 03 47; fax 02 97 67 00 02; infos@moulin-cadillac.com; www.moulin-cadillac.com]** Fr N165 take D140 N to Noyal-Muzillac, turn R at x-rds, site well sp; care on LH hairpin at rd junc 100m fr site. Sh app rd but steep & sharp bends. Med, hdg pitch, terr, shd; wc; chem disp; mv service pnt; baby facs; shwrs inc; el pnts (10A) €3.20; gas; Indtte; shop; tradsmn; rest; bar; playgrnd; htd pool; waterslide; beach 15km; fishing lake; tennis; games area; golf 15km; TV rm; 30% statics; dogs €1.80; phone; adv bkg rec high ssn; quiet; "In wooded valley away fr cr coastal sites; relaxing site." ♦ 1 May-30 Sep. € 16.40 2008*

MUZILLAC *2G3* (7km NE Rural) *47.58261, -2.41582* **Camp Municipal Borgnehue, Le Borg-Nehué, 56190 Le Guerno [02 97 42 99 38 or 02 97 42 94 76 (Mairie); fax 02 97 42 84 36; mairie-leguerno@wanadoo.fr; www.camping-leguerno.com]** Exit N165 onto D139 dir Questembert. In 5km turn L onto D20 dir Muzillac then in 2km R onto D139A to Le Guerno. Just pass vill sp do not foll rd round to R into vill but take C104 strt for 100m, then foll camping sp. Site on R just after leaving Le Guerno. When turning R into site, keep to L. Sm, hdg pitch, pt shd; wc; chem disp (wc); mv service pnt; baby facs; shwrs inc; el pnts (6-10A) €2.04-3.09; Indtte; playgrnd; some statics; phone; adv bkg; quiet. "Warden high ssn only; book in at vill shop or Mairie (site clsd 1300-1600); pitches lge but poss diff lge o'fits - need to unhitch; gd site." 1 Apr-31 Oct. € 7.65 2006*

MUZILLAC *2G3* (8km SW Coastal) *47.51780, -2.55539* **Camping Ty Breiz, 15 Grande Rue, 56750 Kervoyal-Damgan [tel/fax 02 97 41 13 47; info@campingtybreiz.com; www.campingtybreiz.com]** Fr Muzillac on D153 dir Damgan, turn S for Kervoyal; site on L opp church. Med, hdg/mkd pitch, pt shd; wc; shwrs inc; el pnts (6-10A) €3-3.50; Indtte; playgrnd; sand beach 300m; dogs €1.50; Eng spkn; adv bkg rec high ssn; quiet; ccard acc; red low ssn; CCI. "Pleasant, welcoming, family-run site; excel san facs, inc for disabled; quiet low ssn; cycle path to Damgan; mkt Wed; vg." ♦ 26 Apr-19 Oct. € 16.50 2008*

MUZILLAC *2G3* (4km W Coastal) *47.52552, -2.51231* **Camping Le Bédume, Bétahon-Plage, 56190 Ambon-Plages [02 97 41 68 13; fax 02 97 41 56 79; cledelles.ambon@free.fr; www.bedume.com]** Fr N165 take D20 W dir Ambon, foll to Bétahon, site sp. Lge, hdg pitch, pt shd; wc; chem disp; baby facs; shwrs inc; el pnts (5A) inc; Indtte; shop; tradsmn; snacks; bar; BBQ; playgrnd; htd pools; waterslide; sand beach adj; games area; games rm; TV rm; 75% statics; dogs €4.20; Eng spkn; adv bkg req; quiet; ccard acc; red low ssn. ♦ 1 Apr-30 Sep. € 34.10 2006*

NAGES see Lacaune *8E4*

NAJAC *8E4* (Rural) *44.22011, 1.96985* **Camping Le Païsserou, 12270 Najac [05 65 29 73 96; fax 05 65 29 72 29; info@camping-massifcentral.com; www.camping-massifcentral.com/Najac.htm]** Take D922 fr Villefranche-de-Rouergue. Turn R on D39 at La Fouillade to Najac. Site by rv, sp in vill. Or fr A20 exit junc 59 onto D926. At Caylus take D84 to Najac. Med, hdg pitch, shd; wc; chem disp; shwrs inc; el pnts €3; Indtte; shops & rest in vill; tradsmn; snacks; bar; htd, covrd pool adj (free); tennis adj; some statics; dogs €1.50; phone; poss cr; Eng spkn; adv bkg; quiet; red low ssn; CCI. "Conv for Aveyron gorges; friendly owners; ltd facs low ssn; lovely vill; unreliable opening low ssn, phone ahead." 30 Apr-1 Oct. € 22.00 2007*

NALLIERS see Luçon *7A1*

⊞ **NAMPONT ST MARTIN** *3B3* (2km NE Rural) *50.37039, 1.77546* **Camping Auberge des Etangs, 91 Rue Vallée de l'Authie, 62870 Roussent [03 21 81 20 10; www.auberge-des-etangs.fr]** 11km S of Montreuil on D901 (N1), take D139E to Roussent, site on R in vill. Med, mkd pitch, pt sl, pt shd; wc; chem disp; shwrs inc; el pnts (6A) inc; gas; Indtte; shop; rest; snacks; playgrnd; rv fishing 2km; entmnt; TV; mostly statics; site clsd Jan; quiet but noise fr hotel (disco); sm space for tourers. "NH only." € 13.00 2006*

NAMPONT ST MARTIN *3B3* (3km W Rural) *50.33595, 1.71230* **Kawan Village La Ferme des Aulnes, 1 Rue du Marais, Fresne-sur-Authie, 80120 Nampont-St Martin [03 22 29 22 69 or 06 22 41 86 54 (mob LS); fax 03 22 29 39 43; contact@fermedesaulnes.com; www.fermedesaulnes.com]** D901 (N1) S fr Montreuil 13km thro Nampont-St Firmin to Nampont-St Martin; turn R in vill onto D485; site in 3km; sp fr D901. Med, some hdg pitch, pt sl, pt shd; htd wc; chem disp; mv service pnt; shwrs inc; el pnts (6-10A) €6-12; Indry rm; shop 5km; tradsmn, rest, snacks, bar high ssn; BBQ (not elec); playgrnd; htd, covrd pool; beach 10km; archery; golf 1km; games area; entmnt; wifi; TV & cinema rm; mostly statics; dogs €4; poss cr; adv bkg; quiet; CCI. "Attractive site nr Calais; some pitches sm, some v sl; friendly staff; clsd 2200-0800; poss noisy cockerels." ♦ 1 Apr-1 Nov. € 21.00 (3 persons) (CChq acc) 2009*

NANCAY *4G3* (500m NW Rural) *47.35215, 2.18522* **Camp Municipal des Pins, Route de Salbris, La Chaux, 18330 Nançay [02 48 51 81 80 or 02 48 51 81 35 (Mairie); fax 02 48 51 80 60]** Site on D944 fr Salbris twd Bourges clearly sp on L immed bef ent Nançay. Med, mkd pitch, hdstg, shd; htd wc; chem disp; shwrs inc; el pnts (6A) inc; gas; Indtte; shops 1km; playgrnd; tennis; golf 2km; fishing; 50% statics; no twin-axles; adv bkg; quiet; CCI. "Lovely spot in pine woods; friendly recep; clean san facs; poor site lighting; beautiful vill; gd walking." 1 Apr-2 Nov. € 9.00 2009*

NANCY *6E2* (6km SW Rural) *48.65730, 6.14028* **CAMPEOLE Camping Le Brabois, 2301 Ave Paul Muller, 54600 Villers-lès-Nancy [03 83 27 18 28; fax 03 83 40 06 43; brabois@campeole.com; www.camping-brabois.com or www.campeole.com]** Fr A33 exit junc 2b sp Brabois onto D974 dir Nancy; after 400m turn L at 2nd traff lts; at slip rd after 2nd further traff lts turn R on slip rd & site on R; site well sp. Lge, mkd pitch, pt shd; htd wc (some cont); chem disp; mv service pnt; shwrs inc; el pnts (5-15A) €4.10-5.25 (poss rev pol); gas; Indtte; shop; tradsmn; supmkt & petrol 2km; rest; snacks (high ssn); bar; BBQ; playgrnd; games area; TV; dogs €2.60; bus (tickets fr recep); poss cr; Eng spkn; adv bkg; quiet; ccard acc; red low ssn; CCI. "Well-run, popular site with lge pitches; helpful staff; gd, clean san facs; less pitch care low ssn; no twin-axle c'vans over 5.50m (m'vans OK); interesting town; rec arr early; vg NH." ♦ 1 Apr-15 Oct. € 14.20 2009*

NANCY *6E2* (10km NW Rural) *48.74733, 6.05700* **Camping Les Boucles de la Moselle, Ave Eugène Lerebourg, 54460 Liverdun [03 83 24 43 78 or 06 03 27 69 71 (mob); fax 03 83 24 89 47; francis.iung@orange.fr]** Fr A31 exit junc 22 to Frouard. In Frouard bear L onto D90 to Liverdun; cross rv bdge (sp Liverdun); under rlwy bdge L at traff lts, thro town, fork L & foll sp to site by on rvside by sports area. Do not turn L at site exit when towing. Lge, pt shd; htd wc; baby facs; shwrs (0730-1000) inc; el pnts (6A) €3.20; Indtte; shop & 1.5km; rest; snacks; bar; playgrnd; pool; entmnt; some statics; dogs €1.20; quiet except rlwy noise; ccard not acc; CCI. "Lovely site & area; helpful staff; Nancy worth visit." 1 May-30 Sep. € 11.10 2008*

NANS LES PINS *10F3* (1km N Rural) *43.37535, 5.78510* **Camping Village Club La Sainte Baume, Quartier Delvieux Sud, 83860 Nans-les-Pins [04 94 78 92 68; fax 04 94 78 67 37; ste-baume@wanadoo.fr; www.saintebaume.com]** Exit A8 junc 34 dir St Maximin onto N560. Cross N7 & at next lge junc turn R onto D560 then immed L onto D80. Site 600m after sp Nans-les-Pins, then up private rd to site. Lge, mkd pitch, pt sl, shd; wc; chem disp; baby facs; shwrs inc; el pnts (6A) inc; gas; Indtte; shop; rest; snacks; bar; playgrnd; 3 pools; waterslide; jacuzzi; sand beach 35km; horseriding; 90% statics; dogs €5; adv bkg; ccard acc; red low ssn. "Friendly staff; modern san facs; some pitches diff access; ltd facs low ssn; path into pleasant vill; mkt Wed am; excel." ♦ 1 Apr-30 Sep. € 33.00 (CChq acc) 2009*

NANT *10E1* (2km N Rural) *44.03578, 3.29008* **Camping Le Roc Qui Parle, Les Cuns, 12230 Nant [tel/fax 05 65 62 22 05; contact@camping-roc-qui-parle-aveyron.fr; www.camping-roc-qui-parle-aveyron.fr]** Fr Millau take D991E to site passing Val de Cantobre. Fr La Cavalerie take D999E to Nant & at T-junc on o'skts of Nant turn N; Millau & Les Cuns approx 2km; site on R. NB Steep decent into site. Med, hdg/mkd pitch, pt sl, pt shd; wc; serviced pitches; chem disp; mv service pnt; shwrs inc; el pnts (6A) €3.10; Indtte; shop; BBQ; playgrnd; rv sw & fishing on site; dogs free; adv bkg; quiet; no ccard acc; CCI. "Magnificent surroundings; excel, well-run site; v lge pitches with views; warm welcome, friendly & helpful; excel facs; rv walk; rec." ♦ 1 Apr-30 Sep. € 13.50 2009*

NANT *10E1* (4km N Rural) *44.04550, 3.30170* **RCN Camping Le Val de Cantobre, Domaine de Vellas, 12230 Nant [05 65 58 43 00 or 06 80 44 40 63 (mob); fax 05 65 62 10 36; info@rcn-valdecantobre.fr; www.rcn-valdecantobre.fr]** Exit A75 junc 47 (La Cavalerie/Nant); foll sp D999 E dir La Cavalerie/Nant for 12 km. At Nant at T-junc turn L onto D991 sp Val de Cantobre. Site on R in 4km. NB Steep access rd, care req. Lge, mkd pitch, hdstg, terr, pt shd; wc (some cont); chem disp; mv service pnt; baby facs; shwrs inc; el pnts (6A) inc; gas; lndtte; shop; rest; snacks; bar; BBQ; playgrnd; htd pool; paddling pool; waterslide; tennis; games rm; organised walks; entmnt; wifi; games/TV rm; some tour op statics & tents; dogs €6; poss cr; Eng spkn; adv bkg ess; quiet; ccard acc; red low ssn. "Busy, popular, Dutch-owned site in gd position off beaten track - views fr most pitches; helpful, welcoming staff; excel amenities; clean, modern san facs (inc disabled) but long walk fr most pitches; steep site rds & many steps; many pitches sm with no privacy; mkt Tue; excel." ♦ 10 Apr-2 Oct. € 43.50 (CChq acc) ABS - C19 2009*

NANT *10E1* (1km S Rural) *44.01698, 3.30125* **Camping Les Deux Vallées, 12230 Nant [05 65 62 26 89 or 05 65 62 10 40; fax 05 65 62 17 23; www.lesdeuxvallees.com]** Exit A75 junc 47 onto D999 for 14km to Nant; site sp. Med, mkd pitch, pt shd; wc (some cont); own san; chem disp; mv service pnt; some serviced pitches; shwrs inc; el pnts (6A) €2 (poss rev pol); lndtte; tradsmn; rest; snacks; bar; shop 1km; pool 500m; playgrnd; entmnts; rv fishing; TV; dogs €1; phone; quiet; adv bkg; CCI. "Peaceful, well-kept, friendly, scenic site; ltd facs low ssn; 15 mins walk fr vill cent; gd walking; rec." ♦ 1 Apr-31 Oct. € 14.00 2007*

NANT *10E1* (2.5km S Rural) *44.01319, 3.32032* **Camping Castelnau (Gely), 12230 Nant [05 65 62 25 15; isaetdom@aliceadsl.fr; www.campingcastelnau.free.fr]** Fr Nant take D999 E twds Le Vigan; site is sp on L in 2.5km. Last 200m rough rd. Sm, pt shd; wc; chem disp (wc); shwrs inc; el pnts (11A) €2.50 (poss long lead req); lndtte, shop, rest, snacks, bar 2.5km; playgrnd; pool 3km; sw & fishing nr; some statics; dogs free; poss cr; adv bkg; quiet; ccard not acc; CCI. "Spacious CL-type site; lovely location; clean facs; conv Roquefort." ♦ 1 Apr-30 Oct. € 8.00 2009*

NANT *10E1* (500m SW Rural) *44.02105, 3.29390* **Camping Les Vernèdes, Route St Martin-Le Bourg, 12230 Nant [05 65 62 15 19]** Site sp fr vill cent. Sm, shd; wc (some cont); chem disp; shwrs inc; el pnts (10A) inc (long lead req); gas 500m; lndtte; rest adj; BBQ; playgrnd; dogs; Eng spkn; adv bkg; quiet; CCI. "Orchard site - many low branches make access to pitches poss diff; scruffy & unkempt low ssn; boggy after rain; pleasant stroll to Nant cent; gd trout rest adj; gd touring base; helpful owners." 1 Mar-31 Oct. € 10.50 2009*

⊞ **NANTES** *2G4* (3km N Urban) *47.24261, -1.55703* **Camping Le Petit Port, 21 Blvd de Petit Port, 44300 Nantes [02 40 74 47 94; fax 02 40 74 23 06; camping-petit-port@nge-nantes.fr; www.nge-nantes.fr]** Fr ring rd exit Porte de la Chapelle & foll sp Centre Ville, Camping Petit Port or University when ent o'skts of Nantes; site ent opp Hippodrome & nr racecourse & university; well sp. Fr S keep on ring rd & exit Porte de la Chapelle, then as before. Lge, hdg/mkd pitch, all hdstg, shd; wc; serviced pitches; chem disp; mv service pnt; shwrs inc; el pnts (16A) €3.80; gas; lndtte; shop; tradsmn; snacks, rest & bar 100m; BBQ; playgrnd; htd, covrd pool adj; waterslide; cycle hire; TV; 30% statics; dogs €1.60; bus, tram to city cent; twin-axles acc (extra charge); o'night m'van area; poss cr; Eng spkn; adv bkg (groups); quiet; red long stay; ccard acc; CCI. "Vg, well-equipped, functional site in excel location; helpful staff; tram/bus tickets fr recep; conv base for Nantes; ice skating adj." ♦ € 17.00 2009*

⊞ **NANTES** *2G4* (6km E Rural) *47.25416, -1.45361* **Camping Belle Rivière, Rue des Perrières, 44980 Ste Luce-sur-Loire [tel/fax 02 40 25 85 81; belleriviere@wanadoo.fr; www.camping-belleriviere.com]** Fr 'Nantes Périphérique Est' take exit 43 (at Porte d'Anjou) onto A811; exit A811 junc 24 dir Thouaré-sur-Loire on D68; at traff lights turn S & foll sp over rlwy bdge; site sp. Fr E via D68, thro Thouaré dir Ste Luce; at traff lts nr g'ge, S over rlwy bdge twd rv; sp. Med, hdg/mkd pitch, hdstg, pt shd; wc (50% cont); chem disp; shwrs inc; el pnts (3-10A) €2.60-3.70 (extra charge in winter); gas; lndry rm; shops 3km; tradsmn; rest; snacks; bar; BBQ; playgrnd; wifi; 50% statics; dogs €1.35; poss cr; Eng spkn; adv bkg; quiet; red low ssn/CCI. "Beautifully kept site; helpful owners; gd clean san facs; rvside walks; conv Nantes Périphérique & city cent; gd touring base; excel." ♦ € 13.65 2009*

NANTIAT *7B3* (600m W Urban) *46.00471, 1.15300* **Camp Municipal Les Haches, Ave de la Gare, 87140 Nantiat [05 55 53 42 43 (Mairie); fax 05 55 53 56 28]** Turn E off N147 at x-rds in Chamboret onto D711, site 1km on L, sp fr N147. Sm, pt sl, pt shd; wc; chem disp; shwrs inc; el pnts; shops 1km; rest, bar 600m; playgrnd; fishing; rlwy noise; CCI. "Gd, clean site & facs; lovely setting o'looking lake; phone ahead as opening dates not reliable; height barrier 2.50m; conv 'Martyr Village' at Oradour-sur-Glane; gd sh stay/NH." 15 Jun-15 Sep. 2008*

⊞ **NANTUA** *9A3* (1km W Urban) *46.14999, 5.60017* **Camp Municipal Le Signal, 17 Ave du Camping, 01130 Nantua [04 74 75 02 09 or 04 74 75 20 55 (Mairie); campingdusignal@orange.fr]** E on D1084 (N84) fr Pont d'Ain, rd passes alongside Nantua lake on R. At end of lake bef ent town turn R & foll sps. Sm, hdg/mkd pitch, unshd; wc; shwrs inc; el pnts (16A) €2; shops 200m; rest; snacks; playgrnd; lake sw 300m; sports cent nr; dogs €0.50; poss cr; quiet. "Attractive, spacious, well-kept site in lovely setting." € 12.00 2008*

France

⊞ **NAPOULE, LA** *10F4* (2km N Coastal) *43.53913, 6.94273* **Camping Les Cigales, 505 Ave de la Mer, Quartier d'Etang, 06210 Mandelieu-la-Napoule [04 93 49 23 53; fax 04 93 49 30 45; campingcigales@wanadoo.fr; www.lescigales.com]** Take Mandelieu exit junc 40 fr A8 & turn R twice in Mandelieu cent into Ave des Ecureuils, sp Campings. Pass under a'route & in 1km turn L at T-junc into Ave de la Mer. Site in 50m on L. Or on DN7 fr Fréjus turn R at rndabt with fountains app Mandelieu. Or fr coast rd turn inland at bdge over Rv La Siagne into Blvd de la Mer & site in 1km on R. Med, hdg/mkd pitch, hdstg, shd; htd wc; chem disp; mv service pnt; baby facs; shwrs inc; el pnts (6A) €4.50; Indtte; shop 1.5km; rest; snacks; bar; playgrnd; pool; sand beach 800m; solarium; dir access to rv; fishing, sailing & other waterports 800m; entmnt; 50% statics; dogs €1.50; bus adj; poss cr; Eng spkn; adv bkg; some noise fr rd, rlwy, aircraft; ccard acc; red low ssn/long stay. "Excel location; gd san facs; ltd facs low ssn; gd pool." ♦ € 41.50 2008*

NAPOULE, LA *10F4* (2km N Urban) *43.53507, 6.94258* **Camping Les Pruniers, 18 Rue de la Pinéa, 06210 Mandelieu-la-Napoule [04 92 97 00 44 or 04 93 49 99 23; fax 04 93 49 37 45; contact@bungalow-camping.com; www.bungalow-camping.com]** Fr A8 exit junc 40 & turn R twice in Mandelieu cent into Blvd des Ecureuils sp 'Sofitel Royal Casino'. Pass under a'route & in 1km turn L at T-junc into Ave de la Mer. At rndabt bear R & next R sp Pierre-Vacances. Turn R in 50m, site at end of rd. On DN7 fr Fréjus, turn R at rndabt with fountains app Mandelieu. Fr coast rd take slip rd for Mandelieu. Sm, mkd pitch, hdstg; shd; wc; chem disp (in cont wc); shwrs inc; el pnts (5-20A) €4.40; Indtte; shop (high ssn) & 1.2km; snacks, bar in vill; playgrnd; htd pool; sand beach 500m; sea & rv fishing; entmnt; 60% statics (sep area); dogs €5; no twin-axle c'vans & max length c'van 6m, m'van 7m; poss cr; Eng spkn; adv bkg; quiet; red low ssn; ccard acc; CCI. "Delightful, peaceful site on rv opp marina; dated, clean san facs; excel base for area; easy cycling to beach & Cannes." 1 Apr-15 Oct. € 23.00 2006*

NAPOULE, LA *10F4* (3km N Urban/Coastal) *43.5234, 6.9308* **Camping de la Ferme, Blvd du Bon Puits, 06210 Mandelieu-la-Napoule [04 93 49 94 19; fax 04 93 49 18 52; info@campingdelaferme.com; www.campingdelaferme.com]** Fr A8 exit junc 40 & turn L in Mandelieu cent sp Fréjus; 200m after rndabt with palm tree centre, fork R into Ave Maréchal Juin & strt into Blvd du Bon Puits. Avoid La Napoule vill when towing. Med, shd; wc; shwrs €0.50; el pnts (6A) €3; gas; Indtte; shops; rest; snacks; bar; sand beach 700m; some statics; dogs €2; poss v cr; adv bkg; quiet; red low ssn. "Nice atmosphere; some pitches v sm; friendly, helpful staff; dated but clean facs; pleasant bar & sm rest." ♦ 25 Mar-1 Oct. € 20.50 2009*

⊞ **NAPOULE, LA** *10F4* (5km N Urban/Coastal) *43.52547, 6.93354* **Camping L'Argentière, 264 Blvd du Bon-Puits, 06210 Mandelieu-la-Napoule [tel/fax 04 93 49 95 04; www.campingdelargentiere.com]** Fr A8 turn L in Mandelieu cent (sp Fréjus). At rndabt with fountains take 2nd exit, at next rndabt take 2nd exit to L of BP stn, at next rndabt take 2nd exit, site on R in 150m. Avoid La Napoule vill when towing. Med, hdg/mkd pitch, hdstg, pt shd; wc; chem disp; mv service pnt; shwrs inc; el pnts (6A) €3.20; Indtte; shop; hypmkt 1km; rest; snacks; bar; sand beach 800m; fishing; entmnt; TV rm; 80% statics; dogs €3; bus; Eng spkn; adv bkg ess in ssn; poss cr; quiet; CCI. "Clean san facs; lovely local beaches." € 21.00 2007*

NAPOULE, LA *10F4* (10km W Rural) *43.52885, 6.84005* **Camping Les Philippons, 83600 Les Adrets-de-l'Estérel [04 94 40 90 67; fax 04 94 19 35 92; info@philipponscamp.com; www.philipponscamp.com]** Exit A8 at junc 39 Les Adrets (14km fr Cannes). Foll sp Les Adrets on D837 S. In 2km turn L on D237 thro vill, site on L; sm ent. Sm, pt sl, terr, shd; wc; shwrs inc; el pnts (3-10A) €3-5; shop; snacks; bar; playgrnd; pool; sand beach 9km; wifi; poss cr; 90% statics; dogs €3.50; m'van height limit 2.80m; adv bkg; quiet. "Attractive site; diff access for towed c'vans due steep, narr & twisty rd, v ltd turning space." 1 Apr-30 Sep. € 20.50 2007*

NARBONNE *10F1* (10km N Rural) *43.26009, 2.95552* **Camp Municipal, Rue de la Cave Coopérative, 11590 Sallèles-d'Aude [04 68 46 68 46 (Mairie); fax 04 68 46 91 00; ot.sallelesdaude@wanadoo.fr; www.salleles-daude.com]** Fr A9/E15 exit junc 36 onto D64 N & in approx 4km turn L to join D11 W. Cont on this rd for approx 18km, then turn L onto D13 S to Ouveillan. In vill, turn R onto D418 SW to Sallèles-d'Aude. Site in vill. NB Nr Canal du Midi some narr app rds. Sm, hdg/mkd pitch, pt shd; wc; chem disp; el pnts €2.50; shops 1km; BBQ; no statics; dogs; adv bkg; quiet. "Clean site; 16 pitches; nr canal; warden calls am; excel." 1 May-30 Sep. € 11.00 2008*

NARBONNE *10F1* (6km S Rural) *43.13662, 3.02595* **Camping Les Mimosas, Chaussée de Mandirac, 11100 Narbonne [04 68 49 03 72; fax 04 68 49 39 45; info@lesmimosas.com; www.lesmimosas.com]** Leave A9 junc 38 at Narbonne Sud & at rndabt foll sp La Nautique. Turn L opp ent to Camping La Nautique & foll sp Mandirac & site. Lge, hdg/mkd pitch, hdstg, pt shd; htd wc; chem disp; baby facs; fam bthrm; sauna; some serviced pitches; shwrs inc; el pnts (6A) inc; gas; Indtte; shop; rest; snacks; bar; BBQ; playgrnds; 3 pools (1 htd); 4 waterslides; paddling pool; jacuzzi; sand beach 6km; watersports; rv fishing adj; fishing lake 300m; tennis; cycle hire; horseriding adj; gym; cycle hire; games area; games rm; internet; entmnt high ssn; TV rm; 6% statics; dogs €3.50; adv bkg; Eng spkn; quiet; ccard acc; red low ssn/long stay; CCI. "Excel touring base in historic area; excel san facs & pool complex; gd choice of pitches; vg for children; gd birdwatching; cycle path to Narbonne; friendly, helpful staff." ♦ 27 Mar-31 Oct. € 33.00 (CChq acc) ABS - C35 2009*

See advertisement opposite (below)

NARBONNE *10F1* (4km SW Urban) *43.14702, 3.00424* **Camping La Nautique, 11100 Narbonne [04 68 90 48 19; fax 04 68 90 73 39; info@campinglanautique.com; www.campinglanautique.com]** Exit junc 38 fr A9 at Narbonne Sud. After toll take last rndabt exit & foll sp La Nautique. Site on R 2.5km fr A9 exit. Lge, hdg/mkd pitch, some hdstg, pt shd; chem disp; mv service pnt; individ san facs (wc, shwr) on each pitch inc; el pnts (10A) inc; gas; Indtte; shop & 3km; tradsmn; rest, snacks & bar high ssn; BBQ (elec only); playgrnd; htd pool; waterslide; paddling pool; sand beach 10km; lake sw adj; tennis; entmnt; 30% statics; dogs €4; Eng spkn; adv bkg; quiet with some rd noise; ccard acc; red low ssn/long stay; CCI. "Excel, well-run site; helpful, friendly Dutch owners; spotless facs; caution - hot water v hot; some pitches lge but narr; steel pegs req; pitches sheltered but some muddy after heavy rain; special pitches for disabled; excel rest; many sports activities avail; cycle trips; gd walks nrby; highly rec." ♦ 15 Feb-15 Nov. € 42.00 2009*

See advertisement above

France

⊞ **NARBONNE** *10F1* (12km SW Rural) *43.16296, 2.89186* **Camping La Figurotta, Route de Narbonne, 11200 Bizanet [tel/fax 04 68 45 16 26 or 06 88 16 12 30 (mob); info@figurotta.eu; www.figurotta.eu]** Exit A9 at Narbonne Sud onto slip rd N9/D6113 (N113) twd Lézignan-Corbières; in 3km at new rndabt head L twd D613 & then D224 sp Bizanet & site. App fr W not rec due narr D rds. Sm, mkd pitch, hdstg, pt sl, pt terr, shd; htd wc; chem disp; shwrs €0.50; el pnts (4-6A) €2.50-3.50 (poss long lead req); gas; Indtte; sm shop & 2km; tradsmn; rest; snacks; bar; playgrnd; sm pool; sand beach 20km; games area; 5% statics; dogs €1 (sm dogs only); phone; Eng spkn; adv bkg; rd noise; red long stay/low ssn/CCI. "Pleasant, simple, well-run, scenic site; friendly & helpful; gd pool; gusty & stony site - steel pegs req; excel drainage; gd NH en rte Spain; vg." ♦ € 17.00 2009*

NARBONNE PLAGE *10F1* (Coastal) *43.16053, 3.16236* **Camping de la Falaise, 8 Ave des Vacances, 11000 Narbonne-Plage [04 68 49 80 77 or 04 68 49 83 65 (LS); fax 04 68 49 40 44; resacamp@wanadoo.fr; www.campinglafalaise.com]** Exit A9 at Narbonne Est junc 37 onto D168 for 10km to Narbonne-Plage. Site on L at ent to vill. Lge, hdg pitch, shd; wc; chem disp; shwrs inc; el pnts (6A) inc; gas; Indtte; shop; rest; snacks; bar; playgrnd; beach 300m; waterslide 1.5km; games area; cycle hire; TV; some statics; dogs €2; poss cr; adv bkg; poss noise fr open air theatre; red low ssn. "Gd for beach holiday; ltd facs low ssn." 1 Apr-28 Sep. € 22.00 2007*

NARBONNE PLAGE *10F1* (8km NE Coastal) *43.20592, 3.21056* **Camping La Grande Cosse (Naturist), St Pierre-sur-Mer, 11560 Fleury-d'Aude [04 68 33 61 87; fax 04 68 33 32 23; contact@grandecosse.com; www.grandecosse.com]** Exit A9 junc 37 & foll sp Narbonne-Plage. Cont thro Narbonne-Plage to St Pierre-sur-Mer, pass municipal site & turn R twd L'Oustalet, site sp. Lge, hdg/mkd pitch, pt shd; wc; chem disp; serviced pitches; chem disp; mv service pnt; shwrs inc; el pnts (8A) €4; gas; lndtte; shop; rest, snacks; bar high ssn; playgrnd; htd pool; sand beach 300m; tennis; games area; games rm; gym; entmnt; boat hire; fishing; TV rm; 20% statics; dogs €4; phone; poss cr Aug; Eng spkn; adv bkg; red long stay/low ssn; ccard acc; INF card req. "Excel, well-run site; gd pitches; helpful, friendly staff; excel san facs; naturist walk to lovely beach thro lagoons & dunes (poss flooded early ssn); mosquitoes poss problem Jun-Sep; flood risk after heavy rain; gd mkt St Pierre-sur-Mer." ♦ 28 Mar-4 Oct. € 32.50 2009*

NASBINALS *9D1* (1km N Rural) *44.67016, 3.04036* **Camp Municipal, Route de St Urcize, 48260 Nasbinals [02 46 32 51 87 or 04 66 32 50 17; mairie.nasbinals@laposte.net; www.mairie-nasbinals.info]** Fr A75 exit 36 to Aumont-Aubrac, then W on D987 to Nasbinals. Turn R onto D12, site sp. Med, pt sl, pt shd; htd wc; chem disp; mv service pnt; shwrs inc; el pnts (16A) €3; shop, rest in vill; BBQ; dogs; quiet; red CCI. ♦ 15 May-30 Sep. € 6.00 2009*

NAUCELLE *8E4* (1km S Rural) *44.18818, 2.34825* **FLOWER Camping du Lac de Bonnefon (FFCC), L'Etang de Bonnefon, 12800 Naucelle [05 65 69 33 20; fax 05 65 69 33 20; camping-du-lac-de-bonnefon@wanadoo.fr; www.camping-du-lac-de-bonnefon.com or www.flowercamping.com]** N fr Carmaux turn L off N88 Albi-Rodez rd at Naucelle Gare onto D997, sp Naucelle Centre. Site sp in 2km. Med, mkd pitch, pt sl, pt shd; htd wc; chem disp; mv service pnt; shwrs inc; el pnts (6A) €4.20; lndtte; shop 1.5km; rest; snacks; bar, playgrnd; pool; wifi; TV; many statics; dogs €2.50; poss cr; quiet; red low ssn; CCI. "Pleasant, clean site adj lge fishing lake; gd san facs; conv Sauveterre-de-Rouergue." ♦ 1 Apr-23 Oct. € 19.30 2009*

NAUSSANNES see Beaumont du Périgord *7D3*

NAVARRENX *8F1* (200m S Urban) *43.31988, -0.76143* **Camping Beau Rivage, Allée des Marronniers, 64190 Navarrenx [05 59 66 10 00; beaucamping@free.fr; www.beaucamping.com]** Fr E exit A64 junc 9 at Artix onto D281 dir Mourenx, then Navarrenx. Fr N on D947 thro Orthez to Navarrenx (D947 fr Orthez much improved). Med, hdg/mkd pitch, some hdstg, pt sl, terr, pt shd; htd wc; chem disp; mv service pnt; some serviced pitches; baby facs; fam bthrm; shwrs inc; el pnts (8-10A) inc; gas 300m; lndtte; ice; shop, rest & bar 300m; snacks; BBQ; playgrnd; pool; rv fishing; rafting; tennis; cycle hire in town; games rm; wifi; 15% statics; dogs €1.50; phone; Eng spkn; adv bkg; quiet; ccard acc; red low ssn; CCI. "Peaceful, well-run site bet interesting Bastide town & rv; helpful, friendly, British owners; clean san facs; gd area for walking, cycling; rec." ♦ 26 Mar-10 Oct. € 24.00 ABS - D26 2009*

NEBOUZAT *9B1* (1km W Rural) *45.72569, 2.89008* **Camping Les Domes, Les Quatre Routes de Nébouzat, 63210 Nébouzat [04 73 87 14 06 or 04 73 93 21 02 (LS); fax 04 73 87 18 81; camping-les-domes@wanadoo.fr; www.les-domes.com]** Exit 5 fr A75 onto D213 twd Col de la Ventouse; turn L on D2089 (N89) sp Tulle. Do not ent vill of Nébouzat but cont for 1km. Take L onto D216 sp Orcival then immed L. Site on L in 100m. Med, mkd pitch, hdstg, pt shd; wc (mainly cont); chem disp; baby facs; shwrs inc; el pnts (10-15A) €6 (poss long lead req); gas; lndtte; shop; tradsmn; snacks; playgrnd; htd covrd pool; boules areas; walking; sailing; windsurfing; entmnt; TV rm; phone; dogs free; Eng spkn; adv bkg; quiet; red CCI. "Immac site; warm welcome; friendly, helpful staff; sm pitches; gd san facs; conv Vulcania." 4 Apr-15 Sep. € 15.50 2008*

NEMOURS *4F3* (5km S Urban) *48.24073, 2.70389* **FFCC Camping de Pierre Le Sault, Chemin des Grèves, 77167 Bagneaux-sur-Loing [01 64 29 24 44]** Well sp bef town fr both dir off D607 (N7). Med, hdg/mkd pitch, pt shd; wc; shwrs inc; el pnts (3-6A) €2-3.05; gas 2km; lndtte; shop 2km; tradsmn; playgrnd; tennis; 90% statics; poss cr; some Eng spkn; ent barrier clsd 2200-0700; no adv bkg; some rd noise; red low ssn; no ccard acc; CCI. "Lovely site by canal & rv; excel clean facs." ♦ 1 Apr-31 Oct. € 7.40 2008*

NERAC *8E2* (800m SW Rural) *44.09948, 0.31028* **Aire Naturelle Les Contes d'Albret, 47600 Nérac [05 53 65 18 73; fax 05 53 97 18 62; lescontesdalbret@orange.fr; www.albret.com]** Exit A62 junc 7 onto D931 to Laplume. Then turn W onto D15 & D656 to Nérac. Cont on D656 dir Mézin & foll site sp to end of rd in 3km. Sm, pt sl, pt shd; htd wc; chem disp; baby facs; shwrs inc; el pnts €2; farm shop, other shops in vill; rest; playgrnd; pool; kayaking; Eng spkn; adv bkg; quiet. "Vg, peaceful, CL-type site; excel views; glorious garden." 1 May-30 Sep. € 13.00 2009*

NERIS LES BAINS *7A4* (1km E Rural) *46.28577, 2.67487* **Aire Naturelle Camping La Grenouillat (Robin), Route de Commentry, 03310 Néris-les-Bains [04 70 03 17 44]** S fr Montluçon on D2144 thro Néris-les-Bains. At x-rds opp g'ge turn L sp 'Camping La Ferme'. Site 1km down track. Sm, pt shd; wc; chem disp; shwrs; el pnts (8A) inc; lndry rm; shop, rest in vill; lake fishing; dogs €0.50; quiet. "Beautiful, quiet site in scenic area." ♦ 1 Apr-31 Oct. € 8.00 2007*

NERIS LES BAINS *7A4* (1km NW Urban) *46.28695, 2.65215* **Camp Municipal du Lac, Ave Marx Dormoy, 03310 Néris-les-Bains [04 70 03 17 59 or 04 70 03 24 70 (recep); fax 04 70 03 79 99; campingdulac-neris@orange.fr; www.ville-neris-les-bains.fr]** Site on N side of Néris off D2144 (N144). Turn W at rndabt by blue tourist office, opp park, & foll sp round 1 way system to site in 500m. Med, hdg/mkd pitch, hdstg, pt sl, terr, pt shd; wc (some cont); chem disp; shwrs inc; el pnts (10A) inc; gas; shops 1km; tradsmn; snacks; bar; playgrnd; covrd pool 500m; some statics; dogs €0.95; quiet; red long stay. "6 pitches for m'vans at ent to site, charge for el pnts (10A) & water only; space to wait on car park if barrier clsd; pleasant town; vg." 1 Apr-22 Oct. € 13.41 2009*

NESLES LA VALLEE see Beaumont sur Oise *3D3*

NESMY see Roche sur Yon, La *2H4*

NEUF BRISACH *6F3* (6km NE Rural) *48.02724, 7.57230* **Camping de L'Ile du Rhin, 68600 Biesheim [03 89 72 57 95; fax 03 89 72 14 21; info@campingiledurhin.com; www.campingiledurhin.com]** On D415 Colmar to Freiburg (Germany). Site on island in Rv Rhine, on R after French Customs point off D415. Lge, hdstg, pt shd; wc; shwrs inc; el pnts (4-10A) inc; Indtte; shop; snacks; htd, covrd pool adj; rv fishing 100m; tennis; 50% statics; poss cr; Eng spkn; ccard acc. "Excel facs; gates clsd 2000-0700; poss flooding some pitches; gd touring base; vg." ♦ 6 Apr-4 Oct. € 18.85 2009*

NEUF BRISACH *6F3* (1.2km E Urban) *48.01638, 7.53565* **Camp Municipal Vauban, 68600 Neuf-Brisach [tel/fax 03 89 72 54 25 or 03 89 72 51 68 (Mairie)]** Fr D415 (Colmar-Freiburg) at E of Neuf-Brisach turn NE on D1 bis (sp Neuf-Brisach & Camping Vauban). At next junc turn L & immed R into site rd. Med, pt shd; wc; mv service pnt; shwrs €1; el pnts (6A) €2.50; shops in town; playgrnd; pool 3km; 40% statics; dogs; adv bkg; quiet; CCI. "Fascinating ramparts around town; no new arr 1200-1400." 1 Apr-1 Oct. € 9.60 2007*

NEUF BRISACH *6F3* (6km SE Rural) *47.97988, 7.59639* **FFCC Camping L'Orée du Bois, 5 Rue du Bouleau, 68600 Geiswasser [03 89 72 80 13; fax 03 89 72 80 13; valerie.schappler@wanadoo.fr]** Site in vill cent; street name on bungalow; ent bet bungalow & vegetable garden - tight turn, watch out bungalow gutters. Sm, hdg pitch, pt shd; htd wc; chem disp; shwrs inc; el pnts (10A) €2.50; Indtte; BBQ; playgrnd; dogs; Eng spkn; adv bkg; quiet; CCI. "Gd touring base; friendly owner; vg." ♦ 1 May-31 Oct. € 6.60 2006*

NEUFCHATEAU *6E2* (10km N Rural) *48.44364, 5.67616* **Camp Municipal, Chemin de Santilles, 88630 Domrémy-la-Pucelle [03 29 06 90 70; fax 03 29 94 33 77]** Take D164 fr Neufchâteau, site in cent of Domrémy vill, clear sp by stadium, nr Rv Meuse. Sm, unshd; wc (some cont); shwrs €0.80; el pnts (16A) €2; shops adj; rest, bar 500m; tennis; quiet. "Site yourself, warden calls (not Sun); nr birthplace of Joan of Arc." 1 Jun-31 Aug. € 6.70 2009*

NEUFCHATEAU *6E2* (500m NW Urban) *48.35609, 5.68845* **Camp Municipal, Place Pitet, Rue de Moulinot, 88300 Neufchâteau [03 29 94 19 03 or 03 29 94 14 75 (Mairie); fax 03 29 94 33 77; contact@neufchateau-tourisme.com; www.neufchateau-tourisme.com]** Clear sp on ent town next to sports stadium. Sm, pt shd; wc; chem disp; shwrs inc; el pnts (10A) inc; Indry rm; shops 500m; htd pool nr; poss v cr; some rlwy noise. "Sm pitches; gd san facs, ltd low ssn; poss unkempt & untidy low ssn; no twin-axles; NH or sh stay." ♦ 15 Apr-30 Sep. € 15.80 2008*

NEUFCHATEL EN BRAY *3C2* (1km NW Urban) *49.73781, 1.42803* **Camping Sainte Claire, 19 Rue Grande Flandre, 76270 Neufchâtel-en-Bray [02 35 93 03 93 or 06 20 12 20 98 (mob); fancelot@wanadoo.fr; www.camping-sainte-claire.com]** Fr S exit A28 junc 9 onto D928 sp Neufchâtel; in 1.9km at bottom hill, immed after rv bdge (easily missed) turn L into Rue de la Grande Flandre; cont past Leclerc supmkt on L; strt on into Rue Ste Claire. Or Fr N exit A28 junc 7 onto D928 dir Neufchâtel; in approx 5km turn R onto D1 for Dieppe & in 1km turn L at site sp. Med, hdg/mkd pitch, hdstg, pt sl, terr, pt shd; wc (some cont); chem disp; shwrs inc; el pnts (6-10A) €4-6; sm shop; supmkt 500m; tradsmn; bar/rest; snacks; bar; playgrnd; cycle hire; fishing; 30% statics; dogs free low ssn; phone adj; bus 1km; poss cr; Eng spkn; adv bkg; quiet; ccard acc; red long stay; CCI. "Pretty, spacious, well-kept family site by rv; conv Le Havre/Dieppe ferries & a'route; friendly, helpful owner; excel facs (disabled planned for 2010); gd wheelchair access/easy walking; walk along old rlwy track; cycle rte adj; Sat mkt; popular NH." 1 Apr-31 Oct. € 10.10 2009*

France

NEUILLY SUR MARNE see Paris *3D3*

NEUNG SUR BEUVRON *4G3* (500m NE Rural) *47.53893, 1.81488* **FFCC Camp Municipal de la Varenne, 34 Rue de Veilleas, 41210 Neung-sur-Beuvron [tel/fax 02 54 83 68 52 or 06 76 80 88 41 (mob); camping.lavarenne@wanadoo.fr; www.neung-sur-beuvron.fr/camping]** On A10 heading S take Orléans Sud exit & join N20 S. At end of La Ferté-St Aubin take D922 SW twd Romorantin-Lanthenay. In 20km R onto D925 to Neung. Turn R at church pedestrian x-ing in cent of vill ('stade' sp), R at fork (white, iron cross) & site on R in 1km. Site by rvside. Fr A71 exit junc 3 onto D923; turn R onto D925 & as above. Sm, hdg/mkd pitch, pt sl, pt shd; wc; chem disp; mv service pnt; shwrs inc; el pnts (10A) €2.60; gas; Indtte; shops 1km; tradsmn; rest, bar 500m; playgrnd; tennis; few statics; dogs; poss cr (Aug); Eng spkn; adv bkg; v quiet; ccard acc. "Friendly, helpful warden; barrier clsd 2200-0800; gd, immac facs; lge pitches; vg cent for hiking, cycling, birdwatching; mkt Sat." Easter-30 Sep. € 7.40 2008*

NEUSSARGUES MOISSAC see Murat *7C4*

NEUVE LYRE, LA *3D2* (Urban) *48.90750, 0.74486* **Camp Municipal La Salle, Rue de l'Union, 27330 La Neuve-Lyre [02 32 60 14 98 or 02 32 30 50 01 (Mairie); fax 02 32 30 22 37; mairie.la-neuve-lyre@wanadoo.fr]** Fr NE on D830 into vill turn R at church (sp not visible), fr S (Rugles) foll sp. Well sp fr vill. Med, pt shd; wc (some cont) ltd; chem disp (wc); mv service pnt; shwrs €0.75; el pnts (5A) €1.70 (poss long lead req); shops 500m; fishing; 40% statics; dogs; quiet; CCI. "Delightful, peaceful, clean site; site yourself, warden calls; excel sh stay/NH." ♦ 15 Mar-15 Oct. € 3.20 2008*

NEUVEGLISE see Chaudes Aigues *9C1*

NEUVIC (CORREZE) *7C4* (4km N Rural) *45.38245, 2.22901* **Camping Domaine de Mialaret, Route d'Egletons, 19160 Neuvic [05 55 46 02 50; fax 05 55 46 02 65; info@lemialaret.com; www.lemialaret.com]** Fr N on A89 exit 23 twds St Angel then D171 to Neuvic or foll sp fr Neuvic on D991. Med, some hdg pitch, pt sl, pt shd; htd wc; chem disp; mv service pnt; baby facs; shwrs inc; el pnts (10A) €3-4; Indtte; shop; tradsmn; rest in chateau fr May; snacks high ssn; bar; playgrnd; pool (fr mid-Jun); 2 carp fishing pools; watersports nrby; mini-farm; mountain bike routes; walking tours; games rm; entmnt; internet; 30% statics (sep area); dogs free; phone; bus 4km; poss cr; quiet; adv bkg; Eng spkn; red long stay/low ssn; CCI. "Excel site in grounds of chateau; charming owner, friendly staff; facs ltd low ssn; blocks req most pitches; children's mini-zoo & rare sheep breeds nrby." 1 Apr-1 Nov. € 25.00 (CChq acc) 2009*

NEUVIC (CORREZE) *7C4* (4km N Rural) *45.41034, 2.28469* **Camping Le Soustran, Pellachal, 19160 Neuvic [05 55 95 03 71 or 06 47 94 89 34 (mob); info@lesoustran.com; www.lesoustran.com]** N fr Neuvic on D982 dir Ussel for 4km; site on L 300m after bdge. Ent steepish & rough. Med, mkd pitch, terr, pt shd; wc; chem disp; shwrs inc; el pnts (6A) €2.50; Indtte; snacks; bar; BBQ; playgrnd; lake sw 300m; TV rm; dogs €1; Eng spkn; quiet; CCI. "No twin-axles." ♦ 1 May-30 Sep. € 11.00 2006*

NEUVIC (CORREZE) *7C4* (4km N Rural) *45.3972, 2.2875* **FFCC Camping Centre Henri Queuille, Antiges, 19160 Neuvic [05 55 95 81 18; fax 05 55 95 97 48; antiguescamping@orange.fr; www.antiges-camping.com]** Fr Neuvic, D982 N twd Ussel. In 3km turn R onto D20 sp Antiges. Site in 1km. Or fr N/S A89 exit 23 then foll St Angel & take D171. Foll sp. Med, pt sl, pt shd; wc; shwrs; el pnts (10A) €1.85; Indtte; snacks; rest; sand beach; lake sw adj; adv bkg; red low ssn; quiet. "Gd site but basic; pleasant lake views." ♦
12 Apr-12 Oct. € 11.70 2007*

NEUVIC (CORREZE) *7C4* (5km NE Rural) **Camping à la Ferme Chez Père Jules (Van Boshuysen), Prentegarde, 19160 Liginiac [tel/fax 05 55 95 84 49; rob_ykie@hotmail.com]** Exit A89 junc 23 onto D979 dir Bort-les-Orgues; in 5km (just after La Serre) turn R onto D982; in 10km turn L to Liginiac; cont thro vill & then turn R uphill onto D20. Site sp to R in 1.5km. Sm, pt sl, pt shd; wc; chem disp; shwrs inc; el pnts (4A) inc; Indtte; shop 1.5km; sm rest; bar; BBQ; playgrnd; pool; lake sw 2km; 5% statics; dogs; Eng spkn; adv bkg; quiet; CCI. "Beautiful CL-type site; helpful Dutch owners; rallies welcome; mv service pnt in Liginiac; vg." 1 Apr-30 Sep. € 14.00 2009*

⊞ **NEUVIC (CORREZE)** *7C4* (7km NW Rural) *45.42721, 2.20419* **Camping Le Vianon, Les Plaines, 19160 Palisse [05 55 95 87 22; fax 05 55 95 98 45; camping.vianon@wanadoo.fr; www.levianon.com]** Fr Neuvic take D47 twd Pallisse. Site well sp. Med, mkd pitch, pt sl, pt shd; htd wc; chem disp; mv service pnt; baby facs; shwrs inc; el pnts (16A) €3.50; Indtte; shops; tradsmn; rest; snacks; bar; BBQ; playgrnd; pool; lake fishing; sports activities; tennis; entmnt; internet; TV rm; 15% statics; dogs €2; poss cr; Eng spkn; adv bkg; quiet; red 7+ days; CCI. "Woodland walks; friendly Dutch owners; vg rest & bar; clean facs." ♦ € 25.85 2009*

NEUVIC (DORDOGNE) *7C3* (500m N Rural) *45.10571, 0.46930* **Camping Le Plein Air Neuvicois, Ave de Planèze, 24190 Neuvic [05 53 81 50 77; fax 05 53 80 46 50; camp.le.plein.air.neuvicois@libertysurf.fr]** On N89, 26km SW fr Périgueux (Mussidan-Bordeaux rd). After 24km, turn R (D44) at Neuvic. Site clearly sp thro vill, by rv bef bdge, on both sides of rv. Med, pt shd; htf wc; baby facs; shwrs inc; el pnts (6-10A) €3-4; Indtte; shop; tradsmn; snacks; bar; pool; fishing; tennis; games rm; some statics; dogs €0.50; phone; adv bkg; quiet. "Charming owners; beautiful location; vg." 1 Jun-15 Sep. € 11.50 2007*

NEUVILLE SUR SARTHE see Mans, Le *4F1*

NEVACHE *9C3* (6km W Rural) *45.03399, 6.54543* **Camp Municipal de Foncouverte, 05100 Névache [04 92 21 38 21 or 04 92 21 31 01]** Fr Briançon take N94 NE twd Italian border dir Turin, then L onto D994 sp Névache. Rd is narr with passing places. Site is 2nd in vill. Med, pt sl, pt shd; wc; shwrs €1.20; Indry rm; shop; tradsmn; Eng spkn; quiet. "Vg for walkers; diff lge o'fits; no c'vans or m'vans allowed on rds W of Névache 0900-1800 in summer." 1 Jun-28 Sep. € 9.50 2006*

⊞ **NEVERS** *4H4* (10km SE Rural) *46.91324, 3.22249* **Camp Municipal Plan d'Eau Bagnade, Route de Magny-Cours, 58160 Chevenon [03 86 68 71 71 or 03 86 68 72 75; fax 03 86 38 30 33]** Fr N7 site sp at Magny-Cours turn R fr S (L fr N) onto D200, site ent on R just bef Chevenon. Or fr N exit N7 junc 37 to Chevernon; site sp. Med, hdg pitch, terr, pt sl, pt shd; htd wc; shwrs inc; el pnts (6A) inc; Indry rm; shops 1km; playgrnd; lake sw adj; fishing; many statics; quiet; CCI. "Pleasant, peaceful site nr lakes & close to French Grand Prix circuit; site yourself if warden not present; gd, clean san facs; facs & pitches unkempt low ssn." ♦ € 12.90 2009*

NEVERS *4H4* (500m S Rural) *46.98210, 3.16110* **FFCC Camping de Nevers, Rue de la Jonction, 58000 Nevers [06 84 98 69 79; info@campingnevers.com; www.campingnevers.com]** Fr E exit A77 junc 37 & foll dir 'Centre Ville'. Site on R immed bef bdge over Rv Loire. Fr W (Bourges) on D976 foll sp 'Nevers Centre' onto D907. In approx 3km bef bdge turn R, site on L. Med, mkd pitch, hdstg, pt shd; htd wc; chem disp; mv service pnt; baby facs; shwrs inc; el pnts (6-10A) €2.50-4.30; Indtte; supmkt 2km; tradsmn; rest 500m; snacks; bar; playgrnd; pool 200m; sand beach 200m; rv fishing; cycle hire; internet; TV; 3% statics; dogs €2; phone; bus 20m; poss cr; Eng spkn; adv bkg; rd noise; ccard not acc; red low ssn; CCI. "Pleasant, scenic site on bank of Rv Loire; on 2 levels - ltd el pnts on lower; cycle paths along Loire; gd san facs, poss stretched high ssn & ltd low ssn; no twin-axles; poss unkempt low ssn; poss noisy when events at Nevers Magny-Cours racing circuit." ♦ 10 Apr-11 Oct. € 16.30 (CChq acc) 2009*

NEVERS *4H4* (7km NW Urban) *47.01222, 3.07822* **FFCC Camping La Loire, 2 Rue de la Folie, 58600 Fourchambault [03 86 60 81 59; fax 03 86 60 96 24; http://membres.lycos.fr/campingloire]** Fr Nevers on D40 thro town, site on L bef rv bdge. Med, pt shd; wc; chem disp; mv service pnt; shwrs inc; el pnts (6-20A) €3-7; Indtte; shop 500m; rest 100m; snacks; bar; BBQ; htd, covrd pool; rv adj; dogs €1; bus; red long stay/CCI. "Friendly, helpful; san facs need update & poss unclean." ♦ 1 Apr-30 Oct. € 9.00 2006*

NEVEZ see Pont Aven *2F2*

NEXON *7B3* (1km SW Rural) *45.67104, 1.18059* **Camp Municipal de l'Etang de la Lande, 87800 Nexon [05 55 58 35 44 or 05 55 58 10 19 (Mairie); fax 05 55 58 33 50; mairie-nexon@wanadoo.fr; www.chalets-decouverte.com]** S fr Limoges on D704, take D15 W twd Nexon. Exit Nexon by D11 sp Ladignac-le-Long & Camping, site 3km S at junc with D17. Med, mkd pitch, sl, pt shd; htd wc; shwrs; el pnts (5-10A) inc; Indtte; shop; bar; rest, supmkt 1km; playgrnd; lake sw adj; cycle hire; entmnt; TV rm; Eng spkn; quiet. "Excel base for Limoges; site open to adj leisure park." 1 Jun-30 Sep. € 10.00 2007*

NEYDENS see St Julien en Genevois *9A3*

NIBELLE *4F3* (2km E Rural) *48.01610, 2.35030* **Camping Parc de Nibelle, Route de Boiscommun, 45340 Nibelle [02 38 32 23 55; fax 02 38 32 03 87; contact@caravaningnibelle.com; www.parc-nibelle.com]** Fr N60 turn N onto D114 dir Nibelle. Turn R onto D9, site sp. Med, pt shd; wc; shwrs inc; el pnts inc; Indtte; shop; tradsmn; rest; snacks; bar; BBQ; playgrnd; htd, covrd pool; paddling pool; tennis; games area; games rm; cycle hire; entmnt; statics; dogs €3; Eng spkn; adv bkg; quiet; red low ssn. "Excel site; nr Etang de la Vallée; facs ltd low ssn - no facs for water tank filling etc." ♦ 1 Mar-30 Nov. € 31.00 2007*

NICE *10E4* (14km NE Rural) *43.77166, 7.37256* **Camping La Laune, Moulin de Peillon, Blvd de la Vallée, 06440 Peillon [06 75 69 97 00 (mob); campingdelalaune@yahoo.fr]** Leave A8 junc 55 (Nice Est); foll D2204 twds Sospel; cont until R turn at rndbt sp D21 Peillon/Peille; site on R in vill in approx 4km. Sm, mkd pitch, pt shd; wc; chem disp; mv service pnt; shwrs inc; el pnts (12-4A) €2.50-3.50 (rev pol); Indtte; shop, rest, bar in vill; tradsmn; shgl beach 14km; dogs €2.50; phone adj; adv bkg; quiet; no ccard acc; CCI. "Sm family-run site; helpful owner; conv for Monaco, Monte Carlo, Nice; sm pitches; some rd/rlwy noise; ltd facs low ssn." May-Sep. € 21.00 2007*

NIEDERBRONN LES BAINS *5D3* (1.5km N Rural) *48.96221, 7.64522* **Camping Heidenkopf, Route de la Lisière, 67110 Niederbronn-les-Bains [tel/fax 03 88 09 08 46; heidenkopf@tiscali.fr; www.camping-alsace.com/niederbronn/]** Fr Niederbronn NW on D1062/D662 (N62) & foll sp rd R into forest fr mineral spring. NB Last 500m single track - poss diff lge o'fits. Med, pt sl, terr, pt shd; htd wc (some cont); chem disp; mv service pnt; baby facs; shwrs inc; el pnts (6A) €3; gas; Indtte; shops 3km; tradsmn; BBQ; playgrnd; pool 600m; dogs €1.25; adv bkg; quiet; red long stay/low ssn. "V peaceful site; warm welcome; forest walks." ♦ 1 Mar-31 Oct. € 14.10 2009*

NIEDERBRONN LES BAINS *5D3* (1.5km SW Rural) *48.92958, 7.60428* **Camp Municipal L'Oasis, 3 Rue de Frohret, 67110 Oberbronn [03 88 09 71 96; fax 03 88 09 97 87; oasis.oberbronn@laregie.fr; www.camping-alsace.com/oberbronn]** Fr D1062 (N62) turn S on D28 away fr Niederbronn; thro Oberbronn, site sp. Lge, mkd pitch, pt sl, pt shd; wc; chem disp; mv service pnt; sauna; shwrs inc; el pnts (6A) inc; Indtte; shop & 1.5km; tradsmn; rest; snacks; bar; BBQ; playgrnd; htd, covrd pool high ssn; paddling pool; tennis; fitness rm; walking, cycling, horseriding rtes; golf, games rm; fishing 2km; 20% statics; dogs €1.80; clsd 1200-1300; poss cr; adv bkg rec high ssn; quiet; red long stay/low ssn; ccard acc; CCI. "Vg site with views; part of leisure complex; sl area for tourers; some san facs tired; site gravel paths not suitable wheelchair users." ♦ 15 Mar-15 Nov. € 15.90 2007*

⊞ **NIMES** *10E2* (7km NE Urban) *43.88323, 4.48791* **Camping Les Cyprès, 5 Rue de la Bastide, 30320 Bezouce [04 66 75 24 30; fax 04 66 75 64 78; cdavidian@wanadoo.fr]** Sp on N86 Nîmes-Avignon rd. Site not well sp in Bezouce - sign high on wall. Narr site access. Sm, pt shd; wc; chem disp; shwrs; el pnts (4-6A) €3.70; shop, rest, bar in vill; sm pool; mostly statics; dogs; poss cr; adv bkg; rd noise & cockerels. "Facs rustic & basic but clean; friendly & helpful owners; conv Pont-du-Gard, Nîmes, Arles; not rec lge o'fits; closes early evening low ssn; NH only." € 12.20 2008*

France

⊞ **NIMES** *10E2* (4km S Rural) *43.78776, 4.35196* **Camp Municipal Domaine de la Bastide, Allee du Mas de la Bastide, 30900 Nîmes [tel/fax 04 66 62 05 82; info@camping-nimes.com; www.camping-nimes.com]** Fr A9 exit junc 25 dir Arles; then take exit 1on A54 sp St Gilles; turn L sp Caisssargues; at 2nd rndabt turn R onto D135; in 2.5km at rndabt turn R; site on L. Site well sp fr town cent. Lge, hdg/mkd pitch, hdstg, shd; htd wc; chem disp; mv service pnt; baby facs; shwrs inc; el pnts (15A); gas; Indtte; shop; tradsmn; hypmkt nr; rest; snacks; bar; playgrnd; games area; wifi; TV rm; 10% statics; dogs €2.60; phone; bus; Eng spkn; adv bkg; quiet - some rd noise; red low ssn; CCI. "Excel, well-run site; lge pitches; friendly, helpful recep; Nîmes 20 mins by bus fr site." ♦ € 16.60 2009*

NIOZELLES see Brillane, La *10E3*

NOAILLES see Brive la Gaillarde *7C3*

NOCLE MAULAIX, LA *4H4* (W Rural) *46.76666, 3.77521* **Camp Municipal du l'Etang Marnant, Route de Decize, 58250 La Nocle-Maulaix [tel/fax 03 86 30 84 13; mairie-la-nocle-maulaix@wanadoo.fr; http://lanocle.fr.st]** Fr Luzy twd Fours on N81, turn L on D3 & foll sp. Site in 5km at La Nocle-Maulaix by junc with D30. Sm, mkd pitch, pt sl, pt shd; wc; shwrs; el pnts €2.45; shops 400m; Indtte; playgrnd; sports area; fishing; watersports on lake; some statics; adv bkg; quiet. "Take 2nd ent to site; site yourself & warden calls." 15 May-15 Sep. € 9.20 2007*

NOGENT L'ARTAUD *3D4* (1km S Rural) *48.96234, 3.32975* **Camp Municipal des Monts, Route de Rebais, 02310 Nogent-l'Artaud [03 23 70 10 21 or 03 23 70 01 18 (Mairie); fax 03 23 70 10 88]** Site sp W of D222/D11, 1km S fr Nogent-l'Artaud. Sm, hdg/mkd pitch, pt terr, pt shd; wc; chem disp (wc); shwrs inc; el pnts (6A) €2.10; Indtte; shop, rest, bar 500m; playgrnd; table tennis, games area adj; 25% statics; dogs €0.85; phone; quiet; ccard acc; CCI. "Beautiful, garden-type site; gd views; although pt terr, access is easy; vg." 1 Apr-30 Sep. € 7.80 2008*

NOGENT LE ROTROU *4E2* (500m N Urban) *48.32541, 0.81599* **Camp Municipal des Viennes, Rue des Viennes, 28400 Nogent-le-Rotrou [02 37 52 80 51; courriel@ville-nogent-le-rotrou.fr; www.ville-nogent-le-rotrou.fr]** Sp in town off D922 & D103 Ave des Prés. Sm, hdg/mkd pitches, hdstg, pt shd; wc; chem disp; serviced pitch; shwrs inc; el pnts (10A) inc; Indry rm; shops adj; playgrnd; pool adj; adv bkg rec high ssn; quiet; CCI. "Site yourself & report later; helpful staff; pleasant, well-run site." 1 Jun-8 Sep. 2007*

NOGENT SUR SEINE *4E4* (500m NE Rural) *48.50365, 3.50889* **Camp Municipal, Rue Villiers-aux-Choux, 10400 Nogent-sur-Seine [tel/fax 03 25 39 76 67 or 03 25 39 42 00 (Mairie)]** Fr Troyes site sp fr D619 (N19) on app to town & fr S ring rd, Site on rvside. Med, mkd pitch, some hdstg, pt shd; htd wc; shwrs; mv service pnt; el pnts; shop 500m; rest 100m; playgrnd; htd pool adj; tennis; quiet. "Pleasant site; poss many long-stay residents; gd NH." 1 Apr-5 Oct. 2009*

NOGENT SUR SEINE *4E4* (10km NE Rural) **Aire Naturelle Municipale (Cunin), 10400 Pont-sur-Seine [03 25 21 43 44 or 03 25 39 42 00 (Mairie); fax 03 25 21 45 66; mairie.pontseine@wanadoo.fr]** Fr Nogent-sur-Seine take D619 (N19) twd Romilly-sur-Seine. In 10km turn L on D52 to Pont-sur-Seine. Site on L thro vill nr rv. Med, unshd; wc; chem disp (wc); el pnts (6A) inc; rest, shop 750m; quiet; adv bkg; phone. "Peaceful, vg value site; pitch yourself, warden calls; gd facs poss stretched if busy." ♦ 1 May-17 Sep. € 9.00 2006*

NOIRETABLE *9B1* (1km S Rural) *45.80817, 3.76844* **Camp Municipal de la Roche, Route de la Roche, 42440 Noirétable [04 77 24 72 68; fax 04 77 24 92 20]** Leave A72/E70 junc 4 sp Noirétable; thro toll & turn SW onto D53. Ignore narr tourist rte sp to W; cont downhill to T-junc & turn R onto D1089 (N89). Take next L & site on R in 750m. Sm, mkd pitch, hdstg, pt terr, pt sl, pt shd; wc (cont); shwrs; el pnts (10A) inc; snacks, bar nr; playgrnd, lake adj; ccard not acc. 1 Apr-1 Nov. € 8.20 2006*

NOIRMOUTIER EN L'ILE *2H3* (2km E Coastal) *46.99769, -2.22331* **Camp Municipal Le Clair Matin, Les Sableaux, 85330 Noirmoutier-en-l'Ile [02 51 39 05 56; fax 02 51 39 74 36]** Ent Noirmoutier on D948 & foll sp to Les Sableaux. Site well sp. Med, mkd pitch, terr, pt shd; wc; mv service pnt; shwrs €1; el pnts (10A) €3.30; Indtte; shop; rest 500m; bar 150m; playgrnd; pool 2.5km; sand beach adj; fishing; dogs €1.20; adv bkg rec; quiet. "Gd; clean facs; excel cycle paths & beach fishing." ♦ Easter-30 Oct. € 13.00 (3 persons) 2008*

NOIRMOUTIER EN L'ILE *2H3* (2km E Coastal) *46.99697, -2.22057* **Camping Indigo Noirmoutier La Vendette, 23 Rue des Sableaux, 85330 Noirmoutier-en-l'Ile [02 51 39 06 24; fax 02 51 35 97 63; noirmoutier@camping-indigo.com; www.camping-indigo.com]** Ent Noirmoutier on D948, strt on over bdge & foll sp for Bois-de-la-Chaize, then 'campings'. Lge, pt shd; wc; mv service pnt; shwrs inc; el pnts (6-10A) €3.60-5; Indtte; tradsmn; rest; snacks; bar; playgrnd; sand beach adj; fishing; boat-launching; cycle hire; some statics; dogs €2.70; phone; poss cr; adv bkg; quiet; red low ssn; CCI ess. "In pine forest nr salt water marshes; gd for children; shellfish at low tide." 28 Mar-5 Oct. € 18.10 (CChq acc) 2008*

NOIRMOUTIER EN L'ILE *2H3* (10km SE Coastal) *46.94503, -2.18542* **Camp Municipal du Midi, Fief du Moulin, 85630 Barbâtre [02 51 39 63 74; fax 02 51 39 58 63; camping-du-midi@wanadoo.fr]** Cross to island by Passage du Gois D948 (low tide - 2.5 hrs per day) or bdge D38. Turn L after 2.5km off dual c'way to Barbâtre. Site sp N thro vill. V lge, pt sl, shd; wc; baby facs; shwrs; el pnts (5A) inc; gas; Indtte; shop; rest; snacks; bar; BBQ (gas/elec); htd pool; sand beach adj; tennis; entmnt; poss cr; no adv bkg; quiet; ccard acc; red low ssn. ♦ Easter-16 Sep. € 28.00 (3 persons) 2006*

NOIRMOUTIER EN L'ILE *2H3* (4km S Coastal) *46.96621, -2.21623* **Camping Le Caravan'île, 1 Rue de la Tresson, 85680 La Guérinière [02 51 39 50 29; fax 02 51 35 86 85; contact@caravanile.com; www.caravanile.com]** Cross to island on D38, at rndabt foll sp La Guérinière. Site on L. Lge, hdg pitch, pt shd; wc; shwrs; el pnts (5A) inc; Indtte; shop; rest 1km; snacks; playgrnd; 3 pools (1 covrd); waterslide; beach adj; games rm; fitness rm; TV; 50% statics; dogs €2.90; adv bkg; quiet; ccard acc; CCI. "Well-run, popular site; conv cycling, birdwatching, watersports, fishing etc." ♦ 1 Mar-15 Nov. € 22.00 2007*

NOIRMOUTIER EN L'ILE *2H3* (3.5km SW Coastal) *46.98609, -2.28790* **Camp Municipal La Bosse, 85740 L'Epine [02 51 39 01 07]** Fr bdge take D38 to La Guérinière: turn W along D38 to L'Epine & foll camp sp to La Bosse. Lge, pt sl, unshd; wc; chem disp; shwrs inc; el pnts (5A) €2.50-3; Indtte; BBQ; playgrnd; sand beach, boat hire, sw & fishing 100m; entmnt; quiet; adv bkg. "Cheap & cheerful; many pitches sandy & v sl or uneven, others permanently occupied; can get v windy; san facs adequate." ♦ 1 Apr-30 Sep. € 15.00 2009*

NOIRMOUTIER EN L'ILE *2H3* (8km W Coastal) *47.02409, -2.30374* **Camp Municipal La Pointe, L'Herbaudière, 85330 Noirmoutier-en-l'Ile [02 51 39 16 70; fax 02 51 39 74 15]** Fr bdge to island foll sp to Noirmoutier town, then to L'Herbaudière & port. At port turn L, 500m to site. Med, mkd pitch, unshd; wc; chem disp; mv service pnt; shwrs inc; el pnts (10A) €3.50 (long leads poss req); gas; Indtte; shop; rest, snacks & bar in town; beach adj; dogs €1.50; adv bkg; quiet; red low ssn; CCI. "Excel site in beautiful location; poss windy (exposed to sea on 3 sides); helpful staff; clean, adequate facs; gd cycle rtes on island; rec." 1 Apr-29 Sep. € 13.50 2009*

NOLAY *6H1* (9km SW Rural) *46.87406, 4.56743* **Camp Municipal La Gabrelle, La Varenne, 71490 Couches [03 85 45 59 49 or 03 85 98 19 20 (Mairie); fax 03 85 98 19 29; camping-la-gabrelle@orange.fr]** Exit A6 at junc 25 Chalon-sur-Saône Nord onto D978 sp Autun. In 26km at Couches, site NW of vill. Sm, hdg pitch, terr, pt shd; wc; shwrs inc; el pnts (6A) €2.80; Indtte; supmkt 5km; snacks; bar; playgrnd; lake adj; some daytime rd noise. "Attractive countryside nr wine area." ♦ 1 Jun-15 Sep. € 11.20 2008*

⊞ **NOLAY** *6H1* (1km NW Rural) *46.95084, 4.62266* **Camp Municipal La Bruyère, Rue du Moulin Larché, 21340 Nolay [tel/fax 03 80 21 87 59; camping.labruyere@mfcoy.fr; www.nolay.com]** Fr Beaune take D973 W dir Autun. In approx 20km, arr in vill of Nolay & cont on D973 thro vill. Site on L in 1km after vill, opp supmkt. Sm, hdg/mkd pitch, terr, pt shd; htd wc; chem disp; mv service pnt; shwrs inc; el pnts (12A) €3.50; Indtte; shop adj; supmkt, rest & bar 1km; BBQ; phone adj; bus adj; Eng spkn; quiet; ccard acc red low ssn; CCI. "Lovely, peaceful, well-kept site; friendly warden; gd, clean san facs; attractive walk to bustling old town; gd touring base in wine area or NH; poss grape pickers in Sep." ♦ € 13.80 2009*

NONANCOURT *4E2* (4km E Urban) *48.76410, 1.23686* **Camp Municipal du Pré de l'Eglise, Rue Pré de l'Eglise, 28380 St Rémy-sur-Avre [02 37 48 93 87 or 02 37 62 52 00 (LS); fax 02 37 48 80 15; mairiesaintremy2@wanadoo.fr; www.ville-st-remy-sur-avre.fr]** Fr Dreux take N12 W to St Rémy; strt over 1st rndabt & at traff lts complex in 500m turn R & then immed R & foll site sp. Fr Evreux (W) on N12 to St Rémy; after x-ing rv bdge at traff lts complex strt ahead to rndabt (no L turn at traff lts), then immed R at end rv bdge as above. Site clearly sp in vill cent, sp 'Oscar' is for sports cent adj. NB Speed ramps on site app rd. Sm, hdg/mkd pitch (some grouped x 4), pt shd; wc; chem disp; shwrs inc; el pnts (10A) €2.83 (poss rev pol); Indtte (inc dryer); shop, tradsmn; rest 500m; snacks; playgrnd; tennis & trout fishing adj; sat TV; dogs; phone; poss cr; Eng spkn; adv bkg rec high ssn; factory adj poss noisy; ccard not acc; CCI. "Pleasant, popular NH; welcoming, friendly warden; clean facs, some modern, ltd low ssn; no twin-axles (but negotiable); some pitches poss diff access; poss itinerants." ♦ 4 Apr-30 Sep. € 9.43 2009*

NONETTE see Issoire *9B1*

⊞ **NONTRON** *7B3* (7km NE Rural) *45.56185, 0.71979* **Camping Manzac Ferme, Manzac, 24300 Augignac [05 53 56 02 62; info@manzac-ferme.com; www.manzac-ferme.com]** Fr Nontron take D675 N dir Rochechouart & after 7km on ent Augignac turn R sp Abjat-sur-Bandiat then immed R sp Manzac. Site on R 3.5km Sm, mkd pitch, pt hdstg, sl, pt shd; htd wc; chem disp; shwrs inc; el pnts (6A) inc; gas 6km; shops, rest, bar 5km; BBQ; rv fishing; dogs by arrangement; adv bkg; quiet. "Adults only; vg, relaxing CL-type site; ideal for birdwatching & wildlife; helpful British owners; phone ahead in winter." ♦ € 22.00 2008*

NONTRON *7B3* (8km NE Rural) *45.56026, 0.75914* **Camping La Ripole, Route du Stade, 24300 Abjat-sur-Bandiat [tel/fax 05 53 56 38 81 or 06 11 51 90 25 (mob); camping.la.ripole@wanadoo.fr; www.campingripole.info]** Exit D675 at Nontron onto D707 then L onto D85; in 8km turn L onto D96 dir Abjat-sur-Bandiat; in 3km turn L into Route du Stade. Site on L in 2km. Sm, hdg pitch, pt shd; wc; chem disp (wc); shwrs inc; el pnts (6A) €3; Indtte; tradsmn; snacks; bar; BBQ (gas/elec); playgrnd; pool; lake sw; fishing; games area; games rm; entmnt; 60% statics; dogs €1.10; bus 2km; Eng spkn; adv bkg; quiet; ccard acc; CCI. "Excel touring base." ♦ 15 Jun-15 Sep. € 11.30 2007*

France

NONTRON *7B3* (11km NE Rural) *45.55138, 0.79472* **Kawan Village Le Château Le Verdoyer, 24470 Champs-Romain [05 53 56 94 64; fax 05 53 56 38 70; chateau@verdoyer.fr; www.verdoyer.fr]** Fr Limoges on N21 twd Périgueux. At Châlus turn R sp Nontron (D6 bis-D85). After approx 18km turn L twd Champs Romain on D96 to site on L in 2km. Med, terr, pt shd; wc; chem disp; mv service pnt; baby facs; shwrs inc; el pnts (10A) inc (poss rev pol); gas; lndtte; shop; rest, snacks; bar; B&B in chateau; BBQ (charcoal/gas); playgrnd; 2 htd pools (1 covrd); paddling pool; waterslide; lake fishing; tennis; cycle hire; golf 25km; child entmnt; wifi; games/TV rm; 20% statics; dogs €3; phone; poss cr; Eng spkn; adv bkg; quiet; ccard acc; red low ssn; CCI. "Excel, peaceful site in lovely location; friendly staff; superb facs; poss steep access some pitches; highly rec." ♦ 24 Apr-5 Oct. € 34.00 (CChq acc) ABS - D21 2009*

⊞ **NONTRON** *7B3* (1km S Urban) *45.51992, 0.65876* **Camping de Nontron, St Martiel-de-Valette, 24300 Nontron [05 53 56 02 04 or 06 30 66 25 74 (mob); camping-de-nontron@orange.fr; www.campingdenontron.com]** Thro Nontron S twd Brantôme on D675. Site on o'skts of town on L nr stadium. Sp. Med, hdg/mkd pitch, pt shd; htd wc; mv service pnt; shwrs; el pnts (10A) €3.50; gas; lndtte; shops adj; tradsmn; rest, snacks, bar 600m; playgrnd; pool adj; paddling pool; games area; games rm; entmnt; TV rm; statics; dogs €1; site clsd mid-Dec to early Jan; poss cr; Eng spkn; quiet; CCI. "Pleasant owners; excel, modern san facs; gd touring base." € 10.00 2008*

NORDAUSQUES see Ardres *3A3*

NORT SUR ERDRE *2G4* (1km S Rural) *47.42770, -1.49877* **Camp Municipal du Port Mulon, Rue des Mares Noires, 44390 Nort-sur-Erdre [02 40 72 23 57; fax 02 40 72 16 09; camping.nort-sur-erdre@orange.fr; www.nort-sur-erdre.fr]** Sp fr all ents to town; foll 'Camping' & 'Hippodrome' sp. NB: C'vans banned fr town cent, look for diversion sp. Med, shd; wc; chem disp; shwrs inc; el pnts (6A) €2.30; lndtte (inc dryer); supmkt 1.5km; playgrnd; tennis; fishing; boating; dogs €0.80; adv bkg; quiet; CCI. "Delightful site but area not v interesting." 19 Apr-13 Sep. € 8.90 2009*

NOTRE DAME DE RIEZ *2H3* (1km NE Rural) *46.75523, -1.89814* **Camping Domaine des Renardières, 13 Chemin de Chêne Vert, 85270 Notre-Dame-de-Riez [02 51 55 14 17 or 06 20 98 37 46 (mob); fax 02 51 54 96 13; caroline.raffin@free.fr; www.camping-renardieres.com]** On D38 to Notre-Dame-de-Riez. Thro vill, over rv & 1st L over rlwy to site in 1km. Med, pt shd; wc; chem disp; baby facs; shwrs inc; el pnts (6A) inc; gas; lndtte lndry rm; tradsmn; rest; bar; snacks; BBQ; pool; playgrnd; sand beach 5km; TV rm; 20% statics; dogs €3; Eng spkn; adv bkg; quiet phone; 15% red low ssn; ccard not acc; CCI. "Gd picturesque site; helpful owner; rec." ♦ 1 Apr-2 Sep. € 17.50 2006*

NOTRE DAME DE RIEZ *2H3* (2km SW Rural) *46.75020, -1.88079* **Camping Fonteclose, Route de Commequiers, 85270 Notre-Dame-de-Riez [02 51 55 22 22; fax 02 51 55 91 98; la.fonteclose@wanadoo.fr; www.fonteclose.com]** Sp fr D83 & D32. Med, pt shd, wc; baby facs; shwrs inc; el pnts (6A) €3; lndtte; shop; rest; bar; BBQ; BBQ; playgrnd; htd pool; fishing 100m; tennis; games area; entmnt; TV; 60% statics; dogs €2; adv bkg. "Friendly site." 1 Jun-30 Sep. € 15.00 2006*

NOTRE DAME DU TOUCHET see Mortain *2E4*

NOUAN LE FUZELIER *4G3* (S Urban) *47.53328, 2.03508* **Camping La Grande Sologne, Rue Gauchoix, 41600 Nouan-le-Fuzelier [02 54 88 70 22; fax 02 54 88 41 74; camping-lagrande-sologne@wanadoo.fr; www.nouan-le-fuzelier.fr/camping.html]** On E side of D2020 (N20), at S end of Nouan opp rlwy stn. Sp fr town cent & opp rlwy stn. NB Sat nav not rec. Lge, mkd pitch, pt shd; wc (some cont); chem disp; mv service pnt; baby facs; shwrs inc; el pnts (6-10A) inc; gas; lndtte; shops 800m; tradsmn; rest; snacks; bar; playgrnd; htd pool adj; tennis; games area; fishing; golf 15km; dogs €1; poss cr; Eng spkn; adv bkg; quiet; red long stay/low ssn; CCI. "Pretty site adj lake (no sw); some pitches boggy when wet; facs poss stretched high ssn; ltd facs end of ssn & poss unclean; public park at ent to site, but quiet; rec arr early; excel NH." 1 Apr-15 Oct. € 18.40 2009*

NOUVION EN THIERACHE, LE *3B4* (1km S Rural) *50.00538, 3.78292* **Camp Municipal du Lac de Condé, Promenade Henri d'Orléans, Rue de Guise (Le Lac), 02170 Le Nouvion-en-Thiérache [03 23 98 98 58; fax 03 23 98 94 90; mairie.nouvion@orange.fr; www.lenouvion.com]** Sp fr cent of Le Nouvion fr D1043 (N43) on D26, dir Guise opp chateau. Med, hdg/mkd pitch, some hdstg, pt sl, pt shd; wc; chem disp; shwrs inc; el pnts (4A) inc; lndtte (inc dryer); shop 1km; tradsmn; rest, snacks, bar 1km; BBQ; playgrnd; htd pool adj; tennis, canoe hire, horseriding nrby; 10% statics; dogs €0.70; phone; Eng spkn; red long stay/CCI; ccard acc. "Beautiful, spacious, lakeside site; warm welcome; gd san facs; gd for families; busy even low ssn - rec phone ahead; not suitable m'vans due sl pitches; muddy when wet; excel." ♦ 15 Apr-15 Oct. € 11.35 2008*

NOYERS *4G4* (200m S Rural) **Camping Rurale, Promenade du Pré de l'Echelle, 89310 Noyers [03 86 82 83 72; fax 03 86 82 63 41; mairie-de-noyers@wanadoo.fr]** Exit A6 at Nitry & turn R onto D944. In 2km at N edge of Nitry, turn R onto D49 sp Noyers. In 10km in Noyers, turn L onto D86 sp Centre Ville/Camping. Immed after crossing rv & bef gate, turn L bet 2 obelisks. Site at end of track. Sm, mkd pitch, terr, shd; wc; own san; chem disp; shwrs inc; el pnts €1.05; shop, rest, snacks & bar 200m; BBQ; playgrnd; dogs; quiet, except church bells. "Attractive, secluded site nr Rv Serein (6 pitches); ent key fr Mairie on R after going thro town gate; ltd san facs." € 4.30 2008*

⊞ **NOYON** *3C3* (4km E Rural) **FFCC Camping L'Etang du Moulin, 54 Rue du Moulin, 60400 Salency [tel/fax 03 44 09 99 81 or 03 44 43 06 78]** Take D1032 (N32) fr Noyon dir Chauny. On ent Salency turn L & foll site sp. Site in 1km. Sm, pt sl, shd; htd wc; chem disp; mv service pnt; shwrs €2; el pnts (10A) €1.60; gas; shop, rest 4km; tradsmn; bar; BBQ; playgrnd; fishing; tennis; 60% statics; dogs €1; quiet; CCI. "Site unclean (Jan 2009); san facs need maintenance & unclean (Sep 2007)." ♦ € 14.30 2009*

NOYON *3C3* (8km S Rural) *49.50667, 3.01765* **FFCC Camping Les Araucarias, 870 Rue du Général Leclerc, 60170 Carlepont [03 44 75 27 39; fax 03 44 38 12 51; camping-les-araucarias@wanadoo.fr; www.camping-les-araucarias.com]** Fr S, fr A1 exit junc 9 or 10 for Compiègne. There take D130 sp Tracy-le-Val & Carlepont. Site on L 100m fr Carlepont vill sp. Or fr N on D934 Noyon-Soissons rd take D130 dir Carlepont & Tracy-le-Val. Site on R after vill on SW twd Compiegne - not well sp. Sm, mkd pitch, pt sl, pt shd; wc; chem disp; mv service pnt; baby facs; shwrs inc; el pnts (6-10A) €3 (poss rev pol); gas; lndtte; shop, rest, bar 1km; BBQ; playgrnd; 20% statics; dogs €1; poss cr; Eng spkn; adv bkg; quiet; CCI. "Secluded site, previously an arboretum; poss diff when wet; close Parc Astérix & La Mer-de-Sable (theme park); 85km Disneyland; san facs poss scruffy low ssn; vg." ♦ 21 Mar-21 Dec. € 9.04 2009*

NOZAY *2G4* (8km NW Rural) *47.59606, -1.71583* **Camp Municipal La Roche, 44170 Marsac-sur-Don [02 40 87 54 77 (Mairie); fax 02 40 87 51 29; mairie.marsacsurdon@wanadoo.fr]** Fr N137 turn W onto D124 to Marsac-sur-Don. Fr vill take D125 W dir Guénouvry, site sp. Sm, mkd pitch, pt sl, pt shd; wc; shwrs; el pnts €2.10; rest, bar nrby; playgrnd; fishing; games area; walking circuit; quiet; CCI. "Gd basic site; own san rec; vg value."
1 May-30 Sep. € 5.00 2006*

NUITS ST GEORGES *6G1* (3km SW Urban) *47.10323, 4.94148* **Camping Le Moulin de Prissey, 21700 Premeaux-Prissey [03 80 62 31 15; fax 03 80 61 37 29]** Exit Beaune on D974 (N74) twd Nuits-St Georges & Dijon; app Premeaux-Prissey turn R soon after vill sp, under rlwy bdge & foll site sp. Fr A31 exit at Nuits-St Georges & foll camp sp for Saule-Guillaume, thro Premeaux-Prissey & foll site sp. Sm, mkd pitch, pt sl, pt shd; wc (some cont); chem disp (wc); mv service pnt; shwrs inc; el pnts (6A) €3.50; gas; lndtte; shops 3km; tradsmn; snacks; rest, bar 4km; BBQ; playgrnd; dogs €0.90; poss cr; adv bkg; noisy rlwy adj; ccard not acc; CCI. "Arr early; popular NH; sm pitches; access poss diff for lge o'fits; gd cycling." ♦ 1 Apr-15 Oct. € 13.35 2008*

NYONS *9D2* (1km NE Rural) *44.36523, 5.15365* **Camping Les Clos, Route de Gap, 26110 Nyons [04 75 26 29 90; fax 04 75 26 49 44; camping-les-clos@clario.fr; www.campinglesclos.com]** Fr rndabt in town cent take D94 sp Gap & site on R in 1km. Med, hdg/mkd pitch, hdstg, pt shd; wc; chem disp; shwrs inc; baby facs; el pnts (10A) inc; gas; lndtte; shop; rest 1km; snacks; bar; BBQ (gas/elec only); playgrnd; pool; shgl rv beach & fishing; entmnt (ltd); 20% statics; dogs €2.10; phone; poss v cr; Eng spkn; adv bkg; red low ssn; ccard acc; CCI. "Quiet, well-kept site in lovely area; friendly, helpful staff; excel touring base." ♦
15 Mar-15 Oct. € 21.00 2008*

NYONS *9D2* (3km NE Rural) *44.37247, 5.16255* **Camping L'Or Vert, 26110 Aubres [04 75 26 24 85; fax 04 75 26 17 89; camping-or-vert@wanadoo.fr; www.camping-or-vert.com]** Fr Nyons take D94 twd Serre, site on R of rd on rvside. Med, hdg/mkd pitch, hdstg, pt sl, pt shd; wc (cont); chem disp; shwrs inc; el pnts (6A) €3.60; gas; lndtte; shop; snacks; playgrnd; pool 3km; rv adj; fishing; tennis 600m; games area; entmnt; TV; some statics; dogs €1.80 (not acc Jul/Aug); quiet; ccard not acc. "Scenic area; min stay 10 days Jul-Aug; nice rv site; ltd facs low ssn; phone ahead to check opening dates low ssn; clean facs."
1 Apr-1 Oct. € 13.30 2006*

NYONS *9D2* (12km NE Rural) *44.42569, 5.21904* **Camping de Trente Pas, 26110 St Ferréol-Trente-Pas [04 75 27 70 69; contact@campingtrentepas.com; www.campingtrentepas.com]** Exit A7 junc 19 Bollène onto D994 & D94. L on D70 to St Ferréol-Trente-Pas. Site 100m fr vill on banks of stream. Med, shd; wc; shwrs; el pnts (6A) €2.80; lndry rm; sm shop & snacks high ssn; shop 2km; rest 200m; bar; playgrnd; pool; games rm; tennis; cycle hire; horseriding 4km; entmnt; TV; 5% statics; dogs €1.60; quiet. "Scenic area - views fr site; excel value; gd, clean san facs; gd pool; rec." 1 May-31 Aug. € 13.20 2008*

NYONS *9D2* (12km NE Rural) *44.43507, 5.21248* **FFCC Camping Le Pilat, 26110 St Ferréol-Trente-Pas [04 75 27 72 09; fax 04 75 27 72 34; info@campinglepilat.com; www.campinglepilat.com]** Fr D94 N or Nyons turn N at La Bonté onto D70 to St Ferréol, site sp 1km N of vill. Med, hdg pitch, shd; wc (some cont); chem disp; shwrs inc; el pnts (6A) €3.50; lndtte; shop high ssn & 3km; tradsmn; snacks; playgrnd; covrd pool; paddling pool; lake sw adj; games area; entmnt; TV; 25% statics; dogs €1.50; phone; Eng spkn; quiet; red low ssn; CCI. "Site among lavender fields; Thurs mkt Nyons; pleasant, helpful owners; clean facs; gd walking & off-rd cycling; excel." ♦
1 Apr-30 Sep. € 19.50 2008*

NYONS *9D2* (12km E Rural) *44.34319, 5.28357* **Camp Municipal Les Cigales, Allée des Platanes, 26110 Ste Jalle [04 75 27 34 88 or 04 75 27 32 78 (mairie)]** Fr Nyons take D94 dir Serres; in 10 km at Curnier turn R onto D64 to Ste-Jalle. In vill turn R onto D108 dir Buis-les-Baronnies. Site on R in 300m. NB Dist by rd fr Nyons is 20km. Sm, hdg pitch, pt shd; wc; chem disp; shwrs inc; el pnts (10A) €2.20; shop, rest, snacks, bar 300m; playgrnd; 15% statics; dogs; adv bkg. "Vg, quiet site in attractive old vill." 1 May-30 Sep. € 7.40 2006*

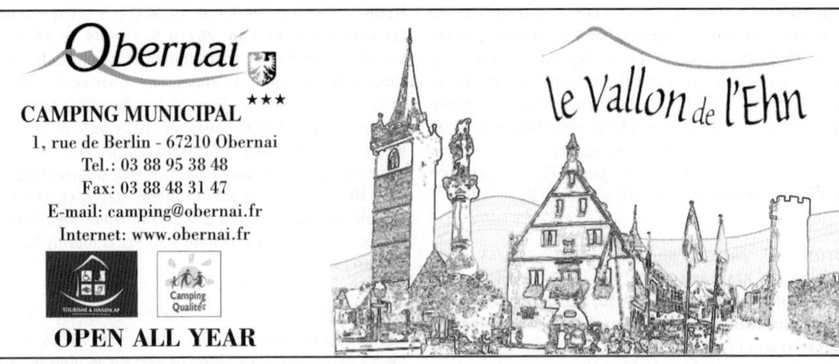

⊞ **NYONS** *9D2* (6km SW Rural) *44.32830, 5.08380* **Camping Domaine Le Sagittaire, Le Pont de Mirabel, 26110 Vinsobres [04 75 27 00 00; fax 04 75 27 00 39; camping.sagittaire@wanadoo.fr; www.le-sagittaire.com or www.camping-franceloc.fr]** Fr Nyons on D94, sp Orange, site on L just after junc with D4, well sp. Lge, hdg pitch, pt shd; htd wc; chem disp; shwrs inc; el pnts (6-10A) €4.70-5.70; gas; Indtte; shop; tradsmn; rest, snacks, bar in ssn; playgrnd; htd, covrd pool; waterslide; tennis; cycle hire; entmnt; TV; 25% statics; dogs €5; poss cr; adv bkg; quiet but some rd noise on edge of site; ccard acc; red long stay/low ssn; CCI. "Part of holiday complex in attractive, uncommercialised area." € 31.00 2009*

NYONS *9D2* (7km SW Rural) **Camp Municipal Chez Antoinette, Champessier, 26110 Vinsobres [04 75 27 61 65 or 04 75 27 64 49 (Mairie); fax 04 75 27 59 20; camping-municipal@club-internet.fr]** Fr Nyons on D94 sp Orange. Turn R 500m after junc with D4 twd Vinsobres vill. Site 500m on L bef vill. Sm, mkd pitch, pt shd; htd wc; chem disp; shwrs inc; el pnts (6A) €2.70; Indry rm; BBQ; playgrnd; adv bkg; quiet; ccard acc; CCI. "Peaceful, v popular site; cramped san facs; steep unhill walk to vill; excel touring area." ♦ Easter-30 Oct. € 8.20 2006*

NYONS *9D2* (4km NW Rural) *44.40829, 5.07993* **Camping Les Terrasses Provençales, Les Barroux-Novezan, 26110 Venterol [tel/fax 04 75 27 92 36; novezan@lesterrasses provencales. com; www.lesterrassesprovencales.com]** Exit A7/E15 at junc 18 sp Nyons. Join D541 E twd Nyons. Site in Venterol, sp bet Valréas & Nyons. Med, hdg/mkd pitch, hdstg, terr, pt shd; wc; chem disp; baby facs; fam bthrm; shwrs inc; el pnts (10A) €3.70 (poss rev pol); gas; Indtte; shop 6km; tradsmn; rest, bar 2km; playgrnd; pool; dogs low ssn only €1.85; poss cr; some Eng spkn; quiet; ccard acc; CCI. "Owner will tow c'van onto terr pitch; excel." ♦ 15 Apr-30 Sep. € 16.00 2007*

OBERNAI *6E3* (10km N Urban) *48.54124, 7.50003* **Camp Municipal de Molsheim, 9 Rue des Sports, 67120 Molsheim [03 88 49 82 45 or 03 88 49 58 58 (LS); fax 03 88 49 58 59; www.mairie-molsheim.fr]** On ent town fr Obernai on D1422 (D422) site sp on R immed after x-ing sm rv bdge. Med, mkd pitch, pt shd; wc; chem disp; mv service pnt; shwrs inc; el pnts €2.50; Indtte; tradsmn; BBQ; pool adj; cycle hire; dogs €1.10; train to Strasbourg 700m; poss cr; Eng spkn; adv bkg; quiet; CCI. "Easy walk to town cent & shops." ♦ 1 May-30 Sep. € 11.30 2007*

⊞ **OBERNAI** *6E3* (1km W Urban) *48.4646, 7.4675* **Camp Municipal Le Vallon de l'Ehn, 1 Rue de Berlin, 67210 Obernai [03 88 95 38 48; fax 03 88 48 31 47; camping@obernai.fr; www.obernai.fr]** Fr Strasbourg SW on D1422 (D422)/A35; leave at junc 11 sp Obernai; on ent town, turn L at 2nd rndabt (McDonalds) sp D426 Ottrott; in 3km after 3rd rndabt turn R at T-junc sp Obernai then almost immed L at camping sp; site on L in 200m, sp but obscure. Look for sp Camping VVF. Fr S on A35, exit at junc 12 sp Obernai. At 3rd rndabt turn L onto D426 Otrott-Mont Ste Odile (look for sp Camping VVF). Lge, mkd pitch, hdstg, pt sl, pt shd; htd wc; chem disp; mv service pnt; 75% serviced pitches; baby facs; shwrs inc; el pnts (16A) €4; gas 1km; Indtte; sm shop & 1km; tradsmn; BBQ; playgrnd; lge pool 200m; tennis, horseriding adj; wifi; dogs €1; bus to Strasbourg & Obernai nr; train; poss cr; Eng spkn; adv bkg; quiet; ccard acc; 10% red C'van Club members low ssn. "Attractive, well-kept, busy site on edge of pictureque town; sm pitches; welcoming, helpful staff; superb, clean facs; no entry after 1930; rec arr early high ssn; c'vans, m'vans & tents all sep areas; excel bus/train links; ideal NH." ♦ € 13.40 2009*

See advertisement

OCTON *10F1* (Rural) *43.66029, 3.32083* **Camping Le Village du Bosc (Naturist), Chemin de Ricazouls, 34800 Octon [04 67 96 07 37; fax 04 67 96 35 75; www.villagedubosc.net]** Exit 54 or 55 fr N9/A75 dir Octon onto D148, foll sp to Ricazouls/site. Med, terr, pt shd; wc; chem disp; shwrs; el pnts (6A) inc; rest; snacks; bar; shop; Indtte; playgrnd; htd pool; lake sw; watersports; 20% statics; dogs €2 (restricted area only); poss cr; adv bkg; INF card. "Lovely, quiet site with wooded walks; friendly owners; clean facs; tight turns on terr access for lge o'fits; Octon vill pretty." ♦ 1 Apr-30 Sep. € 24.70 2009*

OCTON *10F1* (4km E Rural) *43.64838, 3.32235* **Aire Naturelle Les Arcades (Gros-Fromenty), Lac-de-Salagou, 34800 Octon [04 67 96 99 13]** Sp fr Octon. Sm, pt shd; wc; chem disp (wc); shwrs inc; no el pnts; BBQ; fishing nrby; quiet. "Excel clean & tidy; lge pitches under acacia trees; gd views; vg." 15 May-30 Sep. € 14.50 2007*

OCTON *10F1* (600m SE Rural) *43.65100, 3.30877* **Camping Le Mas des Carles, 34800 Octon [04 67 96 32 33]** Leave A75 at junc 54, foll sp for Octon, 100m after vill sp turn L & foll white site sp keeping L. Ent on L opp tel kiosk (sharp turn). Sm, some hdg/mkd pitch, pt sl, terr, pt shd, pt shd; wc; chem disp; shwrs inc; el pnts (6-10A) inc; Indtte; Indry rm; shop 500m; rest adj; playgrnd; pool; boating/watersports in lake 800m; 30% statics; dogs; phone; poss cr; adv bkg; quiet; ccard not acc; CCI. "Pleasant site with views; facs a little tired; helpful owner; take care low branches on pitches - diff for c'vans; Lac de Salagou with abandoned vill of Celles 1km." Easter-30 Sep. € 20.90 2009*

OFFRANVILLE see Dieppe *3C2*

OLARGUES *8F4* (N Rural) **Camp Municipal Le Baoüs, 34390 Olargues [04 67 97 71 26 or 04 67 97 71 50; otsi.olargues@wanadoo.fr; www.olargues.org]** Take D908 W fr Bédarieux, site immed bef ent Olargues. Site sp over sm bdge on L. At end of bdge turn R to site. Last 50m rough track & narr turn into site. Sm, pt shd; wc (cont); chem disp; shwrs inc; el pnts (6A) €2.20; shop 300m; playgrnd; canoeing; cycle hire; internet; adv bkg Jul/Aug; quiet. "Helpful warden; hill climb to services block; site poss flooded by Rv Jaur in spring." 15 May-15 Sep. 2006*

OLLIERES SUR EYRIEUX, LES *9D2* (Rural) *44.80733, 4.62933* **Eyrieux Camping, La Fereyre, 07360 Les Ollières-sur-Eyrieux [04 75 66 30 08; fax 04 75 66 63 76; blotjm@aol.com]** Exit D86 at Beauchastel via D21 to D120. In 15km site on L bef ent Les Ollières. App via 500m of steep, unmade single track rd with unexpected hairpin bend at bottom. For sm vans & experienced drivers only. Med, pt sl, terr, pt shd; wc; chem disp; shwrs inc; baby facs; el pnts (6A) inc; shop & 500m; rest; snacks; bar; playgrnd; pool; rv sw & fishing adj; tennis; games area; cycle hire; entmnt; dogs €2.30; adv bkg; quiet. ♦ Easter-17 Sep. € 21.50 2006*

OLLIERES SUR EYRIEUX, LES *9D2* (500m N Rural) *44.80730, 4.61500* **Camping Le Mas de Champel, Route de La Voulte-sur-Rhône, 07360 Les Ollières-sur-Eyrieux [04 75 66 23 23; fax 04 75 66 23 16; info@masdechampel.com; www.masdechampel.com]** Fr D86 W on D120 at La Voulte-sur-Rhône or D21 at Beauchastel. Rds join at St Laurent-du-Pape. Cont on D120, turn R soon after D2 on ent Les Ollières bef descent into vill. Site sp. Med, terr, unshd; wc; chem disp; shwrs inc; el pnts (10A) inc; Indtte; shops 1km; rest; snacks; bar; playgrnd; pool; paddling pool; fishing; canoeing; guided walks; cycle hire; archery; solarium; entmnt; some statics; poss cr; adv bkg; quiet. "Pleasant site in lovely countryside." ♦ 10 Apr-27 Sep. € 24.00 (CChq acc) 2009*

OLLIERES SUR EYRIEUX, LES *9D2* (1.7km E Rural) *44.80870, 4.63595* **Camping Le Domaine des Plantas, 07360 Les Ollières-sur-Eyrieux [04 75 66 21 53; fax 04 75 66 23 65; plantas.ardeche@wanadoo.fr; www.domainedesplantas.com or www.camping-franceloc.fr]** Exit A7 junc 16, cross Rv Rhône on N304 to Le Pouzin, then turn N thro La Voulte-sur-Rhône. Then take D120 sp St Fortunat, 20km to Les Ollières; over bdge, turn L & foll site sp. Med, hdg/mkd pitch, hdstg, terr, pt shd; wc; chem disp; mv service pnt; baby facs; shwrs inc; el pnts (10A) inc; gas; Indtte; shop & 2km; rest; snacks; bar; playgrnd; htd, covrd pool; rv sw & sand beach adj; fishing; hiking; games rm; 30% statics; dogs €3; Eng spkn; adv bkg ess; quiet; ccard acc; red low ssn; CCI. "Beautiful site in wondrous setting; well wooded; warm-hearted owners; gd san facs; c'vans can only leave when accompanied 0800, 0930 & 1100; 4x4 used to take c'vans up steep exit; excel." ♦ 5 Apr-4 Oct. € 31.00 2007*

OLLIERES SUR EYRIEUX, LES *9D2* (2.5km S Rural) *44.78155, 4.61790* **Camping Le Chambourlas, Chambon de Bavas, 07360 Les Ollières-sur-Eyrieux [04 75 66 24 31; fax 04 75 66 21 22; info@chambourlas.com; www.chambourlas.com]** Fr Privas take D2 dir Le Cheylard; site on R in 14km at Les Ollières. D2 a v slow, twisty rd. Steep site ent. Med, mkd pitch, shd; wc; chem disp; baby facs; shwrs inc; el pnts (10A) inc; gas; Indtte; shop; rest; snacks; bar; BBQ; playgrnd; pool; paddling pool; lake sw & fishing; canoe hire; games area; TV rm; 10% statics; dogs €2.50; adv bkg; ccard acc. "Lovely site; lge pitches; warm welcome; gd walks fr site." ♦ Easter-30 Sep. € 31.50 (CChq acc) 2009*

OLLIERES SUR EYRIEUX, LES *9D2* (10km NW Rural) *44.82895, 4.52295* **L'Ardechois Camping, Le Chambon, 07190 Gluiras [04 75 66 61 87; fax 04 75 66 63 67; ardechois.camping@wanadoo.fr; www.ardechois-camping.fr]** Exit A7 junc 15 or 16 & cross rv onto D86. Turn W at Beauchastel onto D120 dir Le Cheylard to St Sauveur. In St Sauveur foll D102 dir Mézilhac & St Pierreville. Site approx 8km on bank Rv Glueyre. Med, hdg/mkd pitch, terr, shd; htd wc (mainly cont); chem disp; mv service pnt; shwrs inc; el pnts (6-10A) inc; gas; Indtte; shop & 8km; tradsmn; rest high ssn; snacks; bar; playgrnd; htd pool; paddling pool; rv & sand beach adj; cycle hire; games area; internet; TV rm; 70% statics; dogs €4; Eng spkn; adv bkg ess in ssn; ccard acc; red low ssn/snr citizens; CCI. "Wonderful, friendly, family site in glorious countryside; helpful Dutch owners; excel rest; organised walks, picnics." ♦ 25 Apr-30 Sep. € 27.50 (CChq acc) 2008*

OLLIERGUES *9B1* (1.75km E Rural) *45.69008, 3.63289* **Camping Les Chelles, 63880 Olliergues [tel/fax 04 73 95 54 34; info@camping-les-chelles.com; www.camping-les-chelles.com]** Fr Olliergues take D37 N up hill dir Le Brugeron; then sharp L onto D87 dir La Chabasse; site sp. Med, hdg/mkd pitch, terr, shd; wc; chem disp; shwrs inc; el pnts (15A) €2.80; Indtte (inc dryer); shop 5km; rest; snacks; bar; playgrnd; pool; games area; games rm; wifi; TV; dogs €1; phone; Eng spkn; adv bkg; ccard acc. "Facs excel for families with young children; enthusiastic Dutch owners; gd walking; gd touring base; vg." ♦ 1 Apr-31 Oct. € 13.00 2009*

OLONNE SUR MER see Sables d'Olonne, Les *7A1*

OLONZAC *8F4* (6km N Rural) *43.3408, 2.7056* **Camping Le Mas de Lignières (Naturist), Montcélèbre, 34210 Cesseras-en-Minervois [tel/fax 04 68 91 24 86; lemas1@wanadoo.fr; www.lemasdelignieres.com]** Fr Olonzac go N on D182 thro Cesseras & cont N dir Fauzan. Look for R turn to Montcélèbre - site on R behind lge, clsd brown gates (intercom) - not easy to find. Care needed thro Cesseras. Sm, hdg/mkd pitch, hdstg, pt sl, pt shd; wc (some cont); chem disp; baby facs; fam bthrm; shwrs inc; el pnts (6A) inc; gas; Indtte; sm shop & 2km; tradsmn; covrd pool; tennis; library; TV rm; 5% statics; dogs €1.50; phone; poss cr; adv bkg; red 10 days; quiet; ccard acc; INF card ess & avail at site. "Well-run, scenic site in remote location; lge pitches; fair san facs; nearest supmkt in La Redorte (10km); vg walks." ♦ 26 Apr-30 Sep. € 25.50 2009*

⊞ **OLONZAC** *8F4* (9km E Rural) *43.28372, 2.82688* **FFCC Camping Les Auberges, 11120 Pouzols-Minervois [tel/fax 04 68 46 26 50; vero.pradal@neuf.fr; http://pagesperso-orange.fr/xanne/camping]** Fr D5 site 500m S of vill of Pouzols. Sm, mkd pitch, pt shd; wc; chem disp (wc); shwrs inc; el pnts (5A) €3.50; gas adj; Indtte; shop adj; playgrnd; pool; 30% statics; dogs; poss cr; Eng spkn; adv bkg rec; quiet; CCI. "V popular site; friendly owners; sm Sat mkt at 'cave' opp." € 11.50 2008*

OLORON STE MARIE *8F2* (2km W Urban) *43.17886, -0.62328* **Camping-Gîtes du Stade, Chemin de Lagravette, 64400 Oloron-Ste Marie [05 59 39 11 26; fax 05 59 36 12 01; camping-du-stade@wanadoo.fr; www.camping-du-stade.com]** Fr N on ring rd foll sp to Saragosse (Spain); at rndabt take 2nd exit onto D6 still sp Saragosse, site sp on R just after sports field. Fr S on D55 join ring rd & turn W at rndabt by McDonalds; sp. Med, hdg/mkd pitch, pt shd; wc; chem disp; shwrs inc; el pnts (6-10A) €4-6 (some rev pol); Indry rm; tradsmn; supmkt 1km; rest; snacks; playgrnd; pool adj; rv fishing & sw 1km; tennis; cycle hire; entmnts; TV; dogs €1.20; adv bkg; quiet; red low ssn; CCI. "Well-maintained site; lge pitches; clean facs but ltd low ssn & stretched high ssn; helpful staff; barrier clsd 1200-1500; excel base for Pyrenees; gd walking." 1 Apr-30 Sep. € 15.00 2009*

OMONVILLE LA ROGUE see Beaumont Hague *1C4*

ONESSE ET LAHARIE *8E1* (500m N Rural) *44.06344, -1.07257* **FFCC Camping Le Bienvenu, 259 Route de Mimizan, 40110 Onesse-et-Laharie [05 58 07 30 49 or 06 81 32 12 56 (mob); www.camping-onesse.fr]** On N10 Bordeaux-Bayonne rd, turn W onto D38 at Laharie. Site in 5km. Med, mkd pitch, pt shd; wc (some cont); chem disp; mv service pnt; shwrs inc; el pnts (10A) €4; Indtte; shop 100m; rest, bar adj; playgrnd; beach 20km; TV rm; some statics; dogs €1; adv bkg; quiet; red long stay; CCI. "Well-run, family site." 1 Mar-30 Sep. € 13.10 2008*

ONZAIN *4G2* (4km N Rural) *47.52620, 1.18718* **Camping Domaine de Dugny, 45 Route de Chambon-sur-Cisse, 41150 Onzain [02 54 20 70 66; fax 02 54 33 71 69; info@dugny.fr; www.siblu.com/domainededugny]** Exit A10 junc 17 Blois onto D952 (N152) dir Tours. After 16km at rndabt at bdge to Chaumont, turn N dir Onzain. Take D45 N dir Chambon-sur-Cisse to Cabinette. Site sp on a minor rd to L, beside sm lake. Site well sp fr Onzain cent. Lge, hdg/mkd pitch, hdstg, pt sl, pt shd; htd wc; chem disp; mv service pnt; serviced pitches; baby facs; fam bthrm; shwrs inc; el pnts (6-10A) inc; gas; Indtte; shop; tradsmn; rest; snacks; bar; BBQ; playgrnd; htd pool & paddling pool; waterslide; lake sw & 10km; fishing; cycle hire; games rm; games area; golf 8km; boules; boat hire; entmnt high ssn; ultra-light flights; internet; TV rm; 90% statics; dogs €4.50; train 4km; Eng spkn; adv bkg; quiet; ccard acc; red low ssn; CCI. "Peaceful site; v welcoming; clean san facs but v ltd low ssn; gd facs for children; poss diff in wet weather; chateaux close by - World Heritage site; gd NH." ♦ 15 Mar-29 Sep. € 50.00 2008*

ONZAIN *4G2* (1.5km SE Urban) *47.49081, 1.18847* **Camp Municipal, Ave Général de Gaulle, 41150 Onzain [02 54 20 85 15 or 02 54 51 20 40 (Mairie); fax 02 54 20 74 34; marie@ville-onzain.fr; www.ville-onzain.fr]** Fr N of Chaumont-sur-Loire, at rndabt at junc D952 (N152) & D1 take D1 N twds Onzain then take 1st turn on R. Foll sp. Sm, hdg pitch, pt sl, pt shd; wc (some cont); chem disp; shwrs inc; el pnts (10A) €1.95; gas; Indtte; shops 500m; playgrnd; dogs €1.53; no twin-axle vans; gates locked 2000-0800; poss cr; ccard not acc; CCI. "Central for Loire chateaux; clsd 2200-0800." ♦ 1 May-31 Aug. € 7.80 2008*

ONZAIN *4G2* (6km W Rural) *47.51030, 1.10400* **Yelloh! Village Le Parc du Val de Loire, 155 Route de Fleuray, 41150 Mesland [02 54 70 27 18; fax 02 54 70 21 71; parcduvaldeloire@wanadoo.fr; www.parcduvaldeloire.com]** Fr Blois take D952 (N152) SW twd Amboise. Approx 16km outside Blois turn R to Onzain & foll sp to Mesland; go thro Mesland vill & turn L dir Fleuray; site on R after 1.5km. Lge, hdg/mkd pitch, pt sl, pt shd; wc; chem disp; mv service pnt; some serviced pitches; baby facs; shwrs inc; el pnts (10A) inc; gas; Indtte; shop; tradsmn; rest; snacks; bar; BBQ; playgrnd; 2 pools (1 htd, covrd); paddling pool; waterslide; tennis; games area; cycle hire; wine-tasting; entmnt; wifi; games/TV rm; 30% statics; dogs €4; Eng spkn; adv bkg; ccard acc; red low ssn/CCI. "Secluded site; excursions to vineyards; mkt Thu Onzain; excel." ♦ 2 Apr-12 Sep. € 31.00 ABS - L02 2009*

OPIO see Grasse *10E4*

OPPEDE see Cavaillon *10E2*

ORANGE *10E2* (6km N Rural) *44.18303, 4.84985* **Camping La Ferme de Rameyron (Pellegrin), Chemin de Roard, Route de Camaret-sur-Aigues, 84830 Sérignan-du-Comtat [04 90 70 06 48]** Fr Orange on N7 dir Bollène turn R sp Sérignan-du-Comtat. In town cent turn R at x-rds sp Camaret. Turn 3rd R into Chemin de Roard. Site on L in 100m. Sm, pt shd; wc (some cont); chem disp; mv service pnt; shwrs inc; el pnts (10A) €1.50; gas, shops, rest, bar 800m; playgrnd; pool; dogs; poss cr; quiet; ccard acc. "Clean, pleasant, CL-type site but poss run down low ssn & cold shwrs; close to historic vill & autorte." 1 Jun-31 Aug. € 10.00 2006*

ORANGE *10E2* (10km NE Rural) *44.16222, 4.93531* **Aire Naturelle Domaine des Favards, Route d'Orange, 84150 Violès [04 90 70 90 93; fax 04 90 70 97 28; favards@free.fr; www.favards.com]** Fr N exit A7 junc 19 Bollène. Foll D8 dir Carpentras & Violès. In Violès foll dir Orange & look for camp sp. Fr S exit A7 junc 22 sp Carpentras, take dir Avignon, then dir Vaison-la-Romaine to Violès. Avoid cent of Orange when towing. Sm, hdg/mkd pitch, unshd; htd wc (some cont); baby facs; shwrs inc; el pnts (6-10A) €3 (poss rev pol); Indry rm; tradsmn; snacks; bar; playgrnd; pool; dogs €1; poss cr; Eng spkn; adv bkg; quiet; no ccard acc; red low ssn; CCI. "Well-kept site; excel pitches - some v lge (extra charge); superb san facs, poss stretched; wine-tasting on site high ssn; gd touring base; poss dust clouds fr Mistral wind; pitches muddy when wet; gd." ♦ 1 May-30 Sep. € 15.00 2009*

ORANGE *10E2* (8km SE Urban) *44.11472, 4.90314* **Camp Municipal Les Peupliers, Ave Pierre-de-Coubertin, 84150 Jonquières [04 90 70 67 09; fax 04 90 70 59 01]** Exit junc 22 fr A7 onto N7 S. In 2km turn L (E) onto D950. In 5km at rndabt turn L onto D977. In 200m turn L sp Jonquières, site on L in 2km, sp in vill. Site behind sports complex. Sp not obvious. Med, mkd pitch, pt shd; wc; chem disp; shwrs inc; el pnts (10A) €1.40; gas 500m; Indtte; shop, rest, snacks, bar 500m; playgrnd; pool, tennis adj; dogs €2.65; phone; poss cr; Eng spkn; adv bkg; noise fr airfield (week days); ccard not acc; CCI. "Excel, well-run, busy site; friendly & welcoming owners; vg, clean san facs; need care with high o'fits due trees; arr bef 1600; gates close 2200; Roman ruins nrby; popular long stay." 1 May-30 Sep. € 9.60 2008*

ORANGE *10E2* (1.5km NW Urban) *44.14666, 4.79541* **Camping Le Jonquier, 1321 Rue Alexis Carrel, 84100 Orange [04 90 34 49 48; fax 04 90 51 16 97; info@campinglejonquier.com; www.campinglejonquier.com]** Site N of Arc de Triomphe off N7; turn W at traff lts to site in 500m & foll site sp across rndabt, R at next rndabt. Med, hdg/mkd pitch, mostly unshd; wc (some cont); chem disp; baby facs; shwrs inc; el pnts (3-6A) €3-4; Indtte; shop; supmkt 500m; bar; playgrnd; htd pool; tennis; pony rides; some statics; dogs €5; poss cr; Eng spkn; quiet; ccard acc; red low ssn; CCI. "Helpful staff; unkempt low ssn; san facs poss stretched high ssn; ltd drinking water pnts; lge mkt Thurs." ♦ 1 Apr-30 Sep. € 25.50 2009*

ORBEC *3D1* (500m N Urban) *49.02829, 0.40857* **Camp Municipal Les Capucins, Rue des Frères Bigot, 14290 Orbec [02 31 32 76 22]** Exit A28 junc 15 to Orbec; on ent town foll site sp. If app fr D519 or D819 steep drag up to site & care req down to town. Sm, pt shd; wc; chem disp; shwrs inc; el pnts (10A) €2; shops 800m; playgrnd; dogs free; quiet. "Well-kept site; san facs old but clean; no twin-axles; delightful countryside." 24 May-8 Sep. € 7.40 2009*

ORBEY see Munster *6F3*

ORCET see Clermont Ferrand *9B1*

⊞ **ORCIVAL** *7B4* (6km NE Rural) *45.7067, 2.8593* **FFCC Camping La Haute Sioule, Route du Camping, 63210 St Bonnet-près-Orcival [04 73 65 83 32; fax 04 73 65 85 19; info@camping-auvergne.info; www.camping-auvergne.info]** Fr Clermont-Ferrand take N89 S then W twds La Bourboule for approx 20km. At junc with D216 turn L twds Orcival. Site in 4km. Foll site sp. Med, sl, pt shd; wc; mv service pnt; shwrs inc; el pnts (4-13A) €2.70-5.90; gas; Indtte; shops 250m; snacks; playgrnd; rv sw adj; golf; fishing adj; games rm; entmnt; 50% statics; dogs free; poss cr; Eng spkn; CCI. "Owners friendly; pleasant site late ssn but poss untidy; ltd facs low ssn & if no recep site self; poss diff lge o'fits; gd views; fair NH." € 14.00 2008*

ORCIVAL *7B4* (5km W Rural) *45.68388, 2.79926* **Camp Municipal La Buge, 63210 Rochefort-Montagne [04 73 65 84 98 or 04 73 65 82 51; fax 04 73 65 93 69; mairie.rochefort@rochefort-montagne.com]** Fr NE on D2089 (N89). Thro vill L after x-ing bdge. Sp 200m R. Med, pt shd; wc; chem disp; shwrs inc; el pnts (15A) €2.65; Indtte; shop adj; playgrnd; rv 500m; tennis; dogs €0.90; adv bkg. 1 Jun-15 Sep. € 8.80 (3 persons) 2006*

ORINCLES see Bagneres de Bigorre *8F2*

ORLEANS *4F3* (10km E Rural) *47.88830, 2.02744* **Camp Municipal Les Pâtures, 55 Chemin du Port, 45430 Chécy [02 38 91 13 27]** Take D960 E twd Châteauneuf. In Chécy, foll site sp. Access thro town via narr streets. Med, hdg pitch, pt shd; wc; chem disp; mv service pnt; shwrs €0.30/3 mins; el pnts (16A) €3.80; Indtte; shop 1km; BBQ; tennis; fishing; golf 5km; no statics; dogs €1; Eng spkn; adv bkg; some noise fr adj site; CCI. "Superb, well-run site on Rv Loire; vg location; friendly, helpful warden; excel san facs; conv Orléans; poss open bef & after dates given; popular NH." ♦ 28 May-3 Sep. € 12.00 2009*

France

ORLEANS *4F3* (4km S Rural) *47.85603, 1.92555* **Camp Municipal d'Olivet, Rue du Pont-Bouchet, 45160 Olivet [02 38 63 53 94 or 02 38 63 82 82 (Mairie); fax 02 38 63 58 96; campingolivet@wanadoo.fr; www.camping-olivet.org]** To avoid height restriction, best app fr A71 exit junc 2 onto N271 dir Orléans-La Source. Cont on N271 until rd crosses N20 into Rue de Bourges. Pass commercial estate & hotel on L & turn L at traff lts into Rue de Châteauroux. Pass university (Parc Technologique), cross tramway & turn L at traff lts onto D14, Rue de la Source, then in 500m turn R (watch for pharmacy on L & green site sp) into Rue to Pont-Bouchet (narr rd). Sp from Olivet but sps diff to pick out (sm, green). NB Beware height restrictions on junc underpasses in Orléans cent. Med, hdg pitch, pt sl, pt shd; htd wc (some cont); chem disp; shwrs inc; el pnts (16A) €2.30; lndtte; shop 500m; tradsmn; snacks; playgrnd; dogs €2.05; bus/tram 200m (secure car park); poss cr; Eng spkn; adv bkg rec, confirm by tel bef 1800 (booking fee & dep); quiet - poss noisy at w/end; red long stay; CCI. "Well-run, busy, friendly site by Rv Loiret; vg san facs inc disabled; tram service into town; vineyards nr; gd walking." ♦ 1 Apr-15 Oct. € 14.10 2009*

ORLEAT see Thiers *9B1*

ORNANS *6G2* (6km SE Rural) *47.06366, 6.22277* **Camp Municipal Le Pré Bailly, 25840 Vuillafans [03 81 60 91 52; fax 03 81 60 95 68; mairie.vuillafans@wanadoo.fr; www.vuillafans.fr]** Site sp fr D67 adj Rv Loue. Sm, mkd pitch, terr, pt shd; htd wc; shwrs inc; el pnts (4-10A) €2-4.80; shop 300m; rest, bar 200m; playgrnd; fishing; canoeing; phone adj; quiet. "Simple site in pretty vill; gd walks; site yourself, warden calls." 15 Mar-30 Sep. € 8.90 2008*

ORNANS *6G2* (11km SE Rural) *47.04132, 6.26024* **Camp Municipal Le Champaloux, 25930 Lods [03 81 60 90 11 (Mairie); fax 03 81 60 93 86; mairie.lods@wanadoo.fr]** Fr Ornans SE on D67. In Lods turn R across Rv Loue. Site in 150m beside rv. Or N fr Pontarlier on N57/E23 to St Gorgon then W on D67 to Lods. Med, pt shd, hdstg; wc; mv service pnt; shwrs inc; el pnts (16A) €2.80; shop 1.5km; playgrnd; fishing; quiet. "Lovely, peaceful site by rv; on disused rlwy stn in attractive area; friendly, helpful warden; excel shwrs; site yourself, office open eves; vg rest 200m; woodland walks." 15 Jun-16 Sep. € 8.00 2009*

ORNANS *6G2* (1km S Rural) *47.10070, 6.12795* **Camping Domaine Le Chanet, 9 Chemin de Chanet, 25290 Ornans [03 81 62 23 44; fax 03 81 62 13 97; contact@lechanet.com; www.lechanet.com]** Fr Besançon take D67 25km to Ornans. In Ornans at rndabt cont to town cent. Take 1st R, cross Rv Loue then turn R. Foll sp to site in 1km. Look for R turn after school. Med, hdg pitch, steep sl & terr, pt shd; htd wc; chem disp; mv service pnt; baby facs; shwrs inc; el pnts (3-10A) €3-3.50; lndtte; shop; tradsmn; snacks; bar; BBQ; sm playgrnd; htd pool 500m; rv 1km; games area; many statics; dogs €1.50; phone; poss cr; adv bkg; quiet; red low ssn. "Picturesque site; sm pitches; facs poss stretched in ssn." ♦ 28 Mar-25 Oct. € 17.40 2009*

ORPIERRE *9D3* (500m E Rural) *44.31110, 5.69650* **Camping Les Princes d'Orange, Flonsaine, 05700 Orpierre [04 92 66 22 53; fax 04 92 66 31 08; campingorpierre@wanadoo.fr; www.campingorpierre.com]** N75 S fr Serres for 11km to Eyguians. Turn R in Eyguians onto D30, 8km to Orpierre, turn L in vill to site (sp). Med, mkd pitch, hdstg, pt sl, terr, pt shd; wc; chem disp; mv service pnt; baby facs; shwrs inc; el pnts (4A) €3.10; gas; lndtte; shop; snacks; bar; playgrnd; htd pool; waterslide; tennis; games area; entmnt; TV; fishing; some statics; dogs €1.50; adv bkg; red low ssn. "Rock-climbing area; gd walking; beautiful vill." ♦
1 Apr-28 Oct. € 20.00 (3 persons) 2007*

The opening dates and prices on this campsite have changed. I'll send a site report form to the Club for the next edition of the guide.

ORTHEZ *8F1* (1.5km SE Rural) *43.48793, -0.75882* **Camping La Source, Blvd Charles de Gaulle, 64300 Orthez [05 59 67 04 81; fax 05 59 67 02 38; info@camping-orthez.com; www.camping-orthez.com]** Leave Orthez on D817 (N117) twd Pau, turn L at sp Mont-de-Marsan & site on R in 300m. Sm, pt sl, some hdstg, ltd shd; wc; mv service pnt; shwrs inc; chem disp; el pnts (10A) €3.50; tradsmn; snacks; playgrnd; pool 2km; fishing; some statics; dogs €1.50; phone; v quiet; red low ssn; CCI. "Peaceful, basic but well-maintained site; friendly & helpful staff; gd, clean facs; some pitches soft in wet weather; gd security; rec."
1 Apr-31 Oct. € 14.20 2008*

OUILLY DU HOULEY see Lisieux *3D1*

OUISTREHAM *3D1* (1km S Urban) *49.26909, -0.25498* **Camp Municipal Les Pommiers, Rue de la Haie Breton, 14150 Ouistreham [tel/fax 02 31 97 12 66; campingpommiers.orb@wanadoo.fr]** Fr ferry terminal foll sp Caen on D84 (Rue de l'Yser/Ave du Grand Large); in approx 1.5km site sp at rndabt; take 3rd exit. Lge, hdg pitch, pt shd; htd wc; chem disp; mv service pnt; shwrs inc; el pnts (6A) €3; gas; lndry rm; supmkt 500m; tradsmn; playgrnd; pool 1km; sand beach 1.8km; tennis; rv 200m; 80% statics; poss cr; Eng spkn; no adv bkg; some rd noise; ccard acc; CCI. "Conv for late or early ferry (5 mins to terminal); v busy high ssn; sep section for 'Brittany Ferries' tourers; gates open 0700-2300 (open automatic outgoing at other times); friendly, efficient recep; san facs gd but basic, stretched high ssn; walk/cycle along canal to Ouistreham; no twin-axles; mkt Thur; vg NH." 15 Feb-15 Dec. € 12.80 2009*

⊞ **OUISTREHAM** *3D1* (6km S Rural) *49.23838, -0.25763* **FFCC Camping des Capucines, 14860 Ranville [02 31 78 69 82; fax 02 31 78 16 94]** App Caen fr E or W, take Blvd Péripherique Nord, then exit 3a sp Ouistreham car ferry (D515). In approx 8.5km turn R onto D514 sp Cabourg, cross Pegasus Bdge & foll sp Ranville across 2 rndabts; at x-rds in 500m turn L (at sm campsite sp); site in 300m on L. Fr Ouistreham foll D514 dir Caborg to Pegasus Bdge, then as above. Med, hdg/mkd pitch, terr, pt shd; htd wc; chem disp; mv service pnt; baby facs; shwrs inc; el pnts (6-10A) €3.10-3.70 (poss rev pol); gas; Indtte; sm shop; supmkt 2km; rest, bar 1km; playgrnd; sand beach 3km; 60% statics; dogs €1.80; phone; bus 500m; poss cr; some Eng spkn; adv bkg if arr late; quiet; ccard acc; red low ssn/CCI. "Excel site in pleasant position; some pitches sm; gd clean san facs; helpful, friendly owner; barrier open 0600-2400; take care o'hanging trees; conv ferries (if arr late fr ferry, phone in advance for pitch number & barrier code & use intercom at recep); conv Pegasus Bdge, museum & war cemetery; vg." € 15.00 2009*

OUISTREHAM *3D1* (3km SW Urban) *49.24970, -0.27190* **Camping Les Hautes Coutures, Route de Ouistreham, 14970 Bénouville [02 31 44 73 08 or 06 07 25 26 90 (mob LS); fax 02 31 95 30 80; info@campinghautescoutures.com; www.campinghautescoutures.com]** Leave Ouistreham ferry & foll sp Caen & A13 over 2 rndabts. After 2nd rndabt join dual c'way. Leave at 1st exit (D35) sp St Aubin d'Arquenay & ZA de Bénouville. Turn R at end of slip rd, then L at T-junc; site in 200m uphill on R. Or fr Caen twd port on dual c'way, site has own exit shortly after Pegasus Memorial Bdge exit; site clearly visible on R of dual c'way. Med, hdg pitch, pt sl & uneven, pt shd; htd wc; chem disp (wc); baby facs; shwrs inc; el pnts (6A) inc (rev pol)(adaptors avail); Indtte; sm shop; hypmkt at Hérouville; tradsmn; rest, snacks; bar; BBQ; playgrnd; htd pool; beach 2km; fishing; tennis; horseriding, windsurfing 1km; golf 4km; entmnt; wifi; games/TV rm; 90% statics; dogs €1.50; poss cr; Eng spkn; adv bkg; ccard acc; red low ssn; CCI. "Busy, poss noisy site o'verlooking Caen Canal; friendly staff; sm pitches; ltd el pnts; gates clsd 2200-0630 but staff will open for late ferry arrivals; cycle path to Caen; daily mkt in Ouistreham. "Conv NH only; ltd el pnts." ♦ 1 Apr-31 Oct. € 34.10 ABS - N05 2009*

OUISTREHAM *3D1* (7km W Coastal) *49.2915, -0.3017* **Camping des Hautes Sentes, Chemin des Hautes Sentes, 14880 Hermanville [02 31 96 39 12; fax 02 31 96 92 98; leshautessentes@yahoo.fr; www.campingdeshautessentes.fr]** Well sp on D514 W fr Ouistreham. Med, hdg/mkd pitch, pt shd; wc; chem disp; shwrs inc; el pnts (6A) €2; Indtte; tradsmn; snacks; bar; playgrnd; beach 700m; games area; entmnt; TV rm; 90% statics; dogs €1.52; bus 400m; Eng spkn; quiet. "Friendly, pleasant site; clean facs; few tourist pitches." 1 Apr-30 Sep. € 16.70 2009*

OUISTREHAM *3D1* (12km NW Coastal) *49.31799, -0.35824* **Camp Municipal Capricieuse, 2 Rue Brummel, 14530 Luc-sur-Mer [02 31 97 34 43; fax 02 31 97 43 64; info@campinglacapricieuse.com; www.campinglacapricieuse.com]** Fr ferry terminal turn R at 3rd traff lts (D514) into Ave du G. Leclerc. Cont to Luc-sur-Mer; 1st turn L after casino; site on R in 300m. Ave Lecuyer is sp & Rue Brummel is off that rd. Lge, hdg/mkd pitch, terr, pt shd; wc; mv service pnt; chem disp; shwrs inc; el pnts (6-10A) €4.40-5.95; gas; Indtte; shop 300m; tradsmn; playgrnd; sand beach adj; tennis; games rm; entmnt; excursions; wifi; TV rm; dogs €2.35; Eng spkn; adv bkg by wk only; quiet; ccard acc; red low ssn; CCI. "Some lge pitches with easy access; gd position - conv WW2 beaches; clean; ltd facs low ssn; excel site." ♦ 1 Apr-30 Sep. € 14.40 2008*

OUNANS *6H2* (1km N Rural) *47.00290, 5.66550* **Kawan Village La Plage Blanche, 3 Rue de la Plage, 39380 Ounans [03 84 37 69 63; fax 03 84 37 60 21; reservation@la-plage-blanche.com; www.la-plage-blanche.com]** Exit A39 junc 6 sp Dole Centre. Foll N5 SE for 18km dir Pontarlier. After passing Souvans, turn L on D472 sp Mont-sous-Vaudrey. Foll sp to Ounans. Site well sp in vill. Lge, mkd pitch, hdstg, pt shd; wc; chem disp; mv service pnt; shwrs inc; el pnts (10A) €4 (poss rev pol); gas 1km; Indtte; shop 1km; supmkt 4km; tradsmn; rest; snacks; bar; playgrnd; pool; paddling pool; shgl rv beach & sw 500m; trout & carp fishing lake; canoeing; horseriding; entmnt; TV rm; 1% statics; dogs €1.50; Eng spkn; adv bkg rec (bkg fee); quiet; red low ssn; ccard acc; CCI. "Friendly recep; excel san facs; superb rvside pitches; gd rest." ♦ 1 Apr-12 Oct. € 19.00 (CChq acc) 2008*

OURSEL MAISON see Crèvecoeur le Grand *3C3*

OUSSE see Pau *8F2*

OUST *8G3* (2km N Rural) *42.89343, 1.21381* **Camp Municipal La Claire, Rue La Palere, 09140 Soueix-Rogalle [05 61 66 84 88; campinglaclaire@orange.fr]** S fr St Girons take D3/D618; in 13km just bef rndabt turn R onto D32 sp Soueix. Turn R at vill sq & site in 200m. Sm, pt shd; htd wc (cont); shwrs inc; el pnts (10A) €3; Indtte; shop 1.5km; rest 200m; playgrnd; paddling pool; fishing; 10% statics; dogs €1; phone; quiet; CCI. "Pleasant, well-maintained, rvside site; lge pitches." 1 Apr-31 Oct. € 10.00 2008*

⊞ **OUST** *8G3* (9km SE Rural) *42.81105, 1.25558* **Camping Le Montagnou, Route de Seix, Le Trein-d'Ustou, 09140 Ustou [05 61 66 94 97; fax 05 61 66 91 20; campinglemontagnou@wanadoo.fr; www.lemontagnou.com]** Fr Oust SE on D3 & D8 (via Seix) dir Aulus, approx 13km by rd. Site sp. Med, hdg pitch, pt shd; htd wc; chem disp; shwrs inc; el pnts (10A) inc; Indtte; mini shop, tradsmn & snacks (Jul/Aug); rest nr; BBQ; playgrnd; fishing; rv sw 3km; tennis; skiing 9km; 15% statics; dogs €1.50; phone; poss cr; adv bkg; quiet; ccard acc; CCI. "Well-situated, well-run rvside site; mountain views; gd sized pitches; friendly British owners; gd walking; highly rec." ♦ € 16.00 2009*

France

OUST *8G3* (S Rural) *42.87042, 1.21947* **Camping Les Quatre Saisons, Route d'Aulus-les-Bains, 09140 Oust [05 61 96 55 55; camping.ariege@gmail.com; www.camping4saisons.com]** Take D618 S fr St Girons; then D3 to Oust; on N o'skts of town turn L (sp Aulus) onto D32; in 1km site on R nr Rv Garbet. Med, hdg pitch, pt shd; htd wc; chem disp; shwrs inc; el pnts (5-10A) €2.80-5.60; Indtte; shop 200m; bar; playgrnd; pool; games area; TV; 25% statics; dogs €1.50; phone; Eng spkn; adv bkg rec; quiet; ccard acc; red low ssn; CCI. "In beautiful, unspoilt area; friendly site; footpath to vill; excel." 7 Mar-30 Sep. € 17.50 2009*

⊞ **OUST** *8G3* (2.5km S Rural) *42.87085, 1.20663* **Camping Le Haut Salat, La Campagne-d'en Bas, 09140 Seix [05 61 66 81 78; fax 05 61 66 94 17; info@camping-haut-salat.com; www.camping-haut-salat.com]** Take D618 S fr St Girons, at Oust take D3 twds Seix. Site well sp just N of vill nr rv. Med, hdg/mkd pitch, pt shd; htd wc; baby facs; shwrs inc; el pnts (5-10A) inc (long lead req); Indtte; shops 500m; bar; BBQ; htd pool; fishing; games area; games rm; entmnt; TV; 85% statics; dogs; clsd last week Oct, 1st week Nov & last week Dec; adv bkg; quiet; CCI. "Gd facs; gd walking area; pitches poss not open winter, phone ahead." € 20.00 2008*

OYE PLAGE see Calais *3A3*

OYONNAX *9A3* (8km E Rural) *46.25530, 5.55705* **Camping Les Gorges de l'Oignin, Rue du Lac, 01580 Matafelon-Granges [04 74 76 80 97; camping.lesgorgesdeloignin@wanadoo.fr; www.gorges-de-loignin.com]** Exit A404 junc 9 onto D979 dir Bourg-en-Bresse; in 700m turn R onto D18 to Matafelon-Granges; foll sp. NB Fr Oyonnax 22km by rd. Med, hdg/mkd pitch, hdstg, terr, pt shd; htd wc; chem disp; baby facs; shwrs inc; el pnts (10A) €3.10; Indtte; ltd shop or 3km; rest; snacks; bar; BBQ; playgrnd; 3 pools; lake sw adj; games area; wifi; TV rm; 10% statics; dogs €2; phone; Eng spkn; adv bkg; quiet; red low ssn; CCI. "Beautiful site on lake - boat launching; friendly, helpful staff; Jura National Park; Rv Ain gorges; excel." 1 Apr-30 Sep. € 20.20 2009*

PACAUDIERE, LA *9A1* (200m E Rural) *46.17512, 3.87639* **Camp Municipal Beausoleil, Route de Vivans, 42310 La Pacaudière [04 77 64 11 50 or 04 77 64 30 18 (Mairie); fax 04 77 64 14 40; lapacaudiere@wanadoo.fr]** NW on N7 Roanne to Lapalisse; turn R in La Pacaudière, D35; site well sp; fork R in 50m; site ent in 400m. Sm, hdg pitch, hdstg, sl, unshd; wc; chem disp; shwrs inc; el pnts (10A) €2.90; gas; Indtte; shop; supmkt 500m; playgrnd; public pool high ssn; TV rm; quiet. "Pleasant NH in interesting area; ltd facs low ssn; Sat mkt." 1 May-30 Sep. € 8.70 2009*

⊞ **PAIMBOEUF** *2G3* (Urban/Coastal) *47.28907, -2.03964* **Camp Municipal de l'Estuaire, 44560 Paimboeuf [02 40 27 52 12; fax 02 40 27 61 14; info@camping-lestuaire.com; www.camping-lestuaire.com]** Fr St Nazaire on D77; turn L at rndabt imm after town sp; site on L in 300m. Med, pt shd; htd wc; shwrs inc; el pnts (10A) €3.85 (poss rev pol & poss long lead req); Indtte; supmkt 3km; bar; crêperie rest adj; playgrnd; pool; rv adj; cycle hire; entmnt; dogs €1.25; adv bkg; red low ssn; CCI. "Poss itinerants." € 11.50 2007*

PAIMPOL *1D3* (2km SE Coastal) *48.76966, -3.02209* **Camp Municipal Crukin, Ave Crukin, Kérity, 22500 Paimpol [02 96 20 78 47 or 02 96 55 31 70 (Mairie); fax 02 96 20 75 00; camping.cruckin@wanadoo.fr]** On D786 fr St Brieuc/Paimpol, site sp in vill of Kérity 80m off main rd. Med, hdg pitch, pt shd; htd wc; chem disp; mv service pnt; shwrs inc; el pnts (6-12A) €2.40-2.69; Indtte; shops 1km; playgrnd; shgl beach 250m; fishing; watersports; TV rm; 10% statics; dogs €1.12; bus 100m; poss cr; quiet; CCI. "Clean & tidy; excel sh stay/NH." ♦ 1 Apr-30 Sep. € 12.20 2006*

PAIMPOL *1D3* (5km SE Coastal) *48.75993, -2.96233* **FFCC Camping Le Cap Horn, Port-Lazo, 22470 Plouézec [02 96 20 64 28; fax 02 96 20 63 88; lecaphorn@hotmail.com; www.lecaphorn.com]** Site sp fr D786 at Plouézec dir Port-Lazo. Site 3km NE of Plouézec. Med, hdg/mkd pitch, pt sl, terr, pt shd; wc; chem disp; baby facs; shwrs inc; el pnts (6A) inc (poss rev pol); gas; Indtte; shop; rest 1km; snacks; bar; playgrnd; htd pool; paddling pool; direct access to shgl beach 500m; boating; games rm; entmnt; 20% statics; dogs €1; adv bkg; quiet; ccard acc; red low ssn/long stay/CCI. "On 2 levels in valley & hillside; sea views; steep path to beach; gd facs; gd." ♦ 15 Apr-31 Oct. € 25.00 2009*

PAIMPONT see Plélan le Grand *2F3*

PALAU DEL VIDRE see Elne *10G1*

⊞ **PALAVAS LES FLOTS** *10F1* (500m N Coastal) *43.53000, 3.92400* **Aire Communale/Camping-Car Halte, Base Fluviale Paul Riquer, 34250 Palavas-les-Flots [04 67 07 73 45 or 04 67 07 73 48; fax 04 67 50 61 04]** Fr Montpellier on D986 to Palavas. On ent town at 1st rndabt 'Europe' foll sp Base Fluviale & site sp. Med, mkd pitch, hdstg, pt shd; wc; chem disp; mv service pnt; shwrs inc; el pnts (16A) €2; Indtte; shop, rest, snacks, bar adj; sand beach 500m; phone; bus 200m; poss cr; some rd noise; ccard acc; CCI. "M'vans only; special elec cable req - obtain fr recep (dep); some pitches on marina quay; conv Montpellier, Camargue; 3 night max stay." € 10.00 2008*

PALAVAS LES FLOTS *10F1* (1km NE Coastal) *43.53346, 3.94820* **Camping Montpellier Plage, 95 Ave St Maurice, 34250 Palavas-les-Flots [04 67 68 00 91; fax 04 67 68 10 69; camping.montpellier.plage@wanadoo.fr; www.domaine-saint-maurice.com]** Site on D21ES on o'skts of vill twd Carnon. V Lge, pt mkd pitch, pt shd; wc (some cont); chem disp; shwrs inc; mv service pnt; el pnts (4A) inc; gas; Indtte; shops; tradsmn; rest; snacks; bar; BBQ; playgrnd; pool with spa facs; paddling pool; sand beach adj; games area; 50% statics; dogs; poss cr; Eng spkn; adv bking; noisy; CCI. "Gd location; basic san facs but lge pitches & friendliness of site outweigh this; easy walk into Palavas - interesting sm port; flamingoes on adjoining lake; gd." ♦ 14 Apr-9 Sep. € 30.30 2007*

PALAVAS LES FLOTS *10F1* (2km E Urban/Coastal) *43.53867, 3.96076* **Camping Les Roquilles, 267b Ave St Maurice, 34250 Palavas-les-Flots [04 67 68 03 47; fax 04 67 68 54 98; roquilles@wanadoo.fr; www.camping-les-roquilles.fr]** Exit A9 junc 30 onto D986 dir Palavas. In Palavas foll sp Carnon-Plage on D62, site sp. V lge, mkd pitch, hdstg, pt shd; wc (mainly cont); chem disp; mv service pnt; serviced pitches; shwrs inc; el pnts (6A) €3.90; gas 100m; Indtte; rest; snacks; bar; playgrnd; 3 pools (1 htd); waterslide; sand beach 100m; entmnt; TV; 30% statics; no dogs; phone; bus; poss cr; Eng spkn; adv bkg; poss noisy high ssn; ccard acc; red low ssn/long stay; CCI. "Excel pizza bar on site." 15 Apr-15 Sep. € 23.20 2008*

PALAVAS LES FLOTS *10F1* (1.5km SW Coastal) *43.51972, 3.90959* **Camping Palavas, Route de Maguelone, 34250 Palavas-Les-Flots [04 67 68 01 28 or 06 62 42 34 43 (mob); www.palavas-camping.fr]** Exit A9 junc 30 onto D986 dir Palavas-Les-Flots; cross bdge; turn R at rndabt, foll sp Maguelone; sit on L in 1km. Lge, hdg/mkd pitch, hdstg, pt shd; wc; chem disp; m'van water refill; baby facs; shwrs inc; el pnts (6A) inc; Indtte; supmkt; rest; snacks; bar; playgrnd; pool; paddling pool; spa pool; beach adj; games area; games rm; infant club; 30% statics; dogs €2.50; phone adj; bus 1.5km; poss cr; Eng spkn; w/e disco noise some pitches; red low ssn. "Great views; gd pool area; sep car park; vg." 16 Apr-15 Sep. € 38.00 2009*

PALINGES *9A2* (1km N Rural) *46.56118, 4.22516* **Camp Municipal du Lac, Le Fourneau, 71430 Palinges [03 85 88 14 49 or 06 06 88 14 49 (mob); jeroenvs@wxs.nl; http://home.planet.nl/~jeroenvs]** N70 Montceau-les-Mines dir Paray, turn L onto D92 into Palinges cent (4km). By church turn L church onto D128. Site in 1km. Sm, hdg/mkd pitch, pt sl, pt shd; htd wc; chem disp; baby facs; shwrs inc; el pnts (10A) inc; Indtte; shop, rest 1km; snacks; bar; playgrnd; lake fishing adj; cycle hire; tennis; dogs €1.60; adv bkg; Eng spkn; quiet; no ccard acc; CCI. "Excel, immac, friendly site; highly rec." ♦ 1 Apr-30 Oct. € 16.80 2008*

PALME, LA see Sigean *10G1*

PALMYRE, LA see Mathes, Les *7B1*

PALUD SUR VERDON, LA *10E3* (1km E Rural) *43.78042, 6.34882* **Camp Municipal Le Grand Canyon, Route de Castellane, 04120 La Palud-sur-Verdon [tel/fax 04 92 77 38 13 or 02 92 77 30 87 (Mairie); campinglapalud@wanadoo.fr]** W on D952 fr Castellane, site on L (S) of rd just bef vill La Palud (30km W of Castellane, max gradient 1-in-8). Or on D952 fr Moustiers-Ste-Marie site on R (S) after leaving vill La Palud (also with steep & narr sections). App fr Moustiers easier. Med, mkd pitch, pt sl, pt shd; wc (some cont); chem disp; mv service pnt; baby facs; shwrs inc; el pnts (10A €3.20 (poss rev pol); gas 800m; Indtte; shops, rest, snacks, bar 500m; dogs €0.50; phone; poss cr; quiet; ccard not acc. "Basic facs but well-kept; helpful staff; interesting area; conv Gorge du Verdon." ♦ 15 Apr-30 Sep. € 9.70 2008*

PAMIERS *8F3* (800m N Rural) *43.12490, 1.60195* **Camping L'Apamée, Route d'Ecosse, 09100 Pamiers [tel/fax 05 61 60 06 89; nfo@lapamee.com; www.lapamee.com]** Fr N on D820 (N20), at traff lts turn R & cross narr bdge over Rv Ariège, Pont du Jeu du Mail, site sp. Med, shd; htd wc; chem disp; mv service pnt; baby facs; shwrs inc; el pnts (10A) inc; Indtte; shop 800m; tradsmn; snacks; bar; BBQ; playgrnd; htd pool; rv fishing; tennis 100m; games rm; cycle hire; TV rm; 5% statics; dogs €2; phone; o'night area for m'vans; adv bkg; quiet but rd noise; red low ssn; CCI. "Clean, modern facs; helpful staff; unkempt & v ltd facs early ssn; excel." ♦ 22 Mar-31 Oct. € 22.00 (CChq acc) 2008*

PAMPELONNE *8E4* (2km NE Rural) *44.12685, 2.25681* **Camping Thuriès, 81190 Pampelonne [05 63 76 44 01; fax 05 63 76 92 78; campthuries@wanadoo.fr]** N fr Carmaux on N88 turn L onto D78 sp Pampelonne. Site sp & 2km fr town over narr bdge; steep, winding rd. Or S fr Rodez on N88 turn R onto D17 sp Pampelonne. Site bef rv bdge on L. Sm, mkd pitch, shd; htd wc; chem disp; mv service pnt; shwrs inc; el pnts (6A) inc; Indtte; shop & 3km; tradsmn; rest, snacks 3km; dogs; phone; poss cr; Eng spkn; quiet; CCI. "Pleasant site; conv Albi & Rodez." 15 Jun-1 Sep. € 15.70 2009*

PARAY LE MONIAL *9A1* (1km NW Urban) *46.45750, 4.10472* **Camping de Mambré, Route du Gué-Léger, 71600 Paray-le-Monial [03 85 88 89 20; fax 03 85 88 87 81]** Fr N79 Moulin to Mâcon; site at W end of town; just after level x-ing turn NE into Rte du Gué-Léger. Turn R into site after x-ing rv; well sp. Lge, hgd/mkd pitch, pt shd; wc; chem disp; shwrs inc; el pnts (10A) inc; Indtte; sm shop & 500m; rest; snacks in high ssn; bar; playgrnd; pool 200m high ssn; dogs; quiet, but some rd noise; CCI. "Paray is pilgrimage cent; ltd facs low ssn & poss poorly maintained." 15 May-30 Sep. € 18.20 2008*

France

PARCEY see Dole *6H2*

PARENTIS EN BORN *7D1* (2km W Rural) *44.34593, -1.10106* **FFCC Camp Municipal Pipiou, Route du Lac, 40160 Parentis-en-Born [05 58 78 57 25; fax 05 58 78 93 17; pipiou@parentis.com; www.parentis.com]** Site on D43 rd twds lake beach. In vill foll sp 'Lac'. After 2km where rest on R, turn R. Site is 150m on R. Lge, hdg/mkd pitch, pt shd; wc; chem disp; mv service pnt; 100% serviced pitches; baby facs; shwrs inc; el pnts (10A) €3.50 (poss rev pol); gas high ssn; lndtte; shop; rest; snacks; bar; playgrnd; lake sw & sand beach adj, fishing & watersports adj; entmnts; TV; 25% statics; dogs €1.30; phone; poss cr; adv bkg; quiet but pitches adj rd noisy; ccard acc; red low ssn/long stay/CCI. "Lovely lakeside location; phone to check open low ssn; some pitches tight; facs stretched high ssn; cycle tracks thro vill & woods; office not open w/ends low ssn or public hols when access/leaving site not possible; excel." 15 Feb-15 Nov. € 19.00 2009*

PARENTIS EN BORN *7D1* (3km NW Rural) *44.35153, -1.10959* **Camping Calède, Quartier Lahitte, 40160 Parentis-en-Born [05 58 78 44 63; fax 05 58 78 40 13; contact@camping-calede.com; www.camping-calede.com]** Exit N10 junc 17 onto D43 to Parentis-en-Born; then take D652 dir Biscarrosse; site in 3km on L. Sp adj lake. Med, hdg pitch, pt shd; wc; chem disp; baby facs; shwrs inc; el pnts (5A) €3.25; gas; lndtte; shop 3km; tradsmn; snacks; bar; BBQ; playgrnd; lake sw & sand beach adj; sailing; fishing; dogs €0.50; phone; poss cr; Eng spkn; quiet; adv bkg; red low ss; CCI. "Peaceful site in remote location; well-kept pitches & san facs; friendly, helpful staff; site yourself if office clsd; rec." ♦ 1 May-30 Sep. € 17.00 2009*

PARIS *3D3* (12km E Urban) *48.8543, 2.5363* **Camp Municipal La Haute Ile, Rue de l'Ecluse, 93330 Neuilly-sur-Marne [01 43 08 21 21; fax 01 43 08 22 03; camping municipal.nsm@wandadoo.fr]** Fr Périphérique (Porte de Vincennes) foll N34 sp Vincennes. Shortly after passing Château de Vincennes on R, L at fork, sp Lagny. At next major x-rds sharp L (still N34) sp Chelles. Thro Neuilly-Plaisance to Neuilly-sur-Marne. In cent lge x-rds turn R sp N370 Marne-la-Vallée & A4 Paris. In 200m, bef rv bdge, foll Camp Municipal sp (no tent or c'van symbols on sp) turn L. Site at junc of rv & canal. Lge, mkd pitch, pt shd; wc (some cont); shwrs inc; el pnts (10A) inc (check rev pol); gas; lndtte adj; shop; rest adj; BBQ; playgrnd; rv fishing; 25% statics; dogs €2.85; bus/train; poss cr; Eng spkn; adv bkg (rec high ssn); quiet. "Lovely location; wooden posts on pitches poss diff manoeuvring lge o'fits; some sm pitches; soft after rain; gd base & transport for Paris; poss unkempt low ssn; gd dog walks adj; gd NH." 1 Apr-30 Sep. € 18.70 2007*

⊞ **PARIS** *3D3* (15km SE Urban) *48.82963, 2.4772* **Camping Paris Est Le Tremblay, Blvd des Alliés, 94507 Champigny-sur-Marne [01 43 97 43 97; fax 01 48 89 07 94; champigny@campingparis.fr; www.campingparis.fr]** Rec rte for c'vans. Fr A4 (Paris-Reims) exit 5 sp Nogent/Champigny-sur-Marne. D45 dir Champigny to end of dual c'way at traff lts go R on N303 dir St Maur. Join N4 after 1km (traff lts) & take 2nd R (200m). Site sp. NB site also known as 'Camping de Champigny' or 'Camping International/IDF'. Med, hdg/mkd pitch, pt shd; htd wc (some cont); chem disp; mv service pnt; shwrs inc; el pnts (10A) inc; gas; lndtte; shop; rest; snacks; bar; games rm; TV; playgrnd; 20% statics; dogs €2.60; adv bkg; some rd noise; red low ssn; ccard acc; CCI. "Vg site; easy parking nr metro or bus fr camp to rlwy stn direct to city & Disneyland; twin-axle c'vans book ahead or poss extra charge; take care to avoid grounding on kerb to pitches; clsd to cars 0200-0600." ♦ € 29.90 2007*

This is a wonderful site.

I'll fill in a report online and let the Club know – www.caravanclub.co.uk/europereport

⊞ **PARIS** *3D3* (10km W Urban) *48.86843, 2.23471* **Camping Bois de Boulogne, 2 Allée du Bord de l'Eau, 75016 Paris [01 45 24 30 00 or 01 45 24 30 31; fax 01 42 24 42 95; camping@campingparis.fr; www.campingparis.fr]** Site bet bdge of Puteaux & bdge of Suresnes. App fr A1: take Blvd Périphérique W to Bois de Boulogne exit at Porte Maillot; foll camp sp. App fr A6: Blvd Périphérique W to Porte Dauphine exit at Porte Maillot; foll camp sp. App fr Pont de Sèvres (A10, A11): on bdge take R lane & take 2nd rd R mkd Neuilly-sur-Seine; rd runs parallel to Seine; cont to site ent. App fr A13: after St Cloud Tunnel, foll sp twd Paris; immed after x-ing Rv Seine, 1st turn on R sp Bois de Boulogne; foll camp sps; traff lts at site ent. NB Sharp turn to site, poorly sp fr N - watch for lge 'Parking Borne de l'Eau 200m'. V lge, hdg/mkd pitch, hdstg, pt sl, pt shd; htd wc (some cont); chem disp; mv service pnt; baby facs; shwrs inc; el pnts (10A) inc; gas; lndtte; shop, rest & bar in ssn or 1km; pool 1km; TV; Metro Porte Maillot 4km; shuttle bus (May-Sep) to & fr site morn/eve to 2300; some statics; dogs €2; phone; bus to metro; extra €26 per night for twin-axles; poss cr; Eng spkn; adv bkg rec high ssn; rd noise; red low ssn; ccard acc; CCI. "Busy site in excel location; easy access A13; conv cent Paris; some v sm pitches; san facs poss unclean; walk over Suresne bdge for shops, food mkt, supmkt etc; some tour ops on site; gd security; excel." € 37.20 2009*

France

PARIS *3D3* (20km NW Urban) *48.94001, 2.14563* **Camping International Maisons Laffitte, Ile de la Commune, 1 Rue Johnson, 78600 Maisons-Laffitte [01 39 12 21 91; fax 01 39 12 70 50; ci.mlaffitte@wanadoo.fr; www.campint.com]** Easy access fr A13 sp Poissy; take D308 to Maisons-Laffitte; foll site sp bef town cent. Fr A15 take N184 S fr Poissy, foll sp St Germain; approx 6km after x-ing Rv Seine & approx 300m after x-ing lge steel bdge, take L lane ready for L turn onto D308 to Maison-Laffitte; foll camp sp. Or D301 (N1) to St Denis, then A86 exit Bezons, then dir Poissy, Noailles, Sartrouville & Maisons-Laffitte. NB Narr app rd diff due parked cars & high kerbs. Lge, hdg/mkd pitch, pt shd; htd wc; chem disp; mv service pnt; shwrs inc; el pnts (6A) €3.10 (poss rev pol); gas; Indtte; sm shop; tradsmn; hypmkt 5km; rest; snacks; bar; no BBQ; playgrnd; games area; TV rm; 50% statics; dogs €2.60; RER stn 1km; poss cr; Eng spkn; adv bkg; some noise fr rlwy & rv traff; ccard acc; red low ssn; CCI. "V busy, popular site on island in Rv Seine; ideal for visiting Paris (20 min by RER), Disneyland & Versailles; Mobilis ticket covers rlwy, metro & bus for day in Paris; friendly, helpful staff; ltd facs low ssn." ♦ 27 Mar-31 Oct. € 28.00 2009*

See advertisement

PARRANQUET see Villeréal *7D3*

PARTHENAY *4H1* (1km SW Urban) *46.64160, -0.26740* **Kawan Village Camping du Bois Vert, 14 Rue de Boisseau, Le Tallud, 79200 Parthenay [tel/fax 05 49 65 78 43; boisvert@cvtloisirs.fr; www.camping-boisvert.com]** Site on D743 to Niort. Sp fr N & S. Fr S 1km bef town turn L at sp La Roche-sur-Yon immed after rv bdge turn R; site on R in 500m. Med, hdg/mkd pitch, some hdstg, pt sl, pt shd; htd wc (some cont); chem disp; mv service pnt; baby facs; shwrs inc; el pnts (10A) €3.50; Indtte; shops 1km; tradsmn; rest; snacks; bar; playgrnd; pool; boating; fishing; tennis; games rm; wifi;TV; 10% statics; phone; poss cr; adv bkg; noisy nr main rd & bar; ccard not acc; red low ssn; CCI. "Rvside walk to town; basic san facs ltd low ssn, tired high ssn; m'van o'night area adj; Wed mkt; gd NH to Spain; conv Futuroscope." ♦ 1 Apr-30 Sep. € 19.00 (CChq acc) 2008*

PARTHENAY *4H1* (9km W Urban) *46.62214, -0.35139* **Camp Municipal Les Peupliers, 79130 Azay-sur-Thouet [05 49 95 37 13 (Mairie); fax 05 49 70 36 14; mairie-azaysurthouet@cc-parthenay.fr]** Fr Parthenay take D949 dir Secondigny to Azay-sur-Thouet; turn L onto D139 dir St Pardoux; site on L in 200m. Site adj stadium on rvside. Sm, mkd pitch, pt shd; wc; shwrs inc; el pnts (10A) €2.75; shop 250m; BBQ; playgrnd; quiet. "Pleasant, peaceful site; barrier open 0900; inadequate number facs (2009)." 15 Jun-30 Sep. € 8.05 2009*

PARTHENAY *4H1* (10km W Rural) *46.65738, -0.34816* **FFCC Camping La Chagnée (Baudoin), 79450 St Aubin-le-Cloud [05 49 95 31 44 or 06 71 10 09 66 (mob); fax 06 71 10 09 66; gerard.baudoin3@wanadoo.fr; www.cc-parthenay.fr/la-chagnee]** Fr Parthenay on D949 dir Secondigny. Turn R in Azay-sur-Thouet onto D139 dir St Aubin, site on R in 2km, look for 'Gîte' sp. Sm, pt shd; wc; mv service pnt; shwrs; el pnts €3.10; Indtte; shops 1km; pool 1km; fishing; dogs; Eng spkn; quiet. "Charming, CL-type organic farm site o'looking lake; friendly, helpful owners; clean facs; open all yr providing use own san in winter; maps loaned for walking; excel." ♦ 1 Apr-31 Oct. € 10.90 2009*

PASSY see Sallanches *9A3*

PATORNAY see Clairvaux les Lacs *6H2*

PAU *8F2* (3km N Urban) **Camp Municipal de la Plaine des Sports et des Loisirs, Blvd du Cami-Salié, 64000 Pau [05 59 02 30 49; fax 05 59 11 08 19; direction.sport@ville-pau.fr]** Fr S exit Pau on D834 (N134) twd Bordeaux. After 3km turn R on slip rd at traff lts onto Blvd Cami-Salié sp Hippodrome (narr tree-lined avenue). Site on L in 1km adj sports complex. Or fr N cross bdge over A64, at rndabt strt on sp Pau Centre. At x-rds with traff lts turn L into Blvd Cami-Salié. Med, hdg/mkd pitch, shd; htd wc; chem disp; shwrs inc; el pnts (3A) €2.20; Indry rm; supmkt 2km; htd, covrd pool, tennis adj; games area; dogs; phone; bus adj; Eng spkn; adv bkg; quiet but some noise fr rd & sports complex; CCI. "Fair NH." May-Sep. € 11.50 2007*

⊞ **PAU** *8F2* (5km E Rural) *43.28909, -0.26985* **FFCC Camping Les Sapins, Route de Tarbes, 64320 Ousse [05 59 81 79 03 or 05 59 81 74 21 (LS); lessapins64@orange.fr]** Site adj Hôtel des Sapins on S side of D817 (N117) (Pau-Tarbes rd). Sm, pt shd; wc; mv service pnt; shwrs inc; el pnts (4-6A) €2-3; shop adj; rest in hotel adj; fishing; poss cr; noisy; some rd noise. "Popular, pleasant NH; red facs low ssn; helpful owners; NH only." € 9.50 2006*

PAU *8F2* (10km S Rural) **Camping à la Ferme (André), Chemin de Castagnet, Haut de Gan, 64290 Gan [05 59 21 51 84]** S fr Pau on N134 dir Oloron-Ste Marie; approx 8km past Gan turn L sp 'Camping Paysan'; site on R in 150m. Sp diff to spot. Sm, pt shd; wc; chem disp; shwrs; el pnts inc; lndry rm; tradsmn; shop 8km; horseriding nrby; quiet. "Peaceful site in orchard; facs clean; helpful, friendly owners; not suitable lge o'fits; excel touring base inc Lourdes; conv NH to Spain." € 14.20 2008*

⊞ **PAU** *8F2* (6km W Rural) *43.32081, -0.45096* **Camping Le Terrier, Ave du Vert-Galant, 64230 Lescar [05 59 81 01 82; fax 05 59 81 26 83; contact@camping-terrier.com; www.camping-terrier.com]** Fr D817 (N117) at Lescar foll sp S dir Artiguelouve, site at rv bdge. Access via narr lane - no parking or turning space. Med, hdg/mkd pitch, pt shd; wc (own san rec); chem disp; baby facs; shwrs inc; el pnts (3-10A) €2.20-5.50; gas; lndtte; shop 500m; tradsmn; hypmkt 2km; rest, snacks, bar high ssn; playgrnd; htd pool high ssn; rv fishing adj; tennis; car wash; 10% statics; dogs €1.50; poss cr; Eng spkn; adv bkg; quiet; 30% red 30+ days; CCI. "Gd base for Pau & district; some permanent residents; no twin-axles; 2 golf courses nr; poss slighly run-down; gd NH." € 12.50 2008*

PAUILLAC *7C2* (1km S Rural) *45.18515, -0.74218* **FFCC Camp Municipal Les Gabarreys, Route de la Rivière, 33250 Pauillac [05 56 59 10 03 or 05 56 73 30 50; fax 05 56 73 30 68; camping.les.gabarreys@wanadoo.fr; www.pauillac-medoc.com]** On ent Pauillac on D206, turn R at rndabt, sp site. On app Quays, turn R bef 'Maison du Vin'. Site on L in 1km. Med, hdg/mkd pitch, hdstg, pt shd; wc; chem disp; mv service pnt; shwrs inc; el pnts (5A) €3.80; lndtte; shop 1km; tradsmn; BBQ; playgrnd; htd, covrd pool 1km; games rm; TV; 6% statics; dogs €2; Eng spkn; adv bkg; quiet; red low ssn; ccard acc; CCI. "Excel, well-kept, well-equipped, peaceful site on estuary; clean san facs; conv wine chateaux; cycle rtes; mkt Sat." ♦ 3 Apr-10 Oct. € 14.00 2009*

PAULHAGUET *9C1* (500m SE Rural) *45.19900, 3.52000* **Camping La Fridière, 6 Route d'Esfacy, 43230 Paulhaguet [04 71 76 65 54; campingpaulhaguet@wanadoo.fr; www.campingfr.nl]** On SE side of town on D4. Sm, hdg/mkd pitch, pt shd; htd wc; chem disp; mv service pnt; shwrs inc; el pnts (10-16A) €3.50; gas 500m; lndtte; shop, snacks 500m; tradsmn; bar; playgrnd; rv fishing; internet; dogs €1; Eng spkn; quiet; CCI. "Useful NH; vg, clean san facs; lge pitches; friendly owners; popular with young Dutch families; mkt Mon; excel." ♦ 1 Apr-1 Oct. € 13.00 2009*

PAULHIAC see Biron *7D3*

⊞ **PAYRAC** *7D3* (1km N Rural) *44.80574, 1.47479* **Camping Panoramic, Route de Loupiac, 46350 Payrac-en-Quercy [05 65 37 98 45; fax 05 65 37 91 65; info@campingpanoramic.com; www.campingpanoramic.com]** N fr Payrac, site W of D820 (N20) at start of dual c'way, foll sp Loupiac, then site. Sm, pt sl, hdstg pt shd; htd wc; chem disp; baby facs; shwrs inc; el pnts (5A) €3 (poss rev pol); gas; lndtte; shop 1km; tradsmn; rest high ssn; snacks; bar; BBQ; playgrnd; pool 400m; rv sw 5km; canoe hire; cycle hire; wifi; TV rm; 10% statics; phone; poss cr; Eng spkn; adv bkg; quiet; CCI. "Well-run, clean, busy site with excel san facs; poss v muddy in bad weather; friendly, helpful Dutch owner; organised canoe trips & entmnt; gd walking; excel winter NH." ♦ € 10.60 2009*

PAYRAC *7D3* (6km N Rural) *44.82182, 1.46801* **Camping à la Ferme Le Treil (Gatignol), 46350 Loupiac [05 65 37 64 87; francis.gatignol@wanadoo.fr]** Fr N or S on D820 (N20), sp 'A la Ferme'. Sm, sl, pt shd; wc; chem disp (wc); shwrs inc; el pnts (4A) €2 (long lead poss req); lndtte; shops 2km; tradsmn; bar; playgrnd; pool; fishing; boating; tennis; golf 3km; TV; BBQ; poss cr; Eng spkn; adv bkg; quiet; 10% red low ssn. "Pleasant site; mkd ent for c'vans poss diff long o'fits - rec use ent for tents if gd power/weight ratio; friendly owner." 1 May-30 Oct. € 10.00 2006*

PAYRAC *7D3* (6km N Rural) *44.83527, 1.46008* **Camping Les Hirondelles, Al Pech, 46350 Loupiac [05 65 37 66 25; fax 05 65 37 66 65; camp.les-hirondelles@orange.fr; www.les-hirondelles.com]** Fr Souillac foll D820 (N20) for about 12km. Site on R bef dual c'way. Sm, hdg/mkd pitch, pt sl, shd; htd wc; chem disp; baby facs; shwrs inc; el pnts (6A) inc (poss rev pol); gas; lndtte; shop; tradsmn; rest; snacks; bar; playgrnd; htd pool; cycle hire; entmnt; TV; 40% statics; dogs €1.20; phone; poss cr w/end; Eng spkn; adv bkg; quiet; CCI. "Vg friendly, helpful owners; clean site; gd views fr some pitches; excel." ♦ 1 Apr-15 Sep. € 15.00 2006*

PAYRAC *7D3* (500m S Rural) *44.78936, 1.47299* **FLOWER Camping Les Pins, 46350 Payrac-en-Quercy [05 65 37 96 32; fax 05 65 37 91 08; info@les-pins-camping.com; www.les-pins-camping.com or www.flower camping.com]** Exit A20 junc 55 onto D804 dir Souillac; in 2.4km at next rndbt take 3rd exit onto D820 (N20); cont for 16km thro Payrac; site on R in 800m - tight R-hand turn. Med, hdg/mkd pitch, hdstg, terr, pt shd; wc; chem disp; mv service pnt; serviced pitches; shwrs inc; el pnts (10A) inc; gas 1km; lndtte; shop; rest; snacks; bar; BBQ; playgrnd; 2 htd pools; waterslide; paddling pool; tennis; entmnt; wifi; games/TV rm; many statics; dogs €2.50; some rd & disco noise; adv bkg; Eng spkn; rd noise; ccard acc; red low ssn; CCI. "Gd, clean site in interesting area; friendly staff; vg pool; most pitches shd with high firs; trees make access to some pitches diff; low ssn not suitable disabled unless sited nr recep; boggy in wet." ♦ 17 Apr-12 Sep. € 28.50 ABS - D25 2009*

PAYRAC *7D3* (5km NW Rural) *44.80805, 1.41027* **Camping Les Grands Chênes (Naturist), Le Peyronnet, 46350 Lamothe-Fénelon (Postal address 46300 Fajoles) [tel/fax 05 65 41 68 79; camping@les-grands-chenes.com; www.les-grands-chenes.com]** Fr N exit A20 junc 55 onto D820 (N20) dir Payrac; turn R onto minor rd to Lamothe-Fénelon; site on D12, sp in vill. Or fr N on D820 turn R in Payrac onto D36 (best route). Fr S exit junc 56 onto D801, then turn R onto D820 to Payrac. Access rds narr fr Payrac. Sm, mkd pitch, pt sl, pt shd; wc; chem disp; baby facs; shwrs inc; el pnts (6A) €3 (long lead poss req); Indtte; shop; tradsmn; rest 6km; snacks; bar; playgrnd; pool; games area; canoe hire, golf, horseriding nrby; 2% statics; dogs €1.50; poss cr; little Eng spkn; adv bkg; quiet; INF card req; red low ssn. "Charming, peaceful site in woodland; lovely location; attractive, unusual architecture on site; friendly staff; excel san facs; cycling rte on old rlwy; close to Rv Dordogne; excel." ♦ 16 May-12 Sep. € 21.80 2009*

PEGOMAS see Cannes *10F4*

PEIGNEY see Langres *6F1*

PEILLAC *2F3* (1km N Rural) *47.72598, -2.21287* **Camp Municipal du Pont d'Oust, 56220 Peillac [02 99 91 39 33 or 02 99 91 26 76 (Mairie); fax 02 99 91 31 83]** Fr La Gacilly on D777, turn L onto D14 sp Les Fougerêts. Thro vill, site on R opp canal. Med, pt shd; htd wc; shwrs €1.20; el pnts (6A) €2.40; Indtte; shops 1km; rest, bar 300m; BBQ; pool adj; rv adj; quiet. "Vg site nr pretty vill; helpful warden & staff; v flat, ideal for cycling." 1 May-30 Sep. € 5.90 2008*

PEILLON see Nice *10E4*

PEISEY NANCROIX see Bourg St Maurice *9B4*

PENESTIN *2G3* (1.5km N Coastal) *47.47687, -2.45204* **Camping Les Pins, Chemin du Val au Bois de la Lande, 56760 Pénestin [tel/fax 02 99 90 33 13; camping.lespins@wanadoo.fr; www.camping-despins.com]** Fr Roche-Bernard take D34 dir Pénestin, 2km bef town turn L sp Camping Les Pins. Site on R in 1km. Med, hdg/mkd pitch, pt sl, pt shd; htd wc (some cont); chem disp; baby facs; shwrs inc; el pnts (10A) €2.60; gas; Indtte; shop & 2km; tradsmn; snacks; bar; BBQ; playgrnd; htd pool; paddling pool; waterslide; playgrnd; sand beach 3km; cycle hire; games area; games rm; entmnt; TV; 33% statics; dogs €1; phone; bus; Eng spkn; adv bkg; quiet; red low ssn/long stay/CCI. "Sun mkt; excel." ♦ 1 Apr-19 Oct. € 14.40 2008*

PENESTIN *2G3* (1.5km E Rural) *47.47890, -2.45390* **Camping Le Cénic, Route de la Roche-Bernard, 56760 Pénestin-sur-Mer [02 99 90 45 65; fax 02 99 90 45 05; info@lecenic.com; www.lecenic.com]** Fr La Roche-Bernard take N774 sp La Baule. In 1.5km turn R onto D34. At Pénestin turn L opp Intermarché & foll sp to site in 800m. Lge, mkd pitch, pt sl, pt shd; wc; chem disp; mv service pnt; shwrs inc; el pnts (4-6A) €4; Indtte; shop adj; snacks; bar; playgrnd; htd, covrd pool/aquatic park; paddling pool; waterslides; jacuzzi; beach 3km; lake fishing; tennis; games area; games rm; few statics; dogs €2.50; Eng spkn; adv bkg rec high ssn; poss noisy high ssn; red low ssn; CCI. "Vg site nr unspoilt coastline; pleasant staff; take care when pitching due trees." ♦ 4 Apr-19 Sep. € 27.00 2009*

PENESTIN *2G3* (2km S Rural) *47.47150, -2.46695* **Yelloh! Village Le Domaine d'Inly, Route de Couarne, 56760 Pénestin [02 99 90 35 09; inly-info@wanadoo.fr; www.camping-inly.com or www.yellohvillage.com]** Fr Vannes or Nantes on N165, exit junc 15 W onto D34 fr La Roche-Bernard to Pénestin, then onto D201, site sp on L. Lge, hdg pitch, hdstg, pt shd; wc; chem disp; shwrs inc; el pnts (10A) inc; Indtte; shop; rest; snacks; bar; playgrnd; htd, covrd pool; paddling pool; waterslide; sand beach 1.5km; tennis; games area; horseriding; TV; entmnt; 20% statics; dogs €4; Eng spkn; adv bkg; ccard acc; red long stay/low ssn; ccard acc; CCI. "V pleasant, family site." ♦ 4 Apr-20 Sep. € 39.00 2009*

PENESTIN *2G3* (3km S Coastal) *47.44527, -2.48416* **Camping des Iles, La Pointe du Bile, 56760 Pénestin [02 99 90 30 24; fax 02 99 90 44 55; contact@camping-des-iles.fr; www.camping-des-iles.fr]** Fr La Roche Bernard take D34 to Pénestin; cont on D201 for 2.5km & foll site sp. Lge, hdg/mkd pitch, pt shd; wc; chem disp; some serviced pitches; baby facs; shwrs inc; el pnts (6A) inc; gas; Indtte; shop; tradsmn; rest; snacks; bar; BBQ (elec/charcoal); playgrnd; htd pool & paddling pool; waterslide; sand beach adj; fishing adj; tennis; cycle hire; horseriding; entmnt; wifi; games/TV rm; some tour op statics; no c'vans over 7m high ssn; dogs €4; poss cr; Eng spkn; adv bkg; quiet but noisy nr rd; ccard acc; red low ssn; CCI. "Vg quiet site; gd san facs; helpful staff; cliff-top walks; clean beach; dog mess on site; mkt Sun (also Wed in Jul/Aug)." ♦ 2 Apr-17 Oct. € 39.50 (CChq acc) ABS - B06 2009*

PENNE SUR L'OUVEZE, LA see Buis les Baronnies *9D2*

PENVINS see Sarzeau *2G3*

PERIERS *1D4* (5km SE Rural) *49.16638, -1.34916* **FFCC Aire Naturelle Municipale Le Clos Vert, 50190 St Martin-d'Aubigny [02 33 46 57 03 or 02 33 07 73 92 (Mairie); fax 02 33 07 02 53; mairie-st-martin-daubigny@wanadoo.fr]** E fr Périers on D900 dir St Lô; in 4km turn R sp St Martin-d'Aubigny; site on L in 500m adj church. Sm, pt shd; wc; chem disp; shwrs inc; el pnts (6A) €2; Indry rm; shop 5km; rest & bar 500m; BBQ; playgrnd; fishing, tennis & golf 2km; Eng spkn; quiet; CCI. "Easy 70km run to Cherbourg; no twin-axles." ♦ 15 Apr-15 Oct. € 6.60 2008*

⊞ **PERIGUEUX** *7C3* (12km NE Rural) *45.21975, 0.86383* **Camping Le Bois du Coderc, Route des Gaunies, 24420 Antonne-et-Trigonant [05 53 05 99 83; fax 05 53 05 15 93; coderc-camping@wanadoo.fr; www.campinglecoderc.com]** NE fr Périgueux on N21 twd Limoges, thro Antonne approx 1km turn R at x-rds bet car park & Routiers café. Site in 500m. Sm, pt shd; wc; chem disp; baby facs; shwrs inc; el pnts (6-10A) €3.20-5; gas 5km; lndtte (inc dryer); ice; shop 4km; tradsmn; rest 1km; snacks; bar; BBQ; playgrnd; htd pool; rv sw & shgl beach adj; games area; games rm; wifi; TV; some statics; dogs €1; phone; Eng spkn; adv bkg; quiet; ccard acc; red low ssn/CCI. "Secluded site; most pitches spacious; helpful owners; vg clean san facs; rallies welcome; highly rec." ♦ € 12.50 2009*

PERIGUEUX *7C3* (1.5km E Urban) *45.1866, 0.7416* **Camping de Barnabé, 80 Rue des Bains, 24750 Boulazac [05 53 53 41 45; fax 05 53 54 16 62; contact@barnabe-perigord.com; www.barnabe-perigord.com]** 1.5km E on rd to Brive, sp to L. Sp not clear - 2 bdges, site across 2nd bdge. Med, hdg/mkd pitch, pt shd; htd wc; chem disp; shwrs inc; el pnts (5-10A) €3-3.50; shops 500m; supmkt 1km; rest; snacks; bar; rv fishing; no statics; dogs €1.20; poss cr; Eng spkn; adv bkg; quiet; red long stay/low ssn; ccard acc. "Pleasant rvside site; san facs dated & poss unclean low ssn; pitches cramped for lge o'fits; poss clsd low ssn - phone ahead." 1 Mar-31 Oct. € 15.10 2009*

PERIGUEUX *7C3* (10km E Rural) *45.21306, 0.83780* **FFCC Camping au Fil de l'Eau, 6 Allée des Platanes, 24420 Antonne-et-Trigonant [05 53 06 17 88; fax 05 53 08 97 76; campingaufildeleau@wanadoo.fr; http://camping-aufildeleau.monsite.wanadoo.fr]** E fr Périgueux on N21 twd Limoges; sp on R at end of vill; camp 350m along rd to Escoire. Well sp. Sm, pt shd; wc; chem disp; shwrs inc; el pnts (5A) €3; lndtte; shops 1km; tradsmn; snacks; playgrnd; lake sw; canoe hire; fishing; cycle hire; some statics; adv bkg; quiet; CCI. "Pleasant site; gd base for area; helpful owners; clean facs; red facs low ssn; excel." ♦ 15 Jun-15 Sep. € 11.40 2008*

PERIGUEUX *7C3* (7km S Rural) *45.14900, 0.77880* **Camping Le Grand Dague, Route du Grand Dague, 24750 Atur [05 53 04 21 01; fax 05 53 04 22 01; info@legranddague.fr; www.legranddague.fr]** Fr cent Périgueux, take N21 & A89 twd Brive. Fork L onto D2 to Atur (main rd bears R). In Atur turn L after bar/tabac; foll site sp for 2.5km. Med, pt sl, shd; wc; chem disp; baby facs; shwrs inc; el pnts (6A) inc; lndtte; ltd shop; tradsmn; rest; snacks; bar; playgrnd; pool; games rm; entmnt; TV; dogs €2; phone; Eng spkn; adv bkg; quiet; red low ssn; ccard acc; red low ssn; CCI. "Gd family site; friendly owners; lots to do." ♦ 30 May-27 Sep. € 27.00 (CChq acc) 2008*

PERNES LES FONTAINES see Carpentras *10E2*

PERONNE *3C3* (300m NE Urban) *49.93424, 2.94140* **Camp Municipal du Brochet, Rue Georges Clémenceau, 80200 Péronne [03 22 84 02 35 or 03 22 73 31 00; fax 03 22 73 31 01; info@campingdubrochet.com; www.campingdubrochet.com]** Fr N on D1017 (N17) turn R into town. L at lights & L immed after footbdge. 1st R & site on L. Well sp fr all dirs. Go to town cent then foll 'Intn'l Camping Site' sps. Sm, hdstg, pt sl, terr, pt shd; wc; chem disp; mv service pnt; shwrs €1.10; el pnts (16A) €2.20; lndtte; shops & rest 500m; playgrnd; bus 500m; dogs free; phone; poss cr; Eng spkn; adv bkg; quiet; CCI. "Pleasant, basic but clean site nr park & attractive town; san facs need refurb; grass pitches soft when wet; rec arr early high ssn; conv WW1 museum; poss itinerants; vg." ♦ 1 Apr-1 Oct. € 10.90 2008*

⊞ **PERONNE** *3C3* (11km SE Rural) *49.88777, 3.06488* **Camping des Hortensias, 22 Rue Basse, 80240 Vraignes-en-Vermandois [03 22 85 64 68; accueil@campinghortensias.com; www.campinghortensias.com]** Fr N on A1/E15 take exit 13 onto D1029 (N29) sp St Quentin; strt rd 16km until rndabt, take D15 (Vraignes) exit; site sp 1st on R in vill. Or fr S & A26, take junc 10 onto D1029 sp Péronne; after 15km at rndabt take D15 as bef. Sm, hdg pitch, hdstg, pt shd; htd wc; chem disp; shwrs inc; el pnts (4-8A) €2.50-4.50 (poss long lead req); lndtte; shop 2km; tradsmn; red 5km; snack, bar 1.5km; BBQ; a few statics; dogs €1.20; quiet; red long stay; CCI. "Lovely farm site; sm pitches, poss muddy when wet; helpful, friendly owners; vg, clean san facs; conv for Somme battlefields & m'way; excel." € 11.50 2009*

France

PERONNE *3C3* (1km S Rural) *49.91805, 2.93227* **Camping du Port de Plaisance, Route de Paris, 80200 Péronne [03 22 84 19 31; fax 03 22 73 36 37; contact@camping-plaisance.com; www.camping-plaisance.com]** Exit A1/E15 junc 13.1 dir Peronne on D938 to D1017 (N17). Site on R o'looking canal. Well sp fr all dirs. Med, mkd pitch, pt shd; htd wc; chem disp; mv service pnt; shwrs inc; el pnts (6A) €4.10 (some rev pol & long lead poss req); Indtte; sm shop; tradsmn; supmkt nr; snacks high ssn; rest nr; bar; playgrnd; htd pool high ssn; jacuzzi; fishing; wifi; dogs €1.25; poss v cr; Eng spkn; poss some rd noise; red low ssn/long stay; ccard acc. "Pleasant site & popular NH; helpful owners; san facs adequate; gd play park & pool; gates locked 2200-0800 - when clsd, park outside; rec visit to war museum in Péronne castle; popular with ralliers; no twin-axles; poss ltd security." ♦ 1 Mar-31 Oct. € 22.50 (3 persons) 2009*

See advertisement above

PERONNE *3C3* (8km W Rural) *49.94777, 2.84416* **Camping Château de l'Oseraie, 10 Rue du Château, 80200 Feuillères [03 22 83 17 59 or 03 22 84 10 45 (LS); fax 03 22 83 04 14; jsg-bred@wanadoo.fr; www.camping-chateau-oseraie.com]** Fr A1/E15 exit 13.1 Maurepas, R onto D938 & then L onto D146; R at staggered x-rds in Feuillères (by church) & site on R in 500m. Med, hdg/mkd pitch, hdstg, pt shd; wc; chem disp; mv service pnt; shwrs €1.15; el pnts (6A) €2.90 (poss rev pol); gas; Indtte; tradsmn; supmkt 10km; snacks; bar; BBQ; playgrnd; htd pool 8km; fishing; tennis; games area; games rm; wifi; entmnt high ssn; 70% statics; dogs €1.10; Eng spkn; slight rlwy noise; adv bkg rec high ssn; red long stay; CCI. "Excel, well-kept, well-run site; gd sized pitches; clean san facs; friendly staff; conv WW1 battlefields & Disneyland Paris." ♦ 1 Apr-31 Oct. € 13.80 2009*

See advertisement opposite

PERONNE *3C3* (2km NW Rural) *49.94409, 2.90826* **Camping La Tortille, L'Orgibée, 80200 Cléry-sur-Somme [03 22 83 17 59 or 03 22 84 10 45 (LS); fax 03 22 83 04 14; jsg-bred@wanadoo.fr]** Exit A1/E15 junc 13.1 onto D938 to Cléry, dir Peronne. Site sp on rvside in 5km. Med, hdg pitch, hdstg, pt shd; wc; shwrs €1.10; el pnts (6A) €2.85; shop 4km; BBQ; playgrnd; rv fishing; games area; 80% statics; dogs €1; adv bkg; quiet; red long stay; CCI. "Peaceful site; sm pitches poss bet statics; conv for m'way." ♦ 1 Apr-31 Oct. € 12.20 2009*

See advertisement opposite

PERPIGNAN *8G4* (6km S Rural) *42.63754, 2.89819* **Camping Les Rives du Lac, Chemin de la Serre, 66180 Villeneuve-de-la-Raho [04 68 55 83 51; fax 04 68 55 86 37; camping.villeneuveraho@wanadoo.fr]** Fr A9 exit Perpignan Sud, dir Porte d'Espagne. In 3km turn R onto N9 dir Le Boulou. In 1km after Auchan supmkt take slip rd to N91 dir Villeneuve-de-la-Raho. In 2km rd becomes D39, turn R to site, site on L in 1km. Beware ford on D39 in v wet weather (usually dry). Med, mkd pitch, pt sl, hdstg, pt shd; htd wc; chem disp; mv service pnt; shwrs inc; el pnts (6A) inc; Indtte; shop; supmkt 3km; rest; snacks; bar; BBQ (elec/gas); playgrnd; htd pool; lake sw, beach, fishing & watersports 1.5km; tennis 2km; some statics; dogs €1.60; phone; Eng spkn; adv bkg; poss noise fr adj picnic area w/ends; red low ssn; ccard acc; CCI. "Lakeside site with views; poor san facs & insufficient for site size (2008); busy cycling/jogging path adj; conv trips to Spain; busy public beach nr." ♦ 15 Mar-15 Nov. € 17.50 2009*

PERROS GUIREC *1D2* (5km E Coastal) *48.81439, -3.38372* **Camp Municipal Le Palud, Port L'Epine, 22660 Trélévern [02 96 91 73 11 or 02 96 23 71 91 (LS); fax 02 96 91 76 30; www.trelevern.fr]** Fr Lannion on D788 to Perros-Guirec; at rndabt on sea front turn R onto D6 dir Louannec & Trélévern; in 3km turn L to Trélévern. Foll sps Port L'Epine & Camping Municipal. Med, mkd pitch, unshd; wc; chem disp; baby facs; shwrs inc; el pnts (10A) inc; gas 1km; Indtte; sm shop & 1km; tradsmn; rest; snacks; bar; BBQ; playgrnd; beach adj; entmnt; internet; dogs €1.10; phone adj; Eng spkn; adv bkg; quiet; ccard acc; red low ssn; CCI. "V peaceful site with views; many pitches beside sea; rocks & sand adj; excel." ♦ 7 Jun-7 Sep. € 20.55 2008*

PERROS GUIREC *1D2* (10km E Coastal/Rural) *48.81310, -3.38590* **FFCC Camping de Port l'Epine, 10 Venelle de Pors-Garo, 22660 Trélévern [02 96 23 71 94; fax 02 96 23 77 83; camping-de-port-lepine@wanadoo.fr; www.camping-port-lepine.com]** N fr Guingamp on D767 dir Lannion for approx 30km, then D788 dir Perros-Guirec; at rndabt just outside Perros-Guirec turn R onto D38 dir Trélévern. In Trélévern turn L at petrol stn & cont twd beach, sp Port L'Epine & Cmp Municipal; site on L opp Municipal site. NB Park on R at bottom of hill & walk to site to collect check-in information. Med, hdg/mkd pitch, pt sl, pt shd; wc; chem disp; serviced piches; shwrs inc; el pnts (16A) inc (poss rev pol); gas; lndtte; shop; tradsmn; rest; snacks; bar; BBQ; playgrnd; htd pool; paddling pool; dir access shgl beach; cycle hire; games rm; entmnt; 30% statics; dogs €3.50; c'vans over 8m not acc high ssn; poss cr; Eng spkn; adv bkg; quiet; ccard acc; red long stay/low ssn; CCI. "Pleasant, family-run, friendly site; facs poss stretched high ssn; narr site rds; mkt Perros-Guirec Fri; beach front pitches avail at extra cost; barrier clsd 2230-0730." ♦ 8 May-25 Sep. € 30.00 ABS - B18 2009*

PERROS GUIREC *1D2* (1km SE Coastal) *48.79657, -3.42689* **Camp Municipal Ernest Renan, 22700 Louannec [02 96 23 11 78; fax 02 96 23 35 42; mairie-louannec@wanadoo.fr]** 1km W of Louannec on D6. Lge, unshd; wc (some cont); chem disp; mv service pnt; shwrs inc; el pnts (6A) inc; gas; shop high ssn; rest; bar; playgrnd; htd pool; sand beach adj; fishing & watersports adj; games rm; TV; dogs €1.05; poss cr; adv bkg; Eng spkn; traff noise early am (minimal away fr rd). "Well-kept site; pitches on seashore; clean san facs; clsd 1200-1530, little parking space outside; highly rec." ♦ 1 Jun-30 Sep. € 16.55 2008*

PERROS GUIREC *1D2* (1km W Rural) *48.80617, -3.46541* **Camping La Claire Fontaine, Toul ar Lann, 22700 Perros-Guirec [02 96 23 03 55; fax 02 96 49 06 19; www.camping-claire-fontaine.com]** Fr Lannion N on D788 twd Perros-Guirec. At 2nd rndabt W on D11, then N on D6, L fork sp. Med, pt sl, pt shd; wc (some cont); chem disp; mv service pnt; baby facs; shwrs inc; el pnts (4-6A) inc; lndtte; tradsmn; shop; sand beach 800m; playgrnd; TV rm; some statics; dogs €1; Eng spkn; adv bkg rec high ssn; quiet. "Helpful staff." 1 Jun-15 Sep. € 21.00 2008*

PERROS GUIREC *1D2* (3km NW Coastal) *48.82798, -3.47623* **Yelloh! Village Le Ranolien, Ploumanac'h, 22700 Perros-Guirec [02 96 91 65 65; fax 02 96 91 41 90; www.yellohvillage.com]** At Perros-Guirec harbour turn R at Marina foll sp Trégastel. Up hill above coast into Perros Guirec town. Cont strt thro traff lts & into La Clarté vill; strt at traff lts & sharp R at Camping & Le Ranolien sp. Ent shortly on L. Foll Trégastel sp all way. Lge, pt sl, pt shd; wc; mv service pnt; baby facs; shwrs inc; el pnts (16A) inc; lndtte; shop; rest; snacks; bar; 2 pools; waterslide; sand & rock beach; fishing; tennis; golf; horseriding; entmnt; many tour op statics; dogs €2; poss cr; Eng spkn; adv bkg; ccard acc. "Excel beaches; vg coastal walks nrby." ♦ 5 Apr-14 Sep. € 39.00 2006*

⊞ **PERTRE, LE** *2F4* (1km W Rural) *48.03287, -1.03965* **Camp Municipal Le Chardonneret, Rue de Chardonneret, 35370 Le Pertre [02 99 96 99 27; fax 02 99 96 98 92; mariellepertre@lepertre.fr; www.lepertre.fr]** W fr Laval on D57 turn S at La Gravelle onto D43 to Le Pertre. Or exit A81 junc 5 S. Sm, hdg pitch, pt sl, pt shd; htd wc; shwrs; el pt (16A) €1.80; lndry rm; BBQ; 20% statics; dogs; phone; quiet but factory adj & church bells at night. "Warden calls am/pm; o'night area for m'vans; basic shops in town; some run down statics; gd NH." ♦ € 7.00 2009*

⊞ **PERTUIS** *10E3* (8km N Rural) *43.75860, 5.50407* **Camping Etang de la Bonde, 84730 Cabrières-d'Aigues [04 90 77 63 64 or 04 90 77 77 15 (LS); fax 04 90 07 73 04; campingdelabonde@wanadoo.fr; www.campingdelabonde.com]** NE fr Pertuis on D956, fork L onto D9 (sp Cabrières & Etang de la Bonde). At x-rds in 8km turn R onto D27. Site on L in 200m. Med, pt shd; wc (some cont); shwrs; el pnts (6A) €3.20; gas; shop; rest; snacks; playgrnd; pool 8km; lake sw, watersports & fishing; tennis; games area; many statics; dogs €1.80; poss cr; adv bkg; quiet; ccard acc; CCI. "Lovely lakeside & beach; ltd facs low ssn; phone ahead to check site open." € 12.00 2007*

PERTUIS *10E3* (1.5km E Urban) *43.69014, 5.52489* **FFCC Camp Municipal Les Pinèdes, Quartier St Sépulcre, 84120 Pertuis [04 90 79 10 98; fax 04 90 09 03 99; campinglespinedes@free.fr; www.campinglespinedes.com]** Exit Pertuis on D973 twd Manosque. After 1km fr cent of Pertuis turn R foll sp Camping & Piscine. In 2km pass pool to site 100m on brow of hill. Lge, hdg/mkd pitch, hdstg, terr, pt sl, pt shd; wc (cont); own san rec; chem disp; mv service pnt; baby facs; shwrs inc; el pnts (6-10A) €2.40-4.20; gas; lndry rm; shop & 2km; playgrnd; pool 200m; trampolines; entmnt; 5% statics; dogs €2; phone; quiet; red long stay; ccard acc (high ssn); red low ssn; CCI. "Spacious, attractive, well-kept site; san facs need update (2009); gates clsd 2200-0700; poss itinerants; mkt high ssn; vg."
15 Mar-15 Oct. € 11.60 2009*

PERTUIS *10E3* (6km SW Rural) *43.64382, 5.45844* **Camping Messidor (Naturist), Route de St Canadet, 13610 Le Puy-Ste Réparade [04 42 61 90 28; fax 04 42 50 07 08; messidor@online.fr; www.messidor.fr]** S fr Pertuis on D956/D556 twds Aix-en-Provence; after 5km turn R onto D561 twds Le Puy-Ste Réparade & Silvacane. At ent to vill take sp Aix-en-Provence via St Canadet (D13). Cross canal & turn immed 2nd R. Med, terr, pt sl, pt shd; wc; shwrs inc; el pnts (4A) €2.80; lndtte; shop 3km; tradsmn; rest; snacks; bar; pool; rv fishing & watersports; tennis; 50% statics; dogs €2; Eng spkn; adv bkg; quiet; INF card req. "Gd facs & pool; lovely views fr some pitches; sh walk to bus stop for Aix."
1 Apr-30 Sep. € 18.00 2006*

PESMES *6G2* (500m S Rural) *47.27612, 5.56451* **Camp Municipal La Colombière, Route de Dole, 70140 Pesmes [03 84 31 20 15; fax 03 84 31 20 54; campcolombiere@aol.com]** On D475 halfway bet Gray & Dole. S fr Pesmes immed on L after x-ing rv bdge. N fr Dole, site sp on R immed bef rest at rv bdge. Med, some hdg pitch, pt shd; wc; own san rec high ssn; chem disp (wc); shwrs; el pnts (6-10A) €2.30-3.60; Indtte; shop 500m; rest adj; snacks; bar; cycle hire; dogs €1; phone; Eng spkn; adv bkg rec high ssn; quiet; no ccard acc. "Picturesque vill; helpful, friendly staff; vg." 1 Apr-30 Sep. € 8.30 2007*

PETIT PALAIS ET CORNEMPS see St Médard de Guizières *7C2*

PETITE PIERRE, LA *5D3* (2km S Rural) *48.84519, 7.31825* **Camping Imsterfeld, Route Forestière, 67290 La Petite-Pierre [tel/fax 03 88 70 42 12; camping-imsterfeld@wanadoo.fr]** Fr N61 turn E onto D13/D9 to La Petite-Pierre. Sm, hdg/mkd pitch, terr, pt shd; wc; chem disp (wc); shwrs €0.50; el pnts €2; tradsmn; BBQ; 75% statics; dogs; CCI. "Pleasant site with lake view (fenced); gd uphill walks to town." 1 May-30 Sep. € 10.50 2008*

PEUPLINGUES see Calais *3A3*

PEYNIER see Trets *10F3*

PEYRAT LE CHATEAU see Eymoutiers *7B4*

PEYREHORADE *8F1* (7km N Rural) *43.60318, -1.12970* **Camping La Comtesse, Lieu-dit Claquin, 40300 Bélus [05 58 57 69 07; fax 05 58 57 62 50; campinglacomtesse@wanadoo.fr; www.campinglacomtesse.com]** N fr Peyrehorade on D33; in 4km turn R sp Bélus; in 1.5km turn L; site on R in 1.5km, sp. Med, hdg/mkd pitch, pt shd; wc; chem disp; shwrs incl; el pnts (10A) €3.10; Indtte (inc dryer); shops, rests nrby; bar; BBQ; playgrnd; htd pool; games rm; entment; 50% statics; dogs €1.70; phone; adv bkg; red low ssn. "By pretty lake; friendly staff; ltd facs low ssn; vg." ♦ 1 Apr-30 Sep. € 12.90 2009*

PEYRELEAU *10E1* (1km N Rural) *44.19126, 3.20470* **Camp Municipal de Brouillet, 48150 Le Rozier [05 65 62 63 98; fax 05 65 62 60 83; contact@campinglerozier.com; www.camping-lerozier.com]** Fr Millau take D809 (N9) N to Aguessac, onto D907; in Le Rozier, x bdge over Rv Tarn onto D996 & in 200m (opp church); take rd on R to site; sp. Lge, mkd pitch, pt shd; wc (some cont); chem disp (wc); baby facs; shwrs inc; el pnts (6A) €3.50; Indtte; shop 200m; playgrnd; htd pool; poss cr; adv bkg rec high ssn; quiet; red low ssn; CCI. "V pleasant, busy, spacious site adj rv; friendly recep; vg for m'vans; poss facs stretched & unclean; gd base for Tarn Gorges; gd area walking & birdwatching." ♦ 1 Apr-20 Sep. € 15.70 2008*

PEYRELEAU *10E1* (1km N Rural) *44.19111, 3.20486* **Camping Les Peupliers, 48150 Le Rozier [05 65 62 60 85 or 06 74 37 79 72 (mob); peupliers12@orange.fr; www.camping-lespeupliers.com]** Fr Millau take D809 (N9) N to Aguessac, turn R onto D907 to Le Rozier. Cross bdge over Rv Tarn onto D996 & take rd on R to site; sp. Sm, mkd pitch, pt shd; wc; chem disp; shwrs inc; el pnts (6A) €2.50; Indry rm; shop, rest, bar 300m; tradsmn; snacks; BBQ; playgrnd; wifi; dogs free; bus 300m; Eng spkn; adv bkg rec high ssn; quiet; CCI. "Lovely, friendly, little site on Rv Jonte; gd base for walking etc." € 9.00 2009*

PEYRELEAU *10E1* (1km W Rural) *44.19470, 3.20210* **Camping Saint Pal, Route des Gorges du Tarn, 12720 Mostuéjouls [tel/fax 05 65 62 64 46 or 05 65 58 79 82 (LS); saintpal@wanadoo.fr; www.campingsaintpal.com]** Exit A75 exit junc 44.1 onto D29 to Aguessac then L onto D907 to Mostuéjouls. Or fr Millau take D809 (N9) N to Aguessac, turn R onto D907 to Mostuéjouls. Site in 10km 500m fr Rozier bdge. Med, hdg/mkd pitch, shd; wc (some cont); chem disp; mv service pnt; baby facs; fam bthrm; shwrs; el pnts (6A) €3.20; gas; Indtte; shop & 1km; tradsmn; snacks, bar high ssn; BBQ; playgrnd; pool; rv sw & beach adj; games rm; organised walks; TV; 20% statics; dogs €2; phone; poss cr; Eng spkn; adv bkg; quiet; ccard acc; red low ssn/CCI. "Excel site & facs; gd walks, canoeing, fishing & birdwatching, beavers on rv bank opp; poss diff for lge o'fits." ♦ 1 May-30 Sep. € 21.30 2008*

⊞ **PEYRIGNAC** *7C3* (1km W Rural) *45.16048, 1.18594* **Camping La Garenne, La Brousse, 24210 Peyrignac [tel/fax 05 53 50 57 73; s.lagarenne@wanadoo.com; http://membres.lycos.fr/campinglagarenne]** E fr Périgueux on A89. At Peyrignac foll site sp. Narr, steep rd poss diff lge o'fits. Med, mkd pitch, pt sl, shd; htd wc; chem disp; mv service pnt; baby facs; shwrs inc; el pnts (6-10A) €3-5 (poss rev pol); gas; Indtte; shop; tradsmn; snacks; bar; playgrnd; sm pool; games area; 50% statics; dogs €1.50; poss cr; adv bkg; quiet; red low ssn; CCI. "Gd touring base; gd size pitches; clean san facs; v kind owners; vg." ♦ € 15.00 2008*

PEYRILLAC ET MILLAC see Souillac *7C3*

PEZENAS *10F1* (1km NE Urban) *43.46618, 3.42397* **Camping St Christol, Chemin de St Christol, 34120 Pézenas [04 67 98 09 00 or 06 11 39 59 17 (mob); fax 04 67 98 89 61; info@campingsaintchristol.com; www.campingsaintchristol.com]** Exit A75 junc 59 Pézenas N onto N9 by-pass for town cent; turn R immed bef bdge; sp on R in 200m. NB app rds narr. Med, hdg/mkd pitch, hdstg, shd; wc (some cont); chem disp (wc); baby facs; shwrs inc; el pnts (10A) €3.40; gas; Indtte; shop; tradsmn; rest; snacks; BBQ area; playgrnd; pool; fishing; games rm; entmnt; TV; some statics; dogs €1.70; poss cr; adv bkg rec Jul/Aug; quiet; ccard acc; red low ssn; CCI. "Friendly, lively site; lge gravel pitches but hard & dusty; poss diff to manoeuvre due trees; san facs reasonable (2009); rest rec; historic town." ♦ 15 Apr-15 Sep. € 18.00 2009*

France

PEZENAS *10F1* (6km S Rural) *43.38776, 3.42298* **Camping Le Pin Parasol, 34630 St Thibéry [tel/fax 04 67 77 84 29; camping-pin-parasol@wanadoo.fr; www.campinglepinparasol.com]** Fr A9 exit junc 34 onto D13 & foll Pézenas sps; in 2.5km turn R to St Thibéry & site 150m on R. Med, mkd pitch, pt shd; wc; shwrs inc; el pnts (10A) €3.80; snacks; supmkt 200m; tradsmn; playgrnd; pool; sand beach 10km; tennis 1km; games rm; rv sw 1km; fishing; entmnt; TV; 30% statics; dogs €3; poss cr; adv bkg; rd noise; ccard not acc; CCI. "Vg san facs; lovely pool; site poss run down, dusty low ssn; stone quarry & indus units nrby; interesting vill." ♦ 1 Apr-30 Oct. € 16.00 2009*

PEZENAS *10F1* (1km SW Urban) *43.45589, 3.41782* **Camp Municipal de Castelsec, Chemin de Castelsec, 34120 Pézenas [04 67 98 04 02; fax 04 67 98 35 40]** Fr Béziers take N9 to Pézenas; foll Centre Ville sps & take 1st L immed after McDonalds at ent to Champion supmkt; foll Campotel sps; site on L in 300m. Sm, mkd pitch, pt sl, pt terr, pt shd; wc; shwrs inc; el pnts (10A) €2.70; lndtte; shops 500m; playgrnd; pool 1km; tennis adj; TV; 30% statics; dogs €1.60; adv bkg; quiet; red low ssn; CCI. "Pleasant site; clean, dated facs; friendly staff; easy walk/cycle to town; toy museum worth visit." ♦ 1 Apr-30 Oct. € 13.50 2009*

PEZULS see Bugue, Le *7C3*

PHALSBOURG *5D3* (2km N Rural) *48.78300, 7.25020* **FFCC Camping de Bouleaux (CC de F), 5 Rue des Trois Journeaux, 57370 Vilsberg [03 87 24 18 72; fax 03 87 24 46 52; info@campinglesbouleaux.fr; www.campingclub.asso.fr or www.campinglesbouleaux.fr]** Fr A4 exit junc 44 dir Phalsbourg. At x-rds turn L sp D661 Sarreguemines. Site on R in 2km. Lge, pt shd; wc; chem disp; mv service pnt; baby facs; shwrs inc; el pnts (6A) inc; lndtte; shop; tradsmn; BBQ; playgrnd; 15% statics; dogs €2; phone; bus 2km; Eng spkn; adv bkg; quiet; red low ssn; CCI. "Welcoming new owners (2009); barrier clsd 1930; gd facs; clean; conv m'way & NH to/fr Germany/Austria." ♦ 1 Apr-31 Oct. € 17.80 2009*

PHALSBOURG *5D3* (6km SW Rural) *48.71922, 7.22643* **Camping du Plan Incliné, Hoffmuhl, 57820 Henridorff [tel/fax 03 87 25 30 13 or 06 71 21 86 91 (mob); campingplanincline@wanadoo.fr; www.campingplanincline.com]** Exit A4 at junc 44. In Phalsbourg take D38 twds Lutzelbourg; turn R onto D98 dir Arzviller & foll sp to Henridorff & site on R adj rv (narr ent). Med, some hdg/hdstg pitches, pt shd; wc; chem disp; shwrs inc; el pnts (6A) €3; gas; lndtte; shop 2km; tradsmn; rest; snacks; bar; playgrnd; pool high ssn (spring water); rv sw, fishing & boating adj; entmnts; 60% statics; dogs €1; phone; Eng spkn; adv bkg; rlwy noise & some rd & boat noise; red long stay; ccard not acc; CCI. "In wooded valley; friendly, helpful owner; vg rest; grnd soft when wet; cycle path to Strasbourg." ♦ 1 Apr-20 Oct. € 13.00 2008*

PICQUIGNY *3C3* (E Urban) *49.94321, 2.14855* **Camp Municipal, 66 Rue du Marais, 80310 Picquigny [03 22 51 25 83 or 03 22 51 40 31 (Mairie); fax 03 22 51 30 98]** Site sp fr town cent. Med, unshd; wc; chem disp; shwrs inc; el pnts (10A); lndry rm; shop nr; playgrnd; rv & fishing; mainly statics; dogs; quiet; occasional noise fr rlwy line; adv bkg rec high ssn. "Pleasant site; modern san facs; WW1 war cemetery nr town." 1 Apr-31 Oct. 2008*

PIERRE BUFFIERE *7B3* (1.5km S Rural) *45.68937, 1.37101* **Camp Intercommunal Chabanas, 87260 Pierre-Buffière [tel/fax 05 55 00 96 43]** Approx 20km S of Limoges on A20, take exit 40 onto D420 southbound; site on L in 500m. Foll sps for 'Stade-Chabanas'. Med, hdg/mkd pitch (all grass), pt sl, pt shd; htd wc; chemp disp (wc); shwrs inc; el pnts inc (poss rev pol); lndtte; shop & snacks 2 km; playgrnd; fishing; dogs €0.80; phone; adv bkg; quiet but some rlwy noise; red low ssn; CCI. "Clean, quiet site; helpful staff; excel san facs; some pitches diff for lge o'fits; no twin-axles; warden on site 1500-2200, but gate poss locked all day low ssn (code issued); phone ahead; conv Limoges; excel NH fr A20." ♦ 15 May-30 Sep. € 13.50 2009*

PIERREFITTE SUR SAULDRE *4G3* (6km NE Rural) *47.54444, 2.19138* **Parc des Alicourts, Domaine des Alicourts, 41300 Pierrefitte-sur-Sauldre [02 54 88 63 34; fax 02 54 88 58 40; info@lesalicourts.com; www.lesalicourts.com]** Fr S of Lamotte-Beuvron, turn L on D923. After 14km turn R on D24E sp Pierrefitte. After 750m turn L, foll sp to site approx 750m on R. Med, pt shd; wc; mv service pnt; chem disp; baby facs; shwrs inc; el pnts (6A) inc; gas; lndtte; shop; rest; snacks; bar; BBQ; playgrnd; 3 pools; waterslide; tennis; lake sw; kayak/pedalo hire; skating rink; cycle hire; fitness cent; games rm; entmnt; some statics; dogs €7; extra for lakeside pitches; poss cr (but roomy); Eng spkn; adv bkg; quiet; ccard acc; red low ssn; CCI. "Excel, peaceful site; gd, clean facs; v lge pitches." ♦ 28 Apr-8 Sep. € 49.00 2009*

See advertisement

PIERREFONDS *3D3* (500m N Urban) *49.35427, 2.97564* **Camp Municipal de Batigny, Rue de l'Armistice, 60350 Pierrefonds [03 44 42 80 83]** Take D973 fr Compiegne; after 14km site on L adj sp for Pierrefonds at ent to vill. Med, hdg pitch, pt shd; htd wc; chem disp; mv service pnt; 90% serviced pitches; shwrs inc; el pnts (8A) €2.20 (poss rev pol); lndtte; shops 800m; rest in vill; 80% statics; dogs €1; poss cr; adv bkg; quiet but some rd noise; ccard not acc; red long stay; CCI. "Attractive, well-maintained site; facs stretched high ssn; tight pitches for lge o'fits; nr Armistice train & museum; excel." 31 Mar-15 Oct. € 9.00 2009*

PIERREFORT *7C4* (7km SW Rural) *44.85405, 2.77060* **FLOWER Camping La Source, Presqu'ile de Laussac, 12600 Thérondels [05 65 66 05 62; fax 05 65 66 21 00; info@camping-la-source.com; www.camping-la-source.com or www.flowercamping.com]** Fr A75 at St Flour, take D921 to Les Ternes, then D990 thro Pierrefort. Approx 2km after Pierrefort, turn L onto D34. Go thro Paulhenc, site on L after approx 7km. Med, mkd pitch, terr, pt shd; wc; chem disp; mv service pnt; baby facs; shwrs inc; el pnts (6A) inc; gas; lndtte; shop; tradsmn; rest; snacks; bar; playgrnd; htd pool; paddling pool; waterslide; lake sw adj; fishing; watersports; boat hire; tennis; games area; internet; entmnt; TV; dogs €1.60; 35% statics; quiet; adv bkg rec high ssn; red low ssn/long stay; CCI. "Excel lakeside site; poss diff lge o'fits due lge trees." ♦ 16 May-6 Sep. € 26.90 (CChq acc) 2008*

⊞ **PIEUX, LES** *1C4* (6km S Rural) *49.48702, -1.79854* **Camp Municipal, 2 Route du Rozel, 50340 St Germain-le-Gaillard [02 33 52 55 64]** Take D650 fr Cherbourg. 3km beyond Les Pieux turn R sp Le Rozel. Site on R 100m. Sm, hdg pitch, some hdstg, unshd; htd wc; chem disp; shwrs inc; el pnts (15A) €2.60; 4 water stand pnts; lndry rm; shop; playgrnd; pool & sand beach 3km; 85% statics (sep area); dogs €1.30; poss cr; adv bkg. "Modern, clean, well-kept san facs; rec arr early high ssn - ltd touring pitches; poss diff in wet." ♦ € 6.10 2008*

PIEUX, LES *1C4* (3km SW Coastal) *49.49444, -1.84194* **Kawan Village Le Grand Large, 50340 Les Pieux [02 33 52 40 75; fax 02 33 52 58 20; info@legrandlarge.com; www.legrandlarge.com]** Fr ferry at 1st rndabt take 1st exit sp Centre Ville. Closer to town cent foll old N13 sp Caen. In about 1.5km branch R onto D900 then L onto D650 sp Carteret. Foll this rd past Les Pieux, cont on D650 to sp Super U. Turn R & foll site sp onto D517, then D117 for 3km until reaching beach rd to site, site on L in 2km. Lge, hdg/mkd pitch, pt shd; htd wc; chem disp; mv service pnt; baby facs; shwrs inc; el pnts (10A) inc; gas; lndtte; shop; tradsmn; snacks high ssn; bar; BBQ; playgrnd; htd pool; paddling pool; sand beach adj; horseriding 4km; tennis; entmnt; wifi; games/TV rm; 40% statics; dogs; phone; poss cr; Eng spkn; adv bkg; quiet; ccard acc; red low ssn; CCI. "Dir access to superb beach; clean facs; friendly staff; barrier clsd 2100-0900; rec for families; mkt Fri; conv for Cherbourg ferries but arr not rec after dark due sm country lanes; outside pitches avail for early dep for ferries." ♦ 10 Apr-19 Sep. € 35.00 (CChq acc) ABS - N07 2009*

See advertisement

PIEUX, LES *1C4* (4km SW Coastal) *49.48022, -1.84216* **Camping Le Ranch, 50340 Le Rozel [02 33 10 07 10; fax 02 33 10 07 11; contact@camping-leranch.com; www.camping-leranch.com]** S fr Cherbourg on D650 & turn R to Les Pieux, then take D117 to Le Rozel. Turn L thro Rozel, foll sps to site. Site is on R at end rd. Med, pt sl, unshd; wc; chem disp; baby facs; shwrs inc; el pnts (3A) €4.20; lndtte; shop; rest; snacks; bar; playgrnd; htd pool; waterslide; sand beach adj; fishing; watersports; games area; wifi; entmnt; 40% statics; dogs €2.30; quiet; red low ssn/long stay; CCI. 1 Apr-31 Oct. € 25.40 2007*

⊞ **PIEUX, LES** *1C4* (6km NW Coastal) *49.56985, -1.83853* **Camp Municipal Clairefontaine, 5 Rue Alfred Rossel, 50340 Siouville-Hague [02 33 52 42 73]** Take D650 S fr Cherbourg, just bef Les Pieux turn R onto D23 Siouville-Hague, site sp fr beach rd. Lge, mkd pitch, pt shd; wc; shwrs; el pnts (6A) €2.26; lndtte; shops, rest, bar 500m; playgrnd; sand beach 300m; rv adj; quiet; ccard acc. € 6.86 2007*

PINSAC see Souillac *7C3*

PIRIAC SUR MER *2G3* (3.5km E Coastal/Rural) *47.38705, -2.51021* **Camping Parc du Guibel, Route de Kerdrien, 44420 Piriac-sur-Mer [02 40 23 52 67; fax 02 40 15 50 24; camping@parcduguibel.com; www.parcduguibel.com]** Fr Guérande take D99 to La Turballe, D333 to St Sébastien. In St Sébastien turn R to Kerdrien over x-rds & site on R in approx 500m. Lge, mkd pitch, hdstg, pt sl, pt shd; wc (some cont); chem disp; mv service pnt; serviced pitches; shwrs inc; el pnts (3-10A) €2.90-4.30 (poss rev pol); gas; lndtte; shop; rest; snacks; bar; BBQ; playgrnd; htd pool high ssn; paddling pool; mini-waterslide; sand beach 1km; tennis; games area; cycle hire; entmnt; TV rm; 30% statics; dogs €2; phone; adv bkg; ccard acc; CCI. "Helpful owner; lovely, quiet location in woods; gd touring base." ♦ 22 Mar-21 Sep. € 19.50 2008*

PIRIAC SUR MER *2G3* (1km S Rural) *47.37485, -2.53556* **Camping Amor-Héol, Route de Guérande, 44420 Piriac-sur-Mer [02 40 23 57 80; fax 02 40 23 59 42; armor-heol@wanadoo.fr; www.camping-armor-heol.com]** Fr Guérande on D90 & D33, site sp. Lge, mkd pitch, pt shd; wc; chem disp; baby facs; shwrs inc; el pnts (5A) €3.50; gas; lndtte; shops 1km; rest; snacks; bar; BBQ; playgrnd; htd, covrd pool; waterslide; sand beach 700m; tennis; games area; games rm; fitness rm; 40% statics; dogs €4; adv bkg; quiet. "Attractive, well-maintained site; lge pitches." 5 Apr-21 Sep. € 29.75 2007*

PISSOS *7D1* (500m E Rural) *44.30831, -0.76987* **Camp Municipal l'Arriu, 40410 Pissos [05 58 08 90 38 or 05 58 04 41 40 (LS); fax 05 58 08 92 93; mairie.pissos@wanadoo.fr; www.pissos.fr]** Fr N exit N10 junc 18 onto D834 to Pissos; at x-rds turn L onto D43; site on R in 500m, sp. Med, shd; wc; chem disp; shwrs inc; el pnts €2.10; ice; playgrnd; pool 500m; rv fishing 300m; quiet; red long stay. "Lge pitches; excel." 1 Jul-15 -Sep. € 11.50 2009*

France

⊞ **PITHIVIERS** *4F3* (8km S Rural) *48.10365, 2.24142* **Camping Le Clos des Tourterelles, Rue des Rendillons, 45300 Bouzonville-aux-Bois [02 38 33 01 00]** S fr Pithiviers on D921 twds Jargeau; enter Bouzonville; turn R immed bef cafe; site 500m on R; sp in vill. Med, pt shd; htd wc; chem disp; shwrs inc; el pnts (16A) inc; Indtte; shop 8km; playgrnd; 90% statics; adv bkg; quiet; CCI. "Ltd space for tourers - phone ahead rec; friendly, helpful owners; gd NH." ♦ € 11.00 2009*

⊞ **PLA, LE** *8G4* (750m S Rural) *42.71042, 2.07647* **Camp Municipal La Pradaille, 09460 Le Pla [04 68 20 49 14 or 04 68 20 41 37 (Mairie); fax 04 68 20 40 40; mairie.le-pla@wanadoo.fr]** Fr Axat on D117 take D118 S dir Quérigut & foll sp Le Pla. Or fr Mont-Louis take D118/D16 N to Quérigut & cont to Le Pla. Site well sp just S of vill. Med, hdg/mkd pitch, pt sl, pt shd; htd wc; chem disp (wc); shwrs inc; el pnts (16A) €3.20; Indtte; tradsmn; shops etc 5km; BBQ; playgrnd; 30% statics; phone adj; adv bkg; quiet; red low ssn. "Excel walking & mountain biking; 8km winter skiing, 6km x-country skiing; excel." ♦ € 12.50 2008*

PLAINE SUR MER, LA **see Pornic** *2G3*

PLAISANCE (GERS) *8F2* (500m E Rural) *43.60805, 0.05370* **Camping de l'Arros, Allée de Ormeaux, 32160 Plaisance [05 62 69 30 28; infos@plaisance-evasion.com; www.plaisance-evasion.com]** N from Tarbes on D935, approx 25 km N of Maubourguet turn R onto D946 to Plaisance. Foll sp to site on o'skts of town. Sm, mkd pitch; pt sl, pt shd; wc; chem disp; shwrs inc; el pnts (2-5A); Indtte; shops 500m; rest; snacks; bar; gas BBQ only; playgrnd; pool; 40% statics; dogs €2; phone; adv bkg ess high ssn; red low ssn; ccard acc; CCI. "Close to rv; canoes avail." ♦ 1 Apr-30 Sep. € 21.00 2006*

PLANCOET *2E3* (Urban) *48.52035, -2.23213* **Camp Municipal du Verger, 22130 Plancoët [02 96 84 03 42 or 02 96 84 39 70 (Mairie); fax 02 96 84 19 49; mairie.plancoet@wanadoo.fr; www.mairie-plancoet.fr]** On D974 fr Dinan descend to bdge over rlwy lines & site well sp. Med, mkd pitch, pt shd; wc; chem disp; shwrs inc; el pnts (5A) inc; Indtte; shops 50m; sand beach 13km; rv fishing; cycle hire; TV; some statics; adv bkg rec high ssn; quiet; CCI. "Excel sand beach at Pen Guen; adj park & rv with canoeing; poss itinerants/mkt traders." 1 Jun-15 Sep. € 8.60 2006*

PLANCOET *2E3* (4km SW Rural) *48.50269, -2.23313* **Camping Pallieter (Naturist), Le Ville Menier, Bourseul, 22130 Plancoët [02 96 83 05 15; fax 02 96 83 06 13; mail@pallieter.fr; www.pallieter.fr]** NW fr Dinan on D794 to Plancoët. In Plancoët turn L at rndbt opp Hotel Relais de la Source onto D19 dir Plélan-le-Petit. Site in 3km, sp. Med, unshd, mkd pitch; wc; chem disp; shwrs inc; el pnts (6A) €3.50; Indtte; shop 4km; tradsmn; snacks; bar; playgrnd; pool; some statics; dogs €5; Eng spkn; adv bkg; quiet; INF card. "Gd site; min stay 3 nights high ssn." 28 Apr-30 Sep. € 25.00 2007*

PLANCOET *2E3* (8km W Rural) *48.51954, -2.33389* **Camping à la Ferme (Robert), Le Pont-à-l'Ane, 22130 Landébia [tel/fax 02 96 84 47 52]** Fr Plancoët, take D768 twd Lamballe; in 8km turn L at 1st sp to Landébia, farm in 800m on R, sp fr Plancoët. Sm, pt shd; wc; own san; shwrs inc; el pnts (10A) €2.80; shops 1km; tradsmn; playgrnd; pool 8km; dogs €0.60; some Eng spkn; quiet; ccard not acc. "Pleasant CL-type in orchard; facs basic; owners helpful & friendly; gd base for N coast beaches; poss mosquitoes." 1 Apr-31 Oct. € 9.00 2008*

PLELAN LE GRAND *2F3* (400m S Urban) *47.99841, -2.09664* **Camp Municipal, Rue de l'Hermine, 35380 Plélan-le-Grand [02 99 06 81 41 (Mairie)]** Fr Rennes on D224 (N24). Leave D224 at town sp. Site sp on L at W end of town. Sm, shd; wc (some cont); chem disp (wc); mv service pnt; shwrs inc; el pnts; Indtte; shops 400m; playgrnd; htd pool; rv 2km; tennis; dogs; quiet but some traff noise. "Well-organised; gd facs for municipal site; warden calls am & pm, site yourself; gd NH." 2007*

PLELAN LE GRAND *2F3* (7km SW Rural) **Camping du Château d'Aleth, Rue de l'Ecole, 56380 St Malo-de-Beignon [06 78 96 10 62 (mob); contact@camping-aleth.com; www.camping-aleth.com]** Fr D224 (N24) twds Rennes exit N onto D773 to St Malo-de-Beignon in 5km, site L by church. Sm, pt sl, pt shd; wc; chem disp; mv service pnt; shwrs; el pnts (10A) €2.50; Indtte; shop; rest, bar 300m; BBQ; playgrnd; dogs; Eng spkn; quiet. "Pleasant, clean site by lake; clean facs." ♦ 1 Apr-30 Sep. € 9.50 2006*

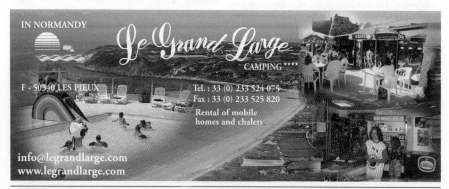

PLELAN LE GRAND *2F3* (8km NW Rural) *48.02403, -2.17282* **Camp Municipal Brocéliande, Rue du Chevalier Lancelot du Lac, 35380 Paimpont [02 99 07 89 16 or 02 99 07 81 18 (Mairie); fax 02 99 07 88 18; mairie. paimport@wanadoo.fr; www.camping-paimpont-broceliande.com]** Sp on N edge of Paimpont vill. On D773 dir St Méen-le-Grand/Concoret, 500m fr Paimpont. Med, hdg/mkd pitch, pt shd; wc (some cont); chem disp; shwrs inc; el pnts (5A) €3; gas 500m; Indtte; playgrnd; rv & lake sw & fishing adj; cycle hire; tennis; entmnts; internet; phone; bus in vill; quiet; red low ssn; CCI. " Pleasant, spacious, clean site; friendly; conv NH; no barrier; gd facs for children; sh walk to attractive vill; excel." ♦ 1 Apr-30 Sep. € 10.00 2009*

PLESTIN LES GREVES *2E2* (2km NE Coastal) *48.66805, -3.60060* **Camp Municipal St Efflam, Rue Lan-Carré, 22310 Plestin-les-Grèves [02 96 35 62 15; fax 02 96 35 09 75; campingmunicipalplestin@wanadoo.fr; www.camping-municipal-bretagne.com]** Fr Morlaix on D786 thro Plestin-les-Grèves; foll D786 sp St Efflam down hill to bay; site on R 850m along bay; sp. Lge, mkd pitch, pt sl, terr, pt shd; wc; chem disp; mv service pnt; shwrs inc; el pnts (7A) €2.50; gas; Indtte; tradsmn; rest; bar; BBQ; playgrnd; sand beach 150m; sw, fishing, boating adj; dogs €1.30; Eng spkn; adv bkg ess high ssn; ccard acc; red low ssn; CCI. "Excel; helpful recep." ♦ 1 Apr-30 Sep. € 11.00 2009*

PLEUBIAN see Tréguier *1D3*

PLEUMEUR BODOU see Trégastel *1D2*

PLEUVILLE see Pressac *7A3*

PLEYBEN *2E2* (5km S Rural) *48.19316, -3.98160* **Camp Municipal de Pont-Coblant, 29190 Pleyben [02 98 73 31 22 or 02 98 26 68 11 (Mairie); fax 02 98 26 38 99; communedepleyben@wanadoo.fr]** On D785 Quimper rd. Turn L immed by phone box on ent Pont-Coblant. Med, mkd pitch, pt shd; wc; shwrs inc; el pnts (6-10A) €3.20; shop 4km; rest, bar adj; canoe & cycle hire; poss cr; quiet but some rd noise. "Beautiful site adj rv/ canal; spacious pitches; dated facs, ltd low ssn; warden visits twice daily (or call at Mairie); poss unkempt low ssn." 15 Jun-15 Sep. € 9.20 2008*

PLOBANNALEC see Pont l'Abbé *2F2*

PLOEMEL see Auray *2F3*

PLOEMEUR see Lorient *2F2*

PLOERMEL *2F3* (3km N Rural) *47.94866, -2.42077* **Camping du Lac, Les Belles Rives, 56800 Taupont-Ploërmel [tel/ fax 02 97 74 01 22; camping-du-lac@wanadoo.fr; www. camping-du-lac-ploermel.com]** Fr Ploërmel cent, take D8 twds Taupont; under narr bdge; foll sp to Lac-au-Duc 3km. Site clearly sp on R on edge of lake. Med, hdg/mkd/ hdstg pitch, terr, pt shd; htd wc; mv service pnt; chem disp; shwrs inc; el pnts (5A) €2.10; gas; Indtte; shop; tradsmn; snacks; bar; BBQ; playgrnd; pool & waterslide nrby; sand beach & lake sw adj; watersports adj; cycle hire nrby; tennis; 10% statics; dogs €0.80; Eng spkn; adv bkg; quiet; ccard acc high ssn; red low ssn; CCI. "V pleasant site; golf & horseriding 1km; interesting area; vg." ♦ 1 Apr-30 Sep. € 11.80 2008*

⊞ **PLOERMEL** *2F3* (6km N Rural) *47.98425, -2.38191* **FFCC Camping Parc Merlin l'Enchanteur, 8 Rue du Pont, Vallée de l'Yvel, 56800 Loyat [02 97 93 05 52 or 02 97 73 89 45; fax 02 97 60 47 77; camelotpark@wanadoo.fr; www. campingmerlin.com]** Fr Ploërmel take D766 N sp St Malo. In 5km turn L to Loyat. Site on L on ent vill opp garage, adj sm lake. Med, hdg/mkd pitch, pt shd; htd wc; chem disp; mv service pnt; shwrs inc; el pnts (6-10A) €4.50-6 (poss rev pol); gas; Indtte; sm shop & other shops 600m; tradsmn high ssn; rest, bar 200m; BBQ; htd covrd pool; sand beach/ lake sw with watersports 4km; fishing; tennis; games area; cycle hire; 10% statics; dogs €1; phone 1km; adv bkg; v quiet; red long stay; ccard acc; red CCI. "Lovely, peaceful site; spacious pitches; welcoming British owners; vg clean facs; poss soggy in winter; excel rest in vill; conv Château Josselin, Lizio & Brocéliande forest with legend of King Arthur; vg." ♦ € 12.00 2009*

PLOERMEL *2F3* (10km S Urban) *47.82479, -2.50182* **Camp Municipal du Pont Salmon, Rue Général de Gaulle, 56460 Sérent [02 97 75 91 98; fax 02 97 75 98 35; mairie.serent@wanadoo.fr; www.serent.fr]** S fr Ploërmel on N166 take D10 W 5km to Sérent. At N end of vill turn L at Pont Salmon, site on R. Med, hdg pitch, pt sl, pt shd; htd wc (male all cont); chem disp; mv service pnt; shwrs inc; el pnts (10A) €2.35 (poss rev pol); Indtte; shops 300m; playgrnd; htd pool; 5% statics; adv bkg; quiet. "Excel, well-kept site; gd san facs; Resistance Museum at St Marcel-Malestroit." ♦ 1 May-30 Sep. € 7.95 2009*

PLOERMEL *2F3* (7km NW Rural) *47.96932, -2.47010* **Camping La Vallée du Ninian, Route du Lac, Le Rocher-Taupont, 56800 Ploërmel [02 97 93 53 01; fax 02 97 93 57 27; infos@camping-ninian.com; www. camping-ninian.com]** Fr Ploërmel cent foll sp to Taupont or Lac au Duc; N on D8. Thro vill Taupont take L hand turn sp La Vallée du Ninian; site on L 1km fr Helléan. Sm, hdg pitch (lge), pt shd; wc; chem disp; shwrs inc; baby facs; el pnts (3-6A) €2-3.50; Indtte; shop; bar; playgrnd; htd pool; paddling pool; lake sw & watersports 4km; sand beach 4km; entmnt; dogs €1; quiet; adv bkg. "Farm produce; helpful owners; v peaceful; gd facs for children; vg." ♦ 4 Apr-19 Sep. € 16.00 2009*

PLOMBIERES LES BAINS *6F2* (10km S Rural) *47.92460, 6.47545* **Camp Municipal Le Val d'Ajol, Chemin des Oeuvres, 88340 Le Val-d'Ajol [03 29 66 55 17]** Fr N on N57 after Plombières-les-Bains turn onto D20 sp Le Val-d'Ajol. Site sps in vill. Sm, hdg pitch, pt shd; wc; chem disp; shwrs inc; el pnts (6A) €2.20; shop 1km; pool adj; TV; dogs; phone; adv bkg; quiet; CCI. "Clean facs; vg touring base; excel site." ♦ 15 Apr-30 Sep. € 8.10 2006*

PLOMBIERES LES BAINS *6F2* (2km W Rural) *47.96731, 6.44656* **Camping de l'Hermitage, 54 Rue du Boulot, 88370 Plombières-les-Bains [03 29 30 01 87; fax 03 29 30 04 01; contact@hermitage-camping.com; www.hermitage-camping.com]** Fr Plombières-les-Bains take D63 N dir Epinal; site sp. Med, hgd/mkd pitch, terr, pt shd; htd wc; chem disp; baby facs; fam bthrm; shwrs inc; gas; el pnts (4-10A) €3.20-5.30; lndtte; tradsmn; snacks; takeaway; BBQ; playgrnd; pool; games area; games rm; TV; 10% statics; dogs €1.60; phone; no twin-axles; poss cr; Eng spkn; adv bkg; quiet; red low ssn/CCI. "Gd, unisex san facs; vg." 1 Apr-15 Oct. € 13.90 2008*

PLOMBIERES LES BAINS *6F2* (4km W Urban) *47.96603, 6.41692* **Camp Municipal du Fraiteux, 81 Rue du Camping, Ruaux, 88370 Plombières-les-Bains [03 29 66 00 71 or 03 29 66 00 24 (Mairie); fax 03 29 30 06 64; campingdufraiteux@tiscali.fr; http://chaletsdufraiteux.chez-alice.fr]** Turn W fr N57 in cent of Plombières-les-Bains onto D20, foll sp to Epinal for 2km then L onto D20B to Ruaux, site on L. Sm, mkd pitch, pt sl; wc; shwrs inc; el pnts (4-10A) €2.70-4; gas; lndtte; shops adj; playgrnd; pool 3km; some statics; dogs €0.70; poss cr; quiet; 20% red CCI. 1 Mar-31 Oct. € 10.60 2007*

PLOMEUR see Pont l'Abbe *2F2*

PLONEOUR LANVERN see Pont l'Abbé *2F2*

PLONEVEZ PORZAY *2E2* (4km W Coastal) *48.11637, -4.26793* **Camping International de Kervel, 29550 Plonévez-Porzay [02 98 92 51 54; fax 02 98 92 54 96; camping.kervel@wanadoo.fr; www.camping-franceloc.fr]** Fr Douarnenez take D107 twd Châteaulin. After 8km turn L to Plage de Kervel & foll sp. Lge, hdg/mkd pitch, hdstg, pt shd; htd wc; chem disp; mv service pnt; baby facs; shwrs inc; el pnts (10A) €3.50; gas; lndtte; shop; rest; snacks; bar; BBQ (gas/charcoal); playgrnd; 3 htd pools (1 covrd); waterslide; sand beach 800m; tennis; games rm; entmnt (Jul & Aug); 30% statics; dogs €5; poss cr; Eng spkn; adv bkg (rec in high ssn); ccard acc; 5% red CCI. "Gd touring base for lovely area; helpful staff; excel, clean san facs." ♦ 28 Apr-30 Sep. € 23.50 2007*

PLONEVEZ PORZAY *2E2* (4km W Coastal) *48.14458, -4.26915* **Camping La Plage de Tréguer, Plage de Ste Anne-la-Palud, 29550 Plonévez-Porzay [02 98 92 53 52; fax 02 98 92 54 89; camping-treguer-plage@wanadoo.fr; www.camping-treguer-plage.com]** On D107 S fr Châteaulin. After 8km turn R to Ste Anne-la-Palud & foll sp. Lge, hdg/mkd pitch, hdstg, pt shd; wc (some cont); chem disp; mv service pnt; shwrs inc; el pnts (6A) €3.40; gas; lndtte; shop; tradsmn; snacks; bar; BBQ; playgrnd; sand beach adj; games area; games rm; entmnt; TV rm; some statics; dogs €2.20; Eng spkn; adv bkg; ccard acc; red low ssn; CCI. "Well-situated touring base; vg, friendly site; excel beach." 4 Apr-27 Sep. € 19.50 2009*

PLONEVEZ PORZAY *2E2* (4km W Coastal) *48.11042, -4.27983* **Camping Trezmalaouen, 20 Route de la Baie, 29550 Plonévez-Porzay [tel/fax 02 98 92 54 24; contact@campingtrezmalaouen.com; www.camping-trezmalaouen.com]** Fr Douarnenez take D107 N dir Plonévez-Porzay, site sp. Med, hdg/mkd pitch, some hdstg, pt shd; wc; chem disp; mv service pnt; shwrs inc; el pnts; lndtte; BBQ; playgrnd; sand beach adj; 75% statics; dogs €1.70; 2 mobile homes for disabled; dogs; adv bkg; ccard acc; red long stay/low ssn/CCI. "Sea views; vg touring base." 15 Mar-15 Oct. € 13.00 2006*

PLOUAY *2F2* (4km NW Rural) *47.96415, -3.42297* **Camping Bois des Ecureuils, 29300 Guilligomarc'h [tel/fax 02 98 71 70 98 or 01202 881602 (UK); bois-des-ecureuils@aliceadsl.fr; www.bois-des-ecureuils.fr]** N fr Plouay on D769 dir Faouet, for 5km; turn L to Guilligomarc'h; site sp. Sm, mkd pitch, pt sl, shd; wc (some cont); chem disp; shwrs inc; el pnts (5A) €2.50; gas; lndtte; shop 3km; tradsmn; playgrnd; rv sw 3km; lake 6km; sand beach 25km; cycle hire; dogs €1; poss cr; Eng spkn; adv bkg; quiet; no ccard acc; CCI. "Friendly British owners; gd walking; excel peaceful site; lge pitches." ♦ 2 Jun-2 Sep. € 11.00 2008*

PLOUESCAT *2E2* (2km W Coastal) *48.65980, -4.21340* **Camping La Baie du Kernic, Rue de Pen-an-Théven, 29430 Plouescat [02 98 69 86 60 or 04 99 57 20 25; fax 04 99 57 21 22; www.village-center.com]** Site sp W of Plouescat fr D10. Lge, hdg/mkd pitch, hdstg, pt shd; wc; chem disp; mv service pnt; sauna; shwrs €2; el pnts (8A) inc; lndtte; shop; rest; tradsmn; snacks; bar; BBQ; playgrnd; htd pools (1 covrd); paddling pool; sand beach adj; watersports; tennis; games area; internet; entmnt; dogs €3; Eng spkn; adv bkg; red low ssn. "Pleasant resort; well-run site with excel facs." ♦ 7 Apr-16 Sep. € 29.00 2007*

PLOUEZEC see Paimpol *1D3*

France

PLOUGASNOU *1D2* (1.5km SE Rural) *48.68548, -3.78530* **Camping Le Trégor, Route de Morlaix, Kerjean, 29630 Plougasnou [02 98 67 37 64; bookings@campingdutregor.com; www.campingdutregor.com]** At junc of D46 to Plougasnou. Site is on L just bef town sp. Sm, hdg/mkd pitch, pt shd; wc; chem disp (wc); shwrs inc; el pnts (6-10A) inc; gas; lndtte; shop 1km; BBQ; playgrnd; sand beach 1.2km; lake sw & watersports 3km; 10% statics; dogs €1; poss cr; adv bkg; quiet; no ccard acc; CCI. "Well-run site in beautiful area; British owners; dated but clean facs; ideal for walking, cycling & fishing; conv Roscoff ferries & Morlaix; phone if req NH after end Oct." Easter-31 Oct. € 15.00 2008*

PLOUGASNOU *1D2* (3km NW Coastal/Urban) *48.71421, -3.81563* **Camp Municipal de la Mer, 29630 Primel-Trégastel [02 98 72 37 06 or 02 98 67 30 06; fax 02 98 67 82 79; primel-tregastel.camping-de-la-mer@wanadoo.fr]** Fr Morlaix take D46 to Plougastel on to Primel-Trégastel. Bear R in vill & 1st L opp cafe to site on R in 100 m. Med, unshd, wc; chem disp; mv service pnt; shwrs €1; el pnts (10A) inc; gas 1.5km; lndtte; shop, rest, bar 500m; tradsmn high ssn; playgrnd; sand beach 500m; dogs €0.90; phone; poss cr; no adv bkg; quiet; no ccard acc; CCI. "Fine coastal views; gd walking & cycling; ltd facs low ssn." ♦ 1 Jun-30 Sep. € 15.60 2008*

⊞ **PLOUGASTEL DAOULAS** *2E2* (4.5km NE Coastal) *48.40134, -4.35419* **Camping St Jean, 29470 Plougastel-Daoulas [02 98 40 32 90 or 02 98 04 23 11; info@campingsaintjean.com; www.campingsaintjean.com]** Fr Brest, take N165 E for approx 12km then leave m'way after Plougastel exit & foll sp. Site in 2km at end of rd by rv. Med, hdg pitch, pt sl, terr, pt shd; wc; chem disp; mv service pnt; baby facs; shwrs; el pnts (6A) inc (poss rev pol); lndtte; shop; rest; snacks; BBQ; playgrnd; htd, covrd pool; entmnt; TV; some statics; dogs €2; poss cr; quiet; red low ssn. "Nice site by rv; steep in places; gd facs." € 22.00 (CChq acc) 2008*

PLOUGONVELIN see Conquet, Le *2E1*

PLOUGOULM see Roscoff *1D2*

PLOUGRESCANT see Tréguier *1D3*

PLOUGUERNEAU *2E2* (3km N Coastal) *48.63048, -4.52402* **Camping La Grève Blanche, St Michel, 29880 Plouguerneau [02 98 04 70 35 or 02 98 04 63 97 (LS); fax 02 98 04 63 97; lroudaut@free.fr; www.campinggreveblanche.com]** Fr Lannilis D13 to Plouguerneau, D32 sp La Grève, St Michel (look out for lorry rte sp). Avoid Plouguerneau vill when towing - tight RH bend. Med, pt sl, terr, unshd; wc; chem disp; mv service pnt; shwrs €1; el pnts (9A) €2.50; bar; shops 3km; playgrnd; sand beach; dogs €1.90; Eng spkn; adv bkg; 10% red low ssn; CCI. "Excel location; sea views; helpful staff; facs clean & well-kept; low ssn recep open eves only; in fog lighthouse sounds all night otherwise quiet." ♦ 7 May-12 Oct. € 10.90 2008*

PLOUGUERNEAU *2E2* (6km N Coastal) *48.63112, -4.44972* **Camping du Vougot, Route de Prat-Leden, 29880 Plouguerneau [tel/fax 02 98 25 61 51; campingduvougot@hotmail.fr; www.campingplageduvougot.com]** Fr N12 at Landerneau exit N onto D770 to Lesneven, then D28/D32 to Plouguerneau. Fr Plouguerneau take D10 dir Guissény then turn W onto D52 dir Grève-du-Vougot, site sp. Med, hdg/mkd pitch, pt shd; wc; chem disp; mv service pnt; shwrs €0.50; el pnts (10A) €3.30; lndtte; shop 6km; tradsmn; snacks; playgrnd; sand beach 250m; watersports nr; entmnt; 30% statics; dogs €2.60; adv bkg; quiet; ccard acc; red long stay; CCI. "Gd walking (GR34); interesting area; excel touring base." ♦ 1 Apr-31 Oct. € 16.00 2009*

See advertisement

PLOUGUERNEAU *2E2* (5km NE Coastal) *48.61032, -4.42817* **Aire Naturalle de Keralloret (Yvinec), 29880 Guissény [02 98 25 60 37; fax 02 98 25 69 88; auberge@keralloret.com jiesan@davidryan@wanadoo.co.uk; www.keralloret.com]** On D10 dir Plouguerneau, site 2.5km after Guissény. Sm, pt shd; wc; chem disp (wc); shwrs inc; el pnts (6A) €2.40 (v long lead req most pitches); tradsmn; rest; snacks; beach 5km; Eng spkn; adv bkg; quiet; ccard acc; CCI. "Delightful, spacious, peaceful CL-type site by sm lake; pleasant owners; ltd hook-ups; sm, dated but clean san facs; vg rest." Easter-1 Nov. € 9.50 2007*

PLOUHA *2E3* (Rural/Coastal) *48.69338, -2.89670* **Camping Domaine de Kerjean, 22580 Plouha [02 96 20 24 75]** Exit N12 at Les Rampes onto D786 N to Plouha. Site sp fr town cent. Lge, mkd pitch, hdstg, pt shd; wc; shwrs inc; el pnts €4; shop 3km; snacks; bar; BBQ (gas/elec); playgrnd; htd, covrd pool nr; sand beach 1km; fishing, sailing 10km; tennis 4km; horseriding 2km; dogs; adv bkg; Eng spkn; quiet. "Well-situated for beautiful beaches; gd walking area; vg." ♦ 15 May-15 Sep. € 18.00 2007*

PLOUHA *2E3* (2km NE Coastal) *48.69022, -2.90930* **Camping Domaine de Keravel, La Trinité, 22580 Plouha [02 96 22 49 13; fax 02 96 22 47 13; keravel@wanadoo.fr; www.keravel.com or www.les-castels.com]** Fr St Brieux, take D786 twd Paimpol. In cent of Plouha at church & traff lts foll sp to Port Moguer. Med, pt sl, terr, hdg pitch, pt shd; wc; chem disp; shwrs inc; el pnts (10A) €3.80 (rev pol); gas; Indtte; shop; snacks; playgrnd; htd pool; paddling pool; beach 1km; tennis; fishing; entmnt; games rm; cycle hire; entmnt; TV rm; dogs €3; adv bkg; quiet; CCI. "V pleasant site; modern san facs; access some pitches tight; helpful staff; lovely grounds." ♦ 26 Apr-27 Sep. € 24.10 2008*

PLOUHA *2E3* (5km NE Coastal) *48.71944, -2.95305* **Camping Le Varquez-sur-Mer, 5 Route de la Corniche, Bréhec-Plage, 22580 Plouha [02 96 22 34 43; fax 02 96 22 68 87; campinglevarquez@wanadoo.fr; www.camping-le-varquez.com]** Sp bet St Quay-Portrieux & Paimpol fr D786. Med, hdg/mkd pitch, hdstg, pt sl, pt shd; wc; chem disp; shwrs; el pnts (10A) €3.70; gas; Indtte; shop 4km; tradsmn; snacks; bar; BBQ; playgrnd; htd pool; paddling pool; sand beach 600m; entmnt; 30% statics; dogs €1.90; Eng spkn; quiet; ccard acc; CCI. "Lovely coast; peaceful, family-run site; adj walking rte GR34." ♦ 4 Apr-4 Oct. € 19.20 2008*

PLOUHARNEL see Carnac *2G3*

PLOUHINEC *2F2* (1km SE Coastal) *47.66489, -3.22105* **Camping Le Moténo, Rue du Passage d'Etel, 56680 Plouhinec [02 97 36 76 63; fax 02 97 85 81 84; info@camping-moteno.com; www.camping-le-moteno.com]** App Auray on D22, take 2nd turn L after Pont Lerois & foll sps. Lge, hdg/mkd pitch, pt shd; wc; chem disp; shwrs inc; el pnts (10A) inc; gas; Indtte; shop; rest; snacks; bar; playgrnd; htd, covrd pool; waterslide; jacuzzi; sand beach 800m; fishing & watersports 100m; cycle hire; games area; games rm; entmnt; TV; some statics; dogs €5; Eng spkn; adv bkg; quiet; red low ssn. "Pleasant site; gd base Carnac & Quiberon Peninsula." ♦ 3 Apr-11 Sep. € 32.00 2009*

PLOUVORN see Landivisiau *2E2*

PLOZEVET *2F2* (500m SW Rural) *47.98006, -4.43071* **Camping La Corniche, Chemin de la Corniche, 29710 Plozévet [02 98 91 33 94 or 02 98 91 32 93; fax 02 98 91 41 53; infos@campinglacorniche.com; www.campinglacorniche.com]** Fr N165 foll sp Audierne onto D784 to Plozévet & foll sps to site. Med, hdg pitch, pt shd; wc; chem disp; mv service pnt; baby facs; shwrs inc; el pnts (10A) €3.20 (poss rev pol); Indtte; shop; tradsmn; playgrnd; pool; beach 2km; wifi; 10% statics; dogs €2.20; red low ssn; CCI. "Clean site; lge pitches; helpful owner; excel facs; gd." ♦ 4 Apr-26 Sep. € 17.00 2009*

PLUMERGAT see Ste Anne d'Auray *2F3*

POET LAVAL, LE *9D2* (E Rural) *44.52961, 5.02227* **Camp Municipal Lorette, 26160 Le Poët-Laval [04 75 91 00 62 or 04 75 46 44 12 (Mairie); fax 04 75 46 46 45; camping.lorette@wanadoo.fr]** Site 4km W of Dieulefit on D540. Med, mkd pitch, pt shd; wc; chem disp (wc); mv service pnt; shwrs inc; el pnts (6A) €2; Indtte; shop; tradsmn; rest 500m; snacks; playgrnd; pool; tennis; no statics; dogs €1.10; bus; phone; quiet; CCI. "Well-kept site with views; lge pitches; clean, modern facs; nr lavender fields (Jun/Jul); mkt in Dieulefit Fri; excel." ♦ 1 May-30 Sep. € 9.60 2009*

POET LAVAL, LE *9D2* (8km W Rural) *44.56423, 4.90788* **Camping à la Ferme des Roures (Gontard), Route de St Gervais, Les Roures, 26160 La Bégude-de-Mazenc [04 75 46 21 80; gitesfrance@ferme-des-roures.com]** Fr Montélimar E on D540 for 15km. Turn L onto D74 dir St Gervais. Foll sp for site. Sm, pt sl, shd; wc; chem disp; shwrs inc; el pnts (10A) €2.20 (poss rev pol); Indtte; gas & shop 4km; dogs €0.75; quiet; CCI. "Site in wood in pleasant area; friendly, helpful owners; clean facs." ♦ 1 May-30 Sep. € 8.00 2006*

POILLY LEZ GIEN see Gien *4G3*

POITIERS For sites convenient for Futuroscope, also see listings under Châtellerault and Jaunay Clan.

POITIERS *7A2* (10km N Rural) *46.65611, 0.30194* **Camping du Futur, 1 Rue des Bois, 86170 Avanton [05 49 54 09 67; fax 05 49 54 09 59; contact@camping-du-futur.com; www.camping-du-futur.com]** Exit A10 junc 28. After toll take 1st exit at rndabt sp Avanton. Site well sp fr Avanton, but care needed thro Martigny & hotel complex. Med, hdg/mkd pitch, pt shd; wc; chem disp (wc); mv service pnt; shwrs inc; el pnts (10A) €3.50; Indtte; shop, rest & snacks 1km; tradsmn; bar; playgrnd; pool (high ssn); games area; games rm; TV; dogs €1.50; c'van storage; adv bkg; quiet; red low ssn; CCI. "Spacious, well-run site; helpful British owners; vg clean san facs; ltd facs early ssn; 5 mins Futuroscope & A10; ideal NH or longer." ♦ 1 Apr-30 Sep. € 19.50 2009*

POITIERS *7A2* (4.5km S Rural) *46.54367, 0.33230* **Camp Municipal de St Benoît, 2 Rue de Passe Lourdain, 86280 St Benoît [05 49 88 48 55; tourisme@ville-saint-benoit.fr; www.ville-saint-benoit.fr]** Fr N or S turn W off D741 to St Benoît, site well sp. Med, mkd pitch, pt shd; wc; shwrs; el pnts (4A) €3; shops, rest, bar in vill; playgrnd; rv fishing & watersports adj; dogs €0.50; poss cr; adv bkg; rlwy noise adj; CCI. 1 Jun-6 Sep. € 12.20 2009*

POIX DE PICARDIE *3C3* (300m SW Rural) *49.77621, 1.97467* **Camp Municipal Le Bois des Pêcheurs, Route de Forges-les-Eaux, 80290 Poix-de-Picardie [03 22 90 11 71 or 03 22 90 32 90 (Mairie); fax 03 22 90 32 91; camping@ville-poix-de-picardie.fr; www.ville-poix-de-picardie.fr]** Fr town cent by D901 dir Beauvais, turn R onto D919 sp Camping. Fr Beauvais, turn L at bottom of steep hill opp Citroen agent, site 500m on R. Med, hdg/mkd pitch, hdstg, pt shd; wc; chem disp; shwrs inc; el pnts (10A) €4; gas 300m; Indtte; shops, supmkt adj; rest, bar 500m; BBQ; playgrnd; htd, covrd pool 800m; rv & fishing adj; tennis 800m; games rm; cycle hire; TV; dogs €1.50; poss cr; Eng spkn; adv bkg; quiet; ccard not acc; red long stay; CCI. "Pleasant, peaceful site in delightful area; friendly; clean facs; gd touring base; vg walking & cycling; train to Amiens; mkt Sun; rec." ♦ 1 Apr-30 Sep. € 12.00 2009*

POLIGNY *6H2* (1km SW Rural) **Camp Communautaire de la Croix du Dan, 39800 Poligny [03 84 37 01 35; fax 03 84 73 77 59; cccgrimont@wanadoo.fr; www.ville-poligny.fr]** Fr SW on N83 turn R at rndabt sp 'Centre'; site on R immed bef town sp Poligny. Fr N & NW take D905 (N5) into & thro town cent (no L turn on N83 S of Poligny), then foll sp Lons-Le Saunier. Site on L bef sportsgrnd - look for m'van sp. Do not overshoot ent, as diff to see. N5 fr E not rec as steep & hairpins. Med, mkd pitch, pt shd; wc (mainly cont); chem disp; shwrs inc; el pnts (10A) €6.40; Indtte; shops 1km; tradsmn; playgrnd; no statics; dogs; phone; poss cr; Eng spkn; quiet; CCI. "Excel, clean, tidy site; helpful warden; gates open 24hrs; twin-axles extra; pretty town." ♦ 15 Jun-20 Sep. € 7.45 2009*

POMMEROL see Rémuzat *9D2*

POMMEUSE *4E4* (1km SW Rural) *48.80860, 2.99300* **Camping Le Chêne Gris, 24 Place de la Gare de Faremoutiers, 77515 Pommeuse [01 64 04 21 80; fax 01 64 20 05 89; info@lechenegris.com; www.lechenegris.com]** Fr A4, take D634 (N34) SE dir Coulommiers, turn R onto D25 sp Pommeuse & Faremoutiers. Site on R after stn at Faremoutiers. Well sp. Lge, hdg pitch, hdstg, terr, pt shd; htd wc; chem disp; mv service pnt; baby facs; shwrs inc; el pnts (10A) inc; Indtte; shop; tradsmn; rest; snacks; bar; playgrnd; 2 pools (1 htd, covrd); paddling pool; games rm; internet; 60% statics; dogs €2.50; phone; Eng spkn; adv bkg; quiet; red low ssn; CCI. "Conv Paris, Disneyland & Parc Astérix; walking dist to trains - direct line to Paris; excel san facs; vg." ♦ 24 Apr-8 Nov. € 37.00 (CChq acc) 2008*

PONCIN see Pont d'Ain *9A2*

⊞ **PONS (CHARENTE MARITIME)** *7B2* (1km NE Rural) *45.59429, -0.53841* **Camping Les Moulins de la Vergne, 9 Route de Colombiers, 17800 Pons [tel/fax 05 46 90 50 84 or 05 46 49 11 49; uffelen@wanadoo.fr; www.moulinsdelavergne.nl]** Fr N on D137 take 1st exit Pons, turn L & foll yellow site sp. Fr S exit A10 junc 36 onto D732 & at rndabt take D137 N dir Saintes. In 4km turn R onto D125(E2) then R (S) onto D234, site sp on L. Fr town cent foll yellow sps in Pons - do not confuse with municipal site Le Paradis. NB c'vans not allowed thro Pons & should stay on by-pass. Med, mkd pitch, pt shd; wc; chem disp; shwrs inc; el pnts (10A) €2.90; Indtte; shops 1km; tradsmn; rest; snacks; bar; BBQ; playgrnd; pool; wifi; dogs €1.76; adv bkg; Eng spkn; rd noise; ccard acc; CCI. "Relaxed, friendly & helpful Dutch owners; clean san facs need update, ltd low ssn; excel rest; grass pitches soft in wet weather - park on site roads off ssn; no site lighting low ssn in touring area; site poss unkempt low ssn & poss mkt traders; conv touring base or NH nr A10 en rte Spain." ♦ € 13.20 2009*

PONS (CHARENTE MARITIME) *7B2* (500m W Urban) *45.57791, -0.55552* **Camp Municipal Le Paradis, 1 Ave de Poitou, 17800 Pons [05 46 91 36 72; fax 05 46 96 14 15; ville.pons@smic17.fr; www.pons-ville.org]** Well sp fr town o'skts. Med, mkd pitch, pt shd; wc; mv service pnt; shwrs inc; el pnts (6-10A) inc; shops adj; tradsmn; pool, waterslide 100m; rv fishing 200m; TV; dogs €1.76. "Excel; attractive grounds; interesting town; conv for Saintes, Cognac, Royan; helpful warden." ♦ 1 May-30 Sep. € 15.00 2007*

⊞ **PONS (CHARENTE MARITIME)** *7B2* (2km W Rural) *45.56976, -0.57906* **FFCC Camping Chardon, 13 Route des Bernards, 17800 Pons [50 46 95 01 25 or 06 62 34 39 44 (mob); camping.chardon@gmail.com; www.camping-chardon.fr]** Fr N or S on A10, exit junc 36 onto D732 (take care as heavy, fast traff). Site sp on R in 1km. Narr ent to rd. Or fr N or S on N137 take D732 twd Gémozac, site on L 2km fr Pons. Site lies to S of D732, bet N137 & A10. Sm, hdg pitch, pt shd; wc; chem disp; serviced pitch; shwrs; el pnts (10A) €3; gas 2km; Indtte; shops 1km; tradsmn; rest; pizzeria; bar; playgrnd; pool 1km; 75% statics; dogs €1.50; adv bkg; quiet; no ccard acc. "Excel basic, rustic site; friendly owners; basic, open-air san facs, ltd low ssn; poor facs for disabled; vg rest; conv Cognac, Saintes & Royan; low ssn phone ahead to check if open; v conv NH A10 or N137." ♦ € 13.00 2009*

PONT AUDEMER *3D2* (8km W Rural) *49.31433, 0.40344* **Camping La Lorie (Lehaye), 5 La Lorie, 27210 Fort-Moville [02 32 57 15 49]** Sm, pt shd; wc; chem disp (wc); shwrs inc; el pnts (10A) inc; BBQ; rest, snacks, bar 2km; playgrnd; 10% statics; dogs; quiet; CCI. "CL-type site in attractive area; basic facs; conv Le Havre, Honfleur." Easter-1 Nov. € 13.50 2008*

France

PONT AUDEMER *3D2* (2km NW Rural) *49.36673, 0.48651* **Camp Municipal Risle-Seine Les Etangs, 19 Route des Etangs, 27500 Toutainville [02 32 42 46 65; fax 02 32 42 24 17; camping@ville-pont-audemer.fr; www.ville-pont-audemer.fr]** Fr Le Havre on A131/E05 cross rv at Pont de Normandie (toll). Take D580 & at junc 3 branch R & take 2nd exit onto D22 sp Beuzeville. At edge of Fiquefleur take D180, then D675 (N175) dir Pont-Audemer. In Toutainville foll site sp, turn L just bef A13 underpass, then immed R. Site approx 2km on R. Med, hdg/mkd pitch, pt shd; wc; chem disp; mv service pnt; serviced pitches; shwrs inc; el pnts (10A) inc; Indtte; shop 1.5km; tradsmn; snacks; bar; BBQ; playgrnd; htd pool & tennis 2km; fishing; canoeing, watersports; cycle hire; games area; wifi; games/TV rm; dogs free; bus; Eng spkn; adv bkg; quiet; red long stay/low ssn; ccard acc. "Lovely, well-run site; spacious pitches; poss school groups at w/end; helpful warden; barrier clsd 2200-0830 but flexible for ferry; many leisure activities; vg for dogs; 1hr Le Havre ferry; Fri mkt Pont-Audemer; conv NH; excel." ♦ 15 Mar-15 Nov. € 16.50
ABS - N13 2009*

See advertisement

PONT AUTHOU see Brionne *3D2*

PONT AVEN *2F2* (10km N Rural) *47.92512, -3.68888* **Camping Les Genêts d'Or, Kermerour 29380 Bannalec [tel/fax 02 98 39 54 35; info@holidaybrittany.com; www.holidaybrittany.com]** Fr Pont Aven/Bannalec exit on N165 N to Bannalec on D4; after rlwy x-ing turn R sp Quimperlé. In 1km turn R, sp Le Trévoux; site on L 500m. Sm, hdg/mkd pitch, pt sl, pt shd; wc; chem disp; shwrs inc; el pnts (6A) €3; Indtte (inc dryer); shop 500m; supmkt 1km; rest; snacks; bar; BBQ; playgrnd; pool 10km; sand beach 15km; games rm; cycle hire; some statics; dogs €1.50; Eng spkn; adv bkg; quiet, some non-intrusive rd/rlwy noise; ccard not acc; red long stay; CCI. "Nice, well-kept, peaceful site in orchard; lge pitches; welcoming British owners; immac san facs; Bannalec in walking dist; excel touring base; rec." ♦ 1 Apr-30 Sep. € 13.00 2009*

PONT AVEN *2F2* (8km SE Coastal) *47.78799, -3.70064* **Camping de l'Ile Percée, Plage de Trénez, 29350 Moëlan-sur-Mer [02 98 71 16 25; contact@camping-ilepercee.com; http://camping-ilepercee.ifrance.com]** App thro Moëlan-sur-Mer, 6km SE of Pont-Aven or 6km SW of Quimperlé - watch for R turn after Moëlan. Take D116 sp to Kerfany. Keep strt at Kergroës, turn L after 500m sp L'Ile Percée. Med, pt sl, unshd; wc (some cont); baby facs; shwrs; el pnts (4-6A) €2.40-3.25; Indtte; snacks; bar; BBQ; playgrnd; sandy/rocky beach adj; sw, fishing & watersports 50m; games area; entmnt; TV; some statics; dogs €1; poss cr; adv bkg; v quiet. "Well-run site; sea views; ent narr & winding; sm pitches; san facs poss stretched high ssn." Easter-17 Sep. € 14.50 2006*

PONT AVEN *2F2* (8km S Coastal) *47.79640, -3.77489* **Camping Les Chaumières, Kerascoët, 29920 Névez [02 98 06 73 06; fax 02 98 06 78 34; campingdeschaumieres@wanadoo.fr]** S fr Pont-Aven thro Névez to Kerascoët. Med, hdg/mkd pitch, pt shd; wc; chem disp; mv service pnt; serviced pitches; shwrs inc; el pnts (4-10A) €2.70-3.60; gas 3km; Indtte; shop 3km; tradsmn high ssn; rest, snacks, bar adj; playgrnd; sand beach 800m; dogs €1; Eng spkn; adv bkg ess; quiet; red low ssn; CCI. "Excel, well-organised site; facs poss stretched high ssn; gd play & games areas; sandy bay/beaches, cliff walks." ♦
15 May-15 Sep. € 14.70 2006*

PONT AVEN *2F2* (10km S Coastal) *47.80492, -3.74510* **Camping Le St Nicolas, Port Manec'h, 29920 Névez [02 98 06 89 75; fax 02 98 06 74 61; info@campinglesaintnicolas.com; www.campinglesaintnicolas.com]** Take D783 W fr Pont-Aven for 2km, turn L onto D77 S thro Névez to Port Manech. Site well sp. Narr app to site. Lge, hdg/mkd pitch, pt sl, pt shd; wc (some cont); chem disp; shwrs inc; el pnts (6-10A) €3.70-4.70; gas; Indtte; tradsmn high ssn; rest, snacks, bar in vill; playgrnd; htd pool; paddling pool; sand beach 200m; watersports; games area; games rm; tennis, horseriding nrby; entmnt; TV rm; dogs €1.70; Eng spkn; adv bkg; quiet; ccard acc; red low ssn; CCI. "Pleasant, wooded site; friendly owners; cliff walks; gd touring base." ♦ 1 May-15 Sep. € 21.50 2009*

PONT AVEN *2F2* (3km SW Rural) *47.84500, -3.79000* **Domaine de Kerlann, Land Rosted, 29930 Pont Aven [02 98 06 01 77; fax 02 98 06 18 50; reservations@ledomainedekerlann.fr; www.siblu.fr/domainedekerlann]** Fr Pont Aven foll sp twd Concarneau. After 1.5km, turn L onto D77 twd Névez. Site approx 1.5km on R. V lge, hdg/mkd pitch, hdstg, pt sl, pt shd; htd wc; chem disp; baby facs; shwrs inc; el pnts (8A) inc; gas; Indtte; shop; rest; snacks; bar; playgrnd; htd pools (1 covrd); waterslide; sand beach 3km; tennis; cycle hire; entmnt; child entmtn; TV rm; 85% statics; Eng spkn; adv bkg ess high ssn; ccard acc; red low ssn/low ssn; CCI. "Wooded site & areas poss muddy after rain; children's club all ssn; teenagers' club Jul/Aug; sports pitch; all facs open all ssn." ♦ 4 Apr-21 Sep. 2009*

PONT AVEN *2F2* (5km SW Rural) *47.81749, -3.79959* **Camping Les Genêts, Route St Philibert, 29920 Névez [02 98 06 86 13 or 02 98 06 72 31; campinglesgenets@aol.com; www.campinglesgenets-nevez.com]** Turn S off D783 onto D77 to Névez. At church in town, bear R & turn immed R to exit Névez with post office on R. Site on L, clearly sp. Med, hdg/mkd pitch, pt shd; wc (some cont); baby facs; shwrs inc; el pnts (3-10A) €2.40-5; gas 500m; Indtte; shops 500m; playgrnd; sand beach; 10% statics; dogs €1; some Eng spkn; adv bkg; quiet; CCI. "Excel beaches adj; vg." 1 Jun-15 Sep. € 10.00 2007*

PONT AVEN *2F2* (6km SW Coastal) *47.79906, -3.79033* **Camping Les Deux Fontaines, Raguenès, 29920 Névez [02 98 06 81 91; fax 02 98 06 71 80; info@les2fontaines.fr; www.les2fontaines.fr]** Leave N165/E60 at Kérampaou foll sp D24 twds Pont Aven. In approx 4.5km turn R (S) foll sp Névez then Raguenès. Site 3km fr Névez. Lge, mkd pitch, pt shd; wc (some cont); shwrs inc; baby facs; el pnts (6A) €3.60; Indtte; shop; rest; bar; sand beach 800m; htd pool; tennis; 80% statics (tour ops); dogs €3.60; o'night facs for m'vans; adv bkg; red low ssn. "Busy high ssn; popular with British families." ♦ 8 May-12 Sep. € 32.50 2009*

PONT AVEN *2F2* (8km SW Coastal) *47.79330, -3.80110* **Airotel Camping Raguenès-Plage, 19 Rue des Îles, 29920 Névez [02 98 06 80 69; fax 02 98 06 89 05; info@camping-le-raguenes-plage.com; www.camping-le-raguenes-plage.com]** Fr Pont-Aven take D783 dir Trégunc; in 2.5km turn L for Névez, foll sps to Raguenès fr Névez. Or fr N165 take D24 at Kérampaou exit; in 3km turn R to Nizon; at church in vill turn R onto D77 to Névez; site on L 3km after Névez. Lge, mkd pitch, hdstg, pt shd; htd wc (some cont); chem disp; mv service pnt; baby facs; sauna; shwrs inc; el pnts (6A) €3.80; gas; Indtte; shop; rest; snacks adj; bar; BBQ; playgrnd; htd, covrd pool & paddling pool; waterslide; sand beach adj; watersports school adj; tennis nr; games rm; cycle hire; trampoline; games area; horseriding; internet; entmnt; 20% statics (sep area); dogs €3.20; Eng spkn; adv bkg rec; quiet; red low ssn; ccard acc; CCI. "Pretty, wooded, family-run site; private path to beach; clean facs; 1st class site." ♦ 1 Apr-30 Sep. € 29.90 2009*

See advertisement above

PONT AVEN *2F2* (8km SW Coastal) *47.7946, -3.79816* **Camping de l'Océan, Impasse des Mouettes, Keroren, Raguenès, 29920 Névez [02 98 06 87 13; fax 02 98 06 78 26; campingocean@orange.fr; www.camping-ocean.fr]** Leave N165 at Kérampaou; foll sp D24 dir Pont Aven; in 4.5km turn R onto D77; foll sp Névez then Raguenès; site 3km fr Névez. Med, hdg/mkd pitch, pt sl, pt shd; wc (some cont); serviced pitches; chem disp; baby facs; shwrs inc; el pnts (4-10A) €3.50-4.70; Indtte; shops 3km; tradsmn; rest, snacks & bar 2km; BBQ; sm playgrnd; htd covrd pool; sand beach 300m; sailing; fishing; games area; games rm; TV; 4% statics; dogs €1.50; phone; bus; poss cr; some Eng spkn; adv bkg rec high ssn; quiet; ccard acc; red low ssn; CCI. "Peaceful, well-run, family-owned site; dir access to beach; excel." ♦ 15 May-15 Sep. € 20.60 2009*

PONT AVEN *2F2* (8km SW Coastal) *47.79597, -3.79877* **Camping Le Vieux Verger - Ty Noul, Raguenès-Plage, 29920 Névez [02 98 06 86 08 or 02 98 06 83 17 (LS); fax 02 98 06 76 74; contact@campingduvieuxverger.com; www.campingduvieuxverger.com]** Fr Pont-Aven take D783 dir Concarneau; in 2.5km L onto D77 to Névez; foll sp Raguenès-Plage; 1st site on R. NB Le Vieux Verger (open Jul/Aug) & Ty Noul are adj sites, same owner. Med, hdg/mkd pitch, pt shd; wc; chem disp (wc); shwrs inc; el pnts (4-10A) €3-4 (poss rev pol); shop (high ssn); rest 500m; playgrnd; sand beach 500m; a few statics; dogs free; phone; poss cr; quiet; red low ssn; CCI. "Le View Verger well-run with pool & waterslides; Ty Noul excel, well-kept site; highly rec low ssn." Easter-27 Sep. € 15.00 2009*

PONT CROIX see Audierne *2F1*

PONT D'AIN *9A2* (6km NE Rural) *46.08969, 5.40557* **Camping Vallée d'Ain, Allée Terres de l'Ain, 01450 Poncin [tel/fax 04 74 37 20 78; camping-vallee-de-lain@laposte.net; http://campingponcin.chez.com]** Fr Pont-d'Ain cent foll D1075 (N75) S & when exit Pont-d'Ain turn L on D1084 (N84) (sp 300m fr vill); site on D81 off D91. Med, pt shd; wc; chem disp; mv service pnt; shwrs inc; el pnts (5-16A) €2.80-4; gas; Indtte; shops adj; rest; snacks; bar; BBQ; playgrnd; htd pool; entmnt; rv adj; canoe, cycle hire; some statics; dogs €1.10; quiet, but some m'way noise; CCI. "Walks by rv, helpful staff; gd san facs." 1 Apr-30 Sep. € 12.20 2007*

PONT D'AIN *9A2* (800m E Urban) *46.04680, 5.34446* **Camping de l'Oiselon, Rue Georges Convert, 01160 Pont-d'Ain [tel/fax 04 74 39 05 23; campingoiselon@libertysurf.fr]** Fr A42 exit Pont-d'Ain foll D90 to vill. In vill cent turn R on D1075 (N75). Turn L immed after x-ing Rv L'Ain. Foll rd passing tennis club on L. Site on L, clearly sp. Lge, pt shd; wc; chem disp; baby facs; shwrs inc; el pnts (6-10A) €2.40-3.10 (poss rev pol); shops; rest; snacks; BBQ; playgrnd; pool; rv sw & beach; fishing; canoeing; tennis adj; horseriding 5km; cycle hire; games area; entmnt; 30% statics; dogs free; poss cr; Eng spkn; adv bkg; quiet (poss some noise fr disco); CCI. "Gd, well-run site with easy access; helpful, friendly staff; gd san facs; NH only." ♦ 21 Mar-11 Oct. € 11.60 2009*

PONT DE L'ARCHE *3D2* (N Urban) *49.3060, 1.1546* **Camp Municipal Eure et Seine, Quai Maréchal Foch, 27340 Pont-de-l'Arche [02 35 23 06 71 or 02 32 98 90 70 (Mairie); fax 02 32 98 90 89; www.pontdelarche.fr]** Fr Rouen S on D6015 (N15) turn 1st L after x-ing rv bdge, drive downhill then L under bdge & strt on for 300m, site on R. Restricted width on app. Sm, mkd pitch, pt shd; wc; chem disp; shwrs inc; el pnts (6-10A) €3.05-3.60; Indtte; shop 200m; rest; bar; playgrnd; rv fishing adj; wifi; 4% statics; dogs €0.95; phone; poss v cr; adv bking; rd noise; ccard acc; red long stay; CCI. "Pleasant, peaceful, clean rvside site in attractive medieval town; sm pitches; gd, modern san facs." ♦ 1 Apr-31 Oct. € 7.90 2009*

⊞ **PONT DE L'ARCHE** *3D2* (3km N Rural) *49.32282, 1.14697* **Camping Les Terrasses, 2 Rue de Rouen, 27460 Igoville [tel/fax 02 35 23 08 15]** Fr A13 exit junc 20 sp Pont-de-l'Arche D321, pass thro town & at intersection of D321 & D6015 (N15) turn L. Cross Rv Seine to Igoville & cont on D6015. Site sp fr D6015 in both dirs. Sm, hdg/mkd pitch, hdstg, terr, pt shd; htd wc (some cont); chem disp; mv service pnt; shwrs inc; el pnts (6A) inc; supmkt 500m; playgrnd; 8% statics; dogs; bus to Rouen; site clsd Xmas & New Year; Eng spkn; adv bkg; quiet; red low ssn; CCI. "Excel views Seine valley; warm welcome; peaceful site." € 10.90 2009*

See advertisement below

⊞ **PONT DE L'ARCHE** *3D2* (10km S Rural) *49.22513, 1.22406* **FFCC Camping Le St Pierre, 1 Rue du Château, 27430 St Pierre-du-Vauvray [tel/fax 02 32 61 01 55; eliane.darcissac@wanadoo.fr; www.lecampingdesaintpierre.com]** Fr S exit A154 junc 3 or A13 junc 18 (Louviers) onto D6155 (N155) E until junc with D6015 (N15). Turn L & in 4km turn R to St Pierre. Fr N on D6015 after x-ing Rv Seine at Pont-de-l'Arche cont for approx 6km & turn L to St Pierre. Do not ent St Pierre fr E on D313 due low bdge under rlwy line. Med, hdg/mkd pitch, pt shd; wc; chem disp; shwrs inc; el pnts (6-10A) €2.30-3.80; Indry rm; shop 1km; BBQ; playgrnd; htd pool; 25% statics; dogs €1.20; site clsd 2 weeks at Xmas/New Year; adv bkg rec; noise fr rlwy adj; CCI. "In grounds sm chateau; TGV rlwy line adj site; conv Giverny; friendly staff; ltd facs; NH only." € 13.10 2008*

France

PONT DE SALARS *7D4* (1.5km N Rural) *44.29150, 2.72571* **Parc Camping du Lac, 12290 Pont-de-Salars [05 65 46 84 86; fax 05 65 46 60 39; camping.du.lac@wanadoo.fr; www.camping-du-lac.fr.st]** Fr Rodez on D911 La Primaube-Millau rd, turn L bef ent Pont-de-Salars. Site sp. Lge, mkd pitch, pt sl, terr, pt shd; wc (some cont); chem disp; baby facs; shwrs inc; el pnts (3-6A) €2.50-3.50; gas; Indtte; shop & 1km; tradsmn; rest; snacks; bar; BBQ; playgrnd; pool; paddling pool; lake sw; sailing; fishing; entmnt; TV; 90% statics; no dogs; phone; poss cr; adv bkg; noisy nr entmnt area; ccard acc; red low ssn. "Beautiful situation; poor for c'vans, OK m'vans; diff lge o'fits; blocks req; site poss unclean end of ssn." ♦ 1 Jun-30 Sep. € 17.00 2009*

PONT DE SALARS *7D4* (4km N Rural) *44.30471, 2.73526* **FLOWER Camping Les Terrasses du Lac, Route du Vibal, 12290 Pont-de-Salars [05 65 46 88 18 or 06 72 89 84 34 (mob); fax 05 65 46 85 38; campinglesterrasses@orange.fr; www.campinglesterrasses.com or www.flowercamping.com]** Fr Rodez S on N2088 to La Primaube. Turn L in La Primaube onto D911 for Pont-de-Salars. Turn L onto D523 by timberyard to Le Vibal & foll sp to site approx 4km fr vill cent. Or fr A75 exit junc 44.1 dir Pont-de-Salars, turn R onto D523 then as above. Lge, hdg pitch, terr, pt shd; wc; chem disp; mv service pnt; some serviced pitches; shwrs inc; el pnts (6A) €4; gas; Indtte; shop; rest; snacks; bar; BBQ; playgrnd; htd pool; sand beach & lake sw adj; boating; fishing; games area; wifi; entmnt; TV; 30% statics; dogs €2; Eng spkn; adv bkg; quiet; ccard acc; red low ssn/long stay; CCI. "Well laid-out site o'looking lake; gd touring base; vg." ♦ 1 Apr-30 Sep. € 22.50 2009*

See advertisement opposite (below)

PONT DE SALARS *7D4* (7km SE Rural) *44.21420, 2.76660* **Camping Le Caussanel, Lac de Pareloup, 12290 Canet-de-Salars [05 65 46 85 19; fax 05 65 46 89 85; info@lecaussanel.com; www.lecaussanel.com or www.les-castels.com]** Exit A75 junc 44.1 onto D911 dir Pont-de-Salars, then D993 Salles-Curan & D538 Canet-de-Salars, dir Lac de Pareloup. In 6km fork R to Le Caussanel: in 100m fork L to site. Fr N88 exit at La Primaube then D911 to Pont-de-Salars, then as above. Lge, mkd pitch, hdstg, pt sl, terr, pt shd; wc; mv service pnt; chem disp; baby facs; shwrs inc; el pnts (5A) inc; shop or 10km; tradsmn; rest; snacks; bar; playgrnd; htd pools; waterslide; fishing; windsurfing & sailing; boat & cycle hire; games rm; entmnt; internet; 20% statics; dogs €3.90; Eng spkn; adv bkg; quiet; red low ssn; CCI. "Beautiful situation, views over lake; friendly owner; vg." ♦ 10 May-11 Sep. € 33.00 (CChq acc) 2009*

PONT DE SALARS *7D4* (8km S Rural) *44.21499, 2.77785* **Camping Le Soleil Levant, Lac de Pareloup, 12290 Canet-de-Salars [05 65 46 03 65; contact@camping-soleil-levant.com; www.camping-soleil-levant.com]** Exit A75 junc 44.1 onto D911 to Pont-de-Salars, then S on D993 dir Salles-Curan. Site in 8km bef bdge on L. Lge, mkd pitch, terr, pt sl, pt shd; htd wc (some cont); chem disp; baby facs; fam bthrm; shwrs inc; el pnts (5A) inc; gas; Indtte; shop 4km; tradsmn; snacks; bar; BBQ; playgrnd; lake sw & sand/shgl beach adj; fishing; watersports; tennis; games area; games rm; wifi; entmnt; internet; TV rm; 10% statics; dogs €2; Eng spkn; adv bkg; quiet; ccard acc; red low ssn/CCI. "Lovely lakeside site; excel san facs." ♦ 1 Apr-30 Sep. € 22.50 2009*

See advertisement opposite (above)

PONT DE VAUX *9A2* (4km NE Rural) *46.44394, 4.98313* **Camping Les Ripettes, Chavannes-sur-Reyssouze, 01190 St Bénigne [03 85 30 66 58; info@camping-les-ripettes.com; www.camping-les-ripettes.com]** Take D2 fr Pont-de-Vaux sp St Trivier-des-Courtes for 3km. Immed after water tower on R turn L onto D58 sp Romenay, then immed L. Site well sp on L in 100m. Med, hdg/mkd pitch, pt sl, pt shd; htd wc; chem disp; mv service pnt; shwrs inc; el pnts (10A) €3; Indtte; shop & 4km; tradsmn; snacks; playgrnd; 2 pools; games area; 1 static; dogs €1.50; phone; Eng spkn; adv bkg rec high ssn; quiet, but some rd noise; ccard acc; red low ssn; CCI. "Pleasant, popular site in beautiful location; spacious pitches; new owners (2009) friendly, helpful; immac facs; gd pool area; gd touring base; hard to beat!" ♦ 1 Apr-30 Sep. € 15.00 2009*

PONT DE VAUX *9A2* (5km W Rural) *46.44710, 4.89890* **Camping aux Rives du Soleil, 01190 Pont-de-Vaux [tel/fax 03 85 30 33 65; info@rivesdusoleil.com; www.rivesdusoleil.com]** Leave D306 (N6) at Fleurville (bet Mâcon & Tournus) & cross Rv Saône on D933A dir Pont-de-Vaux; site on R in 1km. Well sp. Lge, pt shd, wc; chem disp; mv service pnt; baby facs; shwrs inc; el pnts (6A) €3.50; gas; Indtte; shop; rest; snacks; bar; BBQ; playgrnd; pool; paddling pool; rv beach adj; fishing; boating; entmnts; TV; 15% statics; dogs €3; poss cr; Eng spkn; adv bkg; some rlwy noise; red long stay/low ssn. "Pleasant site adj rv & canal; Dutch owners; san facs need update; conv NH fr A6." 25 Apr-30 Sep. € 18.50 2009*

PONT DE VAUX *9A2* (15km W Rural) *46.47686, 4.80908* **Camp Municipal St Pierre, 71260 Lugny [03 85 33 20 25 or 03 85 33 21 96 (Mairie); fax 03 85 33 00 58]** W of A6/N6; take C7 off D56 N out of Lugny; foll sp for Rest St Pierre; site adj & sp fr town. Diff app for lge o'fits. Sm, mkd pitch, pt shd; wc; shwrs inc; el pnts inc; Indry rm; shop 1.5km in Lugny; rest adj; v quiet; ccard not acc. "Simple site; warden calls am & pm; facs clean; gd local walks - steep fr town to site; view of vineyards." 1 May-30 Sep. 2008*

France

PONT D'OUILLY see Condé sur Noireau *3D1*

PONT DU NAVOY see Doucier *6H2*

PONT EN ROYANS *9C2* (Rural) *45.06193, 5.33398* **Camp Municipal Les Seraines, 38680 Pont-en-Royans [04 76 36 06 30 or 04 76 36 03 09 (Mairie); fax 04 76 38 92 37; mairie.pont.en.royans@wanadoo.fr]** App on D531 fr E or D518 fr St Marcellin fr N, site sp on ent town. Sm, hdg pitch, hdstg, pt terr, pt shd; wc (mainly cont); chem disp; mv service pnt; shwrs inc; el pnts (4A) €2.70; Indtte; shops 500m; playgrnd; lake 8km; rv adj; tennis; entmnts; poss cr; statics; dogs; quiet but some rd noise; CCI. "Site in 2 adj parts; helpful warden; rvside walk to town." 15 Apr-30 Sep. € 12.00 2007*

PONT EN ROYANS *9C2* (4km E Rural) *45.06439, 5.39426* **FFCC Camping Le Gouffre de la Croix, 38680 Choranche [tel/fax 04 76 36 07 13; camping.gouffre.croix@wanadoo.fr; www.camping-choranche.com]** App fr Pont-en-Royans only. Site at far end of vill. Ent over narr bdge, OK with care. Sm, mkd pitch, terr, pt shd; wc; chem disp; fam bthrm; shwrs inc; el pnts (6A) €3.50; gas; Indtte; shop 4km; tradsmn; rest 500m; snacks; bar; playgrnd; TV; 4% statics; dogs €2; phone; Eng spkn; adv bkg; quiet; CCI. "Friendly site on trout rv; views fr most pitches; excel walking area; excel." 25 Apr-16 Sep. € 16.00 2008*

PONT FARCY *1D4* (500m N Rural) *47.46810, 4.35709* **Camp Municipal Pont-Farcy, Quai de la Vire, 14380 Pont-Farcy [02 31 68 32 06; fax 02 31 67 94 01; pontfarcy@free.fr; http://pontfarcy.free.fr]** Leave A84 junc 39 onto D21 to Pont-Farcy vill cent; site on L 50m. Med, hdg/mkd pitch, terr, pt shd; wc; chem disp; mv service pnt; shwrs inc; baby facs; el pnts (6-15A) €1.85; shop, rest & bar 500m; playgrnd; rv fishing & boating adj; cycle hire; 30% statics; dogs; phone; adv bkg; quiet; CCI. "Gates poss locked periods during day but parking avail; helpful, friendly warden; clean facs; mosquitoes at dusk." ♦ 1 Apr-30 Sep. € 9.00 2007*

PONT L'ABBE *2F2* (6km S Rural/Coastal) *47.79715, -4.22868* **Camping des Dunes, 67 Rue Paul Langevin, 29740 Lesconil [02 98 87 81 78; fax 02 98 82 27 05]** Fr Pont l'Abbé, S on D102 for 5km to Plobannelec; over x-rds; in 1km turn R, 100m after sports field; green sp to site in 1km. Med, hdg/mkd pitch, pt shd; wc (few cont); chem disp; mv service pnt; baby facs; shwrs inc; el pnts (6-10A) inc; gas 1km; Indtte; shop 1km; tradsmn; snacks; bar; playgrnd; sand beach 200m; trampolines; games rm; games area; dogs €3.15; poss cr high ssn; adv bkg; ccard acc; CCI. "Helpful owner; facs poor low ssn; nr fishing port; gd walking, cycling & birdwatching; site gd for children." ♦ 3 Jun-9 Sep. € 23.30 2006*

PONT L'ABBE *2F2* (7km S Rural) *47.81241, -4.22147* **Yelloh! Village L'Océan Breton/Le Manoir de Kerlut, 29740 Plobannalec-Lesconil [02 98 82 23 89; fax 02 98 82 26 49; info@yellohvillage-manoir-de-kerlut.com; www.domaine manoirdekerlut.com or www.yellohvillage.com]** Fr Pont l'Abbé S on D102 to Plobannalec & head for Lesconil; site on L after supmkt. Lge, hdg/mkd pitch, pt shd; htd wc; serviced pitches; mv service pnt; chem disp; sauna; shwrs inc; el pnts (5A) inc; gas; Indtte; shop; tradsmn; rest; snacks; bar; playgrnd; htd pool; waterslide; sand beach 2km; fitness rm; tennis; games area; 80% statics; dogs €4; phone; Eng spkn; adv bkg; quiet; ccard acc; red long stay/ low ssn; CCI. ♦ 7 May-19 Sep. € 39.00 2009*

PONT L'ABBE *2F2* (5km SW Rural) *47.83264, -4.32630* **Camping Caravaning Pointe de la Torche, 29120 Plomeur [02 98 58 62 82; fax 02 98 58 89 69; info@ campingdelatorche.fr; www.campingdelatorche.fr]** Fr Quimper take D785 to Pont l'Abbé & on to Plomeur. After Plomeur turn W twd La Pointe de la Torche & foll sps for 3km. Lge, pt shd, mkd pitch; wc; chem disp; shwrs inc; baby facs; el pnts (6A) €3.20; gas; Indtte; shop; rest; bar; sand beach 1.5km; pool; playgrnd; tennis, horseriding, fishing, golf, surfing adj; 50% statics; dogs €2; Eng spkn; adv bkg; red low ssn. "V quiet off ssn." 5 Apr-30 Sep. € 19.50 2008*

PONT L'ABBE *2F2* (3km W Rural) *47.86113, -4.26766* **Aire Naturelle Keraluic, 29120 Plomeur [tel/fax 02 98 82 10 22; camping@keraluic.fr; www.keraluic.fr]** Leave Quimper S on D785 to o'skts Pont L'Abbe; turn R at 1st rndabt (junc with D44); strt on at 2nd rndabt (junc with D2); in 1km turn R at 3rd rndabt up narr rd sp St Jean-Trolimon; site on R in 1.5km. Site 2km NE of Plomeur & well sp. Sm, pt shd; wc; chem disp; baby facs; shwrs inc; el pnts €2.90; gas; Indtte; sm shop or 3km; tradsmn; BBQ; playgrnd; surfing 5km; games area; games rm; internet; no dogs high ssn, £1.50 low ssn; no twin-axles; Eng spkn; adv bkg (rec high ssn); quiet; ccard acc; red low ssn; CCI. "Excel, well-kept, family-run site; friendly, helpful Dutch owners; spacious pitches; gd leisure facs; ideal for children; gd walking; gd surfing nrby; facs poss stretched high ssn, highly rec low ssn." ♦ 1 May-31 Oct. € 14.50 2009*

PONT L'ABBE *2F2* (5km NW Urban) *47.90602, -4.28339* **Camp Municipal de Mariano, 29720 Plonéour-Lanvern [02 98 87 74 80; fax 02 98 82 66 09; mairie@ploneour-lanvern.fr; www.ploneour-lanvern.fr]** Fr Pont l'Abbé, take D2 to Plonéour-Lanvern, site sp fr cent town; fr cent L of church & strt to T-junc, turn R 2nd on L. Med, hdg pitch, pt shd; wc; shwrs inc; el pnts (5A) €3; Indtte; shops 400m; pool 6km; playgrnd; sand beach 13km; tennis adj; dogs €1; adv bkg; quiet. "Pleasant site; warden visits am & pm; gd touring base." ♦ 15 Jun-15 Sep. € 9.50 2009*

PONT L'ABBE *2F2* (10km NW Rural) *47.89462, -4.32863* **Camping Kerlaz, Route de la Mer, 29670 Tréguennec [tel/fax 02 98 87 76 79; contact@kerlaz.com; www.kerlaz.com]** Fr Plonéour-Lanvern take D156 SW to Tréguennec. Med, hdg pitch, pt shd; wc; chem disp; mv service pnt; shwrs inc; el pnts (3-10A) €2.40-3.50; Indtte (inc dryer); shop 300m; tradsmn; snacks; BBQ; playgrnd; htd, covrd pool; sand beach 2km; tennis; 10% statics; dogs €1.30; adv bkg; quiet; ccard acc. "Nice, friendly site." 1 Apr-5 Oct. € 15.30 2009*

PONT L'ABBE D'ARNOULT *7B1* (500m E Urban) *45.82592, -0.86568* **Camping Parc de la Garenne, 24 Ave Bernard Chambenoit, 17250 Pont-l'Abbé-d'Arnoult [05 46 97 01 46 or 06 09 43 20 11 (mob); info@lagarenne.net; www.lagarenne.net]** N fr Saintes on N137. In 18km turn L onto D18 to Pont-l'Abbé. In town turn L, foll camp sp to site adj sw pool. Med, shd; wc; chem disp; mv service pnt 150m; baby facs; shwrs inc; el pnts (6-10A) €3.90-4.20; gas; Indtte; shop, rest, snacks & bar 500m; snacks; BBQ (elec only); playgrnd; pool adj; tennis; games area; TV rm; 10% statics; dogs €2; phone; Eng spkn; adv bkg; quiet; CCI. "Well-run site; gd san facs; gd." ♦ 15 May-25 Sep. € 15.00 2006*

PONT LES MOULINS see Baume les Dames *6G2*

PONT L'EVEQUE *3D1* (500m NW Urban) *49.28486, 0.17573* **Camping du Stade, Rue de Beaumont, 14130 Pont l'Evêque [02 31 64 15 03]** Fr town cent take D675 (N175) W twd Caen, turn R at traff lts bef town o'skts to site in 300m. Site sp on R in 300m on D118. Med, mkd pitch, pt shd; wc (some cont); chem disp; shwrs inc; el pnts (6A) €2.80 (poss rev pol); Indry rm; shops in town; tradsmn; playgrnd; beach 12km; rv fishing; tennis; 2% statics; quiet; ccard not acc; CCI. "Basic, clean site; dated san facs; friendly, helpful staff; no hedges - poss noisy high ssn; mkt Mon." ♦ 1 Apr-30 Sep. € 10.20 2008*

PONT ST ESPRIT *9D2* (5km W Rural) *44.27306, 4.57944* **Camping Les Oliviers, Chemin de Tête Grosse, 30130 St Paulet-de-Caisson [04 66 82 14 13; info@camping-lesoliviers.net; www.camping-lesoliviers.net]** Exit A7 junc 19 & foll D994 to Pont-St Esprit, then sp to St Paulet-de-Caisson. Turn R into vill & foll sp to St Julien-de-Peyrolas on D343, site sp 1.5km off narr rd - unsuitable lge o'fits. Sm, hdg/mkd pitch, terr, pt shd; wc; chem disp; shwrs inc; el pnts (4A) €3; Indtte; shops 2km; tradsmn; rest; snacks; bar; pool; playgrnd; rv sw 5km; dogs free; Eng spkn; adv bkg; quiet; CCI. "Ardèche, Roman sites nr; helpful Dutch owners; painting tuition; ltd water points & long way fr lower levels." 1 Apr-30 Sep. € 18.00 2007*

PONT ST ESPRIT *9D2* (6km NW Rural) *44.30388, 4.58443* **Camping Le Pontet, 07700 St Martin-d'Ardèche [04 75 04 63 07 or 04 75 98 76 24; fax 04 75 98 76 59; contact@campinglepontet.com; www.campinglepontet.com]** N86 N of Pont-St Esprit; turn L onto D290 at sp Gorges de l'Ardèche & St Martin-d'Ardèche, site on R after 3km, lge sp. Med, mkd, pt shd; wc; chem disp; mv service pnt; shwrs inc; el pnts (6A) €3.50 (rev pol); gas; lndry rm; tradsmn; shop, rest high ssn; snacks; bar; playgrnd; pool; rv sw 1km; 5% statics; dogs €1; phone; Eng spkn; adv bkg; quiet (poss noisy w/end); ccard not acc; red low ssn; CCI. "Vg; helpful owners; beware low tree branches & falling fruit; access disabled facs thro passage bet shwrs; peaceful out of ssn." ♦ 2 Apr-28 Sep. € 18.90 2007*

⊞ **PONT ST ESPRIT** *9D2* (7km NW Rural) *44.29808, 4.56535* **Camping Les Cigales, 30760 Aiguèze [04 66 82 18 52; fax 04 66 82 25 20; lastridulette@wanadoo.fr]** N fr Pont-St Esprit on D6086 (N86) take D901 NW twd Barjac & D141 to St Martin-d'Ardèche. Site on L bef rv bdge. Avoid app fr St Martin-d'Ardèche over narr suspension bdge. Care at ent. Sm, mkd pitch, shd; wc; mv service pnt; shwrs inc; el pnts (4-6A) €2.60-5.40; gas; lndtte; shops, rest 500m; tradsmn; BBQ; htd pool; rv sw 500m; 25% statics; dogs €1.65; poss cr; adv bkg; rd noise; ccard not acc; CCI. "Helpful owner; easy walk to St Martin-d'Ardèche." € 15.00 2008*

PONT ST ESPRIT *9D2* (7.5km NW Urban) *44.30342, 4.56819* **Camp Municipal Le Village, Rue du Nord, 07700 St Martin-d'Ardèche [04 75 04 65 25; fax 04 75 98 71 38; denislaurent1@sfr.fr]** N on D6086 (N86) fr Pont-St Esprit, turn L onto D290 at St Just. Foll D290 around St Martin-d'Ardèche, look out for site sp. Turn sharp R down under main rd & strt into site - take care if v high outfit. Med, mkd pitch, pt shd; wc; chem disp; shwrs inc; el pnts (4-13A) €1.70-2.80; lndtte; shop, rest, snacks, bar 200m; playgrnd; rv beach adj; fishing; tennis; adv bkg; quiet. "Excel facs, but dusty site; quiet, lovely vill." Easter-30 Sep. € 12.10 2009*

PONT ST ESPRIT *9D2* (7.5km NW Urban) *44.30576, 4.55959* **Camping Le Castelas, Chemin de Tabion, 07700 St Martin-d'Ardèche [tel/fax 04 75 04 66 55; camping-le-castelas@wanadoo.fr; www.camping-le-castelas.com]** N fr Pont-St Esprit on D6086 (N86). At St Just turn W onto D290 sp Ardèche Gorges, St Martin. In 4km take 2nd L sp St Martin-de l'Ardèche & site. In 50m turn R at site sp; site on R in 150m. Med, hdg/mkd pitch, sl, shd; wc; chem disp; shwrs inc; el pnts (3-4A) €1.80-1.90; lndtte; shops 300m; tradsmn; rest, bar 500m; snacks; BBQ; playgrnd; canoeing; fishing; dogs free; poss cr; Eng spkn; adv bkg (ess Jul/Aug - bkg fee); noisy; red low ssn. "V shd pitches; position van with door to S or E in case Mistral blows; helpful, friendly owner; delightful site; views of gorge; gd NH." 24 Mar-11 Nov. € 11.00 2007*

PONT ST ESPRIT *9D2* (8km NW Rural) *44.30043, 4.57069* **Camping Indigo Le Moulin, 07700 St Martin-d'Ardèche [04 75 04 66 20; fax 04 75 04 60 12; moulin@camping-indigo.com; www.camping-indigo.com]** Exit A7 junc 19 to Bollène, then D994 to Pont-St Esprit & D6068/D86 (N86) to St Just. Turn L onto D290 to St Martin in 4km. Site on L on rvside. Med, pt sl, pt shd; htd wc; chem disp; mv service pnt; shwrs inc; el pnts (6A) €3.90; lndtte; shop; rest 5km; snacks; bar; playgrnd; rv sw & beach adj; fishing; canoe hire; tennis 500m; cycle hire; games area; 5% statics; dogs €3; phone; Eng spkn; no adv bkg; ccard acc; quiet. "Friendly site; footpath to vill; rec." ♦ 3 Apr-27 Sep. € 18.50 (CChq acc) 2009*

PONT ST ESPRIT *9D2* (8km NW Rural) *44.28950, 4.58923* **Camping Le Peyrolais, Route de Barjac, 30760 St Julien-de-Peyrolas [04 66 82 14 94; fax 04 66 82 31 70; contact@camping-lepeyrolais.com; www.camping-lepeyrolais.com]** N fr Pont-St. Esprit on D6086 (N86) turn L onto D901 sp Barjac. In 2.5km turn R at site sp, site in 500m up narr track on bank of Rv Ardèche. Med, mkd pitch, pt shd; wc; chem disp; mv waste; shwrs inc; el pnts (3-10A) €2.30-3.80; lndtte; shop & 3km; tradsmn; rest; bar; playgrnd; rv sw adj; fishing; kayaking; cycle & canoe hire; games area; hiking; horseriding; wifi; entmnt; TV rm; dogs €2; phone; poss cr; adv bkg; quiet; ccard acc; CCI. "Attractive, well-maintained site in beautiful location; clean facs; friendly owners; vg." ♦ 4 Apr-2 Oct. € 17.70 2009*

⊞ **PONT ST ESPRIT** *9D2* (8km NW Rural) *44.34423, 4.60434* **FFCC Camping Les Truffières, 201 Route de St Ramèze, 07700 St Marcel-d'Ardèche [04 75 04 68 35 or 06 82 01 28 30 (mob); fax 04 75 98 75 86; soulier.valerie@wanadoo.fr; www.camping-les-truffieres.supersite.fr]** S fr Bourg-St Andéol, turn W on D201; in vill foll sp to site located approx 3km W of vill. Med, mkd pitch, terr, pt shd; htd wc; mv service pnt; shwrs inc; el pnts (6A) €6.60 (poss rev pol); gas; lndtte; shops 3km; rest; snacks; bar; playgrnd; pool; entmnt; 70% statics; dogs €1.60; adv bkg; quiet; red low ssn; CCI. "Friendly owners; glorious views; gd san facs; conv NH nr A7." ♦ € 17.10 2009*

PONT SUR SEINE see Nogent sur Seine *4E4*

PONTAILLER SUR SAONE *6G1* (750m E Rural) *47.30817, 5.42518* **Camping La Chanoie, 46 Rue de la Chanoie, 21270 Pontailler-sur-Saône [03 80 36 10 58; fax 03 80 47 84 42; tourisme-canton-pontailler.com; www.tourisme-canton-pontailler.com]** E fr Pontailler-sur-Saône on D959; pass town hall & tourist office on R; after bdg take 1st L sp Camping; site in 500m. Fr W on D959 turn R bef bdg & bef ent town. Med, hdg/mkd pitch, pt shd; htd wc (some cont); chem disp (wc); mv service pnt; baby facs; shwrs inc; el pnts (6-10A) €2.85-4.10; gas 1km; lndtte; shops 750m; rest; snacks; bar; BBQ; playgrnd; rv sw, water sports & fishing adj; tennis; games area; games rm; dogs €1.55; bus; poss cr; adv bkg; quiet, poss noisy if busy; red long stay; CCI. "Attractive sm town; polite & helpful owner; clean san facs, poss stretched high ssn; vg." ♦ 15 Apr-15 Oct. € 9.30 2007*

PONTAIX *9D2* (2km E Rural) *44.76585, 5.27270* **Aire Naturelle La Condamine (Archinard), 26150 Pontaix [04 75 21 08 19; fax 04 74 04 46 12; aurelie.goderiaux@laposte.net]** W fr Die on D93; site on R just after D129. Fr E, 2km after Pontaix on L. Sm; wc; chem disp; shwrs inc; el pnts (10A) €2.60; Indry rm; shop 8km; rest, snacks, bar 1km; BBQ; rv sw adj; dogs €1; adv bkg; quiet; CCI; excel. "Excel CL-type site by Rv Drôme (2006); helpful owner; Roman remains on site." ♦ 15 Apr-15 Oct. € 9.90 2009*

⊞ **PONTARLIER** *6H2* (1km SE Rural) *46.90024, 6.37425* **FFCC Camping Le Larmont, Rue du Toulombief, 25300 Pontarlier [03 81 46 23 33; fax 03 81 46 23 34; lelarmont.pontarlier@wanadoo.fr; www.camping-pontarlier.fr]** Leave N57 at Pontarlier Gare & foll site sp. Site uphill, turning nr Nestlé factory. Med, some hdstg, terr, unshd; htd wc; chem disp; mv service pnt; shwrs inc; el pnts (10A) €4; gas; Indtte; sm shop; tradsmn; snacks; bar; playgrnd; pool 2km; horseriding adj; skiing winter; wifi; 10-20% statics; dogs €1; Eng spkn; adv bkg; red CCI. "Friendly; easy access; clean san facs; ltd pitches for awnings; pitch yourself out of office hrs." ♦ € 13.90 2009*

PONTARLIER *6H2* (12km S Rural) *46.81176, 6.30326* **Camp Municipal, 8 Rue du Port, 25160 St Point-Lac [03 81 69 61 64 or 03 81 69 62 08 (Mairie); fax 03 81 69 65 74; camping-saintpointlac@wanadoo.fr; www.camping-saintpointlac.com]** Exit Pontarlier on N57 dir Lausanne, turn R on D437, after further 6km turn R on D129. Site on L. Med, mkd pitch, hdstg, unshd; htd wc; chem disp; mv service pnt; chem disp; shwrs inc; el pnts (16A) inc; Indtte; shop; rest, snacks & bar 100m; BBQ; 10% statics; dogs €1; adv bkg rec high ssn; quiet; ccard acc; CCI. "Well-kept, lakeside site in beautiful position; friendly staff; vg san facs; sm pitches; m'van o'night area with facs opp; gd fishing, walking, birdwatching; excel." ♦
1 May-30 Sep. € 15.10 2009*

PONTAUBAULT *2E4* (Urban) *48.62983, -1.35205* **Camping La Vallée de la Sélune, 7 Rue Maréchal Leclerc, 50220 Pontaubault [tel/fax 02 33 60 39 00; campselune@wanadoo.fr]** Foll sp to Pontaubault (well sp fr all dirs). In vill head twd Avranches. Turn L immed bef bdge over Rv Sélune. In 100m turn L, site strt in 100m, well sp. Med, mkd pitch, pt sl, pt shd; wc; chem disp; shwrs inc; el pnts (8-10A) €3; Indtte; shop; tradsmn; supmkt 6km; snacks, bar high ssn; playgrnd; pool 7km; sand beach 10km; tennis adj; fishing adj; horseriding, cycling & golf nrby; 10% statics; dogs €1.30; poss cr; adv bkg rec; rd/rlwy noise; ccard acc; red long stay/CCI. "Relaxing, clean, tidy site; friendly British owner; vg, clean san facs; conv Mont St Michel & Cherbourg ferries; gd NH." ♦ 1 Apr-20 Oct. € 12.00 2008*

PONTAUBAULT *2E4* (4km E Rural) *48.61690, -1.29475* **Camp Municipal La Sélune, Rue de Boishue, 50220 Ducey [02 33 48 46 49 or 02 33 48 50 52; fax 02 33 48 87 59; ducey.tourisme@wanadoo.fr; www.ducey-tourisme.com]** Exit A84 junc 33 onto N176 E fr Pontaubault. In Ducey turn R onto D178 twd St Aubin-de-Terregatte. Ent at sports grnd in 200m. Sm, hdg pitch, pt sl, shd; wc; chem disp; shwrs inc; el pnts (6A) (rev pol) €1.71; gas; Indtte; shop; rest, snacks, bar in vill; playgrnd; pool nr; sand beach 25km; tennis adj; 10% statics; dogs €1.30; phone; bus; poss cr; Eng spkn; adv bkg; quiet; CCI. "Well-maintained." 1 Apr-30 Sep. € 7.38 2008*

PONTAUBAULT *2E4* (6km SW Coastal) *48.59670, -1.41259* **CAMPEOLE Camping St Grégoire, Le Haut Bourg, 50170 Servon [02 33 60 26 03; fax 02 33 60 68 65; saint-gregoire@campeole.com; www.normandie-camping.net or www.campeole.com]** Foll N175 fr Pontaubault twd Pontorson. After 6km site sp on R twd Servon vill. Med, pt shd; wc; shwrs; el pnts (6A) €2.90; Indtte; sm shop; playgrnd; pool; games rm; TV; 30% statics; dogs €2.60; adv bkg; quiet but some rd noise on S side of site; ccard acc; red low ssn; CCI. "Conv ferries." 2 Apr-26 Sep. € 14.00 2006*

PONTCHATEAU *2G3* (4km W Rural) *47.44106, -2.15981* **Camping Le Château du Deffay, Ste Reine-de-Bretagne, 44160 Pontchâteau [02 40 88 00 57; fax 02 40 01 66 55; campingdudeffay@wanadoo.fr; www.camping-le-deffay.com]** Leave N165 at junc 13 onto D33 twd Herbignac. Site on R approx 1.5km after Le Calvaire de la Madeleine x-rds, 270m past Chateau ent. Site sp fr by-pass. Med, some hdg/mkd pitch, pt terr, pt shd; wc; chem disp; mv service pnt; baby facs; shwrs inc; el pnts (6A) inc (take care electrics); Indtte; shop; rest; snacks; bar; BBQ (charcoal/gas); playgrnd; htd, covrd pool; paddling pool; lake fishing; tennis & pedaloes; cycle hire; woodland walks; golf 10km; entmnt; wifi; games/TV rm; 50% statics; dogs €2 (for 2nd dog); Eng spkn; adv bkg; ccard acc (not in rest); red low ssn; CCI. "Friendly, welcoming owners & staff; lakeside pitches not fenced; mkt Mon; vg." ♦ 1 May-30 Sep. € 27.80 (CChq acc) ABS - B25 2009*

See advertisement

PONTCHATEAU *2G3* (2km NW Rural) *47.45490, -2.11053* **Camping Le Bois Beaumard, 1 Rue de la Beaumard, 44160 Pontchâteau [tel/fax 02 40 88 03 36; obocamp@aol.com; www.campingbeaumard.com]** Fr Nantes on N165 by-pass; ignore sp Pontchâteau Est, take 2nd sp & foll site sp. Fr Vannes NW of town exit sp Beaulieu; foll site sp. Site also sp bef Pontchâteau on D773 S fr Redon. Sm, hdg/mkd pitch, pt shd; wc; chem disp; baby facs; shwrs inc; el pnts (10-12A) €3; Indtte; shops 2km; tradsmn; BBQ; playgrnd; TV rm; some statics; dogs €1; Eng spkn; adv bkg; quiet, some rd noise; CCI. "Peaceful, immac site in orchard; red squirrels, bird song; friendly, helpful owners; gd walking." 1 Apr-1 Oct. € 13.50 2009*

PONTET, LE see Avignon *10E2*

PONTGIBAUD *7B4* (3km NE Rural) *45.84436, 2.87672* **Camping Bel-Air, 63230 St Ours [04 73 88 72 14; contact@campingbelair.fr; www.campingbelair.fr]** Exit A89 junc 26 onto D941 dir Pontgibaud; cont past Pontigibaud; in 1.5km turn L onto D943; site in 1.3km on L. Site sp. Med, mkd pitch, pt sl, shd; wc; chem disp; mv service pnt; baby facs; shwrs inc; el pnts (6A) €3.30; gas; Indry rm; shop 1.5km; tradsmn; rest; snacks; bar; BBQ; playgrnd; golf; games area; 5% statics; dogs €1; Eng spkn; adv bkg; quiet, but some rd noise; CCI. "Peaceful, basic site in beautiful area; helpful owner; clean facs, ltd low ssn; vg disabled facs; conv Vulcania; excel." ♦ 1 May-27 Sep. € 13.70 2009*

PONTGIBAUD *7B4* (200m S Rural) *45.82978, 2.84517* **FFCC Camp Municipal La Palle, Route de la Miouze, 63230 Pontgibaud [04 73 88 96 99 or 04 73 88 70 42 (LS); fax 04 73 88 77 77; mairie.pontgibaud@wanadoo.fr; www.ville-pontgiabud.fr]** At W end of Pontgibaud turn S over bdge on D986 & site in 500m on L. Med, hdg/mkd pitch, hdstg, pt shd; htd wc (some cont); chem disp; mv service pnt; shwrs inc; el pnts (10-16A) €2.60-3.10; gas 400m; Indtte; shops 400m; tradsmn; rest; BBQ; playgrnd; lake sw & beach 4km; games area; tennis, cycle hire 400m; entmnt; 5% statics; dogs; Eng spkn; adv bkg; quiet; red long stay/low ssn; CCI. "Pleasant site; helpful staff; gd touring base; conv Vulcania exhibition cent." ♦ 15 Apr-30 Sep. € 8.80 2008*

PONTOISE *3D3* (6km E Urban) **Camp Municipal Bellerive, Chemin de Bellerive, 95430 Auvers-sur-Oise [01 34 48 05 22; fax 01 30 36 70 30; www.auvers-sur-oise.com]** Exit N184 junc 7 sp Méry & Auvers-sur-Oise; in Méry foll sp to Auvers; immed on ent Auvers turn L sp Parking; foll rd (narr in places) to T-junc; turn L; foll Camping sp. Site 300m on L on rvside. Sm, shd; wc (some cont); chem disp (wc); shwrs inc; el pnts (6A) inc (poss rev pol); Indry rm; shop, rest, snacks & bar 1km; BBQ; adv bkg; quiet; CCI. "Easy access to Paris & Disneyland; sh walk to town where Van Gogh buried; gd." 15 Jun-15 Sep. € 14.30 2007*

PONTORSON *2E4* (400m NW Rural) *48.55805, -1.51444* **Kawan Village Haliotis, Chemin des Soupirs, 50170 Pontorson [02 33 68 11 59; fax 02 33 58 95 36; info@camping-haliotis-mont-saint-michel.com; www.camping-haliotis-mont-saint-michel.com]** Exit A84 junc 33 onto N175 dir Pontorson; foll sp Centre Ville/Mont-St-Michel. Site well sp. Med, hdg pitch, pt sl, pt shd; htd wc; chem disp; mv service pnt; baby facs; sauna; shwrs inc; el pnts (10-16A) inc (poss rev pol); gas; Indtte; shop; supmkt 400m; tradsmn; rest 400m; snacks; bar; BBQ; playgrnd; htd pool; paddling pool; spa; rv fishing; boating; tennis; cycle hire; games area; games rm; wifi; 25% statics; dogs €0.50; phone; bus 400m; poss cr; Eng spkn; adv bkg rec; quiet, poss noise till late w/ends; ccard acc; red low ssn; CCI. "Popular, well-kept site; lge pitches; friendly, helpful owners; immac san facs; lovely pool & bar; site locked at night till 0730; cycle rte/bus to Mont St Michel; highly rec." ♦ 1 Apr-6 Nov. € 22.00 (CChq acc) 2009*

PONTRIEUX *2E3* (4km E Rural) **Camp Municipal du Bois d'Amour, 22260 Quemper-Guézennec [02 96 95 13 40 or 02 96 95 62 62; fax 02 96 95 36 07]** Exit N12 at Guincamp Est; D787 twds Pontrieux. At rndabt ent to Pontrieux, turn R & foll rd to indus est over level x-ing. Turn R along rv front, site in approx 200 yrds. Sm, hdg/mkd pitch, pt shd, mkd pitch; wc; shwrs; el pnts (10A) €3; Indtte; sm shop; tradsmn; playgrnd; fishing; 10% statics; ccard not acc; quiet; CCI. "Excel site; some rvside pitches; pay at Marie in town low ssn; clean & roomy san facs; gd touring base." ♦ 15 Jun-15 Sep. € 9.42 2009*

⊞ **PONTRIEUX** *2E3* (500m W Rural) *48.69493, -3.16365* **Camping de Traou Mélédern (Thomas), 22260 Pontrieux [02 96 95 68 72 or 02 96 95 69 27; http://campingpontrieux.free.fr]** N on D787 fr Guingamp; on ent town square turn sharp L sp Traou Mélédern, cross rv bdge & turn R alongside church. Site in 400m. Access poss diff for lge o'fits; steep exit on 1-way system. Med, hdg/mkd pitch, pt sl, pt shd; wc; chem disp; shwrs inc; el pnts (8A) €3; Indtte; shops, supmkt 1km; tradsmn; playgrnd; BBQ; dogs; €0.90; phone; poss cr; Eng spkn; adv bkg; quiet but some daytime factory noise; CCI. "In orchard; excel touring base; friendly owner; steep junc nr site poss problem for lge o'fits; gd." ♦ € 9.40 2007*

France

PONTS DE CE, LES see Angers *4G1*

PORDIC see Binic *2E3*

PORGE, LE *7C1* (9km W Coastal) *44.89430, -1.20181* **Camp Municipal La Grigne, Ave de l'Océan, 33680 Le Porge [05 56 26 54 88; fax 05 56 26 52 07; campingduporge2@wanadoo.fr; www.leporge.fr]** Fr Bordeaux ring rd take N215 twd Lacaneau. In 22km at Ste Hélène D5 to Saumos & onto Le Porge. Site on L of rd to Porge-Océan in approx 9km. V lge, mkd pitch, terr, pt sl, shd; wc; chem disp; shwrs inc; el pnts (10A) €4; gas; shop; lndtte; bar; snacks; playgrnd; beach 600m; tennis; games area; TV; poss cr; adv bkg; quiet. "Vg facs; great beach; excel cycle path network; red long stay/low ssn." ♦ 1 Apr-30 Sep. € 20.30 2009*

PORNIC Caravans are prohibited in Pornic. If app fr E on D751 or fr SE on D13 remain on by-pass to N of Pornic & take D86/D13 exit.

PORNIC *2G3* (700m N Urban) *47.12066, -2.10019* **Camping Bon Accueil, 8 Rue de St Père-en-Retz, 44210 Pornic [06 09 56 84 28 (mob); fax 02 40 82 87 45; bonaccueil44@wanadoo.fr]** Fr D213 exit Pornic cent N on D86. Site on L in 400m. Sm, hdg pitch, pt shd; wc; chem disp; mv service pnt; shwrs inc; lndry rm; shop 1km; rest; snacks; bar; BBQ; playgrnd; sm pool; sand beach 1.5km; 50% statics; dogs; bus adj; quiet; cc acc; CCI. "Nearest site to Pornic cent; facs old but clean; gd/fair." ♦ 1 Apr-30 Sep. € 19.00 2008*

PORNIC *2G3* (10km N Urban) *47.20315, -2.03716* **Camping du Grand Fay, Rue du Grand Fay, 44320 St Père-en-Retz [02 40 21 72 89; fax 02 40 82 40 27; legrandfay@aol.com; www.camping-grandfay.com]** Fr Mairie in cent St Père-en-Retz take D78 E twds Frossay. After 500m turn R into Rue des Sports, after 200m turn L into Rue du Grand Fay. Site on L in 200m adj sports cent. Med, mkd pitch, pt sl, pt shd; wc (some cont); shwrs inc; el pnts (6A) €3.80; lndry rm; tradsmn; supmkt nrby; playgrnd; htd pool; beach 8km; lake fishing adj; games areal some statics; dogs €2; quiet; red low ssn; CCI. "Pleasant site nr sandy beaches." ♦ 1 Apr-15 Oct. € 13.80 2009*

PORNIC *2G3* (9km NE Rural) *47.14057, -2.20334* **Camping La Renaudière, 44770 La Plaine-sur-Mer [02 40 21 50 03; fax 02 40 21 09 41; info@campinglarenaudiere.cor; www.campinglarenaudiere.com]** S fr St Nazaire on D213 twd Pornic, turn onto D96 twd Préfailles. Fr Nantes D751 W to Pornic then D13, dir La Plaine-sur-Mer, then Rte de la Prée. Med, pt shd; wc; chem disp; baby facs; shwrs; el pnts (6-10A) €3.80; gas; lndtte; shop adj; rest; snacks; bar; BBQ; playgrnd; htd pool; beach & watersports 2km; entmnts; TV; some statics; dogs €2.50; adv bkg; CCI. ♦ 1 Apr-15 Sep. € 21.70 2008*

PORNIC *2G3* (2km E Rural) *47.11987, -2.06894* **Camping La Chênaie, 36 Rue du Patisseau, 44210 Pornic [02 40 82 07 31; fax 02 40 27 95 67; la.chenaie44@wanadoo.fr; www.campinglachenaie.com]** Fr Nantes on D751 to Pornic, at 1st rndabt turn R. Fr St Nazaire on D213, foll sp Nantes & Le Clion-sur-Mer to avoid Pornic cent. Med, hdg/mkd pitch, hdstg, pt sl, terr, pt shd; wc; chem disp; mv service pnt; serviced pitch; child/baby facs; shwrs inc; el pnts (6A) €4; lndtte; shop; tradsmn; snacks; bar; BBQ; playgrnd; 3 pools (1 covrd); sand beach 2.5km; horseriding; golf; cycle hire; entmnt; 37% statics; dogs €4; Eng spkn; adv bkg; quiet; ccard acc; red low ssn/long stay; CCI. "Nice, lge pitches; friendly site; gd walking." ♦ 30 Apr-13 Sep. € 14.00 2009*

PORNIC *2G3* (4km E Rural) *47.11885, -2.07296* **Camping Le Patisseau, 29 Rue du Patisseau, 44210 Pornic [02 40 82 10 39; fax 02 40 82 22 81; contact@lepatisseau.com; www.lepatisseau.com]** Fr N or S on D213, take slip rd D751 Nantes. At rndabt take exit sp to Le Patisseau, foll sp. Lge, hdg/mkd pitch, hdstg, pt sl, pt shd; htd wc; chem disp; mv service pnt; sauna; shwrs inc; el pnts (6A) inc; gas; lndtte; shop; tradsmn; rest; snacks; bar; BBQ; playgrnd; 2 htd pools (1 htd, covrd); 2 htd paddling pools (1 covrd); 2 waterslides; sand beach 2.5km; jacuzzi; fitness rm; tennis 1km; games area; games rm; golf 2km; entmnt; TV; 35% statics; dogs €5; Eng spkn; adv bkg rec high ssn; quiet; ccard acc; red low ssn. "Excel, modern, family site; modern san facs block - lovely shwrs; 1hr walk on path fr back of site to Pornic." ♦ 4 Apr-11 Nov. € 39.00 2009*

See advertisement below

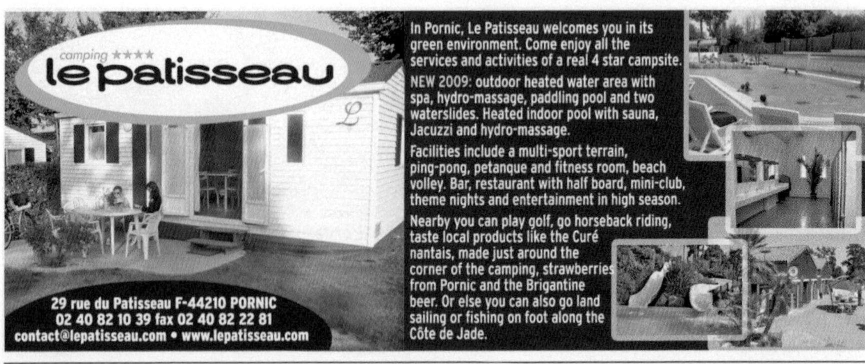

France

PORNIC *2G3* (5km E Coastal) *47.09748, -2.0525* **Airotel Camping Village La Boutinardière, 23 Rue de la Plage, Le Clion-sur-Mer, 44210 Pornic [02 40 82 05 68; fax 02 40 82 49 01; info@laboutinardiere.com; www.camping-boutinardiere.com]** SW fr Nantes on D723; turn L on D751 twd Pornic. Foll dir La Bernerie-en-Retz & site sp. Lge, hdg pitch, pt sl, pt shd; wc; chem disp; mv service pnt; serviced pitches; baby facs; sauna; shwrs inc; el pnts (6-10A) €5-6 (poss rev pol); gas; Indtte; shop; supmkt; rest; snacks; bar; BBQ; playgrnd; 2 pools (1 htd, covrd); paddling pool; waterslide; jacuzzi; sand beach 200m; lake sw 3km; tennis; games rm; golf 5km; cycle hire; entmnt & activities; TV rm; 15% statics; dogs €5; bus nrby; poss cr; Eng spkn; adv bkg; quiet; red low ssn; ccard acc; red long stay/low ssn; CCI. "Excel family site; vg pool complex; v busy high ssn; Pornic interesting town." ♦ 3 Apr-27 Sep. € 37.00 2009*

PORNIC *2G3* (6km SE Rural/Coastal) *47.08450, -2.03650* **Camping Les Ecureuils, 24 Ave Gilbert Burlot, 44760 La Bernerie-en-Retz [02 40 82 76 95; fax 02 40 64 79 52; camping.les-ecureuils@wanadoo.fr; www.camping-les-ecureuils.com]** Fr Pornic take D13 S for 5km, then D66 for 1km; site sp. Lge, hdg pitch, pt sl, pt shd; wc; chem disp; baby facs; shwrs inc; el pnts (6-10A) €4; Indtte; shops 500m; snacks; bar; BBQ area; playgrnd; htd pool; paddling pool; waterslide; sand beach 350m; tennis; golf 5km; entmnt; children's club; 30% statics; dogs (up to 10kg only) €4; Eng spkn; adv bkg; quiet; ccard acc; red low ssn/CCI. "Excel." ♦ 10 Apr-19 Sep. € 30.00 2009*

See advertisement above

PORNIC *2G3* (7km SE Coastal) *47.06945, -2.01407* **Camping de la Plage, 53 Route de la Bernerie, 44580 Les Moutiers-en-Retz [02 40 82 71 43; fax 02 40 82 72 46; bernard.beaujean@wanadoo.fr; www.camping-la-plage.com]** SE fr Pornic dir Bourgneuf, in 5km turn R for La Bernerie. 1st L after church. Site on R in 2km. Foll sps fr cent Les Moutiers. Lge, hdg/mkd pitch, pt sl, pt shd; wc; chem disp; shwrs inc; el pnts (10-16A) €3.60; Indtte; shop; snacks; bar; BBQ; playgrnd; htd pool; beach adj; entmnt; TV; some statics; dogs €1; Eng spkn; adv bkg; red low ssn; ccard acc; CCI. "Vg; diff access to some pitches - manhandling poss req." 1 Apr-30 Sep. € 21.00 2006*

PORNIC *2G3* (9km SE Coastal) *47.06383, -1.99732* **Camping Le Village de la Mer, 18 Rue de Prigny, 44760 Les Moutiers-en-Retz [02 40 64 65 90; fax 02 51 74 63 17; info@village-mer.fr; www.village-mer.fr]** Site sp on D97 dir Bourgneuf, site is 100m to SE of Les Moutiers-en-Retz. Lge, hdg/mkd pitch, pt shd; mv service pnt; chem disp; baby facs; shwrs inc; el pnts (8A) inc; gas; Indtte; shop adj; snacks; bar; BBQ; playgrnd; htd pool; waterpark; sand beach 400m; watersports; tennis; games rm; entmnt; internet; 50% statics; dogs €3; Eng spkn; adv bkg; red low ssn; ccard acc; CCI. "Quiet; ideal for families." ♦ 15 Jun-15 Sep. € 29.00 2008*

PORNIC *2G3* (2km W Coastal/Urban) *47.11866, -2.13023* **Camping du Golf, 40 Rue de la Renaissance, 44210 Pornic [02 40 82 46 17; fax 02 40 27 92 68; contact@campingdugolf.fr; www.campingdugolf.fr]** Fr Nantes, take D751 W dir Ste Marie. App Pornic, take D213 dir St Nazaire & foll sp Ste Marie & site; well sp. Med, mkd pitch, hdstg, pt shd; wc; chem disp; baby facs; fam bthrm; shwrs inc; el pnts (6-10A) €5-6; gas; Indtte; shop 500m; tradsmn; rest, snacks, bar high ssn; BBQ; playgrnd; htd pool; sand beach 800m; lake sw 200m; tennis; games rm; golf 1km; cycle hire; entmnt; TV; 90% statics; dogs €4; Eng spkn; adv bkg; quiet; red low ssn/long stay; ccard acc; CCI. "Conv coastal path; twin-axles not acc; ltd space for tourers." ♦ 1 May-30 Sep. € 20.00 2008*

PORNIC *2G3* (2km W Urban) *47.12219, -2.12780* **Camping Les Coeurés, 28 Rue des Coeurés, Ste Maire, 44210 Pornic [06 87 29 33 62 (mob)]** S fr St Nazaire on D213; turn R bef Pornic onto D286 to Ste Marie; turn R at rndabt onto D13, then 1st L. Site on L in 100m. Med, pt shd; wc (some cont); chem disp (wc); shwrs inc; el pnts (10A) €2.90; shop 300m; sand beach 3km; 10% statics; dogs €0.60; poss cr; quiet. "Excel." 1 May-30 Sep. € 11.70 2009*

PORNIC *2G3* (4km W Coastal) *47.11593, -2.15222* **Camping La Madrague, Chemin de la Madrague, Ste Marie, 44210 Pornic [02 40 82 06 73; fax 02 51 74 11 93; info@madrague.net; www.madrague.net or www.camping-franceloc.fr]** Fr Pornic on D213 foll sp Ste Marie-sur-Mer. Foll D286 then R on D13. Turn L into Rue du Moulin Neuf, then R into Rue des Bougrenets. Cont on Rue Yves Ponceau, then Chemin de la Madrague to site. Lge, hdg/mkd pitch, pt sl, pt shd; htd wc; chem disp; mv service pnt; baby facs; fam bthrm; shwrs inc; el pnts (10A) €4; gas; Indtte; shop; tradsmn; rest; snacks; bar; playgrnd; htd pool; dir access to sand beach 500m; games area; entmnt; 80% statics; dogs €5; phone; bus; poss cr; adv bkg; quiet. "Clean, well-organised site; helpful staff; facs stretched high ssn; excel coastal path walks; gd for dog owners; sea views." ♦ Easter-16 Sep. € 42.00 2008*

PORNIC *2G3* (5km W Coastal) *47.15435, -2.1660* **Camping Le Ranch, Chemin des Hautes Raillères, 44770 La Plaine-sur-Mer [02 40 21 52 62; fax 02 51 74 81 31; info@camping-le-ranch.com; www.camping-le-ranch.com]** S fr St Nazaire on D213 twd Pornic, turn onto D96 twd Préfailles. Site between Tharon-Plage & La Plaine-sur-Mer on D96. Lge, hdg/mkd pitch, pt shd; wc; chem disp; baby facs; shwrs; el pnts (6A) €3.80; gas; Indtte; shop; tradsmn; snacks; bar; BBQ; playgrnd; htd pool; paddling pool; waterslide; sand beach 800m; tennis; games rm; games area; entmnt; dogs €2.50; Eng spkn; adv bkg; quiet; red low ssn; CCI. "Excel, family site." ♦ 1 Apr-30 Sep. € 23.00 2007*

PORNIC *2G3* (5km W Rural) *47.14079, -2.15306* **FFCC Camping La Tabardière, 44770 La Plaine-sur-Mer [02 40 21 58 83; fax 02 40 21 02 68; info@camping-la-tabardiere.com; www.camping-la-tabardiere.com]** Take D13 NW out of Pornic sp Préfailles & La Plaine-sur-Mer. In about 5.5km turn R (nr water tower). Foll sps to site, about 1km fr main rd. Lge, hdg/mkd pitch, hdstg, terr, pt shd; htd wc (some cont); chem disp; mv service pnt; baby facs; shwrs inc; el pnts (8A) inc; gas; Indtte; shop & 3km; tradsmn; snacks; bar; BBQ; playgrnd; htd, covrd pool & paddling pool; waterslides; sand beach 3km; tennis; fishing 3km; horseriding 5km; games area; games rm; entmnt; wifi; TV rm; 40% statics; dogs €3.30; Eng spkn; adv bkg; quiet; ccard acc; red low ssn; CCI. "Excel, peaceful site; vg facs for families; gates clsd 2230-0800." ♦ 3 Apr-26 Sep. € 32.40 (CChq acc) ABS - B31 2009*

See advertisement

PORNIC *2G3* (8km W Coastal) *47.13261, -2.23138* **Camping Eléovic, Route de la Pointe St Gildas, 44770 Préfailles [02 40 21 61 60; fax 02 40 64 51 95; contact@camping-eleovic.com; www.camping-eleovic.com]** W fr Pornic on D13 to La Plaine-sur-Mer, turn S to Préfailles, cont twds Pointe-St Gildas 1km, L site sp. Med, hdg pitch, terr, pt shd; htd wc; chem disp; mv service pnt; serviced pitches; baby facs; shwrs inc; el pnts (6A) €4.15; Indtte; tradsmn; rest; snacks; bar; BBQ; htd, covrd pool; waterslide; playgrnd; sand beach adj; fishing; sailing; TV; entmnt; 20% statics; dogs €3-5.40; phone; Eng spkn; adv bkg; red low ssn/long stay/CCI; ccard acc. "Dir access to coast path; barrier clsd 2200-1000; vg." ♦ 1 Apr-30 Sep. € 31.10 2006*

PORNIC *2G3* (7km NW Coastal) *47.17614, -2.15462* **Camping Bel Essor, Rue de Tharon, 44730 St Michel-Chef-Chef [02 40 27 85 40 or 02 47 38 89 07 (LS); www.campingbelessor.com]** On D123 fr Pornic dir St Nazaire (Route Bleue) turn L sp Tharon-Plage. After 2nd rndabt take next turn R & keep R. Foll sps St Michel & site. Site on L after supmkt ent. Lge, mkd pitch, pt sl, pt shd; wc (some cont); chem disp (wc); shwrs inc; el pnts (6A) €4.20; Indtte; supmkt opp; tradsmn; snacks; bar; playgrnd; sand beach 400m; some statics; dogs €2; phone adj; poss cr in high ssn; Eng spkn; adv bkg; red low ssn; CCI. "Vg site; clean facs; helpful owners." ♦ 25 Apr-20 Sep. € 14.60 2009*

PORNIC *2G3* (8km NW Coastal) *47.17305, -2.15833* **Camping Clos Mer et Nature, 103 Rue Tharon, 44730 St Michel-Chef-Chef [02 40 27 85 71; fax 02 40 39 41 89; info@camping-clos-mer-nature.com; www.camping-clos-mer-nature.com]** Take D213 fr Mindin. After 11km R on D77 sp St Michel-Chef-Chef 2nd R after cent of vill sp Tharon-Plage site on L after 1.5km. Lge, pt sl, pt shd; htd wc; mv service pnt; baby facs; shwrs inc; el pnts (6-10A) €3.50-5; Indtte; shop; supmkt 300m; snacks; playgrnd; pool; waterslide; sand beach 400m; fishing; sailing; windsurfing; tennis; cycle hire; games area; entmnt; some statics; dogs €3; o'night m'van area; adv bkg; quiet. "Vg, modern san facs." ♦ 1 Apr-17 Oct. € 20.00 2009*

PORNIC *2G3* (8km NW Coastal) *47.16007, -2.16274* **Camping Le Vieux Château, Ave du Vieux-Tharon, Tharon-Plage, 44730 St Michel-Chef-Chef [02 40 27 83 47 or 02 33 65 02 96; camping.duvieuxchateau@wanadoo.fr]** Fr Pornic dir St Nazaire, turn W twd Tharon-Plage, site sp. Med, hdg/mkd pitch, terr, pt shd; wc; chem disp; shwrs inc; el pnts (6A) €3.50; Indtte; shop; tradsmn; snacks; bar; BBQ; playgrnd; htd pool; paddling pool; sand beach 400m; playgrnd; games rm; many statics; dogs €1.50; poss cr; Eng spkn; adv bkg; quiet; ccard acc; red long stay; CCI. "Unkempt low ssn; clean facs." ♦ 1 May-15 Sep. € 17.00 2006*

PORNIC *2G3* (10km NW Coastal) *47.15076, -2.19481* **Camping Bernier, 56 Rue de la Cormorane, 44770 La Plaine-sur-Mer [02 40 21 04 31 or 06 63 82 39 91 (mob); fax 02 40 21 08 12; www.camping-lebernier.com]** S fr St Nazaire bdge on D213 twd Pornic, turn R, S of St Michel-Chef-Chef on D96. Cont to junc, turn R, cont to x-rd, turn L. In 500m on R. Or thro La Plaine-sur-Mer on D13, turn R on leaving vill past g'ge twd Port Giraud. Site on L in 1km. Med, some hdg pitch, pt shd; wc; chem disp; some serviced pitches; shwrs inc; el pnts (6A) €3.60; Indtte; shop 300m; snacks; playgrnd; htd pool; sand beach 600m; some statics; dogs €2.80; adv bkg; quiet; 40-50% red low ssn; 5% red CCI. "Excel family site site nr gd beaches." ♦ 1 May-30 Sep. € 19.10 2009*

PORNICHET *2G3* (2km E Coastal) *47.24956, -2.32140* **Camping Bel Air, 150 Ave de Bonne Source, Ste Marguerite, 44380 Pornichet [02 40 61 10 78; fax 02 40 61 26 18; reception@bel-air-pornichet.com; www.belairpornichet.com]** On coast rd fr Pornichet to Ste Margarite; sp. Lge, hdg/mkd pitch, pt sl, pt shd; htd wc; chem disp; mv service pnt; baby facs; fam bthrm; shwrs inc; el pnts some (10A) €4; gas; Indtte; shop; tradsmn; snacks; rest; snacks; bar; BBQ; playgrnd; htd pool; sand beach 50m; multi-sport area; fishing; sailing; cycle hire; internet; TV rm; 50% statics; dogs €1.50; no twin-axles; Eng spkn; adv bkg; quiet; ccard acc; red long stay/low ssn. "Easy access to beach; pleasant town; St Nazaire shipyards worth visit." ♦ 28 Apr-16 Sep. € 35.00 2007*

PORNICHET *2G3* (2km E Urban/Coastal) *47.25280, -2.31910* **Camping du Bugeau, 33 Ave des Loriettes, 44380 Pornichet [02 40 61 02 02 or 02 40 61 15 44 (LS); fax 02 40 61 22 75; info@campingdubugeau.com; www.campingdubugeau.com]** W fr St Nazaire on D92 then L at rndabt at St Marguerite by car showrm; site sp 2nd L, site 500m on L. Med, hdg/mkd pitch, pt shd; htd wc; chem disp; mv service pnt; shwrs inc; el pnts (4-10A) €2.90-3.80; Indtte; shop & 500m; tradsmn; snacks; BBQ; playgrnd; htd, covrd pool; sand beach & watersports 500m; tennis 500m; cycle hire 1km; TV; 30% statics; dogs; Eng spkn; adv bkg; ccard acc. "Gd." ♦ Apr-Sep. € 19.10 2007*

PORNICHET *2G3* (4km E Rural) *47.26912, -2.29401* **Camping au Repos des Forges, 98 Route de la Villès-Blaise, 44380 Pornichet [02 40 61 18 84; fax 02 40 60 11 84; camping@campinglesforges.com; www.campinglesforges.com]** To N of D92 halfway bet St Nazaire & Pornichet. Accessible also fr N171; sp. Med, pt sl, pt shd; wc; chem disp; shwrs inc; el pnts (6-10A) €4-5; gas; Indtte; shop in ssn; snacks; playgrnd; htd pool; beach 3km; games area; games rm; TV rm; 70% statics; dogs €4; Eng spkn; adv bkg; quiet; CCI. "Friendly recep; barrier clsd 2300-0700; excel san facs." ♦ 1 Jul-31 Aug. € 22.00 2008*

PORT DES BARQUES see Rochefort *7B1*

PORT EN BESSIN HUPPAIN *3D1* (500m W Coastal) *49.34693, -0.77095* **Camping Port'land, Chemin du Castel, 14520 Port-en-Bessin [02 31 51 07 06; fax 02 31 51 76 49; campingportland@wanadoo.fr; www.camping-portland.com]** Site sp fr D514 W of Port-en-Bessin. Lge, hdg/mkd pitch, pt shd; htd wc; mv service pnt; chem disp; mv service pnt; shwrs inc; el pnts (16A) inc; gas 1km; Indtte; shop; tradsmn; rest; snacks; bar; BBQ; playgrnd; htd, covrd pool; waterslide; paddling pool; sand beach 4km; tennis 600m; games area; games rm; entmnt; wifi; TV; 30% statics; dogs €3; Eng spkn; adv bkg; ccard acc; red long stay/low ssn; CCI. "Nice site; friendly & helpful; vg san facs; extra charge lger pitches; excel touring base." ♦ 1 Apr-7 Nov. € 39.00 2009*

PORT LA NOUVELLE *10G1* (500M S Urban) *43.01477, 3.04565* **Camp Municipal du Golfe, 406 Blvd Francis Vals, 11210 Port-la-Nouvelle [04 68 48 08 42; fax 04 68 40 37 90]** Exit A9/E15 junc 39 onto D6139 (N139) to Port-la-Nouvelle; at cement works rndbt R into D709; in 1km L over rlwy; L at rndbt; immed L into site. Lge, some hdg/mkd pitch, pt shd; wc; shwrs inc; el pnts (6A) €2.30; Indry rm; shop 500m; playgrnd; sand beach 1km; dogs €1.20; some rlwy & rd noise; red low ssn; CCI. "Useful NH nr A9." ♦ 1 Apr-30 Sep. € 13.00 2007*

France

PORT LA NOUVELLE *10G1* (2km S Coastal) *42.99817, 3.04825* **Camping Côte Vermeille, Chemin des Vignes, 11210 Port-la-Nouvelle [04 68 48 05 80; fax 04 68 27 53 03; infos@camping-cote-vermeille.com; www.camping-franceloc.fr]** Fr N exit A9 junc 39 onto D6139 then D6009 twd La Palme. In 9km turn L onto D709, site in 6km. V lge, mkd pitch, pt shd; wc; chem disp; mv service pnt; el pnts (6A) €4; Indtte; shop; supmkt 3km; rest; snacks; bar; playgrnd; pool; paddling pool; waterslide; sand beach 200m; wifi; entmnt; TV; some statics; adv bkg; CCI. "Superb pool complex." ♦ 4 Apr-27 Sep. € 26.00 2009*

PORT LE GRAND see Abbeville *3B3*

PORT SUR SAONE *6F2* (800m S Rural) *47.68056, 6.03937* **Camp Municipal Parc de la Maladière, 70170 Port-sur-Saône [03 84 91 51 32 or 03 84 78 18 00 (Mairie); fax 03 84 78 18 09; tourisme.portsursaone@wanadoo.fr]** Take D619 (N19) SE fr Langres or NW fr Vesoul. Site sp in vill bet rv & canal off D6 at municipal bathing area. Med, hdg pitch, pt shd; wc (mainly cont); own san facs; chem disp; shwrs inc; el pnts (6A) €2.50 (poss rev pol); Indry rm; shops 1km; tradsmn high ssn; rest, bar; in vill; playgrnd; pool adj; tennis; fishing; adv bkg; ccard acc; quiet; CCI. "Peaceful site on island; rvside cycle path; gd walks; gd sh stay/NH." ♦ 15 May-15 Sep. € 7.50 2006*

⊞ **PORT VENDRES** *10G1* (500m W Urban) *42.51775, 3.11314* **Aire Communale des Tamarins, Route de la Jetée, 66660 Port-Vendres [04 68 82 07 54]** Fr D914 (N114) at Port-Vendres at Banyuls side of town turn N on D86B sp Port de Commerce & Aire de Camping-Cars. Foll sp to site on R in 700m. Sm, hdstg, pt shd; chem disp; mv service pnt; wc (part cont); own san; no el pnts (2009); gas 1km; shop 1km; rest 500m; snacks, bar 1km; playgrnd adj; shgl beach 100m; red low ssn. "NH, m'vans only; walking dist rlwy stn; poss cr even low ssn; a bit run down (Jun 2009)." € 8.40 2009*

PORT VENDRES *10G1* (2km NW Coastal) *42.53147, 3.07167* **Camping Les Amandiers, Plage de l'Ouile, 66190 Collioure [04 68 81 14 69; fax 04 68 81 09 95; contact@camping-les-amandiers.com; www.camping-les-amandiers.com]** On D914 (N114) SE fr Perpignan, leave at junc 13 sp Collioure. After rndabt foll rd to Collioure. Climb coastal rd; site on L, steep descent, not rec lge o'fits. Med, mkd pitch, pt sl, terr, shd; htd wc (some cont); chem disp; mv service pnt; shwrs inc; el pnts (5A) €4; Indtte; gas; sm shop; tradsmn; sm rest, bar high ssn; sm playgrnd; shgl beach 200m; 10% statics; dogs €3; poss cr; Eng spkn; adv bkg; (rec high ssn); some rlwy noise; ccard not acc; CCI. "Site access v diff, espec for lge/med o'fits, manhandling prob req - rec investigation bef ent; sm pitches; facs stretched high ssn; many trees - dusty site; steep site rds; friendly, helpful owners; Collioure historic port; gd." ♦ 1 Apr-30 Sep. € 22.00 2007*

PORTIRAGNES PLAGE *10F1* (Coastal) *43.28003, 3.36396* **Camping Les Sablons, Plage-Est, 34420 Portiragnes-Plage [04 67 90 90 55; fax 04 67 90 82 91; les.sablons@wanadoo.fr; www.les-sablons.com]** Fr A9 exit Béziers Est junc 35 onto N112. Then take D37 S to Portiragnes-Plage & foll sp. V lge, mkd pitch, shd; wc; chem disp; mv service pnt; baby facs; shwrs inc; el pnts (6A) inc; gas; Indtte; shop; rest; snacks; bar; BBQ; playgrnd; 2 htd pools; waterslide; sand beach adj; diving; boating; fishing; tennis; games area; cycle hire; entmnt; 50% statics; dogs €4; phone; poss cr; Eng spkn; adv bkg; ccard acc; quiet. "Gd site on beach; modern san facs; nightly disco but quiet after midnight." ♦ 1 Apr-30 Sep. € 46.00 2007*

PORTIRAGNES PLAGE *10F1* (2km NE Coastal) *43.29138, 3.37333* **Camping Les Mimosas, Port Cassafières, 34420 Portiragnes-Plage [04 67 90 92 92; fax 04 67 90 85 39; info@mimosas.fr or les.mimosas.portiragnes@wanadoo.fr; www.mimosas.com]** Exit A9 junc 35 Béziers Est & take N112 sp Vias, Agde. After 3km at rndabt foll sp Portiragnes & cont along side of Canal du Midi. Cross canal, site sp. Lge, mkd pitch, hdstg, pt shd; wc; sauna; private san facs avail; shwrs inc; el pnts (6-10A) €4; gas; Indtte; shop; supmkt; rest; snacks; bar; BBQ (gas); playgrnd; pools; paddling pool; waterslides; jacuzzi; sand beach 1km; cycle hire; games area; fitness rm; entmnt; 50% statics; dogs €5.50; Eng spkn; adv bkg; quiet; ccard acc; red low ssn. "Excel touring base in interesting area; friendly welcome; vg water park; gd for families." ♦ 22 May-4 Sep. € 35.00 2009*

See advertisement

POUANCE *2F4* (1.5km N Rural) *47.74850, -1.17841* **Camp Muncipal La Roche Martin, 23 Rue des Etangs, 49420 Pouancé [02 41 92 43 97 or 02 41 92 41 08 (Mairie); fax 02 41 92 62 30]** Take D6 (sp St Aignan) N fr town. After level x-ing turn L onto D72 (sp La Guerche-de-Bretagne). In 300m, site on L. Sm, mkd pitch, pt terr, pt sl; wc; mv service pnt; shwrs; el pnts (10A); gas; shops 1km; rest, bar 100m; playgrnd; direct access to lake; watersports; tennis; games area; tennis; poss cr; adv bkg. "Well-kept, friendly site o'looking lge lake; noise fr rd & sailing school." 1 Apr-30 Sep. 2007*

POUGUES LES EAUX *4H4* (1km N Urban) *47.08430, 3.09349* **Camp Municipal Les Chanternes, Ave du Paris, 58320 Pougues-les-Eaux [03 86 68 86 18 or 03 86 90 96 00 (Mairie); www.ville-pouguesleseaux.fr]** On side of D907 (N7) in Pougues-les-Eaux at rear of open-air pool & thro same ent. Med, mkd pitch, pt shd; htd wc (some cont); mv service pnt; shwrs inc; el pnts; shops, rest & snacks in vill; pool adj; adv bkg; rd & rlwy noise; CCI. 1 Jun-30 Sep. 2006*

France

POUILLY EN AUXOIS *6G1* (NW Urban) *47.26534, 4.54804* **FFCC Camping Le Vert Auxois, 15 Voûte du Canal du Bourgogne, 21320 Pouilly-en-Auxois [03 80 90 71 89; fax 03 80 90 77 58; vert.auxois@wanadoo.fr; http://camping.vertauxois.free.fr]** Exit A6 at Dijon/Pouilly-en-Auxois onto A38. Exit A38 at junc 24. Thro vill & turn L after church on R, site sp adj Burgandy canal. Med, hdg pitch, pt shd; wc; mv service pnt; shwrs inc; el pnts (6-10A) €3.80-4.50; gas; Indtte; shop 400m; tradsmn; rest 400m; snacks, bar high ssn; playgrnd; rv fishing adj; lake 5km; wifi; TV rm; quiet; bus 300m; ccard not acc; CCI. "Beautiful position; lge pitches; gd facs; friendly owner; gd cycling; excel." 1 May-15 Sep. € 9.30 2009*

POUILLY SUR LOIRE *4G3* (1km N Rural) *47.28742, 2.94427* **Camp Municipal Le Malaga, Rue des Champs-sur-Loire, Les Loges, 58150 Pouilly-sur-Loire [tel/fax 03 86 39 14 54 or 03 86 58 74 38 (LS); www.ot-pouillysurloire.fr]** Fr S exit A77 junc 26 onto D28a, turn L onto D59/D4289 W, bef rv bdge turn R, site in 1km on rv. Fr N on ent vill turn R at site sp into narr rd. Turn R along rv as above. Med, pt shd; wc; chem disp; shwrs inc; el pnts (10A) inc (poss long lead req & poss rev pol); Indry rm; shop & 1km; tradsmn; snacks; bar; BBQ; playgrnd; dogs €1; phone; no twin-axles or o'fits over 5m; poss cr; Eng spkn; quiet, but some rlwy noise & poss noisy w/end. "Excel, busy NH; spacious but uneven pitches; mixed reports san facs; poss youth groups; beautiful area; poss mosquitoes." ♦ 1 Jun-1 Sep. € 11.00 2008*

POULDU, LE *2F2* (N Urban/Coastal) *47.76850, -3.54540* **Camping Les Embruns, Rue du Philosophe Alain, 29360 Le Pouldu [02 98 39 91 07; fax 02 98 39 97 87; camping-les-embruns@wanadoo.fr; www.camping-les-embruns.com]** Exit N165 dir Quimperlé Cent, onto D16/D24 to Clohars-Carnoët. Foll sp Le Pouldu & site on R on ent 1-way traff system. Lge, hdg/mkd pitch, hdstg, terr, pt shd; wc; chem disp; mv service pnt; all serviced pitches; baby facs; fam bthrm; shwrs inc; el pnts (10A) inc; gas; Indtte; shop; rest; snacks; bar; BBQ; playgrnd; 2 pools (1 htd, covrd); sand beach 200m; watersports; tennis 200m; fishing; cycle hire; horseriding nr; games area; games rm; TV rm; 50% statics; dogs €23; adv bkg; quiet; ccard acc; red low ssn; CCI. "Excel family-run site; gd location - town was home of Paul Gauguin; luxury pitches extra charge; vg, clean san facs; gd walking along coastal paths." ♦ 4 Apr-13 Sep. € 29.90 2008*

POULDU, LE *2F2* (2km N Rural) *47.78669, -3.55110* **Camping du Quinquis, 29360 Le Pouldu [02 98 39 92 40; fax 02 98 39 96 56; andrew.munro@clara.co.uk; www.campingquinquis.com]** On D16 fr Quimperlé, 2km S of x-rds with D224. Or fr N165 exit Guidel junc 45; foll sps to Le Pouldu & zoo adj to site. Med, hdg pitch, pt sl, pt shd; wc; shwrs; el pnts (10A) inc; gas; Indtte; sm shop; snacks; bar; playgrnd; pool & paddling pool; sand beach 2km; tennis; cycle hire; games rm; entmnt; TV; 80% statics; dogs; phone; poss cr; quiet; red low ssn. "Vg, peaceful, British-owned site." ♦ 23 May-5 Sep. € 21.00 2009*

POULDU, LE *2F2* (500m NE Rural) *47.77274, -3.54433* **Camping Keranquernat, 29360 Keranquernat [02 98 39 92 32; fax 02 98 39 99 84; camping.keranquernat@wanadoo.fr; www.camping-keranquernat.com]** Fr Quimperlé D16 to Clohars-Carnoët, then D24 to Le Pouldu - twd port; turn R at x-rds nr Ar Men Résidence; site ent immed on R. Fr S on N165 exit junc 45 sp Guidel; in 1km turn W onto D162/D224, then foll sp Le Pouldu; site sp at town ent. Med, hdg/mkd pitch, pt shd; wc (some cont); chem disp; baby facs; shwrs; el pnts (3-5A) €3-3.50; Indtte; shops 300m; tradsmn; rest & bar nrby; BBQ; playgrnd; htd pool; paddling pool; sand beach 700m; fishing; sailing; tennis; cycle hire; games rm; TV; dogs €0.50; adv bkg; quiet; red low ssn; CCI. "Beautifully-kept, pretty site; welcoming owners; highly rec." 1 May-6 Sep. € 16.50 2008*

POULDU, LE *2F2* (2km E Rural/Coastal) *47.77466, -3.50616* **Camping Les Jardins de Kergal, Route des Plages, 56520 Guidel [06 83 46 53 08 (Mob); fax 02 97 32 88 27; contact@camping-lorient.com; www.camping-lorient.com]** Fr N165 Brest-Nantes take Guidel exit; thro Guidel & onto Guidel-Plages; camp sp in 1km. Lge, hdg/mkd pitch, pt sl, pt shd; wc; chem disp; baby facs; shwrs inc; el pnts (10A) inc; Indtte; gas; shops 2km; tradsmn high ssn; rest, snacks, bar high ssn; BBQ; playgrnd; pool; waterslide; sand beach 1.5km; tennis; entmnt; cycle hire; games area; wifi; 75% statics; dogs €3; adv bkg; quiet but poss noisy youth groups high ssn; red low ssn; CCI. "Friendly, helpful, welcoming staff; well-run, peaceful site; conv beaches & touring; most pitches triangular - poss diff." ♦ 1 Apr-30 Sep. € 29.70 2008*

POULE LES ECHARMEAUX *9A2* (1.5km W Rural) *46.15028, 4.45419* **Camp Municipal Les Echarmeaux, 69870 Poule-les-Echarmeaux [06 89 90 33 64 (mob) or 04 74 03 60 98; fax 04 74 03 68 71; www.poulelesecharmeaux.eu]** Turn E off D385 to Poule-les-Echarmeaux, site sp. Sm, hdg pitch, terr, pt shd; wc; shwrs inc; el pnts inc; shop 500m; playgrnd; adv bkg. "Beautifully situated site adj lake; nr Beaujolais wine area; excel sh stay." 1 May-30 Sep. € 11.20 2009*

POULIGUEN, LE *2G3* (Urban/Coastal) *47.27130, -2.43012* **Camp Municipal du Clein, Ave de Kerdun, 44510 Le Pouliguen [02 40 42 43 99 or 02 40 15 08 08 (Mairie); fax 02 40 15 14 60; leclein@mairie-lepouliguen.fr]** Fr La Baule (W end) take coast rd to Le Pouliguen & foll sps. Lge, pt shd; wc; shwrs; el pnts (6-10A) €3-3.50; playgrnd; sand beach, fishing, sailing 500m; windsurfing 1.50m; dogs €2; poss cr; red low ssn. Easter-15 Sep. € 12.00 2008*

POULIGUEN, LE *2G3* (SW Urban/Coastal) *47.27183, -2.44025* **Camp Municipal Les Mouettes, 45 Blvd de l'Atlantique, 44510 Le Pouliguen [tel/fax 02 40 42 43 98 or 06 37 09 21 66 (mob); lesmouettes@mairie-lepouliguen.fr]** Fr La Boule (W end) take coast rd to Le Pouliguen & foll sps to site on D45. Lge, mkd pitch, unshd; htd wc; baby facs; mv service pnt; shwrs; el pnts (6A) €3; Indtte; shop, supmkt 200m; rest; snacks; bar; playgrnd; beach 800m; fishing; sailing; cycle hire 200m; games area; entmnt; TV; dogs €2; no adv bkg. "Poss resident workers." 1 Apr-15 Oct. € 12.80 2008*

POULLAN SUR MER see Douarnenez *2E2*

⊞ **POUZAUGES** *2H4* (1.5km W Rural) *46.78150, -0.85326* **Camping du Lac, L'Espérance, 85700 Pouzauges [tel/fax 02 51 91 37 55; campingpouzauges@tele2.fr; www.campingpouzauges.com]** W fr Pouzauges on D960B, turn R in 1km onto unclass rd, site in 1km. Sp fr all dir. Sm, hdg/mkd pitch, pt sl, shd; wc; shwrs; el pnts (6-10A) €4 (poss rev pol); Indtte; shops 1.5km; tradsmn; rest 1.5km; snacks; bar; lake sw & fishing adj; boat hire; play & picnic area adj; some statics; dogs €3; c'van storage; poss cr; adv bkg; quiet; CCI. "Excel site; friendly, helpful British owners; san facs ltd when site full; gd local walks & cycling; conv Puy de Fou." ♦ € 13.00 2009*

PRADEAUX, LES see Issoire *9B1*

⊞ **PRADES** *8G4* (500m N Urban) *42.62141, 2.42272* **Camp Municipal Plaine St Martin, 66500 Prades [04 68 96 29 83 or 04 68 05 41 00 (Mairie); prades-leconflent@wanadoo.fr; www.leconflent.net/camping]** Site sp on ent town on N116 fr both dirs. Med, hdg/mkd pitch, pt sl, shd; wc (some cont); chem disp; 50% serviced pitches; shwrs inc; el pnts (6-10A) €2.80; gas 500m; Indtte; shop, rest, snacks & bar 500m; playgrnd; htd, covrd pool; fishing; 30% statics; dogs €1.35; phone; poss cr; adv bkg; quiet; ccard acc; CCI. "Lge pitches; facs old but clean; poss unkempt low ssn; excel touring base; music festival in Jul; mkt Tues; NH." € 9.80 2009*

PRADES *8G4* (7km E Rural) *42.61722, 2.50111* **Camping Le Canigou, 66320 Espira-de-Conflent [04 68 05 85 40; fax 04 68 05 86 20; canigou@yahoo.com; www.canigou-espira.com]** On N116 Andorra-Perpignan, 2km after Marquixanes, R at sm site sp also sp 'Espira-de-Conflent'. Or, fr Perpignan on N116, turn L 7km bef Prades onto D25 & foll sp for 3.5km. Med, hdg/mkd pitch, pl sl, terr, shd; wc; chem disp; mv service pnt; shwrs inc; el pnts (6A) inc; Indtte; shop; tradsmn; rest; snacks; bar; playgrnd; rv pool; lake & watersports 5km; 5% statics; dogs €1.50; Eng spkn; adv bkg; quiet; red long stay/low ssn; ccard acc; CCI. "Beautiful rvside site; youth groups in summer; some noise; narr site rds not rec for lge o'fits." ♦ 1 Feb-31 Oct. € 23.90 2009*

PRADES *8G4* (2km SW Rural) *42.60308, 2.39841* **Camping Bellevue, Rue de St Jean, 66500 Ria-Sirach [tel/fax 04 68 96 48 96; bellevue.camping@wanadoo.fr; www.camping-bellevue-riasirach.com]** W on N116 fr Perpignan, thro Prades. In 1km at far edge of vill of Ria, turn L on D26A & foll sps to site. Access steep. Med, mkd pitch, pt sl, terr, shd; wc; baby facs; shwrs inc; el pnts (3-6A) €5.90-6.80; Indtte; shop 500m; bar; playgrnd; rv sw & fishing 500m; dogs €1; adv bkg; quiet; red CCI. "Peaceful with gd views." ♦ 1 Apr-30 Sep. € 10.00 2009*

PRADES *8G4* (5km W Rural) *42.58019, 2.35057* **Camping Mas de Lastourg, Serdinya, 66500 Villefranche-de-Conflent [04 68 05 35 25; maslastourg@aol.com; www.camping-lastourg.com]** W fr Prades on N116. Site on L of main rd 2km after Villefranche, turn L 100m after start of dual c'way. Med, hdg/mkd pitch, pt shd; wc; chem disp (wc); baby facs; shwrs inc; el pnts (6-10A) €3-5; Indtte; sm shop & 2km; tradsmn; rest; snacks; bar; BBQ; playgrnd; sm pool; a few statics; dogs €1; phone; poss cr; Eng spkn; adv bkg; quiet but some rd/rlwy noise; ccard acc; red low ssn; CCI. "Lovely site; easy access; nice pitches; conv 'Little Yellow Train'; poss clsd low ssn - phone ahead to check; excel." ♦ 1 Apr-15 Nov. € 17.50 2009*

PRALOGNAN LA VANOISE *9B4* (500m S Rural) *45.37692, 6.72375* **Camp Municipal Le Chamois, Route de l'Isertan, 73710 Pralognan-la-Vanoise [04 79 08 71 54; fax 04 79 08 78 77; camping@pralognan.com]** Fr Moûtiers take D915 to Pralognan. Pass under concrete bdge, turn SW & foll camping sp; keep L past recep of bigger Iseran site. Lge, mkd pitch, terr, pt sl, unshd; htd wc (some cont); chem disp (wc); shwrs inc; el pnts (2-10A) €2.30-3.90; Indtte; shops 500m; htd pool 300m; rv fishing; dogs; poss cr; quiet. "Peaceful site in beautiful area; vg walks; friendly staff; cable car up mountain." 1 Jun-15 Sep & 15 Dec-8 May. 2006*

PRALOGNAN LA VANOISE *9B4* (500m S Rural) *45.37667, 6.72236* **Camping Le Parc Isertan, Route de l'Isertan, 73710 Pralognan-la-Vanoise [04 79 08 75 24; fax 04 79 08 76 13; camping@camping-isertan.com; www.camping-isertan.com]** Fr Moûtiers, take D915 E to Pralognan. Pass under concrete bdge & foll camping sp. Site behind pool adj municipal site. Lge, hdstg, terr, pt shd; htd wc; chem disp; mv service pnt; baby facs; shwrs inc; el pnts (10A) €5.50; gas 500m; tradsmn; shop 500m; rest; snacks; bar; BBQ; playgrnd; htd, covrd pool, sports cent adj; horseriding 500m; some statics; dogs €1; phone; poss cr; Eng spkn; adv bkg; quiet; ccard acc; red low ssn/ CCI. "Superb scenery; wonderful walking; cable car in vill; v peaceful." ♦ 21 Dec-19 Apr & 24 Jun-27 Oct. € 18.00 2007*

PRATS DE CARLUX see Sarlat la Canéda *7C3*

PRATS DE MOLLO LA PRESTE *8H4* (11km E Rural) *42.38892, 2.60620* **Camp Municipal Verte Rive, Place de l'Ile, 66260 St Laurent-de-Cerdans [04 68 39 54 64 or 04 68 39 50 04 (Mairie); fax 04 68 39 59 59; contact@ville-saint-laurent-de-cerdans.fr; www.ville-saint-laurent-de-cerdans.fr]** Fr Le Boulou, take D115 twd Prats-de-Mollo, turn L on D3 twd St Laurent. Site 4km fr Spanish border. Med, mkd pitch, pt sl, pt shd; htd wc; shwrs inc; el pnts (5A) €2.75; lndtte; shop 1.5km; playgrnd; pool adj; some statics; poss cr; adv bkg; CCI. "Conv NH." ♦ 1 May-31 Oct. € 5.40 2006*

PRATS DE MOLLO LA PRESTE *8H4* (12km E Rural) *42.41200, 2.61800* **Camping Domaine Le Clols (Naturist), 66260 St Laurent-de-Cerdans [04 68 39 51 68; info@leclols.com; www.leclols.com]** Fr A9 at Le Boulou take D115 dir Prats-de-Mollo; 6km past Arles-sur-Tech take D3 on L sp St Laurent-de-Cerdans; at La Forge-del-Mitg turn sharp L sp Le Clols; site on R in 3km (narr, winding rd). Sm, pt sl, pt shd; wc (some cont); chem disp (wc); shwrs inc; el pnts (5-10A) €3-3.95; gas; lndtte; shop; snacks; playgrnd; pool; TV; some statics; dogs €2; adv bkg; quiet; red 10+ days; CCI. "Gd views; friendly British owners; gd walks fr site." ♦ 1 May-30 Sep. € 22.00 2009*

PRE EN PAIL *4E1* (200m N Urban) *48.46094, -0.20140* **Camp Municipal Alain Gerbault, Rue des Troènes, 53140 Pré-en-Pail [02 43 03 04 28; camping.preenpail@wanadoo.fr]** Fr E on N12, turn R at major rndabt (sp D176 Domfront). Turn R twd sports cent & well sp fr there on N edge of vill. Sm, mkd pitch, pt shd; wc (some cont); chem disp; shwrs inc; el pnts (16A) €2.60; shop 250m; rest; snacks; bar; playgrnd; htd pool adj; dogs €1.10; phone; CCI. "Pleasant wooded region; poss mkt traders on site; OK as touring base." Easter-30 Sep. € 7.40 2006*

PRECY SOUS THIL *6G1* (8km S Rural) *47.32309, 4.33086* **Camping Le Village, 21210 La Motte-Ternant [tel/fax 03 80 84 30 11; campinglamotteternant@wanadoo.fr; www.campinglamotteternant.eu]** Exit A6 junc 23 onto D980 to Précy-sous-Thil; then take D36 to Fontangy; turn R onto D26 to La Motte-Ternant. Fr Saulieu take D26 to La Motte-Ternant. Site in 10km. Site sp, but diff to see fr S (obscured by building). Sm, pt sl, shd; wc; chem disp (wc); shwrs inc; el pnts (16A) €3.75; tradsmn; shop & bar 800m; tradsmn; BBQ; dogs free; Eng spkn; adv bkg; quiet; ccard acc. "Delightful, friendly site with views; helpful Dutch owners; hot water poss extremely hot - children take care; gd." 1 Apr-1 Nov. € 11.25 2008*

PRECY SOUS THIL *6G1* (W Rural) *47.38721, 4.30645* **Camp Municipal, Rue de l'Hôtel de Ville, 21390 Précy-sous-Thil [03 80 64 57 18 (Mairie); fax 03 80 64 43 37]** Exit A6 at junc 23 Bierre-lès-Semur exit onto D980 to Précy. Site sp in vill. Sm, pt sl, pt shd; wc; shwrs inc; el pnts (4A) €2.40; lndtte; shops 150m; rest & bar 300m; playgrnd; rv adj; tennis nr; horseriding; entmnt; TV; some statics; dogs €1.30; quiet. "In grnds of Town Hall; conv NH on way S." Easter-1 Nov. € 8.10 2008*

PREFAILLES see Pornic *2G3*

PREIXAN see Carcassonne *8F4*

PREMEAUX PRISSEY see Nuits St Georges *6G1*

PREMERY *4G4* (500m NW) *47.17804, 3.33692* **Camp Municipal Le Plan D'eau (Les Prés de la Ville), 58700 Prémery [03 86 37 99 42 or 03 86 68 12 40 (Mairie); fax 03 86 37 98 72; mairie-premery@wanadoo.fr]** N fr Nevers on D977 to Prémery; turn R after 2nd rndabt. Site sp on D977. Med, pt shd; wc (some cont); chem disp (wc); shwrs inc; el pnts (8-10A) €1-1.80; shops 500m; lake & rv adj with sand beach, sw, fishing & boating; tennis adj; adv bkg; quiet; 10% red 10+ days. "Lovely, well-run lakeside site in town park; popular NH; interesting town; poss market traders; excel value." ♦ 25 Apr-30 Sep. € 8.00 2009*

PREMIAN see St Pons de Thomières *8F4*

PRESILLY see St Julien en Genevois *9A3*

PRESSAC *7A3* (7km E Rural) *46.12342, 0.65975* **FFCC Camp Municipal Le Parc, 86460 Availles-Limouzine [05 49 48 51 22; fax 05 49 48 66 76; camping.leparc@wanadoo.fr; http://monsite.wanadoo.fr/campingleparc]** Fr Confolens N on D948 & turn R on D34 to Availles-Limouzine. Site on Rv Vienne by town bdge. Med, pt shd; wc; chem disp; mv service pnt; shwrs inc; el pnts (10A) inc; gas; shops 750m; playgrnd; lge paddling pool; dogs €2.65; poss cr; Eng spkn; adv bkg; quiet; CCI. "Attractive, well-run site in beautiful position; rv views; friendly, helpful warden lives on site; excel san facs; vg playgrnd; barrier clsd 2200-0800; poss scruffy low ssn; vg value; excel." ♦ 1 May-30 Sep. € 11.50 2009*

France

⊞ **PRESSAC** *7A3* (6km SW Rural) *46.09696, 0.48081* **Camping Rural des Marronniers, La Bussière, 16490 Pleuville [05 45 31 03 45; ssmpooleman1@aliceadsl.fr; www.conkertreefarmcampsite.bravehost.com]** S fr Poitiers on D741 to Pressac; turn R onto D34 to Pleuville; site on D30 dir Charroux. Sm, terr, pt shd; htd wc; chem disp; fam bathrm; shwrs inc; el pnts (6A) €2; gas; lndtte; shop 1km; rest 8km; snacks; bar 1km; BBQ; playgrnd; pool; games rm; dogs; adv bkg; quiet. "British-owned, CL-type farm site; gd touring base; excel." ♦ € 8.00 2006*

PRESSIGNAC see Rochechouart *7B3*

PREUILLY see Mehun sur Yevre *4H3*

PREUILLY SUR CLAISE *4H2* (SW Urban) *46.85113, 0.92892* **Camp Municipal Bord de Claise, 37290 Preuilly-sur-Claise [02 47 94 50 04 (Mairie); fax 02 47 94 63 26]** Fr E on D725 descend hill into vill. At T-junc opp town hall turn R & in 30m take 2nd L sp Camping & Piscine - poss diff turn long o'fits due narr rd. Site adj pool in 300m. Sm, hdg pitch, pt shd; wc; chem disp (wc); shwrs inc; el pnts (6A) €3.20; lndtte; shop, rest, bar in vill; BBQ; playgrnd; htd pool adj; rv fishing adj; poss cr; quiet. "No twin-axles allowed." 1 May-15 Sep. € 7.50 2008*

The opening dates and prices on this campsite have changed. I'll send a site report form to the Club for the next edition of the guide.

PRIVAS *9D2* (8km NE Rural) *44.75721, 4.71298* **Camping L'Albanou (formerly Pampelonne), Quartier Pampelonne, 07000 St Julien-en-St Alban [04 75 66 00 97; camping.albanou@wanadoo.fr; www.camping-albanou.com]** Fr A7 exit junc 16 at Loriol dir Le Pouzin, go thro Le Pouzin on D104 (N304) dir Privas/Aubenas. Site in 6km on L just bef vill of St Julien-en-St Alban. Med, hdg/mkd pitch, pt sl, pt shd; wc; chem disp; mv service pnt; baby facs; shwrs inc; el pnts (6A) €3.50; lndtte; shops 1km; tradsmn; snacks; playgrnd; pool; rv fishing adj; some statics; dogs €2; Eng spkn; adv bkg; quiet; red low ssn; CCI. "Well-run, clean site by rv; gd sized pitches; friendly, helpful owners; super pool; excel." 28 Apr-22 Sep. € 19.00 2009*

PRIVAS *9D2* (3km E Rural) *44.73615, 4.62390* **Camping Le Moulin d'Onclaire, 07000 Coux [04 75 64 51 98; moulin@onclaire.com; www.onclaire.com]** Fr Privas take D104 (N304) E twds Le Pouzin, sp Valence. Site on R after passing narr bdge to Coux. Sm, pt shd; wc; shwrs inc; el pnts (5A) €3; shop; snacks; rest & bar adj; BBQ; pool 3km; tennis; some statics; dogs €2; Eng spkn; adv bkg; CCI. "NH only." 1 Apr-6 Oct. € 13.00 2008*

PRIVAS *9D2* (1.5km S Urban) *44.72668, 4.59730* **Kawan Village Ardèche Camping, Blvd de Paste, Quartier Ouvèze, 07000 Privas [04 75 64 05 80; fax 04 75 64 59 68; jcray@wanadoo.fr; www.ardechecamping.fr]** Exit A7 junc 16 dir Privas. App Privas cross rv bdge & at rndabt take 2nd exit. Site ent opp supmkt, sp. Lge, mkd pitch, pt sl, pt shd; wc (mainly cont); chem disp; mv service pnt; baby facs; shwrs inc; el pnts (5-10A) €3.50; lndtte; shops adj; supmkt 100m; rest; snacks; bar; BBQ; playgrnd; htd pool; rv fishing; tennis adj; internet; entmnt; TV rm; 80% statics; dogs €3; Eng spkn; adv bkg; quiet, but some rd noise fr D2; ccard acc; red low ssn; CCI. "Well-run, clean site; san facs need update (2008); gd touring base; m'vans beware low canopy on service stn at Intermarché opp." ♦ 1 Apr-30 Sep. € 22.50 (CChq acc) 2009*

PRIVEZAC *7D4* (1km E Rural) *44.40930, 2.20155* **Aire Naturelle Municipale Les Malénies, Plan d'Eau, 12350 Privezac [05 65 81 92 80; fax 05 65 81 96 77]** N fr Villefranche-de-Rouergue on D1 dir Rodez, at Lanuéjouls turn onto D614 & D48 to Privezac. In vill foll sp 'Plan d'Eau', site sp in 1km by lake. Sm, hdg pitch, pt shd; wc; shwrs inc; el pnts €1.50; bar; playgrnd; sand beach & lake sw adj; fishing; canoeing; 10% statics; dogs; quiet. "Fair sh stay." ♦ 1 Jun-15 Sep. 2006*

PROISSANS see Sarlat la Canéda *7C3*

PROVINS *4E4* (1km NE Rural) *48.57000, 3.30611* **Camping MJC de Fontaine Riante, Route de la Ferté Gaucher, 77483 Provins [01 64 00 53 62; fax 01 64 00 57 55; mjc.provins@wanadoo.fr; http://mjc.provins.free.fr/camping]** App Provins fr N D403, foll sp at rndabt NE of town. After 200m turn R for site. Sm, pt sl, terr, pt shd; wc; own san; chem disp (wc); shwrs inc; el pnts (4-6A) €3-4; gas, lndtte, shop, rest etc 1km; dogs €1.60; poss cr; quiet. "Facs old & poss used by itinerants fr adj field; avoid town cent narr rds; sh, steep gravel slopes bet terr levels." 1 Apr-31 Oct. € 9.40 2006*

PRUNIERES see Chorges *9D3*

PUGET SUR ARGENS see Fréjus *10F4*

PUGET THENIERS *10E4* (9km E Rural) *43.94526, 7.01194* **Camping L'Amitie, 06710 Touët-sur-Var [tel/fax 04 93 05 74 32; camping-de-lamitie@wanadoo.fr]** Site sp at both end of vill on N202. Fr Nice turn L off N202, site in 800m immed after x-ing rv & sp fr town cent. App v difficult - narr app rds, rv bdge v narr & site ent req tight turn; imposs for m'vans +6m long & 2m wide & c'vans 4+m long. Exit fr site also narr, twisting & steep. Sm, mkd pitch, pt shd; wc; chem disp; mv service pnt; shwrs €1.30; el pnts (3-16A) inc; gas; lndtte; shop; tradsmn; snacks; bar; BBQ; playgrnd; rv sw & fishing adj; horseriding; cycle hire; games area; entmnts; TV; dogs €2; 30% statics; adv bkg (ess high ssn); CCI. "Fair NH; steam train ride down valley to coast." ♦ 1 Apr-30 Sep. € 16.40 2007*

PUGET THENIERS *10E4* (8km W Rural) *43.96163, 6.79830* **Camping Le Brec, 04320 Entrevaux [tel/fax 04 93 05 42 45; info@camping-dubrec.com; www.camping-dubrec.com]** Site sp on R just after bdge 2km W of Entrevaux on N202. Rd (2km) to site narr with poor surface, passing places & occasional lge lorries. Med, mkd pitch, pt sl, pt shd; htd wc; chem disp; mv service pnt; baby facs; shwrs inc; el pnts (10A) €3 (poss long lead req); Indtte; tradsmn; snacks; BBQ; watersports cent, rv sw, fishing & boating adj; wifi; TV; 10% statics; dogs €1; phone; Eng spkn; adv bkg; quiet; ccard acc; red CCI. "In beautiful area; friendly Dutch owners; popular with canoeists; easy rv walk to town." 15 Mar-31 Oct. € 17.00 2009*

PUGET THENIERS *10E4* (2km NW Rural) *43.95801, 6.85980* **Camping L'Origan (Naturist), 06260 Puget-Théniers [04 93 05 06 00; fax 04 93 05 09 34; origan@wanadoo.fr; www.origan-village.com]** On N202 fr Entrevaux (dir Nice) at Puget-Théniers, immed turn L at rlwy x-ing (sp), site approx 1km up track. Med, hdg/mkd pitch, hdstg, pt sl, terr, pt shd; htd wc; sauna; shwrs inc; el pnts (6A) €4; gas 2km; Indtte; shop; tradsmn; rest; snacks; bar; BBQ; playgrnd; htd pool; paddling pool; waterslide; fishing; tennis; archery; wifi; TV rm; 50% statics; dogs €2.50; phone; train to Nice; adv bkg; Eng spkn; ccard acc; red low ssn; INF card. "Sm pitches not suitable o'fits over 6m; hilly site but pitches level; facs run down early ssn (2009); interesting area." ♦ 18 Apr-4 Oct. € 37.00 (CChq acc) 2009*

PUIMOISSON see Riez *10E3*

PUIVERT *8G4* (500m S Rural) *42.91596, 2.0441* **FFCC Camping de Puivert (formerly Camp Municipal de Fontclaire), Fontclaire, 11230 Puivert [04 68 20 00 58; fax 04 68 20 82 29; camping-de-puivert@orange.fr]** Take D117 W fr Quillan twd Lavelanet for 16km. Site by lake well sp. Med, hdg pitch, pt sl, pt shd; wc; chem disp (wc); mv service pnt; shwrs; el pnts (10A) €3; Indtte; shops in vill 500m; snacks; lake sw & fishing; entmnt; internet; quiet. "Attractive area; v sm pitches, poss diff lge o'fits." 24 Apr-27 Sep. € 12.00 2009*

PUTANGES PONT ECREPIN *4E1* (1km W Rural) *48.76067, -0.24564* **Camp Municipal Le Val d'Orne, Le Friche, 61210 Putanges-Pont-Ecrepin [02 33 35 00 25 (Mairie); fax 02 33 35 49 50]** S fr Falaise on D909 to Putanges. Ent Putanges cross Rv L'Orne & ignore camping sp immed on L (Grand Rue). Go thro vill for approx 1km, turn L sp camping 200m. Site on R. Sm, hdg/mkd pitch, pt shd; wc; shwrs inc; el pnts (6A) inc; shops & rest 5 mins walk via rv bank; rv fishing; playgrnd; dogs €0.85; adv bkg; quiet. "Site yourself, warden visits am & pm; excel, clean, well-run rvside site; ltd facs." 1 Apr-30 Sep. € 7.70 2006*

PUY EN VELAY, LE *9C1* (500m N Urban) *45.05014, 3.88044* **Camping Bouthezard, Chemin de Bouthezard, Ave d'Aiguilhe, 43000 Le Puy-en-Velay [04 71 09 55 09 or 06 15 08 23 59 (mob); www.ot-lepuyenvelay.fr]** Fr Le Puy heading NW on N102 to city cent; look for sp Clermont & Vichy; turn R at traff lts in Place Carnot at sp for Valence; site on L on bank of rv. Site ent immed opp Chapel St Michel & 200m fr volcanic core. Med, some hdg pitches, pt shd; wc; chem disp; mv service pnt; shwrs inc; el pnts (6A) inc (rev pol); Indtte; sm shop; shop 200m & supmkt 500m; snacks; playgrnd adj; pool & tennis adj; games rm; dogs €0.85; poss cr; Eng spkn; adv bkg; noise of church bells (not night-time); ccard not acc; CCI. "Popular, well-located, well-kept, busy site - rec arr early; efficient staff; gd facs; gates clsd 2100-0700 low ssn; no twin-axles; may flood in v heavy rain; unreliable opening dates - phone ahead low ssn; vg touring base on pilgrim rte to Spain." ♦ 15 Mar-31 Oct. € 14.50 2009*

PUY EN VELAY, LE *9C1* (9km N Rural) *45.12473, 3.92177* **Camp Municipal Les Longes, Route des Rosières, 43800 Lavoûte-sur-Loire [04 71 08 18 79; fax 04 71 08 16 96; mairie.lavoutesurloire@wanadoo.fr; www.cc-emblavez.fr]** Fr Le Puy take N on D103 sp Lavoûte & Retournac. In Lavoûte turn R onto D7 bef rv bdge, site on L in 1km on rvside. Med, mkd pitch, pt shd; wc; shwrs €1; el pnts (6A) €1.90; Indtte; shops 9km; bread 1km; tradsmn (high ssn); playgrnd; pool 1km; rv sw, fishing 50m; tennis; dogs €1.50; quiet. "Gd; walking; scenic views." ♦ 1 May-15 Sep. € 8.25 2007*

PUY EN VELAY, LE *9C1* (3km E Urban) *45.04431, 3.93030* **Camp Municipal d'Audinet, Ave des Sports, 43700 Brives-Charensac [tel/fax 04 71 09 10 18; camping.audinet@wanadoo.fr; www.camping-audinet.fr]** Fr Le Puy foll green sp E twd Valence. Fr S on N88 foll sp twd Valence & on E side of town foll white sp. Lge, pt shd; wc (mostly cont); chem disp; mv service pnt; baby facs; shwrs inc; el pnts (6A) €3; Indtte; sm shop & shops 500m; supmkt 1.5km; rest; snacks; bar; BBQ; playgrnd; rv & lake sw/fishing; internet; bus to town; quiet; red low ssn/long stay. "Spacious site on rvside; friendly, helpful staff; poss itinerants - but not a prob; gd san facs, poss stretched high ssn; no twin-axles; vg." ♦ 30 Apr-21 Sep. € 10.50 2009*

PUY EN VELAY, LE *9C1* (9km E Rural) *45.06020, 3.95660* **Camping Le Moulin de Barette, Le Pont de Sumène, 43540 Blavozy [04 71 03 00 88; fax 04 71 03 00 51; hotel@lemoulindebarette.com; www.lemoulindebarette.com]** Take N88 dir St Etienne. Exit after 7km at D156 Blavozy. At rndabt foll sp for Rosières & 1st L to Moulin-de-Barette. Med, mkd pitch, pt sl, pt shd; wc; chem disp; mv service pnt; shwrs inc; el pnts €4; Indtte; shop; rest; bar; pool (high ssn); playgrnd; tennis; cycle hire; TV rm; few statics; dogs €1; quiet; red long stay; ccard acc. "Part of hotel complex; dated san facs in need of refurb; v quiet low ssn." ♦ € 14.70 2008*

France

PUY EN VELAY, LE *9C1* (7km S Rural) *44.99369, 3.90345* **Camping Comme au Soleil, Route du Plan d'Eau, 43700 Coubon [tel/fax 04 71 08 32 55; dumoulin-patrick@club-internet.fr; www.camping-le-puy.com]** S fr Puy-en-Velay on N88, turn E onto D38 to Coubon, site sp. Sm, pt shd; htd wc; chem disp; baby facs; shwrs inc; el pnts (10A) €3.50; lndtte (inc dryer); ice; tradsmn; rest; snacks; bar; BBQ; playgrnd; pool; games area; cycle hire; 5% statics; dogs €1; bus; some Eng spkn; adv bkg; quiet; red low ssn; CCI. "Well-kept site; helpful owners; clean facs; vg rest; excel." ♦ 15 Apr-15 Oct. € 10.50 2009*

PUY EN VELAY, LE *9C1* (11km S Rural) **Camp Municipal, Le Monastier, 43370 Solignac-sur-Loire [04 71 03 11 46 (Mairie); fax 04 71 03 12 77; maire.solignacsurloire@wanadoo.fr]** Fr Le Puy S on N88 twd Mende; after about 7km at Les Baraques turn L on D27 dir Solignac & foll camping sp. Sm, hdg/mkd pitch, pt shd, pt sl; wc; shwrs inc; el pnts (6-10A) €2.06; lndry rm; shops 1km; playgrnd; quiet; CCI. "Site yourself; warden calls am & pm; gd views; excel facs; clean & tidy; no twin-axle c'vans, but mkt traders poss tolerated." ♦ 15 Jun-15 Sep. € 7.80 2006*

⊞ **PUY GUILLAUME** *9B1* (6km SW Rural) **Camping à la Ferme (Lehalper), Les Marodons, 63290 Noalhat [04 73 94 11 68; l.lehaper@libertysurf.fr]** Fr D906 turn W at La Croix-St Bonnet onto D44 to Noalhat, site sp. Sm, shd; wc; shwrs; el pnts (10A) €1.50; lndtte; games area; fishing, rv sw nr; dogs; quiet. "Friendly; san facs fair; phone ahead rec; poss diff lge o'fits." € 9.00 2008*

PUY GUILLAUME *9B1* (1km W Rural) *45.96231, 3.46632* **Camping de la Dore (formerly Municipal), 86 Rue Joseph Claussat, 63290 Puy-Guillaume [04 73 94 78 51 or 06 70 14 56 10 (mob); contact@camping-auvergne-63.com; www.camping-auvergne-63.com]** N fr Thiers on D906 as far as Puy-Guillaume; at ent to town (lge sculpture on rndabt), turn L at rndabt onto D343 (which joins D63); then L again at next rndabt onto D63. Site on R by rv. Med, pt shd; wc (some cont); chem disp; some serviced pitches; shwrs inc; el pnts (6A) €3.65; lndtte; shops 1km; rest; snacks; bar; playgrnd; pool; rv fishing adj; dogs; phone adj; bus 1km; adv bkg (rec high ssn); ccard acc; CCI. "Neat, tidy site in pleasant location; friendly staff; clean san facs; excel." ♦ 1 May-15 Sep. € 11.60 2009*

PUY L'EVEQUE *7D3* (2.5km S Rural) *44.47780, 1.14214* **FFCC Village-Camping Les Vignes, Le Méoure, Le Cayrou, 46700 Puy-l'Evêque [tel/fax 05 65 30 81 72; villagecamping.lesvignes@wanadoo.fr]** App fr E on D911 dir Villeneuve-sur-Lot, just bef ent Puy-l'Evêque turn L, foll sp for 3km. Site adj Rv Lot. Avoid town cent while towing. Med, shd; wc; baby facs; shwrs; el pnts; (10A) €2.70; gas; lndtte; shops 3km; tradsmn; snacks; bar; playgrnd; pool; tennis; games area; fishing; cycle hire; entmnt high ssn; TV; dogs €1.50; quiet; red over 55s/low ssn. "Lovely, well-kept site in beautiful countryside; warm welcome, friendly owners; gd san facs." 1 Apr-30 Sep. € 13.60 2009*

PUY L'EVEQUE *7D3* (6km W Rural) *44.49636, 1.08220* **Club de Vacances Duravel, Route de Vire, 46700 Duravel [05 65 24 65 06 or 0031 74 2666499 (LS-N'lands); fax 05 65 24 64 96 or 0031 74 2668205 (LS-N'lands); www.clubdevacances.net]** Fr D811 Puy-l'Evêque to Fumel rd at Duravel town cent, opp Mairie turn S onto D58 sp Vire-sur-Lot. Site in 2.5km. Lge, hdg/mkd pitch, pt sl, pt shd; wc (some cont); chem disp; mv service pnt; shwrs inc; el pnts (10A) €3.15; gas; lndtte; shop; tradsmn; rest; snacks; bar; playgrnd; 2 pools (1 htd); waterslide; beach nr; tennis; games area; canoeing; fishing; cycle hire; entmnt; 12% statics; poss cr; Eng spkn; adv bkg; quiet; 10% red low ssn; ccard acc; CCI. "Vg site; friendly staff; lovely situation; all sps on site in Dutch - enquire at recep for info in Eng." ♦ 29 Apr-23 Sep. € 23.35 2006*

PUYCELCI *8E3* (4km W Rural) *43.99254, 1.65140* **Centre Naturiste Le Fiscalou (Naturist), 1 Route de Montclar, 81140 Puycelci [05 63 30 45 95; fax 05 62 30 32 88; fiscalou@orange.fr; www.fiscalou.com]** Fr Bruniquel D964 S twd Castelnau. Take D1 sp Monclar-de-Quercy. Site on L after 4km. Sm, pt sl, pt shd; wc; chem disp; shwrs inc; el pnts (3A) €3.75 (poss long lead req); tradsmn; rest; bar; playgrnd; pool; some statics; dogs €3.15; Eng spkn; adv bkg; quiet; red long stay. "Pleasant, rustic site; excel touring base." 1 May-30 Sep. € 22.50 2008*

PYLA SUR MER *7D1* (7km S Coastal) *44.58130, -1.21234* **Camping La Dune, Route de Biscarrosse, 33115 Pyla-sur-Mer [tel/fax 05 56 22 72 17; reception@campingdeladune.fr; www.campingdeladune.fr]** Fr Bordeaux app Arcachon; at rndabt foll sp Dune du Pilat & 'campings'; at T-junc turn L & foll 'plage' & camping sp on D218; site on R. Lge, pt sl, pt shd; htd wc (some cont for men); shwrs inc; el pnts inc; gas; lndtte; shop; rest; snacks; bar; playgrnd; pool; sand beach 500m; tennis; cycle hire; entmnt; TV rm; dogs €4; poss cr; adv bkg (ess Jul/Aug); quiet; "Poss diff pitches for c'vans; sm, unlevel, narr access; site dominated by sand dunes." 1 May-30 Sep. € 32.00 2006*

PYLA SUR MER *7D1* (7km S Coastal) *44.58517, -1.20868* **Camping La Forêt, Route de Biscarosse, 33115 Pyla-sur-Mer [05 56 22 73 28; fax 05 56 22 70 50; www.village-center.com]** Fr Bordeaux app Arcachon on A660 by-pass rd; at La Teste-de-Buch at rndabt foll sp for Dune du Pilat & 'campings'. At T-junc in 4km turn L; foll 'plage' & camping sp on D218. Site on R. Lge, hdg/mkd pitch, sl, shd; wc; chem disp; mv service pnt; shwrs inc; el pnts (6A) inc; lndtte; shop; rest; snacks; bar; BBQ; playgrnd; pool; sand beach 600m; solarium; tennis; cycle hire; many statics (sep area); dogs €2; adv bkg; red low ssn; ccard acc; CCI. "Forest setting at foot of sand dune; well-organised; many facs; hang-gliding, surfing, sailing, cycle rtes nrby." ♦ 26 Apr-14 Sep. € 34.00 2008*

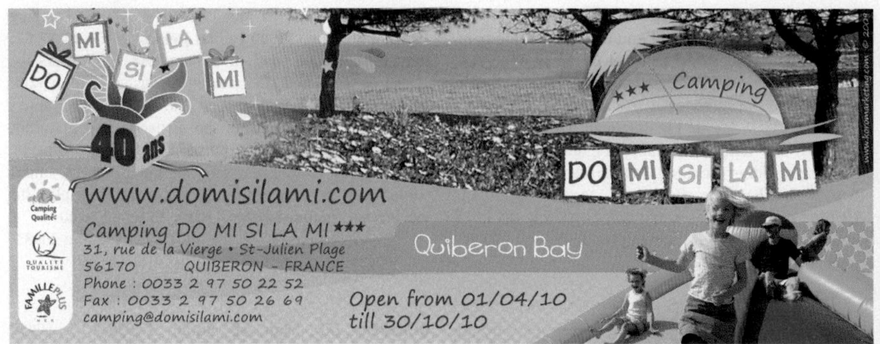

PYLA SUR MER *7D1* (7km S Coastal) *44.57243, -1.22030* **Camping Le Petit Nice, Route de Biscarosse, 33115 Pyla-sur-Mer [05 56 22 74 03; fax 05 56 22 14 31; info@petitnice.com; www.petitnice.com]** Fr Bordeaux on app Arcachon foll sp for Dune-du-Pilat & 'campings'. At T-junc turn L; foll 'plage' & camping sp on D218. Site on R. Lge, pt sl, shd; wc; chem disp; mv service pnt; baby facs; shwrs inc; el pnts (5A) inc; gas; Indtte; shop; rest; snacks; bar; playgrnd; htd pool; paddling pool; sand beach adj; tennis; entmnt; TV rm; 50% statics; dogs €5; poss cr; adv bkg; quiet but poss noisy disco; red low ssn/long stay. "Open beach with steep wooden steps." 1 Apr-30 Sep. € 39.00 2008*

PYLA SUR MER *7D1* (7km S Coastal/Rural) *44.57474, -1.22217* **Yelloh! Village Panorama du Pyla, Route de Biscarosse, 33115 Pyla-sur-Mer [05 56 22 10 44; fax 05 56 22 10 12; mail@camping-panorama.com; www.camping-panorama.com or www.yellohvillage.com]** App Arcachon fr Bordeaux on A63/A660, at rndabt foll sp for Dune-du-Pilat & 'campings'. Foll sp for 'plage' & 'campings' on D218. Site on R next to Camping Le Petit Nice. Lge, mkd pitch, pt sl, terr, pt shd; wc (some cont); chem disp; mv service pnt; sauna; shwrs inc; el pnts (3-10A) inc; gas; rest; snacks; bar; shop; playgrnd; htd pool; sand beach adj; tennis; TV; entmnt; dogs €5; Eng spkn; adv bkg; quiet; red low ssn; CCI. "Pleasant site on wooded dune; direct steep access to excel beach; site rds v narr; ltd pitches for v lge o'fits; some pitches sandy & unsuitable m'vans; gd facs; paragliding adj." ♦ 20 Apr-15 Sep. € 40.00 2007*

QUEAUX see Lussac les Châteaux *7A3*

QUESTEMBERT see Muzillac *2G3*

QUETTEHOU *1C4* (2.5km E Urban/Coastal) *49.58520, -1.26858* **Camping La Gallouette, Rue de la Gallouette, 50550 St Vaast-la-Hougue [02 33 54 20 57; fax 02 33 54 16 71; contact@camping-lagallouette.fr; www.lagallouette.com]** E fr Quettehou on D1, site sp in St Vaast-la-Houge to S of town. Lge, hdg/mkd pitch, pt shd; wc; chem disp; mv service pnt; baby facs; shwrs; el pnts (6-10A) €3.80-4.60; gas; Indtte; shop; tradsmn; rest; snacks; bar; BBQ; playgrnd; htd pool; sand beach 300m; games area; games rm; 10% statics; dogs €1.80; phone; poss cr; adv bkg; quiet; CCI. "Lovely friendly site; some lge pitches; gd range of facs; sh walk to interesting town; excel site." ♦ 1 Apr-30 Sep. € 22.30 2009*

QUETTEHOU *1C4* (2km S Coastal) *49.57960, -1.30760* **Camping Le Rivage, Route de Morsalines, 50630 Quettehou [02 33 54 13 76; fax 02 33 43 10 42; info@camping-lerivage.com]** Fr Quettehou on D14, sp on L. Med, unshd; wc; shwrs inc; el pnts (6A) €3.90; Indtte; shop; snacks; bar; BBQ; playgrnd; htd pool; paddling pool; sand beach 400m; 50% statics; dogs €2; Eng spkn; adv bkg rec high ssn; quiet. "Gd clean site." 1 Apr-30 Sep. € 18.00 2006*

QUIBERON *2G3* (1.5km N Coastal) *47.49978, -3.12021* **Camping Do Mi Si La Mi, 31 Rue de la Vierge, St Julien-Plage, 56170 Quiberon [02 97 50 22 52; fax 02 97 50 26 69; camping@domisilami.com; www.domisilami.com]** Take D768 down Quiberon Peninsular, 3km after St Pierre-Quiberon & shortly after sp for rlwy level x-ing turn L into Rue de la Vierge, site on R in 400m. Lge, hdg/mkd pitch, pt sl, pt shd; wc (some cont); chem disp; mv service pnt; baby facs; serviced pitches; shwrs inc; el pnts (3-10A) €2.80-4.20; gas; Indtte; shop, snacks, bar adj; BBQ; playgrnd; sand/shgl beach 100m; games area; cycle hire; sailing, horseriding, tennis nr; 40% statics; dogs €2.30; poss cr; Eng spkn; quiet; red low ssn; ccard acc; CCI. "Gd touring base; vg." ♦ 1 Apr-30 Oct. € 21.00 2009*

See advertisement

QUIBERON *2G3* (800m SE Urban) *47.47919, -3.10090* **Camping Les Joncs du Roch, Rue de l'Aérodrome, 56170 Quiberon [02 97 50 24 37 or 02 97 50 11 36 (LS)]** Foll sp to aerodrome. Site ent opp. Lge, pt shd; wc (some cont); chem disp; shwrs inc; el pnts (4-10A) €2.50-3.50; gas; shops 1km; sand beach 1km; dogs €2; poss cr; quiet, but minimal aircraft noise. "Well-maintained, clean, friendly, sheltered site gd facs; easy access town/beach; vg." 3 Apr-25 Sep. € 18.60 2008*

QUIBERON *2G3* (1.5km SE Coastal/Rural) *47.47641, -3.10441* **Camping Le Bois d'Amour, Rue St Clément, 56170 Quiberon [02 97 50 13 52 or 04 42 20 47 25 (LS); fax 02 97 50 42 67; info@homair.com; www.homair.com]** Exit N165 at Auray onto D768. In Quiberon foll sp 'Thalassothérapie', site sp. Lge, hdg/mkd pitch, pt shd; wc; mv service pnt; chem disp; baby facs; shwrs inc; el pnts (10A) €5; gas; Indtte; shop; rest; snacks; bar; BBQ; playgrnd; htd pool; beach 200m; games area; tennis; horseriding; cycle hire; entmnt; dogs €5; adv bkg; quiet; Eng spkn; red low ssn; ccard acc; CCI. ♦ 3 Apr-2 Oct. € 36.00 2006*

QUIBERON *2G3* (1.5km SE Coastal) *47.47690, -3.09246* **Camping Le Conguel, Blvd de la Teignouse, 56175 Quiberon [02 97 50 19 11; fax 02 97 30 46 66; info@campingduconguel.com; www.campingduconguel.com]** On D768 fr N, turn E at rlwy stn on ent Quiberon, foll sps for Pointe du Conguel, site sp. Lge, mkd pitch, pt sl, unshd; wc; baby facs; sauna; shwrs; el pnts €3.65; gas; Indtte; shop; rest; snacks; bar; playgrnd; htd pool; paddling pool; waterslide; sand beach adj; watersports; tennis; games area; games rm; fitness rm; cycle hire; entmnt; internet; TV rm; adv bkg; quiet; red low ssn. "Beautiful, varied coastline; excel family site." ♦ 4 Apr-31 Oct. € 43.30 2009*

See advertisement on page 518

QUIBERON *2G3* (1km S Coastal) *47.47424, -3.10563* **Camp Municipal Le Goviro, Blvd du Goviro, 56170 Quiberon [02 97 50 13 54]** Fr D768 at Quiberon foll sp Port Maria & 'Centre Thalassothérapie'. Site 1km on L nr Sofitel. Lge, hdg/mkd pitch, terr, pt shd; wc; chem disp; mv service pnt; shwrs; el pnts (13A) €3; gas; Indtte; rest adj; playgrnd; sand beach, fishing & watersports adj; dogs €1.65; poss cr; quiet. "Gd sea views & coastal path; clean san facs, ltd low ssn; quiet." ♦ 1 Apr-12 Oct. € 10.80 2008*

QUIBERVILLE PLAGE see Veules les Roses *3C2*

QUILLAN *8G4* (W Urban) *42.87358, 2.17565* **FFCC Camp Municipal La Sapinette, 21 Ave René Delpech, 11500 Quillan [04 68 20 13 52; fax 04 68 20 27 80; contact@camping-la-sapinette.com; www.villedequillan.fr]** Foll D118 fr Carcassonne to Quillan; turn R at 2nd traff lts in town cent; site sp in town. Med, hdg/mkd pitch, some hdstg, sl, terr, pt shd; htd wc; chem disp; mv service pnt; shwrs inc; el pnts (16A) €3.30; Indtte; shops 400m; playgrnd; pool; leisure cent 500m in town; TV; 25% statics; dogs €1.55; poss cr; adv bkg; quiet; ccard acc; red low ssn/CCI. "Gd touring base; sm pitches; early arr rec; helpful staff; san facs OK; excel pool; site poss tired end ssn; mkt Wed & Sat; vet adj; highly rec." 1 Apr-30 Nov. € 18.85 2009*

QUILLAN *8G4* (8km NW Rural) *42.89296, 2.10464* **Camping Le Fontaulié-Sud, 11500 Nébias [tel/fax 04 68 20 17 62; www.fontauliesud.com]** In Quillan take D117 twd Foix. Turn L at sp immed after leaving Nébias vill. Site in 1km. NB Steep rd to site. Med, pt sl, pt shd; wc; chem disp; shwrs inc; el pnts (4A) €2; Indtte; shop; snacks; bar; playgrnd; pool; paddling pool; tennis, horseriding, watersports nr; TV rm; some statics; dogs €1; adv bkg; quiet; CCI. "Beautiful scenery & many mkd walks; owners friendly, helpful; ltd facs low ssn; gd touring base." 1 May-15 Sep. € 16.00 2008*

QUIMPER *2F2* (9km SE Rural) *47.93811, -3.99959* **Camping Vert de Creac'h-Lann (Hemidy), 202 Route de Concarneau, 29170 St Evarzec [02 98 56 29 88 or 06 68 46 97 25 (mob); contact@campingvertcreachlann.com; www.campingvertcreachlann.com]** S fr Quimper on D783, 1.5km fr St Evarzec rndabt at brow of hill (easily missed). Sm, hdg pitch, pt sl, pt shd; wc; chem disp; shwrs; el pnts (4-13A) €2.80-3.70 (not on all pitches, 2009); Indtte; shop, rest, snacks & bar 3km; playgrnd; sand beach 5km; 50% statics; dogs; poss cr; Eng spkn; adv bkg; quiet; ccard not acc. "Lovely spacious site; lge pitches; friendly, helpful owner; gd playgrnd; poss to stay after end Sep by arrangement; lovely old town; gd touring base; daily mkt; excel." 15 May-30 Sep. € 9.70 2009*

QUIMPER *2F2* (2km S Rural) *47.97685, -4.11060* **Camping L'Orangerie de Lanniron, Château de Lanniron, 29000 Quimper [02 98 90 62 02; fax 02 98 52 15 56; camping@lanniron.com; www.lanniron.com or www.les-castels.com]** Fr Rennes/Lorient: on N165 Rennes-Quimper, Quimper-Centre, Quimper-Sud exit, foll dir Pont l'Abbé on S bypass until exit sp Camping de Lanninon on R. At top of slip rd turn L & foll site sp, under bypass then 2nd R to site. Recep at Old Farm 500m before site. Lge, pt shd; wc; chem disp; some serviced pitches; baby facs; shwrs inc; el pnts (10A) inc; gas; Indtte; shop; supmkt adj; rest; snacks; bar; BBQ; playgrnd; htd pool & paddling pool; aquatic park; fishing; beach 12km; tennis; cycle hire; entmnt; wifi; games/TV rm; golf; 25% statics; dogs €4.50; bus; phone; poss cr; Eng spkn; adv bkg; ccard acc; red low ssn; CCI. "Excel, family-run site with vg leisure facs; well-spaced pitches; vg san facs." ♦ 15 May-15 Sep. € 42.40 (CChq acc) ABS - B21 2009*

⊞ **QUIMPER** *2F2* (1km W Urban) *47.99198, -4.12536* **Camp Municipal Bois du Séminaire, Ave des Oiseaux, 29000 Quimper [tel/fax 02 98 55 61 09; camping-municipal@quimper.fr; www.mairie-quimper.fr]** Fr E on D765 to Quimper, bear L on 1-way system along rv. In 1km bear R over rv into Blvd de Boulguinan - D785. In 500m turn R onto Blvd de France (lge junc). In 1km bear R into Ave des Oiseaux, site on R in front of Auberge de Jeunesse. Med, hdg pitch, terr, pt shd; wc; chem disp (wc); shwrs inc; el pnts (5A) €3; Indry facs; shops, rest, snacks, bar 500m; BBQ; pool nr; sand beach 15km; 10% statics; phone; bus adj; poss cr; quiet; ccard acc; CCI. "Conv NH/sh stay." ♦ € 9.95 2008*

QUIMPER *2F2* (12km W Rural) *48.00126, -4.26925* **Camping La Rocaille, Kérandoaré, 29710 Plogastel-St Germain [02 98 54 58 13 or 06 72 34 73 13 (mob)]** Fr N165 exit Quimper Sud & foll sp dir Audierne onto D784; in 9km turn R at Kérandoaré; site sp in 200m. NB Avoid Quimper town cent. Sm, hdg/mkd pitch, terr, pt shd; wc (some cont); shwrs inc; el pnts (6A) inc; Indtte; shop 500m; tradsmn; beach 10km; Eng spkn; quiet. "Lovely touring area; friendly, helpful owner; vg san facs; poss diff m'vans if wet."
1 Jun-15 Sep. € 13.00 2009*

QUIMPERLE *2F2* (7km NE Rural) *47.90468, -3.47477* **Camping Le Ty-Nadan, Route d'Arzano, 29310 Locunolé [02 98 71 75 47; fax 02 98 71 77 31; info@tynadan-vacances.fr; www.tynadan-vacances.fr or www.les-castels.com]** To avoid Quimperlé cent exit N165 dir Quimperlé. As ent town turn R onto D22 dir Arzano. In 9km turn L in Arzano (un-numbered rd) sp Locunolé & Camping Ty Nadan; site on L just after x-ing Rv Elle. Or fr Roscoff on D69 S join N165/E60 but take care at uneven level x-ing at Pen-ar-Hoat 11km after Sizun. Lge, hdg/mkd pitch, shd; htd wc; chem disp; mv service pnt; sauna; serviced pitches; baby facs; shwrs inc; el pnts (10A) inc (long lead poss req); gas; Indtte; shop; rest; snacks; bar; BBQ; playgrnd; htd pools (1 covrd); waterslides; paddling pool; sand beach 18km; rv fishing, canoeing adj; tennis; cycle hire; horseriding; archery; rock-climbing; excursions; adventure park; games area; entmnt; wifi; sat TV/games rm; 40% statics; dogs €5.80; c'vans over 8.50m not acc high ssn; Eng spkn; adv bkg; ccard acc; red low ssn/CCI. "Excel, peaceful site by rv; lge pitches; friendly staff; excel touring base." ♦ 27 Mar-2 Sep. € 46.00 (CChq acc)
ABS - B20 2009*

See advertisement

QUIMPERLE *2F2* (1.5km SW Urban) *47.87250, -3.56952* **Camp Municipal de Kerbertrand, Rue du Camping, 29300 Quimperlé [02 98 39 31 30 or 02 98 96 04 32 (TO); fax 02 98 96 16 12; contact@quimperletourisme.com; www.quimperletourisme.com]** Exit N165 at Kervidanou junc SW of town. Foll sp 'Centre Ville' along Rue de Pont-Aven. In 1km turn L bef supmkt, sp v sm. Sm, hdg pitch, pt shd; wc; shwrs; el pnts €1.70; playgrnd; TV; dogs. "Delightful site; helpful warden." 1 Jun-15 Sep. € 8.00 2007*

QUINGEY *6H2* (Urban) *47.10431, 5.88821* **Camp Municipal Les Promenades, Bord de la Loue, 25440 Quingey [03 81 63 74 01 or 03 81 63 63 25 (Mairie); fax 03 81 63 63 25; www.campingquingey.fr]** Site sp off N83 by-pass, then in Quingey. Thro vill, immed on L after bdge over Rv Loue. Sm, pt shd; wc (some cont); chem disp; shwrs inc; el pnts (6A) €3; Indtte; shop; snacks; rest; playgrnd; fishing, sailing; canoeing, tennis, cycle hire & archery adj; dogs €1; quiet but some daytime rd noise."Excel NH or sh stay." ♦ 1 May-30 Sep. € 11.20 2009*

QUINSON *10E3* (Rural) *43.69715, 6.04044* **Village Center Les Prés du Verdon, 04500 Quinson [0810 122 813 or 04 99 57 21 21; www.village-center.com]** Site sp fr D11. Lge, mkd pitch, pt shd; wc; shwrs inc; el pnts (6A) inc; Indtte; shop; snacks; bar; playgrnd; pool; paddling pool; lake fishing adj; entmnt; statics; dogs €3; Eng spkn; adv bkg; ccard acc. "Beautiful area; vg site." ♦ 10 Apr-13 Sep. € 16.00 2007*

QUINTIN *2E3* (NE Urban) **Camp Municipal Le Vélodrome, Route de la Roche Longue, 22800 Quintin [02 96 74 92 54 or 02 96 74 84 01 (Mairie); fax 02 96 74 06 53]** Fr N exit D790 at rndabt; foll Centre Ville; at 2nd rndabt site sp; site on L 200m after 5th ped x-ing (narr rd, easy to miss). Fr S on D790 do not take slip rd (D7) but cont to rndabt - narr rds in town; then as above. Site N (100m) of town gardens & boating lake. Sm, pt sl, pt shd; wc (some cont); mv service pnt; shwrs; el pnts (6A) €2.80; BBQ; shops, rest, snacks, bar 500m; playgrnd; fishing; quiet. "Fair site; interesting town." ♦ 15 Apr-30 Sep. € 8.52 2008*

RABASTENS *8E3* (2km NW Rural) *43.83090, 1.69805* **Camp Municipal des Auzerals, Route de Grazac, 81800 Rabastens [05 63 33 70 36 or 06 12 90 14 55 (mob); fax 05 63 33 64 05; mairie.rabastens@libertysurf.fr]** Exit A68 junc 7 onto D12. In Rabastens town cent foll sp dir Grazac, site sp. Sm, hdg/mkd pitch, pt sl, terr, pt shd; wc (mainly cont); chem disp; shwrs inc; el pnts (10-12A) inc; Indtte; shop 2km; rest 2km; playgrnd; pool adj high ssn; quiet; adv bkg ess high ssn; CCI. "Attractive lakeside site; facs old but clean; warden on site am & pm otherwise height barrier in place; conv m'way NH; highly rec." 1 May-15 Sep. € 9.90 2008*

France

RAGUENES see Pont Aven *2F2*

RAMATUELLE see St Tropez *10F4*

RAMBOUILLET *4E3* (3km SE Rural) *48.6252, 1.84495* **Camping Huttopia Rambouillet, Route du Château d'Eau, 78120 Rambouillet [01 30 41 07 34; fax 01 30 41 00 17; rambouillet@huttopia.com; www.huttopia.com]** Fr N exit D910 at 'Rambouillet Eveuses' & foll sp to site in 2.5km. Fr S exit at 'Rambouillet Centre' & foll sp to site back onto D910 (in opp dir), exit 'Rambouillet Eveuses' as above. Avoid Rambouillet town cent. Lge, hdg pitch, pt shd; htd wc (some cont); mv service pnt; chem disp; baby facs; shwrs inc; el pnts (6-10A) €4.60-6.80 (poss rev pol); lndtte; shop; tradsmn, rest; snacks; bar; BBQ (gas/elec); playgrnd; fishing adj; some statics; dogs €4; phone; sep car park; Eng spkn; adv bkg (rec high ssn); quiet; ccard acc; red low ssn; CCI. "Excel, busy, wooded site; conv Paris by train - parking at stn 3km; gd cycling rtes; interesting town." ♦ 3 Apr-5 Nov. € 25.20 2009*

RANG DU FLIERS see Berck *3B2*

RANVILLE see Ouistreham *3D1*

RAON L'ETAPE *6E3* (10km NE Rural) *48.45490, 6.94722* **Camping des Lacs, 88110 Celles-sur-Plaine [03 29 41 28 00; fax 03 29 41 18 69; info@paysdeslacs.com; www.paysdeslacs.com]** Fr Raon-l'Etape turn onto D392A to Celles-sur-Plaine, site sp. Med, hdg/mkd pitch, hdstg, pt sl, pt shd; htd wc (some cont); solarium; chem disp; shwrs inc; el pnts (4-10A) inc; lndtte; shop; tradsmn; snacks; bar; playgrnd; htd pool; sand beach & lake sw 400m; fishing; windsurfing; tennis; 10% statics; dogs €1.50; Eng spkn; adv bkg; quiet; ccard acc; red low ssn/long stay; CCI. "Poss unkempt & facs unclean low ssn, otherwise vg." ♦ 1 Apr-30 Sep. € 19.00 2008*

RAON L'ETAPE *6E3* (10km E Rural) *48.35281, 6.98903* **Camping des 7 Hameaux, 1 La Fontenelle, 88210 Ban-de-Sapt [03 29 58 95 75; camping7hameaux@wanadoo.fr; http://camping7hameaux.monsite.orange.fr]** Fr St Dié NE on D49 to St Jean-d'Ormont (turn R after cathedral in St Dié). Then D32 sp 'Saales' to Ban-de-Sapt. Turn L onto D49 to La Fontenelle. Site on R 1km past sp to military cemetery. Or fr N59 take D424 sp Senones. In 3.3km in Moyenmoutiers turn R onto D37 sp Ban-de-Sapt. In 6.1km join D49. site on L in 1.3km. Sm, pt sl; wc; chem disp; shwrs €1; el pnts (6A) €2; rest, bar & shop 1km; tradsmn; pool 10km; quiet; adv bkg; ccard not acc; CCI. "Walks, cycle rtes; farm produce; friendly; vg." 1 Apr-31 Oct. € 9.50 2008*

⊞ **RAON L'ETAPE** *6E3* (5km SE Rural) *48.39474, 6.86232* **Camping Vosgina, 1 Rue la Cheville, 88420 Moyenmoutier [tel/fax 03 29 41 47 63; camping-vosgina@wanadoo.fr; www.vosges-camping.com]** On N59 St Dié-Lunéville rd, take exit mkd Senones, Moyenmoutier. At rndabt take rd twd St Blaise & foll camping sp. Site is on minor rd parallel with N59 bet Moyenmoutier & Raon. Med, hdg pitch, terr, shd; wc; shwrs inc; el pnts (4-10A) €2.20-5.50; gas; lndtte; sm shop & 3km; tradsmn; snacks; bar; 20% statics; dogs €1.50; Eng spkn; quiet but some rd noise; CCI. "Gd site for quiet holiday in a non-touristy area of Alsace; friendly recep; lovely countryside; many cycle/walking routes in area; barrier clsd 2200-0700." € 12.30 2008*

⊞ **RAON L'ETAPE** *6E3* (6km SE Rural) *48.36355, 6.83861* **Camping Beaulieu-sur-l'Eau, 41 Rue de Trieuche, 88480 Etival-Clairefontaine [tel/fax 03 29 41 53 51; camping-beaulieu-vosges@orange.fr; www.camping-beaulieu-vosges.com]** SE fr Baccarat on N59 turn R in vill of Etival-Clairefontaine on D424 sp Rambervillers & Epinal & foll sp for 3km. Ent on L. Med, mkd pitch, terr, pt shd; htd wc; mv service pnt; shwrs inc; el pnts (4-10A) €3.05-7.90; gas; shop; rest 400m; bar; playgrnd; rv sw & beach 400m; 10% statics; adv bkg rec high ssn; quiet; CCI. "Lovely, peaceful, clean site." € 10.50 2008*

RAUZAN *7D2* (200m N Rural) *44.78237, -0.12712* **Camping du Vieux Château, 33420 Rauzan [05 57 84 15 38; fax 05 57 84 18 34; hoekstra.camping@wanadoo.fr; www.vieux-chateau.com]** Fr Libourne S on D670, site is on D123 about 1.5km fr D670, sp. Sm, mkd pitch, shd; wc; chem disp; baby facs; shwrs inc; el pnts (6A) €3.30 (poss rev pol); gas; lndtte; shop, tradsmn; rest 200m; snacks; sm bar & in 200m; playgrnd; pool; tennis; rv/lake 5km; cycle hire; horseriding; wine-tasting; entmnt; TV; 10% statics; dogs €2; poss cr; Eng spkn; adv bkg; quiet; red low ssn; ccard acc; CCI. "Lovely site but take care tree roots on pitches; helpful owners; basic san facs - ltd low ssn & poss not well-maintained, & poss stretched high ssn; access to some pitches diff when wet; conv vineyards." ♦ 29 Mar-11 Oct. € 18.50 2008*

RAVENOVILLE PLAGE see Ste Mere Eglise *1C4*

REALMONT *8E4* (2km SW Rural) *43.77092, 2.16336* **Camp Municipal de la Batisse, Route de Graulhet, 81120 Réalmont [05 63 55 50 41 or 05 63 45 50 68; fax 05 63 55 65 62; camping-realmont@wanadoo.fr; www.realmont.fr]** On D612 (N112) fr Albi heading S thro Réalmont. On exit Réalmont turn R on D631 where site sp. Site 1.5km on L on Rv Dadou. Sm, pt shd; wc; shwrs; el pnts (3A) inc; gas; shops, rest, snacks, bar 2km; playgrnd; rv adj; fishing; some statics; quiet. "Pleasant, peaceful, well-kept site; friendly warden; nr Albi-Castres cycle rte; excel value; mkt Wed; gd." 1 Apr-30 Sep. € 9.00 2009*

RECOUBEAU JANSAC see Luc en Diois *9D3*

REDON *2F3* (1km SW Rural) *47.63384, -2.09851* **Camp Municipal de la Goule d'Eau, Rue de la Goule d'Eau, 35600 Redon [02 99 72 14 39 or 02 99 71 05 27 (Mairie)]** Foll sp in town. Sm, shd; wc; shwrs inc; el pnts (10A) inc; shop; supmkt 1km; playgrnd; fishing; sailing; Eng spkn; quiet; CCI. "Lge pitches; friendly staff; clean, modern san facs; rvside walk to town; vg value." 15 Jun-15 Sep. € 10.00 2007*

REGUINY *2F3* (1km S Urban) *47.96928, -2.74083* **Camp Municipal de l'Etang, 56500 Réguiny [02 97 38 66 11; fax 02 97 38 63 44; mairie.requiny@wanadoo.fr; www.reguiny.com]** On D764 fr Pontivy to Ploërmel, turn R into D11 to Réguiny then foll sp. Med, pt shd; wc; chem disp; mv service pnt; baby facs; shwrs inc; el pnts (10A) €2.50; Indtte; shop 2km; rest, bar 1km; playgrnd; htd pool 500m; dogs €2; phone; Eng spkn; quiet; ccard acc. "Gd facs; gd touring base." 14 Jun-15 Sep. € 8.60 2008*

I'm going to fill in some site report forms and post them off to the Club; we could win a ferry crossing – it's here on page 12.

REGUSSE *10E3* (1.5km NW Rural) *43.66031, 6.15103* **Village-Camping Les Lacs du Verdon, Domaine de Roquelande, 83630 Régusse [04 94 70 17 95; fax 04 94 70 51 79; info@leslacsduverdon.com; www.leslacsduverdon.com]** Fr W exit A8 junc 34 at St Maximin onto D560 Barjols, Tavernes, Montmeyan then D30 to Régusse. At rndabt in Régusse turn L twd St Jean & foll sp. Fr E exit A8 junc 36 Le Muy then Draguignan then D557 to Villecroze, Aups & Régusse. At rndabt turn R twd St Jean & foll sp. Lge, mkd pitch, pt shd; wc; chem disp; mv service pnt; shwrs inc; el pnts (6A) €4; gas; Indtte; shop; rest; snacks; bar; BBQ; playgrnd; pool; tennis; entmnt; internet; TV rm; 10% statics; dogs €3; poss cr; Eng spkn; adv bkg ess high ssn; quiet; ccard acc; CCI. "Beautiful area; mainly gravel pitches under pine trees; diff lge outfits without mover due to trees; gd facs slightly scruffy low ssn; recep closes 1800." ♦ 29 Apr-23 Sep. € 27.00 2006*

REHAUPAL see Tholy, Le *6F3*

REILLANNE *10E3* (2km W Rural) *43.86875, 5.63639* **Camping le Vallon des Oiseaux (Naturist), 04110 Reillanne [04 92 76 47 33; fax 04 92 76 44 64; info@levallon.com; www.levallon.com]** Fr Apt take D900 (N100) twd Céreste. Approx 2km after Céreste sharp turn L onto minor rd. Site sp. Med, pt sl, pt shd; wc; chem disp; shwrs inc; el pnts (4A) €3; Indtte; shop 2km; tradsmn; rest; snacks; bar; playgrnd; pool; TV rm; 5% statics; dogs €3; phone; poss cr; Eng spkn; adv bkg; quiet; red low ssn; INF card. "Friendly, helpful staff." ♦ 29 Mar-18 Oct. € 24.00 2008*

REIMS *3D4* (16km SE Rural) *49.16687, 4.21416* **Camp Municipal, 8 Rue de Routoir Courmelois, 51360 Val-de-Vesle [03 26 03 91 79; fax 03 26 03 28 22; valdevesle.mairie@wanadoo.fr]** Fr Reims twd Châlons-en-Champagne on D944 (N44), turn L by camp sp on D326 to Val-de-Vesle, foll camp sp; look for tall grain silos by canal. NB do not turn L bef D326 due narr lane. Med, shd; wc; chem disp; shwrs inc; el pnts (6-10A) €3 (long lead poss req); Indtte; tradsmn; BBQ; playgrnd; rv fishing; dogs €0.80; poss cr; adv bkg; some rlwy noise; ccard acc over €15; CCI. "Charming, well-kept, busy site; friendly, helpful staff; vg, immac san facs; site yourself if office clsd; informal pitching; poss mosquito prob; cycle rte to Reims along canal; gd touring base or NH." ♦ 1 Apr-15 Oct. € 10.00 2009*

REMIREMONT *6F2* (8km SE Rural) *47.94799, 6.63296* **Camping Le Pont de Maxonchamp, Rue du Camping, 88360 Rupt-sur-Moselle [03 29 24 30 65]** Fr Remiremont SE on N66/E51; site clearly sp to L; also visible 300m down lane. Sm, pt shd; wc; chem disp; shwrs €1; el pnts (10A) €2.50; shop 3km; playgrnd; rv sw adj; 20% statics; dogs €0.50; poss cr; quiet; CCI. "Vg, attractive rvside site." ♦ 1 Apr-31 Oct. € 5.00 2009*

REMOULINS *10E2* (1.5km S Rural) *43.92655, 4.56445* **Camping Domaine de la Soubeyranne, Route de Beaucaire, 30210 Remoulins [04 66 37 03 21; fax 04 66 37 14 65; soubeyranne@franceloc.fr; www.soubeyranne.com or www.camping-franceloc.fr]** Exit A9 for Remoulins onto D986. On D6086 (N86) Remoulins to Nîmes rd turn L after x-ing bdge fr Remoulins. Site on L in 1km. Lge, hdg pitch, shd; wc; chem disp; baby facs; shwrs inc; el pnts (6A) €4.70; gas; Indtte; shop; rest; snacks; bar; BBQ; playgrnd; htd, covrd pool; paddling pool; fishing; tennis; TV rm; some statics; dogs €5; adv bkg; some rd & rlwy noise; CCI. "Gd site." 4 Apr-27 Sep. € 26.50 2009*

REMOULINS *10E2* (2km NW Rural) *43.94805, 4.54583* **Camping La Sousta, Ave du Pont de Gard, 30210 Remoulins [04 66 37 12 80; fax 04 66 37 23 69; info@lasousta.fr; www.lasousta.fr]** Fr A9 exit Remoulins, foll sp for Nîmes, then sp 'Pont du Gard par Rive Droite' thro town. Immed over rv bdge turn R sp 'Pont du Gard etc'; site on R 800m fr Pont du Gard. Lge, mkd pitch, hdstg, shd; wc; chem disp; mv service pnt; baby facs; shwrs inc; el pnts (6A) €3; gas; Indtte; shop; tradsmn; rest adj; snacks; bar; BBQ in sep area; playgrnd; pool; tennis; rv sw adj; watersports; fishing; cycle hire; wifi; entmnt; TV; 20% statics; dogs €2; poss cr; Eng spkn; adv bkg; quiet; ccard acc; CCI. "Friendly, helpful staff; poss diff for lge o'fits due trees; excel touring base; walking dist Pont-du-Gard; vg." ♦ 1 Mar-31 Oct. € 25.00 2009*

France

REMOULINS *10E2* (4km NW Rural) *43.95594, 4.51588* **Camping International Les Gorges du Gardon, Chemin de la Barque Vieille, Route d'Uzès, 30210 Vers-Pont-du-Gard [04 66 22 81 81; fax 04 66 22 90 12; camping.international@wanadoo.fr; www.le-camping-international.com]** Exit A9 junc 23 Remoulins & head NW twd Uzès on D981. Pass turn for Pont-du-Gard & site on L in 1.5km. Or fr E on N100 turn N onto D6086 (N86) then D19A to Pont-du-Gard (avoiding Remoulins cent). Lge, hdg/mkd pitch, pt shd; wc; chem disp; mv service pnt; baby facs; shwrs inc; el pnts (6A) €3.30; gas; lndtte; shop; tradsmn; rest; snacks; bar; playgrnd; htd pool; rv sw & private beach adj; boating; fishing; tennis; games area; games rm; entmnt; internet; TV rm; 10% statics; dogs €2; no twin-axles or o'fits over 5m; Eng spkn; adv bkg; quiet; ccard acc; red low ssn/long stay; CCI. "Beautiful location; many sm pitches - some lge pitches to back of site; friendly, cheerful owners; excel san facs, ltd low ssn; beavers in rv; site poss subject to flooding & evacuation; superb." ♦ 15 Mar-30 Sep. € 19.50 2008*

REMOULINS *10E2* (7km NW Rural) *43.95788, 4.48716* **Camping Le Barralet, 30210 Collias [04 66 22 84 52 or 06 11 56 01 21 (mob); fax 04 66 22 89 17; camping@barralet.fr; www.barralet.fr]** W off A9 on D981 to Uzès; thro Remoulins; foll camp sp; turn S on D112 D3 to Collias; sp in 4km on L past quarry on bend; turn L up narr rd & site in 50m on R. Med, pt shd; wc; shwrs inc; el pnts €3.50 (adaptors supplied free); lndtte; shop; rest; snacks; bar; pool; playgrnd; fishing & canoe/kayak hire adj; tennis nr; games area; dogs €2; phone; quiet; ccard acc; CCI. "Gd location; gd rvside walks & cycling; sm pitches; poss lge youth groups use activity cent; site run down (2009)." ♦ 1 Apr-20 Sep. € 18.50 2009*

REMUZAT *9D2* (8km N Rural) *44.48192, 5.37882* **Camp Municipal Le Village, Chemin du Piscine, 26470 La Motte-Chalancon [04 75 27 22 95 or 04 75 27 20 41 (Mairie); fax 04 75 27 20 38; mairie@lamottechalancon.com; www.lamottechalancon.com]** S fr Die on D93 dir Luc-en-Diois for 18km, turn R onto D61 S twd La Motte-Chalancon for 19km. In La Motte, just bef rv bdge & Citroën garage on L, turn sharp L. Site sp in 500m on L adj Rv L'Oule. Med, pt shd; wc (cont); chem disp; mv service pnt; shwrs inc; el pnts (5-10A) inc; lndtte; shops, rest 500m; snacks; bar; playgrnd; pool; paddling pool; rv sw, beach 2km; dogs €0.80; phone; poss noisy; ccard acc; CCI. "Beautiful views; attractive vill." Easter-30 Sep. € 14.00 2007*

REMUZAT *9D2* (9km NE Rural) *44.44598, 5.45913* **Aire Naturelle de Pommerol (Morin), Quartier Lemoulin, 26470 Pommerol [04 75 27 25 63 or 04 75 98 26 25 (LS); fax 04 75 27 25 63; camping.pommerol@wanadoo.fr]** Fr Rémuzat, take D61 N dir La Motte-Chalancon. In vill, turn R & cont on D61 for 6km dir La Charce, then turn R onto D138 sp Montmorin/Pommerol. In 1km bear R onto D338 to Pommerol. Site sp in 2km on R. Sm, terr, pt shd; htd wc; chem disp; shwrs inc; el pnts €2 (long lead req); gas 10km; lndtte; shops 10km; rest, snacks, bar, (high ssn only or 10km); BBQ; playgrnd; htd pool 10km; lake sw, beach 12km; dogs €2; Eng spkn; adv bkg; quiet; CCI. "Superb views; access diff for lge o'fits; adv bkg ess high ssn." 1 Apr-30 Oct. € 10.00 2006*

REMUZAT *9D2* (S Rural) *44.41036, 5.35272* **Camp Municipal Les Aires, 26510 Rémuzat [04 75 27 81 43 or 04 75 25 85 78 (Mairie); www.remuzat.com]** Fr Rosans take D94 W for approx 10km; then R onto D61 to Rémuzat; site on R at ent to vill, on rvside. Sm, hdg/mkd pitch, pt shd; wc; chem disp; baby facs; shwrs inc; el pnts (10A) €3.65; lndtte; shop nr; BBQ; dogs €1; poss v cr if rallies; quiet; CCI. "Beautiful site, vill & area; some sm pitches; helpful warden; san facs old but clean; excel." ♦ 30 May-15 Sep. € 10.10 2009*

REMUZAT *9D2* (10km W Rural) *44.41670, 5.27294* **Camp Municipal Les Oliviers, Quartier St Jean, 26510 Sahune [04 75 27 40 40; fax 04 75 27 44 48]** Take N94 fr Nyons dir Serres. In 16km at Sahune turn R over bdge & foll sp to site. Sm, pt shd; wc; chem disp (wc); shwrs inc; el pnts (4-10A) €1.70-2.70; gas 500m; lndtte; shop, rest, snacks, bar 500m; Eng spkn; quiet; CCI. 15 May-15 Sep. 2007*

REMUZAT *9D2* (10km W Rural) *44.41257, 5.26188* **Camping La Vallée Bleue, La Plaine-du-Pont, 26510 Sahune [04 75 27 44 42 or 06 81 19 94 22 (mob); lavallee.bleue0711@orange.fr; www.lavalleebleue.com]** On D94 well sp. Med, pt shd; wc; chem disp; shwrs; el pnts (6A) inc; lndtte; shop 500m; tradsmn; rest; snacks; bar; playgrnd; pool; 5% statics; dogs €1.50; phone; poss cr; adv bkg; quiet; CCI. "Golf & fishing nrby." ♦ 1 Apr-30 Sep. € 21.00 2008*

⊞ **RENNES** *2F4* (2km NE Urban) *48.13456, -1.64923* **Camp Municipal des Gayeulles, Rue du Professor Maurice Audin, 35700 Rennes [02 99 36 91 22; fax 02 23 20 06 34; info@camping-rennes.com; www.camping-rennes.com]** Exit Rennes ring rd N136 junc 14 dir Maurepas & Maison Blanche, follow sp 'Les Gayeules' & site. Narr app to site. Med, mkd pitch, hdstg, pt sl, pt shd; wc; chem disp; mv service pnt; baby facs; shwrs; el pnts (10A) €3.30; lndtte (inc dryer); shops 500m; tradsmn; snacks; BBQ; playgrnd; pool 500m; tennis, archery & mini-golf nrby; internet; dogs €1; phone; bus to city; m'van o'night area; Eng spkn; adv bkg; quiet; red low ssn/long stay; ccard acc; CCI. "Lovely, well-kept, well-run site; friendly, helpful staff; lge pitches; slight sl for m'vans; 1st class facs, inc disabled; park adj; excel." ♦ € 15.40 2009*

RENNES LES BAINS *8G4* (S Rural) *42.91364, 2.31839* **Camping La Bernède, 11190 Rennes-les-Bains [04 68 69 86 49; fax 04 68 74 09 31; camping.renneslesbains@wanadoo.fr; www.renneslesbains.org]** S fr Carcassonne or N fr Quillan on D118, turn E at Couiza on D613. In 5km turn R onto D14 to Rennes-les-Bains in 3km. Drive thro vill, then turn L over bdge sp Sougraigne, then immed L. Sm, mkd pitch, pt shd; wc; chem disp (wc); shwrs inc; el pnts (5A) €2.55; lndtte; shop; tradsmn; rest in vill; bar; playgrnd; rv adj; fishing; 10% statics; dogs €1.15; adv bkg; quiet; CCI. "10 mins walk into town with thermal spa; vg." ♦ 10 May-30 Sep. € 11.55 2008*

REOLE, LA *7D2* (S Urban) *44.57778, -0.03360* **Camp Municipal La Rouergue, Bords de Garonne, 33190 La Réole [05 56 61 13 55; fax 05 56 61 89 13; lareole@entredeuxmers.com; www.entredeuxmers.com]** On N113 bet Bordeaux & Agen or exit A62 at junc 4. In La Réole foll sps S on D9 to site on L immed after x-ing suspension bdge. Med, pt shd; wc; shwrs inc; el pnts (3A) inc; gas; shop; tradsmn; snacks; pool 500m; fishing, boating; dogs €2; some rd noise. "Resident warden; 2m barrier clsd 1200-1500; Sat mkt on rv bank." 15 May-15 Oct. € 14.00 2009*

RETHEL *5C1* (14km E Urban) *49.48234, 4.57589* **Camp Municipal Le Vallage, 38 Chemin de l'Assaut, 08130 Attigny [03 24 71 23 06 or 03 24 71 20 68; fax 03 24 71 94 00; mairie-d-attigny@wanadoo.fr]** E on D983 fr Rethel to Attigny; fr town cent take D987 twd Charleville; over rv bdge; 2nd turn on L; sp. Med, hdg/mkd pitch, hdstg, pt shd; wc; chem disp; shwrs inc; el pnts (10A) inc; Indry rm; shop 1km; tradsmn; pool & sports facs adj; playgrnd; fishing; tennis; 50% statics; dogs; phone; CCI. "Lovely quiet site; lge pitches; helpful staff; gd facs." 19 Apr-30 Sep. € 11.00 2009*

REVEL *8F4* (500m E Urban) *43.45454, 2.01515* **Camp Municipal Le Moulin du Roy, Rue de Sorèze, 31250 Revel [05 61 83 32 47 or 05 62 18 71 40 (Mairie); mairie@mairie-revel.fr]** Fr Revel ring rd take D85 dir Sorèze, site sp. Med, hdg pitch, pt shd; mv service pnt; shwrs inc; el pnts €3; shop 500m; supmkt 1km; playgrnd; htd pool adj; lake sw & beach 2.5km; tennis adj; dogs €0.50; phone; bus; Eng spkn; quiet; red CCI. "Pleasant, immac site; helpful staff; Sat mkt; vg." 15 Jun-15 Sep. € 9.40 2009*

REVEL *8F4* (5.5km E Urban) *43.45446, 2.06953* **Camping Saint Martin, 81540 Sorèze [tel/fax 05 63 73 28 99; mary@campingsaintmartin.com; www.campingsaintmartin.com]** Fr Revel take D85 sp Sorèze; site sp outside vill; turn L at traff lts; site on R in 100m. Sm, hdg/mkd pitch; pt shd; wc; chem disp; shwrs inc; el pnts (4-13A) €3.15-6.12; sm shop & rest 500m; snacks; bar; playgrnd; pool; lake sw 3km; TV; 20% statics; dogs €1; quiet; CCI. "Fascinating medieval town; nr Bassin de St Ferréol; friendly staff; barrier clsd 2230-7000; excel mkt in Revel; vg." 15 Jun-15 Sep. € 14.30 2006*

REVEL *8F4* (8km SE Rural) *43.40780, 2.08640* **Camping La Rigole, 81540 Les Cammazes [tel/fax 05 63 73 28 99; mary@campingdlr.com; http://campingdlr.free.fr]** Fr Revel take D629 E to Les Cammazes. Thro vill 300m take 1st L. Site well sp, 1km fr vill. Med, mkd pitch, hdstg, terr, pt sl, terr, pt shd; wc; chem disp; shwrs inc; el pnts (4A) inc; Indtte; shop &1km; tradsmn; rest; snacks; bar; BBQ; playgrnd; pool; lake sw 5km; games area; TV rm; dogs €1; bus 3km; phone; poss cr; Eng spkn; adv bkg; v quiet; red low ssn; CCI. "Pretty, well laid-out, immac site; welcoming, helpful staff; help req to access some pitches; gd san facs; gd disabled facs but wheelchair movement on site impossible unaided & diff at best due slope; phone ahead to check open low ssn; excel." ♦ 15 Apr-1 Oct. € 18.50 2008*

REVEL *8F4* (4km S Rural) *43.43415, 2.01662* **Camping En Salvan, 31350 St Ferréol [05 61 83 55 95; lvt-en-salvan@wanadoo.fr; www.camping-ensalvan.com]** Fr Revel head S on D629 up long hill. At lake at top turn R for 2km, site on R. Sm, mkd pitch, hdstg, shd; shwrs; mv service pnt; el pnts (3-10A) €2-3.90; Indtte; shop; BBQ; playgrnd; pool; paddling pool; games area; 20% statics; dogs €1; poss cr; quiet; red low ssn. "Pleasant site; sm pitches; tired end of ssn (2008); poss school parties low ssn." 5 Apr-31 Oct. € 12.50 2008*

REVIGNY SUR ORNAIN *5D1* (250m S Urban) *48.82663, 4.98412* **Camp Municipal du Moulin des Gravières, Rue du Stade, 55800 Revigny-sur-Ornain [tel/fax 03 29 78 73 34 or 03 29 70 50 55 (Mairie); contact@ot-revigny-ornain.fr; www.ot-revigny-ornain.fr]** N fr Bar-le-Duc on D994 to Revigny-sur-Ornain; fr town cent take D995 twd Vitry-le-François. Site on R, sp. Sm, hdg/mkd pitch, pt shd; wc (some cont); chem disp; mv service pnt; baby facs; shwrs inc; el pnts (6A) €3; Indtte (inc dryer); supmkt 500m; snacks; playgrnd; tennis & cycle hire in town; TV rm; 40% statics; dogs; Eng spkn; adv bkg; v quiet; ccard not acc; CCI. "Pleasant, well-maintained site; lge pitches but poss mkt traders/itinerants on lgest; vg, modern facs; trout stream runs thro site; mkt Wed adj; highly rec." ♦ 1 May-30 Sep. € 10.35 2008*

REVIN *5C1* (N Rural) *49.94420, 4.63138* **Camp Municipal Les Bateaux, Quai Edgar Quinet, 08500 Revin [03 24 40 15 65 or 03 24 40 19 59 (LS); fax 03 24 40 21 98; camping.les.bateaux-revin@wanadoo.fr; www.ville-revin.fr]** Fr Fumay take D988 to Revin, or fr Charleville take D989/988 (23km) or take rte D1 E fr Rocroi. On ent Revin turn L after narr bdge (1-way) over Rv Meuse. Fr cent of Revin foll sp Montherme; at Total g'ge R fork, then 1st L. At rv turn L, 500m to site, sp. Med, hdg/mkd pitch, pt shd; htd wc; chem disp; baby facs; shwrs; el pnts (6A) €2.65 (poss rev pol); Indtte; shop; supmkt 1km; tradsmn; playgrnd; rv fishing; paragliding nrby; games rm; TV rm; 5% statics; dogs €0.90; adv bkg; quiet; CCI. "Peaceful, clean, rvside site; lge pitches; excel san facs, inc for disabled; if office clsd site self & book in later; helpful warden; gd walks; excel." ♦ Easter-30 Oct. € 8.55 2007*

RHINAU *6E3* (500m NW Rural) *48.32123, 7.69788* **Camping Ferme des Tuileries, 1 Rue des Tuileries, 67230 Rhinau [03 88 74 60 45; fax 03 88 74 85 35; camping.fermetuileries@neuf.fr; www.fermedestuileries.com]** S on D468 at Boofzheim, turn L at sp Rhinau, D5. Site 2.4km after L turn. Ent Rhinau site 3rd turn R. Lge, mkd pitch, some hdstg; pt shd; wc; chem disp; mv service pnt; baby facs; shwrs inc; el pnts (2-6A) €1.40-3.20; gas; Indtte; shops 500m; tradsmn; rest & snacks (Jul/Aug); playgrnd; sm htd pool; lake sw; tennis; cycle hire; games area; entmnt; 50% statics; no dogs; poss cr; quiet. "Spacious site with excel facs; regimented; free ferry across Rv Rhine adj; vg." ♦ 1 Apr-30 Sep. € 9.90 2008*

France

RHINAU *6E3* (2.5km NW Rural) *48.32823, 7.69115* **Camping du Ried, 1 Rue du Camping, 67860 Boofzheim [03 88 74 68 27; fax 03 88 74 62 89; info@camping-ried.com; www.camping-ried.com]** Site sp fr D5, 1km E of Boofzheim. Lge, hdg/mkd pitch, pt shd; htd wc; mv service pnt; shwrs; el pnts (5A) €4; Indtte; shop 200m; snacks; bar; BBQ; playgrnd; 2 htd pools (1 covrd); paddling pool; lake sw; watersports; fishing; games area; cycle hire; entmnt; TV rm; 20% statics; dogs €4; phone; adv bkg; quiet; red low ssn; ccard acc. "Conv Strasbourg, Colmar & Europ Park theme park; vg site." ♦ 1 Apr-30 Sep. € 17.50 2007*

RIBEAUVILLE *6E3* (2km E Urban) *48.19490, 7.33648* **Camp Municipal Pierre-de-Coubertin, Rue de Landau, 68150 Ribeauville [tel/fax 03 89 73 66 71; camping.ribeauville@wanadoo.fr; www.camping-alsace.com]** Exit N83 at Ribeauville, turn R on D106 & foll rd to o'skts, at traff lts turn R & then immed R again. Site on R in 750m. Camp at sports grnd nr Lycée. Lge, mkd pitch, pt sl, pt shd; htd wc; chem disp; baby facs; shwrs inc; el pnts (16A) inc (rev pol & poss long lead req); gas; Indtte; sm shop; pool adj; wifi; dogs €1; poss cr; quiet; red low ssn; CCI. "Well-run site; friendly, helpful managers; park outside site bef checking in; clean san facs; resident storks; gd touring base; mkt Sat; highly rec." ♦ 15 Mar-15 Nov. € 16.50 2009*

RIBEAUVILLE *6E3* (4.5km S Rural) *48.16200, 7.31691* **Camp Intercommunal, 1 Route des Vins, 68340 Riquewihr [03 89 47 90 08; fax 03 89 49 05 63; camping.riquewihr@wanadoo.fr]** Fr Strasbourg on N83/E25, take junc 21 (fr opp dir take junc 22) to Blebenheim/Riquewihr. D416 & D3 thro Blebenheim. At T-junc turn R onto D1B, site on R at rndabt. Lge, hdg/mkd pitch, some hdstg, pt sl, pt shd; htd wc; chem disp; mv service pnt; baby facs; shwrs inc; el pnts (6A) €3.50 (poss rev pol); gas; Indtte (inc dryer); shops 5km; tradsmn in ssn; snacks; playgrnd; tennis; games area adj; dogs €1.20; poss cr; adv bkg; noise fr main rd; ccard acc; CCI ess. "Rec arr early; friendly staff; san facs clean; gd for sm children; lovely town; m'van o'night area." ♦ 10 Apr-31 Dec. € 12.00 2008*

RIBEAUVILLE *6E3* (8km W Rural) *48.19610, 7.22336* **FFCC Camp Municipal de la Ménère, 68150 Aubure [03 89 73 92 99; aubure@cc-ribeauville.fr]** Take D416 W fr Ribeauville for 7km, then turn L to Aubure; foll rd to vill for 5km; site 200m S of vill. Or take D416 E fr Ste Marie-aux-Mines; then turn R onto D11 to Aubure (gd rd, resurfaced 2007). For info: D11 gd rd S fr Aubure over hills to N415. Med, mkd pitch, terr, pt shd; wc; chem disp; mv service pnt; shwrs inc; el pnts (6A) €2.65; gas; Indry rm; shops 12km; playgrnd 50m; no statics; dogs €0.50; phone; Eng spkn; adv bkg; quiet; CCI. "Highest vill in Alsace (800m); fresh, pleasant, peaceful site; walking & cycling rtes nrby." 8 May-15 Sep. € 10.55 2007*

RIBERAC *7C2* (500m N Rural) *45.25668, 0.34280* **Camp Municipal La Dronne, Route d'Angoulême, 24600 Ribérac [05 53 90 50 08 or 05 53 90 03 10; fax 05 53 91 35 13; ot.riberac@perigord.tm.fr]** Site on L of main rd D709 immed N of bdge over Rv Dronne on o'skts of Ribérac. Med, some hdg pitches, pt shd; wc (cont for men); shwrs inc; el pnts (10A) €2.50; Indtte; supmkt 500m; tradsmn; snacks; playgrnd; pool 1km; dogs €0.50; no twin-axles; quiet. "Vg, well-run site; pitches in cent hdgd & shady; facs gd & clean but inadequate high ssn; Fri mkt." ♦ 1 Jun-15 Sep. € 8.00 2008*

RICHELIEU *4H1* (500m S Rural) *47.00774, 0.32078* **Camp Municipal, 6 Ave de Schaafheim, 37120 Richelieu [02 47 58 15 02 or 02 47 58 10 13 (Mairie); fax 02 47 58 16 42; commune-de-richelieu@wanadoo.fr]** Fr Loudun, take D61 to Richelieu, D749 twd Châtellerault; site sp. Sm, hdg/mkd pitch, pt shd; wc; chem disp; shwrs inc; el pnts (5-15A) €1.50-3.10; shop 1km; playgrnd; pool 500m; fishing; tennis; quiet; CCI. "Phone ahead to check site open low ssn; clean, gd facs but need updating; poss itinerants." ♦ 15 May-15 Sep. € 6.70 2006*

RIEL LES EAUX *6F1* (1.8km W Rural) *47.97050, 4.64990* **Camp Municipal du Plan d'Eau, 21570 Riel-les-Eaux [tel/fax 03 80 93 72 76; bar-camping-du-marais@wanadoo.fr]** NE fr Châtillon-sur-Seine on D965 twd Chaumont: after 6km turn N onto D13 at Brion-sur-Ource; cont thro Belan-sur-Ource. Site almost opp junc with D22 turning to Riel-les-Eaux; site well sp. Sm, hdg pitch, pt shd; wc; chem disp; shwrs inc; el pnts (6A) €3; tradsmn; snacks; bar; playgrnd; lake adj; fishing; Eng spkn; quiet; CCI. "Conv Champagne area; excel." ♦ 1 Apr-31 Oct. € 8.60 2009*

RIEZ *10E3* (5km N Rural) **Camp Municipal Le Touires, 04410 Puimoisson [04 92 74 71 49]** N fr Riez on D953 to Puimoisson in 5km; turn L onto D56; site in 1km on R. Med, mkd pitch, pt shd; wc (cont) (own san rec); shwrs inc; shop, rest & snacks 1km; dogs €1.50; quiet; ccard not acc; CCI. "Pleasant, clean site; mountain views; ramp to gd basic facs; conv Gorges du Verdon & Lac de Ste Croix - gd sw & beach; gd walking & cycling." ♦ 1 Jun-30 Sep. € 9.40 2009*

RIEZ *10E3* (500m SE Urban) *43.81306, 6.09931* **Camping Rose de Provence, Rue Edouard Dauphin, 04500 Riez [tel/fax 94 92 77 75 45; info@rose-de-provence.com; www.rose-de-provence.com]** Exit A51 junc 18 onto D82 to Gréoux-les-Bains then D952 to Riez. On reaching Riez strt across rndabt, at T-junc turn L & immed R, site sp. Med, mkd pitch, pt shd; wc; chem disp; shwrs inc; el pnts (6A) €3; Indtte; rest, snacks, bar 500m; playgrnd; jacuzzi; lake sw 10km; tennis adj; 5% statics; dogs €1.45; phone; adv bkg; red low ssn; CCI. "Clean site; gd san facs; helpful, friendly owners; conv Verdon Gorge." ♦ 5 Apr-5 Oct. € 13.80 2007*

RIEZ *10E3* (10km S Rural) *43.74773, 6.09843* **Camping Le Côteau de la Marine, 04500 Montagnac-Montpezat [04 92 77 53 33; fax 04 92 77 59 34; www.village-center.com]** A51 exit 18, D82 to Gréoux-les-Bains, then D952 & D11 & Montagnac, Montpezat & site sp. (Steep incline bef ent to site) Lge, hdg/mkd pitch, hdstg, pt sl, terr, pt shd; wc; chem disp; mv service pnt; 50% serviced pitch; shwrs inc; el pnts (10A) inc; gas; lndtte; shop; tradsmn; rest; snacks; bar; playgrnd; pool; fishing; boating; tennis; games area; games rm; entmnt; internet & wifi; TV; dogs €3; statics; Eng spkn; adv bkg ess high ssn; quiet but poss noise fr night-flying helicopters in gorge; ccard acc; CCI. "Helpful staff; gd facs; gravel pegs req for awnings; mountain views; excel." ♦ 21 Apr-16 Sep. € 30.00 2007*

RILLE *4G1* (4km W Rural) *47.45750, 0.21840* **Camping Huttopia Rillé, Base de Loisirs de Pincemaille, Lac de Rillé, 37340 Rillé [02 47 24 62 97; fax 02 47 24 63 61; rille@huttopia.com; www.huttopia.com]** Fr N or S D749 to Rillé, foll sp to Lac de Pincemaille, site sp on S side of lake. Med, shd; htd wc; chem disp; mv service pnt; baby facs; fam bthrm; shwrs inc; el pnts (6-10A) €4.20-6.20; shop; rest; snacks; bar; playgrnd; htd pool; lake sw & beach adj; fishing; watersports; tennis; games rm; some statics; dogs €3.50; sep car park; adv bkg. "Peaceful site; vg walking; excel." 24 Apr-5 Nov. € 24.00 2008*

RIOM *9B1* (5km NW Rural) *45.90614, 3.06041* **Camping de la Croze, St Hippolyte, 63140 Châtelguyon [04 73 86 08 27 or 06 87 14 43 62 (mob); fax 04 73 86 08 51; info@campingcroze.com; www.campingcroze.com]** Fr A71 exit junc 13; ring rd around Riom sp Châtelguyon to Mozac, then D227. Site L bef ent St Hippolyte. Fr Volvic on D986 turn L at rndabt after Leclerc supmkt & L again to D227. NB Avoid diff ent to site by going ahead 1km, doing U-turn in St Hippolyte & then R turn to site. Not rec to tow thro Riom. Lge, mkd pitch, pt sl, pt shd; htd wc; chem disp; shwrs inc; el pnts (6-10A) €2.50; lndtte; shops 2km; tradsmn; playgrnd; htd pool; 10% statics; dogs €1.30; quiet; CCI. "Gd sightseeing area; poss diff for British c'vans on sl pitches; vg." 1 May-20 Oct. € 9.50 2007*

RIOM *9B1* (6km NW Rural) *45.91593, 3.07684* **Camping Clos de Balanède, Route de la Piscine, 63140 Châtelguyon [04 73 86 02 47; fax 04 73 86 05 64; clos-balanede.sarl-camping@wanadoo.fr; www.balanede.com]** Fr Riom take D227 to Châtelguyon, site on R on o'skts of town. Tight turn into ent. Lge, pt sl, pt shd; wc; shwrs inc; el pnts (5-10A) inc; gas; lndtte; shop; rest; snacks; bar; playgrnd; 3 pools; tennis; dogs €1.60; poss cr; Eng spkn; adv bkg; quiet; poss open until 31 Dec; red low ssn/long stay. "Nice, clean, well-organised site; gd facs; sh walk to town; m'vans/campers not allowed up to Puy-de-Dôme - must use bus provided." ♦ 10 Apr-1 Oct. € 17.60 2009*

RIOM ES MONTAGNES *7C4* (500m NE Rural) *45.28214, 2.66707* **Camp Municipal Le Sédour, 15400 Riom-ès-Montagnes [04 71 78 05 71]** Site on W of D678 Riom N to Condat rd, 500m out of town over bdge, sp fr all dirs, opp Clinique du Haut Cantal. Med, mkd pitch, pt shd; wc; shwrs inc; el pnts (2-10A); lndtte; supmkt 200m; playgrnd; pool 5km; games area; TV rm; Eng spkn; adv bkg; some rd noise top end of site. "Vg." 1 May-30 Sep. 2007*

RIOM ES MONTAGNES *7C4* (10km SW Rural) *45.24821, 2.53650* **Camp Municipal Le Pioulat, 15400 Trizac [04 71 78 64 20 or 04 71 78 60 37 (Mairie); fax 04 71 78 65 40; mairie.trizac@wanadoo.fr]** D678 W fr Riom-ès-Montagnes to Trizac. Site on R after leaving vill S twd Mauriac. Sm, hdg pitch, pt sl, pt shd; htd wc; chem disp; el pnts (5A) €2.30; gas, tradsmn, rest, bar, shops 1km; BBQ; lndtte; playgrnd; tennis nr; sand beach; lake sw; quiet; Eng spkn; adv bkg; phone; CCI. "Beautiful site, lovely scenery; friendly staff; clean facs; vg walking area; highly rec." ♦ 16 Jun-15 Sep. € 7.80 2008*

RIOZ *6G2* (E Rural) *47.42397, 6.07342* **Camp Municipal du Lac, Rue de la Faïencerie, 70190 Rioz [03 84 91 91 59 or 03 84 91 84 84 (Mairie); fax 03 84 91 90 45; mairierioz@wanadoo.fr]** Site sp off D15. Med, some hdg pitch, some hdstg, pt shd; htd wc; baby facs; shwrs inc; el pnts (16A) €2.50; gas; shops 500m; rests in vill; playgrnd; pool adj; dogs €1.50; quiet, but some rd noise. "Site yourself, warden calls; some lge pitches; gd facs; footpath to vill shops." 1 Apr-30 Sep. € 10.40 2009*

RIOZ *6G2* (7km S Rural) *47.35873, 6.07855* **Camping L'Esplanade, Rue du Pont, 70190 Cromary [03 84 91 82 00 or 03 84 91 85 84 (LS); benttom@hotmail.com; www.lesplanade.nl]** Fr S on N57 take D14 E thro Devecey. At Vielley turn L onto D412. Site on L over rv. Fr N on N57 by-pass Rioz & take slip rd onto D15 sp Sorans. Turn L in vill, pass under N57 to They, then foll sp Cromary & site. Sm, hdg/mkd pitch, pt shd; wc (some cont); chem disp; shwrs inc; el pnts (4-8A) €2.10-3.10; lndtte; shop 3km; tradsmn; snacks; BBQ; playgrnd; rv sw adj; 40% statics; dogs €0.50; Eng spkn; adv bkg; quiet; ccard acc. "Well-kept site; welcoming Dutch owners; v muddy after heavy rain (no tractor help); many itinerants (Jul 08)." ♦ 1 Apr-30 Nov. € 10.30 2008*

RIQUEWIHR see Ribeauville *6E3*

RISCLE *8E2* (500m N Urban) *43.66324, -0.08180* **FFCC Camp Municipal Le Pont de l'Adour, 32400 Riscle [05 62 69 72 45 or 06 08 55 36 89 (mob); fax 05 62 69 72 45; camping.dupondeladour@wanadoo.fr]** On ent Riscle fr N on D935, site on L immed after x-ing Rv Adour. Med, pt shd, hdg pitch; wc (some cont); chem disp; mv service pnt; shwrs inc; el pnts (5-6A) inc; lndtte; shop; rest; snacks; pool adj; playgrnd; entmnt; TV; dogs €1.52; quiet; red low ssn; CCI. "V quiet low ssn." ♦ 1 Apr-15 Oct. € 15.00 2006*

RIVIERE SAAS ET GOURBY see Dax *8E1*

RIVIERE SUR TARN *10E1* (Rural) *44.20319, 3.15806* **FFCC Camping Le Pont, Boyne, 12640 Rivière-sur-Tarn [05 65 62 61 12]** Fr Millau head N on N9, R after 7km onto D907 sp Gorges du Tarn, site in 9km on R on ent to vill. Sm, pt shd; wc (some cont); chem disp; mv service pnt; shwrs inc; el pnts (4A) €2.50; lndry rm; shops, rest adj; playgrnd; sw pool 2km; rv sw & fishing adj; dogs €1; quiet; CCI. "Gd base for Tarn gorges; canoeing & climbing nrby; facs dated but spotlessly clean; helpful owner has tourist info; excel." 1 Jun-30 Sep. € 9.00 2006*

France

RIVIERE SUR TARN *10E1* (2km E Rural) *44.19100, 3.15675* **FLOWER Camping Le Peyrelade, Route des Gorges du Tarn, 12640 Rivière-sur-Tarn [05 65 62 62 54; fax 05 65 62 65 61; campingpeyrelade@wanadoo.fr; www.campingpeyrelade.com or www.flowercamping.com]** Exit A75 junc 44.1 to Aguessac, then take D907 N thro Rivière-sur-Tarn to site in 2km. Fr Millau drive N on N9 to Aguessac, then onto D907 thro Rivière-sur-Tarn, & site sp on R. Lge, hdg/mkd pitch, terr, shd; wc; chem disp; mv service pnt; baby facs; shwrs inc; el pnts (6A) €4; gas; Indtte; shop; tradsmn; rest; snacks; bar; BBQ; playgrnd; htd pool; rv beach & sw adj; canoeing; games rm; cycle hire 100m; entmnt; TV; dogs €2; adv bkg; quiet; ccard acc; red low ssn; CCI. "Excel touring base in interesting area; rvside pitches extra charge." ♦ 15 May-6 Sep. € 25.00 2008*

RIVIERE SUR TARN *10E1* (2.5km E Rural) *44.20083, 3.15944* **Camping du Moulin de la Galinière, Boyne, 12640 Rivière-sur-Tarn [05 65 62 65 60 or 05 65 62 61 81; fax 05 65 62 69 84; moulindelagaliniere@orange.fr; www.moulindelagaliniere.com]** Exit A75 junc 44.1 La Gamasse onto D29 & foll sp Gorges du Tarn. Site ent bef Boyne vill, other side of bdge to Camping Le Pont, bef R turn. Site on bank Rv Tarn. Med, pt shd; wc; baby facs; shwrs inc; el pnts (6A) €3; Indtte; shops adj; snacks; playgrnd; shgl beach; rv sw & fishing; dogs €1; quiet. "Excel, clean facs, poss tired low ssn; pleasant owners." 1 Jul-31 Aug. € 12.00 2006*

RIVIERE SUR TARN *10E1* (250m SE Rural) *44.18680, 3.13650* **Camping Le Papillon, Les Canals, 12640 La Cresse [tel/fax 05 65 59 08 42; info@campinglepapillon.com; www.campinglepapillon.com]** Fr N on A75 exit junc 44.1 onto D29 to Aguessac; then turn L onto D547/D907; in 3km turn R sp La Cresse on D187. Site sp. Rivière-sur-Tarn on W bank of rv, site on E bank; Rivière-sur-Tarn 2km by rd. Rec app fr S. Sm, hdg/mkd pitch, terr, shd, pt shd; htd wc; chem disp; baby facs; fam bthrm; shwrs inc; el pnts (10A) €3; gas; Indtte; ice; tradsmn; rest; snacks; bar; BBQ (not charcoal); playgrnd; rv sw 150m; TV; 5% statics; dogs €2; Eng spkn; adv bkg; quiet; red long stay/low ssn; CCI. "Pleasant site, amazing views; new helpful Dutch owner (2009); excel facs; rec." 25 Apr-12 Sep. € 18.50 2009*

RIVIERE SUR TARN *10E1* (SW Rural) *44.1853, 3.1306* **Camping Les Peupliers, Rue de la Combe, 12640 Rivière-sur-Tarn [05 65 59 85 17; fax 05 65 61 09 03; lespeupliers12640@orange.fr; www.campinglespeupliers.fr]** Heading N on N9 turn R dir Aguessac onto D907 twd Rivière-sur-Tarn. Site on R bef vill. Or fr A75 exit junc 44.1 sp Aguessac/Gorges du Tarn. In Aguessac, foll sp Rivière-sur-Tarn for 5km, site clearly sp. NB Take care speed humps bet main rd & site. Med, hdg/mkd pitch, some hdstg, pt shd; wc (some cont); chem disp; mv service pnt; baby facs; fam bthrm; shwrs inc; el pt (6A) inc; gas; Indtte; shop 200m; tradsmn; rest; snacks, bar high ssn; BBQ; playgrnd; pool; waterslide; rv sw & shgl beach adj; fishing; canoeing; watersports; horseriding; games area; entmnt; wifi; TV rm; some statics; dogs €2.50; phone; Eng spkn; adv bkg (rec high ssn); quiet; red low ssn; ccard acc; CCI. "Pleasant, peaceful site; busy low ssn; narr access rds; lge, well-shaded pitches, but some sm & diff lge o'fits; friendly staff; clean san facs; beavers in rv; picturesque vill nrby." ♦ 1 Apr-30 Sep. € 28.00 (CChq acc) 2009*

ROANNE *9A1* (12km S Rural) *45.91576, 4.06108* **Camping Le Mars, La Presqu'île de Mars, 42123 Cordelle [04 77 64 94 42 or 06 81 17 87 88 (mob); campingdemars@orange.fr; www.camping-de-mars.fr]** On D56 fr Roanne foll dir Lac Villarest; cross barrage & site 4.5km S of Cordelle well sp just off D56. Fr junc 70 on N7 to St Cyr-de-Favières. Foll sp to Château de la Roche on D17 & site on D56. Fr S take D56 immed after Balbigny; single track app, with restricted visibility. Or fr N82 exit for Neulise onto D26 to Jodard, then D56 twd Cordelle. Site on L in 11km. Med, pt sl, terr, pt shd, hdg pitch; wc; chem disp; serviced pitch; mv service pnt; shwrs; child/baby facs; el pnts (6A) inc; Indtte; shop; tradsmn; snacks; bar; playgrnd; pool; lake sw, fishing & watersports 500m; entmnts; 40% statics; Eng spkn; adv bkg rec high ssn; quiet; red long stay; CCI. "Peaceful; lovely views; poss run down, scruffy low ssn." ♦ 15 Mar-31 Oct. € 19.50 2009*

ROANNE *9A1* (5km SW Rural) *45.98830, 4.04531* **Camping L'Orée du Lac, Le Barrage, 42300 Villerest [tel/fax 04 77 69 60 88; camping@loreedulac.net; www.loreedulac.net]** Take D53 SW fr Roanne to Villerest; site sp in vill. Sm, mkd pitch, pt sl, pt shd; wc; chem disp (wc); shwrs inc; el pnts (6A) €3.50; shop 400m; rest; snacks; bar; playgrnd; pool; rv 300m; lake 100m; fishing; watersports; entmnt; TV; dogs €2; phone; Eng spkn; adv bkg rec high ssn; quiet; red low ssn; CCI. "Attractive site nr medieval vill; much of site diff lge/med o'fits; lower part of site diff when wet." Easter-30 Sep. € 14.10 2009*

ROCAMADOUR *7D3* (1km E Rural) *44.80508, 1.63228* **Camping Les Cigales, L'Hospitalet, Route de Rignac, 46500 Rocamadour [05 65 33 64 44; fax 05 65 33 69 60; camping.cigales@wanadoo.fr; www.camping-cigales.com]** Fr N on D840 (N140) Brive-Gramat turn W on D36 approx 5.5km bef Gramat; in 3km site on R at L'Hospitalet. Med, mkd pitch, shd; wc (some cont); chem disp; mv service pnt; baby facs; shwrs inc; el pnts (6A) €3; gas; Indtte; shop; rest; snacks; bar; playgrnd; pool & paddling pool; rv, canoeing 10km; games rm; entmnt; TV; dogs €2; adv bkg; CCI. "Busy, family site; facs poss stretched; gd pool." ♦ 1 Apr-31 Oct. € 15.50 2007*

ROCAMADOUR *7D3* (1km E Rural) *44.80427, 1.62755* **Le Relais du Campeur, L'Hospitalet, 46500 Rocamadour [05 65 33 63 28; fax 05 65 10 68 21; contact@relais-du-campeur.com; www.ww.lerelaisducampeur.fr]** Fr S exit D820 (N20) (Brive-la-Gaillarde to Cahors) at Payrac; R on D673, 21km to L'Hospitalet. Fr N exit D820 at Cressensac for D840 (N140) to Figeac & Rodez; turn R at D673; site at x-rds after 4km; site behind grocer's shop on L. Avoid app fr W thro Rocamadour (acute hair-pin & rd 2.2m wide). Med, pt sl, pt shd; wc (some cont); shwrs inc; el pnts (6A) €2.60; gas; shops; tradsmn; BBQ; playgrnd; pool; cycling; sailing; dogs €1; adv bkg; quiet; ccard acc; red low ssn. "Busy site, even low ssn; dated facs, insufficient high ssn & ltd low ssn; poss special deal for m'vans high ssn; vg." Easter-1 Nov. € 13.00 2008*

ROCAMADOUR *7D3* (1km NW Rural) *44.81040, 1.61615* **FFCC Aire Naturelle Les Campagnes (Branche), Route de Souillac, 46500 Rocamadour [05 65 33 63 37; camping fermebranche@yahoo.fr; www.campingfermebranche.com]** Site on D247, 1km N of Rocamadour. Sm, pt shd; wc; (some cont); mv service pnt; shwrs inc; el pnts (6A) €1.80; Indtte; shop 1km; BBQ; playgrnd; dogs free; phone; quiet. "Lovely, open, spacious site; gd, clean facs; ltd el pnts; gd for dogs." 1 Apr-15 Nov. € 7.00 2009*

ROCHE BERNARD, LA *2G3* (500m S Urban) *47.51946, -2.30517* **Camp Municipal Le Patis, Chemin du Patis, 56130 La Roche-Bernard [02 99 90 60 13 or 02 99 90 60 51 (Mairie); fax 02 99 90 88 28; mairie-lrb@wanadoo.fr; www.camping-larochebernard.com]** Leave N165 junc 17 (fr N) junc 15 (fr S) & foll marina sp. NB Arr/exit OK on market day (Thurs) if avoid town cent. Med, mkd pitch, hdstg, pt shd; wc; chem disp; mv service pnt; shwrs inc; el pnts (6A) €4; Indtte; shops & snacks 500m; playgrnd; pool 1km; sand beach 18km; rv adj; sailing, boating at marina adj; dogs €1.50; m'van o'night area; poss cr; Eng spkn; adv bkg; quiet but some rd noise; ccard acc; red long stay. "Excel clean site in lovely spot on rv bank; helpful staff; facs poss stretched high ssn; grass pitches poss soft - heavy o'fits phone ahead in wet weather; Thurs mkt." ♦ 1 Apr-30 Sep. € 14.00 2009*

ROCHE CHALAIS, LA *7C2* (500m S Rural) *45.14892, -0.00245* **Camp Municipal Gerbes, Rue de la Dronne, 24490 La Roche-Chalais [05 53 91 40 65; fax 05 53 90 32 01; camping.la.roche.chalais@wanadoo.fr]** Fr S on D674 turn sharp L in vill at site sp. Site on R in 500m. Fr N take Coutras-Libourne rd thro vill; site sp on L beyond sm indus est. Med, mkd pitch, terr, pt shd; wc; shwrs inc; el pnts (5-10A) €2.40-3.40; Indtte; tradsmn; shops 500m; playgrnd; rv sw, fishing, boating & canoeing adj; leisure pk 5km; adv bkg; rlwy & factory noise; red long stay; CCI. "Pleasant, well-kept, well-run site; clean san facs; some rvside pitches; rec pitch N side of site to avoid factory noise/smell; rec." ♦ 15 Apr-30 Sep. € 7.60 2009*

ROCHE DE GLUN, LA see Valence *9C2*

ROCHE DES ARNAUDS, LA see Veynes *9D3*

ROCHE POSAY, LA *4H2* (1.5km N Rural) *46.79951, 0.80933* **Camp Municipal Le Riveau, Route de Lésigny. 86270 La Roche-Posay [05 49 86 21 23; info@camping-le-riveau.com; www.camping-le-riveau.com]** Fr both E & W take new by-pass around N of town on D725; turn N onto D5; foll 'Hippodrome & Camping' sp; site on R 100m after D5/D725 junc; avoid town cent. Fr S bear L in town bef arch & foll sp. Lge, hdg/mkd pitch, shd; htd wc; mv service pnt; shwrs inc; el pnts (16A) inc (check pol); gas; Indtte; shops 1km; rest; snacks; bar; BBQ (gas/elec); playgrnd; pool; rv sw & fishing 1.5km; tennis; cycle hire; entmnt; 10% statics; dogs €1; poss cr; Eng spkn; adv bkg; quiet; red low ssn/long stay; CCI. "Excel, popular, well-maintained site; 1st class facs; barrier locks automatically 2300; parking avail outside; walk to town on busy rd with no pavement; spa town." ♦ 29 Mar-18 Oct. € 18.40 2008*

ROCHE POSAY, LA *4H2* (3km E Rural) *46.78274, 0.86942* **Camp Municipal Les Bords de Creuse, Rue du Pont, 37290 Yzeures-sur-Creuse [tel/fax 02 47 94 48 32 or 02 47 94 55 01 (Mairie)]** Fr Châtellerault take D725 E twds La Roche-Posay; after x-ing Rv Creuse, turn L onto D750 twds Yzeures-sur-Creuse; at traff lts in vill turn S onto D104; site on R in 200m at T-junc. Med, mkd pitch, pt sl, pt shd; wc; chem disp; shwrs inc; el pnts (6A) inc; Indtte; shop 500m BBQ; pool, rv sw, tennis adj; games rm; dogs; quiet. ♦ 15 Jun-15 Sep. € 10.30 2009*

ROCHE SUR YON, LA *2H4* (8km S Rural) *46.59340, -1.43839* **Camping La Venise du Bocage, Le Chaillot, 85310 Nesmy [tel/fax 02 51 98 01 20; contact@la-venise-du-bocage.com; www.la-venise-du-bocage.com]** Fr N take D747 dir La Tranche-sur-Mer. Take D36 twd Nesmy & site sp on R after 500m. Sm, mkd pitch, pt shd; wc (some cont); chem disp; baby facs; shwrs inc; el pnts (6-10A) €2.80-3.70; Indtte; ltd shop or 3km; rest & bar 3km; playgrnd; pool; tennis; horseriding, golf 3km; 25% statics; dogs €1.70; phone; poss cr; adv bkg; quiet; red low ssn. "Helpful, friendly owner; gd san facs; poss untidy end of ssn; poss barrier down & staff not avail to open for arr; NH only." ♦ 1 Apr-30 Sep. € 10.60 2009*

ROCHEBRUNE *9D3* (S Rural) *44.45967, 6.16798* **Camping Les Trois Lacs, Les Plantiers, 05190 Rochebrune [04 92 54 41 52; fax 04 92 54 16 14; direction@camping les3lacs.com; www.campingles3lacs.com]** On D900b fr Serre-Ponçon to Tallard, 2km after Espinasses turn L onto D951 & look for site sp. Turn R onto D56 after x-ing Rv Durance. Site on R in 2km. Sm, mkd/hdstg pitch, pt sl, shd; wc (some cont); chem disp; baby facs; shwrs inc; el pnts (2-6A) €2.50-4.70; gas; Indtte; shop 5km & supmkt 8km; tradsmn high ssn; rest; snacks; bar; playgrnd; lake sw adj; fishing; tennis nrby; paragliding; go-karting; entmnt; 20% statics; dogs €3; poss cr; adv bkg; quiet; red long stay/low ssn; ccard acc high ssn only; CCI. "Site in pine trees, poss diff for lge o'fits. ♦ 1 Apr-30 Oct. € 15.00 2007*

ROCHECHOUART *7B3* (1km S Rural) *45.81498, 0.82208* **Camping de la Météorite (formerly Municipal Lac de Bois Chenu), Boischenu, 87600 Rochechouart [05 55 03 65 96; fax 05 55 05 97 62; campingdelameteorite@orange.fr; www.campingmeteorite.fr]** S fr Rochechouart on D675. Turn R onto D10 them immed L by lake into park. Site ent at far end of park by snack bar. Med, mkd pitch, pt sl, terr, shd; wc; chem disp; mv service pnt; shwrs inc; el pnts (10A) €3 (poss long lead req); gas; sm shop & 3km; tradsmn; rest adj; BBQ; playgrnd; htd pool; lake sw & fishing; cycle hire; games area; games rm; entmnt; internet; TV; 10% statics; dogs free; phone; poss cr; Eng spkn; adv bkg; quiet; ccard acc; red low ssn. "Delightful, wooded site o'looking fishing lake; renovated (2009); helpful owner; clean, modern san facs; gd pool (unfenced 2009); some v steep (10ft) terraces with no retaining walls (2009)." ♦ 23 Mar-31 Oct. € 18.00 2009*

CAMPING SAINT OFFANGE
Tel/Fax: 0241788211
www.camping-rochefort49.0rg.fr • stoffange@hotmail.com
Address: Route de Savennières. 49190 Rochefort sur Loire.
UNESCO heritage site, Rental of mobile homes and bungalow tents. Kayak base. Bivouac and hiking on the Loire. Swimming allowed at 50 meters under parental supervision. Leisure packages, Animations, Games, Mini-golf, Petanque, Bar
www.loire-canoe-kayak.com

ROCHECHOUART *7B3* (4km SW Rural) *45.80385, 0.70623* **Camping des Lacs, Le Guerlie, 16150 Pressignac [05 45 31 17 80; fax 05 56 70 15 01; aquitaine@relaisoleil.com; www.relaisoleil.com/pressignac]** W fr Rochechouart on D161, then D160 dir La Guerlie & lake. Lge, hdg/mkd pitch, terr, pt shd; wc; chem disp; mv service pnt; el pnts (10A) €3.70; gas; Indtte; sm shop & 4km; rest 100m; bar; playgrnd; 2 pools (1 htd, covrd); paddling pool; lake sw 500m; watersports; games area; games rm; wifi; entmnt; 5% statics; dogs €3.15; adv bkg; Eng spkn; ccard acc; red low ssn; CCI. "Peaceful site; superb walking; excel touring base." ♦ 28 Jun-30 Aug. € 20.20 2007*

⊞ **ROCHECHOUART** *7B3* (13km SW Rural) *45.73390, 0.68070* **Camping Chez Rambaud, 87440 Les Salles-Lavauguyon [05 55 00 08 90; fax 05 55 00 08 90; camping@chez-rambaud.com; www.chez-rambaud.com]** Fr Rochechouart on D675 then D10 dir Videix & Verneuil, turn L sp Les Salles-Lavauguyon for 2km. Leave vill on D34 sp Sauvagnac; in 100m turn L sp Chez Rambaud, site on L in 1.5km. Sm, hdg/mkd pitch, pt sl, pt shd; htd wc; chem disp; shwrs inc; el pnts (10A) €3.50; Indtte; ice; BBQ; lake sw & sand beach 10km; dogs €1.50; Eng spkn; adv bkg; quiet; no ccard acc; CCI. "Tranquil, CL-type site; views over wooded valley; friendly, helpful British owners; excel immac facs; gd touring base; gd walking & cycling; Richard The Lion Heart rte in vill; mkt in Rochechouart Sat; excel." ♦ € 13.00 2009*

ROCHEFORT *7B1* (1.5km N Coastal) *45.94986, -0.99499* **Camping Le Bateau, Rue des Pêcheurs d'Islande, 17300 Rochefort [05 46 99 41 00; fax 05 46 99 91 65; lebateau@wanadoo.fr; www.campinglebateau.com]** Exit A837/E602 at junc 31 & take D733 dir Rochefort. At 1st rndabt by McDonalds, take D733 dir Royan. At next rndabt 1st R onto Rue des Pêcheurs d'Islande. Site at end of rd on L. Med, hdg pitch, pt shd; wc; chem disp; shwrs inc; el pnts (10A) €4; Indtte; shop; tradsmn; rest; snacks; bar; playgrnd; pool; waterslide; watersports; fishing; tennis; games rm; entmnt; 25% statics; dogs €1.70; quiet; red low ssn; CCI. "Helpful staff; poss scruffy low ssn - ducks & geese on site (Jun 2008); basic san facs, ltd low ssn; no twin-axles; gd cycling, walking; mkt Tues & Sat." 1 Apr-1 Nov. € 14.00 2009*

ROCHEFORT *7B1* (8km W Coastal) *45.94828, -1.09592* **Camp Municipal de la Garenne, Ave de l'Ile-Madame, 17730 Port-des-Barques [05 46 84 80 66 or 06 08 57 08 75 (mob); fax 05 46 84 98 33; camping@ville-portdesbarques.fr; www.ville-portdesbarques.fr]** Fr Rochefort S on D773, cross Rv Charente bdge & take 1st exit sp Soubise & Ile Madame. Cont strt thro Port-des-Barques, site on L opp causeway to Ile Madame. Lge, mkd pitch, unshd; wc; chem disp; mv service pnt; baby facs; shwrs inc; el pnts (10A) inc; Indtte; shop 1km; rest 500m; snacks; bar 1km; playgrnd; htd pool; sand/shgl beach adj; 25% statics; dogs €1.06; phone; bus adj; poss cr; adv bkg; quiet; ccard acc; CCI. "Pleasant site; lge pitches; clean facs." ♦ 15 Mar-15 Oct. € 15.90 2008*

ROCHEFORT EN TERRE *2F3* (600m Rural) *47.69217, -2.34794* **Camping du Moulin Neuf, Chemin de Bogeais, Route de Limerzel, 56220 Rochefort-en-Terre [02 97 43 37 52; fax 02 97 43 35 45]** Fr Redon W on D775 twd Vannes, approx 23km turn R onto D774 sp Rochefort-en-Terre; immed after vill limit sp, turn sharp L up slope to ent; avoid vill. Med, hdg/mkd pitch, terr, pt sl, pt shd; mv service pnt; wc; chem disp; shwrs inc; el pnts ltd (10A) €4.50; Indtte; shops in vill; tradsmn; rest nr; BBQ; play area; htd pool high ssn; lake beach & sw 500m; some statics; dogs €3; poss cr; adv bkg; quiet; ccard acc; CCI. "Peaceful base for touring area; helpful owners; no vehicle movements 2200-0700; no twin-axles; excel." ♦ 13 May-13 Sep. € 20.60 2009*

ROCHEFORT EN TERRE *2F3* (8km NE) *47.74455, -2.25997* **Camp Municipal La Digue, 56200 St Martin-sur-Oust [02 99 91 55 76 or 02 99 91 49 45; fax 02 99 91 42 94; st-martin-oust@wanadoo.fr]** On D873 14km N of Redon at Gacilly, turn W onto D777 twd Rochefort-en-Terre; site sp in 10km in St Martin. Med, pt shd; wc; shwrs; el pnts (3-5A) €2.40; Indtte; shops adj; BBQ; playgrnd; rv fishing 50m; dogs €0.30; adv bkg; quiet. "Towpath walks to vill & shops; clean facs but ltd low ssn; well-maintained site; site yourself, warden calls am & eve." 1 May-30 Sep. € 7.30 2009*

ROCHEFORT MONTAGNE see Orcival *7B4*

ROCHEFORT SUR LOIRE *4G1* (500m N Rural) *47.36028, -0.65593* **Camping Saint Offange, Route de Savennières, 49190 Rochefort-sur-Loire [tel/fax 02 41 78 82 11; stoffange@hotmail.com; www.camping-rochefort49.org.fr]** S fr Angers on A87, exit junc 24 onto D54/160 N. Foll sp Rochefort-sur-Loire & site on D106. Med, hdg/mkd pitch, pt shd; wc; chem disp; mv service pnt; shwrs inc; el pnts (10A) €2.70; Indtte; shop; bar; BBQ; playgrnd; pool adj; rv sw & sand beach adj; fishing; canoeing; games area; games rm; entmnt; 10% statics; dogs €1.80; extra for twin-axles; adv bkg; quiet. "Helpful owners, excel." ♦ 10 Jun-15 Sep. € 11.50 2009*

See advertisement opposite

ROCHEFORT SUR NENON see Dole *6H2*

ROCHEFOUCAULD, LA *7B2* (500m N Rural) *45.74495, 0.38123* **Camping des Flots, Rue des Flots, 16110 La Rochefoucauld [05 45 63 07 45; fax 05 45 63 08 54; camping.larochefoucauld@wanadoo.fr]** Foll camping sp on app to Rochefoucauld; site next to rv. Sm, shd; wc (cont); chem disp; shwrs inc; el pnts; shops 500m in town; playgrnd; pool & tennis 300m; rv fishing 200m; dogs; adv bkg; quiet; CCI. "Site run by fire brigade, use adj phone to ring fire stn for site key if no-one on site; pitch nr recep as other end adj to sewage plant; excel clean san facs; chateau & cloisters worth visit." 15 May-15 Sep. 2007*

⊞ **ROCHEFOUCAULD, LA** *7B2* (6km E Rural) **Camping La Rose Blanche (Gannicott), 16110 Yvrac-et-Malleyrand [tel/fax 05 45 63 07 56; gannicott@wanadoo.fr]** Take D13 E fr La Rochefoucauld, after 7km turn R onto D62 sp Malleyrand. Site in vill cent L past fire hydrant 100m. Sm, hdstg, pt sl, unshd; wc; chem disp; shwrs inc; el pnts (16A) inc; BBQ; lake sw nr; dogs (on lead only); adv bkg; quiet. "Friendly, helpful British owners; phone ahead rec; CL-type site with vg views; vg san facs." € 15.00 2007*

ROCHELLE, LA *7A1* (12km N Rural/Coastal) *46.25239, -1.11972* **Camp Municipal Les Misottes, 46 Rue de l'Océan, 17137 Esnandes [05 46 35 04 07 or 05 46 01 32 13 (Mairie); lesmisottes@yahoo.fr; www.campinglesmisottes.blogspot.com]** Fr N on D938 or N1327 turn W at Marans onto D105. In 7.5km turn S onto D9 then D202 to Esnandes. Enter vill, at x-rds strt, site on R in 200m. Fr La Rochelle D105 N to cent Esnandes, site sp. Med, mkd pitch, pt shd; wc (cont); shwrs inc; el pnts (10A) €2.85; Indtte; shops 500m; rest, bar 200m; snacks; playgrnd; pool; shgl beach 2km; canal fishing; 5% statics; dogs €1.60; poss cr; Eng spkn; adv bkg; quiet; CCI. "Site on the edge of marshlands; poor san facs (2009); liable to flood; vg." 1 Apr-15 Oct. € 8.70 2009*

ROCHELLE, LA *7A1* (3km S Coastal) *46.1160, 1.1230* **Camping de la Plage, La Lizotière, 66 Route de la Plage, 17440 Aytré [05 46 44 19 33; fax 05 46 45 78 21; contact@campingdelaplage17.com; www.campingdelaplage17.com]** S fr La Rochelle on N137 twd Rochefort; take exit sp Aytré & head for coast rd. Med, shd; wc; baby facs; shwrs inc; el pnts (6A) €3.50; Indtte; rest, snacks, bar 200m; playgrnd; htd, covrd pool; waterslide; sand beach adj; games area; entmnt; some statics; dogs €2; poss cr; quiet. "Some sm pitches; gd cycling." 1 Feb-30 Nov. € 18.50 2007*

ROCHELLE, LA *7A1* (8km S Coastal) *46.10409, -1.13093* **Camping Les Chirats-La Platère, Route de la Platère, 17690 Angoulins-sur-Mer [05 46 56 94 16; fax 05 46 56 65 95; contact@campingleschirats.fr; www.campingleschirats.fr]** Turn off N137 S of La Rochelle & go thro Angoulins-sur-Mer. Foll site sp fr vill N twd Aytré. After 300m turn L across rlwy at stn. Foll sp 'plage' & site. Lge, hdg/mkd pitch, hdstg, pt sl, pt shd; wc (some cont); chem disp; sauna; serviced pitches; shwrs inc; el pnts (6-10A) inc; gas; Indtte; shop & 2km; tradsmn; rest; snacks; bar; playgrnd; pools (1 htd, covrd); paddling pool; waterslide; jacuzzi; sand beach adj; fishing; fitness rm; games area; horseriding 1km; tennis 500m; TV rm; 10% statics; dogs €2.45; phone; poss cr; Eng spkn; adv bkg; quiet; ccard acc; CCI. "Gd facs; well-run site; aquarium worth a visit." ♦ Easter-30 Sep. € 24.70 2009*

See advertisement below

ROCHELLE, LA *7A1* (500m SW Urban/Coastal) *46.15050, -1.15859* **Camp Municipal Le Soleil, Ave Michel Crépeau, 17000 La Rochelle [05 46 44 42 53 or 05 46 51 51 25 (Mairie)]** App La Rochelle on N11, prepare to take L turn sp Port des Minimes when 2 lge concrete water towers come into view. Foll Port des Minimes to rlwy stn (clock tower). Turn R for site over mini-rndabt then L, then L again onto Quai Georges Simenon. Turn L onto Rue Sénac de Meilan, then turn onto Ave Michel Crépeau, site on L, sp. Or fr S on N137 take D937 sp Port des Minimes & rest as above. Lge, mkd pitch, unshd, some hdstg; wc; chem disp; mv service pnt adj; shwrs inc; el pnts (6A) €3.65; shops 1km; tradsmn; BBQ area; beach 1km; some Eng spkn; adv bkg; some noise fr rd & port; CCI. "Walking dist cent La Rochelle & marina; sm pitches, facs basic; ltd space for tourers; free m'van o'night area opp site ent; daily mkt in town; site poss full by 1400 - rec arr early; NH only." 15 May-29 Sep. € 13.10 2009*

⊞ **ROCHELLE, LA** *7A1* (2km W Urban) *46.16041, -1.18578* **Camp Municipal de Port Neuf, Blvd Aristide Rondeau, Port Neuf, 17000 La Rochelle [05 46 43 81 20 or 05 46 51 51 25 (Mairie); camping-portneuf@orange.fr]** On ring rd fr N on N11 turn R onto N237 sp Ile-de-Ré, after sp to city cent, foll sp 'Port Neuf & Ile-de-Ré' & site. Well sp on promenade rd on N side of harbour. If app fr airport side take care to avoid Ile-de-Ré tollbooth. Lge, some hdstg, pt shd; wc (some cont); chem disp; baby facs; shwrs inc; el pnts (6-10A) €3.45-4.15 (poss rev pol); gas; lndttes nr; pool 2km; sand beach 1.5km; dogs €2.25; bus; poss cr; Eng spkn; rd noise; red low ssn; CCI. "Busy site in gd location; clean facs but ltd low ssn; phone ahead to check space high ssn or open low ssn, espec mid-winter; when office clsd some parking along rd adj football pitch; min stay 2 nights high ssn; poss itinerants; m'vans not allowed in old part of town; gd cycle path along seafront." € 10.85 2009*

ROCHELLE, LA *7A1* (3km NW Urban) *46.19190, -1.15853* **Camp Municipal Le Parc, Rue du Parc, 17140 Lagord [05 46 67 61 54 or 05 46 00 62 12 (Mairie); fax 05 46 00 62 01; contact@marie-lagord.fr]** On N237 ring-rd N of La Rochelle, take D104 exit for Lagord. At rndabt in approx 800m turn L then 3rd L, site on L. Med, hdg/mkd pitch, pt shd; wc; chem disp; shwrs inc; el pnts (3-10A) inc (poss rev pol); lndtte; supmkt 2km; BBQ (gas only); playgrnd; beach 4km; few statics; dogs €1.10; bus; Eng spkn; adv bkg; quiet; CCI. "Gd facs & pitches; red facs low ssn; helpful staff; conv Ile de Ré; bus & cycle path to La Rochelle; twin axles extra; excel." ♦ 1 Jun-15 Sep. € 12.00 2009*

ROCHELLE, LA *7A1* (5km NW Rural/Coastal) *46.19583, -1.1875* **Camping au Petit Port de l'Houmeau, Rue des Sartières, 17137 L'Houmeau [05 46 50 90 82; fax 05 46 50 01 33; info@aupetitport.com; www.aupetitport.com]** On ring rd N237 twd Ile-de-Ré, take exit Lagord, across rndabt, after 300m turn R onto D104 to L'Houmeau. At T-junc in L'Houmeau turn R on D106, at 2nd boulangerie turn L & foll 1-way system/sp 'camping' thro vill (modern housing est). Site on L immed after sharp R-hand bend. Med, hdg/mkd pitch, hdstg, terr, shd; wc; chem disp; mv service pnt; baby facs; shwrs inc; el pnts (5-10A) €3.50-4.20; tradsmn; shops & rest 400m; snacks; bar; BBQ (gas); playgrnd; shgl beach 1.5km; cycle hire; games rm; internet; dogs €2.50; bus 400m; poss cr; Eng spkn; adv bkg rec; quiet; red low ssn; ccard acc; CCI. "Pleasant, friendly site; helpful owners; clean facs; no vehicle access 2230-0730; gd cycling; conv Ile de Ré bdge; excel." ♦ 1 Apr-30 Sep. € 17.00 2009*

⊞ **ROCROI** *5C1* (3km SE Rural) *49.89446, 4.53770* **Camping La Murée, 35 Rue Catherine-de-Clèves, 08230 Bourg-Fidèle [tel/fax 03 24 54 24 45; campingdelamuree@wanadoo.fr; www.campingdelamuree.com]** Site sp fr Rocroi on R. Sm, some hdstg, pt shd; wc; chem disp; baby facs; shwrs inc; el pnts (10A) €4; lndtte; shops 3km; rest; bar; playgrnd; lake sw 4km; 40% statics; dogs €1.50; some Eng spkn; adv bkg; quiet; ccard acc; CCI. "Two fishing lakes on site; pleasant site; gd sh stay/NH." ♦ € 14.50 2009*

⊞ **ROCROI** *5C1* (8km SE Rural) *49.87200, 4.60446* **Camp Départemental du Lac des Vieilles Forges, 08500 Les Mazures [03 24 40 17 31; fax 03 24 41 72 38; cmpingvieillesforges@cg08.fr]** Fr Rocroi take D1 & D988 for Les Mazures/Renwez. Turn R D40 at sp Les Vieilles Forges. Site on R nr lakeside. Lge, mkd pitch, hdstg, pt sl, shd; htd wc; mv service pnt; shwrs inc; el pnts (6-10A) €2.50-4.30; lndtte; shop; tradsmn; snacks; playgrnd; shgl beach & lake sw; boating, fishing; tennis; cycle hire; entmnt high ssn; TV; 20% statics; dogs €1; poss cr; adv bkg; quiet. "Attractive walks; lake views fr some pitches; vg site." ♦ € 13.00 2009*

RODEZ *7D4* (1km NE Urban) *44.35323, 2.58708* **Camp Municipal de Layoule, 12000 Rodez [05 65 67 09 52; fax 05 65 67 11 43; contact@mairie-rodez.fr; www.mairie-rodez.fr]** Clearly sp in Rodez town cent & all app rds. Access at bottom steep hill thro residential area. Med, hdg/mkd pitches, hdstg, pt shd; wc (poss cont only low ssn); chem disp; mv service pnt; shwrs inc; el pnts (6A) €3; lndry rm; shop 1km; tradsmn; playgrnd; pool, golf, tennis nrby; no statics; no dogs; phone; quiet; CCI. "Gd sized pitches; helpful warden; clean facs; steep walk to historic town; gates clsd 2000-0700; 2 exits fr site, 1 uphill & poss v diff; excel." ♦ 1 Jun-30 Sep. € 13.00 (3 persons) 2009*

ROESCHWOOG *5D3* (1km W Rural) *48.83215, 8.01916* **Camping du Staedly, 30 Rue de l'Etang, 67480 Roeschwoog [tel/fax 03 88 86 42 18; cc-uffried@cc-uffried.com]** Exit A35 junc 53 or 55 onto D468. Fr traff lts in cent of Roeschwoog go W sp Leutenheim into Rue de la Gare twd rlwy stn, cross rlwy & turn L immed to site. Med, mkd pitch, pt shd; htd wc; chem disp; shwrs inc; el pnts (6A) €3.10; Indtte; shop 2km; snacks; bar; lake sw; games area; TV; many statics; adv bkg; noisy Fri & Sat (bar). 1 Apr-31 Oct. € 9.00 2008*

ROHAN *2F3* (200m NW Rural) *48.07078, -2.75525* **Camp Municipal du Val d'Oust, Rue de St Gouvry, 56580 Rohan [02 97 51 57 58 or 02 97 51 50 33 (Mairie); fax 02 97 51 52 11; mairie.rohan@wanadoo.fr]** Rue de St Gouvry runs NW fr Rohan parallel to D11, but other side of canal. Sm, mkd pitch, pt shd; wc; chem disp (wc); shwrs inc; el pnts €2.70; Indtte; shop, rest, snacks & bar 200m; BBQ; playgrnd; dogs €0.90; phone; adv bkg; CCI. "Pleasant site beside Nantes/Brest canal; gd cycling." ♦ 15 Jun-15 Sep. € 8.70 2008*

ROMAGNE SOUS MONTFAUCON see Dun sur Meuse *5C1*

ROMANSWILLER see Wasselonne *6E3*

ROMIEU, LA *8E2* (300m NE Rural) *43.98299, 0.50183* **Kawan Village Le Camp de Florence, 32480 La Romieu [05 62 28 15 58; fax 05 62 28 20 04; info@lecampdeflorence.com; www.lecampdeflorence.com]** Take D931 N fr Condom & turn R onto D41, where La Romieu sp next to radio mast. Go thro La Romieu & turn L at sp just bef leaving vill. Lge, hdg pitch, some hdstg, pt shd; wc; chem disp; mv service pnt; baby facs; shwrs inc; el pnts (10A) inc (poss rev pol); Indtte; shops in vill; tradsmn; rest in 16thC farmhouse; snacks; bar; BBQ; playgrnd; pool; paddling pool; waterslide; jacuzzi; leisure complex 500m; tennis; cycle hire; games area; archery; clay pigeon-shooting; entmnt, excursions high ssn; wifi; TV/games rm; many statics; dogs €2.25; Eng spkn; adv bkg ess; quiet; ccard acc; red low ssn; CCI. "Peaceful Dutch-run site in pleasant location; welcoming, helpful staff; gd sized pitches, most with views; poss muddy when wet; clean san facs, ltd low ssn - 2nd block in need of renovation (2008); some noise fr disco, ask for pitch away fr bar; facs some dist fr touring pitches; nice pool but take care sl ent; mkt Wed Condom." ♦ 1 Apr-10 Oct. € 31.90 (CChq acc) ABS - D19 2009*

⊞ **ROMILLY SUR SEINE** *4E4* (4km W Rural) *48.5259, 3.6646* **Camping du Domaine de la Noue des Rois, Chemin des Brayes, 10100 St Hilaire-sous-Romilly [03 25 24 41 60; fax 03 25 24 34 18; contact@lanouedesrois.com; www.lanouedesrois.com]** Site sp fr D619 (N19), on rvside. Lge, mkd pitch, pt shd; htd wc; mv service pnt; baby facs; shwrs; el pnts (16A) €3.50-5; gas; Indtte; shop; tradsmn; rest; bar; playgrnd; htd, covrd pool; paddling pool; waterslide; fishing; sailing; watersports; tennis; games area; entmnt; 90% statics; dogs (on lead) €3.50; Eng spkn; adv bkg; quiet; ccard acc; red long stay/low ssn; CCI. "Gd situation in wooded area; conv Paris & Disneyland; ltd pitches/facs for tourers." ♦ € 30.00 2009*

ROMORANTIN LANTHENAY *4G2* (500m E Urban) *47.35486, 1.75586* **Camping de Tournefeuille, Rue de Long Eaton, 41200 Romorantin-Lanthenay [02 54 76 16 60; fax 02 54 76 00 34; camping.romo@wanadoo.fr; www.jmonnet-romorantin.com/camping/]** Fr town cent on D724 to Salbis, foll sp thro several traff lts over bdge turn R into Rue de Long-Eaton, site sp. Med, pt shd; htd wc; shwrs inc; el pnts (6A) €2.50; gas; shop 500m; snacks; pool adj; playgrnd; fishing; cycle hire; quiet. "Rv walk to town rec." 1 Apr-30 Sep. € 13.00 (3 persons) 2007*

RONCE LES BAINS see Tremblade, La *7B1*

RONDE, LA see Courçon *7A2*

ROQUE D'ANTHERON, LA see Cadenet *10E3*

ROQUE GAGEAC, LA see Sarlat la Canéda *7C3*

ROQUEBRUN *10F1* (300m SE Rural) *43.49775, 3.02834* **Camp Municipal Le Nice, Rue du Temps Libre, 34460 Roquebrun [04 67 89 61 99 or 04 67 89 79 97; fax 04 67 89 78 15; camping-campotel@wanadoo.fr; www.camping-lenice.com]** N112 to St Chinian & take D20 dir Cessenon-sur-Orb, turn L onto D14 twd Roquebrun; site on L bef bdge over rv. Sm, mkd pitch, some hdstg, pt sl, terr, pt shd; wc (some cont); chem disp; mv service pnt; shwrs inc; el pnts (6A) €2.50; Indtte; shops, rest, snack, bar 1km; playgrnd; rv sw & shgl beach adj; rv sw, fishing, sailing, canoe hire adj; tennis; entmnt; 15% statics; dogs €1.30; phone; poss cr; adv bkg; quiet; ccard acc; CCI. "Excel cent for walking & cycling; beautiful scenery; ltd touring pitches; some gd, modern san facs." 10 Mar-10 Nov. € 12.00 2009*

ROQUEBRUNE SUR ARGENS see Fréjus *10F4*

ROQUEFORT *8E2* (2.5km S Rural) *44.02093, -0.31032* **Camp Municipal, Route de Pau, 40120 Sarbazan [05 58 45 64 93 (Mairie); fax 05 58 45 69 91]** Fr Roquefort take D934 S twd Villeneuve-de-Marsan & Pau. In 2km camp sp on L in Sarbazan. Sm, mkd pitch, pt sl, shd; wc (some cont); shwrs inc; el pnts (5A) €1.60-2.40 (poss rev pol); Indtte; shops 2.5km; tradsmn; BBQ; playgrnd; tennis; dogs; quiet; red low ssn; CCI. "Peaceful, friendly; site yourself, warden calls am & pm; dated, clean san facs; some pitches soft after heavy rain; nr arena; highly rec." ♦ 1 Apr-30 Oct. € 9.00 2009*

ROQUELAURE see Auch *8F3*

ROQUES see Toulouse *8F3*

ROQUETTE SUR SIAGNE, LA see Cannes *10F4*

France

ROSANS *9D3* (1.5km N Rural) *44.39547, 5.46094* **Camping Tamier Naturiste (Naturist), Route du Col de Pomerol, Tamier 05150 Rosans [04 92 66 61 55 or 06 80 23 64 81 (mob); fax 04 92 87 47 24; tamier@wanadoo.fr; www.naturisme-tamier.fr]** Off D94/D994 Serres to Nyons rd; turn N onto D25 at Rosans. Site sp in vill. Med, mkd pitch, terr, pt shd; htd wc; chem disp; shwrs inc; el pnts (6A) inc; lndtte; shop; tradsmn; rest; snacks; bar; playgrnd; pool; games area; some statics; TV; adv bkg; quiet; ccard acc; red low ssn. "Wonderful scenery; friendly owners; v steep access rd; suggest park in upper car park nr ent bef going to recep." 15 Apr-15 Oct. € 23.40 2009*

ROSANS *9D3* (4km W Rural) *44.38523, 5.42540* **Aire Naturelle Le Gessy (Cagossi), 26510 Verclause [tel/fax 04 75 27 80 39 or 06 84 14 69 01 (mob); legessy@hotmail.com]** Site sp fr vill; 2km up steep, narr, winding rd. Sm, hdstg, sl, terr, pt shd; wc; chem disp (wc); shwrs inc; el pnts(6-10A) €2.50; supmkt & rest 2km; snacks; playgrnd; pool; 10% statics; dogs €2; Eng spkn; adv bkg; quiet; CCI. "Spacious pitches; gd views; vg." 1 Apr-15 Oct. € 12.50 2006*

ROSCANVEL *2E1* (500m S Coastal) *48.30893, -4.55851* **Camp Municipal Le Kervian, Route du Camping, 29570 Roscanvel [02 98 27 43 23 or 02 98 27 48 51 (Mairie); fax 02 98 27 41 10]** Fr Crozon foll D355 dir Le Fret/Roscanvel. After Le Fret x-rds foll Municipal sp. Turn L just bef Roscanvel. Sm, mkd pitch, terr, unshd; wc (some cont); chem disp (wc); shwrs inc; el pnts (10A) €3.18; gas 1km; lndry rm; shop & bar 1km; tradsmn; playgrnd; sand beach 800m; horseriding nrby; some statics; dogs €1.06; phone adj; Eng spkn; quiet; ccard not acc; CCI. "Gd views; gd." 15 Jun-15 Sep. € 8.00 2006*

ROSCOFF *1D2* (7km SW Coastal/Rural) *48.67142, -4.05088* **Camp Municipal du Bois de la Palud, 29250 Plougoulm [02 98 29 81 82 or 02 98 29 90 76 (Mairie); mairie-de-plougoulm@wanadoo.fr]** Fr D58 turn W on D10 sp Cléder/Plouescat; after 3km on ent Plougoulm foll sp to site. Sm, hdg/mkd pitch, terr, pt shd; wc; chem disp; shwrs inc; el pnts (8A) €3.50; lndry rm; shop 800m; sand beach 500m; playgrnd; phone; some Eng spkn; adv bkg; quiet; ccard acc; CCI. "Clean, tidy site in delightful area; conv ferry; if arr late, site yourself; warden calls am & pm; access all hrs with c'van; walk in first, turning diff inside; sh walk to vill; excel." ♦ 14 Jun-6 Sep. € 12.50 2009*

ROSCOFF *1D2* (10km SW Coastal) *48.69033, -4.13879* **Camping Village de Roguennic, 29233 Cléder [02 98 69 63 88; fax 02 98 61 95 45; semcleder@wanadoo.fr; www.campingvillageroguennic.com]** Fr D10 bet St Pol-de-Léon & Lesneven, take coast rd at either Plouescat or Cléder, foll Camping sp twd sea. Site sp. Lge, mkd pitch, pt sl, pt shd; wc; mv service pnt; shwrs inc; el pnts (6A) €2.15; gas; lndtte; shop, rest, snacks, bar (high ssn); playgrnd; htd pool (high ssn); sand beach adj; tennis; games area; sailing school nr; entment; statics sep area; dogs €1; phone; bus; adv bkg; quiet; ccard acc; CCI. "Holiday vill, lovely early ssn; direct access to beach." ♦ 1 May-15 Sep. € 13.10 2006*

ROSCOFF *1D2* (3.5km W Coastal) *48.71411, -4.00866* **Camping aux Quatre Saisons, Perharidy, Le Ruguel, 29680 Roscoff [02 98 69 70 86; fax 02 98 61 15 74; camping.roscoff@wanadoo.fr; www.camping-aux4saisons.com]** Fr dock foll exit & camping sps; at rndbt exit N on D169 twd cent ville; in 800m turn W dir Santec, foll camping sps, pass travellers' site. Lge, hdg pitch, unshd; wc; chem disp; shwrs inc; baby facs; el pnts (4-8A) €2.70-4.30; lndtte; shops 2km; BBQ; playgrnd; sand beach; windsurfing; fishing; sailing; entmnt; dogs €1; poss cr; adv bkg rec high ssn; red low ssn; quiet. "Will open low ssn if bkd in adv; conv for ferry; cheap & cheerful." ♦ 1 Apr-11 Oct. € 11.50 2007*

ROSIERES *9D2* (4km S Rural) *44.46423, 4.27278* **Camping Arleblanc, 07260 Rosières [04 75 39 53 11; fax 04 75 39 93 98; info@arleblanc.com; www.arleblanc.com]** S fr Aubenas on D104, turn L at Intermarché, site in 2.8km down lane to site by Rv Baume. Lge, mkd pitch, shd; wc (some cont); chem disp; shwrs inc; el pnts (10A) €3.75; gas; lndtte; shop; tradsmn; rest; bar; playgrnd; pool; canoeing; tennis; entmnt; TV rm; 40% statics; dogs free; poss cr; adv bkg; v quiet; CCI. "Excel family-run site; lge pitches." ♦ 15 Mar-31 Oct. € 23.00 2008*

ROSIERS SUR LOIRE, LES *4G1* (1km N Rural) *47.35908, -0.22500* **FLOWER Camping Val de Loire, 6 Rue Ste Baudruche, 49350 Les Rosiers-sur-Loire [02 41 51 94 33; fax 02 41 51 89 13; contact@camping-valdeloire.com; www.camping-valdeloire.com or www.flowercamping.com]** Take D952 fr Saumur in dir Angers. Site on D59 1km N of vill cent on L dir Beaufort-en-Vallée. Med, hdg/mkd pitch, hdstg, pt shd; wc; chem disp; mv service pnt; baby facs; 50% serviced pitch; shwrs inc; el pnts (10A) €4.50; gas; lndtte; tradsmn; rest; snacks; bar; BBQ; playgrnd; htd pool; paddling pool; lake sw 15km; waterslide; tennis; games rm; internet; entmnt; TV rm; 15% statics; dogs €2.50; Eng spkn; adv bkg; quiet; red long stay/low ssn; CCI. "Close to Rv Loire; lge pitches; friendly, helpful staff; excel san facs; gd touring base for chateaux region; excel." ♦ 1 Apr-30 Sep. € 21.00 2009*

ROSIERS SUR LOIRE, LES *4G1* (6km NW Rural) *47.39231, -0.27381* **Camping Port St Maur, 49250 La Ménitré [02 41 45 60 80; fax 02 41 45 65 65; info@loiredelumiere.com; www.loiredelumiere.com]** Exit Les Rosiers on D952 sp Angers. Site on L by rv. Med, mkd pitch, pt shd; wc; shwrs inc; el pnts (5A) €2.30; lndtte; shops 1km; rest; snacks; bar; playgrnd; games area; entmnt; boat trips on Loire; some statics; dogs €1; some rd & rlwy noise. "Access to san facs by steps; helpful warden." ♦ 1 May-15 Sep. € 7.60 2008*

⊞ **ROSNAY** *4H2* (500m N Rural) *46.70647, 1.21161* **Camp Municipal Les Millots, Route de St Michel-en-Brenne, 36300 Rosnay [02 54 37 80 17 (Mairie); fax 02 54 37 02 86; rosnay-mairie@wanadoo.fr]** NE on D27 fr Le Blanc to Rosnay; site sp 500m N of Rosnay on D44. Sm, some mkd pitch, pt shd; htd wc; chem disp; baby facs; shwrs inc; el pnts (3-6A) €1.90-3.20 (rev pol); lndry rm; rest & shop 500m; BBQ; playgrnd;lake fishing; cycling; tennis; dogs; phone; poss cr; adv bkg; quiet; CCI. "Lovely, well-kept, tranquil, popular site; excel, clean san facs; warden collects fees twice daily; lakeside walks; birdwatching; excel." ♦ € 7.50 2008*

ROSPORDEN *2F2* (8km W) *47.95025, -3.96744* **Village Center Le Bois de Pleuven, 29140 St Yvi [02 98 94 70 47; www.village-center.com]** Site sp fr Rosporden-Quimper D765, or Concarneau-Quimper D783. Turn S at St Yvi & turn R at x-rds; foll site sp. Lge, mkd pitch, shd; wc; baby facs; shwrs inc; el pnts (6A) inc; gas; lndtte; shop; snacks; bar; playgrnd; htd pool; beach 5km; tennis; cycle hire; entmnt; TV rm; 90% statics; dogs €0.50; adv bkg; red low ssn; quiet. "Site in woodland." 1 Apr-15 Oct. € 20.00 2007*

⊞ **ROSTRENEN** *2E2* (2km S Rural) *48.23063, -3.29881* **Camping Fleur de Bretagne, Kerandouaron, 22110 Rostrenen [02 96 29 16 45 or 02 96 29 15 45; fax 02 96 29 16 45; info@fleurdebretagne.com; www.fleurde bretagne.com]** Fr Rostrenen town cent foll dir Champion supmkt & take next R turn sp D31 Silfiac. In approx 1km turn L, site sp. Med, mkd pitch, pt sl, terr, pt shd; wc; chem disp; mv service pnt; shwrs inc; el pnts (6A) €3; lndry rm; shop 2km; snacks; bar; BBQ; playgrnd; pool; fishing lake; watersports, horseriding nr; dogs €2; phone; Eng spkn; adv bkg; quiet; red long stay; CCI. "Helpful British owners; wooded walks; ltd opening Nov-Mar - phone ahead; facs in need of refurb." ♦ € 12.00 2007*

ROUEN *3C2* (4km N Urban) *49.47009, 1.04669* **Camp Municipal, Rue Jules Ferry, 76250 Déville-lès-Rouen [02 35 74 07 59 or 02 32 82 34 80 (Mairie)]** Fr Rouen take A150 N twd Dieppe; in Déville turn L at traff lts immed after Hôtel de Ville, foll sp to site. Fr Le Havre at Barentin, turn R onto old N15, thro Maromme, turn R after 3 traff lts. Med, unshd, gravel pitch; wc; chem disp; mv service pnt; shwrs inc; el pnts (10A) €2.30; supmkt 500m; playgrnd; pool 300m; some statics; dogs €1; bus to Rouen; poss cr; adv bkg; noise fr adj factory & rd. "Facs poss tired/unclean but upgrade planned; narr pitches; site office clsd w/end & pubic hols; poss mkt traders; phone ahead to check site open low ssn; NH only." 1 Mar-31 Oct. € 12.40 2009*

⊞ **ROUEN** *3C2* (5km E Urban) *49.43154, 1.15387* **Camping L'Aubette, 23 Rue du Vert Buisson, 76160 St Léger-du-Bourg-Denis [tel/fax 02 35 08 47 69]** Fr Rouen E on N31 dir Darnétal & Beauvais; in 1km cont strt on onto D42/D138 dir St Léger-du-Bourg-Denis; in 400m turn L onto Rue du Vert Buisson; site on L in 800m. Site well sp as 'Camping' fr Rouen cent. Med, pt sl, terr, pt shd; wc (mainly cont); shwrs €1.60; el pnts (3-10A) €1.50-3; shops 400m; 50% statics; poss cr. "In attractive rv valley; conv city cent." € 9.10 2007*

ROUEN *3C2* (13km NW Rural) *49.50553, 0.98409* **Camping Les Nenuphars, 765 Rue des Deux Tilleuls, Le Bout du Haut, 76480 Roumare [02 35 33 80 75; camping.les.nenuphars@wanadoo.fr; http://camping-les-nenuphars.ifrance.com]** S on D6015/A150 dir Rouen, foll sp Roumare & site. Fr Rouen take N15/D6015 N to St Jean-du-Cardonnay; turn L to Roumare; site sp. 500m bef Roumare. Med, hdg/mkd pitch, unshd; htd san facs; el pnts (5-10A) €2.50-3; lndtte; playgrnd; 50% statics; site clsd 16 Feb-29 Mar; dogs €1; adv bkg; quiet. "Member reported site neglected (2009); NH only." € 12.00 2007*

ROUFFACH *6F3* (W Urban) *47.9557, 7.2964* **Camp Municipal, 4 Rue de la Piscine, 68250 Rouffach [03 89 49 78 13; fax 03 89 78 03 09; campingmunicipal.rouffach@orange.fr]** On D83 (N83) S fr Colmar bet Colmar & Cernay. Foll sp 'Sport, Loisirs, Piscine'. Sm, pt shd; htd wc; chem disp; mv service pnt; shwrs €1.50; el pnts (6A) €2.50; lndry rm; shop 500m; pool nr; quiet; CCI. "Clean site; pitch self, contact office when open; vg NH." 1 May-30 Sep. € 6.40 2009*

ROUFFIGNAC *7C3* (300m N Rural) *45.05473, 0.98708* **Camping Bleu Soleil, Domaine Touvent, 24580 Rouffignac-St-Cernin-de-Reilhac [05 53 05 48 30; fax 05 53 05 27 87; infos@bleusoleil.com; www.camping-bleusoleil.com]** On D6 in Rouffignac, take D31 NE twd Thenon. Site clearly sp on R after 300m. Med, hdg/mkd pitch, pt sl, terr, pt shd; wc; chem disp; 75% serviced pitches; shwrs inc; el pnts (6-10A) €2.90; lndtte; shop; tradsmn; rest, snacks & bar high ssn; BBQ; playgrnd; htd pool; tennis; games rm; TV rm; 10% statics; dogs €1.50; phone; Eng spkn; adv bkg; quiet; red low ssn; ccard acc; CCI. "Relaxing site with views nr pretty vill; friendly, helpful owners; ltd facs low ssn; poss diff for lge o'fits; excel." ♦ 1 Apr-30 Sep. € 16.10 2007*

ROUFFIGNAC *7C3* (6km SW Rural) **Camping Le Coteau de l'Herm (Naturist), Route du Château de l'Herm, 24580 Rouffignac [05 53 46 67 77; fax 05 53 05 74 87; info@naturisme-dordogne.com; www.naturisme-dordogne.com]** Exit A89 junc 17 onto D6089 to Thenon; 1km past Thenon turn L onto D31 sp Rouffignac. In approx 10km turn R dir Prisse, site on L in 2km. Sm, mkd pitch, terr, pt sl, pt shd; htd wc; chem disp; shwrs inc; el pnts (4-10A) €3.50-4.50; gas; lndtte; shop; tradsmn; bar; snacks; BBQ; playgrnd; pool; cycle hire; dogs €3.75; Eng spkn; adv bkg; quiet; red long stay; CCI. "Excel site & facs; gd access; helpful Dutch owners; delightful location." ♦ 15 May-16 Sep. € 23.00 2008*

ROUSSET see Chorges *9D3*

ROUSSET, LE *9A2* (1.5km N Rural) *46.57866, 4.45033* **Camping du Lac de Rousset, 71220 Le Rousset [03 85 24 68 74; fax 03 85 24 68 00]** Fr Montceau-les-Mines S on D980; in 10 km turn R onto D33; well sp. Sm, mkd pitch, pt sl, pt shd; wc, chem disp; shwrs inc; el pnts (6A) €2; snacks (high ssn); playgrnd; lake sand beach adj; no statics; quiet; CCI. "Lakeside, CL-type site in beautiful location; basic facs; fair." 3 Mar-10 Oct. € 9.00 2007*

France

ROUSSILLON *10E2* (2.5km SW Rural) *43.88973, 5.27596* **Camping L'Arc-en-Ciel, Route de Goult, 84220 Roussillon [04 90 05 73 96; campingarcenciel@wanadoo.fr]** Take D900 (N100) W out of Apt, then R on D201 sp Roussillon, then R on D4 for 1.5km, then L on D104 twd Roussillon. Take L fork twd Goult, site well sp 2.5km on L. No access for c'vans & m'vans in Roussillon vill. Med, mkd pitch, hdstg, pt sl, terr, pt shd; wc (some cont); chem disp; shwrs inc; el pnts (4A) €3.30; gas; Indry rm; sm shop & 2.5km (uphill); tradsmn; snacks; bar; playgrnd; pool; children's pool; games area; phone; adv bkg; quiet; CCI. "Tranquil site in former ochre quarry; helpful staff; gd san facs; beware rd humps & drainage channels on site access rds; worth a detour; vg." ♦ 15 Mar-31 Oct. € 12.50 2009*

ROYAN *7B1* (6km NE Rural) *45.64796, -0.95847* **FFCC Camping Le Bois Roland, 82 Route de Royan, 17600 Médis [tel/fax 05 46 05 47 58; bois.roland@wanadoo.fr; www.le-bois-roland.com]** On N150 Saintes-Royan rd, site sp on R 100m beyond Médis vill sp. Med, pt shd; wc (some cont); chem disp; shwrs inc; el pnts (5-10A) €4.20-5; gas; Indtte (inc dryer); shop & 600m; tradsmn; snacks; bar; playgrnd; pool; paddling pool; sand beach 4km; entmnt; TV; dogs €2.80; phone; poss cr; adv bkg; Eng spkn; quiet; ccard acc; CCI. "Attractive, family-run wooded site; facs poss stretched high ssn; vg." ♦ 11 Apr-30 Sep. € 18.50 2009*

ROYAN *7B1* (5km E Rural) *45.62991, -0.94626* **Camping Le Clos Fleuri, 8 Impasse du Clos Fleuri, 17600 Médis [05 46 05 62 17; fax 05 46 06 75 61; clos-fleuri@wanadoo.fr; www.le-clos-fleuri.com]** On N150 Saintes-Royan rd turn S in Médis dir Semussac. Well sp. Med, hdg/mkd pitch, shd; wc (cont); baby facs; fam bathrm; sauna; shwrs inc; el pnts (5-10A) €4.50-5.80; Indtte; shop in ssn & 2km; tradsmn; rest, snacks & bar in ssn; playgrnd; pool; sand beach 7km; games area; ltd entmnt; TV; 10% statics; dogs €3.50; phone; Eng spkn; adv bkg; quiet; ccard acc; red low ssn; CCI. "Lovely, peaceful, family-run site; san facs clean but dated; rec for young families; access poss diff lge o'fits; some pitches dark due o'hanging trees; excel, under-used site." ♦ 1 Jun-15 Sep. € 26.50 2008*

⊞ **ROYAN** *7B1* (1.7km SE Coastal) *45.61817, -1.00425* **Camping La Triloterie, 44 ter, Ave Aliénor d'Aquitaine, 17200 Royan [05 46 05 26 91; fax 05 46 06 20 74; info@campingroyan.com; www.campingroyan.com]** Fr Royan PO, foll sp Bordeaux N730, on E of rd. Med, shd; htd wc; chem disp; mv service pnt; baby facs; shwrs inc; el pnts (4-12A) €3.50-5.50 (poss rev pol); shops 500m; BBQ; playgrnd; waterslide; sand beach 900m; wifi; entmnt; some statics; dogs €1.50; phone; poss cr/noisy high ssn; some rd noise; red low ssn. € 21.00 2009*

ROYAN *7B1* (6km SE Coastal) *45.58345, -0.98720* **Camping Bois-Soleil, 2 Ave de Suzac, 17110 St Georges-de-Didonne [05 46 05 05 94; fax 05 46 06 27 43; camping.bois.soleil@wanadoo.fr; www.bois-soleil.com]** Fr A10 exit junc 35 dir Saintes & Royan; on app Royan foll St Georges-de-Didonne sp onto bypass D25/D730/D25/D25E; go over 2 rndabts (with underpass between); at 3rd rndabt turn L sp Meschers-sur-Gironde; site on R in 500m. Site well sp. Lge, hdg/mkd pitch, hdstg, terr, pt shd; htd wc (some cont); chem disp; mv service pnt; baby facs; shwrs inc; el pnts (6A) inc (poss rev pol); gas; Indtte; shop; tradsmn; rest; snacks; bar; BBQ (gas); playgrnd; htd pool; paddling pool; dir access to sand beach adj; tennis; games area; wifi; entmnt; TV rm; 30% statics; dogs €3 (not acc end Jun-Aug inc); phone; poss cr; Eng spkn; adv bkg rec (ess Jul/Aug); ccard acc; red low ssn; CCI. "Superb wooded site in vg location nr beach; popular & busy; pitches sm & poss tight for lge o'fits, some sandy; excel, clean san facs; vg shop & rest." ♦ 3 Apr-10 Oct. € 40.00 (3 persons) (CChq acc) 2009*

See advertisement

ROYAN *7B1* (6km SE Coastal) *45.59253, -0.98713* **Camping Idéal, Ave de Suzac, 17110 St Georges-de-Didonne [05 46 05 29 04; fax 05 46 06 32 36; info@ideal-camping.com; www.ideal-camping.com]** Fr Royan foll coast rd sp St Georges-de-Didonne. Site sp on D25 2km S of St Georges, opp Cmp Bois-Soleil. Lge, mkd pitch, shd; wc (some cont); chem disp; shwrs inc; el pnts (6-10A) €4.10-4.90; gas; lndtte; shop; tradsmn; rest; snacks; bar; playgrnd; htd pool; paddling pool; waterslide; jacuzzi; sand beach 200m; tennis 500m; games area; games rm; cycle hire; horseriding 300m; entmnt; phone; some statics; no dogs; poss noisy (bar); ccard acc; red low ssn; CCI. ♦ 7 May-6 Sep. € 26.70 (3 persons) 2008*

ROYAN *7B1* (10km SE) *45.55713, -0.94655* **Camping Soleil Levant, Allée de la Langée, 17132 Meschers-sur-Gironde [05 46 02 76 62; fax 05 46 02 50 56; info@camping-soleillevant.com; www.camping-soleillevant.com]** Take D145 coast rd fr Royan to Talmont. At Meschers turn R foll camp sp twd port; sp. Med, pt shd; wc (some cont); chem disp; shwrs inc; el pnts (10A) €4.60; gas 1km; lndtte; snacks; bar; shop; playgrnd; sand beach 1.5km; free pool & paddling pool; watersports & horseriding adj; 20% statics; dogs €3; adv bkg; quiet; ccard acc; CCI. "Gd, busy site; sm pitches, some diff to get into; san facs poss unclean (2009); port & rest 300m; vill shop & daily mkt 500m; visits to Cognac & Bordeaux distilleries." 1 Apr-30 Sep. € 17.70 2009*

ROYAN *7B1* (2km SW Coastal/Urban) *45.61509, -0.99472* **Village Center - Les Catalpas, 45 Chemin d'Enlias, 17110 St Georges-de-Didonne [05 46 05 84 97 or 04 99 57 20 25; fax 04 99 57 21 22; www.village-center.com]** Site sp in St Georges-de-Didonne. Med, mkd pitch, pt shd; wc; chem disp; baby facs; shwrs; el pnts (6A) inc; gas; lndtte; shop; tradsmn; supmkt 500m; rest; snacks; bar; playgrnd; htd pool; sand beach 1.5km; entmnt; 7% statics; dogs €3; Eng spkn; adv bkg; quiet. ♦ 28 Apr-16 Sep. € 23.00 2007*

ROYAN *7B1* (2km NW Urban) *45.64470, -1.04160* **Camping Le Royan, 10 Rue des Bleuets, 17200 Royan [05 46 39 09 06; fax 05 46 38 12 05; camping.le.royan@wanadoo.fr; www.le-royan.com]** Take D25 by-pass fr Royan dir La Palmyre. Site sp. Lge, mkd pitch, hdstg, pt sl, pt shd; wc (some cont); chem disp; mv service pnt; baby facs; some serviced pitches; shwrs inc; el pnts (10A) inc; gas; lndtte; shop; rest; snacks; bar; BBQ; playgrnd; htd pool; paddling pool; waterslide; spa; sand beach 2.5km; lake sw 3km; solarium; games area; games rm; cycle hire; entmnt; TV; 25% statics; dogs €3; poss cr; adv bkg; quiet; ccard acc; red low ssn/long stay/CCI. "Friendly, helpful owners; excel pool complex." ♦ 1 Apr-10 Oct. € 30.50 (3 persons) 2006*

ROYAN *7B1* (4km NW Urban/Coastal) *45.6309, -1.0498* **CAMPEOLE Camping Clairefontaine, 6 Rue du Colonel Lachaud, 17200 Royan-Pontaillac [05 46 39 08 11; fax 05 46 38 13 79; clairefontaine@campeole.com; www.camping-clairefontaine.com or www.campeole.com]** Foll Pontaillac sp fr Royan. Site sp in Clairefontaine (& Pontaillac). Lge, mkd pitch, pt shd; wc (some cont); chem disp; mv service pnt; fam bthrm; serviced pitches; shwrs inc; el pnts (5A) €4.10; gas; lndtte; tradsmn; shop; rest; snacks; bar; BBQ; playgrnd; 2 pools; sand beach 300m; tennis; casino 300m; TV rm; many statics; dogs €3; phone; Eng spkn; adv bkg (fee + dep req); quiet; ccard acc; red low ssn; CCI. "Gd for family holiday; ltd touring pitches; gd security; site poss dusty." ♦ 2 Apr-26 Sep. € 26.70 (3 persons) 2009*

ROYBON *9C2* (1km S Rural) *45.24639, 5.24806* **Camping de Roybon, Route de St Antoine, 38940 Roybon [04 76 36 23 67; fax 04 76 36 33 02; info@campingroybon.com; www.campingroybon.com]** Fr Roybon go S on D71 & foll sp. Med, mkd pitch, pt sl, pt shd; wc; chem disp; shwrs inc; el pnts (6A) €3.50; shops 1km; playgrnd; sw & watersports in lake adj; dogs €2.65; adv bkg; quiet; red low ssn. "V peaceful; gd, modern facs new; vg." ♦ 15 Apr-15 Oct. € 16.80 2009*

ROYERE DE VASSIVIERE *7B4* (6km SW Rural) *45.78869, 1.89855* **Camping Les Terrasses du Lac, Vauveix, 23460 Royère-de-Vassivière [05 55 64 76 77; fax 05 55 64 76 78; http://lesterrasses.camping.free.fr]** Fr Eymoutiers take D43 for approx 10km then take D36 to Vauveix & foll sp. Med, hdg/mkd pitch, terr, pt shd; htd wc; chem disp; shwrs inc; el pnts (10A) €3 (poss rev pol); lndtte; rest, bar 300m; snacks 500m; sand beach, sw & watersports adj; horseriding; walking; cycling; TV rm; dogs; phone 50m; quiet; CCI. "Helpful staff; lovely setting." ♦ 1 Apr-15 Oct. € 12.50 2006*

ROZIER, LE see Peyreleau *10E1*

RUE *3B2* (7km N Rural) *50.31367, 1.69472* **Kawan Village Le Val d'Authie, 20 Route de Vercourt, 80120 Villers-sur-Authie [03 22 29 92 47; fax 03 22 29 92 20; camping@valdauthie.fr; www.valdauthie.fr]** Best access via Rue or via D85/D485 fr D1001 (N1). Rd fr Vron to Villers-sur-Authie is narr single track across fields. Lge, hdg/mkd pitch, pt sl, pt shd; htd wc; chem disp; mv service pnt; sauna; steam rm; shwrs inc; baby facs; el pnts (6-10A) €5-8 (rev pol); gas; lndtte; shop; tradsmn; rest; snacks; bar; playgrnd; htd, covrd pool; paddling pool; sand beach 10km; tennis; games area; games rm; fitness rm; internet; entmnt; TV rm; 60% statics; dogs €1.50; phone; poss cr; Eng spkn; adv bkg; quiet but poss noise fr chalets/statics; ccard acc; red low ssn; CCI. "Set in pleasant countryside; helpful, friendly owners; clean, unisex facs & spacious shwrs; sm sep area for tourers, but many touring pitches bet statics (2009); poss diff for lge o'fits; gd pool; v cr & noisy high ssn; excel." ♦ 1 Apr-11 Oct. € 25.00 (3 persons) (CChq acc) 2009*

France

⊞ **RUFFEC** *7A2* (5km NE Rural) *46.07505, 0.26055* **Camping Rural La Renardière, 16700 Taizé-Aizie [05 45 71 74 59; la-renardiere@club-internet.fr; www.la-renardiere.eu]** Fr N, leave Civray on D1/D8; in 8km pass x-rds (L turn sp Lizant, R turn sp Voulème); take next L turn (dir Le Gros Chêne) bef x-ing Rv Charente; foll sm rd up hill; site in 1km on R bef hamlet of Le Gros Chêne. Sm, some hdg/mkd pitch, hdstg, pt shd; htd wc; fam bthrm; shwrs inc; el pnts (10A) €4; Indtte; tradsmn; snacks & meals; BBQ; playgrnd; pool; lake sw & fishing 3km; cycle hire; games area; games rm; wifi; dogs €1; clsd 3-12 Dec; adv bkg; quiet; ccard acc; red low ssn/long stay; CCI. "CL-type site with views; friendly British owners; basic san facs low ssn; vg pool; excel." ♦ € 11.00 2009*

RUFFEC *7A2* (3km SE Rural) *46.01500, 0.21304* **Camping Le Réjallant, Les Grands Champs, 16700 Condac [05 45 31 29 06 or 05 45 31 07 14; fax 05 45 31 34 76; cdc-ruffec-charente@wanadoo.fr]** Site sp fr N10 & fr town. App 1km fr turn-off. Med, hdg/mkd pitch, pt sl, shd; wc; chem disp (wc); shwrs inc; el pnts (10A) inc; Indtte; tradsmn; snacks; rest & bar 100m; sm playgrnd; rv sw, fishing 100m; dogs; Eng spkn; quiet; ccard not acc; CCI. "Some pitches v lge; clean facs - water poss v hot; shwrs ltd; gates open 0700-2100 high ssn; no entry/exit 1100-1600 low ssn; great for families." 15 May-15 Sep. € 13.00 2009*

⊞ **RUFFEC** *7A2* (10km W Rural) *46.00722, 0.09664* **Camping à la Ferme (Peloquin), Chassagne, 16240 Villefagnan [05 45 31 61 47; fax 05 45 29 55 87]** Exit N10 onto D740 W to Villefagnan. Site 1.8km SE of vill on D27. Sm, pt sl, pt shd; wc; chem disp (wc); shwrs; el pnts (10A) inc; Indtte; farm produce; shop, rest, snacks, bar 1.8km; playgrnd; pool high ssn; gites avail; dogs; poss cr; adv bkg; quiet. "Vg CL-type site; excel pool; gd cycle rtes." ♦ € 12.50 2008*

RUFFIEUX *9B3* (500m W Rural) *45.84932, 5.83441* **Camping Le Saumont, 73310 Ruffieux [04 79 54 26 26; camping.saumont@wanadoo.fr; www.campingsaumont.com]** N fr Aix-les-Bains take D991 N to Ruffieux, sp just bef Ruffieux at junc with D904. Sm, hdg/mkd pitch, pt shd; wc; chem disp; serviced pitch; shwrs; el pnts (6A) inc; Indtte; shop 1.5km; snacks; bar; BBQ; playgrnd; 2 pools; lake & rv sw 2.5km; tennis; cycle hire; 10% statics; dogs €1.80; adv bkg; quiet; red low ssn. "Dusty rd thro site when hot & dry; muddy after rain." 1 May-26 Sep. € 20.00 2009*

RUFFIEUX *9B3* (4km W Rural) *45.85255, 5.79274* **Camping Le Colombier, Ile de Verbaou, 01350 Culoz [tel/fax 04 79 87 19 00; camping.colombier@free.fr; http://camping.colombier.free.fr]** W fr Ruffieux or N fr Belley on D904, site sp off rndabt 1km E of Culoz. Med, hdg/mkd pitch, hdstg, pt shd; wc (some cont); chem disp; mv service pnt; baby facs; shwrs inc; el pnts (10A) €3; Indtte; shop 1km; tradsmn; rest; snacks; bar; playgrnd; lake sw adj; tennis; cycle hire; TV; some statics; dogs €1; phone; Eng spkn; adv bkg; quiet; ccard acc; red CCI. "Gd touring base; conv Annecy." ♦ 10 Apr-27 Sep. € 15.00 2007*

RUMILLY *9B3* (4km N Rural) *45.90229, 5.92738* **Camping Les Charmilles, Route de Seyssel, 74150 Vallières [04 50 62 10 60; fax 04 50 62 19 45; lescharmilles.camping@wanadoo.fr; www.campinglescharmilles.com]** Exit A41 junc 15 at Alby onto D3 to Rumilly; 4km N of Rumilly in Vallières exit D910 on D14 sp Seyssel. Site on L in 500m. Med, mkd pitch, pt shd; wc; baby facs; shwrs inc; el pnts (6A) €3.50; gas; Indtte; shops 500m; tradmsn; rest; snacks; bar; BBQ; playgrnd; pool; paddling pool; games area; entmnt; TV; dogs €1.50; phone; adv bkg; quiet; red low ssn. "Gd, modern san facs; pleasant situation." ♦ 1 Apr-30 Oct. € 15.00 2007*

RUOMS *9D2* (2km N Rural) *44.47655, 4.35858* **Camping Les Coudoulets, Chemin de l'Ardèche, 07120 Pradons [04 75 93 94 95; fax 04 79 39 65 89; camping@coudoulets.com; www.coudoulets.com]** Site sp fr D579. Med, mkd pitch, shd; wc; chem disp; mv service pnt; baby facs; shwrs inc; el pnts (6A) €4; Indtte; shop 300m; rest; snacks; bar; playgrnd; htd pool; paddling pool; rv fishing nr; games area; 5% statics; dogs €2.50; Eng spkn; adv bkg; quiet. "Site o'looks Rv Ardèche; friendly, careful owners; excel pool." ♦ 18 Apr-19 Sep. € 25.00 2009*

RUOMS *9D2* (3km N Rural) *44.47375, 4.35325* **Camping du Pont des Champs des Souliers, Route de Chauzon, Chemin du Cirque de Gens, 07120 Pradons [04 75 93 93 98; campingdupont07@wanadoo.fr; www.campingdupontardeche.com]** S fr Aubenas on D104, on o'skts of town take D579 to Pradons. Thro vill, bef end vill sp turn R onto D308 opp Netto supmkt to Chauzon. Site 300m on L, site sp. Med, hdg/mkd pitch, pt shd; wc (some cont); chem disp; shwrs inc; el pnts (6-10A) €3.80 Indtte; shop 100m; rest 300m; snacks; bar; BBQ; playgrnd; htd pool; rv sw & sand beach adj; canoe hire; games area; wifi; TV; 15% statics; dogs €2.20; phone; bus; Eng spkn; adv bkg; quiet; CCI. "Friendly owners; lovely, rugged area; vg." ♦ 15 Mar-30 Sep. € 21.50 2007*

RUOMS *9D2* (2km S Rural) *44.4375, 4.3419* **FFCC Camping Le Mas de Barry, Bévennes, 07120 Ruoms [04 42 54 27 68; fax 04 42 53 43 19; masdebarry@wanadoo.fr; www.masdebarry.com]** By-pass Ruoms on D579 sp Vallon-Pont-d'Arc. On D579, 100m N of junc with D111. Site on R. Med, mkd pitch, sl, pt shd; wc; baby facs; shwrs; el pnts (6A); gas; Indtte; shop; snacks; rest in ssn; bar; playgrnd; pool; some statics; no dogs; poss cr; Eng spkn; adv bkg; rd noise; ccard acc; CCI. "Quiet site in busy area; clean facs; helpful, welcoming manager." ♦ Apr-Oct. 2008*

RUOMS *9D2* (3km S Rural) *44.42761, 4.33561* **Yelloh! Village La Plaine, 07120 Ruoms [04 75 39 65 83; fax 04 75 39 74 38; camping.la.plaine@wanadoo.fr; www.camping-la-plaine.com or www.yellohvillage.com]** Exit Ruoms S on D579 dir Vallon-Pont-d'Arc; at junc in 2km turn S onto D111 dir St Ambroix. Site on L. Lge, mkd pitch, pt sl, pt shd; wc; baby facs; shwrs inc; el pnts (6A) inc; Indtte; shop; rest; snacks; bar; BBQ; playgrnd; rv sw, fishing & private beach; dogs €5; red low ssn; CCI. 5 Apr-14 Sep. € 40.00 2007*

RUOMS *9D2* (4km SW) *44.43101, 4.32945* **Camping La Chapoulière, 07120 Ruoms [tel/fax 04 75 39 64 98 or 04 75 93 90 72; camping@lachapouliere.com; www.lachapouliere.com]** Exit Ruoms S on D579. At junc 2km S, foll D111 sp St Ambroix. Site 1.5km fr junc. Med, mkd pitch, pt sl, shd; wc; mv service pnt; baby facs; shwrs inc; el pnts (6A) €4; gas; Indtte; shop in ssn & 3km; rest; snacks; bar; pool; paddling pool; rv sw & fishing adj; canoeing; tennis 2km; games area; entmnts; wifi; TV; dogs €2.50; Eng spkn; adv bkg rec high ssn; quiet; red low ssn. "Beautiful pitches on rv bank; friendly; ltd facs low ssn; vg." ♦ Easter-30 Sep. € 27.00 2008*

RUOMS *9D2* (7km SW Rural) *44.41350, 4.27195* **Camping Sunêlia Le Ranc Davaine, 07120 St Alban-Auriolles [04 75 39 60 55; fax 04 75 39 38 50; camping.ranc.davaine@wanadoo.fr; www.camping-ranc-davaine.fr]** Leave A7/E15 at Montélimar/Aubenas exit, foll sp twd Aubenas on N102. Just past Villeneuve-de-Berg turn L onto D103, thro St Germain, then join D579 to Ruoms. S of Ruoms leave D579 sp Gorges de l'Ardèche & join D111 twd Grospierres. At Les Tessiers turn R onto D246, sp St Alban-Auriolles. After x-ing Rv Chassezac turn L twd Chandolas, in approx 800m turn left at site sp. Lge, shd; wc; chem disp; baby facs; sauna; steam rm; shwrs inc; el pnts (6-10A) inc; Indtte; shop; rest; snacks; bar; BBQ (el only); playgrnd; pool complex (inc 1 htd, covrd); waterslide; paddling pool; fishing; tennis; archery; fitness cent; entmnt; wifi; games/TV rm; 75% statics; dogs €4.90; adv bkg; quiet; ccard acc. "Helpful staff; conv Gorges de l'Ardèche; public rd divides site; excel pool complex & playgrnd; mkt Mon." ♦
4 Apr-13 Sep. € 42.00 2008*

RUPT SUR MOSELLE see Remiremont *6F2*

RUSSEY, LE see Maîche *6G3*

RUYNES EN MARGERIDE *9C1* (4km E Rural) **Camping à la Ferme (Rolland), 15320 Clavières [04 71 23 45 50]** Fr St Flour, S on N9. After 7km turn L onto D4 thro Clavières & foll sps. Site in Chirol, foll Chirol sp. Sm, wc; shwrs inc; el pnts (long lead req); farm food avail; shops 2.5km; playgrnd; rv 2.5km; pool, tennis, golf, horseriding 10km; sailing, fishing 15km; quiet. "Isolated, with beautiful views, gd facs for a basic site; pay at old white house in Chirol." 1 Jun-30 Sep. € 4.57 2006*

RUYNES EN MARGERIDE *9C1* (300m SW Rural) *44.99910, 3.21893* **Camp Municipal du Petit Bois, 15320 Ruynes-en-Margeride [tel/fax 04 71 23 42 26; contact@revea-vacances.com; www.revea-vacances.fr/campings]** Fr St Flour S on N9. After 7km turn L onto D4. Site in 7km, sp. Or exit junc 30 fr A75, turn R into vill & foll sp. Lge, pt sl, pt shd; wc (some cont); chem disp; mv service pnt; baby facs; shwrs inc; el pnts (6-10A) €3.50; gas; Indtte; shops, rest, bar 500m; playgrnd; pool adj; some log cabins; dogs €1.50; phone; Eng spkn; adv bkg; quiet; ccard acc; CCI. "Scenic; v few flat pitches; excel san facs; barrier clsd 1200-1500; gd cent for walking, horseriding & fishing; used as field work cent in term time; gd." ♦ 5 May-16 Sep. € 14.70 (CChq acc) 2008*

SAALES *6E3* (W Rural) *48.34730, 7.09968* **Camp Municipal Rové, Route de la Grande Fosse, 67420 Saales [03 88 97 70 26 (Mairie); fax 03 88 97 77 39; www.mairie-saales.fr]** Fr St Dié take D420 twd Strasbourg, turn onto D32 in vill. Site on R just bef football pitch, well sp. Med, pt sl, terr, pt shd; wc; chem disp; shwrs inc; el pnts inc; shop & rest 500m; tennis, fishing adj; 40% statics; quiet. "Site yourself, warden calls." ♦ 15 Jun-15 Sep. 2007*

SABLE SUR SARTHE *4F1* (10km NE Rural) *47.86677, -0.20869* **Camp Municipal des Deux Rivières, 72430 Avoise [02 43 95 32 07 or 02 43 92 76 12; fax 02 43 95 62 48]** Fr Sablé take D309 twd Le Mans, after 10km thro vill of Parcé-sur-Sarthe, cont twds Le Mans & cross bdge over Rv Sarthe; sp for Avoise & camping sp on L; in cent Avoise on L 3rd car park. Site adj rv. Sm, hdg pitch, pt shd; wc; shwrs inc; el pnts inc (poss rev pol); gas; shops adj; Eng spkn; adv bkg; quiet; CCI. "Vg, pleasant, clean site; off beaten track." 4 Jun-4 Sep. € 6.30 2006*

SABLE SUR SARTHE *4F1* (500m S Rural) *47.83101, -0.33177* **Camp Municipal de l'Hippodrome, Allée du Québec, 72300 Sable-sur-Sarthe [02 43 95 42 61; fax 02 43 92 74 82; camping-sable@wanadoo.fr; www.sable-sur-sarthe.com]** Sp in town (foll sm, white sp with c'van symbols or Hippodrome). Suggested rte: foll Rue St Denis, Ave de Montreaux & Ave de la Vaige to Allée du Québec. Med, hdg pitch, pt shd; wc; shwrs inc; el pnts (15A) inc; gas; BBQ; Indry rm; sm shop; tradsmn; snacks; playgrnd; pool; rv fishing; boat & cycle hire; canoeing; entmnt; TV rm; Eng spkn; quiet; ccard acc; red long stay/low ssn. "Excel site; gd, clean facs; helpful staff; some pitches by rv, some diff for lge fits." ♦ 28 Mar-4 Oct. € 11.90 2009*

SABLES D'OLONNE, LES *7A1* (4km N Rural) *46.54738, -1.80518* **Camping de Sauveterre, 3 Rue des Amis de la Nature, 85340 Olonne-sur-Mer [02 51 33 10 58; fax 02 51 21 33 97; info@campingsauveterre.com; www.campingsauveterre.com]** Fr Les Sables-d'Olonne take D32 N to Olonne-sur-Mer; then D80 twds St Gilles-Croix-de-Vie for 3.5km; after 2nd rndabt site is on L. Med, mkd pitch, pt shd; wc (some cont); chem disp; shwrs inc; el pnts (6A) inc; gas; Indtte; shop; rest; snacks; bar; playgrnd; htd pool; paddling pool; waterslide; sand beach 1.5km; many statics; dogs €2.10; poss cr; adv bkg rec high ssn; quiet; red low ssn; CCI. "Gd walking/cycling." 1 Apr-30 Sep. € 20.80 2008*

SABLES D'OLONNE, LES *7A1* (4km N Rural) *46.53320, -1.79379* **Camping Nid d'Eté, 2 Rue de la Vigne Verte, 85340 Olonne-sur-Mer [02 51 95 34 38; fax 02 51 95 34 64; info@leniddete.com; www.leniddete.com]** Fr Les Sables-d'Olonne take D32 N to Olonne-sur-Mer. L onto D80 twd St Gilles-Croix-de-Vie. Immed over rlwy bdge turn L, site on L. Med, pt hdg/mkd pitch, pt shd; wc; chem disp; baby facs; shwrs inc; el pnts (6A) €3.80; Indtte; shop & 2km; snacks; playgrnd; htd, covrd pool high ssn; beach 3km; entmnt; few statics; dogs €2.50; c'van winter storage; adv bkg; v quiet; red low ssn; CCI. "Pleasant site; excel." 4 Apr-26 Sep. € 23.80 2009*

SABLES D'OLONNE, LES *7A1* (5km N Urban) *46.53166, -1.75843* **Camping Le Trianon, 95 Rue du Maréchal Joffre, 85340 Olonne-sur-Mer [02 51 23 61 61; fax 02 51 90 77 70; campingletrianon@wanadoo.fr; www.camping-le-trianon.com]** S on D160 La Roche-sur-Yon twd Les Sables-d'Olonne; at Pierre Levée turn R onto D80 sp Olonne-sur-Mer. Also sp fr D80 N. V lge, hdg/mkd pitch, pt shd, serviced pitches; wc; chem disp; shwrs inc; el pnts (6A) inc (extra for 10-16A); Indtte; shop; rest; snacks; bar; playgrnd; htd, covrd pool; waterslide; sand beach 5km; fishing & watersports 4km; tennis; golf; games area; entmnt; 40% statics; dogs €4.30; poss cr; adv bkg; quiet; red low ssn. "Pleasant situation; high kerbs into sm pitches; friendly, helpful staff; excel facs for families." ♦ 28 Mar-30 Sep. € 36.90 2009*

See advertisement on previous page

SABLES D'OLONNE, LES *7A1* (5km N Coastal) *46.54613, -1.80591* **Camping La Loubine, 1 Route de la Mer, 85340 Olonne-sur-Mer [02 51 33 12 92; fax 02 51 33 12 71; info@la-loubine.fr; www.la-loubine.fr]** Fr Les Sables-d'Olonne take D32 N to Olonne-sur-Mer then D80 dir St Gilles-Croix-de-Vie for 3.5km; turn L at junc to Plage-de-Sauveterre; ent to site immed on L after turn. Lge, hdg/mkd pitch, pt sl, pt shd; wc; chem disp; serviced pitches; shwrs inc; el pnts (5A) €3.65; gas; Indtte; shop; rest; snacks; bar; playgrnd; 2 htd pools (1 covrd); sand beach 1.8km; tennis; entmnt; TV; 50% statics; no dogs; poss cr; Eng spkn; adv bkg; noise fr rd & nightclub; ccard acc; CCI. "Site lit & guarded at night; lge car park for late arrivals; excel." ♦
4 Apr-30 Sep. € 27.00 2009*

See advertisement opposite

SABLES D'OLONNE, LES *7A1* (8km N Rural) *46.54934, -1.80654* **Camping Domaine de l'Orée, Route des Amis de la Nature, 85340 Olonne-sur-Mer [02 51 33 10 59; fax 02 51 33 15 16; www.l-oree.com]** Fr Les Sables-d'Olonne take D80 twd St Gilles-Croix-de-Vie for 4km - site on L after traff lts in Olonne-sur-Mer, well sp. Lge, hdg/mkd pitch, pt shd; wc; baby facs; shwrs inc; el pnts (6A) €4; gas; Indtte; shop; snacks; bar; playgrnd; htd pool; waterslide; sand beach 3km; tennis; horseriding; cycle hire; games area; games rm; entmnt; 90% statics; dogs €2.50; phone; Eng spkn; adv bkg; quiet; CCI. "Pleasant walk (30-40 mins) thro forest to vg beach; c'vans & tents for hire; helpful owner."
♦ 1 Apr-30 Nov. € 25.00 2007*

SABLES D'OLONNE, LES *7A1* (2km E Rural) *46.48098, -1.73146* **Camping Le Puits Rochais, 25 Rue de Bourdigal, 85180 Château-d'Olonne [02 51 21 09 69; fax 02 51 23 62 20; info@puitsrochais.com; www.puitsrochais.com]** Fr Les Sables-d'Olonne take D949 twd La Rochelle. Pass rndabt with lge hypermrkt 'Magasin Géant' & turn R at 1st traff lts at Mercedes g'ge, then 1st L to site. Med, hdg/mkd pitch, pt shd; wc; chem disp; baby facs; shwrs inc; el pnts (6-10A) inc; Indtte; shop; supmkt 1km; rest; snacks; bar; BBQ (gas); playgrnd; htd pool; paddling pool; waterslide; sand beach 2km; tennis; cycle hire; games area; games rm; internet; entmnt; TV; 60% statics; dogs €3.30; phone; adv bkg; quiet; ccard acc; red low ssn/CCI. "Friendly, welcoming site; gd for families." ♦
4 Apr-30 Sep. € 31.95 2009*

See advertisement above

SABLES D'OLONNE, LES *7A1* (SE Urban/Coastal) *46.49171, -1.76536* **CHADOTEL Camping Les Roses, Rue des Roses, 85100 Les Sables-d'Olonne [02 51 95 10 42 or 02 51 33 05 05 (LS); fax 02 51 33 94 04; chadotel@wanadoo.fr; www.chadotel.com]** Fr town cent foll dir Niort, turn down Blvd Ampère by Total petrol stn to Rue des Roses. Site opp take-away cafe & adj to hospital, lying bet D949 & sea front. Lge, hdg/mkd pitch, pt shd; htd wc; chem disp; shwrs inc; el pnts (6A) inc; gas 1.5km; Indtte; tradsmn; rest 500m; snacks (high ssn); bar; BBQ (gas); playgrnd; htd pool; waterslide; sand beach 500m; entmnt; cycle hire; games rm; TV rm; 70% statics; dogs €3; phone; poss cr; Eng spkn; adv bkg; quiet; ccard acc; CCI. "Conv for town & beach; close by harbour, shops, museums & salt marshes; shuttle buses; excel." ♦ 5 Apr-9 Nov. € 28.90 2008*

SABLES D'OLONNE, LES *7A1* (2km SE Urban) *46.47932, -1.74123* **Camping Les Fosses Rouges, La Pironnière, 8 Rue des Fosses Rouges, 85180 Château-d'Olonne [02 51 95 17 95; info@camping-lesfossesrouges.com; www.camping-lesfossesrouges.com]** Take D949 La Rochelle. At lge rndabt turn R, sp La Pironnière. Camp clearly sp on L in 1km. Lge, mkd pitch, shd; wc; shwrs inc; el pnts (10A) €3.60; gas; Indtte; shop & 500m; snacks; bar; playgrnd; htd pool; sand beach 1.5km; cycle hire; entmnt; internet; TV; 70% statics; dogs €1.60; poss cr; adv bkg; quiet; red low ssn. "Attractive site on o'skts fishing port; some pitches poss diff lge o'fits; gd pool." ♦ 8 Apr-30 Sep. € 16.00 2009*

SABLES D'OLONNE, LES *7A1* (4km SW Coastal) *46.51193, -1.81398* **CHADOTEL Camping La Dune des Sables, La Paracou, 85100 Les Sables-d'Olonne [02 51 32 31 21 or 02 51 33 05 05 (LS); fax 02 51 33 94 04; chadotel@wanadoo.fr; www.chadotel.com]** Foll D160 to Les Sables-d'Olonne. Fr town foll sps to La Chaume & Les Dunes. Lge, mkd pitch, pt sl, unshd; htd wc; serviced pitches; shwrs inc; el pnts (6A) inc; gas; Indtte; shop; snacks; bar; BBQ (gas); playgrnd; pool; waterslide; sand beach 100m; tennis; cycle hire; games rm; entmnt; 75% statics; dogs €3; Eng spkn; adv bkg rec high ssn; red low ssn; CCI. "Great for family beach holiday; helpful warden." ♦ 5 Apr-27 Sep. € 29.90 2008*

SABLES D'OR LES PINS *2E3* (4km NE Coastal) *48.65158, -2.35647* **Camp Municipal Pont de l'Etang, Pléhérel-Plage, 22240 Fréhel [02 96 41 40 45 or 02 96 41 40 12 (Mairie); otfrehel@wanadoo.fr; www.frehelcamping.bzh.bz]** Best app fr D786 via D34 to Sables d'Or; then D34A to Pléhérel-Plage; just N of vill, sp. V lge, pt sl, pt shd; wc (some cont); chem disp; mv service pnt; shwrs inc; el pnts (6A) inc; Indry rm; mobile shops in high ssn; tradsmn; snacks; playgrnd; sand beach 200m; horseriding, tennis adj; v few statics; dogs €0.60; phone; poss cr; Eng spkn; poss noisy; CCI. "Lovely site amongst sand dunes; ideal for children; ltd facs low ssn." ♦ 1 Apr-30 Sep. € 13.00 2008*

SABLES D'OR LES PINS *3E2* (5.5km NE Coastal) *48.66418, -2.34260* **Camp Municipal Cap Fréhel/Les Grèves d'en Bas, 22240 Plévenon [02 96 41 43 34 or 02 96 29 60 51 (Mairie); mairie.plevenon.capfrehel@wanadoo.fr]** W fr St Malo on D168/D786; in 30km turn R onto D34 or D341 dir Cap Fréhel; site on R 2.5km bef Cap Fréhel. Med, pt hdg/mkd pitch, pt sl, pt shd; wc; chem disp; shwrs inc; el pnts (5A) €2.05; tradsmn; rest 2km; sand beach adj; 10% statics; dogs €0.75; quiet. "Access to coast path fr site; gd." Apr-Nov. € 9.75 2009*

SABLES D'OR LES PINS *2E3* (1.2km NW Coastal/Rural) *48.63230, -2.41229* **Camp Municipal La Saline, Rue du Lac, 22240 Plurien [02 96 72 17 40 or 02 96 72 17 23 (Mairie)]** Fr D786 turn N at Plurien onto D34 to Sables-d'Or. In 1km turn L & site on L after 200m. Med, pt sl, terr, pt shd; wc (some cont); chem disp; shwrs inc; el pnts (6A) inc; Indtte; shops 500m; playgrnd; sand beach 400m; dogs €0.50; phone; poss cr; Eng spkn; adv bkg; quiet; CCI. "Lovely hillside, family site; some sea views; vg san facs; gates clsd 2200-0700." ♦ 1 Jun-15 Sep. € 12.35 2008*

SACQUENAY *6G1* (500m S Rural) *47.58924, 5.32178* **Aire Naturelle La Chênaie (Méot), 16 Rue du 19 Mars, 21260 Sacquenay [eric.meot@wanadoo.fr]** S on D974 (N74) turn L onto D171A sp Occey & Sacquenay, site sp. Sm, pt sl, pt shd; wc; shwrs inc; el pnts (6A); shop 400m; Indtte; playgrnd; poss cr; Eng spkn; adv bkg; quiet; red 10+ days; CCI. "Peaceful site in orchard." 1 Apr-1 Oct. € 12.20 2007*

SAHUNE see Rémuzat *9D2*

SAILLANS *9D2* (Rural) *44.69511, 5.18124* **Camping Les Chapelains, 26340 Saillans [04 75 21 55 47; info@camping.saillans.com]** Fr W on D93 turn onto D493. Site well sp just bef Saillans vill boundary adj Rv Drôme. Sm, hdg/mkd pitch, pt shd; wc; shwrs inc; el pnts (4-10A) €2.30-4; gas; Indtte; sm shop; rest; tradsmn; snacks; bar; playgrnd; shgl beach; dogs €1; Eng spkn; adv bkg; quiet; ccard not acc; CCI. "Attractive, well-run rvside site; some v sm pitches; san facs need updating; friendly, helpful warden; rv walk to vill; rest open low ssn." 1 Apr-30 Sep. € 7.50 2006*

SAILLANS *9D2* (4km NE Rural) *44.71636, 5.26440* **Camping Les Tuillères, Route de Die, 26340 Vercheny [04 75 21 18 86; fax 04 75 21 29 34; contact@campinglestuilleres.com; www.camping-les-tuilleres.com]** On D93, 1km E of Vercheny. Med, pt shd; wc; chem disp; shwrs inc; el pnts (6A) €3; Indtte; shop 6km; tradsmn; rest & bar 1km; snacks; playgrnd; pool; rv sw adj; dogs €1.60; phone; Eng spkn; adv bkg; quiet; red low ssn; ccard acc; CCI. "Beautiful location by rv; helpful owner; highly rec." ♦ 24 Apr-30 Sep. € 13.50 2007*

SAILLANS *9D2* (3km E Rural) *44.69579, 5.30393* **Camping Le Pont d'Espénel, 26340 Espénel [04 75 21 72 70; fax 04 75 21 71 10; reservation@camping-du-pont.com; www.camping-du-pont.com]** Fr Crest dir Die on D93, dir access to site on R, adj Rv Drôme. Med, mkd pitch, pt sl, pt shd; wc; chem disp; shwrs inc; el pnts (6A) €2.60; Indtte; rest; bar; playgrnd; rv sw adj; canoeing; dogs €1.40; phone; Eng spkn; ccard acc; CCI. "Excel." 1 Apr-15 Oct. € 9.80 2006*

SAILLANS *9D2* (8km E Rural) *44.69579, 5.30393* **Camp Municipal La Colombe, 26340 Aurel [04 75 21 76 29 or 04 75 21 71 88; fax 04 75 21 71 89]** E of Saillans on D93, in vill of Vercheny turn S onto D357. Bef vill of Aurel turn R by war memorial. Sm, mkd pitch, terr, shd; wc (cont); shwrs inc; el pnts; Indtte; shops 4km; rest; snacks; bar; playgrnd; pool; rv sw & fishing 5km; games area; some statics; v quiet. "Peaceful, mountain site; beautiful views." 1 May-30 Sep. 2006*

SAILLY LE SEC see Albert *3B3*

SAINTES *7B2* (1km N Urban) *45.75511, -0.62871* **Camp Municipal au Fil de l'Eau, 6 Route de Courbiac, 17100 Saintes [05 46 93 08 00; fax 05 46 93 61 88; info@camping-saintes-17.com; www.camping-saintes-17.com]** Well sp as 'Camping Municipal' fr rndbts on by-pass N & S on D150 & D137 (thro indus area), adj rv. NB 1st Mon in month street mkt & many rds clsd. Lge, hdg/mkd pitch, pt shd; wc; chem disp; shwrs inc; el pnts (10A) €3.57; Indtte; shop; snacks; rest high ssn; bar; playgrnd; sm pool; rv sw, fishing & boating adj; some statics; dogs €0.85; Eng spkn; ccard acc; red low ssn; CCI. "Excel site; gd san facs - low ssn ltd & poss unclean; ground poss boggy when wet; gd tourng base; poss itinerants; mkt Wed & Sat." ♦ 20 Apr-15 Oct. € 13.50 2009*

ST AFFRIQUE *8E4* (1km E Urban) *43.95025, 2.89248* **Camp Municipal, Parc des Sports, La Capelle Basse, 12400 St Affrique [05 65 98 20 00; fax 05 65 49 02 29]** Site on D99 Albi-Millau rd to St Affrique sp fr all dir in E end of town. Nr stn & sports complex. Med, pt shd; wc (some cont); shwrs; el pnts €2.75; shop 1km; rest, snacks & bar 1km; pool; rv fishing & sw; tennis; adv bkg; quiet. "Gd clean facs." 14 Jun-13 Sep. € 10.00 2008*

ST AGNAN *4G4* (Rural) *47.31812, 4.09520* **Camping du Lac, Le Château, 58230 St Agnan [03 86 78 73 70 or 01772 700531 (UK tel LS); fax 03 86 78 74 94; info@campingburgundy.co.uk; www.campingburgundy.co.uk]** Exit A6 junc 22 onto D646 then D906 (N6) dir Saulieu; at La Roche-en-Brenil turn R onto D226 to St Agnan. Site ent on R opp junc. Fr Saulieu leave town S on D980 sp Autun; on o'skts turn W onto D26B to Eschamps then D106 to St Agnan. Med, pt sl, pt shd; wc (some cont); chem disp; shws inc; el pnts (6A) €3; Indtte; shop; tradsmn; rest; snacks; bar; BBQ; playgrnd; lake sw adj; kayak & pedalo hire nr; games rm; dogs €1; Eng spkn; adv bkg; quiet; ccard acc; CCI. "Pretty, British-owned site in grnds of chateau; v ltd facs low ssn." 15 Apr-15 Oct. € 12.90 2008*

ST AIGNAN SUR CHER *4G2* (2km SE Rural) *47.26530, 1.38875* **Camping Les Cochards, 1 Rue du Camping, Seigy, 41110 St Aignan-sur-Cher [02 54 75 15 59 or 06 83 79 45 44 (mob); fax 02 54 75 44 72; camping@lesclochards.com; www.lescochards.com]** On D17 heading SE fr St Aignan twd Seigy on S bank of Rv Cher. Lge, mkd pitch, pt shd; htd wc; chem disp; mv service pnt; baby facs; shwrs inc; el pnts (5A) €3.60; Indtte; sm shop & 3km; rest; snacks; bar; BBQ; playgrnd; pool; rv sw adj; rv fishing; canoeing; horseriding 3km; archery; entmnt; TV rm; 20% statics; dogs €1.20; phone; Eng spkn; quiet; ccard acc; red low ssn; CCI. "Attractive, open site; young, enthusiastic, helpful owners; gd san facs; recep clsd 2000; some pitches waterlogged after rain; excel." ♦ 27 Mar-15 Oct. € 19.50 (CChq acc) 2009*

ST AIGNAN SUR CHER *4G2* (4km NW Rural) *47.29411, 1.33041* **Camp Municipal Le Port, Place de l'Eglise, 41110 Mareuil-sur-Cher [tel/fax 02 54 32 79 51 or 02 54 75 21 78; leportdemareuil@orange.fr; www.campingleportdemareuil.com]** Fr St Aignan take D17 twd Tours (on S bank of Cher); site in 4km in vill of Mareuil-sur-Cher behind church, thro new archway, on Rv Cher. By Mareuil chateau. Or fr A85 sp. Sm, mkd pitch, pt shd; htd wc; chem disp; shwrs inc; el pnts (10A) inc; ice/gas 50m; shop & baker 100m; supmkt adj; rest 4km; playgrnd; rv sw (shgl beach); fishing; canoe hire; internet at supmkt; dogs €1; Eng spkn; quiet, but some rd noise & poss events in chateau; no ccard acc; CCI. "Beautiful, simple, rvside site; friendly staff; clean san facs but ltd; opening/closing dates variable, phone ahead to check; if office clsd enquire at supmkt adj (same owners); no access 1300-1500; diff lge o'fits; no twin-axles; m'vans extra; gd touring area." ♦ 7 Apr-30 Sep. € 11.90 2009*

ST ALBAN AURIOLLES see Ruoms *9D2*

ST ALBAN DE MONTBEL see Chambéry *9B3*

ST ALBAN SUR LIMAGNOLE see St Chély d'Apcher *9D1*

ST AMAND DE COLY see Montignac *7C3*

ST AMAND EN PUISAYE *4G4* (500m NE Urban) *47.53294, 3.07333* **Camp Municipal La Vrille, Route de St Sauveur, 58310 St Amand-en-Puisaye [03 86 39 72 21 or 03 86 39 63 72 (Mairie); fax 03 86 39 64 97; saintam.mairie@wanadoo.fr; www.ot-puisaye-nivernaise.fr]** Fr N7 take D957 Neuvy-sur-Loire to St Amand, at rd junc in vill take D955 sp St Sauveur-en-Puisaye, site on R in 500m; clearly sp on all app to vill. Sm, mkd pitch, pt shd; wc (some cont); shwrs inc; el pnts €2.30; shop, rest, bar 500m; sailing & fishing in adj reservoir. "Vg simple site; gates clsd 2200-0700." 1 Jun-30 Sep. € 8.40 2008*

France

ST AMAND LES EAUX *3B4* (3.5km SE Rural) *50.43535, 3.46290* **Camping du Mont des Bruyères, 806 Rue Basly, 59230 St Amand-les-Eaux [tel/fax 03 27 48 56 87]** Exit A23 m'way at junc 5 or 6 onto ring rd D169, site sp. Fr N exit E42 junc 31 onto N52/N507 then D169. Avoid St Amand cent. Med, hdg/mkd pitch, pt sl, terr, shd; htd wc; shwrs inc; el pnts (6A) €3.70; Indtte; shop; bar; playgrnd; pool 7km; 60% statics; adv bkg; quiet; CCI. "Attractive site on forest edge; most touring pitches under trees; access to some pitches diff due slopes; dated facs clean but tired; gd cycling; excel birdlife on site; ltd facs & poss unkempt low ssn; fair." 15 Mar-15 Nov. € 14.00 2008*

ST AMAND LES EAUX *3B4* (7km NW Rural) *50.46313, 3.34428* **FFCC Camping La Gentilhommière, 905 Rue de Beaumetz, 59310 Saméon [tel/fax 03 20 61 54 03]** Fr A23 Paris-Lille, exit junc 3, sp St Amand, then L at rndabt foll sp Saméon. Site on R 300m. Med, hdg pitch, shd; htd wc; chem disp; shwrs inc; el pnts (3A) inc; gas; Indtte; shop 8km; tradsmn; snacks; bar; BBQ; playgrnd; fishing; tennis; 90% statics; dogs €0.80; poss cr; quiet; CCI. "Well-kept site; 5 touring pitches only; charming owner; gd local rest; gd for Lille (park & ride fr a'route); 1km to train to Lille with Piscine Roubaix museum." ♦ 1 Apr-30 Oct. € 11.00 2009*

ST AMAND MONTROND *4H3* (3km SW Rural) *46.71808, 2.49159* **Camp Municipal La Roche, Rue de la Roche, 18200 St Amand-Montrond [tel/fax 02 48 96 09 36; camping-la-roche@wanadoo.fr; www.st-amand-tourisme.com]** Exit A71/E11 junc 8 dir St Amand-Montrond on D300. Then foll sp to Montluçon on D2144 (N144). Site sp on far side of town. Med, shd, pt sl; htd wc (some cont); shwrs inc; chem disp (wc); el pnts (5A) €2.70 (poss rev pol); Indtte (inc dryer); shops 900m; playgrnd; pool nr; rv fishing; tennis; entmnt; dogs; phone; quiet; CCI. "Clean facs; helpful warden; pleasant town; popular NH, rec arr by 1700 high ssn; gd." ♦ 1 Apr-30 Sep. € 9.90 2009*

See advertisement

ST AMAND MONTROND *4H3* (8km NW Rural) *46.77033, 2.42907* **FFCC Camping Les Platanes, 18200 Bruère-Allichamps [02 48 61 06 69 or 02 48 61 02 68 (Mairie)]** Site on N edge of town on rvside. Sm, pt shd; wc; chem disp; shwrs €1; el pnts (10A) inc; shops adj; tradsmn; snacks; playgrnd; rv fishing; quiet. "Lovely surroundings; san facs dated but clean; friendly staff; level walk to interesting vill; excel." 1 Apr-30 Sep. € 8.70 2009*

ST AMANS DES COTS *7D4* (5km S Rural) *44.66690, 2.68001* **Camping Les Tours, 12460 St Amans-des-Cots [05 65 44 88 10 or 04 99 57 20 25; fax 05 65 44 83 07; www.camping-les-tours.com or www.village-center.com]** Foll D34/D97 fr Entraygues to St Amans, sp in vill. Site on Lac de la Selves. Or fr S, D97 fr Estaing. V lge, hdg/mkd pitch, hdstg, terr, pt shd; wc (some cont); chem disp; mv service pnt; serviced pitches; baby facs; fam bthrm; shwrs inc; el pnts (6A) inc; gas; Indtte; sm shop & 5km; rest; snacks; bar; BBQ; playgrnd; htd pool complex; paddling pool; waterslide; lake & rv sw; windsurfing, boating on lake; tennis; horseriding; fishing; golf; gym; entmnt; TV; 20% statics; dogs €3; adv bkg; quiet; red low ssn; ccard acc. "Beautiful site on lake; some unshd pitches - book early (Xmas) for shd pitch; 600m altitude so cold nights; steep slope to san facs." ♦ 30 Apr-13 Sep. € 37.00 2007*

ST AMANT ROCHE SAVINE see Ambert *9B1*

ST AMBROIX *9D2* (3km S Rural) *44.23748, 4.20163* **Camping Beau Rivage, Route de Uzès, Le Moulinet, 30500 St Ambroix [04 66 24 10 17; marc@camping-beau-rivage.fr; www.camping-beau-rivage.fr]** N on D904, after Les Mages in 5km. Camping sp on R. Foll sp approx 2-3km. Site off D37 twd Le Moulinet. Med, hdg/mkd pitch, pt sl, terr, pt sl, shd; wc (some cont); chem disp; shwrs inc; el pnts (6A); €3.50; gas; Indtte; shop 1km; tradsmn; rest, snacks 2km; bar 1km; playgrnd; pool; paddling pool; canoeing; wifi; no statics; dogs; poss cr; adv bkg; quiet; red low ssn; CCI. "Lovely location." ♦ 1 May-1 Sep. € 20.00 2009*

ST AMBROIX *9D2* (200m W Rural) *44.26234, 4.19598* **Camping Le Clos, Place de l'Eglise, 30500 St Ambroix [04 66 24 10 08 or 06 07 54 57 66 (mob); fax 04 66 60 25 62; campingleclos@wanadoo.fr; www.camping-le-clos.fr]** Fr S on D904, in St Amboix turn L immed bef church. Site in 300m. Foll intn'l camping sp. Sm, mkd pitch, pt shd; wc; chem disp; shwrs inc; el pnts (6-10A) €3-5; lndtte; snacks; bar; playgrnd; pool; paddling pool; fishing; sailing; cycle hire; TV rm; 20% statics; dogs €2; adv bkg; quiet. "Well-kept san facs; access poss diff for lge o'fits." ♦ 1 Apr-31 Oct. € 17.00 2007*

ST AMBROIX *9D2* (12km NW Rural) *44.29104, 4.06840* **Camping des Drouilhedes, Peyremale-sur-Cèze, 30160 Bessèges [04 66 25 04 80; fax 04 66 25 10 95; info@campingcevennes.com; www.camping-drouilhedes.com]** Leave D904 at St Ambroix onto D51 sp Bessèges. In Bessèges turn L over bdge sp Peyremale & in approx 1km turn R & foll camping sp. Med, hdg/mkd pitch, pt shd; wc (some cont); chem disp; baby facs; shwrs inc; el pnts (6A) €4.20; gas; lndtte; shop; tradsmn; rest; snacks; bar; BBQ (gas only); playgrnd; rv sw adj; tennis; games area; TV rm; 10% statics; dogs; phone; poss cr; Eng spkn; quiet; ccard acc; CCI. "Well-run, scenic site with excel facs; ideal for children; helpful Dutch owners." ♦ 1 Apr-30 Sep. € 21.85 2008*

ST AMOUR *9A2* (SW Urban) *46.43048, 5.33941* **Camp Municipal, 4 Ave des Sports, 39160 St Amour [03 84 48 71 68 or 03 84 44 02 00; fax 03 84 48 88 15]** Sp S & N of vill. Ent by pool & tennis courts. Narr app. Med, pt sl, pt shd, some hdstdg; wc; chem disp; el pnts (6A) €4.50; shwrs; shops 400m; playgrnd; pool adj; tennis; rv 5km; quiet but some rlwy noise at night. "Site in public park; office open ltd hrs, site yourself; well-kept san facs; gd cycling; gd NH or longer." 15 Jun-30 Sep. € 12.30 2007*

STE ANASTASIE SUR ISSOLE see Brignoles *10F3*

ST ANDIOL see Cavaillon *10E2*

ST ANDRE DE CUBZAC *7C2* (4km NW Rural) *45.00703, -0.47724* **FFCC Camping Le Port Neuf, 33240 St André-de-Cubzac [tel/fax 05 57 43 16 44; camping.port@neuf.fr; http://camping.port.neuf.fr]** Fr A10 or N10 take exit sp St André. Well sp fr St André (narr rds) on D669. Med, pt shd; wc; chem disp; mv service pnt; shwrs inc; el pnts (10A) €2.50 (poss long lead req); bar; playgrnd; pool; cycle hire; trout-fishing & boating in sm lake + rv 100m; many statics; dogs €1; quiet; Eng spkn; red CCI. "San facs clean; gd NH only." 1 May-1 Oct. € 12.00 2009*

ST ANDRE DE LIDON see Cozes *8B1*

ST ANDRE DE SEIGNANX see Bayonne *8F1*

ST ANDRE DES EAUX see Baule, La *2G3*

⊞ **ST ANDRE LES ALPES** *10E3* (6km NE Rural) *44.00668, 6.55815* **FFCC Camping L'Adrech, Route du Pont d'Allons, 04170 La Mure-Argens [04 92 89 17 81; contact@adrech.com; www.adrech.com/camping]** Fr E or W on N202 to St André-les-Alpes, turn N onto D955 dir Colmars, Site on R. Do not app fr N fr Barcelonette via Col d'Allos. Sm, mkd pitch, pt sl, pt shd; wc; chem disp (wc); shwrs inc; el pnts (3-6A) €3.50; snacks; bar; BBQ; watersports, lake sw nrby; wifi; 25% statics; dogs €1; Eng spkn; adv bkg; ccard acc; CCI. "Family-run site; helpful, friendly; gd touring base in interesting area." € 12.50 2008*

ST ANDRE LES ALPES *10E3* (500m S Urban) *43.96101, 6.50871* **Camp Municipal Les Iscles, Route de Nice, 04170 St André-les-Alpes [04 92 89 02 29; fax 04 92 89 02 56; mairie.st-andre.les.alpes@wanadoo.fr; www.saint-andre-les-alpes.fr]** Exit St André-les-Alpes SE on N202 to Nice turn E at edge of vill on wide service rd. Site almost immed on L fronted by lge car-park. Med, mkd pitch, shd; wc (some cont); chem disp; serviced pitches; shwrs inc; el pnts (4A) €2; lndtte; supmkt adj; BBQ; TV/games rm; trains to Nice etc nrby; Eng spkn; quiet. "Gd welcome; gd site in scenic area in pine woods; rough stony ground." 1 May-30 Sep. € 10.90 2007*

ST ANGEAU see Mansle *7B2*

STE ANNE D'AURAY *2F3* (6km N Rural) *47.72889, -2.95349* **FFCC Aire Naturelle Nerhouit, 56400 Plumergat [02 97 57 70 62; nerhouit@tromp.net]** Fr N165 turn N on D17 to Plumergat; site 3km W of Plumergat, sp. Sm, pt shd; wc; chem disp (wc); shwrs €0.50; el pnts (6A) inc (poss long lead req); lndry rm; shop, rest, bar 3km; playgrnd; dogs; Eng spkn; adv bkg; quiet; CCI. "Pitches on lge grassy area; friendly Dutch owner; own cider avail; gd touring base." ♦ 1 Jun-15 Sep. € 12.50 2006*

STE ANNE D'AURAY *2F3* (500m SW Rural) *47.69842, -2.96226* **Camp Municipal du Motten, Allée des Pins, 56400 Ste Anne-d'Auray [02 97 57 60 27]** Fr W on N165 take D17bis N to St Anne-d'Auray; then L onto D19 to town. This rte avoids Pluneret. Foll site sp. Med, mkd pitch, pt shd; wc; chem disp; mv service pnt; shwrs inc; el pnts (10A) €3.10; lndtte; shops 1km; snacks; playgrnd; sand beach 12km; tennis; games area; TV; adv bkg; poss cr; quiet; "Peaceful, well-kept site; best pitches immed R after ent; v welcoming; san facs poss stretched high ssn." ♦ 1 Jun-30 Sep. € 9.80 2009*

ST ANTOINE D'AUBEROCHE see Thenon *7C3*

ST ANTOINE DE BREUILH see Ste Foy la Grande *7C2*

ST ANTONIN NOBLE VAL *8E4* (1.5km N Rural) *44.1595, 1.7564* **FFCC Camp Municipal Le Ponget, Route de Caylus, 82140 St Antonin-Noble-Val [05 63 68 21 13 or 05 63 30 60 23 (Mairie); camping-leponget@wanadoo.fr]** Fr Caylus take D19 S to St Antonin; site on R, well sp. Sm, hdg pitch, pt shd; htd wc; mv service pnt; shwrs inc; el pnts (3-6A) €2.50-3.70; gas; lndtte; shops, rest, snacks, bar 1km; playgrnd; sw 1km; dogs €1.20; phone; quiet; ccard not acc; CCI. "Well-maintained site adj sports field; modern san facs; poss diff lge o'fits; gd walking." ♦ 2 May-30 Sep. € 11.70 2009*

ST ANTONIN NOBLE VAL *8E4* (6km N Rural) *44.19265, 1.69570* **FFCC Camping Les Trois Cantons, Vivens, 82140 St Antonin-Noble-Val [05 63 31 98 57; fax 05 63 31 25 93; info@3cantons.fr; www.3cantons.fr]** Fr Caussade take D926 dir Villefranche (do not take D5 or D19 sp St Antonin.) Site is on C5, sp. Fr St Antonin foll dir Caylus on D19. Just outside vill, after sm bdge where rd turns to R, turn L up hill. Foll this rd for 6km - narr rd. NB Hill steep & continuous. Med, mkd pitch, hdstg, pt sl, pt shd; htd wc (some cont); chem disp; mv service pnt; shwrs inc; el pnts (3-10A) €2.65-6.70; gas; lndtte; shop; supmkt 8km; BBQ; playgrnd; htd, covrd pool; rv sw 8km; tennis; cycle hire; horseriding nr; canoeing; entmnt; TV rm; dogs €1.25; poss cr; Eng spkn; adv bkg; quiet; ccard acc; red low ssn; CCI. "Peaceful, clean, well-managed, family site in oak forest; unspoilt region; helpful Dutch owners; gravel pitches muddy in wet; gd." ♦ 15 Apr-30 Sep. € 19.35 (CChq acc) 2007*

ST ANTONIN NOBLE VAL *8E4* (1km E Rural) *44.15192, 1.77152* **FLOWER Camping des Gorges de L'Aveyron, Marsac Bas, 82140 St Antonin-Noble-Val [05 63 30 69 76; fax 05 63 30 67 61; info@camping-gorges-aveyron.com; www.camping-gorges-aveyron.com or www.flowercamping.com]** Fr Caussade on D926 dir Caylus for approx 5km; after Septfords take D5 then D958 to St Antonin-Noble-Val; on ent to vill cont over rv & L thro tunnel onto D115 dir Féneyrols & Cordes-sur-Ciel. Site in 1.5km on L. Med, hdg pitch, pt shd; wc; chem disp; mv service pnt; shwrs inc; el pnts (6A) inc (poss rev pol); lndtte; shops; tradsmn; snacks; bar; playgrnd; fishing rv adj; canoeing; wifi; 5% statics; dogs €2.50; poss cr; adv bkg; quiet; red long stay/low ssn; CCI. "Neat, tidy site - best in area; lge, shady pitches; friendly owners; gd san facs; gd walking & cycling." ♦ 28 Mar-4 Oct. € 20.90 (CChq acc) 2009*

ST APOLLINAIRE see Chorges *9D3*

ST ARNOULT see Deauville *3D1*

ST ASTIER *7C3* (600m E Rural) *45.14735, 0.53308* **Camp Municipal Le Pontet, Route de Montanceix, 24110 St Astier [05 53 54 14 22; fax 05 53 04 39 36; camp.lepontet@wanadoo.fr; www.ville-saint-astier.fr]** Take D6089 (N89) SW fr Périgueux; in 14km turn R sp St Astier; site on R on D41 on banks of Rv Isle. Med, mkd pitch, shd; wc; chem disp; shwrs inc; el pnts (6A) €2.55; gas; lndtte; shops 400m; snacks; BBQ; playgrnd; pool; paddling pool; sand beach adj; fishing; canoeing; entmnt; statics; dogs; poss cr; adv bkg; v quiet; CCI. "Some areas soft in wet weather." 1 Apr-30 Sep. € 12.00 2007*

ST AUBAN *10E4* (300m S Rural) *43.84509, 6.73452* **Camping La Pinatelle, 269 Chemin St Auban, 06850 St Auban [04 93 60 40 46; fax 04 93 60 42 45; contact@camping-saintauban.com; www.camping-saintauban.com]** Fr D6085 (N85) take D2211, site well sp on R just bef vill. Sm, mkd pitch, hdstg, pt shd; wc; chem disp; mv service pnt; shwrs; el pnts (6A) inc; lndtte; supmkt 1km; tradsmn; rest; snacks; bar; playgrnd; sm pool; games area; 15% statics; dogs €1; phone; Eng spkn; adv bkg; quiet; CCI. "Family-run CL-type site in beautiful countryside; friendly, helpful owners; excel facs; gd walking, cycling." ♦ 14 Apr-16 Sep. € 16.00 2008*

ST AUBAN *10E4* (2km NW Rural) *43.86421, 6.73386* **Camping Le Haut Chandelalar (Naturist), 06850 Briançonnet [04 93 60 40 09; fax 04 93 60 49 64; info@le-haut-chandelalar.com; www.le-haut-chandelalar.com]** Exit D6085 (N85) Gasse-Castellane rd onto D2211; site bet St Auban & Briançonnet. Or fr Nice on N202 dir Digne-les-Bains; at Puget-Théniers turn L onto D2211 dir St Auban; 1.5km after Briançonnet turn R at site sp; site on L in 900m. Med, mkd pitch, hdstg, pt sl, terr, pt shd; wc (some cont); chem disp (wc); baby facs; shwrs inc; el pnts (6A) inc; gas; lndtte; shop; tradsmn; rest; snacks; bar; BBQ; playgrnd; htd pool; entmnt; internet; TV rm; some statics; no dogs; phone; poss cr high ssn; adv bkg; Eng spkn; quiet; ccard acc; CCI. "Peaceful, secluded site with views; pleasant owners; some pitches poss diff access for lge o'fits - steep site rds with sharp bends & poss diff after heavy rain; gd touring base; gd walking; excel." ♦ 1 May-30 Sep. € 25.20 2008*

ST AUBIN DE LUIGNE see Chalonnes sur Loire *2G4*

ST AUBIN DU CORMIER *2E4* (E Urban) *48.25990, -1.39609* **Camp Municipal, Rue de l'Etang, 35140 St Aubin-du-Cormier [06 83 38 93 63 (mob) or 02 99 39 10 42 (Mairie); fax 02 99 39 23 25; mairie@ville-staubinducormier.fr]** NE fr Rennes on A84; in 20km exit junc 28 dir St Aubin-du-Cormier. Foll sp 'Centre Ville' then site sp. Poss diff for lge o'fits - narr app. Sm, pt sl, pt shd; wc; shwrs €1.05; el pnts (6-10A) inc; shops adj; supmkt 1km; lake fishing; 10% statics; dogs €0.65; poss cr; adv bkg; quiet; CCI. "Pleasant site adj lake; friendly; forest walks & around lake; pretty vill; vet 1km; excel." 1 Apr-30 Sep. € 12.05 2009*

ST AUBIN SUR MER see Caen *3D1*

ST AUGUSTIN (CHARENTE MARITIME) see St Palais sur Mer *7B1*

ST AVERTIN see Tours *4G2*

ST AVIT DE VIALARD see Bugue, Le *7C3*

⊞ **ST AVOLD** *5D2* (1km N Urban) *49.10772, 6.70924* **FFCC Camping Le Felsberg, Centre International de Séjour, 57500 St Avold [03 87 92 75 05; fax 03 87 92 20 69; cis.stavold@wanadoo.fr; www.camping-moselle.com]** Fr N on A4 exit junc 39 onto D633 to St Avold, stay in L hand lane at 2nd traff lts & turn L; pass under D603 (N3) for 2km & turn R. Site well sp in & around town; app up steep incline. Sm, hdg/mkd pitch, hdstg, pt sl, pt shd; wc; chem disp; mv service pnt; shwrs inc; el pnts (6-10A) €3-5; Indtte; tradsmn; hypmkt 1.5km; rest, bar high ssn; playgrnd; 50% statics; dogs €1; poss cr; adv bkg; ccard acc; red long stay; CCI. "German border 10km; sm pitches; gd facs; coal mine & archaeological park nrby worth visit; awkward, heavy duty security gate at site ent; conv NH nr m'way; gd." ♦ € 14.00 2009*

ST AYGULF *10F4* (500m N Coastal) *43.39151, 6.72648* **Camping de St Aygulf Plage, 270 Ave Salvarelli, 83370 St Aygulf [04 94 17 62 49; fax 04 09 81 03 16; camping.cote.d.azur.plage@wanadoo.fr; www.camping-cote-azur.com]** Fr Roquebrunne on D7 at rndabt 100m after vill sp St Aygulf take 3rd exit leading to Rue Roger Martin du Gard. Keep turning L. Fr Fréjus on D559 (N98), rd bends R after bdge over beach access, turn R bef rd climbs to L. V lge, mkd pitch, shd; wc; chem disp; shwrs inc; el pnts (5A) €3.50; gas; Indtte; shop; rest; snacks; bar; playgrnd; sand beach adj; watersports & sports facs nr; fishing; games area; entmnt; statics; dogs €3-3.50; adv bkg; ccard acc; red 28+ days; CCI. "Facs dated but clean; gd." 28 Apr-30 Sep. € 26.00 2007*

ST AYGULF *10F4* (4km S Coastal) *43.40963, 6.72491* **Camping Le Pont d'Argens, 83370 St Aygulf [04 94 51 14 97; fax 04 94 51 29 44]** Well sp fr D559 (N98) bet Fréjus & St Aygulf. Situated by Rv Argens. If app fr W pass site on R & return via next rndbt. Lge, mkd pitch, pt shd; htd wc; chem disp; mv service pnt; baby facs; shwrs; el pnts (6A) €2; gas; Indtte; shop; tradsmn; hypmkt 1km; rest; snacks; bar; playgrnd; pool; sand beach adj; cycle hire; TV rm; 5% statics; dogs €2.50; poss cr; Eng spkn; adv bkg; some rd noise; ccard acc; CCI. "Excel, well-run site by rv; sh walk to uncrowded beach (pt naturist); excel facs & pool; cycle track to St Aygulf & pt way to Fréjus." 1 Apr-15 Oct. € 30.00 2008*

ST AYGULF *10F4* (2km W Rural) *43.40691, 6.70923* **Camping Les Lauriers Roses, Route de Roquebrune, 83370 St Aygulf [04 94 81 24 46 or 04 94 81 03 58 (LS); fax 04 94 81 79 63; lauriersroses@cs.com; www.info-lauriersroses.com]** Exit A8 at junc 37 Puget-sur-Argens onto DN7 to Fréjus. At 1st rndabt after Fréjus town sp, turn R to St Aygulf at junc immed after rndabt. Pass under rlwy bdge & turn R onto D8. After bdge with traff lts foll rd up to junc & turn L onto D7, site in 1.5km on R. Med, mkd pitch, pt sl, terr, pt shd; wc; chem disp; baby facs; shwrs inc; el pnts (6A) €3.50; gas; Indtte; shop 500m; snacks; bar; BBQ (gas only); playgrnd; htd pool & paddling pool; sand beach 2km; games rm; entmnt; internet; 10% statics; dogs €1.85; Eng spkn; adv bkg; quiet; ccard not acc; CCI. "Excel, family-run, wooded site on hillside; diff acc some pitches for lge o'fits (max 8m) - owner assists with siting c'vans; mkt Tue & Fri; no arrivals bet 1230-1500." ♦ 19 Apr-27 Sep. € 27.50 2007*

ST AYGULF *10F4* (2.5km W Coastal) *43.36566, 6.71264* **Camping Au Paradis des Campeurs, La Gaillarde-Plage, 83380 Les Issambres [04 94 96 93 55; fax 04 94 49 62 99; www.paradis-des-campeurs.com]** Exit A8/E80 junc 37 at Puget-sur-Argens onto DN7 to by-pass Fréjus, then onto D559 (N98) twd Ste Maxime. Site on R 2km after passing thro St Aygulf, on LH bend bef hill. Or exit junc 36 onto D125 to Ste Maxime, then D559 dir Fréjus. Site on L after ent Les Issambres. Med, mkd pitch, hdstg, pt sl, terr, pt shd; htd wc; chem disp; mv service pnt; baby facs; fam bthrm; 30% serviced pitches (extra charge); shwrs inc; el pnts (6A) €4 (poss rev pol); gas 2km; Indtte; shop; tradsmn; rest; snacks; bar; BBQ; playgrnd; sand beach adj; cycle hire; golf 4km; games rm; internet; TV rm; dogs €3; poss cr; Eng spkn; quiet; ccard acc; red low ssn; CCI. "V popular low ssn; direct access via underpass to beach; excel san facs; superb views fr top level pitches - worth extra; gates shut at night & guarded; helpful owners; old rd to St Aygulf suitable for cycling; excel." ♦ 27 Mar-16 Oct. € 23.00 (3 persons) 2009*

ST AYGULF *10F4* (5km NW Rural) *43.41626, 6.70598* **Camping L'Etoile d'Argens, Chemin des Etangs, 83370 St Aygulf [04 94 81 01 41; fax 04 94 81 21 45; info@etoiledargens.com; www.etoiledargens.com]** Exit A8 at junc 37 Puget-sur-Argens onto DN7 to Fréjus & D559 (N98) to St Aygulf, or fr DN7 take D7 to St Aygulf by-passing Fréjus & turn onto D8 to site. Lge, hdg/mkd pitch, shd; 25% serviced pitches; wc; chem disp; baby facs; shwrs inc; el pnts (10A) inc; gas; Indtte; shop; tradsmn; rest; snacks; bar; no BBQ; playgrnd; htd pool; sand beach 3km; rv fishing; tennis; archery; golf 1.5km; entmnt; wifi; 40% statics; dogs €5; poss cr; Eng spkn; adv bkg; quiet; ccard acc; red low ssn; CCI. "Friendly, helpful owners; gd facs, poss unclean low ssn; excel pool complex; ferry down rv to beach in ssn; vg." ♦ 1 Apr-30 Sep. € 52.00 2009*

⊞ **ST BEAT** *8G3* (8km SE Rural) *42.87122, 0.73629* **Camp Municipal, 31440 Fos [05 61 79 35 94 or 05 61 79 41 61 (Mairie); mairie.fos@wanadoo.fr]** S fr St Béat on N125 foll camping sp on site alongside Rv Garonne. Ring bell at recep to alert warden of arr. Sm, mkd pitch, unshd; htd wc; chem disp (wc); shwrs inc; el pnts (12A) inc; rest, bar 400m; playgrnd; tennis 300m; dogs; phone; CCI. "Basic facs; gd NH en route Spain; suitable sm o'fits only; have right money - warden never has change!" € 10.80 2008*

⊞ **ST BEAT** *8G3* (500m S Rural) *42.91030, 0.69098* **Camp Municipal Clef de France, 31440 St Béat [05 61 94 35 39]** On N125 at S exit to town, sp on L on rvside. Med, mkd pitch, pt shd; htd wc; shwrs inc; el pnts (5A) inc; shops, rest, bar 500m; playgrnd; pool 200m; fishing; boating; 95% statics; dogs free; quiet. "Facs ltd low ssn; long walk to san facs; conv Spanish border; NH/sh stay only." € 10.45 2006*

ST BENOIT DES ONDES see Cancale *2E4*

ST BENOIT SUR LOIRE *4F3* (500m SE Rural) *47.80711, 2.29528* **FFCC Camping Le Port, Rue du Port, 45730 St Benoît-sur-Loire [02 38 35 79 00; fax 02 38 35 77 19]** Fr Orléans take N60 & bypass Châteauneuf-sur-Loire. Take D60 twd Sully-sur-Loire to St Benoît-sur-Loire. Foll sp fr vill, site on L side of 1-way street. Sm, pt sl, shd; wc; mv service pnt; shwrs inc; el pnts (13A) €2.50; gas 4km; shop, rest 1.5km; BBQ; playgrnd; sand beach adj; rv sw, fishing, canoeing adj; dogs; phone; poss cr; Eng spkn; quiet; CCI. "Gd cycling, walking; pleasant town." ♦ 1 Apr-30 Sep. € 11.00 2007*

ST BERTRAND DE COMMINGES see Montréjeau *8F3*

ST BOIL *6H1* (1.5km S Rural) *46.64621, 4.69480* **Camping Moulin de Collonge, Route des Vins, 71940 St Boil [03 85 44 00 40 or 03 85 44 00 32; fax 03 85 44 00 40; millofcollonge@wanadoo.fr; www.moulindecollonge.com]** S on A6 take N80 at Chalon-Sud; W dir Le Creusot; 9km turn S on D981 thro Buxy to St Boil; sp on L thro vill. Sm, hdg/mkd pitch, pt shd; wc (few cont); baby facs; shwrs inc; el pnts (6A) €3.50 (poss no earth or rev pol); gas; Indtte; sm shop & 2km; tradsmn; rest; snacks; bar; BBQ; playgrnd; htd, covrd pool; lake fishing; cycle hire; entmnt; wifi; some statics; dogs; v cr high ssn; some Eng spkn; adv bkg; quiet; ccard acc; red low ssn; CCI. "Busy but quiet site; clean, dated san facs; uneven pitches & some sm - poss muddy when wet; gd cycling." ♦ 1 Apr-29 Sep. € 19.00 2009*

ST BOMER LES FORGES see Domfront *4E1*

ST BONNET PRES ORCIVAL see Orcival *7B4*

ST BONNET TRONCAIS see Cérilly *4H3*

⊞ **ST BREVIN LES PINS** *2G3* (N Coastal) **Camping de Mindin (formerly Municipal), 32-40 Ave du Bois, 44250 St Brévin-les-Pins [02 40 27 46 41; fax 02 40 39 20 53; info@camping-de-mindin.com; www.camping-de-mindin.com]** On beach rd at N end of St Brevin. Med, shd; htd wc; chem disp; baby facs; shwrs inc; el pnts (6A) €5.05; Indtte; shop; rest; snacks; bar; playgrnd; htd pool; paddling pool; sand beach adj; mainly statics; dogs €2.35; poss cr; adv bkg; ccard acc; red low ssn; CCI. "Sm, sandy pitches; gd san facs." € 15.70 2008*

⊞ **ST BREVIN LES PINS** *2G3* (1km S Coastal) *47.23800, -2.17030* **Camping La Courance (formerly Municipal), 100-110 Ave Maréchal Foch, 44250 St Brévin-les-Pins [02 40 27 22 91; fax 02 40 27 24 59; francecamping@wanadoo.fr; www.campinglacourance.fr]** Take Ave Foch fr cent of St Brevin, site on R, clearly sp. Lge, pt sl, shd; htd wc; baby facs; shwrs inc; el pnts (5A) inc (poss long lead req); gas; Indtte; shops 1km; rest; snacks; bar; beach adj; 90% statics; dogs €2.20; quiet; red low ssn. "Well-maintained; steep, poss slippery paths." € 14.20 2008*

ST BREVIN LES PINS *2G3* (2km S Coastal) *47.21375, -2.15409* **Camping Les Rochelets, Chemin des Grandes Rivières, 44250 St Brévin-les-Pins [02 40 27 40 25; fax 02 40 27 15 55; rochelets@wanadoo.fr; www.rochelets.com]** Fr N or S on D213 exit sp Les Rochelets, site sp. Lge, hdg/mkd pitch, pt shd; wc (some cont); shwrs; el pnts (6A) €4; Indtte; tradsmn; rest; snacks; bar; playgrnd; htd pool; beach 100m; games area; games rm; entmnt & 30% statics; dogs €2.05; adv bkg; quiet; ccard acc; red low ssn. "Gd site for families." 1 Apr-30 Oct. € 19.00 2006*

ST BREVIN LES PINS *2G3* (2.4km S Coastal) *47.23514, -2.16739* **Camping Sunêlia Le Fief, 57 Chemin du Fief, 44250 St Brévin-les-Pins [02 40 27 23 86; fax 02 40 64 46 19; camping@lefief.com; www.lefief.com]** Fr Nantes dir St Nazaire. After St Nazaire bdge S on D213. Pass Leclerc & exit sp St Brévin-l'Océan/La Courance. At rndabt foll sp Le Fief. Lge, mkd pitch, hdstg, pt shd; wc; chem disp; mv service pnt; baby facs; sauna; shwrs inc; el pnts (6A) €6; gas; Indtte; shop; tradsmn; rest; snacks; bar; BBQ (gas/charcoal); playgrnd; htd, covrd pool; waterslide; jacuzzi; sand beach 800m; waterpark & waterslide etc adj; tennis; games area; games rm; wellness cent; fitness rm; cycle hire nr; gym; wifi; entmnt; TV rm; 30% statics; dogs €7; Eng spkn; adv bkg; quiet; ccard acc; red low ssn/long stay/CCI. "Excel for families; vg leisure facs." ♦ 3 Apr-3 Oct. € 37.00 2009*

See advertisement

ST BREVIN LES PINS *2G3* (5km S Coastal) *47.20441, -2.15773* **Camping Les Pierres Couchées, Ave des Pierres Couchées, L'Ermitage, 44250 St Brévin-les-Pins [02 40 27 85 64; fax 02 40 64 97 03; www.siblu.com/lespierrescouchees]** Sp fr D213 in St Brévin-l'Ermitage. Lge, mkd pitch, terr, pt shd; htd wc (some cont); baby facs; shwrs inc; el pnts (10A); Indtte; shop & 3km; tradsmn; rest; snacks; bar; BBQ; playgrnd; htd pool; paddling pool; waterslide; sand beach 300m; tennis; games area; games rm; fitness rm; cycle hire; horseriding 300m; golf 12km; entmnt; TV; 75% statics; dogs; Eng spkn; adv bkg; quiet; ccard acc; red low ssn; CCI. "Vg facs for families; friendly, helpful staff." ♦ 4 Apr-26 Sep. € 28.00 2009*

ST BRIAC SUR MER *2E3* (Urban/Coastal) *48.62765, -2.13056* **FFCC Camping Emeraude, 7 Chemin de la Souris, 35800 St Briac-sur-Mer [tel/fax 02 99 88 34 55; camping.emeraude@wanadoo.fr; www.camping-emeraude.com]** SW fr Dinard to St Lunaire on N786, after passing Dinard golf course, site is sp to L. Lge, pt shd; wc; chem disp; shwrs inc; el pnts (6A) €3.80; gas; Indtte; sm shop & 200m; tradsmn; snacks; bar; playgrnd; htd pool & paddling pool; water park; beach 700m & sand beach 1.5km; games area; entmnt; 40% statics; dogs €2.30; poss cr; adv bkg. "Excel, well-run site." ♦ 3 Apr-29 Sep. € 19.00 2006*

ST BRIAC SUR MER *2E3* (400m S Coastal) *48.61420, -2.12780* **Camping Le Pont Laurin, La Vallée Gatorge, 35800 St Briac-sur-Mer [02 99 88 34 64 or 06 12 88 56 39 (mob); lepontlaurin@ouest-camping.com; www.ouest-camping.com]** Fr St Briac, 500m S on D3. Lge, hdg/mkd pitch, a few hdstg, pt shd; wc; chem disp; mv service pnt; shwrs inc; el pnts (10A) €3.60 (poss rev pol); Indtte; shop & 400m; tradsmn; snacks; playgrnd; sand beach 900m; sailing; canoe hire; sports cent adj; many statics (sep area); dogs €1.50; Eng spkn; adv bkg; quiet; CCI. "Peaceful site; welcoming, helpful staff; clean, modern san facs; excel beaches; gd walking; interesting town; highly rec." 1 Mar-15 Nov. € 16.00 2008*

ST BRIAC SUR MER *2E3* (500m SW Coastal) *48.60422, -2.15616* **Camp Municipal des Mielles, Rue Jules Jeunet, 22770 Lancieux [02 96 86 22 98 or 02 96 86 22 19; fax 02 96 86 28 20; campinglesmielles@orange.fr; www.mairie-lancieux.fr]** Fr S on D786 at 500m past windmill turn L into Rue du Fredy. Site on R in 300m, sp. Lge, mkd pitch, unshd; wc (some cont); chem disp; shwrs inc; el pnts (6A) €3.20; Indtte; shop 500m; playgrnd; sand beach 400m; watersports 150m; tennis; entmnts; wifi; 2% statics; dogs €1.70; poss cr; CCI. "Well-managed, popular site; gd security in ssn; excel facs; hot water ltd low ssn." ♦ 1 Apr-30 Sep. € 10.50 2009*

ST BRICE SUR VIENNE see St Junien *7B3*

ST BRIEUC *2E3* (5km E Coastal) *48.53311, -2.67193* **FFCC Camping Bellevue Mer, Pointe de Guettes, 22120 Hillion [02 96 32 20 39 or 02 96 31 25 05 (HS); fax 02 96 32 20 39; contact@bellevuemer.com; www.bellevuemer.com]** Fr St Brieuc twds Dinan on N12 turn N at exit St René onto D712 to Hillion, then rd to Lermot. Site well sp. Narr, winding app rd. Med, unshd; wc; chem disp; mv service pnt; shwrs €0.15; el pnts (4-10A) €2-3 (poss rev pol); Indtte; shops 1.5km; tradsmn; bar; playgrnd; dogs €0.50; quiet; red low ssn. "Sea views fr most pitches; well-maintained site; welcoming, friendly owners; facs basic; narr site rds poss diff lge o'fits; vg." 1 Apr-30 Sep. € 12.50 2008*

France

ST BRIEUC *2E3* (2km S Rural) *48.50066, -2.75938* **Camping des Vallées, Blvd Paul-Doumer, 22000 St Brieuc [tel/fax 02 96 94 05 05; campingdesvallees@wanadoo.fr; www.mairie-saint-brieuc.fr]** Fr N12 take exit sp D700 Trégueux, Pleufragan & foll sp 'Des Vallées'. Site nr Parc de Brézillet Med, hdg pitch, some hdstg, pt shd; wc (some cont); chem disp; mv service pnt; baby facs; shwrs inc; el pnts (10A) €4; Indtte; shop; snacks; bar; playgrnd; htd pool, waterslide adj; sand beach 3km; 25% statics; dogs €2.40; adv bkg; CCI. "High kerbs to pitches." ♦ Easter-30 Oct. € 15.20 2008*

ST CALAIS *4F2* (500m N Urban) *47.92691, 0.74413* **Camp Municipal du Lac, Rue du Lac, 72120 St Calais [02 43 35 04 81]** Leave D357 (N157) at R angle bend by Champion supmkt; site in 100m. Site by lake on N edge of town, well sp fr cent. Ent easy to miss. Med, hdg/mkd pitch, pt shd; wc; chem disp; mv service pnt; shwrs inc; el pnts (3-6A) inc; Indtte; shops 500m; rest; snacks/bar adj; BBQ; playgrnd; pool adj; lake sw adj; some statics; dogs; poss cr; adv bkg; quiet; no ccard acc; CCI. "Delightful, well-kept site; friendly, helpful warden; spacious pitches espec nr lake; gd touring base." ♦ 1 Apr-15 Oct. € 10.80 2009*

ST CANNAT *10F2* (3km NW Rural) *43.63882, 5.27625* **Provence Camping, Chemin des Ponnes, 13410 Lambesc [04 42 57 05 78; fax 04 42 92 98 02; provencecamping@wanadoo.fr; www.provencecamping.com]** Fr N on D7n (N7), at end of Lambesc by-pass turn R onto D15; site on L in 150m. Sm, mkd pitch, pt sl, terr, shd; wc; mv service pnt; shwrs inc; el pnts (5-10A) €2.50-3.50; gas; Indtte; shop; bar; playgrnd; pool; games area; horseriding; entmnt; TV; some statics; dogs €2; red low ssn; CCI. "Kerbs to pitches; stays of 3+ nights preferred to o'nighters." ♦ 1 Apr-15 Oct. € 15.00 2007*

ST CAST LE GUILDO *2E3* (Coastal) *48.62732, -2.25403* **Camping Les Mielles, Blvd de la Vieux Ville, 22380 St Cast-le-Guildo [02 96 41 87 60; info@campings-vert-bleu.com; www.campings-vert-bleu.com]** Fr D786 at Matignon turn onto D13 into St Cast. Cross over staggered x-rds foll site sp down long gentle hill. R at next x-rds & site on R in 200m. Lge, unshd; wc (mainly cont); chem disp; baby facs; shwrs inc; el pnts (3-10A) €4.45-6.20; Indtte; shop; snacks; bar; playgrnd; htd pool; sand beach 350m; entmnt; 95% statics; dogs €2.40; poss cr; poss noisy; red low ssn. "Plenty of facs for teenagers; gd san facs; ltd space for tourers." 15 Mar-2 Jan. € 19.95 2009*

ST CAST LE GUILDO *2E3* (500m N Coastal) *48.64203, -2.25616* **Camping La Crique, Rue La Mare, 22380 St Cast-Le-Guildo [02 96 41 89 19; fax 02 96 81 04 77; info@campings-vert-bleu.com; www.campings-vert-bleu.com]** On ent town foll site sp. Med, mkd pitch, unshd; wc; chem disp; shwrs inc; el pnts (6A) €3.85; Indtte; snacks; bar; playgrnd; beach 200m; some statics (sep area); dogs €1.85; poss cr; adv bkg; quiet; CCI. "Site on top of low cliff with path to beach; vg." 15 Jun-15 Sep. € 14.60 2006*

ST CAST LE GUILDO *2E3* (500m N Coastal) *48.63690, -2.26900* **Camping Le Chatelet, Rue des Nouettes, 22380 St Cast-le-Guildo [02 96 41 96 33; fax 02 96 41 97 99; info@lechatelet.com; www.lechatelet.com]** Site sp fr all dir & in St Cast-le-Guildo but best rte: fr D786 at Matignon take D13 into St Cast-le-Guildo, turn L after Intermarché supmkt on R; foll sm site sp. Or app on D19 fr St Jaguel. Care needed down ramp to main site. (NB Avoid Matignon cent Wed due to mkt.) Lge, hdg/mkd pitch, pt sl, terr, pt shd; wc; chem disp; mv service pnt; baby facs; shwrs inc; el pnts (8A) inc (50m cable req); gas; Indtte; shop; snacks; bar; BBQ (gas/elec); playgrnd; htd pool & paddling pool; dir access sand beach 300m (via steep steps); fishing; tennis; cycle hire 500m; games rm; golf 2km; entmnt; wifi; TV; 10% statics (tour ops); dogs €4; adv bkg; ccard acc; red low ssn. "O'looking coast; extra for sea view pitches; gates clsd 2230-0730; helpful staff; access to some pitches diff lge o'fits; steep climb to beaches; mkt Mon." ♦ 24 Apr-11 Sep. € 39.00 ABS - B11 2009

The opening dates and prices on this campsite have changed. I'll send a site report form to the Club for the next edition of the guide.

ST CAST LE GUILDO *2E3* (1km S Coastal) *48.61337, -2.25627* **Camping Les Blés d'Or, La Chapelle, 22380 St Cast-le-Guildo [02 96 41 99 93; fax 02 96 81 04 63; camping-les-bles-dor@wanadoo.fr; www.camping-les-bles-dor.com]** App St Cast fr S on D19. Site sp opp beach N of Pen-Guen. Med, hdg/mkd pitch, pt shd; wc; chem disp; 30 pitches with individ san facs €25 per night, el pnts inc; shwrs inc; el pnts (10A) €3; gas; Indtte; supmkt 900m; tradsmn; rest 700m; snacks high ssn; bar; BBQ; playgrnd; htd pool; sand beach 700m; games rm; 30% statics; dogs free; phone; adv bkg; quiet; red low ssn; ccard acc; CCI. "Excel site; warm welcome." ♦ 1 Apr-31 Oct. € 15.00 2007*

ST CAST LE GUILDO *2E3* (3.5km S Rural) *48.58441, -2.25691* **Camping Le Château de Galinée, 22380 St Cast-le-Guildo [02 96 41 10 56; fax 02 96 41 03 72; contact@chateaudegalinee.com; www.chateaudegalinee.com or www.les-castels.com]** W fr St Malo on D168 thro Ploubalay. At La Ville-es-Comte branch onto D786 & go thro Notre Dame-du-Guildo. Approx 2km after Notre Dame-du-Guildo turn 3rd L into Rue de Galinée & foll sp to site. Do not go into St Cast. Med, hdg/mkd pitch, pt shd; wc; chem disp; baby facs; fam bthrm; shwrs inc; el pnts (10A) inc; Indtte; sm shop; snacks; bar; BBQ; playgrnd; htd pool complex inc covrd pool; waterslide; new covrd pool; paddling pool; sand beach 4km; fishing pond; tennis; games area; horseriding 6km; golf 3km; entmnt; wifi; games/TV rm; 30% statics; dogs €4; Eng spkn; adv bkg; quiet; ccard acc; red low ssn/long stay/CCI. "Excel, peaceful, family site in lovely area; spacious, well laid-out pitches; friendly, helpful staff; modern, clean san facs; pitches poss muddy after rain; excel rest; mkt Fri & Mon; highly rec." ♦ 7 May-11 Sep. € 37.00 (CChq acc) ABS - B27 2009*

ST CAST LE GUILDO *2E3* (6km SW Rural) *48.59111, -2.29578* **Camping Le Vallon aux Merlettes, Route de Lamballe, 22550 Matignon [02 96 41 11 61 or 06 70 31 03 22 (mob); giblanchet@orange.fr; www.camping-matignon.com]** Fr E & W take D786 to Matignon; 500m fr town cent turn SW on D13 twds Lamballe. Med, pt sl, pt shd; wc (cont); chem disp; mv service pnt; shwrs inc; el pnts (8A) €3.10; gas; lndtte; shop; snacks; playgrnd; pool 4km; tennis; sand beach 6km; some statics; dogs €0.75; adv bkg rec; quiet; ccard not acc; CCI. "Lovely site on playing fields outside attractive town; vg clean facs." ♦ Easter-30 Oct. € 12.70 2009*

ST CAST LE GUILDO *2E3* (2km NW Coastal) *48.63268, -2.27847* **Camping de la Fontaine, La Ville Norme, 22380 St Cast-le-Guildo [02 96 41 95 64 or 06 78 22 42 24 (mob); camping.la-fontaine@orange.fr]** Exit D786 at Matignon onto D13. Site well sp fr all dir. Take rd to beach of La Fresnaye (500m). Med, terr; unshd; wc; chem disp; mv service pnt; shwrs inc; el pnts (10A) €2.80-3.50 (poss long lead req); gas; lndtte; shop 3km; rest 1.5km; playgrnd; sand/shgl beach 500m; 90% statics; phone; poss cr; Eng spkn; adv bkg (rec Jul/Aug); quiet; CCI. "Sea views; clean modern san facs; coastal path & sm coves; spectacular sunsets; gd." ♦ 1 Apr-30 Sep. € 12.60 2008*

STE CATHERINE DE FIERBOIS see Ste Maure de Touraine *4H2*

STE CECILE see Chantonnay *2H4*

ST CERE *7C4* (SE Rural) *44.85792, 1.89761* **Camping Le Soulhol, Quai Salesses, 46400 St Céré [tel/fax 05 65 38 12 37; info@campinglesoulhol.com; www.campinglesoulhol.com]** Fr S on D940 twds St Céré turn onto D48 (Leyme); in 300m turn L (sp not easily seen); site in 200m. Site sp fr all dirs to St Céré. Lge, pt shd; wc; chem disp; mv service pnt; baby facs; shwrs; el pnts (10A) €3.10; gas; lndtte; sm shop, tradsmn (high ssn); shops, rests in town 1km; snacks; use of microwave; pool; tennis; cycles loan (free); Eng library; internet; entmnts; TV rm; 10% statics; dogs €1.50; phone; quiet; red low ssn; ccard not acc; red low ssn; CCI. "Spacious site; lge pitches; friendly, helpful staff; gd clean san facs; far end of site bet 2 rvs v quiet; poss flooding after heavy rain; mkt alt Weds; excel." ♦ 1 May-26 Sep. € 14.40 2009*

ST CHAMARAND *7D3* (2km SE Rural) *44.67259, 1.47733* **Camping Plage du Relais, Pont de Rhodes, 46310 St Chamarand [tel/fax 05 65 31 21 42 or 06 73 65 06 94 (mob); campingplagedurelais@wanadoo.fr; www.camping-plage-relais.com]** Exit A20 junc 56 onto D801 to join D820 dir Cahors. Site on R of D820 1km N of Frayssinet. Sm, mkd pitch, pt shd; wc; chem disp; mv service pnt; shwrs inc; el pnts (6A) €2.70; lndtte; shops adj; snacks; bar; BBQ; playgrnd; pool; lake fishing; tennis; games rm; entmnt; some statics; dogs €1; Eng spkn; adv bkg; quiet; CCI. "Pleasant, helpful owners; swing close to recep to get in gate." 1 Mar-31 Oct. € 14.40 2007*

ST CHELY D'APCHER *9D1* (N Rural) *44.81644, 3.27074* **Camp Municipal Croix des Anglais, 48200 St Chély-d'Apcher [04 66 31 03 24 or 04 66 31 00 67 (Mairie); fax 04 66 31 30 30; contact@ot.saintchelydapcher.com; www.ot-saintchelydapcher.com]** On E side of D809 (N9) to N end of town. Med, hdg pitch, unshd; wc; shwrs; el pnts (10A) inc; shops, rest bar 2km; playgrnd; htd pool 1km; TV; some statics; dogs €1; poss cr; Eng spkn; adv bkg; quiet. "Friendly site; gd walks; gd NH." 15 Jun-15 Sep. € 10.00 2007*

ST CHELY D'APCHER *9D1* (8km E Rural) *44.77506, 3.37203* **FFCC Camping Le Galier, Route de St Chély, 48120 St Alban-sur-Limagnole [04 66 31 58 80; fax 04 66 31 41 83; campinglegalier48@wanadoo.fr]** Exit A75 junc 34 onto D806 (N106), then E on D987 for 3km. Site 1.5km SW of St Alban on rvside. Sm, mkd pitch, pt sl; htd wc (some cont); shwrs inc; el pnts (6A) €3.70; lndtte; shop 1.5km; snacks; bar; BBQ; playgrnd; pool; some statics; dogs €1.60; poss cr; Eng spk; adv bkg; quiet; red low ssn/CCI. "Lovely setting by rv; friendly owners; clean san facs - stretched high ssn, ltd low ssn; gd walking, fishing; vg NH." ♦ 1 Mar-15 Nov. € 16.70 (3 persons) 2008*

⊞ **ST CHERON** *4E3* (3km SE Rural) *48.54435, 2.13840* **Camping Héliomonde (Naturist), La Petite Beauce, 91530 St Chéron [01 64 56 61 37; fax 01 64 56 51 30; helio@heliomonde.fr; www.heliomonde.fr]** N20 S to Arpajon; then D116 to St Chéron. Site bet Arpajon & Dourdan. Sp in town. Med, shd; htd wc (most cont); chem disp; mv service pnt; sauna; shwrs inc; el pnts (10A) €3.50; lndtte; shop; supmkt 3km; rest; snacks; bar; playgrnd; htd pool; paddling pool; tennis; games area; fitness rm; wifi; entmnt; mainly statics; dogs €3; train (Paris) 2km; adv bkg; quiet. "Open site; ltd facs; gd rest; conv Versailles, Paris; gd." € 25.00 (CChq acc) 2009*

ST CHERON *4E3* (3.5km SE Rural) *48.54341, 2.13791* **Camping Le Parc des Roches, La Petite Beauce, 91530 St Chéron [01 64 56 65 50; fax 01 64 56 54 50; contact@parcdesroches.com; www.parcdesroches.com]** N20 S to Arpajon; then D116 to St Chéron. Site bet Arpajon & Dourdan. Sp in town. Lge, hdg/mkd pitch, hdstg, pt shd; htd wc; chem disp; baby facs; shwrs inc; el pnts (4A) €2.60; gas 200m; lndtte; shop 3lkm; tradsmn; rest; snacks; bar; BBQ; playgrnd; htd pool; paddling pool; tennis; solarium; games area; games rm; 70% statics; dogs €1.70; train 3km; Eng spkn; adv bkg; quiet but poss noisy high ssn; ccard acc; CCI. "Pleasant, wooded site; helpful, friendly owner; o'night pitches lge & nr ent; san facs need refurb (2008); gd walking." ♦ 1 Apr-15 Oct. € 20.80 (CChq acc) 2008*

ST CHINIAN *10F1* (1km W) *43.42199, 2.93361* **Camp Municipal Les Terrasses, Route de St Pons, 34360 St Chinian [04 67 38 28 28 (Mairie); fax 04 67 38 28 29; mairie@saintchinian.fr]** On main Béziers-St Pons rd, D612 (N112), heading W on o'skts of St Chinian. Site on L. Med, terr, unshd; wc; shwrs inc; el pnts €2.15; shops 1km; poss cr; quiet. "Attractive site with gd views; sm pitches; diff access some pitches." 7 Jul-31 Aug. € 7.50 2009*

France

⊞ **ST CIRQ LAPOPIE** *7D3* (2km N Rural) *44.46926, 1.68135* **Camping La Plage, 46330 St Cirq-Lapopie [05 65 30 29 51; fax 05 65 30 23 33; camping.laplage@wanadoo.fr; www.campingplage.com]** Exit Cahors on D653, in Vers take D662 sp Cajarc. In 20km turn R at Tour-de-Faure over narr bdge, sp St Cirq-Lapopie, site 100m on R beside Rv Lot. Med, mkd pitch, shd; wc; baby facs; shwrs inc; el pnts (6-16A) €4-5; Indtte; shop; rest; snacks; bar; BBQ; playgrnd; pool; canoeing; watersports; wifi; entmnt; 5% statics; dogs €2; adv bkg; quiet; CCI. "Clean, tidy site rvside site; v shady; low ssn site yourself, pay later; friendly staff; gd walking; excel." ♦ € 17.00 2009*

ST CIRQ LAPOPIE *7D3* (2.5km S Rural) *44.44871, 1.67468* **FFCC Camping La Truffière, Route de Concots, 46330 St Cirq-Lapopie [05 65 30 20 22; fax 05 65 30 20 27; contact@camping-truffiere.com; www.camping-truffiere.com]** Take D911, Cahors to Villefranche rd; in 20km turn N onto D42 at Concots dir St Cirq for 8km - site clearly sp. NB Do not app fr St Cirq-Lapopie. Med, pt sl, terr, shd; htd wc; chem disp; mv service pnt; shwrs inc; el pnts (6A) €3.50; Indtte; ltd shop & 4km; rest; snacks; bar; playgrnd; htd pool; paddling pool; fishing 3km; cycle hire; entmnt; TV; dogs €1.50; phone; Eng spkn; adv bkg; quiet; 10% red low ssn; ccard acc; CCI. "Well-kept site in gd location; friendly owners; excel facs, ltd low ssn; most pitches in forest clearings; lovely pool; excel." ♦ 1 Apr-30 Sep. € 18.20 (CChq acc) 2009*

ST CIRQ LAPOPIE *7D3* (7km W Rural) *44.46991, 1.58701* **Camp Municipal, 46330 St Géry [05 65 31 40 08 (Mairie); fax 05 65 31 45 65]** Fr St Cirq foll N side Rv Lot on D662. Thro St Géry & after rlwy x-ing turn R bef petrol stn. Sp. Sm, pt sl, shd; wc (cont); el pnts (10A) inc (poss long lead req); shop 2km; rv & fishing adj; quiet. "Clean facs; warden calls eve." 1 Jul-5 Sep. € 8.80 2006*

ST CLAR *8E3* (4km NE Rural) *43.89797, 0.81114* **Camping Les Roches (Naturist), Le Nèri, 32380 Mauroux [tel/fax 05 62 66 30 18; campinglesroches@wanadoo.fr; www.campinglesroches.net]** Fr Fleurance take D953 to St Clar then D167 for 3km to site on L. Well sp on D167. Sm, hdg pitch, pt sl, pt shd; wc; chem disp; mv service pnt; sauna; shwrs; el pnts (6A) €4; Indtte; shops; tradsmn; rest; snacks; bar; pool; lake fishing; entmnt; TV rm; some statics; dogs €1.80; phone; Eng spkn; adv bkg; quiet; red low ssn/long stay; INF card. "Beautiful site in remote location; pleasant, helpful owners; gd sized pitches; gd walking; excel." ♦ 1 May-15 Sep. € 18.50 2009*

⊞ **ST CLAR** *8E3* (8km E Rural) *43.89075, 0.82837* **FFCC Centre Naturiste de Devèze (Naturist), 32380 Gaudonville [05 62 66 43 86; fax 05 62 66 42 02; camping.deveze@wanadoo.fr; www.deveze.eu]** Fr Fleurance to St Clar on D953; then take D40 sp Valence; in 700m take D13 sp Mauroux; in 700m take D167 to site in 4km on L. Lge, hdg pitch, pt sl, terr, pt shd; wc; chem disp; mv service pnt; 80% serviced pitches; shwrs inc; el pnts (5A) €4; gas; Indtte; shop; tradsmn; rest, snacks high ssn; bar; playgrnd; pool; lge lake; fishing; tennis; cycle hire; entmnt; TV rm; 15% statics; dogs €1.80; phone; Eng spkn; adv bkg; quiet; ccard acc; red low ssn; INF card req. "Lovely site; highly rec. "♦ € 19.20 2008*

ST CLAUDE *9A3* (2km SE Rural) *46.37153, 5.87171* **Camp Municipal du Martinet, Route de Genève, 39200 St Claude [03 84 45 00 40 or 03 84 41 42 62 (LS); fax 03 84 45 11 30]** On ent town foll 1-way, under bdge mkd 4.1m high, then take R turn 'Centre Ville' lane to next traff lts. Turn R then immed L sp Genève, turn R 300m after Fiat g'ge onto D290, site on R. Med, pt shd; wc (cont); chem disp; shwrs inc; el pnts (5A) €2.30; gas; Idntte; shops 1km; rest; htd pool adj; tennis; fishing; poss cr; adv bkg; quiet; red low ssn; CCI. "Warden calls am & pm only low ssn; ltd facs low ssn; excel walking; v attractive town; poss funfair on site in Jun - no prob; gd." 1 May-30 Sep. € 9.40 2008*

ST COLOMBAN DES VILLARDS *9C3* (700m SW Rural) *45.29015, 6.22091* **Camping La Perrière, Route du Col du Glandon, 73130 St Colomban-des-Villards [04 79 59 16 07; fax 04 79 59 15 17; camping.laperriere@wanadoo.fr]** Exit A43 junc 26 onto D927. Site at end of vill. Access rd narr & winding in places - not rec long o'fits. Sm, mkd pitch, hdstg, terr, pt shd; w; mv service pnt; shwrs inc; el pnts €4; Indtte; shop 200m; BBQ; playgrnd; games area; phone; quiet. "Excel." ♦ 10 Jun-9 Sep. € 15.00 2006*

ST COULOMB see St Malo *2E4*

ST CREPIN ET CARLUCET see Sarlat la Canéda *7C3*

STE CROIX EN PLAINE see Colmar *6F3*

ST CYBRANET see Sarlat la Canéda *7C3*

ST CYPRIEN (DORDOGNE) *7C3* (1km S Rural) *44.85547, 1.03788* **Camping du Garrit, Le Garrit, 24220 St Cyprien [05 53 29 20 56; pbecheau@aol.com; www.campingdugarritendordogneperigord.com]** Fr W on D703 turn R bef town sp; cross rlwy & bear R; then sharp R at rv. Sp on D703 fr St Cyprien as 'Le Garrit'. Med, hdg/mkd pitch, pt shd; wc; chem disp; baby facs; shwrs inc; el pnts (6A) €3; Indtte; shop; BBQ; playgrnd; pool; canoeing; sailing; boat hire; fishing; dogs €1; phone; Eng spkn; adv bkg; rd & rlwy noise some pitches; CCI. "Lovely, rvside site; lge pitches; excel san facs; gd touring base for prehistoric caves; NH or sh stay." 1 May-15 Sep. € 15.00 2009*

ST CYPRIEN PLAGE *10G1* (3km S Coastal) *42.59939, 3.03761* **Camping Cala Gogo, Ave Armand Lanoux, Les Capellans, 66750 St Cyprien-Plage [04 68 21 07 12; fax 04 68 21 02 19; camping.calagogo@wanadoo.fr; www.campmed.com]** Exit A9 at Perpignan Nord onto D617 to Canet-Plage, then D81; site sp bet St Cyprien-Plage & Argelès-Plage dir Les Capellans. V lge, hdg/mkd pitch, pt shd; htd wc (some cont); chem disp; mv service pnt; baby facs; shwrs inc; el pnts (6A) €3.40; Indtte; supmkt; rest; snacks; bar; playgrnd; 2 pools; paddling pool; sand beach adj; tennis; games area; entmnt; TV rm; 30% statics; dogs €3.70; Eng spkn; adv bkg; red low ssn; ccard acc; CCI. "Excel site; gd pitches; lovely beach; suitable for partially-sighted." ♦ 10 May-20 Sep. € 29.80 2008*

ST CYPRIEN PLAGE *10G1* (1.5km SW Urban/Coastal) *42.61851, 3.01582* **CHADOTEL Camping Le Roussillon, Chemin de la Mer, 66750 St Cyprien [04 68 21 06 45 or 02 51 33 05 05 (LS); fax 02 51 33 94 04; chadotel@wanadoo.fr; www.chadotel.com]** Exit A9 junc 42 Perpignan Sud onto D914 (N114) to Elne, D40 to St Cyprien. Site sp. Lge, hdg/mkd pitch, unshd; htd wc; baby facs; shwrs inc; el pnts (6A) inc; gas; Indtte; shop; snacks; bar; BBQ (gas); playgrnd; htd pool; waterslide; sand beach 1km; cycle hire; games rm; TV rm; entmnt; bus to beach; dogs €3; Eng spkn; adv bkg; red long stay/low ssn; ccard acc. "Vg family site; gd touring base." ♦ 5 Apr-27 Sep. € 29.90 2008*

ST CYPRIEN PLAGE *10G1* (3km W Rural) *42.62360, 3.00094* **Camp Municipal Bosc d'en Roug, 66750 St Cyprien [04 68 21 07 95; fax 04 68 21 55 43; www.camping-saint-cyprien.com]** Exit A9 junc 42 & foll sp Argelès-sur-Mer on D914. Turn off onto D40 dir Elne & foll sp St Cyprien. Site sp. V lge, mkd pitch, pt shd; wc; chem disp; mv waste; shwrs inc; (10A) inc; gas; Indtte; shop; rest; snacks; bar; playgrnd; htd pool; sand beach 3km; entmnt; 50% statics; dogs €2; phone; poss cr; Eng spkn; adv bkg; quiet. "Gd shady site in nice location on edge well-kept vill; gd rest & entmnt; helpful, friendly staff; no twin-axle c'vans." ♦ 5 Apr-20 Sep. € 11.00 2007*

ST CYPRIEN SUR DOURDOU see Conques *7D4*

ST CYR (VIENNE) see Jaunay Clan *4H1*

ST CYR SUR MER (VAR) see Bandol *10F3*

ST DENIS DU PAYRE see Luçon *7A1*

ST DIE *6E3* (10km E Rural) *48.25367, 7.08275* **Camp Municipal Le Violu, 88520 Gemaingoutte [03 29 57 70 70 (Mairie); fax 03 29 51 72 60; mairie gemaingoutte@wanadoo.fr]** Take D459 (N59) Rte du Col fr St Dié twd Ste Marie-aux-Mines. Site on L at ent to Gemaingoutte, 1km after junc with D23. Sm, pt sl, pt shd, mkd pitch; wc (some cont); chem disp; shwrs inc; el pnts (5A) €2.20; Indtte; shops 2.5km; tradsmn; playgrnd; rv adj; dogs €0.80; quiet; CCI. "Peaceful site on Rte du Vin." ♦ 1 Apr-31 Oct. € 8.50 2007*

⊞ **ST DIE** *6E3* (1km SE Urban) *48.28605, 6.96990* **Camping La Vanne de Pierre, 5 Rue du Camping, 88100 St Dié-des-Vosges [03 29 56 23 56; fax 03 29 42 22 23; vanne depierre@wanadoo.fr; www.vannedepierre.com]** Fr any dir twd town cent foll 'Stade du Breuil Camping' sp. Med, hdg/mkd pitch, terr, pt shd; htd wc (some cont); chem disp; shwrs inc; el pnts (6-10A) €6-7; Indtte (inc dryer); shops 2km; tradsmn; rest in town; snacks; bar; playgrnd; pool; rv fishing; tennis 500m; entmnt; internet; TV rm; 15% statics; dogs €3; poss cr; adv bkg rec; quiet but some rd noise; ccard acc; red low ssn; CCI. "Gd, clean san facs; lge pitches; well-kept site; helpful owners." ♦ € 24.00 (CChq acc) 2009*

ST DONAT SUR L'HERBASSE *9C2* (6km N Rural) *45.14631, 5.02140* **FFCC Camping Les Falquets, Route de Margès, 26260 Charmes-sur-l'Herbasse [04 75 45 75 57 or 04 75 45 27 44 (LS); fax 04 75 45 66 17; info@lesfalquets.com; www.lesfalquets.com]** Exit A7 junc 13 onto D532 dir Romans-sur-Isère; at Chanos-Curson turn N onto D67 to Charmes (via St Donat-sur-l'Herbasse), then D121 dir Margès. Site sp in vill on rvside. Med, shd; wc (some cont); chem disp; shwrs inc; el pnts (6-10A) €2.80-3.50; Indtte; shop 3km; bar; playgrnd; lake sw, waterslide, windsurfing & tennis 3km; 25% statics; dogs free; phone; Eng spkn; adv bkg rec high ssn; quiet; red low ssn; CCI. "Pleasant, well-kept site; old facs but clean; helpful warden; sh walk to vill; gd." ♦ 1 May-31 Aug. € 13.00 2009*

ST DONAT SUR L'HERBASSE *9C2* (500m S Rural) *45.11916, 4.99290* **Camping Domaine Les Ulèzes, Route de Romans, 26260 St Donat-sur-l'Herbasse [tel/fax 04 75 47 83 20; contact@domaine-des-ulezes.com; www.domaine-des-ulezes.com]** Exit A7 junc 13 onto D532 dir Romans-sur-Isère. In 5km turn N onto D67 thro St Donat. Site on edge of vill off D53 dir Peyrins, well sp. Med, hdg/mkd pitch, pt shd; wc; chem disp; mv service pnt; shwrs inc; el pnts (6-10A) €3.50-4.50; gas 1km; Indtte; ice; shop; tradsmn; rest; snacks; bar; BBQ (gas/elec); playgrnd; htd pool; games area; games rm; entmnt; wifi; TV; 10% statics; dogs €2; no twin-axles; Eng spkn; adv bkg; quiet; ccard acc; red low ssn; CCI. "Lovely rvside site; gd size pitches; welcoming, friendly owners; canal-side walk to town; gd touring base; vg." ♦ 1 Apr-31 Oct. € 18.50 2009*

ST ELOY LES MINES *7A4* (S Rural) *46.15144, 2.83321* **Camp Municipal La Poule d'Eau, Rue de la Poule d'Eau, 63700 St Eloy-les-Mines [04 73 85 45 47; fax 04 73 85 07 75; selm.maire@wanadoo.fr; www.sainteloylesmines.com]** On D2144 (N144) fr S turn W at 1st rndabt at St Eloy-les-Mines (Vieille Ville) onto D110; site 200m clearly sp. Fr Montluçon/Montaigut, last rndabt; site by 2 lakes. Med, mkd pitch, pt sl, shd; wc; shwrs; el pnts (6A) inc; shop adj; tradsmn; playgrnd; lake sw, fishing & watersports adj; entmnt; adv bkg; quiet. "Barrier clsd 1200-1600; nice location; warden v proud of his site; excel sh stay/NH." 1 Jun-30 Sep. € 8.48 2008*

ST EMILION *7C2* (3km N Rural) *44.91695, -0.14160* **Camping Domaine de la Barbanne, Route de Montagne, 33330 St Emilion [05 57 24 75 80; fax 05 57 24 69 68; barbanne@wanadoo.fr; www.camping-saint-emilion.com]** NB Trailer c'vans not permitted in cent of St Emilion. Fr A10 exit junc 39a sp Libourne onto D670. In Libourne turn E on D243 twd St Emilion. On o'skts of St Emilion turn L onto D122 dir Lussac & Montagne; site on R by lake in 3km. Or fr S, foll site sp off D670 to Libourne, nr Les Bigaroux. NB D122 S of St Emilion unsuitable for c'vans. NB Do not use D1089 (N89) N of Libourne - width restriction. Lge, hdg/mkd pitch, hdstg, shd; wc (some cont); chem disp; mv service pnt; baby facs; shwrs inc; el pnts (10A) inc; gas; lndtte; sm shop; tradsmn; rest, snacks high ssn; BBQ; playgrnd; htd pool; paddling pool; waterslide; fishing; watersports nr; tennis; cycle hire; horseriding 8km; games/ TV rm; wifi; entmnt; 20% statics; dogs €4; phone; poss cr; Eng spkn; adv bkg; quiet; ccard acc; red low ssn; CCI. "Lovely, peaceful, family site; well-run; owners friendly & helpful; clean, modern san facs - poss stretched high ssn & ltd low ssn; muddy when wet; facs used by long-dist coach firms; free bus/taxi service to St Emilion; tree fluff a minor irritation in May (gone by Jun); gd cycle rtes; excel." ♦ 2 Apr-21 Sep. € 35.00 (CChq acc) ABS - D08 2009*

⊞ **ST EMILION** *7C2* (4km SE Rural) **Aire St Emilion Domaine du Château Gerbaud, 33000 St Peu-d'Armens [06 03 27 00 32 (mob); fax 05 57 47 10 53; contact@ chateau-gerbaud.com; www.chateau-gerbaud.com]** Fr Libourne SE on D670/D936 dir Castillon-la-Bataille. In St Pey-d'Armens at bar/tabac foll sp Château Gerbaud vineyard. Parking & service pnt for m'vans for max 48 hours; no charge if wine purchased. "Friendly, Eng-speaking owners." 2006*

STE ENGRACE *8F1* (5km NW Rural) *43.01600, -0.85786* **FFCC Camping Ibarra, Quartier Les Casernes, 64560 Ste Engrâce [05 59 28 73 59; maryse@ibarra-chantina. com; www.ibarra-chantina.com]** D918 S fr Tardets-Sorholus; in 2km turn R onto D26; in 6km to L onto D113 sp Ste Engrâce; site on R in 5km. Site clearly sp just bef La Caserne. NB not suitable car+c'van. Sm, mkd pitch, pt shd; wc (some cont); chem disp; shwrs inc; el pnts (5A) €1.80; lndry rm; tradsmn; snacks 500m; bar; BBQ (sep area); playgrnd; 8% statics; dogs; quiet; CCI. "Pleasant site on rv bank; scenic views; spectacular Kakuetta gorges nrby; vg." ♦ 1 Apr-30 Sep. € 10.20 2008*

STE ENIMIE *9D1* (1.5km SW Rural) *44.35378, 3.40155* **Camp Couderc, Route de Millau, 48210 Ste Enimie [04 66 48 50 53; fax 04 66 48 58 59; campingcouderc@ orange.fr; www.campingcouderc.fr]** Leave Ste Eminie on D907B in dir Millau, site on L bank of Rv Tarn. Med, mkd pitch, pt sl, terr, pt shd; wc; chem disp; mv service pnt; baby facs; shwrs inc; el pnts (6A) €3; gas; shop; snacks; bar; playgrnd; pool; canoeing; dogs free; Eng spkn; quiet; red low ssn; CCI. "Rd along gorge narr & twisting; busy, friendly, lovely site; gd modern facs." ♦ 1 Apr-30 Sep. € 18.00 2009*

ST ETIENNE DE BAIGORRY *8F1* (500m N Rural) *43.18370, -1.33569* **Camp Municipal L'Irouleguy, 64430 St Etienne-de-Baïgorry [05 59 37 43 96 or 05 59 37 40 80; fax 05 59 37 48 20; comstetiennebaigorry@wanadoo.fr]** W on D15 fr St Jean-Pied-de-Port to St Etienne-de-Baigorry; site on R 300m bef junc with D948; ent next to wine co-operative. Fr N on D948, on ent St Etienne-de-Baïgorry turn L onto D15; site in 300m on L. Med, shd; wc; chem disp; shwrs inc; el pnts (6A) €2.70; lndtte; gas, shop 100m; htd pool adj; tennis adj; troutfishing; birdwatching; poss cr; adv bkg; quiet. "Scenic; gd hill walking cent; out of ssn call at Mairie to open site for NH." ♦ 1 Mar-15 Dec. € 10.80 2008*

ST ETIENNE DE FONTBELLON see Aubenas *9D2*

⊞ **ST ETIENNE DE MONTLUC** *2G4* (200m N Rural) *47.28002, -1.77967* **Camp Municipal de la Coletterie, Rue de Tivoli, 44360 St Etienne-de-Montluc [02 40 86 97 44 or 02 40 86 80 26 (Mairie)]** Well sp fr N165 (E60) in both dirs. Sm, hdg/mkd pitch, pt sl, pt shd; htd wc; chem disp; shwrs inc; baby facs; el pnts (15A) €3.50; lndtte (inc dryer); shop, rest, bar 500m; playgrnd; fishing; games area; dogs €1.05; phone; adv bkg; quiet; CCI. "Vg." ♦ € 7.40 2009*

ST ETIENNE DE VILLEREAL see Villeréal *7D3*

ST ETIENNE DU BOIS (VENDEE) see Legé *2H4*

STE EULALIE EN BORN *7D1* (W Rural) *44.30607, -1.17867* **Camp Municipal du Lac, 1590 Route du Lac, 40200 Ste Eulalie-en-Born [05 58 09 70 10 or 05 58 09 73 48 (Mairie); fax 05 58 09 76 89; contact@ lecampingdulac.com; www.lecampingdulac.com]** N fr Mimizan on D87/D652. Pass Ste Eulalie & turn W at water tower, site sp. Med, mkd pitch, pt shd; wc; chem disp; mv service pnt; baby facs; shwrs inc; el pnts (10A) €3.90; gas; lndtte; snacks; bar; pool; lake sw & beach adj; boat hire; games area; some statics; dogs €2.10; phone; poss cr; Eng spkn; adv bkg; quiet; ccard acc; CCI. "On Lake Biscarrosse; vg for familes; do not confuse with site of similar name on Lac Aureilhan, 2km N of Mimizan." 1 Apr-30 Oct. € 17.50 2009*

ST EUSTACHE see Annecy *9B3*

ST EVARZEC see Quimper *2F2*

ST EVROULT NOTRE DAME DU BOIS see Aigle, L' *4E2*

ST FARGEAU *4G4* (6km SE Rural) *47.60941, 3.11961* **Camp Municipal La Calangue, 89170 St Fargeau [tel/fax 03 86 74 04 55]** Fr St Fargeau take D85 dir of St Sauveur-en-Puisaye. In 4.5km turn R sp Etang/Réservoir de Bourdon. Site on N shore of lake, well sp. Lge, mkd pitch, shd; htd wc (some cont)(own san rec Jul 2007); shwrs inc; el pnts (6-10A) €2-2.60; lndtte; shop, rest, snacks, bar adj; playgrnd; lake sw & sand beach adj; fishing; canoeing; horseriding nr; 10% statics; poss cr; quiet (noisy nr lake); adv bkg rec high ssn; CCI. "Pleasant site in woods; tight manoeuvring round trees; sm pitches; gd." ♦ Easter-30 Sep. € 8.20 2007*

ST FELIX DE REILLAC see Douze, La *7C3*

ST FERREOL TRENTE PAS see Nyons *9D2*

ST FLORENT SUR CHER *4H3* (7km SE Rural) *46.93663, 2.27071* **Camp Intercommunal, 6 Rue de l'Abreuvoir, 18400 Lunery [02 48 68 07 38 or 02 48 23 22 08; fax 02 48 55 26 78; fercher@fr-oleane.com]** Fr N151 turn S onto D27 at St Florent-sur-Cher, cont for 7km, site in vill cent of Lunery. Sm, hdg/mkd pitch, pt shd; wc; chem disp; mv service pnt; shwrs inc; el pnts (6A) €3.50 (poss rev pol); shop, rest in vill; playgrnd; fishing; tennis nr; no statics; bus 200m, train in vill; phone 100m; Eng spkn; red long stay; CCI. "Charming, peaceful, rvside site; quiet even high ssn; gd clean san facs; liable to flood low ssn - phone ahead to check open; gd." ♦ 15 Apr-15 Sep. € 15.00 2009*

ST FLORENTIN *4F4* (1km S Rural) *47.99252, 3.73450* **Camping L'Armançon, 89600 St Florentin [tel/fax 03 86 35 11 86; ot.saint-florentin@wanadoo.fr; www.saint-florentin-tourisme.fr]** N fr Auxerre on N77 site on R app rv bdge S of town. Fr N pass traff islands, exit town up slope, x-ing canal & rv. Site immed on S side of rv bdge - turn R immed at end of bdg then under bdg to site. Site well sp fr all dirs. Med, hdg pitch, pt sl, pt shd; wc (cont); chem disp; shwrs inc; el pnts (13A) €2.30; gas; Indtte; shop; café/bar; snacks; playgrnd; fishing; dogs €0.20; poss cr; some rd noise at night. "Well-kept site; excel pitches; friendly manager; dated but clean san facs; diff, steep exit to main rd; gd." 11 Apr-1 Oct. € 9.30 2009*

ST FLOUR *9C1* (2km N Rural) *45.05120, 3.10778* **Camping International La Roche Murat, 15100 St Flour [04 71 60 43 63; fax 04 71 60 02 10; courrier@camping-saint-flour.com; www.camping-saint-flour.com]** Fr N or S on A75 exit junc 28; sp off rndabt on St Flour side of m'way. Site ent visible 150m fr rndabt. Med, hdg/mkd pitch, terr, pt shd; htd wc; chem disp; mv service pnt; shwrs inc; el pnts (10A) inc; gas; Indry rm; shops 4km; tradsmn; playgrnd; pool 2km; dogs; Eng spkn; adv bkg; quiet, v little rd noise; ccard not acc; CCI. "Busy site; conv NH fr A75; gd views; sunny & secluded pitches; helpful warden; gd, clean facs; some pitches sm; when pitches waterlogged use site rds; old town high on hill worth visit; excel touring cent; vg." ♦ 1 Apr-1 Nov. € 14.30 2009*

ST FLOUR *9C1* (SW Urban) *45.03313, 3.08306* **Camp Municipal Les Orgues, 19 Ave Dr Maillet, 15100 St Flour [04 71 60 44 01]** On A75 to St Flour, foll sps for 'ville haute'; at x-rds in town cent turn L (dir Aurillac). Ent in 250m, narr & steep on L bet houses, site sp opp poss obscured by parked cars. NB Site ent is on busy main rd & has 2m high barrier. If c'van over 2m, stop at barrier (c'van sticking out into rd), walk down to office & ask warden to unlock barrier - poss v dangerous. Med, mkd pitch, pt sl, pt shd; wc; shwrs inc; el pnts (6A) inc; shops, rest; bar 1km; playgrnd; covrd pool 1km; tennis; quiet; poss cr; CCI. "Friendly recep; gd pitches; gd NH." ♦ 1 Jun-1 Sep. € 11.85 2008*

ST FORT SUR GIRONDE *7B2* (4km SW Rural) *45.43278, -0.75185* **Camping Port Maubert, 8 Rue de Chassillac, 17240 St Fort-sur-Gironde [05 46 04 78 86; fax 05 46 04 16 79; bourdieu.jean-luc@wanadoo.fr; www.campingportmaubert.com]** Exit A10 junc 37 onto D730 dir Royan. Foll sp Port Maubert & site. Sm, hdg/mkd pitch, shd; wc (some cont); chem disp; mv service pnt; shwrs inc; el pnts (10A) €3.50; gas; Indtte; shop 4km; tradsmn; bar; BBQ; playgrnd; pool; sand beach 25km; cycle hire; games rm; TV; some statics; dogs €2; Eng spkn; adv bkg; quiet; ccard acc; red long stay/CCI. "Pleasant, well-run site." 1 May-30 Sep. € 12.40 2009*

France

STE FOY LA GRANDE *7C2* (1.5km NE Rural) *44.84426, 0.22468* **Camping de la Bastide, Allée du Camping, 2 Les Tuileries, Pineuilh, 33220 Ste Foy-la-Grande [tel/fax 05 57 46 13 84; contact@camping-bastide.com; www.camping-bastide.com]** Fr W go thro town & turn off at D130 to site, well sp on Rv Dordogne. Med, mkd pitch, pt shd; wc; chem disp; mv service pnt; baby facs; shwrs inc; el pnts (10A) inc (poss rev pol); Indtte; tradsmn; shops, snacks & bar 500m, playgrnd; pool; jacuzzi; fishing, canoeing; games rm; wifi; 10% statics; dogs €2; phone; poss cr; Eng spkn; adv bkg; v quiet; ccard acc; red low ssn; CCI. "Pretty, well-cared for site; sm pitches; helpful British owners; immac, modern san facs; high kerb stones onto pitches - poss diff lge o'fits; no twin-axles; mkt Sat; vg." ♦ 1 Apr-31 Oct. € 20.00 2009*

STE FOY LA GRANDE *7C2* (6km W Rural) *44.82954, 0.12290* **FLOWER Camping La Rivière Fleurie, St Aulaye, 24230 St Antoine-de-Breuilh [tel/fax 05 53 24 82 80; info@la-riviere-fleurie.com; www.la-riviere-fleurie.com or www.flowercamping.com]** Turn S off D936 at W end of St Antoine-de-Breuilh; site 2.7km fr main rd in vill of St Aulaye adj Rv Dordogne. Well sp. Med, mkd pitch, pt shd; wc; chem disp; baby facs; shwrs inc; el pnts (4-10A) €3.10-€4.50; gas; Indtte; shops 4km; hypmkt 5km; tradsmn; rest; bar; BBQ; playgrnd; htd pool; paddling pool; games rm; rv sw adj; tennis, horseriding; golf; canoeing & fishing nrby; entmnt; wifi; 10% statics; dogs €2; phone; Eng spkn; adv bkg; quiet; red low ssn/long stay; CCI. "Peaceful, well-maintained site; spacious pitches; welcoming, helpful owners; excel san facs; church bells during day; vg cycling; mkt Sat in Ste Foy; highly rec." ♦ 10 Apr-20 Sep. € 18.50 2008*

STE FOY LA GRANDE *7C2* (10km W Rural) *44.82486, 0.06127* **Camping La Plage, 24230 St Seurin-de-Prats [tel/fax 05 53 58 61 07; enquiries@dordognecamping.co.uk; www.dordognecamping.co.uk]** Fr D936 W of Ste Foy take D11 at Les Réaux twrds Pessac. Site on R of D11 immed bef x-ing Rv Dordogne into Pessac. Sm, pt sl, pt shd; wc; chem disp (wc); mv service pnt nrby; shwrs inc; el pnts (15A) €4; Indry service; shops 500m; rest; snacks; bar; BBQ (gas); playgrnd; pool; rv & shgl beach adj; canoeing; fishing; games area; sat TV; twin-axles & RVs acc (must book in advance); no statics: dogs €2 (max 2 per o'fit); bus & train in walking dist; adv bkg; quiet; CCI. "Beautiful, spacious rvside site with mature trees; peaceful; friendly, helpful British owners; gd clean san facs; lovely pool; suitable v lge o'fits; golf, horseriding, aquapark nrby; excel." 1 Jun-15 Sep. € 18.50 2009*

STE FOY L'ARGENTIERE *9B2* (7km SE Rural) *45.65185, 4.56315* **Camp Municipal Les Verpillières, Les Plaines, 69850 St Martin-en-Haut [04 78 48 62 16; http://saintmartin.decideur.net]** Fr Craponne on W o'skts of Lyon SW on D11 to cent of St Martin-en-Haut. W of St Martin on D311 dir St Symphorien turn L dir Ste Catherine, site on L in 3km. Fr St Foy take D489 SE to Duerne, D34 to St Martin-en-Haut, then as above. This app not for lge o'fits, two 7-12% climbs out of St Foy & hairpins after Duerne. Med, mkd pitch, pt sl, shd; htd wc; shwrs; el pnts (10A) €3.75; Indtte; shops 500m; snacks; bar; playgrnd; tennis 300m; entmnt; 75% statics; poss cr; adv bkg; quiet. "Lovely wooded site with red squirrels; busy at w/end." 1 Apr-31 Oct. € 7.00 2008*

ST FRAIMBAULT see Domfront *4E1*

ST GALMIER *9B2* (2km E Rural) *45.59266, 4.33528* **CAMPEOLE Camping Le Val de Coise, Route de la Thiéry, 42330 St Galmier [04 77 54 14 82; fax 04 77 54 02 45; val-de-coise@campeole.com;www.camping-valdecoise.com or www.campeole.com]** Fr St Etienne take D1082 (N82) N. In 7km turn R onto D12 sp St Galmier; after x-ing rv bdge on outskirts of vill turn R & foll Camping sp for 2km. Or fr N on D1082 look for sp to St Galmier about 1.5km S of Montrond-les-Bains & turn L onto D6 to St Galmier. On D12 in St Galmier at floral rndabt with fountain if app fr N go L & fr S go R, uphill & foll site sp. Site approx 1.5km fr rndabt. Med, mkd pitch, hdstg, pt sl, pt shd; wc; chem disp; baby facs; shwrs inc; el pnts (16A) €4.10; gas; Indtte; sm shop & 2km; tradsmn; rest & snacks 2km; BBQ; playgrnd; htd pool; paddling pool; fishing; tennis 2km; cycle hire; games area; games rm; wifi; entmnt; TV rm; 20% statics; dogs €2.60; phone; Eng spkn; adv bkg; v quiet; ccard acc; red low ssn; CCI. "Pleasant rvside site; helpful staff; facs poss stretched high ssn; highly rec." ♦ 10 Apr-17 Oct. € 15.00 2009*

See advertisement above

ST GAUDENS *8F3* (1km W Rural) *43.11000, 0.70839* **Camp Municipal Belvédère des Pyrénées, Rue des Chanteurs du Comminges, 31800 St Gaudens [05 62 00 16 03; www.st-gaudens.com]** Foll camping sp fr St Gaudens town cent on D817 (N117) dir Tarbes. Site ent at top of hill on N side. Last rd sp is 'Belvédère'. Med, pt shd; htd wc; mv service pnt; shwrs inc; el pnts (4-13A) €2.75-5.35; gas; rest nrby; playgrnd; dogs €1.50; no adv bkg; some rd noise; ccard not acc. "Pleasant site; facs clean; gates clsd 1200-1500 & 2300-0700." 1 Jun-30 Sep. € 14.70 2007*

ST GAULTIER *4H2* (S Rural) *46.63235, 1.42145* **Camp Municipal L'Illon, Rue de Limage, 36800 St Gaultier [02 54 47 11 22 or 02 54 01 66 00 (Mairie); fax 02 54 01 66 09; st-gaultier.mairie@wanadoo.fr; www.mairie-saintgaultier.fr]** Site well sp in town. V narr thro town - best app fr W. NB App down short, steep hill with sharp R turn into site ent. Med, mkd pitch, pt sl, pt shd; wc (some cont); shwrs inc; el pnts €2; gas; shops 500m; playgrnd; rv & fishing 50m; quiet. "Lovely, peaceful setting; nr rv; pitch yourself, warden calls; site ent poss too narr for twin-axles/lge o'fits." Easter-30 Sep. € 7.20 2008*

ST GENIEZ D'OLT *9D1* (750m NE Rural) *44.46861, 2.98166* **CAMPEOLE Camping La Boissière, Route de la Cascade, 12130 St Geniez-d'Olt [05 65 70 40 43; fax 05 65 47 56 39; boissiere@campeole.com; www.camping-aveyron.info or www.campeole.com]** Exit A75 junc 40 onto D998 dir St Geniez-d'Olt. Site sp on R on E edge of town. Lge, hdg/mkd pitch, hdstg, pt sl, pt shd; htd wc; chem disp; baby facs; shwrs inc; el pnts (6-10A) inc; Indtte (inc dryer); shop; supmkt nr; tradsmn; rest; snacks; bar; BBQ; playgrnd; htd pool; paddling pool; tennis adj; fishing & canoeing nrby; games area; games rm; wifi; entment; some statics; dogs €2.80; phone; Eng spkn; adv bkg; quiet; ccard acc; red low ssn; CCI. "Pleasant, tranquil site & town in Lot Valley." ♦ 17 Apr-19 Sep. € 24.50 2009*

See advertisement opposite

ST GENIEZ D'OLT *9D1* (500m W Rural) *44.46210, 2.96240* **Kawan Village Marmotel, 12130 St Geniez-d'Olt [05 65 70 46 51; fax 05 65 47 41 38; info@marmotel.com; www.marmotel.com]** Exit A75 at junc 41 onto D37 dir Campagnac. Then onto D202, D45 & D988. Site situated on W of vill by Rv Lot on D19. Lge, hdg pitch, pt shd; wc; chem disp; mv service pnt; some pitches with individual san facs; baby facs; sauna; shwrs inc; el pnts (10A) inc; gas; Indtte; shop 500m; tradsmn; rest, bar high ssn; BBQ; playgrnd; htd pool; paddling pool; waterslide; tennis; games area; cycle hire; entmnt; TV rm; some statics; dogs €1.50; Eng spkn; adv bkg; quiet; red low ssn; ccard acc; CCI. "Highly rec; some pitches poss tight lge o'fits; poss muddy when wet; gd pool & rest." ♦ 10 May-14 Sep. € 26.30 (CChq acc) 2008*

ST GENIS LAVAL see Lyon *9B2*

ST GEORGES (PAS DE CALAIS) see Hesdin *3B3*

ST GEORGES DE DIDONNE see Royan *7B1*

ST GEORGES DE LEVEJAC see Vignes, Les *9D1*

ST GEORGES DU VIEVRE *3D2* (3km E Rural) **Camping La Brettonnière (Séjourne), 27450 St Grégoire-du-Vièvre [02 32 42 82 67; www.stgeorgesvievre.fr]** At traff lts on D130 in Pont Authou turn W onto D137 twd St Georges-du-Vièvre; after 7km turn L, sp Camping Rural; site in 1km. NB Steep rdway down & narr terrs poss unsuitable for c'vans. Sm, mkd pitch, terr, shd; wc; chem disp; shwrs inc; el pnts €4; shop 1km; playgrnd; pool 4km; adv bkg; quiet; CCI. "CL-type farm site; vg." 1 May-31 Oct. € 14.60 2007*

ST GEORGES DU VIEVRE *3D2* (200m W Rural) *49.24248, 0.58040* **Camp Municipal du Vièvre, Route de Noards, 27450 St Georges-du-Vièvre [02 32 42 76 79 or 02 32 56 34 29 (LS); fax 02 32 57 52 90; camping.stgeorgesduvievre@wanadoo.fr; www.camping-normand.com]** Fr traff lts on D130 in Pont Authou turn W onto D137 to St Georges-du-Vièvre; in town sq at tourist info turn L uphill sp camping; site 200m on L. If app fr S on N138 at Bernay take D834 sp Le Havre to Lieurey. Turn R onto D137 to St Georges, then turn R at camping sp by sw pool. Sm, hdg pitch, pt shd; wc; chem disp; serviced pitches; shwrs inc; el pnts (5A) €2.20; gas 200m; Indry rm; shops 200m; playgrnd; pool 150m; tennis 50m; sw 100m; cycle hire; wifi at TO; dogs; Eng spkn; adv bkg (rec high ssn); quiet; CCI. "Peaceful; gd facs & pitches; well-run site; interesting area; gd cycling; vg." ♦ 1 Apr-30 Sep. € 8.10 2009*

ST GEORGES SUR LAYON see Doué la Fontaine *4G1*

ST GEOURS DE MAREMNE *8E1* (500m W Rural) *43.68981, -1.23376* **Camping Les Platanes, 3 Route de Lecoume, 40230 St Geours-de-Maremne [tel/fax 05 58 57 45 35; info@platanes.com; www.platanes.com]** Fr N10 take junc sp St Geours-de-Maremne. Site sp fr town cent. Med, pt sl, pt shd; htd wc; chem disp; shwrs inc; el pnts (6A) €4.10; gas; Indtte; shop nr; tradsmn; rest; snacks; bar; BBQ; playgrnd; pool (high ssn); sand beach 8km; tennis; games area; wifi; TV; 50% statics; dogs €1.40; phone; poss cr; adv bkg; quiet; ccard acc; red low ssn/long stay; CCI. "Friendly British owners; diff to site on lower level; OK upper level; low ssn poss long walk to san facs in dark; muddy pitches if wet; useful NH on N10." 1 Mar-15 Nov. € 17.95 2006*

ST GERAUD DE CORPS see Montpon Ménestérol *7C2*

ST GERMAIN see Aubenas *9D2*

ST GERMAIN DU BEL AIR see Gourdon *7D3*

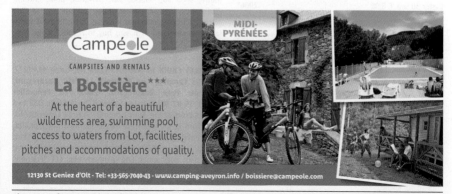

ST GERMAIN DU BOIS *6H1* (500m S Rural) *46.74661, 5.24613* **Camp Municipal de l'Etang Titard, Route de Louhans, 71330 St Germain-du-Bois [03 85 72 06 15 or 03 85 72 01 47; fax 03 85 72 03 38; mairie-71330-saint-germain-du-bois@wanadoo.fr]** Fr Chalon-sur Saône E on N78, exit at Thurey onto D24 to St Germain. Site sp on D13 adj lake. Sm, mkd pitch, terr, pt shd; wc; chem disp; mv service pnt; shwrs inc; el pnts (6A); lndtte; shop, rest, bar 300m; BBQ; playgrnd, htd, covrd pool in sports grnd adj; fishing; dogs; adv bkg; quiet; CCI. "Lge pitches; friendly warden; no sw in lake; pleasant town; gd cycling area." ♦ 1 May-15 Sep. € 7.60 2009*

ST GERMAIN LES BELLES see Masseret *7B3*

ST GERMAIN L'HERM *9B1* (500m W Rural) *45.45663, 3.54823* **Camping St Eloy, Route de la Chaise-Dieu, 63630 St Germain-l'Herm [04 73 72 05 13 or 04 73 34 75 53 (LS)); fax 04 73 34 70 94; sogeval@wanadoo.fr]** Take D906 S fr Ambert to Arlanc, turn R onto D300 (D999A) to St Germain, site sp on app to vill. Med, mkd pitch, pt sl, terr, pt shd; wc (some cont); chem disp; mv service pnt; el pnts (8A) €3; lndry rm; shop 500m; tradsmn; rest 500m; BBQ; playgrnd; pool; 10% statics; dogs €1.50; phone; adv bkg; quiet. "Pleasant views; cycle & walking tracks fr vill; vg." ♦ 15 Jun-30 Sep. € 12.00 2008*

ST GERVAIS D'AUVERGNE *7A4* (500m N Rural) *46.03706, 2.81733* **Camp Municipal L'Etang Philippe, 63390 St Gervais-d'Auvergne [tel/fax 04 73 85 74 84; info@camping-loisir.com; www.camping-loisir.com]** Fr N144 3km S of St Eloy-les-Mines, take D987 S to St Gervais. Site on R just bef town. Lge, hdg pitch, pt shd; wc; chem disp; mv service pnt; shwrs inc; el pnts (10A) inc; lndtte; shop 500m; tradsmn (Jul/Aug); playgrnd; lake sw & beach adj; cycle hire; tennis; archery; entmnt; some statics; dogs €0.50; Eng spkn; adv bkg; quiet; CCI. "Popular, well-maintained site; clean facs; poss untidy low ssn & ltd facs; vg." ♦ Easter-30 Sep. € 8.90 2006*

ST GERVAIS D'AUVERGNE *7A4* (8km E Rural) *46.02741, 2.89894* **Camp Municipal Les Prés Dimanches, 63390 Châteauneuf-les-Bains [04 73 86 41 50 or 04 73 86 67 65 (LS); fax 04 73 86 41 71; mairie-chat-les-bains@wanadoo.fr]** Fr Montaigut take N144 S twd Riom & Clermont-Ferrand. In 9km at La Boule S onto D987 to St Gervais. Take D227 E to Chateuneuf-les-Bains. In 7km L onto D109. Site thro vill on R. Sm, pt shd, hdg/mkd pitch; htd wc; shwrs inc; el pnts (6A) inc; lndtte; shop 250m; rest adj; playgrnd; fishing, tennis, canoeing nrby; spa baths 500m; quiet; adv bkg; excel; CCI. "Lovely, well-kept site; helpful warden." ♦ 30 Apr-15 Oct. € 12.00 2008*

ST GERVAIS LES BAINS *9B4* (10km SE Rural) *45.80275, 6.72207* **Camping Le Pontet, 2485 Route de Notre-Dame-de-la-Gorge, 74170 Les Contamines-Montjoie [04 50 47 04 04; fax 04 50 47 18 10; welcome@campinglepontet.fr; www.campinglepontet.fr]** Fr St Gervais take D902 to Les Contamines-Montjoie (sp); go thro vill & foll sp to Notre Dame-de-la-Gorge; site in 2km on L, clearly sp. Lge, mkd pitch, hdstg, pt shd; htd wc; chem disp; baby facs; shwrs inc; el pnts (2-10A) €3-9.90; lndtte; shops 2km; tradsmn; rest; snacks; playgrnd; fishing; lake adj; leisure/sports park adj; tennis; horseriding; skilift 200m; dogs free; phone; Eng spkn; adv bkg; quiet; ccard acc. "Mkd alpine walks." ♦ 1 May-26 Sep & 1 Dec-30 Apr. € 15.00 2009*

ST GERVAIS LES BAINS *9B4* (2km S Rural) *45.87333, 6.72000* **Camping Les Dômes de Miage, 197 Route des Contamines, 74170 St Gervais-les-Bains [04 50 93 45 96; info@camping-mont-blanc.com; www.camping-mont-blanc.com]** Exit A40 junc 21; fr N thro St Gervais, at fork take L sp Les Contamines onto D902, site 2km on L. Med, mkd pitch, pt shd; htd wc (some cont); chem disp; mv service pnt; baby facs; shwrs inc; el pnts (3-10A) €2.90-3.90 (poss rev pol); gas; lndtte (inc dryer); shop; tradsmn; supmkt 7km; rest, bar adj; snacks; BBQ; playgrnd; htd pool, tennis 800m; fishing 1km; cycle hire; games area; wifi; TV rm; no statics; dogs €2; bus adj; train 5.5km; Eng spkn; adv bkg (bkg fee); quiet; ccard acc; red low ssn; CCI. "Superb, well-maintained, family-owned site in beautiful location; welcoming, helpful & friendly; immac san facs (poss long walk); conv Tramway du Mont Blanc tunnel & trips; mkt Thurs." ♦ 1 May-12 Sep. € 21.20 (CChq acc) 2009*

ST GERY see St Cirq Lapopie *7D3*

ST GILDAS DE RHUYS see Sarzeau *2G3*

ST GILLES *10E2* (Urban) *43.67569, 4.42946* **Camping de la Chicanette, Rue de la Chicanette, 30800 St Gilles [04 66 87 28 32; fax 04 66 87 49 85; camping.la.chicanette@libertysurf.fr]** Site on D6572 (N572) W fr Arles, sp in cent of town, behind Auberge de la Chicanette. Narr app rd, tight turn to ent. Med, hdg pitch, pt shd; wc; chem disp; shwrs inc; el pnts (6A) inc (rev pol); lndtte; shop adj; snacks; bar; playgrnd; pool; entmnt; 20% statics; dogs €2; poss cr; quiet; red low ssn; CCI. "Sm pitches; site poss unkempt low ssn; interesting old town; facs poss stretched high ssn; bus to Nîmes." 1 Apr-Nov. € 21.00 2007*

ST GILLES CROIX DE VIE *2H3* (3km NE Rural) *46.71217, -1.90613* **Camping Aire Naturelle Le Petit Beauregard, Rue du Petit Beauregard, 85800 Le Fenouiller [02 51 55 07 98]** N fr Les Sables d'Olonne take D38 twd St Gilles Croix-de-Vie. Turn R onto D754 sp Le Fenouiller for 3km. Turn R; site well sp in 500m. Sm, mkd pitch, pt shd; wc; chem disp; shwrs inc; el pnts (6A) €3; lndtte; shop 1km; tradsmn; rest nr; BBQ; playgrnd; pool; sand beach 3km; few statics; dogs; quiet; Eng spkn; adv bkg; CCI. "Friendly, helpful owner; excel, clean san facs; gd beaches nrby; St Gilles busy & cr." ♦ 1 Apr-30 Sep. € 13.50 2009*

ST GILLES CROIX DE VIE *2H3* (3km NE) *46.71201, -1.91457* **Camping Le Chatelier, Route de Nantes, 85800 Le Fenouiller [tel/fax 02 28 10 50 75]** Fr St Gilles-Croix-de-Vie D754 NE, sp to Le Fenouiller, site on L. Med, mkd pitch, pt shd; wc; chem disp; shwrs inc; baby facs; el pnts (6A) (rec long lead); gas; lndtte; tradsmn; shops 2km; snacks; bar; BBQ; playgrnd; htd pool high ssn; sand beach 3km; entmnt adj; TV rm; 50% statics; dogs €2.20; quiet. "Friendly owners; sm san facs block." ♦ Easter-15 Oct. € 18.50 2006*

ST GILLES CROIX DE VIE *2H3* (5km E Rural) *46.69480, -1.85310* **Camping Europa, Le Bois Givrand, 85800 Givrand [02 51 55 32 68; fax 02 72 22 06 71; contact@europacamp.com; www.europacamp.com]** App site fr 'Leclerc' rndabt at St Gilles-Croix-de-Vie, take D6 exit dir Coëx & Aizenay; at 1st & 2nd rndabts go straight on; at 3rd rndabt take 1st exit; site on right in 150m, opp boat builders. Lge, mkd pitch, pt shd; wc (some cont); chem disp; serviced pitches; baby facs; shwrs inc; el pnts (10A) inc; gas; lndtte; shop 3km; rest, snacks, bar high ssn; BBQ; playgrnd; pool complex; waterslide; sand beach 5km; rv fishing, boat hire adj; fishing, watersports, cycle hire & horseriding 5km; golf nr; tennis; entmnt; wifi; games/TV rm; 60% statics (sep area); dogs €2.60; adv bkg; ccard acc; red low ssn. "Vg; pleasant site but facs stretched high ssn." ♦ 15 Jun-15 Sep. € 29.60 ABS - A13 2009*

ST GILLES CROIX DE VIE *2H3* (8km E Rural) *46.69665, -1.83395* **Camping Le Pont Rouge, Ave Georges Clémenceau, 85220 St Révérend [tel/fax 02 51 54 68 50; camping.pontrouge@wanadoo.fr; www.camping-lepont rouge.com]** W fr Aizenay on D6 rd for St Gilles-Croix-de-Vie, turn R just past water tower into St Révérend. Foll sp to site. Med, hdg pitch, pt sl, pt shd; htd wc; chem disp; mv service pnt; baby facs; shwrs inc; el pnts (6A) €3; lndtte; shop 1km; tradsmn; rest 3km; snacks; playgrnd; htd pool; sand beach 8km; golf course with rest 3km; games area; entmnt; TV; 50% statics; dogs €2.50; poss cr; Eng spkn; adv bkg; quiet; red low ssn; CCI. "Attractive, secluded site; modern, clean san facs; working windmill (with tours) 1km; vg." ♦ 29 Mar-5 Nov. € 17.50 2008*

ST GILLES CROIX DE VIE *2H3* (3km SE Coastal) *46.66748, -1.90213* **Camping du Jaunay, 102 Route des Sables, 85800 Givrand [02 51 55 14 77; buro@campingduejaunay.com; www.campingdujaunay.com]** S fr St Gilles-Croix-de-Vie on D38 or B38b; site on R 200m after 2nd rndabt (1st rndabt joins D38 with D38b, 2nd rndabt 400m further on). Sm, mkd pitch, pt shd; htd wc; chem disp; shwrs inc; el pnts (6A) €3; lndtte; shop or 3km; tradsmn; rest; snacks; bar; BBQ; playgrnd; htd pool; canoe hire; fishing; sand beach 1.2km; TV; 30% statics; dogs €1.60; phone; adv bkg; red low ssn; CCI. "Vg site; lge pitches; friendly, helpful owner; vg cycle paths adj." Apr-Sep. € 14.00 2009*

ST GILLES CROIX DE VIE *2H3* (4km SE Rural) **Camping à la Ferme Petit Bois, 85800 Givrand [06 21 55 26 89 (mob)]** W fr Aizenay on D6 for 20km; turn L at rndabt sp Givrand; site on L in 1km. Sm, hdg/mkd pitch, shd; htd wc; chem disp; shwrs inc; el pnts (6A) €3; lndtte; shop 2km; BBQ; sand beach 4km; dogs free; poss cr; Eng spkn; quiet; CCI. "Well-kept site; lge pitches; friendly owner; site yourself, owners calls eves; many cycle tracks; gd access to coast; excel." 1 May-30 Sep. € 15.00 (3 persons) 2009*

ST GILLES CROIX DE VIE *2H3* (4km SE Urban/Coastal) *46.67113, -1.90356* **CHADOTEL Le Domaine de Beaulieu, Route des Sables-d'Olonne, 85800 Givrand [02 51 55 59 46 or 02 51 33 05 05 (LS); chadotel@wanadoo.fr; www.chadotel.com]** S on D38 fr St Gilles Croix-de-Vie, site sp on L. Lge, hdg/mkd pitch, pt shd; htd wc; serviced pitches; baby facs; shwrs inc; el pnts (6A) inc; gas; lndtte; shop; snacks; bar; BBQ (gas); playgrnd; 2 pools; waterslide; sand beach 1km; tennis; entmnt; golf 5km; TV; dogs €3; adv bkg; quiet; red long stay/low ssn; ccard acc; CCI. "Gd for families; red facs low ssn." ♦ 5 Apr-27 Sep. € 28.90 2008*

ST GILLES CROIX DE VIE *2H3* (1km S Coastal) *46.67095, -1.90874* **Camping Les Cyprès, 41 Rue du Pont du Jaunay, 85800 St Gilles-Croix-de-Vie [02 51 55 38 98; fax 02 51 54 98 94; contact@campinglescypres.com; www.campinglescypres.com]** Site on S end of St Gilles-Croix-de-Vie off D38, after rndabt sp Le Jaunay turn sharp L - hard to spot. Lge, hdg pitch, shd; wc; chem disp, mv service pnt, shwrs inc; el pnts (10A) inc; gas; lndtte; shop, tradsmn; rest; snacks; bar; playgrnd; htd, covrd pool & jacuzzi; sand beach 600m; 12% statics; dogs €3.50; rv 100m; Eng spkn; adv bkg €7.62 fee; quiet; ccard acc; red long stay/low ssn; CCI. "Excel for family hols; family-run site; red facs low ssn." ♦ 1 Apr-15 Sep. € 23.00 2007*

ST GILLES CROIX DE VIE *2H3* (2km S Coastal) *46.67819, -1.91561* **CHADOTEL Camping Le Bahamas Beach, 168 Route des Sables, 85800 St Gilles-Croix-de-Vie [02 51 54 69 16 or 02 51 33 05 05 (LS); fax 02 51 33 94 04; chadotel@wanadoo.fr; www.chadotel.com]** S fr St Gilles-Croix-de-Vie on Rte des Sables (D38), sp. Lge, hdg/mkd pitch, unshd; wc; chem disp (wc); shwrs inc; el pnts (6A) €4.70; gas; lndtte; sm shop (high ssn) & 3km; tradsmn; rest, snacks & bar (high ssn); BBQ (gas); playgrnd; htd covrd pool; waterslide; sand beach 800m; watersports; excursions; cycle hire; games area; games rm; entmnt; internet; TV rm; many statics; dogs €3; phone; poss cr; Eng spkn; adv bkg; quiet; red long stay/low ssn; ccard acc; CCI. "Gd for children; superb pool; san facs need update (2007) & low ssn ltd; facs far fr some pitches; excel cycle rtes along coast." ♦ 5 Apr-27 Sep. € 24.20 2008*

France

ST GIRONS *8G3* (3km N Rural) *43.00731, 1.18409* **Camping Audinac Les Bains, 09200 Montjoie-en-Couserans [tel/fax 05 61 66 44 50; accueil@audinac.com; www.audinac.com]** E fr St Girons take D117 twd Foix; after 2km uphill turn L onto D627; foll sp. Med, terr, pt shd; htd wc; chem disp (wc); mv service pnt; shwrs inc; el pnts (10A) €3.50; gas; Indtte (inc dryer); shops 5km; tradsmn; rest in ssn; playgrnd; pool high ssn; statics; dogs €1; no twin-axles; Eng spkn; adv bkg ess; quiet; ccard acc; red low ssn; CCI. "Spacious, attractive, well-appointed site; facs ltd low ssn." ♦ 1 May-30 Sep. € 16.00 2008*

⊞ **ST GIRONS** *8G3* (2km SE Rural) *42.97400, 1.16582* **FFCC Camping Parc de Palétès, Route de Lacourt, 09200 St Girons [05 61 66 06 79 or 06 07 02 40 24 (mob); fax 05 61 66 76 86; contacts@parcdepaletes.com; www.parcdepaletes.com]** Fr S loop of D117 in St Girons at rndabt take D3 dir Lacourt (D3 runs parallel to D618 on E of rv & starts as Ave des Evadés de France); site sp on L in 1.5km. Note: D618 runs on W side of rv - cannot cross it bef Lacourt. Sm, pt sl, pt shd; wc; chem disp; mv service pnt; shwrs inc; el pnts (10A) €4; gas; Indry rm; shop; tradsmn; rest; snacks; bar; BBQ; playgrnd; pool; wifi; dogs €1.50; bus; phone; poss cr; Eng spkn; adv bkg; quiet; red low ssn; m'vans all year, c'vans 1 Jun-30 Sep; CCI. "Gd site." ♦ € 17.00 2009*

ST GIRONS PLAGE *8E1* (Coastal) *43.95440, -1.35672* **CAMPEOLE Camping Les Tourterelles, 40560 St Girons-Plage [05 58 47 93 12; tourterelles@campeole.com; www.camping-tourterelles.com or www.campeole.com]** Exit N10 at Castets & take D42 W to St Girons, then to St Girons-Plage. Lge, pt sl, shd; wc; shwrs inc; el pnts (6A) €3.90; Indtte; shops 1km; BBQ; playgrnd; sand beach 200m; games area; games rm; entmnt; dogs €1; poss cr; quiet; red low ssn. "Site in pine trees; footpath to dunes & beach." 15 Mar-15 Oct. € 20.20 2007*

ST GIRONS PLAGE *8E1* (Coastal) *43.95105, -1.35276* **Camping Eurosol, Route de la Plage, 40560 St Girons-Plage [05 58 47 90 14 or 05 58 56 54 90; fax 05 58 47 76 74; contact@camping-eurosol.com; www.camping-eurosol.com]** Turn W off D652 at St Girons on D42. Site on L in 4km. Lge, pt sl, pt shd; wc; chem disp; baby facs; serviced pitches; shwrs inc; el pnts (6-10A) inc; gas; Indtte; shop; rest; snacks; playgrnd; 2 pools; paddling pool; sand beach 700m; tennis; games area; games rm; horseriding adj; cycle hire; entmnt; TV rm; some statics; dogs €2.50; poss cr; red low ssn; quiet. "Pitches poss tight for long vans." ♦ 10 May-13 Sep. € 45.00 (4 persons) 2008*

STE HERMINE *2H4* (11km NE Rural) *46.59555, -0.97247* **FFCC Camping Le Colombier (Naturist), 85210 St Martin-Lars [02 51 27 83 84; fax 02 51 27 87 29; lecolombier.nat@wanadoo.fr; www.lecolombier-naturisme.com]** Fr junc 7 of A83 take D137 N; 3km past Ste Hermine turn R onto D52 to Le Poteau; turn L onto D10 to St Martin-Lars; 150m past St Martin-Lars turn R sp Le Colombier. Site ent on L in 200m. Lge, pt sl, pt shd; wc; chem disp; shwrs inc; sauna; el pnts (6A) €3.70; Indtte; shops 2km; tradsmn; rest; snacks; bar; playgrnd; pool; lake sw; wifi; 2% statics to let; dogs €3.70; poss cr; Eng spkn; adv bkg; quiet; ccard acc. "Excel, well-run site; diff areas diff character; lge pitches; vg facs; friendly Dutch owners; gd walking in site grnds & local area; conv Mervent National Park; excel." ♦ 1 Apr-31 Oct. € 19.00 2009*

STE HERMINE *2H4* (500m SW Rural) *46.54928, -1.06337* **Camp Municipal La Smagne, 85210 Ste Hermine [02 51 27 35 54]** On D137 500m S of vill cent. Med, mkd pitch; pt shd, wc; chem disp; serviced pitches; mv service pnt; shwrs inc; el pnts (5A) €1.50; gas; Indtte; shops 500m; rest, bar 200m; playgrnd; htd pool adj; tennis; quiet but some rd noise. "Nice site; pleasant vill; conv location just off A83; phone ahead to check open low ssn." 15 Jun-15 Sep. 2007*

ST HILAIRE DE LUSIGNAN **see Agen** *8E3*

ST HILAIRE DE RIEZ *2H3* (Coastal) *46.72289, -1.97931* **Camp Municipal de La Plage de Riez, Allée de la Plage de Riez, Ave des Mimosas, 85270 St Hilaire-de-Riez [02 51 54 36 59; fax 02 51 60 07 84; www.souslespins.com]** Fr St Hilaire take D6A sp Sion-sur-l'Océan. Turn R at traff lts into Ave des Mimosas, site 1st L. V lge, mkd pitch, pt sl, shd; wc; some serviced pitch; shwrs inc; el pnts (10A) €3.40; gas; Indtte; shop; rest; snacks; bar; playgrnd; pool 5km; sand beach adj; cycle hire; internet; entmnt; TV; 30% statics; dogs €3.90; poss cr; Eng spkn; red low ssn. "Vg for dogs; exceptionally helpful manager." 30 Mar-31 Oct. € 21.80 2007*

ST HILAIRE DE RIEZ *2H3* (Coastal) *46.74458, -2.00423* **Camping La Ningle, Chemin des Roselières, 85270 St Hilaire-de-Riez [02 51 54 07 11 or 02 51 54 16 65 (LS); fax 02 51 54 99 39; campingdelaningle@wanadoo.fr; www.campinglaningle.com]** Fr St Hilaire, take rd sp Sion-sur-l'Océan. At traff lts/rndabt, foll sp 'Autres Campings' until site sp is seen. Med, hdg/mkd pitch, pt shd, wc; chem disp; serviced pitches; shwrs inc; el pnts (6A) inc; gas; Indtte; shop; tradsmn; bar; playgrnd; pool; sand beach 500m; tennis; fitness rm; poss cr; adv bkg; dogs €1.90; Eng spkn; red low ssn; CCI. "Highly rec; friendly, helpful staff; gd sized pitches; well-maintained; excel." ♦ 20 May-10 Sep. € 24.40 2006*

France

ST HILAIRE DE RIEZ *2H3* (2km N Urban/Coastal) *46.73566, -1.97519* **Camping Cap Natur (Naturist), 151 Ave de la Faye, 85270 St Hilaire-de-Riez [02 51 60 11 66; fax 02 51 60 17 48; info@cap-natur.com; www.cap-natur.com]** Ent St Hilaire fr N via D69, turn R at 1st rndabt; R at next rndabt; fork R in approx 300m; site on L approx 600m. Med, hdg/mkd pitch, pt sl, pt terr, pt shd; htd wc; chem disp; mv service pnt; baby facs; sauna; shwrs inc; el pnts (10A) €4.40; gas; Indtte; shop & 1km; tradsmn; rest; snacks; bar; BBQ; playgrnd; 2 htd pools (1 covrd); sand/shgl beach 800m (naturist beach 6km); games area; games rm; cycle hire; golf 10km; entmnt; many statics; dogs €2.50; poss cr; Eng spkn; adv bkg; quiet; 20% red 20+ days/low ssn; ccard acc; INF card req (can purchase on site). "Excel, busy site in gd location; sm pitches; gd facs; friendly staff; interesting area." ♦ 31 Mar-14 Oct. € 28.70 2007*

ST HILAIRE DE RIEZ *2H3* (6km N Rural) *46.76270, -1.96045* **Camping La Puerta del Sol, 7 Chemin des Hommeaux, 85270 St Hilaire-de-Riez [02 51 49 10 10; fax 02 51 49 84 84; info@campinglapuertadelsol.com; www.campinglapuertadelsol.com]** N on D38 fr Les Sables-d'Olonne; exit onto D69 sp Soullans, Challans, Le Pissot. At next rndabt take 3rd exit & foll lge sp to site. Site on R in 1.5km. Lge, hdg/mkd pitch, pt sl, pt shd; wc; chem disp; serviced pitches; baby facs; shwrs inc; el pnts (10A) inc (poss rev pol); Indtte; shop, rest, snacks, bar high ssn; BBQ (gas/elec); playgrnd; htd pool; paddling pool; waterslide; sand beach 4.5km; watersports 5km; fishing 2km; tennis; horseriding; golf; cycle hire; games area; entmnt; wifi; games/TV rm; 50% statics; dogs €4; Eng spkn; adv bkg; quiet; ccard acc; red low ssn; CCI. "Vg; red facs low ssn; sm pitches not rec twin-axles." ♦ 1 Apr-30 Sep. € 32.00 ABS - A19 2009*

ST HILAIRE DE RIEZ *2H3* (1km W Coastal) *46.71649, -1.97199* **Camp Municipal de Sion, Ave de la Forêt, Sion-sur-l'Océan, 85270 St Hilaire-de-Riez [02 51 54 34 23; fax 02 51 60 07 84; sion85@free.fr; www.souslespins.com]** Fr St Hilaire, take D6A sp Sion-sur-l'Océan, strt at traff lts. Site 200m on R. Lge, mkd pitch, pt shd; wc; chem disp; mv service pnt; shwrs inc; el pnts (10A) inc; Indtte; shop, rest, snacks, bar 400m; BBQ; playgrnd; pool 1km; sand beach adj; games rm; 15% statics; dogs €2.70; phone; Eng spkn; adv bkg rec high ssn; quiet; CCI. "Gd for family holidays." ♦ 30 Mar-31 Oct. € 26.90 2007*

ST HILAIRE DE RIEZ *2H3* (5km NW Coastal) *46.73970, -1.98410* **Camping La Parée Préneau, 23 Ave de la Parée Préneau, 85270 St Hilaire-de-Riez [02 51 54 33 84; fax 02 51 55 29 57; camplapareepreneau@wanadoo.fr; www.campinglapareepreneau.com]** Fr N on D38 a rndabt foll sp Sion-sur-l'Océan & St Hilaire-de-Riez cent. At next rndabt take 1st exit (petrol stn on R) & foll sp La Parée Préneau; site on L in 2km. Or fr S on D38, go thro St Gilles-Croix-de-Vie & pass St Hilaire-de-Riez; at rndabt turn L sp Sion-sur-l'Océan & St Hilaire-de-Riez cent, then as above. Lge, hdg pitch, pt sl, shd; wc (some cont); baby facs; shwrs inc; el pnts (6A) inc; Indtte; sumpkt nrby; tradsmn; bar; BBQ (charcoal/gas); playgrnd; 2 pools (1 htd/covrd); paddling pool; jacuzzi; sand beach 1km; fishing 1km; windsurfing 5km; entmnt; TV/games rm; dogs €2.50; c'vans over 7m not acc; Eng spkn; adv bkg; ccard acc; red low ssn; CCI. "Gd, simple site; some pitches poss tight lge o'fits; mkt Thu & Sun." ♦ 1 May-11 Sep. € 25.50 ABS - A29 2009*

ST HILAIRE DU HARCOUET *2E4* (1km W Urban) *48.58105, -1.09771* **FFCC Camp Municipal de la Sélune, 50600 St Hilaire-du-Harcouët [02 33 49 43 74 or 02 33 49 70 06; fax 02 33 49 59 40; info@st-hilaire.fr; www.st-hilaire.fr]** Sp on N side of N176 twd Mont St Michel/St Malo/Dinan, on W side of town; well sp. Med, hdg pitch, pt sl, pt shd; wc; chem disp; shwrs inc; el pnts (6A) €1.85; Indry rm; shops 1km; snacks 500m; playgrnd; pool 300m; dogs; gate locked 2200-0730; red long stay/CCI. "Easy access; helpful, pleasant warden; excel." 1 Apr-15 Sep. € 7.85 2007*

ST HILAIRE LA FORET *7A1* (4km SW Rural) *46.44836, -1.52860* **Camping Les Batardières, Rue des Bartardières, 85440 St Hilaire-la-Forêt [02 51 33 33 85]** Fr Sables d'Olonne take D949 twd Avrillé. 7km after Talmont-St-Hilaire fork R on D70 to St Hilaire-la-Forêt. In 3km turn R on ent vill. Site 70m on L. Med, hdg pitch, pt shd; wc; chem disp; serviced pitches; shwrs inc; el pnts (6A) €3.50; Indtte; shop adj; playgrnd; sand beach 5km; free tennis; cycling; no statics; dogs €1.50; adv bkg; quiet; CCI. "Excel; spacious pitches; clean facs; excel for families; rec." 1 Jul-2 Sep. € 19.50 2007*

ST HILAIRE LA FORET *7A1* (1km NW Rural) *46.44846, -1.52643* **Camping La Grand' Métairie, 8 Rue de la Vineuse-en-Plaine, 85440 St Hilaire-la-Forêt [02 51 33 32 38; fax 02 51 33 25 69; info@camping-grandmetairie.com; www.la-grand-metairie.com]** Fr D949 turn S onto D70, sp St Hilaire-la-Forêt, or fr Avrillé take D19. Site at ent to vill. Lge, hdg/mkd pitch, pt shd; wc; chem disp; serviced pitches; sauna; shwrs inc; el pnts (10A) inc (poss rev pol); gas; Indtte (inc dryer); shop; tradsmn; rest; snacks; bar; playgrnd; htd, covrd pool; paddling pool; sand beach 3km; tennis; jacuzzi; fitness rm; games rm; cycle hire; golf 15km; entmnt; wifi; 80% statics; dogs €4; poss cr; Eng spkn; adv bkg; quiet; red low ssn/long stay; ccard acc; red CCI. "Gd base for beaches, La Rochelle, Ile de Ré; friendly, helpful owners; cycle rtes fr site; excel." ♦ 17 Apr-10 Sep. € 39.00 2009*

See advertisement on previous page

ST HILAIRE LA PALUD *7A2* (5km NW Rural) *46.28386, -0.74344* **Camping Indigo Le Lidon, Le Lidon, 79210 St Hilaire-la-Palud [05 49 35 33 64; fax 05 49 35 32 63; info@le-lidon.com; www.le-lidon.com]** Exit A10 junc 33 onto E601 then N248 & N11 S. At Epannes foll D1 N to Sansais, then D3 to St Hilaire-la-Palud. Foll sp Canal du Mignon & site. NB Access to site over narr angled bdge, extreme care needed - v diff lge o'fits. Med, hdg/mkd pitch, pt shd; wc; chem disp; mv service pnt; baby facs; fam bthrm; shwrs inc; el pnts (10A) €5; gas 4km; Indtte; ice; shop; tradsmn; rest; snacks; bar; playgrnd; htd pool; paddling pool; fishing; canoe hire; cycle hire; entmnt; 5% statics; dogs €2.50; some Eng spkn; adv bkg; quiet; ccard acc; red low ssn; CCI. "Secluded, quiet site in Marais Poitevin Regional Park (marsh land); good sized pitches; excel clean san facs; gd walking, cycling, birdwatching; vg." ♦ 4 Apr-30 Sep. € 20.40 (CChq acc) 2009*

There aren't many sites open at this time of year. We'd better phone ahead to check that the one we're heading for is open.

ST HILAIRE ST FLORENT see Saumur *4G1*

ST HONORE LES BAINS *4H4* (W Urban) *46.90413, 3.83919* **Camp Municipal Plateau du Guet, 13 Rue Eugène Collin, 58360 St Honoré-les-Bains [03 86 30 76 00 or 03 86 30 74 87 (Mairie); fax 03 86 30 73 33; mairie-de-st-honore-les-bains@wanadoo.fr; www.st-honore-les-bains.com]** On D985 fr Luzy to St Honoré-les-Bains. In cent vill turn L on D106 twd Vandenesse. Site on L in 150m. Or N fr Château-Chinon 27km. Then D985 to St Honoré. Med, mkd pitch, pt hdstg, pt terr, pt shd; htd wc; mv service pnt; shwrs inc; el pnts (10A) €2.90; Indtte; shop, rest, snacks, bar 300m; playgrnd; htd pool 300m; adv bkg; quiet; CCI. "Gd, modern san facs; pleasant, conv site but town rather run down." ♦ 1 Apr-26 Oct. € 8.60 2008*

ST HONORE LES BAINS *4H4* (1km W Rural) *46.90680, 3.82843* **Camping Les Bains, 15 Ave Jean Mermoz, 58360 St Honoré-les-Bains [03 86 30 73 44; fax 03 86 30 61 88; camping-les-bains@wanadoo.fr; www.campinglesbains.com]** Fr St Honoré-les-Bains foll site sp as 'Village des Bains' fr town cent on D106 twd Vandenesse. Med, hdg/mkd pitch, some hdstg, pt sl, shd; wc (some cont); chem disp; baby facs; shwrs inc; el pnts (6A) inc; gas; Indtte; shop 1km; rest; snacks; bar; BBQ; playgrnd; pool; waterslide; paddling pool; fishing; tennis; horseriding 300m; cycle hire; entmnt; internet; games/TV rm; dogs €1.50; c'vans over 8m not acc; Eng spkn; adv bkg; quiet low ssn; ccard acc; CCI. "Helpful staff; poor maintenance & san facs need refurb (May 2008); gd walking; sm pitches & poss waterlogged after rain; mkt Thu." ♦ 1 Apr-31 Oct. € 16.00 (CChq acc) 2008*

ST JACQUES DES BLATS *7C4* (Rural) *45.05181, 2.71377* **Camp Municipal Les Blats, Route de la Gare, 15800 St Jacques-des-Blats [04 71 47 06 00 or 04 71 47 05 90 (Mairie); fax 04 71 47 07 09; i-tourisme-st-jacques@wanadoo.fr]** Sp fr N122, 3km SW of Lioran Tunnel in vill of St Jacques-des-Blats; 300m fr N122 down steep app rd; sp in vill adj rv. Sm, hdg pitch, pt shd; htd wc; chem disp; shwrs; el pnts (10A); Indtte; shops 200m; rest 200m; bar; BBQ; playgrnd; TV; 30% statics; quiet; CCI. "Gd walking trails fr site; lift to summit Plomb du Cantal." 1 May-30 Sep. € 9.00 2009*

ST JANS CAPPEL see Bailleul *3A3*

ST JEAN D'ANGELY *7B2* (500m W Rural) *45.94868, -0.53645* **Camping Val de Boutonne, Quai de Bernouet, 17400 St Jean-d'Angély [05 46 32 26 16; fax 05 46 32 29 54; info@valba.net; www.valba.net]** Exit A10 at junc 34; head SE on D939; turn R at 1st rndabt into town. Site sp. Med, mkd pitch, shd; wc (some cont); chem disp; mv service pnt; shwrs inc; el pnts (10A) €3.50; Indtte; sm shop; tradsmn; rest, snacks, bar 200m; playgrnd; aquatic cent 500m; TV rm; 10% statics; dogs €1.20; phone adj; Eng spkn; adv bkg; quiet; ccard acc; red long stay; CCI. "Pleasant, friendly, clean site by Rv Boutonne; helpful owners; gd san facs; poss open in Oct - phone ahead; vg." ♦ 1 Apr-30 Sep. € 13.00 2009*

ST JEAN DE CEYRARGUES see Alès *10E1*

ST JEAN DE COUZ see Echelles, Les *9B3*

ST JEAN DE LOSNE *6H1* (800m E Rural) *47.10232, 5.27521* **Camp Municipal Les Herlequins, 21170 St Jean-de-Losne [03 80 39 22 26; fax 03 80 29 05 48; www.saintjeandelosne.com]** Site sp on ent town fr N on D968. Access fr town on Quai National & Rue du Port-Bernard on N bank of Rv Saône. Med, hdg/mkd pitch, hdstg, pt shd; wc (some cont); shwrs; el pnts (10A); shop 1km; rest; snacks; bar; BBQ; playgrnd; sand beach; poss cr; adv bkg; quiet. 1 May-30 Sep. 2008*

ST JEAN DE LUZ *8F1* (3km N Coastal) *43.40549, -1.64222* **Camping Bord de Mer, Erromardie, 64500 St Jean-de-Luz [tel/fax 05 59 26 24 61]** Exit A63 junc 3 onto D810 (N10) dir St Jean-de-Luz. In 1km cross rlwy & immed turn sharp R sp Erromardie. Site on sharp turn L bef beach. Ent by plastic chain fence bef ent to prom, but easy to miss. App poss diff lge o'fits due hairpin turn - drive on to car park where may be poss to turn. Med, hdg pitch, pt sl; terr; wc (mainly cont); chem disp; mv service pnt; shwrs inc; el pnts (10A) €4; Indy rm; tradsmn; snacks; bar; BBQ; sand beach adj; dogs; quiet. "Nice site in excel position; basic facs in basement need update; sm, inadequate shwr cubicles; owner connects el pnts; cliff walk to town; NH en route Spain." ♦ 1 Mar-30 Oct. € 21.50 2009*

ST JEAN DE LUZ *8F1* (3km N Urban/Coastal) *43.40777, -1.63777* **Camping International Erromardie, Ave de la Source, 64500 St Jean-de-Luz [05 59 26 07 74; fax 05 59 51 12 11; camping-international@wanadoo.fr; www.erromardie.com]** Fr A63 exit junc 3 sp St Jean-de-Luz. At traff lts at end of slip rd turn L onto D810 (N10) sp St Jean; in 1km cross rlwy & immed turn sharp R sp Erromardie, site on R in 1km opp beach. Lge, hdg/mkd pitch, pt sl, shd; wc (some cont); chem disp (wc); shwrs inc; el pnts (5A) inc; Indtte; shop; rest; snacks; bar; BBQ (charcoal); playgrnd; pool; sand/shgl beach adj; fishing 2km; watersports 3km; golf, entmnt; TV rm; many statics; dogs €3; c'vans over 7m not acc high ssn; adv bkg; quiet; ccard acc. "Facs & office poss clsd after 1800 low ssn; poss poor security; twin-axle c'vans acc;mkd Tue & Fri." 7 Apr-30 Sep. € 29.00 2007*

ST JEAN DE LUZ *8F1* (1.5km NE Coastal) *43.40472, -1.64111* **Camping Iratzia, Chemin d'Erromardie, 64500 St Jean-de-Luz [05 59 26 14 89; fax 05 59 26 69 69]** Fr A63 exit St Jean-de-Luz Nord. Join D810 (N10) twds St Jean; after Shell g'ge cross rlwy bdge & immed turn R sp Erromardie. Site on R in 500m. Lge, pt terr, pt sl, pt shd; wc; shwrs inc; el pnts (6A) €3.50; Indry rm; shop; rest; bar; playgrnd; sand beach 300m; TV; entmnt; dogs €1; phone; poss cr; adv bkg; red low ssn; CCI. "Many pitches diff access for long o'fits; friendly, well-kept, clean site." 1 May-30 Sep. 2006*

ST JEAN DE LUZ *8F1* (2km NE Coastal) *43.40563, -1.64216* **Camping de la Ferme Erromardie, 40 Chemin d'Erromardie, 64500 St Jean-de-Luz [05 59 26 34 26; fax 05 59 51 26 02; contact@camping-erromardie.com; www.camping-erromardie.com]** Exit A63 junc 3 onto D810 (N10) sp St Jean-de-Luz. After 1km x rlwy and turn immed sharp R sp Erromardie. Site ent on R in 1km just bef rest/bar. Lge, hdg/mkd pitch, shd; wc; chem disp; mv service pnt; baby facs; shwrs inc; el pnts (4-6A) €3-3.70; gas; Indtte; tradsmn; rest; snacks; bar; playgrnd; sand beach adj; many statics; dogs €0.60; poss cr; Eng spkn; adv bkg; CCI. "Well-run site; cheerful, helpful staff; modern san facs; coastal walk into St Jean-de-Luz; lovely, sandy beaches; Basque museum nrby." 15 Mar-9 Oct. € 21.50 2009*

ST JEAN DE LUZ *8F1* (3km NE Coastal) *43.41472, -1.61694* **Camping Itsas-Mendi, Acotz, 64500 St Jean-de-Luz [05 59 26 56 50; fax 05 59 26 54 44; itsas@wanadoo.fr; www.itsas-mendi.com]** Exit A63 junc 3 sp St Jean-de-Luz; take D810 (N10) dir Biarritz; in 3km turn L sp Acotz Plage & Camping; site well sp. Lge, hdg pitch, pt sl, terr, shd; htd wc; chem disp; mv service pnt; sauna; shwrs inc; fam bthrm; el pnts (10A) inc; Indtte; shop; rest; snacks; bar; playgrnd; htd pools; waterslides & aquatic area; paddling pool; tennis; games area; beach 500m; internet; TV rm; dogs €2.20; phone; poss cr; Eng spkn; quiet but rlwy adj; red low ssn; CCI. "Excel." ♦ 5 Apr-28 Sep. € 34.50 (CChq acc) 2008*

France

ST JEAN DE LUZ *8F1* (4km NE Rural) *43.41527, -1.61666* **Camping Atlantica, Quartier Acotz, 64500 St Jean-de-Luz [05 59 47 72 44; fax 05 59 54 72 27; info@campingatlantica.com; www.campingatlantica.com]** Exit A63 at junc 3 sp St Jean-de-Luz-Nord. Take D810 (N10) twd Biarritz & at top of hill foll sp Acotz Plage; site well sp. Lge, mkd pitch, pt sl, pt shd; wc; mv service pnt; shwrs inc; baby facs; el pnts (6A) €4.20; Indtte; shop; rest; snacks; bar; playgrnd; pool; paddling pool; beach 500m; entmnt; games/TV rm; 35% statics; dogs €2.50; bus; poss cr; Eng spkn; adv bkg; some rd & rlwy noise; ccard acc; CCI. "Vg pool; gd san facs; excel." ♦ 1 Apr-30 Sep. € 26.00 2008*

ST JEAN DE LUZ *8F1* (4km NE Coastal) *43.41674, -1.62274* **Camping Duna-Munguy, Quartier Acotz, 64500 St Jean-de-Luz [05 59 47 70 70; fax 05 59 47 78 82; camping-duna-munguy@wanadoo.fr; www.camping-dunamunguy.com]** Exit A63 at junc 3 St Jean-de-Luz Nord. Take D810 (N10) twd Biarritz, turn L at 2nd rise then R at T-junc & down hill under rlwy bdge sp Acotz Plages. Site well sp. NB Steep downhill app. Sm, mkd pitch, hdstg, pt shd; htd wc; chem disp; shwrs inc; jacuzzi; el pnts (10A) €4 (poss rev pol); Indtte; playgrnd; sm pool; sandy beach 300m; golf 5km; TV; 80% statics; dogs €4; phone; bus 1km (at top of hill); poss cr; Eng spkn; adv bkg; quiet but rlwy noise; ccard not acc; CCI. "Steep app poss diff long o'fits; sm pitches - poss liable to flood; gd san facs with smart shwrs; helpful owner; no sea views but sheltered in storms; gd coastal walks; rec." ♦ 14 Feb-14 Nov. € 26.00 2008*

ST JEAN DE LUZ *8F1* (4km NE Coastal) *43.41861, -1.62320* **Camping Merko Lacarra, 820 Route des Plages, Plage d'Acotz, 64500 St Jean-de-Luz [05 59 26 56 76; fax 05 59 54 73 81; contact@merkolacarra.com; www.merkolacarra.com]** Exit A63 at junc 3 St Jean-de-Luz Nord. Take D810 (N10) twd Biarritz, turn L at 2nd rise then R at T-junc & down hill under rlwy bdge sp Acotz Plages, site on L. NB steep downhill app. Med, pt sl, pt shd; wc; chem disp; shwrs; el pnts (16A) £4; Indtte; shop; snacks; bar; sand beach over rd; wifi; 15% statics; dogs €1.50; m'van o'night sep area; Eng spkn; quiet; ccard acc; CCI. "Lovely walking/cycling; well-kept site; some pitches awkward due trees/bushes; poss cr high ssn." ♦ 28 Mar-17 Oct. € 27.00 2009*

ST JEAN DE LUZ *8F1* (5km NE Coastal) *43.41418, -1.62644* **Camping Caravaning Playa, Quartier Acotz, 64500 St Jean-de-Luz [tel/fax 05 59 26 55 85; www.camping-playa.com]** Fr St Jean-de-Luz take D810 (N10) twd Biarritz. Before Guéthary turn L at sp Acotz-Plages. Turn L at T-junc & foll rd to site. Med, mkd pitch, terr, pt shd; wc; chem disp; shwrs inc; el pnts (6A) €3; Indtte; shop; rest; snacks; bar; sand/shgl beach adj; fishing; boating; 95% statics; dogs €1.80; poss cr; noisy nr rd; ccard acc; CCI. "V pretty site o'looking lovely beach." ♦ 1 Apr-30 Oct. € 22.00 2006*

ST JEAN DE LUZ *8F1* (5km NE Coastal) *43.41791, -1.62397* **Camping Les Tamaris Plage, Quartier Acotz, 64500 St Jean-de-Luz [05 59 26 55 90; fax 05 59 47 70 15; contact@tamaris-plage.com; www.tamaris-plage.com]** Fr A63 take St Jean-de-Luz Nord exit. Turn R sp Guéthary. After 1km turn L sp Acotz, Campings-Plages. Then foll sps to Tamaris Plage. Med, hdg/mkd pitch, pt sl, pt shd; wc (some cont); chem disp; mv service pnt; baby facs; shwrs inc; el pnts (7A) €3; gas; Indtte; shop, rest, snacks, bar 1.5km; BBQ; playgrnd; beach adj; games rm; games area; entmnt; TV rm; 50% statics; dogs €5; phone; poss cr; poss noisy; Eng spkn; red low ssn; CCI. "Luxurious facs block has fountain & flowers; excel." ♦ 21 Mar-5 Nov. € 24.00 2008*

ST JEAN DE LUZ *8F1* (5km NE Coastal) *43.41640, -1.62482* **Camping-Plage Soubelet, Quartier Acotz, 64500 St Jean-de-Luz [05 59 26 51 60; www.soubelet-plage.com]** Fr St Jean take D810 (N10) twd Biarritz. Bef Guéthary turn L to Acotz/Plages. Turn R down hill, under rlwy bdge & turn L. Site on R in 300m. Lge, mkd pitch, hdstg, pt shd; htd wc; chem disp; baby facs; shwrs inc; el pnts (15A) €4; Indtte; shop; snacks; playgrnd; sand beach adj; 5% statics; dogs free; poss cr; Eng spkn; quiet. "Gd sea views; poss ltd san facs low ssn & stretched high ssn, conv Bidart for rests, shops etc." ♦ 1 Apr-15 Oct. € 22.50 2008*

⊞ **ST JEAN DE LUZ** *8F1* (6km SE Rural) *43.34591, -1.61724* **Camping Chourio, Luberriaga, 64310 Ascain [05 59 54 06 31 or 05 59 54 04 32]** Fr St Jean-de-Luz take D918 sp Ascain. In 6km turn R at traff lts, in 250m over rv bdge & turn L at mini-rndabt. Site sp in town. Med, pt shd; wc; chem disp; mv service pnt; shwrs inc; el pnts (6A) €2.40; tradsmn; rest, snacks, bar 1km; phone; poss cr; quiet; CCI. "Friendly, family-owned, relaxed site in lovely countryside; conv Spanish border; Tues & Sat mkt St Jean-de-Luz; vg." € 9.50 2009*

ST JEAN DE LUZ *8F1* (10km SE Rural) *43.35748, -1.57465* **Camping d'Ibarron, 64310 St Pée-sur-Nivelle [05 59 54 10 43; fax 05 59 54 51 95; camping.dibarron@wanadoo.fr; www.camping-ibarron.com]** Fr St Jean take D918 twd St Pée, site 2km bef St Pée on R of rd. Lge, shd; wc (mainly cont); chem disp; mv service pnt; shwrs inc; el pnts (6A) €3.90; gas 3km; Indtte; shop, tradsmn, snacks high ssn; supmkt adj; playgrnd; pool; sand beach 10km; 5% statics; dogs €1.60; phone; Eng spkn; adv bkg; quiet; red low ssn; CCI. "Spacious pitches; helpful, pleasant owner; ltd facs low ssn; on main rd & no footpath to vill; excel." ♦ 1 May-30 Sep. € 19.10 2008*

ST JEAN DE LUZ *8F1* (10km SE Rural) *43.36288, -1.56638* **Camping Goyetchea, Route d'Ahetze, 64310 St Pée-sur-Nivelle [05 59 54 19 59; info@camping-goyetchea.com; www.camping-goyetchea.com]** Fr St Jean-de-Luz take D918 twd St Pée-sur-Nivelle. Turn L at Hotel Bonnet at Ibarron D855. Site on R in 800m. Med, pt shd; wc (some cont); chem disp; baby facs; shwrs inc; el pnts (6A) €3.50; gas; Indry rm; shop; supmkt 800m; tradsmn; rest; snacks; BBQ; playgrnd; pool; sand beach 10km; lake sw 4km; games area; entmnt; TV rm; 10% statics; dogs €1.50; adv bkg; quiet; ccard acc; red low ssn; CCI. "Pleasant, quiet site; vg." ♦ 3 Jun-16 Sep. € 18.50 2006*

⊞ **ST JEAN DE LUZ** *8F1* (3km SW Rural) *43.37064, -1.68629* **Camping Larrouleta, 210 Route de Socoa, 64122 Urrugne [05 59 47 37 84; fax 05 59 47 42 54; info@larrouleta.com; www.larrouleta.com]** Exit A63 junc 2 St Jean-de-Luz Sud. Pass under D810 (N10) & take 1st L sp Urrugne. Loop back up to N10 & turn R, site sp in 500m. Or fr S on D810, 2km beyond Urrugne vill (by-pass vill), turn L into minor rd, site 50m on R. Lge, hdg/mkd pitch, hdstg, pt shd; htd wc; chem disp; baby facs; shwrs inc; el pnts (5A) €2.50 (poss rev pol); gas; Indtte; shop; hypmkt 1.5km; tradsmn; rest (Jul/Aug); snacks; bar; playgrnd; htd, covrd pool; lake sw, fishing & boating; sand beach 3km; tennis; games; wifi; entmnt; no statics (2009); dogs €2; phone; bus 200m; poss cr; some Eng spkn; adv bkg ess high ssn; ccard acc; red low ssn; CCI. "Pleasant, well-kept, well-run site nr lake; excel san facs (unisex low ssn) & pool; friendly & helpful (ask for dir on dep to avoid dangerous bend); some pitches unreliable in wet but can park on site rds/hdstg; poss ltd facs low ssn & unclean; poor facs for disabled; conv A63, Biarritz & en rte Spain; excel." ♦ € 17.50 2009*

ST JEAN DE LUZ *8F1* (4km SW Coastal) *43.39320, -1.69310* **Camping Juantcho, Route de la Corniche, Socoa, 64122 Urrugne [tel/fax 05 59 47 11 97; camping.juantcho@wanadoo.fr; www.camping-juantcho.com]** Leave A63 at junc 2. Keep to L lane & immed after passing toll booth take exit to Socoa, site on R on cliff top rd - busy & steep. Lge, mkd pitch, terr, pt shd; wc; chem disp; shwrs inc; el pnts (5A) €3.80; Indtte; shop & snacks in ssn; playgrnd; beach 500m; fishing, watersports; entmnts 500m; some statics; dogs €2; poss cr; quiet; CCI. "Helpful staff; beautiful beach; ferry fr Socoa to St Jean; ltd facs low ssn." 1 May-30 Sep. € 16.80 2006*

ST JEAN DE LUZ *8F1* (7km SW Rural) *43.33277, -1.68527* **Camping Sunêlia du Col d'Ibardin, Route d'Ascain, 64122 Urrugne [05 59 54 31 21; fax 05 59 54 62 28; info@col-ibardin.com; www.col-ibardin.com]** Turn L off D810 (N10) onto D4; at rndbt foll sp Col d'Ibardin Ascain; site on R immed past minor rd to Col d'Ibardin. Med, hdg/mkd pitch, pt sl, pt terr, pt shd; 5% serviced pitch; wc; chem disp; baby facs; shwrs inc; el pnts (5A) inc (poss rev pol); gas; Indtte; shop; tradsmn; supmkt 5km; rest, snacks & bar in ssn; BBQ; playgrnd; htd pool; paddling pool; sand beach 6km; tennis; TV; 5% statics; dogs €2.50; phone; Eng spkn; adv bkg; quiet; ccard acc; red low ssn; CCI. "Lovely, well-run site in woodland; fair sized pitches; helpful, friendly owner; gd san facs; pleasant bar/rest; mountain rlwy nr; gd touring base for Pyrenees & N Spain; excel." ♦ 21 Mar-30 Sep. € 30.00 2008*

ST JEAN DE MAURIENNE *9C3* (Urban) *45.27034, 6.35023* **Camp Municipal des Grands Cols, 422 Ave du Mont-Cenis, 73300 St Jean-de-Maurienne [tel/fax 04 79 64 28 02 or 06 64 09 77 48 (mob); info@campingdesgrandscols.com; www.campingdesgrandscols.com]** Site sp fr D1006 (N6) in St Jean-de-Maurienne; site behind shops 100m fr town cent behind trees/parking. Med, hdg/mkd pitch, hdstg, pt sl, pt shd; wc; chem disp; mv service pnt; 20% serviced pitches; shwrs inc; el pnts (16A) €3; Indtte; supmkt 1km; tradsmn; snacks; bar; playgrnd; pool 1.5km; lake 3km; games rm; TV; dogs €1; Eng spkn; quiet; ccard not acc; red low ssn; CCI. "Warm welcome; helpful staff; clean san facs; interesting town; excel for serious cycling; gd NH for Fréjus tunnel; excel." 26 Apr-30 Sep. € 16.00 2009*

ST JEAN DE MONTS *2H3* (2km N Coastal) *46.80666, -2.09970* **Camping La Davière Plage, Route de Notre-Dame, 85160 St Jean-de-Monts [tel/fax 02 51 58 27 99; info@daviereplage.com; www.daviereplage.com]** Site on L off D38 Rte de Notre Dame fr St Jean & 2km W of Notre-Dame. Well sp. Med, hdg/mkd pitch, pt shd; wc; chem disp; shwrs; el pnts (10A) €3.90; gas; Indry rm; shops adj; tradsmn; rest; snacks; bar; playgrnd; sand beach, watersports 700m; sports area; entmnt; TV rm; dogs €3.15; CCI. "Gd family site close to amenities; mkd cycle & walking trails; o'night area for m'vans." 1 May-30 Sep. € 18.65 2007*

ST JEAN DE MONTS *2H3* (SE Urban/Coastal) *46.78029, -2.05629* **CAMPEOLE Camping Les Sirènes, Ave des Demoiselles, 85160 St Jean-de-Monts [02 51 58 01 31; fax 02 51 59 03 67; sirenes@campeole.com; www.vendee-camping.info or www.campeole.com]** Site in town cent; ent town on D753 fr Challans, turn R at junc, then 1st L at church. Take 2nd L (Ave des Demoiselles). Site on L. V lge, pt sl, shd; wc (some cont); chem disp; shwrs inc; el pnts (10A) inc; gas; Indtte; sm shop adj or 2km; rest; snacks; bar; playgrnd; pool; sand beach 500m; fishing, watersports 500m; cycle hire; games area; entmnt; dogs €2.50; adv bkg ess high ssn; quiet; red low ssn. "Vg." ♦ 2 Apr-12 Sep. € 20.30 2007*

ST JEAN DE MONTS *2H3* (2km SE Urban) *46.78841, -2.03008* **Camping Le Bois Masson, 149 Rue des Sables, 85167 St Jean-de-Monts [02 51 58 62 62 or 05 56 07 90 17; fax 02 51 58 29 97; boismasson@siblu.fr; www.siblu.com/leboismasson]** Fr Challans pass thro Le Perrier to St Jean-de-Monts. At 1st rndabt take last exit dir Les Sables-d'Olonne. Foll Les Sables at next rndabts & at 4th rndabt turn R, site on R shortly after Camping Le Bois Dormant. V lge, hdg/mkd pitch, pt shd; htd wc; chem disp; baby facs; shwrs inc; el pnts (6A) inc; gas; Indtte; shop; rest; snacks; bar; BBQ (gas); playgrnd; 2 htd pools (1 covrd); waterslide; sand beach 2.5km; fishing, windsurfing, watersports nrby; entmnt; internet; TV; 4% statics; no dogs; Eng spkn; adv bkg; quiet; 20% red low ssn. "Excel, busy, popular, family site; narr access rds; mkt Sat." ♦ 4 Apr-20 Sep. 2009*

ST JEAN DE MONTS *2H3* (3km SE Coastal) *46.78160, -2.01810* **Camping Zagarella, Route des Sables, Le Puy Blanc, 85160 St Jean-de-Monts [02 51 58 19 82; fax 02 51 59 35 28; zagarella@wanadoo.fr; www.zagarella.fr or www.camping-franceloc.fr]** On D38, S fr St Jean-de-Monts. Med, hdg/mkd pitch, pt shd; wc; chem disp; baby facs; shwrs inc; el pns (16A) inc; gas; Indtte (inc dryer); shop; tradsmn; rest; snacks; bar; playgrnd; htd pool; cycle hire; fitness rm; aqua gym; games rm; entmnt; children's club Jul/Aug; wifi; TV; 50% statics; dogs €3.30; phone; poss cr; Eng spkn; adv bkg; red low ssn; CCI. "Gd, clean site; gd pool; vg." ♦ 5 May-13 Sep. € 37.20 2008*

ST JEAN DE MONTS *2H3* (6km SE Coastal) *46.75655, -2.00770* **Camping La Yole, Chemin des Bosses, Orouët, 85160 St Jean-de-Monts [02 51 58 67 17; fax 02 51 59 05 35; contact@la-yole.com; www.la-yole.com]** Take D38 S fr St Jean-de-Monts dir Les Sable d'Olonne & Orouet. At Orouet turn R at L'Oasis rest dir Mouette; in 1.5km turn L at campsite sp; site on L. Situated bet D38 & coast, 1km fr Plage des Mouettes. On arr, park in carpark on R bef registering. Lge, hdg/mkd pitch, shd; wc; chem disp; serviced pitch; baby facs; jacuzzi; shwrs inc; el pnts (10A) inc; Indtte; shop; rest; snacks; bar; BBQ (gas only); playgrnd; 2 pools (1 htd covrd); paddling pool; waterslide; jacuzzi; sand beach 2km; tennis; fishing; horseriding 3km; watersports 6km; entmnt; wifi; games/TV; many statics (tour ops); sm dogs €5; c'vans over 6m not acc high ssn; poss cr; Eng spkn; adv bkg ess; ccard acc; red low ssn; CCI. "Vg, well-run, busy site; friendly staff; facs clean but need update; excel cycle paths; mkt Wed & Sat." ♦ 2 Apr-24 Sep. € 30.50 (CChq acc) ABS - A23 2009*

ST JEAN DE MONTS *2H3* (2km S Rural/Coastal) *46.78638, -2.03538* **Camping Les Verts, 177 Ave Valentin, 85160 St Jean-de-Monts [tel/fax 02 51 58 47 63]** Sp on D38 & coast rd. Lge, hdg/mkd pitch, pt sl, pt shd; wc; shwrs inc; el pnts (3-6A) inc; gas; Indtte; shop high ssn; rest 2km; snacks; bar; playgrnd; TV; htd pool; sand beach 1.6km; 10% statics; dogs €1.50; poss cr; adv bkg; red low ssn; CCI. "Excel beach, v welcoming; Itd facs low ssn; some pitches narr & rough." ♦ 1 May-30 Sep. € 18.90 (3 persons) 2006*

ST JEAN DE MONTS *2H3* (1km W Coastal) *46.79931, -2.07378* **Camping Le Bois Joly, 46 Route de Notre Dame-de-Monts, 85165 St Jean-de-Monts [02 51 59 11 63; fax 02 51 69 11 06; contact@camping-leboisjoly.com; www.camping-leboisjoly.com]** N on D38 circular around St Jean-de-Monts; at rndabt past junc with D51 turn R dir Notre Dame-de-Monts, site on R in 300m. Lge, hdg/mkd pitch, pt shd; wc; chem disp; baby facs; sauna; shwrs inc; el pnts (6A) inc; Indtte; shops 1km; rest, snacks, bar high ssn; playgrnd; 2 pools (1 htd, covrd); waterslide; sand beach 1km; games area; entmnt; TV rm; 25% statics; dogs €2.50; phone; poss cr; Eng spkn; adv bkg; ccard acc; CCI. "Ideal for families; gd san facs; lge pitches; coastal & inland cycleways nrby; excel." ♦ 5 Apr-28 Sep. € 26.00 2006*

ST JEAN DE MONTS *2H3* (1km NW Rural) *46.80083, -2.08013* **Camping La Buzelière, 79 Rue de Notre Dame, 85169 St Jean-de-Monts [02 51 58 64 80; fax 02 28 11 03 61; buzeliere@aol.com; www.buzeliere.com]** Take D38 fr St Jean-de-Monts to Notre Dame-de-Monts. Site on L. Med, hdg/mkd pitch, pt sl, pt shd; wc; chem disp; baby facs; fam bthrm; shwrs inc; el pnts (10A) inc; gas; lndtte; shop 1km; tradsmn; snacks; bar; BBQ; playgrnd; htd pool; sand beach 1km; games area; games rm; TV; 20% statics; dogs €1.50; phone adj; Eng spkn; adv bkg; quiet; ccard acc; red low ssn; CCI. "Many sports inc golf nr; clean san facs; red facs low ssn; excel." ♦ 1 May-30 Sep. € 26.00 2008*

ST JEAN DE MONTS *2H3* (3km NW Coastal) *46.80389, -2.09452* **Camping Le Fief, 168 Rue de Moulin Cassé, 85160 St Jean-de-Monts [02 51 58 63 77]** Fr St Jean on D38 NW, after 3km take L to le Fief-Haut / Route du Fief, then L again, sp immed on L. Rue de Moulin Cassé runs parallel to D38, nearer coast. Sm, pt shd; wc (cont); shwrs inc; el pnts (6A) €2.50; lndtte; shop & 3km; tradsmn; sand beach 2km; some statics; poss cr; adv bkg (rec high ssn); quiet; red low ssn. "Helpful owners; gd value for area; gd." ♦ May-Sep. € 13.00 2008*

ST JEAN DE MONTS *2H3* (3.5km NW Urban/Coastal) *46.80825, -2.10461* **Camping Les Amiaux, 223 Rue de Notre-Dame-de-Monts, 85160 St Jean-de-Monts [02 51 58 22 22; fax 02 51 58 26 09; accueil@amiaux.fr; www.amiaux.fr]** Site on D38 mid-way bet St Jean-de-Monts & Notre-Dame-de-Monts. V lge, hdg/mkd pitches, pt shd; htd wc; chem disp; serviced pitches; baby facs; shwrs inc; el pnts (10A) inc; gas; lndtte; sm shop; rest; snacks; bar; BBQ (gas & elec); playgrnd; htd, covrd pool; waterslides; sand beach 700m; tennis; cycle hire; horseriding 2km; golf 4km; games area; games rm; entmnt; wifi; TV rm; 50% statics; dogs €2.50; Eng spkn; adv bkg; ccard acc; red low ssn; CCI. "Excel, family site; gd facs; conv Puy du Fou theme park; rec long stay." ♦ 3 May-30 Sep. € 26.50 2009*

ST JEAN DE MONTS *2H3* (4km NW Coastal) *46.80926, -2.11045* **Camping aux Coeurs Vendéens, 251 Route de Notre Dame-de-Monts, 85160 St Jean-de-Monts [02 51 58 84 91; fax 02 28 11 20 75; infocoeursvendeens.com; www.coeursvendeens.com]** Take D38 fr St Jean-de-Monts to Fromentine, site on L after 4km. Med, hdg pitch, shd; wc; shwrs inc; el pnts (10A) €3.30; lndtte; shop; rest; snacks; bar; playgrnd; htd pool; sand beach 700m; cycle hire; sailing & windsurfing 700m; entmnt; TV rm; 10% statics; dogs €2.90; late night car park; poss cr; adv bkg rec high ssn; quiet; red low ssn. ♦ 1 May-20 Sep. € 25.50 2007*

ST JEAN DE MONTS *2H3* (6km NW Coastal) *46.81831, -2.13006* **Camping La Forêt, 190 Chemin de la Rive, 85160 St Jean-de-Monts [02 51 58 84 63; camping-la-foret@wanadoo.fr; www.hpa-laforet.com]** Fr St Jean-de-Monts, take D38 twd Notre-Dame-de-Monts for 6km, over rndabt then turn L (last turning bef Notre-Dame-de-Monts) sp Pont d'Yeu, then immed L, site on L in 200m, on parallel rd to main rd. Med, hdg/mkd pitch, pt shd; wc; chem disp; shwrs inc; el pnts (6A) €3.80; gas; lndtte; shop; tradsmn; snacks; pool; playgrnd; htd pool; sand beach 500m; horseriding nrby; TV; 30% statics; dogs €2.50; phone; poss cr; Eng spkn; adv bkg; quiet; Eng spkn; BBQ; CCI. "Friendly, helpful owners; clean san facs; not suitable twin-axles; some pitches diff c'vans; excel." ♦ 2 May-20 Sep. € 27.00 2009*

ST JEAN DE MUZOLS see Tournon sur Rhône *9C2*

ST JEAN DU GARD *10E1* (1.5km N Rural) *44.11346, 3.89208* **Camping Les Sources, Route du Mialet, 30270 St Jean-du-Gard [04 66 85 38 03; fax 04 66 85 16 09; camping-des-sources@wanadoo.fr; www.camping-des-sources.fr]** Fr Alès take D907 twd Anduze & St Jean-du-Gard. Take by-pass twd Florac. R at traff lts on D983, foll camp sp. NB: Do not enter town cent when towing - narr rds. Med, hdg pitch, terr, shd; htd wc (some cont); chem disp; shwrs inc; el pnts (6A) inc; gas; shop; tradsmn; snacks; bar; playgrnd; pool; dogs €1.80; Eng spkn; adv bkg ess Jul/Aug; quiet. "Lovely, well laid-out site; pitches sm, not rec for lge o'fits; friendly, helpful family owners; modern san facs, ltd low ssn; conv National Park of Cévennes." ♦ 1 Apr-30 Sep. € 22.00 2008*

ST JEAN DU GARD *10E1* (5km N Rural) *44.13187, 3.89025* **Camping La Forêt, 30270 Falguières [04 66 85 37 00; fax 04 66 85 07 05; laforet30@aol.com; www.campingalaforet.com]** Fr D907 turn N fr by-pass onto D983, then D50. Foll sp to Falguières & site sp on narr winding rd for 2.5km. Med, pt sl, pt shd; wc; baby facs; shwrs inc; el pnts (4-6A) €2.70-3.70; gas; lndtte; shop; rest 5km; bar; playgrnd; pool; paddling pool; rv sw 400m; 15% statics; adv bkg; quiet. "Wooded hill country; friendly family owners; walking rtes fr site." 1 May-15 Sep. € 18.10 2006*

ST JEAN DU GARD *10E1* (2km W Rural) *44.11241, 3.86023* **Camping à la Ferme le Petit Baigneur (Rossel), Les Deux Chemins, 30270 St Jean-du-Gard [04 66 85 32 05; fax 04 66 85 35 48; http://pagesperso-orange.fr/le-petit-baigneur]** Site on S side of D907 at W end of St Jean-du-Gard by-pass & 250m beyond D907/260 junc. If app fr W go past site ent & make U turn at layby opp D907/260 junc - due acute angle of site ent. Sm, pt shd; wc; chem disp (wc); shwrs inc; el pnts (6A) €1.50; lndtte; shop 1.5km; tradsmn; rest, snacks, bar 1.5km; BBQ; playgrnd; rv & shgl beach adj; fishing; TV; no statics; dogs; phone; some rd noise; red low ssn; CCI. "Family-run, simple, pleasant site by rv; san facs dated but clean; tourist steam train 1.5km; mkt Tues." ♦ Easter-15 Sep. € 11.85 2008*

ST JEAN EN ROYANS *9C2* (6km NE Rural) *45.05917, 5.25353* **FFCC Camp Municipal, 26190 St Nazaire-en-Royans [04 75 48 41 18 or 04 75 48 40 63 (Mairie); contact@saint-nazaire-en-royans.com]** Exit A49 onto D1532 (N532) to St Nazaire-en-Royans, site is on E edge of vill on D76, 700m fr cent, well sp. Med, hdg pitch, pt sl, pt shd; wc (some cont); chem disp; shwrs inc; el pnts (3-6A) €2.60-3.50; Indtte; shops & rest 700m; playgrnd; dogs €1.22; quiet; CCI. "Clean facs; helpful warden; gate clsd 2200-0700; conv mountains of Vercors; aquaduct on Rv Isère worth seeing; excel." ♦ 1 May-30 Sep. € 8.10 2009*

ST JEAN EN ROYANS *9C2* (500m SW Urban) *45.01132, 5.28609* **Camp Municipal, Ave de Provence, 26190 St Jean-en-Royans [04 75 47 74 60]** Exit A49 junc 8 onto D1532 (N532) to St Nazaire-en-Royans. Shortly after passing under high rlwy arch in St Nazaire turn R on D76 to St Jean-en-Royans. Site at S end of St Jean; sp (different site fr Camp Municipal St Nazaire). Med, hdg pitch, pt shd; wc; chem disp; mv service pnt; shwrs inc; some el pnts (10A) €2; Indtte; shops 500m; playgrnd; rv fishing 50m; some statics; dogs €1; daytime factory noise. "Pleasant, relaxing, under-used site in semi-parkland; dated, clean san facs; lge pitches; no twin-axle vans; rec use drinking water fr san facs, not fr old water pumps; gd walking." 1 May-30 Sep. € 8.60 2008*

ST JEAN FROIDMENTEL see Cloyes sur le Loir *4F2*

ST JEAN PIED DE PORT *8F1* (3km E Rural) *43.17763, -1.21317* **Aire Naturelle La Paix des Champs (Jasses), Ferme Asoritzia, Route de Jaxu, 64220 St Jean-le-Vieux [05 59 37 02 63]** E fr St Jean-Pied-de-Port on D933. In 2km turn L onto D22 sp Jaxu, site on R in 1km. Sm, pt shd, wc; chem disp (wc); shwrs inc; el pnts (3A) €1.80; Indry facs; supmkt 1km; playgrnd; pool 2km; trout-fishing; dogs €0.50; quiet; CCI. "Tranquil & beautiful; mountain views; san facs stretched high ssn; site needs maintenance (9/07); run down low ssn; interesting town on pilgrim rte to Spain." ♦ 15 Apr-30 Sep. € 9.00 2008*

ST JEAN PIED DE PORT *8F1* (200m S Urban) *43.16126, -1.23662* **Camp Municipal de Plaza Berri, Ave de Fronton, 64220 St Jean-Pied-de-Port [05 59 37 11 19 or 05 59 37 00 92; fax 05 59 37 99 78; mairie.stjeanpieddeport@wanadoo.fr]** Fr N on D933 thro town & cross rv. In 50m bear L at sm rndabt, site in 200m, sp. Enquire at Hôtel de Ville (Town Hall) off ssn. Narr app rds. Med, some mkd pitch; pt sl, pt shd; wc; chem disp; mv service pnt; shwrs inc; el pnts (5A) €2.50 (poss rev pol); shops 400m; pool 500m; quiet; CCI. "Busy site - arr early; if recep unmanned, site yourself & report later; facs well-kept & clean; mkt Mon; poss open until mid-Nov; gd NH - used by walkers on pilgrim rte." ♦ Easter-1 Nov. € 10.00 2009*

ST JEAN PIED DE PORT *8F1* (1.5km W Rural) *43.17304, -1.25416* **Europ Camping, 64220 Ascarat [05 59 37 12 78; fax 05 59 37 29 82; europcamping64@orange.fr; www.europ-camping.com]** Site on D918 bet Uhart-Cize & Ascarat. Well sp. Med, hdg/mkd pitch, pt shd; wc; chem disp; serviced pitch; sauna; shwrs inc; el pnts (6A) €4 (check pol); Indtte; shop 2km; tradsmn; rest; snacks; bar; playgrnd; pool; paddling pool; games area; games rm; 30% statics; dogs €2.50; adv bkg; quiet; ccard acc; red low ssn; CCI. "Beautiful location; helpful staff; ltd facs low ssn; only basic food in bar/rest; ground v soft when wet; vg." ♦ 1 Apr-30 Sep. € 23.00 2009*

ST JEAN PIED DE PORT *8F1* (3km W Rural) *43.17745, -1.25970* **Camping Narbaïtz, Route de Bayonne, 64220 Ascarat [05 59 37 10 13 or 05 59 37 09 22 (LS); fax 05 59 37 21 42; camping-narbaitz@wanadoo.fr; www.camping-narbaitz.com]** Site on L of D918 St Jean to Bayonne 3km fr St Jean, sp. Med, hdg/mkd pitch, pt sl, pt shd; htd wc (some cont); chem disp; mv service pnt; baby facs; shwrs inc; el pnts (6-10A) €4-5 (poss rev pol); Indtte; shop, snacks & bar in ssn; tradsmn; playgrnd; htd pool; trout-fishing; canoeing; kayaking; cycling; entmnt; internet; 5% statics; dogs free; phone; poss cr; Eng spkn; adv bkg; quiet; ccard acc high ssn; red low ssn; CCI. "Attractive, clean, family-run site; lovely views; helpful owners; vg facs; rec m'vans use top of site when wet; nr Spanish border (cheaper petrol); excel." ♦ 4 Apr-19 Sep. € 22.00 (CChq acc) 2009*

ST JORIOZ see Annecy *9B3*

ST JORY DE CHALAIS see Thiviers *7C3*

ST JOUAN DES GUERETS see St Malo *2E4*

ST JOUIN DE MARNES *4H1* (Rural) **Camping Clos-aux-Pères, 18 Rue des Gentils-Lieux, 79600 St Jouin-de-Marnes [05 49 67 44 50; fax 05 49 67 47 89; p.panneau@tiscali.fr; www.clos-aux-peres.fr.st]** S of Thouars on D37 in dir Poitiers, site on L on ent to vill. Sm, hdg pitch, pt shd; wc; chem disp; shwrs inc; el pnts (10A) €2.50; Indtte; tradsmn; shop, rest, bar in vill; BBQ; playgrnd; pool; lake nr; phone; quiet; CCI. "Welcoming, CL-type site." 1 Jun-30 Sep. € 12.00 2006*

ST JULIEN DE LAMPON see Sarlat la Canéda *7C3*

ST JULIEN DE PEYROLAS see Pont St Esprit *9D2*

ST JULIEN DES LANDES see Mothe Achard, La *2H4*

ST JULIEN EN BEAUCHENE *9D3* (7km N Rural) *44.66440, 5.70742* **Camping Le Champ La Chèvre, 26620 Lus-La-Croix-Haute [04 92 58 50 14; fax 04 92 58 55 92; info@campingchamplachevre.com; www.campingchamplachevre.com]** Turn E off D1075 (N75) thru Lus vill, site SE of vill nr sw pool on D505. Med, mkd pitch, pt sl, terr, pt shd; wc; chem disp; shwrs €1; el pnts (6A) €4.05; gas; Indtte; shops 300m; snacks; playgrnd; htd pool adj; fishing; some statics; dogs €2.65; poss cr; adv bkg; quiet; ccard acc; CCI. "Mountain views; helpful staff; excel pool; many waymkd walks; vg." ♦ 27 Apr-30 Sep. € 16.40 2009*

ST JULIEN EN GENEVOIS *9A3* (5km SE Rural) *46.12015, 6.10565* **Kawan Village La Colombière, Chef-Lieu, 74160 Neydens [04 50 35 13 14; fax 04 50 35 13 40; la.colombiere@wanadoo.fr; www.camping-la-colombiere.com]** Exit A40 junc 13 onto D1201 (N201) dir Cruseilles; in 1.75km turn L to Neydens; turn R at church; site on R in 200m. Site sp. NB: Do not go into St Julien-en-Genevois when towing. Med, hdg/mkd pitch, hdstg, pt sl, pt shd; htd wc; chem disp; mv service pnt; baby facs; shwrs inc; el pnts (6A) inc, extra for 15A; gas; Indtte; shops 500m; farm produce; rest; snacks; bar; BBQ (gas/elect/charcoal); playgrnd; 2 pools (1 sm htd, covrd); paddling pool; lake fishing 1km; cycle hire; archery; entmnt; wifi; games/TV rm; 10% statics; dogs €2; park & ride bus; poss cr; Eng spkn; adv bkg; quiet; ccard acc; red low ssn; CCI. "Excel, clean, well-managed, family-run site; vg san facs; friendly, helpful staff; boggy after heavy rain; open for m'vans all year; conv Geneva - excel guided tours high ssn; gd NH." ♦ 1 Mar-12 Nov. € 31.00 (CChq acc) ABS - M08 2009*

ST JULIEN EN GENEVOIS *9A3* (6km S Rural) *46.09921, 6.08357* **Camping Le Terroir, 184 Chemin de Clairjoie, 74160 Présilly [04 50 04 42 07; fax 04 50 04 55 53; camping.le.terroir@wanadoo.fr; www.camping-le-terroir.fr]** Fr St Julien-en-Genevois S on D1201 (N201) for 5km. At traff lts after rndabt junc with D18, turn R twd Présilly, Route de Viry. Site on L past vill on D18. Sm, mkd pitch, pt shd; htd wc; chem disp; shwrs inc; el pnts (5-10A) €3-3.50; Indtte; tradsmn; rest 5km; snacks, bar 2km; BBQ; playgrnd; htd pool 6km; TV rm; some statics; dogs; poss cr; Eng spkn; adv bkg; quiet; CCI. "Gd touring base." 1 May-15 Sep. € 10.50 2008*

ST JULIEN EN ST ALBAN see Privas *9D2*

ST JUNIEN *7B3* (500m Urban) *45.89616, 0.89979* **Camp Municipal de la Glane, Allée des Pommiers, Ave Corot, 87200 St Junien [05 55 02 34 86; fax 05 55 02 34 88; sports@mairie-saint-junien.fr; www.mairie-saint-junien.fr]** Fr Limoges take D941/N141 W to St Junien. Or 9km NE Rochechouart on D675. Site in town, well sp. Med, hdg pitch, sl, shd; wc; chem disp; mv service pnt; shwrs inc; el pnts (10A) €3.40; playgrnd; htd pool 300m; rv fishing 200m; dogs; adv bkg. "Modern san facs; many sloping pitches, some boggy after rain; vg." 15 May-19 Sep. € 6.90 2008*

ST JUNIEN *7B3* (4km E Rural) *45.88078, 0.96539* **FFCC Camp Municipal de Chambery, 87200 St Brice-sur-Vienne [05 55 02 18 13; mairiest-brice@wanadoo.fr]** Fr Limoges on D941/N141 turn L at rndabt 5km fr St Junien sp St Brice. In vill turn L onto D32; in 1.5km (on outskirts of vill) turn L & foll site sp; site on L in 500m. Or fr St Junien take D32 E sp St Brice & St Victurnien, site sp on L on E edge of vill. Sm, hdg/mkd pitch, hdstg, pt sl, pt shd; htd wc; chem disp; mv service pnt; serviced pitches; shwrs inc; el pnts (6A) inc; Indtte; shop in vill; playgrnd; rv nr; dogs; adv bkg; CCI. "Peaceful, clean site in park; spacious pitches o'look lake & countryside; site yourself, warden calls early eve; barrier clsd 2200-0700; conv Oradour-sur-Glane; vg." ♦ 26 Apr-15 Sep. € 9.40 2009*

ST JURS see Moustiers Ste Marie *10E3*

ST JUST (CANTAL) *9C1* (Urban) *44.88997, 3.21028* **FFCC Camp Municipal, 15320 St Just [04 71 73 72 57, 04 71 73 70 48 or 06 31 47 05 15 (mob); fax 04 71 73 71 44; info@saintjust.com; www.saintjust.com]** Exit junc 31 fr A75, foll sp St Chély-d'Apcher D909; turn W onto D448 twds St Just (approx 6km); sp with gd access. Med, mkd pitch, pt sl, terr, pt shd; htd wc; chem disp; mv service pnt; shwrs inc; el pnts (10A) €2.10; Indtte; shop; snacks; bar; pool high ssn; fishing; tennis; cycle hire; v quiet; red low ssn/long stay. "Friendly warden; ltd facs low ssn; gd touring base; area for m'vans." Easter-30 Sep. € 9.50 2009*

ST JUST EN CHEVALET *9B1* (1km NW Rural) *45.91459, 3.84026* **Camp Municipal Le Verdillé, 42430 St Just-en-Chevalet [tel/fax 04 77 65 17 82 or 04 77 65 00 62 (Mairie); jpallut@tele2.fr]** Exit A72 at junc 4, join D53 NE twd St Just-en-Chevalet. Foll sp in town to camping/piscine. Due to steep gradients avoid D1 when towing. Med, hdg pitch, pt sl, pt shd; wc (mainly cont); chem disp; mv service pnt; shwrs inc; el pnts (16A) €3; Indtte; shops & supmkt 500m; rest 500m; snacks, bar adj; htd pool & tennis adj; 10% statics; dogs €1.70; phone; Eng spkn; adv bkg; quiet; CCI. "Friendly owners." 15 Apr-15 Oct. € 8.50 2008*

ST JUST LUZAC see Marennes *7B1*

ST JUSTIN *8E2* (2km NW Rural) *44.00166, -0.23502* **Camping Le Pin, Route de Roquefort, 40240 St Justin [tel/fax 05 58 44 88 91; campinglepin@wanadoo.fr; www.campinglepin.com]** Fr St Justin on D933, take D626 twd Roquefort. Site on L in 2km, well sp fr town. Sm, shd; wc; shwrs inc; el pnts (6A) €3; Indtte; shop & 2km; rest; snacks; bar; playgrnd; pool; rv fishing 2km; cycle hire; horseriding; games area; entmnt; TV; some statics; dogs €1.50; poss cr; adv bkg; quiet; red low ssn/snr citizens; CCI. "Pleasant, spacious site; facs old but clean & poss stretched when site full; beautiful vill." ♦ 1 Apr-30 Sep. € 18.00 2009*

ST LAGER BRESSAC see St Vincent de Barrès *9D2*

ST LAMBERT DU LATTAY *4G1* **FFCC Camp Municipal La Coudraye, Rue de la Coudray, 49190 St Lambert-du-Lattay [02 41 78 49 31 or 02 41 78 44 26 (Mairie); miche.rip@wanadoo.fr]** Fr Angers on D160 thro vill cent dir Chemillé. Site sp on L adj wine museum in 200m. Poor sp fr N. Sm, hdg pitch, pt sl, pt shd; wc (some cont); chem disp; mv service pnt; shwrs inc; el pnts (10A) €2.40-4.20; gas; Indry rm; playgrnd; rv 500m; fishing 50m; entmnt; dogs €0.70; adv bkg. "Lovely, quiet site; wine museums worth visiting; site yourself, warden calls am & pm; gd walking; fair NH." ♦ 1 Apr-30 Oct. € 6.90 2007*

ST LARY SOULAN *8G2* (Rural) *42.81538, 0.32329* **Camp Municipal La Lanne, 65170 St Lary-Soulan [05 62 39 41 58 or 05 62 40 87 85 (LS); fax 05 62 40 01 40; camping@saintlary-vacances.com; www.saintlary-vacances.com]** On Bielsa-Aragnouet rd, sp on on ent vill. Site in side street E of main rd & ent not sp. Look for ent with tall trees at each side. Med, mkd pitch, pt sl, shd; htd wc; chem disp; shwrs inc; el pnts (2-10A) €3-7; gas; Indtte; shop 250m; rest, snacks, bar 400m; playgrnd; htd pool adj; TV rm; adv bkg; quiet; red low ssn. "Vg san facs." ♦ 30 Nov-30 Sep. € 15.00 2008*

⊞ **ST LARY SOULAN** *8G2* (2km N Rural) *42.8400, 0.33983* **Camping Le Rioumajou, 65170 Bourisp [05 62 39 48 32; fax 05 62 39 58 27; info@camping-le-rioumajou.com; www.camping-le-rioumajou.com]** On W side of D929 2km N of St Lary-Soulon & 500m N of Bourisp. Lge, hdg/mkd pitch, hdstg, shd; wc; chem disp; shwrs inc; el pnts (10A) €6; gas; Indtte; shop; tradsmn; rest; snacks; bar; htd pool; playgrnd; tennis; entmnt; TV rm; phone; dogs €1.50; poss cr; Eng spkn; adv bkg; quiet; CCI. "Conv Bielsa tunnel; St Lary-Soulan attractive; gd walking & watersports." € 17.30 2008*

⊞ **ST LARY SOULAN** *8G2* (4km NE Rural) *42.84482, 0.33836* **Camping Le Lustou, Agos, 65170 Vielle-Aure [05 62 39 40 64; contact@lustou.com; www.lustou.com]** Exit A64 junc 16 & head S on D929. Thro Arreau & Guchen turn R onto D19 dir Vielle-Aure. Site on R just bef Agos. Med, mkd pitch, pt sl, pt shd; htd wc; chem disp; baby facs; shwrs inc; el pnts (6-10A) €5.50-6.50; gas; Indtte; shop 2km; snacks; bar; playgrnd; htd, covrd pool; fishing, canoeing, tennis nrby; TV rm; dogs €1.60; phone; adv bkg; some rd noise; CCI. "Family-owned site; excel walking, skiing; immac facs." ♦ € 12.20 (3 persons) 2007*

ST LAURENT DE CERDANS see Prats de Mollo la Preste *8H4*

⊞ **ST LAURENT DE CERIS** *7B3* (2km NE Rural) *45.96037, 0.52855* **Camping Le Fournet (Dyson), Le Fournet, 16450 St Laurent-de-Céris [05 45 31 78 28; info@lefournet.com; www.lefournet.com]** Fr St Laurent-de-Céris on D345; take 2nd turning to L sp Ambernac; in 2km site on R. Or fr N on D951, take D15 dir St Laurent-de-Céris, then take D345 dir Ambernac. Sm, pt sl, pt shd; wc; chem disp, shwrs inc; el pnts (10A) €2; Indtte; tradsmn; BBQ; pool; fishing; internet; dogs €0.50; Eng spkn; adv bkg; quiet; red long stay. "Peaceful, well-kept CL-type site; friendly & helpful British owners; san facs clean; excel." € 8.00 2008*

ST LAURENT DE NESTE see Montréjeau *8F3*

ST LAURENT DU PAPE see Voulte sur Rhône, La *9D2*

ST LAURENT DU PONT see Echelles, Les *9B3*

ST LAURENT DU VAR see Cagnes sur Mer *10E4*

ST LAURENT DU VERDON *10E3* (1.5km N Rural) *43.73386, 6.07838* **Camping La Farigoulette, Lac de St Laurent, 04500 St Laurent-du-Verdon [04 92 74 41 62; fax 04 92 74 00 86; info@camping-la-farigoulette.com; www.camping-la-farigoulette.com]** Fr Riez SE on D11; in 15km turn L onto D311 to St Laurent-du-Verdon; on ent vill turn L at shrine onto C1 dir Montpezat; site on R in 1km. Fr Quinson take D11 & in 2km turn R onto D311; cont thro vill & take R fork at shrine onto C1 dir Montpezat, site on R in 1km. Lge, pt sl, shd; wc; mv service pnt; shwrs inc; el pnts (5A) €3.50; Indtte; shop; rest; snacks; bar; BBQ; playgrnd; 2 pools; lake sw adj; canoeing, watersports; fishing; tennis; cycle hire; entmnt; TV; some statics; dogs €2; poss cr; red low ssn. 15 May-30 Sep. € 20.00 2007*

ST LAURENT DU VERDON *10E3* (2km W Rural) *43.71066, 6.05789* **Domaine Naturiste d'Enriou (Naturist), 04500 St Laurent-du-Verdon [04 92 74 41 02; fax 04 92 74 01 20; domaine.enriou@voila.fr; www.domainedenriou.com]** Fr Riez foll D11 S, site on D311 to St Laurent-du-Verdon & sp fr D11/D311 junc immed N of Quinson. Med, shd; wc; chem disp; shwrs inc; el pnts (3-6A) €3.60-4; gas; shops; rest; snacks; playgrnd; 2 pools; sw lake 500m; canoes; archery; fishing; entmnt; TV; few statics; dogs €3.80; adv bkg; v quiet; INF card req. "Vg, friendly, peaceful site; lovely spot; conv Gorges du Verdon." 15 May-30 Sep. € 26.50 2009*

ST LAURENT EN BEAUMONT see Mure, La (Isere) *9C3*

ST LAURENT EN GRANDVAUX *6H2* (500m SE Rural) *46.57645, 5.96214* **Camp Municipal Le Champs de Mars, Rue du Camping, 39150 St Laurent-en-Grandvaux [03 84 60 19 30 or 06 03 61 06 61; fax 03 84 60 19 72; champmars.camping@wanadoo.fr; www.st-laurent39.fr]** E thro St Laurent on N5 twd Morez, site on R, sp `Caravaneige' at ent. Med, mkd pitch, hdstg, pt sl, pt shd; htd wc; chem disp; mv service pnt; shwrs inc; some serviced pitches; el pnts (4-10A) €3.60-5-90; Indtte; shops & supmkt in vill; playgrnd; TV rm; 20% statics; dogs; phone; adv bkg; quiet; red low ssn; CCI. "Gd site, peaceful low ssn." ♦ 16 Dec-30 Sep. € 11.25 2008*

ST LAURENT EN GRANDVAUX *6H2* (10km W Rural) *46.59689, 5.87163* **Camping L'Abbaye, 2 Route du Lac, 39130 Bonlieu [03 84 25 57 04; fax 03 84 25 50 82; camping.abbaye@wanadoo.fr; www.camping-abbaye.com]** Site on L of D678 (N78), 1km bef vill of Bonlieu, sp. Med, mkd pitch, pt sl, pt shd; wc; chem disp; baby facs; shwrs inc; el pnts (6A) €3; Indtte; shop 4km; rest; snacks; bar; BBQ; playgrnd; games area; dogs €1; Eng spkn; adv bkg; quiet; CCI. "Pleasant site in attractive area; bar/rest open low ssn; modern san facs; access to disabled facs fr first (upper) terrace; blocks req for most lge pitches; gd walks; gd dog walks; Lac de Bonlieu 1km." ♦ 1 May-30 Sep. € 13.50 2008*

France

ST LAURENT MEDOC *7C1* (2km N Rural) *45.17499, -0.83893* **Camping Le Paradis, 8 Rue Fournon, 33112 St Laurent-Médoc [tel/fax 05 56 59 42 15 or 06 87 73 66 36 (mob); www.leparadismedoc.com]** On W side of D1215 (N215) at Ballac. Med, mkd pitch, pt shd; wc; chem disp; mv service pnt; baby facs; shwrs inc; el pnts (10A) €4; Indtte; tradsmn; snacks; bar; playgrnd; pool; paddling pool; games area; entmnt; TV; some statics; dogs €2.60; adv bkg; quiet. "Excel site; helpful staff." 1 Apr-17 Sep. € 14.00 2006*

ST LAURENT NOUAN see Beaugency *4F2*

ST LAURENT SUR SEVRE *2H4* (5km S Rural) *46.92452, -0.87406* **Camp Municipal La Vallée de Poupet, 85590 St Malô-du-Bois [02 51 92 31 45; fax 02 51 92 38 65; camping@valleedepoupet.com; www.valleedepoupet.com]** Fr N on N149 turn S onto D752 at La Trique. At St Malô-du-Bois (4km) foll sp for 4.5km. Fr S fr Mauléon on N149 turn L onto D11 twd Mallièvre; 4km after Mallièvre turn R onto D752. After 2.5km turn R & foll sp. Steep app to site. Med, mkd pitch, pt shd; wc; chem disp; mv service pnt; baby facs; shwrs inc; el pnts (6A) €2.60; Indtte; shops 2km; tradsmn; rest; bar 500m; playgrnd; htd, covrd pool; fishing; entmnt; 10% statics; dogs €1; phone adj; Eng spkn; adv bkg; quiet; CCI. "Excel rvside site." ♦ 15 May-15 Sep. € 14.00 2006*

⊞ **ST LAURENT SUR SEVRE** *2H4* (1km W Rural) *46.95790, -0.90290* **Camping Le Rouge Gorge, Route de la Verrie, 85290 St Laurent-sur-Sèvre [02 51 67 86 39; fax 02 51 67 73 40; info@lerougegorge.com; www.lerougegorge.com]** Fr Cholet on N160 dir La Roche-sur-Yon; at Mortagne-sur-Sèvre take N149 to St Laurent-sur-Sèvre. In St Laurent foll sp La Verrie on D111. Site on R at top of hill. Or take 762 S fr Cholet to St Laurent. Site sp in town. Med, hdg/mkd pitch, pt sl, pt shd; htd wc; chem disp; mv service pnt; baby facs; shwrs inc; el pnts (4-13A) €2.30-5.60; Indtte; shop; snacks; bar; playgrnd; pool; paddling pool; rv & lake fishing 800m; games area; golf 15km; 30% statics; dogs €1.75; adv bkg; quiet; red low ssn; CCI. "Peaceful family site; woodland walks & mountain biking; attractive sm town." ♦ € 16.80 (CChq acc) 2009*

ST LEGER DE FOUGERET see Château-Chinon *4H4*

ST LEGER DU BOURG DENIS see Rouen *3C2*

⊞ **ST LEGER LES MALEZES** *9D3* (300m E Rural) *44.64551, 6.20436* **Camping La Pause, Route du Barry, 05260 St Léger-les-Mélèzes [04 92 50 44 92; fax 04 92 50 77 59; valerie.portier@wanadoo.fr; www.camping-la-pause.com]** Fr N85 Route Napoléon turn E onto D14 St Laurent-du Cros. At La Plaine take D113 to St Léger, site sp. Med, pt shd; htd wc; baby facs; chem disp; mv service pnt; shwrs inc; el pnts (2-10A) €2-10; gas; Indtte; shop 100m; rest; snacks; bar; BBQ; playgrnd; htd pool; tennis; horseriding; games area; games rm; wintersports; entmnt; 60% statics; dogs €1.50; adv bkg; quiet. € 13.00 2006*

ST LEGER SOUS BEUVRAY *4H4* (1km N Rural) *46.93180, 4.09861* **Camping La Boutière, 71990 St Léger-sous-Beuvray [03 85 82 48 86 or 03 85 82 39 73 (LS); camping@la-boutiere.com; www.la-boutiere.com]** Take N81 SW fr Autun dir Bourbon-Lancy & in approx 10km, turn R onto D61 to St Léger. Site sp in vill. Sm, mkd pitch, pt sl, pt shd; wc; chem disp; shwrs inc; el pnts (6-10A) inc; shops 1km; 5% statics; dogs €1.50; phone; twin-axle c'vans €75; poss cr; quiet; CCI. "Simple site; gd facs; popular with Dutch; vg." 1 Apr-30 Sep. € 18.30 2008*

ST LEON SUR VEZERE see Montignac *7C3*

ST LEONARD DE NOBLAT *7B3* (12km N Rural) *45.94311, 1.51459* **Camp Municipal du Pont du Dognon, 87240 St Laurent-les-Eglises [05 55 56 57 25; fax 05 55 56 55 17; mairie-st-laurent-les-eglises@wanadoo.fr]** Take D941 (N141) fr St Léonard-de-Noblat; after 1.5km turn L (N) on D19 thro Le Châtenet-en-Dognon. Site in approx 4km, bef St Laurent-les-Eglises. Med, mkd pitch, terr, pt shd; htd wc; shwrs inc; el pnts (5A) €2.62; gas; Indtte; shop & 3km; rest; snacks; BBQ; pool; shgl beach; canoeing; tennis; cycle hire; entmnt; dogs €0.90; adv bkg; quiet. "Vg site." 15 Apr-15 Oct. € 11.25 2009*

ST LEONARD DE NOBLAT *7B3* (9km SE Rural) *45.80125, 1.62774* **Camp Municipal du Lac, Ste Helène, 87460 Bujaleuf [tel/fax 05 55 69 54 54; tourisme@bujaleuf.fr]** Fr St Léonard take D13, D14 to Bujaleuf. Site 500m N of town on D16. Med, terr, pt shd; htd wc; shwrs inc; el pnts (5A) €2; Indtte; shops 1km; tradsmn; playgrnd; poss cr; adv bkg; quiet; red low ssn. "No warden Sun or Mon; el pnts on lower terr; modern san facs; Bujaleuf sm mkt town." 15 May-30 Sep. € 8.00 2007*

ST LEONARD DE NOBLAT *7B3* (2km S Rural) *45.82300, 1.49200* **Camping de Beaufort, 87400 St Léonard-de-Noblat [05 55 56 02 79; info@campingdebeaufort.com; www.campingdebeaufort.com]** Leave A20 S-bound at junc 34 dir St Léonard, onto D941 (N141). In 18km on ent St Léonard, 300m after x-ing Rv Vienne, fork R (sp). Site on R in 2km. Med, hdg pitch, pt sl, pt shd; htd wc; chem disp (wc); shwrs inc; el pnts (15A) €3; Indtte; shop & 4km; tradsmn; bar; playgrnd; fishing; dogs €1.50; phone; poss cr; adv bkg; ccard acc; CCI. ♦ 15 Jun-15 Sep. € 14.00 2009*

ST LEONARD DES BOIS *4E1* (Rural) *48.35353, -0.07669* **Camp Municipal Les Alpes Mancelles, Le Bourg, 72130 St Léonard-des-Bois [02 43 33 81 79; fax 02 43 34 49 02; campalpesmancelles@free.fr; www.ot-alpes-mancelles.com]** SW of Alençon on D1/D121 to Gesvres; turn L onto D149 to St Léonard-des-Bois; site sp on Rv Sarthe. Or easy access fr Fresnay-sur-Sarthe N on D15/D112. Med, mkd pitch, pt sl, pt shd; wc; shwrs inc; el pnts (6A) inc (poss rev pol); lndry rm; shop, snacks & bar nrby; playgrnd; rv watersports; dogs €0.50; phone; CCI. "Pretty, well-run, basic site by rv; gd san facs; well-marked walks; gd touring base; interesting vill; vg." 1 Apr-30 Sep. € 11.40 2009*

ST LEU D'ESSERENT see Chantilly *3D3*

ST LOUIS *6G3* (2km N Rural) *47.59428, 7.58930* **Camp Municipal au Petit Port, 10 Allée des Marronniers, 68330 Huningue [tel/fax 03 89 69 05 25; www.ville-huningue.fr]** S fr Mulhouse on A35, exit onto D105 & foll sps to Huningue; after level x-ing site sp on rvside. Sm, shd; wc; mv service pnt; shwrs inc; el pnts (4A) €1.50; shop 1km; rest, bar 500m; htd pool 2km; 50% statics; dogs; bus to Basle; poss cr; quiet. "Poss diff access lge o'fits; helpful warden; gd." ♦ 15 Apr-15 Oct. € 10.00 2007*

ST LUNAIRE see Dinard *2E3*

ST LYPHARD *2G3* (500m W Rural) *47.39688, -2.30146* **Camping Les Brières du Bourg, Route d'Herbignac, 44410 St Lyphard [02 40 91 43 13 or 01 40 33 93 33 (LS); fax 02 51 74 06 62; cledelles.reservations@wanadoo.fr; www.lescledelles.com]** Fr Nantes on N165 dir Vannes, exit junc 15 dir La Roche-Bernard then in 2km turn L onto D574 then D774 sp Herbignac, Guérande. At Herbignac fork L onto D47. Pass 1st sp on R to St Lyphard, site on L in 1km. Med, hdg/mkd pitch, pt sl, shd; wc; chem disp; mv service pnt; baby facs; serviced pitch; shwrs inc; el pnts (6A) €5; gas; lndtte; shops 1km; tradsmn; rest 1km; snacks; bar; playgrnd; pool; lake sw adj; fishing; tennis; cycle hire; games rm; entnmt; TV; 10% statics; dogs €2.30; phone; Eng spkn; adv bkg; quiet; red long stay/low ssn; CCI. "Delightful vill; sports complex adj." ♦ 1 Apr-30 Sep. € 15.00 2007*

ST MAIXENT L'ECOLE *7A2* (SW Urban) *46.40836, -0.21856* **Camp Municipal du Panier Fleuri, Rue Paul Drévin, 79400 St Maixent-l'Ecole [05 49 05 53 21 or 05 49 76 13 77 (Mairie)]** Take D611 (N11) twd Niort, at 2nd set of traff lts nr top of hill out of town turn L. Foll camping sps into ent. Med, mkd pitch, pt sl, pt shd; wc (some cont); mv service pnt; shwrs inc; el pnts (10A) €1.45-5; tradsmn; rest, snacks, bar 1km; playgrnd; pool adj; tennis; dogs €0.55; quiet; ccard not acc. "Warden on site am & eve, if office locked go to house nr wc block; ltd/basic facs low ssn in Portakabin; poss itinerants; interesting town; NH en rte Spain." 1 Apr-31 Oct. € 7.30 2006*

ST MALO *2E4* (500m Urban/Coastal) *48.63558, -2.02731* **Camp Municipal Cité d'Alet, Allée Gaston Buy, 35400 St Malo [02 99 81 60 91 or 02 99 40 71 11 (LS); fax 02 99 40 71 37; camping@ville-saint-malo.fr; www.ville-saint-malo.fr/campings]** Fr ferry terminal go twd St Malo, site sp at rndabt immed past docks. Fr all other dir foll sp for port/ferry, then site sp. Site off Place St Pierre, St Servan-sur-Mer. App thro old part of city poss diff for lge o'fits. Lge, mkd pitch, pt sl, pt shd; wc; chem disp; mv service pnt; shwrs inc; el pnts (10A) €4.25 (poss rev pol & long elec cable poss req); lndtte; shops, tradsmn, rest, snacks 500m; bar; playgrnd; sand beach 500m; dogs €2.35; bus; phone; poss v cr; Eng spkn; adv bkg; quiet; ccard acc; CCI. "Nice views over harbour to old city; staff helpful & courteous; sm pitches; access to some pitches diff lge o'fits; san facs basic but OK; WW2 museum on site; noise fr harbour when foggy; mkt Fri." ♦ 1 May-28 Sep. € 13.00 2009*

ST MALO *2E4* (2km NE Coastal) *48.68173, -1.97748* **Camp Municipal Le Nicet, Ave de la Varde, 35400 St Malo [02 99 40 26 32; fax 02 99 21 92 62; camping@ville-saint-malo.fr]** Fr St Malo take coast (busy & narr) rd Ave JF Kennedy twd Cancale; pass Camping Nielles on L bef district of Rotheneuf; turn L at camping sp just after sm g'ge on L; turn L at T-junc; site in view. Lge, mkd pitch, pt sl, pt terr, unshd; wc; chem disp, shwrs inc; el pnts (5-10A) inc (rev pol); lndtte; shops 800m; tradsmn; playgrnd; sand beach adj; dogs €2.20; poss cr & noisy high ssn; Eng spkn; adv bkg; ccard acc; CCI. "Clean, well-run site on cliff top; can be exposed if pitched nr edge with sea view; secluded beach via steep steps; some pitches sm." ♦ 1 Jul-1 Sep. € 15.50 2006*

ST MALO *2E4* (8km NE Coastal) *48.69000, -1.94200* **Camping des Chevrets, La Guimorais, 35350 St Coulomb [02 99 89 01 90; fax 02 99 89 01 16; campingdeschevrets@wanadoo.fr; www.campingdeschevrets.fr]** St Malo to Cancale coast rd D201; La Guimorais on L 3km E of Rothéneuf, strt thro vill; fairly narr app. V lge, hdg/mkd pitch, pt sl, pt shd; wc; chem disp; mv service pnt; baby facs; shwrs inc; el pnts (6A) €3.35 (poss rev pol); gas; lndtte; shop; rest; snacks; bar; BBQ; playgrnd; sand beach adj; games area; cycle hire; internet; entmnt; 50% statics; dogs; poss cr; Eng spkn; adv bkg; quiet; ccard acc; red low ssn/long stay; CCI. "Vg location with 2 bays; vg site." ♦ 6 Apr-1 Nov. € 21.95 2009*

ST MALO *2E4* (1km E Coastal) *48.66737, -1.98486* **Camp Municipal Les Nielles, 47 Ave du Président Kennedy, Paramé, 35400 St Malo [02 99 40 26 35; fax 02 99 21 92 62; camping@ville-saint-malo.fr; www.ville-saint-malo.fr/campings/]** Fr cent of St Malo (avoiding old walled town) E on D201 parallel & adj to coast; few site sp & poss not easy to find. Med, mkd pitch, unshd; wc (some cont); shwrs inc; el pnts (10A) inc; shop 900m; rest, bar 500m; playgrnd; sand beach adj; fishing; dogs €2.40; poss cr; some rd noise. "Excel for beach & ferry; pitches nr beach v exposed if weather bad." ♦ 1 Jul-31 Aug. € 17.25 2009*

France

⊞ **ST MALO** *2E4* (5km E Urban) *48.65762, -1.95932* **Camping La Fontaine, 40 Rue de la Fontaine aux Pèlerins, 35400 St Malo [02 99 81 62 62; fax 02 99 81 68 95; contact@campinglafontaine.com; www.campinglafontaine.com]** N fr Rennes on D137 turn R onto D301 sp Cancale. Turn R onto D155 sp Mont-St Michel, site in L in 100m. Med, hdg/mkd pitch, pt shd; htd wc; chem disp; mv service pnt; baby facs; fam bthrm; shwrs; el pnts (10A) €3.80 (poss rev pol); gas; lndtte; shop & 250m; tradsmn; rest; snacks; bar; BBQ; htd pool; sand beach 5km; cycle hire; games area; entmnt; wifi; 80% statics; dogs €2.50; phone; poss cr; quiet; ccard acc; red low ssn; CCI. "Gd touring base; conv ferry; gd." € 21.60 2009*

ST MALO *2E4* (5km SE Rural) *48.60916, -1.98663* **Camping Le P'tit Bois, La Chalandouze, 35430 St Jouan-des-Guérets [02 99 21 14 30; fax 02 99 81 74 14; camping.ptitbois@wanadoo.fr; www.ptitbois.com]** Fr St Malo take D137 dir Rennes; after o'skts of St Malo turn R twd St Jouan-des-Guérets, site sp. Lge, hdg/mkd pitch, pt shd; wc (some cont); chem disp; mv service pnt; baby facs; shwrs inc; el pnts (10A) inc; gas; lndtte; shop; rest; snacks; bar; BBQ (gas/elec); playgrnd; 2 htd pools; (1 covrd); waterslides; paddling pool; jacuzzi; turkish bath; sand beach 2km; tidal rv sw, fishing, watersports 2km; tennis; entmnt; wifi; games/TV rm; 50% tour ops/statics; dogs €6; adv bkg; ccard acc; (3 persons min 3/7-21/8); red low ssn/CCI. "Well-run site; friendly, helpful recep; gd for families; pitches poss soggy for heavy m'vans when wet; conv Le Mont-St Michel & ferries; excel." ♦ 2 Apr-11 Sep. € 48.00 (3 persons) ABS - B03 2009*

See advertisement

ST MALO *2E4* (3km S Rural) *48.61469, -1.98663* **Camping Domaine de la Ville Huchet, Rue de la Passagère, Quelmer, 34500 St Malo [02 99 81 11 83; fax 02 99 81 51 89; info@lavillehuchet.com; www.lavillehuchet.com]** Fr ferry port, foll sps for D137 dir Rennes; site sp fr "Madeleine" rndabt on leaving St Malo. Or fr S on D137 take D301 sp St Malo centre. Take 1st exit at next 2 rndabts (thro indus est) & cont on this rd past sharp R-hand bend, then under bdge, site on R. Lge, hdg/mkd pitch, pt sl, pt shd; wc; chem disp; baby facs; shwrs inc; el pnts (6A) inc; lndtte; shop; rest; snacks; bar; playgrnd; waterpark; sand beach 3km; cycle hire; games area; entmnt; TV; 40% statics; dogs €3; poss cr; Eng spkn; adv bkg; quiet, but some rd noise; red low ssn. "Spacious site; helpful owner; modern san facs; excel pool; some pitches v shady; ltd facs low ssn & site 'tired'." ♦ 10 Apr-12 Sep. € 32.00 ABS - B32 2009*

ST MALO DU BOIS see St Laurent sur Sèvre *2H4*

ST MARCEL D'ARDECHE see Pont St Esprit *9D2*

ST MARCELLIN *9C2* (7km E Rural) *45.12122, 5.33775* **Camping Château de Beauvoir, 38160 Beauvoir-en-Royans [04 76 64 01 79; fax 04 76 38 49 60; chateaudebeauvoir@wanadoo.fr]** On D1092 (N532) Romans to Grenoble, turn into narr uphill rd D518 to vill; L into site, sp. Care needed on app rd & ent gate narr. Sm, shd; htd wc; shwrs inc; el pnts (10A) €2; lndtte; shop 6km; bar; rest 2km; 10% statics; dogs; adv bkg rec; quiet. "Vg site on château lawn; gd walking." 1 Apr-31 Oct. € 11.60 2008*

⊞ **STE MARIE AUX MINES** *6E3* (1km E Urban) *48.23520, 7.16995* **FFCC Camping Les Reflets du Val d'Argent, 20 Rue d'Untergrombach, 68160 Ste Marie-aux-Mines [03 89 58 64 83; fax 03 89 58 64 31; reflets@calixo.net; www.les-reflets.com]** Fr Sélestat N59 into Ste Marie. Go thro vill to traff lts & turn L. 1km to site; sp. Med, hdg/mkd pitch, pt sl, pt shd; htd wc; chem disp; mv service pnt; shwrs inc; el pnts (5-15A) €3.30-9.90; lndtte; shop & 1km; tradsmn; rest; snacks; bar; BBQ; playgrnd; pool; games rm; TV; 5% statics; dogs €3.50; phone; adv bkg; quiet; red low ssn; CCI. "Pleasant site but facs run down & need refurb; winter skiing 5km." ♦ € 17.20 2008*

STE MARIE DU MONT *1D4* (6km NE Coastal) *49.41935, -1.18118* **Camping Utah Beach, La Madeleine, 50480 Ste Marie-du-Mont [02 33 71 53 69; fax 02 33 71 07 11; contact@camping-utahbeach.com; www.camping-utahbeach.com]** 50km S of Cherbourg on N13 turn L onto D913 to Ste Marie-du-Mont. Foll D913 to coast & sp to Utah Beach Memorial - approx 4km. Site on beach rd D421. Med, hdg/mkd pitch, pt sl, pt shd; wc; chem disp; mv service pnt; shwrs inc; el pnts (6A) inc; gas; lndtte; shop; tradsmn; snacks; bar; playgrnd; htd pool; sand beach 50m; water/beach sports; tennis; games rm; archery; internet; entmnt; excursions; 55% statics; dogs €2.90; phone; quiet; adv bkg; red low ssn; ccard acc; red low ssn; red CCI. "Well-kept site; gd touring base; site of US landing in 1944; gd birdwatching." 1 Apr-20 Sep. € 24.30 2008*

STE MARIE DU MONT *1D4* (3km SE Coastal) *49.36564, -1.17721* **Camping La Baie des Veys, Le Grand Vey, 50480 Ste Marie-du-Mont [02 33 71 56 90 or 06 09 82 61 82 (mob); jerome.etasse@orange.fr; www.campinglabaiedesveys.com]** N of Carentan exit N13 onto D913 thro Ste Marie-du-Mont. At lge calvary 2km after vill, turn R onto D115 sp Le Grand Vey. Turn R at sea edge, site on R in 100m. Med, hdg/mkd pitch, pt shd; wc; chem disp (wc); shwrs inc; el pnts (6A) €3; lndtte; shop & 6km; snacks; bar; BBQ; cycle hire; wifi; 10% statics; dogs free;; adv bkg; quiet. "Friendly site beside salt flats; gd birdwatching, fishing; conv Utah Beach, D-Day museums etc." ♦ 1 Apr-30 Sep. € 14.50 2009*

⊞ **STES MARIES DE LA MER** *10F2* (1km E Coastal) *43.45633, 4.43576* **Camping La Brise, Rue Marcel Carrière, 13460 Stes Maries-de-la-Mer [04 90 97 84 67; fax 04 90 97 72 01; labrise@saintesmaries.com; www.saintesmariesdelamer.com]** Sp on o'skts on all rds. Take N570 fr Arles or D58 (N570) fr Aigues-Mortes. V lge, unshd; htd wc (mainly cont); mv service pnt; shwrs inc; el pnts (10A) €4.70; Indtte; sm shop & 500m; 3 htd pools; beach adj; fishing; entmnt; dogs €4.60; clsd mid Nov to mid Dec; red low ssn. "Under same ownership as Le Clos du Rhône & can use their facs; v cr Aug; poss unkempt low ssn; poss mosquitoes; m'vans can use free municipal car park with facs; gd security; vg winter NH." ♦ € 20.20 2008*

STES MARIES DE LA MER *10F2* (2km W Coastal) *43.45014, 4.40163* **Camping Le Clos du Rhône, Route d'Aigues-Mortes, 13460 Stes Maries-de-la-Mer [04 90 97 85 99; fax 04 90 97 78 85; leclos@saintesmaries.com; www.saintesmariesdelamer.com]** Fr Arles take D570 to Stes Maries; fr Aigues Mortes, D58/D570. Lge, unshd; wc; some serviced pitches; chem disp; shwrs inc; el pnts (6-10A) €4.50; gas; Indtte; shop; rest; snacks; playgrnd; htd pool; sand beach; entmnt; dogs; horseriding adj; poss cr; quiet; adv bkg; ccard acc. "Excel pool & facs; san facs poss ltd & stretched low ssn; popular with families; private gate to beach; mosquitoes."♦ 20 Mar-3 Nov. € 29.20 2007*

ST MARTIAL DE NABIRAT see Gourdon *7D3*

ST MARTIAL ENTRAYGUES see Argentat *7C4*

ST MARTIN D'ARDECHE see Pont St Esprit *9D2*

ST MARTIN DE CRAU *10F2* (W Urban) *43.63750, 4.80570* **Camping La Crau, 4 Ave de St Roch, 13310 St Martin-de-Crau [04 90 47 17 09; fax 04 90 47 09 92; contact@campingdelacrau.com; www.campingdelacrau.com]** Fr W take D453 sp St Martin-de-Crau. L at 1st traff lts. Fr E take D453 thro town & R at traff lts by Hotel. Site behind Hôtel de la Crau, 50m up side rd running N off D453 on D83b. Fr N (St Rémy) on D27 turn R in town & as bef. Med, hdg/mkd pitch, shd; wc (some cont); chem disp; mv service pnt; shwrs inc; el pnts (6A) inc; Indtte; shop & 300m; tradsmn; rest; snacks; bar; playgrnd; pool (high ssn); TV rm; dogs €2; Eng spkn; adv bkg; poss noise fr local airfield; red long stay/low ssn; ccard acc (Visa); CCI. "Site run by adj hotel; poss itinerants; facs dated (plans for upgrading); special private pitch extra; noisy nr pool; under-staffed low ssn; gd birdwatching; mkt Fri." ♦ Apr-Oct. € 22.00 2008*

ST MARTIN DE LONDRES *10E1* (10km N Rural) *43.88865, 3.73631* **Camping Les Muriers, Chemin de Sauzèdes, 34190 Bauzille-de-Putois [04 67 73 73 63; fax 04 67 73 31 84 (Mairie)]** Fr S on D986 twd Ganges turn L at rndabt on ent Bauzille-de-Putois & foll sp. Site in 500m on L. Med, pt shd; wc (cont); chem disp (wc); mv service pnt; shwrs inc; el pnts (5A) €3; Indtte; tradsmn; snacks; BBQ; playgrnd; sw rv & canoe hire 500m; dogs; phone; bus 500m; poss cr; quiet; ccard not acc; CCI. "Gd." 1 May-30 Aug. € 10.00 2007*

ST MARTIN DE LONDRES *10E1* (2km E Rural) *43.79180, 3.73911* **FFCC Camping Le Pic St-Loup, 34380 St Martin-de-Londres [04 67 55 00 53; fax 04 67 55 00 04; depelchinp@aol.com]** Fr Ganges take D986 S. In St Martin turn L onto D122, site sp. Med, some hdg/mkd pitch, pt sl, pt shd; wc; chem disp; shwrs inc; el pnts (6A) inc; gas; Indtte; shop; rest; snacks; bar; playgrnd; htd covrd pool; 10% statics; poss cr; adv bkg; quiet but some rd noise; ccard not acc; red long stay; CCI. "Friendly, helpful owner; some pitches sm for van, awning & car; lger pitches on lower terr; dated san facs; excel pool; lower field muddy when wet." 1 Apr-30 Sep. € 20.00 2009*

ST MARTIN DE SEIGNANX see Bayonne *8F1*

ST MARTIN DE VALAMAS *9C2* (500m N Rural) *44.94249, 4.36779* **Camp Municipal La Teyre, 07310 St Martin-de-Valamas [04 75 30 47 16]** At N end of vill across single-track bdge. Well sp. Sm, mkd pitch, pt shd; wc (cont); chem disp (wc); shwrs inc; el pnts (6A) inc; Indry rm; playgrnd; games area; quiet. "Lge pitches; vg." ♦ 1 May-30 Sep. € 12.00 2009*

ST MARTIN DES BESACES *1D4* (W Rural) *49.00923, -0.85738* **Camping Le Puits, La Groudière, 14350 St Martin-des-Besaces [tel/fax 02 31 67 80 02; camping.le.puits@wanadoo.fr; www.lepuits.com]** Fr Caen SW on A84 dir Rennes, Villers-Bocage & exit junc 41 to St Martin-des-Besaces. At traff lts in vill turn R & foll site sp, site on L at end of vill in 500m. Fr Cherbourg foll sp St Lô onto m'way. After Torini-sur-Vire at junc with A84 foll sp Caen & exit junc 41, then as above. Sm, hdg/mkd pitch, pt sl, pt shd; wc; chem disp; mv service pnt; shwrs inc; el pnts (6A) €5 (poss rev pol); gas; Indtte; shop 500m; tradsmn; rest 500m; snacks; bar; BBQ; sm playgrnd; pool 10km; sand beach 35km; lake adj; fishing; cycling; equestrian trails; entmnt; no statics; dogs €1; adv bkg; quiet; red low ssn; ccard acc; CCI. "Pleasant CL-type orchard site; welcoming, helpful Irish owners; no arr bef 1400; lge pitches with garden; san facs ltd; B&B in farmhouse; suitable for rallies up to 30 vans; c'van storage; war museum in vill; conv Caen ferries; gd." ♦ 1 Mar-31 Oct. € 17.00 2008*

ST MARTIN EN CAMPAGNE *3B2* (3km N Coastal) *49.96679, 1.20444* **Camping Domaine Les Goélands, Rue des Grèbes, 76370 St Martin-en-Campagne [02 35 83 82 90; fax 02 35 83 21 79; g4sdomaine@wanadoo.fr; www.lesdomaines.org]** Fr Dieppe foll D925 twd Le Tréport & Abbeville. Turn L at rndabt on D113 twd St Martin-en-Campagne. Cont thro vill to St Martin-Plage (approx 3km) & foll 'Camping' sp to site on L. Lge, hdg/mkd pitch, hdstg, pt sl, terr, pt shd, hdstg; htd wc; 100% serviced pitches; chem disp; baby facs; shwrs inc; el pnts (16A) inc (poss rev pol); gas; Indtte; shop 1km; tradsmn; snacks (& in vill), bar high ssn; BBQ; playgrnd; htd pool & waterslide 1km; sand/shgl beach 500m; fishing; tennis; cycle hire; golf 20km; horseriding, archery 15km; TV; 40% statics; dogs €1.50; Eng spkn; adv bkg; quiet; ccard acc; red CCI. "Gd touring area; ltd recep hrs low ssn; no late arrivals area; poss resident workers low ssn; mkt Dieppe Sat; vg site." ♦ 1 Apr-31 Oct. € 27.00 2006*

ST MARTIN EN HAUT see Ste Foy l'Argentiere *9B2*

ST MARTIN EN VERCORS see Chapelle en Vercors, La *9C3*

ST MARTIN LARS see Ste Hermine *2H4*

ST MARTIN SUR LA CHAMBRE *9B3* (Rural) *45.36146, 6.31300* **Camping Le Bois Joli, 73130 St Martin-sur-la-Chambre [04 79 56 21 28; fax 04 79 56 29 95; camping.le.bois.joli@wanadoo.fr; www.campingleboisjoli.com]** Leave A43 at junc 26 onto D213 sp La Chambre & Col de la Madeleine; foll camping sp (rd narr & winding in places); site on L. Med, mkd pitch, terr, pt sl, pt shd; wc (some cont); chem disp; baby facs; shwrs inc; el pnts (10A) €3.50; gas; Indtte; shop, snacks, bar 3km; tradsmn; rest; BBQ; playgrnd; pool; fishing; guided walks; entmnt; dogs €1; 20% statics; poss cr; quiet; Eng spkn; adv bkg; red long stay; phone; CCI. "Helpful staff; mountain scenery; gd walking, skiing; ltd facs low ssn; conv Fréjus Tunnel." ♦ 15 Apr-30 Oct. € 13.00 2007*

⊞ **ST MARTIN SUR LA CHAMBRE** *9B3* (2km N Rural) *45.36883, 6.31458* **Camping Le Petit Nice, Notre Dame-de-Cruet, 73130 St Martin-sur-la-Chambre [tel/fax 04 79 56 37 72 or 06 76 29 19 39 (mob); camping lepetitnice@wanadoo.fr; www.camping-petitnice.com]** Fr N on A43 exit junc 26 & foll sp to cent of La Chambre, thro town to rndabt & turn R into Rue Notre Dame-du-Cruet. Foll site sp & in 2km turn R thro housing, site on L in 200m. Sm, terr, pt shd; htd wc; chem disp; shwrs inc; el pnts (3-10A) €3; Indtte; shop & 2km; rest; snacks; bar; playgrnd; pool; wifi; 80% statics; dogs €1; poss cr; Eng spkn; adv bkg; quiet; CCI. "By stream with mountain views; clean, modern san facs." ♦ € 13.00 2009*

ST MARTIN SUR OUST see Rochefort en Terre *2F3*

ST MATHIEU *7B3* (3km E Rural) *45.71413, 0.78835* **Camp Municipal Le Lac, Les Champs, 87440 St Mathieu [05 55 00 30 26 (Mairie); fax 05 55 48 80 62]** On D699 heading E in dir of Limoges 1.8km fr vill turn on L (N). Sp fr vill cent. Med, hdg/mkd pitch, pt shd; wc; baby facs; shwrs; el pnts €2.60; Indtte; shops 3km; rest adj; playgrnd; lake sw & beach; crazy golf; quiet. "Attractive, well-kept site nr lake; lge pitches; site yourself, warden calls; beautiful lake with lots of activities, inc windsurfing." 1 May-15 Sep. € 9.30 2009*

ST MATHIEU *7B3* (9.5km SW Rural) *45.67752, 0.63937* **Camp Municipal St Martial, Le Cros de l'Ouvrage, 24360 Busserolles [tel/fax 05 53 60 53 04; mairie.busserolles@wanadoo.fr; www.campingbusserolles.com]** Fr S on D675 turn W onto D90 to Busserolles. Fr N turn off at St Mathieu onto D699 & then S onto D88. Site sp in Busserolles. Sm, hdg/mkd pitch, pt sl, pt shd; wc; chem disp (wc); shwrs inc; el pnts inc; Indtte; shop 10km; BBQ; playgrnd; lake sw adj; games area; dogs €1; adv bkg; quiet; CCI. "Peaceful site in sm vill; vg." 15 Jun-15 Sep. € 11.00 2008*

STE MAURE DE TOURAINE *4H2* (6km NE Rural) *47.14831, 0.65453* **Camping Le Parc de Fierbois, 37800 Ste Catherine-de-Fierbois [02 47 65 43 35; fax 02 47 65 53 75; parc.fierbois@wanadoo.fr; www.fierbois.com or www.les-castels.com]** S on D910 (N10) fr Tours, thro Montbazon & cont twd Ste Maure & Châtellerault. About 16km outside Montbazon nr vill of Ste Catherine look for site sp. Turn L off main rd & foll sp to site. Or fr Ste Maure-de-Tourane take D910 sp Tours; in 3km turn R to Ste Catherine-de-Fierbois; site on L 1.5km past vill. Lge, hdg/mkd pitch, pt shd; wc; chem disp; mv service pnt; baby facs; shwrs inc; el pnts (4A) inc; Indtte; shop; rest; bar; BBQ; playgrnd; htd, pool & covrd pool; paddling pool; waterslide; sand/shgl beach at lake; boating; fishing; tennis; games area; games rm; entmnt; wifi; TV; statics; dogs free; poss cr; Eng spkn; adv bkg; ccard acc; red low ssn; CCI. "Excel, family site; peaceful low ssn; helpful staff; check el pnts; rec site." ♦ 10 May-10 Sep. € 46.50 ABS - L20 2009*

STE MAURE DE TOURAINE *4H2* (1.5km SE Rural) *47.10483, 0.62574* **Camp Municipal Marans, Rue de Toizelet, 37800 Ste Maure-de-Touraine [02 47 65 44 93]** Fr A10 take Ste Maure exit junc 25 & foll D760 twd Loches. At 4th rndabt turn L & then immed R. Site on R in 500m. Site sp fr m'way. Med, mkd pitch, pt shd; wc; chem disp; mv service pnt; shwrs inc; el pnts (10A) €2.60 (poss long cables req); supmkt 500m; shops, rest, bar 1km; BBQ; playgrnd; pool 1.5km; fishing; tennis; roller blade court; dogs €1.35; phone; Eng spkn; adv bkg; quiet. "Well-kept, basic site; cheerful staff; gd, clean facs inc disabled; facs poss stretched when busy; if office clsd site yourself; barrier down 2200-0700; late arrival area outside barrier; no twin-axles; poss itinerants in sep area; vg." ♦ 10 Apr-30 Sep. € 7.80 2009*

⊞ **STE MAURE DE TOURAINE** *4H2* (1.5km S Rural) *47.10861, 0.61440* **Aire de Service Camping-Cars Bois de Chaudron, 37800 Ste Maure-de-Touraine [02 47 34 06 04]** Fr S on D910 dir Tours, as ent town, site on R adj junc at traff lts; sm sp on dual-c'way. Sm; wc; mv service pnt; shwrs; el pnts €2 (on only some pitches); Indtte; wifi; m'vans only. "New Aire de Service (2009); warden calls; conv N/S journeys." € 5.00 2009*

STE MAURE DE TOURAINE *4H2* (6km W Rural) *47.10705, 0.51016* **Camping du Château de la Rolandière, 37220 Trogues [tel/fax 02 47 58 53 71; contact@larolandiere.com; www.larolandiere.com]** Exit A10 junc 25 onto D760 dir Chinon & L'Ile-Bouchard. Site sp on S side of rd in 5.5km. Sm, hdg/mkd pitch, pt shd; wc; chem disp; baby facs; shwrs inc; el pnts (10A) €4 (poss long lead req); gas 6km; Indtte (inc dryer); shop 4km; supmkt 9km; tradsmn; snacks; bar; BBQ; playgrnd; htd pool; paddling pool; rv & sand beach 4km; games area; games rm; wifi; TV rm; dogs €3; Eng spkn; adv bkg; quiet; red low ssn; CCI. "Beautiful, well-maintained, family-run site in chateau grnds; friendly welcome; helpful; gd clean san facs; excel for young families; gd dog walking; conv Loire chateaux." ♦ Easter-30 Sep. € 23.50 2009*

STE MAURE DE TOURAINE *4H2* (6km W Rural) *47.09904, 0.50353* **Camping Parc des Allais, Les Allais, 37220 Trogues [02 47 58 60 60; fax 02 47 95 24 04; www.parc-des-allais.com or www.village-center.com]** Exit A10 junc 25 onto D760 dir Chinon. At Noyant turn S onto D58 to Pouzay. In Pouzay turn W for 1km to site, sp. Lge, hdg/mkd pitch, pt shd; htd wc; chem disp; mv service pnt; baby facs; shwrs inc; el pnts (10A) inc; Indtte; shop; tradsmn; snacks; bar; BBQ; playgrnd; htd, covrd pool; waterslide; rv sw 2km; fishing; tennis; cycle hire; games area; games rm; fitness rm; internet; entmnt; TV; 40% statics; dogs €3; phone; Eng spkn; adv bkg; ccard acc; red long stay/CCI. "Pleasant site; superb pool complex; easy access a'route & Futuroscope; conv Loire chateaux." ♦ 5 Apr-13 Sep. € 34.00 2007*

ST MAURICE D'ARDECHE **see Aubenas** *9D2*

ST MAURICE DE LIGNON *9C1* (1km E Rural) *45.22299, 4.15156* **FFCC Camping du Sabot, 813 Route du Stade, 43200 St Maurice-de-Lignon [04 71 65 32 68; campingdusabot@aol.com; www.campingdusabot.fr]** Take N88 N fr Yssingeaux or S fr St Etienne. Site well sp in St Maurice. Med, mkd pitch, pt terr, pt shd; htd wc (some cont); chem disp; mv service pnt; shwrs; el pnts (6A) €3.60; Indtte; shops; rest, snacks 250m: BBQ; playgrnd; games area; 50% statics; dogs €1; phone; poss cr; Eng spkn; adv bkg; quiet. "Warm welcome; helpful owner; mkd walks fr site; ltd touring pitches, blocks poss needed." 15 Apr-15 Oct. € 11.00 2009*

⊞ **ST MAURICE LES CHARENCEY** *4E2* (Rural) *48.64747, 0.75575* **Camp Municipal de la Poste, 61190 St Maurice-lès-Charencey [02 33 25 72 98]** Vill on N12 halfway bet Verneuil-sur-Avre & Mortagne-au-Perche. Site in vill cent, adj post office. Sm, mkd pitch, pt sl, pt shd; wc; shwrs inc; el pnts (5A) €2 (poss rev pol); lake adj; fishing; 50% statics; phone; rd noise. "Phone ahead low ssn to check open; helpful warden; facs basic but adequate; gd NH." ltd. € 6.00 2007*

⊞ **ST MAURICE SUR MOSELLE** *6F3* (4.5km NE Urban) *47.88868, 6.85728* **Camping Domaine de Champé, 14 Rue des Champs Navés, 88540 Bussang [03 29 61 61 51; fax 03 29 61 56 90; info@domaine-de-champe.com; www.domaine-de-champe.com]** Fr N66/E512 in Bussang, site sp from town sq. Med, hdg/mkd pitch, pt sl, pt shd; wc; chem disp; mv service pnt; baby facs; sauna; shwrs; el pnts (6-10A) €5-6; Indtte; shop, tradmsn; rest; snacks; bar; BBQ; playgrnd; pool; paddling pool; rv 1km; tennis; cycle hire; games area; games rm; w/end activities; wifi; TV; 10% statics; dogs €3; phone; bus 1km; poss cr; Eng spkn; quiet; adv bkg; red low ssn; CCI. "Excel site behind hospital; lovely views; welcoming, helpful owners; vg facs; excel walks." ♦ € 25.00 (CChq acc) 2009*

France

ST MAURICE SUR MOSELLE *6F3* (10km E Rural) *47.88170, 6.94435* **Camp Municipal Bénélux-Bâle, Rue de la Scierie, 68121 Urbès [03 89 82 78 76 or 03 89 82 60 91 (Mairie); fax 03 89 82 16 61; mairie.urbes@wanadoo.fr; www.urbes.fr.st]** Site off N66 on N side of rd at foot of hill rising W out of Urbès. At foot of Col de Bessang. Lge, hgd/mkd pitch, pt shd; wc; chem disp; shwrs; el pnts (4-10A); Indtte; bar; playgrnd; rv & lake sw & fishing adj; dogs; 60% statics; adv bkg rec high ssn; quiet; CCI. "Gd sh stay/NH; beautiful area." 1 Apr-31 Oct. 2008*

ST MAURICE SUR MOSELLE *6F3* (W Rural) *47.8555, 6.8117* **Camping Les Deux Ballons, 17 Rue du Stade, 88560 St Maurice-sur-Moselle [03 29 25 17 14; stan@camping-deux-ballons.fr; www.camping-deux-ballons.fr]** On N66 on E side of rd in vill, site on L before petrol stn. Clearly sp. Lge, mkd pitch, pt sl, pt shd; wc; chem disp; mv service pnt; baby facs; shwrs inc; el pnts (4-15A) €4.15-5.20; gas; Indtte; shop 500m; snacks; bar; pool; waterslide; tennis; games rm; internet; TV rm; dogs €3.20; phone; poss cr; Eng spkn; adv bkg; quiet; red low ssn; ccard not acc; CCI. "Some pitches sm; excel site; cycle path fr site." ♦ 17 Apr-27 Sep. € 20.30 2008*

STE MAXIME *10F4* (2.5km N Rural) *43.32536, 6.62213* **Camping La Beaumette-Imbert, Route du Plan de la Tour, 83120 Ste Maxime [04 94 96 10 92 or 04 94 96 14 35 (LS); fax 04 94 96 35 38; camping@labeaumette.com; www.labeaumette.com]** Leave Ste Maxime on D25 dir Le Muy, site on L. Med, shd; wc (own san rec); chem disp; shwrs inc; el pnts (6A) €5; Indry rm; shop 500m; pool; beach 1km; dogs; 50% statics; dogs €1; phone; quiet; adv bkg; CCI. "Vg site; open to end Oct if gd weather but liable to flood in severe weather." ♦ 1 Apr-30 Sep. € 21.00 2008*

STE MAXIME *10F4* (5km NE Coastal) *43.33028, 6.66800* **Camping Les Cigalons, La Nartelle, 83120 Ste Maxime [04 94 96 05 51; fax 04 94 96 79 62; contact@campingcigalon.fr; www.campingcigalon.fr]** Site on D559 (N98) E of Ste Maxime, go thro La Nartelle & turn L into lane immed after seafood rest. Site on L after 25m. Med, mkd pitch, pt sl, shd; wc; chem disp; shwrs; el pnts (6A) €3.60; Indtte; sm shop; rest, snacks, bar adj; paddling pool; sand beach 50m; dogs €2.50poss cr; adv bkg; v quiet. "Friendly owners; gd position; sm v hard compacted earth pitches; car parking poss diff." ♦ 1 Apr-13 Oct. € 23.00 2006*

⊞ **ST MAXIMIN LA STE BAUME** *10F3* (3km S Rural) *43.42848, 5.86498* **Camping Caravaning Le Provencal, Chemin de Mazaugues, 83470 St Maximin-la-Ste Baume [04 94 78 16 97; fax 04 94 78 00 22; camping.provencal@wanadoo.fr]** Exit St Maximin on N560 S twd Marseilles. After 1km turn L onto D64. Site on R after 2km. Lge, mkd pitch, pt sl, shd; wc; mv service pnt; shwrs inc; el pnts (6-10A) €3.40-4.40; gas; Indtte; shop & 3km; rest high ssn; snacks; bar; playgrnd; pool; TV; some statics; adv bkg; CCI. € 16.10 2009*

ST MAYEUX see Mur de Bretagne *2E3*

ST MEDARD DE GUIZIERES *7C2* (500m N Rural) *45.01989, -0.05876* **Camp Municipal Le Gua, 33230 St Médard-de-Guizières [tel/fax 05 57 69 82 37]** On N89 bet Libourne & Montpon-Ménestérol; in St Médard foll sp 'Base de Loisirs'; site adj sw pool. Med, mkd pitch, shd; wc (some cont); chem disp (wc); shwrs inc; el pnts €2.60; shop, rest, snacks, bar 500m; playgrnd; pool adj; rv fishing adj; quiet. "Conv Bordeaux, St Emillion & vineyards; vg." ♦ 15 Jun-15 Sep. € 7.00 2006*

⊞ **ST MEDARD DE GUIZIERES** *7C2* (4km S Rural) *44.99694, -0.06330* **FLOWER Camping Le Pressoir, Queyrai, 33570 Petit-Palais-et-Cornemps [05 57 69 73 25; fax 05 57 69 77 36; contact@campinglepressoir.com; www.campinglepressoir.com or www.flowercamping.com]** Leave A89/E70 junc 11 onto D1089 (N89) E to St Médard-de-Guizières; then take D21 S & foll site sp 'Le Pressoir' (site bef Petit-Palais). Fr Castillon-la-Bataille on D936 Bergerac-Bordeaux rd take D17/D21 sp St Médard & foll site sp. Take care on access & exit. Med, hdg/mkd pitch, pt sl, pt shd; htd wc; chem disp; shwrs inc; el pnts (10A) inc; gas; Indtte; shop; tradsmn; rest; snacks; bar; BBQ; playgrnd; htd pool; cycle hire; games area; entmnt; wifi; TV rm; 30% statics; dogs €1.90; Eng spkn; adv bkg; quiet; ccard acc; red low ssn; CCI. "Close to vineyards; basic san facs; gd rest." ♦ € 26.50 2009*

STE MENEHOULD *5D1* (1km E Rural) *49.08937, 4.90969* **Camp Municipal de la Grelette, Chemin de l'Alleval, 51800 Ste Menéhould [03 26 60 80 21 (Mairie); fax 03 26 60 62 54; mairie@ste-menehould.fr; www.ville-sainte-menehould.fr]** Exit A4 junc 29 to Ste Menéhould; take N3 (D3) E; turn R over 1st bdge after rlwy stn; foll sp for La Piscine; site on R after pool. Sp fr town. Sm, mkd pitch, pt sl, pt shd; wc; shwrs inc; chem disp; el pnts (4A) €3.10; tradsmn; supmkt 500m; rest, snacks, bar 1km; pool adj; dogs €0.85; poss cr; adv bkg; Eng spkn; no ccard acc; CCI. "Delightful site; helpful warden arrives in mins if absent; do not site self; vg, clean san facs; interesting old town." 26 Apr-30 Sep. € 5.80 2008*

STE MERE EGLISE *1C4* (9.5km NE Coastal) *49.46650, -1.23540* **Camping Le Cormoran, 2 Rue du Cormoran, 50480 Ravenoville-Plage [02 33 41 33 94; fax 02 33 95 16 08; lecormoran@wanadoo.fr; www.lecormoran.com]** NE on D15 fr Ste Mère-Eglise to Ravenoville, turn L onto D14 then R back onto D15 to Ravenoville Plage. Turn R on D421, Rte d'Utah Beach, site on R in 1km. Or fr N13 sp C2 Fresville & ent Ste Mère-Eglise, then take D15. Lge, hdg/mkd pitch, some hdstg, unshd; wc; chem disp; mv service pnt; baby facs; shwrs inc; el pnts (6A) inc; gas; Indtte; shop; tradsmn; snacks; bar; BBQ (not elec); playgrnd; htd covrd pool; paddling pool; jacuzzi; sand beach adj; sea fishing; tennis; cycle hire; horseriding; games area; archery; entmnt; wifi; TV/games rm; 60% statics; dogs €3; poss cr; Eng spkn; adv bkg; quiet; ccard acc; red low ssn; CCI. "Excel, family-run site with vg facs for children; warm welcome; helpful recep; lge pitches; poss tired san facs end of ssn; poss v windy; special pitches for early dep for ferry; m'van o'night area." ♦ 3 Apr-26 Sep. € 32.00 (CChq acc) ABS - N12 2009*

STE MERE EGLISE *1C4* (500m E Urban) *49.41006, -1.31078* **Camp Municipal, 6 Rue due 505eme Airborne, 50480 Ste Mère-Eglise [02 33 41 35 22; fax 02 33 41 79 15; www.sainte-mere-eglise.info/camping.html]** Fr Cherbourg S on N13 to cent of Ste Mère-Eglise (avoiding by-pass); at vill sq turn L on D17 to site, next adj sports grnd. Med, some hdstg, pt sl, pt shd, wc (some cont); chem disp (wc); shwrs inc; el pnts (10A) €3 (poss rev pol); gas 500m; lndtte; shop & bar 500m; rest, snacks, BBQ; playgrnd; sand beach 10km; tennis; 5% statics; dogs €1; phone; poss cr; little Eng spkn; adv bkg; CCI. "Nice, basic site; clean facs; friendly warden; if warden absent site yourself & pay later; conv ferries & D-Day beaches etc; gates open 6am for early dep; rec." ♦ 15 Mar-30 Sep. € 9.00 2009*

ST MICHEL CHEF CHEF see Pornic *2G3*

⊞ **ST MICHEL DE MAURIENNE** *9C3* (500m SE Rural) *45.21276, 6.47858* **Camping Le Marintan, 1 Rue de la Provalière, 73140 St Michel-de-Maurienne [04 79 59 17 36; fax 04 79 59 17 86; lemarintan@orange.fr; www.lemarintan.com]** Fr D1006 (N6) foll sp in town to 'Centre Touristique' & 'Maison Retraite'. Rue de la Provalière is a L turn fr D1006 immed bef rlwy bdge. Sm, hdg pitch, unshd; htd wc; chem disp; shwrs inc; el pnts €4.70; shops in town; rest; bar; pool; some statics; dogs €1.20; quiet. "Gd touring base, but no character." € 16.70 2009*

ST MICHEL EN GREVE *2E2* (1km N Coastal) *48.69150, -3.55630* **Camping Les Capucines, Kervourdon, Trédez-Locquémeau, 22300 St Michel-en-Grève [02 96 35 72 28; fax 02 96 35 78 98; les.capucines@wanadoo.fr; www.lescapucines.fr]** Fr Lannion on D786 SW twd St Michel-en-Grève, sp Morlaix; in approx 700m, after steep descent & 'Landebouch' sp, turn R & R again in 100m at x-rds. Fr Roscoff take D58 to join N12 at junc 17; NE of Morlaix at next junc turn onto D786 twd Lannion; site down narr app rd on L on leaving St Michel-en-Grève, then R at x-rds. Med, hdg/mkd pitch, pt sl, pt shd; wc; chem disp; 100% serviced pitches; baby facs; shwrs inc; el pnts (7A) inc; gas; lndtte; shop & 1km; tradsmn; rest 2km; snacks; bar; BBQ (charcoal/gas); playgrnd; htd, covrd pool; paddling pool; sand beach 8km; watersports 1km; cycle hire; wifi; games/TV rm; 7% statics; dogs €2; phone; c'van max length 8m high ssn; Eng spkn; adv bkg; quiet; ccard acc; red low ssn/long stay; CCI. "Excel, peaceful, well-kept site; gd sized pitches; helpful owners; immac san facs; gd pool; gd touring base; mkt Lannion Thu." ♦ 29 Mar-3 Oct. € 27.00 ABS - B13 2009*

ST MICHEL ESCALUS see Léon *8E1*

ST MIHIEL *5D2* (14km NE Rural) *48.94111, 5.71704* **Camp Municipal Les Passons Madine 2, 55210 Heudicourt [03 29 89 36 08; fax 03 29 89 35 60; lacmadine@wanadoo.fr]** Fr St Mihiel, take D901 NE to Chaillon. Turn R on D133 to Heudicourt. Bear L out of vill, still on D133 & after 1km turn R to Nonsard. Site on R in 1.5km, immed after sailing school at N end of Lake Madine. Lge, mkd pitch, pt sl, pt shd; wc (mainly cont); shwrs inc; el pnts £2.50; rest; shop; lndry rm; lake sw adj; nautical sports & fishing; horseriding school & sailing school adj; many statics; CCI. "Gd location by Lake Madine; a little run down low ssn; sm, cramped pitches; san facs clean but need updating; fair NH." 1 Apr-30 Sep. € 13.80 2006*

ST MIHIEL *5D2* (1km NW Rural) *48.90209, 5.53978* **Camping Base de Plein Air, Chemin du Gué Rappeau, 55300 St Mihiel [03 29 89 03 59; fax 03 29 89 07 18; base.de.plein.air@wanadoo.fr]** Site on W bank of rv. Sp app St Mihiel. Fr town cent take rd sp Bar-le-Duc (D901) 1st R after rv bdge. Med, mkd pitch, pt shd; htd wc (mainly cont); chem disp; mv service pnt; shwrs inc; el pnts (10A) €2.60; lndtte; shops, rest, bar 1km; tradsmn; playgrnd; htd pool 1km; canoeing & sailing; games area; TV; 10% statics; bus 1km; adv bkg; quiet; CCI; "Site developed as youth cent; facs clean but tired; pleasant scenery; lge pitches." 1 Apr-1 Nov. € 8.70 2008*

STE NATHALENE see Sarlat la Canéda *7C3*

ST NAZAIRE *2G3* (6km SW Urban/Coastal) *47.24163, -2.26731* **Camping Yakudi Village de l'Eve, Route du Fort, St Marc-sur-Mer, 44600 St Nazaire [02 40 91 90 65 or 05 46 22 38 22; fax 02 40 91 76 59 or 05 46 23 65 10; camping-de-leve@wanadoo.fr; www.yukadivillages.com]** At St Nazaire (Ouest) stay on D213 (N171) La Baule rd. Exit D213 on D492 (Pornichet/La Baule) & cont to junc with D92 (end of D492); at lge island immed after Géant superstore & Big Mac sp, take 4th exit sp Université/Camping de l'Eve. In 1km turn R at traff lts sp Camping de l'Eve; site on R in 2km. Lge, hdg/mkd pitch, pt sl, shd; wc; chem disp; baby facs; fam bthrm; shwrs inc; el pnts (5A) €5.10 (poss rev pol); gas; lndtte; shop; tradsmn; supmkt 2km; snacks; rest, bar high ssn; playgrnd; htd pool; paddling pool; waterslide; sand beach (via subway); tennis; entmnt; 65% statics; dogs €4; bus; poss cr; Eng spkn; adv bkg; quiet; red low ssn; CCI. "Vg facs; few flat pitches; pleasant vill; lovely coastal walks." ♦ 17 May-7 Sep. € 27.00 2007*

ST NAZAIRE EN ROYANS see St Jean en Royans *9C2*

ST NAZAIRE LE DESERT *9D2* (200m E Rural) *44.56952, 5.27750* **Camp Municipal, 26340 St Nazaire-le-Désert [04 75 26 42 99 or 04 75 27 52 31 (LS); info@camping-stnazaire.com; www.camping-stnazaire.com]** Well sp in St Nazaire-le-Désert. Med, mkd pitch, terr, shd; wc (own san rec); chem disp (wc); shwrs inc; el pnts €3; shops nrby; rest; snacks; bar; BBQ; playgrnd; htd pool; games rm; entment; wifi; dogs; phone; no twin-axles; poss cr; Eng spkn; adv bkg rec high ssn. "Busy, friendly site in beautiful location; v lge o'fits poss diff to pitch; gd." 1 May-30 Sep. € 10.00 2009*

ST NECTAIRE *9B1* (1km SE Rural) *45.57971, 3.00173* **Camping Le Viginet, 63710 St Nectaire [04 73 88 53 80 or 08 25 80 14 40; fax 04 73 88 41 93; info@camping-massifcentral.com; www.camping-massifcentral.com]** Exit A75/E11 junc 14 onto D996 dir Mont-Doré. In E side of St Nectaire (opp Ford g'ge) turn sharp L up v steep hill; rd widens after 100m; site on R after bends. Car park at site ent. Med, hdg/mkd pitch, pt sl, pt shd; wc; chem disp; mv service pnt; baby facs; shwrs inc; el pnts (10A) €3.60; gas; lndry rm; shops, rest & bar 1.5km; snacks; playgrnd; pool; 30% statics; dogs €1.50; poss cr; adv bkg; quiet; ccard not acc; CCI. "Nice pitches; gd views; maintenance needed (Jun 2007) & san facs scruffy; nice sm pool." ♦ 7 Apr-30 Sep. € 17.80 2007*

ST NECTAIRE *9B1* (2km SE Rural) *45.57174, 3.01368* **Camping La Hutte des Dômes, Saillant, 63710 St Nectaire [04 73 88 50 22]** Exit 6 fr A75 S of Clermont-Ferrand. Take D978 to Champeix. Turn R onto D996 sp St Nectaire. Site on L in Saillant, ent easily missed. Sm, mkd pitch, pt sl, pt shd; wc (some cont); chem disp; shwrs inc; el pnts (4-6A) €2.50-3; shops 2km; tradsmn; dogs €0.50. "Quiet, peaceful site; clean." 1 Jun-31 Aug. € 9.10 2006*

ST NECTAIRE *9B1* (500m S Rural) *45.57556, 3.00169* **Camping La Clé des Champs, Les Sauces, Route des Granges, 63710 St Nectaire [04 73 88 52 33; camping cledechamps@free.fr; www.campingcledeschamps.com]** S bound exit A75 at junc 6 to join D978 sp Champeix; N bound exit junc 14 to join D996 sp Champeix/St Nectaire. In St Nectaire turn L at VW/Audi g'ge on L (site sp); site 300m on L. Med, hdg/mkd pitch, pt sl, pt shd; wc (some cont); chem disp; mv service pnt; shwrs inc; el pnts (2-6A) €2.10-3.50 (rev pol); gas; lndtte; shops 1km; playgrnd; pool; some statics; dogs €1; poss cr; adv bkg; poss noisy high ssn; CCI. "Well-kept, clean site; helpful owner; facs stretched in high ssn; extra charge for water." ♦ Easter-30 Sep. € 16.00 2007*

ST NECTAIRE *9B1* (1km S Rural) *45.57541, 2.99942* **Camping La Vallée Verte, Route des Granges, 63710 St Nectaire [04 73 88 52 68; lavalleeverte@neuf.fr; www.campinglavalleeverte.com]** Fr A75 exit junc 6 onto D978 & D996 to St Nectaire. On ent o'skts St Nectaire turn L immed at site sp, site in 300m. Med, pt shd; htd wc; chem disp; mv service pnt; fam bthrm; shwrs inc; el pnts (5-8A) inc; lndtte (inc dryer); shop; tradsmn; snacks; bar; playgrnd; lake sw 5km; 20% statics; dogs €1.50; phone; Eng spkn; adv bkg; quiet; CCI. "Vg, friendly, well-maintained, family-run site." ♦ 15 Apr-15 Sep. € 14.00 2009*

ST NIC *2E2* (1.5km SW Coastal) *48.19373, 4.30157* **Camping Domaine de Ker-Ys, Pentrez-Plage, 29550 St Nic [02 98 26 53 95; fax 02 98 26 52 48; camping-kerys@wanadoo.fr; www.ker-ys.com]** Turn W off D887 onto D108 & into St Nic, & foll sp Pentrez-Plage & site. Lge, pt shd; wc; chem disp; baby facs; shwrs inc; el pnts (10A) €3.20; gas; lndtte; shop; snacks; BBQ; bar; htd pool complex; waterslide; sand beach adj; watersports; tennis; games area; entmnt; TV rm; some statics; dogs €2.50; adv bkg; ccard acc; red low ssn. "Gd family site in lovely location; vg beach; friendly, helpful staff." ♦ 1 May-15 Sep. € 22.00 2006*

ST NICOLAS DU PELEM *2E3* (1.5km SW Rural) *48.30983, -3.17923* **Camp Municipal de la Piscine, Croas-Cussuliou, Rue de Rostrenen, 22480 St Nicolas-du-Pélem [02 96 29 51 27; fax 02 96 29 59 73]** Fr Rostrenen, take D790 NE twd Corlay. In 11km, turn L sp St Nicolas-du-Pélem. Site in 500m on R, opp pool. Med, pt shd; wc (some cont); chem disp (wc); shwrs inc; el pnts (5A) €1.51; gas, shops 1.5km; htd pool opp; dogs; quiet; CCI. "Clean, well-kept site; choose own pitch, warden will call." ♦ 15 Jun-15 Sep. € 5.00 2009*

ST NIZIER LE DESERT *9A2* (E Rural) *46.05447, 5.15911* **Camp Municipal La Niziere, 01320 St Nizier-le-Désert [04 74 30 35 16 or 06 74 33 13 48 (mob); fax 04 74 30 32 78; laniziere@cc-chalamont.com]** Fr Bourg-en-Bresse take D1083 (N83) SW for 4km, L onto D22 dir Dompièrre-sur-Veyle (13km). Turn R onto D90 at Les Brires at camping sp, site in 2km on R by lakeside. Med, mkd pitch, shd; wc (mostly cont); mv service pnt; shwrs inc; el pnts (6A) €2; lndry rm; shop 500m; playgrnd; fishing; tennis; 75% statics; quiet. "Unspoilt, peaceful site; off beaten track; access poss diff for c'vans; gd cycling." 15 Apr-31 Aug. € 10.00 2008*

ST OMER *3A3* (8km NE Rural) *50.80152, 2.33924* **Camping La Chaumière, 529 Langhemast Straete, 59285 Buysscheure [03 28 43 03 57; camping.lachaumiere@wanadoo.fr; www.campinglachaumiere.com]** Take D928 fr St Omer (see NOTE) twd Bergues & Watten & foll sp St Momelin. Stay on rd until Lederzeele & turn R onto D26 twds Cassel. After approx 2km turn R just bef rlwy bdge sp Buysscheure & site. Turn L after church, R, then site on L 500m. Single-track rd after church. NOTE on D928 fr St Omer height limit 3m; use adj level x-ing sp rte for vehicles over 3m. NB app fr Cassel diff, especially for wide or long o'fits; also rd thro Cassel cobbled & poss more diff to find. Sm, hdg/mkd pitch, hdstg; pt sl, unshd; wc; chem disp; mv service pnt; baby facs; shwrs inc; el pnts (6A) inc; lndry rm; shop 1km; rest; snacks; bar; BBQ; playgrnd; htd pool; paddling pool; fishing lake; cycle hire; archery; entmnt; TV; dogs €1; Eng spkn; adv bkg; quiet, but some rlwy noise; red long stay; ccard not acc; CCI. "Lovely, well-kept, efficient family-run site; conv ferries; gd sized pitches; gd san facs, ltd in number; office open 0800-2100 - arr & dep outside these hours not poss; close to WW1/WW2 sites; owner can book local vet; excel." ♦ 1 Apr-30 Sep. € 18.00 2009*

ST OMER *3A3* (10km E Rural) *50.73490, 2.37463* **FFCC Camping Le Bloem Straete, 1 Rue Bloemstraete, 59173 Renescure [03 28 49 85 65; lebloemstraete@yahoo.fr; www.lebloemstraete.fr]** E fr St Omer on D642 (N42) thro Renescure dir Hazebrouck; turn L (site sp) onto D406 Rue André Coo on bend on leaving Renescure; over level x-ing; site on L thro gates. Sm, hdg pitch, hdstg, pt shd; htd wc; chem disp (wc); shwrs inc; el pnts (2-6A) €2.50 (poss rev pol); lndtte; shop, rest, snack & bar 1km; playgrnd; tennis; games rm; wifi; 70% statics; dogs; poss cr; Eng spkn; quiet; adv bkg; CCI. "Lovely, peaceful site; excel san facs; v pleasant owners; m'van area; conv Calais ferry & tourist sites; excel." ♦ 15 Apr-15 Oct. € 15.00 2009*

ST OMER *3A3* (3km SE Urban) *50.74612, 2.30566* **Camp Municipal Beauséjour, Rue Michelet, 62510 Arques [tel/fax 03 21 88 53 66; camping-arques@wanadoo.fr; www.ville-arques.fr]** Fr junc 4 of A26 foll sp Arques to town cent. Foll sp Hazebrouck. Ater x-ring canal site sp 'Camping ***' on L. NB Drive 25m bef correct turning to site. Med, hdg/mkd pitch; wc; chem disp; mv service pnt; shwrs inc; el pnts (6A) €3 (poss rev pol); Indtte; shops 1.5km; playgrnd; lake fishing; 80% statics; dogs; phone; adv bkg; some noise fr rlwy & mill across lake; ccard acc; CCI. "Neat, tidy site; lge pitches; friendly, helpful warden; excel, clean facs; no twin-axles; m'van o'night area adj (no el pnts); site boggy when wet; conv visit to Cristal d'Arques; gd cycling along canal; useful NH." ♦ 1 Apr-31 Oct. € 11.80 2009*

ST OMER *3A3* (5km NW Rural) *50.78310, 2.18790* **Camping Le Frémont, 62910 Serques [03 21 39 86 55; campinglefremont@aol.com]** Fr D943 (N43) Calais-St Omer, site on L 1.5km SE of Moulle past Tilques exit just over brow of hill on D943 - don't overshoot. Med, sl, terr, pt shd; wc; chem disp; shwrs €1.35; el pnts (10A) inc; Indtte; shop; rest, snacks 2km; bar; pool 5km; golf 4km; 90% statics; adv bkg; some noise. "Basic site (6 pitches); conv Calais ferry; gd san facs; gd NH." ♦ 1 Apr-15 Oct. € 16.30 2008*

ST OMER *3A3* (10km NW Rural) *50.81890, 2.17870* **Kawan Village Château du Gandspette, 133 Rue du Gandspette, 62910 Eperlecques [03 21 93 43 93 or 03 21 12 89 08 (LS); fax 03 21 95 74 98; contact@chateau-gandspette.com; www.chateau-gandspette.com]** Fr Calais SE on A26/E15 exit junc 2 onto D943 (N43) foll sp Nordausques-St Omer. 1.5km after Nordausques turn L onto D221 twd Eperlecques; site 5km on L. Do not ent Eperlecques. (Larger o'fts should cont on D943 fr Nordausques to Tilques; at rndabt foll sp for Dunkerque (D300) then D221 dir Eperlecques, site on R. Med, hdg/mkd pitch, pt hdstg, pt sl, pt shd; wc; chem disp; mv service pnt; baby facs; shwrs inc; el pnts (6A) inc (some rev pol); gas; Indtte; supmkt 800m; tradsmn; rest (high ssn); snacks; bar; BBQ (not el); playgrnd; 2 pools (1 htd); fishing 3km; tennis; cycle hire; horseriding, golf 3km; wifi; games/TV rm; 15% statics; dogs €1; phone; poss cr; Eng spkn; adv bkg; quiet; ccard acc; red low ssn; CCI. "Well-kept, busy site; spacious, mainly sl pitches; superb, clean san facs; charming owners; vg pool; easy access all o'fit sizes, but narr app on woodland track to far tourer field; site poss muddy in wet; early departures catered for; poss poor security; gd for dogs; vet 1.5km; conv Tunnel." ♦
1 Apr-30 Sep. € 27.00 (CChq acc) ABS - P08 2009*

ST PABU *2E1* (Coastal) *48.57643, -4.62854* **Camp Municipal de L'Aber Benoît, Corn ar Gazel, 29830 St Pabu [02 98 89 76 25]** E fr Ploudalmézeau on D28; in 5km L to St Pabu. Site sp in vill. Med, hdg pitch, pt shd; wc; chem disp (wc); shwrs inc; el pnts (6A) €2.30; Indtte; shop, rest (high ssn); snacks; BBQ; playgrnd; beach 100m; TV rm; 10 statics; dogs €1; poss cr; CCI. "Facs stretched high ssn; vg." Easter-15 Oct. € 9.00 2006*

ST PAIR SUR MER see Granville *1D4*

ST PALAIS (GIRONDE) see Mirambeau *7C2*

ST PALAIS SUR MER *7B1* (1km N Rural/Coastal) *45.65163, -1.10898* **Camping Le Logis, 22 Rue des Palombes, 17420 St Palais-sur-Mer [05 46 23 20 23 or 05 46 22 38 22; fax 05 46 23 10 61 or 05 46 23 65 10; lelogis@yukadivillages.com; www.yukadivillages.com]** On rd N out of Royan, after vill of St Palais-sur-Mer, site sp on R after petrol stn. V lge, pt sl, shd; htd wc (some cont); chem disp; shwrs inc; el pnts (6A) €5.10; gas 2km; Indtte; shop & 2km; tradsmn; snacks; bar; playgrnd; pool; paddling pool; waterslide; aquapark; shgl beach 1km; tennis; games area; entmnt; TV; 35% statics; dogs €4.60; poss cr; Eng spkn; adv bkg; red low ssn. "La Palmyre zoo nr; excel water park."
16 May-9 Sep. € 30.00 2006*

ST PALAIS SUR MER *7B1* (7km N Rural) *45.67550, -1.09670* **Camping Le Logis du Breuil, 17570 St Augustin [05 46 23 23 45 or 05 46 23 23 45 (LS); fax 05 46 23 44 33; camping.logis-du-breuil@wanadoo.fr; www.logis-du-breuil.com]** N150 to Royan, then D25 dir St Palais-sur-Mer. Strt on at 1st rndabt & 2nd rndabt; at next rndabt take 2nd exit dir St Palais-sur-Mer. At next traff lts turn R dir St Augustin onto D145; site on L. Lge, mkd pitch, pt shd, pt sl; wc (some cont); chem disp; baby facs; shwrs inc; el pnts (6A) inc (50m cable poss req); gas; Indtte; shop; supmkt; rest; snacks; bar; BBQ (gas/elec); playgrnd; pool; paddling pool; sand beach 5km; fishing 1km; tennis; games area; cycle hire; archery; horseriding 400m; golf 3km; excursions; entmnt; wifi; games/TV rm; 10% statics; dogs €2.35; phone; poss cr; Eng spkn; adv bkg; ccard acc; red low ssn; CCI. "Lge pitches in wooded area; quiet & peaceful; gd alt to cr beach sites; friendly owner; san facs dated but clean; excel." ♦ 15 May-30 Sep. € 25.75
ABS - A04 2009*

ST PALAIS SUR MER *7B1* (8km N Rural) *45.68888, -1.11034* **Camping Les Vignes, 3 Rue des Ardilliers, 17570 St Augustin [tel/fax 05 46 23 23 51; campinglesvignes17@alicepro.fr; www.campinglesvignes17.com]** On app Royan on D733, after x-ing D14 turn R sp St Palais (by-pass Royan cent). At rndabt on D25 foll sp St Augustin. Site on R. Med, mkd pitch, pt shd; wc (some cont); shwrs; el pnts (5-10A) €3.90-4.70; gas; Indtte; shop; tradsmn; rest; snacks; bar; playgrnd; pool, paddling pool 200m; waterslides; cycle hire; entmnt; wifi; 70% statics; dogs €1.50; phone; adv bkg; red long stay/low ssn; CCI. "Remote, peaceful, welcoming site; basic facs, ltd low ssn; immac pools." ♦ Easter-1 Nov.
€ 15.70 2009*

ST PALAIS SUR MER *7B1* (500m NE Coastal) *45.64245, -1.07677* **Camping de Bernezac, 2 Ave de Bernezac, 17420 St Palais-sur-Mer [05 46 39 00 71; fax 05 46 38 14 46; acccf-ber@wanadoo.fr; http://acccf.com]** Foll sp off Royan-St Palais coast rd. Med, pt shd; wc; chem disp; mv service pnt; 50% serviced pitches; baby facs; shwrs inc; el pnts (6-16A) €3.50 (poss rev pol); Indtte; shop; rest; snacks; BBQ; playgrnd; htd pool; beach adj; lake fishing 1km; entmnt; TV; 30% statics; dogs €1; Eng spkn; adv bkg; quiet. "Helpful, friendly staff." 15 Mar-15 Oct. € 19.60 2007*

France

ST PALAIS SUR MER *7B1* (1.5km E Rural/Coastal) *45.64656, -1.07300* **Camping Les Ormeaux, 44 Ave de Bernezac, 17420 St Palais-sur-Mer [05 46 39 02 07; fax 05 46 38 56 66; campingormeaux@aliceadsl.fr; www.camping-ormeaux.com]** Foll sp fr D25 Royan-St Palais rd. Rec app ent fr R. Ent & camp rds narr. Lge, pt shd; wc; baby facs; shwrs inc; el pnts (6A) €7.50; gas; lndtte; shop; snacks; bar; playgrnd; htd pool; sand beach 800m; entmnt; TV; 98% statics; dogs €4; quiet; red low ssn. "Ltd touring area & access diff for lge o'fits or m'vans - tents or sm m'vans only." ♦ 1 Apr-31 Oct. € 27.00 (3 persons) 2009*

ST PALAIS SUR MER *7B1* (2km E Coastal) *45.63990, -1.06790* **Camping Le Val Vert, 108 Ave Frédéric Garnier, 17640 Vaux-sur-Mer [05 46 38 25 51; fax 05 46 38 06 15; camping-val-vert@wanadoo.fr; www.val-vert.com]** Fr Saintes on N150 dir Royan; join D25 dir St Palais-sur-Mer; turn L at rndabt sp Vaux-sur-Mer & Centre Hospitaliers; at traff lts turn L; at rndabt take 3rd exit & then turn immed R. Site on R in 500m. Lge, hdg pitch; wc; chem disp; baby facs; shwrs inc; el pnts (10A) inc; gas; lndtte; shop; rest; snacks; bar; gas/elec BBQ (gas/elec); playgrnd; htd pool; paddling pool; sand beach 900m; watersports; fishing; tennis 400m; horseriding, golf 5km; entmnt; games rm; wifi; dogs €2.90; no c'vans over 6.50m high ssn; adv bkg; ccard acc; red low ssn. "Gd clean site; no twin-axles; gd local shops; daily mkt in Royan." ♦ 9 Apr-21 Sep. € 33.40 (3 persons) ABS - A25 2009*

ST PALAIS SUR MER *7B1* (2km SE Coastal/Urban) *45.64272, -1.07183* **Camping Nauzan-Plage, 39 Ave de Nauzan-Plage, 17640 Vaux-sur-Mer [05 46 38 29 13; fax 05 46 38 18 43; info@campinglenauzanplage.com; www.campinglenauzanplage.com]** Take either coast rd or inland rd fr Royan to Vaux-sur-Mer; site not well sp. Lge, mkd pitch, pt shd; wc; chem disp; baby facs; shwrs inc; el pnts (10A) €5; gas; lndtte; shop; supmkt 1km; rest; snacks; bar; playgrnd; sm pool; sand beach 450m; tennis 200m; games/TV rm; 10% statics (sep area) dogs €5; adv bkg (rec Jul/Aug); quiet; red low ssn; CCI. "Gd site; helpful staff."♦ 1 Apr-30 Sep. € 30.00 (3 persons) 2009*

ST PALAIS SUR MER *7B1* (3km NW Coastal) *45.6500, -1.1193* **Camping La Côte de Beauté, 157 Ave de la Grande Côte, 17420 St Palais-sur-Mer [05 46 23 20 59; fax 05 46 23 37 32; campingcotedebeaute@wanadoo.fr; www.camping-cote-de-beaute.com]** Fr St Palais-sur-Mer foll sp to La Tremblade & Ronce-les-Bains. Site on D25, 50m fr beach, look for twin flagpoles of Camping Le Puits de l'Auture & lge neon sp on R; site in 50m. Med, hdg pitch, shd; htd wc; baby facs; shwrs inc; el pnts (6A) €4; lndtte; supmkt adj; tradsmn; rest; snacks; bar; playgrnd; sand beach 200m across rd; tennis, cycle hire adj; golf 2km; some statics; dogs €2.50; adv bkg; quiet. "Friendly staff; clean, tidy site; steep descent to beach opp - better beach 600m twd La Tremblade; cycle track to St Palais & Pontaillac." 1 May-30 Sep. € 23.00 (3 persons) 2008*

ST PALAIS SUR MER *7B1* (3km NW Coastal) *45.6482, -1.1108* **Camping La Grande Côte, 167 Ave de la Grande Côte, 17420 St Palais-sur-Mer [tel/fax 05 46 23 20 18; info@campinglagrandecote.com; www.campinglagrandecote.com]** Fr Royan, take D25 thro St Palais, site on R where rd runs close to sea. Look for flags. Med, mkd pitch, pt shd; htd wc; baby facs; shwrs inc; el pnts (6A) €4.20; gas; lndtte; rest adj; bar; BBQ; sand beach 200m; dogs €3; bus; quiet; CCI. "Helpful staff; excel site." ♦ 1 May-12 Sep. € 23.60 2009*

ST PALAIS SUR MER *7B1* (3km NW Coastal) *45.64930, -1.11785* **Camping Le Puits de l'Auture, La Grande Côte, 17420 St Palais-sur-Mer [05 46 23 20 31; fax 05 46 23 26 38; camping-lauture@wanadoo.fr; www.camping-puitsdelauture.com]** Fr Royan take D25 onto new rd past St Palais foll sp for La Palmyre. At 1-way section turn back L sp La Grande Côte & site is 800m; rd runs close to sea, flags at ent. Lge, pt shd; htd wc; serviced pitches; baby facs; shwrs inc; el pnts (10A) inc; gas; lndtte; shop; snacks; bar; playgrnd; htd pool; sand beach opp & 500m; fishing; games area; internet; 25% statics; no dogs; poss cr; Eng spkn; adv bkg rec; quiet; red low ssn; ccard acc; CCI. "Well-maintained, well laid-out, excel site; san facs stretched high ssn & 'tired'; poss cr but carefully controlled; friendly, helpful staff." ♦ 1 May-30 Sep. € 31.00 (3 persons) 2008*

ST PANTALEON *7D3* (4km NE Rural) *44.36760, 1.30634* **Camping des Arcades, Moulin de St Martiel, 46800 St Pantaléon [05 65 22 92 27 or 06 80 43 19 82 (mob); fax 05 65 31 98 89; info@des-arcades.com; www.des-arcades.com]** Fr N20 3km S of Cahors take D653 sp Montcuq, after 17km site in hamlet of St Martial on L. Med, mkd pitch, pt sl, pt shd; wc; chem disp; shwrs inc; el pnts (6A) 3; lndtte; sm shop; tradsmn; rest; snacks; bar; BBQ; playgrnd; htd pool; paddling pool; lake sw & fishing adj; 5% statics; dogs €1.50; Eng spkn; adv bkg; quiet; red low ssn; ccard acc; CCI. "Vg Dutch-owned site with restored 13thC windmill; sm lake; clean facs." ♦ 28 Apr-30 Sep. € 20.00 2007*

ST PARDOUX *9A1* (4km SW Rural) *46.03752, 2.95436* **Camping Elan, Route de Villemorie, 63440 Blot-l'Eglise [04 73 97 51 70 or 06 10 21 40 58 (mob); info@camping-elan.com; www.camping-elan.com]** Fr N on N144 take D16 to Blot, fr S take D50, foll site sp. Sm, hdg/mkd pitch, pt shd; wc; chem disp (wc); shwrs inc; el pnts (5-10A) €2.50-4.50; gas 200m; lndry rm; shop 200m; rest; snacks; bar; playgrnd; tennis; games area; TV; dogs €1; no twin-axles; Eng spkn; adv bkg; quiet; red low ssn/long stay/CCI. "In beautiful area; lge pitches; friendly Dutch owners; clean but basic san facs; site open low ssn by arrangement; gd touring base; conv Vulcania; gd." 1 Apr-30 Sep. € 12.50 2009*

ST PARTHEM see Decazeville *7D4*

ST PAUL DE FENOUILLET *8G4* (7km E Rural) *42.80782, 2.60579* **Camp Municipal Les Oliviers, 66460 Maury [04 68 59 15 24 (Mairie); fax 04 68 59 08 74]** Heading W on D117. Site immed after level x-ing on R 500m bef Maury. Sm, mkd pitch, shd; wc (cont); shwrs inc; el pnts; shop, rest, bar 1km; playgrnd; CCI. "Some rd noise fr level x-ing." 15 Jun-15 Sep. € 11.00 2007*

⊞ **ST PAUL DE FENOUILLET** *8G4* (S Rural) *42.80762, 2.50235* **Camp Municipal de l'Agly, Ave 16 Août 1944, 66220 St Paul-de-Fenouillet [04 68 59 09 09; fax 04 68 59 11 04; contact@camping-agly.com; www.camping-agly.com]** Heading W on D117; turn L at traff lts in St Paul; site on R in 200m, well sp. Sm, hdg/mkd pitch, pt sl, pt shd; wc; chem disp; shwrs inc; el pnts (16A) €3.90; gas & supmkt 500m; pool 1km; rv sw 500m; quiet; red low ssn; CCI. "Gd site; friendly warden; mountain scenery; gd climbing & cycling." ♦ € 14.30 2009*

ST PAUL DE VARAX see Bourg en Bresse *9A2*

ST PAUL DE VEZELIN *9B1* (N Rural) *45.91159, 4.06615* **Camping d'Arpheuilles, Lac de Villerest, 42590 St-Paul-de-Vézelin [04 77 63 43 43; arpheuilles@wanadoo.fr; www.camping-arpheuilles.com]** Take D53 fr Roanne 10km. Turn L onto D8 twd St German-Laval. Turn L at Dancé onto D112 to St-Paul-de-Vézelin. Turn L on ent to vill. Or fr A72 exit junc 5 onto D8, then D26. V diff single track fr vill (3km) - v steep in places. Med, mkd pitch, pt sl, pt shd; wc (some cont); chem disp; mv service pnt; shwrs inc; el pnts (5/6A) €3; gas; lndtte; shop; tradsmn; rest; snacks; bar; BBQ; playgrnd; pool; paddling pool; lake sw & sand beach adj; TV; few statics; dogs; phone; Eng spkn; adv bkg; 20% red 3+ days; quiet. "Beautiful location; helpful owner; well-managed with gd facs; various sports facs." 1 May-10 Sep. € 17.00 2006*

ST PAUL EN FORET see Fayence *10E4*

ST PAUL LE GAULTIER *4E1* (S Rural) *48.32039, -0.10928* **Camp Municipal Le Lac, 72590 St Paul-le-Gaultier [02 43 33 58 55 or 02 43 97 27 12 (Mairie)]** Located on D15, St Paul-le-Gaultier is 25km SW of Alençon. Sm, mkd pitch; shwrs free; el pnts (4A) inc; playgrnd; fishing; quiet. "Tranquil lakeside site." 1 Apr-30 Sep. 2007*

ST PAULIEN *9C1* (2.5km SW Rural) *45.12041, 3.79357* **Camping de la Rochelambert, 43350 St Paulien [04 71 00 54 02; fax 04 71 00 54 32; infos@camping-rochelambert.com; www.camping-rochelambert.com]** Fr St Paulien take D13; turn L onto D25 sp La Rochelambert; site on L in 1.5km. Med, mkd pitch, terr, pt shd; wc (some cont); chem disp; mv service pnt; shwrs inc; el pnts (10A) €2.90; lndtte; shop 3km; tradsmn; snacks; bar; BBQ; playgrnd; pools; paddling pool; tennis; 15% statics; dogs; phone; poss cr; Eng spkn; adv bkg; quiet; CCI. "Improving site; gd walking & fishing; app poss diff lge/long o'fits; gd touring base; gd." ♦ 29 Apr-30 Sep. € 14.95 2007*

ST PEE SUR NIVELLE see St Jean de Luz *8F1*

⊞ **ST PEREUSE** *4H4* (SE Rural) *47.0572, 3.8158* **Camping Le Manoir de Bezolle, 58110 St Péreuse-en-Morvan [03 86 84 42 55; fax 03 86 84 43 77; info@camping-bezolle.com; www.camping-bezolle.com or www.les-castels.com]** 9km W of Château-Chinon on D978 Autun-Nevers. Site sp; ent on N side of D978 on D11. Med, pt sl, pt terr, pt shd; wc; chem disp; mv service pnt; shwrs inc; el pnts (10A) inc (long lead poss req & avail on loan); gas; lndtte; vg shop; rest; snacks; bar; playgrnd; 2 pools; lakeside walks; fishing; tennis; horseriding; entmnt; wifi; TV rm; 25% statics; dogs €2; quiet; ccard acc; red low ssn; CCI. "Gd views fr upper pitches; steep access & site rds, poss in poor condition; friendly recep; lge pitches extra; gd touring base Burgundy." ♦ € 31.00 ABS - L19 2009*

The opening dates and prices on this campsite have changed. I'll send a site report form to the Club for the next edition of the guide.

ST PHILBERT DE GRAND LIEU *2H4* (N Rural) *47.04202, -1.64021* **Camping La Boulogne, 1 Ave de Nantes, 44310 St Philbert-de-Grand-Lieu [32 40 78 88 79; fax 32 40 78 76 50; contact@campinglaboulogne.fr; www.campinglaboulogne.fr]** Fr Nantes on A83 exit junc 1 or 2 onto D178 - D117 dir St Philbert; turn L onto D65 (Ave de Nantes) to St Philbert; site on R in 500m adj rv & sp. Or fr Machecoul take bypass to St Philbert & then D65 as narr rds thro town. Med, hdg/mkd pitch, pt shd; wc; chem disp; baby facs; shwrs inc; el pnts (6A) inc; lndtte; shops 500m; tradsmn; snacks; bar; BBQ; playgrnd; htd, covrd pool 200m; lake adj; fishng 4km; entment; internet; 10% statics; dogs €1; phone; bus adj; no twin-axles; Eng spkn; adv bkg; quiet; ccard acc; CCI. "Gd." ♦ 6 Apr-30 Sep. € 12.50 2007*

ST PIERRE A CHAMP *4H1* (S Rural) **Camping Skorski, 26 Rue de Acacias, 79290 St Pierre-à-Champ [05 49 66 41 28; skorski.anthony@wanadoo.fr; www.campingalaskorski.com]** Leave Doué-la-Fontaine S on D69/D32; in 15km turn L in St Pierre-à-Champ onto D61 dir Thouars; site in 100m on R. Sm, unshd; wc; chem disp; shwrs inc; baby facs; el pnts (16A) €2; lndtte; tradsmn; rest & bar 200m; BBQ; playgrnd; swimming & fishing nrby; dogs; phone & bus 200m; adv bkg; quiet. "Relaxing, British owned site; will open any time by arrangement; gd cycling; conv Futuroscope; more el pnts & shade planned (2007); rec." ♦ Easter-31 Oct. € 9.50 2007*

France

ST PIERRE D'ALBIGNY see Montmelian *9B3*

ST PIERRE D'ARGENCON see Aspres sur Buëch *9D3*

ST PIERRE DE CHARTREUSE *9C3* (2km S Rural) *45.32570, 5.79700* **Camping de Martinière, Route du Col de Porte, 38380 St Pierre-de-Chartreuse [04 76 88 60 36; fax 04 76 88 69 10; camping-de-martiniere@orange.fr; www.campingdemartiniere.com]** Take D520 S fr Les Echelles to St Laurent-du-Pont, D512 thro Gorge-du-Guiers-Mort to St Pierre-de-Chartreuse. Site clearly sp on D512 rd to Grenoble. Med, mkd pitch, pt shd; htd wc (mainly cont); chem disp; mv service pnt; baby facs; shwrs inc; el pnts (2-6A) €3.90; gas; Indtte (inc dryer); shop; tradsmn; rest; snacks; bar; BBQ; playgrnd; pool; paddling pool; fishing; library; 15% statics; dogs €1.50; phone; poss cr; Eng spkn; adv bkg; quiet; red low ssn; ccard acc; red low ssn; CCI. "Site being developed (2008); lge pitches; friendly owner; excel mountain/hill walking, cycling; Grand Chartreuse Monastery 4km; vg." 1 May-13 Sep. € 18.00 (CChq acc) 2008*

ST PIERRE DU VAUVRAY see Pont de l'Arche *3D2*

ST PIERRE LAFEUILLE see Cahors *7D3*

ST PIERRE LE MOUTIER *4H4* (7km W Rural) *46.75722, 3.03328* **Camp Municipal de St Mayeul, 03320 Le Veurdre [04 70 66 40 67 (Mairie); fax 04 70 66 42 88]** Fr N7 at St Pierre-le-Moûtier SW onto D978A to Le Veurdre. Site sp on far side of Le Veurdre. Sm, pt shd; wc; shwrs inc; el pnts €3.20; shops 500m; no statics; quiet. "Pleasant spot; site yourself, warden calls; friendly staff; clean, basic facs." 1 Jun-15 Sep. € 6.80 2009*

ST PIERRE LE MOUTIER *4H4* (8km NW Rural) *46.81730, 3.02746* **Camp Municipal La Bruyère, 18600 Mornay-sur-Allier [02 48 74 50 75 or 06 32 34 97 15 (mob)]** Fr W on D2076 (N76) turn R onto D45 & foll sp. Site just bef x-ing Rv Allier. Sm, pt shd; wc; shwrs inc; el pnts (12A) €1.50; quiet. "Tidy site with clean facs, run by volunteers; pitch self & warden collects fees; excel NH." 1 May-15 Sep. € 6.15 2006*

ST PIERRE QUIBERON *2G3* (1.5km SE Coastal) *47.50400, -3.12028* **Camp Municipal du Petit Rohu, Rue des Men-Du, 56510 St Pierre-Quiberon [02 97 50 27 85 or 02 97 30 92 00 (Mairie)]** On D768 dir Quiberon, 1km past exit for St Pierre-Quiberon turn L at camp sp. Turn R in 200m & L after 250m at T-junc sp Le Petit Rohu. Site on R in 50m on beach. Well sp. Med, mkd pitch, pt sl, unshd; wc; shwrs; mv service pnt; el pnts (10A) inc; gas; Indtte; shop; snacks adj; playgrnd; sand beach adj; boating; fishing; sports area; some statics; dogs; poss cr; quiet. "Vg, clean site; excel location on beach front; gd facs; gd cycling; button on wall to open barrier; vg." ♦ 3 Apr-3 Oct. € 14.00 2008*

ST PIERRE QUIBERON *2G3* (3km SE Coastal) *47.53981, -3.13417* **Camp Municipal de Kerhostin, Allée du Camping, 56510 St Pierre-Quiberon [02 97 30 95 25 or 02 97 30 92 00 (Mairie); fax 02 97 30 87 20; mairie.saintpierrequiberon@wanadoo.fr; www.saintpierrequiberon.fr]** Off D768 turn SE onto Rue des Goélettes by rlwy x-ing (no thro rd sp), turn L at 1st sm island, turn L at end, site 300m on R. Med, mkd pitch, pt shd; wc; shwrs inc; el pnts (10A) €1.69; Indtte; shops adj; rest, snacks, bar 500m; playgrnd; pool 2km; sand beach 200m; dogs €0.86; poss cr; no adv bkg; red low ssn. 28 Apr-2 Sep. € 14.38 2006*

This is a wonderful site.

I'll fill in a report online and let the Club know – www.caravanclub.co.uk/europereport

ST PIERRE QUIBERON *2G3* (W Coastal) *47.53400, -3.14000* **FLOWER Camping St Joseph de l'Océan, 16 Ave de Groix, Kerhostin, 56510 St Pierre-Quiberon [02 97 30 91 29; fax 02 97 30 80 18; info@relaisdelocean.com; www.relaisdelocean.com or www.flowercamping.com]** S on D768 fr Carnac at traff lts in Kerhostin turn R into Rue de Sombreuil then Ave de Groix, site sp. Lge, hdg/mkd pitch, pt shd; wc; chem disp; baby facs; shwrs inc; el pnts (10A) €3.80; gas; Indtte; shop 1km; tradsmn; rest; snacks; bar; BBQ; playgrnd; sand beach adj; games area; games rm; cycle hire; golf 15km; entmnt; TV; 20% statics; dogs €2.15; Eng spkn; adv bkg; quiet; ccard acc; red low ssn/CCI. "Pleasant site; gd sized pitches; gd amenities; staff helpful; gd for families; popular with surfers; vg." ♦ 1 Apr-15 Oct. € 15.00 2006*

ST POINT see Cluny *9A2*

ST POINT LAC see Pontarlier *6H2*

ST POL DE LEON *1D2* (2km E Coastal) *48.69103, -3.9673* **Camping Ar Kleguer, Plage de Ste Anne, 29250 St Pol-de-Léon [02 98 69 18 81; fax 02 98 29 12 84; info@camping-ar-kleguer.com; www.camping-ar-kleguer.com]** In St Pol-de-Léon foll Centre Ville sp. At cathedral sq (2 towers) with cathedral on L descend hill & in 150m, bef church with tall belfry, turn L foll Plage & camping sp. On reaching sea turn L (N); site at end, well sp. NB Narr, busy rds in town. Med, mkd pitch, terr, pt sl, pt shd; wc (some cont); chem disp; mv service pnt; baby facs; shwrs inc; el pnts (10A) €3.60 (long lead poss req); Indtte; shops 500m; tradsmn; snacks; bar; htd pool; waterslide; beach adj; tennis; games rm; 40% statics; dogs €2; poss cr; adv bkg; poss noisy; CCI. "Well-kept, attractive site; modern facs; gd views; conv Roscoff ferry." 1 Apr-30 Sep. € 18.70 2007*

ST POL DE LEON *1D2* (2km E Coastal) *48.69355, -3.96930* **Camping de Trologot, Grève du Man, 29250 St Pol-de-Léon [02 98 69 06 26 or 06 62 16 39 30 (mob); fax 02 98 29 18 30; camping-trologot@wanadoo.fr; www.camping-trologot.com]** Fr E take N12/E50 twd Morlaix & join D58 to St Pol-de-Léon. In St Pol foll sps 'Plages, Port, La Mer' along seafront for approx 600m. Site after a sharp L-hand bend, opp Grève du Man beach. Fr Roscoff on D58 turn L onto D769 sp St Pol. In town cent veer R & pass church on L then in 200m turn L at bell tower sp Morlaix & Carantec. At cemetary turn L & foll sp 'Campings', 'Plages' & 'Port'; then turn L at seafront, then as above. NB Narr, busy rds in town. Med, hdg/mkd pitch, unshd; wc (some cont); chem disp; mv service pnt; baby facs; shwrs inc; el pnts (10A) inc; lndtte; shop & 600m; tradsmn; snacks; bar; BBQ (gas/charcoal only); playgrnd; htd pool; paddling pool; shgl beach adj; entmnt; wifi; games/TV rm; 20% statics; dogs free; no c'vans over 7m high ssn; poss cr; adv bkg; quiet; ccard acc; red long stay/low ssn/CCI. "Ideal NH for Roscoff ferry; gd sized pitches; helpful owners; clean, modern san facs; highly rec." ♦ 1 May-30 Sep. € 21.00 (CChq acc) ABS - B29 2009*

ST POL DE LEON *1D2* (2km SE Rural) *48.64912, -3.92126* **Camping Les Hortensias, Kermen, 29660 Carantec [02 98 67 08 63; contact@leshortensias.fr; www.leshortensias.fr]** Fr Roscoff on D58 dir Morlaix. Turn L after approx 10km on D173, turn R at 1st rndabt for site sp. Sm, unshd; wc; chem disp; mv service pnt; shwrs inc; el pnts (10A) €2; gas 3km; lndtte (inc dryer); shop 3km; playgrnd; htd, covrd pool 6km; beach 2.5km; dogs €1; adv bkg; quiet; CCI. "Gd touring base; conv ferry." ♦ 1 May-30 Sep. € 10.60 2008*

ST POL DE LEON *1D2* (5km SE Coastal) *48.65805, -3.92805* **Yelloh! Village Les Mouettes, La Grande Grève, 29660 Carantec [02 98 67 02 46; fax 02 98 78 31 46; camping@les-mouettes.com; www.les-mouettes.com or www.yellohvillage.com]** Fr Morlaix take D58 N sp Roscoff; at lge rndabt turn R sp Carantec on D173; turn L at 1st rndabt; strt on at 2nd rndabt; turn L at 3rd rndabt; site on L. Or fr Roscoff take D58 sp Mortaix, then D173 to Carantec; foll sp town cent, then site. Lge, mkd pitch, pt shd; wc; chem disp; mv service pnt; baby facs; shwrs inc; el pnts (6A) inc (poss rev pol); gas; lndtte; shop; snacks; bar; BBQ (charcoal/gas only); playgrnd; htd pool & paddling pool; waterslide; sand/shgl beach 1km; fishing; tennis; entmnt; wifi; games/TV rm; 50% statics; dogs €4; poss cr; Eng spkn; adv bkg; noise fr boatyard; ccard acc; red low ssn; CCI. "Sea views; mkt Thu." ♦ 11 May-12 Sep. € 42.00 ABS - B14 2009*

ST POL DE LEON *1D2* (6km S Urban) *48.63476, -3.92962* **Camp Municipal de Kerilis, Menez Izella, 29670 Henvic [02 98 62 82 10; fax 02 98 62 81 56; commune-henvic@wanadoo.fr]** Exit D58 (St Pol-de-Léon to Morlaix rd) at Henvic; foll sp. Site 800m after exit main rd, behind football stadium. NB 2m height barrier open 0830-1230 & 1300-2000, so unsuitable late arrivals/early departures. Med, pt shd; wc; shwrs inc; el pnts €2.10 (poss long lead req); lndry rm; supmkt nr; playgrnd; sand beach 8km; quiet; CCI. "Pleasant, simple, well-run site; helpful warden." 1 Jul-31 Aug. € 9.45 2009*

⊞ **ST POL DE LEON** *1D2* (7km W Coastal) *48.68972, -4.08396* **Camp du Theven, Moguériec, 29250 Sibiril [02 98 29 96 86; fax 02 98 61 23 30; roudaut.theven.29@wanadoo.fr; http://pagesperso-orange.fr/camping.theven.29]** Fr Roscoff ferry on D58, at junc with D10 take Sibiril/Cléder turn. In Sibiril pass church & turn R past water tower, foll sp Port de Moguériec, site sp. Sm, hdg/mkd pitch, terr, pt shd; wc; shwrs €1; el pnts (4-6A) €3; lndtte; shop; supmkt 5km; snacks; bar; BBQ; playgrnd; sand/rocky beach adj; fishing; boat hire; entmnt; 6% statics; dogs €1; Eng spkn; adv bkg; quiet; CCI. "Friendly, helpful owner; liable to close for 10 day periods low ssn - phone ahead to check open; ltd facs low ssn, poss no hot water." € 11.70 2007*

⊞ **ST POL SUR TERNOISE** *3B3* (5km NW Rural) *50.38465, 2.28429* **Camping du Ternoise, Rue d'en Haut, 62130 Croix-en-Ternois [tel/fax 03 21 03 39 87 or 03 21 03 43 12]** W fr St Pol-sur-Ternoise on D939 (N39) then into Croix-en-Ternois; foll camp sp. Sm, hdg pitch, pt shd; wc; shwrs €1.50; el pnts (6A) inc; shop 5km; bar; BBQ; playgrnd; fishing & horseriding nr; 50% statics; dogs; adv bkg; poss noise fr motorbike circuit. "Pleasant, quiet site; clean, smart san facs; site yourself; gd walks & cycling; vg." ♦ € 20.00 2007*

ST PONS DE THOMIERES *8F4* (4km N Rural) *43.51223, 2.75289* **Aire Naturelle La Borio de Roque, Route de la Salvetat, 34220 St Pons-de-Thomières [04 67 97 10 97; fax 04 67 97 21 61; info@borioderoque.com; www.borioderoque.com]** On D907, R at sp, foll track for 1.2km to site. Sm, hdg pitch, terr, shd; wc; chem disp; shwrs inc; el pnts (10A) €3; lndtte; tradsmn; bar; playgrnd; pool; Eng spkn; some statics; dogs €2; adv bkg rec high ssn; CCI. "Excel, welcoming, clean, secluded site; diff access lge/underpowered o'fits down single, dirt track - no turning/passing." ♦ 15 May-15 Sep. € 20.25 2008*

ST PONS DE THOMIERES *8F4* (8km NE Rural) *43.52181, 2.83027* **Camping Les Terrasses du Jaur, Chemin de Notre Dame, 34390 Prémian [04 67 97 27 85; fax 04 67 97 06 40]** Go E on D908 fr St Pons-de-Thomières twd Olargues for 8km. Imposs to turn R over rv to site, cont on D908, turn round & app fr E, turn L into site. Sm, hdg pitch, pt sl, terr, pt shd; wc; chem disp; shwrs inc; el pnts (3A) €1.50; lndry rm; shop; fishing 100m; quiet; 30% statics; adv bkg; CCI. "Improving site now private (2007); poss pitching all year with ltd facs." 15 May-15 Oct. 2007*

⊞ **ST PONS DE THOMIERES** *8F4* (2km E Rural) *43.49055, 2.78527* **Camping Village Les Cerisiers du Jaur, Route de Bédarieux, 34220 St Pons-de-Thomières [04 67 95 30 33; fax 04 67 23 09 96; lescerisiersdujaur@orange.fr; www.cerisierdujaur.com]** Fr Castres on D612 (N112) to St Pons; go thro town cent under rlwy bdge; turn L onto D908 sp Olargues. Site on R in 500m. Med, hdg/mkd pitch, terr, pt shd; wc; chem disp; mv service pnt; baby facs; shwrs inc; el pnts (10A) €3.50; lndtte; ltd shop; tradsmn; snacks; playgrnd; pool; cycle hire; dogs €1.50; phone; poss cr; Eng spkn; quiet; ccard acc; red low ssn; CCI. "Excel site nr Rv Jaur; welcoming, friendly, helpful owner; vg san facs, inc disabled; an oasis!." ♦ € 22.00 (CChq acc) 2009*

ST PONS DE THOMIERES *8F4* (11km W Rural) **Camp Municipal de Cabanes, Route de St Pons, 81270 Labastide-Rouairoux [05 63 98 49 74 or 05 63 98 07 58; tourisme@labastide-rouairoux.com; www.labastide-rouairoux.com]** E fr Labastide-Rouairoux twd St Pons on D612 (N112). Site adj D612 immed after leaving Labastide vill. Sm, hdg/mkd pitch, terr, pt shd; wc; chem disp; shwrs; el pnts inc; shop 1km; tradsmn; adv bkg; some rd noise; CCI. "Lovely site; poss diff lge o'fits due to terr."
15 Jun-15 Sep. € 11.00 2009*

ST POURCAIN SUR SIOULE *9A1* (E Urban) *46.30643, 3.29207* **Camp Municipal Ile de la Ronde, Quai de la Ronde, 03500 St Pourçain-sur-Sioule [04 70 45 45 43; hdv.st.pourcain.s.sioule@wanadoo.fr; www.ville-saint-pourcain-sur-sioule.com]** On D2009 (N9), 31km S of Moulins; in St Pourçain-sur-Sioule town cent turn R immed bef rv bdge; site ent on L in 100m. NB Sp in town easily missed. Med, hdg pitch, pt shd; wc; chem disp; mv service pnt; shwrs; el pnts (6A) €2.20; lndtte; shops adj; playgrnd; pool 1km; dogs; adv bkg; quiet; CCI. "Clean, well-run, busy site in pretty town; extra charge for lger pitches; barrier clsd 2000-0800; gd rest nr; mkt Sat; great value; excel."
2 May-30 Sep. € 8.05 2009*

⊞ **ST PRIVAT** *7C4* (400m N) *45.14382, 2.09938* **Aire Communale Les Chanaux, 19220 St Privat [tel/fax 05 55 28 28 77 (Mairie); francois-michel.perrier@wanadoo.fr]** Fr Argentat on D980 for 17km dir Pleaux & Mauriac, rd steep & winding in parts. Sm, chem disp; mv service pnt; water fill €2 for 100 litres; el pnts (10A) €2; shops, rests in vill; m'vans only. 2006*

ST PRIVAT *7C4* (4km N Rural) *45.14557, 2.03467* **Camp Municipal du Lac de Feyt, 19220 Servières-le-Château [05 55 28 25 42; fax 05 55 28 29 08; campingserviereslechateau@orange.fr]** Fr Argentat take D980 & D75 dir Servières-le-Château. Thro Servières to site in 4km on lakeside, sp. Med, hdg pitch, pt shd; wc (cont); mv service pnt; shwrs inc; el pnts (5A) €2.35; lndtte; shops 4km; tradsmn; playgrnd; lake sw; tennis adj; fishing; sailing; some statics; poss cr; adv bkg; quiet. "Beautiful countryside; vg site." 29 Mar-27 Sep. € 9.45 2007*

ST PRIVAT D'ALLIER see Monistrol d'Allier *9C1*

ST QUAY PORTRIEUX *2E3* (600m NW Coastal) *48.66269, -2.84550* **Camping Bellevue, 68 Blvd du Littoral, 22410 St Quay-Portrieux [02 96 70 41 84; fax 02 96 70 55 46; campingbellevue22@orange.fr; www.campingbellevue.net]** Foll D786 thro St Quay-Portrieux twd Paimpol; turn R at traff lts sp St Quay-Portrieux; foll site sp; site in 2.5km. Lge, hdg/mkd/pitch, hdstg, terr, pt shd; wc (some cont); chem disp; mv service pnt; baby facs; shwrs inc; el pnts (6A) €3; gas; lndtte; shop; tradsmn; snacks; BBQ; playgrnd; pool; paddling pool; sand beach adj & 600m; games area; TV; dogs; Eng spkn; adv bkg; quiet; ccard acc; red low ssn; CCI. "Beautiful position with sea views; direct access to sm cove; friendly staff; gd, clean facs; vg." ♦ 30 Apr-18 Sep. € 18.50 2009*

ST QUENTIN *3C4* (SE Urban) *49.85536, 3.31033* **Camp Municipal, 91 Blvd Jean Bouin, 02100 St Quentin [03 23 06 94 05]** Fr all app rds foll sp Centre Ville/Auberge de Jeunesse (c'van on sign). Poss diff to find - foll canal rd. Sp 'Terrain de Camping'. Press intercom at barrier for ent. Sm, mkd pitch, hdstg, pt shd; htd wc (most cont); chem disp; shwrs inc; el pnts (6-10A) €2.35-7; supmkt 1km; pool adj; dogs free; bus adj; some rd noise; ccard acc; CCI. "Usefully placed site; easy access to lge, gritty pitches; helpful staff; gd clean san facs; gates clsd 2200-0700; pleasant canal walk adj; poss itinerants; vg." ♦
1 Mar-30 Nov. € 6.40 2009*

ST QUENTIN *3C4* (10km SW Urban) *49.78222, 3.21333* **Camping Le Vivier aux Carpes, 10 Rue Charles Voyeux, 02790 Seraucourt-le-Grand [03 23 60 50 10; fax 03 23 60 51 69; camping.du.vivier@wanadoo.fr; www.camping-picardie.com]** Fr A26 take exit 11 St Quentin/Soissons; S 4km on D1 dir Tergnier/Soissons. Fork R onto D8 to Essigny-le-Grand & in vill foll camping sp W to Seraucourt. Fr St Quentin, S 10km on D930 to Roupy, E on D32 5km to Seraucourt-le-Grand. Site N of Seraucourt on D321. Med, hdg/mkd pitch, some hdstg, pt shd; wc; chem disp; mv service pnt; baby facs; shwrs inc; el pnts (6A) inc (poss rev pol); gas; lndtte; shop & supmkt 200m; tradsmn; snacks; BBQ; playgrnd; pool nr; angling; golf, tennis, horseriding adj; games rm; wifi; 30% statics; dogs €1; c'van storage; Eng spkn; adv bkg; quiet; CCI. "Delightful, well-run, busy site - rec arr early; peaceful low ssn; gd, lge pitches; gd clean san facs; ltd hdstg; friendly, helpful staff - can arrange vet; poss flooding; vg angling; mosquito probs; Disneyland 90 mins; conv Channel ports; warn staff night bef if v early dep; excel." ♦ 1 Mar-31 Oct. € 18.50 2009*

ST QUENTIN EN TOURMONT *3B2* (500m S Rural) *50.26895, 1.60263* **Camping Le Champ Neuf, 8 Rue du Champ Neuf, 80120 St Quentin-en-Tourmont [03 22 25 07 94; fax 03 22 25 09 87; contact@camping.lechampneuf.com; www.camping-lechampneuf.com]** Exit D1001 (N1) or A16 onto D32 to Rue, take D940 around Rue & foll sp St Quentin-en-Tourmont, Parc Ornithologique & Domaine du Marquenterre to site. Site sp fr D204. Lge, hdg/mkd pitch, pt shd; wc; chem disp; mv service pnt; baby facs; shwrs inc; el pnts (5-10A) €3.40-3.80; lndtte; shop; snacks; bar; BBQ; playgrnd; htd, covrd pool complex; paddling pool; beach 2km; games area; cycle hire; horseriding 500m; wifi; entmnt high ssn; many statics; dogs €1.20; adv bkg; quiet; ccard acc. "Excel Ornithological Park adj; well-kept, pleasant site; friendly, helpful owner; gd cycle paths." ♦ 1 Apr-1 Nov. € 16.00 2009*

See advertisement

ST QUENTIN EN TOURMONT *3B2* (1km S Rural) *50.26978, 1.59855* **Camping des Crocs, 2 Chemin des Garennes, 80120 St Quentin-en-Tourmont [03 22 25 73 33; fax 03 22 25 75 17; contact@campingdescrocs.com; www.campingdescrocs.com]** Exit D1001 (N1) or A16 onto D32 to Rue. When W of Rue turn off onto D4 heading W. In 2km turn R onto D204 & foll sp Le Bout des Crocs, then Parc Ornithologique. Site on R. Med, hdg/mkd pitch, unshd; wc; chem disp; baby facs; shwrs €1; el pnts (6A) €3; Indtte; tradsmn; playgrnd; TV rm; 80% statics; dogs €0.50; CCI. "V quiet site; nr Marquenterre bird reserve; immac facs, but poss long walk; cycle tracks to beach & inland; mosquitoes poss problem; vg." 1 Apr-1 Nov. € 14.00 2009*

ST QUENTIN LA POTERIE see Uzès *10E2*

ST RAMBERT D'ALBON *9C2* (Urban) *45.29992, 4.80722* **Camping des Claires, 26140 St Rambert-d'Albon [tel/fax 04 75 31 01 87; info@camping-des-claires.com; www.camping-des-claires.com]** Fr A7 exit junc 12 dir Chanas, turn S onto N7. In 1km turn R to St Rambert, turn R at rndabt by rlwy stn, under rlwy bdge & foll site sp. Med, pt sl, shd; wc; chem disp (wc); baby facs; shwrs inc; el pnts (6A) €3.80; gas; Indtte; tradsmn; rest; snacks; bar in vill; BBQ; playgrnd; pool; sports area; entmnt; 50% statics; dogs €1.40; phone adj; Eng spkn; some rlwy noise; CCI. "Excel NH." 1 Apr-15 Oct. € 14.80 2007*

ST RAMBERT D'ALBON *9C2* (3km N Rural) *45.31421, 4.82481* **Camping Beauséjour, Route de Grenoble, 38150 Chanas [04 74 84 21 38 or 04 74 84 31 01; jvernet@campingbeausejour.fr; www.campingbeausejour.fr]** Exit A7 junc 12 onto D519 dir Grenoble; site on R in 3km. Med, mkd pitch; pt sh; wc; chem disp; shwrs inc; Indry rm; el pnts (6A) €3.20; playgrnd; sm pool; shops 1km; games rm; no statics; some rd noise fr D519; red CCI; no ccard acc; CCI. "Gd NH off A7/N7; fair." 15 Apr-30 Sep. € 12.40 2007*

ST RAMBERT D'ALBON *9C2* (8km NE Rural) *45.32400, 4.90510* **Camping Le Temps Libre, Quartier Font Rozier, 38150 Bougé-Chambalud [04 74 84 04 09; fax 04 74 84 15 71; info@temps-libre.fr; www.temps-libre.fr or www.camping-franceloc.fr]** Fr A7 take exit junc 12 Chanas onto D519, dir Grenoble for 8km. Or fr N7 take exit D519 E sp Grenoble. Site sp at 1st rndabt & well sp in vill. Med, hdg/mkd pitch, hdstg, pt sl, terr, pt shd; wc; chem disp; serviced pitches; shwrs inc; el pnts (9A) €5.70 Indtte; shop in ssn & supmkt 10km; tradsmn; rest high ssn; snacks; bar high ssn; playgrnd; 3 htd pools with chutes (1 covrd); tennis; fishing; pedal boats; wifi; 50% statics; dogs €4.50; Eng spkn; adv bkg; poss noisy; red low ssn; ccard acc; CCI. "Useful NH S of Lyon; ltd facs low ssn; busy w/end; excel pools; poss flooding in heavy rain; excel." ♦ 29 Mar-27 Sep. € 22.50 2008*

I'm going to fill in some site report forms and post them off to the Club; we could win a ferry crossing – it's here on page 12.

ST RAPHAEL See also sites listed under Agay.

ST RAPHAEL *10F4* (4.5km N Rural) *43.44611, 6.80610* **Kawan Village Douce Quiétude, 3435 Blvd Jacques Baudino, 83700 St Raphaël [04 94 44 30 00; fax 04 94 44 30 30; info@douce-quietude.com; www.douce-quietude.com]** Exit A8 at junc 38 onto D37 then D100 sp Agay. Foll sp Valescure-Boulouris, site sp. NB c'vans not permitted on St Raphaël seafront. Lge, pt sl, pt shd; wc; chem disp; serviced pitches; shwrs; el pnts (6A) inc; gas; Indtte; shop; rest; bar; BBQ (gas only); playgrnd; pool; sand beach 6km; entmnt; excursions; TV; many tour ops statics; dogs €4; phone; poss v cr; ccard acc. "Noisy disco nightly high ssn; excel facs; sm touring pitches mostly amongst statics." ♦ 1 Apr-14 Oct. € 49.50 (3 persons) (CChq acc) 2007*

France

ST REMEZE see Vallon Pont d'Arc *9D2*

ST REMY DE PROVENCE *10E2* (500m NE) *43.79870, 4.83823* **FFCC Camping Le Mas de Nicolas, Ave Plaisance-du-Touch, 13210 St Rémy-de-Provence [04 90 92 27 05; fax 04 90 92 36 83; camping-mas-de-nicolas@wanadoo.fr; www.camping-masdenicolas.com]** S fr Avignon on D571, at rndabt just bef St Rémy turn L onto D99 sp Cavaillon; at next rndabt turn L, site sp on L in 500m. Well sp fr all dirs & in town. Site ent narr. NB Avoid ent St Rémy. Med, mkd/hdg pitch, pt sl, terr, pt shd/unshd; htd wc (some cont); chem disp; mv service pnt; baby facs; shwrs inc; el pnts (6A) €3.50; gas 2km; Indtte; sm shop or supmkt 1km, snacks; bar in ssn; BBQ; pool; playgrnd; games area; games rm; entmnt; wifi; sat TV; 20% statics; dogs €1.80; phone 400m; bus 1km; poss cr; Eng spkn; adv bkg ess; quiet; ccard acc; red low ssn; CCI. "Family-owned site; gd clean san facs; some pitches diff access long o'fits; excel'." ♦ 1 Mar-31 Oct. € 20.50 2009*

ST REMY DE PROVENCE *10E2* (500m E Urban) *43.78836, 4.84093* **Camping Pégomas, Ave Jean Moulin, 13210 St Rémy-de-Provence [tel/fax 04 90 92 01 21; contact@campingpegomas.com; www.campingpegomas.com]** On D99 fr W dir Cavaillon, ignore R fork to St Rémy 'Centre Ville' (& sat nav!). Pass twin stone sculptures on rndabt, at 2nd rndabt turn into Ave Jean Moulin , site on R in 400m - v sharp turn into site. Fr E Exit A7 junc 25 on D99 W dir St Rémy. Ignore sp 'Centre Ville', pass under aquaduct & across rndabt. At next rndabt turn L into Ave Jean Moulin, then as above. Do not attempt to tow thro town. Med, hdg/mkd pitch, shd; htd wc (mainly cont); chem disp; mv service pnt; baby facs; shwrs inc; el pnts (6A) €3.50 (poss rev pol & long lead req); gas; Indtte; shop 300m; tradsmn; snacks; bar; playgrnd; pool & paddling pool high ssn; entmnt; TV; dogs €1.70; phone; poss cr; Eng spkn; adv bkg; quiet; ccard acc; red low ssn/long stay; CCI. "Well-run, busy site; lge o'fits poss diff some sm pitches; gd pool; san facs clean; gates clsd 2000/2100-0800 mkt Wed; gd touring base." ♦ 1 Mar-31 Oct. € 20.00 2009*

ST REMY DE PROVENCE *10E2* (1km NW Rural) *43.7967, 4.82378* **Camping Monplaisir, Chemin Monplaisir, 13210 St Rémy-de-Provence [04 90 92 22 70; fax 04 90 92 18 57; reception@camping-monplaisir.fr; www.camping-monplaisir.fr]** Exit D99 at St Rémy onto D5 going NW dir Maillane, in 110m turn L & foll sp in 500m. Avoid going thro town. Med, hdg/mkd pitch, hdstg, pt shd; htd wc; chem disp; mv service pnt; baby facs; fam bthrm; shwrs inc; el pnts (10A) €3.60; gas; Indtte; shop; supmkt 500m; tradsmn; snacks, bar high ssn; BBQ (gas/elec); playgrnd; pool; paddling pool; cycle hire; entmnt; wifi; dogs €2; phone; bus 1km; Eng spkn; adv bkg; quiet; ccard acc; red long stay/low ssn; CCI. "Immac, well-run site; clean, modern san facs; some pitches poss diff lge o'fits; gd touring base; highly rec." ♦ 6 Mar-31 Oct. € 23.00 2009*

See advertisement above

ST REMY SOUS BARBUISE see Arcis sur Aube *4E4*

ST RENAN *2E1* (2km NW Urban) *48.43899, -4.62959* **Camp Municipal Lokournan, Route de l'Aber, 29290 St Renan [02 98 84 37 67 or 02 98 84 20 08 (Mairie); fax 02 98 32 43 20]** On D27 fr St Renan dir Lanildut, site sp in 2km. Sm, hdg pitch, pt sl, pt shd; wc; chem disp; shwrs; el pnts €2.70; shop 1km; no statics; dogs €0.80; adv bkg; CCI. "Vg." ♦ 1 Jun-15 Sep. € 7.00 2006*

ST REVEREND see St Gilles Croix de Vie *2H3*

ST ROMAIN DE JALIONAS see Cremieu *9B2*

ST ROME DE DOLAN see Severac le château *9D1*

France

⊞ **ST ROME DE TARN** *8E4* (300m N Rural) *44.05302, 2.89978* **Camping de la Cascade des Naisses, Route du Pont, 12490 St Rome-de-Tarn [05 65 62 56 59; fax 05 65 62 58 62; contact@camping-cascade-aveyron.com; www.camping-cascade-aveyron.com]** Fr Millau take D992 to St Georges-de-Luzençon, turn R onto D73 & foll sp to St Rome. In St Rome turn R along Ave du Pont-du-Tarn, site sp. Diff, steep app for sm/underpowered car+c'van o'fits. Med, hdg/mkd pitch, hdstg, terr, pt shd; htd wc; own san; chem disp; mv service pnt; baby facs; shwrs inc; el pnts (6A) inc; Indtte; shop; rest; bar; playgrnd; pool; paddling pool; rv sw, fishing, boating; tennis; cycle hire; wifi; entmnt; 40% statics; dogs €6; Eng spkn; adv bkg; quiet; CCI. "Lovely rvside pitches; pleasant vill; friendly, helpful staff; each level has a wc but steep walk to shwr block; owners will site vans; conv Millau viaduct; excel tranquil, scenic site." ♦ € 27.00 2009*

See advertisement below

ST ROME DE TARN *8E4* (10km W Rural) *44.05131, 2.82865* **FFCC Camping La Tioule, 12400 St Victor-et-Melvieu [05 65 62 51 93; carriere.nic@wanadoo.fr; http://pagesperso-orange.fr/campinglatioule/]** Fr Millau or St Affrique on D999 at Lauras take D23 sp Tiergues, then D250/D50 sp St Victor-et-Melvieu. Other app not rec due narr, winding rds. Sm, mkd pitch, pt sl, terr, pt shd; wc; chem disp; mv service pnt; shwrs inc; el pnts (16A) €2.80; Indtte; tradsmn; BBQ; playgrnd; pool; dogs; adv bkg; quiet; CCI. "Beautiful area; vg site." 1 Jul-31 Aug. € 12.00 2008*

ST SATURNIN (PUY DE DOME) *9B1* (Rural) *45.68442, 3.06163* **Domaine La Serre de Portelas (Naturist), 63450 St Saturnin [04 73 39 35 25 or 04 73 91 21 31 (LS); fax 04 73 39 35 76; ffn-laserre@ifrance.com; www.ffn-laserre.com]** On A75 S fr Clermont-Ferrand exit junc 5 onto D213 W-bound sp Tallende. In 4km turn N on D96 sp Chadrat. Site on L about 3.5km after Chadrat. Turn acute L at end of tel posts. Or take N89 S fr Clermont-Ferrand twd Theix, turn S onto D96 & foll rd to site, sp. Sm, pt sl, pt shd; wc; chem disp; shwrs inc; el pnts (6A) €3.20; gas; Indtte; sm shop & 6km; tradsmn; snacks; BBQ; playgrnd; pool; paddling pool; tennis; games area; wifi; 35% statics; dogs; phone; quiet; red low ssn/long stay; INF card req. "Lovely site with views; friendly owners; gd facs; gd base Auvergne; excel." 15 Jun-15 Sep. € 15.00 2008*

ST SATURNIN (PUY DE DOME) *9B1* (9km W Rural) *45.66977, 3.00054* **Camping La Clairière, Rouillas-Bas, 63970 Aydat [tel/fax 04 73 79 31 15; info@campinglaclairiere.com; www.campinglaclairiere.com]** S fr Clermont-Ferrand exit A75 junc 5 onto D213 W & foll sp Lac d'Aydat. At x-rds at end Rouillas-Bas turn L, site 100m on L. Sm, hdg pitch, terr, pt shd; htd wc; chem disp; shwrs inc; el pnts (10A) €3.50 (poss rev pol); Indtte; shop 600m; rest 250m; snacks high ssn; playgrnd; wifi; 10% statics; dogs €1; Eng spkn; adv bkg rec high ssn; quiet; red low ssn. "V pleasant site; friendly, helpful owner; clean facs poss stretched when site full; excel walking." 15 Apr-30 Sep. € 13.00 2009*

ST SAUVEUR EN PUISAYE *4G4* (2km N Rural) *47.63076, 3.19231* **FFCC Camping Les Joumiers, Route de Mézilles, 89520 St Sauveur-en-Puisaye [03 86 45 66 28; fax 03 86 45 60 27; biotic@wanadoo.fr; www.camping-motel-joumiers.com]** Fr A6 S, exit at sp Joigny-Toucy onto D955 thro Aillant-sur-Tholon to Toucy, then cont to St Sauveur. Or N fr St Sauveur on D7 sp Mézilles, site on R in 1.5km. Site well sp at main x-rds in town. Med, hdg/mkd pitch, pt shd; htd wc; chem disp; shwrs inc; el pnts (5-10A) €2.80-3.80; gas; Indry rm; tradsmn; rest; snacks; bar 2km; BBQ; playgrnd; htd pool; lake sw & beach adj; fishing; games area; cycle hire; 6 statics; dogs €1.25; phone; poss cr; no adv bkg; quiet; ccard acc; 5% red long stay/CCI. "Helpful staff; lge pitches with lake views." ♦ 15 Mar-15 Nov. € 12.00 2006*

ST SAUVEUR LE VICOMTE see Haye du Puits, La *1D4*

ST SAVIN *7A3* (1km N Rural) **Camp Municipal Moulin de la Gassotte, 10 Rue de la Gassotte, 86310 St Savin-sur-Gartempe [05 49 48 18 02; fax 05 49 48 28 56; saint.savin@ag86.fr]** E fr Chauvigny on D951 (N151) to St Savin; fr St Savin N on D11; well sp. Fr S on D5 cross rv; meet D951, turn R & site on R. Fr S on D11 use 'poids lourds' (heavy vehicles) rec rte to meet D951. Sm, pt shd; wc; chem disp; mv service pnt; shwrs inc; el pnts (12A) €2.50; Indry rm; shop, rests & bars 500m; tradsmn; playgrnd; rv fishing adj; TV; quiet; CCI. "Beautiful, peaceful site by rv; helpful warden; san facs old but clean; sh walk to vill; murals in Abbey restored by UNESCO." ♦ 13 May-15 Sep. € 6.75 2009*

ST SAVINIEN *7B2* (1km S Rural) *45.87789, -0.68441* **Camping L'Ile aux Loisirs (La Grenouillette), 17350 St Savinien [05 46 90 35 11; fax 05 46 91 65 06; ileauxloisirs@wanadoo.fr; www.ileauxloisirs.com]** Fr St Jean-d'Angély take D18 to St Savinien. Site on S side of town; cross rv bdge in vill; site on L after 300m. Med, pt shd; wc; shwrs inc; el pnts (6A) €4.50; (rev pol); Indtte; shop; bar; snacks; playgrnd; pool adj; tennis & mini-golf nrby; entmnt; dogs €1; adv bkg; quiet, some rd noise; red low ssn; ccard acc. "Pleasant, well-run site; attractive town." 1 Apr-22 Sep. € 16.10 2009*

⊞ **ST SEBASTIEN** *7A3* (1km SW Rural) *46.38871, 1.52249* **Camp Municipal La Garenne, Route de la Garenne, 23160 St Sébastien [05 55 63 50 39]** Exit A20 junc 20 & foll sp dir La Souterraine on D5. In 4km turn L to St Sébastien. On ent vill turn R, R again, site on L just after equestrian cent. Sm, mkd pitch, pt sl, terr, pt shd; wc; shwrs inc; el pnts inc; shop, rest 500m; quiet. "Gd NH nr A20; gd touring base." € 6.20 2006*

ST SEINE L'ABBAYE *6G1* (N Rural) *47.44073, 4.79236* **Camp Municipal, Rue de la Foire aux Vaches, 21440 St Seine-l'Abbaye [03 80 35 00 09 or 03 80 35 01 64 (Mairie]** On D971 (N71) in vill of St Seine-l'Abbaye, turn N onto D16. Turn R uphill, sp camping & turn R thro gateway in high stone wall. Narr streets in vill. Or fr N on D974 (N74), avoiding Dijon, turn R onto D959 at Til-Châtel, then D901 Moloy/Lamargelle. Turn L in Lamargelle onto D16 St Seine-l'Abbaye. Turn L uphill at edge of vill & as above (avoids narr streets). Sm, pt sl, unshd; wc (cont); chem disp; shwrs inc; el pnts (10A) €2.50 (rev pol); shops 500m; pool 4km; rv 500m; dogs; v quiet; CCI. "V pleasantly situated site; conv for Dijon or as NH; fees collected fr 1900 hrs; basic but immac facs; excel." 1 May-30 Sep. € 8.40 2008*

ST SEURIN DE PRATS see Ste Foy la Grande *7C2*

ST SEVER *8E2* (1km N Urban) *43.76570, -0.56312* **FFCC Camping Les Rives de l'Adour, Ave René Crabos, 40500 St Sever [05 58 76 04 60; camping.deladour@orange.fr; www.camping-lesrivesdeladour.com]** S on D933 fr Mont-de-Marsan, cross D924 then bdge over Rv Adour. Look immed for access rd on L bef rlwy x-ing & steep climb up to St Sever. Site sp adj Parc des Sports. Med, hdg/mkd pitch, shd; htd wc; mv service pnt; shwrs inc; el pnts (13A) €2.50; sm shop & 1km; Indtte (inc dryer); playgrnd; pool nrby inc; tennis; sailing; fishing; cycle hire; games rm; wifi; TV; dogs €1.50; quiet; red low ssn/long stay. "Gd san facs; gd."
1 Apr-31 Oct. € 12.50 2008*

ST SEVER CALVADOS *1D4* (1km SE Rural) *48.83271, -1.03845* **Camp Municipal, Route du Vieux Château, 14380 St Sever-Calvados [02 31 68 82 63 (Mairie); fax 02 31 67 95 15]** Fr A84 exit junc 37 or 38 E onto D924 or fr Vire W on D524, site sp on SE dir Champ-du-Boult. Med, sl, pt shd; wc; chem disp; shwrs inc; el pnts (5A) €2.50; shops 1km; snacks; bar; playgrnd; htd pool 1km; sand beach 30km; fishing; boating; tennis adj; dogs; adv bkg rec high ssn; quiet. "Peaceful, clean site in wooded area; gd walking; gd for young children; barrier open 1200-1330 & 1700-2100 only." 1 Apr-31 Oct. € 6.30 2007*

STE SEVERE SUR INDRE *7A4* (200m N Urban) *46.48843, 2.06902* **Camp Municipal, Route de l'Auvergne, 36160 Ste Sévère-sur-Indre [02 54 30 50 28 (Mairie); fax 02 54 30 63 39]** On D917 fr La Châtre, site on R 200m after g'ge on L. Sm, pt shd; wc (some cont); mv service pnt; shwrs inc; el pnts (10A) €1.70; gas, shop, rest, bar 500m; playgrnd adj; fishing; dogs; quiet. "Tiny site in pleasant vill; gd facs; associations with Jacques Tati & Georges Sand; vg NH." Easter-1 Nov. € 6.80 2008*

STE SEVERE SUR INDRE *7A4* (6km SE Rural) **Camping Pérassay, Le Bourg, 36160 Pérassay [02 54 30 63 25; camping@the-french-connection.net; www.the-french-connection.net]** Fr Ste Sévère take D917 S & after approx 6km turn L onto D71 sp Pérassay. Site on L in cent of vill opp tabac. Sm, pt sl, pt shd; wc; chem disp (wc); shwrs inc; el pnts (16A) €2.50; Indtte; BBQ; lake sw 10km; 1 static; dogs €2.50; adv bkg; quiet; red low ssn. "Lovely CL-type site in quiet location; friendly British owner; vg san facs; vg." ♦
1 Apr-31 Oct. € 15.00 2009*

STE SIGOLENE see Monistrol sur Loire *9C1*

ST SORNIN see Marennes *7B1*

ST SOZY see Souillac *7C3*

ST SYLVESTRE (HAUTE VIENNE) *7B3* (4.5km W Rural) *46.00561, 1.33551* **Camping Les Roussilles, La Crouzille, 87240 St Sylvestre [05 55 71 32 54; contact@campinglesroussilles.nl; www.campinglesroussilles.nl]** Fr N on A20 exit junc 25, fr S take exit 26; site approx 1.5km N of Le Crouzille. Med, mkd pitch, pt sl, shd; wc; chem disp; shwrs inc; el pnts (6A) inc; Indtte; shop 5km; tradsmn; rest high ssn; snacks; bar; playgrnd; pool; wifi; poss cr; adv bkg; quiet; CCI. "Excel pool; basic facs; phone ahead low ssn to check open." ♦ 1 Mar-31 Dec. € 15.00 2006*

ST SYLVESTRE SUR LOT see Villeneuve sur Lot *7D3*

⊞ **ST SYMPHORIEN** *7D2* (1km S Rural) *44.41831, -0.49232* **FFCC Camping La Hure, Route de Sore, 33113 St Symphorien [tel/fax 05 56 25 79 54 or 06 86 77 09 27 (mob); campingdelahure@wanadoo.fr; http://monsite.wanadoo.fr/campingdelahure/]** S thro Langon on app to . Foll sp Villandraut, St Symphorien. Sp fr vill 1km S on D220, opp Intermarché. Med, shd; htd wc; chem disp; mv service pnt; shwrs inc; el pnts (5A) €2.50; Indtte; shops; rest; snacks; playgrnd; pool adj; tennis; rv fishing; many statics; dogs €1.30; adv bkg; red low ssn. "Helpful staff; basic facs; site in pinewoods; gd cycling, walks, beaches." € 9.10 2009*

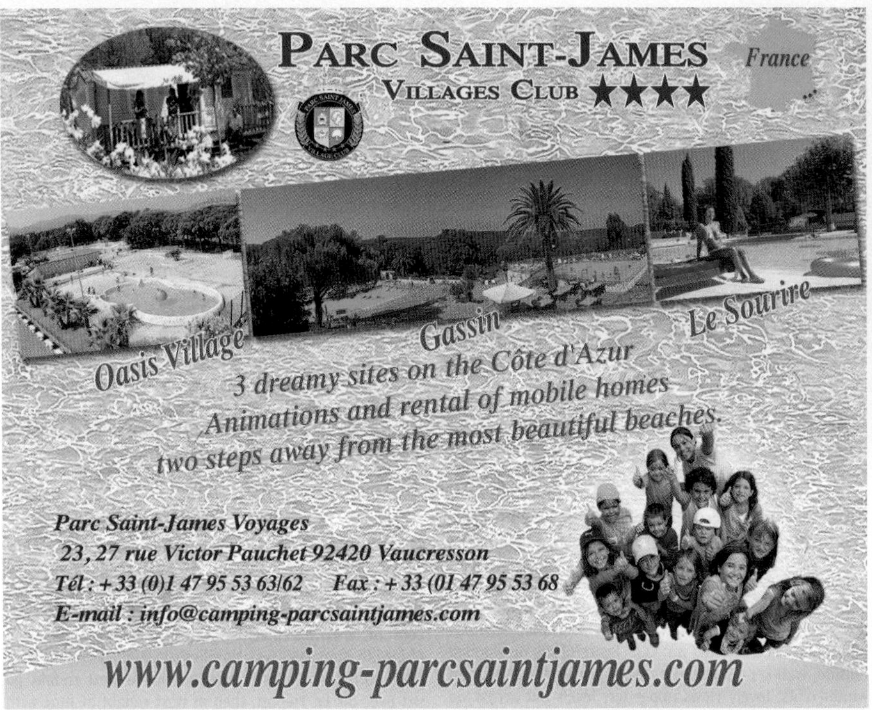

ST THEOFFREY *9C3* (E Rural) *44.99990, 5.77920* **FFCC Camping Ser-Sirant, Petichet, 38119 St Théoffrey [04 76 83 91 97; fax 04 76 30 83 69; campingsersirant@wanadoo.fr; www.euro-campsite.com]** N fr La Mure on N85 dir Grenoble. At traff lts in Petichet turn E, site on lakeside in 500m. Med, mkd pitch, pt terr, pt shd; wc; chem disp; mv service pnt; shwrs inc; el pnts (6-10A) €3-4.50; Indtte; shop 8km; tradsmn; rest 1km; snacks; sm playgrnd; lake sw & beach adj; watersports; dogs €1.50; phone; bus 1km; Eng spkn; adv bkg; quiet; CCI. "Gd site with views; most pitches req blocks; helpful owners; excel walking & cycling; highly rec." 1 May-Oct. € 16.90 2009*

ST THIBERY see Pézenas *10F1*

ST TROPEZ *10F4* (7km S Rural) *43.21442, 6.63914* **CAMPEOLE Camping La Croix du Sud, Loumède, Route des Plages, 83350 Ramatuelle [04 94 79 89 21; fax 04 94 79 89 21; croix-du-sud@campeole.com; www.camping-saint-tropez.com or www.campeole.com]** App St Tropez fr W on D98A, turn R at traff lts at W o'skts onto D93 sp Ramatuelle. Site on R in 7km opp filling stn. Med, mkd pitch, pt sl, terr, pt shd; wc; baby facs; shwrs; el pnts (6A) €4.10; gas; Indtte; shop; tradsmn; rest; snacks; playgrnd; htd pool; sand beach 1.7km; games area; entmnt; TV; 50% statics; dogs €3.90; poss cr; Eng spkn; quiet; red low ssn; CCI. "Sm pitches, access poss diff." 2 Apr-2 Oct. € 38.90 2009*

ST TROPEZ *10F4* (7km S Rural) *43.24092, 6.57404* **Parc Saint James Gassin, Route de Bourrian, 83580 Gassin [04 94 55 20 20; fax 04 94 56 34 77; gassin@camping-parcsaintjames.com; www.camping-parcsaintjames.com]** Exit A8 at junc 36 St Tropez; after Port-Grimaud foll sp Cavalaire-sur-Mer S on D559 where clearly sp. V lge, hdg/mkd pitch, hdstg, terr, pt shd; htd wc; shwrs inc; el pnts (6A) €5; Indtte; shop; rest; snacks; bar; BBQ; playgrnd; htd pool; paddling pool; spa/jacuzzi; beach 4km; tennis; games area; games rm; entmnt (child & adult); internet; golf 12km; 50% statics; dogs €5; phone; Eng spkn; adv bkg ess high ssn; quiet but some rd noise; ccard acc; red long stay/low ssn. "Conv St Tropez; scenic drives; vg." ♦ 9 Jan-20 Nov. € 33.00 2009*

See advertisement

ST TROPEZ *10F4* (7km S Coastal) *43.23198, 6.65924* **Riviera Villages Kon-Tiki, Plage de Pampelonne, 83350 Ramatuelle [04 94 55 96 96; fax 04 94 55 96 95; kontiki@riviera-villages.com; www.riviera-villages.com]** Foll Ramatuelle on D93 sp fr St Tropez; site sp on L. V lge, mkd pitch, pt sl, pt shd; wc; chem disp; baby facs; shwrs inc; el pnts (6A) inc; gas; Indtte; shop; rest; snacks; bar; playgrnd; sand beach adj; watersports; tennis; archery; entmnt; TV; mainly statics; dogs; poss cr; adv bkg ess high ssn; quiet; red low ssn; ccard acc; CCI. "Touring area sm & poss a bit unkempt end of ssn; some sm pitches; coastal walks; conv St Tropez & hill vills." 1 Apr-31 Oct. € 40.00 2009*

PRIVILEGE CAMPING TICKET
LE WALRIC
Present this Privilege camping ticket at reception and you will only pay 18€ per night for a pitch with electricity up to 3 persons.
Except in July and August.
Saint Valery sur Somme, season 2010
Suggested by: Camping Le Walric
Camping ★★★★ Le Walric Route d'eu
80230 Saint-Valéry-sur-somme
Tel.: 0033 80)322 268 197
Fax: 0033 80)322 607 726
www.campinglewalric.com
Open from
01/04 till 01/11

ST TROPEZ *10F4* (8km S Rural) *43.20596, 6.65083* **Yelloh! Village Les Tournels, Route de Camarat, 83350 Ramatuelle [04 94 55 90 90; fax 04 94 55 90 99; info@tournels.com; www.tournels.com or www.yellohvillage.com]** Exit A8 at Le Muy dir St Maxime, St Tropez. Take D61 dir Ramatuelle then foll sp 'La Plage' & Camarat lighthouse. V lge, mkd pitch, terr, shd; htd wc (some cont); chem disp; mv service pnt; some serviced pitches; sauna; shwrs inc; el pnts (5A) inc; gas; Indtte; shops; rest; snacks; bar; playgrnd; htd pool; paddling pool; sand beach 1.5km; (shuttle bus high ssn); tennis; games area; fitness rm; cycle hire; entmnt; TV; 90% statics; dogs €4; Eng spkn; adv bkg; quiet; ccard acc; red low ssn; CCI. "Peaceful site on wooded hillside; well-kept & well-run; lower pitches full long term winter o'fits; lovely views upper terr levels but access via steep, narr rd - poss diff long o'fits, mechanical help avail." 16 Mar-9 Jan. € 48.00 2009*

ST VAAST LA HOUGUE see Quettehou *1C4*

ST VALERY EN CAUX *3C2* (500m NE Coastal) *49.86838, 0.71636* **Camp Municipal Falaise d'Amont, Rue Traversière, 76460 St Valery-en-Caux [02 35 97 05 07; servicetourisme@ville-saint-valery-en-caux.fr]** SW fr Dieppe on D925 to St Valery-en-Caux; site sp on R off D925 500m fr town cent. App rd v steep, not rec lge o'fits - 18% gradient. Sm, mkd pitch, terr, unshd; htd wc; chem disp; shwrs inc; el pnts (6A) €2.15; Indtte; shop 1km; rest, bar 200m; playgrnd; shgl beach 500m; quiet; CCI. "Gd views; conv WW2 memorials; unsuitable towed c'vans due terrs." 16 Mar-15 Nov. € 6.00 2007*

⊞ **ST VALERY EN CAUX** *3C2* (SW Coastal) *49.85853, 0.70450* **Camp Municipal d'Etennemare, Rue Traversière, 76460 St Valery-en-Caux [tel/fax 02 35 97 15 79; servicetourisme@ville-saint-valery-en-caux.fr]** Fr Dieppe on D925 foll camping sp on ent town. Med, mkd pitch, pt shd; htd wc; chem disp; baby facs; shwrs inc; el pnts (10A) €2.15; Indtte; shop; tradsmn; rest 800m; playgrnd; htd pool & tennis in town; shgl beach; adv bkg; quiet; ccard acc; CCI. "Site poss clsd low ssn - phone to check; clean, tidy site." ♦ € 13.40 2006*

⊞ **ST VALERY EN CAUX** *3C2* (W Coastal) **Aire Communale, Plage Ouest, 76460 St Valery-en-Caux [02 35 97 00 63 or 02 35 97 00 63 (TO)]** Sp fr cent of St Valery-en-Caux along rv/seafront to harbour. Sm, chem disp; mv service pnt; water fill €3; el pnts €3; Indtte, shops, rests nr; phone; free parking for 48 hrs. M'vans only. "Rec arr early." € 3.00 2007*

ST VALERY SUR SOMME *3B2* (2km S Rural) *50.15333, 1.63583* **Camping Le Domaine du Château de Drancourt, 80230 Estréboeuf [03 22 26 93 45; fax 03 22 26 85 87; chateau.drancourt@wanadoo.fr; www.chateau-drancourt.com or www.les-castels.com]** Exit A28/E402 junc 1 at Abbeville onto D40 twd Noyelles-sur-Mer. At rndabt with D940 turn L sp St Valéry-sur-Somme. At next rndabt go strt over dir Le Tréport, then at next rndabt at junc with D48 take last exit (sp Estréboeuf), turn immed L & foll sps to site. NB.1-way system at recep area. Lge, mkd pitch, pt sl, pt shd; wc; chem disp; mv service pnt; baby facs; shwrs inc; el pnts (6A) inc (poss rev pol); gas; Indtte; shop; rest; snacks; bar; BBQ; playgrnd; 2 htd pools + paddling pool; sand beach 8km; fishing adj; watersports 2km; tennis; new games hall (for 2008); cycle hire; horseriding 12km; entmnt; 80% statics; dogs free; poss cr & noisy; Eng spkn; adv bkg; ccard acc; red low ssn; CCI. "Conv, busy, popular NH; friendly staff; red facs low ssn; chem disp long walk fr site; gd." ♦ 1 Apr-2 Nov. € 35.00 ABS - P06 2009*

ST VALERY SUR SOMME *3B2* (1km SW Urban/Coastal) *50.18331, 1.61786* **Camping Le Walric, Route d'Eu, 80230 St Valery-sur-Somme [03 22 26 81 97; fax 03 22 60 77 26; info@campinglewalric.com; www.campinglewalric.com]** Ringrd round St Valery D940 dir Le Tréport. Cont to 3rd rndabt (1st rndabt Carrefour supmkt on L) 3km & take 1st exit (R) sp St Valery & Cap Hornu D3. Site on R in 2km at ent to town sp. Lge, hdg/mkd pitch, pt shd; wc; chem disp; mv service pnt; baby facs; shwrs inc; el pnts (6A) inc; gas; Indtte; shop; tradsmn; bar; BBQ; playgrnd; htd pool; paddling pool; beaches nr; fishing; boat & cycle hire; tennis; games area; games rm; entmnt; 70% statics; dogs €3; phone; Eng spkn; adv bkg; quiet; ccard acc; red low ssn; CCI. "Well-kept, well-run site in excel location; excel clean facs; cycle rtes, canal track; steam train; delightful medieval town; mkt Sun; rec." ♦ 1 Apr-1 Nov. € 29.00 (3 persons) 2009*

See advertisement

ST VALERY SUR SOMME *3B2* (3km SW Rural) *50.17632, 1.58969* **Camping de la Baie, Routhiaville, 80230 Pendé [03 22 60 72 72]** Just off D940 twd Tréport, well sp. Sm, hdg pitch; wc (some cont); chem disp; shwrs inc; el pnts (6A) €2; lndtte; shop 2km; tradsmn; playgrnd; 95% statics; adv bkg; quiet; red low ssn; CCI. "Well-run, clean, tidy site & san facs; friendly, helpful owners; low trees in places need care; cycle rte to St Valery." Easter-15 Oct. € 15.00 2009*

ST VALERY SUR SOMME *3B2* (1km W Urban) *50.18447, 1.62263* **Camping de la Croix l'Abbé, Place de la Croix l'Abbé, 80230 St Valery-sur-Somme [03 22 60 81 46; w.a.georges@wanadoo.fr]** Ringrd round St Valery D940 dir Le Tréport. Cont to 2nd rndabt (1st rndabt Champion supmkt on L) 3km & take 1st exit (R) sp St Valery & Cap Hornu D3. Site 250m beyond Camping Le Walric. Lge, hdg/mkd pitch, pt sl, unshd; wc (some cont); chem disp; shwrs inc; el pnts (10A) inc; shop 1km; tradsmn; rest; snacks; bar; playgrnd; htd, covrd pool; sand/shgl beach 1km TV rm; 85% statics; bus adj; poss cr; Eng spkn; quiet. "San facs need update; gd location for walk to town; sh stay/NH only." 1 Apr-30 Nov. € 20.00 2009*

ST VALLIER *9C2* (400m N Rural) *45.18767, 4.81225* **Camp Municipal Les Iles de Silon, 26240 St Vallier [04 75 23 22 17 or 04 73 23 07 66]** On N7 just N of town, clearly sp in both dirs on rvside. Med, hdg pitch, pt shd; wc; chem disp; shwrs inc; el pnts (10A) €2.30 (poss long cable req); lndtte; shop & 500m; snacks; BBQ; playgrnd; pool 1km; watersports; tennis adj; some statics; dogs €1.30; Eng spkn; adv bkg; quiet but some rlwy noise; ccard acc; CCI. "Views over rv; friendly warden; immac facs; rec arr bef 1600 high ssn; c'vans over 5.50m not acc." ♦ 15 Mar-15 Nov. € 7.40 2009*

ST VALLIER *9C2* (5km W Rural) *45.17917, 4.73960* **Camping L'Oasis, Le Petit Chaléat, 07370 Eclassan [04 75 34 56 23; fax 04 75 34 47 94; oasis.camp@wanadoo.fr; www.oasisardeche.com]** Leave N7 at St Vallier, cross Rhône to Sarras. Then across D86 onto D6 sp St Jeure-d'Ay, in 7km turn R foll sp to site. App rd twisting & narr, many sharp bends & no passing places. Sm, hdg/mkd pitch, terr, pt shd, 80% serviced pitch; wc; chem disp; shwrs inc; el pnts (3-6A) €3.10-3.60; gas; lndtte; shop; tradsmn; rest; snacks; bar; playgrnd; pool; rv adj; archery; golf 10km; 20% statics; dogs €2; Eng spkn; adv bkg; quiet; ccard not acc; CCI. "Lovely setting by rv; tractor tow to pitch; not rec NH due diff app." 15 Apr-30 Sep. € 18.00 2006*

ST VALLIER DE THIEY see Grasse *10E4*

ST VARENT *4H1* (2km S Rural) *46.89741, -0.24147* **Camp Municipal La Grande Versenne, 79330 St Varent [05 49 67 62 11 (Mairie); fax 05 49 67 67 87; villestvarent@wanadoo.fr]** Site sp on D938 at Bouillé-St Varent. Sm, hdg pitch, pt shd; wc; baby facs; shwrs inc; el pnts (10A) €2.50; supmkt nr; playgrnd; rv nrby; no statics; dogs €0.50; adv bkg; quiet. "Friendly staff; gd NH." ♦ 1 Apr-31 Oct. € 9.50 2007*

ST VICTOR ET MELVIEU see St Rome de Tarn *8E4*

ST VINCENT DE BARRES *9D2* (5km N Rural) *44.69272, 4.71634* **FFCC Camp Municipal Les Civelles d'Ozon, 07210 St Lager-Bressac [04 75 65 01 86; fax 04 75 65 13 02; tour-a@wanadoo.fr; www.camping-ardeche-lescivelles.com]** S fr Privas on D2 dir Montélemar; site well sp on L. S fr Valence on N86; turn R onto D22; site sp to L, narr rd - or cont to rndabt, turn L onto D2 to Montélimar & as above. Sm, hdg/mkd pitch, pt sl, pt shd; serviced pitches; wc; chem disp; shwrs inc; el pnts (10A) inc (poss rev pol); lndtte; shops 3km; playgrnd; pools & paddling pool adj inc (Jul/Aug); tennis; games rm; dogs €2.50; adv bkg; quiet; red low ssn; CCI. "Helpful warden; rec arr early espec at w/e; popular NH; excel." ♦ 1 Apr-30 Sep. € 17.00 2008*

France

ST VINCENT DE BARRES *9D2* (1km SW Rural) *44.65659, 4.69330* **Camping Le Rieutord, 07210 St Vincent-de-Barrès [04 75 65 07 73; moncamping@wanadoo.fr; www.ardeche-sud-camping.com]** Fr N exit A7 junc 16 Loriol onto D104 (N304) & foll sp Le Pouzin then Chomérac (do not foll 1st sp St Vincent-de-Barrès - narr rd). At rndabt foll D2 dir Le Teil-Montélimar for 6km. When arr at St Vincent (vill on L), turn R & foll site sp for 1.5km. Fr S exit junc 18 Montélimar Sud, foll sps Montélimar then Privas. Cross Rv Rhône, go thro Rochemaure sp Privas. At Meysse turn L after bdge dir Privas. Foll D2 for 4.5km then turn L dir St Bauzile to site in 3km. Med, hdg pitch, pt sl, pt shd; htd wc; shwrs inc; el pnts (16A) €3; lndtte; shop; snacks; bar; cooking facs; playgrnd; pool; paddling pool; waterslide; games area; some statics; €2; no c'vans over 6m or twin-axles; Eng spkn; adv bkg; quiet CCI. "Tranquil site in beautiful setting nr old walled town; pleasant owners; gd touring base." 28 Apr-30 Sep. € 15.00 2006*

ST VINCENT DE COSSE see Sarlat la Canéda *7C3*

ST VINCENT DE PAUL see Dax *8E1*

ST VINCENT LES FORTS *9D3* (1km N Rural) *44.45682, 6.36529* **CAMPEOLE Camping Le Lac, Le Fein, 04340 St Vincent-les-Forts [04 92 85 51 57; fax 04 92 85 57 63; lac@campeole.com; www.campeole.com]**
W fr Barcelonnette on D900/D900b, past St Vincent-les-Forts dir Le Lautaret. Turn R onto D7 & foll winding rd to end, site sp o'looking lake. Lge, mkd pitch, terr, sl, pt shd; wc; chem disp; mv service pnt; baby facs; shwrs inc; el pnts (6A) €4.10; lndtte (inc dryer); shop; tradsmn; rest; snacks; bar; BBQ; playgrnd; pool; paddling pool; lake sw & beach 500m; fishing; watersports; tennis; horseriding; games area; games rm; wifi; child entmnt; 30% statics; dogs €3.50; phone; Eng spkn; adv bkg; quiet; ccard acc; red low ssn; CCI. "Superb, scenic location; many leisure activities; vg walking in area; vg, simple site." ♦
30 Apr-26 Sep. € 22.50 2009*

See advertisement on next page

ST VINCENT SUR JARD see Jard sur Mer *7A1*

ST YORRE *9A1* (500m SW Rural) *46.06056, 3.46014* **Camping Les Gravières, Rue de la Gravière, 03270 St Yorre [04 70 59 21 00 or 06 27 35 14 26 (mob); fax 04 70 59 20 09; camping-st-yorre@orange.fr; www.camping-vichy.com]** Fr A71 exit junc 12 sp Gannat. At Bellerive turn R onto D131 sp Hauterive. L over bdge to St Yorre. Foll camping sp. C'vans banned fr St Yorre town cent. Med, hdg pitch, pt shd; wc (some cont); chem disp; baby facs; shwrs inc; el pnts (4-10A) inc; dry rm; shops 1km; tradsmn; snacks; BBQ; playgrnd; pool & sports cent adj; fishing; games area; dogs; phone adj; adv bkg; quiet; CCI. "Gd touring base." ♦ 1 May-30 Sep. € 14.70 2008*

ST YRIEIX LA PERCHE *7B3* (1.7km N Rural) *45.52793, 1.20021* **Camping Plan d'Eau d'Arfeuille, 87500 St Yrieix-la-Perche [05 55 75 08 75; fax 05 55 75 26 08; camping@saint-yrieix.fr]** Site well sp on L on D704 fr St Yrieix-la-Perche N dir Limoges. Med, hdg pitch, terr, pt shd; htd wc; chem disp; mv service pnt; baby facs; shwrs; el pnts (10A) inc; lndtte (inc dryer); rest; bar; playgrnd; pool; waterslide; lake sw & beach adj; fishing; canoeing; games area; entmnt; adv bkg; quiet. "Pleasant situation; friendly staff." 1 Jun-15 Sep. € 12.40 2009*

⊞ **ST YRIEIX LA PERCHE** *7B3* (8km W Rural) *45.55460, 1.11867* **FFCC Camping Les Vigères, 87500 Le Chalard [05 55 09 37 22; fax 05 55 09 93 39; infovigeres@aol.com; www.lesvigeres.com]** Take N20 to Limoges then N704 to St Yrieix. In St Yrieix turn W on D901 to Châlus. 1st vill is Le Chalard & site is 1km after vill. Sm, hdg/mkd pitch, pt shd; wc; chem disp; shwrs inc; el pnts (3-10A) €3-4; lndtte; shops 2km; BBQ; playgrnd; pool; lake sw & sand beach adj; fishing; library; adv bkg; v quiet; 10% red low ssn; CCI. "Vg, peaceful site; welcoming British owners; clean san facs, ltd low ssn; poss unkempt low ssn; historic area; rec." ♦ € 14.50 2009*

ST YRIEIX LA PERCHE *7B3* (12km NW Rural) *45.59175, 1.11131* **Camp Municipal de Bel Air, 87500 Ladignac-le-Long [05 55 09 39 82 or 05 55 09 30 02 (Mairie); fax 05 55 09 39 80; camping-ladignac@wanadoo.fr; www.ladignac.com]** Exit Limoges S on N21 to Châlus. Turn E on D901 sp St Yrieix to Ladignac. Turn N to lakes at sp. Site on R. Med, pt shd, hdg pitch; wc; chem disp; mv service pnt; shwrs inc; el pnts (6A) €2.65; lndtte; shop & 1km; tradsmn; playgrnd; lake sw 500m; games/TV rm; 10% statics; dogs; phone; no twin-axles; Eng spkn; adv bkg; quiet; red low ssn; CCI. "Beautiful lakeside site; spacious pitches; clean san facs; barrier with card operation - early ssn apply to Mairie in vill sq for card; cycling; walking; excel." 1 May-31 Oct. € 10.40 2008*

ST YRIEIX SUR CHARANTE see Angouleme *7B2*

SALBRIS *4G3* (500m NE Urban) *47.43055, 2.05461* **Camping de Sologne, 8 Allée de la Sauldre, Route de Pierrefitte, 41300 Salbris [02 54 97 06 38; fax 02 54 97 33 13; campingdesologne@wanadoo.fr; www.campingdesologne.com]** Exit A71 junc 4; take D724 bypass, then take D2020 (N20) N (Do not take D724 into town); turn E onto D55 (Route de Pierrefitte); Impasse de la Sauldre leading to Allée de la Sauldre is 2nd turning on R in 200m (narr & easy to miss). Med, hdg/mkd pitch, pt shd; wc; chem disp; baby facs; shwrs inc; el pnts (10A) inc (some rev pol); gas; lndtte; shop 200m; hypmkt 1km; rest; snacks; bar high ssn; playgrnd; lake adj; fishing; boat hire; karting 6km; TV rm; 25% statics; dogs €1; phone; poss cr; Eng spkn; adv bkg; some noise fr rlwy, rd & motor circuit; ccard acc; red low ssn; CCI. "Excel, well-kept site in pleasant lakeside location; friendly, helpful owners; gd san facs poss stretched if site busy & ltd low ssn; poss scruffy early ssn (2009); gd rest; gd dog walks adj; conv NH." ♦ 1 Apr-30 Sep. € 17.00 2009*

SALERNES *10F3* (4km E Rural) *43.55360, 6.29781* **Camping Club Le Ruou, Les Esparrus, 83690 Villecroze-les-Grottes [04 94 70 67 70; fax 04 94 70 64 65; camping.leruou@wanadoo.fr; www.leruou.com]** Fr Draguignan take D557 thro Flayosc, then D560 dir Salernes. Site sp on L. Med, mkd pitch, terr, shd; htd wc; chem disp; mv service pnt; baby facs; el pnts (6-10A) €3.50-5.50; gas; lndtte; shop; rest; snacks; bar; BBQ: playgrnd; htd pool; paddling pool; waterslide; fishing; games area; archery; games/TV rm; adv bkg; 35% statics; dogs €2.70; adv bkg; quiet. ♦
1 Apr-31 Oct. € 25.20 (CChq acc) 2008*

SALERNES *10F3* (W Rural) *43.56606, 6.22561* **Camp Municipal Les Arnauds, 83690 Salernes [04 94 67 51 95; fax 04 94 70 75 57; lesarnauds@ville-salernes.fr; www.ville-salernes.fr]** W fr Draguignan on D557 thro Salernes; site sp on L on W o'skts of town; to avoid town cent turn R at rndabt on E o'skts sp Villecroze; take 1st L at next 2 rndabts & foll site sp. Med, hdg/mkd pitch, pt shd; wc; chem disp; baby facs; shwrs; el pnts (10A) inc; lndtte; bar; playgrnd; rv sw adj; tennis; dogs €1.80; Eng spkn; adv bkg; quiet; red low ssn; CCI. "Excel, rvside site & san facs; warm welcome; gd night lighting; some sm pitches poss diff lge o'fits; no twin-axles; no entry 1200-1500; take torch into shwrs, lights on sh time switch." 2 May-30 Sep. € 22.55 2006*

SALERNES *10F3* (5km NW Rural) *43.57302, 6.18816* **Camping Le Relais de la Bresque, Chemin de la Piscine, 83690 Sillans-la-Cascade [04 94 04 64 89; fax 04 94 77 19 54; info@lerelaisdelabresque.com; www.lerelaisdelabresque.com]** Fr W on D560 to Sillans-la-Cascade & take D22 N to site, 1.5km on R. Med, shd, mkd pitch; htd wc; chem disp; shwrs inc; el pnts (5-10A) €3-5; lndtte; ltd shop; tradsmn; rest; takeaway; bar; playgrnd; pool; rv 1.5km; cycle hire; horseriding; archery, fitness course; games area; games rm; entmnt; wifi; TV; 65% statics; dogs €2; Eng spkn; quiet; adv bkg rec; red low ssn. "Well-run, clean site; lovely walk to vill; unreliable opening dates - phone ahead low ssn." 1 Apr-27 Oct. € 20.00 2008*

SALERS *7C4* (800m NE Rural) *45.14756, 2.49857* **Camp Municipal Le Mouriol, Route de Puy-Mary, 15410 Salers [04 71 40 73 09 or 04 71 40 72 33 (Mairie); fax 04 71 40 76 28]** Take D922 SE fr Mauriac dir Aurillac; turn onto D680 E dir Salers; site 1km NE of Salers on D680 dir Puy Mary, opp Hôtel Le Gerfaut; sp fr all dir. Med, hdg/mkd pitch, sl, pt shd, wc (some cont); chem disp; shwrs inc; el pnts (16A) inc (long lead poss req); lndtte; shops, rest, snacks & bar 1km; BBQ; playgrnd; tennis; hill-walking; dogs; bus 1km; phone; poss cr; no adv bkg; quiet; 10% red 10 days; CCI. "Generous pitches; san facs stretched if site full; peaceful low ssn; excel cycling & walking; beautiful medieval vill; vg." ♦ 15 May-15 Oct. € 16.40 2009*

SALERS *7C4* (800m W Rural) **Camping à la Ferme (Fruquière), Apcher, 15140 Salers [04 71 40 72 26]** D922 S fr Mauriac for 17km; L on D680 sp Salers; in lane on R sp Apcher - immed after passing Salers town sp. Sm, pt shd; wc (some cont), chem disp (wc); shwrs inc; el pnts (10A) €2.20; shop 300m; dogs; poss cr; quiet; CCI. "Sm farm site; gd." 1 May-30 Sep. € 8.60 2008*

SALERS *7C4* (7km W Rural) *45.11625, 2.42343* **Camp Municipal Les Moulin du Teinturier, 9 Rue de Montjoly,15140 St Martin-Valmeroux [04 71 69 43 12 or 04 71 69 20 32 (Mairie); fax 04 71 69 24 52; mairie.saint-martin-valmeroux@wanadoo.fr]** Fr Mauriac S on D922; sp on D37 E; 500m on L on Rv Maronne. Med, hdg pitch, pt shd; wc; serviced pitch; shwrs; el pnts (6A) €2.70; lndtte; shop; rest; BBQ; playgrnd; rv fishing; walking; tennis, horseriding & pool adj; TV; quiet. "Site on Rv Maronne; gd walking; ideal exploring Auvergne."♦ 15 Jun-15 Sep. € 10.20 2008*

SALIES DE BEARN *8F1* (2km NW Urban) *43.47639, -0.9382* **Camp Municipal de Mosquéros, Ave Al Cartéro, 64270 Salies-de-Béarn [05 59 38 12 94; mairie-salies@wanadoo.fr]** Leave A64 at exit 7 onto D430 S sp Salies de Béarn. After 500m take D330 on R sp 'Casino' & turn R onto D17 at rndabt. Site sp in town, on D17 Bayonne rd NW of town. Site next to 'Base Plein Aire des Mosquéros'. NB Avoid town - narr streets & diff when busy. Med, hdg/mkd pitch, pt sl, terr, pt shd; wc; chem disp; shwrs inc; el pnts inc (10A) inc; lndtte; shops 2km; rest, snacks, bar 1km; pool, sports facs adj; fishing 1km; golf 2km; horseriding 3km; TV; quiet; "Excel site; excel serviced pitches; helpful warden; old but clean san facs; levelling blocks req some pitches; poss diff lge o'fits; barrier clsd 2200-0700; mkt Thu." ♦
15 Mar-15 Oct. € 14.30 2009*

SALIES DU SALAT *8F3* (2km S Rural) *43.07621, 0.94683* **Complex Touristique de la Justale, Chemin de St Jean, 31260 Mane [05 61 90 68 18; fax 05 61 97 40 18; contact@village-vacances-mane.fr; www.village-vacances-mane.fr]** Fr A64 exit 20 onto D117, turn R in vill at sp 'Village de Vacances'. Site on R in approx 500m. Sm, pt shd; wc; chem disp; mv service pnt; shwrs inc; el pnts (6A) €2.30 (poss rev pol); lndtte; shops 500m; playgrnd; pool; fishing; tennis; horseriding; internet; TV rm; dogs €1.20; phone' adv bkg. "Lovely, peaceful site; lge pitches; helpful staff; excel facs." 1 Apr-31 Oct. € 11.60 2009*

SALIGNAC EYVIGNES see Sarlat la Canéda *7C3*

SALINS LES BAINS *6H2* (500m N Rural) *46.94650, 5.87896* **Camp Municipal, 39110 Salins-les-Bains [03 84 37 92 70; campingsalins.kanak.fr]** SE fr Besançon on N83. At Mouchard take D472 E to Salins. Turn L at rndabt at N of Salins, well sp nr old stn. If app fr E take 2nd exit fr rndabt (blind app). Sm, pt shd; wc; shwrs inc; el pnts (10A) inc; lndry rm; supmkt 500m; playgrnd; htd pool adj; adv bkg; quiet but some rd noise at 1 end & primary school at other. "Well-run site; clean, modern san facs; excel touring base N Jura; not often visited by British; far end of site quieter; gd NH." ♦ 1 Apr-30 Sep. € 15.80 2009*

France

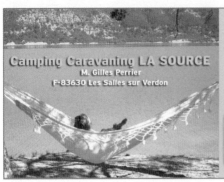

SALLANCHES *9A3* (2km SE Rural) *45.92470, 6.65528* **Camping Miroir du Mont Blanc, 1213 Chemin de Mont-Blanc-Plage, 74700 Sallanches [04 50 58 14 28 or 04 50 58 12 04 (LS); fax 04 50 93 95 23; beatrice.brosse2@wanadoo.fr]** Fr Geneva on D1205 (N205) into Sallanches. Take 1st L after 2nd set of traff lts (by post office) sp 'Hôpital'. Foll rd thro traff lits & over rndabt when rd turns sharp R & runs alongside m'way. In 2km site ent on R beside rndabt. Or exit A41 junc 21 or 22 dir Lac de Passy, site sp. Med, mkd pitch, shd; wc; shwrs inc; el pnts (6A) €2.50; gas 2km; lndry rm; shops 2km; tradsmn; rest; snacks; bar; playgrnd; pool & paddling pool 200m; waterslide; lake sw & sand/shgl beach adj; tennis; fishing; sailing; windsurfing 50m; entmnt; adv bkg rec; rd noise; red low ssn. "Situated bet m'way & rlwy." 15 May-15 Sep. € 13.00 2009*

SALLANCHES *9A3* (2km SE Rural) *45.92723, 6.64710* **Camping Mont Blanc Village L'Ecureuil, 490 Route des Follieux, 74700 Sallanches [04 50 58 43 67; fax 04 50 58 44 61; contact@camping-ecureuil.com; www.camping-ecureuil.com]** App fr Chamonix on D1205 (N205), turn R opp Ford g'ge ent Sallanches; strt on thro traff lts, over sleeping policemen, under rlwy bdge & fork R at Braconne rest; strt at next junc to site in 200m. Med, shd; wc; chem disp; mv service pnt; shwrs inc; el pnts (10A) €2.50; gas; lndtte (inc dryer); shops 1km; tradsmn; rest (not every day); bar; playgrnd; pool nr; lake sw & sand/shgl beach; games area; games rm; TV; some statics; dogs €1; poss cr; quiet; ccard acc; red low ssn; CCI. "Gd, clean, spacious site; mountain views; well drained after rain; excel." Easter-15 Oct. € 15.60 2009*

SALLANCHES *9A3* (4km SE Rural) *45.92388, 6.65042* **Camping des Iles, 245 Chemin de la Cavettaz, 74190 Passy [04 50 58 45 36 or 04 99 57 21 21; www.village-center.com]** On D1205 (N205) dir Chamonix t turn L (1st into filter to turn L) onto D199 3km after Sallanches. Turn L immed bef level x-ing. Site at end of rd. Lge, hdg/mkd pitch, pt shd; wc (some cont); baby facs; shwrs inc; el pnts (8A) inc; lndtte; shop & 3km; snacks; playgrnd; htd pool; shgl lake beach & sw adj; fishing; entmnt; statics; dogs €3; phone; Eng spkn; adv bkg; quiet; ccard acc high ssn; CCI. "Mountain views; conv Chamonix; vg site." ♦ 2 Jun-16 Sep. € 18.00 2007*

SALLELES D'AUDE see Narbonne *10F1*

SALLES (GIRONDE) *7D1* (Urban) *44.54475, -0.87506* **FFCC Camping Parc du Val de l'Eyre, 8 Route du Minoy, 33770 Salles [05 56 88 47 03; fax 05 56 88 47 27; levaldeleyre2@wanadoo.fr; www.valdeleyre.com]** Exit junc 21 fr A63, foll dir to Salles on D3. On edge of Salles turn L on D108 at x-rds. Ent to site on L after rv opp Champion supmkt building. Lge, pt shd; wc; chem disp; mv service pnt; baby facs; shwrs inc; el pnts (6A) inc (poss rev pol); gas; lndtte; shops adj; supmkt nr; rest; snacks; bar; BBQ; playgrnd; sports area; lake & rv sw; fishing; canoeing; tennis 500km; horseriding 8km; entmnt; dogs €2.80; quiet but entmnt poss noisy; ccard acc; red low ssn. "Attractive site; gd san facs but poss stretched when site busy." ♦ 1 Apr-30 Sep. € 26.80 2008*

SALLES (GIRONDE) *7D1* (8km S Rural) *44.45244, -0.94505* **Camping La Cypréa, 33830 Lugos [05 57 71 93 30]** S fr Bordeaux on N10 to cent Belin-Béliet; turn R onto D110; camp sp on wall facing you; stay on this rd thro pine forest. Camp on L just bef sp for Lugos (Gare). Sm, pt shd; wc; mv service pnt; shwrs €1; el pnts inc (2A) €2.50; lndtte; tradsmn; playgrnd; pool; games area; no dogs; quiet; CCI. "Friendly owner; lovely sm pool." 1 Jul-1 Sep. € 10.00 2006*

⊞ **SALLES (GIRONDE)** *7D1* (4km SW Rural) *44.52039, -0.89631* **Camping Le Bilos, 37 Route de Bilos, 33770 Salles [05 56 88 45 14 or 05 56 88 36 53; fax 05 56 88 45 14; http://lebilos.com]** Exit A63 junc 21. Foll sp Salles on D3. Turn L onto D108/D108E3 sp Lanot, pass Carrefour supmkt on R; in 2km bear R & site on R in 2km. Med, pt shd; htd wc; chem disp; shwrs inc; el pnts (3-10A) €2.50.30; gas; lndtte; shop; supmkt 2.5km; BBQ sep area; playgrnd; 80% statics; dogs; adv bkg; quiet. "Pleasant, peaceful site in pine forest; sm, well-drained pitches; ltd space for tourers; friendly owners; vg NH en rte Spain; old but clean san facs, ltd low ssn; cycle lane thro forest." € 7.90 2009*

SALLES CURAN *8E4* (2km NW Rural) *44.18933, 2.76693* **Camping Les Genêts, Lac de Pareloup, 12410 Salles-Curan [05 65 46 35 34 or 05 65 42 06 46; fax 05 65 78 00 72; contact@camping-les-genets.fr; www.camping-les-genets.fr]** Fr D911 Rodez-Millau rd take D993 S for approx 9km, then R onto D577, site sp on R by lake. Lge, pt sl, shd; wc; shwrs; el pnts (6A) inc; lndtte; shop; rest; pizzeria; bar; htd pool; cycle hire; sailing; fishing; lake sw & beach; 40% statics; dogs €4; adv bkg; red long stay/low ssn. "Beautiful area; ltd facs low ssn." ♦ 25 May-12 Sep. € 33.00 (CChq acc) 2008*

SALLES LAVAUGUYON, LES see Rochechouart *7B3*

SALLES SUR VERDON, LES *10E3* (N Rural) *43.78129, 6.21298* **Camp Municipal Les Ruisses, 83630 Les Salles-sur-Verdon [04 98 10 28 15; fax 04 98 10 28 16; lesruissescamping@orange.fr; www.sallessurverdon.com]** Fr Moustiers foll D957, site on L just bef Les Salles. Lge, mkd pitch, pt shd; wc (some cont); baby facs; shwrs inc; el pnts (6A) €3.20; lndtte; shop, snacks, bar high ssn; playgrnd; shgl beach & lake nr; fishing; dogs €1.15; no adv bkg; quiet; ccard acc; CCI. "Pleasant site; ltd facs low ssn but gd hot shwrs & clean facs." ♦ 15 Feb-15 Nov. € 11.05 2009*

SALLES SUR VERDON, LES *10E3* (2km E Rural) *43.77574, 6.24561* **FFCC Camping L'Aigle, Quartier St Pierre, 83630 Aiguines [tel/fax 04 94 84 23 75; contact@camping-aigle.fr; www.camping-aigle.fr]** Fr D957 fr Les Salles or Moustiers turn onto D19 & cont for approx 7km. Site sp 1km beyond vill. Rd steep, winding & with hairpins & vill narr for lge o'fits. Med, sl, terr, pt shd; wc; mv service pnt; baby facs; shwrs inc; el pnts (2-10A) €2.50-3.70; lndtte; shops, rest 300m; BBQ; playgrnd; ent barrier; dogs €1.70; phone; Eng spkn; quiet; ccard acc; CCI. "Lake views; clean, modern facs; steep, twisting access to terr pitches poss diff lge o'fits; highly rec." Easter-30 Sep. € 12.00 2006*

SALLES SUR VERDON, LES *10E3* (3km E Rural) *43.79653, 6.24315* **Camp Municipal Le Galetas, Quartier Vernis, 83630 Aiguines [tel/fax 04 94 70 20 48; campinglegaletas@aol.com; www.aiguines.com/galetas.html]** Fr S foll D957 twd Moustiers-Ste Marie then take D71 to Aguines & foll sp. Lge, pt shd; wc; chem disp; mv service pnt; shwrs inc; el pnts (6A) €2.50; lndtte; shop; snacks; bar; lake sw; watersports; some statics; dogs €1; quiet. "Views of lake." 1 Apr-15 Oct. € 14.60 2008*

SALLES SUR VERDON, LES *10E3* (500m W Rural) *43.77552, 6.20719* **Camping La Source, Lac de Sainte Croix, Quartier Margaridon, 83630 Les Salles-sur-Verdon [04 94 70 20 40; fax 04 94 70 20 74; contact@camping-la-source.eu; www.camping-la-source.eu]** Fr Moustiers on D957, foll sp Camping Les Pins (adj) via rd round vill. Med, hdg/mkd pitch, hdstg, pt terr; pt shd; wc (some cont); chem disp; child/baby facs; serviced pitches; shwrs inc; el pnts (10A) €3.60 (poss rev pol); gas; lndtte; shop, rest, snacks, bar 500m; BBQ; playgrnd; dir access to lake; lake sw & shgl beach adj; watersports; canoe hire; TV rm; dogs €2; phone; Eng spkn; adv bkg; quiet; ccard acc; red low ssn; CCI. "Excel facs; superb situation; well-run site conv Gorges du Verdon; friendly, helpful owners; gates clsd 2200-0700; some sm pitches - manhandling poss req; highly rec." ♦ 1 Apr-10 Oct. € 16.90 2009*

See advertisement

SALLES SUR VERDON, LES *10E3* (500m W Rural) *43.77628, 6.2090* **Camping Les Pins, Lac de Sainte Croix, 83630 Les Salles-sur-Verdon [04 98 10 23 80; fax 04 94 84 23 27; camping.les.pins@wanadoo.fr; www.campinglespins.com]** Fr Moustiers on D957 to Les Salles-sur-Verdon. Site clearly sp in vill on lakeside, via track round vill. Med, hdg/mkd pitch, hdstg, terr, pt shd; wc; chem disp; mv service pnt; serviced pitches; baby facs; shwrs inc; el pnts (6A) inc; gas; lndtte; shop 200m, tradsmn; bar; playgrnd; shgl beach & lake sw 200m; fishing; canoe hire; watersports; dogs €1.80; Eng spkn; adv bkg; quiet; ccard acc; red low ssn/CCI. "Lovely views; gd touring base; excel, friendly site." ♦ 1 Apr-17 Oct. € 21.80 2008*

SALON DE PROVENCE *10E2* (12km SE) *43.72125, 5.20495* **FFCC Camping Durance et Luberon, Domaine du Vergon, 13370 Mallemort [04 90 59 13 36; fax 04 90 57 46 62; duranceluberon@aol.com; www.campingduranceluberon.com]** Fr Salon take N538 (N) for approx 6km; turn E onto D17/D23 twd Mallemort; go strt at N7 rnabt, into Mallemort cent; site sp fr there. Med, hdg/mkd pitch, pt shd; wc (some cont); chem disp (wc); mv service pnt; shwrs inc; el pnts inc (6-10A) €3-3.60; gas; lndtte; sm shop & 3km; tradsmn; rest adj; snacks; bar; BBQ; playgrnd; htd pool; paddling pool; tennis; cycle hire; horseriding adj; rv fishing 1km; 5% statics; dogs €1.70; phone; Eng spkn; adv bkg; quiet; 10% red long stays; ccard not acc; CCI. "Lge pitches; clean, modern san facs; friendly owners; gd touring base; excel." 1 Apr-15 Oct. € 17.00 2006*

SALON DE PROVENCE *10E2* (5km NW Rural) *43.67820, 5.06480* **Camping Nostradamus, Route d'Eyguières, 13300 Salon-de-Provence [04 90 56 08 36; fax 04 90 56 65 05; gilles.nostra@orange.fr; www.camping-nostradamus.com]** Exit A54/E80 junc 13 onto D569 N sp Eyguières. After approx 1.5km turn R opp airfield onto D72d, site on R in approx 4km just bef T-junc. Or fr N exit A7 junc 26 dir Salon-de-Provence. Turn R onto D17 for 5km dir Eyguières, then L onto D72, site on L. Med, hdg/mkd pitch, pt shd; wc; chem disp; mv service pnt; baby facs; shwrs inc; el pnts (4-6A) €2.95-5.40; gas; lndtte; shop; tradsmn; rest; snacks; bar; BBQ; playgrnd; pool; paddling pool; games area; entmnt; wifi; TV; 15% statics; dogs €2.80; phone; Eng spkn; adv bkg (bkg fee); quiet; ccard acc; red low ssn; CCI. "Pleasant site; welcoming owner with vg sense of humour!; san facs dated & poor (Apr 2008); poss diff access for lge o'fits; gd walking." ♦ 1 Mar-30 Oct. € 17.10 (CChq acc) 2008*

SALORNAY SUR GUYE see Cluny *9A2*

⊞ **SALSES LE CHATEAU** *10G1* (1km N Rural) *42.84420, 2.92778* **FFCC Camp International du Roussillon, 66600 Salses-le-Château [04 68 38 60 72; fax 04 68 52 75 46; camping-roussillon@orange.fr; www.camping-roussillon.com]** Fr N on A9 exit junc 40 on D6009/D900 (N9) dir Perpignan; site on R, N of town. Fr S exit A9 junc 41. Site has hotel, rest & camping. Med, hdg pitch, hdstg, pt shd; wc; chem disp; shwrs inc; el pnts (5-6A) €3 (poss rev pol); gas; lndtte; shops 2km; tradsmn; rest; snacks; pizza adj low ssn; bar; BBQ (no elec); playgrnd; pool; 40% statics; dogs €3; phone; Eng spkn; adv bkg; some rd & rlwy noise; red long stay; ccard acc; CCI. "Helpful, friendly owners; red facs low ssn & poss unkempt pitches; gd access for lge m'vans; mosquitoes; popular NH." ♦ € 22.00 2009*

SALVETAT SUR AGOUT, LA *8F4* (N Rural) *43.60321, 2.70310* **Camping de la Blaquière, Route de Lacaune, 34330 La Salvetat-sur-Agout [tel/fax 04 67 97 61 29 or 04 67 24 71 08; jerome@campingblaquiere.com; www.blaquiere.fr.st]** Fr Lacaune S on D607 to site in La Salvetat. Sp on ent to vill. Fr S heading N on D907 foll site sps thro vill, site on L on rvside just after sm supmkt. Med, mkd pitch, shd; wc; chem disp (wc); baby facs; shwrs inc; el pnts €2.80; ice lndtte; shop, rest etc in vill; BBQ; playgrnd; rv sw adj; lake sw, fishing, watersports 3km; tennis; horseriding; 5% statics; adv bkg; quiet; CCI. "Spectacular scenery; friendly owner." 1 Jun-31 Aug. € 9.50 2006*

SALVETAT SUR AGOUT, LA *8F4* (4km N Rural) *43.62739, 2.67919* **Camping Goudal, Route de Lacaune, La Gâche, 34330 La Salvetat-sur-Agout [04 67 97 60 44; fax 04 67 97 62 68; info@goudal.com; www.goudal.com]** Fr St Pons-de-Thomières take D907 N dir Lacaune. Go thro La Salvetat, site sp. Med, mkd pitch, pt sl, terr, pt shd; wc; chem disp; mv service pnt; baby facs; shwrs inc; el pnts (4-6A) €4; gas; lndtte; shop; rest high ssn; BBQ; playgrnd; entmnt; some statics; dogs €2; poss cr; Eng spkn; adv bkg; quiet; CCI. "Friendly Dutch owners; spacious site in woodland; vg." 1 May-30 Sep. € 17.35 2009*

SALVETAT SUR AGOUT, LA *8F4* (10km E Rural) *43.60653, 2.77940* **Camping Le Pioch, 34330 Fraisse-sur-Agout [04 67 97 61 72; NICO-OUDHOF@wanadoo.fr; www.lepioch.nl/fr/]** Fr Salvetat take D14 E twd Fraisse-sur-Agout. In 6km look for sp on L (2km bef Fraise). Site is up narr, steep rd but with passing places. Med, pt sl, pt shd; wc; shwrs inc; el pnts (6A) €2.50; gas; lndtte; shop; tradsmn; rest; snacks; bar; BBQ; playgrnd; dogs €1.50; Eng spkn; adv bkg; quiet; CCI. "Excel walking area; views fr site." 1 May-30 Sep. € 12.50 2009*

When we get home I'm going to post all these site report forms to the Club for next year's guide. The deadline's September.

SAMOENS *9A3* (5km SE Rural) *46.07392, 6.83768* **Camp Municipal Le Pelly, 74740 Sixt-Fer-à-Cheval [04 50 34 12 17; fax 04 50 89 51 02; mairie@sixtferacheval.com]** Take D907 NE fr Sixt. Site sp on R after 6km bef bdge over Rv Giffre. Med, pt sl, pt shd; wc; chem disp; shwrs inc; el pnts (10A) €2.90; lndry rm; tradsmn; shop & 6km; snacks; bar; BBQ; playgrnd; horseriding 500m; dogs €1.55; phone; quiet. "Gd walking; alpine flowers & wildlife; helpful wardens." 1 Jun-10 Sep. € 8.50 2006*

⊞ **SAMOENS** *9A3* (750m S Rural) *46.07731, 6.71851* **Camping Caravaneige Le Giffre, La Glière, 74340 Samoëns [04 50 34 41 92; fax 04 50 34 98 84; camping@samoens.com; www.camping-samoens.com]** Leave A40 at junc 15 sp Fillinges/St Jeoire. Foll D907 thro Taninges E for 11km, sp Samoëns. At W town boundary turn R immed after wooden arch over rd, foll sp to Parc des Loisirs. Site on R after sw pool & park. Lge, mkd pitch, pt shd; htd wc (few cont); chem disp; shwrs inc; el pnts (6-10A) €3-4.50; gas 3km; lndtte; shops 750m; tradsmn; rest, snacks adj; playgrnd; htd pool adj; fishing lake adj; drying rm; htd ski storage rm; Samoëns ski gondola 150m; tennis; 5% statics; dogs €2; phone; poss cr; adv bkg ess high ssn; quiet; ccard acc; red CCI. "Friendly staff; some facs ltd low ssn; on arr, park on rdside bef checking in; excel winter site." € 17.90 (CChq acc) 2008*

⊞ **SAMOENS** *9A3* (5km W Rural) *46.08944, 6.67874* **Camp Municipal Lac et Montagne, 74440 Verchaix [04 50 90 10 12; fax 04 50 54 39 60]** Fr Taninges take D907 sp Samoëns for 6km, site to R of main rd in Verchaix. Med, shd; shwrs; el pnts (10A) €7.40; lndtte; shops nr; rest, bar adj; playgrnd; rv & lake adj; tennis; some statics; adv bkg; quiet. "Gd touring base." ♦ € 8.30 2007*

SAMOREAU see Fontainebleau *4E3*

SAMPZON see Vallon Pont d'Arc *9D2*

SANARY SUR MER *10F3* (4km NE Urban) *43.13147, 5.81483* **Campasun Mas de Pierredon, 652 Chemin Raoul Coletta, 83110 Sanary-sur-Mer [04 94 74 25 02; fax 04 94 74 61 42; pierredon@campasun.com; www.campasun-pierredon.fr]** Take D11 fr Sanary, cross m'way & 1st L. Site on R in approx 1km. Med, shd; htd wc; chem disp; mv service pnt; shwrs inc; el pnts (10A) inc; lndtte; shop; supmkt 800m; rest; snacks; bar; playgrnd; htd pool; paddling pool; waterslides; beach 3km; tennis; wifi; entmnt; TV; dogs €4; poss cr; adv bkg rec; rd noise; red low ssn; red CCI. "Gd family site." ♦ 1 Apr-30 Sep. € 35.00 2007*

SANARY SUR MER *10F3* (1.5km W Coastal) *43.12400, 5.78695* **Campasun Parc Mogador, Chemin de Beaucours, 83110 Sanary-sur-Mer [04 94 74 53 16; fax 04 94 74 10 58; mogador@campasum.eu; www.campasun-mogador.eu]** Fr A50 exit junc 12 dir Bandol. Camping sp on R bef Sanary (for 2 sites). Lge, pt shd; htd wc; mv service pnt; shwrs inc; el pnts (10A) inc; gas; lndtte; ltd shop; rest; snacks; bar; playgrnd; htd pool; paddling pool; shgl beach 800m; fishing, watersports 1km; games area; entmnt; TV; 40% statics; dogs €4 (not acc Jul/Aug); bus nrby; adv bkg rec; quiet; red low ssn. "Busy site; gd sized pitches; narr site rds poss diff lge o'fits; excel, modern san facs; poss muddy after heavy rain; attractive port." 15 Feb-31 Dec. € 37.10 (CChq acc) 2009*

SANCERRE *4G3* (4km N Rural) *47.34215, 2.86571* **Camping Le René Foltzer, 18300 St Satur [02 48 54 04 67 or 02 48 54 02 61 (Mairie); fax 02 48 54 01 30; aquadis1@wanadoo.fr; www.aquadis-loisirs.com]** Fr Sancerre on D955 thro cent St Satur & St Thibault. Turn L immed bef Loire bdge. Site on R in 100m. Med, hdg pitch, shd; wc; chem disp; shwrs inc; el pnts (10A) inc; gas; lndtte; shop 500m; rest 500m; playgrnd; pool 500m; rv sw, canoe hire adj; tennis; entmnt; golf 1km; 50% statics; dogs €1.50; poss cr; some Eng spkn; adv bkg; quiet; CCI. "Friendly & helpful staff; gd san facs; some sm pitches, some with rv view; gates clsd 2200-0700; poss itinerants; rvside walks; gd touring cent; vg." ♦ 1 May-30 Sep. € 12.00 2009*

SANCHEY see Epinal *6F2*

SANDUN see Guérande *2G3*

SANGUINET *7D1* (3km N Rural) *44.49915, -1.07911* **Camping Lou Broustaricq, Route de Langeot, 40460 Sanguinet [05 58 82 74 82; fax 05 58 82 10 74; loubrousta@wanadoo.fr; www.lou-broustaricq.com]** Take Arcachon exit off Bordeax-Bayonne m'way. After 5km twd S on D3 & D216 to Sanguinet. Site sp in town off Bordeaux rd. V lge, mkd pitch, pt shd; htd wc (some cont); chem disp; shwrs inc; el pnts (10A) €3.65; lndtte; shop, rest, snacks, bar high ssn; BBQ; playgrnd; pool; waterslide; lake sw & sand beach 500m; watersports; sailing school; tennis; walking tracks; games area; cycle hire; entmnt; golf nr; TV rm; 60% statics; no dogs; Eng spkn; adv bkg; quiet; red low ssn; ccard acc; CCI. "In lovely wooded area; gd cycle tracks; gd for children; facs poss unclean low ssn; vg." ♦ 16 Mar-15 Nov. € 29.10 2006*

SANGUINET *7D1* (1.5km S Rural) *44.48372, -1.09449* **CAMPEOLE Camping Le Lac Sanguinet, 526 Rue de Pinton, 40460 Sanguinet [05 58 82 70 80; fax 05 58 82 14 24; lac-sanguinet@campeole.com; www.campeole.com]** Foll Le Lac sp at rndabt in Sanguinet, turn L on lakeside, site on L in 600m. Lge, mkd pitch, pt shd; wc; mv service pnt; shwrs inc; el pnts (6-10A) €4.10; lndtte; shops 500m; tradsmn; snacks; bar; BBQ (not charcoal); playgrnd; htd pool; paddling pool; sand beach, lake sw & sailing nrby; watersports; games area; games rm; cycle hire; wifi; entmnt; some statics; dogs €3.10; extra €26 for twin-axles; poss cr; quiet; red low ssn; CCI. "Spacious site in pine woods; cycle path around lake; san facs poss run down low ssn; friendly, helpful staff." 30 Apr-19 Sep. € 26.50 2009*

SANGUINET *7D1* (2km SW Rural) *44.48402, -1.09098* **Camping Les Grands Pins, Ave de Losa, Route du Lac, 40460 Sanguinet [05 58 78 61 74; fax 05 58 78 69 15; info@campinglesgrandspins.com; www.campinglesgrandspins.com]** Foll Le Lac sp at rndabt in Sanguinet. Turn L at lakeside. Site on L in 450m opposite yacht club. Lge, hdg pitch, shd; wc; chem disp; (wc); shwrs inc; child/baby facs; el pnts (3-10A) inc; lndtte; rest; snacks; bar; playgrnd; pool; sand beach & lake sw adj; boating; windsurfing; fishing, canoeing; tennis; cycle hire; TV; 50% statics; dogs €2; poss cr; Eng spkn; adv bkg; poss noisy; red low ssn; CCI. "Clean site; rest & bar poss clsd low ssn; parking for m'vans adj." ♦ 1 Apr-31 Oct. € 37.00 2008*

⊞ **SARLAT LA CANEDA** *7C3* (12km N Rural) *44.97450, 1.18832* **Camping Les Tailladis, 24200 Marcillac-St Quentin [05 53 59 10 95; fax 05 53 29 47 56; info@tailladis.com; www.tailladis.com]** N fr Sarlat on D704 dir Montignac. After 7km turn L & foll sp to site. Med, hdg pitch, pt sl, terr, pt shd; wc; chem disp; mv service pnt; shwrs inc; el pnts (6-10A) €3.60; gas; lndtte; shop; rest, snacks & bar (Apr-Oct); pool; lake sw; fishing; canoeing; 6% statics; dogs €2; phone; poss cr; Eng spkn; adv bkg; ccard acc; red low ssn. "Friendly & helpful Dutch owners; clean san facs; c'van storage; vg." ♦ € 17.65 2009*

SARLAT LA CANEDA *7C3* (6km NE Rural) **Camping Le Val d'Ussel, 24200 Proissans [05 53 59 28 73; fax 05 53 29 38 25; www.homair.com]** Fr Sarlat, take D704 N & foll sps to Proissans. Fr Périgueux, take N89 to Thenon, D67 to Chambon, D704 to sps to Proissans. Fr Brive, N89 twd Périgueux, D60 S. Med, pt sl, pt shd; wc; chem disp; shwrs inc; baby facs; el pnts (6-10A); gas; lndtte; tradsmn; rest; snacks; bar; BBQ; playgrnd; 2 htd pools; lake adj; fishing; shgl beach 15km; tennis; games area; cycle hire; entmnt; TV; many statics; dogs; adv bkg; quiet; red low ssn. 27 Apr-7 Sep. 2008*

France

SARLAT LA CANEDA *7C3* (6km NE Rural) *44.90404, 1.28210* **Camping Les Grottes de Roffy, 24200 Ste Nathalène [05 53 59 15 61; fax 05 53 31 09 11; contact@roffy.fr; www.roffy.fr]** Fr N end of Sarlat take D47 NE for Ste Nathalène. Site on R 1km bef vill. Or fr A20 exit junc 55 onto ND804/D703 dir Carlux. Turn R onto D61B then D47 to Ste Nathalène, site thro vill on L. Lge, hdg/mkd pitch, terr, pt shd; htd wc; chem disp; baby facs; shwrs inc; el pnts (6A) €3; gas; Indtte; shop; tradsmn; rest; snacks; bar; BBQ; playgrnd; 4 pools inc paddling pool; canoeing; tennis; games area; games rm; cycle hire; entmnt; 40% statics (inc tour ops); dogs €2.10; extra for 'comfort' pitches; Eng spkn; adv bkg (ess Jul/Aug); CCI. "Excel rest & shop; helpful staff; lovely site." ♦ 17 Apr-19 Sep. € 25.30 2009*

See advertisement

SARLAT LA CANEDA *7C3* (8km NE Rural) *44.90030, 1.29700* **Camping La Châtaigneraie, 24370 Prats-de-Carlux [05 53 59 03 61 or 05 53 30 29 03 (LS); fax 05 53 29 86 16; lachataigneraie@orange.fr; www.lachataigneraie24.com]** Fr Sarlat take D704 E twd Souillac, after 3km turn L onto D704A/D703. At Rouffillac turn L opp rv bdge onto D61 sp Carlux. In Carlux fork L onto D47B & in 4km turn L at site sp, site on R in 500m. Med, hdg/mkd pitch, terr, pt shd; wc; chem disp; baby facs; shwrs inc; el pnts (10A) inc (poss rev pol); gas; Indtte; shop; rest; snacks; sm bar; BBQ (gas only); playgrnd; htd covrd pool; paddling pool; waterslide; fishing; tennis; entmnt & child entmnt (Jul/Aug); wifi; games/TV rm; dogs €2.30; max van length high ssn 7m; poss cr; quiet; ccard acc; red low ssn. "Excel site; friendly & helpful owners; vg san facs; some pitches diff due position of trees; vg pool area; mkt Sarlat Wed & Sat am." ♦ 1 May-15 Sep. € 29.90 ABS - D13 2009*

SARLAT LA CANEDA *7C3* (8km NE Rural) *44.91328, 1.26469* **Camping Maillac, 24200 Ste Nathalène [05 53 59 22 12; fax 05 53 29 60 17; campingmaillac@wanadoo.fr; www.campingmaillac.fr]** Take D47 out of Sarlat to Ste Nathalène. After 4km turn L at x-rds (if missed next 2 turnings also lead to site), v well sp. Med, mkd pitch, pt sl, pt shd; wc; chem disp; mv service pnt; shwrs inc; el pnts (6-10A) €3-4.50; gas; Indtte; shop; rest; snacks; bar; BBQ; playgrnd; pool; paddling pool; games rm; entmnt; 10% statics; dogs €1.20; poss cr Jul/Aug; some Eng spkn; adv bkg; quiet; red low ssn; ccard acc; CCI. "Family-run site; spacious pitches; lovely area." 15 May-30 Sep. € 15.80 2007*

SARLAT LA CANEDA *7C3* (9km NE Rural) **Camping La Palombière, 24200 Ste Nathalène [05 53 59 42 34; fax 05 53 28 45 40; la.palombiere@wanadoo.fr; www.lapalombiere.fr]** Take D47 fr Sarlat to Ste Nathalène, thro vill, past Mill Rest, fork L on o'skts by cemetary. Site sp on R in 300m - sharp R turn & access poss diff. Med, terr, shd; wc; chem disp; baby facs; shwrs inc; el pnts (10A) €3; Indtte; shop; rest; snacks; bar; BBQ; htd pools; waterslide; tennis; gym; games rm; games area; entmnt; TV; 70% statics (tour ops); dogs €2; Eng spkn; adv bkg; quiet; 10% red low ssn. "Lovely, well-run site; friendly owners; immac san facs; vg rest with views; poss diff for lge o'fits due trees, narr site rds & pitch sizes; highly rec." ♦ 30 Apr-13 Sep. € 25.70 2009*

SARLAT LA CANEDA *7C3* (10km NE Rural) *44.95778, 1.27280* **Camping Les Péneyrals, Le Poujol, 24590 St Crépin-et-Carlucet [05 53 28 85 71; fax 05 53 28 80 99; camping.peneyrals@wanadoo.fr; www.peneyrals.com]** Fr Sarlat N on D704; D60 E dir Salignac-Eyvignes to Le Poujol; S to St Crépin. Site sp. Lge, hdg pitch, pt sl, terr, pt shd; htd wc; chem disp; mv service pnt; all serviced pitch; baby facs; shwrs inc; el pnts (5-10A) €3.10-3.70; Indtte; shop; rest; snacks; bar; playgrnd; 4 pools (1 htd, covrd); paddling pool; waterslide; fishing; tennis; games area; boules; entmnt; 50% statics; dogs €2; phone adj; Eng spkn; adv bkg; quiet; red low ssn; ccard acc; red low ssn. "Friendly owners; superb family & touring site." ♦ 15 May-15 Sep. € 25.90 2006*

SARLAT LA CANEDA *7C3* (12km NE Rural) *44.96347, 1.32817* **FLOWER Camping Le Temps de Vivre, Route de Carlux, 24590 Salignac-Eyvignes [tel/fax 05 53 28 93 21; contact@temps-de-vivre.com; www.temps-de-vivre.com or www.flowercamping.com]** Fr Sarlat N on D704, bear R onto D60 to Salignac-Eyvigues. Fr Salignac take D61 S dir Carlux, site sp in 1.5km on R. Sm, hdg/mkd pitch, terr, pt shd; wc; chem disp; mv service pnt; baby facs; fam bthrm; shwrs inc; el pnts (10A) €3; gas; Indtte; shop; tradsmn; BBQ; supmkt 2km; rest & bar (high ssn); snacks; pool; playgrnd; games area; golf; tennis; fishing; dogs €2; 40% statics; poss cr; quiet; phone; adv bkg (fee); Eng spkn; ccard acc; CCI. "Attractive, clean, well-kept site; friendly, helpful owners; highly rec." ♦ 29 Mar-1 Nov. € 18.50 2007*

SARLAT LA CANEDA *7C3* (1km E Rural) *44.89328, 1.22756* **Camping Les Périères, Rue Jean Gabin/Route de la Croix d'Allon, 24200 Sarlat-la-Canéda [05 53 59 05 84; fax 05 53 28 57 51; les-perieres@wanadoo.fr; www.lesperieres.com]** Site on R of D47 to Proissans & Ste Nathalène. NB steep access rds. Med, mkd pitch, terr, shd; wc; mv service pnt; sauna; baby facs; shwrs inc; el pnts (6A) €3.90; gas; Indry rm; shop; tradsmn; bar; BBQ (gas/charcoal); playgrnd; 2 pools (1 htd covrd); games rm; tennis; dogs; poss cr; Eng spkn; adv bkg; quiet; ccard acc +2% charge; red low ssn. "In grounds of holiday vill; friendly, helpful staff; san facs clean but poss too few; excel pool complex; poss not suitable disabled as steep site rds; access poss diff med & lge o'fits; excel." ♦ 1 Apr-30 Sep. € 27.50 (3 persons) 2009*

SARLAT LA CANEDA *7C3* (10km E Rural) *44.8674, 1.3578* **Camping Les Ombrages de la Dordogne, Rouffillac, 24370 Carlux [05 53 28 62 17; fax 05 53 28 62 18; ombrages@perigord.com; www.ombrages.fr]** 12km W thro Souillac on D703. Turn L at x-rds in Rouffillac & immed turn L bef rv bdge into site. Med, some mkd pitch, pt shd; wc; chem disp; shwrs inc; el pnts (6A) €2.70; gas 1km; Indtte; shop 1km; tradsmn (high ssn); rest 500m; snacks; bar; BBQ; playgrnd; pool adj; rv sw adj; fishing; tennis; games area; cycle & canoe hire; internet; TV rm; 2% statics; dogs €2; phone; poss cr; Eng spkn; adv bkg; quiet but some rd noise; ccard acc; red low ssn; CCI. "Pleasant, well-kept, rvside site; enthusiastic owners live on site; pitching poss diff due trees; san facs (open air) poss stretched high ssn; cycle track; vg." 15 Apr-15 Oct. € 13.10 2009*

France

SARLAT LA CANEDA *7C3* (12km E Rural) *44.86419, 1.35998* **Camp Municipal Le Bourniou, 24370 St Julien-de-Lampon [05 53 29 83 39 or 05 53 29 46 11 (Mairie); fax 05 53 29 46 12; camping-le-bourniou@wanadoo.fr; www.camping-bourniou.com]** Fr Sarlat-la-Canéda take D704/703 E, cross rv at Rouffillac sp St Julien-de-Lampon. Site on L on rvside 200m after bdge. Med, mkd pitch, pt shd; wc; chem disp; shwrs inc; el pnts (6A) €2.50; Indtte; shop 500m; tradsmn; rest, snacks & bar 200m; playgrnd; rv sw adj; fishing; canoe hire; tennis 500m; some statics; dogs; phone; Eng spkn; quiet; CCI. "Lovely location with mature trees; poss tight pitches for lge o'fits; football stadium on site & public use rest, bar & picnic area; site is NH for canoe safaris; gd walking." 1 Jun-15 Sep. € 12.60 2007*

SARLAT LA CANEDA *7C3* (12km E Rural) *44.86345, 1.37350* **Camping Le Mondou, Le Colombier, 24370 St Julien-de-Lampon [tel/fax 05 53 29 70 37; lemondou@camping-dordogne.info; www.camping-dordogne.info]** Fr Sarlat-la-Canéda take D704/D703 E; cross rv at Rouffillac, ent St Julien-de-Lampon & turn L at x-rds; site sp on R in 2km. Med, hdg/mkd pitch, pl, pt shd; wc; chem disp; mv service pnt; baby facs; shwrs inc; el pnts (6A) €2.75; gas 700m; Indtte; shop 2km; tradsmn; rest; snacks; bar; BBQ; playgrnd; pool & paddling pool; rv sw, fishing & waterports 300m; games rm; games area; cycle hire; internet; 10% statics; dogs €1; phone; poss cr; Eng spkn; adv bkg; quiet. "Beautiful views; friendly, helpful owners; sm, uneven pitches; gd cycle paths." ♦ 1 May-15 Oct. € 14.00 2008*

SARLAT LA CANEDA *7C3* (5km SE Rural) *44.85480, 1.23760* **Camping Les Acacias, Route de Cahors, 24200 Sarlat-la-Canéda [05 53 31 08 50; fax 05 53 59 29 30; camping-acacias@wanadoo.fr; www.acacias.fr]** Foll sp La Canéda vill & site fr D704 S fr Sarlat. NB Last few metres of app v narr rd. Med, hdg/mkd pitch, pt sl, shd; wc; chem disp; mv service pnt; baby facs; shwrs inc; el pnts (6A) €3; gas; Indtte; supmkt 3km; tradsmn; rest; snacks; bar; playgrnd; 2 pools; games area; entmnt; some statics; dogs €1.50; phone; bus; adv bkg; quiet; ccard acc; red CCI. "Clean, modern san facs; helpful, enthusiastic owners; ideal touring base; mkt Wed & Sat." 1 Apr-30 Sep. € 16.00 2009*

SARLAT LA CANEDA *7C3* (7km SE Rural) *44.86696, 1.27945* **Camping Aqua Viva, 24200 Carsac-Aillac [05 53 31 46 00 or 04 99 57 20 25; www.aquaviva.fr or www.village-center.com]** Fr N or S take N20/A20 to Souillac; the foll D703 beside Rv Dordogne twd Sarlat-la-Caneda. Just past Calviac-en-Périgord, turn R onto D704a; site on L in 3km. Ent easily missed; app with care as busy rd. Lge, mkd pitch, pt terr, pt sl, pt shd; wc; chem disp; baby facs; shwrs inc; el pnts (10A) inc (poss rev pol); gas; Indtte; shop; rest; snacks; bar; BBQ; playgrnd; pool; sw & boating in sm lake; fishing; cycle hire; games rm; internet; many statics; dogs €3; poss cr; Eng spkn; adv bkg ess; ccard acc; CCI. "Friendly staff; excel, lively site for families; basic but gd value rest; gd sports facs; facs stretched high ssn & ltd low ssn." ♦ 15 Apr-23 Sep. € 30.00 2007*

SARLAT LA CANEDA *7C3* (8km SE Rural) *44.86340, 1.29727* **Camping Les Chênes Verts, Route de Sarlat, 24370 Calviac-en-Périgord [05 53 59 21 07; fax 05 53 31 05 51; chenes-verts@wanadoo.fr; www.chenes-verts.com]** S fr Châteauroux on A20 leave at Souillac exit. Join D703 heading W twd Sarlat; branch R onto D704a soon after Calviac-en-Périgord, site on R in 2km. Or take D704/704A SE fr Sarlat. Site in 8km on L; clearly sp & flags at ent. Med, hdg/mkd pitch, pt sl, pt shd; wc; chem disp; mv service pnt; baby facs; shwrs inc; el pnts (6A) inc (25m cable rec); gas; Indtte; sm shop; tradsmn; rest; snacks; bar; BBQ (gas/charcoal only); playgrnd; 2 pools (1 htd, covrd); paddling pool; canoeing; cycle hire; golf 7km; games area; games rm; entmnt; TV; 70 statics (sep area); no dogs; Eng spkn; adv bkg; quiet but some noise fr bar; red long stay; ccard acc; CCI. "Pleasant, peaceful site; gd sized pitches but sandy, so muddy when wet; new owners updating facs (2008); excel pool; mkt Sat Sarlat." ♦ 1 Apr-30 Sep. € 30.30 2008*

SARLAT LA CANEDA *7C3* (9km SE Rural) *44.81939, 1.21488* **Camping La Butte, 24250 La Roque-Gageac [tel/fax 05 53 28 30 28; contact@camping-la-butte.com; www.camping-la-butte.com]** On D703 1km fr Vitrac bet Vitrac & Cénac. Med, hdg pitch, shd; wc; shwrs inc; el pnts (4-10A) €2.90-3.50; gas; Indtte; shop; rest; snacks; bar; BBQ; pool; fishing; boating; dogs €1/70; poss cr; adv bkg; red low ssn. "Beautiful area." 1 Apr-30 Sep. € 16.20 2007*

SARLAT LA CANEDA *7C3* (10km SE Rural) *44.8289, 1.2667* **Camping Le Rocher de la Cave, 24200 Carsac-Aillac [05 53 28 14 26; fax 05 53 28 27 10; rocher.de.la.cave@wanadoo.fr; www.rocherdelacave.com]** Fr Sarlat-la-Canéda take D704 S twd Carsac-Aillac & turn L bef vill. Follow sp. Med, hdg/mkd pitch, pt shd; wc; shwrs inc; el pnts (10A) €3; gas; lndtte; shop; tradsmn; rest; snacks; bar; playgrnd; pool; paddling pool; canoe hire; tennis 500m; games area; entmnt; 5% statics; dogs; phone; quiet; red low ssn. "Rvside sitel; gd." ♦ 1 May-15 Sep. € 16.80 2008*

SARLAT LA CANEDA *7C3* (10km SE Rural) *44.81536, 1.29245* **Camping Les Granges, 24250 Groléjac [05 53 28 11 15; fax 05 53 28 57 13; contact@lesgranges-fr.com; www.lesgranges-fr.com]** Fr Sarlat take D704 SE, sp Gourdon. Site sp nr cent of Groléjac on R. Care on acute corner after rlwy bdge. Med, hdg, terr, pt shd; wc; chem disp; baby facs; serviced pitches; shwrs inc; el pnts (6A) €7.30; gas; lndtte; shop; rest; snacks; bar; playgrnd; htd pool; paddling pool; cycle hire; entmnt; rv & lake fishing 1km; TV; 40% statics; dogs €3; poss cr; Eng spkn; adv bkg; ccard acc; red low ssn; CCI. "Historical & beautiful area; vg site & facs."
25 Apr-13 Sep. € 23.95 2009*

See advertisement on page 518

SARLAT LA CANEDA *7C3* (13km SE Rural) *44.80227, 1.29448* **Camping du Lac de Groléjac (formerly Camp Municipal Le Roc Percé), Plan d'Eau, 24250 Groléjac [05 53 59 48 70; fax 05 53 29 39 74; contact@camping-dulac-dordogne.com; www.camping-dulac-dordogne.com]** On D704 SE fr Sarlat twd Goudon, Groléjac in 11km. In vill cent, foll sp 'Plan d'Eau'; pass thro vill & turn R in front of Le Marais Rest, in 100m turn L dir Nabirat. Site on L in 500m. Med, hdg pitch, pt shd; wc; chem disp; baby facs; shwrs; el pnts (10A) €3; gas; lndtte; sm shop; sm rest; snacks; bar; playgrnd; sand beach & lake sw; fishing; watersports; cycle hire; wifi; dogs €1.50; Eng spkn; adv bkg; quiet; ccard acc; CCI. "Popular site on created lake with artificial sand beach; excel." ♦ 15 Apr-15 Oct. € 11.50 2009*

SARLAT LA CANEDA *7C3* (6km S Rural) *44.82375, 1.25080* **Camping La Bouysse de Caudon, 24200 Vitrac [05 53 28 33 05; fax 05 53 30 38 52; info@labouysse.com; www.labouysse.com]** S fr Sarlat on D46 dir Vitrac. At Vitrac 'port' bef bdge turn L onto D703 sp Carsac. In 2km turn R & foll site sp, site on L. Well sp. Med, hdg/mkd pitch, pt shd; wc; chem disp; baby facs; shwrs inc; el pnts (6-10A) €3.40-3.90; gas; lndtte; shop; tradsmn; rest; snacks; bar; BBQ; playgrnd; pool; rv sw & shgl beach; fishing; canoe hire; tennis; games area; internet; entmnt; 8% statics; dogs €1.70; phone; poss cr; Eng spkn; adv bkg (dep); quiet; ccard acc; red low ssn; CCI. "Excel, family-run site on Rv Dordogne; helpful staff; plenty of gd, clean san facs; many Bastides in area." ♦ 1 Apr-30 Sep. € 18.50 2007*

SARLAT LA CANEDA *7C3* (8km S Rural) *44.82500, 1.25388* **Camping Domaine de Soleil-Plage, Caudon-par-Montfort, 24200 Vitrac [05 53 28 33 33 or 06 07 33 96 54 (mob LS); fax 05 53 28 30 24; info@soleilplage.fr; www.soleilplage.fr]** On D46, 6km S of Sarlat twd Vitrac, turn L onto D703, to Château Montfort, R to site dir Caudon, sp. Site beyond Camping La Bouysse on rvside, 2km E of Vitrac. If coming fr Souillac on D703, when app Montfort rd v narr with overhanging rock faces. Narr access rds on site. Med, hdg pitch, pt shd; wc; chem disp; mv service pnt; baby facs; serviced pitches; shwrs inc; el pnts (10A) €3.50; gas; lndtte; shop; rest; snacks; bar; BBQ; playgrnd; htd pool; paddling pool; waterslide; rv sw & sand beach adj; fishing; canoeing; tennis; cycle hire; golf 1km; horseriding 5km; games rm; internet; TV; 45% statics; dogs €3.50; phone; Eng spkn; adv bkg ess Jul/Aug; quiet; ccard acc; red low ssn/groups; CCI. "Lovely site in beautiful location; friendly, welcoming owner; variety of pitches - extra for serviced/rvside; san facs clean; superb aquatic complex; v shd pitches by rv; poss muddy when wet; excel." ♦ 4 Apr-27 Sep. € 27.90 (CChq acc) 2009*

See advertisement below

SARLAT LA CANEDA *7C3* (9km S Rural) *44.81628, 1.21508* **Camping Beau Rivage, Gaillardou, 24250 La Roque-Gageac [05 53 28 32 05; fax 05 53 29 63 56; camping.beau.rivage@wanadoo.fr; www.camping-beau-rivage.com]** On S side of D703, 1km W of Vitrac adj Rv Dordogne. Lge, mkd pitch, shd; htd wc (some cont); chem disp; baby facs; shwrs inc; el pnts (6A) €2; gas; Indtte; shop; rest 200m; snacks; bar; playgrnd; pool; rv sw & beach; canoeing; tennis; games area; cycle hire; horseriding; archery; golf 2km; entmnt; TV; some statics; dogs €3; phone; poss cr; adv bkg rec high ssn; quiet. ♦ 4 Apr-10 Sep. € 22.00 2009*

See advertisement on page 518

SARLAT LA CANEDA *7C3* (9km S Rural) *44.82442, 1.16939* **Camping La Plage, 83 Près La Roque-Gageac, 24220 Vézac [05 53 29 50 83; fax 05 53 30 31 63; campinglaplage24@orange.fr; www.camping-laplage.fr]** On banks of Rv Dordogne, 500m W of La Roque-Gageac on D703. Med, mkd pitch, shd; wc; chem disp (wc); shwrs inc; el pnts (3-10A) €2.30-4.50; gas; sm shop 1km; BBQ; playgrnd; shgl beach & rv sw; fishing; canoeing; some statics; poss cr; adv bkg; quiet; red CCI. "Attractive site; excel pitches; basic san facs but clean; ltd facs low ssn; kind, helpful owners; highly rec." 1 Apr-30 Sep. € 14.00 2007*

SARLAT LA CANEDA *7C3* (9km S Rural) *44.78648, 1.20930* **Camping Le Pech de Caumont, 24250 Cénac-et-St-Julien [05 53 28 21 63 or 05 53 28 30 67; fax 05 53 29 99 73; jmilhac@pech-de-caumont.com; www.pech-de-caumont.com]** D46 fr Sarlat to Cénac, cross rv & cont on D46 thro Cénac; site ent on L 500m past End of Vill sp. Do not go thro Domme. Med, hdg/mkd pitch, pt sl, terr, pt shd; wc; chem disp; shwrs inc; el pnts (6A) €3.10; Indtte; shops 1km; snacks & sm bar (high ssn); BBQ; playgrnd; pool; rv sw 2km; TV rm; 20% statics; dogs; phone; poss cr; Eng spkn; adv bkg; quiet; ccard acc; red low ssn; CCI. "Views fr most pitches; modern, clean san facs; helpful owners; popular, tidy, family-run site; excel." 1 Apr-30 Sep. € 15.45 2008*

SARLAT LA CANEDA *7C3* (10km S Rural) *44.80436, 1.20589* **Camp Municipal, 24250 Cénac-et-St Julien [05 53 28 31 91 or 05 53 31 41 31 (Mairie)]** D46 fr Sarlat to Vitrac then Cénac; cross rv & site on L on ent Cénac. Med, mkd pitch, pt shd; wc; chem disp; shwrs inc; el pnts (6A) inc (poss long lead req); Indry rm; shop, rest, snacks, bar 200m; rv sw, boating & fishing adj; dogs; phone; adv bkg; quiet; no ccard acc. "Pleasant site in excel rvside location; clean facs but dated & ltd low ssn; ground rather rough; site opens earlier if demand; poss flooding after heavy rain; vg NH." 1 Jun-15 Sep. € 11.47 2008*

SARLAT LA CANEDA *7C3* (10km S Rural) *44.81521, 1.22362* **Camping La Rivière de Domme, 24250 Domme [05 53 28 33 46; fax 05 53 29 56 04; contact@camping-riviere-domme.com; www.camping-riviere-domme.com]** Fr Sarlat take D46 to Vitrac. Cross rv bdge on D46E. In 1km at T-junc turn R on D50 & in 1km turn R at sp into site. Sm, pt shd; wc; chem disp; shwrs inc; el pnts (10A) €2.50 (poss rev pol); Indtte; shops 4km; playgrnd; pool; games area; few statics; Eng spkn; adv bkg; quiet; red low ssn. "Generous pitches; pleasant owner; modern san facs; excel disabled facs; many walks fr site." ♦ 4 Apr-3 Oct. € 10.80 2009*

SARLAT LA CANEDA *7C3* (10km S Rural) *44.82181, 1.22587* **Camping Le Bosquet, La Rivière, 24250 Domme [05 53 28 37 39; fax 05 53 29 41 95; info@lebousquet.com; www.lebosquet.com]** Fr Sarlat take D46 S to Vitrac cross rv on D46E. Sp at junc, site 500m on R. Sm, hdg/mkd pitch, pt shd, wc; chem disp; shwrs inc; el pnts (6A) €2.50 (long lead poss req); gas; Indtte; sm shop; tradsmn; snacks; pool; rv sw & fishing 500m; wifi; 50% statics; dogs €2; Eng spkn; adv bkg; quiet; CCI. "Friendly, helpful owners; excel clean facs but poss stretched high ssn; gd shd but sm pitches." ♦ 1 Apr-26 Sep. € 12.50 2009*

SARLAT LA CANEDA *7C3* (10km S Rural) *44.81725, 1.21944* **Camping Le Perpetuum, 24250 Domme [05 53 28 35 18; fax 05 53 29 63 64; leperpetuum.domme@wanadoo.fr; www.campingleperpetuum.com]** Fr Sarlat take D46 to Vitrac; cross rv bdge to D46E; in 1km turn R onto D50, R again in 1km at site sp. Med, hdg/mkd pitch, hdstg, pt shd; wc; chem disp; mv service pnt; baby facs; shwrs inc; el pnts (10A) €3.50; Indtte; sm shop (farm produce); supmkt 3km; tradsmn; snacks; bar; BBQ; playgrnd; pool; rv sw & beach adj (Rv Dordogne); canoeing; games area; entmnt; TV rm statics; dogs €1; poss cr; some Eng spkn; adv bkg; quiet; ccard acc; red low ssn/CCI. "Site fronts rv; busy high ssn; relaxed, friendly atmosphere; gd sized pitches; cheerful, helpful owners; gd san facs; gd pool; gd local walks; late arr area at ent." ♦ 1 May-10 Oct. € 17.20 2009*

SARLAT LA CANEDA *7C3* (12km S Rural) *44.79175, 1.16266* **Camping Bel Ombrage, 24250 St Cybranet [05 53 28 34 14; fax 05 53 59 64 64; belombrage@wanadoo.fr; www.belombrage.com]** Fr Sarlat take D46 sp Bergerac, rd then conts as D57; after 8km turn L at Vézac sp Castelnaund. After 1.6km at T-junction turn L onto D703 & in 180m turn R onto D57. Cont thro Castelnaund on D57; site on L in 3km. Lge, hdg pitch, shd; wc; chem disp; shwrs inc; el pnts (10A) inc; gas 800m; Indtte; tradsmn; shop 800m; rest, snacks & bar 100m; BBQ; playgrnd; 3 pools; paddling pool; rv sw & beach; fishing, canoeing, tennis, cycle hire & horseriding 3km; games area; wifi; games/TV rm; library; dogs free; c'vans over 8m not acc high ssn; adv bkg; quiet; ccard not acc; CCI. "Attractive, well-managed site; popular with British; peaceful early ssn; ideal base for Dordogne; mkt Thu; excel." ♦ 1 Jun-5 Sep. € 21.80 ABS - D01 2009*

SARLAT LA CANEDA *7C3* (4km SW Rural) *44.86500, 1.18750* **Camping Domaine de Loisirs Le Montant, Negrelat, Route de Bergerac, 24200 Sarlat-la-Canéda [05 53 59 18 50; fax 05 53 59 37 73; contact@camping-sarlat.com; www.camping-sarlat.com]** Leave Sarlat on D57 dir Bergerac. Turn R opp school 'Pré de Cordy', site in 2.3km, sp. Med, hdg/mkd pitch, hdstg, terr, pt shd; htd wc; chem disp; mv service pnt; baby facs; fam bthrm; shwrs inc; el pnts (6-10A) €3.60; lndtte; shop 3km; tradsmn; rest; snacks; bar; BBQ; playgrnd; htd, covrd pool; waterslide; paddling pool; jacuzzi; games area; games rm; golf nr; wifi; entmnt; TV rm; 1% statics; dogs €1; Eng spkn; adv bkg rec high ssn; quiet; ccard acc; red low ssn; CCI. "Vg, pleasant site; many sports activities & excursions." ♦ 1 May-20 Sep. € 22.50 2008*

⊞ **SARLAT LA CANEDA** *7C3* (8km SW Rural) *44.83560, 1.15873* **Camping Les Deux Vallées, 24220 Vézac [05 53 29 53 55; fax 05 53 31 09 81; les2v@perigord.com; www.les-2-vallees.com]** Exit A20 junc 55 onto D804 dir Sarlat-la-Caneda; cont onto D703/D704A/D704 to Sarlat; then take D57 SW to Vézac; immed after sp for vill take 1st R to site. Or fr E leave D703 onto D57; 250m after junc with D49 turn L & foll sp to site. Med, hdg/mkd pitch, hdstg, pt shd; htd wc; chem disp; baby facs; shwrs inc; el pnts (6-10A) €3.50; gas; lndtte (inc dryer); ice; shop; tradsmn; rest; snacks; bar; BBQ; 2 playgrnds; 3 pools; rv 500m, shgl beach; cycle hire; games area; games rm; entmnt & child entment July/Aug; TV; 6% statics; dogs €2; poss cr; Eng spkn; adv bkg ess Jul/Aug; quiet but rlwy adj; ccard acc; red low ssn/long stay; CCI. "Excel site; helpful, friendly Dutch owners; ltd san facs low ssn; poss muddy when wet; gd local walks." ♦ € 19.15 2009*

SARLAT LA CANEDA *7C3* (9km SW Rural) *44.82585, 1.15322* **Camping La Cabane, 24220 Vézac [05 53 29 52 28; fax 05 53 59 09 15; contact@lacabanedordogne.com; www.lacabanedordogne.com]** Fr Sarlat-La-Canéda take D57 thro Vézac. On leaving Vézac turn L immed bef rlwy bdge, site sp on R on bank of Rv Dordogne. Lge, hdg/mkd pitch, pt shd; wc; shwrs inc; el pnts (6-10A) €2;60-3.20; gas; lndtte; shop high ssn; rest & snacks 3km; BBQ; playgrnd; htd covrd pool; rv sw & shgl beach adj; TV rm; internet; some statics; dogs €1 (fee low ssn); phone; poss cr; Eng spkn; adv bkg; quiet; ccard acc; CCI. "Well-shaded, rvside site; lge pitches; clean facs; friendly, helpful family owners; rvside walk to Beynac Château; gd." ♦ 1 Apr-30 Sep. € 11.60 2008*

SARLAT LA CANEDA *7C3* (10km SW Rural) *44.83819, 1.14846* **Camping Le Capeyrou, 24220 Beynac-et-Cazenac [05 53 29 54 95; fax 05 53 28 36 27; lecapeyrou@wanadoo.fr; www.campinglecapeyrou.com]** Fr W on D703 on R (opp sm supmkt & baker) immed past vill of Beynac. Or fr N on D57 fr Sarlat; in vill immed on L on rv. Med, hdg pitch, some hdstg, pt shd; wc; chem disp; mv service pnt; baby facs; shwrs inc; el pnts (6-10A) €3.20-4; lndtte; shop & rest adj; snacks; bar; playgrnd; pool; wifi; dogs €1.60: poss cr; Eng spkn; adv bkg; some rd & rlwy noise; ccard acc; red low ssn. "View of chateau most pitches; rvside walk to attractive vill; helpful, friendly owners; clean san facs; excel lge pool; excel NH." ♦ Easter-30 Sep. € 17.70 2009*

SARLAT LA CANEDA *7C3* (10km SW Rural) *44.80519, 1.15852* **Camping-Caravaning Maisonneuve, Vallée de Céou, 24250 Castelnaud-la-Chapelle [05 53 29 51 29; fax 05 53 30 27 06; campmaison@orange.fr or contact@campingmaisonneuve.com; www.campingmaisonneuve.com]** Take D57 SW fr Sarlat sp Beynac. Cross Rv Dordogne at Castelnaud; site sp 500m on L out of Castelnaud on D57 twd Daglan. Foll narr rd across bdge (or alt ent - cont on D57 for 2km, sp on L for c'vans). Med, hdg/mkd pitch, some hdstg, pt shd; htd wc (some cont); chem disp; mv service pnt; child/baby facs; fam bthrm; shwrs inc; el pnts (6-10A) €4-4.90; gas; lndtte; shop, rest, snacks & bar high ssn; BBQ; playgrnd; pool; paddling pool; rv & shgl beach; fishing; tennis 2km; cycle hire; games rm; entmnt; wifi; TV rm; 10% statics; dogs €2; Eng spkn; adv bkg ess high ssn; quiet; ccard acc; red low ssn/CCI. "Vg, spacious site with modern facs; helpful owners; gd walking, cycling." ♦ 27 Mar- 2 Nov. € 19.70 2009*

SARLAT LA CANEDA *7C3* (12km SW Rural) *44.83760, 1.11296* **Camping Le Tiradou, Chemin du Grand-Fosse, 24220 St Vincent-de-Cosse [05 53 30 30 73; fax 05 53 31 16 24; contact@camping-le-tiradou.com; www.camping-le-tiradou.com]** Take D703 fr La Roque-Gageac thro Beynac & onto St Vincent; site is 2km fr Beynac on R. Med, hdg/mkd pitch, shd; wc; chem disp (wc); shwrs inc; el pnts (6A) inc; lndtte (inc dryer); shop; tradsmn; snacks; bar; BBQ; playgrnd; pool; paddling pool; rv fishing, boating, watersports & beach adj; cycle hire; wifi; TV; some statics; dogs €1.80; phone; Eng spkn; adv bkg; quiet; ccard acc. "Gd touring base along Rv Dordogne." ♦ 5 Apr-25 Oct. € 22.60 2008*

France

SARLAT LA CANEDA *7C3* (18km SW Rural) *44.83610, 1.06230* **Domaine Le Cro Magnon, La Raisse, 24220 Allas-les-Mines [05 53 29 13 70; fax 05 53 29 15 79; contact@domaine-cro-magnon.com; www.domaine-cro-magnon.com]** Fr Sarlat two Bergerac/Le Buisson on D57/D703 turn L after St Cyprien & rv x-ing onto D48 sp site & Berbiguières. Approx 1.5km after Berbiguières turn L at site sp. Do not foll any earlier sp to site as rds impassable to c'vans & m'vans. App steep, narr & twisting but gd surface. NB App via Berbiguières only. Med, pt shd; wc; chem disp; baby facs; sauna; shwrs inc; el pnts (6A) inc; gas; Indtte; shop; rest; snacks; bar; BBQ; playgrnd; 2 pools (1 htd covrd); paddling pool; rv fishing 800m; watersports; tennis; cycle hire; games area; entmnt; wifi; games/TV rm; dogs €3.60; adv bkg; quiet; ccard acc; red low ssn. ♦ 12 Jun-11 Sep. € 30.20 ABS - D24 2009*

The opening dates and prices on this campsite have changed. I'll send a site report form to the Club for the next edition of the guide.

SARLAT LA CANEDA *7C3* (9km W Rural) *44.90805, 1.11527* **Camping Le Moulin du Roch, Le Roch, Route des Eyzies, 24200 Sarlat-la-Canéda [05 53 59 20 27; fax 05 53 59 20 95; moulin.du.roch@wanadoo.fr; www.moulin-du-roch.com]** Fr A20 take exit 55 at Souillac dir Sarlat. At rndabt in Sarlat (just under rlwy viaduct) take 1st exit & foll sp thro Sarlat dir Périgueux. As come to end of Sarlat turn L onto D6 dir Les Eyzies (becomes D47 in 2km). Site on L in approx 9 km on D47. Fr N on D704 to Sarlat, turn R at hypmkt, then as above. Lge, hdg/mkd pitch, terr, pt shd; htd wc; chem disp; baby facs; some serviced pitches; shwrs inc; el pnts (6A) inc; gas; Indtte; shop; rest; snacks; bar; BBQ (gas/charcoal only); playgrnd; htd pool; paddling pool with mini waterslide; fishing lake; lake sw 8km; tennis; horseriding; canoeing 10km; wifi; entmnt; internet; games/TV rm; 45% static tents/vans; no dogs; Eng spkn; adv bkg rec Jun-Aug; quiet; ccard acc; red low ssn/long stay; CCI. "Well-run site; lge pitches; clean facs but poss long, steep walk; gd rest & pool; m'vans poss not acc after prolonged heavy rain due soft ground; mkt Sat." ♦ 10 May-17 Sep. € 34.00 (CChq acc) ABS - D02 2009*

SARLAT LA CANEDA *7C3* (4km NW) *44.90929, 1.18738* **FFCC Camping Le Rivaux, Route de Périgueux, 24200 Sarlat-la-Canéda [05 53 59 04 41]** Fr Sarlat take D47 sp Les Eyzies & Périgueux; after approx 2km, take D6. Site on R after approx 300m. Med, hdg/mkd pitch, pt sl, pt shd; wc; chem disp; shwrs inc; el pnts (2-6A) €1.50-2.80; gas; Indry rm; shops 3km; tradsmn high ssn; BBQ; playgrnd; pool 4km; games rm; dogs; phone; quiet; adv bkg rec high ssn; CCI. "Spacious pitches; gd touring base; vg." ♦ 1 Apr-30 Sep. € 11.00 2009*

SARZEAU *2G3* (10km E Coastal) *47.51903, -2.64915* **Camp Municipal Roch Ventur, Rue de la Plage de Rouvran, 56370 Le Tour-du-Parc [02 97 67 30 88; fax 02 97 67 39 02]** On N165 fr Vannes dir Nantes, exit sp Sarzeau onto D780. Just S of St Armel turn L onto D199 & in 3km onto D199A for Le Tour-du-Parc, then foll sp for site. Med, mkd pitch, pt sl, pt shd; wc; chem disp (wc); shwrs inc; el pnts (5A) €3; gas; Indtte; Indry rm; tradsmn; shop; rest; snacks 1km; playgrnd; sand beach adj; watersports adj; tennis; cycle hire & routes; 5% statics; dogs €0.80; phone adj; poss cr; Eng spkn; adv bkg; quiet; CCI. "Little shade; gd san facs; fair." ♦ 1 Apr-15 Sep. € 9.00 2007*

SARZEAU *2G3* (10km E Coastal) *47.52045, -2.65737* **Camping Le Cadran Solaire, Kerjambet, 56370 Le Tour-du-Parc [02 97 67 30 40; fax 02 97 67 40 28; cadran solaire56@yahoo.fr]** Take N165 fr Vannes twds Nantes, turn R for Sarzeau (D780), nr St Armel turn L on D199 & in 3.2km on D199A for Le Tour-du-Parc. In Le Tour-du-Parc turn R at water tower onto D324 sp Sarzeau, site on R in 1km. Med, hdg pitch, pt shd; wc; chem disp; shwrs inc; el pnts (6A) €2.80; Indtte; shop; playgrnd; lake shgl beach adj; tennis; some statics; phone; poss cr; quiet; ccard acc; CCI. "Vg san block." ♦ 1 Apr-30 Sep. € 12.30 2007*

SARZEAU *2G3* (7km SE Coastal) *47.50551, -2.68308* **Camping Manoir de Ker An Poul, 1 Route de la Grée, Penvins, 56370 Sarzeau [02 97 67 33 30; fax 02 97 67 44 83; manoirdekeranpoul@wanadoo.fr; www.manoirdekeranpoul.com]** Fr E exit N165 1km E of Muzillac, sp Sarzeau D20 & cont approx 20km to junc of D20 & D199, S on D199 sp Penvins. Fr W, 6km E of Vannes, exit N165 onto N780 sp Sarzeau, in 9.5km S onto D199 sp Penvins. Lge, hdg pitch, pt sl, pt shd; wc (some cont); chem disp; baby facs; shwrs inc; el pnts (6A) €4; Indtte; shop; rest adj; snacks; bar; BBQ; playgrnd; htd pool; sand beach 700m; tennis; games area; cycle hire; wifi; entmnt; TV rm; 30% statics; dogs €4; poss cr; Eng spkn; adv bkg; quiet; red low ssn; CCI. "Spacious pitches; warm welcome; lovely situation in grnds of chateau." ♦ 4 Apr-26 Sep. € 25.00 2009*

See advertisement opposite

SARZEAU *2G3* (2.5km S Coastal) *47.50720, -2.76083* **Camping La Ferme de Lann Hoëdic, Rue Jean de la Fontaine, Route de Roaliguen, 56370 Sarzeau [02 97 48 01 73; contact@camping-lannhoedic.fr; www.camping-lannhoedic.fr]** Fr Vannes on N165 turn onto D780 dir Sarzeau. Do not ent Sarzeau, but at Super U rndabt foll sp Le Roaliguen. After 1.5km turn L to Lann Hoëdic. Med, mkd pitch, pt shd; htd wc; chem disp; mv service pnt; baby facs; fam bthrm; shwrs inc; el pnts (10A) €3; gas; Indtte; shop 800m; tradsmn; rest 2km; snacks; bar 1km; playgrnd; sand beach 800m; cycle hire; wifi; 10% statics; dogs €1.90; phone; Eng spkn; adv bkg; quiet; CCI. "Peaceful, well managed, family-run site; warm welcome; excel, clean facs inc disabled; beautiful coastline - beaches & dunes; highly rec." ♦ 1 Apr-31 Oct. € 16.90 (CChq acc) 2009*

See advertisement on next page

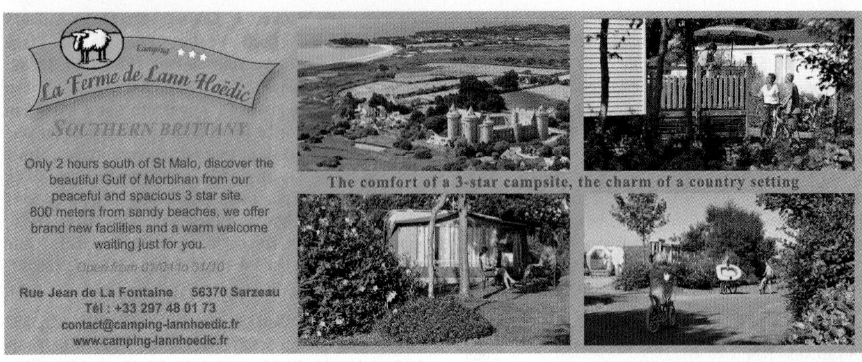

Camping ★★★
La Ferme de Lann Hoëdic
SOUTHERN BRITTANY
Only 2 hours south of St Malo, discover the beautiful Gulf of Morbihan from our peaceful and spacious 3 star site.
800 meters from sandy beaches, we offer brand new facilities and a warm welcome waiting just for you.
Open from 01/04 to 31/10
Rue Jean de La Fontaine 56370 Sarzeau
Tél : +33 297 48 01 73
contact@camping-lannhoedic.fr
www.camping-lannhoedic.fr
The comfort of a 3-star campsite, the charm of a country setting

SARZEAU *2G3* (4km S Coastal/Rural) *47.50589, -2.77139* **Camping An Trest, Route de la Plage de Roaliguen, 56370 Sarzeau [02 97 41 79 60; fax 02 97 41 36 21; letreste@campingletreste.com; www.an-trest.com]** Fr E on D780 turn L at 1st rndabt nr Super U supmkt sp Le Roaliguen, site sp on L. NB ignore R turn to Sarzeau after sp Port Navalo. Lge, hdg/mkd pitch, pt sl, pt shd; wc (some cont); chem disp; baby facs; shwrs inc; el pnts (10A) €3.30; gas; lndtte; supmkt 2km; tradsmn; snacks; bar in ssn; playgrnd; htd pool & paddling pool; waterslide; sand beach 800m; tennis, horseriding, golf 3km; TV rm; 5% statics; dogs €1.50; phone; Eng spkn; adv bkg; quiet; 20% red low ssn; ccard acc; CCI. "Pleasant, well-run site; gd touring base; helpful owners." ♦ 1 May-14 Sep. € 20.70 2006*

SARZEAU *2G3* (2km SW Rural) *47.52255, -2.79713* **Camping Domaine Le Bohat, Le Haut Bohat, Route d'Arzon, 56370 Sarzeau [02 97 41 78 68; fax 02 97 41 71 97; contact@domainelebohat.com; www.domainelebohat.com]** Fr Vannes on N165, exit onto D780 to Sarzeau. Do not turn off this main rd to Sarzeau (town not suitable for m'vans or c'vans) but cont twd Arzon; 1km after 2nd rndabt turn L for Le Bohat & Spernec, then take 1st R. Fr S on N165 take D20 at Muzillac, thro Surzur & cont to join D780 to Sarzeau. Then as above. Lge, hdg/mkd pitch, pt shd; wc (some cont); chem disp; mv service pnt; baby facs; shwrs inc; el pnts (10A) inc; gas; lndtte; shop; tradsmn; rest; snacks; bar; BBQ (gas/charcoal); playgrnd; htd pool, htd covrd pool & paddling pool; waterslide; sand beach, watersports 4km; cycle hire 2km, golf 6km; horseriding 2km; entmnt; wifi; games/TV rm; 4% statics; dogs €3.50; phone; c'vans over 7.50m not acc high ssn; poss cr; Eng spkn; adv bkg; quiet; ccard acc; red low ssn; CCI. "Busy, Dutch-owned site; lge pitches; excel, helpful staff; cycle tracks; mkt Thu; vg." ♦ 25 Apr-25 Sep. € 32.20 ABS - B07 2009*

SARZEAU *2G3* (3km SW Coastal) *47.50941, -2.80747* **Camping à la Ferme L'Abri-Côtier (Rio), 90 Route de Sarzeau, 56730 St Gildas-de-Rhuys [02 97 45 27 42; contact@abri-cotier.com; www.abri-cotier.com]** Fr Sarzeau take D198 sp St Gildas-de-Rhuys. Site in 3km. Med, hdg/mkd pitch, pt shd; wc; chem disp; baby facs; fam bthrm; shwrs inc; el pnts €3; gas; lndtte; shop, rest & bar 2km; tradsm; snacks; BBQ (charcoal/gas); beach adj; games area; wifi; TV; dogs €1; bus 100m; Eng pkn; adv bkg; v quiet; ccard acc. "Well-run, clean, reliable site; lge pitches; friendly staff; cannot fault!" ♦ 1 Apr-30 Sep. € 14.00 2008*

SARZEAU *2G3* (5km SW Coastal) *47.48976, -2.80075* **Camping Saint Jacques, 1 Rue Pratel Vihan, 56370 Sarzeau [02 97 41 79 29; fax 02 97 48 04 45; info@camping-stjacques.com; www.camping-stjacques.com]** Fr Sarzeau on D780, at 2nd rndabt foll dir St Jacques, site sp. Lge, mkd pitch, pt shd; wc (come cont); chem disp; baby facs; shwrs inc; el pnts (4-6A) €2.55; gas; lndtte; shop; snacks; bar; BBQ; playgrnd; sand beach adj; tennis; fishing; sailing school; cycle hire; entmnt; 10% statics; dogs €1; Eng spkn; adv bkg; quiet; red low ssn; ccard acc; CCI. "Poss untidy site; many long-stay c'vans; excel beach & dunes; gd sea sw; NH only." ♦ 1 Apr-30 Sep. € 13.55 2009*

SARZEAU *2G3* (6km W Coastal) *47.52865, -2.84772* **Camping du Menhir, La Saline, 56730 St Gildas-de-Rhuys [02 97 45 22 88; contact@camping-bretagnesud.com; www.camping-bretagnesud.com]** Take D780 Vannes-Port Navalo rd; 6km after Sarzeau turn L sp La Saline & Camping Menhir. Lge, mkd pitch, pt shd; wc; baby facs; shwrs inc; el pnts (6-10A) €4-5; gas; lndtte (inc dryer); sm shop high ssn or 3km; tradsmn; rest; snacks; bar; playgrnd; htd pool; waterslides; paddling pool; sand beach 1km; tennis; games area; games rm; dogs €3; adv bkg; quiet; red low ssn. "Lge pitches; gd san facs; excel." ♦ 26 May-6 Sep. € 29.50 2009*

SAUCHY LESTREE see Marquion *3B4*

SAUGNACQ ET MURET *7D1* (4km W Rural) *44.40946, -0.82623* **Camping Le Muretois, 40410 Saugnacq-et-Muret [tel/fax 05 58 09 62 14]** Exit A63/N10 junc 18 at Le Muret, site within 500m of N10 at junc with D20, sp. Nr Hotel Le Caravaniers. Sm, mkd pitch, pt shd; wc (own san rec); chem disp (wc); shwrs; el pnts (10A) (some rev pol); lndtte; shop 500m; rest 100m; snacks; bar; playgrnd; rv fishing 3km; tennis; cycle hire; dogs; phone; poss cr; adv bkg rec high ssn; quiet; CCI. "Friendly, basic site; gd NH; take care el pnts; unreliable opening dates - phone ahead to check!" 1 Apr-30 Sep. € 10.00 2008*

SAUGUES *9C1* (500m W Rural) *44.9586, 3.5417* **Camp Municipal de la Seuge, Ave du Gévaudan, 43170 Saugues [04 71 77 80 62 or 06 65 15 04 32; fax 04 71 77 66 40; camping@mairie-saugues.com; www.mairie-saugues.com]** 500m W fr Saugues on D589 twd Paulhac, turn R into Ave de Gévaudan. Site on L in 100m. Well sp. Med, mkd pitch, pt shd; htd wc; chem disp; mv service pnt; baby facs; shwrs inc; el pnts (10A) €2.50; Indtte; shop; snacks; bar; playgrnd; BBQ; fishing; boating; canoeing; sports area; adv bkg; ccard not acc; CCI. "Gd cent for gorges of Allier & Le Puy-en-Velay; barriers clsd at night; lge grass pitches." 15 Apr-15 Oct. € 10.60 2008*

SAUJON *7B1* (2km N Rural) *45.68646, -0.94000* **Aire Naturelle Le Logis de la Lande (Renouleau), Route de l'Ilatte, 17600 Saujon [05 46 02 84 31 or 06 77 38 62 98 (mob); christianerenouleau@wanadoo.fr; http://camping-lalande.monsite.wanadoo.fr]** Fr N150 Saujon by-pass turn onto D1 dir Le Gua. At 1st rndabt turn L, pass fire stn & sports grnd on L. Site on R immed after R bend. Sm, pt sl, pt shd; wc; chem disp; shwrs; el pnts (6A) €4; Indry rm; shop, rest, snacks & bar 2km; playgrnd; beach 12km; dogs €2 poss cr; v quiet. "Pleasant, well-kept CL-type site; san facs clean but ltd in number; inland fr crowded coast, not full peak ssn; excel." Apr-Oct. € 11.80 2009*

SAUJON *7B1* (2km N Rural) *45.68326, -0.93741* **FFCC Camping du Lac du Saujon, Aire de la Lande, Voie des Tourterelles, 17600 Saujon [05 46 06 82 99; fax 05 46 06 83 66; info@campingdulac.net; www.campingdulac.net]** Fr N150 Saujon by-pass turn onto D1 dir Le Gua. Foll sp to site. Med, mkd pitch, pt shd; wc; chem disp; mv service pnt; shwrs inc; el pnts (6-10A) €4-6; Indtte; shop & 2km; rest; snacks; bar; playgrnd; htd, covrd pool adj; fishing; tennis; cycle hire; jogging course, horseriding nr; entmnt; 33% statics; dogs €2.60; phone; poss cr; Eng spkn; adv bkg; red low ssn; CCI. "Excel site." ♦ 1 Apr-15 Nov. € 15.80 2006*

SAULCE, LA *9D3* (2km E Rural) *44.42559, 6.02944* **Camping Le Lac, Route Napoléon, 05110 Curbans [04 92 54 23 10; fax 04 92 54 23 11; info@au-camping-du-lac.com; www.au-camping-du-lac.com]** S fr Gap on N85 twd Sisteron for 16km; R to La Saulce over ; in vill turn L onto D19 & over canal. Turn L again. Site 1km on L. Med, pt shd; wc; chem disp; shwrs inc; el pnts (6A) €3; Indtte; shop 2km; tradsmn; rest; bar; playgrnd; pool; paddling pool; fishing; 10% statics; dogs €2; poss cr; Eng spkn; adv bkg; quiet; CCI. "Enthusiastic family owners; lge pitches." ♦ 1 Apr-10 Oct. € 19.00 2008*

SAULIAC SUR CELE *7D4* (1km N Rural) *44.52609, 1.71944* **Camping Mas de Nadal (Naturist), 46330 Sauliac-sur-Célé [05 65 31 20 51; fax 05 65 31 20 57; info@masdenadal.com; www.masdenadal.com]** Fr Cahors take D653 E. After 35km turn R onto D40 S, sp Blars. Fr Blars cont S for 2km to site ent on R. Sm, mkd pitch, pt sl, pt shd; wc; shwrs inc; el pnts (3-9A) €4; Indtte; shops 2km; tradsmn; rest; bar; playgrnd; pool; canoe hire; games area; phone; dogs €4.50; poss cr; Eng spkn; adv bkg; quiet; CCI/INF card req. "Secluded wooded hillside; ltd rough pitches not suitable lge o'fits; rec phone ahead to check avail; suitable for m'vans." 1 Apr-30 Sep. € 21.00 2009*

SAULIEU *6G1* (1km N Rural) *47.28936, 4.22401* **Camp Municipal Le Perron, Route de Paris, 21210 Saulieu [tel/fax 03 80 64 16 19 or 03 80 64 09 22 (Mairie); camping.salieu@wanadoo.fr]** On D906 (N6) on L of rd on ent fr N. Sp. Lge, hdg/mkd pitch, pt sl, pt shd; htd wc; chem disp; shwrs inc; el pnts (10A) €2.50; gas; Indtte; sm shop; tradsmn; rest in ssn; bar; playgrnd; pool; tennis; dogs €1; adv bkg; quiet, but rd noise; red low ssn; CCI. "No twin-axle c'vans; gates clsd 2200-0700; gd touring base; lake fishing; gd walking area." ♦ 5 Apr-20 Sep. € 12.50 2006*

SAULT *10E3* (2km NE Rural) *44.10165, 5.42260* **Camp Municipal du Defends, Route de St Trinit, 84390 Sault [04 90 64 07 18 or 04 90 64 02 30 (Mairie); camping sault@wanadoo.fr]** NE fr Sault on D950 dir St Trinit; site on R in 2km. Med, some mkd pitch, shd; wc; chem disp; shwrs inc; el pnts (6A) €2.60 (poss long lead req); gas 1km; supmkt 1km; BBQ; playgrnd; 10% statics; dogs; phone adj; poss cr; Eng spkn; CCI. "Site in woodland; conv Mont Ventoux & Gorges de la Nesque; gd cycling; gd." 7 Apr-30 Sep. € 10.75 2009*

⊞ **SAULXURES SUR MOSELOTTE** *6F3* (1.5km W Rural) *47.95284, 6.75115* **Camping Le Lac de la Moselotte, 336 Route des Amias, 88290 Saulxures-sur-Moselotte [03 29 24 56 56; fax 03 29 24 58 31; lac-moselotte@ville-saulxures-mtte.fr; www.ville-saulxures-mtte.fr]** Sp fr D43. Med, hdg/mkd pitch, pt sl, pt shd; htd wc; chem disp; shwrs inc; el pnts (10A) €5 (poss rev pol); Indtte; shop; tradsmn; snacks; bar; playgrnd; lake sw & sand beach adj; watersports; canoe & cycle hire; fishing; games rm; entmnt; TV; 5% statics; dogs €1; phone; Eng spkn; adv bkg; quiet; ccard acc; red long stay/CCI. "Pleasant, well-situated site; lake fenced off." ♦ € 15.00 2007*

SAUMUR See also sites listed under Bourgueil, Coutures, Doué-la-Fontaine, Montsoreau, Les Rosiers-sur-Loire and Vernantes.

SAUMUR *4G1* (1km N Urban) *47.25990, -0.06440* **Camping L'Ile d'Offard, Rue de Verden, 49400 Saumur [02 41 40 30 00; fax 02 41 67 37 81; iledoffard@cvtloisirs.fr; www.cvtloisirs.com]** Exit A85 junc 3 onto N347; ent town past rlwy stn & cross Rv Loire bdge; turn L immed over bdge & foll sp Chinon alongside rv. At rndabt turn L & take 1st L to site; foll sp. Site on island facing Saumur castle. Lge, hdg/mkd pitch, hdstg, pt sl, pt shd; htd wc; chem disp; mv service pnt; shwrs inc; el pnts (6-10A) €4 (poss rev pol); gas; Indtte; shops in ssn; tradsmn; rest; snacks, bar; playgrnd; htd pool; covrd pool adj; paddling pool; rv sw & fishing, boating adj; tennis; cycle hire; games area; entmnt; wifi; TV rm; 20% tour ops statics; dogs €1.50; poss cr; Eng spkn; adv bkg (non-refundable bkg fee); some rlwy noise; ccard acc; red low ssn/CCI. "Pleasant, busy, well-managed site; hdstg pitches in winter; poss unkempt/scruffy low ssn; helpful staff; gd, clean san facs, ltd low ssn; most pitches lge but some v sm pitches bet statics - lge o'fits check in advance; can be muddy when wet; gd access to Saumur; gd cycle rtes." ♦ 1 Mar-15 Nov. € 25.50 (CChq acc) 2009*

SAUMUR *4G1* (7km NE Rural) *47.29937, -0.01218* **Camping Le Pô Doré, 49650 Allonnes [tel/fax 02 41 38 78 80; camping.du.po.dore@wanadoo.fr; www.camping-lepodore.com]** NE fr Saumur on N347 & turn R onto D10. Site 3km W of Allonnes on R. Med, hdg/mkd pitch, some hdstg; pt shd; wc; chem disp; mv service pnt; shwrs inc; el pnts (6-10A) €2.70-3.80 (poss rev pol); Indtte; tradsmn; rest; snacks; bar; playgrnd; htd pool; cycle hire; entmnt; 25% statics; dogs €1.10; phone; poss cr; some Eng spkn; some rlwy noise; ccard acc; red low ssn; CCI. "Conv NH/sh stay for wine rtes, caves & museums & a'route." ♦
15 Mar-1 Nov. € 14.70 2008*

SAUMUR *4G1* (6km E Rural) *47.24755, -0.00033* **Camping L'Etang de la Brèche, 5 Impasse de la Brèche, 49730 Varennes-sur-Loire [02 41 51 22 92; fax 02 41 51 27 24; mail@etang-breche.com; www.etang-breche.com or www.les-castels.com]** Exit Saumur on N152 twd Tours & site sp fr either dir. Site on N side of rd (6km W of Varennes) app fr lge lay-by giving easy ent. Lge, hdg pitch, pt shd; wc; chem disp; mv service pnt; 20% serviced pitch; baby facs; shwrs inc; el pnts (10A) €3.50; gas; Indtte; shop; tradsmn; rest; snacks; bar; playgrnd; 2 htd pools (no shorts); waterslide; cycle hire; tennis; games rms; entmnt; internet; TV rm; 30% statics; dogs; phone; Eng spkn; adv bkg (ess Jul/Aug); quiet but rd noise in some areas; ccard acc; red low ssn; CCI. "Spacious site & pitches; well-organised; excel facs; auto barrier clsd 2300-0700; helpful staff; excel." ♦
30 Apr-15 Sep. € 33.00 2009*

SAUMUR *4G1* (5km NW Rural) *47.29440, -0.14120* **Camping de Chantepie, Route de Chantepie, 49400 St Hilaire-St Florent [02 41 67 95 34; fax 02 41 67 95 85; info@campingchantepie.com; www.campingchantepie.com]** Fr Saumer take D751 on S bank of Rv Loire sp Gennes. Site on L bet Le Pointrineau & La Croix. Or fr N after x-ing rv on N347, take turn sp St Hilaire-St-Florent & join D751 for Gennes; site is 3km N of St Hilaire-St Florent, well sp fr D751. NB Easy to miss turning. Lge, hdg/mkd pitch, pt shd; wc; chem disp; mv service pnt; baby facs; shwrs inc; el pnts (10A) inc (poss rev pol); gas; Indtte; shop; tradsmn; rest/snacks; bar; BBQ; playgrnd; 2 pools (1 htd, covrd); paddling pool; rv beach 200m; fishing; tennis 2km; cycle hire; golf 2km; horseriding, boating 5km; entmnt; wifi; games/TV rm; 10% statics; dogs €4; c'vans over 8m not acc; Eng spkn; adv bkg; quiet; ccard acc; red low ssn; CCI. "Excel site with rv views; well-spaced, lge pitches; care with access to pitches for lge o'fits; friendly, helpful staff; excel san facs, inc for disabled; conv Loire cycle rte; mkt Sat Saumur." ♦
15 May-11 Sep. € 30.00 ABS - L06 2009*

SAUMUR *4G1* (8km NW Rural) *47.31033, -0.14508* **Camping La Croix Rouge, Rue de la Croix Rouge, 49160 St Martin-de-la-Place [02 41 38 09 02 or 06 32 17 14 61 (mob); fax 02 41 45 65 65; campinglacroixrouge@laposte.net; http://campinglacroixrouge.cabanova.fr]** Fr Saumur, take N347 N across rv then turn L onto D952 dir Angers. At St Martin-de-la-Place foll sp for site. Med, mkd pitch, pt shd; wc; chem disp; mv service pnt; shwrs; el pnts (5A) €3; Indry rm; shop 600m; sm rest, bar 200m; playgrnd; rv sw, sailing adj; dogs €1; bus 150m; adv bkg; quiet; ccard not acc; CCI. "Beautiful, tranquil site on Rv Loire; views fr some pitches; 26 steps to clean spacious san facs (2009); disabled facs at grnd level; barrier clsd 2200-0700; no twin-axles; conv Saumur; excel." ♦ 21 May-15 Oct. € 8.50 2009*

SAUSHEIM see Mulhouse *6F3*

SAUVETERRE DE BEARN *8F1* (S Rural) *43.39518, -0.94416* **Camping du Gave, Ave de la Gare, 64390 Sauveterre-de-Béarn [05 59 38 53 30; fax 05 59 36 19 88; camping-du-gave@wanadoo.fr; www.bearn-gaves.com/camping-du-gave]** Site on D933 on S side of town. Ent immed off rndabt at end of rv bdge. Med, mkd pitch, shd; wc (some cont); chem disp (wc); shwrs; el pnts (6A) inc; Indtte; shop & 200m; tradsmn; rest 1km; snacks; bar; playgrnd; rv sw adj; canoeing; 10% statics; dogs; poss cr; adv bkg; quiet. "Facs poss stretched in ssn; friendly management; footpath to medieval town." ♦ 1 Apr-30 Sep. € 12.80 2008*

SAUVETERRE DE GUYENNE *7D2* (8km NW Rural) *44.72564, -0.15066* **Camping Château Guiton (Naturist), 33760 Frontenac [05 56 23 52 79; fax 05 56 23 99 40; accueil@chateau-guiton.com; www.chateau-guiton.com]** N of Sauveterre-de-Guyenne turn W onto D123 sp Frontenac. Turn L just bef vill sp Château Guiton. Sm, mkd pitch, pt sl, pt shd; wc; chem disp; sauna; shwrs; el pnts (6-10A) €3.50; Indtte; shop; tradsmn; rest & bar 4km; playgrnd; pool; gym; TV rm; dogs €2; phone; Eng spkn; adv bkg; quiet; ccard acc; red low ssn; IFN card req. "Part-wooded site in cent wine region; friendly owner; gd cycling; conv Bordeaux; gd."
15 May-30 Sep. € 23.50 2009*

SAUVETERRE LA LEMANCE see Villefranche du Périgord *7D3*

SAUVIAN see Valras Plage *10F1*

SAUXILLANGES *9B1* (500m SW Rural) *45.54578, 3.36451* **Camping Sauxillanges, Chemin des Prairies, 63490 Sauxillanges [04 73 96 86 26; chateau@lagrangefort.com; www.lagrangefort.com]** Exit A75 (E11) at junc 13 to D996, head E twd Sauxillanges. Turn R 100m after Gendarmerie in vill. Sp. Med, mkd pitch, shd; wc (some cont); chem disp; some serviced pitches; shwrs inc; el pnts (6A) €2.50 (poss rev pol); Indtte; shop; playgrnd; pool adj (Jul/Aug); tennis; fishing adj; 5% statics; dogs €1.35; Eng spkn; adv bkg ess high ssn; quiet; ccard acc. "Charming, interesting town; excel." ♦ 15 Jun-15 Sep. € 13.00 2008*

SAVENAY *2G3* (2km E Rural) *47.35651, -1.92136* **Camp Municipal du Lac, La Moëre, 44260 Savenay [02 40 58 31 76; fax 02 40 58 39 35]** Site well sp in Savenay. Med, mkd pitch, terr, pt shd; htd wc; shwrs inc; el pnts (5A); gas adj; lndtte; tradsmn; snacks; sm playgrnd; pool adj; fishing; quiet. "Vg, clean site in attractive lakeside park; lge pitches." ♦ 1 May-30 Sep. 2009*

SAVERNE *6E3* (1.3km SW Urban) *48.73148, 7.35561* **FFCC Camping de Saverne, Rue du Père Libermann, 67700 Saverne [tel/fax 03 88 91 35 65; info@campingsaverne.com; www.campingsaverne.com]** Take Saverne exit fr A4, junc 45. Site well sp nr town cent. Med, hdg/mkd pitch, hdstg, pt sl, pt shd; htd wc; chem disp; mv service pnt; shwrs inc; el pnts (6-10A) €3-5 (poss rev pol); lndry rm; supmkt 1.5km; playgrnd; pool 1km; 20% statics; dogs €1.35; poss cr; adv bkg; quiet; ccard acc; red low ssn/CCI. "Pleasant, busy, well-run site; warm welcome, friendly staff; excel san facs; m'van aire de service nr ent; trains to Strasbourg fr town; gd." ♦ 1 Apr-30 Sep. € 12.00 2009*

SAVERNE *6E3* (5km SW Rural) *48.69172, 7.32958* **Camping au Paradis Perdu, Rue de Hirschberg, St Gall, 67440 Thal-Marmoutier [03 88 70 60 59]** Fr Saverne, use minor rds rather than by-pass; foll sp Thal-Marmoutier then foll camp sps to St Gall & site; access thro archway - poss tight for lge vans. Sm, pt sl, pt shd; wc; chem disp; shwrs; el pnts (3-6A) €1.85-€3.70; shops 3km; rest; snacks; bar; playgrnd; 30% statics; dogs €1.20; adv bkg; quiet. "Pleasant setting at rear of rest; facs basic but gd." 1 Apr-15 Oct. € 10.30 2006*

SAVIGNY EN VERON *4G1* (500m W Rural) *47.20059, 0.13932* **FFCC Camping La Fritillaire, Rue Basse, 37420 Savigny-en-Véron [02 47 58 03 79; fax 02 47 58 03 81; lafritillaire.veron@ffcc.fr; www.camp-in-france.com]** Fr Montsoreau on D751 or D7 on S bank of Rv Loire, foll sp to Savigny-en-Véron & site. Med, mkd pitch, pt shd; htd wc; chem disp; mv service pnt; baby facs; shwrs inc; el pnts (10A) €3.20; lndtte; rest, snacks & bar 500m; BBQ; playgrnd; htd, covrd pool 4km; games area (under-7s); tennis; cycle hire; horseriding; some statics; dogs €1; Eng spkn; adv bkg; quiet; red low ssn; CCI. "Excel, peaceful site; friendly owners; gd clean facs, ltd low ssn; gd touring base Loire chateaux; vg cycle rtes; poss workers staying on site (2009)." ♦ 1 Apr-30 Sep. € 10.10 2009*

SAVINES LE LAC *9D3* (2km SW Rural) *44.51812, 6.38445* **Camp Municipal Les Eygoires, 05160 Savines-le-Lac [04 92 44 20 48 or 04 92 44 20 03 (Mairie); fax 04 92 44 39 71; camping.municipal.savinelelac@wanadoo.fr]** Take N94 to Savines. Site on D954 on N side of rd. Lge, terr, pt shd; wc (some cont); baby facs; shwrs; el pnts (5A) €3.30; lndtte; shop; snacks; bar; playgrnd; lake sw & shgl beach; sailing; some statics; dogs €1; adv bkg; quiet. 1 Jun-30 Sep. € 11.60 2006*

SAVINES LE LAC *9D3* (5km SW Rural) *44.49924, 6.34545* **Camping La Palatrière, 05160 Le Sauze-du-Lac [tel/fax 04 92 44 20 98; lapalatriere@wanadoo.fr; www.lapalatriere.com]** Take N94 fr Gap thro Chorges, turn R after bdge at Savines-le-Lac onto D954 for 5km twds Le Sauze-du-Lac. Sm, mkd pitch, terr, pt shd; wc; shwrs inc; el pnts (6A) inc; lndtte; shop; rest; snacks; bar; BBQ; playgrnd; lake sw; 25% statics; dogs €1; entmnt; TV; ccard acc. "Lovely, family-run site on hillside; beautiful views; unsuitable lge o'fits due steep site rds; some pitches soft after rain." 1 May-30 Nov. € 20.00 2007*

I'm going to fill in some site report forms and post them off to the Club; we could win a ferry crossing – it's here on page 12.

SCAER *2F2* (200m E Rural) *48.0265, -3.6970* **Camp Municipal de Kérisole, Rue Pasteur, 29390 Scaër [02 98 57 60 91 or 02 98 59 42 10 (LS); fax 02 98 57 66 89; mairie.scaer@altica.com; www.ville-scaer.fr]** Fr N165 take D70 to Rosporden, then N on D782, site well sp in Scaër. Thro town foll sp to site. Med, mkd pitch, pt shd; wc; chem disp; mv service pnt; baby facs; shwrs; el pnts (13A) €2.35; lndtte; shop; tradsmn; rest; snacks; bar 250m; playgrnd; pool; fishing; few statics; dogs; phone; Eng spkn; adv bkg; quiet; CCI. "Vg site at ent to forest; excel san facs." ♦ 15 Jun-15 Sep. € 8.00 2008*

SECONDIGNY *4H1* (S Rural) *46.60486, -0.41599* **Camp Municipal du Moulin des Effres, 79130 Secondigny [05 49 95 61 97 or 05 49 63 70 15 (Mairie); fax 05 49 63 55 48; secondigny@marie-secondigny.fr]** D949 to Secondigny, S onto D748. Site sp 800m on L immed after lake. Med, mkd pitch, pt sl, pt shd; wc (some cont); shwrs inc; el pnts (6A) €2.80; rest 400m; snacks; shops 500m; lndry rm; pool; tennis; TV; entmnt; lake fishing adj; poss cr; quiet; CCI. "Warden calls pm; in pleasant surroundings nr attractive vill." 1 Jun-15 Sep. € 8.60 2006*

SEDAN *5C1* (11km SE Rural) *49.66265, 5.04718* **Camp Municipal du Lac, Route de Mouzon, 08140 Douzy [03 24 26 31 19 or 03 24 26 31 48 (Mairie); fax 03 24 26 84 01; aubergedulac@free.fr]** On N43 fr Sedan-Metz to Douzy. Turn R (S) at traff lts in Douzy & site in 500m on L. Clearly sp. Med, few hdstg, pt shd; few hdstg; wc; 60% serviced pitch; shwrs inc; el pnts (6A) inc; gas 1km; lndtte; shops 1km; tradsmn; rest adj; snacks; bar; playgrnd; shgl beach & lake sw adj; waterslides; tennis; dogs €1.50; poss cr; Eng spkn; adv bkg; some rd & light aircraft noise; red long stay; CCI. "Helpful staff; pitches mostly uneven; modern san facs; ltd facs low ssn; excel." ♦ 1 May-30 Sep. € 13.50 2008*

SEDAN *5C1* (1km W Urban) *49.69868, 4.93848* **Camp Municipal, Prairie de Torcy, Blvd Fabert, 08200 Sedan [tel/fax 03 24 27 13 05 or 03 24 27 73 42]** Fr A34(A203) exit junc 4 dir Sedan cent. Cont strt thro town & over rlwy bdge; in 500m cont over viaduct, site visible on R, turn R at next traff lts at end of viaduct, site 100m on R. Easy to find. Med, pt shd; no hdstg; wc (some cont); chem disp; mv service pnt; shwrs inc; el pnts (10A) €3; lndtte; shop 300m; rest, snacks & bar 500m; BBQ; sm playgrnd; pool 500m; dogs €1; phone; poss cr; adv bkg; some traff noise; red long stay; CCI. "Pleasant, peaceful site by rv; friendly, helpful staff; uneven pitches; san facs clean, too few & need refurb (own san facs rec); poss muddy when wet; market traders for fair mid Sep; vg." ♦ 1 Apr-30 Sep. € 7.55 2009*

SEDERON *9D3* (2km E Rural) *44.19184, 5.55616* **Camping Les Routelles (Naturist), 26560 Séderon [04 75 28 54 54; fax 04 75 28 53 14; infos@routelles.com; www.routelles.com]** Best app fr E fr Sisteron on D946. Immed bef Séderon turn R onto D225B (opp Renault g'ge), & foll sp 2km. At ent owner will tow up steep track to pitch. Med, sl, terr, pt shd; wc; chem disp; sauna; shwrs inc; el pnts (6A) €2.50; tradsmn; rest; snacks; bar; BBQ (subject to pitch); playgrnd; pool; TV rm; dogs €0.70;phone; some Eng spkn; adv bkg; quiet; red low ssn. "Excel site with views; clean san facs; friendly, helpful owner - pitches vans with 4x4; highly rec; unsuitable for disabled." 1 Apr-1 Nov. € 22.50 2006*

SEES *4E1* (S Urban) *48.59875, 0.17103* **Camp Municipal Le Clos Normand, Rue du 8 Mai 1945, 61500 Sées [02 33 28 87 37 or 02 33 28 74 79 (LS); fax 02 33 28 18 13; sees.tourisme@wanadoo.fr; www.camping-clos-normand.fr]** C'vans & lge m'vans best app fr S - twd rndabt at S end of by-pass (rec use this rndabt as other rtes diff & narr). Well sp. Narr ent. Sm, hdg pitch, pt shd; wc; chem disp; mv service pnt; shwrs inc; el pnts (6A) €2.50; gas; lndtte; supmkt opp; snacks & bar 100m; rest 500m; playgrnd; pool 2km; fishing; 10% statics; no twin axles; dogs €1.15; some Eng spkn; adv bkg; slight rd noise; CCI. "Spacious, well-cared for pitches; helpful, friendly warden; gd san facs, poss stretched if site full; excel mv service pnt; gates clsd 2100 (2000 low ssn)." ♦ 1 May-30 Sep. € 10.10 2009*

SEGRE *2F4* (7km NW Rural) *47.71003, -0.95165* **Camping Parc de St Blaise, 49520 Noyant-la-Gravoyère [02 41 61 93 09; direction@laminebleue.com; www.campingsaintblaise.fr]** Fr Segré take D775 (N162) dir Pouancé to Noyant, site/park sp in vill on R. Sm, hdg pitch, terr, pt shd; wc; chem disp (wc); shwrs inc; el pnts (6A) inc; shop & 1km; tradsmn; rest; bar; playgrnd; lake sw adj; aquatic park; fishing; horseriding; entmnt; dogs; phone; CCI. "Clean, well-maintained site in leisure park; gd views; slate mine worth visit (not an eyesore)." ♦ 15 Jun-30 Oct. € 17.00 2008*

SEIGNOSSE see Hossegor *8E1*

SEILHAC *7C4* (4km SW Rural) *45.35018, 1.64642* **Camp Municipal du Pilard, La Barthe, 19700 Lagraulière [05 55 73 71 04; fax 05 55 73 25 28; mairie.lagrauliere@wanadoo.fr; www.lagrauliere.correze.net]** Exit A20 junc 46 onto D34 to Lagraulière, site sp. NB Lge o'fits rec take D44 & D167E fr Seilhac. Sm, mkd pitch, pt shd; wc; chem disp (wc); shwrs inc; el pnts (3-6A) €2; gas 2km, shop 700m; rest, snacks, bar 1km; BBQ; playgrnd; htd pool adj; tennis; dogs €0.75; phone adj; Eng spkn; quiet; CCI. "Quiet, clean site nr pleasant vill; warden calls." ♦ 15 Jun-15 Sep. € 5.80 2007*

SEILHAC *7C4* (2.5km NW Rural) *45.37750, 1.70227* **Camp Municipal Le Lac de Bournazel, 19700 Seilhac [05 55 27 05 65; fax 04 73 93 71 00]** Fr Seilhac W on D1120 (N120) for 1.5km turn R at rndabt for 1km, clearly sp. Lge, mkd pitch, terr, pt shd; wc; chem disp; mv service pnt; baby facs; shwrs inc; el pnts (6-10A) €3.05; lndtte; shop in ssn; rest, bar; snacks 100m; BBQ; playgrnd; lakeside beach & sw adj; 25% statics; dogs €1.10; Eng spkn; adv bkg; CCI. "Clean site with public access; lge pitches." 1 Apr-30 Sep. € 13.85 2009*

SELESTAT *6E3* (4km N Rural) **Camping à la Ferme St Paul (Loos), 67600 Ebersheim [03 88 85 71 80; fax 03 88 85 71 05; fermest.paul@orange.fr]** Exit Sélestat on N83 to N & site on R in approx 4km, sp. Sm, pt shd; wc; chem disp; mv service pnt; shwrs €1; el pnts €2; gas 1km; lndtte; shops 1km; snacks; rest & bar Sat eve; playgrnd; horseriding, tennis 1km; dogs €1; adv bkg; quiet; CCI. "CL-type site; friendly owner." 1 Apr-30 Oct. € 7.00 2009*

SELESTAT *6E3* (5km N Rural) **Camping Rural (Weiss), 17 Rue du Buhl, 67600 Ebersheim [03 88 85 72 97; elizabeth.trau@wanadoo.fr]** Fr S or N on N83 in vill of Ebersheim foll green Camping Rural sps. Sm, pt shd; wc; shwrs inc; el pnts inc; shop 500m; cooking facs; quiet; adv bkg; ccard not acc; CCI. "Gd touring base; friendly, helpful warden." ♦ 15 Jun-15 Sep. € 9.40 2007*

SELESTAT *6E3* (6km N Rural) *48.32600, 7.42510* **Camping de l'Ours, Route d'Ebersheim, 67650 Dambach-la-Ville [06 77 11 16 48 (mob); camping-de-l-ours@orange.fr; www.pays-de-barr.com]** Exit A35 at junc 16 for D1422 (formerly N422) dir Obernai. After approx 2km take D210 for Dambach-la-Ville & foll sp. Med, mkd pitch, pt shd; wc; chem disp; shwrs inc; el pnts (5A) €3.30; lndtte; shop, rest, snacks, bar 1km; BBQ; playgrnd; sports area; tennis adj; dogs €1.90; quiet. "Attractive medieval town; recep clsd 1200-1430; no access/waiting when barrier down as rd too narr." ♦ Easter-1 Nov. € 11.70 2008*

SELESTAT *6E3* (S Urban) *48.25470, 7.44781* **Camp Municipal Les Cigognes, Rue de la 1ère D.F.L, 67600 Sélestat [03 88 92 03 98 or 03 88 58 87 20; fax 03 88 92 88 63; accueil@selestat-tourisme.com; www.selestat-tourisme.com]** Site sp D1083 (N83) & D424. Fr S town cent turn E off D1083 & foll sps to site adj schools & playing fields. Med, mkd pitch, pt shd; wc; mv service pnt; chem disp; shwrs inc; el pnts (5-16A) inc; gas; lndtte; shops; rest, snacks, bar 500m; playgrnd; pool 300m; rv & lake nrby; entmnt; dogs €1; train to Strasbourg nrby; poss cr; Eng spkn; adv bkg rec high ssn; quiet but some noise fr local football area; CCI. "Well-run site; helpful staff; clean san facs; easy walk to old town; mkt Sat; excel value; rec." ♦ 15 Apr-30 Sep. € 14.20 (3 persons) 2009*

SELESTAT *6E3* (12km W Rural) *48.27287, 7.29052* **Camping du Haut-Koenigsbourg, Rue de la Vancelle, 68660 Lièpvre [03 89 58 43 20; fax 03 89 58 98 29; camping.haut-koenigsbourg@orange.fr; www.camping-alsace.com/liepvre]** Fr Sélestat W on N59 twd Lièpvre vill then R at factory car park & foll site sps. Fr Ste Marie-aux-Mines on N59 turn L at rndabt after tunnel. Med, mkd pitch, pt sl, pt shd; htd wc; mv service pnt; shwrs inc; el pnts (4-8A) €2.50-3.50; lndtte; shop 1km; tradsmn; bar; BBQ; playgrnd; TV rm; 10% statics; dogs €1.50; poss cr; quiet; CCI. ♦ 15 Mar-15 Nov. € 9.50 2008*

SELESTAT *6E3* (5km NW Rural) *48.28915, 7.41787* **Aire Naturelle (Palmer), 11 Rue Faviers 67759 Scherwiller [03 88 92 94 57; fax 03 88 82 05 39; campingpalmer@yahoo.fr; www.campingpalmer.fr]** Fr N foll N83 to Ebersheim then D81 to Scherwiller. Site sp off D35 at N end vill. Sm, pt shd; wc; chem disp; shwrs €2.05; el pnts (6A) €2.50; gas 1km; tradsmn; shop, rest, snacks & bar 1km; BBQ; pool 5km; dogs €1; quiet; ccard acc; CCI. "Friendly site on wine route; British owner; easy walk to vill; easy access to Rhine/Germany; vg." 1 May-30 Sep. € 9.50 2009*

⊞ **SELLES SUR CHER** *4G2* (4km S Rural) **Camping Ch'ti-mi, 57 Route de Valençay, 36600 La Vernelle [02 54 97 52 95]** S fr Selles-sur-Cher on D956, site on L at S end of La Vernelle. Med, pt shd; wc; shwrs inc; el pnts (10A) inc; lndtte; shop, rest, bar 300m; htd pool; games area; quiet. "Useful NH; fair site." € 12.00 2008*

SELONGEY *6G1* (500m SW Rural) *47.58248, 5.18408* **Camp Municipal Les Courvelles, Rue Henri Jevain, 21260 Selongey [03 80 75 52 38 or 03 80 75 70 74 (Mairie); fax 03 80 75 56 65; mairie.selongey@wanadoo.fr; www.selongey.com]** Exit A31 junc 5 N of Dijon onto D974 (N74) N for 3km to Orville: turn W in Orville sp Selongey & site; site in approx 2km. Sm, some hdstg, unshd; wc; shwrs inc; el pnts (6A) €2; shop 1km; tennis; quiet; CCI. "Clean, friendly site; warden calls am & eve; rec arr bef 1600 & site yourself if req hdstg; no twin-axles; poss itinerants; conv m'way/NH; excel." ♦ 1 May-30 Sep. € 11.00 2009*

SELTZ *5D4* (1km S Rural) *48.88269, 8.10001* **Camping Die Grüne Les Peupliers, 67470 Seltz [03 88 86 52 37; peupliers@ville-seltz.fr]** Fr Seltz on D468, turn L in 1km at sp. Lge, pt shd; wc; chem disp; mv service pnt; shwrs; el pnts (6A) €3; rest; bar; playgrnd; lake fishing & boating adj; 85% statics; dogs €1.50; ccard acc; CCI. "Sm pitches." ♦ 1 Apr-30 Sep. € 17.70 2008*

SEMUR EN AUXOIS *6G1* (3.5km S Rural) *47.46812, 4.35589* **FFCC Camping Lac de Pont, 16 Rue du Lac, 21140 Pont-et-Massène [03 80 97 01 26 or 03 80 97 01 26 (LS); campinglacdepont@orrange.fr; www.campinglacdepont.fr]** Exit A6 junc 23 twd Semur-en-Auxois on D980; after sh dist turn R sp 'Lac de Pont' D103. Med, some hdg pitch, pt sl, pt shd; wc; chem disp; mv service pnt; baby facs; shwrs inc; el pnts (6A) €3.50; gas; lndtte; shop; tradsmn; rest 500m; snacks; bar; BBQ; playgrnd; lake sw, sand beach adj; diving platform; watersports on lake; tennis; games area; games rm; cycle hire; 30% statics; dogs €1.70; phone; poss cr; Eng spkn; quiet; ccard acc; CCI. "Warm welcome, helpful owners; generous pitches, some shady; san facs dated; vg for teenagers - games/meeting rm; 'Petit Train' goes round site & into Semur; cycle rte/walks adj; gd touring base; nr A6 m'way; walled, medieval town; superb." 30 Apr-3 Oct. € 14.80 2009*

SENERGUES see Conques *7D4*

SENNECEY LE GRAND *6H1* (6km E Rural) *46.65480, 4.94461* **Kawan Village du Château de L'Epervière, Rue du Château, 71240 Gigny-sur-Saône [03 85 94 16 90; fax 03 85 94 16 97; info@domaine-eperviere.com; www.domaine-eperviere.com]** Fr N exit A6 junc 26 (Chalon Sud) onto N6 dir Mâcon & Tournus; at Sennecey-le-Grand turn E onto D18 sp Gigny-sur-Saône; site sp 1km S of Gigny-sur-Saône. Or fr S exit A6 junc 27 (Tournus) onto N6 N to Sennecey-le-Grand, then as above. NB Diff to find signs fr main rd. Lge, hdg/mkd pitch, pt shd; htd wc; chem disp; baby facs; jacuzzi/sauna; shwrs inc; el pnts (10A) inc; gas; lndtte; sm shop; tradsmn; rest; snacks; pizzeria; bar high ssn; BBQ; playgrnd; 2 pools (1 htd, covrd); paddling pool; lake & rv nr; fishing; tennis 400m; cycle hire; entmnt; wifi; games/TV rm; tour op statics & chalets; dogs €3; poss v cr; Eng spkn; adv bkg; quiet; ccard acc; red low ssn; CCI. "Top-quality, busy site; lge pitches; boggy when wet; warm welcome, pleasant staff; gd clean san facs; highly rec." ♦ 1 Apr-30 Sep. € 33.50 (CChq acc) ABS - L12 2009*

SENNECEY LE GRAND *6H1* (5km NW Rural) *46.67160, 4.83301* **Camping La Héronnière, Les Lacs de Laives, 71240 Laives [tel/fax 03 85 44 98 85; contact@camping-laheronniere.com; www.camping-laheronniere.com]** Exit A6 junc 26 (fr N) or junc 27 (fr S) onto N6. Turn W at Sennecey-le-Grand to Laives. Foll sp 'Lacs de Laives'. Sp on D18. Med, hdg/mkd pitch, some hdstg, pt shd; wc; chem disp; shwrs inc; el pnts (6A) €4.30; lndtte; shop; rest 300m; snacks; playgrnd; sm htd pool; lake sw & beach nrby; fishing; windsurfing; watersports; cycle hire; dogs €1.50; Eng spkn; adv bkg; quiet, but some rd noise fr A6; CCI. "Lovely, level, lakeside site; excel, busy NH; may fill up after 1500; gd shwrs; rest at lakeside (high ssn); popular with bikers; vg." ♦ 26 Apr-16 Sep. € 18.20 2009*

SENONCHES *4E2* (500m S Rural) *48.55569, 1.03851* **Camping Huttopia Senonches, Ave de Badouleaux, 28250 Senonches [04 37 64 22 35 or 02 37 37 81 40 (reservations); fax 04 72 85 08 02; senonches@huttopia.com; www.huttopia.com]** Fr Senonches cent take D155 dir Etang de Badouleaux, site sp. Med, pt shd; htd wc; baby facs; shwrs; el pnts (6-10A) €4.60-6.80; rest; snacks; bar; playgrnd; pool; tennis adj; cycle hire; games area; entmnt; internet; TV rm; some statics; dogs €4; adv bkg; quiet. ♦ 3 Jul-5 Nov. € 18.00 2009*

SENS *4F4* (1km S Urban) *48.18312, 3.28803* **Camp Municipal Entre Deux Vannes, Ave de Senigallia, 89100 Sens [03 86 65 64 71; fax 03 86 95 39 41]** Fr NW on D606 (N6) to Sens; site bet on E side of D606 (N360); foll sp. Med, mkd pitch, pt shd; wc (some cont); chem disp (wc); mv service pnt; baby facs; shwrs inc; el pnts (16A) €1.50; Indtte; shops 1km; tradsmn high ssn; rest nrby; playgrnd; adv bkg rec; some noise fr rd & commercial premises nrby during day; ccard acc; CCI. "Friendly, helpful warden; san facs old but clean; gate locked 2200." 15 May-15 Sep. € 10.60 2008*

SEPPOIS LE BAS see Altkirch *6F3*

⊞ **SEPTEMES LES VALLONS** *10F3* (1km NE Urban) *43.40688, 5.36185* **Camping Le Verdière, 4 Chemin de la Haute Bédoule, 13240 Septèmes-les-Vallons [04 91 65 59 98 or 06 28 19 20 25 (mob); fax 04 91 65 59 98; camping.laverdiere@wanadoo.fr; www.camping-la-verdiere.com]** Exit A51 junc 1 onto D543 dir Septèmes-les-Vallons; at 5-pnt rndabt in 1km take 2nd exit; at next rndabt in 800m turn R under m'way; immed turn R again (on other side m'way) into Chemin de la Haute Bédoule; site on L in 800m. Sm, pt shd; wc; el pnts; shops nrby; supmkt 1km; bar; pool; 40% statics; dogs €3; bus & train 1km; Eng spkn. "OK." € 17.00 2009*

SERAUCOURT LE GRAND see St Quentin *3C4*

SERENT see Ploermel *2F3*

SERIGNAC *7D3* (5km W Rural) *44.43103, 1.06902* **Camping Le Clos Barrat (Naturist), 46700 Sérignac [05 65 31 97 93; fax 05 65 31 91 17; contact@leclosbarrat.com; www.leclosbarrat.fr]** Fr Fumel by-pass turn S on D139 to Montayral, rd cont but becomes D4. Site sp bet Mauroux & St Matré. Med, pt shd, mkd pitch; wc; chem disp; shwrs inc; el pnts (6A) inc; gas; Indtte; shop; tradsmn; rest; snacks; playgrnd; pool; paddling pool; entmnt; dogs €1.60; quiet; ccard acc. "Nr Rv Lot; INF card req - can be bought on site; helpful staff; excel." 1 Apr-30 Sep. € 22.10 2006*

SERIGNAC PEBOUDOU see Cancon *7D3*

SERIGNAN DU COMTAT see Orange *10E2*

SERIGNAN PLAGE *10F1* (300m W Coastal) *43.26741, 3.33473* **Yelloh! Village Aloha, 34410 Sérignan-Plage [04 67 39 71 30; fax 04 67 32 58 15; www.yellohvillage-aloha.com]** Exit A9 at Béziers Est; take D64 then D37E to Sérignan-Plage; turn R at Centre Commercial. Lge, hdg/mkd pitch, shd; htd wc; chem disp; mv service pnt; baby facs; shwrs inc; el pnts (10A) inc; gas; Indtte (inc dryer); shop; rest; snacks; bar; BBQ; playgrnd; 3 htd pools; 2 waterslides; sand beach adj; watersports; tennis; games area; games rm; entmnt; children's club high ssn; wifi; TV; 50% statics; dogs €3; phone; bus adj; Eng spkn; adv bkg; quiet; ccard acc; red low ssn; CCI. "Nice family site; gd." ♦ 26 Apr-14 Sep. € 43.00 2008*

SERIGNAN PLAGE *10F1* (500m W Coastal) *43.26715, 3.33051* **Camping Village Le Beauséjour, 34410 Sérignan-Plage [04 67 39 50 93; fax 04 67 32 01 96; contact@camping-beausejour.com; www.camping-beausejour.com]** Fr A9/E15, exit Béziers Est junc 35 onto D64 S. In 4km turn L onto D37E to Sérignan-Plage. Site on R just bef shops. Lge, hdg/mkd pitch, pt shd; wc; chem disp; mv service pnt; shwrs inc; el pnts (10A) inc; gas; Indtte; shop; hypmkt nr; rest; snacks; bar; BBQ; playgrnd; htd pool; paddling pool; waterslide; sand beach adj; games rm; entmnt; 50% statics; dogs €3.50; poss cr; Eng spkn; adv bkg; quiet; ccard acc; red long stay/low ssn;; CCI. "Excel beach; weekly mkts in vill; vg site; excel facs." ♦ 1 Apr-30 Sep. € 41.00 2009*

See advertisement

SERIGNAN PLAGE *10F1* (1km W Coastal) *43.26398, 3.3210* **Yelloh! Village Le Sérignan Plage, Les Orpelières, 34410 Sérignan-Plage [04 67 32 35 33; fax 04 67 32 26 36; info@leserignanplage.com; www.leserignanplage.com or www.yellohvillage.com]** Exit A9 junc 35. After toll turn L at traff lts onto N112 & at 1st rndabt strt on to D64. In 5km turn L onto D37E Sérignan-Plage, turn R on narr 1-way rd to site. Adj to Camping Sérignan-Plage Nature (Naturist site). V lge, hdg pitch, pt shd; wc (some cont); chem disp (wc); mv service pnt; baby facs; shwrs inc; el pnts (5A) inc; gas; Indtte; shop; hypmkt 6km; rest; snacks; bar; playgrnd; htd, covrd pool; Club Nautique - sw, sailing & water-ski tuition on private beach; tennis; horseriding; disco; entmnt; TV; many statics; dogs €3; use of naturist private beach & facs adj; poss v cr; Eng spkn; adv bkg; poss noisy; red low ssn; no ccard acc; CCI. "Busy, even low ssn: excel pool but poss v cr; some tourers amongst statics & sm sep touring area." 26 Apr-23 Sep. € 42.00 2006*

SERIGNAN PLAGE *10F1* (1.5km W Coastal) *43.26154, 3.32131* **Camping Le Clos de Ferrand (Naturist), 33 Ave de Beziers, 34410 Sérignan-Plage [04 67 32 14 30; fax 04 67 32 15 59; centrenaturiste.closferrand@wanadoo.fr; www.leclosferrand-centrenaturiste.fr]** Exit A9 junc 35 onto D64 dir Valras-Plage. At Sérignan town turn L on D37E to Sérignan-Plage 5km, site sp. Med, hdg/mkd pitch, pt shd; wc; chem disp; shwrs inc; el pnts (2-6A) €4-5; Indtte; shop; snacks; rest; bar; playgrnd; TV rm; beach adj; rv 1km; fishing; boat hire; no dogs; adv bkg; quiet; ccard not acc; INF card req; CCI. "Direct access to beach; gd sized pitches; reported run down (Aug 2007)." ♦ 10 May-20 Sep. € 38.00 2008*

France

SERIGNAN PLAGE *10F1* (1.6km W Coastal) *43.26403, 3.3203* **Camping Le Sérignan-Plage Nature (Naturist), Les Orpelières, 34410 Sérignan-Plage [04 67 32 09 61; fax 04 67 32 26 36; info@leserignannature.com; www.leserignannature.com]** Exit A9 junc 36 Beziers Est onto D64. At Sérignan town turn L on D37E to Sérignan-Plage. After 4km turn R on single-lane dual c'way. At T-junc turn L & immed L again in 50m to site. Lge, mkd pitch, pt shd; wc (some cont); chem disp; mv service pnt; shwrs inc; el pnts (5A) inc (poss rev pol); gas; Indry rm; shop; rest; snacks; bar; playgrnd; pool complex; sand beach; golf 15km; beauty cent; wifi; TV rm; 75% statics; dogs €4; poss cr; Eng spkn; adv bkg rec; quiet, but some noise fr disco (quiet by 2330); red long stay/low ssn; CCI. "Lovely, clean site & facs; helpful staff; Cmp Le Sérignan Plage (non-naturist) adj with use of same private beach & facs; pool also shared - for naturists' use 1000-1200 only; cycle rtes adj; excel." 21 Apr-24 Sep. € 42.00 (CChq acc) 2008*

SERIGNAN PLAGE *10F1* (5km W Rural) *43.26965, 3.28631* **FFCC Camping Le Paradis, Route de Valras-Plage, 34410 Sérignan [tel/fax 04 67 32 24 03; http://camping-leparadis.com]** Exit A9 junc 35 Béziers Est onto D64 dir Valras-Plage. Site on L on rndabt at S end of Sérignan by-pass, 1.5km S of Sérignan. Med, mkd pitch, pt shd; wc; chem disp; shwrs; el pnts (6A) inc; gas; Indtte; shop; supmkt opp; rest, snacks & bar high ssn; snacks; playgrnd; pool (high ssn); sand beach 2km; no dogs; poss cr; Eng spkn; adv bkg rec; quiet except for twice weekly disco (high ssn only) to 0030 & some rd noise; red low ssn/CCI. "Excel, well-kept, family-run site; immac san facs; nr gd beaches; vg value low ssn." ♦ 1 Apr-30 Sep. € 30.00 2009*

SERIGNAN PLAGE *10F1* (800m NW Coastal) *43.27119, 3.32921* **Camping La Maïre, Route de Sérignan-Plage, 34410 Sérignan-Plage [04 67 39 72 00; fax 04 67 32 56 16; richard.berge@wanadoo.fr; www.camping-lamaire.fr]** Exit A9 junc 35 onto D64 dir Sérignan; bef vill turn L onto D37E11 to Sérignan-Page; site on L after ent vill. Lge, hdg/mkd pitch, pt shd; wc; chem disp; shwrs inc; el pnts (6A) inc; gas; Indtte; shop; rest; snacks; bar; BBQ (sep area); playgrnd; pool; sand beach 1km; cycle hire; horseriding adj; games rm; 20% statics; dogs €0.50; phone adj; no twin-axles; poss cr; quiet; ccard acc. "V lge pitches; excel, clean san facs; excel." 15 Apr-15 Sep. € 30.00 2007*

SERRES *9D3* (2km SE Rural) *44.42124, 5.72884* **Camping Domaine des Deux Soleils, 05700 Serres [04 92 67 01 33; fax 04 92 67 08 02; contact@domaine-2soleils.com; www.domaine-2soleils.com]** Take D1075 (N75) S fr Serres dir Sisteron, then turn L to Super-Serres thro wood & up winding mountainside rd, site sp. Med, mkd pitch, sl, terr, pt shd; wc; shwrs inc; el pnts (6A) €3.35; Indtte; shop; rest; snacks; playgrnd; pool; paddling pool; waterslide; fishing, horseriding adj; archery; games area; guided walks; entmnt; TV; dogs €2; phone; adv bkg; quiet. "Some lge pitches; pleasant site & area." 1 May-30 Sep. € 19.10 2007*

SERRIERES *9C2* (3km W Rural) *45.30872, 4.74622* **Camping Le Bas Larin, 88 Route de Larin Le Bas, 07340 Félines [tel/fax 04 75 34 87 93 or 06 74 75 96 07 (mob); camping.baslarin@wanadoo.fr; www.bas-larin.com]** Exit A7 junc 12 Chanas or fr N7, exit at Serrières onto D1082; cross canal & rv; cont over rndabt up winding hill, camp on L nr hill top. Sp fr N7 & D1082, but easily missed - foll sp Safari de Peaugres. Med, terr, shd; wc; chem disp; shwrs inc; el pnts (4-10A) €2.50-3.50; Indtte; shops 2km; rest adj; playgrnd; pool; paddling pool; dogs; Eng spkn; some rd noise; CCI. "Friendly, family-run site; helpful staff; easy access pitches; beautiful views; popular with Dutch; excel." ♦ 1 Apr-30 Sep. € 14.00 2006*

SERVON see Pontaubault *2E4*

SETE *10F1* (11km SW Coastal) *43.34194, 3.58440* **Camping Le Castellas, Cours Gambetta, 34200 Sète [04 67 51 63 00; fax 04 67 53 63 01; www.le-castellas.com www.village-center.com]** On D612/N112 bet Agde and Sète. Foll sp for 'Plages-Agde'. Lge, hdg pitch, pt shd; wc; chem disp; shwrs inc; el pnts (6A) inc; gas; Indtte; shop; rest; snacks; bar; playgrnd; 2 htd pools; sand beach 150m (across busy rd); tennis; games area; cycle hire; entmnt; dogs €3; poss cr; Eng spkn; adv bkg; rd & rlwy noise; red low ssn/long stay; CCI. "Bull-fighting in ssn; superb beach; twin-axles welcome." 4 Apr-20 Sep. € 40.00 2009*

SEURRE *6H1* (600m W Rural) *47.00022, 5.13702* **Camp Municipal La Piscine, Route de Dijon, 21250 Seurre [03 80 20 49 22; fax 03 80 20 34 01; ot.seurre@wanadoo.fr; www.tourisme-seurre]** Exit Seurre on D973 Dijon/Beaune rd; site on R over bdge adj municipal pool. Lge, hdstg, pt shd; wc; chem disp; shwrs inc; el pnts (10A) (rev pol); gas; Indtte; shops 600m; rest; snacks; bar; playgrnd; pool adj; 25% statics; dogs; adv bkg ess high ssn; quiet; CCI. "Vg san facs but inadequate when full; twin-axles acc." ♦ 15 May-15 Sep. 2007*

SEURRE *6H1* (3km NW Rural) *47.01563, 5.12780* **Camping Les Sables, Chemin de la Plage, 21250 Pouilly-sur-Saône [03 80 20 43 50; les.sables@tiscali.fr]** Exit A36 at junc 1 onto D976 for Seurre then onto D973 to D996 to Pouilly-sur-Saône. Fr A31 exit junc Nuits-St Georges & take D35 dir Gerland & Bagnot. At D996 turn R for Pouilly in 7km. Site well sp. Sm, mkd pitch, pt shd; wc; chem disp (wc); shwrs inc; el pnts (6A) inc; shop 5km; tradsmn; BBQ; playgrnd; pool 2km; fishing adj; dogs €0.80; Eng spkn; adv bkg; quiet; CCI. "Excel CL-type site nr Rv Saône; helpful British owners; facs basic but clean." ♦ 1 Jun-31 Aug. € 13.80 2007*

SEVERAC LE CHATEAU *9D1* (1km SE Urban) *44.31841, 3.06412* **FFCC Camping Les Calquières (formerly Municipal), Ave Jean Moulin, 12150 Sévérac-le-Château [05 65 47 64 82; contact@camping-calquieres.com; www.camping-calquieres.com]** Exit A75 junc 42 sp Sévérac & Rodez; foll 'Camping' sps to avoid narr town rds. Med, hdg pitch, pt shd; wc (some cont); 50% serviced pitches; shwrs inc; el pnts (6A) €3.30; (poss long lead req); Indry rm; shop 250m; tradsmn; rest; snacks; bar; playgrnd; pool; games area; fishing; tennis; wifi; some statics; dogs €1.50; adv bkg; quiet, but poss noise fr sports facs adj; red long stay/low ssn; CCI. "Lovely, spacious site with gd views; lge pitches; friendly owners; main san facs block vg, other needs updating but clean; if office clsd site self; gd touring base; conv A75; busy NH, espec w/end." ♦ 1 Apr-15 Oct. € 16.60 2009*

SEVERAC LE CHATEAU *9D1* (15km SE Rural) *44.27302, 3.21538* **Camp Municipal, 48500 St Rome-de-Dolan [tel/fax 04 66 44 03 81 or 04 66 48 83 59; mairie-stromededolan@wanadoo.fr; www.st-rome-de-dolan.com/fr/camping.htm]** Exit A75 junc 42 to Sévérac, then take D995 fr Séverac-le-Château then E thro Le Massegros to St Rome-de-Dolan. Site on R at ent to vill, sp. Sm, pt sl, pt terr, pt shd; wc; chem disp; shwrs inc; el pnts (6A) €2.20; Indtte; shop 5km; tradsmn; rest, snacks, bar 5km; BBQ; playgrnd; rv sw 5km; dogs €0.80; phone 50m; Eng spkn; adv bkg; quiet; CCI. "Well-run, simple, scenic site nr Gorges du Tarn; friendly, helpful warden; spotless san facs; birdwatching; walking; highly rec." ♦ 1 May-30 Sep. € 10.00 2009*

SEVRIER see Annecy *9B3*

SEYNE *9D3* (800m S Rural) *44.34270, 6.35896* **Camping Les Prairies, Haute Gréyère, 04140 Seyne-les-Alpes [04 92 35 10 21; fax 04 92 35 26 96; info@campinglesprairies.com; www.campinglesprairies.com]** Fr Digne-les-Bains, take D900 N to Seyne. Turn L on ent Seyne onto D7, site sp beside Rv La Blanche. Med, mkd pitch, pt shd; htd wc; chem disp; mv service pnt; baby facs; shwrs inc; el pnts (10A) €3.50; gas; Indtte; shop 800m; tradsmn; rest 800m; snacks; BBQ; playgrnd; htd pool; tennis 300m; horseriding 500m; dogs €2; phone; Eng spkn; adv bkg; quiet; ccard acc; red low ssn; CCI. "Immac, tidy, peaceful site." 18 Apr-12 Sep. € 19.00 2009*

SEYSSEL *9B3* (400m N Urban) *45.96324, 5.83574* **Camping Le Nant Matraz, 15 Route de Genève, 74910 Seyssel [04 50 59 03 68]** On L of D992 sp Frangy. Lge supmkt opp. Med, own san; mkd pitch, pt shd; wc (some cont); chem disp; mv service pnt; shwrs inc; el pnts (6A) inc; Indtte; shop adj; snacks; bar; BBQ; playgrnd; pool in town; boat hire; rv fishing; games rm; dogs; Eng spkn; adv bkg; rd/rlwy noise; ccard acc. "On banks of Rv Rhône; san facs well worn." 11 Apr-30 Sep. € 13.70 2006*

⊞ **SEZANNE** *4E4* (6km SW Rural) *48.70328, 3.65230* **Aire de Loisirs La Traconne, 4 Impasse de Rouge Coq, 51120 Le Meix-St Epoing [03 26 80 70 76; fax 03 26 42 74 98; info@camping-traconne.com; www.camping-traconne.com]** Turn S off N4 at Beauvais about 12km W of Sézanne. Foll sp to vill/site on D239, site sp. Exit fr N4 at Moeurs-Verday via v narr rd - not rec. Med, hdg/mkd pitch, pt shd; htd wc; chem disp; mv service pnt; baby facs; shwrs inc; el pnts (6A) €3.50 (poss rev pol); gas; Indtte; shops 5km; tradsmn; rest 5km; BBQ; playgrnd; pool & waterslide 5km; fishing adj; games rm; 30% statics; dogs €2; Eng spkn; adv bkg; quiet; CCI. "Peaceful site in forest; lge pitches; friendly owners; excel cycling & walking." ♦ € 12.00 2009*

SEZANNE *4E4* (500m NW Rural) *48.72115, 3.70247* **Camp Municipal, Route de Launat, 51120 Sézanne [03 26 80 57 00; campingdesezanne@wanadoo.fr]** W'bound on N4 Sézanne by-pass onto D373 & foll site sp. No access fr N4 E'bound. If app fr S foll camping sps, but avoid town cent, turn L immed after 2nd set of traff lts. Foll sps 'Camping' & 'Piscine'. Med, mainly sl, pt shd; serviced pitches; wc (some cont); shwrs inc; shop, el pnts (10A) inc; shop 500m; rest in town 1km; sm playgrnd; pool adj; waterslide; dogs €0.95; some rd noise; no ccard acc; CCI. "Clean, tidy site; helpful manager; immac san facs; levelling blocks ess for m'vans, but work in hand to level some pitches (2008); request for gate opening/closing at back bungalow of 2 opp site; vg." ♦ 1 Apr-1 Oct. € 9.70 2008*

SIBIRIL see St Pol de Léon *1D2*

⊞ **SIGEAN** *10G1* (5km N Rural) *43.06633, 2.94100* **Camping La Grange Neuve, Route de la Réserve Africaine, 11130 Sigean [tel/fax 04 68 48 58 70; info@camping-sigean.com; www.camping-sigean.com]** Exit junc 39 fr A9; foll sp La Réserve Africaine. Med, hdg/mkd pitch, hdstg, pt sl, terr, pt shd; wc; chem disp; shwrs inc; el pnts (6A) €4; Indtte; shop; rest; snacks, bar; playgrnd; pool; waterslide; sand beach 5km; TV rm; 5% statics; dogs €3; poss cr; adv bkg; quiet but some rd noise; red low ssn; CCI. "Easy access; gd san facs; excel pool; ltd facs low ssn; phone ahead to check open low ssn; gd NH." ♦ € 28.00 2009*

SIGEAN *10G1* (8km SE Rural) *42.95800, 2.99586* **Camping Le Clapotis (Naturist), 11480 La Palme [04 68 48 15 40; info@leclapotis.com; www.leclapotis.com]** On D6009 (N9) S fr Narbonne turn L 8km S of Sigean. After 350m turn R at camping sp. Site in 150m. Final app rd narr but negotiable for lge vans. Lge, mkd pitch, pt shd; wc (cont); shwrs inc; el pnts (4A) €4; gas; rest & bar in ssn; pool; sm lake beach; tennis; games area; internet; many statics; dogs €2; poss cr; Eng spkn; adv bkg; quiet; red low ssn; Naturists INF card req; ccard acc; red low ssn. "Pleasant, basic, friendly site; sm pitches; helpful owners; san facs dated but clean; gd pool; poss strong winds - gd windsurfing; La Palme vill 15 mins walk." 15 Mar-15 Oct. € 22.00 2009*

SIGNY L'ABBAYE *5C1* (N Urban) *49.70123, 4.41971* **Camp Municipal de l'Abbaye, 08460 Signy-l'Abbaye [03 24 52 87 73; mairie-signy-l.abbaye@wanadoo.fr]** Take D985 N twd Belgium fr Rethel to Signy-l'Abbaye. Foll sp fr town cent to Stade & Camping. Site by sports stadium. Sm, some hdg/hdstg pitch, pt sl, pt shd; htd wc; chem disp; shwrs inc; el pnts (10A) €2.90 (poss rev pol); Indry rm; shops, rest 500m; playgrnd; sports cent adj; rv fishing adj; dogs €0.60; little Eng spkn; adv bkg; v quiet; CCI. "Lovely site in gd location; friendly warden; san facs excel (shared with public fr sports cent); strong awning pegs req on gravel hdg pitches, or can park on open grassed area." ♦ 1 May-30 Sep. € 6.40 2009*

SIGOULES *7D2* (1.5km N Rural) *44.77135, 0.41076* **Camp Municipal La Gardonnette, Les Coteaux de Sigoulès, 24240 Pomport-Sigoulès [tel/fax 05 53 58 81 94; campingdelagardonnette@wanadoo.fr]** S fr Bergerac take D933 S. After 6km at top of hill turn R by La Grappe d'Or Rest onto D17 sp Pomport/Sigoulès. Thro Pomport, site at bottom of hill on R by lake. Med, mkd pitch, pt sl, shd; wc; chem disp; shwrs inc; el pnts (6A); Indtte; shop, snacks, bar 1km; playgrnd; lake sw adj; fishing; canoeing; tennis; games area; entmnt; TV; 25% statics; dogs; phone; Eng spkn; adv bkg; ccard acc; CCI. "Barrier ent; facs clean but well worn & in need of refurb; gd security." 1 Apr-30 Sep. 2009*

SILLE LE GUILLAUME *4F1* (3km N Rural) *48.20928, -0.13444* **FFCC Camping La Forêt, Sillé-Plage, 72140 Sillé-le-Guillaume [02 43 20 11 04; fax 02 43 20 84 82; info@campingsilleplage.com; www.campingsilleplage.com]** Exit Sillé on D304 sp Mayenne. After 2km at x-rds turn R; across next x-rds & turn L at next x-rds; sp Sillé-Plage; site on R in 500m, visible. Sp fr other dir. Lge, pt shd; wc; mv service pnt; shwrs inc; el pnts (10A) €2.50; gas; shop; tradsmn; playgrnd; tennis; boating; lake sw; fishing; 40% statics; dogs €1.10; poss cr; rd noise; CCI. "Pleasant lakeside & forest scenery (some pitches amongst trees); highly rec." 31 Mar-31 Oct. € 9.00 2008*

SILLE LE GUILLAUME *4F1* (3km N Rural) *48.20352, -0.12774* **Indigo Camping Les Mollières, Sillé-Plage, 72140 Sillé-le-Guillaume [02 43 20 16 12; molieres@camping-indigo.com]** Fr Sillé-le-Guillaume take D5 N, D203 to site. Med, shd; wc; chem disp; shwrs inc; el pnts (13A) inc; Indtte; shop; playgrnd; lake sw; fishing; watersports; games area; dogs; quiet; ccard acc. "Site in pine forest." 1 Jun-31 Aug. € 13.30 (CChq acc) 2009*

SILLE LE GUILLAUME *4F1* (2km NW Rural) *48.18943, -0.14130* **Camping Les Tournesols, Route de Mayenne, Le Grez, 72140 Sillé-le-Guillaume [02 43 20 12 69 or 06 98 04 74 29 (mob); campinglestournesols@wanadoo.fr; www.campinglestournesols.com]** Exit Sillé on D304/D35 sp Mayenne; in 2km at x-rds turn R; site in 150m on L, easily visible & sp. Med, hdg/mkd pitch, pt sl, pt shd; wc; chem disp; mv service pnt; shwrs inc; el pnts (6A) inc (poss long lead req); Indtte (inc dryer); shop; tradsmn; snacks; bar; BBQ (gas); playgrnd; rv/lake sw & canoeing 2km; fishing 1km; cycle hire; entmnt; internet; TV; 20% statics; dogs €2; no twin-axles; Eng spkn; adv bkg; quiet; ccard acc; red long stay; CCI. "Beautiful site; friendly, helpful owners; pleasant town; conv Le Mans; gd." ♦ 1 May-30 Sep. € 18.00 2009*

SILLE LE PHILIPPE *4F1* (2km SW Rural) *48.10880, 0.33730* **Camping Le Château de Chanteloup, 72460 Sillé-le-Philippe [02 43 27 51 07 or 02 43 89 66 47; fax 02 43 89 05 05; chanteloup.souffront@wanadoo.fr; www.chateau-de-chanteloup.com or www.les-castels.com]** Leave A11/E50 at junc 7 Sp Le Mans Z1 Nord. After toll turn L onto N338. Foll this & turn L onto D313 sp Coulaines, Mamers & Ballon. Take D301 (at lge supmkt) & in approx 13km site is sp just after ent to Sillé-le-Philippe. Avoid cent Sillé-le-Philippe. Med, some mkd pitch, pt sl, pt shd; wc; chem disp; baby facs; shwrs inc; el pnts (8A) inc (poss rev pol); Indtte; ltd shop & 2km; tradsmn; rest high ssn; snacks; bar; BBQ; playgrnd; pool; paddling pool; lake fishing; tennis; horseriding & golf 10km; games area; entmnt; wifi; games/TV rm; dogs free; c'vans over 8m not acc; sep o'night area with elec & water; poss v cr; Eng spkn; adv bkg; higher charge during Le Mans events; quiet; ccard acc; red low ssn; CCI. "Lovely, tranquil, spacious site; pleasant, helpful staff; dated, clean san facs - but far fr pitches; gd rest; gd for Le Mans; rest & shop poss clsd after Le Mans w/end; excel." ♦ 1 Jun-31 Aug. € 34.80 ABS - L13 2009*

France

SINGLES *7B4* (900m SE Rural) *45.54310, 2.54278* **Camping Le Moulin de Serre, 63690 Singles [04 73 21 16 06; fax 04 73 21 12 56; moulin-de-serre@wanadoo.fr; www.moulindeserre.com]** N fr Bort-les-Orgues on D922; in 14km at Les Quatre-Vents turn L onto D25; at Larodde turn R onto D73. Site well sp fr D922. NB Diff access for v lge o'fits due bends on app rds. Med, hdg/mkd pitch, pt shd; htd wc; chem disp; mv service pnt; shwrs inc; el pnts (5-10A) €3.70-4.70; Indtte (inc dryer); shop; tradsmn; snacks; bar; BBQ (sep areas); playgrnd; pool; fishing & canoeing on lake nrby; games area; TV; 40% statics; dogs €1.80; phone; adv bkg; ccard acc; red low ssn; CCI. "Lovely site; friendly staff; vg." ♦ 12 Apr-14 Sep. € 17.85 2008*

SIREUIL see Angouleme *7B2*

SISTERON *10E3* (2.5km N Rural) *44.21467, 5.93643* **Camp Municipal Les Prés Hauts, 44 Chemin des Prés Hauts, 04200 Sisteron [tel/fax 04 92 61 00 37 or 04 92 61 19 69; contact@camping-sisteron.com; www.sisteron.com]** On W of D951. Lge, hdg pitch, pt sl, pt shd; wc; chem disp; serviced pitches; shwrs inc; el pnts (6A) €4 (poss rev pol); Indtte; shop & 1.5km; playgrnd; pool; tennis; fishing; entmnt; dogs €1; Eng spkn; quiet; ccard acc; red low ssn; CCI. "Pleasant, well-kept site; gd views; lge pitches; helpful, friendly warden; site yourself low ssn; vg facs, ltd low ssn; pleasant old town, gd mkt; vg." ♦ 1 Mar-31 Oct. € 19.00 2009*

SIVRY SUR MEUSE see Dun sur Meuse *5C1*

SIXT SUR AFF see Gacilly, La *2F3*

SIZUN *2E2* (Rural) *48.40038, -4.07635* **Camp Municipal du Gollen, 29450 Sizun [02 98 24 11 43 or 02 98 68 80 13 (Mairie); fax 02 98 68 86 56]** Fr Roscoff take D788 SW onto D69 to Landivisiau, D30 & D764 to Sizun. In Sizun take D18 at rndabt. At end of by-pass, at next rndabt, take 3rd exit. Site adj pool. Sm, pt shd; wc (some cont); shwrs inc; el pnts (10A) €4 (poss rev pol); Indry rm; shops 500m; playgrnd; htd pool adj high ssn; phone; no twin-axles; poss cr; no adv bkg; quiet; ccard not acc; CCI. "Lovely litte site; simple & restful by rv in nature park; friendly recep; site yourself if warden not avail; vg." Easter-30 Sep. € 10.10 2009*

⊞ **SOISSONS** *3D4* (1km N Urban) *49.39295, 3.32701* **Camp Municipal, Ave du Mail, 02200 Soissons [03 23 74 52 69; fax 03 23 75 05 21; officedetourisme@ville-soissons.fr; www.ville-soissons.fr]** Fr N on D1; foll town cent sp to 1st rndabt; turn R, cross rv & immed R into Ave du Mail. Foll sp 'Camping Piscine'. Site well sp beside sw pool. Rd humps & tight ent on last 500m of access rd. (Poss to avoid tight ent by going 150m to rndabt & returning.) Med, hdg/mkd pitch, hdstg, pt shd; htd wc; chem disp (wc); shwrs inc; el pnts (6A) €3 (poss rev pol); Indtte (inc dryer); shop; rest; snacks; bar 1km; BBQ; playgrnd; pool adj; cycle hire; 5% statics; dogs €1; phone; poss cr; quiet; ccard acc; CCI. "Pleasant, well-run site in interesting area; gd sized pitches, some nr rv; poss muddy, park on site rds in winter; helpful, friendly staff; gd clean san facs; rvside walks/cycling; gate clsd 2200-0700; poor security; poss motor rallies nrby; vet nrby; mkt Wed & Sat; vg winter NH." ♦ € 15.00 2009*

SOLIGNAC SUR LOIRE see Puy en Velay, Le *9C1*

SOMMIERES *10E1* (2km SE Rural) *43.77550, 4.09280* **Camping Domaine de Massereau, 1990 Route d'Aubais, 30250 Sommières [04 66 53 11 20 or 06 03 31 27 21 (mob); fax 04 66 73 32 29; info@massereau.fr; www.massereau.fr or www.les-castels.com]** Exit A9 junc 26 at Gallargues, foll sp Sommières; site sp on D12. NB Danger of grounding at ent fr D12. Use this route 24/7 - 03/08 (due to festival in Sommières). Otherwise exit A9 junc 27 onto D34 to Sommières, foll sps to "Centre Historique" dir Aubias; cross bdge (sharp turn) & turn R onto D12; site on L in 3km. Med, hdg/mkd pitch; pt sl, pt shd; wc (some cont); chem disp; mv service pnt; baby facs; serviced pitch; sauna; shwrs inc; el pnts (16A) inc; gas; Indtte; shop; tradsmn; rest; snacks; bar; BBQ (gas/elec only); playgrnd; pool; waterslide; rv sw 500m; tennis; cycle hire; games area; games rm; entmnt; wifi; TV; 50% statics; dogs €4.20; phone; poss cr; Eng spkn; adv bkg; quiet; ccard acc; red low ssn; CCI. "Lovely, tranquil, well-run site adj vineyard; pleasant staff; modern san facs; narr site rds, sl/uneven pitches & trees diff lge o'fits; tight ents, diff without mover; excel." ♦ 28 Mar-10 Nov. € 38.40 ABS - C33 2009*

SOMMIERES *10E1* (3km SE Rural) *43.76120, 4.11961* **Camping Les Chênes, Les Teullières Basses, 30250 Junas [04 66 80 99 07 or 06 03 29 36 32 (mob); fax 04 66 51 33 23; chenes@wanadoo.fr; www.camping-les-chenes.com]** Fr Sommières take D12 S (sp Gallargues) 3km to junc with D140 L (N) for 1km. Site on R 300m up side rd. Sp. Med, pt sl, shd; wc (cont); chem disp; shwrs inc; el pnts (3-10A) €3-4.20 (long lead poss req); Indtte; shops 1km; playgrnd; pool; beach & rv sw 2km; games area; wifi; some statics; dogs €3; phone; sep car park; adv bkg; quiet; red low ssn; CCI. "Gd shade; gd san facs; friendly, helpful staff; vg." 5 Apr-12 Oct. € 12.20 2008*

SOMMIERES *10E1* (500m NW Urban) *43.78672, 4.08702* **Camp Municipal Le Garanel, Rue Eugène Rouché, 30250 Sommières [tel/fax 04 66 80 33 49; campingmunicipal.sommieres@wanadoo.fr]** Fr S on A9 exit junc 27 N & foll D34 then take D610 (N110) twd Sommières. By-pass town on D610, over rv bdge; turn R for D40, Rue Condamine. After L turn for Nîmes pull out to make sharp R turn sp 'Camping Arena'. At T-junc turn R, site thro car park. Fr N on D610 turn L at 4th junc sp 'Ville Vieille' & site adj rv. Site sp fr D610 fr N. Sm, hdg/mkd pitch, pt shd; wc (some cont); chem disp; mv service pnt; shwrs inc; el pnts (10A) inc; Indtte; shops, rest, snacks 300m; tradsmn; bar 200m; BBQ; pool; beach 25km; tennis adj; dogs €2; bus 500m; twin-axle restrictions; poss cr; Eng spkn; adv bkg; quiet but noise fr vill car park; CCI. "Great location near town cent; some open views; friendly, helpful warden; well-kept, dated facs; rv walks; Voie Verte cycle rte; Sat mkt; site subject to flooding any time of year." 1 Apr-30 Sep. € 12.00 2009*

SONZAY *4G1* (500m W Rural) *47.52620, 0.45070* **Kawan Village L'Arada Parc, 88 Rue de la Baratière, 37360 Sonzay [02 47 24 72 69; fax 02 47 24 72 70; info@laradaparc.com; www.laradaparc.com]** Exit A28 junc 27 to Neuillé-Pont-Pierre; then D766 & D6 to Sonzay; turn R in town cent. Site on R on o'skirts immed past new houses; sp. Med, hdg/mkd pitch, pt sl, pt shd; wc; chem disp; mv service pnt; 20% serviced pitches; child/baby facs; shwrs inc; el pnts (10A) €3.60 (poss rev pol); gas; lndtte; shop; tradsmn; rest; snacks; bar; BBQ; playgrnd; htd pool; covrd pool; paddling pool; spa; gym; tennis; lake sw 9km; rv fishing 500m; cycle hire; games area; entmnt; internet; TV rm; 15% statics; dogs €1.50; phone; bus to Tours; Eng spkn; adv bkg; quiet; red long stay/low ssn; ccard acc; CCI. "Peaceful, well-maintained site; friendly, helpful owners; clean, modern facs; gd views; poss diff for lge o'fits when site full/cr; barrier clsd 2300-0800; 60km fr Le Mans circuit; excel." ♦ 22 Mar-25 Oct. € 20.50 (CChq acc) 2009*

SOREDE see Argelès sur Mer *10G1*

⊞ **SORGUES** *10E2* (1km NE Urban) *44.02083, 4.89166* **Camping La Montagne, 944 Chemin de la Montagne, 84700 Sorgues [04 90 83 36 66; fax 04 90 39 82 94; contact@campinglamontagne.com; www.campinglamontagne.com]** Exit A7 at Avignon Nord junc 23 twd Carpentras on D942, then N on D6 to Sorgues; site sp fr a'route but foll `Zone Industrielle' sps. App via steep ramp. Med, shd; wc; shwrs inc; el pnts (15A) €4.50; lndtte; shop; rest; snacks; bar; playgrnd; pool; internet; entmnt; TV; 10% statics; dogs €2.50; adv bkg; quiet but m'way noise. "Ltd facs low ssn." € 18.50 2008*

SOSPEL *10E4* (4km NW Rural) *43.89702, 7.41685* **Camping Domaine Ste Madeleine, Route de Moulinet, 06380 Sospel [04 93 04 10 48; fax 04 93 04 18 37; camp@camping-sainte-madeleine.com; www.camping-sainte-madeleine.com]** Take D2566 fr Sospel NW to Turini & site 4km on L; sp fr town. Rd to site fr Menton steep with many hairpins. Med, mkd pitch, pt sl, pt terr, shd; wc; chem disp; mv service pnt; shwrs €0.50; el pnts (10A) €2.90; gas; lndtte; pool; beach 20km; rv 3km; dogs €1.40; Eng spkn; adv bkg rec high ssn; quiet; 10% red low ssn; CCI. "Friendly, busy site; gd facs; gd pool but has no shallow end; stunning scenery." 1 Apr-30 Sep. € 19.00 2006*

SOUBES see Lodève *10E1*

SOUILLAC *7C3* (5km SE Rural) *44.85503, 1.52257* **Camp Municipal Beauregard, 46200 Pinsac [05 65 37 85 83 or 05 65 37 06 02]** S on D820 (N20) thro Souillac, turn L on o'skts onto D43 immed bef Rv Dordogne. Site in 5km. Sm, pt shd; wc; shwrs inc; el pnts (5A) €2.90; lndry rm; shop 1km; rest & bar 100m; snacks; fishing; dogs €0.70; Eng spkn; quiet. "Useful rvside NH/sh stay espec low ssn; warden calls pm; basic facs." 1 Jun-30 Sep. € 9.00 2008*

SOUILLAC *7C3* (7km SE Rural) *44.87716, 1.57361* **Camping Les Borgnes, 46200 St Sozy [05 65 32 21 48; info@campinglesborgnes.fr; www.campinglesborgnes.fr]** Exit A20 junc 55; foll sp Martel on D803; in 5km turn R onto D15 to St Sozy; site just bef rv bdge. Med, pt shd; wc (some cont); chem disp; shwrs inc; el pnts €3; gas; lndtte; shop nr; tradsmn; rest; snacks; bar; BBQ; playgrnd; pool; paddling pool; rv sw adj; canoe hire; 60% statics; dogs €1; phone; Eng spkn; adv bkg; quiet, some rd noise; ccard acc; red CCI. "New, helpful British owners (2008) working hard to improve site; gd." ♦ 1 May-30 Sep. € 12.00 2008*

SOUILLAC *7C3* (1km S Rural) *44.88197, 1.48253* **Camp Municipal du Pont, 46200 Lanzac [05 65 37 02 58; fax 05 65 37 02 31]** S on D820 (N20) thro Souillac; immed after x-ing Rv Dordogne site visible on R of D820. Sm, shd; wc (mainly cont); chem disp; shwrs inc; el pnts (6-10A); gas; shops 1km; tradsmn; rest; snacks; playgrnd; fishing; canoe hire; TV; some statics; dogs; adv bkg; CCI. "Easy stroll into Souillac along rv; lovely location but poss itinerants; facs tired high ssn; freestyle pitching; unreliable opening dates - phone ahead." ♦ 15 Jun-15 Sep. 2009*

SOUILLAC *7C3* (5km S Rural) *44.86602, 1.49715* **Camping Verte Rive, 46200 Pinsac [05 65 37 85 96 or 06 65 37 85 96 (mob); fax 05 65 32 67 69; chalet-dordogne@orange.fr; www.location-dordogne-chalet.com]** Fr Souillac S on D820 (N20). Turn L immed bef Dordogne rv bdge on D43 to Pinsac. Site on R in 2km on rvside. Med, hdg/mkd pitch, shd; wc (some cont); chem disp; baby facs; shwrs inc; el pnts (10A) €3; gas; lndtte; shop & 1km; rest; snacks; bar; playgrnd; pool; canoeing; games rm; 20% statics; dogs €2; poss cr; Eng spkn; adv bkg ess high ssn; quiet; ccard acc; red low ssn; CCI. "Pleasant, peaceful, wooded site on Rv Dordogne; gd san facs; poss mosquitoes by rv; gd pool." ♦ 27 Apr-30 Sep. € 16.50 2009*

⊞ **SOUILLAC** *7C3* (300m SW Urban) *44.89150, 1.47654* **Aire Communale, Rue de la Pomme, 46200 Souillac [05 65 32 71 00]** Take D820 (N20) to Souillac cent then D804/D703 dir Sarlat. In 200m turn L, site ent on R at Parking Baillot. Sm, hdstg, unshd; chem disp; wc; water & el pnts €2; shop, rest 300m; free parking for m'vans only. 2007*

SOUILLAC *7C3* (5km SW Rural) *44.87340, 1.43389* **Camp Municipal La Borgne, 24370 Cazoulès [05 53 29 81 64 or 05 53 31 45 25 (Mairie); fax 05 53 31 45 26; camping cazoules@orange.fr; http://pagesperso-orange.fr/cazoules]** Fr Souillac, take D804/D703 twd Sarlat. In 4km in vill of Cazoulès turn L & foll site sps. Site on R just bef rv bdge & adj Rv Dordogne. Lge, pt shd; wc; baby facs; shwrs inc; el pnts (10A) €2.50; lndtte; sm shop; supmkt 4km; BBQ; playgrnd; pool; paddling pool; canoe trips; boat hire; fishing; tennis adj; 15% statics; dogs €0.80; quiet. "Poss mosquito problem; helpful staff." ♦ 15 Jun-15 Sep. € 14.50 2009*

France

SOUILLAC *7C3* (1km W Urban) *44.88895, 1.47418* **Camping Les Ondines, Ave de Sarlat, 46200 Souillac [05 65 37 86 44 or 06 33 54 32 00; fax 05 65 32 61 15; www.souillac-sur-dordogne.fr]** Turn W off D820 (N20) in cent Souillac onto D804/D703 sp Sarlat. In 200m turn L at sp into narr rd. Ent 400m on R adj rv. Lge, mkd pitch, pt sl, pt shd; wc; chem disp; shwrs inc; el pnts (5A) €2.30; Indtte; shop; rest 1km; BBQ; playgrnd; htd pool & aquatic park nrby; tennis; fishing; canoeing; tennis; horseriding; entmnt; some statics; dogs; phone; Eng spkn; quiet; red long stay; CCI. "Clean facs; dedicated staff; conv NH Rocamadour & caves; vg." ♦ 1 May-30 Sep. € 9.70 2009*

SOUILLAC *7C3* (6km W Rural) *44.88577, 1.40678* **Camping à la Ferme (Levet), La Périgourdine, 24370 Peyrillac-et-Millac [05 53 29 72 12]** Fr cent of Souillac, W on D804 then D703 to Peyrillac-et-Millac; in vill turn L at sp to site. Drive past farmhouse, ent 75m on R. Sm, pt shd; htd wc; shwrs inc; el pnts (16A) €2.50; Indry rm; shop, rest, bar etc 5km; BBQ; playgrnd; pool; rv 2km; dogs €1.50; adv bkg; quiet; no ccard acc; CCI. "Excel CL-type site; gd touring cent & gd NH en rte Spain; friendly & helpful; ltd facs low ssn; not suitable lge o'fits as access narr, sloping & sharp bend; gd cycle rtes." € 12.00 2008*

SOUILLAC *7C3* (6km W Rural) *44.89841, 1.40486* **Camping au P'tit Bonheur, 24370 Peyrillac-et-Millac [tel/fax 05 53 29 77 93; auptitbonheur@wanadoo.fr; www.camping-auptitbonheur.com]** Exit Souillac by D804/D703 sp Sarlat. At Peyrillac turn R to Millac, about 2km on minor & narr rd uphill (13%) to plateau. Well sp fr D703. Med, terr, hdg/mkd pitch, pt shd; wc (some cont); chem disp; shwrs inc; el pnts (10A) €3.60; gas; shops 2km; tradsmn; snacks; bar; playgrndhtd pool; 5% statics; dogs €2; Eng spkn; adv bkg; quiet; red low ssn; ccard acc high ssn only; CCI. "Peaceful, well-run site; owners pleasant; app rd steep mostly single track; many pitches diff for twin-axles & lge o'fits; site may close bef 30 Sep; excel." ♦ 1 Apr-30 Sep. € 16.40 2007*

SOUILLAC *7C3* (7km NW Rural) *44.93599, 1.43743* **Camping La Draille, La Draille, 46200 Souillac [05 65 32 65 01; fax 05 65 37 06 20; la.draille@wanadoo.fr; www.ladraille.com]** Leave Souillac on D15 sp Salignac-Evvigues; at Bourzoles in 6km take D165; site sp in 500m on L. Med, hdg pitch, pt sl, pt shd; wc; chem disp; baby facs; shwrs inc; el pnts (4A) €2.50; Indtte; shop; rest; snacks; bar; BBQ; pool; 25% statics; dogs €2.50; phone; poss cr; Eng spkn; adv bkg; quiet; ccard acc; CCI. "Lovely location; friendly; gd walks; highly rec." ♦ 22 Apr-13 Oct. € 20.50 2007*

SOUILLAC *7C3* (8km NW Rural) *44.94510, 1.44140* **Camping Le Domaine de la Paille Basse, 46200 Souillac [05 65 37 85 48; fax 05 65 37 09 58; info@lapaillebasse.com; www.lapaillebasse.com or www.les-castels.com]** Exit Souillac by D15 sp Salignac, turn onto D165 at Bourzolles foll sp to site in 3km. NB Narr app, few passing places. Lge, hdg pitch, terr, pt shd; wc; chem disp; mv service pnt 800m; shwrs inc; el pnts (3-10A) €4-6; gas; Indtte; shop; rest; snacks; bar; playgrnd; pool; paddling pool; waterslides; games rm; tennis; sports area; golf 5km; organised outdoor activities; entmnt; wifi; TV/cinema rm; dogs €4; adv bkg; quiet; ccard acc; red low ssn. "Excel site in remote location; friendly, helpful staff; clean facs; some shwrs unisex; restored medieval vill." ♦ 15 May-15 Sep. € 24.80 (CChq acc) 2009*

SOULAC SUR MER *7B1* (1km S Coastal) *45.50136, -1.13185* **Camping Le Palace, 65 Blvd Marsan-de-Montbrun, Forêt Sud, 33780 Soulac-sur-Mer [05 56 09 80 22; fax 05 56 09 84 23; info@camping-palace.com; www.camping-palace.com]** Fr ferry at Le Verdon-sur-Mer S on D1215, site sp. Or fr S on D101. V lge, hdg/mkd pitch, shd; wc; mv service pnt; baby facs; shwrs inc; el pnts; Indtte; shop; rest; snacks; bar; BBQ; playgrnd; htd, covrd pool; paddling pool; waterslide; sand beach 400m; cycle hire; internet; entmnt; 65% statics; dogs €3; adv bkg; quiet. "Ideal for family beach holiday." 1 May-27 Sep. € 25.00 2008*

We can fill in site
report forms on the
Club's website –
www.caravanclub.co.uk/
europereport

SOULAC SUR MER *7B1* (2km S Rural) *45.48568, -1.11909* **Camping Club de Soulac Le Lilhan, 8 Allée Michel Montaigne, 33780 Soulac-sur-Mer [tel/fax 05 56 09 78 78; contact@lelilhan.com; www.lelilhan.com]** Fr S on D1215 dir Le Verdon, turn W dir Lilhan & L'Amélie-sur-Mer, site sp. Lge, hdg/mkd pitch, pt shd; htd wc; chem disp; mv service pnt; sauna; shwrs; el pnts (10A) inc; Indtte; shop; supmkt 3m; rest; snacks; bar; playgrnd; pool; sand beach 2km; tennis; some statics; dogs €2.95; adv bkg; quiet. ♦ 1 Apr-30 Sep. € 25.00 (CChq acc) 2009*

SOULAC SUR MER *7B1* (13km S Coastal) *45.43357, -1.14519* **Camp Municipal du Gurp, 51 Route de l'Océan, 33590 Grayan-et-L'Hôpital [05 56 09 44 53; fax 05 56 09 54 73]** Take D101 fr Soulac. Turn R after 5km sp Grayan & R at x-rds. Site clearly sp. V lge, mkd pitch, hdstg, shd; wc; chem disp; baby facs; shwrs inc; el pnts (4-10A) inc; Indtte; shop; rest; snacks; bar; playgrnd; sand beach adj; tennis; games area; games rm; entmnt; TV; dogs; poss cr; quiet. "In pine forest; gd, vast beaches." 1 Jun-15 Sep. € 19.90 2009*

SOULAC SUR MER *7B1* (13km S Coastal) *45.41600, -0.12930* **Centre Naturiste Euronat La Dépée (Naturist), 33590 Grayan-et-L'Hôpital [05 56 09 33 33; fax 05 56 09 30 27; info@euronat.fr; www.euronat.fr]** Fr Soulac, take D101 twd Montalivet, turn W at camp sp onto rd leading direct to site. Fr Bordeaux, take D1215 sp Le Verdon-sur-Mer. Approx 8km after Lesparre-Médoc turn L onto D102. In Venday-Montalivet bear R onto D101. In 7.5km turn L sp Euronat. V lge, mkd pitch, hdstg, shd; wc (some htd); chem disp; all serviced pitches; shwrs inc; el pnts (10A) inc; gas; lndtte; shop; rest; snacks; bar; BBQ; playgrnd; htd, covrd pool; thalassotherapy cent; sand beach adj; tennis; horseriding; cinema; archery; cycle hire; golf driving range; internet; TV; 30% statics; dogs €3; phone; Eng spkn; adv bkg; quiet; red low ssn; INF card req. "Expensive, but well worth it; lge pitches; excel." ♦ 27 Mar-1 Nov. € 45.00 (CChq acc) 2009*

SOULAC SUR MER *7B1* (1.5km SW Coastal) *45.49958, -1.13899* **Camping Les Sables d'Argent, Blvd de l'Amélie, 33780 Soulac-sur-Mer [05 56 09 82 87; fax 05 56 09 94 82; sables@lelilhan.com; www.sables-d-argent.com]** Drive S fr Soulac twd L'Amélie-sur-Mer. Clearly sp on R. Med, mkd pitch, pt sl, pt shd; wc; shwrs inc; el pnts (10A) inc (poss long lead req); lndtte; shop; rest; snacks; bar; private sand beach adj; fishing; tennis; internet; entmnt; TV; 60% statics; dogs €2.95; poss cr; red low ssn. "Nice area, but major erosion of coast so no access to beach (2009); poss diff lge o'fits; old san facs (2009); Soulac sm, lively mkt town." 1 Apr-30 Sep. € 24.95 2009*

SOULAC SUR MER *7B1* (3km SW Coastal) *45.48068, -1.14538* **Camping L'Océan, 62 Allée de la Négade, L'Amélie-sur-Mer, 33780 Soulac-sur-Mer [05 56 09 76 10; fax 05 56 09 74 75; camping.ocean@wanadoo.fr; http://pagesperso-orange.fr/camping.ocean]** Fr S on D1215 dir Soulac-sur-Mer; turn L onto D102 to Vendays-Montalivet; then turn N onto D101 Soulac-sur-Mer; in 14km turn L onto D101E2 sp L'Amélie-sur-Mer; in 2km at sp Camping L'Océan turn L into Allée de la Négade. Site on R. Lge, mkd pitch, pt shd; wc; chem disp; shwrs inc; el pnts (10A) €4; lndtte; shop; rest 500m; snacks; bar; BBQ (charcoal, sep area); playgrnd; sand beach 600m; cycle hire; tennis; games area; games rm; initernet; TV; dogs €2.10; adv bkg; ccard not acc; red low ssn; CCI. "Several cycle tracks; vg." ♦ 1 Jun-15 Sep. € 21.00 2008*

SOULAINES DHUYS *6E1* (500m N Rural) *48.37661, 4.73829* **Camping La Croix Badeau, 6 Rue Croix Badeau, 10200 Soulaines-Dhuys [03 25 27 05 43 or 03 26 82 35 31 (LS); responsable@croix-badeau.com; www.croix-badeau.com]** 500m N of junc D960 & D384, behind lge church of Soulaines-Dhuys, well sp. Sm, hdg/mkd pitch, hdstg, pt shd; wc (some cont); chem disp; shwrs inc; el pnts (10A) €2.50; lndtte; shop 500m; playgrnd; tennis; rv 300m; dogs €1; phone; Eng spkn; quiet; CCI. "Excel, clean site in interesting vill; hourly church bells (not o'night)." 1 Apr-15 Oct. € 11.00 2008*

SOULLANS *2H3* (500m NE Urban) *46.79840, -1.89647* **Camp Municipal Le Moulin Neuf, Rue St Christophe, 85300 Soullans [02 51 68 00 24 (Mairie); fax 02 51 68 88 66; camping-soullans@wanadoo.fr]** Fr Challans ring rd take D69 sp Soullans. Site sp on L just bef town cent. Med, hdg/mkd pitch, pt shd; wc (some cont); shwrs inc; el pnts (4A) inc; gas 500m; lndtte; shop 500m; playgrnd; beach 12km; tennis; phone adj; poss cr; adv bkg; quiet; CCI. "Simple site; lovely walks & cycling; vg." 15 Jun-15 Sep. € 8.80 2008*

SOURAIDE see Cambo les Bains *8F1*

SOURSAC *7C4* (1km NE Rural) *45.28066, 2.20999* **Camp Municipal de la Plage, Centre Touristique du Pont Aubert, 19550 Soursac [05 55 27 55 43 or 05 55 27 52 61 (Mairie); fax 05 55 27 63 31; vvpontaubert@correze.net; www.vvpontaubert.correze.net]** Fr Mauriac take D678 to Chalvignac. Bear R onto D105 at 3km (12% descent) to cross Barrage de l'Aigle & 2km 12% ascent on D105E/D16, winding rd. In further 3km pass junc to Latronche, 1st R to site. Med, mkd pitch, terr, pt sl, shd; wc; mv service pnt; baby facs; shwrs inc; el pnts (6A) €2.50; lndtte; shop 1km; rest; snacks; bar; playgrnd; lake sw & waterslide nrby; fishing; archery; cycle hire; games area; entmnt; TV; some statics; dogs €1.50; adv bkg; quiet; "Attractive site by lake; well worth detour; gd, clean san facs; excel." ♦ 15 Jun-15 Sep. € 15.00 2008*

SOUSTONS *8E1* (6km NE Rural) *43.79193, -1.29455* **Camping Le Tuc, 155 Rue Henri Goalard, 40140 Azur [05 58 48 22 52; fax 05 58 48 33 53; campingletuc@wanadoo.fr; www.campingletuc.fr]** Exit N10 junc 11 at Magescq onto D150 dir Azur; site on R 1km SE fr Azur. Site sp fr Azur. Med, hdg pitch, pt shd; wc; chem disp; shwrs inc; el pnts (6-10A) €2.30; gas; lndtte; shop, tradsmn (high ssn); playgrnd; pool; tennis; games area; lake water sports & fishing 2km; TV rm; 50% statics; dogs €1.60; poss cr; adv bkg; quiet; red low ssn; CCI. "Woodland walks; excel." ♦ 1 Apr-15 Sep. € 11.50 2006*

SOUSTONS *8E1* (6km NE Rural) *43.78694, -1.30861* **Camping Village La Paillotte, 40140 Azur [05 58 48 12 12; fax 05 58 48 10 73; info@paillotte.com; www.paillotte.com or www.camping-franceloc.fr]** Exit N10 junc 11; cont thro Magescq & Azur on D16. Turn L by church, after 1.5km site sp on L. Lge, mkd pitch, pt shd; wc (some cont); chem disp; baby facs; shwrs inc; el pnts (10A) inc; lndtte; shop; rest; snacks; bar; BBQ (gas/elec); playgrnd; htd pool; paddling pool; waterslide; lake sw & sand beach adj; hot springs; dinghy sailing; windsurfing; fishing; cycle hire; tennis; horseriding 7km; entmnt; wifi; games/TV rm; statics (tour ops); no dogs; bus; adv bkg; ccard acc; red low ssn; CCI. "Lakeside site; facs ltd low ssn; mkt Soustons Mon." ♦ 24 Apr-26 Sep. € 39.00 ABS - A22 2009*

France

SOUSTONS *8E1* (6.5km NE Rural) *43.78430, -1.30473* **Camping Azu'Rivage, 720 Route des Campings, 40140 Azur [tel/fax 05 58 48 30 72; info@campingazurivage.com; www.campingazurivage.com]** Exit m'way A10 at exit Magescq & take D150 W for 8km to Azur, site sp fr church adj La Paillotte. Med, pt shd; wc; baby facs; shwrs inc; el pnts (10A) inc; lndtte; sm shop & 6km; rest; snacks; playgrnd; pool; paddling pool; sand beach & lake sw; tennis; boating; watersports; entmnt; TV rm; dogs €1.70; poss cr; adv bkg; ccard acc; red long stay; quiet. "Delightful forest setting adj lake; rec." ♦ 15 Jun-15 Sep. € 22.00 2009*

SOUSTONS *8E1* (2km W Rural) *43.75438, -1.35195* **Camp Municipal L'Airial, 61 Ave de Port d'Albret, Quartier Nicot, 40140 Soustons [05 58 41 12 48; fax 05 58 41 53 83; contact@camping-airial.com; www.camping-airial.com]** On D652 (Mimizan/Labenne), opp Etang de Soustons. Foll site sp fr Soustons. Lge, mkd pitch, shd; wc; chem disp; shwrs inc; el pnts (10-16A) €4.90; lndtte; shop; rest; snacks; bar; BBQ; playgrnd; htd, covrd pool; sand beach 7km; boating; watersports; fishing; cycle hire; wifi; entmnt; TV rm; dogs €3.20; phone; poss cr; adv bkg; quiet; red low ssn. "V pleasant site; gd shade & many birds; gd, clean facs but ltd low ssn." 1 Apr-15 Oct. € 19.80 2007*

⊞ **SOUTERRAINE, LA** *7A3* (2km NE Rural) *46.24368, 1.50606* **Camping Suisse Océan, Etang-du-Cheix, 23300 La Souterraine [05 55 63 33 32 or 05 55 63 59 71; fax 05 55 63 21 82]** Fr N145/E62 take D72 sp La Souterraine. Strt over 1st rndabt, at 2nd rndabt turn R, then L to L'Etang de Cheix. Fr N exit A20 junc 22 onto D912 sp La Souterraine; at T-junc turn L & foll outer rd D912b; at rndabt turn L to Etang-du-Cheix; in 50m turn L to site. Sp fr D912b. Sm, hdg/mkd pitch, hdstg, pt sl, terr, pt shd; htd wc (some cont); chem disp; mv service pnt; shwrs inc; el pnts (10A) €3.50; lndtte; sm shop & 2km; tradsmn; rest; snacks; bar; playgrnd; sand lake beach, fishing, sailing adj; diving (summer); tennis; 10% statics; dogs €1.20; poss cr; Eng spkn; adv bkg; quiet but night noise fr factory nrby; CCI. "Superb location by lake; lge pitches; sl rds on site could ground lge o'fits - walk site bef pitching; san facs in Portacabin; ltd facs low ssn inc el pnts & inadequate when site full; pleasant sm town; mkt Thur & Sat; site fair." ♦ € 11.40 2008*

SOUTERRAINE, LA *7A3* (6km E Rural) *46.24534, 1.59083* **Camp Municipal Etang de la Cazine, 23300 Noth [05 55 63 72 21; fax 05 55 63 13 12; mairiedenoth@wanadoo.fr]** Exit A20 junc 23 onto N145 dir Guéret; turn L on D49 sp Noth. Site opp lake. Sm, shd; wc, chem disp; shwrs inc; el pnts (10A) €1.60; ltd snacks; bar; lake fishing & sw adj; quiet; CCI. "Gd touring base; gd." 1 Jun-30 Sep. € 7.40 2006*

SOUTERRAINE, LA *7A3* (10km S Rural) *46.15129, 1.51059* **Camp Municipal, 23290 St Pierre-de-Fursac [05 55 63 65 69 or 05 55 63 61 28 (Mairie); fax 05 55 63 68 20]** Exit A20 at junc 23.1 onto D1 S twd St Pierre-de-Fursac. Site on L at ent to vill dir 'Stade'. Sm, mkd pitch, pt sl, pt shd; wc; shwrs inc; el pnts (6A) €2 (poss rev pol); shop 500m; playgrnd; phone; quiet. "Pleasant, well-kept site o'looking vill; san facs basic but clean; fine NH; gd." ♦ 15 Jun-15 Sep. € 6.00 2008*

STELLA PLAGE see Touquet Paris Plage, Le *6B2*

⊞ **STENAY** *5C1* (250m W Urban) *49.49083, 5.18333* **Port de Plaisance - Motor Caravan Parking Area, Rue du Port, 55700 Stenay [03 29 80 64 22 or 03 29 74 87 54; fax 03 29 80 62 59; otsistenayaccueil@orange.fr]** Off D947 fr town cent. Foll sp to rv port. NB M'vans only. Sm, hdstg; mv service pnt; shwrs inc; shop 600m; rest 300m; quiet. "Adj to rv; excel san facs; NH only." ♦ € 6.00 2008*

⊞ **STRASBOURG** *6E3* (3km W Urban) *48.57525, 7.71730* **FFCC Camping La Montagne Verte, 2 Rue Robert Forrer, 67000 Strasbourg [03 88 30 25 46; fax 03 88 27 10 15; aquadis1@wanadoo.fr; www.aquadis-loisirs.com]** Fr A35 about 2km S of Strasbourg exit junc 4 for Montagne-Verte. Foll camp sp, 1st R to site on R in approx 1km. Sp off D1004 (N4) & D392 to W of city, 1km fr town side of Boulevard de Lyon. Fr town cent foll sp for St Dié/Colmar as camp sp intermittent. NB Fr S on D392 height limit 3.3m on app rd to site. Lge, mkd pitch, pt shd; wc; chem disp; baby facs; shwrs inc; el pnts (6A) inc (poss rev pol); gas; lndry rm; shop 200m; rest 250m; tradsmn; bar; BBQ; playgrnd; covrd pool; tennis; games area; few statics; dogs €1.90; bus/tram to city; Eng spkn; noise fr aircraft, rlwy & church clock; ccard acc; red CCI. "Well-kept site adj rv; mixed reports early ssn; san facs need update, poss unclean; pitches v soft after rain; gates clsd 1900-0700 & 1200-1530 low ssn; easy access to city inc cycle tracks; poss itinerants; gd dog walks." € 18.20 2009*

SUEVRES see Blois *4G2*

⊞ **SUHESCUN** *8F1* (Rural) **Camping à la Ferme (Bachoc), Maison Etchemendigaraya, 64780 Suhescun [05 59 37 60 83; bruno.bachoc@wanadoo.fr; www.chez.com/mendi]** Fr D933 fr St Palais to St Jean-Pied-de-Port, take D22 twd Suhescun. Site sp. Sm, pt sl, pt shd; wc; shwrs inc; el pnts (3A) €2; lndry rm; shop 3km; farm produce for sale; sand beach 45km; watersports nr; cycle hire; internet; statics; adv bkg; quiet; red CCI. "CL-type site on working farm; vg family atmosphere; welcoming owners; conv en rte Spain." € 10.00 2007*

⊞ **SULLY SUR LOIRE** *4F3* (2km N Rural) *47.77180, 2.36200* **Camping Hortus - Le Jardin de Sully, 1 Route d'Orléans, St Père-sur-Loire, 45600 Sully-sur-Loire [tel/fax 02 38 36 35 94; info@camping-hortus.com; www.camping-hortus.com]** Fr N on D948 to Sully then turn R at rndabt immed bef x-ing bdge over Rv Loire onto D60 in St Père-sur-Loire, dir Châteauneuf-sur-Loire. Sp to site in 200m. Fr S thro Sully on D948, cross Rv Loire & turn L at rndabt onto D60. Well sp fr town. Med, hdg/mkd pitch, hdstg, pt shd; htd wc (some cont); chem disp; mv service pnt; baby facs; serviced pitches; shwrs inc; el pnts (10A) inc (poss rev pol); gas; Indtte; shop; tradsmn; snacks; pizzeria; bar; BBQ; playgrnd; games rm; cycle hire; internet; sat TV; dogs €2; phone; bus; Eng spkn; adv bkg rec; quiet; ccard acc; red low ssn; CCI. "Well laid-out site on rvside adj nature reserve; warm welcome, helpful & friendly; some sm pitches; gd cycling; gd dog walks; vg winter site; gd NH en rte S; fairy-tale chateau in Sully." ♦ € 12.50 2009*

See advertisement

SURGERES *7A2* (500m S Urban) *46.10180, -0.75376* **Camping La Gères, 10 Rue de la Gères, 17700 Surgères [05 46 07 79 97 or 06 64 03 89 32 (mob); fax 05 46 27 16 78; christian.Michallet-Ferrier@wanadoo.fr; www.campingdelageres.com]** Site sp in Surgères, on banks of Rv Gères, & fr Surgères by-pass. Sm, mkd pitch, pt shd; wc (cont); mv service pnt; shwrs; el pnts (6A) €3.50; Indtte (inc dryer); shop 300m; rest, snacks & bar 800m; pool & tennis 800m; dogs €1.50; phone; poss cr; ccard acc; CCI. "Adj to park; m'vans extra charge; poss itinerants; NH only." 1 Apr-30 Sep. € 16.50 2009*

SURIS *7B3* (1km N Rural) *45.85925, 0.63739* **Camping La Blanchie, 16270 Suris [tel/fax 05 45 89 33 19 or 06 12 15 66 03 (mob); lablanchie@wanadoo.fr; www.lablanchie.co.uk]** Fr N141 halfway bet Angoulême & Limoges take D52 S at La Péruse to Suris; in 3km turn E up a narr lane to site. Sm, some hdstg, pt sl, pt shd; wc; chem disp; shwrs inc; el pnts (10A) €3; Indtte; playgrnd; pool; lake/rv sw & sand beach 2.5km; tennis, golf, Futuroscope nrby; some statics; dogs free; c'van storage; adv bkg; quiet; red long stay; CCI. "Welcoming British owners; clean site in lovely area; ltd facs; gd touring base." ♦ 14 Mar-31 Oct. € 13.40 2009*

⊞ **SURTAINVILLE** *1C4* (1km W Coastal) *49.46447, -1.82919* **Camp Municipal Les Mielles, 80 Route des Laguettes, 50270 Surtainville [tel/fax 02 33 04 31 04; camping.lesmielles@wanadoo.fr; www.surtainville.com]** S fr Cherbourg on D650, take D66 W thro Surtainville, site on R. Med, pt sl, unshd; htd wc (male cont); chem disp; shwrs inc; el pnts (4A) €2.50; Indtte; playgrnd; sand beach 100m; 30% statics; dogs €1; adv bkg; quiet; CCI. "Excel beach." ♦ € 8.70 2009*

SUSSAC *7B4* (S Rural) *45.66225, 1.65304* **Camp Municipal Beauséjour, Plan d'Eau, 87130 Sussac [05 55 69 62 41; fax 05 55 69 36 80; mairiesussac@wanadoo.fr]** Fr Eymoutiers take D30 dir Chamberet & turn R onto D43 at Chouviat for Sussac. Cont for approx 9 km & foll sp. Site adj lake. Sm, mkd pitch, terr, pt shd; wc (cont); chem disp; shwrs inc; el pnts €2.30; Indtte; shops 500m; snacks; bar; playgrnd; lake adj; Eng spkn; adv bkg; quiet. "Gd site; gd walks, fishing." 15 Jun-15 Sep. € 8.00 2007*

SUSSAC *7B4* (S Rural) *45.65140, 1.67854* **Camping Les Saules (Naturist), 87130 Sussac [05 55 69 64 36 or 0031-2068-25077 (LS); janjansen@lessaules.com; www.lessaules.com]** SE fr Limoges on D979; in 33km turn R to Châteauneuf-la-Forêt; then sharp L turn onto D39 to Sussac. Site sp. Sm, hdg/mkd pitch, terr, pt shd; wc; shwrs inc; el pnts (6A) €3.50; Indtte; shop 10km; tradsmn; snacks; bar; BBQ; playgrnd; lake sand beach; games area; dogs free; Eng spkn; adv bkg; quiet. "Natural site with wild life & flowers; friendly Dutch owners; facs poss stretched when full; sep car park; vg." 16 Jun-31 Aug. € 16.60 2007*

SUZE LA ROUSSE see Bollène *9D2*

TADEN see Dinan *2E3*

⊞ **TAIN L'HERMITAGE** *9C2* (5km NE Rural) *45.10715, 4.89105* **Camping Chante-Merle, 26600 Chantemerle-les-Blés [04 75 07 49 73; fax 04 75 07 45 15; camping chantemerle@wanadoo.fr]** Exit A7 at Tain-l'Hermitage. After exit toll turn L twd town, next turn R (D109) to Chantemerle; site sp. Cont for 5km, site on L. Sm, hdg/mkd pitch, pt shd; htd wc; chem disp; serviced pitches; baby facs; shwrs inc; el pnts (10A) €3.90; Indtte; shops 300m; tradsmn; rest & snacks high ssn; bar; playgrnd; pool; tennis 500m; wifi; 10% statics; dogs €2; site clsd Jan; adv bkg ess; quiet but some rd noise; CCI. "Helpful manager; popular site; excel facs." ♦ € 16.10 2008*

TAIN L'HERMITAGE *9C2* (500m SE Urban) *45.06988, 4.83913* **Camp Municipal Les Lucs, 24 Ave du Président Roosevelt, 26600 Tain l'Hermitage [04 75 08 32 82 or 04 75 08 30 32; fax 04 75 08 32 06; camping. tainlhermitage@wanadoo.fr; http://pagesperso-orange. fr/leslucs]** Fr S on N7 cont twd town cent; at fuel station on R & Netto supmkt sp prepare to turn L in 80m; ent to site in 35m. Fr N on N7 prepare to turn R after Shell fuel station on R. Site alongside Rv Rhône via gates (locked o'night). Well sp adj sw pool/petrol stn. Med, hdg/mkd pitch, pt shd; wc (some cont); chem disp; mv service pnt; shwrs inc; el pnts (10A) €1.30 (poss rev pol); Indtte; shops, snacks adj; playgrnd; pool adj; dogs €1.40; phone; no twin-axles; Eng spkn; some rd/rlwy noise; red low ssn; ccard not acc; CCI. "Pretty, immac, well-run site by Rhône; popular NH; secure site; friendly staff; gd, clean san facs; excel pool complex; no twin-axles, no c'vans over 5.50m & no m'vans over 6m; rvside walk to town; mkt Sat; highly rec." ♦ 15 Mar-15 Oct. € 17.00 2009*

TALLARD see Gap *9D3*

⊞ **TANINGES** *9A3* (1km S Rural) *46.09899, 6.58806* **Camp Municipal des Thézières, Les Vernays-sous-la-Ville, 74440 Taninges [04 50 34 25 59; fax 04 50 34 39 78; camping. taninges@wanadoo.fr; www.taninges.com]** Take D902 N fr Cluses; site 1km S of Taninges on L - just after 'Taninges' sp on ent town boundary; sp Camping-Caravaneige. Lge, pt shd; htd wc (some cont); chem disp; mv service pnt; shwrs inc; el pnts (6-10A) inc; Indtte; ltd shop; shops, rest, snacks, bar 1km; BBQ; playgrnd; pool at Samoens 11km; tennis; wifi; TV rm; dogs €1.10; phone; poss cr; Eng spkn; quiet; ccard acc; CCI. "Conv for N Haute Savoie & Switzerland to Lake Geneva; splendid site with magnificent views; lge pitches; excel facs; friendly, helpful staff." ♦ € 11.25 2009*

⊞ **TARADEAU** *10F3* (3km S Rural) *43.44116, 6.42766* **Camping La Vallée de Taradeau, Chemin La Musardière, 83460 Taradeau [tel/fax 04 94 73 09 14; campingdetaradeau@hotmail.com; www.camping detaradeau.com]** Exit A8 junc 13 & take DN7 (N7) to Vidauban. Opp Mairie take D48 dir Lorgues then D73 N twd Taradeau for 1.5km. Site sp - rough app rd - on rvside. Med, mkd pitch, shd; htd wc; mv service pnt; shwrs inc; el pnts (2-10A) €2.30-6.50; Indtte; rest; snacks; bar; playgrnd; pool; caneoing; games area; games rm; wifi; entmnt; some statics; dogs €2; adv bkg; quiet; CCI. "Pleasantly situated site; friendly, helpful staff; vg pool." € 17.00 2007*

TARASCON *10E2* (6km N Rural) *43.85503, 4.62556* **Camping Lou Vincen, 30300 Vallabrègues [04 66 59 21 29; fax 04 66 59 07 41; campinglouvincen@wanadoo.fr; www. campinglouvincen.com]** N fr Tarascon on D81A, then D183A. Med, hdg/mkd pitch, hdstg, shd; htd wc (some cont); chem disp; mv service pnt; shwrs inc; el pnts (6A) €3.40; gas; Indtte; shop, rest, snacks, bar 100m; playgrnd; pool; tennis; fishing; horseriding 3km; TV; dogs €1.30; adv bkg; quiet but noise fr skateboarders opp; ccard acc; red long stay/low ssn/CCI. "Pitches poss sm for lge o'fits; ltd facs low ssn; attractive vill; gd base for Camargue." 1 Apr-30 Oct. € 15.80 2008*

⊞ **TARASCON** *10E2* (5km SE) *43.78638, 4.71789* **Camp Municipal, Ave Docteur Barberin, 13150 St Etienne-du-Grès [04 90 49 00 03 or 06 14 62 04 34 (mob); camping municipaldugres@wanadoo.fr]** Fr Arles take N570 dir Avignon D99 E dir St Rémy. Site sp on o'skts of St Etienne. Sm, hdg pitch, pt shd; wc (some cont); chem disp; mv service pnt; shwrs inc; el pnts (6A) €2.80; shop 1km; no statics; dogs €1; quiet; CCI. "Gd, peaceful site; gd grass pitches, poss muddy when wet." € 10.00 2008*

TARASCON *10E2* (5km SE Rural) *43.76744, 4.69331* **Camping St Gabriel, 13150 Tarascon [tel/fax 04 90 91 19 83; contact@campingsaintgabriel.com; www.campingsaint gabriel.com]** Take D970 fr Tarascon, at rndabt take D33 sp Fontvieille, site sp 100m on R. Med, hdg pitch, shd; htd wc; chem disp; shwrs inc; el pnts (6A) €3; gas; Indtte; shop; rest adj; snacks; bar; playgrnd; htd pool; games rm; wifi; 30% statics; dogs €2; bus 3km; adv bkg; quiet but some rd noise; CCI. "Excel base for Camargue & Arles; modern san facs; sm pitches poss not suitable lge o'fits; gd." ♦ 1 Mar-30 Nov. € 16.00 2009*

TARASCON SUR ARIEGE *8G3* (4km N Rural) *42.87910, 1.62829* **Camping du Lac, 1 Promenade du Camping, 09400 Mercus-Garrabet [tel/fax 05 61 05 90 61 or 06 86 07 24 18 (mob); info@campinglac.com; www. campinglac.com]** N20 S fr Foix, after 10km exit Mercus over N20 sp, cross rlwy line. At T-junc turn R thro Mercus, site of R over level x-ing. Tight bend into site off long, narr ent drive. Med, hdg/mkd pitch, terr, shd; wc (some cont); chem disp; baby facs; shwrs inc; el pnts (6-10A) €3.40-4.90; Indtte; shop; tradsmn; supmkt 4km; rest, bar 1km; BBQ; htd pool; rv & lake sw, fishing & watersports adj; games rm; 20% statics; dogs €2; phone; some Eng spkn; adv bkg (fee); some rd & rlwy noise; red long stay: CCI. "Clean facs; friendly owners; diff ent for long c'vans; sm pitches; 60km Andorra; a real find!." ♦ 11 Apr-19 Sep. € 23.00 2008*

TARASCON SUR ARIEGE *8G3* (1.5km SE Rural) *42.83981, 1.61215* **FFCC Camping Le Pré-Lombard, Route d'Ussat, 09400 Tarascon-sur-Ariège [05 61 05 61 94; fax 05 61 05 78 93; leprelombard@wanadoo.fr; www.prelombard.com]** Travelling S twd Andorra join N20 to Tarascon. Approx 15km S of Foix after 3 rndabts & x-ing a bdge, at 4th rndabt turn L & foll site sp after rlwy. This rte avoids cent of Tarascon. Lge, mkd pitch, pt shd; htd wc; chem disp; mv service pnt; shwrs inc; el pnts (10A) inc; gas; Indtte; shop & snacks high ssn only; rest & supmkt in town; bar; BBQ (gas/elec/charcoal); playgrnd; htd pool; paddling pool; rv fishing, watersports & sw adj; tennis 1km; archery; entmnt; wifi; games/TV rm; 50% statics; dogs €2.50; Eng spkn; adv bkg rec high ssn; quiet; ccard acc; red low ssn; CCI. "Busy, well-run family site in lovely location; spacious pitches; helpful owner; gd san facs; excel winter NH en rte to Spain; poss noisy at night; poss rallies low ssn; excel." ♦ 27 Mar-11 Nov. € 32.00 (CChq acc) ABS - D23 2009*

TARASCON SUR ARIEGE *8G3* (2km S Rural) *42.8167, 1.6347* **Camping Ariège Evasion, 09400 Ornolac-Ussat-Les-Bains [tel/fax 05 61 05 11 11; contact@ariege-evasion.com; www.ariege-evasion.com]** S on N20 fr Foix to Tarascon-sur-Ariège then 2km to Ornalac-Ussat-Les-Bains. Foll camp sp over narr bdge & R at T-junc. In 750m turn L & immed R at staggered x-rds, site in 100m. Med, hdg/mkd pitch, pt shd; wc (cont); chem disp; mv service pnt; shwrs inc; el pnts (3-10A) €2-4; gas 1km; Indtte; shop 1km; tradsmn; rest; snacks; playgrnd; trout-fishing; canoe hire; 5% statics; Eng spkn; adv bkg; quiet; red low ssn; CCI. "Prehistoric caves nr." 14 Apr-15 Oct. € 15.00 2007*

⊞ **TARASCON SUR ARIEGE** *8G3* (1.5km NW Rural) *42.85606, 1.58861* **Camping Le Sédour, Florac, 09400 Surba [05 61 05 87 28; fax 05 61 01 49 33; info@campinglesedour.com; www.campinglesedour.com]** Fr rndbt 1km N of Tarascon take 1st R sp Massat. Turn R in 100m, site on L in Surba vill. Med, hdg/mkd pitch, pt sl, pt shd; wc; chem disp; some serviced pitches; shwrs inc; el pnts (10A) inc; Indtte; supmkt 1km; tradsmn; rest, bar 300m; playgrnd; 60% statics; dogs €2; poss cr; some Eng spkn; adv bkg; quiet; red long stay; CCI. "Friendly, helpful owners; gd facs; poss diff access lge o'fits; conv for Ariège valleys & prehistoric park; mountain views." ♦ € 20.00 2009*

TARDETS SORHOLUS *8F1* (1km S Rural) *43.11143, -0.86362* **Camping du Pont d'Abense, 64470 Tardets-Sorholus [tel/fax 05 59 28 58 76 or 06 78 73 53 59 (mob); camping.abense@wanadoo.fr; www.camping-pontabense.com]** Take D918 S to Tardets, turn R to cross bdge onto D57. Site sp on R. Tardets cent narr. Med, shd; wc; chem disp; shwrs inc; el pnts (3A) €3.20; lndry rm; shop, rest, snacks & bar 500m; tradsmn; rv & beach nrby; fishing; some statics; dogs €2; quiet; adv bkg; red low ssn; CCI. "Informal pitching; facs old & poss unclean (2007); gd birdwatching." Easter-Mid Nov. € 14.70 2008*

TARDETS SORHOLUS *8F1* (1km W Rural) *43.11364, -0.88122* **Camping à la Ferme Carrique (Iriart), 64470 Alos-Sibas-Abense [05 59 28 50 25; carrique64@hotmail.fr; www.campingcarrique.wordpress.com]** S fr Mauléon on D918 to Tardets-Sorholus. Turn W on D24 to Alos over single c'way bdge. Site 500m on L after Alos. Sm, pt shd; wc; shwrs inc; el pnts (3A) €2; Indtte; shops 2km; tradsmn; rv sw 2km; dogs €0.50; quiet. "CL-type farm site; friendly family; clean facs; excel." ♦ 1 Jun-31 Oct. € 9.00 2007*

TAUPONT see Ploërmel *2F3*

TAUTAVEL see Estagel *8G4*

TEILLET *8E4* (S Rural) *43.83186, 2.33832* **Camping Le Relais de l'Entre-Deux-Lacs, Route de Lacaune, 81120 Teillet [05 63 55 74 45; fax 05 63 55 75 65; contact@camping-entredeuxlacs.com; www.campingdutarn.com]** Fr Albi by-pass take D81 SE to Teillet. Site on R at S end of vill. Med, hdstg, terr, shd; wc; chem disp; mv service pnt; shwrs inc; el pnts inc (10A) inc (poss no earth & long lead poss req); gas; Indtte; shops 200m; rest, snacks, bar high ssn; BBQ; playgrnd; pool high ssn; games area; archery; guided walks; 10% statics; dogs €2; adv bkg; quiet; red low ssn. "Friendly; steep site rds; few water points; heavily wooded." ♦ 1 Apr-31 Oct. € 22.00 2007*

TELGRUC SUR MER *2E2* (1km S Coastal) *48.22386, -4.37223* **Camping Le Panoramic, 130 Route de la Plage, 29560 Telgruc-sur-Mer [02 98 27 78 41; fax 02 98 27 36 10; info@camping-panoramic.com; www.camping-panoramic.com]** Fr D887 Crozon-Châteaulin rd, turn W on D208 twd Trez-Bellec Plage, site sp on R in approx 1.5km. Med, hdg/mkd pitch, terr, pt shd, wc (some cont); chem disp; mv service pnt; baby facs; shwrs inc, el pnts (6-10A) €3.10-4.50; Indtte; shop; rest; snacks; bar; BBQ; playgrnd; covrd pool; jacuzzi; sand beach 700m; tennis; cycle hire; games rm; TV rm; some statics; dogs €2; adv bkg; quiet; ccard acc; red low ssn; CCI. "Vg, well-run, welcoming site; access to pitches poss diff due trees & narr site rds." ♦ 1 May-12 Sep. € 22.00 2009*

See advertisement on next page

TELGRUC SUR MER *2E2* (2km S Coastal) *48.21003, -4.36881* **Camping Pen-Bellec, Trez Bellec, 29560 Telgruc-sur-Mer [02 98 27 31 87 or 02 98 27 76 55; camping.penbellec@wanadoo.fr; www.camping-telgruc.fr]** Fr D887 turn S onto D208 for Telgruc-sur-Mer. In Telgruc take rd mkd 'Plage Trez Bellec' & cont to far end where rd rises & turns inland. Sm, mkd pitch, unshd; wc; mv service pnt; shwrs €1.50; el pnts (3A) €3; Indtte; shop & 2km; tradsmn; rest 3km; playgrnd; sand beach adj; watersports adj; cycle hire; games area; dogs €1.50; poss cr; Eng spkn; adv bkg; poss noisy. "Clean, well-situated site with views (exposed in bad weather); friendly, helpful owners; san facs satisfactory; gd cliff walking; gd touring base; highly rec." Jun-Sep. € 11.00 2008*

LE PANORAMIC ****
Campsite of the "SITES et PAYSAGES de FRANCE" chain

TELGRUC SUR MER *2E2* (1km W Coastal) *48.22696, -4.36844* **Camping Les Mimosas, Kergreis, 106 Rue de la Plage, 29560 Telgruc-sur-Mer [tel/fax 02 98 27 76 06; campingmimosa@wanadoo.fr; www.campingmimosa.com]** Fr D887 Crozon-Châteaulin rd turn SW onto D208 into Telgruc. Fr town sq foll sp Trez-Bellec-Plage. In 900m, after exiting town, turn L & L, site clearly sp. Med, hdg/mkd pitch, terr, pt shd; wc; chem disp; shwrs inc; el pnts (10A) €1.80; Indtte; shop 600m; sand beach 1km; playgrnd; tennis; dogs €0.80; poss cr; adv bkg rec high ssn; quiet; CCI. "Gd." 1 Apr-30 Sep. € 10.20 2009*

TENDE *10E4* (500m NE Rural) *44.09185, 7.59843* **Camp Municipal St Jacques, Route de la Pia, 06430 Tende [04 93 04 76 08; fax 04 93 04 35 09]** Fr N on D6204 (N204) site sp on L on ent Tende. Cross rv & foll site sp. Sm, hdstg, shd; htd wc; chem disp; shwrs inc; shops 500m; el pnts (10A) inc; gas; Indtte; shop, rest, snacks, bar in town; TV rm; bus; phone; quiet. "Clean site; gd walking & touring base." 1 May-30 Sep. € 13.40 2007*

TENDE *10E4* (9km S Rural) *44.00746, 7.55448* **Camp Municipal, Quartier Barnabin, 06540 Fontan [04 93 04 52 02 or 04 93 04 50 01 (Mairie)]** Site is on D6204 (N204) 200m N of Fontan. Sm, pt sl, pt shd; wc (some cont); shwrs inc; el pnts; Indtte; shop, rest, snacks, bar 200m; dogs; phone; adv bkg; some rd noise; CCI. "Pleasant site nr scenic vill of Saorge; site yourself if recep shut (ltd open hrs)." 1 Apr-30 Sep. 2006*

TERRASSON LAVILLEDIEU *7C3* (4km W Rural) *45.12344, 1.26797* **Camping La Salvinie, Bouillac-Sud, 24120 Terrasson-Lavilledieu [05 53 50 06 11 or 06 03 61 55 72; camping.lasalvinie@orange.fr; www.camping-salvinie.com]** Exit A89 junc 18 onto D6089 dir Terrasson-Lavilledieu. Cross Rv Vézère & turn immed L, site in 4km sp. Med, hdg/mkd pitch, shd; wc; chem disp; mv service pnt; shwrs; el pnts (6A) €2.60; gas; Indtte; shop & 4km; tradsmn; ice; supmkt 3km; rest; snacks; bar; BBQ; playgrnd; pool; games area; games rm; wifi; 10% statics; dogs €1; no twin-axles; poss cr; Eng spkn; adv bkg; quiet; ccard acc. "Excel, scenic site; friendly owners; Terrasson interesting town; mkt Thurs." ♦ 1 Apr-31 Oct. € 11.10 2009*

TEUILLAC *7C2* (Rural) **Camp Municipal, 33710 Teuillac [05 57 64 34 55; fax 05 57 64 22 25; accueil@mairie-teuillac.com; www.teuillac.a3w.fr/]** Fr D137 turn onto D134 at Le Poteau twd Teuillac, site in 2km adj Mairie. Sm, pt shd; wc; baby facs; shwrs; el pnts €2; snacks; pool; fishing nr; quiet. "Pleasant, basic site; useful NH, conv Bordeaux." 1 May-30 Sep. € 6.00 2008*

THANN *6F3* (7km NW Rural) *47.85071, 7.03058* **FFCC Camping La Mine d'Argent, Rue des Mines, 68690 Moosch [03 89 82 30 66 or 03 89 60 34 74; fax 03 89 42 15 12; moosch@camping-la-mine-argent.com; http://camping-la-mine-argent.com]** Turn L off N66 Thann-Thillot rd in cent of Moosch opp church; foll sps for 1.5km, ent on R, narr app. Med, mkd pitch, pt sl, pt terr, pt shd; wc; chem disp; mv service pnt; shwrs inc; el pnts (6A) inc; gas; Indtte; tradsmn; shops 1.5km; playgrnd; 10% statics; dogs €0.60; phone; adv bkg; quiet; ccard acc; red low ssn/CCI. "In wooded valley; clean, well-kept site; helpful staff; excel walking; busy w/end; highly rec." 18 Apr-17 Oct. € 11.40 2009*

THARON PLAGE see Pornic *2G3*

THEIX see Vannes *2F3*

THENON *7C3* (3km SE Rural) *45.11883, 1.09119* **Camping Le Verdoyant (formerly Camping Jarry-Carrey), Route de Montignac, 24210 Thenon [05 53 05 20 78; fax 05 67 34 05 00; contact@campingleverdoyant.fr; campingleverdoyant.fr; www.lejarrycarrey.fr]** Sp fr A89, take D67 fr Thenon to Montignac. Site on R in 4km. Med, mkd pitch, pt sl, terr, pt shd; wc; chem disp (wc); shwrs inc; el pnts (10A) €3.15; shops 2km; tradsmn; snacks; bar; gas; Indtte; playgrnd; pool; lake fishing; dogs €1.60; adv bkg; quiet; 20% statics; dogs €1.65; Eng spkn; quiet; red low ssn; CCI. "Beautiful setting away fr tourist bustle; excel base for area; friendly owners; site unkempt & lacking in care early ssn (May 2008)." ♦ 1 Apr-30 Sep. € 13.65 2009*

THENON *7C3* (10km W Rural) *45.13165, 0.92867* **Camping de la Pélonie, La Bourgie, 24330 St Antoine-d'Auberoche [05 53 07 55 78; fax 05 53 03 74 27; www.lapelonie.com]** Fr Périgueux on A89 twd Brive; 5km past St Pierre-de-Chignac, site sp on L; turn L at picnic area - go under rlwy bdge; site ent on L. Med, mkd pitch, pt shd; wc; chem disp; shwrs inc; el pnts (6A) €3.10 (poss req long cable); Indtte; gas; shop; tradsmn; rest; snacks; bar; playgrnd; htd pool; paddling pool; wifi; TV; 20% statics; dogs €2; phone; poss cr; Eng spkn; adv bkg; quiet; ccard acc; red low ssn; CCI. "Delightful site; pleasant, welcoming owners; gd, clean facs; excel facs for children; some pitches diff lge o'fits; gd touring base." ♦ 11 Apr-17 Oct. € 16.30 2009*

THERONDELS see Pierrefort *7C4*

THIEMBRONNE *3A3* (500m NW Urban) *50.62114, 2.05424* **Camping Les Pommiers, 1 Route des Desvres, 62560 Thiembronne [03 21 39 50 19 or 03 21 66 25 47 (LS); fax 03 21 95 79 20]** SW fr St Omer for 25km on D928 to Fauquembergues. NW on D158 for 4km past water tower. Site sp. Med, sl, shd; wc; chem disp; shwrs €0.30; el pnts (4A) €2.60; Indtte; shop 1km; snacks; playgrnd; pool; games area; entmnt; TV; 75% statics; poss cr; adv bkg; quiet. 15 Mar-15 Oct. € 15.40 2006*

THIERS *9B1* (6km NE Rural) *45.89874, 3.59888* **Camping Les Chanterelles, 63550 St Rémy-sur-Durolle [04 73 94 31 71; fax 04 73 93 71 00; contact@revea-vacances.com; www.revea-vacances.fr]** On A72/E70 W dir Clermont-Ferrand, exit at junc 3 sp Thiers. Foll sp twd Thiers on N89 into L Monnerie. Fr vill, take D20 & foll sp St Rémy. In St Rémy, foll 'Camping' sp. Do not app thro Thiers as narr rds v diff for lge o'fits. Med, terr, pt shd; htd wc; chem disp; mv service pnt; shwrs inc; el pnts (10A) €3.50; gas; Indtte; shop; tradsmn; BBQ; playgrnd; htd pool; lake sw 600m; windsurfing; tennis 600m; TV rm; some statics; dogs €1.50; adv bkg; quiet; ccard acc; CCI. "Beautiful situation with views; modern, clean facs; some noise at w/end fr statics; excel." ♦ 1 May-13 Sep. € 13.70 (CChq acc) 2008*

THIERS *9B1* (8km W Rural) *45.86845, 3.47616* **Camp Municipal Pont Astier, 63190 Orléat [tel/fax 04 73 53 64 40; mairie.orleat@orleat.com]** On A72 take exit 2 onto D906 S for 2.5km. Turn R on N89 for Clermont-Ferrand. Turn R at Pont-de-Dore onto D224. Site 3km on R. Med, hdg pitch, pt sl, pt shd; wc (some cont); chem disp; shwrs inc; el pnts (10A) €4; Indtte; shop 3km; tradsmn; snacks; bar; BBQ; playgrnd; pool; fishing; tennis; dogs €0.90; Eng spkn; adv bkg; red low ssn; CCI. "By Rv Dore; lge pitches, but some damp; poss mosquito prob; site ent poss diff; unreliable opening dates." ♦ 1 May-30 Sep. € 12.00 2009*

THIERS *9B1* (4km NW Rural) *45.87168, 3.48538* **Camping Base de Loisirs Iloa, Courty, 63300 Thiers [04 73 80 92 35 or 04 73 80 14 90; fax 04 73 80 88 81; http://ville-thiers.fr]** Exit A72 junc 2 for Thiers; at rndabt turn L sp Vichy but take D44 sp Dorat; pass under m'way, site beyond Courty on L sp Les Rives-de-Thiers. Sm, mkd pitch, pt shd; wc (some cont); chem disp; mv service pnt; some serviced pitches; shwrs inc; el pnts (6A) inc; gas 5km; Indtte; supmkt 5km; tradsmn; playgrnd; pool & sports adj; lake fishing; tennis; entmnt; TV rm; dogs; CCI. "Well-maintained; vg, clean san facs; friendly warden; quiet low ssn; vg NH." ♦ 5 May-16 Sep. € 14.10 (3 persons) 2009*

THIEZAC see Vic sur Cère *7C4*

⊞ **THILLOT, LE** *6F3* (1km NW Rural) *47.88893, 6.75683* **Camp Municipal Clos des Chaume, 36 Rue de la Chaume, 88160 Le Thillot [03 29 25 10 30; fax 03 29 25 25 87; campingmunicipal@ville-lethillot88.fr; www.ville-lethillot88.fr]** Site sp on N o'skts of town N on N66, on R behind sports cent. Med, pt sl, pt shd; htd wc; shwrs inc; el pnts (6A) €1.80; gas; Indtte; shops 1km; playgrnd; pool & tennis adj; few statics; adv bkg; quiet. "Attractive, well-maintained site; friendly staff; vg san facs; excel touring base." € 6.10 2009*

THILLOT, LE *6F3* (2.5km NW Rural) *47.89322, 67.3803* **Camping Le Clos Martin, 5 Rue du Clos-Martin, 88160 Ramonchamp [03 29 25 05 38]** At Ramonchamp on N66 (travelling E) turn R & foll sp. Sm, pt shd; wc; chem disp; shwrs €1.30; el pnts (6A) €2 (poss rev pol); Indtte; shops, rest 200m; BBQ; playgrnd; rv fishing; dogs €0.50; phone; quiet; CCI. "Pleasant site; helpful owners; gd walking & cycling." 1 Apr-15 Sep. € 7.30 2008*

THIONVILLE *5C2* (NE Urban) *49.36127, 6.17534* **Camp Municipal, 6 Rue du Parc, 57100 Thionville [03 82 53 83 75; fax 03 82 53 91 27]** Exit A31 at sp Thionville Cent; foll sp 'Centre Ville'; foll site sp dir Manom. Sm, mkd pitch, some hdstg, pt shd; wc; chem disp; mv service pnt; shwrs inc; el pnts (3-10A) inc; shop 250m; rest snacks, bar 250m; playgrnd; pool 1km; boating; fishing; poss cr; Eng spkn; adv bkg; quiet; CCI. "Well-kept site, poss untidy low ssn; friendly warden; gd san facs; some rvside pitches; no hdstg until Jun due to rv conditions; rec arr early high ssn; vg." ♦ 1 May-30 Sep. € 12.25 2009*

⊞ **THIVIERS** *7C3* (10km N Rural) *45.50261, 0.91478* **Camping Le Touroulet, Moulin du Tourelet, 24800 Chaleix [tel/fax 05 53 55 23 59 or 05 53 62 07 90; touroulet@hotmail.com; www.camping-touroulet.com]** Fr Limoges on N21 S twd Périgueux, thro vill of La Coquille, in about 4.5km turn R onto D98 twd St Jory-de-Chalais & Chaleix. In 4km turn L to vill & site 1km further on. Take care narr bdge & site ent. Sm, pt sl, some hdstg, pt shd; pt htd wc; chem disp; shwrs inc; el pnts (8A) €3; Indtte; shop 1.5km; tradsmn; rest; bar; BBQ; fishing; games rm; entmnt; internet; dogs €0.50; adv bkg; quiet; CCI. "Beautiful, spacious, well-kept, rvside site; welcoming, helpful British owners; basic, ltd san facs, stretched high ssn; hdstg pitches sl & uneven; Xmas package; vg." € 12.00 2009*

France

THIVIERS *7C3* (10km N Rural) *45.49950, 0.90690* **Camping Maisonneuve, 1 Chemin de Maisonneuve, 24800 St Jory-de-Chalais [tel/fax 05 53 55 10 63; camping.maisonneuve@wanadoo.fr; www.camping-maisonneuve.com]** N fr Thiviers on N21 for 6km; turn L on D98 thro Chaleix; site on L bef ent St Jory. Other rtes v narr. Sm, hdg/mkd pitch, hdstg, pt sl, pt shd; wc (some cont); chem disp; mv service pnt; sauna; shwrs inc; el pnts (10A) €3.50; Indtte; shop 500m; rest; snacks; bar; playgrnd; pool; fishing lake; games rm; TV; 10% statics; dogs €1; Eng spkn; adv bkg; quiet; red low ssn/long stay/CCI. "Pretty site in attractive countryside; lge pitches, some v shaded; helpful, welcoming owners; excel." ♦ 1 Apr-31 Oct. € 20.00 2008*

⊞ **THIVIERS** *7C3* (2km E Rural) *45.41299, 0.93209* **Camping Le Repaire (formerly Municipal), Ave de Verdun, 24800 Thiviers [tel/fax 05 53 52 69 75; camping.le.repaire@gmail.com; www.camping-thiviers-perigord.com]** N21 to Thiviers; at rndabt take D707 E dir Lanouaille; site in 1.5km on R. Med, hdg/mkd pitch, pt sl, terr, pt shd; htd wc; chem disp; mv service pnt; shwrs inc; el pnts (12A) €3; Indtte; shop 2km; snacks; BBQ; playgrnd; covrd pool; lake fishing; entmnt; games rm; TV rm; 5% statics; dogs €1.60; phone; no twin-axles; poss cr; Eng spkn; adv bkg; quiet; red low ssn; CCI. "Lovely site - one of best in area; friendly owners; clean san facs; some pitches unrel in wet weather; excel." ♦ € 14.00 2009*

THOISSEY *9A2* (1km SW Rural) *46.16512, 4.79257* **Camp Municipal Plage International, Le Port, 01140 Thoissey [04 74 04 02 97 or 06 65 20 44 05 (mob); fax 04 74 69 76 13; campingthoissey@orange.fr; http://ladombes.free.fr/Camping/Thoissey.htm]** S on D306 (N6) turn L onto D9. Turn sharp R on Plage immed after x-ing Rv Saône. Lge, mkd pitch, pt shd; wc (mainly cont); shwrs inc; el pnts (6-10A) inc; Indtte; shop; rest; snacks; bar; playgrnd; htd pool (high ssn); watersports; tennis; rv beach & sw adj; TV; 75% statics; dogs €1.50; phone; poss cr; quiet; CCI. "Lge pitches; san facs need refurb & poss unclean (2008); site muddy when wet." ♦ 15 Apr-15 Sep. € 13.40 2008*

THOLY, LE *6F3* (6km N Rural) *48.12005, 6.73181* **Camping Le Barba, 45 Le Village, 88640 Rehaupal [03 29 66 35 57; barba@campingdubarba.com; www.campingdubarba.com]** Fr Gérardmer on D417 after 8km site sp on R 2km bef Le Tholy. Foll sp to Rehaupal, site on R on ent to vill. Sm, mkd pitch, pt shd; wc; chem disp; shwrs inc; el pnts (3-6A) €2.50-3.50; gas; Indtte; shop adj; tradsmn; rest; some statics; dogs €1; Eng spkn; quiet. "Friendly owner; scenic site; vg walking." 1 May-30 Sep. € 10.00 2008*

THOLY, LE *6F3* (1.3km NW Rural) *48.08897, 6.72869* **Camping de Noirrupt, 15 Chemin de L'Etang, 88530 Le Tholy [03 29 61 81 27; fax 03 29 61 83 05; info@jpvacances.com; www.jpvacances.com]** Fr Gérardmer, take D417 W, turn R in Le Tholy up hill onto D11. Site on L on secondary rd to Epinal & sp. Med, terr, pt shd; wc (some cont); chem disp; baby facs; sauna; shwrs inc; el pnts (2-6A) €3-5; gas; Indtte; shops 1km; snacks; bar; BBQ; htd pool; tennis; entmnt; TV rm; some statics; dogs €1.50; poss cr; some rd noise; red long stay. "Pleasant, well laid-out site in lovely area; sm pitches; vg." 15 Apr-15 Oct. € 20.30 2009*

THONAC see Montignac *7C3*

THONNANCE LES MOULINS *6E1* (2km W Rural) *48.40630, 5.27110* **Camping La Forge de Ste Marie, 52230 Thonnance-les-Moulins [03 25 94 42 00; fax 03 25 94 41 43; info@laforgedesaintemarie.com; www.laforgedesaintemarie.com or www.les-castels.com]** Fr N67 exit sp Joinville-Est, foll D60 NE sp Vaucouleurs. In 500m turn R onto D427 sp Poissons & Neufchâteau. Site on R in 11km. NB Swing wide at turn into site fr main c'way, not fr what appears to be a run in. Site ent narr. Med, hdg/mkd pitch, pt sl, pt terr, shd; wc; chem disp; serviced pitches; baby facs; shwrs inc; el pnts (6A) inc; gas; Indtte; shop; tradsmn; rest; snacks; bar; BBQ; htd, covrd pool & paddling pool; lake; boating; freshwater fishing; cycle hire; gd walking; entmnt; wifi; games/TV rm; 25% statics; dogs €1.50; phone; Eng spkn; adv bkg; ccard acc; red low ssn; CCI. "Vg, well-kept, busy site; friendly, helpful owners; access poss diff to some terr pitches/sharp bends on site rds; muddy after rain; vg rest; mkt Fri." ♦ 24 Apr-10 Sep. € 29.90 (CChq acc) ABS - J04 2009*

THONON LES BAINS *9A3* (3km NE Rural) *46.39944, 6.50416* **Camping Le Saint Disdille, Vongy, 117 Ave de St Disdille, 74200 Thonon-Les-Bains [04 50 71 14 11; fax 04 50 71 93 67; camping@disdille.com; www.disdille.com]** Exit A41/A40 junc 14 Annemasse onto D1005 (N5) & foll sp Thonon twd Evian. At Vongy rndabt foll sp St Disdille & site. Site 200m fr Lake Geneva. V lge, mkd pitch, shd; wc; shwrs; el pnts (6-10A) €4; gas; Indtte; shop; rest; snacks; bar; playgrnd; lake sw & beach 200m; fishing; watersports; tennis; cycle hire; games area; games rm; wifi; entmnt; 30% statics; dogs €2; adv bkg ess; ccard acc; CCI. "Well-situated, well-equipped site." ♦ 1 Apr-30 Sep. € 19.70 2009*

See advertisement

⊞ **THONON LES BAINS** *9A3* (9km SE Rural) *46.37058, 6.55146* **Camping La Prairie, Rue de Savoie, 74500 Champanges [04 50 81 02 08; fax 04 50 73 40 68; www.champanges.fr]** Rec rte for c'vans & lge m'vans: D32 fr Thonon & foll sp Marin & Vallée d'Abondance/Champanges. Turn R into vill, site on R. Med, pt sl, terr, pt shd; htd wc; chem disp (wc); mv service pnt; baby facs; shwrs inc; el pnts (6A) €2.75; Indtte; shop 200m; rest; snacks; bar; BBQ; playgrnd; lake sw in Thonon; tennis; games area; entmnt; TV rm; 40% statics; dogs €0.60; CCI. "Gd walking." ♦ € 8.10 2006*

THONON LES BAINS *9A3* (10km W Rural) *46.35638, 6.35250* **CAMPEOLE Camping La Pinède, 74140 Excenevex [04 50 72 85 05 or 04 50 72 81 27 (Mairie); fax 04 50 72 93 00; pinede@campeole.com; www.camping-lac-leman.info or www.campeole.com]** On D1005 (N5) to Geneva, 10km fr Thonon, turn R at Camping sp. V lge, htd/mkd pitch, shd; htd wc; child facs; shwrs inc; chem disp; mv service pnt; child facs; el pnts (10A) €4.10; gas; Indtte; shop; rest; snacks; bar; BBQ; playgrnd; sports area; tennis; lake sw, fishing, watersports & sand beach adj; horseriding 1km; entmnt; internet; TV; 75% statics; dogs €3.50; poss cr; adv bkg; quiet; red low ssn. "Excel lakeside site; friendly & efficient staff." 2 Apr-10 Sep. € 21.40 2009*

THORE LA ROCHETTE see Vendôme *4F2*

THORENS GLIERES *9A3* (2km N Rural) *46.01642, 6.24394* **Camping Nantizel, 135 Route de Nantizel, 74570 Thorens-Glières [04 50 22 43 42]** Fr A410 exit 19. Take D1203 (N203) twd Annecy. In 10km after S-bend take D5 E to Thorens-Glières & foll camping sp to site. Sm, pt sl, pt shd; wc; own san rec; chem disp; shwrs inc; el pnts (3A) €2.30; shops 4km; playgrnd; dogs €1.30; v quiet. "Scenic CL-type site on alpine farm; highly rec." 15 Jun-15 Sep. € 12.00 2008*

THORENS GLIERES *9A3* (3km SE Rural) *45.98416, 6.27153* **Camping Rural Les Combes d'Usillon, 461 Chemin des Combes d'Usillon, 74570 Thorens-Glières [04 50 22 81 10; campingville@aol.com]** Fr Thorens-Glières take D5 S twd Aviernoz. In 1km turn L twd La Louvatière. Site sp Camping Rural in 2km on rvside. Sm, pt shd; shwrs inc; el pnts €1.85; Indtte; shop 2.5km; rest; dogs; v quiet. "Quiet, scenic site 'away-from-it-all'; site yourself; pleasant owner; drinking water fr owner's house; gd walking." 15 May-15 Sep. € 10.00 2008*

THORENS GLIERES *9A3* (3km NW Rural) *46.00200, 6.19190* **Aire Naturelle Le Moulin Dollay, 206 Rue du Moulin Dollay, 74570 Groisy [tel/fax 04 50 68 00 31; moulin.dollay@orange.fr; www.moulin.dollay@orange.fr]** Fr Annecy take D1203 (N203) N. At Champion supmkt fork L to Groisy. Thro Groisy & over rv bdge, turn R sp La Roche-sur-Foron, site on L. Sm, mkd pitch, pt shd; htd wc; chem disp; mv service pnt; baby facs; fam bthrm; shwrs inc; el pnts (6A) €3; gas 1km; Indtte (inc dryer); shops 1km; tradsmn; snacks; BBQ; bar 5km; playgrnd; rv sw adj; TV rm; no dogs; train 500m; phone; o'night m'van area; adv bkg; quiet; red long stay. "Excel site with immac san facs; friendly owner." ♦ 1 May-15 Sep. € 16.00 2008*

THOUARCE *4G1* (SW Rural) *47.26524, -0.50747* **Camp Municipal de l'Ecluse, Ave des Trois Ponts, 49380 Thouarcé [02 41 54 14 36 (Mairie); fax 02 41 54 09 11; mairie.thouarce@wanadoo.fr]** Exit A87 junc 24 onto D160/D55 dir Beaulieu-sur-Layon & Thouarcé. Site sp adj Rv Layon. Sm, pt shd; wc (cont for men); shwrs inc; el pnts €1.70; gas; shops & supmkt 400m; playgrnd; pool, tennis nr; fishing; no adv bkg; quiet; CCI. 15 Apr-15 Sep. € 3.20 2006*

THOUARS *4H1* (500m E Rural) *46.98044, -0.21967* **Camp Municipal Le Clos Imbert, Rue de la Grande-Côte-de-Crevant, 79100 Thouars [05 49 66 17 99 or 05 49 68 22 80 (Mairie); fax 05 49 66 16 09; camping@ville-thouars.fr; www.ville-thouars.fr]** Sp fr cent of town & fr D938. Ent down 1 in 5 (20%) hill, narr & winding; access should not be attempted by lge o'fits. Site adj Rv Thouet. Sm, pt shd; wc; shwrs; el pnts (5-10A) €2.15-3.20; snacks; playgrnd; fishing; sports facs nr; quiet. "Pleasant little site." ♦ 9 Jun-28 Sep. € 8.60 2008*

THUEYTS *9D2* (4km E Rural) *44.66846, 4.28329* **Camping Le Ventadour, Pont de Rolandy, 07380 Meyras [tel/fax 04 75 94 18 15; info@leventadour.com; www.leventadour.com]** Sp fr N102. Med, pt shd; htd wc; shwrs inc; el pnts (6-10A) €3-3.50 (poss rev pol); Indtte; shop; supmkt 5km; snacks; bar; gas BBQ; playgrnd; fishing; some statics; dogs €1.50; Eng spkn; adv bkg; quiet. "Helpful owners; easy access; gd, clean facs; attractive site." 1 Apr-30 Sep. € 14.00 2006*

France

THURY HARCOURT *3D1* (500m NE Rural) *48.98930, -0.46966* **FFCC Camping Vallée du Traspy, Rue du Pont Benoît, 14220 Thury-Harcourt [02 31 79 61 80 or 02 31 52 53 54; fax 02 31 84 76 19]** App fr N on D562 fr Caen, take L fork into town after pool complex. In 100m turn L at Hôtel de la Poste, 1st L to site, clearly sp adj Rv Orne. Med, mkd pitch, terr, pt shd; wc (some cont); chem disp; mv service pnt; shwrs inc; el pnts (6-10A) €3.90-4.90; gas; lndtte; shop 1km; tradsmn; snacks; bar; BBQ; playgrnd; htd pool nr; rv adj & lake nrby; fishing; canoeing; entmnt; 20% statics; dogs €2.80; phone; poss cr; Eng spkn; adv bkg rec high ssn; quiet; CCI. "Friendly owners; o'night area for m'vans; gd walking." ♦ 1 Apr-30 Sep. € 14.40 2009*

TIL CHATEL *6G1* (2km E Rural) *47.53042, 5.18700* **Camping Les Sapins, 21120 Til-Châtel [03 80 95 16 68]** Leave A31 junc 5 onto D974 (N74) dir Til-Châtel. Site on R in 500m adj Rest Les Sapins. Sm, pt sl, pt shd, serviced pitch; wc (some cont); shwrs inc; el pnts (10A) inc; shops 2km; rest; snacks; bar; poss v cr; Eng spkn; adv bkg; minimal rd noise; CCI. "Clean, comfortable site; gd rest; no twin-axles; conv NH fr a'route." 1 Apr-30 Sep. € 16.50 2009*

TINTENIAC *2E4* (500m N Rural) *48.33111, -1.83315* **Camp Municipal du Pont L'Abbesse, Rue du 8 Mai 1945, 35190 Tinténiac [02 99 68 09 91 or 02 99 68 02 15 (Mairie); fax 02 99 68 05 44]** Fr D137 turn E onto D20 to Tinténiac; go strt thro vill to canal; sp just bef canal bdge; turn L. Site behind Brit Hôtel La Guinguette, on Canal d'Ille et Rance. Sm, hdg/mkd pitch, pt sl, pt shd; htd wc; shwrs; el pnts inc; shops, rest, snacks & bar adj; playgrnd; fishing; few statics; quiet; CCI. "Lovely walks/cycling along canal; san facs OK." ♦ 1 Mar-31 Oct. € 8.00 2009*

TINTENIAC *2E4* (2km S Rural) *48.31058, -1.82027* **Camping Les Peupliers, Manoir de la Besnelais, 35190 Tinténiac [02 99 45 49 75; fax 02 99 45 52 98; camping.les.peupliers@wanadoo.fr; www.les-peupliers-camping.fr]** On D137 Rennes to St Malo rd; after Hédé foll rd to Tinténiac about 2km; site on main rd on R, sp. Med, hdg/mkd pitch, pt sl, pt shd; wc (some cont); chem disp; mv service pnt; shwrs inc; el pnts (6A) €2.70 (poss rev pol); lndtte; shops 2km; tradsmn high ssn; rest; snacks; bar; playgrnd; htd pool; lake fishing; tennis; games area; TV rm; 30% statics; dogs €1.60; phone; adv bkg; CCI. "Quiet, clean, tidy site in fir trees; gd pool & park; on pilgrim rte to Spain." ♦ 1 Apr-30 Sep. € 17.40 2007*

TONNEINS *7D2* (500m SE Urban) *44.38161, 0.31822* **Camp Municipal Le Robinson, 47400 Tonneins [05 53 79 02 28; fax 05 53 79 83 01; tonneins@valdegaronne.com; www.valdegaronne.com]** On N113, bet Marmande & Agen. Sm, mkd pitch, pt shd, hdstg; wc; shwrs inc; el pnts inc; lndtte; hypermkt 3km; dogs; phone; quiet, some rd & rlwy noise. ♦ 1 Jun-30 Sep. € 10.25 2006*

TONNERRE *4F4* (600m N Urban) *47.86003, 3.98429* **Camp Municipal de la Cascade, Ave Aristide Briand, 89700 Tonnerre [03 86 55 15 44 or 03 86 55 22 55 (Mairie); fax 03 86 55 30 64; ot.tonnerre@wandoo.fr; www.tonnerre.fr]** Best app via D905 (E by-pass); turn at rndabt twd town cent L after x-ing 1st rv bdge. Foll site sp to avoid low bdge (height 2.9m, width 2.4m). Or fr D444 strt over rndabt in town cent, over canal bdge & site on L. On banks of Rv Armançon & nr Canal de l'Yonne, 100m fr junc D905 & D944. Med, pt shd; htd wc; chem disp; mv service pnt; baby facs; shwrs inc; el pnts (6-10A) €2.70-3.70; lndtte (inc dryer); shop; tradsmn; rest; snacks; bar; playgrnd; htd pool 1km; rv sw adj; fishing; entmnt; TV rm; 5% statics; Eng spkn; adv bkg; quiet, but some rlwy noise; ccard acc; CCI. "Pleasant, spacious, shady site in parkland; friendly warden; lge pitches; excel san facs; no twin-axles; interesting town; gd cycling/walking along canal - 500m to hypmkt; excel." ♦ 1 Apr-2 Nov. € 11.05 2009*

TONNOY *6E2* (500m SW Rural) *48.54966, 6.24343* **Camp Municipal Le Grand Vanné, 54210 Tonnoy [03 83 26 62 36; fax 03 83 26 66 05; mairie-de-tonnoy@wanadoo.fr]** On A330 S fr Nancy sp Epinal, exit junc 7 onto D570 sp Flavigny. Site on L on banks of Rv Moselle in 5km. Med, pt shd; wc (cont); shwrs inc; el pnts (3-6A) inc; shops 500m; snacks; BBQ; playgrnd; fishing; 50% statics; dogs; poss cr; quiet. "Gd." 15 Apr-30 Sep. € 11.30 2006*

⊞ **TORCY** *3D3* (3km N Urban) *48.85921, 2.65057* **Camping Le Parc de la Colline, Route de Lagny, 77200 Torcy [01 60 05 42 32; fax 01 64 80 05 17; camping.parc.de.la.colline@wanadoo.fr; www.camping-de-la-colline.com]** Exit A104 junc 10 W onto D10 sp Torcy/Noisiel. Site on L in 1km. Lge, hdg/mkd pitch, terr, pt shd; htd wc (some cont); chem disp; mv service pnt; shwrs inc; el pnts (6A) €3; lndtte; shop; hypmkt 3km; playgrnd; htd pool; waterslide; lake beach & sw 1km; tennis; internet; TV rm; some statics; dogs €4.50; poss cr; Eng spkn; adv bkg; ccard acc; CCI. "Conv Disneyland, Parc Astérix, Paris; conv RER by site minibus; helpful staff; steep app to pitches but tow avail." ♦ € 24.80 2006*

TORIGNI SUR VIRE *1D4* (1km S Rural) *49.02833, -0.97194* **Camping Le Lac des Charmilles, Route de Vire, 50160 Torigni-sur-Vire [02 33 56 91 74; contact@camping-lacdescharmilles.com; www.camping-lacdescharmilles.com]** Exit A84 junc 40 onto N174 dir Torigni-sur-Vire/St Lô; site on R in 4km. Opp municipal stadium. Med, hdg/mkd pitch, hdstg, pt sl, pt shd; htd wc; chem disp; mv service pnt; baby facs; fam bthrm; shwrs inc; el pnts (16A) €4 (long lead poss req); lndtte; shop; tradsmn; rest; snacks; bar; BBQ; playgrnd; htd pool; lake sw adj; cycle hire; games area; games rm; TV; 30% statics; dogs €1.50; phone; poss cr; Eng spkn; adv bkg; quiet; ccard acc; red low ssn; CCI. "Lovely, well-laid out site; clean, modern san facs; interesting town; vg." ♦ 1 Apr-15 Oct. € 18.80 (CChq acc) 2009*

See advertisement on page 634

France

TORREILLES PLAGE *10G1* (Coastal) *42.76750, 3.02972* **Camping Sunêlia Les Tropiques, Blvd de la Méditerranée, 66440 Torreilles-Plage [04 68 28 05 09; fax 04 68 28 48 90; contact@campinglestropiques.com; www.campinglestropiques.com]** Exit A9 junc 41 onto D83 E dir Le Barcarès, then D81 dir Canet-Plage. At 1st rndabt turn L onto D11 sp Torreilles-Plage, site sp. Lge, hdg/mkd pitch, shd; wc; chem disp; mv service pnt; baby facs; shwrs inc; el pnts (6A) inc; gas; lndtte; shops; rest; snacks; bar; 2 playgrnds; 2 pools; paddling pool; waterslide; sand beach 400m; tennis; cycle hire; games area; gym; internet; entmnt; TV rm; 80% statics; dogs €4; poss cr; Eng spkn; ccard acc; red low ssn/long stay/CCI. "Vg family site; excel leisure & san facs." ♦ 3 Apr-2 Oct. € 44.00 2009*

See advertisement

TORREILLES PLAGE *10G1* (Coastal) *42.76556, 3.02710* **CHADOTEL Camping Le Trivoly, Blvd des Plages, 66440 Torreilles-Plage [04 68 28 20 28 or 02 51 33 05 05 (LS); fax 04 68 28 16 48; chadotel@wanadoo.fr; www.chadotel.com]** Torreilles-Plage is sp fr D81, site in vill cent. Lge, hdg/mkd pitch, pt shd; htd wc; serviced pitches; shwrs inc; el pnts (6A) inc; gas; lndtte; shop; snacks; bar; playgrnd; htd pool; waterslide; sand beach 800m; tennis; cycle hire; watersports; games rm; TV rm; entmnt; dogs €3; Eng spkn; adv bkg; quiet; ccard acc. "Gd walking in Pyrenees; vg." ♦ 5 Apr-27 Sep. € 29.90 2008*

TORREILLES PLAGE *10G1* (N Coastal) *42.76760, 3.02820* **Camping Le Calypso, Blvd de la Plage, 66440 Torreilles-Plage [04 68 28 09 47; fax 04 68 28 24 76; info@camping-calypso.com; www.camping-calypso.com]** Take D617 fr Perpignan sp Canet-Plage & D81 to St Laurent. 1.7km prior to St Laurent on R hand side of rd. 2nd site on L on way to beach. Lge, mkd pitch, shd; wc; chem disp; baby facs; shwrs; private san facs avail; el pnts (6A) inc; gas; lndtte; supmkt; rest; snacks; bar; playgrnd; htd pool complex; sand beach 300m; games area; games rm; cycle hire; entmnt; wifi; TV; 40% statics; dogs €4; poss cr; adv bkg rec high ssn; quiet; ccard acc. "Trips to vineyards; many activities; superb pool complex." ♦ 1 Apr-30 Sep. € 37.00 2009*

TORREILLES PLAGE *10G1* (8km N Coastal) *42.76503, 3.02841* **Camping La Palmeraie, Blvd de la Plage, 66440 Torreilles-Plage [04 68 28 20 64; fax 04 68 59 67 41; info@camping-la-palmeraie.com; www.camping-la-palmeraie.com]** Exit A9/E15 junc 41 at Perpignan Nord onto D83 twd Le Barcarès for 10km. At int'chge turn R at junc 9 onto D81 dir Canet-Plage, cont for 3km to lge rndabt & turn L sp Torreilles-Plage, site on R. Lge, hdg/mkd pitch, shd; wc; chem disp; shwrs inc; el pnts (5-10A) €4-7; gas; lndtte; shop; rest; snacks; bar; BBQ (gas only); playgrnd; pool; sand beach 600m; tennis, horseriding nr; games area; games rm; entmnt; TV rm; some statics; dogs €5; Eng spkn; adv bkg; quiet; red low ssn; ccard acc; CCI. "Attractive site; friendly, helpful staff." ♦ 11 Apr-26 Sep. € 28.00 2008*

TORTEQUESNE see Douai *3B4*

TOUCY *4F4* (300m S Urban) *47.73159, 3.29677* **Camping des Quatre Merlettes, Rue du Pâtis, 89130 Toucy [03 86 44 13 84; fax 03 86 44 28 42; campingdetoucy@wanadoo.fr]** On D3, 25km SW of Auxerre to Toucy. After rv x-ing take 1st L sp 'Base de Loisirs'. Site on S bank of Rv Quanne. Med, pt shd; wc; mv service pnt; shwrs inc; el pnts (3A) €3; shops 500m; htd pool; fishing; some statics; dogs; poss cr; adv bkg; quiet. "Pleasant vill; mkt Sat; no twin-axles." 1 Apr-15 Oct. € 7.60 2008*

TOUL *6E2* (7km E Rural) *48.65281, 5.99260* **Camping de Villey-le-Sec, 34 Rue de la Gare, 54840 Villey-le-Sec [tel/fax 03 83 63 64 28; info@campingvilleylesec.com; www.campingvilleylesec.com]** Exit Toul E on D909 or exit A31 junc 15 ondo D400 (W, in dir Hôpital Jeanne d'Arc); at rndabt turn L onto D909 to Villey-le-Sec; in vill site S by Rv Moselle, sp. V steep app rd. Med, hdg/mkd pitch, hdstg, pt shd; wc; chem disp; mv service pnt; baby facs; shwrs inc; el pnts (6-10A) €3.60-4.50; gas; lndtte; shop; hypmkt nr; rest; snacks; bar; BBQ; playgrnd; games area; dogs €1.70; phone; Eng spkn; no adv bkg; quiet; ccard acc; red long stay/low ssn. "Clean, friendly site on rvside; lge pitches; vg san facs, poss stretched; cycle paths; popular NH, rec arr early high ssn; excel." ♦ 1 Apr-30 Sep. € 14.90 2009*

TOULON SUR ARROUX *4H4* (500m W Urban) *46.69419, 4.13233* **Camp Municipal Le Val d'Arroux, Route d'Uxeau, 71320 Toulon-sur-Arroux [03 85 79 51 22 or 03 85 79 42 55 (Mairie); fax 03 85 79 62 17]** Fr Toulon-sur-Arroux NW on D985 over rv bdge; rturn L in 100m, site sp. Med, pt shd; wc; chem disp; mv service pnt; shwrs inc; el pnts (6A) €3; Indtte; shops 500m; playgrnd; rv sw adj; 30% statics; dogs; quiet but some rd noise. "Rvside site; boules park adj; beautiful Buddhist temple 6km; gd." ♦ 16 Apr-15 Oct. € 9.00 2009*

⊞ **TOULOUSE** *8F3* (5km N Urban) *43.6562, 1.4158* **Camping Le Rupé, 21 Chemin du Pont de Rupé, 31000 Toulouse [05 61 70 07 35; fax 05 61 70 93 17; campinglerupe31@wanadoo.fr]** N fr Toulouse on N20, sp. Poss tricky app fr N for long vans, suggest cont past Pont de Rupé traff lts to next rndabt & double back to turn. Fr S on ring rd exit junc 33A (after junc 12), turn immed R & foll sp. Lge, hdg/mkd pitch, hdstg, pt shd; htd wc (cont); chem disp; mv service pnt; baby facs; shwrs inc; el pnts (6-10A) €3.50-4.70; Indtte; shop; rest; snacks; playgrnd; lake fishing; games rm; TV; 90% statics; dogs €1; phone; bus; poss cr (esp public hols); Eng spkn; adv bkg; ccard acc; CCI "Poss unkempt & poor facs low ssn; many shabby statics & poss itinerants low ssn; NH only." € 14.00 (CChq acc) 2007*

TOULOUSE *8F3* (10km S Rural) *43.50879, 1.37567* **FFCC Camp Municipal du Ramier, 31120 Roques [05 61 72 56 07; fax 05 61 72 57 52]** Exit junc 35 fr A64 S of Toulouse onto D817 to Roques. Site on banks of Rv Garonne. Med, mkd pitch, pt shd; wc (most cont); mv service pnt; shwrs inc; el pnts (6-10A) inc; Indtte; shop 1km; rest, bar 100m; playgrnd; bus to city; poss cr; rd noise. "Poss itinerants & workers on site; poss light aircraft noise; quiet at night; NH only." 1 Jun-31 Oct. € 13.50 2007*

TOUQUES see Deauville *3D1*

⊞ **TOUQUET PARIS PLAGE, LE** *3B2* (5km N Rural) *50.55270, 1.61887* **Camping La Dune Blanche, Route de Camiers, 62176 Camiers [03 21 09 78 48 or 06 86 15 69 32 (mob); fax 03 21 09 79 59; duneblanche@wanadoo.fr; www.lesdomaines.org]** Leave A16 junc 26 dir Etaples or junc 27 dir Neufchâtel onto D940 dir Etables, Le Touquet. Site well sp. Lge, mkd pitch, pt sl, shd; wc; chem disp; baby facs; shwrs inc; el pnts (6A) €6; gas; Indtte; shops 2km; tradsmn; bar; BBQ; playgrnd; sand beach 3km; entmnt; TV; 90% statics; dogs €2.50; phone; bus to beach at Ste Cécile; poss cr; adv bkg; quiet; red long stay; ccard acc; CCI. "Amongst trees; remote, quiet by rlwy line; staff friendly & helpful; site poss scruffy; san facs need upgrade." ♦ € 15.00 2007*

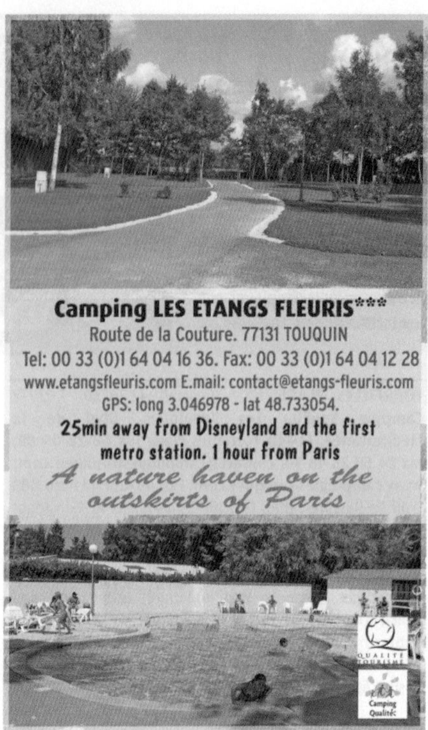

Camping LES ETANGS FLEURIS***
Route de la Couture. 77131 TOUQUIN
Tel: 00 33 (0)1 64 04 16 36. Fax: 00 33 (0)1 64 04 12 28
www.etangsfleuris.com E.mail: contact@etangs-fleuris.com
GPS: long 3.046978 - lat 48.733054.
25min away from Disneyland and the first metro station. 1 hour from Paris
A nature haven on the outskirts of Paris

TOUQUET PARIS PLAGE, LE *3B2* (1km S Coastal) *50.51091, 1.58867* **Camping Caravaning Municipal Stoneham, Ave François Godin, 62520 Le Touquet-Paris-Plage [03 21 05 16 55; fax 03 21 05 06 48; caravaning.stoneham@letouquet.com; www.letouquet.com]** Fr Etaples on D939 (N39); stay in L-hand lane at traff lts dir airport & cont strt on (Ave du Général de Gaulle); L at traff lts sp Golf (Ave du Golf); foll rd to rndabt; turn R onto Ave François Godin (site sp); at next rndabt site on R. Lge, hdg pitch, pt shd; wc; shwrs inc; el pnts (6A) €4.80 (poss rev pol); Indtte; shops 1km; tradsmn; playgrnd; htd pool 2km; sand beach 1km; 95% statics; dogs €1.50; poss cr even low ssn; adv bkg rec; CCI. "Pleasant site; excel facs; helpful staff; mkt Sat; m'van 'aires' nr harbour & equestrian cent; excel." 1 Feb-15 Nov. € 16.60 2009*

TOUQUET PARIS PLAGE, LE *3B2* (5km S Coastal) *50.47238, 1.57717* **Camp Municipal de la Mer, Cours des Champs Elysées, 62780 Stella-Plage [03 21 84 60 60; fax 03 21 94 13 55; info@campingdelamer.com; www.campingdelamer.com]** S fr Etaples on D940, in 4km turn R dir Stella-Plage; at lge rndabt by sea front turn L to site; sp at end of rd. Lge, unshd; wc; el pnts (10A) €4.60; Indtte; shops etc nrby; direct access to beach 200m; tennis nrby; aqualand, golf & horseriding in Le Touquet; some statics; dogs €0.70; quiet. "Interesting, sandy site sheltered by dunes; busy high ssn; san facs clean." ♦ 15 Jun-15 Sep. € 15.00 2009*

TOUQUIN *4E4* (2.5km W Rural) *48.73305, 3.04697* **Camping Les Etangs Fleuris, Route de la Couture, 77131 Touquin [01 64 04 16 36; fax 01 64 04 12 28; contact@etangs-fleuris.com; www.etangsfleuris.com or www.paris-camping.com]** On D231 fr Provins, turn R to Touquin. Turn sharp R in vill & foll sp to site on R in approx 2km. Or fr Coulommiers, take D402 SW twd Mauperthuis, after Mauperthuis L twd Touquin. Foll sp in vill. Med, hdg/mkd pitch, hdstg, pt shd; htd wc; chem disp; mv service pnt; shwrs inc; el pnts (10A) inc; gas; Indtte; sm shop & 2.5km; tradsmn; snacks; bar; BBQ; playgrnd; htd pool; paddling pool; fishing; games area; games rm; wifi; entmnt; TV rm; 20% statics (inc tour ops); dogs €1.50; phone; adv bkg; quiet; ccard acc; red CCI. "Peaceful site; no twin-axle c'vans high ssn; conv Paris & Disneyland." 15 Apr-15 Sep. € 19.00 2009*

See advertisement

TOUR DU MEIX, LA see Clairvaux les Lacs *6H2*

TOUR DU PARC, LE see Sarzeau *2G3*

TOURNAN EN BRIE *4E3* (1km S Rural) *48.73317, 2.76069* **Caravaning Fredland, Parc de Combreux, 77220 Tournan-en-Brie [01 64 07 96 44; fax 01 64 42 00 61; fred.chauvineau@wanadoo.fr]** Foll N4 E fr Paris. 15km beyond junc with N104 turn R onto D10 sp Liverdy. Site immed on R on lakeside Med, mkd pitch, pt sl, pt shd; wc; chem disp; shwrs inc; el pnts (6A) inc; Indtte; rest; snacks; bar; BBQ; playgrnd; htd pool; fishing; games area; 75% statics; poss cr; Eng spkn; adv bkg; quiet. "Conv for Paris; 10 min walk to stn; dated san facs; nice site." 1 Mar-31 Oct. € 24.00 2008*

TOURNEHEM SUR LA HEM see Ardres *3A3*

🏠 **TOURNIERES** *1D4* (500m S Rural) *49.23017, -0.93256* **Camping Le Picard, 14330 Tournières [02 31 22 82 44; fax 02 31 51 70 28; paul.palmer@wanadoo.fr; www.camp-france.com]** Fr Bayeux foll D5/D15 W to Tournières, 5km past Le Molay-Littry. Fr N13 Cherbourg-Bayeux, E of Carentan turn S onto N174 then E on D15 to Tournières. Site sp opp Tournières church. Sm, pt shd, hdg pitch; htd wc; chem disp; serviced pitches; shwrs inc; el pnts (10A) €3.50; shop 5km; tradsmn; rest; snacks; bar; playgrnd; htd pool; boating; fishing; wifi; no dogs; phone; adv bkg; quiet; ccard acc; CCI. "Delightful, British-owned site; conv Normandy beaches, Bayeux, Cherbourg ferry; helpful owners bake croissants & will do laundry; san facs need refurb/update; c'van storage." ♦ € 18.00 2008*

🏠 **TOURNON SUR RHONE** *9C2* (N Rural) *45.07000, 4.83000* **Camping de Tournon HPA, 1 Promenade Roche-de-France, 07300 Tournon-sur-Rhône [tel/fax 04 75 08 05 28; camping@camping-tournon.com; www.camping-tournon.com]** Fr Tain l'Hermitage cross Rhône, turn R onto D86. In approx 1km R at end of car park. Turn L after 50m, site on R on Rv Rhône. Med, shd; htd wc (some cont); chem disp; mv service pnt; shwrs inc; el pnts (6-10A) €3-5; gas; Indtte; shop, rest, snacks & bar nr; playgrnd; pool 1km; canoeing; internet; some statics; dogs €2; phone; m'van o'night area; c'van storage avail; poss cr; Eng spkn; adv bkg rec; ccard not acc high ssn; red long stay/low ssn; CCI. "Nice site in wooded location; rvside pitches; friendly owners; clean, dated san facs (unisex low ssn); some sm pitches & narr site rds poss diff lge o'fits; fr mid-Jun rock concerts poss held nrby at w/end; gd." ♦ € 13.00 2009*

TOURNON SUR RHONE *9C2* (6km N Rural) *45.12116, 4.80023* **FFCC Camping L'Iserand, Rue Royal, 07610 Vion [04 75 08 01 73; fax 04 75 08 55 82; iserand@tele2.fr; www.iserandcampingardeche.com]** Take D86 N fr Tournon, site 1km N of Vion on L. Med, hdg/mkd pitch, sl, terr, pt shd; htd wc (some cont); chem disp; mv service pnt; baby facs; shwrs inc; el pnts (10A) €3; gas; Indtte; shop & 1km; tradsmn; rest 1km; snacks; bar; BBQ; playgrnd; pool; beach; cycle hire; canoeing 1km; entmnt; TV rm; 20% statics; dogs €3; bus 1km; phone; poss cr; adv bkg; Eng spkn; rd & rlwy noise; red low ssn; CCI. "Excel site; friendly owner lives on site - will take low ssn visitors." 7 Apr-30 Sep. € 16.00 2009*

TOURNON SUR RHONE *9C2* (2.5km W Rural) *45.06591, 4.79446* **Camping Les Acacias, 190 Route de Lamastre, 07300 Tournon-sur-Rhône [tel/fax 04 75 08 83 90; info@acacias-camping.com; www.acacias-camping.com]** Fr D86 Tournon turn W onto D532 dir Lamastre, site on R in approx 2km. Med, pt shd; wc (some cont); chem disp; shwrs; el pnts (6A) €3.30; gas; Indtte; rest; shop 2km; playgrnd; pool; dogs €2.20; poss cr; Eng spkn; rd noise; adv bkg; red low ssn; CCI. "Nr steam rlwy; gd pitches; some noise fr sawmill; vg, friendly site." ♦ 1 Apr-30 Sep. € 15.96 2008*

TOURNON SUR RHONE *9C2* (3km W Rural) *45.06650, 4.78830* **FFCC Camping Le Manoir, 222 Route de Lamastre, 07300 Tournon-sur-Rhône [04 75 08 02 50 or 06 70 00 06 13 (mob); fax 04 75 08 57 10; info@lemanoir-ardeche.com; www.lemanoir-ardeche.com]** Leave Tournon on D532 just bef x-ing rv, dir Lamastre. Site on R after 3km (4th site). Med, mkd pitch, pt shd; wc (50% cont); chem disp; mv service pnt; shwrs inc; el pnts (10A) €3; Indtte; shop 2.5km; tradsmn; snacks; bar; BBQ; playgrnd; pool; rv adj; TV rm; entmnt; 70% statics; dogs; phone; poss cr; adv bkg; quiet but some rd noise; ccard acc; red CCI. "Pleasant, family-run, rvside site; friendly, hard-working staff; gd facs; gd walking,vineyard tours; vg." ♦ 1 Apr-30 Sep. € 16.00 2007*

France

TOURNON SUR RHONE *9C2* (4km W Rural) *45.06786, 4.78516* **Camping Le Castelet, 113 Route du Grand Pont, 07300 St Jean-de-Muzols [04 75 08 09 48; fax 04 75 08 49 60; courrier@camping-lecastelet.com; www.camping-lecastelet.com]** Exit Tournon on D86 N; in 500m turn L on D532 twd Lamastre; in 4km turn R on D532 over bdge & turn immed R into site. Med, mkd pitch, terr, pt shd; wc (some cont); chem disp; baby facs; shwrs inc; el pnts (5A) €3.20; gas; Indtte; shop & supmkt 4km; tradsmn; bar; playgrnd; pool; paddling pool; entmnt; dogs; adv bkg; quiet, but some rd noise; red low ssn; ccard not acc. "Steam rlwy adj; owner will arrange to have train stop; clean san facs." 1 Apr-13 Sep. € 14.50 2007*

TOURNUS *9A2* (1km N Urban) *46.57244, 4.90854* **Camping de Tournus, 14 Rue des Canes, 71700 Tournus [03 85 51 16 58; reception@camping-tournus.com; www.camping-tournus.com]** Fr N6 at N of town turn E opp rlwy stn & rest 'Le Terminus;' foll site sp. Med, some mkd pitch, hdstg, pt sl, pt shd; wc (some cont); chem disp; mv service pnt; shwrs inc; el pnts (10A) €4.40 (long lead poss req); gas; Indtte; shops; BBQ; playgrnd; htd pools adj; wifi; TV; dogs €2.30; Eng spkn; quiet but rd & rlwy noise some pitches; red low ssn; CCI. "Peaceful, rvside site; popular NH conv A6 - rec arr early; helpful staff; clean facs but stretched high ssn & ltd low ssn; poss extra charge twin-axles; rv walk into town; gd cycling nrby; abbey worth visit." ♦ 28 Mar-30 Sep. € 18.70 (CChq acc) 2009*

TOURNUS *9A2* (9km S Rural) *46.48768, 4.91286* **FFCC Camping International d'Uchizy - Le National 6, 71700 Uchizy [tel/fax 03 85 40 53 90; camping.uchizylen6@wanadoo.fr; www.camping-lenational6.com]** Exit A6 junc 27 & foll N6 S; sp on L, turn L over rwly bdge on lane to site on L. Adj Rv Saône. Med, shd; wc; shwrs inc; el pnts (6A) €3.90; gas; shop; snacks; playgrnd; pool; fishing; boat hire; dogs €1; poss cr; adv bkg; quiet; red low ssn. "Attractive, well-maintained site; gd, modern san facs; pitches soft & muddy in rain: arr early for rvside pitch." 1 Apr-30 Sep. € 13.90 2008*

TOURNUS *9A2* (10km W Rural) *46.59182, 4.77746* **Aire Naturelle de Camping à la Ferme de Malo (Goujon), Champlieu, 71240 Etrigny [03 85 92 21 47 or 03 85 92 23 40; fax 03 85 92 22 13; fam@aubergemalo.com; www.aubergemalo.com]** S on N6 to Tournus; after rwly stn turn R onto D14; after passing under rlwy DO NOT fork L to foll D14 - cont strt onto D215 dir St Gengoux-le-National. In 8km, in Nogent, turn R at lge stone drinking trough onto D159; at 2nd x-rds turn L onto D459 (sp Champlieu); at 1st x-rds turn L into Champlieu; site on L 500m after vill, bef rv. Sm, pt shd; wc (cont); chem disp (wc); shwrs inc; el pnts (6-10A) €3 (long lead poss req); Indtte; tradsmn; rest 1km; playgrnd; tennis 3km; horseriding; dogs; adv bkg ess high ssn; quiet; no ccard acc; CCI. "Pitch yourself, owner calls 1800; san facs poss stretched high ssn; additional pitches & pool opp main site; adj to Rv Grison." 1 May-1 Nov. € 9.80 2006*

⊞ **TOURS** *4G2* (6km E Rural) *47.40226, 0.77845* **Camping Les Acacias, Rue Berthe Morisot, 37700 La Ville-aux-Dames [02 47 44 08 16 or 02 62 19 18 08 (LS); fax 02 47 46 26 65; camplvad@orange.fr; www.camplvad.com]** Fr Tours take D751 E sp Amboise; after 6km at rndabt where La Ville-aux-Dames sp to R, go strt on for 200m, then turn R, site sp. Med, shd; htd wc; chem disp; mv service pnt; serviced pitch; shwrs; el pnts (4-10A) €2.90-4.60; gas; Indtte; sm shop; supmkt 1km; rest nrby; playgrnd; pool 500m; tennis 600m; fitness trail, mountain bike circuit, fishing 100m; dogs €1.90; bus nr; adv bkg; rd & rlwy noise; CCI. "Helpful, friendly owners; excel san facs, ltd low ssn; conv town cent; recep clsd at w/end Oct-Apr - no ent without key pass during this period; many long-term residents; gd site." ♦ € 11.70 2009*

TOURS *4G2* (5km SE Urban) *47.37070, 0.72305* **Camping Les Rives du Cher, 61 Rue de Rochepinard, 37550 St Avertin [02 47 27 27 60; fax 02 47 25 82 89; contact@camping-lesrivesducher.com; www.camping-lesrivesducher.com]** Fr Tours, take D976 (N76) S of rv sp Bléré/Vierzon into St Avertin vill. Take next L at traff lts over 1st of 2 bdges. Site on R in 450m, not well sp. Med, hdg/mkd pitch, some hdstg, pt shd; wc (some cont); chem disp; mv service pnt; shwrs inc; el pnts (4-10A) €3.30-5.30 (poss rev pol); Indtte; shops 400m; rest, snacks & bar adj; playgrnd; htd pool adj; tennis; fishing; dogs €1.30; bus nrby; phone; adv bkg; quiet; ccard acc; red long stay; CCI. "Friendly owner; site needs modernising; tired low ssn; some resident workers; pitches nr noisy rd in morning rush hour; poss late night noise fr adj parks & clubs; frequent bus to Tours." ♦ 1 Apr-15 Oct. € 15.30 2009*

TOURS *4G2* (8km SW Urban) *47.35530, 0.63401* **Camping La Mignardière, 22 Ave des Aubépines, 37510 Ballan-Miré [02 47 73 31 00; fax 02 47 73 31 01; info@mignardiere.com; www.mignardiere.com]** Fr A10 exit junc 24 onto N585 & D37 by-pass. At exit for Joué-lès-Tours foll sp Ballan-Miré onto D751. Turn R at 1st set traff lts & foll site sp to W of lake. Lge, hdg/mkd pitch, hdstg, pt shd; htd wc; chem disp; mv service pnt; 10% serviced pitch; baby facs; shwrs inc; el pnts (6-10A) €3.50; Indtte; sm shop; tradsmn; snacks; bar 200m; BBQ; playgrnd; htd, covrd pool; windsurfing & fishing 1km; tennis; cycle hire; squash; internet; entmnt; TV rm; dogs; phone; Eng spkn; adv bkg; quiet, but some rd/rlwy noise; red low ssn; CCI. "Conv Loire valley & chateaux; friendly, helpful staff; unisex facs low ssn; gd cycle paths; vg site; rec." ♦ 22 Mar-23 Sep. € 22.00 (CChq acc) 2009*

TOURS *4G2* (8km W Rural) *47.38950, 0.59616* **Camping L'Islette, 23 Rue de Vallières, 37230 Fondettes [02 47 42 26 42]** Foll D952 (N152) W fr Tours twd Saumur. In approx 6km turn R at traff lts onto D276 at Port-de-Vallières. Site on L in approx 2km. Sm, hdg pitch, pt shd; wc (some cont); mv service pnt; shwrs inc; el pnts (10A) €2; shop 2km; playgrnd; pool 4km; dogs; bus; poss cr; adv bkg; quiet; CCI. "Pleasant site; helpful owners; facs poss stretched if site full; poss boggy when wet." ♦ 1 Apr-31 Oct. € 8.00 2009*

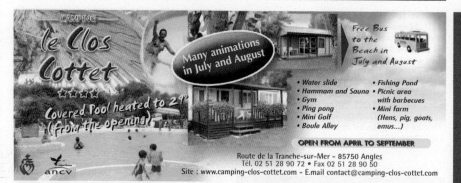

TOURS *4G2* (10km W Rural) *47.38110, 0.55830* **Camping Club Les Granges, Le Bourg, 37230 Luynes [02 47 55 79 05 or 01 76 61 65 94; fax 02 47 40 92 43; reception@campinglesgranges.fr; www.campinglesgranges.fr]** W fr Tours on D952 (N152) dir Saumur; in 9km turn R at Le Port-de-Luynes dir Luynes, site on R in 500m. Med, hdg/mkd pitch, pt shd; htd wc; mv service pnt; baby facs; shwrs inc; el pnts (10A) €3.70; Indtte; shops; tradsmn; snacks; bar; BBQ; playgrnd; pool; fishing 500m; tennis 700m; games area; games rm; wifi; TV; some statics; dogs €2.50; adv bkg; quiet; ccard acc. "Pleasant site; gd touring base Loire valley." ♦ 2 May-27 Sep. € 20.00 2009*

TOURS *4G2* (10km W Rural) *47.35054, 0.54964* **Camping de la Confluence, Route de Bray, 37510 Savonnières [02 47 50 00 25; fax 02 47 50 15 71; camping@tourisme-en-confluence.com; www.villandry-tourisme.com]** Fr Tours take D7 on S of Rv Cher. Site on R on ent Savonnières on rvside. Med, hdg/mkd pitch, hdstg, pt shd; wc (some cont); chem disp; mv service pnt; baby facs; shwrs inc; el pnts (10A) inc; Indtte; shops 500m; tradsmn; rest 100m; bar adj; BBQ; playgrnd; canoe hire; tennis adj; dogs €1.20; phone; bus 200m; Eng spkn; adv bkg; quiet; red 15 days; CCI. "Rv views; clean, well-kept site; efficient, friendly staff; modern san facs; lovely vill with gd facs; gd touring base; gd birdwatching, cycling; highly rec." ♦ 15 May-15 Sep. € 15.60 2008*

TOURY *4F3* (SW Urban) *48.19361, 1.93260* **Camp Municipal, Rue de Boissay, 28310 Toury [02 37 90 50 60 (Mairie); fax 02 37 90 58 61; mairie-toury@wanadoo.fr]** Fr Orléans take N20 N. Site well sp. Sm, shd; wc; chem disp; shwrs inc; el pnts (6A) inc; gas 1km; shop 800m; rest 200m; bar 100m; BBQ; playgrnd; dogs; poss cr' rd & rlwy noise. "NH only; warden calls; clean san facs; arrive bef 1600 to ensure pitch." 1 Apr-15 Oct. € 10.00 2009*

TOUSSAINT see Fécamp *3C1*

TOUTAINVILLE see Pont Audemer *3D2*

TOUZAC see Fumel *7D3*

TRANCHE SUR MER, LA *7A1* (500m N Urban/Coastal) *46.34563, -1.44296* **Camp Municipal Le Vieux Moulin, Ave Maurice Samson, 85360 La Tranche-sur-Mer [tel/fax 02 51 28 93 48; campinglevieuxmoulin@latranchesurmer.fr; www.latranchesurmer.org]** On ent town foll sp for Gendarmerie, sp adj supmkt. Lge, mkd pitch, some hdstg, pt sl, pt shd; wc (chem closet); own san; chem disp; baby facs; shwrs inc; el pnts (6A) inc; Indry rm; shop 400m; sand beach 350m; 50% statics; dogs €2.50; poss cr; adv bkg (dep); quiet; CCI. "Some sm pitches; town cent & beach 5 mins walk." 15 Mar-12 Oct. € 19.40 2008*

TRANCHE SUR MER, LA *7A1* (2km NE Coastal) *46.39206, -1.40199* **Camping Le Clos Cottet, Route de la Tranche-sur-Mer, 85750 Angles [02 51 28 90 72; fax 02 51 28 90 50; contact@camping-clos-cottet.com; www.camping-clos-cottet.com]** Fr N on D747 twd La Tranche-sur-Mer, site is on R sp after passing Angles, sp. Lge, hdg/mkd pitch, pt shd; htd wc (some cont); chem disp; mv service pnt; serviced pitch; baby facs; shwrs; el pnts (5A) inc; gas; Indtte; shop; rest; snacks; bar; BBQ; playgrnd; 2 pools (1 htd, covrd); paddling pool; waterslide; jacuzzi; sand beach 4km (free bus high ssn); lake fishing; games area; games rm; fitness rm; wifi; entmnt; 60% statics; dogs €3; Eng spkn; adv bkg; quiet; red CCI. "Excel family site; vg facs; helpful, friendly staff." ♦ 3 Apr-20 Sep. € 25.00 2009*

See advertisement

TRANCHE SUR MER, LA *7A1* (2.6km NE) *46.36286, -1.41936* **Camping Les Blancs Chênes, Route de la Roche-sur-Yon, 85360 La Tranche-sur-Mer [02 51 30 41 70 or 02 51 27 37 80 (res); fax 02 51 28 84 09; info@camping-vagues.oceanes.com; www.camping-vagues-oceanes.com]** Site sp on rd D747 Lge, mkd pitch, pt shd; mv service pnt; wc; baby facs; shwrs inc; el pnts (6A) €5.50 gas; Indtte; shop; tradsmn; rest; snacks; bar; BBQ; playgrnd; htd, covrd pool; paddling pool; waterslide; sand beach 1.8km; tennis; games area; games rm; entmnt; statics; dogs €2.60; shuttle bus to beach; quiet; Eng spkn; adv bkg; ccard acc; red low ssn; CCI. "Superb pool complex." ♦ Easter-15 Sep. € 23.00 2006*

France

TRANCHE SUR MER, LA *7A1* (3km NE Rural) *46.37250, -1.41528* **Camping Les Almadies, La Charrière des Bandes, Route de la Roche-sur-Yonne, 85360 La Tranche-sur-Mer [02 51 30 36 94; fax 02 51 30 37 04; info@lesalmadies.com; www.lesalmadies.com]** S fr La Roche-sur-Yonne on D747, site sp. Lge, mkd pitch, pt shd; wc; chem disp; baby facs; shwrs; el pnts (10A) €3.65; Indtte; shop; rest; snacks; bar; BBQ; htd pool; paddling pool; waterslides; sand beach 3km; bus to beach high ssn; cycle hire; games area; entmnt; internet; TV; dogs; adv bkg; quiet; red low ssn. "Pleasant site; vg facs for children; helpful, friendly staff." 4 Apr-27 Sep. € 25.30 2008*

When we get home I'm going to post all these site report forms to the Club for next year's guide.
The deadline's September.

TRANCHE SUR MER, LA *7A1* (500m E Coastal) *46.34611, -1.43225* **Camping La Baie d'Aunis, 10 Rue de Pertuis-Breton, 85360 La Tranche-sur-Mer [02 51 27 47 36; fax 02 51 27 44 54; info@camping-baiedaunis.com; www.camping-baiedaunis.com]** Fr La Roche-sur-Yon on D747 to La Tranche-sur-Mer; at 1st rndabt turn R, at 2nd rndabt (by Super U) turn L, at 3rd rndabt turn R - (all sp Centre Ville); ahead at min-rndabt & site on L in 100m. Med, hdg/mkd pitch, hdstg, pt shd; htd wc; chem disp; mv service pnt; baby facs; shwrs inc; el pnts (10A) €5; gas; Indtte; shop 600m; tradsmn; rest; snacks; bar; BBQ; playgrnd; htd pool; sand beach adj; sailing; sea-fishing; watersports; tennis 500m; cycle hire adj; games rm; entmnt; TV; 10% statics; dogs (not Jul/Aug) €2.30; Eng spkn; adv bkg (ess Jul/Aug); quiet; ccard acc; red low ssn; CCI. "Vg, friendly site; excel facs & rest; lovely area, gd beaches; poss diff ent for lge o'fits." ♦ 30 Apr-19 Sep. € 27.50 2009*

See advertisement below

TRANCHE SUR MER, LA *7A1* (3km E Coastal) *46.34810, -1.38730* **Camping du Jard, 123 Blvd du Lattre de Tassigny, 85360 La Tranche-sur-Mer [02 51 27 43 79; fax 02 51 27 42 92; info@campingdujard.fr; www.campingdujard.fr]** Foll D747 S fr La Roche-sur-Yon twd La Tranche on D747; at rndabt on outskirts of La Tranche turn L onto D46 sp La Faute-sur-Mer; cont for approx 5km. At rndabt turn R sp La Faute-sur-Mer 'par la côte'; then R at next rndabt onto D46 sp La Tranche-sur-Mer 'par la côte' & La Grière-Plage (ignore all previous La Grière sps); site on R in 1km. Rough app rd. Lge, hdg pitch, unshd; wc (some cont); chem disp; serviced pitch; baby facs; sauna; shwrs inc; el pnts (10A) inc; Indtte; shop; rest; snacks; bar; BBQ (charcoal); playgrnd; 2 pools (1 htd, covrd); paddling pool; waterslide; sand beach 700m; tennis; games area; fitness cent; cycle hire; horseriding 10km; golf 20km; entmnt; wifi; games/TV rm; 30% statics (tour ops); no dogs; c'vans over 10m not acc high ssn; adv bkg; rd noise; ccard acc; red low ssn/CCI. "Clean, tidy, well-run site; pitches liable to flood in wet weather; some sm pitches; gd pool; mkt Tue & Sat." ♦ 15 May-12 Sep. € 34.90 ABS - A03 2009*

See advertisement opposite

TREBES see Carcassonne *8F4*

TREBEURDEN *1D2* (4km N Coastal) *48.79078, -3.55787* **Camping L'Espérance, Penvern, 22560 Trébeurden [02 96 91 95 05; fax 02 96 91 98 12; loro-alain@wanadoo.fr; www.camping-esperance.com]** Fr Lannion on D65 to Trébeurden, then D788 sp Trégastel, site in 5km. Med, hdg/mkd pitch, pt shd; wc (some cont); chem disp; mv service pnt; baby facs; shwrs inc; el pnts (5-10A) €2.80-3.50; gas; Indtte; shop 2km; playgrnd; sand beach adj; golf adj; TV; 10% statics; dogs €1.50; bus; Eng spkn; adv bkg; quiet; ccard not acc; CCI. "Pleasant site; nr GR34 long dist walking rte." ♦ 1 Apr-30 Sep. € 14.20 2009*

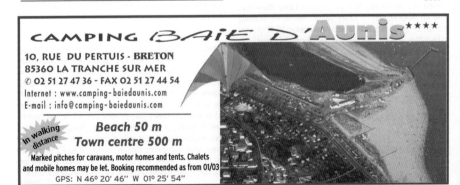

France

TREBEURDEN *1D2* (1km S Coastal) *48.76450, -3.56185* **Camping Armor Loisirs, Pors-Mabo, Rue de Kernévez, 22560 Trébeurden [02 96 23 52 31; fax 02 96 15 40 36; info@armorloisirs.com; www.armorloisirs.com]** N fr Lannion twds Trébeurden on D65. Turn L at 1st mini rndabt, then immed fork R into Rue de Kernévez, site on R in 800m, foll sp Pors-Mabo. Med, hdg/mkd pitch, pt sl, pt shd; wc; chem disp; baby facs; fam bthrm; serviced pitches; shwrs; el pnts (10A) inc; gas; Indtte; shop; tradsmn; snacks; bar; BBQ; playgrnd; htd pool; sand beach 500m; watersports; fishing; games rm; entmnt; internet; TV; 50% statics; dogs €2; Eng spkn; adv bkg; quiet; ccard acc; red low ssn/long stay/CCI. "Peaceful, well-run site; steep 'sleeping policemen'; some pitches poss diff for long o'fits; gd sea views; vg." ♦ 1 Apr-30 Sep. € 22.50 2007*

TREDION *2F3* (1.5km S Rural) *47.78295, -2.59060* **Camp Municipal l'Etang aux Biches, Route d'Elven, 56350 Trédion [02 97 67 14 06; fax 02 97 67 13 41]** E fr Vannes on N166 for 15km to Elven; in town foll sps N on D1 for Trédion. Site on L in 5km. Sm, hdg/mkd pitch, pt sl, pt shd; wc; shwrs €1.10; el pnts (3A) €1.90; shop 1.5km; tradsmn; playgrnd; quiet. "Peaceful; inland fr v busy coast." ♦ 1 Jul-31 Aug. € 5.40 2006*

TREGASTEL *1D2* (1.5km N Coastal) *48.82549, -3.49135* **Tourony Camping, 105 Rue de Poul-Palud, 22730 Trégastel [02 96 23 86 61; fax 02 96 15 97 84; contact@camping-tourony.com; www.camping-tourony.com]** On D788 fr Trébeurden dir Perros Guirec, site on R immed after exit Trégastel town sp & immed bef bdge over Traouieros inlet, opp Port de Ploumanac'h. Med, hdg/mkd pitch, pt shd; wc (some cont); chem disp; mv service pnt; baby facs; shwrs inc; el pnts (6A) €3; gas; Indtte; shop 400m; tradsmn; snacks; bar; BBQ; playgrnd; sand beach adj; lake fishing; tennis; cycle hire; games area; golf, horseriding nrby; entmnt; TV; 15% statics; dogs €1.50; Eng spkn; adv bkg; quiet; ccard acc; red long stay/low ssn; CCI. "Pleasant site in gd location; friendly, helpful staff; gd touring base Granit Rose coast." ♦ 4 Apr-25 Sep. € 17.40 2009*

TREGASTEL *1D2* (4km SW Coastal) *48.79905, -3.58386* **Camp Municipal Le Dourlin, L'Île Grande, 22560 Pleumeur-Bodou [02 96 91 92 41 or 02 96 23 91 17 (Mairie)]** Off D788 SW of Trégastel. Foll minor rd thro vill to site on coast. Well sp. Med, mkd pitch, unshd; wc; chem disp; shwrs inc; el pnts (6-13A) €2.20-4.40; Indtte; shops 500m; rest; snacks; bar; BBQ; playgrnd; sand/shgl beach; sailing; fishing; sports area; dogs; phone; bus; poss cr; Eng spkn; quiet; CCI. "Fine sea views; gd walking, cycling; ornithological cent nr; gd." ♦ 15 May-16 Sep. € 8.05 2006*

TREGASTEL *1D2* (4km W Coastal/Rural) *48.80995, -3.54140* **Camping du Port, 3 Chemin des Douaniers, Landrellec, 22560 Pleumeur-Bodou [02 96 23 87 79; fax 02 96 15 30 40; renseignements@camping-du-port.com or vive-la-mer49@hotmail.fr; www.camping-du-port-22.com]** Turn off D788 to Landrellec & foll rd thro vill past shop for 100m, take care tight turn L. Site in 500m. Med, hdg/mkd pitch, pt sl, pt shd; htd wc; chem disp; mv service pnt; serviced pitches; baby facs; shwrs inc; el pnts (10A) €2.90; gas; Indtte (inc dryer); shop; tradsmn; rest; snacks; bar; BBQ; playgrnd; pool 2km; direct access to sandy/rocky beach; fishing, boating, waterskiing; cycle hire; games rm; entmnt; wifi; TV rm; 25% statics; dogs €2.50; Eng spkn; adv bkg; quiet; ccard acc; red low ssn; CCI. "Immac, family-owned site; beautiful location; direct access beach; coastal path runs thro site; narr pitches by shore; telecoms museum worth visit." ♦ 3 Apr-3 Oct. € 13.80 2009*

See advertisement on next page

TREGUENNEC see Pont l'Abbé *2F2*

TREGUIER *1D3* (8km N Coastal) *48.84877, -3.21065* **Camp Municipal de Beg-Ar-Vilin, 22820 Plougrescant [02 96 92 56 15 or 02 96 92 51 18 (Mairie); fax 02 96 92 59 26; mairie.plougrescant@wanadoo.fr]** Take D8 N out of Tréguier to Plougrescant. At St Gonéry/Plougrescant turn R foll sp. Site 1.5km NE of Plougrescant. Med, mkd pitch, pt shd; wc; shwrs inc; Indtte; shops 2km; el pnts; beach sand/rock adj; phone; quiet. "Gd; busy, cr site high ssn." ♦ 15 Jun-15 Sep. 2008*

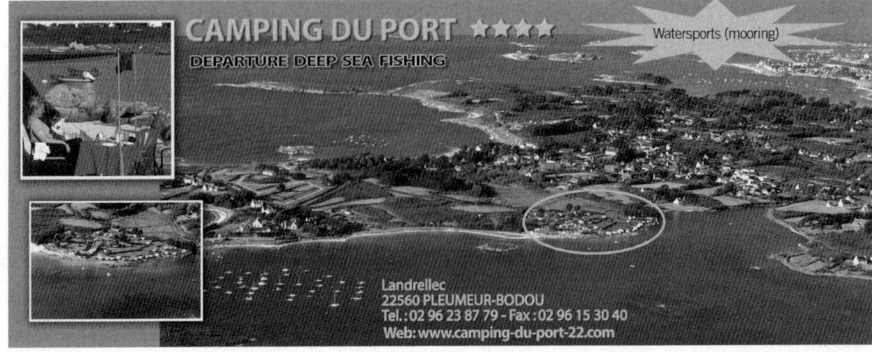

CAMPING DU PORT ★★★★
DEPARTURE DEEP SEA FISHING
Watersports (mooring)
Landrellec
22560 PLEUMEUR-BODOU
Tel.: 02 96 23 87 79 - Fax: 02 96 15 30 40
Web: www.camping-du-port-22.com

TREGUIER *1D3* (10km N Coastal) *48.85810, -3.22013* **FFCC Camping Le Varlen, 4 Pors-Hir, 22820 Plougrescant [02 96 92 52 15; fax 02 96 92 50 34; www.levarlen.com]** Take D8 N out of Tréguier to Plougrescant. Go past old chapel then immed bef church turn R sp Pors-Hir to site in 1km on R. Sm, mkd pitch, pt sl, pt shd; wc; mv service pnt; baby facs; shwrs inc; el pnts (6-10A) €3-3.70 (poss rev pol); lndtte; shop; tradsmn; bar; playgrnd; sports area; shgl beach 300m; 90% statics; dogs €1.30; adv bkg; quiet; ccard acc; red low ssn. "Friendly, helpful owners; some pitches sm & poss diff lge o'fits/m'vans; coastal walks." 1 Mar-15 Nov. € 13.80 2008*

TREGUIER *1D3* (9km NE Coastal) *48.85060, -3.12810* **Camping Port La Chaîne, 22610 Pleubian [02 96 22 92 38; fax 02 96 22 87 92; info@portlachaine.com; www.portlachaine.com]** Fr Paimpol take old D786 W & pick up new D786 over estuary & thro Lézardrieux. After 3km at x-rds turn R (N) onto D33 thro Pleumeur-Gautier to Pleubian; then D20 twds Larmor-Pleubian; turn L after 2km twd coast & foll site sp. Lge, mkd pitch, pt sl, pt shd; wc (some cont); chem disp; serviced pitch; baby facs; shwrs inc; el pnts (6A) inc; gas; lndtte; shop; tradsmn; rest; snacks; bar; BBQ (charcoal); playgrnd; pool; paddling pool; shgl beach adj; watersports nr; fishing; cycle hire in vill; entmnt; wifi; games/TV rm; 30% statics; dogs €2.90; poss cr; Eng spkn; adv bkg ess; quiet; ccard acc; red low ssn. "Lovely, peaceful site; excel views fr some pitches; helpful owners; gd facs." ♦ 43 Apr-19 Sep. € 25.50 ABS - B23 2009*

⊞ **TREGUNC** *2F2* (3km SE Rural) *47.82974, -3.79967* **Camping Fleuri, Route de Névez, Kervec, 29910 Trégunc [02 98 96 74 76; ulrike.kuster@orange.fr]** Fr D783 turn S onto D77 dir Névez. At rndabt turn R onto D177, site in 500m on R. Sm, hdg pitch, pt shd; htd wc; chem disp (wc); mv service pnt; shwrs inc; el pnts (6A) €2.20; gas; lndtte; supmkt 500m; playgrnd; sand beach 3km; 70% statics; dogs €1; phone; poss cr; Eng spkn; adv bkg; quiet; ccard acc; CCI. "Wooded site; friendly, helpful owners; gd san facs; gd coastal walking & beaches; conv Concarneau & Pont-Aven; gd." ♦ € 9.70 2007*

TREGUNC *2F2* (3km S Coastal) *47.81065, -3.85091* **Camping des Etangs de Trévignon, Kerlin, 29910 Trégunc [tel/fax 02 98 50 00 41; camp.etangdetrevignon@wanadoo.fr; www.camping-etangs.com]** Exit N165/E60 at Kérampaou. S on D122 to Trégunc, then cont S on D1 to Trévignon. Site in 3km. Foll sp. Lge, hdg/mkd pitch, pt shd; wc (some cont); chem disp; baby facs; shwrs inc; el pnts (5A) €3.20; gas; lndtte; shop 2km; tradsmn; rest 3km; snacks; bar; BBQ; playgrnd; htd, covrd pool high ssn; waterslide; sand beach 800m; cycle hire; TV rm; 5% statics; dogs €1.80; phone; Eng spkn; adv bkg; quiet; red low ssn/long stay; ccard acc; red CCI. "In nature reserve with bird sanctuary nr; excel." ♦ 1 Jun-15 Sep. € 20.50 2009*

TREGUNC *2F2* (4km S Coastal) *47.79706, -3.82701* **Camping Le Suroît, Plage de Karidan, 29128 Trégunc [tel/fax 02 98 50 01 76 or 02 98 97 65 42 (LS)]** Fr Concarneau take D783 to Trégunc; D1 S for 3km dir La Pointe de Trévignon & turn L & foll sps for 3.5km. Med, mkd pitch, pt sl, pt shd; wc; chem disp; shwrs inc; el pnts (4-10A) €2.60; lndtte; shop 2km; rest; snacks; bar; BBQ; sand beach adj; 50% statics; dogs €0.50; poss cr; adv bkg; quiet; CCI. "Simple site; sm, modern san facs block, poss stretched high ssn; pleasant owner; lovely sand beach across rd; gd." 15 Apr-30 Sep. € 12.50 2007*

TREGUNC *2F2* (5.5km S Coastal) *47.80705, -3.83863* **Camping La Pommeraie, St Philibert, 29910 Trégunc [02 98 50 02 73; fax 02 98 50 07 91; info@campingdelapommeraie.com; www.campingdelapommeraie.com]** Fr D783 bet Concarneau & Pont-Aven, turn S in Trégunc onto D1 twd Pointe de Trévignon. In 5.5km look for site sp. Turn L to St Philibert & Névez. Ent immed on L. Lge, hdg/mkd pitch, pt shd; wc (some cont); chem disp; shwrs inc; mv service pnt; some serviced pitches; el pnts (10A) €2; gas; lndtte; shop & 250m; rest; snacks; bar; playgrnd; htd pool; paddling pool; sand beach 1km; boating; fishing; games rm; cycle hire; entmnt; TV; 60% statics; dogs €3.50; Eng spkn; adv bkg; quiet; ccard acc; red low ssn; CCI. "Pleasant site in apple orchard; warm welcome." ♦ 1 May-26 Sep. € 29.00 2009*

TREGUNC *2F2* (3.5km SW Coastal) *47.83384, -3.89173* **Camping La Plage Loc'h Ven, Plage de Pendruc, 29910 Trégunc [02 98 50 26 20; fax 02 98 50 27 63; contact@lochven.com; www.lochven.com]** Fr N165 exit at Kérampaou sp Trégunc. At rndbt W of Trégunc foll Loc'h Ven sp thro Lambell, site on coast. Med, hdg/mkd pitch, pt sl, pt shd; htd wc; chem disp; baby facs; shwrs inc; el pnts (4-10A) €3-4.60; gas; Indtte; shop 4km; tradsmn; rest, snacks, bar 4km; playgrnd; sand/shgl beach adj; games area; TV; 40% statics; dogs free; poss cr; Eng spkn; adv bkg; quiet. "Easy walk to beach, rock pools & coastal footpath; helpful owners." 28 Apr-20 Sep. € 15.00 2008*

TREIGNAC *7B4* (4.5km N Rural) *45.56023, 1.81369* **Camping La Plage, Les Barriousses, 19260 Treignac [05 55 98 08 54; fax 05 55 98 16 47; info@laplage camping.com; www.laplagecamping.com]** On D940 opp Lac des Barriousses. Med, mkd pitch, pt sl, terr, shd; htd wc; chem disp; mv service pnt; shwrs inc; el pnts (6A) €2.80; Indtte; sm shop & 4.5km; rest 500m; snacks; lake sw, boating, fishing adj; 5% statics; dogs €1.20; poss cr; adv bkg; quiet; CCI. "Beautiful area & outlook; friendly; facs unclean low ssn (Sep 2007)." ♦ 1 May-16 Sep. € 12.70 2007*

TREIGNAC *7B4* (10km SE Rural) *45.50262, 1.86911* **Camping Le Fayard, Cors, 19260 Veix [05 55 94 00 20 or 0031 113301245 (N'lands); veen514@zonnet.nl; www. le-fayard.com]** Fr Treignac take D16 dir Lestards. 1km after Lestards take D32 dir Cors, site sp. Sm, mkd pitch, pt sl, pt shd; wc; chem disp; baby facs; fam bthrm; shwrs inc; el pts (6A) €2.95; Indtte; shop 7km; tradsmn; rest 10km; bar; playgrnd; htd pool; games area; dogs €1.60; adv bkg; quiet; CCI. "Friendly Dutch owners; relaxing site in National Park of Limousin." ♦ 12 May-1 Oct. € 15.00 2006*

TREIGNAC *7B4* (10km NW Rural) *45.57956, 1.70852* **Camp Municipal Le Merle/Badinage, 19370 Chamberet [05 55 98 30 12 (Mairie); fax 05 55 98 79 34; mairie. chamberet@wanadoo.fr; www.chamberet-correze.net]** S fr Eymoutiers on D30 or N fr Treignac on D16. In Chamberet foll sp Camping Badinage, opp lake take rd up past some houses, site 250m at end. Sm, mkd pitch, hdstg, pt sl, terr, shd; wc; chem disp (wc); mv service pnt at stadium; shwrs inc; el pnts (6A) €1.50; gas 1km; Indtte (inc dryers); shop, rest & bar 1km; BBQ; playgrnd; pool & lake sw 250m; cycle hire; dogs; quiet; CCI. "Peaceful site; pay at Camping du Bois Combet opp (tel 05 55 98 96 83); vg." ♦ 15 Jun-15 Sep. € 9.90 2009*

TREIN D'USTOU, LE see Oust *8G3*

TRELEVERN see Perros Guirec *1D2*

TREMBLADE, LA *7B1* (2km N Rural) *45.77302, -1.16686* **Camping La Clairière, Rue des Roseaux, Ronce-les-Bains, 17390 La Tremblade [05 46 36 36 63; fax 05 46 36 06 74; info@camping-la-clairiere.com; www. camping-la-clairiere.com]** Fr N on A10 exit Saintes, foll sp La Tremblade; site sp. Med, pt shd; wc; baby facs; shwrs; el pnts (6A) €4.80; Indtte; shop; rest; snacks; bar; BBQ (gas); playgrnd; 2 htd pools; paddling pool; waterslide; beach 2.5km; fishing; watersports; tennis; cycle hire; games area; entmnt; TV; statics; dogs €3; poss cr; adv bkg; quiet. 1 May-15 Sep. € 25.00 2007*

TREMBLADE, LA *7B1* (3km W Rural) *45.75849, -1.17420* **Camping Le Pacha, Rue Bouffard, 17390 La Tremblade [05 46 36 14 44 or 06 16 38 45 46]** Sp from D25 bypass around La Tremblade. Med, shd; wc; shwrs inc; el pnts (10A); tradsmn; snacks; bar; playgrnd; pool; beach 5km; entmnt; TV; some statics; dogs; quiet. "Peaceful site amongst pine trees; san facs old, could be cleaner (2009); Viaduct de la Seudre 3km." Easter-15 Oct. € 22.00 2009*

TREMOLAT see Bugue, Le *7C3*

TREPORT, LE *3B2* (N Urban) *50.05805, 1.38860* **Camp Municipal Les Boucaniers, Rue Pierre Mendès-France, 76470 Le Tréport [02 35 86 35 47; fax 02 35 86 55 82; camping@ville-le-treport.fr; www.ville-le-treport.fr]** Fr Eu take minor rd sp to Le Tréport under low bdge. On ent o'skts of Le Tréport, turn R at traff lts, camp ent 100m on R. Site nr stadium. Lge, pt shd; htd wc; shwrs inc; el pnts (6A) €4.30; Indtte; shop; rest; snacks; bar; playgrnd; sand beach 2km; games rm; entmnt; TV; 10% statics; dogs; quiet; red facs low ssn. "Gd, clean san facs; gd sep m'van area; excel." ♦ 1 Apr-30 Sep. € 12.35 2009*

TREPORT, LE *3B2* (1km S Coastal) *50.05311, 1.36623* **Camp International du Golf, 102 Route de Dieppe, 76470 Le Tréport [02 27 28 01 50; fax 02 27 28 01 51; evergreen2@wanadoo.fr]** Fr Dieppe, take D925 NE twd Le Tréport for 20km bef taking D940 sp Floques/Le Tréport. Site on L at top of hill on o'skts of Le Tréport. Foll sp. Lge, mkd pitch, shd; wc; chem disp; mv service pnt; 30% serviced pitches; shwrs inc; el pnts (5A) €4.60; shop 1km; rest, snacks, bar 500m; playgrnd; shgl beach 600m; fishing; sailing; windsurfing; 10% statics; dogs €3; poss cr; adv bkg; quiet; red low ssn; ccard acc; CCI. "Site neglected (2009); san facs need update; more suitable tents only; fairly steep hill down fr site to town." 1 Apr-20 Sep. € 15.00 2009*

TREPT *9B2* (2.5km E Rural) *45.68701, 5.35190* **Domaine Les Trois Lacs du Soleil, 38460 Trept [04 74 92 92 06; fax 04 74 92 93 35; info@les3lacsdusoleil.com; www. les3lacsdusoleil.com]** Exit A432 at junc 3 or 3 & head twd Crémieu then Morestel. Trept bet these 2 towns on D517, site sp by lakes. Lge, pt shd; wc; baby facs; shwrs inc; el pnts (6A) inc; Indtte; shop; rest; snacks; bar; BBQ (gas); playgrnd; pool complex; waterslides; lake sw & beach adj; fishing; tennis; archery; horseriding 2km; entmnt; internet; TV rm; 5% statics; dogs €1.50; adv bkg; Eng spkn; quiet; ccard acc; red low ssn. "Modest rest; OK NH." ♦ 1 May-16 Sep. € 31.00 2006*

France

⊞ **TRETS** *10F3* (4km SW Rural) *43.44178, 5.62847* **Camping Le Devançon, Chemin de Pourachon, 13790 Peynier [04 42 53 10 06; fax 04 42 53 04 79; infos@ledevancon.com; www.ledevancon.com]** Leave A8 at Canet or Pas-de-Trets or leave D6 at Trets & take D908 to Peynier. In vill cont on D908 sp Marseille. Site on R at end vill after g'ge. Med, mkd pitch, all hdstg, pt sl, shd; htd wc; chem disp; mv service pnt; shwrs inc; el pnts (3-10A) €3-5; gas; Indtte; shop; tradsmn; snacks; rest & bar (high ssn) BBQ; playgrnd; pool; paddling pool; sand beach 30km; tennis; entmnt; TV rm; 50% statics; dogs €2; some Eng spkn; adv bkg; quiet; ccard acc; red long stay/CCI. "Excel facs & site; helpful owner; poss diff manoeuvring onto pitches for lge o'fits; few water points; ltd facs low ssn; gd touring area." ♦ € 19.00 2006*

TREVIERES *1D4* (Rural) *49.31308, -0.90578* **Camp Municipal Sous Les Pommiers, Rue du Pont de la Barre, 14710 Trévières [02 31 22 57 52 or 02 31 92 89 24; fax 02 31 22 19 49; mairie@ville-trevieres.fr]** Turn S off N13 onto D30 sp Trévières. Site on R on ent to vill. Med, hdg/mkd pitch, pt shd; wc (cont); chem disp; mv service pnt; shwrs inc; el pnts (10A) €3.50; Indtte; shops 500m; rest; playgrnd; sand beach 10km; rv fishing adj; poss cr; adv bkg rec high ssn; quiet; CCI. "Delightful site in apple orchard; lge pitches; vg san facs; conv D-Day beaches." ♦ 1 Apr-30 Sep. € 10.60 2009*

TREVIERES *1D4* (3km NE Rural) *49.32530, -0.86480* **Camping La Roseraie, Rue de l'Eglise, 14710 Surrain [tel/fax 02 31 21 17 71; camping.laroseraie@neuf.fr; www.camping-laroseraie.com]** Take N13 fr Bayeux twds Cherbourg. In approx 12km take D208 sp Surrain. Site sp in vill. Med, mkd pitch, pt sl, pt shd; wc; el pnts (6A) €4.60; Indtte; shop; snacks; playgrnd; htd pool; tennis; entmnt; 50% statics; dogs €2.50; Eng spkn; adv bkg; quiet. "Friendly recep; touring pitches bet statics; access rds restricted; conv Bayeux & D-Day Museums." ♦ 1 Apr-20 Sep. € 17.30 2009*

TREVOUX see Villefranche sur Saône *9B2*

TRIE SUR BAISE *8F2* (2.5km NE Rural) **Camping Fontrailles, Le Quartier Lanorbe, 65220 Fontrailles [05 62 35 62 52; detm.paddon@orange.fr; www.fontraillescamping.com]** Fr N on N21 leave Mirande & turn L (S) at end of town sp Trie-sur-Baïse onto D939; after St Michel look out for silos on R after 7km, site sp. Fr S at Miélan turn onto D3/D17 sp Trie-sur-Baïse to Fontrailles. Sm, pt sl, pt shd; wc; chem disp (wc); shwrs inc; el pnts (9A) €2; shop, rest, snacks & bar 3km; BBQ; playgrnd; pool; tennis; fishing; dogs; Eng spkn; adv bkg; quiet; red long stay; CCI. "Delightful, well-kept CL-type site in orchard; friendly, helpful British owners; excel pool & tennis nrby; gd walking; conv Lourdes, Pyrenees & Spain; mkt Trie-sur-Baïse Tues." 1 Jul-30 Sep. € 14.00 2008*

TRINITE SUR MER, LA see Carnac *2G3*

TRIZAC see Riom ès Montagnes *7C4*

TROCHE see Uzerche *7B3*

TROGUES see Ste Maure de Touraine *4H2*

TROYES *4E4* (2km NE Urban) *48.31150, 4.09630* **Camp Municipal de Troyes, 7 Rue Roger Salengro, 10150 Pont-Ste Marie [tel/fax 03 25 81 02 64; info@troyescamping.net; www.troyescamping.net]** Fr Troyes N on D677 (N77) (en rte Nancy on D960); on o'skts of town on L opp Stadium & adj Esso g'ge. Fr N site on R on D677, just pass junc with D960. Pont-Ste-Marie & site 'municipal' well sp fr all dirs & in town. NB Queues form onto rd outside site, use Esso g'ge or supmkt to turn if queue too long. Med, some hdg/mkd pitch, some hdstg, pt shd; wc; chem disp; mv service pnt; shwrs inc; el pnts (5A) €2.80 (long lead poss req); gas; Indtte (inc dryer); shop; tradsmn; supmkt adj; rest nrby; snacks; BBQ; playgrnd; htd pool; cycle hire; games area; games rm; wifi; TV; dogs €1; bus opp; poss cr; Eng spkn; adv bkg; ccard acc; red 3+ nights low ssn; CCI. "Busy, popular, transit site in parkland - rec arr early; vg pool; some lge pitches; twin-axles acc at recep's discretion; red facs low ssn; Troyes Cathedral, museums & old quarter worth visit; Lac d'Orient & Lac du Temple nrby; conv NH." ♦ 1 Apr-15 Oct. € 15.50 2009*

TROYES *4E4* (16km E Rural) *48.28998, 4.28279* **Camping La Fromentelle, Ferme Fromentelle, 10220 Dosches [tel/fax 03 25 41 52 67]** Exit A26 junc 23 onto D619 (N19) dir Bar-sur-Aube. In 8.5km turn L onto D1 sp Géraudot (take care bends). Site on L in 5km. Sm, mkd pitch, pt sl, pt shd; htd wc; chem disp; mv service pnt; shwrs inc; el pnts (6A) €3 (long lead poss req)(poss rev pol); BBQ; playgrnd; sand beach 5km; lake sw 5km; games area; dogs €0.60; adv bkg; quiet, poss noise fr workers in statics leaving for work 6am; CCI. "Lovely but remote farm/CL-type site in old orchard; well-kept; warm welcome; gd san facs; gd for birdwatching, sailing, watersports on lakes; excel cycle tracks; nr nature reserve; conv A26." ♦ 30 Apr-30 Sep. € 11.50 2009*

TROYES *4E4* (10km SE Rural) *48.20106, 4.16620* **FFCC Camping Plan d'Eau des Terres Rouges, 10390 Clérey [03 25 46 04 45; fax 03 25 46 05 86; terres-rouges@wanadoo.fr; www.terres-rouges.fr.st]** Exit A5 junc 21 onto D671 (N71) S dir Bar-sur-Seine & Dijon; site on R in 2km. Or SE fr Troyes on D671 (N71) dir Bar-sur-Seine, foll sp Clérey; then as bef. Site well sp. Sm, hdstg, pt shd; wc (1 cont); chem disp; shwrs €1; el pnts (5-10A) €2.60 (poss rev pol); shops 4km; tradsmn; rest; snacks; bar; playgrnd; lake sw; tennis; lakes for fishing, waterskiing, boating; 10% statics; dogs; phone; adv bkg; quiet; no ccard acc; CCI. "Gd, basic NH; san facs clean; friendly, helpful owners; gate opens 0600; conv fr a'route to Calais." Mid Apr-30 Sep. € 11.00 2009*

TUFFE *4F1* (1km N Urban) *48.11866, 0.51148* **FFCC Camping du Lac, Plan d'Eau, Route de Prévelles, 72160 Tuffé [02 43 93 88 34; fax 02 43 93 43 54; camping.tuffe@wanadoo.fr]** Site on D33, sp. Med, hdg/mkd pitch, pt shd; htd wc; chem disp; mv service pnt; baby facs; fam bthrm; shwrs inc; el pnts (6A) €2.50; Indtte; snacks; bar; BBQ; playgrnd; fishing; TV; lake sw adj; 10% statics; dogs €2; Eng spkn; adv bkg; CCI. "Well-kept, pretty lakeside site; adj tourist train; clean san facs; friendly staff." 1 Apr-30 Sep. € 9.30 2008*

TULETTE *9D2* (2.2km S Rural) *44.26485, 4.93180* **Camping Les Rives de L'Aygues, Route de Cairanne, 26790 Tulette [tel/fax 04 75 98 37 50; camping.aygues@wanadoo.fr; www.lesrivesdelaygues.com]** Exit D94 at Tulette onto D193 S; site in 2.2km on L. Site sp. Med, hdg/mkd pitch, hdstg, shd; wc; chem disp; shwrs inc; el pnts (6A) €3.90; gas; tradsmn; snacks; bar; playgrnd; htd pool; direct access to rv; games area; internet; 5% statics; dogs €2.50; phone; Eng spkn; adv bkg; quiet; ccard acc; red low ssn; CCI. "Peaceful, woodland site amongst vineyards by Rv Aygue; excel." ♦ 27 Apr-30 Sep. € 18.00 2009*

TULLE *7C4* (3km NE Rural) *45.28330, 1.78673* **Camp Municipal Bourbacoup, Ave du Lieutenant-Colonel Faro, 19000 Tulle [05 55 26 75 97; fax 05 55 21 73 62]** Fr Tulle, take D1120 (N120) NW dir Limoges. Turn R onto D23 & foll site sp. Med, mkd pitch, pt shd; wc (some cont); shwrs inc; el pnts inc; supmkt 3km; rest, bar 1km; pool 1km; rv adj; dogs; quiet. "Pretty rvside site; easy cycle ride to town; dated but clean san facs." ♦ 1 Jul-31 Aug. € 10.50 2007*

TULLE *7C4* (4km SE Rural) *45.24992, 1.78948* **Camping Le Pré du Moulin, 19150 Laguenne [tel/fax 05 55 26 21 96; lepredumoulin@wanadoo.fr; www.lepredumoulin.com]** Exit Tulle on D1120 (N120) twd Aurillac, pass ATAC commercial cent on R, cross bdge & 1st L to camp site. Last 1km on unmade rd, but not diff. Sm, pt sl, pt shd; wc; chem disp; shwrs inc; el pnts (6A) €2.50; gas; lndtte; shops 2km; tradsmn; snacks; pool; rv fishing adj; cycle hire; €1.50; adv bkg rec high ssn; quiet; CCI. "Attractive, peaceful, well-kept British-owned site; steep climb to adequate san facs - diff for disabled." 1 Apr-1 Oct. € 15.50 2009*

TURBALLE, LA see Guérande *2G3*

TURCKHEIM see Colmar *6F3*

TURSAC see Eyzies de Tayac, Les *7C3*

UCHIZY see Tournus *9A2*

UGINE *9B3* (7km NW Rural) *45.76141, 6.33702* **Camping Champ Tillet, 28 Rue Chenevier, 74210 Marlens [04 50 44 40 07; fax 04 50 32 51 92; duchamptillet@wanadoo.fr; www.champtillet.com]** D1508 (N508) S fr Annecy after leaving Lake. Take by-pass past Faverges dir Ugine. After rndabt, site on R at junc bef Marlens, sp. Med, pt shd; wc (some cont); chem disp (wc); shwrs inc; el pnts (3-10A) €3.40 (poss rev pol); lndtte; shops adj; supmkts 3km; rest; snacks; bar; playgrnd; pool; rv 500m; statics; some rd noise - adj extensive cycle track; red low ssn; ccard acc. "Gd walks; lovely views; barrier clsd 2300-0700." ♦ 1 Apr-30 Oct. € 20.00 2009*

URBES see St Maurice sur Moselle *6F3*

URCAY *4H3* (6km NE Rural) *46.6430, 2.6620* **Camping Champ de la Chapelle, St Bonnet-Tronçais, 03360 Braize [04 70 06 15 45; champdelachapelle@wanadoo.fr; www.champdelachapelle.com]** Fr D2144 (N144) take D978A for Tronçais. 1.5km on L fr Rond-de-Montaloyer. Site sp. Med, mkd pitch, pt sl, pt shd; wc; chem disp; shwrs; el pnts (10A) €3.50; lndtte; shop; tradsmn; rest 5km; snacks; bar; playgrnd; pool; lake & rv sw 5km; games area; some statics; dogs €1; Eng spkn; adv bkg; ccard acc; red low ssn/CCI. "Excel walking & flora/fauna in ancient oak forest; some lge pitches." 2 Apr-31 Oct. € 14.50 2009*

URCAY *4H3* (500m W Rural) *46.62713, 2.58580* **Camp Municipal La Plage du Cher, Rue de la Gare, 03360 Urçay [04 70 06 96 91 or 04 70 06 93 30 (Mairie); fax 04 70 06 96 78; mairie-urcay@pays-allier.com]** S fr Bourges on D2144 or N fr Montluçon to Urçay. Site by rv to W of Urçay, sp fr both N & S. Sm, mkd pitch, pt shd; wc (some cont); shwrs inc; el pnts (5A) €3; shops 500m; rest, snacks & bar in vill; playgrnd; fishing; phone; train 200m; adv bkg; quiet; ccard not acc; CCI. "Clean, basic rvside site; ltd facs; pleasant situation; site yourself, warden calls; gd cycling." 15 May-15 Sep. € 8.00 2007*

URDOS *8G2* (500m N Rural) *42.87705, -0.55670* **Camp Municipal Le Gave d'Aspe, 64490 Urdos [05 59 34 88 26; fax 05 59 34 88 86; guittonb@hotmail.com]** Turn W off N134 onto site access rd by disused Urdos stn approx 1km bef vill, clear sp. Other access rds in vill v diff lge o'fits. Sm, mkd pitch, pt sl, pt shd; wc; chem disp; mv service pnt; shwrs inc; el pnts (30A) €2.40; lndtte; shop, rest, bar 500m; tradsmn; BBQ; playgrnd; paddling pool; rv phone; poss cr; Eng spkn; adv bkg; quiet; ccard acc; CCI. "Adj Rv Aspe; 14km fr Col du Somport/Tunnel; surrounded by mountains; conv x-ing into Spain; ltd facs; vg." 1 May-15 Sep. € 10.00 2007*

URRUGNE see St Jean de Luz *8F1*

⊞ **URT** *8F1* (E Rural) *43.49353, -1.27960* **Camping Ferme Mimizan, 64240 Urt [tel/fax 05 59 56 21 51; campinglafermedemimizan@wanadoo.fr; www.lafermedemimizan.fr]** E fr Bayonne on A64/E80, exit junc 4 sp Urt; in vill turn sharp R at PO & foll sps; site on R in 1km. Fr N on D12 cross Rv Adour by metal bdge & turn L immed past church, site on R in 1.5km. Med, pt shd; wc; shwrs inc; el pnts (10A) €3.50; playgrnd; pool; paddling pool; some statics; adv bkg; poss noise fr static residents; red low ssn; CCI. "V peaceful out of ssn; friendly owners; gd walking & cycling; conv coast & Pyrenees; gd NH." € 19.50 2009*

URT *8F1* (500m S Rural) *43.49165, -1.29677* **Camping Etche Zahar, Allée des Mesplès, 64240 Urt [05 59 56 27 36; fax 05 59 56 29 62; camping.etche-zahar@wanadoo.fr; www.etche-zahar.fr]** Exit A64 at junc 4 dir Urt. Fr N on N10 exit junc 9 at St Geours-de-Maremne onto D12 S to Urt, site sp. Fr town cent head W, L at rndabt, L again to site. Sm, hdg pitch, pt sl, pt shd; wc; chem disp; shwrs inc; el pnts (10A) €3.20; lndtte; shop 500m; tradsmn; snacks; bar; BBQ; rest 500m; playgrnd; pool; paddling pool; fishing; games area; cycle hire; entmnt; internet; 25% statics; dogs €2.10; phone; site clsd 1 Jan-7 Feb; Eng spkn; adv bkg; quiet; CCI. "Peaceful site; welcoming, pleasant owners; gd walking & cycling." ♦ 24 Mar-5 Nov. € 17.00 2006*

USTOU see Oust *8G3*

UZER *9D2* (3km SE Rural) *44.50819, 4.32119* **Camping La Turelure, Fontanne, 07110 Uzer [04 75 89 29 21 or 06 79 74 40 53 (mob)]** S fr Aubenas on D104, 1km S of Uzer. Site well sp; app rd narr. Sm, hdg/mkd pitch, pt shd; wc (some cont); chem disp; mv service pnt; shwrs; el pnts (3-6A) €2.30-3.50; gas; lndtte; shop 1km; tradsmn high ssn; rest 1km; snacks 5km; BBQ; playgrnd; fishing; canoeing; games area; 10% statics; dogs free; phone; poss cr; some Eng spkn; adv bkg; quiet; red low ssn; ccard not acc; CCI. "Pleasant, peaceful, scenic site in orchard bet vineyard & rv; friendly owner; vg touring base." ♦ 1 Apr-31 Oct. € 14.00 2007*

UZER *9D2* (4km SW Rural) *44.49964, 4.30621* **FLOWER Camping St Amand, 07110 Laurac-en-Vivrais [04 75 36 84 45; st-amand@wanadoo.fr; www.campingsaintamand.com]** S fr Aubenas on D104 to Uzer; cont past vill; turn L 400m after junc with D4. Med, pt shd; wc (some cont); chem disp; shwrs; baby facs; el pnts (6A) inc; lndtte; tradsmn; rest; snacks; BBQ (gas); playgrnd; pool; paddling pool; games area; entmnt; 30% statics; dogs €1.50; Eng spkn; adv bkg; quiet; ccard acc; red low ssn; CCI. "Vg touring base; gd walking; peaceful, family site." 4 Apr-19 Sep. € 17.90 2008*

UZERCHE *7B3* (8km NE Rural) *45.45200, 1.65056* **Camping Aimée Porcher (Naturist), 19140 Eyburie [05 55 73 20 97 or 0031 264 436285 (N'lands) (LS); fax 0031 264 436285; info@aimee-porcher.com; www.aimee-porcher.com]** Fr Uzerche take D3 NE to Eyburie & in Eyburie turn R at site sp (Cheyron/Pingrieux). In 1km turn L at site sp; site at end of narr lane. Sm, mkd pitch, terr, pt shd; wc; chem disp; shwrs inc; baby facs; el pnts (6A) €3.50 (poss long lead req); lndtte; tradsmn; snacks; bar; BBQ; playgrnd; lake sw adj; no statics; dogs €2; Eng spkn; adv bkg; quiet; red long stay; CCI. "Beautiful views; friendly, helpful Dutch owners; spacious pitches; basic, clean facs - stretched if site full." ♦ 1 Jun-1 Sep. € 31.50 2006*

UZERCHE *7B3* (200m SE Rural) *45.42148, 1.56592* **Camp Municipal La Minoterie, Route de la Minoterie, 19140 Uzerche [05 55 73 12 75 or 05 55 73 17 00 (Mairie); fax 05 55 98 44 55; www.uzerche.fr]** Fr N exit A20 at junc 44 for Uzerche on D920; proceed thro tunnel & cross town bdge. Site clearly sp on ent to town on rvside. Steep app rd & sharp bend. NB Narr app rd used by lorries fr nrby quarry. Site well sp. Sm, mkd pitch, pt sl, shd; wc; chem disp; shwrs inc; el pnts (10A) €2.90; lndtte; shops 200m; tradsmn; playgrnd; fishing; kayak hire; white water sports cent; rock-climbing; tennis; games rm; TV; Eng spkn; quiet; CCI. "Lovely pitches on river's edge; helpful warden; not suitable lge o'fits or lge m'vans; sh walk along rv to beautiful old vill; gd local walks; poss risk of flooding; v quiet end of ssn; conv NH; excel." 1 May-2 Oct. € 10.00 2009*

UZERCHE *7B3* (9km SW Rural) *45.36861, 1.53849* **Camp Municipal du Lac du Pontcharal, 19410 Vigeois [05 55 98 90 86 or 05 55 98 91 93 (Mairie); fax 05 55 98 99 79; mairievigeois@wanadoo.fr; www.vigeois.com]** Fr A20 exit 45 onto D3 to Vegeois then D7. Site is 2.5km SE of Vigeois. Med, pt sl, shd; wc; chem disp; shwrs inc; el pnts (15A) €3 (poss rev pol); gas; lndtte; shop; rest; snacks; bar; playgrnd; lake sw & beach; fishing; watersports; games area; tennis 2km; entmnt; TV; dogs €0.90; adv bkg; quiet. "Delightful, well-kept site; excel san facs." ♦ 1 Jun-15 Sep. € 8.70 2008*

UZERCHE *7B3* (9km SW Rural) *45.40833, 1.47898* **FFCC Camping à la Ferme Domaine Vert (Broeks), Les Magnes, 19230 Troche [tel/fax 05 55 73 59 89; www.ledomainevert.nl]** Exit A20 junc 45 onto D3 to Vigeois, 2km after Vigeois turn R onto D50 sp Lubersac. After 5km (ignore sp to Troche) foll site sp to R. Sm, pt sl, pt shd; wc; shwrs; lndry rm; el pnts €2.50 (poss rev pol); meals avail; fishing 4km; canoeing nr, lake sw; dogs €1.50; Eng spkn; quiet; red CCI. "Peaceful, clean, farm site; many pitches v sl; welcoming, friendly Dutch owners; adv bkg ess high ssn; lovely lake; vg." 1 Apr-1 Oct. € 16.00 2009*

UZERCHE *7B3* (12km SW Rural) *45.34632, 1.51493* **Aire Naturelle du Bois Coutal (Veysseix), Perpezac-le-Noir, 19410 Vigeois [05 55 73 71 93; fax 05 55 73 27 66; boiscoutal@wanadoo.fr]** Exit A20/E09 S fr Uzerche at junc 46 onto D920 N & foll sp Perpezac le-Noir. Go thro Perpezac on D156 N dir Vigeois & foll site sp. Site in 4km. Sm, sl, pt shd; wc; chem disp; shwrs inc; el pnts inc (6A) €2.50; lndtte; shop, rest, snacks, bar 3km; playgrnd; pool; games rm; entmnt; few statics; dogs; poss cr; Eng spkn; adv bkg; v quiet. "Friendly, helpful owner; clean facs; gd NH." 15 Apt-15 Oct. € 9.00 2009*

UZES *10E2* (800m N Rural) *44.02231, 4.42087* **Camping La Paillotte, Quartier de Grézac, 30700 Uzès [04 66 22 38 55; fax 04 66 22 26 66; http://lapailloteuzes.monsite.wanadoo.fr/]** Exit A9 junc 23 sp Remoulins. Fr Remoulins take D981 to Uzès. Aim for town cent 1-way ring rd. Site sp clearly. Narr rds for 800m passing cemetery. Med, mkd pitch, terr, shd; wc; shwrs inc; el pnts (10A) inc; gas; lndtte; shop; tradsmn; rest high ssn; snacks; bar; playgrnd; pool; paddling pool; cycle hire; games area; games rm; entmnt; some statics; adv bkg; quiet; CCI. "Facs clean but water temperature poss variable." 20 Mar-30 Sep. € 35.00 2007*

UZES *10E2* (2km E Rural) *44.03202, 4.45557* **Camping Le Moulin Neuf, 30700 St Quentin-la-Poterie [04 66 22 17 21; fax 04 66 22 91 82; lemoulinneuf@yahoo.fr; www.le-moulin-neuf.com]** Take D982 out of Uzès, after 3km turn N, site in 400m. Med, mkd pitch, pt shd; wc; chem disp; mv service pnt; shwrs inc; el pnts (5A) €2.60; lndtte; shop & 2km; snacks; bar; playgrnd; htd pool; fishing; tennis; cycle hire; horseriding; 10% statics; dogs €1.50; o'night m'van area; poss cr; v quiet. "Site off beaten track; conv touring base; barrier clsd 2230-0700; poss mosquito problem."♦ 1 Apr-23 Sep. € 16.90 2008*

UZES *10E2* (3km SW Rural) *43.99843, 4.38424* **Camping Le Mas de Rey, Route d'Anduze, 30700 Arpaillargues [tel/fax 04 66 22 18 27; info@campingmasderey.com; www.campingmasderey.com]** Sp fr Uzès. Exit by D982 sp Anduze. After 2.5km cross narr bdge, turn L in 100m on site app rd. Med, hdg/mkd pitch, hdstg, pt sl, pt shd; wc; chem disp; fam bthrm; shwrs inc; el pnts (10A) €3.50 (rev pol); Indtte; shop & 3km; tradsmn; rest, snacks; bar; BBQ; playgrnd; pool; TV rm; dogs €2; phone; poss cr; Eng spkn; adv bkg; quiet; red low ssn/snr citizens; CCI. "Helpful Dutch owners; some v lge pitches; gd for sm children; excel cycling; Uzès interesting." ♦ 1 Apr-15 Oct. € 20.00 2009*

VACQUEYRAS see Carpentras *10E2*

VAISON LA ROMAINE *9D2* (500m NE Urban) *44.24518, 5.07886* **Camping du Théâtre Romain, Quartier des Arts, Chemin du Brusquet, 84110 Vaison-la-Romaine [04 90 28 78 66; fax 04 90 28 78 76; info@camping-theatre.com; www.camping-theatre.com]** Fr town cent foll sp for Théâtre Romain & site. Ent to Chemin du Busquet on rndabt at Théâtre Romain. Or site sp off Orange-Nyons rd thro town (do not ent town cent). Med, hdg/mkd pitch, pt shd; wc; chem disp (wc); mv service pnt; serviced pitches; baby facs; shwrs inc; el pnts (5-10A) €3-4; gas 500m; Indtte; shop 500m; tradsmn; bar; BBQ; playgrnd; pool; wifi; some statics; dogs €2; Eng spkn; adv bkg ess high ssn (bkg fee); quiet; ccard acc; red low ssn; CCI. "Excel, well-kept site; busy even low ssn - rec arr early or adv book; mainly gd sized pitches; suitable m'vans; clean unisex san facs; attractive town; mkt Tues; highly rec." ♦ 15 Mar-5 Nov. € 20.80 2009*

The opening dates and prices on this campsite have changed. I'll send a site report form to the Club for the next edition of the guide.

VAISON LA ROMAINE *9D2* (4km NE Rural) *44.26240, 5.12950* **Camping L'Ayguette, 84110 Faucon [04 90 46 40 35 or 06 18 47 33 42 (mob); fax 04 90 46 46 17; info@ayguette.com; www.ayguette.com]** Exit Vaison NE on D938, R on D71, thro St Romain-en-Viennois. Then R onto D86 sp Faucon. Site on R, well sp. Med, mkd pitch, terr, shd; htd wc; chem disp; baby facs; shwrs inc; el pnts (10A) €2.50 (poss long lead req); Indtte; shop, supmkt 4km; tradsmn; snacks; bar; BBQ; playgrnd; htd pool; wifi; dogs €1.80; adv bkg; quiet; ccard acc; red low ssn/long stay; CCI. "Excel, well-run site; lge pitches in forest setting; friendly, helpful owners; excel mod facs inc hairdryers & children's shwrs; tractor tow available." 1 Apr-30 Sep. € 22.00 2009*

VAISON LA ROMAINE *9D2* (4km NE Rural) *44.26806, 5.10651* **Camping Le Soleil de Provence, Route de Nyons, Quartier Trameiller, 84110 St Romain-en-Viennois [04 90 46 46 00; fax 04 90 46 40 37; info@camping-soleil-de-provence.fr; www.camping-soleil-de-provence.fr]** Leave A7 at junc 19 Bollène onto D94 dir Nyons. After Tullette turn R onto D20 & then D975 to Vaison-la-Romaine; fr Vaison take D938 sp Nyons; in 4km R & in 150m L to site; well sp. Lge, terr, hdg/mkd pitch, pt shd; htd wc; chem disp; some serviced pitches; shwrs inc; el pnts (10A) €4; gas; Indtte; shop; tradsmn; rest high ssn; snacks; bar; playgrnd; pool; paddling pool; entmnt; wifi; dogs: poss cr; adv bkg; quiet, but weekly disco eves; ccard not acc; red low ssn; CCI. "Popular, scenic, family-run site; gd pools; lovely town; poss strong Minstral winds Sep; mkt Tues; excel." ♦ 15 Mar-31 Oct. € 23.00 2009*

France

⊞ **VAISON LA ROMAINE** *9D2* (800m SE Rural) *44.23440, 5.08955* **FFCC Camping Club International Carpe Diem, Route de St Marcellin, 84110 Vaison-la-Romaine [04 90 36 02 02; fax 04 90 36 36 90; contact@camping-carpe-diem.com; www.camping-carpe-diem.com or www.camping-franceloc.fr]** S on A7 exit Orange; foll sp to Vaison; at Vaison on Nyons rd (D938) turn S at rndabt by supmkt dir Carpentras. In 1km turn L at junc to St Marcellin, site immed on L. Lge, hdg/mkd pitch, terr, pt shd; wc (some cont); chem disp; mv service pnt; shwrs inc; el pnts (6-10A) €4.70-5.70; gas; Indtte; shop & 800m; tradsmn; pizzeria, snacks, bar high ssn; playgrnd; 2 pools; paddling pool; waterslide; entmnt; internet; TV rm; 10% statics; dogs €5; site clsd 21 Dec-16 Jan; poss cr; Eng spkn; adv bkg; red low ssn; ccard acc; CCI. "Lively site; helpful staff; poss dust from nrby quarry; poss muddy pitches; gd san facs; gd cent for Provence." ♦ € 30.00 2009*

VAISON LA ROMAINE *9D2* (6km SE Rural) *44.23728, 5.14959* **Camping Les Trois Rivières, Quarter des Jonches, 84340 Entrechaux [04 90 46 01 72; fax 04 90 46 00 75; doc@camping-3rivieres.com; www.camping-les3rivieres.com]** Take D938 fr Vaison twd Malaucène for 3.5km. Turn E onto D54 to Entrechaux; site well sp at rndabts at both ends of vill. Narr app rd. Med, pt sl, shd; wc; shwrs inc; el pnts (3-10A) €2.50-4.50; gas; Indtte; shop 2km; rest; snacks; bar; playgrnd; rv shgl beach, sw & fishing; horseriding; games rm; some statics; wifi; entmnt; TV; some statics; dogs €2; poss cr; quiet; adv bkg; red low ssn. "Access poss diff for lge o'fits; quiet & shd." 1 Apr-30 Sep. € 14.50 2009*

VAISON LA ROMAINE *9D2* (5km NW Rural) *44.26446, 5.05242* **Camping Domaine de La Cambuse, Route de Villedieu, 84110 Vaison-la-Romaine [04 90 36 14 53 or 06 32 18 15 54 (mob); dom.lacambuse@wanadoo.fr; www.domainelacambuse.com]** Fr Vaison-la-Romaine N on D51 sp Villedieu. After 4km fork R onto D94 sp Villedieu. Site on R after 300m. Sm, terr, pt shd; wc (some cont); chem disp; shwrs inc; el pnts (15A) €2.35; gas 4km; tradsmn; snacks, bar in ssn; pool; paddling pool; 5% statics; dogs €1.52; phone; poss cr; quiet; CCI. "Site in vineyard on hillside; friendly, helpful owners." 1 May-15 Oct. € 10.70 2007*

VAL ANDRE, LE *2E3* (3km S Coastal) *48.58944, -2.55083* **CAMPEOLE Camping Les Monts Colleux, 26 Rue Jean Le Brun, 22370 Pléneuf-Val-André [02 96 72 95 10; fax 02 96 63 10 49; monts-colleux@campeole.com; www.camping-montscolleux.com or www.campeole.com]** Site 800m off D786 & off D78, sp fr Pléneuf town cent. Rec app only fr Pléneuf centre; at traff lts turn towards Les Plages, then site sp - adj municipal pool. Med, hdg/mkd pitch, hdstg, pt sl, pt shd; htd wc; chem disp; mv service pnt; shwrs inc; el pnts (6-10A) inc (poss rev pol); Indtte (inc dryer); shops, rest nr; tradsmn; bar; BBQ; playgrnd; covrd pool adj; sand/shgl beach 300m; tennis; games area; golf 1km; wifi; entment; TV rm; 40% statics; dogs €2.60; phone; Eng spkn; adv bkg; quiet; ccard ac; red low ssn/CCI. "Pleasant combination of gd beach, port & vill with mkt; san facs basic but clean." ♦ 1 Apr-30 Sep. € 22.00 2009*

See advertisement

VAL D'AJOL, LE see Plombières les Bains *6F2*

VAL DE VESLE see Reims *3D4*

VAL D'ISERE *9B4* (1km E Rural) *45.44622, 6.99218* **Camping Les Richardes, Le Laisinant, 73150 Val-d'Isère [tel/fax 04 79 06 26 60; campinglesrichardes@free.fr; http://campinglesrichardes.free.fr]** Leave Val d'Isère going E twds Col de l'Iseran on D902, site on R 1.5km bef Le Fornet vill. Med, pt sl, unshd; wc; shwrs €1; el pnts (3-6A) €1.90-3.80; pool 1.5km; dogs €0.50; quiet; CCI. "Peaceful site; delightful owner." 15 Jun-15 Sep. € 9.96 2009*

This is a
wonderful
site.

VALENCAY *4H2* (1km W Urban) *47.15656, 1.55202* **Camp Municipal Les Chênes, Route de Loches, 36600 Valençay [tel/fax 02 54 00 03 92 or 02 54 00 32 32]** App town fr E on D960 or N/S on D956, foll sp for D960 Luçay-le-Mâle. Ignore 1st sp for camping (Veuil); D960 is next L in town. Foll sp for pool & camping. Site adj pool mkd by flags. Sm, hdg/mkd pitch, pt shd; wc; chem disp; shwrs inc; el pnts (6A) €3.20 (poss rev pol); Indtte; shop; tradsmn; BBQ; playgrnd; htd pool adj (high ssn); tennis adj; fishing; TV rm; dogs; adv bkg; quiet; red long stay; CCI. "Excel site in parkland with lake; lge pitches; gd, clean facs; poss muddy after heavy rain; gate clsd 2200-0700; day's drive to Calais or Le Havre ferries." ♦ 1 May-30 Sep. € 11.94 2009*

VALENCE *9C2* (12km SE Rural) *44.91560, 5.06520* **Camping Sunêlia Le Grand Lierne, 26120 Chabeuil [04 75 59 83 14; fax 04 75 59 87 95; grand-lierne@franceloc.fr; www.grandlierne.com or www.camping-franceloc.fr]** Fr A7 S take Valence Sud exit dir Grenoble. After 8km take D68 on R twd Chabeuil. Turn L at rndabt on o'skts of vill & foll site sp on by-pass; do not go into vill. On arr, park in lay-by at end of app rd & walk to recep to book in. Or app off D125 NE of Chabeuil. Med, some mkd pitch, shd; wc; chem disp; baby facs; shwrs inc; el pnts (6-10A) €4.70-5.70; gas; Indtte; shop; rest; snacks; bar; BBQ (gas & el only); playgrnd; pool & whirlpool; paddling pool; archery; golf 3km; games area; entmnt; wifi; games/TV rm; many statics; dogs €2.50 (no dogs Jul/Aug): poss cr; Eng spkn; adv bkg rec; poss noisy high ssn; ccard acc; red low ssn; CCI. "Site in oak forest; friendly staff; gd facs & all-round entmnt; some sm pitches - poss diff lge o'fits; no twin-axles; gd for families; barrier clsd 2200-0700; mkt Chabeuil Tue, mkt Valence Thur; gd but regimented!" ♦ 18 Apr-27 Sep. € 30.90 ABS - M04 2009*

⊞ **VALENCE** *9C2* (2km S Urban) *44.91871, 4.87561* **Camp Municipal de l'Epervière, Chemin de l'Epervière, 26000 Valence [04 75 42 32 00; fax 04 75 56 20 67; eperviere26@orange.fr; www.valence-espaces-evenements.com]** Exit A7 at Valence Sud & turn N onto N7, site well sp fr N7. When app fr S on N7 turn L at traff lts 500m after Géant supmkt. Fr N on N7 look for R turn 2km S of Valence. Lge, hdg pitch, hdstg, pt shd; htd wc; mv service pnt; shwrs inc; el pnts (10A) €4.90 (poss rev pol); Indtte; supmkt 500m; rest adj; rest; snacks; bar; playgrnd; htd pool; fishing in Rv Rhône; watersports cent adj; games area; TV; 30% statics; site clsd mid-Dec to mid-Jan; poss cr; Eng spkn; no adv bkg; rd noise; ccard acc; red low ssn; CCI. "Generous pitches; clean, dated san facs; office opp side of rd behind other buildings & up steps; poss unkempt low ssn; poss itinerants." ♦ € 18.00 2009*

VALENCE *9C2* (9km NW Rural) *45.00726, 4.84862* **Camp Municipal Les Vernes, 26600 La Roche-de-Glun [04 75 84 54 11 or 04 75 84 60 52 (Mairie); mairie.rdg@wanadoo.fr]** Turn W off N7 at Pont-d'Isère. On ent La Roche-de-Glun foll camping sp. Sm, hdg/mkd pitch, shd; wc (some cont); serviced pitches; chem disp; shwrs inc; el pnts (10A) inc; Indtte; shop 500m; BBQ; htd pool adj in ssn inc; sports cent adj; 50% statics; phone; poss cr; adv bkg; quiet; no ccard acc; red low ssn; CCI. "Pleasant site; gd, clean san facs; resident warden; barrier clsd 2200-0700." ♦
1 May-30 Sep. € 14.90 2009*

VALENCE D'AGEN *8E3* (1km S Rural) *44.09663, 0.88986* **Camp Municipal Val de Garonne, Route des Charretiers, 82400 Valence-d'Agen [05 63 39 61 67; tourisme.valencedagen@wanadoo.fr]** Exit town on D953 sp Auch, turn R after x-ing rv 1st L. Site sp behind pool on R. Sm, pt shd; wc (cont); shwrs; el pnts inc; shops 1km; rest, snacks adj; playgrnd; games area; poss cr; quiet. "Height barrier to car park opened by warden; no external water pnts for m'vans." 1 Jul-31 Aug. € 10.00 2008*

VALLABREGUES see Tarascon *10E2*

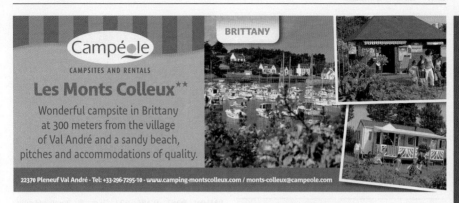

VALLERAUGUE *10E1* (2km NW Rural) *44.08553, 3.61688* **Camping Le Pied de l'Aigoual, Domaine de Pateau, 30570 Valleraugue [04 67 82 24 40; fax 04 67 82 24 23]** Fr Le Vigan, take D999 E to Pont L'Hérault then take D896 N. Site on R. Well sp. Med, mkd pitch, shd; wc; shwrs inc; chem disp; el pnts (3-6A) €3-3.50; lndtte; shops in vill; snacks; bar; playgrnd; pool; fishing; tennis 2km; 4% statics; dogs €1.20; phone; bus; Eng spkn; adv bkg; quiet; CCI. "Excel touring base 1 hr fr Mediterranean; pretty vill." 1 Jun-15 Sep. € 13.50 2006*

VALLIERES see Rumilly *9B3*

VALLOIRE *9C3* (500m N Rural) *45.17000, 6.42960* **Camp Caravaneige Municipal Ste Thècle, Route des Villards, 73450 Valloire [04 79 83 30 11; fax 04 79 83 35 13; camping-caravaneige@valloire.net]** Exit A43 junc 29 onto D306 (N6) to St Michel-de-Maurienne, then onto D902 to Valloire. At vill mkt turn R over rv to site. Climb fr valley 15% gradient max. Med, mkd pitch, some hdstg, unshd; htd wc (cont); chem disp; mv service pnt; baby facs; fam bthrm; shwrs €1; el pnts (13A) €2.20; gas 1km; lndtte; shop 300m; rest 500m; bar 200m; playgrnd; skiing, iceskating, pool nr; TV rm; dogs; phone 100m; bus; Eng spkn; adv bkg; quiet; red long stay; ccard acc. "Superb mountain scenery for walking & cycling; excel." ♦ 22 Dec-20 Apr & 1 Jun-30 Sep. € 15.70 2006*

VALLON EN SULLY *7A4* (500m S Rural) *46.53019, 2.61447* **Camp Municipal Les Soupirs, Allée des Soupirs, 03190 Vallon-en-Sully [04 70 06 50 96 or 04 70 06 50 10 (LS); fax 04 70 06 51 18; mairie.vallonensully@wanadoo.fr; www.vallonensully.com]** N fr Montluçon on N144; in 23km at traff lts where D11 crosses N144 turn L & foll camping sp for Vallon-en-Sully. After bdge over Rv Cher turn L in 50m. Site in 100m. If N or S on A71 exit at junc 9 Vallon-en-Sully; turn N on N144; in 3km at traff lts turn L. Med, pt shd; wc (cont); chem disp (wc); shwrs; el pnts (6-20A) €2-4; shops 500m; rest, snacks, bar adj; TV rm; dogs; bus 500m; adv bkg; quiet. "Peaceful, spacious site on banks of rv & canal; immac san facs; lge pitches; risk of flooding in wet; gd cycling along canal; gd NH; vg." 13 Jun-12 Sep. € 6.00 2009*

VALLON PONT D'ARC *9D2* (9km E Rural) *44.39146, 4.51057* **Camping Carrefour de l'Ardèche, Route de Bourg-St Andéol, Quartier Gourdaud, 07700 St Remèze [04 75 04 15 75; fax 04 75 04 35 05; carrefourardeche@yahoo.fr; www.ardechecamping.net]** D4 E fr Vallon-Pont-d'Arc. Site on L on bend after St Remèze vill. Med, mkd pitch, pt shd; wc; chem disp; baby facs; shwrs inc; el pnts (6A) €3.50; gas; lndtte; shop; snacks; bar; playgrnd; pool; cycle hire; canoeing; fishing 5km; entmnt; TV; dogs €2.50; adv bkg; quiet; ccard acc. "Surrounded by vineyards; vg." ♦ 15 Apr-30 Sep. € 20.00 2009*

VALLON PONT D'ARC *9D2* (1km SE Rural) *44.39783, 4.40005* **Camping Le Provençal, Route des Gorges, 07150 Vallon-Pont-d'Arc [04 75 88 00 48; fax 04 75 88 02 00; camping.le.provencal@wanadoo.fr; www.camping-le-provencal.fr]** Fr Aubenas take D579 thro Vallon-Pont-d'Arc to S. Turn L on D290 N of rv; site on R in 500m (middle of 3 sites). Fr Alès, N on D904/D104, turn R onto D111 & D579 to Vallon-Pont-d'Arc. Lge, pt shd; htd wc; shwrs inc; el pnts (8A) €3.90; gas; lndtte; shop; rest; snacks; bar; playgrnd; htd pool; canoeing; fishing; sailing; tennis; internet; some statics; dogs €4; poss cr; Eng spkn; adv bkg; quiet; ccard acc. "Friendly, helpful staff; site at NW end of spectacular Gorges de l'Ardèche." ♦ Easter-20 Sep. € 29.50 2008*

VALLON PONT D'ARC *9D2* (1km SE Rural) *44.39777, 4.39861* **Camping Nature Park L'Ardéchois, Route des Gorges de l'Ardèche, 07150 Vallon-Pont-d'Arc [04 75 88 06 63; fax 04 75 37 14 97; ardecamp@bigfoot.com; www.ardechois-camping.com or www.les-castels.com]** Fr Vallon take D290 Rte des Gorges & site on R bet rd & rv. Lge, mkd pitch, hdstg, pt sl, shd; htd wc; chem disp; mv service pnt; baby facs; fam bthrm; serviced pitch (extra charge); private bthrm €16 (by reservation); shwrs inc; el pnts (6-10A) inc; gas; lndtte; shop; tradsmn; rest; snacks; bar; BBQ; playgrnd; htd pool & paddling pool; tennis; canoeing; games area; cycle hire; internet; entmnt; TV rm; dogs €7.20; Eng spkn; adv bkg; quiet; ccard acc; red low ssn; CCI. "Spectacular scenery; excel rvside site; helpful staff; price depends on size of pitch; gd san facs." ♦ 1 Apr-30 Sep. € 44.00 2009*

See advertisement on next page

VALLON PONT D'ARC *9D2* (1.5km SE Rural) *44.39467, 4.39909* **Mondial Camping, Route des Gorges, 07150 Vallon-Pont-d'Arc [04 75 88 00 44; fax 04 75 37 13 73; reserv-info@mondial-camping.com; www.mondial-camping.com]** Fr N exit A7 Montélimar Nord junc 17 dir Le Teil, Villeneuve-de-Berg, Vogüé, Ruoms then Vallon-Pont-d'Arc. Take D290, Rte des Gorges de l'Ardèche to site in 1.5km. Fr S exit A7 junc 19 at Bollène, dir Bourg-St Andéol, then D4 to St Remèze & Vallon-Pont-d'Arc. Lge, hdg/mkd pitch, shd; htd wc; chem disp; mv service pnt; serviced pitches (extra charge); baby facs; shwrs inc; el pnts (6-10A) inc; gas; Indtte; shop; rest; snacks; bar; playgrnd; 2 htd pools; waterslides & aqua park; canoeing; tennis adj; games rm; entmnt; internet; TV; some statics; dogs €4.50; poss cr; Eng spkn; adv bkg; quiet; ccard acc; red low ssn/snr citizens; CCI. "Dir access to rv, Ardèche gorges & canoe facs; gd touring base; excel site." ♦ 20 Mar-30 Sep. € 40.00 2009*

See advertisement opposite

VALLON PONT D'ARC *9D2* (2km SW Rural) *44.39591, 4.38008* **Camping Le Casque Roi, Route de Vallon-Pont-d'Arc, 07150 Salavas [04 75 88 04 23; fax 04 75 37 18 64; casqueroi@orange.fr; www.casqueroi.com]** Take D579 S fr Vallon-Pont-d'Arc; site on R 500m after bdge over Ardèche. Sm, mkd pitch, shd; htd wc (some cont); baby facs; shwrs inc; el pnts (10A) inc; Indtte; shop; snacks; bar; playgrnd; pool; rv 1km; cycle hire; entmnt; 10% statics; dogs €4; poss cr; quiet; CCI. "Canoeing & guided walks." 1 Apr-12 Nov. € 27.00 2007*

VALLON PONT D'ARC *9D2* (800m W Rural) *44.40509, 4.37827* **Camping La Roubine, Route de Ruoms, 07150 Vallon-Pont-d'Arc [tel/fax 04 75 88 04 56; roubine.ardeche@wanadoo.fr; www.camping-roubine.com]** Site on W side of Vallon-Pont-d'Arc off D579, well sp by rvside. Med, hdg/mkd pitch, pt shd; htd wc; chem disp; mv service pnt; baby facs; shwrs inc; el pnts (10A) €4.50; gas; Indtte; shop; rest; snacks; bar; BBQ (gas) playgrnd; htd pool; sm waterslide; rv & sand beach adj; fishing; canoeing; tennis; cycle hire; games area; entmnt; wifi; TV rm; 15% statics; dogs €4; Eng spkn; adv bkg; quiet; ccard acc. "Excel, well-run site in lovely area; excel rest; guided walks high ssn." ♦ 26 Apr-16 Sep. € 43.00 2009*

VALLON PONT D'ARC *9D2* (2km W Rural) *44.4086, 4.3542* **Camping La Plage Fleurie, Les Mazes, 07150 Vallon-Pont-d'Arc [04 75 88 01 15; fax 04 75 88 11 31; info@laplagefleurie.com; www.laplagefleurie.com]** Site on main 'Route Touristique' of Ardèche: D579, 4.5km SE of Ruoms turn R at sp La Plage Fleurie in 1.5km. Fr N sp easily missed; no sp fr S. Lge, mkd pitch, pt sl, terr, shd; wc; baby facs; shwrs inc; chem disp; el pnts (10A) €4.20; gas; Indtte; shop & 1.5km; tradsmn; snacks; rest; bar; BBQ; playgrnd; pool; sand beach & rv; canoe hire; fishing; sailing; entmnt; TV rm; 10% statics; dogs €4; Eng spkn; adv bkg rec high ssn; quiet; red low ssn; CCI. "Conv Gorges de l'Ardèche; gd position on rvside; excel san facs." ♦ 24 Apr-13 Sep. € 29.90 2008*

VALLON PONT D'ARC *9D2* (2km W Rural) *44.41251, 4.35018* **Camping L'Arc en Ciel, Route de Ruoms, Les Mazes, 07150 Vallon-Pont-d'Arc [04 75 88 04 65; fax 04 75 37 16 99; info@arcenciel-camping.com; www.arcenciel-camping.com]** Take D579 W fr Vallon. After 1.1km bear L for Les Mazes. Pass thro vill & in about 1.7km bear L at camp sp. Lge, pt sl, pt shd; wc; baby facs; shwrs; el pnts (6A) €3.50; Indtte; shop; rest; snacks; bar; playgrnd; pool; paddling pool; shgl beach & rv; fishing; tennis, horseriding nr; games rm; entmnt; some statics; dogs €3; poss cr; adv bkg; quiet; ccard acc. "Pleasant site on rv bank; excel." ♦ 16 May-9 Sep. € 23.50 2006*

VALLON PONT D'ARC *9D2* (2km W Rural) *44.40645, 4.36448* **Camping Le Beau Rivage, Les Mazes, 07150 Vallon-Pont-d'Arc [tel/fax 04 75 88 03 54; campingbeaurivage@wanadoo.fr; www.beaurivage-camping.com]** Take D579 W fr Vallon. After approx 1km bear L for Les Mazes at rndabt. After 800m turn L down side rd for site. Med, mkd pitch, terr, shd; wc (some cont); chem disp; baby facs; shwrs; el pnts (6A) €3.90; gas; Indry rm; shop & 2km; tradsmn; rest 2km; bar; BBQ; playgrnd; htd pool; fishing; sailing; canoe hire; entmnt; TV rm; 5% statics; dogs €2; phone; poss cr; Eng spkn; ccard acc; red low ssn; CCI. "Vg quality, clean, family site; dir access to rv; friendly owners; poss diff access some pitches for lge o'fits due trees; excel." 1 May-13 Sep. € 24.00 2009*

VALLON PONT D'ARC *9D2* (3km W Rural) *44.42332, 4.31565* **Camping Le Chassezac, Route d'Alès, 07120 Sampzon [04 75 39 60 71 or 06 81 96 68 76 (mob); fax 04 75 39 76 35; info@campinglechassezac.com; www.campinglechassezac.com]** Fr Aubenas S on D579. Approx 2.5km past Ruoms at rndabt, turn R onto D111. Foll sp 2km to site on R. Med, mkd pitch, pt shd; wc (some cont); chem disp; mv service pnt; baby facs; shwrs inc; el pnts (6A) €3.90; Indtte; shop; rest; snacks; bar; BBQ (gas only); playgrnd; pool; rv adj; fishing; cycle & canoe hire; horseriding; TV; 15% statics; dogs €2; phone; o'night m'van area; poss cr; Eng spkn; adv bkg; quiet; CCI. "Friendly, helpful staff; vg." ♦ 1 Apr-30 Sep. € 20.50 2008*

VALLON PONT D'ARC *9D2* (5km NW Rural) *44.42958, 4.35528* **Yelloh! Village Soleil Vivarais, 07120 Sampzon [04 75 39 67 56 or 04 66 73 97 39; fax 04 75 39 64 69; info@soleil-vivarais.com; www.soleil-vivarais.com or www.yellohvillage.com]** Take D579 fr Vallon-Pont-d'Arc. After 6km turn L onto D161, cross narr bdge over Rv Ardèche. Site immed on R. Lge, hdg/mkd pitch, shd; wc; chem disp; mv service pnt; baby facs; shwrs inc; el pnts (10A) inc; gas; Indtte; shop; rest; snacks; bar; playgrnd; htd pool; shgl beach & rv 500m; canoe hire; tennis; games rm; entmnt Jul/Aug; TV; 50% statics; dogs €3; poss cr; Eng spkn; adv bkg; quiet; ccard acc. "Interesting area; busy site in gd location; sm pitches poss diff lge o'fits; gd entmnt." ♦ 5 Apr-15 Sep. € 42.00 2008*

VALLON PONT D'ARC *9D2* (5km NW Rural) *44.42900, 4.35515* **FLOWER Camping Le Riviera, 07120 Sampzon [04 75 39 67 57; fax 04 75 93 95 57; leriviera@wanadoo.fr; www.campingleriviera.com or www.flowercamping.com]** Take D579 W fr Vallon-Pont-d'Arc. After 6.5km cross narr bdge over Ardèche on D161. Site immed on L. Lge, mkd pitch, pt shd; wc; chem disp; mv service pnt; shwrs inc; el pnts (10A) inc; gas; Indry rm; shop 100m; rest; snacks; bar; BBQ; playgrnd; pool; paddling pool; rv adj; shgl beach; tennis; games rm; cycle hire; horseriding; entmnt; TV rm; some statics; dogs €3; poss cr; some rd noise. "Attractive pools." 1 Apr-30 Sep. € 36.00 2007*

VALLON PONT D'ARC *9D2* (6km NW Rural) *44.42279, 4.3224* **Camping La Bastide en Ardèche, Route de Gros-Pierres, 07120 Sampzon [04 75 39 64 72; fax 04 75 39 73 28; info@rcn-labastideenardeche.fr; www.rcn-campings.fr]** Fr Vallon take D579 W & turn L onto D111. Cross rv, site sp on L. Lge, mkd pitch, pt shd; htd wc; chem disp; sauna; shwrs; el pnts (3-5A) inc; gas; Indtte; shop high ssn; tradsmn; rest, snacks, bar high ssn; BBQ (gas); playgrnd; 2 htd pools; canoeing; fishing; sailing; tennis; games area; entmnt; horseriding; entmnt; TV rm; 70% statics; dogs €4; Eng spkn; adv bkg; quiet; ccard acc; red low ssn; CCI. "Well-run site." ♦ 22 Mar-25 Oct. € 43.50 2007*

VALLORCINE *9A4* (1km SE Rural) *46.0242, 6.92370* **Camping des Montets, Le Buet, 74660 Vallorcine [04 50 54 60 45 or 04 50 54 24 13 (LS); fax 04 50 54 01 34; camping.des.montets@wanadoo.fr; www.vallorcine.com]** N fr Chamonix on D1506 (N506) via Col de Montets; Le Buet 2km S of Vallorcine; site sp nr Le Buet stn. Fr Martigny (Switzerland) cross border via Col de la Forclaz; then D1506 to Vallorcine; cont to Le Buet in 1km. Med, hdg/mkd pitch, pt shd; wc (some cont); chem disp (wc); shwrs inc; el pnts (3-6A) €2-3; lndtte; shops 1km; tradsmn; snacks; tennis adj; no statics; dogs; train 500m; Eng spkn; quiet; CCI. "Excel walking direct fr site; free train pass to Chamonix; immac facs; vg." ♦ 1 Jun-15 Sep. € 13.10 2007*

VALLOUISE see Argentière La Bessée, L' *9C3*

VALOGNES *1C4* (1km N Urban) *49.51154, -1.47534* **Camp Municipal Le Bocage, Rue Neuve, 50700 Valognes [02 33 95 82 01 or 06 10 84 59 33 (mob); environement@mairie-valognes.fr; www.mairie-valognes.fr]** Off N13 Cherbourg to Carentan take 1st exit to Valonges, turn L just past Champion at Lidl sp; site sp bef & in town. Fr Carentan dir, take 3rd R after 4th set traff lts. Sm, hdg/mkd pitch, hdstg, pt shd; wc (cont); chem disp (wc); shwrs inc; el pnts (6-10A) €2.10-3.50 (poss rev pol); gas; supmkt 100m; rest, snacks, bar nr; dogs €0.50; poss cr; quiet; ccard not acc; CCI. "Excel, gem of a site; clean san facs; friendly staff; conv Cherbourg ferries (17km); poss itinerants; warden calls 1900-2000, site self if office clsd; gates clsd 2200-0600; ideal NH." ♦ 1 Apr-15 Oct. € 9.00 2009*

VALRAS PLAGE *10F1* (500m N Urban/Coastal) *43.25416, 3.28861* **Camping Le Levant, Ave Charles Cauquil, 34350 Valras-Plage [04 67 32 04 45; www.campingdulevant.com]** Exit A9 junc 35 onto D64 twd Valras-Plage. At rndabt junc with D19, turn L into Ave Charles Cauquil, site sp. Med, mkd pitch, pt shd; htd wc; chem disp; mv service pnt; baby facs; shwrs inc; el pnts (10A) inc; lndtte; shops; snacks; bar; BBQ; playgrnd; htd pool; paddling pool; sand beach 800m; games area; 40% statics; dogs €4; adv bkg; quiet. "Pleasant family site; gd facs; friendly, helpful staff." 11 Apr-13 Sep. € 30.00 2008*

VALRAS PLAGE *10F1* (1km N Coastal) *43.25670, 3.28480* **Camping Les Sables du Midi (formerly L'Occitanie), Chemin de Querelles, 34350 Valras-Plage [04 67 32 33 86; www.siblu.fr/lessablesdumidi]** Fr A9/E15 exit junc 35 at Béziers Est & join D64 sp Valras-Plage. Site is immed on L after rndabt at ent to Valras-Plage Est. Lge, hdg/mkd pitch, hdstg, pt sl, shd; htd wc; chem disp; mv service pnt; baby facs; shwrs inc; el pnts (5A) inc (poss rev pol); lndtte; shop 1km; tradsmn; rest; snacks; bar; BBQ (gas/charcoal only); playgrnd; pool; paddling pool; waterslide; sand beach 1km; sailing; fishing; games area; entmnt; wifi; games/TV rm; 75% statics; no dogs; c'van/m'van max 7m Jul/Aug; poss cr; Eng spkn; adv bkg; quiet; ccard acc; red low ssn/long stay; CCI. "Lively town; mkt Mon & Fri am." ♦ 1 Jun-11 Sep. € 48.00 2009*

VALRAS PLAGE *10F1* (3km SW Coastal) *43.23750, 3.26166* **Camping Domaine de la Yole, 34350 Valras-Plage [04 67 37 33 87; fax 04 67 37 44 89; info@campinglayole.com; www.campinglayole.com]** Leave A9/E15 at Béziers-Ouest; foll D64 twd coast dir Valras-Plage, then Valras-Plage-Ouest & site sp. V lge, hdg/mkd pitch, hdstg, shd; wc (some cont); chem disp; baby facs; shwrs inc; el pnts (5A) inc; gas; lndtte; supmkt; rest; snacks; bar; BBQ (charcoal/gas); playgrnd; 2 pools & paddling pool; waterslide; sand beach 400m; tennis; cycle hire; fishing, horseriding 3km; games area; games rm; entmnt; wifi; TV; tour ops statics; dogs €4.50 (not on beach); poss cr; Eng spkn; adv bkg; quiet but some rd noise; ccard acc; red low ssn; CCI. "Excel; gd for all age groups; mkt Mon & Fri." ♦ 24 Apr-18 Sep. € 48.00 ABS - C03 2009*

VALRAS PLAGE *10F1* (3km SW Coastal) *43.23101, 3.25330* **Camping Sunêlia Les Vagues, Chemin des Montilles, 34350 Vendres-Plage [04 67 37 33 12; fax 04 67 37 50 36; contact@lesvagues.net; www.lesvagues.net]** Exit A9 junc 36 onto D64 to Valras-Plage then Vendres-Plage. Site sp. Lge, pt shd; wc; baby facs; shwrs inc; el pnts inc; lndtte; shop; rest; snacks; bar; playgrnd; htd pool complex; paddling pool; waterslides; jacuzzi; sand beach 300m; games area; horseriding 5km; entmnt; TV rm; 75% statics; dogs €6; adv bkg; red low ssn. "Recep helpful; clean san facs; excel." ♦ 1 Apr-30 Sep. € 42.00 (CChq acc) 2007*

VALRAS PLAGE *10F1* (2.5km W Urban/Coastal) *43.22750, 3.24329* **Camping Blue Bayou, Vendres-Plage-Ouest, 34350 Valras-Plage [04 67 37 41 97; fax 04 67 37 53 00; bluebayou@infonie.fr; www.bluebayou.fr]** Exit Béziers Ouest fr A9 twd Valras-Plage & Vendres-Plage-Ouest. Lge, mkd pitch, pt shd; wc; baby facs; shwrs inc; el pnts inc; gas; lndtte; shop; rest; snacks; bar; playgrnd; 2 htd pools; waterslide; sand beach 300m; Rv Aude 1km; tennis; games area; games rm; entmnt; 30% statics; dogs €5; adv bkg; quiet; CCI. "Poss dusty/windy end Jul/Aug, gd beach & pool." 1 May-30 Sep. € 38.00 2006*

VALRAS PLAGE *10F1* (3.5km W Rural) *43.25925, 3.27562* **Camping Domaine Les Vignes d'Or, Route de Valras, 34350 Valras-Plage [04 67 32 37 18; fax 04 67 32 00 80; info@vignesdor.com; www.vignesdor.com or www.camping-franceloc.fr]** Exit A9 junc 35 Béziers Est onto D64 to Sérignan then dir Valras-Plage; site sp. Med, hdg/mkd pitch, pt shd; wc; baby facs; shwrs inc; el pnts (6A) €3.70; lndtte; tradsmn; rest; snacks; bar; playgrnd; pool; beach 2.5km; games area; entmnt; 95% statics; dogs €4.30; quiet; red long stay; CCI. "Ltd touring pitches; gd NH only." ♦ 1 Apr-30 Sep. € 26.00 2007*

VALRAS PLAGE *10F1* (5km W Coastal) *43.2260, 3.24433* **Camping Les Foulègues, 34350 Valras-Plage [04 67 37 33 65; info@campinglesfoulegues.com; www.campinglesfoulegues.com]** Exit fr A9 junc 36 onto D64 dir Valras-Plage; then foll sp Valras-Plage Ouest, by-passing town. Site sp. Lge, hdg/mkd pitch, shd; wc (some cont); chem disp; shwrs inc; el pnts (6A) inc; gas; lndtte; shop; snacks; bar; BBQ (sep area); playgrnd; pool; paddling pool; sand beach 500m; watersports; cycle hire; tennis; games area; entmnt; internet; 80% statics; dogs €4; phone; bus adj; poss cr; Eng spkn; adv bkg; ccard acc; CCI. "Quiet, family site opp nature reserve; gd pitches; welcoming owner; excel beaches; mkt nrby; gd." 1 Jun-25 Sep. € 37.50 2007*

VALRAS PLAGE *10F1* (5km NW Rural) *43.29273, 3.26710* **Camping La Gabinelle, 7 Rue de la Grille, 34410 Sauvian [04 67 39 50 87 or 04 67 32 30 79; info@lagabinelle.com; www.lagabinelle.com]** Exit A9 at Béziers Ouest, turn R twd beaches sp S to Sauvian on D19. Site 500m on L thro town. Med, pt shd; wc; chem disp; shwrs inc; el pnts (5A) €3; lndtte; shops, rest, snacks adj; bar; playgrnd; pool; sand beach 5km; fishing 1km; canoeing 2km; tennis; games area; games rm; entmnt; TV; dogs €3.50; adv bkg; quiet, but poss noise fr bar; red low ssn/long stay. "Friendly; suitable lge m'vans; low ssn ltd san facs & poss unkempt; sh walk to delightful old vill." ♦ 12 Apr-12 Sep. € 19.00 2009*

VALREAS *9D2* (1km N Rural) *44.39264, 4.99245* **Camping La Coronne, Route de Pègue, 84600 Valréas [04 90 35 03 78; fax 04 90 35 26 73]** Fr Nyons take D538 W to Valréas. Exit town on D10 rd to Taulignan, immed after x-ing bdge over Rv Coronne turn R into D196 sp Le Pègue. Site on R in 100m on rvside. Sp app fr E but easy to miss; app fr W; well sp in Valréas. Med, hdg/mkd pitch, pt shd; wc (some cont); chem disp; mv service pnt; shwrs inc; el pnts (3-10A) inc; gas; lndtte; shop; tradsmn; rest; snacks; bar; BBQ; playgrnd; pool; paddling pool; fishing; entmnt; TV; dogs €0.80; phone; poss cr; Eng spkn; adv bkg; quiet; ccard acc; CCI. "Sm pitches; excel pool; facs need refurb & poss unclean; site clsd 2200-0700." ♦ 1 Mar-30 Sep. € 15.00 2006*

VALREAS *9D2* (7km NE Rural) **Camp Municipal La Rochecourbière, Ave du Grillon, 26230 Grignan [04 75 46 50 06; fax 04 75 46 93 13; mairie.grignan@wanadoo.fr]** Sp at E end of D541 bypass of Grignan; Ave du Grillon runs NE off D541; site in 100m. Do not go into town. Sm, hdg/mkd pitch, pt sl, pt shd; wc (some cont); chem disp (wc); shwrs inc; el pnts inc; dogs; quiet. "Unspoilt, simple site outside ramparts of historic town; clean, modern san facs; if office clsd site self or contact Mairie; gd." ♦ 1 Jul-31 Aug. € 12.00 2008*

VALREAS *9D2* (8km SE Rural) *44.31230, 4.93569* **Camping de l'Hérein, Route de Bouchet, 84820 Visan [04 90 41 95 99; fax 04 90 41 91 72; acceuil@camping-visan.com; www.camping-visan.com]** E fr Bollène on D94/D994 twd Nyons; after Tulette turn L (N) onto D576 dir Visan & Valréas; sp in vill opp PO; turn L onto D161 Bouchet rd; site on L in 800m just over sm bdge. Med, hdg/mkd pitch, pt shd; wc; chem disp; shwrs inc; el pnts (6-10A) €3-3.50; gas; lndtte; shop & 1km; tradsmn; snacks; bar; playgrnd; pool; dogs €1.50; quiet; adv bkg rec; ccard acc; CCI. "Lge pitches; well-wooded site; poss unkempt low ssn; facs poss stretched high ssn; friendly staff; vg." ♦15 Mar-15 Oct. € 14.50 2007*

I'm going to fill in some site report forms and post them off to the Club; we could win a ferry crossing – it's here on page 12.

VALREAS *9D2* (8km W Rural) *44.41131, 4.89112* **Camping Les Truffières, 1100 Chemin de Bellevue-d'Air, Nachony, 26230 Grignan [tel/fax 04 75 46 93 62; info@lestruffieres.com; www.lestruffieres.com]** Fr A7 take D133 E twds Grignan. On W o'skts of vill turn S on D71. In 1km turn L at sp. Site is 200m on R. Fr Nyons take D538 W to Grignan. Sm, mkd pitch, shd; wc; chem disp; mv service pnt; shwrs inc; el pnts (10A) €4.20; gas; lndtte; shop 1km; tradsmn, rest, snacks high ssn; bar; communal BBQ only; playgrnd; pool; fishing; 5% statics; no dogs; Eng spkn; adv bkg; quiet; red low ssn; CCI. "Pleasant owners; 20 min stroll to town; immac san facs; gd pool; some pitches diff access; well-wooded site, poss dusty; excel." ♦ 20 Apr-20 Sep. € 17.00 2009*

VANDENESSE EN AUXOIS *6G1* (3km NE Rural) *47.23661, 4.62880* **Camping Le Lac de Panthier, 21320 Vandenesse-en-Auxois [03 80 49 21 94; fax 03 80 49 25 80; info@lac-de-panthier.com; www.lac-de-panthier.com]** Exit A6 junc 24 (A38) at Pouilly-en-Auxois; foll D16/D18 to Vandenesse; turn L on D977bis, cross canal bdge & cont strt for 3km to site on L. Fr SW (Autun) on D981 approx 12km after Arnay-le-Duc turn R onto D994 sp Châteauneuf. At x-rds cont onto D977bis then as above. Lge, hdg/mkd pitch, pt sl, terr, pt shd; wc; chem disp (wc); sauna; shwrs inc; el pnts (6A) inc (some rev pol); lndtte; shop & 6km; rest; snacks; bar; playgrnd; 2 pools (1 htd, covrd); waterslide; lake beach 50m; fishing; cycle hire; entmnt; sat TV; dogs €3; adv bkg ess; Oct open Fri, Sat & Sun; CCI. "Lovely area; views fr higher pitches; well-run site operating with Les Voiliers adj; lge pitches, most sl & blocks req; facs poss stretched high ssn; gd cycling & walks round lake; popular NH; vg." ♦ 5 Apr-12 Oct. € 25.00 (CChq acc) 2008*

VANDIERES see Dormans *3D4*

France

⊞ **VANNES** *2F3* (5km N Rural) *47.73035, -2.72795* **Camping du Haras, Kersimon Vannes-Meucon, 56250 Monterblanc [02 97 44 66 06 or 06 71 00 05 59 (mob LS); fax 02 97 44 49 41; contact@campingvannes.com; www.campingvannes.com]** App fr N165 turn L onto D767 sp Airport. Go N for 7km & turn R onto D778 for 1km & turn R again. After 1km approx, turn L onto Airport Perimeter Rd, site sp on W side. App fr N on D767, join D778 & as above. Med, hdg/mkd pitch, hdstg, pt shd; htd wc; chem disp; mv service pnt; fam bthrm; shwrs inc; el pnts (4-10A) €3-6; gas; Indtte; sm shop; tradsmn; snacks; bar; BBQ; playgrnd; htd pools; paddling pool; waterslide; sand beach 12km; lake sw 3km; fishing; tennis; horseriding 300m; trampoline; cycle hire; games rm; 30% statics; dogs €4; Eng spkn; adv bkg; quiet with minimal aircraft noise; ccard acc; red long stay/long ssn/CCI. "Lovely site; basic facs; ltd space for tourers; pitches soft in wet." ♦ € 19.00 2009*

VANNES *2F3* (10km SE Rural) *47.64045, -2.65437* **Camping La Peupleraie, Le Marais, 56450 Theix [tel/fax 02 97 43 09 46; contact@camping-lapeupleraie.com; www.camping-lapeupleraie.com]** Exit N165 into Theix foll sp dir Treffléan, site off D116/D104 2.5km NE of Theix, well sp. Med, shd; wc; chem disp; shwrs inc; el pnts (5A) €2 (rev pol); Indtte; shops 3km; tradsmn; playgrnd; games area; mainly statids; dogs €1; adv bkg; quiet; 10% red CCI. "San facs in need of update; gd NH for Vannes." 15 Apr-15 Oct. € 11.50 2006*

VANNES *2F3* (3km S Rural) *47.62754, -2.74117* **FFCC Camping Moulin de Cantizac, 2 Rue des Orchidées, 56860 Séné [tel/fax 02 97 66 90 26; info@camping-vannes.com; www.camping-vannes.com]** S fr Vannes on D199 twds Séné. Site on L at rndabt beside rv. Med, hdg pitch, pt sl, pt shd; wc (some cont); shwrs inc; el pnts (6A) €3.40; Indtte; tradsmn; sand beach 4km; boating; wifi; 10% statics; dogs €1.80; quiet. "Superb cent for birdwatching." 1 May-15 Oct. € 8.50 2008*

VANNES *2F3* (3km SW Coastal) *47.63365, -2.78008* **FFCC Camp Municipal de Conleau, 188 Ave Maréchal Juin, 56000 Vannes [02 97 63 13 88; fax 02 97 40 38 82; camping@mairie-vannes.fr; www.mairie-vannes.fr]** Exit N165 at Vannes Ouest junc; Conleau sp on R. Site twd end of rd on R. If on N165 fr Auray take 1st exit sp Vannes & at 2nd rndabt R (sp) to avoid town cent. C'vans not allowed thro town cent. Lge, mkd pitch, pt sl, pt shd; wc; chem disp; mv service pnt; shwrs; el pnts (6A) €3.50 (some rev pol); Indtte; tradsmn; playgrnd; sea water pool nr; sand beach 300m; entmnt; TV; dogs €1.50; bus adj; adv bkg; quiet; ccard acc. "Most pitches sl; sep area for m'vans by rd - little shd & poss long walk to san facs." ♦ 1 Apr-30 Sep. € 17.30 2008*

VANNES *2F3* (5km SW Coastal) *47.62206, -2.80110* **Camping de Penboch, 9 Chemin de Penboch, 56610 Arradon [02 97 44 71 29; fax 02 97 44 79 10; camping.penboch@wanadoo.fr; www.camping-penboch.fr]** Exit Brest-Nantes N165 Vannes by-pass onto D101 & foll sp Arradon. Site well sp. Lge, hdg/mkd pitch, pt shd; wc (some cont); chem disp; mv service pnt; baby facs; shwrs inc; el pnts (6-10A) €3.50-4.50 (poss rev pol); gas; Indtte; sm shop & 2km; tradsmn; snacks; bar; BBQ; playgrnd; covrd htd pool; waterslide; sand beach 200m; games rm; wifi; TV rm; some statics; dogs €3.50 (high ssn); Eng spkn; adv bkg rec high ssn; quiet; rccard acc; red low ssn; CCI. "Gd san facs; steel pegs req; o'verflow area with facs; plenty for youngsters; gd coast walks; excel." ♦ 4 Apr-26 Sep. € 34.80 2009*

VANNES *2F3* (6km SW Coastal) *47.62108, -2.84025* **Camping de l'Allée, 56610 Arradon [02 97 44 01 98; fax 02 97 44 73 74; www.camping-allee.com]** Fr Vannes take D101 & D101A to Arradon. Take by-pass & take 1st exit at rndabt & foll sp. Site to SW of Arradon. Fr Auray on D101 turn R on C203 immed after Moustoir. Med, some hdg/mkd pitch, pt sl, pt shd; wc; chem disp; baby facs; shwrs inc; el pnts (6-10A) €2.80-4.20 (poss long leads req); gas; Indtte; sm shop & 2km; tradsmn; snacks; playgrnd; htd pool (high ssn); shgl beach 600m; games/TV rm; 5% statics; dogs €1.60; poss cr; Eng spkn; adv bkg; quiet; 20% red low ssn; CCI. "Delightful, family-run site in orchard; site yourself if office clsd; modern san facs; gd walks; gd touring base." ♦ 1 Apr-30 Sep. € 18.40 2009*

VANS, LES *9D1* (2.5km E Rural) *44.40953, 4.16768* **Camping Domaine des Chênes, 07140 Chassagnes-Haut [04 75 37 34 35; fax 04 75 37 20 10; reception@domaine-des-chenes.fr; www.domaine-des-chenes.fr]** Fr town cent take D104A dir Aubenas. After Peugeot g'ge turn R onto D295 at garden cent twd Chassagnes. Site on L after 2km; sp adj Rv Chassezac. Med, terr, pt sl, pt shd; wc (some cont); mv service pnt; baby facs; shwrs inc; el pnts (10A) inc; Indtte; shop; rest; snacks; bar; BBQ; playgrnd; pool; rv fishing 500m; 80% statics; dogs €2.50; poss cr; adv bkg; quiet; ccard acc; CCI. "Lovely shady site; ideal for birdwatchers." 1 Apr-30 Sep. € 24.00 2007*

VANS, LES *9D1* (3.5km NW Rural) *44.41613, 4.09229* **Camping Le Mas du Serre, 07140 Gravières [04 75 37 33 84; camping-le-mas-du-serre@wanadoo.fr; www.campinglemasduserre.com]** NW fr Les Vans on D901 dir Villefort; in 2km turn R onto D113 dir Gravières; in 1.5km turn R bef bdge. NB Awkward turn downhill. Foll site sp. Recep in cent of site. Med, pt sl, pt terr, hdstg, shd; wc (some cont); chem disp (wc); shwrs inc; el pnts (6A) €3 (long lead poss req); supmkt 4km; snacks; bar; pool; paddling pool; boating on rv nrby; canyoning & caves nrby; games area; entmnt; 10% statics; dogs €1.50; adv bkg; quiet; red low ssn. "Beautiful scenery; san facs clean but ltd; gd walking." 1 Apr-1 Oct € 18.50 2009*

VANS, LES *9D1* (5km NW Rural) *44.43722, 4.08028* **Camping Les Gorges de Chassezac, Champ d'Eynes, 07140 Malarce-sur-la-Thines [04 75 39 45 12; campinggorgeschassezac@wanadoo.fr; www.campinggorgeschassezac.com]** Fr Les Vans cent, dir Gravière, approx 5km thro Gravière cont, site on L. Med, mkd pitch, pt sl, terr, shd; wc (many cont); chem disp; shwrs; el pnts (6A) €3; gas; lndtte; shop; tradsmn; snacks; bar; playgrnd; rv adj; TV; dogs €1; entmnt; poss cr; Eng spkn; adv bkg; quiet; CCI. "Peaceful site." ♦ 1 May-31 Aug. € 13.00 2006*

VARADES see Ancenis *2G4*

VARCES ALLIERES ET RISSET see Grenoble *9C3*

VARENNES EN ARGONNE *5D1* (N Rural) *49.22935, 5.03424* **Camp Municipal Le Pâquis, Rue St Jean, 55270 Varennes-en-Argonne [03 29 80 71 01 (Mairie); fax 03 29 80 71 43; mairievarennesenargonne@wanadoo.fr]** On D946 Vouziers/Clermont-en-Argonne rd; sp by bdge in vill, on banks of Rv Aire, 200m N of bdge. NB Ignore sp by bdge to Camping Lac Vert (not nr). Med, pt shd; wc; shwrs inc; el pnts (3-6A) €2.90; lndtte; shops adj; BBQ; playgrnd; rv fishing; dog €0.40; quiet. "Pleasant site with gd facs; gd (hilly) cycle ride taking in US WWI cemetary." 24 Apr-1 Oct. € 7.90 2009*

VARENNES SUR ALLIER *9A1* (3km NW Rural) *46.33273, 3.38836* **Camping Le Château de Chazeuil, Route de Moulins, 03150 Varennes-sur-Allier [tel/fax 04 70 45 83 26; camping-dechazeuil@hetnet.nl; www.camping-dechazeuil.eu]** Ent to chateau grounds 200m N of rndabt at junc of N7 & D46. (E & immed L bet tall iron gates). Med, pt shd; wc (some cont); chem disp; mv service pnt; shwrs inc; el pnts (6A) €3 (long lead poss req); lndtte; shops, rest, snacks & bar 2km; tradsmn; BBQ; playgrnd; pool; fishing; games rm; games area; horseriding; internet; dogs €1; Eng spkn; adv bkg; quiet; CCI. "Superb, quiet site; friendly owners; excel pool & san facs, but ltd wcs & el pnts; rec." ♦ 1 Apr-15 Oct. € 18.75 2008*

VARENNES SUR LOIRE see Saumur *4G1*

⊞ **VARILHES** *8G3* (Urban) *43.04714, 1.63096* **Camp Municipal du Parc du Château, Ave de 8 Mai 1945, 09120 Varilhes [05 61 67 42 84 or 05 61 60 55 54 (TO); marie-line.bordin165@orange.fr; www.camping-ariege-pyrenees.com]** Exit N20/E9 at sp Varilhes. Turn N in town on D624. Site 250m on L (sp) just bef leisure cent adj Rv Ariège. Med, mkd pitch, terr, pt shd; htd wc; shwrs inc; el pnts (5-10A) €5.90-6.40; lndtte; shops adj & 200m; tradsmn; rest 200m; snacks; bar 300m; playgrnd; pool adj; rv fishing adj; games area; 20% statics; dogs; adv bkg; quiet. € 11.50 2007*

⊞ **VARILHES** *8G3* (3km NW Rural) *43.06258, 1.62101* **FFCC Camping Les Mijeannes, Route de Ferriès, 09120 Rieux-de-Pelleport [05 61 60 82 23; fax 05 61 67 74 80; lesmijeannes@wanadoo.fr; www.campinglesmijeannes.com]** Exit N20 sp Varilhes; on app Varilhes cent join 1-way system; 1st R at Hôtel de Ville; over rv bdge; foll camp sps; site 2km on R. Med, hdg pitch, pt shd; wc; chem disp; shwrs inc; el pnts (10A) €4.10; tradsmn; bar; BBQ; playgrnd; pool; fishing; games area; TV; dogs €1.10; some Eng spkn; adv bkg; quiet; red low ssn; CCI. "Peaceful site by rv; helpful owner; gd size pitches; poss ltd facs low ssn; weekly theme nights high ssn; excel." € 17.80 2009*

VARREDDES see Meaux *3D3*

VARZY *4G4* (1km N Rural) *47.37242, 3.38311* **Camp Municipal du Moulin Naudin, 58210 Varzy [03 86 29 43 12; fax 03 86 29 72 73]** Fr N151 in Varzy, turn N onto D5, site sp. Sm, pt shd; some hdg pitch; wc; shwrs inc; el pnts (5A) €2.10; tradsmn; shops 1.5km; fishing; tennis nrby; quiet. 1 May-30 Sep. € 8.60 2007*

VATAN *4H3* (8km N Rural) *47.13479, 1.85121* **Camp Municipal St Phalier, 2 Chemin Trompe-Souris, 18310 Graçay [02 48 51 24 14 or 02 48 51 42 07 (Mairie); fax 02 48 51 25 92; camping-gracay@wanadoo.fr; www.camping.gracay.info]** Leave A20 at junc 9 & take D83 to Graçay. On o'skts of vill turn L & immed turn L foll sp to Cent Omnisport & site. Sm, mkd pitch, pt shd; wc (some cont); chem disp; shwrs €1; el pnts (10A) €2.56; rest, bar & shop 1km; tradsmn; playgrnd & pool adj; fishing; dogs €1; phone; Eng spkn; quiet; CCI. "A lovely little site; well-kept; plenty of space lge o'fits - site yourself; excel clean san facs; sm lake & park adj; vill in walking dist; gd NH fr A20." 1 Apr-15 Sep. € 9.30 2009*

VATAN *4H3* (1km S Rural) *47.06540, 1.80043* **Camping Le Moulin de la Ronde (Naturist), Route de la Ronde, 36150 Vatan [02 54 49 83 28; www.moulindelaronde.com]** Fr town cent take D136 S twds A20; at supmkt turn R; site on L 500m; sp. Sm, hdg/mkt pitch, pt shd; htd wc; chem disp; shwrs inc; el pnts (10A) €2.50 (long lead poss req); gas 1km; supmkt 400m; tradsmn; snacks; bar; BBQ; playgrnd; pool; games area; games rm; dogs €1.60; adv bkg; quiet; INF card req. "Pleasant, simple site; helpful owners; dated & modern san facs; take great care with el pnts; mkt Wed; gd NH." 1 Apr-30 Sep. € 14.90 2008*

VATAN *4H3* (W Urban) *47.07131, 1.80573* **Camp Municipal de la Ruelle au Loup, Rue du Collège, 36150 Vatan [02 54 49 91 37 or 02 54 49 76 31 (Mairie); fax 02 54 49 93 72; vatan-mairie1@wanadoo.fr; www.vatan-en-berry.com]** Exit A20 junc 10 onto D922 to town cent. Take D2 dir Guilly & foll site sp - 2nd on L (easily missed). Med, hdg/mkd pitch, pt shd; wc; mv service pnt; shwrs inc; el pnts (10A) €2 (rev pol); lndtte; shops, rests 200m; playgrnd; pool adj; adv bkg; quiet; ccard not acc; CCI. "Pleasant, clean, well-kept site in park; spacious pitches; basic but clean san facs; twin-axles extra; easy access fr a'route; conv Loire chateaux." ♦ 5 May-15 Sep. € 8.00 2009*

France

VAUVERT *10E2* (5km SE Rural) *43.65440, 4.29610* **FLOWER Camping Le Mas de Mourgues, Gallician, 30600 Vauvert [tel/fax 04 66 73 30 88; info@masdemourgues.com; www.masdemourgues.com or www.flowercamping.com]** Exit A9 junc 26 onto D6313 (N313)/D6572 (N572). Site on L at x-rds with D779 sp to Gallician & Stes Marie-de-la-Mer. Med, mkd pitch, pt shd; wc; chem disp; mv service pnt; shwrs inc; el pnts (6A) €2.50; Indtte; shop; snacks; BBQ; pool; games area; internet; 15% statics; dogs €2; phone; Eng spkn; adv bkg; rd & farming noise; ccard acc; CCI. "Enthusiastic, helpful British owners; some diff, long narr pitches; ground stony; clean facs but poss stretched high ssn; excel pool; excel cycling; gd." ♦ 1 Apr-30 Sep. € 16.60 2008*

VAUX SUR MER see St Palais sur Mer *7B1*

VAYRAC *7C4* (3.5km S Rural) *44.93462, 1.67981* **FFCC Camping Les Granges, Les Granges-de-Mezel, 46110 Vayrac [05 65 32 46 58; fax 05 65 32 57 94; info@les-granges.com; www.les-granges.com]** App Vayrac on D803; turn S at square in town sp "Campings"; site in 3.5km on banks of Rv Dordogne. Sp in Vayrac. Alt rte fr D803 in St Denis-les-Martel on D80 S - shorter on narr rds; site sp. Lge, pt shd; wc (some cont); shwrs; el pnts (10A) €4; gas; Indtte; shop; rest; snacks; bar; playgrnd; pool; paddling pool; fishing; canoeing; cycling; games area; entmnt; TV; dogs €1.60; adv bkg; quiet; red low ssn. "Vg children's amenities; facs fair; poss mosquitoes." 8 May-20 Sep. € 15.30 2008*

VEDENE see Avignon *10E2*

VEIGNE see Montbazon *4G2*

VEIX see Treignac *7B4*

VELLES see Châteauroux *4H2*

VENAREY LES LAUMES *6G1* (600m W Urban) *47.54448, 4.45043* **Camp Municipal Alésia, Rue du Docteur Roux, 21150 Venarey-les-Laumes [03 80 96 07 76 or 03 80 96 01 59 (Mairie); fax 03 80 96 02 19; camping@ville-venareyleslaumes.fr; www.venareyleslaumes.fr]** SE fr Montbard on D905, site well sp fr Venarey on D954. Med, hdg/mkd pitch, hdstg, pt shd, some hdstg; htd wc; chem disp; shwrs inc; el pnts (16A) €2.50; Indtte; shops 1km; tradsmn; BBQ; playgrnd; sand beach & lake sw; cycle hire; TV rm; some statics; dogs €0.50; phone; poss cr; Eng spkn; adv bkg; red low stay; ccard acc; CCI. "Well-kept site in scenic area; lge pitches; friendly, helpful warden; gd, clean san facs; barrier clsd 2200-0700; cycle tracks to Canal de Bourgogne." ♦ 1 Apr-15 Oct. € 9.00 2009*

VENCE *10E4* (3km W Rural) *43.7117, 7.0905* **Camping Domaine La Bergerie, 1330 Chemin de la Sine, 06140 Vence [04 93 58 09 36; fax 04 93 59 80 44; info@camping-domainedelabergerie.com; www.camping-domainedelabergerie.com]** Fr A8 exit junc 47 & foll sp Vence thro Cagnes-sur-Mer. Take detour to W around Vence foll sp Grasse/Tourrettes-sur-Loup. At rndabt beyond viaduct take last exit, foll site sp S thro La Sine town; long, narr rd to site, up driveway on R. Lge, mkd pitch, hdstg, pt sl, shd; wc; chem disp; mv service pnt; shwrs inc; el pnts (5A) inc; gas; Indtte; shop & 5km; tradsmn; rest; snacks; bar; playgrnd; pool; tennis; dogs; poss cr; Eng spkn; adv bkg; quiet; 5-10% red 10-20+ days; ccard acc; CCI. "Helpful owner; access to san facs diff for disabled & many pitches long way fr san facs; no twin-axles or c'vans over 5m; site poss neglected & scruffy low ssn; Vence lovely & excel touring base." 23 Mar-15 Oct. € 31.50 (CChq acc) 2009*

VENCE *10E4* (6km W Rural) *43.69958, 7.00785* **Camping Les Rives du Loup, Route de la Colle, 06140 Tourrettes-sur-Loup [04 93 24 15 65; fax 04 93 24 53 70; info@rivesduloup.com; www.rivesduloup.com]** Exit A8 junc 47 at Cagnes-sur-Mer. Foll sp La Colle-sur-Loup, then Bar-sur-Loup (D6). Site in Gorges-du-Loup valley, 3km bef Pont-du-Loup. Sm, pt shd; wc; baby facs; shwrs inc; el pnts (5A) €3.50 (poss rev pol); Indtte; shop; rest; snacks; bar; playgrnd; pool; fishing; tennis; guided walks; horseriding 5km; internet; 60% statics; dogs €3.50; adv bkg; quiet. "Many activities avail; beautiful location." Easter-30 Sep. € 23.50 2006*

VENDAYS MONTALIVET *7C1* (6km NE Rural) *45.39875, -1.04828* **Camping du Vieux Moulin, 15 Route du Moulin, 33590 Vensac [tel/fax 05 56 09 45 98; postmaster@campingduvieuxmoulin.fr; www.campingduvieuxmoulin.fr]** Turn off D1215 sp Vensac. Well sp in vill adj windmill. Med, pt shd, mkd pitch; wc; chem disp; shwrs inc; el pnts (10A) €3; Indtte; shop; tradsmn; rest; snacks; bar; playgrnd; pool; sand beach 8km; entmnt; TV; 50% statics; dogs €1.50; Eng spkn; adv bkg; quiet. "Excel ambiance; ltd facs low ssn; tourers in sep field." 1 May-31 Oct. € 13.00 2007*

VENDAYS MONTALIVET *7C1* (1km S Rural) *45.35285, -1.05985* **Camping Les Peupliers, 17 Route de Sarnac, 33930 Vendays-Montalivet [tel/fax 05 56 41 70 44; lespeupliers33@hotmail.com; www.camping-montalivet-lespeupliers.com]** NW fr Lesparre-Médoc on D1215 for 9km. Then W on D102 to Vendays-Montalivet. In town cent foll D101 twd Hourtin. Turn L in 100m (sp), site on L in 200m. Med, mkd pitch, shd; wc; chem disp; baby facs; shwrs inc; el pnts (4-6A) €2.80-3.50; gas; Indtte; shop 400m; tradsmn; snacks; BBQ; playgrnd; pool; sand beach 10km; entmnt; fitness rm; TV rm; cycle hire; 10% statics; dogs €2; phone; Eng spkn; adv bkg; quiet; red long stay/low ssn; ccard acc; CCI. "Friendly owners; excel san facs; poss ltd el pnts high ssn; excel cycle paths adj; conv Médoc vineyards." ♦ 1 May-30 Sep. € 15.00 2008*

VENDAYS MONTALIVET *7C1* (3km W Rural) *45.36698, -1.09885* **Camping du Mérin, 7 Route de Mérin, 33930 Vendays-Montalivet [tel/fax 05 56 41 78 64; www.campinglemerin.com]** NW fr Lesparre-Médoc on D1215 for 9km; then W on D102 to Vendays-Montalivet. Cont on D102 twds Montalivet-les-Bains. Site on L in 3km. Lge, hdg pitch, pt shd; wc; shwrs; el pnts (6-10A) inc; lndtte; shop 3km; tradsmn in ssn; playgrnd; sand beach 4km; fishing; cycle hire; entmnt; 5% statics; dogs €0.80; adv bkg; CCI. "Working farm; basic facs." 1 Apr-31 Oct. € 12.65 2006*

VENDAYS MONTALIVET *7C1* (6km W Coastal) *45.37040, -1.14442* **Camp Municipal de Montalivet, Ave de l'Europe, 33930 Vendays-Montalivet [05 56 09 33 45; fax 05 56 09 33 12; campingmunicipal-vendays@wanadoo.fr]** Take D101 fr Soulac to Vendays, D102 to Montalivet-les-Bains. Site sp bef ent to Montalivet. Turn L at petrol stn, site 500m on L. V lge, mkd pitch, shd; wc; chem disp; mv service pnt; shwrs inc; el pnts inc; lndtte; shop; rest; snacks; bar; playgrnd; paddling pool; beach 700m; dogs €1.87; quiet; adv bkg. "Site in pine forest; gd mkt 1km; naturist beaches N & S of Montalivet." ♦ 1 May-30 Sep. € 14.70 2007*

⊞ **VENDAYS MONTALIVET** *7C1* (6km W Coastal) *45.36325, -1.14496* **Camping CHM Montalivet (Naturist), 46 Ave de l'Europe, 33340 Vendays-Montalivet [05 56 73 26 81 or 05 56 73 73 73; fax 05 56 09 32 15; infos@chm-montalivet.com; www.chm-montalivet.com]** D101 fr Soulac to Vendays-Montalivet; D102 to Matalivet-les-Bains; site bef ent to vill; turn L at petrol stn; site 1km on R. V lge, mkd pitch, pt sl, pt shd; wc; chem disp (wc); el pnts €4.70; gas; lndry rm; shop; rest; snacks; bar; playgrnd; htd pool; sand beach adj; 50% statics; dogs €6.70; poss cr; Eng spkn; adv bkg; quiet; red long stay; ccard acc; INF card. "Peaceful; dated facs; lge naturist beach adj." ♦ € 30.35 2007*

⊞ **VENDOIRE** *7B2* (3km W Rural) *45.40860, 0.28079* **Camping du Petit Lion, 24320 Vendoire [05 53 91 00 74; info@lepetitlion.co.uk; www.dordogne-camping.info]** S fr Angoulême on D939 or D674, take D5 to Villebois-Lavalette, then D17 to Gurat. Then take D102 to Vendoire, site sp. Sm, hdg pitch, some hdstg, pt shd; htd wc; shwrs inc; el pnts (10A) €2.50; lndtte; shop & 7km; rest; snacks; bar; playgrnd; pool; paddling pool; lake fishing; tennis; internet; 10% statics; dogs €2; rally fields; British owners; adv bkg; quiet; CCI. ♦ € 10.00 2006*

VENDOME *4F2* (500m E Urban) *47.79122, 1.07586* **Camp Municipal Les Grands Prés, Rue Geoffroy-Martel, 41100 Vendôme [02 54 77 00 27 or 02 54 89 43 51; fax 02 54 89 41 01; campings@cpvendome.com; www.vendome.eu]** Fr N10 by-pass foll sp for town cent. In town foll sp Loisirs & Sports. Site adj to pool 500m. Or fr D957 N of town foll sp to Loisirs & Sports for 2km. Lge, mkd pitch, pt shd; wc; chem disp; baby facs; shwrs inc; el pnts (4-6A) €3.30-4.70; lndtte; rest in town; snacks; BBQ; playgrnd; htd pool adj; rv fishing adj; entmnt; 5% statics; dogs €1.10; phone; poss cr; adv bkg rec high ssn; quiet but some rd noise; CCI. "Pleasant rvside setting; friendly staff; clean san facs - a trek fr outer pitches; sports cent, pool & theatre adj; poss itinerants; vg." ♦ 22 May-7 Sep. € 12.40 2009*

VENDOME *4F2* (8km W Rural) *47.80206, 0.95835* **Camp Municipal de la Bonne Aventure, Route de Cunaille, 41100 Thoré-la-Rochette [02 54 72 00 59; fax 02 54 89 41 01; camping@cpvendome.com]** Fr Vendôme take D917 twd Montoire. After 6km turn R onto D82 for Thoré; thro vill & cont to vill exit sign, foll site sp. NB: there are 2 rds to Montoire - foll sp to vill. Med, pt shd; wc; chem disp; shwrs; el pnts (5A) €2.70 (long lead poss req); lndtte; shop 2km; tradsmn; snacks; fishing & watersports adj; playgrnd; tennis; entmnts; games area; dogs €1; Eng spkn; adv bkg; CCI. "Peaceful, pretty site by Rv Loir; well-kept facs; helpful warden; gd." 6 Jun-1 Sep. € 10.00 2009*

France

VENOSC see Bourg d'Oisans, Le *9C3*

VENSAC see Vendays Montalivet *7C1*

VERCHAIX see Samoëns *9A3*

VERDON SUR MER, LE *7B1* (Rural/Coastal) *45.54068, -1.09335* **Camping Le Royannais, 88 Route de Soulac, 33123 Le Verdon-sur-Mer [05 56 09 61 12; fax 05 56 73 70 67; camping.le.royannais@wanadoo.fr; www.royannais.com]** Fr Bordeaux on D1215 (N215) dir Le Verdon-sur-Mer (Royan); on o'skts of Verdon, 100m beyond sp 'Royan Ahead, Verdon Right' turn R dir Verdon (by large buoy); site on L in 200m. Med, mkd pitch, hdstg, pt shd; htd wc; chem disp; baby facs; serviced pitches; shwrs inc; el pnts (4-6A) €4.70-5.80; gas; lndtte; shop; snacks; bar; BBQ; playgrnd; pool complex; waterslide; beach 400m; cycle hire; 40% statics; dogs €2.80; phone; bus; Eng spkn; adv bkg; quiet; red long stay; CCI. "Charming wooded site; gd shwrs; ferry to Royan 30 mins." ♦ 1 Apr-15 Oct. € 19.00 2008*

VERDUN *5D1* (1km SW Urban) *49.15428, 5.36598* **Camping Les Breuils, 8 Allée des Breuils, 55100 Verdun [03 29 86 15 31; fax 03 29 86 75 76; contact@camping-lesbreuils.com; www.camping-lesbreuils.com]** Fr W (Paris) on A4/E50 exit junc 30 sp Verdun, fr E (Metz) exit junc 31. Site sp nr Citadel. Avoid Verdun town cent due to 1-way streets. Allée des Breuils runs parallel to D34 on E side of rwly. Site well sp fr D603 (N3) & all other directions. Steepish ent. Lge, hdg/mkd pitch, some hdstg, pt sl, pt shd; wc; chem disp; mv service pnt; baby facs; shwrs inc; el pnts (6A) €4 (some rev pol); gas; lndtte; sm shop & 3km; tradsmn, rest, snacks & bar (high ssn); playgrnd; pool; waterslide; cycle hire; fishing; sports cent; wifi; dogs €1.80; phone; poss cr; Eng spkn; adv bkg rec high ssn; ccard acc; red low ssn/long stay; CCI. "Pleasant, well-kept, busy, family-run site; grass pitches beside lge pond, some lge; modern san block, poss stretched if site full; poss long walk to water taps; some site rds tight for lge o'fits; gd pool; poss v lge youth groups Sep - phone ahead to check; cycle rtes around WWI battlefields; excel." ♦ 1 Apr-30 Sep. € 16.60 2009*

VERDUN *5D1* (6km NW Rural) *49.20998, 5.36567* **FFCC Camp Municipal sous Le Moulin, 55100 Charny-sur-Meuse [03 29 84 28 35 or 03 29 86 67 06 (LS); fax 03 29 84 67 99; mairie.charny.sur.meuse@wanadoo.fr]** N fr Verdun on D964; turn L onto D115 to Charny-sur-Meuse; site sp. Med, pt sl, pt shd; wc (all cont) (own san rec); mv service pnt; shwrs inc; el pnts (6A) €2.40; fishing; dogs €1; CCI. "CL-type site; open pitches round lake; facs adequate; useful touring base; conv WWI sites; gd." 1 May-30 Sep. € 7.00 2009*

VERDUN SUR GARONNE *8E3* (300m N Rural) **FFCC Camping Le Grand Gravier, Chemin des Allées, 82600 Verdun-sur-Garonne [05 63 64 32 44 or 05 63 26 30 64; camping@garonne-gascogne.com; www.garonne-gascogne.com]** Exit A20/E09 at junc 68 onto A72 & exit junc 10 onto D820 (N20) S to Grisolles. At rndabt turn R onto D813 (N113) NW for 3km, then L at rndabt onto D6 W sp Verdun-sur-Garonne. Cross rv bdge; site sharp R in 200m. Med, hdg pitch, pt shd; wc (mainly cont); shwrs inc; el pnts (6A) €2.80; shop 1km; BBQ; playgrnd; rv fishing; tennis; games rm; 30% statics; dogs €1; adv bkg; quiet; red long stay; CCI. "Pleasant, interesting site; next to fast flowing rv, poss floods in wet weather; gd modern facs." 23 May-5 Sep. € 9.40 2007*

VERDUN SUR LE DOUBS *6H1* (500m W Rural) *46.90259, 5.01777* **Camp Municipal La Plage, 71350 Verdun-sur-le-Doubs [03 85 91 55 50 or 03 85 91 52 52; fax 03 85 91 90 91; mairie.verdunsurledoubs@wanadoo.fr]** SE on D970 fr Beaune to Verdun-sur-le-Doubs & foll sp in town. Or on D973 or N73 twd Chalon fr Seurre, turn R onto D115 to Verdun; site on bank of Rv Saône. Lge, mkd pitch, pt sl, shd; wc (some cont); chem disp; shwrs inc; el pnts (15A) €1.80; shops 500m; rest, snacks & bar 500m; BBQ; playgrnd; pool adj; waterslide; fishing; phone; quiet. "Lovely rvside location; interesting sm town; lge pitches; excel." 1 May-30 Sep. € 8.10 2006*

VERMENTON *4G4* (500m W Rural) *47.65897, 3.73087* **Camp Municipal Les Coullemières, 89270 Vermenton [03 86 81 53 02; fax 03 86 81 63 95; camping.vermenton@orange.fr; www.camping-vermenton.com]** Lies W of D606 (N6) - turn off D606 into Rue Pasteur (tight turn & narr rd), strt on at x-rds into Ave de la Gare. Turn R at stn, L over level x-ing. Well sp in vill adj to rv but sps low down & easy to miss. Med, hdg/mkd pitch, pt shd; htd wc (some cont); chem disp; shwrs inc; el pnts (6A) €2.50; lndtte; shop 500m; rest 200m; playgrnd; tennis; fishing, boating; cycle hire; TV rm; 5% statics; dogs €1; bus; adv bkg rec high ssn; quiet; ccard acc. "Peaceful, clean, well-run, rvside site; gd facs; no twin-axle vans; weight limit on access rds & pitches; gd walks & cycling; beautiful town with 12thC church." ♦ 1 Apr-30 Sep. € 10.50 2008*

VERMENTON *4G4* (2km W Rural) *47.66199, 3.70493* **Camp Municipal Le Moulin Jacquot, Route de Bazarnes, 89460 Accolay [tel/fax 03 86 81 56 48 or 03 86 81 56 87 (Mairie); mairie.accolay@wanadoo.fr]** N fr Vermenton on N6 dir Auxerre; in 2km turn L onto D39 sp Accolay. Cross bdge, turn R thro vill; site on R at 200m adj Canal du Nivernais. Sm, mkd pitch, shd; wc; chem disp; mv service pnt; shwrs inc; el pnts (6A) €2.20; lndtte; shops, rest 300m; bar 200m; playgrnd; adv bkg; quiet; ccard not acc; red long stay; CCI. "Site yourself; grassy pitches poss boggy; pleasant sm vill; caves 11km; gd, flat cyling along canal." ♦ 1 Apr-1 Oct. € 8.20 2009*

VERNANTES *4G1* (2km E Rural) **Camping Intercommunal de la Grande Pâture, Route de Vernoil, 49390 Vernantes [02 41 51 45 39; fax 02 41 51 57 20]** Fr Saumur on N147. Take D767 to Vernantes then D58 dir Vernoil. Site sp. Sm, pt shd; wc; shwrs inc; el pnts (10A) €2.29; shop 200m; playgrnd; tennis, fishing adj; adv bkg; quiet; CCI. 15 Jun-30 Sep. € 7.71 2006*

VERNANTES *4G1* (4km E Rural) *47.38310, 0.10036* **Camping La Sirotière, La Sablonnière, 49390 Vernoil-le-Fourrier [02 41 67 29 32; ann.bullock@orange.fr]** Fr Vernantes foll sp Vernoil & Super U; at rndabt (Super U on L) strt over & at end vill (at Barthelemy sp on L) turn R sp La Sablonnière. Foll rd up hill & turn R 300m after 2nd x-rds sp, & foll long drive to site. If coming fr Noyant (N) on D767 do not use satnav after Noyant, but foll dirs above. Fr A85 exit junc 2 onto D53 to St Philbert & Vernantes, then as above. Sm, pt sl, pt shd; htd wc; chem disp; shwrs inc; el pnts (10A) inc; lndtte; shop & bar 1km; rest 2km; cycle hire; dogs by request; Eng spkn; adv bkg; quiet; no ccard acc. "Peaceful CL-type site; British owners; adults only; site yourself if no reply at bell; vg." 1 Mar-31 Dec. € 13.00 2009*

⊞ **VERNANTES** *4G1* (4km NW Rural) *47.43700, 0.00600* **Camping La Fortinerie, La Fortinerie, 49390 Mouliherne [02 41 67 59 76; john.north.a@gmail.com; www.lafortinerie.com]** Fr Vernantes take D58 dir Mouliherne; opp Château Loroux (Plaissance) turn L; at x-rds turn R, site over 1km on L. Sm, pt shd; wc; chem disp; mv service pnt; shwrs inc; el pnts €5; ice; lndtte; shop 4km; rest & bar 3km; BBQ; no statics; dogs; B&B avail; adv bkg; quiet. "CL-type site; helpful, friendly British owners; beautiful chateau town; conv Loire valley; only sound is crickets!" € 10.00 2009*

⊞ **VERNANTES** *4G1* (9km NW Rural) *47.4304, 0.0397* **Camping Le Chant d'Oiseau, 49390 Mouliherne [02 41 67 09 78; info@loire-gites.com; www.loire-gites.com]** Fr Saumur take D767 twd Noyant. Turn L in Vernantes then R onto D58 twd Mouliherne. Foll this rd to gatehouse of Chateau du Louroux then 1st R opp 'Plaisance' farm. Foll rd for 1km. Site on R. Fr Mouliherne on D58 for 3km, turn L at x-rds with wooden cross. Fork R in 700m, site on L. NB App by bumpy forest road. Sm, pt sl, pt shd; wc; chem disp; shwrs inc; el pnts (6A) €5; BBQ; pool; cycle hire; some statics; dogs (low ssn only); Eng spkn; quiet. "Wonderful CL-type site; helpful, friendly British owners; gd facs but poss unkempt & not suitable winter stay; gd birdwatching." ♦ € 18.50 2008*

VERNET see Auterive *8F3*

VERNET LES BAINS *8G4* (1km N Rural) *42.55506, 2.37756* **Camping L'Eau Vive, Chemin de St Saturnin, 66820 Vernet-les-Bains [04 68 05 54 14; fax 04 68 05 78 14; info@leau-vive.com; www.leau-vive.com]** On app to town cent on D116 turn R over rv & site 1st R 1km at end of rd. Med, mkd pitch, terr, pt shd; wc; chem disp; serviced pitch; mv service pnt; shwrs inc; el pnts (10A) €3.50; Indtte; shop 1km; tradsmn; rest; snacks; bar; BBQ; playgrnd; lake sw; waterslide; tennis 500m; games area; TV rm; 40% statics; dogs €2.50; Eng spkn; quiet; red low ssn. "Helpful, friendly Dutch owners; beautiful area; gd walking; excel." ♦ 1 Mar-31 Oct. € 21.50 (3 persons) 2008*

VERNET LES BAINS *8G4* (2km N Rural) *42.56598, 2.38864* **Camping Las Closes, Route de Fillois, 66820 Corneilla-de-Conflent [04 68 05 66 48 or 06 81 85 14 46 (mob); www.las-closes.fr]** Exit N116 at Villefranche-de-Conflent onto D116 dir Vernet-Les-Bains; in 2km turn L into Corneilla-de-Conflent. Foll sp, site approx 1km. Med, mkd pitch, pt sl, terr, pt shd; wc (some cont); chem disp; shwrs inc; el pnts (10A) €2.80; Indtte; shop 500m; playgrnd; pool; dogs free; phone; adv bkg; CCI. "Beautiful views; helpful owners; interesting area." ♦ 1 Apr-30 Sep. € 11.40 2009*

VERNET LES BAINS *8G4* (2km NE Rural) *42.56567, 2.41984* **Camping Les Sauterelles, Col de Millères, 66820 Fillols [tel/fax 04 68 05 63 72]** Fr Perpignan take N116 to Prades, then D27 S. Foll sps to Chalet des Cortalets. Suitable for sm o'fits. Med, pt sl, pt shd; wc (cont); mv service pnt; shwrs; el pnts (5A) €3; shop; snacks; bar; BBQ; playgrnd; pool; no dogs; phone; adv bkg; quiet. "Attractive site; friendly owners; mountain walking, caves, vineyards; historical locations; gd views." ♦ 1 Jun-30 Sep. € 11.00 2008*

VERNET LES BAINS *8G4* (3km NW Rural) *42.56255, 2.36050* **Camping Le Rotja, Ave de la Rotja, 66820 Fuilla [tel/fax 04 68 96 52 75; info@camping-lerotja.com; www.camping-lerotja.com]** Take N116 fr Prades dir Mont-Louis, 500m after Villefranche-de-Conflens turn L onto D6 sp Fuilla. In 3km just bef church, turn R at sp to site. Sm, mkd pitch, pt sl, terr, pt shd; htd wc; chem disp; baby facs; shwrs inc; el pnts (10A) inc; gas; Indtte; shop 2km; rest 100m; snacks; BBQ (gas); playgrnd; pool; rv adj; 10% statics; dogs €2; phone; Eng spkn; adv bkg; quiet; ccard acc; red long stay; CCI. "Views of Mount Canigou; peaceful site; friendly Dutch owners; gd hiking." ♦ 1 May-31 Oct. € 20.50 2007*

VERNET, LE *9D3* (800m N Rural) *44.28170, 6.39080* **Camping Lou Passavous, Route de Roussimat, 04140 Le Vernet [04 92 35 14 67; fax 04 92 35 09 35; lou passavous@wanadoo.fr; www.loupassavous.com]** Fr N on A51 exit junc 21 Volonne onto N85 sp Digne. Fr Digne N on D900 to Le Vernet; site on R. Fr S exit A51 junc 20 Les Mées onto D4, then N85 E to Digne, then as above. Sm, pt sl, pt shd; htd wc; chem disp; baby facs; shwrs inc; el pnts (6A) €3.50; Indtte; shop; tradsmn; rest; snacks; bar; playgrnd; pool; fishing; games area; entmnt; TV; dogs €1; poss cr; Eng spkn; adv bkg; quiet; ccard acc; CCI. "Scenic location; gd facs for size; Dutch owners; gd walking." ♦ 15 Apr-15 Sep. € 15.00 2007*

⊞ **VERNEUIL SUR AVRE** *4E2* (1km W Rural) *48.73880, 0.90910* **Camping Le Vert Bocage, Ave Edmond Demolins, 27130 Verneuil-sur-Avre [tel/fax 02 32 32 26 79; www.camping-le-vert-bocage.com]** On ent Verneuil-sur-Avre join ring rd & foll sp for D926 to L'Aigle & Argentan. Site clearly sp on o'skts on L. Sm, hdg/mkd pitch, pt shd; htd wc; chem disp; baby facs; shwrs inc; el pnts (6A) inc; gas; Indtte (inc dryer); shops 1km; tradsmn; rest, snacks, bar & pool 200m; playgrnd; fishing adj; tennis; sports in town; games rm; TV rm; 25% statics; dogs; phone; site poss clsd Jan; adv bkg; quiet but some traff noise; red long stay; CCI. "Clean san facs; gd NH." ♦ € 14.80 2008*

VERNEUIL SUR SEINE *3D3* (1.5km N Rural) *48.99567, 1.95681* **Camping-Caravaning 3* du Val de Seine, Chemin du Rouillard, 78480 Verneuil-sur-Seine [01 39 71 88 34 or 01 39 28 16 20; fax 01 39 71 18 60; vds78@orange.fr; www.vds78.com]** Exit A13 junc 8 & foll sp to Verneuil; site sp twd rvside. Med, mkd pitch, hdstg, pt shd; htd wc; shwrs inc; chem disp; mv service pnt; el pnts (6A) €4.25; Indtte; shop & 1km; rest; snacks; BBQ; playgrnd; lake sw & beach 600m; fishing; watersports; horseriding; games area; some statics; dogs €2; Paris 20 mins by train; Eng spkn; quiet; ccard acc; red low ssn. "V pleasant site adj Rv Seine; friendly, helpful staff; gd facs & activities." ♦ 15 Apr-30 Sep. € 13.90 2008*

VERNIOZ see Auberives sur Varèze *9B2*

VERNON *3D2* (2km W Rural) *49.09631, 1.43827* **Camping Les Fosses Rouges, Chemin de Réanville, 27950 St Marcel [02 32 51 59 86; fax 02 32 53 30 45; camping@cape27.fr; www.cape-tourisme.fr]** Exit A13/E5 junc 16 dir Vernon onto D181; in 2km at rndabt turn L onto D64e dir St Marcel; in 2km at 5-exit rndabt take 1st R onto Chemin de Réanville (D64) & foll camping sp; site in 500m on L. NB Easy to miss site ent - sp appears to point strt on when you should turn L. Med, mkd pitch, pt sl, pt shd; htd wc (some cont); chem disp; shwrs inc; el pnts (6-10A) €2.60-3.40 (poss rev pol); gas; shops 600m; tradsmn; BBQ; playgrnd; pool 4km; some statics; dogs free; adv bkg; quiet; no ccard acc; CCI. "Well-kept, scenic site; friendly, helpful owner; gd san facs; clsd 1100-1600; no new arrivals after 2000 hrs; parking for m'vans at Giverny - cont past site over rndabt for 900m, turn sharp L past hotel on R & parking on R; lovely little vill." ♦ 1 Mar-31 Oct. € 8.10 2009*

VERRUYES *7A2* (500m NE Rural) *46.52073, -0.28431* **Camping Etang de la Fragnée, 79310 Verruyes [tel/fax 05 49 63 21 37; contact@campinglafragnee.com; www.campinglafragnee.com]** Fr D743 S fr Parthenay turn SE onto D24 at Mazières-en-Gâtine for Verruyes; sp `Verruyes Plan d'Eau'. Med, mkd pitch, shd; wc; chem disp; shwrs inc; el pnts (6A) €2.80; Indtte; gas; shop; tradsmn; rest; snacks; bar; playgrnd; sand beach & lake sw; fishing; tennis; cycle hire; entmnt; dogs €1.30; Eng spkn; adv bkg; quiet; ccard acc. "Friendly site; pitches muddy when wet." 15 Apr-15 Oct. € 10.60 2006*

France

VERS *7D3* (Rural) *44.48442, 1.55380* **Camp Municipal de l'Arquette, 46090 Vers [05 65 31 42 59 (Mairie) or 06 33 65 06 23 (mob); mairie-vers@wanadoo.fr; www.commune-de-vers.net]** Fr Cahors foll D653 on N side Rv Lot to Vers; in vill turn R over bdge onto D662 sp St Cirq-Lapopie; turn R in 100m, foll site sp. Use this rte to avoid low bdge 2.9m. Med, mkd pitch, shd; wc; chem disp; mv service pnt; shwrs inc; el pnts (10A) €4 (rev pol); lndry rm; shop & rest 200m; playgrnd adj; dogs €1.50; phone; poss cr; Eng spkn; adv bkg; ccard not acc; CCI. "Attractive rvside site; friendly staff; excel san facs; gd walks; poss flood risk; poss noisy youth groups w/ends; conv Pech-Merle cave paintings." 1 May-30 Sep. € 12.00 2009*

VERS *7D3* (1.5km S Rural) *44.46787, 1.54482* **Camping La Chêneraie, Le Cuzoul, 46090 Vers [05 65 31 40 29; fax 05 65 31 41 70; lacheneraie@free.fr; www.cheneraie.com]** Exit Cahors on D653 sp Figeac. In Vers turn L at rlwy x-ing, site on R in 50m, clearly sp. App steep & siting lge o'fits poss diff. Sm, mkd pitch, pt sl, pt shd; wc; chem disp (wc); mv service pnt; shwrs inc; el pnts (10A) €4; gas; lndtte; rest 2km; snacks; bar; playgrnd; pool; tennis; entmnt; some statics; dogs; phone; Eng spkn; adv bkg ess high ssn; quiet; ccard acc; CCI. "Well-run, scenic, friendly site in Lot Valley." 1 May-31 Oct. € 17.00 2007*

VERS PONT DU GARD see Remoulins *10E2*

VERSAILLES *4E3* (3km E Urban) *48.79455, 2.16038* **Camping Huttopia Versailles, 31 Rue Berthelot, Porchefontaine, 78000 Versailles [01 39 51 23 61; fax 01 39 53 68 29; versailles@huttopia.com; www.huttopia.com]** Foll sp to Château de Versailles; fr main ent take Ave de Paris dir Porchefontaine & turn R immed after twin gate lodges; sp. Narr access rd due parked cars & sharp bends. Lge, mkd pitch, pt sl, terr, pt shd; htd wc; chem disp; mv service pnt; baby facs; shwrs inc; el pnts inc (6-10A) €4.60-6.80; gas; lndtte; shop 500m; tradsmen; rest; snacks; bar; BBQ; playgrnd; htd pool; games area; cycle hire; TV rm; 20% statics; dogs €4; bus 500m; Eng spkn; adv bkg; quiet; ccard acc; red low ssn/long stay; CCI. "Pretty, renovated, well-run, wooded site; sm, sl, uneven pitches poss diff lge o'fits; friendly, helpful staff; excel, clean san facs, stretched high ssn; conv Paris trains & Versailles Château." ♦ 3 Apr-4 Nov. € 32.00 2009*

VERTEILLAC *7C2* (600m NE Urban) *45.35064, 0.37010* **Camp Municipal Le Pontis Sud-Est, 24320 Verteillac [05 53 90 37 74; fax 05 53 90 77 13; j-c.rouvel@wanadoo.fr; www.camping-le-pontis.com]** N fr Ribérac on D708 dir Angoulême; leaving Verteillac turn R at 'Camping' sp, then L at gendarmerie, then 1st R. Site adj stadium. Sm, hdg pitch, sl, unshd; wc, chem disp (wc); mv service pnt; shwrs inc; el pnts (6A) €1.90; lndry rm; shop, rest, snacks, bar nrby; BBQ; pool 500m; wifi; 70% statics; dogs €0.50; quiet; CCI. "Easy access to pitches; m'van pitches sm; facs modern but ltd & in need of maintenance (2009); ltd el pnts; attractive vill; Ribérac mkt Fri." ♦ 4 Apr-15 Nov. € 8.10 2009*

VERTEILLAC *7C2* (8km NW Rural) *45.39629, 0.29338* **Camping Petit Vos (Hutchinson), 24320 Nanteuil-Auriac-de-Bourzac [05 53 90 39 46; petitvos@aol.com]** On D674 S fr Angoulême to Libourne, turn L at Montmoreau-St Cybard onto D24 to Salles-Lavalette (11km), then take D1 to Nanteuil-Auriac (4.5km). Go thro vill & foll sp 'Petit Vos' up to x-rds. Turn R sp Vendoire, then 2nd R. Site immed on R. Sm, pt sl, pt shd; wc; chem disp (wc); shwrs inc; el pnts (10A) inc; lndtte; shops & bar 4.5km; rest 2km; BBQ; rv & sand beach 15km; dogs €1; lge m'vans & children not acc; adv bkg ess; quiet; CCI. "Scenic, peaceful, CL-type, British owned site; excel facs but ltd." € 8.50 2006*

VERVINS *3C4* (7km N Rural) *49.90676, 3.91977* **FFCC Camping Le Val d'Oise, Route de Mont-d'Origny, 02580 Etréaupont [03 23 97 48 04]** Site to E of Etréaupont off N2, Mons-Reims rd. Site adj football pitch on banks of Rv Oise. Well sp fr main rd. Sm, /hdg/mkd pitches, pt shd; wc (some cont); shwrs inc; el pnts (6A) €3.25 (poss rev pol); shops 500m; tradsmn; playgrnd; tennis; sports field adj; rv & fishing adj; dogs €0.30; quiet. "Pretty, tidy site; warm welcome; clean san facs; uninspiring vill; conv rte to Zeebrugge ferry (approx 200km); gd walking & cycling; site self if recep clsd; gd." 1 Apr-30 Oct. € 9.15 2009*

VESDUN see Culan *7A4*

VESOUL *6G2* (1.5km W Rural) *47.63026, 6.12858* **Camping International du Lac, Ave des Rives du Lac, 70000 Vesoul [03 84 76 22 86; fax 03 84 75 74 93; camping_dulac@yahoo.fr; www.camping-vesoul.com]** 2km fr D619 (N19), sp fr W end of by-pass, pass indus est to lge lake on W o'skts. Ent opp Peugeot/Citroën factory on lakeside. Lge, mkd pitch, pt shd; htd wc; mv service pnt; baby facs; shwrs inc; el pnts (10A) €2; gas; lndtte; shops 2km; rest; bar; playgrnd; pool, paddling pool, waterslides 300m; fishing; tennis; games area; some statics; dogs €1.80; adv bkg; ccard acc; red CCI. "Super site screened fr indus est by trees; gd size pitches but poss soft after rain; excel aqua park nr; gd cycle rtes." ♦ 1 Mar-31 Oct. € 12.85 2008*

VEULES LES ROSES *3C2* (3.5km E Rural) *49.88351, 0.85188* **Camp Municipal Le Mesnil, Route de Sotteville, 76740 St Aubin-sur-Mer [tel/fax 02 35 83 02 83]** On D68 2km W of St Aubin-sur-Mer. Med, hdg pitch, terr, unshd; mv service pnt; htd wc; shwrs inc; el pnts (10A) €3.70; lndtte; shop; tradsmn; playgrnd; sand beach 1.5km; ccard acc; CCI. ♦ 1 Apr-31 Oct. € 16.00 2007*

VEULES LES ROSES *3C2* (6km E Rural) *49.86083, 0.89079* **Camping Les Garennes de la Mer, 12 Route de Luneray, 76740 Le Bourg-Dun [02 35 83 10 44; camping_lesgarennesdelamer@hotmail.com]** Fr Veules-les-Roses, take D925 twd Dieppe. Site sp in Le Bourg-Dun - 1km SE. Sm, mkd pitch, pt sl, pt shd; wc; shwrs inc; el pnts (16A) €3.50; gas; lndtte; shops 250m; supmkt 5km; tradsmn; shgl beach 3km; 60% statics; Eng spkn; poss cr; adv bkg; quiet; ccard acc; CCI. "Well-kept site; vg san facs." ♦ 1 Apr-15 Oct. € 13.50 2009*

VEULES LES ROSES *3C2* (10km E Coastal) *49.90558, 0.92787* **Camp Municipal de la Plage, 123 Rue de la Saâne, 76860 Quiberville-Plage [02 35 83 01 04 or 02 35 04 21 33 (Mairie); fax 02 35 85 10 25; camping plage3@wanadoo.fr; www.campingplagequiberville.com]** Fr Dieppe on D75, site sp in Quiberville-Plage on D127. Lge, hdg/mkd pitch, unshd; wc; mv service pnt; shwrs; el pnts (6-10A) €4.10-4.80; Indtte; rest in vill; playgrnd; beach adj; tennis adj; games area; dogs €1.40; phone; adv bkg; quiet. "Conv Dieppe ferry; pleasant site." ♦ 1 Apr-31 Oct. € 19.30 2009*

VEULES LES ROSES *3C2* (500m S Coastal/Rural) *49.87586, 0.80314* **Camping Les Mouettes, 7 Ave Jean Moulin, 76980 Veules-les-Roses [02 35 97 61 98; fax 02 35 97 33 44; camping-les-mouettes@wanadoo.fr; www.camping-les mouettes-normandie.com]** On ent vill fr Dieppe on D925, turn R onto D68, site in 500m up hill (14%). Lge, mkd pitch, pt shd; htd wc; chem disp; baby facs; shwrs inc; el pnts (6A) inc; gas; Indtte; shop; tradsmn; snacks; bar; htd pool; sand beach 300m; cycle hire; games area; games rm; wifi; TV; 10% statics; dogs €1.50; adv bkg; Eng spkn; quiet; ccard acc; red long stay/low ssn/CCI. "Pleasant area." ♦ 1 Apr-15 Nov. € 19.80 2009*

See advertisement on page 226

VEURDRE, LE see St Pierre le Moûtier *4H4*

VEYNES *9D3* (6km NE Rural) *44.56866, 5.88326* **Camping Mon Repos, Le Cadillon, 05400 Montmaur [04 92 58 03 14; campings@alpes-campings.com]** Fr D994 Veynes-Gap rd, foll D937 N, turning R at bdge to keep on D937. Site sp. Sm, pt sl, shd; wc; chem disp; mv service pnt 6km; shwrs inc; el pnts (2-5A) €2-3; gas; Indtte; shop; tradsmn; snacks; playgrnd; pool 6km; entmnt; TV rm; 30% statics; dogs €1; quiet; Eng spkn; CCI. "Friendly, family-run site; excel walking." ♦ 1 Apr-30 Sep. € 10.00 2006*

⊞ **VEYNES** *9D3* (15km NE Rural) *44.55003, 5.95114* **Camping au Blanc Manteau, Route de Céüze, Mantayer, 05400 La Roche-des-Arnauds [02 97 57 82 56]** Take D994 fr Veynes twd Gap; site sp in vill of La Roche-des-Arnauds on D18 in 1km. Sm, pt shd; htd wc (some cont); chem disp; baby facs; shwrs inc; el pnts (10A) €5.35; Indtte; shops 750m; snacks; bar; playgrnd; pool; tennis; adv bkg. "Gd sized pitches; some daytime rd noise; pleasant owner." ♦ € 16.00 2007*

VEYNES *9D3* (2km SW Rural) *44.51889, 5.79880* **Camping Les Rives du Lac, Les Iscles, 05400 Veynes [04 92 57 20 90; contact@camping-lac.com; www.camping-lac.com]** Off D994. Sp on lakeside. Med, mkd pitch, hdstg, pt sl, pt shd; wc; chem disp; mv service pnt; baby facs; shwrs; el pnts (10A) €3.50; Indtte; snacks; bar; BBQ; playgrnd; pool; lake sw & beach adj; watersports; mountain biking; climbing; wifi; dogs €2.50; bus 500m; phone; adv bkg; quiet, occasional rlwy noise; ccard acc; CCI. "V attractive, well-managed, clean site on shore of sm lake; san facs excel; welcoming staff." 1 May-20 Sep. € 19.00 2009*

VEZAC see Sarlat la Canéda *7C3*

VEZELAY *4G4* (3km N Rural) *47.48280, 3.75904* **Camp Municipal Le Pâtis, Route de Givry, 89450 Asquins [03 86 33 30 80; mairie.asquins@wanadoo.fr]** Fr Vézelay take D951 N to Asquins, & turn R to site on rvside - tight turn. Site sp. Sm, pt shd; htd wc; chem disp (wc); baby facs; shwrs inc; el pnts €3; shop 500m; BBQ; playgrnd; dogs; poss cr; quiet; CCI. 1 Jun-30 Sep. € 8.00 2008*

VEZELAY *4G4* (2km SE Rural) *47.45879, 3.77150* **Camp Municipal, 89450 St Père [03 86 33 36 58 or 03 86 33 26 62 (Mairie); fax 03 86 33 34 56; mairie-saint-pere@wanadoo.fr; www.saint-pere.fr]** Fr Vézelay take D957, turn onto D36 to St Père. Site sp. Med, pt shd; wc (cont); shwrs inc; el pnts (10A) €2 (poss rev pol); shops 500m; playgrnd; rv adj; fishing; canoeing; tennis; some statics; poss cr; quiet. "Pleasant site; conv Morvan National Park; warden comes am & pm; basic san facs; gd walking area." Easter-30 Sep. € 6.60 2008*

VEZELAY *4G4* (600m S Rural) *47.45675, 3.78768* **FFCC Camping de Vézelay L'Ermitage, Route de l'Étang, 89450 Vézelay [tel/fax 03 86 33 24 18]** Foll sp fr cent of Vézelay to 'Camping Vézelay' & Youth Hostel. Sm, pt sl, pt shd; wc; chem disp; mv service pnt; some serviced pitches; shwrs inc; el pnts (4-6A) €2.50 (rev pol); shops 500m; tradsmn (high ssn); poss cr; Eng spkn; quiet; no ccard acc; CCI. "Pleasant, peaceful, scenic site; welcoming; gd, clean facs; blocks req; some pitches diff lge o'fits; recep eve only - site self & sign in when open; some pitches muddy after heavy rain; superb abbey in Vézelay; excel." 1 Apr-31 Oct. € 7.50 2009*

⊞ **VIAS** *10F1* (2km S Coastal) *43.29235, 3.39961* **Camping Cap Soleil, 34450 Vias-Plage [04 67 21 64 77; fax 04 67 21 70 66; cap.soleil@wanadoo.fr; www.capsoleil.fr]** D612 (N112) W fr Agde to Vias. Turn S in town & foll sps for Vias-Plage over canal bdge & sps to site. Lge, mkd pitch; shd; wc; chem disp; mv service pnt; baby facs; shwrs inc; el pnts (10A) €3.50; Indtte; shop in ssn; rest; snacks; bar; BBQ; playgrnd; htd pool; waterslide; naturist pool 1/7-31/8; sand beach 800m; rv 600m; tennis; entmnt; TV rm; 90% statics; dogs €5; private washrms avail; adv bkg; quiet; red low ssn. "Sm pitches; open NH winter but ltd facs & poss unclean." € 39.00 2007*

VIAS *10F1* (3km S Coastal) *43.29055, 3.39863* **Camping Californie Plage, 34450 Vias-Plage [04 67 21 64 69; fax 04 67 21 54 62; californie-plage@wanadoo.fr; www.californie-plage.fr]** W fr Agde on D612 (N112) to Vias; turn S in town & foll sps 'Mer' over canal bdge & sp to site. Lge, mkd pitch, shd; wc; chem disp; shwrs inc; el pnts (5-10A) €1.50-3.50; gas; Indtte; supmkt; rest; snacks; bar; playgrnd; htd/covrd pool; paddling pool; waterslide; sand beach adj; cycle hire; internet; entmnt; TV rm; 10% statics; dogs €4.60; Eng spkn; adv bkg; ccard acc; CCI. ♦ 1 Apr-30 Oct. € 33.00 2008*

France

VIAS *10F1* (3km S Coastal) *43.29800, 3.41750* **Camping Les Salisses, Route de la Mer, 34450 Vias-Plage [04 67 21 64 07; fax 04 67 21 76 51; info@salisses.com; www.salisses.com]** Turn S off D612 (N112) (Agde-Béziers rd) in Vias & foll sp to Vias-Plage. Cross Canal du Midi bdge & site on R. Lge, mkd pitch, pt shd; wc; chem disp; shwrs inc; el pnts (6A) inc; gas; Indtte; shop; rest; snacks; bar; playgrnd; 3 pools (1 htd, covrd); waterslide; sand beach 1km; tennis; cycle hire; horseriding; TV rm; 80% statics; dogs €5; quiet; ccard acc. "Vg family hols; interesting town & mkt in Agde." Easter-19 Sep. € 31.00 (CChq acc) 2006*

VIAS *10F1* (3km S Coastal) *43.29083, 3.41861* **Yelloh! Village Le Club Farret, Farinette-Plage, 34450 Vias-Plage [04 67 21 64 45; fax 04 67 21 70 49; farret@wanadoo.fr; www.camping-farret.com or www.yellohvillage.com]** Fr A9, exit Agde junc 34. Foll sp Vias-Plage on D137. Sp fr cent of Vias-Plage on L, immed after Gendarmerie. V lge, mkd pitch, pt shd; wc; chem disp; mv service pnt; baby facs; shwrs inc; el pnts (6A) inc; gas; Indtte; shop; rest; snacks; bar; playgrnd; htd pool; sand beach adj; watersports; tennis; cycle hire; fitness rm; games area; games rm; entmnt; TV; some statics; dogs €4; Eng spkn; adv bkg; quiet; ccard acc; red low ssn; CCI. "Excel facs, entmnt, excursions; gd security." ♦ 25 Mar-25 Sep. € 47.00 2009*

See advertisement

VIAS *10F1* (5km SW Coastal) *43.29708, 3.42072* **Camping La Carabasse, Route de Farinette, 34450 Vias-Plage [04 67 21 64 01; fax 04 67 21 76 87; lacarabasse@siblu.fr; www.lacarabasse.fr]** Fr S on A9 exit 34 & take 1st exit onto N312 sp Vias & Agde. After 8km take RH lane twd Béziers on D612 (N112). Branch R to Vias-Plage & at rndabt foll sp for Vias-Plage on D137. Site 1km on L. V lge, hdg/mkd pitch, pt shd; htd wc; chem disp; baby facs; shwrs inc; some pitches with indiv san facs; el pnts (6A) inc (poss rev pol); gas; Indtte; shop; rest; snacks; bar; BBQ; playgrnd; 2 htd pools; waterslide; sand beach 800m; tennis; watersports; golf 10km; entmnt; TV; 80% statics; no dogs; Eng spkn; adv bkg ess; quiet but poss noisy high ssn; red low ssn; CCI. "Vg local produce inc wines; organised activities; pitches poss tight med/lge o'fits due trees; many excel facs - vg for young families." ♦ 4 Apr-19 Sep. 2009*

VIAS *10F1* (5km SW Coastal) *43.29093, 3.40383* **Camping Les Flots Bleus, Côte Ouest, 34450 Vias-Plage [04 67 21 64 80; fax 04 67 01 78 12; camping lesflotsbleus@wanadoo.fr; www.camping-flotsbleus.com]** Fr D612 (N112) at Vias, take D137 sp Vias-Plage. After x-ing Canal du Midi turn R sp Côte Ouest, site sp. Lge, some hdg/mkd pitch, hdstg, pt shd; wc (some cont); chem disp; mv service pnt; baby facs; shwrs inc; el pnts (6A) inc; Indtte; shop; tradsmn; rest; snacks; bar; playgrnd; htd pool complex; waterslide; sand beach adj; games area; cycle hire; entmnt; 50% statics; dogs €3.50; adv bkg; quiet; red low ssn; CCI. "Facs clean but poss stretched high ssn; gd." 7 Apr-16 Sep. € 32.00 2009*

VIAS *10F1* (3km W Rural) *43.31222, 3.36320* **Camping Sunêlia Le Domaine de la Dragonnière, 34450 Vias [04 67 01 03 10; fax 04 67 21 73 39; dragonniere@ wanadoo.fr; www.dragonniere.com]** Exit A9 junc 35 onto D64 twd Valras, then D612 (N112) dir Agde & Vias. Site on R bef Vias. Or exit junc 34 onto N312. At Vias turn R onto D612 (N112) sp Béziers, site on L. NB Take care high speed humps at sh intervals. V lge, hdg/mkd pitch, pt shd; wc; chem disp; mv service pnt; sauna; shwrs inc; el pnts (6A) inc; gas; Indtte; shop; tradsmn; rest; snacks; bar; BBQ; playgrnd; htd pool complex; paddling pool; sand beach 3km (free shuttle high ssn); tennis; games area; cycle hire; entmnt; internet; TV rm; 80% statics; dogs €5; phone; poss cr; Eng spkn; adv bkg; traff & aircraft noise; ccard acc; red low ssn; CCI. "Vg site in botanical reserve; excel for children & teenagers high ssn; Canal du Midi nrby; opp Béziers airport; site poss flooded after heavy rain." ♦ 4 Apr-26 Sep. € 42.00 (3 persons) (CChq acc) 2008*

VIC LE COMPT *9B1* (500m NE Rural) *45.64568, 3.23683* **Camp Municipal La Croix de Vent, 63270 Vic-le-Comte [04 73 69 22 63 or 04 73 69 02 12 (Mairie)]** Fr N exit A75 junc 5 onto D213/D225 to Vic-le-Comte & foll sp for camping or sw pool, 'piscine'. Fr S exit A75 junc 8 onto D229 to Vic. Sm, pt shd; wc; shwrs; el pnts (16A) €2; Indry rm; shops 500m; pool adj; tennis; adv bkg; quiet. "Friendly, helpful staff; gd san facs; pleasant old town; conv NH." 1 Jul-31 Aug. € 8.70 2008*

VIC SUR CERE *7C4* (6km NE Rural) *45.01325, 2.67043* **Camp Municipal La Bédisse, Route de Raulhac, 15800 Thiézac [04 71 47 00 41 or 04 71 47 01 21 (Mairie); fax 04 71 47 02 23; otthiezac@wanadoo.fr]** Sp fr N122 on D59. Med, mkd pitch, pt shd; wc (some cont); shwrs inc; el pnts (10A) €2.20; Indry rm; shops 500m; playgrnd adj; pool 3km; tennis; poss cr; quiet. "Gd walking in Cantal; helpful owner; clean facs." 15 Jun-15 Sep. € 7.80 2007*

VIC SUR CERE *7C4* (1km E Rural) *44.98136, 2.62930* **Camp Municipal du Carladez, Ave des Tilleuls, 15800 Vic-sur-Cère [04 71 47 51 04 or 04 71 47 51 75 (Mairie); fax 04 71 47 50 59; vic-sur-cere@wanadoo.fr; www.vicsur cere.com]** Fr Aurillac on N122 site sp on ent Vic-sur-Cère on R. Lge, pt shd; wc (some cont); shwrs inc; el pnts (6A) €2.50; supmkt 100m; pool 500m; playgrnd, tennis & mini-golf nrby; rv fishing; poss cr; adv bkg; quiet. "Gate clsd 2000; office clsd Sun; no pitching without booking in; plenty of rm high ssn (2007); helpful warden; clean facs." ♦ 1 Apr-30 Sep. € 8.40 2007*

VIC SUR CERE *7C4* (1.5km SE Rural) *44.97142, 2.63319* **Camping La Pommeraie, 15800 Vic-sur-Cère [04 71 47 54 18; fax 04 71 49 63 30; pommeraie@ wanadoo.fr; www.camping-la-pommeraie.com]** Fr Vic-sur-Cère take D54 twd Pierrefort & Chaudes-Aigues, initially sp Salvanhac. Foll yellow site sp over rv, under rlwy bdge. Foll D154 up steep, narr, winding hill for 1.5km. Foll camp sp R into narr lane. Med, terr, pt shd; wc (some cont); baby facs; serviced pitches; shwrs inc; el pnts (6A) €4; Indtte; shop high ssn; rest; snacks; bar; no BBQ; playgrnd; pool; paddling pool; fishing; tennis; wifi; entmnt; TV rm; many statics; dogs €2.50; poss cr; adv bkg rec; ccard acc. "Peaceful, scenic site; best pitches at top but steep access; not suitable elderly or infirm; mkt Tue, Fri." ♦ 1 May-12 Sep. € 25.00 2009*

VICHY *9A1* (1km SW Rural) *46.11648, 3.42560* **Camping Les Acacias, Rue Claude Decloître, 03700 Bellerive-sur-Allier [04 70 32 36 22; fax 04 70 32 88 52; camping-acacias03@orange.fr; www.camping-acacias.com]** Cross bdge to Bellerive fr Vichy & foll Hauterive sp onto D1093. Strt over at 1st rndabt & turn L at 2nd rndabt onto D131 dir Hauterive. At 3rd rndabt turn L sp 'piscine'. Foll sm camping sps along rv side. Or fr S leave D906 at St Yorre & cross Rv Allier, then foll sp to Bellerive. Site sp at rndabt on app to Bellerive adj Rv Allier. On final app, at sp showing site in either dir, keep L & foll site sp along rv bank to recep. NB Many other sites in area, foll sp carefully. Med, hdg/mkd pitch, shd; wc; chem disp; baby facs; shwrs inc; el pnts (10A) €3; gas; shops 1km; snacks; BBQ; playgrnd; pool; fishing; boating; TV; 20% statics; dogs €1; adv bkg; ccard acc; red low ssn; CCI. "Well-run site; helpful owner; gd san facs; lovely town." 1 Apr-15 Oct. € 16.00 2009*

VICHY *9A1* (1.5km SW Rural) *46.11555, 3.43006* **Camping Beau Rivage, Rue Claude Decloître, 03700 Bellerive-sur-Allier [04 70 32 26 85; fax 04 70 32 03 94; camping-beaurivage@wanadoo.fr; www.camping-beaurivage.com]** Fr Vichy take D2209 dir Gannat. After x-ing bdge over Rv Allier, turn L at rndabt foll sp Camping, sp to Beau Rivage. Site on L on rv bank. Med, shd; wc (mainly cont); chem disp; mv service pnt; baby facs; shwrs inc; el pnts (10A) €3; gas; Indtte; shop; supmkt 1km; rest; BBQ; playgrnd; 2 pools; waterslide; fishing; canoeing; cycle hire; games area; tennis 2km; archery; entmnt; wifi; TV; some statics; dogs €1; poss cr; quiet; red low ssn. ♦ 1 Apr-15 Oct. € 16.00 (CChq acc) 2009*

VICHY *9A1* (5km SW Rural) *46.07961, 3.38213* **FLOWER Camping La Roseraie, 1093 Route de Randan, 03700 Brugheas [04 70 32 43 33; fax 04 70 32 26 23; campinglaroseraie@wanadoo.fr; www.campinglaroseraie. com or www.flowercamping.com]** Fr Vichy on D1093, foll sp to Brugheas. Site well sp. Med, hdg/mkd pitch, pt shd; wc; chem disp; baby facs; shwrs inc; el pnts (6A) €2.50; gas; Indtte; shop 3km; tradsmn; snacks, bar high ssn; BBQ; playgrnd; pool; TV rm; games area; 10% statics; dogs; adv bkg; quiet; red long stay; CCI. "Lovely pool." ♦ 1 Apr-30 Oct. € 12.60 2006*

France

VIELLE ST GIRONS see Léon *8E1*

⊞ **VIELMUR SUR AGOUT** *8F4* (S Rural) *43.62094, 2.09293* **FFCC Camping Le Pessac, 14 Quartier du Pessac, 81570 Vielmur-sur-Agout [tel/fax 05 63 74 30 24; info@camping-lepessac.com; www.camping-lepessac.com]** W on D112 fr Castres, after 13km turn L D92 S. 200m after level x-ing turn L, site in 100m, sp. Med, mkd pitch, pt shd; wc; mv service pnt; shwrs; el pnts (6A) €3.30; Indtte; shop; bar; playgrnd; pool; paddling pool; fishing; tennis nr; entmnt; 20% statics; dogs €1; red low ssn; CCI. "Clean site; helpful, pleasant staff; extension to site & new san facs in progress (2008); pool upgraded." € 10.70 2008*

VIERZON *4G3* (2.5km SW Urban) *47.20937, 2.08079* **Camp Municipal de Bellon, Route de Bellon, 18100 Vierzon [02 48 75 49 10 or 02 48 53 06 11; fax 02 48 71 40 94; campingmunicipal-vierzon@wanadoo.fr; www.ville-vierzon.fr]** Fr N on A71 take A20 dir Châteauroux, leave at junc 7 onto D2020 & then D27 dir Bourges; pass Intermarché supmkt on L, after next traff lts turn L into Route de Bellon; site in 1km on R, sp. NB Do not go into town cent. Med, hdg pitch, pt sl, pt shd; wc (some cont); chem disp; mv service pnt; shwrs inc; el pnts (6A) €2.35 (some rev pol); gas; Indry rm; shop 500m; rest; snacks; playgrnd; fishing; boat hire; internet; phone; poss cr; Eng spkn; adv bkg; quiet but some rlwy noise; no ccard acc; CCI. "Attractive, well-kept site by rv; gd sized pitches but some poss diff to negotiate; gd, clean facs; gates clsd 2300-0700; warden on site 1700-2200; poss itinerants; vg." ♦ 1 May-30 Sep. € 9.15 2009*

⊞ **VIERZON** *4G3* (5km NW Rural) **Aire Communale, Place de la Mairie, 18100 Méry-sur-Cher [02 48 75 38 18; mairie-mery-sur-cher@wanadoo.fr]** Fr Vierzon on D2076 (N76) dir Tours. Site clearly sp on L on ent Méry-sur-Cher. Sm, mkd pitch, hdstg, ltd shd; wc; chem disp; mv service pnt; el pnts inc; shop 100m; dogs; phone; bus; rd noise; m'vans only - max 48 hrs. "Well-maintained site; pay at machine on ent (credit cards only); excel NH." € 5.00 2009*

VIEUX BOUCAU LES BAINS *8E1* (800m N Coastal) *43.79309, -1.40607* **Camp Municipal Les Sablères, Bldv du Marensin, 40480 Vieux-Boucau-les-Bains [05 58 48 12 29 or 05 58 48 13 22; fax 05 58 48 20 70; camping-lessableres@wanadoo.fr; www.les-sableres.com]** Foll sps fr cent of vill twd beach, site sp fr D652. V lge, mkd pitch, pt sl, shd; wc (some cont); chem disp; mv service pnt; baby facs; shwrs inc; el pnts (5-10A) €3.10-4.30; Indtte; shops, rest & snack 1km; BBQ; playgrnd; sand/surf beach 300m (sw not rec due dangerous currents); lake sw nrby; games area; 20% statics; dogs €1.80; phone; poss cr; Eng spkn; adv bkg; quiet; CCI. "Site by lge sand dune; vg." ♦ 1 Apr-15 Oct. € 16.00 2007*

VIGAN, LE (GARD) *10E1* (2km E Rural) *43.99141, 3.63760* **Camping Le Val de l'Arre, Route du Pont de la Croix, 30120 Le Vigan [04 67 81 02 77 or 06 82 31 79 72 (mob); fax 04 67 81 71 23; valdelarre@wanadoo.fr; www.valdelarre.com]** E fr Le Vigan on D999. Turn R at 1st rndabt over bdge. Turn L immed after bdge; site in 400m, well sp. Height limit 3.5m. Med, mkd pitch, pt sl, pt shd; wc (some cont); chem disp; shwrs inc; el pnts inc (10A) €3.50; gas & 2km; Indtte; tradsmn; shop & 2km; rest; snacks; playgrnd; htd pool; fishing 4km; entmnt; games rm; TV; dogs €2; phone; Eng spkn; adv bkg; some rd noise; ccard acc; red low ssn; CCI. "Peaceful, well-run rvside site; friendly, helpful owners; gd touring base; rec for nature lovers." ♦ 1 Apr-30 Sep. € 16.00 2009*

VIGAN, LE (GARD) *10E1* (7km S Rural) *43.92896, 3.59061* **Camp Municipal, 30120 Montdardier [04 67 81 52 16 or 04 67 81 52 46 (Mairie); fax 04 67 81 53 22]** Fr D999 in Le Vigan turn S onto D48 dir Aveze to Montdardier in 5km; site on W of D48. Site sp (sm brown) in Mondardier. NB D48 narr & steep with hairpins - not rec lge o'fits. Sm, pt sl, pt shd; wc; shwrs; el pnts (6A) €1-1.50; shop 300m; playgrnd; poss cr; quiet; adv bkg. "Warden calls." 1 Mar-31 Oct. € 9.70 2006*

VIGAN, LE (LOT) see Gourdon *7D3*

VIGEOIS see Uzerche *7B3*

VIGNEAUX, LES see Argentiere la Bessee, L' *9C3*

VIGNES, LES *9D1* (4.5km N Rural) **Aire Naturelle de Camping à la Ferme (Bonnal), Le Bouquet, 48500 St Georges-de-Lévéjac [04 66 48 81 82; campingbonnal@orange.fr; www.cardoule.com/lebouquet]** Exit A75 junc 42 onto D955 to Le Massegros; turn L onto D32 sp La Canourgue; at next x-rds turn L to Le Bouquet. Site sp at x-rds. Sm, pt sl, pt shd; wc; chem disp (wc); shwrs inc; el pnts (10A) €2.30; dogs; phone; adv bkg; quiet. "Site is lge field on a farm; v peaceful, nr Gorge du Tarn; all basic facs; owners helpful." ♦ 1 May-30 Sep. € 9.00 2006*

VIGNES, LES *9D1* (6km NE Rural) *44.30424, 3.26858* **Camping La Blaquière, 48210 Les Vignes [tel/fax 04 66 48 54 93; campingblaquiere@wanadoo.fr; www.campingblaquiere.fr]** On Gorges du Tarn D907b fr Le Rozier to St Enimie, camp is on R 6km after Les Vignes on rvside. Sm, mkd pitch, terr, shd; wc; chem disp; baby facs; shwrs inc; el pnts (6A) €2.50; Indtte; shop; tradsmn; rest; snacks; BBQ; playgrnd; rv & beach; fishing; entmnt; 50% statics; dogs €1.60; phone; Eng spkn; quiet; red low ssn. "Superb rvside location." ♦ 1 May-10 Sep. € 12.60 2007*

⊞ **VIHIERS** *4G1* (10km SE Rural) *47.07419, -0.41104* **Camping Le Serpolin, St Pierre-à-Champ, 49560 Cléré-sur-Layon [02 41 52 43 08; fax 02 41 52 39 18; info@loirecamping.com; www.loirecamping.com]** Take D748 S fr Vihiers by-pass sp Argenton Château. In 2km turn L at sp Cléré-sur-Layon onto D54. Cont thro vill to 1st mkd x-rd, turn R, site last house along this lane. Sm, hdstg, pt shd; htd wc; chem disp; shwrs inc; el pnts (6A) €4; Indtte; BBQ; playgrnd; pool; fishing; cycle hire; wifi; dogs free; Eng spkn; adv bkg rec; quiet; red low ssn; CCI. "Peaceful, CL-type site; clean san facs; helpful British owners; rallies by arrangement; conv chateaux; Futuroscope; vg." € 13.00 2008*

VIHIERS *4G1* (1km W Rural) *47.14647, -0.54090* **Camp Municipal La Vallée du Lys, Route du Voide, 49310 Vihiers [02 41 75 00 14 or 02 41 75 80 60 (Mairie); fax 02 41 75 58 01; ville.vihiers@wanadoo.fr; http://vihiers.free.fr]** W of Vihiers leave D960 onto D54 twds Valanjou, & in 150m bear L at 1st fork in rd. Sm, mkd pitch, pt shd; wc; shwrs inc; el pnts (6A) €1.91; Indry rm; shop; playgrnd; coarse fishing; games area; 15% statics; some rd noise; CCI. "Twin-axles extra; san facs excel; warden helpful; narr ent to some pitches; rec." ♦ 25 May-1 Sep. € 6.55 2007*

VILLARD DE LANS *9C3* (800m N Rural) *45.07750, 5.55620* **Camping Caravaneige L'Oursière, 38250 Villard-de-Lans [04 76 95 14 77; fax 04 76 95 58 11; info@camping-oursiere.fr; www.camping-oursiere.fr]** Site clearly visible on app to town fr D531 Gorges d'Engins rd (13km SW Grenoble). App fr W on D531 not rec for c'vans. Lge, terr, unshd; htd wc (some cont); chem disp; mv service pnt; baby facs; shwrs inc; el pnts (6-10A) €4-6.50; gas; Indtte; shops; snacks; rest; BBQ; playgrnd; pool, waterspark 800m; drying rm; 20% statics; dogs €0.90; poss cr; adv bkg; quiet; ccard acc; CCI. "Excel all winter sports; friendly, helpful owners; excel." ♦ 5 Dec-27 Sep. € 16.00 2009*

⊞ **VILLARD DE LANS** *9C3* (10km N Rural) *45.12951, 5.53215* **Camping Caravaneige Les Buissonnets, 38112 Méaudre [04 76 95 21 04; fax 04 76 95 26 14; camping-les-buissonnets@wanadoo.fr; www.camping-les-buissonnets.com]** NE o'skts of Méaudre off D106, approx 30km SW of Grenoble by rd & 18km as crow flies. Med, sl, unshd; htd wc; chem disp; mv service pnt; shwrs inc; el pnts (2-10A) €2.20-8; Indtte; shops 500m; snacks; rest 500m; pool 300m; playgrnd; games area; bus to ski slopes; site clsd 5 Nov to mid-Dec; Eng spkn; quiet; higher price in winter. "Gd skiing cent; conv touring Vercours; levellers ess; highly rec." ♦ € 14.00 2008*

VILLARDONNEL see Carcassonne *8F4*

VILLARS COLMARS see Colmars *9D4*

VILLARS LES DOMBES *9A2* (S Urban) *45.99763, 5.03163* **Camp Municipal Les Autières, Ave des Nations, 01330 Villars-les-Dombes [04 74 98 00 21; fax 04 74 98 05 82; autieres@campingendombes.fr; www.campingendombes.fr]** N fr Lyon on N83, site in town cent on R by sw pool. Lge, pt shd; wc; shwrs inc; el pnts inc; Indtte; shop; rest; snacks; BBQ; playgrnd; htd pool adj inc; tennis; rv adj; entmnts; 60% static; dogs €2.50. "Gd site & facs; popular NH; gd security; bird park 10 mins walk." ♦ 1 May-14 Sep. € 18.50 2009*

VILLECROZE LES GROTTES see Salernes *10F3*

VILLEDIEU LES POELES *1D4* (500m S Urban) *48.83638, -1.21694* **Camping Les Chevaliers, 2 Impasse Pré de la Rose, 50800 Villedieu-les-Poêles [02 33 61 02 44; contact@camping-deschevaliers; www.camping-des chevaliers.com]** Exit A84 junc 38 onto D999 twd Villedieu, then R onto D975 (N175) & R onto D924 to avoid town cent. Foll sp fr car park on R after x-ing rv. Med, hdg/mkd pitch, pt shd; wc; chem disp; mv service pnt; shwrs inc; baby facs; el pnts (6A) inc; Indtte; shop 500m; supmkt 2km; rest; snacks; bar; playgrnd; htd pool; rv fishing; boating; tennis; entmnt; TV rm; dogs €1.50; phone; poss cr; Eng spkn; adv bkg; quiet; red low ssn; CCI. "Peaceful site; lge pitches but kerbs poss diff lger o'fits; gd, modern san facs; site gates clsd 2200-0700; site yourself if office clsd; interesting historic town; avoid arr Tue am due mkt; conv A84 & Cherbourg ferry; vg." ♦ 1 Apr-15 Oct. € 22.80 2009*

See advertisement

VILLEFAGNAN see Ruffec *7A2*

France

VILLEFORT (LOZERE) *9D1* (3.4km N Rural) *44.46133, 3.92736* **Camping du Lac, Morangiès, 48800 Pourcharesses [04 66 46 81 27 or 06 84 12 11 18 (mob); fax 04 66 69 77 49; contact@camping-lac-cevennes.com; www.camping-lac-cevennes.com]** Well sp on D906 nr Villefort dir Pourcharesses. Steep access rd. Med, hdg/mkd pitch, terr, pt shd; wc; chem disp (wc); baby facs; shwrs inc; el pnts €1.50; Indtte; tradsmn; playgrnd; pool; lake sw; some statics; dogs €1.50; poss cr; Eng spkn; adv bkg, ess high ssn. "Diff access to terr (with view) for lge o'fits, but worth effort; excel." 1 May-30 Sep. € 12.50 2009*

VILLEFORT (LOZERE) *9D1* (600m S Rural) **Camp Municipal Les Sédaries, Route d'Alès, 48800 Villefort [04 66 46 84 33; fax 04 66 46 89 66; sedaries.villefort@wanadoo.fr; www.villefort-cevennes.com http://sedaries.villefort-cevennes.com/]** On D906 heading S fr Villefort twd Alès. Sm, terr, pt shd; wc; chem disp (wc); shwrs inc; el pnts (6A) €2; Indtte; shops, rest, bar in town; BBQ; lake sw, fishing 2km; dogs €1; phone; poss cr; quiet; CCI. "Attractive, scenic site; bureau clsd 1000-1830." 1 Jun-30 Sep. € 9.00 2009*

VILLEFRANCHE DE CONFLENT see Prades *8G4*

⊞ **VILLEFRANCHE DE LAURAGAIS** *8F3* (8km SW Rural) *43.35498, 1.64862* **Camping Le Lac de la Thésauque, Nailloux, 31560 Montgeard [05 61 81 34 67; fax 05 61 81 00 12; camping-thesauque@caramail.com; www.camping-thesauque.com]** Fr S exit A61 at Villefrance-de-Lauragais junc 20 onto D622, foll sp Auterive then Lac after Gardouch vill, site sp. Fr N turn off A61 at 1st junc after tolls S of Toulouse onto A66 (sp Foix). Leave A66 at junc 1 & foll sp Nailloux. Turn L on ent vill onto D662 & in 2km turn R onto D25 & immed R to site, sp. Med, mkd pitch, hdstg, terr, pt shd; htd wc; chem disp; shwrs inc; el pnts (6-10A) €3.30-4.30; Indtte; shop; rest; snacks; bar; BBQ; playgrnd; fishing; boating; 70% statics; dogs €1.50; poss cr; red low ssn; CCI. "Scenic, peaceful location; conv NH for A61; helpful owners; ltd facs low ssn; gd security; steep app to sm terr pitches poss diff lge o'fits." € 14.90 2009*

VILLEFRANCHE DE ROUERGUE *7D4* (9km SE Rural) *44.26695, 2.11575* **Camping Le Muret, 12200 St Salvadou [05 65 81 80 69 or 05 65 29 84 87; info@lemuret.com; www.lemuret.com]** Fr Villefranche on D911 twd Millau, R on D905A sp camping & foll camping sp 7km. Sm, hdg/mkd pitch, shd; wc; shwrs inc; el pnts (16A) €4.50; gas & ice at farm; Indtte; shops 9km; tradsmn; rest; snacks; bar; lake adj; fishing; dogs €2; phone; adv bkg; v quiet; red long stay; CCI. "Lovely setting; gd sized pitches; san facs sub-standard 2008 (owners aware)." ♦ 5 Apr-22 Oct. € 14.50 2008*

VILLEFRANCHE DE ROUERGUE *7D4* (1km SW Urban) *44.34207, 2.02731* **FFCC Camping du Rouergue, 35b Ave de Fondies, Le Teulel, 12200 Villefranche-de-Rouergue [tel/fax 05 65 45 16 24; campingrouergue@wanadoo.fr; www.campingdurouergue.com]** Best app fr N on D922, then D47 dir Monteils & Najac; avoid 1-way system in town; ent thro sports stadium. Site well sp. Med, hdg/mkd pitch, hdstg, shd; wc (some cont); chem disp; mv service pnt; baby facs; serviced pitches; shwrs inc; el pnts (16A) €3; Indtte; shop; tradsmn; rest; snacks; bar; playgrnd; pool; sports stadium adj; tennis 1km; entmnt; TV rm; 15% statics; dogs €1; bus high ssn; extra for twin-axles; Eng spkn; adv bkg (30% dep); quiet; ccard acc; red low ssn/long stay/CCI. "Well-kept, peaceful site; pleasant, friendly owner; lge pitches; excel san facs; gd security; m'van services outside site; rec." ♦ 13 Apr-30 Sep. € 14.00 2009*

⊞ **VILLEFRANCHE DE ROUERGUE** *7D4* (10km W Rural) *44.38404, 1.88802* **Camping Le Moulin de Bannac, 12200 Martiel [05 65 29 44 52; fax 05 65 29 43 84; contact@bannaclelac.com; www.bannaclelac.com]** On rd D911 to S bet Martiel & Limogne. Med, hdg/mkd pitch, pt sl, pt shd; wc; chem disp; mv service pnt; shwrs inc; el pnts (16A) inc; gas; Indtte; shop 1km; rest; snacks; bar; BBQ; playgrnd; pool; fishing; entmnt; internet; 6% statics; dogs €1.50; adv bgk; quiet; Eng spkn; CCI. "Wooded setting & lake." ♦ € 13.00 2008*

VILLEFRANCHE DU PERIGORD *7D3* (1km E Urban) *44.62794, 1.08249* **FFCC Camping La Bastide, Route de Cahors, 24550 Villefranche-du-Périgord [05 53 28 94 57; fax 05 53 29 47 95; campinglabastide@wanadoo.fr; www.camping-la-bastide.com]** On N660 fr Villefranche-du-Périgord dir Cahors; site past Post Office on R nr top of hill on town o'skts. Med, hdg/mkd pitch, terr, pt shd; wc; chem disp; mv service pnt; baby facs; shwrs inc; el pnts (6-10A) €3-4; Indtte; shops 300m; rest; snacks; bar; playgrnd; pool; tennis 300m; fishing; entmnt; 25% statics; dogs €1; poss cr; adv bkg; quiet; red low ssn; CCI. "Steep, terr site but easy access; charming owners; excel touring base; vg." ♦ 5 Apr-8 Nov. € 17.00 2008*

VILLEFRANCHE DU PERIGORD *7D3* (6km SW Rural) *44.59025, 1.04799* **FLOWER Camping Moulin du Périé, 47500 Sauveterre-la-Lémance [05 53 40 67 26; fax 05 53 40 62 46; moulinduperie@wanadoo.fr; www.camping-moulin-perie.com or www.flowercamping.com]** FrN fr Villefranche-du-Périgord take D710 S dir Fumel. At Sauveterre-la-Lémance turn L at traff lts, cross level x-ing & in 400m turn L sp Loubejac & site; site on R in 4km. Tight ent bet tall hedges 2.6m apart for 30m. Fr E fr Cahors on D660 & turn L onto D46 sp Loubejac. Cont thro Loubejac & turn L at T-junc, foll sp Sauveterre. Site on R in 4km. Med, pt sl, pt shd; wc; chem disp; mv service pnt; baby facs; shwrs inc; el pnts (10A) inc (poss rev pol); gas; Indtte; shop; rest; snacks; bar; BBQ; playgrnd; pool; paddling pool; sm lake & beach; trout fishing; tennis 3km; cycle hire; archery; organised activities; microlight flying; games/TV rm; 25% statics; dogs €4.40; poss cr; Eng spkn; adv bkg rec; quiet; ccard acc; red low ssn; CCI. "Beautiful, well-run, welcoming site; friendly family owners; san facs clean; red facs low ssn; vg rest; gd touring base; site rds narr; not suitable v lge o'fits." ♦ 15 May-19 Sep. € 30.00 (CChq acc) ABS - D09 2009*

VILLEFRANCHE DU QUEYRAN see Casteljaloux *7D2*

VILLEFRANCHE SUR CHER *4G3* (9km SE Rural) *47.26917, 1.86265* **Camp Municipal Val Rose, Rue du Val Rose, 41320 Mennetou-sur-Cher [02 54 98 11 02 or 02 54 98 01 19 (Mairie)]** Site sp fr D976/D2076 (N76) fr Villefranche (sm white sp); site on R in W side of vill of Mennetou. Sm, pt shd; htd wc; chem disp; shwrs inc; el pnts (6A) inc; Indtte; snacks & shops adj; rest in town; playgrnd; htd pool adj; rv adj; adv bkg; quiet. "Well-kept, clean site; friendly warden; excel san facs; barrier clsd 2200-0700; pretty, walled town 5 mins walk along canal; mkt Thurs." ♦ 15 May-31 Aug. € 8.50 2009*

VILLEFRANCHE SUR CHER *4G3* (10km SE Rural) *47.26248, 1.90823* **Camp Municipal Les Saules, 41320 Châtres-sur-Cher [02 54 98 04 55 or 02 54 98 03 24 (Mairie); fax 02 54 98 09 57; chatres-sur-cher@cg41.fr]** Site off D976 (N76) in Châtres-sur-Cher bet Villefranche & Vierzon. Med, pt shd; wc; shwrs inc; el pnts (5A) €1.80; shops & rests nrby; playgrnd; sand beach & rv adj; fishing & watersports; 10% statics; adv bkg; quiet; CCI. "Lovely, well-kept site on rv; friendly warden; facs old but clean; gd NH." 1 May-31 Aug. € 6.25 2007*

VILLEFRANCHE SUR SAONE *9B2* (10km E Rural) *45.99104, 4.81802* **Camp Municipal le Bois de la Dame, 01480 Ars-sur-Formans [04 74 00 77 23 or 04 74 00 71 84 (Mairie); fax 04 74 08 10 62; mairie.ars-sur-formans@wanadoo.fr]** Exit A6 junc 31.1 or 31.2 onto D131/D44 E dir Villars-les-Dombes. Site 500m W of Ars-sur-Formans on lake, sp. Med, mkd pitch, pt sl, terr, pt shd; wc (cont); chem disp; shwrs inc; el pnts (6A) €2; Indtte; playgrnd; fishing lake; 60% statics; dogs €1.22; poss cr; adv bkg rec high ssn; CCI. "Ltd facs low ssn; twin-axle vans not acc; excel." ♦ 1 Apr-30 Sep. € 8.00 2007*

VILLEFRANCHE SUR SAONE *9B2* (3km SE Rural) *45.97243, 4.75237* **Camp Municipal La Plage Plan d'Eau, 2788 Route de Riottier, 69400 Villefranche-sur-Saône [04 74 65 33 48; fax 04 74 60 68 18; camping villefranche@voila.fr]** Exit A6 junc 31.2 Villefranche. Fr N turn R at rndabt, cross over a'route & str over next rndabt; cont to site on R bef Rv Saône. Or fr S turn R at rndabt & cont to site as above. Look for sp on rndabt. Med, shd; wc (some cont); chem disp; mv service pnt; shwrs inc; el pnts (6A) inc; gas; Indry rm; shop 1km; tradsmn; snacks in ssn; bar; lake sw adj; fishing; 10% statics; adv bkg; quiet; ccard acc; CCI. "Busy site in gd position; easy access & nr m'way but quiet; a bit run down & san facs not v clean (2008); gd walking; NH only." ♦ 30 Apr-30 Sep. € 16.60 2009*

VILLEFRANCHE SUR SAONE *9B2* (6km SE Rural) *45.93978, 4.76811* **Camp Municipal La Petite Saône, Rue Robert Baltié, 01600 Trévoux [04 74 00 14 16 or 04 74 08 73 73 (Mairie); fax 04 74 00 17 10; mairie.trevoux@wanadoo.fr; http://ladombes.free.fr/Camping/Trevoux.htm]** Fr Villefranche take D306 (N6) S to Anse. Turn L onto D39/D6 for Trévoux, site sp in town, on bank of Rv Saône. Lge, pt shd; wc (mainly cont); shwrs; el pnts (10A) inc; shops 1km; playgrnd; rv fishing & sw adj; entmnts; 75% statics; adv bkg high ssn; quiet; red/CCI. "Spacious rvside site nr vill; helpful staff; clean facs; access poss diff lge o'fits due statics; Trévoux interesting history." 1 Apr-30 Sep. € 13.80 2009*

VILLEFRANCHE SUR SAONE *9B2* (5km S Rural) *45.94050, 4.72680* **Camping Les Portes du Beaujolais, Ave Jean Vacher, 69480 Anse [04 74 67 12 87; fax 04 74 09 90 97; campingbeaujolais@wanadoo.fr; www.camping-beaujolais.com]** Exit A6 junc 31.2 at Villefranche & foll D306 S to Anse (foll sp Champion supmkt). Site well sp off D39, on banks of Rvs Saône & L'Azergues. Lge, hdg/mkd pitch, hdstg, pt shd; htd wc (some cont); chem disp; mv service pnt; shwrs inc; el pnts (6-10A) €3.20; Indtte; shop; snacks; bar; playgrnd; pool; lake sw; cycle hire; wifi; TV rm; 10% statics; dogs €; phone; Eng spkn; adv bkg; rd noise fr A6 nrby; CCI. "Pleasant, friendly site; vg pitches but some sm, uneven & diff lge o'fits & muddy when wet; ltd facs low ssn; rvside walk; Anse 10 min walk - bus to Lyons; narr gauge rlwy adj; conv NH." ♦ 1 Mar-31 Oct. € 18.90 (CChq acc) 2009*

VILLEFRANCHE SUR SAONE *9B2* (8km NW Rural) *46.04751, 4.66041* **Camping Domaine de la Maison Germain, Route de Salles, Impasse de Charpenay, 69460 Blaceret [04 74 67 56 36; info@bossan.tk; www.bossan.tk]** Exit A6 junc 31.1 onto D43 dir Arnas. Cont to Blaceret then turn L onto D20. In 500m turn R into lane, recep on R but site strt on. Sm, hdg pitch, pt shd; wc; shwrs inc; el pnts (10A) inc; rest; Eng spkn; adv bkg; quiet. "CL-type site - conv NH; san facs clsd in cold weather but site open - phone in advance." 1 Apr-31 Oct. € 15.50 2007*

France

VILLENEUVE DE BERG *9D2* (2km N Rural) *44.57251, 4.51041* **Camping Domaine Le Pommier, 07170 Villeneuve-de-Berg [04 75 94 82 81; fax 04 75 94 83 90; info@campinglepommier.com; www.campinglepommier.com]** Site off rndabt at E end of by-pass to Villeneuve-de-Berg on N102. If app fr Aubenas do not go thro town. Steep incline, poss req tractor. Lge, mkd pitch, hdstg, terr, pt sl, pt shd; htd wc; chem disp; mv service pnt; baby facs; fam bthrm; shwrs inc; el pnts (6A) €4; lndtte; supmkt; rest; snacks; bar; BBQ (gas); playgrnd; htd pools; waterslides; paddling pool; tennis; games area; games rm; cycle hire; wifi; entmnt; sound-proofed disco high ssn; TV rm; 30% statics; dogs €4; Eng spkn; adv bkg; quiet; ccard acc; red low ssn/long stay; CCI. "Vg Dutch-owned site; superb pool complex; excel san facs." ♦ 25 Apr-30 Sep. € 30.50 2009*

See advertisement

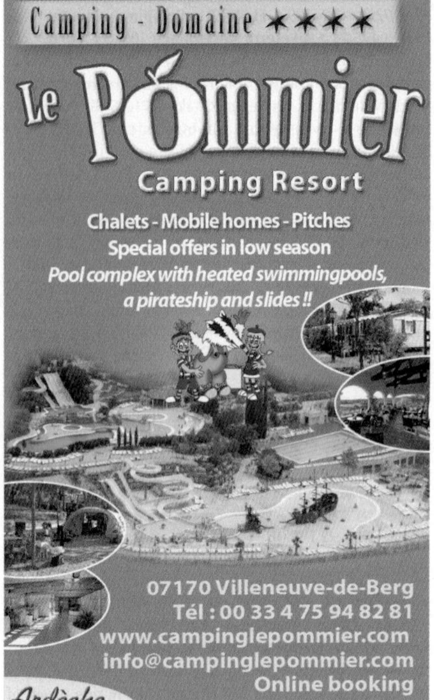

VILLENEUVE DE LA RAHO see Perpignan *8G4*

VILLENEUVE LES GENETS see Bléneau *4G3*

VILLENEUVE LOUBET see Cagnes sur Mer *10E4*

⊞ **VILLENEUVE SUR LOT** *7D3* (7km E Rural) *44.39590, 0.78664* **Camping Le Sablon, 47140 St Sylvestre-sur-Lot [05 53 41 37 74; campinglesablon@wanadoo.fr]** Fr Villeneuve E on D911 sp Cahors, after 5km on ent St Sylvestre site on R behind supmkt. Sm, hdg/mkd pitch, shd; htd wc; shwrs; el pnts (6-10A) €2.50-3.50; lndry rm; snacks; playgrnd; pools & paddling pool; waterslide; fishing; 25% statics; quiet. "Pleasant, family-owned site; gd facs but run down low ssn; muddy when wet - no hdstg; poss itinerants; barrier clsd 1200-1400." € 10.00 2006*

VILLENEUVE SUR LOT *7D3* (8km E Urban) **Camping Les Berges du Lot, Place de la Mairie, 47140 St Sylvestre-sur-Lot [05 53 41 22 23 or 05 53 41 24 58 (Mairie)]** Exit Villeneuve on D911 sp Cahors. Site in cent of St Sylvestre-sur-Lot. Foll Camping sp to rear of La Mairie (Town Hall) & adj car park to R of main rd. Sm, mkd pitch, pt shd; wc; chem disp; shwrs inc; el pnts (16A) €2.50; shops & supmkt adj; rest, bar 1km; sm pool; boating; fishing; birdwatching; Eng spkn; quiet. "Popular, comfortable, scenic site; clean facs; helpful staff; adv bkg rec high ssn; many long term residents, inc British; rec." ♦ 15 May-30 Sep. € 7.50 2009*

VILLENEUVE SUR LOT *7D3* (1.5km S Urban) *44.39446, 0.71504* **Camp Municipal du Rooy, Rue de Rooy, 47300 Villeneuve-sur-Lot [05 53 70 24 18 or 05 53 36 17 30; tourisme.villeneuve-sur-lot@wanadoo.fr]** Site sp to E of N21. Med, mkd pitch, pt sl, terr, pt shd; wc (some cont); chem disp; shwrs inc; el pnts (6-10A) €1.50-2.30; lndtte; shops 2km; tradsmn; BBQ; pool nrby; rv 5m; 15% statics; dogs €0.30; phone; poss cr; no ccard acc; quiet, but rlwy noise; CCI. "Nice, friendly site; helpful warden; some pitches poss flooded in bad weather (keep to L of site); san facs old but clean; conv NH or visit old city." 15 Apr-30 Sep. € 8.10 2009*

VILLEREAL *7D3* (2km N Rural) *44.65723, 0.72820* **Camping Château de Fonrives, Route d'Issigeac, Rives, 47210 Villeréal [05 53 36 63 38; fax 05 53 36 09 98; contact@campingchateaufonrives.com; www.campingchateaufonrives.com]** Fr Bergerac take N21 S for 8km, turn L onto D14 thro Issigeac; site is just outside vill of Rives in grounds of chateau. Med, pt sl, pt shd; wc; baby facs; shwrs inc; el pnts (6A) inc; gas; lndtte; shop; rest; bar; BBQ; playgrnd; 2 pools (1 htd, covrd); waterslide; lake sw; fishing; golf; cycle hire; games rm; entmnt; some statics; dogs €3; Eng spkn; adv bkg; quiet but some noise fr weekly disco; ccard acc; CCI. "Spacious site; gd, lge pool; van poss manhandled on some shady pitches; easier access pitches without shade; friendly owners; B&B avail; interesting town; mkt Sat." ♦ 4 Apr-3 Oct. € 33.50 2008*

VILLEREAL *7D3* (7km NE Rural) *44.65331, 0.80953* **Camping Le Moulin de Mandassagne, 47210 Parranquet [tel/fax 05 53 36 04 02; isabelle.pimouguet@orange.fr; www.haut-agenais-perigord.com]** Fr D104/D2 bet Villeréal & Monpazier turn N sp Parranquet, site sp. Sm, mkd pitch, pt shd; wc; chem disp; shwrs inc; el pnts (6A) inc; gas; lndry rm; shop adj; snacks; playgrnd; pool; fishing; tennis; entmnt; TV; poss cr; Eng spkn; adv bkg; v quiet. "Lovely countryside; friendly owners." ♦ 1 Apr-1 Oct. € 15.00 2008*

VILLEREAL *7D3* (3km SE Rural) *44.61000, 0.76256* **Camping Les Ormes, Fauquié-Haut, 47210 St Etienne-de-Villeréal [05 53 36 60 26; fax 05 53 36 69 90; info@campinglesormes.com; www.campinglesormes.com]** Take D255 SE fr Villeréal. At fork in rd in 1km, take RH rd sp St Etienne-de-Villeréal. Site on R in 2km. Med, mkd pitch, pt shd; wc; chem disp; baby facs; shwrs inc; el pnts (4A) €3; gas; lndtte; shop; tradsmn; rest; snacks; bar; BBQ; playgrnd; pool; lake fishing; tennis; games rm; entmnt; TV; 10% statics; dogs €3 (not acc high ssn); phone; poss cr; Eng spkn; adv bkg; quiet; red low ssn; CCI. "Excel site; highly rec early & late summer; busy high ssn." 29 Apr-30 Sep. € 22.00 2007*

VILLEREAL *7D3* (10km SE Rural) *44.61426, 0.81889* **Camping Fontaine du Roc, Les Moulaties, 47210 Dévillac [05 53 36 08 16; fax 05 53 61 60 23; fontaine.du.roc@wanadoo.fr; www.fontaineduroc.com]** Fr Villeréal take D255 sp Dévillac, just beyond Dévillac at x-rds turn L & L again sp Estrade; site on L in 500m. Med, hdg/mkd pitch, hdstg, pt shd; wc; chem disp; shwrs inc; el pnts (5A) €3 gas; lndtte; shop 7km; tradsmn; rest; snacks; bar; BBQ; playgrnd; pool; paddling pool; cycle hire; games rm; TV; 2% statics; dogs €3; phone; Eng spkn; adv bkg; quiet; red low ssn/long stay; no ccard acc; CCI. "Peaceful, well-cared for site; helpful owner; lge pitches." 1 May-30 Sep. € 17.00 2006*

⊞ **VILLEREAL** *7D3* (4km W Rural) *44.64001, 0.68725* **Aire Naturelle Ferme de Bourgade Holidays (Taylor-Block), 47210 Bournel [05 53 36 67 15; bourgade47@libertysurf.fr; www.bourgade-holidays.co.uk]** Exit N21 at Castillonnès onto D2 dir Villeréal; in 7.5km turn L dir Mazières & La Ferme Bourgade; in 800m turn L again; farm in 300 on L; site sp. Or fr Villeréal on D2 dir Castillonnès; in 2.2km turn R (nr Courbarieu); site on L in 2.4km. Site N of D2, Bournel S of D2. Sm, pt shd; wc; shwrs inc; el pnts inc; BBQ; dogs; CCI. "Delightful, quiet farm site; friendly, British owners; basic, adequate san facs; mkt Villeréal Sat am; vg." € 14.00 2009*

VILLEREAL *7D3* (3km NW Rural) *44.65253, 0.72375* **Aire Naturelle de Bergougne (Bru), 47210 Rives [05 53 36 01 30; fax 05 53 36 05 41; info@camping-de-bergougne.com; www.camping-de-bergougne.com]** Fr Villeréal, take D207 NW sp Issigeac/Bergerac. In 1km turn L onto D250 W sp Doudrac. Foll sm green sp to site. Sm, hdg pitch, pt sl, unshd; wc; chem disp; shwrs inc; el pnts (6A) inc; lndtte; rest, bar 3km; snacks; playgrnd; pool; fishing; games area; games rm; dogs €2; adv bkg. 15 May-30 Sep. € 14.70 2007*

VILLEROUGE LA CREMADE see Lezignan Corbieres *8F4*

VILLERS BOCAGE *3D1* (7km S Urban) *49.02530, -0.62515* **Camp Municipal La Closerie, Rue de Caen, 14260 Aunay-sur-Odon [02 31 77 32 46; fax 02 31 77 70 07; mairie.aunay.sur.odon@wanadoo.fr]** Exit A84 junc 43 sp Villers-Bocage/Aunay & take D6 twd Aunay. In approx 5km bef Aunay town sp, turn L sp 'Zone Industrielle', in 200m turn R at rndabt. Site on R in 100m. Sm, mkd pitch, pt sl, pt shd; wc; chem disp; shwrs inc; el pnts inc; gas, shops 500m; games area; dogs €1.55; quiet; CCI. "Warden calls." ♦ 1 Jul-31 Aug. € 15.00 2007*

VILLERS BOCAGE *3D1* (6km SW Rural) *49.07150, -0.74210* **Centre de Loisirs de la Vallée de Crahan, 14240 Cahagnes [02 31 73 02 26 or 06 72 12 10 40 (mob)]** Fr cent Cahagnes on D54 then take D193 for 2km; sp fr town sq; 1.5km narr app rd is 1-way. Med, pt sl, pt shd; wc; shwrs inc; el pnts (6A) €1.80; lndry rm; shops 3km; snacks; fishing; boating; 30% statics; quiet. "Peaceful, scenic site; resident wardens, but still site yourself; friendly welcome; dated san facs." 1 Jun-30 Sep. € 10.00 2008*

VILLERS LES NANCY see Nancy *6E2*

VILLERS SIRE NICOLE see Maubeuge *3B4*

VILLERS SUR AUTHIE see Rue *3B2*

VILLES SUR AUZON see Mormoiron *10E2*

⊞ **VILLEVAUDE** *3D3* (2km E Rural) *48.91258, 2.67025* **Camping Le Parc de Paris, Rue Adèle Claret, Montjay-la-Tour, 77410 Villevaudé [01 60 26 20 79; fax 01 60 27 02 75; info@campingleparc.fr; www.campingleparc.fr]** Fr N, A1 twds Paris, then A104 to Marne-la-Vallée, exit at junc 6B (Paris Bobigny), then D105 to Villevaudé, then to Montjay & site sp. Fr S exit A104 at junc 8 to Meaux & Villevaudé. Lge, hdg/mkd pitch, pt sl, pt shd; htd wc; serviced pitches; chem disp; mv service pnt; baby facs; shwrs inc; el pnts (10A) €3; lndtte (inc dryers); shop 5km; tradsmn; rest high ssn; snacks; bar; playgrnd; lake sw & sand beach 5km; tennis 200m; games area; games rm; entmnt; wifi; TV rm; 50% statics; dogs €5; phone; Eng spkn; adv bkg; ccard acc; CCI. "Conv Disneyland, Paris, Parc Astérix (Disney tickets fr recep); helpful staff; gd san facs; twin-axles acc if adv bkg; minibus fr site to local stn, shuttle service to Disneyland; vg." ♦ € 26.00 2009*

See advertisement on next page

VILLIERS CHARLEMAGNE see Chateau Gontier *4F1*

VILLIERS LE MORHIER see Maintenon *4E2*

⊞ **VILLIERS SUR ORGE** *4E3* (600m SE Urban) *48.65527, 2.30409* **Camping Le Beau Village, 1 Voie des Prés, 91700 Villiers-sur-Orge [01 60 16 17 86; le-beau-village@wanadoo.fr; www.beau-village.com]** Rec app fr N20, exit sp La Ville-du-Bois & Carrefour. Take rd for Villiers-sur-Orge & turn R at traff lts with sm Renault g'ge. Site sp 200m on L. Care needed on app due to narr rds. Med, hdg pitch, pt shd, htd wc; chem disp; mv service pnt; shwrs inc; el pnts (10A) inc (poss rev pol); gas; lndtte; shops 700m; tradsmn; bar; playgrnd; kayaking; games rm; dogs €2; phone; train 700m; recep clsd w/ends Dec to Feb; poss cr; quiet; red low ssn. "Pleasant, well-run site; conv Paris; ltd space for lge o'fits." € 18.00 2009*

VIMOUTIERS *3D1* (700m N Urban) *48.93236, 0.19646* **Camp Municipal La Campière, Ave Dr Dentu, 61120 Vimoutiers [02 33 39 30 29 or 02 33 39 18 86 (Mairie); fax 02 33 36 51 43; campingmunicipalvimoutiers@wanadoo.fr]** App on D579 or D916 or D979 bet Lisieux & Argental. Site nr stadium. Sm, hdg pitch, pt shd; htd wc; chem disp; shwrs inc; el pnts (6A) €2.10; Indry rm; shop 200m; rest, snacks 800m; playgrnd adj; pool & sports facs 2km; rv fishing, sw & boating 2km; tennis; cycle hire; 10% statics; dogs €1.15; poss cr; adv bkg; noise fr nrby factory; red low ssn; CCI. "Excel, well-maintained, pretty site at cent of Camembert cheese industry; helpful, friendly warden; vg, clean san facs; attractive town." ♦ 1 Mar-29 Oct. € 10.00 2008*

VINCELLES see Auxerre *4F4*

VINSOBRES see Nyons *9D2*

VIOLES see Orange *10E2*

VION see Tournon sur Rhône *9C2*

When we get home I'm going to post all these site report forms to the Club for next year's guide. The deadline's September.

⊞ **VIRIEU LE GRAND** *9B3* (5km NE Rural) *45.87483, 5.68428* **Camping Le Vaugrais, Chemin de Vaugrais, 01510 Artemare [04 79 87 37 34; fax 04 79 87 37 46; contact@camping-le-vaugrais.fr; www.camping-le-vaugrais.fr]** N fr Belley on D1504 (N504) then D904 to Artemare; sp in vill. Well sp fr D904 on rvside. Sm, pt shd, hdg pitch; wc (some cont); chem disp (wc); baby facs; shwrs inc; el pnts (5A) €2.40; Indtte; shop 500m; tradsmn; snacks; bar; BBQ; playgrnd; pool; fishing; wifi; 1% statics; dogs €1; Eng spkn; adv bkg; quiet; CCI. "Charming site; lge pitches with views; friendly owner; clean san facs, poss inadequate high ssn; Artemare within walking dist; excel." ♦ € 12.00 2007*

VIRIEU LE GRAND *9B3* (2.5km S Rural) *45.82954, 5.64432* **Camping Le Lac, 01510 Virieu-le-Grand [tel/fax 04 79 87 82 02 or 06 80 33 43 06 (mob); campingvirieu@orange.fr; www.campingvirieu.com]** Fr S on D904 site sp on R. Uneven app. Med, hdg pitch, terr, pt shd; wc; mv service pnt; shwrs inc; el pnts (6A) €3; tradsmn; shops 4km; snacks; BBQ; playgrnd; lake beach, sw & fishing; cycle hire; wifi; some statics; dogs €3.10; some rd & rlwy noise. "Clean, pleasant, scenic, lakeside site; clean facs; helpful owner." 7 Apr-28 Sep. € 14.60 2008*

VISAN see Valréas *9D2*

VITRAC see Sarlat la Canéda *7C3*

VITRE *2F4* (N Rural) *48.23090, -1.18087* **Camp Municipal du Lac, 35210 Châtillon-en-Vendelais [02 99 76 06 32 or 02 99 76 06 22 (Mairie); fax 02 99 76 12 39]** Take D178 fr Vitré to Fougères. In 11km branch L onto D108, sp Châtillon-en-Vendelais. Foll sp thro vill & turn R immed after level x-ing & bef bdge; site in 1km. Med, pt sl, pt shd; wc; shwrs inc; el pnts (6A) €3.10 (poss rev pol); Indtte; shop & 1km; playgrnd; tennis; lake adj; fishing; 10% statics; quiet; CCI. "Pleasant site; clean san facs; warden on site 0900-1000 only; levelling blocks req most pitches; quiet low ssn; gd walks; nature reserve (birds) nr." 15 May-30 Sep. € 7.30 2009*

VITRE *2F4* (2km SE Urban) *48.10889, -1.19823* **Camp Municipal Ste Etienne, Route d'Argentré-du-Plessis, 35500 Vitré [02 99 75 25 28 or 02 99 74 43 53; fax 02 99 74 04 12; www.ot-vitre.fr]** Exit A11 at junc 5 onto D857 twd Vitré. Take Vitré ring rd twd Rennes; 500m fr ring rd S on D88 twd Argentré-du-Plessis & foll camp sp. Sm, hdg pitch, pt sl, shd; wc (some cont); chem disp (wc); mv service pnt; shwrs inc; el pnts (10A) inc; shop 1km; supmkt 800m; sports complex adj; 25% statics; dogs; quiet but some rd & military aircraft noise; ccard not acc; CCI. "Peaceful site; gd size pitches but access to some poss diff; pitch yourself, warden calls am & eves - friendly & helpful; facs dated but clean; no security; poss unkempt low ssn; poss itinerants." 1 Apr-31 Oct. € 9.90 2008*

VITRY AUX LOGES *4F3* (3.5km N Rural) *47.95851, 2.28107* **Camping Hortus - Etang de la Vallée, Seichebrières, 45530 Vitry-aux-Loges [tel/fax 02 38 36 35 94; info@camping-hortus.com; www.camping-hortus.com]** Fr junc of N60, E60 & D952 N of Châteauneuf-sur-Loire take D10 N. In Vitry-aux-Loges foll sp Seichbrières, site sp on R just outside vill. Lge, mkd pitch, shd; htd wc; chem disp (wc); shwrs inc; el pnts (10A) €4; Indtte; tradsmn; snacks, bar 100m; lake sw 100m; fishing; watersports; phone; adv bkg; quiet; CCI. "Gd forest walking; conv Orléans." ♦
1 Apr-30 Sep. € 11.40 2009*

VITRY LE FRANCOIS *6E1* (4km SE Rural) *48.69673, 4.63039* **Aire Naturelle Camping Nature (Scherschell), 13 Rue de l'Evangile, 51300 Luxémont-et-Villotte [03 26 72 61 14 or 06 83 42 83 53 (mob)]** Fr Châlons sp on N44, site sp at E end of Vitry-le-François by-pass (N4); foll sp to R, then foll 3km to site. Fr S take exit for Vitry-le-François & pass lorry park; in approx 1km, turn L at rndabt; foll sp to Luxémont-et-Villotte; site in vill on R. Sm, pt sl, pt shd; wc (some cont); chem disp; mv service pnt; shwrs inc; el pnts (6A) inc (poss rev pol & long lead poss req); gas 2km; shop 6km; tradsmn; BBQ; playgrnd; lake sw 500m; fishing; adv bkg; quiet; CCI. "Delightful, CL-type site; well-kept & immac; helpful, friendly owners; no twin-axles; san facs stretched high ssn; excel." 1 May-1 Oct. € 13.00 2009*

VITRY LE FRANCOIS *6E1* (2km W Urban) *48.73020, 4.58114* **Camp Municipal La Peupleraie, Quai des Fontaines, 51300 Vitry-le-François [03 26 74 20 47 or 03 26 41 22 77 (Mairie); fax 03 26 41 22 88; camping@vitry-le-francois.net]** Fr N on N44 turn R at lge gate (sp Paris) & cont on dual c'way for approx 1km. Turn R on side rd, site sp nr lge parking area. Med, hdg pitch, pt shd; wc; shwrs inc; el pnts (5A) €2.13; gas; shops adj; rest, snacks, bar 500m; dogs €2.13; quiet, but some rd noise. "Delightful site; tight ent poss diff lge o'fits; no twin-axles." 1 Jun-30 Sep. € 12.18 2008*

VITTEAUX *6G1* (1km W Rural) *47.40134, 4.52951* **Camp Municipal La Gare, 21350 Vitteaux [03 80 49 60 87 or 03 80 49 61 25 (Mairie)]** Sp fr vill nr Hippodrome. Sm, hdg pitch, shd; wc; chem disp (wc); shwrs inc; el pnts (6A) €2.50; Indry rm; rest, snacks & bar 1km; BBQ; playgrnd; htd covrd pool nr; dogs €1; quiet. "Part of sports complex; warden calls am & pm; pick your spot; no security barrier." ♦ 1 Apr-15 Sep. € 8.00 2008*

VITTEFLEUR see Cany Barville *3C2*

VITTEL *6F2* (1km NE Urban) *48.20762, 5.95531* **Camping de Vittel, 270 Rue Claude Bassot, 88800 Vittel [03 29 08 02 71; aquadis1@wanadoo.fr; www.aquadis-loisirs.com]** Fr Chaumont/Dijon at traff lts take Epinal/Nancy rd into Place Gen de Gaulle; turn L over bdge & foll sp. Fr Epinal turn R over bdge at Place Gen de Gaulle & foll sp. Med, hdg/mkd pitch, hdstg, pt shd; htd wc (mainly cont); chem disp; shwrs inc; el pnts (10A) €2; Indtte; shop 1km; tradsmn; pool. Tennis 2km; dogs €3.10; poss cr; Eng spkn; adv bkg; quiet; CCI. "Interesting town; on Tour de France rte; walking & cycling rtes; san facs unclean (2008 & 2009)." 1 Apr-17 Oct. € 16.00 2009*

VIVIER SUR MER, LE see Dol de Bretagne *2E4*

VIVIERS *9D2* (1.2km N Urban) *44.48963, 4.67696* **Camping Rochecondrie, Quartier Rochecondrie, 07220 Viviers [tel/fax 04 75 52 74 66; campingrochecondrie@wanadoo.fr; www.campingrochecondrie.com]** Site on E side of D86. Fr N on D86 ent for S'bound traff tricky - rec cont past site to junc with D107, turn W (dir Aubenas) & turn around; app fr S as bef. Med, mkd pitch, pt shd; wc (mainly cont); chem disp; el pnts (6-10A) €3-5; gas; Indtte; BBQ; rest; bar; playgrnd; pool; fishing; 30% statics; dogs €1; phone; Eng spkn; rlwy noise; red low ssn; ccard acc; CCI. "Resident llamas; sm shwr cubicles; nr to Ardèche gorges; interesting medieval vill; site v neglected (2009)." ♦
1 Apr-15 Oct. € 18.00 2007*

VIVONNE *7A2* (500m E Rural) *46.42511, 0.26409* **Camp Municipal, Chemin de Prairie, 86370 Vivonne [05 49 43 25 95 or 05 49 43 41 05 (Mairie); fax 05 49 43 34 87; vivonne@cg86.fr]** Exit N10 where it by-passes Vivonne & ent town. Site in municipal park to E of town. Med, pt shd; wc; shwrs €1.95; el pnts €2.25; Indtte; playgrnd; pool; waterslide adj; noise fr rlwy, quieter w/end. "Welcoming, helpful resident warden; clean facs; gd for wheelchair users; sh walk to town cent; worth a visit; gd." ♦ May-Sep. € 7.50 2009*

VIZILLE *9C3* (500m N Urban) *45.08660, 5.76814* **FFCC Camping Le Bois de Cornage, Chemin du Camping, 38220 Vizille [tel/fax 04 76 68 12 39; campingvizille@wanadoo.fr; www.campingvizille.com]** Site sp at x-rds of Rte Napoléon, N85 & Rte de Briançon D1091 (N91). Site on N outskirts of town. Well sp. Med, hdg/mkd pitch, pt sl, terr, shd; wc; chem disp; mv service pnt; baby facs; shwrs inc; el pnts (6-10A) €2.80-3.30 (long lead poss req); gas 500m; Indtte; shops 200m; supmkt 500m; tradsmn; rest; snacks; bar; playgrnd; htd pool; gd cycling & climbing nrby; 10% statics; dogs €0.80; no vans over 5m acc; poss v cr; Eng spkn; adv bkg rec high ssn; quiet; red long stay/low ssn; CCI. "Helpful owner; excel clean facs; mkd walks nrby; poss mosquitoes; vg." 25 Apr-30 Sep. € 13.90 2007*

VIZILLE *9C3* (7km S Rural) *45.02055, 5.77522* **Camp Municipal Les Grands Sagnes, 38220 Laffrey [04 76 73 10 21 or 04 76 73 11 37]** Exit Grenoble on N85. S thro Vizille to Laffrey. Steep climb on narr rd. Site 200m S of vill at top of steep hill on Rte Napoléon. Site sp fr town. Med, pt sl, pt shd; wc; shwrs inc; el pnts (6A) €3.10; shop in ssn; snacks; lake sw & watersports; dogs €1; some rd noise. "Gd sized pitches." 15 Jun-15 Sep. € 10.80 2006*

VOGUE see Aubenas *9D2*

VOLONNE see Château Arnoux *10E3*

France

VOLSTROFF *5D2* (1.5km SE Rural) *49.29772, 6.26989* **FFCC Camp du Centre de Loisirs et Culture de Volstroff, Route de Luttange, 57940 Volstroff [03 82 56 93 40; fax 03 82 50 39 90; campingvol@aol.com; www.campingvol.com]** Exit A31 junc 37.2 E onto D918; in 5km at end vill of Stuckange turn R sp Volstroff, Luttange. Go thro Volstroff, site in R in 3km. Med, hdg/mkd pitch,hdstg, pt sl, shd; wc (some cont); chem disp; mv service pnt; baby facs; shwrs inc; el pnts (8A) €2.30; gas; lndtte (inc dryer); shop; rest; snacks; bar; playgrnd; pool; lake sw adj; waterslide; water sports; horseriding; tennis; cycle hire; child entmnt; wifi; dogs; phone; Eng spkn; adv bkg; poss cr; ccard acc; red low ssn; CCI. "Lovely lake adj site; many facs for children; excel." ♦ 11 Apr-25 Oct. € 18.00 (4 persons) 2009*

VOLVIC *9B1* (E Urban) *45.87213, 3.04381* **Camp Municipal Pierre et Sources, Rue de Chancelas, 63530 Volvic [04 73 33 50 16; fax 04 73 33 54 98; camping@ville-volvic.fr; www.ville-volvic.fr]** Exit Riom on D986: foll sp for Pontgibaud & Volvic. Site sp to R on app to town. Sm, shd; htd wc; chem disp; mv service pnt; shwrs inc; el pnts (10A) €3.50; lndtte; sm shop; tradsmn; some statics; dogs €1.50; adv bkg; quiet. 15 Apr-31 Oct. € 13.00 2007*

VONNAS *9A2* (300m NW Rural) *46.22152, 4.98805* **Camp Municipal Le Renom, Rue de Verdemont, 01540 Vonnas [tel/fax 04 74 50 02 75; campingvonnas@wanadoo.fr; www.vonnas.com]** Fr Bourg-en-Bresse take D1079 (N79) W sp Mâcon. In 15km take D26 or D47 S to Vonnas; turn R in town cent (ignore sp on o'skts of town) & site on R in 300m by leisure cent. Med, hdg/mkd pitch, pt shd; wc; chem disp; baby facs; shwrs inc; el pnts (10A) €3; lndtte; shop 300m; BBQ; htd pool, tennis adj; rv fishing; 30% statics; dogs €1; quiet. "Warm welcome; interesting town; mkt Thurs." ♦ 15 Apr-5 Oct. € 13.00 2008*

VOREY *9C1* (4km NE Rural) *45.20305, 3.94464* **Camping Domaine du Pra de Mars, Le Chambon de Vorey, 43800 Vorey-sur-Arzon [tel/fax 04 71 03 40 86; leprademars@wanadoo.fr; www.leprademars.com]** On D103 dir Retournac. Med, hdg/mkd pitch, pt sl, pt shd; htd wc (some cont); chem disp; some serviced pitches; mv service pnt; baby facs; fam bthrm; shwrs inc; el pnts (5A) €3; lndtte; rest; snacks; bar; BBQ; htd pool; dogs €1.50; bus; phone; Eng spkn; adv bkg; quiet; ccard acc; CCI. "Beautiful rvside setting; welcoming owners; facs clean but need update (2009); vg." 3 Apr-27 Sep. € 13.50 2009*

VOREY *9C1* (500m SW Rural) *45.18576, 3.90679* **Camping Les Moulettes, Chemin de Félines, 43800 Vorey-sur-Arzon [04 71 03 70 48; fax 04 71 03 72 06; contact@camping-les-moulettes.fr; www.camping-les-moulettes.fr]** Fr Le Puy take D103 sp Vorey. Site sp in vill; L in main sq. Sm, hdg pitch, pt shd; wc; shwrs inc; el pnts (10A) €2.90; lndtte; shops in vill; snacks; bar; playgrnd; pool, waterslide, fishing adj; games area; some statics; dogs €1.50; Eng spkn; adv bkg; quiet. ♦ 1 May-15 Sep. € 12.50 2006*

VOUECOURT *6E1* (Rural) *48.26774, 5.13671* **Camp Municipal Rives de Marne, 52320 Vouécourt [03 25 01 39 58 or 03 25 02 44 46 (Mairie); camping-vouecourt@wanadoo.fr]** N fr Chaumont on N67; sp to site in 17km; thro vill by Rv Marne; site on L bef main rv bdge, almost opp Mairie; well sp. Sm, mkd pitch; pt shd; wc (some cont); chem disp; shwr; el pnts (10A) €2.20 (poss rev pol); gas; shop 5km; rest 1km; tradsmn; playgrnd; fishing; adv bkg; CCI. "Lovely, peaceful, rvside site; gd sized pitches; friendly warden calls pm; clean, dated san facs; rv poss floods in winter; forest walks & cycling; excel." 15 Apr-15 Oct. € 10.00 2009*

VOUILLE *4H1* (Urban) *46.63968, 0.16488* **Camp Municipal, Chemin de la Piscine; 86190 Vouillé [05 49 51 90 10 (after 1800) or 05 49 54 20 30 (Mairie); fax 05 49 51 14 47; vouille@cg86.fr]** Fr Parthenay take N149 twds Vouillé; go thro Vouillé & turn R onto D43 by Super U. At bottom of hill turn R twds town cent; site sp behind Cheval Blanc rest nr rvside. Sm, mkd pitch, shd; wc; chem disp (wc); shwrs inc; el pnts (3A) €2; lndry rm; shop; supmkt 1km; rest 500m; bar; playgrnd adj; fishing; quiet. "Site yourself; useful NH; ideal Futuroscope." ♦ 15 May-30 Aug. € 6.00 2008*

VOULTE SUR RHONE, LA *9D2* (4km N Rural) *44.82663, 4.76171* **Camping La Garenne, Quartier La Garenne, 07800 St Laurent-du-Pape [tel/fax 04 75 62 24 62; info@lagarenne.org; www.lagarenne.org]** Well sp fr La Voulte. Fr Valence S on D86 La Voulte, approx 15km turn W onto D120; 300m after St Laurent-du-Pape cent, turn R bef PO. Med, pt terr, pt shd; wc; chem disp; shwrs inc; el pnts (4A) inc (poss rev pol); gas; lndtte; shop; rest; snacks; bar; playgrnd; pool; cycle hire; programme of activities; wifi; dogs €2.50; poss v cr; Eng spkn; adv bkg; quiet; red low ssn/long stay; CCI. "Popular site; friendly, helpful Dutch owners; views fr terr pitches; gd clean san facs; sh walk to vill; vg." ♦ 1 Mar-1 Nov. € 30.50 2009*

VOULTE SUR RHONE, LA *9D2* (4km NE Rural) *44.82004, 4.81960* **Camp Municipal Les Voiliers, 07800 Beauchastel [04 75 62 24 04; fax 04 75 62 42 32]** Site 30km S of Tournon on D86, 500m E of Beauchastel sp in town, over canal, past hydro. Med, terr, shd; htd wc (cont); snacks; shwrs inc; el pnts (5A) inc; lndtte; shops 500m; snacks; bar; BBQ; playgrnd; pool; 15% statics; dogs €1.07; poss cr; quiet. "Friendly; gd san facs." 1 Apr-31 Oct. € 13.50 2006*

VOUVRAY *4G2* (500m S Rural) *47.40867, 0.79626* **Camp Municipal du Bec de Cisse, 37210 Vouvray [02 47 52 68 81; fax 02 47 52 67 76]** Fr Tours E on D952 (N152); in 6km turn R at traff lts in Vouvray; site in 200m. Do not turn L into town cent. Sm, hdg/mkd pitch, pt shd; wc; chem disp; shwrs; el pnts (10A) €3.60; gas; lndtte; shop 500m; tradsmn; rest, snacks, bar 300m; playgrnd; sw 1km; dogs €1.30; Eng spkn; adv bkg rec high ssn; quiet but some traff noise; CCI. "Pleasant, well-kept, well-run site; clean san facs; gd cycling; vg." ♦ 30 Apr-28 Sep. € 11.20 2009*

VRAIGNES EN VERMANDOIS see Péronne *3C3*

VUILLAFANS see Ornans *6G2*

WACQUINGHEN see Marquise *3A3*

WASSELONNE *6E3* (1km W Urban) *48.63739, 7.43209* **FFCC Camp Municipal, Route de Romanswiller, 67310 Wasselonne [tel/fax 03 88 87 00 08 or 03 88 59 12 27; camping-wasselonne@wanadoo.fr]** Fr D1004 (N4) take D244 to site. Med, mkd pitch, terr, pt shd; wc; mv service pnt; shwrs inc; el pnts (5-10A) €2.30-3.70; gas; Indtte; shop; rest; snacks; bar; playgrnd; htd, covrd pool high ssn; 30% statics; dogs €0.60; quiet; CCI. "Pleasant town; facs OK; cycle rte to Strasbourg; gd NH." 15 Apr-15 Oct. € 11.10 2007*

WASSELONNE *6E3* (5km NW Urban) *48.64487, 7.39953* **Camp Municipal, 67310 Romanswiller [tel/fax 03 88 87 45 54 or 03 88 87 05 57 (Mairie)]** Fr Saverne take D1004 (N4) twd Strasbourg. 1km N of Wasselonne turn R onto D260 & cont twd town cent, turn R onto D224 sp Romanswiller & 'Camping Piscine'. 2km N at o'skts turn L into 'Centre des Loisirs'. Sm, hdg pitch, pt shd; wc; chem disp; all serviced pitches; shwrs inc; el pnts (10A) inc; Indry rm; shops 2km; rest; snacks; BBQ; playgrnd; htd pool 5km; games area; cycle hire; 90% statics; dogs; poss cr; some Eng spkn; poss noisy; CCI. "Well-kept, scenic site; pleasant town." 1 May-15 Sep. € 12.00 2006*

WATTEN *3A3* (W Urban) *50.83353, 2.21005* **Camping Le Val Joly, Rue de l'Aa, 59143 Watten [03 21 88 23 26 or 03 21 88 24 75]** NW fr St Omer on D943 (N43); N of Tilques turn N on D300; in 5km turn R to D207 sp Watten; at T-junc turn L; cross rv; thro town; site sp on L nr L'Aa canal. Site sp fr N & S on D943. Fr N on D300 take slip rd sp Watten & foll sp to town cent for short dist - site sp on R. Med, pt shd; wc; chem disp; shwrs €1.85; el pnts (3A) €3; shops adj; supmkt nr; playgrnd; fishing & cycling along rv/canal; 90% statics; dogs; quiet but some rd & rlwy noise; CCI. "Spacious, attractive, well-kept site; conv NH for ferries; friendly, helpful, welcoming warden - call at house; basic, clean san facs; secure gates; few touring pitches - arr early or phone ahead high ssn; glass works at Arques; vet nr; gd." 1 Apr-31 Oct. € 9.00 2009*

WATTWILLER see Cernay *6F3*

⊞ **WIMEREUX** *3A2* (5km N Rural) *50.81938, 1.63082* **Camping Le Beaucamp, 10 Rue de Ferquent, Raventhun, 62164 Ambleteuse [03 21 32 62 10; fax 03 21 30 63 77; le.beaucamp@wanadoo.fr; www.le-beaucamp.fr.st]** Exit A16 junc 36 onto D191E dir Ambleteuse, site in 6km in R. Lge, hdg pitch, unshd; htd wc; chem disp; shwrs €1.70; el pnts (10A) €4; gas; Indtte; shop; rest; snacks; bar; BBQ; playgrnd; sand beach 1.5km; entmnt; 98% statics; dogs €3; quiet; ccard acc; CCI. "Gd NH; sep field for tourers but sharp R-angle turns to ent & poss reverse to exit so diff lge o'fits - owners will tractor tow if necessary; basic facs; poor value in low ssn." € 21.00 2007*

WIMEREUX *3A2* (1km S Coastal) *50.76131, 1.60769* **Camp Municipal Olympic, 49 Rue de la Libération, 62930 Wimereux [03 21 32 45 63]** A16 exit 32 & foll sp Wimereux Sud to vill; turn R at rndabt to site. Or N fr Boulogne on D940, at vill sp Wimereux & rndabt, turn R. Med, hdg/mkd pitch, pt sl, unshd; wc; chem disp; baby facs; shwrs inc; el pnts (4A) inc; BBQ; Indry rm; shop adj; tradsmn; rest; playgrnd; pool 4km; beach 800m; sailing; fishing; mainly statics; dogs €2; Eng spkn; some noise fr rds & rlwy; ccard acc; CCI. "Conv Boulogne & NH; basic, clean facs, stretched high ssn; hot water runs out early; gd vet in attractive seaside town; poor security, take care thieves at night (2009); useful NH only." 15 Mar-28 Oct. € 16.00 2009*

⊞ **WIMEREUX** *3A2* (1.5km S Coastal) *50.75277, 1.60722* **Caravaning L'Eté Indien, Hameau de Honvault, 62930 Wimereux [03 21 30 23 50; fax 03 21 30 17 14; ete.indien@wanadoo.fr; www.eteindien-wimereux.com]** Fr Calais on A16 exit junc 32 sp Wimereux Sud. Thro Terlincthun R after x-ing rlwy, site in 700m on R - narr, v rough rd. Med, pt sl, terr, unshd; htd wc; chem disp; mv service pnt; serviced pitches; baby facs; shwrs inc; el pnts (10A) inc; gas; Indtte (inc dryer); shop; snacks; bar; BBQ (gas); playgrnd; htd pool; paddling pool; sandy beach 1.5km; games area; games rm; entmnt; wifi; 98% statics; dogs €2; phone; poss cr; Eng spkn; adv bkg; some rlwy noise; red low ssn/long stay. "Pleasant site; conv A16, Calais ferries; rec low ssn phone to check site open; ltd touring pitches & poss steep; improvements in hand (2008/09); rlwy runs along one side of site; NH only." ♦ € 20.00 2009*

WINGEN SUR MODER *5D3* (W Rural) *48.91565, 7.36934* **Camp Municipal/Aire Naturelle, Rue de Zittersheim, 67290 Wingen-sur-Moder [03 88 89 71 27 (Mairie); fax 03 88 89 86 99; mairie@wingen-moder.com; www.wingen-moder.com]** W fr Haguenau on D919 to W end Wingen-sur-Moder. Site sp by rlwy arch. Sm, mkd pitch, terr, pt shd; wc; chem disp; shwrs inc; el pnts (13A) inc; shop 500m; rest nr; Eng spkn; adv bkg; quiet; CCI. "Excel, peaceful site but adj sports field poss used by youth groups/motorbikers high ssn; clean facs; warden calls am & pm; gd walking/cycling." 1 May-30 Sep. € 11.40 2009*

WISSANT *3A2* (6km NE Coastal/Rural) *50.91853, 1.71039* **Camping Côte d'Opale Le Blanc Nez, 18 Rue de la Mer, 62179 Escalles [tel/fax 03 21 85 27 38; camping.blancnez@laposte.net; http://camping.blancnez.free.fr]** Fr A16 take junc 40 to Cap Blanc-Nez. Site situated on W edge of Escalles on D940 twd sea. Med, mkd pitch, pt sl, pt shd; wc; chem disp; mv service pnt; shwrs €1; el pnts (4A) inc (long lead poss req); gas; Indry rm; shop; tradsmn; rest; snacks; bar; playgrnd; sand/shgl beach 1km; 25% statics; dogs €1.50; phone; bus 100m; poss cr; adv bkg; quiet; ccard acc; CCI. "Busy site; clean, basic san facs; ltd hot shwrs/hot water, espec low ssn; diff access for lge o'fits due parked cars; sm pitches; elec linked to pitch number - no choice; gd location & walking; gd NH." 15 Mar-15 Nov. € 17.50 2009*

France

WISSANT *3A2* (6km NE Coastal) *50.91226, 1.72054* **Camping Les Erables, 17 Rue du Château d'Eau, 62179 Escalles [03 21 85 25 36; boutroy.les-erables@wanadoo.fr]** Fr A16 take exit 40 onto D243 thro Peuplingues. Site sp to L on ent Escalles (on sharp R bend). Steep ent. Don't be put off by No Entry signs - 1-way system for c'vans on app rd. Sm, mkd pitch, hdstg, terr, unshd; htd wc; chem disp; mv service pnt; shwrs €1; el pnts (6-10A) €3 (poss rev pol); Indtte; shop 2km; tradsmn; rest & snacks 500m; BBQ; sand beach 2km; dogs; phone; poss cr/noisy at w/end; Eng spkn; adv bkg; CCI. "Lovely, well-kept, family-owned, open site with views; spacious pitches but poss haphazard pitching; welcoming staff; immac, modern facs; gates open 0600-2200; 2 pitches for disabled visitors with san facs; conv tunnel & ferries; excel." ♦ 1 Apr-11 Nov. € 12.50 2009*

XONRUPT LONGEMER see Gérardmer *6F3*

YCHOUX *7D1* (10km E Rural) *44.33060, -0.97975* **Camp Municipal du Lac des Forges, 40160 Ychoux [05 58 82 35 57 or 05 58 82 36 01 (Mairie); fax 05 58 82 35 46]** Fr Bordeaux take N10 S & turn onto D43 at Liposthey W twd Parentis-en-Born. Site in 8km on R, past vill of Ychoux. Sm, pt sl, pt shd; wc; chem disp; mv service pnt; shwrs; el pnts (5-10A) €3.50 (rev pol); Indtte; shops 1km; rest; bar; playgrnd; TV rm; lake adj; fishing; sailing; dogs €1.50; quiet. "Levelling blocks poss req; pitches nr rd poss noisy." 15 Jun-10 Sep. € 12.00 2008*

YENNE *9B3* (4km E Rural) *45.69471, 5.82380* **FLOWER Camping des Lacs, 73170 St Jean-de-Chevelu [04 79 36 72 21 or 04 79 36 90 76; camping-des-lacs@wanadoo.fr; www.camping-lacs-savoie.com or www.flowercamping.com]** Fr Yenne, take D1504, D210 to St Jean-de-Chevelu. Med, pt shd; wc; mv service pnt; shwrs inc; el pnts (6A) inc; Indtte; shop; rest; snacks; bar; playgrnd; lake sw, sand beach; boating; fishing; games rm; dogs €3; quiet."V peaceful." 2 Jun-1 Sep. € 18.00 2007*

YENNE *9B3* (300m NW Rural) *45.70591, 5.75319* **Camping du Flon, Ave du Rhône, 73170 Yenne [04 79 36 82 70 or 06 10 22 23 38 (mob); fax 04 79 36 92 72; jpmollard@wanadoo.fr; www.avant-pays-savoyard.com]** Fr D1504 (N504) ent Yenne, site visible. E on rd to Tunnel du Chat, site sp on banks Rv Rhône. Med, mkd pitch, shd; wc (cont); shwrs inc; el pnts; shops 500m; rest, snacks, bar 500m; playgrnd; fishing; canoeing; dogs; adv bkg; some rd noise. 1 May-30 Sep. € 9.00 2007*

YPORT *3C1* (1km SW Coastal) *49.73746, 0.30959* **Camping Le Rivage, Rue Hottières, 76111 Yport [tel/fax 02 35 27 33 78]** Fr D940 bet Etretat & Fécamp take D11 2km NE of Les Loges, meeting up with D211 & head twd Yport. Site on D211. Or foll sp fr Yport. Med, pt sl, terr, unshd; wc; chem disp; shwrs; el pnts (6A) inc (poss long lead req); shops 1km; snacks; bar; shgl beach 300m; games rm; TV rm; phone; adv bkg; quiet. "Well-situated, o'looking sea; steep descent to beach; san facs inadequate high ssn & long walk fr most pitches; rec stop at top of site & walk to recep bef pitching, as turning poss diff lge o'fits." 12 Apr-21 Sep. € 14.00 2006*

The opening dates and prices on this campsite have changed. I'll send a site report form to the Club for the next edition of the guide.

YSSINGEAUX *9C1* (300m SE Urban) *45.13251, 4.12522* **Camp Municipal de Choumouroux, 43200 Yssingeaux [04 71 65 53 44 or 04 71 59 01 13 (Mairie); fax 04 71 65 19 35]** N88 Le Puy to St Etienne on R bef Yssingeaux; ent next to school, opp petrol stn. Sm, pt shd; wc (cont); chem disp; mv service pnt; shwrs inc; el pnts (10A) inc; shops 500m; playgrnd; fishing; dogs €1.20; quiet. "Gd location amongst extinct volcanoes; well-maintained." 1 May-30 Sep. € 10.20 2008*

YVETOT *3C2* (10km N Rural) *49.69494, 0.69652* **Camp Municipal de la Durdent, Route du Moulin Bleu, 76560 Héricourt-en-Caux [02 35 96 38 08 or 02 35 96 42 12 (Mairie); fax 02 32 70 02 59; camping.hericourt@orange.fr; www.ot-caux-fleurdelin.fr]** Fr Le Havre on D6015 (N15) L at traff lts in Yvetot on D131 sp Cany to Héricourt. After passing thro vill turn L on D149. Site on L in 300m. Or exit A29 junc 8 dir Fécamp. After 3.5km at rndabt outside Fauville turn R sp Héricourt 10km. Site visible on R below rd on ent vill. Sm, mkd pitch, pt sl, unshd; wc (some cont); shwrs inc; el pnts (6A) €2.30; Indry rm; shops 500m; quiet but some rd noise in day; ccard not acc; CCI. "Delightful site by stream; pitch yourself, warden calls; basic facs but well-maintained; poss closes bef end Sep - phone to check." 15 Apr-30 Sep. € 9.05 2009*

YVOIRE see Douvaine *9A3*

YVRAC ET MALLEYRAND see Rochefoucauld, La *7B2*

YVVRE L'EVEQUE see Mans, Le *4F1*

CORSICA

AJACCIO *10H2* (4km W Coastal) *41.91029, 8.68377* **Camping Château de Barbicaggia, Route des Sanguinaires, 20000 Ajaccio [04 95 52 01 17]** Fr Ajaccio take D111 twds Iles Sanguinaires. Site on R after 4km. Med, hdg/mkd pitch, hdstg, terr, shd; wc (some cont); chem disp; shwrs inc; el pnts €2.40; Indtte; sand beach 200m; 5% statics; dogs €1.50; phone adj; bus 200m; poss v cr; Eng spkn. "Sea views over bay; steep ent not suitable lge o'fits; rec check pitch bef ent site." ♦ € 16.70 2007*

AJACCIO *10H2* (3km NW Coastal) *41.93725, 8.72851* **Camping Les Mimosas, Route d'Alata, 20000 Ajaccio [04 95 20 99 85; fax 04 95 10 01 77; camping mimosas@wanadoo.fr; www.camping-lesmimosas.com]** Foll N194 round N of Ajaccio & then directions to Super U; 1st R off rndabt immed after Super U; after rndabt site in 1km up narr rd. Med, hdg/mkd pitch, hdstg, pt sl, shd; wc; chem disp; mv service pnt; serviced pitches; shwrs inc; el pnts (5-10A) €2.80; gas 1km; Indtte (inc dryer); sm shop & 1km; tradsmn; rest; snacks; bar; playgrnd; shgl beach 1km; 5% statics; no dogs; phone; adv bkg; quiet; 10% red low ssn/CCI. "Conv Ajaccio; gd rest on site." ♦ 1 Apr-18 Oct. € 17.60 2008*

ALERIA *10H2* (7km N Coastal) *42.16155, 9.55265* **Camping-Village Riva-Bella (Naturist), 20270 Aléria [04 95 38 81 10; fax 04 95 38 91 29; riva-bella@ wanadoo.fr; www.rivabella-corsica.com]** Fr Bastia S on N198 for 60km, site sp to L. Med, pt shd; wc; mv service pnt; steam rm; sauna; shwrs; el pnts €4; Indtte; shop; rest; snacks; bar; playgrnd; sand beach adj; fishing; watersports; tennis; cycle hire; fitness rm; internet; entmnt; TV rm; 10% statics; dogs €3; adv bkg; quiet; red low ssn; INF card. ♦ 30 Mar-2 Oct. € 34.00 (CChq acc) 2009*

ALERIA *10H2* (3km E Coastal) *42.11123, 9.55122* **Camping Marina d'Aléria, 20270 Aléria [04 95 57 01 42; fax 04 95 57 04 29; info@marina-aleria.com; www.marina-aleria.com]** S fr Bastia on N198; in Aléria turn L at x-rds onto N200 to Plage de Padulone. Lge, hdg pitch, pt shd, wc; mv service pnt; shwrs inc; el pnts (6A) €3.70; Indtte; shop; rest; snacks; bar; BBQ; playgrnd; sand beach adj; tennis; cycle hire; entmnt; TV; some statics; dogs €3; ccard acc. "Superb site on sea shore; Roman ruins in Aléria." Easter-15 Oct. € 27.50 2007*

ALGAJOLA *10G2* (800m E Coastal) *42.60844, 8.87409* **Camping de la Plage en Balagne, 20220 Algajola [tel/fax 04 95 60 71 76; campingalgajola@wanadoo.fr; www. camping-de-la-plage-en-balagne.com]** Site 6km W fr L'Ile-Rousse on N197 (D199) dir Algajola. On R opp Hotel Pascal Paoli bef Algajola. Med, pt shd; htd wc (some cont); chem disp; mv service pnt; shwrs inc; el pnts (6A) €3; Indtte; shop; rest; snacks; bar; playgrnd; sand beach adj; games area; gym; entmnt; some statics; dogs €1.50; tram; poss cr; adv bkg; quiet; ccard acc. "Rest, snacks & bar on beach - poss clsd low ssn; tram to l'Ile-Rousse & Calvi fr site gd for touring inland; gd." 15 Mar-15 Nov. € 20.60 2007*

BASTIA *10G2* (5km N Coastal) **Camping Les Orangers, Licciola, 20200 Miomo [04 95 33 24 09; fax 04 95 33 23 65]** Foll main coast rd D80 N 4km fr ferry. Site well sp on L of rd. Sm, shd; wc; shwrs; el pnts; shop; tradsmn; rest; snacks; bar; TV; sandy/shgl beach adj; quiet; CCI. "Poss run down low ssn; friendly owners; vg rest; site ent tight for lge o'fits; poss unreliable opening dates." 1 Apr-1 Sep. 2007*

BASTIA *10G2* (11km S Coastal) *42.62922, 9.46835* **Camping San Damiano, Lido de la Marana, 20620 Biguglia [04 95 33 68 02; fax 04 95 30 84 10; san.damiano@ wanadoo.fr; www.campingsandamiano.com]** S fr Bastia on N193 for 4km. Turn SE onto Lagoon Rd (sp Lido de Marana). Site on L in 7km. Lge, pt shd; wc; chem disp; baby facs; shwrs inc; el pnts (6A) €3.40; Indtte; shop; rest; playgrnd; pool; sandy beach adj; cycle path; games area; games rm; dogs €0.90; Eng spkn; ccard acc; red long stay'/low ssn; CCI. "San facs basic but clean." ♦ 1 Apr-30 Oct. € 22.00 2008*

BIGUGLIA see Bastia *10G2*

BONIFACIO *10H2* (15km N Coastal) *41.47326, 9.26318* **Camping Rondinara, Suartone, 20169 Bonifacio [04 95 70 43 15; fax 04 95 70 56 79; reception@ rondinara.fr; www.rondinara.fr]** Fr Bonifacio take N198 dir Porte-Vecchio for 10km, then turn R onto D158 dir Suartone (lge camp sp at turning). Site in 5km. NB D158 single track, many bends & hills. Med, pt sl, pt shd; wc; mv service pnt; shwrs inc; el pnts (6A) €3.60; Indtte; shop; rest; snacks; bar; BBQ; playgrnd; pool; sand beach 400m; watersports; games area; games rm; some statics; dogs €2.60; poss cr; Eng spkn; no adv bkg; quiet; red low ssn; ccard acc; CCI. "Excel rest; idyllic location by bay." 15 May-30 Sep. € 26.70 2009*

BONIFACIO *10H2* (3km NE Rural) *41.41842, 9.17898* **Pertamina Village U Farniente, 20169 Bonifacio [04 95 73 05 47; fax 04 95 73 11 42; pertamina@ wanadoo.fr; www.camping-pertamina.com]** Fr Bonifacio take RN198 N, site on R in 4km. Med, hdg/mkd pitch, pt sl, pt shd; wc (some cont); chem disp; mv service pnt; baby facs; shwrs inc; el pnts (6A) inc; gas; Indtte; shop; rest; snacks; bar; playgrnd; htd pool; waterslide; beach 3km; tennis; fitness rm; entmnt; TV rm; 50% statics; dogs; poss cr; adv bkg; ccard acc; CCI. "Access to pitches diff; excel." ♦ 1 Apr-15 Oct. € 33.00 (CChq acc) 2009*

BONIFACIO *10H2* (4km NE Rural) *41.39986, 9.20141* **Camping Pian del Fosse, Route de Sant' Amanza, 20169 Bonifacio [tel/fax 04 95 73 16 34; camping@piandel fosse.com; www.piandelfosse.com]** Leave Bonifacio on D58 dir Sant' Amanza, site on L in 4km. Sm, hdg/mkd pitch, terr, shd; wc; chem disp; mv service pnt; baby facs; shwrs inc; el pnts (4A) €3.80; Indtte; shop; tradsmn; snacks; BBQ; playgrnd; sand/shgl beach 3km; 20% statics; dogs €2.50; poss cr; Eng spkn; quiet; red snr citizens/long stay. "Pitches poss diff lge m'vans due o'hanging trees; vg." ♦ Easter-15 Oct. € 24.20 2008*

France
Corsica

CALVI *10G2* (1.8km SE Coastal) *42.55228, 8.76423* **Camping Paduella, Route de Bastia, 20260 Calvi [04 95 65 13 20 or 04 95 65 06 16; fax 04 95 65 17 50]** On N197 fr Calvi; on R 200m after rndabt by Casino supmkt. Med, mkd pitch, pt sl, terr, pt shd; wc chem disp; baby facs; shwrs inc; el pnts (6A) €3.65; Indtte; shop/supmkt; snacks; bar; playgrnd; sand beach 300m; 25% statics; dogs; poss cr; Eng spkn; quiet; CCI. "Poss best site in Calvi; immac san facs but slippery when wet, especially disabled ramp; vg." ♦ 15 May-15 Oct. € 21.00 2008*

CALVI *10G2* (4km SE Coastal) *42.55403, 8.78879* **Camping La Dolce Vita, Ponte Bambino, Route de Bastia, 20260 Calvi [04 95 65 05 99; fax 04 95 65 31 25; www.dolce-vita.org]** N197 twd L'Ile Rousse. Site on L, by rest, immed after x-ing rv bdge. Adj Bastia-Calvi. Lge, shd; wc; baby facs; shwrs inc; el pnts (10A) €4; gas; Indtte; shop; rest; snacks; bar; playgrnd; sand beach 150m; TV rm; dir access to rv; fishing; sailing windsurfing; poss cr; quiet, but some aircraft & rlwy noise. 1 May-30 Sep. € 24.70 2008*

CALVI *10G2* (1.6km SW Coastal) *42.55290, 8.76870* **Camping La Pinède, Route de la Pinède, 20260 Calvi [04 95 65 17 80; fax 04 95 65 19 60; info@camping-calvi.com; www.camping-calvi.com]** S fr L'Ile-Rousse on N197; well sp ent Calvi; 1st ent on R to Rte de la Pinède, 2nd ent 1km after 1st. Lge, shd; wc; chem disp; mv service pnt; shwrs; el pnts (6A) €3.50; Indtte; shop; supmkt nrby; rest; snacks; bar; playgrnd; pool; beach 250m; tennis; games area; dogs €2; train to Calvi & Ile-Rousse 250m; ccard acc. "Too much shd; clean facs; superb beach." 1 Apr-31 Oct. € 27.50 2008*

CARGESE *10H2* (4km N Coastal) *42.1625, 8.59791* **Camping Le Torraccia, Bagghiuccia, 20130 Cargèse [tel/fax 04 95 26 42 39; contact@camping-torraccia.com; www.camping-torraccia.com]** N fr Cargèse twd Porto on D81 for 3km. Site on L. Med, terr, pt shd; wc; baby facs; shwrs inc; ltd el pnts (6A) €3.10; Indrtte; shop; rest 4km; snacks; bar; playgrnd; pool; sand beach 1km; games area; internet; no adv bkg; red low ssn. "Nearest site to Porto without diff traffic conditions." 21 Apr-30 Sep. € 20.10 2008*

CERVIONE *10G2* (7km NE Coastal) *42.36326, 9.52978* **Camping Merendella, Moriani-Plage, 20230 San Nicolao [04 95 38 53 47 or 04 95 38 50 54; fax 04 95 38 44 01; merendel@club-internet.fr; www.merendella.com]** Site 44km S of Bastia at Moriani-Plage; foll N193 & N198 fr Bastia to Moriani Plage, on E (beach side) of N198, 700m after supmkt. Med, hdg/mkd pitch, shd; wc; chem disp; mv service pnt; shwrs inc; el pnts (5A) €4.30; Indtte; shop & supmkt 1km; rest; bar; playgrnd; dir access to beach adj; tennis 500m; TV rm; no dogs; adv bkg; quiet; ccard acc; CCI. "Idyllic beachside pitches; friendly, helpful, efficient staff; easy access; excel." ♦ 1 Jun-30 Sep. € 21.95 2007*

CERVIONE *10G2* (6km SE Coastal) *42.32155, 9.54546* **Camping Calamar, Prunete, 20221 Cervione [04 95 38 03 54 or 04 94 38 00 94 (LS); fax 04 95 31 17 09; contact@campingcalamar.eu; www.campingcalamar.eu]** On N198 S fr Prunete for 6km. Turn L at x-rds, site in 500m beside beach, sp. Sm, pt shd; wc; shwrs inc; el pnts €2.50; Indtte; shop 500m; tradsmn; snacks; bar; BBQ; sand beach adj; sailing; watersports; games area; dogs free; Eng spkn; adv bkg; quiet; red low ssn. "Friendly owner; pleasant site with trees & shrubs; excel." 1 Apr-31 Oct. € 13.00 2006*

CORBARA see Ile Rousse L' (Corsica) *10G2*

CORTE *10G2* (500m S Rural) *42.30109, 9.15098* **FFCC Camping Le Restonica, Quartier Porette, Faubourg St Antoine, 20250 Corte [tel/fax 04 95 46 11 59; vero.camp@worldonline.fr]** Fr N193 Ajaccio to Corte, twd cent of town. Pass petrol stn on R then sharp turn R before x-ing bdge (acute angle). Site on R in 200m opp Chapelle St Antoine. Sharp turn down hill to ent. Med; wc; shwrs inc; el pnts €3.50; gas; shops 200m; rest; sports complex 150m; adv bkg; quiet. "Beautiful old town; gd walking & horseriding." 1 May-15 Oct. € 17.00 2008*

CORTE *10G2* (500m SW Rural) *42.30023, 9.14783* **Aire Naturelle Camping U Sognu, Route de la Restonica, 20250 Corte [04 95 46 09 07]** At rndabt turn W off N193 sp Centre Ville. Immed L after bdge onto D623 sp La Restonica & site. Site on R in 200m. Med, pt shd; wc; shwrs inc; el pnts (6A); shop; tradsmn; rest; bar; rv & lake 200m; sw & fishing; poss v cr; ccard not acc. "Gd views; clean but inadequate facs high ssn; conv walking Restonica & Tavignano gorges." 1 Apr-25 Oct. 2007*

GHISONACCIA *10H2* (4km E Coastal) *41.99850, 9.44220* **Camping Arinella Bianca, Route de la Mer, Bruschetto, 20240 Ghisonaccia [04 95 56 04 78; fax 04 95 56 12 54; arinella@arinellabianca.com; www.arinellabianca.com]** S fr Bastia on N193/N198 approx 70km to Ghisonaccia. At Ghisonaccia foll sp opp pharmacy to beach (plage) & Rte de la Mer. In 3km turn R at rndabt & site well sp. NB When towing keep to main, coastal rds. Lge, hdg/mkd pitch, shd; wc (some cont); chem disp; mv service pnt; baby facs; shwrs inc; el pnts (6A) €5.50 (rev pol); gas; Indtte; shop; tradsmn; rest; snacks; bar; BBQ; playgrnd; pool; sand beach adj; fishing; watersports & activities; tennis; horseriding adj; cycle hire; games rm; internet; entmnt; TV rm; 45% statics; dogs €6; Eng spkn; adv bkg; red low ssn; ccard acc; CCI. "Clean, well-run site; attractive lake in cent; trees make access to pitches diff; helpful owner & staff." ♦ 11 Apr-30 Sep. € 38.00 (CChq acc) 2009*

GHISONACCIA *10H2* (4km E Coastal) *41.9998, 9.44731* **Camping Marina d'Erba Rossa, Route de la Mer, 20240 Ghisonaccia [04 95 56 25 14 or 04 95 56 21 18; fax 04 95 56 27 23; info@marina-erbarossa.com; www.marina-erbarossa.com]** Drive into town on N198. Site sp down D144 (easy to miss). Take D144 E to coast & site on R after 5km. Lge, hdg/mkd pitch, shd; wc; chem disp; shwrs; el pnts (5-6A) inc (long lead rec); Indtte; shop; rest; pizzeria; snacks; playgrnd; pool; private sand beach; watersports; tennis; cycle hire; horseriding; entmnt; some statics; dogs €4; adv bkg; quiet. ♦ 5 Apr-25 Oct. € 37.20 2008*

ILE ROUSSE, L' *10G2* (7km SE Rural) *42.62706, 9.01081* **Camping Le Clos des Chênes, Route de Belgodère, 20226 Lozari [04 95 60 15 13 or 04 95 60 41 27 (LS); fax 04 95 60 21 16; cdc.lozari@wanadoo.fr; www.closdeschenes.fr]** E on fr L'Ile Rousse on N197 E twd Bastia. After 7km turn S at Lozari onto N197 sp Belgodère; site on R after 1.5km. Lge, sl, pt shd; wc; chem disp; baby facs; shwrs inc; el pnts (4-10A) €3.80-6.50 (long cable req); gas; Indtte; shop; tradsmn; rest; bar; pizzeria; BBQ; playgrnd; pool; paddling pool; waterslide; sand beach 1.5km; tennis; games rm; 10% statics; dogs €3.50; poss cr; some Eng spkn; adv bkg; red low ssn; ccard acc; CCI. "Tranquil site; most pitches haphazard amongst oaks, some with views; ltd facs low ssn; gd touring cent; daily mkt." ♦ 1 May-30 Sep. € 26.45 2008*

ILE ROUSSE, L' *10G2* (500m S Urban/Coastal) *42.63111, 8.95236* **Camping Les Oliviers, Route de Bastia, 20220 Monticello [04 95 60 19 92; fax 04 95 60 30 91; contact@camping-oliviers.com; www.camping-oliviers.com]** Fr L'Ile Rousse take N197 dir Bastia. Site on L in 500m. Lge, mkd pitch (some), pt sl, pt shd; wc; chem disp; mv service pnt; shwrs inc; el pnts (6A); gas 800m; Indtte; shop 800m; tradsmn; rest; snacks; bar; shgl beach 500m; 5% statics; dogs; phone; tram 1km; poss cr; adv bkg; quiet but some rd noise; ccard acc. "Pleasant site but facs stretched & cr high ssn; ltd el pnts; gd location; coastal path to town." ♦ 1 Apr-30 Sep. 2007*

ILE ROUSSE, L' *10G2* (6km SW Coastal) *42.60753, 8.88790* **Aire Naturelle Balanéa (Savelli de Guido), Route d'Algajola, 20256 Corbara [tel/fax 04 95 60 06 84 or 04 95 60 11 77 (ssn); contact@balanea.net; www.balanea.net]** Off N197, site sp. Med, pt shd; wc; shwrs inc; el pnts €3; Indtte; shops 5km; snacks; beach 1km; dogs €1.50; CCI. ♦ Easter-30 Sep. € 18.50 2007*

LECCI *10H2* (8km S Rural) *41.67200, 9.30152* **Camping Mulinacciu, 20137 Lecci [04 95 71 47 48; fax 04 95 71 54 82; infos@campingmulinacciu@.com; www.camping-mulinacciu.com]** N fr Porto-Vecchio on N198 for approx 10km. Cross double bdge over Rv Oso & turn L onto unmade rd opp D668 dir San Ciprianu. Site sp down this rd. Med, pt shd; wc; shwrs inc; el pnts (5A) €3.50; Indtte; shop; playgrnd; pool; waterslide; sand beach 7km; fishing; tennis; games area; TV; some statics; dogs €2; Eng spkn; quiet. "Access to rv; friendly owners." 15 Jun-15 Sep. € 20.20 2006*

LOZARI see Ile Rouse, L' *10G2*

OLMETO *10H2* (3km S Coastal) *41.69803, 8.89667* **Camping Vigna Maggiore, 20113 Olmeto-Plage [04 95 76 02 07; fax 04 95 74 62 02; vignamaggiore@wanadoo.fr; www.vignamaggiore.com]** Site is approx 5km N of Propriano at junc N196 & D157 Med, terr, pt shd; wc; chem disp; mv waste; shwrs inc; el pnts €3.60; Indtte; rest; bar; playgrnd; pool; sand beach 1km; games area; some statics; poss cr; no adv bkg; CCI. 1 Apr-30 Sep. € 20.90 2009*

This is a
wonderful
site.

I'll fill in a report online and let the Club know – www.caravanclub.co.uk/europereport

OLMETO *10H2* (5km SW Coastal) *41.69563, 8.88866* **Camping Village Esplanade, Tour de la Calanca, 20113 Olmeto-Plage [04 95 76 05 03; fax 04 95 76 16 22; campinglesplanade@club-internet.fr; www.campingesplanade.com]** S fr Olmeto on N196 twd Propriano; turn R onto D157; site in 1km. Med, mkd pitch, pt sl, terr, shd; wc; shwrs inc; el pnts (6-10A) €3; Indtte; shop; rest; snacks; bar; playgrnd; pool; paddling pool; sand beach adj; games rm; some statics; dogs free; sep car park; Eng spkn; adv bkg; quiet; ccard acc. "Pleasant, shady site in gd location." 1 Apr-15 Oct. € 22.70 2008*

PIANA *10G2* (11.5km W Coastal) *42.21087, 8.58610* **Camping La Plage d'Arone, 20115 Piana [tel/fax 04 95 20 64 54]** Tho SW of Porto, rec c'vans arr fr Cargèse in S. Fr Cargèse head N on D81 to Piana. Turn L in vill onto D824 (sp), site on R in 11km. Med, pt shd; wc; chem disp; shwrs inc; el pnts; Indtte; shop high ssn; supmkt in Piana; tradsmn; playgrnd; sand beach 500m; dogs; quiet; CCI. "Access fr site to excel sandy bay with 2 rests/bars; delightful little site." ♦ 15 May-30 Sep. 2007*

PIANOTTOLI CALDARELLO *10H2* (3.5km SE Coastal) *41.47272, 9.04327* **Camping Kevano Plage, 20131 Pianottoli-Caldarello [04 95 71 83 22; fax 04 95 71 83 83; info@camping-kevano.com; www.camping-kevano.com]** Turn off N196 in Pianottoli at x-rds onto D122 for 1km. Turn R in Caldarello, site on L in 2km. Med, mkd pitch, pt sl, terr, pt shd; wc; chem disp; mv service pnt; shwrs inc; el pnts (4-6A) €2.50; Indtte; shop; tradsmn; pizzeria; rest; snacks; bar; playgrnd; sand beach 400m; entmnt; TV; some statics; dogs €1; phone; poss cr; Eng spkn; adv bkg rec high ssn; quiet; ccard acc; CCI. "Beautiful, family-run site in macchia amongst huge boulders; san facs tired but clean; no dogs on beach Jul/Aug." ♦ 27 Apr-30 Sep. € 29.60 2007*

PIETRACORBARA *10G2* (4km SE Coastal) *42.83908, 9.4736* **Camping La Pietra, Marine de Pietracorbara, 20233 Pietracorbara [04 95 35 27 49; fax 04 95 35 28 57; www.la-pietra.com]** Fr Bastia on D80 N. In 20km ent vill & turn L onto D232. Site on R in 1km at marina beach. Well sp. Med, hdg/mkd pitch, shd; wc; baby facs; shwrs inc; el pnts (20A) €3.50; Indtte; shop; tradsmn; rest on beach; bar; playgrnd; pool; sand beach 300m; tennis; dogs €2.50; bus nr; Eng spkn; red low ssn; ccard acc; CCI. "Excel facs; beautiful pool; generous pitches; helpful owners; low ssn, site yourself; site poss clsd early Apr." ♦ 1 Apr-15 Oct. € 28.40 (CChq acc) 2008*

PORTO *10G2* (1km E Rural) *42.26275, 8.7102* **Camping Sole e Vista, Rue d'Ota, 20150 Porto [04 95 26 15 71; fax 04 95 26 10 79; www.camping-sole-e-vista.com]** On D81 Ajaccio-Calvi rd, turn E onto D124. Ent thro Spar/Timy supmkt car park in Porto. NB rd fr Calvi diff for c'vans. Lge, mkd pitch, terr, pt sl, shd; wc; chem disp; mv service pnt; shwrs inc; el pnts (16A) €3.80; gas; Indtte; shop adj; snacks; bar; BBQ; playgrnd; shgl beach 1.5km; some statics; poss cr; Eng spkn; adv bkg; quiet; red CCI. "Vg." 1 Apr-31 Oct. € 15.50 2006*

PORTO *10G2* (1.5km E Coastal) *42.26211, 8.71011* **Camping Les Oliviers, 20150 Porto [04 95 26 14 49; fax 04 95 26 12 49; lesoliviersporto@wanadoo.fr; www.campinglesoliviers.com]** On D81 fr Porto on R bank of Rv Porto nr Pont de Porto. Site nr rv a sh distance downhill fr Cmp Sole e Vista. Check for access, poss ltd space for c'vans. Lge, terr, shd; wc; baby facs; shwrs; el pnts (5A) inc; Indry rm; shop high ssn; tradsmn; snacks; bar; BBQ; playgrnd; beach 1km; rv sw adj; sailing & windsurfing 1km; tennis; cycle hire; archery; entmnt; TV; no dogs high ssn; quiet; ccard acc. "Gd, clean, modern facs; ent to site upper levels v steep." 1 Apr-10 Nov. € 27.50 2008*

PORTO POLLO *10H2* (500m E Coastal) *41.71126, 8.80485* **Camping Alfonsi-U-Casselo, 20140 Serra-di-Ferro [04 95 74 01 80; fax 04 95 74 07 67]** Turn W onto D157 off N196 Propriano-Olmeto rd sp Porto-Pollo. After narr rv bdge turn L on D757. Site in 4km on L bef Porto-Pollo vill. Med, pt shd; wc; mv service pnt; shwrs; el pnts (10A) €3.40; Indtte; shop high ssn; supmkt in vill; rest high ssn; snacks; beach; poss cr; poss noisy; CCI. "Pleasant site." ♦
1 Jun-15 Oct. € 21.40 2006*

PORTO VECCHIO *10H2* (5km N Rural/Coastal) *41.63275, 9.29288* **Camping La Vetta, Ste Trinité, 20137 Porto-Vecchio [04 95 70 09 86; fax 04 95 70 43 21; info@campinglavetta.com; www.campinglavetta.com]** On L (W) of N198 N of Ste Trinité. Sp in advance fr N & S. Med, pt sl, shd; wc; shwrs inc; el pnts (10A) €3; gas; Indtte; shop 800m; supmkt 3km; rest; snacks; playgrnd; games area; pool; sand beach 3km; Eng spkn; quiet but some rd noise; ccard acc. "Excel bay for snorkelling, sw & windsurfing."
1 Jun-1 Oct. € 21.50 2008*

PORTO VECCHIO *10H2* (5km NE Coastal) *41.62273, 9.2997* **Camping Les Ilots d'Or, Ste Trinité, Route de Marina di Fiori, 20137 Porto-Vecchio [04 95 70 01 30 or 04 95 36 91 75; fax 04 95 70 01 30; info@campinglesilotsdor.com; www.campinglesilotsdor.com]** Turn E off N198 5km N of Porto-Vecchio at Ste Trinité twd San Ciprianu. In 1km fork R, site in 1km. Med, pt sl, pt terr, shd; wc (cont); shwrs inc; el pnts (6A) €3; gas; Indtte; shop; rest; snacks; bar; sand beach adj; poss cr; quiet. "Well-organised site; helpful family owners; many vg beaches in easy reach." 15 Apr-15 Oct. € 19.00 2007*

PORTO VECCHIO *10H2* (7km SE Rural) *41.58976, 9.33181* **Camping U Pirellu, Route de Palombaggia, 20137 Porto-Vecchio [04 95 70 23 44; fax 04 95 70 60 22; u.pirellu@wanadoo.fr; www.u-pirellu.com]** On N198 fr Porto-Vecchio 2km S, L on rte de Palombaggia & site in 6km. Med, hdg pitch, terr, pt sl, pt shd; wc; chem disp; shwrs; el pnts (6A) €3.50; Indtte; shop; rest; snacks; bar; playgrnd; pool; sand beach 3km; tennis; TV; some statics; no dogs; red low ssn; CCI. "Steep slope fr ent gate; pleasant site amongst oak trees." 15 Apr-30 Sep. € 20.50 2007*

PORTO VECCHIO *10H2* (2km S Rural) *41.57084, 9.27609* **Camping U-Stabiacciu, Route de Palombaggia, 20137 Porto-Vecchio [04 95 70 37 17; fax 04 95 70 62 59; stabiacciu@wanadoo.fr; www.stabiacciu.com]** Foll ring-rd N198 to S Porto-Vecchio, take 1st L sp Palombaggia. Site in 50m. Med, shd; wc (some cont); mv service pnt; shwrs inc; el pnts (10A) €3; Indtte; shop in ssn; tradsmn; rest; snacks; bar; BBQ; playgrnd; jacuzzis; sand beach 4km; 3% statics; dogs; phone; Eng spkn; ccard acc; CCI. "Excel beaches; gd touring base." 1 Apr-14 Oct. € 19.10 2006*

PORTO VECCHIO *10H2* (8km W Coastal) *41.59336, 9.35718* **Camping Club La Chiappa (Naturist), 20137 Porto-Vecchio [04 95 70 00 31; fax 04 95 70 07 70; chiappa@wanadoo.fr; www.chiappa.com]** On N198 fr Bastia heading S thro Porto-Vecchio. 2km S turn L to Pointe de la Chiappa & foll camp sp. Lge, pt shd; wc; chem disp; shwrs; el pnts inc; Indtte; sauna; shop; rest; bar; playgrnd; pool; watersports; private sand beach adj; tennis; horseriding; entmnt; TV rm; 10% statics; dogs €5; adv bkg; quiet; red low ssn. "Lovely setting in naturist reserve; vg facs." 12 May-6 Oct. € 34.00 2007*

SAGONE *10H2* (2km N Rural) *42.13030, 8.70550* **Sagone Camping, Route de Vico, 20118 Sagone [04 95 28 04 15; fax 04 95 28 08 28; sagone.camping@wanadoo.fr; www.camping-sagone.com]** Fr Sagone dir Cargèse then D70 dir Vico, site sp. Lge, mkd pitch, pt shd; wc; baby facs; shwrs inc; el pnts €3.15; Indtte; shop; rest; snacks; bar; BBQ; playgrnd; pool; beach 1.5km; tennis 100m; horseriding 1km; entmnt; TV rm; 10% statics; dogs €2.10; adv bkg; quiet. ♦
1 May-30 Sep. € 24.15 (CChq acc) 2008*

ST FLORENT *10G2* (1km SW Coastal) *42.67394, 9.29205* **Camping U Pezzo, Route de la Roya, 20217 St Florent [tel/fax 04 95 37 01 65; contact@upezzo.com; www.upezzo.com]** Exit St Florent for L'Ile-Rousse on D81 then N199 Route de la Plage. After 2km sharp R immed after x-ing bdge. Med, terr, pt shd; wc; mv service pnt; baby facs; shwrs; el pnts (10A) €3.50; Indtte; shop; rest; snacks; bar; sand beach adj; fishing; sailing; windsurfing; waterslide; horseriding; mini-farm for children; adv bkg; quiet; red low ssn; CCI. "Pleasant site." 15 Apr-15 Oct. € 17.00 2007*

I'm going to fill in some site report forms and post them off to the Club; we could win a ferry crossing – it's here on page 12.

ST FLORENT *10G2* (2.5km W Coastal) *42.67334, 9.29693* **Camping Kalliste, Route de la Plage, 20217 St Florent [04 95 37 03 08; fax 04 95 37 19 77; www.camping-kalliste.com]** Fr St Florent twd L'Ile-Rousse on N199, after 2km sharp R immed after x-ing bdge. Site sp in 500m. Lge, hdg pitch, unshd; wc; mv service pnt; shwrs inc; el pnts (10A) €3.40; Indtte; shop high ssn; rest; snacks; bar; tennis; horseriding; sand beach adj; fishing; sailing; windsurfing; games area; TV; poss cr; adv bkg; CCI. 1 Apr-31 Oct. € 20.50 2006*

SERRA DI FERRO (CORSICA) see Porto Pollo *10H2*

VENACO *10G2* (3km E Rural) *42.22388, 9.19364* **Camping La Ferme de Peridundellu, 20231 Venaco [tel/fax 04 95 47 09 89; campingvenaco@wanadoo.fr; http://campingvenaco.monsite.wanadoo.fr]** S on N200 fr Corte for 15km; R on D143; at bdge keep R towards Venaco; site on L in 1.5km on bend. Sm, pt sl, pt shd; htd wc; chem disp (wc); shwrs inc; el pnts (6-10A) €3.50; Indtte; shop 2km; tradsmn; rest adj; snacks & bar 2km; quiet; ccard acc; CCI. "CL-type site; beautifully situated; gd walking country; friendly owner." Apr-Sep. € 15.00 2008*

VIVARIO *10G2* (5km N Rural) *42.15311, 9.15148* **Aire Naturelle Le Soleil (Marietti), 20219 Tattone [04 95 47 21 16; www.corte-tourisme.com]** N fr Ajaccio on N193 twds Corte. Well sp by stn in Tattone. Sm, hdstg, terr, shd; wc; chem disp; shwrs; el pnts inc; pizzeria; bar; fishing; quiet. "Nice, clean site; superb views; friendly owners; sm area for tourers; facs poss stretched high ssn; ring ahead low ssn; train to Corte & Ajaccio stops on request; ideal walking." 1 May-15 Oct. € 17.00 2007*

ILE DE RE

ARS EN RE *7A1* (400m S Coastal) *46.20395, -1.52014* **Camping du Soleil, 57 Route de la Grange, 17590 Ars-en-Ré [05 46 29 40 62; fax 05 46 29 41 74; contact@campdusoleil.com; www.campdusoleil.com]** On ent Ars-en-Ré on D735, pass Citroën g'ge & in 700m take 3rd L dir Plage de la Grange. Site sp. Med, hdg/mkd pitch, mainly shd; wc; chem disp; mv service pnt; baby facs; fam bthrm; shwrs inc; el pnts (10A) €4.56; Indtte; shop; rest; snacks; bar; BBQ (gas/elec); playgrnd; htd pool; paddling pool; sand beach 400m; tennis; games area; cycle hire; wifi; TV rm; 35% statics; dogs €3; phone; adv bkg; CCI. "Pleasant, pretty site; helpful, friendly staff; gd cycling & walking." ♦ 15 Mar-15 Nov. € 31.90 2008*

ARS EN RE *7A1* (800m SW Coastal) *46.20282, -1.52733* **Camping ESSI, Route de la Pointe de Grignon, 17590 Ars-en-Ré [05 46 29 44 73 or 05 46 29 46 09 (LS); fax 05 46 37 57 78; camping.essi@wanadoo.fr; www.campingessi.com]** D735 to Ars-en-Ré; do not enter town; turn L at supmkt. Site sp. Med, hdg pitch, pt shd; htd wc; chem disp; baby facs; shwrs inc; el pnts (5-10A) €3.95-5.60; Indtte; shop; tradsmn; rest; snacks; bar; BBQ; playgrnd; pool; watersports; cycle hire; 7% statics; dogs €2.10; phone; bus 800m; adv bkg; quiet; red low ssn; CCI. "Attractive waterfront town; excel beaches 2km; gd cycling; gd oysters; vg." ♦ 31 Mar- 31 Oct. € 22.10 (3 persons) 2007*

ARS EN RE *7A1* (300m NW Coastal) *46.21130, -1.53017* **Airotel Camping Le Cormoran, Route de Radia, 17590 Ars-en-Ré [05 46 29 46 04; fax 05 46 29 29 36; info@cormoran.com; www.cormoran.com]** Fr La Rochelle take D735 onto Ile-de-Ré, site sp fr Ars-en-Ré. Med, hdg/mkd pitch, hdstg, pt shd; wc; chem disp; mv service pnt; baby facs; sauna; shwrs inc; el pnts (10A) €5; Indtte; shop 800m; tradsmn; rest; snacks; bar; playgrnd; htd pool; beach 500m; tennis; cycle hire; games area; games rm; golf 10km; entmnt; some statics; dogs €5.50; Eng spkn; adv bkg; quiet; ccard acc; red low ssn; CCI. "Delightful vill; vg site." ♦ 1 Apr-30 Sep. € 40.00 (3 persons) 2007*

COUARDE SUR MER, LA *7A1* (4km SE Coastal) *46.17733, -1.38629* **CAMPEOLE Camping Les Amis de la Plage, Ave Pas des Boeufs, 17580 Le Bois-Plage-en-Ré [tel/fax 05 46 09 24 01; contact@les-amis-de-la-plage.com; www.les-amis-de-la-plage.com or www.campeole.com]** Fr toll bdge fr La Rochelle foll D201 to Le Bois-Plage-en-Ré; on ent vill take 1st L sp 'Plage-des-Boeufs' & 'Municipal'. Site on R at end of rd. Lge, pt sl, pt shd; wc; chem disp (wc); mv service pnt; baby facs; shwrs inc; el pnts (10A) €4; Indtte; shops & mkt 1km; tradsmn; rest & snacks adj; BBQ; playgrnd; sand beach adj; pool adj; 5% statics; dogs €2; phone; bus 1km; poss cr; Eng spkn; quiet; ccard acc; red low ssn; CCI. "Friendly, easy-going site; pitches on sand/soil/dry grass; vg." 1 Apr-30 Sep. € 19.00 (3 persons) 2009*

France
Ile De Re

COUARDE SUR MER, LA *7A1* (4km SE Coastal) *46.17850, -1.38320* **Camping Les Varennes, Raise Maritaise, 17580 Le Bois-Plage-en-Ré [05 46 09 15 43; fax 05 46 09 47 27; les-varennes@wanadoo.fr; www.les-varennes.com]** Fr toll bdge at La Rochelle, foll D201 to Gros-Jonc (1km bef Le Bois-Plage-en-Ré cent); turn L at rndabt; after 350m turn R; site on R in 500m. Med, mkd pitch, shd; htd wc (some cont); chem disp; mv service pnt; baby facs; shws inc; el pnts (10A) €5.30; Indtte; shop & rest 1km; snacks; bar; BBQ (sep area); playgrnd; htd, covrd pool; sand beach 300m; cycle hire; wifi; TV; 70% statics; dogs €6; poss cr; Eng spkn; adv bkg; quiet; ccard acc; red low ssn/long stay; CCI. "Excel, site; many cycle tracks; vg." ♦ 1 Apr-30 Sep. € 38.00 (3 persons) 2008*

COUARDE SUR MER, LA *7A1* (4km SE Coastal) *46.17405, -1.37865* **Sunêlia Parc Club Interlude, Plage de Gros-Jonc, 17580 Le Bois-Plage-en-Ré [05 46 09 18 22; fax 05 46 09 23 38; infos@interlude.fr; www.interlude.fr]** Fr toll bdge at La Rochelle foll D201 to Gros-Jonc. Turn L at rndabt at site sp. Site 400m on L. Lge, mkd pitch, hdstg, pt shd; htd wc; chem disp; mv service pnt; baby facs; fam bthrm; sauna; some serviced pitches; shwrs inc; el pnts (10A) inc; gas; Indtte; shop; rest; snacks; bar; BBQ; playgrnd; 2 pools (1 htd, covrd); sand beach; watersports; jacuzzi; solarium; tennis nr; games area; boat & cycle hire; fitness rm; TV rm; 45% statics; dogs €7; poss cr; Eng spkn; o'night area for m'vans; adv bkg ess; quiet. "Excel, relaxing, well-run, busy site; vg facs; some sm, sandy pitches - extra for lger; nrby beaches excel." ♦ 1 Apr-11 Nov. € 42.00 2006*

COUARDE SUR MER, LA *7A1* (5km SE Coastal) *46.16793, -1.36351* **Camping Antioche, Route de Ste Marie, 17580 Le Bois-Plage-en-Ré [05 46 09 23 86; fax 05 46 09 43 34; camping.antioche@wanadoo.fr; www.antioche.com]** Fr toll bdge fr La Rochelle, at 1st rndabt take D201 sp Le Bois-Plage. In about 9km, site on L. Med, hdg/mkd pitch (sandy), pt sl, pt shd; wc; chem disp; mv service pnt; shwrs inc; el pnts (6A) inc; Indtte; shop & 3km; playgrnd; snacks; bar; BBQ; cooking facs; sand beach adj; entmnt; some statics; dogs €6; phone; poss cr; Eng spkn; adv bkg; ccard acc; red low ssn/long stay/CCI. "Lovely site with gd sized pitches; direct access to beach & cycle path; friendly staff; clean facs." ♦ 4 Apr-19 Sep. € 37.00 (3 persons) 2009*

COUARDE SUR MER, LA *7A1* (2km W Coastal) *46.20296, -1.45505* **Camping Le Bois Henri IV, Route d'Ars, 17670 La Couarde-sur-Mer [tel/fax 05 46 29 87 01]** On D735 W fr La Couarde-sur-Mer. Easy to miss site ent. Med, hdg/mkd pitch, pt shd; wc; shwrs inc; chem disp (wc); el pnts; Indtte; playgrnd; beach 200m; some statics; Eng spkn; quiet; red low ssn; CCI. "Long, sandy beaches; birdwatching in salt marshes; 100km of flat cycling, pathways vg; san facs oldish but clean; friendly owner; gd." 1 Apr-30 Sep. € 20.00 2008*

COUARDE SUR MER, LA *7A1* (800m NW Coastal) *46.20408, -1.46740* **Camping de l'Océan, 50 Route d'Ars, 17670 La Couarde-sur-Mer [05 46 29 87 70; fax 05 46 29 92 13; campingdelocean@wanadoo.fr; www.campingocean.com]** Fr La Rochelle take D735 over bdge to Ile de Ré. Past St Martin-de-Re & La Couarde twd Ars-en-Ré. Site on R, 2.5km after La Couarde. Lge, hdg/mkd pitch, shd; wc; chem disp; mv service pnt; baby facs; fam bthrm; shwrs inc; el pnts (5-10A) €3.50-5.20; Indtte; shop; rest, snacks & bar high ssn; no BBQ; playgrnd; 2 pools (1 htd); paddling pool; sand beach adj; watersports; tennis; games area; cycle hire; horseriding 1.5km; golf 6km; entmnt; wifi; 40% statics; dogs €4.64; phone; poss cr; Eng spkn; adv bkg; rd noisy; red low ssn; CCI. "Popular site in superb location; some sm pitches with diff access; site rds & ent to pitches narr; gd, clean san facs; friendly staff; twin-axles not rec; gd walking & cycling; excel." ♦ 5 Apr-28 Sep. € 38.90 (3 persons) (CChq acc) 2008*

COUARDE SUR MER, LA *7A1* (2km NW Coastal) *46.20473, -1.44470* **Camping La Tour des Prises, Chemin de la Grifforine, Route d'Ars, 17670 La Couarde-sur-Mer [05 46 29 84 82; fax 05 46 29 88 99; camping@lesprises.com; www.lesprises.com]** Fr toll bdge foll D735 or D201 to La Couarde, then Rte d'Ars for 1.8km to R turn; site sp & 200m on R. Med, hdg/mkd pitch, pt shd; htd wc (some cont); chem disp; mv service pnt; baby facs; shwrs inc; el pnts (16A) €5; Indtte; shop; tradsmn; snacks; playgrnd; htd, covrd pool; beach 600m; sailing school; games rm; cycle hire; 30% statics; dogs €3; Eng spkn; adv bkg; quiet; ccard acc; red low ssn; CCI. "Excel, well-managed, clean site; lge indiv pitches, mixed sizes; helpful owner & staff; excel pool; many cycle/walking tracks; beach 10 mins walk; ideal for families." ♦ 1 Apr-30 Sep. € 35.00 (3 persons) 2009*

PORTES EN RE, LES *7A1* (800m E Urban/Coastal) *46.24657, -1.48627* **Camping La Providence, Route de la Trousse-Chemise, 17880 Les Portes-en-Ré [05 46 29 56 82; fax 05 46 29 61 80; campingprovidence@wanadoo.fr; www.campingprovidence.com]** On N11 & N137 to La Rochelle foll sp to Ile de Ré. Cross toll bdge & foll D735 to Les Portes-en-Ré at far end of island. Site adj to Plage de la Redoute. Lge, hdg/mkd pitch, pt shd; htd wc (few cont); chem disp; mv service pnt; baby facs; shwrs inc; el pnts (10A) €5; gas; Indtte; shop; rest; snacks; bar; playgrnd; sand beach adj; sailing, watersports, tennis, golf nrby; cycle hire; games rm; 50% statics; dogs €4; poss cr; Eng spkn; adv bkg; CCI. "Lge pitches; gd, flat cycling on island & across bdge to mainland." ♦ 1 Apr-15 Oct. € 27.00 (3 persons) 2007*

RIVEDOUX PLAGE *7A1* (N Coastal) *46.16017, -1.27682* **Camping Les Tamaris, 4 Rue du Comte-d'Hastrel, 17940 Rivedoux-Plage [05 46 09 81 28; www.rivedoux-plage.fr]** Cross bdge to island on D735 & bear L onto D201. Site sp. Med, mkd pitch, pt shd; wc; chem disp; shwrs inc; el pnts (10A) €3.60 (long lead poss req); Indtte; shop, rest, snacks, bar nrby; sand beach adj; sat TV; dogs €1.20; phone; poss cr; quiet; red low ssn; CCI. "Friendly, helpful owners; facs basic but clean." 1 May-30 Sep. € 13.00 2007*

ST CLEMENT DES BALEINES *7A1* (500m N Coastal) *46.24120, -1.55335* **Airotel Camping La Plage, 408 Rue du Chaume, 17590 St Clément-des-Baleines [05 46 29 42 62; fax 05 46 29 03 39; info@la-plage.com; www.la-plage.com]** Fr La Rochelle on D735 to far end of Ile de Ré; site 500m fr Baleines lighthouse, sp. Med, hdg/mkd pitch, hdstg, unshd; htd wc (some cont); chem disp; mv service pnt; baby facs; fam bthrm; shwrs inc; el pnts (10A) €5; gas 1km; Indtte; shop 1.5km; tradsmn; rest; snacks; bar; playgrnd; htd pool; paddling pool; sand beach adj; games area; games rm; cycle hire; wifi; entmnt; dogs €5.50; Eng spkn; adv bkg; quiet; ccard acc; red low ssn; CCI. "Delightful vill; excel facs for families; vg." ♦ Easter-30 Sep. € 40.00 (3 persons) 2007*

ST CLEMENT DES BALEINES *7A1* (S Coastal) *46.22567, -1.54424* **Camping La Côte Sauvage, 336 Rue de la Forêt, 17590 St Clément-des-Baleines [04 73 77 05 05; fax 04 73 77 05 06; contact@lesbalconsverts.com; www.lesbalconsverts.com]** Fr cent of vill, foll sp to site at edge of forest. Lge, mkd pitch, pt sl, pt shd; wc; chem disp; mv service pnt; baby facs; shws inc; el pnts (10A) inc (poss long lead req); shop 300m; tradsmn; snacks; shgl beach adj; cycle routes adj; sw; wifi; dogs €3; phone; Eng spkn; quiet; red low ssn; CCI. "Gd location; some pitches uneven; san facs old but OK; poss unreliable opening dates; gd." ♦ 1 Apr-10 Oct. € 20.00 2009*

STE MARIE DE RE *7A1* (Coastal) *46.14504, -1.31509* **Camp Municipal La Côte Sauvage, La Basse Benée 17740 Ste Marie-de-Ré [05 46 30 21 74; fax 05 46 30 15 64; info@mairie-sainte-marie-de-re.fr; www.mairie-sainte-marie-de-re.fr]** Site sp fr main rd. V narr rds thro town. Med, mkd pitch, pt shd; wc; chem disp; mv service pnt; shwrs inc; el pnts (16A) €3; shop; supmkt 2km snacks; bar; playgrnd; sand beach adj; fishing; quiet; ccard acc; CCI. "Excel location but poss windy; helpful owners; free parking for m'vans adj; highly rec." 1 May-21 Sep. € 11.70 2008*

ST MARTIN DE RE *7A1* (4km E Coastal/Urban) *46.18194, -1.33110* **Camp Municipal de Bel Air, Route de la Noué, 17630 La Flotte [05 46 09 63 10]** Fr toll bdge take D735 to La Flotte. Turn R at rndabt to town into Route de la Noué, site sp.. Lge, hdg/mkd pitch, pt shd; wc (some cont); chem disp; mv service pnt; shwrs inc; el pnts (6A) €3.84; Indtte; rest; snacks; bar; playgrnd; beach 800m; tennis; games rm; entmnt; phone; adv bkg; quiet. "Walk to shops, harbour, beach etc; gd." ♦ 1 Apr-30 Sep. € 13.64 2007*

ST MARTIN DE RE *7A1* (2km SE Coastal) *46.18370, -1.30820* **FFCC Camping Les Peupliers, 17630 La Flotte [05 46 09 62 35; fax 05 46 09 59 76; camping@lespeupliers.com; www.les-peupliers.com]** Site sp fr D735, the main rd on Ile-de-Ré. Lge, hdg pitch, pt shd, wc; chem disp; mv service pnt; shwrs inc; el pnts (5A) inc; Indtte; shop; tradsmn; rest; snacks; bar; playgrnd; htd pool; paddling pool; sand beach 3km; games area; entmnt; internet; TV rm; 80% statics; dogs €5; phone; Eng spkn; adv bkg rec; quiet; ccard acc; CCI. "Sea views; some pitches sm; ltd touring ptiches; poss cr low ssn; gd sports facs." ♦ 25 Apr-18 Sep. € 28.00 (3 persons) (CChq acc) 2008*

ST MARTIN DE RE *7A1* (5km SE Rural) *46.18740, -1.34390* **Camping La Grainetière, Route St Martin, 17630 La Flotte [05 46 09 68 86; fax 05 46 09 53 13; lagrainetiere@free.fr; www.la-grainetiere.com]** 10km W fr toll bdge, site sp on La Flotte ring rd. Med, pt shd; wc; chem disp; mv service pnt; baby facs; shwrs inc; el pnts (10A) €4; gas; Indtte; shop; tradsmn; playgrnd; htd pool; sand beach 3km; cycle hire; wifi; TV rm; 70% statics; dogs €3; poss cr; Eng spkn; adv bkg; rd noise; red low ssn; CCI. "Beautiful, clean, wooded site; lge pitches; gd san facs; helpful owners; daily mkt." ♦ 4 Apr-30 Sep. € 26.00 2009*

ST MARTIN DE RE *7A1* (800m S Urban) *46.19913, -1.36682* **Camp Municipal Les Remparts, Rue Les Remparts, 17410 St Martin-de-Ré [05 46 09 21 96; fax 05 46 09 94 18; camping.stmartindere@wanadoo.fr; www.saint-martin-de-re.fr]** Foll D735 fr toll bdge to St Martin; sp in town fr both ends. Med, hdg/mkd pitch, pt sl, pt shd; wc; chem disp; mv service pnt; shwrs inc; el pnts (10A) €3.60; Indtte; shop; snacks; BBQ; playgrnd; pool 3km; sand beach 1.3km; dogs €1.70; Eng spkn; adv bkg; quiet; ccard acc; red low ssn; CCI. "Busy site in brilliant location; san facs dated but clean; gd basic rest; some pitches boggy when wet; gd cycling; site poss unkempt end ssn." ♦ 7 Mar-13 Nov. € 16.60 (3 persons) 2009*

ILE D'OLERON

BREE LES BAINS, LA *7A1* (Coastal) *46.01892, -1.35540* **Camp Municipal Le Planginot, Allée du Gai Séjour, 17840 La Brée-les-Bains [05 46 47 82 18; fax 05 46 75 90 74; camping.planginot@orange.fr; www.leplanginot.com]** N fr St Pierre d'Oléron on D734, turn R for La Brée on D273, site sp. Lge, mkd pitch, pt shd; htd wc; chem disp; mv service pnt; shwrs inc; el pnts (10A) €3.60; Indtte; snacks; rest in high ssn; playgrnd; beach adj; dogs €2; Eng spkn; adv bkg; quiet; red low ssn. "Well kept site in quiet location; friendly, helpful staff; immac san facs; daily mkt adj; excel value low ssn; vg." ♦ 15 Mar-15 Oct. € 12.80 2008*

BREE LES BAINS, LA *7A1* (3km NW Coastal) *46.03855, -1.37521* **Camp Municipal, 10 Blvd d'Antioche, 17650 St Denis-d'Oléron [05 46 47 85 62; fax 05 46 47 81 51; camping-municipal-st-denis-doleron@wanadoo.fr; www.st-denis-oleron.com]** Clear sp fr D734 in St Denis-d'Oléron town cent. 300m fr port. Lge, mkd pitch, pt sl, pt shd; htd wc; chem disp; mv service pnt; shwrs inc; el pnts (6A) €3.90; gas; Indtte; shop; rest nrby; snacks; playgrnd; sand beach adj; fishing; tennis; dogs €2.50; phone; poss cr; Eng spkn; quiet; CCI. "Some sea views; gd facs; some pitches v soft; ideal for beach holiday with children; gd." 15 Apr-15 Oct. € 13.20 (3 persons) 2006*

France
Ile D'Oleron

CHATEAU D'OLERON, LE *7B1* (Urban/Coastal) *45.88970, -1.20028* **Camping Les Remparts, Blvd Philippe-Daste, 17480 Le Château-d'Oléron [05 46 47 61 93; fax 05 46 47 73 65; camping@les-remparts.com; www.les-remparts.com]** Fr cent Le Château-d'Oléron take D734 dir Dolus d'Oléron rd. After x-ing ramparts/moat turn R at next rndabt, site on R Lge, pt sl, pt shd; wc (mainly cont); mv service pnt; shwrs inc; el pnts (5A) €3.90; Indtte; shop nrby; tradsmn; rest, snacks, bar nrby; playgrnd; sand beach adj; some statics; dogs €2; phone; quiet; red low ssn/long stay. "Pleasant site for NH/sh stay." 1 Mar-30 Nov. € 17.50 (3 persons) 2009*

CHATEAU D'OLERON, LE *7B1* (1km W Coastal) *45.88207, -1.20648* **Airotel Camping Domaine d'Oléron, Domaine de Montravail, 17480 Le Château-d'Oléron [05 46 47 61 82; fax 05 46 47 79 67; info@camping-airotel-oleron.com; www.camping-airotel-oleron.com]** Clearly sp fr D734 after x-ing bdge. Not well sp fr N of island. Ent to site thro stables & horseriding cent. Med, mkd pitch, pt shd; wc; shwrs inc; el pnts (10A) €3.90 (poss rev pol); gas; Indtte; shop & 500m; snacks; bar; BBQ; playgrnd; htd pool; sand beach 1km; fishing; tennis; equestrian centre; games area; cycle hire; some statics; dogs €2.50; poss cr; Eng spkn; adv bkg; quiet; red low ssn/CCI. "Site poss unkempt early ssn; easy walk to town." ♦ 1 Apr-31 Oct. € 22.50 2009*

CHATEAU D'OLERON, LE *7B1* (2.5km NW Coastal) *45.90415, -1.21525* **Camping La Brande, Route des Huîtres, 17480 Le Château-d'Oléron [05 46 47 62 37; fax 05 46 47 71 70; info@camping-labrande.com; www.camping-labrande.com]** Cross bdge on D26, turn R & go thro Le Château-d'Oléron. Foll Rte des Huîtres to La Gaconnière to site. Lge, shd; wc; mv service pnt; baby facs; sauna; steam room; shwrs inc; el pnts (6-10A) €3.20-4; gas; Indtte; shop; rest in ssn; snacks; bar; BBQ; playgrnd; 3 pools (1 htd, covrd); waterslide; sand beach 300m; tennis; cycle hire; games area; golf 6km; entmnt; wifi; TV rm; 60% statics; dogs €2.50; sep car park; Eng spkn; adv bkg; red low ssn. "Pleasant owners; 10 min cycle ride into town; pitches at far end adj oyster farm - noise fr pumps & poss mosquitoes." ♦ 15 Mar-15 Nov. € 30.00 (CChq acc) 2008*

ST DENIS D'OLERON (ILE D'OLERON) see Brée les Bains, La *7A1*

ST GEORGES D'OLERON *7A1* (5km E Coastal) *45.98738, -1.29347* **Camping La Gautrelle (CC de F), Plage des Saumonards, 17190 St Georges-d'Oléron [05 46 47 21 57; fax 05 46 75 10 74; lagautrelle.ccdf@wanadoo.fr; www.campingclub.asso.fr]** Fr viaduct, take D734 to St Pierre. At 3rd traff lts, turn R to Sauzelle, thro vill & L for St Georges & immed to R sp CCDF La Gautrelle. Site at end of lane in approx 1.5km & adj to beach. Lge, mkd pitch, shd; wc; shwrs inc; el pnts (6A) inc (long cable req); shops adj; sand beach; fishing; some statics; dogs €2.32; adv bkg; quiet; CCI. "Splendid beaches; forest walks, fishing; ltd el pnts." ♦ 1 Apr-30 Sep. € 19.85 2009*

ST GEORGES D'OLERON *7A1* (6km E Coastal) *45.96820, -1.24483* **Camping Signol, Ave des Albatros, Boyardville, 17190 St Georges-d'Oléron [05 46 47 01 22; fax 05 46 47 23 46; contact@signol.com; www.signol.com]** Cross bdge onto Ile d'Oléron & cont on main rd twd St Pierre-d'Oléron. Turn R at Dolus-d'Oléron for Boyardville & foll sp in vill. Lge, hdg/mkd pitch, pt sl, pt shd; wc (most cont)(own san facs rec); mv service pnt; chem disp; baby facs; shwrs inc; el pnts (6A) €4.60; gas; Indtte; shops adj; tradsmn; bar; playgrnd; htd pool; paddling pool; sand beach 800m; many statics; no dogs Jul/Aug, low ssn €4; Eng spkn; adv bkg; red low ssn. "Fine site but san facs poor & inadequate for size of site & stretched peak ssn; size & quality of pitches variable, poss far fr san facs; poss flooding in wet weather." ♦ 1 May-30 Sep. € 29.80 2008*

ST GEORGES D'OLERON *7A1* (800m SE Rural) *45.97310, -1.32020* **CHADOTEL Camping Le Domaine d'Oléron, La Jousselinière, 17190 St Georges-d'Oléron [05 46 76 54 97 or 02 51 33 05 05 (LS); fax 02 51 33 94 04; chadotel@wanadoo.fr; www.chadotel.com]** After x-ing Viaduct (bridge) onto island foll sp dir St Pierre d'Oléron & St Georges-d'Oléron on D734; turn R on rndabt immed see Leclerc supmkt on R; at next rndabt turn L sp 'Le Bois Fleury'; pass airfield 'Bois 'Fleury' on R; take next R & then immed L. Site on L in 500m. Med, mkd pitch, terr, pt shd; wc; chem disp; mv service pnt; baby facs; shwrs inc; el pnts (6A) inc; gas; Indtte (inc dryers); shop; rest; snacks; bar; BBQ (gas only) sep area; playgrnd; pool; waterslide; paddling pool; sand beach 3km; cycle hire; games area; entmnt; child entmnt; wifi; games/TV rm; 40% statics; dogs €3; Eng spkn; adv bkg ess high ssn; ccard acc; red long stay/low ssn; CCI. "Popular, well-organised, clean site; friendly, helpful staff; lovely pool; cycle paths; excel." ♦ 3 Apr-25 Sep. € 29.90 ABS - A41 2009*

ST GEORGES D'OLERON *7A1* (2km SE Rural) *45.97126, -1.31757* **Camping Verébleu, La Jousselinière, 17190 St Georges-d'Oléron [05 46 76 57 70; fax 05 46 76 70 56; verebleu@wanadoo.fr; www.verebleu.tm.fr]** Foll D734 thro St Pierre-d'Oléron. On NW o'skts of town at St Gilles turn R (sp La Jousselinière), cross over D273. After 1km take 1st turn L (sp St Georges, La Jousselinière). Site 500m on L. Lge, hdg/mkd pitch, some hdstg, pt shd; wc (some cont); chem disp; mv service pnt; baby facs; shwrs inc; el pnts (4-8A) €3.50-€6; gas; Indtte; sm shop; supmkt 1.5km; rest; snacks; bar; playgrnd; htd pool; waterslide; sand beach 3km; tennis; entmnt; 30% statics; no dogs; poss cr; adv bkg ess high ssn; quiet; ccard acc; CCI. "V efficient management; excel; Oléron is a sm, unspoilt island; lovely beaches; gd for families." ♦ 2 Jun-16 Sep. € 29.00 2007*

ST GEORGES D'OLERON *7A1* (4km SW Coastal) *45.95386, -1.37932* **Camping Les Gros Joncs, Les Sables Vigniers, 17190 St Georges-d'Oléron [05 46 76 52 29; camping.gros.joncs@wanadoo.fr; www.les-gros-joncs.fr]** Fr Ile d'Oléron toll bdge, by-passing Le Château-d'Oléron, NW on D734 to St Pierre-d'Oléron & St Georges-d'Oléron. At Chéray, foll sps to site. V lge, pt shd; wc; shwrs; el pnts (10A) €3; Indtte; shop; rest; snacks; bar; playgrnd; htd pool; paddling pool; jacuzzi; rocky beach 200m; sand beach 1km; games area; TV; some statics; dogs €3; adv bkg; quiet. ♦ 23 Mar-23 Oct. € 42.50 (3 persons) 2009*

ST GEORGES D'OLERON *7A1* (3km W Coastal) *45.94756, -1.37386* **Camping Le Suroit, L'Ileau, 17190 St Georges-d'Oléron [05 46 47 07 25 or 06 80 10 93 18 (mob); fax 05 46 75 04 24; camping@lesuroit.fr; www.camping-lesuroit.com]** Fr Domino cent foll sp for beach, turn L for L'Ileau. Strt at x-rds. Fork L for La Cotinière, site on R in 150m. Lge, mkd pitch, shd; htd wc; baby facs; shwrs inc; el pnts (10A) €4; gas; Indtte; shop; rest; snacks; bar; playgrnd; htd, covrd pool; sand beach adj; tennis; games area; cycle hire; entmnt; TV; some statics; dogs €3; adv bkg; quiet; red low ssn. "Excel, well-organised site." ♦ 1 Apr-30 Sep. € 22.00 2008*

ST GEORGES D'OLERON *7A1* (3km W Coastal) *45.96119, -1.37032* **Camping Les Grosses Pierres, Les Sables Vigniers, 17190 St Georges-d'Oléron [05 46 76 52 19 or 02 51 27 37 80 (reservation); fax 05 46 76 54 85 or 02 51 28 84 09; vagues-oceanes@wanadoo.fr; www.camping-vagues-oceanes.com]** Site sp fr D734. Lge, mkd pitch, terr, pt shd; wc; shwrs inc; el pnts (5A) €6; gas; Indtte; shop; rest; snacks; bar; playgrnd; 2 pools (1 htd, covrd); waterslide; sand beach 900m; 95% statics; dogs €4; Eng spkn; adv bkg; ccard acc; CCI. 15 Apr-30 Sep. € 24.00 2006*

ST PIERRE D'OLERON *7B1* (Coastal) *45.92394, -1.34273* **FFCC Camp Municipal La Fauche Prère, Ave des Pins, La Cotinière, 17310 St Pierre d'Oléron [05 46 47 10 53; fax 05 46 75 23 44; camping@saint-pierre-oleron.com; www.saint-pierre-oleron.com]** Fr bdge foll D734 N to St Pierre-d'Oléron. Turn L onto D274 for La Cotinière, site bef vill on L, sp. Med, mkd pitch, pt sl, shd; wc; chem disp (wc); mv service pnt; baby facs; shwrs €0.80; el pnts (12A) €3.10; Indtte; shop; playgrnd; sand beach adj; dogs €1.55; poss cr; CCI. "Direct access to beach; most pitches sandy; gd." 1 Apr-30 Sep. € 12.40 (3 persons) 2006*

ST PIERRE D'OLERON*7B1* (400m N Rural) *45.94706, -1.31251* **Camping La Pierrière, 18 Route de St Georges, 17310 St Pierre-d'Oléron [05 46 47 08 29; fax 05 46 75 12 82; info@camping-la-pierriere.com; www.camping-la-pierriere.com]** On island foll sp into St Pierre. Turn R at 3rd traff lts then L. Clear sp to La Pierriere-Piscine. Med, mkd pitch, pt shd; some serviced pitch; wc; chem disp; shwrs inc, el pnts (4-10A) €3.50-5; Indtte; rest; snacks; bar; playgrnd; htd pool; sand beach 4km; some statics; dogs €2; poss cr; Eng spkn; adv bkg; quiet; ccard acc; CCI. "Gd for cycling; daily mkt in town; some facs clsd Sep." ♦ 5 Apr-19 Sep. € 22.00 2006*

ST PIERRE D'OLERON *7B1* (3km W Coastal) *45.90164, -1.30266* **Camping La Perroche Leitner, 18 Rue de Renclos de la Perroche, 17310 St Pierre-d'Oléron [05 46 75 37 33; fax 05 49 85 12 57]** Site about 10km fr bdge on W coast of Ile d'Oléron. Fr bdge foll sp to Grande Village/Vert-Bois/La Remigeasse & La Perroche. Well sp. Med, hdg/mkd pitch, hdstg, terr, pt shd; wc; mv service pnt; shwrs inc; el pnts (5-10A) €4.90-5.90; gas; Indtte; shop; tradsmn; playgrnd; direct access sand beach 200m; games area; dogs €2.20; Eng spkn; quiet; ccard acc. "Superb site; site staff connect/disconnect el pnts." ♦ 1 Apr-15 Sep. € 20.20 2006*

ST TROJAN LES BAINS *7B1* (1.5km SW Coastal) *45.83159, -1.21389* **Camp Municipal Les Martinets, 11 Ave des Bris, 17370 St Trojan-les-Bains [05 46 76 02 39; fax 05 46 76 42 95; lesmartinets@wanadoo.fr; http://monsite.wanadoo.fr/lesmartinets]** Fr D26 cont on toll bdge rd then L onto D126 to St Trojan-les-Bains. Foll sp for 'Campings' & 'Plage' then sp for Gatseau-Plage. Lge, mkd pitch, pt sl, terr, pt shd; wc (few cont); chem disp; mv service pnt; shwrs inc; el pnts (6A) €3.40 (poss long lead req); gas 500m; Indtte; shops 300m; tradsmn; snacks high ssn; playgrnd; sand beach 1km; cycle hire; 5% statics; dogs €1.40; phone; Eng spkn; adv bkg; ccard acc; red low ssn; CCI. "Some sm pitches & some on sand; fair." ♦ 15 Jan-15 Nov. € 12.50 2008*

ST TROJAN LES BAINS *7B1* (1.5km SW Rural) *45.82947, -1.21632* **Camping La Combinette, 36 Ave des Bris, 17370 St Trojan-les-Bains [05 46 76 00 47; fax 05 46 76 16 96; la-combinette@wanadoo.fr; www.combinette-oleron.com]** Fr toll bdge stay on D26 for 1km, L onto D275 & L onto D126 to St Trojan-les-Bains. Strt ahead at rndabt with figure sculpture, then R at next rndabt sp Campings. In 1km turn L at rd fork, site on R in 1km. Lge, shd; wc; baby facs; shwrs inc; el pnts (5-10A) €3-3.90; gas; Indtte; shop; rest; snacks; playgrnd; beach 2km; games area; cycle hire; entmnt; dogs €2.20; poss cr; quiet. "Gd touring base; facs poss stretched high ssn." ♦ 1 Apr-31 Oct. € 15.30 2006*

Sites in Andorra

⊞ **ANDORRA LA VELLA** *8G3* (7km NE Urban) *42.53333, 1.57527* **Camping Internacional, Ctra de Vila s/n, AD200 Encamp [tel/fax 831 609; info@campinginternacional.com; www.campinginternacional.com]** On rd thro Encamp turn at traff lts & motor museum. Med, mkd pitch, pl sl, pt shd; wc; chem disp; mv service pnt; shwrs inc; el pnts (6A) €4.20; lndtte; shop; supmkt 100m; tradsmn; snacks; bar; htd pool; TV rm; 40% statics; dogs; phone; bus; skilift 12km; adv bkg; poss v cr; Eng spkn; quiet; CCI. "Sm pitches; gd rests nr; friendly, family-run." € 20.80 2008*

⊞ **ANDORRA LA VELLA** *8G3* (600m S Urban) *42.50166, 1.51527* **Camping Valira, Ave de Salou, AD500 Andorra-la-Vella [tel/fax 722 384; campvalira@andorra.ad; www.campvalira.com]** Site on E site of main rd S fr Andorra-la-Vella; behind sports stadium; clearly sp. Lge, hdstg, terr, pt shd; htd wc; chem disp; mv service pnt; shwrs inc; el pnts (3-10A) €3-5.35 (no earth); gas; lndtte; shop; rest; snacks; bar; playgrnd; covrd pool; dogs €2; Eng spkn; adv bkg; quiet; CCI. "Conv NH for shopping; excel facs; vg rest; beware of sudden storms blowing up." ♦ € 21.40 2006*

⊞ **ANDORRA LA VELLA** *8G3* (3km SW Rural) *42.46136, 1.48949* **Camping Huguet, Ctra de Fontaneda, AD600 St Julià de Lòria [tel 843 718; fax 843 803; renepujol@hotmail.com]** Site at S end of St Julià. NE fr Spain site 2km fr frontier. After petrol stn & Mamot supmkt turn L over sm rv bdge. Sp & visible fr main rd. Sm, pt shd; wc; chem disp; shwrs inc; el pnts (6A) inc (no earth); lndtte; shop high ssn; supmkt 100m; rest, snacks, bar 1km; pool; playgrnd; rv fishing; tennis; games rm; cycle hire; dogs; Eng spkn; adv bkg; quiet; ccard acc; CCI. "Excel facs; take care with el pnts; poor value for money high ssn." € 25.35 2007*

⊞ **CANILLO** *8G3* (Urban) *42.56740, 1.60235* **Camping Pla, Ctra General s/n, AD100 Canillo [tel 851 333; fax 851 280; campingpla@cyberandorra.com; www.campingpla.cyberandorra.com]** App Canillo fr S, pass Tarrado petrol stn on R; take 1st exit at 2nd rndabt opp lge hotel, over bdge & turn L to site. Med, mkd pitch, pt shd; htd wc; chem disp; baby facs; shwrs inc; el pnts (5-10A) €3; gas; lndtte; rest, snacks in town; bar; playgrnd; htd, covrd pool & sports facs in town; skilift 100m; 75% statics; dogs; bus adj; Eng spkn; adv bkg; ccard not acc. "Excel location for skiing but poss unkempt/untidy low ssn." € 14.50 2008*

MASSANA, LA *8G3* (2km N Rural) *42.56601, 1.52448* **Camping Borda d'Ansalonga, Ctra del Serrat, AD400 Ordino [tel 850 374; fax 735 400; campingansalonga@andorra.ad; www.campingansalonga.com]** Fr Andorra-la-Vella foll sp La Massana & Ordino. Turn L twd El Serrat, site on R, well sp. Lge, pt shd; htd wc; chem disp; baby facs; shwrs inc; el pnts (10A) €4.80; gas; lndtte; shop; tradsmn; rest; bar; BBQ; playgrnd; pool; games rm; winter statics for skiers; dogs; phone; Eng spkn; quiet; CCI. "Statics moved to storage area in summer; quieter than sites on main thro rte." 27 Oct-1 May & 15 Jun-15 Sep. € 17.50 2007*

⊞ **MASSANA, LA** *8G3* (2km NW Rural) *42.55361, 1.48916* **Camping Xixerella, Ctra de Pal, AD400 Erts [tel 836 613; fax 839 113; c-xixerella@campingxixerella.com; www.campingxixerella.com]** Fr Andorra la Vella take rd for La Massana; fr there foll sps for Xixerella & vill of Pal. Site on L. Med, terr, pt shd; htd wc; chem disp; htd shwrs; el pnts (3-6A) €5.70 (poss no earth); lndtte; shop; rest; bar; playgrnd; pool; crazy golf; entmnt; some statics; dogs; phone; Eng spkn; adv bkg; quiet; ccard acc; red long stay; CCI. "Lovely site; clean, modern facs; helpful staff; no drying rm for ski gear; gd mountain walks; long walk to dispose of rubbish; site poss untidy/unkempt low ssn." ♦ € 24.80 2008*

France

Distances are shown in kilometres and are calculated from town/city centres along the most practical roads, although not necessarily taking the shortest route.
1km = 0.62miles

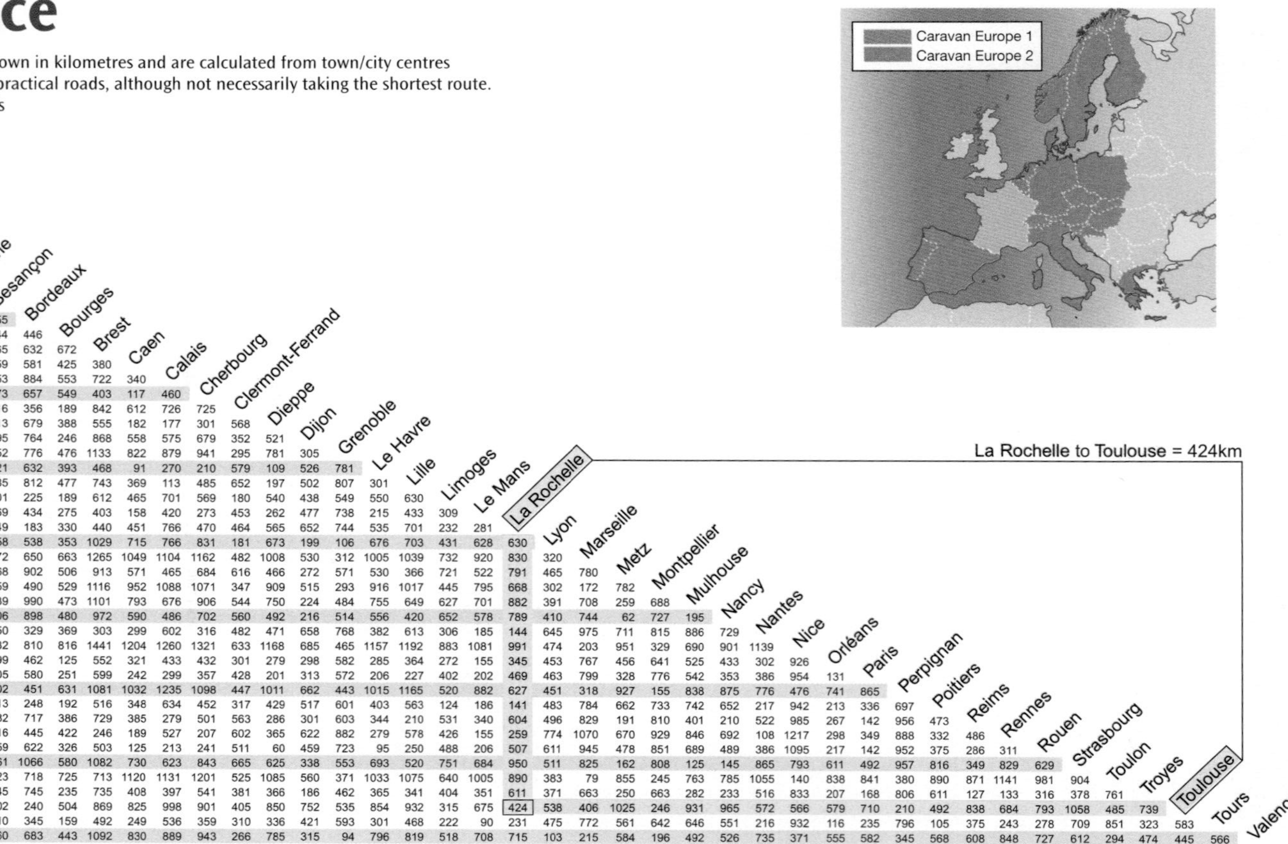

La Rochelle to Toulouse = 424km

	Andorra-la-Vella	Annecy	Bayonne	Besançon	Bordeaux	Bourges	Brest	Caen	Calais	Cherbourg	Clermont-Ferrand	Dieppe	Dijon	Grenoble	Le Havre	Lille	Limoges	Le Mans	La Rochelle
Annecy	701																		
Bayonne	415	912																	
Besançon	861	230	1042																
Bordeaux	432	691	190	855															
Bourges	678	505	630	544	446														
Brest	1051	1092	822	965	632	672													
Caen	1026	790	775	659	581	425	380												
Calais	1141	832	1067	653	884	553	722	340											
Cherbourg	1085	910	843	773	657	549	403	117	460										
Clermont-Ferrand	591	332	545	416	356	189	842	612	726	725									
Dieppe	1052	751	863	613	679	388	555	182	177	301	568								
Dijon	783	263	955	95	764	246	868	558	575	679	352	521							
Grenoble	601	106	821	352	776	476	1133	822	879	941	295	781	305						
Le Havre	1051	754	823	621	632	393	468	91	270	210	579	109	526	781					
Lille	1105	756	1003	585	812	477	743	369	113	485	652	197	502	807	301				
Limoges	516	580	409	501	225	189	612	465	701	569	180	540	438	549	550	630			
Le Mans	873	709	624	569	434	275	403	158	420	273	453	262	477	738	215	433	309		
La Rochelle	627	782	375	749	183	330	440	451	766	470	464	565	652	744	535	701	232	281	
Lyon	615	143	828	258	538	353	1029	715	766	831	181	673	199	106	676	703	431	628	630
Marseille	477	401	695	572	650	663	1265	1049	1104	1162	482	1008	530	312	1005	1039	732	920	830
Metz	1084	528	1099	268	902	506	913	571	465	684	616	466	272	571	530	366	721	522	791
Montpellier	320	383	533	559	490	529	1116	952	1088	1071	347	909	515	293	916	1017	445	795	668
Mulhouse	989	358	1183	139	990	473	1101	793	676	906	544	750	224	484	755	649	627	701	882
Nancy	1013	472	1081	206	898	480	972	590	486	702	560	492	216	514	556	420	652	578	789
Nantes	762	886	522	750	329	369	303	299	602	316	482	471	658	768	382	613	306	185	144
Nice	641	529	850	732	810	816	1441	1204	1260	1321	633	1168	685	465	1157	1192	883	1081	991
Orléans	748	532	651	399	462	125	552	321	433	432	301	279	298	582	285	364	272	155	345
Paris	875	542	769	405	580	251	599	242	299	357	428	201	313	572	206	227	402	202	469
Perpignan	158	533	491	702	451	631	1081	1032	1235	1098	447	1011	662	443	1015	1165	520	882	627
Poitiers	663	629	436	613	248	192	516	348	634	452	317	429	517	601	403	563	124	186	141
Reims	989	557	911	382	717	386	729	385	279	501	563	286	301	603	344	210	531	340	604
Rennes	871	846	634	716	445	422	246	189	527	207	602	365	622	882	279	578	426	155	259
Rouen	995	690	812	559	622	326	503	125	213	241	511	60	459	723	95	250	488	206	507
Strasbourg	1093	452	1256	261	1066	580	1082	730	623	843	665	625	338	553	693	520	751	684	950
Toulon	551	480	760	623	718	725	713	1120	1131	1201	525	1085	560	371	1033	1075	640	1005	890
Troyes	967	411	911	245	745	235	735	408	397	541	381	366	186	462	365	341	404	351	611
Toulouse	203	626	295	802	240	504	869	825	998	901	405	850	752	535	854	932	315	675	424
Tours	771	623	538	510	345	159	492	249	536	359	310	336	421	593	301	468	222	90	231
Valence	519	178	729	360	683	443	1092	830	889	943	266	785	315	94	796	819	518	708	715

	Lyon	Marseille	Metz	Montpellier	Mulhouse	Nancy	Nantes	Nice	Orléans	Paris	Perpignan	Poitiers	Reims	Rennes	Rouen	Strasbourg	Toulon	Troyes	Toulouse	Tours
Marseille	320																			
Metz	465	780																		
Montpellier	302	172	782																	
Mulhouse	391	708	259	688																
Nancy	410	744	62	727	195															
Nantes	645	975	711	815	886	729														
Nice	474	203	951	329	690	901	1139													
Orléans	453	767	456	641	525	433	302	926												
Paris	463	799	328	776	542	353	386	954	131											
Perpignan	451	318	927	155	838	875	776	476	741	865										
Poitiers	483	784	662	733	742	652	217	942	213	336	697									
Reims	496	829	191	810	401	210	522	985	267	142	956	473								
Rennes	774	1070	670	929	846	692	108	1217	298	349	888	332	486							
Rouen	611	945	478	851	689	489	386	1095	217	142	952	375	286	311						
Strasbourg	511	825	162	808	125	145	865	793	611	492	957	816	349	829	629					
Toulon	383	79	855	245	763	785	1055	140	838	841	380	890	871	1141	981	904				
Troyes	371	663	250	663	282	233	516	833	207	168	806	611	127	133	316	378	761			
Toulouse	538	406	1025	246	931	965	572	566	579	710	210	492	838	684	793	1058	485	739		
Tours	475	772	561	642	646	551	216	932	116	235	796	105	375	243	278	709	851	323	583	
Valence	103	215	584	196	492	526	735	371	555	582	345	568	608	848	727	612	294	474	445	566

Regions and Departments of France

ALSACE
67 Bas-Rhin
68 Haut-Rhin

AQUITAINE
24 Dordogne
33 Gironde
40 Landes
47 Lot-et-Garonne
64 Pyrénées-Atlantiques

AUVERGNE
03 Allier
15 Cantal
43 Haute-Loire
63 Puy-de-Dôme

BOURGOGNE
21 Côte-d'Or
58 Nièvre
71 Saône-et-Loire
89 Yonne

BRETAGNE
22 Côtes-d'Armor
29 Finistère
35 Ille-et-Vilaine
56 Morbihan

CENTRE
18 Cher
28 Eure-et-Loir
36 Indre
37 Indre-et-Loire
41 Loir-et-Cher
45 Loiret

CHAMPAGNE-ARDENNE
08 Ardennes
10 Aube
51 Marne
52 Haute-Marne

CORSE
02A Corse-du-Sud
02B Haute-Corse

FRANCHE-COMTE
25 Doubs
39 Jura
70 Haute-Saône
90 Territoire-de-Belfort

LANGUEDOC-ROUSSILLON
11 Aude
30 Gard
34 Hérault
48 Lozère
66 Pyrénées-Orientales

LIMOUSIN
19 Corrèze
23 Creuse
87 Haute-Vienne

LORRAINE
54 Meurthe-et-Moselle
55 Meuse
57 Moselle
88 Vosges

MIDI-PYRENEES
09 Ariège
12 Aveyron
31 Haute-Garonne
32 Gers
46 Lot
65 Hautes-Pyrénées
81 Tarn
82 Tarn-et-Garonne

NORD/PAS-DE-CALAIS
59 Nord
62 Pas-de-Calais

NORMANDIE
14 Calvados
27 Eure
50 Manche
61 Orne
76 Seine-Maritime

PARIS-ILE DE FRANCE
75 Paris
77 Seine-et-Marne
78 Yvelines
91 Essonne
92 Haut-de-Seine
93 Seine-St-Denis
94 Val-de-Marne
95 Val-d'Oise

PAYS DE LA LOIRE
44 Loire-Atlantique
49 Maine-et-Loire
53 Mayenne
72 Sarthe
85 Vendée

PICARDIE
02 Aisne
60 Oise
80 Somme

POITOU-CHARENTES
16 Charente
17 Charente-Maritime
79 Deux-Sèvres
86 Vienne

PROVENCE-COTE D'AZUR
04 Alpes-de-Haute-Provence
05 Hautes-Alpes
06 Alpes-Maritimes
13 Bouches-du-Rhône
83 Var
84 Vaucluse

RHONE-ALPS
01 Ain
07 Ardèche
26 Drôme
38 Isère
42 Loire
69 Rhône
73 Savoie
74 Haute-Savoie

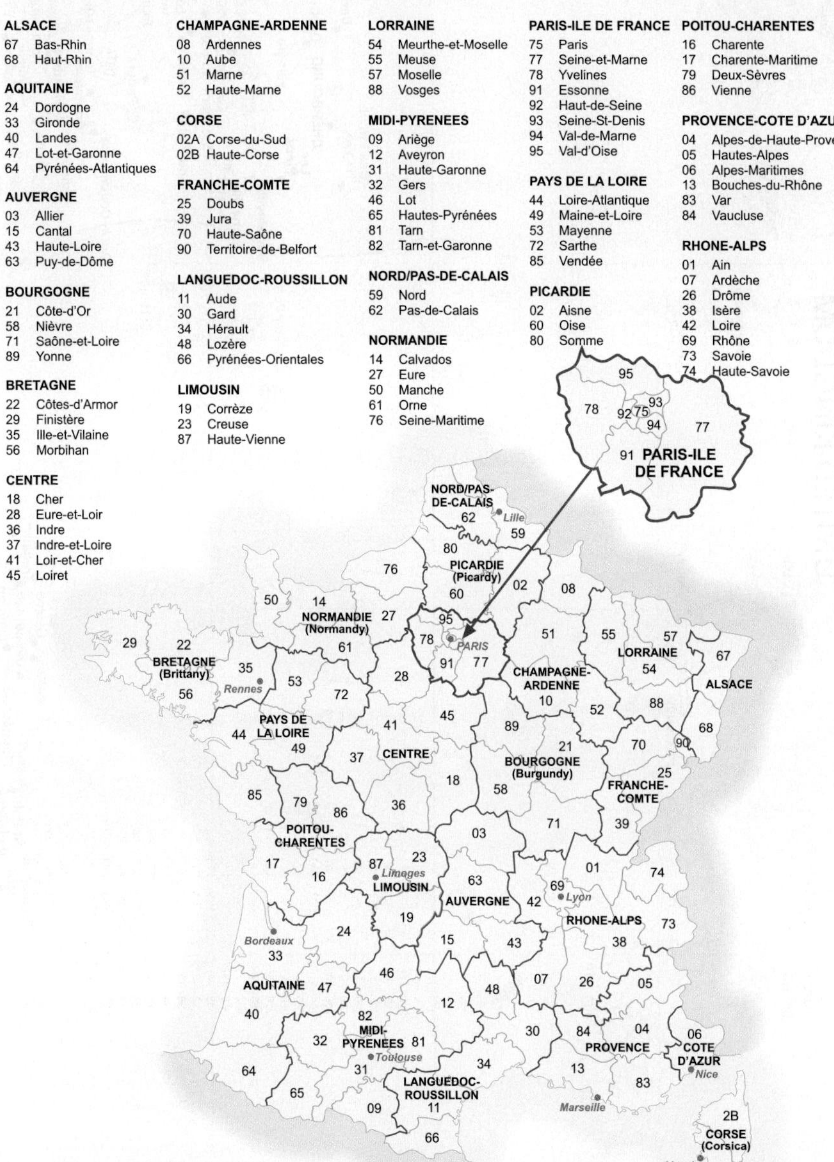

The first two digits of a French postcode correspond to the number of the department in which that town or village is situated

Source : French Government Tourist Office

Map 1

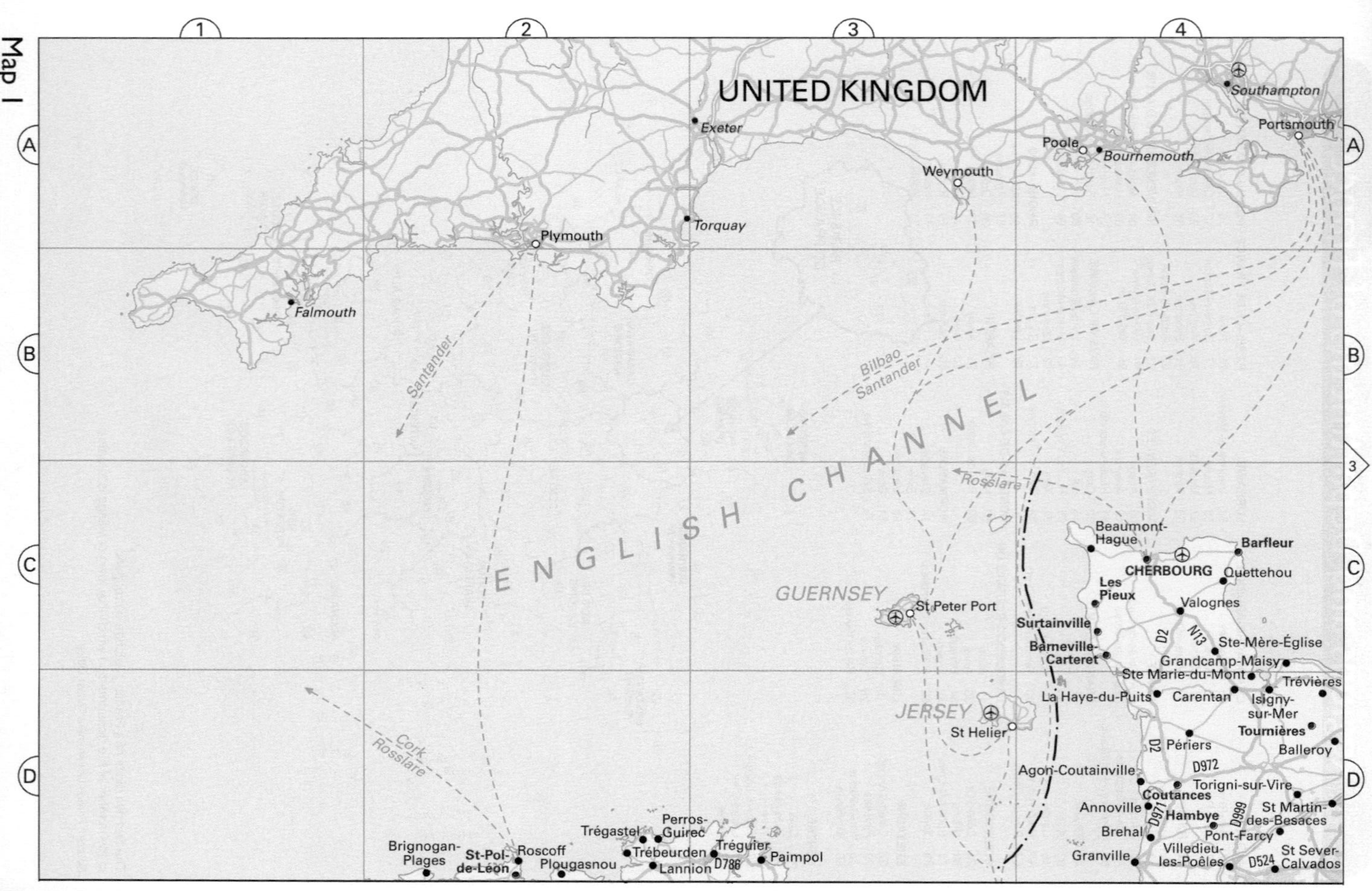

UNITED KINGDOM
ENGLISH CHANNEL
GUERNSEY
JERSEY
Southampton
Portsmouth
Poole
Bournemouth
Weymouth
Exeter
Torquay
Plymouth
Falmouth
Santander
Bilbao
Santander
Rosslare
Cork
Rosslare
St Peter Port
St Helier
Beaumont-Hague
Barfleur
CHERBOURG
Quettehou
Les Pieux
Valognes
Surtainville
D2
N13
Ste-Mère-Église
Barneville-Carteret
Grandcamp-Maisy
Ste Marie-du-Mont
Trévières
La Haye-du-Puits
Carentan
Isigny-sur-Mer
Tournières
Périers
Balleroy
D2
D972
Agon-Coutainville
Torigni-sur-Vire
Coutances
St Martin-des-Besaces
Annoville
Hambye
D999
D971
Brehal
Pont-Farcy
Granville
Villedieu-les-Poêles
D524
St Sever-Calvados
Brignogan-Plages
St-Pol-de-Léon
Roscoff
Plougasnou
Trégastel
Perros-Guirec
Trébeurden
Lannion
Tréguier
D786
Paimpol
1
2
3
4
A
B
C
D
3

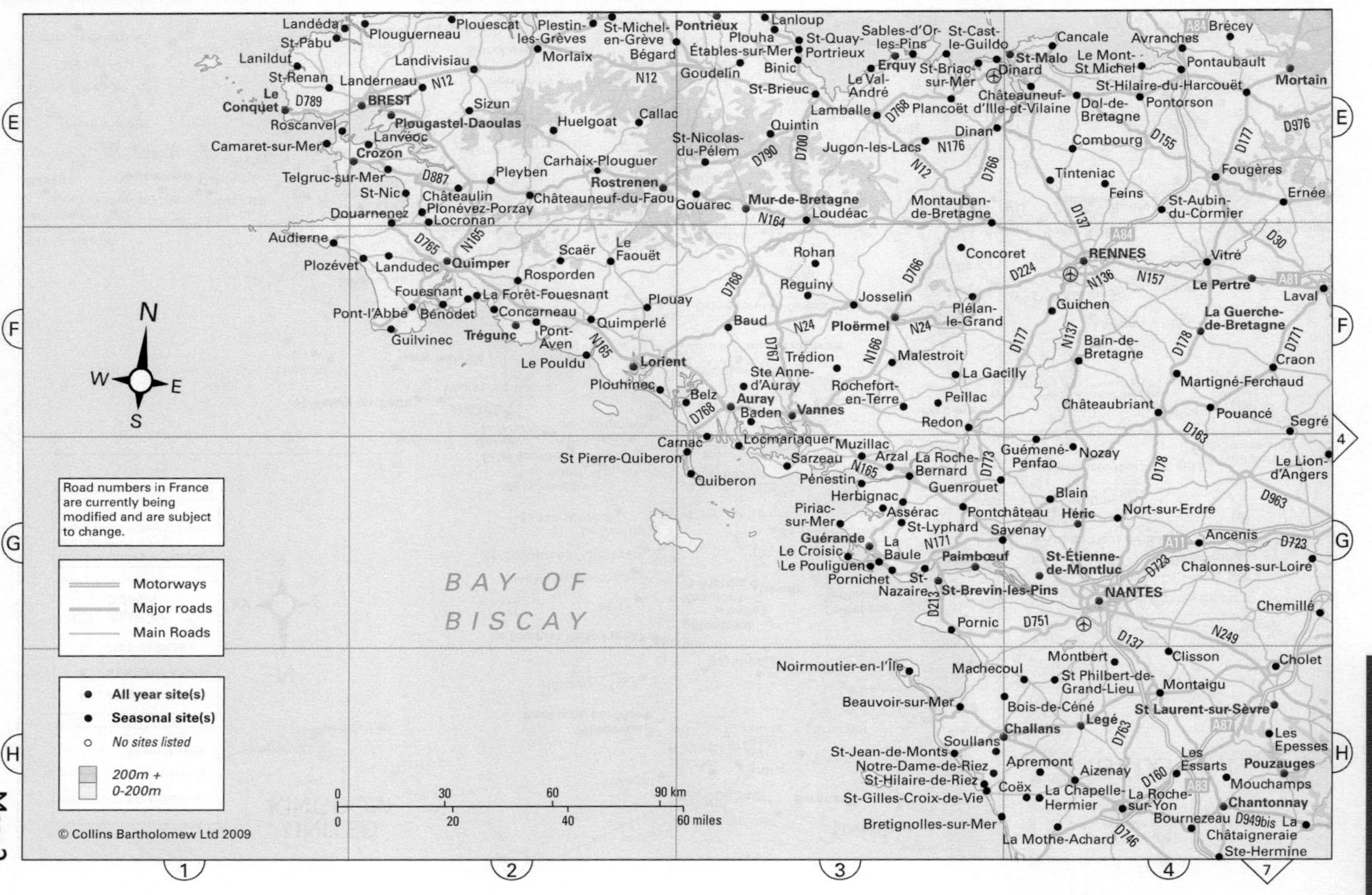
E
F
G
H
1
2
3
4
7
BAY OF BISCAY
Road numbers in France are currently being modified and are subject to change.
Motorways
Major roads
Main Roads
All year site(s)
Seasonal site(s)
No sites listed
200m +
0-200m
N
E
S
W
0
30
60
90 km
0
20
40
60 miles
© Collins Bartholomew Ltd 2009
Landéda
Plouguerneau
Plouescat
Plestin-les-Grèves
St-Michel-en-Grève
Pontrieux
Lanloup
Plouha
St-Quay-Portrieux
Sables-d'Or-les-Pins
St-Cast-le-Guildo
Cancale
Avranches
Brécey
St-Pabu
Lanildut
Morlaix
Bégard
Étables-sur-Mer
Binic
Erquy
St-Briac-sur-Mer
St-Malo
Dinard
Le Mont-St Michel
Pontaubault
Mortain
St-Renan
Le Conquet
Landivisiau
Landerneau
BREST
Goudelin
St-Brieuc
Le Val-André
Lamballe
Plancoët
Châteauneuf-d'Ille-et-Vilaine
Dol-de-Bretagne
St-Hilaire-du-Harcouët
Pontorson
Roscanvel
Plougastel-Daoulas
Sizun
Huelgoat
Callac
Quintin
Dinan
Combourg
Camaret-sur-Mer
Lanvéoc
Crozon
St-Nicolas-du-Pélem
Jugon-les-Lacs
Tinteniac
Feins
Fougères
Ernée
Telgruc-sur-Mer
Pleyben
Carhaix-Plouguer
Rostrenen
St-Nic
Châteaulin
Plonévez-Porzay
Châteauneuf-du-Faou
Gouarec
Mur-de-Bretagne
Loudéac
Montauban-de-Bretagne
St-Aubin-du-Cormier
Douarnenez
Locronan
Audierne
Plozévet
Landudec
Quimper
Scaër
Le Faouët
Rohan
Concoret
RENNES
Vitré
Le Pertre
Laval
Rosporden
Fouesnant
La Forêt-Fouesnant
Pont-l'Abbé
Bénodet
Concarneau
Plouay
Reguiny
Josselin
Plélan-le-Grand
Guichen
La Guerche-de-Bretagne
Guilvinec
Trégunc
Pont-Aven
Quimperlé
Baud
Ploërmel
Bain-de-Bretagne
Craon
Le Pouldu
Lorient
Trédion
Malestroit
La Gacilly
Martigné-Ferchaud
Plouhinec
Belz
Ste Anne-d'Auray
Auray
Baden
Vannes
Rochefort-en-Terre
Peillac
Châteaubriant
Pouancé
Redon
Segré
Carnac
Locmariaquer
Muzillac
St Pierre-Quiberon
Sarzeau
Arzal
La Roche-Bernard
Guémené-Penfao
Nozay
Le Lion-d'Angers
Quiberon
Pénestin
Guenrouet
Herbignac
Blain
Piriac-sur-Mer
Assérac
Pontchâteau
Héric
Nort-sur-Erdre
St-Lyphard
Savenay
Guérande
La Baule
Ancenis
Le Croisic
Le Pouliguen
Paimbœuf
St-Étienne-de-Montluc
Chalonnes-sur-Loire
Pornichet
St-Nazaire
St-Brevin-les-Pins
NANTES
Chemillé
Pornic
Montbert
Clisson
Cholet
Noirmoutier-en-l'Île
Machecoul
St Philbert-de-Grand-Lieu
Montaigu
Beauvoir-sur-Mer
Bois-de-Céné
St Laurent-sur-Sèvre
Legé
Challans
Les Epesses
Soullans
St-Jean-de-Monts
Apremont
Les Essarts
Pouzauges
Notre-Dame-de-Riez
Aizenay
St-Hilaire-de-Riez
Coëx
La Chapelle-Hermier
La Roche-sur-Yon
Mouchamps
St-Gilles-Croix-de-Vie
Chantonnay
Bournezeau
La Châtaigneraie
Bretignolles-sur-Mer
La Mothe-Achard
Ste-Hermine
A84
D789
N12
D887
D765
N165
D790
D700
N176
D768
D766
N164
D155
D177
D976
D137
D224
N136
N157
A81
D767
N24
N166
D177
N137
D178
D771
D163
D773
D178
D963
N171
A11
D723
D213
D751
D137
N249
D763
A87
D160
A83
D949bis
D746

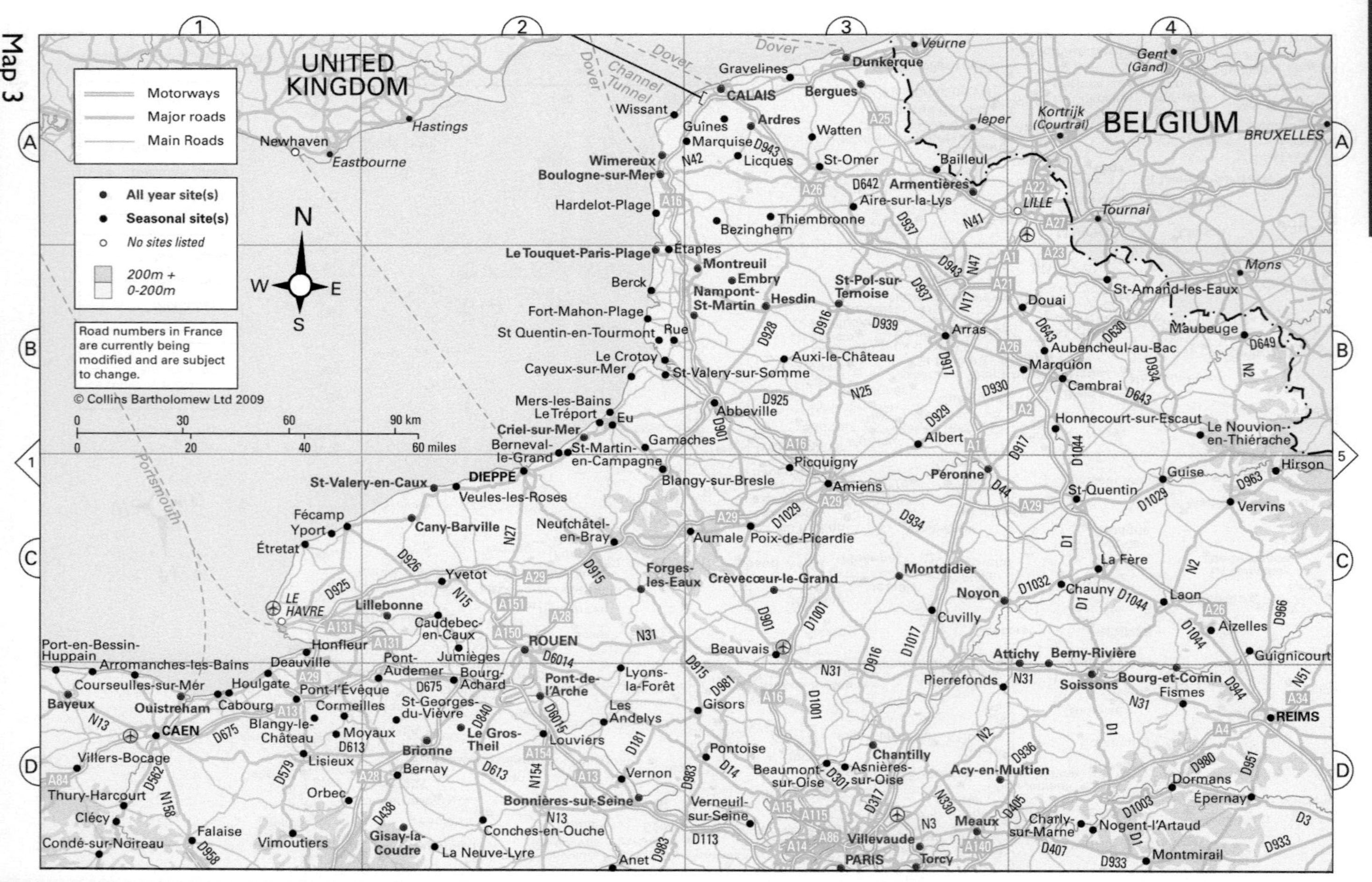

Motorways
Major roads
Main Roads
All year site(s)
Seasonal site(s)
No sites listed
200m +
0-200m
Road numbers in France are currently being modified and are subject to change.
© Collins Bartholomew Ltd 2009
0 30 60 90 km
0 20 40 60 miles
N
E
S
W
UNITED KINGDOM
BELGIUM
BRUXELLES
Gent (Gand)
Kortrijk (Courtrai)
Ieper
Veurne
Tournai
Mons
Hastings
Eastbourne
Newhaven
Dover
Channel Tunnel
Portsmouth
Dunkerque
Bergues
Gravelines
CALAIS
Wissant
Guînes
Marquise
Ardres
Licques
Watten
St-Omer
Wimereux
Boulogne-sur-Mer
Hardelot-Plage
Bezinghem
Thiembronne
Aire-sur-la-Lys
Armentières
Bailleul
LILLE
Douai
Arras
St-Amand-les-Eaux
Maubeuge
Le Nouvion-en-Thiérache
Hirson
Vervins
Guise
St-Quentin
Cambrai
Marquion
Aubencheul-au-Bac
Honnecourt-sur-Escaut
Le Touquet-Paris-Plage
Étaples
Montreuil
Embry
Berck
Nampont-St-Martin
Hesdin
St-Pol-sur-Ternoise
Auxi-le-Château
Fort-Mahon-Plage
St Quentin-en-Tourmont
Rue
Le Crotoy
St-Valery-sur-Somme
Cayeux-sur-Mer
Abbeville
Albert
Péronne
Amiens
Picquigny
Mers-les-Bains
Le Tréport
Eu
Gamaches
Criel-sur-Mer
Berneval-le-Grand
St-Martin-en-Campagne
Blangy-sur-Bresle
DIEPPE
Veules-les-Roses
St-Valery-en-Caux
Cany-Barville
Fécamp
Yport
Étretat
LE HAVRE
Aumale
Poix-de-Picardie
Neufchâtel-en-Bray
Forges-les-Eaux
Crèvecœur-le-Grand
Montdidier
Noyon
Cuvilly
Chauny
La Fère
Laon
Aizelles
Guignicourt
REIMS
Yvetot
Lillebonne
Caudebec-en-Caux
Jumièges
ROUEN
Pont-Audemer
Bourg-Achard
Pont-de-l'Arche
Louviers
Les Andelys
Lyons-la-Forêt
Gisors
Beauvais
Pontoise
Beaumont-sur-Oise
Asnières-sur-Oise
Chantilly
Pierrefonds
Attichy
Berny-Rivière
Soissons
Bourg-et-Comin
Fismes
Acy-en-Multien
Meaux
Charly-sur-Marne
Nogent-l'Artaud
Dormans
Épernay
Montmirail
Torcy
Villevaude
PARIS
Verneuil-sur-Seine
Vernon
Anet
Bonnières-sur-Seine
Le Gros-Theil
St-Georges-du-Vièvre
Brionne
Bernay
Conches-en-Ouche
La Neuve-Lyre
Gisay-la-Coudre
Orbec
Lisieux
Moyaux
Cormeilles
Pont-l'Évêque
Honfleur
Deauville
Houlgate
Cabourg
Blangy-le-Château
Vimoutiers
Arromanches-les-Bains
Port-en-Bessin-Huppain
Courseulles-sur-Mer
Ouistreham
CAEN
Bayeux
Villers-Bocage
Thury-Harcourt
Clécy
Condé-sur-Noireau
Falaise

Map 3

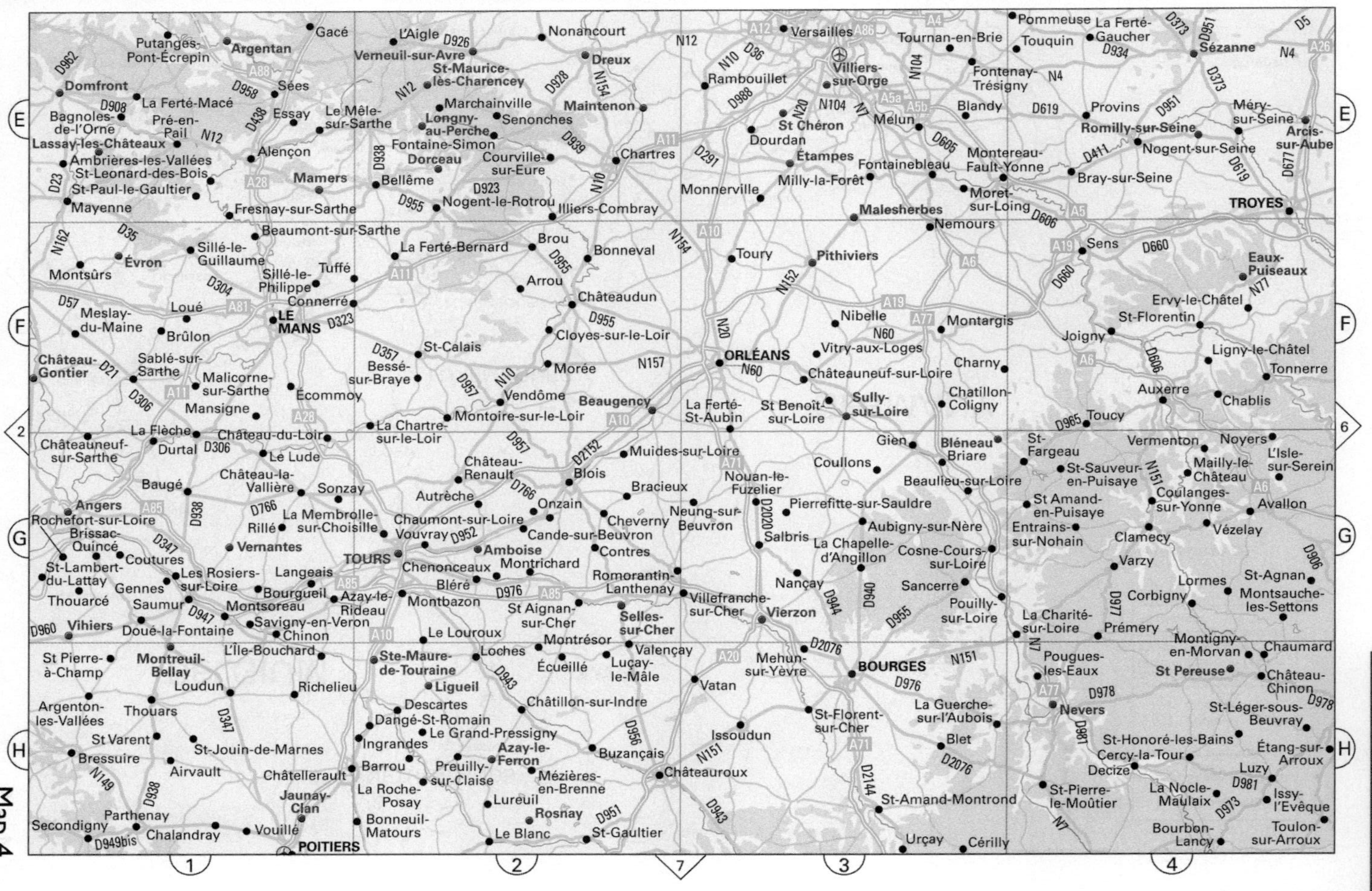

E
F
G
H
1
2
3
4
6
7
TROYES
ORLÉANS
LE MANS
TOURS
BOURGES
POITIERS
Pommeuse
La Ferté-Gaucher
Sézanne
Méry-sur-Seine
Arcis-sur-Aube
Touquin
Provins
Romilly-sur-Seine
Nogent-sur-Seine
Bray-sur-Seine
Tournan-en-Brie
Fontenay-Trésigny
Blandy
Montereau-Fault-Yonne
Moret-sur-Loing
Melun
Fontainebleau
Nemours
Versailles
Villiers-sur-Orge
St Chéron
Étampes
Milly-la-Forêt
Malesherbes
Rambouillet
Dourdan
Monnerville
Sens
Eaux-Puiseaux
Ervy-le-Châtel
St-Florentin
Joigny
Ligny-le-Châtel
Tonnerre
Chablis
Auxerre
Toucy
Pithiviers
Toury
Montargis
Nibelle
Vitry-aux-Loges
Châteauneuf-sur-Loire
Sully-sur-Loire
St Benoît-sur-Loire
Charny
Châtillon-Coligny
La Ferté-St-Aubin
Gien
Bléneau
Briare
St-Fargeau
St-Sauveur-en-Puisaye
Vermenton
Noyers
L'Isle-sur-Serein
Mailly-le-Château
Coulanges-sur-Yonne
Avallon
Vézelay
Clamecy
St Amand-en-Puisaye
Entrains-sur-Nohain
Varzy
Corbigny
Lormes
St-Agnan
Montsauche-les-Settons
Beaulieu-sur-Loire
Coullons
Aubigny-sur-Nère
Cosne-Cours-sur-Loire
Sancerre
Pouilly-sur-Loire
La Charité-sur-Loire
Prémery
Nouan-le-Fuzelier
Pierrefitte-sur-Sauldre
La Chapelle-d'Angillon
Salbris
Nançay
Vierzon
Mehun-sur-Yèvre
Pougues-les-Eaux
Nevers
St Pereuse
Montigny-en-Morvan
Chaumard
Château-Chinon
St-Léger-sous-Beuvray
St-Honoré-les-Bains
Étang-sur-Arroux
Luzy
Issy-l'Évêque
Toulon-sur-Arroux
Cercy-la-Tour
Decize
La Nocle-Maulaix
Bourbon-Lancy
St-Pierre-le-Moûtier
La Guerche-sur-l'Aubois
Blet
St-Amand-Montrond
Cérilly
Urçay
St-Florent-sur-Cher
Issoudun
Châteauroux
Vatan
Nonancourt
Dreux
Maintenon
Chartres
L'Aigle
Verneuil-sur-Avre
St-Maurice-lès-Charencey
Senonches
Marchainville
Longny-au-Perche
Courville-sur-Eure
Fontaine-Simon
Dorceau
Bellême
Nogent-le-Rotrou
Illiers-Combray
Bonneval
Brou
Châteaudun
Arrou
Cloyes-sur-le-Loir
Morée
Beaugency
La Ferté-Bernard
St-Calais
Vendôme
Montoire-sur-le-Loir
Bessé-sur-Braye
La Chartre-sur-le-Loir
Muides-sur-Loire
Blois
Bracieux
Cheverny
Neung-sur-Beuvron
Contres
Romorantin-Lanthenay
Villefranche-sur-Cher
Selles-sur-Cher
Valençay
Luçay-le-Mâle
Onzain
Cande-sur-Beuvron
Château-Renault
Autrèche
Chaumont-sur-Loire
Amboise
Montrichard
Chenonceaux
Bléré
Vouvray
St Aignan-sur-Cher
Montrésor
Écueillé
Montbazon
Le Louroux
Loches
Châtillon-sur-Indre
Buzançais
Ligueil
Descartes
Le Grand-Pressigny
Azay-le-Ferron
Mézières-en-Brenne
Preuilly-sur-Claise
Lureuil
Rosnay
Le Blanc
St-Gaultier
La Roche-Posay
Bonneuil-Matours
Ste-Maure-de-Touraine
Dangé-St-Romain
Ingrandes
Barrou
Gacé
Argentan
Sées
Essay
Le Mêle-sur-Sarthe
Alençon
Mamers
Fresnay-sur-Sarthe
Beaumont-sur-Sarthe
Sillé-le-Guillaume
Sillé-le-Philippe
Tuffé
Connerré
Écommoy
Château-du-Loir
Le Lude
Sonzay
La Membrolle-sur-Choisille
Château-la-Vallière
Vernantes
Rillé
Langeais
Azay-le-Rideau
Savigny-en-Veron
Chinon
Bourgueil
Montsoreau
Richelieu
L'Île-Bouchard
Châtellerault
Jaunay-Clan
Vouillé
Putanges-Pont-Écrepin
Domfront
La Ferté-Macé
Bagnoles-de-l'Orne
Pré-en-Pail
Lassay-les-Châteaux
Ambrières-les-Vallées
St-Léonard-des-Bois
St-Paul-le-Gaultier
Mayenne
Évron
Montsûrs
Meslay-du-Maine
Loué
Brûlon
Sablé-sur-Sarthe
Malicorne-sur-Sarthe
Mansigne
Château-Gontier
La Flèche
Durtal
Baugé
Châteauneuf-sur-Sarthe
Angers
Brissac-Quincé
Coutures
Les Rosiers-sur-Loire
Rochefort-sur-Loire
St-Lambert-du-Lattay
Gennes
Saumur
Thouarcé
Doué-la-Fontaine
Vihiers
Montreuil-Bellay
Loudun
St-Jouin-de-Marnes
Thouars
Airvault
St Pierre-à-Champ
Argenton-les-Vallées
St Varent
Bressuire
Parthenay
Chalandray
Secondigny

Map 4

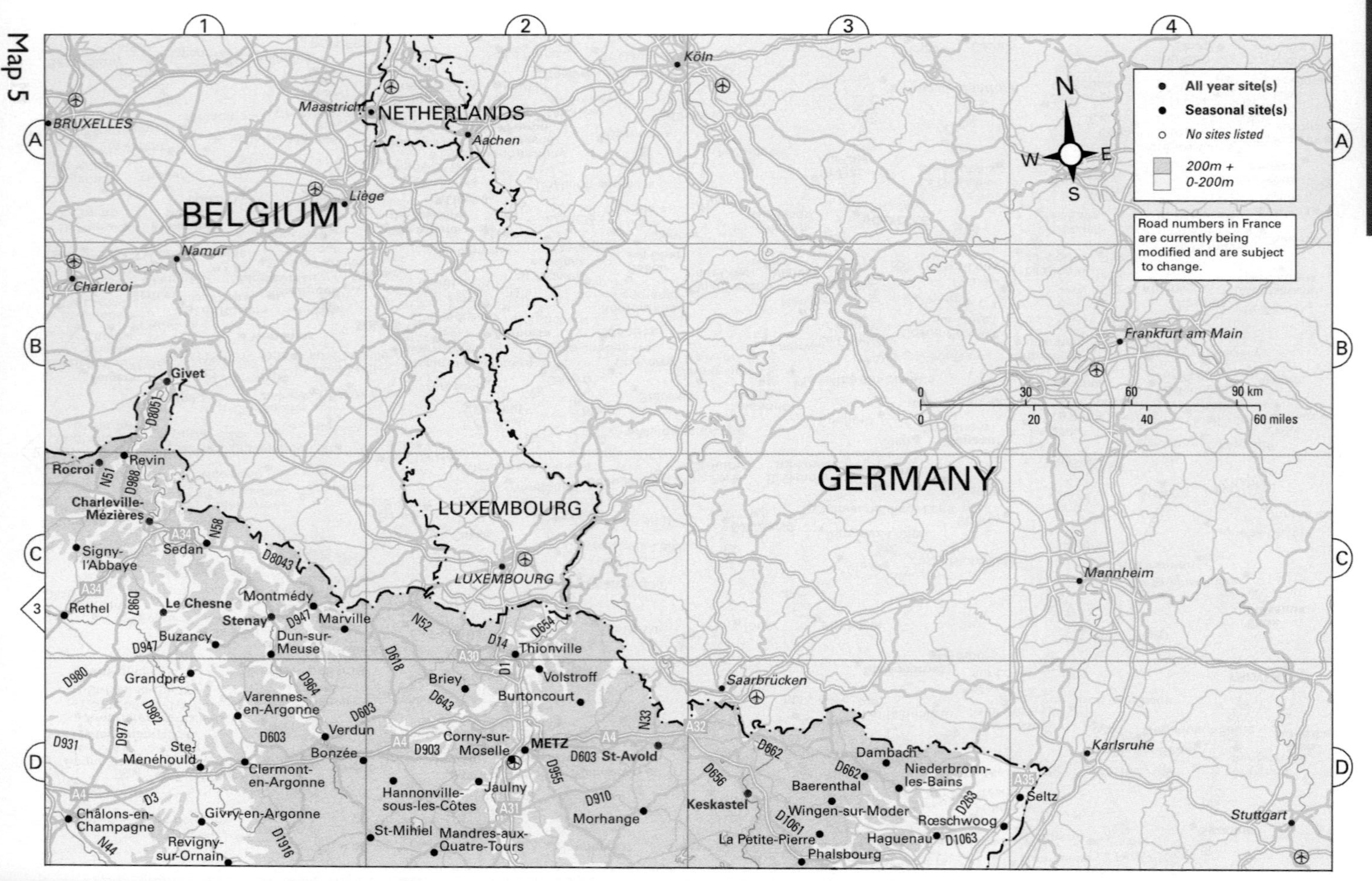
All year site(s)
Seasonal site(s)
No sites listed
200m +
0-200m
Road numbers in France are currently being modified and are subject to change.
0 30 60 90 km
0 20 40 60 miles
N
E
S
W
BELGIUM
NETHERLANDS
LUXEMBOURG
GERMANY
BRUXELLES
Charleroi
Namur
Liège
Maastricht
Aachen
Köln
Frankfurt am Main
Mannheim
Karlsruhe
Stuttgart
Saarbrücken
LUXEMBOURG
Givet
Revin
Rocroi
Charleville-Mézières
Signy-l'Abbaye
Rethel
Sedan
Le Chesne
Buzancy
Grandpré
Stenay
Montmédy
Dun-sur-Meuse
Marville
Varennes-en-Argonne
Clermont-en-Argonne
Ste Menehould
Verdun
Bonzée
Briey
Thionville
Volstroff
Burtoncourt
Corny-sur-Moselle
METZ
Jaulny
Hannonville-sous-les-Côtes
St-Mihiel
Mandres-aux-Quatre-Tours
St-Avold
Morhange
Keskastel
La Petite-Pierre
Phalsbourg
Baerenthal
Wingen-sur-Moder
Dambach
Niederbronn-les-Bains
Haguenau
Rœschwoog
Seltz
Châlons-en-Champagne
Givry-en-Argonne
Revigny-sur-Ornain
A4
A30
A31
A32
A34
A35
N33
N44
N51
N52
N58
D1
D3
D14
D654
D603
D643
D618
D903
D955
D910
D656
D662
D862
D1061
D1063
D263
D8043
D947
D964
D1916
D977
D982
D987
D988
D8051
D931
D980

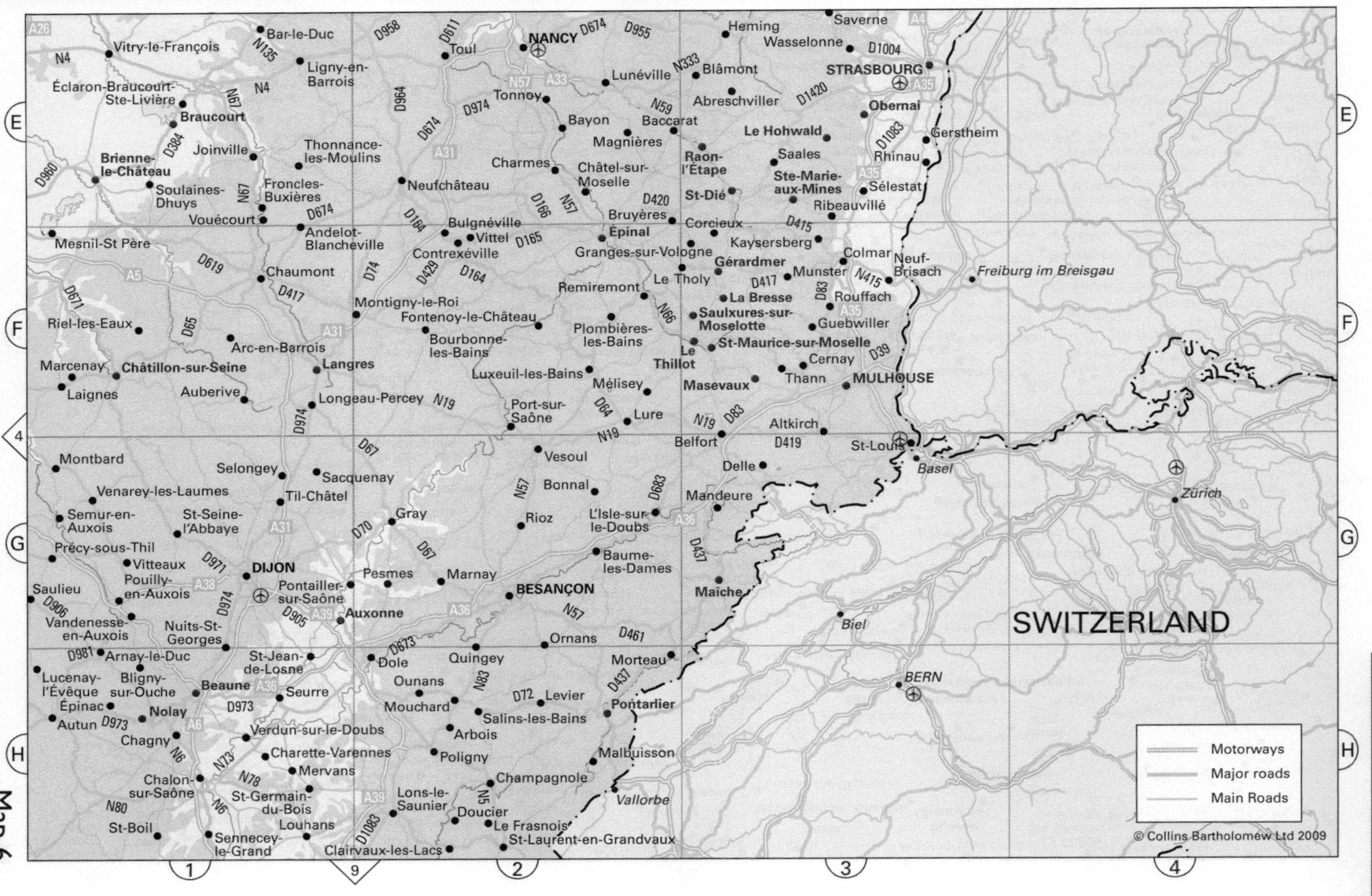

SWITZERLAND
STRASBOURG
NANCY
MULHOUSE
BESANÇON
DIJON
BERN
Zürich
Basel
Biel
Freiburg im Breisgau
Motorways
Major roads
Main Roads
© Collins Bartholomew Ltd 2009
Vitry-le-François
Bar-le-Duc
Ligny-en-Barrois
Toul
Heming
Saverne
Wasselonne
Blâmont
Lunéville
Tonnoy
Éclaron-Braucourt-Ste-Livière
Braucourt
Abreschviller
Obernai
Bayon
Baccarat
Le Hohwald
Gerstheim
Joinville
Thonnance-les-Moulins
Magnières
Raon-l'Étape
Saales
Rhinau
Brienne-le-Château
Charmes
Châtel-sur-Moselle
Ste-Marie-aux-Mines
Sélestat
Soulaines-Dhuys
Froncles-Buxières
Neufchâteau
St-Dié
Ribeauvillé
Vouécourt
Bruyères
Corcieux
Mesnil-St Père
Andelot-Blancheville
Bulgnéville
Vittel
Épinal
Kaysersberg
Contrexéville
Granges-sur-Vologne
Colmar
Neuf-Brisach
Gérardmer
Chaumont
Le Tholy
Munster
Remiremont
La Bresse
Rouffach
Montigny-le-Roi
Saulxures-sur-Moselotte
Fontenoy-le-Château
Plombières-les-Bains
Guebwiller
Riel-les-Eaux
Arc-en-Barrois
Bourbonne-les-Bains
Le Thillot
St-Maurice-sur-Moselle
Cernay
Marcenay
Châtillon-sur-Seine
Langres
Luxeuil-les-Bains
Thann
Laignes
Auberive
Mélisey
Masevaux
Longeau-Percey
Port-sur-Saône
Lure
Altkirch
Belfort
St-Louis
Montbard
Selongey
Sacquenay
Vesoul
Delle
Venarey-les-Laumes
Til-Châtel
Bonnal
Mandeure
Semur-en-Auxois
St-Seine-l'Abbaye
Gray
Rioz
L'Isle-sur-le-Doubs
Précy-sous-Thil
Baume-les-Dames
Vitteaux
Pouilly-en-Auxois
Pesmes
Marnay
Maîche
Saulieu
Pontailler-sur-Saône
Vandenesse-en-Auxois
Nuits-St-Georges
Auxonne
Ornans
Arnay-le-Duc
St-Jean-de-Losne
Dole
Quingey
Morteau
Lucenay-l'Évêque
Bligny-sur-Ouche
Beaune
Seurre
Ounans
Levier
Épinac
Nolay
Mouchard
Pontarlier
Autun
Salins-les-Bains
Chagny
Verdun-sur-le-Doubs
Arbois
Charette-Varennes
Poligny
Malbuisson
Mervans
Champagnole
Chalon-sur-Saône
St-Germain-du-Bois
Lons-le-Saunier
Vallorbe
Doucier
Louhans
Le Frasnois
St-Boil
Sennecey-le-Grand
Clairvaux-les-Lacs
St-Laurent-en-Grandvaux
E
F
G
H
1
2
3
4
9

Map 6

Map 7

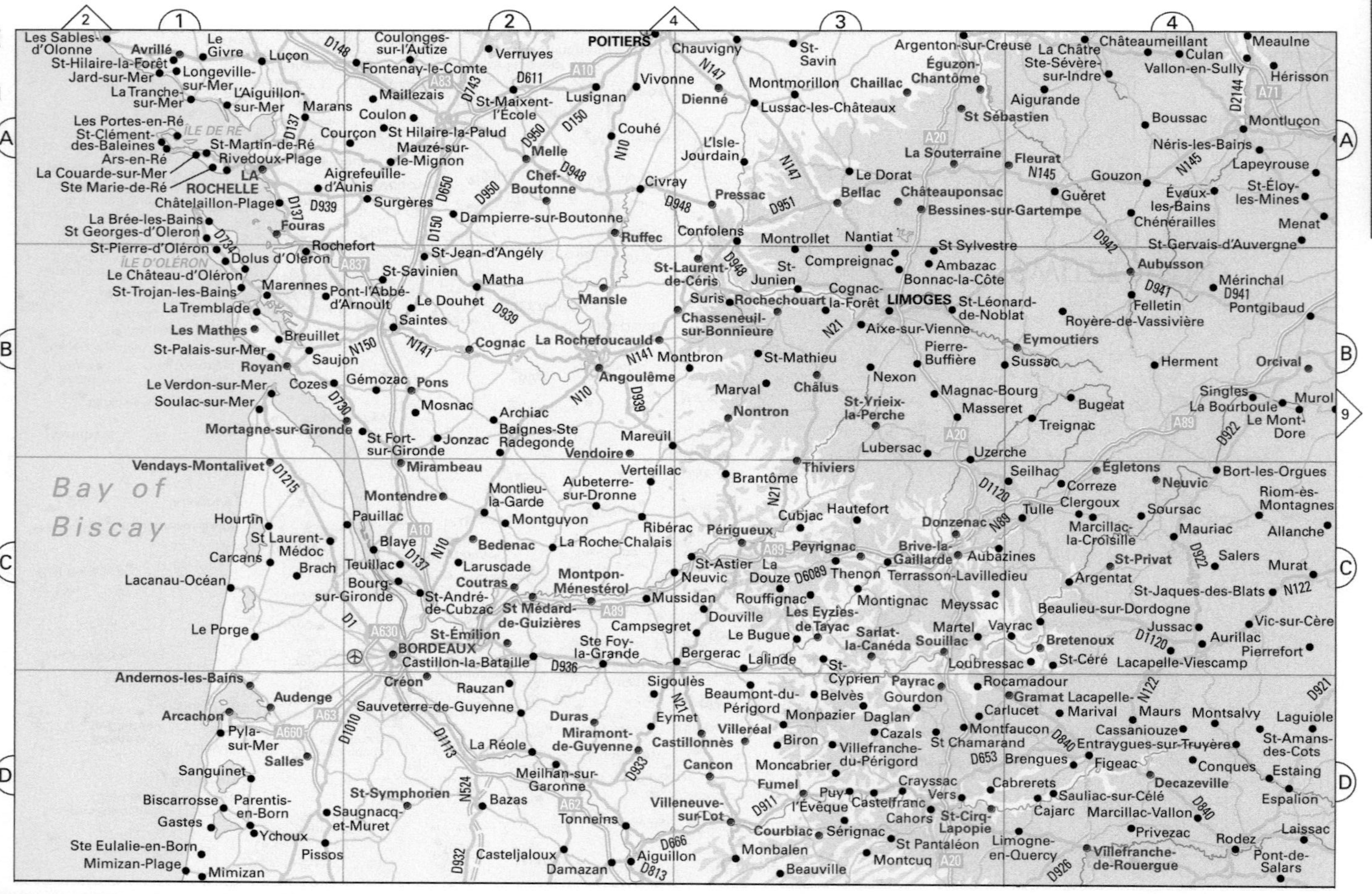

Bay of Biscay
POITIERS
LIMOGES
BORDEAUX
LA ROCHELLE
ÎLE DE RÉ
ÎLE D'OLÉRON
Les Sables-d'Olonne
Avrillé
Le Givre
Luçon
St-Hilaire-la-Forêt
Jard-sur-Mer
Longeville-sur-Mer
La Tranche-sur-Mer
L'Aiguillon-sur-Mer
Marans
Les Portes-en-Ré
St-Clément-des-Baleines
St-Martin-de-Ré
Rivedoux-Plage
Ars-en-Ré
La Couarde-sur-Mer
Ste Marie-de-Ré
Châtelaillon-Plage
La Brée-les-Bains
St Georges-d'Oleron
Fouras
Rochefort
St-Pierre-d'Oléron
Dolus d'Oleron
Le Château-d'Oléron
St-Trojan-les-Bains
Marennes
Pont-l'Abbé-d'Arnoult
La Tremblade
Les Mathes
Breuillet
St-Palais-sur-Mer
Saujon
Royan
Le Verdon-sur-Mer
Soulac-sur-Mer
Cozes
Gémozac
Pons
Mosnac
Mortagne-sur-Gironde
St Fort-sur-Gironde
Jonzac
Archiac
Baignes-Ste Radegonde
Coulonges-sur-l'Autize
Fontenay-le-Comte
Verruyes
Maillezais
Coulon
Courçon
St Hilaire-la-Palud
Mauzé-sur-le-Mignon
Aigrefeuille-d'Aunis
Surgères
St-Maixent-l'École
Melle
Chef-Boutonne
Dampierre-sur-Boutonne
St-Jean-d'Angély
St-Savinien
Matha
Le Douhet
Saintes
Cognac
Lusignan
Couhé
Vivonne
Civray
Ruffec
Mansle
La Rochefoucauld
Angoulême
Montbron
Mareuil
Vendoire
Chauvigny
Dienné
St-Savin
Montmorillon
Lussac-les-Châteaux
L'Isle-Jourdain
Pressac
Confolens
St-Laurent-de-Céris
St-Junien
Suris
Rochechouart
Chasseneuil-sur-Bonnieure
Montrollet
Nantiat
Compreignac
Cognac-la-Forêt
Le Dorat
Bellac
Argenton-sur-Creuse
Chaillac
Éguzon-Chantôme
St Sébastien
La Souterraine
Châteauponsac
Bessines-sur-Gartempe
St Sylvestre
Ambazac
Bonnac-la-Côte
St-Léonard-de-Noblat
Aixe-sur-Vienne
St-Mathieu
Marval
Châlus
Nontron
Nexon
Pierre-Buffière
St-Yrieix-la-Perche
Magnac-Bourg
Masseret
Lubersac
La Châtre
Ste-Sévère-sur-Indre
Aigurande
Fleurat
Guéret
Royère-de-Vassivière
Eymoutiers
Sussac
Bugeat
Treignac
Uzerche
Châteaumeillant
Culan
Vallon-en-Sully
Meaulne
Hérisson
Boussac
Montluçon
Néris-les-Bains
Gouzon
Lapeyrouse
Évaux-les-Bains
St-Éloy-les-Mines
Chénérailles
Menat
St-Gervais-d'Auvergne
Aubusson
Mérinchal
Felletin
Pontgibaud
Herment
Orcival
Singles
La Bourboule
Murol
Le Mont-Dore
Vendays-Montalivet
Mirambeau
Montendre
Montlieu-la-Garde
Aubeterre-sur-Dronne
Verteillac
Montguyon
Ribérac
Hourtin
Pauillac
St Laurent-Médoc
Carcans
Brach
Blaye
Teuillac
Bourg-sur-Gironde
Bedenac
Laruscade
Coutras
La Roche-Chalais
Lacanau-Océan
St-André-de-Cubzac
Montpon-Ménestérol
St Médard-de-Guizières
Le Porge
St-Émilion
Castillon-la-Bataille
Ste Foy-la-Grande
Campsegret
Mussidan
Neuvic
St-Astier
Brantôme
Périgueux
Cubjac
Hautefort
Thiviers
La Douze
Rouffignac
Douville
Le Bugue
Les Eyzies-de-Tayac
Bergerac
Lalinde
Peyrignac
Thenon
Montignac
Sarlat-la-Canéda
St-Cyprien
Donzenac
Brive-la-Gaillarde
Aubazines
Terrasson-Lavilledieu
Meyssac
Martel
Souillac
Vayrac
Loubressac
Seilhac
Corrèze
Égletons
Tulle
Clergoux
Marcillac-la-Croisille
Neuvic
Soursac
St-Privat
Argentat
Beaulieu-sur-Dordogne
Bretenoux
St-Céré
Bort-les-Orgues
Riom-ès-Montagnes
Allanche
Mauriac
Salers
Murat
St-Jaques-des-Blats
Jussac
Aurillac
Vic-sur-Cère
Pierrefort
Lacapelle-Viescamp
Andernos-les-Bains
Audenge
Arcachon
Pyla-sur-Mer
Salles
Sanguinet
Biscarrosse
Parentis-en-Born
Gastes
Ychoux
Ste Eulalie-en-Born
Mimizan-Plage
Mimizan
Pissos
Saugnacq-et-Muret
St-Symphorien
Créon
Rauzan
Sauveterre-de-Guyenne
La Réole
Meilhan-sur-Garonne
Bazas
Casteljaloux
Damazan
Tonneins
Aiguillon
Duras
Miramont-de-Guyenne
Sigoulès
Eymet
Castillonnès
Villeréal
Cancon
Villeneuve-sur-Lot
Beaumont-du-Périgord
Monpazier
Biron
Moncabrier
Fumel
Puy-l'Évêque
Courbiac
Monbalen
Beauville
Belvès
Daglan
Cazals
Villefranche-du-Périgord
Payrac
Gourdon
Crayssac
Castelfranc
Cahors
Sérignac
St Pantaléon
Montcuq
Vers
St-Cirq-Lapopie
Rocamadour
Gramat
Carlucet
Montfaucon
St Chamarand
Cabrerets
Limogne-en-Quercy
Lacapelle-Marival
Brengues
Figeac
Cajarc
Sauliac-sur-Célé
Marcillac-Vallon
Villefranche-de-Rouergue
Maurs
Cassaniouze
Entraygues-sur-Truyère
Montsalvy
Decazeville
Conques
Privezac
Laguiole
St-Amans-des-Cots
Estaing
Espalion
Rodez
Laissac
Pont-de-Salars

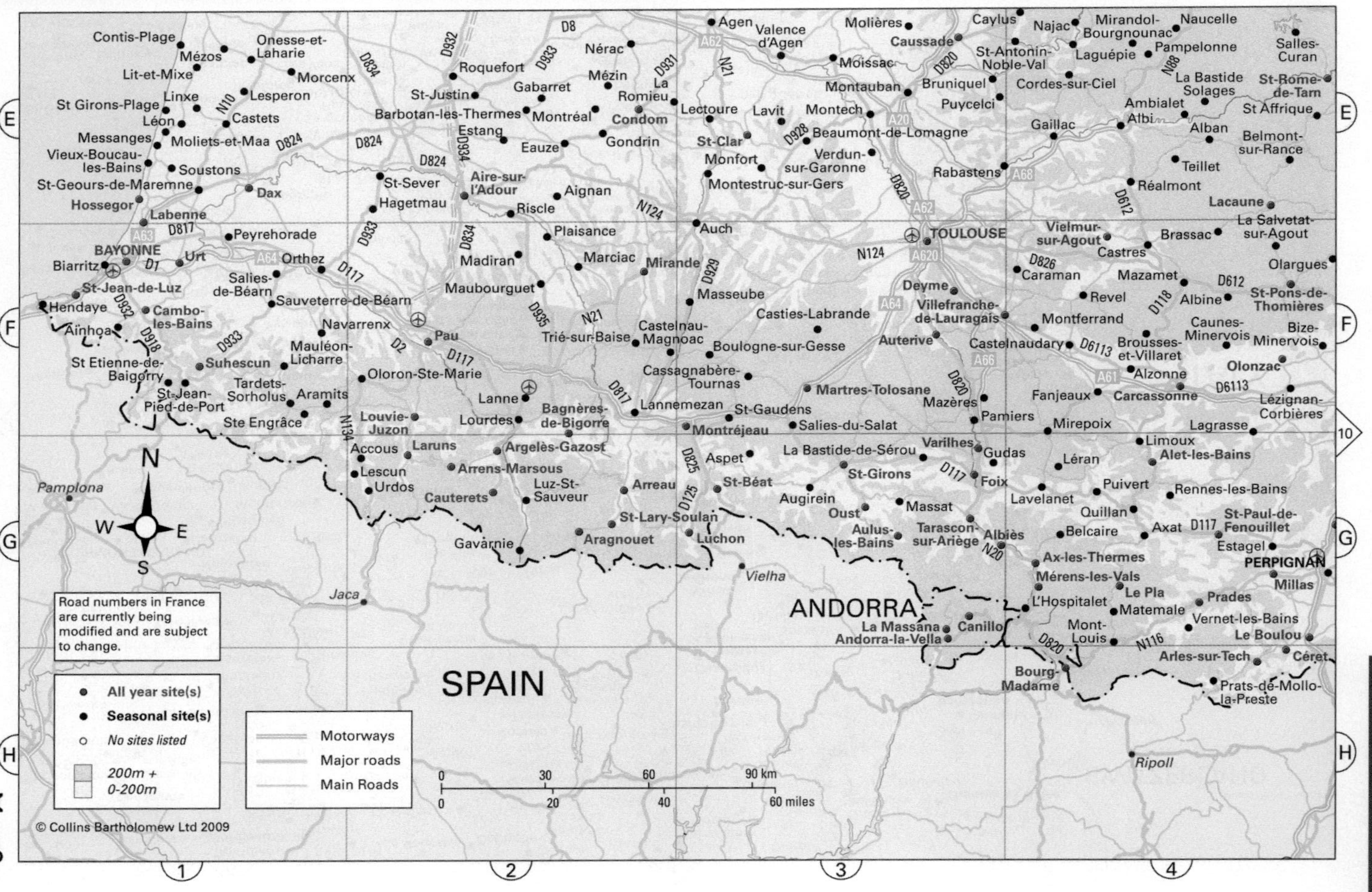
Contis-Plage
Mézos
Onesse-et-Laharie
Morcenx
Lit-et-Mixe
Linxe
Lesperon
St Girons-Plage
Léon
Castets
Messanges
Moliets-et-Maa
Vieux-Boucau-les-Bains
Soustons
St-Geours-de-Maremne
Dax
Hossegor
Labenne
Peyrehorade
BAYONNE
Biarritz
Urt
Orthez
St-Jean-de-Luz
Salies-de-Béarn
Hendaye
Cambo-les-Bains
Sauveterre-de-Béarn
Aïnhoa
Navarrenx
St Etienne-de-Baigorry
Suhescun
Mauléon-Licharre
St-Jean-Pied-de-Port
Tardets-Sorholus
Aramits
Ste Engrâce
Oloron-Ste-Marie
Louvie-Juzon
Accous
Laruns
Lescun
Urdos
Pau
Arrens-Marsous
Cauterets
Luz-St-Sauveur
Argelès-Gazost
Gavarnie
Lanne
Lourdes
Bagnères-de-Bigorre
Roquefort
St-Justin
Gabarret
Barbotan-les-Thermes
Montréal
Estang
Eauze
St-Sever
Aire-sur-l'Adour
Hagetmau
Riscle
Aignan
Madiran
Plaisance
Marciac
Maubourguet
Trié-sur-Baïse
Nérac
Mézin
La Romieu
Condom
Gondrin
Agen
Valence d'Agen
Lectoure
Lavit
St-Clar
Monfort
Montestruc-sur-Gers
Auch
Mirande
Masseube
Castelnau-Magnoac
Cassagnabère-Tournas
Boulogne-sur-Gesse
Casties-Labrande
Lannemezan
Arreau
St-Lary-Soulan
Aragnouet
Montréjeau
St-Gaudens
Aspet
St-Béat
Luchon
Salies-du-Salat
Martres-Tolosane
Molières
Moissac
Caussade
Montauban
Montech
Beaumont-de-Lomagne
Verdun-sur-Garonne
TOULOUSE
Deyme
Villefranche-de-Lauragais
Auterive
Mazères
Pamiers
La Bastide-de-Sérou
St-Girons
Augirein
Oust
Aulus-les-Bains
Massat
Varilhes
Gudas
Foix
Tarascon-sur-Ariège
Caylus
St-Antonin-Noble-Val
Najac
Bruniquel
Puycelci
Cordes-sur-Ciel
Gaillac
Rabastens
Mirandol-Bourgnounac
Laguépie
Naucelle
Pampelonne
La Bastide Solages
Ambialet
Albi
Alban
Teillet
Réalmont
Lacaune
Salles-Curan
St-Rome-de-Tarn
St Affrique
Belmont-sur-Rance
Brassac
La Salvetat-sur-Agout
Olargues
Vielmur-sur-Agout
Castres
Caraman
Revel
Mazamet
Albine
St-Pons-de-Thomières
Montferrand
Castelnaudary
Brousses-et-Villaret
Caunes-Minervois
Bize-Minervois
Olonzac
Alzonne
Carcassonne
Fanjeaux
Mirepoix
Lézignan-Corbières
Lagrasse
Limoux
Alet-les-Bains
Léran
Puivert
Lavelanet
Quillan
Belcaire
Rennes-les-Bains
Axat
St-Paul-de-Fenouillet
Estagel
PERPIGNAN
Millas
Prades
Vernet-les-Bains
Le Boulou
Céret
Arles-sur-Tech
Prats-de-Mollo-la-Preste
Albiès
Ax-les-Thermes
Mérens-les-Vals
L'Hospitalet
Le Pla
Matemale
Mont-Louis
Bourg-Madame
Canillo
La Massana
Andorra-la-Vella
ANDORRA
SPAIN
Pamplona
Jaca
Vielha
Ripoll
Road numbers in France are currently being modified and are subject to change.
All year site(s)
Seasonal site(s)
No sites listed
200m +
0-200m
Motorways
Major roads
Main Roads
0 30 60 90 km
0 20 40 60 miles
N
S
E
W
© Collins Bartholomew Ltd 2009

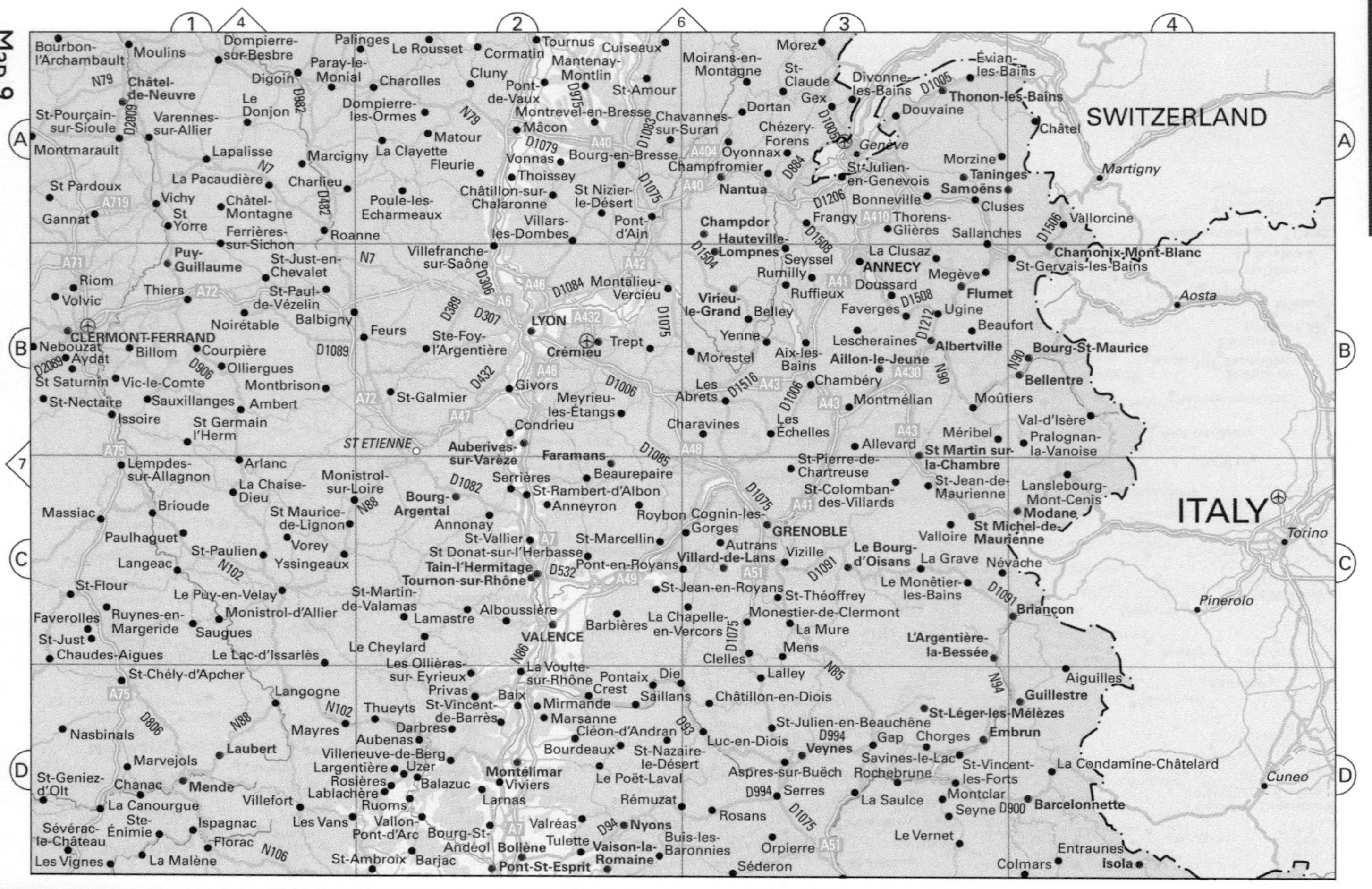
SWITZERLAND
ITALY
Genève
Torino
Aosta
Martigny
Pinerolo
Cuneo
LYON
GRENOBLE
VALENCE
CLERMONT-FERRAND
ST ETIENNE
ANNECY
Chambéry
Chamonix-Mont-Blanc
Albertville
Bourg-St-Maurice
Briançon
Embrun
Gap
Montélimar
Vichy
Mâcon
Roanne
Bourg-en-Bresse
Thonon-les-Bains
Mende

Map 9

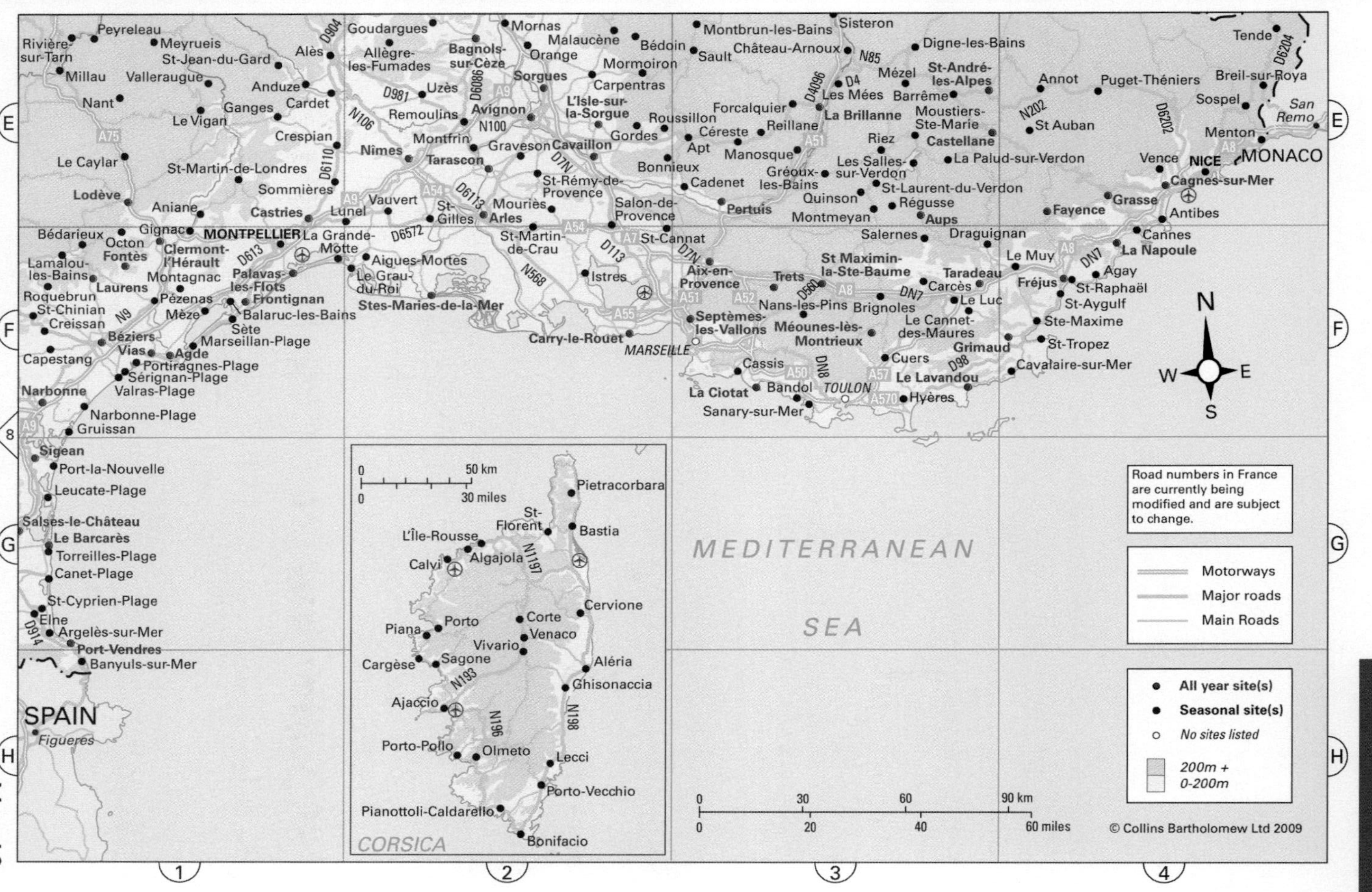

Road numbers in France are currently being modified and are subject to change.
Motorways
Major roads
Main Roads
All year site(s)
Seasonal site(s)
No sites listed
200m +
0-200m
© Collins Bartholomew Ltd 2009
MEDITERRANEAN
SEA
CORSICA
SPAIN
Figueres
MONACO
NICE
MONTPELLIER
MARSEILLE
TOULON
San Remo
N
E
S
W
0
30
60
90 km
0
20
40
60 miles
0
50 km
0
30 miles
E
F
G
H
1
2
3
4
8
Rivière-sur-Tarn
Peyreleau
Meyrueis
St-Jean-du-Gard
Millau
Valleraugue
Nant
Le Vigan
Ganges
Anduze
Cardet
Alès
Goudargues
Allègre-les-Fumades
Bagnols-sur-Cèze
Mornas
Malaucène
Bédoin
Orange
Sorgues
Mormoiron
Carpentras
Uzès
Remoulins
Avignon
L'Isle-sur-la-Sorgue
Roussillon
Gordes
Crespian
Montfrin
Nîmes
Tarascon
Graveson
Cavaillon
Bonnieux
Le Caylar
St-Martin-de-Londres
Sommières
St-Rémy-de-Provence
Lodève
Aniane
Castries
Lunel
Vauvert
St-Gilles
Mouriès
Arles
Salon-de-Provence
Montbrun-les-Bains
Sisteron
Sault
Château-Arnoux
Digne-les-Bains
Mézel
St-André-les-Alpes
Les Mées
Barrême
Forcalquier
La Brillanne
Moustiers-Ste-Marie
Céreste
Reillanne
Riez
Castellane
Apt
Manosque
Les Salles-sur-Verdon
La Palud-sur-Verdon
Cadenet
Gréoux-les-Bains
St-Laurent-du-Verdon
Quinson
Régusse
Pertuis
Montmeyan
Aups
Annot
Puget-Théniers
Tende
Breil-sur-Roya
Sospel
St Auban
Menton
Vence
Cagnes-sur-Mer
Fayence
Grasse
Antibes
Bédarieux
Gignac
Octon
Fontès
Clermont-l'Hérault
La Grande-Motte
Lamalou-les-Bains
Montagnac
Palavas-les-Flots
Aigues-Mortes
Le Grau-du-Roi
Laurens
Roquebrun
Pézenas
Frontignan
St-Chinian
Mèze
Balaruc-les-Bains
Stes-Maries-de-la-Mer
Creissan
Sète
Béziers
Vias
Agde
Marseillan-Plage
Capestang
Portiragnes-Plage
Sérignan-Plage
Valras-Plage
Narbonne
Narbonne-Plage
Gruissan
St-Martin-de-Crau
Istres
St-Cannat
Aix-en-Provence
Trets
Septèmes-les-Vallons
Carry-le-Rouet
Salernes
Draguignan
St Maximin-la-Ste-Baume
Taradeau
Carcès
Nans-les-Pins
Brignoles
Le Luc
Méounes-lès-Montrieux
Le Cannet-des-Maures
Grimaud
Cassis
Cuers
La Ciotat
Bandol
Le Lavandou
Hyères
Sanary-sur-Mer
Le Muy
Cannes
La Napoule
Agay
Fréjus
St-Raphaël
St-Aygulf
Ste-Maxime
St-Tropez
Cavalaire-sur-Mer
Sigean
Port-la-Nouvelle
Leucate-Plage
Salses-le-Château
Le Barcarès
Torreilles-Plage
Canet-Plage
St-Cyprien-Plage
Elne
Argelès-sur-Mer
Port-Vendres
Banyuls-sur-Mer
Pietracorbara
St-Florent
Bastia
L'Île-Rousse
Algajola
Calvi
Cervione
Piana
Porto
Corte
Venaco
Vivario
Cargèse
Sagone
Aléria
Ghisonaccia
Ajaccio
Porto-Pollo
Olmeto
Lecci
Porto-Vecchio
Pianottoli-Caldarello
Bonifacio
A75
A9
A54
A7
A51
A52
A55
A8
A50
A57
A570
N9
N106
N100
N568
N85
N202
N1197
N193
N196
N198
D904
D981
D6086
D6110
D613
D6572
D6113
D7N
D113
D560
DN7
DN8
D98
D4096
D4
D6202
D6204
D914

Portugal

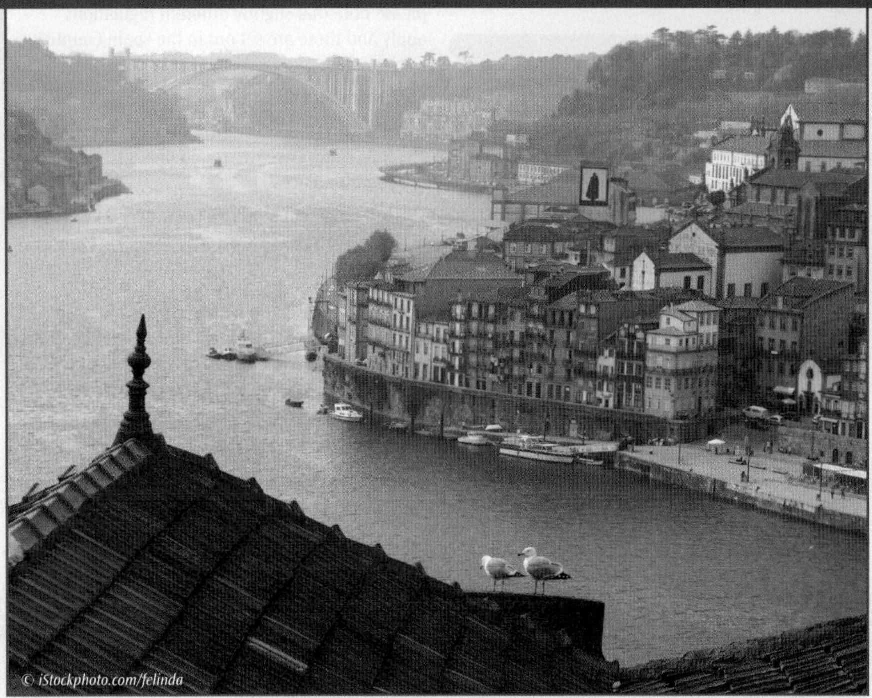

Porto

Population: 10.6 million

Capital: Lisbon (population 2.7 million)

Area: 92,951 sq km (inc Azores and Madeira)

Bordered by: Spain

Terrain: Rolling plains in south; mountainous and forested north of River Tagus

Climate: Temperate climate with no extremes of temperature; wet winters in the north influenced by the gulf stream; elsewhere Mediterranean with hot, dry summers and short, mild winters

Coastline: 1,793 km

Highest Point (mainland Portugal): Monte Torre 1,993 m

Language: Portuguese

Local Time: GMT or BST, ie the same as the UK all year

Currency: Euro divided into 100 cents; £1 = €1.10, €1 = 90 pence (September 2009)

Telephoning: From the UK dial 00351 for Portugal. All numbers have 9 digits, including the area code which starts with a 2 and which must be dialled even for local calls. To call the UK dial 0044, omitting the initial zero of the area code

Emergency numbers: Police 112; Fire brigade 112; Ambulance 112

Public Holidays 2010

Jan 1; Feb 16 (Carnival); Apr 2, 25 (Day of Liberty); May 1; Jun 3, 10 (Portugal Day); Aug 15; Oct 5 (Republic Day); Nov 1; Dec 1 (Independence Day), 8 (Immaculate Conception), 25. Other holidays and saints' days are celebrated according to region, eg June 13 in Lisbon (St Anthony), School summer holidays run from the end of June to the end of August

Tourist Office

PORTUGUESE TOURIST OFFICE
11 BELGRAVE SQUARE
LONDON SW1X 8PP
Tel: 0845 3551212
www.visitportugal.com
info@visitportugal.com

The following chapter should be read in conjunction with the important information contained in the Handbook chapters at the front of this guide.

Camping and Caravanning

There are more than 300 campsites in Portugal, many of which are situated along the coast. Sites are rated from 1 to 4 stars. A further category 'P' refers to private sites such as those belonging to the Portuguese Camping Federation and other clubs. A Camping Card International (CCI) is essential in lieu of a passport at these sites, and may entitle the holder to a reduction in price.

There are 21 privately owned sites in the Orbitur chain. They are open to all and caravanners can join the Orbitur Camping Club to obtain generous discounts off current rates. Senior citizens may join this Club free, otherwise the cost is €15. Membership can be arranged via any Orbitur site or on the Orbitur website. Their head office is at:

RUA DIOGO DO COUTO 1-8° Fte
P-1149-042 LISBOA
Tel: 00351 21 8117000 Fax: 00351 21 8117034
www.orbitur.com
info@orbitur.pt

Motor Caravanners

A number of local authorities now provide dedicated or short stay areas for motor caravanners called 'Áreas de Serviçio'. A guide entitled 'All the Aires – Spain and Portugal' is published by Vicarious Books, www.vicariousbooks.co.uk, tel 0131 208 3333. It is rare that yours will be the only motor caravan staying on such areas, but take sensible precautions and avoid any that are isolated.

Casual/wild camping is not permitted.

Country Information

Cycling

In Lisbon there are cycle lanes in Campo Grande gardens, also from Torre de Belém to Cais do Sodré (7 km) along the River Tagus, and between Cascais and Guincho. Elsewhere in the country there are few cycle lanes.

Transportation of Bicycles

Legislation stipulates that the exterior dimensions of a vehicle should not be exceeded and, in practice, this means that only caravans or motor caravans are allowed to carry bicycles/motorbikes at the rear of the vehicle. Bicycles may not extend beyond the width of the vehicle or more than 45 cms from the back. However, bicycles may be transported on the roof of cars provided that an overall height of 4 metres is not exceeded. Cars carrying bicycles/motorbikes on the back may be subject to a fine.

If you are planning to travel from Spain to Portugal please note that slightly different regulations apply and these are set out in the Spain Country Introduction.

Electricity and Gas

Usually current on campsites varies between 6 and 15 amps. Plugs have two round pins. CEE connections are commonplace.

The full range of Campingaz cylinders is available.

*See **Electricity and Gas** in the section **DURING YOUR STAY.***

Entry Formalities

Holders of British and Irish passports may visit Portugal for up to 90 days without a visa. Registration formalities are carried out by campsite reception staff.

Regulations for Pets

*See **Pet Travel Scheme** under **Documents** in the section **PLANNING AND TRAVELLING.***

Medical Services

For treatment of minor conditions go to a pharmacy (farmacia). Staff are generally well-trained and are qualified to dispense drugs which may only be available on prescription in Britain. In large towns there is usually at least one pharmacy whose staff speak English, and all have information posted on the door indicating the whereabouts of the nearest pharmacy open at night.

All municipalities have a health centre. A doctor will charge you for treatment but basic emergency hospital treatment is free on production of a European Health Insurance Card (EHIC). You will have to pay for items such as X-rays, laboratory tests and prescribed medicines as well as dental treatment. Nationals of other EU countries resident in the UK will also require an EHIC.

For serious illness you can obtain the name of an English-speaking doctor from the local police station or tourist office or from a British or American consulate. There is a private British hospital at Campo de Ourique, Rua Saraiva de Carvalho 49, 1269-098 Lisbon. Private treatment is expensive.

Normal precautions should be taken to avoid mosquito bites, including the use of insect repellents, especially at night.

You are strongly recommended to obtain comprehensive travel and medical insurance before travelling to Portugal, such as the Caravan Club's Red Pennant Overseas Holiday Insurance – see www.caravanclub.co.uk/redpennant

*See **Medical Matters** in the section **DURING YOUR STAY.***

Opening Hours

Banks – Mon-Fri 8.30am-3pm; some banks in city centres also open 6pm-11pm Mon-Sat.

Museums – Tue-Sun 10am-5pm; closed Monday.

Post Offices – Mon-Fri 9am-6pm; in main towns open on Saturday morning.

Shops – Mon-Fri 9am-1pm & 3pm-7pm, Sat 9am-1pm; supermarkets open Mon-Sat until 10pm & on Sunday.

Safety and Security

The crime rate is comparatively low but pickpocketing, bag-snatching and thefts from cars are common in major tourist areas. Be particularly vigilant on public transport, at crowded tourist sites and in public parks where it is wise to go in pairs. Keep car windows closed and doors locked while driving in urban areas at night. Pedestrians, particularly the elderly, are advised not to wear valuable jewellery or watches in public areas.

Take extra care when crossing busy roads, especially late at night. This warning also applies to zebra crossings which are often badly lit and poorly marked.

Do not leave valuables in an unattended car. Thieves often target foreign-registered and hire cars.

Take care of your belongings at all times. Do not leave your bag on the chair beside you, under the table or hanging on your chair while you eat in a restaurant or café. Thieves often work in groups and create distractions with the aim of stealing.

Forest fires occasionally cause road and rail closures. You should be aware of this and be prepared for possible delays. Be extremely careful when visiting isolated areas in any affected regions and be guided by local fire service authorities at all times. No smoking is allowed in woodland areas and barbecues should be avoided. If you see the onset of a forest fire call the emergency services on 112 or 117.

Don't waste water during your visit.

Death by drowning occurs every year on Portuguese beaches. Warning flags should be taken very seriously. A red flag indicates danger and you should not enter the water when it is flying. If a yellow flag is flying you may paddle at the water's edge, but you may not swim. A green flag indicates that it is safe to swim, and a chequered flag means that the lifeguard is temporarily absent. The police are entitled to fine bathers who disobey warning flags. Do not swim from beaches which are not manned by lifeguards.

Portugal shares with the rest of Europe an underlying threat from international terrorism. Attacks could be indiscriminate and against civilian targets in public places including tourist sites.

*See **Safety and Security** in the section **DURING YOUR STAY.***

British Embassy

RUA DE SÃO BERNARDO 33,
P-1249-082 LISBOA
Tel: 21 3924000
www.ukinportugal.gov.uk
Lisbon.Consulate@fco.gov.uk

There are also British Consulates/Honorary Consulates in Porto and Portimão.

Irish Embassy

RUA DA IMPRENSA A ESTRELA 1-4,
P-1200-684 LISBOA
Tel: 21 3929440
www.embassyofireland.pt

Customs Regulations

Alcohol and Tobacco

For import allowances for alcohol and tobacco products see ***Customs Regulations*** in the section ***PLANNING AND TRAVELLING.***

Caravans and Motor Caravans

Dimensions must not exceed 4 metres in height, 2.50 metres in width, 12 metres in length and combined length of car + caravan 18 metres.

Documents

The Portuguese authorities stipulate that proof of identity bearing the holder's photograph and signature, eg a passport, should be carried at all times. Failure to do so may incur a fine.

All valid UK driving licences should be accepted in Portugal but holders of an older all-green style licence are advised to update it to a photocard licence before travelling in order to avoid any local difficulties. Alternatively carry an International Driving Permit.

When driving you must carry your vehicle registration certificate (V5C), proof of insurance and MOT certificate (if applicable). There are heavy on-the-spot fines for those who fail to do so.

*See **Documents** in the section **PLANNING AND TRAVELLING.***

Money

Travellers' cheques may be cashed in banks and are accepted as a means of payment in shops, hotels and restaurants displaying the appropriate logo or sign. Commission charges can be high.

The major credit cards are widely accepted and there are cash machines (Multibanco) throughout the country. A tax of €0.50 is added to credit card transactions.

Cardholders are recommended to carry their credit card issuers'/banks' 24-hour UK contact numbers in case of loss or theft.

Recent visitors report that small change appears to be in short supply and you may well be asked for it in shops.

Motoring

Many Portuguese drive erratically and vigilance is advised. By comparison with the UK, the accident rate is high. Particular blackspots are the N125 along the south coast, especially in the busy holiday season, and the coast road between Lisbon and Cascais. In rural areas you may encounter horse-drawn carts and flocks of sheep or goats. Otherwise there are no special difficulties in driving except in Lisbon and Porto, which are unlimited 'free-for-alls'.

Alcohol

The maximum permitted level of alcohol is 50 milligrams in 100 millilitres of blood, ie lower than permitted in the UK (80 milligrams). It is advisable to adopt the 'no drink-driving' rule at all times.

Breakdown Service

The Automovel Club de Portugal (ACP) operates a 24-hour breakdown service covering all roads in mainland Portugal. Its vehicles are coloured red and white. Emergency telephones are located at 2 km intervals on main roads and motorways. To contact the ACP breakdown service call +351 219 429113 from a mobile phone or 707 509510 from a landline.

The service is available to members of AIT and FIA affiliated clubs, such as the Caravan Club, and comprises on-the-spot repairs taking up to a maximum of 45 minutes and, if necessary, the towing of vehicles. The charges for breakdown assistance and towing vary according to distance, time of day and day of the week, plus motorway tolls if applicable. Payment by credit card is accepted.

Alternatively, on motorways breakdown vehicles belonging to the motorway companies (their emergency numbers are displayed on boards along the motorways) and police patrols (GNR/Brigada de Trânsito) can assist motorists.

Essential Equipment

Reflective Jackets

A driver whose vehicle is immobilised on the carriageway must wear a reflective jacket or waistcoat when getting out of the vehicle. Sensibly, any passenger who gets out to assist should also wear one. This rule does not apply to foreign-registered vehicles, but as you will need to buy a reflective jacket to comply with Spanish law while driving through Spain to Portugal, it would be sensible to observe the rule in Portugal.

Seat Belts

All passengers must wear a seat belt at all times. Children under 12 years and less than 1.5m (5 feet) in height are not allowed to travel in the front passenger seat.

Warning Triangles

Use a warning triangle if, for any reason, a stationary vehicle is not visible for at least 100 metres. In addition, hazard warning lights must be used if a vehicle is causing an obstruction or danger to other road users.

*See **Motoring – Equipment** in the section **PLANNING AND TRAVELLING.***

Fuel

Unleaded petrol and diesel are readily available throughout the country. 'Super' petrol with a lead substitute has replaced leaded petrol. Credit cards are accepted at most filling stations but a small extra charge may be made. There are no automatic petrol pumps. LPG (gáz liquido) is widely available – see www.portugalmania.com/transports/gpl

*See also **Fuel** under **Motoring – Advice** in the section **PLANNING AND TRAVELLING.***

Mountain Roads and Passes

There are no mountain passes or tunnels in Portugal. Roads through the Serra da Estrela near Guarda and Covilha may be temporarily obstructed for short periods after heavy snow; otherwise motorists will encounter no difficulties in winter.

Parking

Vehicles must be parked facing in the same direction as moving traffic. On-street parking is very limited in the centre of main towns and cities and 'blue zone' parking schemes operate. Illegally parked vehicles may be towed away or clamped. Parking in Portuguese is 'estacionamento'.

*See also **Parking Facilities for the Disabled** under **Motoring – Advice** in the section **PLANNING AND TRAVELLING.***

Priority

In general, at intersections and road junctions road users must give way to vehicles approaching from the right unless signs indicate otherwise. At roundabouts vehicles already on the roundabout have right of way.

Do not pass stationary trams at a tram stop until you are certain that all passengers have finished entering or leaving the tram and/or have reached the pavement at the side of the road.

Roads

Roads are surfaced with asphalt, concrete or stone setts. Main roads generally are well-surfaced and may be three lanes wide, the middle lane being used for overtaking in either direction. Roads in the south of the country are generally in good condition, but, despite recent extensive road improvement schemes, some sections in the north may still be in a poor state. All roads, with the exception of motorways, should be treated with care; even a good section may suddenly deteriorate and potholes may be a hazard. Roads in many towns and villages are often cobbled and rough.

Drivers entering Portugal from Zamora in Spain will notice an apparently shorter route on the CL527/N221 road via Mogadouro. Although this is actually the signposted route, the road surface is poor in places and this route is not recommended for trailer caravans. The recommended route is via the N122/IP4 to Bragança.

Road Signs and Markings

Road signs conform to international standards. Road markings are white or yellow. Roads are classified as follows:

AE	Motorways
IP	Principal routes
IC	Complementary routes
EN	National roads
EM	Municipal roads
CM	Other municipal roads

Signs you might encounter are as follows:

Atalho – *Detour*

Entrada – *Entrance*

Estacão de gasolina – *Petrol station*

Estacão de policia – *Police station*

Estacionamento – *Parking*

Estrada con portagem – *Toll road*

Saida – *Exit*

Speed Limits

*See **Speed Limits Table** under **Motoring – Advice** in the section **PLANNING AND TRAVELLING.***

Exceptions

Drivers must maintain a speed between 40 km/h (25 mph) and 60 km/h (37 mph) on the 25th April Bridge over the River Tagus in Lisbon. Speed limits are electronically controlled.

Motor caravans over 3,500 kg are restricted to 50 km/h (31 mph) in built-up areas, 70/80 km/h (44/50 mph) on the open road, and 90 km/h (56 mph) on motorways.

Visitors who have held a driving licence for less than one year must not exceed 90 km/h (56 mph).

It is prohibited to use a radar detector or to have one installed in a vehicle. For maps showing the location of fixed speed cameras in and around major towns in Portugal see www.fixedspeedcamera.com

Towing

Motor caravans are permitted to tow a car on a four-wheel trailer, ie with all four wheels off the ground. Towing a car on an A-frame (two back wheels on the ground) is not permitted.

Traffic Jams

Traffic jams are most likely to be encountered around the two major cities of Lisbon and Porto and on roads to the coast, such as the A1 Lisbon-Porto and the A2 Lisbon-Setúbal motorways, which are very busy on Friday evenings and Saturday mornings. The peak periods for holiday traffic are the last weekend in June and the first and last weekends in July and August.

Around Lisbon bottlenecks occur on the bridges across the River Tagus, the N6 to Cascais, the A1 to Vila Franca de Xira, the N8 to Loures and on the N10 from Setúbal via Almada.

Around Porto you may encounter traffic jams on the IC1 on the Arribada Bridge and at Vila Nova de Gaia, the A28/IC1 from Póvoa de Varzim and near Vila de Conde, and on the N13, N14 and the N15.

Major motorways are equipped with suspended signs which indicate the recommended route to take when there is traffic congestion.

Traffic Lights

There is no amber signal after the red. A flashing amber light indicates 'caution' and a flashing red light indicates 'stop'. In Lisbon there are separate traffic lights in bus lanes.

Violation of Traffic Regulations

Speeding, illegal parking and other infringements of traffic regulations are heavily penalised. You may incur a fine for crossing a continuous single or double white or yellow line in the centre of the road when overtaking or when executing a left turn into or off a main road, despite the lack of any other 'no left turn' signs. If necessary, drive on to a roundabout or junction to turn, or turn right as directed by arrows.

The police are authorised to impose on-the-spot fines and a receipt must be given. Most police vehicles are now equipped with portable credit card machines to facilitate immediate payment of fines.

Motorways

Portugal has more than 2,400 km of motorways (auto-estradas) and tolls (portagem) are payable on most sections. Take care not to use the 'Via Verde' green lanes reserved for motorists who subscribe to the automatic payment system.

It is permitted to spend the night on a motorway rest or service area with a caravan, although the Caravan Club does not recommend this practice for security reasons. It should be noted that toll tickets are only valid for 12 hours and fines are incurred if this period of time is exceeded.

Motorway Tolls

Class 1 Vehicle with or without trailer with height from front axle less than 1.10 m.

Class 2 Vehicle with or without trailer with height from front axle over 1.10 m.

Class 3 Vehicle or vehicle combination with 3 axles with height from front axle over 1.10 m.

Class 4* Vehicle or vehicle combination with 4 or more axles with height from front axle over 1.10 m.

* Drivers of high vehicles of the Range Rover/Jeep variety, together with some MPVs, and towing a twin-axle caravan pay Class 4 tolls.

Road No.	Route	km	Class 1	Class 2	Class 3	Class 4
A1	Lisbon to Porto	304	19.75	33.85	43.85	48.65
A2	Lisbon to Algarve	238	19.40	34.10	44.65	48.55
A3	Porto to Valença	108	9.25	18.85	20.05	22.75
A4	Porto to Amarente	54	5.55	9.65	12.50	13.85
A5	Lisbon to Cascais	25	2.45	4.80	4.80	4.80
A6	A2 to A6 Caia (Spanish border)	156	11.90	20.85	26.70	29.70
A7	Póvoa de Varzim (A28-IC1) to Vila Pouca de Aguiar (N206)	76	9.35	16.35	21.00	23.30
A8	Lisboa to Leiria	131	8.50	14.85	19.20	21.35
A9-A1-A5	Alverca to A5 (Estádio Nacional)	33	2.95	5.10	6.55	7.25
A10	A9 to A10 Carregado	23	6.25	11.05	14.15	15.75
A11	A11-A28 Braga (A3) to Guimarães (A7) to A4	61	7.00	12.25	15.85	17.55
A12	Setúbal to Montijo (Vasco de Gama Bridge)	25	1.90	3.30	4.20	4.65
A13	Santa Estevão to Marateca	76	6.75	11.85	15.15	16.85
A14	Figueira da Foz to Coimbra (A1)	38	2.20	3.90	5.05	5.55
A15	Caldas da Rainha to Santarém (A1)	42	3.55	6.10	7.85	8.65
A17	Marinha Grande Este (A8) to Mira	90	7.95	13.95	17.75	19.90
A21	Malveira (A80) to Ericeira	17	0.60	1.00	1.30	1.40
	Vasco da Gama Bridge, Lisbon (S to N)	17	2.35	5.40	8.05	10.45
	25 April Bridge, Lisbon (S to N)	2	1.35	3.25	4.70	6.15

Toll charges (2009) in euros. Credit cards accepted on the following motorways: A1, A2, A3, A4, A5, A6, A9, A10, A12, A13, A14, otherwise payment in cash. Some exits have automatic toll booths.

Other stretches of motorway totalling several hundred miles are toll-free.

Toll Bridges

25th April Bridge and Vasco da Gama Bridge

The 2 km long 25th April Bridge in Lisbon crosses the River Tagus. Tolls are charged for vehicles travelling in a south-north direction only. Tolls also apply on the Vasco da Gama Bridge, north of Lisbon, but again only to vehicles travelling in a south-north direction.

In case of breakdown, or if you need assistance, you must keep as near to the right-hand side as possible and wait inside your vehicle until a patrol arrives. It is prohibited to carry out repairs, to push vehicles physically or to walk on the bridges. If you run out of petrol, you must wait for a patrol vehicle.

Touring

Some English is spoken in large cities and tourist areas. Elsewhere a knowledge of French could be useful.

A Lisboa Card valid for 24, 48 or 72 hours entitles the holder to free unrestricted access to public transport, including trains to Cascais and Sintra, free entry to a number of museums, monuments and other places of interest in Lisbon and surrounding areas, and discounts in shops and places offering services to tourists. It is obtainable from tourist information offices, travel agents, some hotels and Carris ticket booths, or from www.europeancitycards.com

Portuguese cuisine is rich and varied and makes the most of abundant, locally grown produce; seafood is particularly good. The national speciality is bacalhau – dried, salted cod – for which there are 365 recipes, one for each day of the year. Aside from port, many excellent and inexpensive wines are produced, both red and white, including the famous vinho verde (verde means young and fresh, not green!)

Do ensure when eating out that you understand exactly what you are paying for; appetisers put on the table are not free. Service is included in the bill, but it is customary to tip 5 to 10% of the total if you have received good service. Rules on smoking in restaurants and bars vary according to the area available. The areas where clients are allowed to smoke are indicated by signs and there must be adequate ventilation.

Each town in Portugal devotes several days in the year to local celebrations which are invariably lively and colourful. Carnivals and festivals during the period before Lent, during Holy Week and at wine harvest can be particularly spectacular.

During the summer months bullfights are generally held each Sunday. In Portugal the bull is not killed.

Local Travel

A passenger and vehicle ferry crosses the River Sado estuary from Setúbal to Tróia and there are frequent ferry and catamaran services for cars and passengers across the River Tagus from various points in Lisbon including Belém and Cais do Sodré.

Both Lisbon and Porto have metro systems operating from 6am to 1am. For routes and fares information see www.metrolisboa.pt and www.metrodoporto.pt (English versions).

Throughout the country buses are cheap, regular and mostly on time, with every town connected. In Lisbon the extensive bus and tram network is operated by Carris, together with one lift and three funiculars which tackle the city's steepest hills. Buy single journey tickets on board from bus drivers or buy a re-chargeable 'Sete Colinas' card for use on buses and the metro.

In Porto buy a 'Euro' bus ticket, which can be charged with various amounts, from metro stations and transport offices. Validate tickets for each journey at machines on the buses. Also available is an 'Andante' ticket which is valid on the metro and on buses. Porto also has a passenger lift and a funicular which allows you to avoid the steep walk to and from the riverside.

Taxis are usually cream in colour. In cities they charge a standard, metered fare; outside they may run on the meter or charge a flat rate and are entitled to charge for the return fare.

All place names used in the Site Entry listings which follow can be found in Michelin's Touring & Motoring Atlas for Spain & Portugal, scale 1:400,000 (1 cm = 4 km).

Sites in Portugal

⊞ **ABRANTES** *B3* (4km S Urban) *39.44897, -8.19238* **Clube de Campismo de Abrantes, Travessa do Cavaco, 2205-059 Rossio ao Sul do Tejo [241 331743; parquecampismo abrantes@iol.pt; www.parquecampismoabrantes.pt]** Exit A23 sp Abrantes & foll sp Abrantes, then Rossio. Keep strt for 4km to rndabt with elaborate olive press in cent. Exit slightly L for 'Sul Ponte'. Keep strt & cross Rv Tejus on N2. At rndabt immed after bdge take exit sharp L down hill to rv. Site in 200m on R behind wall. Sm, pt shd; wc (own san rec); chem disp (wc); shwrs inc; el pnts (9A) €1.50; lndry rm; shop, rest, snacks, bar 200m; BBQ; playgrnd; pool 200m; rv adj; fishing; canoeing; entmnt high ssn; TV rm; no statics; bus 300m, rlwy stn 600m; poss cr; rd noise; red snr citizens; CCI. "Friendly, helpful owners; unmkd pitches; modern san facs." € 8.00 2008*

ALANDROAL *C3* (13km S Rural) *38.60645, -7.34674* **Camping Rosário, Monte das Mimosas, Rosário, 7250-999 Alandroal [268 459566; info@campingrosario.com; www.campingrosario.com]** Fr E exit IP7/A6 at Elvas W junc 9; at 3rd rndabt take exit sp Espanha, immed 1st R dir Juromenha & Redondo. Onto N373 until exit Rosário. Fr W exit IP7/A6 junc 8 at Borba onto N255 to Alandroal, then N373 E sp Elvas. After 1.5km turn R to Rosário & foll sp to site. Sm, hdstg, pt sl, pt shd; wc; chem disp; shwrs inc; el pnts (6A) €2.35; gas 2km; lndtte; shop 2km; tradsmn; rest; bar; playgrnd; pool; lake sw adj; boating; fishing; TV; no statics; dogs €1 (not acc Jul/Aug); Eng spkn; adv bkg; quiet; red long stay/low ssn; CCI. "Remote site being developed by enthusiastic young Dutch couple beside Alqueva Dam; excel touring base; ltd to 50 people max." 1 Mar-1 Oct. € 14.10 2009*

⊞ **ALBUFEIRA** *B4* (1.5km NE Urban) *37.10617, -8.25395* **Camping Albufeira, Estrada de Ferreiras, 8200-555 Albufeira [289 587629 or 587630; fax 289 587633; geral@campingalbufeira.net; www.campingalbufeira.net]** Exit IP1/E1 sp Albufeira onto N125/N395 dir Albufeira; camp on L, sp. V lge, some mkd pitch, pt sl, pt shd, wc; chem disp; mv service pnt; shwrs inc; el pnts (10-12A) €2.90; gas; lndtte; shop; supmkt; rest; snacks; bar; playgrnd; 3 pools; sand beach 1.5km; tennis; sports park; cycle hire; games area; games rm; disco (soundproofed); entmnt; TV; 20% statics; dogs; phone; bus adj; car wash; cash machine; security patrols; poss v cr; Eng spkn; no adv bkg; quiet; ccard acc; red long stay/low ssn/CCI. "Friendly, secure site; excel pool area/rest/bar; some pitches lge enough for US RVs; pitches on lower part of site prone to flooding in heavy rain; conv beach & town; poss lge rallies during Jan-Apr; camp bus to town high ssn." ♦ € 23.90 2007*

⊞ **ALBUFEIRA** *B4* (10km W Urban) *37.11916, -8.35083* **Camping Canelas, Alcantarilha, 8365-908 Armação de Pêra [282 312612; fax 282 314719; turismovel@mail.telepac.pt; www.camping-canelas.com]** Fr Lagos take N125, turn R (S) at Alcantarilha twd Armação de Pêra, site in 1.5km on R. Fr IP1/A22 Algarve coastal m'way, take Alcantarilha exit & turn L on N125 into vill, turn R at rndabt. Site on R in 1.5km just bef 2nd rndabt. V lge, hdg pitch, pt sl, shd; wc; chem disp; mv service pnt; shwrs; el pnts (5-12A) €2.75-3.50; gas; lndtte; shop; tradsmn; rest high ssn; snacks; bar; BBQ; playgrnd; 3 solar htd pools; sand beach 1.5km; tennis; games area; games rm; entmnt; TV rm; 5% statics; dogs; bus; phone; poss cr; Eng spkn; red low ssn/long stay; CCI. "Spacious, shady, much improved site; v popular in winter; vg security at ent; excel cent for Algarve." ♦ € 19.00 2009*

See advertisement opposite (below)

⊞ **ALBUFEIRA** *B4* (10.5km W Urban/Coastal) *37.10916, -8.35333* **Camping Armação de Pêra, 8365-184 Armação de Pêra [282 312260; fax 282 315379; camping_arm_pera@hotmail.com; www.roteiro-campista.pt/Faro/armpera.htm]** Fr Lagos take N125 coast rd E. At Alcantarilha turn S onto N269-1 sp Armação de Pêra & Campismo. Site at 3rd rndabt in 2km on L. V lge, hdg pitch, pt sl, shd; wc; chem disp; mv service pnt; shwrs inc; el pnts (6-10A) €2.50-4; gas; lndtte (inc dryer); shop; rest; snacks; bar; playgrnd; pool & paddling pool; sand beach 500m; tennis; cycle hire; games area; games rm; entmnt; TV rm; 25% statics; phone; bus adj; car wash; poss cr; Eng spkn; quiet; red low ssn; CCI. "Friendly, popular & attractive site; hot water to shwrs only; gd pool; min stay 3 days Oct-May; easy walk to town; interesting chapel of skulls at Alcantarilha; birdwatching in local lagoon." ♦ € 20.50 2009*

See advertisement above

⊞ **ALCACER DO SAL** *B3* (1km NW Rural) *38.38027, -8.51583* **Parque de Campismo Municipal de Alcácer do Sal, Olival do Outeiro, 7580-125 Alcácer do Sal [265 612303; fax 265 610079; cmalcacer@mail.telepac.pt; www.m-alcacerdosal.pt]** Heading S on A2/IP1 turn L twd Alcácer do Sal on N5. Site on R 1km fr Alcácer do Sal. Sp at rndabt. Site behind supmkt. Sm, hdg/mkd pitch, pt sl, pt shd; wc; chem disp; mv service pnt; shwrs inc; el pnts (6-12A) €1.50; lndtte; shops 100m, rest, snacks & bar 50m; BBQ; playgrnd; pool, paddling pool adj; rv 1km; sand beach 24km; games area; internet; dogs; phone; bus 50m; clsd mid-Dec to mid-Jan; poss cr; Eng spkn; quiet; red low ssn; ccard acc; CCI. "Excel, clean facs; in rice growing area - major mosquito prob; historic town; spacious pitches; poss full in winter - rec phone ahead." ♦ € 10.40 2009*

⊞ **ALCOBACA** *B2* (N Urban) *39.5525, -8.97805* **Campismo Municipal de Alcobaça, Avda Joaquim V Natividade, 2460-071 Alcobaça [262 582265]** Turn W off A8/IC1at junc 21 onto N8 twd Alcobaça. Site on L on ent town, well sp. Med, hdg pitch, hdstg, pt sl, terr, shd; wc; chem disp; shwrs inc; el pnts (3-6A) €0.90-1.50; gas; lndtte; shop 100m, tradsmn; rest, snacks 200m; bar; playgrnd; pool 200m; TV; some statics; bus 250m; site clsd Jan; poss cr; Eng spkn; some rd noise; quiet; red low ssn/CCI. "Well-run, clean, tidy site; excel touring base; friendly staff; vg facs; Batalha & monastery worth a visit; fascinating Mon mkt nrby; pleasant sm town with gd rests; bus service to Lisbon." ♦ € 9.30 2008*

Portugal

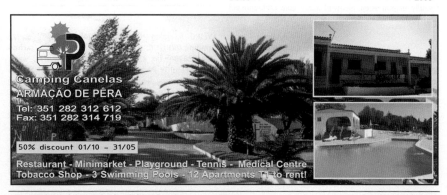

ALCOBACA *B2* (3km S Rural) *39.52611, -8.96583* **Camping Silveira, Capuchos, 2460-479 Alcobaça [262 509573; silveira.capuchos@clix.pt; www.camping silveira.com]** S fr Alcobaça on N 8-6 sp Evora de Alcobaça. Site on L in 3km after Capuchos. Med, hdg pitch, pt shd; wc; shwrs inc; el pnts (6A) €1.50; gas; lndtte; shops 1.5km; rest, snacks, bar 1km; playgrnd; pool 3km; sand beach 10km; games rm; no statics; dogs free; bus 500m; Eng spkn; quiet; CCI. "Vg, wooded, CL-type site; friendly owner; gd views; excel facs; excel touring base." 1 May-30 Sep. € 13.00 2008*

⊞ **ALJEZUR** *B4* (3.5km N Rural) *37.33972, -8.81277* **Camping Serrão, Herdade do Serrão, 8670-121 Aljezur [282 990220; fax 282 990229; info@parque-campismo-serrao.com; www.parque-campismo-serrao.com]** Site off N120 sp Praia Amoreira & Campsite. Driving fr N 4km after Rogil turn by café on R on slight bend. Lge sp 200m bef turn. Driving fr S ignore 1st L turn sp Praia Amereira, 4km after Aljezur (camp sp 1.3km), turn on L by café. V lge, hdstg, shd; wc (some cont); chem disp; mv service pnt; shwrs inc; el pnts (6A) €2.60; lndtte; shop; tradsmn; rest; bar; playgrnd; pool; sand beach 3.5km; fishing; tennis; games area; cycle hire; entmnt; TV; some statics; dogs; phone; quiet; no adv bkg; ccard acc; red low ssn/long stay/CCI. "No mkd pitches, pitch between lines of trees; helpful owner; gd san facs; much quieter area than S coast; lovely beaches." ♦ € 22.50 2008*

ALVOR see Portimao *B4*

AMARANTE *C1* (1.5km NE Rural) *41.27805, -8.07027* **Camping Penedo da Rainha, Rua Pedro Alveollos, Gatão, 4600-099 Amarante [255 437630; fax 255 437353; ccporto@sapo.pt]** Fr IP4 Vila Real to Porto foll sp to Amarante & N15. On N15 cross bdge for Porto & immed take R slip rd. Foll sp thro junc & up rv to site. Lge, some hdstg, pt sl, terr, shd; wc; chem disp; mv service pnt; shwrs inc; el pnts (4A) €1.50; gas 2km; lndtte; shop in ssn & 2km; rest; snacks 100m; bar; playgrnd; sm pool & 3km; rv adj; fishing; canoeing; cycling; games rm; entmnt; TV; dogs; phone; bus to Porto fr Amarante; some Eng spkn; adv bkg; quiet; red low ssn/CCI. "Well-run site in steep woodland/ parkland - take advice or survey rte bef driving to pitch; excel facs but some pitches far fr facs; few touring pitches; friendly, helpful recep; plenty of shade; conv Amarante old town & Douro Valley; Sat mkt." ♦ 1 Feb-30 Nov. € 12.50 2009*

⊞ **ARGANIL** *C2* (3km NE Rural) *40.2418, -8.06746* **Camp Municipal de Arganil, 3300-432 Sarzedo [235 205706; fax 235 200134; camping@mail.telepac.pt; www.cm-arganil.pt]** Fr Coimbra on N17 twd Guarda; after 50km turn S sp Arganil on N342-4; site on L in 4km in o'skts of Sarzedo bef rv bdge; avoid Góis to Arganil rd fr SW. Med, terr, shd; wc (some cont); mv service pnt; shwrs inc; el pnts (5-15A) €2.40; gas; lndtte; shop 100m; rest; snacks; bar; playgrnd; fishing & canoeing adj; ski in Serra da Estrela 50km Dec/ Jan; TV; phone; Eng spkn; quiet; red low ssn/long stay/snr citizens; ccard acc; CCI. "Vg, well-run site; friendly owner; fine views; gd cent for touring." € 10.60 2007*

ARMACAO DE PERA see Albufeira *B4*

⊞ **AVEIRO** *B2* (5.5km SW Coastal) *40.62480, -8.71315* **Parque de Campismo Gafanha da Nazaré, Rua dos Balneários do G Desportivo, 3830-640 Gafanha da Nazaré [234 366565; fax 234 365789; mail.gdg@clix.pt]** SW fr Aveiro on IP5/A25; exit at site sp on L. Foll Campismo sp. Lge, hdstg, pt shd; wc; own san rec; shwrs inc; el pnts (4A) €1.05; gas; shop 1km; rest; snacks; bar; playgrnd; pool 2km; sand beach 3km; fishing; canoeing; cycle hire; entmnt; TV; 90% statics; quiet; CCI. "Gd security; dated, shabby facs; NH only." ♦ € 6.82 2007*

⊞ **AVEIRO** *B2* (6km SW Coastal) *40.59960, -8.74981* **Camping Costa Nova, Estrada da Vagueira, Quinta dos Patos, 3830 Ílhavo [234 393220; fax 234 394721; info@ campingcostanova.com; www.campingcostanova.com]** Site on Barra-Vagueira coast rd 1km on R after Costa Nova. V lge, mkd pitch, unshd; htd wc; chem disp; mv service pnt; shwrs inc; el pnts (2-6A) €2.30; gas; lndtte; shop & 1.5km; tradsmn; rest in ssn; snacks; bar; BBQ; playgrnd; pool 4km; sand beach; fishing; cycle hire; games area; games rm; entmnt; internet; TV rm; some statics; dogs €1.55; phone; site clsd 1st two weeks Jan; Eng spkn; adv bkg; quiet; ccard acc; red long stay; CCI. "Peaceful, tidy site adj nature reserve; helpful staff; gd, modern facs; hot water to shwrs only; vg." ♦ € 17.25 2007*

⊞ **AVEIRO** *B2* (10km W Coastal) *40.63861, -8.74500* **Parque de Campismo Praia da Barra, Rua Diogo Cão 125, Praia da Barra, 3830-772 Gafanha da Nazaré [tel/fax 234 369425; barra@cacampings.com; www. cacampings.com]** Fr Aveiro foll sp to Barra on A25/IP5; foll sp to site. Lge, mkd pitch, shd; wc (some cont); chem disp; mv service pnt; baby facs; shwrs inc; el pnts (6A) €2.50; gas; lndtte (inc dryer); shop; rest; bar; BBQ; playgrnd; pool 400m; sand beach 200m; cycle hire; games area; games rm; internet; entmnt; TV rm; some statics; dogs €1.60; phone; bus adj; recep open 0900-2200; Eng spkn; adv bkg; quiet; red low ssn; CCI. "V pleasant, well-situated site with pitches in pine trees; vg." ♦ € 15.10 2009*

See advertisement on page 694

AVEIRO *B2* (8km NW Coastal/Rural) *40.70277, -8.7175* **Camping ORBITUR, N327, Km 20, 3800-901 São Jacinto [234 838284; fax 234 838122; info@orbitur.pt; www. orbitur.com]** Fr Porto take A29/IC1 S & exit sp Ovar onto N327. (Note long detour fr Aveiro itself by road - 30+ km.) Site in trees to N of São Jacinto. Lge, mkd pitch, hdstg, terr, shd; wc; chem disp; mv service pnt; baby facs; shwrs inc; el pnts (5-15A) €3-4 (poss rev pol); gas; lndtte; sm shop & 5km; tradsmn; rest; snacks; bar; BBQ; playgrnd; pool 5km; sand beach 2.5km; fishing; TV; some statics; dogs €1.50; phone; bus; car wash; Eng spkn; adv bkg; quiet; red low ssn/long stay/snr citizens; ccard acc; CCI. "Excel site; best in area; gd children's park; 15 min to (car) ferry; gd, clean san facs." ♦ 1 Jan-10 Oct. € 20.70 2009*

⊞ **AVIS** *C3* (1km SW Rural) *39.05638, -7.91138* **Parque de Campismo da Albufeira do Maranhão, Clube Náutico de Avis, Albufeira do Maranhão, 7480-999 Avis [242 412452; fax 242 410099; parque_campismo@cm-avis.pt; www.cm-avis.pt/parquecampismo]** Fr N exit A23/IP6 at Abrantes onto N2 dir Ponte de Sor, then N244 to Avis. Fr S exit A6/IP7 N at junc 7 Estremoz or junc 4 Montemor onto N4 to Arraiolos, then onto N370 to Pavia & Avis. Site sp. V lge, mkd pitch, terr, pt shd; wc; chem disp; mv service pnt; shwrs inc; el pnts (16A) €2.60; gas 1km; lndry rm; shop 1km; rest adj; snacks; bar; playgrnd; pool complex adj; lake fishing & shgl beach adj; watersports; tennis; games area; games rm; TV; dogs €1; bus 1km; Eng spkn; adv bkg; quiet; red long stay; CCI. "V pleasant site on lakeside; interesting, historic town; gd walking area." ♦ € 14.00 2009*

See advertisement

AVO see Oliveira do Hospital *C2*

⊞ **BEJA** *C4* (500m S Urban) *38.00777, -7.86222* **Parque de Campismo Municipal de Beja, Avda Vasco da Gama, 7800-397 Beja [tel/fax 284 311911; www.cm-beja.pt]** Fr S (N122) take 1st exit strt into Beja. In 600m turn R at island then L in 100m into Avda Vasco da Gama & foll sp for site on R in 300m - narr ent. Fr N on N122 take by-pass round town then 1st L after Intermarche supmkt, then as above. Lge, hdstg, shd, gravel pitches; wc; chem disp; shwrs inc; el pnts (6A) €1.85; supmkt 500m; rest 500m; snacks 200m; bar adj; pool, tennis & football stadium adj; bus 300m; rlwy stn 1.5km; Eng spkn; poss noisy in ssn; red low ssn/CCI. "C'van storage facs; helpful staff; san facs old but clean; NH only." ♦ € 10.40 2009*

⊞ **BRAGA** *B1* (1km S Urban) *41.53831, -8.42208* **Parque Municipal da Ponte, São Lazaro, 4710 Braga [253 273355; fax 253 613387]** Fr Porto N14 N to Braga, then fr ring rd exit junc 2 onto N101 dir Guimarães. After Guimarães bear L for underpass sp hospital & other rtes. Site by old football stadium 200m on R (do not confuse with new stadium). Fr N drive thro city, foll sp Guimarães, bear L for underpass (no max height shown) sp hospital & other rtes. Sm, hdstg, pt sl, terr, pt shd; chem disp; wc; own san rec; shwrs inc; el pnts (16A) €1.65; gas; shop 200m; rest 500m; playgrnd; pool, tennis adj; no adv bkg; rd noise. "Not rec for disabled; terr pitches steep for vans, check site/pitch bef driving in; poss scruffy pitches & unclean shwrs; conv Porto, Gêres National Park; easy walk to city cent; NH only." € 12.00 2008*

BRAGANCA *D1* (6km N Rural) *41.84361, -6.74722* **Inatel Campismo de Bragança (formerly Municipal), Estrada de Rabal, 5300-671 Meixedo [tel/fax 273 329409; pc.braganca@inatel.pt]** Fr Bragança N for 6km on N103.7 twd Spanish border. Site on R, sp Inatel. Med, hdstg, pt sl, terr, pt shd; wc; chem disp; shwrs inc; el pnts (6A) inc; gas; lndry rm; shop & 6km; tradsmn; rest in ssn; snacks; bar; playgrnd; fishing; cycle hire; dogs; bus; poss cr; Eng spkn; quiet but barking dogs. "On S boundary of National Park; rv runs thro site; Bragança citadel worth visit; friendly staff; gd rest; vg facs." 1 Apr-30 Sep. € 10.40 2009*

BRAGANCA *D1* (10km W Rural) *41.84879, -6.86120* **Cepo Verde Camping, Gondesende, 5300-561 Bragança [273 999371; fax 273 323577; cepoverde@bragancanet.pt; www.bragancanet.pt/cepoverde]** Fr IP4 fr W take N103 fr Bragança for 8km. Site sp fr IP4 ring rd. R off N103, foll lane & turn R at sp. NB Camping sp to rd 103-7 leads to different site (Sabor) N of city. Med, mkd pitch, hdstg, terr, pt shd; wc; chem disp; shwrs inc; el pnts (6A) €1.40 (poss rev pol & long lead poss req); lndtte; shop; rest; snacks; bar; playgrnd; pool; dogs; phone; bus 1km; Eng spkn; adv bkg; quiet; CCI. "Remote, friendly, v pleasant, scenic site adj Montesinho National Park; clean, modern facs; vg value." ♦ 1 Apr-30 Sep. € 10.20 2007*

BUDENS see Vila do Bispo *B4*

CABANAS TAVIRA see Tavira *C4*

CABRIL see Geres *C1*

⊞ **CALDAS DA RAINHA** *B3* (8km W Rural/Coastal) *39.43083, -9.20083* **Camping ORBITUR, Rua Maldonado Freitas, 2500-516 Foz do Arelho [262 978683; fax 262 978685; info@orbitur.pt; www.orbitur.com]** Take N360 fr Caldas da Raina twds Foz do Arelho. Site on L; well sp. Lge, mkd pitch, terr, shd; wc; chem disp; mv service pnt; shwrs; el pnts (5-15A) €3-4; gas; lndtte; shop; tradsmn; rest high ssn; snacks; bar; BBQ; playgrnd; htd pool high ssn; sand beach 2km; tennis; cycle hire; games rm; entmnt; wifi; cab/sat TV; 25% statics; dogs €1.50; car wash; Eng spkn; adv bkg; quiet; ccard acc; red low ssn; CCI. "Óbidos Lagoon nr; interesting walled town; attractive area; well-maintained, well-run site; excel san facs; excel touring base.." ♦ € 25.60 2009*

⊞ **CAMINHA** *B1* (4.5km NE Rural) *41.89361, -8.79861* **Camping Parque Natural Vilar de Mouros, 4910 Vilar de Mouros [tel/fax 258 727472; geral@casa-da-anta.com; www.casa-da-anta.com]** Fr Caminha take N13 NE twd Valença. In approx 5km, after Seixas, turn R onto rd sp Vilar de Mouros (Camping 1.5km). Foll camping sp, site on R. Lge, pt sl, terr, pt shd; wc; chem disp; shwrs inc; el pnts (10A) €2.30; lndtte; shop; rest; snacks; playgrnd; pool; fishing; tennis; entmnt; poss cr; 10% statics; phone; bus 1km; site clsd 1-25 Dec; adv bkg; quiet; ccard acc; CCI. "Excursion to mountains; mosquito repellant fr recep; site looking tired." € 14.50 2007*

⊞ **CAMINHA** *B1* (2km SW Coastal) *41.86611, -8.85888* **Camping ORBITUR-Caminha, Mata do Camarido, N13, Km 90, 4910-180 Caminha [258 921295; fax 258 921473; info@orbitur.pt; www.orbitur.com]** Foll seafront rd N13/E1 fr Caminha dir Viana/Porto, at sp Foz do Minho turn R, site in approx 1km. Long o'fits take care at ent. Med, terr, shd; wc; mv service pnt; chem disp; shwrs inc; el pnts (5-15A) €3-4; gas; lndtte; shop (high ssn); tradsmn; rest (high ssn); snacks; bar; playgrnd; pool 2.5km; sand beach 150m; fishing; cycle hire; wifi; TV rm; 5% statics; dogs €1.50; Eng spkn; adv bkg; fairly quiet; ccard acc; red low ssn/long stay/snr citizens; CCI. "Pleasant, woodland site; care in shwrs - turn cold water on 1st as hot poss scalding; Gerês National Park & Viana do Castelo worth visit; poss to cycle to Caminha; vg site." ♦ € 24.00 2009*

⊞ **CAMPO MAIOR** *C3* (4km W Rural) *39.00589, -7.13051* **Parque de Campismo de Campo Maior, Barragem do Caia, 7370 Campo Maior [268 689493; info@parqueverde.pt; www.parqueverde.pt]** Fr Elvas on N373 or Badajoz on N371 turn L on edge of Campo Maior onto N243 sp Barragem do Caia. Site on R in 4km just bef reservoir, sp Faisão Rest. V lge, hdstg, terr, pt shd; wc; chem disp; shwrs inc; el pnts (6A) €1.95 (long lead poss req); lndtte; rest; snacks; bar; shop; pool 4km; lake sw adj; playgrnd; games area; boating; fishing; 98% statics; dogs; phone; poss cr/noisy high ssn & w/end; CCI. "Gd welcome; superb views fr top terrs; poss muddy pitches or soft patches." ♦ € 13.75 2007*

CANDEMIL see Vila Nova de Cerveira *B1*

⊞ **CASCAIS** *A3* (5km NW Coastal/Urban) *38.72166, -9.46666* **Camping ORBITUR-Guincho, N247-6, Lugar de Areia, Guincho, 2750-053 Cascais [214 870450 or 871014; fax 214 857410; fernanda.botelho@orbitur.pt; www.orbitur.com]** Fr Lisbon take A5 W, at end m'way foll sp twd Cascais. At 1st rndabt turn R sp Birre & Campismo. Foll sp for 2.5km. Steep traff calming hump - care needed. V lge, some hdg/mkd pitch, terr, shd; wc; chem disp; mv service pnt; baby facs; shwrs inc; el pnts (6A) €3-4; gas; lndtte; supmkt & 500m; rest; snacks; bar; BBQ; playgrnd; pool; sand beach 800m; watersports & fishing 1km; tennis; cycle hire; horseriding 500m; golf 3km; entmnt in ssn; games rm; wifi; cab/sat TV; 50% statics; dogs on lead €1.50; phone; car wash; Eng spkn; adv bkg; some rd noise; ccard acc; red low ssn/long stay/snr citizens; CCI. "Buses to Cascais for train to Lisbon; sandy, wooded site behind dunes; open pitches with views; gd value rest; ltd facs in winter; charge for awnings; busy high ssn; vg low ssn but poss windy; steep rd to beach." ♦ € 25.60 ABS - E10 2009*

CASTELO BRANCO *C2* (2.5km N Rural) *39.85777, -7.49361* **Camp Municipal Castelo Branco, 6000-113 Castelo Branco [272 322577; fax 272 322578; albigec@sm-castelobranco.pt]** Fr IP2 take Castelo Branco Norte, exit R on slip rd, L at 1st rndabt, site sp at 2nd rndabt. Turn L at T junc just bef Modelo supmkt, site 2km on L, well sp. Lge, pt sl, shd; wc; shwrs; chem disp; mv service pnt; el pnts (12A) €2.25; gas; lndtte; shop, rest, bar 2km; playgrnd; pool 4km; lake 500m; bus 100m; Eng spkn; quiet but some rd noise; CCI. "Useful NH on little used x-ing to Portugal; gd site but rds to it poor." 2 Jan-15 Nov. € 9.25 2009*

⊞ **CASTELO DE VIDE** *C3* (3km SW Rural) *39.39805, -7.48722* **Camping Quinta do Pomarinho, N246, Km 16.5, Castelo de Vide [965-755341 (mob); info@pomarinho.co.uk; www.pomarinho.com]** On N246 at km 16.5 by bus stop, turn into dirt track. Site in 500m. Sm, mkd pitch, hdstg, unshd; wc; chem disp; shwrs inc; el pnts (6-10A) €2.50-3.50; lndtte; shop 5km; tradsmn; pool; cycle hire; wifi; dogs; bus adj; Eng spkn; adv bkg; quiet. "On edge of Serra de São Mamede National Park; gd walking, fishing, birdwatching, cycling; vg." € 14.00 2009*

⊞ **CELORICO DE BASTO** *C1* (500m NW Rural) *41.39026, -8.00581* **Parque de Campismo da Celorico de Basto, Adaufe-Gemeos, 4890-361 Celorico de Basto [(255) 323340 or 964-064436 (mob); fax (255) 323341; geral@celoricodebastocamping.com; www.celoricodebastocamping.com]** E fr Guimarães exit A7/IC5 S sp Vila Nune (bef x-ing rv). Foll sp Fermil & Celorico de Basto, site sp. Med, mkd pitch, some hdstg, shd; wc; chem disp; mv service pnt; shwrs inc; el pnts (6-16A) €2-3.20; gas; lndtte (inc dryer); shop; tradsmn; rest; bar; BBQ; playgrnd; pool 500m; rv sw & fishing adj; games area; wifi; entmnt; TV rm; some statics; dogs €1.80; phone; quiet; ccard acc; red long stay/CCI. "Peaceful, well-run site; gd facs; gd cycling & walking; vg." ♦ € 12.90 2009*

See advertisement

⊞ **CHAVES** *C1* (4km S Rural) *41.70166, -7.50055* **Camp Municipal Quinta do Rebentão, Vila Nova de Veiga, 5400-764 Chaves [tel/fax 276 322733; cccchaves@sapo.pt]** Fr o'skts Chaves take N2 S. After about 3km in vill of Vila Nova de Veiga turn E at sp thro new estate, site in about 500m. Med, hdstg, terr, pt shd; wc; chem disp; mv service pnt; shwrs inc; el pnts (6A) €1.50; gas 4km; Indry rm; shop 1km; rest; snacks; bar; BBQ; pool adj; rv sw & fishing 4km; cycle hire; dogs; phone; bus 800m; site clsd Dec; Eng spkn; adv bkg; red CCI. "Gd site in lovely valley but remote; helpful staff; facs block quite a hike fr some terr pitches; Chaves interesting, historical Roman town." ♦ € 12.50 2009*

The opening dates and prices on this campsite have changed. I'll send a site report form to the Club for the next edition of the guide.

⊞ **COIMBRA** *B2* (1km SE Urban) *40.18888, -8.39944* **Camping Municipal Parque de Campismo de Coimbra, Rua de Escola, Alto do Areeiro, Santo António dos Olivais, 3030-011 Coimbra [tel/fax 239 086902; coimbra@cacampings.com; www.cacampings.com]** Fr S on AP1/IP1 at junc 11 turn twd Lousa & in 1km turn twd Coimbra on IC2. In 9.5km turn R at rndabt onto Ponte Rainha, strt on at 3 rndabts along Avda Mendes Silva. Then turn R along Estrada des Beiras & cross rndabt to Rua de Escola. Or fr N17 dir Beira foll sp sports stadium/campismo. Fr N ent Coimbra on IC2, turn L onto ring rd & foll Campismo sps. V lge, terr, hdstg, pt sl, pt shd; htd wc; chem disp; mv service pnt; sauna; baby facs; shwrs inc; el pnts (20A) €2.70; gas; Indtte; shop; tradsmn; rest; snacks; bar; BBQ; playgrnd; pool adj; rv sw 300m; health club; tennis; cycle hire; games area; games rm; internet; TV rm; 10% statics; dogs €2.20; bus 100m; poss cr; Eng spkn; adv bkg; ccard acc; red long stay/low ssn/CCI. "Vg site & facs; v interesting, lively university town." ♦ € 16.10 2009*

See advertisement on page 694

⊞ **COIMBRAO** *B2* (Rural) *39.90027, -8.88805* **Camping Coimbrão, 185 Travessa do Gomes, 2425-452 Coimbrão [tel/fax 244 606007; campingcoimbrao@web.de]** Site down lane in vill cent. Care needed lge outfits, but site worth the effort. Sm, unshd; wc; chem disp; mv service pnt; shwrs inc; el pnts (6-10A) €2-3; Indry rm; tradsmn; shop & snacks 300m; playgrnd; pool; sw, fishing, canoeing 4km; TV; no dogs; bus 200m; Eng spkn; quiet; office open 0800-1200 & 1500-2200; red long stay. "Excel site; helpful & friendly staff; gd touring base." ♦ € 11.10 2006*

CORTEGACA see Espinho *B1*

COSTA DE CAPARICA see Lisboa *B3*

⊞ **COVILHA** *C2* (4km NW Rural) *40.28750, -7.52722* **Clube de Campismo do Pião, 6200-036 Covilhã [tel/fax 275 314312; campismopiao@hotmail.com; www.clubecampismocovilha.com]** App Covilhã, foll sp to cent, then sp to Penhas da Saúde/Seia; after 4km of gd but twisting climbing rd; site on L. Lge, terr, pt shd; wc; shwrs inc; el pnts (4A) €1.40; gas; shop; rest; snacks; bar; playgrnd; 2 pools; tennis; entmnt; many statics; phone; bus adj; poss cr; Eng spkn; CCI. "Gd walking fr site; few touring pitches." ♦ € 11.30 2006*

DARQUE see Viana do Castelo *B1*

ELVAS *C3* (1.5km W Urban) *38.87305, -7.1800* **Parque de Campismo da Piedade, 7350-901 Elvas [268 628997 or 622877; fax 268 620729]** Exit IP7/E90 junc 9 or 12 & foll site sp dir Estremoz. Med, mkd pitch, hdstg, mostly sl, pt shd; wc; chem disp; shwrs inc; el pnts (16A) inc; gas; Indry rm; shop 200m; rest; snacks; bar; BBQ; playgrnd; dogs; phone; bus 500m; poss cr; CCI. "Attractive aqueduct & walls; Piedade church & relics adj; traditional shops; pleasant walk to town; v quiet site, even high ssn; adequate san facs; conv NH en rte Algarve." 1 Apr-15 Sep. € 16.50 2009*

ENTRE AMBOS OS RIOS see Ponte da Barca *B1*

Portugal

⊞ **ERICEIRA** *B3* (1km N Coastal) *38.98055, -9.41861* **Camp Municipal Mil Regos, 2655-319 Ericeira [261 862706; fax 261 866798; info@ericeiracamping.com; www.ericeiracamping.com]** On N247 coast rd, well sp N of Ericeira. V lge, pt sl, pt shd; wc (some cont); own san rec; shwrs inc; el pnts (10A) €3.50; gas; shop; rest; playgrnd; 2 pools adj; beach 200m; fishing; internet; entmnt; 75% statics; phone; bus adj; quiet. "Busy site with sea views; improvements in hand (2009); uneven, sl pitches." ♦ € 24.50 2009*

⊞ **ERMIDAS SADO** *B4* (7km NW Rural) *38.01805, -8.48500* **Camping Monte Naturista O Barão (Naturist), Foros do Barão, 7566-909 Ermidas-Sado [936710623 (mob); info@montenaturista.com; www.montenaturista.com]** Fr A2 turn W onto N121 thro Ermidas-Sado twd Santiago do Cacém. Nr Arelãos turn N at bus stop (km 17.5) dir Barão. Site in 1km along dirt rd. Sm, pt shd; wc; chem disp; mv service pnt; baby facs; fam bthrm; shwrs inc; el pnts (6A) €3.20; Indtte; tradsmn; meals on request; bar; pool; 10% statics; dogs €1; Eng spkn; adv bkg; quiet; red long stay. "Gd site in beautiful wooded area; spacious pitches - sun or shd." ♦ € 15.10 2007*

⊞ **ESPINHO** *B1* (Urban) *41.01413, -8.63741* **Camp Municipal de Espinho, Rua Nova da Praia, 4500-083 Espinho [227 335871; fax 227 322680; campismo@c.m-espinho.pt]** Foll N109 fr Porto to Espinho; on app town site sp at junc on R. V lge, sl, pt shd; wc; chem disp; mv service pnt; shwrs inc; el pnts (10A) €1.68; gas; shop; snacks; bar; playgrnd; pool; paddling pool; sand beach 800m; fishing; no dogs; bus 600m; poss cr; adv bkg; rd noise; red CCI. "Sep secure area for cars; if pitched at bottom of site must climb to get to facs; frequent trains to Porto 800m." € 14.07 2007*

⊞ **ESPINHO** *B1* (10km S Coastal) *40.9400, -8.65833* **Camping Os Nortenhos, Praia de Cortegaça, 3885-278 Cortegaça [256 752199; fax 256 755177; clube.nortenhos@netvisao.pt; http://cccosnortenhos.cidadevirtual.pt]** Fr Espinho foll rd thro Esmoriz twd Aveiro to Cortegaça vill. Turn R to beach (Praia), site on L at beach, sp fr vill. V lge, pt shd; wc (cont); shwrs; el pnts (6A); gas; shop; snacks; bar; playgrnd; sand beach adj; entmnt; TV; 95% statics; no dogs; phone; bus 500m; poss cr; quiet; ccard acc; CCI. "V helpful, friendly staff; v ltd tourer pitches & poss v cr high ssn; facs ltd at w/end; conv Porto; guarded at ent; sun shelters over pitches." ♦ € 13.70 2007*

ESTELA see Povoa De Varzim *B1*

⊞ **EVORA** *C3* (2km SW Urban) *38.55722, -7.92583* **Camping ORBITUR, Estrada das Alcaçovas, Herdade Esparragosa, 7005-706 Évora [266 705190; fax 266 709830; info@orbitur.pt; www.orbitur.com]** Fr N foll N18 & by-pass, then foll sps for Lisbon rd at each rndabt or traff lts. Fr town cent take N380 SW sp Alcaçovas, foll site sp, site in 2km. NB Narr gate to site. Med, mkd pitch, hdstg, pt sl, pt shd; wc; chem disp; mv service pnt; shwrs inc; el pnts (5-15A) €3-4 (long lead poss req); gas; Indtte; shop; supmkt 500m; tradsmn; snacks; bar; playgrnd; pool; tennis; games area; TV rm; dogs €1.50; phone; car wash; bus; rlwy stn 2km; Eng spkn; adv bkg ess; quiet; ccard acc; red low ssn/long stay/snr citizens; red CCI. "Conv town cent, Évora World Heritage site with wealth of monuments & prehistoric sites nrby; cycle path to town; free car parks just outside town walls; poss flooding some pitches after heavy rain." ♦ € 25.60 2009*

⊞ **FAO** *B1* (1km S Urban/Coastal) *41.50780, -8.77830* **Parque de Campismo de Fão, Rua São João de Deus, 4740-380 Fão [253 981777; fax 253 817786; contacto@cccbarcelos.com; www.cccbarcelos.com]** Exit A28/IC1 junc 8 fr S or junc 9 fr N onto N13 thro Fão twd coast. Site sp off rd M501. Sm, pt shd; wc; chem disp; mv service pnt; shwrs inc; el pnts (3A) €2.60; gas; shop, snacks, bar high ssn; playgrnd; pool 2km; sand beach 800m; entmnt; TV; many statics; no dogs; bus 800m; quiet. "Gd site; Barcelos mkt Thurs." € 15.40 2006*

FERRAGUDO see Portimao *B4*

FERREIRA DO ZEZERE *B2* (1.5km E Rural) *39.70083, -8.27805* **Camping Quinta da Cerejeira, 2240-333 Ferreira do Zêzere [tel/fax 249 361756; info@cerejeira.com; www.cerejeira.com]** Fr Serta (N) take N238 twd Tomar & turn E to Ferreira do Zêzere. Thro Ferreira dir Vila de Rei, turn L at blue site sp in 1km. Sm, terr, pt shd; wc; chem disp (wc); shwrs inc; el pnts (6A) €2.25; gas 1.5km; Indtte; tradsmn; rest, snacks & bar 1.5km; BBQ; pool 1km; TV rm; bus 1.5km; Eng spkn; adv bkg; red long stay; CCI.
1 Feb-30 Nov. € 12.75 2008*

⊞ **FIGUEIRA DA FOZ** *B2* (4km S Coastal/Urban) *40.11861, -8.85666* **Camping ORBITUR-Gala, N109, Km 4, Gala, 3090-458 Figueira da Foz [233 431492; fax 233 431231; info@orbitur.pt; www.orbitur.com]** Fr Figueira da Foz on N109 dir Leiria for 3.5km. After Gala site on R in approx 400m. Ignore sp on R 'Campismo' after long bdge. Lge, mkd pitch, hdstg, terr, shd; wc; chem disp; mv service pnt; shwrs; el pnts (6-10A) €3-4; gas; Indtte; shop; tradsmn; rest; snacks; bar; BBQ; playgrnd; htd pool high ssn; sand beach 400m; fishing 1km; tennis; games rm; entmnt; wifi; TV rm; many statics; dogs €1.50; phone; car wash; Eng spkn; adv bkg; red low ssn/long stay/snr citizens; ccard acc; CCI. "Gd, renovated site adj busy rd; luxury san facs (furthest fr recep); excel pool." ♦ € 25.60 2009*

FIGUEIRA DA FOZ *B2* (6km S Coastal) *40.14055, -8.86277* **Camping Foz do Mondego, Cabedelo-Gala, 3080-661 Figueira da Foz [233 402740/2; fax 233 402749; foz.mondego@fcmportugal.com; www.fcmportugal.com]** Fr S on N109 turn L bef bdge sp Gala. Foll site sp. V lge, mkd pitch; htd wc; chem disp; mv service pnt; baby facs; shwrs inc; el pnts (2A) inc; gas; lndtte; shop 2km; rest; snacks; bar; BBQ; playgrnd; sand beach adj; fishing; surfing; TV; 40% statics; dogs €0.50; phone; bus 1km; CCI. "Wonderful sea views but indus est adj; NH only." ♦ 14 Jan-13 Nov. € 16.40 2009*

FOZ DO ARELHO see Caldas da Rainha *B3*

⊞ **FUNDAO** *C2* (3km SW Urban) *40.13276, -7.51205* **Camping Quinta do Convento, 6234-909 Fundão [275 753118; fax 275 771368]** Fr N thro town cent; when almost thro town take L fork at triangle dir Silvares; site 1km uphill on L - steep. Site well sp fr A23. Med, hdstg, terr, shd; wc (some cont); chem disp; mv service pnt; shwrs inc; el pnts (4-10A) €2; lndtte; shop; rest; snacks; bar; playgrnd; pool; entmnt; TV; bus 1.5km; adv bkg; quiet. "Guarded; no vehicle access after 2300; gd, friendly site with nice atmosphere; narr site rds & pitches diff to access - rec arr early for easy pitching." ♦ € 10.30 2007*

FUZETA see Olhao *C4*

GAFANHA DA NAZARE see Aveiro *B2*

⊞ **GERES** *C1* (1km N Rural) *41.76305, -8.19111* **Parque de Campismo de Cerdeira, Campo do Gerês, 4840-030 Terras do Bouro [253 351005; fax 253 353315; info@parquecerdeira.com; www.parquecerdeira.com]** Fr N103 Braga-Chaves rd, 28km E of Braga turn N onto N304 at sp to Poussada. Cont N for 18km to Campo de Gerês. Site in 1km; well sp. V lge, shd; wc; chem disp; shwrs inc; el pnts (5-10A) €2.50-3.75; gas; lndry service; rest; bar; shop; playgrnd; lake sw; TV rm; cycle hire; fishing 2km; canoeing; few statics; no dogs; bus 500m; entmnt; poss cr; quiet; Eng spkn; ccard acc; CCI. "Beautiful scenery; unspoilt area; fascinating old vills nrby & gd walking; ltd facs low ssn." ♦ € 20.70 2008*

GERES *C1* (2km N Rural) *41.73777, -8.15805* **Vidoeiro Camping, Lugar do Vidoeiro, 4845-081 Gerês [253 391289; aderepg@mail.telepac.pt; www.adere-pg.pt]** NE fr Braga take N103 twds Chaves for 25km. 1km past Cerdeirinhas turn L twds Gerês onto N308. Site on L 2km after Caldos do Gerês. Steep rds with hairpins. Cross bdge & reservoir, foll camp sps. Lge, mkd pitch, hdstg, terr, pt shd; wc; chem disp; shwrs inc; el pnts (12A) €1.20; lndry rm; tradsmn; rest, bar 500m; BBQ; pool 500m, lake sw 500m; dogs €0.60; phone; quiet. "Attractive, wooded site in National Park; gd, clean facs; thermal spa in Gerês." ♦ 15 May-15 Oct. € 14.00 2009*

GERES *C1* (10km E Rural) *41.71529, -8.03071* **Camping Outeiro Alto, Eiredo-Cabril, 5470-013 Cabril [tel/fax 253 659860; outeiro_alto@hotmail.com; www.geocities.com/campingouteiroalto]** Fr N103 turn N dir Ferral, Paradela & Cabril, site sp. App poss difficult. Med, terr, pt shd; wc; shwrs inc; el pnts (12A) €1.50; lndtte; shop 800m; rest 500m; snacks; bar; BBQ; fishing; boating; entmnt; TV rm; dogs €1; Eng spkn; quiet. "A white knuckle app; spectacular scenery; sm area for tourers." 1 Mar-30 Oct. € 13.00 2006*

⊞ **GOIS** *C2* (1km S Rural) *40.15400, -8.11409* **Camp Municipal do Castelo, Castelo, 3330-309 Góis [235 778585; fax 235 770129; reservas@goistur.com; www.goistur.com]** Fr Coimbra take N17/N2 E to Góis, site sp to W of rv. Steep access rd. Med, terr, shd; wc (some cont); chem disp; baby facs; shwrs inc; el pnts (4-16A) €1.60-2.30; gas; lndry rm; shop; tradsmn; rest 150m; snacks; bar; BBQ; playgrnd; sand beach 15km; rv sw 500m; fishing; canoeing; tennis; cycle hire; entmnt; some chalets; dogs €1.40; bus 100m; poss cr; Eng spkn; adv bkg; quiet; red low ssn/CCI. "Quiet, clean site in beautiful wooded countryside; ltd pitches for lge o'fits; helpful owners; highly rec." ♦ € 12.40 2007*

⊞ **GOUVEIA** *C2* (6km NE Rural) *40.52083, -7.54149* **Camping Quinta das Cegonhas, Nabaínhos, 6290-122 Melo [tel/fax 238 745886; cegonhas@cegonhas.com; www.cegonhas.com]** Turn S at 114km post on N17 Seia-Celorico da Beira. Site sp thro Melo vill. Sm, pt shd; wc; chem disp; mv service pnt; shwrs; el pnts (4A) €2.20; lndtte; shop 300m; rest; snacks; bar; playgrnd; pool; entmnt; TV; dogs €0.75; bus 400m; Eng spkn; adv bkg; quiet; red low stay/low ssn; CCI. "Vg, well-run, busy site in grounds of vill manor house; friendly Dutch owners; beautiful location conv Torre & Serra da Estrella; gd walks; highly rec." ♦ € 12.60 2008*

⊞ **GUARDA** *C2* (500m SW Urban) *40.53861, -7.27944* **Camp Municipal da Guarda, Avda do Estádio Municipal, 6300-705 Guarda [271 221200; fax 271 210025]** Exit A23 junc 35 onto N18 to Guarda. Foll sp cent & sports centre. Site adj sports cent off rndabt. Med, hdstg, sl, shd; wc (some cont, own san rec); chem disp (wc); shwrs inc; el pnts (15A) €1.40; gas; lndry rm; shop; rest, snacks, bar high ssn; BBQ; playgrnd; pool 2km; TV; phone; bus adj; Eng spkn; poss noise fr rd & nrby nightclub; CCI. "Access to some pitches diff for c'vans, OK for m'vans; poss run down facs & site poss neglected low/mid ssn; walking dist to interesting town - highest in Portugal & poss v cold at night; music festival 1st week Sep." ♦ € 10.05 2007*

Portugal

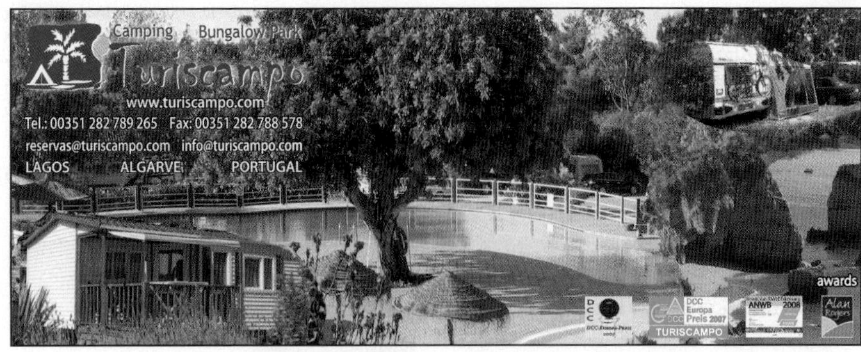

GUIMARAES *B1* (6km SE Rural) *41.42833, -8.26861* **Camping Parque da Penha, Penha-Costa, 4800-026 Guimarães [tel/fax 253 515912 or 253 515085; geral@turipenha.pt; www.turipenha.pt]** Take N101 SE fr Guimarães sp Felgueiras. Turn R at sp for Nascente/Penha. Site sp. Lge, hdstg, pt sl, terr, shd; wc; shwrs inc; el pnts (6A) €1.80; gas; shop; rest adj; snacks; bar; playgrnd; pool; fishing; no statics; no dogs; phone; bus 200m, teleferic (cable car) 200m; car wash; poss cr; Eng spkn; adv bkg; poss noisy; CCI. "Excel staff; gd san facs; lower terrs not suitable lge o'fits; densely wooded hilltop site; conv Guimarães World Heritage site." ♦ 1 Apr-30 Sep. € 10.40 2008*

⊞ **IDANHA A NOVA** *C2* (8km NE Rural) *39.95027, -7.18777* **Camping ORBITUR, N354-1, Km 8, Barragem de Idanha-a-Nova, 6060 Idanha-a-Nova [277 202793; fax 277 202945; info@orbitur.pt; www.orbitur.com]** Exit IP2 at junc 25 sp Lardosa & foll sp Idanha-a-Nova on N18, then N233, N353. Thro Idanha & cross Rv Ponsul onto N354 to site. Avoid rte fr Castelo Branco via Ladoeiro as rd narr, steep & winding in places. V lge, mkd pitch, hdstg, terr, shd; wc; chem disp; mv service pnt; shwrs inc; el pnts (6A) €3-4; gas; lndtte; shop; tradsmn; rest; snacks; bar; BBQ; playgrnd; htd pool; lake sw, fishing; watersports 150m; tennis; games rm; entmnt; wifi; cab/sat TV; 10% statics; dogs €1.50; phone; car wash; Eng spkn; adv bkg; quiet; red long stay/low ssn/snr citizens; ccard acc. "Uphill to town & supmkts; hot water to shwrs only; pitches poss diff - a mover req; excel." ♦ € 20.70 2009*

ILHAVO see Aveiro *B2*

⊞ **LAGOS** *B4* (1km SW Urban/Coastal) *37.09469, -8.67218* **Parque de Campismo da Trinidade, Rossio da Trindade, 8601-908 Lagos [282 763893; fax 282 762885; cfelagos@clix.pt; www.campingtrindade.com]** Fr Faro on N125 app Lagos, foll sp for Centro; drive 1.5km along front past BP stn, up hill to traff lts; turn L & foll Campismo sp to L. Cont to traff island & foll to bottom of hill, ent on R. Site adj football stadium Sm, hdstg, terr, pt shd; wc; own san facs; chem disp; shwrs inc; el pnts (12A) €3.50; gas; lndtte; shop; rest; snacks; bar; playgrnd; pool 500m; sand beach 500m; phone; poss cr; Eng spkn; rd noise; ccard acc; red long stay; CCI. "Gd beaches & cliff walks; conv walk into Lagos." ♦ € 16.70 2007*

⊞ **LAGOS** *B4* (4km W Rural/Coastal) *37.10095, -8.73220* **Camping Turiscampo, N125 Espiche, 8600-109 Luz-Lagos [282 789265; fax 282 788578; info@turiscampo.com or reservas@turiscampo.com; www.turiscampo.com]** Exit A22/IC4 junc 1 to Lagos then N125 fr Lagos dir Sagres, site 3km on R. Lge, hdg/mkd pitch, some hdstg, pt sl, terr, shd; htd wc; chem disp; mv service pnt; baby facs; shwrs inc; el pnts (6-10A) €3.20-5; gas; lndtte; supmkt; tradsmn; rest; snacks; bar; playgrnd; pool; paddling pool; solarium; sand beach 2km; fishing 2.5km; cycle hire; games rm; games area; entmnt; wifi; TV rm; 20% statics; dogs €1.50; phone; bus 100m; Eng spkn; adv bkg; quiet; ccard acc; red long stay/low ssn/CCI. "Superb, busy site refurbished to high standards; v popular for long winter stays; winter rallies; gd san facs; helpful staff; lovely vill, beach & views; varied & interesting area, Luz worth visit." ♦ € 26.15 (CChq acc) 2009*

See advertisement

⊞ **LAGOS** *B4* (7km W Coastal/Urban) *37.10111, -8.71777* **Camping ORBITUR-Valverde, Estrada da Praia da Luz, Valverde, 8600-148 Lagos [214 857400; fax 214 857410; fernanda.botelho@orbitur.pt; www.orbitur.com]** Foll coast rd N125 fr Lagos to Sagres for 3km. Turn L at traff lts sp Luz, site 2km on R, well sp. V lge, hdg/mkd pitch, hdstg, terr, pt shd; wc; chem disp; mv service pnt; baby facs; shwrs inc; el pnts (6A) €3-4; gas; lndtte; supmkt; tradsmn; rest; snacks; bar; BBQ: playgrnd; 2 pools; sand beach 3km; tennis; sports facs; games area; games rm; entmnt; wifi; cab/sat TV; some statics; dogs €1.50; bus; car wash; Eng spkn; adv bkg; quiet; ccard acc; red low ssn/long stay/snr citizens/Orbitur card; CCI. "Well-run site; friendly staff; gd, clean san facs; access to pitches tight due trees; poss muddy in wet weather; spacious low ssn; narr, busy rd to beach/town; lovely beach & town." ♦ € 29.50 ABS - E09 2009*

⊞ **LAMAS DE MOURO** *C1* (1km S Rural) *42.04166, -8.20833* **Camping Lamas de Mouro, 4960-170 Lamas de Mouro [251 465129; info@versana.pt; www.versana.pt]** Fr N202 at Melgaco foll sp Peneda National Park, site sp in Lamas de Mouro. Med, pt shd; wc; chem disp; mv service pnt; shwrs inc; el pnts (10A) €2.30; lndry rm; shop; tradsmn; rest; snacks; bar; cooking facs; playgrnd; natural pool; phone; bus 1km; poss cr; quiet; CCI. "Ideal for walking in National Park." € 14.80 2007*

LAVRA see Porto *B1*

⊞ **LISBOA** *B3* (10km SW Coastal) *38.65111, -9.23777* **Camping ORBITUR-Costa de Caparica, Ave Afonso de Albuquerque, Quinta de S. António, 2825-450 Costa de Caparica [212 901366 or 903894; fax 212 900661; info@orbitur.pt; www.orbitur.com]** Take A2/IP7 S fr Lisbon; after Rv Tagus bdge turn W to Costa de Caparica. At end of rd turn N twd Trafaria, & site on L. Well sp fr a'strada. Lge, hdg/mkd pitch, terr, shd; wc; chem disp; mv service pnt; shwrs inc; el pnts (6A) €3; gas; lndtte; shop; tradsmn; rest; snacks; bar; BBQ; playgrnd; pool 800m; sand beach 1km; fishing; tennis; games rm; entmnt; wifi; TV; 25% statics; dogs €1.50; phone; car wash; bus to Lisbon; Eng spkn; adv bkg; some rd noise; ccard acc; red low ssn/long stay/snr citizens/Orbitur card; CCI. "Site fine but san facs need refurb; beach adequate, app on foot; heavy traff into city; rec use free parking at Monument to the Discoveries & tram to city cent; ferry to Belém; ltd facs low ssn; pleasant, helpful staff." ♦ € 25.60 2009*

⊞ **LISBOA** *B3* (5km NW Urban) *38.72472, -9.20805* **Parque Municipal de Campismo de Monsanto, Estrada da Circunvalação, 1400-061 Lisboa [217 623100; fax 217 623105; info@lisboacamping.com; www.lisboacamping.com]** Fr W on A5 foll sp Parque Florestal de Monsanto/Buraca. Fr S on A2, cross toll bdge & foll sp for Sintra; join expressway, foll up hill; site well sp; stay in RH lane. Fr N on A1 pass airport, take Benfica exit & foll sp under m'way to site. Site sp fr all major rds. Avoid rush hours! V lge, mkd pitch, hdstg, pt sl, terr, pt shd; htd wc (cont); chem disp; mv service pnt; 80% serviced pitches; baby facs; fam bthrm; shwrs inc; el pnts (6-16A) inc; gas; lndtte; shop; tradsmn; rest; snacks; bar; playgrnd; pool; sand beach 10km; tennis; entmnt; bank; post office; car wash; TV rm; 5% statics; dogs free; frequent bus to city; rlwy station 3km; poss cr; Eng spkn; adv bkg; some rd noise; red low ssn; ccard acc; red CCI. "Well laid-out, spacious, guarded site in trees; ltd mv service pnt; take care hygiene at chem disp/clean water tap; facs poss badly maintained & stretched when site full; friendly, helpful staff; in high ssn some o'fits placed on sloping forest area (quiet); few pitches take awning; excel excursions booked at tourist office on site." ♦ € 26.00 2009*

LOURICAL *B2* (4km SW Rural) *39.99149, -8.78880* **Campismo O Tamanco, Rua do Louriçal, Casas Brancas, 3105-158 Louriçal [tel/fax 236 952551; campismo.o.tamanco@mail.telepac.pt; www.campismo-o-tamanco.com]** S on N109 fr Figuera da Foz S twds Leiria foll sp at rndabt Matos do Corrico onto N342 to Louriçal. Site 800m on L. Med, hdg/mkd pitch, pt shd; wc; chem disp; shwrs inc; el pnts inc (6-16A) €2.25-3.50; gas; lndtte; shop; tradsmn; rest; snacks; bar; pool; sand beach 12km; lake sw adj; cycle hire; entmnt; TV; dogs €0.60; bus 500m; poss cr; Eng spkn; adv bkg; rd noise; red low ssn/low stay; CCI. "Excel; friendly Dutch owners; chickens & ducks roaming site; superb mkt on Sun at Louriçal; a bit of real Portugal; gd touring base." 1 Feb-31 Oct. € 13.15 2007*

⊞ **LUSO** *B2* (1.5km S Rural) *40.38222, -8.38583* **Camping Luso, N336, Pampilhosa, Quinta do Vale do Jorge, 3050-246 Luso [231 930916; fax 231 930917; info@orbitur.pt]** S fr Luso on N336, sp. Lge, hdstg, pt sl, pt shd; wc; chem disp; mv service pnt; shwrs inc; el pnts (5-15A) €2.50; gas; lndtte; shop; tradsmn; rest; snacks; bar; playgrnd; pool 1km; sand beach 35km; tennis; games rm; TV rm; some statics; dogs €1.30; car wash; adv bkg; Eng spkn; quiet; red low ssn/long stay/snr citizens; ccard acc; CCI. "Excel site in wooded valley; vg san facs; some sm pitches unsuitable for c'vans + awnings; internet in vill; sh walk to interesting spa town; conv Coimbra." ♦ € 17.50 2007*

MARTINCHEL see Tomar *B2*

MEDAS GONDOMAR see Porto *B1*

MELO see Gouveia *C2*

⊞ **MIRA** *B2* (3km W Rural) *40.44728, -8.75723* **Camping Vila Caia, Lagoa de Mira, 3070-176 Mira [231 451524; fax 231 451861; vlcaia@portugalmail.com; www.vilacaia.com]** S fr Aveiro on N109 for 29km; at Mira take N334 for 5km. Site sp on R 500m W of Lagoa de Mira. Lge, hdstg, pt shd; wc (some cont); chem disp; mv service pnt; shwrs inc; el pnts (4A) €2.50; gas; lndtte; shop; rest; snacks; bar; playgrnd; pool; paddling pool; sand beach 3km; fishing; tennis; cycle hire; entmnt; TV; some statics; no dogs; phone; bus adj; site clsd Dec; Eng spkn; no adv bkg; quiet, but poss noisy entmnt high ssn; ccard acc; red low ssn; CCI. "Gd site." ♦ € 16.10 2006*

MIRA *B2* (7km NW Coastal/Urban) *40.44472, -8.79888* **Camping ORBITUR-Mira, E Florestal 1, Km 2, Dunas de Mira, 3070-792 Praia de Mira [231 471234; fax 231 472047; info@orbitur.pt; www.orbitur.com]** Fr N109 in Mira turn W to Praia de Mira, foll site sp. Lge, hdg pitch, hdstg, shd; wc; chem disp; mv service pnt; shwrs inc; el pnts (5-15A) €3-4 (poss rev pol); gas; lndtte; shop (in ssn); tradsmn; rest, snacks, bar high ssn; playgrnd; pool 7km; sandy, surfing beach & dunes 800m; entmnt; fishing; boating; TV rm; 5% statics; dogs €1.50; phone; site clsd Dec; Eng spkn; adv bkg; poss noisy w/end; red low ssn/long stay/snr citizens; ccard acc; CCI. "Friendly, helpful staff; gd, clean, attractive site; excel surfing beach nr; suitable for cycling; nature reserve opp site." ♦ 1 Jan-10 Oct. € 24.00 2009*

MIRANDA DO DOURO *D1* (500m W Rural) *41.49861, -6.28444* **Campismo Municipal Santa Lúzia, Rua do Parque de Campismo, 5210-190 Miranda do Douro [273 431273 or 430020; fax 273 431075; mirdouro@mail.telepac.pt; www.cm-mdouro.pt]** Fr Spain on ZA324/N221, cross dam & thro town, site well sp. Do not enter walled town. Lge, pt sl, terr, pt shd; wc; chem disp; shwrs inc; el pnts (5A) €1.25; shop, rest & 1km; snacks, bar; playgrnd; pool 100m; phone; bus 500m; Eng spkn; quiet; CCI. "Simple, peaceful site; interesting ent into N Portugal; old walled town; spectacular rv gorge; boat trips." ♦ 1 Jun-30 Sep. € 9.50 2007*

Parque de Campismo da Quinta da Agueira
Tel. +351 279 340 230
Between the castle and
the mountain range...

⊞ **MIRANDELA** *C1* (4km N Rural) *41.50690, -7.19685* **Camping Três Rios Maravilha, 5370-555 Mirandela [tel/fax 278 263177; clube.ccm@oninet.pt]** Fr IP4 take Mirandela N exit twd town. Foll camping sp at 1st rndabt. At 2nd rndabt take 1st exit, site on L in approx 2km, adj Rv Tuela. Site well sp. Lge, mkd pitch, pt shd; wc (some cont); chem disp; shwrs inc; el pnts (12-16A) €2 (poss rev pol); gas; Indtte; tradsmn; rest; snacks; bar; playgrnd; pool; canoeing; fishing; tennis; entmnt; TV; 60% statics; dogs; phone; bus, train 2km; Eng spkn; poss cr & noisy; red low ssn/CCI. "V pleasant situation by rv; busy site but v quiet low ssn; friendly owner; attractive pool." ♦ € 14.00 2007*

MOGADOURO *D1* (1km S Rural) *41.33527, -6.71861* **Parque de Campismo da Quinta da Agueira, Complexo Desportivo, 5200-244 Mogadouro [279 340230 or 936-989202 (mob); fax 279 341874; cameramogadouro@mail.telepac.pt]** Fr Miranda do Douro on N221 or fr Bragança on IP2 to Macedo then N216 to Mogadouro. Site sp adj sports complex. Lge, shd; wc; chem disp; mv service pnt; shwrs inc; el pnts (15A) €2; gas; Indry rm; shop 1km; rest 200m; snacks; bar; BBQ; playgrnd; pool adj; waterslide; beach 15km; tennis; car wash; entmnt; internet; TV; dogs €1.50; phone; bus 300m; Eng spkn; adv bkg; quiet. "In lovely area; gd touring base." ♦ 1 Apr-30 Sep. € 11.50 2009*

See advertisement above

MONCARAPACHO see Olhao *C4*

⊞ **MONCHIQUE** *B4* (6km S Rural) **Parque Rural Caldas de Monchique, Barracão 190, 8550-213 Monchique [282 911502; fax 282 911503; valedacarrasqueira@sapo.pt; www.valedacarrasqueira.com]** Fr S exit A22 N onto N266, site sp on R in 11km. Fr N on N266 dir Portimão, thru Monchique, site on L. Well sp. M'vans only. Sm, mkd pitch, hdstg, unshd; wc; chem disp; mv waste; all serviced pitches; shwrs inc; el pnts (16A) inc; Indtte; bar; BBQ; pool; dogs; no adv bkg; Eng spkn; quiet. "Excel, peaceful, scenic, clean site; excel san facs; helpful staff; poss taking c'vans in future." € 15.00 2006*

⊞ **MONTARGIL** *B3* (5km N Rural) *39.10083, -8.14472* **Camping ORBITUR, N2, 7425-017 Montargil [242 901207; fax 242 901220; info@orbitur.pt; www.orbitur.com]** Fr N251 Coruche to Vimiero rd, turn N on N2, over dam at Barragem de Montargil. Fr Ponte de Sor S on N2 until 3km fr Montargil. Site clearly sp bet rd & lake. Med, mkd pitch, hdstg, terr, pt shd; wc; chem disp; mv service pnt; shwrs inc; el pnts (6-10A) €3-4; gas; Indtte; shop & 3km; tradsmn; rest; snacks; bar; playgrnd; pool; rv beach adj; boating; watersports; fishing; tennis; games rm; entmnt; wifi; cab/sat TV; 60% statics; dogs €1.50; phone; car wash; Eng spkn; adv bkg; some rd noise; ccard acc; red low ssn/long stay/snr citizens; CCI. "Friendly site in beautiful area." ♦ € 24.00 2009*

⊞ **NAZARE** *B2* (2km N Rural) *39.62036, -9.05630* **Camping Vale Paraíso, N242, 2450-138 Nazaré [262 561800; fax 262 561900; info@valeparaiso.com; www.valeparaiso.com]** Site thro pine reserve on N242 fr Nazaré to Leiria. V lge, mkd pitch, hdstg, terr, shd; wc (some cont); chem disp; mv service pnt; baby facs; shwrs inc; el pnts (4-10A) €2.50; gas; Indtte; supmkt; rest; snacks & takeaway; bar; playgrnd; 2 pools; sand beach 2km; lake 1km; fishing; games area; games rm; cycle hire; internet; TV; 20% statics; dogs €2; bus; site clsd 20-24 Dec; Eng spkn; adv bkg; quiet; ccard acc; red low ssn/long stay; CCI. "Gd, clean site; gd security; pitches vary in size & price, & divided by concrete walls, poss not suitable lge o'fits." ♦ € 17.50 (CChq acc) 2007*

NAZARE *B2* (2km E Rural) *39.59777, -9.05611* **Camping ORBITUR-Valado, Rua dos Combatentes do Ultramar 2, EN8, Km 5, Valado, 2450-148 Nazaré-Alcobaca [262 561111; fax 262 561137; info@orbitur.pt; www.orbitur.com]** Site on N of rd to Alcobaça & Valado (N8-4), opp Monte de São Bartolomeu. Lge, mkd pitch, terr, sl, shd; wc; chem disp; mv service pnt; shwrs inc; el pnts (6A) €3; gas; Indtte; shop & 2km; tradsmn;rest; snacks; bar; BBQ; playgrnd; pool 3km; sand beach 1.8km; tennis; wifi; TV rm; 10% statics; dogs €1.50; phone; car wash; Eng spkn; adv bkg; red low ssn/long stay/snr citizens; ccard acc. "Pleasant site in pine trees; v soft sand - tractor avail; helpful manager; visits to Fátima, Alcobaça, Balhala rec." ♦ 1 Jan-10 Oct. € 20.70 2009*

⊞ **ODECEIXE** *B4* (1.5km NE Rural) *37.43826, -8.75596* **Camping São Miguel, 7630-592 São Miguel [282 947145; fax 282 947245; camping.sao.miguel@mail.telepac.pt; www.campingsaomiguel.com]** Fr N120 site ent 1.5km NE of Odeceixe. V lge, pt sl, shd; wc; chem disp; mv service pnt; shwrs inc; el pnts (6A) €2.75; gas; Indtte; shop, rest, snacks bar high ssn; BBQ; playgrnd; pool; paddling pool; sand beach 5km; tennis; games rm; TV; bus 500m; no dogs; phone; site clsd midnight-0800; adv bkg; quiet; red low ssn/long stay. "Gd, clean facs." ♦ € 25.50 2007*

⊞ **ODEMIRA** *B4* (7km W Rural) *37.60422, -8.73142* **Zmar Eco Camping Resort, Herdade A-de-Mateus, N393/1, San Salvador, 7630 Odemira [707 200626; info@zmar.eu; www.zmar.eu]** Fr S on N120 via Aljezur, take N393 dir Zambujeira do Mar & foll sp to site. Fr N on A2, then IC33 dir Sines. Fr Sines take IC4 to Cercal then foll sp dir Zambujeira do Mar on N393, site sp. Med, mkd pitch, hdstg, pt shd; wc; chem disp; mv service pnt; baby facs; fam bthrm; sauna; shwrs inc; private bthrms avail; el pnts (10A) inc; Indtte (inc dryer); shop; rest; snacks; bar; 2 pools (1 htd, covrd); paddling pool; sand beach 7km; tennis; cycle hire; games area; wellness cent; fitness rm; internet; entmnt; TV rm; 17% statics; adv bkg; dogs €2.50; quiet; red low ssn. "Superb new site (eco resort) with excel facs; in national park; vg touring base." ♦ € 50.00 (4 persons) (CChq acc) 2009*

See advertisement below

⊞ **ODIVELAS** *B3* (3km NE Rural) *38.18361, -8.10361* **Camping Markádia, Barragem de Odivelas, 7920-999 Alvito [284 763141; fax 284 763102; markadia@hotmail.com]** Fr Ferreira do Alentejo on N2 N twd Torrão. After Odivelas turn R onto N257 twd Alvito & turn R twd Barragem de Odivels. Site in 7km, clearly sp. Med, hdstg, pt sl, pt shd; wc; chem disp; mv service pnt; shwrs inc; el pnts (16A) €2.60; gas; Indtte; shop; tradsmn; rest; snacks; bar; playgrnd; pool 50m; sand beach, lake sw 500m; boating; fishing; horseriding; tennis; no dogs Jul-Aug; phone; car wash; adv bkg; v quiet; red low ssn/CCI. "Exceptionally beautiful, superb, secluded site on banks of reservoir; spacious pitches; site lighting low but san facs well lit; excel walking, cycling, birdwatching." ♦ € 20.80 2009*

⊞ **OLHAO** *C4* (10km NE Rural) **Camping Caravanas Algarve, Sitio da Cabeça Moncarapacho, 8700-618 Moncarapacho [289 791669]** Exit IP1/A22 sp Moncarapacho. In 2km turn L sp Fuzeta. At traff lts turn L & immed L opp supmkt in 1km. Turn R at site sp. Site on L. Sm, hdstg, pt sl, unshd; wc; chem disp; shwrs inc; el pnts (6A) inc; Indtte; shop, rest, snacks, bar 1.5km; sand beach 4km; 10% statics; dogs; poss cr; Eng spkn; adv bkg; quiet; 10% red CCI. "Situated on a farm in orange groves; pitches ltd in wet conditions; gd, modern san facs; gd security; Spanish border 35km; National Park Ria Formosa 4km." € 10.00 2008*

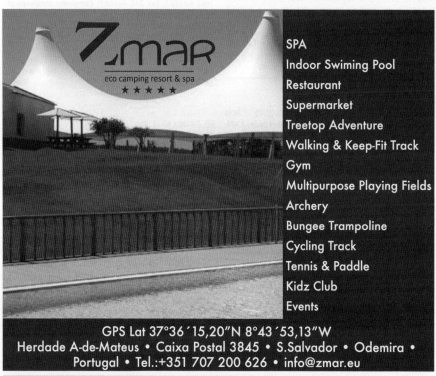

Portugal

⊞ **OLHAO** *C4* (10km NE Rural) **Campismo Casa Rosa, 8700 Moncarapacho [289 794400; fax 289 792952; casarosa@sapo.pt; www.casarosa.com.pt]** Fr A22 (IP1) E twd Spain, leave at exit 15 Olhão/Moncarapacho. At rndabt take 2nd exit dir Moncarapacho. Cont past sp Moncarapacho Centro direction Olhão. In 1km at Lagoão, on L is Café Da Lagoão with its orange awning. Just past café is sp for Casa Rosa. Foll sp. Sm, hdstg, terr, unshd; htd wc; chem disp; shwrs inc; el pnts (6A) inc; gas 3km; lndtte; rest; pool; shgl beach 6km; rv sw 6km; sat TV; no dogs; Eng spkn; adv bkg; noise fr construction yard adj; CCI. "Excel CL-type site adj holiday apartments; adults only; helpful, friendly, Norwegian owners; evening meals avail; ideal for touring E Algarve; conv Spanish border; rec." ♦ € 13.00 2009*

⊞ **OLHAO** *C4* (1.5km E Rural) *37.03527, -7.82250* **Camping Olhão, Pinheiros do Marim, 8700-912 Olhão [289 700300; fax 289 700390 or 700391; parque.campismo@sbsi.pt; www.sbsi.pt]** Turn S twd coast fr N125 1.5km E of Olhão by filling stn. Clearly sp on S side of N125, adj Ria Formosa National Park. V lge, hdg/mkd pitch, pt sl, shd; wc; chem disp; mv service pnt; shwrs inc; el pnts (6A) €1.80; gas; lndtte inc dryers; supmkt; tradsmn; rest; bar; playgrnd; pool; paddling pool; beach 1.5km; tennis; games rm; games area; cycle hire; horseriding 1km; internet; TV; 75% statics; dogs €1.50; phone; bus adj; rlwy station 1.5km; sep car park for some pitches; car wash; security guard; Eng spkn; adv bkg; some rlwy noise; ccard acc; red long stay/low ssn; CCI. "Pleasant, helpful staff; excel pool; gd san facs; v popular long stay low ssn; many sm sandy pitches, some diff access for lge o'fits; gd for cycling, bird-watching; ferry to islands." ♦ € 19.10 2009*

See advertisement

⊞ **OLHAO** *C4* (9km E Coastal/Urban) *37.05277, -7.7450* **Parque Campismo de Fuzeta, 2 Rua do Liberdade, 8700-019 Fuzeta [289 793459; fax 289 794034; camping@jf-fuseta.pt]** Fr N125 Olhão-Tavira rd, turn S at traff lts at Alfandanga sp Fuzeta & foll sp to site. Lge, some hdstg, pt shd; wc; chem disp; shwrs €0.25; el pnts (6A) inc; gas; lndtte; shop & 1km; rest adj; snacks; bar; BBQ; playgrnd adj; sand beach adj; 5% statics; dogs; phone; train 500m; Eng spkn; no adv bkg; noise fr rd & adj bars; red long stay. "Pleasant staff; popular with long-stay m'vanners; haphazard pitching; elec cables run across site rds; poss flooding after heavy rain; areas of soft sand; clean san facs; gd security; attractive area." ♦ € 14.50 2009*

⊞ **OLIVEIRA DE AZEMEIS** *B2* (1.5km E Rural) *40.8436, -8.4664* **Camping La Salette, 3720-222 Oliveira de Azeméis [256 674373]** Fr N1 turn E onto N224 to Vale de Cambra, foll sp Parque La Salette. Med, shd; wc; shwrs €0.75; el pnts (6A) €0.75 (poss rev pol); gas; lndtte; shop 100m; rest, snacks, bar adj; BBQ; playgrnd 300m; pool adj; TV; phone; bus 200m; quiet. "Picturesque area; friendly site; clean facs; gd NH." ♦ € 8.50 2008*

⊞ **OLIVEIRA DO HOSPITAL** *C2* (9km SE Rural) *40.34647, -7.80747* **Parque de São Gião, 3400-570 São Gião [238 691154; fax 238 692451]** Fr N17 Guarda-Coimbra rd turn S almost opp N230 rd to Oliveira do Hospital, dir Sandomil. Site on R in about 3km over rv bdge. Lge, shd; wc; chem disp; shwrs; el pnts (6A) €1.50; gas; lndtte; shop; rest; snacks; bar; BBQ; playgrnd; pool 7km; fishing; phone; 50% statics; no dogs; bus adj; quiet. "Facs basic but clean; working water mill; app/exit long, steep, narr, lane." € 10.50 2006*

⊞ **OLIVEIRA DO HOSPITAL** *C2* (15km S Rural) *40.30708, -7.87151* **Parque de Campismo Ponte Das Três Entradas, Santa Ovaia, 3400-591 Avô [238 670050; fax 238 670055; ponte3entradas@mail.telepac.pt]** On N17 Guarda-Coimbra rd after town of Oliveira do Hospital turn S at Pousada sp onto N230. Site sp by Rv Alva 4km bef Avô. Med, pt shd; wc; shwrs inc; el pnts (4A) €2.50; gas; lndtte; shop; rest; snacks; bar; BBQ; playgrnd; fishing; tennis; games area; cycle hire; entmnt; TV; some statics; phone; quiet; ccard acc; red low ssn/long stay; CCI. "Pretty site in mountains." ♦ € 9.00 2006*

⊞ **OLIVEIRA DO HOSPITAL** *C2* (10km NW Rural) *40.40550, -7.93100* **Camping Quinta das Oliveiras (Naturist), Rua de Estrada Nova, Andorinha, 3405-498 Travanca de Lagos [962 621287; fax 235 466007; campismo.nat@sapo.pt; www.quinta-das-oliveiras.com]** Fr Oliveira do Hospital foll N230 & N1314 to Travanca de Lagos. Then take N502 twd Midões. After 2km turn R on N1313 to Andorinha. Site on R 1.5km after Andorinha. Sm, pt sl, terr, pt shd; wc; chem disp; shwrs inc; el pnts (6A) €3.50; tradsmn; BBQ; playgrnd; pool; dogs €1.50; poss cr; Eng spkn; adv bkg; quiet; INF card. € 16.15 2006*

⊞ **ORTIGA** *C3* (1.5km SE Rural) *39.48277, -8.00305* **Parque Campismo de Ortiga, Estrada da Barragem, 6120-525 Ortiga [241 573464; fax 241 573482; campismo@cm-macao.pt; www.cm-macao.pt]** Exit A23/IP6 junc 12 S to Ortiga. Thro Ortiga & foll site sp for 1.5km. Site beside dam. Sm, mkd pitch, hdstg, terr, pt shd; wc; chem disp; shwrs inc; el pnts (10A) €1.50; lndtte; shop 1km; rest, snacks, bar adj; BBQ; playgrnd; lake sw 100m; watersports; TV; 50% statics; dogs free; bus 1.5km; poss cr; Eng spkn; quiet; CCI. "Vg." ♦ € 10.90 2008*

⊞ **OURIQUE** *B4* (10km S Rural) *37.5675, -8.2644* **Camping Serro da Bica, Horta da Bica, Aldeia de Palheiros, 7670-202 Ourique [tel/fax 286 516750; info@serrodabica.com; www.serrodabica.com]** Fr N of IC1 turn R at km post 679.4 & foll sp to site. Fr S go past km post & do U-turn at turn off for Castro da Cola, then as above. Sm, terr, pt shd; wc; chem disp; shwrs inc; el pnts (10A) €2.50; gas; lndtte; tradsmn; bar; rv nrby; wifi; no statics; bus 800m; Eng spkn; adv bkg; quiet; red long stay; CCI. "Pretty site; gd walking; excel." € 13.00 2008*

PENACOVA *B2* (3km N Rural) *40.27916, -8.26805* **Camp Municipal de Vila Nova, Rua dos Barqueiros, Vila Nova, 3360-204 Penacova [239 477946; fax 239 474857; penaparque2@iol.pt]** IP3 fr Coimbra, exit junc 11, cross Rv Mondego N of Penacova & foll to sp to Vila Nova & site. Med, pt shd; wc; shwrs inc; el pnts (6A) €1; shop 50m; rest 150m; snacks; bar; BBQ; playgrnd; rv sw 200m; fishing; cycle hire; TV; no dogs; phone; bus 150m; Eng spkn; red CCI. "Open, attractive site." 1 Apr-30 Sep. € 8.10 2006*

PENACOVA *B2* (1km S Rural) *40.26666, -8.27833* **Camping Penacova, Estrada da Carvoeira, 3360 Penacova [tel/fax 239 477464; penacova@fcmportugal.com; www.fcmportugal.com]** On N2 S of Penacova on E bank of rv. Fairly steep app needing care. Lge, pt shd; wc; chem disp; shwrs inc; el pnts (6A) €3; gas 500m; shop; rest/snacks; bar; playgrnd; fishing; canoeing; entmnt; 70% statics; dogs €0.60; phone; bus 1km; quiet but poss noisy w/end; red low ssn; CCI. "Impeccable; lovely site; friendly helpful owner; pretty, rural area; heavily wooded; strenuous trek up to Penacova." ♦ 13 Jan-11 Nov. € 15.00 2007*

PENELA *B2* (500m SE Rural) *40.02501, -8.38900* **Parque Municipal de Campismo de Panela, Rua de Coimbra, 3230-284 Penela [239 569256; fax 239 569400]** Fr Coimbra S on IC2, L at Condeixa a Nova, IC3 dir Penela. Thro vill foll sp to site. Sm, hstg, pt sl, terr, pt shd; wc; chem disp; shwrs €0.50; el pnts (6A) €0.50; shop, rest, snacks, bar 200m pool 500m; some statics; no dogs; bus adj; some traff noise; CCI. "Attractive sm town; restful, clean, well-maintained site." ♦ 1 Jun-30 Sep. € 4.50 2006*

⊞ **PENICHE** *B3* (3km E Coastal) *39.35388, -9.36111* **Camp Municipal de Peniche, Avda Monsenhor M Bastos, 2520-206 Peniche [262 789696; fax 262 789529; campismo-peniche@sapo.pt; www.cm-peniche.pt]** Site 2km E fr Lourinha after N114 (fr Obidos) joins N247; rd crosses bdge & site on R. V lge, terr, pt shd; wc; shwrs inc; el pnts (4A) €1.35; gas; lndtte; shop; rest; bar; playgrnd; pool adj; beach 200m; fishing; tennis; TV; 40% statics; phone; bus 500m; red low ssn; v quiet; ccard acc. "Friendly staff; interesting area; gd NH." ♦ € 11.20 2008*

⊞ **PENICHE** *B3* (1.5km NW Urban/Coastal) *39.36944, -9.39194* **Camping Peniche Praia, Estrada Marginal Norte, 2520 Peniche [262 783460; fax 262 789447; penichepraia@hotmail.com; www.penichepraia.pt]** Travel S on IP6 then take N114 sp Peniche; fr Lisbon N on N247 then N114 sp Peniche. Site on R on N114 1km bef Peniche. Med, hdg/mkd pitch, hdstg, unshd; wc; chem disp; mv service pnt; shwrs inc; el pnts (6A) inc; lndtte; shop 1.5km; tradsmn; rest, snacks, bar high ssn; BBQ; playgrnd; covrd pool; paddling pool; sand beach 1.5km; games rm; cycle hire; internet; entmnt; TV; 30% statics; phone; bus 2km; car wash; poss cr; Eng spkn; adv bkg rec; red long stay/low ssn/CCI. "Vg site in lovely location; some sm pitches; rec, espec low ssn." € 14.75 2008*

POCO REDONDO see Tomar *B2*

PONTE DA BARCA *B1* (4km N Rural) *41.90199, -8.31510* **Camping Travança, Lugar de Bouças Donas, Cabana Maior, 4970-094 Arcos de Valdevez [258 526105 or 258 452280; fax 258 452450; aderepg@mail.telepac.pt; www.adere-pg.pt]** Fr Arcos de Valdevez on N202 twd Mezio, turn L sp Bouças Donas. Foll sp National Park & site. Sm, hdstg, pt shd; wc (some cont); baby facs; showrs inc; el pnts (16A) €1.20; shop; tradsmn; bar; BBQ; playgrnd; TV rm; no statics; dogs €0.60; phone; no adv bkg; quiet. "In National Park high up in glorious country; vg walking." 1 Jul-31 Aug. € 12.40 2007*

PONTE DA BARCA *B1* (11km E Rural) *41.82376, -8.31723* **Camping Entre-Ambos-os-Rios, Lugar da Igreja, Entre-Ambos-os-Rios, 4980-613 Ponte da Barca [258 588361; fax 258 452450; aderepg@mail.telepac.pt; www.adere-pg.pt]** N203 E fr Ponte da Barca, pass ent sp for vill. Site sp N twd Rv Lima, after 1st bdge. Lge, pt sl, shd; wc; shwrs inc; el pnts (12A) €1.20; gas; lndry rm; shop, rest 300m; snacks; bar; playgrnd; canoeing; fishing; entmnt; TV; dogs €0.60; phone; bus 100m; adv bkg; CCI. "Beautiful, clean, well-run site in pine trees, well situated for National Park." 15 May-30 Sep. € 12.10 2009*

Portugal

⊞ **PORTIMAO** *B4* (3km SE Coastal) *37.11305, -8.51083* **Camping Ferragudo, 8400-280 Ferragudo [282 461121; fax 282 461355; geral@clubecampismolisboa.pt; www.clubecampismolisboa.pt]** Leave N125 at sp Ferraguda, turn L at traff lts at end of Parchal vill onto N539. Foll sp to site. V lge, terr, pt shd; cont wc; shwrs inc; el pnts (4-6A) inc; gas; lndry rm; shop; rest; snacks; bar; playgrnd; pool; sw & fishing 800m; entmnt; TV; no dogs; phone; bus 100m; v cr Jul/Aug; CCI. "Helpful staff; bus to Portimão at ent; shop/recep 1.5km fr pitches; unsuitable lge m'vans; housing bet site & beach." € 26.00 2009*

⊞ **PORTIMAO** *B4* (10km SW Urban) *37.13500, -8.59027* **Parque de Campismo da Dourada, 8500-053 Alvor [282 459178; fax 282 458002; campingdourada@hotmail.com]** Turn S at W end of N125 Portimão by-pass sp Alvor. Site on L in 4km bef ent town. V lge, pt sl, terr, shd; wc; chem disp; shwrs €0.50; el pnts (6A) €2.50; gas; lndtte; shop high ssn; rest; snacks; bar; playgrnd; pool; paddling pool; sand beach 1km; fishing; sports area; entmnt; TV rm; dogs €1.75; bus adj; poss noisy; red long stay/low ssn; CCI. "Friendly & helpful family-run site; office frequently unattended in winter & ltd facs; excel rest; lovely town & beaches." ♦ € 17.00 2008*

⊞ **PORTO** *B1* (11km N Coastal) *41.2675, -8.71972* **Camping ORBITUR-Angeiras, Rua de Angeiras, Matosinhos, 4455-039 Lavra [229 270571 or 270634; fax 229 271178; info@orbutur.pt; www.orbitur.com]** Fr ICI/A28 take turn-off sp Lavra, site sp at end of slip rd. Site in approx 3km - app rd potholed & cobbled. Lge, pt sl, shd; wc (some cont); chem disp; mv service pnt; shwrs inc; el pnts (6A) €3 (check earth); gas; lndtte; shop; tradsmn; rest; snacks; bar; BBQ; playgrnd; pool; sand beach 400m; tennis; fishing; games area; games rm; wifi; cab/sat TV; 70% statics; dogs €1.50; phone; bus to Porto at site ent; car wash; Eng spkn; adv bkg; red low ssn/long stay/snr citizens; ccard acc; CCI. "Friendly & helpful staff; clean, dated san facs; gd rest; gd pitches in trees at end of site but ltd space lge o'fits; fish & veg mkt in Matosinhos." ♦ € 25.60 2009*

⊞ **PORTO** *B1* (16km SE Rural) *41.03972, -8.42666* **Campidouro Parque de Medas, Lugar do Gavinho, 4515-397 Medas-Gondomar [224 760162; fax 224 769082; geral@campidouro.pt]** Take N12 dir Gondomar off A1. Almost immed take R exit sp Entre-os-Rios. At rndabt pick up N108 & in approx 14km. Sp for Medas on R, thro hamlet & forest for 3km & foll sp for site on R. Long, steep app. New concrete access/site rds. Lge, mkd pitch, hdstg, terr, pt shd; wc; chem disp; mv service pnt; serviced pitches; shwrs inc; el pnts (3-6A) €2.73 (poss rev pol); gas; lndtte; shop, rest (w/end only low ssn); bar; playgrnd; pool & paddling pool; rv sw, fishing, boating; tennis; games rm; entmnt; TV rm; 90% statics; phone; bus to Porto; poss cr; quiet; ccard acc; red CCI. "Beautiful site on Rv Douro; helpful owners; gd rest; clean facs; sm level area (poss cr by rv & pool) for tourers - poss noisy at night & waterlogged after heavy rain; bus to Porto rec as parking diff (ltd buses at w/end)." € 17.10 2008*

⊞ **PORTO** *B1* (6km SW Coastal) *41.11055, -8.66083* **Camping Marisol, Rua Alto das Chaquedas 82, Canidelo, 400-356 Vila Nova de Gaia [227 135942; fax 227 126351]** Fr Porto ring rd IC1 take N109 exit sp Espinho. In 1km take exit Madalena. Site sp on coast rd. Med, hdg pitch, pt shd; wc; chem disp; mv service pnt; shwrs inc; el pnts (6A) €2.50; gas; lndry rm; shop; rest; bar; BBQ; playgrnd; pool 800m; sand beach adj; games area; car wash; TV; 50% statics; dogs €1.80; bus 150m; poss cr; Eng spkn. "Conv for Porto; gd." ♦ € 13.50 2009*

⊞ **PORTO** *B1* (10km SW Coastal/Urban) *41.10777, -8.65611* **Camping ORBITUR-Madalena, Rua do Cerro 608, Praia da Madalena, 4405-736 Vila Nova de Gaia [227 122520 or 122524; fax 227 122534; info@orbitur.pt; www.orbitur.com]** Fr Porto ring rd IC1/A44 take A29 exit dir Espinho. In 1km take exit slip rd sp Madalena opp Volvo agent. Watch for either 'Campismo' or 'Orbitur' sp to site along winding, cobbled rd. Lge, terr, pt sl, pt shd; wc (some cont); chem disp; mv service pnt; baby facs; shwrs inc; el pnts (6A) €3; gas; lndtte; shop; tradsmn; rest, snacks, bar in ssn; BBQ; playgrnd; pool; sand beach 250m; tennis; games area; entmnt; games rm; wifi; TV rm; 40% statics; dogs €1.50; phone; bus to Porto; car wash; Eng spkn; adv bkg; ccard acc; red low ssn/long stay/snr citizens; CCI. "Site in forest; restricted area for tourers; slight aircraft noise; some uneven pitches; poss ltd facs low ssn; excel bus to Porto cent fr site ent - do not take c'van into Porto." ♦ € 25.60 2009*

PORTO COVO see Sines *B4*

This is a wonderful site.

⊞ **POVOA DE VARZIM** *B1* (13km N Coastal) *41.46277, -8.77277* **Camping ORBITUR-Rio Alto, EN13, Km 13, Lugar do Rio Alto, Estela, 4570-275 Póvoa de Varzim [252 615699; fax 252 615599; info@orbitur.pt; www.orbitur.com]** Fr A28 exit Póvoa onto N13 N; turn L 1km N of Estela at yellow Golf sp by hotel, in 2km (cobbles) turn R to camp ent. V lge, some hdg/mkd pitch, shd; wc; chem disp; mv service pnt; baby facs; shwrs inc; el pnts (5-15A) €3-4; gas; lndtte; shop; tradsmn; rest; snacks; bar; BBQ; playgrnd; pool high ssn; sand beach 150m; tennis; games area; games rm; golf adj; entmnt; wifi; cab/sat TV; 50% static/semi-statics; dogs €1.50; phone; bus 2km; car wash; poss cr; Eng spkn; adv bkg; poss cr; red low ssn/long stay/snr citizens; ccard acc; CCI. "Excel facs; helpful staff; vg rest on site; direct access to vg beach (steep sl); strong NW prevailing wind; excel touring base." ♦ € 28.00 2009*

PRAIA DE MIRA see Mira *B2*

PRAIA DE QUIAIOS *B2* (2km W Coastal) *40.2200, -8.88666* **Camping ORBITUR, Praia de Quiaios, 3080-515 Quiaios [233 919995; fax 233 919996; info@orbitur.pt; www.orbitur.com]** Fr N109 turn W onto N109-8 dir Quiaios, foll sp 3km to Praia de Quiaios & site. Lge, some mkd pitch, pt shd; wc; chem disp; mv service pnt; shwrs inc; el pnts (10A) €3; gas; lndtte; supmkt; tradsmn; rest; snacks; bar; BBQ; playgrnd; pool 500m; sand beach 500m; tennis; cycle hire; games rm; TV; entmnt; 20% statics; dogs €1.50; phone; car wash; Eng spkn; adv bkg; quiet; ccard acc; red low ssn/snr citizens/long stay; CCI. "Interesting historical area; vg touring base; peaceful site; hot water to shwrs only; care needed some pitches due soft sand." ♦ 1 Jan-10 Oct. € 20.70 2009*

I'm going to fill in some
site report forms and post
them off to the Club;
we could win a ferry
crossing – it's here on
page 12.

⊞ **QUARTEIRA** *C4* (2km N Coastal/Urban) *37.06722, -8.08666* **Camping ORBITUR-Quarteira, Estrada da Fonte Santa, Ave Sá Carneira, 8125-618 Quarteira [289 302826 or 302821; fax 289 302822; info@orbitur.pt; www.orbitur.com]** Fr E & IP1/A22 take exit junc 12 at Loulé onto N396 to Quarteira; in 8.5km at rndabt by g'ge L along dual c'way. In 1km at traff lts fork R into site. No advance sp to site. V lge, mkd pitch, pt sl, terr, pt shd; wc; chem disp; mv service pnt; shwrs inc; el pnts (6A) €3 (long lead req some pitches); gas; lndtte; supmkt 200m; tradsmn; rest; snacks; bar; BBQ; playgrnd; pool; waterslide; sand beach 600m; tennis; games rm; wifi; entmnt; TV rm; 5% statics (tour ops); dogs €1.50; phone; bus 50m; car wash; Eng spkn; adv bkg; aircraft noise fr Faro; red low ssn/long stay/snr citizens; ccard acc; CCI. "Lovely site; popular winter long stay; narr site rds & tight turns; some o'hanging trees; some pitches diff lge o'fits; gd san facs; caterpillar problem Jan-Mar; easy walk to town; mkt Wed." ♦ € 29.30 2009*

ROSARIO see Alandroal *C3*

⊞ **SAGRES** *B4* (2km W Coastal) *37.02305, -8.94555* **Camping ORBITUR, Cerro das Moitas, 8650-998 Vila de Sagres [282 624371; fax 282 624445; info@orbitur.pt; www.orbitur.com]** On N268 to Cape St Vincent; well sp. Lge, hdg/mkd pitch, hdstg, pt shd; wc; chem disp; mv service pnt; shwrs inc; el pnts (6-10A) €3-4; gas; lndtte; shop; rest; snacks; bar; BBQ; playgrnd; sand beach 2km; cycle hire; games rm; TV rm; dogs €1.50; car wash; Eng spkn; adv bkg; quiet; red long stay/low ssn/snr citizens; ccard acc. "Vg, clean, tidy site in pine trees; hot water to shwrs only; cliff walks." ♦ € 24.00 2009*

⊞ **SANTO ANTONIO DAS AREIAS** *C3* (1km SE Rural) *39.41000, -7.34000* **Camping Asseiceira, Asseiceira, 7330-204 Santo António das Areias [tel/fax 245 992940; gary-campingasseiceira@hotmail.com; www.campingasseiceira.com]** Fr N246-1 turn off sp Marvão/Santo António das Areias. Turn L to Santo António das Areias then 1st R on ent town then immed R again, up sm hill to rndabt. At rndabt turn R then at next rndabt cont straight on. There is a petrol stn on R, cont down hill for 400m. Site on L. Sm, pt sl, pt shd; wc; chem disp; shwrs inc; el pnts (16A) €4; gas 500m; shop, rest 3km; snacks; bar; pool; wifi; no statics; dogs €1; bus 1km; quiet; CCI. "Attractive area; peaceful, well-equipped, remote site among olive trees; clean, tidy; new san facs planned 2009; gd for walking, birdwatching; helpful, friendly, British owners; interesting vills; nr Spanish border; excel." ♦ € 14.00 2009*

SAO JACINTO see Aveiro *B2*

⊞ **SAO MARCOS DO SERRA** *B4* (3km S Rural) *37.3350, -8.3467* **Campismo Rural Quinta Odelouca, Vale Grande de Baixo, CxP 644-S, 8375-215 São Marcos da Serra [282 361718; info@quintaodelouca.com; www.quintaodelouca.com]** Fr N (Ourique) on IC1 pass São Marcos da Serra & in approx 2.5km turn R & cross blue rlwy bdge. At bottom turn L & at cont until turn R for Vale Grande (paved rd changes to unmade). Foll sp to site. Fr S exit A22 junc 9 onto IC1 dir Ourique. Pass São Bartolomeu de Messines & at km 710.5 turn L & cross blue rlwy bdge, then as above. Sm, terr, pt shd; wc; chem disp; baby facs; shwrs inc; el pnts (10A) €2.10; lndtte; shop 3km; tradsmn; rest 2km; bar; BBQ; pool; lake sw; wifi; dogs €1; Eng spkn; adv bkg; quiet; CCI. "Helpful, friendly Dutch owners; phone ahead bet Nov & Feb; beautiful views; gd walks; vg." € 13.10 2009*

⊞ **SAO MARTINHO DO PORTO** *B2* (1.5km NE Coastal) *39.52280, -9.12310* **Parque de Campismo Colina do Sol, Serra dos Mangues, 2460-697 São Martinho do Porto [262 989764; fax 262 989763; parque.colina.sol@clix.pt; www.colinadosol.net]** Leave A8/IC1 SW at junc 21 onto N242 W to São Martinho, by-pass town on N242 dir Nazaré. Site on L. Lge, mkd pitch, hdstg, terr, pt shd; wc; chem disp; mv service pnt; shwrs inc; el pnts (6A) €2.75; gas; lndtte; shop high ssn; rest; snacks; bar; BBQ; playgrnd; pool; paddling pool; sand beach 2km; fishing; games area; games rm; TV; mobile homes/c'vans for hire; dogs €1; phone; bus 2km; site clsd at Xmas; poss cr; Eng spkn; adv bkg; quiet; ccard acc; CCI. "Gd touring base on attractive coastline; gd walking, cycling; excel site; vg san facs." ♦ € 18.00 2009*

See advertisement on next page

Portugal

⊞ **SAO PEDRO DE MOEL** *B2* (N Urban/Coastal) *39.75861, -9.02583* **Camping ORBITUR, Rua Volta do Sete, São Pedro de Moel, 2430 Marinha Grande [244 599168; fax 244 599148; info@orbitur.pt; www.orbitur.com]** Site at end of rd fr Marinha Grande to beach; turn R at 1st rndabt on ent vill. Site S of lighthouse. V lge, some hdg/mkd pitch, hdstg, pt terr, shd; wc; chem disp; mv service pnt; shwrs inc; el pnts (6A) €3 (poss rev pol); gas; Indtte; shop; tradsmn; rest; snacks; bar; BBQ; playgrnd; htd pool; waterslide; sand beach 500m (heavy surf); fishing; tennis; cycle hire; games rm; entmnt; wifi; cab/sat TV; some statics; dogs €1.50; phone; car wash; poss cr; Eng spkn; adv bkg; quiet; red low ssn/long stay/snr citizens; ccard acc; CCI. "Friendly, well-run, clean site; easy walk to shops, rests; site in pinewoods; gd cycling to beaches; São Pedro smart resort; ltd facs low ssn." ♦ € 25.60 2009*

⊞ **SAO PEDRO DE MOEL** *B2* (2km N Coastal) *39.7650, -9.0303* **Inatal Parque de Campismo, Avda do Farol, 2430-502 São Pedro de Moel [244 599289; fax 244 599550; pc.spmoel@inatel.pt; www.inatel.pt]** Site 100m N of lighthouse on rd to Praia de Vieira. Lge, hdg/mkd pitch, hdstg, shd; wc (some cont); chem disp (wc); shwrs inc; el pnts (4A) inc; shop high ssn; rest, snacks, bar high ssn & 2km; playgrnd; pool 500m; sand beach adj; TV; 25% statics; no dogs; bus 300m; poss cr; quiet. "Tidy site; basic san facs." € 15.65 2007*

⊞ **SAO TEOTONIO** *B4* (7km W Coastal) *37.49497, -8.78667* **Camping Monte Carvalhal da Rocha, Praia do Carvalhal, Brejão, 7630-569 São Teotónio [282 947293; fax 282 947294; geral@montecarvalhalr-turismo.com; www.montecarvalhaldarocha.com]** Turn W off N120 dir Brejão & Carvalhal; site in 4.5km. Site sp. Med, shd; wc; shwrs inc; el pnts (16A) inc; gas; Indtte; shop, rest, snacks, bar high ssn; BBQ; playgrnd; sand beach 500m; fishing; cycle hire; TV; some statics; no dogs; phone; bus 2km; car wash; Eng spkn; adv bkg; quiet; ccard acc; red low ssn. "Beautiful area; friendly, helpful staff." € 26.00 2009*

⊞ **SAO TEOTONIO** *B4* (7km W Coastal) *37.52560, -8.77560* **Parque de Campismo da Zambujeira, Praia da Zambujeira, 7630-740 Zambujeira do Mar [283 961172; fax 283 961320; www.campingzambujeira.com.sapo.pt]** S on N120 twd Lagos, turn W when level with São Teotónio on unclassified rd to Zambujeira. Site on L in 7km, bef vill. V lge, pt sl, pt shd; wc; chem disp; mv service pnt; shwrs inc; el pnts (6-10A) €3; gas; shop, rest, snacks & bar high ssn; playgrnd; sand beach 1km; tennis; TV; dogs €3; phone; bus adj; site clsd Nov; Eng spkn; some rd noise; red low ssn/long stay. "Welcoming, friendly owners; in pleasant rural setting; hot water to shwrs only; sh walk to unspoilt vill with some shops & rest; cliff walks." € 20.00 2009*

SATAO *C2* (10km N Rural) *40.82280, -7.6961* **Camping Quinta Chave Grande, Casfreires, Ferreira d'Aves, 3560-043 Sátão [232 665552; fax 232 665352; chave-grande@sapo.pt; www.chavegrande.com]** Leave IP5 Salamanca-Viseu rd onto N229 to Sátão, site sp in Satão - beyond Lamas. Med, terr, pt shd; wc; chem disp; baby facs; shwrs inc; el pnts (6A) €3; gas; Indtte; shop 3km; tradsmn; rest 3km; snacks; bar; playgrnd; pool; paddling pool; tennis; games area; games rm; internet; TV; dogs €1.50; Eng spkn; quiet; red long stay. "Warm welcome fr friendly Dutch owners; gd facs; well organised BBQs - friendly atmosphere; gd touring base; gd walks fr site; excel." 15 Mar-31 Oct. € 17.00 2009*

⊞ **SERPA** *C4* (1km SE Urban) *37.94105, -7.60421* **Parque Municipal de Campismo Serpa, Largo de São Pedro, 7830-303 Serpa [284 544290; fax 284 540109]** Fr N260 take 1st sp for town; site well sp fr most directions - opp sw pool. Do not ent walled town. Med, pt sl, pt shd; wc; chem disp; shwrs inc; el pnts (6A) €1.25; gas; Indtte; shop 100m; rest, snacks, bar 50m; BBQ; daily mkt 500m; supmkt nr; pool adj; rv sw 5km; 20% statics; dogs; phone; adv bkg; poss noise fr rd & barking dogs; no ccard acc; CCI. "Popular site; simple, high quality facs; interesting town, developing rapidly; historic centre nrby." ♦ € 7.75 2007*

⊞ **SESIMBRA** *B3* (1.5km W Coastal) *38.43580, -9.11658* **Camp Municipal Forte do Cavalo, Porto de Abrigo, 2970 Sesimbra [212 288508; fax 212 288265; decl_dtc_st@mun-sesimbra.pt; www.mun-sesimbra.pt]** Fr Lisbon S on A2/IP7 turn S onto N378 to Sesimbra. Turn R immed after town ent sp Campismo & Porto. Fork R again sp Porto; L downhill at traff lts to avoid town cent. Turn R at sea front to site by lighthouse. Steep uphill app. V lge, pt sl, terr, shd; wc; shwrs inc; el pnts (6A) €2.10; gas; shop, rest 1km; snacks, bar 500m; BBQ; playgrnd; beach 800m; fishing; boating; no dogs; phone; bus 100m; poss cr; Eng spkn; no adv bkg; quiet; CCI. "Pitches ltd for tourers; gd views; lovely, unique fishing vill; castle worth visit; unreliable opening dates (poss not open until Jun) - phone ahead." € 11.50 2006*

⊞ **SESIMBRA** *B3* (12km W Coastal) *38.46356, -9.18936* **Parque Campismo Campimeco, Praia das Bicas, 2970-066 Aldeia do Meco [212 683374; fax 212 683844]** Fr Sesimbra take N379 twd Azóia & Cabo Espichel. Turn R in Azóia, then L in Aldeia do Meco at x-rds, site sp. V lge, pt sl, pt shd; wc; chem disp (wc); shwrs inc; el pnts (5A) €1.90; Indry rm; shop; rest, snacks, bar 2km; playgrnd; pool; sand beach adj; tennis; 98% statics; dogs; bus 2km; poss cr; quiet; CCI. "Vg low ssn; steep descent to beach (dogs not allowed); ltd touring pitches." € 10.90 2007*

⊞ **SETUBAL** *B3* (4km W Coastal) *38.50299, -8.92909* **Parque de Campismo do Outão, Estrada de Rasca, 2900-182 Setúbal [265 238318; fax 265 228098]** Fr Setúbal take coast rd W twd Outão, site on L. V lge, mkd pitch, hdstg, pt shd; wc (some cont); chem disp; shwrs inc; el pnts (5A) €2.40; gas; shop; rest; bar; playgrnd; sand beach adj; 90% statics; dogs €1.50; poss cr; Eng spkn; some rd noise; red low ssn/CCI. "Few pitches for tourers; hdstg not suitable for awning." ♦ € 14.00 2006*

⊞ **SINES** *B4* (15km SE Rural) *37.85272, -8.78788* **Parque de Campismo de Porto Covo, Estrada Municipal 554, 7250-437 Porto Covo [269 905136; fax 269 905239; camping-portocovo@gmail.com]** S fr Sines on N120 twd Cercal, turn R after 13km dir Porto Covo & site 200m bef vill. V rough app rd to site. Med, hdstg, pt sl, unshd; wc (cont); chem disp; mv service pnt; shwrs inc; el pnts (4-10A) €3.05; gas; Indtte; shop; rest; snacks; bar; BBQ; playgrnd; pool; sand beach 400m; games area; cycle hire; boat trips; TV; mostly statics; dogs; phone; bus 300m; poss cr; adv bkg; poss noisy high ssn; red low ssn. "Not rec for tourers, few touring pitches & v sm, diff access; pleasant site; lovely vill." ♦ € 18.40 2007*

⊞ **TAVIRA** *C4* (5km E Rural/Coastal) *37.14506, -7.60223* **Camping Ria Formosa, Quinta da Gomeira, 8800-591 Cabanas Tavira [281 328887; fax 281 326087; info@campingriaformosa.com; www.campingriaformosa.com]** Fr N125 turn S at Conceição dir 'Cabanas Tavira' & 'Campismo'. Cross rlwy line & turn L to site, sp. V lge, mkd pitch, hdstg, terr, pt shd; htd wc; chem disp; mv service pnt; shwrs inc; el pnts (16A) €3; gas; Indtte; shop; tradsmn; rest; snacks; bar; BBQ; playgrnd; pool; paddling pool; cycle hire; sand beach 1.2km; games area; wifi; dogs €2; bus 100m; car wash; Eng spkn; adv bkg; quiet; ccard acc; red long stay/CCI. "Excel new site; friendly, welcoming owner & staff; vg, modern san facs; cycle path to Tavira." ♦ € 15.00 2009*

See advertisement below

⊞ **TOCHA** *B2* (7.5km W Coastal) *40.32777, -8.84027* **Camping Praia da Tocha, Rua dos Pescadores, Nossa Sra da Tocha, Praia da Tocha, 3060-691 Tocha [231 447112; tocha@cacampings.com; www.cacampings.com]** Fr N or S on N109, turn W onto N335 to Praia da Tocha, site sp. Med, pt shd; wc; chem disp; baby facs; shwrs; el pnts (4-6A) €1.85; gas; Indtte (inc dryer); shop, rest, snacks, bar high ssn; playgrnd; sand beach 200m; watersports; cycle hire; internet; TV rm; dogs €1.55; phone; bus adj; Eng spkn; adv bkg; quiet; CCI. "Well-maintained, pleasant site; helpful staff." ♦ € 11.80 2009*

See advertisement on next page

Portugal

⊞ **TOMAR** *B2* (Urban) **Campismo Parque Municipal, 2300 Tomar [249 329824; fax 249 322608; camping@cm-tomar.pt; www.cm-tomar.pt]** Fr S on B110 ent town & cross Ponte Veilha (old, 2nd bdge) over Rv Nabao. Turn immed sharp L, site at far end of stadium. Fr N (Coimbra) on N110 turn R immed bef bdge. Site well sp fr all dirs. Med, mkd pitch, pt shd; wc; chem disp; mv service pnt; baby facs; shwrs inc; el pnts (10A) €1.40; shop, rest, snacks, bar in town; playgrnd; pool adj; TV; dogs; phone; Eng spkn; quiet; red low ssn; ccard acc; CCI. "Useful base for touring Alcobaca, Batatha & historic monuments in Tomar; conv Fatima; Convento de Cristo worth visit; vg, popular site; improvements planned (2009/10)." € 10.55 2009*

TOMAR *B2* (7km NE Rural) *39.63833, -8.33694* **Camping Pelinos 77, 2300-093 Tomar [249 301814]** N fr Tomar on N110, turn R to Calçadas at traff lts opp g'ge, foll site sp. Steep descent to site. Sm, terr, pt shd; wc; shwrs inc; el pnts (12A) €2; Indtte; rest; snacks; bar; BBQ (winter only); playgrnd; pool; lake sw, watersports, fishing 7km; TV; dogs; phone; bus 100m; Eng spkn; adv bkg; quiet; red low ssn; CCI. "Owner will assist taking o'fits in/out; vg." 15 Jan-15 Nov. € 11.50 2006*

⊞ **TOMAR** *B2* (10km E Rural) *39.62527, -8.32194* **Camping Redondo, Rua do Casal Rei 6, 2300-035 Poço Redondo [tel/fax 249 376421; info@campingredondo.co.uk; www.campingredondo.com]** Fr N or S on N110, take IC3 for Tomar, then take 1st exit sp Albufeira do Castelo do Bode/Tomar. Foll site sp (red hearts) for 7km. Steep drop at site ent. Sm, pt sl, pt shd; wc; chem disp; mv service pnt; shwrs inc; el pnts (4-6A) €2-2.30; Indtte; shop 2km; rest; snacks; bar; playgrnd; pool; waterslide; lake beach 4.5km; TV rm; few statics; dogs €1; phone; bus; poss cr; Eng spkn; adv bkg; red low ssn; CCI. "Due steep drop at ent, site owner tows c'vans out." € 13.60 2009*

TOMAR *B2* (10km SE Rural) *39.53963, -8.31895* **Camping Castelo do Bode, 2200 Martinchel [241 849262; fax 241 849244; castelo.bode@fcmportugal.com]** S fr Tomar on N110, in approx 7km L onto N358-2 dir Barragem & Castelo do Bode. Site on L in 6km immed after dam; steep ent. Med, mkd pitch, hdstg, terr, pt shd; wc (some cont); chem disp; shwrs inc; el pnts (6A) inc; gas; supmkt 6km; tradsmn; rest, snacks 2km; bar; playgrnd; lake sw adj; boating; fishing; dogs €0.60; phone; bus to Tomar 1km; no adv bkg; quiet; CCI. "Site on edge of 60km long lake with excel watersports; old san facs, but clean; helpful staff; lge car park on ent Tomar - interesting town." ♦ 13 Jan-11 Nov. € 12.25 2009*

⊞ **VAGOS** *B2* (8km W Rural) *40.55805, -8.74527* **ORBITUR Camping Vagueira, Rua do Parque de Campismo, 3840-254 Gafanha da Boa-Hora [234 797526; fax 234 797093; info@orbitur.pt; www.orbitur.pt]** Fr Aveiro take N109 S twd Figuera da Foz. Turn R in Vagos vill. After 6km along narr poor rd, site on R bef reaching Vagueira vill. V lge, mkd pitch, shd; wc; chem disp; mv service pnt; baby facs; shwrs inc; el pnts (6-16A) €3-4; gas; Indtte; supmkt, tradsmn, rest, bar high ssn; playgrnd; pool 1km; sand beach 1.5km; fishing 1km; tennis; games area; cycle hire; entmnt; wifi; 90% statics; dogs €1.50; bus 500m; Eng spkn; adv bkg; quiet; ccard acc; red low ssn/snr citizens; CCI. "V pleasant & well-run; friendly staff; poss diff access to pitches for lge o'fits; areas soft sand; gd touring base." ♦ € 20.70 2009*

VALHELHAS *C2* (1km W Rural) *40.40388, -7.40611* **Camp Municipal Rossio de Valhelhas, 6300-235 Valhelhas [275 487160; fax 275 487372; jfvalhelhas@clix.pt; www.valhelhas.com]** Fr Manteigas, site is on R of N232 on ent Valhelhas. Lge, shd; wc; shwrs inc; el pnts (5-10A) €1 (long lead req); Indry rm; shop 150m; rest 300m; snacks; bar; playgrnd; rv adj; fishing; games area; few statics; phone; bus 100m; poss cr; quiet; ccard not acc; CCI. "Pleasant, woodland site; conv for touring Serra da Estrela; rv dammed to make natural sw pool; friendly, helpful staff." 1 May-30 Sep. € 9.75 2008*

⊞ **VALPACOS** *C1* (6km E Rural) *41.63254, -7.24794* **Campismo Rabaçal-Valpaços, Rua Gago Coutinho 14, 5430 Valpaços [278 759354]** Fr E82/IP4 turn N onto N213 to Valpaços, turn R onto N206, site sp. Lge, pt shd; wc; mv service pnt; shwrs inc; el pnts (6A) €1.20; gas; Indtte; rest; bar; BBQ; playgrnd; fishing adj; phone; quiet; red CCI. "Friendly staff; beautiful rvside setting." ♦ € 8.50 2006*

VALVERDE see Lagos *B4*

⊞ **VIANA DO CASTELO** *B1* (3km S Coastal) **Parque de Campismo Inatel do Cabedelo, Avda dos Trabalhadores, 4900-164 Darque [258 322042; fax 258 331502; pc.cabedelo@inatel.pt; www.inatel.pt]** Exit IC1 junc 11 to W sp Darque, Cabedelo, foll sp to site. Lge, mkd pitch, hdstg, pt sl, pt shd; wc (some cont); shwrs inc; el pnts (6A) inc; gas; Indtte; shop high ssn; tradsmn; snacks; bar; sand beach adj; entmnt; 30% statics; no dogs; phone; bus 100m; site clsd mid-Dec to mid-Jan; adv bkg; quiet; CCI. "V secure; gd for children; hourly ferry to Viana; spacious pitches under pines; poss poor facs low ssn & in need of refurb." ♦ € 12.50 2007*

⊞ **VIANA DO CASTELO** *B1* (2km SW Coastal/Urban) *41.67888, -8.82583* **Camping ORBITUR-Viana do Castelo, Rua Diogo Álvares, Cabedelo, 4935-161 Darque [258 322167; fax 258 321946; info@orbitur.pt; www.orbitur.com]** Exit IC1 junc 11 to W sp Darque, Cabedelo, foll sp to site in park. Lge, mkd pitch, pt sl, shd; wc; chem disp; mv service pnt; shwrs inc; el pnts (5-15A) €3-4; gas; Indtte; shop; tradsmn; rest; snacks; bar; BBQ; playgrnd; htd pool; lge sand beach adj; surfing; fishing; entmnt; wifi; TV; dogs €1.50; phone; car wash; Eng spkn; adv bkg; quiet; red low ssn/long stay/snr citizens; ccard acc; CCI. "Site in pine woods; friendly staff; gd facs; plenty of shade; major festival in Viana 3rd w/end in Aug; lge mkt in town Fri; sm passenger ferry over Rv Lima to town high ssn; Santa Luzia worth visit." ♦ € 25.60 2009*

VIEIRA DO MINHO *C1* (800m SE Urban) *41.63333, -8.13583* **Parque de Campismo de Cabreira, 4850 Vieira do Minho [253 648665; fax 253 648395; bina.vc@mail.telepac.pt; www.vieiraminhoturismo.com]** Take N103 E fr Braga for 30km; foll sp to Vieira Do Minho, site sp in Vieira. Lge, pt shd; wc; chem disp (wc); shwrs inc; el pnts (5A) €2.50; gas; Indtte; shop; rest; snacks; bar; playgrnd; 2 pools adj; rv adj; tennis; sports area; cycle hire; entmnt; phone; bus 1km; Eng spkn; quiet; CCI. "Gd, level grassy site; conv Gerês National Park." ♦ 1 Feb-31 Oct. € 14.50 2008*

⊞ **VILA DO BISPO** *B4* (8km SE Coastal/Rural) *37.07542, -8.83133* **Parque de Campismo Quinta dos Carriços (Part Naturist), Praia de Salema, 8650-196 Budens [282 695201; fax 282 695122; quintacarrico@oninet.pt; www.quintadoscarricos.com]** Take N125 out of Lagos twd Sagres. In approx 14km at sp Salema, turn L & again immed L twd Salema. Site on R 300m. Lge, pt terr (tractor avail), pt shd; htd wc; chem disp; mv service pnt; shwrs €0.65; el pnts (6-10A) €3 (metered for long stay); gas; Indtte; shop; rest; snacks; bar; playground; pool 1km; sand beach 1km; golf 1km; TV; 8% statics; dogs €2.45; phone; bus; Eng spkn; adv bkg (ess high ssn); noise fr adj quarry; ccard acc; red long stay/CCI. "Naturist section in sep valley; apartments avail on site; ltd pitches for lge o'fits; friendly Dutch owners; tractor avail to tow to terr; area of wild flowers in spring; no music allowed; beach 30 mins walk; buses pass ent for Lagos, beach & Sagres; excel." ♦ € 23.10 2008*

⊞ **VILA FLOR** *C1* (2.5km SW Rural) *41.29420, -7.17180* **Camp Municipal de Vila Flor, Barragem do Peneireiro, 5360-303 Vila Flor [278 512350; fax 278 512380; cm.vila.flor@mail.telepac.pt; www.cm-vilaflor.espigueiro.pt]** Site is off N215, sp fr all dirs. V bumpy app rd - 12km. V lge, terr, pt shd; wc; chem disp (wc); shwrs inc; el pnts (16A) €1.50; gas; Indry rm; shop; snacks; bar; BBQ; playgrnd; pool adj; tennis adj; TV rm; 10% statics; dogs; phone; clsd 2300-0700 (1800-0800 low ssn); poss v cr; adv bkg; noisy high ssn; CCI. "Friendly staff; access to pitches diff." ♦ € 9.40 2006*

VILA NOVA DE CACELA see Vila Real de Santo Antonio *C4*

VILA NOVA DE CERVEIRA *B1* (5km E Rural) *41.94362, -8.69365* **Parque de Campismo Convívio, Rua de Badão, 1 Bacelo, 4920-020 Candemil [251 794404; convivio@vodafone.pt; http://convivio.planetaclix.pt]** Fr Vila Nova de Cerveira dir Candemil on N13/N302, turn L at Bacelo, site sp. Sm, terr, pt shd; wc; chem disp; shwrs inc; el pnts (6A) €2.50; Indtte; shop 2km; tradsmn; rest 4km; snacks; bar; BBQ; htd pool; games rm; no statics; dogs €0.85; phone; bus/train 5km; poss cr; Eng spkn; adv bkg; quiet; red long stay; CCI. "No twin-axle c'vans acc; site open Oct-Mar for adv bkgs only." 1 Apr-1 Oct. € 13.00 2007*

VILA NOVA DE GAIA see Porto *B1*

⊞ **VILA NOVA DE MILFONTES** *B4* (Coastal) *37.72933, -8.78308* **Camping Campiférias, 7645-301 Vila Nova de Milfontes [283 996409; fax 283 996581; novaferias@oninet.pt]** S fr Sines on N120/IC4 for 22km; turn R at Cercal on N390 SW for Milfontes on banks of Rio Mira; clearly sp on edge of town opp mkt. If driving thro Vila Nova twd coast, look out for site sp on R. App rds bumpy - care needed. Site well sp. V lge, pt shd; wc (cont); chem disp; mv service pnt; shwrs inc; el pnts (5A) €2.30; shop 50m; rest; snacks; bar; playgrnd; beach 800m; entmnt; TV; 50% statics; no dogs; bus 500m; phone; site clsd 3-25 Dec; adv bkg; quiet; red low ssn. "V clean site but san facs need upgrade; trees may make pitching diff; conv for beach & shops; mkt opp; leaving site poss diff - rec plan rte in advance." ♦ € 16.00 2007*

⊞ **VILA NOVA DE MILFONTES** *B4* (1km N Coastal) *37.73194, -8.78277* **Camping Milfontes, 7645-300 Vila Nova de Milfontes [283 996140; fax 283 996104; geral@parquemilfontes.com; www.campingmilfontes.com]** S fr Sines on N120/IC4 for 22km; turn R at Cercal on N390 SW for Milfontes on banks of Rio Mira; clear sp. V lge, hdg/mkd pitch, pt shd; wc; chem disp; mv service pnt; shwrs inc; el pnts (6A) €2 (long lead poss req); gas; lndtte; shop; supmkt & mkt 5 mins walk; rest, snacks, bar high ssn; playgrnd; sand beach 800m; TV; many statics; phone; bus 600m; poss cr; quiet; ccard acc; red CCI. "Pitching poss diff for lge o'fits due trees & statics; nr fishing vill at mouth Rv Mira with beaches & sailing on rv; nice site." ♦ € 18.00 2009*

⊞ **VILA NOVA DE MILFONTES** *B4* (8km N Coastal) *37.77844, -8.78977* **Sitava Camping, Brejo da Zimbreira, 7645-017 Vila Nova de Milfontes [283 890100; fax 283 890109; sitava@camping.sitave.pt; www.sitava.pt]** S fr Sines on N120/IC4. At Cercal take dir Vila Nova de Milfontes. At Brunheiras turn R at site sp; site in 4km on L. V lge, mkd pitch, pt sl, pt shd; wc; chem disp; shwrs inc; el pnts (6A) €2.15; gas; lndtte; shop high ssn; tradsmn; rest; snacks; bar; BBQ; playgrnd; pool; sand beach 600m; tennis; games area; games rm; entmnt; TV; 60% statics; no dogs; phone; bus 100m; poss cr; Eng spkn; adv bkg; quiet; red low ssn/CCI. "Friendly staff; bus to beach; excel facs but ltd low ssn; vg security." ♦ € 13.60 2007*

VILA PRAIA DE ANCORA *B1* (7km S Coastal) *41.80255, -8.84821* **Parque de Campismo do Paço, 4910-024 Vila Praia de Âncora [tel/fax 258 912697; geral@campingpaco.com; www.campingpaco.com]** Fr N13 Caminha-Viana do Castelo, site sp 1km S of Âncora, km 81. Med, pt shd; wc; chem disp; mv service pnt; shwrs inc; el pnts (6A) €2.25; gas; lndtte; shop; tradsmn; rest; snacks; bar; BBQ; playgrnd; pool 1.5km; sand beach 1km; fishing; canoeing; games area; TV; phone; bus 600m; car wash; adv bkg; Eng spkn; quiet; ccard acc; red CCI. "Pleasant staff; excel san facs; vg touring base; gd beaches nr." 15 Apr-30 Sep. € 14.70 2007*

VILA REAL *C1* (500m NE Urban) *41.30361, -7.73694* **Camping Vila Real, Rua Dr Manuel Cardona, 5000-558 Vila Real [259 324724]** On IP4/E82 take Vila Real N exit & head S into town. At Galp g'ge rndabt, turn L & in 30m turn L again Site at end of rd in 400m. Site sp fr all dirs. Lge, pt sl, terr, pt shd; wc; chem disp; baby facs; shwrs inc; el pnts (6A) €1.75; gas; sm shop adj; tradsmn; rest; snacks; bar; BBQ; playgrnd; pool complex adj; tennis; 10% statics; dogs; phone; bus 150m; poss cr; red CCI. "Conv upper Douro; gd facs ltd when site full; gd mkt in town." ♦ 1 Mar-30 Nov. € 16.15 2009*

⊞ **VILA REAL DE SANTO ANTONIO** *C4* (3km W Coastal) *37.17972, -7.44361* **Parque Municipal de Campismo, 8900 Monte Gordo [281 510970; fax 281 510977; cmvrsa@mail.telepac.pt]** Fr Faro on N125 turn R sp Monte Gordo. Site on sea front in 500m. Or fr Spain over bdge at border, exit junc 9 to Vila Real over rlwy line. Strt over rndabt & turn R at T-junc, site sp just bef ent town. V lge, pt sl, shd; wc (some cont); chem disp; shwrs inc; el pnts (10A) €1.90 (long cable poss req); gas; lndtte; shop & 1km; tradsmn; rest; snacks; bar; BBQ; playgrnd; sand beach 100m; canoeing; TV; 10% statics; dogs €3; phone; bus; train to Faro 3km; poss v cr; Eng spkn; no adv bkg; quiet; ccard acc; red low ssn/long stay/snr citizens; CCI. "V lge pitches but poss v overcr high ssn; many long stay c'vans; caution soft sand makes some pitches unreliable, esp in wet; ground poss too soft for lge o'fits; san facs plentiful & clean; lovely area; gd security." ♦ € 13.50 2008*

⊞ **VILA REAL DE SANTO ANTONIO** *C4* (10km W Rural) *37.18649, -7.55003* **Camping Caliço Park, Sitio do Caliço, 8900-907 Vila Nova de Cacela [281 951195; fax 281 951977; transcampo@mail.telepac.pt]** On N side of N125 Vila Real to Faro rd. Sp on main rd & in Vila Nova de Cacela vill, visible fr rd. Rds have been re-surfaced for 95% of the way. Lge, pt sl, shd; wc; chem disp; shwrs inc; el pnts (6A) €2.60; gas; lndtte; shop; rest; snacks; bar; playgrnd; pool; sand beach 4km; cycle hire; many statics; dogs €1.30; phone; bus/train 2km; Eng spkn; adv bkg; noisy in ssn & rd noise; ccard acc; red long stay/low ssn; CCI. "Friendly staff; gd NH." € 15.60 2007*

VILAR DE MOUROS see Caminha *B1*

⊞ **VOUZELA** *C2* (2km E Rural) *40.71638, -8.09250* **Parque Campismo Municipal Vouzela, Monte da Senhora do Castelo, 3670-250 Vouzela [232 740020; fax 232 711513; parquecampismo@cm-vouzela.pt; www.cm-vouzela.pt]** Fr Vouzela foll N228; turn R sp Sra do Castelo. Site well sp fr town cent. Steep app. V lge, pt sl, terr, pt shd; wc; chem disp; mv service pnt; shwrs inc; el pnts (6-15A) €1.30; gas; lndry rm; shop; rest; snacks; bar; playgrnd; pool; tennis; cycle hire; entmnt; TV; 95% statics; dogs €1; phone; bus 3km; quiet except w/end; CCI. "Lovely location; poss diff to find pitch bet statics; access to higher terrs by steep hill." ♦ € 9.00 2008*

ZAMBUJEIRA DO MAR see Sao Teotonio *B4*

Portugal

Distances are shown in kilometres and are calculated from town/city centres along the most practical roads, although not necessarily taking the shortest route.
1km = 0.62miles

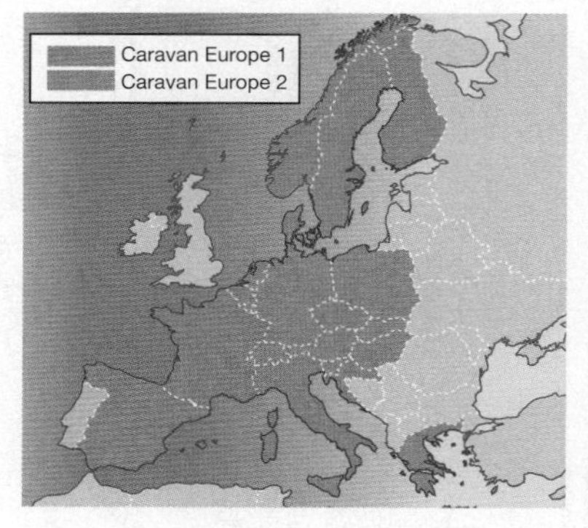

Miranda do Douro to Vila Real de Santo António = 688km

	Aveiro	Beja	Braga	Bragança	Castelo Branco	Chaves	Coimbra	Elvas	Évora	Faro	Fundão	Guarda	Leiria	Lisboa (Lisbon)	Miranda do Douro	Mourão	Portalegre	Portimão	Porto	Sagres	Santarém	Setúbal	Sines	Valença	Viana do Castelo	Vila Formoso	Vila Real	Vila Real de Santo António	Vila Verde de Ficalho
Beja	408																												
Braga	129	500																											
Bragança	285	558	214																										
Castelo Branco	225	274	318	288																									
Chaves	235	630	140	106	341																								
Coimbra	77	339	186	298	156	260																							
Elvas	379	162	478	445	155	496	253																						
Évora	325	77	432	485	198	513	258	84																					
Faro	535	164	639	732	442	723	468	328	245																				
Fundão	227	317	263	253	43	175	150	198	239	483																			
Guarda	163	361	263	200	92	240	156	247	290	538	57																		
Leiria	143	276	248	368	174	327	77	252	201	417	199	230																	
Lisboa (Lisbon)	273	179	383	503	247	480	206	206	131	295	300	362	146																
Miranda do Douro	320	572	280	76	287	180	313	442	487	732	252	195	387	607															
Mourão	365	110	490	533	260	575	322	101	66	276	303	356	265	193	552														
Portalegre	258	180	365	382	94	440	191	64	105	351	136	185	167	216	382	173													
Portimão	508	105	607	680	379	725	443	267	185	61	465	476	381	295	682	215	288												
Porto	74	445	65	219	261	170	121	364	372	578	208	209	191	317	254	407	303	552											
Sagres	556	153	655	728	407	773	491	315	233	109	513	524	429	343	730	263	336	48	600										
Santarém	205	198	310	426	177	388	140	174	120	338	220	292	78	80	445	186	148	336	251	384									
Setúbal	309	144	418	525	261	500	240	171	96	260	347	391	182	47	576	161	195	260	355	308	113								
Sines	390	99	497	609	305	570	323	193	109	201	348	397	262	162	592	209	214	140	433	147	184	119							
Valença	180	560	66	280	373	208	241	529	487	696	365	316	297	436	352	544	418	658	116	706	364	466	548						
Viana do Castelo	147	520	50	264	342	192	196	437	446	651	314	283	263	395	340	509	379	625	77	673	322	423	507	51					
Vila Formoso	193	400	290	226	135	269	190	290	271	575	111	44	259	428	175	336	228	507	240	555	333	439	380	358	342				
Vila Real	163	560	95	119	268	643	190	425	448	641	222	166	262	412	188	510	363	660	100	708	321	432	506	165	150	200			
Vila Real de Santo António	594	120	693	688	396	815	529	284	200	66	560	492	463	350	688	234	308	126	639	174	400	312	264	761	728	535	742		
Vila Verde de Ficalho	465	60	560	626	334	680	399	222	140	230	377	430	338	241	627	68	246	182	511	230	261	204	160	622	583	460	614	183	
Viseu	84	445	191	220	171	173	89	326	341	547	77	77	161	330	234	401	259	650	132	698	219	321	404	255	237	107	99	562	501

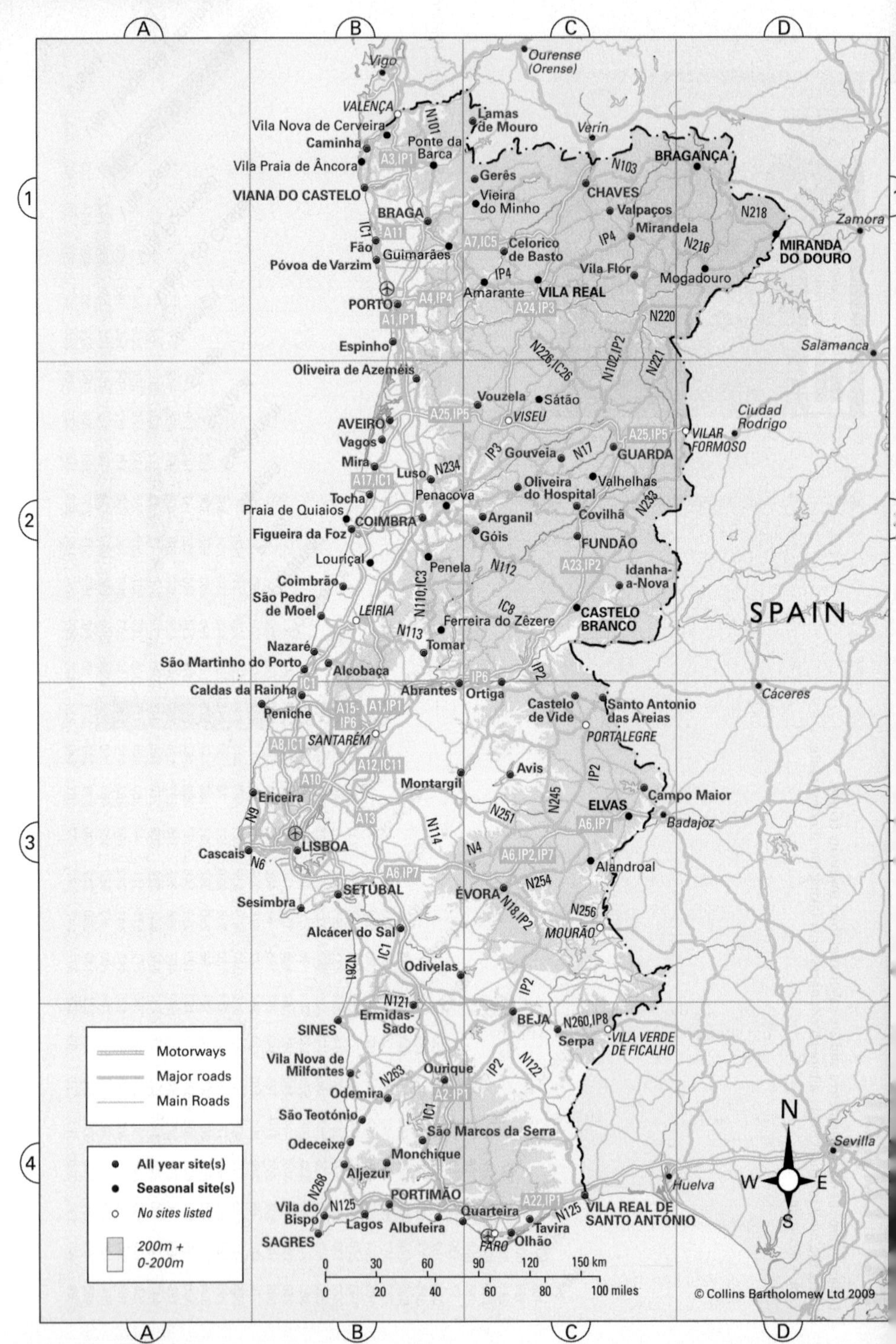

Vigo
Ourense (Orense)
VALENÇA
Vila Nova de Cerveira
Lamas de Mouro
Caminha
Ponte da Barca
Vila Praia de Âncora
Verín
BRAGANÇA
Gerês
VIANA DO CASTELO
CHAVES
Vieira do Minho
Valpaços
BRAGA
Mirandela
Zamora
Fão
Celorico de Basto
MIRANDA DO DOURO
Póvoa de Varzim
Guimarães
Vila Flor
Mogadouro
Amarante
VILA REAL
PORTO
Espinho
Salamanca
Oliveira de Azeméis
Vouzela
Sátão
AVEIRO
VISEU
Ciudad Rodrigo
VILAR FORMOSO
Vagos
Gouveia
GUARDA
Mira
Luso
Oliveira do Hospital
Valhelhas
Tocha
Penacova
Praia de Quiaios
COIMBRA
Arganil
Covilhã
Figueira da Foz
Góis
FUNDÃO
Louriçal
Penela
Idanha-a-Nova
Coimbrão
São Pedro de Moel
LEIRIA
CASTELO BRANCO
SPAIN
Ferreira do Zêzere
Tomar
Nazaré
São Martinho do Porto
Alcobaça
Abrantes
Ortiga
Cáceres
Caldas da Rainha
Peniche
Castelo de Vide
Santo Antonio das Areias
SANTARÉM
PORTALEGRE
Avis
Montargil
Ericeira
Campo Maior
ELVAS
Badajoz
LISBOA
Cascais
Alandroal
SETÚBAL
ÉVORA
Sesimbra
MOURÃO
Alcácer do Sal
Odivelas
Ermidas-Sado
SINES
BEJA
Serpa
VILA VERDE DE FICALHO
Vila Nova de Milfontes
Ourique
Odemira
São Teotónio
São Marcos da Serra
Odeceixe
Monchique
Aljezur
Sevilla
Huelva
PORTIMÃO
Vila do Bispo
Lagos
Albufeira
Quarteira
Tavira
VILA REAL DE SANTO ANTÓNIO
SAGRES
FARO
Olhão
N101
A3,IP1
N103
N218
IC1
A11
A7,IC5
IP4
N216
A4,IP4
A24,IP3
A1,IP1
N220
N226,IC26
N102,IP2
N221
A25,IP5
IP3
N17
N234
A17,IC1
N233
N112
A23,IP2
N110,IC3
IC8
N113
IP2
IP6
A15-IP6
A8,IC1
A12,IC11
A10
N245
N251
N9
A13
N114
A6,IP7
N6
N4
A6,IP2,IP7
N254
N18,IP2
N256
N261
N121
N260,IP8
N122
N263
A2-IP1
N268
N125
A22,IP1
Motorways
Major roads
Main Roads
All year site(s)
Seasonal site(s)
No sites listed
200m +
0-200m
0 30 60 90 120 150 km
0 20 40 60 80 100 miles
N
W
E
S
A B C D
1 2 3 4

Spain

Alhambra Garden, Granada

Population: 45 million

Capital: Madrid (population 3.3 million)

Area: 510,000 sq km (inc Balearic & Canary Islands)

Bordered by: Andorra, France, Portugal

Terrain: High, rugged central plateau, mountains to north and south

Climate: Temperate climate; hot summers, cold winters in the interior; more moderate summers and cool winters along the northern and eastern coasts; very hot summers and mild/warm winters along the southern coast

Coastline: 4,964 km

Highest Point (mainland Spain): Mulhacén (Granada) 3,478 m

Languages: Castilian Spanish, Catalan, Galician, Basque

Local Time: GMT or BST + 1, ie 1 hour ahead of the UK all year

Currency: Euro divided into 100 cents; £1 = €1.10, €1 = 90 pence (September 2009)

Telephoning: From the UK dial 0034 for Spain. All numbers have 9 digits, starting with 9, which incorporate the area code. Mobile phone numbers start with a 6. To call the UK dial 0044, omitting the initial zero of the area code. To call Gibraltar dial 00350

Emergency numbers: Police 112; Fire brigade 112; Ambulance (SAMUR) 112. Operators speak English. Civil Guard 062

Public Holidays 2010

Jan 1, 6; Apr 1, 2, 5; May 1; Aug 15; Oct 12 (National Holiday); Nov 1; Dec 6 (Constitution Day), 8 (Immaculate Conception), 25. Several other dates are celebrated for fiestas according to region. School summer holidays stretch from mid-June to mid-September

Tourist Office

SPANISH TOURIST OFFICE
P.O. BOX 4009, LONDON W1A 6NB
Tel: 0845 9400180 (brochure requests) or 020 7486 8077
(Visits by appointment only)
www.spain.info/uk
info.londres@tourspain.es

The following introduction to Spain should be read in conjunction with the important information contained in the Handbook chapters at the front of this guide.

Camping and Caravanning

There are more than 1,200 campsites in Spain with something to suit all tastes – from some of the best and biggest holiday parks in Europe, to a wealth of attractive small sites offering a personal, friendly welcome. Most campsites are located near the Mediterranean, especially on the Costa Brava and Costa del Sol, as well as in the Pyrenees and other areas of tourist interest. Campsites are indicated by blue road signs. In general pitch sizes are small at about 80 square metres.

Recent visitors report that many popular, coastal sites favoured for long winter stays may contain tightly packed pitches whose long-term residents erect large awnings, umbrellas and other secondary structures. Many sites allow pitches to be reserved from year to year which can result in a tight knit community possibly biased to one nationality. As a result the availability of pitches to short term tourists may be restricted to the smaller or less favoured areas of the site. If planning to stay on sites in the popular coastal areas between late spring and October, or in January and February, it is advisable to arrive early in the afternoon or to book in advance.

Although many sites claim to be open all year this cannot always be relied on and if planning a visit out of season it is advisable to check first. It is commom for many 'all year' sites to open only at the weekends during the winter and facilities may be very limited.

A Camping Card International (CCI), while not compulsory, is recommended and is increasingly required when checking into sites. Failing that, provide reception staff with a photocopy of your passport for registration purposes rather than leave your passport for later collection. Senior citizens may be eligible for discounted prices at some sites on presentation of proof of age.

Motor Caravanners

A number of local authorities now provide dedicated or short stay areas for motor caravanners called 'Áreas de Servicio'. For details see the websites www.lapaca.org (click on the motor caravan symbol) or www.viajarenautocaravana.com (click on 'Donde parar' under 'Preparando una salida') for a list of Spanish regions/towns which have at least one of these dedicated areas.

The French website, www.campingcar-infos.com also contains comprehensive information on 'áreas de servicio' in Spain and Portugal. In addition, a guide entitled 'All the Aires – Spain and Portugal' is published by Vicarious Books, www.vicariousbooks.co.uk, tel 0131 208 3333.

It is rare that yours will be the only motor caravan staying on such areas, but take sensible precautions and avoid any that are isolated.

Some motor caravan service points are situated in motorway service areas. Use these only as a last resort and do not be tempted to park overnight. The risk of a break-in is high.

Recent visitors to tourist areas on Spain's Mediterranean coast report that the parking of motor caravans on public roads and, in some instances in public parking areas, may be prohibited in an effort to discourage 'wild camping'. Specific areas where visitors have encountered this problem include Alicante, Dénia, Palamós and the Murcian coast. Police are frequently in evidence moving parked motor caravans on and it is understood that a number of owners of motor caravans have been fined for parking on sections of the beach belonging to the local authority.

Country Information

Cycling

There are more than 1,700 km of dedicated cycle paths in Spain, many of which follow disused railway tracks. Known as 'Vias Verdes' (Green Ways) they can be found mainly in northern Spain, in Andalucia, around Madrid and inland from the Costa Blanca. For more information see the website www.viasverdes.com or contact the Spanish Tourist Office.

There are cycle lanes in major cities and towns such as Barcelona, Bilbao, Córdoba, Madrid, Seville and Valencia. Madrid alone has over 100 km of cycle lanes

It is compulsory for all cyclists, regardless of age, to wear a safety helmet on all roads outside built-up areas. At night, in tunnels or in bad weather, bicycles must have front and rear lights, together with reflectors at the rear and on wheels and pedals. Cyclists must also wear a reflective waistcoat or jacket while riding at night on roads outside built-up areas (to be visible from a distance of 150 metres) or when visibility is bad.

Strictly speaking, cyclists have right of way when motor vehicles wish to cross their path to turn left or right, but great care should be taken. Do not proceed unless you are sure that a motorist is giving way.

Transportation of Bicycles

Spanish regulations stipulate that motor cycles or bicycles may be carried on the rear of a vehicle providing the rack to which the motorcycle or bicycle is fastened has been designed for the purpose. Lights, indicators, number plate and any signals made by the driver must not be obscured and the rack should not compromise the carrying vehicle's stability.

An overhanging load, such as bicycles, should not extend beyond the width of the vehicle but may exceed the length of the vehicle by up to 10% (up to 15% in the case of indivisible items). The load must be indicated by a 50 cm square panel with reflective red and white diagonal stripes. These panels may be purchased in the UK from motor caravan or caravan dealers/accessory shops. There is currently no requirement for bicycle racks to be certified or pass a technical inspection.

If you are planning to travel from Spain to Portugal please note that slightly different official regulations apply which are set out in the Portugal Country Introduction.

Electricity and Gas

Usually the current on campsites is 4 amps or more. Plugs have two round pins. Many campsites do not yet have CEE connections.

Campingaz is widely available in 901 and 907 cylinders. The Cepsa Company sells butane gas cylinders and regulators, which are available in large stores and petrol stations, and the Repsol Company sells butane cylinders at their petrol stations throughout the country. It is understood that Repsol and Cepsa depots will refill cylinders, but the Caravan Club does not recommend this practice.

French and Spanish butane and propane gas cylinders are understood to be widely available in Andorra.

*See **Electricity and Gas** in the section **DURING YOUR STAY.***

Entry Formalities

Holders of valid British and Irish passports are permitted to stay up to 90 days without a visa.

EU residents planning to stay longer are required to register in person at the Oficina de Extranjeros (Foreigners' Office) in their province of residence or at a designated police station. You will be issued with a certificate confirming that the registration obligation has been fulfilled.

Regulations for Pets

*See **Pet Travel Scheme** under **Documents** in the section **PLANNING AND TRAVELLING.***

Dogs must be kept on a lead in public places and in a car they should be isolated from the driver by means of bars or netting.

Medical Services

Basic emergency health care is available free from practitioners in the Spanish National Health Service on production of a European Health Insurance Card (EHIC). Some health centres offer both private and state-provided health care and you should ensure that staff are aware which service you require. In some parts of the country you may have to travel some distance to attend a surgery or health clinic operating within the state health service. In any event, it is probably quicker and more convenient to use a private clinic, but the Spanish health service will not refund any private health care charges.

In an emergency go to the casualty department (urgencias) of any major public hospital. Urgent treatment is free in a public ward on production of an EHIC; for other treatment you will have to pay a proportion of the cost.

Medicines prescribed by health service practitioners can be obtained from any pharmacy (farmacia) and are free to EU pensioners. In all major towns there is a 24 hour pharmacy.

Dental treatment is not generally provided under the state system and you will have to pay for treatment.

The EHIC is not accepted in Andorra.

You are strongly recommended to obtain comprehensive travel and medical insurance before travelling to Spain, such as the Caravan Club's Red Pennant Overseas Holiday Insurance – see www.caravanclub.co.uk/redpennant

*See **Medical Matters** in the section **DURING YOUR STAY.***

Opening Hours

Banks – Mon-Fri 9am-2pm, Sat 9am-1pm.

Museums – Tue-Sat 10am-8pm, Sun 10am-2pm; closed Monday.

Post Offices – Mon-Fri 8.30am-2/2.30pm & 5pm-8pm, Sat 9am-1pm.

Shops – Mon-Sat 10am-1pm & 3pm-8pm; department stores and shopping centres do not close for lunch.

Safety and Security

Street crime is common in many Spanish towns and holiday resorts and is occasionally accompanied by violence. Avoid carrying passports, credit cards, travel tickets and money all together in handbags or pockets and keep all valuable personal items such as cameras or jewellery out of sight. The authorities have stepped up the police presence in tourist areas but nevertheless, you should remain alert at all times (including at airports, train and bus stations, and even in supermarkets and their car parks).

In Madrid particular care should be taken in the Puerto de Sol and surrounding streets, including the Plaza Mayor, Retiro Park and Lavapies, and on the metro. This advice also applies to the Ramblas, Monjuic, Plaza Catalunya, Port Vell and Olympic Port areas of Barcelona. Be wary of approaches by strangers either asking directions or offering any kind of help. These approaches are sometimes ploys to distract attention while they or their accomplices make off with valuables and/or take note of credit card numbers for future illegal use. Beware muggers who use children or babies to distract your attention while you are being robbed.

The incidence of rape and sexual assault is very low; nevertheless attacks occur and are often carried out by other British nationals. Visitors are advised not to lower their personal security awareness because they are on holiday. You should also be alert to the availability and possible use of 'date rape' drugs. Purchase your own drinks and keep sight of them at all times to make sure they cannot be spiked.

Motorists travelling on motorways – particularly those north and south of Barcelona, in the Alicante region, on the M30, M40 and M50 Madrid ring roads and on the A4 and A5 – should be wary of approaches by bogus policemen in plain clothes travelling in unmarked cars. In all traffic-related matters police officers will be in uniform. Unmarked vehicles will have a flashing electronic sign in the rear window reading 'Policía' or 'Guardia Civil' and normally have blue flashing lights incorporated into their headlights, which are activated when the police stop you. In non-traffic related matters police officers may be in plain clothes but you have the right to ask to see identification. Genuine officers may ask you to show them your documents but would not request that you hand over your bag or wallet. If in any doubt, converse through the car window and telephone the police on 112 or the Guardia Civil on 062 and ask them for confirmation that the registration number of the vehicle corresponds to an official police vehicle.

On the A7 motorway between the La Junquera and Tarragona toll stations be alert for 'highway pirates' who flag down foreign-registered and hire cars (the latter have a distinctive number plate), especially those towing caravans. Motorists are sometimes targetted in service areas, followed and subsequently tricked into stopping on the hard shoulder of the motorway. The usual ploy is for the driver or passenger in a passing vehicle, which may be 'official-looking', to suggest by gesture that there is something seriously wrong with a rear wheel or exhaust pipe (a tyre having been punctured earlier, for example, at a petrol station). The Club has received reports of the involvement of a second vehicle whose occupants also indicate a problem at the rear of your vehicle and gesture that you should pull over onto the hard shoulder. If flagged down by other motorists or a motorcyclist in this way, be extremely wary. Within the Barcelona urban area thieves may also employ the 'punctured tyre' tactic at traffic lights.

In instances such as this, the Spanish Tourist Office advises you not to pull over but to wait until you reach a service area or toll station. If you do get out of your car when flagged down take care it is locked while you check outside, even if someone is left inside. Car keys should never be left in the ignition. Be suspicious when parked in lay-bys or picnic areas of approaches by other motorists asking for help.

A few incidents have been reported of visitors being approached by a bogus uniformed police officer asking to inspect wallets for fake euro notes, or to check their identity by keying their credit card PIN into an official-looking piece of equipment carried by the officer. If in doubt ask to see a police officer's official indentification, refuse to comply with the request and offer instead to go to the nearest police station.

Spanish police have set up an emergency number for holidaymakers employing English-speaking staff and offering round-the-clock assistance – 902-10 21 12. An English-speaking operator will take a statement about the incident, translate it into Spanish and fax or email it to the nearest police station. You still have to report in person to a police station if you have an accident, or have been robbed or swindled, and the helpline operator will advise you where to find the nearest one.

The Basque terrorist organisation, ETA, announced an end to its ceasefire with effect from June 2007. There is a very real threat of terrorism – real or hoax – in Spain and, while British tourists are not a target for ETA, attacks could be indiscriminate and against civilian targets and you may be caught in an attack. You should be vigilant and follow the instructions of local police and other authorities.

Coast guards operate a beach flag system to indicate the general safety of beaches for swimming: red – do not enter the water; yellow – take precautions;

green – all clear. Coast guards operate on most of the popular beaches, so if in doubt, ask. During the summer months stinging jellyfish frequent Mediterranean coastal waters.

There is a high risk of forest fires during the hottest months and you should avoid camping in areas with limited escape routes. Take care to avoid actions that could cause a fire, eg careless disposal of cigarette ends. It is possible that the Spanish government will introduce a total prohibition on the lighting of fires (including barbecues) in forest areas throughout Spain.

Respect Spanish laws and customs. Parents should be aware that Spanish law defines anyone under the age of 18 as a minor, subject to parental control or adult supervision. Any unaccompanied minor coming to the attention of the local authorities for whatever reason is deemed to be vulnerable under the law and faces being taken into a minors' centre for protection until a parent or suitable guardian can be found.

Andorra

For Consular help while in Andorra contact the British Consulate-General in Barcelona – see below.

*See **Safety and Security** in the section **DURING YOUR STAY.***

British Embassy & Consulate-General

TORRE ESPACIO, PASEO DE LA CASTELLANA 259D
E-28046 MADRID
Tel: 917-14 64 00
http://ukinspain.fco.gov.uk/en/
Madrid.Consulate@fco.gov.uk

British Consulate-General

AVDA DIAGONAL 477-13º, E-08036 BARCELONA
Tel: 933-66 62 00
Barcelona.Consulate@fco.gov.uk

There are also British Consulates in Bilbao, Alicante and Málaga.

Irish Embassy

IRELAND HOUSE, PASEO DE LA CASTELLANA 46-4
E-28046 MADRID
Tel: 914-36 40 93
www.embassyofireland.es

There are also Irish Honorary Consulates in Alicante, Barcelona, Bilbao, El Ferrol, Malaga and Seville.

Customs Regulations

Alcohol and Tobacco

For import allowances for alcohol and tobacco products see ***Customs Regulations*** in the section ***PLANNING AND TRAVELLING.***

Under Spanish law the number of cigarettes which may be exported from Spain is set at eight hundred. Anything above this amount is regarded as a trade transaction which must be accompanied by the required documentation. If travellers are apprehended with more than 800 cigarettes but without the necessary paperwork, they face seizure of the cigarettes and a large fine.

Duty-Free Imports from Andorra

Duty-free shopping is permitted in Andorra, which is not a member of the EU, but there are strict limits on the amount of goods which can be imported into Spain and France from Andorra free of duty or tax, as follows:

1.5 litre of spirits or 3 litres fortified wine

5 litres of table wine

16 litres beer

300 cigarettes or 150 cigarillos or 75 cigars or 400 gm of tobacco

Other items, including perfume, up to the value of €525

Alcohol and tobacco allowances apply only to persons aged 17 or over.

Customs checks are frequently made when entering Spain or France from Andorra but there are no Customs formalities when entering Andorra from either country.

Caravans and Motor Caravans

The maximum permitted height of a caravan or motor caravan is 4 metres, width 2.55 metres and length of motor vehicle, caravan or trailer, 12 metres. Maximum combined length of car + caravan 18.75 metres.

A vehicle or vehicle combination exceeding 12 metres in length must display two yellow reflectors at the rear of the towed vehicle – see information under ***Essential Equipment*** later in this chapter.

Documents

Visitors must be able to show some form of identity if requested to do so by the police. Carry your passport, or other form of photographic ID such as a photocard driving licence at all times.

The British EU-format pink driving licence is recognised in Spain. Holders of the old-style all-green driving licence are advised to replace it with a photocard version. Alternatively, the old-style licence may be accompanied by an International Driving Permit available from the AA, Green Flag or the RAC.

At all times when driving in Spain it is compulsory to carry your driving licence, vehicle registration certificate (V5C), insurance certificate and MOT certificate, if applicable. Vehicles imported by a person other than the owner must have a letter of authority from the owner.

*See also **Documents** and **Insurance** in the section **PLANNING AND TRAVELLING.***

Money

All bank branches offer foreign currency exchange, as do many hotels and travel agents. Travellers' cheques are widely accepted as a means of payment in hotels, shops and restaurants and can be changed at banks and bureaux de change. However, recent visitors continue to report difficulties cashing euro travellers' cheques and you should not rely on them for your immediate cash needs.

The major credit cards are widely accepted as a means of payment in shops, restaurants and petrol stations. Smaller retail outlets in non-commercial areas may not accept payments by credit card – check before buying. When shopping carry your passport or photocard driving licence if paying with a credit card as you will almost certainly be asked for photographic proof of identity.

Cardholders are recommended to carry their credit card issuers'/banks' 24-hour UK contact numbers in case of loss or theft.

Keep a supply of loose change as you could be asked for it frequently in shops and at kiosks.

Motoring

Drivers should take particular care as driving standards can be erratic, eg excessive speed and dangerous overtaking, and the accident rate is higher than in the UK. Pedestrians should take particular care when crossing roads (even at zebra crossings) or walking along unlit roads at night.

Accidents

The Central Traffic Department runs an assistance service for victims of traffic accidents linked to an SOS telephone network along motorways and some roads. Motorists in need of help should ask for 'auxilio en carretera' (road assistance). The special ambulances used are connected by radio to hospitals participating in the scheme.

Alcohol

The maximum permitted level of alcohol is 50 milligrams in 100 millilitres of blood, ie less than in the UK (80 milligrams) and it reduces to 30 milligrams for drivers with less than two years' experience and for drivers of vehicles over 3,500 kg. After a traffic accident all road users involved have to undergo a breath test. Penalties for refusing a test or exceeding the legal limit are severe and may include immobilisation of vehicles, a large fine and suspension of your driving licence. This limit applies to cyclists as well as drivers of private vehicles.

Breakdown Service

The motoring organisation, Real Automóvil Club de España (RACE), operates a breakdown service and assistance may be obtained 24 hours a day by telephoning the national centre in Madrid on 915-94 93 47. After hearing a message in Spanish press the number 1 to access the control room where English is spoken.

RACE's breakdown vehicles are blue and yellow and display the words 'RACE Asistencia' on the sides. There are assistance points throughout mainland and insular Spain and vehicles patrol the main roads and towns. This service provides on-the-spot minor repairs and towing to the nearest garage. Charges vary according to type of vehicle and time of day, but payment for road assistance must be made in cash.

Essential Equipment

Glasses

Spanish drivers wearing glasses to drive must carry a spare pair at all times when driving. Visiting motorists are advised to do the same in order to avoid any local difficulties.

Lights

Dipped headlights should be used in built-up areas, in tunnels and at night on motorways and fast roads, even if they are well lit. Spare bulbs and fuses should be carried, together with the tools to fit them.

Dipped headlights must be used at all times on 'special' roads, eg temporary routes created at the time of road works such as the hard shoulder, or in a contra-flow lane.

Hazard warning lights should be used if you are unable to reach the minimum required speed on a motorway – 60 km/h (37 mph) – or to alert drivers behind you to danger ahead.

Mirrors

The law requires all vehicles towing caravans to be fitted with extension mirrors

Reflective Jacket

If your vehicle is immobilised on the carriageway outside a built-up area at night, or in poor visibility, you must wear a reflective jacket or waistcoat when getting out of your vehicle. This rule also applies to passengers who may leave the vehicle, for example, to assist with a repair.

Reflectors for Caravans

Any vehicle or vehicle combination, ie car+caravan over 12 metres in length must display at the rear of the towed vehicle two yellow reflectors with a red outline. These must be positioned between 50 cm and 150 cm off the ground and must be 565 mm x 200 mm in size. Alternatively a single reflector may be used measuring 1,130 mm x 200 mm. To buy these reflectors contact www.freightproducts.co.uk, tel 01926 641222.

Warning Triangles

Foreign-registered vehicles are recommended to carry two triangles (as required by Spanish drivers) in order to avoid any local difficulties which may arise. Warning triangles should be placed 50 metres behind and in front of broken-down vehicles.

*See also **Motoring – Equipment** in the section **PLANNING AND TRAVELLING.***

Fuel

Credit cards are accepted at most petrol stations, but you should be prepared to pay cash if necessary in remote areas.

Leaded petrol is not available.

LPG (Autogas) can be purchased from some Repsol filling stations. Details of approximately 25 sales outlets throughout mainland Spain can be found on www.spainautogas.com or on www.repsolypf.com. Alternatively you will find them listed in 'LPG Gids', a guide sold by Vicarious Books – call 0131 208 3333 or see www.vicariousbooks.co.uk

*See also **Fuel** under **Motoring – Advice** in the section **PLANNING AND TRAVELLING.***

Mountain Passes and Tunnels

Some passes are occasionally blocked in winter following heavy falls of snow. Check locally for information on road conditions.

*See **Mountain Passes and Tunnels** in the section **PLANNING AND TRAVELLING.***

Parking

Yellow road markings indicate parking restrictions. Vehicles must be parked on the right-hand side of the carriageway except in one-way streets where parking is allowed on both sides. Illegally parked vehicles may be towed away or clamped but, despite this, you will frequently encounter double and triple parking.

In large cities there are parking meters patrolled by traffic wardens. Signs indicate blue zones (zona azul); the maximum period of parking is 90 minutes between 8am and 9pm. Parking discs are available from town halls, hotels and travel agents. In the centre of some towns there is a 'zona ORA' where parking is permitted for up to 90 minutes against tickets bought in tobacconists.

*See also **Parking Facilities for the Disabled** under **Motoring – Advice** in the section **PLANNING AND TRAVELLING.***

Pedestrians

Jaywalking is not permitted. In main towns pedestrians may not cross a road unless a traffic light is at red against the traffic, or a policeman gives permission. Offenders may be fined.

Priority and Overtaking

As a general rule traffic coming from the right has priority at intersections but when entering a main road from a secondary road drivers must give way to traffic from both directions. Traffic already on a roundabout (ie from the left) has priority over traffic joining it. Trams and emergency vehicles have priority at all times over other road users and you must not pass trams which are stationary while letting passengers on or off.

Motorists must give way to cyclists on a cycle lane, cycle crossing or other specially designated cycle track. They must also give way to cyclists when turning left or right.

You must use your indicators when overtaking. If a vehicle comes up behind you signalling that it wants to overtake and if the road ahead is clear, you must use your right indicator to acknowledge the situation.

Roads

There are approximately 14,000 km of highways and dual carriageways. Roads marked AP (autopista) are toll roads and roads marked A (autovía) or N (nacional) are dual carriageways with motorway characteristics – but not necessarily with a central reservation – and are toll-free. In recent years some major national roads have become dual carriageways and, therefore, have two identifying codes or have changed codes, eg the N-I from Madrid to Irún near the French border is now known as the A1 or Autovía del Norte. Autovías are often as fast as autopistas and are generally more scenic.

Local roads managed by regional or local authorites are prefixed with the various identification letters such as C, CV, GR, L or T.

All national roads and roads of interest to tourists are in good condition and well-signposted, and driving is straightforward. Hills often tend to be longer and steeper than in parts of the UK and some of the coastal roads are very winding, so traffic flows at the speed of the slowest lorry.

As far as accidents are concerned the N340 coast road, especially between Málaga and Fuengirola, is notorious, as are the Madrid ring roads, and special vigilance is necessary.

Road humps are making an appearance on Spanish roads and recent visitors report that they may be high, putting low stabilisers at risk.

Andorra

The main road to Barcelona from Andorra is the C14/C1412/N141b via Ponts and Calaf. It has a good surface and avoids any high passes. The N260 along the south side of Andorra via Puigcerda and La Seo de Urgel also has a good surface.

Road Signs and Markings

Road signs conform to international standards. Lines and markings are white. Place names may appear both in standard (Castilian) Spanish and in a local form, eg Gerona/Girona, San Sebastián/ Donostia, Jávea/Xàbio, and road atlases and maps usually show both.

You may encounter the following signs:

Carretera de peaje – *Toll road*

Ceda el paso – *Give way*

Cuidado – *Caution*

Curva peligrosa – *Dangerous bend*

Despacio – *Slow*

Desviación – *Detour*

Dirección única – *One-way street*

Embotellamiento – *Traffic jam*

Estacionamiento prohibido – *No parking*

Estrechamiento – *Narrow lane*

Gravillas – *Loose chippings/gravel*

Inicio – *Start*

Obras – *Roadworks*

Paso prohibido – *No entry*

Peligro – *Danger*

Prioridad – *Right of way*

Salida – *Exit*

Todas direcciones – *All directions*

Many non-motorway roads have a continuous white line on the near (verge) side of the carriageway. Any narrow lane between this line and the side of the carriageway is intended primarily for pedestrians and cyclists and not for use as a hard shoulder.

A continuous line also indicates 'no stopping' even if it is possible to park entirely off the road and it should be treated as a double white line and not crossed except in a serious emergency. If your vehicle breaks down on a road where there is a continuous white line along the verge, it should not be left unattended as this is illegal and an on-the-spot fine may be levied.

Many road junctions have a continuous white centre line along the main road. This line must not be crossed to execute a left turn, despite the lack of any other 'no left turn' signs. If necessary, drive on to a 'cambio de sentido' (change of direction) sign to turn.

Turning permitted

Change direction only as shown

Traffic police are keen to enforce both the above regulations.

Watch out for traffic lights which may be mounted high above the road and hard to spot. Green, amber and red arrows are used on traffic lights at some intersections. Two red lights mean no entry.

Speed Limits

*See **Speed Limits Table** under **Motoring – Advice** in the section **PLANNING AND TRAVELLING.***

In built-up areas, speed is limited to 50 km/h (31 mph) except where signs indicate a lower limit. Reduce your speed to 20 km/h (13 mph) in residential areas. On motorways and dual carriageways in built-up areas, speed is limited to 80 km/h (50 mph) except where indicated by signs.

Outside built-up areas motor caravans of any weight are limited to 90 km/h (56 mph) on motorways and dual carriageways, to 80 km/h (50 mph) on other main roads with more than one lane in each direction, and to 70 km/h (44 mph) on secondary roads.

It is prohibited to own, transport or use radar detectors. For the location of fixed speed cameras in Spain see www.fixedspeedcamera.com. Drivers are not allowed to make signals to warn other drivers of the presence of police, eg headlight-flashing.

Towing

Motor caravans are prohibited from towing a car unless the car is on a special towing trailer with all four wheels off the ground.

Any towing combination in excess of 10 metres in length must keep at least 50 metres from the vehicle in front except in built-up areas, on roads where overtaking is prohibited or where there are several lanes in the same direction.

Traffic Jams

Roads around the large Spanish cities such as Madrid, Barcelona, Zaragoza, Valencia and Seville are extremely busy on Friday afternoons when residents leave for the mountains or coast, and again on Sunday evenings when they return. The coastal roads along the Costa Brava and the Costa Dorada may also be congested. The coast road south of Torrevieja is frequently heavily congested as a result of extensive holiday home construction.

Summer holidays extend from mid-June to mid-September and the busiest periods are the last weekend in July, the first weekend in August and the period around the Assumption holiday in mid-August.

Traffic jams occur on the busy AP7 from the French border to Barcelona during the peak summer holiday period. An alternative route now exists from Malgrat de Mar along the coast to Barcelona using the C32 where tolls are lower than on the AP7.

The Autovía de la Cataluña Central (C25) provides a rapid east-west link between Gerona and Lleida via Vic, Manresa and Tàrrega. There is fast access from Madrid to La Coruña in the far north-west via the A6/AP6.

Information on road conditions, traffic delays etc. can be found (in English) on http://infocar.dgt.es/etraffic

Violation of Traffic Regulations

The police are empowered to impose on-the-spot fines. There is usually a 30% reduction for immediate settlement; an official receipt should be obtained. An appeal may be made within 15 days and there are instructions on the back of the form in English. RACE can provide legal advice – tel 902-40 45 45.

Motorways

The Spanish motorway system has been subject to considerable expansion in recent years with more under construction or planned. The main sections of motorway are along the Mediterranean coast, across the north of the country and around Madrid. Tolls are charged on most autopistas but many sections are toll-free, as are autovias. Exits on autopistas are numbered consecutively from Madrid. Exits on autovias are numbered according to the kilometre point from Madrid.

Many different companies operate within the motorway network, each setting their own tolls which may vary according to the time of day, and classification of vehicles. For an overview of the motorway network (in English) see www.aseta.es. This website has links to the numerous motorway companies where you will be able to view routes and tolls (generally shown in Spanish only). Tolls are payable in cash or by credit card.

Avoid signposted 'Via T' lanes showing a circular sign with a white capital T on a blue background where toll collection is by electronic device only. Square 'Via T' signs are displayed above mixed lanes where other forms of payment are also accepted.

Rest areas with parking facilities, petrol stations and restaurants or cafés are strategically placed and are well-signposted. Emergency telephones are located at 2 km intervals.

Motorway signs near Barcelona are confusing. To avoid the city traffic when heading south, follow signs for Barcelona but the moment signs for Tarragona appear follow these and ignore Barcelona signs.

Touring

One of Spain's greatest attractions is undoubtedly its cuisine. Spanish cooking is rich and varied with many regional specialities and traditional dishes which have achieved worldwide fame, such as paella, gazpacho and tapas. Seafood in particular is excellent and plentiful. A fixed-price menu or 'menu del dia' invariably offers good value. Spain is one of the world's top wine producers, enjoying a great variety of high quality wines of which rioja and sherry are probably the best known. Local beer is low in alcohol content and is generally drunk as an aperitif to accompany tapas. Service is generally included in restaurant bills but a tip of approximately €1 per person up to 10% of the bill is appropriate if you have received good service. Smoking is not allowed in public places, including most bars, restaurants and cafés. In small bars and restaurants smoking may be allowed at the owner's discretion in designated areas.

Perhaps due to the benign climate and long hours of sunshine, Spaniards tend to get up later and stay out later at night than their European neighbours. Out of the main tourist season and in 'non-touristy' areas it may be difficult to find a restaurant open in the evening before 9pm. Taking a siesta is still common practice, although it is now usual for businesses to stay open during the traditional siesta hours.

Spain's many different cultural and regional influences are responsible for the variety and originality of fiestas held each year. Over 200 have been classified as 'of interest to tourists' while others have gained international fame. A full list can be obtained from the Spanish Tourist Office in London, from Real Automóvil Club de Espana (RACE) or from provincial tourist offices.

The Madrid Card, valid for one, two or three days, gives free use of public transport, free entry to various attractions and museums, including the Prado, Reina Sofia and Thyssen-Bornesmisza collection, as well as free tours and discounts at restaurants and shows. You can buy the card from www.madridcard.com, or by visiting the City Tourist Office in Plaza Mayor, or on Madrid Visión tour buses. Similar generous discounts can be obtained with the Barcelona Card, valid from one to five days, which can be purchased from tourist offices or online at www.barcelonaturisme.com. Other tourist cards are available in Burgos, Córdoba, Seville and Zaragoza.

Bullfighting is still a very popular entertainment in Spain and fights take place in the bullrings or plazas of main towns during the summer. In addition, every year each town celebrates its local Saint's Day which is always a very happy and colourful occasion.

The region of Valencia and the Balearic Islands are prone to severe storms and torrential rainfall between September and November and are probably best avoided at that time. Monitor national and regional weather on http://worldweather.wmo.int/

Gibraltar

For information on Gibraltar contact:

GIBRALTAR GOVERNMENT TOURIST OFFICE
150 STRAND
LONDON WC2R 1JA
Tel: 020 7836 0777
www.gibraltar.gi or www.gibraltar.gov.uk
info@gibraltar.gov.uk

There are no campsites on the Rock, the nearest being at San Roque and La Línea de la Concepción in Spain. The only direct access to Gibraltar from Spain is via the border at La Línea which is open 24 hours a day. You may cross on foot and it is also possible to take cars or motor caravans to Gibraltar.

A valid British passport is required for all British nationals visiting Gibraltar. Nationals of other countries should check entry requirements with the Gibraltar Government Tourist Office.

There is currently no charge for visitors to enter Gibraltar but Spanish border checks can cause delays and you should be prepared for long queues. As roads in the town are extremely narrow and bridges low, it is advisable to park on the outskirts. Visitors advise against leaving vehicles on the Spanish side of the border owing to the high risk of break-ins.

An attraction to taking the car into Gibraltar is English-style supermarkets and a wide variety of competitively priced goods free of VAT. The currency is sterling and British notes and coins circulate alongside Gibraltar pounds and pence, but note that Gibraltar notes and coins are not accepted in the UK. Scottish and Northern Irish notes are not generally accepted in Gibraltar. Euros are accepted but the exchange rate may not be favourable.

Disabled visitors to Gibraltar may obtain a temporary parking permit from the police station on production of evidence confirming their disability. This permit allows parking for up to two hours (between 8am and 10pm) in parking places reserved for disabled people.

Violence or street crime is rare but there have been reports of people walking from La Línea to Gibraltar at night being attacked and robbed.

If you need emergency medical attention while on a visit to Gibraltar, treatment at primary health care centres is free to UK passport holders under the local medical scheme. Non-UK nationals need a European Health Insurance Card (EHIC). You are not eligible for free treatment if you go to Gibraltar specifically to be treated for a condition which arose elsewhere, eg in Spain.

Local Travel

Year-round ferry services from Spain to North Africa, the Balearic Islands and the Canary Islands are operated by Acciona Trasmediterranea. All enquiries should be made through their UK agent:

SOUTHERN FERRIES
30 CHURTON STREET
VICTORIA
LONDON SW1V 2LP
Tel: 0844 8157785, Fax: 0844 815 7795
www.southernferries.co.uk
mail@southernferries.co.uk

Madrid boasts an extensive and efficient public transport network including a metro system, suburban railways and bus routes. You can purchase a pack of ten tickets which offer better value than single tickets. In addition, tourist travel passes for use on all public transport are available from metro stations, tourist offices and travel agencies and are valid for one to seven days – you will need to present your passport when buying them. Single tickets must be validated before travel. Metro systems also operate in Barcelona, Bilbao, Seville and Valencia.

A few cities operate tram services including La Coruña, Valencia, Barcelona and Bilbao. The Valencia service links Alicante, Benidorm and Dénia.

All place names used in the Site Entry listings which follow can be found in Michelin's Tourist & Motoring Atlas for Spain & Portugal, scale 1:400,000 (1 cm = 4 km).

Sites in Spain

ABEJAR *3C1* (800m NW Rural) *41.81645, -2.78869* **Camping El Concurso, Ctra Abejar-Molinos de Duero s/n, Km 1, N234, 42146 Abejar (Soria) [975-37 33 61; fax 975-37 33 96; info@campingelconcurso.com; www.campingzelconcurso.com]** N234 W fr Soria to Abejar. Turn onto rd CL117 dir Molinos de Duero, site on L. Lge, mkd pitch, pt sl, pt shd; wc; chem disp; mv service pnt; shwrs inc; el pnts (5A) inc; gas; Indtte; shop & 500m; tradsmn; rest; snacks; bar; BBQ; playgrnd; pool; paddling pool; lake 2km; some statics; dogs; phone; poss cr & noisy in ssn; ccard acc; CCI. "Nr lake & National Park; v beautiful; gd san facs; not suitable m'van due slope." ♦ Easter-12 Oct. € 19.50 2009*

🀫 **ABIZANDA** *3B2* (Rural) *42.28087, 0.19740* **Fundación Liguerré de Cinca, Ctra A138, Km 28, 22393 Abizanda (Huesca) [974-50 08 00; fax 974-50 08 30; icinca@aragon.ugt.ore; www.liguerredecinca.com]** A138 N fr Barbastro, site sp at km 29 or S fr Ainsa, site sp at km 27, 18 km S of Ainsa. Med, mkd pitch, terr, shd; wc; chem disp; shwrs inc; baby rm; el pnts (10A) €4.60; gas; Indtte; shop, rest, snacks, bar high ssn; playgrnd; pool; lake sw 1km; watersports; tennis; games rm; horseriding; cycle hire; car wash; 10% statics; dogs; phone; poss cr; Eng spkn; adv bkg; quiet; ccard acc; red long stay; CCI. "Excel facs, ltd low ssn; highly rec; site in 2 parts sep by ravine, bottom terr muddy in wet; trees may be diff for lge o'fits; helpful staff; lovely site; nearest shops at Ainsa; conv Ordesa & Monte Perdido National Park." € 19.90 2006*

🀫 **AGER** *03B2* (300m W Rural) *42.00277, 0.76472* **Camping Val d'Àger, Calle Afores s/n, 25691 Ager (Lleida) [973-45 52 00; fax 973-45 52 02; iniciatives@valldager.com; www.campingvalldager.com/]** Fr C13 turn W onto L904/C12 twd L'Ametlla & Àger. Cross Rv Noguera, site sp on L. Med, terr, pt shd; wc; chem disp; shwrs inc; el pnts €5.70; Indtte; shop & 800m; rest; snacks; bar; BBQ; playgrnd; pool high ssn; paddling pool; games area; games rm; wifi; some statics; dogs €3.60; adv bkg; quiet. "Mountain views; high o'fits rec to park nr recep (due trees); vg, peaceful site." ♦ € 22.10 2009*

🀫 **AGUILAR DE CAMPOO** *1B4* (3km W Rural) *42.78694, -4.30222* **Monte Royal Camping, Ave Virgen del Llano, s/n, 34800 Aguilar de Campóo (Palencia) [979-12 30 83]** App site fr S on N611 fr Palencia. At Aguilar de Campóo turn W at S end of rv bdge at S end of town. Site on L in 3km; sp at edge of reservoir. Fr N take 3rd exit fr rndabt on N611. Do not tow thro town. Lge, mkd pitch, pt sl, shd; wc; chem disp (wc); baby facs; shwrs €0.60; el pnts (2A) €3.30; gas; Indtte; shops 3km; rest in ssn; bar; playgrnd; sand beach nr lake; watersports; horseriding; fishing; TV; 20% statics; dogs; phone; ccard acc; CCI. "Useful, peaceful NH 2 hrs fr Santander; ltd/basic facs low ssn & poss stretched high ssn; barking dogs poss problem; friendly staff; gd walking, cycling & birdwatching in National Park; unreliable opening dates low ssn." ♦ € 18.32 2008*

🀫 **AGUILAS** *4G1* (4km NE Rural) *37.42638, -1.55083* **Camping Águilas, Ctra Cabo Cope, Los Geráneos, 30880 Águilas (Murcia) [968-41 92 05; fax 968-41 92 82; campingaquilas@hotmail.com]** Fr A7 N of Lorca take C3211 dir Águilas. On joining N332 turn L & foll sp L to Calabardina/Cabo Cope; site on L within 3km. Med, mkd pitch, hdstg, pt shd; wc; chem disp; shwrs inc; el pnts (10A) inc; gas; Indtte; shop high ssn; rest; snacks; bar; playgrnd; pool; sand beach 4km; tennis; 30% statics; phone; site clsd last 2 weeks May & Sep; Eng spkn; adv bkg; quiet; red low ssn/long stay; ccard acc; CCI. "All pitches shaded with trees or netting; clean facs; helpful warden popular winter long stay; excel." € 20.00 2006*

🀫 **AGUILAS** *4G1* (2km SW Coastal) *37.3925, -1.61111* **Camping Bellavista, Ctra de Vera, Km 3, 30880 Águilas (Murcia) [tel/fax 968-44 91 51; info@campingbellavista.com; www.campingbellavista.com]** Site on N332 Águilas to Vera rd on R at top of sh, steep hill, 100m after R turn to El Cocon. Well marked by flags. Fr S by N332 on L 400m after fuel stn, after v sharp corner. Sm, hdg pitch, hdstg, pt sl, pt shd; wc; chem disp; shwrs inc; el pnts (10A) €4.60 or metered; gas; Indtte; sm shop; tradsmn; rest adj; snacks; BBQ; playgrnd; sand beach 500m; cycle hire; wifi; some statics; dogs €0.90; poss cr; Eng spkn; adv bkg; quiet; ccard acc; red long stay/low ssn; CCI. "Gd autumn/winter stay; clean, tidy, improving site with excel facs; pool planned for 2009; ltd pitches for lge o'fits; helpful owner; fine views; rd noise at 1 end; excel town & vg beaches." € 19.80 2008*

There aren't many sites open at this time of year. We'd better phone ahead to check that the one we're heading for is open.

🀫 **AINSA** *3B2* (2.5km N Rural) *42.43555, 0.13583* **Camping Pena Montanesa, Ctra Ainsa-Bielsa, Km 2.3, 22360 Labuerda (Huesca) [974-50 00 32; fax 974-50 09 91; info@penamontanesa.com; www.penamontanesa.com]** E fr Huesca on N240 for approx 50km, turn N onto N123 just after Barbastro twd Ainsa. In 8km turn onto A138 N for Ainsa & Bielsa. Or fr Bielsa Tunnel to A138 S to Ainsa & Bielsa, site sp. NB: Bielsa Tunnel sometimes clsd bet Oct & Easter due to weather. Lge, mkd pitch, shd; htd wc; chem disp; mv service pnt; baby facs; sauna; shwrs inc; el pnts (10A) inc; gas; Indtte; supmkt; rest; snacks; bar; BBQ (gas/elec only); playgrnd; htd pools (1 covrd); paddling pool; lake sw 2km; canoeing; tennis; cycle hire; horseriding; games area; entmnt; wifi; TV; 20% statics; dogs €4.15; phone; adv bkg; quiet; ccard acc; red low ssn; CCI. "Friendly staff; gd, clean facs; pitches poss tight due trees; beautiful medieval town & Ordesa National Park; excel." ♦ € 38.00 ABS - E12 2009*

See advertisement on next page

Spain

AINSA *3B2* (1km E Rural) *42.41944, 0.15111* **Camping Ainsa, Ctra Ainsa-Campo, 22330 Ainsa (Huesca) [tel/fax 974-50 02 60; info@campingainsa.com; www.campingainsa.com]** Fr Ainsa take N260 E dir Pueyo de Araguás, cross rv bdge, site sp L in 200m. Foll lane to site. Sm, terr, pt shd; wc; baby facs; shwrs inc; el pnts €4.75; gas; lndtte; shop 1km; rest, snacks bar high ssn; playgrnd; pool; games rm; wifi; TV; 50% statics; dogs €2.20; phone; poss cr; some indus noise mornings; ccard acc; red low ssn; CCI. "Pleasant, welcoming, well-maintained site; fine view of old city & some pitches mountain views; vg san facs; not suitable lge o'fits; gd pool." Holy Week-30 Oct. € 22.25 2009*

⊞ **AINSA** *3B2* (6km NW Rural) *42.43004, 0.07881* **Camping Boltaña, Ctra N260, Km 442, Ctra Margudgued, 22340 Boltaña (Huesca) [974-50 23 47; fax 974-50 20 23; info@campingboltana.com; www.campingboltana.com]** Fr Ainsa head twd Boltaña, turn L over rv & foll sp. Site is 2km E of Boltaña, final 300m on single track rd. Med, mkd pitch, pt sl, terr, pt shd; htd wc; chem disp; baby facs; shwrs inc; el pnts (4-10A) inc; gas; lndtte; shop & 2km; tradsmn; rest; snacks; bar; playgrnd; pool; paddling pool; fishing 600m; tennis 1km; horseriding 500m; games area; cycle hire; adventure sports; 60% statics; dogs €2.90; phone; clsd 15 Dec-15 Jan; poss cr; Eng spkn; adv bkg; poss noisy; ccard acc; red low ssn. "Conv Ordesa National Park; poss diff for disabled travellers; san facs stretched high ssn; friendly, helpful staff; Ainsa old town worth visit; excel." ♦ € 35.00 (CChq acc) 2008*

ALBANYA *3B3* (W Rural) *42.30630, 2.70970* **Camping Bassegoda Park, Camí Camp de l'Illa, 17733 Albanyà (Gerona) [972-54 20 20; fax 972-54 20 21; info@bassegodapark.com; www.bassegodapark.com]** Fr France exit AP7/E15 junc 3 onto GI510 to Albanyà. At end of rd turn R, site on rvside. Fr S exit AP7 junc 4 dir Terrades, then Albanyà. App poss diff for lge o'fits Med, hdg pitch, hdstg, pt shd; htd wc; chem disp; mv waste; baby facs; shwrs inc; el pnts (10A) €5.95; lndtte; shop; rest; snacks; bar; playgrnd; pool; fishing; trekking; hill walking; mountain biking; games area; games rm; entmnt; 8% statics; dogs €4.25 (1 only); phone; Eng spkn; adv bkg; quiet; red low ssn/snr citizens/CCI. "Excel site surrounded by woods, rvs & streams; excel san facs, espec for disabled; well worth a detour." ♦ 1 Mar-11 Dec. € 26.20 2009*

ALBARRACIN *3D1* (2km E Rural) *40.41228, -1.42788* **Camp Municipal Ciudad de Albarracín, Camino de Gea s/n, 44100 Albarracín (Teruel) [tel/fax 978-71 01 97 or 657-49 84 33 (mob); www.campingalbarracin.com]** Fr Teruel take A1512 to Albarracín. Go thro vill, foll camping sps. Med, pt sl, pt shd; wc; chem disp; baby facs; shwrs inc; el pnts (16A) €2.90; gas; lndtte; shop & adj; tradsmn; rest; snacks; bar; BBQ; playgrnd; pool in ssn; some statics; dogs; phone; poss cr; adv bkg; quiet; ccard acc; CCI. "Excel site; immac san facs; narr pitches poss diff for lge o'fits; sports cent adj; gd touring base & gd walking fr site; rec." 1 Mar-2 Nov. € 13.70 2008*

ALBERCA, LA *1D3* (2km N Rural) *40.50915, -6.12312* **Camping Al-Bereka, Ctra Salamanca-La Alberca, Km 75.6, 37624 La Alberca (Salamanca) [923-41 51 95; www.albereka.com]** Fr Salamanca S on N630/E803 take C515 to Mogarraz, then SA202 to La Alberca. Site on L at km 75.6 bef vill. Rte fr Ciudad Real OK but bumpy in places. Med, mkd pitch, terr, shd; wc; chem disp; shwrs inc; el pnts (3-6A) €3.50; lndtte; shop; rest; snacks; bar; BBQ; playgrnd; pool; paddling pool; TV; some statics; dogs; quiet; ccard acc; CCI. "Gd, quiet site; helpful owner; beautiful countryside; La Alberca medieval vill with abbey." ♦ 15 Mar-31 Oct. € 21.40 2009*

ALBERCA, LA *1D3* (6km N Rural) *40.52112, -6.13756* **Camping Sierra de Francia, Ctra Salamanca-La Alberca, Km 73, El Caserito, 37623 Nava de Francia (Salamanca) [923-45 40 81; fax 923-45 40 01; www.campingsierradefrancia.com]** Fr Cuidad Rodrigo take C515. Turn R at El Cabaco, site on L in approx 2km. Med, shd; wc; shwrs; el pnts €3.75; gas; lndtte; shop; rest; bar; playgrnd; pool; horseriding; cycle hire; some statics; dogs; quiet; ccard acc. "Conv 'living history' vill of La Alberca & Monasterio San Juan de la Peña; excel views." ♦ 1 Apr-30 Sep. € 18.88 2006*

⊞ **ALCALA DE LOS GAZULES** *2H3* (4km E Rural) *36.46403, -5.66482* **Camping Los Gazules, Ctra de Patrite, Km 4, 11180 Alcalá de los Gazules (Cádiz) [956-42 04 86; fax 956-42 03 88; losgazules@hotmail.com; www.campinglosgazules.com]** Fr N exit A381 at 1st junc to Alcalá, proceed thro town to 1st rndabt & turn L onto A375/A2304 dir Ubriqu, site sp strt ahead in 1km onto CA2115 dir Patrite on v sharp L. Fr S exit A381 at 1st sp for Acalá. At rndabt turn R onto A375/A2304 dir Ubrique. Then as above. Med, mkd pitch, pt sl, pt shd; wc; chem disp (wc); mv service pnt; shwrs inc; el pnts (10A) €4.50 (poss rev pol); lndtte; shop; rest; bar; playgrnd; pool; cycle hire; TV rm; 90% statics; phone; adv bkg; red long stay/low ssn; CCI. "Well-maintained, upgraded site; take care canopy frames; sm pitches & tight turns & kerbs on site; friendly, helpful staff; attractive town with v narr streets, leave car in park at bottom & walk; gd walking, birdwatching; ltd facs low ssn; ltd touring pitches." € 20.00 2008*

ALCANAR *3D2* (3km N Coastal) *40.59500, 0.56998* **Camping Los Alfaques, 43530 Alcanar Platja (Tarragona) [977-74 05 61; fax 977-74 25 95; info@alfaques.com; www.alfaques.com]** Fr N exit AP7 junc 41 onto N340 thro Amposta, site sp on N340 approx 2km S of Sant Carles de la Ràpita. Lge, mkd pitch, pt sl, shd; wc; chem disp (wc); shwrs inc; el pnts (5A) €5; gas; lndtte; shop & 2km; rest; snacks; bar; playgrnd; pool 200m; steep, shgl beach adj; fishing; internet; entmnt; 30% statics; dogs €3; phone; rd noise. "Sm, cr pitches - seafront pitches rec; conv ancient town of Morella; no twin-axles; NH only." 1 Apr-30 Sep. € 26.00 2008*

ALCANTARA *2E2* (4km NW Rural) *39.74126, -6.89520* **Camping Puente de Alcántara, Ctra EX117, Km 36, Finca Los Cabezos, 10980 Alcántara (Cáceres) [927-39 09 47; recepcion@campingalcantara.com; www.campingalcantara.com]** W fr Alcántara to Roman bdge over Rv Tagus. Turn R at camping sp over cattle grid. Med, pt sl, unshd; wc; chem disp; shwrs inc; el pnts (5A) €4; gas; lndtte; shop; snacks; bar; playgrnd; pool; watersports; tennis; adv bkg; quiet; ccard acc; CCI. "Nice views; attractive vill with many storks; gd birdwatching area; friendly owner; ltd facs low ssn." ♦ 15 Mar-30 Sep. € 18.00 2008*

⊞ **ALCARAZ** *4F1* (6km E Rural) *38.67301, -2.40462* **Camping Sierra de Peñascosa, Ctra Peñascosa-Bogarra, Km 1, 02313 Peñascosa (Albacete) [967-38 25 21; info@campingsierrapenascosa.com; www.campingsierrapenascosa.com]** Fr N322 turn E bet km posts 279 & 280 sp Peñascosa. In vill foll site sp for 1km beyond vill. Gravel access track & narr ent. Sm, mkd pitch, hdstg, terr, shd; wc; chem disp; shwrs; el pnts (6A) €4; gas; lndtte; shop; rest high ssn; snacks; bar; playgrnd; pool; cycle hire; dogs €2; open w/end in winter; v quiet; ccard acc; CCI. "Not suitable lge o'fits or faint-hearted; pitches sm, uneven & amongst trees - care needed when manoeuvring; historical sites nr." ♦ € 21.00 2009*

⊞ **ALCOSSEBRE** *3D2* (2.5km NE Coastal/Rural) *40.27030, 0.30670* **Camping Ribamar, Partida Ribamar s/n, 12579 Alcossebre (Castellón) [964-76 11 63; fax 964-76 14 84; info@campingribamar.com; www.campingribamar.com]** Exit AP7 at junc 44 into N340 & foll sp to Alcossebre, then dir Serra d'Irta & Las Fuentes. Turn in dir of sea & foll sp to site in 2km. Med, hdg/mkd pitch, hdstg, pt sl, terr, pt shd; wc; chem disp; mv service pnt; baby facs; shwrs inc; el pnts (10A) €4.30; gas; lndtte (inc dryer); shop; tradsmn; supmkt 2km; rest; bar; playgrnd; pool; sand beach 100m; paddling pool; tennis; games area; games rm; wifi; entmnt; TV rm; 25% statics; dogs €1.60; poss cr; Eng spkn; adv bkg; quiet; red long stay/low ssn; CCI. "Excel, refurbished site in 'natural park'; warm welcome; realistic pitch sizes; variable prices; excel san facs; beware caterpillars in spring - poss dangerous for dogs." ♦ € 40.00 2009*

See advertisement on next page

⊞ **ALCOSSEBRE** *3D2* (2.5km S Coastal) *40.22138, 0.26888* **Camping Playa Tropicana, 12579 Alcossebre (Castellón) [964-41 24 63; fax 964 41 28 05; info@playatropicana.com; www.playatropicana.com]** Fr AP7 exit junc 44 onto N340 dir Barcelona. After 3km at km 1018 turn on CV142 twd Alcossebre. Just bef ent town turn R sp 'Platjes Capicorb', turn R at beach in 2.5km, site on R. Lge, mkd pitch, pt terr, pt shd; htd wc; chem disp; baby facs; some serviced pitches; shwrs inc; el pnts (6A) inc; gas; lndtte; shop; rest; snacks; bar; playgrnd; pool; sand beach adj; watersports; cycle hire; games area; cinema rm; wifi; TV; car wash; 10% statics; no dogs; poss cr; adv bkg rec high ssn; quiet; ccard acc; red low ssn/long stay & special offers; various pitch prices. "Excel facs & security; superb well-run site; vg low ssn; poss rallies Jan-Apr; management v helpful; poss flooding after heavy rain; pitch access poss diff lge o'fits due narr access rds & high kerbs; take fly swat!" ♦ € 68.00 (CChq acc) 2009*

⊞ **ALGAMITAS** *2G3* (3km SW Rural) *37.01934, -5.17440* **Camping El Peñon, Ctra Algámitas-Pruna, Km 3, 41661 Algámitas (Sevilla) [955-85 53 00; info@campingalgamitas.com]** Fr A92 turn S at junc 41 (Arahal) to Morón de la Frontera on A8125. Fr Morón take A406 & A363 dir Pruna. At 1st rndabt at ent Pruna turn L onto SE9225 to Algámitas. Site on L in approx 10km - steep app rd. Sm, hdg/mkd pitch, hdstg, pt shd; wc; chem disp (wc); mv service pnt; shwrs inc; el pnts (16A) €3.32; gas; lndtte (inc dryer); shop 3km; rest; bar; BBQ; playgrnd; pool; games area; 50% statics; dogs; site clsd 13-24 Nov; adv bkg; quiet; cc acc; CCI. "Conv Seville, Ronda & white vills; walking, hiking & horseriding fr site; excel rest; excel, clean san facs; vg site - worth effort to find." ♦ € 15.10 2009*

⊞ **ALHAMA DE MURCIA** *4F1* (6km NW Rural) *37.88888, -1.49333* **Camping Sierra Espuña, El Berro, 30848 Alhama de Murcia (Murcia) [968-66 80 38; fax 968-66 80 79; info@campingelberro.com; www.campingsierraespuna.com]** Exit A7 junc 627 or 631 to Alhama de Murcia & take C3315 sp Gebas & Mula. Ignore 1st sp to site & after Gebas foll sp to site sp El Berro, site on edge of vill. 15km by rd fr Alhama - narr, twisty & steep in parts, diff for lge o'fits & m'vans over 7.5m. Med, hdstg, terr, pt shd; wc; chem disp; baby facs; shwrs; el pnts (6A) €4.28 (poss rev pol); gas; lndtte; shop 200m; rest in vill; snacks; bar; playgrnd; pool; tennis; minigolf; organised activities; wifi; 30% statics; dogs €2.14; phone; adv bkg; quiet but poss noise w/end; red long stay; ccard acc; CCI. "In Sierra Espuña National Park on edge of unspoilt vill; gd walking, climbing, mountain biking area; friendly staff; highly rec." ♦ € 17.20 2009*

⊞ **ALHAURIN DE LA TORRE** *2H4* (4km W Rural) *36.65174, -4.61064* **Camping Malaga Monte Parc, 29130 Alhaurín de la Torre (Málaga) [tel/fax 951-29 60 28; info@malagamonteparc.com; www.malagamonteparc.com]** W fr Málaga on AP7 or N340 take exit for Churriana/Alhaurín de la Torre. Thro Alhuarín de la Torre take A404 W sp Alhaurín el Grande, site on R, sp. Sm, hdg/mkd pitch, hdstg, pt sl, shd; htd wc (cont); chem disp; shwrs inc; el pnts (6A) inc; lndtte; shop 4km; rest; snacks; bar; BBQ; pool; golf nrby; wifi; TV; some statics; dogs €1.70; bus 200m; Eng spkn; adv bkg; quiet; ccard acc; red low ssn; CCI. "Vg site; well-appointed, clean san facs; friendly Welsh owner." ♦ € 24.70 2009*

⊞ **ALICANTE** *4F2* (10km NE Coastal) *38.41333, -0.40556* **Camping Bon Sol, Camino Real de Villajoyosa 35, Playa Muchavista, 03560 El Campello (Alicante) [tel/fax 965-94 13 83; bonsol@infonegocio.com; www.infonegocio.com/bonsol]** Exit AP7 N of Alicante at junc 67 onto N332 sp Playa San Juan; on reaching coast rd turn N twds El Campello; site sp. Sm, mkd pitch, hdstg, pt shd, all serviced pitches; wc; chem disp; shwrs; el pnts (4A) €4.50; lndtte; shop; rest; bar; sand beach; 50% statics; adv bkg; ccard acc; red long stay/low ssn; CCI. "Diff ent for long o'fits; helpful staff; noisy at w/end; poss cold shwrs; vg." ♦ € 31.50 2008*

⊞ **ALICANTE** *4F2* (10km NE Coastal) *38.43638, -0.3887* **Camping Costa Blanca, Calle Convento 143, 03560 El Campello (Alicante) [tel/fax 965-63 06 70; info@campingcostablanca.com; www.campingcostablanca.com]** Exit AP7/E15 junc 67 onto N332, site visible on L at turn for El Campello. Med, hdg pitch, hdstg, shd; htd wc; chem disp; mv service pnt; shwrs inc; baby facs; el pnts (6A) €4.30; gas; lndtte; shop; rest; snacks; bar; playgrnd; pool; waterslides; sand beach 500m; watersports; tennis 800m; horseriding 1km; golf 3km; TV cab/sat; 80% statics; dogs free; train 1km; sep car park; poss cr; adv bkg; some noise fr rlwy; red long stay; CCI. "Pleasant site nr archaeological site & fishmkt; modern facs; friendly, helpful staff; not suitable RVs & lge o'fits due narr access to pitches; pitches sm & low canvas awnings; gd security; v popular low ssn." ♦ € 28.10 2008*

⊞ **ALLARIZ** *1B2* (1.5km W Rural) *42.18443, -7.81811* **Camping Os Invernadeiros, Ctra Allariz-Celanova, Km 3, 32660 Allariz (Ourense) [988-44 01 26; fax 988-44 20 06; reatur@allariz.com]** Well sp off N525 Orense-Xinzo rd & fr A52. Steep descent to site off rd OU300. Height limit 2.85m adj reception - use gate to R. Sm, pt shd; wc; shwrs inc; el pnts €3.21; gas; lndtte; shop; snacks; bar; playgrnd; pool 1.5km; horseriding; cycle hire; some statics; dogs €1.61; bus 1.8km; Eng spkn; quiet; red long stay; ccard acc; CCI. "Vg; site combined with horseriding stable; rv walk adj." € 19.81 2008*

ALMAYATE see Torre del Mar *2H4*

⊞ **ALMERIA** *4G1* (23km SE Coastal/Rural) *36.80187, -2.24471* **Camping Cabo de Gata, Ctra Cabo de Gata s/n, Cortijo Ferrón, 04150 Cabo de Gata (Almería) [950-16 04 43; fax 950-52 00 03; info@campingcabo degata.com; www.campingcabodegata.com]** Exit m'way N340/344/E15 junc 460 or 467 sp Cabo de Gata, foll sp to site. Lge, hdg/mkd pitch, shd; wc; chem disp; baby facs; shwrs inc; el pnts (6-16A) metered; gas; Indtte; supmkt high ssn; tradsmn; rest; snacks; bar; playgrnd; pool; diving cent; sand beach 900m; tennis; games area; games rm; excursions; cycle hire; wifi; TV; some statics; dogs €2.80; bus 1km; Eng spkn; adv bkg; quiet; ccard acc; red long stay/low ssn/CCI. "M'vans with solar panels/TV aerials take care sun shades; occasional power cuts & poss restricted drinking water supply; poss long walk to water point; gd cycling, birdwatching esp flamingoes; popular at w/end; isolated, dry area of Spain with many interesting features; warm winters; excel." ♦ € 24.85 2009*

See advertisement below

⊞ **ALMERIA** *4G1* (4km W Coastal) *36.82560, -2.51685* **Camping La Garrofa, Ctra N340a, Km 435.4, 04002 Almería [tel/fax 950-23 57 70; info@lagarrofa.com; www.lagarrofa.com]** Site sp on coast rd bet Almería & Aguadulce. Med, mkd pitch, pt sl, shd; wc; chem disp; mv service pnt; shwrs inc; el pnts (6-10A) €4.30-4.90; gas; Indtte; shop; rest; snacks; bar; playgrnd; shgl beach adj; games area; wifi; 10% statics; dogs €2.40; phone; bus adj; sep car park; quiet; red low ssn/long stay; CCI. "V pleasant site adj eucalyptus grove; helpful staff; modern, clean facs; sm pitches, not rec lge o'fits; vg." ♦ € 20.50 2009*

See advertisement above

⊞ **ALMERIA** *4G1* (10km W Coastal) *36.79738, -2.59128* **Camping Roquetas, Ctra Los Parrales s/n, 04740 Roquetas de Mar (Almería) [950-34 38 09; fax 950-34 25 25; info@ campingroquetas.com; www.campingroquetas.com]** Fr A7 take exit 429; ahead at rndabt A391 sp Roquetas. Turn L at rndabt sp camping & foll sp to site. V lge, pt shd; wc; chem disp; mv service pnt; shwrs inc; el pnts (5-15A) €4.60-7.30; gas; Indtte; shop; snacks; bar; 2 pools; paddling pool; shgl beach 400m; tennis; TV rm; 10% statics; dogs €2.25; phone; bus 1km; Eng spkn; adv bkg rec all year; quiet; ccard acc; red low ssn/long stay/CCI. "Double-size pitches in winter; helpful staff; gd clean facs; tidy site but poss dusty; artificial shade; many long term visitors in winter." ♦ € 18.40 2008*

Spain

ALMUNECAR *2H4* (6km W Coastal) *36.73954, -3.75358* **Nuevo Camping La Herradura, Paseo Andrés Segovia (Peña Parda), 18690 La Herradura (Granada) [958-64 06 34; fax 958-64 06 42; laherradura@neuvo camping.com]** Turn S off N340 sp La Herradura & foll rd to seafront. Turn R to end of beach rd. Avoid town cent due narr rds. Med, mkd pitch, pt terr, pt shd; wc; chem disp; mv service pnt; serviced pitches; shwrs inc; el pnts (5A) €3.75; gas 500m; Indtte; shop, rest, snacks, bar adj; playgrnd; shgl beach adj; 20% statics; dogs €1.10; phone; bus 300m; poss v cr; adv bkg; quiet; red low ssn/long stay; CCI. "Friendly site in avocado orchard; untidy but attractive; mountain views some pitches; height restriction lge m'vans; some sm pitches - v tight to manoeuvre; vg san facs but ltd low ssn; popular winter long stay." ♦ 1 Apr-28 Oct. € 21.00
2008*

⊞ **ALTEA** *4F2* (4km S Coastal) *38.57751, -0.06440* **Camping Cap-Blanch, Playa de Albir, 03530 Altea (Alicante) [965-84 59 46; fax 965-84 45 56; capblanch@ ctv.es; www.camping-capblanch.com]** Exit AP7/E15 junc 64 Altea-Collosa onto N332, site bet Altea & Benidorm, dir Albir. 'No entry' sps on prom rd do not apply to access to site. Lge, pt shd, hdstg; wc; chem disp; mv service pnt; baby facs; shwrs inc; el pnts (5A) €5.35; gas; shop 100m; Indtte; rest; bar; playgrnd; shgl beach adj; watersports; tennis; golf 5km; TV; some statics; carwash; poss cr; Eng spkn; adv bkg; quiet; ccard acc; red low ssn/long stay. "V cr in winter with long stay campers; Altea mkt Tues; buses to Benidorm & Altea; most pitches hdstg on pebbles." ♦ € 39.59
2006*

⊞ **AMETLLA DE MAR, L'** *3C2* (2.5km S Coastal) *40.86493, 0.77860* **Camping L'Ametlla Village Platja, Paratge Stes Creus s/n, 43860 L'Ametlla de Mar (Tarragona) [977-26 77 84; fax 977-26 78 68; info@campingametlla. com; www.campingametlla.com]** Exit AP7 junc 39, fork R as soon as cross m'way. Foll site sp for 3km - 1 v sharp, steep bend. Lge, hdg/mkd pitch, hdstg, terr, pt shd; htd wc; chem disp; mv service pnt; baby facs; shwrs inc; el pnts (5A) inc; gas; Indtte; shop high ssn; rest; snacks; bar; BBQ; playgrnd; pool; paddling pool; shgl beach 400m; diving cent; games area; games rm; fitness rm; cycle hire; wifi; entmnt; TV rm; some statics; dogs free; phone; Eng spkn; adv bkg; some rd & rlwy noise; ccard acc; red low ssn/long stay; CCI. "Conv Port Aventura & Ebro Delta National Park; excel site & facs." ♦ € 35.20 2008*

⊞ **ARACENA** *2F3* (3km S Rural) *37.88105, -6.52101* **Camping Aracena Sierra, Ctra Sevilla-Lisboa, Km 83, 21200 Aracena (Huelva) [959-50 10 05]** Fr N on N433, site sp on rd to Corteconcepción, down hill on R. No sp fr S. Med, terr, pt shd; wc (cont); chem disp; shwrs inc; el pnts (10A) €3.65; rest; snacks; bar; BBQ; playgrnd; pool; 40% statics; dogs; Eng spkn; adv bkg; poss noisy at w/end; CCI. "Fair site; dated facs; Aracena busy, sm town." € 25.15 2009*

⊞ **ARANDA DE DUERO** *1C4* (3km N Rural) *41.70138, -3.68666* **Camping Costajan, Ctra A1/E5, Km 164-165, 09400 Aranda de Duero (Burgos) [947-50 20 70; fax 947-51 13 54; campingcostajan@camping-costajan.com]** Sp on A1/E5 Madrid-Burgos rd, N'bound exit km 164 Aranda Norte, S'bound exit km 165 & foll sp to Aranda & site 500m on R. Med, pt sl, shd; htd wc; chem disp; mv service pnt; shwrs inc; el pnts (10A) €4.85 (poss rev pol &/ or no earth); gas; Indtte; shop; tradsmn; supmkt 3km; rest high ssn; snacks; bar; BBQ; playgrnd; pool high ssn; tennis; games area; 10% statics; dogs €2; phone; bus 2km; Eng spkn; adv bkg; quiet, but some traff noise; red low ssn but ltd facs; CCI. "Lovely site under pine trees; poultry farm adj; diff pitch access due trees & sandy soil; v friendly, helpful owner; site poss clsd low ssn - phone ahead to check; many facs clsd low ssn & gate clsd o'night until 0800; recep poss open evening only; excel facs for disabled; poss cold/tepid shwrs low ssn; gd winter NH but unhtd san facs." € 23.30
2009*

⊞ **ARANJUEZ** *1D4* (1.5km NE Rural) *40.04222, -3.59944* **Camping International Aranjuez, Calle Soto del Rebollo s/n, 28300 Aranjuez (Madrid) [918-91 13 95; fax 918-92 04 06; info@campingaranjuez.com; www. campingaranjuez.com]** Fr N (Madrid) turn off A4 exit 37 onto M305. After ent town turn L bef rv, after petrol stn on R. Take L lane & watch for site sp on L, also mkd M305 Madrid. Site in 500m on R. (If missed cont around cobbled rndabt & back twd Madrid.) Fr S turn off A4 for Aranjuez & foll Palacio Real sp. Join M305 & foll sp for Madrid & camping site. Site on Rv Tajo. Warning: rd surface rolls, take it slowly on app to site & ent gate tight. Med, mkd pitch, pt sl, pt shd; htd wc; chem disp; mv service pnt; some serviced pitches; shwrs inc; el pnts (16A) €3.75 (poss no earth, rev pol); gas; Indtte; shop; hypmkt 3km; rest; snacks; bar; playgrnd; pool & paddling pool; rv fishing; canoe & cycle hire; games area; wifi; entmnt; some statics; dogs free; phone; quiet; ccard acc; red low ssn/long stay; CCI. "Well-maintained site; gd san facs; some lge pitches - access poss diff due trees; some uneven pitches - care req when pitching; pleasant town - World Heritage site; conv Royal Palace & gardens & Madrid by train." ♦ € 25.70
2009*

See advertisement

ARBON *1A3* (S Rural) *43.48141, -6.70376* **Camping La Cascada, 33718 Arbón (Asturias) [985-62 50 81; campinglacascada@hotmail.com]** Approx 20km W of Luarca on N634, turn S onto AS25 for approx 10km. Immed bef town of Navía, site sp. Winding rd. Med, sl, pt shd; wc; chem disp (wc); shwrs inc; el pnts (3-4A) €2.70; gas; shop & 1km; snacks; bar; BBQ; playgrnd; pool; sand beach 12km; 15% statics; dogs; phone; bus 1km; Eng spkn; adv bkg; quiet; CCI. "V friendly, family-run site in beautiful area; excel info fr local tourist office." Easter-15 Sep. € 14.00
2008*

🕂 **ARCOS DE LA FRONTERA** *2G3* (1km E Rural) *36.75222, -5.78722* **Camping Lago de Arcos, 11630 Arcos de la Frontera (Cádiz) [956-70 83 33; fax 956-70 80 00; lagodearcos@campings.net]** Exit A382 junc 29 S to Arcos A372. Turn L at sp El Santiscal & site, site on R. Med, pt shd; wc; shwrs inc; el pnts (5A) €3.53; gas; lndtte; sm shop; snacks; bar; playgrnd; pool high ssn; dogs; phone; poss cr; quiet; ccard acc; CCI. "Noisy at Easter due Running Bull Festival; unkempt low ssn & poss itinerants; tel to check open in low ssn; busy w/end; friendly staff; most pitches have canopy frames; sh walk to lake." ♦ € 17.61 2008*

🕂 **ARENAS DEL REY** *2G4* (5km N Rural) *36.99439, -3.88064* **Camping Los Bermejales, Km 360, Embalse Los Bermejales, 18129 Arenas del Rey (Granada) [958-35 91 90; fax 958-35 93 36; camping@losbermejales.com; www.losbermejales.com]** On A44/E902 S fr Granada, exit at junc 139 dir La Malahá onto A385. In approx 10km, turn L onto A338 dir Alhama de Granada & foll sp for site. Fr A92 foll sp Alhama de Granada, then Embalse Los Bermejales. Med, mkd pitch, hdstg, terr, pt shd; wc; chem disp; mv service pnt; shwrs inc; el pnts (9A) €2.67; gas; lndtte; shop; rest; snacks; bar; BBQ; playgrnd; pool; lake sw & sand/shgl beach adj; fishing (licence req); pedalos; tennis; TV rm; 50% statics; dogs; phone; poss cr high ssn; little Eng spkn; adv bkg; quiet. "Ideal base for touring Granada; Roman baths 12km at Alhama de Granada; vg disabled facs." ♦ € 16.70 2007*

ARENAS, LAS *1A4* (1km E Rural) *43.30083, -4.80500* **Camping Naranjo de Bulnes, Ctra Cangas de Onís-Panes, Km 32.5, 33554 Arenas de Cabrales (Asturias) [tel/fax 985-84 65 78]** Fr Unquera on N634, take N621 S to Panes, AS114 23km to Las Arenas. Site E of vill of Las Arenas de Cabrales, both sides of rd. V lge, mkd pitch, pt sl, pt terr, pt shd; wc; chem disp; baby facs; shwrs inc; el pnts (10A) €3.50 (poss rev pol); gas; lndtte; shop; rest; snacks; bar; playgrnd; internet; TV rm; poss cr; adv bkg; rd noise; ccard acc. "Beautifully-situated site by rv; delightful vill; attractive, rustic-style san facs - hot water to shwrs only; wcs up steps; poss poor security; conv Picos de Europa; mountain-climbing school; excursions; walking; excel cheese festival last Sun in Aug." Holy Week-4 Nov. € 25.60 2009*

ARIJA *1A4* (1km N Rural) *43.00064, -3.94492* **Camping Playa de Arija, Avda Gran Via, 09570 Arija (Burgos) [942-77 33 00; fax 942-77 32 72; dptocomercial@campingplayadearija.com; www.campingplayadearija.com]** Fr W on A67 at Reinosa along S side of Embalse del Ebro. Go thro Arija & take 1st L after x-ing bdge. Go under rlwy bdge, site well sp on peninsula N of vill on lakeside. Or fr E on N623 turn W onto BU642 to Arija & turn R to peninsula & site. NB Rd fr W under repair 2009 & in poor condition. Lge, unshd; wc; chem disp; mv service pnt; baby facs; shwrs inc; el pnts (5A) €3; lndtte; shop; rest; bar; BBQ; playgrnd; lake sw & beach; watersports; games area; 10% statics; dogs; phone; bus 1km; quiet; CCI. "Gd new site; gd birdwatching." Easter-15 Sep. € 17.50 2009*

🕂 **ARNES** *3C2* (1km NE Rural) *40.9186, 0.2678* **Camping Els Ports, Ctra Tortosa T330, Km 2, 43597 Arnes (Tarragona) [tel/fax 977-43 55 60; elsports@hotmail.com]** Exit AP7 at junc Tortosa onto C12 sp Gandesa. Turn W onto T333 at El Pinell de Brai, then T330 to site. Med, pt shd; htd wc; shwrs inc; el pnts €4.20; lndtte; rest; bar; pool; paddling pool; games area; cycle hire; horseriding 3km; entmnt; TV rm; some statics; no dogs; phone; bus 1km; quiet; ccard acc. "Nr nature reserve & many sports activities; excel walking/mountain cycling; basic san facs; poss smells fr adj pig units (2009); rock pegs req." ♦ € 18.40 2009*

AURITZ *3A1* (3km SW Rural) *42.97302, -1.35248* **Camping Urrobi, Ctra Pamplona-Valcarlos, Km 42, 31694 Aurizberri-Espinal (Navarra) [tel/fax 948-76 02 00; info@campingurrobi.com; www.campingurrobi.com]** NE fr Pamplona on N135 twd Valcarlos thro Erro; 1.5km after Auritzberri (Espinal) turn R on N172. Site on N172 at junc with N135 opp picnic area. Med, pt shd; wc; chem disp; mv service pnt; shwrs inc; el pnts (5A) €4.35; gas; lndtte; shop; tradsmn; supmkt 1.5km; rest; snacks; bar; BBQ; playgrnd; pool; rv adj; tennis; cycle hire; horseriding; wifi; 20% statics; phone; Eng spkn; adv bkg; quiet; ccard acc; CCI. "Excel site & facs; solar htd water - hot water to shwrs only; walks in surrounding hills; ltd facs low ssn." ♦ 1 Apr-31 Oct. € 17.85 2007*

Spain

AVIN see Cangas de Onis *1A3*

⊞ **AYERBE** *3B2* (1km NE Rural) *42.28211, -0.67536* **Camping La Banera, Ctra Loarre Km.1, 22800 Ayerbe (Huesca) [tel/fax 974-38 02 42; labanera@gmail.com; www.labanera.turincon.com]** Take A132 NW fr Huesca dir Pamplona. Turn R at 1st x-rds at ent to Ayerbe sp Loarre & Camping. Site 1km on R on A1206. Med, mkd pitch, terr, pt shd; wc; chem disp (wc); baby facs; fam bthrm; shwrs inc; el pnts (6A) €2.50; gas; lndtte; shop 1km; rest; snacks; bar; cooking facs; TV rm; dogs; some Eng spkn; adv bkg; quiet; ccard acc; red long stay; CCI. "Friendly, pleasant, well-maintained, peaceful, family-run site; facs clean; pitches poss muddy after rain; helpful owners; wonderful views; close to Loarre Castle; care req by high o'fits as many low trees." ♦ € 12.50 2008*

AYERBE *3B2* (10km NE Rural) *42.31989, -0.61848* **Camping Castillo de Loarre, 22809 Loarre (Huesca) [974-38 27 23; fax 974-38 27 22; info@campingloarre.com; www.campingloarre.com]** NW on A132 fr Huesca, turn R at ent to Ayerbe to Loare sp Castillo de Loarre. Pass 1st site on R (La Banera) & foll sp to castle past Loarre vill on L; site on L. App rd steep & twisting. Med, pt sl, pt shd; wc; chem disp; shwrs inc; el pnts (6A) €3.50; gas; lndtte; shop; tradsmn; rest; snacks; bar; playgrnd; sm pool; cycle hire; 10% statics; dogs; phone; poss cr; Eng spkn; quiet; ccard acc; CCI. "Elevated site in almond grove; superb scenery & views, esp fr pitches on far L of site; some pitches ltd el pnts; excel birdwatching - many vultures/eagles; gd touring area; site open w/end in winter; busy high ssn & w/ends; pitching poss diff lge o'fits due low trees; worth the journey." ♦ 9 Apr-4 Nov. € 12.50 2007*

BAIONA *1B2* (5km NE Urban/Coastal) *42.13861, -8.80916* **Camping Playa América, Ctra Vigo-Baiona, Km 9.250, 36350 Nigrán (Pontevedra) [986-36 54 03 or 986-36 71 61; fax 986-36 54 04; oficina@campingplaya america.com; www.campingplayaamerica.com]** Sp on rd PO552 fr all dirs (Vigo/Baiona) nr beach. Med, mkd pitch, pt shd; wc; chem disp; mv service pnt; baby facs; shwrs inc; el pnts (6A) €4.50; gas; lndtte; shop; tradsmn; rest; snacks; bar; BBQ; playgrnd; pool; paddling pool; sand beach 300m; cycle hire; 60% statics; dogs; bus 500m; poss cr; Eng spkn; adv bkg; CCI. "Friendly staff; pleasant, wooded site; gd." ♦ 16 Mar-15 Oct. € 24.60 2008*

⊞ **BAIONA** *1B2* (1km E Coastal) *42.11416, -8.82611* **Camping Bayona Playa, Ctra Vigo-Baiona, Km 19, Sabarís, 36393 Baiona (Pontevedra) [986-35 00 35; fax 986-35 29 52; campingbayona@bme.es; www.camping bayona.com]** Fr Vigo on PO552 sp Baiona. Or fr A57 exit Baiona & foll sp Vigo & site sp. Site clearly sp for 25km around. Lge, mkd pitch, pt shd; wc (some cont); chem disp; mv service pnt; shwrs inc; el pnts (3A) €3.95; gas; lndtte; shop; rest; snacks; bar; playgrnd; pool; waterslide; sand beach adj; 50% statics; dogs; phone; poss cr; adv bkg (ess high ssn); quiet; red low ssn/long stay; CCI. "Area of o'stndg natural beauty with sea on 3 sides; gd cycle track to town; well-organised site; excel, clean san facs; avoid access w/end as v busy; ltd facs low ssn; sm pitches." ♦ € 25.90 2008*

BAIONA *1B2* (7km S Coastal) *42.08642, -8.89129* **Camping Mougás (Naturist), As Mariñas 20B, Ctra Baiona-A Guarda, Km 156, 36309 Mougás (Pontevedra) [986-38 50 11; fax 986-38 29 90; campingmougas@campingmougas.com]** Fr Baiona take coastal rd PO552 S; site sp. Med, pt shd; wc; chem disp; shwrs; el pnts €4.65; lndtte; supmkt; rest; snacks; bar; BBQ; playgrnd; pool; fishing; tennis; games rn; entmnt; some statics; phone; ccard acc; red low ssn; CCI. "Excel staff; lovely site on rocky coast; gd for watching sunsets; gd NH." ♦ Holy Week-15 Sep. € 25.00 2008*

⊞ **BALAGUER** *3C2* (8km N Rural) *41.86030, 0.83250* **Camping La Noguera, Partida de la Solana s/n, 25615 Sant Llorenç de Montgai (Lleida) [973-42 03 34; fax 973-42 02 12; jaume@campinglanoguera.com; www.campinglanoguera.com]** Fr Lleida, take N11 ring rd & exit at km 467 onto C13 NE dir Andorra & Balaguer. Head for Balaguer town cent, cross rv & turn R onto LV9047 dir Gerb. Site on L in 8km thro Gerb. App fr Camarasa not rec. Lge, mkd pitch, hdstg, terr, pt shd; wc; chem disp; mv service pnt; baby facs; shwrs inc; el pnts (6A) €5.15; gas; lndtte; supmkt; tradsmn; rest; snacks; bar; BBQ; playgrnd; pool; games area; TV rm; 80% statics; dogs €3.50; phone; poss cr; Eng spkn; adv bkg; quiet; ccard acc; red long stay; CCI. "Next to lake & nature reserve; gd cycling; poss diff lge o'fits." ♦ € 20.60 2008*

BANOS DE FORTUNA see Fortuna *4F1*

BANOS DE MONTEMAYOR see Béjar *1D3*

⊞ **BANYOLES** *3B3* (2km W Rural) *42.12071, 2.74690* **Camping Caravaning El Llac, Ctra Circumvallació de l'Estany s/n, 17834 Porqueres (Gerona) [tel/fax 972-57 03 05; info@campingllac.com; www.campingllac.com]** Exit AP7 junc 6 to Banyoles. Go strt thro town (do not use by-pass) & exit town at end of lake in 1.6km. Use R-hand layby to turn L sp Porqueres. Site on R in 2.5km. Lge, mkd pitch, pt shd; chem disp; htd wc; shwrs; el pnts €4.60; lndtte; shop; snacks; bar; pool; lake sw; wifi; 80% statics; dogs €2.30; bus 1km; site clsd mid-Dec to mid-Jan; poss cr; quiet but noisy rest/disco adj in high ssn; red long stay/low ssn. "Immac, ltd facs low ssn & stretched high ssn; sm pitches bet trees; pleasant walk around lake to town; site muddy when wet." ♦ € 22.10 2009*

BARBATE see Vejer de la Frontera *2H3*

BARCELONA See sites listed under El Masnou, Gavà and Sitges.

BARREIROS/REINANTE see Foz *1A2*

⊞ **BECERREA** *1B2* (15km E Rural) *42.86138, -7.12000* **Camping Os Ancares, Ctra NV1, Liber, 27664 Mosteiro-Cervantes (Lugo) [tel/fax 982-36 45 56; www.campingosancares.com]** Fr A6 exit Becerreá S onto LU722 sp Navia de Suarna. After 10km in Liber turn R onto LU723 sp Doiras, site in 7km just beyond Mosteiro hamlet; site sp. Site ent steep & narr - diff lge o'fits & lge m'vans. Med, terr, shd; wc; shwrs inc; el pnts (6A) €3; gas; lndry rm; rest; snacks; bar; playgrnd; pool; fishing; horseriding; some statics; dogs €1; poss cr; quiet; CCI. "Isolated, scenic site; gd rest & san facs; ltd facs low ssn; low trees some pitches; gd walking." € 14.20 2008*

BEGUR *3B3* (2km N Coastal) *41.9686, 3.2099* **Camping El Maset, Playa Sa Riera, 17255 Begur (Gerona) [972-62 30 23; fax 972-62 39 01; info@campingelmaset.com; www.campingelmaset.com]** Fr Begur take rd N twd Sa Riera. Med, shd; wc; chem disp; mv service pnt; baby facs; shwrs inc; el pnts (4-6A) €3.40-4.50; gas; lndtte; shop; rest; snacks; bar; playgrnd; pool; sand beach 300m; games area; games rm; internet; phone; no dogs; ccard acc; quiet. "Pleasant site in gd location." ♦ 1 Apr-25 Sep. € 26.30 2006*

BEGUR *3B3* (1.5km S Rural) *41.94040, 3.19890* **Camping Begur, Ctra d'Esclanyà, Km 2, 17255 Begur (Gerona) [972-62 32 01; fax 972-62 45 66; info@campingbegur.com; www.campingbegur.com]** Exit AP7/E15 junc 6 Gerona onto C66 dir La Bisbal & Palamós. At x-rds to Pals turn L dir Begur then turn R twd Esclanyà, site on R, clearly sp. Slope to site ent. Lge, mkd pitch, hdstg, shd; wc; chem disp; mv service pnt; baby facs; serviced pitches; shwrs inc; el pnts (10A) inc; lndtte; supmkt; rest; snacks; bar; BBQ; playgrnd; pool; paddling pool; sand/shgl beach 2km; tennis; cycle hire; games area; games rm; gym; wifi; entmnt; 14% statics; dogs €5.90; phone; bus adj; Eng spkn; adv bkg; red long stay/snr citizens/CCI. "Excel, peaceful site; narr site rds poss diff lge o'fits; adj castle & magnificent views; excel touring base." ♦ 1 Apr-26 Sep. € 47.10 2008*

BEJAR *1D3* (6km S Rural) *40.36344, -5.74918* **Camping Cinco Castaños, Ctra de la Sierra s/n, 37710 Candelario (Salamanca) [923-41 32 04; fax 923-41 32 82; profetur@candelariohotel.com; www.candelariohotel.com]** Fr Béjar foll sp Candelario on C515/SA220, site sp on N side of vill. Steep bends & narr app rd. Sm, mkd pitch, pt sl, pt shd; htd wc; chem disp (wc); baby facs; shwrs inc; el pnts (6A) €3.15; gas; lndtte; shop 500m; rest; bar; playgrnd; pool high ssn; no dogs; bus 500m; phone; quiet; CCI. "Mountain vill; friendly owner; no facs in winter; no lge o'fits as steep site." ♦ Holy Week-15 Oct. € 18.50 2007*

⊞ **BEJAR** *1D3* (15km SW Rural) *40.28560, -5.88182* **Camping Las Cañadas, Ctra N630, Km 432, 10750 Baños de Montemayor (Cáceres) [927-48 11 26; fax 927-48 13 14; info@campinglascanadas.com; www.campinglascanadas.com]** Fr S turn off A630 m'way at 437km stone to Heruns then take old N630 twd Béjar. Site at 432km stone, behind 'Hervas Peil' (leather goods shop). Fr N exit A66 junc 427 thro Baños for 3km to site at km432 on R. Lge, mkd pitch, pt sl; shd (net shdg); htd wc; chem disp; mv service pnt; baby facs; shwrs inc; el pnts (5A) €3.20; gas; lndtte; shop; rest; snacks; bar; playgrnd; pool in high ssn; paddling pool; fishing; tennis; games area; TV rm; 60% statics; dogs; poss cr; Eng spkn; quiet but rd noise; ccard acc; red long stay/low ssn/CCI. "Gd san facs but poss cold shwrs; high vehicles take care overhanging trees; gd walking country; NH/sh stay." ♦ € 15.66 (CChq acc) 2007*

⊞ **BELLVER DE CERDANYA** *3B3* (2km E Rural) *42.37163, 1.80674* **Camping Bellver, Ctra N260, Km 193.7, 17539 Isòvol (Gerona) [973-51 02 39; fax 973-51 07 19; campingbellver@campingbellver.com; www.campingbellver.com]** On N260 fr Puigcerdà to Bellver; site on L, well sp. Lge, mkd pitch, shd; htd wc; chem disp (wc); shwrs inc; el pnts (5A) €3.50; gas; lndtte; rest; snacks; bar; playgrnd; pool; 90% statics; dogs; phone; poss cr; Eng spkn; quiet; ccard acc; CCI. "Friendly, helpful staff; lovely pitches along rv; san facs immac; v quiet low ssn; gd NH for Andorra." € 19.20 2007*

⊞ **BELLVER DE CERDANYA** *3B3* (1km W Rural) *42.37110, 1.73625* **Camping La Cerdanya, Ctra N260, Km 200, 25727 Prullans (Lleida) [973-51 02 62; fax 973-51 06 72; cerdanya@prullans.net; www.prullans.net/camping]** Fr Andorra frontier on N260, site sp. Lge, mkd pitch, shd; wc; baby facs; mv service pnt; shwrs inc; el pnts (4A) €5.15; gas; lndtte; shop; rest; snacks; playgrnd; pool; paddling pool; games area; internet; entmnt; 80% statics; dogs €3.45; phone; bus 1km; poss cr; adv bkg; quiet; red long stay; ccard acc. ♦ € 20.60 2007*

BELLVER DE CERDANYA *3B3* (1km W Rural) *42.37299, 1.76042* **Camping Solana del Segre, Ctra N260, Km 198, 25720 Bellver de Cerdanya (Lleida) [973-51 03 10; fax 973-51 06 98; info@solanadelsegre.com; www.solanadelsegre.com]** Take N260 fr Puigcerdà to Seo de Urgell, site at km 198 after Bellver de Cerdanya on L. Lge, pt sl, pt shd; wc; chem disp; shwrs inc; baby facs; el pnts (5A) €4.20; lndtte; shop; rest (w/end only low ssn); snacks; bar; BBQ; playgrnd; pool; games area; games rm; wifi; entmnt; 80% statics; dogs €5; phone; bus 500m; poss cr; adv bkg; quiet; ccard acc; red low ssn. "Steep site rds & exit fr site to main rd; poss diff for cars under 2L; conv NH nr Cadí Tunnel." ♦ 1 Jul-31 Aug. € 37.00 2008*

BENABARRE *3B2* (500m N Urban) *42.1103, 0.4811* **Camping Benabarre, 22580 Benabarre (Huesca) [974-54 35 72; fax 974-54 34 32; aytobenabarre@aragon.es]** Fr N230 S, turn L after 2nd camping sp over bdge & into vill. Ignore brown camping sp (part of riding cent). Med, some hdstg, pt shd; wc; shwrs inc; el pnts (10A) inc; shops 500m; bar; pool; tennis; no statics; bus 600m; phone; quiet. "Excel, friendly, simple site; gd facs; gd value for money; v quiet low ssn; warden calls 1700; mkt on Fri; lovely vill with excel chocolate shop; conv Graus & mountains - a real find." 1 Apr-30 Sep. € 14.00 2008*

BENAMAHOMA see Ubrique *2H3*

⊞ **BENASQUE** *3B2* (3km N Rural) *42.62420, 0.54478* **Camping Aneto, 22440 Benasque (Huesca) [974-55 11 41; fax 974-55 16 63; info@campinganeto.com; www.campinganeto.com]** Fr Vielha N230 then N260 to Castejón de Sos, foll sp to Benasque, site on L in 3km. Med, pt sl, pt shd; wc; chem disp; shwrs inc; el pnts (10A) €4.60; gas; lndtte; shop in ssn & 3km; tradsmn; rest in ssn; snacks; bar; BBQ; playgrnd; sw 3km; trekking; poss cr; Eng spkn; 75% statics; site clsd Nov; phone; quiet; ccard acc; CCI. "Friendly owners; access to pitches poss diff lge o'fits; unspoilt countryside; stunning app via gorges fr S; gd walking, wildflowers." € 25.00 2008*

⊞ **BENICARLO** *3D2* (1.5km NE Urban/Coastal) *40.42611, 0.43777* **Camping La Alegría del Mar, Ctra N340, Km 1046, Calle Playa Norte, 12580 Benicarló (Castellón) [964-47 08 71; info@campingalegria.com; www.campingalegria.com]** Sp off main N340 app Benicarló. Take slip rd mkd Service, go under underpass, turn R on exit & cont twd town, then turn at camp sp by Peugeot dealers. Sm, mkd pitch, pt shd; htd wc; shwrs; el pnts (4-6A) €4.70; gas; lndtte; shop 500m; rest; snacks; bar; playgrnd; sm pool; beach adj; games rm; wifi; some statics; dogs; phone; bus 800m; poss cr; quiet but rd noise at night & poss cockerels!; red long stay/low ssn; ccard acc. "British owners; access to pitches variable, poss diff in ssn; vg, clean san facs; Xmas & New Year packages; phone ahead to reserve pitch; excel." € 22.00 2009*

⊞ **BENICASSIM** *3D2* (500m NE Coastal) *40.05709, 0.07429* **Camping Bonterra Park, Avda de Barcelona 47, 12560 Benicàssim (Castellón) [964-30 00 07; fax 964 30 00 08; info@bonterrapark.com; www.bonterrapark.com]** Fr N exit AP7 junc 45 onto N340 dir Benicàssim. In approx 7km turn R to Benicàssim/Centro Urba; strt ahead to traff lts, then turn L, site on L 500m after going under rlwy bdge. Lge, mkd pitch, hdstg, pt sl, shd; htd wc; chem disp; mv service pnt; baby facs; shwrs inc; el pnts (10A) inc; gas; lndtte; shop adj; rest; snacks; bar; BBQ; playgrnd; 2 pools (1 covrd & htd); paddling pool; sand beach 300m; tennis; cycle hire; entmnt; games area; wifi; games/TV rm; 15% statics; dogs €2.22 (not acc Jul/Aug); phone; train; sep car park; Eng spkn; adv bkg; poss noisy; ccard acc; red long stay/low ssn/CCI. "Busy, popular site in gd location; clean & well-managed; winter festival 3rd wk Jan; access to some pitches poss diff due trees; sun shades some pitches; lovely beach; highly rec." ♦ € 53.72 ABS - E19 2009*

See advertisement

⊞ **BENICASSIM** *3D2* (4.5km NW Coastal) *40.05908, 0.08515* **Camping Azahar, Ptda Villaroig s/n, 12560 Benicàssim (Castellón) [964-30 31 96; fax 964-30 25 12; campingazahar@yahoo.es]** Fr AP7 junc 45 take N340 twd València; in 5km L at top of hill (do not turn R to go-karting); foll sp. Turn R under rlwy bdge opp Hotel Voramar. Lge, mkd pitch, pt sl, terr, unshd; htd wc; chem disp; mv service pnt; baby facs; shwrs inc; el pnts (4-6A) €2.90 (long leads poss req); gas; lndtte; rest; snacks; bar; playgrnd; pool; sand beach 300m across rd; tennis at hotel; cycle hire; 25% statics; dogs €4.07; phone; bus adj; poss cr high ssn; Eng spkn; bus adj; adv bkg; ccard acc; red long stay/low ssn/snr citizens; CCI. "Popular site, esp in winter; poss noisy high ssn; access poss diff for m'vans & lge o'fits; poss uneven pitches; organised events; gd walking & cycling; gd touring base." ♦ € 27.10 2009*

⊞ **BENIDORM** *4F2* (1km N Coastal) *38.5514, -0.09628* **Camping Arena Blanca, Avda Dr Severo Ochoa 44, 03503 Benidorm (Alicante) [965-86 18 89; fax 965-86 11 07; info@camping-arenablanca.es; www.camping-arenablanca.es]** Fr AP7 exit junc 65 onto N332 dir Playa Levante. Site sp. Med, terr, pt shd; wc; chem disp; some serviced pitches; shwrs inc; el pnts (16A) €3; gas; lndtte; supmkt; rest; snacks; bar; playgrnd; pool; paddling pool; sand beach 1km; cash machine; sat TV conn all pitches; 30% statics; dogs free; phone; bus 200m; adv bkg; quiet; red long stays; ccard acc; red CCI. ♦ € 27.00 2008*

⊞ **BENIDORM** *4F2* (1.5km NE Urban) *38.54833, -0.09851* **Camping El Raco, Avda Dr Severo Ochoa s/n, Racó de Loix, 03500 Benidorm (Alicante) [965-86 85 52; fax 965-86 85 44; info@campingraco.com; www.campingraco.com]** Turn off A7 m'way at junc 65 then L onto A332; take turning sp Benidorm Levante Beach; ignore others; L at 1st traff lghts; strt on at next traff lts, El Raco 1km on R. Lge, hdg/mkd pitch, hdstg, pt sl, pt shd; wc; chem disp; 50% serviced pitches; baby facs; shwrs inc; el pnts (10A) €3; gas; lndtte; shop; bar; BBQ; rest; playgrnd; 2 pools (1 htd, covrd); beach 1.5km; games area; TV (UK channels); 30% statics; bus; poss v cr in winter; quiet; red low ssn; CCI. "Excel site; popular winter long stay but strictly applied rules about leaving c'van unoccupied; el pnts metered for long stay." ♦ € 26.00 2006*

⊞ **BENIDORM** *4F2* (3km NE Urban) *38.56024, -0.09844* **Camping Benisol, Avda de la Comunidad Valenciana s/n, 03500 Benidorm (Alicante) [965-85 16 73; fax 965-86 08 95; campingbenisol@yahoo.es; www.campingbenisol.com]** Exit AP7/E15 junc 65 onto N332. Foll sp Benidorm, Playa Levante (avoid by-pass). Dangerous rd on ent to sit; site ent easy to miss. Lge, hdg pitch, hdstg, shd; wc; chem disp; serviced pitches; shwrs inc; el pnts (4-6A) €2.80; gas; lndtte; shop & rest (high ssn); snacks; bar; playgrnd; pool (hgh ssn); sand beach 4km; TV; 85% statics; dogs; phone; bus to Benidorm; poss cr; Eng spkn; adv bkg with dep; some rd noise; red long stay/low ssn; CCI. "Helpful staff; well-run, clean site; many permanent residents." ♦ € 27.20 2007*

☐ **BENIDORM** *4F2* (3km NE Coastal) *38.54438, -0.10325* **Camping La Torreta, Avda Dr Severo Ochoa s/n, 03500 Benidorm (Alicante) [965-85 46 68; fax 965-80 26 53]** Exit AP7/E15 junc 65 onto N332. Foll sp Playa Levante, site sp. Lge, mkd pitch, hdstg, pt sl, terr, pt shd (bamboo shades); wc (some cont); mv service pnt; shwrs inc; el pnts (10A) €3.30; gas; Indtte; shop; rest; bar; playgrnd; pool & paddling pool; sand beach 1km; 10% statics; dogs; bus; no adv bkg; quiet; red long stay; CCI. "Take care siting if heavy rain; some pitches v sm; popular with long stay winter visitors." ♦ € 24.90 2006*

☐ **BENIDORM** *4F2* (1km E Coastal) *38.5449, -0.10696* **Camping Villasol, Avda Bernat de Sarriá 13, 03500 Benidorm (Alicante) [965-85 04 22; fax 966-80 64 20; info@camping-villasol.com; www.camping-villasol.com]** Leave AP7 at junc 65 onto N332 dir Alicante; take exit into Benidorm sp Levante. Turn L at traff lts just past Camping Titus, then in 200m R at lts into Avda Albir. Site on R in 1km. Care - dip at ent, poss grounding. V lge, mkd pitch, hdstg, shd; htd wc; chem disp; baby facs; shwrs inc; el pnts (5A) €4.28; Indtte; supmkt; rest; snacks; bar; playgrnd; 2 pools (1 htd, covrd); sand beach 300m; games area; wifi; sat TV all pitches; medical service; currency exchange; 5% statics; no dogs; phone; adv bkg; Eng spkn; quiet; ccard acc; red low ssn/long stay. "Excel, well-kept site especially in winter; some sm pitches; friendly staff." ♦ € 34.55 2008*

☐ **BERCEO** *1B4* (200m SE Rural) *42.33565, -2.85335* **Camping Berceo, El Molino s/n, 26327 Berceo (La Rioja) [941-37 32 37; fax 941-37 32 01]** Fr E on N120 foll sp Tricio, San Millan de la Cogolla on LR136/LR206. Fr W foll sp Villar de Torre & San Millan. In Berceo foll sp sw pools & site. Med, hdg/mkd pitch, hdstg, pt sl, shd; htd wc; chem disp; fam bthrm; shwrs inc; el pnts (7A) €3.20; Indtte; shop; tradsmn; rest; snacks; bar; playgrnd; pool; paddling pool; cycle hire; TV; 50% statics; phone; bus 200m; adv bkg; quiet; red long stay; CCI. "Excel base for Rioja vineyards; gd site." ♦ € 24.00 2006*

BESALU *3B3* (2km E Rural) *42.20952, 2.73682* **Camping Masia Can Coromines, Ctra N260, Km 60, 17851 Maià del Montcal (Gerona) [tel/fax 972-59 11 08; coromines@grn.es; www.cancoromines.com]** NW fr Gerona on C66 to Besalú. Turn R sp Figueras (N260) for 2.5km. At 60km sp turn into driveway on L opp fountain for approx 300m. Narr app & ent. Site is 1km W of Maià. Narr site ent poss diff lge o'fits. Sm, pt shd; wc; serviced pitch; shwrs €0.50; el pnts (10-15A) €3; gas; Indtte; shop 2.5km; rest high ssn; snacks; bar; playgrnd; pool; cycle hire; internet; some statics; dogs €2.90; Eng spkn; adv bkg; quiet with some rd noise; ccard acc; CCI. "Friendly, family-run site in beautiful area; gd walks; facs poss stretched when site full." ♦
1 Apr-4 Nov. € 20.40 2007*

Spain

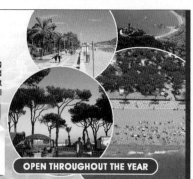

BIELSA *3B2* (8km W Rural) *42.65176, 0.14076* **Camping Pineta, Ctra del Parador, Km 7, 22350 Bielsa (Huesca) [974-50 10 89; fax 974-50 11 84; www.campingpineta.com]** Fr A138 in Beilsa turn W & foll sp for Parador Monte Perdido & Valle de Pineta. Site on L after 8km (ignore previous campsite off rd). Lge, terr, pt sl, pt shd; wc; chem disp; baby facs; shwrs inc; el pnts (6A) €4.17 (poss rev pol); gas; Indtte; shop & 8km; rest; snacks; bar; BBQ; playgrnd; pool; games area; cycle hire; some statics; phone; ccard acc; CCI. "Well-maintained site; clean facs; glorious location in National Park." Easter-10 Dec. € 17.48 2006*

⊞ **BIESCAS** *3B2* (1km SE Rural) *42.61944, -0.30416* **Camping Gavín, Ctra N260, Km 503, 22639 Gavín (Huesca) [974-48 50 90 or 659-47 95 51; fax 974-48 50 17; info@campinggavin.com; www.campinggavin.com]** Take N330/A23/E7 N fr Huesca twd Sabiñánigo then N260 twd Biescas & Valle de Tena (do not take 1st sp Biescas fr Huesca). Bear R on N260 at g'ge on app to Biescas & foll sp Gavín & site, well sp. Site is at km 503 fr Huesca, bet Biescas & Gavín. Lge, mkd pitch, terr, pt shd; htd wc; chem disp; mv service pnt; baby facs; fam bthrm; shwrs inc; el pnts (10A) inc; gas; Indtte; shop; tradsmn; rest; snacks; bar; playgrnd; pool; tennis; cycle hire in National Park; wifi; TV rm; 20% statics; dogs free; phone; bus 1km; adv bkg; quiet; CCI. "Wonderful, scenic site nr Ordesa National Park; poss diff access to pitches for lge o'fits & m'vans; immac san facs; excel." ♦ € 34.60 (CChq acc) 2009*

⊞ **BILBAO** *1A4* (14km N Coastal) *43.38916, -2.98444* **Camping Sopelana, Ctra Bilbao-Plentzia, Km 18, Playa Atxabiribil 30, 48600 Sopelana (Vizcaya) [946-76 19 81; fax 944-21 50 10; recepcion@campingsopelana.com; www.campingsopelana.com]** In Bilbao cross rv by m'way bdge sp to airport, foll 637/634 N twd & Plentzia. Cont thro Sopelana & foll sp on L. Med, hdg pitch, sl, terr; wc (some cont); own san; chem disp; mv service pnt; baby facs; shwrs; el pnts (10A) €3.50; gas; Indtte; shop, rest (w/end only low ssn); snacks; bar; playgrnd; pool; sand beach 200m; 70% statics; metro 2km; poss cr; Eng spkn; adv bkg ess high ssn; quiet but noise fr disco adj; red long stay; CCI. "Poss stong sea winds; ltd space for tourers; pitches sm, poss flooded after heavy rain & poss diff due narr, steep site rds; ltd facs low ssn & poss v unclean; poss no hot water for shwrs; helpful manager; site used by local workers; poor security in city cent/Guggenheim car park; NH/sh stay only." ♦ € 31.50 2009*

The opening dates and prices on this campsite have changed. I'll send a site report form to the Club for the next edition of the guide.

BILBAO *1A4* (3km NW Urban) *43.27600, -2.96700* **Camp Municipal Caravaning Bilbao, Ribera de Zorrozaurre 2, 48014 Bilbao (Vizcaya) [944-79 57 60; informacion@bilbaoturismo.net; www.bilbao.net/bilbaoturismo]** Exit A8 junc 117; foll sps to Plaza Sagrado Corazón; at rndabt (with column) take exit at 11 o'clock to Euskalduna Bdge across rv; at next rndabt take last exit along rv. Site in 1.6km. Lock-up g'ge on R. NB A drive thro busy city cent with only occasional yellow sps 'Caravannes Parking'. Rec download Michelin map bef travel. Sm, hdstg, shd; htd wc; chem disp; mv service pnt; shwrs inc; el pnts inc; bus adj to metro; some rd & rlwy noise; max stay 3 days. "Unconventional site v conv for Bilbao; gd san facs; lock-up g'ge facs for 10-15 o'fits; gd." 15 Jul-15 Sep. € 10.00 2008*

BLANES *3C3* (1km S Coastal) *41.65944, 2.77972* **Camping Bella Terra, Avda Vila de Madrid 35-40, 17300 Blanes (Gerona) [972-34 80 17 or 972-34 80 23; fax 972-34 82 75; info@campingbellaterra.com; www.campingbellaterra.com]** Exit A7 junc 9 via Lloret or junc 10 via Tordera. On app Blanes, all campsites are sp at rndabts; all sites along same rd. V lge, mkd pitch, hdstg, pt sl, shd; wc; chem disp; mv service pnt; baby facs; shwrs inc; el pnts (5A) inc; gas; lndtte; shop; tradsmn; rest; snacks; bar; BBQ; playgrnd; pools; sand beach adj; tennis; games area; games rm; cycle hire; entmnt; internet; TV rm; 15% statics; dogs €4.50; Eng spkn; quiet; ccard acc; red long stay/CCI. "Split site - 1 side has pool, 1 side adj beach; some pitches poss diff for lge o'fits - pitches on pool side lger; vg site with excel facs." ♦ 27 Mar-26 Sep. € 42.40 2009*

See advertisement opposite (below)

⊞ **BLANES** *3C3* (1km S Coastal) *41.65933, 2.77000* **Camping Blanes, Avda Vila de Madrid 33, 17300 Blanes (Gerona) [972-33 15 91; fax 972-33 70 63; info@campingblanes.com; www.campingblanes.com]** Fr N on AP7/E15 exit junc 9 onto NII dir Barcelona & foll sp Blanes. Fr S to end of C32, then NII dir Blanes. On app Blanes, foll camping sps & Playa S'Abanell - all campsites are sp at rndabts; all sites along same rd. Site adj Hotel Blau-Mar. Lge, mkd pitch, shd; wc; chem disp; mv service pnt; shwrs inc; shop; el pnts (5A) inc; gas; lndtte; supmkt; snacks high ssn; bar; playgrnd; pool; dir access to sand beach; watersports; cycle hire; games rm; wifi; entmnt; dogs; phone; bus; poss cr; Eng spkn; quiet; ccard acc; red low ssn. "Some sm pitches with low-hanging trees; narr site rds; easy walk to town cent; trains to Barcelona & Gerona; helpful owner; excel, espec low ssn." ♦ € 35.10 2009*

See advertisement opposite (above)

BLANES *3C3* (1km S Coastal) *41.6550, 2.77861* **Camping El Pinar Beach, Avda Villa de Madrid s/n, 17300 Blanes (Gerona) [972-33 10 83; fax 972-33 11 00; camping@elpinarbeach.com; www.elpinarbeach.com]** Exit AP7/E15 junc 9 dir Malgrat. On app Blanes, all campsites are sp at rndabts; all sites along same rd. V lge, mkd pitch, shd; wc; chem disp; mv service pnt; baby facs; shwrs inc; el pnts (5A) inc; lndtte; shop; rest; snacks; bar; BBQ; playgrnd; pool; paddling pool; sand beach adj; games area; entmnt; excursions; internet; TV; 10% statics; dogs €2; phone; adv bkg; ccard acc; red long stay/low ssn/CCI. "V pleasant site; gd facs; lovely beach; lots to do." ♦ 4 Apr-4 Oct. € 35.30 2009*

See advertisement below

⊞ **BLANES** *3C3* (1km S Coastal) *41.66408, 2.78249* **Camping S'Abanell, Avda Villa de Madrid 7-9, 17300 Blanes (Gerona) [972-33 18 09; fax 972-35 05 06; info@sabanell.com; www.sabanell.com]** Take coast rd S fr cent Blanes. Site well sp on L in 1km. Lge, mkd pitch, pt sl, shd; wc; chem disp; serviced pitches; shwrs; el pnts (6A) €3; gas; lndtte; shop; rest; snacks; bar; sand beach adj; 5% statics; dogs €1; phone; site clsd 25 Dec-6 Jan; poss cr; adv bkg; rd noise; red low ssn/snr citizens; CCI. "Friendly, helpful staff; lge o'fits may need manhandling due pitch layout." € 32.90 2008*

⊞ **BLANES** *3C3* (1.5km SW Urban/Coastal) *41.66305, 2.78083* **Camping La Masia, Calle Cristòfor Colon 44, 17300 Blanes (Gerona) [972-33 10 13; fax 972-33 31 28; info@campinglamasia.com; www.campinglamasia.com]** Fr A7 exit junc 9 sp Lloret de Mar, then Blanes. At Blanes foll sp Blanes Sur (Playa) & Campings, site immed past Camping S'Abanell, well sp. V lge, hdstg, pt shd; htd wc; chem disp; mv service pnt; 25% serviced pitches; sauna; steam rm; shwrs inc; el pnts (3-5A) inc; Indtte; shop; rest; snacks; bar; playgrnd; 2 pools (1 htd, covrd); sand beach nrby; watersports; tennis 500m; weights rm; wellness cent; games area; games rm; entmnt; TV rm; 90% statics; dogs; site clsd mid-Dec to mid-Jan; poss cr; Eng spkn; adv bkg; poss noisy at w/ends; red long stay/low ssn; CCI. "Well-maintained site; excel, clean facs; helpful staff." ♦ € 38.50 (CChq acc) 2009*

BLANES *3C3* (1.5km SW Coastal) *41.66206, 2.78046* **Camping Solmar, Calle Cristòfor Colom 48, 17300 Blanes (Gerona) [972-34 80 34; fax 972-34 82 83; campingsolmar@campingsolmar.com; www.campingsolmar.com]** Fr N on AP7/E15 exit junc 9 onto NII dir Barcelona & foll sp Blanes. Fr S to end of C32, then NII dir Blanes. On app Blanes, foll camping sps. Lge, hdg/mkd pitch, shd; wc; chem disp; mv service pnt; baby facs; shwrs inc; el pnts (6A) inc; Indtte (inc dryer); shop; rest; snacks; bar; BBQ; playgrnd; 2 pools; paddling pool; sand beach 150m; tennis; games area; games rm; wifi; entmnt; some statics; dogs free; bus 100m; adv bkg; quiet; ccard acc; red long stay/low ssn/CCI. "Excel site & facs." ♦ 1 Apr-12 Oct. € 39.00 2009*

See advertisement

BOCA DE HUERGANO see Riaño *1A3*

⊞ **BOCAIRENT** *4F2* (9km E Rural) *38.75332, -0.54957* **Camping Mariola, Ctra Bocairent-Alcoi, Km 9, 46880 Bocairent (València) [962-13 51 60; fax 962-13 50 31; info@campingmariola.com; www.campingmariola.com]** Fr N330 turn E at Villena onto CV81. N of Banyeres & bef Bocairent turn E sp Alcoi up narr, steep hill with some diff turns & sheer drops; site sp. Lge, hdstg, pt shd; htd wc (cont); mv service pnt; shwrs inc; el pnts (6A) €4; Indtte; shop; rest; snacks; bar; BBQ; cooking facs; playgrnd; pool; paddling pool; games area; internet; 50% statics; phone; ccard acc; CCI. "In Mariola mountains; gd walking." € 17.55 2007*

BOLTANA see Ainsa *3B2*

BONANSA see Pont de Suert *3B2*

⊞ **BOSSOST** *3B2* (3km SE Rural) *42.74921, 0.70071* **Camping Prado Verde, Ctra de Lleida a Francia, N230, Km 173, 25551 Era Bordeta/La Bordeta de Vilamòs (Lleida) [973-64 71 72; fax 973-64 04 56; joseluisperise@hotmail.com; www.campingpradoverde.es]** On N230 at km 173 on banks of Rv Garona. Med, shd; wc; baby facs; mv service pnt; shwrs; el pnts €4.80; Indtte; shop & 3km; rest; snacks; bar; playgrnd; pool; fishing; cycle hire; TV; some statics; no dogs; bus 1km; quiet; ccard acc; CCI. "V pleasant NH." € 20.40 2006*

BOSSOST *3B2* (4km S Rural) *42.75122, 0.69677* **Camping Bedura Park, Ctra N230, Km 174.5, 25551 Era Bordeta (Lleida) [tel/fax 973-64 82 93; info@bedurapark.com; www.bedurapark.com]** Fr N on N230, R over rv behind Camping Forcanada. Fr S on N230, 10km fr Viela, L turn over rv. Site is 12km fr French border. Med, mkd pitch, terr, pt shd; wc; chem disp; baby facs; shwrs; el pnts (5A) €4.25; gas; Indtte; shop; rest; BBQ; playgrnd; htd pool; fishing; cycle hire; 20% statics; no dogs; phone; bus 200m; poss cr; Eng spkn; adv bkg; CCI. "Skiing, walking in area; excel." ♦ Holy Week-30 Sep. € 28.50 2008*

BROTO *3B2* (1km N Rural) *42.63194, -0.11194* **Camping Rió Ara, Ctra Ordesa s/n, 22376 Torla (Huesca) [974-48 62 48; campingrioara@ordesa.com; www.ordesa.net/camping-rioara]** Leave N260/A135 on bend approx 2km N of Broto sp Torla & Ordesa National Park. Drive thro Torla; as leaving vill turn R sp Rió Ara. Steep, narr rd down to & across narr bdge (worth it). Med, pt sl, pt shd; wc; chem disp; baby facs; shwrs inc; el pnts (5A) €4.39; Indtte; shop; tradsmn; rest 500m; bar; no statics; phone; bus; 500m; ccard not acc; CCI. "Attractive, well-kept, family-run site; mainly tents; conv for Torla; bus to Ordesa National Park (high ssn); not rec for lge o'fits due to steep app; gd walking & birdwatching; excel." Easter-31 Oct. € 19.10 2008*

⊞ **BROTO** *3B2* (5km N Rural) *42.63948, -0.10948* **Camping Ordesa, 22376 Torla (Huesca) [974-48 61 25; fax 974-48 63 81; info@hotelordesa.com; www.hotelordesa.com]** Fr Ainsa on N260 twd Torla. Pass Torla turn R onto A135 (Valle de Ordesa twd Ordesa National Park). Site 2km N of Torla, adj Hotel Ordesa. Med, pt shd; wc; chem disp; serviced pitch; baby facs; shwrs; el pnts (6A) €3.80; gas 2km; Indtte; shop 2km, tradsmn; rest high ssn; bar; playgrnd; pool; tennis; some statics (sep area); phone; bus 1km; poss cr; Eng spkn; adv bkg (ess Jul/Aug); quiet; red low ssn; ccard acc; CCI. "V scenic; recep in adj Hotel Ordesa; excel rest; v helpful staff; facs poss stretched w/end; long, narr pitches & lge trees on access rd poss diff lge o'fits; ltd facs low ssn; no access to National Park by car Jul/Aug, shuttlebus fr Torla." € 22.00 2008*

BROTO *3B2* (1.2km W Rural) *42.59779, -0.13072* **Camping Oto, Afueras s/n, 22370 Oto-Broto (Huesca) [974-48 60 75; fax 974-48 63 47; info@campingoto.com; www.campingoto.com]** On N260 foll camp sp on N o'skts of Broto. Diff app thro vill but poss. Lge, pt sl, pt shd; wc; chem disp; baby facs; shwrs inc; el pnts (10A) €3.80 (poss no earth); gas; Indtte; shop; snacks; bar; BBQ; playgrnd; pool; paddling pool; entmnt; adv bkg; quiet; ccard acc. "Excel, clean san facs; excel bar & café; friendly owner; pitches below pool rec; some noise fr adj youth site; conv Ordesa National Park." 6 Mar-14 Oct. € 16.70 2008*

⊞ **BROTO** *3B2* (6km W Rural) *42.61576, -0.15432* **Camping Viu, Ctra N260, Biescas-Ordesa, Km 484.2, 22378 Viu de Linás (Huesca) [974-48 63 01; fax 974-48 63 73; info@campingviu.com; www.campingviu.com]** Lies on N260, 4km W of Broto. Fr Broto, N for 2km on rd 135; turn W twd Biesca at junc with Torla rd; site approx 4km on R. Med, sl, pt shd; htd wc; chem disp; mv service pnt; shwrs inc; el pnts (5-8A) €4.20; gas; Indtte; shop; rest; BBQ; playgrnd; games rm; cycle hire; horseriding; walking, skiing & climbing adj; car wash; phone; adv bkg; quiet; ccard acc; CCI. "Friendly owners; gd home cooking; fine views; highly rec; clean, modern san facs; poss not suitable for lge o'fits." € 17.40 2007*

BURGO DE OSMA, EL *1C4* (17km N Rural) *41.7292, -3.0481* **Camping Cañón del Rió Lobos, Ctra El Burgo de Osma-San Leonardo, 42317 Ucero (Soria) [tel/fax 975-36 35 65]** On SO 920 17km N fr El Burgo de Osma or S fr San Leonardo de Yagüe. Site 1km N of Ucero. Care needed over narr bdge in vill cent. Med, hdg/mkd pitch, hdstg & grass, shd; wc; chem disp; mv service pnt; shwrs inc; el pnts (6A) €4.85; Indtte; rest; snacks; bar; BBQ; playgrnd; pool; no dogs; quiet; no ccard acc; CCI. "Sm pitches/tight turning - help avail; heart of canyon of Rv Lobos; v pretty location; gd base walking, cycling, climbing; bird watchers' paradise; poss w/end only until beginning Jun." Easter-30 Sep. € 22.50 2008*

⊞ **BURGOS** *1B4* (2.5km E Rural) *42.34111, -3.65777* **Camp Municipal Fuentes Blancas, Ctra Cartuja Miraflores, Km 3.5, 09193 Burgos [tel/fax 947-48 60 16; info@campingburgos.com; www.campingburgos.com]** E or W on A1 exit junc 238 & turn R sp Cortes. Cont to rndabt & go strt on for Burgos town cent. Look for yellow sps to site. Lge, mkd pitch, shd; some htd wc; chem disp; mv service pnt; baby facs; shwrs inc; el pnts (6A) inc; gas; Indtte; shop high ssn & 3km; rest; snacks; bar; playgrnd; pool high ssn; games area; wifi; 10% statics; dogs €2.25; phone; bus at gate; poss cr; Eng spkn; quiet; ccard acc; CCI. "Clean facs & plenty of hot water; neat, roomy site but some sm pitches & poorly maintained el pnts & shwrs; ltd facs low ssn, poss unkempt & poss itinerants; poss v muddy in wet; vg recep open 0800-2200; easy access town car parks or cycle/rv walk; Burgos lovely town; gd NH." € 24.10 2009*

CABO DE GATA see Almería *4G1*

⊞ **CABRERA, LA** *1D4* (4km S Rural) *40.82124, -3.63729* **Camping d'Oremor, Ctra Cabanillas-Bustarviejo, 28721 Cabanillas de la Sierra (Madrid) [918-43 90 34; fax 918-43 90 09; doremor@doremor.com; www.doremor.com]** Fr Madrid N on A1/E5 exit junc 50 onto M608; in 500m turn N parallel to E5/N1. Site clearly sp in 3km. Med, shd; htd wc; chem disp; mv service pnt; shwrs inc; el pnts €4.70; gas; Indtte; shop; rest; snacks; bar; playgrnd; pool; lake sw & fishing adj; tennis; mainly statics; dogs; bus 700m; poss cr; adv bkg; quiet; ccard acc. "Ltd facs low ssn & site run down, untidy; dated facs; check el pnts carefully; windsurfing on lake & skiing in area in winter; take care marble floor tiles in shwrs - v slippery when wet; NH only." ♦ € 19.70 2007*

⊞ **CABRERA, LA** *1D4* (1km SW Rural) *40.85797, -3.61580* **Camping Pico de la Miel, Ctra N1, Km 58, Finca Prado Nuevo, 28751 La Cabrera (Madrid) [918-68 80 82 or 918-68 95 07; fax 918-68 85 41; pico-miel@picomiel.com; www.picodelamiel.com]** Fr Madrid on A1/E5, exit junc 57 sp La Cabrera. Turn L at rndabt, site sp. Lge, mkd pitch, pt sl, pt shd; htd wc; chem disp; shwrs inc; el pnts (10A) €4.45; gas; Indtte (inc dryer); shop high ssn; supmkt 1km; rest, snacks, bar high ssn & w/end; playgrnd; Olympic-size pool; paddling pool; sailing; fishing; windsurfing; tennis; games area; squash; mountain-climbing; car wash; 75% statics; dogs; phone; v cr high ssn & w/end; some Eng spkn; adv bkg; quiet; ccard acc; red long stay/low ssn/CCI. "Attractive walking country; conv Madrid; ltd touring area not v attractive; some pitches have low sun shades; excel san facs; ltd facs low ssn." ♦ € 24.00 2008*

⊞ **CABRERA, LA** *1D4* (15km SW Rural) *40.80821, -3.69106* **Camping Piscis, Ctra Guadalix de la Sierra a Navalafuente, Km 3, 28729 Navalafuente (Madrid) [918-43 22 68; fax 918-43 22 53; campiscis@campiscis.com; www.campiscis.com]** Fr A1/E5 exit junc 50 onto M608 dir Guidalix de la Sierra, foll sp to Navalafuente & site. Lge, hdg pitch, hdstg, pt sl, pt shd; wc; chem disp; shwrs €0.30; el pnts (5A) €3.40 (long lead req); gas; Indtte; shop 6km; rest; snacks; bar; playgrnd; pool; paddling pool; watersports 10km; tennis; games area; 75% statics; quiet; adv bkg; Eng spkn; ccard acc; red low ssn; CCI. "Mountain views; walking; bus to Madrid daily outside gate, 1 hr ride; spacious pitches but uneven; rough site rds; v ltd facs, poss unclean low ssn & poss no hot water." ♦ € 21.40 2007*

⊞ **CACERES** *2E3* (2km NW Urban) *39.48861, -6.41277* **Camp Municipal Ciudad de Cáceres, Ctra N630, Km 549.5, 10080 Cáceres [tel/fax 927-23 31 00; info@campingcaceres.com; www.campingcaceres.com]** Fr Cáceres ring rd take N630 dir Salamanca. At 1st rndbt turn R sp Via de Servicio with camping symbol. Foll sp 500m to site. Or fr N exit A66 junc 545 onto N630 twd Cáceres. At 2nd rndabt turn L sp Via de Servicio, site on L adj football stadium. Med, mkd pitch, hdstg, terr, unshd; wc; chem disp; mv service pnt; individ san facs each pitch; shwrs inc; el pnts (10-16A) €3.20; gas; Indtte; shop; rest; snacks; bar; BBQ; playgrnd; pool high ssn; paddling pool; games area; wifi; TV; 15% statics; dogs; bus 500m over footbdge; Eng spkn; adv bkg; distant noise fr indus est nrby; ccard acc; red low ssn/CCI. "Vg, well-run site; excel facs; vg value rest; gd for disabled access." € 22.00 2009*

CADAQUES *3B3* (1km N Coastal) *42.28833, 3.28194* **Camping Cadaqués, Ctra Port Lligat 17, 17488 Cadaqués (Gerona) [972-25 81 26; fax 972-15 93 83; info@campingcadaques.com]** At ent to town, turn L onto tarmac rd thro narr streets, site in about 1.5km on L. NB App to Cadaqués on busy, narr mountain rds, not suitable lge o'fits. If raining, roads only towable with 4x4. Lge, mkd pitch, hdstg, sl, pt shd; wc; chem disp; shwrs; el pnts (5A) €5.15; gas; Indtte; shop; rest; snacks; bar; playgrnd; pool; paddling pool; shgl beach 600m; no dogs; sep car park; poss cr; Eng spkn; no adv bkg; quiet; ccard acc. "Cadaqués home of Salvador Dali; sm pitches; medical facs high ssn; san facs poss poor low ssn; fair." Easter-17 Sep. € 30.35 2007*

CADAVEDO see Luarca *1A3*

⊞ **CALATAYUD** *3C1* (15km N Rural) *41.44666, -1.55805* **Camping Saviñan Parc, Ctra El Frasno-Mores, Km 7, 50299 Saviñan (Zaragoza) [tel/fax 976-82 54 23]** Exit A2/E90 (Zaragoza-Madrid) at km 255 to T-junc. Turn R to Saviñan for 6km, foll sps to site 1km S. Lge, hdstg, terr, pt shd; wc; chem disp; mv service pnt; shwrs inc; el pnts (6-10A) €4.20; gas; Indry rm; shop 1.5km; playgrnd; pool high ssn; tennis; horseriding; phone; 50% statics; dogs €2.70; site clsd Jan; quiet; ccard acc; CCI. "Beautiful scenery & views; some sm narr pitches; rec identify pitch location to avoid stop/start on hill; terr pitches have steep, unfenced edges; many pitches with sunscreen frames & diff to manoeuvre long o'fits; modern facs block but cold in winter & poss stretched high ssn; hot water to some shwrs only; gates poss clsd low ssn - use intercom; site poss clsd Feb." € 21.00 2008*

CALATAYUD *3C1* (3km E Rural) *41.36247, -1.60505* **Camping Calatayud, Ctra Madrid-Barcelona, Km 239, 50300 Calatayud (Zaragoza) [976-88 05 92; fax 976-36 07 76; rsanramon237@msn.com]** Fr W exit A2 sp Calatayud; site on S side of old N11 (parallel to new dual c'way) at km stone 239a. Med, pt shd; wc; chem disp; shwrs inc; el pnts (5-10A) €5.35 (poss rev pol); gas; Indtte; snacks; shop 2km; pool; dogs; some rd noise; ccard acc; CCI. "Site area bleak; clean, refurbished san facs & pool; easy to manoeuvre twin-axles; interesting town; much improved NH."
15 Mar-30 Oct. € 21.40 2009*

⊞ **CALDES DE MONTBUI** *3C3* (2km N Rural) *41.6442, 2.1564* **Camping El Pasqualet, Ctra Sant Sebastià de Montmajor, Km 0.3, 08140 Caldes de Montbui (Barcelona)[938-65 46 95; fax 938-65 38 96; elpasqualet@elpasqualet.com; www.elpasqualet.com]** N fr Caldes on C59 dir Montmajor, site sp on L off rd BV1243. Med, terr, pt shd; wc; chem disp; mv service pnt; baby facs; shwrs inc; el pnts (4A) €5; gas; Indtte (inc dryer); shop 2km; tradsmn; rest; snacks; bar; playgrnd; pool; games area; TV rm; 80% statics; dogs €2.15; bus 2km; site clsd mid-Dec to mid-Jan; poss cr; adv bkg; quiet. "Beautiful area; ltd touring pitches; facs poss stretched high ssn." ♦
€ 29.00 2008*

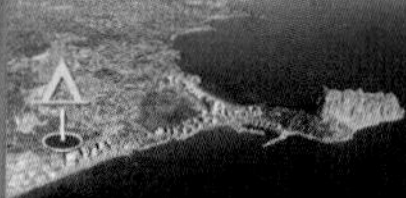

CALELLA *3C3* (2km NE Coastal) *41.61774, 2.67680* **Camping Caballo de Mar, Passeig Maritim s/n, 08397 Pineda de Mar (Barcelona) [937-67 17 06; fax 937-67 16 15; info@caballodemar.com; www.caballodemar.com]** Fr N exit AP7 junc 9 & immed turn R onto NII dir Barcelona. Foll sp Pineda de Mar & turn L twd Paseo Maritimo. Fr S on C32 exit 122 dir Pineda de Mar & foll dir Paseo Maritimo. Lge, mkd pitch, shd; wc; chem disp; baby facs; shwrs inc; el pnts (3-6A) €3.40-4.40; gas; lndtte; shop; tradsmn; rest; snacks; bar; BBQ; playgrnd; pool; sand beach adj; games area; games rm; entmnt; internet; 10% statics; dogs €2.20; rlwy stn 2km (Barcelona 30 mins); Eng spkn; adv bkg; quiet; ccard acc; red long stay/CCI. "Excursions arranged; gd touring base & conv Barcelona; gd, modern facs; excel." ♦ 31 Mar-30 Sep. € 25.60 2007*

⊞ **CALELLA** *3C3* (1km S Coastal) *41.6069, 2.6392* **Camping Botànic Bona Vista Kim, Ctra N11, Km 665, 08370 Calella de la Costa (Barcelona) [937-69 24 88; fax 937-69 58 04; info@botanic-bonavista.net; www.botanic-bonavista.net]** A19/C32 exit sp Calella onto NII coast rd, site is sp S of Calella on R. Care needed on busy rd & sp almost on top of turning (adj Camp Roca Grossa). Lge, mkd pitch, hdstg, terr, pt shd; shwrs inc; wc; chem disp; mv service pnt; sauna; shwrs inc; el pnts (6A) €6.42 (rev pol); lndtte; supmkt; rest; snacks; bar; BBQ/picnic area; playgrnd; pool; sand beach adj; solarium; jacuzzi; TV; 20% statics; dogs €4.81; phone; poss cr; Eng spkn; adv bkg; some rd noise; CCI. "V steep access rd to site - owner prefers to tow c'vans with 4x4; poss diff v lge m'vans; all pitches have sea view; v friendly owner; spotless facs; train to Barcelona fr St Pol (2km)." ♦ € 25.46 2006*

CALELLA *3C3* (1km SW Coastal) *41.60635, 2.63890* **Camping Roca Grossa, Ctra N-11, Km 665, 08370 Calella (Barcelona) [937-69 12 97; fax 937-66 15 56; rocagrossa@rocagrossa.com; www.rocagrossa.com]** Situated off rd N11 at km stone 665, site sp. V steep access rd to site. Lge, sl, terr, shd; wc; chem disp; mv service pnt; shwrs inc; el pnts (6A) €6; gas; lndtte; shop; rest; snacks; bar; games rm; TV rm; pool; playgrnd; beach adj; windsurfing; tennis; statics; phone; dogs €4.20; adv bkg; Eng spkn; ccard acc. "V friendly, family-run site; steep site - tractor pull avail; modern facs; excel pool & playgrnd on top of hill; scenic drive to Tossa de Mar; conv for Barcelona." 1 Apr-30 Sep. € 28.40 2009*

CALONGE see Playa de Aro *3B3*

⊞ **CALPE** *4F2* (1km N Urban/Coastal) *38.6542, 0.0681* **Camping La Merced, Ctra de la Cometa, 03710 Calpe (Alicante) [965-83 00 97]** Exit A7/E15 at junc 63 & foll sp Calpe Norte down hill to traff lts & turn L. Foll dual c'way round Calpe, past Peñón de Ifach. Pass Cmp Levante on L, at next rndabt turn L, site on R in 400m. Med, mkd pitch, hdstg, pt terr, shd; htd wc; chem disp; mv service pnt; shwrs inc; el pnts (10A) €3.50 (poss long cable req); gas; lndtte; shop; supmkt 400m; rest 150m; snacks; bar; BBQ; sand beach 400m; TV rm; 10% statics; dogs €2.50; phone; bus 50m; poss cr; Eng spkn; adv bkg; poss noisy; red long stay/low ssn; CCI. "Gd san facs but dated; improved site; log fire in bar in winter; fair site; unkempt low ssn." ♦ € 25.60 2008*

⊞ **CALPE** *4F2* (1km N Urban/Coastal) *38.64781, 0.07172* **Camping Levante, Avda de la Marina s/n, 03710 Calpe (Alicante) [tel/fax 965-83 22 72; info@campinglevantecalpe.com; www.campinglevantecalpe.com]** Fr N332 (Alicante-València) take slip rd sp Calpe. Foll dual c'way round Calpe past Peñón-de-Ifach. Pass site on L, cont to rndabt & back to site. Sm, hdstg, shd; wc; chem disp; shwrs inc; el pnts (6A) inc; lndtte; shop; rest; snacks; bar; sand beach 100m; 10% statics; dogs; bus; Eng spkn; adv bkg; quiet; ccard acc; red long stay; CCI. "Well-run, clean, tidy site; liable to flood after heavy rain; pleasant town & promenade." € 25.20 2008*

⊞ **CALPE** *4F2* (300m NE Urban/Coastal) *38.64488, 0.05604* **Camping CalpeMar, Calle Eslovenia 3, 03710 Calpe (Alicante) [tel/fax 965-87 55 76; info@campingcalpemar.com; www.campingcalpemar.com]** Exit AP7/E15 junc 63 onto N332 & foll sp, take slip rd sp Calpe Norte & foll dual c'way CV746 round Calpe twd Peñón d'Ifach. At rndabt nr police stn with metal statues turn L, then L at next rndabt, over next rndabt, site 100m on R. Med, hdg/mkd pitch, hdstg, unshd; htd wc; chem disp; baby facs; fam bthrm; all serviced pitches; shwrs inc; el pnts (10A) inc; lndtte; ice; shop 500m; tradsmn; rest; snacks; bar; BBQ; playgrnd; pool; sand beach 300m; games area; games rm; entmnt; car wash; dog wash; internet; TV; 3% statics; dogs free; phone; bus adj; sep car park; Eng spkn; adv bkg; quiet; ccard acc; red long stay/low ssn; CCI. "New, high standard site 2008; gd security; excel." ♦ € 35.00 2009*

See advertisement

⊞ **CAMARASA** *3B2* (23km N Rural) *42.00416, 0.86583* **Camping Zodiac, Ctra C13, Km 66, La Baronia de Sant Oïsme, 25621 Camarasa (Lleida) [tel/fax 973-45 50 03; zodiac@campingzodiac.com; www.campingzodiac.com]** Fr C13 Lleida to Balaguer. N of Balaguer take C13 & foll sp for Camarasa, then dir Tremp & site. Steep, winding but scenic app rd. Med, hdstg, pt sl, terr, pt shd; wc; chem disp; baby facs; shwrs; el pnts (5A) €4.60; shop; lndtte; rest; snacks; bar; playgrnd; pool; rv sw adj; tennis; TV; 90% statics; phone; Eng spkn; quiet; ccard acc. "Site on reservoir; poss untidy, shabby low ssn; some sm pitches diff due trees; excel views & walks; Terradets Pass 2km." ♦ € 18.80 2007*

CAMBRILS See also Salou.

⊞ **CAMBRILS** *3C2* (1km N Rural) *41.07928, 1.06661* **Camping Àmfora d'Arcs, Ctra N340, Km 1145, 43391 Vinyols i Els Arcs (Tarragona) [977-36 12 11; fax 977-79 50 75; info@amforadarcs.com; www.amforadarcs.com]** Exit AP7 junc 37 onto N340 E & watch for km sps, site bet 1145 & 1146km. Lge, hdg pitch, hdstg, pt shd; wc; chem disp; shwrs inc; el pnts (5A) inc; gas; lndtte; supmkt opp; rest high ssn; bar; playgrnd; pool; beach 1.5km; 60% statics; dogs €4.50; phone; bus 300m; site poss clsd Xmas; poss cr; Eng spkn; adv bkg; noisy espec at w/end; ccard acc; red long stay/low ssn; CCI. "Sm pitches." € 34.50 2009*

Spain

CAMBRILS *3C2* (1.5km N Urban/Coastal) *41.06500, 1.08361* **Camping Playa Cambrils Don Camilo, Carrer de Oleastrum, Ctra Cambrils-Salou, Km 1.5, 43850 Cambrils (Tarragona) [977-36 14 90; fax 977-36 49 88; camping@ playacambrils.com; www.playacambrils.com]**
Exit A7 junc 37 dir Cambrils & N340. Turn L onto N340 then R dir port then L onto coast rd. Site sp on L at rndabt after rv bdge 100m bef watch tower on R, approx 2km fr port. V lge, hdg/mkd pitch, shd; wc; chem disp; baby facs; shwrs inc; el pnts (5A) inc; gas; Indtte; supmkt; rest; snacks; bar; playgrnd; htd pool; sand beach adj; tennis; games rm; boat hire; cycle hire; watersports; entmnt; children's club; cinema; TV rm; 25% statics; bus to Port Aventura; cash machine; doctor; 24-hour security; dogs €4.20; Eng spkn; adv bkg ess high ssn; some rd & rlwy noise; ccard acc; red long stay/low ssn/CCI. "Helpful, friendly staff; sports activities avail; Port Aventura 5km." ♦ 15 Mar-12 Oct. € 41.40 2009*

See advertisement below

CAMBRILS *3C2* (5km N Rural) *41.11132, 1.04558* **Vinyols Camp, Camí de Berenys s/n, 43391 Vinyols i Els Arcs [977-85 04 09; fax 977-76 84 49; info@vinyolscamp.com; www.vinyolscamp.com]** Exit AP7 junc 37 N onto T312 dir Montbrió del Camp for 4km. Turn R at rndabt onto T314 dir Vinyols; site at ent to vill. Med, pt shd; el pnts (4A); shop 200m; rest; snacks; bar; pool; paddling pool; sand beach 5km; internet; entmnt; some statics; dogs €2.50; adv bkg; quiet. "Peaceful, ecological, farm site." 7 Mar-2 Nov. € 17.20 2008*

⊞ **CAMBRILS** *3C2* (S Urban/Coastal) *41.06550, 1.04460* **Camping La Llosa, Ctra N340, Km 1143, 43850 Cambrils (Tarragona) [977-36 26 15; fax 977-79 11 80; info@ camping-lallosa.com; www.camping-lallosa.com]**
Exit A7/E15 at junc 37 & join N340 S. Head S into Cambrils (ignore L turn to cent) & at traff lts turn R. Site sp on L within 100m. Fr N exit junc 35 onto N340. Strt over at x-rds, then L over rlwy bdge at end of rd, strt to site. V lge, hdstg, shd; wc; shwrs inc; el pnts (5A) €5; gas; Indtte; shop; rest; snacks; bar; playgrnd; pool; sand beach; entmnt high ssn; car wash; 50% statics; dogs €2.50; phone; bus 500m; poss cr; Eng spkn; some rd & rlwy noise; ccard acc; red long stay/low ssn. "Interesting fishing port; gd facs; excel pool; gd supmkt nrby; poss diff siting for m'vans due low trees; excel winter NH." ♦ € 27.30 2009*

CAMBRILS *3C2* (2km S Coastal) *41.05533, 1.02333* **Camping Joan, Urbanització La Dorada, Passeig Marítim 88, 43850 Cambrils (Tarragona) [977-36 46 04; fax 977-79 42 14; info@campingjoan.com; www.camping joan.com]** Exit AP7 junc 37 onto N340, S dir València. Turn off at km 1.141 & Hotel Daurada, foll site sp. Lge, hdg/mkd pitch, hdstg, terr, shd; htd wc; chem disp; mv service pnt; baby facs; shwrs inc; el pnts (5A) €4.40; gas; Indtte; supmkt; rest; snacks; bar; BBQ; playgrnd; pool & paddling pool; sand beach adj; watersports; fishing; cycle hire; games area; games rm; entmnt; wifi; sat TV; 16% statics; dogs €3.10; phone; currency exchange; car wash; Eng spkn; adv bkg; quiet; red low ssn/long stay/CCI. "Conv Port Aventura; gd family site; v clean san facs; friendly welcome; some sm pitches; gd beach; vg." ♦ 27 Mar-5 Nov. € 29.95 2009*

See advertisement opposite

CAMBRILS *3C2* (5km SW Coastal) *41.04694, 1.00361* **Camping Oasis Mar, Ctra de València N340, Km 1139, 43892 Montroig (Tarragona) [977-17 95 95; fax 977-17 95 16; info@oasismar.com; www.oasismar.com]** Fr AP7 exit 37; N340 Tarragona-València rd, at Montroig, km 1139. Lge, mkd pitch, pt shd; wc; chem disp; shwrs inc; baby facs; el pnts (5A) €5; gas; Indtte; shop; rest; snacks; bar; BBQ; playgrnd; pool; sand beach adj; watersports; 30% statics; dogs €5.08 Eng spkn; red long stay/low ssn. "Excel site by super beach; friendly, helpful owners; gd facs; busy at w/end when statics occupied; vg." 1 Mar-31 Oct. € 30.00 2009*

CAMBRILS *3C2* (7km SW Coastal) *41.04011, 0.98061* **Camping Els Prats - Marius, Ctra N340, Km 1137, Montroig del Camp, 43892 Miami Playa (Tarragona) [977-81 00 27; fax 977-17 09 01; info@campingelsprats. com; www.campingelsprats.com]** Exit AP7 junc 37 onto N340 twds València. At km 1137 turn dir Camping Marius, under rlwy bdge & turn R to site. Lge, mkd pitch, shd; wc; chem disp; mv service pnt; baby facs; shwrs; el pnts (5A) €4.50; Indtte; shop; rest; snacks; bar; playgrnd; pool; sand beach adj; watersports; games area; tennis 100m; horseriding 3km; golf 6km; cycle hire; entmnt; TV; 20% statics; dogs €2.50 (not acc end Jun-mid Aug); adv bkg; quiet; ccard acc. "Pleasant, well-run, family site." ♦ 6 Mar-12 Oct. € 32.00 2008*

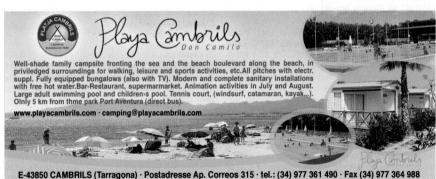

CAMBRILS *3C2* (8km SW Coastal) *41.03333, 0.96777* **Playa Montroig Camping Resort, N340, Km1.136, 43300 Montroig (Tarragona) [977-81 06 37; fax 977-81 14 11; info@playamontroig.com; www.playamontroig.com]** Exit AP7 junc 37, W onto N340. Site has own dir access onto N340 bet Cambrils & L'Hospitalet de L'Infant, well sp fr Cambrils. V lge, mkd pitch, pt sl, shd; htd wc; chem disp; mv service pnt; serviced pitches; baby facs; shwrs inc; el pnts (10A) inc; gas; lndtte; supmkt; rest; snacks; bars; playgrnd; 3 htd pools; sand beach adj; tennis; games area; games rm; skateboard track; many sports; cycle hire; golf 3km; cash machine; doctor; wifi; entmnt; 30% statics; no dogs; phone; Eng spkn; adv bkg; some rd & rlwy noise; ccard acc; red snr citizens/low ssn/CCI. "Magnificent, clean, secure site; private, swept beach; some sm pitches & low branches; 4 grades pitch/price; highly rec." ♦ 19 Mar-31 Oct. € 61.50 2009*

CAMBRILS *3C2* (8km W Coastal) *41.03807, 0.97478* **Camping La Torre del Sol, Ctra N340, Km 1136, Miami-Playa, 43300 Montroig Del Camp (Tarragona) [977-81 04 86; fax 977-81 13 06; info@latorredelsol.com; www.latorredelsol.com]** Leave A7 València/Barcelona m'way at junc 37 & foll sp Cambrils. After 1.5km join N340 coast rd S for 6km. Watch for site sp 4km bef Miami Playa. Fr S exit AP7 junc 38, foll sp Cambrils on N340. Site on R 4km after Miami Playa. Site ent narr, alt ent avail for lge o'fits. Lge, hdg/mkd pitch, shd; wc; chem disp; mv service pnt; baby facs; sauna; shwrs inc; el pnts (6A) inc (10A avail); gas; lndtte; supmkt; tradsmn; rest; snacks; bar; BBQ; luxury playgrnd; 3 pools; whirlpool; private sand beach; tennis; squash; cycle hire; horseriding; gym; skateboard zone; golf 4km; cinema; disco; wifi; entmnt & child entmt; live shows high ssn; day-care cent for children; excursions; doctor; cash machine; hairdresser; wifi; TV; 40% statics; no dogs; poss v cr; Eng spkn; adv bkg; quiet, but some rd/rlwy noise & disco; ccard acc; red low ssn. "Attractive site for all ages; gd, clean facs; well-guarded; radios/TVs to be used inside vans only; conv Port Aventura, Aquaparc, Aquopolis; no c'vans over 7m high ssn; excel." ♦ 15 Mar-31 Oct. € 51.50 (CChq acc) ABS - E14 2009*

See advertisement on bookmark at front of guide

⊞ **CAMPELL** *4E2* (1km S Rural) *38.77672, -0.10529* **Camping Vall de Laguar, Carrer Sant Antoni 24, 03791 La Vall de Laguar (Alicante) [965-57 74 90 or 699-77 35 09; info@campinglaguar.com; www.campinglaguar.com]** Exit A7 junc 62 sp Ondara. Turn L to Orba onto CV733 dir Benimaurell & foll sp to Vall de Laguar. In Campell vill (narr rds) fork L & foll site sp uphill (narr rd). Steep ent to site. Lge o'fits ignore sp in vill & turn R to Fleix vill. In Fleix turn L to main rd, downhill to site sp at hairpin. Diff app. Med, mkd pitch, hdstg, terr, pt shd; htd wc; chem disp; shwrs inc; el pnts (5-10A) €2.75; gas; lndtte; shop 500m; rest; snacks; bar; BBQ; pool; sand beach 18km; 50% statics; dogs €1.30; phone; Eng spkn; adv bkg; quiet; ccard acc; red low ssn/long stay; CCI. "Sm pitches diff for lge o'fits; m'vans 7.50m max; excel home-cooked food in rest; ideal site for walkers; mountain views; friendly owners live on site; excel but rec sm o'fits & m'vans only." ♦ € 21.50 2009*

CAMPELLO, EL see Alicante *4F2*

⊞ **CAMPRODON** *3B3* (2km S Rural) *42.29010, 2.36230* **Camping Vall de Camprodón, Les Planes d'en Xenturri, Ctra Ripoll-Camprodón, C38, Km 7.5, 17867 Camprodón [972-74 05 07; fax 972-13 06 32; info@valldecamprodon.net; www.valldecamprodon.net]** Fr Gerona W on C66/C26 to Sant Pau de Segúries. Turn N onto C38 to Camprodón, site sp. Access over bdge weight limit 3,5000 kg. Lge, mkd pitch, pt shd; htd wc; mv service pnt; baby facs; shwrs; el pnts (4-10) €3.60-7.45 (poss rev pol); lndtte; shop; rest (w/end & public hols) & 2km; snacks; bar; playgrnd; pool; paddling pool; tennis; games area; horseriding; wifi; entmnt; TV; 90% statics; dogs €5.50; bus 200m; o'night m'van area (no san facs); adv bkg; quiet. "Camprodón attractive vill; lovely scenery; peaceful site; helpful staff; ltd facs low ssn." ♦ € 29.45 (CChq acc) 2008*

CANDAS see Gijon *1A3*

CANDELARIO see Béjar *1D3*

Spain

CANET DE MAR *3C3* (E Coastal) *41.59086, 2.59195* **Camping Globo Rojo, Ctra N11, Km 660.9, 08360 Canet de Mar (Barcelona) [tel/fax 937-94 11 43; camping@globo-rojo.com; www.globo-rojo.com]** On N11 500m N of Canet de Mar. Site clearly sp on L. Gd access. Med, hdg/mkd pitch, hdstg, shd; wc; chem disp; baby facs; shwrs; el pnts (10A) €4.25; gas; lndtte; shop; tradsmn; rest; snacks; bar; BBQ; playgrnd; pool; paddling pool; shgl beach & watersports adj; tennis; games area; horseriding 2km; cycle hire; internet; TV rm; 80% statics; dogs €5.35; phone; sep car park; Eng spkn; adv bkg; rd noise; ccard acc; red low ssn/CCI. "Excel facs; friendly, family-run site; busy w/end; slightly run down area; conv Barcelona by train (40km)." ♦ 1 Apr-30 Sep. € 30.80 2007*

⊞ **CANGAS DE ONIS** *1A3* (16km E Rural) *43.33527, -4.94777* **Camping Picos de Europa, Ctra Cangas de Onís-Cabrales, Km 17, 33556 Avín (Asturias) [985-84 40 70; fax 985-84 42 40; info@picos-europa.com; www.picos-europa.com]** N625 fr Arriondas to Cangas, then AS114 dir Panes for approx 16km. Go thro Avín vill, site on R at 17km marker - sp fr both dirs. Med, terr, pt shd; wc; chem disp; baby facs; shwrs inc; el pnts (6A) €3.75; gas; lndtte (inc dryer); shop; rest; snacks; bar; pool; beach 20km; horseriding; canoeing on local rvs; some statics; phone; poss cr; Eng spkn; adv bkg; some rd noise & goat bells; ccard acc; CCI. "Owners v helpful; beautiful, busy, well-run site; vg value rest; modern san facs; poss diff access due narr site rds & cr; some sm pitches - lge o'fits may need 2; conv local caves, mountains, National Park, beaches; vg rest." € 19.70 2009*

CANGAS DE ONIS *1A3* (3km SE Rural) *43.34715, -5.08362* **Camping Covadonga, 33589 Soto de Cangas (Asturias) [tel/fax 985-94 00 97; info@camping-covadonga.com; www.camping-covadonga.com]** N625 fr Arriondas to Cangas de Onis, then AS114 twds Covadonga & Panes, cont thro town sp Covadonga. At rndabt take 2nd exit sp Cabrales, site on R in 100m. Access tight. Med, mkd pitch, pt shd; wc; chem disp; shwrs; el pnts (10A) €3.50 (no earth); lndtte (inc dryer); shop; supmkt in town; rest; snacks; bar; bus adj; poss cr; adv bkg; quiet, but slight rd noise; red long stay; CCI. "V sm pitches (approx 5 x 6m); take care with access; site rds narr; 17 uneven steps to san facs; conv for Picos de Europa; owner's dog fouls site." Holy Week & 15 Jun-30 Sep. € 21.20 2009*

CAPMANY see Figueres *3B3*

CARAVIA ALTA see Colunga *1A3*

⊞ **CARBALLO** *1A2* (6km N Coastal) *43.29556, -8.65528* **Camping Baldayo, Rebordelos, 15684 Carballo (La Coruña) [981-73 95 29]** On AC552 fr La Coruña dir Carballo, turn R approx 3km bef Carballo sp Noicela 8km. In Noicela fork R sp Caión, next L & site sp when app dunes. App fr Arteijo diff for lge vans. Sm, pt sl, terr, pt shd; wc; chem disp; shwrs; el pnts €1.50; lndtte; shop; snacks; bar; playgrnd; sand beach 500m; 95% statics; no dogs; phone; poss cr; quiet. "Sm pitches & narr camp rds poss diff lge o'fits; poss unkempt low ssn." € 15.20 2008*

CARBALLO *1A2* (10km N Coastal) *43.29305, -8.62239* **Camping As Nevedas, Ctra Carballo-Caión, Km.8.5, Noicela, 15100 Carballo (La Coruña) [tel/fax 981-73 95 52; info@asnevedas.com; www.asnevedas.com]** On AC552 fr La Coruña dir Carballo, turn R approx 3km bef Carballo sp Noicela 8km. Site on L in vill. Sm, hdg pitch, pt sl, pt shd; wc; chem disp (wc); serviced pitch; shwrs inc; el pnts (5A) €2.60; gas; lndtte; shop; tradsmn; rest; bar; BBQ; playgrnd; pool; sand beach 2km; golf 2km; 20% statics; dogs; bus fr ent; phone; poss cr; Eng spkn; adv bkg; quiet; red long stay; ccard acc; CCI. "Santiago de Compostela 45km; water amusement park 15km; friendly staff; facs slightly run-down low ssn; mkt Sun Carballo; excel." 1 Apr-29 Sep. € 17.94 2008*

CARCHUNA see Motril *2H4*

CARIDAD, LA (EL FRANCO) *1A3* (1km SE Coastal) *43.54795, -6.80701* **Camping Playa de Castelló, Ctra N634, Santander-La Coruña, Km 532, 33758 La Caridad (El Franca) (Asturias) [985-47 82 77; camping_castello@hotmail.com]** On N634/E70 Santander dir La Coruña, turn N at km 532. Site in 200m fr N634, sp fr each direction. Sm, mkd pitch, pt shd; wc; chem disp; baby facs; shwrs inc; el pnts (2-5A) €2; gas; lndtte; shop, tradsmn, bar high ssn only; shgl beach 800m; internet; some statics; dogs €1; bus 200m; Eng spkn; adv bkg; quiet; red long stay/CCI. "A green oasis with character; gd." Holy Week & 1 Jun-30 Sep. € 13.00 2006*

⊞ **CARLOTA, LA** *2G3* (1km NE Rural) *37.68285, -4.91980* **Camping Carlos III, Ctra de Madrid-Cádiz Km 430.5, 14100 La Carlota (Córdoba) [957-30 03 38; fax 957-30 06 97; camping@campingcarlosiii.com; www.campingcarlosiii.com]** Approx 25km SW of Córdoba on A4/E5, exit at km 432 turning L under autovia. Turn L at rndabt on main rd, site well sp on L in 800m. Lge, mkd pitch, hdstg, pt sl, pt shd; htd wc (some cont); chem disp; shwrs inc; el pnts (5-10A) €3.90; gas; lndtte; shop; rest; bar; BBQ; playgrnd; pool; horseriding; 30% statics; dogs; phone; Eng spkn; adv bkg; ccard acc; red long stay; CCI. "V efficient, well-run site; less cr than Córdoba municipal site; excel pool; gd, clean facs; if pitched under mulberry trees, poss staining fr berries; bus to Córdoba every 2 hrs."♦ € 20.30 2009*

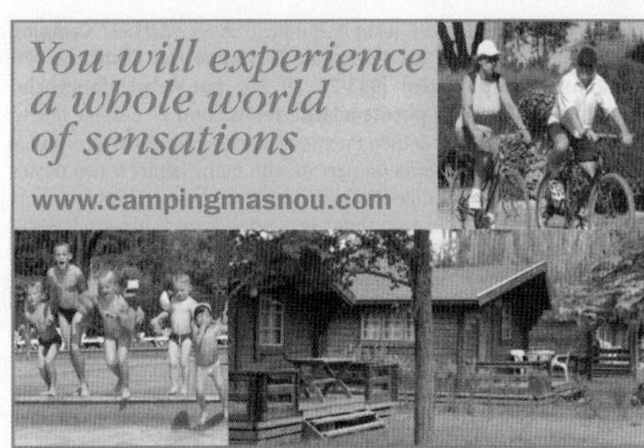

⊞ **CARRION DE LOS CONDES** *1B4* (W Rural) *42.33694, -4.60638* **Camping El Edén, Ctra Vigo-Logroño, Km 200, 34120 Carrión de los Condes (Palencia) [979-88 11 52]** Exit A231 to Carrión, turn L immed onto N120 sp Burgos & ent town fr NE. Site sp E & W ents to town off N120 adj Rv Carrión at El Plantio. App poorly sp down narr rds to rv. Suggest park nr Café España & check rte on foot. Med, mkd pitch, pt shd; wc; shwrs; mv service pnt; el pnts (5A) €3.50; gas; Indtte; rest; bar; playgrnd; dogs; bus 500m; ccard acc. "Pleasant walk to town; basic rvside site; recep in bar/rest; site open w/ends only low ssn; fair NH." ♦ € 14.90 2008*

⊞ **CARTAGENA** *4G1* (10km SW Coastal/Rural) *37.58611, -1.0675* **Camping Naturista El Portús (Naturist), 30393 Cartagena (Murcia) [968-55 30 52; fax 968-55 30 53; elportus@elportus.com; www.elportus.com]** Fr N332 Cartagena to Mazarrón rd take E20 to Canteras. In Canteras turn R onto E22 sp Isla Plana & in 500m turn L onto E21 sp Galifa/El Portús. In 2km at rndabt, site ent on L. Lge, mkd pitch; some hdstg, pt shd; wc; chem disp; mv service pnt; shwrs inc; el pnts (6A) inc; gas; Indtte (inc dryer); shop; rest; snacks; bar; playgrnd; htd, covrd pool & paddling pool; shgl beach adj; tennis; games area; gym; spa; golf 15km; internet; entmnt; 30% statics; dogs €4.80; phone; bus 1km; poss cr; Eng spkn; ccard acc; red low ssn/long stay; INF card req. "Restful low ssn; gd situation; many long-stay winter visitors; helpful staff; random pitching & poss untidy site; Cartagena interesting old town." ♦ € 40.80 2009*

CASPE *3C2* (12km NE Rural) *41.28883, 0.05733* **Lake Caspe Camping, Ctra N211, Km 286.7, 50700 Caspe (Zaragoza) [976-63 41 74 or 689-99 64 30 (mob); fax 976-63 41 87; lakecaspe@lakecaspe.com; www.lakecaspe.com]** Fr E leave AP2 or N11 at Fraga & foll N211 dir Caspe to site. Fr W take N232 fr Zaragoza then A1404 & A221 E thro Caspe to site in 16km on L at km 286.7, sp. Med, hdg/mkd pitch, hdstg, pt shd; wc; chem disp; baby facs; shwrs inc; el pnts (5-10A) €5.15; gas; Indtte; shop; rest; snacks; bar; playgrnd; pool high ssn; fishing; sailing; 10% statics; dogs €3.75; phone; poss cr; Eng spkn; adv bkg; quiet; CCI. "Gd, well-run, scenic site but isolated (come prepared); avoid on public hols; site rds gravelled but muddy after rain; sm pitches nr lake; gd watersports; mosquitoes." 15 Mar-9 Nov. € 20.05 2008*

CASTANARES DE LA RIOJA see Haro *1B4*

CASTELLBO see Seo de Urgel *3B3*

CASTELLO D'EMPURIES *3B3* (4km NE Rural) *42.26460, 3.10160* **Camping Mas Nou, Ctra Mas Nou 7, Km 38, 17486 Castelló d'Empúries (Gerona) [972-45 41 75; fax 972-45 43 58; info@campingmasnou.com; www.campingmasnou.com]** On m'way A7 exit 3 if coming fr France & exit 4 fr Barcelona dir Rosas (E) C260. Site on L at ent to Empuriabrava - use rndabt to turn. Lge, shd, mkd pitch; wc; chem disp; baby facs; shwrs inc; el pnts (10A) €4.60; Indtte; shops 200m; rest; snacks; bar; BBQ; playgrnd; pool; beach 2.5km; tennis; games area; wifi; entmnt; TV; car wash; 5% statics; dogs €2.30; phone; Eng spkn; red long stay/low ssn; ccard acc; CCI. "Aqua Park 4km, Dali Museum 10km; gd touring base; helpful staff; well-run site; excel, clean san facs; sports activities & children's club; gd cycling; excel." ♦ 27 Mar-26 Sep. € 38.30 (CChq acc) 2009*

See advertisement

CASTELLO D'EMPURIES *3B3* (4km SE Coastal) *42.20725, 3.10026* **Camping Nautic Almatá, Aiguamolls de l'Empordà, 17486 Castelló d'Empúries (Gerona) [972-45 44 77; fax 972-45 46 86; info@almata.com; www.almata.com]** Fr A7 m'way exit 3; foll sp to Rosas. After 12km turn S for Sant Pere Pescador & site on L in 5km. Site clearly sp on rd Castelló d'Empúries-Sant Pere Pescador. Lge, pt shd; wc; chem disp; shwrs inc; el pnts (10A) inc; rest; gas; shop; Indtte; playgrnd; pool; sand beach adj; sailing school; tennis; games area; horseriding; cycle hire; TV; disco bar on beach; entmnt; dogs €6.40; poss cr; adv bkg; quiet; red low ssn. "Excel, clean facs; ample pitches; sports facs inc in price; helpful staff; direct access to nature reserve; waterside pitches rec." ♦ 16 May-20 Sep. € 53.50 2009*

CASTELLO D'EMPURIES *3B3* (1km S Coastal) *42.25563, 3.13791* **Camping Castell Mar, Ctra Rosas-Figueres, Km 40.5, Playa de la Rubina, 17486 Castelló d'Empúries (Gerona) [972-45 08 22; fax 972-45 23 30; cmar@camping parks.com; www.campingparks.com or www.campeole. com]** Exit A7 at junc 3 sp Figueres; turn L onto C260 sp Rosas, after traff lts cont twd Rosas, turn R down side of rest La Llar for 1.5km, foll sp Playa de la Rubina. Lge, hdg/mkd pitch, pt shd; wc; chem disp; serviced pitches; baby facs; shwrs inc; el pnts (6A) inc; gas; Indtte; shop; tradsmn; rest; snacks; bar; BBQ; playgrnd; pool; sand beach 100m; games rm; entmnt; excursions; TV; 30% statics; dogs; phone; Eng spkn; adv bkg; quiet; red low ssn; CCI. "Sm pitches, poss unsuitable lge o'fits; excel for families." ♦ 22 May-19 Sep. € 42.00 2006*

CASTELLO D'EMPURIES *3B3* (5km S Coastal) *42.23735, 3.12121* **Camping-Caravaning Laguna, Platja Can Turias, 17486 Castelló d'Empúries (Gerona) [972-45 05 53; fax 972-45 07 99; info@campinglaguna.com; www.camping laguna.com]** Exit AP7 junc 4 dir Roses. After 12km at rndabt take 3rd exit, site sp. Site in 4km; rough app track. V lge, mkd pitch, pt shd; wc; chem disp; mv service pnt; some serviced pitches (inc gas); baby facs; shwrs inc; el pnts (5A) €4; gas; Indtte; supmkt; rest; snacks; bar; playgrnd; htd pool; sand beach; sailing; watersports; tennis; games area; multisports area; cycle hire; horseriding; entmnt; wifi; 4% statics; dogs free; Eng spkn; adv bkg; quiet; red snr citizens/long stay/low ssn; ccard acc; CCI. "Clean, modern san facs; gd birdwatching; excel." ♦ 23 Mar-18 Oct. € 35.80 2009*

CASTRO URDIALES *1A4* (1km N Coastal) *43.39000, -3.24194* **Camping de Castro, Barrio Campijo, 39700 Castro Urdiales (Cantabria) [942-86 74 23; fax 942-63 07 25; info@camping.castro.com]** Fr Bilbao turn off A8 at 2nd Castro Urdiales sp, km 151. Camp sp on R by bullring. V narr, steep lanes to site - no passing places, great care req. Lge, pt sl, pt terr, unshd; wc; shwrs inc; el pnts (6A) €3; Indtte; shop; rest; bar; playgrnd; pool; sand beach 1km; 90% statics; dogs; phone; bus; poss cr; Eng spkn; adv bkg; quiet; CCI. "Gd, clean facs; conv NH for ferries; ltd touring pitches." ♦ Easter & 1 Jun-30 Sep. € 19.50 2008*

CASTROJERIZ *1B4* (1km NE Rural) *42.29194, -4.13361* **Camping Camino de Santiago, Calle Virgen del Manzano s/n, 09110 Castrojeriz (Burgos) [947-37 72 55 or 658-96 67 43 (mob); fax 947-37 72 56; info@camping camino.com; www.campingcamino.com]** Exit A62/E80 junc 40 dir Los Balbases, Vallunquera & Castrojeriz - narr, uneven rd. In 16 km ent Castrojeriz, site well sp off BU404 under ruined castle. Med, hdg/mkd pitch, pt sl, shd; wc (some cont); chem disp (wc); shwrs inc; el pnts (5-10A) €3.50 (poss no earth); Indtte (inc dryer); shop 1km; rest; snacks; bar; games area; games rm; internet; TV rm; dogs €2; bus 200m; some Eng spkn; quiet; CCI. "Lovely site; helpful owner; pilgrims' refuge on site (40 beds); vg." ♦ 1 Mar-30 Nov. € 18.00 2009*

CASTROPOL see Ribadeo *1A2*

CAZORLA *2F4* (6km E Rural) *37.9059, -2.93597* **Camping Puente de las Herrerías, El Vadillo del Castril, 23470 Cazorla (Jaén) [953-72 70 90; puenteh@infonegocio. com; www.puentedelasherrerias.com]** Fr Cazorla foll sp for Parador & then Puente de la Herrerías. Driving distance 25km fr Cazorla on narr rd with many bends & two passes - not rec trailer c'vans. Lge, pt shd; wc; shwrs; el pnts (16A) €3.10; gas; shop; rest; snacks; bar; playgrnd; pool; horseriding; cycle hire; phone; quiet. "Stunning scenery in National Park." Easter-15 Oct. € 20.64 2008*

CAZORLA *2F4* (2km SW Rural) *37.90444, -3.01416* **Camping San Isicio, Camino de San Isicio s/n, 23470 Cazorla (Jaén) [tel/fax 953-72 12 80; campingcortijo@hotmail. com]** Fr W on A319, turn R bef Cazorla, foll sp. Sm, pt shd; wc; shwrs; el pnts €2.50; playgrnd; pool; dogs free; quiet. "Perched on steep hill; towing service for c'vans but really only suitable sm m'vans; ltd facs but a gem of a site." 1 Mar-1 Nov. € 16.60 2008*

CEE *1A1* (6km NW Coastal) *42.94555, -9.21861* **Camping Ruta Finisterre, Ctra La Coruña-Finisterre, Km 6, Playa de Estorde, 15270 Cée (La Coruña) [tel/fax 981-74 63 02; www.rutafinisterre.com]** Foll sp thro Cée & Corcubión on rd AC445 twd Finisterre; site easily seen on R of rd (no thro rd). Lge, mkd pitch, terr, shd; wc; chem disp; shwrs inc; el pnts (10A) €3.50; gas; Indtte; shop & 1km; rest; snacks; bar; playgrnd; sand beach 100m; dogs €3.70; phone; bus adj; poss cr; Eng spkn; adv bkg; some rd noise; ccard acc; CCI. "Family-run site in pine trees - check access to pitch & el pnts bef positioning; gd, clean facs; 5km to Finisterre; clean beach adj; peaceful." ♦ Holy Week & 15 Jun-15 Sep. € 21.50 2008*

CERVERA DE PISUERGA *1B4* (500m W Rural) *42.87135, -4.50332* **Camping Fuentes Carrionas, La Bárcena s/n, 34840 Cervera de Pisuerga (Palencia) [979-87 04 24; fax 979-12 30 76]** Fr Aguilar de Campóo on CL626 pass thro Cervera foll sp CL627 Potes. Site sp on L bef rv bdge. Med, mkd pitch, pt shd; wc; chem disp; shwrs inc; el pnts €2.73; Indtte; shop 500m; rest 500m; bar; games area; 80% statics; bus 100m; quiet; CCI. "Gd walking in nature reserve; conv Casa del Osos bear info cent." ♦ 13 Apr-30 Sep. € 23.11 2006*

⊞ **CHILCHES** *4E2* (1km S Coastal) *39.75722, -0.16333* **Camping Mediterráneo, Avda Mare Nostrum s/n, 12592 Chilches (Castellón) [tel/fax 964-58 32 18; informacion@ mediterraneocamping.com]** Exit AP7 junc 49 onto N340 S, exit junc 947-948 twds Chilches. Fr Chilches take CV2280 to coast & turn S, site sp. Lge, mkd pitch, hdstg, shd; wc; chem disp; shwrs inc; el pnts inc; gas; Indtte; shop; tradsmn; rest; snacks; bar; playgrnd; pool; sand beach 500m; solarium; TV rm; some statics; dogs; phone; bus 1km; poss cr; adv bkg; ccard acc; red long stay/CCI. ♦ € 32.10 2008*

⊞ **CIUDAD RODRIGO** *1D3* (1km SW Rural) *40.59206, -6.53445* **Camping La Pesquera, Ctra Cáceres-Arrabal, Km 424, 37500 Ciudad Rodrigo (Salamanca) [923-48 13 48; campinglapesquera@hotmail.com; www.campingla pesquera.com]** Fr Salamanca on A62/E80 exit junc 332. Look for tent sp on R & turn R, then 1st L & foll round until site on rvside. Med, mkd pitch, pt shd; wc; shwrs inc; el pnts (6A) €3; lndtte; shop; snacks; rv sw, fishing adj; wifi; TV; dogs free; phone; poss cr; no adv bkg; noisy; ccard acc; CCI. "Medieval walled city worth visit - easy walk over Roman bdge; gd, modern san facs; gd, improved site." ♦ € 12.80 2009*

⊞ **CLARIANA** *3B3* (4km NE Rural) *41.95878, 1.60361* **Camping La Ribera, Pantà de Sant Ponç, 25290 Clariana de Cardener (Lleida) [tel/fax 973-48 25 52; info@ campinglaribera.com; www.campinglaribera.com]** Fr Solsona S on C55, turn L onto C26 at km 71. Go 2.7km, site sp immed bef Sant Ponç Dam. Lge, mkd pitch, hdstg, pt shd; wc; chem disp; baby facs; shwrs; el pnts (4-10A) €3.30-6.60; lndtte; shop; snacks; bar; playgrnd; pool; paddling pool; lake sw & beach 500m; tennis; games area; TV; 95% statics; dogs; bus 2.5km; phone; quiet. "Excel facs; gd site; narr pitches." ♦ € 26.60 2008*

COLERA see Llançà *3B3*

COLOMBRES see Unquera *1A4*

COLUNGA *1A3* (1km N Coastal) *43.49972, -5.26527* **Camping Costa Verde, Playa La Griega de Colunga, 33320 Colunga (Asturias) [tel/fax 985-85 63 73]** N632 coast rd, fr E turn R twd Lastres in cent of Colunga; site 1km on R. Med, mkd pitch, unshd; wc; chem disp; mv service pnt; baby facs; shwrs; el pnts (5A) €3.50 (poss rev pol); gas; lndtte; shop; rest; bar; BBQ; playgrnd; sand beach 500m; games area; cycle hire; 50% statics; dogs €3; bus 500m; adv bkg; quiet but some rd noise; ccard acc; CCI. "Beautiful sandy beach; lovely views to mountains & sea; some site access rds used for winter storage; gd, plentiful facs; ltd hot water low ssn; friendly, welcoming staff; pleasant town." Easter & 1 Jun-30 Sep. € 19.25 2009*

COLUNGA *1A3* (8km E Coastal) *43.47160, -5.18434* **Camping Arenal de Moris, Ctra de la Playa s/n, 33344 Caravia Alta (Asturias) [985-85 30 97; fax 985-85 31 37; camoris@desdeasturias.com; www.arenaldemoris.com]** Fr E70/A8 exit junc 337 onto N632 to Caravia Alta, site clearly sp. Lge, mkd pitch, terr, pt shd; wc; chem disp; shwrs inc; el pnts (5A) €4.50; lndtte; shop; rest; snacks; bar; playgrnd; pool; sand beach 500m; tennis; 10% statics; bus 1.5km; adv bkg; quiet but rd noise; ccard acc; CCI. "Lovely views to mountains & sea; well-kept, well-run site; excel, clean san facs." Easter-20 Sep. € 24.00 2009*

COMA RUGA see Vendrell, El *3C3*

COMILLAS *1A4* (1km E Coastal) *43.38583, -4.28444* **Camping de Comillas, 39520 Comillas (Cantabria) [942-72 00 74; fax 942-21 52 06; info@campingcomillas.com; www. campingcomillas.com]** Site on coast rd CA131 at E end of Comillas by-pass. App fr Santillana or San Vicente avoids town cent & narr streets. Lge, hdg/mkd pitch, pt sl, pt shd; wc; chem disp; shwrs inc; el pnts (5A) €3.85; lndtte (inc dryer); shop; rest 1km; snacks; bar; playgrnd; sand beach 800m; TV; dogs; phone; poss cr; adv bkg; quiet; CCI. "Clean, ltd facs low ssn (hot water to shwrs only); vg site in gd position with views; easy walk to interesting town; gd beach across rd; helpful owner." 1 Jun-30 Sep. € 25.20 2009*

COMILLAS *1A4* (3km E Rural) *43.38328, -4.24689* **Camping El Helguero, 39527 Ruiloba (Cantabria) [942-72 21 24; fax 942-72 10 20; reservas@ampingelhelguero.com; www.campingelhelguero.com]** Exit A8 junc 249 dir Comillas onto CA135 to km 7. Turn dir Ruiloba onto CA359 & thro Ruiloba & La Iglesia, fork R uphill. Site sp. Lge, mkd pitch, pt sl, pt shd; htd wc; chem disp; mv service pnt; shwrs inc; el pnts (6A) €3.80; lndtte; shop, rest, snacks, bar in ssn; playgrnd; pool; paddling pool; sand beach 3km; tennis 300m; cycle hire; many statics; dogs; night security; poss v cr high ssn; Eng spkn; poss noisy high ssn; ccard acc; CCI. "Attractive site, gd touring cent; v clean facs; helpful staff; sm pitches poss muddy in wet." ♦ 1 Apr-30 Sep. € 21.00 (CChq acc) 2009*

⊞ **COMILLAS** *1A4* (3km W Rural/Coastal) *43.3858, -4.3361* **Camping Rodero, Ctra Comillas-St Vicente, Km 5, 39528 Oyambre (Cantabria) [942-72 20 40; fax 942-72 26 29; info@campingrodero.es; www.campingrodero.es]** Exit A8 dir San Vicente de la Barquera, cross bdge over estuary & take R fork nr km27.5. Site just off C131 bet San Vicente & Comillas, sp. Lge, mkd pitch, pt sl, terr, pt shd; wc; chem disp; mv service pnt; shwrs inc; el pnts (6A) €3; gas; lndtte; shop; tradsmn; rest; snacks; bar; playgrnd; pool; sand beach 200m; games area; wifi; 10% statics; no dogs; phone; bus 200m; poss v cr; adv bkg; ccard acc; CCI. "Lovely views; friendly owners; site noisy but happy - owner puts Dutch/ British in quieter part; sm pitches; poss run down low ssn & prob clsd in winter - phone ahead to check." ♦ € 29.00 2009*

CONIL DE LA FRONTERA *2H3* (3km N Coastal) *36.30206, -6.13082* **Camping Cala del Aceite (Naturist), Ctra del Puerto Pesquero, Km 4, 11140 Conil de la Frontera (Cádiz) [956-44 29 50; fax 956-44 09 72; info@caladel aceite.com; www.caladelaceite.com]** Exit A48 junc 26 dir Conil. In 2km at rndabt foll sp Puerto Pesquero along CA3208 & CA4202. Site sp. V lge, mkd pitch, pt shd; wc; chem disp; fam bthrm; sauna; shwrs inc; el pnts (10A) €5.50; gas; lndtte; supmkt; rest; snacks; bar; playgrnd; pool; sand beach 200m; 20% statics; dogs €3; phone; poss cr; Eng spkn; adv bkg; quiet; red long stay; CCI. "Friendly, helpful staff; interesting region; gd cliff-top walking; lge pitches; gd, modern san facs." ♦ Holy Week-31 Oct. € 36.10 2009*

Spain

⊞ **CONIL DE LA FRONTERA** *2H3* (3km NE Rural) *36.31061, -6.11276* **Camping Roche, Carril de Pilahito s/n, N340km 19.2, 11149 Conil de la Frontera (Cádiz) [956-44 22 16; fax 956-44 30 02; info@campingroche.com; www.campingroche.com]** Exit A48 junc 15 Conil Norte. Site sp on N340 dir Algeciras. Lge, mkd pitch, hdstg, pt shd; wc; chem disp; mv service pnt; el pnts (5A) €5; Indtte; shop; rest; snacks; bar; BBQ low ssn; playgrnd; pool; paddling pool; sand beach 2.5km; tennis; games area; games rm; TV; 20% statics; dogs €3.75; Eng spkn; adv bkg; quiet; ccard acc; red low ssn/long stay; special monthly rates. "V pleasant, peaceful site in pine woods; friendly, helpful staff; spotless san facs; superb beaches nr." ♦ € 27.50 2009*

See advertisement

⊞ **CONIL DE LA FRONTERA** *2H3* (1.3km NW Rural/ Coastal) *36.29340, -6.09626* **Camping La Rosaleda, Ctra del Pradillo, Km 1.3, 11140 Conil de la Frontera (Cádiz) [956-44 33 27; fax 956-44 33 85; info@campinglarosaleda.com; www.campinglarosaleda.com]** Exit A48 junc 26 dir Conil. In 2km at rndabt foll sp Puerto Pesquero along CA3208. Site sp on R. Lge, mkd pitch, some hdstg, pt sl, terr, pt shd; wc; chem disp; mv service pnt; shwrs inc; el pnts (5-10A) inc; gas; Indtte; shop & 1.3km; tradsmn; rest; snacks; bar; playgrnd; pool; sand beach 1.3km; entmnt; internet; 10% statics; no dogs 15 Jun-15 Sep, otherwise in sep area €5; phone; car wash; Eng spkn; adv bkg; quiet; red low ssn/long stay; CCI. "Well-run site; friendly, helpful staff; gd social atmosphere; poss noisy w/end; sm pitches not suitable lge o'fits but double-length pitches avail; poss itinerants; pitches soft/muddy when wet; poss cold & windy in winter; lge rally on site in winter; gd walking & cycling; sea views; historical, interesting area; conv Seville, Cádiz, Jerez, day trips Morocco." ♦ € 37.00 2009*

⊞ **CORDOBA** *2F3* (8km N Rural) *37.96138, -4.81361* **Camping Los Villares, Ctra Los Villares, Km 7.5, 14071 Córdoba (Córdoba) [957-33 01 45; fax 957-33 14 55; campingvillares@latinmail.com]** Best app fr N on N432: turn W onto CP45 1km N of Cerro Muriano at km 254. Site on R after approx 7km shortly after golf club. Last 5-6km of app rd v narr & steep, but well-engineered. Badly sp, easy to miss. Or fr city cent foll sp for Parador until past municipal site on R. Shortly after, turn L onto CP45 & foll sp Parque Forestal Los Villares, then as above. Sm, hdstg, sl, shd; wc; chem disp; shwrs inc; el pnts (15A) €4.30 (poss rev pol); gas; lndry rm; shop; rest & bar (high ssn); some statics; no dogs; bus 1km; quiet; red long stay; CCI. "In nature reserve; peaceful; cooler than Córdoba city with beautiful walks, views & wildlife; sm, close pitches; basic facs (v ltd & poss unclean low ssn); mainly sl site in trees; strictly run; take care electrics; poss no drinking water/hot water." ♦ € 17.70 2009*

⊞ **CORDOBA** *2F3* (1km NW Urban) *37.90063, -4.7875* **Camp Municipal El Brillante, Avda del Brillante 50, 14012 Córdoba [957-40 38 36; fax 957-28 21 65; elbrillante@campings.net; www.campingelbrillante.com]** Fr N1V take Badejoz turning N432. Take rd Córdoba N & foll sp to Parador. Turn R into Paseo del Brilliante which leads into Avda del Brilliante; white grilleblock wall surrounds site. Alt, foll sp for 'Macdonalds Brilliante.' Site on R 400m beyond Macdonalds on main rd going uphill away fr town cent. Site poorly sp. Med, hdg/mkd pitch, hdstg, pt shd; wc; chem disp; mv service pnt; serviced pitches; shwrs inc; el pnts (6-10A) €5 (poss no earth); gas; Indtte (inc dryer); shop; tradsmn; hypmkt nrby; rest, snacks high ssn; bar; playgrnd; pool adj in ssn; dogs free; phone; bus adj; poss cr; Eng spkn; no adv bkg; quiet but traff noise & barking dogs off site; ccard not acc; CCI. "Well-run, busy, clean site; rec arr bef 1500; friendly staff; sun shades over pitches; easy walk/gd bus to town; poss cramped pitches - diff lge o'fits; poss itinerants low ssn (noisy); gd for wheelchair users; highly rec." ♦ € 31.90 2009*

CORUNA, A see Coruña, La *1A2*

⊞ **CORUNA, LA** *1A2* (5km E Coastal) *43.34305, -8.35722* **Camping Bastiagueiro, Playa Bastiagueiro, 15110 Oleiros (La Coruña) [981-61 48 78; fax 981-26 60 08]** Exit La Coruña by NVI twd Betanzos. After bdge, take AC173 sp Santa Cruz. At 3rd rndabt, take 3rd exit sp Camping. In 100m, turn R up narr rd. Site on R in 150m. Sm, pt shd; wc (some cont); chem disp; shwrs inc; el pnts (6A) €3.18; gas; Indtte; shop; snacks; bar; playgrnd; sand beach 500m; dogs; phone; bus 300m; poss cr; adv bkg; quiet; CCI. "Friendly owners; lovely views of beach; care req going thro narr ent gate; poss feral cats on site & facs poss unclean in winter." € 19.00 2007*

CORUNA, LA *1A2* (9km E Rural) *43.34806, -8.33592* **Camping Los Manzanos, Olieros, 15179 Santa Cruz (La Coruña) [981-61 48 25; info@camping-losmanzanos.com; www.camping-losmanzanos.com]** App La Coruña fr E on NVI, bef bdge take AC173 sp Santa Cruz. Turn R at 2nd traff lts in Santa Cruz cent (by petrol stn), foll sp, site on L. Fr AP9/E1 exit junc 3, turn R onto NVI dir Lugo. Take L fork dir Santa Cruz/La Coruña, then foll sp Meiras. Site sp. Lge, pt shd; wc; chem disp; shwrs; el pnts (6A) €4.50; gas; Indtte (inc dryer); shop; rest; snacks; bar; playgrnd; pool; TV; 10% statics; dogs free; phone; adv bkg (day bef arr only); ccard acc; CCI. "Lovely site; steep slope into site; helpful owners; hilly 1km walk to Santa Cruz for bus to La Coruña or park at Torre de Hércules (lighthouse) & take tram; conv for Santiago de Compostela; excel." Easter-30 Sep. € 24.90 2009*

⊞ **COTORIOS** *4F1* (500m Rural) *38.04807, -2.85128* **Camping Chopera, Cazorla-Cotoríos, Km 21, Santiago Pontones, 23478 Cotoríos (Jaén) [tel/fax 953-71 30 05]** Fr Jaén-Albacete rd N322 turn onto A1305, nr Villanueva del Arzobispo, sp El Tranco. In 26km at app to El Tranco lake (sh distance after exit fr tunnel), turn R & cross over embankment. Cotoríos at km 52-53, approx 25km on shore of lake & Río Guadalquivir. Warning, if towing c'van, do not app via Cazorla as rds are tortuous. Only app & return fr Villanueva as rd well surfaced, but still some steep sections. Med, shd; wc; shwrs; el pnts (16A) €3; Indtte; gas; shop; snacks; bar; playgrnd; rv adj; dogs; phone; car wash; ccard acc; red low ssn. "In cent of beautiful National Park; lots of wildlife." ♦ € 15.55 2008*

⊞ **COTORIOS** *4F1* (2km E Rural) *38.05255, -2.83996* **Camping Llanos de Arance, Ctra Sierra de Cazorla/Beas de Segura, Km 22, 23478 Cotoríos (Jaén) [953-71 31 39; fax 953-71 30 36; arancell@inicia.es; www.llanosdearance.com]** Fr Jaén-Albecete rd N322 turn E onto A1305 N of Villanueva del Arzobispo sp El Tranco. In 26km to El Tranco lake, turn R & cross over embankment. Cotoríos at km stone 53, approx 25km on shore of lake & Río Guadalaquivir. App fr Cazorla or Beas definitely not rec if towing. Lge, shd; wc; shwrs; el pnts (5A) €3.21; gas; shops 1.5km; rest; snacks; bar; BBQ; playgrnd; pool; 2% statics; no dogs; phone; poss cr; quiet; ccard acc; red low ssn; CCI. "Lovely site; excel walks & bird life, boar & wild life in Cazorla National Park." € 17.75 2008*

⊞ **COVARRUBIAS** *1B4* (500m E Rural) *42.05944, -3.51527* **Camping Covarrubias, Ctra Hortigüela, 09346 Covarrubias (Burgos) [947-40 64 17; fax 983-29 58 41; proatur@proatur.com; www.proatur.com]** Take N1/E5 or N234 S fr Burgos, turn onto BU905 after approx 35km. Site sp on BU905. Med, mkd pitch, pt sl, pt shd; wc; shwrs; el pnts (12A) €3.42; gas; Indtte; shop 500m; rest; bar; playgrnd; pool & paddling pool; 50% statics; phone; poss cr; ccard acc. "Ltd facs low ssn; pitches poss muddy after rain; charming vill; poss vultures!" € 19.35 2008*

CREIXELL *3C3* (Coastal) *41.16338, 1.45878* **Camping La Plana, Ctra N340, Km 1182, 43839 Creixell (Tarragona) [977-80 03 04; fax 977-66 36 63]** Site sp at Creixell off N340. Med, hdstg, shd; wc; chem disp; shwrs inc; el pnts inc; gas; Indtte; shop; rest; snacks; bar; sand beach adj; poss cr; Eng spkn; adv bkg; some rlwy noise. "Vg, v clean site; v helpful & pleasant owners." 1 May-30 Sep. € 21.00 2007*

CREIXELL *3C3* (Coastal) *41.16390, 1.44682* **Camping La Sirena Dorada, Ctra N340, Km 1181, 43839 Creixell (Tarragona) [977-80 13 03; fax 977-80 12 15; info@sirenadorada.com; www.sirenadorada.com]** Fr N exit AP7 at junc 31, foll N340 sp Tarragona, site 200m past Roman arch on L. Fr S exit junc 32 onto N340 to Creixall. Lge, pt shd; wc; shwrs inc; mv service pnt; el pnts (5A) €5.40; gas; Indtte; shop; rest; bar; playgrnd; pool; waterslide; sand beach 200m; games area; wifi; entmnt; 15% statics; poss cr; adv bkg; quiet; CCI. "Unreliable opening dates - low ssn phone to check open." ♦ 1 Mar-1 Nov. € 32.50 2008*

CREIXELL *3C3* (1km S Coastal) *41.15714, 1.44137* **Camping Gavina Platja, Ctra N340, Km 1181, Platja Creixell, 43839 Creixell de Mar (Tarragona) [977-80 15 03; fax 977-80 05 27; info@gavina.net; www.gavina.net]** Exit AP7 junc 31 (Coma-Ruga) onto N340 dir Tarragona. At km 1181 turn R twd Playa de Creixel via undergnd passage. Site 1km S of Creixell, adj beach - foll sp Creixell Platja. Lge, mkd pitch, pt shd; wc; chem disp; baby facs; fam bthrm; shwrs inc; el pnts (6A) €3.80; gas; Indtte; shop; rest; snacks; bar; playgrnd; sand beach adj; watersports; tennis; entmnt; wifi; car wash; 20% statics; dogs; poss cr; adv bkg rec Jul/Aug; some train noise; ccard acc; red long stay; CCI. "Rest o'looks beach; Port Aventura 20km." ♦ 30 Mar-31 Oct. € 28.30 (CChq acc) 2007*

CREVILLENT see Elche *4F2*

Spain

⊞ **CUBILLAS DE SANTA MARTA** *1C4* (4km S Rural) *41.80511, -4.58776* **Camping Cubillas, Ctra N620, Km 102, 47290 Cubillas de Santa Marta (Valladolid) [983-58 50 02; fax 983-58 50 16; info@campingcubillas.com; www.campingcubillas.com]** A62 Valladolid-Palencia, turn W at km 102. Site on L. Lge, some hdg/mkd pitch, pt sl, unshd; wc; chem disp; mv service pnt; shwrs inc; el pnts (2-5A) €3.85; gas; Indtte; sm shop; tradsmn; rest; snacks & bar in ssn; BBQ; playgrnd; pool; entmnt; 50% statics; dogs €1.80; phone; site clsd 10 Dec-10 Jan; Eng spkn; ccard acc; red long stay/low ssn; CCI. "Ltd space for tourers; conv visit Palencia & Valladolid; rd, rlwy & disco noise at w/end until v late; v ltd facs low ssn; NH only." ♦ € 23.30 2009*

CUDILLERO *1A3* (2.5km SE Rural) *43.55416, -6.12944* **Camping Cudillero, Ctra Playa de Aguilar, Aronces, 33150 El Pito (Asturias) [tel/fax 985-59 06 63; info@campingcudillero.com; www.campingcudillero.com]** Exit N632 (E70) sp El Pito. Turn L at rndabt sp Cudillero & in 300m at end of wall turn R at site sp, cont for 1km, site on L. Do not app thro Cudillero; streets v narr & steep; much traffic. Med, hdg/mkd pitch, pt shd; wc; chem disp; baby facs; shwrs inc; el pnts (3-5A) €3.75; gas; Indtte; shop; snacks high ssn; bar; playgrnd; htd pool; sand beach 1.2km; games area; entmnt high ssn; internet; TV; no statics; dogs €2.15; phone; bus 1km; adv bkg; quiet; CCI. "Well-maintained & well laid-out site; sm pitches; gd san facs; steep walk to beach & vill." ♦ Holy Week & 1 May-15 Sep. € 22.50 2009*

CUDILLERO *1A3* (2km S Rural) *43.55555, -6.13777* **Camping L'Amuravela, El Pito, 33150 Cudillero (Asturias) [tel/fax 985-59 09 95; camping@lamuravela.com; www.lamuravela.com]** Exit N632 (E70) sp El Pito. Turn L at rndabt sp Cudillero & in approx 1km turn R at site sp. Do not app thro Cudillero; streets v narr & steep; much traffic. Med, mkd pitch, pt sl, unshd; wc; chem disp; mv service pnt; shwrs inc; el pnts €3; gas; shop; snacks; bar; pool; paddling pool; sand beach 2km; 50% statics (sep area); dogs €1; poss cr; ccard acc high ssn. "Hillside walks into Cudillero, attractive fishing vill with gd fish rests; gd clean facs; red facs low ssn." 1 Mar-30 Nov. € 20.10 2007*

CUENCA *3D1* (8km N Rural) *40.12694, -2.14194* **Camping Cuenca, Ctra Cuenca-Tragacete, Km 7, 16147 Cuenca [tel/fax 969-23 16 56; info@campingcuenca.com; www.campingcuenca.com]** Fr Madrid take N400/A40 dir Cuenca & exit sp 'Ciudad Encantada' & Valdecabras on CM2105. In 7km rd splits, take CM2105 to site in 1km on L. Lge, pt sl, pt terr, pt shd; wc; chem disp; mv service pnt; shwrs inc; el pnts (6-10A) €4; gas; Indtte; shop; snacks; bar; playgrnd; pool high ssn; jacuzzi; tennis; games area; 15% statics; dogs €1.07; phone; poss cr esp Easter w/end; Eng spkn; adv bkg; quiet; CCI. "Pleasant, well-kept, green site; gd touring cent; friendly, helpful staff; excel san facs but ltd low ssn; interesting rock formations at Ciudad Encantada." ♦ 19 Mar-11 Oct. € 20.80 2009*

CUEVAS DEL ALMANZORA see Garrucha *4G1*

CULLERA see Sueca *4E2*

DEBA *3A1* (6km E Coastal) *43.29436, -2.32853* **Camping Itxaspe, N634, Km 38, 20829 Itziar (Guipúzkoa) [tel/fax 943-19 93 77; itxaspe@campingitxaspe.com; www.campingitxaspe.com]** Exit A8 junc 13 dir Deba; at main rd turn L up hill, in 400m at x-rds turn L, site in 2km - narr, winding rd. NB Do not go into Itziar vill. Sm, mkd pitch, pt sl, pt shd; wc; chem disp; baby facs; shwrs; el pnts (5A) €3.15; gas; shop; rest, bar adj; BBQ; playgrnd; pool; solarium; shgl beach 4km; wifi; some statics; bus 2km; adv bkg; quiet; red low ssn; CCI. "Excel site; helpful owner; w/ends busy; sea views." ♦ 1 Apr-30 Sep. € 20.00 2009*

DEBA *3A1* (5km W Coastal) *43.30577, -2.37789* **Camping Aitzeta, Ctra Deba-Guernica, Km. 3.5, C6212, 20930 Mutriku (Guipúzkoa) [943-60 33 56; fax 943-60 31 06; www.campingseuskadi.com/aitzeta]** On N634 San Sebastián-Bilbao rd thro Deba & on o'skts turn R over rv sp Mutriku. Site on L after 3km on narr & winding rd up short steep climb. Med, mkd pitch, terr, pt shd; wc; chem disp (wc); shwrs inc; el pnts (4A) €3; gas; Indry rm; sm shop; rest 300m; snacks; bar; playgrnd; sand beach 1km; dogs; bus 500m; phone; quiet; CCI. "Easy reach of Bilbao ferry; gd views; gd, well-run, clean site; not suitable lge o'fits; ltd pitches for tourers; helpful staff." ♦ 1 May-30 Sep. € 21.00 2009*

⊞ **DEBA** *3A1* (7km W Rural) *43.31340, -2.39459* **Camping Santa Elena, Ctra Deba-Gernika, Km 5, 20830 Mutriku (Guipúzkoa) [tel/fax 943-60 39 82; www.campingseuskadi.com/santaelena]** On N634 San Sebastián-Bilbao rd, thro Deba on o'skts turn R over rv bdge, thro Mutriku & at end of town slowly under narr bdge, 30m after turn R sp Galdonamendi, 2km up hill. Med, sl, terr, shd; wc; shwrs; el pnts €3.50; Indtte; shop; rest; playgrnd; sand beach 4km; 80% statics; phone; poss cr w/end; adv bkg; quiet. "Blocks ess for levelling; gd views; sm pitches & narr site rds." € 21.50 2008*

DELTEBRE *3D2* (8km E Coastal) *40.72041, 0.84849* **Camping L'Aube, Afores s/n, 43580 Deltebre (Tarragona) [977-26 70 66; fax 977-26 75 05; campinglaube@hotmail.com; www.campinglaube.com]** Exit AP7 junc 40 or 41 onto N340 dir Deltebre. Fr Deltebre foll T340 sp Riumar for 8km. At info kiosk branch R, site sp 1km on R. Lge, mkd pitch, hdstg, pt shd; wc; chem disp; mv service pnt; shwrs inc; el pnts (3-10A) €2.80-5; Indtte; shop; rest; bar; snacks; pool; playgrnd; phone; sand beach adj; 40% statics; poss cr low ssn; red long stay; CCI. "At edge of Ebro Delta National Park; excel birdwatching; ltd facs in winter." ♦ 1 Mar-31 Oct. € 16.00 2008*

DELTEBRE *3D2* (10km SE Coastal) *40.65681, 0.77971* **Camping Eucaliptus, Playa Eucaliptus s/n, 43870 Amposta (Tarragona) [tel/fax 977-47 90 46; eucaliptus@campingeucaliptus.com; www.campingeucaliptus.com]** Exit AP7/E15 at junc 41. Foll sp to Amposta but do not go into town. Take sp for Els Muntells on TV3405 then Eucaliptus beach. Site on R 100m fr beach. Lge, mkd pitch, pt shd; wc; chem disp; shwrs; el pnts (5A) €4.30; gas; Indtte; shops; rest; snacks; bar; BBQ area; playgrnd; pool; paddling pool; sand beach adj; fishing; watersports; cycling; entmnt; 40% statics; dogs €2.40; poss cr; adv bkg; noisy w/end & high ssn; red long stay; CCI. "Vg, well-run, peaceful site; gd facs; gd bar/rest; excel birdwatching; poss mosquito prob." ♦ Holy Week-27 Sep. € 24.10 2009*

DENIA *4E2* (2km SE Coastal) *38.83203, 0.13895* **Camping Tolosa, Camí d´Urios 32, Les Rotes, 03700 Dénia (Alicante) [965-78 72 94; info@campingtolosa.com; www.campingtolosa.com]** Fr E end of Dénia Harbour take Jávea/Les Rotes rd. In approx 2km keep L at fork exit Jávea rd on R. In approx 1km site app clearly sp on L; site 300m twd sea. Med, mkd pitch, hdstg, pt shd; wc; chem disp; shwrs inc; el pnts (6A) €3; gas; shop; supmkt adj; bar; BBQ; shgl beach adj; 40% statics; dogs; phone; bus 300m; poss cr; quiet; red long stay. "Well-managed site; pleasant staff; sm pitches." Holy Week & 1 Apr-30 Sep. € 26.00 2008*

⊞ **DENIA** *4E2* (3.5km SE Coastal) *38.82968, 0.14767* **Camping Los Pinos, Ctra Dénia-Les Rotes, Km 3, Les Rotes, 03700 Dénia (Alicante) [tel/fax 965-78 26 98; lospinosdenia@gmail.com]** Fr N332 foll sp to Dénia then dir Les Rotes/Jávea, site sp. Narr access rd poss diff lge o'fits. Med, mkd pitch, pt shd; wc; chem disp; shwrs inc; el pnts (6-10A) €3.20; gas; Indtte; shop adj; tradsmn; BBQ; cooking facs; playgrnd; shgl beach adj; internet; TV rm; 25% statics; dogs €3; phone; bus 100m; poss cr; Eng spkn; adv bkg; quiet; red long stays/low ssn; ccard acc; CCI. "Friendly, well-run, clean, tidy site but san facs a little 'tired' (Mar 09); excel value; access some pitches poss diff due trees - not suitable lge o'fits or m'vans; many long-stay winter residents; cycle path into Dénia; social rm with log fire; naturist beach 1km, private but rocky shore." ♦ € 25.40 2009*

⊞ **DENIA** *4E2* (9km W Rural/Coastal) *38.86750, -0.01615* **Camping Los Llanos, Cami de les Deveses, 03700 Dénia (Alicante) [965-75 51 88 or 649-45 51 58; fax 965-75 54 25; losllanos@losllanos.net; www.losllanos.net]** Exit AP7 junc 62 dir Dénia onto CV725. At lge rndabt turn L & foll sp to site along N332a. Med, pt shd; wc; chem disp; mv service pnt; shwrs inc; el pnts (10A) €3.50; Indtte; shop & 2km; rest 500m; snacks; bar; playgrnd; pool; paddling pool; sand beach 150m; wifi; 30% statics; dogs €2; phone; bus 100m; poss cr; adv bkg; quiet; ccard acc; red long stay. "Pleasant site; gd, modern san facs; gd touring base; friendly, helpful staff; vg." € 25.00 2009*

See advertisement

⊞ **DOS HERMANAS** *2G3* (1km W Urban) *37.27756, -5.93642* **Camping Villsom, Ctra Sevilla/Cádiz A4, Km 554.8, 41700 Dos Hermanas (Sevilla) [tel/fax 954-72 08 28; campingvillsom@hotmail.com]** Fr AP4/E5 Sevilla-Cádiz, exit junc 553 on SE3205 dir Dos Hermanas Centro, site on L immed bef L fork & bdge for Dos Hermanas. Lge, hdg/mkd pitch, hdstg, pt sl, pt shd; wc (some cont); chem disp; shwrs inc; el pnts (8A) €3.20 (poss no earth); gas; Indtte; sm shop; hypmkt 1km; snacks in ssn; bar; playgrnd; pool in ssn; wifi; bus to Seville 300m (over bdge & rndabt); site clsd 24 Dec-9 Jan; poss cr; Eng spkn; adv bkg; rd noise; ccard acc; CCI. "Adv bkg rec Holy Week; sm pitches - diff access lge o'fits; helpful staff; clean, tidy, well-run site; vg, san facs, ltd low ssn; height barrier at Carrefour hypmkt - ent via deliveries." € 23.90 2009*

⊞ **ELCHE** *4F2* (10km SW Urban) *38.24055, -0.81194* **Camping Las Palmeras, Ctra Murcia-Alicante, Km 45.3, 03330 Crevillent (Alicante) [965-40 01 88 or 966-68 06 30; fax 966-68 06 64; laspalmeras@laspalmeras-sl.com; www.laspalmeras-sl.com]** Exit A7 junc 726/77 onto N340 to Crevillent. Immed bef traff lts take slip rd into restaurant parking/service area. Site on R, access rd down side of rest. Med, mkd pitch, hdstg, pt shd; wc; chem disp; shwrs inc; el pnts (6A) inc; Indtte; supmkt adj; rest; snacks; bar; pool; paddling pool; 10% statics; dogs free; ccard acc; CCI. "Useful NH; report to recep in hotel; helpful staff; gd cent for touring Murcia; gd rest in hotel; gd, modern san facs; excel." € 26.00 2008*

Spain

ERRATZU *3A1* (E Rural) *43.18055, -1.45166* **Camping Baztan, Ctra Francia s/n, 31714 Erratzu (Navarra) [948-45 31 33; fax 948-45 30 85; campingbaztan@campingbaztan.com; www.campingbaztan.com]** Fr N121B km 62 marker take NA2600 sp Erratzu. In vill strt on at staggered x-rds & foll sp dir France, site on R outside vill 100m after Y junc. App rd thro vill narr with tight turns. Med, hdg/mkd pitch, shd; wc; chem disp; shwrs inc; el pnts inc; lndtte; shop; rest; playgrnd; pool; dogs €4; poss cr; adv bkg; quiet; ccard acc. "Site manned w/end only low ssn; gd walking; lovely scenery." ♦ 9 Apr-31 Oct. € 33.10 2008*

⊞ **ESCALA, L'** *3B3* (2km SE Coastal) *42.11048, 3.16378* **Camping Cala Montgó, Avda Montgó s/n, 17130 L'Escala (Gerona) [972-77 08 66; fax 972-77 43 40; calamontgo@betsa.es; www.betsa.es]** Exit AP7 junc 4 Figueres onto C31 dir Torroella de Montgri. Foll sp L'Escala & Montgó to site. V lge, pt sl, pt shd; wc; chem disp; baby facs; shwrs inc; el pnts (5A) €4.10; gas; lndtte; shop; tradsmn; rest; bar; playgrnd; pool; paddling pool; sand beach 200m; fishing; sports area; cycle hire; 30% statics; dogs; poss cr; adv bkg; quiet; ccard not acc; red low ssn; CCI. "Nr trad fishing vill; facs ltd/run down; quiet low ssn; exposed, poss windy & dusty site." ♦ € 36.00 2009*

ESCALA, L' *3B3* (500m S Urban/Coastal) *42.1211, 3.1346* **Camping L'Escala, Camí Ample 21, 17130 L'Escala (Gerona) [972-77 00 84; fax 972-77 00 08; info@campinglescala.com; www.campinglescala.com]** Exit AP7 junc 5 onto GI623 dir L'Escala; at o'skts of L'Escala, at 1st rndabt (with yellow sign GI623 on top of rd direction sp) turn L dir L'Escala & Ruïnes Empúries; at 2nd rndabt go str on dir L'Escala-Riells; 3rd rndabt shows site sp (to R); 4th rndabt also shows site sp (to L); site in sh dist. Do not app thro town. Med, hdg/mkd pitch, pt shd; wc (wc); chem disp; all serviced pitches; shwrs inc; el pnts (6A) inc; gas; shop; tradsmn; rest 100m; snacks; bar; BBQ; playgrnd; beach 300m; TV; 20% statics; dogs €2.50; phone; car wash; poss cr; Eng spkn; adv bkg; quiet; red low ssn; CCI. "Access to sm pitches poss diff lge o'fits; helpful, friendly staff; san facs poss unclean; no facs for dogs; Empúrias ruins 5km; vg." ♦ Easter-30 Sep. € 29.70 2008*

ESCALA, L' *3B3* (1km S Coastal) *42.1134, 3.1443* **Camping Maite, Avda Montó, Playa de Riells, 17130 L'Escala (Gerona) [tel/fax 972-77 05 44; rmaite@campings.net; www.campingmaite.com]** Exit A7 junc 5 dir L'Escala. Thro town dir Riells to rndabt with supmkts on each corner, turn R to site. Lge, mkd pitch, some terr, shd; wc; chem disp; mv service pnt; shwrs inc; el pnts (6A) €4.30; gas; shop adj; rest; bar; playgrnd; beach 200m; TV; bus 1km; adv bkg; red long stay; ccard acc; CCI. "Well-run site; quiet oasis in busy resort; steep site rds; some pitches narr access." ♦ 1 Jun-15 Sep. € 20.80 2007*

ESCALA, L' *3B3* (2km S Coastal) *42.11027, 3.16555* **Camping Illa Mateua, Ave Montgó 260, 17130 L'Escala (Gerona) [972-77 02 00 or 77 17 95; fax 972-77 20 31; info@campingillamateua.com; www.campingillamateua.com]** On N11 thro Figueras, approx 3km on L sp C31 L'Escala; in town foll sp for Montgó & Paradis. Lge, terr, pt shd; wc; chem disp; mv service pnt; baby facs; shwrs inc; el pnts (5A) inc; gas; lndtte; shop; rest; bar; playgrnd; 2 pools; sand beach adj; watersports; tennis; games area; entmnt; 5% statics; dogs €3.60; Eng spkn; adv bkg ess high ssn; quiet; red low ssn/long stay; CCI. "V well-run site; spacious pitches; excel san facs; gd beach; no depth marking in pool." ♦ 15 Mar-10 Oct. € 41.20 2007*

ESCALA, L' *3B3* (3km S Coastal) *42.10512, 3.15843* **Camping Neus, Cala Montgó, 17130 L'Escala (Gerona) [972-77 04 03 or 972-20 86 67; fax 972-77 27 51 or 972-22 24 09; info@campingneus.com; www.campingneus.com]** Exit AP7 junc 5 twd L'Escala then turn R twd Cala Montgó & foll sp. Med, mkd pitch, pt sl, pt terr, shd; wc; chem disp; mv service pnt; baby facs; shwrs inc; el pnts (6A) €4; gas; lndtte; shop; snacks; bar; playgrnd; pool; paddling pool; sand beach 850m; fishing; tennis; car wash; internet; entmnt; TV rm; 15% statics; dogs €2; phone; bus 500m; Eng spkn; adv bkg; quiet; ccard acc; red low ssn/long stay; CCI. "Pleasant, clean site in pine forest; gd san facs; lge pitches; vg." 28 May-19 Sep. € 39.00 2009*

⊞ **ESCORIAL, EL** *1D4* (6km NE Rural) *40.62630, -4.09970* **Camping-Caravaning El Escorial, Ctra Guadarrama a El Escorial, Km 3.5, 28280 El Escorial (Madrid) [918-90 24 12 or 902-01 49 00; fax 918-96 10 62; info@campingelescorial.com; www.campingelescorial.com]** Exit AP6 NW of Madrid junc 47 El Escorial/Guadarrama, onto M505 & foll sp to El Escorial, site on L at km stone 3,500 - long o'fits rec cont to rndabt (1km) to turn & app site on R. V lge, mkd pitch, some hdstg, pt shd; htd wc; chem disp; baby facs; shwrs inc; el pnts (5A) inc (long cable rec); gas; lndtte; shop; rest, bar in ssn & w/end; hypmkt 5km; snacks; BBQ; playgrnd; 3 pools high ssn; tennis; horseriding 7km; games rm; wifi; TV; 25% statics (sep area); dogs free; cash machine; adv bkg; some Eng spkn; poss cr & noisy at w/end; ccard acc. "Excel base for sightseeing; clean facs; helpful staff; gd security; sm pitches poss diff to access due trees; facs ltd low ssn; overhead canopies, strong awning pegs rec; day trips to Segovia & Ávila (high ssn); trains & buses to Madrid nr; Valle de Los Caídos & Palace at El Escorial well worth visit; gd views of mountains; easy parking in town for m'vans if go in early; mkt Wed." ♦ € 33.25 ABS - E13 2009*

See advertisement

ESCULLOS, LOS see Nijar *4G1*

ESPINAL see Auritz *3A1*

⊞ **ESPONELLA** *3B3* (500m N Rural) *42.1817, 2.7949* **Camping Esponellà, Ctra Banyoles-Figueres, Km 8, 17832 Esponellà (Gerona) [972-59 70 74; fax 972-59 71 32; informa@campingesponella.com; www.campingesponella.com]** Heading S fr French frontier, turn R (W) at Figueras on N260. After 13km turn L at junc to Banyoles, site in 6.5km. Fr S foll C66 N fr Gerona, then in 17km turn R twds Figueres. Lge, hdg pitch, pt shd; htd wc (some cont); chem disp; shwrs inc; rest; el pnts (5A) €4.70 (check earth); Indtte; shop; rest; bar; BBQ; playgrnd; 2 htd covrd pools; tennis; games area; cycle hire; rv fishing; horseriding; entmnt; 40% statics; dogs €2; quiet; red long stay/CCI. "Excel facs but ltd low ssn; v busy w/end; lovely site but poss not suitable lge o'fits due trees; gd walks." € 28.15 2008*

ESPOT *3B2* (500m SE Rural) *42.95916, 1.14916* **Camping Sol I Neu, Ctra Sant Maurici s/n, 25597 Espot (Lleida) [973-62 40 01; fax 973-62 41 07; camping@solineu.com; www.solineu.com]** N fr Sort on C13 turn L to Espot on rd LV5004, site on L in approx 6.5km by rvside. Med, mkd pitch, pt shd; wc; chem disp; baby facs; shwrs inc; el pnts (6-10A) €5.15; gas; Indtte; shop, bar high ssn; playgrnd; pool; paddling pool; TV; dogs €3.60; quiet; ccard acc; CCI. "Excel facs; beautiful site nr National Park (Landrover taxis avail - no private vehicles allowed in Park); suitable sm o'fits only; poss unreliable opening dates." 24 Jun-15 Sep. € 23.70 2008*

ESPOT *3B2* (1km W Rural) *42.58527, 1.0750* **Camping Voraparc, Ctra Sant Maurici s/n, Prat del Vedat, 25597 Espot (Lleida) [973-62 41 08 or 973-25 23 24; fax 973-62 41 43; info@voraparc.com; www.voraparc.com]** Fr Sort N on C13 N. At sp turn L for Espot, go thro vill then turn R for National Park. Site in 1.5km on R. Well sp. Med, mkd pitch, pt sl, shd; wc; chem disp (wc); mv service pnt; baby facs; shwrs inc; el pnts (6A) €4.25 (poss rev pol); gas; Indtte; shop; tradsmn; snacks; bar; BBQ; playgrnd; htd pool; watersports nrby; walks; cycle hire; TV/games rm; no statics; dogs; phone; bus 1km; Eng spkn; adv bkg; quiet; red long stay; ccard acc; CCI. "Friendly owners; clean facs; access rd narr & needs care; National Park in walking/cycling distance; gd birdwatching; excel." ♦ Holy Week & 1 May-30 Sep. € 20.60 2008*

ESTARTIT L' *3B3* (W Coastal) *42.05333, 3.19277* **Camping Rifort, Ctra de Torroella s/n, Km 5.5, 17258 L'Estartit (Gerona) [972-75 04 06; fax 972-75 17 22; campingrifort@campingrifort.com; www.campingrifort.com]** Site on rndabt at ent to L'Estartit. Med, hdg/mkd pitch, terr, pt shd; wc; chem disp; mv service pnt; shwrs; baby facs; el pnts €4.15; gas; Indtte; shop 50m; snacks; bar; pool; sand beach 500m; tennis 150m; watersports; internet; some statics; dogs €2.15; phone; bus adj; Eng spkn; adv bkg; noise fr adj main rd & entmnt; red low ssn; ccard acc. "Family-run; excel, immac facs." ♦ 7 Apr-12 Oct. € 22.10 2008*

ESTARTIT, L' *3B3* (500m Urban/Coastal) *42.04808, 3.1871* **Camping La Sirena, Calle La Platera s/n, 17258 L'Estartit (Gerona) [972-75 15 42; fax 972-75 09 44; info@camping-lasirena.com; www.camping-lasirena.com]** Fr Torroella foll sp to L'Estartit on rd GI641. On o'skts of vill turn R at Els Jocs amusements, site on L 200m. Lge, pt shd; wc; chem disp; baby facs; shwrs inc; el pnts (6-10A) €4.80 (poss long lead req); gas; Indtte (inc dryer); shop; rest; snacks; bar; BBQ; playgrnd; htd pool; paddling pool; sand beach adj; scuba diving; internet; money exchange; car wash; TV; 10% statics; dogs €2.35; bus adj; Eng spkn; quiet; red long stay/low ssn; CCI. "Sm pitches, diff lge o'fits; poss long walk to beach; v ltd facs low ssn; gd value boat trips; nature reserve adj." ♦ Easter-12 Oct. € 24.00 2009*

ESTARTIT, L' *3B3* (1km S Coastal) *42.04972, 3.18416* **Camping El Molino, Camino del Ter, 17258 L'Estartit (Gerona) [tel/fax 972-75 06 29]** Fr N11 junc 5, take rd to L'Escala. Foll sp to Torroella de Montgri, then L'Estartit. Ent town & foll sp, site on rd GI 641. V lge, hdg pitch, pt sl, pt shd; wc; mv service pnt; shwrs; el pnts (6A) €3.60; gas; Indtte; supmkt high ssn & 2km; rest; bar; playgrnd; sand beach 1km; games rm; internet; bus 1km; poss cr; adv bkg. "Site in 2 parts - 1 in shd, 1 at beach unshd; gd facs; quiet location outside busy town." 1 Apr-30 Sep. € 21.00 2009*

Spain

⊞ **ESTARTIT, L'** *3B3* (2km S Coastal) *42.04250, 3.18333* **Camping Les Medes, Paratge Camp de l'Arbre s/n, 17258 L'Estartit (Gerona) [972-75 18 05; fax 972-75 04 13; info@campinglesmedes.com; www.campinglesmedes.com]** Fr Torroella foll sp to L'Estartit. In vill turn R at town name sp (sp Urb Estartit Oeste), foll rd for 1.5km, turn R, site well sp. Lge, mkd pitch, shd; htd wc; chem disp; mv service pnt; serviced pitches; baby facs; sauna; shwrs inc; el pnts (6-10A) €4.50 (poss no earth); gas; Indtte; shop; rest; snacks; bar; playgrnd; htd indoor/outdoor pools; sand beach 800m; watersports; solarium; tennis; games area; horseriding 400m; cycle hire; car wash; games rm; wifi; entmnt; TV; 7% statics; no dogs high ssn otherwise €2.50; phone; site clsd Nov; poss cr; Eng spkn; adv bkg; quiet; red long stay/low ssn (pay on arrival); CCI. "Excel, family-run & well organised site; welcome pack; gd clean facs & constant hot water; gd for children; no twin-axle vans high ssn - by arrangement low ssn; conv National Park; well mkd foot & cycle paths." ♦ € 34.90 2009*

See advertisement below

ESTARTIT, L' *3B3* (W Coastal) *42.05035, 3.18023* **Camping Castell Montgri, Ctra de Torroella, Km 4.7, 17258 L'Estartit (Gerona) [972-75 16 30; fax 972-75 09 06; cmontgri@campingparks.com; www.campingparks.com or www.campeole.com]** Exit A7 junc 5 onto GI 623 dir L'Escala. Foll sp on rd C252 fr Torroella de Montgri to L'Estartit. Site on L clearly sp. V lge, hdg pitch, terr, hdstg, shd; wc; mv service pnt; chem disp; baby facs; shwrs inc; el pnts (6A) inc; gas; Indtte; shop; rest; snacks; bar; playgrnd; 3 pools; waterslide; beach 1km; tennis; games area; watersports; entmnt; excursions; internet; TV; car wash; money exchange; 30% statics; dogs free; phone; poss cr; adv bkg; red long stay/low ssn. "Gd views; help given to get to pitch; excel." ♦ 15 May-16 Sep. € 44.00 2006*

ESTARTIT, L' *3B3* (W Coastal) *42.05670, 3.19785* **Camping Estartit, Calle Villa Primevera 12, 17258 L'Estartit (Gerona) [972-75 19 09; fax 972-75 09 91; www.campingestartit.com]** Exit AP7 junc 6 onto C66, then take G642 dir Torroella de Montgri & L'Estartit; fork L on ent L'Estartit, foll site sps. Med, pt sl, shd; htd wc; chem disp; baby facs; shwrs ; el pnts (6A) €3.73; gas; Indtte; shop; rest adj; snacks; bar; playgrnd; htd pool; paddling pool; sand beach 400m; entmnt; 15% statics; no dogs 20/6-20/8; phone; poss cr; Eng spkn; red long stay. "Friendly staff; 100m fr vill cent; gd security; gd walks adj nature reserve; bar/rest & night club adj; facs poss stretched high ssn." 1 Apr-30 Sep. € 23.90 2009*

ESTARTIT, L' *3B3* (1km W Coastal) *42.04907, 3.18385* **Camping L'Empordà, Ctra Torroella-L'Estartit, Km 4.8, 17258 L'Estartit (Gerona) [972-75 06 49; fax 972-75 14 30; info@campingemporda.com; www.campingemporda.com]** Exit AP7 junc 5 onto GI623 dir L'Escala. Bef L'Escala turn S onto C31 dir Torroella de Montgri, then at Torroella take rd GI641 dir L'Estartit. Site bet L'Estartit & Torroella, opp Castell Montgri. Lge, hdg/mkd pitch, pt shd; wc; chem disp; shwrs inc; baby facs; el pnts (6A) €4.40; gas; Indtte; shop; snacks; bar; playgrnd; pool; paddling pool; sand beach 1km; tennis; entmnt; organised walks; wifi; TV; dogs €2.50; phone; bus 70m; car wash; site clsd 21 Dec-31 Jan; poss cr; adv bkg; quiet; red low ssn/long stay; CCI. "Family-run, pleasant & helpful; easy walking dist town cent; lge pitches." ♦ 4 Apr-12 Oct. € 24.20 2009*

See advertisement above

⊞ **ESTELLA** *3B1* (2km S Rural) *42.65695, -2.01761* **Camping Lizarra, Ordoiz s/n, 31200 Estella (Navarra) [948-55 17 33; fax 948-55 47 55; info@campinglizarra.com; www.campinglizarra.com]** N111 Pamplona to Logroño. Leave N111 sp Estella, turn R at T-junc, bear R at traff lts & turn R immed after rd tunnel, site sp. Pass factory, site on L in 1.5km. Well sp thro town. Lge, mkd pitch, wide terr, pt sl, unshd; htd wc; chem disp; mv service pnt; baby facs; shwrs inc; el pnts (6A) inc; gas; Indtte; shop high ssn; rest; snacks; bar; BBQ; playgrnd; pool; 80% w/end statics; phone; bus at w/end; poss cr; Eng spkn; noisy; ccard acc; CCI. "Poss school parties; no hdstg; poss muddy when wet; poss smell fr nrby factory; interesting old town; excel birdwatching in hills; on rte Camino de Compostella." ♦ € 20.20 2006*

⊞ **ESTEPAR** *1B4* (2km NE Rural) *42.29233, -3.85097* **Camping Cabia, Ctra Burgos-Valladolid, Km 17, 09192 Cabia/Cavia (Burgos) [947-41 20 78]** Site 15km SW of Burgos on N side of A62/E80, adj Hotel Rio Cabia. Ent via Campsa petrol stn, W'bound exit 17, E'bound exit 16, cross over & re-join m'way. Ignore camp sp at exit 18 which leads up narr service rd. Med, pt shd; wc; chem disp; shwrs inc; el pnts (6A) €2.20; shops 15km & basic supplies fr rest; rest; bar; playgrnd; few statics; dogs; constant rd noise; ccard acc; CCI. "Friendly, helpful owner; gd rest; conv for m'way for Portugal but poorly sp fr W; poss v muddy in winter; poorly maintained, run down san facs; NH only." € 11.60 2009*

⊞ **ESTEPONA** *2H3* (7km E Coastal) *36.45436, -5.08105* **Camping Parque Tropical, Ctra N340, Km 162, 29680 Estepona (Málaga) [tel/fax 952-79 36 18; parquetropicalcamping@hotmail.com; www.campingparquetropical.com]** On N side of N340 at km 162, 200m off main rd. Med, hdg/mkd pitch, terr, pt shd; wc; chem disp; mv service pnt; serviced pitch; shwrs inc; el pnts (10A) €4; gas; Indtte; shop; rest; snacks; bar; sm playgrnd; htd, covrd pool; sand/shgl beach 1km; golf, horseriding nrby; wildlife park 1km; 60% statics; dogs €3; phone; bus 400m; poss cr; Eng spkn; adv bkg; rd noise; red low ssn/long stay; CCI. "Site run down (Feb 09); facs poorly maintained & in need of update." ♦ € 27.00 2009*

ETXARRI ARANATZ *3B1* (2km N Rural) *42.91255, -2.07919* **Camping Etxarri, Parase Dambolintxulo, 31820 Etxarri-Aranatz (Navarra) [tel/fax 948-46 05 37; info@campingetxarri.com; www.campingetxarri.com]** S on AP15, turn W at Irurtzun onto N240A/N1 dir Vitoria/Gasteiz. Go thro Etxarri vill, turn L & cross bdge, then take rd over rlwy. Turn L, site sp. Med, hdg pitch, pt shd; wc; chem disp; shwrs inc; el pnts (6A) €5; gas; Indtte; shop; rest; bar; BBQ; pool; playgrnd; sports area; archery; horseriding; cycling; entmnt; wifi; 50% statics; dogs €2.15; phone; poss cr; Eng spkn; ccard acc; red low ssn; CCI. "Gd, wooded site; gd walks; interesting area; helpful owner; lge pitches - easy access lge o'fits; conv NH to/fr Pyrenees; youth hostel on site." 1 Apr-3 Oct. € 20.10 2009*

EUSA see Pamplona *3B1*

FARGA DE MOLES, LA see Seo de Urgel *3B3*

🅃 **FIGUERES** *3B3* (1km N Urban) *42.28340, 2.94960* **Camping Pous, Ctra N11A, Km 8.5, 17600 Figueres (Gerona) [972-67 54 96; fax 972-67 50 57; hostalandrol@wanadoo.es; www.androl.internet-park.net]** Fr N exit AP7/E15 at junc 3 & join N11. Then foll N11A S twd Figueres. Site on L in 2km, ent adj Hostal Androl. From S exit junc 4 onto NII to N of town. At rndabt (access to AP7 junc 3) foll NII S, then as above. Site recep in hotel. No access to N11A fr junc 4. Med, mkd pitch, pt sl, shd; wc; chem disp; shwrs inc; el pnts (10A) €3; shop 1km; rest; snacks; bar; playgrnd; few statics; dogs €2.50; bus adj; Eng spkn; quiet with some rd noise; ccard acc. "Gd, clean site but san facs slightly run down & ltd/unisex low ssn; easy access; pleasant owner; excel rest; 30 min walk to town (busy main rd, no pavements) & Dali museum; 18km fr Rosas on coast." ♦ € 34.00 2009*

🅃 **FIGUERES** *3B3* (12km N Rural) *42.37305, 2.91305* **Camping Les Pedres, Calle Vendador s/n, 17750 Capmany (Gerona) [972-54 91 92 or 686 01 12 23 (mob); recep@campinglespedres.com; www.campinglespedres.net]** S fr French border on N11, turn L sp Capmany, L again in 2km at site sp & foll site sp. Med, mkd pitch, pt sl, pt shd; htd wc; chem disp; shwrs inc; el pnts (6-10A) €4.15; lndry rm; shop 1km; rest; snacks; bar; pool; sand beach 25km; 20% statics; dogs; phone; Eng spkn; adv bkg; quiet; ccard acc; red low ssn; CCI. "Helpful Dutch owner; lovely views; gd touring & walking cent; gd winter NH." ♦ € 24.00 2009*

FIGUERES *3B3* (8km NE Rural) *42.33902, 3.06758* **Camping Vell Empordà, Ctra Rosas-La Jonquera s/n, 17780 Garriguella (Gerona) [972-53 02 00 or 972-57 06 31 (LS); fax 972-55 23 43; vellemporda@vellemporda.com; www.vellemporda.com]** On A7/E11 exit junc 3 onto N260 NE dir Llançà. Nr km 26 marker, turn R sp Garriguella, then L at T-junc N twd Garriguella. Site on R shortly bef vill. Lge, hdg/mkd pitch, hdstg, terr, shd; htd wc; chem disp; mv service pnt; baby facs; shwrs inc; el pnts (6-10A) inc; gas; lndtte; shop; rest; snacks; bar; BBQ; playgrnd; pool; paddling pool; sand beach 6km; games area; games rm; entmnt; internet; TV; 20% statics; dogs €4.50; phone; Eng spkn; adv bkg; quiet; ccard acc; red long stay/low ssn; CCI. "Conv N Costa Brava away fr cr beaches & sites; 20 mins to sea, at Llançà; overhanging trees poss diff high vehicles; excel." ♦ 1 Feb-15 Dec. € 32.00 2009*

See advertisement

🅃 **FIGUERES** *3B3* (15km NW Rural) *42.31444, 2.77638* **Camping La Fradera, Pedramala, 17732 Sant Llorenç de la Muga (Gerona) [tel/fax 972-54 20 54; camping.fradera@teleline.es; www.terra.es/personal2/camping.fradera]** Fr cent Figueres take N260 W dir Olot. After 1km turn R at mini-rndabt (supmkt on L), pass police stn to rd junc, strt on & cross over A7 m'way & pass thro Llers & Terrades to Sant Llorenç. Site 1km past vill on L. Med, mkd pitch, pt shd; wc; chem disp; shwrs inc; el pnts (6A) €2.67; lndtte; shop 2km; tradsmn; snacks; rest in vill; playgrnd; htd pool; rv sw 1km; few statics; poss cr; Eng spkn; adv bkg; quiet; ccard acc; red long stay. "Vg site in delightful vill in foothills of Pyrenees; fiesta 2nd w/end Aug; v pleasant staff; gates clsd low ssn - phone owner." ♦ € 19.26 2007*

FORNELLS DE LA SELVA see Gerona *3B3*

🅃 **FORTUNA** *4F1* (3km N Rural) *38.20562, -1.10712* **Camping Fuente, Camino de la Bocamina s/n, 30709 Baños de Fortuna (Murcia) [tel/fax 968-68 51 25; info@campingfuente.com; www.campingfuente.com]** Fr Murcia on A7/E15 turn L onto C3223 sp Fortuna. After 19km turn onto A21 & foll sp Baños de Fortuna, then sp 'Complejo Hotelero La Fuente'. Avoid towing thro vill, if poss. Med, mkd pitch, hdstg, pt sl, unshd; htd wc; chem disp; indiv san facs some pitches; shwrs; el pnts (10-16A) €2 or metered; gas; lndtte; shop; tradsmn; rest; snacks; bar; BBQ; playgrnd; htd pool, spa, jacuzzi; internet; some statics; dogs €1; phone; bus 200m; adv bkg; ccard acc; red long stay; CCI. "Gd san facs; excel pool & rest; secure o'flow parking area; many long-stay winter visitors - adv bkg rec; ltd recep hrs low ssn; poss sulphurous smell fr thermal baths." ♦ € 18.50 2009*

🅃 **FORTUNA** *4F1* (3km N Rural) *38.20666, -1.11194* **Camping Las Palmeras, 30709 Baños de Fortuna (Murcia) [tel/fax 968-68 60 95]** Exit A7 junc 83 Fortuna; cont on C3223 thro Fortuna to Los Baños; turn R & foll sp. Concealed R turn on crest at beg of vill. Med, mkd pitch, pt shd; wc; chem disp (wc); shwrs; el pnts (6-10A) €2.20-3; gas; lndtte; shops 300m; tradsmn; rest; snacks; bar; natural hot water mineral pool 200m; some statics; dogs €0.50; poss cr; quiet; adv bkg acc; red long stay; ccard acc; CCI. "Gd value, friendly site; gd, modern san facs; gd rest; lge pitches; poss tatty statics; thermal baths also at Archena (15km)." ♦ € 10.50 2009*

🅃 **FOZ** *1A2* (7km E Coastal) *43.55416, -7.17000* **Camping Playa Reinante Anosa Casa, Estrada da Costa 42, 27279 Barreiros/Reinante (Lugo) [tel/fax 982-13 40 05; info@campinganosacasa.com; www.campinganosacasa.com]** E fr Barreiros on N634, exit rd at Reinante opp Hotel Casa Amadora, turn R at beach, site on R. Sm, unshd; wc; chem disp; shwrs €1; el pnts €4.50; gas; lndtte; shop, rest, snacks, bar 500m; BBQ; sand beach adj; wifi; 10% statics; dogs €5; bus/train 900m; quiet. "Owners & location make up for basic facs in need of upgrading; excel coastal walking fr site." ♦ € 18.00 2009*

🅃 **FOZ** *1A2* (8km E Coastal) **Camping Benquerencia, 27792 Benquerencia-Barreiros (Lugo) [982-12 44 50 or 679-15 87 88 (mob); contactol@campingbenquerencia.com; www.campingbenquerencia.com]** Fr junc of N642 & N634 S of Foz; E twd Ribadeo; in 1km past Barreiros at km stone 566 turn L at site sp. Site on R in 1.5km. Med, mkd pitch, pt sl, pt shd; wc; shwrs inc; el pnts (6A) €3.50; gas; lndtte; shop in ssn & 2km; rest; bar; playgrnd; sand beach 400m; tennis; games area; phone; quiet; ccard acc; CCI. "Hot water to shwrs only; NH only." € 18.50 2009*

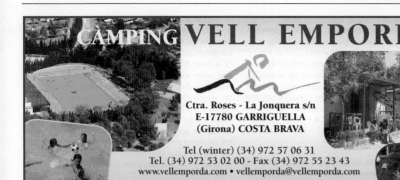

FOZ *1A2* (2.5km NW Coastal/Rural) *43.58678, -7.28356* **Camping San Rafael, Playa de Peizas, 27789 Foz (Lugo) [tel/fax 982-13 22 18; info@campingsanrafael.com; www.campingsanrafael.com]** N fr Foz on N642, site sp on R. Med, pt sl, unshd; wc; chem disp; mv service pnt; shwrs inc; el pnts (5A) €4.50; gas; Indtte; shop; tradsmn; rest; snacks; bar; sand beach adj; games area; wifi; dogs €1; bus 200m; poss cr; adv bkg; quiet; 15% red long stay; ccard acc; CCI. "Peaceful, spacious site; basic facs; hot water to shwrs only; take care electrics; pay night bef departure." 1 Apr-30 Sep. € 17.55 2009*

⊞ **FRAGA** *3C2* (1km SE Urban) *41.51738, 0.35553* **Camping Fraga, Ctra N11-Seros, Km 437, Ptda Vincanet s/n, 22520 Fraga (Huesca) [974-34 52 12; info@campingfraga.com; www.campingfraga.com]** Fr W pass thro Fraga town on N11. After about 500m turn R into indus est just past petrol stn. Turn R again in indus est, foll site sp. Fr E turn L into indus est just bef petrol stn. NB steep app poss not suitable c'vans. Sm, mkd pitch, hdstg, terr, pt shd; wc; chem disp; mv service pnt; shwrs inc; el pnts (6A) €3.20 (rev pol & poss long lead req); Indtte; hypmkt 1km; tradsmn; rest; snacks; bar; playgrnd; pool; TV rm; some statics; dogs €2.70; phone; bus 1km; poss cr; adv bkg; red low ssn; CCI. "Conv NH bet Zaragoza & Tarragona; unspoilt town in beautiful area; rec not to hook-up if in transit - ltd reliable el pnts." ♦ € 22.60 2009*

FRANCA, LA *1A4* (1km NW Coastal) *43.39250, -4.57722* **Camping Las Hortensias, Ctra N634, Km 286, 33590 Playa de la Franca (Asturias) [985-41 24 42; fax 985-41 21 53; lashortensias@campinglashortensias.com; www.campinglashortensias.com]** Fr N634 on leaving vill of La Franca, at km286 foll sp 'Playa de la Franca' & cont past 1st site & thro car park to end of rd. Med, mkd pitch, pt sl, pt terr, pt shd; wc; chem disp; baby facs; shwrs inc; el pnts (6-10A) €4.40; gas; Indtte; shop; rest, snacks, bar adj; playgrnd; sand beach adj; tennis; cycle hire; phone; dogs (but not on beach) €5; bus 800m; poss cr; Eng spkn; adv bkg; ccard acc; red CCI. "Beautiful location nr scenic beach; sea views fr top terr pitches; vg." 5 Jun-30 Sep. € 26.35 2009*

FRESNEDA, LA *3C2* (2.5km SW Rural) *40.90705, 0.06166* **Camping La Fresneda, Partida Vall del Pi, 44596 La Fresneda (Teruel) [978-85 40 85; info@campinglafresneda.com; www.campinglafresneda.com]** Fr Alcañiz S on N232 dir Morella; in 15km turn L onto A231 thro Valjunquera to La Fresneda; cont thro vill; in 2.5km turn R onto site rd. Site sp fr vill. Sm, hdg/mkd pitch, terr, unshd; wc; chem disp; baby facs; shwrs inc; el pnts (6A) inc; gas 2.5km; Indtte; tradsmn; rest; snacks; bar; plunge pool; wifi; no dogs; poss cr; Eng spkn; quiet; ccard acc; red long stay; CCI. "Narr site rds, poss diff lge o'fits; various pitch sizes; gd." ♦ 15 Mar-1 Nov. € 22.47 2009*

FRIAS *1B4* (3km NW Rural) *42.77097, -3.29686* **Camping Friás, Ctra Quintana-Martin, 09211 Galíndez-Friás (Burgos) [947-35 71 98; fax 947-35 71 99; info@campingfrias.com; www.campingfrias.com]** Fr AP1 take N232 & N629 NW to Trespaderne. Turn sharp R (dir Miranda) & E for 10km. Foll site sp at Friás. Site on R in 3km bef rv bdge. Med, mkd pitch, pt shd; wc; chem disp; mv service pnt; shwrs €0.60; el pnts (5A) €3.50; shop; rest; bar; 3 pools; rv adj; fishing; archery; cycle hire; 95% statics; dogs €3; phone; poss cr w/end; quiet; ccard acc. "Open w/end only in winter, but phone ahead to check; sh stay/NH only; interesting vill with castle & Roman bdge." 1 Apr-30 Sep. € 20.50 2008*

⊞ **FUENGIROLA** *2H4* (2km SW Coastal) *36.5207, 4.6306* **Camping Fuengirola, Ctra Cádiz-Málaga Km 207, 29640 Fuengirola (Málaga) [tel/fax 952-47 41 08]** On R of N340 Málaga-Algeciras rd opp hotel immed at km stone 207. Go slowly down service stn exit (if missed, next rndabt is 2km). Lge, shd; wc; chem disp; serviced pitches; shwrs inc; el pnts (6A) €2.75; gas; Indtte; shop; rest; bar; playgrnd; pool; sand beach adj; watersports; TV; adv bkg; Eng spkn; some rd noise; red long stay; ccard acc; CCI. "Sea views; clean facs; helpful staff; take care tree sap - can eat into lacquer finish of cars!" € 29.00 2008*

Spain

⊞ **FUENGIROLA** *2H4* (9km W Coastal) *36.48943, -4.71813* **Camping Los Jarales, Ctra N340, Km 197 Calahonda, 29650 Mijas-Costa (Málaga) [tel/fax 952-93 00 03]** Fr Fuengirola take N340 W twd Marbella, turn at km 197 stone; site located to N of rd. Lge, mkd pitch, hdstg, pt sl, pt shd; wc; chem disp; serviced pitch; shwrs inc; el pnts (5A) €3.15; gas; Indtte; shop adj; rest; snacks; bar; playgrnd; pool; sand beach 400m; tennis; TV; no dogs; bus adj; poss cr; Eng spkn; adv bkg; rd noise; red long stay/CCI. "Well-run site; buses to Marbella & Fuengirola." ♦ € 23.00 2007*

⊞ **FUENTE DE PIEDRA** *2G4* (700m S Rural) *37.12905, -4.73315* **Camping Fuente de Pedra, Calle Campillos 88-90, 29520 Fuente de Piedra (Málaga) [952-73 52 94; fax 952-73 54 61; info@camping-rural.com; www.camping-rural.com]** Turn off A92 at km 132 sp Fuente de Piedra. Sp fr vill cent. Or to avoid town turn N fr A384 just W of turn for Bobadilla Estación, sp Sierra de Yeguas. In 2km turn R into nature reserve, cont for approx 3km, site on L at end of town. Sm, mkd pitch, hdstg, pt sl, terr, pt shd; wc; shwrs inc; el pnts (10A) €5; gas; Indry rm; shop; rest; snacks; bar; BBQ; playgrnd; pool in ssn; internet; 25% chalets; dogs €3; phone; bus 500m; Eng spkn; poss noise fr adj public pool; ccard acc; red long stay/low ssn/CCI. "Mostly sm, narr pitches, but some avail for o'fits up to 7m; gd rest; san facs dated & poss stretched; adj lge lake with flamingoes; gd." ♦ € 22.00 2009*

FUENTE DE SAN ESTABAN, LA *1D3* (1km E Rural) *40.79128, -6.24384* **Camping El Cruce, Ctra A62, Km 291 (E80), 37200 La Fuente de San Estaban (Salamanca) [923-44 01 30; campingelcruce@yahoo.es]** On A62/E80 (Salamanca-Portugal) km stone 291 immed behind hotel on S side of rd. Fr E watch for sp 'Cambio de Sentido' to cross main rd. Med, pt shd; wc; chem disp; shwrs; el pnts (6A) €3 (poss no earth); rest adj; snacks; bar; playgrnd; Eng spkn; some rd noise; ccard acc; CCI. "Conv NH/sh stay en rte Portugal; friendly." 15 Jun-30 Sep. € 14.00 2006*

⊞ **FUENTEHERIDOS** *2F3* (600m SW Rural) *37.9050, -6.6742* **Camping El Madroñal, Ctra Fuenteheridos-Castaño del Robledo, Km 0.6, 21292 Fuenteheridos (Huelva) [959-50 12 01; castillo@campingelmadronal.com; www.campingelmadronal.com]** Fr Zafra S on N435n turn L onto N433 sp Aracena, ignore first R to Fuenteheridos vill, camp sp R at next x-rd 500m on R. At rndabt take 2nd exit. Avoid Fuenteheridos vill - narr rds. Med, mkd pitch, pt sl, pt shd; wc; chem disp; shwrs; el pnts €3.20; gas; Indry rm; shop & 600m; snacks, bar high ssn; BBQ; 2 pools; cycle hire; horseriding; 80% statics; dogs; phone; bus 1km; car wash; quiet; CCI. "Tranquil site in National Park of Sierra de Aracena; pitches among chestnut trees - poss diff lge o'fits or m'vans & poss sl & uneven; o'hanging trees on site rds." € 14.20 2008*

GALENDE see Puebla de Sanabria *1B3*

⊞ **GALLARDOS, LOS** *4G1* (4km N Rural) *37.18448, -1.92408* **Camping Los Gallardos, 04280 Los Gallardos (Almería) [950-52 83 24; fax 950-46 95 96; reception@campinglosgallardos.com; www.campinglosgallardos.com]** Fr N leave A7/E15 at junc 525; foll sp to Los Gallardos; pass under a'route after 800m; turn L into site ent. Med, mkd pitch, hdstg, pt shd; wc; chem disp; serviced pitch; mv service pnt; shwrs inc; el pnts (10A) €3; gas; Indtte; supmkt; rest (clsd Thurs); snacks; bar; pool; sand beach 10km; 2 grass bowling greens; golf; tennis adj; dogs €2.25; 40% statics; poss v cr; m'way noise; adv bkg; reds long stay/low ssn; ccard acc; CCI. "British owned; 90% British clientele low ssn; gd social atmosphere; sep drinking water supply nr recep; prone to flooding wet weather." ♦ € 17.60 2007*

⊞ **GANDIA** *4E2* (2km N Coastal) *38.98613, -0.16352* **Camping L'Alqueria, Avda del Grau s/n; 46730 Grao de Gandía (València) [962-84 04 70; fax 962-84 10 63; info@campinggandia.es; www.lalqueria.com]** Fr N on A7/AP7 exit 60 onto N332 dir Grao de Gandía. Site sp on rd bet Gandía & seafront. Fr S exit junc 61 & foll sp to beaches. Lge, mkd pitch, hdstg, pt shd; htd wc; chem disp; mv service pnt; baby facs; shwrs inc; el pnts (10A) €5.50; gas; Indtte; shop; rest adj; snacks; bar; playgrnd; htd, covrd pool; jacuzzi; sand beach 1km; games area; cycle hire; wifi; entmnt; 30% statics inc disabled accessible; sm dogs (under 10kg) €1.90; phone; bus; adv bkg; quiet; ccard acc; red long stay/snr citizens; CCI. "Pleasant site; helpful family owners; lovely pool; easy walk to town & stn; excel beach nrby; bus & train to Valencia." ♦ € 33.28 2009*

⊞ **GARGANTILLA DEL LOZOYA** *1C4* (2km SW Rural) *40.9503, -3.7294* **Camping Monte Holiday, Ctra C604, Km 8.8, 28739 Gargantilla del Lozoya (Madrid) [918-69 50 65; fax 918-69 52 78; monteholiday@monteholiday.com; www.monteholiday.com]** Fr N on A1/E5 Burgos-Madrid rd turn R on M604 at km stone 69 sp Rascafría; in 8km turn R immed after rlwy bdge & then L up track in 300m, foll site sp. Do not ent vill. Lge, terr, pt sl, pt shd; wc; chem disp; baby facs; shwrs inc; el pnts (7A) €4 (poss rev pol); Indtte; shop 6km; rest; bar; pool; 80% statics; bus 500m; phone; little Eng spkn; adv bkg; quiet; ccard acc; red CCI. "Interesting, friendly site; vg san facs; gd views; easy to find; some facs clsd low ssn; lovely area but site isolated in winter & poss heavy snow; conv NH fr m'way & for Madrid & Segovia." ♦ € 24.00 2008*

GARRIGUELLA see Figueres *3B3*

⊞ **GARRUCHA** *4G1* (6km N Coastal) *37.23785, -1.79911* **Camping Cuevas Mar, Ctra Garrucha-Villaricos s/n, 04618 Palomares-Cuevas de Almanzora (Almería) [tel/fax 950-46 73 82; cuevasmar@arrakis.es; www.campingcuevasmar.com]** Exit A7 at junc 537 sp Cuevas del Almanzora & take A1200 sp Vera. In 2km turn L onto AL7101 (ALP118) sp Palomares & take 2nd exit at rndabt immed bef Palomares, site on L in 1.5km. Fr S exit A7 at junc 520, by-pass Garrucha, site on L in 6km. Med, hdg/mkd pitch, hdstg, pt shd; wc; chem disp; mv service pnt; baby facs; shwrs inc; el pnts (6A) €4.20; gas 3km; Indtte (inc dryer); shop; tradsmn; rest 500m; bar; BBQ; playgrnd; pool; jacuzzi; sand/shgl beach 350m; wifi; 10% statics; dogs €2; bus adj; poss cr; adv bkg; red low ssn/long stay; CCI. "Immac, well-maintained site; lge pitches; friendly owner; vg san facs; only 1 tap for drinking water; cycle track adj; beautiful coastline; mosquito problem; Fri mkt Garrucha; popular long stay site." ♦ € 22.60 2009*

⊞ **GARRUCHA** *4G1* (4km E Coastal) *37.22793, -1.80459* **Camping Almanzora (Naturist), Ctra Garrucha-Palomares, 04620 Vera (Almería) [950-46 74 74; fax 950-46 74 25; www.campingalmanzora.com]** SE on N340 Murcia-Almería rd, exit Vera, foll sp Garrucha. In 5km L & foll site sp. At junc with Garrucha & Villaricos rd turn L, then R at Vera Playa Hotel. Site on L at rndabt on hotel access rd. Lge, pt shd, wc; chem disp; mv service pnt; shwrs inc; baby facs; el pnts (16A) €3.50 (rec long lead); gas; Indtte; shop; tradsmn; rest; snacks; bar; playgrnd; pools; sand beach 300m; tennis; phone; few statics; dogs €2.25; phone; poss cr; adv bkg rec; quiet; ccard acc; red long stay; CCI. "Excel site but part o'looked fr main rd; many long-stay winter visitors; naturist beach adj; many pitches have shade awnings but sm & poss diff for lge o'fits; Friday mkt at Garrucha." € 23.00 2008*

GATA *1D3* (4km W Rural) *40.21145, -6.64208* **Camping Sierra de Gata, Ctra EX109 a Gata, Km 4.100, 10860 Gata (Cáceres) [927-67 21 68; fax 927-67 22 11; cgata@turiex.com; www.turiex.com/cgata]** Foll sp Gata fr rd EX109/C526, site sp on unmkd rd on rvside. Med, shd; wc; chem disp; shwrs; el pnts (5-10A) €4.25; gas; Indtte; shop; rest 100m; snacks; bar; playgrnd; pool; fishing; paddling pool; tennis; games area; cycle hire; entmnt; TV; statics; dogs €2; phone; quiet. "Peaceful, family-run site in beautiful area." ♦ 15 Feb-14 Mar. € 17.00 2008*

GAVA *3C3* (5km S Coastal) *41.27245, 2.04250* **Camping Tres Estrellas, C31, Km 186.2, 08850 Gavà (Barcelona) [936-33 06 37; fax 936-33 15 25; fina@camping3estrellas.com; www.camping3estrellas.com]** Fr S take C31 (Castelldefels to Barcelona), exit 13. Site at km 186.2 300m past rd bdge. Fr N foll Barcelona airport sp, then C31 junc 13 Gavà-Mar slip rd immed under rd bdge. Cross m'way, turn R then R again to join m'way heading N for 400m. Lge, mkd pitch, pt sl, pt shd; htd wc; chem disp; mv service pnt; shwrs inc; el pnts (6A) €5.40 (poss rev pol &/or no earth); gas; Indtte; shop; rest; snacks; bar; playgrnd; htd pool; sand beach adj; tennis; entmnt; internet; TV; 20% statics; dogs €5.40; phone; bus to Barcelona 400m; poss cr; Eng spkn; adv bkg; aircraft & rd noise & w/e noise fr disco nrby; ccard acc; red snr citizens/CCI. "20 min by bus to Barcelona cent; poss smells fr stagnant stream in corner of site; poss mosquitoes." ♦ 15 Mar-15 Oct. € 32.65 (CChq acc) 2008*

GERONA *3B3* (8km S Rural) *41.9224, 2.82864* **Camping Can Toni Manescal, Ctra de la Barceloneta, 17458 Fornells de la Selva (Gerona) [972-47 61 17; fax 972-47 67 35; campinggirona@campinggirona.com; www.campinggirona.com]** Fr N leave AP7 at junc 7 onto N11 dir Barcelona. In 2km turn L to Fornells de la Selva; in vill turn L at church (sp); over rv; in 1km bear R & site on L in 400m. NB Narr rd in Fornells vill not poss lge o'fits. Sm, mkd pitch, pt sl, pt shd; wc; chem disp; baby facs; shwrs inc; el pnts (5A) inc (poss long lead req); gas; Indtte; shop, rest 2km; snacks, bar 4km; playgrnd; pool; sand beach 23km; dogs; bus 1.5km; train nr; Eng spkn; adv bkg; quiet; ccard acc; CCI. "V pleasant, open site on farm; gd base for lovely medieval city Gerona - foll bus stn sp for gd, secure m'van parking; welcoming & helpful owners; lge pitches; ltd san facs; excel cycle path into Gerona, along old rlwy line; Gerona mid-May flower festival rec; gd touring base away fr cr coastal sites." 1 Jun-30 Sep. € 23.00 2009*

GETAFE see Madrid *1D4*

⊞ **GIJON** *1A3* (4km E Rural) *43.51365, -5.59896* **Camping Deva-Gijón, Parroquia de Deva, 33394 Deva (Asturias) [985-13 38 48; fax 985-13 38 89; info@campingdeva-gijon.com; www.campingdeva-gijon.com]** Exit A8 junc 382 N. Site nr km marker 65 - foll sp carefully. Lge, mkd pitch; pt sl, terr, pt shd; serviced pitches; wc; chem disp; shwrs inc; el pnts (16A) €3.30; Indtte; shop, rest, snacks in ssn; bar; pool & paddling pool; sand beach 4km; tennis; cycle hire; golf 3km; internet; 50% statics; bus nr; car wash; sep car park; poss cr; noisy visitors & nr rd; ccard acc €40 min; CCI. "Gd touring base for 2 National Parks; facs ltd low ssn & v open san facs not rec winter." ♦ € 23.60 2008*

⊞ **GIJON** *1A3* (9.5km NW Coastal) *43.58333, -5.7566* **Camping Perlora, Ctra Candás, Km 12, Perán, 33491 Candás (Asturias) [tel/fax 985-87 00 48; www.campings.com/perlora]** Exit A8 junc 404 dir Candás (take care staggered junc). In 9km at rndabt turn R sp Perlora (AS118). At sea turn L sp Candás, site on R. Avoid Sat mkt day. Med, mkd pitch, pt sl, terr, unshd; wc; chem disp; mv service pnt; some serviced pitches; shwrs inc; el pnts (5A) €3.50; gas; lndtte (inc dryer); shop; rest; playgrnd; sand beach 1km; tennis; watersports; fishing; 80% statics; dogs free; phone; bus adj; poss cr; Eng spkn; quiet; ccard not acc; red long stay. "Excel; helpful staff; lovely, immac site on dramatic headland; ltd space for tourers; superb san facs, ltd low ssn; easy walk to Candás." ♦ € 18.60 2009*

GIJON *1A3* (13km NW Coastal) *43.57575, -5.74530* **Camping Buenavista, Ctra Dormon-Perlora s/n, Carreño, 33491 Perlora (Asturias) [tel/fax 985-87 17 93; buenavista@campingbuenavista.com; www.campingbuenavista.com]** Fr Gijón take AS19 sp Tremañes & foll rd for approx 5km. On sharp L bend take exit on R (Avilés) & immed L onto AS239 sp Candás/Perlora, site sp. Med, terr, pt shd; wc; chem disp; shwrs; el pnts inc; gas; lndtte; shop; rest; snacks; bar; playgrnd; sand beach 500m; 70% statics; bus 200m; site open w/end only out of ssn & clsd Dec & Jan; poss cr; noisy; CCI. "Oviedo historic town worth a visit; quite steep pull-out, need gd power/weight ratio." 15 Jun-15 Sep. € 22.70 2007*

GIRONELLA *3B3* (500m S Rural) *42.01378, 1.87849* **Camping Gironella, Ctra C16/E9, Km 86.750 Entrada Sud Gironella, 08680 Gironella (Barcelona) [938-25 15 29; fax 938-22 97 37; informacio@campinggironella.com; www.campinggironella.cat]** Site is bet Berga & Puig-reig on C16/E9. Well sp. Med, hdg/mkd pitch, hdstg, pt shd; wc; chem disp; serviced pitch; baby facs; shwrs inc; el pnts (3-10A) €2.75-7; gas; lndtte; shop; tradsmn; rest; snacks; bar; playgrnd; htd pool; games rm; entmnt; TV rm; 90% statics; dogs €1; phone; bus 600m; poss cr; Eng spkn; adv bkg; quiet; CCI. "Pleasant site; friendly staff; ltd touring pitches (phone ahead); conv NH." ♦ Holy Week, 1 Jul-15 Sep & w/e low ssn. € 18.00 2007*

GORLIZ *1A4* (700m N Coastal) *43.41782, -2.93626* **Camping Arrien, Uresarantze Bidea, 48630 Gorliz (Bizkaia) [946-77 19 11; fax 946-77 44 80; arrien@teleline.es; www.campingarrien.com]** Fr Bilbao foll m'way to Getxo, then 637/634 thro Sopelana & Plentzia to Gorliz. In Gorliz turn L at 1st rndabt, pass tourist office on R, then R at next rndabt, strt over next, site on L adj sports cent/running track. Not sp locally. Lge, pt sl, pt shd; wc; chem disp; shwrs inc; el pnts (3-5A) €3.95; lndtte; gas; shop; rest; snacks; bar; BBQ; playgrnd; sand beach 700m; 60% statics; dogs €1; phone; bus 150m; poss cr; Eng spkn; ccard acc; red long stay/CCI. "Useful base for Bilbao & ferry (approx 1hr); bus to Plentzia every 20 mins, fr there can get metro to Bilbao; friendly, helpful staff; poss shortage of hot water." 1 Mar-31 Oct. € 22.90 2008*

GRANADA *2G4* (4km N Rural) *37.24194, -3.63333* **Camping Granada, Cerro de la Cruz s/n, 18210 Peligros (Granada) [tel/fax 958-34 05 48; pruizlopez1953@yahoo.es]** S on A44 fr Jaén twd Granada; take exit 121 & foll sp Peligros. Turn L at rndabt after 1km by Spar shop, site access rd 300m on R. Single track access 1km. Med, hdstg, terr, pt shd; wc; chem disp; shwrs inc; el pnts (5A) €4.32; gas; lndtte; shop; rest; bar; playgrnd; pool; tennis; dogs €1.30; bus 1km; poss cr; some Eng spkn; adv bkg; quiet; ccard acc; CCI. "Friendly, helpful owners; well-run site in olive grove; vg facs; superb views; gd access for m'vans but poss diff for v lge o'fits; pitches poss uneven & muddy after rain; site rds & access steep; conv Alhambra - book tickets at recep." ♦ Holy Week & 1 Jul-30 Sep. € 24.62 2009*

The opening dates and prices on this campsite have changed. I'll send a site report form to the Club for the next edition of the guide.

GRANADA *2G4* (4km N Urban) *37.19916, -3.61361* **Camping Motel Sierra Nevada, Avda de Madrid 107, 18014 Granada [958-15 00 62; fax 958-15 09 54; campingmotel@terra.es; www.campingsierranevada.com]** App Granada S-bound on A44 & exit at junc 123, foll dir Granada. Site on R in 1.5km just beyond bus stn & opp El Campo supmkt, well sp. Lge, shd; wc; chem disp; mv service pnt; baby facs; shwrs inc; el pnts (6A) €4.20; gas; lndtte (inc dryer); supmkt opp; rest; snacks; BBQ; playgrnd; 2 pools adj; sports facs; wifi; dogs; bus to city cent 500m; poss cr (arr early); Eng spkn; noisy at w/end; ccard acc; CCI. "V helpful staff; excel san facs, but poss ltd low ssn; motel rms avail; can book Alhambra tickets at recep (24 hrs notice); conv city." ♦ 1 Mar-31 Oct. € 25.60 2009*

⊞ **GRANADA** *2G4* (13km E Rural) *37.16085, -3.45388* **Camping Las Lomas, 11 Ctra de Güejar-Sierra, Km 6.5, 18160 Güejar-Sierra (Granada) [958-48 47 42; fax 958-48 40 00; laslomas@campings.net; www.campinglaslomas.com]** Fr A44 exit onto by-pass 'Ronda Sur', then exit onto A395 sp Sierra Nevada. In approx 4km exit sp Cenes, turn under A395 to T-junc & turn R sp Güejar-Sierra, Embalse de Canales. After approx 3km turn L at sp Güejar-Sierra & site. Site on R 6.5km up winding mountain rd. Med, hdg/mkd pitch, terr, pt shd; htd wc; chem disp; mv service pnt; baby facs; fam bthrm; shwrs inc; el pnts (10A) €3.50 (poss no earth/rev pol); gas; lndtte; shop; rest; snacks; bar; playgrnd; pool; waterskiing nrby; internet; dogs free; bus adj; poss cr; Eng spkn; adv bkg ess; quiet; red long stay; ccard acc; CCI. "Helpful, friendly owners; well-run site; conv Granada (bus at gate); access poss diff for lge o'fits; excel san facs; gd shop & rest; beautiful mountain scenery; excel site." ♦ € 26.00 2009*

⊞ **GRANADA** *2G4* (3km SE Urban) *37.12444, -3.58611* **Camping Reina Isabel, Calle de Laurel de la Reina, 18140 La Zubia (Granada) [958-59 00 41; fax 958-59 11 91; info@reinaisabelcamping.com; www.reinaisabelcamping.com]** Exit A44 nr Granada at junc sp Ronda Sur, dir Sierra Nevada, Alhambra, then exit 2 sp La Zubia. Foll site sp approx 1.2km on R; narr ent set back fr rd. Med, hdg pitch, hdstg, pt shd; htd wc; chem disp; mv service pnt; baby facs; shwrs inc; el pnts (5A) €2.90 (poss rev pol); gas; Indtte; shop; supmkt 1km; tradsmn; snacks; bar; pool high ssn; internet; TV; dogs free; phone; bus to Granada cent; Eng spkn; poss cr; adv bkg rec at all times; quiet except during festival in May; ccard acc; red long stay/low ssn; red CCI. "Well-run, busy site; poss shwrs v hot/cold - warn children; helpful staff; ltd touring pitches & sm; poss student groups; conv Alhambra (order tickets at site)." ♦ € 21.00 2009*

⊞ **GRANADA** *2G4* (12km S Rural) *37.06785, -3.65176* **Camping Suspiro del Moro, 107 Avda de Madrid, 18630 Otura (Granada) [tel/fax 958-55 54 11; info@campingsuspirodelmoro.com; www.campingsuspirodelmoro.com]** On A44/E902 dir Motril, exit junc 139. Foll camp sp fr W side of rndabt; site visible at top of slight rise on W side of A44, 1km S of Otura. Med, mkd pitch, hdstg, shd; wc; chem disp; mv service pnt; shwrs inc; el pnts (5A) €3 (poss no earth); gas; Indry rm; shop; snacks & rest in ssn; bar; playgrnd; lge pool; tennis; games area; 10% statics; phone; bus to Granada adj; Eng spkn; rd noise & noisy rest at w/end; red low ssn; ccard acc; CCI. "Decent site; reasonable pitches; quiet low ssn; clean facs but inadequate for site this size." ♦ € 19.10 2007*

⊞ **GRANADA** *2G4* (10km W Rural) *37.19150, -3.65444* **Camping Maria Eugenia, Avda Andalucia 190, Santa Fé, 18014 Granada [958-20 06 06; fax 958-20 63 17; campingmariaeugenia@gmail.com; www.campingmariaeugenia.com]** On A329/A92G fr Granada dir Antequera.Fr W exit A92 junc 230 dir Granada. By-pass Santa Fé, site on R in 3km, nr airport - sps last minutes only. Sm, mkd pitch, pt shd; wc; chem disp; mv service pnt; shwrs inc; el pnts (10-16A) €3.60-4.60; Indtte; shop; rest; snacks; bar; BBQ; pool; TV; 30% statics; dogs; phone; bus fr site ent; poss cr; rd noise. "Friendly, family-run site; unkempt low ssn; conv Granada, bus adj; NH only." € 19.60 2008*

⊞ **GRAUS** *3B2* (6km S Rural) *42.13069, 0.30980* **Camping Bellavista & Subenuix, Embalse de Barasona, Ctra Graus N123, Km 23, 22435 La Puebla de Castro (Huesca) [974-54 51 13; fax 974 34 70 71; info@hotelcampingbellavista.com; www.hotelcampingbellavista.com]** Fr E on N230/N123 ignore 1st sp for Graus. Cont to 2nd sp 'El Grado/Graus' & turn R. Site on L in 1km adj hotel. Med, mkd pitch, terr, pt shd; htd wc; chem disp; shwrs inc; el pnts (10A) €3.50; gas; Indry rm; shop; rest; snacks; bar; playgrnd; pool; lake sw adj; watersports; fishing; tennis; horseriding; entmnt; internet; TV rm; 50% statics; dogs €1.50; phone; Eng spkn; adv bkg; noisy at w/end; red low ssn; ccard acc; CCI. "V helpful staff; sm pitches; excel rest; beautiful position above lake; mountain views." € 17.90 2006*

GRAUS *3B2* (5km SW Rural) *42.13130, 0.30871* **Camping Lago Barasona, Ctra N123A, Km 25, 22435 La Puebla de Castro (Huesca) [974-54 51 48 or 974-24 69 06; fax 974-54 52 28; info@lagobarasona.com; www.lagobarasona.com]** Fr E on N123, ignore 1st sp for Graus. Cont to 2nd sp 'El Grado/Graus/Benasque' & turn R. Site on L in 2km. Lge, hdg/mkd pitch, hdstg, sl, terr, shd; htd wc; chem disp; mv service pnt; shwrs inc; el pnts (6A) €5.60 gas; Indry rm; shop; tradsmn; rest; snacks; bar; BBQ; playgrnd; 2 pools; lake beach & sw 100m; watersports; sailing; tennis; horseriding 1km; entmnt; TV rm; 15% statics; dogs €2.80; Eng spkn; adv bkg; quiet; ccard acc; red long stay; CCI. "Excel, well-equipped site; lge pitches; v helpful staff; adj reservoir water levels likely to drop; highly rec." ♦ 1 Mar-10 Dec. € 23.60 (CChq acc) 2008*

GUADALUPE *2E3* (1.5km S Rural) *39.44232, -5.31708* **Camping Las Villuercas, Ctra Villanueva-Huerta del Río, Km 2, 10140 Guadalupe (Cáceres) [927-36 71 39; fax 927-36 70 28]** Exit A5/E90 at junc 178 onto EX118 to Guadalupe. Do not ent town. Site sp on R at rndabt at foot of hill. Med, shd; wc; shwrs; el pnts €2.50 (poss no earth/rev pol); Indtte; shop; rest; bar; playgrnd; pool; tennis; ccard acc. "Vg; helpful owners; ltd facs low ssn; some pitches sm & poss not avail in wet weather; nr famous monastery." 1 Mar-15 Dec. € 12.50 2007*

⊞ **GUARDA, A** *1B2* (2km E Coastal) *41.89876, -8.84703* **Camping Santa Tecla, Ctra Tui-La Guardía, Salcidos, 36780 A Guarda (Pontevedra) [986-61 30 11; fax 986-61 30 63; campingstatecla@telefonica.net; www.campingsantatecla.com]** S fr Vigo on PO552 coast rd. Site well sp thro A Guarda. Lge, mkd pitch, pt shd; wc; chem disp; mv service pnt; shwrs; el pnts €3.70; gas; Indtte; shop; rest; bar; playgrnd; pool; rv sw adj; games area; dogs; bus 1km; Eng spkn; quiet; red low ssn. "Views across estuary to Portugal; 2km fr ferry; excel san facs; ltd facs low ssn; unreliable opening low ssn - poss w/end only - phone ahead." ♦ € 22.50 2008*

⊞ **GUARDAMAR DEL SEGURA** *4F2* (2km N Rural/Coastal) *38.10916, -0.65472* **Camping Marjal, Ctra N332, Km 73.4, 03140 Guardamar del Segura (Alicante) [966-72 70 70 or 966-72 50 22; fax 966-72 66 95; camping@marjal.com; www.campingmarjal.com]** Fr N exit A7 junc 72 sp Aeropuerto/Santa Pola; in 5km turn R onto N332 sp Santa Pola/Cartagena, U-turn at km 73.4, site sp on R at km 73.5. Fr S exit AP7 at junc 740 onto CV91 twd Guardamar. In 9km join N332 twd Alicante, site on R at next rndabt. Lge, hdg/mkd pitch, hdstg, pt shd; all serviced pitches; wc; chem disp; baby facs; sauna; shwrs inc; el pnts (16A) €3 or metered; gas; Indtte; supmkt; rest; snacks & bar; BBQ; playgrnd; 2 htd pools (1 covrd); sand beaches 1km (inc naturist); lake sw 15km; tennis; sports cent; cycle hire; entmnt; internet; TV rm; 18% statics; dogs €2.20; phone; recep 0800-2300; adv bkg rec; Eng spkn; quiet; red long stay/low ssn; ccard acc; CCI. "Gd facs; friendly, helpful staff; excel family entmnt & activities; excel." ♦ € 63.00 2009*

See advertisement on next page

Spain

GUARDAMAR DEL SEGURA *4F2* (1km S Coastal) *38.07298, -0.65294* **Camping Palm-Mar, 03140 Guardamar del Segura (Alicante) [tel/fax 965-72 88 56; admin@camping palmmar.es; www.campingpalmmar.es]** Foll site sp fr N332 at x-rds, twds sea. Med, hdg/mkd pitch, pt shd; wc; chem disp; mv service pnt; baby facs; shwrs inc; el pnts (3A) €5; Indtte; shop; rest; snacks; bar; BBQ; playgrnd; sand beach adj; internet; TV rm; 20% statics; dogs; bus adj; no adv bkg; quiet; red long stay." 1 Jun-30 Sep. € 30.00 2008*

GUARDIOLA DE BERGUEDA *3B3* (3.5km SW Rural) *42.21602, 1.83705* **Camping El Berguedà, Ctra B400, Km 3.5, 08694 Guardiola de Berguedà (Barcelona) [938-22 74 32; campingbergueda@gmail.com; www.campingbergueda.com]** On C16 S take B400 W dir Saldes. Site is approx 10km S of Cadí Tunnel. Med, mkd pitch, some hdstg, terr, pt shd; wc; chem disp; baby facs; shwrs; el pnts (6A) €3.90 (poss rev pol); gas; Indtte; shop; tradsmn; rest; snacks; bar; BBQ; playgrnd; pool; paddling pool; games area; games rm; TV; some statics; phone; dogs; Eng spkn; quiet; CCI. "V helpful staff; vg san facs; beautiful, remote situation; gd walking; poss open w/ends in winter; a gem!" ♦ Easter-30 Nov. € 18.20 2008*

GUEJAR SIERRA see Granada *2G4*

GUITIRIZ *1A2* (1km N Rural) **Camping El Mesón, 27305 Guitiriz (Lugo) [982-37 32 88]** On A6 NW fr Lugo, exit km 535 sp Guitiriz, site sp. Sm, pt sl, pt shd; wc; chem disp (wc); shwrs inc; el pnts (6A) €3.30; gas; supmkt 1km; rest; bar; playgrnd; pool 6km; rv sw 500m; phone; bus adj; quiet. 15 Jun-15 Sep. € 15.00 2008*

⊞ **HARO** *1B4* (600m N Urban) *42.57916, -2.85583* **Camping de Haro, Avda Miranda 1, 26200 Haro (La Rioja) [941-31 27 37; fax 941-31 20 68; campingdeharo@fer.es; www.campingdeharo.com]** Fr N or S on N124 take exit sp Haro. In 500m at rndabt take 1st exit, under rlwy bdge, cont to site on R immed bef rv bdge. Fr AP68 exit junc 9 to town; at 2nd rndabt turn L onto LR111 (sp Logroño). Immed after rv bdge turn sharp L & foll site sp. Avoid cont into town cent. Med, hdg/mkd pitch, pt shd; htd wc; chem disp; mv service pnt; shwrs inc (am only in winter); el pnts (5-6A) €3.85; gas; Indtte (inc dryer); shop & 600m; snacks; bar; playgrnd; htd pool high ssn; wifi; 70% statics; dogs €2.40; phone; bus 800m; car wash; site clsd 8 Dec-10 Jan; poss cr; Eng spkn; adv bkg; quiet (not w/end), some rv noise; red low ssn; ccard acc; CCI. "Clean, tidy site but dusty rds & poss untidy low ssn; friendly owner; some sm pitches & diff turns; excel facs; statics busy at w/ends; conv Rioja 'bodegas'; conv Bilbao & Santander ferries; conv NH." ♦ € 19.80 (CChq acc) 2009*

⊞ **HARO** *1B4* (10km SW Rural) *42.53017, -2.92173* **Camping De La Rioja, Ctra de Haro/Santo Domingo de la Calzada, Km 8.5, 26240 Castañares de la Rioja (La Rioja) [941-30 01 74; fax 941-30 01 56; info@camping delarioja.com]** Exit AP68 junc 9, take rd twd Santo Domingo de la Calzada. Foll by-pass round Casalarreina, site on R nr rvside just past vill on rd LR111. Lge, hdg pitch, pt shd; htd wc; chem disp; shwrs; el pnts (4A) €3.90 (poss rev pol); gas; Indtte (inc dryer); sm shop; rest; snacks; bar; pool high ssn; tennis; cycle hire; entmnt; dogs; clsd 10 Dec-8 Jan; 90% statics; dogs; bus adj; site clsd 9 Dec-11 Jan; poss cr; adv bkg; noisy high ssn; ccard acc. "Fair site but fairly isolated; basic san facs but clean; ltd facs in winter; sm pitches; conv for Rioja wine cents; Bilbao ferry." € 26.80 2009*

⊞ **HECHO** *3B1* (8km N Rural) *42.7878, -0.7300* **Camping Borda Bisáltico, Ctra Gabardito, Km 2, 22720 Hecho (Huesca) [974-37 53 88; info@bordabisaltico.com; www. bordabisaltico.com]** Fr Jaca W on N240 dir Pamplona, after 25km at Puente La Reina turn R onto A176 then take HU210. Foll sp. Site in 8km. Take care, 1.5km narr, winding, potholed rd. Med, sl, terr, pt shd; wc; chem disp; mv service pnt; baby facs; shwrs inc; el pnts (3A) €4; gas; Indtte; tradsmn; rest; bar; no statics; site clsd 2-30 Nov; dogs; phone; bus; quiet; CCI. "Well-organised site; friendly owners; beautiful views; excel, modern san facs; gd walking, climbing, birdwatching; poss erratic elec supply (generator) & pitches not level; phone ahead to check open low ssn; excel." € 17.50 2008*

This is a wonderful site.

I'll fill in a report online and let the Club know – www.caravanclub.co.uk/europereport

⊞ **HECHO** *3B1* (1km S Rural) *42.73222, -0.75305* **Camping Valle de Hecho, Ctra Puente La Reina-Hecho s/n, 22720 Hecho (Huesca) [974-37 53 61; fax 976-27 78 42; www. campinghecho.com]** Leave Jaca W on N240. After 25km turn N on A176 at Puente La Reina de Jaca. Site on W of rd, o'skts of Hecho/Echo. Med, mkd pitch, pt sl, pt shd; htd wc; chem disp; mv service pnt; shwrs inc; el pnts (5-15A) €4.70; gas; Indtte; shop; rest; snacks; bar; playgrnd; pool; games area; 50% statics; dogs; phone; bus 200m; quiet; ccard acc; CCI. "Pleasant site in foothills of Pyrenees; excel, spotless facs but poss inadequate hot water; gd birdwatching area; Hecho fascinating vill; shop & bar clsd low ssn except w/end; v ltd facs & poss neglected low ssn." € 19.50 2008*

HERRADURA, LA see Almuñécar *2H4*

HONDARRIBIA see Irun *3A1*

⊞ **HORCAJO DE LOS MONTES** *2E4* (200m E Rural) *39.32440, -4.6358* **Camping El Mirador de Cabañeros, Calle Cañada Real Segoviana s/n, 13110 Horcajo de los Montes (Ciudad Real) [926-77 54 39; fax 926-77 50 03; camping-cabaneros@hortur.com; www.campingcabaneros.com]** At km 53 off CM4103 Horcajo-Alcoba rd, 200m fr vill. CM4106 to Horcajo fr NW poor in parts. Med, mkd pitch, hdstg, terr, pt shd; htd wc; chem disp; mv service pnt; baby facs; shwrs; el pnts (6A) €3.50; gas; shop 500m; rest; bar; BBQ; playgrnd; pool; rv sw 12km; games area; games rm; tennis 500m; cycle hire; entmnt; TV; 10% statics; phone; adv bkg rec high ssn; quiet; red long stay/low ssn; ccard acc; CCI. "Beside Cabañeros National Park; beautiful views." ♦ € 19.50 2009*

HORNOS *4F1* (9km SW Rural) *38.18666, -2.77277* **Camping Montillana Rural, Ctra Tranco-Hornos A319, km 78.5, 23292 Hornos de Segura (Jaén) [953-12 61 94 or 680-15 21 10 (mob); www.campingmontillana.com]** Fr N on N322 take A310 then A317 S then A319 dir Tranco & Cazorla. Site nr km 78.5, ent by 1st turning. Fr S on N322 take A6202 N of Villanueva del Arzobispo. In 26km at Tranco turn L onto A319 & nr km 78.5 ent by 1st turning up slight hill. Sm, mkd pitch, hdstg, terr, pt shd; wc; chem disp; shwrs inc; el pnts (10A) €3.20; Indtte; shop; tradsmn; rest; snacks; bar; pool; lake adj; 5% statics; dogs; phone; some Eng spkn; adv bkg; quiet; CCI. "Beautiful area; conv Segura de la Sierra, Cazorla National Park; much wildlife; friendly, helpful staff; gd site." 19 Mar-15 Oct. € 14.00 2008*

HOSPITAL DE ORBIGO *1B3* (N Urban) *42.4664, -5.8836* **Camp Municipal Don Suero, 24286 Hospital de Órbigo (León) [987-36 10 18; fax 987-38 82 36; camping@ hospitaldeorbigo.com; www.hospitaldeorbigo.com]** N120 rd fr León to Astorga, km 30. Site well sp fr N120. Narr streets in Hospital. Med, hdg pitch, pt shd; wc; shwrs; el pnts (6A) €1.90; Indtte (inc dryer); shop, bar high ssn; rest adj; BBQ; pool adj; bus to León nr; 50% statics; dogs; bus 1km; poss open w/end only mid Apr-May; phone; poss cr; Eng spkn; ccard acc; CCI. "Statics v busy w/ends, facs stretched; poss noisy; phone ahead to check site open if travelling close to opening/closing dates." ♦ Holy Week-30 Sep. € 14.40 2009*

⊞ **HOSPITALET DE L'INFANT, L'** *3C2* (2km S Coastal) *40.97750, 0.90361* **Camping Cala d'Oques, Via de Augusta s/n, 43890 L'Hospitalet de l'Infant (Tarragona) [977-82 32 54; fax 977-82 06 91; eroller@tinet.org; www. usuaris.tinet.org/eroller]** Exit AP7 junc 38 onto N340. Take rd sp L'Hospitalet de l'Infant at km 1123. Lge, terr, shd; htd wc; mv service pnt; baby facs; shwrs; el pnts (5-10A) €4.30; gas; Indtte; shop; rest; bar; playgrnd; sand/shgl beach adj (naturist beaches nr); internet; entmnt; dogs €2.95; phone; poss cr; Eng spkn; some rlwy & rd noise; ltd facs low ssn; red snr citizens/long stay/low ssn; CCI. "Winter NH; friendly, relaxing; facs outdated; site poss unkempt low ssn; vg rest; sea views; poss v windy; conv Aquapolis & Port Aventura." € 36.40 2008*

Spain

HOSPITALET DE L'INFANT, L' *3C2* (2km S Coastal) *40.97722, 0.90083* **Camping El Templo del Sol (Naturist), Polígon 14-15, Playa del Torn, 43890 L'Hospitalet de l'Infant (Tarragona) [977-82 34 34; fax 977-82 34 64; info@eltemplodelsol.com; www.eltemplodelsol.com]** Leave A7 at exit 38 or N340 twds town cent. Turn R (S) along coast rd for 2km. Ignore 1st camp sp on L, site 200m further on L. Lge, hdg/mkd pitch, pt sl, pt shd; wc; chem disp; serviced pitch; shwrs inc; el pnts (6A) inc; gas; lndtte; shop; rest; snacks; bar; playgrnd; pools; solar-energy park; jacuzzi; official naturist sand/shgl beach adj; cinema/theatre; TV rm; 5% statics; poss cr; Eng spkn; adv bkg (dep); some rlwy noise rear of site; ccard acc; red long stay/low ssn. "Excel naturist site; no dogs, radios or TV on pitches; lge private wash/shwr rms; pitches v tight; conv Port Aventura; mosquito problem; poss strong winds - take care with awnings." ♦ 22 Mar-22 Oct. € 40.45 2007*

⊞ **HOSPITALET DE L'INFANT, L'** *3C2* (8km S Coastal) *40.94024, 0.85688* **Camping La Masia, Playa de l'Almadrava, Km 1121, N340, 43890 L'Hospitalet de l'Infant (Tarragona) [977-82 31 02 or 82 05 88; fax 977-82 33 54]** Site sp on sea side of N340 at km 1121. Med, hdstg, sl, terr, pt shd; wc; chem disp (wc); jaccuzi; baby facs; sauna; shwrs inc; el pnts (5A) €4; lndtte; shop; rest; bar; BBQ; playgrnd; pool; beach adj; gym; tennis; games area; squash; minigolf; cycle hire; horseriding 5km; golf 6km; entmnt; games/TV rm; internet; 80% statics; phone; site clsd Jan; poss cr; rlwy noise. "Not rec lge o'fits due poss diff access to pitches." ♦ € 31.50 2008*

HOYOS DEL ESPINO *1D3* (4km E Rural) *40.34313, -5.13131* **Camping Navagredos, Ctra de Valdecasas, 05635 Navarredonda de Gredos (Ávila) [920-20 74 76; fax 983-29 58 41; proatur@proatur.com]** Fr N take N502 S. Then W on C500 twd El Barco. Site sp in Navarredonda on L in 2km, just bef petrol stn. Med, pt sl, pt shd; wc; chem disp; mv service pnt; baby facs; shwrs inc; el pnts (10A) €2.73; lndry rm; shops 2km; tradsmn; rest & snacks in ssn; bar; phone; quiet. "Excel walking in Gredos mountains; some facs poorly maintained low ssn; steep slope to san facs; rd on app to site steep with bends; site open w/ends until mid-Nov." ♦ Easter-12 Oct. € 12.65 2006*

HOYOS DEL ESPINO *1D3* (1.5km S Rural) *40.34055, -5.17527* **Camping Gredos, Ctra Plataforma, Km.1.8, 05634 Hoyos del Espino (Ávila) [920-20 75 85; campingredos@campingredos.com; www.campingredos.com]** Fr N110 turn E at El Barco onto AV941 for approx 41km; at Hoyos del Espino turn S twd Plataforma de Gredos. Site on R in 1.8km. Or fr N502 turn W onto AV941 dir Parador de Gredos to Hoyos del Espino, then as above. Sm, pt sl, pt shd; wc; chem disp; shwrs inc; el pnts €2.90; gas; lndtte; shop 1km; snacks; playgrnd; rv sw adj; cycle hire; horseriding; adv bkg; quiet; CCI. "Lovely mountain scenery." ♦ Holy Week & 1 May-1 Oct. € 12.20 2007*

⊞ **HUELVA** *2G2* (8km SE Coastal) *37.12527, -6.79944* **Camping Playa de Mazagón, Calle Cuesta de la Barca, s/n, 21130 Mazagón (Huelva) [959-37 62 08; fax 959-53 62 56; info@campingplayamazagon.com; www.campingplayamazagon.com]** Best app fr A494 fr Matalascañas, site clearly sp. Of fr A49 ent Huelva & eventually pick up & foll sp twds indus zone. Head for coast, keep sea on R; over bdge & strt on twds Mazagón; site on R clearly sp off rd up hill. Lge, mkd pitch, pt shd; wc; chem disp; shwrs inc; el pnts (10A) €9; gas; lndtte; shop; rest; snacks; bar; playgrnd; pool; paddling pool; sand beach adj; 75% statics; dogs €3.20; phone; bus adj; poss cr; quiet; ccard acc; red low ssn/CCI. "Close to Doñana National Park; poss exposed low ssn; poss unclean; some pitches v soft; not suitable m'vans 3,000 kg & over; fair sh stay/NH only." € 34.75 2009*

HUESCA *3B2* (1.5km SW Urban) *42.13725, -0.41900* **Camping San Jorge, Calle Ricardo del Arco s/n, 22004 Huesca [tel/fax 974-22 74 16; contacto@campingsanjorge.com; www.campingsanjorge.com]** Exit A23 S of town at km 568 & head N twd town cent. Site well sp adj municipal pool & leisure facs. Med, shd; wc; chem disp (wc); shwrs inc; el pnts (10A) €3.40; lndtte; shop; snacks; bar; 2 pools; internet; dogs; bus 300m; ccard acc; CCI. "Grassy pitches poss flooded after heavy rain; san facs gd but poss stretched high ssn; vg pool; friendly; conv town cent; gd supmkt 250m; gd NH." 1 Apr-15 Oct. € 15.90 2009*

⊞ **IRUN** *3A1* (2km N Rural) *43.36638, -1.80436* **Camping Jaizkibel, Ctra Guadalupe Km 22, 20280 Hondarribia (Guipúzkoa) [943-64 16 79; fax 943-64 26 53; jaizkibel@campingseuskadi.com; www.campingseuskadi.com/jaizkibel]** Fr Hondarribia/Fuenterrabia inner ring rd foll sp to site below old town wall. Do not ent town. Med, hdg pitch, pt hdstg, terr, pt shd; wc; baby facs; shwrs; el pnts (2-6A) €3.62 (check earth); lndtte; tradsmn; rest; bar; BBQ; playgrnd; sand beach 1.5km; tennis; 90% statics; no dogs; phone; bus 1km; adv bkg; quiet; red low ssn; ccard acc; CCI. "Easy 20 mins walk to historic town; v scenic area; gd walking; gd touring base but ltd space on site for tourers; clean facs; gd rest & bar." € 16.10 2007*

⊞ **IRUN** *3A1* (3km S Rural) *43.31540, -1.87419* **Camping Oliden, Ctra NI Madrid-Irún, Km 470, 20180 Oiartzun (Guipúzkoa) [943-49 07 28; oliden@campingseuskadi.com; www.campingseuskadi.com/oliden]** On S side of N1 at E end of vill. Lge, pt sl, pt shd; wc; chem disp; shwrs; el pnts (5A) €3.40; lndtte; shops adj; bar; playgrnd; pool in ssn; beach 10km; rlwy & factory noise; red CCI. "Steps to shwrs, diff access for disabled; san facs old but clean; grass pitches v wet low ssn; NH only." € 19.60 2006*

⊞ **ISABA** *3B1* (13km E Rural) *42.86607, -0.81195* **Camping Zuriza, Ctra Anso-Zuriza, Km 14, 22728 Anso (Huesca) [974-37 01 96; www.lospirineos.info/campingzuriza]** On NA 137 N fr Isaba, turn R 4km onto NA 2000 to Zuriza. Foll sp to site. Fr Ansó, take HU 2024 N to Zuriza. Foll sp to site; narr, rough rd not rec for underpowered o'fits. Lge, pt sl, pt shd; wc; some serviced pitches; shwrs inc; el pnts €3.75; Indry rm; shop; tradsmn; rest; bar; playgrnd; 50% statics; phone; quiet; ccard acc; CCI. "Beautiful, remote valley; no vill at Zuriza, nearest vills Isaba & Ansó; no direct route to France; superb location for walking." € 16.85 2006*

ISLA *1A4* (4km SW Rural) *43.46446, -3.60773* **Camping Los Molinos de Bareyo, 39190 Bareyo (Cantabria) [942-67 05 69; losmolinosdebareyo@ceoecant.es; www.campingsonline.com/molinosdebareyo/]** Exit A8 at km 185 & foll sp for Beranga, Noja. Bef Noja at rndabt take L for Ajo, site sp on L up hill. Do not confuse with Cmp Los Molinos in Noja. V lge, mkd pitch, terr, pt shd; htd wc; chem disp; shwrs inc; el pnts (3A) €3; Indtte; shop; rest; snacks; bar; BBQ; playgrnd; htd pool; sand beach 4km; tennis; games area; TV rm; 60% statics; dogs; phone; bus 1km; site clsd mid Dec-end Jan; poss cr; Eng spkn; adv bkg; CCI. "Vg site on hill with views of coast; lively but not o'crowded high ssn." ♦ Easter & 1 Jun-30 Sep. € 20.50 2008*

ISLA *1A4* (1km NW Coastal) *43.50261, -3.54351* **Camping Playa de Isla, Calle Ardanal 1, 39195 Isla (Cantabria) [tel/fax 942-67 93 61; consultas@playadeisla.com; www.playadeisla.com]** Turn off A8/E70 at km 185 Beranga sp Noja & Isla. Foll sp Isla. In town to beach, site sp to L. Then in 100m keep R along narr seafront lane (main rd bends L) for 1km (rd looks like dead end). Med, mkd pitch, pt sl, terr, pt shd; wc; chem disp; shwrs inc; el pnts (3A) €4.50; gas; Indtte; shop & 1km; snacks; bar; playgrnd; sand beach adj; 90% statics; no dogs; phone; bus 1km; poss cr; quiet; ccard acc; CCI. "Beautiful situation; ltd touring pitches; busy at w/end." Easter-30 Sep. € 28.25 2009*

⊞ **ISLA CRISTINA** *2G2* (1.5km E Coastal) *37.19976, -7.30075* **Camping Giralda, Ctra La Antilla, Km 1.5, 21410 Isla Cristina [959-34 33 18; fax 959-34 32 84; campinggiralda@infonegocia.com; www.campinggiralda.com]** Exit A49 sp Isla Cristina & go thro town heading E (speed bumps in town). Or exit A49 at km 117 sp Lepe. In Lepe turn S on H4116 to La Antilla, then R on coast rd to Isla Cristina & site. V lge, mkd/hdstg/sandy pitches; shd, wc; chem disp; mv service pnt; baby facs; shwrs inc; el pnts €5.90; gas; Indtte; shop; rest; snacks; bar; playgrnd; pool high ssn; paddling pool; sand beach nrby; windsurfing; TV rm; 20% statics; dogs €2.60; poss cr, even low ssn; Eng spkn; red long stay/low ssn; ccard acc. "V helpful staff; some pitches uneven & muddy in wet weather; unkempt low ssn; san facs OK, irreg cleaning low ssn; diff for lge o'fits; narr site rds, some high kerbs; gd winter stay." ♦ € 25.70 2008*

⊞ **ISLA CRISTINA** *2G2* (4km E Coastal) *37.20555, -7.26722* **Camping Playa Taray, Ctra La Antilla-Isla Cristina, Km 9, 21430 La Redondela (Huelva) [959-34 11 02; fax 959-34 11 96; www.campingtaray.com]** Fr W exit A49 sp Isla Cristina & go thro town heading E. Fr E exit A49 at km 117 sp Lepe. In Lepe turn S on H4116 to La Antilla, then R on coast rd to Isla Cristina & site. Lge, pt shd; wc; mv service pnt; shwrs; el pnts (10) €4.28; gas; Indtte; shop; bar; rest; playrnd; sand beach adj; some statics; phone; dogs; bus; quiet; ccard acc; red long stay/low ssn; CCI. "Gd birdwatching, cycling; less cr than other sites in area in winter; poss untidy low ssn & ltd facs; poss diff for lge o'fits; friendly, helpful owner." ♦ € 19.10 2007*

⊞ **ISLA CRISTINA** *2G2* (7km E Coastal) *37.20796, -7.25222* **Camping Luz, Ctra La Antilla-Isla Cristina, Km 5, 21410 Isla Cristina (Huelva) [959-34 11 42; fax 059-48 64 54]** Fr W exit A49 sp Isla Cristina & go thro town heading E. Fr E exit A49 at km 117 sp Lepe. In Lepe turn S on H4116 to La Antilla, then R on coast rd to Isla Cristina & site. Med, pt sl, pt shd; wc; shwrs inc; el pnts (5A) inc; gas; Indtte; shop & 3km; tradsmn; rest; snacks; bar; BBQ; playgrnd; pool; beach 200m; 40% statics; dogs; phone; bus 50m; poss cr; rd noise/noisy at w/end; red long stay; CCI. "V friendly staff, well-managed; vg shwrs; ltd facs low ssn; uneven pitches; poss diff for lge o'fits." € 35.00 (3 persons) 2008*

ISLA PLANA see Puerto de Mazarrón *4G1*

ISLARES see Oriñón *1A4*

ITZIAR see Deba *3A1*

⊞ **IZNATE** *2G4* (1km NE Rural) *36.78449, -4.17442* **Camping Iznate, Ctra Iznate-Benamocarra s/n, 29792 Iznate (Málaga) [952-03 06 06; fax 952-55 61 93; info@campingiznate.com; www.campingiznate.com]** Exit A7/E15 junc 265 dir Cajiz & Iznate. Med, mkd pitch, hdstg, unshd; wc; chem disp; shwrs; el pnts (15A) €3 (poss no earth); gas; Indtte; shop; rest; snacks; bar; pool; shgl beach 8km; no statics; dogs €2; bus adj; Eng spkn; quiet; red long stay. "Beautiful scenery & mountain villages; conv Vélez-Málaga & Torre del Mar; pleasant owners." € 17.30 2007*

⊞ **JACA** *3B2* (2km W Urban) *42.56416, -0.57027* **Camping Victoria, Avda de la Victoria 34, 22700 Jaca (Huesca) [974-35 70 08; fax 974-35 70 09; campingvictoria@eresmas.com; www.campingvictoria.es]** Fr Jaca cent take N240 dir Pamplona, site on R. Med, mkd pitch, pt shd; wc; chem disp; mv service pnt; shwrs inc; el pnts (10A) €5; Indtte; snacks; bar; BBQ; playgrnd; htd pool high ssn; 80% statics; dogs; bus adj; quiet. "Basic facs, but clean & well-maintained; friendly staff; conv NH/sh stay Somport Pass." € 20.00 2009*

Spain

JARANDILLA DE LA VERA *1D3* (2km W Rural) *40.12723, -5.69318* **Camping Yuste, N501, Km 47, 10440 Aldeaneuva de la Vera (Cáceres) [927-57 26 59]** Fr Plasencia head E on EX203 following sp for Parador, site at km stone 47 in Aldeaneuva de la Vera. Clearly sp down narr rd. Med, shd; wc; shwrs; el pnts €3.20; gas; snacks; bar; pool; tennis; bus 500m; phone; quiet. "Simple, well-maintained, attractive site." 1 Apr-30 Sep. € 12.90 2006*

⊞ **JAVEA/XABIA** *4E2* (1km S Rural) *38.78333, 0.17294* **Camping Jávea, Camí de la Fontana 10, 03730 Jávea (Alicante) [965-79 10 70; fax 966-46 05 07; info@camping-javea.com; www.camping-javea.com]** Exit N332 for Jávea on A132, cont in dir Port on CV734. At rndabt & Lidl supmkt, take slip rd to R immed after rv bdge sp Arenal Platjas & Cap de la Nau. Strt on at next rndabt to site sp & slip rd 100m sp Autocine. If you miss slip rd go back fr next rndabt. Lge, mkd pitch, pt shd; wc; chem disp; baby facs; shwrs inc; el pnts (8A) €4.50 (long lead rec); gas; Indtte; shop 500m; tradsmn; rest; snacks; bar; BBQ; playgrnd; pool; paddling pool; sand beach 1.5km; tennis; games area; internet; 15% statics; dogs €2; adv bkg; quiet; red low ssn/long stay; ccard acc; CCI. "Excel site & rest; variable pitch sizes/prices; some lge pitches - lge o'fits rec phone ahead; gd, clean san facs; mountain views; helpful staff; m'vans beware low trees; gd cycling." ♦ € 29.20 2009*

See advertisement below

⊞ **JAVEA/XABIA** *4E2* (3km S Coastal) *38.77058, 0.18207* **Camping El Naranjal, Cami dels Morers 15, 03730 Jávea (Alicante) [965-79 29 89; fax 966-46 02 56; delfi@campingelnaranjal.com; www.campingelnaranjal.com]** Exit A7 junc 62 or 63 onto N332 València/Alicante rd. Exit at Gata de Gorgos to Jávea. Foll sp Camping Jávea/Camping El Naranjal. Access rd by tennis club, foll sp. Med, mkd pitch, hdstg, pt shd; htd wc; chem disp; mv service pnt; baby facs; shwrs inc; el pnts (10A) €4 (poss rev pol); gas; Indtte; shop; tradsmn; rest; snacks; bar; BBQ; playgrnd; pool; paddling pool; sand beach 300m; tennis 300m; cycle hire; games rm; golf 3km; wifi; TV rm; 35% statics; dogs free; phone; bus 500m; adv bkg; Eng spkn; quiet; ccard acc; red long stay/low ssn/CCI. "Gd scenery & beach; pitches poss tight lge o'fits; excel rest; immac facs; tourist info - tickets sold; rec." ♦ € 26.00 2009*

See advertisement above

I'm going to fill in some site report forms and post them off to the Club; we could win a ferry crossing – it's here on page 12.

⊞ **JIMENA DE LA FRONTERA** *2H3* (NW Rural) *36.44299, -5.45985* **Camping Los Alcornocales, Ctra CC3331/A369, 11330 Jimena de la Frontera (Cádiz) [956-64 00 60; fax 956-64 12 90; alcornocales@terra.es]** Site sp fr A369 Ronda to Algeciras rd. Rec app fr N onto C3331, turn L at camping sp at top of bank, site on R in 100m. Do not enter Jimena - narr rds. Med, hdg/mkd pitch, pt sl, terr, shd; wc; chem disp; shwrs inc; el pnts €3.85; gas; lndtte; shop; rest; bar; cycle hire; excursions; 90% statics; dogs; phone; adv bkg; quiet; ccard acc; red CCI. "V friendly owner; poss unkempt & ltd facs low ssn; unsuitable lge o'fits; conv Gibraltar; 5 mins walk to attractive hill town; wonderful flora, fauna & scenery in National Park." ♦ € 17.37 2008*

LABUERDA see Ainsa *3B2*

LAREDO *1A4* (500m W Urban/Coastal) *43.40888, -3.43277* **Camping Carlos V, Avnda Los Derechos Humanos 15, Ctra Residencial Playa, 39770 Laredo (Cantabria) [tel/fax 942-60 55 93]** Leave A8 at junc 172 to Laredo, foll yellow camping sp, site on W side of town. Med, mkd pitch, pt shd; wc; mv service pnt; baby facs; shwrs inc; el pnts €2.60; gas; lndtte; shop & 100m; rest; bar; playgrnd; sand beach 200m; dogs €2.14; bus 100m; poss cr; noisy; CCI. "Well sheltered & lively resort; sm area for tourers; gd, clean, modern facs." 6 May-30 Sep. € 25.14 2009*

LAREDO *1A4* (2km W Coastal) *43.41441, -3.44800* **Camping Laredo, Calle Rep de Filipinas s/n, 39770 Laredo (Cantabria) [942-60 50 35; fax 942-61 31 80; info@campinglaredo.com; www.campinglaredo.com]** Fr A8 exit junc 172 sp Laredo; cont N at rndabt into Laredo Playa, L at traff lts & foll sp hospital & site. Lge, mkd pitch, pt shd; wc; chem disp; mv service pnt; baby facs; shwrs; el pnts (6A) €3.25; gas; lndtte; shop (high ssn) snacks; bar; playgrnd; pool (caps essential); sand beach 500m; cycle hire; horseriding; TV; 20% statics; no dogs; phone; bus 300m; poss cr; noisy; adv bkg; red CCI. Holy Week & 1 Jun-15 Sep. € 23.60 2008*

LAREDO *1A4* (2km W Coastal) *43.41176, -3.45329* **Camping Playa del Regatón, El Sable 8, 39770 Laredo (Cantabria) [tel/fax 942-60 69 95; info@campingplayaregaton.com; www.campingplayaregaton.com]** Fr W leave A8 junc 172, under m'way to rndabt & take exit sp Calle Rep Colombia. In 800m turn L at traff lts, in further 800m turn L onto tarmac rd to end, passing other sites. Fr E leave at junc 172, at 1st rndabt take 2nd exit sp Centro Comercial N634 Colindres. At next rndabt take exit Calle Rep Colombia, then as above. Lge, mkd pitch; pt shd; wc; chem disp; mv service pnt; shwrs inc; el pnts (6A) €3.21; gas; lndtte; shop; rest; bar; sand beach adj & 3km; horseriding mr; wifi; 75% statics; no dogs; bus 600m; Eng spkn; adv bkg; quiet; ccard acc; red long stay/CCI. "Clean site; sep area for tourers; wash up facs (cold water) every pitch; gd, modern facs; gd NH/sh stay (check opening times of office for el pnt release)." ♦ 1 Apr-28 Sep. € 19.15 2008*

⊞ **LASPAULES** *3B2* (Rural) *42.47149, 0.59917* **Camping Laspaúles, Ctra N260, Km 369, 22471 Laspaúles (Huesca) [974-55 33 20; camping@laspaules.com; www.laspaules.com]** Approx 20km NW Pont de Suert, in cent of vill adj rv. Med, pt shd; wc; baby facs; shwrs; el pnts (6A) €4.90; gas; lndry rm; shop & in vill; tradsmn; snacks; bar; playgrnd; pool; paddling pool; TV; some statics; quiet; ccard acc; red long stay/low ssn; CCI. "V pleasant; pitches well back fr rd." € 19.60 2008*

⊞ **LEKEITIO** *3A1* (3km S Coastal) *43.35071, -2.49260* **Camping Leagi, Calle Barrio Leagi s/n, 48289 Mendexa (Vizcaya) [tel/fax 946-84 23 52; leagi@campingleagi.com; www.campingleagi.com]** Fr San Sebastian leave A8/N634 at Deba twd Ondarroa. At Ondarroa do not turn into town, but cont on BI633 beyond Berriatua, then turn R onto BI3405 to Lekeitio. Fr Bilbao leave A8/N634 at Durango & foll B1633 twd Ondarroa. Turn L after Markina onto BI3405 to Lekeitio - do not go via Ondarroa. Steep climb to site & v steep tarmac ent to site. Only suitable for o'fits with v high power/weight ratio. Med, mkd pitch, pt sl, unshd; wc; chem disp; mv service pnt; serviced pitch; shwrs inc; el pnts (5A) €3.60 (rev pol); lndtte; shop; rest; snacks; bar; playgrnd; sand beach 1km; many statics; dogs; bus 1.5km; cr & noisy high ssn; ccard acc (over €50); CCI. "Ltd facs low ssn; tractor tow avail up to site ent; beautiful scenery; excel local beach; lovely town; gd views; gd walking." € 22.80 2007*

LEKUNBERRI *3A1* (500m SE Rural) *43.00043, -1.88831* **Aralar Camping, Plazaola 9, 31870 Lekunberri (Navarra) [tel/fax 948-50 40 11 or 948-50 40 49; info@campingaralar.com; www.campingaralar.com]** Exit fr AP15 at junc 124 dir Lukunberri & foll sp for site. Site on R after v sharp downhill turn. Med, all hdstg, pt sl, terr, pt shd; htd wc; chem disp; shwrs inc; el pnts (5A) €4.65; gas; lndtte; shop; rest; snacks; bar; playgrnd; pool; cycle hire; horseriding; TV; dogs €2.95; 70% statics; phone; some Eng spkn; quiet; ccard acc. "Beautiful scenery & mountain walks; only 14 sm touring pitches; v pleasantly arranged site; avoid Pamplona mid-Aug during bull-run; site also open at w/end & long w/end all year except Jan/Feb." Holy Week & 1 Jun-30 Sep. € 22.50 2009*

LEON *1B3* (3km SE Urban) *42.5900, -5.5331* **Camping Ciudad de León, Ctra N601, 24195 Golpejar de la Sobarriba [tel/fax 987-26 90 86; camping_leon@yahoo.es; www.vivaleon.com/campingleon.htm]** SE fr León on N601 twds Valladolid, L at top of hill at rndabt & Opel g'ge & foll site sp Golpejar de la Sobarriba; 500m after radio masts turn R at site sp. Narr track to site ent. Sm, pt sl, shd; wc; chem disp; shwrs inc; el pnts inc (4A) €3.25; gas; lndry rm; shop; rest; snacks; bar; playgrnd; pool; paddling pool; tennis; cycle hire; dogs €1.50; bus 200m; quiet; adv bkg; poss cr; Eng spkn; CCI. "Clean, pleasant site; helpful, welcoming staff; access some sm pitches poss diff; easy access to León; building work around site." ♦ 1 Jun-20 Sep. € 18.30 2009*

Spain

LEON *1B3* (14km SE Rural) *42.50370, -5.41540* **Camp Municipal Esla, N601, Km 310, 24210 Mansilla de las Mulas (León) [987-31 00 89; fax 987-31 18 10; info@ayto-mansilla.org; www.ayto-mansilla.org]** N601 SE fr León, turn W onto N625 twd Mansilla. In 200m, turn L onto slip rd sp to site. Site in 1km. Heading N on N601 twd León, exit junc 21 sp León. Turn L into Mansilla & drive thro town. Site sp on R immed after bdge. Med, pt shd; wc; chem disp; shwrs inc; el pnts €1.90; Indtte; rest; bar; playgrnd; rv sw nrby; adv bkg; quiet; ccard acc; CCI. "Gd base for León." 18 Jun-11 Sep. € 9.85 2007*

LEON *1B3* (12km SW Urban) *42.51250, -5.77472* **Camping Camino de Santiago, Ctra N120, Km 324.4, 24392 Villadangos del Páramo (León) [tel/fax 987-68 02 53; info@campingcaminodesantiago.com; www.camping caminodesantiago.com]** Access fr N120 to W of vill, site sp on R (take care fast, o'taking traff). Fr E turn L in town & foll sp to site. Lge, mkd pitch, pt shd; wc; chem disp; mv service pnt; baby facs; shwrs inc; el pnts €3.75; gas; Indtte; shop; rest; snacks; bar; pool; wifi; 50% statics; dogs; phone; bus 300m; poss cr; adv bkg; rd noise; ccard acc; red long stay; CCI. "Poss no hot water low ssn; facs tired; pleasant, helpful staff; mosquitoes; vill church worth visit; gd NH." ♦ Easter-28 Sep. € 18.20 2009*

⊞ **LINEA DE LA CONCEPCION, LA** *2H3* (S Urban/Coastal) *36.19167, -5.3350* **Camping Sureuropa, Camino de Sobrevela s/n, 11300 La Línea de la Concepción (Cádiz) [956-64 35 87; fax 956-64 30 59; info@campingsureuropa.com; www.campingsureuropa.com]** Fr S on E5/N340 onto N351 coast rd. Just bef Gibraltar turn R up lane, in 200m turn L into site. Fr N on AP7, exit junc 124 onto A383 dir La Línea; foll sp Santa Margarita thro to beach. Foll rd to R along sea front, site in approx 1km - no advance sp. App rd to site off coast rd poss floods after heavy rain. Med, hdg/mkd pitch, hdstg, pt shd; wc; chem disp (wc); shwrs inc; el pnts €3.50; Indtte; bar; sand beach 500m; sports club adj; some statics; clsd 21 Dec-7 Jan; no dogs; phone; bus 1.5km; poss cr; Eng spkn; adv bkg; quiet but noise fr adj sports club; no ccard acc; CCI. "Clean, flat, pretty site (gd for disabled); vg, modern san facs; sm pitches & tight site rds poss diff twin-axles & l'ge o'fits; ideal for Gibraltar 4km; stay ltd to 4 days." ♦ € 15.00 2008*

LLAFRANC see Palafrugell *3B3*

⊞ **LLANCA** *3B3* (500m N Coastal) *42.37083, 3.15388* **Camping L'Ombra, Ctra Bisbal-Portbou, Km 16.5, 17490 Llançà (Gerona) [tel/fax 972-12 02 61; campinglombra@terra.es]** Fr Figueres on N260 dir Portbou, site on L 500m N of traff lts at Llançà turn off. Med, mkd pitch, pt sl, pt shd; wc; chem disp; shwrs inc; el pnts €4; Indtte; shop; supmkt 1km; bar; playgrnd; beach 1km; internet; 75% statics; dogs €1.50; bus 500m; train 1km; quiet; red low ssn. "Useful winter base for coastal towns when other sites clsd." € 27.00 2008*

LLANCA *3B3* (4km N Coastal) *42.40320, 3.14580* **Camping Caravaning Sant Miquel, Pozo 22, 17469 Colera (Gerona) [tel/fax 972-38 90 18; info@campingsantmiquel.com; www.campingsantmiquel.com]** Take main rd fr Portbou to Cadaqués. After 7km turn L into Colera vill, then 1st R over bdge, turn L into site in 200m, well sp. Lge, mkd pitch, pt shd; wc; chem disp; shwrs inc; el pnts (6-10A) €4.45; gas; Indtte; shop; rest; snacks; bar; playgrnd; htd pool; shgl beach 1km; watersports; diving; cycle hire; entmnt; TV rm; 10% statics; dogs €2; poss cr; Eng spkn; adv bkg; quiet; ccard acc; CCI. "Friendly site; gd rest & pool; poss v cr high ssn with students; conv local fishing ports & Dali Museum." ♦ 15 Mar-30 Sep. € 21.10 2008*

LLANES *1A4* (8km E Coastal) *43.39948, -4.65350* **Camping La Paz, Ctra N634, Km 292, 33597 Playa de Vidiago (Asturias) [tel/fax 985-41 12 35; delfin@campinglapaz.com; www.campinglapaz.com]** Take Fr A8/N634/E70 turn R at sp to site bet km stone 292 & 293 bef Vidiago.Site access via narr 1km lane. Stop bef bdge & park on R, staff will tow to pitch. Narr site ent & steep access to pitches. Lge, mkd pitch, terr, shd; wc; chem disp; mv service pnt; baby facs; shwrs inc; el pnts (9A) €4.25 (poss rev pol); gas; Indtte; shop; rest; bar; BBQ; playgrnd; sand beach adj; fishing; watersports; horseriding; mountain sports; games rm; no statics; dogs €2.25; phone; poss cr w/end; Eng spkn; adv bkg; quiet; ccard acc; CCI. "Exceptionally helpful owner & staff; sm pitches; gd, modern san facs; excel views; cliff top rest; superb beaches in area." ♦ Easter-30 Sep. € 28.25 2009*

See advertisement

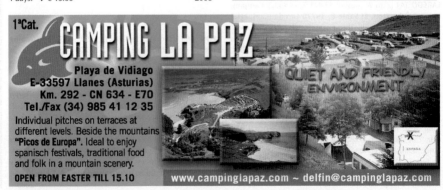

LLANES *1A4* (1.5km W Coastal) *43.4242, 4.7876* **Camping Las Conchas de Póo, Ctra General, 33509 Póo de Llanes (Asturias) [985-402 290]** Exit A8/E70 at Llanes West junc 307 & foll sp. Med, sl, terr, pt shd; wc; chem disp; baby facs; shwrs; el pnts (5A) €2.50; Indtte; shop; rest; bar; playgrnd; sand beach adj; 50% statics; no dogs; phone; bus; quiet. "Pleasant site; footpath to lovely beach." 1 Jun-30 Sep. € 15.00 2006*

LLANES *1A4* (5km W Coastal) *43.43471, -4.81810* **Camping Playa de Troenzo, Ctra de Celerio-Barro, 33595 Celorio (Asturias) [985-40 16 72; fax 985-74 07 23; troenzo@telepolis.com]** Fr E take E70/A8 past Llanes & exit at junc 307 to Celorio. At T-junc with AS263 turn L dir Celorio & Llanes. Turn L on N9 (Celorio) thro vill & foll sp to Barro. Site on R after 500m (after Maria Elena site). Lge, terr, pt shd; wc; chem disp; mv service pnt; shwrs inc; el pnts (6A) €2.51; gas; Indtte; shop; rest; snacks; bar; playgrnd; sand beach 400m; 90% statics; dogs; phone; poss cr; Eng spkn; adv bkg; CCI. "Lovely, old town; most pitches sm; for pitches with sea views go thro statics to end of site; gd, modern facs; gd rests in town; nr harbour." 16 Feb-19 Dec. € 19.10 2007*

LLAVORSI *3B2* (3km N Rural) *42.50415, 1.20272* **Camping Riberies, Ctra Vall d'Arau 55, 25595 Llavorsí (Lleida) [973-62 21 51; fax 973-62 20 02; consulta@camping riberies.com; www.campingriberies.com]** On C113 3km N of Llavorsí. Fr S site is immed bef rv bdge on ent Riberies. Med, shd; wc; shwrs; el pnts €4.20; Indtte; shop in vill; rest adj; bar; playgrnd; kayaking; rafting; phone; bus 500m; quiet but some rd noise. 15 Mar-30 Oct. € 17.20 2006*

LLAVORSI *3B2* (8km N Rural) *42.56004, 1.22810* **Camping Del Cardós, Ctra Llavorsí-Tavascan, Km 85, 25570 Ribera de Cardós (Lleida) [973-62 31 12; fax 973-62 31 83; info@campingdelcardos.com; www.campingdelcardos.com]** Take L504 fr Llavorsi dir Ribera de Cardós for 9km; site on R on ent vill. Med, mkd pitch, pt shd; wc; chem disp; mv service pnt; shwrs; el pnts (4-6A) €5.30; gas; Indtte (inc dryer); shop; tradsmn; rest; playgrnd; pool; 2 paddling pools; fishing; games area; TV rm; 5% statics; dogs €3.60; Eng spkn; quiet; CCI. "By side of rv, v quiet low ssn; excel." 1 Apr-20 Oct. € 24.00 2009*

⊞ **LLAVORSI** *3B2* (9km N Rural) *42.56890, 1.23040* **Camping La Borda del Pubill, Ctra de Tavescan, Km 9.5, 25570 Ribera de Cardós (Lleida) [973-62 30 80; fax 973-62 30 28; info@campinglabordadelpubill.com; www.campinglabordadelpubill.com]** Fr France on A64 exit junc 17 at Montréjeau & head twd Spanish border. At Vielha turn E onto C28/C1412 to Llavorsí, then L504 to Ribera. Fr S take N260 fr Tremp to Llavorsí, then L504 to site. Lge, pt shd; htd wc; baby facs; shwrs; el pnts €5.30; gas; Indtte; shop, rest high ssn; snacks; bar; playgrnd; htd pool; paddling pool; rv sw & fishing; kayaking; trekking; adventure sports; quad bike hire; horseriding; skiing 30km; games area; games rm; TV; 10% statics; dogs €3; phone; car wash; adv bkg; quiet; ccard acc. "In beautiful area; excel walking; gd rest." ♦ € 24.10 2009*

LLORET DE MAR *3B3* (1km S Coastal) *41.6973, 2.8217* **Camping Tucan, Ctra Blanes-Lloret, 17310 Lloret de Mar (Gerona) [972-36 99 65; fax 972-36 00 79; info@campingtucan.com; www.campingtucan.com]** Fr N exit AP7 junc 9 onto C35 twd Sant Feliu then C63 on R sp Lloret de Mar. At x-rds foll sp Blanes, site on R. Fr S take last exit fr C32 & foll sp Lloret de Mar, site on L, sp. Lge, mkd pitch, terr, shd; wc; chem disp; baby facs; shwrs inc; el pnts (3-6A) €3.40-4.40; gas; Indtte; shop; rest; snacks; bar; BBQ; playgrnd; pool; paddling pool; sand beach 600m; games area; golf 500m; entmnt; internet; TV rm; 25% statics; dogs €2; phone; bus; car wash; Eng spkn; adv bkg; quiet; ccard acc; red long stay/snr citizens/CCI. "Well-appointed site; friendly staff." ♦ 1 Apr-30 Sep. € 27.80 2007*

⊞ **LLORET DE MAR** *3B3* (1km SW Coastal) *41.6984, 2.8265* **Camping Santa Elena-Ciutat, Ctra Blanes/Lloret, 17310 Lloret de Mar (Gerona) [972-36 40 09; fax 972-36 79 54; santaelana@betsa.es; www.betsa.es]** Exit A7 junc 9 dir Lloret. In Lloret take Blanes rd, site sp at km 10.5 on rd GI 682. V lge, pt sl; wc; baby facs; shwrs; el pnts (5A) €3.90; gas; Indtte; shop; rest; snacks; bar; playgrnd; pool; paddling pool; shgl beach 600m; games area; phone; cash machine; poss cr; Eng spkn; quiet low ssn; red facs low ssn; CCI. "Ideal for teenagers." ♦ € 34.60 2007*

⊞ **LOBOS, LOS** *4G1* (2km NE Rural) **Camping Hierbabuena, Los Lobos, 04610 Cuevas del Almanzora (Almería) [tel/fax 950-16 86 97 or 629-68 81 53 (mob)]** S fr Lorca on A7; at Cuevas del Almanzora turn L onto A332 to Los Lobos - do not ent vill; 400m after junc with A1201 (dir El Largo & Pulpí) turn L & foll gravel rd to site in 1km. Sm, mkd pitch, hdstg, pt shd; htd wc; chem disp; baby facs; shwrs inc; el pnts (6-10A) inc; gas (Spanish only); Indtte; supmkt & rest 5km; snacks & bar 500m; BBQ; playgrnd; sand beach 5km; 75% statics (sep area); dogs free; Eng spkn; adv bkg; quiet; ccard not acc; red long stay. "Gd for long winter stay; friendly British owners; lge pitches; pretty & interesting area; excel choice of beaches; gd walking, cycling & sightseeing; vg security; excel." ♦ € 25.45 2009*

LOGRONO *3B1* (500m N Urban) *42.47187, -2.45164* **Camping La Playa, Avda de la Playa 6, 26006 Logroño (La Rioja) [941-25 22 53; fax 941-25 86 61; info@campinglaplaya.com; www.campinglaplaya.com]** Leave Logroño by bdge 'Puente de Piedra' on N111, then turn L at rndabt into Camino de las Norias. Site well sp in town & fr N111, adj sports cent Las Norias, on N side of Rv Ebro. Med, hdg pitch, shd; wc; shwrs inc; el pnts (5A) €3; gas; Indtte; shop; snacks, bar in ssn; playgrnd; pool; rv sw adj; tennis; 80% statics; no dogs; red CCI. "Sh walk to town cent; ltd facs low ssn & site poss clsd; vg." 1 Apr-30 Sep. € 18.50 2007*

Spain

⊞ **LOGRONO** *3B1* (10km W Rural) *42.41613, -2.55169* **Camping Navarrete, Ctra La Navarrete-Entrena, Km 1.5, 26370 Navarrete (La Rioja) [941-44 01 69; fax 941-44 06 39; campingnavarrete@fer.es; www.fer.es/campings]** Fr AP68 exit junc 11, at end slip rd turn L onto LR137 to Navarette. Foll sp thro town for Entrena (S) on LR137 dir Entrena. Site 1km on R. Lge, mkd pitch, pt shd; wc; chem disp; mv service pnt; baby facs; shwrs inc; el pnts (5A) €4; gas; lndtte; shop; snacks; bar; BBQ; playgrnd; pool & paddling pool; tennis; horseriding; car wash; wifi; 95% statics; dogs €2.40; site clsd 11 Dec-11 Jan; bus 1.3km; Eng spkn; noisy at w/end; ccard acc; red low ssn/long stay. "Professionally run, v clean, tidy site; excel san facs; helpful staff; some sm pitches; local wine sold at recep; Bilbao ferry 2 hrs via m'way; interesting area." € 22.25 2009*

⊞ **LORCA** *4G1* (8km W Rural) *37.62861, -1.74888* **Camping La Torrecilla, Ctra Granada-LaTorrecilla, 30817 Lorca (Murcia) [tel/fax 968-44 21 96; campinglatorrecilla@hotmail.com]** Leave A7/E15 at junc 585. In 1km turn L, site well sp. Med, mkd pitch, hdstg, pt sl, pt shd; htd wc; chem disp; mv service pnt; shwrs inc; el pnts (6A) €3.21; gas; lndtte; shop 2km; tradsmn; rest; snacks; bar; BBQ; playgrnd; pool; tennis; games area; TV rm; 95% statics; dogs; phone; bus 1km; poss cr; Eng spkn; quiet; ccard acc; red long stay. "V ltd touring pitches; ltd el pts; friendly, helpful staff; excel pool; vg san facs." ♦ € 14.30 2009*

⊞ **LUARCA** *1A3* (1km NE Coastal) *43.54914, -6.52426* **Camping Los Cantiles, Ctra N634, Km 502.7, 33700 Luarca (Asturias) [tel/fax 985-64 09 38; cantiles@campingloscantiles.com; www.campingloscantiles.com]** Fr E leave N632 sp Luarca onto N634 S, then take exit to Barcia/Almuña onto rd 754 to sea; site sp (easily missed - look out for R turn with railings). Not rec to ent town fr W. Cont on N634/N632 to exit for Oviedo (N634) then take exit to Barcia/Almuña, then as for app fr E. On leaving site, retrace to main rd - do not tow thro Luarca. Med, hdg pitch, pt shd; wc; chem disp; baby facs; shwrs inc; el pnts inc (3-6A) €2-2.50; gas; lndtte; shop; tradsmn; rest high ssn; snacks; bar; pool 300m; shgl beach at foot of cliff; phone; poss cr; Eng spkn; adv bkg; quiet; red long stay; CCI. "Site on cliff top; san facs ltd & run down (8/09); some narr site rds; pitches soft after rain; steep climb down to beach." ♦ € 18.10 2009*

⊞ **LUARCA** *1A3* (12km E Rural/Coastal) *43.54898, -6.38420* **Camping La Regalina, Ctra de la Playa s/n, 33788 Cadavedo (Asturias) [tel/fax 985-64 50 56; info@laregalina.com]** Fr N632 dir Cadavedo, km126. Site well sp. Med, pt shd; wc; chem disp; shwrs inc; el pnts (5-8A) €2.30; gas; shop; rest; snacks; bar; pool; beach 1km; TV; 10% statics; dogs €3; phone; bus 600m; adv bkg; quiet; ccard acc high ssn; red long stay. "Scenic area; pretty vill; ltd facs low ssn; gd." € 21.10 2009*

LUARCA *1A3* (2km W Coastal) *43.55116, -6.55310* **Camping Playa de Taurán, 33700 Luarca (Asturias) [tel/fax 985-64 12 72 or 619-88 43 06; tauran@campingtauran.com; www.campingtauran.com]** Fr Luarca, take N634 W & turn R at rndabt, sp El Chano. If missed, another sp in 1km. Cont 3.5km on long, narr, rough access rd. Rd thro Luarca unsuitable for c'vans. Med, some hdg pitch, pt sl, pt shd; wc; chem disp; mv service pnt; baby facs; shwrs inc; el pnts (15A) €3.50; gas; lndtte; shop; tradsmn; rest; snacks; bar; BBQ; pool; paddling pool; shgl beach 200m; sand beach 2km; cycle hire; phone; dogs €1; quiet; red long stays. "Superb sea views & mountain views; off beaten track; conv fishing & hill vills; v peaceful, restful, attractive, well-kept site; steep access to beach; excel." Holy Week-30 Sep. € 18.50 2009*

LUMBIER *3B1* (500m W Rural) *42.6500, -1.3119* **Camping Iturbero, Ctra N240 Pamplona-Huesca, 31440 Lumbier (Navarra) [948-88 04 05; fax 948-88 04 14; iturbero@campingiturbero.com; www.campingiturbero.com]** SE fr Pamplona on N240 twds Yesa Reservoir. In 30km L on NA150 twds Lumbier. In 3.5km immed bef Lumbier turn R at rndabt then over bdge, 1st L to site, adj sw pool. Well sp fr N240. Med, hdg/mkd pitch, some hdstg, pt shd; wc; chem disp; mv service pnt; shwrs inc; el pnts (5A) €4.95; gas; lndtte; shop 1km; rest; snacks; bar; BBQ; playgrnd; pool 100m; tennis; hang-gliding; 25% statics; dogs; bus 1km; quiet; CCI. "Beautiful, well-kept site; clean, basic facs; excel touring base; open w/end only Dec-Easter (poss fr Sep) but clsd 19 Dec-19 Feb; eagles & vultures in gorge & seen fr site; helpful staff; Lumbier lovely sm town." Holy Week-8 Dec. € 22.30 2008*

⊞ **LUMBRALES** *1C3* (6km NE Rural) *40.95750, -6.65611* **Camping La Hojita, Ctra de Fregeneda, Km 89, 37240 Lumbrales (Salamanca) [923-16 92 68 or 655-91 95 80 (mob); camping_la_hojita@hotmail.com; www.campinglahojita.com]** Fr Salamanca or fr Portuguese border, site sp on CL517. Sm, mkd pitch, shd; wc; chem disp; mv service pnt; baby facs; shwrs inc; el pnts (10A) €3.15; lndtte; shop 2km; rest; snacks; bar; BBQ; playgrnd; pool; some statics; Eng spkn; quiet; red long stay. "Excel, tranquil site." 1 Apr-1 Nov. € 18.00 2009*

⊞ **MADRID** *1D4* (8km NE Urban) *40.45361, -3.60333* **Camping Osuna, Calle de los Jardines de Aranjuez, Avda de Logroño s/n, 28042 Madrid [917-41 05 10; fax 913-20 63 65; camping.osuna.madrid@microgest.es]** Fr M40, travelling S clockwise (anti-clockwise fr N or E) exit junc 8 at Canillejas sp 'Avda de Logroño'. Turn L under m'way, then R under rlwy, immed after turn R at traff lts. Site on L corner - white painted wall. Travelling N, leave M40 at junc 7 (no turn off at junc 8) sp Avda 25 Sep, U-turn at km 7, head S to junc 8, then as above. Med, hdg/mkd pitch, pt sl, pt shd; wc; chem disp; shwrs inc; el pnts (5A) €4.85 (long lead rec); lndtte; shop 600m; playgrnd; metro to town 600m; 10% statics; dogs free; phone; poss cr; rd & aircraft noise; Eng spkn; red low ssn; CCI. "Sm pitches poss diff lge o'fits; helpful staff; conv city cent; clean site but poss neglected low ssn & facs tired; poss itinerants." ♦ € 25.40 2009*

⊞ **MADRID** *1D4* (13km S Urban) *40.31805, -3.68888* **Camping Alpha, Ctra de Andalucía N-IV, Km 12.4, 28906 Getafe (Madrid) [916-95 80 69; fax 916-83 16 59; info@campingalpha.com; www.campingalpha.com]** Fr S on A4/E5 twd Madrid, leave at km 12.4 to W dir Ocaña & foll sp. Fr N on A4/E5 at km 13b to change dir back onto A4; then exit 12b sp 'Poligono Industria Los Olivos' to site. Lge, hdstg, hdg pitch, pt shd; wc; chem disp; mv service pnt; shwrs inc; el pnts (15A) €5.90 (poss no earth); Indtte; shop; rest; snacks; bar; playgrnd; pool high ssn; tennis; games area; 20% statics; dogs; phone; poss cr; Eng spkn; adv bkg; ccard acc; 10% red CCI. "Lorry depot adj; poss vehicle movements 24 hrs but minimal noise; bus & metro to Madrid 30-40 mins; sm pitches poss tight for space; clean facs but need update; ltd hot water low ssn; v helpful staff; NH only." € 27.40 2008*

⊞ **MADRIGAL DE LA VERA** *1D3* (500m E Rural) *40.14864, -5.35769* **Camping Alardos, Ctra Madrigal-Candeleda, 10480 Madrigal de la Vera (Cáceres) [tel/fax 927-56 50 66; mirceavd@hotmail.com; www.campingalardos.com]** Fr Jarandilla take EX203 E to Madrigal. Site sp in vill nr rv bdge. Med, mkd pitch, pt shd; wc; chem disp; shwrs inc; el pnts (6-10A) €4; Indtte; shop & 1km; rest; snacks; bar; BBQ; playgrnd; pool; rv sw adj; TV; 10% statics; no dogs; phone; poss cr Jul/Aug; Eng spkn; adv bkg; ccard not acc. "Friendly owners; superb site; ltd facs low ssn; beautiful scenery; excel touring area; ancient Celtic settlement at El Raso 5km." € 23.30 2009*

⊞ **MALGRAT DE MAR** *3C3* (500m SW Coastal) *41.63161, 2.72061* **Camping Bon Repós, Pg Maritim s/n, 08398 Santa Susanna (Barcelona) [937-67 84 75; fax 937-76 85 26; info@campingbonrepos.com; www.campingbonrepos.com]** App fr Gerona on rd N11, site sp. Track leaves on L of N11; foll camp sp for 680m & turn R at sea-front T-junc. Cont thro Santa Susanna, down underpass & turn L in middle, app rd to site on beach behind rlwy stn; sp. NB Heavy rain may cause flooding of underpass; alt exit max 2.5m height. V lge, shd; wc; chem disp; baby facs; shwrs inc; el pnts (5A) €9; gas; Indtte; supmkt; rest; bar; playgrnd; 2 pools; beach adj; watersports; tennis; entmnt; 10% statics; dogs €2.50; train to Barcelona 400m; poss cr; poss noisy; ccard acc; red low ssn. "Some sm pitches, some at water's edge; vg site." ♦ € 37.50 2008*

⊞ **MAMOLA, LA** *2H4* (500m W Coastal) *36.74062, -3.29976* **Camping Castillo de Baños, Castillo de Baños, 18750 La Mamola (Granada) [958-82 95 28; fax 958-82 97 68; info@campingcastillo.com; www.campingcastillo.com]** Fr E on A7/E15 exit km 360.4 sp Camping/Rest El Paraiso/Castillo de Baños, site on L after rest at ent to vill. Fr W exit km 359.3. Lge, mkd pitch, hdstg, pt shd; wc; chem disp; mv service pnt; shwrs inc; el pnts (5A) €4; gas; Indtte; shop; tradsmn; rest; snacks; bar; playgrnd; pool; private shgl beach adj; fishing; cycle hire; entmnt; internet; Eng spkn; dogs €1.95; adv bkg; ccard acc; quiet; red low ssn/CCI. "Poss rallies low ssn." ♦ € 23.50 2008*

⊞ **MANGA DEL MAR MENOR, LA** *4G2* (2km W Coastal) *37.62455, -0.74300* **Camping La Manga, Ctra El Algar/Cabo de Palos, Km 12, 30386 La Manga del Mar Menor (Murcia) [968-56 30 14 or 56 30 19; fax 968-56 34 26; lamanga@caravaning.es; www.caravaning.es]** Leave MU312 junc 11 sp Playa Honda; over dual c'way then turn R. Site sp fr La Manga. Ent visible beside dual c'way with flags flying. V lge, hdg/mkd pitch, hdstg, pt shd; htd wc; chem disp; mv service pnt; sauna; serviced pitches; shwrs inc; el pnts (10A) inc; gas; Indtte; supmkt; rest; snacks; bar; BBQ; playgrnd; 2 pools - 1 htd, covrd Oct-Mar; paddling pool; sand beach adj; fishing; windsurfing; jacuzzi, gym (Oct-Mar); tennis; open-air cinema high ssn; games rm; wifi; cab TV/TV rm; 30% statics; dogs €1.35; phone; recep 0700-2300; poss cr; Eng spkn; adv bkg ess; ccard acc; red long stay/low ssn. "Immac, busy, popular winter site; poss lge rallies on site Dec-Mar; Mar Menor shallow & warm lagoon; gd for families; 2 pitch sizes - sm ones unsuitable o'fits over 5m; some narr site rds & trees - rec park in car park on arr & walk to find pitch; additional area for m'vans; site liable to flood Sep/Oct; regional park 3km; gd walking; mountain biking; bird sanctuary; conv Roman ruins Cartagena, Murcia, Alicante; excel." ♦ € 29.00 (CChq acc) ABS - E16 2009*

See advertisement

Spain

⊞ **MANZANARES EL REAL** *1D4* (8km NE Rural) *40.74278, -3.81583* **Camping La Fresneda, Ctra M608, Km 19.5, 28791 Soto del Real (Madrid) [tel/fax 918-47 65 23]** Fr AP6/NV1 turn NE at Collado-Villalba onto M608 to Cerceda & Manzanares el Real. Foll rd round lake to Soto del Real, site sp at km 19.5. Med, shd; wc; chem disp; baby facs; shwrs €0.15; el pnts (6A) €3.50; gas; lndtte; shop; snacks; bar; playgrnd; pool; tennis; dogs €3; phone; rd noise; ccard acc. ♦ € 24.00 2009*

⊞ **MANZANARES EL REAL** *1D4* (3km NW Rural) *40.74165, -3.87509* **Camping El Ortigal, Montañeros 19, La Pedriza, 28410 Manzanares el Real (Madrid) [918-53 01 20]** Fr AP6/NV1 turn NE at Collado-Villalba onto M608 to Cerceda & Manzanares el Real. In 6km take L sp to Manzanares, cross rv & immed L. Sp at this junc; site further 3km - speed humps. Not many sp to site or Pedriza. Lge, pt sl; wc; shwrs; el pnts (10A) €3.85 (poss rev pol); gas; shop; rest; bar; playgrnd; 99% statics/chalets; phone; red low ssn. "Sm area for tourers - rec arr early; warm welcome; san facs dated; attractive country & views; excel walking in adj National Park." ♦ € 25.70 2008*

⊞ **MANZANERA** *3D2* (1km NE Rural) *40.06333, -0.8250* **Camping Villa de Manzanera, Partida Las Bateas s/n, Ctra 1514, Km 10.5, 44420 Manzanera (Teruel) [978-78 18 19 or 978-78 17 48; fax 978-78 17 09; reservas@campingmanzanera.com; www.camping manzanera.com]** Fr A23/N234 Teruel-Sagunto, turn S at km 980 slip rd onto N234 dir Sarrión. Nr Mora turn onto A1514 at site sp. Site on L by petrol stn bef vill. Med, mkd pitch, unshd; htd wc; chem disp; shwrs inc; el pnts (10A) €4.30; gas; lndtte; shop 1km; rest; snacks; bar; playgrnd; pool; 80% statics; no dogs; phone; bus 300m; poss cr; poss noisy; ccard acc; CCI. "Site much enlarged but a little run down; popular with young tenters; nr wintersports area; obliging staff; excel san facs but poss stretched high ssn; ltd touring pitches - some pitches worn & uneven; excel, gd value rest; ltd facs in winter; pay at filling stn adj." ♦ € 13.80 2008*

⊞ **MARBELLA** *2H3* (7km E Coastal) *36.50259, -4.80413* **Camping La Buganvilla, Ctra N340, Km 188.8, 29600 Marbella (Málaga) [952-83 19 73 or 952-83 19 74; fax 952-83 19 74; info@campingbuganvilla.com; www. campingbuganvilla.com]** E fr Marbella for 6km on N340/E15 twds Málaga. Pass site & cross over m'way at Elviria & foll site sp. Fr Málaga exit R off autovia immed after 189km marker. Lge, terr, shd; wc; chem disp; shwrs; el pnts (10A) €4.80; gas; lndtte; shop & 250m; rest; bar & sun terr; playgrnd; pool; sand beach 350m; games rm; wifi; TV; phone; dogs €4 (not acc Jul/Aug); Eng spkn; adv bkg; poss noisy at w/end; 15% red long stay/snr citizens; ccard acc; CCI. "Relaxed, conv site; helpful staff; excel beach." ♦ € 28.50 2009*

⊞ **MARBELLA** *2H3* (10km E Coastal) *36.49111, -4.76416* **Camping Marbella Playa, Ctra N340, Km 192.8, 29600 Marbella (Málaga) [952-83 39 98; fax 952-83 39 99; recepcion@campingmarbella.com; www.camping marbella.com]** Fr Marbella on A7/N340 coast rd (not AP7/E15 toll m'way) & site is on R bef 193 km stone & just bef pedestrian bdge over A7/N340, sp 'to beach'. Fr Málaga U-turn on m'way as follows: pass 192km mark & immed take R slip rd to Elviria to turn L over bdge, back onto A7/N340. Turn R bef next bdge. Lge, mkd pitch, hdstg, pt shd; wc; chem disp; mv service pnt; baby facs; shwrs; el pnts (10A) inc; gas; supmkt; rest; snacks; bar; BBQ; playgrnd; pool; sand beach adj; watersports; tennis 50m; wifi; TV; dogs; phone; bus nr; poss v cr; rd noise; ccard acc; red low ssn/long stay/snr citizens/CCI. "Pitches tight; clean facs but tired; gd supmkt; friendly, helpful manager; gd base Costa del Sol; noisy peak ssn & w/ends, espec Sat nights." ♦ € 31.19 2008*

⊞ **MARBELLA** *2H3* (12km E Coastal) *36.48881, -4.74294* **Camping Cabopino, Ctra N340/A7, Km 194.7, 29600 Marbella (Málaga) [tel/fax 952-83 43 73; info@camping cabopino.com; www.campingcabopino.com]** Fr E site is on N side of N340/A7; turn R at km 195 'Salida Cabopino' past petrol stn, site on R at rndabt. Fr W on A7 turn R at 'Salida Cabopino' km 194.7, go over bdge to rndabt, site strt over. NB Do not take sm exit fr A7 immed at 1st Cabopino sp. Lge, mkd pitch, pt sl, pt shd; wc; chem disp; mv service pnt; baby facs; shwrs inc; el pnts (10A) inc (poss long lead req); lndtte; shop; rest; snacks; bar; BBQ; playgrnd; 2 pools (1 covrd); sand beach/dunes 200m; watersports; marina 300m; games area; archery; golf driving range; wifi; games/TV rm; 50% statics; dogs €1.70; bus 100m; Eng spkn; rd noise & lge groups w/enders; ccard acc; red low ssn; CCI. "Popular low ssn; busy w/end; tourers ltd to lower half of site - flooding danger in heavy rain & access to some diff due drops; blocks req some pitches; sm pitches; gd, clean san facs; feral cats on site; v nice site." ♦ € 34.50 (CChq acc) ABS - E21 2009*

⊞ **MARIA** *4G1* (8km W Rural) *37.70823, -2.23609* **Camping Sierra de María, Ctra María a Orce, Km 7, Paraje La Piza, 04838 María (Málaga) [950-16 70 45 or 660-26 64 74 (mob); fax 950-48 54 16; info@camping sierrademaria.com; www.campingsierrademaria.com]** Exit A92 at junc 408 to Vélez Rubio, Vélez Blanco & María. Foll A317 to María & cont dir Huéscar & Orce. Site on R. Med, mkd pitch, pt sl, pt shd; wc; chem disp; shwrs; el pnts (6-10A) €3.75; shop high ssn; rest; bar; cycle hire; horseriding; some statics; dogs; adv bkg; quiet; ccard acc; CCI. "Lovely, peaceful, ecological site in mountains; much wildlife; variable pitch sizes; facs poss stretched high ssn; v cold in winter. ♦ € 16.20 2007*

⊞ **MARINA, LA** *4F2* (1.5km S Coastal) *38.12972, -0.65000* **Camping Internacional La Marina, Ctra N332a, Km 76, 03194 La Marina (Alicante) [965-41 92 00; fax 965-41 91 10; info@campinglamarina.com; www.campinglamarina.com]** Fr N332 S of La Marina turn E twd sea at rndabt onto Camino del Cementerio. At next rndabt turn S onto N332a & foll site sp along Avda de l'Alegría. V lge, hdg/mkd pitch, hdstg, terr, shd; htd wc; chem disp; mv service pnt; 50% serviced pitches; baby facs; fam bthrm; sauna; solarium; shwrs inc; el pnts (10A) €3.21; gas; Indtte; supmkt; rest; snacks; bars; playgrnd; 2 pools (1 htd/covrd); waterslides; sand beach 500m; fishing; watersports; tennis; games area; games rm; fitness cent; entmnt; disco; wifi; TV rm; 10% statics; dogs €2.14; phone; bus 50m; car wash; security; Eng spkn; adv bkg; ccard acc; varying pitch size & price; red long stay/low ssn; CCI. "Almost full late Feb; v busy w/end; spotless, high quality facs; popular winter site; bus fr gate; gd security; gd rest; discount if booking/paying on site's website." ♦ € 59.40 2009*

See advertisement on next page

⊞ **MASNOU, EL** *3C3* (750m W Coastal) *41.4753, 2.3033* **Camping Masnou, Ctra NII, Km 633, Carrer de Camil Fabra 33, 08320 El Masnou (Barcelona) [tel/fax 935-55 15 03; masnou@campingsonline.es]** App site fr N on N11. Pass El Masnou rlwy station on L & go strt on at traff lts. Site on R on N11 after km 633. Not clearly sp. Med, pt sl, shd; wc; mv service pnt; shwrs inc; el pnts €5.88; shop, snacks, bar high ssn; BBQ; playgrnd; pool high ssn; sand beach opp; internet; dogs; phone; bus 300m; train to Barcelona nr; poss v cr; Eng spkn; rd & rlwy noise; ccard acc (€100 +); CCI. "Blocks of flats either side of site; gd pitches, no awnings; some sm pitches, poss shared; facs vg, though poss stretched when site busy; no restriction on NH vehicle movements; well-run, friendly site but a little 'tired'; gd service low ssn." ♦ € 33.70 2009*

MATARO *3C3* (3km E Coastal) *41.55060, 2.48330* **Camping Barcelona (formerly Playa Sol), Ctra NII, Km 650, 08304 Mataró (Barcelona) [937-90 47 20; fax 937-41 02 82; info@campingbarcelona.com; www.campingbarcelona.com]** Exit AP7 onto C60 sp Mataró. Turn N onto NII dir Gerona, site sp on L after rndabt. Lge, mkd pitch, hdstg, shd; wc; chem disp; mv service pnt; baby facs; shwrs inc; el pnts (6A) €5.50; gas; Indtte; shop; rest; snacks; bar; playgrnd; pool; paddling pool; sand beach 1.5km; games area; games rm; animal farm; wifi; entmnt; TV; 5% statics; dogs €4.25; shuttle bus to beach & town; Eng spkn; adv bkg; rd noise; ccard acc; red long stay/low ssn; CCI. "Conv Barcelona 28km; pleasant site; friendly, welcoming staff." ♦ 5 Mar-1 Dec. € 45.80 2009*

MAZAGON see Huelva *2G2*

⊞ **MAZAGON** *2G2* (10km E Coastal) *37.09855, -6.72650* **Camping Doñana Playa, Ctra San Juan del Puerto-Matalascañas, Km 34.6, 21130 Mazagón (Huelva) [959-53 62 81; fax 959-53 63 13; info@campingdonana.com; www.campingdonana.com]** Fr A49 exit junc 48 at Bullullos del Condado onto A483 sp El Rocio, Matalascañas. At coast turn R sp Mazagón, site on L in 16km. V lge, mkd pitch, hdstg, pt shd; wc; chem disp; shwrs inc; el pnts (6A) €5.20; shop; rest; snacks; bar; playgrnd; pool; sand beach 300m; watersports; tennis; games area; cycle hire; entmnt; some statics; dogs €4.10; bus 500m; site clsd 14 Dec-14 Jan; adv bkg; quiet but v noisy Fri/Sat nights; red low ssn; CCI. "Pleasant site amongst pine trees but lack of site care low ssn; basic san facs, ltd low ssn; lge pitches but poss soft sand." ♦ € 30.40 2009*

MENDEXA see Lekeitio *3A1*

⊞ **MENDIGORRIA** *3B1* (500m SW Rural) *42.62416, -1.84277* **Camping El Molino, Ctra Larraga, 31150 Mendigorría (Navarra) [948-34 06 04; fax 948-34 00 82; info@campingelmolino.com; www.campingelmolino.com]** Fr Pamplona on N111 turn L at 25km in Puente la Reina onto NA601 sp Mendigorría. Site sp thro vill dir Larraga. Med, some mkd pitch, pt shd; wc; chem disp; mv service pnt; serviced pitches; baby facs; shwrs inc; el pnts (6A) inc; gas; Indtte; shop; tradsmn; rest; snacks; bar; BBQ; playgrnd; pool; canoe hire; tennis; games area; wifi; TV; statics (sep area); dogs; phone; poss cr at w/end; clsd 23 Dec-5 Jan & poss Mon-Thurs fr Nov to Feb; adv bkg; poss v noisy at w/end; ccard acc; CCI. "Gd clean facs; solar water heating - water poss only warm; vg leisure facs; ltd facs low ssn; for early am dep low ssn, pay night bef & obtain barrier key; friendly, helpful staff; lovely medieval vill; excel." ♦ € 24.70 (CChq acc) 2009*

MEQUINENZA *3C2* (Urban) *41.37833, 0.30555* **Camp Municipal Octogesa, Ctra N211 s/n, Km 314, 50170 Mequinenza (Zaragoza) [974-46 44 31; fax 974-46 50 31; rai@fuibol.e.telefonica.net; www.fuibol.net]** Exit AP2 junc 4 onto N211 S. On ent Mequinenza just past wooded area on L, turn L thro break in service rd, site well sp. Tight ent poss unsuitable lge o'fits. Med, hdg/mkd pitch, terr, pt shd; wc; chem disp (wc); shwrs inc; el pnts (6A) €3.90; Indtte; shop 1km; rest; snacks; bar; BBQ; playgrnd; 2 pools high ssn; tennis; dogs; phone; Eng spkn; adv bkg; quiet but noise fr arr of fishing parties; ccard acc; CCI. "Site part of complex on bank of Rv Segre; base for fishing trips - equipment supplied; sm pitches unsuitable lge o'fits; NH only." 15 Feb-15 Nov. € 17.20 2009*

Spain

⊞ **MERIDA** *2E3* (2km SE Urban) *38.93558, -6.30426* **Camping Mérida, Avda de la Reina Sofia s/n, 06800 Mérida (Badajoz) [924-30 34 53; fax 924-30 03 98; proexcam@jet.es; www.pagina.de/campingmerida]** Fr E on A5/E90 exit junc 333/334 to Mérida, site on L in 2km. Fr W on A5/E90 exit junc 346, site sp. Fr N exit A66/E803 at junc 617 onto A5 E. Leave at junc 334, site on L in 1km twd Mérida. Fr S on A66-E803 app Mérida, foll Cáceres sp onto bypass to E; at lge rndabt turn R sp Madrid; site on R after 2km. Med, mkd pitch, pt sl, pt shd; wc; chem disp; shwrs inc; el pnts (6A) inc (long lead poss req & poss rev pol); gas; Indtte; ltd shop high ssn & 3km; hypmkt 6km; rest; snacks; bar; 2 free pools; TV; some statics; dogs; phone; no bus; quiet but some rd noise; CCI. "Roman remains & National Museum of Roman Art worth visit; poss diff lge o'fits manoeuvring onto pitch due trees & soft ground after rain; facs tired; gd seafood rest; ltd facs low ssn; conv NH; warden calls to collect fees." ♦ € 24.40 2009*

⊞ **MIAJADAS** *2E3* (10km SW Rural) *39.09599, -6.01333* **Camping-Restaurant El 301, Ctra Madrid-Lisbon, Km 301, 10100 Miajadas (Cáceres) [927-34 79 14; camping301@hotmail.com]** Leave A5/E90 just bef km stone 301 & foll sp 'Via de Servicio' with rest & camping symbols; site in 500m. Med, pt shd; wc; chem disp; shwrs inc; el pnts (8A) €4 (poss no earth); gas; Indtte; shop; rest; snacks; bar; playgrnd; pool; TV; phone; m'way noise & dogs; ccard acc; CCI. "Well-maintained, clean site; grass pitches; OK wheelchair users but steps to pool; gd NH." € 16.20 2009*

MIJAS COSTA see Fuengirola *2H4*

MIRANDA DEL CASTANAR *1D3* (500m S Rural) *40.47527, -5.99833* **Camping El Burro Blanco, Camino de las Norias s/n, 37660 Miranda del Castañar (Salamanca) [tel/fax 923-16 11 00; el.burro.blanco@hotmail.com; www.elburroblanco.net]** Fr Ciudad Rodrigo take SA220 to El Cabaco then foll sp for 2km to Miranda del Castañar. In 2km turn L onto concrete/dirt rd for 700m. Site on R. Sm, mkd pitch, terr, pt shd; wc; chem disp; shwrs inc; el pnts (2-10A) €1.50-4.80; Indtte; shop, rest, snacks 1km; tradsmn; bar; pool; no statics; dogs; phone 1km; Eng spkn; quiet; 10% red 3+ days; CCI. "Nice scenery, set in oak wood; medieval hill-top town 500m; tight ent to some pitches, manhandling req; excel." 1 Apr-1 Oct. € 18.80 2008*

MOANA *1B2* (3km W Coastal) *42.26991, -8.75202* **Camping Tiran, Ctra Cangas-Moaña, Km 3, 36957 Moaña (Pontevedra) [986-31 01 50; fax 986-44 72 04]** Exit AP9 junc 146 & foll sp Moaña/Cangas. Site beyond Moaña. Med, hdg pitch, terr, pt shd; wc; shwrs inc; el pnts (6A) inc; lndry rm; shop; tradsmn; rest; snacks; bar; playgrnd; beach adj; TV; 80% statics; no dogs; phone; adv bkg; quiet. "Site on v steep hill - only suitable m'vans & single-axle c'vans with powerful tow car; gd touring base S Galicia." 3 Apr-5 Oct. € 25.00 2008*

MOIXENT *4E2* (12km N Rural) *38.96488, -0.79917* **Camping Sierra Natura (Naturist), Finca El Tejarico, Ctra Moixent-Navalón, Km 11.5, 46810 Enguera (València) [962-25 30 26; fax 962-25 30 20; info@sierranatura.com; www.sierranatura.com]** Exit A35 fr N exit junc 23 or junc 23 fr S onto CV589 sp Navalón. At 11.5km turn R sp Sierra Natura - gd rd surface but narr & some steep, tight hairpin bends (owners arrange convoys on request). Fr E on N340 exit junc 18 (do not take junc 14). Sm, pt sl, pt shd; wc; chem disp; baby facs; sauna; shwrs inc; el pnts (10A) €5.20; lndry rm; shop & 12 km; rest; snacks; bar; playgrnd; pool; 10% statics; dogs €4.55; phone; poss cr; Eng spkn; adv bkg; quiet; red long stay. "Tranquil, family-run site in remote area; unusual architecture; stunning mountain scenery; nature walks on site; excel pool & rest complex." ♦ 1 Mar-30 Oct. € 19.16 2008*

⊞ **MOJACAR** *4G1* (3.5km S Coastal) *37.12656, -1.83250* **Camping El Cantal di Mojácar, Ctra Garrucha-Carboneras, 04638 Mojácar (Almería) [950-47 82 04; fax 950-47 83 34]** Fr N on coast rd AL5105, site on R 800m after Parador, opp 25km sp.Or exit A7 junc 520 sp Mojácar Parador. Foll Parador sps by-passing Mojácar, to site. Med, hdstg, pt shd; wc; chem disp; mv service pnt; shwrs inc; el pnts (15A) €3; gas; lndry rm; shop 500m; tradsmn; shops adj; rest; snacks; bar adj; BBQ; sand beach adj; 5% statics; dogs; phone; bus; poss v cr; some rd noise; red long stay/low ssn; CCI. "Pitches quite lge, not mkd; lge o'fits rec use pitches at front of site." ♦ € 22.20 2009*

⊞ **MOJACAR** *4G1* (9km S Rural) *37.06536, -1.86864* **Camping Sopalmo, Sopalmo, 04638 Mojácar (Almería) [950-47 84 13; fax 950-47 30 02; info@campingsopalmoelcortijillo.com; www.campingsopalmoelcortijillo.com]** Exit A7/E15 at junc 520 onto AL6111 sp Mojácar. Fr Mojácar turn S onto A1203/AL5105 dir Carboneras, site sp on W of rd about 1km S of El Agua del Medio. Sm, mkd pitch, hdstg, pt shd; wc; chem disp (wc); shwrs; el pnts (15A) €3; gas; lndtte; sm shop (high ssn); tradsmn; rest, snacks 6km; bar; shgl beach 1.7km; internet; 10% statics; dogs €1; Eng spkn; adv bkg; some rd noise; ccard not acc; red low ssn; CCI. "Clean, pleasant, popular site; remote & peaceful; friendly owner; gd walking in National Park." ♦ € 19.70 2008*

⊞ **MOJACAR** *4G1* (4km SW Coastal) *37.08888, -1.85599* **Camping Cueva Negra, Camino Lotaza, 2, 04638 Mojácar (Almería) [950-47 58 55; fax 950-47 57 11; info@campingcuevanegra.es; www.campingcuevanegra.es]** Leave N340/E15 at junc 520 for AL151 twd Mojácar Playa. Turn R onto coastal rd. Site 500m fr Hotel Marina on R. App rd diff lge o'fits.m'vans due grounding. Take care dip at site ent. Med, hdg/mkd pitch, all hdstg, terr, unshd; wc; chem disp; mv service pnt; shwrs inc; el pnts (22A) €3.30; gas; lndtte; shop; tradsmn; rest; snacks; bar; covrd pool; jacuzzi; sand beach adj; entmnt; TV; 5% statics; dogs €1.90; poss cr; adv bkg; quiet; red 30+ days; CCI. "Well-kept, beautifully laid-out site; clean san facs but some basic; pleasant atmosphere; gd touring base; facs stretched when site full." ♦ € 28.60 2007*

⊞ **MOJACAR** *4G1* (500m W Rural) *37.14083, -1.85916* **Camping El Quinto, Ctra Mojácar-Turre, 04638 Mojácar (Almería) [950-47 87 04; fax 950-47 21 48; campingelquinto@hotmail.com]** Fr A7/E15 exit 520 sp Turre & Mojácar. Site on R in approx 13km at bottom of Mojácar vill. Sm, hdg/mkd pitch, hdstg, pt shd; wc; chem disp; mv service pnt; shwrs inc; el pnts (6-10A) €3.21; gas; lndtte; shop; tradsmn; rest 3km; snacks; bar; BBQ; playgrnd; pool; sand beach 3km; dogs €1; phone; poss cr; Eng spkn; adv bkg; quiet but some rd noise; red long stay; CCI. "Neat, tidy site; mkt Wed; close National Park; excel beaches; metered 6A elect for long winter stay; popular in winter, poss cr & facs stretched; security barrier; poss mosquitoes; drinking water ltd to 5L a time." ♦ € 20.50 2007*

⊞ **MOJACAR** *4G1* (5km W Rural) **Canada Camping, 04639 Turre (Almería) [627-76 39 08 (mob); canadacampingmojacar@yahoo.co.uk]** Exit A7/E15 at junc 525 & foll sp Los Gallardos on N340A. After approx 3km turn L at sp Turre & Garrucha on A370. In 3.5km slow down at green sp 'Kapunda' & turn R in 300m at sp 'Casa Bruns'. Site in 100m. Sm, hdg/mkd pitch, hdstg, unshd; wc (cont); chem disp; mv service pnt; shwrs inc; el pnts (6A) inc; lndry rm; no statics; dogs; adv bkg; quiet; CCI. "Gd, adults-only site; friendly atmosphere." € 12.00 2009*

⊞ **MONASTERIO DE RODILLA** *1B4* (800m NE Rural) *42.4604, -3.4581* **Camping Picon del Conde, Ctra N1 Madrid-Irún, Km 263, 09292 Monasterio de Rodilla (Burgos) [tel/fax 947-59 43 55]** Fr A1 join N1 at exit 2 or 3, site is on N1 at km marker 263 - behind motel. Easy to miss in heavy traff. Med, hdg/mkd pitch, shd; htd wc; chem disp; shwrs inc; el pnts (5A) €3.60; gas; lndry rm; shop; rest; snacks; bar; playgrnd; pool; 75% statics; dogs; phone; rd noise; ccard acc; CCI. "Ltd facs low ssn; poss migrant workers; caution el pnts; new grnd floor san facs 2009; site muddy in wet weather; friendly staff; 2 hrs drive fr Bilbao ferry; gd NH." ♦ € 14.60 2009*

Spain

⊞ **MONCOFA** *3D2* (2km E Coastal/Urban) *39.80861, -0.12805* **Camping Monmar, Camino Serratelles s/n, 12593 Platja de Moncófa (Castellón) [tel/fax 964-58 85 92; campingmonmar@terra.es]** Exit 49 fr A7 or N340, foll sp Moncófa Platja passing thro Moncófa & foll sp beach & tourist info thro 1-way system. Site sp, adj Aqua Park. Lge, hdg pitch, hdstg, pt shd; htd wc; chem disp; all serviced pitches; baby facs; shwrs inc; el pnts (6A) inc; gas; Indtte; shop & 1km; tradsmn; rest; snacks; bar; BBQ; playgrnd; pool; sand/shgl beach 200m; entmnt; internet; 80% statics; no dogs; phone; bus 300m; poss cr; Eng spkn; adv bkg; quiet; ccard acc; red low ssn/long stay; CCI. "V helpful owner & staff; rallies on site Dec-Apr; poss v cr; mini-bus to stn & excursions; sunshades over pitches poss diff high o'fits; excel clean, tidy site." ♦ € 35.00 2009*

⊞ **MONCOFA** *3D2* (2km S Coastal) *39.78138, -0.14888* **Camping Los Naranjos, Camino Cabres, Km 950.8, 12593 Moncófa (Castellón) [964-58 03 37; fax 964-76 62 37; info@campinglosnaranjos.com]** Fr N340 at km post 950.8 turn L at site sp, site 1km on R. Med, mkd pitch, hdstg, pt shd; wc; chem disp; mv service pnt; shwrs inc; el pnts (10A) €4.40; gas; Indtte; shop; tradsmn; rest; snacks; bar; playgrnd; pool; paddling pool; beach 300m; games area; 20% statics; phone; bus 1.5km; poss cr; adv bkg; quiet; red low ssn/long stay. "Gd." € 24.09 2008*

MONTAGUT I OIX *3B3* (2km N Rural) *42.24538, 2.59943* **Camping Montagut, Ctra de Sadernes, Km 2, 17855 Montagut I Oix (Gerona) [972-28 72 02; fax 972-28 72 01; info@campingmontagut.com; www.campingmontagut.com]** Exit AP7 junc 4 onto N260 W; join A26 & approx 10km past Besalú at Sant Jaume turn R twd Montagut i Oix on GIP5233. At end of vill turn L twd Sadernes on GIV5231, site in 2km, sp. Med, hdg/mkd pitch, terr; shd; htd wc; chem disp; mv service pnt; baby facs; shwrs inc; el pnts (6A) €3.90; gas; Indtte; shop; tradsmn; rest (w/end); bar; playgrnd; pool; paddling pool; no statics; quiet; red low ssn/long stay. "Excel, peaceful, scenic site; high standard san facs; helpful staff; gd walks nrby." ♦ 15 Mar-19 Oct. € 19.20 2008*

⊞ **MONTBLANC** *3C2* (1.5km NE Rural) *41.37743, 1.18511* **Camping Montblanc Park, Ctra Prenafeta, Km 1.8, 43400 Montblanc (Tarragona) [977-86 25 44; fax 977-86 05 39; info@montblancpark.com; www.montblancpark.com]** Exit AP2 junc 9 sp Montblanc; foll sp Montblanc/Prenafeta/TV2421; site on L on TV2421. Med, hdg pitch, pt sl, terr, pt shd; htd wc; chem disp; mv service pnt; baby facs; shwrs inc; el pnts (10A) inc; Indtte; shop; tradsmn; rest; snacks; bar; BBQ; playgrnd; pool; paddling pool; wifi; entmnt; 50% statics; dogs €4.50; phone; Eng spkn; adv bkg; ccard acc; red long stay/snr citizens; CCI. "Excel site; superb san facs; lovely area; Cistercian monestaries nrby; conv NH Andorra." ♦ € 34.50 2009*

MONTERROSO *1B2* (1km S Rural) *42.78720, -7.84414* **Camp Municipal de Monterroso, A Pineda, 27569 Monterroso (Lugo) [982-37 75 01; fax 982-37 74 16; aged@cinsl.es; www.campingmonterroso.com]** Fr N540 turn W onto N640 to Monterroso. Fr town cent turn S on LU212. In 100m turn sharp R then downhill for 1km; 2 sharp bends to site. Sm, hdg/mkd pitch, pt sl, pt shd; wc; chem disp; shwrs inc; el pnts (10A) €3.50; shop; tradsmn; rest, snacks, bar 500m; pool adj; games area; internet; dogs; Eng spkn; quiet; CCI. "Helpful staff; v quiet & ltd facs low ssn; vg." ♦
1 Apr-30 Sep. € 15.00 2008*

MONTROIG see Cambrils *3C2*

⊞ **MORAIRA** *4F2* (1.5km SW Coastal) *38.68576, 0.11930* **Camping Moraira, Camino del Paellero 50, 03724 Moraira-Teulada (Alicante) [965-74 52 49; fax 965-74 53 15; campingmoraira@campingmoraira.com; www.campingmoraira.com]** Fr A7 exit junc 63. Foll sp Teulada & Moraira. Turn W 1km S of Moraira at km post 1.2, then site 500m up hill. Med, mkd pitch, hdstg, terr, shd; wc; chem disp; 15% serviced pitches; baby facs; shwrs inc; el pnts (6A) €4.28; Indtte (inc dryer); shop & 650m; tradsmn; rest; snacks; bar; htd pool; sand beach 1km; internet; some statics; dogs; phone; bus 500m; Eng spkn; adv bkg; poss noisy w/end high ssn; red low ssn/long stay; ccard acc; CCI. "Coastal town with harbour; modern site; gd touring base; ltd facs low ssn, san facs stretched high ssn; pitching poss diff for lge o'fits due trees & walls." ♦ € 31.00 2008*

⊞ **MORATALLA** *4F1* (8km NW Rural) *38.21162, -1.94444* **Camping La Puerta, Ctra del Canal, Paraje de la Puerta, 30440 Moratalla (Murcia) [tel/fax 968-73 00 08; lapuerta@forodigital.es; www.campinglapuerta.com]** Fr Murcia take C415 dir Mula & Caravaca. Foll sp Moratalla & site. Lge, shd; htd wc; shwrs inc (poss cold); el pnts (10A) €4.95; gas; Indtte; shop; rest; bar; BBQ; playgrnd; pool; tennis; games area; internet; TV rm; statics; dogs €1.10; site clsd 22 Dec-6 Jan; adv bkg; quiet; ccard acc. "Busy at w/ends." ♦ € 17.80 (CChq acc) 2008*

⊞ **MORELLA** *3D2* (2km NE Rural) *40.62401, -0.09141* **Motor Caravan Parking, 12300 Morella (Castellón)** Exit N232 at sp (m'van emptying). Sm, hdstg, pt shd; chem disp; mv service pnt; water; quiet. "Free of charge; stay up to 72 hrs; clean; superb location; lge m'vans acc." 2009*

MOSTEIRO CERVANTES see Becerreá *1B2*

⊞ **MOTRIL** *2H4* (12km SE Coastal) *36.70066, -3.44032* **Camping Don Cactus, N340, Km 343, 18730 Carchuna (Granada) [958-62 31 09; fax 958-62 42 94; camping@doncactus.com; www.doncactus.com]** On N340 SE fr Motril 1km W of Calahonda. Foll site sp. Lge, hdstg, shd; wc; chem disp; mv service pnt; shwrs; el pnts (5A) €4.50 (no earth); gas; lndtte; supmkt; rest; snacks; bar; BBQ; playgrnd; pool; shgl beach adj; tennis; archery; golf 6km; entmnt; wi-fi internet; TV rm; 60% statics; dogs €2.50 (not acc Jul & Aug); poss cr; no adv bkg; quiet; ccard acc; red long stay/low ssn; CCI. "Many greenhouses around site (unobtrusive); some sm pitches not rec lge o'fits; dated but clean san facs; gd pool & rest; helpful staff; popular winter long stay; gd NH." ♦ € 28.50 2008*

⊞ **MOTRIL** *2H4* (3km SW Urban/Coastal) *36.71833, -3.54616* **Camping Playa de Poniente de Motril, 18600 Motril (Granada) [958-82 03 03; fax 958-60 41 91; camplapo@infonegocio.com]** Turn off coast rd N340 to port bef flyover; at rndabt take rd for Motril. Turn R in town, site sp. Lge, pt shd; htd wc; chem disp; mv service pnt; baby facs; shwrs; el pnts (6-10) €3.35; gas; lndtte; shop; supmkt 4km; rest, bar in ssn; beach adj; pool; playgrnd; golf; tennis; horseriding; cycle hire; 70% statics; dogs €1.50; bus; Eng spkn; adv bkg; ccard acc; red low ssn/long stay. "Well-appointed site but surrounded by blocks of flats; gd, clean facs; helpful recep; gd shop; access diff for lge o'fits; poss lge flying beetles; excel long stay winter." ♦ € 23.50 2008*

⊞ **MUNDAKA** *3A1* (1km N Coastal) *43.4094, -2.7003* **Camping Portuondo, Ctra Amorebieta-Bermeo, Km 43, 48360 Mundaka (Bilbao) [946-87 77 01; fax 946-87 78 28; recepcion@campingportuondo.com; www.campingportuondo.com]** Leave E70 E of Bilbao onto B1631 to Bermeo. Keep on coast rd dir Mundaka, site 1km on L. Ess to app fr Bermeo due to steep ent. Do not drive past recep until booked in due steep access. Med, terr, pt shd; wc; shwrs inc; el pnts (6A) €3.25; lndtte; rest; snacks; bar; playgrnd; pool; paddling pool; beach 500m; 30% statics; site clsd mid Dec-mid Jan; dogs; train 800m; poss v cr w/ends; adv bkg rec; ccard acc. "Clean, modern facs; pitches tight; popular with surfers; conv Bilbao by train; site suitable sm m'vans only." € 22.90 2008*

⊞ **MURCIA** *4F1* (10km SW Rural) *37.95444, -1.26166* **Camping La Paz, Ctra 340 Murcia-Granada, Km 321, 30835 Sangonera La Seca (Murcia) [968-89 39 29; fax 968-80 13 37; horepa_@hotmail.com]** Tourist complex La Paz off A7 on W of junc 647; site sp visible both dirs. Med, hdg/mkd pitch, hdstg, unshd; htd wc; chem disp; serviced pitches; shwrs inc; el pnts inc (poss rev pol); lndtte; sm shop adj; tradsmn; rest; snacks; bar; BBQ; playgrnd; pool; tennis; games area; TV; 95% statics; dogs; phone; cash machine; bus 600m; Eng spkn; adv bkg; rd noise; red long stay/low ssn; ccard acc; CCI. "Gd NH but v ltd number touring pitches - rec walking to find pitch." ♦ € 17.36 2008*

MUROS *1B1* (500m W Coastal/Rural) *42.76176, -9.07365* **Camping San Francisco, Camino de Convento 21, 15291 Louro-Muros (La Coruña) [981-82 61 48; fax 981-57 19 16; campinglouro@yahoo.es; www.campinglouro.com]** Fr Muros cont on C550 coast rd for 3km to San Francisco vill. Site sp to R up narr rd. Med, mkd pitch, pt shd; htd wc; chem disp; mv service pnt; shwrs; el pnts (5-8A) inc; gas; lndtte; rest; snacks; bar; sand beach 200m; playgrnd; dogs; phone; bus 300m; Eng spkn; adv bkg; quiet; ccard acc; CCI. "Pleasant site in walled monastery garden; gd, clean facs; vg sm rest; sh walk to lovely beach; excel security; unspoilt area." ♦ 22 Jun-7 Sep. € 27.60 2009*

MUROS *1B1* (7km W Coastal) *42.76100, 9.11100* **Camping Ancoradoiro, Ctra Corcubión-Muros, Km.7.2, 15250 Louro (La Coruña) [981-87 88 97; fax 981-87 85 50; wolfgang@mundo-r.com]** Foll AC550 W fr Muros. Site on L (S), well sp. Immed inside ent arch, to thro gate on L. Med, hdg/mkd pitch, terr, pt shd; wc; chem disp; shwrs inc; el pnts (6A) €3.74; lndtte; shop adj; rest; snacks, bar adj; playgrnd; sand beach 500m; watersports; entmnt; no statics; no dogs; phone; poss cr; adv bkg; quiet; CCI. "Well-run site; excel rest; beautiful beaches; scenic area; vg." 15 Mar-15 Sep. € 20.75 2008*

MUTRIKU see Deba *3A1*

⊞ **MUXIA** *1A1* (10km E Coastal) *43.1164, -9.1583* **Camping Playa Barreira Leis, Playa Berreira, Leis, 15124 Camariñas-Muxia (La Coruña) [tel/fax 981-73 03 04]** Fr Ponte do Porto turn L sp Muxia; foll camp sp. Site is 1st after Leis vill on R. Med, mkd pitch, terr, pt shd; wc; chem disp; shwrs inc; el pnts €3.50; lndtte; shop; rest; bar; BBQ; playgrnd; sand beach 100m; dogs €1; TV; quiet; ccard acc; CCI. "Beautiful situation on wooded hillside; dir acces to gd beach; ltd, poorly maintained facs low ssn; mkt in Muxia Thurs." € 15.80 2008*

NAJERA *3B1* (500m S Urban) *42.41183, -2.73168* **Camping El Ruedo, San Julián 24, 26300 Nájera (La Rioja) [941-36 01 02; www.campingelruedo.es.vg]** Take Nájera town dirs off N120. In town turn L bef x-ing bdge. Site sp. Sm, pt shd; htd wc; chem disp; shwrs inc; el pnts (10-16A) €3 (rev pol & poss no earth); gas; lndtte; shop; rest; snacks; bar; playgrnd; pool 1km; entmnt; TV; phone; bus 200m; poss cr; adv bkg; quiet; ccard acc; CCI. "Pleasant site in quiet location, don't be put off by 1st impression of town; monastery worth visit." 1 Apr-10 Sep. € 19.00 2008*

⊞ **NAVAJAS** *3D2* (1km W Rural) *39.87489, -0.51034* **Camping Altomira, Ctra Navajas/Pantano del Regajo, 12470 Navajas (Castellón) [964-71 32 11 or 964-71 09 46; fax 964-71 35 12; reservas@campingaltomira.com; www.campingaltomira.com]** Exit A23/N234 at junc 33 to rndabt & take CV214 dir Navajas. In approx 2km turn L onto CV213, site on L just past R turn into vill, sp. Med, hdstg, terr, pt shd; htd wc; chem disp; mv service pnt; serviced pitches; baby facs; shwrs; el pnts (3-6A) €3.70; gas; Indtte; shop; tradsmn; rest; snacks; bar; playgrnd; pool; paddling pool; tennis; cycle hire; wifi; 70% statics; dogs; phone; bus 500m; adv bkg; poss noisy w/end & public hols; ccard acc; red low ssn/long stay/CCI. "Superb welcome; friendly staff; panoramic views fr upper level but not rec for lge o'fits due tight bends & ramped access; gd birdwatching; walking/cycling rte adj; ltd facs low ssn; steep app to touring pitches on upper levels & kerbs to some pitches; excel san facs but stretched if site full; some sm pitches poss diff for lge o'fits without motor mover; poss clsd low ssn - phone ahead to check; useful NH & longer; excel." ♦ € 22.10 (CChq acc) 2009*

NAVALAFUENTE see Cabrera, La *1D4*

NAVARREDONDA DE GREDOS see Hoyos del Espino *1D3*

NAVARRETE see Logroño *3B1*

⊞ **NEGRAS, LAS** *4G1* (1km N Coastal) *36.87243, -2.00674* **Camping Náutico La Caleta, Parque Natural Cabo de Gata, 04116 Las Negras (Almería) [tel/fax 950-52 52 37; campinglacaleta@arrakis.es]** Exit N344 at km stone 487 twd Las Negras. Site sp at ent to vill on R. Med, hdg pitch, hdstg, shd; wc; chem disp; mv service pnt; shwrs inc; el pnts (10A) €4.50; gas; Indtte; shop & 1km; tradsmn; rest; snacks; bar; playgrnd; pool (high ssn); sand/shgl beach adj; cycle hire; dogs €3; phone; poss cr; quiet; red long stay/low ssn; CCI. "Lge o'fits need care on steep app rd; vans over 2.50m take care sun shades on pitches; gd walking area; vg." ♦ € 24.30 2008*

⊞ **NERJA** *2H4* (4km E Rural) *36.76035, -3.83490* **Nerja Camping, Ctra Vieja Almeria, Km 296.5, Camp de Maro, 29787 Nerja (Málaga) [952-52 97 14; fax 952-52 96 96; nerjacamping5@hotmail.com]** On N340, cont past sp on L for 200m around RH corner, bef turning round over broken white line. Foll partly surfaced rd to site on hillside. Fr Almuñécar on N340, site on R approx 20km. Med, pt sl, terr, pt shd; wc; chem disp; shwrs inc; el pnts (5A) €3.75 (check earth); gas; Indry rm; shops; tradsmn; rest; snacks; bar; playgrnd; sm pool; sand beach 2km; cycle hire; site clsd Oct; Eng spkn; adv bkg rec; rd noise; red long stay/low ssn/CCI. "5 mins to Nerja caves; mkt Tue; annual carnival 15 May; diff access lge o'fits; gd horseriding; site rds steep but gd surface; gd views; friendly owners." ♦ € 23.80 2007*

⊞ **NIJAR** *4G1* (23km SE Coastal) *36.80298, -2.07768* **Camping Los Escullos, Paraje de los Escullos s/n, 04118 San José-Nijar (Almería) [950-38 98 11 or 950-38 98 10; fax 950-38 98 10; info@losescullossanjose.com; www.losescullossanjose.com]** Fr E on E15/A7 exit 479 sp San Isidro; fr W exit junc 471 sp San José. Foll sp San José on AL3108 & after passing La Boca de los Frailes turn L onto AL4200 sp Los Escullos & site. After 3km turn R to site, ent on R in 1km - take care unmarked speed bumps. Lge, mkd pitch, hdstg, pt sl, shd; wc; chem disp; mv service pnt; baby facs; sauna; shwrs inc; el pnts (10A) €4.95; gas; Indtte; shop; rest; snacks; bar; playgrnd; pool; beach 700m; watersports; diving; tennis; cycle hire; fitness rm; entmnt; excursions arranged; wifi; TV rm; 40% statics; dogs €2.50; Eng spkn; adv bkg; ccard acc; red long stay/CCI. "Well-run, rustic, attractive site in National Park; many secluded beaches & walks; excel for watersports; vg pool & rest; clean facs; helpful staff; pitches poss flood in heavy rain." ♦ € 29.00 (CChq acc) 2009*

⊞ **NOIA** *1B2* (5km SW Coastal) *42.77198, -8.93761* **Camping Punta Batuda, Playa Hornanda, 15970 Porto do Son (La Coruña) [981-76 65 42; camping@puntabatuda.com; www.puntabatuda.com]** Fr Santiago take C543 twd Noia, then AC550 5km SW to Porto do Son. Site on R approx 1km after Boa. Lge, mkd pitch, terr, pt shd; htd wc; chem disp; shwrs inc; el pnts (3A) €3.74 (poss rev pol); gas; Indtte; shop; rest w/end only; snacks; bar; tradsmn; playgrnd; htd pool w/end only; sand beach adj; tennis; 50% statics; some Eng spkn; adv bkg; quiet; red long stay/low ssn; CCI. "Wonderful views; exposed to elements & poss windy; ltd facs low ssn; hot water to shwrs only; some pitches v steep &/or sm; gd facs for disabled; naturist beach 5km S." ♦ € 21.40 2008*

NOJA *1A4* (N Coastal) *43.48525, -3.53918* **Camping Los Molinos, Playa del Ris, 39180 Noja (Cantabria) [942-63 04 26; fax 942-63 07 25; losmolinos@ceoecant.es; www.campinglosmolinos.com]** Exit A8 at km 185. Go N & foll sp to Noja, then L at Playa del Ris. Site sp. V lge, hdg pitch, pt shd; wc; chem disp; mv service pnt; shwrs; baby facs; el pnts (3A) €3; gas; Indtte; shop; rest; snacks; bar; BBQ; playgrnd; pool; paddling pool; sand beach 500m; tennis; car wash; entmnt; 75% statics; dogs; poss cr; Eng spkn; adv bkg; ccard not acc; CCI. "Gd site; lovely beach; some noise fr karting circuit until late evening but noise levels strictly curtailed at midnight." ♦ Holy Week & 1 Jun-30 Sep. € 24.00 2007*

NOJA *1A4* (700m N Coastal) *43.49011, -3.53636* **Camping Playa Joyel, Playa del Ris, 39180 Noja (Cantabria) [942-63 00 81; fax 942-63 12 94; playajoyel@telefonica.net; www.playajoyel.com]** Fr Santander or Bilbao foll sp A8/E70 (toll-free). Approx 15km E of Solares exit m'way junc 185 at Beranga onto CA147 N twd Noja & coast. On o'skirts of Noja turn L sp Playa de Ris, foll rd approx 1.5km to rndabt, site sp to L, 500m fr rndabt. Fr Santander take S10 for approx 8km, then join A8/E70. V lge, mkd pitch, pt sl, pt shd; wc; chem disp; mv service pnt; baby facs; shwrs inc; el pnts (6A) €4.80; gas; Indtte; supmkt; tradsmn; rest; snacks; bar; BBQ (gas/charcoal); playgrnd; pool; paddling pool; jacuzzi; sand beach adj; windsurfing; sailing; tennis; hairdresser; car wash; cash dispenser; wifi; entment; games/TV rm; 15% statics; no dogs; phone; recep 0800-2200; poss v cr w/end & high ssn; Eng spkn; adv bkg; ccard not acc; red low ssn/snr citizens; CCI. "Well-organised site on sheltered bay; gd, clean facs; superb pool & beach; pleasant staff; ltd facs low ssn & ltd site lighting; some narr site rds with kerbs; midnight silence enforced; Wed mkt outside site; highly rec." ♦ 26 Mar-25 Sep. € 40.90
ABS - E05 2009*

NUEVALOS *3C1* (N Rural) *41.21846, -1.79211* **Camping Lago Park, Ctra De Alhama de Aragón a Cillas, Km 39, 50210 Nuévalos (Zaragoza) [tel/fax 976-84 90 38; info@campinglagopark.com; www.campinglagopark.com]**
Fr E on A2/E90 exit junc 231 to Nuévalos, turn R sp Madrid. Site 1.5km on L when ent Nuévalos. Fr W exit junc 204, site well sp. Steep ent fr rd. V lge, mkd pitch, terr, pt shd; wc; chem disp; child/baby facs; shwrs inc; el pnts (10A) €5.20; gas; Indtte; shop, rest, snacks high ssn; bar 500m; BBQ; playgrnd; pool; lake nrby; fishing; boating; some statics; dogs free; bus 500m; poss cr; adv bkg; quiet but noisy w/end high ssn; red long stay; CCI. "Nr Monasterio de Piedra & Tranquera Lake; excel facs on top terr, but stretched high ssn & poss long, steepish walk; ltd facs low ssn; gd birdwatching; only site in area; gd." 1 Apr-30 Sep. € 26.30
2008*

⊞ **OCHAGAVIA** *3A1* (500m S Rural) *42.90777, -1.08750* **Camping Osate, Ctra Salazar s/n, 31680 Ochagavia (Navarra) [tel/fax 948-89 01 84; info@campingsnavarra.com; www.campingsnavarra.com]** On N135 SE fr Auritz, turn L onto NA140 & cont for 24km bef turning L twd Ochagavia on NA140. Site sp in 2km on R, 500m bef vill. Lge, mkd pitch, pt shd; wc; chem disp; some serviced pitches; shwrs inc; el pnts (4A) €5.50; gas; Indtte; shop; rest high ssn; snacks; bar; BBQ; 50% statics; dogs €2; quiet but poss noise fr bar (open to public). "Attractive, remote vill; gd, well-maintained site; touring pitches under trees, sep fr statics; facs ltd & poss stretched high ssn; site clsd 3 Nov-15 Dec & rec phone ahead low ssn." € 19.40 2008*

⊞ **OLITE** *3B1* (2km S Rural) *42.48083, -1.67756* **Camping Ciudad de Olite, Ctra N115, Tafalla-Peralta, Km 2.3, 31390 Olite [948-74 10 14; fax 948-74 06 04; info@campingdeolite.com; www.campingdeolite.com]** Fr Pamplona S on AP15 exit 50 twd Olite. At rndabt turn L, then in 300m turn R onto NA115, site sp on L past Netto in 2km. Lge, mkd pitch, pt shd; wc; chem disp; mv service pnt; serviced pitches; baby facs; shwrs inc; el pnts (5A) inc; Indtte; shop 2km; rest; bar; playgrnd; htd pool (caps ess); tennis; entmnt; games area; 95% statics; dogs €1; poss cr; Eng spkn; phone; poss noisy at w/ends; ccard acc; CCI. "Close to m'way; ltd space & facs for tourers; site mostly used by Spanish for w/end; site bleak in winter; narr site rds; Olite historic vill with fairytale castle; poss neglected facs (2009); NH only." ♦ € 21.50 2009*

⊞ **OLIVA** *4E2* (2km E Coastal) *38.93250, -0.09750* **Camping Kiko Park, Calle Assagador de Carro 2, 46780 Playa de Oliva (València) [962-85 09 05; fax 962-85 43 20; kikopark@kikopark.com; www.kikopark.com]** Exit AP7/E15 junc 61; fr toll turn R at T-junc onto N332. Site sp on L (by iron monoliths) around seaboard side of town. Do not drive thro Oliva. Access poss diff on app rds due humps. Lge, hdg/mkd pitches, hdstg, shd; htd wc; chem disp; mv service pnt; some serviced pitches; baby facs; fam bthrm; shwrs inc; el pnts (16A) inc; gas; Indtte; supmkt; rest; bar; BBQ; playgrnd; 2 pools (1 covrd); sand beach adj; watersports; windsurfing school; fishing; tennis 1km; games area; cycle hire; entmnt; games rm; wifi; dogs €2.90; phone; pitch price variable; Eng spkn; adv bkg; quiet; ccard acc; red snr cititzens/long stay/low ssn; red CCI. "Excel rest in Michelin Guide; v helpful staff; gd family-run site; lots to do in area." ♦ € 46.50 ABS - E20 2009*

See advertisement on previous page

The opening dates and prices on this campsite have changed. I'll send a site report form to the Club for the next edition of the guide.

⊞ **OLIVA** *4E2* (4km E Coastal) *38.90759, -0.06722* **Camping Azul, 46780 Playa de Oliva (València) [962-85 41 06; fax 962-85 40 96; campingazul@ctv.es; www.campingazul.com]** Exit A7/E15 junc 61; fr toll turn R at T-junc onto N332. Drive S thro Oliva, site sp, turn twds sea at km 209.8. Narr access rd. Med, mkd pitch, pt shd; wc; mv service pnt; shwrs inc; el pnts (10A) €3.20; gas; Indtte; shop; rest; bar; playgrnd; cycle hire; games area; golf 1km; wifi; entmnt; 20% statics; dogs free; no adv bkg; ccard acc; red long stay/low ssn. "Gd site but constant barking dogs fr adj houses; san facs tired." ♦ € 24.90 2008*

⊞ **OLIVA** *4E2* (3km SE Coastal) *38.90555, -0.06666* **Eurocamping, Ctra València-Oliva, Aptdo 7, Partida Rabdells s/n, 46780 Playa de Oliva (València) [962-85 40 98; fax 962-85 17 53; info@eurocamping-es.com; www.eurocamping-es.com]** Fr N exit AP7/E15 junc 61 onto N332 dir Alicante. Drive S thro Oliva & exit N332 km 209.9 sp 'urbanización'. At v lge hotel Oliva Nova Golf take 3rd exit at rndabt sp Oliva & foll camping sp to site. Fr S exit AP7 junc 62 onto N332 dir València, exit at km 209 sp 'urbanización', then as above. Lge, hdg/mkd pitch, hdstg, pt shd; htd wc; chem disp; mv service pnt; baby facs; shwrs inc; el pnts (6-10A) €4.30-6.70; gas; Indtte; shop; tradsmn; rest; snacks; bar; BBQ; playgrnd; sand beach adj; cycle hire; wifi; entmnt; TV; dogs €2; phone; poss cr; quiet but some noise fr adj bar; ccard acc; red long stay/low ssn/CCI. "Gd facs; busy, well-maintained, clean site adj housing development; helpful British owners; beautiful clean beach; gd rest; gd beach walks; cycle rte thro orange groves to town; pitch far fr recep if poss, night noise fr generators 1700-2400; recep clsd 1400-1600; highly rec." ♦ € 41.10 (CChq acc) 2008*

⊞ **OLIVA** *4E2* (3km S Coastal) *38.89444, -0.05361* **Camping Olé, Partida Aigua Morta s/n, 46780 Playa de Oliva (València) [tel/fax 962-85 75 16 or 962-85 75 17; campingole@hotmail.com; www.camping-ole.com]** Exit AP7/E15 junc 61 onto N332 dir Valencia/Oliva. At km 209 (bef bdge) turn R sp 'Urbanización. At 1st rndabt, take 2nd exit past golf club ent, then 1st exit at next rndabt, turn L sp ' Camping Olé' & others. Site down narr rd on L. Lge, hdg/mkd pitch, hdstg, pt shd; htd wc; chem disp; baby facs; shwrs inc; el pnts (6-10A) €5.02; gas; Indtte; supmkt; rest; snacks; bar; BBQ; playgrnd; pool; sand beach adj; fishing; tennis 600m; cycle hire; horseriding 2km; golf adj; wifi; entmnt; 15% statics; dogs €2.75; phone; Eng spkn; adv bkg; quiet; ccard acc; red long stay/low ssn; CCI. "Many sports & activities; direct access to beach; excel." ♦ € 21.70 2009*

See advertisement opposite

⊞ **OLIVA** *4E2* (5km S Coastal) *38.89503, -0.05422* **Camping Pepe, 46780 Playa de Oliva (València) [962-85 75 19; fax 962-85 75 22; campingpepe@telefonica.net; www.campingpepe.com]** Exit A7 junc 61; fr toll turn R at T-junc onto N332 dir Valencia/Oliva. Drive S thro Oliva & in 3.5km at km 209, move R to service rd sp 'Urbanización'. Cont past service stn & across flyover. At 1st rndabt, take 2nd exit past golf club ent, then 1st exit at next rndabt, turn L sp ' Camping Pepe' & others. Site down narr rd on L. Lge, hdg/mkd pitch, hdstg, pt shd; wc; chem disp; baby facs; shwrs; el pnts (5A) €4.70; gas; Indtte; shop & 1km; tradmn; rest high ssn; snacks; bar; BBQ; playgrnd; sand beach adj; golf club nr; 30% statics; dogs €2; phone; poss cr; Eng spkn; quiet; red long stay/low ssn; CCI. "Well-managed, friendly, busy site; 5 san facs blocks; hot water avail all day for all needs; high kerb to some pitches; barrier locked at night; beautiful beach; vg for winter stay." ♦ € 25.50 2008*

⊞ **OLIVA** *4E2* (7km S Coastal) *38.88611, -0.03972* **Camping Rió Mar, Ctra N332, Km 207, 46780 Playa de Oliva (València) [962-85 40 97; fax 962-83 91 32; riomar@campingriomar.com; www.campingriomar.com]** Exit A7/E15 junc 61; fr toll turn R at T-junc onto N332. Drive S thro Oliva, site sp at km 207. Med, hdstg, shd; wc; chem disp; shwrs; el pnts (6A) €4.60; gas; Indtte; supmkt high ssn; rest, bar high ssn; playgrnd; sand beach adj; 20% statics; dogs €2.10; phone; poss cr; adv bkg; quiet; ccard acc; red snr citizens; CCI. "Friendly, clean, family-run site; facs in need of refurb; sm pitches but lge o'fits use sandy area bet site & beach; Fri mkt in Oliva." € 26.70 2008*

⊞ **OLOT** *3B3* (3km SE Rural) *42.15722, 2.51694* **Camping Fageda, Batet de la Serra, Ctra Olot-Santa Pau, Km 3.8, 17800 Olot (Gerona) [tel/fax 972-27 12 39; info@campinglafageda.com; www.campinglafageda.com]** Fr Figueras exit A26 sp Olot E twd town cent. Pick up & foll so Santa Pau on rd GI524. Site in 3.8km. Med, mkd pitch, pt sl, terr, pt shd; htd wc; chem disp; shwrs inc; el pnts (10A) €5.05 (poss rev pol); gas; Indtte; shop; snacks; rest & bar high ssn; playgrnd; htd pool high ssn; 90% statics (sep area); dogs; phone; adv bkg (dep); quiet; ccard acc; CCI. "Situated in beautiful area with extinct volcanoes & forests; walks fr site; diff access to water pnts for m'vans; isolated, pretty site, few visitors low ssn; v friendly, helpful staff." ♦ € 19.90 2009*

ORGANYA *3B2* (500m NW Rural) *42.21527, 1.33222* **Camping Organyà, Calle Piscines s/n, Partida Lloredes, 25794 Organyà (Lleida) [973-38 20 39; fax 973-38 35 36]** Site sp to E of C14 adj sports cent/football pitch. Sharp rise off rd & narr access, not rec for lge o'fits. Med, pt shd; wc; shwrs; el pnts (3A) €4.30; shop, rest 1km; bar; playgrnd; pools adj; tennis; paragliding tuition avail; mainly statics; dogs €2; phone; some rd noise; CCI. "Excel mountain scenery & interesting vill; gd, clean san facs; pleasant pools adj; NH only - phone ahead low ssn to check site open." Holy Week & 22 Jun-11 Sep. € 17.65 2008*

⊞ **ORGIVA** *2G4* (2km S Rural) *36.88852, -3.41837* **Camping Órgiva, Ctra A348, Km 18.9, 18400 Órgiva (Granada) [tel/fax 958-78 43 07; campingorgiva@descubrelaalpujarra.com; www.descubrelaalpujarra.com]** Fr N or S on Granada-Motril rd suggest avoid A348 via Lanjarón (narr & congested). Fr N323/A44 turn E nr km 179, 1km S of lge dam sp Vélez de Benaudalla, over multi-arch bdge, turn L sp Órgiva. Foll rd (easy climb) turn L after sh tunnel over rv bdge; site 2nd building on R. Sm, pt sl, pt shd; wc; chem disp; serviced pitches; baby facs; shwrs inc; el pnts (10A) €2.70 (rev pol); gas; Indtte; supmkt 2km; rest; snacks; bar; playgrnd; pool; shgl beach 30km; bus 2km; adv bkg; ccard acc; some Eng spkn; red low ssn/long stay; ccard acc; red long stay/CCI. "Immac san facs; excel, friendly site; some sm pitches; vg value rest open all yr; magnificent scenery; gd base for mountains & coast; Thurs mkt in town; fiesta 27 Sep-1 Oct; pleasant walk thro orange & almond groves to vill." ♦ € 17.50 2008*

⊞ **ORGIVA** *2G4* (2km NW Rural) *36.90420, -3.43880* **Camping Puerta de la Alpujarra, Ctra Lanjarón-Órgiva (Las Barreras), 18418 Órgiva (Granada) [tel/fax 958-78 44 50; puertadelaalpujarra@campings.net; www.campingpuertadelaalpujarra.com]** Fr Órgiva take A348 to Lanjarón. Site on L in 2km. Lanjarón poss diff for long o'fits. Med, mkd pitch, hdstg, terr, pt shd; wc; chem disp; mv service pnt; shwrs inc; el pnts (16A) €3.50; gas 2km; Indtte; shop; rest; bar; playgrnd; pool, paddling pool high ssn; entmnt; few statics; dogs free; phone; bus adj; poss cr; Eng spkn; adv bkg; quiet; ccard acc; 10% red 7+ days. "Scenic area with gd views fr site; steepish access to pitches; excel walking." ♦ € 20.00 2008*

ORIHUELA DEL TREMEDAL *3D1* (1km S Rural) *40.54784, -1.65095* **Camping Caimodorro, Camino Fuente de los Colladillos s/n, 44366 Orihuela del Tremedal (Teruel) [978-71 43 55; caimodorro@suone.com; www.caimodorro.com]** Fr Albarracin on A1512 head twd Orihuela. Turn R twd vill & R after petrol stn, sp. Sm, unshd; wc; shwrs; el pnts €2.20; Indtte; shop; bar; pool; dogs; phone; bus 600m; Eng spkn; ccard acc. "Elevated, breezy situation o'looking mountain vill; lovely scenery; gd touring base; friendly owner; v quiet low ssn." 1 Apr-31 Oct. € 11.60 2006*

Spain

ORINON *1A4* (2km E Coastal) *43.40361, -3.31027* **Camping Playa Arenillas, Ctra Santander-Bilbao, Km 64, 39798 Islares (Cantabria) [tel/fax 942-86 31 52; cueva@mundivia.es; www.campingplayaarenillas.com]** Exit A8 at km 156 Islares. Turn W on N634. Site on R at W end of Islares. Steep ent & sharp turn into site, exit less steep. Lge, mkd pitch, pt shd; wc; chem disp; baby facs; shwrs inc; el pnts (3-5A) €4.14 (poss no earth); gas; Indtte; shop; tradsmn; rest adj; snacks; bar; BBQ; playgrnd; sand beach 100m; horseriding; cycle hire; games area; TV; 40% statics; no dogs; phone; bus 500m; poss cr; adv bkg rec Jul/Aug; some rd noise; ccard acc; CCI. "Facs ltd low ssn & stretched in ssn; facs constantly cleaned; hot water to shwrs only; rec arr early for choice of own pitch; conv Guggenheim Museum; excel NH for Bilbao ferry." 1 Apr-30 Sep. € 21.40 2009*

ORINON *1A4* (500m NW Rural/Coastal) *43.39944, -3.32805* **Camping Oriñón, 39797 Oriñón (Cantabria) [tel/fax 942-87 86 30; info@campingorinon.com; www.campingorinon.com]** Exit A8/E70 at km 160 to Oriñón. Adj holiday vill. Med, mkd pitch, pt sl, unshd; wc; chem disp; mv service pnt; shwrs inc; el pnts (4A) €4; gas; Indtte (inc dryer); shop; rest; snacks; bar; playgrnd; sand beach adj; internet; TV; 90% statics; dogs; phone; bus 1km; Eng spkn; quiet; red long stay. "Excel surfing beach adj; clean site; no hot water to wash basins; helpful staff; conv Bilbao ferry." ♦ Holy Week & 1 Jun-30 Sep. € 20.00 2009*

ORIO see Zarautz *3A1*

⊞ **OROPESA** *3D2* (3km NE Coastal) *40.12786, 0.16088* **Camping Torre La Sal 1, Camí L'Atall s/n, 12595 Ribera de Cabanes (Castellón) [964-31 95 96; fax 964-31 96 29; info@campingtorrelasal.com; www.campingtorrelasal.com]** Leave AP7 at exit 45 & take N340 twd Tarragona. Foll camp sp fr km 1000.1 stone. Do not confuse with Torre La Sal 2 or Torre Maria. Lge, hdg/mkd pitch, hdstg, pt shd; htd wc; chem disp; baby facs; shwrs inc; el pnts (10A) €4.20; gas; Indtte; shop adj; rest, snacks, bar; BBQ; playgrnd; htd, covrd pool; sand/shgl beach adj; tennis; games area; wifi; Tv rm; 10% statics; dogs (except Jul/Aug); phone adj; bus 1.5km; poss cr; Eng spkn; adv bkg; quiet; ccard acc; red long stay/snr citizens; CCI. "Clean, well-maintained, peaceful site; elec metered for long stays; night security guard." ♦ € 30.00 2009*

⊞ **OROPESA** *3D2* (3.5km NE Coastal) *40.1275, 0.15972* **Camping Torre La Sal 2, Cami L'Atall s/n, 12595 Ribera de Cabanes (Castellón) [964-31 95 67; fax 964-31 97 44; camping@torrelasal2.com; www.torrelasal2.com]** Leave AP7 at exit 45 & take N340 twd Tarragona. Foll camp sp fr km 1000 stone. Site adj Torre La Sal 1. Lge, hdg/mkd pitch, hdstg, pt shd; htd wc; chem disp; sauna; serviced pitch; shwrs inc; el pnts (10A) €6.10; gas; Indtte; shop; tradsmn; supmkt adj & 1km; rest; snacks; bar; playgrnd; shgl beach adj; 4 pools (2 htd & covrd); tennis; games area; wifi; entmnt; library; wifi; TV rm; some statics; dogs free; Eng spkn; adv bkg; quiet; red long stay/low ssn/snr citizens; CCI. "Vg, clean, peaceful, well-run site; lger pitches nr pool; poss diff for lge o'fits & m'vans; excel rest; excel beach with dunes." ♦ € 29.50 2009*

⊞ **OSSA DE MONTIEL** *4E1* (10km SW Rural) *38.93717, -2.84744* **Camping Los Batanes, Ctra Lagunas de Ruidera, Km 8, 02611 Ossa de Montiel (Albacete) [926-69 90 76; fax 926-69 91 71; camping@losbatanes.com; www.losbatanes.com]** Fr Munera twd Ossa de Montiel on N430. In Ossa foll sp in vill to site in 10km. Fr Manzanares on N430 app to Ruidera, cross bdge; turn immed R alongside lagoon, camp at 12km. Lge, pt shd; htd wc; chem disp; mv service pnt; shwrs; el pnts (5A) €3.10; Indtte; shops 10km; tradsmn; rest 200m; snacks; bar; playgrnd; pool, paddling pool high ssn; lake sw adj; cycle hire; TV; 10% statics; dogs €2; phone; site clsd 28 Dec-2 Jan; Eng spkn; adv bkg; noisy at w/end; ccard acc; 10% red CCI. "Lovely area of natural lakes; excel birdwatching & walking; friendly owners; low ssn phone to check open." ♦ € 23.90 2007*

OTURA see Granada *2G4*

PALAFRUGELL *3B3* (5km E Coastal) *41.9005, 3.1893* **Kim's Camping, Calle Font d'en Xeco s/n, 17211 Llafranc (Gerona) [972-30 11 56; fax 972-61 08 94; info@campingkims.com; www.campingkims.com]** Exit AP7 at junc 6 Gerona Nord if coming fr France, or junc 9 fr S dir Palamós. Foll sp for Palafrugell, Playa Llafranc. Site is 500m N of Llafranc. Lge, hdg/mkd pitches, hdstg, pl sl, terr, shd; wc; chem disp; baby facs; shwrs inc; el pnts (6A) inc; gas; Indtte; shop; rest; snacks; bar; BBQ (gas only); playgrnd; 2 pools; sand beach 500m; watersports; tennis 500m; games rm; games area; cycle hire 500m; golf 10km; internet; entmnt; excursions; TV; 10% statics; dogs; phone; guarded; poss cr; Eng spkn; adv bkg; quiet; ccard acc; red low ssn/long stay; red CCI. "Excel, well-organised, friendly site; steep site rds; high ssn w/end noise fr adj site; excel, modern san facs inc for disabled; ltd facs low ssn." ♦ Easter-30 Sep. € 39.00 (CChq acc) 2007*

PALAFRUGELL *3B3* (5km SE Rural) *41.8971, 3.1824* **Camping La Siesta, Chopitea 110, 17210 Calella de Palafrugell (Gerona) [972-61 51 16; fax 972-61 44 16; info@campinglasiesta.com; www.campinglasiesta.com]** On main rd to Gerona-Palamós turn L (E) at rndabt onto GI654 & foll sp Calella. Site on R just bef Calella dir Llafranc. V lge, mkd pitch, pt sl, pt shd; wc; chem disp; shwrs inc; el pnts inc; gas; Indtte; shops; rest; snacks; 2 bars; no BBQ; playgrnd; 2 lge pools; beach 1.3km; tennis; horseriding; entmnt; statics; no dogs; bus; site open w/ends Nov-March & clsd Xmas to 8 Jan; Eng spkn; adv bkg; noisy at w/end; red low ssn. "Excel beaches at Llafranc & Calella de Palafrugell; mkt at Palafrugell; many beaches & coves adj; narr, winding paths thro pines to pitches; most vans have to be manhandled onto pitches; twin-axles acc." Easter-31 Oct. € 40.90 2006*

PALAFRUGELL *3B3* (5km S Coastal) *41.88831, 3.18013* **Camping Moby Dick, Carrer de la Costa Verda 16-28, 17210 Calella de Palafrugell (Gerona) [972-61 43 07; fax 972-61 49 40; info@campingmobydick.com; www.campingmobydick.com]** Fr Palafrugell foll sps to Calella. At rndabt just bef Calella turn R, then 4th L, site clearly sp on R. Med, hdstg, sl, terr, pt shd; wc; chem disp; mv service pnts; baby facs; shwrs inc; el pnts (6-10A); €4.05; Indtte; shop; supmkt 100m; rest 100m; snacks; bar; playgrnd; shgl beach 100m; TV; 15% statics; dogs €3.30; phone; bus 100m; poss cr; Eng spkn; adv bkg; quiet; ccard acc; CCI. ♦ 1 Apr-30 Sep. € 23.40 2009*

PALAMOS *3B3* (1km N Coastal) *41.85695, 3.13801* **Camping Internacional de Palamós, Camí Cap de Planes s/n, 17230 Palamós (Gerona) [972-31 47 36; fax 972-31 76 26; info@internacionalpalamos.com; www.internacionalpalamos.com]** Fr N leave AP7 at junc 6 to Palamós on C66. Fr Palafrugell turn L 16m after o/head sp to Sant Feliu-Palamós at sm sp La Fosca & camp sites. Winding app thro La Fosca. Fr S, take exit 9 dir Sant Feliu & Lloret, then C65/C31 to Santa Christina-Palamós, then La Fosca. Lge, pt shd; wc (mainly cont); chem disp; mv service pnt; baby facs; serviced pitches; private bthrms avail; shwrs inc; el pnts; (5A) inc; Indtte; shop; rest; snacks; bar; playgrnd; pool; paddling pool; sand beach 600m; solarium; mini-golf 200m; windsurfing, sailing & diving 1km; golf 15km; TV rm; car wash; 20% statics; phone; bus 600m; quiet. "Attractive site; superb san facs; some sm pitches on steep access rds - check bef pitching; highly rec; lovely area." ♦ 4 Apr-30 Sep. € 38.90 (CChq acc) 2008*

PALAMOS *3B3* (1km N Coastal) *41.85044, 3.13873* **Camping Palamós, Ctra La Fosca 12, 17230 Palamós (Gerona) [972-31 42 96; fax 972-60 11 00; campingpal@grn.es; www.campingpalamos.com]** App Palamós on C66/C31 fr Gerona & Palafrugell turn L 16m after o/head sp Sant Feliu-Palamós at sm sp La Fosca & campsites. Lge, pt sl, terr, pt shd; wc; shwrs; baby facs; el pnts (4A) €2.70; gas; Indtte; shop; rest 400m; playgrnd; 2 htd pools; shgl/rocky beach adj; tennis; golf; internet; 30% statics; dogs €2; phone; ccard acc. ♦ 27 Mar-30 Sep. € 31.90 2007*

PALAMOS *3B3* (2km N Coastal) *41.87277, 3.15055* **Camping Benelux, Paratge Torre Mirona s/n, 17230 Palamós (Gerona) [972-31 55 75; fax 972-60 19 01; cbenelux@cbenelux.com; www.cbenelux.com]** Turn E off Palamós-La Bisbal rd (C66/C31) at junc 328. Site in 800m on minor metalled rd, twd sea at Playa del Castell. Lge, hdstg, pt sl, pt shd; wc; chem disp; mv service pnt; shwrs inc; el pnts (6A) €4.30; gas; Indtte; shop; tradsmn; supmkt; rest (w/end only low ssn); snacks; bar; playgrnd; pool; sand beach 1km; safe dep; car wash; currency exchange; TV; 50% statics; dogs; poss cr; Eng spkn; adv bkg; noisy at w/end; red low ssn/long stay; ccard acc; CCI. "In pine woods; many long stay British/Dutch; v friendly owner; clean facs poss ltd low ssn; poss flooding in heavy rain; poss diff for disabled, rough ground." ♦ Easter-30 Sep. € 28.45 2008*

PALAMOS *3B3* (3km N Coastal) *41.89194, 3.14388* **Camping Relax Ge, Barrio Roqueta s/n, 17253 Mont-Ràs (Gerona) [972-30 15 49 or 972-31 42 06 (LS); fax 972-60 11 00; info@campingrelaxge.com; www.campingrelaxge.com]** C31 Palafrugell-Palamós rd at km 38.7, site sp. Med, mkd pitch, pt shd; wc; chem disp; shwrs (5A) €3; gas; Indtte; shop; rest; snacks; bar; playgrnd; htd pool & paddling pool; sand beach 1km; 10% statics; dogs €2.50; adv bkg; quiet; ccard acc; CCI. "Friendly, family-run site; exceptional beaches; conv Gerona, Barcelona." 1 Jun-31 Aug. € 28.90 2008*

PALAMOS *3B3* (6.5km N Rural) *41.89166, 3.15583* **Camping Relax-Nat (Naturist), Barrio Roqueta s/n, 17253 Mont-Ràs (Gerona) [972-30 08 18; fax 972-60 11 00; info@campingrelaxnat.com; www.campingrelaxnat.com]** Exit C31 Palafrugell-Palamós rd at sp Mont-Ràs (exit 249), cross under carriageway to 2nd rndabt & take last exit. Lge, pt shd; wc; chem disp; shwrs; el pnts (2A) €3; Indtte; shop; rest; snacks; bar; playgrnd; sand beach 4km; pool; playgrnd; tennis; games area; entmnt; some statics; no dogs; adv bkg; quiet. "Naturist families & mixed groups min 2 people; diff pitch access for lge o'fits." ♦ 15 Mar-28 Sep. € 31.50 2008*

Spain

PALAMOS *3B3* (3km SW Coastal) *41.84598, 3.09460* **Camping Costa Brava, Avda Unió s/n, 17252 Sant Antoni de Calonge (Gerona) [tel/fax 972-65 02 22; campingcosta brava@campingcostabrava.net; www.campingcosta brava.net]** Foll sp St Antoni de Calonge fr C31, site sp. Lge, mkd pitch, shd; wc; chem disp; baby facs; shwrs inc; el pnts (4A) €3.80; Indtte; shop adj; rest; snacks; bar; BBQ; playgrnd; pool & child pool; sand beach 300m; watersports; games rm; entmnt; car wash; dogs; phone; bus; poss cr; adv bkg; quiet; ccard acc. "Well-managed, family-run site; sm pitches; clean san facs; rec arr early high ssn to secure pitch; pleasant, helpful owners." ♦ 1 Jun-15 Sep. € 22.75 2007*

PALAMOS *3B3* (2.5km W Rural) *41.88194, 3.14083* **Camping Castell Park, Ctra C31 Palamós-Palafrugell, Km 328, 17253 Vall-Llobrega (Gerona) [tel/fax 972-31 52 63; info@ campingcastellpark.com; www.campingcastellpark.com]** Exit m'way at junc 6 & take C66/C31 to Palamós. Site on R sp after 40km marker. Lge, mkd pitch, terr, shd; wc (some cont); chem disp; baby facs; shwrs inc; el pnts (3A) inc; gas; Indtte; supmkt; rest; snacks; bar; BBQ; playgrnd; pool; paddling pool; sand beach 2.5km; cycle hire; golf 11km; games rm; internet; entmnt; TV rm; some statics; dogs; bus 700m; Eng spkn; adv bkg; quiet; red long stay/low ssn/ snr citizens; CCI. "Pleasant, quiet family site with friendly atmosphere & gd welcome; rallies & single c'vanners welcome; c'van storage avail." ♦ 27 Mar-12 Sep. € 34.00 2009*

PALAMOS *3B3* (3km W Coastal) *41.84700, 3.09861* **Eurocamping, Avda Catalunya 15, 17252 Sant Antoni de Calonge (Gerona) [972-65 08 79; fax 972-66 19 87; info@euro-camping.com; www.euro-camping.com]** Exit A7 junc 6 dir Palamós on C66 & Sant Feliu C31. Take exit Sant Antoni; on ent Sant Antoni turn R at 1st rndabt. Visible fr main rd at cent of Sant Antoni. V lge, hdg/mkd pitch, shd; wc; chem disp; mv service pnt; 20% serviced pitches; baby facs; shwrs inc; el pnts (5A) inc; Indtte; supmkt; rest; snacks; bar; BBQ; playgrnd; 2 pools & paddling pool; sand beach 300m; waterpark 5km; tennis; cycle hire 200m; golf 7km; games area; games rm; fitness rm; doctor Jul & Aug; car wash; entmnt high ssn; wifi; TV rm; 15% statics; dogs €3.75; phone; Eng spkn; adv bkg; quiet; ccard acc; red long stay/low ssn; CCI. "Excel facs for families; lots to do in area; excel." ♦ 24 Apr-19 Sep. € 45.25 2009*

See advertisement on previous page

PALS *3B3* (2km NE Coastal) *41.98132, 3.20125* **Camping Inter Pals, Avda Mediterránea s/n, Km 45, 17256 Playa de Pals (Gerona) [972-63 61 79; fax 972-66 74 76; interpals@interpals.com; www.interpals.com]** Exit A7 junc 6 dir Palamós onto C66. Turn N sp Pals & foll sp Playa/Platja de Pals, site clearly sp. Lge, pt sl, terr, shd; htd wc; chem disp; mv service pnt; baby facs; shwrs inc; el pnts (5-10A) inc; Indtte; rest; snacks; bar; playgrnd; pool; sand beach 600m (naturist beach 1km); watersports; tennis; games area; golf 1km; internet; TV; 5% statics; dogs €3.30; phone; adv bkg; quiet; 10% red CCI. "Lovely site in pine forest; poss diff lge o'fits; modern, well-maintained facs." ♦ 26 Mar-26 Sep. € 40.00 (CChq acc) 2009*

⊞ **PALS** *3B3* (1km E Rural) *41.95541, 3.15780* **Camping Resort Mas Patoxas Bungalow Park, Ctra Torroella-Palafrugell, Km 339, 17256 Pals (Gerona) [972-63 69 28; fax 972-66 73 49; info@campingmaspatoxas.com; www. campingmaspatoxas.com]** AP7 exit 6 onto C66 Palamós/La Bisbal, turn L via Torrent to Pals. Turn R & site on R almost opp old town of Pals on rd to Torroella de Montgri. Or fr Palafrugell on C31 turn at km 339. Lge, mkd pitch, terr, shd; htd wc; 30% serviced pitches; chem disp; mv service pnt; baby facs; shwrs inc; el pnts (5A) inc; gas; Indtte; supmkt; tradsmn; rest; snacks; bar; playgrnd; pool; sand beach 4km; games area; entmnt; tennis; cycle hire; golf 4km; TV; dogs €3.60; phone; site clsd 21 Dec-15 Jan; recep clsd Monday low ssn; Eng spkn; adv bkg ess high ssn; quiet; red long stay/low ssn; gd security; ccard acc; CCI. "Excel." ♦ € 47.00 2008*

PALS *3B3* (4km E Rural) *41.98555, 3.18194* **Camping Cypsela, Rodors 7, 17256 Playa de Pals (Gerona) [972-66 76 96; fax 972-66 73 00; info@cypsela.com; www.cypsela.com]** Exit AP7 junc 6, rd C66 dir Palamós. 7km fr La Bisbal take dir Pals & foll sp Playa/Platja de Pals, site sp. V lge, hdg/mkd pitch, hdstg, shd; wc; chem disp; mv service pnt; 25% serviced pitches; child/baby facs; private bthrms avail; shwrs inc; el pnts (6A) inc; gas; Indtte; supmkt; rest; snacks; bar; BBQ; playgrnd; pool; sand beach 1.5km; tennis; mini-golf & other sports; cycle hire; golf 1km; games rm; entmnt; wifi; TV rm; free bus to beach; 30% statics; no dogs; Eng spkn; adv bkg; ccard acc; red long stay/CCI. "Noise levels controlled after midnight; excel san facs; 4 grades of pitch/price (highest price shown); vg site." ♦ 15 May-15 Sep. € 76.40 2009*

See advertisement opposite

⊞ **PAMPLONA** *3B1* (7km N Rural) *42.85776, -1.62250* **Camping Ezcaba, Ctra N121, Km 7, 31194 Eusa-Oricain (Navarre) [948-33 03 15; fax 948-33 13 16; info@ campingszcaba.com; www.campingezcaba.com]** Fr N leave AP15 onto NA30 (N ring rd) to N121A sp Francia/Iruña. Pass Arre & Oricáin, turn L foll site sp 500m on R dir Berriosuso. Site on R in 500m - fairly steep ent. Or fr S leave AP15 onto NA32 (E by-pass) to N121A sp Francia/Iruña, then as above. Med, mkd pitch, pt sl, pt shd; wc; shwrs inc; el pnts €4.60; gas; Indtte; shop; rest; snacks; bar; pool; horseriding; tennis; wifi; dogs €2.60; phone; bus 1km; poss cr; adv bkg; rd noise; red low ssn. "Helpful, friendly staff; sm pitches unsuitable lge o'fits & poss diff due trees, esp when site full; attractive setting; gd pool, bar & rest; ltd facs low ssn & poss long walk to san facs; in winter use as NH only; phone to check open low ssn." ♦ € 21.40 2009*

⊞ **PANCORBO** *1B4* (3km NE Rural) *42.63305, -3.11138* **Camping El Desfiladero, Ctra Madrid-Irún, Km 305, 09280 Pancorbo (Burgos) [tel/fax 947-35 40 27; hceldesfiladero@teleline.es]** Fr AP1/E5 exit junc 4 onto N1 dir Vitoria/Gasteiz, site on L in 2km at hostel. Med, hdg pitch, some hdstg, terr, pt shd; wc; chem disp; shwrs; el pnts (8A) €3.40; Indtte; shop 3km; rest; snacks; bar; playgrnd; pool; tennis; 25% statics; dogs; train 3km; some rd & rlwy noise; ccard acc; red CCI. "Access diff lge o'fits due steep ent; recep in hostel rest low ssn; friendly, helpful owner; facs tired; sh stay/NH only." ♦ € 16.00 2008*

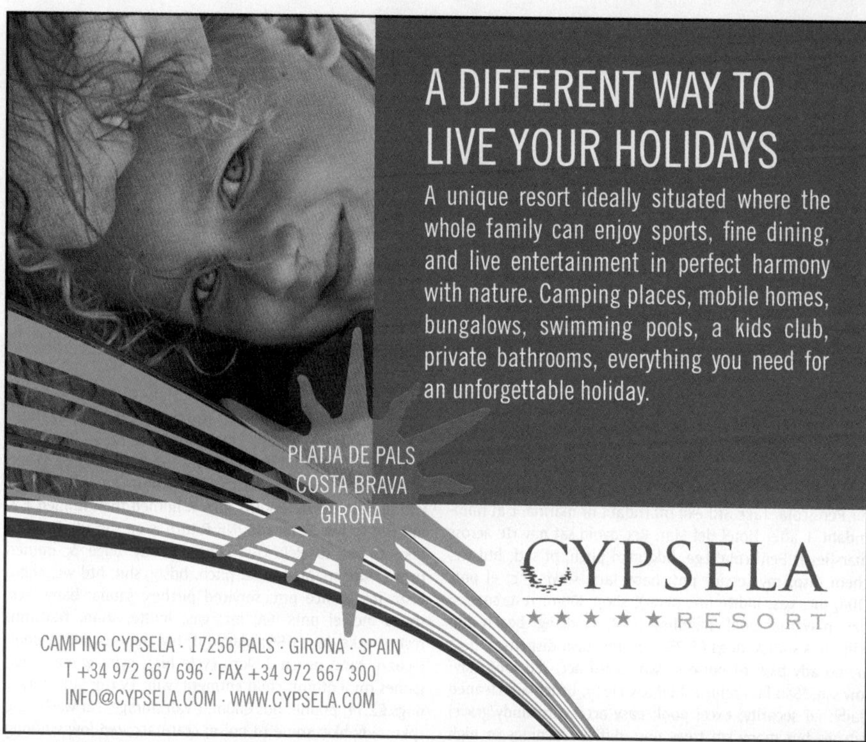

PEDROSILLO EL RALO see Salamanca *1C3*

PELIGROS see Granada *2G4*

PENAFIEL *1C4* (2km SW Rural) *41.59538, -4.12811* **Camping Riberduero, Avda Polideportivo 51, 47300 Peñafiel [tel/fax 983-88 16 37; camping@campingpenafiel.com; www.campingpenafiel.com]** Fr Valladolid 56km or Aranda de Duero 38km on N122. In Peñafiel take VA223 dir Cuéllar, foll sp to sports cent/camping. Med, mkd pitch, hdstg, shd; htd wc; chem disp; mv service pnt; baby facs; fam bthrm; shwrs inc; el pnts (5A) €3.50; gas; Indtte; shop; rest; snacks; bar; playgrnd; pool; rv 1km; cycle hire; TV; 20% statics; dogs €1.50; phone; bus 1km; site open w/end only low ssn; poss cr; Eng spkn; adv bkg; quiet; ccard acc; 10% red 15 days. "Excel, well-kept site; interesting, historical area; ideal for wheelchair users." ♦ Holy Week & 1 Apr-30 Sep. € 18.60 2008*

PENASCOSA see Alcaraz *4F1*

⊞ **PENISCOLA** *3D2* (500m N Coastal) *40.37694, 0.39222* **Camping El Cid, Azagador de la Cruz s/n, 12598 Peñíscola (Castellón) [964-48 03 80; fax 964-46 76 02; info@campingelcid.com; www.campingelcid.com]** Exit A7 at junc 43. Take N340 sp València for sh distance, turn L sp Peñíscola. Approx 2km look for yellow sp to site. Narr site ent - rec loop o'fit rnd in rd & ent thro R-hand site of security barrier. Med, mkd pitch, shd; wc; chem disp; shwrs inc; el pnts (10A) €4.50; gas; Indtte; shop; supmkt; rest; snacks; bar; playgrnd; pool; paddling pool; sand beach 500m; 50% statics; poss cr; ccard acc; red long stay/low ssn; CCI. "Vg, well-run site; popular with Spanish families; friendly staff." € 27.00 2009*

⊞ **PENISCOLA** *3D2* (500m N Coastal) *40.36222, 0.39583* **Camping Ferrer, Avda de la Estación 27, 12598 Peñíscola (Castellón) [964-48 92 23; fax 964-48 91 44; campingferrer@campingferrer.com; www.campingferrer.com]** Exit AP7 onto CV141 twd Peñíscola, site sp on R, adj Consum supmkt. Med, hdstg, terr, pt shd; htd wc; chem disp; mv service pnt; baby facs; shwrs inc; el pnts (6A) €3; Indry rm; shop adj; rest; snacks; bar; BBQ; playgrnd; pool; sand beach 500m; games rm; entmnt; wifi; some statics; dogs; bus 700m; adv bkg; poss rd noise; cc acc; red long stay; CCI. "Conv NH; vg, family run site; level pitches." € 22.00 2009*

Spain

⊞ **PENISCOLA** *3D2* (1km N Coastal) *40.37152, 0.40269* **Camping El Edén, Ctra CS501 Benicarló-Peñíscola Km 6, 12598 Peñíscola (Castellón) [964-48 05 62; fax 964-48 98 28; camping@camping-eden.com; www. camping-eden.com]** Exit AP7 junc 43 onto N340 & CV141 dir Peñíscola. Take 3rd exit off rndabt nr marina, L at mini-rndabt, L after Hotel del Mar. Rec avoid sat nav rte across marshes fr Peñíscola. Lge, hdg/mkd pitch, pt shd; htd wc; chem disp; mv service pnt; baby facs; shwrs inc; el pnts (10A) inc; gas; Indtte (inc dryer); shop 300m; rest, snacks; bar; playgrnd; pool; paddling pool; sand/shgl beach adj; wifi; 40% statics; dogs €0.75; bus adj; cash dispenser; poss cr; no adv bkg; rd noise in ssn; ccard acc; red long stay/ low ssn. "San facs refurbished & v clean; beach adj cleaned daily; gd security; excel pool; easy access to sandy/gravel pitches but many sm trees poss diff for awnings or high m'vans; poss vicious mosquitoes at dusk; easy walk/cycle to town; 4 diff sizes of pitch (some with tap, sink & drain) with different prices; ltd facs low ssn; excel." ♦ € 49.65 2009*

⊞ **PENISCOLA** *3D2* (2km W) *40.37916, 0.38833* **Camping Los Pinos, Calle Abellars s/n, 12598 Peñíscola (Castellón) [tel/fax 964-48 03 79; info@campinglospinos.com; www. campinglospinos.com]** Exit A7 junc 43 or N340 sp Peñíscola. Site sp on L. Med, pt shd; wc; chem disp; mv service pnt; baby facs; shwrs; el pnts €5.62; gas; Indtte; shop; rest; snacks; bar; BBQ; playgrnd; pool; phone; bus fr site; red low ssn. "Narr site rds, lots of trees; poss diff access some pitches." € 22.67 2008*

⊞ **PENISCOLA** *3D2* (2km NW Rural) *40.40158, 0.38116* **Camping Spa Natura Resort (formerly Camping Azahar), Partida Villarroyos s/n, Playa Montana, 12598 Peñíscola-Benicarló (Castellón) [tel/fax 964-47 54 80; info@spanatura resort.com; www.spanaturaresort.com]** Exit AP7 junc 43, within 50m of toll booths turn R immed then immed L & foll site sp twd Benicarló (NB R turn is on slip rd). Fr N340 take CV141 to Peñíscola. Cross m'way bdge & immed turn L; site sp. Med, mkd pitch, hdstg, shd; htd wc; chem disp; mv service pnt; serviced pitches; sauna; baby facs; shwrs inc; el pnts (6A) inc; gas; Indtte; shop; tradsmn; rest; snacks; bar; BBQ; playgrnd; htd pool; paddling pool; jacuzzi; sand beach 2.5km; cycle hire; gym; games area; games rm; entmnt; child entment; wifi; TV rm; 50% statics; dogs €2.14; phone; bus 600m; c'van storage; car wash; Eng spkn; adv bkg; some rd noise; ccard acc; red low ssn/long stay/snr citizens/ CCI. "Helpful, enthusiastic staff & owners; vg site; gd cycling." ♦ € 53.07 (CChq acc) ABS - E23 2009*

PINEDA DE MAR see Calella *3C3*

PINEDA, LA see Salou *3C2*

PITRES *2G4* (500m SW Rural) *36.93178, -3.33268* **Camping El Balcón de Pitres, Ctra Órgiva-Ugijar, Km 51, 18414 Pitres (Granada) [958-76 61 11; fax 958-80 44 53; info@balcondepitres.com; www.balcondepitres.com]** S fr Granada on A44/E902, turn E onto A348 for 22km. At Órgiva take A4132 dir Trevélez to Pitres to site. Ask at rest in vill for dirs. Sm, terr, shd; wc; chem disp; el pnts (10A) €4.28; gas; Indtte; shop; rest; snacks; bar; playgrnd; pool; cycle hire; some statics; bus 600m; poss cr Aug; adv bkg; quiet; red long stay; ccard acc; CCI. "Site in unspoilt Alpujarras region of Sierra Nevada mountains; fine scenery & wildlife; site on steep hillside, poss diff lge o'fits; san facs at top of hill - own san facs saves climb." 1 Mar-31 Oct. € 32.10 (3 persons) 2007*

PLASENCIA *1D3* (4km NE Urban) *40.04348, -6.05751* **Camping La Chopera, Ctra N110, Km 401, Valle del Jerte, 10600 Plasencia (Caceras) [tel/fax 927-41 66 60]** In Plasencia on N630 turn E on N110 sp Ávila & foll sp indus est & sp to site. Med, shd; wc; serviced pitches; chem disp; baby facs; shwrs inc; el pnts (6A) inc; gas; Indtte; shop; rest; bar; BBQ; playgrnd; 2 pools in ssn; tennis; cycle hire; dogs; quiet but w/end disco; ccard acc; CCI. "Peaceful & spacious; much birdsong; conv Manfragüe National Park (breeding of black/Egyptian vultures, black storks, imperial eagles); excel pool & modern facs; helpful owners." ♦ 1 Mar-30 Sep. € 15.40 2006*

⊞ **PLASENCIA** *1D3* (10km SE Rural) *39.94361, -6.08444* **Camping Parque Natural Monfragüe, Ctra Plasencia-Trujillo, Km 10, 10680 Malpartida de Plasencia (Cáceres) [tel/fax 927-45 92 33; contact@campingmonfrague.com; www.campingmonfrague.com]** Fr N on A66/N630 by-pass town, 5km S of town at flyover junc take EXA1 (EX108) sp Navalmoral de la Mata. In 6km turn R onto EX208 dir Trujillo, site on L in 5km. Med, hdg pitch, pt sl, terr, pt shd; htd wc; chem disp; mv service pnt; baby facs; shwrs inc; el pnts (5-15A) €3; gas; Indtte; shop; tradsmn; rest; snacks; bar; BBQ; playgrnd; pool high ssn; tennis; games area; archery; cycle hire; rambling; 4x4 off-rd; horseriding; wifi; TV rm; 10% statics; dogs; phone; Eng spkn; no adv bkg; quiet; ccard acc; red long stay/cash/CCI. "Friendly staff; vg, clean facs; gd rest; clean, tidy, busy site but poss dusty - hoses avail; 10km to National Park (birdwatching trips); excel winter base." ♦ € 16.40 (CChq acc) 2009*

PLAYA DE ARO *3B3* (1km N Coastal) *41.83666, 3.08722* **Camping Treumal, Ctra Playa de Aro/Palamós, C253, Km 47.5, 17250 Playa de Arro (Gerona) [972-65 10 95; fax 972-65 16 71; info@campingtreumal.com; www.campingtreumal.com]** Exit m'way at junc 6, 7 or 9 dir Sant Feliu de Guixols to Playa de Aro; site is sp at km 47.5 fr C253 coast rd SW of Palamós. Lge, mkd pitch, terr, shd; wc; baby facs; shwrs inc; chem disp; mv service pnt; el pnts (10A) inc; gas; Indtte; supmkt; tradsmn; rest; snacks; bar; playgrnd; sm pool; sand beach adj; fishing; tennis 1km; games rm; sports facs; cycle hire; golf 5km; wifi; entmnt; 25% statics; no dogs; phone; car wash; Eng spkn; adv bkg; quiet; ccard acc; red low ssn; CCI. "Peaceful site in pine trees; excel san facs; manhandling poss req onto terr pitches; gd beach." ♦ 27 Mar-30 Sep. € 46.40 2009*

See advertisement opposite (below)

PLAYA DE ARO *3B3* (2km N Coastal) *41.83116, 3.08366* **Camping Cala Gogo, Avda Andorra 13, 17251 Calonge (Gerona) [972-65 15 64; fax 972-65 05 53; calagogo@calagogo.es; www.calagogo.es]** Exit AP7 junc 6 dir Palamós/Sant Feliu. Fr Palamós take C253 coast rd S twd Sant Antoni, site on R 2km fr Playa de Aro, sp. Lge, pt sl, pt terr, pt shd; wc; chem disp; mv service pnt; serviced pitch; baby facs; shwrs inc; el pnts (10A) inc; gas; Indtte; supmkt; rest; snacks; bar; BBQ; playgrnds; htd pool; paddling pool; sand beach adj; boat hire; diving school; games area; games rm; tennis; cycle hire; golf 4km; entmnt; internet; TV; no dogs 1/7-22/8 (otherwise €2); Eng spkn; adv bkg; quiet; red long stay/low ssn. "Clean, airy facs; site terraced into pinewood on steep hillside; some manhandling may be req when siting; excel family site." 24 Apr-26 Sep. € 47.95 2009*

See advertisement opposite (above)

⊞ **PLAYA DE ARO** *3B3* (2km N Coastal) *41.83333, 3.08416* **Camping Internacional de Calonge, Avda d'Andorra s/n, Ctra 253, Km 47, 17251 Calonge (Gerona) [972-65 12 33 or 972-65 14 64; fax 972-65 25 07; info@intercalonge.com; www.intercalonge.com]** Fr A7 exit junc 6 onto C66 dir La Bisbal, Palamós & Playa de Aro; 3km bef Palamós foll sp St Antoni de Calonge. At 2nd rndbt bear R onto C253 dir Sant Feliu, site on R in 3km. V lge, mkd pitch, terr, shd; htd wc; chem disp; mv service pnt; some serviced pitches; baby facs; shwrs inc; el pnts (5A) inc; gas; Indtte; supmkt; rest; snacks; bar; BBQ; playgrnd; 2 pools; paddling pool; solarium; sand/shgl beach adj; tennis; extensive sports facs; entmnt; wifi; TV rm; 30% statics; phone; dogs €4.20; Eng spkn; adv bkg; poss noisy high ssn; red low ssn/long stay; ccard acc; CCI. "On side of steep hill - parking poss diff at times; conv Dali Museum; Roman ruins; excel site; gd security." ♦ € 46.30 2009*

See advertisement on next page

PLAYA DE ARO *3B3* (2km N Rural) *41.81116, 3.01821* **Yelloh! Village Mas Sant Josep, Ctra Santa Cristina-Playa de Aro, Km 2, 17246 Santa Cristina de Aro (Gerona) [972-83 51 08; fax 972-83 70 18; info@campingmassantjosep.com; www.campingmassantjosep.com or www.yellohvillage.com]** Fr A7/E15 take exit 7 dir Sant Feliu de Guixols to Santa Christina town. Take old rd dir Playa de Aro, site in 2km. V lge, mkd pitch, shd; htd wc; chem disp; mv service pnt; baby facs; serviced pitches; sauna; shwrs inc; el pnts (10A) inc; gas; Indtte (inc dryer); shop; rest; snacks; bar; BBQ; playgrnd; lge pools; sand beach 3.5km; tennis; games rm; games area; mini-golf & assorted sports; cycle hire; entmnt; golf 4km; internet; TV rm; 60% statics; dogs; Eng spkn; adv bkg; quiet; ccard acc; red low ssn; CCI. "Generous pitches; excel." ♦ 22 May-13 Sep. € 44.00 2008*

Spain

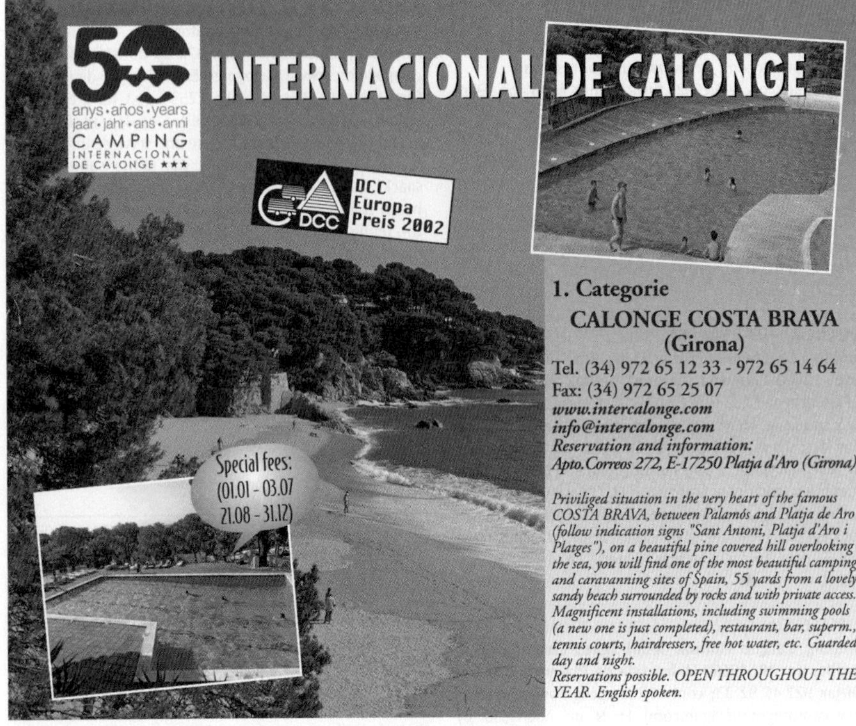

50
anys • años • years
jaar • jahr • ans • anni
CAMPING
INTERNACIONAL
DE CALONGE ★★★
INTERNACIONAL DE CALONGE
DCC
DCC
Europa
Preis 2002
Special fees:
(01.01 - 03.07
21.08 - 31.12)
1. Categorie
CALONGE COSTA BRAVA
(Girona)
Tel. (34) 972 65 12 33 - 972 65 14 64
Fax: (34) 972 65 25 07
www.intercalonge.com
info@intercalonge.com
Reservation and information:
Apto.Correos 272, E-17250 Platja d'Aro (Girona)
Priviliged situation in the very heart of the famous COSTA BRAVA, between Palamós and Platja de Aro (follow indication signs "Sant Antoni, Platja d'Aro i Platges"), on a beautiful pine covered hill overlooking the sea, you will find one of the most beautiful camping and caravanning sites of Spain, 55 yards from a lovely sandy beach surrounded by rocks and with private access. Magnificent installations, including swimming pools (a new one is just completed), restaurant, bar, superm., tennis courts, hairdressers, free hot water, etc. Guarded day and night.
Reservations possible. OPEN THROUGHOUT THE YEAR. English spoken.

PLAYA DE ARO *3B3* (1km S Coastal) *41.81416, 3.04444* **Camping Valldaro, Carrer del Camí Vell 63, 17250 Playa de Aro (Gerona) [972-81 75 15; fax 972-81 66 62; info@valldaro.com; www.valldaro.com]** Exit A7 junc 7 onto C65 dir Sant Feliu. Turn L onto C31 for Playa de Aro thro Castillo de Aro & site on R, 1km fr Playa at km 4.2. V lge, pt shd; wc; chem disp; mv service pnt; baby facs; shwrs inc; el pnts (5A) inc; gas; Indtte; shop; rest; snacks; bar; playgrnd; 2 pools; waterslides; beach 1km; watersports; tennis; horseriding 2km; golf 3km; games area; cycle hire; wifi; entmnt; 50% statics; dogs €2.80; phone; adv bkg; red long stay. "Gd family site; some lge pitches; many facs." ♦ 26 Mar-26 Sep. € 44.60 (CChq acc) 2009*

PLAYA DE ARO *3B3* (2km S Coastal) *41.8098, 3.0466* **Camping Riembau, Calle Santiago Rusiñol s/n, 17250 Playa de Aro (Gerona) [972-81 71 23; fax 972-82 52 10; camping@riembau.com; www.riembau.com]** Fr Gerona take C250 thro Llagostera, turn for Playa de Aro. Fr Playa de Aro take C253 twd Sant Feliu. Site access rd 2km on R. V lge, pt shd; wc; chem disp; baby facs; shwrs inc; el pnts (5A) inc; gas; Indtte; rest; snacks; bar; shop; beach 800m; 2 pools (1 indoor); playgrnd; tennis; fitness cent; games area; games rm; entmnt; internet; 40% statics; phone; adv bkg; some rd noise. ♦ Easter-30 Sep. € 35.90 2007*

PLAYA DE ARO *3B3* (2km S Urban/Coastal) *41.80472, 3.06333* **Camping Vall d'Or, Avda Verona-Teruel s/n, 17250 Playa de Aro (Gerona) [972-81 75 85; fax 972-67 44 95; valldor@betsa.es; www.betsa.es]** Exit A7 junc 7 onto C65 dir Sant Feliu de Guixols, then C31 to Playa de Aro. V lge, pt shd; wc; chem disp; shwrs inc; el pnts (5A) €4.15; gas; Indtte; shop; rest; bar; playgrnd; sand beach adj; TV; 50% statics; dogs; phone; poss cr; adv bkg. "Gd family site." Easter-2 Nov. € 31.80 2008*

PLAYA DE OLIVA see Oliva *4E2*

PLAYA DE PALS see Pals *3B3*

PLAYA DE PINEDO see Valencia *4E2*

PLAYA DE VIDIAGO see Llanes *1A4*

PLAYA TAMARIT see Tarragona *3C3*

POBLA DE SEGUR, LA *3B2* (3km NE Rural) *42.2602, 0.9862* **Camping Collegats, Ctra N260, Km 306, 25500 La Pobla de Segur (Lleida) [973-68 07 14; fax 973-68 14 02; camping@collegats.com; www.collegats.com]** Fr Tremp N to La Pobla on N260. Site sp in town at traff lts, turn R onto N260 dir Sort. Ent by hairpin bend. Last section of rd narr & rough. Med, mkd pitch, shd; wc; chem disp; shwrs; el pnts €5; gas; lndtte; shop & 4km; tradsmn; snacks; bar; BBQ; playgrnd; pool; games area; some statics (sep area); dogs; poss cr; Eng spkn; quiet; CCI. "Clean facs; site not suitable lge o'fits; twin-axle vans not acc; conv NH." ♦ 1 Apr-31 Oct. € 20.00 2007*

⊞ **POBOLEDA** *3C2* (SW Rural) *41.23298, 0.84305* **Camping Poboleda, Plaça Les Casetes s/n, 43376 Poboleda (Tarragona) [tel/fax 977-82 71 97; poboleda@campingsonline.com; www.campingpoboleda.com]** By-pass Reus W of Tarragona on T11/N420 then turn N onto C242 sp Les Borges del Camp. Go thro Alforja over Col d'Alforja & turn L onto T207 to Poboleda & foll camping sp in vill. Med, mkd pitch, terr, pt shd; htd wc; chem disp; baby facs; fam bthrm; el pnts (4A) inc; lndry rm; shop, rest, snacks, bar in vill; pool; lake sw 8km; tennis; wifi; TV; no statics; dogs; phone; Eng spkn; quiet; ccard acc; CCI. "In heart of welcoming vill in lovely mountain setting; v friendly, helpful owner; not suitable lge o'fits as access thro vill." ♦ € 25.00 2007*

POLA DE SOMIEDO *1A3* (250m E Rural) *43.09222, -6.25222* **Camping La Pomerada de Somiedo, 33840 Pola de Somiedo (Asturias) [985-76 34 04; csomiedo@infonegocio.com]** W fr Oviedo on A63, turn S onto AS15/AS227 to Augasmestas & Pola de Somiedo. Site adj Hotel Alba, sp fr vill. Route on steep, winding, mountain rd - suitable sm, powerful o'fits only. Sm, mkd pitch, pt shd; wc; chem disp; mv service pnt; shwrs inc; el pnts €4.20; shop, rest bar in vill; quiet. "Mountain views; nr national park." 1 Apr-31 Dec. € 19.00 2009*

⊞ **PONFERRADA** *1B3* (10km W Rural) *42.56160, 6.74590* **Camping El Bierzo, 24550 Villamartín de la Abadia (León) [tel/fax 987-56 25 15; rafcadma@lesein.es]** Exit A6 junc 399 dir Carracedelo; after rndabt turn onto NV1 & foll sp Villamartín. Bef ent Villamartín turn L & foll site sp. Med, pt shd; wc; chem disp; mv service pnt (ltd); shwrs inc; el pnts €3.75; shops 2km; rest; bar; playgrnd; no statics; dogs €1.73; phone; bus 1km; adv bkg; quiet; ccard not acc; CCI. "Attractive, rvside site in pleasant area; gd facs; friendly, helpful owner takes pride in his site; Roman & medieval attractions nr." ♦ € 15.00 2009*

PONT D'ARROS see Vielha *3B2*

⊞ **PONT DE BAR, EL** *3B3* (2.6km E Rural) *42.37458, 1.63687* **Camping Pont d'Ardaix, N260, Km 210, 25723 El Pont de Bar (Lleida) [973-38 40 98; fax 973-38 41 15; pontdardaix@clior.es; www.pontdardaix.com]** On Seo de Urgel-Puigcerdà rd, N260, at rear of bar/rest Pont d'Ardaix. Med, terr, pt shd; wc; mv service pnt; shwrs inc; el pnts (3-5A) €5.10-7.10; gas; lndtte; shop & 4km; rest; bar; playgrnd; pool; 80% statics; dogs €5.30; phone; Eng spkn; quiet; CCI; "In pleasant valley on bank of Rv Segre; touring pitches on rv bank; site poss scruffy & unkempt low ssn; gd NH." ♦ € 20.40 2008*

PONT DE SUERT *3B2* (4km N Rural) *42.43083, 0.73861* **Camping Can Roig, Ctra De Boí, Km 0.5, 25520 Pont de Suert (Lleida) [973-69 05 02; fax 973-69 12 06; info@campingcanroig.com; www.campingcanroig.com]** N of Pont de Suert on N230 turn NE onto L500 dir Caldes de Boí. Site in 1km. App narr for 100m. Med, mkd pitch, hdstg, pt sl, pt shd; wc; chem disp; shwrs inc; el pnts (5A) €3.75; gas; lndtte; shop & 3km; snacks; bar; playgrnd; paddling pool; 5% statics; dogs €1.95; adv bkg; quiet; ccard acc. "NH en rte S; beautiful valley." 1 Mar-31 Oct. € 15.60 2007*

⊞ **PONT DE SUERT** *3B2* (5.5km N Rural) *42.44833, 0.71027* **Camping Alta Ribagorça, Ctra Les Bordes s/n, Km 131, 25520 Pont de Suert (Lleida) [973-69 05 21; fax 973-69 06 97; ana.uma@hotmail.com]** Fr N on N230 site sp S of Vilaller on L. Sm, mkd pitch, terr, pt shd; htd wc; chem disp; shwrs inc; el pnts (5A) inc; lndtte; rest; bar; playgrnd; pool; 10% statics; dogs; Eng spkn; rd noise. "Fair NH." € 19.50 2009*

⊞ **PONT DE SUERT** *3B2* (16km NE Rural) *42.51900, 8.84600* **Camping Taüll, Ctra Taüll s/n, 25528 Taüll (Lleida) [973 69 61 74; www.campingtaull.com]** Fr Pont de Suert 3km N on N230 then NE on L500 dir Caldes de Boí. In 13km turn R into Taüll. Site sp on R. Sm, pt sl, terr, pt shd; htd wc; chem disp; baby facs; shwrs inc; el pnts €6; lndry rm; shop, rest, bar 300m; 30% statics; dogs €3; clsd 15 Oct-15 Nov; poss cr; quiet; CCI. "Excel facs; taxis into National Park avail; ltd touring pitches; suitable sm m'vans only." € 21.50 2007*

⊞ **PONT DE SUERT** *3B2* (5km NW Rural) *42.43944, 0.69860* **Camping Baliera, Ctra N260, Km 355.5, Castejón de Sos, 22523 Bonansa (Huesca) [974-55 40 16; fax 974-55 40 99; info@baliera.com; www.baliera.com]** N fr Pont de Suert on N230 turn L opp petrol stn onto N260 sp Castejón de Sos. In 1km turn L onto A1605 sp Bonansa, site on L immed over rv bdge. Site sp fr N230. Lge, mkd pitch, pt sl, terr, shd; htd wc; chem disp; mv service pnt; baby facs; shwrs inc; el pnts (5-10A) €4.50; gas; lndtte; shop; tradsmn; rest in ssn; snacks; bar; BBQ; playgrnd; pool (high ssn); lrv fishing; ake sw 10km; horseriding 4km; golf 4km; weights rm; internet; sat TV; 50% statics; dogs €2.40; phone; site clsd Nov & Xmas; poss cr; Eng spkn; quiet; ccard acc; red low ssn; CCI. "Excel, well-run, peaceful site in parkland setting; walking in summer, skiing in winter; excel cent for touring; conv Vielha tunnel; all facs up steps; part of site v sl; helpful owner proud of his site; spotless facs." ♦ € 25.60 (CChq acc) 2008*

Spain

PONTEAREAS *1B2* (1.5km N Rural) **Camping A Freixa, 36866 Ribadetea (Pontevedra) [986-64 02 99]** On N120 fr Vigo & Porriño, turn L at fountain bef bdge at ent to Ponteareas. In 1.5km at tall chimney on L, turn R & site in 200m adj Rv Tea. Med, sl, pt shd; wc; shwrs; el pnts €3.60; lndtte; shop; rest; bar; playgrnd; sand beach & rv sw; tennis; phone; bus 700m; quiet. Holy Week & 1 Jul-30 Aug. € 19.10 2008*

PORT DE LA SELVA, EL *3B3* (2km N Coastal) *42.34222, 3.18333* **Camping Port de la Vall, Ctra Port de Llançà, 17489 El Port de la Selva (Gerona) [972-38 71 86; fax 972-12 63 08; portdelavall@terra.es]** On coast rd fr French border at Llançà take GI612 twd El Port de la Selva. Site on L, easily seen. Lge, pt shd; wc; shwrs; el pnts (3-5A) €5.65; gas; lndtte; shop; rest; snacks; bar; playgrnd; shgl beach adj; internet; some statics; dogs €2.95; phone; poss cr; adv bkg; poss noisy; ccard acc; red low ssn. "Easy walk to harbour; gd site; sm pitches & low branches poss diff - check bef siting." 1 Mar-15 Oct. € 43.00 (4 persons) 2008*

PORT DE LA SELVA, EL *3B3* (1km S Coastal) *42.32641, 3.20480* **Camping Port de la Selva, Ctra Cadaqués s/n, Km 1, 17489 El Port de la Selva (Gerona) [972-38 72 87; fax 972-38 73 86; info@campingselva.com; www.campingselva.com]** Exit A7 junc 3 or 4 onto N260 to Llança, then take GI 612 to El Port de la Selva. On ent town turn R twd Cadaqués, site in R in 1km. Med, mkd pitch, pt shd; wc; chem disp (wc); shwrs inc; el pnts €3.70 (poss no earth); lndtte; shop on site & 1km; rest, snacks, bar 1km; playgrnd; pool; sand/shgl beach 1km; games area; TV; 25% statics; dogs €2.85; poss cr; adv bkg; quiet; ccard not acc; red low ssn; CCI. "Excel for coastal & hill walking; well-run site; gd, clean facs; gd beach; pleasant, attractive vill; poss diff for lge m'vans due low branches." 1 Jun-15 Sep. € 31.00 2008*

POTES *1A4* (1.5km W Rural) *43.15527, -4.63694* **Camping La Viorna, Ctra Santo Toribio, Km 1, Mieses, 39570 Potes (Cantabria) [942-73 20 21; fax 942-73 21 01; info@campinglaviorna.com; www.campinglaviorna.com]** Exit N634 at junc 272 onto N621 dir Panes & Potes - narr, winding rd (passable for c'vans). Fr Potes take rd to Fuente Dé sp Espinama; in 1km turn L sp Toribio. Site on R in 1km, sp fr Potes. Med, mkd pitch, terr, pt shd; htd wc; chem disp; mv service pnt; baby facs; shwrs inc; el pnts (6A) €3.20 (poss rev pol); lndtte (inc dryer); shop & 2km; tradsmn; rest; snacks; bar; BBQ; playgrnd; pool high ssn; paddling pool; cycle hire; wifi; bus 1km; Eng spkn; adv bkg; quiet; ccard acc; CCI; "Lovely views; gd walks; friendly, family-run, clean, tidy site; gd pool; ideal Picos de Europa; conv cable car, 4x4 tours, trekking; mkt on Mon; festival mid-Sep v noisy; some pitches diff in wet & diff lge o'fits; excel." ♦ 1 Apr-31 Oct. € 24.70 2009*

POTES *1A4* (3km W Rural) *43.15742, -4.65617* **Camping La Isla-Picos de Europa, Ctra Potes-Fuente Dé, 39586 Turieno (Cantabria) [tel/fax 942-73 08 96; campicoseuropa@terra.es; www.liebanaypicosdeeuropa.com/guia-i/laisla.htm]** Take N521 W fr Potes twd Espinama, site on R in 3km thro vill of Turieno (app Potes fr N). Med, mkd pitch, pt sl, shd; wc; chem disp; mv service pnt; shwrs inc; el pnts (6A) €3.25 (poss rev pol); gas; lndtte; shop; tradsmn; rest; bar; BBQ; playgrnd; pool; walking; horseriding; cycling; 4x4 touring; hang-gliding; mountain treks in area; wifi; some statics; phone; poss cr; Eng spkn; adv bkg; poss noisy high ssn; ccard acc; red long stay; CCI. "Delightful, family-run site; friendly, helpful owners; gd san facs; conv cable car & mountain walks (map fr recep); many trees & low branches; rec early am departure to avoid coaches on gorge rd; highly rec." Easter-31 Oct. € 18.90 2009*

POTES *1A4* (5km W Rural) *43.15527, -4.68333* **Camping San Pelayo, Ruta Potes-Fuente Dé, Km 5, 39587 San Pelayo (Cantabria) [tel/fax 942-73 30 87 or 942-73 31 64; www.campingsanpelayo.com]** Take CA185 W fr Potes twd Espinama, site on R in 5km, 2km past Camping La Isla. Med, mkd pitch, pt sl, pt shd; wc; chem disp; shwrs inc; el pnts (6A) inc; lndtte; shop; rest; snacks; bar; playgrnd; pool; cycle hire; games rm; poss cr; adv bkg; quiet, but noise fr bar; ccard acc high ssn; 20% red 5+ days; CCI. "Friendly, helpful owner; some sm pitches; conv mountain walking; excel pool." Easter-15 Oct. € 16.00 2006*

POZO ALCON *2G4* (7km N Rural) *37.75873, -2.91403* **Camping La Bolera, Ctra Castril, Km 8, Pantano Bolera, 23485 Pozo Alcón (Jaén) [953-73 90 05]** Fr Pozo Alcón take A326 N dir Castril. Site on L. Med, pt sl, pt shd; wc; chem disp; shwrs inc; el pnts (5A) €3; gas; lndtte; shop; rest; bar; BBQ; playgrnd; some statics; dogs €1.50; bus adj; quiet; ccard acc; CCI. "Excel scenery & wildlife." 1 Apr-14 Dec. € 14.40 2008*

PRADES see Vilanova de Prades *3C2*

PUEBLA DE CASTRO, LA see Graus *3B2*

PUEBLA DE SANABRIA *1B3* (500m S Rural) *42.04930, -6.63068* **Camping Isla de Puebla, Pago de Barregas s/n, 49300 Puebla de Sanabria (Zamora) [980-56 79 54 or 617-66 23 57; fax 980-56 79 55; c.isladepuebla@hotmail.com; www.isladepuebla.com]** Fr Portugal border on C622, at ent to Puebla de Sanabria foll sp down short track twd rv. Fr N525 ent vill & foll sp Isla de Puebla. Med, mkd pitch, pt shd; wc; chem disp;mv service pnt; shwrs inc; el pnts (10A) €2.73; gas; lndtte (inc dryer); shop; rest; snacks; bar; playgrnd; pool; trout-fishing; some statics; dogs; bus 200m; adv bkg; quiet; red long stay; ccard acc; CCI. "Vg, modern san facs; interesting town; vg for nature lovers; friendly, helpful staff; facs ltd low ssn." Holy Week-30 Sep. € 16.70 2008*

PUEBLA DE SANABRIA *1B3* (10km NW Rural) *42.13111, -6.70111* **Camping El Folgoso, Ctra Puebla de Sanabria-San Martin de Castañeda, Km 13, 49361 Vigo de Sanabria (Zamora) [980-62 67 74; fax 980-62 68 00; camping@elfolgoso.com]** Exit A52 sp Puebla de Sanabria & foll sp for Lago/Vigo de Sanabria thro Puente de Sanabria & Galende; site 2km beyond vill of Galende; sp. Med, pt sl, terr, shd; wc; chem disp; shwrs €1; el pnts (5A) €2.50; gas; Indtte; shop high ssn; rest high ssn; snacks; bar; playgrnd; cycle hire; statics; phone; ccard acc. "Lovely setting beside lake; v cold in winter." ♦ 1 Apr-31 Oct. € 16.80 2008*

PUEBLA DE SANABRIA *1B3* (10km NW Rural) *42.11778, -6.69116* **Camping Peña Gullón, Ctra Puebla de Santabria-Ribadelago, Km 11.5, Lago de Sanabria, 49360 Galende (Zamora) [980-62 67 72]** Fr Puebla de Sanabria foll sp for Lago de Sanabria. Site 3km beyond vill of Galende clearly sp. Lge, pt shd; wc; shwrs inc; el pnts (15A) €2.51; gas; Indtte; shop in ssn; rest; playgrnd; lake adj; poss cr; quiet; red long stay; CCI. "Site in nature park 35km fr Portugal's Montesinho Park; rec arr by 1200; beautiful area; excel site." 28 Jun-31 Aug. € 17.00 2007*

⊞ **PUERTO DE MAZARRON** *4G1* (3km NE Rural/Coastal) *37.58981, -1.22881* **Camping Las Torres, Ctra N332, Cartagena-Mazarrón, Km 29, 30860 Puerto de Mazarrón (Murcia) [tel/fax 968-59 52 25; info@campinglastorres.com; www.campinglastorres.com]** Fr N on A7/E15 exit junc 627 onto MU602, then MU603 to Mazarrón. At junc with N322 turn L to Puerto de Mazarrón & foll Cartagena sp until site sps. Lge, hdg/mkd pitch, terr, hdstg, pt shd; wc; chem disp; mv service pnt; 40% serviced pitch (€1.80 extra); baby facs; shwrs inc; el pnts (6A) inc; gas; Indtte; rest (w/end only); snacks; bar; sm shop & 3km; playgrnd; htd, covrd pool; sand/shgl beach 2km; tennis; cycle hire; sat TV; 60% statics; dogs; phone; Eng spkn; adv bkg rec in winter; poss noisy; ccard acc; red low ssn/long stay; CCI. "Unspoilt coastline; busy at w/end; well-managed, family site; poss full in winter; excel pool; sm pitches." ♦ € 20.00 2006*

⊞ **PUERTO DE MAZARRON** *4G1* (5km NE Coastal) *37.5800, -1.1950* **Camping Los Madriles, Ctra a la Azohía 60, Km 4.5, 30868 Isla Plana (Murcia) [968-15 21 51; fax 968-15 20 92; camplosmadriles@terra.es; www.campinglosmadriles.com]** Fr Cartegena on N332 dir Puerto de Mazarrón. Turn L at rd junc sp La Azohía (32km). Site in 4km sp. Fr Murcia on E15/N340 dir Lorca exit junc 627 onto MU603 to Mazarrón, then foll sp. (Do not use rd fr Cartegena unless powerful tow vehicle/gd weight differential - use rte fr m'way thro Mazarrón.) Lge, hdg/mkd pitch, hdstg, pt sl, pt shd; wc; chem disp; mv service pnt; serviced pitches; shwrs inc; el pnts (10A) €3.85; gas; Indtte; shop; rest high ssn; bar; playgrnd; 2 htd pools; jacuzzi; shgl beach 500m; games area; wifi; no dogs; bus; poss cr; Eng spkn; adv bkg (fr Oct for min 2 months only); quiet; ccard acc high ssn; red long stay/low ssn/CCI. "Clean, v popular winter site; adv bkg ess fr Oct; some sm pitches, some with sea views; poss not suitable for disabled due to sl bet terrs; 3 days min stay high ssn; excel." ♦ € 30.50 2009*

⊞ **PUERTO DE MAZARRON** *4G1* (2km E Rural/Coastal) *37.56777, -1.2300* **Camping Los Delfines, Ctra Isla Plana-Playa El Mojon, 30860 Puerto de Mazarrón (Murcia) [tel/fax 968-59 45 27; www.campinglosdelfines.com]** Fr N332 turn S sp La Azohía & Isla Plana. Site on L in 3km. Med, mkd pitch, hdstg, pt sl, pt shd; htd wc; chem disp; mv service pnt; serviced pitches; baby facs; private san facs avail; shwrs inc; el pnts (5A) €3; gas; Indtte; tradsmn; snacks & bar high ssn; BBQ; playgrnd; shgl beach adj; TV; 5% statics; dogs €3; quiet; poss cr; Eng spkn; phone; red long stay; CCI. "Gd sized pitches; popular low ssn." ♦ € 40.80 2009*

⊞ **PUERTO DE MAZARRON** *4G1* (5km SW Coastal) *37.56388, -1.30388* **Camping Playa de Mazarrón, Ctra Mazarrón-Bolnuevo, Bolnuevo, 30877 Mazarrón (Murcia) [968-15 06 60; fax 968-15 08 37; camping@playamazarron.com; www.playamazarron.com]** Take Bolnuevo rd fr Mazarrón, at rndabt go strt, site immed on L. Lge, mkd pitch, hdstg, pt shd; wc; 90% serviced pitches; chem disp; mv service pnt; shwrs inc; el pnts (5A) €3.70; gas; Indtte; shop, rest (high ssn); snacks, bar; playgrnd; sand beach adj; tennis; games area; internet; TV; dogs free; bus; phone; poss v cr; adv bkg; red long stay/low ssn; ccard acc. "Some lge pitches but tight turning for lge o'fits; friendly staff; metal-framed sunshades in ssn on most pitches but low for m'vans; poss poor daytime security; gd for wheelchair users; popular & v cr in winter - many long stay visitors." ♦ € 26.00 2008*

⊞ **PUERTO DE SANTA MARIA, EL** *2H3* (2km SW Coastal) *36.58768, -6.24092* **Camping Playa Las Dunas de San Antón, Paseo Maritimo La Puntilla s/n, 11500 El Puerto de Santa María (Cádiz) [956-87 22 10; fax 956-86 01 17; info@lasdunascamping.com; www.lasdunascamping.com]** Fr N or S exit A4 at El Puerto de Sta María. Foll site sp carefully to avoid narr streets of town cent. Site 2-3km S of marina & leisure complex of Puerto Sherry. Alternatively, fr A4 take Rota rd & look for sp to site & Hotel Playa Las Dunas. Site better sp fr this dir & avoids town. Lge, pt sl, pt shd; wc; chem disp; mv service pnt; shwrs inc; el pnts (5-10A) €3.10-6.30; gas; Indtte; shop (high ssn); tradsmn; snacks; bar; playgrnd; pool adj; sand beach 50m; sports facs; internet; 30% statics; phone; guarded; poss cr; adv bkg rec; poss noisy disco w/end; red facs low ssn; ccard acc; red low ssn; CCI. "Friendly staff; conv Cádiz & Jerez sherry region, birdwatching areas & beaches; conv ferry or catamaran to Cádiz; facs poss stretched high ssn; hot water to shwrs only; pitches quiet away fr rd; take care caterpillars in spring - poss dangerous to dogs; dusty site but staff water rds." ♦ € 19.90 2009*

⊞ **PUERTO DE SANTA MARIA, EL** *2H3* (12km W Coastal) *36.67111, -6.40611* **Camping Playa Aguadulce, Ctra Rota-Chipiona, Km 21, Pago Aguadulce, 11520 Rota (Cádiz) [956-84 70 78; fax 956-84 71 94; cpa@playaaguadulce.com; www.playaaguadulce.com]** W fr El Puerto on A491, twd Chipiona. Ignore sp Rota & take last exit rndabt sp Costa Ballena (camping sp). Foll site sp & narr track for 1km. Med, hdg pitch, hdstg, shd; wc; chem disp; mv service pnt; baby facs; shwrs inc; el pnts (6-10A) inc; gas; lndtte; shop & 7km; tradsmn; rest; snacks; bar; playgrnd; sand beach adj; wifi; 25% statics; dogs; noisy; adv bkg; Eng spkn; ccard acc; CCI. "Well-kept, attractive site; adj to excel beach; noisy at w/end & school holidays; v helpful owners; sm pitches poss diff lge o'fits; site rds narr & restricted by trees/bushes." € 27.69 2008*

⊞ **PUERTO LUMBRERAS** *4G1* (1km E Urban) *37.57473, -1.79531* **Camping Los Ángeles, Ctra Cádiz-Barcelona, Km 580, 30890 Puerto Lumbreras (Murcia) [968-40 27 82]** Exit 580 fr new dual c'way section of N340 at rndabt dir Lorca. Site 200m on R, ent beside rest, at rear. Steep driveway. Sm, hdstg, pt shd; wc; mv service pnt; shwrs inc; el pnts (6A) €3.20 (poss no earth); gas; shop 1km; rest/bar adj high ssn; playgrnd; htd pool; internet; dogs €2.15; phone; no adv bkg; quiet; CCI. "Site run down low ssn, but fair NH; site yourself." ♦ € 15.00 2007*

PUIGCERDA *3B3* (2km NE Rural) *42.44156, 1.94174* **Camping Stel, Ctra de Llívia s/n, 17520 Puigcerdà (Gerona) [972-88 23 61; fax 972-14 04 19; puigcerda@stel.es; www.stel.es]** Fr France head for Bourg-Madame on N820 (N20) or N116. Cross border dir Llívia on N154, site is 1km after rndabt on L. Lge, mkd pitch, terr, pt shd; htd wc; chem disp; mv service pnt; baby facs; shwrs; el pnts (7A) €4.20; lndtte; shop; rest; snacks; bar; playgrnd; htd pool; canoeing; watersports; archery; cycle hire; games area; golf 4km; internet; entmnt; TV rm; 10% statics; dogs; site open w/ends only in winter; Eng spkn; adv bkg; some rd noise; ccard acc. "Pitches on upper terr quieter; superb scenery; sep area for campers with pets; gd walking, cycling." ♦ 30 May-28 Sep. € 34.50 (CChq acc) 2008*

QUEVEDA see Santillana del Mar *1A4*

RIANO *1A3* (7km E Rural) *42.97361, -4.92000* **Camping Alto Esla, Ctra León-Santander, 24911 Boca de Huérgano (León) [987-74 01 39; camping@altoesla.eu; www.altoesla.eu]** SW on N621 fr Potes just past junc with LE241 at Boca de Huérgano. Site on L. (See Picos de Europa in Mountain Passes & Tunnels in the section Planning & Travelling at front of guide.) Sm, pt sl, pt shd; wc; chem disp; mv service pnt; el pnts (5A) €2.68 (poss rev pol); lndtte; shops 500m; bus 300m; bar; phone; quiet; ccard acc; CCI. "Lovely setting; superb views; attractive site; ltd el pnts; excel san facs; lots of storks!" ♦ 26 Jun-8 Sep. € 15.50 2009*

⊞ **RIAZA** *1C4* (1km W Rural) *41.26995, -3.49750* **Camping Riaza, Ctra de la Estación s/n, 40500 Riaza (Segovia) [tel/fax 921-55 05 80; info@camping-riaza.com; www.camping-riaza.com]** Fr N exit A1/E5 junc 104, fr S exit 103 onto N110 N. In 12km turn R at rndabt on ent to town, site on L. Lge, hdg pitch, unshd; htd wc; chem disp; mv service pnt; baby facs; shwrs inc; el pnts (15A) €4.20; lndtte (inc dryer); shop; rest; snacks; bar; BBQ; playgrnd; pool; paddling pool; games area; games rm; internet; some statics; dogs; phone; bus 900m; Eng spkn; adv bkg; quiet. "Vg site; various pitch sizes - some lge; excel san facs; easy access to/fr Santander or Bilbao; beautiful little town." ♦ € 23.40 2009*

RIBADEO *1A2* (4km E Coastal) *43.55097, -6.99699* **Camping Playa Peñarronda, Playa de Peñarronda-Barres, 33794 Castropol (Asturias) [tel/fax 985-62 30 22; campingpenarrondacb@hotmail.com; www.campingplayapenarronda.com]** Fr N634 turn S onto N640 dir Lugo. Immed take 1st R, then foll site sp for 2km. Take care due ongoing rd works. Med, mkd pitch, shd; wc; chem disp; mv service pnt; shwrs inc; el pnts (6A) €3.80 (poss rev pol); gas; lndtte; shop; rest; snacks; bar; BBQ; playgrnd; sand beach adj; games area; cycle hire; some statics; phone; Eng spkn; quiet; red long stay; CCI. "Beautifully-kept, clean, friendly, family-run site on 'Blue Flag' beach; rec arr early to get pitch; facs clean; gd cycling along coastal paths & to Ribadeo; ltd facs low ssn, sm pitches." Holy Week-25 Sep. € 20.70 2009*

⊞ **RIBADEO** *1A2* (4km E Coastal) *43.54587, -6.99613* **Camping Vegamar, Ctra Playa de Peñarronda-Barres, 33794 Castropol (Asturias) [985-62 39 48; rlopezo@terra.es]** Fr E on E70/N634 turn L at junc (rndabt) N640 & N634 dir Vegadeo. Immed take 1st R & immed R under main rd. Site sp 500m. Med, pt shd; wc; chem disp; mv service pnt; shwrs; el pnts €2.57; gas; lndtte; shop; rest; snacks; bar; playgrnd; pool; sand beach 400m; games are; 60% statics; dogs; bus 1km; adv bkg; quiet; CCI. "Excel facs; family-run site; unreliable opening low ssn; excel NH." ♦ € 15.10 2008*

RIBADEO *1A2* (3km W Rural) *43.53722, -7.08472* **Camping Ribadeo, Ctra Ribadeo-La Coruña, Km 2, 27700 Ribadeo (Lugo) [982-13 11 68; fax 982-13 11 67; www.campingribadeo.com]** W fr Ribadeo on N634/E70 twd La Coruña, in 2km pass sp Camping Ribadeo. Ignore 1st camping sp, take next L in 1.4km. Lge, mkd pitch, pt shd; wc; chem disp; mv service pnt; shwrs inc; el pnts (3A) €3.20 (rev pol); gas 4km; lndtte; shop; tradsmn; rest; snacks; bar; BBQ; playgrnd; pool; sand beach 3km; no dogs; bus 500m; quiet; red for 10+ days; CCI. "Gd NH; friendly, family owners; gd san facs, request hot water for shwrs; everything immac; highly rec; many interesting local features." Holy Week & 1 Jun-30 Sep. € 16.65 2007*

RIBADESELLA *1A3* (4km W) *43.46258, -5.08725* **Camping Ribadesella, Sebreño s/n, 33560 Ribadesella (Asturias) [tel/fax 985-85 82 93; camping.reservas@fade.es; www.camping-ribadesella.com]** W fr Ribadesella take N632. After 2km fork L up hill. Site on L after 2km. Poss diff for lge o'fits & alternative rte fr Ribadesella vill to site to avoid steep uphill turn can be used. Lge, mkd pitch, pt sl, pt terr, pt shd; wc; chem disp; baby facs; shwrs inc; el pnts (5A) €3.20; gas; lndtte; shop, rest, snacks, bar; BBQ; playgrnd; pool high ssn; sand beach 4km; tennis; sports facs; poss cr; adv bkg; quiet; ccard acc; red low ssn/long stay; CCI. "Clean san facs; some sm pitches; attractive fishing vill; prehistoric cave paintings nrby." ♦ Easter-14 Sep. € 21.61 2006*

RIBADESELLA *1A3* (8km W Coastal/Rural) *43.47472, -5.13416* **Camping Playa de Vega, Vega, 33345 Ribadesella (Asturias) [985-86 04 06; fax 985-85 76 62; campingplayadevega@hotmail.com; www.campingplayadevega.com]** Fr A8 exit junc 333 sp Ribadesella W, thro Bones. At rndabt cont W dir Caravia, turn R opp quarry sp Playa de Vega. Fr cent of Ribadesella (poss congestion) W on N632. Cont for 5km past turning to autovia. Turn R at sp Vega & site. Med, hdg pitch, pt terr, pt shd; wc; chem disp; serviced pitch; shwrs inc; el pnts €3.50; lndtte; shop; beach rest; snacks; bar; BBQ; sand beach 400m; TV; dogs; bus 700m; phone; quiet; ccard acc; CCI. "Sh walk to vg beach thro orchards; sm pitches not suitable lge o'fits; poss overgrown low ssn." 1 Jul-15 Sep. € 19.10 2009*

⊞ **RIBEIRA** *1B2* (7km N Rural) *42.62100, -8.98600* **Camping Ría de Arosa II, Oleiros, 15993 Santa Eugenia (Uxía) de Ribeira (La Coruña) [902-33 30 40; fax 981-86 55 55; info@camping.riadearosa.com; www.campingriadearosa.com]** Exit AP9 junc 93 Padrón & take N550 then AC305/VG11 to Ribeira. Then take AC550 to Oleiros to site, well sp. Med, hdg/mkd pitch, shd; htd wc; chem disp; mv service pnt; baby facs; shwrs inc; el pnts (6A) inc; gas; lndtte; supmkt; rest; snacks; bar; BBQ; playgrnd; pool; sand beach 7km; fishing; tennis; games area; games rm; wifi; TV; some statics; dogs €2.50; phone; Eng spkn; adv bkg; quiet; ccard acc; red low ssn; CCI. "Beautiful area; helpful, friendly staff; excel." ♦ € 25.90 2008*

⊞ **RIBEIRA** *1B2* (8km NE Coastal) *42.58852, -8.92465* **Camping Playa Ría de Arosa I, Playa de Cabío s/n, 15940 Puebla (Pobra) do Caramiñal (La Coruña) [981-83 22 22; fax 981-83 32 93; playa@campingriadearosa.com; www.campingriadearosa.com]** Exit AP9/E1 junc 93 at Padrón onto VG11 along N side of Ría de Arosa into Puebla d0 Caramiñal. Site is 1.5km S of Puebla, sp fr town. Lge, pt shd; wc; chem disp; mv service pnt; shwrs; el pnts (6A) €4.10; gas; lndtte; shop; rest; snacks; bar; playgrnd; sand beach; cycle hire; TV; some statics; dogs €2.50; phone; poss cr; adv bkg; quiet; ccard acc. € 22.10 (CChq acc) 2009*

RIBEIRA *1B2* (2km E Coastal) *42.5700, -8.97138* **Camping Coroso, Playa de Coroso, 15950 Santa Eugenia (Uxía) de Ribeira (La Coruña) [981-83 80 02; fax 981-83 85 77; info@campingcoroso.com; www.campingcoroso.com]** Fr Padrón on N550 or AP9 6km S of Santiago de Compostela take VRG11 (fast rd) to Ribeira (approx 40km), then foll sp to site on L on ent Ribeira. Lge, some hdg/mkd pitches, hdstg, pt sl, terr, pt shd; wc; chem disp; baby facs; fam bthrm; shwrs inc; el pnts (10A) inc; gas; lndtte; shop in ssn; café in ssn; snacks; bar; BBQ; sandy beach; sailing; tennis; bus; Eng spkn; poss cr; adv bkg; fairly quiet; red 15+ days; ccard acc; CCI. "Marvellous views; gd coastal walks; friendly staff; gd rest." 1 Apr-30 Sep. € 25.10 2008*

RIBERA DE CARDOS see Llavorsí *3B2*

⊞ **RIBES DE FRESER** *3B3* (500m NE Rural) *42.31260, 2.17570* **Camping Vall de Ribes, Ctra de Pardines, Km 0.5, 17534 Ribes de Freser (Gerona) [tel/fax 972-72 88 20; info@campingvallderibes.com; www.campingvallderibes.com]** N fr Ripoll on N152; turn E at Ribes de Freser; site beyond town dir Pardines. Site nr town but 1km by rd. App rd narr. Med, mkd pitch, terr, pt shd; htd wc; chem disp; shwrs inc; el pnts (6A) €4.20; lndry rm; shop 500m; rest; bar; playgrnd; pool; 50% statics; dogs €3; train 500m; quiet; CCI. "Gd, basic site; steep footpath fr site to town; 10-20 min walk to stn; cog rlwy train to Núria a 'must' - spectacular gorge, gd walking & interesting exhibitions; sm/med o'fits only; poss unkempt statics low ssn." € 20.00 2007*

⊞ **RIPOLL** *3B3* (2km N Rural) *42.21995, 2.17505* **Camping Ripollés, Ctra Barcelona/Puigcerdà, Km 109.3, 17500 Ripoll (Gerona) [972-70 37 70; fax 972-70 35 54]** At km 109.3 up hill N fr town; well sp. Steep access rd. Med, mkd pitch, pt sl, pt shd; htd wc; chem disp; mv service pnt; baby facs; shwrs inc; el pnts €4; lndtte; shop 2km; rest; snacks; bar; BBQ; playgrnd; pool; tennis; 20% statics; dogs €2.80; phone; adv bkg; quiet; ccard acc; CCI. "V pleasant; gd bar/rest; not suitable med/lge o'fits." ♦ € 19.00 2007*

RIPOLL *3B3* (2km S Rural) *42.18218, 2.19552* **Camping Solana del Ter, Ctra Barcelona-Puigcerdà, C17, Km 92.5, 17500 Ripoll (Gerona) [972-70 10 62; fax 972-71 43 43; hotel@solanadelter.com; www.solanadelter.com]** Site sp S of Ripoll behind hotel & rest. Med, mkd pitch, hdstg, pt shd; htd wc; chem disp; baby facs; shwrs inc; el pnts (4A) €5; lndtte; shop; rest; snacks; bar; playgrnd; pool; tennis; TV; Eng spkn; phone; some rd & rlwy noise; ccard acc; CCI. "Historic monastery in town; scenic drives nr; expensive for standard of site." 1 Apr-30 Oct. € 23.10 2006*

⊞ **RIPOLL** *3B3* (6km NW Rural) *42.23522, 2.11797* **Camping Molí Serradell, 17530 Campdevànol (Gerona) [tel/fax 972-73 09 27; calrei@teleline.es]** Fr Ripoll N on N152; L onto GI401 dir Gombrèn; site on L in 4km. NB 2nd site. Sm, pt shd; htd wc; chem disp; mv service pnt; shwrs inc; el pnts €4.50; lndtte (in dryer); shop; tradsmn; rest; 75% statics; poss cr; quiet; red low ssn; CCI. € 25.40 2009*

⊞ **ROCIO, EL** *2G3* (1km N Rural) *37.14194, -6.49250* **Camping La Aldea, Ctra del Rocío, Km 25, 21750 El Rocío (Huelva) [959-44 26 77; fax 959-44 25 82; info@campinglaaldea.com; www.campinglaaldea.com]** Fr A49 turn S at junc 48 onto A483 by-passing Almonte, site sp just bef El Rocío rndabt. Fr W (Portugal) turn off at junc 60 to A484 to Almonte, then A483. Lge, hdg/mkd pitch, hdstg, pt shd; htd wc; chem disp; mv service pnt; baby facs; shwrs inc; el pnts (10A) €5.50; gas; lndtte (inc dryer); shop; tradsmn; rest; snacks; bar; BBQ; playgrnd; htd pool high ssn; sand beach 16km; horseriding nrby; van washing facs; wifi; 30% statics; dogs €3; phone; bus 500m; poss cr; Eng spkn; adv bkg; rd/motocross noise; red long stay/low ssn; ccard acc; CCI. "Well-appointed & maintained site; winter rallies; excel san facs; friendly, helpful staff; tight turns on site; most pitches have kerb or gully; pitches soft after rain; gd birdwatching (lagoon 1km) & cycling; interesting town; avoid festival (2nd week May) when town cr & site charges higher; poss windy; excel birdwatching nrby." ♦ € 26.00 2009*

RODA DE BARA *3C3* (2km E Coastal) *41.17003, 1.46427* **Camping Stel, Ctra N340, Km 1182, 43883 Roda de Barà (Tarragona) [977-80 20 02; fax 977-80 05 25; rodadebara@stel.es; www.stel.es]** Exit AP7 junc 31, foll sps for Tarragona on N340. Site on L immed after Arco de Barà. Lge, mkd pitch, pt shd; wc; chem disp; baby facs; htd private bthrms avail; shwrs inc; el pnts (5A) inc; gas; lndtte; shop; rest; snacks; bar; playgrnd; htd pool; waterslides; sand beach adj; watersports; tennis; sports & entmnt; golf 20km; internet; TV; 10% statics; no dogs; phone; poss cr; adv bkg; some rd/rlwy noise; red long stay/low ssn; CCI. "Some sm pitches." ♦ 2 Apr-27 Sep. € 45.00 (CChq acc) 2009*

⊞ **RODA DE BARA** *3C3* (3km E Coastal/Rural) *41.17034, 1.46708* **Camping Arc de Barà, N340, Km 1182, 43883 Roda de Barà (Tarragona) [977-80 09 02; fax 977-80 15 52; camping@campingarcdebara.com; www.campingarcdebara.com]** Exit AP7 junc 31 or 32, foll sp Arc de Barà on N340 dir Tarragona. Site on L after 5km shortly after Camping Park Playa Barà. NB When app fr N ess to use 'Cambia de Sentido' just after Arc de Barà (old arch). Lge, shd; htd wc; chem disp; baby facs; shwrs inc; el pnts (5A) €3.40; gas; lndtte; shop high ssn; supmkt 200m; rest; snacks; bar; BBQ; pool; sand beach adj; 75% statics in sep area; dogs €2.50; phone; bus adj; site clsd Nov; poss cr; Eng spkn; rlwy noise; ccard acc; CCI. "Ltd number sm touring pitches; gd, clean NH en rte Alicante; phone ahead winter/low ssn to check open." ♦ € 28.40 (3 persons) 2006*

RODA DE BARA *3C3* (3km E Coastal) *41.17277, 1.46916* **Camping Park Playa Barà, Ctra N340, Km 1.183, 43883 Roda de Barà (Tarragona) [977-80 27 01; fax 977-80 04 56; info@barapark.es; www.barapark.es]** Exit AP7 junc 31 onto N340, cont to Barà Roman Arch. Turn halfway bet El Vendrell & Torredembarra at km 1183. V lge, hdg/mkd pitch, terr, shd; htd wc; 100% serviced pitches; chem disp; mv service pnt; baby facs; shwrs inc; el pnts (5A) €3.50; gas; lndtte; supmkt; rest; snacks; bar; playgrnd; htd pool; sand beach adj; watersports; jacuzzi; solarium; tennis; games area; cycle hire; horseriding; entmnt; wifi; sat TV; doctor; car wash; cash machine; 10% statics; dogs free; bus; adv bkg; Eng spkn; quiet; red long stay/low ssn/snr citizens; red CCI (only for min 10 nights' stay high ssn). "Beautiful surroundings; conv Port Aventura; excel site; vg rest - red for snr citizens low ssn." ♦ 19 Mar-26 Sep. € 37.60 2009*

RONDA *2H3* (4km NE Rural) *36.76600, -5.11900* **Camping El Cortijo, Ctra Campillos, Km 4.5, 29400 Ronda (Málaga) [952-87 07 46; fax 952-87 30 82; elcortijo@hermanosmacias.com; www.hermanosmacias.com]** Fr Ronda by-pass take A367 twd Campillos. Site on L after 4.5km opp new development 'Hacienda Los Pinos'. Med, mkd pitch, pt shd; wc; chem disp; mv service pnt; serviced pitches; baby facs; shwrs inc; el pnts inc; lndtte; shop; rest; bar; playgrnd; pool; tennis; games area; cycle hire; 5% statics; dogs; phone; Eng spkn; some rd noise; CCI. "Friendly, helpful owner; conv NH." ♦ 1 Apr-15 Oct. € 16.00 2007*

⊞ **RONDA** *2H3* (6km NE Rural) *36.78691, -5.11241* **Camping El Abogao, Ctra Ronda-Campillos, Km 5, 29400 Ronda (Málaga) [952-87 58 44; fax 952 19 02 67]** Fr Marbella take A376 NW twds Ronda (NB: This rte is v mountainous); turn R onto A367 twds Campillos; site on R in 6km. Sm, pt shd, mkd pitch; wc; chem disp; shwrs inc; el pnts (6A) €4; gas; lndtte; shop 6km; rest; bar; pool; cycle hire; some statics; dogs; phone; adv bkg; quiet; ccard acc; CCI. "Narr ent, tight corners; poss diff access to pitches for long o'fits; sandy & soft after rain; take care low level obstructions when manoeuvring." € 15.00 2008*

⊞ **RONDA** *2H3* (1km S Rural) *36.72111, -5.17166* **Camping El Sur, Ctra Ronda-Algeciras Km 1.5, 29400 Ronda (Málaga) [952-87 59 39; fax 952-87 70 54; info@campingelsur.com; www.campingelsur.com]** Site on W side of A369 dir Algeciras. Do not tow thro Ronda. Med, mkd pitch, hdstg, terr, pt shd; htd wc; chem disp; mv service pnt; baby facs; shwrs inc; el pnts (5-10A) €4.30-5.35 (poss rev pol &/or no earth); lndtte; shop; rest adj; snacks; bar; playgrnd; pool high ssn; internet; dogs €1.70; phone; poss cr; Eng spkn; adv bkg; quiet; red long stay/low ssn; CCI. "Gd rd fr coast with spectacular views; long haul for lge o'fits; busy family-run site in lovely setting; rather regimented; conv National Parks & Pileta Caves; poss diff access some pitches due trees & high kerbs; hard, rocky ground; san facs poss stretched high ssn; easy walk to town; friendly staff; vg rest; excel." ♦ € 22.50 2009*

ROQUETAS DE MAR see Almería *4G1*

ROSAS *3B3* (200m SW Coastal) *42.26888, 3.1525* **Camping Rodas, Calle Punta Falconera 62,17480 Rosas (Gerona) [972-25 76 17; fax 972-15 24 66; info@campingrodas.com; www.campingrodas.com]** On Figueras-Rosas rd, at o'skts of Rosas sp on R after supmkt. Lge, hdg/mkd pitch, pt shd; wc; chem disp; serviced pitches; shwrs inc; el pnts inc; gas; rest; snacks; bar; Indtte; shop adj; tradsmn; sm playgrnd; htd pool; sand beach 600m; bus 1km; poss cr; Eng spkn; adv bkg; quiet; ccard acc; CCI. "Gd pool & children's pool; site rds all tarmac; Rosas gd cent for region; well-run site; gates clsd at midnight." 1 Jun-30 Sep. € 28.00 2007*

ROSAS *3B3* (1km W Urban/Coastal) *42.26638, 3.16305* **Camping Joncar Mar, Ctra Figueres s/n, 17480 Rosas (Gerona) [tel/fax 972-25 67 02; info@campingjoncarmar.com; www.campingjoncarmar.com]** At Figueres take C260 W for Rosas. On ent Rosas turn sharp R at last rndabt at end of dual c'way. Site on both sides or rd - go to R (better) side, park & report to recep on L. Lge, pt sl, pt shd; htd wc; chem disp; baby facs; shwrs; el pnts (6-10A) €4.20 (poss no earth); gas; Indtte; shop; rest; bar; playgrnd; pool; sand beach 150m; golf 15km; entmnt; games rm; internet; 15% statics; dogs €2.40; phone; bus 500m; poss cr; Eng spkn; adv bkg; rd noise; ccard acc; red low ssn/long stay. "Conv walk into Rosas; hotels & apartment blocks bet site & beach; poss cramped/tight pitches; narr rds; vg value low ssn; new san facs under construction 2009." 1 Apr-31 Oct. € 26.70 2009*

⊞ **ROSAS** *3B3* (2km W Coastal) *42.26638, 3.15611* **Camping Salatà, Port Reig s/n, 17480 Rosas (Gerona) [972-25 60 86; fax 972-15 02 33; info@campingsalata.com; www.campingsalata.com]** App Rosas on rd C260. On ent Rosas take 1st R after Rosas sign & Caprabo supmkt. Lge, mkd pitch, hdstg, pt shd; htd wc; chem disp; baby facs; shwrs inc; el pnts (6A) inc; gas; Indtte (inc dryer); shop; tradsmn; rest; snacks; bar; playgrnd; htd pool high ssn; sand beach 200m; wifi; 10% statics; dogs €2.70; phone; site clsd Jan to mid-Feb; poss cr; Eng spkn; adv bkg (bkg fee); red long stay/low ssn; ccard acc; CCI. "Vg area for sub-aqua sports; vg clean facs; red facs low ssn; pleasant walk/cycle to town; excel winter site - min 2 night stay low ssn, 7 nights Sat-Sat high ssn." ♦ € 38.60 2009*

ROTA see Puerto de Santa María, El *2H3*

RUILOBA see Comillas *1A4*

⊞ **SABINANIGO** *3B2* (6km N Rural) *42.55694, -0.33722* **Camping Valle de Tena, Ctra N260, Km 512.6, 22600 Senegüe (Huesca). [974-48 09 77; fax 974-48 25 51; correo@campingvalledetena.com; www.campingvalledetena.com]** Fr Jaca take N330, in 12km turn L onto N260 dir Biescas. In 5km ignore site sp Sorripas, cont for 500m to site on L - new ent at far end. Lge, mkd pitch, terr, unshd; htd wc; chem disp; mv service pnt; serviced pitches; baby facs; shwrs inc; el pnts (6A) inc; Indtte; shop; rest; snacks; bar; playgrnd; pool; sports facs; hiking & rv rafting nr; entmnt; internet; TV rm; 60% statics; phone; Eng spkn; adv bkg; rd noise during day but quiet at night. "Helpful staff; steep, narr site rd; sm pitches; excel, busy NH to/fr France; beautiful area." € 20.00 2009*

⊞ **SABINANIGO** *3B2* (1km NE Urban) *42.52739, -0.35923* **Camping Aurín, Ctra C330, Circunvalación Sabiñánigo-Francia, s/n, 22600 Sabiñánigo (Huesca) [974-48 34 45; fax 974-48 32 80; recep.sabi@trhhoteles.com]** On Sabiñánigo by-pass (N330) 1km SE of junc with N260. Fr Jaca (S) site on L, go past to turning point in 800m. Site well sp behind & beside TRH Sabinanigo Hotel. Lge, mkd pitch, pt shd; htd wc; mv service pnt; chem disp; baby facs; shwrs inc; el pnts (5A) €6; gas; Indtte; shop 2km; supmkt opp; rest, bar in hotel; snacks; playgrnd; 2 pools; tennis; watersports; car wash; 95% statics; no dogs; bus 400m; site clsd 1 Nov-19 Dec; poss cr; Eng spkn; quiet excl w/end; ccard acc. "V sm, cr area for tourers; pitches poss soft; lge o'fits park adj pool low ssn; san facs gd - plenty hot water; site poss scruffy early ssn; mountain walking; skiing; all hotel facs avail to campers; conv NH; CCI not acc." ♦ € 24.00 2009*

⊞ **SACEDON** *3D1* (500m E Rural) *40.48148, -2.72700* **Camp Municipal Ecomillans, Camino Sacedón 15, 19120 Sacedón (Guadalajara) [949-35 10 18; fax 949-35 10 73; ecomillans63@hotmail.com]** Fr E on N320 exit km220, foll Sacedón & site sp; site on L. Fr W exit km222. Med, mkd pitch, hdstg, pt sl, shd; wc (cont); shwrs; el pnts €3.75; Indry rm; shop 500m; lake sw 1km; quiet. "NH only in area of few sites; sm pitches; low ssn phone to check open." ♦ € 13.70 2007*

⊞ **SAGUNTO** *4E2* (7km NE Coastal) *39.72027, -0.19166* **Camping Malvarrosa de Corinto, Playa Malvarrosa de Corinto, 46500 Sagunto (València) [962-60 89 06; fax 962-60 89 43; camalva@ctv.es; www.malvacorinto.com]** Exit 49 fr A7 onto N340, foll dir Almenara-Casa Blanca. Turn E twd Port de Sagunto & Canet d'en Berenguer on CV320. Site poorly sp. Lge, pt shd; wc; chem disp; sauna; shwrs inc; el pnts (5-10A) €4.30; gas; Indtte; shop & 5km; rest; snacks; bar; BBQ; playgrnd; sand & shgl beach adj; tennis; horseriding; gym; 85% statics; dogs €2.70; phone; poss cr; Eng spkn; quiet; red ow ssn/long stay; CCI. "Lovely site under palm trees; friendly, helpful owners; gd facs; feral cats & owners' dogs on site; excel pitches adj beach; ltd touring pitches but access to some poss diff; ltd facs & poss neglected low ssn; no local transport." € 23.40 2009*

Spain

SALAMANCA *1C3* (4km N Rural) *41.02805, -5.67472* **Camping La Capea, Ctra N630, Km 384, 37189 Aldeaseca de la Armuña (Salamanca) [923-25 10 66; campingla capea@hotmail.com]** Close to km post 333 on N630. Site sp fr both dirs. Ent on brow of a hill on W side of rd. Med, hdg/mkd pitch, hdstg, shd; wc; chem disp; mv service pnt; shwrs inc; el pnts (10A) €3.45; lndtte; shop; snacks; bar; playgrnd; pool; TV; 10% statics; dogs; some Eng spkn; some rd noise; CCI. "Friendly; variety of pitch sizes but most not suitable c'vans 6m & over; site poss untidy, unkempt low ssn; conv NH." 1 Apr-30 Sep. € 13.80 2008*

SALAMANCA *1C3* (4.5km NE Rural) *40.97611, -5.60472* **Camping Don Quijote, Ctra Salamanca-Aldealengua, Km 4, 37193 Cabrerizos (Salamanca) [tel/fax 923-20 90 52; info@campingdonquijote.com; www.campingdonquijote.com]** Fr Madrid or fr S cross Rv Tormes by most easterly bdge to join inner ring rd. Foll Paseo de Canalejas for 800m to Plaza España. Turn R onto SA804 Avda de los Comuneros & strt on for 5km. Site ent 2km after town boundary sp. Fr other dirs, head into city & foll inner ring rd to Plaza España. Site well sp fr rv & ring rd. Med, hdg pitch, pt shd; wc; chem disp; mv service pnt; baby facs; shwrs inc; el pnts (10A) €3.45; lndtte; shop; supmkt 3km; rest; snacks; bar; playgrnd; pool; paddling pool; rv fishing; 10% statics; dogs; phone; bus; poss cr w/end; adv bkg; quiet; red CCI. "Gd rv walks; conv city cent; v basic facs." ♦ 1 Mar-31 Oct. € 14.80 2008*

⊞ **SALAMANCA** *1C3* (12km NE Rural) *41.05805, -5.54611* **Camping Olimpia, Ctra de Gomecello, Km 3.150, 37427 Pedrosillo el Ralo (Salamanca) [923-08 08 54 or 619-00 45 18; fax 923-35 44 26; info@campingolimpia.com; www.campingolimpia.com]** Exit A62 junc 225 dir Pedrosillo el Ralo & La Vellés, strt over rndabt, site sp. Sm, hdg pitch, pt shd; htd wc; chem disp; mv service pnt; shwrs inc; el pnts €3; lndtte (inc dryer); tradsmn; rest; snacks; bar; no statics; dogs €1; phone; bus 300m; Eng spkn; adv bkg; some rd noise. "V helpful owner; gd site." € 15.00 2009*

⊞ **SALAMANCA** *1C3* (4km E Urban) *40.94722, -5.6150* **Camping Regio, Ctra Ávila-Madrid, Km 4, 37900 Santa Marta de Tormes (Salamanca) [923-13 88 88; fax 923-13 80 44; recepcion@campingregio.com; www.campingregio.com]** Fr E on SA20/N501 outer ring rd, pass hotel/camping sp visible on L & exit Sta Marta de Tormes, site directly behind Hotel Regio. Foll sp to hotel. Lge, mkd pitch, pt sl, pt shd; wc; chem disp; mv service pnt; baby facs; shwrs inc; el pnts (10A) €3.95 (no earth); gas; lndtte; shop & 1km; hypmkt 3km; rest, snacks in hotel; bar; playgrnd; hotel pool high ssn; cycle hire; wifi; TV; 5% statics; dogs; phone; bus to Salamanca; car wash; poss cr; Eng spkn; quiet; ccard acc; CCI. "In low ssn stop at 24hr hotel recep; poss v cold in winter; poss no hdstg in wet conditions; conv en rte Portugal; refurbished facs to excel standard; site poss untidy low ssn & itinerants, ltd security; spacious pitches but some poss tight for lge o'fits; take care lge brick markers when reversing; excel pool; vg." ♦ € 19.70 2009*

SALAMANCA *1C3* (4km NW Rural) *40.99945, -5.67916* **Camping Ruta de la Plata, Ctra de Villamayor, 37184 Villares de la Reina (Salamanca) [tel/fax 923-28 95 74; recepcion@campingrutadelaplata.com; www.campingrutadelaplata.com]** Fr N or S on A62/E80 Salamanca by-pass exit junc 238 & foll sp Villamayor. Site on R about 800m after rndabt at stadium 'Helmántico'. Avoid SA300 - speed bumps. Med, some hdg/mkd pitch, terr, pt sl, pt shd; htd wc; chem disp; mv service pnt; shwrs inc; el pnts (6A) €3.50; gas; lndtte; shop & 1km; tradsmn; snacks; bar; playgrnd; pool high ssn; golf 3km; TV rm; dogs €1.50; bus to city at gate; poss cr; rd noise; red snr citizen/CCI. "Family-owned site; gd, modern san facs; ltd facs low ssn; less site care low ssn; conv NH." ♦ 1 Feb-30 Nov. € 15.60 (CChq acc) 2009*

⊞ **SALDANA** *1B4* (250m S Urban) *42.51568, -4.73888* **Camping El Soto, Avda del Instituto, 34100 Saldaña (Palencia) [979-89 20 10; mordax@iespana.es]** Cross rv bdge S of Saldana twds Carrión de los Condes. Turn R immed & then immed R again, site not sp. Med, pt shd; wc; chem disp; shwrs; el pnts (10A) €1.80; lndtte; shop in vill; tradsmn; snacks; bar; 20% statics; dogs; phone; quiet; ccard acc; CCI. "Gd base for Roman mosaics at Villa La Olmeda, Pedrosa de la Vega." € 11.70 2006*

I'm going to fill in some site report forms and post them off to the Club; we could win a ferry crossing – it's here on page 12.

⊞ **SALDES** *3B3* (3km E Rural) *42.2280, 1.7594* **Camping Repos del Pedraforca, Ctra B400, Km 13.5, 08697 Saldes (Barcelona) [938-25 80 44; fax 938-25 80 61; pedra@campingpedraforca.com; www.campingpedraforca.com]** S fr Puigcerdà on C1411 for 35km, turn R at B400, site on L in 13.5km. Med, mkd pitch, pt sl, shd; htd wc; chem disp; mv service pnt; baby facs; sauna; shwrs inc; el pnts (3-5A) €4.50-5.40; lndtte; shop; tradsmn; rest, snacks high ssn; bar; playgrnd; 2 htd pools (1 covrd); cycle hire; gym; entmnt; TV rm; 50% statics; dogs €2.50; phone; Eng spkn; some rd noise; adv bkg; red 14+ days; ccard acc; CCI. "Tow to pitches avail; vg walking; in heart of nature reserve; poss diff ent long o'fits; excel." € 29.30 (CChq acc) 2009*

SALOU *3C2* (Urban/Coastal) *41.07805, 1.14000* **Camping La Siesta, Carrer del Nord 37, 43840 Salou (Tarragona) [977-38 08 52; fax 977-38 31 91; info@camping-lasiesta.es; www.campinglasiesta.es]** Site in cent of town, well sp. Lge, mkd pitch, pt sl, shd; wc; chem closet; chem disp; baby facs; shwrs; el pnts (10A) €4; gas; lndtte; shop; rest; snacks; bar; pool; paddling pool; sand beach 300m; cycle hire; sports area; 30% statics; poss cr; adv bkg ess; some rd noise & disco; adv bkg; ccard acc; CCI. "Gd cycle path by beach to Cambrils; site guarded; conv for beach & Port Aventura." ♦ 10 Mar-3 Nov. € 35.20 2007*

⊞ **SALOU** *3C2* (2km NE Coastal) *41.08858, 1.18224* **Camping La Pineda de Salou, Ctra Tarragona-Salou, Km 5, 43481 La Pineda-Vilaseca (Tarragona) [977-37 30 80; fax 977-37 30 81; info@campinglapineda.com; www.campinglapineda.com]** Exit A7 junc 35 dir Salou, Vilaseca & Port Aventura. Foll sp Port Aventura then La Pineda/Platjes on rd TV 3148. Med, mkd pitch, pt shd; wc; baby facs; chem disp; sauna; shwrs; el pnts (5A) €3.50; gas; Indtte; shop; rest; snacks; bar; playgrnd; pool & paddling pool; spa cent; beach 400m; watersports; fishing; tennis; horseriding; cycle hire; mini club; tourist info; entmnt; TV; some statics; dogs €2.90; phone; ccard acc; red low ssn. "Conv Port Aventura & Tarragona." € 32.20 2006*

SALOU *3C2* (1km S Urban/Coastal) *41.0752, 1.1176* **Camping Sanguli-Salou, Paseo Miramar-Plaza Venus, 43840 Salou (Tarragona) [977-38 16 41; fax 977-38 46 16; mail@sanguli.es; www.sanguli.es]** Exit AP7/E15 junc 35. At 1st rndbt take dir to Salou (Plaça Europa), at 2nd rndabt foll site sp. V lge, mkd pitch, hdstg, pt sl, shd; htd wc; chem disp; mv service pnt; some serviced pitches; baby facs; shwrs inc; el pnts (10A) inc; gas; Indtte; shop; 2 supmkts; rest; snacks; bar; BBQ; playgrnd; 3 pools & 3 paddling pools; waterslide; jacuzzi; sand beach 50m; games area; tennis; games rm; fitness rm; entmnt; excursions; cinema; youth club; mini-club; amphitheatre; internet; TV; dogs; 35% statics; phone; bus; car wash; Eng spkn; adv bkg rec Jul-Aug; some rlwy noise; red low ssn/long stay/snr citizens; ccard acc; CCI. "Quiet end of Salou nr Cambrils & 3km Port Aventura; lge o'fits take care manoeuvring on some pitches & overhanging trees; excel, well-maintained site." ♦ 19 Mar-1 Nov. € 59.00 2009*

See advertisement on previous page

SALOU *3C2* (2km W Coastal) *41.07665, 1.10960* **Camping Cambrils Park, Avda Mas Clariana s/n, 43850 Cambrils (Tarragona) [977-35 10 31; fax 977-35 22 10; mail@cambrilspark.es; www.cambrilspark.es]** Exit AP7 junc 35 & foll sp Salou; at 1st rndabt foll sp Cambrils; after 2km site sp to L at rndabt. V lge, mkd pitch, hdstg, pt sl, shd; htd wc; chem disp; mv service pnt; baby facs; some serviced pitches; shwrs inc; el pnts (10A) inc; gas; Indtte; shop; rest; snacks; bar; BBQ; playgrnd; lge pool complex; sand beach 400m; tennis; child mini-club; entmnt; excursions; games rm; internet; TV rm; car wash; 50% statics; no dogs; phone; Eng spkn; adv bkg rec; quiet; ccard acc; red low ssn/long stay/snr citizens; CCI. "Superb, busy site; excel, clean facs; helpful staff; access to some pitches poss diff long o'fits; walk along sea front to Salou or Cambrils; conv Port Aventura; bus to Tarragona nrby or walk to Salou for train; excel site rest & pools." ♦ 26 Mar-12 Oct. € 61.00 (CChq acc) 2009*

SAN MIGUEL DE SALINAS see Torrevieja *4F2*

⊞ **SAN ROQUE** *2H3* (6km E Rural) *36.25055, -6.66166* **Camping La Casita, Ctra N340, Km 126.2, 11360 San Roque (Cádiz) [tel/fax 956-78 00 31]** Site sp 'Via de Servicio' parallel to AP7/E15. Access at km 119 fr S, km 127 fr N. Site visible fr rd. Med, pt sl, pt terr, pt shd, wc; chem disp; mv service pnt; shwrs; el pnts (10A) €4.54; shop; rest; bar; playgrnd; pool; sand beach 3km; horseriding; entmnt; 90% statics; dogs €2.67; bus 100m; phone; poss cr; Eng spkn; adv bkg ess; noisy; ccard acc; red long stay/low ssn; CCI. "Shwrs solar htd - water temp depends on weather (poss cold); san facs poss unclean; friendly staff; conv Gibraltar & Morocco; daily buses to La Línea & Algeciras; ferries to N Africa (secure parking at port)." ♦ € 39.50 2008*

⊞ **SAN SEBASTIAN/DONOSTIA** *3A1* (5km NW Rural) *43.30458, -2.04588* **Camping Igueldo, Paseo Padre Orkolaga 69, 20008 San Sebastián (Guipúzkoa) [943-21 45 02; fax 943-28 04 11; info@campingigueldo.com; www.campingigueldo.com]** Fr W on A8, leave m'way at junc 9 twd city cent, take 1st R & R at rndabt onto Avda de Tolosa sp Ondarreta. At sea front turn hard L at rndabt sp to site (Avda Satrústegui) & foll sp up steep hill 4km to site. Fr E exit junc 8 then as above. Site sp as Garoa Camping Bungalows. Steep app poss diff for lge o'fits. Lge, hdg/mkd pitches, terr, pt shd, 40% serviced pitches; wc; chem disp; baby facs; shwrs inc; el pnts (5A) inc; gas; Indtte; shop; rest, bar high ssn; playgrnd; pool 5km; sand beach 5km; TV; phone; bus to city adj; poss cr/noisy; Eng spkn; red long stay/low ssn; CCI. "Gd, clean facs; sm pitches poss diff; spectacular views; pitches muddy when wet; excel rest 1km (open in winter)." ♦ € 30.50 2009*

SAN VICENTE DE LA BARQUERA *1A4* (1km E Coastal) *43.38901, -4.3853* **Camping El Rosal, Ctra de la Playa s/n, 39540 San Vicente de la Barquera (Cantabria) [942-71 01 65; fax 942-71 00 11; info@campingelrosal.com; www.campingelrosal.com]** Fr A8 km 264, foll sp San Vicente. Turn R over bdge then 1st L (site sp) immed at end of bdge; keep L & foll sp to site. Med, mkd pitch, pt sl, pt shd; wc; chem disp; shwrs; el pnts (6A) €3.37; gas; Indtte; shop; rest; snacks; bar; sand beach adj; wifi; phone; poss cr; Eng spkn; adv bkg; quiet; ccard acc; red low ssn/long stay; CCI. "Site in pine wood o'looking bay; surfing beach; some modern, clean facs; helpful staff; vg rest; easy walk or cycle ride to interesting town; Sat mkt." ♦ Easter & 1 Jun-15 Sep. € 28.00 2009*

SAN VICENTE DE LA BARQUERA *1A4* (5km E Coastal) *43.38529, -4.33831* **Camping Playa de Oyambre, Finca Peña Gerra, 39540 San Vicente de la Barquera (Cantabria) [942-71 14 61; fax 942-71 15 30; camping@oyambre.com; www.oyambre.com]** Fr N634 foll sp to La Revilla. Site on L in 3km. Lge, mkd pitch, terr, pt sl, pt shd; wc; chem disp; mv service pnt; shwrs inc; el pnts (10A) €4.55; gas; Indtte; shop & 5km; tradsmn; rest; snacks; bar; pool; beach 800m; wifi; 40% statics; bus 200m; Eng spkn; adv bkg; ccard acc; CCI. "V well-kept site; clean, dated san facs; helpful owner; quiet week days low ssn; gd base for N coast & Picos de Europa; 4x4 avail to tow to pitch if wet; some sm pitches & rd noise some pitches; conv Santander ferry." 1 Apr-30 Sep. € 20.30 2009*

SANGONERA LA SECA see Murcia *4F1*

SANGUESA *3B1* (500m S Urban) *42.57087, -1.28403* **Camping Cantolagua, Camino de Cantolagua, 31400 Sangüesa (Navarra) [948-43 03 52; fax 948-87 13 13; camping.sanguesa@meganet.es]** Turn off N240 fr Pamplona onto N127 to Sangüesa. Turn into town over bdge, foll sp, 2nd R up thro town, R at Bull Ring then L, then 1st R. Site well sp in town. Med, hdg pitch, pt shd; wc; chem disp (wc); mv service pnt; some serviced pitches; shwrs inc; el pnts (8A) €3.40; Indtte; shops 1km; tradsmn; rest; snacks; bar; BBQ; htd pool adj; playgrnd; horseriding; tennis; cycle hire; TV rm; phone; poss cr; Eng spkn; 10% statics; quiet; ccard acc; CCI. "Serviced pitches not suitable for m'vans; facs clean; lovely historic unspoilt town; adequate NH." ♦ 1 Feb-31 Oct. € 14.50 2006*

SANT ANTONI DE CALONGE see Palamós *3B3*

SANT FELIU DE GUIXOLS *3B3* (1km N Urban/Coastal) *41.78611, 3.04111* **Camping Sant Pol, Ctra Dr Fleming 1, 17220 Sant Feliu de Guixols (Gerona) [972-32 72 69 or 972-20 86 67; fax 972-32 72 11 or 972-22 24 09; info@campingsantpol.cat; www.campingsantpol.cat]** Exit AP7 junc 7 onto C31 dir Sant Feliu. At km 312 take dir S'Agaro; at rndabt foll sp to site. Med, hdg/mkd pitch, terr, shd; htd wc; chem disp; mv service pnt; some serviced pitches; baby facs; shwrs inc; el pnts (10A) €4; Indtte; shop; rest; bar; BBQ; playgrnd; 3 htd pools; sand beach 350m; games rm; cycle hire; wifi; 30% statics; dogs €2; sep car park; Eng spkn; adv bkg; quiet - some rd noise; ccard acc; red long stay/snr citizens/CCI. "Vg, well-run site; excel facs; lovely pool; cycle track to Gerona." ♦ 26 Mar-12 Dec. € 53.00 2009*

SANT JOAN DE LES ABADESSES see Sant Pau de Segúries *3B3*

SANT LLORENC DE LA MUGA see Figueres *3B3*

⊞ **SANT PAU DE SEGURIES** *3B3* (500m S Rural) *42.26292, 2.36913* **Camping Els Roures, Avda del Mariner 34, 17864 Sant Pau de Segúries (Gerona) [972-74 70 00; fax 972-74 71 09; info@elsroures.com; www.elsroures.com]** On C38/C26 Camprodón S twd Ripoll for 6km. In Sant Pau turn L 50m after traff lts. Site on R after 400m. Lge, mkd pitch, terr, shd; wc; mv service pnt; baby facs; shwrs inc; el pnts (4-8A) €3.20-6.50; gas; Indtte; shop; rest; bar; playgrnd; 2 pools; tennis; cinema; games rm; gym; internet; 80% statics; dogs €3.50; phone; bus 200m; poss cr; some noise; CCI. "Gd." ♦ € 26.00 2007*

⊞ **SANT PAU DE SEGURIES** *3B3* (4km SW Rural) *42.25549, 2.35081* **Camping Abadesses, Ctra Camprodón, Km 14.6, 17860 Sant Joan de les Abadesses (Gerona) [630-14 36 06; fax 972-70 20 69; info@campingabadesses.com; www.campingabadesses.com]** Fr Ripoll take C26 in dir Sant Joan, site approx 4km on R after vill. Steep access. Sm, mkd pitch, terr, unshd; htd wc; baby facs; shwrs; el pnts (6A) €2.88; gas; Indtte; shop; snacks; bar; playgrnd; pool; games area; wifi; 70% statics; dogs €3.21; bus 150m; quiet; ccard acc. "Vg facs; gd views fr most pitches; steep access to recep; poss diff access around terraces." ♦ € 21.90 2007*

SANT PERE PESCADOR *3B3* (200m E Rural) *42.18747, 3.08891* **Camping Riu, Ctra de la Playa s/n, 17470 Sant Pere Pescador (Gerona) [972-52 02 16; fax 972-55 04 69; info@campingriu.com; www.campingriu.com]** Fr N exit AP7 junc 4 dir L'Escala & foll sp Sant Pere Pescador, then turn L twds coast, site on L. Fr S exit AP7 junc 5 dir L'Escala, then as above & turn R to beaches & site. Lge, mkd pitch, shd; wc; chem disp; baby facs; shwrs inc; el pnts (5A) €3.90; gas; Indtte; shop & 300m; rest; snacks; bar; BBQ; playgrnd; pool; sand beach 2km; rv fishing adj; kayak hire; games area; entmnt; internet; 5% statics; dogs €3.40; Eng spkn; adv bkg; quiet; ccard acc; red long stay; CCI. "Excel boating facs & fishing on site; gd situation; site rec." ♦ 4 Apr-19 Sep. € 38.00 2009*

SANT PERE PESCADOR *3B3* (1km E Coastal) *42.18908, 3.1080* **Camping La Gaviota, Ctra de la Playa s/n, 17470 Sant Pere Pescador (Gerona) [972-52 05 69; fax 972-55 03 48; info@lagaviota.com; www.lagaviota.com]** Exit 5 fr A7 dir Sant Martí d'Empúries, site at end of beach rd. Med, hdg/mkd pitch, pt shd; wc; chem disp; baby facs; shwrs inc; el pnts (5A) €3.70; gas; Indtte; shop; rest; bar; playgrnd; direct access sand beach 50m; games rm; internet; 20% statics; phone; dogs €4; poss cr; Eng spkn; adv bkg; quiet; ccard acc; red long stay; CCI. "V friendly owners; gd, clean site; excel facs & constant hot water; some sm pitches & narr site rds; poss ltd access for lge o'fits; take care o'hanging trees; poss mosquito problem." ♦ 19 Mar-24 Oct. € 38.00 2009*

SANT PERE PESCADOR *3B3* (1km SE Coastal) *42.18180, 3.10403* **Camping L'Àmfora, Avda Josep Tarradellas 2, 17470 Sant Pere Pescador (Gerona) [972-52 05 40 or 972-52 05 42; fax 972-52 05 39; info@campingamfora.com; www.campingamfora.com]** Fr N exit junc 3 fr AP7 onto N11 fro Figueres/Roses. At junc with C260 foll sp Castelló d'Empúries & Roses. At Castelló turn R at rndabt sp Sant Pere Pescador then foll sp to L'Amfora. Fr S exit junc 5 fr AP7 onto GI 623/GI 624 to Sant Pere Pescador. V lge, hdg/mkd pitch, pt shd; htd wc; chem disp; mv service pnt; serviced pitches; baby facs; shwrs inc; el pnts (10A) inc; gas; Indtte; ice; shop; supmkt; rest; snacks; bar; BBQ (charcoal/elec); playgrnd; 4 pools; waterslide; paddling pool; sand beach adj; windsurf school; fishing; tennis; horseriding 5km; cycle hire; entmnt; children's club; wifi; games/TV rm; 15% statics; dogs €4.80; phone; adv bkg; Eng spkn; quiet; ccard not acc; red long stay/low ssn/snr citizens/CCI. "Excel, well-run, clean site; helpful staff; choice of 3 pitch sizes; lger pitches have own san facs & may be shared to reduce cost; immac san facs; gd rest, shop & evening entmnt; poss flooding on some pitches when wet; Parque Acuatico 18km; gd." ♦ 29 Mar-30 Sep. € 53.00 (CChq acc) ABS - E22 2009*

See advertisement above

SANT PERE PESCADOR *3B3* (2km SE Coastal) *42.16194, 3.10888* **Camping Las Dunas, 17470 Sant Pere Pescador (Gerona) (Postal Address: Aptdo Correos 23, 17130 L'Escala) [972-52 17 17 or 01205 366856 (UK); fax 972-55 00 46; info@campinglasdunas.com or callaway@campinglasdunas.com; www.campinglasdunas.com]** Exit AP7 junc 5 dir Viladamat & L'Escala; 2km bef L'Escala turn L for Sant Martí d'Empúries, turn L bef ent vill for 2km, camp sp. V lge, mkd pitch, pt sl, pt shd; wc; chem disp; mv service pnt; baby facs; serviced pitches; shwrs inc; el pnts (10A) inc; gas; Indtte; kiosk; supmkt; souvenir shop; rest; snacks; bar; BBQ; 2 pools; sand beach adj; playgrnd; tennis & sports; entmnt; TV; money exchange; cash machines; doctor; 5% statics; dogs €4.50; phone; quiet; adv bkg (ess high ssn); Eng spkn; red low ssn; CCI. "Greco-Roman ruins in Empúries; gd sized pitches - extra for serviced; busy, popular site; excel, clean facs." ♦ 21 May-17 Sep. € 52.50 2009*

See advertisement on inside back cover

SANT PERE PESCADOR *3B3* (3km SE Coastal) *42.17701, 3.10833* **Camping Aquarius, Camí Sant Martí d'Empúries, 17470 Sant Pere Pescador (Gerona) [972-52 00 03; fax 972-55 02 16; camping@aquarius.es; www.aquarius.es]** Fr AP7 m'way exit 3, foll sp to Roses. Join C260, after 7km bear R to Sant Pere Pescador. Cross rv bdge in vill, take 1st L & foll camp sp. Turn R at next rndabt, site on R in 1.5km. Lge, pt shd; wc; chem disp; mv service pnt; serviced pitches; baby facs; fam bthrm; shwrs; el pnts (6A) €3.70; gas; Indtte; supmkt; rest; snacks; bar; 2 playgrnds; sand beach adj; nursery in ssn; games rm; games area; car wash; internet; some statics; dogs €3.85; phone; cash point; poss cr; Eng spkn; adv bkg (ess Jul/Aug); quiet; red low ssn/long stay/snr citizens (except Jul/Aug)/CCI. "Immac, well-run site; helpful staff; vg rest; windsurfing; vast beach; recycling facs; excel." ♦ 15 Mar-31 Oct. € 47.00 2009*

SANT PERE PESCADOR *3B3* (1.3km S Coastal) *42.18816, 3.10265* **Camping Las Palmeras, Ctra de la Platja 9, 17470 Sant Pere Pescador (Gerona) [972-52 05 06; fax 972-55 02 85; info@campinglaspalmeras.com; www.campinglaspalmeras.com]** Exit AP7 junc 3 or 4 at Figueras onto C260 dir Rosas/Cadaqués rd. After 8km at Castelló d'Empúries turn S for Sant Pere Pescador & cont twd beach. Site on R of rd. Lge, mkd pitch, shd; wc; chem disp; mv service pnt; some serviced pitches; baby facs; shwrs inc; el pnts (5-16A) €4 (check for earth); gas; Indtte; shop; rest; snacks; bar; playgrnd; htd pool; paddling pool; sand beach 200m; tennis; cycle hire; games area; games rm; internet; entmnt; TV; 10% statics; dogs €4.30; phone; cash point; poss cr; Eng spkn; adv bkg; quiet; red CCI. "Pleasant site; helpful, friendly staff; superb, clean san facs; gd cycle tracks; nature reserve nrby; excel." ♦ 27 Mar-23 Oct. € 46.00 2009*

See advertisement below

SANT PERE PESCADOR *3B3* (4km S Rural/Coastal) *42.15222, 3.11166* **Camping La Ballena Alegre, Ctra Sant Martí d'Empúries, 17470 Sant Pere Pescador (Gerona) [902-51 05 20; fax 902 51 05 21; infb2@ballena-alegre.es; www.ballena-alegre.com]** Fr A7 exit 5, dir L'Escala to rd GI 623, km 18.5. At 1st rndabt turn L dir Sant Martí d'Empúries, site on R in 1km. V lge, mkd pitch, hdstg, terr, unshd; htd wc; chem disp; some serviced pitches; baby facs; shwrs inc; el pnts (10A) €4.70; gas; Indtte; supmkt; tradsmn; rest; snacks; bar; BBQ; playgrnd; 3 pools; sand beach adj; watersports; tennis; games area; games rm; fitness rm; cycle hire; money exchange; surf shop; doctor; entmnt; wifi; TV rm; 10% statics; dogs €4.70; poss cr; Eng spkn; adv bkg; quiet; red low ssn/snr citizens/long stay; CCI. "Excel site; superb facs." ♦ 14 May-20 Sep. € 54.50 2009*

See advertisement on next page

⊞ **SANT QUIRZE SAFAJA** *3C3* (2km E Rural) *41.72297, 2.16888* **Camping L'Illa, Ctra Sant Feliu de Codines-Centelles, Km 3.9, 08189 Sant Quirze Safaja (Barcelona) [938-66 25 26; fax 935-72 96 21; info@campinglilla.com; www.campinglilla.com]** N fr Sabadell on C1413 to Caldes de Montbui; then twds Moià on C59. Turn R at golf club, site 2km on R. Lge, mkd pitch, hdstg, terr, pt shd; wc; shwrs inc; el pnts (6A) €4.10; gas; Indtte; rest; sm shop; playgrnd; pool; paddling pool; 50% statics; dogs €4.50; bus 100m; site clsd mid-Dec to mid-Jan; adv bkg; CCI. "Easy drive to Barcelona; poss open w/end only low ssn." € 22.00 2007*

⊞ **SANTA CILIA DE JACA** *3B2* (3km W Rural) *42.55556, -0.75616* **Camping Los Pirineos, Ctra Pamplona N240, Km 300.5, 22791 Santa Cilia de Jaca (Huesca) [tel/fax 974-37 73 51; pirineos@pirinet.com; www.pirinet.com/pirineos]** Fr Jaca on N240 twd Pamplona. Site on R after Santa Cilia de Jaca, clearly sp. Lge, hdg/mkd pitch, hdstg, terr, shd; wc; chem disp; mv service pnt; baby facs; shwrs inc; el pnts (5A) €4.96 (check for earth); gas; Indtte; shop, rest high ssn; snacks; bar high ssn; playgrnd; pool in ssn; tennis; 90% statics; dogs; site clsd Nov; Eng spkn; adv bkg; some rd noise; ccard acc; red low ssn; CCI. "Excel site in lovely area; ltd access for tourers & some pitches diff lge o'fits; gd bar/rest on site; on Caminho de Santiago pilgrim rte; conv NH." ♦ € 25.11 2008*

Spain

SANTA CRISTINA DE ARO see Playa de Aro *3B3*

SANTA CRUZ see Coruña, La *1A2*

⊞ **SANTA ELENA** *2F4* (N Rural) *38.34305, -3.53611* **Camping Despeñaperros, Calle Infanta Elena s/n, Junto a Autovia de Andulucia, Km 257, 23213 Santa Elena (Jaén) [953-66 41 92; fax 953-66 19 93; info@camping despenaperros.com; www.campingdespenaperros.com]** Leave A4/E5 at junc 257 or 259, site well sp to N side of vill nr municipal leisure complex. Med, mkd pitch, hdstg, pt shd; wc; chem disp; mv service pnt; all serviced pitches; shwrs inc; el pnts (10A) €3.75 (poss rev pol); gas; Indtte; sm shop; tradsmn; rest high ssn; snacks; bar; playgrnd; pool; internet; TV & tel points all pitches; dogs free; phone; bus 500m; adv bkg; poss noisy w/end high ssn; ccard acc; red long stay/CCI. "Gd winter NH in wooded location; gd size pitches but muddy if wet; gd walking area; friendly, helpful staff; clean san facs; disabled facs (wc only) only useable with manual wheelchair; conv national park & m'way; gd rest; sh walk to vill & shops." ♦ € 17.80 2009*

SANTA MARINA DE VALDEON *1A3* (500m N Rural) *43.13638, -4.89472* **Camping El Cares, El Cardo, 24915 Santa Marina de Valdeón (León) [tel/fax 987-74 26 76; cares@elcares.com]** Fr S take N621 to Portilla de la Reina. Turn L onto LE243 to Santa Marina. Turn L thro vill, just beyond vill turn L at camping sp. Vill street is narr & narr bdge 2.55m on app to site. Do not attempt to app fr N if towing - 4km of single track rd fr Posada. Med, terr, pt shd; wc; chem disp; shwrs; el pnts (5A) €3.20; Indtte; shop; tradsmn; rest; bar; 10% statics; dogs €2.10; phone; bus 1km; quiet; ccard acc; CCI. "Site high in mountains; gd base for Cares Gorge; friendly, helpful staff; gd views; tight access - not rec if towing or lge m'van; poss only cold shwrs." ♦ Holy Week & 15 Jun-16 Sep. € 18.85 2009*

SANTA MARTA DE TORMES see Salamanca *1C3*

I'll go online and tell the Club what we think of the campsites we've visited – www.caravanclub.co.uk/ europereport

⊞ **SANTA PAU** *3B3* (2km E Rural) *42.15204, 2.54713* **Camping Ecológic Lava, Ctra Olot-Santa Pau, Km 7, 17811 Santa Pau (Gerona) [972-68 03 58; fax 972-68 03 15; vacances@i-santapau.com; www.i-santapau.com]** Take rd GI 524 fr Olot, site at top of hill, well sp & visible fr rd. Lge, mkd pitch, pt shd; wc; chem disp (wc); shwrs inc; baby facs; el pnts €4.20; gas; Indtte; shop 2km; tradsmn; rest; snacks; bar; playgrnd; pool; horseriding adj; dogs; phone; Eng spkn; adv bkg; quiet; ccard acc. "V helpful staff; gd facs; v interesting, unspoilt area & town; in Garrotxa Parc Naturel volcanic region; v busy with tourists all ssn; walks sp fr site; Pyrenees museum in Olot; tourist train fr site to volcano; excel rests in medieval town." € 24.50 2007*

⊞ **SANTA POLA** *4F2* (1km NW Urban/Coastal) *38.20105, -0.56983* **Camping Bahía de Santa Pola, Ctra de Elche s/n, Km 38, 03130 Santa Pola (Alicante) [965-41 10 12; fax 965-41 67 90; campingbahia@santapola.com; www.santapola.com]** Exit A7 junc 72 dir airport, cont to N332 & turn R dir Cartagena. At rndabt take exit sp Elx/Elche onto CV865, site 100m on R. Lge, mkd pitch, hdstg, pt shd; htd wc; chem disp; mv service pnt; baby facs; shwrs inc; el pnts (10A) €2.50; gas; Indtte; shop; supmkt; rest; playgrnd; pool; sand beach 1km; sat TV; 50% statics; phone; bus adj; Eng spkn; adv bkg; rd noise; ccard acc; red long stay/low ssn/CCI. "Helpful, friendly manager; well-organised site; recep in red building facing ent; excel san facs; site rds steep; attractive coastal cycle path." ♦ € 21.00 2009*

⊞ **SANTAELLA** *2G3* (5km N Rural) *37.62263, -4.85950* **Camping La Campiña, La Guijarrosa-Santaella, 14547 Santaella (Córdoba) [957-31 53 03; fax 957-31 51 58; info@campinglacampina.com; www.campinglacampina.com]** Fr A4/E5 leave at km 441 onto A386 rd dir La Rambla to Santaella for 11km, turn L onto A379 for 5km & foll sp. Sm, mkd pitch, hdstg, pt sl, pt shd; wc; chem disp; baby facs; shwrs inc; el pnts (5A) €3.20; gas; Indtte; shop & 6km; rest; snacks; bar; BBQ; playgrnd; pool; TV; dogs €2; bus at gate to Córdoba; Eng spkn; adv bkg; rd noise; ccard acc; red long stay/low ssn; CCI. "Fine views; friendly, warm welcome; popular, family-run site; many pitches sm for lge o'fits; guided walks; poss clsd winter - phone to check." ♦ € 17.10 2006*

SANTANDER *1A4* (4km E Coastal) *43.45638, -3.72138* **Camping Latas, Barrio Arna, s/n, 39140 Somo (Cantabria) [tel/fax 942-51 06 31]** Exit A8 junc 11 dir Pedreña/Heres, thro Somo up hill; L at 2nd rndabt (sp Loredo NOT Laredo); turn L after camp sp; call at bar for access on R. Med, hdg pitch, pt sl, terr, pt shd; wc; chem disp; mv service pnt; baby facs; shwrs inc; el pnts (2-6A) €4.30; gas; Indtte; shop; rest; snacks; bar; playgrnd; pool; sand beach nr; watersports; tennis; 50% statics; phone; bus 200m; poss cr; adv bkg; poss noisy; no ccard acc; CCI. "Noisy until midnight then strict silence." ♦ Holy Week & 15 Jun-9 Sep. € 22.60 2007*

⊞ **SANTANDER** *1A4* (12km E Rural) *43.44777, -3.72861* **Camping Somo Parque, Ctra Somo-Suesa s/n, 39150 Suesa-Ribamontán al Mar (Cantabria) [tel/fax 942-51 03 09; somoparque@somoparque.com; www.somoparque.com]** Fr car ferry foll sp Bilbao. After approx 8km turn L over bdge sp Pontejos & Somo. After Pedreña climb hill at Somo Playa & take 1st R sp Suesa. Foll site sp. Med, pt shd; wc; chem disp; shwrs & bath; el pnts (6A) €3 (poss rev pol); gas; shop; snacks; bar; playgrnd; beach 1.5km; 99% statics; site clsd 16 Dec-31 Jan; some Eng spkn; quiet; CCI. "Friendly owners; peaceful rural setting; sm ferry bet Somo & Santander; poss unkempt low ssn; NH only." € 17.80 2009*

SANTANDER *1A4* (6km W Coastal) *43.47611, -3.95944* **Camping Virgen del Mar, Ctra Santander-Liencres, San Román-Corbán s/n, 39000 Santander (Cantabria) [942-34 24 25; fax 942-32 24 90; cvirdman@ceoecant.es; www.campingvirgenmar.com]** Fr ferry turn R, then L up to football stadium, L again leads strt into San Román. If app fr W, take A67 (El Sardinero) then S20, leave at junc 2 dir Liencres, strt on. Site well sp. Lge, mkd pitch, pt shd; wc; chem disp; mv service pnt; shwrs; el pnts (4-10A) €4; Indtte; shop; supmkt 2km; rest; snacks; bar; playgrnd; pool; sand beach 300m; no dogs; bus 500m; adv bkg; quiet; red long stay; CCI. "Basic facs, poss ltd hot water; some sm pitches not suitable lge o'fits; site adj cemetary; phone in low ssn to check site open; expensive low ssn." ♦ 1 Mar-10 Dec. € 28.00 2009*

⊞ **SANTANDER** *1A4* (2km NW Coastal) *43.46888, -3.85111* **Camping Costa San Juan, Avda San Juan de la Canal s/n, 39110 Soto de la Marina (Cantabria) [tel/fax 942-57 95 80 or 629-30 36 86; hotelcostasanjuan@yahoo.es; www.hotelcostasanjuan.com]** Fr A67 exit junc 197 to Liencres. In 5km turn R onto CA231 thro Soto de la Marina. Turn L at Irish pub on R & site in 500m behind hotel. Sm, pt shd; wc; chem disp; shwrs €2; el pnts (3-6A) €3.20; Indry rm; rest; bar; sand beach 400m; TV rm; 90% statics; dogs; poss cr; quiet. "Gd NH for ferry; poss diff lge o'fits; gd coastal walks." € 22.50 2009*

SANTANDER *1A4* (6km NW Coastal) *43.48916, -3.79361* **Camping Cabo Mayor, Avda. del Faro s/n, 39012 Santander (Cantabria) [tel/fax 942-39 15 42; info@cabomayor.com; www.cabomayor.com]** Sp thro town but not v clearly. On waterfront (turn R if arr by ferry). At lge junc do not foll quayside, take uphill rd (resort type prom) & foll sp for Faro de Cabo Mayor. Site 200m bef lighthouse on L. Lge, mkd pitch, terr, unshd; wc; chem disp (wc); baby facs; shwrs inc; el pnts (5A) inc; gas; Indtte; shop; rest; snacks; bar; playgrnd; pool high ssn; many beaches adj; TV; 10% statics; no dogs; phone; poss cr; Eng spkn; no ccards; CCI. "San facs old but clean; v sm pitches; site popular with lge youth groups high ssn; shwrs clsd 2200-0800 & stretched in high ssn; poss run down end of ssn (2008); conv ferry; nice coastal walk to Sardinero beachs; NH only." ♦ 1 Apr-14 Oct. € 27.80 2008*

Spain

⊞ **SANTIAGO DE COMPOSTELA** *1A2* (2km E Urban) *42.88972, -8.52444* **Camping As Cancelas, Rua 25 do Xullo 35, 15704 Santiago de Compostela (La Coruña) [981-58 02 66 or 981-58 04 76; fax 981-57 55 53; info@campingascancelas.com; www.campingascancelas.com]** Exit AP9 junc 67 & foll sp Santiago. At rndabt with lge service stn turn L sp 'camping' & foll sp to site turning L at McDonalds. Site adj Guardia Civil barracks - poorly sp. Lge, mkd pitch, terr, pt sl, shd; wc; chem disp; baby facs; shwrs inc; el pnts (5-10A) €4.50; gas; Indtte; shop, rest, snacks & bar in ssn; BBQ; playgrnd; pool & paddling pool high ssn; wifi; entmnt; TV; dogs; phone; bus 100m; poss v cr; Eng spkn; quiet; red low ssn; CCI. "Busy site - conv for pilgrims; rec arr early high ssn; some sm pitches poss diff c'vans & steep ascent; clean san facs but stretched when site busy; gd rest; bus 100m fr gate avoids steep 15 min walk back fr town (low ssn adequate car parks in town); poss interference with car/c'van electrics fr local transmitter - if problems report to site recep; in winter recep in bar." ♦ € 25.20 2009*

SANTIAGO DE COMPOSTELA *1A2* (4km E Urban) *42.88694, -8.49027* **Camping Monte do Gozo, Ctra Aeropuerto, Km 2, 15820 Santiago de Compostela (La Coruña) [981-55 89 42; fax 981-56 28 92; info@cvacaciones-montedogozo.com; www.montedogozo.com]** Site sp on 'old' rd N634 (not new autovia) into town fr E, nr San Marcos. Do not confuse with pilgrim site nr to city. Foll sp 'Ciudad de Vacaciones'. Lge, pt sl, shd; wc; chem disp; shwrs; el pnts €5 (poss rev pol); gas; Indtte; shop; rest; bar; playgrnd; 2 pools; tennis; cycle hire; 20% statics; no dogs; phone; bus 1km; ccard acc. 1 Jul-31 Aug. € 21.95 2007*

SANTILLANA DEL MAR *1A4* (3km E Rural) *43.38222, -4.08305* **Camping Altamira, Barrio Las Quintas s/n, 39314 Queveda (Cantabria) [942-84 01 81; fax 942-26 01 55; altamiracamping@yahoo.es; www.campingaltamira.com]** Clear sp to Santillana fr A67; site on R 3km bef vill. Med, mkd pitch, pt sl, terr, unshd; wc; shwrs; el pnts (3A) €3.20 (poss rev pol); gas; Indtte; sm shop; rest; bar; pool; sand beach 8km; horseriding; TV rm; 30% statics; bus 100m; poss cr; Eng spkn; adv bkg ess high ssn; ccard acc in ssn; CCI. "Ltd facs low ssn; nr Altimira cave paintings; easy access Santander ferry on m'way; gd coastal walks; open w/end only Nov-Mar - rec phone ahead; excel." 19 Mar-8 Dec. € 20.00 2008*

⊞ **SANTILLANA DEL MAR** *1A4* (500m W Rural) *43.39333, -4.11222* **Camping Santillana del Mar, Ctra de Comillas s/n, 39330 Santillana del Mar (Cantabria) [942-81 82 50; fax 942-84 01 83; complejosantillana@cantabria.com; www.cantabria.com/complejosantillana]** Exit A8 junc 230 Santillana-Comillas, then foll sp Santillana & site on rd CA131. Lge, sl, terr, pt shd; wc; chem disp (wc); mv service pnt; baby facs; shwrs inc; el pnts (5A) inc (poss rev pol); gas; Indtte; shop high ssn; rest; snacks; bar; playgrnd; pool & paddling pool; beach 5km; tennis; cycle hire; horseriding; golf 15km; entmnt; internet; car wash; cash machine; 20% statics; dogs; bus 300m; phone; poss cr; Eng spkn; some rd noise; CCI. "Gd, clean facs but ltd low ssn; diff access to fresh water & to mv disposal point; take care poss v hot shwrs; care needed to some pitches due narr, winding access rds - not rec lge o'fits or twin-axles; poss muddy low ssn; poss itinerants; gd views; vg." ♦ € 31.30 (CChq acc) 2009*

SANXENXO *1B2* (2km E Coastal) *42.39638, -8.77777* **Camping Airiños do Mar, Playa de Areas, O Grove, 36960 Sanxenxo (Pontevedra) [tel/fax 986-72 31 54]** Fr Pontevedra take P0308 W twd Sanxenxo & O Grove. Turn L at km post 65; site sp on S side of rd. Access rd needs care in negotiation. Sm, mkd pitch, pt shd; wc; shwrs inc; el pnts (16A) €4.81; gas; Indtte; shop; rest; bar; beach adj; bus adj; poss cr; Eng spkn; adv bkg; quiet. "Not suitable for m'vans over 2.50m high; c'vans over 6m long may need help of staff at ent; bar & rest overlook beach; lovely views." 1 Jun-30 Sep. € 24.60 2007*

SANXENXO *1B2* (4km W Rural/Coastal) *42.39944, -8.85472* **Camping Suavila, Playa de Montalvo 76-77, 36970 Portonovo (Pontevedra) [tel/fax 986-72 37 60; suavila@terra.es; www.suavila.com]** Fr Sanxenxo take P0308 W; at km 57.5 site sp on L. Med, mkd pitch, shd; wc; serviced pitches; baby facs; shwrs inc; el pnts (6A) €3.75; gas; Indtte; shop; tradsmn; rest; snacks; bar; BBQ; playgrnd; sand beach; TV rm; phone; adv bkg; ccard acc; red long stay; quiet; CCI. "Warm welcome; v friendly owner; sm pitches in 1 part of site." ♦ Holy Week-30 Sep. € 19.00 2007*

⊞ **SANXENXO** *1B2* (3km NW Coastal) *42.41777, -8.87555* **Camping Monte Cabo, Soutullo 174, 36990 Noalla (Pontevedra) [tel/fax 986-74 41 41; info@montecabo.com; www.montecabo.com]** Fr AP9 exit junc 119 onto upgraded VRG4.1 dir Sanxenxo. Ignore sp for Sanxenxo until rndabt sp A Toxa/La Toja, where turn L onto P308. Cont to Fontenla supmkt on R - minor rd to site just bef supmkt. Rd P308 fr AP9 junc 129 best avoided. Sm, mkd pitch, terr, pt shd; wc; chem disp; shwrs inc; el pnts €3.40; Indtte; shop & 500m; tradsmn; rest; snacks; bar; playgrnd; sand beach 250m; TV; 10% statics; phone; bus 700m; poss cr; Eng spkn; adv bkg; quiet; ccard acc; red long stay/low ssn; CCI. "Peaceful, friendly site set above sm beach (access via steep path); beautiful coastline & interesting historical sites; vg." € 16.05 2007*

Spain

SANXENXO *1B2* (3km NW Coastal) *42.39254, -8.84517* **Camping Playa Paxariñas, Ctra C550, Km 2.3 Lanzada-Portonovo, 36960 Sanxenxo (Pontevedra) [986-72 30 55; fax 986-72 13 56; info@campingpaxarinas.com; www.campingpaxarinas.com]** Fr Pontevedra W on P0308 coast rd; 3km after Sanxenxo. Site thro hotel on L at bend. Site poorly sp. Fr AP9 fr N exit junc 119 onto VRG41 & exit for Sanxenxo. Turn R at 3rd rndabt for Portonovo to site in dir O Grove. Do not turn L to port area on ent Portonovo. Lge, mkd pitch, pt sl, terr, shd; wc (some cont); chem disp; mv service pnt; serviced pitches; baby facs; shwrs inc; el pnts (5A) €4.60; gas; Indtte (inc dryer); shop & 2km; tradsmn; rest; snacks; bar; playgrnd; sand beach adj; wifi; TV; 25% statics; dogs; phone; Eng spkn; adv bkg; quiet; red long stay/CCI. "Vg site in gd position; secluded beaches; views over estuary; take care high kerbs on pitches; v ltd facs low ssn & poss clsd." ♦ Easter-15 Oct. € 26.15 2009*

SAVINAN see Calatayud *3C1*

SAX *4F2* (5km NW Rural) **Camping Gwen & Michael, Colonia de Santa Eulalia 1, 03630 Sax (Alicante) [965-47 44 19 or 01202 291587 (UK)]** Exit A31 at junc 48 & foll sp for Santa Eulalia, site on R just bef vill square. Rec phone prior to arr. Sm, hdg pitch, hdstg, unshd; wc; chem disp; fam bthrm; shwrs inc; el pnts (3A) €1; Indtte; shops 6km; bar 100m; no statics; dogs; quiet. "Vg CL-type site; friendly British owners; beautiful area; gd NH & touring base." 15 Mar-30 Nov. € 14.00 2009*

SEGOVIA *1C4* (2km SE Urban) *40.93138, -4.09250* **Camping El Acueducto, Avda Don Juan de Borbón 49, 40004 Segovia [tel/fax 921-42 50 00; campingsg@navegalia.com; www.campingacueducto.com]** Turn off Segovia by-pass at La Granja exit, but head twd Segovia. Site in approx 500m off dual c'way just bef Restaurante Lago. If coming fr Madrid via N603 turn L twd Segovia onto N601 fr La Granja. Lge, mkd pitch, pt sl, pt shd; wc; chem disp; mv service pnt; shwrs inc; el pnts (6-10A) €4.50; gas; Indtte; sm shop; mkt 1km; rest adj; bar; BBQ; playgrnd; pool & paddling pool high ssn; cycle hire; dogs; phone; bus 150m; poss cr; m'way noise; CCI. "Excel; v helpful staff; lovely views; v clean facs; gates locked 0000-0800; city a 'must' to visit; gd bus service; some pitches sm & diff for lge o'fits." ♦ 1 Apr-30 Sep. € 27.80 2009*

SENEGUE see Sabiñánigo *3B2*

⊞ **SEO DE URGEL** *3B3* (8km N Rural) *42.42777, 1.46333* **Camping Frontera, Ctra de Andorra, Km 8, 25799 La Farga de Moles (Lleida) [973-35 14 27; fax 973-35 33 40; info@fronterapark.com; www.fronterapark.com]** Sp on N145 about 300m fr Spanish Customs sheds. Access poss diff. Suggest app fr N - turn in front Customs sheds if coming fr S. Lge, mkd pitch, hdstg, pt sl, pt shd; htd wc; chem disp; mv service pnt; shwrs inc; el pnts (10A) €4.25; gas; Indtte; hypmkt 2km; tradsmn; rest; snacks; bar; playgrnd; 2 pools; internet; TV rm; 90% statics; dogs €3.60; phone; car wash; poss cr; adv bkg; noisy; CCI. "Ideal for shopping in Andorra; winter skiing; beautiful situation but poss dusty; sm pitches; v helpful owners." ♦ € 23.65 (CChq acc) 2008*

⊞ **SEO DE URGEL** *3B3* (3km SW Urban) *42.34777, 1.43055* **Camping Gran Sol, Ctra N260, Km 230, 25711 Montferrer (Lleida) [973-35 13 32; fax 973-35 55 40; info@campingransol.com; www.campingransol.com]** S fr Seo de Urgel on N260/C1313 twds Lerida/Lleida. Site approx 3km on L fr town. Med, pt shd; wc; chem disp (wc); shwrs inc; el pnts (2-6A) €4.25; gas; Indtte; shop; rest; playgrnd; pool; dogs €3.60; bus 100m; some Eng spkn; adv bkg; some rd noise; CCI. "Gd site & facs (poss stretched if full); conv for Andorra; beautiful vills & mountain scenery; in low ssn phone to check site open; gd NH." ♦ € 23.65 2007*

SEO DE URGEL *3B3* (8.5km NW Rural) *42.37388, 1.35777* **Camping Castellbò-Buchaca, Ctra St Joan de l'Erm, 25712 Castellbò (Lleida) [973-35 21 55]** Leave Seo de Urgel on N260/1313 twd Lerida. In approx 3km turn N sp Castellbò. Site on L, well sp. Sm, mkd pitch, pt sl, pt shd; wc; chem disp (wc); shwrs inc; el pnts (5A) €5.15; Indtte; shop; snacks; playgrnd; pool; dogs €3.60; phone; poss cr; adv bkg; quiet. "CL-type site in beautiful surroundings; v friendly recep; poss diff access lge o'fits." 1 May-30 Sep. € 20.60 2008*

SEVILLA See sites listed under Dos Hermanas and Alcalá de Guadaíra

⊞ **SITGES** *3C3* (2km SW Urban/Coastal) *41.23351, 1.78111* **Camping El Garrofer, Ctra C246a, Km 39, 08870 Sitges (Barcelona) [938-94 17 80; fax 938-11 06 23; info@garroferpark.com; www.garroferpark.com]** Fr AP7/E15 exit junc 28 or 29 dir Sitges. Thro Sitges & under rlwy arch, then turn R twd Vilanova/Tarragona. Site on L twd Vilanova, sp. V lge, hdg/mkd pitch, hdstg, pt shd; htd wc; chem disp; mv service pnt; baby facs; shwrs inc; serviced pitches; el pnts (5-10A) inc (poss rev pol); gas; Indtte; shop; rest; snacks; bar; playgrnd; pool; shgl beach 900m; windsurfing; tennis 800m; horseriding; cycle hire; games area; games rm; car wash; wifi; entmnt; TV; 10% statics; dogs €2.60; phone; bus adj (to Barcelona); recep open 0800-2100; site clsd 20 Dec-28 Jan to tourers; poss cr; Eng spkn; adv bkg; ccard acc; red snr citizen/low ssn; CCI. "Gd location, conv Barcelona; sep area for m'vans; v busy site espec w/ends." ♦ € 34.90 2009*

See advertisement

SITGES *3C3* (1.5km W Urban/Coastal) *41.2328, 1.78511* **Camping Sitges, Ctra C31, Km 38, 08870 Sitges (Barcelona) [938-94 10 80; fax 938-94 98 52; info@campingsitges.com; www.campingsitges.com]** Fr AP7/E15 exit junc 28 or 29 dir Sitges. Site on R after El Garrofer, sp. If app fr Sitges go round rndabt 1 more exit than sp, & immed take slip rd - avoids a L turn. Lge, mkd pitch, hdstg, pt shd; wc; chem disp; baby facs; shwrs inc; el pnts (6A) €4.50; gas; Indtte; shop; rest; snacks; bar; BBQ; playgrnd; pool high ssn; paddling pool; sand beach 800m; 30% statics; dogs; phone; bus 300m; train 1.5km; poss cr; Eng spkn; quiet but some rlwy noise; ccard acc; red long stay. "Friendly staff; excel, clean san facs; well-maintained, clean site but poss dusty; some pitches v sm; m'vans with trailers not acc; gd pool & shop; rec arr early as v popular & busy." ♦
1 Mar-20 Oct. € 26.00 2009*

⊞ **SOLSONA** *3B3* (2km N Rural) *42.01271, 1.51571* **Camping El Solsonès, Ctra St Llorenç, Km 2, 25280 Solsona (Lleida) [973-48 28 61; fax 973-48 13 00; info@campingsolsones.com; www.campingsolsones.com]** Fr Solsona to St Llorenç site on R in 2km well sp. Ignore new rd sp St Llorenç. Lge, mkd pitch, pt sl, pt shd; wc; chem disp; shwrs; el pnts (4-10A) €3.65-6.75; Indtte; shops & 2km; snacks; pool; 25% statics; clsd mid- Dec to mid-Jan; no dogs; poss cr w/end; quiet off peak; ccard acc; red CCI. "Helpful staff." € 21.60 2007*

SOMO see Santander *1A4*

SOPELANA see Bilbao *1A4*

SORIA *3C1* (2km SW Rural) *41.74588, -2.48456* **Camping Fuente de la Teja, Ctra Madrid-Soria, Km 223, 42004 Soria [tel/fax 975-22 29 67; camping@fuentedelateja.com; www.fuentedelateja.com]** Fr N on N111 (Soria by-pass) 2km S of junc with N122 (500m S of Km 223) take exit for Quintana Redondo, site sp. Fr Soria on NIII dir Madrid sp just past km 223. Turn R into site app rd. Fr S on N111 site sp fr 2 exits. Med, mkd pitch, pt sl, pt shd; wc; chem disp; baby facs; shwrs inc; el pnts (6A) €3 (poss no earth); gas; Indtte; hypmkt 3km; tradsmn; rest; snacks; bar; playgrnd; pool high ssn; TV rm; many statics; dogs; bus 500m; phone; poss cr; adv bkg; some rd noise; ccard acc; CCI. "Excel, busy NH; vg san facs; interesting town; phone ahead to check site poss open bet Oct & Easter." ♦
1 Mar-30 Sep & 10 Oct-30 Nov. € 23.80 2009*

SOTO DEL REAL see Manzanares el Real *1D4*

SOTOSERRANO *1D3* (3km E Rural) *40.43138, -5.93138* **Camping Vega de Francia, Ctra Sotoserrano-Béjar, Paraje Vega de Francia, 37657 Sotoserrano (Salamanca) [tel/fax 923-16 11 04; info@vegadefrancia.com; www.vegadefrancia.com]** Fr Sotoserrano take Ctra de Béjar E sp Colmenar de Montemayor. Bef Roman bdge turn L onto rd sp Camping Vega de Francia for 500m to site. Single track in places. Sm, hdg pitch, hdstg, terr, shd; wc; chem disp; mv service pnt; baby facs; shwrs inc; el pnts (3A) €3; Indtte inc dryer; shop; tradsmn; rest; snacks; bar; BBQ; playgrnd; rv sw adj; TV rm; 50% statics; dogs; phone; Eng spkn; adv bkg; quiet; 20% red 15+ days; ccard acc. "Friendly, family-run site; excel bar-rest popular with locals; gd walking & views; approach poss not suitable lge o'fits." ♦
1 Mar-31 Oct. € 17.50 2008*

The opening dates and prices on this campsite have changed. I'll send a site report form to the Club for the next edition of the guide.

⊞ **SUECA** *4E2* (5km NE Coastal) *39.30354, -0.29270* **Camping Les Barraquetes, Playa de Sueca, Mareny Barraquetes, 46410 Sueca (València) [961-76 07 23; fax 963-20 93 63; info@barraquetes.com; www.barraquetes.com]** Exit AP7 junc 58 dir Sueca onto N332. In Sueca take CV500 to Mareny Barraquetes. Or S fr València on CV500 coast rd. Foll sp for Cullera & Sueca. Site on L. Lge, mkd pitch, shd; wc; chem disp; mv service pnt; baby facs; shwrs inc; el pnts (10A) €5.88; gas; Indtte; shop; bar; BBQ; playgrnd; pool; paddling pool; waterslide; sand beach 350m; windsurfing school; tennis; games area; entmnt; TV rm; 5% statics; dogs €4.28; phone; bus 500m; site clsd Dec to mid-Jan; poss cr; Eng spkn; ccard acc; red long stay/snr citizens; CCI. "Quiet, family atmosphere; conv touring base & València." ♦
€ 28.35 2008*

Spain

⊞ **SUECA** *4E2* (6km SE Coastal) *39.17711, -0.24403* **Camping Santa Marta, Ctra Cullera-Faro, Km 2, Playa del Raço, 46400 Cullera (València) [961-72 14 40; fax 961-73 08 20; info@santamartacamping.com; www.santamartacamping.com]** On N332 ent Cullera & foll sp. Turn up steep lane beside bullring (white building). Lge, terr, pt sl, shd; wc; chem disp; baby facs; shwrs; el pnts (10A) €5.88; lndtte; shop; tradsmn; rest; bar; no BBQ; playgrnd; pool; sand beach 100m; windsurfing school; cycle hire; entmnt; 5% statics; dogs €4.28; phone; site clsd mid-Dec to mid-Jan; Eng spkn; quiet; ccard acc; red long stay; CCI. "Pleasant site amongst pine trees; pitching poss diff on steep terrs; beach across busy rd; vg." ♦ € 28.35 2008*

⊞ **TABERNAS** *4G1* (8km E Rural) **Camping Oro Verde, Piezas de Algarra s/n, 04200 Tabernas (Almería) [687-62 99 96 or 01434 320495 (UK); info@romanwallcamping.co.uk; www.oroverde.co.uk/contdata6.htm]** Fr N340A turn S onto ALP112 sp Turrillas. Turn R in 100m into narr tarmac lane bet villas, site on L in 600m, not well sp. Sm, pt shd; wc; chem disp; shwrs inc; el pnts (6-10A) inc (poss long lead req); gas; lndtte; shop 1km; rest, bar nrby in hotel; BBQ; pool; sand beach 40km; dogs; adv bkg; quiet; red long stay; CCI. "In sm olive grove; beautiful views; pitches muddy in wet; basic san facs; friendly British owners; 'Mini-Hollywood' 7km where many Westerns filmed; conv Sorbas & Guadix caves; excel." ♦ € 16.00 2008*

TALARN see Tremp *3B2*

TAMARIT see Tarragona *3C3*

⊞ **TAPIA DE CASARIEGO** *1A3* (2km W Rural) *43.54870, -6.97436* **Camping El Carbayin, La Penela-Serantes, 33740 Tapia de Casariego (Asturias) [tel/fax 985-62 37 09]** Foll N634/E70 E fr Ribadeo for 2km to Serantes. Site on R 400m fr rd, well sp. Sm, mkd pitch, pt sl, pt shd; wc; chem disp; baby facs; shwrs inc; el pnts (3A) €3; lndtte; shop; rest; bar; playgrnd; sand beach 1km; fishing; watersports; some statics; bus 400m; phone; adv bkg; quiet; ccard acc; CCI. "Gd for coastal walks & trips to mountains; excel." ♦ € 16.50 2007*

TAPIA DE CASARIEGO *1A3* (3km W Coastal) *43.56394, -6.95247* **Camping Playa de Tapia, La Reburdia, 33740 Tapia de Casariego (Asturias) [985-47 27 21]** Fr E on N634 go past 2 exits sp Tapia de Casariego; then 500m on R foll sp over x-rd to site on L. Med, hdg/mkd pitch, pt sl, pt shd; wc; chem disp; shwrs inc; el pnts (16A) €4.06; gas; lndtte; shop; rest; bar; sand beach 500m; bus 800m; phone; Eng spkn; adv bkg; quiet; CCI. "Gd access; busy, well-maintained, friendly site; harbour & coastal views; walking dist to town." ♦ Holy Week & 1 Jun-15 Sep. € 22.10 2009*

TARAZONA *3B1* (8km SE Rural) *41.81890, -1.69230* **Camping Veruela Moncayo, Ctra Vera-Veruela, 50580 Vera de Moncayo (Zaragoza) [976-64 91 54 or 639-34 92 94 (mob); antoniogp@able.es]** Fr Zaragoza, take AP68 or N232 twd Tudela/Logroño; after approx. 50km, turn L to join N122 (km stone 75) twd Tarazona; cont 30km & turn L twd Vera de Moncayo; go thro town cent; site on R; well sp. Lge, hdg pitch, pt sl, unshd; wc; shwrs inc; el pnts €5.35; gas; rest, snacks, bar & shop 300m; playgrnd adj; pool 500m; cycle hire; dogs; adv bkg; CCI. "Quiet site adj monastery; NH only." ♦ Holy Week & 15 Jun-15 Oct. € 14.50 2008*

⊞ **TARIFA** *2H3* (11km W Coastal) *36.07027, -5.69305* **Camping El Jardín de las Dunas, Ctra N340, Km 74, 11380 Punta Paloma (Cádiz) [956-68 91 01; fax 956-69 91 06; recepcion@campingjdunas.com; www.campingjdunas.com]** W on N340 fr Tarifa, L at sp Punta Paloma. Turn L 300m after Camping Paloma, site in 500m. Lge, hdg pitch, pt shd; wc; chem disp; serviced pitches; baby facs; shwrs inc; el pnts (6A) €3.37; lndtte; shop; rest; snacks; bar; playgrnd; beach 50m; entmnt; TV rm; no dogs; phone; noisy; ccard acc; red low ssn. "Poss strong winds; unsuitable lge o'fits due tight turns & trees." ♦ € 30.38 2008*

⊞ **TARIFA** *2H3* (3km NW Coastal) *36.04277, -5.62972* **Camping Rió Jara, 11380 Tarifa (Cádiz) [tel/fax 956-68 05 70; campingriojara@terra.es]** Site on S of N340 Cádiz-Algeciras rd at km post 81.2; 3km after Tarifa; clearly visible & sp. Med, mkd pitch, pt shd; wc (some cont); chem disp; mv service pnt; shwrs inc; el pnts (10A) €4; gas; lndtte; shop; tradsmn; rest; snacks; bar; playgrnd; sand beach 200m; fishing; wifi; dogs €3.50; poss cr; adv bkg; rd noise; ccard acc; red low ssn; CCI. "Clean, well-kept site; friendly recep; long, narr pitches diff for awnings; daily trips to N Africa; gd windsurfing nrby; poss strong winds; mosquitoes in summer." ♦ € 32.00 2008*

TARIFA *2H3* (6km NW Coastal) *36.05468, -5.64977* **Camping Tarifa, N340, Km 78.87, Los Lances, 11380 Tarifa (Cádiz) [tel/fax 956-68 47 78; info@campingtarifa.es; www.campingtarifa.es]** Site on R of Cádiz-Málaga rd N340. Med, mkd pitch, hdstg, shd; wc; chem disp; mv service pnt; serviced pitch; baby facs; shwrs inc; el pnts (5A) €3.50; gas; lndtte; shop; rest; snacks; bar; playgrnd; pool; sand beach adj; no dogs; phone; car wash; site clsd Nov; Eng spkn; adv bkg; quiet; red long stay & low ssn; ccard acc. "Vg; ideal for windsurfing; immed access to beach; lovely site with beautiful pool; v secure - fenced & locked at night; some pitches sm & poss diff access due bends, trees & kerbs; conv ferry to Morocco; poss strong winds." ♦ 1 Mar-31 Oct. € 33.20 (CChq acc) 2009*

⊞ **TARIFA** *2H3* (7km NW Coastal) *36.06055, -5.66083* **Camping Torre de la Peña 1, Ctra Cádiz, 11380 Tarifa (Cádiz) [956-68 49 03; fax 956-68 14 73; informacion@campingtp.com; www.campingtp.com]** Site at km 79 on both sides of N340, sp. Steep access fr fast main rd. Lge, terr, pt sl, pt shd; wc; shwrs; el pnts (5A) €3.50; gas; lndtte; shop; rest; bar; pool; sand beach adj (via tunnel under rd); dogs €2.70 (Aug not acc); few statics; poss cr; adv bkg; quiet; red long stay/low ssn. "Excel; upper level poss diff lge o'fits; helpful staff; superb views to Africa; conv for Gibraltar & Tangiers; poss strong winds." € 30.60 2008*

⊞ **TARIFA** *2H3* (11km NW Coastal) *36.07621, -5.69336* **Camping Paloma, Ctra Cádiz-Málaga, Km 74, Punta Paloma, 11380 Tarifa (Cádiz) [956-68 42 03; fax 956-68 18 80; campingpaloma@yahoo.es; www.camping paloma.com]** Fr Tarifa on N340, site on L at 74km stone sp Punta Paloma, site on R. Lge, mkd pitch, hdstg, pt sl, terr, pt shd; wc (some cont); chem disp; mv service pnt; shwrs inc; el pnts (6A) €4.28; gas; Indtte; shop; rest; snacks; bar; playgrnd; pool high ssn; sand beach 1km; waterspsorts; windsurfing; horseriding; cycle hire; 20% statics; bus 200m; poss cr; Eng spkn; no adv bkg; quiet; ccard acc; red long stay/low ssn; CCI. "Well-run site; vg facs; peaceful away fr busy rds; lge o'fits poss diff due low tree; trips to N Africa & whale-watching; mountain views." ♦ € 21.47 2009*

TARRAGONA *3C3* (4km NE Coastal) *41.13082, 1.30345* **Camping Las Salinas, Ctra N340, Km 1168, Playa Larga, 43007 Tarragona [977-20 76 28]** Access via N340 bet km 1167 & 1168. Med, shd; wc; shwrs; el pnts €3.74; gas; Indtte; shop; snacks; bar; beach adj; some statics; bus 200m; poss cr; rlwy noise. Holy Week & 15 May-30 Sep. € 29.20 2007*

TARRAGONA *3C3* (5km NE Coastal) *41.13019, 1.31170* **Camping Las Palmeras, N340, Km 1168, 43080 Tarragona [977-20 80 81; fax 977-20 78 17; laspalmeras@ laspalmeras.com; www.laspalmeras.com]** Exit AP7 at junc 32 (sp Altafulla). After about 5km on N340 twd Tarragona take sp L turn at crest of hill. Site sp. V lge, mkd pitch, pt shd; wc; chem disp; shwrs inc; el pnts (6A) inc; gas; Indtte; shop; rest; snacks; bar; playgrnd; pool; sand beach adj; naturist beach 1km; tennis; games area; some statics; dogs €3; phone; poss cr; rlwy noise; ccard acc; red long stay/low ssn; CCI. "Gd beach, ideal for families; poss mosquito prob; many sporting facs; gd, clean san facs; friendly, helpful staff." ♦ 28 Mar-12 Oct. € 44.00 (CChq acc) 2008*

TARRAGONA *3C3* (7km NE Coastal) *41.12887, 1.34415* **Camping Torre de la Mora, Ctra N340, Km 1171, 43080 Tarragona-Tamarit [977-65 02 77; fax 977-65 28 58; info@torredelamora.com; www.torredelamora.com]** Fr AP7 exit junc 32 (sp Altafulla), at rndabt take La Mora rd. Then foll site sp. After approx 1km turn R, L at T-junc, site on R. Lge, hdstg, terr, pt shd; wc; chem disp; mv service pnt; baby facs; shwrs inc; el pnts (6A) €4.30; gas; Indtte; shop & 1km; tradsmn; rest; snacks; bar; playgrnd; pool; sand beach adj; tennis; sports club adj; golf 2km; entmnt; internet; 50% statics; dogs €2.90; bus 200m; Eng spkn; adv bkg; quiet away fr rd & rlwy; ccard acc; red long stay; CCI. "Improved, clean site set in attractive bay with fine beach; excel pool; conv Tarragona & Port Aventura; sports club adj; various pitch sizes, some v sm; private bthrms avail." ♦ 28 Mar-31 Oct. € 42.00 2008*

TARRAGONA *3C3* (7km NE Coastal) *41.1324, 1.3604* **Camping-Caravaning Tamarit Park, Playa Tamarit, Ctra N340, Km 1172, 43008 Playa Tamarit (Tarragona) [977-65 01 28; fax 977-65 04 51; tamaritpark@tamarit. com; www.tamarit.com]** Fr A7/E15 exit junc 32 sp Altafulla/ Torredembarra, at rndabt join N340 by-pass sp Tarragona. At rndabt foll sp Altafulla, turn sharp R to cross rlwy bdge to site in 1.2km, sp. V lge, hdg pitch, some hdstg, pt sl, shd; htd wc; chem disp; mv service pnt; serviced pitches; baby facs; fam bthrm; private bthrms avail; shwrs inc; el pnts (10A) inc; gas; Indtte; supmkt; rest; snacks; bar; BBQ; playgrnd; htd pool; paddling pool; sand/shgl beach adj; watersports; tennis; games area; entmnt; internet; TV; 30% statics; dogs €4; phone; cash machine; car wash; adv bkg (rec Jul/Aug); Eng spkn; ccard acc; red long stay/ snr citizens/low ssn; CCI. "Well-maintained, secure site with family atmosphere; excel beach; superb pool; best site in area but poss noisy at night & w/end; variable pitch prices; beachside pitches avail; take care overhanging trees; Altafulla sh walk along beach worth visit." ♦ 3 Apr-13 Oct. € 62.00 2008*

TAULL see Pont de Suert *3B2*

TAVASCAN *3B2* (5km NW Rural) *42.67021, 1.23501* **Camping Masia Bordes de Graus, Ctra Pleta del Plat, Km 5, Pallars Sobirà, 25577 Tavascan (Lleida) [973-62 32 46; info@bordesdegraus.com; www.bordesde graus.com]** N fr Llavorsí on L504. In approx 20km at Tavascan foll site sp along single track rd. Sm, mkd pitch, pt sl, pt shd; htd wc; chem disp; shwrs inc; el pnts (6A) €5.15; Indtte; tradsmn; rest; snacks; bar; BBQ; playgrnd; games area; games rm; some statics; dogs €3.60; adv bkg; quiet; CCI. "Vg site at high altitude; gd mountain walking & climbing; not rec towed c'vans/lge m'vans." ♦ Holy Week & 24 Jun-11 Sep. € 20.60 2008*

This is a wonderful site.

TIEMBLO, EL *1D4* (8km W Rural) *40.40700, 4.57400* **Camping Valle de Iruelas, Las Cruceras, 05110 Barraco (Ávila) [920-28 72 50; fax 918-62 53 95; iruelas@valle deiruelas.com; www.valledeiruelas.com]** Fr N403 turn off at sp Reserva Natural Valle de Iruelas. After x-ing dam foll sp Las Cruceras & camping. In 5km foll sp La Rinconada, site in 1km. Med, hdg/mkd pitch, terr, shd; wc; chem disp; baby facs; shwrs inc; el pnts inc; Indtte; supmkt; rest; bar; playgrnd; pool; canoeing; horseriding; bird hide; quiet; CCI. "Pleasant, woodland site with wildlife." ♦ Easter-31 Aug. € 30.00 2006*

Spain

⊞ **TOLEDO** *1D4* (2km W Rural) *39.86416, -4.04694* **Camping El Greco, Ctra Pueblo Montalban, Km.97, 45004 Toledo [tel/fax 925-22 00 90; campingelgreco@telefonica.net; www.campingelgreco.ya.st]** Site on CM4000 fr Toledo dir La Puebla de Montalbán & Talavera. When app, avoid town cent, keep to N outside of old town & watch for camping sp. Or use outer ring rd. Med, hdg/mkd pitch, hdstg, pt sl, pt shd; htd wc; chem disp; mv service pnt; shwrs inc; el pnts (6A) €4.24 (poss rev pol); gas; Indtte; shop; tradsmn; bar; BBQ; playgrnd; pool; paddling pool; games area; dogs; bus to town; train to Madrid fr town; phone; Eng spkn; ccard acc; CCI. "Clean & tidy; all pitches on gravel; easy parking on o'skts - adj Puerta de San Martín rec - or bus; some pitches poss tight; excel san facs but could be cleaner - stretched if site full; lovely, scenic situation; friendly, helpful owners." € 25.00 2008*

TORDESILLAS *1C3* (1km SW Urban) *41.49653, -5.00614* **Camping El Astral, Camino de Pollos 8, 47100 Tordesillas (Valladolid) [tel/fax 983-77 09 53; info@campingelastral.com; www.campingelastral.com]** Fr NE on A62/E80 thro town turn L at rndabt over rv & immed after bdge turn R dir Salamanca & in 500m R again into narr gravel track (bef Parador) & foll rd to site; foll camping sp & Parador. Poorly sp. Fr A6 exit sp Tordesillas & take A62. Cross bdge out of town & foll site sp. Med, hdg/mkd pitch, hdstg, pt shd; wc; chem disp; mv service pnt; baby facs; shwrs inc; el pnts (5A) €3.60 (rev pol); gas; Indtte; shop; supmkt in town; rest; snacks; bar; playgrnd; pool in ssn; rv fishing; tennis; cycle hire; excursions; TV rm; 10% statics; dogs €2.35; phone; site open w/end Mar & Oct; Eng spkn; quiet, but some traff noise; ccard acc; CCI. "Helpful owners; easy walk to interesting town; v nice site by rv; popular NH; gd, modern san facs." ♦ 1 Apr-30 Sep. € 25.30 (CChq acc) 2009*

TORLA see Broto *3B2*

⊞ **TORRE DEL MAR** *2H4* (1km SW Coastal) *36.7342, -4.1003* **Camping Torre del Mar, Paseo Maritimo s/n, 29740 Torre del Mar (Málaga) [952-54 02 24; fax 952-54 04 31]** Fr N340 coast rd, at rndabt at W end of town with 'correos' on corner turn twds sea sp Faro, Torre del Mar. At rndabt with lighthouse adj turn R, then 2nd R, site adj big hotel, ent bet lge stone pillars (no name sp). Lge, hdg/mkd pitch, hdstg, shd; wc; chem disp; mv service pnt; serviced pitches; shwrs inc; el pnts (10A) €4 (long lead req); gas; Indtte; shop & 500m; rest, snacks, bar nrby in ssn; playgrnd; pool & paddling pool; sandy/shgl beach 50m; tennis; sat TV; 39% statics; phone; poss cr all year; quiet but noise fr adj football pitch; red low ssn/long stay; CCI. "Tidy, clean, friendly, well-run site; some sm pitches; site rds tight; gd san facs; popular low ssn." ♦ € 21.20 2008*

⊞ **TORRE DEL MAR** *2H4* (1km W Coastal) *36.72976, -4.10285* **Camping Laguna Playa, Prolongación Paseo Maritimo s/n, 29740 Torre del Mar (Málaga) [952-54 06 31; fax 952-54 04 84; info@lagunaplaya.com; www.lagunaplaya.com]** Fr N340 coast rd, at rndabt at W end of town with 'correos' on corner turn twds sea sp Faro, Torre del Mar. At rndabt with lighthouse adj turn R, then 2nd R, site sp in 400m. Med, pt shd; wc; chem disp; mv service pnt; shwrs inc; el pnts (5-10A) €3.70; gas; Indtte; shop; rest; snacks; bar; playgrnd; pool; sand beach 1km; 80% statics; dogs; poss cr; Eng spkn; adv bkg; quiet; red low ssn. "Popular low ssn; sm pitches; excel, clean san facs; gd location, easy walk to town; NH only." € 19.80 2008*

⊞ **TORRE DEL MAR** *2H4* (2km W Coastal) *36.72660, -4.11330* **Camping Naturista Almanat (Naturist), Ctra de la Torre Alta, Km 269, 29749 Almayate (Málaga) [952-55 64 62; fax 952-55 62 71; info@almanat.de; www.almanat.de]** Exit E15/N340 junc 274 sp Vélez Málaga for Torre del Mar. Exit Torre del Mar on coast rd sp Málaga. In 2km bef lge black bull on R on hill & bef water tower turn L at sp. If rd not clear cont to next turning point & return in dir Torre del Mar & turn R to site at km 269. Site well sp. Lge, hdg/mkd pitch, hdstg (gravel), pt shd; htd wc; chem disp; mv service pnt (on request); sauna; shwrs inc; el pnts (10-16A) €3.90; gas; Indtte; shop; rest; bar; BBQ; playgrnd; pool; jacuzzi; sand/shgl beach adj; tennis; wifi; entmnt; cinema; games area; gym; golf 10km; some statics; dogs €2.70; phone; bus 500m; poss cr; Eng spkn; adv bkg; quiet but poss noise fr birdscarer; ccard acc; red long stay/low ssn/snr citizens up to 50%; INF card. "Superb facs; popular & highly rec; reasonable dist Seville, Granada, Córdoba; easy walk/cycle to town; emergency exit poss kept locked; sm pitches & narr site rds diff for lge o'fits." ♦ € 21.00 2009*

TORRE DEL MAR *2H4* (3km W Coastal) *36.72526, -4.13532* **Camping Almayate Costa, Ctra N340, Km 267, 29749 Almayate Bajo (Málaga) [952-55 62 89; fax 952-55 63 10; almayatecosta@campings.net; www.campings.net/almayatecosta]** E fr Málaga on N340/E15 coast rd. Exit junc 258 dir Almería, site on R 3km bef Torre del Mar. Easy access. Lge, mkd pitch, hdstg, shd; wc; chem disp; mv service pnt; shwrs inc; el pnts (10A) inc; gas; Indtte; supmkt; bar; BBQ; playgrnd; pool & paddling pool; sand beach adj; games rm; golf 7km; no dogs; car wash; phone; Eng spkn; adv bkg; quiet but some rd noise; ccard acc; red long stay/low ssn; CCI. "Helpful manager; pitches nr beach tight for lge o'fits & access rds poss diff; vg resort." ♦ 12 Mar-28 Sep. € 45.00 (4 persons) 2007*

⊞ **TORREMOLINOS** *2H4* (3km NE Coastal) *36.64666, -4.48888* **Camping Torremolinos, Loma del Paraíso 2, 29620 Torremolinos (Málaga) [952-38 26 02; campingtorrole@telefonica.net]** Fr Málaga by-pass heading W take exit sp 'aeropuerto' & foll sp Torremolinos & site. Med, hdstg; terr, pt sl, pt shd; wc (some cont); shwrs; el pnts (5A) €3.90; gas; Indtte; shop; rest 200m; snacks; bar; sand beach 700m; golf 500m; no dogs; buses & trains nrby; no adv bkg; noise fr rd, rlwy & aircraft; red CCI. "V helpful staff; v clean site; gd san facs." € 44.00 2008*

TORREVIEJA *4F2* (4.5km S Urban) *37.94762, -0.71500* **Camping La Campana, Ctra Torrevieja-Cartagena, Km 4.5, 03180 Torrevieja (Alicante) [965-71 21 52]** Take N332 S fr Torrevieja. Site ent dir off rndabt for Rocío del Mar at S end of Torrevieja by-pass. Med, mkd pitch, hdstg, pt shd; wc; chem disp; shwrs; el pnts (6A) €3.20; gas; 500m; lndtte; shop; rest; snacks; bar; playgrnd; pool; shgle beach 1km; 80% statics; dogs €2.15; phone adj; bus 50m; poss cr; Eng spkn; noisy; red low ssn/CCI. "OK NH." ♦
1 Apr-30 Sep. € 24.60 2008*

I'm going to fill in some site report forms and post them off to the Club; we could win a ferry crossing – it's here on page 12.

TORROELLA DE MONTGRI *3B3* (6km SE Coastal) *42.01111, 3.18833* **Camping El Delfin Verde, Ctra Torroella de Montgrí-Palafrugell, Km 4, 17257 Torroella de Montgrí (Gerona) [972-75 84 54; fax 972-76 00 70; info@eldelfinverde.com; www.eldelfinverde.com]** Fr N leave A7 at junc 5 dir L'Escala. At Viladamat turn R onto C31 sp La Bisbal. After a few km turn L twd Torroella de Montgrí. At rndabt foll sp for Pals (also sp El Delfin Verde). At the flags turn L sp Els Mas Pinell. Foll site sp for 5km. Lge, mkd pitch, pt sl, pt shd; wc; chem disp; mv service pnt; baby facs; shwrs inc; el pnts (6A) inc; gas; lndtte; supmkt; rests; snacks; 3 bars; BBQ; playgrnd; pool; sand beach adj; fishing; tennis; horseriding 4km; cycle hire; windsurfing; sportsgrnd; hairdresser; money exchange; games rm; entmnt; disco; wifi; TV; 40% statics (sep area); winter storage; no dogs 11/7-14/8, at low ssn €4; poss cr; quiet; ccard acc; red low ssn; CCI. "Superb, gd value site; excel pool; all water de-salinated fr fresh water production plant; bottled water rec for drinking & cooking; mkt Mon."
♦ 24 Apr-26 Sep. € 54.00 ABS - E01 2009*

See advertisement on next page

⊞ **TORREVIEJA** *4F2* (7km SW Rural) *37.97500, -0.75111* **Camping Florantilles, Ctra San Miguel de Salinas-Torrevieja, 03193 San Miguel de Salinas (Alicante) [965-72 04 56; fax 966-72 32 50; florantilles@terra.es]** Exit AP7 junc 758 onto CV95, sp Orihuela, Torrevieja Sud. Turn R at rndabt & after 300m turn R again, site immed on L. Or if travelling on N332 S past Alicante airport twd Torrevieja. Leave Torrevieja by-pass sp Torrevieja, San Miguel. Turn R onto CV95 & foll for 3km thro urbanisation 'Los Balcones', then cont for 500m, under by-pass, round rndabt & up hill, site sp on R. Lge, hdg/mkd, hdstg, terr, pt shd; wc; chem disp; mv service pnt; shwrs inc; el pnts (10A) inc; gas; lndtte; supmkt; snacks; bar; BBQ; pool & paddling pool (high ssn); sand beach 5km; horseriding 10km; fitness studio; 80% statics; no dogs; recep clsd 1330-1630; poss cr in winter; adv bkg; rd noise; ccard acc; red low ssn; CCI. NB: Sm number of touring pitches ONLY avail if booked through The Caravan Club, rest avail for 12-month rental only. "Popular, British owned site; friendly staff; many long-stay visitors & all year c'vans; own transport ess." ♦
€ 29.74 ABS - E11 2009*

⊞ **TORROX COSTA** *2H4* (N Urban) *36.73944, -3.94972* **Camping El Pino, Urbanización Torrox Park s/n, 29793 Torrox Costa (Málaga) [952-53 00 06; fax 952-53 25 78; info@campingelpino.com; www.campingelpino.com]** Exit A7 at km 285, turn S at 1st rndabt, turn L at 2nd rndabt & foll sp Torrox Costa N340; in 1.5km at rndabt turn R to Torrox Costa, then L onto rndabt sp Nerja, site well sp in 4km. App rd steep with S bends. Fr N340 fr Torrox Costa foll sp Torrox Park, site sp. V lge, mkd pitch, hdstg, terr, shd; wc; chem disp; shwrs inc; el pnts €3.80 (long lead req); gas; lndtte; shop; rest, snacks adj; bar; BBQ; playgrnd; 2 pools; sand beach 800m; games area; golf 8km; wifi; 35% statics; dogs €2.50; phone; car wash; Eng spkn; red low ssn/long stay; CCI. "Gd size pitches but high kerbs; gd hill walks; conv Malaga; Nerja caves, Ronda; gd touring base." ♦
€ 18.50 2009*

See advertisement below

TOSSA DE MAR *3B3* (500m N Coastal) *41.72885, 2.92584* **Camping Can Martí, Avda Pau Casals s/n, 17320 Tossa de Mar (Gerona) [972-34 08 51; fax 972-34 24 61; camping canmarti@terra.es; www.campingcanmarti.net]** Exit AP7 junc 9 dir Vidreras & take C35 dir Llagostera. Turn R at rndabt onto GI681 to coast, then GI682 to site. Mountain rd fr Sant Feliu not rec. V lge, mkd pitch, pt shd; wc; chem disp; baby facs; shwrs inc; el pnts (10A) €3; gas; Indtte; shop; rest; snacks; bar; playgrnd; pool & paddling pool; shgl beach 500m; fishing; tennis; horseriding; 10% statics; dogs free; phone; car wash; sep car park; Eng spkn; no adv bkg; quiet; red long stay/low ssn/CCI. "Helpful, friendly staff; facs clean." ♦ 15 May-15 Sep. € 32.00 2009*

TOSSA DE MAR *3B3* (4km NE Coastal) *41.73627, 2.94683* **Camping Pola, Ctra Tossa-Sant Feliu, Km 4, 17320 Tossa de Mar (Gerona) [972-34 10 50; campingpola@giverola.es; www.camping-pola.es]** Exit AP7 junc 9 onto C35 dir Sant Feliu de Guíxols. In approx 9km turn R onto GI681 dir Tossa de Mar. In Tossa take GI GE682 dir Sant Feliu. Narr, winding rd but gd. Site sp. Lge, pt sl, pt shd; wc; shwrs inc; el pnts (15A) inc; gas; Indtte (inc dryer); shop; rest; bar; playgrnd; pool; paddling pool; sand beach adj; tennis; games area; entmnt; some statics; dogs €3.50; bus 500m; sep car park high ssn; adv bkg; ccard acc. "Site deep in narr coastal inlet with excel beach; few British visitors; san facs old but clean; gd." 1 Jun-30 Sep. € 44.80 2009*

⊞ **TOTANA** *4G1* (2km SW Rural) *37.74645, -1.51933* **Camping Totana, Ctra N340, Km 614, 30850 Totana (Murcia) [tel/fax 968-42 48 64; info@campingtotana.es; www.campingtotana.es]** Fr N340/E15 exit at km 612 fr N. Fr S exit km 609. Foll Totana rd, site 2km on R. Sl ent. Sm, hdg/mkd pitch, hdstg, terr, pt shd; wc; chem disp; shwrs inc; el pnts (6A) €3; shop & 4km; rest, bar high ssn; BBQ; playgrnd; pool high ssn; games rm; entmnt; 80% statics; dogs; Eng spkn; red long stay; CCI. "Access to sm pitches tight due trees; helpful owners; tidy site; ltd privacy in shwrs; vg NH." € 16.00 2009*

TREMP *3B2* (4km N Rural) *42.18872, 0.92152* **Camping Gaset, Ctra C13, Km 91, 25630 Talarn (Lleida) [973-65 07 37; fax 973-65 01 02; campingaset@pallarsjussa.net; www.pallarsjussa.net/gaset/]** Fr Tremp, take C13/N260 N sp Talarn. Site clearly visible on R by lake. Lge, pt sl, terr, pt shd; wc; shwrs; el pnts (4A) €3.90; Indtte; shop; rest 4km; snacks; bar; playgrnd; pool; paddling pool; sand beach & lake sw; fishing; tennis; 15% statics; dogs; phone; poss cr; quiet; ccard acc. "Picturesque setting; some sm pitches." 1 Apr-15 Oct. € 19.20 2006*

⊞ **TREVELEZ** *2G4* (1km E Rural) *36.99195, -3.27026* **Camping Trevélez, Ctra Órgiva-Trevélez, Km 1, 18417 Trevélez (Granada) [tel/fax 958-85 87 35 or 625-50-27-69 (mob); info@campingtrevelez.net; www.campingtrevelez.net]** Fr Granada on A44/E902 exit junc 164 onto A348 dir Lanjarón, Pampaneira. Cont for approx 50km to on A4132 to Trevélez, site sp. Med, mkd pitch, terr, pt shd; htd wc; chem disp; mv service pnt; shwrs inc; el pnts (9A) €3.50; gas; Indtte; shop; tradsmn; rest; snacks; bar; playgrnd; pool; rv 1km; entmnt; few statics; dogs; phone; bus adj; poss cr; Eng spkn; adv bkg; quiet; red long stay. "Excel site; helpful, welcoming owners; access to Mulhacén (highest mountain mainland Spain); lots of hiking." ♦ € 17.80 2008*

TURIENO see Potes *1A4*

UBRIQUE *2H3* (15km N Rural) *36.76898, -5.46043* **Camping Los Linares, Calle Nacimiento s/n, 11679 Benamahoma (Cádiz) [956-71 62 75; fax 956-71 64 73; parque@camping loslinares.com; www.campingloslinares.com]** N fr Ubrique to El Bosque, turn E dir Benamahoma & Grazalema. Site well sp in vill. To avoid narr streets ent fr El Bosque end of vill. Med, mkd pitch, unshd; wc; chem disp; shwrs inc; el pnts inc; shop 500m; rest; snacks; bar; playgrnd; pool; some statics; no dogs; bus 300m; poss cr; CCI. "Gd walking/ birdwatching area in National Park; narr vill streets poss diff lge o'fits; open w/end & public hols all year." ♦ 1 Mar-31 Oct. € 28.00 2008*

UCERO see Burgo de Osma, El *1C4*

UNQUERA *1A4* (3km N Coastal) *43.39127, -4.50986* **Camping Las Arenas, Ctra Unquera-Pechón, Km. 2, 39594 Pechón (Cantabria) [tel/fax 942-71 71 88; info@ campinglasarenas.com; www.campinglasarenas.com]** Exit A8/E70 at km 272 sp Unquera. At rndabt foll CA380 sp Pechón, climb narr winding rd to site ent at top on L. Lge, mkd pitch, pt sl, terr, pt shd; wc; chem disp; shwrs inc; el pnts (8A) €3.60; gas; Indtte; rest; shop & 3km; bar; playgrnd; pool; shgl beach adj; fishing; cycle hire; internet; no statics; dogs; poss cr; Eng spkn; quiet; ccard acc; CCI. "Magnificent position on terr cliffs; peaceful, well-kept & clean; immac, modern san facs." 1 Jun-30 Sep. € 27.55 2009*

UNQUERA *1A4* (3km S Rural) *43.3750, -4.56416* **Camping El Mirador de Llavandes, Vegas Grandes, 33590 Colombres (Asturias) [tel/fax 985-41 22 44; info@ campingelmiradordellavandes.com; www.camping elmiradordellavandes.com]** Fr N634 12km W of San Vicente de la Barquera turn at km 283/284 dir Noriega, site in 1.3km. Med, mkd pitch, terr, unshd; wc; chem disp; shwrs inc; el pnts (3A) €3.20; Indtte; shop & 2km; playgrnd; sand beach 1km; TV; some statics; dogs €2.15; phone; no adv bkg; quiet; red CCI. "Peaceful setting; excel for touring Picos." ♦ Holy Week & 15 Jun-15 Sep. € 20.00 2008*

⊞ **VALDEAVELLANO DE TERA** *3B1* (1km NW Rural) *41.94523, -2.58837* **Camping Entrerrobles, 42165 Valdeavellano de Tera (Soria) [975-18 08 00; fax 975-18 08 76; entrerobbles@hotmail.com; www. entrerrobles.freeservers.com]** S fr Logroño on N111, after Almarza turn R onto SO-820 to Valdeavellano. In 10km turn R at site sp, site on R in 1km. Med, mkd pitch, pt sl, pt shd; htd wc; chem disp; baby facs; shwrs inc; el pnts (6A) €5; Indtte (inc dryer); tradsmn; rest; snacks; bar; playgrnd; pool; games area; cycle hire; TV rm; 8% statics; dogs; phone; Eng spkn; adv bkg; quiet; ccard acc; red CCI. "Excel touring base; attractive area but isolated (come prepared); friendly staff; new san facs (2008)." ♦ € 19.00 2009*

VALDOVINO *1A2* (700m W Coastal) *43.61222, -8.14916* **Camping Valdoviño, Ctra Ferrol-Cedeira, Km 13, 15552 Valdoviño (La Coruña) [981-48 70 76; fax 981-48 61 31]** Fr Ortigueira on C642; turn W onto C646 sp Cadeira then Ferrol; turn R at camping sp, down hill R again, site on R almost on beach. Med, terr, pt shd; wc; chem disp; baby facs; shwrs inc; el pnts (15A) inc; gas; Indtte; shop; rest; bar; snacks; playgrnd; sand beach adj; playgrnd; wifi; TV; some statics; no dogs; bus adj; poss cr; quiet; Eng spkn; CCI. "Pleasant, busy site nr lge beach with lagoon & cliffs but poss windy; locality run down; vg rest." ♦ 10 Apr-30 Sep. € 28.50 2009*

VALENCIA *4E2* (9km S Coastal) *39.39638, -0.33250* **Camping Coll Vert, Ctra Nazaret-Oliva, Km 7.5, 46012 Playa de Pinedo (València) [961-83 00 36; fax 961-83 00 40; info@collvertcamping.com; www.collvertcamping.com]** Fr S on V31 turn R onto V30 sp Pinedo. After approx 1km turn R onto V15/CV500 sp El Salar to exit El Salar Platjes. Turn L at rndabt, site on L in 1km. Fr N bypass València on A7/E15 & after junc 524 turn N twd València onto V31, then as above. Turn L at rndabt, site in 1km on L. Med, hdg/ mkd pitch, shd; wc; shwrs inc; el pnts €4.81; gas; Indtte; shop; bar; BBQ; playgrnd; pool; paddling pool; sand beach 500m; games area; entmnt; 5% statics; dogs €4.28; phone; bus to city & marine park; car wash; poss cr; Eng spkn; adv bkg; quiet; some rd noise; ccard acc; red long stay. "Hourly bus service fr outside site to cent of València & marine park; helpful, friendly staff. ♦ 16 Feb-14 Dec. € 31.32 2009*

⊞ **VALENCIA** *4E2* (9.5km S Urban/Coastal) **Camping Park, Ctra del Riu 548, 46012 El Saler (València) [961-83 02 44]** Fr València foll coast rd or V15 to El Saler. Site adj rndabt just N of El Saler. Med, hdg/mkd pitch, hdstg, pt shd; wc; chem disp; shwrs inc; el pnts (6A) inc; Indtte; shop; rest; bar; pool; sand beach 300m; 50% statics; dogs; phone; bus at gate; poss cr; rd noise; CCI. "V conv València - hourly bus." € 25.00 2007*

⊞ **VALENCIA** *4E2* (16km S Rural) *39.32302, -0.30940* **Camping Devesa Gardens, Ctra El Saler, Km 13, 46012 València [961-61 11 36; fax 961-61 11 05; alojamiento@devesagardens.com; www.devesagardens.com]** S fr València on CV500, site well sp on R 4km S of El Saler. Med, mkd pitch, hdstg, pt shd; htd wc; chem disp; mv service pnt; baby facs; el pnts (7-15A) €5.35; gas; lndtte; supmkt (high ssn) & 4km; rest; bar; BBQ; playgrnd; pool; beach 700m; tennis; lake canoeing; horseriding; 70% statics; no dogs; phone; bus to València; quiet; adv bkg; ccard acc. "Friendly staff; warden needed to connect to el pt; site has own zoo; excel." ♦ € 23.53 2008*

VALENCIA DE DON JUAN see Villamañán *1B3*

VALL LLOBREGA see Palamós *3B3*

⊞ **VALLE DE CABUERNIGA** *1A4* (1km NE Rural) *43.22800, 4.28900* **Camping El Molino de Cabuérniga, Sopeña, 39510 Cabuérniga (Cantabria) [942-70 62 59; fax 942-70 62 78; cmcabuerniga@campingcabuerniga.com; www.campingcabuerniga.com]** Fr A8/E70 take exit 249 onto N634 Cabezón de la Sal. Turn R onto CA180 sp Valle de Cabuérniga & Rionansa. After 11km turn L into vill of Sopeña. Foll sm green or blue sp to apartments & site - v narr rds. Med, shd; wc; shwrs inc; el pnts (3A) €2.67 (check earth); gas; lndtte; sm shop; snacks; bar; playgrnd; rv 200m; fishing; tennis; dogs €1.50; phone; bus 500m; adv bkg; quiet; ccard acc; CCI. "Excel site & facs on edge of vill; no shops in vicinity, but gd location." ♦ € 20.00 2008*

VECILLA, LA *1B3* (1km N Rural) *42.85806, -5.41155* **Camping La Cota, Ctra Valdelugueros, LE321, Km 19, 24840 La Vecilla (León) [987-74 10 91; lacota@campinglacota.com; www.campinglacota.com]** Fr N630 turn E onto CL626 at La Robla, 17km to La Vecilla. Site sp in vill. Med, mkd pitch, shd; wc; chem disp; baby facs; shwrs inc; el pnts €3; lndry rm; snacks; bar; games area; wifi; 50% statics; open w/ends out of ssn; train nr; quiet. "Pleasant site under poplar trees; gd walking, climbing nr." 1 Apr-30 Sep. € 15.50 2009*

VEJER DE LA FRONTERA *2H3* (4km SE) *36.25456, -5.93518* **Camping Vejer, 11150 Vejer de la Frontera (Cádiz) [tel/fax 956-45 00 98; campingvejer@terra.es; www.campingvejer.com]** App fr Málaga dir on N340, at km stone 39.5, exit to L, bet 2 rests, site in 100m. Do not take o'fit into Vejer. Sm, pt sl, terr, pt shd; wc; chem disp; shwrs; el pnts (10A) €3; lndtte; shop; snacks; bar; playgrnd; pool; sand beach 9km; golf 2km; cycle hire; internet; 10% statics; dogs €1; phone; adv bkg; quiet; ccard acc; red low ssn; CCI. "In wooded area away fr main rd; v ltd, neglected facs low ssn." 13 Apr-30 Sep. € 27.00 2008*

⊞ **VEJER DE LA FRONTERA** *2H3* (10km SE Coastal) *36.12320, -5.83555* **Camping Bahía de la Plata, Ctra de Atlanterra s/n, 11393 Zahara de los Atunes (Cádiz) [956-43 90 40; fax 956-43 90 87; info@campingbahiadelaplata.com; www.campingbahiadelaplata.com]** Fr Vejer de la Frontera, take A314 twds Barbate; thro town & onto A2231 coastal rd twds Zahara de los Atunes; go thro Zahara, foll lorry rte to avoid narr streets & sharp corners of cent twds Atlanterra; site sp. Lge, mkd pitch, shd; wc; chem disp; shwrs inc; el pnts (16A) inc; lndtte; shop; rest; snacks; bar; playgrnd; beach adj; cycle hire; entmnt; TV; some statics; no dogs; phone; ccard acc. "Site opens onto beach; well-equipped & managed." ♦ € 21.10 2006*

VEJER DE LA FRONTERA *2H3* (10km S Coastal) *36.20141, -6.03549* **Camping Caños de Meca, Ctra de Vejer-Los Caños de Meca, Km 10, 11160 Barbate (Cádiz) [956-43 71 20; fax 956-43 71 37; info@camping-canos-de-meca.com; www.camping-canos-de-meca.com]** Fr A48/N340 exit junc 36 onto A314 to Barbate, then foll dir Los Caños de Meca. Turn R at seashore rd dir Zahora. Site on L 2km beyond town. Med, mkd pitch, shd; wc; chem disp; shwrs inc; el pnts (5A) inc; gas; lndtte; shop; rest; snacks; bar; playgrnd; pool; sand beach 600m; watersports; cycle hire; 20% statics; no dogs Jul/Aug; phone; poss cr; adv bkg; ccard acc; red low ssn; CCI. "Vg." ♦ 26 Mar-12 Oct. € 39.60 (3 persons) 2008*

⊞ **VEJER DE LA FRONTERA** *2H3* (10km S Coastal) *36.20084, -6.03506* **Camping Pinar San José, Ctra de Vejer-Caños de Meca, Km 10.2, Zahora 17, 11159 Barbate (Cadiz) [956-43 70 30; fax 956-43 71 74; info@campingpinarsanjose.com; www.campingpinarsanjose.com]** Fr A48/N340 exit junc 36 onto A314 to Barbate, then foll dir Los Caños de Meca. Turn R at seashore rd dir Zahora. Site on L 2km beyond town. Med, mkd pitch, shd; wc; chem disp; mv service pnt; fam bthrm; shwrs; el pnts; lndtte; shop; rest; playgrnd; pool; paddling pool; sand beach 700m; tennis; games area; wifi; sat TV; some statics; dogs €2.50 (low ssn only); adv bkg; quiet. "New site 2008; excel, modern facs." ♦ € 28.40 2008*

⊞ **VELEZ BLANCO** *4G1* (1km S Rural) *37.65394, -2.07845* **Camping El Pinar del Rey, Paseo de los Sauces 5, 04830 Vélez Blanco (Almería) [950-41 55 00 or 649-90 16 80 (mob); camping@pinardelrey.es; www.pinardelrey.es]** Fr A92N turn off at Vélez Rubio & foll sp Vélez Blanco on A317. Site on R bef vill. Sm, hdstg, pt shd; htd wc; chem disp (wc); mv service pnt; shwrs inc; el pnts (10A) inc; rest; snacks; bar; playgrnd; pool; TV rm; no statics; site open w/end only low ssn; poss cr; adv bkg; CCI. "Beautiful area; clean mountain air; friendly staff; site poss untidy; gd, clean facs." ♦ € 20.00 2008*

VENDRELL, EL *3C3* (2km S Coastal) *41.18312, 1.53593* **Camping Sant Salvador, Avda Palfuriana 68, 43880 Sant Salvador (Tarragona) [tel/fax 977-68 08 04; campingsantsalvador@troc.es; www.campingsantsalvador.com]** Exit A7 junc 31 onto N340, after 1km turn L. Site bet Calafell & Coma-Ruga. Lge, pt shd; wc; chem disp; baby facs; shwrs inc; el pnts (4A) €4; gas; Indtte; shop; rest; bar; playgrnd; beach; 75% statics; dogs €1.50; bus adj; poss cr; ccard acc; red long stay/low ssn; CCI. "Secure site; not suitable lge o'fits; conv Safari Park & Port Aventura." ♦ 30 Mar-30 Sep. € 24.80 2007*

VENDRELL, EL *3C3* (7km SW Coastal) *41.17752, 1.50132* **Camping Francàs, Ctra N340, Km 1185.5, 43880 Coma-Ruga, (Tarragona) [977-68 07 25; fax 977-68 47 73; info@campingfrancas.net; www.campingfrancas.net]** Exit N340 at km stone 303 to Comarruga. Lge, mkd pitch, shd; wc; chem disp; baby facs; shwrs; el pnts €3.30; Indtte; shop; rest; snacks; bar; BBQ; playgrnd; sand beach adj; watersports; fishing; games area; entmnt; dogs; bus 100m; car wash; adv bkg; quiet. "Pleasant site." ♦ Easter-30 Sep. € 21.20 2007*

VERA see Garrucha *4G1*

VIELHA *3B2* (6km N Rural) *42.73638, 0.76083* **Camping Artiganè, Ctra N230, Km 171, Val d'Arán, 25537 Pont d'Arròs (Lleida) [tel/fax 973-64 03 38; info@campingartigane.com; www.campingartigane.com]** Fr French border head S on N230 for 15km. Fr Vielha head N to France & turn L at Pont d'Arròs. Site on main rd by rv. Lge, pt sl, pt shd; wc; chem disp; baby facs; shwrs inc; el pnts (10A) €4.50; gas; Indry rm; shop; rest, snacks, bar in high ssn; BBQ; playgrnd; htd pool; games area; golf; 5% statics; dogs €3.25; bus adj; phone; poss cr; quiet; CCI. "Scenic area - wild flowers, butterflies; friendly warden; low ssn site yourself - warden calls; simple/v basic facs, poss stretched when site full." ♦ Holy Week-15 Oct. € 24.10 2009*

VIELHA *3B2* (7km N Rural) *42.73649, 0.74640* **Camping Verneda, Ctra Francia N230, Km 171, 25537 Pont d'Arròs (Lleida) [973-64 10 24; fax 973-64 32 18; info@campingverneda.com; www.campingverneda.com]** Fr Lerida N on N230 twd Spain/France border, site on R adj N230, 2km W of Pont d'Arròs on rvside, 1km after Camping Artigane. Med, pt shd; wc; chem disp; baby facs; shwrs inc; el pnts (4A) €3.90; gas; Indtte; rest; snacks; bar; playgrnd; pool; horseriding; games rm; cycle hire; entmnt; TV; 10% statics; dogs €2.50; adv bkg; Eng spkn; ccard acc; CCI. "Gd area for walking; site open w/end rest of year; well-run site; gd facs." 1 May-15 Oct. € 21.80 2007*

VIELHA *3B2* (6km SE Rural) *42.70005, 0.87060* **Camping Era Yerla D'Arties, Ctra C142, Vielha-Baquiera s/n, 25599 Arties (Lleida) [973-64 16 02; fax 973-64 30 53; yerla@coac.net; www.aranweb.com/yerla]** Fr Vielha take C28 dir Baquiera, site sp. Turn R at rndabt into Arties, site in 30m on R. Med, shd; htd wc; chem disp; baby facs; shwrs inc; el pnts (4-10A) €4.25-5.15; gas; Indtte; shop & rest nrby; snacks; bar; pool; skiing nr; some statics; bus 200m; phone; quiet; ccard acc; CCI. "Pleasant site; ideal for ski resort; clean facs; gd walking." 1 Dec-14 Sep. € 23.65 2008*

VILAGARCIA DE AROUSA *1B2* (4km NE Coastal) *42.63527, -8.75555* **Camping Río Ulla, Bamio, 36612 Vilagarcía de Arousa (Pontevedra) [tel/fax 986-50 54 30; 986505430@telefonica.net; www.campingrioulla.com]** Fr N exit A9 at km 93 dir Pontecesures & take PO548 twd Vilagarcía de Arousa. Thro Catoira & in 5km turn R at traff lts at top of hill, site in 500m. Med, hdg/mkd pitch, pt shd; wc; chem disp; mv service pnt; baby facs; shwrs inc; el pnts (10A) €4; Indtte; shop; rest; snacks; bar; BBQ; playgrnd; pool; paddling pool; sand beach adj; games area; TV; 10% statics; bus 200m; Eng spkn; adv bkg; rd & rlwy noise; ccard acc; CCI. "Helpful owners; excel, clean facs." ♦ Holy Week & 1 Jun-15 Sep. € 20.00 2009*

⊞ **VILALLONGA DE TER** *3B3* (500m NW Rural) *42.33406, 2.30705* **Camping Conca de Ter, Ctra Setcases s/n, Km 5.4, 17869 Vilallonga de Ter (Gerona) [972-74 06 29; fax 972-13 01 71; concater@concater.com; www.concater.com]** Exit C38 at Camprodón; at Vilallonga de Ter do NOT turn off into vill but stay on main rd; site on L. Lge, mkd pitch, hdstg, pt shd; wc; chem disp; shwrs inc; el pnts (5-15A) €3.50-6.54; Indtte; rest; bar; pool; skilift 15km; 95% statics; dogs €2; poss cr; Eng spkn; ccard acc; CCI. "Pitches sm & cr together; rest w/end only low ssn & then only after 2100; gd." ♦ € 24.00 2006*

⊞ **VILANOVA DE PRADES** *3C2* (500m NE Rural) *41.34890, 0.95860* **Camping Parc de Vacances Serra de Prades, Calle Sant Antoni s/n, 43439 Vilanova de Prades (Tarragona) [tel/fax 977-86 90 50; info@serradeprades.com; www.serradeprades.com]** Fr AP2 take exit 8 (L'Albi) or 9 (Montblanc), foll C240 to Vimbodi. At km 47.5 take TV7004 for 10km to Vilanova de Prades. Site ent on R immed after rndabt at ent to vill. Lge, some hdg/mkd pitch, terr, pt shd; wc; chem disp; mv service pnt; baby facs; shwrs inc; el pnts (6A) €5.80 (poss long lead req) gas; Indtte; basic shop & 8km; tradsmn; rest; snacks; bar; playgrnd; htd pool; lake sw 20km; tennis; games area; games rm; TV rm; many statics; dogs; phone; Eng spkn; adv bkg high ssn; quiet; red long stay/CCI. "Well-maintained, well-run, scenic, friendly site; clean facs; sm pitches; access some pitches diff due steep, gravel site rds & storm gullies; conv Barcelona; vg touring base/NH." ♦ € 27.20 (CChq acc) 2009*

Spain

⊞ **VILANOVA DE PRADES** *3C2* (4km S Rural) *41.31129, 0.98020* **Camping Prades, Ctra T701, Km 6.850, 43364 Prades (Tarragona) [977-86 82 70; fax 977-86 82 79; camping@campingprades.com; www.campingprades.com]** Fr S take N420 W fr Reus, C242 N to Albarca, T701 E to Prades. Fr N exit AP2/E90 junc 9 Montblanc; N240 to Vimbodi; TV7004 to Vilanova de Prades; L at rndabt to Prades; go thro town, site on R in 500m. Narr rds & hairpins fr both dirs. Lge, mkd pitch, pt shd; wc; chem disp; mv service pnt; baby facs; shwrs; el pnts (3A) €4.40; gas; Indtte; shop; tradsmn; rest; snacks; bar; playgrnd; pool; cycle hire; wifi; 60% statics; phone; bus 200m; poss cr; adv bkg; ccard acc; CCI. "Beautiful area; in walking dist of lovely, tranquil old town; excel." ♦ € 21.80 2006*

VILANOVA I LA GELTRU *3C3* (5km SW Coastal) *41.19988, 1.64339* **Camping La Rueda, Ctra C31, Km 146.2, 08880 Cubelles (Barcelona) [938-95 02 07; fax 938-95 03 47; larueda@la-rueda.com; www.la-rueda.com]** Exit A7 junc 29 then take C15 dir Vilanova onto autopista C32 & take exit 13 dir Cunit. Site is 2.5km S of Cubelles on C31 at km stone 146.2. Lge, mkd pitch, shd; htd wc; chem disp; mv service pnt; shwrs inc; el pnts (4A) €6.85; gas; Indtte; shop; rest; snacks; bar; sand beach 100m; playgrnd; pool; tennis; horseriding; watersports; fishing; entmnt; car wash; 12% statics; dogs €3.65; phone; bus; train; Eng spkn; adv bkg; quiet; red long stay/low ssn; ccard acc; red CCI. "Conv Port Aventura & Barcelona; vg family site." 27 Mar-12 Sep. € 34.20 2009*

⊞ **VILANOVA I LA GELTRU** *3C3* (3km NW Urban) *41.23190, 1.69075* **Camping Vilanova Park, Ctra Arboç, Km 2.5, 08800 Vilanova i la Geltru (Barcelona) [938-93 34 02; fax 938-93 55 28; info@vilanovapark.com or reservas@vilanovapark.com; www.vilanovapark.com]** Fr N on AP7 exit junc 29 onto C15 dir Vilanova; then take C31 dir Cubelles. Leave at 153km exit dir Vilanova Oeste/L'Arboç to site. Fr W on C32/A16 take Vilanova-Sant Pere de Ribes exit. Take C31 & at 153km exit take BV2115 dir L'Arboc to site. Fr AP7 W leave at exit 31 onto the C32 (A16); take exit 16 (Vilanova-L'Arboc exit) onto BV2115 to site. Parked cars may block loop & obscure site sp. V lge, hdg/mkd pitch, hdstg, terr, pt shd; htd wc (some cont); chem disp; mv service pnt; some serviced pitches; baby facs; fam bthrm; sauna; shwrs inc; el pnts (10A) inc (poss rev pol); gas; Indtte; supmkt; tradsmn; rest; snacks; bar; BBQ (charcoal); playgrnd; 3 pools (1 htd covrd); jacuzzi; fitness cent; sand beach 3km; lake sw 2km; fishing; cycle hire; tennis; horseriding 500m; golf 1km; games rm; cash point; wifi; entmnt; TV; 40% statics; dogs €7; phone; bus/train; recep 0800-2300 high ssn; poss cr; Eng spkn; adv bkg ess high ssn; poss noisy nights & w/end high ssn; ccard acc; red snr citizens/low ssn/long stay; CCI. "Gd for children; excel san facs; gd winter facs; helpful staff; gd security; some sm pitches with diff access due trees; poss diff pitch access on terr due ramps; gd rest & bar; conv Barcelona, Tarragona & Port Aventura; gd bus (with guide) & train service; gd sat TV; mkt Sat; excel site." ♦ € 46.00 (CChq acc) ABS - E08 2009*

See advertisement

VILLADANGOS DEL PARAMO see León *1B3*

⊞ **VILLAFRANCA DE CORDOBA** *2F4* (1km W Rural) *37.95333, -4.54710* **Camping La Albolafia, Camino de la Vega s/n, 14420 Villafranca de Córdoba (Córdoba) [tel/fax 957-19 08 35; informacion@campingalbolafia.com; www.campingalbolafia.com]** Exit A4/E5 junc 377, cross rv & at rndabt turn L & foll sp to site in 2km. Med, hdg/mkd pitch, hdstg, pt shd; wc; chem disp; mv service pnt; shwrs inc; el pnts (10A) €4.20 (long lead poss req); Indtte (inc dryer); shop; rest; snacks; bar; BBQ; playgrnd; pool; wifi; TV; some statics; dogs €2.80; bus to Córdoba 500m; phone; Eng spkn; quiet; CCI. "V pleasant, well-run, clean site; watersports park nrby." ♦ € 20.00 2009*

⊞ **VILLAJOYOSA** *4F2* (1km SW Coastal) *38.50000, -0.24888* **Camping Playa Paraíso, Ctra Valencia-Alicante, Km 136, 03570 Villajoyosa (Alicante) [966-85 18 38; fax 966-85 07 98; info@campingplayaparaiso.com]** Exit AP7 junc 65A onto N332 & foll sp Villajoyosa Sud. Site on R in approx 1km, just past Campsa g'ge. Med, pt shd; htd wc; chem disp; baby facs; shwrs inc; el pnts (16A) €4.20; Indtte (inc dryer); shop; rest 500m; snacks; bar; BBQ; playgrnd; pool; beach adj; games area; games rm; wifi; 5% statics; dogs; phone; bus adj; Eng spkn; adv bkg; ccard acc; red long stay/low ssn; CCI. " Gd." € 29.50 2008*

⊞ **VILLAMANAN** *1B3* (1km SE Rural) *42.31403, -5.57290* **Camping Palazuelo, 24680 Villamañán (León) [tel/fax 987-76 82 10]** Fr N630 Salamanca-León turn SE at Villamañán onto C621 dir Valencia de Don Juan. Site on R in 1km behind hotel. Med, pt shd; wc; shwrs inc; el pnts (10A) €2.50; Indtte; shop 1km; rest; snacks; pool; quiet but some rd noise; ccard acc. "NH only; neglected & run down low ssn, poss unclean; ltd privacy in shwrs; Valencia de Don Juan worth visit." € 19.00 2009*

VILLAMANAN *1B3* (6km SE Rural) *42.29527, -5.53777* **Camping Pico Verde, Ctra Mayorga-Astorga, Km 27.6, 24200 Valencia de Don Juan (León) [tel/fax 987-75 05 25; campingpicoverd@terra.es]** Fr N630 S, turn E at km 32.2 onto C621 sp Valencia de Don Juan. Site in 4km on R. Med, mkd pitch, mkd pitch; wc; shwrs inc; el pnts (6A) inc; Indtte; shop & 1km; rest; snacks 1km; playgrnd; covrd pool; paddling pool; tennis; 25% statics; dogs free; quiet; red CCI. "Friendly, helpful staff; conv León; picturesque vill; phone ahead to check site open if travelling close to opening/closing dates." ♦ 15 Jun-8 Sep. € 17.60 2008*

VILLAMARTIN DE LA ABADIA see Ponferrada *1B3*

VILLANANE *1B4* (3km S Rural) *42.84221, -3.06867* **Camping Angosto, Ctra Villanañe-Angosto 2, 01425 Villanañe (Gipuzkoa) [945-35 32 71; fax 945-35 30 41; info@camping-angosto.com; www.camping-angosto.com]** S fr Bilbao on AP68 exit at vill of Pobes & take rd to W sp Espejo. Turn L 2.4km N of Espejo dir Villanañe, lane to site 400m on R. Med, some mkd pitch, pt shd; htd wc; chem disp; baby facs; shwrs inc; el pnts €4.15 (long cable poss req - supplied by site); lndtte; shop; rest; snacks; bar; BBQ; playgrnd; htd, covrd pool; entmnt; TV; 50% statics; dogs; phone; poss cr w/ends; Eng spkn; quiet. "Beautiful area; friendly staff; open site - mkd pitches rec if poss; gd rest; conv NH fr Bilbao; vultures!" ♦ 15 Feb-30 Nov. € 20.10 2009*

⊞ **VILLANUEVA DE TAPIA** *2G4* (2km S Rural) **Camping Cortijo La Alegria, Cortijo La Alegria 36, 29315 Villanueva de Tapia (Málaga) [952-75 04 19; cabinning@yahoo.co.uk]** Exit A92 junc 175 onto A333 to Villanueva de Tapia. Turn L into layby at 63km opp Hotel/Rest La Paloma. Sm, pt sl, unshd; fam bthrm; lndtte; tradsmn; lake sw & beach 11km; Eng spkn; quiet. "Vg CL-type site with superb mountain views; phone in advance; v steep ent suited m'vans & sm o'fits only." € 10.00 2008*

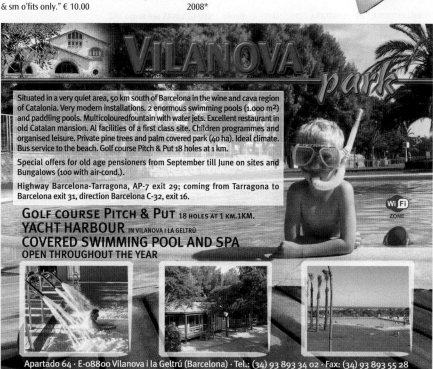

⊞ **VILLARGORDO DEL CABRIEL** *4E1* (3km NW Rural) *39.5525, -1.47444* **Kiko Park Rural, Ctra Embalse Contreras, Km 3, 46317 Villargordo del Cabriel (València) [962-13 90 82; fax 962-13 93 37; kikopark rural@kikopark.com; www.kikopark.com/rural]** A3/E901 València-Madrid, exit junc 255 to Villargordo del Cabriel, foll sp to site. Med, mkd pitch, hdstg, terr, pt shd; wc; chem disp; mv service pnt; some serviced pitches; shwrs inc; el pnts (6A) €3.35; gas; lndtte; shop; tradsmn; rest; snacks; bar; pool; lake sw 1km; canoeing; watersports; fishing; horseriding; white water rafting; cycle hire; TV; some statics; dogs €0.70; Eng spkn; adv bkg rec high ssn; some rlwy noise; ccard acc; red long stay/low ssn/snr citizens; red CCI. "Beautiful location; superb, well-run, peaceful site; lge pitches; gd walking; vg rest; many activities." ♦ € 26.60 2009*

See advertisement on page 763

VILLAVICIOSA *1A3* (8km NE Rural) *43.50900, -5.33600* **Camping La Rasa, Ctra La Busta-Selorio, 33316 Villaviciosa (Asturias) [985-89 15 29; info@campinglarase.com; www.campinglarasa.com]** Fr A8 exit km 353 sp Lastres/Venta del Pobre. In approx 500m foll site sp, cross bdge over m'way to site. Lge, hdg/mkd pitch, sl, unshd; wc; chem disp; mv service pnt; serviced pitches; shwrs inc; el pnts (6A) €3.10; Indtte; sm shop; snacks; bar; playgrnd; pool; sand beach 7km; 60% statics; dogs €2.80; phone; site open w/end low ssn/winter; Eng spkn; red low ssn; CCI. "Pleasant, friendly site; beautiful countryside; conv m'way & coast; tight access rds to sm pitches." ♦
15 Jun-15 Sep. € 22.80 2009*

VILLAVICIOSA *1A3* (15km NW Rural) *43.5400, -5.52638* **Camping Playa España, Playa de España, Quintes, 33300 Villaviciosa (Asturias) [tel/fax 985-89 42 73; camping@campingplayaespana.es; www.campingplayaespana.es]** Exit A8 onto N632/AS256 dir Quintes then Villaverde. Site approx 12km fr Villaviciosa & 10km fr Gijón. Last 3km of app rd narr & steep with sharp bends. Med, pt shd; wc; chem disp; shwrs; el pnts €4.25 (poss rev pol); gas; Indtte; shop; snacks; bar; beach 200m; phone; quiet; ccard acc. "Gd site; lovely coast & scenery with mountains behind; clean; vg san facs." Holy Week & 15 Jun-15 Sep. € 20.45 2008*

⊞ **VILLAVICIOSA DE CORDOBA** *2F3* (8km E Rural) *38.08127, -4.92761* **Camping Puente Nuevo, Ctra A3075, Km 8.5, 14300 Villaviciosa de Córdoba (Córdoba) [tel/fax 957-36 07 27; info@campingpuentenuevo.com; www.campingpuentenuevo.com]** Exit A4/E5 onto N432 dir Badajoz. In 32km turn L onto A3075, site in 8.5km. Med, hdg pitch, hdstg, sl, pt shd; wc; chem disp; shwrs inc; el pnts (16A) €4.28; Indtte; shop; tradsmn; rest; bar; BBQ; playgrnd; pool; lake sw 3km; games area; cycle hire; 40% statics; dogs €2; phone; bus 500m; poss cr; adv bkg; CCI. "Pitches poss tight lge o'fits; levellers needed all pitches; area well worth visit." ♦ € 19.92 2008*

⊞ **VINAROS** *3D2* (5km N Coastal) *40.49363, 0.48504* **Camping Vinarós, Ctra N340, Km 1054, 12500 Vinarós (Castellón) [tel/fax 964-40 24 24; info@campingvinaros.com; www.campingvinaros.com]** Fr N exit AP7 junc 42 onto N238 dir Vinarós. At junc with N340 turn L dir Tarragona, site on R at km 1054. Fr S exit AP7 junc 43. Lge, hdg/mkd pitch, hdstg, pt shd; htd wc; chem disp; mv service pnt; 85% serviced pitches; baby facs; shwrs inc; el pnts (6A) €6; gas; Indtte; shop 500m; tradsmn; rest adj; snacks; bar; playgrnd; pool; sand/shgl beach 1km; wifi; 15% statics; dogs €3; phone; bus adj; currency exchange; poss cr; Eng spkn; adv bkg - rec high ssn; quiet but some rd noise; ccard acc; red long stay/low ssn; CCI. "Excel gd value, busy, well-run site; many long-stay winter residents; spacious pitches; vg clean, modern san facs; el volts poss v low in evening; gd rest; friendly, helpful staff; rec use bottled water; Peñíscola Castle & Morello worth a visit; site set amongst orange groves; easy cycle to town." ♦ € 25.00 2009*

VINUESA *3B1* (2km N Rural) *41.9272, -2.7650* **Camping Cobijo, Ctra Laguna Negra, Km 2, 42150 Vinuesa (Soria) [tel/fax 975-37 83 31; recepcion@campingcobijo.com; www.campingcobijo.com]** Travelling W fr Soria to Burgos, at Abejar R on SO840. by-pass Abejar cont to Vinuesa. Well sp fr there. Lge, pt sl, pt shd; wc; chem disp; baby facs; shwrs inc; el pnts (3-6A) €4-5.70 (long lead poss req); gas; Indtte; shop; rest, snacks, bar high ssn; BBQ; playgrnd; pool; cycle hire; internet; 10% statics; dogs; phone; poss cr w/end; Eng spkn; phone; quiet; ccard acc; CCI. "Friendly staff; clean, attractive site; some pitches in wooded area poss diff lge o'fits; special elec connector supplied (deposit); ltd bar & rest low ssn, excel rests in town; gd walks." ♦
Holy Week-2 Nov. € 17.10 2009*

⊞ **VITORIA/GASTEIZ** *3B1* (3km W Rural) *42.8314, -2.7225* **Camping Ibaya, Arbolado de Acacias en la N102, Km 346.5, 01195 Zuazo de Vitoria/Gasteiz (Alava) [945-14 76 20]** Fr A1 take exit 343 sp A3302. At rndabt foll sp N102 Vitoria/Gasteiz. At next rndabt take 3rd exit & immed turn L twd filling stn. Site ent on R in 100m, sp. Sm, mkd pitch, pt sl, pt shd; wc; chem disp; shwrs inc; el pnts (10A) €3.50; gas; Indry rm; sm shop; supmkt 2km; tradsmn; rest adj; bar; playgrnd; 5-10% statics; phone; poss cr; rd noise; CCI. "NH only; gd, modern san facs; phone ahead to check open low ssn." € 17.30 2009*

VIU DE LINAS see Broto *3B2*

VIVEIRO *1A2* (500m NW Coastal) *43.66812, -7.59998* **Camping Viveiro, Cantarrana s/n, Covas, 27850 Viveiro (Lugo) [982-56 00 04; fax 982-56 00 84]** Fr E twd El Ferrol on rd LU862, turn R in town over rv bdge & bear R & foll yellow camping sp. Site in 500m adj football stadium in Covas, sp. Fr W go into town on 1-way system & re-cross rv on parallel bdge to access rd to site. Foll stadium sp. Med, shd; wc; chem disp; shwrs inc; el pnts (10A) €4; Indtte; shop & 1.5km; snacks; beach 500m; phone; bus adj; ccard acc. "Gd clean site; uninspiring town." Easter & 1 Jun-30 Sep. € 16.00 2007*

VIVER *3D2* (3.5km W Rural) *39.90944, -0.61833* **Camping Villa de Viver, Camino Benaval s/n, 12460 Viver (Castellón) [964-14 13 34; info@campingviver.com; www.campingviver.com]** Fr Sagunto on A23 dir Terual, approx 10km fr Segorbe turn L sp Jérica, Viver. Thro vill dir Teresa, site sp W of Viver at end of single track lane in approx 2.8km (yellow sp) - poss diff for car+c'van, OK m'vans. Med, hdg pitch, terr, pt shd; htd wc; chem disp; mv service pnt; some serviced pitches; shwrs inc; el pnts (6A) €3.80; Indtte; shop 3.5km; tradsmn; rest; snacks; bar; playgrnd; pool; TV; 10% statics; dogs €3; phone; Eng spkn; adv bkg; quiet; red long stay; ccard acc; CCI. "Improved site; lovely situation - worth the effort." ♦ 15 Feb-15 Dec. € 21.85 2009*

ZAHARA DE LOS ATUNES see Vejer de la Frontera *2H3*

ZAMORA *1C3* (2.5km SE Urban) *41.4853, -5.7233* **Camping Ciudad de Zamora, Ctra Zamora-Fuentesaúco, Km 2.5, 49021 Zamora (Zamora) [980-53 72 95; fax 980-52 14 29; info@campingzamora.com; www.campingzamora.com]** Fr N630 fr N or S, turn onto C605 dir Fuentesaúco, site sp. Med, mkd pitch, pt shd; wc; chem disp; mv service pnt; baby facs; shwrs inc; el pnts (6A) €4.16; gas; Indry service; shop; tradsmn; rest high ssn; snacks; bar; BBQ; playgrnd; pool high ssn; rv & sand beach 3km; TV; dogs €1; phone; bus 2km; Eng spkn; adv bkg; quiet; ccard acc; red long stay/low ssn; ccard acc; red CCI. "Clean, well-run, conv site for town cent; excel san facs; friendly, helpful owners; gd cycling; ltd facs low ssn." ♦ Holy Week-15 Sep. € 19.20 2009*

⊞ **ZARAGOZA** *3C1* (3km S Urban) *41.63766, -0.94227* **Camping Ciudad de Zaragoza, Calle San Juan Bautista de la Salle s/n, 50112 Zaragoza [876-24 14 95; fax 876-24 12 86; info@campingzaragoza.com; www.campingzaragoza.com]** Fr S on A23 foll Adva Gómez Laguna, turn L at 2nd rndabt, in 500m bear R in order to turn L at rndabt, site on R in 750m, sp. Fr all other dirs take Z40 ring rd dir Teruel, then Adva Gómez Laguna twd city, then as above. Med, mkd pitch, hdstg, pt sl, unshd; htd wc; chem disp; mv service pnt; baby facs; shwrs inc; el pnts (10A) €4.30; Indtte (inc dryer); shop; rest; snacks; bar; BBQ; playgrnd; pool; tennis; games area; some statics; dogs €2.70; poss cr; Eng spkn; adv bkg; poss noisy (campers & daytime aircraft). "New site 2008 in suburbs; gd modern san facs; not rec high summer until trees grow & provide shade." € 21.00 2009*

⊞ **ZARAUTZ** *3A1* (2.5km E Coastal) *43.28958, -2.14603* **Gran Camping Zarautz, Monte Talaimendi s/n, 20800 Zarautz (Guipúzkoa) [943-83 12 38; fax 943-13 24 86; info@grancampingzarautz.com; www.grancampingzarautz.com]** Exit A8 junc 11 Zarautz, turn R at 2nd rndbt onto N634 to site sp on L in 200m. On N634 fr San Sebastián to Zarautz, thro Orio & turn R 300m bef m'way exit foll sps. Long, steep app (approx 1km). Lge, hdg/mkd pitch, hdstg, pt sl, terr, pt shd; htd wc; chem disp; mv service pnt; shwrs inc; el pnts (6A) €3.50; gas; Indry rm; shop; tradsmn; rest; bar; BBQ; playgrnd; beach 1km (steep walk); games rm; golf 1km; TV rm; 50% statics; phone; train/bus to Bilbao & San Sebastian; poss cr; Eng spkn; no adv bkg; ccard acc; CCI. "Site on cliff o'looking bay; excel beach, gd base for coast & mountains; helpful staff; some pitches sm with steep access & o'looked fr terr above; old san facs block in need of upgrade - new OK - all clean; excel disabled facs; pitches poss muddy; NH for Bilbao ferry; rec arr early to secure pitch." ♦ € 28.70 (CChq acc) 2009*

ZARAUTZ *3A1* (4km E Coastal) *43.27777, -2.12305* **Camping Playa de Orio, 20810 Orio (Guipúzkoa) [943-83 48 01; fax 943-13 34 33; kanpina@terra.es; www.oriora.com]** Fr E on A8 exit junc 33 & at rndabt foll sp Orio, Kanpin & Playa. Site on R. Or to avoid town cent cross bdge & foll N634 for 1km, turn L at sp Orio & camping, turn R at rndabt to site. Lge, mkd pitch, pt sl, pt shd; wc; chem disp; mv service pnt; baby facs; shwrs inc; el pnts (5A) inc; gas; Indtte (inc dryer); shop high ssn; tradsmn; rest adj; snacks; bar; playgrnd; pool high ssn; paddling pool; sand beach adj; tennis; 50% statics (sep area); no dogs; phone; car wash; poss cr at w/end; Eng spkn; adv bkg; quiet; red low ssn; ccard acc; CCI. "Busy site; flats now built bet site & beach & new marina adj - now no sea views; walks; gd facs; friendly staff; useful NH bef leaving Spain." ♦ 1 Mar-1 Nov. € 32.50 2009*

ZUBIA, LA see Granada *2G4*

Spain

Spain

Distances are shown in kilometres and are calculated from town/city centres along the most practical roads, although not necessarily taking the shortest route.
1km = 0.62miles

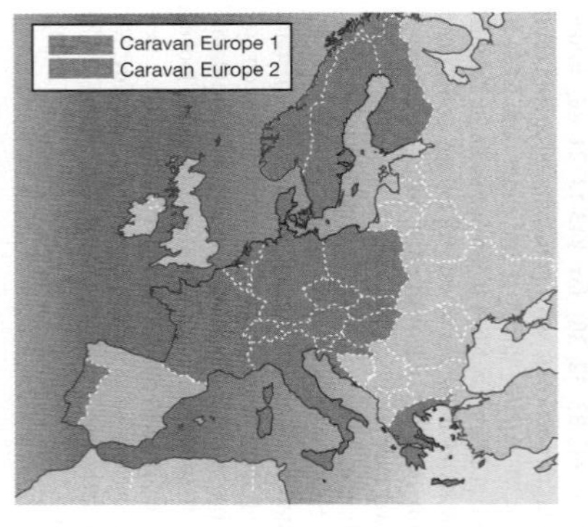

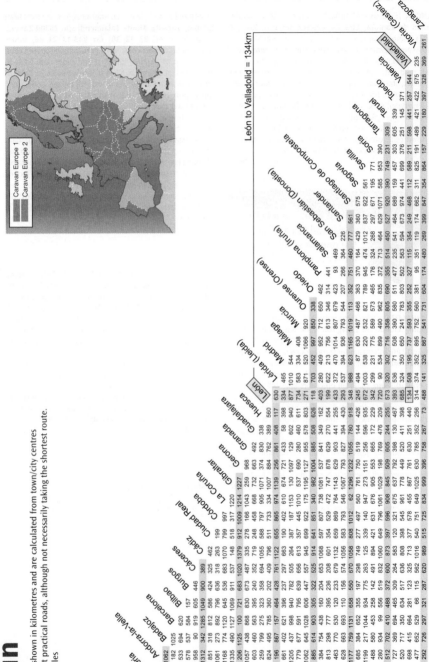

León to Valladolid = 134km

	Albacete	Alicante	Almeria	Andorra-la-Vella	Badajoz	Barcelona	Bilbao	Burgos	Cáceres	Cádiz	Ciudad Real	Córdoba	La Coruña	Gibraltar	Gerona	Granada	Guadalajara	Huesca	León	Lérida (Lleida)	Madrid	Málaga	Murcia	Ourense (Orense)	Oviedo	Pamplona (Iruña)	Salamanca	San Sebastián (Donostia)	Santander	Santiago de Compostela	Segovia	Sevilla	Soria	Tarragona	Teruel	Toledo	Valencia	Valladolid	Vitoria (Gasteiz)
Alicante	172																																						
Almeria	370	296																																					
Andorra-la-Vella	711	686	998																																				
Badajoz	523	694	605	1062																																			
Barcelona	539	516	810	182	1025																																		
Bilbao	645	818	959	533	694	620																																	
Burgos	489	657	799	578	537	584	157																																
Cáceres	503	675	652	958	90	919	605	446																															
Cádiz	619	688	848	1312	342	1285	1049	900	389																														
Ciudad Real	208	379	408	851	318	812	586	424	325	462																													
Córdoba	355	524	333	1061	273	892	796	636	318	263	199																												
La Coruña	863	1029	1170	1168	774	1120	645	536	683	1070	799	997																											
Gibraltar	603	612	349	1335	490	1127	1069	911	537	148	518	317	1220																										
Gerona	642	615	908	206	1125	100	721	683	1020	1379	912	1009	1214	1227																									
Granada	362	354	167	1057	438	868	830	673	487	335	278	166	1043	259	968																								
Guadalajara	308	483	619	603	460	563	395	240	352	719	248	458	668	732	663	492																							
Huesca	494	570	828	259	799	275	323	358	694	1055	588	797	905	1071	374	830	338																						
León	583	756	898	824	495	785	360	202	409	796	511	733	334	1007	884	762	389	560																					
Lérida (Lleida)	514	491	801	196	867	157	464	428	761	1122	655	865	974	1139	256	861	408	117	630																				
Madrid	251	423	563	661	402	621	396	237	297	663	190	402	610	674	721	433	58	398	334	465																			
Málaga	475	481	218	1205	437	998	940	782	505	264	387	187	1153	130	1097	129	602	940	877	1010	544																		
Murcia	151	76	220	779	677	591	795	639	656	613	357	445	1010	537	690	280	460	611	734	583	334	408																	
Ourense (Orense)	773	944	1085	1062	645	1028	606	447	557	945	699	922	175	1195	1127	955	578	803	271	871	520	1066	920																
Oviedo	700	873	1015	885	614	903	305	322	525	914	641	851	340	982	1004	885	508	626	118	703	452	997	850	338															
Pamplona (Iruña)	601	675	971	384	754	438	160	204	653	1068	597	807	738	1081	537	841	349	162	403	280	409	952	712	650	462														
Salamanca	462	633	762	813	298	777	395	236	208	601	354	529	472	747	878	629	270	554	199	622	213	756	613	346	314	441													
San Sebastián (Donostia)	692	767	1031	463	770	530	120	233	679	1132	659	869	764	1143	629	903	441	255	433	372	470	1014	807	679	423	93	469												
Santander	642	816	957	628	663	693	110	156	574	1056	583	793	546	1067	793	827	394	430	293	537	394	936	793	544	207	266	364	226											
Santiago de Compostela	871	1045	1184	1177	759	1131	658	550	670	1058	808	1012	62	1296	1232	1055	780	918	348	988	623	1165	1019	113	352	751	460	777	561										
Segovia	339	511	651	685	384	652	355	197	298	749	277	497	560	761	750	519	144	426	245	494	87	630	487	466	363	370	164	429	360	575									
Sevilla	490	609	423	1199	217	1044	934	775	263	125	339	140	947	273	1151	256	596	935	672	1003	538	220	532	821	789	945	474	1012	837	922	561								
Soria	472	549	795	488	580	453	258	142	491	894	421	631	676	905	553	665	172	229	342	299	231	775	589	573	465	176	324	268	297	671	195	771							
Tarragona	442	417	710	280	934	99	556	519	832	1060	649	796	1061	1029	198	769	476	209	720	90	534	899	490	962	835	372	713	464	629	1071	585	953	390						
Teruel	243	317	578	512	702	410	488	372	600	873	397	596	908	845	509	605	244	255	573	320	302	716	358	805	690	355	514	450	527	920	390	749	231	309					
Toledo	241	411	526	727	369	694	465	309	264	583	120	321	675	637	792	398	130	467	393	536	71	508	390	580	511	477	235	541	464	689	159	457	303	605	339				
Valencia	192	167	461	520	717	350	634	517	636	808	398	545	961	778	449	520	411	398	685	324	350	650	241	783	803	502	563	594	673	974	441	699	376	251	145	371			
Valladolid	445	614	757	698	415	664	281	123	325	713	377	578	455	867	761	630	251	440	134	508	195	737	593	355	252	327	115	354	249	468	112	589	211	598	441	257	544		
Vitoria (Gasteiz)	603	741	916	477	652	529	66	115	562	1016	540	751	649	1025	630	785	352	256	314	374	352	895	752	560	381	95	351	119	174	662	311	825	191	489	421	422	575	235	
Zaragoza	424	500	758	292	726	297	321	287	620	989	515	725	834	999	396	758	267	73	488	141	325	867	541	731	604	174	480	269	399	847	354	864	157	229	180	397	328	369	261

Regions and Provinces of Spain

ANDALUCIA
4 Alméria
11 Cádiz
14 Córdoba
18 Granada
21 Huelva
23 Jaén
29 Málaga
41 Sevilla

ARAGON
22 Huesca
44 Teruel
50 Zaragoza

ASTURIAS
33 Asturias

BALEARIC ISLANDS
7 Balearic Islands

CANARY ISLANDS
35 Las Palmas
38 Sta. Cruz de Tenerife

CANTABRIA
39 Cantabria

CASTILLA-LA MANCHA
2 Albacete
13 Cuidad Real
16 Cuenca
19 Guadalajara
45 Toledo

CASTILLA Y LEON
5 Ávila
9 Burgos
24 León
34 Palencia
37 Salamanca
40 Segovia
42 Soria
47 Valladolid
49 Zamora

CATALUÑA
8 Barcelona
17 Gerona
25 Lérida
43 Tarragona

COMUNIDAD VALENCIANA
3 Alicante
12 Castellón
46 Valencia

EXTREMADURA
6 Badajoz
10 Cáceres

GALICIA
15 La Coruña
27 Lugo
32 Ourense
36 Pontevedra

LA RIOJA
26 La Rioja

MADRID
28 Madrid

MURCIA
30 Murcia

NAVARRA
31 Navarra

PAIS VASCO
1 Álava
20 Guipúzcua
48 Vizcaya

SPANISH ENCLAVES
51 Ceuta
52 Melilla

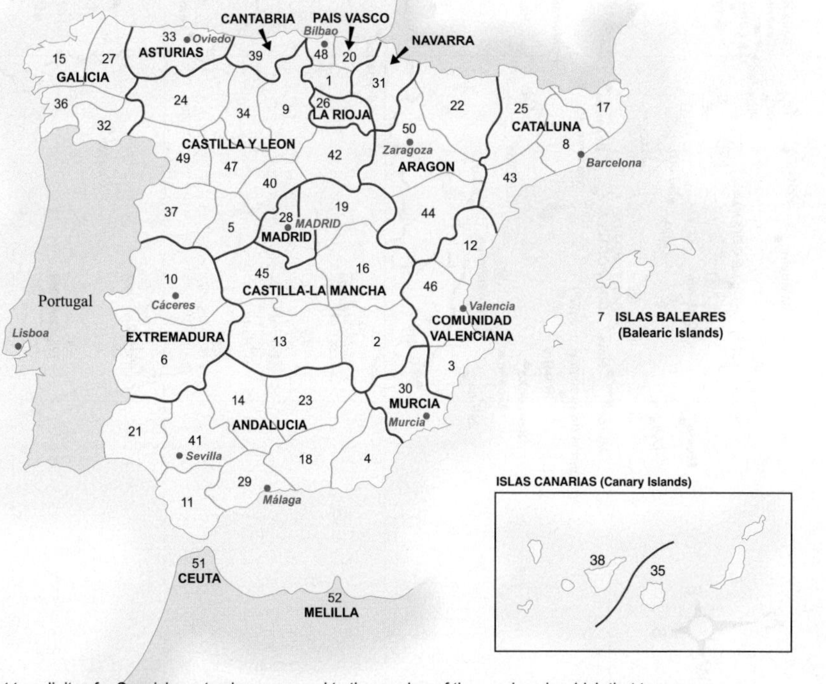

The first two digits of a Spanish postcode correspond to the number of the province in which that town or village is situated

Source : Spanish National Tourist Office

Map 1

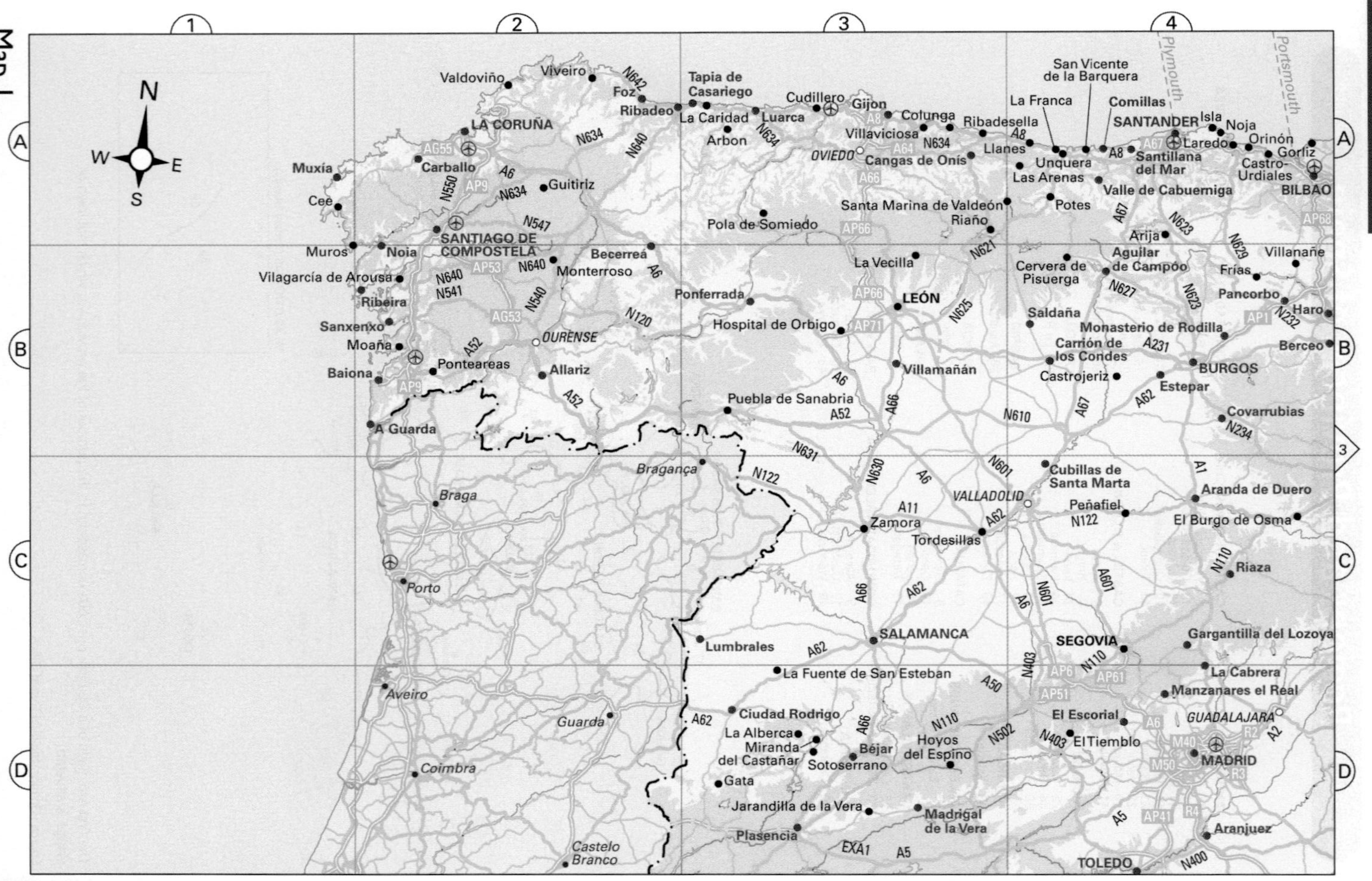

1
2
3
4
A
B
C
D
N
E
S
W
Plymouth
Portsmouth
Valdoviño
Viveiro
Foz
Ribadeo
Tapia de Casariego
La Caridad
Arbon
Luarca
Cudillero
Gijon
Colunga
Villaviciosa
OVIEDO
Cangas de Onís
Ribadesella
Llanes
La Franca
Unquera
Las Arenas
San Vicente de la Barquera
Comillas
SANTANDER
Santillana del Mar
Isla
Noja
Laredo
Orinón
Gorliz
Castro-Urdiales
BILBAO
Valle de Cabuerniga
Potes
Santa Marina de Valdeón
Riaño
Pola de Somiedo
LA CORUÑA
Muxía
Carballo
Guitiriz
Cee
SANTIAGO DE COMPOSTELA
Muros
Noia
Vilagarcía de Arousa
Ribeira
Sanxenxo
Moaña
Baiona
Pontearreas
A Guarda
Becerreá
Monterroso
OURENSE
Allariz
Ponferrada
Hospital de Orbigo
La Vecilla
LEÓN
Villamañán
Puebla de Sanabria
Arija
Aguilar de Campóo
Cervera de Pisuerga
Saldaña
Carrión de los Condes
Castrojeriz
Monasterio de Rodilla
BURGOS
Estepar
Covarrubias
Villanañe
Frías
Pancorbo
Haro
Berceo
Bragança
Braga
Porto
Cubillas de Santa Marta
VALLADOLID
Peñafiel
Aranda de Duero
El Burgo de Osma
Zamora
Tordesillas
Riaza
Lumbrales
SALAMANCA
SEGOVIA
Gargantilla del Lozoya
La Cabrera
Manzanares el Real
La Fuente de San Esteban
Aveiro
Guarda
Ciudad Rodrigo
La Alberca
Miranda del Castañar
Béjar
Sotoserrano
Hoyos del Espino
El Escorial
El Tiemblo
GUADALAJARA
MADRID
Coimbra
Gata
Jarandilla de la Vera
Madrigal de la Vera
Plasencia
Aranjuez
Castelo Branco
TOLEDO
N642
N634
N640
AG55
AP9
N550
A6
N547
AP53
N640
N541
AG53
N540
A52
A8
A64
N634
A66
AP66
AP71
N621
N625
N120
A6
A52
A66
N631
N122
N630
A11
A6
N601
A62
N610
A67
N627
N623
N629
A231
AP1
N232
A62
N234
A1
N122
N110
A601
N601
A66
A62
A6
N403
AP6
AP61
N110
AP51
A50
A62
A66
N110
N502
N403
A6
A2
M40
M50
R2
R3
R4
AP41
A5
N400
EXA1
AP68
A67

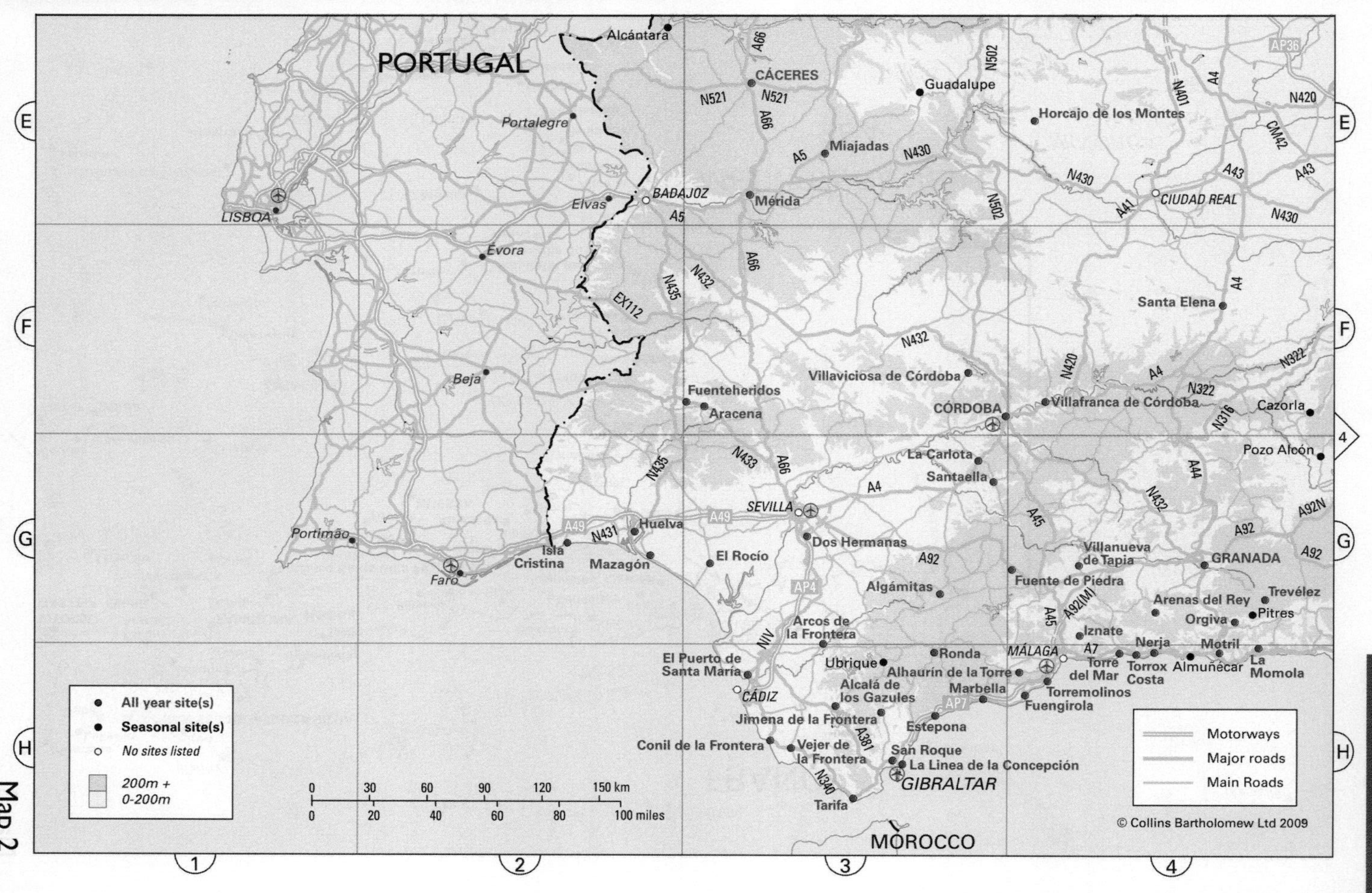
PORTUGAL
Alcántara
CÁCERES
Guadalupe
Horcajo de los Montes
Portalegre
Miajadas
LISBOA
Elvas
BADAJOZ
Mérida
CIUDAD REAL
Évora
Santa Elena
Beja
Villaviciosa de Córdoba
Fuenteheridos
Aracena
CÓRDOBA
Villafranca de Córdoba
Cazorla
La Carlota
Pozo Alcón
Santaella
SEVILLA
Portimão
Huelva
Dos Hermanas
Isla Cristina
Faro
Mazagón
El Rocío
Villanueva de Tapia
GRANADA
Trevélez
Algámitas
Fuente de Piedra
Arenas del Rey
Pitres
Orgiva
Iznate
Arcos de la Frontera
Nerja
Motril
MÁLAGA
Ronda
El Puerto de Santa María
Ubrique
Alhaurín de la Torre
Torre del Mar
Torrox Costa
Almuñécar
La Mamola
CÁDIZ
Alcalá de los Gazules
Marbella
Torremolinos
Fuengirola
Jimena de la Frontera
Estepona
Conil de la Frontera
Vejer de la Frontera
San Roque
La Linea de la Concepción
GIBRALTAR
Tarifa
MOROCCO
A4
A5
A7
A41
A43
A44
A45
A49
A66
A92
A92N
A92(M)
A381
AP4
AP7
AP36
CM42
EX112
N316
N322
N340
N401
N420
N430
N431
N432
N433
N435
N502
N521
NIV
All year site(s)
Seasonal site(s)
No sites listed
200m +
0-200m
0
30
60
90
120
150 km
0
20
40
60
80
100 miles
Motorways
Major roads
Main Roads
© Collins Bartholomew Ltd 2009
E
F
G
H
1
2
3
4

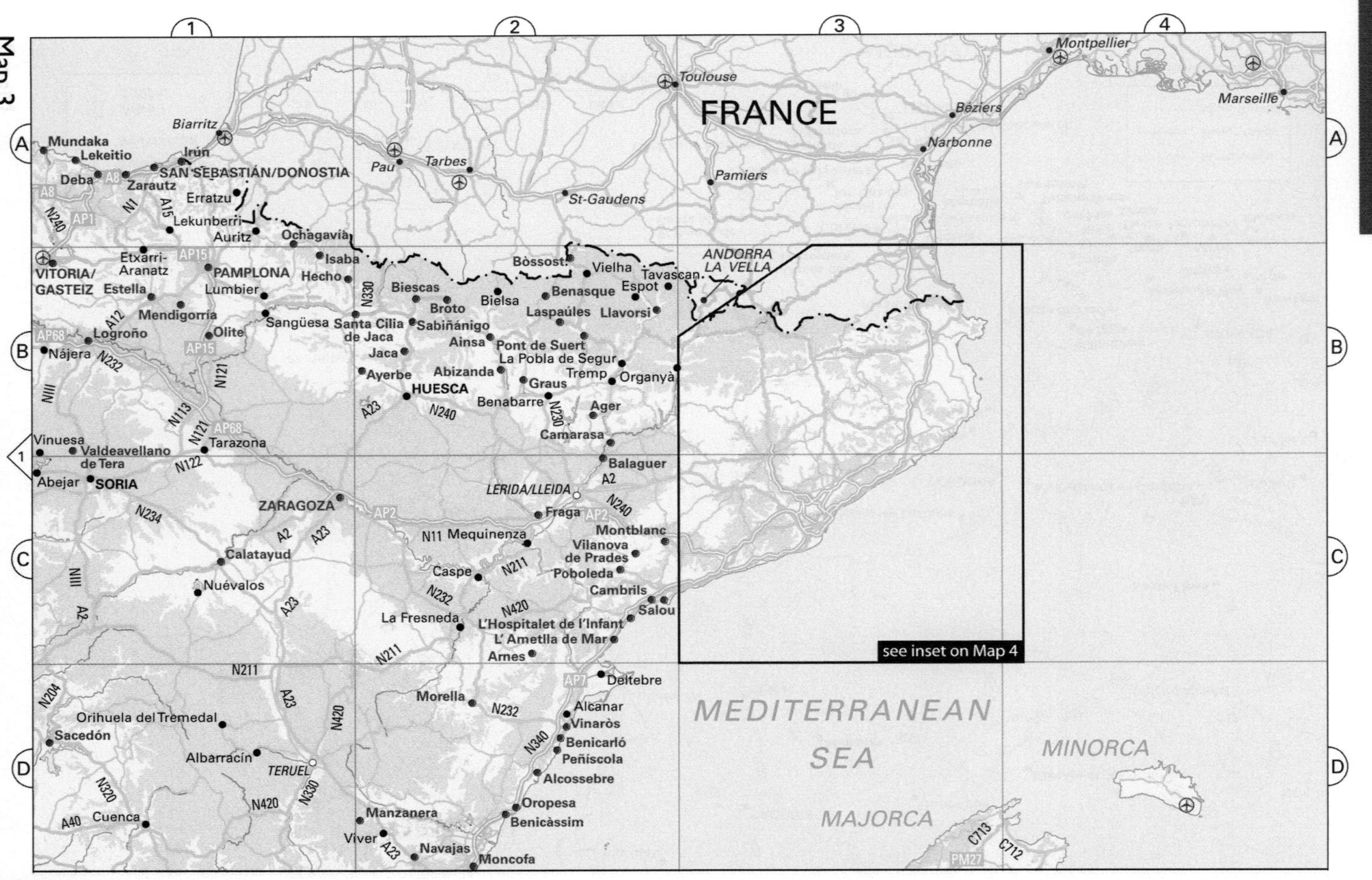
FRANCE
MEDITERRANEAN SEA
MINORCA
MAJORCA
see inset on Map 4
ANDORRA LA VELLA
Toulouse
Montpellier
Marseille
Béziers
Narbonne
Pamiers
St-Gaudens
Tarbes
Pau
Biarritz
Irún
SAN SEBASTIÁN/DONOSTIA
Erratzu
Lekunberri
Auritz
Ochagavía
Isaba
Hecho
PAMPLONA
Lumbier
Sangüesa
Olite
Mendigorría
Estella
Etxarri-Aranatz
VITORIA/GASTEIZ
Zarautz
Deba
Lekeitio
Mundaka
Logroño
Nájera
Tarazona
Valdeavellano de Tera
Vinuesa
Abejar
SORIA
ZARAGOZA
Calatayud
Nuévalos
Santa Cilia de Jaca
Jaca
Ayerbe
Biescas
Broto
Sabiñánigo
HUESCA
Abizanda
Ainsa
Bielsa
Benabarre
Graus
Pont de Suert
La Pobla de Segur
Laspaúles
Benasque
Bòssost
Vielha
Espot
Tavascan
Llavorsí
Organyà
Tremp
Ager
Camarasa
Balaguer
LERIDA/LLEIDA
Fraga
N11 Mequinenza
Caspe
La Fresneda
Montblanc
Vilanova de Prades
Poboleda
Cambrils
Salou
L'Hospitalet de l'Infant
L' Ametlla de Mar
Arnes
Deltebre
Alcanar
Vinaròs
Benicarló
Peñíscola
Alcossebre
Oropesa
Benicàssim
Morella
Moncofa
Navajas
Viver
Manzanera
TERUEL
Albarracín
Orihuela del Tremedal
Sacedón
Cuenca
A
B
C
D
1
2
3
4
A2
A8
A12
A15
A23
A40
AP1
AP2
AP7
AP15
AP68
N1
N113
N121
N122
N204
N211
N230
N232
N234
N240
N320
N330
N340
N420
NIII
C712
C713
PM27

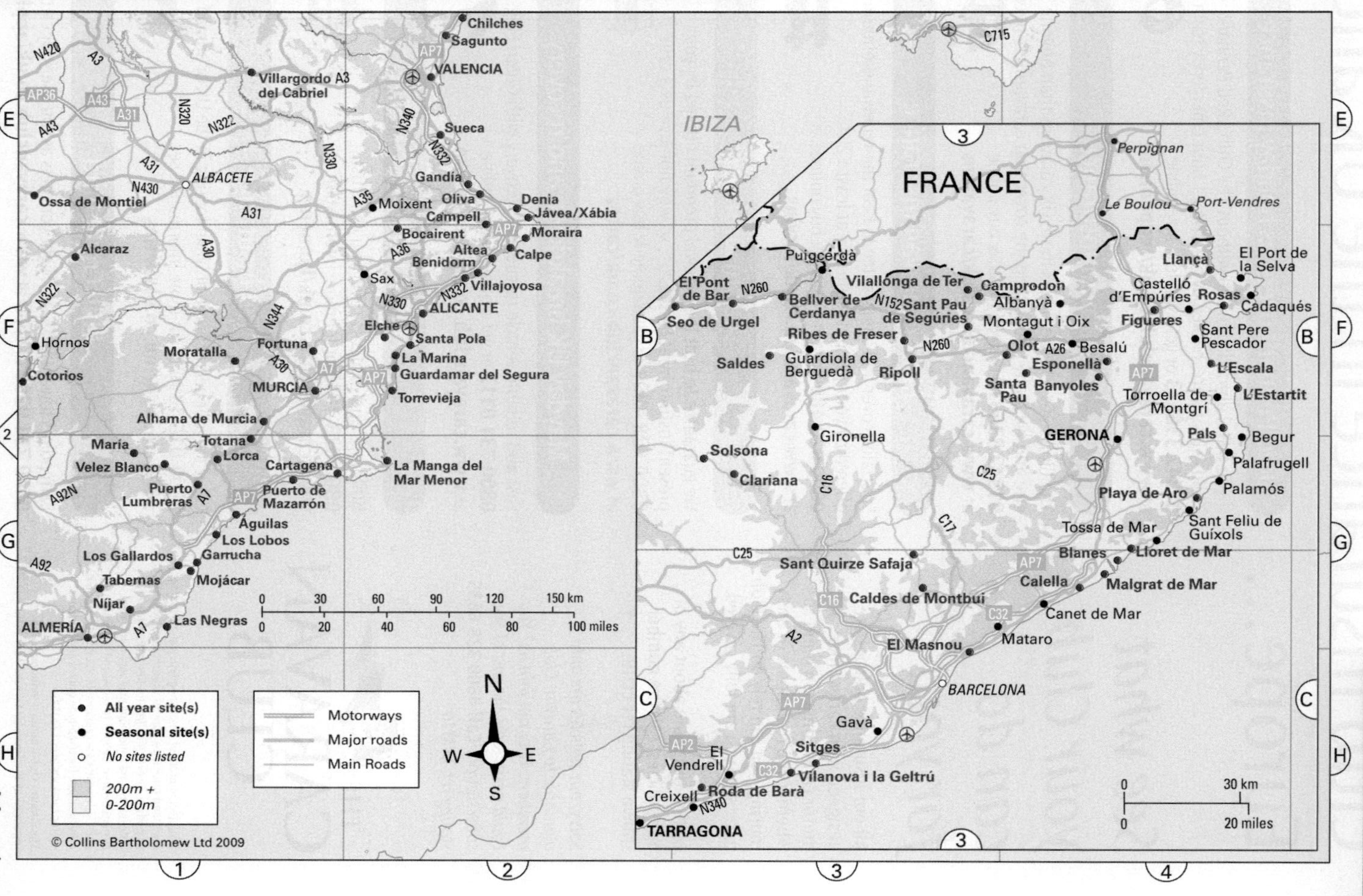
Chilches
Sagunto
VALENCIA
Villargordo del Cabriel
Sueca
ALBACETE
Ossa de Montiel
Gandía
Moixent
Oliva
Denia
Jávea/Xábia
Campell
Bocairent
Moraira
Alcaraz
Altea
Calpe
Benidorm
Sax
Villajoyosa
ALICANTE
Elche
Santa Pola
Hornos
Moratalla
Fortuna
La Marina
Guardamar del Segura
Cotorios
MURCIA
Torrevieja
Alhama de Murcia
María
Totana
Lorca
Velez Blanco
Cartagena
La Manga del Mar Menor
Puerto Lumbreras
Puerto de Mazarrón
Águilas
Los Lobos
Los Gallardos
Garrucha
Tabernas
Mojácar
Níjar
ALMERÍA
Las Negras
IBIZA
FRANCE
Perpignan
Le Boulou
Port-Vendres
Puigcerdà
Llançà
El Port de la Selva
El Pont de Bar
Vilallonga de Ter
Camprodon
Castelló d'Empúries
Rosas
Cadaqués
Seo de Urgel
Bellver de Cerdanya
Sant Pau de Segúries
Albanyà
Montagut i Oix
Figueres
Sant Pere Pescador
Ribes de Freser
Olot
Besalú
Saldes
Guardiola de Berguedà
Ripoll
Esponellà
L'Escala
Santa Pau
Banyoles
Torroella de Montgrí
L'Estartit
Gironella
GERONA
Pals
Begur
Solsona
Palafrugell
Clariana
Playa de Aro
Palamós
Tossa de Mar
Sant Feliu de Guíxols
Blanes
Lloret de Mar
Sant Quirze Safaja
Calella
Malgrat de Mar
Caldes de Montbui
Canet de Mar
Mataro
El Masnou
BARCELONA
Gavà
Sitges
El Vendrell
Vilanova i la Geltrú
Creixell
Roda de Barà
TARRAGONA
0 30 60 90 120 150 km
0 20 40 60 80 100 miles
0 30 km
0 20 miles
N
E
S
W
All year site(s)
Seasonal site(s)
No sites listed
200m +
0-200m
Motorways
Major roads
Main Roads
© Collins Bartholomew Ltd 2009

Caravan Europe Site Report Form **

If campsite is already listed, complete only those sections of the form where changes apply

Please print, type or tick in the white areas

Sites not reported on for 5 years may be deleted from the guide

Year of guide used	20..........	Is site listed?	Listed on page no.	Unlisted	Date of visit	......../........./.........

A – CAMPSITE NAME AND LOCATION

Country		Name of town/village site listed under *(see Sites Location Maps)*			
Distance & direction from centre of town site is listed under *(in a straight line)*	...................km	eg N, NE, S, SW	Urban	Rural	Coastal
Site open all year?	Y / N	Period site is open *(if not all year)*	................./................. to ..../..................		
Site name				Naturist site	Y / N
Site address					
Telephone		Fax			
E-mail		Website			

B – CAMPSITE CHARGES

Charge for car, caravan + 2 adults in local currency	PRICE		EL PNTS inc in this price?	Y / N	Amps ....

C – DIRECTIONS

Brief, specific directions to site (in km) *To convert miles to kilometres multiply by 8 and divide by 5 or use Conversion Table in guide*	
GPS	Latitude...*(eg 12.34567)* Longitude...*(eg 1.23456 or -1.23456)*

D – CAMPSITE DESCRIPTION

SITE size ie number of pitches	Small Max 50	SM	Medium 51-150	MED	Large 151-500	LGE	Very large 500+	V LGE	Unchanged
PITCH size	*eg small, medium, large, very large, various*								Unchanged
Pitch features if **NOT** open-plan/grassy	Hedged	HDG PITCH	Marked or numbered	MKD PITCH	Hardstanding or gravel	HDSTG			Unchanged
If site is **NOT** level, is it	Part sloping	PT SL	Sloping	SL	Terraced	TERR			Unchanged
Is site shaded?	Shaded	SHD	Part shaded	PT SHD	Unshaded	UNSHD			Unchanged

E – CAMPSITE FACILITIES

WC	Heated	HTD WC	Continental	CONT	Own San recommended	OWN SAN REC
Chemical disposal point	CHEM DISP		Dedicated point		WC only	
Motor caravan waste discharge and water refill point			MV SERVICE PNT			
Child / baby facilities (bathroom)	CHILD / BABY FACS		Family bathroom		FAM BTHRM	
Hot shower(s)	SHWR(S)		Inc in site fee?	Y / N	Price..................*(if not inc)*	
ELECTRIC HOOK UP *if not included in price above*	EL PNTS		Price......................................		Amps..	
Supplies of bottled gas	GAS		On site	Y / N	Or in .... Kms	
Launderette / Washing Machine	LNDTTE		Inc dryer Y / N		LNDRY RM *(if no washing machine)*	

** *You can also complete forms online: www.caravanclub.co.uk/europereport*

CUT ALONG DOTTED LINE

F – FOOD & DRINK

Shop(s) / supermarket	SHOP(S) / SUPMKT	On site		or	.... kms
Bread / milk delivered	TRADSMN				
Restaurant / cafeteria	REST	On site		or	.... kms
Snack bar / take-away	SNACKS	On site		or	.... kms
Bar	BAR	On site		or	.... kms
Barbecue allowed	BBQ	Charcoal	Gas	Elec	Sep area
Cooking facilities	COOKING FACS				

G – LEISURE FACILITIES

Playground	PLAYGRND					
Swimming pool	POOL	On site		or ....km	Heated	Covered
Beach	BEACH	Adj		or ....km	Sand	Shingle
Alternative swimming *(lake)*	SW	Adj		or ....km	Sand	Shingle
Games /sports area / Games room	GAMES AREA	GAMES ROOM				
Entertainment in high season	ENTMNT					
Internet use by visitors	INTERNET	Wifi Internet		WIFI		
Television room	TV RM	Satellite / Cable to pitches		TV CAB / SAT		

H – OTHER INFORMATION

% Static caravans / mobile homes / chalets / cottages / fixed tents on site					................% STATICS
Dogs allowed	DOGS		Y / N	Price per night .... *(if allowed)*	
Phone	PHONE		On site	Adj	
Bus / tram / train	BUS / TRAM / TRAIN		Adj	or .... km	
Twin axles caravans allowed?	TWIN AXLES Y / N		Possibly crowded in high season		POSS CR
English spoken	ENG SPKN				
Advance bookings accepted	ADV BKG		Y / N		
Noise levels on site in season	NOISY	QUIET	If noisy, why?		
Credit card accepted	CCARD ACC		Reduction low season		RED LOW SSN
Camping Card International accepted in lieu of passport	CCI		INF card required *(If naturist site)*		Y / N
Facilities for disabled	Full wheelchair facilities	♦	Limited disabled facilities		♦ ltd

I – ADDITIONAL REMARKS AND/OR ITEMS OF INTEREST

Tourist attractions, unusual features or other facilities, eg waterslide, tennis, cycle hire, watersports, horseriding, separate car park, walking distance to shops etc	YOUR OPINION OF THE SITE:
	EXCEL
	VERY GOOD
	GOOD
	FAIR / POOR
	NIGHT HALT ONLY
Your comments & opinions may be used in future editions of the guide, if you do not wish them to be used please tick	

J – MEMBER DETAILS

ARE YOU A:	Caravanner		Motor caravanner		Trailer-tenter?
NAME:	CARAVAN CLUB MEMBERSHIP NO:				
	POST CODE:				
DO YOU NEED MORE BLANK SITE REPORT FORMS?	YES		NO		
Address *(Non-members only please complete this section)*					

Please use a separate form for each campsite and do not send receipts. Owing to the large number of site reports received, it is not possible to enter into correspondence. Please return completed form to:

The Editor, Caravan Europe, The Caravan Club
FREEPOST, PO Box 386, (RRZG-SXKK-UCUJ)
East Grinstead RH19 1FH

(This address to be used when mailing within the UK only)

Caravan Europe Site Report Form **

If campsite is already listed, complete only those sections of the form where changes apply

Please print, type or tick in the white areas

Sites not reported on for 5 years may be deleted from the guide

Year of guide used	20.........	Is site listed?	Listed on page no.	Unlisted	Date of visit	......../......../.........

A – CAMPSITE NAME AND LOCATION

Country		Name of town/village site listed under *(see Sites Location Maps)*			
Distance & direction from centre of town site is listed under *(in a straight line)*	..................km	eg N, NE, S, SW	Urban	Rural	Coastal
Site open all year?	Y / N	Period site is open *(if not all year)*	................./.................	to	................./.................
Site name				Naturist site	Y / N
Site address					
Telephone		Fax			
E-mail		Website			

B – CAMPSITE CHARGES

Charge for car, caravan + 2 adults in local currency	PRICE		EL PNTS inc in this price?	Y / N	Amps ....

C – DIRECTIONS

Brief, specific directions to site (in km) *To convert miles to kilometres multiply by 8 and divide by 5 or use Conversion Table in guide*	
GPS	Latitude..*(eg 12.34567)* Longitude..*(eg 1.23456 or -1.23456)*

D – CAMPSITE DESCRIPTION

SITE size ie number of pitches	Small Max 50	SM	Medium 51-150	MED	Large 151-500	LGE	Very large 500+	V LGE	Unchanged

PITCH size	*eg small, medium, large, very large, various*	Unchanged

Pitch features if **NOT** open-plan/grassy	Hedged	HDG PITCH	Marked or numbered	MKD PITCH	Hardstanding or gravel	HDSTG	Unchanged
If site is **NOT** level, is it	Part sloping	PT SL	Sloping	SL	Terraced	TERR	Unchanged
Is site shaded?	Shaded	SHD	Part shaded	PT SHD	Unshaded	UNSHD	Unchanged

E – CAMPSITE FACILITIES

WC	Heated	HTD WC	Continental	CONT	Own San recommended	OWN SAN REC

Chemical disposal point	CHEM DISP	Dedicated point		WC only
Motor caravan waste discharge and water refill point		MV SERVICE PNT		
Child / baby facilities (bathroom)	CHILD / BABY FACS	Family bathroom		FAM BTHRM
Hot shower(s)	SHWR(S)	Inc in site fee?	Y / N	Price...................*(if not inc)*
ELECTRIC HOOK UP *if not included in price above*	EL PNTS	Price..................................		Amps..................................
Supplies of bottled gas	GAS	On site	Y / N	Or in .... Kms
Launderette / Washing Machine	LNDTTE	Inc dryer Y / N		LNDRY RM *(if no washing machine)*

** *You can also complete forms online: www.caravanclub.co.uk/europereport*

CUT ALONG DOTTED LINE

F – FOOD & DRINK

Shop(s) / supermarket	SHOP(S) / SUPMKT	On site		or	.... kms
Bread / milk delivered	TRADSMN				
Restaurant / cafeteria	REST	On site		or	.... kms
Snack bar / take-away	SNACKS	On site		or	.... kms
Bar	BAR	On site		or	.... kms
Barbecue allowed	BBQ	Charcoal	Gas	Elec	Sep area
Cooking facilities	COOKING FACS				

G – LEISURE FACILITIES

Playground	PLAYGRND					
Swimming pool	POOL	On site		or ....km	Heated	Covered
Beach	BEACH	Adj		or ....km	Sand	Shingle
Alternative swimming *(lake)*	SW	Adj		or ....km	Sand	Shingle
Games /sports area / Games room	GAMES AREA	GAMES ROOM				
Entertainment in high season	ENTMNT					
Internet use by visitors	INTERNET	Wifi Internet		WIFI		
Television room	TV RM	Satellite / Cable to pitches		TV CAB / SAT		

H – OTHER INFORMATION

% Static caravans / mobile homes / chalets / cottages / fixed tents on site				................% STATICS
Dogs allowed	DOGS	Y / N	Price per night .... *(if allowed)*	
Phone	PHONE	On site	Adj	
Bus / tram / train	BUS / TRAM / TRAIN	Adj	or .... km	
Twin axles caravans allowed?	TWIN AXLES Y / N	Possibly crowded in high season		POSS CR
English spoken	ENG SPKN			
Advance bookings accepted	ADV BKG	Y / N		
Noise levels on site in season	NOISY / QUIET	If noisy, why?		
Credit card accepted	CCARD ACC	Reduction low season		RED LOW SSN
Camping Card International accepted in lieu of passport	CCI	INF card required *(If naturist site)*		Y / N
Facilities for disabled	Full wheelchair facilities	♦	Limited disabled facilities	♦ ltd

I – ADDITIONAL REMARKS AND/OR ITEMS OF INTEREST

Tourist attractions, unusual features or other facilities, eg waterslide, tennis, cycle hire, watersports, horseriding, separate car park, walking distance to shops etc	YOUR OPINION OF THE SITE:
	EXCEL
	VERY GOOD
	GOOD
	FAIR / POOR
	NIGHT HALT ONLY
Your comments & opinions may be used in future editions of the guide, if you do not wish them to be used please tick	

J – MEMBER DETAILS

ARE YOU A:	Caravanner		Motor caravanner		Trailer-tenter?	
NAME:	CARAVAN CLUB MEMBERSHIP NO:					
	POST CODE:					
DO YOU NEED MORE BLANK SITE REPORT FORMS?		YES		NO		
Address *(Non-members only please complete this section)*						

Please use a separate form for each campsite and do not send receipts. Owing to the large number of site reports received, it is not possible to enter into correspondence. Please return completed form to:

The Editor, Caravan Europe, The Caravan Club
FREEPOST, PO Box 386, (RRZG-SXKK-UCUJ)
East Grinstead RH19 1FH

(This address to be used when mailing within the UK only)

Caravan Europe Site Report Form **

If campsite is already listed, complete only those sections of the form where changes apply

Please print, type or tick in the white areas

Sites not reported on for 5 years may be deleted from the guide

Year of guide used	20..........	Is site listed?	Listed on page no.	Unlisted	Date of visit	......./........./.........

A – CAMPSITE NAME AND LOCATION

Country		Name of town/village site listed under *(see Sites Location Maps)*			
Distance & direction from centre of town site is listed under *(in a straight line)*	..................km	eg N, NE, S, SW	Urban	Rural	Coastal
Site open all year?	Y / N	Period site is open *(if not all year)*	................./.................	to	................../.................
Site name				Naturist site	Y / N
Site address					
Telephone		Fax			
E-mail		Website			

B – CAMPSITE CHARGES

Charge for car, caravan + 2 adults in local currency	PRICE		EL PNTS inc in this price?	Y / N	Amps ....

C – DIRECTIONS

Brief, specific directions to site (in km) *To convert miles to kilometres multiply by 8 and divide by 5 or use Conversion Table in guide*	
GPS	Latitude...(*eg 12.34567*) Longitude...(*eg 1.23456 or -1.23456*)

D – CAMPSITE DESCRIPTION

SITE size ie number of pitches	Small Max 50	SM	Medium 51-150	MED	Large 151-500	LGE	Very large 500+	V LGE	Unchanged

PITCH size	*eg small, medium, large, very large, various*	Unchanged

Pitch features if **NOT** open-plan/grassy	Hedged	HDG PITCH	Marked or numbered	MKD PITCH	Hardstanding or gravel	HDSTG	Unchanged
If site is **NOT** level, is it	Part sloping	PT SL	Sloping	SL	Terraced	TERR	Unchanged
Is site shaded?	Shaded	SHD	Part shaded	PT SHD	Unshaded	UNSHD	Unchanged

E – CAMPSITE FACILITIES

WC	Heated	HTD WC	Continental	CONT	Own San recommended	OWN SAN REC

Chemical disposal point	CHEM DISP	Dedicated point		WC only
Motor caravan waste discharge and water refill point		MV SERVICE PNT		
Child / baby facilities (bathroom)	CHILD / BABY FACS	Family bathroom		FAM BTHRM
Hot shower(s)	SHWR(S)	Inc in site fee?	Y / N	Price...................(*if not inc*)
ELECTRIC HOOK UP *if not included in price above*	EL PNTS	Price..		Amps..
Supplies of bottled gas	GAS	On site	Y / N	Or in .... Kms
Launderette / Washing Machine	LNDTTE	Inc dryer Y / N		LNDRY RM *(if no washing machine)*

** *You can also complete forms online: www.caravanclub.co.uk/europereport*

F – FOOD & DRINK

Shop(s) / supermarket	SHOP(S) / SUPMKT	On site		or	.... kms
Bread / milk delivered	TRADSMN				
Restaurant / cafeteria	REST	On site		or	.... kms
Snack bar / take-away	SNACKS	On site		or	.... kms
Bar	BAR	On site		or	.... kms
Barbecue allowed	BBQ	Charcoal	Gas	Elec	Sep area
Cooking facilities	COOKING FACS				

G – LEISURE FACILITIES

Playground	PLAYGRND					
Swimming pool	POOL	On site		or ....km	Heated	Covered
Beach	BEACH	Adj		or ....km	Sand	Shingle
Alternative swimming *(lake)*	SW	Adj		or ....km	Sand	Shingle
Games /sports area / Games room	GAMES AREA	GAMES ROOM				
Entertainment in high season	ENTMNT					
Internet use by visitors	INTERNET	Wifi Internet		WIFI		
Television room	TV RM	Satellite / Cable to pitches		TV CAB / SAT		

H – OTHER INFORMATION

% Static caravans / mobile homes / chalets / cottages / fixed tents on site				................% STATICS
Dogs allowed	DOGS	Y / N	Price per night .... *(if allowed)*	
Phone	PHONE	On site	Adj	
Bus / tram / train	BUS / TRAM / TRAIN	Adj	or .... km	
Twin axles caravans allowed?	TWIN AXLES Y / N	Possibly crowded in high season		POSS CR
English spoken	ENG SPKN			
Advance bookings accepted	ADV BKG	Y / N		
Noise levels on site in season	NOISY / QUIET	If noisy, why?		
Credit card accepted	CCARD ACC	Reduction low season		RED LOW SSN
Camping Card International accepted in lieu of passport	CCI	INF card required *(If naturist site)*		Y / N
Facilities for disabled	Full wheelchair facilities	♦	Limited disabled facilities	♦ ltd

I – ADDITIONAL REMARKS AND/OR ITEMS OF INTEREST

Tourist attractions, unusual features or other facilities, eg waterslide, tennis, cycle hire, watersports, horseriding, separate car park, walking distance to shops etc	YOUR OPINION OF THE SITE:
	EXCEL
	VERY GOOD
	GOOD
	FAIR / POOR
	NIGHT HALT ONLY
Your comments & opinions may be used in future editions of the guide, if you do not wish them to be used please tick	

J – MEMBER DETAILS

ARE YOU A:	Caravanner		Motor caravanner		Trailer-tenter?	
NAME:	CARAVAN CLUB MEMBERSHIP NO:					
	POST CODE:					
DO YOU NEED MORE BLANK SITE REPORT FORMS?		YES		NO		
Address *(Non-members only please complete this section)*						

Please use a separate form for each campsite and do not send receipts. Owing to the large number of site reports received, it is not possible to enter into correspondence. Please return completed form to:

The Editor, Caravan Europe, The Caravan Club
FREEPOST, PO Box 386, (RRZG-SXKK-UCUJ)
East Grinstead RH19 1FH

(This address to be used when mailing within the UK only)

Caravan Europe **
Abbreviated Site Report Form

Use this abbreviated Site Report Form if you have visited a number of sites and there are no changes (or only insignificant changes) to their entries in the guide. If reporting on a new site, or reporting several changes, please use the full version of the report form. **If advising prices,** these should be for a car, caravan and 2 adults for one night's stay. **Please indicate high or low season prices and whether electricity is included.**

Remember, if you don't tell us about sites you have visited, they may eventually be deleted from the guide.

Year of guide used	20.........	Page No.	....	Name of town/village site listed under		
Site Name					Date of visit	...... /...... /.......
GPS	Latitude.......................................(*eg 12.34567*) Longitude.......................................(*eg 1.23456 or -1.23456*)					
Site is in: Andorra / Austria / Belgium / Croatia / Czech Republic / Denmark / Finland / France / Germany / Greece / Hungary / Italy / Luxembourg / Netherlands / Norway / Poland / Portugal / Slovakia / Slovenia / Spain / Sweden / Switzerland						
Charge for car, caravan & 2 adults in local currency	High Season	Low Season	Elec inc in price?	Y / N	...........amps	
			Price of elec (if not inc)		...........amps	

Year of guide used	20.........	Page No.	....	Name of town/village site listed under		
Site Name					Date of visit	...... /...... /.......
GPS	Latitude.......................................(*eg 12.34567*) Longitude.......................................(*eg 1.23456 or -1.23456*)					
Site is in: Andorra / Austria / Belgium / Croatia / Czech Republic / Denmark / Finland / France / Germany / Greece / Hungary / Italy / Luxembourg / Netherlands / Norway / Poland / Portugal / Slovakia / Slovenia / Spain / Sweden / Switzerland						
Charge for car, caravan & 2 adults in local currency	High Season	Low Season	Elec inc in price?	Y / N	...........amps	
			Price of elec (if not inc)		...........amps	

Year of guide used	20.........	Page No.	....	Name of town/village site listed under		
Site Name					Date of visit	...... /...... /.......
GPS	Latitude.......................................(*eg 12.34567*) Longitude.......................................(*eg 1.23456 or -1.23456*)					
Site is in: Andorra / Austria / Belgium / Croatia / Czech Republic / Denmark / Finland / France / Germany / Greece / Hungary / Italy / Luxembourg / Netherlands / Norway / Poland / Portugal / Slovakia / Slovenia / Spain / Sweden / Switzerland						
Charge for car, caravan & 2 adults in local currency	High Season	Low Season	Elec inc in price?	Y / N	...........amps	
			Price of elec (if not inc)		...........amps	

Your comments & opinions may be used in future editions of the guide, if you do not wish them to be used please tick ....

Name...   Do you need more blank Site Report Forms?   Yes ☐   No ☐

Membership No................................ or postcode   Caravanner ☐   Motor caravanner ☐   Trailer-tenter ☐

Please return completed form to:
The Editor, Caravan Europe, The Caravan Club
FREEPOST, PO Box 386 (RRZG-SXKK-UCUJ)
East Grinstead RH19 1FH
(This address to be used when mailing within UK only)

** *You can also complete forms online: www.caravanclub.co.uk/europereport*

CUT ALONG DOTTED LINE

Year of guide used	20..........	Page No.	....	Name of town/village site listed under	
Site Name				Date of visit	.... /....... /.......
GPS	Latitude...(eg 12.34567) Longitude...(eg 1.23456 or -1.23456)				
Site is in: Andorra / Austria / Belgium / Croatia / Czech Republic / Denmark / Finland / France / Germany / Greece / Hungary / Italy / Luxembourg / Netherlands / Norway / Poland / Portugal / Slovakia / Slovenia / Spain / Sweden / Switzerland					
Charge for car, caravan & 2 adults in local currency	High Season	Low Season	Elec inc in price?	Y / N	............amps
			Price of elec (if not inc)		............amps

Year of guide used	20..........	Page No.	....	Name of town/village site listed under	
Site Name				Date of visit	.... /....... /.......
GPS	Latitude...(eg 12.34567) Longitude...(eg 1.23456 or -1.23456)				
Site is in: Andorra / Austria / Belgium / Croatia / Czech Republic / Denmark / Finland / France / Germany / Greece / Hungary / Italy / Luxembourg / Netherlands / Norway / Poland / Portugal / Slovakia / Slovenia / Spain / Sweden / Switzerland					
Charge for car, caravan & 2 adults in local currency	High Season	Low Season	Elec inc in price?	Y / N	............amps
			Price of elec (if not inc)		............amps

Year of guide used	20..........	Page No.	....	Name of town/village site listed under	
Site Name				Date of visit	.... /....... /.......
GPS	Latitude...(eg 12.34567) Longitude...(eg 1.23456 or -1.23456)				
Site is in: Andorra / Austria / Belgium / Croatia / Czech Republic / Denmark / Finland / France / Germany / Greece / Hungary / Italy / Luxembourg / Netherlands / Norway / Poland / Portugal / Slovakia / Slovenia / Spain / Sweden / Switzerland					
Charge for car, caravan & 2 adults in local currency	High Season	Low Season	Elec inc in price?	Y / N	............amps
			Price of elec (if not inc)		............amps

Year of guide used	20..........	Page No.	....	Name of town/village site listed under	
Site Name				Date of visit	.... /....... /.......
GPS	Latitude...(eg 12.34567) Longitude...(eg 1.23456 or -1.23456)				
Site is in: Andorra / Austria / Belgium / Croatia / Czech Republic / Denmark / Finland / France / Germany / Greece / Hungary / Italy / Luxembourg / Netherlands / Norway / Poland / Portugal / Slovakia / Slovenia / Spain / Sweden / Switzerland					
Charge for car, caravan & 2 adults in local currency	High Season	Low Season	Elec inc in price?	Y / N	............amps
			Price of elec (if not inc)		............amps

Caravan Europe **
Abbreviated Site Report Form

Use this abbreviated Site Report Form if you have visited a number of sites and there are no changes (or only insignificant changes) to their entries in the guide. If reporting on a new site, or reporting several changes, please use the full version of the report form. **If advising prices, these should be for a car, caravan and 2 adults for one night's stay. Please indicate high or low season prices and whether electricity is included.**

Remember, if you don't tell us about sites you have visited, they may eventually be deleted from the guide.

Year of guide used	20.........	Page No.	....	Name of town/village site listed under		
Site Name					Date of visit	.... /....... /.......
GPS	Latitude...(eg 12.34567) Longitude...(eg 1.23456 or -1.23456)					
Site is in: Andorra / Austria / Belgium / Croatia / Czech Republic / Denmark / Finland / France / Germany / Greece / Hungary / Italy / Luxembourg / Netherlands / Norway / Poland / Portugal / Slovakia / Slovenia / Spain / Sweden / Switzerland						

Charge for car, caravan & 2 adults in local currency	High Season	Low Season	Elec inc in price?	Y / N	............amps
			Price of elec (if not inc)		............amps

Year of guide used	20.........	Page No.	....	Name of town/village site listed under		
Site Name					Date of visit	.... /....... /.......
GPS	Latitude...(eg 12.34567) Longitude...(eg 1.23456 or -1.23456)					
Site is in: Andorra / Austria / Belgium / Croatia / Czech Republic / Denmark / Finland / France / Germany / Greece / Hungary / Italy / Luxembourg / Netherlands / Norway / Poland / Portugal / Slovakia / Slovenia / Spain / Sweden / Switzerland						

Charge for car, caravan & 2 adults in local currency	High Season	Low Season	Elec inc in price?	Y / N	............amps
			Price of elec (if not inc)		............amps

Year of guide used	20.........	Page No.	....	Name of town/village site listed under		
Site Name					Date of visit	.... /....... /.......
GPS	Latitude...(eg 12.34567) Longitude...(eg 1.23456 or -1.23456)					
Site is in: Andorra / Austria / Belgium / Croatia / Czech Republic / Denmark / Finland / France / Germany / Greece / Hungary / Italy / Luxembourg / Netherlands / Norway / Poland / Portugal / Slovakia / Slovenia / Spain / Sweden / Switzerland						

Charge for car, caravan & 2 adults in local currency	High Season	Low Season	Elec inc in price?	Y / N	............amps
			Price of elec (if not inc)		............amps

Your comments & opinions may be used in future editions of the guide, if you do not wish them to be used please tick ....

Name.. Do you need more blank Site Report Forms? Yes ☐ No ☐

Membership No................................ or postcode Caravanner ☐ Motor caravanner ☐ Trailer-tenter ☐

Please return completed form to:
The Editor, Caravan Europe, The Caravan Club
FREEPOST, PO Box 386 (RRZG-SXKK-UCUJ)
East Grinstead RH19 1FH
(This address to be used when mailing within UK only)

*** You can also complete forms online: www.caravanclub.co.uk/europereport*

CUT ALONG DOTTED LINE

Year of guide used	20..........	Page No.	....	Name of town/village site listed under		
Site Name					Date of visit	.... /....... /........
GPS	Latitude..(eg 12.34567) Longitude..(eg 1.23456 or -1.23456)					
Site is in: Andorra / Austria / Belgium / Croatia / Czech Republic / Denmark / Finland / France / Germany / Greece / Hungary / Italy / Luxembourg / Netherlands / Norway / Poland / Portugal / Slovakia / Slovenia / Spain / Sweden / Switzerland						
Charge for car, caravan & 2 adults in local currency	High Season	Low Season	Elec inc in price?	Y / N	............amps	
			Price of elec (if not inc)		............amps	

Year of guide used	20..........	Page No.	....	Name of town/village site listed under		
Site Name					Date of visit	.... /....... /........
GPS	Latitude..(eg 12.34567) Longitude..(eg 1.23456 or -1.23456)					
Site is in: Andorra / Austria / Belgium / Croatia / Czech Republic / Denmark / Finland / France / Germany / Greece / Hungary / Italy / Luxembourg / Netherlands / Norway / Poland / Portugal / Slovakia / Slovenia / Spain / Sweden / Switzerland						
Charge for car, caravan & 2 adults in local currency	High Season	Low Season	Elec inc in price?	Y / N	............amps	
			Price of elec (if not inc)		............amps	

Year of guide used	20..........	Page No.	....	Name of town/village site listed under		
Site Name					Date of visit	.... /....... /........
GPS	Latitude..(eg 12.34567) Longitude..(eg 1.23456 or -1.23456)					
Site is in: Andorra / Austria / Belgium / Croatia / Czech Republic / Denmark / Finland / France / Germany / Greece / Hungary / Italy / Luxembourg / Netherlands / Norway / Poland / Portugal / Slovakia / Slovenia / Spain / Sweden / Switzerland						
Charge for car, caravan & 2 adults in local currency	High Season	Low Season	Elec inc in price?	Y / N	............amps	
			Price of elec (if not inc)		............amps	

Year of guide used	20..........	Page No.	....	Name of town/village site listed under		
Site Name					Date of visit	.... /....... /........
GPS	Latitude..(eg 12.34567) Longitude..(eg 1.23456 or -1.23456)					
Site is in: Andorra / Austria / Belgium / Croatia / Czech Republic / Denmark / Finland / France / Germany / Greece / Hungary / Italy / Luxembourg / Netherlands / Norway / Poland / Portugal / Slovakia / Slovenia / Spain / Sweden / Switzerland						
Charge for car, caravan & 2 adults in local currency	High Season	Low Season	Elec inc in price?	Y / N	............amps	
			Price of elec (if not inc)		............amps	

Caravan Europe **
Abbreviated Site Report Form

Use this abbreviated Site Report Form if you have visited a number of sites and there are no changes (or only insignificant changes) to their entries in the guide. If reporting on a new site, or reporting several changes, please use the full version of the report form. **If advising prices,** these should be for a car, caravan and 2 adults for one night's stay. **Please indicate high or low season prices and whether electricity is included.**

Remember, if you don't tell us about sites you have visited, they may eventually be deleted from the guide.

Year of guide used	20..........	Page No.	....	Name of town/village site listed under	
Site Name				Date of visit	.... /....... /........
GPS	Latitude...(eg 12.34567) Longitude...(eg 1.23456 or -1.23456)				
Site is in: Andorra / Austria / Belgium / Croatia / Czech Republic / Denmark / Finland / France / Germany / Greece / Hungary / Italy / Luxembourg / Netherlands / Norway / Poland / Portugal / Slovakia / Slovenia / Spain / Sweden / Switzerland					
Charge for car, caravan & 2 adults in local currency	High Season	Low Season	Elec inc in price?	Y / N	.............amps
			Price of elec (if not inc)		.............amps

Year of guide used	20..........	Page No.	....	Name of town/village site listed under	
Site Name				Date of visit	.... /....... /........
GPS	Latitude...(eg 12.34567) Longitude...(eg 1.23456 or -1.23456)				
Site is in: Andorra / Austria / Belgium / Croatia / Czech Republic / Denmark / Finland / France / Germany / Greece / Hungary / Italy / Luxembourg / Netherlands / Norway / Poland / Portugal / Slovakia / Slovenia / Spain / Sweden / Switzerland					
Charge for car, caravan & 2 adults in local currency	High Season	Low Season	Elec inc in price?	Y / N	.............amps
			Price of elec (if not inc)		.............amps

Year of guide used	20..........	Page No.	....	Name of town/village site listed under	
Site Name				Date of visit	.... /....... /........
GPS	Latitude...(eg 12.34567) Longitude...(eg 1.23456 or -1.23456)				
Site is in: Andorra / Austria / Belgium / Croatia / Czech Republic / Denmark / Finland / France / Germany / Greece / Hungary / Italy / Luxembourg / Netherlands / Norway / Poland / Portugal / Slovakia / Slovenia / Spain / Sweden / Switzerland					
Charge for car, caravan & 2 adults in local currency	High Season	Low Season	Elec inc in price?	Y / N	.............amps
			Price of elec (if not inc)		.............amps

Your comments & opinions may be used in future editions of the guide, if you do not wish them to be used please tick ....

Name.. Do you need more blank Site Report Forms? Yes ☐ No ☐

Membership No................................ or postcode Caravanner ☐ Motor caravanner ☐ Trailer-tenter ☐

Please return completed form to:
The Editor, Caravan Europe, The Caravan Club
FREEPOST, PO Box 386 (RRZG-SXKK-UCUJ)
East Grinstead RH19 1FH
(This address to be used when mailing within UK only)

*** You can also complete forms online: www.caravanclub.co.uk/europereport*

Year of guide used	20..........	Page No.	....	Name of town/village site listed under	
Site Name				Date of visit	.... /....... /........
GPS	Latitude...(eg 12.34567) Longitude...(eg 1.23456 or -1.23456)				
Site is in: Andorra / Austria / Belgium / Croatia / Czech Republic / Denmark / Finland / France / Germany / Greece / Hungary / Italy / Luxembourg / Netherlands / Norway / Poland / Portugal / Slovakia / Slovenia / Spain / Sweden / Switzerland					
Charge for car, caravan & 2 adults in local currency	High Season	Low Season	Elec inc in price?	Y / N	.............amps
			Price of elec (if not inc)		.............amps

Year of guide used	20..........	Page No.	....	Name of town/village site listed under	
Site Name				Date of visit	.... /....... /........
GPS	Latitude...(eg 12.34567) Longitude...(eg 1.23456 or -1.23456)				
Site is in: Andorra / Austria / Belgium / Croatia / Czech Republic / Denmark / Finland / France / Germany / Greece / Hungary / Italy / Luxembourg / Netherlands / Norway / Poland / Portugal / Slovakia / Slovenia / Spain / Sweden / Switzerland					
Charge for car, caravan & 2 adults in local currency	High Season	Low Season	Elec inc in price?	Y / N	.............amps
			Price of elec (if not inc)		.............amps

Year of guide used	20..........	Page No.	....	Name of town/village site listed under	
Site Name				Date of visit	.... /....... /........
GPS	Latitude...(eg 12.34567) Longitude...(eg 1.23456 or -1.23456)				
Site is in: Andorra / Austria / Belgium / Croatia / Czech Republic / Denmark / Finland / France / Germany / Greece / Hungary / Italy / Luxembourg / Netherlands / Norway / Poland / Portugal / Slovakia / Slovenia / Spain / Sweden / Switzerland					
Charge for car, caravan & 2 adults in local currency	High Season	Low Season	Elec inc in price?	Y / N	.............amps
			Price of elec (if not inc)		.............amps

Year of guide used	20..........	Page No.	....	Name of town/village site listed under	
Site Name				Date of visit	.... /....... /........
GPS	Latitude...(eg 12.34567) Longitude...(eg 1.23456 or -1.23456)				
Site is in: Andorra / Austria / Belgium / Croatia / Czech Republic / Denmark / Finland / France / Germany / Greece / Hungary / Italy / Luxembourg / Netherlands / Norway / Poland / Portugal / Slovakia / Slovenia / Spain / Sweden / Switzerland					
Charge for car, caravan & 2 adults in local currency	High Season	Low Season	Elec inc in price?	Y / N	.............amps
			Price of elec (if not inc)		.............amps

Index

Index